SCARECROW CONCORDANCES

1. Doyle, Paul A. A Concordance to the Collected Poems of James Joyce. 1966.

2. Borrello, Alfred. A Concordance to the Poetry in English of Gerard Manley Hopkins. 1969.

3. Lane, Gary. A Concordance to the Poems of Theodore Roethke. 1972.

4. Landry, Hilton & Elaine. A Concordance to the Poems of Hart Crane. 1973.

5. Lane, Gary. A Concordance to the Poems of Dylan Thomas. 1976.

A CONCORDANCE
TO THE POEMS OF
DYLAN THOMAS

by

GARY LANE

Scarecrow Concordances, No. 5

The Scarecrow Press, Inc.

Metuchen, N.J.   1976

Library of Congress Cataloging in Publication Data

Lane, Gary, 1943-
    A concordance to The poems of Dylan Thomas.

    (Scarecrow concordances ; 5)
    Keyed to the 1971 ed. of The poems of Dylan Thomas,
edited by D. Jones.
    1. Thomas, Dylan, 1914-1953--Concordances.
I. Thomas, Dylan, 1914-1953. The poems of Dylan Thomas.
II. Title.
PR6039.H52Z49 1976   821'.91'2   76-18078
ISBN 0-8108-0971-0

CONTENTS

Preface   v

Concordance   (A-Z)   1

Components of Hyphenated Compounds   640

Table of Word Frequencies   665

PREFACE

The 1971 publication of <u>The Poems of Dylan Thomas</u> at last brought us an extensive collection of the Welshman's work. The new volume, issued nineteen years after Thomas gathered and ordered ninety of his lyrics for the miscalled <u>Collected Poems</u>, adds 102 more poems to the original group and sets all the work in the chronological order of its composition. It is to this volume that the present concordance is keyed. With its aid, the user can pursue a variety of poetic inquiries. He can more fully and carefully than was previously possible examine the linguistic and symbolic textures of Thomas' work; too, because of the poems' chronological ordering, he can easily investigate matters of poetic development.

The concordance, compiled on a UNIVAC 1106 computer, is in three parts. The first, pages 1-639, lists all the words and numbers, with their occurrences, in Thomas' poetry. Part two, pages 640-663, lists separately the components of the poet's hyphenated compounds, providing a cross reference to uses that might otherwise be missed. Thus, the investigator of Thomas' similes will find in the first part of the book, under "like," 151 occurrences of the word. If he turns to the second section, he will discover, again under "like," four additional examples, "leaf-like," "cloud-like," "grief-like," "shroud-like." (The observer of "Prologue" 's extended rhyme scheme may wonder for a moment whether Thomas planned this effect also!) The concordance's final section, pages 664-697, lists all the poet's words in descending order of frequency.

The format is straightforward. Beside each line is listed the page number in <u>The Poems of Dylan Thomas</u> on which it appears, the title of the poem to which it belongs (or a shortened version thereof), and its line number within the poem. Poem titles are designated by a T in the column for line number. In order to save space I have suppressed the listing of the words below, all of which, I think, are unlikely to interest. A suppressed word is followed not by the lines that use it but by a single, parenthesized number, its frequency of occurrence. My choices are of course somewhat arbitrary--I have, for example, fully listed "I," "me," and "my," the lyric poet's avowal of selfhood--but I preferred to list rather than suppress in cases that seemed in any way debatable.

Suppressed Words

a	for	is	she	to
am	from	it	that	us
an	had	its	the	was
and	has	no	their	we
are	have	nor	them	were
at	he	not	these	with
be	her	of	they	you
been	him	on	this	your
but	his	or	those	
by	in	our	through	

In preparing this volume I have silently corrected a number of misprints that have clung to Thomas' poems through their printing history, and corrected also a few errors that crept into the new collection.   Otherwise, I have followed exactly the text of Daniel Jones's The Poems of Dylan Thomas.   Most of Thomas' poems have titles too long for exact listing in my format, and for these I have tried to devise shortened titles evocative of the original ones.   The following table lists those poems whose titles in the concordance and The Poems of Dylan Thomas are not identical.

Concordance	Poems of Dylan Thomas	DT Page
A PROCESS IN	A process in the weather of the heart	88
A WAR OF WITS	Out of a war of wits	42
AFTER FUNERAL	After the funeral	136
AIR BREATHE	The air you breathe	11
ALL ALL AND	All all and all the dry worlds lever	106
ALL THAT I OWE	All that I owe the fellows of the grave	80
ALMANAC TIME	The almanac of time	79
ALTARWISE	Altarwise by owl-light	116
BEAUTY TO DUST	When you have ground such beauty down to dust	25
BEFORE KNOCKED	Before I knocked	68
BELOW A TIME	Once below a time	151
BEWILDERED WAY	Although through my bewildered way	21
BOYS OF SUMMER	I see the boys of summer	91
BREAD I BREAK	This bread I break	86
BREATH SHED	Poem (Your breath was shed)	176
CLOWN IN MOON	Clown in the Moon	225
COLOUR OF SAY	Once it was the colour of saying	144
CONVERS PRAYER	The Conversation of Prayer	193
COOL, OH NO	Cool, oh no cool	10
COUNTRY HEAVEN	In Country Heaven	215
COUNTRY SLEEP	In Country Sleep	197
CRAFT OR ART	In my craft or sullen art	196
DAWN RAID	Among those Killed in the Dawn Raid was a Man Aged a Hundred	172
DEATHS AND ENT	Deaths and Entrances	160
EARS IN TURRET	Ears in the turrets hear	62
ENCOMPASSED	To be encompassed by the brilliant earth	20
EUNUCH DREAMS	Our eunuch dreams	89

FACES SHONE	Their faces shone under some radiance	43
FAIRY TALES	We have the fairy tales by heart	59
FELLOWED SLEEP	I fellowed sleep	101
FIRE RAID	Ceremony after a Fire Raid	173
FIVE & COUNTRY	When all my five and country senses see	138
FOR LEDA	The morning, space for Leda	14
FOSTER LIGHT	Foster the light	123
FURIOUS MOTION	When your furious motion	232
GAS FADES	Before the gas fades	38
GIANT'S THIGH	In the White Giant's Thigh	203
GODS THUMP	Shall gods be said to thump the clouds	65
GREEK PLAY	Greek Play in a Garden	56
GRIEF THIEF	Grief thief of time	107
HAND SIGNED	The hand that signed the paper	66
HELD-OUT HAND	Upon your held-out hand	32
HERE IN SPRING	Here in this spring	58
HERE LIE BEAST	Here lie the beasts	81
HOLD HARD	Hold hard, these ancient minutes in the cuckoo's month	122
HOW MY ANIMAL	How shall my animal	134
I DREAMED MY	I dreamed my genesis	102
I, FIRST NAMED	I, the first named	141
I, IN IMAGE	I, in my intricate image	108
I MAKE THIS IN	I make this in a warring absence	131
IDYLL UNFORGET	Idyll of Unforgetfulness	223
IF HEAD HURT	'If my head hurt a hair's foot'	145
IMAGES IN AIR	Conceive these images in air	19
IN BEGINNING	In the beginning	93
IN GARDENS	Walking in gardens	33
IN OBLIVION	It's not in misery but in oblivion	16
INCARNATE DEVL	Incarnate devil	121
INTO HER HEAD	Into her lying down head	157
LANTERNS SHINE	Should lanterns shine	116
LASHED RINGS	Through these lashed rings	76
LET A FAITH	Let for one moment a faith statement	66
LET BE KNOWN	Let it be known	36
LETTER TO AUNT	A Letter to my Aunt Discussing the Correct Approach to Modern Poetry	83
LIFT UP FACE	Lift up your face	35
LIGHT BREAKS	Light breaks where no sun shines	82
LIGHT, I KNOW	Light, I know, treads the ten million stars	48
LONG, SKELETON	Too long, skeleton	29
LONGED TO MOVE	I have longed to move away	43
LONG-LEGGED	Ballad of the Long-legged Bait	161
LORD RED HAIL	Not forever shall the Lord of the red hail	73
LOVE IN ASYLUM	Love in the Asylum	169
LOVE'S FEVER	From love's first fever to her plague	78
MAKE ME A MASK	O make me a mask	133
MAKES INTERVALS	It's light that makes the intervals	238
MARRIAGE VIRG	On the Marriage of a Virgin	170
MEAT ON BONES	'Find meat on bones'	60
MIDNIGHT ROAD	The midnight road	36
MINUTE'S HOUR	I know this vicious minute's hour	9
MY BEGGAR ARM	Last night I dived my beggar arm	175
MY HERO BARES	My hero bares his nerves	75

MY NEOPHYTE	Then was my neophyte	128
NATURAL DAY	The natural day and night	17
NO DOMINION	And death shall have no dominion	49
NO MAN BELIEVE	No man believes	54
NO, PIGEON	No, pigeon, I'm too wise	234
NO THOUGHT	No thought can trouble my unwholesome pose	233
NO WINGS	Children of darkness got no wings	28
NO WORK WORDS	On no work of words	140
NOT DESPAIR	You shall not despair	228
NOT FATHER ME	Do you not father me	112
NOT FROM ANGER	Not from this anger	134
NOT GO GENTLE	Do not go gentle into that good night	207
NOW, SAY NAY	Now (Now, Say nay)	127
OBLIVIOUS DARK	Never to reach the oblivious dark	27
OCTOBER WIND	Especially when the October wind	98
ON QUIET NIGHT	Since, on a quiet night	22
OUR SANCTITY	We will be conscious of our sanctity	230
OUT OF SIGHS	Out of the sighs	31
PAIN BE MUSIC	Your pain shall be a music	87
PAPER & STICKS	Paper and sticks	149
PERSONAL EPIT	Written for a Personal Epitaph	26
PLEASURE-BIRD	Because the pleasure-bird whistles	144
PLOUGHMAN GONE	The ploughman's gone	45
POEM IN OCT	Poem in October (It was my thirtieth year)	176
POEM ON B'DAY	Poem on his Birthday (In the mustardseed sun)	208
RAIN CUTS	Rain cuts the place we tread	13
REALM OF FLESH	You are the ruler of this realm of flesh	67
REFUSAL MOURN	A Refusal to Mourn the Death, by Fire, of a Child in London	191
RETURN	The Countryman's Return	154
RUB OF LOVE	If I were tickled by the rub of love	94
RUNNING GRAVE	When, like a running grave	99
SAINT TO FALL	A saint about to fall	141
SECRET WIND	We see rise the secret wind	69
SEE, SAYS LIME	See, says the lime	85
SEED-AT-ZERO	The seed-at-zero	125
SERVANT SUN	How soon the servant sun	113
SIDE OF TRUTH	This side of the truth	192
SINNERS' BELL	It is the sinners' dust-tongued bell	130
SIR JOHNS HILL	Over Sir John's hill	201
SKY'S BRIGHT	Sometimes the sky's too bright	12
SLEEP BECALMED	Lie still, sleep becalmed	194
SLENDER WIND	To a Slender Wind	225
SONG: LOVE ME	Song (Love me, not as the dreaming nurses)	75
SONG OF DOG	The Song of the Mischievous Dog	221
SPIRE CRANES	The spire cranes	15
SPRING-SPIRIT	To the Spring-Spirit	227
SUN BURNS	The sun burns the morning	74
TAKE NEEDLES	Take the needles and the knives	70
THE FORCE THAT	The force that through the green fuse drives the flower	77
THE HUNCHBACK	The hunchback in the park	171
THE NEOPHYTE	The neophyte, baptized in smiles	19
THE ONLY DEAD	They are the only dead who did not love	23
THERE'S PLENTY	There's plenty in the world	25

Concordance	Poems of Dylan Thomas	DT Page
THIRST PARCHES	Now the thirst parches lip and tongue	34
TIME TO ROT	Time enough to rot	16
TO ARCHITECTS	Praise to the architects	57
TO FOLLOW FOX	To follow the fox	44
TO LEDA	Request to Leda	159
TO OTHERS	To Others than You	146
TODAY, INSECT	Today, this insect	124
TOMBSTONE TOLD	The tombstone told when she died	139
TWILIGHT LOCKS	When once the twilight locks no longer	97
TWINING HEAD	The rod can lift its twining head	240
UNLUCKILY FOR	Unluckily for a death	147
VISION, PRAYER	Vision and Prayer	180
WAS A SAVIOUR	There was a saviour	152
WAS THERE TIME	Was there a time	40
WE BY SEASAND	We lying by seasand	54
WE MOTHERNAKED	Before we mothernaked fall	73
WEDDING ANNIV	On a Wedding Anniversary	161
WHERE ONCE THE	Where once the waters of your face	90
WHY EAST WIND	Why east wind chills	55
WINDMILLS TURN	With windmills turning wrong directions	36
WINTER'S TALE	A Winter's Tale	187
WOMAN SPEAKS	The Woman Speaks	63
WOMAN TAPESTRY	Woman on Tapestry	234
WORLD PYRAMID	My World is Pyramid	103
YOUNG ARE OLD	'We who are young are old'	40
YOUR VOICE	I have come to catch your voice	231
YOUTH CALLS	Youth Calls to Age	30
24 YEARS	Twenty-four years	143

I have been fortunate in having expert and expeditious assistance always at hand. For technical advice, I am grateful to Carole Saurino, Dick Sandifer, and Bob Simon; for financial support, to a University of Miami Faculty Humanities Grant. Esther Maria Vidaurreta keypunched and helped proofread, always graciously and precisely. And Bonnie, Baron, and Heathcliff offered patience, encouragement, and love.

Gary Lane
University of Texas at San Antonio
May 1976

                                              PAGE   TITLE   LINE
A (974)
AARON
     WAS WHO WAS FOLDED ON THE ROD THE AARON   115   A GRIEF AGO   13
ABADDON
     ABADDON IN THE HANGNAIL CRACKED FROM ADAM, ... 116   ALTARWISE   3
     THE HORIZONTAL CROSS-BONES OF ABADDON, ... 117   ALTARWISE   21
ABASING
     AND WEEPS ON THE ABASING HILL, ... 215   COUNTRY HEAVEN   5
ABED
     AND THE LOVERS LIE ABED   197   CRAFT OR ART   4
ABOUT
     FEELING THE WIND ABOUT OUR HEADS THAT DOES NOT COOL,   26   THERE'S PLENTY   18
     THE ANGELS' WINGS BEATING ABOUT YOUR HEAD   33   HELD-OUT HAND   4
     ABOUT YOU, FLESH WILL PERISH, AND BLOOD   39   GAS FADES   31
     THE MOTHER'S CRY HAS FUMED ABOUT THE WINDS;   64   WOMAN SPEAKS   53
     WHEN NO MOUTH STIRRED ABOUT THE HANGING FAMINE,   ...   78   LOVE'S FEVER   5
     THERE ROUND ABOUT YOUR STONES THE SHADES   91   WHERE ONCE THE   16
     MY HOUSE WOULD FALL LIKE BREAD ABOUT MY HOMAGE;   ...   96   TWELVE   11
     NOR DAMNED THE SEA THAT SPED ABOUT MY FIST, ...   97   TWILIGHT LOCKS   3
     THE SECRET CHILD, I SHIFT ABOUT THE SEA   105   WORLD PYRAMID   59
     A SAINT ABOUT TO FALL   141   SAINT TO FALL   T
     A SAINT ABOUT TO FALL, ... 141   SAINT TO FALL   1
     ABOUT THE SAINT IN SHADES WHILE THE ENDLESS BREVIARY 148   UNLUCKILY FOR   26
     ABOUT THE SOILED UNDEAD   176   BREATH SHED   3
     OF MOVING ABOUT YOUR DEATH   192   SIDE OF TRUTH   14
     THE CONVERSATION OF PRAYERS ABOUT TO BE SAID 193   CONVERS PRAYER   1
     THE SOUND ABOUT TO BE SAID IN THE TWO PRAYERS 194   CONVERS PRAYER   9
     THE CONVERSATION OF PRAYERS ABOUT TO BE SAID 194   CONVERS PRAYER   13
     ABOUT THE LILTING HOUSE AND HAPPY AS THE GRASS WAS
        GREEN, ... 195   FERN HILL   2
     ABOUT THE HAPPY YARD AND SINGING AS THE FARM WAS
        HOME, ... 195   FERN HILL   11
     I HAVE KNOWN THE MYSTERY OF THE SEA TO BE MANTLED
        ABOUT ME;   223   IDYLL UNFORGET   18
     FIERCE COLOURS FLED ABOUT THE BRANCHES, ... 226   THE OAK   1
     CLOSES ABOUT YOUR CLASPED FINGERS   229   MY RIVER   25
     YOUR STEP WILL REMAIN ABOUT TO FALL.   232   FURIOUS MOTION   4
ABOVE
     ABOVE A BOAT OF LEAVES AND WEEDS.   14   RAIN CUTS   24
     THRUST OUT OUR HEADS ABOVE THE BRANCHES   31   BEING BUT MEN   9
     ABOVE THEM POISE THE SWOLLEN CLOUDS   36   MIDNIGHT ROAD   12
     ABOVE THE WASTE ALLOTMENTS THE DAWN HALTS.   82   LIGHT BREAKS   30
     AND SLEEP ROLLS MUTE ABOVE THE BEDS   98   TWILIGHT LOCKS   28
     ABOVE THE FARMS AND THE WHITE HORSES   177   POEM IN OCT   13
     ABOVE HER FOLDED HEAD, AND THE SOFT FEATHERED VOICE 189   WINTER'S TALE   82
     THE NIGHT ABOVE THE DINGLE STARRY, ... 195   FERN HILL   3
     NIGHT AND THE REINDEER ON THE CLOUDS ABOVE THE
        HAYCOCKS   199   COUNTRY SLEEP   64
     ABOVE ALL HE LONGED FOR HIS MOTHER'S BREAST   216   ELEGY   9
     SLEEP ABOVE IN THE GLOW OF A FADING SUNSET;   222   FOREST PICTURE   7
ABRAHAM-MAN
     UP ROSE THE ABRAHAM-MAN, MAD FOR MY SAKE, ... 112   NOT FATHER ME   19
ABROAD
     AND WALKED ABROAD IN A SHOWER OF ALL MY DAYS.   177   POEM IN OCT   16
     BAY. NO-GOOD IS ABROAD. I UNHARDY CAN   179   NEW QUAY   8
ABSCESSES
     VESSEL OF ABSCESSES AND EXULTATION'S SHELL, ... 134   HOW MY ANIMAL   3
ABSENCE
     I MAKE THIS IN A WARRING ABSENCE   131   I MAKE THIS IN   T
     I MAKE THIS IN A WARRING ABSENCE WHEN   131   I MAKE THIS IN   1

	PAGE	TITLE	LINE
ABSENCE (CONTINUED)			
AND A SILK PIGEON'S GUILT IN HER PROUD ABSENCE, ...	131	I MAKE THIS IN	17
ABSTRACT			
OF CHURCHES MADE FROM ABSTRACT AND CONCRETE.	51	OUT OF THE PIT	28
ABSTRACTED			
ABSTRACTED ALL THE LETTERS OF THE VOID;	94	IN BEGINNING	21
ACCIDENT			
HEAR BY DEATH'S ACCIDENT THE CLOCKED AND DASHED-DOWN SPIRE	130	SINNERS' BELL	11
ACHE			
BUT DO NOT ACHE.	13	SKY'S BRIGHT	30
HE'LL ACHE TOO LONG	32	OUT OF SIGHS	13
ACHE ON THE LOVELORN PAPER	75	MY HERO BARES	7
BEND, IF MY JOURNEY ACHE, DIRECTION LIKE AN ARC OR MAKE	145	IF HEAD HURT	14
THE ACHE RETURN.	239	MAKES INTERVALS	26
ACHES			
ACHES TILL THE METAL MEETS THE MARROW, ...	47	POET: 1935	50
SO I HAVE COME TO KNOW, BUT KNOWLEDGE ACHES;	64	WOMAN SPEAKS	48
ACID			
THE ACID POURS AWAY, THE ACID DRIPS	34	THIRST PARCHES	8
THE ACID POURS AWAY, THE ACID DRIPS	34	THIRST PARCHES	8
THE MILKY ACID ON EACH HINGE, ...	97	TWILIGHT LOCKS	5
A NITRIC SHAPE THAT LEAPS HER, TIME AND ACID;	115	A GRIEF AGO	34
ACORN			
THE OAK IS FELLED IN THE ACORN	167	LONG-LEGGED	155
ACORNED			
AND HIS RUNAWAY BELOVED CHILDLIKE LAID IN THE ACORNED SAND.	157	INTO HER HEAD	23
ACQUAINT			
ACQUAINT THE FLESH WITH A REMEMBERED ITCH, ...	80	ALL THAT I OWE	12
ACQUAINTED			
ACQUAINTED WITH THE SALT ADVENTURE	69	BEFORE KNOCKED	33
ACQUAINTING			
ACQUAINTING ME WITH MY DIVINITY;	77	LASHED RINGS	15
ACQUAINTS			
A HOLY VOICE ACQUAINTS ME WITH HIS GLORY.	76	LASHED RINGS	6
ACRE			
THERE SHALL BE NO MUTE MOURNING OVER HIS ACRE, ...	64	WOMAN SPEAKS	38
LEFT BY THE DEAD WHO, IN THEIR MOONLESS ACRE, ...	79	LOVE'S FEVER	35
AND FATHER ALL NOR FAIL THE FLY-LORD'S ACRE, ...	123	FOSTER LIGHT	13
ACRES			
WHAT OF A BAMBOO MAN AMONG YOUR ACRES?	118	ALTARWISE	49
ACRID			
IT'S ACRID IN THE STREETS;	16	TIME TO ROT	10
THAT SPILL SUCH ACRID BLOOD.	32	OUT OF SIGHS	16
ACRITUDES			
OLD IN ILLUSIONS TURNED TO ACRITUDES, ...	20	THE NEOPHYTE	23
ACROSS			
CRY, MULTITUDES OF ARKS! ACROSS	5	PROLOGUE	93
HE GOES ACROSS THE SKY, ...	13	RAIN CUTS	19
YOU'RE THE PERVERSE TO LIE ACROSS, ...	21	BEWILDERED WAY	15
HER LONELINESS ACROSS THE EMPTY WAVES	22	ON QUIET NIGHT	10
SPELLING ACROSS THE SKY HIS DEVIL'S NEWS, ...	29	NEARLY SUMMER	5
STEPPING ON CLOUDS ACROSS THE GOLDEN SKY, ...	30	YOUTH CALLS	2
YOUTH CALLS TO AGE ACROSS THE TIRED YEARS:	30	YOUTH CALLS	13
ACROSS THE SUN WAS SPREAD A CRAZY SMILE.	50	OUT OF THE PIT	11
AND MY HEART IS CRACKED ACROSS;	61	MEAT ON BONES	18
ONE SMILE OF LIGHT ACROSS THE EMPTY FACE;	93	IN BEGINNING	2
ONE BOUGH OF BONE ACROSS THE ROOTING AIR, ...	93	IN BEGINNING	3

	PAGE	TITLE	LINE
ACROSS (CONTINUED)			
AND BEAR THOSE TENDRIL HANDS I TOUCH ACROSS	134	NOT FROM ANGER	6
FLASHED FIRST ACROSS HIS THUNDERCLAPPING EYES.	160	DEATHS AND ENT	24
THE SKY IS TORN ACROSS	161	WEDDING ANNIV	1
ACT			
IS A BURNING AND CRESTED ACT, ...	3	PROLOGUE	25
WITH UNFORGETTABLY SMILING ACT, ...	146	TO OTHERS	11
EARTH, AIR, WATER, FIRE, SINGING INTO THE WHITE ACT,	200	COUNTRY SLEEP	87
AND ALONE IN THE NIGHT'S ETERNAL, CURVING ACT	203	GIANT'S THIGH	9
TO-DAY, IF ALL MY SENSES ACT, ...	238	MAKES INTERVALS	9
ACTIONS			
UNTHINKING ACTIONS GIVEN CAUSES	38	THE GOSSIPERS	4
ACTIONS'			
THE ACTIONS' END.	101	RUNNING GRAVE	45
AND, WHEN IT QUICKENS, ALTER THE ACTIONS' PACE	116	LANTERNS SHINE	12
ACTORS			
THAT MADDEN BOTH WATCHERS AND ACTORS.	33	HELD-OUT HAND	16
ACTS			
THE BRAIN ACTS TO THE LEGAL DEAD.	67	REALM OF FLESH	9
ADAM			
OF BUD OF ADAM THROUGH HIS BOXY SHIFT, ...	101	RUNNING GRAVE	38
HIS SEA-SUCKED ADAM IN THE HOLLOW HULK, ...	103	WORLD PYRAMID	2
ABADDON IN THE HANGNAIL CRACKED FROM ADAM, ...	116	ALTARWISE	3
RUNG BONE AND BLADE, THE VERTICALS OF ADAM, ...	117	ALTARWISE	23
ROSE MY BYZANTINE ADAM IN THE NIGHT.	118	ALTARWISE	62
CROSS-STROKED SALT ADAM TO THE FROZEN ANGEL	119	ALTARWISE	67
ADAM, TIME'S JOKER, ON A WITCH OF CARDBOARD	119	ALTARWISE	81
WHO SUCKS THE BELL-VOICED ADAM OUT OF MAGIC, ...	119	ALTARWISE	93
'ADAM I LOVE, MY MADMEN'S LOVE IS ENDLESS, ...	125	TODAY, INSECT	23
ADAM OR EVE, THE ADORNED HOLY BULLOCK	174	FIRE RAID	34
O ADAM AND EVE TOGETHER	174	FIRE RAID	42
OF ADAM AND EVE IS NEVER FOR A SECOND	174	FIRE RAID	48
AND UPRIGHT ADAM	182	VISION, PRAYER	89
SHINING, IT WAS ADAM AND MAIDEN, ...	196	FERN HILL	30
ADAM'S			
STALE OF ADAM'S BRINE UNTIL, VISION	103	I DREAMED MY	27
I, IN A WIND ON FIRE, FROM GREEN ADAM'S CRADLE, ...	111	I, IN IMAGE	95
THAT ADAM'S WETHER IN THE FLOCK OF HORNS, ...	117	ALTARWISE	31
ADD			
THAT THE SUM SANITY MIGHT ADD TO NAUGHT	96	TWELVE	1
ADD ONE MORE NAIL OF PRAISE ON TO THE CROSS, ...	96	TWELVE	7
ADDER			
PUFF TILL THE ADDER IS, ...	22	HIGH ON A HILL	9
SLY AS AN ADDER, RID OF FLEAS.	29	LONG, SKELETON	6
ADDERS			
AND LOOSED THE BRAIDING ADDERS FROM THEIR HAIRS;	104	WORLD PYRAMID	22
ADMIRE			
MADE, FOR THE BATHERS TO ADMIRE, ...	34	IN GARDENS	12
AND MAY I YET LIVE TO ADMIRE	85	LETTER TO AUNT	65
ADMIRING			
ON TUMBLING HILLS ADMIRING THE SEA, ...	48	POET: 1935	61
ADMIT			
ADMIT THE SUN	240	ADMIT THE SUN	T
ADMIT THE SUN INTO YOUR HIGH NEST	240	ADMIT THE SUN	1
ADMITS			
WHO ADMITS THE DELUSIVE LIGHT THROUGH THE BOUNCING			
WALL, ...	170	LOVE IN ASYLUM	11
ADOLESCENCE			
THE THIEF OF ADOLESCENCE, ...	158	INTO HER HEAD	31

	PAGE	TITLE	LINE
ADORATION			
AND THE LIGHTNINGS OF ADORATION	181	VISION, PRAYER	60
ADORE			
BUT LEAVE BUT STILL ADORE	11	AIR BREATHE	8
ADORE MY WINDOWS FOR THEIR SUMMER SCENE?	112	NOT FATHER ME	8
ADORED			
THE ADORED	183	VISION, PRAYER	129
HAVE NOT ADORED MY BODY AS IT SOFTLY SMOOTHED THEIR			
SKIN.	223	IDYLL UNFORGET	16
ADORERS			
TO YOUNG ADORERS DYING ON A KISS.	81	ALL THAT I OWE	18
ADORNED			
ADAM OR EVE, THE ADORNED HOLY BULLOCK	174	FIRE RAID	34
ADORNERS			
ADORNERS OF THE CITY'S FOREHEAD, ...	70	SECRET WIND	9
ADORNING			
WITH DRY FLESH AND EARTH FOR ADORNING AND BED.	152	BELOW A TIME	43
ADVANCE			
I ADVANCE FOR AS LONG AS FOREVER IS.	143	24 YEARS	9
ADVENTURE			
ACQUAINTED WITH THE SALT ADVENTURE	69	BEFORE KNOCKED	33
SAIL ON THE LEVEL, THE DEPARTING ADVENTURE, ...	109	I, IN IMAGE	35
ADVICE			
ALL THINGS ARE KNOWN: THE STARS' ADVICE	56	WHY EAST WIND	16
LION OR LOUSE? TAKE YOUR OWN ADVICE;	58	TO ARCHITECTS	17
AEGEAN			
AND NO AEGEAN WIND COOL HER CRACKED HEART;	57	GREEK PLAY	10
AESOP			
I YOUNG AESOP FABLING TO THE NEAR NIGHT BY THE DINGLE	202	SIR JOHNS HILL	35
AFFECTIONATE			
THE AFFECTIONATE PICKPOCKET	155	RETURN	50
WHISPERED THE AFFECTIONATE SAND	162	LONG-LEGGED	9
AFFECTIONS			
MAKING OUR AFFECTIONS FAST;	230	OUR SANCTITY	18
AFLAME			
JUAN AFLAME AND SAVAGELY YOUNG KING LEAR, ...	157	INTO HER HEAD	11
AFLOAT			
IN THE THROAT, BURNING AND TURNING. ALL NIGHT AFLOAT	194	SLEEP BECALMED	2
AFRAID			
AFRAID, LETTING OUR SYLLABLES BE SOFT	31	BEING BUT MEN	2
I HAVE LONGED TO MOVE AWAY BUT AM AFRAID;	44	LONGED TO MOVE	11
AT THE POINT OF LOVE, FORSAKEN AND AFRAID.	188	WINTER'S TALE	30
AFTER			
TIME AFTER TIME.	22	ON QUIET NIGHT	11
STILL'S VAIN TO ARGUE AFTER DEATH;	27	OBLIVIOUS DARK	10
AND, AFTER THE SOFT ASCENT, ...	31	BEING BUT MEN	8
AND THAT IS TRUE AFTER PERPETUAL DEFEAT.	32	OUT OF SIGHS	9
AFTER SUCH FIGHTING AS THE WEAKEST KNOW, ...	32	OUT OF SIGHS	10
CONTENT SHALL COME AFTER A TWISTED NIGHT	35	LIFT UP FACE	25
AND THAT IS LIES THAT, AFTER THE OLD MEN DIE, ...	36	LET BE KNOWN	5
DECLARE THEIR SOULS, LET CHILDREN KNOW, LIVE AFTER.	36	LET BE KNOWN	6
PLAY PATIENCE IN THE PARLOUR AFTER DARK.	40	YOUNG ARE OLD	14
THE LIVING AFTER, THE FILLED WITH FEAR, ...	41	YOUNG ARE OLD	36
TO PURGE AFTER THE WITS' FIGHT, ...	42	A WAR OF WITS	6
NOT STUMPS, AFTER THE HOUR OF BATTLE, ...	42	A WAR OF WITS	9
PRAISE THAT ONLY THE WITS ARE HURT AFTER THE WITS'			
FIGHT.	42	A WAR OF WITS	11
AFTER THE PERILS OF FRIENDS' TALK	42	A WAR OF WITS	15
AFTER A VOLLEY OF QUESTIONS AND REPLIES	42	A WAR OF WITS	17
AND, AFTER IT HAS SUNK, THE SANE MOON, ...	42	A WAR OF WITS	21

	PAGE	TITLE	LINE
AFTER (CONTINUED)			
AND AFTER CAME THE IMPRINTS ON THE WATER, ...	94	IN BEGINNING	9
NOT FROM THIS ANGER, ANTICLIMAX AFTER	134	NOT FROM ANGER	1
NOT FROM THIS ANGER AFTER	134	NOT FROM ANGER	11
AFTER THE FUNERAL	136	AFTER FUNERAL	T
AFTER THE FUNERAL, MULE PRAISES, BRAYS, ...	136	AFTER FUNERAL	1
AFTER THE FEAST OF TEAR-STUFFED TIME AND THISTLES ..	136	AFTER FUNERAL	10
O WAKE TO SEE, AFTER A NOBLE FALL, ...	142	SAINT TO FALL	43
NIGHT AFTER NIGHT THEIR HANDS IMPLORE	143	THE MOLLS	3
BECAUSE THE PLEASURE-BIRD WHISTLES AFTER THE HOT			
WIRES, ...	144	PLEASURE-BIRD	1
THAT THE PHOENIX' BID FOR HEAVEN AND THE DESIRE AFTER	148	UNLUCKILY FOR	45
AFTER A WATER-FACE WALK, ...	150	WHEN I WOKE	18
BIRD AFTER DARK AND THE LAUGHING FISH	166	LONG-LEGGED	126
AFTER THE LOCKS AND CHAINS	172	THE HUNCHBACK	36
AFTER THE RAILINGS AND SHRUBBERIES	172	THE HUNCHBACK	38
CEREMONY AFTER A FIRE RAID	173	FIRE RAID	T
TO GLOW AFTER THE GOD STONING NIGHT	186	HOLY SPRING	11
HIM UP AND HE RAN LIKE A WIND AFTER THE KINDLING			
FLIGHT	190	WINTER'S TALE	89
AFTER THE FIRST DEATH, THERE IS NO OTHER.	192	REFUSAL MOURN	24
SO IT MUST HAVE BEEN AFTER THE BIRTH OF THE SIMPLE			
LIGHT	196	FERN HILL	33
YOUNG AS THEY IN THE AFTER MILKING MOONLIGHT LAY	204	GIANT'S THIGH	16
TEACH ME THE LOVE THAT IS EVERGREEN AFTER THE FALL			
LEAVED	205	GIANT'S THIGH	53
GRAVE, AFTER BELOVED ON THE GRASS GULFED CROSS IS			
SCRUBBED	205	GIANT'S THIGH	54
IT WAS THE MAGPIE, AFTER, ...	238	PILLAR BREAKS	17
AFTERNOON			
IN THE AFTERNOON WASTERS	154	RETURN	24
AFTER'S			
THOUGH, AFTER'S DONE, I	24	LITTLE PROBLEM	15
AGAIN			
SHE IS ON DANCING TOES AGAIN, ...	12	CABARET	18
BY WAVES WHICH GROW AGAIN	14	RAIN CUTS	33
THEY HARDEN AND TAKE SHAPE AGAIN	19	IMAGES IN AIR	11
INTO THE VOID AGAIN OF THIS BEWILDERMENT AND THAT			
INSANITY	21	BEWILDERED WAY	25
AND THEN AGAIN: THERE WAS A CHILD	22	ON QUIET NIGHT	15
THE SUICIDES PARADE AGAIN, NOW RIPE FOR DYING.	43	FACES SHONE	14
REVOLVES OVER AND OVER AGAIN	46	PLOUGHMAN GONE	28
THOUGH THEY SINK THROUGH THE SEA THEY SHALL RISE			
AGAIN;	49	NO DOMINION	7
SAID ALL THE USUAL THINGS OVER AND AGAIN;	52	OUT OF THE PIT	71
AND THEN RAISE UP THE SKELETON AGAIN, ...	55	NO MAN BELIEVE	20
THE SYLLABLES BE SAID AND SAID AGAIN:	80	ALMANAC TIME	14
I DREAMED MY GENESIS AND DIED AGAIN, SHRAPNEL	103	I DREAMED MY	13
OR LIKE THE TIDE-LOOPED BREASTKNOT REEFED AGAIN ...	131	I MAKE THIS IN	11
THE OLD MUD HATCH AGAIN, THE HORRID	142	SAINT TO FALL	44
AGAIN, A COLLECTED POET	155	RETURN	30
STREAMED AGAIN A WONDER OF SUMMER	178	POEM IN OCT	43
MILD. TURNED AGAIN, WORTHINGTON. NEVER WHISKY.	179	NEW QUAY	12
AND I MUST ENTER AGAIN THE ROUND	191	REFUSAL MOURN	7
THE SKY GATHERED AGAIN	196	FERN HILL	31
DAWS SIR JOHN'S JUST HILL DONS, AND AGAIN THE GULLED			
BIRDS HARE	201	SIR JOHNS HILL	15
WE GRIEVE AS THE BLITHE BIRDS, NEVER AGAIN, LEAVE			
SHINGLE AND ELM, ...	202	SIR JOHNS HILL	33
YOU SHALL BE TAKEN SWEETLY AGAIN	228	NOT DESPAIR	12

	PAGE	TITLE	LINE
AGAIN (CONTINUED)			
DOING MY LITTLE TRICKS OF SPEECH AGAIN	234	NO, PIGEON	20
BUILD, BUILD AGAIN!	238	PILLAR BREAKS	27
I'LL HAVE TO BREAK IN THOUGHT AGAIN, ...	239	MAKES INTERVALS	27
AGAINST			
BREATHE AGAINST AIR, ...	16	TIME TO ROT	4
WILL FIND SUCH LOVE AGAINST THE GRAIN, ...	16	TIME TO ROT	8
SET AGAINST GRANITE, ...	19	IMAGES IN AIR	3
NO USE TO RUN YOUR HEAD AGAINST THE WALL	27	OBLIVIOUS DARK	11
FIND HARD TO DART AGAINST A CLOUD, ...	37	WINDMILLS TURN	8
AGAINST THE RUSTY SWORD AND THE OLD HORSE	45	PLOUGHMAN GONE	8
'REBEL AGAINST THE BINDING MOON	61	MEAT ON BONES	9
REBEL AGAINST THE FLESH AND BONE, ...	61	MEAT ON BONES	14
REBEL AGAINST MY FATHER'S DREAM	61	MEAT ON BONES	27
UNDER THE CLOUD AGAINST LOVE IS CAUGHT AND HELD AND			
KISSED	147	UNLUCKILY FOR	17
AND LAID YOUR CHEEK AGAINST A CLOUD-FORMED SHELL:	153	WAS A SAVIOUR	23
AGAINST THE FRUIT MACHINE, ...	155	RETURN	34
A CLOUD AGAINST THE GLASSY SUN FLUTTERS HIS	179	NEW QUAY	5
RAGE, RAGE AGAINST THE DYING OF THE LIGHT.	207	NOT GO GENTLE	3
RAGE, RAGE AGAINST THE DYING OF THE LIGHT.	208	NOT GO GENTLE	9
RAGE, RAGE AGAINST THE DYING OF THE LIGHT.	208	NOT GO GENTLE	15
RAGE, RAGE AGAINST THE DYING OF THE LIGHT.	208	NOT GO GENTLE	19
AGAINST THIS SIDE.	229	MY RIVER	20
AND SHOWS THEM FAIR AGAINST THE DARK, ...	238	MAKES INTERVALS	3
AGAMEMNON			
OF AGAMEMNON AND HIS KINGLY BLOOD	56	GREEK PLAY	7
AGAPE			
AGAPE, WITH WOE	4	PROLOGUE	65
AGE			
AGE COME TO YOU--YOU'RE BRIGHT AND USELESS, ...	21	BEWILDERED WAY	4
AND YET, MAD WITH YOUNG BLOOD OR STAINED WITH AGE,	26	THERE'S PLENTY	16
YOUTH CALLS TO AGE	30	YOUTH CALLS	T
YOUTH CALLS TO AGE ACROSS THE TIRED YEARS:	30	YOUTH CALLS	13
'WHAT YOU HAVE FOUND,' AGE ANSWERS THROUGH HIS TEARS,	30	YOUTH CALLS	15
AGE SOURS BEFORE YOUTH'S TASTED IN THE MOUTH	40	YOUNG ARE OLD	2
I KNOW THAT AGE IS SNOW UPON THE HAIR, ...	64	WOMAN SPEAKS	49
IN HIS AGE THE LASS'S CLAY.	75	SONG: LOVE ME	3
DRIVES MY GREEN AGE; THAT BLASTS THE ROOTS OF TREES	77	THE FORCE THAT	2
THE TIME FOR BREAST AND THE GREEN APRON AGE	78	LOVE'S FEVER	4
THE CALENDAR OF AGE HANGS IN THE HEART, ...	80	ALMANAC TIME	6
BY YOUTH AND AGE, THE MORTAL STATE AND THOUGHT	80	ALMANAC TIME	9
WARMS YOUTH AND SEED AND BURNS THE SEEDS OF AGE;	82	LIGHT BREAKS	8
IN THIS OUR AGE THE GUNMAN AND HIS MOLL, ...	89	EUNUCH DREAMS	11
COMES, LIKE A SCISSORS STALKING, TAILOR AGE, ...	100	RUNNING GRAVE	6
(MY SHAPE OF AGE NAGGING THE WOUNDED WHISPER.)	118	ALTARWISE	46
THE MORNING IS FLYING ON THE WINGS OF HIS AGE	173	DAWN RAID	13
LEAVES IS DANCING. LINES OF AGE ON THE STONES WEAVE			
IN A FLOCK.	189	WINTER'S TALE	78
BACK. LINES OF AGE SLEEP ON THE STONES TILL			
TRUMPETING DAWN.	191	WINTER'S TALE	118
THE GRAINS BEYOND AGE, THE DARK VEINS OF HER MOTHER,	192	REFUSAL MOURN	21
OLD AGE SHOULD BURN AND RAVE AT CLOSE OF DAY;	207	NOT GO GENTLE	2
HIS DRIFTWOOD THIRTY-FIFTH WIND TURNED AGE;	208	POEM ON B'DAY	8
SUMMER IS HEAVY WITH AGE, AND LEANS UPON AUTUMN.	221	FOREST PICTURE	4
IN THE AGE OF LADY FRANKINCENSE	240	ADMIT THE SUN	13
AGED			
AMONG THOSE KILLED IN THE DAWN RAID WAS A MAN AGED A			
HUNDRED	172	DAWN RAID	T

	PAGE	TITLE	LINE
AGEING			
AGEING BOTH DAY AND NIGHT.	80	ALMANAC TIME	10
WAX CLOTHES THAT WAX UPON THE AGEING RIBS;	81	ALL THAT I OWE	26
AGELESS			
GREEK IN THE IRISH SEA THE AGELESS VOICE:	125	TODAY, INSECT	22
AGENT			
HAIRS OF YOUR HEAD, THEN SAID THE HOLLOW AGENT, ...	117	ALTARWISE	25
AGES			
IN THE TAKEN BODY AT MANY AGES, ...	158	INTO HER HEAD	40
ROUND THE GRIEFS OF THE AGES, ...	197	CRAFT OR ART	18
AGHAST			
WHO RAZED MY WOODEN FOLLY STANDS AGHAST, ...	113	NOT FATHER ME	22
AGLOW			
AND HONEY STEAL FROM FLOWERS AGLOW.	228	TRIOLET	6
AGO			
A GRIEF AGO	114	A GRIEF AGO	T
A GRIEF AGO, ...	114	A GRIEF AGO	1
IN THE LONG AGO LAND THAT GLIDED THE DARK DOOR WIDE	189	WINTER'S TALE	67
OF FIELDS. FOR LOVE, THE LONG AGO SHE BIRD RISES.			
LOOK.	189	WINTER'S TALE	80
IN THE FAR AGO LAND THE DOOR OF HIS DEATH GLIDED WIDE	190	WINTER'S TALE	105
TO LABOUR AND LOVE THOUGH THEY LAY DOWN LONG AGO.	203	GIANT'S THIGH	5
AGONIZED			
THE AGONIZED, TWO SEAS.	134	NOT FROM ANGER	7
AGONY			
BEFORE THE AGONY; THE SPIRIT GROWS, ...	31	OUT OF SIGHS	3
HE, TOO, HAS KNOWN THE AGONY IN THE GARDEN, ...	52	OUT OF THE PIT	54
THE STOCKED HEART IS FORCED, AND AGONY HAS ANOTHER			
MOUTH TO FEED.	142	SAINT TO FALL	42
AGROUND			
DAWN SHIPS CLOUTED AGROUND, ...	211	POEM ON B'DAY	79
AH			
AH, NIGHTINGALE, MY VOICE	234	NO, PIGEON	8
AHOY			
AHOY, OLD, SEA-LEGGED FOX, ...	5	PROLOGUE	98
AIM			
HIS AIM AND DESTINATION.	26	PERSONAL EPIT	18
IS THE AIM AND THE END.	31	BEING BUT MEN	16
AIR			
THE AIR YOU BREATHE	11	AIR BREATHE	T
THE AIR YOU BREATHE ENCROACHES	11	AIR BREATHE	1
BREATHE AGAINST AIR, ...	16	TIME TO ROT	4
CONCEIVE THESE IMAGES IN AIR	19	IMAGES IN AIR	T
CONCEIVE THESE IMAGES IN AIR, ...	19	IMAGES IN AIR	1
OF WATER, FLAME, OR AIR.	20	THE NEOPHYTE	17
SHUT IN THE MADHOUSE CALL FOR COOL AIR TO BREATHE.	26	THERE'S PLENTY	13
DRAMATIC GESTURES IN THE AIR.	34	IN GARDENS	13
FROM THERE ARE GHOSTS IN THE AIR	43	LONGED TO MOVE	8
AND, CRACKLING INTO THE AIR, LEAVE ME HALF-BLIND.	44	LONGED TO MOVE	14
OR CATCH ALL DEATH THAT'S IN THE AIR.	47	POET: 1935	46
DRUM HARSHLY ON THE AIR, THE LIGHTNING SWORDS	51	OUT OF THE PIT	15
RIDING ON GIRDERS OF THE AIR, LOOKS DOWN	52	OUT OF THE PIT	47
RADIO'S A BUILDING IN THE AIR;	58	TO ARCHITECTS	5
OR LAME THE AIR WITH LEAPING FROM ITS HEATS;	92	BOYS OF SUMMER	21
ONE BOUGH OF BONE ACROSS THE ROOTING AIR, ...	93	IN BEGINNING	3
THEN ALL THE MATTER OF THE LIVING AIR	102	FELLOWED SLEEP	21
THE HALVES THAT PIERCE THE PIN'S POINT IN THE AIR,	104	WORLD PYRAMID	26
THAT SHAPES EACH BUSHY ITEM OF THE AIR	123	FOSTER LIGHT	5
WE MAKE ME MYSTIC AS THE ARM OF AIR, ...	128	NOW, SAY NAY	34
CUDGEL GREAT AIR, WRECK EAST, AND TOPPLE SUNDOWN,	132	I MAKE THIS IN	33

		PAGE	TITLE	LINE
AIR (CONTINUED)				
AND THOUGH MY LOVE PULLS THE PALE, NIPPLED AIR,	...	133	I MAKE THIS IN	66
HEAVEN FELL WITH HIS FALL AND ONE CROCKED BELL BEAT THE LEFT AIR.	......	142	SAINT TO FALL	25
BEFORE I RUSH IN A CROUCH THE GHOST WITH A HAMMER, AIR,	......	145	IF HEAD HURT	9
YOU MY FRIEND THERE WITH A WINNING AIR	......	146	TO OTHERS	3
WHILE YOU DISPLACED A TRUTH IN THE AIR,	......	147	TO OTHERS	17
WORDS ON THE AIR AS THE FIRE CATCHES	......	149	PAPER & STICKS	17
A VOICE IN THE ERECTED AIR,	......	150	WHEN I WOKE	25
BODY AND AIR AND BUILDING;	......	156	RETURN	82
OPEN AS TO THE AIR TO THE NAKED SHADOW	......	159	INTO HER HEAD	63
LEADS THEM AS CHILDREN AND AS AIR	......	167	LONG-LEGGED	149
AND DOWN THE OTHER AIR AND THE BLUE ALTERED SKY	...	178	POEM IN OCT	42
THOUGH NO SOUND FLOWED DOWN THE HAND FOLDED AIR	...	188	WINTER'S TALE	40
FIELDS HIGH AS THE HOUSE, THE TUNES FROM THE CHIMNEYS, IT WAS AIR	......	195	FERN HILL	20
EARTH, AIR, WATER, FIRE, SINGING INTO THE WHITE ACT,		200	COUNTRY SLEEP	87
AND AIR SHAPED HEAVEN WHERE SOULS GROW WILD	......	210	POEM ON B'DAY	74
THAN OUR LAUGHTER AT THE AIR	......	230	OUR SANCTITY	13
AND GO INTO THE AIR,	......	231	OUR SANCTITY	34
STROKING THE AIR AND HOLDING LIGHT.	......	235	WOMAN TAPESTRY	30
AND THE ROOTS OF THE TREES CLIMBED THROUGH THE AIR		235	WOMAN TAPESTRY	31
OUT OF THE AIR IT STRIKES.	......	241	ADMIT THE SUN	22
AIR-DRAWN				
AN AIR-DRAWN WINDMILL ON A WOODEN HORSE,	......	124	TODAY, INSECT	20
AIRY				
I EYE THE RING OF EARTH, THE AIRY CIRCLE,	......	76	LASHED RINGS	2
THEIR AIRY LOVERS, NOR THE MERMAIDEN	......	76	SONG: LOVE ME	6
AND EARTH AND SKY WERE AS ONE AIRY HILL,	......	78	LOVE'S FEVER	8
AISLE				
TIME MARKS A BLACK AISLE KINDLE FROM THE BRAND OF ASHES,	......	130	SINNERS' BELL	4
AISLES				
PARADED UP THE AISLES AND IN THE CRYPT	......	51	OUT OF THE PIT	27
OF DAY, IN THE THISTLE AISLES, TILL THE WHITE OWL CROSSED	......	204	GIANT'S THIGH	32
ALBATROSS				
HACK OF THE COUGH, THE HANGING ALBATROSS,	......	107	GRIEF THIEF	10
ALBINO				
THE FLYING LOOSE, ALBINO EYED, WING SINGED,	......	41	YOUNG ARE OLD	38
ALCOVE				
ALCOVE OF WORDS OUT OF CICADA SHADE,	......	54	WE BY SEASAND	4
ALIGHT				
THAT SET ALIGHT THE WEATHERS FROM A SPARK,	......	94	IN BEGINNING	14
SOON SETS ALIGHT A LONG STICK FROM THE CRADLE;	....	117	ALTARWISE	20
ALIVE				
ALIVE WITHIN HIS CRANING THROAT--	......	14	FOR LEDA	7
TOO LONG, SKELETON, DEATH'S ALL ALIVE	......	29	LONG, SKELETON	4
THE REDHAIRED CANCER STILL ALIVE,	......	97	TWILIGHT LOCKS	20
ALONE ALIVE AMONG HIS MUTTON FOLD,	......	118	ALTARWISE	40
OVER THE SEA-GUT LOUDENING, SETS A ROCK ALIVE;	....	122	HOLD HARD	15
A GIRL ALIVE WITH HIS HOOKS THROUGH HER LIPS;	.....	162	LONG-LEGGED	22
AND TERRIBLY LEAD HIM HOME ALIVE	......	168	LONG-LEGGED	198
SANG ALIVE	......	178	POEM IN OCT	59
TO-NIGHT SHALL FIND NO DYING BUT ALIVE AND WARM	...	194	CONVERS PRAYER	15
ALL				
ALL SEASONS WITH THE SAME METICULOUS POWER,	......	17	IN OBLIVION	13
AND ALL MY THIN PREROGATIVE OF TASTE.	......	18	NATURAL DAY	18
BREATHING ON ALL SIDES PUNGENTLY	......	20	ENCOMPASSED	2

		PAGE	TITLE	LINE
ALL (CONTINUED)				
DEATH TO THE MAGICAL WHEN ALL IS DONE,	....	21	BEWILDERED WAY	3
IN TIME, LIKE ALL, THROUGH MY UNREASON	....	21	BEWILDERED WAY	7
WHERE ALL IS WELL,	....	21	BEWILDERED WAY	11
OF ALL THE MYSTERY THERE IS IN LIFE	....	22	ON QUIET NIGHT	3
AND ALL THE MASTERY THERE IS IN DEATH,	....	22	ON QUIET NIGHT	4
ALL LOVE AND SWEAT	....	26	PERSONAL EPIT	15
ALL HOLD THE SUM, NOTHING TO NOTHING,	....	27	OBLIVIOUS DARK	21
WAITING ALL VAINLY THIS WE KNOW.	....	28	NO WINGS	26
TOO LONG, SKELETON, DEATH'S ALL ALIVE	....	29	LONG, SKELETON	4
ALL THAT IS BEAUTIFUL BUT BORN TO DIE,	....	30	YOUTH CALLS	6
ALL HE HAS REAPED IN WONDER.	....	30	NEARLY SUMMER	18
ALL THAT IS NOT ALREADY BROKEN,	....	30	NEARLY SUMMER	22
ALL COULD NOT DISAPPOINT;	....	32	OUT OF SIGHS	6
THE HOLLOW WORDS COULD BEAR ALL SUFFERING	....	32	OUT OF SIGHS	22
FOR ALL THERE IS TO GIVE I OFFER:	....	32	OUT OF SIGHS	28
AND DROWN ALL SORROWS IN THE GROSS CATASTROPHE.	...	34	THIRST PARCHES	15
FOR ALL THE INCONVENIENCE THEY MAKE,	....	38	THE GOSSIPERS	14
CROSS ALL DIRECTIONS, BRACKEN POINTS TO THE SKIES,		44	TO FOLLOW FOX	9
ON THE CANVAS SKY, AND ALL HOT COLOURS MELT	....	46	POET: 1935	19
AMONG ALL LIVING MEN IS A SAD GHOST.	....	47	POET: 1935	24
OR CATCH ALL DEATH THAT'S IN THE AIR.	....	47	POET: 1935	46
WHO ON HIS CLOUD HEARS ALL MY WISHES,	....	48	LIGHT, I KNOW	15
ROLLED DOWN ALL IMAGES INTO THE PITS	....	50	OUT OF THE PIT	3
SPLIT ALL ENDS UP THEY SHAN'T CRACK;	....	50	NO DOMINION	17
ALL REASON BROKE, AND HORROR WALKED THE ROADS.	....	51	OUT OF THE PIT	18
SAID ALL THE USUAL THINGS OVER AND AGAIN;	....	52	OUT OF THE PIT	71
NOW HE IS ONE WITH MANY, ONE WITH ALL,	....	53	OUT OF THE PIT	98
OF ALL ORESTES' CONTINENT OF PRIDE	....	56	GREEK PLAY	5
THE CHILD SHALL QUESTION ALL HIS DAYS,	....	56	WHY EAST WIND	7
ALL THINGS ARE KNOWN: THE STARS' ADVICE	....	56	WHY EAST WIND	16
TELL, IF AT ALL, THE WINTER'S STORMS	....	58	HERE IN SPRING	10
PECKING AND NESTLING ALL THE TIME OF NIGHT.	....	63	WOMAN SPEAKS	18
ALL THAT WAS LOVED AND LOVED MADE THE FOWLS' FOOD,		64	WOMAN SPEAKS	31
THE SADDEST DUST IN ALL THIS HOLLOW WORLD.	....	64	WOMAN SPEAKS	41
WITH TONGUES THAT TALK ALL TONGUES.	....	66	GODS THUMP	14
BUT ALL THIS LAND GIVES OFF A CHARNEL STENCH,	.....	67	REALM OF FLESH	4
ALL THE CABINNED FAITHS DENY	....	71	TAKE NEEDLES	15
THREAD AND TORTURE ALL THE DAY;	....	72	TAKE NEEDLES	53
OUR CLAIM IS STAKED FOR ONCE AND ALL	....	73	WE MOTHERNAKED	5
WHERE ALL THE HIDDEN STONES ARE GOLD,	....	74	WE MOTHERNAKED	10
THAT UTTERS ALL LOVE HUNGER	....	75	MY HERO BARES	9
ALL WORLD WAS ONE, ONE WINDY NOTHING,	....	78	LOVE'S FEVER	6
ALL THAT I OWE THE FELLOWS OF THE GRAVE	....	80	ALL THAT I OWE	T
ALL THAT I OWE THE FELLOWS OF THE GRAVE	....	80	ALL THAT I OWE	1
AND ALL THE DEAD BEQUEATH FROM PALE ESTATES	....	80	ALL THAT I OWE	2
O ALL I OWE IS ALL THE FLESH INHERITS,	....	80	ALL THAT I OWE	5
O ALL I OWE IS ALL THE FLESH INHERITS,	....	80	ALL THAT I OWE	5
ALL SUCH DISEASE I DOCTOR IN MY BLOOD,	....	81	ALL THAT I OWE	19
AND ALL SUCH LOVE'S A SHRUB SOWN IN THE BREATH.	...	81	ALL THAT I OWE	20
ALL NIGHT AND DAY I EYE THE RAGGED GLOBE	....	81	ALL THAT I OWE	23
ALL NIGHT AND DAY I WANDER IN THESE SAME	....	81	ALL THAT I OWE	25
ALL NIGHT MY FORTUNE SLUMBERS IN ITS SHEET.	....	81	ALL THAT I OWE	27
ALL NIGHT MY FORTUNE SLUMBERS IN ITS SHEET.	....	81	ALL THAT I OWE	30
(ALL MODERN PAINTERS USE THEIR FEET	....	83	LETTER TO AUNT	20
(AND WHAT A PART) IN ALL GOOD ART.	....	84	LETTER TO AUNT	47
OUR EUNUCH DREAMS, ALL SEEDLESS IN THE LIGHT,	.....	89	EUNUCH DREAMS	1
THE SHADES OF GIRLS, ALL FLAVOURED FROM THEIR SHROUDS,	....	89	EUNUCH DREAMS	7
TILL ALL OUR SEA-FAITHS DIE.	....	91	WHERE ONCE THE	24

ALL

	PAGE	TITLE	LINE
ALL (CONTINUED)			
ABSTRACTED ALL THE LETTERS OF THE VOID;	94	IN BEGINNING	21
AND ALL THE HERRINGS SMELLING IN THE SEA, ...	95	RUB OF LOVE	33
AND ALL THE DRY SEABED UNLOCKED, ...	97	TWILIGHT LOCKS	8
ALL ISSUE ARMOURED, OF THE GRAVE, ...	97	TWILIGHT LOCKS	19
ALL BUT THE BRISKEST RIDERS THROWN, ...	98	TWILIGHT LOCKS	41
THE SIGNAL GRASS THAT TELLS ME ALL I KNOW	99	OCTOBER WIND	22
ALL, MEN MY MADMEN, THE UNWHOLESOME WIND	101	RUNNING GRAVE	46
THROUGH ALL THE IRONS IN THE GRASS, METAL	102	I DREAMED MY	7
THEN ALL THE MATTER OF THE LIVING AIR	102	FELLOWED SLEEP	21
ALL ALL AND ALL THE DRY WORLDS LEVER	106	ALL ALL AND	T
ALL ALL AND ALL THE DRY WORLDS LEVER	106	ALL ALL AND	T
ALL ALL AND ALL THE DRY WORLDS LEVER	106	ALL ALL AND	T
ALL ALL AND ALL THE DRY WORLDS LEVER, ...	106	ALL ALL AND	1
ALL ALL AND ALL THE DRY WORLDS LEVER, ...	106	ALL ALL AND	1
ALL ALL AND ALL THE DRY WORLDS LEVER, ...	106	ALL ALL AND	1
ALL FROM THE OIL, THE POUND OF LAVA.	106	ALL ALL AND	3
ALL ALL AND ALL, THE CORPSE'S LOVER, ...	106	ALL ALL AND	10
ALL ALL AND ALL, THE CORPSE'S LOVER, ...	106	ALL ALL AND	10
ALL ALL AND ALL, THE CORPSE'S LOVER, ...	106	ALL ALL AND	10
ALL OF THE FLESH, THE DRY WORLDS LEVER.	106	ALL ALL AND	12
ALL ALL AND ALL THE DRY WORLDS COUPLE, ...	107	ALL ALL AND	25
ALL ALL AND ALL THE DRY WORLDS COUPLE, ...	107	ALL ALL AND	25
ALL ALL AND ALL THE DRY WORLDS COUPLE, ...	107	ALL ALL AND	25
ALL THAT SHAPES FROM THE CAUL AND SUCKLE, ...	107	ALL ALL AND	28
FLOWER, FLOWER, ALL ALL AND ALL.	107	ALL ALL AND	36
FLOWER, FLOWER, ALL ALL AND ALL.	107	ALL ALL AND	36
FLOWER, FLOWER, ALL ALL AND ALL.	107	ALL ALL AND	36
ALL SHALL REMAIN AND ON THE GRAVEWARD GULF	108	GRIEF THIEF	27
AM I NOT ALL OF YOU BY THE DIRECTED SEA	112	NOT FATHER ME	13
YOU ARE ALL THESE, SAID SHE WHO GAVE ME THE LONG			
SUCK, ...	112	NOT FATHER ME	17
ALL THESE, HE SAID WHO SACKED THE CHILDREN'S TOWN,	112	NOT FATHER ME	18
UNSHELVE THAT ALL MY GRISTLES HAVE A GOWN	113	SERVANT SUN	6
LIE ALL UNKNOWING OF THE GRAVE SIN-EATER.	113	NOT FATHER ME	32
ALL NERVES TO SERVE THE SUN, ...	114	SERVANT SUN	15
AND ALL SWEET HELL, DEAF AS AN HOUR'S EAR, ...	114	SERVANT SUN	33
SHAPE ALL HER WHELPS WITH THE LONG VOICE OF WATER,	115	A GRIEF AGO	29
DEATH IS ALL METAPHORS, SHAPE IN ONE HISTORY;	117	ALTARWISE	15
A BIBLE-LEAVED OF ALL THE WRITTEN WOODS	119	ALTARWISE	86
I BY THE TREE OF THIEVES, ALL GLORY'S SAWBONES, ...	120	ALTARWISE	109
ALL HEAVEN IN A MIDNIGHT OF THE SUN, ...	122	INCARNATE DEVL	17
AND FATHER ALL NOR FAIL THE FLY-LORD'S ACRE, ...	123	FOSTER LIGHT	13
FROM ALL MY MORTAL LOVERS WITH A STARBOARD SMILE;	123	FOSTER LIGHT	21
ALL LEGENDS' SWEETHEARTS ON A TREE OF STORIES, ...	125	TODAY, INSECT	25
KNEW ALL HIS HORRIBLE DESIRES	128	MY NEOPHYTE	10
AND ALL LOVE'S SINNERS IN SWEET CLOTH KNEEL TO A			
HYLEG IMAGE, ...	130	SINNERS' BELL	28
BUT I, ANN'S BARD ON A RAISED HEARTH, CALL ALL	136	AFTER FUNERAL	21
WHEN ALL MY FIVE AND COUNTRY SENSES SEE	138	FIVE & COUNTRY	T
WHEN ALL MY FIVE AND COUNTRY SENSES SEE, ...	138	FIVE & COUNTRY	1
IN ALL LOVE'S COUNTRIES, THAT WILL GROPE AWAKE; ...	139	FIVE & COUNTRY	12
TO TAKE TO GIVE IS ALL, RETURN WHAT IS HUNGRILY GIVEN	140	NO WORK WORDS	4
THAT WILL RAKE AT LAST ALL CURRENCIES OF THE MARKED			
BREATH	140	NO WORK WORDS	8
CUT CHRISTBREAD SPITTING VINEGAR AND ALL	141	SAINT TO FALL	16
WILDE WORDS, ALL BUTTERED, BADLY BRED, ...	143	THE MOLLS	10
THAT ALL THE CHARMINGLY DROWNED ARISE TO COCKCROW			
AND KILL.	144	COLOUR OF SAY	6
'ALL GAME PHRASES FIT YOUR RING OF A COCKFIGHT: ...	145	IF HEAD HURT	6

	PAGE	TITLE	LINE
ALL (CONTINUED)			
NOR WHEN ALL PONDEROUS HEAVEN'S HOST OF WATERS BREAKS.	146	IF HEAD HURT	20
ALL LOVE BUT FOR THE FULL ASSEMBLAGE IN FLOWER	148	UNLUCKILY FOR	40
ALL I COULD SEE WERE HIS BROWN EYES BURNING	149	PAPER & STICKS	8
UNCLENCHED, ARMLESS, SILK AND ROUGH LOVE THAT BREAKS ALL ROCKS.	154	WAS A SAVIOUR	40
THE SPONGEBAG LET THEM ALL MELT.	155	RETURN	36
ALL THE HYPNOTISED CITY'S	156	RETURN	62
BURY ALL RUBBISH AND LOVE SIGNS	156	RETURN	90
JEALOUSY CANNOT FORGET FOR ALL HER SAKES,	158	INTO HER HEAD	34
ALL BLOOD-SIGNED ASSAILINGS AND VANISHED MARRIAGES IN WHICH HE HAD NO LOVELY PART	158	INTO HER HEAD	43
ALL THE FISHES WERE RAYED IN BLOOD,	162	LONG-LEGGED	23
OH ALL THE WANTING FLESH HIS ENEMY	165	LONG-LEGGED	91
AND ALL THE LIFTED WATERS WALK AND LEAP.	165	LONG-LEGGED	112
ALL THE HORSES OF HIS HAUL OF MIRACLES	168	LONG-LEGGED	187
HER HEART ALL EARS AND EYES, LIPS CATCHING THE AVALANCHE	170	MARRIAGE VIRG	10
WHEN ALL THE KEYS SHOT FROM THE LOCKS, AND RANG.	172	DAWN RAID	8
MADE ALL DAY UNTIL BELL TIME	172	THE HUNCHBACK	31
ALL NIGHT IN THE UNMADE PARK	172	THE HUNCHBACK	37
AND WALKED ABROAD IN A SHOWER OF ALL MY DAYS.	177	POEM IN OCT	16
BUT ALL THE GARDENS	177	POEM IN OCT	35
ALL MEN	183	VISION, PRAYER	128
TO KNOW ALL	184	VISION, PRAYER	159
PRAISE THAT THE SPRING TIME IS ALL	186	HOLY SPRING	14
AND ALL THE WOKEN FARM AT ITS WHITE TRADES,	187	WINTER'S TALE	25
BY LOSING HIM ALL IN LOVE, AND CAST HIS NEED	188	WINTER'S TALE	52
AND ALL THE ELEMENTS OF THE SNOW FALL REJOICED	189	WINTER'S TALE	84
ALL NIGHT LOST AND LONG WADING IN THE WAKE OF THE SHE-	190	WINTER'S TALE	98
FATHERING AND ALL HUMBLING DARKNESS	191	REFUSAL MOURN	3
THAT ALL IS UNDONE,	192	SIDE OF TRUTH	5
AND THE SOULS OF ALL MEN	193	SIDE OF TRUTH	19
AND ALL YOUR DEEDS AND WORDS,	193	SIDE OF TRUTH	34
IN THE THROAT, BURNING AND TURNING. ALL NIGHT AFLOAT	194	SLEEP BECALMED	2
THE VOICES OF ALL THE DROWNED SWAM ON THE WIND.	194	SLEEP BECALMED	8
ALL THE SUN LONG IT WAS RUNNING, IT WAS LOVELY, THE HAY	195	FERN HILL	19
ALL THE MOON LONG I HEARD, BLESSED AMONG STABLES, THE NIGHTJARS	195	FERN HILL	25
WITH THE DEW, COME BACK, THE COCK ON HIS SHOULDER: IT WAS ALL	195	FERN HILL	29
IN ALL HIS TUNEFUL TURNING SO FEW AND SUCH MORNING SONGS	196	FERN HILL	43
WITH ALL THEIR GRIEFS IN THEIR ARMS,	197	CRAFT OR ART	5
FOR EVER OF ALL NOT THE WOLF IN HIS BAAING HOOD	198	COUNTRY SLEEP	36
LEAPING! THE GOSPEL ROOKS! ALL TELL, THIS NIGHT, OF HIM	200	COUNTRY SLEEP	80
EVER AND EVER BY ALL YOUR VOWS BELIEVE AND FEAR	201	COUNTRY SLEEP	107
ALL PRAISE OF THE HAWK ON FIRE IN HAWK-EYED DUSK BE SUNG,	202	SIR JOHNS HILL	27
HILL. WHO ONCE IN GOOSESKIN WINTER LOVED ALL ICE LEAVED	203	GIANT'S THIGH	12
MAKES ALL THE MUSIC; AND I WHO HEAR THE TUNE OF THE SLOW,	203	SIR JOHNS HILL	57
ALL BIRDS AND BEASTS OF THE LINKED NIGHT UPROAR AND CHIME	204	GIANT'S THIGH	35
ALL THE GREEN LEAVED LITTLE WEDDINGS' WIVES	206	LAMENT	11

	PAGE	TITLE	LINE
ALL (CONTINUED)			
I WHISTLED ALL NIGHT IN THE TWISTED FLUES, ...	206	LAMENT	18
AND ALL THE DEADLY VIRTUES PLAGUE MY DEATH!	207	LAMENT	60
WITH ALL THE LIVING, PRAYS, ...	210	POEM ON B'DAY	66
HUMBLE IN ALL HIS PLANETS, ...	215	COUNTRY HEAVEN	4
OR STILL ALL THE NUMBERLESS DAYS OF HIS DEATH, THOUGH	216	ELEGY	8
ABOVE ALL HE LONGED FOR HIS MOTHER'S BREAST	216	ELEGY	9
ALL HIS BONES CRYING, AND POOR IN ALL BUT PAIN, ...	217	ELEGY	21
ALL HIS BONES CRYING, AND POOR IN ALL BUT PAIN, ...	217	ELEGY	21
O DEEPEST WOUND OF ALL THAT HE SHOULD DIE	217	ELEGY	37
YET IN SPITE OF ALL THIS, I HAVE MOMENTS OF BLISS,	221	SONG OF DOG	9
ALL THE LAND IS RIPE. THERE IS NO MOTION	222	FOREST PICTURE	5
ALL THINGS REST IN THE WILL OF PURPOSE TRIUMPHANT.	222	FOREST PICTURE	8
AND COVERING ALL HAS BEEN A QUIETUDE, AND A SINGING			
FROM FLAKE-BARE THROATS.	224	IDYLL UNFORGET	35
GREEN-SHADOWED PANOPLY ENVELOPING ALL ITS			
STRANGENESS AND SOFTNESS OF STEALTH.	224	IDYLL UNFORGET	45
FOR ALL THINGS ARE LEAF-LIKE	225	OF ANY FLOWER	2
AND ALL MY GRIEF FLOWS FROM THE RIFT	225	CLOWN IN MOON	3
FOR ALL THINGS ARE GRIEF-LIKE	225	OF ANY FLOWER	5
THEY ARE ALL GODDESSES;	226	THE ELM	1
I'M ALL FOR GROUND, ...	234	NO, PIGEON	17
WITH ALL MY USUAL CARE.	234	NO, PIGEON	21
TO-DAY, IF ALL MY SENSES ACT, ...	238	MAKES INTERVALS	9
ALL-HOLLOWED			
ALL-HOLLOWED MAN WEPT FOR HIS WHITE APPAREL.	111	I, IN IMAGE	102
ALL-IN			
OR ALL-IN WRESTLING FOR TORN LIMBS TO HEAL, ...	51	OUT OF THE PIT	31
ALLOTMENT			
BEFORE THE ALLOTMENT IS WEEDED AND SOWN, ...	38	GAS FADES	5
ALLOTMENTS			
ABOVE THE WASTE ALLOTMENTS THE DAWN HALTS.	82	LIGHT BREAKS	30
ALLOWS			
THE LAW ALLOWS	29	NEARLY SUMMER	9
AND NOTHING I CARED, AT MY SKY BLUE TRADES, THAT			
TIME ALLOWS	196	FERN HILL	42
ALMANAC			
THE ALMANAC OF TIME	79	ALMANAC TIME	T
THE ALMANAC OF TIME HANGS IN THE BRAIN;	79	ALMANAC TIME	1
ALMOST			
ON ALMOST THE INCENDIARY EVE	160	DEATHS AND ENT	1
ON ALMOST THE INCENDIARY EVE	160	DEATHS AND ENT	13
ON ALMOST THE INCENDIARY EVE	160	DEATHS AND ENT	25
ALONE			
WE WILL RIDE OUT ALONE, AND THEN, ...	5	PROLOGUE	91
IT IS GOOD TO STEP ONTO THE EARTH, ALONE, ...	43	A WAR OF WITS	24
HE ALONE IS FREE, AND, FREE, MOANS TO THE SKY.	46	POET: 1935	13
I AM ALONE, ALONE COMPLAIN TO THE STARS.	48	POET: 1935	62
I AM ALONE, ALONE COMPLAIN TO THE STARS.	48	POET: 1935	62
VERY ALONE, HE PLOUGHED THE ONLY WAY.	53	OUT OF THE PIT	86
PITY THE LIVING WHO ARE LOST, ALONE;	57	GREEK PLAY	21
ALONE TILL THE DAY I DIE	62	EARS IN TURRET	6
HEIR TO THE TELLING SENSES THAT ALONE	80	ALL THAT I OWE	11
ALONE ALIVE AMONG HIS MUTTON FOLD, ...	118	ALTARWISE	40
AND, PRIDE IS LAST, IS LIKE A CHILD ALONE	131	I MAKE THIS IN	13
I STAND, FOR THIS MEMORIAL'S SAKE, ALONE	136	AFTER FUNERAL	12
AN ENAMOURED MAN ALONE BY THE TWIGS OF HIS EYES, TWO			
FIRES, ...	144	PLEASURE-BIRD	7
NOW SEE, ALONE IN US, ...	153	WAS A SAVIOUR	36
ALONE WITH MY BOUNCING BAG, ...	155	RETURN	45

	PAGE	TITLE	LINE
ALONE (CONTINUED)			
OCEANIC LOVER ALONE	158	INTO HER HEAD	33
O SHE LIES ALONE AND STILL,	159	INTO HER HEAD	64
HE STANDS ALONE AT THE DOOR OF HIS HOME,	169	LONG-LEGGED	215
WAKING ALONE IN A MULTITUDE OF LOVES WHEN MORNING'S LIGHT	170	MARRIAGE VIRG	1
HER DEEPSEA PILLOW WHERE ONCE SHE MARRIED ALONE,	170	MARRIAGE VIRG	9
ALONE BETWEEN NURSES AND SWANS	171	THE HUNCHBACK	26
FOR ME ALONE BUT ONLY A ROCKED DRUM	175	MY BEGGAR ARM	3
BUT DARK ALONE	180	VISION, PRAYER	14
THAT UNCALM STILL IT IS SURE ALONE TO STAND AND SING	186	HOLY SPRING	21
ALONE IN THE HUSK OF MAN'S HOME	186	HOLY SPRING	22
TORN AND ALONE IN A FARM HOUSE IN A FOLD	187	WINTER'S TALE	15
AND THE DUCK POND GLASS AND THE BLINDING BYRES ALONE	188	WINTER'S TALE	35
ALONE AND NAKED IN THE ENGULFING BRIDE,	188	WINTER'S TALE	53
THAT A MAN KNELT ALONE IN THE CUP OF THE VALES,	189	WINTER'S TALE	85
AND ALONE IN THE NIGHT'S ETERNAL, CURVING ACT	203	GIANT'S THIGH	9
HE, ON THE EARTH OF THE NIGHT, ALONE	210	POEM ON B'DAY	65
AND MY SHINING MEN NO MORE ALONE	211	POEM ON B'DAY	107
ALONE'S			
ALONE'S UNHURT, SO THE BLIND MAN SEES BEST.	40	WAS THERE TIME	9
ALONG			
COURSING ALONG THE CHANNELS	17	IN OBLIVION	10
THAT CRIES ALONG HER VEINS. NO SUN OR MOON	56	GREEK PLAY	8
HERE IN THIS SPRING, STARS FLOAT ALONG THE VOID;	58	HERE IN SPRING	1
MY HERO BARES HIS NERVES ALONG MY WRIST	75	MY HERO BARES	1
LIKE SENNA STIRS ALONG THE RAVAGED ROOTS.	80	ALL THAT I OWE	4
THE KNOBBLY APE THAT SWINGS ALONG HIS SEX	96	RUB OF LOVE	37
SO, PLANING-HEELED, I FLEW ALONG MY MAN	101	FELLOWED SLEEP	4
THAT BURNS ALONG MY EYES.	134	NOT FROM ANGER	14
ALONG HER INNOCENCE GLIDED	157	INTO HER HEAD	10
ALONG THE BORDERS OF THE GARDEN-WALKS.	223	IN DREAMS	12
ALOUD			
CRYING ALOUD IN PAIN,	18	NATURAL DAY	32
CRIES NOT ALOUD BLIND AS A BAT,	54	NO MAN BELIEVE	2
CURLEWS ALOUD IN THE CONGERED WAVES	209	POEM ON B'DAY	13
COUNT MY BLESSINGS ALOUD:	211	POEM ON B'DAY	81
ALPHABET			
STRIP TO THIS TREE: A ROCKING ALPHABET,	119	ALTARWISE	87
ALPS			
WHALES IN THE WAKE LIKE CAPES AND ALPS	163	LONG-LEGGED	49
ALREADY			
ALL THAT IS NOT ALREADY BROKEN,	30	NEARLY SUMMER	22
CRUNCHING THE ALREADY BROKEN,	45	TO FOLLOW FOX	21
THAT THE EYES ARE ALREADY MURDERED,	142	SAINT TO FALL	41
GROWING THEIR WOUNDS ALREADY,	154	RETURN	13
ALSO			
GLORY ALSO THIS STAR, BIRD	4	PROLOGUE	40
RAPE GULP AND BE MARRY, HE ALSO SERVES	138	O CHATTERTON	26
ALTAR			
YOU WHO BOW DOWN AT CROSS AND ALTAR,	69	BEFORE KNOCKED	43
GRIEF WITH DISHEVELLED HANDS TEAR OUT THE ALTAR GHOST	130	SINNERS' BELL	5
ON THE ALTAR OF LONDON,	174	FIRE RAID	38
ALTARWISE			
ALTARWISE BY OWL-LIGHT	116	ALTARWISE	T
ALTARWISE BY OWL-LIGHT IN THE HALF-WAY HOUSE	116	ALTARWISE	1
ALTER			
AND, WHEN IT QUICKENS, ALTER THE ACTIONS' PACE	116	LANTERNS SHINE	12
ALTERED			
OF NEOPHYTES TAKE ALTERED ROADS.	37	WINDMILLS TURN	33

	PAGE	TITLE	LINE
ALTERED (CONTINUED)			
AND DOWN THE OTHER AIR AND THE BLUE ALTERED SKY ...	178	POEM IN OCT	42
ALTHOUGH			
ALTHOUGH THROUGH MY BEWILDERED WAY	21	BEWILDERED WAY	T
ALTHOUGH THROUGH MY BEWILDERED WAY	21	BEWILDERED WAY	1
ALTHOUGH IT IS SO STRAIGHT AND UNBENDING;	231	YOUR VOICE	5
ALTHOUGH YOUR ANGER IS NOT A SLIGHT THING, ...	232	YOUR VOICE	13
ALTHOUGH YOUR CAGE IS STRONG.	239	LET ME ESCAPE	8
ALWAYS			
AND THERE IS ALWAYS DAY, THE SHINING OF SOME SUN,	49	LIGHT, I KNOW	18
HER HOLY UNHOLY HOURS WITH THE ALWAYS ANONYMOUS			
BEAST.	158	INTO HER HEAD	46
AND ALWAYS KNOWN MUST LEAVE	160	DEATHS AND ENT	4
ALWAYS GOOD-BYE TO THE LONG-LEGGED BREAD	165	LONG-LEGGED	94
ALWAYS GOOD-BYE TO THE FIRES OF THE FACE, ...	165	LONG-LEGGED	98
IS ALWAYS LOST IN HER VAULTED BREATH, ...	165	LONG-LEGGED	116
ALWAYS GOOD-BYE, CRIED THE VOICES THROUGH THE SHELL,	166	LONG-LEGGED	121
GOOD-BYE ALWAYS FOR THE FLESH IS CAST	166	LONG-LEGGED	122
ALWAYS GOOD LUCK, PRAISED THE FINNED IN THE FEATHER	166	LONG-LEGGED	125
THE SKY STRIDE OF THE ALWAYS SLAIN	182	VISION, PRAYER	94
IN THE ALWAYS DESIRING CENTRE OF THE WHITE	188	WINTER'S TALE	48
IN THE MOON THAT IS ALWAYS RISING, ...	196	FERN HILL	48
NOR WILL BE EVER IS ALWAYS TRUE, ...	210	POEM ON B'DAY	51
ALWAYS WHEN HE, IN COUNTRY HEAVEN, ...	215	COUNTRY HEAVEN	1
AM (31)			
AMBASSADOR			
I SENT MY OWN AMBASSADOR TO LIGHT;	98	TWILIGHT LOCKS	33
AMBITION			
NOT FOR AMBITION OR BREAD	197	CRAFT OR ART	7
AMBULANCE			
THE HEAVENLY AMBULANCE DRAWN BY A WOUND	172	DAWN RAID	10
AMBUSH			
DESERVES NO BRUSH, BUT A FOOL'S AMBUSH.	44	TO FOLLOW FOX	6
TOILS TOWARDS THE AMBUSH OF HIS WOUNDS;	209	POEM ON B'DAY	17
AMEN			
AND THE KNOWN DARK OF THE EARTH AMEN.	185	VISION, PRAYER	187
AMID			
SOMEHOW IT SEEMS, AMID THE EVENING HAZE, ...	223	IN DREAMS	8
AMONG			
NOBLE AMONG A CROWD OF LIGHTS.	21	BEWILDERED WAY	12
LEAVES IT AMONG THE CIGARETTE ENDS AND THE GLASSES.	30	NEARLY SUMMER	23
MOVES, AMONG MEN CAUGHT BY THE SUN, ...	46	POET: 1935	11
EVEN AMONG HIS OWN KIN IS HE LOST, ...	47	POET: 1935	22
AMONG ALL LIVING MEN IS A SAD GHOST.	47	POET: 1935	24
LEPER AMONG A CLEAN PEOPLE	47	POET: 1935	26
O LONELY AMONG MANY, THE GODS' MAN, ...	47	POET: 1935	47
WHERE, WHAT'S MY GOD AMONG THIS CRAZY RATTLING	51	OUT OF THE PIT	33
WHERE, WHAT'S MY GOD AMONG THIS TAXI STEPPING, ...	52	OUT OF THE PIT	49
STILL, IN HIS HUT, HE BROODS AMONG HIS BIRDS.	53	OUT OF THE PIT	101
A WOMAN WAILS HER DEAD AMONG THE TREES, ...	56	GREEK PLAY	1
AMONG THE TREES THE LANGUAGE OF THE DEAD	57	GREEK PLAY	13
AMONG THE GARDEN TREES A PIGEON CALLS, ...	57	GREEK PLAY	29
HALT AMONG EUNUCHS, AND THE NITRIC STAIN	100	RUNNING GRAVE	24
LIMP IN THE STREET OF SEA, AMONG THE RABBLE	104	WORLD PYRAMID	15
AND, FROM HIS FORK, A DOG AMONG THE FAIRIES, ...	117	ALTARWISE	4
ALONE ALIVE AMONG HIS MUTTON FOLD, ...	118	ALTARWISE	40
WHAT OF A BAMBOO MAN AMONG YOUR ACRES?	118	ALTARWISE	49
NAKED AMONG THE BOW-AND-ARROW BIRDS	123	FOSTER LIGHT	23
AMONG MEN LATER I HEARD IT SAID	139	TOMBSTONE TOLD	16
LAPPED AMONG HERODS WAIL	142	SAINT TO FALL	39

	PAGE	TITLE	LINE
AMONG (CONTINUED)			
OR A NACREOUS SLEEP AMONG SOFT PARTICLES AND CHARMS	146	IF HEAD HURT	17
SAINT CARVED AND SENSUAL AMONG THE SCUDDING	147	UNLUCKILY FOR	5
TIME AMONG WALKING PINTABLES	154	RETURN	10
AMONG THE HARDLY POSSESSED.	156	RETURN	65
CAUGHT AMONG NEVER ENOUGH	156	RETURN	67
THE WASTEFUL HUSHES AMONG TREES.	157	RETURN	99
SHE LONGS AMONG HORSES AND ANGELS, ...	163	LONG-LEGGED	33
WEEPS LIKE THE RISEN SUN AMONG	167	LONG-LEGGED	163
AND THE BAIT IS DROWNED AMONG HAYRICKS, ...	169	LONG-LEGGED	208
WHILE THE BOYS AMONG WILLOWS	171	THE HUNCHBACK	27
AMONG THOSE KILLED IN THE DAWN RAID WAS A MAN AGED A HUNDRED	172	DAWN RAID	T
AMONG THE STREET BURNED TO TIRELESS DEATH	173	FIRE RAID	4
AND BUTTON UP. HE MINCES AMONG KNICKERS, ...	179	NEW QUAY	23
HE SNUGGLES DEEP AMONG THE CHAPEL THIGHS, ...	179	NEW QUAY	30
WARNING AMONG THE FOLDS, AND THE FROZEN HOLD	187	WINTER'S TALE	8
WHEN COLD AS SNOW HE SHOULD RUN THE WENDED VALES AMONG	188	WINTER'S TALE	45
AND HONOURED AMONG WAGONS I WAS PRINCE OF THE APPLE TOWNS	195	FERN HILL	6
AND AS I WAS GREEN AND CAREFREE, FAMOUS AMONG THE BARNS	195	FERN HILL	10
ALL THE MOON LONG I HEARD, BLESSED AMONG STABLES, THE NIGHTJARS	195	FERN HILL	25
AND HONOURED AMONG FOXES AND PHEASANTS BY THE GAY HOUSE	196	FERN HILL	37
AND STAVED, AND RIVEN AMONG PLUMES MY RIDER WEEP.	198	COUNTRY SLEEP	16
OF BIRDS! AMONG THE COCKS LIKE FIRE THE RED FOX ...	199	COUNTRY SLEEP	69
OF PSALMS AND SHADOWS AMONG THE PINCERED SANDCRABS PRANCING	202	SIR JOHNS HILL	24
IN HIS HOUSE ON STILTS HIGH AMONG BEAKS	208	POEM ON B'DAY	4
YOUNG AMONG THE LONG FLOCKS, AND NEVER LIE LOST ...	216	ELEGY	7
PROWLS FLAMING AMONG THE COCKERELS	216	COUNTRY HEAVEN	28
HERE AMONG THE LIGHT OF THE LORDING SKY	217	ELEGY	29
AMONG THE QUIET TREES. AND HAND IN HAND	227	SPRING-SPIRIT	11
WE STRANGELY SANG AMONG THE FEATHERY FLOWERS.	227	SPRING-SPIRIT	12
AMORIST			
AND WHO SHALL TELL THE AMORIST	17	IN OBLIVION	27
RAPES, LEAVES FOR LOST (THE AMORIST!), ...	30	NEARLY SUMMER	16
AMPLIFY			
LUST BEARS LIKE VOLTS, WHO'LL AMPLIFY, AND STRANGE	159	TO LEDA	8
AN (58)			
ANACHRONISTIC			
IN THIS ANACHRONISTIC SCENE	156	RETURN	92
ANAL			
A CRUDE, UNHAPPY, ANAL CRAMP.	143	THE MOLLS	8
ANATOMIST			
COMES LOVE'S ANATOMIST WITH SUN-GLOVED HAND	132	I MAKE THIS IN	44
ANATOMY			
DON'T HURT THE CHIC ANATOMY	18	NATURAL DAY	9
ANCESTRALLY			
OR RENT ANCESTRALLY THE ROPED SEA-HYMEN, ...	131	I MAKE THIS IN	12
ANCHOR			
SHIPS ANCHOR OFF THE BAY.	62	EARS IN TURRET	20
SHIPS ANCHOR OFF THE BAY, ...	62	EARS IN TURRET	27
THE DEADROCK BASE THE BLOW THE FLOWERED ANCHOR, ...	127	NOW, SAY NAY	5
BOAT WITH ITS ANCHOR FREE AND FAST	162	LONG-LEGGED	6
WHERE THE ANCHOR RODE LIKE A GULL	163	LONG-LEGGED	37
THE ANCHOR DIVES THROUGH THE FLOORS OF A CHURCH.	169	LONG-LEGGED	212

	PAGE	TITLE	LINE
ANCHORED			
BE BY THE SHIPS' SEA BROKEN AT THE MANSTRING ANCHORED	111	I, IN IMAGE	86
HARBOURS MY ANCHORED TONGUE, SLIPS THE QUAYSTONE,	131	I MAKE THIS IN	3
ANCHORGROUND			
IN THAT BRIGHT ANCHORGROUND WHERE I LAY LINENED,	132	I MAKE THIS IN	48
ANCIENT			
OVER THE ANCIENT WINTER,	17	IN OBLIVION	4
NEITHER BY NIGHT'S ANCIENT FEAR,	44	LONGED TO MOVE	15
TO HERMITS' HUTS, AND TALKED TO ANCIENT MEN.	53	OUT OF THE PIT	91
THE MUMMY CLOTHS EXPOSE AN ANCIENT BREAST.	116	LANTERNS SHINE	8
HOLD HARD, THESE ANCIENT MINUTES IN THE CUCKOO'S MONTH	122	HOLD HARD	T
HOLD HARD, THESE ANCIENT MINUTES IN THE CUCKOO'S MONTH,	122	HOLD HARD	1
EACH ANCIENT, STONE-NECKED MINUTE OF LOVE'S SEASON	131	I MAKE THIS IN	2
ANCIENT WOODS OF MY BLOOD, DASH DOWN TO THE NUT OF THE SEAS	140	NO WORK WORDS	11
THE WOUNDWARD FLIGHT OF THE ANCIENT	182	VISION, PRAYER	92
AND (1955)			
ANDROGYNOUS			
IN THE ANDROGYNOUS DARK,	148	UNLUCKILY FOR	30
ANEMONE			
SING AND HOWL THROUGH SAND AND ANEMONE	165	LONG-LEGGED	89
ANEW			
TO SHADE AND KNIT ANEW THE PATCH OF WORDS	79	LOVE'S FEVER	34
ANGEL			
BEFORE THE ARRIVAL OF ANGEL OR DEVIL,	39	GAS FADES	15
THE ARTERIAL ANGEL.	104	WORLD PYRAMID	24
SUFFER, MY TOPSY-TURVIES, THAT A DOUBLE ANGEL	111	I, IN IMAGE	77
CROSS-STROKED SALT ADAM TO THE FROZEN ANGEL	119	ALTARWISE	67
A HILL TOUCHES AN ANGEL. OUT OF A SAINT'S CELL	198	COUNTRY SLEEP	27
HAS STOPPED, (ANGEL, YOU'RE PROUD),	237	PILLAR BREAKS	3
ANGELIC			
'BUT THIS WE TREAD BEARS THE ANGELIC GANGS,	102	FELLOWED SLEEP	13
ON THE ANGELIC ETNA OF THE LAST WHIRRING FEATHERLANDS,	141	SAINT TO FALL	11
ANGELS			
HERE LIES THE BEAST OF MAN AND HERE HIS ANGELS,	81	HERE LIE BEAST	7
OF PUTREFYING ANGELS WHO	84	LETTER TO AUNT	54
AS, BLOWING ON THE ANGELS, I WAS LOST	102	FELLOWED SLEEP	17
SHE LONGS AMONG HORSES AND ANGELS,	163	LONG-LEGGED	33
IN THE COAL BLACK SKY AND SHE BORE ANGELS!	207	LAMENT	55
MORE SPANNED WITH ANGELS RIDE	211	POEM ON B'DAY	104
AND THE ANGELS WHIRR LIKE PHEASANTS	215	COUNTRY HEAVEN	9
ANGELS'			
THE ANGELS' WINGS BEATING ABOUT YOUR HEAD	33	HELD-OUT HAND	4
ANGEL'S			
THE CREATURE WITH THE ANGEL'S FACE	12	SKY'S BRIGHT	12
THE ANGEL'S HURT IS LEFT;	12	SKY'S BRIGHT	18
BINDING MY ANGEL'S HOOD.	105	WORLD PYRAMID	54
ANGELUS			
WAVE'S SILENCE, WEPT WHITE ANGELUS KNELLS.	209	POEM ON B'DAY	38
ANGER			
THAT TURNED ON AND LIFTED IN ANGER	39	GAS FADES	25
AND LOUD HIS ANGER STAMP UPON THE HILL.	73	LORD RED HAIL	6
BRAND OF THE LILY'S ANGER ON HER RING,	115	A GRIEF AGO	19
FORSAKE, THE FOOL, THE HARDINESS OF ANGER.	127	NOW, SAY NAY	7
NOT FROM THIS ANGER	134	NOT FROM ANGER	T
NOT FROM THIS ANGER, ANTICLIMAX AFTER	134	NOT FROM ANGER	1
NOT FROM THIS ANGER AFTER	134	NOT FROM ANGER	11

		PAGE	TITLE	LINE
ANGER (CONTINUED)				
ALTHOUGH YOUR ANGER IS NOT A SLIGHT THING,	....	232	YOUR VOICE	13
ANGLE				
STAR-SET AT JACOB'S ANGLE,	....	111	I, IN IMAGE	81
THIS WAS THE SKY, JACK CHRIST, EACH MINSTREL ANGLE		120	ALTARWISE	105
TONGUE AND EAR IN THE THREAD, ANGLE THE TEMPLE-BOUND		135	HOW MY ANIMAL	26
ANGRILY				
YOUR SPORT IS SUMMER AS THE SPRING RUNS ANGRILY.		123	HOLD HARD	24
ANGUISH				
TO THE ANGUISH AND CARRION, TO THE INFANT FOREVER UNFREE,	....	146	IF HEAD HURT	22
HE SINGS TOWARDS ANGUISH; FINCHES FLY	....	209	POEM ON B'DAY	20
ANIMAL				
AT NIGHTBREAK BORN IN THE FAT SIDE, FROM AN ANIMAL BED	....	130	SINNERS' BELL	26
HOW SHALL MY ANIMAL	....	134	HOW MY ANIMAL	T
HOW SHALL MY ANIMAL	....	134	HOW MY ANIMAL	1
CURL-LOCKED AND ANIMAL CAVEPOOLS OF SPELLS AND BONE,		135	HOW MY ANIMAL	27
MAN, ANIMAL, OR BIRD	....	153	WAS A SAVIOUR	13
SANCTUM SANCTORUM THE ANIMAL EYE OF THE WOOD	......	198	COUNTRY SLEEP	30
SHE BECAME LIKE A DANCER OR A PRETTY ANIMAL	....	235	WOMAN TAPESTRY	20
ANIMALS				
BUT ANIMALS THICK AS THIEVES	....	5	PROLOGUE	74
WITH BIRDS AND ANIMALS	....	167	LONG-LEGGED	168
AND ANIMALS AND BIRDS,	....	193	SIDE OF TRUTH	31
ANKLING				
NOW ON SIR JOHN'S HILL. THE HERON, ANKLING THE SCALY		203	SIR JOHNS HILL	55
ANN				
IN THE SNIVELLING HOURS WITH DEAD, HUMPED ANN	.....	136	AFTER FUNERAL	13
AND SCULPTURED ANN IS SEVENTY YEARS OF STONE.	.....	137	AFTER FUNERAL	35
ANNIVERSARY				
ON A WEDDING ANNIVERSARY	....	161	WEDDING ANNIV	T
THIS RAGGED ANNIVERSARY OF TWO	....	161	WEDDING ANNIV	2
ANNOUNCED				
CLOSE AND FAR SHE ANNOUNCED THE THEFT OF THE HEART		158	INTO HER HEAD	39
ANN'S				
BUT I, ANN'S BARD ON A RAISED HEARTH, CALL ALL	....	136	AFTER FUNERAL	21
ANONYMOUS				
OF A LACK-A-HEAD GHOST I FEAR TO THE ANONYMOUS END.		141	I, FIRST NAMED	4
HER HOLY UNHOLY HOURS WITH THE ALWAYS ANONYMOUS BEAST.	....	158	INTO HER HEAD	46
ANOTHER				
AND TAKE ANOTHER NIBBLE AT MY FLASK.	....	137	O CHATTERTON	16
THE STOCKED HEART IS FORCED, AND AGONY HAS ANOTHER MOUTH TO FEED.	....	142	SAINT TO FALL	42
ANOTHER WITH HERS UNDER HER BELT,	....	155	RETURN	39
YOUR POLESTAR NEIGHBOUR, SUN OF ANOTHER STREET,	...	160	DEATHS AND ENT	17
TIME IS BEARING ANOTHER SON.	....	167	LONG-LEGGED	153
OF THE DEATH IN A BED IN ANOTHER COUNTRY.	....	176	MY BEGGAR ARM	8
ANOTHER'S				
OUT OF THE FULLNESS OF ANOTHER'S HEART	....	23	THE ONLY DEAD	21
ANSWER				
SHALL A WHITE ANSWER ECHO FROM THE ROOFTOPS.	......	56	WHY EAST WIND	15
AND 'KNOW NO ANSWER', AND I KNOW	....	56	WHY EAST WIND	23
NO ANSWER TO THE CHILDREN'S CRY	....	56	WHY EAST WIND	24
OF ECHO'S ANSWER AND THE MAN OF FROST	....	56	WHY EAST WIND	25
ANSWER: SHALL A MOTHER LIE	....	72	TAKE NEEDLES	59
ANSWER: WHEN HER BABE DENIES HER.	....	72	TAKE NEEDLES	62
ANSWER: WHEN THE GREEN LEAVES PRIZE HER.	....	72	TAKE NEEDLES	64
LOVE'S HOUSE, THEY ANSWER, AND THE TOWER DEATH	....	113	NOT FATHER ME	31

	PAGE	TITLE	LINE
ANSWER (CONTINUED)			
THE YES TO DEATH, THE YESMAN AND THE ANSWER, ...	127	NOW, SAY NAY	12
ANSWERING			
INTO THE ANSWERING SKIES FROM THE GREEN GROUND, ...	193	CONVERS PRAYER	7
ANSWERS			
'WHAT YOU HAVE FOUND,' AGE ANSWERS THROUGH HIS TEARS,	30	YOUTH CALLS	15
HIS LIGHTNING ANSWERS MY	185	VISION, PRAYER	201
VOICES HAVE CALLED, AND THE ANSWERS LEMURAL WHISPERS			
FROM THE SEA;	224	IDYLL UNFORGET	34
ANTICLIMAX			
NOT FROM THIS ANGER, ANTICLIMAX AFTER	134	NOT FROM ANGER	1
ANTICS			
THE EYES REMARK THE ANTICS OF THE HAWK.	63	WOMAN SPEAKS	10
ANTIPODES			
SAID THE ANTIPODES, AND TWICE SPRING CHIMED.	118	ALTARWISE	42
AN UPRIGHT MAN IN THE ANTIPODES	145	PLEASURE-BIRD	23
ANTISEPTIC			
THE TRAY OF KNIVES, THE ANTISEPTIC FUNERAL, ...	110	I, IN IMAGE	54
ANTLERED			
AND FAST THROUGH THE DRIFTS OF THE THICKETS ANTLERED			
LIKE DEER, ...	190	WINTER'S TALE	95
ANTLERS			
COMBING WITH ANTLERS, COLUMBUS ON FIRE, ...	152	BELOW A TIME	37
ANVILS			
(A CLASH OF ANVILS FOR MY	5	PROLOGUE	71
ANY			
TO ANY LIGHTER STATE	19	IMAGES IN AIR	13
ANY MAN'S TROUBLES NOT YOUR OWN--	27	OBLIVIOUS DARK	3
AND ANY SWEETNESS THAT IT HAS	40	YOUNG ARE OLD	3
MARY, VIRGIN, OR ANY OTHER.	41	YOUNG ARE OLD	48
COOLS ANY ARDOUR THEY MAY HAVE	47	POET: 1935	33
WHEN ANY LIGHT GOES OUT, AND LIFE IS DEATH.	55	NO MAN BELIEVE	6
WOULD WITHER UP, AND ANY BOY OF LOVE	116	LANTERNS SHINE	3
WITH ANY FURTHER	192	REFUSAL MOURN	17
CLUNG TO THE PITCHING CLOUDS, OR GAY WITH ANY ONE	204	GIANT'S THIGH	15
OF ANY FLOWER	225	OF ANY FLOWER	T
NOR THE PETALS OF ANY FLOWER DROP.	232	YOUR VOICE	16
ANYTHING			
IF HUNTING MEANS ANYTHING MORE THAN THE CHASE	44	TO FOLLOW FOX	18
APART			
NOT FOR THE PROUD MAN APART	197	CRAFT OR ART	12
TERROR WILL RAGE APART	210	POEM ON B'DAY	43
YOU STAND A LITTLE APART, ...	229	MY RIVER	6
APE			
THE KNOBBLY APE THAT SWINGS ALONG HIS SEX	96	RUB OF LOVE	37
APOSTLES'			
OF THE TWELVE APOSTLES' TOWNS RING IN HIS NIGHT;	216	COUNTRY HEAVEN	26
APPAREL			
ALL-HOLLOWED MAN WEPT FOR HIS WHITE APPAREL.	111	I, IN IMAGE	102
APPARELLED			
I WOULD ENFORCE THE BLACK APPARELLED CRIES, ...	96	TWELVE	5
APPEARS			
SO THAT SHE APPEARS ENTERTAINING	236	WOMAN TAPESTRY	38
APPETITE			
DEATH'S APPETITE IS SHARPENED BY THE BULLET'S THUMB;	64	WOMAN SPEAKS	34
APPLE			
I WOULD NOT FEAR THE APPLE NOR THE FLOOD	95	RUB OF LOVE	6
IN SHAPES OF SIN FORKED OUT THE BEARDED APPLE, ...	121	INCARNATE DEVL	4
NOW AS I WAS YOUNG AND EASY UNDER THE APPLE BOUGHS	195	FERN HILL	1

	PAGE	TITLE	LINE
APPLE (CONTINUED)			
AND HONOURED AMONG WAGONS I WAS PRINCE OF THE APPLE TOWNS	195	FERN HILL	6
MILLED DUST OF THE APPLE TREE AND THE POUNDED ISLANDS	199	COUNTRY SLEEP	59
APPLE SEED GLIDES,	199	COUNTRY SLEEP	61
APPLES			
AND DROWN THE CARGOED APPLES IN THEIR TIDES.	91	BOYS OF SUMMER	6
WITH APPLES	178	POEM IN OCT	44
APPLE'S			
THE WALKER'S APPLE'S BLACK AS SIN;	16	TIME TO ROT	15
APPROACH			
A LETTER TO MY AUNT DISCUSSING THE CORRECT APPROACH TO MODERN POETRY	83	LETTER TO AUNT	T
APPROACHING			
LIKE AN APPROACHING WAVE I SPRAWL TO RUIN.	132	I MAKE THIS IN	38
APRIL			
CRACK LIKE A SPRING IN A VICE, BONE BREAKING APRIL,	122	HOLD HARD	17
APRON			
THE TIME FOR BREAST AND THE GREEN APRON AGE	78	LOVE'S FEVER	4
APT			
THE RAINBOW'S FOOT IS NOT MORE APT	11	AIR BREATHE	5
APTITUDE			
MY APTITUDE FOR SIN.	240	TWINING HEAD	12
ARAN			
SPROUT FROM THE STONY LOCKERS LIKE A TREE ON ARAN.	111	I, IN IMAGE	78
ARBOUR			
I HAVE MADE MY THROAT AN ARBOUR FOR FORGOTTEN SONGS.	224	IDYLL UNFORGET	20
ARC			
UNDER THE ARC OF THE SKY THEY ARE UNSAFE.	40	WAS THERE TIME	5
BEND, IF MY JOURNEY ACHE, DIRECTION LIKE AN ARC OR MAKE	145	IF HEAD HURT	14
AS THE ARC OF THE BILLHOOKS THAT FLASHED THE HEDGES LOW	205	GIANT'S THIGH	48
ARCHED			
GALLOP THROUGH THE ARCHED, GREEN FARMS,	168	LONG-LEGGED	188
ARCHES			
LONDON'S ARCHES ARE FALLING	154	RETURN	26
ARCHITECTS			
PRAISE TO THE ARCHITECTS	57	TO ARCHITECTS	T
PRAISE TO THE ARCHITECTS;	57	TO ARCHITECTS	1
PRAISE TO THE ARCHITECTS;	58	TO ARCHITECTS	4
PRAISE TO THE ARCHITECTS;	58	TO ARCHITECTS	10
PRAISE TO THE ARCHITECTS;	58	TO ARCHITECTS	14
PRAISE TO THE ARCHITECTS.	58	TO ARCHITECTS	18
ARCHIVES			
FROM THE ORACULAR ARCHIVES AND THE PARCHMENT,	120	ALTARWISE	113
ARC-LAMPED			
ARC-LAMPED THROWN BACK UPON THE CUTTING FLOOD.	118	ALTARWISE	56
ARCLAMPS			
THEY DANCE BETWEEN THEIR ARCLAMPS AND OUR SKULL,	89	EUNUCH DREAMS	17
ARCS			
SHOT IN THE WIND, BY TILTED ARCS,	129	MY NEOPHYTE	26
ARCTIC			
THE ARCTIC SCUT, AND BASIN OF THE SOUTH,	105	WORLD PYRAMID	44
ARDOUR			
COOLS ANY ARDOUR THEY MAY HAVE	47	POET: 1935	33
BUT I HAVE KNOWN THE STILL ARDOUR OF EQUABILITY;	223	IDYLL UNFORGET	17
ARDOUROUSLY			
IMMUTABLE, AND ARDOUROUSLY CONSECRATED;	223	IDYLL UNFORGET	2
ARE (126)			

	PAGE	TITLE	LINE
ARENºT			
THE PHRASES ON THE WOOD ARENºT HERS;	14	FOR LEDA	5
ARGUE			
STILLºS VAIN TO ARGUE AFTER DEATH;	27	OBLIVIOUS DARK	10
WHERE MEN WOULD ARGUE TILL THE STARS BE GREEN, ...	43	A WAR OF WITS	23
ARGUMENT			
ARGUMENT OF THE HEWN VOICE, GESTURE AND PSALM, ...	137	AFTER FUNERAL	37
ARISE			
THAT ALL THE CHARMINGLY DROWNED ARISE TO COCKCROW			
AND KILL. •••••••••••••••••••••••••••••••••	144	COLOUR OF SAY	6
NEVER TO AWAKE AND ARISE •••••••••••••••••••••••••	184	VISION, PRAYER	168
TURNS IN THE DARK ON THE SOUND THEY KNOW WILL ARISE	193	CONVERS PRAYER	6
ARISING			
MY ARISING PRODIGAL •••••••••••••••••••••••••••••	186	HOLY SPRING	18
ARK			
I BUILD MY BELLOWING ARK •••••••••••••••••••••••••	4	PROLOGUE	44
MY ARK SINGS IN THE SUN •••••••••••••••••••••••••	5	PROLOGUE	100
SHAPED MY CLAYFELLOW, AND THE HEAVENºS ARK	124	FOSTER LIGHT	26
ARKS			
CRY, MULTITUDES OF ARKS! ACROSS •••••••••••••••••	5	PROLOGUE	93
ARM			
DO YOU NOT FATHER ME, NOR THE ERECTED ARM	112	NOT FATHER ME	1
WE MAKE ME MYSTIC AS THE ARM OF AIR, ...	128	NOW, SAY NAY	34
ON MY CLEAVING ARM AS I BLASTED IN A WAVE.	152	BELOW A TIME	48
UNDER HIS DOWNY ARM YOU SIGHED AS HE STRUCK, ...	153	WAS A SAVIOUR	19
BOLTING THE NIGHT OF THE DOOR WITH HER ARM HER PLUME.	169	LOVE IN ASYLUM	4
FOR A MAN SLEEPS WHERE FIRE LEAPT DOWN AND SHE			
LEARNS THROUGH HIS ARM •••••••••••••••••••••••	170	MARRIAGE VIRG	13
LAST NIGHT I DIVED MY BEGGAR ARM •••••••••••••••	175	MY BEGGAR ARM	T
LAST NIGHT I DIVED MY BEGGAR ARM •••••••••••••••	175	MY BEGGAR ARM	1
TO THRUST YOUR ARM INTO THE EARTH •••••••••••••••	229	MY RIVER	10
TO MAIM OR STING MY ARM, •••••••••••••••••••••••••	240	TWINING HEAD	2
ARMIES			
LET THE TINY ARMIES LAP, •••••••••••••••••••••••••	71	TAKE NEEDLES	10
ARMLESS			
UNCLENCHED, ARMLESS, SILK AND ROUGH LOVE THAT BREAKS			
ALL ROCKS. •••••••••••••••••••••••••••••••••	154	WAS A SAVIOUR	40
ARMOUR			
FELT THUD BENEATH MY FLESHºS ARMOUR, ...	68	BEFORE KNOCKED	9
WHO TOOK MY FLESH AND BONE FOR ARMOUR	69	BEFORE KNOCKED	45
MY EGYPTºS ARMOUR BUCKLING IN ITS SHEET, ...	104	WORLD PYRAMID	34
MY HALF GHOST IN ARMOUR HOLD HARD IN DEATHºS			
CORRIDOR, •••••••••••••••••••••••••••••••••••	108	I, IN IMAGE	5
SHAPED IN OLD ARMOUR AND OAK THE COUNTENANCE OF A			
DUNCE •••••••••••••••••••••••••••••••••••••••	133	MAKE ME A MASK	7
ARMOURED			
ALL ISSUE ARMOURED, OF THE GRAVE, •••••••••••••••	97	TWILIGHT LOCKS	19
ARMPITS			
STINK OF CIGARETTES AND ARMPITS, •••••••••••••••	28	NO WINGS	16
VOLES AT HIS ARMPITS, DOWN THE SAD CANAL ••••••••	51	OUT OF THE PIT	40
FEED IN THE ARMPITS OF DROWNED GIRLS, IºVE SWUM ...	52	OUT OF THE PIT	69
ARMS			
TO WALES IN MY ARMS. •••••••••••••••••••••••••••	4	PROLOGUE	52
AND MANY ARMS TO RAISE •••••••••••••••••••••••••	12	CABARET	20
UNDER THE SKYSIGNS THEY WHO HAVE NO ARMS ••••••••	40	WAS THERE TIME	7
REACH ASKING ARMS UP TO THE MILKY SKY, ••••••••••	42	A WAR OF WITS	16
WITH WOODEN ARMS REVOLVING IN THE WIND ••••••••••	45	PLOUGHMAN GONE	7
FOLD IN THEIR ARMS. •••••••••••••••••••••••••••	89	EUNUCH DREAMS	6
TO A HAYCOCK COUCH AND THE SCYTHES OF HIS ARMS	157	INTO HER HEAD	17
AND TAKEN BY LIGHT IN HER ARMS AT LONG AND DEAR LAST	170	LOVE IN ASYLUM	16

	PAGE	TITLE	LINE
ARMS (CONTINUED)			
THE MOTHER DUG, AND ITS ARMS FULL OF FIRES.	173	FIRE RAID	8
WITH ALL THEIR GRIEFS IN THEIR ARMS, ...	197	CRAFT OR ART	5
BUT FOR THE LOVERS, THEIR ARMS	197	CRAFT OR ART	17
AND HOURS MADE LITTLE I HAVE DIPPED MY ARMS IN THEIR			
RAPTURE;	224	IDYLL UNFORGET	31
LIKE THE ARMS OF A CLEAN WOMAN	236	WOMAN TAPESTRY	39
IN THE FOLD OF HER ARMS	236	WOMAN TAPESTRY	64
ARMY			
YOUR MONSTROUS OFFICERS AND THE DECAYING ARMY, ...	110	I, IN IMAGE	56
OVER THE BARBED AND SHOOTING SEA ASSUMED AN ARMY	186	HOLY SPRING	6
AROSE			
AND YOU AROSE FROM DEPTHS OF GRASS	227	SPRING-SPIRIT	5
AROUND			
WON'T HARM THE TENT AROUND HIM, ...	17	IN OBLIVION	24
AROUND OUR LITTLE SELVES	24	THE ONLY DEAD	32
SPEWING ITS SAPLESS LEAVES AROUND, ...	26	THERE'S PLENTY	10
WIND CARVEN LINES AROUND THE DROOPING MOUTH;	64	WOMAN SPEAKS	50
OF SKIN AND VEIN AROUND THE WELL	69	BEFORE KNOCKED	26
TO THAT UNENDING SEA AROUND MY ISLAND	76	LASHED RINGS	8
SEE, SAYS THE LIME, AROUND THESE WRECKS	86	SEE, SAYS LIME	25
TOWNS AROUND ON A WHEEL OF FIRE.	106	ALL ALL AND	6
AND RIVERS OF THE DEAD AROUND MY NECK.	120	ALTARWISE	126
AND WOULD A-WOOING GO AROUND THE GRAVES.	138	O CHATTERTON	28
AROUND SOME COFFIN CARRYING	152	BELOW A TIME	30
HIS FAITH AROUND HER FLEW UNDONE	158	INTO HER HEAD	26
AWAY BUT THE WEATHER TURNED AROUND.	178	POEM IN OCT	40
AWAY BUT THE WEATHER TURNED AROUND. AND THE TRUE	178	POEM IN OCT	62
HARPIES AROUND ME OUT OF HER WOMB!	207	LAMENT	56
OF MINNOWS WREATHING AROUND THEIR PRAYER;	209	POEM ON B'DAY	29
WHICH GOES AROUND ME EASILY	236	WOMAN TAPESTRY	54
AND TWINE THE LIMBS AROUND MY HANDS.	239	MAKES INTERVALS	24
AROUSE			
EXILED IN US WE AROUSE THE SOFT, ...	154	WAS A SAVIOUR	39
ARRIVAL			
BEFORE THE ARRIVAL OF ANGEL OR DEVIL, ...	39	GAS FADES	15
CAN WE FEND OFF ROCK ARRIVAL, ...	54	WE BY SEASAND	22
TO THE SEA-BLOWN ARRIVAL.	109	I, IN IMAGE	36
ARROW			
AND HEAVEN CRIER, ARROW NOW OF ASPIRING	148	UNLUCKILY FOR	38
ARROWS'			
FREE FROM THEIR BURNING NESTS THE ARROWS' BROOD.	73	LORD RED HAIL	4
ARROWY			
FAINT ARROWY MOONSTONE ON A TEAR-CULLED CADENCE,	225	SLENDER WIND	3
ARSE			
WATER FROM NOSE AND ARSE, A SANGER'S SHOW	51	OUT OF THE PIT	26
ART			
WORK ART AND THE MOONSHINE	5	PROLOGUE	84
(AND WHAT A PART) IN ALL GOOD ART.	84	LETTER TO AUNT	47
THE CONVULSIONS OF YOUR ART, ...	84	LETTER TO AUNT	59
IN MY CRAFT OR SULLEN ART	196	CRAFT OR ART	T
IN MY CRAFT OR SULLEN ART	196	CRAFT OR ART	1
NOR HEED MY CRAFT OR ART.	197	CRAFT OR ART	20
ARTERIAL			
THE ARTERIAL ANGEL.	104	WORLD PYRAMID	24
TURN THE LONG SEA ARTERIAL	110	I, IN IMAGE	46
ARTERY			
WEANS ON AN ARTERY THE GENDER'S STRIP;	117	ALTARWISE	18
AS			
LIKE LEAVES OF TREES AND AS SOON	3	PROLOGUE	31

		PAGE	TITLE	LINE
AS (CONTINUED)				
MY DABBED BAY'S DUSK, AS I HACK	....	4	PROLOGUE	36
AS THE FLOOD BEGINS,	....	4	PROLOGUE	46
CLANGOUR AS I HEW AND SMITE	....	5	PROLOGUE	70
BUT ANIMALS THICK AS THIEVES	....	5	PROLOGUE	74
POOR PEACE AS THE SUN SETS	....	5	PROLOGUE	89
NOT, AS A SYMBOL, STONE/ SPEAKING OR NO,	....	9	MINUTE'S HOUR	15
AS THAT HER HEEL WAS LIFTED,	....	12	CABARET	15
AND, AS WE WATCH, THE RAINBOW'S FOOT	....	13	RAIN CUTS	15
THE WALKER'S APPLE'S BLACK AS SIN;	....	16	TIME TO ROT	15
AS DROWN, OVER AND OVER, THIS FEVER.	....	17	IN OBLIVION	18
AND, ON THE GROUND, GYRATES AS EASILY	....	19	THE NEOPHYTE	7
AS THOUGH THE SUN WERE SPINNING UP THROUGH IT.	....	19	THE NEOPHYTE	8
AS SIGNS I'VE NOT BROUGHT DOWN	....	19	IMAGES IN AIR	12
AS EDGES OFF YOUR NERVES TO MINE,	....	20	ENCOMPASSED	5
OR, WHITE AS MILK, OUT OF THE SEEPING DARK,	....	20	ENCOMPASSED	11
THE DROOPING AS YOU CLOSE ME IN	....	20	ENCOMPASSED	12
OBLIVION IS AS LOVERLESS;	....	22	ON QUIET NIGHT	13
OBLIVION IS AS LOVERLESS.	....	22	ON QUIET NIGHT	14
OF SUCH GREAT GOODNESS AS IS OURS.	....	23	THE ONLY DEAD	18
OBLIVION IS AS BLIND,	....	23	ON QUIET NIGHT	19
OBLIVION IS AS BLIND,	....	23	ON QUIET NIGHT	20
AS YOU, ORIGINAL, DERIVE.	....	24	LITTLE PROBLEM	25
AS FLIES BEFORE THE BREATH	....	25	BEAUTY TO DUST	2
ONLY AS WRONG; BUT SHAN'T THE GENIUS FAIL,	....	28	NO WINGS	7
SLY AS AN ADDER, RID OF FLEAS.	....	29	LONG, SKELETON	6
AS RAPED AND REAPED, THE FINAL EMBLEM.	....	29	LONG, SKELETON	8
RATHER THAN CHARNEL-HOUSE AS SYMBOL	....	29	LONG, SKELETON	12
YOU, WHO ARE OLD, HAVE LOVED AND LOST AS I	....	30	YOUTH CALLS	5
KNOWING SUCH JOY AS I.	....	30	YOUTH CALLS	11
THE WELCOME DEVIL COMES AS GUEST,	....	30	NEARLY SUMMER	14
OUT OF CONFUSION, AS THE WAY IS,	....	31	BEING BUT MEN	11
FEEL, AS THE PULSE GROWS TIRED,	....	32	HELD-OUT HAND	3
AFTER SUCH FIGHTING AS THE WEAKEST KNOW,	....	32	OUT OF SIGHS	10
AS MEANINGLESS AS THE BELLS (OH CHANGE THE LIFE!),	..	33	HELD-OUT HAND	9
AS MEANINGLESS AS THE BELLS (OH CHANGE THE LIFE!),	..	33	HELD-OUT HAND	9
HAVE CLEANEST HANDS, AND, AS THE HEARTLESS GHOST	..	40	WAS THERE TIME	8
WITH HALF-AVERTED HEADS, AS IF TO LISTEN,	....	40	YOUNG ARE OLD	13
FELL HARD AS WHIPS ON AN OLD WOUND,	....	42	A WAR OF WITS	3
GROWING MORE TERRIBLE AS THE DAY	....	43	LONGED TO MOVE	4
TO FOLLOW, WILD AS THE CHICKEN STEALER,	....	44	TO FOLLOW FOX	3
AS THE HANDS THAT HELD THEM IN MY FATHER'S TIME.	..	45	PLOUGHMAN GONE	11
YOU SHALL GO AS THE OTHERS HAVE GONE,	....	45	PLOUGHMAN GONE	16
THAT THUNDERS AS HEART THUNDERS, SLOWS AS HEART SLOWS.	....	46	POET: 1935	6
THAT THUNDERS AS HEART THUNDERS, SLOWS AS HEART SLOWS.	....	46	POET: 1935	6
THE SAME TUNE AS IN MY FATHER'S TIME:	....	46	PLOUGHMAN GONE	29
YOU SHALL GO AS THE OTHERS HAVE GONE,	....	46	PLOUGHMAN GONE	30
DRIP FROM MY OPEN EYES AS HONEY	....	48	LIGHT, I KNOW	9
AS CLEARLY AS THE LIGHT OF MY OWN BRAIN,	....	49	LIGHT, I KNOW	28
AS CLEARLY AS THE LIGHT OF MY OWN BRAIN,	....	49	LIGHT, I KNOW	28
THOUGH THEY BE MAD AND DEAD AS NAILS,	....	50	NO DOMINION	24
HE, TOO, HAS SEEN THE WORLD AS BOTTOM ROTTEN,	.....	52	OUT OF THE PIT	56
CRIES NOT ALOUD BLIND AS A BAT,	....	54	NO MAN BELIEVE	2
THAT'S GRAVE AND GAY AS GRAVE AND SEA	....	54	WE BY SEASAND	7
SOUNDS WITH THE GRAINS AS THEY HURRY	....	54	WE BY SEASAND	15
THOUGH WHAT THE STARS ASK AS THEY ROUND	....	56	WHY EAST WIND	18
AVOID CHURCH AS A RAT;	....	59	FAIRY TALES	5
BUT WHEN THE LADIES ARE COLD AS STONE	....	60	MEAT ON BONES	7

		PAGE	TITLE	LINE
AS (CONTINUED)				
FEAR DEATH AS LITTLE AS THE THUNDER'S SHOT,	....	60	FAIRY TALES	40
FEAR DEATH AS LITTLE AS THE THUNDER'S SHOT,	....	60	FAIRY TALES	40
COOL AS THE WAX-RED FOUNTAINS OF THE VEINS;	....	63	WOMAN SPEAKS	5
A HAND RULES PITY AS A HAND RULES HEAVEN;	....	66	HAND SIGNED	15
AND GODS BE CHANGED AS OFTEN AS THE SHIFT.	....	67	LET A FAITH	8
AND GODS BE CHANGED AS OFTEN AS THE SHIFT.	....	67	LET A FAITH	8
GOD IS THE SAME THOUGH HE BE PRAISED AS MANY,	.....	67	LET A FAITH	9
I WHO WAS SHAPELESS AS THE WATER	....	68	BEFORE KNOCKED	3
AS YET WAS IN A MOLTEN FORM,	....	68	BEFORE KNOCKED	10
AS YET UNGOTTEN, I DID SUFFER;	....	68	BEFORE KNOCKED	19
AS FIRE FALLS, TWO HEMISPHERES DIVIDE,	....	73	LORD RED HAIL	7
LOVE ME, NOT AS THE DREAMING NURSES	....	75	SONG: LOVE ME	1
MY FALLING LUNGS, NOR AS THE CYPRESS	....	75	SONG: LOVE ME	2
LOVE ME, NOT AS THE GIRLS OF HEAVEN	....	76	SONG: LOVE ME	5
LOVE ME, NOT AS THE RUFFLING PIGEON	....	76	SONG: LOVE ME	9
THE WATER-SPIRIT MOVES AS IT IS HIDDEN,	....	76	LASHED RINGS	9
THE TOPS OF TREES, NOR AS THE LEGION	....	76	SONG: LOVE ME	10
LOVE ME, AS LOVES THE MOLE HIS DARKNESS	....	76	SONG: LOVE ME	13
AND EARTH AND SKY WERE AS ONE AIRY HILL,	....	78	LOVE'S FEVER	8
THE EARTH AND SKY WERE AS TWO MOUNTAINS MEETING.	..	78	LOVE'S FEVER	15
AND THE FOUR WINDS, THAT HAD LONG BLOWN AS ONE,	...	78	LOVE'S FEVER	19
AS FORKS MY EYE;	....	79	LOVE'S FEVER	47
HIS GRAPH IS MEASURED AS THE PAGE OF PAIN	....	80	ALMANAC TIME	4
I ROUND THIS HERITAGE AS ROUNDS THE SUN	....	80	ALL THAT I OWE	13
HIS WINY SKY, AND, AS THE CANDLE'S MOON,	....	80	ALL THAT I OWE	14
BRIGHT AS A FIG;	....	82	LIGHT BREAKS	11
PERHAPS IT WOULD BE JUST AS WELL,	....	84	LETTER TO AUNT	30
AS BELLY, GENITALS, AND ----,	....	84	LETTER TO AUNT	45
THE BLOOD GOT UP AS RED AS WAX	....	85	SEE, SAYS LIME	13
THE BLOOD GOT UP AS RED AS WAX	....	85	SEE, SAYS LIME	13
AS KISSES FROZE THE WAXING THOUGHT,	....	85	SEE, SAYS LIME	14
AS MILK SHALL BE A MUSIC IN THE PAPS	....	87	PAIN BE MUSIC	14
DRIVES IN A DEATH AS LIFE LEAKS OUT.	....	88	A PROCESS IN	9
AND SPEAK THEIR MIDNIGHT NOTHINGS AS THEY SWELL;	..	89	EUNUCH DREAMS	14
THAT SHROUDED MEN MIGHT MARROW AS THEY FLY.	....	90	EUNUCH DREAMS	30
OUR STRIPS OF STUFF THAT TATTER AS WE MOVE	....	90	EUNUCH DREAMS	32
AND LETS THEIR TRASH BE HONOURED AS THE QUICK.	....	90	EUNUCH DREAMS	35
AND WHO REMAIN SHALL FLOWER AS THEY LOVE,	....	90	EUNUCH DREAMS	41
DRY AS A TOMB, YOUR COLOURED LIDS	....	91	WHERE ONCE THE	19
AS SUNLIGHT PAINTS THE SHELLING OF THEIR HEADS.	...	92	BOYS OF SUMMER	18
WHERE, PUNCTUAL AS DEATH, WE RING THE STARS;	......	92	BOYS OF SUMMER	27
NOR BLOWS BACK MOON-AND-MIDNIGHT AS SHE BLOWS.	....	92	BOYS OF SUMMER	30
HEAVEN AND HELL MIXED AS THEY SPUN.	....	93	IN BEGINNING	6
O SEE THE POLES ARE KISSING AS THEY CROSS.	....	93	BOYS OF SUMMER	54
THREE-SYLLABLED AND STARRY AS THE SMILE;	....	94	IN BEGINNING	8
A THREE-EYED, RED-EYED SPARK, BLUNT AS A FLOWER;	..	94	IN BEGINNING	15
IF THE RED TICKLE AS THE CATTLE CALVE	....	95	RUB OF LOVE	4
WOULD LEAVE ME COLD AS BUTTER FOR THE FLIES,	......	95	RUB OF LOVE	26
THE SEA OF SCUMS COULD DROWN ME AS IT BROKE	....	95	RUB OF LOVE	27
AS FLEECED AS THEY BOW LOWLY WITH THE SHEEP,	......	96	TWELVE	10
AS FLEECED AS THEY BOW LOWLY WITH THE SHEEP,	......	96	TWELVE	10
MY BUSY HEART WHO SHUDDERS AS SHE TALKS	....	98	OCTOBER WIND	7
AND MOTHER MILK WAS STIFF AS SAND,	....	98	TWILIGHT LOCKS	32
I FLED THAT GROUND AS LIGHTLY AS A FEATHER.	....	101	FELLOWED SLEEP	10
I FLED THAT GROUND AS LIGHTLY AS A FEATHER.	....	101	FELLOWED SLEEP	10
HAPPY CADAVER'S HUNGER AS YOU TAKE	....	101	RUNNING GRAVE	49
AS MOTOR MUSCLE ON THE DRILL, DRIVING	....	102	I DREAMED MY	3
AS, BLOWING ON THE ANGELS, I WAS LOST	....	102	FELLOWED SLEEP	17
HALF OF THE FELLOW FATHER AS HE DOUBLES	....	103	WORLD PYRAMID	1

	PAGE	TITLE	LINE
AS **(CONTINUED)**			
HALF OF THE FELLOW MOTHER AS SHE DABBLES	103	WORLD PYRAMID	3
THE FELLOW HALF WAS FROZEN AS IT BUBBLED	104	WORLD PYRAMID	7
THE FELLOW SEED AND SHADOW AS IT BABBLED	104	WORLD PYRAMID	9
THE PATCHWORK HALVES WERE CLOVEN AS THEY SCUDDED	104	WORLD PYRAMID	19
ROTATING HALVES ARE HORNING AS THEY DRILL	104	WORLD PYRAMID	23
THE GHOST THAT HATCHED HIS HAVOC AS HE FLEW	104	WORLD PYRAMID	29
THE STRAWS OF ASIA, LOSE ME AS I TURN	105	WORLD PYRAMID	47
THE FELLOW HALVES THAT, CLOVEN AS THEY SWIVEL	105	WORLD PYRAMID	49
THE TONGUES OF HEAVEN GOSSIP AS I GLIDE	105	WORLD PYRAMID	53
SKINNY AS SIN, THE FOAMING MARROW, ...	106	ALL ALL AND	11
BRIGHT AS HER SPINNING-WHEELS, THE COLIC SEASON ...	108	I, IN IMAGE	8
AS THEY DIVE, THE DUST SETTLES, ...	110	I, IN IMAGE	43
AS THEY DROWN, THE CHIME TRAVELS, ...	110	I, IN IMAGE	61
AND, AS FOR OILS AND OINTMENTS ON THE FLYING GRAIL,	111	I, IN IMAGE	101
DO YOU NOT MOTHER ME, NOR, AS I AM, ...	112	NOT FATHER ME	3
FOR MY TALL TURRETS CARRY AS YOUR SIN?	112	NOT FATHER ME	6
DO YOU NOT BROTHER ME, NOR, AS YOU CLIMB, ...	112	NOT FATHER ME	7
TELLS YOU AND YOU, MY MASTERS, AS HIS STRANGE	113	SERVANT SUN	13
A LEG AS LONG AS TREES, ...	114	SERVANT SUN	29
A LEG AS LONG AS TREES, ...	114	SERVANT SUN	29
AND ALL SWEET HELL, DEAF AS AN HOUR'S EAR, ...	114	SERVANT SUN	33
AS TARRED WITH BLOOD AS THE BRIGHT THORNS I WEPT;	120	ALTARWISE	101
AS TARRED WITH BLOOD AS THE BRIGHT THORNS I WEPT;	120	ALTARWISE	101
BLACK AS THE BEAST AND PALER THAN THE CROSS.	121	INCARNATE DEVL	12
GREEN AS BEGINNING, LET THE GARDEN DIVING	121	ALTARWISE	137
AS THE GREEN BLOOMS RIDE UPWARD, TO THE DRIVE OF			
TIME;	122	HOLD HARD	3
THE GREENWOOD DYING AS THE DEER FALL IN THEIR TRACKS,	122	HOLD HARD	11
HURDLES AND GUNS AND RAILINGS, AS THE BOULDERS HEAVE,	122	HOLD HARD	16
O RING OF SEAS, NOR SORROW AS I SHIFT	123	FOSTER LIGHT	20
YOUR SPORT IS SUMMER AS THE SPRING RUNS ANGRILY.	123	HOLD HARD	24
NOW MAKE THE WORLD OF ME AS I HAVE MADE	124	FOSTER LIGHT	29
WE MAKE ME MYSTIC AS THE ARM OF AIR, ...	128	NOW, SAY NAY	34
MOONFALL AND SAILING EMPEROR, PALE AS THEIR			
TIDE-PRINT, ...	130	SINNERS' BELL	10
PROUD AS A SUCKED STONE AND HUGE AS SANDGRAINS. ...	131	I MAKE THIS IN	23
PROUD AS A SUCKED STONE AND HUGE AS SANDGRAINS. ...	131	I MAKE THIS IN	23
AND, MILD AS PARDON FROM A CLOUD OF PRIDE, ...	133	I MAKE THIS IN	59
DRUNK AS A VINEYARD SNAIL, FLAILED LIKE AN OCTOPUS,	134	HOW MY ANIMAL	7
LOPS, AS A BUSH PLUMED WITH FLAMES, THE RANT OF THE			
FIERCE EYE, ...	135	HOW MY ANIMAL	38
HER FLESH WAS MEEK AS MILK, BUT THIS SKYWARD STATUE	136	AFTER FUNERAL	27
TAKING JEYES' FLUID AS NARCOTIC;	137	O CHATTERTON	3
AS THEIR BLADE MARCHES IN	142	SAINT TO FALL	40
AND OFFER AS THE LAST DELIGHT	143	THE MOLLS	7
I ADVANCE FOR AS LONG AS FOREVER IS.	143	24 YEARS	9
I ADVANCE FOR AS LONG AS FOREVER IS.	143	24 YEARS	9
NOR EVER, AS THE WILD TONGUE BREAKS ITS TOMBS, ...	144	PLEASURE-BIRD	11
WHOM NOW I CONJURE TO STAND AS THIEF	146	TO OTHERS	9
THE GRAVE AND MY CALM BODY ARE SHUT TO YOUR COMING			
AS STONE, ...	146	IF HEAD HURT	29
AS MUCH AS FOR THEIR GOOD, ...	147	TO OTHERS	19
AS MUCH AS FOR THEIR GOOD, ...	147	TO OTHERS	19
I TALK TO HIM AS I CLEAN THE GRATE	149	PAPER & STICKS	10
TO TAKE ME AWAY AS YOU WHISPERED AND WROTE	149	PAPER & STICKS	12
WORDS ON THE AIR AS THE FIRE CATCHES	149	PAPER & STICKS	17
SLASHED DOWN THE LAST SNAKE AS THOUGH	150	WHEN I WOKE	13
IN COMMON CLAY CLOTHES DISGUISED AS SCALES, ...	151	BELOW A TIME	15
AS A HE-GOD'S PADDLING WATER SKIRTS, ...	151	BELOW A TIME	16

		PAGE	TITLE	LINE
AS	(CONTINUED)			
WITH MY CHERRY CAPPED DANGLER GREEN AS SEAWEED	....	152	BELOW A TIME	45
ON MY CLEAVING ARM AS I BLASTED IN A WAVE.	....	152	BELOW A TIME	48
AS QUIET AS A BONE.	....	152	BELOW A TIME	51
AS QUIET AS A BONE.	....	152	BELOW A TIME	51
UNDER HIS DOWNY ARM YOU SIGHED AS HE STRUCK,	....	153	WAS A SAVIOUR	19
NIGHT, AND ENJOYED AS HE WOULD.	....	158	INTO HER HEAD	36
OPEN AS TO THE AIR TO THE NAKED SHADOW	....	159	INTO HER HEAD	63
AS A BIRD HOOKING OVER THE SEA,	....	162	LONG-LEGGED	7
SAILS DRANK THE WIND, AND WHITE AS MILK	....	162	LONG-LEGGED	13
IS OLD AS WATER AND PLAIN AS AN EEL;	....	165	LONG-LEGGED	93
IS OLD AS WATER AND PLAIN AS AN EEL;	....	165	LONG-LEGGED	93
THE BLIND, CLAWED STARE IS COLD AS SLEET.	....	165	LONG-LEGGED	101
AS THE SAILS DRANK UP THE HAIL OF THUNDER	....	166	LONG-LEGGED	127
AS THE BOAT SKIMS ON WITH DRINKING WINGS!	....	166	LONG-LEGGED	134
DRY AS ECHOES AND INSECT-FACED,	....	167	LONG-LEGGED	146
LEADS THEM AS CHILDREN AND AS AIR	....	167	LONG-LEGGED	149
LEADS THEM AS CHILDREN AND AS AIR	....	167	LONG-LEGGED	149
A GIRL MAD AS BIRDS	....	169	LOVE IN ASYLUM	3
AT LARGE AS THE DEAD,	....	169	LOVE IN ASYLUM	8
WAS MIRACULOUS VIRGINITY OLD AS LOAVES AND FISHES,		170	MARRIAGE VIRG	5
STRAIGHT AS A YOUNG ELM	....	172	THE HUNCHBACK	33
AND THE WILD BOYS INNOCENT AS STRAWBERRIES	....	172	THE HUNCHBACK	40
AS THE GRAINS BLOW, AS YOUR DEATH GROWS, THROUGH OUR HEART.	....	173	FIRE RAID	24
AS THE GRAINS BLOW, AS YOUR DEATH GROWS, THROUGH OUR HEART.	....	173	FIRE RAID	24
WHITE AS THE SKELETON	....	174	FIRE RAID	45
BARE AS THE NURSERIES	....	175	FIRE RAID	59
A DARK AS DEEP	....	176	BREATH SHED	9
MY LOVE AS A ROUND WAVE	....	176	BREATH SHED	10
OF THE TOWN CLOSED AS THE TOWN AWOKE.	....	177	POEM IN OCT	20
BROWN AS OWLS	....	177	POEM IN OCT	34
HEAR THEIR LAUGHTER SLY AS GONOCOCCI.	....	179	NEW QUAY	18
BEHIND THE WALL THIN AS A WREN'S BONE?	....	180	VISION, PRAYER	9
STILL AS STONE	....	180	VISION, PRAYER	20
AND I AM STRUCK AS LONELY AS A HOLY MAKER BY THE SUN.		186	HOLY SPRING	12
AND I AM STRUCK AS LONELY AS A HOLY MAKER BY THE SUN.		186	HOLY SPRING	12
GABRIEL AND RADIANT SHRUBBERY AS THE MORNING GROWS JOYFUL	....	186	HOLY SPRING	15
ON A STAR OF FAITH PURE AS THE DRIFTING BREAD,	....	187	WINTER'S TALE	12
AS THE FOOD AND FLAMES OF THE SNOW, A MAN UNROLLED		187	WINTER'S TALE	13
AND THE DUNG HILLS WHITE AS WOOL AND THE HEN	....	187	WINTER'S TALE	18
WHEN COLD AS SNOW HE SHOULD RUN THE WENDED VALES AMONG	....	188	WINTER'S TALE	45
AS A DUST OF PIGEONS. EXULTING, THE GRAVE HOOVED		189	WINTER'S TALE	73
LEAP, AS TO TRUMPETS. CALLIGRAPHY OF THE OLD	......	189	WINTER'S TALE	77
WAS FLYING THROUGH THE HOUSE AS THOUGH THE SHE BIRD PRAISED	....	189	WINTER'S TALE	83
IN A CHOIR OF WINGS, AS THOUGH SHE SLEPT OR DIED,		191	WINTER'S TALE	122
SHALL DROWN IN A GRIEF AS DEEP AS HIS MADE GRAVE,		194	CONVERS PRAYER	18
SHALL DROWN IN A GRIEF AS DEEP AS HIS MADE GRAVE,		194	CONVERS PRAYER	18
NOW AS I WAS YOUNG AND EASY UNDER THE APPLE BOUGHS		195	FERN HILL	1
ABOUT THE LILTING HOUSE AND HAPPY AS THE GRASS WAS GREEN,	....	195	FERN HILL	2
AND AS I WAS GREEN AND CAREFREE, FAMOUS AMONG THE BARNS	....	195	FERN HILL	10
ABOUT THE HAPPY YARD AND SINGING AS THE FARM WAS HOME,	....	195	FERN HILL	11

	PAGE	TITLE	LINE
AS (CONTINUED)			
FIELDS HIGH AS THE HOUSE, THE TUNES FROM THE CHIMNEYS, IT WAS AIR	195	FERN HILL	20
AND FIRE GREEN AS GRASS.	195	FERN HILL	22
AS I RODE TO SLEEP THE OWLS WERE BEARING THE FARM AWAY, ...	195	FERN HILL	24
UNDER THE NEW MADE CLOUDS AND HAPPY AS THE HEART WAS LONG, ...	196	FERN HILL	38
OH AS I WAS YOUNG AND EASY IN THE MERCY OF HIS MEANS,	196	FERN HILL	52
AND MIRE OF LOVE, BUT THE THIEF AS MEEK AS THE DEW.	198	COUNTRY SLEEP	38
AND MIRE OF LOVE, BUT THE THIEF AS MEEK AS THE DEW.	198	COUNTRY SLEEP	38
AND SLY AS SNOW AND MEEK AS DEW BLOWN TO THE THORN,	199	COUNTRY SLEEP	50
AND SLY AS SNOW AND MEEK AS DEW BLOWN TO THE THORN,	199	COUNTRY SLEEP	50
EVER AND EVER HE FINDS A WAY, AS THE SNOW FALLS,	199	COUNTRY SLEEP	56
AS THE RAIN FALLS, HAIL ON THE FLEECE, AS THE VALE MIST RIDES	199	COUNTRY SLEEP	57
AS THE RAIN FALLS, HAIL ON THE FLEECE, AS THE VALE MIST RIDES	199	COUNTRY SLEEP	57
THROUGH THE HAYGOLD STALLS, AS THE DEW FALLS ON THE WIND-	199	COUNTRY SLEEP	58
OF THE MORNING LEAVES, AS THE STAR FALLS, AS THE WINGED	199	COUNTRY SLEEP	60
OF THE MORNING LEAVES, AS THE STAR FALLS, AS THE WINGED	199	COUNTRY SLEEP	60
AS THE WORLD FALLS, SILENT AS THE CYCLONE OF SILENCE.	199	COUNTRY SLEEP	63
AS THE WORLD FALLS, SILENT AS THE CYCLONE OF SILENCE.	199	COUNTRY SLEEP	63
WHO COMES AS RED AS THE FOX AND SLY AS THE HEELED WIND.	200	COUNTRY SLEEP	81
WHO COMES AS RED AS THE FOX AND SLY AS THE HEELED WIND.	200	COUNTRY SLEEP	81
WHO COMES AS RED AS THE FOX AND SLY AS THE HEELED WIND.	200	COUNTRY SLEEP	81
YOUR FAITH AS DEATHLESS AS THE OUTCRY OF THE RULED SUN.	201	COUNTRY SLEEP	111
YOUR FAITH AS DEATHLESS AS THE OUTCRY OF THE RULED SUN.	201	COUNTRY SLEEP	111
DEATH CLEAR AS A BUOY'S BELL:	202	SIR JOHNS HILL	26
WE GRIEVE AS THE BLITHE BIRDS, NEVER AGAIN, LEAVE SHINGLE AND ELM, ...	202	SIR JOHNS HILL	33
WHERE BARREN AS BOULDERS WOMEN LIE LONGING STILL	203	GIANT'S THIGH	4
AS THE SNAPT FEATHERS SNOW, ...	203	SIR JOHNS HILL	50
YOUNG AS THEY IN THE AFTER MILKING MOONLIGHT LAY	204	GIANT'S THIGH	16
ROUGH AS COWS' TONGUES AND THRASHED WITH BRAMBLES THEIR BUTTERMILK	204	GIANT'S THIGH	25
OR RIPPLING SOFT IN THE SPINNEY MOON AS THE SILK	204	GIANT'S THIGH	27
AS THE ARC OF THE BILLHOOKS THAT FLASHED THE HEDGES LOW	205	GIANT'S THIGH	48
I SKIPPED IN A BLUSH AS THE BIG GIRLS ROLLED	206	LAMENT	6
DIPPING MOON AND DRUNK AS A NEW DROPPED CALF, ...	206	LAMENT	17
AND SERVE ME RIGHT AS THE PREACHERS WARN, ...	207	LAMENT	38
PLENTY AS BLACKBERRIES IN THE WOODS	210	POEM ON B'DAY	53
AS HORSES IN THE FOAM:	210	POEM ON B'DAY	75
AS I SAIL OUT TO DIE.	211	POEM ON B'DAY	108
EVEN AS A BABY HE HAD NEVER CRIED;	217	ELEGY	26
HE CRIED AS HE DIED, FEARING AT LAST THE SPHERES'	217	ELEGY	33
IS AS RARE AS A DONKEY THAT'S RED.	221	SONG OF DOG	8
IS AS RARE AS A DONKEY THAT'S RED.	221	SONG OF DOG	8
THESE WERE MY DESIRES, ETERNAL AS MOUNTAINS, ...	223	IDYLL UNFORGET	9
HAVE NOT ADORED MY BODY AS IT SOFTLY SMOOTHED THEIR SKIN.	223	IDYLL UNFORGET	16

	PAGE	TITLE	LINE
AS (CONTINUED)			
OF THE PALE-GREEN, DELICATE FISHES, SILVER AS SIGHS;	224	IDYLL UNFORGET	39
AS THE MOUTH OF THE TIGER-LILY	229	MY RIVER	24
THAT RIPENS AS WE DEVELOP	230	OUR SANCTITY	2
ASCEND			
'SEE,' DRUMMED THE TAUT MASKS, 'HOW THE DEAD ASCEND:	132	I MAKE THIS IN	52
ASCENDING			
AM I NOT FATHER, TOO, AND THE ASCENDING BOY,	112	NOT FATHER ME	9
ASCENSION			
O SPIRAL OF ASCENSION	182	VISION, PRAYER	79
ASCENT			
AND, AFTER THE SOFT ASCENT,	31	BEING BUT MEN	8
ASH			
AND HER TONGUE, LOOK, ASH,	10	COOL, OH NO	15
WITH STONES OF ODYSSEY FOR ASH AND GARLAND	120	ALTARWISE	125
ASH-BINS			
KICKED, WITH A CLATTER, ASH-BINS MARKED VERBOTEN,	52	OUT OF THE PIT	57
ASHEN			
TURNS IN THE EARTH THAT TURNS THE ASHEN	106	ALL ALL AND	5
ASHES			
TIME MARKS A BLACK AISLE KINDLE FROM THE BRAND OF ASHES,	130	SINNERS' BELL	4
BUILD FROM THE ASHES!	238	PILLAR BREAKS	25
ASHPIT			
ON THE SNAPPING RIMS OF THE ASHPIT,	151	BELOW A TIME	8
ASIA			
THE STRAWS OF ASIA, LOSE ME AS I TURN	105	WORLD PYRAMID	47
A CLIMBING SEA FROM ASIA HAD ME DOWN	118	ALTARWISE	65
THE CENTRAL PLAINS OF ASIA IN HIS GARDEN,	121	INCARNATE DEVL	2
ASIDE			
DINNED ASIDE THE COILING CROWD,	150	WHEN I WOKE	3
OR CAST YOUR LOVE ASIDE;	228	NOT DESPAIR	3
ASK			
THOUGH NO ASK BRINGS IT	24	LITTLE PROBLEM	22
WHEN COMETH JACK FROST? THE CHILDREN ASK.	56	WHY EAST WIND	10
THOUGH WHAT THE STARS ASK AS THEY ROUND	56	WHY EAST WIND	18
ASK THE TALL FISH SWEPT FROM THE BIBLE EAST,	121	ALTARWISE	134
AND UP AND DOWN LOVE'S QUESTIONS ASK;	138	O CHATTERTON	23
ASKING			
REACH ASKING ARMS UP TO THE MILKY SKY,	42	A WAR OF WITS	16
ASKS			
UNLESS FOR POETRY, WHICH, IF IT ASKS ME	24	LITTLE PROBLEM	17
ASLEEP			
OVER THE WOUND ASLEEP	4	PROLOGUE	50
I HAVE NOT LAIN AN HOUR ASLEEP	22	ON QUIET NIGHT	5
WHERE DEATH LIES DEAD ASLEEP, ONE BRIGHT EYE OPEN,	41	YOUNG ARE OLD	20
BY TRICK OR CHANCE HE FELL ASLEEP	98	TWILIGHT LOCKS	34
WHO SHOWS TO THE SELVES ASLEEP	165	LONG-LEGGED	103
HIS GOLDEN YESTERDAY ASLEEP UPON THE IRIS	170	MARRIAGE VIRG	3
IN THE LAND OF THE HEARTHSTONE TALES, AND SPELLED ASLEEP,	197	COUNTRY SLEEP	2
THE HAYGOLD HAIRED, MY LOVE ASLEEP, AND THE RIFT BLUE	200	COUNTRY SLEEP	88
ASPIRING			
AND HEAVEN CRIER, ARROW NOW OF ASPIRING	148	UNLUCKILY FOR	38
ASS			
WINGED LIKE A SABBATH ASS THIS CHILDREN'S PIECE	124	TODAY, INSECT	16
ASSAILINGS			
ALL BLOOD-SIGNED ASSAILINGS AND VANISHED MARRIAGES IN WHICH HE HAD NO LOVELY PART	158	INTO HER HEAD	43

	PAGE	TITLE	LINE
ASSASSINS			
WITH PRIEST'S GRAVE FOOT AND HAND OF FIVE ASSASSINS	131	I MAKE THIS IN	25
ASSEMBLAGE			
ALL LOVE BUT FOR THE FULL ASSEMBLAGE IN FLOWER	148	UNLUCKILY FOR	40
ASSEMBLED			
ASSEMBLED AT HIS TONGUE	152	WAS A SAVIOUR	5
ASSEMBLING			
ASSEMBLING WAITS FOR THE SPADE'S RING ON THE CAGE.	172	DAWN RAID	11
ASS'S			
I MAKE A WEAPON OF AN ASS'S SKELETON	132	I MAKE THIS IN	31
ASSUMED			
OVER THE BARBED AND SHOOTING SEA ASSUMED AN ARMY	186	HOLY SPRING	6
ASSUMING			
BUT WHEN THE STARS, ASSUMING SHAPE, ...	97	TWILIGHT LOCKS	16
ASTONISH			
I ROCKETED TO ASTONISH	151	BELOW A TIME	25
ASTOUNDED			
I ASTOUNDED THE SITTING TAILORS, ...	151	BELOW A TIME	17
ASTRIDE			
OR FLOWER UNDER THE TIME DYING FLESH ASTRIDE.	188	WINTER'S TALE	55
THE FIELDS OF SEED AND THE TIME DYING FLESH ASTRIDE,	190	WINTER'S TALE	103
ASUNDER			
AND SHARPER IF I BREAK ASUNDER	10	COOL, OH NO	6
ASYLUM			
THE NEW ASYLUM ON THE HILL	33	HELD-OUT HAND	18
THROUGH THE DARK ASYLUM, ...	142	SAINT TO FALL	38
LOVE IN THE ASYLUM	169	LOVE IN ASYLUM	T
ASYLUMS			
IN LAIRS AND ASYLUMS OF THE TREMENDOUS SHOUT.	153	WAS A SAVIOUR	16
AT (137)			
ATE			
DEATH ON THE MOUTH THAT ATE THE GAS.	103	I DREAMED MY	16
ATLANTIC			
THROUGH THE ATLANTIC CORN.	105	WORLD PYRAMID	48
ATLAS			
NEVER SHALL BEAST BE BORN TO ATLAS THE FEW SEAS ...	135	HOW MY ANIMAL	32
ATLAS-EATER			
THE ATLAS-EATER WITH A JAW FOR NEWS, ...	117	ALTARWISE	5
ATLASWISE			
ATLASWISE HOLD HALF-WAY OFF THE DUMMY BAY	121	ALTARWISE	128
ATONE			
MYSELVES GRIEVE NOW, AND MIRACLES CANNOT ATONE. ...	173	FIRE RAID	16
ATTENTIVE			
OR PRAY FOR DAY TO SOME ATTENTIVE GOD	48	LIGHT, I KNOW	14
ATTIC			
O CHATTERTON AND OTHERS IN THE ATTIC	137	O CHATTERTON	1
AUCTION			
THY PLACE IS FILLED, BONES BID FOR AUCTION, ...	29	LONG, SKELETON	9
AUDEN			
A PINCH OF AUDEN IS THE LION'S FEAST;	58	TO ARCHITECTS	13
AUDEN'S			
AND FEW YOUNG AUDEN'S CODED CHATTER;	84	LETTER TO AUNT	38
AUNT			
A LETTER TO MY AUNT DISCUSSING THE CORRECT APPROACH TO MODERN POETRY	83	LETTER TO AUNT	T
TO YOU, MY AUNT, WHO WOULD EXPLORE	83	LETTER TO AUNT	1
FIE ON YOU, AUNT, THAT YOU SHOULD SEE	83	LETTER TO AUNT	7
FIE ON YOU, AUNT! I'LL SHOW YOU HOW	83	LETTER TO AUNT	11
TAKE COURAGE, AUNT, AND SEND YOUR STUFF	85	LETTER TO AUNT	63

	PAGE	TITLE	LINE
AUSTERE			
SOMETHING AUSTERE HIDES, SOMETHING UNCERTAIN	226	THE OAK	5
AUSTRIAN			
RED IN AN AUSTRIAN VOLLEY.	105	WORLD PYRAMID	39
AUTOCRACY			
AUTOCRACY OF NIGHT AND DAY,	61	MEAT ON BONES	12
AUTOMATIC			
SWEET, AUTOMATIC ME KNOWS BEST.	10	COOL, OH NO	18
AUTUMN			
INTO THE BROWNS OF AUTUMN AND THE SHARP WHITES OF WINTER,	47	POET: 1935	20
IN AUTUMN TEACH THREE SEASONS' FIRES	58	HERE IN SPRING	7
IN RAINY AUTUMN	177	POEM IN OCT	15
SUMMER IS HEAVY WITH AGE, AND LEANS UPON AUTUMN.	221	FOREST PICTURE	4
AUTUMNAL			
(SOME LET ME MAKE YOU OF AUTUMNAL SPELLS,	99	OCTOBER WIND	26
AVALANCHE			
HER HEART ALL EARS AND EYES, LIPS CATCHING THE AVALANCHE	170	MARRIAGE VIRG	10
AVENUES			
DOWN THESE FANTASTIC AVENUES PASS LIKE SHADOWS.	222	FOREST PICTURE	12
AVIARY			
THE SPIRE CRANES. ITS STATUE IS AN AVIARY.	15	SPIRE CRANES	1
AVOID			
AVOID CHURCH AS A RAT;	59	FAIRY TALES	5
AWAKE			
TO KISS AWAKE	15	FOR LEDA	18
HE'S NOT AWAKE TO THE GRAVE	17	IN OBLIVION	15
SHALL FALL AWAKE WHEN CURES AND THEIR ITCH	89	EUNUCH DREAMS	22
AWAKE, MY SLEEPER, TO THE SUN,	98	TWILIGHT LOCKS	37
IN SHAPING-TIME THE CIRCLE STUNG AWAKE,	121	INCARNATE DEVL	3
IN ALL LOVE'S COUNTRIES, THAT WILL GROPE AWAKE;	139	FIVE & COUNTRY	12
'NOW TO AWAKE HUSKED OF GESTURES AND MY JOY LIKE A CAVE	146	IF HEAD HURT	21
AWAKE	184	VISION, PRAYER	145
NEVER TO AWAKE AND ARISE	184	VISION, PRAYER	168
AND THEN TO AWAKE, AND THE FARM, LIKE A WANDERER WHITE	195	FERN HILL	28
AWAKING			
HE COMES TO LEAVE HER IN THE LAWLESS SUN AWAKING	201	COUNTRY SLEEP	105
AWARE			
WATCHING, NOT TOO AWARE	13	RAIN CUTS	9
AWAY			
ETERNAL WATERS AWAY	3	PROLOGUE	18
TRICKLE AWAY THROUGH THOUGHT,	19	IMAGES IN AIR	6
FOR, IF I COULD, I'D FLY AWAY,	21	BEWILDERED WAY	22
FOR IF I COULD, I'D FLY AWAY	21	BEWILDERED WAY	23
TICKING THE WORLD AWAY,	26	THERE'S PLENTY	12
THE ACID POURS AWAY, THE ACID DRIPS	34	THIRST PARCHES	8
THAT LEAD AWAY TO DIRTY TOWNS	37	WINDMILLS TURN	14
IS SUCKED AWAY.'	40	YOUNG ARE OLD	4
I HAVE LONGED TO MOVE AWAY	43	LONGED TO MOVE	T
I HAVE LONGED TO MOVE AWAY	43	LONGED TO MOVE	1
I HAVE LONGED TO MOVE AWAY	43	LONGED TO MOVE	6
I HAVE LONGED TO MOVE AWAY BUT AM AFRAID;	44	LONGED TO MOVE	11
WATCH YELLOW, WISH FOR WIND TO BLOW AWAY	54	WE BY SEASAND	19
SAYS THE WORLD WEARS AWAY?	59	HERE IN SPRING	17
RAIN SHALL DEFILE AND COVER, WIND BEAR AWAY	64	WOMAN SPEAKS	40
TOIL AWAY TILL MUSIC DIES.	70	TAKE NEEDLES	4
SHALL FALL AWAY, AND LEAVE ONE SINGING SHELL.	73	LORD RED HAIL	12

	PAGE	TITLE	LINE
AWAY (CONTINUED)			
IMPOSE THEIR SHOTS, SHOWING THE NIGHTS AWAY;	89	EUNUCH DREAMS	18
THAT WIPES AWAY NOT CROW'S-FOOT NOR THE LOCK	95	RUB OF LOVE	23
WEARING THE QUICK AWAY.	95	RUB OF LOVE	35
THE WHISPERING EARS WILL WATCH LOVE DRUMMED AWAY	138	FIVE & COUNTRY	6
WIPE IT AWAY, WIPE A CRUMB	138	O CHATTERTON	38
TO TAKE ME AWAY AS YOU WHISPERED AND WROTE	149	PAPER & STICKS	12
SWEEP AWAY LIKE A CREAM CLOUD;	156	RETURN	89
HAS MELTED AWAY AND IS LOST	165	LONG-LEGGED	115
THE HILLS HAVE FOOTED THE WAVES AWAY,	168	LONG-LEGGED	184
O KEEP HIS BONES AWAY FROM THAT COMMON CART,	173	DAWN RAID	12
AWAY BUT THE WEATHER TURNED AROUND.	178	POEM IN OCT	40
IT TURNED AWAY FROM THE BLITHE COUNTRY	178	POEM IN OCT	41
AWAY BUT THE WEATHER TURNED AROUND. AND THE TRUE	178	POEM IN OCT	62
BLOW AWAY LIKE BREATH,	193	SIDE OF TRUTH	17
AS I RODE TO SLEEP THE OWLS WERE BEARING THE FARM AWAY,	195	FERN HILL	24
THOUGH THE NAMES ON THEIR WEED GROWN STONES ARE RAINED AWAY,	203	GIANT'S THIGH	8
THE DARKEST WAY, AND DID NOT TURN AWAY,	216	ELEGY	2
CANNOT WEAR YOUR EDGE AWAY,	228	MY RIVER	3
THEN TAKE THEM AWAY QUICKLY	229	MY RIVER	23
AND TAKES THE HEAT AWAY.	230	MY RIVER	43
AND TAKE AWAY YOUR EXOTIC PLUMAGE,	232	YOUR VOICE	12
WENT AWAY FROM THE BRIGHT PLACE.	237	WOMAN TAPESTRY	78
REND THE BRIGHT FLESH AWAY,	239	MAKES INTERVALS	23
AWAY'S			
AND FAR AWAY'S TOO SHARP A SUN	12	SKY'S BRIGHT	3
AWHILE			
AWHILE, A LITTLE,	23	THE ONLY DEAD	20
AWKWARD			
HIS AWKWARD HEART INTO SOME SYMMETRY.	77	LASHED RINGS	17
AWOKE			
OF THE TOWN CLOSED AS THE TOWN AWOKE.	177	POEM IN OCT	20
A-WOOING			
AND WOULD A-WOOING GO AROUND THE GRAVES.	138	O CHATTERTON	28
AXE			
I WOULD NOT FEAR THE GALLOWS NOR THE AXE	95	RUB OF LOVE	13
AXLE			
SHALL YOU TURN COCKWISE ON A TUFTED AXLE.	123	FOSTER LIGHT	24
AZURE			
AND IS AZURE;	226	SLENDER WIND	8
BAAING			
FOR EVER OF ALL NOT THE WOLF IN HIS BAAING HOOD	198	COUNTRY SLEEP	36
BABBLE			
LET THE WAX DISK BABBLE	110	I, IN IMAGE	70
BABBLE LIKE A BELLBUOY OVER THE HYMNING HEADS,	136	AFTER FUNERAL	23
BABBLED			
THE FELLOW SEED AND SHADOW AS IT BABBLED	104	WORLD PYRAMID	9
BABBLING			
WHERE BIRD AND SHELL ARE BABBLING IN MY TOWER?	112	NOT FATHER ME	14
BABE			
FLESH AND SPIRIT, BABE AND DAM,	71	TAKE NEEDLES	30
IN THE DARKNESS DAM AND BABE	71	TAKE NEEDLES	33
ANSWER: WHEN HER BABE DENIES HER.	72	TAKE NEEDLES	62
(BUT NOTHING BORE, NO MOUTHING BABE TO THE VEINED HIVES	205	GIANT'S THIGH	42
BABEL			
FROM HARLEM, BEDLAM, BABEL, AND THE GHETTO,	41	YOUNG ARE OLD	40

	PAGE	TITLE	LINE
BABIES			
HAS STOLEN THE STARVED BABIES FROM THEIR LAPS, ...	96	TWELVE	4
BABY			
HERE A MILD BABY SPEAKS HIS FIRST WORD	74	SUN BURNS	9
EVEN AS A BABY HE HAD NEVER CRIED;	217	ELEGY	26
BABY'S			
SINCE THE FIRST WOMB SPAT FORTH A BABY'S CORPSE,	64	WOMAN SPEAKS	52
THE ITCH OF MAN UPON THE BABY'S THIGH, ...	95	RUB OF LOVE	12
BACK			
BUT COOLER WHEN I TAKE IT BACK, ...	10	COOL, OH NO	5
THOSE CRANING BIRDS ARE CHOICE FOR YOU, SONGS THAT JUMP BACK	16	SPIRE CRANES	9
THE PICCADILLY MEN, THE BACK STREET DRUNKS, ...	41	YOUNG ARE OLD	41
ON A MARE'S BACK OF A MARE'S NEST OR A GOOSE, ...	45	TO FOLLOW FOX	19
SITS BACK AND SMILES, A TINY CORPSE	49	LIGHT, I KNOW	24
BEFORE DEATH TAKES YOU, O TAKE BACK THIS.	61	MEAT ON BONES	41
BLOWING THE OLD DEAD BACK; OUR SHOTS SHALL SMACK	90	EUNUCH DREAMS	38
NOR BLOWS BACK MOON-AND-MIDNIGHT AS SHE BLOWS.	92	BOYS OF SUMMER	30
CALL BACK THE CASTAWAYS	107	GRIEF THIEF	7
CAST BACK THE BONE OF YOUTH	107	GRIEF THIEF	11
BLASTS BACK THE TRUMPET VOICE.	114	SERVANT SUN	34
ARC-LAMPED THROWN BACK UPON THE CUTTING FLOOD.	118	ALTARWISE	56
NOR HAMMER BACK A SEASON IN THE FIGS, ...	123	FOSTER LIGHT	8
DOUBLED, TO FORK HIM BACK, THROUGH THE LOCKJAW BED	132	I MAKE THIS IN	50
OR THAT RAINY TONGUE BEAT BACK	139	TOMBSTONE TOLD	13
THE LOVELY GIFT OF THE GAB BANGS BACK ON A BLIND SHAFT.	140	NO WORK WORDS	6
THE BREATH DRAW BACK LIKE A BOLT THROUGH WHITE OIL	142	SAINT TO FALL	46
PACK BACK THE DOWNED BONE. IF THE UNPRICKED BALL OF MY BREATH	145	IF HEAD HURT	2
RAGE ME BACK TO THE MAKING HOUSE. MY HAND UNRAVEL	145	IF HEAD HURT	12
I SET BACK THE CLOCK FACED TAILORS, ...	151	BELOW A TIME	18
AND SEAR JUST RIDERS BACK, ...	161	DEATHS AND ENT	34
FOR MY SAKE SAIL, AND NEVER LOOK BACK, ...	162	LONG-LEGGED	11
THE CENTURIES THROW BACK THEIR HAIR	167	LONG-LEGGED	151
TELL HIS STREET ON ITS BACK HE STOPPED A SUN	172	DAWN RAID	6
DARKNESS KINDLED BACK INTO BEGINNING	173	FIRE RAID	12
BEGINNING CRUMBLED BACK TO DARKNESS	175	FIRE RAID	58
BACK TO CLACK SILENCE MELT AND MOURN	181	VISION, PRAYER	61
I WOULD TURN BACK AND RUN	185	VISION, PRAYER	191
BACK. LINES OF AGE SLEEP ON THE STONES TILL TRUMPETING DAWN.	191	WINTER'S TALE	118
WITH THE DEW, COME BACK, THE COCK ON HIS SHOULDER: IT WAS ALL	195	FERN HILL	29
YOU BATTER BACK MY FEET), ...	237	PILLAR BREAKS	5
IT IS A WEAPON THAT CAN TURN BACK	241	ADMIT THE SUN	20
BACKS			
OR PAINTINGS ON THE BACKS OF VESTS, ...	83	LETTER TO AUNT	27
BACKWARDS			
WE HAVE THE STORIES BACKWARDS, ...	60	FAIRY TALES	31
OR WRITTEN BACKWARDS IN WELSH VERSE, ...	83	LETTER TO AUNT	26
BAD			
BEFORE GOOD OR BAD LUCK.	39	GAS FADES	18
AND THIS WAY LEADS TO GOOD AND BAD, ...	45	TO FOLLOW FOX	22
BUT NO GOD ROSE. I HAVE SEEN BAD AND WORSE, ...	52	OUT OF THE PIT	77
NOR THE BAD BLOOD OF SPRING.	95	RUB OF LOVE	7
AND COUNT THE TAKEN, FORSAKEN MYSTERIES IN A BAD DARK.	140	NO WORK WORDS	9
YOU WITH A BAD COIN IN YOUR SOCKET, ...	146	TO OTHERS	2
GOD IN BED, GOOD AND BAD, ...	150	WHEN I WOKE	17

	PAGE	TITLE	LINE
BAD (CONTINUED)			
MADE HIS BAD BED IN HER GOOD	158	INTO HER HEAD	35
GOOD AND BAD, TWO WAYS	192	SIDE OF TRUTH	13
DEATH, AND BAD DEATH, AND THEN	193	SIDE OF TRUTH	22
BADINAGE			
TOUCHING OUR SEPARATE LOVE WITH BADINAGE	24	THE ONLY DEAD	33
BADLY			
WILDE WORDS, ALL BUTTERED, BADLY BRED,	143	THE MOLLS	10
BAG			
ALONE WITH MY BOUNCING BAG,	155	RETURN	45
BAGPIPE-BREASTED			
THE BAGPIPE-BREASTED LADIES IN THE DEADWEED	119	ALTARWISE	83
BAGS			
AND BAGS OF BLOOD LET OUT THEIR FLIES;	97	TWILIGHT LOCKS	23
BAIT			
BALLAD OF THE LONG-LEGGED BAIT	161	LONG-LEGGED	T
TO THE BAIT THAT STALKED OUT OF THE SACK,	162	LONG-LEGGED	20
BUT HEARD HIS BAIT BUCK IN THE WAKE	162	LONG-LEGGED	29
DEEP THE GREAT BUSHED BAIT WITH RAINING LIPS	163	LONG-LEGGED	51
THE LONG-LEGGED BEAUTIFUL BAIT THEIR WIVES.	164	LONG-LEGGED	70
AND THE BAIT IS DROWNED AMONG HAYRICKS,	169	LONG-LEGGED	208
BALANCE			
TO BALANCE ON MY PALMS	13	RAIN CUTS	4
TIME'S SHIP-RACKED GOSPEL ON THE GLOBE I BALANCE:	121	ALTARWISE	129
ON THE BALANCE OF HER DARK FOOT,	235	WOMAN TAPESTRY	22
BALD			
FROM BALD PAVILIONS AND THE HOUSE OF BREAD	120	ALTARWISE	96
BALL			
YOUR GOLDEN BALL OF BLOOD;	16	TIME TO ROT	3
PICK THE WORLD'S BALL OF WAVE AND FROTH	93	BOYS OF SUMMER	40
BALL OF THE FOOT DEPENDING FROM THE SUN,	101	RUNNING GRAVE	43
THE HORN AND BALL OF WATER ON THE FROG	115	A GRIEF AGO	15
THE BALL I THREW WHILE PLAYING IN THE PARK	116	LANTERNS SHINE	18
SO THE BALL FAIL,	128	NOW, SAY NAY	25
WOUND LIKE A BALL OF LAKES	129	MY NEOPHYTE	33
AND THE GOLDEN BALL SPINS OUT OF THE SKIES;	134	NOT FROM ANGER	10
PACK BACK THE DOWNED BONE. IF THE UNPRICKED BALL OF MY BREATH	145	IF HEAD HURT	2
SPUN ON A SPOUT LIKE A LONG-LEGGED BALL	163	LONG-LEGGED	56
BALLAD			
BALLAD OF THE LONG-LEGGED BAIT	161	LONG-LEGGED	T
BALL-PRYING			
AT WHOSE BALL-PRYING EVEN DEATH'LL SQUIRM	179	NEW QUAY	22
BAMBOO			
WHAT OF A BAMBOO MAN AMONG YOUR ACRES?	118	ALTARWISE	49
BAND			
THE BAND WAS PLAYING ON THE BLACONY.	11	CABARET	10
BANDAGE			
DEATH FROM A BANDAGE, RANTS THE MASK OF SCHOLARS	120	ALTARWISE	120
BANDAGED			
BROKE THROUGH HER STRAWS, BREAKING MY BANDAGED STRING,	94	RUB OF LOVE	3
BANGED			
LOVING ON THIS SEA BANGED GUILT	147	UNLUCKILY FOR	15
BANGS			
THE LOVELY GIFT OF THE GAB BANGS BACK ON A BLIND SHAFT.	140	NO WORK WORDS	6
BAPTISM			
BOWS NO BAPTISM	180	VISION, PRAYER	13

	PAGE	TITLE	LINE
BAPTIZED			
THE NEOPHYTE, BAPTIZED IN SMILES	19	THE NEOPHYTE	T
THE NEOPHYTE, BAPTIZED IN SMILES, ...	19	THE NEOPHYTE	1
BAR			
AND LEANT ON STILES AND ON THE GOLDEN BAR, ...	52	OUT OF THE PIT	66
BARBED			
MAN'S MARROW BARBED, AND BREAST RIPPED WITH A STEEL,	64	WOMAN SPEAKS	30
THE SKULL OF THE EARTH IS BARBED WITH A WAR OF			
BURNING BRAINS AND HAIR.	142	SAINT TO FALL	34
OVER THE BARBED AND SHOOTING SEA ASSUMED AN ARMY	186	HOLY SPRING	6
MANES, UNDER HIS QUENCHLESS SUMMER BARBED GOLD TO			
THE BONE, ...	204	GIANT'S THIGH	26
IN THE BARBED EARTH, ...	237	WOMAN TAPESTRY	72
BARD			
BUT I, ANN'S BARD ON A RAISED HEARTH, CALL ALL	136	AFTER FUNERAL	21
BARE			
GAG OF A DUMBSTRUCK TREE TO BLOCK FROM BARE ENEMIES	133	MAKE ME A MASK	4
SHE CRIED HER WHITE-DRESSED LIMBS WERE BARE	139	TOMBSTONE TOLD	17
AND I FELT WITH MY BARE FALL	140	TOMBSTONE TOLD	28
NOW SHOWN AND MOSTLY BARE I WOULD LIE DOWN, ...	152	BELOW A TIME	49
QUEEN CATHERINE HOWLING BARE	157	INTO HER HEAD	12
BARE AS THE NURSERIES	175	FIRE RAID	59
CROUCHED BARE	182	VISION, PRAYER	70
MAY HIS HUNGER GO HOWLING ON BARE WHITE BONES	188	WINTER'S TALE	33
HUGGED, AND BARREN AND BARE ON MOTHER GOOSE'S GROUND	205	GIANT'S THIGH	43
THERE HE MIGHT WANDER BARE	210	POEM ON B'DAY	55
BARED			
AND BARED YOUR HEAD BENEATH THE LIVING SKY, ...	30	YOUTH CALLS	9
BARENAVELED			
AN OLD CHATTERBOX, BARENAVELED AT NICE, ...	58	TO ARCHITECTS	8
BARER			
OF LOVE AM BARER THAN CADAVER'S TRAP	100	RUNNING GRAVE	8
BARES			
MY HERO BARES HIS NERVES	75	MY HERO BARES	T
MY HERO BARES HIS NERVES ALONG MY WRIST	75	MY HERO BARES	1
MY HERO BARES MY SIDE AND SEES HIS HEART	75	MY HERO BARES	11
THE TERRIBLE WORLD MY BROTHER BARES HIS SKIN.	133	I MAKE THIS IN	60
BARK			
SOAR, WITH ITS TWO BARK TOWERS, TO THAT DAY	121	ALTARWISE	138
BENEATH THE DEEP BARK CALLS AND MAKES QUIET MUSIC.	226	THE OAK	6
BARKED			
SANG TO MY HORN, THE FOXES ON THE HILLS BARKED CLEAR			
AND COLD, ...	195	FERN HILL	16
BARLEY			
FOR THE SURGE IS SOWN WITH BARLEY, ...	168	LONG-LEGGED	182
TRAIL WITH DAISIES AND BARLEY	195	FERN HILL	8
AND GONE THAT BARLEY DARK WHERE THEIR CLOGS DANCED			
IN THE SPRING, ...	205	GIANT'S THIGH	40
BARN			
CRUMBS, BARN, AND HALTER.	32	OUT OF SIGHS	29
BARNROOFS			
AND BARNROOFS COCKCROW WAR!	5	PROLOGUE	81
BARNS			
PAST THE BLIND BARNS AND BYRES OF THE WINDLESS FARM.	190	WINTER'S TALE	90
AND AS I WAS GREEN AND CAREFREE, FAMOUS AMONG THE			
BARNS	195	FERN HILL	10
BARREN			
LAY THE GOLD TITHINGS BARREN, ...	91	BOYS OF SUMMER	2
MAN IN HIS MAGGOT'S BARREN.	93	BOYS OF SUMMER	50
WHERE BARREN AS BOULDERS WOMEN LIE LONGING STILL	203	GIANT'S THIGH	4

	PAGE	TITLE	LINE
BARREN (CONTINUED)			
HUGGED, AND BARREN AND BARE ON MOTHER GOOSE'S GROUND	205	GIANT'S THIGH	43
BASE			
THE DEADROCK BASE THE BLOW THE FLOWERED ANCHOR,	127	NOW, SAY NAY	5
THE SCUDDING BASE OF THE FAMILIAR SKY,	142	SAINT TO FALL	29
DEEP IN ITS BLACK, BASE BONES,	211	POEM ON B'DAY	88
BASES			
THAT FROM THE SOLID BASES OF THE LIGHT	94	IN BEGINNING	20
AND FROM THE CLOUDY BASES OF THE BREATH	94	IN BEGINNING	22
BASIN			
THE ARCTIC SCUT, AND BASIN OF THE SOUTH,	105	WORLD PYRAMID	44
THE NURSE OF GIANTS BY THE CUT SEA BASIN,	113	SERVANT SUN	10
IN THE FOUNTAIN BASIN WHERE I SAILED MY SHIP	171	THE HUNCHBACK	10
BASKETS			
AND DARKNESS HUNG THE WALLS WITH BASKETS OF SNAKES,	158	INTO HER HEAD	27
BASS			
BRANDY AND RIPE IN MY BRIGHT, BASS PRIME,	206	LAMENT	28
BAT			
CRIES NOT ALOUD BLIND AS A BAT,	54	NO MAN BELIEVE	2
BATHE			
HE'LL BATHE HIS RAINING BLOOD IN THE MALE SEA	160	DEATHS AND ENT	19
WHICH BATHE THEMSELVES IN A RAVISHMENT OF SNOW;	223	IDYLL UNFORGET	14
BATHER			
NO TIDY FLOWER MOVED, NO BATHER GRACEFULLY	34	IN GARDENS	19
BATHERS			
OF MARBLE BATHERS TOEING THE GARDEN PONDS,	33	IN GARDENS	2
MADE, FOR THE BATHERS TO ADMIRE,	34	IN GARDENS	12
BATTER			
YOU BATTER BACK MY FEET),	237	PILLAR BREAKS	5
BATTLE			
NOT STUMPS, AFTER THE HOUR OF BATTLE,	42	A WAR OF WITS	9
SHALL DROWN THE BOYS OF BATTLE IN THEIR SWILL,	73	LORD RED HAIL	8
IN BATTLE! THE HAPPENING	182	VISION, PRAYER	95
BATTLING			
AND HAND TO BUTTOCK, MAN TO ENGINE, BATTLING,	51	OUT OF THE PIT	36
BAY			
DRINKING NOAH OF THE BAY,	5	PROLOGUE	85
SHIPS ANCHOR OFF THE BAY.	62	EARS IN TURRET	20
SHIPS ANCHOR OFF THE BAY,	62	EARS IN TURRET	27
MARKING THE FLESH AND SUMMER IN THE BAY?	112	NOT FATHER ME	11
ATLASWISE HOLD HALF-WAY OFF THE DUMMY BAY	121	ALTARWISE	128
BAY. NO-GOOD IS ABROAD. I UNHARDY CAN	179	NEW QUAY	8
AND GALLOWS, UP THE RAYS OF HIS EYES THE SMALL BIRDS OF THE BAY	201	SIR JOHNS HILL	4
GREEN CHICKENS OF THE BAY AND BUSHES CLUCK, 'DILLY DILLY,	202	SIR JOHNS HILL	31
PLEADING IN THE WADED BAY FOR THE SEED TO FLOW	203	GIANT'S THIGH	7
THEIR FRAIL DEEDS MIGHT HAVE DANCED IN A GREEN BAY,	208	NOT GO GENTLE	8
WITH THE SPIRITS OF THE HORSESHOE BAY	210	POEM ON B'DAY	56
BAYING			
AND AT THEIR BAYING MOVE A TAILOR'S INCH	44	TO FOLLOW FOX	2
STREAM WITH BELLS AND BAYING WATER BOUNDS. THE DEW RINGS	189	WINTER'S TALE	62
BAYONET			
THE STOCK AND STEEL THAT BAYONET FROM THE MUD,	73	LORD RED HAIL	9
THE BAYONET TONGUE IN THIS UNDEFENDED PRAYERPIECE,	133	MAKE ME A MASK	5
BAYS			
DOWN THE LONG BAYS OF BLUE THAT THOSE CLOUDY HEADLANDS	222	FOREST PICTURE	6

	PAGE	TITLE	LINE
BAY'S			
MY DABBED BAY'S DUSK, AS I HACK	4	PROLOGUE	36
THIS SANDGRAIN DAY IN THE BENT BAY'S GRAVE	208	POEM ON B'DAY	6
BE (147)			
BEACH			
THE BEACH OF FLESH, AND WIND HER BLOODRED PLAIT;	75	MY HERO BARES	13
DOWN BREEZE AND SHELL TO A DISCORDANT BEACH,	138	FIVE & COUNTRY	7
BEACH, HEARING RISE SLIMY FROM THE WELSH LECHERED	179	NEW QUAY	16
LYING UPON THE YELLOW BEACH.	229	MY RIVER	40
BEAD			
ZION OF THE WATER BEAD	191	REFUSAL MOURN	8
BEADS			
IN THE RAIN TELLING ITS BEADS, AND THE GRAVEST GHOST	198	COUNTRY SLEEP	31
BEAK			
HEARD HER SPEAK THROUGH THE CHIPPED BEAK	140	TOMBSTONE TOLD	24
COLD NANSEN'S BEAK ON A BOAT FULL OF GONGS,	152	BELOW A TIME	40
FROM SALT-LIPPED BEAK TO THE KICK OF THE STERN	164	LONG-LEGGED	81
AND THE BEAK OF SLIME	183	VISION, PRAYER	114
WITH HIS PINK BEAK,	231	OUR SANCTITY	25
BEAKED			
YET OUT OF THE BEAKED, WEB DARK AND THE POUNCING BOUGHS	199	COUNTRY SLEEP	48
BEAKS			
IN YOUR BEAKS, ON THE GABBING CAPES!	4	PROLOGUE	66
IN HIS HOUSE ON STILTS HIGH AMONG BEAKS	208	POEM ON B'DAY	4
BEAMS			
BUT THE HOT BEAMS ROB ME OF SPEECH,	42	A WAR OF WITS	14
SO THE BETRAYED MIGHT LEARN IN THE SUN BEAMS	176	MY BEGGAR ARM	7
BEAR			
THE HOLLOW WORDS COULD BEAR ALL SUFFERING	32	OUT OF SIGHS	22
THE HARDER TO BEAR AND THE STRONGER.	39	GAS FADES	29
RAIN SHALL DEFILE AND COVER, WIND BEAR AWAY	64	WOMAN SPEAKS	40
BY WASTE SEAS WHERE THE WHITE BEAR QUOTED VIRGIL	119	ALTARWISE	69
AND BEAR THOSE TENDRIL HANDS I TOUCH ACROSS	134	NOT FROM ANGER	6
THE SHE MULES BEAR THEIR MINOTAURS,	148	UNLUCKILY FOR	32
THEN, BUSHILY SWANKED IN BEAR WIG AND TAILS,	151	BELOW A TIME	19
HARDLY BEAR THE DIN OF NO-GOOD WRACKED DRY ON	179	NEW QUAY	9
UNTIL YOU COULD BEAR IT NO LONGER	232	FURIOUS MOTION	12
BEARD			
WHOSE BEARD WAGS IN EGYPTIAN WIND.	116	LANTERNS SHINE	15
AND HIS SCARVING BEARD FROM A BOOK,	150	WHEN I WOKE	12
BEARDED			
IN SHAPES OF SIN FORKED OUT THE BEARDED APPLE,	121	INCARNATE DEVL	4
SUSANNAH'S DROWNED IN THE BEARDED STREAM	165	LONG-LEGGED	107
BEARDING			
BEARDING THE UNBORN DEVIL,	105	WORLD PYRAMID	51
BEARDLESSLY			
BEARDLESSLY WAGGING IN DEAN STREET,	156	RETURN	72
BEARER			
AND A GREEN INCH BE HIS BEARER;	126	SEED-AT-ZERO	32
AND A HIGH SPHERE BE HIS BEARER;	126	SEED-AT-ZERO	39
BEARING			
TIME IS BEARING ANOTHER SON.	167	LONG-LEGGED	153
AND BEARING	183	VISION, PRAYER	108
AS I RODE TO SLEEP THE OWLS WERE BEARING THE FARM AWAY,	195	FERN HILL	24
BEARS			
'BUT THIS WE TREAD BEARS THE ANGELIC GANGS,	102	FELLOWED SLEEP	13
LUST BEARS LIKE VOLTS, WHO'LL AMPLIFY, AND STRANGE	159	TO LEDA	8

	PAGE	TITLE	LINE
BEAST			
HERE LIES THE BEAST OF MAN AND HERE HIS ANGELS, ...	81	HERE LIE BEAST	7
BLACK AS THE BEAST AND PALER THAN THE CROSS.	121	INCARNATE DEVL	12
JOHN'S BEAST, JOB'S PATIENCE, AND THE FIBS OF VISION,	125	TODAY, INSECT	21
HIS BEAST HEEL CLEFT IN A SANDAL, ...	130	SINNERS' BELL	3
THESE ARE HER CONTRARIES: THE BEAST WHO FOLLOWS ...	131	I MAKE THIS IN	24
BENT LIKE A BEAST TO LAP THE SINGULAR FLOODS	134	NOT FROM ANGER	3
NEVER SHALL BEAST BE BORN TO ATLAS THE FEW SEAS ...	135	HOW MY ANIMAL	32
LIE DRY, REST ROBBED, MY BEAST.	135	HOW MY ANIMAL	42
CONVENIENT BIRD AND BEAST LIE LODGED TO SUFFER	144	PLEASURE-BIRD	3
HER HOLY UNHOLY HOURS WITH THE ALWAYS ANONYMOUS			
BEAST.	158	INTO HER HEAD	46
TILL EVERY BEAST BLARED DOWN IN A SWERVE	163	LONG-LEGGED	57
BIRD BEAST AND FLOWER	191	REFUSAL MOURN	2
AND THE BLACK BEAST OF THE BEETLES' PEWS, ...	206	LAMENT	14
BEASTHOOD			
(HAIL TO HIS BEASTHOOD).	5	PROLOGUE	76
BEASTS			
BEASTS WHO SLEEP GOOD AND THIN, ...	5	PROLOGUE	77
SPIED MOON-MAD BEASTS CAROUSING ON THE HILL, ...	50	OUT OF THE PIT	9
HERE LIE THE BEASTS	81	HERE LIE BEAST	T
HERE LIE THE BEASTS OF MAN AND HERE I FEAST, ...	81	HERE LIE BEAST	1
ALL BIRDS AND BEASTS OF THE LINKED NIGHT UPROAR AND			
CHIME	204	GIANT'S THIGH	35
THEN IN THE DELIGHT AND GROVE OF BEASTS AND BIRDS	215	COUNTRY HEAVEN	6
BEAT			
UNSOUNDING, THEY BEAT SO SOFT.	33	HELD-OUT HAND	5
WITH SIGHTLESS EYES AND HEARTS THAT DO NOT BEAT,	39	GAS FADES	36
OR THAT RAINY TONGUE BEAT BACK	139	TOMBSTONE TOLD	13
HEAVEN FELL WITH HIS FALL AND ONE CROCKED BELL BEAT			
THE LEFT AIR.	142	SAINT TO FALL	25
BEDSITTING GIRLS ON THE BEAT	155	RETURN	58
OF THE WOOD! PASTORAL BEAT OF BLOOD THROUGH THE			
LACED LEAVES!	199	COUNTRY SLEEP	71
BEATING			
THE ANGELS' WINGS BEATING ABOUT YOUR HEAD	33	HELD-OUT HAND	4
GREED ON MAN BEATING NEAR THE FIRE NEIGHBOUR	153	WAS A SAVIOUR	30
AND THE BEATING DUST BE BLOWN	184	VISION, PRAYER	150
WITH RAVENS BEATING ON THE ROOF:	237	PILLAR BREAKS	13
BEATS			
RAIN BEATS THE SAND AND SLATES.	62	EARS IN TURRET	28
BEAUTIFUL			
AND THE BEAUTIFUL NOISE IS QUELLED, ...	18	NATURAL DAY	22
ALL THAT IS BEAUTIFUL BUT BORN TO DIE, ...	30	YOUTH CALLS	6
THE LONG-LEGGED BEAUTIFUL BAIT THEIR WIVES.	164	LONG-LEGGED	70
IT IS SO SAD AND BEAUTIFUL, ...	225	CLOWN IN MOON	7
AND IS MORE BEAUTIFUL THAN THE DRIFT OF LEAVES. ...	226	SLENDER WIND	9
FRIENDLY AND BEAUTIFUL TO YOU;	228	NOT DESPAIR	8
STRONG AND BEAUTIFUL ENOUGH	229	MY RIVER	9
YOUR HANDS ARE BEAUTIFUL HANDS	229	MY RIVER	27
BEAUTIFUL ROOTS	230	OUR SANCTITY	8
DEATH COMES TO THE BEAUTIFUL.	236	WOMAN TAPESTRY	41
BEAUTIFULLY			
BEAUTIFULLY LITTLE LIKE CLOUDS:	226	THE ELM	9
BUT BEAUTIFULLY FLAKE YOUR HEAD	227	SPRING-SPIRIT	3
BEAUTY			
WHEN YOU HAVE GROUND SUCH BEAUTY DOWN TO DUST	25	BEAUTY TO DUST	T
WHEN YOU HAVE GROUND SUCH BEAUTY DOWN TO DUST	25	BEAUTY TO DUST	1
NOR WHEN HE FINDS A BEAUTY IN THE BREAST	96	RUB OF LOVE	40
THEIR PALE, ETHEREAL BEAUTY SEEMS TO BE	222	IN DREAMS	3

	PAGE	TITLE	LINE
BEAUTY (CONTINUED)			
THEY OF THE PALE, SEA-WAN BEAUTY, THEY OF THE HOME	224	IDYLL UNFORGET	38
FOR LILACS IN THEIR BEAUTY BLOW	227	TRIOLET	2
FOR LILACS IN THEIR BEAUTY BLOW.	228	TRIOLET	8
BECALMED			
LIE STILL, SLEEP BECALMED	194	SLEEP BECALMED	T
LIE STILL, SLEEP BECALMED, SUFFERER WITH THE WOUND	194	SLEEP BECALMED	1
LIE STILL, SLEEP BECALMED, HIDE THE MOUTH IN THE THROAT, ...	194	SLEEP BECALMED	13
BECAME			
SHE BECAME LIKE A DANCER OR A PRETTY ANIMAL	235	WOMAN TAPESTRY	20
BECAUSE			
BECAUSE LAID DOWN	26	PERSONAL EPIT	3
BECAUSE THE PLEASURE-BIRD WHISTLES	144	PLEASURE-BIRD	T
BECAUSE THE PLEASURE-BIRD WHISTLES AFTER THE HOT WIRES, ...	144	PLEASURE-BIRD	1
BECAUSE THERE STANDS, ONE STORY OUT OF THE BUM CITY,	144	PLEASURE-BIRD	13
BECAUSE THEIR WORDS HAD FORKED NO LIGHTNING THEY	208	NOT GO GENTLE	5
BECAUSE I HAVE FORSAKEN YOU	228	NOT DESPAIR	2
BECAUSE THEY ARE UNDER THE SURFACE	230	OUR SANCTITY	9
WHO FLEW HIMSELF BECAUSE THE BOAT REMAINED	238	PILLAR BREAKS	19
BECKON			
THE MORNING BECKON	176	POEM IN OCT	5
HIDDEN IN DELICATE DRIFTS OF MIST ARE THEY THAT BECKON, ...	224	IDYLL UNFORGET	37
BECKONED			
HER WOVEN HANDS BECKONED ME, ...	234	WOMAN TAPESTRY	1
BED			
INTO A DOUBLE OR A SINGLE BED, ...	28	NO WINGS	18
AND ON THE SWEETHEARTS' BED TO LIE AND GRIN, ...	34	THIRST PARCHES	12
A GIRL WHOSE SINGLE BED HELD TWO	38	THE GOSSIPERS	9
LAY YOUR HEAD ON A HARD BED OF STONE, ...	45	PLOUGHMAN GONE	17
LAY YOUR HEAD ON A HARD BED OF STONE, ...	46	PLOUGHMAN GONE	31
CERECLOTH OF WEED, AND BUILD AN ORDURED BED.	64	WOMAN SPEAKS	27
WILL BE BREATHING BY MY BED.	72	TAKE NEEDLES	48
HERE SLIPS THE GHOST WHO MADE OF MY PALE BED	81	HERE LIE BEAST	11
I BLEW THE DREAMING FELLOWS TO THEIR BED	102	FELLOWED SLEEP	19
IN THE GLASS BED OF GRAPES WITH SNAIL AND FLOWER,	109	I, IN IMAGE	29
LOVE LIKE A MIST OR FIRE THROUGH THE BED OF EELS.	111	I, IN IMAGE	90
AND SHARE MY BED WITH CAPRICORN AND CANCER.	117	ALTARWISE	14
WITH PRIEST AND PHARAOH BED MY GENTLE WOUND, ...	120	ALTARWISE	123
AT NIGHTBREAK BORN IN THE FAT SIDE, FROM AN ANIMAL BED	130	SINNERS' BELL	26
DOUBLED, TO FORK HIM BACK, THROUGH THE LOCKJAW BED	132	I MAKE THIS IN	50
BEFORE SHE LAY ON A STRANGER'S BED	139	TOMBSTONE TOLD	11
FLICKED FROM THE CARBOLIC CITY PUZZLE IN A BED OF SORES	142	SAINT TO FALL	28
PEACOCKSTAIN'S POEMS ON MY BED.	143	THE MOLLS	12
WHEN YOU SEW THE DEEP DOOR. THE BED IS A CROSS PLACE.	145	IF HEAD HURT	13
'NO. NOT FOR CHRIST'S DAZZLING BED	146	IF HEAD HURT	16
WHEN IN OUR BED I WAS TOSSING AND TURNING	149	PAPER & STICKS	7
GOD IN BED, GOOD AND BAD, ...	150	WHEN I WOKE	17
WITH DRY FLESH AND EARTH FOR ADORNING AND BED.	152	BELOW A TIME	43
HIS ENEMIES ENTERED BED, ...	157	INTO HER HEAD	2
MADE HIS BAD BED IN HER GOOD	158	INTO HER HEAD	35
TWO SAND GRAINS TOGETHER IN BED, ...	158	INTO HER HEAD	47
OLD IN HER CRUEL BED.	164	LONG-LEGGED	84
STRAIT IN THE MAZED BED	169	LOVE IN ASYLUM	5
OF THE DEATH IN A BED IN ANOTHER COUNTRY.	176	MY BEGGAR ARM	8
OUT OF A BED OF LOVE	186	HOLY SPRING	2

	PAGE	TITLE	LINE
BED (CONTINUED)			
INHUMAN CRADLE AND THE BRIDE BED FOREVER SOUGHT ...	188	WINTER'S TALE	49
BURNING IN THE BRIDE BED OF LOVE, IN THE WHIRL- ...	191	WINTER'S TALE	127
BY THE CHILD GOING TO BED AND THE MAN ON THE STAIRS	193	CONVERS PRAYER	2
FROM THE MAN ON THE STAIRS AND THE CHILD BY HIS BED.	194	CONVERS PRAYER	8
OR, BUTTER FAT GOOSEGIRLS, BOUNCED IN A GAMBO BED,	204	GIANT'S THIGH	37
AND I LIE DOWN BUT TO SLEEP IN BED, ...	206	LAMENT	35
I PRAYED IN THE CROUCHING ROOM, BY HIS BLIND BED,	216	ELEGY	13
BEDDED			
FOR THE BIRD LAY BEDDED	191	WINTER'S TALE	121
BEDFELLOWS			
THE WITHERED WOMEN WIN THEM BEDFELLOWS.	38	THE GOSSIPERS	16
BEDLAM			
FROM HARLEM, BEDLAM, BABEL, AND THE GHETTO, ...	41	YOUNG ARE OLD	40
TO THE JUDGE BLOWN BEDLAM	182	VISION, PRAYER	74
BEDS			
SKIRTING THE ORDERED BEDS OF PAINT-BOX FLOWERS, ...	33	IN GARDENS	3
STRANGLE THE LITTLE CHILDREN IN THEIR BEDS;	64	WOMAN SPEAKS	46
THE BONES OF MEN, THE BROKEN IN THEIR BEDS, ...	89	EUNUCH DREAMS	9
THERE SHALL BE CORALS IN YOUR BEDS, ...	91	WHERE ONCE THE	22
AND SLEEP ROLLS MUTE ABOVE THE BEDS	98	TWILIGHT LOCKS	28
LOVERS IN THE DIRT OF THEIR LEAFY BEDS, ...	144	COLOUR OF SAY	9
OTHERS WHOSE SINGLE BEDS HOLD TWO	155	RETURN	60
AND THE SIZZLING BEDS OF THE TOWN CRIED, QUICK!--	206	LAMENT	20
BEDSITTING			
BEDSITTING GIRLS ON THE BEAT	155	RETURN	58
BEDTIME			
I DIED BEFORE BEDTIME CAME	140	TOMBSTONE TOLD	26
BEDWARD			
AND SALT-EYED STUMBLE BEDWARD WHERE SHE LIES	107	GRIEF THIEF	12
BEECHES			
SOME LET ME MAKE YOU OF THE VOWELLED BEECHES, ...	99	OCTOBER WIND	13
BEEN (12)			
BEES			
AND THAT BEES NEVER WORK IN THEIR HIVES.	221	SONG OF DOG	4
THE BEES ARE GLAD THE LIVELONG DAY, ...	227	TRIOLET	1
THE BEES ARE GLAD THE LIVELONG DAY, ...	228	TRIOLET	4
THE BEES ARE GLAD THE LIVELONG DAY, ...	228	TRIOLET	7
BEES'			
AND THIS IS PLENTY, THEN, CLOVES AND SWEET OILS, THE BEES' HONEY, ...	36	MIDNIGHT ROAD	5
BEETLE			
I, SAID THE BEETLE, OUT OF MY THIN BLACK WOMB, ...	18	NATURAL DAY	26
BEETLES'			
AND THE BLACK BEAST OF THE BEETLES' PEWS, ...	206	LAMENT	14
BEFORE			
BEFORE THE LAST LIGHT IS BLOWN	21	BEWILDERED WAY	24
AS FLIES BEFORE THE BREATH	25	BEAUTY TO DUST	2
BEFORE THE AGONY; THE SPIRIT GROWS, ...	31	OUT OF SIGHS	3
THAT STOOD BEFORE MY WINDOW, ...	33	HELD-OUT HAND	13
BEFORE THE GAS FADES	38	GAS FADES	T
BEFORE THE GAS FADES WITH A HARSH LAST BUBBLE, ...	38	GAS FADES	1
BEFORE THE LAST FAG AND THE SHIRT SLEEVES AND SLIPPERS, ...	38	GAS FADES	3
BEFORE THE ALLOTMENT IS WEEDED AND SOWN, ...	38	GAS FADES	5
BEFORE CIVILIZATION RISES OR ROTS, ...	39	GAS FADES	9
BEFORE THE ARRIVAL OF ANGEL OR DEVIL, ...	39	GAS FADES	15
BEFORE EVIL OR GOOD, LIGHT OR DARK, ...	39	GAS FADES	16
BEFORE WHITE OR BLACK, THE RIGHT OR LEFT SOCK, ...	39	GAS FADES	17
BEFORE GOOD OR BAD LUCK.	39	GAS FADES	18

	PAGE	TITLE	LINE
BEFORE (CONTINUED)			
BEFORE THE WORLD STEADIES, STOPS ROCKING, IS STEADY,	39	GAS FADES	33
OR ROCKS, SWINGS AND ROCKS, BEFORE THE WORLD TOTTERS.	39	GAS FADES	34
AGE SOURS BEFORE YOUTH'S TASTED IN THE MOUTH	40	YOUNG ARE OLD	2
WE HAVE GROWN WEAK BEFORE WE COULD GROW STRONG, ...	40	YOUNG ARE OLD	7
MEN OLD BEFORE THEIR TIME INTO DARK VALLEYS	41	YOUNG ARE OLD	19
BEFORE THE MOON SHIFTED AND THE SAP RAN OUT, ...	43	FACES SHONE	10
BEFORE THE LADIES' BREASTS ARE HAGS	60	MEAT ON BONES	4
BEFORE DEATH TAKES YOU, O TAKE BACK THIS.	61	MEAT ON BONES	41
BEFORE I KNOCKED	68	BEFORE KNOCKED	T
BEFORE I KNOCKED AND FLESH LET ENTER, ...	68	BEFORE KNOCKED	1
MY THROAT KNEW THIRST BEFORE THE STRUCTURE	69	BEFORE KNOCKED	25
BEFORE WE MOTHERNAKED FALL	73	WE MOTHERNAKED	T
BEFORE WE MOTHERNAKED FALL	73	WE MOTHERNAKED	1
BEFORE THE PROMISES FULFILL	74	WE MOTHERNAKED	7
BEFORE OUR BLOOD;	74	WE MOTHERNAKED	12
AND YOU, BEFORE THE BREATH IS COLD	74	WE MOTHERNAKED	14
A FINAL WORD: BEFORE YOU START	84	LETTER TO AUNT	58
BEFORE THE BLOOD AND FLAME WERE TWINED	86	SEE, SAYS LIME	23
MOVE LIKE TWO GHOSTS BEFORE THE EYE.	88	A PROCESS IN	18
BEFORE THE PITCH WAS FORKING TO A SUN;	94	IN BEGINNING	27
BEFORE THE VEINS WERE SHAKING IN THEIR SIEVE, ...	94	IN BEGINNING	28
RISE BEFORE DARK.	115	A GRIEF AGO	32
I TELL HER THIS: BEFORE THE SUNCOCK CAST	115	A GRIEF AGO	35
LOOK TWICE BEFORE HE FELL FROM GRACE.	116	LANTERNS SHINE	4
A CROCODILE BEFORE THE CHRYSALIS, ...	124	TODAY, INSECT	14
BEFORE THE FALL FROM LOVE THE FLYING HEARTBONE, ...	124	TODAY, INSECT	15
BEFORE I HEARD IN MY MOTHER'S SIDE	139	TOMBSTONE TOLD	6
BEFORE SHE LAY ON A STRANGER'S BED	139	TOMBSTONE TOLD	11
I DIED BEFORE BEDTIME CAME	140	TOMBSTONE TOLD	26
BEFORE I RUSH IN A CROUCH THE GHOST WITH A HAMMER,			
AIR, ...	145	IF HEAD HURT	9
BEFORE THE CROWING MORNING CLIMBED;	157	INTO HER HEAD	19
BEFORE THE LIPS BLAZE AND BLOOM	183	VISION, PRAYER	121
BEFORE YOU MOVE TO MAKE	192	SIDE OF TRUTH	8
IS CAST BEFORE YOU MOVE, ...	193	SIDE OF TRUTH	33
BEFORE THE CHILDREN GREEN AND GOLDEN	196	FERN HILL	44
TO COURT THE HONEYED HEART FROM YOUR SIDE BEFORE			
SUNRISE	198	COUNTRY SLEEP	13
THE OWL AT ITS KNELLING. FOX AND HOLT KNEEL BEFORE			
BLOOD.	198	COUNTRY SLEEP	32
BEFORE THE LUNGE OF THE NIGHT, THE NOTES ON THIS			
TIME-SHAKEN	203	SIR JOHNS HILL	59
BEFORE CHAINS BREAK TO A HAMMER FLAME	210	POEM ON B'DAY	44
IN THE MUTED HOUSE, ONE MINUTE BEFORE	216	ELEGY	14
INFINITE SHADOWY ISLES LIE SILENT BEFORE ME, ...	221	FOREST PICTURE	3
BURNING ITS SWEET PATH CLEARER THAN BEFORE.	232	FURIOUS MOTION	17
BEGAN			
MY BIRTHDAY BEGAN WITH THE WATER-	177	POEM IN OCT	11
BEGGAR			
LAST NIGHT I DIVED MY BEGGAR ARM	175	MY BEGGAR ARM	T
LAST NIGHT I DIVED MY BEGGAR ARM	175	MY BEGGAR ARM	1
BEGGARS			
BEGGARS, ROBBERS, INVEIGLERS, ...	155	RETURN	52
BEGIN			
BEGIN	173	FIRE RAID	9
FOR MY VOYAGE TO BEGIN TO THE END OF MY WOUND, ...	194	SLEEP BECALMED	11
BEGINNING			
IN THE BEGINNING	93	IN BEGINNING	T
IN THE BEGINNING WAS THE THREE-POINTED STAR, ...	93	IN BEGINNING	1

		PAGE	TITLE	LINE
BEGINNING (CONTINUED)				
IN THE BEGINNING WAS THE PALE SIGNATURE,	....	94	IN BEGINNING	7
IN THE BEGINNING WAS THE MOUNTING FIRE	....	94	IN BEGINNING	13
IN THE BEGINNING WAS THE WORD, THE WORD	....	94	IN BEGINNING	19
IN THE BEGINNING WAS THE SECRET BRAIN.	....	94	IN BEGINNING	25
BEGINNING WITH DOOM IN THE BULB, THE SPRING UNRAVELS,		108	I, IN IMAGE	7
BEGINNING WITH DOOM IN THE GHOST, AND THE SPRINGING MARVELS,	....	109	I, IN IMAGE	13
THIS WAS THE GOD OF BEGINNING IN THE INTRICATE SEAWHIRL,	....	112	I, IN IMAGE	107
TIME, MILK, AND MAGIC, FROM THE WORLD BEGINNING.		119	ALTARWISE	94
GREEN AS BEGINNING, LET THE GARDEN DIVING	....	121	ALTARWISE	137
AND BREAKS HIS SHELL IN THE LAST SHOCKED BEGINNING;		124	TODAY, INSECT	13
AND THE ENDLESS BEGINNING OF PRODIGIES SUFFERS OPEN.'		146	IF HEAD HURT	30
HURLING INTO BEGINNING LIKE CHRIST THE CHILD.	.....	149	UNLUCKILY FOR	52
DARKNESS KINDLED BACK INTO BEGINNING	....	173	FIRE RAID	12
BEGINNING CRUMBLED BACK TO DARKNESS	....	175	FIRE RAID	58
DOWN THE BEGINNING OF PLANTS	....	193	SIDE OF TRUTH	30
BEGINS				
AS THE FLOOD BEGINS,	....	4	PROLOGUE	46
BEGUN				
DRESSED TO DIE, THE SENSUAL STRUT BEGUN,	....	143	24 YEARS	6
BEHEADED				
STORM HER SPED HEART, HANG WITH BEHEADED VEINS	....	132	I MAKE THIS IN	34
BEHIND				
BRED IN THE DARK BEHIND THE SKIRTING-BOARD,	....	28	NO WINGS	21
AND NOW BEHIND THE SCREEN ARE VIXEN VOICES,	....	36	MIDNIGHT ROAD	9
STIR THEIR OLD BONES BEHIND CUPBOARD AND CURTAIN.		38	THE GOSSIPERS	5
AND HID BEHIND THE FORTRESS OF THE RIBS	....	63	WOMAN SPEAKS	7
WE SEE RISE THE SECRET WIND BEHIND THE BRAIN,	.....	69	SECRET WIND	1
WE HEAR RISE THE SECRET WIND BEHIND THE BRAIN,	....	70	SECRET WIND	19
THE FIELDS YET UNDIVIDED BEHIND THE SKULL.	....	73	LORD RED HAIL	10
DAWN BREAKS BEHIND THE EYES;	....	82	LIGHT BREAKS	13
BEHIND A POT OF FERNS THE WAGGING CLOCK	....	99	OCTOBER WIND	17
MY CROSS OF TALES BEHIND THE FABULOUS CURTAIN.'	...	125	TODAY, INSECT	26
BEHIND MY HEAD A SQUARE OF SKY SAGS OVER	....	134	NOT FROM ANGER	8
SHALL HER SMILE BREED THAT MOUTH, BEHIND THE MIRROR,		134	NOT FROM ANGER	13
BEHIND A FACE OF HANDS,	....	141	SAINT TO FALL	10
GENTLY THEY SIGH TO MY BEHIND	....	143	THE MOLLS	9
BEHIND THE WALL THIN AS A WREN'S BONE?	....	180	VISION, PRAYER	9
BEHIND THE WALL'S WREN	....	183	VISION, PRAYER	123
FLOW UNEASILY BEHIND YOU.	....	232	FURIOUS MOTION	8
BEING				
BEING BUT MEN	....	31	BEING BUT MEN	T
BEING BUT MEN, WE WALKED INTO THE TREES	....	31	BEING BUT MEN	1
BEING BUT MEN, WE WALKED INTO THE TREES.	....	31	BEING BUT MEN	17
IF LOVE HE CAN BEING NO WOMAN'S MAN.	....	47	POET: 1935	35
LOVING AND BEING LOTH;	....	90	EUNUCH DREAMS	33
NOT GIRL FOR BIRD (GOURD BEING MAN) BREAKS ROOT.		159	TO LEDA	4
BEING INNOCENT, HE DREADED THAT HE DIED	....	217	ELEGY	22
BELFRIES				
HEARS THE BELFRIES AND THE COBBLES	....	215	COUNTRY HEAVEN	25
BELIEVE				
BELIEVE, BELIEVE AND BE SAVED, WE CRY, WHO HAVE NO FAITH.	....	42	YOUNG ARE OLD	57
BELIEVE, BELIEVE AND BE SAVED, WE CRY, WHO HAVE NO FAITH.	....	42	YOUNG ARE OLD	57
BELIEVE AND BE SAVED. NO MAN BELIEVES	....	55	NO MAN BELIEVE	13
FEAR OR BELIEVE THAT THE WOLF IN A SHEEPWHITE HOOD		197	COUNTRY SLEEP	3
BELL BELIEVE OR FEAR THAT THE RUSTIC SHADE OR SPELL		198	COUNTRY SLEEP	22

	PAGE	TITLE	LINE
BELIEVE (CONTINUED)			
EVER AND EVER BY ALL YOUR VOWS BELIEVE AND FEAR ...	201	COUNTRY SLEEP	107
LET ME BELIEVE IN THE CLEAN FAITH OF THE BODY, ...	235	WOMAN TAPESTRY	24
LET ME BELIEVE IN THE CLEAN FAITH OF THE BODY, ...	237	WOMAN TAPESTRY	79
BELIEVED			
HEAD, DECEIVED, I BELIEVED, MY MAKER, ...	152	BELOW A TIME	34
BELIEVER			
BY THE BELIEVER LOST AND THE HURLED OUTCAST OF LIGHT.	188	WINTER'S TALE	50
BELIEVERS			
YOUR DEATH THAT MYSELVES THE BELIEVERS	173	FIRE RAID	20
BELIEVES			
NO MAN BELIEVES	54	NO MAN BELIEVE	T
NO MAN BELIEVES WHO, WHEN A STAR FALLS SHOT, ...	54	NO MAN BELIEVE	1
NO MAN BELIEVES WHO CRIES NOT, GOD IS NOT, ...	55	NO MAN BELIEVE	7
NO MAN BELIEVES WHO DOES NOT WONDER WHY.	55	NO MAN BELIEVE	12
BELIEVE AND BE SAVED. NO MAN BELIEVES	55	NO MAN BELIEVE	13
BELIEVES WHO DOES NOT LANCE HIS FAITH, ...	55	NO MAN BELIEVE	16
BELIEVING			
FIXED FAITH, BELIEVING AND WORSHIPPING TOGETHER ...	41	YOUNG ARE OLD	46
BELL			
A SMILE LET LOOSE A DEVIL, A BELL STRUCK.	51	OUT OF THE PIT	19
SWEETLY THE DIVER'S BELL IN THE STEEPLE OF SPINDRIFT	110	I, IN IMAGE	62
UNDER THE BELL OF ROCKS, ...	128	MY NEOPHYTE	3
IT IS THE SINNERS' DUST-TONGUED BELL	130	SINNERS' BELL	T
IT IS THE SINNERS' DUST-TONGUED BELL CLAPS ME TO CHURCHES	130	SINNERS' BELL	1
FROM THE EMERALD, STILL BELL; AND FROM THE PACING WEATHER-COCK	130	SINNERS' BELL	17
REFUSAL STRUCK LIKE A BELL UNDER WATER	134	NOT FROM ANGER	12
HEAVEN FELL WITH HIS FALL AND ONE CROCKED BELL BEAT THE LEFT AIR.	142	SAINT TO FALL	25
UNTIL THE SUNDAY SOMBRE BELL AT DARK	171	THE HUNCHBACK	6
MADE ALL DAY UNTIL BELL TIME	172	THE HUNCHBACK	31
BELL BELIEVE OR FEAR THAT THE RUSTIC SHADE OR SPELL	198	COUNTRY SLEEP	22
THIS NIGHT AND EACH VAST NIGHT UNTIL THE STERN BELL TALKS	199	COUNTRY SLEEP	51
MIGHT CROSS ITS PLANETS, THE BELL WEEP, NIGHT GATHER HER EYES, ...	200	COUNTRY SLEEP	92
DEATH CLEAR AS A BUOY'S BELL:	202	SIR JOHNS HILL	26
WHO HEARD THE TALL BELL SAIL DOWN THE SUNDAYS OF THE DEAD	205	GIANT'S THIGH	51
WHO TOLLS HIS BIRTHDAY BELL, ...	209	POEM ON B'DAY	16
TO HIS NIMBUS BELL COOL KINGDOM COME	211	POEM ON B'DAY	85
BELLADONNA			
TO VEIL BELLADONNA AND LET THE DRY EYES PERCEIVE	133	MAKE ME A MASK	10
BELLBUOY			
BABBLE LIKE A BELLBUOY OVER THE HYMNING HEADS, ...	136	AFTER FUNERAL	23
BELLED			
THAT BELLED AND BOUNDED WITH THE FOSSIL AND THE DEW REBORN.	191	WINTER'S TALE	120
WHITE, GOD'S BRIGHT, FLOCKS, THE BELLED LAMBS LEAPING, ...	215	COUNTRY HEAVEN	21
BELLMETAL			
STRIKE THE SEA HOUR THROUGH BELLMETAL.	130	SINNERS' BELL	12
BELLOWED			
A SQUALL OF BIRDS BELLOWED AND FELL, ...	163	LONG-LEGGED	39
BELLOWING			
I BUILD MY BELLOWING ARK	4	PROLOGUE	44
BUT MY WOMB WAS BELLOWING	140	TOMBSTONE TOLD	27

	PAGE	TITLE	LINE
BELLOWS			
SAFE BE AND SMOOTH FROM THE BELLOWS OF THE RUSHY BROOD.	198	COUNTRY SLEEP	20
BELLS			
ONLY THE DROWNED DEEP BELLS	5	PROLOGUE	87
TO THE BUILT VOICE, OR FLY WITH WINTER TO THE BELLS,	16	SPIRE CRANES	10
AS MEANINGLESS AS THE BELLS (OH CHANGE THE LIFE!),	33	HELD-OUT HAND	9
THERE, IN HIS NIGHT, THE BLACK-TONGUED BELLS	92	BOYS OF SUMMER	28
THE VANISHING OF THE MUSICAL SHIP-WORK AND THE CHUCKED BELLS,	141	SAINT TO FALL	8
BIRDS AND CLOCKS AND CROSS BELLS	150	WHEN I WOKE	2
NO TIME, SPOKE THE CLOCKS, NO GOD, RANG THE BELLS,	150	WHEN I WOKE	28
STREAM WITH BELLS AND BAYING WATER BOUNDS. THE DEW RINGS	189	WINTER'S TALE	62
I LIE DOWN THIN AND HEAR THE GOOD BELLS JAW--	207	LAMENT	53
THIRTY-FIVE BELLS SING STRUCK	209	POEM ON B'DAY	39
BELL-SPIRE			
MY MAST IS A BELL-SPIRE,	164	LONG-LEGGED	76
BELL-VOICED			
WHO SUCKS THE BELL-VOICED ADAM OUT OF MAGIC,	119	ALTARWISE	93
BELLY			
TO HIDE WHAT DRAGS ITS BELLY FROM THE EGG,	19	THE NEOPHYTE	6
AND THE BELLY IS EMPTY,	39	GAS FADES	28
MY HEART KNEW LOVE, MY BELLY HUNGER;	69	BEFORE KNOCKED	29
AS BELLY, GENITALS, AND ----,	84	LETTER TO AUNT	45
BELLY OF THE RICH YEAR AND THE BIG PURSE OF MY BODY	140	NO WORK WORDS	2
RAZOR MAN AND BELLY KING,	155	RETURN	32
BELLYFUL			
SHALL SHE RECEIVE A BELLYFUL OF WEEDS	134	NOT FROM ANGER	5
BELONG			
TIME SHALL BELONG TO MAN.	80	ALMANAC TIME	15
I PRAY THOUGH I BELONG	183	VISION, PRAYER	115
BELOVED			
AND HIS RUNAWAY BELOVED CHILDLIKE LAID IN THE ACORNED SAND.	157	INTO HER HEAD	23
GRAVE, AFTER BELOVED ON THE GRASS GULFED CROSS IS SCRUBBED	205	GIANT'S THIGH	54
BELOW			
TURNS OF YOUR PRAYED FLESH, NOR SHALL I SHOO THE BIRD BELOW ME:	148	UNLUCKILY FOR	27
ONCE BELOW A TIME	151	BELOW A TIME	T
ONCE BELOW A TIME	151	BELOW A TIME	1
THOUGH THE TOWN BELOW LAY LEAVED WITH OCTOBER BLOOD.	178	POEM IN OCT	67
AND ONCE BELOW A TIME I LORDLY HAD THE TREES AND LEAVES	195	FERN HILL	7
IN THE RIVER TOWY BELOW BOWS HIS TILTED HEADSTONE.	201	SIR JOHNS HILL	12
BELT			
ANOTHER WITH HERS UNDER HER BELT,	155	RETURN	39
BEND			
BEND, IF MY JOURNEY ACHE, DIRECTION LIKE AN ARC OR MAKE	145	IF HEAD HURT	14
THE RAINBOW-FISH BEND IN HER JOYS,	163	LONG-LEGGED	34
BENDS			
ON HOW THE GALLIC LETTER BENDS;	84	LETTER TO AUNT	51
THE ROD BENDS LOW, DIVINING LAND,	167	LONG-LEGGED	165
BENEATH			
IS LAUGHING BOY BENEATH HIS OATH,	19	THE NEOPHYTE	2
SAWDUST BENEATH THE SKIRTS;	27	OBLIVIOUS DARK	17
AND BARED YOUR HEAD BENEATH THE LIVING SKY,	30	YOUTH CALLS	9
I STAND BENEATH THE CLOUDS' CONFESSIONAL,	42	A WAR OF WITS	13

	PAGE	TITLE	LINE
BENEATH (CONTINUED)			
AND YOUNG GUTS DRY BENEATH THE SICKENED SUN.	63	WOMAN SPEAKS	15
FELT THUD BENEATH MY FLESH'S ARMOUR, ...	68	BEFORE KNOCKED	9
THE GRAINS OF LIFE MUST SEETHE BENEATH THE SUN, ...	80	ALMANAC TIME	13
I SIT AND WATCH THE WORM BENEATH MY NAIL	95	RUB OF LOVE	34
BENEATH MY LIFE, THAT SIGHS FOR THE SEDUCER'S COMING	147	UNLUCKILY FOR	13
MOUNTAINS AND GALLERIES BENEATH	164	LONG-LEGGED	86
BENEATH THE DEEP BARK CALLS AND MAKES QUIET MUSIC.	226	THE OAK	6
OR CRUSH THEIR VIPER HEADS BENEATH MY FOOT.	239	LET ME ESCAPE	5
BENEDICTION			
WHISPER A BENEDICTION FOR THE DEAD.	222	MISSING	6
BENEFIT			
NOT BENEFIT FROM THAT?	60	FAIRY TALES	38
BENT			
MY YOUTH IS BENT BY THE SAME WINTRY FEVER.	77	THE FORCE THAT	5
BENT LIKE THREE TREES AND BIRD-PAPPED THROUGH HER			
SHIFT, ...	120	ALTARWISE	103
CHILD IN WHITE BLOOD BENT ON ITS KNEES	128	MY NEOPHYTE	2
BENT LIKE A BEAST TO LAP THE SINGULAR FLOODS	134	NOT FROM ANGER	3
TOWARDS THE STUDDED MALE IN A BENT, MIDNIGHT BLAZE	135	HOW MY ANIMAL	13
CREEP AND HARP ON THE TIDE, SINKING THEIR CHARMED,			
BENT PIN	135	HOW MY ANIMAL	24
BLESS HER BENT SPIRIT WITH FOUR, CROSSING BIRDS.	136	AFTER FUNERAL	26
THIS SANDGRAIN DAY IN THE BENT BAY'S GRAVE	208	POEM ON B'DAY	6
AND BENT UNDER IT, ...	232	FURIOUS MOTION	13
BEQUEATH			
AND ALL THE DEAD BEQUEATH FROM PALE ESTATES	80	ALL THAT I OWE	2
BEREFT			
IN THE BODY BEREFT.	174	FIRE RAID	30
BERRY			
HEIGH HO THE BLOOD AND BERRY, ...	93	BOYS OF SUMMER	44
GROW LARKED AND GREENER AT BERRY BROWN	211	POEM ON B'DAY	101
BESIDE			
AND PUT BESIDE HER A RAM ROSE.	61	MEAT ON BONES	24
BEST			
TO THE BEST OF MY LOVE	4	PROLOGUE	45
SWEET, AUTOMATIC ME KNOWS BEST.	10	COOL, OH NO	18
NEW MAN BEST WHOSE BLOOD RUNS THICK, ...	29	LONG, SKELETON	11
STEALS WHAT IS BEST--THE BODY'S SPLENDOUR--	30	NEARLY SUMMER	15
ALONE'S UNHURT, SO THE BLIND MAN SEES BEST.	40	WAS THERE TIME	9
PERHAPS IT WOULD BE BEST IF YOU	83	LETTER TO AUNT	23
WHEN ONE AT THE GREAT LEAST OF YOUR BEST LOVED	160	DEATHS AND ENT	3
BETHELS			
CAWING FROM THEIR BLACK BETHELS SOARING, THE HOLY			
BOOKS	199	COUNTRY SLEEP	68
BETHEL-WORM			
THAT HYMNING GOOSEBERRY, THAT BETHEL-WORM	179	NEW QUAY	21
BETRAY			
OTHERS BETRAY THE LAMENTING LIES OF THEIR LOSSES	133	MAKE ME A MASK	11
BETRAYAL			
LIBIDINOUS BETRAYAL, ...	158	INTO HER HEAD	54
WOULD PLUNGE MY BETRAYAL FROM SHEET TO SKY	175	MY BEGGAR ARM	6
BETRAYED			
SO THE BETRAYED MIGHT LEARN IN THE SUN BEAMS	176	MY BEGGAR ARM	7
BETTER			
BETTER NOR US CAN'T GAINSAY WALKING, ...	28	NO WINGS	9
A WORM TELLS SUMMER BETTER THAN THE CLOCK, ...	59	HERE IN SPRING	14
LIFE NEAT'S A BETTER POISON THAN IN BOTTLE, ...	137	O CHATTERTON	5
A BETTER VENOM SEETHES IN SPITTLE	137	O CHATTERTON	6
WINGS. IT WOULD BE BETTER IF THE SHUTTERS IS	179	NEW QUAY	6

	PAGE	TITLE	LINE
BETWEEN			
BETWEEN THE MOON AND SUN	15	FOR LEDA	15
BETWEEN THE RISING AND THE FALLING	15	FOR LEDA	20
THOUGH THERE ARE YEARS BETWEEN US, THEY ARE NAUGHT;	30	YOUTH CALLS	12
WE HAVE NO FAITH TO SET BETWEEN OUR TEETH.	42	YOUNG ARE OLD	56
BETWEEN THE STREET-LAMPS AND THE ILL-LIT SKY, ...	52	OUT OF THE PIT	61
AND THUS, BETWEEN THE SEASONS, HEARD HIM CRY:	52	OUT OF THE PIT	62
RIBBED BETWEEN DESERT AND WATER STORM, ...	54	WE BY SEASAND	11
A SECRET NIGHT DESCENDS BETWEEN	69	SECRET WIND	4
BETWEEN THE RAID AND THE RESPONSE	73	WE MOTHERNAKED	3
THEY DANCE BETWEEN THEIR ARCLAMPS AND OUR SKULL,	89	EUNUCH DREAMS	17
IS CELEBRATED THERE, AND COMMUNION BETWEEN SUNS.	148	UNLUCKILY FOR	24
INNOCENT BETWEEN TWO WARS, ...	159	INTO HER HEAD	65
PROPPED BETWEEN TREES AND WATER	171	THE HUNCHBACK	3
ALONE BETWEEN NURSES AND SWANS	171	THE HUNCHBACK	26
AND CAUGHT BETWEEN TWO NIGHTS, BLINDNESS AND DEATH.	217	ELEGY	36
BETWEEN THE PYRAMIDS SO LARGE, ...	238	MAKES INTERVALS	2
BEWILDERED			
ALTHOUGH THROUGH MY BEWILDERED WAY	21	BEWILDERED WAY	T
ALTHOUGH THROUGH MY BEWILDERED WAY	21	BEWILDERED WAY	1
BEWILDERMENT			
INTO THE VOID AGAIN OF THIS BEWILDERMENT AND THAT			
INSANITY	21	BEWILDERED WAY	25
BEYOND			
PERPLEXED BEYOND PERPLEXION, ...	37	WINDMILLS TURN	25
FAITH FIXED BEYOND THE SPINNING STARS, ...	41	YOUNG ARE OLD	45
FAITH FIXED LIKE A STAR BEYOND THE STARS, ...	42	YOUNG ARE OLD	50
BEYOND THIS ISLAND BOUND	62	EARS IN TURRET	10
'REST BEYOND CHOICE IN THE DUST-APPOINTED GRAIN,	146	IF HEAD HURT	26
OF SHADES, SYMBOL OF DESIRE BEYOND MY HOURS	148	UNLUCKILY FOR	35
CHILD BEYOND COCKCROW, BY THE FIRE-DWARFED	174	FIRE RAID	28
BEYOND THE BORDER AND UNDER THE LARK FULL CLOUD.	177	POEM IN OCT	37
THE CLOUD, THE NEED, THE PLANTED STARS, THE JOY			
BEYOND	190	WINTER'S TALE	102
THE GRAINS BEYOND AGE, THE DARK VEINS OF HER MOTHER,	192	REFUSAL MOURN	21
ON THE EDGE BEYOND YOUR REACH;	230	OUR SANCTITY	5
BIBLE			
ASK THE TALL FISH SWEPT FROM THE BIBLE EAST, ...	121	ALTARWISE	134
BIBLE-LEAVED			
A BIBLE-LEAVED OF ALL THE WRITTEN WOODS	119	ALTARWISE	86
BID			
THY PLACE IS FILLED, BONES BID FOR AUCTION, ...	29	LONG, SKELETON	9
THAT THE PHOENIX' BID FOR HEAVEN AND THE DESIRE AFTER	148	UNLUCKILY FOR	45
BIDDEN			
AND THE BIDDEN DUST UPSAILING	182	VISION, PRAYER	77
BIDE			
THE COUNTRY IS HOLY: O BIDE IN THAT COUNTRY KIND,	198	COUNTRY SLEEP	39
BIDING			
THE DEATH BIDING TWO LIE LONELY.	148	UNLUCKILY FOR	28
TO THE SULTRY, BIDING HERDS, I SAID, ...	206	LAMENT	33
BIG			
THE CHAMELEON COATS OF THE BIG BUGS AND SHOTS,) ...	39	GAS FADES	13
NOW IN THE CLOUD'S BIG BREAST LIE QUIET COUNTRIES,	133	I MAKE THIS IN	61
BELLY OF THE RICH YEAR AND THE BIG PURSE OF MY BODY	140	NO WORK WORDS	2
I SKIPPED IN A BLUSH AS THE BIG GIRLS ROLLED	206	LAMENT	6
BILLHOOK			
WHILE A MAN OUTSIDE WITH A BILLHOOK, ...	150	WHEN I WOKE	8
BILLHOOKS			
AS THE ARC OF THE BILLHOOKS THAT FLASHED THE HEDGES			
LOW	205	GIANT'S THIGH	48

	PAGE	TITLE	LINE
BILLS			
AND THE TALL GRAINS FOAMED IN THEIR BILLS;	165	LONG-LEGGED	97
BIND			
BRANDED FOREHEAD, THAT COULD BIND	147	UNLUCKILY FOR	9
BINDING			
THE SILLY BINDING	21	BEWILDERED WAY	19
'REBEL AGAINST THE BINDING MOON	61	MEAT ON BONES	9
BINDING MY ANGEL'S HOOD.	105	WORLD PYRAMID	54
BINDING ME WITH PAIN, ...	236	WOMAN TAPESTRY	62
BIRD			
GLORY ALSO THIS STAR, BIRD	4	PROLOGUE	40
HEAR AND AM STILL THE LITTLE BIRD.	9	MINUTE'S HOUR	7
A FISHING BIRD HAS NOTES OF IVORY	14	FOR LEDA	6
TILL THE BIRD HAS BURST HIS SHELL, ...	22	HIGH ON A HILL	12
YOU TOO HAVE SEEN THE SUN A BIRD OF FIRE	30	YOUTH CALLS	1
CRIES NOT IN TERROR WHEN A BIRD IS DRAWN	54	NO MAN BELIEVE	3
THIS SUMMER BURIES A SPRING BIRD.	58	HERE IN SPRING	4
HERE IS A SAVIOUR WHO SINGS LIKE A BIRD, ...	74	SUN BURNS	7
WHERE BIRD AND SHELL ARE BABBLING IN MY TOWER?	112	NOT FATHER ME	14
THE VOICE OF BIRD ON CORAL PRAYS.	130	SINNERS' BELL	18
FUMED LIKE A TREE, AND TOSSED A BURNING BIRD;	133	I MAKE THIS IN	56
WITH CARVED BIRD, SAINT, AND SUN, THE WRACKSPIKED			
MAIDEN MOUTH	135	HOW MY ANIMAL	37
OF THE STONE BIRD GUARDING HER:	140	TOMBSTONE TOLD	25
CONVENIENT BIRD AND BEAST LIE LODGED TO SUFFER	144	PLEASURE-BIRD	3
TURNS OF YOUR PRAYED FLESH, NOR SHALL I SHOO THE			
BIRD BELOW ME:	148	UNLUCKILY FOR	27
AND THE VAULTING BIRD BE STILL. O MY TRUE LOVE, HOLD			
ME.	149	UNLUCKILY FOR	54
MAN, ANIMAL, OR BIRD	153	WAS A SAVIOUR	13
NOT GIRL FOR BIRD (GOURD BEING MAN) BREAKS ROOT.	159	TO LEDA	4
A SHE BIRD SLEEPING BRITTLE BY	159	INTO HER HEAD	56
AS A BIRD HOOKING OVER THE SEA, ...	162	LONG-LEGGED	7
BIRD AFTER DARK AND THE LAUGHING FISH	166	LONG-LEGGED	126
AND THE DUST SHALL SING LIKE A BIRD	173	FIRE RAID	23
HIS HEAD'S IN A NEST WHERE NO BIRD LAYS HER EGG.	179	NEW QUAY	27
A SHE BIRD ROSE AND RAYED LIKE A BURNING BRIDE. ...	189	WINTER'S TALE	69
A SHE BIRD DAWNED, AND HER BREAST WITH SNOW AND			
SCARLET DOWNED.	189	WINTER'S TALE	70
OF FIELDS. FOR LOVE, THE LONG AGO SHE BIRD RISES.			
LOOK.	189	WINTER'S TALE	80
WAS FLYING THROUGH THE HOUSE AS THOUGH THE SHE BIRD			
PRAISED	189	WINTER'S TALE	83
BIRD THROUGH THE TIMES AND LANDS AND TRIBES OF THE			
SLOW FLAKES.	190	WINTER'S TALE	99
THE SKY, THE BIRD, THE BRIDE, ...	190	WINTER'S TALE	101
AND THE BIRD DESCENDED.	190	WINTER'S TALE	106
BIRD BEAST AND FLOWER	191	REFUSAL MOURN	2
FOR THE BIRD LAY BEDDED	191	WINTER'S TALE	121
BIRD, HE WAS BROUGHT LOW, ...	191	WINTER'S TALE	126
OF BLOOD! THE BIRD LOUD VEIN! THE SAGA FROM MERMEN	200	COUNTRY SLEEP	78
AND THE FRESH-WATER BIRD	231	OUR SANCTITY	24
WAITING FOR THE BIRD WHO SHALL SAY, ...	231	OUR SANCTITY	28
LIKE A BIRD IN ITS LIGHTNESS, ...	233	NO THOUGHT	17
WITH BRANCHES WAITING FOR A SINGING BIRD, ...	234	NO, PIGEON	14
NO BIRD FOR ME:	234	NO, PIGEON	22
THE YELLOW BIRD TO SHOW HIS COLOUR.	238	MAKES INTERVALS	5
BIRD ON THE MAST, (HE CONTEMPLATED), ...	238	PILLAR BREAKS	18
WHERE THE EAGLE IS A STRONG BIRD	240	ADMIT THE SUN	2

	PAGE	TITLE	LINE
BIRDLESS			
BRANCH AND LEAF THE BIRDLESS ROOFS;	156	RETURN	83
BIRDMAN			
BIRDMAN OR TOLD GHOST I HUNG.	152	BELOW A TIME	31
BIRD-PAPPED			
BENT LIKE THREE TREES AND BIRD-PAPPED THROUGH HER SHIFT,	120	ALTARWISE	103
BIRDS			
THE FIRE OF BIRDS IN	3	PROLOGUE	26
OR HAS TOO MANY CLOUDS OR BIRDS,	12	SKY'S BRIGHT	2
CARVED BIRDS BLUNT THEIR STRIKING THROATS ON THE SALT GRAVEL,	15	SPIRE CRANES	3
THOSE CRANING BIRDS ARE CHOICE FOR YOU, SONGS THAT JUMP BACK	16	SPIRE CRANES	9
BY MESSENGERS, THE FLIGHT OF BIRDS	29	NEARLY SUMMER	4
SNARING THE WHISTLES OF THE BIRDS	46	POET: 1935	8
MAD BIRDS IN TREES, AND MAD FISH IN A POOL.	50	OUT OF THE PIT	10
ECHO A HUNDRED TIMES, THE FLIGHT OF BIRDS	50	OUT OF THE PIT	14
AND TOOK TO FEEDING BIRDS WITH BROKEN CRUMBS	53	OUT OF THE PIT	84
STILL, IN HIS HUT, HE BROODS AMONG HIS BIRDS.	53	OUT OF THE PIT	101
NO BIRDS OR FLYING FISH	62	EARS IN TURRET	15
THE BIRDS MAKE HIM HIS CEREMENTS OF PLUMES,	64	WOMAN SPEAKS	26
TELL ME OF HIM WHO FEEDS THE RAGING BIRDS.	65	WOMAN SPEAKS	65
HOLD UP THE NOISY SEA AND DROP HER BIRDS,	93	BOYS OF SUMMER	39
BY THE SEA'S SIDE, HEARING THE NOISE OF BIRDS,	98	OCTOBER WIND	5
BY THE SEA'S SIDE HEAR THE DARK-VOWELLED BIRDS.	99	OCTOBER WIND	32
MAN WAS THE SCALES, THE DEATH BIRDS ON ENAMEL,	111	I, IN IMAGE	97
LIE THIS FIFTH MONTH UNSKATED, AND THE BIRDS HAVE FLOWN;	122	HOLD HARD	9
GOLDEN GLAMORGAN STRAIGHTENS, TO THE FALLING BIRDS.	123	HOLD HARD	23
NAKED AMONG THE BOW-AND-ARROW BIRDS	123	FOSTER LIGHT	23
DESTRUCTION, PICKED BY BIRDS, BRAYS THROUGH THE JAW-BONE,	132	I MAKE THIS IN	36
BLESS HER BENT SPIRIT WITH FOUR, CROSSING BIRDS.	136	AFTER FUNERAL	26
THE DUCK-BILLED PLATYPUS BROODY IN A MILK OF BIRDS.	148	UNLUCKILY FOR	33
BIRDS AND CLOCKS AND CROSS BELLS	150	WHEN I WOKE	2
WHERE BIRDS RIDE LIKE LEAVES AND BOATS LIKE DUCKS	150	WHEN I WOKE	22
IN GROTTOES I WORKED WITH BIRDS,	151	BELOW A TIME	9
BLACKENED WITH BIRDS TOOK A LAST LOOK	161	LONG-LEGGED	2
A SQUALL OF BIRDS BELLOWED AND FELL,	163	LONG-LEGGED	39
OH THE SHEARWATER BIRDS AND THEIR BOATSIZED BROOD	164	LONG-LEGGED	67
FOR THE SALTY BIRDS FLUTTERED AND FED	165	LONG-LEGGED	96
WITH BIRDS AND ANIMALS	167	LONG-LEGGED	168
A GIRL MAD AS BIRDS	169	LOVE IN ASYLUM	3
LIKE THE PARK BIRDS HE CAME EARLY	171	THE HUNCHBACK	13
THE BIRDS THE GRASS THE TREES THE LAKE	172	THE HUNCHBACK	39
BIRDS AND THE BIRDS OF THE WINGED TREES FLYING MY NAME	177	POEM IN OCT	12
BIRDS AND THE BIRDS OF THE WINGED TREES FLYING MY NAME	177	POEM IN OCT	12
OF THE BIRDS OF BURDEN	183	VISION, PRAYER	105
THE PUFFED BIRDS HOPPING AND HUNTING, THE MILKMAIDS	187	WINTER'S TALE	23
HUNGER OF BIRDS IN THE FIELDS OF THE BREAD OF WATER, TOSSED	188	WINTER'S TALE	42
PADDOCKS IN THE FARMS OF BIRDS. THE DEAD OAK WALKS FOR LOVE.	189	WINTER'S TALE	75
AND THE SKY OF BIRDS IN THE PLUMED VOICE CHARMED	190	WINTER'S TALE	88
WHEN BLACK BIRDS DIED LIKE PRIESTS IN THE CLOAKED HEDGE ROW	190	WINTER'S TALE	92
THAT ONCE CUT THE FIGURES OF BIRDS ON THE DEEP BREAD	190	WINTER'S TALE	114

	PAGE	TITLE	LINE
BIRDS (CONTINUED)			
AND ANIMALS AND BIRDS,	193	SIDE OF TRUTH	31
OF BIRDS! AMONG THE COCKS LIKE FIRE THE RED FOX	199	COUNTRY SLEEP	69
BURNING! NIGHT AND THE VEIN OF BIRDS IN THE WINGED, SLOE WRIST	199	COUNTRY SLEEP	70
AND GALLOWS, UP THE RAYS OF HIS EYES THE SMALL BIRDS OF THE BAY	201	SIR JOHNS HILL	4
DAWS SIR JOHN'S JUST HILL DONS, AND AGAIN THE GULLED BIRDS HARE	201	SIR JOHNS HILL	15
WE GRIEVE AS THE BLITHE BIRDS, NEVER AGAIN, LEAVE SHINGLE AND ELM,	202	SIR JOHNS HILL	33
OF THE LED-ASTRAY BIRDS WHOM GOD, FOR THEIR BREAST OF WHISTLES,	202	SIR JOHNS HILL	43
STONE FOR THE SAKE OF THE SOULS OF THE SLAIN BIRDS SAILING.	203	SIR JOHNS HILL	60
ALL BIRDS AND BEASTS OF THE LINKED NIGHT UPROAR AND CHIME	204	GIANT'S THIGH	35
AND PALAVERS OF BIRDS	208	POEM ON B'DAY	5
THEN IN THE DELIGHT AND GROVE OF BEASTS AND BIRDS	215	COUNTRY HEAVEN	6
AND BLUE-TIPPED BIRDS HAVE RIPPLED IT,	224	IDYLL UNFORGET	22
BIRDS'			
AND FOUR BIRDS' NOTES.	58	HERE IN SPRING	8
AND COUNT BY BIRDS' EGGS AND LEAVES	157	RETURN	97
AND CUT THE BIRDS' BOUGHS THAT THE MINSTREL SAP RAN RED.	205	GIANT'S THIGH	49
BIRD'S			
OUT OF A BIRD'S WING WRITING ON A CLOUD	48	POET: 1935	53
LUCIFER THAT BIRD'S DROPPING	165	LONG-LEGGED	113
BIRTH			
OF BIRTH AND DEATH, THE TWO SAD KNAVES OF THIEVES,	75	MY HERO BARES	18
FIRST CHARACTERS OF BIRTH AND DEATH.	94	IN BEGINNING	24
AND POWER WAS CONTAGIOUS IN MY BIRTH, SECOND	103	I DREAMED MY	21
IN THE BIRTH BLOODY ROOM UNKNOWN	180	VISION, PRAYER	10
TO THE BIRTH BLOODY ROOM	183	VISION, PRAYER	122
SO IT MUST HAVE BEEN AFTER THE BIRTH OF THE SIMPLE LIGHT	196	FERN HILL	33
BIRTHDAY			
MY BIRTHDAY BEGAN WITH THE WATER-	177	POEM IN OCT	11
MY BIRTHDAY	178	POEM IN OCT	39
AND THERE COULD I MARVEL MY BIRTHDAY	178	POEM IN OCT	61
POEM ON HIS BIRTHDAY	208	POEM ON B'DAY	T
WHO TOLLS HIS BIRTHDAY BELL,	209	POEM ON B'DAY	16
BISCAY			
OH THE BULLS OF BISCAY AND THEIR CALVES	164	LONG-LEGGED	68
BISCUIT			
AND THOUGH DOUBTFUL OF BISCUIT, I'M WILLING TO RISK IT,	221	SONG OF DOG	11
BISECTED			
BISECTED SHADOWS ON THE THUNDER'S BONE	103	WORLD PYRAMID	5
BISHOP'S			
NO LONGER TREMBLE AT A BISHOP'S HAT,	59	FAIRY TALES	2
BIT			
BIT OUT THE MANDRAKE WITH TO-MORROW'S SCREAM.	117	ALTARWISE	6
TILL THE SWEET TOOTH OF MY LOVE BIT DRY,	146	TO OTHERS	7
CUT-TO-MEASURE FLESH BIT,	151	BELOW A TIME	3
WHEN I WAS A WINDY BOY AND A BIT	205	LAMENT	1
NOT A BOY AND A BIT IN THE WICK-	206	LAMENT	16
BITCHES			
(SIGHED THE OLD RAM ROD, DYING OF BITCHES),	206	LAMENT	15

	PAGE	TITLE	LINE
BITE			
OH MIRACLE OF FISHES! THE LONG DEAD BITE!	166	LONG-LEGGED	140
BUT MY GREATEST DELIGHT IS TO TAKE A GOOD BITE	221	SONG OF DOG	13
AND IF I INDULGE IN A BITE AT A BULGE, ...	221	SONG OF DOG	15
BITER'S			
WITH BITER'S TOOTH AND TAIL	176	BREATH SHED	7
BITES			
YOU RULE THE THUDDING HEART THAT BITES THE SIDE;	67	REALM OF FLESH	7
THESE STOLEN BUBBLES HAVE THE BITES OF SNAKES	108	GRIEF THIEF	23
BITING			
LET THE SOIL SQUEAL I AM THE BITING MAN	114	SERVANT SUN	20
BITS			
TRAMPLING TO DUST THE BITS AND PIECES	34	IN GARDENS	9
AND THE STATE FALLS TO BITS, ...	39	GAS FADES	7
OF OLD DIVINITIES, SPLIT BITS OF NAMES.	53	OUT OF THE PIT	85
ENTICED WITH TWINKLING BITS OF THE EYE	146	TO OTHERS	6
BITTEN			
THAT BURN THE BITTEN DECKS, ...	128	MY NEOPHYTE	9
TRAILING THE FROST BITTEN CLOTH, ...	151	BELOW A TIME	23
BITTER			
OUT OF THE BITTER CONSCIENCE AND THE NERVES, ...	20	THE NEOPHYTE	15
THE BITTER, THE WICKED, THE LONGLYING LEISURE, ...	39	GAS FADES	21
AND MAKE YOU BITTER WITH MY COLD, ...	233	NO THOUGHT	6
BITTERLY			
THAT HER FOND WOUNDS ARE MENDED BITTERLY.	139	FIVE & COUNTRY	9
I BITTERLY TAKE TO TASK MY POVERTY AND CRAFT:	140	NO WORK WORDS	3
BITTERNESS			
YOUR BITTERNESS IS MASKED WITH SMILES, ...	236	WOMAN TAPESTRY	50
THERE WILL BE A NEW BITTERNESS	236	WOMAN TAPESTRY	61
BLACK			
OUT THERE, CROW BLACK, MEN	3	PROLOGUE	12
THE WALKER'S APPLE'S BLACK AS SIN;	16	TIME TO ROT	15
THE BLACK SHADOW COMES DOWN, ...	18	NATURAL DAY	21
I, SAID THE BEETLE, OUT OF MY THIN BLACK WOMB, ...	18	NATURAL DAY	26
OUT OF MY THIN BLACK LIPS, ...	18	NATURAL DAY	27
BEFORE WHITE OR BLACK, THE RIGHT OR LEFT SOCK, ...	39	GAS FADES	17
NOT BLACK OR WHITE OR LEFT OR RIGHT.	39	GAS FADES	39
THE WHITE, THE BLACK, THE YELLOW AND MULATTO	41	YOUNG ARE OLD	39
TELLING IT THIS, PATTING ITS BLACK NOSE:	45	PLOUGHMAN GONE	15
PLUNGED IN BLACK WATERS, UNDER HAIL AND FIRE, ...	51	OUT OF THE PIT	42
BOTH QUENCH HIS THIRST HE'LL HAVE A BLACK REPLY. ...	56	WHY EAST WIND	9
BLACK NIGHT STILL MINISTERS THE MOON, ...	61	MEAT ON BONES	33
I WOULD ENFORCE THE BLACK APPARELLED CRIES, ...	96	TWELVE	5
BRING OUT THE BLACK PATROL, ...	110	I, IN IMAGE	55
YOU BY THE CAVERN OVER THE BLACK STAIRS, ...	117	ALTARWISE	22
THE BLACK RAM, SHUFFLING OF THE YEAR, OLD WINTER,	118	ALTARWISE	39
PIN-LEGGED ON POLE-HILLS WITH A BLACK MEDUSA	119	ALTARWISE	68
BLACK AS THE BEAST AND PALER THAN THE CROSS.	121	INCARNATE DEVL	12
TIME MARKS A BLACK AISLE KINDLE FROM THE BRAND OF ASHES, ...	130	SINNERS' BELL	4
'A LIZARD DARTING WITH BLACK VENOM'S THREAD	132	I MAKE THIS IN	49
THE BLACK, BURST SEA REJOICE, ...	135	HOW MY ANIMAL	19
GRAVE'S FOOT, BLINDS DOWN THE LIDS, THE TEETH IN BLACK, ...	136	AFTER FUNERAL	4
AND THE STRUTTING FERN LAY SEEDS ON THE BLACK SILL.	137	AFTER FUNERAL	40
AND HER RED LIPS WERE KISSED BLACK, ...	139	TOMBSTONE TOLD	18
WITH A STUB OF BLACK BUDS, ...	142	SAINT TO FALL	21
AND A BLACK AND WHITE PATCH OF GIRLS GREW PLAYING;	144	COLOUR OF SAY	4
THE BLACK MAN BLEACHED TO HIS TIDE	155	RETURN	40
BREAK THE BLACK NEWS AND PAINT ON A SAIL	164	LONG-LEGGED	71

	PAGE	TITLE	LINE
BLACK (CONTINUED)			
CHARRED ON THE BLACK BREAST OF THE GRAVE	173	FIRE RAID	7
SEED OF SONS IN THE LOIN OF THE BLACK HUSK LEFT.	174	FIRE RAID	32
THE PEBBLES. IT IS TIME FOR THE BLACK LION	179	NEW QUAY	10
THERE STINKS A SNOOP IN BLACK. I'M THINKING IT	179	NEW QUAY	19
ON THE BLACK PLUME	183	VISION, PRAYER	113
BY THE SPIT AND THE BLACK POT IN THE LOG BRIGHT LIGHT	188	WINTER'S TALE	27
BY THE SPIT AND THE BLACK POT IN THE LOG BRIGHT LIGHT.	190	WINTER'S TALE	87
WHEN BLACK BIRDS DIED LIKE PRIESTS IN THE CLOAKED HEDGE ROW	190	WINTER'S TALE	92
CAWING FROM THEIR BLACK BETHELS SOARING, THE HOLY BOOKS	199	COUNTRY SLEEP	68
THE STREAM FROM THE PRIEST BLACK WRISTED SPINNEY AND SLEEVES	200	COUNTRY SLEEP	72
AND A BLACK CAP OF JACK-	201	SIR JOHNS HILL	14
AND THE BLACK SPIT OF THE CHAPEL FOLD,	205	LAMENT	2
IN THE COAL BLACK BUSH AND LET THEM GRIEVE.	206	LAMENT	12
AND THE BLACK BEAST OF THE BEETLES' PEWS,	206	LAMENT	14
BLACK NIGHT, I LEFT MY QUIVERING PRINTS.	206	LAMENT	24
AND THE BLACK CROSS OF THE HOLY HOUSE,	206	LAMENT	26
FOR MY SULKING, SKULKING, COAL BLACK SOUL!	206	LAMENT	36
BUT A BLACK SHEEP WITH A CRUMPLED HORN,	207	LAMENT	42
AND I SHOVED IT INTO THE COAL BLACK SKY	207	LAMENT	47
AND A BLACK REWARD FOR A ROARING LIFE,	207	LAMENT	50
IN THE COAL BLACK SKY AND SHE BORE ANGELS!	207	LAMENT	55
INNOCENCE SWEETENS MY LAST BLACK BREATH,	207	LAMENT	58
DEEP IN ITS BLACK, BASE BONES,	211	POEM ON B'DAY	88
IN THE BLACK BURIED SPINNEYS	215	COUNTRY HEAVEN	17
RISING ON BLACK WINGS.	229	MY RIVER	33
BLACKAMOOR			
OVER THE BLACKAMOOR SHIRES	215	COUNTRY HEAVEN	24
BLACK-BACKED			
ILLUMINATION OF MUSIC! THE LULLED BLACK-BACKED	200	COUNTRY SLEEP	82
BLACKBERRIES			
PLENTY AS BLACKBERRIES IN THE WOODS	210	POEM ON B'DAY	53
BLACKBIRDS			
BLACKBIRDS AND THE SUN OF OCTOBER	177	POEM IN OCT	23
BLACKED			
TWO PROUD, BLACKED BROTHERS CRY,	153	WAS A SAVIOUR	25
BLACKENED			
BLACKENED WITH BIRDS TOOK A LAST LOOK	161	LONG-LEGGED	2
BLACKHEAD			
MARK, TRUMPET LIPPED AND BLACKHEAD	155	RETURN	41
BLACKNESS			
BUT LUNAR NIGHT WILL NOT GLOW IN MY BLACKNESS,	49	LIGHT, I KNOW	22
BLACK-TONGUED			
THERE, IN HIS NIGHT, THE BLACK-TONGUED BELLS	92	BOYS OF SUMMER	28
BLACK-TONGUED AND TIPSY FROM SALVATION'S BOTTLE.	118	ALTARWISE	61
BLACONY			
THE BAND WAS PLAYING ON THE BLACONY.	11	CABARET	10
BLADDER			
CHOKE THE BLADDER WITH A STONE,	71	TAKE NEEDLES	13
BLADDERS			
OF TIDE-TONGUED HEADS AND BLADDERS IN THE DEEP,	104	WORLD PYRAMID	16
BLADE			
THE TRIGGER AND SCYTHE, THE BRIDAL BLADE,	106	ALL ALL AND	17
RUNG BONE AND BLADE, THE VERTICALS OF ADAM,	117	ALTARWISE	23
BLUNT SCYTHE AND WATER BLADE.	129	MY NEOPHYTE	39
AS THEIR BLADE MARCHES IN	142	SAINT TO FALL	40

	PAGE	TITLE	LINE
BLADE (CONTINUED)			
THERE THE DARK BLADE AND WANTON SIGHING HER DOWN	157	INTO HER HEAD	16
A BLADE OF GRASS LONGS WITH THE MEADOW, ...	159	INTO HER HEAD	61
THE BLADE OF YOUR LONG FOOT, ...	229	MY RIVER	16
BLADES			
HIS NARROW HOUSE IS WALLED WITH BLADES OF GRASS,	64	WOMAN SPEAKS	24
OF HEMLOCK AND THE BLADES, RUST	103	I DREAMED MY	18
BLAME			
WHO DO I BLAME	26	PERSONAL EPIT	2
WHO DO I BLAME?	26	PERSONAL EPIT	6
MOTHER I BLAME	26	PERSONAL EPIT	7
MOTHER I BLAME.	26	PERSONAL EPIT	12
BLANK			
RULE THE BLANK SHEET OF SLEEP, ...	66	LET A FAITH	2
FROM BLANK AND LEAKING WINTER SAILS THE CHILD IN			
COLOUR, ...	130	SINNERS' BELL	22
BLANKNESS			
TO FIND A SWEET BLANKNESS IN THE BLOOD AND SHELL,	27	OBLIVIOUS DARK	12
BLARED			
TILL EVERY BEAST BLARED DOWN IN A SWERVE	163	LONG-LEGGED	57
BLASPHEME			
NOR BLASPHEME DOWN THE STATIONS OF THE BREATH	192	REFUSAL MOURN	16
BLAST			
THE LOCKS YAWNED LOOSE AND A BLAST BLEW THEM WIDE,	172	DAWN RAID	3
BLASTED			
THE SALT PERSON AND BLASTED PLACE	145	PLEASURE-BIRD	20
ON MY CLEAVING ARM AS I BLASTED IN A WAVE.	152	BELOW A TIME	48
BLASTS			
DRIVES MY GREEN AGE; THAT BLASTS THE ROOTS OF TREES	77	THE FORCE THAT	2
BLASTS BACK THE TRUMPET VOICE.	114	SERVANT SUN	34
BLAZE			
TOWARDS THE STUDDED MALE IN A BENT, MIDNIGHT BLAZE	135	HOW MY ANIMAL	13
BEFORE THE LIPS BLAZE AND BLOOM	183	VISION, PRAYER	121
BLIND EYES COULD BLAZE LIKE METEORS AND BE GAY, ...	208	NOT GO GENTLE	14
BLAZING			
BLIND IN THE COIL SCRAMS ROUND THE BLAZING OUTLINE,	124	TODAY, INSECT	11
A BLAZING RED HARSH HEAD TEAR UP	140	TOMBSTONE TOLD	29
OF HIS BLAZING	182	VISION, PRAYER	72
BLEACHED			
THE BLACK MAN BLEACHED TO HIS TIDE	155	RETURN	40
BLEATING			
LOPING AND BLEATING ROUGHLY AND BLITHELY SHALL LEAP,	197	COUNTRY SLEEP	4
BLEED			
BLEED FROM MY BURNING FORK AND SMELL MY HEELS.	105	WORLD PYRAMID	52
AND THE SCYTHED BOULDERS BLEED, AND THE LAST	210	POEM ON B'DAY	69
THAN SIT HERE WASTING, WHILE I BLEED, ...	240	TWINING HEAD	11
BLEEDING			
AND CANNOT MOUNT A CLOTHESHORSE WITHOUT BLEEDING.	40	YOUNG ARE OLD	10
BLESS			
BLESS HER BENT SPIRIT WITH FOUR, CROSSING BIRDS.	136	AFTER FUNERAL	26
CURSE, BLESS, ME NOW WITH YOUR FIERCE TEARS, I PRAY.	208	NOT GO GENTLE	17
HERONS, STEEPLE STEMMED, BLESS.	209	POEM ON B'DAY	18
FOR THAT HE LOVED THEE, SEEK THOU HIM AND BLESS ...	222	MISSING	2
BLESSED			
WITHIN THE HALLOWED GLAND, BLOOD BLESSED THE HEART,	78	LOVE'S FEVER	18
WHEN, PRAISE IS BLESSED, HER PRIDE IN MAST AND			
FOUNTAIN	131	I MAKE THIS IN	4
WITH THE WILD BREAST AND BLESSED AND GIANT SKULL	136	AFTER FUNERAL	28
BUT BLESSED BY SUCH HEROIC HOSTS IN YOUR EVERY	148	UNLUCKILY FOR	21
BUT BLESSED BE HAIL AND UPHEAVAL	186	HOLY SPRING	20

	PAGE	TITLE	LINE
BLESSED (CONTINUED)			
ALL THE MOON LONG I HEARD, BLESSED AMONG STABLES, THE NIGHTJARS	195	FERN HILL	25
AND STAR: HELD AND BLESSED, THOUGH YOU SCOUR THE HIGH FOUR	199	COUNTRY SLEEP	45
HIGH RIDING, HELD AND BLESSED AND TRUE, AND SO STILLY	200	COUNTRY SLEEP	90
WITH BLESSED, UNBORN GOD AND HIS GHOST,	210	POEM ON B'DAY	60
BLESSING			
BOTH SHALL FAIL IF I BOW NOT TO YOUR BLESSING	148	UNLUCKILY FOR	47
BLESSING AND COUNTING THE BUSTLING	156	RETURN	73
BLESSING ON	180	VISION, PRAYER	15
IN A BLESSING OF THE SUDDEN	185	VISION, PRAYER	189
AND THIS LAST BLESSING MOST,	211	POEM ON B'DAY	90
BLESSINGS			
COUNT MY BLESSINGS ALOUD:	211	POEM ON B'DAY	81
BLEST			
ROARED, SEA BORN, MAN TORN, BLOOD BLEST.	4	PROLOGUE	41
WING, AND BLEST SHALL	202	SIR JOHNS HILL	29
BLEW			
WHERE BLEW A FLOWER MAY A FLOWER NO MORE	50	NO DOMINION	22
A MEASURE ON THE LAWN WHERE CUPIDS BLEW	51	OUT OF THE PIT	25
HE BLEW LIKE POWDER TO THE LIGHT	97	TWILIGHT LOCKS	14
I BLEW THE DREAMING FELLOWS TO THEIR BED	102	FELLOWED SLEEP	19
THE SEA-HALVED FAITH THAT BLEW TIME TO HIS KNEES,	107	GRIEF THIEF	4
WHICH SIXTH OF WIND BLEW OUT THE BURNING GENTRY?	118	ALTARWISE	47
TILL TALLOW I BLEW FROM THE WAX'S TOWER	119	ALTARWISE	79
BLEW OUT THE BLOOD GAUZE THROUGH THE WOUND OF MANWAX.	119	ALTARWISE	84
A CLOUD BLEW THE RAIN FROM ITS THROAT;	163	LONG-LEGGED	40
HE WHO BLEW THE GREAT FIRE IN	167	LONG-LEGGED	157
THE LOCKS YAWNED LOOSE AND A BLAST BLEW THEM WIDE,	172	DAWN RAID	3
BLIND			
IS BLIND WITH TEARS TOO FRAIL TO TASTE.	15	FOR LEDA	33
OBLIVION IS AS BLIND,	23	ON QUIET NIGHT	19
OBLIVION IS AS BLIND,	23	ON QUIET NIGHT	20
LIFT UP THE BLINDS OVER THE BLIND EYES.	35	LIFT UP FACE	17
ALONE'S UNHURT, SO THE BLIND MAN SEES BEST.	40	WAS THERE TIME	9
CRIES NOT ALOUD BLIND AS A BAT,	54	NO MAN BELIEVE	2
WOE FROM THE RABBLE OF THE BLIND	70	SECRET WIND	8
TURNING A PETROL FACE BLIND TO THE ENEMY	110	I, IN IMAGE	47
BLIND IN THE COIL SCRAMS ROUND THE BLAZING OUTLINE,	124	TODAY, INSECT	11
BY MAGNET WINDS TO HER BLIND MOTHER DRAWN,	131	I MAKE THIS IN	14
AND WHEN BLIND SLEEP DROPS ON THE SPYING SENSES,	139	FIVE & COUNTRY	13
THE LOVELY GIFT OF THE GAB BANGS BACK ON A BLIND SHAFT.	140	NO WORK WORDS	6
SHALL THE BLIND HORSE SING SWEETER?	144	PLEASURE-BIRD	2
THEN INTO BLIND STREETS I SWAM	155	RETURN	44
EXALTATION OF THE BLIND,	156	RETURN	87
MADE HER LIMBS BLIND BY LUMINOUS CHARMS,	157	INTO HER HEAD	21
HE WAS BLIND TO THE EYES OF CANDLES	162	LONG-LEGGED	27
THE BLIND, CLAWED STARE IS COLD AS SLEET.	165	LONG-LEGGED	101
WHEN THE CAUGHT TONGUE NODDED BLIND,	173	FIRE RAID	13
BLIND HOST TO SLEEP	184	VISION, PRAYER	141
THAT THE SNOW BLIND TWILIGHT FERRIES OVER THE LAKES	187	WINTER'S TALE	2
OF HIS SNOW BLIND LOVE AND RUSH IN THE WHITE LAIRS.	188	WINTER'S TALE	38
PAST THE BLIND BARNS AND BYRES OF THE WINDLESS FARM.	190	WINTER'S TALE	90
KING OF YOUR HEART IN THE BLIND DAYS,	193	SIDE OF TRUTH	16
AND I GAVE MY SOUL A BLIND, SLASHED EYE,	207	LAMENT	45
BLIND EYES COULD BLAZE LIKE METEORS AND BE GAY,	208	NOT GO GENTLE	14
AND TO-MORROW WEEPS IN A BLIND CAGE	209	POEM ON B'DAY	42
THE SHOOTING STAR HAWK STATUED BLIND IN A CLOUD	215	COUNTRY HEAVEN	23

	PAGE	TITLE	LINE
BLIND (CONTINUED)			
TOO PROUD TO DIE, BROKEN AND BLIND HE DIED	216	ELEGY	1
THE DARKEST JUSTICE OF DEATH, BLIND AND UNBLESSED.	216	ELEGY	11
I PRAYED IN THE CROUCHING ROOM, BY HIS BLIND BED,	216	ELEGY	13
AN OLD TORMENTED MAN THREE-QUARTERS BLIND, ...	217	ELEGY	18
OPENING IN THE BLIND CLOUD OVER OUR HEADS;	231	OUR SANCTITY	44
BLINDING			
NOW I AM LOST IN THE BLINDING	185	VISION, PRAYER	203
AND THE DUCK POND GLASS AND THE BLINDING BYRES ALONE	188	WINTER'S TALE	35
IN THE BLINDING COUNTRY OF YOUTH, ...	192	SIDE OF TRUTH	4
GRAVE MEN, NEAR DEATH, WHO SEE WITH BLINDING SIGHT	208	NOT GO GENTLE	13
BLINDLY			
(THOUGH THIS FOR HER IS A MONSTROUS IMAGE BLINDLY	136	AFTER FUNERAL	16
ON TO THE BLINDLY TOSSING TOPS;	167	LONG-LEGGED	150
BLINDNESS			
THE BONES OF BLINDNESS; AND THE WOMB	88	A PROCESS IN	8
AND CAUGHT BETWEEN TWO NIGHTS, BLINDNESS AND DEATH.	217	ELEGY	36
BLINDS			
LIFT UP THE BLINDS OVER THE BLIND EYES.	35	LIFT UP FACE	17
BLINDS THEIR CLOUD-TRACKING EYE.	104	WORLD PYRAMID	30
GRAVE'S FOOT, BLINDS DOWN THE LIDS, THE TEETH IN			
BLACK, ...	136	AFTER FUNERAL	4
BLINDS MY	181	VISION, PRAYER	67
BLISS			
OUT OF THE CHAOS WOULD COME BLISS.	31	BEING BUT MEN	13
YET IN SPITE OF ALL THIS, I HAVE MOMENTS OF BLISS,	221	SONG OF DOG	9
BLISTERED			
IN LOVE TORN BREECHES AND BLISTERED JACKET	151	BELOW A TIME	7
BLITHE			
IT TURNED AWAY FROM THE BLITHE COUNTRY	178	POEM IN OCT	41
WE GRIEVE AS THE BLITHE BIRDS, NEVER AGAIN, LEAVE			
SHINGLE AND ELM, ...	202	SIR JOHNS HILL	33
BLITHELY			
LOPING AND BLEATING ROUGHLY AND BLITHELY SHALL LEAP,	197	COUNTRY SLEEP	4
AND BLITHELY THEY SQUAWK	201	SIR JOHNS HILL	8
BLOCK			
GAG OF A DUMBSTRUCK TREE TO BLOCK FROM BARE ENEMIES	133	MAKE ME A MASK	4
BLOND			
ROOFED WITH THE SKY AND PATTERNED WITH BLOND BONES;	64	WOMAN SPEAKS	25
BLOOD			
ROARED, SEA BORN, MAN TORN, BLOOD BLEST.	4	PROLOGUE	41
IT IS A SOUR MOTION IN THE BLOOD, ...	9	MINUTE'S HOUR	2
TOO FULL WITH BLOOD TO LET MY LOVE FLOW IN.	9	MINUTE'S HOUR	12
OR TOO MUCH BLOOD;	13	SKY'S BRIGHT	21
AND SEE THE BLOOD IS MINE, ...	13	SKY'S BRIGHT	23
YOUR GOLDEN BALL OF BLOOD;	16	TIME TO ROT	3
THE LOVE WE HAD AND GLORY IN HIS BLOOD	17	IN OBLIVION	9
FEEL THE SAME SOFT BLOOD FLOW THOROUGHLY, ...	23	THE ONLY DEAD	11
AND YET, MAD WITH YOUNG BLOOD OR STAINED WITH AGE,	26	THERE'S PLENTY	16
TO FIND A SWEET BLANKNESS IN THE BLOOD AND SHELL,	27	OBLIVIOUS DARK	12
NEW MAN BEST WHOSE BLOOD RUNS THICK, ...	29	LONG, SKELETON	11
THAT SPILL SUCH ACRID BLOOD.	32	OUT OF SIGHS	16
WERE THAT ENOUGH, BONE, BLOOD, AND SINEW, ...	32	OUT OF SIGHS	24
ABOUT YOU, FLESH WILL PERISH, AND BLOOD	39	GAS FADES	31
RARER DELIGHT SHOOTS IN THE BLOOD	48	POET: 1935	55
AND HEARD THE TEETH OF WEASELS DRAWING BLOOD.	52	OUT OF THE PIT	58
FEELING THE PINPRICKS OF THE BLOOD, I'VE SAID	53	OUT OF THE PIT	80
BREAKS, O MY HEART'S BLOOD, LIKE A HEART AND HILL.	54	WE BY SEASAND	24
OF AGAMEMNON AND HIS KINGLY BLOOD	56	GREEK PLAY	7
WHY NIGHT-TIME RAIN AND THE BREAST'S BLOOD	56	WHY EAST WIND	8

	PAGE	TITLE	LINE
BLOOD (CONTINUED)			
THE QUEEN IS SLAIN; ORESTES' HANDS DRIP BLOOD;	57	GREEK PLAY	15
AT FLESH THAT PERISHES AND BLOOD THAT'S SPILT	57	GREEK PLAY	19
STAINED A BLOOD COLOUR;	59	FAIRY TALES	19
THE WORD OF THE BLOOD, THE WILY SKIN, ...	61	MEAT ON BONES	15
SWEET IS THE WAXEN BLOOD, HONEY THE FALLING FLESH;	63	WOMAN SPEAKS	3
COULD IN A DAY BE SICK WITH SO MUCH BLOOD;	63	WOMAN SPEAKS	13
OLD MEN WHOSE BLOOD IS HINDERED IN THEIR VEINS, ...	64	WOMAN SPEAKS	42
AND THEIR RIVERS OF BLOOD TURNED TO ICE.	68	REALM OF FLESH	16
UNFAILING TILL THE BLOOD RUNS FOUL;	69	BEFORE KNOCKED	28
HOLD IN HIS VELVET HAND THE CAN OF BLOOD;	73	LORD RED HAIL	2
HERE IN MY WILDERNESS WANDERS THE BLOOD;	74	SUN BURNS	3
BEFORE OUR BLOOD;	74	WE MOTHERNAKED	12
DRIVES MY RED BLOOD; THAT DRIES THE MOUTHING STREAMS	77	THE FORCE THAT	7
LOVE DRIPS AND GATHERS, BUT THE FALLEN BLOOD	77	THE FORCE THAT	17
WITHIN THE HALLOWED GLAND, BLOOD BLESSED THE HEART,	78	LOVE'S FEVER	18
LIES IN THE FORTUNED BONE, THE FLASK OF BLOOD, ...	80	ALL THAT I OWE	3
MY BROTHERS' BLOOD THAT SALTS MY OPEN WOUNDS.	80	ALL THAT I OWE	8
HERE SPRING THE SILENT VENOMS OF HIS BLOOD, ...	81	HERE LIE BEAST	4
ALL SUCH DISEASE I DOCTOR IN MY BLOOD, ...	81	ALL THAT I OWE	19
FROM POLES OF SKULL AND TOE THE WINDY BLOOD	82	LIGHT BREAKS	14
AND BLOOD JUMPS IN THE SUN;	82	LIGHT BREAKS	29
AND ELBOWED VEINS THAT, NUDGING BLOOD, ...	85	SEE, SAYS LIME	3
THE BLOOD GOT UP AS RED AS WAX	85	SEE, SAYS LIME	13
ONCE IN THIS WINE THE SUMMER BLOOD	86	BREAD I BREAK	6
THIS FLESH YOU BREAK, THIS BLOOD YOU LET	86	BREAD I BREAK	11
BEFORE THE BLOOD AND FLAME WERE TWINED	86	SEE, SAYS LIME	23
WHOSE FLAMING BLOOD SHALL RUB IT AT THE RIMS	87	PAIN BE MUSIC	8
THAT DROPS TO MAKE A MUSIC IN YOUR BLOOD	87	PAIN BE MUSIC	20
FLESH BLOOD AND BONE	87	PAIN BE MUSIC	23
TURNS NIGHT TO DAY; BLOOD IN THEIR SUNS	88	A PROCESS IN	5
HEIGH HO THE BLOOD AND BERRY, ...	93	BOYS OF SUMMER	44
THE BLOOD THAT TOUCHED THE CROSSTREE AND THE GRAIL	94	IN BEGINNING	11
BLOOD SHOT AND SCATTERED TO THE WINDS OF LIGHT	94	IN BEGINNING	29
NOR THE BAD BLOOD OF SPRING.	95	RUB OF LOVE	7
AND BAGS OF BLOOD LET OUT THEIR FLIES;	97	TWILIGHT LOCKS	23
SHEDS THE SYLLABIC BLOOD AND DRAINS HER WORDS.	98	OCTOBER WIND	8
OF CHEMIC BLOOD, WARNED OF THE COMING FURY.	99	OCTOBER WIND	31
WHEN BLOOD, SPADE-HANDED, AND THE LOGIC TIME	100	RUNNING GRAVE	13
DESPAIR OF BLOOD, FAITH IN THE MAIDEN'S SLIME, ...	100	RUNNING GRAVE	23
THE INCHES MONKEYED BY THE BLOOD OF MAN.	102	FELLOWED SLEEP	28
MY BLOOD UPON THE TEMPERED DEAD, FORCING	103	I DREAMED MY	19
AND A BLOOD PARHELION.	104	WORLD PYRAMID	36
FEAR NOT THE FLAT, SYNTHETIC BLOOD, ...	106	ALL ALL AND	14
SOCKET AND GRAVE, THE BRASSY BLOOD, ...	107	ALL ALL AND	35
SHE THREADS OFF THE SAP AND NEEDLES, BLOOD AND BUBBLE	108	I, IN IMAGE	10
FOR LOSS OF BLOOD I FELL ON ISHMAEL'S PLAIN, ...	118	ALTARWISE	63
BLEW OUT THE BLOOD GAUZE THROUGH THE WOUND OF MANWAX.	119	ALTARWISE	84
AS TARRED WITH BLOOD AS THE BRIGHT THORNS I WEPT;	120	ALTARWISE	101
STALKING MY CHILDREN'S FACES WITH A TAIL OF BLOOD,	122	HOLD HARD	20
CHILD IN WHITE BLOOD BENT ON ITS KNEES	128	MY NEOPHYTE	2
ONCE WHERE THE SOFT SNOW'S BLOOD WAS TURNED TO ICE.	133	I MAKE THIS IN	65
AND CLAP ITS GREAT BLOOD DOWN;	135	HOW MY ANIMAL	31
ANCIENT WOODS OF MY BLOOD, DASH DOWN TO THE NUT OF THE SEAS	140	NO WORK WORDS	11
THE SWEET, FISH-GILLED BOATS BRINGING BLOOD	142	SAINT TO FALL	22
UP TO HIS HEAD IN HIS BLOOD, ...	150	WHEN I WOKE	9
HE'LL BATHE HIS RAINING BLOOD IN THE MALE SEA	160	DEATHS AND ENT	19
ALL THE FISHES WERE RAYED IN BLOOD, ...	162	LONG-LEGGED	23
THE WHIRLED BOAT IN THE BURN OF HIS BLOOD	164	LONG-LEGGED	65

	PAGE	TITLE	LINE

BLOOD (CONTINUED)

THAT OTHER SUN, THE JEALOUS COURSING OF THE UNRIVALLED BLOOD.	170	MARRIAGE VIRG	14
TILL THE BLOOD SHALL SPURT,	173	FIRE RAID	22
THOUGH THE TOWN BELOW LAY LEAVED WITH OCTOBER BLOOD.	178	POEM IN OCT	67
AND THE BLOOD DROP'S GARDEN	184	VISION, PRAYER	139
FLY LIKE THE STARS' BLOOD,	193	SIDE OF TRUTH	24
TO THE SEA SOUND FLOWING LIKE BLOOD FROM THE LOUD WOUND	194	SLEEP BECALMED	6
SHALL HARROW AND SNOW THE BLOOD WHILE YOU RIDE WIDE AND NEAR,	198	COUNTRY SLEEP	23
THE OWL AT ITS KNELLING. FOX AND HOLT KNEEL BEFORE BLOOD.	198	COUNTRY SLEEP	32
OF THE WOOD! PASTORAL BEAT OF BLOOD THROUGH THE LACED LEAVES!	199	COUNTRY SLEEP	71
OF BLOOD! THE BIRD LOUD VEIN! THE SAGA FROM MERMEN	200	COUNTRY SLEEP	78
OH, TIME ENOUGH WHEN THE BLOOD CREEPS COLD,	206	LAMENT	34
TO KILL AND THEIR OWN TIDE DAUBING BLOOD	209	POEM ON B'DAY	35
A SENSITIVE CONFUSION IN THE BLOOD,	235	WOMAN TAPESTRY	28
MIX THEIR WILD BLOOD	236	WOMAN TAPESTRY	57

BLOOD-COUNTING

THE WOUND-DOWN COUGH OF THE BLOOD-COUNTING CLOCK	141	SAINT TO FALL	9

BLOODILY

GLAMOUR OF THE BLOODILY BOWED,	156	RETURN	86

BLOODRED

THE BEACH OF FLESH, AND WIND HER BLOODRED PLAIT;	75	MY HERO BARES	13

BLOOD-RED

SLAPPED DOWN THE GUILLOTINE, THE BLOOD-RED DOUBLE	124	TODAY, INSECT	6

BLOOD'S

BLOWING WITH THE BLOOD'S EBB,	22	HIGH ON A HILL	14
MY GREAT BLOOD'S IRON SINGLE	111	I, IN IMAGE	93

BLOOD-SIGNED

ALL BLOOD-SIGNED ASSAILINGS AND VANISHED MARRIAGES IN WHICH HE HAD NO LOVELY PART	158	INTO HER HEAD	43

BLOODY

UNDER THE MASK AND THE ETHER, THEY, MAKING BLOODY	110	I, IN IMAGE	53
ON NO WORK OF WORDS NOW FOR THREE LEAN MONTHS IN THE BLOODY	140	NO WORK WORDS	1
STRIKE LIGHT, AND BLOODY A LOUD ROOM.	145	IF HEAD HURT	10
IN THE BIRTH BLOODY ROOM UNKNOWN	180	VISION, PRAYER	10
TO THE BIRTH BLOODY ROOM	183	VISION, PRAYER	122

BLOOM

THE CRUMPLED PACKS FLED PAST THIS GHOST IN BLOOM,	133	I MAKE THIS IN	58
BEFORE THE LIPS BLAZE AND BLOOM	183	VISION, PRAYER	121
WHO ONCE WERE A BLOOM OF WAYSIDE BRIDES IN THE HAWED HOUSE	204	GIANT'S THIGH	29

BLOOMING

OF SPRING AND SUMMER WERE BLOOMING IN THE TALL TALES	177	POEM IN OCT	36

BLOOMS

AND BLOOMS IN THE HESPERIDES. LIGHT STIRS	48	LIGHT, I KNOW	2
AS THE GREEN BLOOMS RIDE UPWARD, TO THE DRIVE OF TIME;	122	HOLD HARD	3
THE LOUDER THE SUN BLOOMS	211	POEM ON B'DAY	93
HER GARDEN BLOOMS WITH IRIS, AND IT SEEMS	223	IN DREAMS	13

BLOSSOMED

THESE THE IMAGININGS, TENDER AND BLOSSOMED WITH FUTILITY,	223	IDYLL UNFORGET	11

BLOSSOMS

THEY TO MY BLOSSOMS WING THEIR WAY,	228	TRIOLET	5

	PAGE	TITLE	LINE
BLOT			
WHY BLOT THE PICTURES	60	FAIRY TALES	28
BLOW			
WATCH YELLOW, WISH FOR WIND TO BLOW AWAY	54	WE BY SEASAND	19
I BLOW THE STAMMEL FEATHER IN THE VEIN.	105	WORLD PYRAMID	56
NOR WEATHER WINDS THAT BLOW NOT DOWN THE BONE,	123	FOSTER LIGHT	2
THE DEADROCK BASE THE BLOW THE FLOWERED ANCHOR,	127	NOW, SAY NAY	5
AS THE GRAINS BLOW, AS YOUR DEATH GROWS, THROUGH OUR HEART.	173	FIRE RAID	24
WIND BLOW COLD	177	POEM IN OCT	29
BLOW AWAY LIKE BREATH,	193	SIDE OF TRUTH	17
WHO KNOWS THE ROCKETING WIND WILL BLOW	210	POEM ON B'DAY	67
BUSHES AND OWLS BLOW OUT LIKE CANDLES,	215	COUNTRY HEAVEN	18
FOR LILACS IN THEIR BEAUTY BLOW	227	TRIOLET	2
FOR LILACS IN THEIR BEAUTY BLOW.	228	TRIOLET	8
BLOWCLOCK			
AND BY THIS BLOWCLOCK WITNESS OF THE SUN	120	ALTARWISE	111
BLOWING			
BLOWING WITH THE BLOOD'S EBB,	22	HIGH ON A HILL	14
STIRS THE QUICKSAND; THAT ROPES THE BLOWING WIND	77	THE FORCE THAT	12
BLOWING THE OLD DEAD BACK; OUR SHOTS SHALL SMACK	90	EUNUCH DREAMS	38
AS, BLOWING ON THE ANGELS, I WAS LOST	102	FELLOWED SLEEP	17
BLOWN			
BEFORE THE LAST LIGHT IS BLOWN	21	BEWILDERED WAY	24
THE WIND HAS CHANGED, BLOWN INSIDE OUT	37	WINDMILLS TURN	27
HAVE BLOWN SKY HIGH THE NURSERY OF FAIRIES;	59	FAIRY TALES	23
AND THE FOUR WINDS, THAT HAD LONG BLOWN AS ONE,	78	LOVE'S FEVER	19
SPOT THE BLOWN WORD, AND ON THE SEAS I IMAGE	121	ALTARWISE	131
AND OPIUM HEAD, CROW STALK, PUFFED, CUT, AND BLOWN,	131	I MAKE THIS IN	10
THE PRESENT MOUTH, AND THE SWEETLY BLOWN TRUMPET OF LIES,	133	MAKE ME A MASK	6
TO THE JUDGE BLOWN BEDLAM	182	VISION, PRAYER	74
AND THE BEATING DUST BE BLOWN	184	VISION, PRAYER	150
AND SLY AS SNOW AND MEEK AS DEW BLOWN TO THE THORN,	199	COUNTRY SLEEP	50
HOLLOWS, A GRASSBLADE BLOWN IN CUPPED HANDS, IN THE LOOTED ELMS	203	SIR JOHNS HILL	52
LEAF DRIFTWOOD THAT HAS BLOWN.	226	THE ELM	10
BLOWS			
GUIDES AND BLOWS WICKEDLY, FOR LARKS	37	WINDMILLS TURN	7
THE CHANGED WIND BLOWS, AND THERE'S A CHOICE OF SIGNS	37	WINDMILLS TURN	31
LIFT ITS HEAD TO THE BLOWS OF THE RAIN;	50	NO DOMINION	23
A PROCESS BLOWS THE MOON INTO THE SUN,	88	A PROCESS IN	22
SPUN TO MY SCREWS, YOUR DRY GHOST BLOWS,	90	WHERE ONCE THE	2
NOR BLOWS BACK MOON-AND-MIDNIGHT AS SHE BLOWS.	92	BOYS OF SUMMER	30
NOR BLOWS BACK MOON-AND-MIDNIGHT AS SHE BLOWS.	92	BOYS OF SUMMER	30
WHO BLOWS DEATH'S FEATHER? WHAT GLORY IS COLOUR?	105	WORLD PYRAMID	55
MAN MORROW BLOWS THROUGH FOOD.	113	SERVANT SUN	14
UNCREDITED BLOWS JERICHO ON EDEN.	124	TODAY, INSECT	17
A CALM WIND BLOWS THAT RAISED THE TREES LIKE HAIR	133	I MAKE THIS IN	64
SLEEPS TILL SILENCE BLOWS ON A CLOUD	165	LONG-LEGGED	111
BLUE			
AND THE DUMB SWANS DRUB BLUE	4	PROLOGUE	35
WHO MOONS HER BLUE NOTES FROM HER NEST	4	PROLOGUE	62
MAKE DEADLY WHOOPEE IN THE BLUE.	84	LETTER TO AUNT	55
ON THESE BLUE LIPS, THE LIME REMARKS,	85	SEE, SAYS LIME	9
SCALES THE BLUE WALL OF SPIRITS;	130	SINNERS' BELL	21
I LOVED HIS BODY AND HIS NAVY BLUE WEALTH	149	PAPER & STICKS	5
AND THE GROVES WERE BLUE WITH SAILORS	172	THE HUNCHBACK	30
AND DOWN THE OTHER AIR AND THE BLUE ALTERED SKY	178	POEM IN OCT	42
KING OF YOUR BLUE EYES	192	SIDE OF TRUTH	3

	PAGE	TITLE	LINE
BLUE (CONTINUED)			
AND NOTHING I CARED, AT MY SKY BLUE TRADES, THAT			
TIME ALLOWS	196	FERN HILL	42
THE HAYGOLD HAIRED, MY LOVE ASLEEP, AND THE RIFT BLUE	200	COUNTRY SLEEP	88
DOWN THE LONG BAYS OF BLUE THAT THOSE CLOUDY			
HEADLANDS	222	FOREST PICTURE	6
BURROW OUR WAY UPWARDS INTO THE BLUE SKY;	231	OUR SANCTITY	35
LET ME CHANGE TO BLUE, ...	238	MAKES INTERVALS	7
BLUE-HUED			
TO HAVE KNOWN THEM IN THEIR BLUE-HUED VALIANCE, ...	223	IDYLL UNFORGET	3
BLUE-TIPPED			
AND BLUE-TIPPED BIRDS HAVE RIPPLED IT, ...	224	IDYLL UNFORGET	22
BLUFF			
GRAFT, POISON, AND BLUFF, ...	39	GAS FADES	11
BLUNT			
WHY IS MY HAND TOO BLUNT	12	SKY'S BRIGHT	5
CARVED BIRDS BLUNT THEIR STRIKING THROATS ON THE			
SALT GRAVEL, ...	15	SPIRE CRANES	3
A THREE-EYED, RED-EYED SPARK, BLUNT AS A FLOWER;	94	IN BEGINNING	15
BLUNT SCYTHE AND WATER BLADE.	129	MY NEOPHYTE	39
TO SHIELD THE GLISTENING BRAIN AND BLUNT THE			
EXAMINERS, ...	133	MAKE ME A MASK	8
AND THE MOLE SNOUT BLUNT UNDER HIS PILGRIMAGE OF			
DOMES, ...	204	GIANT'S THIGH	36
THE WIND CANNOT BLUNT	229	MY RIVER	15
BLUSH			
I SKIPPED IN A BLUSH AS THE BIG GIRLS ROLLED	206	LAMENT	6
BOARDS			
ON THE MADHOUSE BOARDS WORN THIN BY MY WALKING TEARS.	170	LOVE IN ASYLUM	15
BOAT			
WE SAIL A BOAT UPON THE PATH, ...	13	RAIN CUTS	6
ABOVE A BOAT OF LEAVES AND WEEDS.	14	RAIN CUTS	24
OUR BOAT IS MADE TO RISE	14	RAIN CUTS	32
COLD NANSEN'S BEAK ON A BOAT FULL OF GONGS, ...	152	BELOW A TIME	40
BOAT WITH ITS ANCHOR FREE AND FAST	162	LONG-LEGGED	6
MILES OVER THE MOONSTRUCK BOAT	163	LONG-LEGGED	38
THE WHIRLED BOAT IN THE BURN OF HIS BLOOD	164	LONG-LEGGED	65
THE BOAT SWIMS INTO THE SIX-YEAR WEATHER, ...	166	LONG-LEGGED	129
AS THE BOAT SKIMS ON WITH DRINKING WINGS!	166	LONG-LEGGED	134
IN DEATHBEDS OF ORCHARDS THE BOAT DIES DOWN	169	LONG-LEGGED	207
THROW WIDE TO THE WIND THE GATES OF THE WANDERING			
BOAT	194	SLEEP BECALMED	10
BOAT CANNOT GO.	237	PILLAR BREAKS	6
WHO FLEW HIMSELF BECAUSE THE BOAT REMAINED	238	PILLAR BREAKS	19
BOATS			
THE SWEET, FISH-GILLED BOATS BRINGING BLOOD	142	SAINT TO FALL	22
WHERE BIRDS RIDE LIKE LEAVES AND BOATS LIKE DUCKS	150	WHEN I WOKE	22
THEN SWIFT FROM A BURSTING SEA WITH BOTTLECORK BOATS	151	BELOW A TIME	13
AND THE KNOCK OF SAILING BOATS ON THE NET WEBBED WALL	177	POEM IN OCT	7
BOAT'S			
BOAT'S BROKEN, TOO, AND MAGPIE'S STILL;	238	PILLAR BREAKS	26
BOATSIDE			
TOPPLING UP THE BOATSIDE IN A SNOW OF LIGHT!	166	LONG-LEGGED	138
BOATSIZED			
OH THE SHEARWATER BIRDS AND THEIR BOATSIZED BROOD	164	LONG-LEGGED	67
BODICE			
BUTTON YOUR BODICE ON A HUMP OF SPLINTERS, ...	118	ALTARWISE	51
BODIES			
COILED INTO THEIR BODIES LIKE SNAKES, ...	237	WOMAN TAPESTRY	76

	PAGE	TITLE	LINE
BODILESS			
BRASS AND THE BODILESS IMAGE, ON A STICK OF FOLLY	111	I, IN IMAGE	80
BODY			
AND SEES MY BODY GO	12	SKY'S BRIGHT	14
SPARKLING A TWELVE-LEGGED BODY	12	CABARET	19
BUT IN THE BODY OF THE TREES AND STONES,	25	BEAUTY TO DUST	13
PRAISE THAT MY BODY BE WHOLE, I'VE LIMBS,	42	A WAR OF WITS	8
ONE DAY MY WOMAN'S BODY WILL BE COLD.	64	WOMAN SPEAKS	47
THE BODY PROSPERED, TEETH IN THE MARROWED GUMS,	78	LOVE'S FEVER	16
AND NEED NO DRUID OF HER BROKEN BODY).	136	AFTER FUNERAL	20
BELLY OF THE RICH YEAR AND THE BIG PURSE OF MY BODY	140	NO WORK WORDS	2
THE GRAVE AND MY CALM BODY ARE SHUT TO YOUR COMING AS STONE,	146	IF HEAD HURT	29
MY HOLY LUCKY BODY	147	UNLUCKILY FOR	16
I LOVED HIS BODY AND HIS NAVY BLUE WEALTH	149	PAPER & STICKS	5
BODY AND AIR AND BUILDING;	156	RETURN	82
IN THE TAKEN BODY AT MANY AGES,	158	INTO HER HEAD	40
IN THE BODY BEREFT.	174	FIRE RAID	30
THE CURELESS COUNTED BODY,	186	HOLY SPRING	4
HAVE NOT ADORED MY BODY AS IT SOFTLY SMOOTHED THEIR SKIN.	223	IDYLL UNFORGET	16
YOUR BODY CANNOT GLADDEN ME,	228	NOT DESPAIR	9
UNTIL I FELT THE RHYTHM OF HER BODY	234	WOMAN TAPESTRY	4
LET ME BELIEVE IN THE CLEAN FAITH OF THE BODY,	235	WOMAN TAPESTRY	24
A COMPASSION SPRINGING FROM THE DEEP BODY,	236	WOMAN TAPESTRY	53
LIKE THE BODY OF A GIRL.	236	WOMAN TAPESTRY	55
LET ME BELIEVE IN THE CLEAN FAITH OF THE BODY,	237	WOMAN TAPESTRY	79
BUT IF IT STINGS MY BODY DEAD	240	TWINING HEAD	3
BODY'S			
STEALS WHAT IS BEST--THE BODY'S SPLENDOUR--	30	NEARLY SUMMER	15
FOR THE BODY'S BRITTLE AND THE SKIN'S WHITE.	42	A WAR OF WITS	10
BOILING			
SOUR THE BOILING HONEY;	92	BOYS OF SUMMER	8
AND IN THE PINCERS OF THE BOILING CIRCLE,	111	I, IN IMAGE	91
BOLT			
BOLT FOR THE SALT UNBORN.	103	WORLD PYRAMID	6
THE BREATH DRAW BACK LIKE A BOLT THROUGH WHITE OIL	142	SAINT TO FALL	46
BOLTING			
BOLTING THE NIGHT OF THE DOOR WITH HER ARM HER PLUME.	169	LOVE IN ASYLUM	4
BOLTS			
WHEEL-WINDERS AND FIXERS OF BOLTS.	70	SECRET WIND	18
BONE			
WERE THAT ENOUGH, BONE, BLOOD, AND SINEW,	32	OUT OF SIGHS	24
NOW IS DECAY IN BONE AND SINEW,	34	THIRST PARCHES	3
REBEL AGAINST THE FLESH AND BONE,	61	MEAT ON BONES	14
AND A BONE COAST,	62	EARS IN TURRET	12
AND THIS HILL OF BONE AND HAIR	67	REALM OF FLESH	2
WHO TOOK MY FLESH AND BONE FOR ARMOUR	69	BEFORE KNOCKED	45
FIRMAMENT OF FLESH AND BONE	72	TAKE NEEDLES	38
HERE IS A UNIVERSE BRED IN THE BONE,	74	SUN BURNS	6
LIES IN THE FORTUNED BONE, THE FLASK OF BLOOD,	80	ALL THAT I OWE	3
THE WORD OF TIME LIES ON THE CHAPTERED BONE,	80	ALMANAC TIME	11
DAY LIGHTS THE BONE;	82	LIGHT BREAKS	21
FLESH BLOOD AND BONE	87	PAIN BE MUSIC	23
A WEATHER IN THE FLESH AND BONE	88	A PROCESS IN	16
ONE BOUGH OF BONE ACROSS THE ROOTING AIR,	93	IN BEGINNING	3
THE WINGING BONE THAT SPROUTED IN THE HEELS,	95	RUB OF LOVE	11
AN OLD MAN'S SHANK ONE-MARROWED WITH MY BONE,	95	RUB OF LOVE	32
THAT GLOBE ITSELF OF HAIR AND BONE	97	TWILIGHT LOCKS	10
OF THE BONE INCH,	100	RUNNING GRAVE	10

		PAGE	TITLE	LINE
BONE (CONTINUED)				
BISECTED SHADOWS ON THE THUNDER'S BONE	....	103	WORLD PYRAMID	5
I SCRAPE THROUGH RESIN TO A STARRY BONE	....	104	WORLD PYRAMID	35
KNOW, O MY BONE, THE JOINTED LEVER,	....	106	ALL ALL AND	22
CAST BACK THE BONE OF YOUTH	....	107	GRIEF THIEF	11
(FOG HAS A BONE	....	113	SERVANT SUN	4
A CLAW I QUESTION FROM THE MOUSE'S BONE,	....	114	SERVANT SUN	17
HER BONE TO FIRE,	....	115	A GRIEF AGO	36
RUNG BONE AND BLADE, THE VERTICALS OF ADAM,	....	117	ALTARWISE	23
DIPPED ME BREAST-DEEP IN THE DESCENDED BONE;	......	118	ALTARWISE	38
CRACK LIKE A SPRING IN A VICE, BONE BREAKING APRIL,		122	HOLD HARD	17
NOR WEATHER WINDS THAT BLOW NOT DOWN THE BONE,	....	123	FOSTER LIGHT	2
OUT OF THE FONT OF BONE AND PLANTS AT THAT STONE				
TOCSIN	....	130	SINNERS' BELL	20
CURL-LOCKED AND ANIMAL CAVEPOOLS OF SPELLS AND BONE,		135	HOW MY ANIMAL	27
THAT BREAKS ONE BONE TO LIGHT WITH A JUDGMENT CLOUT,		136	AFTER FUNERAL	9
PACK BACK THE DOWNED BONE. IF THE UNPRICKED BALL OF				
MY BREATH	....	145	IF HEAD HURT	2
AS QUIET AS A BONE.	....	152	BELOW A TIME	51
TILL EVERY BONE IN THE RUSHING GRAVE	....	163	LONG-LEGGED	59
TIME AND PLACES GRIP HER BREAST BONE,	....	168	LONG-LEGGED	175
OF THE GOLDEN GHOST WHO RINGED WITH HIS STREAMS HER				
MERCURY BONE,	....	170	MARRIAGE VIRG	11
BEHIND THE WALL THIN AS A WREN'S BONE?	....	180	VISION, PRAYER	9
BY THE WREN BONE	....	180	VISION, PRAYER	21
BONE WRITHES DOWN	....	181	VISION, PRAYER	37
THE INMOST MARROW OF MY HEART BONE	....	183	VISION, PRAYER	118
BONE AND BE DUMB	....	183	VISION, PRAYER	124
NO HEART BONE	....	184	VISION, PRAYER	146
MANES, UNDER HIS QUENCHLESS SUMMER BARBED GOLD TO				
THE BONE,	....	204	GIANT'S THIGH	26
THERE'LL BE MY BONE TO GO:	....	239	MAKES INTERVALS	21
BONEBOUND				
THEN LOOK, MY EYES, UPON THIS BONEBOUND FORTUNE	...	81	ALL THAT I OWE	21
BONERAILED				
A STEEPLEJACK TOWER, BONERAILED AND MASTERLESS,	...	109	I, IN IMAGE	20
BONES				
THY PLACE IS FILLED, BONES BID FOR AUCTION,	....	29	LONG, SKELETON	9
STIR THEIR OLD BONES BEHIND CUPBOARD AND CURTAIN.		38	THE GOSSIPERS	5
OVER A ROAD THICK WITH THE BONES OF WORDS.	....	44	TO FOLLOW FOX	17
WHEN THEIR BONES ARE PICKED CLEAN AND THE CLEAN				
BONES GONE,	....	49	NO DOMINION	4
WHEN THEIR BONES ARE PICKED CLEAN AND THE CLEAN				
BONES GONE,	....	49	NO DOMINION	4
WHO IN THE BONES FINDS NOT NEW FAITH,	....	55	NO MAN BELIEVE	22
'FIND MEAT ON BONES'	....	60	MEAT ON BONES	T
'FIND MEAT ON BONES THAT SOON HAVE NONE,	....	60	MEAT ON BONES	1
ROOFED WITH THE SKY AND PATTERNED WITH BLOND BONES;		64	WOMAN SPEAKS	25
THE RACK OF DREAMS MY LILY BONES	....	68	BEFORE KNOCKED	20
OF FLESH AND BONES,	....	73	WE MOTHERNAKED	4
THE GROWING BONES, THE RUMOUR OF MANSEED	....	78	LOVE'S FEVER	17
FILE THROUGH THE FLESH WHERE NO FLESH DECKS THE				
BONES.	....	82	LIGHT BREAKS	6
OF GROWING BONES THE MUSCLES SLID;	....	86	SEE, SAYS LIME	26
THE BONES OF BLINDNESS; AND THE WOMB	....	88	A PROCESS IN	8
THE BONES OF MEN, THE BROKEN IN THEIR BEDS,	....	89	EUNUCH DREAMS	9
A CREATURE IN MY BONES I	....	103	I DREAMED MY	10
STREWING THEIR VOWELS FROM A HILL OF BONES,	....	105	WORLD PYRAMID	41
WITH BONES UNBUTTONED TO THE HALF-WAY WINDS,	......	117	ALTARWISE	9
THAT DID NOT NURSE OUR BONES,	....	153	WAS A SAVIOUR	34

	PAGE	TITLE	LINE
BONES (CONTINUED)			
STRAIGHT AND TALL FROM HIS CROOKED BONES	172	THE HUNCHBACK	34
O KEEP HIS BONES AWAY FROM THAT COMMON CART, ...	173	DAWN RAID	12
MAY HIS HUNGER GO HOWLING ON BARE WHITE BONES	188	WINTER'S TALE	33
THE BONES OUT OF THE HILLS, ...	210	POEM ON B'DAY	68
DEEP IN ITS BLACK, BASE BONES, ...	211	POEM ON B'DAY	88
DOWN THE CHEEK BONES AND WHINNYING	215	COUNTRY HEAVEN	14
ALL HIS BONES CRYING, AND POOR IN ALL BUT PAIN, ...	217	ELEGY	21
FOR I CHERISH A PASSION FOR BONES, ...	221	SONG OF DOG	10
BONES'			
THE STOVED BONES' VOYAGE DOWNWARD	111	I, IN IMAGE	87
BONEYARDS			
CORSET THE BONEYARDS FOR A CROOKED BOY?	118	ALTARWISE	50
BONFIRE			
WHO BORE HIM WITH A BONFIRE IN	181	VISION, PRAYER	43
BONY			
BONY AND SPAVINED, RICH WITH FLEAS.	45	PLOUGHMAN GONE	9
BOOK			
HE IN A BOOK OF WATER TALLOW-EYED	119	ALTARWISE	72
AND ONE LIGHT'S LANGUAGE IN THE BOOK OF TREES.	119	ALTARWISE	89
GRIEF WITH DRENCHED BOOK AND CANDLE CHRISTENS THE CHERUB TIME	130	SINNERS' BELL	16
AND HIS SCARVING BEARD FROM A BOOK, ...	150	WHEN I WOKE	12
BOOKS			
THERE WAS A TIME THEY COULD CRY OVER BOOKS, ...	40	WAS THERE TIME	3
CAWING FROM THEIR BLACK BETHELS SOARING, THE HOLY BOOKS	199	COUNTRY SLEEP	68
THE STICKS OF THE HOUSE WERE HIS; HIS BOOKS HE OWNED.	217	ELEGY	25
BORDER			
OVER THE BORDER	177	POEM IN OCT	18
BEYOND THE BORDER AND UNDER THE LARK FULL CLOUD.	177	POEM IN OCT	37
BORDERS			
ALONG THE BORDERS OF THE GARDEN-WALKS.	223	IN DREAMS	12
BORE			
THE LITERARY CHANKLEY BORE, ...	83	LETTER TO AUNT	2
WHO BORE HIM WITH A BONFIRE IN	181	VISION, PRAYER	43
THAT BORE	183	VISION, PRAYER	126
(BUT NOTHING BORE, NO MOUTHING BABE TO THE VEINED HIVES	205	GIANT'S THIGH	42
IN THE COAL BLACK SKY AND SHE BORE ANGELS!	207	LAMENT	55
BORED			
NOR CITY TAR AND SUBWAY BORED TO FOSTER	100	RUNNING GRAVE	34
BORED AND VICIOUSLY WAITING	154	RETURN	22
BORN			
ROARED, SEA BORN, MAN TORN, BLOOD BLEST.	4	PROLOGUE	41
ALL THAT IS BEAUTIFUL BUT BORN TO DIE, ...	30	YOUTH CALLS	6
AN IMAGE BORN OUT OF THE UPROARIOUS SPRING	47	POET: 1935	36
I, BORN OF FLESH AND GHOST, WAS NEITHER	69	BEFORE KNOCKED	37
BORN OF THE SENSUAL ROOT AND SAP;	86	BREAD I BREAK	14
MY JACK OF CHRIST BORN THORNY ON THE TREE?	96	RUB OF LOVE	45
AT NIGHTBREAK BORN IN THE FAT SIDE, FROM AN ANIMAL BED	130	SINNERS' BELL	26
NEVER SHALL BEAST BE BORN TO ATLAS THE FEW SEAS ...	135	HOW MY ANIMAL	32
WHO IS BORN	180	VISION, PRAYER	3
UNTIL THE TURBULENT NEW BORN	180	VISION, PRAYER	27
BORN SEA	182	VISION, PRAYER	86
IN THE SUN BORN OVER AND OVER, ...	196	FERN HILL	39
THIS NIGHT AND EACH NIGHT SINCE THE FALLING STAR YOU WERE BORN, ...	199	COUNTRY SLEEP	55
SINCE YOU WERE BORN:	201	COUNTRY SLEEP	109

	PAGE	TITLE	LINE
BORROW			
BORROW MY EYES. THE DARKENING SEA FLINGS LEA	179	NEW QUAY	2
BOSOM			
IN THE BOSOM, OR THE EMPTY CHANNELS.	17	IN OBLIVION	21
BOTH			
AND MOUTH. BOTH NOTE AND PLUME PLUNGE FROM THE SPIRE'S HOOK.	16	SPIRE CRANES	8
HE WHOSE LOVERS WERE BOTH WISE AND SENSIBLE	25	BEAUTY TO DUST	18
THAT MADDEN BOTH WATCHERS AND ACTORS.	33	HELD-OUT HAND	16
BOTH QUENCH HIS THIRST HE'LL HAVE A BLACK REPLY.	56	WHY EAST WIND	9
BOTH MIND AND MATTER AT THE SCALDING WORD	73	LORD RED HAIL	11
AGEING BOTH DAY AND NIGHT.	80	ALMANAC TIME	10
BOTH SHALL FAIL IF I BOW NOT TO YOUR BLESSING	148	UNLUCKILY FOR	47
BOTTLE			
BLACK-TONGUED AND TIPSY FROM SALVATION'S BOTTLE.	118	ALTARWISE	61
LIFE NEAT'S A BETTER POISON THAN IN BOTTLE, ...	137	O CHATTERTON	5
BOTTLECORK			
THEN SWIFT FROM A BURSTING SEA WITH BOTTLECORK BOATS	151	BELOW A TIME	13
BOTTOM			
HE, TOO, HAS SEEN THE WORLD AS BOTTOM ROTTEN, ...	52	OUT OF THE PIT	56
IN BOTTOM GEAR THROUGH NIGHT-GEARED MAN.	103	I DREAMED MY	12
OF THE UNCAGED SEA BOTTOM	182	VISION, PRAYER	75
BOUGH			
ONE BOUGH OF BONE ACROSS THE ROOTING AIR, ...	93	IN BEGINNING	3
IT WERE A WAND OR SUBTLE BOUGH, ...	150	WHEN I WOKE	14
BOUGHS			
NOW AS I WAS YOUNG AND EASY UNDER THE APPLE BOUGHS	195	FERN HILL	1
YET OUT OF THE BEAKED, WEB DARK AND THE POUNCING BOUGHS	199	COUNTRY SLEEP	48
AND CUT THE BIRDS' BOUGHS THAT THE MINSTREL SAP RAN RED.	205	GIANT'S THIGH	49
SHAKEN SILKILY FROM STAR-SCALED BOUGHS.	226	SLENDER WIND	5
BOUGHT			
FOR WHEN I BOUGHT YOU FOR A THOUGHT, (YOU COST NO MORE)	10	COOL, OH NO	8
BOULDER			
THEY WITH THE SIMPLE JACKS WERE A BOULDER OF WIVES)--	205	GIANT'S THIGH	44
BOULDERS			
HURDLES AND GUNS AND RAILINGS, AS THE BOULDERS HEAVE,	122	HOLD HARD	16
WHERE BARREN AS BOULDERS WOMEN LIE LONGING STILL	203	GIANT'S THIGH	4
AND THE SCYTHED BOULDERS BLEED, AND THE LAST	210	POEM ON B'DAY	69
BOUNCED			
O MY LOST LOVE BOUNCED FROM A GOOD HOME;	146	IF HEAD HURT	23
OR, BUTTER FAT GOOSEGIRLS, BOUNCED IN A GAMBO BED,	204	GIANT'S THIGH	37
BOUNCING			
WITH A BOUNCING AND SILVER SPOONED KID	149	PAPER & STICKS	15
ALONE WITH MY BOUNCING BAG, ...	155	RETURN	45
WHO ADMITS THE DELUSIVE LIGHT THROUGH THE BOUNCING WALL, ...	170	LOVE IN ASYLUM	11
I HEAR THE BOUNCING HILLS	211	POEM ON B'DAY	100
BOUND			
BOUND BY A SOVEREIGN STRIP, WE LIE, ...	54	WE BY SEASAND	18
BEYOND THIS ISLAND BOUND	62	EARS IN TURRET	10
AND HIS NAMELESS NEED BOUND HIM BURNING AND LOST	188	WINTER'S TALE	44
BOUNDED			
THAT BELLED AND BOUNDED WITH THE FOSSIL AND THE DEW REBORN.	191	WINTER'S TALE	120
BOUNDS			
STREAM WITH BELLS AND BAYING WATER BOUNDS. THE DEW RINGS	189	WINTER'S TALE	62

```
                                           PAGE      TITLE        LINE
BOW
    YOU WHO BOW DOWN AT CROSS AND ALTAR,  ..............  69   BEFORE KNOCKED  43
    AS FLEECED AS THEY BOW LOWLY WITH THE SHEEP,  ......  96   TWELVE          10
    BOW DOWN THE WALLS OF THE FERNED AND FOXY WOODS  ... 136   AFTER FUNERAL   24
    BOTH SHALL FAIL IF I BOW NOT TO YOUR BLESSING  ..... 148   UNLUCKILY FOR   47
    TOO FULL TO BOW TO THE DIM  ........................ 155   RETURN          46
BOW-AND-ARROW
    NAKED AMONG THE BOW-AND-ARROW BIRDS  .............. 123   FOSTER LIGHT     23
BOWED
    GLAMOUR OF THE BLOODILY BOWED,  .................... 156   RETURN          86
    HIS NAKED NEED STRUCK HIM HOWLING AND BOWED  ....... 188   WINTER'S TALE   39
BOWELS
    THE BOWELS TURN TURTLE,  ........................... 135   HOW MY ANIMAL   20
BOWER
    THAT OUT OF A BOWER OF RED SWINE  ..................  61   MEAT ON BONES   28
BOWING
    BOWING ON ITS MOSSY KNEES,  ........................  72   TAKE NEEDLES    50
    ON THE LORD'S-TABLE OF THE BOWING GRASS. FEAR MOST  198   COUNTRY SLEEP   35
BOWL
    OR, MASTED VENUS, THROUGH THE PADDLER'S BOWL  ...... 114   A GRIEF AGO      7
    NAILED WITH AN OPEN EYE, IN THE BOWL OF WOUNDS AND
        WEED  ......................................... 135   HOW MY ANIMAL   29
BOWLER
    A BOWLER THING WITH ONE OR TWO  ...................  83   LETTER TO AUNT  17
BOWS
    THE BOWS GLIDED DOWN, AND THE COAST  .............. 161   LONG-LEGGED      1
    WITH FUMING BOWS AND RAM OF ICE,  ................. 163   LONG-LEGGED     42
    BOWS NO BAPTISM  .................................. 180   VISION, PRAYER  13
    IN THE RIVER TOWY BELOW BOWS HIS TILTED HEADSTONE. 201   SIR JOHNS HILL  12
BOX
    WHERE FIFTY FLOWERS BREED IN A FRUIT BOX,  ........  47   POET: 1935      31
    DRAMATIC SHADOWS IN A TIN BOX;  ...................  57   TO ARCHITECTS    2
    HE HOLDS THE WIRE FROM THIS BOX OF NERVES  ........  75   MY HERO BARES   16
BOXED
    THE COUNTRY-HANDED GRAVE BOXED INTO LOVE,  ........ 115   A GRIEF AGO     31
BOXY
    OF BUD OF ADAM THROUGH HIS BOXY SHIFT,  ........... 101   RUNNING GRAVE   38
BOY
    WITH NO FOUNTAIN BOY BUT ME  ......................  13   RAIN CUTS        3
    IS LAUGHING BOY BENEATH HIS OATH,  ................  19   THE NEOPHYTE     2
    BOY SUCKS NO SWEETNESS FROM THE WILLING MOUTH,  ...  19   THE NEOPHYTE     9
    THE BOY SHE DROPPED FROM DARKNESS AT HER SIDE  ....  78   LOVE'S FEVER    26
    AM I NOT FATHER, TOO, AND THE ASCENDING BOY,  ..... 112   NOT FATHER ME    9
    THE BOY OF WOMAN AND THE WANTON STARER  ........... 112   NOT FATHER ME   10
    WOULD WITHER UP, AND ANY BOY OF LOVE  ............. 116   LANTERNS SHINE   3
    CORSET THE BONEYARDS FOR A CROOKED BOY?  .......... 118   ALTARWISE       50
    AND THE MASKED, HEADLESS BOY.  .................... 129   MY NEOPHYTE     30
    SHAKES A DESOLATE BOY WHO SLITS HIS THROAT  ....... 136   AFTER FUNERAL    7
    ONCE I HAD A RICH BOY FOR MYSELF  ................. 149   PAPER & STICKS   4
    I HAD A HANDSOME AND WELL-OFF BOY  ................ 149   PAPER & STICKS  13
    TO THE BOY OF COMMON THREAD,  ..................... 152   BELOW A TIME    41
    WHERE A BOY  ...................................... 178   POEM IN OCT     54
    WHEN I WAS A WINDY BOY AND A BIT  ................. 205   LAMENT           1
    NOT A BOY AND A BIT IN THE WICK-  ................. 206   LAMENT          16
BOYS
    GEESE NEARLY IN HEAVEN, BOYS  ......................   3   PROLOGUE        15
    SHALL DROWN THE BOYS OF BATTLE IN THEIR SWILL,  ...  73   LORD RED HAIL    8
    I SEE THE BOYS OF SUMMER  .........................  91   BOYS OF SUMMER   T
    I SEE THE BOYS OF SUMMER IN THEIR RUIN  ...........  91   BOYS OF SUMMER   1
    THESE BOYS OF LIGHT ARE CURDLERS IN THEIR FOLLY,  .  92   BOYS OF SUMMER   7
```

	PAGE	TITLE	LINE
BOYS (CONTINUED)			
I SEE THAT FROM THESE BOYS SHALL MEN OF NOTHING ...	92	BOYS OF SUMMER	19
WE SUMMER BOYS IN THIS FOUR-WINDED SPINNING, ...	93	BOYS OF SUMMER	37
O SEE THE POLES OF PROMISE IN THE BOYS.	93	BOYS OF SUMMER	48
I SEE YOU BOYS OF SUMMER IN YOUR RUIN.	93	BOYS OF SUMMER	49
AND BOYS ARE FULL AND FOREIGN IN THE POUCH.	93	BOYS OF SUMMER	51
MALE SHAPES, GIRL-LIPPED, BUT CLAD LIKE BOYS:	143	THE MOLLS	2
WHEN I WHISTLED WITH MITCHING BOYS THROUGH A RESERVOIR PARK	144	COLOUR OF SAY	7
LIKE THE MAULED PICTURES OF BOYS?	145	PLEASURE-BIRD	19
THE TRUANT BOYS FROM THE TOWN	171	THE HUNCHBACK	16
WHILE THE BOYS AMONG WILLOWS	171	THE HUNCHBACK	27
AND THE WILD BOYS INNOCENT AS STRAWBERRIES	172	THE HUNCHBACK	40
IN A SPINNEY OF RINGED BOYS AND GANDERS, SPIKE AND BURN, ...	198	COUNTRY SLEEP	14
PETTICOATS GALED HIGH, OR SHY WITH THE ROUGH RIDING BOYS, ...	204	GIANT'S THIGH	18
BOYS'			
WHACK THEIR BOYS' LIMBS, ...	89	EUNUCH DREAMS	3
BRACKEN			
CROSS ALL DIRECTIONS, BRACKEN POINTS TO THE SKIES,	44	TO FOLLOW FOX	9
WHERE THE HAY RIDES NOW OR THE BRACKEN KITCHENS RUST	205	GIANT'S THIGH	47
BRACKET			
LINKED IN ONE GAS BRACKET	137	O CHATTERTON	2
BRAIDING			
AND LOOSED THE BRAIDING ADDERS FROM THEIR HAIRS;	104	WORLD PYRAMID	22
BRAIN			
BUT WE, SHUT IN THE HOUSES OF THE BRAIN, ...	26	THERE'S PLENTY	8
STAINING THE BROKEN BRAIN	27	OBLIVIOUS DARK	8
THE TWISTED BRAIN, THE FAIR-FORMED LOIN, ...	32	OUT OF SIGHS	25
AND THE GHOSTS OF THE BRAIN, ...	35	LIFT UP FACE	5
MY BRAIN CAME CRYING INTO THE FRESH LIGHT, ...	42	A WAR OF WITS	4
OVERWHELMED BY THE SUN, WITH A TORN BRAIN	42	A WAR OF WITS	12
AS CLEARLY AS THE LIGHT OF MY OWN BRAIN, ...	49	LIGHT, I KNOW	28
THE BRAIN ACTS TO THE LEGAL DEAD.	67	REALM OF FLESH	9
WE SEE RISE THE SECRET WIND BEHIND THE BRAIN, ...	69	SECRET WIND	1
WE HEAR RISE THE SECRET WIND BEHIND THE BRAIN, ...	70	SECRET WIND	19
THE SUN BURNS THE MORNING, A BUSH IN THE BRAIN; ...	74	SUN BURNS	1
THE ALMANAC OF TIME HANGS IN THE BRAIN;	79	ALMANAC TIME	1
INTO THE STONY IDIOM OF THE BRAIN, ...	79	LOVE'S FEVER	33
IN THE BEGINNING WAS THE SECRET BRAIN.	94	IN BEGINNING	25
THE BRAIN WAS CELLED AND SOLDERED IN THE THOUGHT	94	IN BEGINNING	26
THAT, SEWN TO ME BY NERVE AND BRAIN, ...	97	TWILIGHT LOCKS	11
I FELLOWED SLEEP WHO KISSED ME IN THE BRAIN, ...	101	FELLOWED SLEEP	1
MASTER THE NIGHT NOR SERVE THE SNOWMAN'S BRAIN	123	FOSTER LIGHT	4
TO SHIELD THE GLISTENING BRAIN AND BLUNT THE EXAMINERS, ...	133	MAKE ME A MASK	8
AND THE DOORS BURN IN THEIR BRAIN.	161	WEDDING ANNIV	12
BRAINS			
ROSE IN OUR OUTWORN BRAINS. WE SPOKE OUR LINES, ...	34	IN GARDENS	11
THE SNIPER LAID HIM LOW AND STREWED HIS BRAINS; ...	63	WOMAN SPEAKS	11
AND BRAMBLES IN THE WRINGING BRAINS.	68	BEFORE KNOCKED	24
REMOVE YOUR BRAINS, TAKE OUT YOUR HEART;	84	LETTER TO AUNT	60
AND BRAINS TURNED SOUR;	85	SEE, SAYS LIME	12
THE BRAINS OF DEATH UNDID THE KNOT	86	SEE, SAYS LIME	22
THE SKULL OF THE EARTH IS BARBED WITH A WAR OF BURNING BRAINS AND HAIR.	142	SAINT TO FALL	34
BRAMBLED			
AND, IN THAT BRAMBLED VOID, ...	210	POEM ON B'DAY	52

	PAGE	TITLE	LINE
BRAMBLES			
AND BRAMBLES IN THE WRINGING BRAINS.	68	BEFORE KNOCKED	24
ROUGH AS COWS' TONGUES AND THRASHED WITH BRAMBLES			
THEIR BUTTERMILK	204	GIANT'S THIGH	25
BRANCH			
BRANCH AND LEAF THE BIRDLESS ROOFS;	156	RETURN	83
BRANCHES			
BRANCHES A MILLION SHADES, ...	14	RAIN CUTS	22
THRUST OUT OUR HEADS ABOVE THE BRANCHES	31	BEING BUT MEN	9
UNDER THE HANGING BRANCHES HEAR THE WINDS' HARPS.	46	POET: 1935	15
IN THAT PROUD SAILING TREE WITH BRANCHES DRIVEN ...	131	I MAKE THIS IN	6
FIERCE COLOURS FLED ABOUT THE BRANCHES, ...	226	THE OAK	1
OUR BRANCHES AND HOLY LEAVES	230	OUR SANCTITY	4
WITH BRANCHES WAITING FOR A SINGING BIRD, ...	234	NO, PIGEON	14
THEIR SILKEN BRANCHES UNMOVING, ...	235	WOMAN TAPESTRY	7
OR THE BRANCHES OF A GREEN TREE.	236	WOMAN TAPESTRY	40
BRAND			
BRAND OF THE LILY'S ANGER ON HER RING, ...	115	A GRIEF AGO	19
TIME MARKS A BLACK AISLE KINDLE FROM THE BRAND OF			
ASHES, ...	130	SINNERS' BELL	4
WHEN HIS VIPERISH FUSE HANGS LOOPED WITH FLAMES			
UNDER THE BRAND	202	SIR JOHNS HILL	28
BRANDED			
BRANDED FOREHEAD, THAT COULD BIND	147	UNLUCKILY FOR	9
BRANDY			
INTO THE WINE BURNING LIKE BRANDY, ...	175	FIRE RAID	71
BRANDY AND RIPE IN MY BRIGHT, BASS PRIME, ...	206	LAMENT	28
BRASS			
BRASS AND THE BODILESS IMAGE, ON A STICK OF FOLLY	111	I, IN IMAGE	80
BRASSILY			
BRASSILY AT MY SHYEST SECRET, ...	146	TO OTHERS	5
BRASSY			
SOCKET AND GRAVE, THE BRASSY BLOOD, ...	107	ALL ALL AND	35
FORGED IN MAN'S MINERALS, THE BRASSY ORATOR	108	I, IN IMAGE	2
BRAVE			
BRAVE DEATHS OF ONLY ONES BUT NEVER FOUND, ...	153	WAS A SAVIOUR	35
A COLD KIND MAN BRAVE IN HIS NARROW PRIDE	216	ELEGY	3
AN OLD KIND MAN BRAVE IN HIS BURNING PRIDE.	217	ELEGY	24
BRAWL			
THOUGH THE BRAWL OF THE KISS HAS NOT OCCURRED	147	UNLUCKILY FOR	7
BRAWNED			
SPLIT UP THE BRAWNED WOMB'S WEATHERS, ...	92	BOYS OF SUMMER	14
BRAYS			
DESTRUCTION, PICKED BY BIRDS, BRAYS THROUGH THE			
JAW-BONE, ...	132	I MAKE THIS IN	36
AFTER THE FUNERAL, MULE PRAISES, BRAYS, ...	136	AFTER FUNERAL	1
BREAD			
THIS BREAD I BREAK	86	BREAD I BREAK	T
THIS BREAD I BREAK WAS ONCE THE OAT, ...	86	BREAD I BREAK	1
ONCE IN THIS BREAD	86	BREAD I BREAK	8
MY WINE YOU DRINK, MY BREAD YOU SNAP.	86	BREAD I BREAK	15
MY HOUSE WOULD FALL LIKE BREAD ABOUT MY HOMAGE; ...	96	TWELVE	11
FROM BALD PAVILIONS AND THE HOUSE OF BREAD	120	ALTARWISE	96
BREAD AND MILK MANSION IN A TOOTHLESS TOWN.	131	I MAKE THIS IN	15
WITH BRIDEBAIT OF GOLD BREAD, I WITH A LIVING SKEIN,	135	HOW MY ANIMAL	25
ALWAYS GOOD-BYE TO THE LONG-LEGGED BREAD	165	LONG-LEGGED	94
EATING BREAD FROM A NEWSPAPER	171	THE HUNCHBACK	7
INTO THE BREAD IN A WHEATFIELD OF FLAMES, ...	175	FIRE RAID	70
ON A STAR OF FAITH PURE AS THE DRIFTING BREAD, ...	187	WINTER'S TALE	12
AND THE CUP AND THE CUT BREAD IN THE DANCING SHADE,	188	WINTER'S TALE	28

	PAGE	TITLE	LINE
BREAD (CONTINUED)			
HUNGER OF BIRDS IN THE FIELDS OF THE BREAD OF WATER, TOSSED	188	WINTER'S TALE	42
AND THERE OUTSIDE ON THE BREAD OF THE GROUND	189	WINTER'S TALE	68
ON A BREAD WHITE HILL OVER THE CUPPED FARM	190	WINTER'S TALE	107
THAT ONCE CUT THE FIGURES OF BIRDS ON THE DEEP BREAD	190	WINTER'S TALE	114
NOT FOR AMBITION OR BREAD	197	CRAFT OR ART	7
BREAD-SIDED			
STILLS SNAPPED BY NIGHT IN THE BREAD-SIDED FIELD,	118	ALTARWISE	54
BREAK			
AND SHARPER IF I BREAK ASUNDER	10	COOL, OH NO	6
RAVAGE AND BREAK,	10	COOL, OH NO	12
AND BREAK THROUGH DARK;	16	TIME TO ROT	9
I TOUCH AND BREAK,	20	ENCOMPASSED	14
I TOUCH AND BREAK.	20	ENCOMPASSED	15
WHO'LL BREAK OUR NECKS UPON THE PAVEMENT	28	NO WINGS	10
CATCH THE ROOKS SLEEPING, AND BREAK NO TWIG,	31	BEING BUT MEN	7
THAT WAIT FOR BREAKING AND THAT NEVER BREAK,	36	MIDNIGHT ROAD	13
STRAPPED TO A WHEEL, YET THEY SHALL NOT BREAK;	49	NO DOMINION	14
OR WAVES BREAK LOUD ON THE SEASHORES;	50	NO DOMINION	21
BREAK IN THE SUN TILL THE SUN BREAKS DOWN,	50	NO DOMINION	26
NO MAN WHO DOES NOT BREAK AND MAKE,	55	NO MAN BELIEVE	21
WHO DOES NOT BREAK AND MAKE HIS FINAL FAITH.	55	NO MAN BELIEVE	24
THIS BREAD I BREAK	86	BREAD I BREAK	T
THIS BREAD I BREAK WAS ONCE THE OAT,	86	BREAD I BREAK	1
THIS FLESH YOU BREAK, THIS BLOOD YOU LET	86	BREAD I BREAK	11
BREAK ON THE LOVEBEDS OF THE WEEDS;	91	WHERE ONCE THE	14
HERE BREAK A KISS IN NO LOVE'S QUARRY.	93	BOYS OF SUMMER	47
THE HEART IS SENSUAL, THOUGH FIVE EYES BREAK.	139	FIVE & COUNTRY	14
NOW BREAK A GIANT TEAR FOR THE LITTLE KNOWN FALL,	153	WAS A SAVIOUR	32
BREAK THE BLACK NEWS AND PAINT ON A SAIL	164	LONG-LEGGED	71
BUT LET IT BREAK	184	VISION, PRAYER	147
BEFORE CHAINS BREAK TO A HAMMER FLAME	210	POEM ON B'DAY	44
NO WEEPING THROUGH THAT DEEP REPOSE CAN BREAK.	222	MISSING	9
MY NET THAT TAKES TO BREAK	233	NO THOUGHT	7
A RHYTHM I CANNOT BREAK	235	WOMAN TAPESTRY	29
AND I WILL BREAK YOUR PACING LIGHT.	239	MAKES INTERVALS	16
BUT IF YOU BREAK I SUFFER,	239	MAKES INTERVALS	20
I NEVER BREAK BUT FEEL THE SUDDEN PAIN,	239	MAKES INTERVALS	25
I'LL HAVE TO BREAK IN THOUGHT AGAIN,	239	MAKES INTERVALS	27
WHO DO NOT BREAK?	241	ADMIT THE SUN	18
BREAKERS			
HEAR THEY THE SALT GLASS BREAKERS AND THE TONGUES OF BURIAL.	110	I, IN IMAGE	66
BREAKING			
OF LADIES' NEEDLES WORN TO BREAKING POINT	18	NATURAL DAY	10
BREAKING, STARE AT THE SKY	35	LIFT UP FACE	2
THAT WAIT FOR BREAKING AND THAT NEVER BREAK,	36	MIDNIGHT ROAD	13
HAND, THE BREAKING OF THE HAIR,	78	LOVE'S FEVER	11
BROKE THROUGH HER STRAWS, BREAKING MY BANDAGED STRING,	94	RUB OF LOVE	3
I DREAMED MY GENESIS IN SWEAT OF SLEEP, BREAKING	102	I DREAMED MY	1
CRACK LIKE A SPRING IN A VICE, BONE BREAKING APRIL,	122	HOLD HARD	17
CRY MY SEA TOWN WAS BREAKING.	150	WHEN I WOKE	27
SHE IS BREAKING WITH SEASONS AND CLOUDS;	168	LONG-LEGGED	176
TELLS WITH SILENCE THE LAST LIGHT BREAKING	191	REFUSAL MOURN	4
BREAKNECK			
ON A BREAKNECK OF ROCKS	3	PROLOGUE	5
BREAKS			
THEY CRY TO BE TAKEN, AND THE DEVIL BREAKS	30	NEARLY SUMMER	21

	PAGE	TITLE	LINE
BREAKS (CONTINUED)			
BREAK IN THE SUN TILL THE SUN BREAKS DOWN, ...	50	NO DOMINION	26
BREAKS, O MY HEART'S BLOOD, LIKE A HEART AND HILL.	54	WE BY SEASAND	24
LIGHT BREAKS WHERE NO SUN SHINES	82	LIGHT BREAKS	T
LIGHT BREAKS WHERE NO SUN SHINES;	82	LIGHT BREAKS	1
DAWN BREAKS BEHIND THE EYES;	82	LIGHT BREAKS	13
LIGHT BREAKS ON SECRET LOTS, ...	82	LIGHT BREAKS	25
BREAKS ON UNANGLED LAND.	88	A PROCESS IN	12
BREAKS WITH THE WORMY WINTER THROUGH THE EYE.	99	OCTOBER WIND	23
AND BREAKS HIS SHELL IN THE LAST SHOCKED BEGINNING;	124	TODAY, INSECT	13
LOVE'S IMAGE TILL MY HEARTBONE BREAKS	129	MY NEOPHYTE	35
THAT BREAKS ONE BONE TO LIGHT WITH A JUDGMENT CLOUT,	136	AFTER FUNERAL	9
NOR EVER, AS THE WILD TONGUE BREAKS ITS TOMBS, ...	144	PLEASURE-BIRD	11
NOR WHEN ALL PONDEROUS HEAVEN'S HOST OF WATERS BREAKS.	146	IF HEAD HURT	20
UNCLENCHED, ARMLESS, SILK AND ROUGH LOVE THAT BREAKS ALL ROCKS.	154	WAS A SAVIOUR	40
NOT GIRL FOR BIRD (GOURD BEING MAN) BREAKS ROOT.	159	TO LEDA	4
THE SINGING BREAKS IN THE SNOW SHOED VILLAGES OF WISHES	190	WINTER'S TALE	113
PILLAR BREAKS	237	PILLAR BREAKS	T
PILLAR BREAKS, AND MAST IS CLEFT	237	PILLAR BREAKS	1
BREAST			
I TEAR HER BREAST, ...	13	SKY'S BRIGHT	22
AND HID HER UNCOVERED BREAST.	15	FOR LEDA	27
NO CRADLE'S WARMER THAN THIS PERISHED BREAST, ...	63	WOMAN SPEAKS	6
MAN'S MARROW BARBED, AND BREAST RIPPED WITH A STEEL,	64	WOMAN SPEAKS	30
A CROSS IS TATOOED ON THE BREAST OF THE CHILD, ...	74	SUN BURNS	12
THE TIME FOR BREAST AND THE GREEN APRON AGE	78	LOVE'S FEVER	4
ONE BREAST GAVE SUCK THE FEVER'S ISSUE;	79	LOVE'S FEVER	43
AND SILENTLY I MILK THE DEVIL'S BREAST.	81	HERE LIE BEAST	3
NOR WHEN HE FINDS A BEAUTY IN THE BREAST	96	RUB OF LOVE	40
AND SWALLOWED DRY THE WATERS OF THE BREAST.	97	TWILIGHT LOCKS	6
THE MUMMY CLOTHS EXPOSE AN ANCIENT BREAST.	116	LANTERNS SHINE	8
NOW IN THE CLOUD'S BIG BREAST LIE QUIET COUNTRIES,	133	I MAKE THIS IN	61
AND DUG YOUR GRAVE IN MY BREAST.	135	HOW MY ANIMAL	44
WITH THE WILD BREAST AND BLESSED AND GIANT SKULL	136	AFTER FUNERAL	28
AT THE BREAST STORED WITH SEAS. NO RETURN	146	IF HEAD HURT	27
OPENED MY BREAST AND INTO	155	RETURN	35
TIME AND PLACES GRIP HER BREAST BONE, ...	168	LONG-LEGGED	175
CHARRED ON THE BLACK BREAST OF THE GRAVE	173	FIRE RAID	7
UNDER THE SAD BREAST OF THE HEAD STONE	174	FIRE RAID	44
DAYS DEEP IN HER BREAST THAT WORE NO HEART	175	MY BEGGAR ARM	2
BREAST I SHALL WAKEN	182	VISION, PRAYER	73
A SHE BIRD DAWNED, AND HER BREAST WITH SNOW AND SCARLET DOWNED.	189	WINTER'S TALE	70
OF THE LED-ASTRAY BIRDS WHOM GOD, FOR THEIR BREAST OF WHISTLES, ...	202	SIR JOHNS HILL	43
THEIR BREAST, THE VAULTING DOES ROISTER, THE HORNED BUCKS CLIMB	204	GIANT'S THIGH	33
WHENEVER I DOVE IN A BREAST HIGH SHOAL, ...	206	LAMENT	21
CROSSES THE BREAST OF THE PRAISING EAST, AND KNEELS,	215	COUNTRY HEAVEN	3
ABOVE ALL HE LONGED FOR HIS MOTHER'S BREAST	216	ELEGY	9
BREASTBONE'S			
I CHALKED UPON THE BREASTBONE'S SLATE	86	SEE, SAYS LIME	27
BREAST-DEEP			
DIPPED ME BREAST-DEEP IN THE DESCENDED BONE;	118	ALTARWISE	38
BREASTED			
IN THE BREASTED SUMMER LONGS NOT FOR SPRING, ...	55	NO MAN BELIEVE	9
NO BREASTED GIRL, NO MAN WHO, YOUNG	55	NO MAN BELIEVE	10

	PAGE	TITLE	LINE
BREASTED (CONTINUED)			
THE WOMAN BREASTED AND THE HEAVEN HEADED	191	WINTER'S TALE	125
HER ROBIN BREASTED TREE, THREE MARYS IN THE RAYS.	198	COUNTRY SLEEP	29
BREASTKNOT			
OR LIKE THE TIDE-LOOPED BREASTKNOT REEFED AGAIN ...	131	I MAKE THIS IN	11
BREASTS			
NIGHTLY UPON THEIR WRINKLED BREASTS	38	THE GOSSIPERS	17
BEFORE THE LADIES' BREASTS ARE HAGS	60	MEAT ON BONES	4
MY BREASTS ARE THIN.	61	MEAT ON BONES	21
POINT THEIR LITTLE BREASTS AT ME;	138	O CHATTERTON	32
THEIR BREASTS FULL OF HONEY, UNDER THEIR GANDER KING	205	GIANT'S THIGH	38
SMOOTH THE PRISMS OF YOUR BREASTS.	229	MY RIVER	18
AND THE CONTACT WITH HER BREASTS	236	WOMAN TAPESTRY	65
FEEL YOUR WOMAN'S BREASTS RISE UP LIKE FLOWERS	238	MAKES INTERVALS	12
BREAST'S			
WHY NIGHT-TIME RAIN AND THE BREAST'S BLOOD	56	WHY EAST WIND	8
BREATH			
AND DREW MY SPIRAL BREATH	11	CABARET	7
AND BREATH ON BREATH OF INDIGO.	14	RAIN CUTS	39
AND BREATH ON BREATH OF INDIGO.	14	RAIN CUTS	39
HE'LL LIE DOWN, AND OUR BREATH	17	IN OBLIVION	5
NOTHING BUT POISON FROM THE BREATH, ...	19	THE NEOPHYTE	10
AS FLIES BEFORE THE BREATH	25	BEAUTY TO DUST	2
YOUNG MEN WITH FALLEN CHESTS AND OLD MEN'S BREATH,	41	YOUNG ARE OLD	27
FIVE SOVEREIGN FINGERS TAXED THE BREATH, ...	66	HAND SIGNED	2
LONG BREATH THAT CARRIED TO MY FATHER	69	BEFORE KNOCKED	41
AND YOU, BEFORE THE BREATH IS COLD	74	WE MOTHERNAKED	14
AND ALL SUCH LOVE'S A SHRUB SOWN IN THE BREATH. ...	81	ALL THAT I OWE	20
AND FROM THE CLOUDY BASES OF THE BREATH	94	IN BEGINNING	22
CLIPS SHORT THE GESTURE OF BREATH.	135	HOW MY ANIMAL	39
MY NOSTRILS SEE HER BREATH BURN LIKE A BUSH.	139	FIVE & COUNTRY	10
THAT WILL RAKE AT LAST ALL CURRENCIES OF THE MARKED			
BREATH	140	NO WORK WORDS	8
THE BREATH DRAW BACK LIKE A BOLT THROUGH WHITE OIL	142	SAINT TO FALL	46
PACK BACK THE DOWNED BONE. IF THE UNPRICKED BALL OF			
MY BREATH	145	IF HEAD HURT	2
WE HID OUR FEARS IN THAT MURDERING BREATH, ...	153	WAS A SAVIOUR	14
LIONS AND FIRES OF HIS FLYING BREATH, ...	160	DEATHS AND ENT	5
IS ALWAYS LOST IN HER VAULTED BREATH, ...	165	LONG-LEGGED	116
YOUR BREATH WAS SHED	176	BREATH SHED	1
THE PALE BREATH OF CATTLE AT THE STEALTHY SAIL, ...	187	WINTER'S TALE	5
NOR BLASPHEME DOWN THE STATIONS OF THE BREATH	192	REFUSAL MOURN	16
BLOW AWAY LIKE BREATH, ...	193	SIDE OF TRUTH	17
INNOCENCE SWEETENS MY LAST BLACK BREATH, ...	207	LAMENT	58
LAST SOUND, THE WORLD GOING OUT WITHOUT A BREATH:	217	ELEGY	34
THE FRAIL AND DELICATE BREATH OF EVEN-TIME.	222	IN DREAMS	4
IS A PETAL THAT HAS DELICATE BREATH	226	SLENDER WIND	7
HE IS A FRIEND WITH FRESH BREATH	236	WOMAN TAPESTRY	42
BREATHE			
THE AIR YOU BREATHE	11	AIR BREATHE	T
THE AIR YOU BREATHE ENCROACHES	11	AIR BREATHE	1
BREATHE AGAINST AIR, ...	16	TIME TO ROT	4
OUR EVIL, WHEN WE BREATHE IT, ...	17	IN OBLIVION	22
BREATHE TILL THE SNAKE IS HOME, ...	22	HIGH ON A HILL	10
SHUT IN THE MADHOUSE CALL FOR COOL AIR TO BREATHE.	26	THERE'S PLENTY	13
HASTENS THE TIME OF THE GERANIUM TO BREATHE;	47	POET: 1935	37
'THESE ARE BUT DREAMING MEN. BREATHE, AND THEY FADE.'	102	FELLOWED SLEEP	15
TODAY, THIS INSECT, AND THE WORLD I BREATHE, ...	124	TODAY, INSECT	1
AND THRILL AND BREATHE AND MOVE	236	WOMAN TAPESTRY	59

	PAGE	TITLE	LINE
BREATHED			
THESE ONCE-BLIND EYES HAVE BREATHED A WIND OF VISIONS,	132	I MAKE THIS IN	54
BREATHES			
A SEPARATE RIVER BREATHES AND RUNS;	168	LONG-LEGGED	180
BREATHING			
BREATHING NO POISON FROM THE OVAL MOUTH,	19	THE NEOPHYTE	3
BREATHING ON ALL SIDES PUNGENTLY	20	ENCOMPASSED	2
HE COULD HEAR WOMEN BREATHING IN THE DARK,	51	OUT OF THE PIT	20
WILL BE BREATHING BY MY BED.	72	TAKE NEEDLES	48
BREATH'S			
IS CORNER-CAST, BREATH'S RAG, SCRAWLED WEED, A VAIN	131	I MAKE THIS IN	9
BREATH-WHITE			
AND THE BREATH-WHITE, CURTAINED MOUTH OF SEED.'	132	I MAKE THIS IN	51
BRED			
BRED IN THE DARK BEHIND THE SKIRTING-BOARD,	28	NO WINGS	21
THE HAND THAT SIGNED THE TREATY BRED A FEVER,	66	HAND SIGNED	9
HERE IS A UNIVERSE BRED IN THE BONE,	74	SUN BURNS	6
WILDE WORDS, ALL BUTTERED, BADLY BRED,	143	THE MOLLS	10
BREECHES			
IN LOVE TORN BREECHES AND BLISTERED JACKET	151	BELOW A TIME	7
BREED			
WHERE FIFTY FLOWERS BREED IN A FRUIT BOX,	47	POET: 1935	31
BUT WISHES BREED NOT, NEITHER	54	WE BY SEASAND	21
SHALL HER SMILE BREED THAT MOUTH, BEHIND THE MIRROR,	134	NOT FROM ANGER	13
BREEZE			
LET THE SAP LEAK IN THE BREEZE.	72	TAKE NEEDLES	52
DOWN BREEZE AND SHELL TO A DISCORDANT BEACH,	138	FIVE & COUNTRY	7
THE PINE IS THE TREE OF THE BREEZE,	227	THE PINE	2
BREEZE-SERENE			
THE SEA HAS BEEN BREEZE-SERENE SAPPHIRE,	224	IDYLL UNFORGET	21
BRETHREN			
BRETHREN FOR JOY HAS MOVED WITHIN	183	VISION, PRAYER	117
BREVIARY			
ABOUT THE SAINT IN SHADES WHILE THE ENDLESS BREVIARY	148	UNLUCKILY FOR	26
BRIARED			
FOR HIS BRIARED HANDS TO HOIST THEM	184	VISION, PRAYER	137
BRIDAL			
THE TRIGGER AND SCYTHE, THE BRIDAL BLADE,	106	ALL ALL AND	17
BRIDE			
GRAFTS ON ITS BRIDE ONE-SIDED SKINS OF TRUTH;	90	EUNUCH DREAMS	28
NUTMEG, CIVET, AND SEA-PARSLEY SERVE THE PLAGUED GROOM AND BRIDE	131	SINNERS' BELL	29
TRESPASSER AND BROKEN BRIDE	158	INTO HER HEAD	41
THE LONG, LAID MINUTE'S BRIDE DRIFTS ON	164	LONG-LEGGED	83
O BRIDE AND BRIDE GROOM	174	FIRE RAID	41
O BRIDE AND BRIDE GROOM	174	FIRE RAID	41
INHUMAN CRADLE AND THE BRIDE BED FOREVER SOUGHT	188	WINTER'S TALE	49
ALONE AND NAKED IN THE ENGULFING BRIDE,	188	WINTER'S TALE	53
A SHE BIRD ROSE AND RAYED LIKE A BURNING BRIDE.	189	WINTER'S TALE	69
THE SKY, THE BIRD, THE BRIDE,	190	WINTER'S TALE	101
AND THROUGH THE THIGHS OF THE ENGULFING BRIDE,	191	WINTER'S TALE	124
BURNING IN THE BRIDE BED OF LOVE, IN THE WHIRL-	191	WINTER'S TALE	127
BRIDEBAIT			
WITH BRIDEBAIT OF GOLD BREAD, I WITH A LIVING SKEIN,	135	HOW MY ANIMAL	25
BRIDES			
GROOM THE DARK BRIDES, THE WIDOWS OF THE NIGHT	89	EUNUCH DREAMS	5
IS DUMB AND GONE WITH HIS FLAME OF BRIDES.	165	LONG-LEGGED	106
WHO ONCE WERE A BLOOM OF WAYSIDE BRIDES IN THE HAWED HOUSE	204	GIANT'S THIGH	29

		PAGE	TITLE	LINE
BRIDGED				
THAT BRIDGED THE HUMAN HALVES,	....	108	GRIEF THIEF	26
BRIDLES				
WITH WILD SEA FILLIES AND SOAKING BRIDLES	....	168	LONG-LEGGED	185
BRIGHT				
SOMETIMES THE SKY'S TOO BRIGHT	....	12	SKY'S BRIGHT	T
SOMETIMES THE SKY'S TOO BRIGHT,	....	12	SKY'S BRIGHT	1
PERHAPS THE SKY'S TOO BRIGHT;	....	13	SKY'S BRIGHT	26
BRIGHT, WELL-HELD HEAD,	....	14	FOR LEDA	9
AGE COME TO YOU--YOU'RE BRIGHT AND USELESS,	....	21	BEWILDERED WAY	4
WHERE DEATH LIES DEAD ASLEEP, ONE BRIGHT EYE OPEN,		41	YOUNG ARE OLD	20
MAKE BRIGHT ITS CORNERS WHERE A SKELETON	....	49	LIGHT, I KNOW	23
BRIGHT AS A FIG;	....	82	LIGHT BREAKS	11
BRIGHT AS HER SPINNING-WHEELS, THE COLIC SEASON	...	108	I, IN IMAGE	8
AS TARRED WITH BLOOD AS THE BRIGHT THORNS I WEPT;		120	ALTARWISE	101
IN THAT BRIGHT ANCHORGROUND WHERE I LAY LINENED,		132	I MAKE THIS IN	48
THE BRIGHT PRETENDER, THE RIDICULOUS SEA DANDY	....	152	BELOW A TIME	42
CARRION, PARADISE, CHIRRUP MY BRIGHT YOLK.	....	159	INTO HER HEAD	60
TO BRIGHT	....	180	VISION, PRAYER	33
BY THE SPIT AND THE BLACK POT IN THE LOG BRIGHT LIGHT		188	WINTER'S TALE	27
BY THE SPIT AND THE BLACK POT IN THE LOG BRIGHT LIGHT.	....	190	WINTER'S TALE	87
BRANDY AND RIPE IN MY BRIGHT, BASS PRIME,	....	206	LAMENT	28
GOOD MEN, THE LAST WAVE BY, CRYING HOW BRIGHT	.....	208	NOT GO GENTLE	7
WHITE, GOD'S BRIGHT, FLOCKS, THE BELLED LAMBS LEAPING,	....	215	COUNTRY HEAVEN	21
OR RUB YOUR BRIGHT STONE.	....	228	MY RIVER	5
MY RIVER CANNOT RUB YOUR BRIGHT STONE,	....	230	MY RIVER	41
AND WHEN THE BRIGHT WHEEL OF YOUR TURNING VOICE IS STILLED,	....	232	FURIOUS MOTION	3
WENT AWAY FROM THE BRIGHT PLACE.	....	237	WOMAN TAPESTRY	78
REND THE BRIGHT FLESH AWAY,	....	239	MAKES INTERVALS	23
AND THE HEAD OF THE BRIGHT POPPY.	....	240	ADMIT THE SUN	11
BRIGHT-EYED				
THE BRIGHT-EYED WORM ON DAVY'S LAMP,	....	92	BOYS OF SUMMER	35
BRILLIANT				
TO BE ENCOMPASSED BY THE BRILLIANT EARTH	....	20	ENCOMPASSED	T
TO BE ENCOMPASSED BY THE BRILLIANT EARTH	....	20	ENCOMPASSED	1
BRIMMING				
CLOUD AND THE ROADSIDE BUSHES BRIMMING WITH WHISTLING		177	POEM IN OCT	22
BRIMSTONE				
HE SHALL BE WISE AND LET HIS BRIMSTONE SPILL,	.....	73	LORD RED HAIL	3
BRINE				
STALE OF ADAM'S BRINE UNTIL, VISION	....	103	I DREAMED MY	27
BRING				
YOU'LL BRING THE PLACE TO ME	....	21	BEWILDERED WAY	10
IN WINDS THAT BRING THE FRUIT AND RIND	....	55	WHY EAST WIND	4
BRING OUT THE BLACK PATROL,	....	110	I, IN IMAGE	55
BRINGING				
THE SWEET, FISH-GILLED BOATS BRINGING BLOOD	....	142	SAINT TO FALL	22
BRINGS				
THOUGH NO ASK BRINGS IT	....	24	LITTLE PROBLEM	22
BRISKEST				
ALL BUT THE BRISKEST RIDERS THROWN,	....	98	TWILIGHT LOCKS	41
BRITTLE				
THAT'LL MAKE, IT'S BRITTLE, DIAPHRAGM	....	24	LITTLE PROBLEM	8
FOR THE BODY'S BRITTLE AND THE SKIN'S WHITE.	......	42	A WAR OF WITS	10
A SHE BIRD SLEEPING BRITTLE BY	....	159	INTO HER HEAD	56
BROAD				
UPON BROAD WINGS	....	231	OUR SANCTITY	33

	PAGE	TITLE	LINE
BROKE			
ALL REASON BROKE, AND HORROR WALKED THE ROADS.	51	OUT OF THE PIT	18
FILL THE VEINS THE FEVERS BROKE, ...	71	TAKE NEEDLES	14
LAID THE CROPS LOW, BROKE THE GRAPE'S JOY.	86	BREAD I BREAK	5
MAN BROKE THE SUN, PULLED THE WIND DOWN.	86	BREAD I BREAK	10
BROKE THROUGH HER STRAWS, BREAKING MY BANDAGED STRING, ...	94	RUB OF LOVE	3
THE SEA OF SCUMS COULD DROWN ME AS IT BROKE	95	RUB OF LOVE	27
TELLING THE HEART I BROKE OF A GOOD HABIT	175	MY BEGGAR ARM	4
AND WHEN THE SALT SHEET BROKE IN A STORM OF SINGING	194	SLEEP BECALMED	7
WHILE ITS VIOLET SHELLS BROKE AND PARTED.	232	FURIOUS MOTION	14
BROKEN			
A SEDGE OF BROKEN STALKS AND SHELLS.	14	RAIN CUTS	28
UNTIL THE DAY'S BROKEN--	22	HIGH ON A HILL	6
STAINING THE BROKEN BRAIN	27	OBLIVIOUS DARK	8
ALL THAT IS NOT ALREADY BROKEN, ...	30	NEARLY SUMMER	22
BROKEN BY CHOKING, ...	39	GAS FADES	23
THE CAUGHT IN THE CAGE, THE BROKEN WINGED, ...	41	YOUNG ARE OLD	37
CRUNCHING THE ALREADY BROKEN, ...	45	TO FOLLOW FOX	21
AND TOOK TO FEEDING BIRDS WITH BROKEN CRUMBS	53	OUT OF THE PIT	84
AND, BROKEN GHOSTS WITH GLOW-WORMS IN THEIR HEADS,	82	LIGHT BREAKS	4
THE BONES OF MEN, THE BROKEN IN THEIR BEDS, ...	89	EUNUCH DREAMS	9
THE BROKEN HALVES ARE FELLOWED IN A CRIPPLE, ...	104	WORLD PYRAMID	13
BE BY THE SHIPS' SEA BROKEN AT THE MANSTRING ANCHORED	111	I, IN IMAGE	86
AND NEED NO DRUID OF HER BROKEN BODY).	136	AFTER FUNERAL	20
THAT CLOUTS THE SPITTLE LIKE BUBBLES WITH BROKEN ROOMS, ...	144	PLEASURE-BIRD	6
HER CONSTANT, NOR THE WINDS OF LOVE BROKEN WIDE ...	147	UNLUCKILY FOR	10
TRESPASSER AND BROKEN BRIDE	158	INTO HER HEAD	41
A STAR WAS BROKEN	173	FIRE RAID	14
TOO PROUD TO DIE, BROKEN AND BLIND HE DIED	216	ELEGY	1
POOR, BROKEN WEBS TO STRIKE THE SKY!	238	PILLAR BREAKS	16
TEMPLE'S BROKEN AND POOR RAVEN'S DEAD;	238	PILLAR BREAKS	24
BOAT'S BROKEN, TOO, AND MAGPIE'S STILL;	238	PILLAR BREAKS	26
BRONZE			
MY MAN OF LEAVES AND THE BRONZE ROOT, MORTAL, UNMORTAL, ...	109	I, IN IMAGE	16
BROOD			
BROOD ON EACH HOTHOUSE PLANT	26	THERE'S PLENTY	9
THE MIDNIGHT FIGURES OF A SULPHUROUS BROOD	36	MIDNIGHT ROAD	10
FREE FROM THEIR BURNING NESTS THE ARROWS' BROOD. ..	73	LORD RED HAIL	4
OH THE SHEARWATER BIRDS AND THEIR BOATSIZED BROOD	164	LONG-LEGGED	67
SAFE BE AND SMOOTH FROM THE BELLOWS OF THE RUSHY BROOD.	198	COUNTRY SLEEP	20
BROODS			
STILL, IN HIS HUT, HE BROODS AMONG HIS BIRDS.	53	OUT OF THE PIT	101
BROODY			
THE DUCK-BILLED PLATYPUS BROODY IN A MILK OF BIRDS.	148	UNLUCKILY FOR	33
BROOM			
A PAPER WITCH UPON HER SULPHURED BROOM	16	TIME TO ROT	11
BROOMED			
FROM THE BROOMED WITCH'S SPUME YOU ARE SHIELDED BY FERN	198	COUNTRY SLEEP	17
BROOMSTICKS			
GIRLS TAKE TO BROOMSTICKS WHEN THE THIEF OF NIGHT	96	TWELVE	3
BROTHER			
GO SILLY AND BE CHRIST'S GOOD BROTHER, ...	25	BEAUTY TO DUST	17
WAS BROTHER TO MNETHA'S DAUGHTER	68	BEFORE KNOCKED	5
DO YOU NOT BROTHER ME, NOR, AS YOU CLIMB, ...	112	NOT FATHER ME	7
THE TERRIBLE WORLD MY BROTHER BARES HIS SKIN.	133	I MAKE THIS IN	60

	PAGE	TITLE	LINE
BROTHER (CONTINUED)			
WITH THE INCESTUOUS SECRET BROTHER IN THE SECONDS TO PERPETUATE THE STARS,	159	INTO HER HEAD	66
BROTHERHOOD			
SALUTING THE BUSY BROTHERHOOD	70	SECRET WIND	11
BROTHERLESS			
HAVE BROTHERLESS HIS SISTER ON THE HANDSAW.	127	NOW, SAY NAY	14
BROTHERS			
TWO PROUD, BLACKED BROTHERS CRY,	153	WAS A SAVIOUR	25
BROTHERS DODGING THROUGH THE FOG	155	RETURN	49
BROTHERS'			
MY BROTHERS' BLOOD THAT SALTS MY OPEN WOUNDS.	80	ALL THAT I OWE	8
BROUGHT			
AS SIGNS I'VE NOT BROUGHT DOWN	19	IMAGES IN AIR	12
WHO HAVE BROUGHT FORTH THE URCHIN GRIEF.	131	SINNERS' BELL	30
BIRD, HE WAS BROUGHT LOW,	191	WINTER'S TALE	126
BROW			
FOR SHE WHO SPRINKLED ON YOUR BROW	20	THE NEOPHYTE	20
THE CRUSTED WOUND NOR STROKE THE BROW;	66	HAND SIGNED	14
AND THE SWEAT ON THE BROW MAKES A SIGN,	74	SUN BURNS	4
TO ELEVATE YOUR MIDDLE BROW,	83	LETTER TO AUNT	12
DECEMBER'S THORN SCREWED IN A BROW OF HOLLY.	121	ALTARWISE	132
BROWN			
THAT HER LOVE SING AND SWING THROUGH A BROWN CHAPEL,	136	AFTER FUNERAL	25
ALL I COULD SEE WERE HIS BROWN EYES BURNING	149	PAPER & STICKS	8
BROWN AS OWLS	177	POEM IN OCT	34
GROW LARKED AND GREENER AT BERRY BROWN	211	POEM ON B'DAY	101
BROWNS			
INTO THE BROWNS OF AUTUMN AND THE SHARP WHITES OF WINTER,	47	POET: 1935	20
BROWSE			
AND BROWSE UPON THE POSTURES OF THE DEAD;	81	ALL THAT I OWE	22
BROWSING			
DOWNS INTO THE LOW BROWSING DARK.	215	COUNTRY HEAVEN	15
BRUISES			
DRIVE CHILDREN UP LIKE BRUISES TO THE THUMB,	100	RUNNING GRAVE	14
BRUISING			
BRUISING, WHERE'S GOD'S MY SHEPHERD, GOD IS LOVE?	51	OUT OF THE PIT	37
BRUISING THE TIRED FEATHERS.	240	ADMIT THE SUN	8
BRUIT			
DESIRE IS PHOSPHORUS: THE CHEMIC BRUIT	159	TO LEDA	7
BRUSH			
TO BRUSH UPON THE WATERS OF THE POND.	34	IN GARDENS	21
DESERVES NO BRUSH, BUT A FOOL'S AMBUSH.	44	TO FOLLOW FOX	6
A MADMAN WITH A BRUSH HAS SLAPPED A FACE	137	O CHATTERTON	13
I HAVE FELT THE SILK WIND BRUSH MY LIPS;	224	IDYLL UNFORGET	19
BRUTE			
A BRUTE LAND IN THE COOL TOP OF THE COUNTRY DAYS	135	HOW MY ANIMAL	15
BRYNS			
HULOO, ON PLUMBED BRYNS,	4	PROLOGUE	57
BUBBLE			
BEFORE THE GAS FADES WITH A HARSH LAST BUBBLE,	38	GAS FADES	1
SHE THREADS OFF THE SAP AND NEEDLES, BLOOD AND BUBBLE	108	I, IN IMAGE	10
BUT THE OIL AND BUBBLE OF THE MOON,	163	LONG-LEGGED	45
BUBBLED			
THE FELLOW HALF WAS FROZEN AS IT BUBBLED	104	WORLD PYRAMID	7
BUBBLES			
WITH SWAG OF BUBBLES IN A SEEDY SACK	108	GRIEF THIEF	17
THESE STOLEN BUBBLES HAVE THE BITES OF SNAKES	108	GRIEF THIEF	23

	PAGE	TITLE	LINE
BUBBLES (CONTINUED)			
THAT CLOUTS THE SPITTLE LIKE BUBBLES WITH BROKEN ROOMS,	144	PLEASURE-BIRD	6
BUMP ON A SPOUT LET THE BUBBLES JUMP OUT.	145	IF HEAD HURT	3
BUCK			
BUT HEARD HIS BAIT BUCK IN THE WAKE	162	LONG-LEGGED	29
BUCKLE			
BUCKLE TO LINT AND CLOTH THEIR NATRON FOOTSTEPS,	120	ALTARWISE	116
BUCKLEY'S			
BUT THERE IS ONLY BUCKLEY'S UNFRISKY	179	NEW QUAY	11
BUCKLING			
MY EGYPT'S ARMOUR BUCKLING IN ITS SHEET,	104	WORLD PYRAMID	34
BUCKS			
THEIR BREAST, THE VAULTING DOES ROISTER, THE HORNED BUCKS CLIMB	204	GIANT'S THIGH	33
BUD			
A MILLION MINDS GAVE SUCK TO SUCH A BUD	79	LOVE'S FEVER	46
AND CURLING ROUND THE BUD THAT FORKS HER EYE.	95	RUB OF LOVE	31
OF BUD OF ADAM THROUGH HIS BOXY SHIFT,	101	RUNNING GRAVE	38
O LIGHT IN ZENITH, THE COUPLED BUD,	107	ALL ALL AND	32
WRENCHED BY MY FINGERMAN, THE LEADEN BUD	115	A GRIEF AGO	11
OF PARADISE, IN THE SPUN BUD OF THE WORLD.	191	WINTER'S TALE	129
BUDS			
AND BUDS IN YOU.	9	MINUTE'S HOUR	4
THAT RISES AND THEN FALLS, BUDS BUT TO WITHER;	25	THERE'S PLENTY	3
WITH A STUB OF BLACK BUDS,	142	SAINT TO FALL	21
BUGLE			
NEVER NEVER OH NEVER TO REGRET THE BUGLE I WORE	152	BELOW A TIME	47
BUGS			
THE CHAMELEON COATS OF THE BIG BUGS AND SHOTS,)	39	GAS FADES	13
BUILD			
I BUILD MY BELLOWING ARK	4	PROLOGUE	44
CERECLOTH OF WEED, AND BUILD AN ORDURED BED.	64	WOMAN SPEAKS	27
AND I WILL BUILD MY LIQUID WORLD,	74	WE MOTHERNAKED	13
AND A FELLOW WHO JESTS THAT A MARE CAN BUILD NESTS	221	SONG OF DOG	7
BUILD FROM THE ASHES!	238	PILLAR BREAKS	25
BUILD, BUILD AGAIN!	238	PILLAR BREAKS	27
BUILD, BUILD AGAIN!	238	PILLAR BREAKS	27
I BUILD A FORTRESS FROM A HEAP OF FLOWERS;	240	ADMIT THE SUN	9
BUILDING			
RADIO'S A BUILDING IN THE AIR;	58	TO ARCHITECTS	5
A POME'S A BUILDING ON A PAGE;	58	TO ARCHITECTS	11
BODY AND AIR AND BUILDING;	156	RETURN	82
BUILDINGS			
OUT OF THE BUILDINGS OF THE DAY I'VE STEPPED	53	OUT OF THE PIT	90
LIFTING HER SMELL OVER THE CITY BUILDINGS.	240	ADMIT THE SUN	14
BUILDS			
WHEN THE WORM BUILDS WITH THE GOLD STRAWS OF VENOM	121	ALTARWISE	139
BUILT			
TO THE BUILT VOICE, OR FLY WITH WINTER TO THE BELLS,	16	SPIRE CRANES	10
BULB			
BEGINNING WITH DOOM IN THE BULB, THE SPRING UNRAVELS,	108	I, IN IMAGE	7
BULGE			
AND IF I INDULGE IN A BITE AT A BULGE,	221	SONG OF DOG	15
BULL			
BUT A HILLOCKY BULL IN THE SWELTER	206	LAMENT	31
OR HICKORY BULL IN MILKY GRASS	207	LAMENT	41
BULLDANCE			
WHALEBED AND BULLDANCE, THE GOLD BUSH OF LIONS,	131	I MAKE THIS IN	22

	PAGE	TITLE	LINE
BULLET'S			
DEATH'S APPETITE IS SHARPENED BY THE BULLET'S THUMB;	64	WOMAN SPEAKS	34
BULLIES			
BULLIES INTO ROUGH SEAS YOU SO GENTLE	142	SAINT TO FALL	49
BULLOCK			
ADAM OR EVE, THE ADORNED HOLY BULLOCK	174	FIRE RAID	34
BULLRING			
A THUNDERING BULLRING OF YOUR SILENT AND GIRL-CIRCLED ISLAND.	142	SAINT TO FALL	51
BULLS			
OH THE BULLS OF BISCAY AND THEIR CALVES	164	LONG-LEGGED	68
BULL'S-EYE			
BULL'S-EYE THE OUTLAW THROUGH A EUNUCH CRACK	108	GRIEF THIEF	19
BULLY			
THAN BULLY ILL LOVE IN THE CLOUTED SCENE.	145	IF HEAD HURT	5
BULWARKS			
AND THE BULWARKS OF THE DAZZLED QUAY.	162	LONG-LEGGED	10
BUM			
BECAUSE THERE STANDS, ONE STORY OUT OF THE BUM CITY,	144	PLEASURE-BIRD	13
BUMP			
BUMP ON A SPOUT LET THE BUBBLES JUMP OUT.	145	IF HEAD HURT	3
BUNCHED			
'IF MY BUNCHED, MONKEY COMING IS CRUEL	145	IF HEAD HURT	11
BUNTING			
IN MORALS AND FULL MARRIAGE BUNTING,	38	THE GOSSIPERS	12
BUOYANT			
TO STIR THE WATER WITH A BUOYANT FOOT,	14	FOR LEDA	2
BUOYS			
CHIMES OF THE ROCKED BUOYS.	163	LONG-LEGGED	36
BUOY'S			
DEATH CLEAR AS A BUOY'S BELL:	202	SIR JOHNS HILL	26
BURDEN			
OF THE BIRDS OF BURDEN	183	VISION, PRAYER	105
BURIAL			
HEAR THEY THE SALT GLASS BREAKERS AND THE TONGUES OF BURIAL.	110	I, IN IMAGE	66
SHAKES, IN CRABBED BURIAL SHAWL, BY SORCERER'S INSECT WOKEN,	130	SINNERS' BELL	23
ENDURE BURIAL UNDER THE SPELLING WALL,	134	HOW MY ANIMAL	4
UNDER THE BURIAL SONG	183	VISION, PRAYER	104
BURIED			
AND SILENTLY I MILK T UR WE .	81	HERE LIE BEAST	9
AND SILENTLY I MILK THE BURIED FLOWERS.	81	HERE LIE BEAST	9
THE DREAM THAT KICKS THE BURIED FROM THEIR SACK	90	EUNUCH DREAMS	34
DUST IN THE BURIED WOOD, FLIES ON THE GRAINS OF HER WINGS	189	WINTER'S TALE	58
IN THE BLACK BURIED SPINNEYS	215	COUNTRY HEAVEN	17
BURIES			
THIS SUMMER BURIES A SPRING BIRD.	58	HERE IN SPRING	4
EXULTATION LIES DOWN. TIME BURIES THE SPRING WEATHER	191	WINTER'S TALE	119
BURN			
BURN OUT THE LASTING ROT,	60	FAIRY TALES	39
AND THROUGH THESE EARS HE HARKS MY FIRE BURN	77	LASHED RINGS	16
THAT BURN THE BITTEN DECKS,	128	MY NEOPHYTE	9
MY NOSTRILS SEE HER BREATH BURN LIKE A BUSH.	139	FIVE & COUNTRY	10
IF I TAKE TO BURN OR RETURN THIS WORLD WHICH IS EACH MAN'S WORK.	140	NO WORK WORDS	12
AND THE DOORS BURN IN THEIR BRAIN.	161	WEDDING ANNIV	12
THE WHIRLED BOAT IN THE BURN OF HIS BLOOD	164	LONG-LEGGED	65
TO THE BURN AND TURN OF TIME	180	VISION, PRAYER	11
I TURN THE CORNER OF PRAYER AND BURN	185	VISION, PRAYER	188

		PAGE	TITLE	LINE
BURN (CONTINUED)				
IN A SPINNEY OF RINGED BOYS AND GANDERS, SPIKE AND				
BURN,	....	198	COUNTRY SLEEP	14
OLD AGE SHOULD BURN AND RAVE AT CLOSE OF DAY;	.....	207	NOT GO GENTLE	2
BURNED				
AND BURNED SEA SILENCE ON A WICK OF WORLDS.	....	119	ALTARWISE	74
AND PROPHETS LOUD ON THE BURNED DUNES;	....	168	LONG-LEGGED	173
AMONG THE STREET BURNED TO TIRELESS DEATH	....	173	FIRE RAID	4
THAT HIS TEARS BURNED MY CHEEKS AND HIS HEART MOVED				
IN MINE.	....	178	POEM IN OCT	52
THE SCROLLS OF FIRE THAT BURNED IN HIS HEART AND				
HEAD,	....	187	WINTER'S TALE	14
BURNING				
IS A BURNING AND CRESTED ACT,	....	3	PROLOGUE	25
OUT OF THE OLD LIE BURNING ON THE GROUND,	....	44	LONGED TO MOVE	13
FREE FROM THEIR BURNING NESTS THE ARROWS' BROOD.		73	LORD RED HAIL	4
AND, BURNING CIPHERS ON THE ROUND OF SPACE,	....	93	IN BEGINNING	5
BLEED FROM MY BURNING FORK AND SMELL MY HEELS.	....	105	WORLD PYRAMID	52
WHICH SIXTH OF WIND BLEW OUT THE BURNING GENTRY?		118	ALTARWISE	47
FARMER IN TIME OF FROST THE BURNING LEAGUES,	....	123	FOSTER LIGHT	10
FUMED LIKE A TREE, AND TOSSED A BURNING BIRD;	.....	133	I MAKE THIS IN	56
THE SKULL OF THE EARTH IS BARBED WITH A WAR OF				
BURNING BRAINS AND HAIR.	....	142	SAINT TO FALL	34
TOPPLING AND BURNING IN THE MUDDLE OF TOWERS AND				
GALLERIES	....	145	PLEASURE-BIRD	18
ALL I COULD SEE WERE HIS BROWN EYES BURNING	....	149	PAPER & STICKS	8
MAN WAS THE BURNING ENGLAND SHE WAS SLEEP-WALKING,				
AND THE ENAMOURING ISLAND	....	157	INTO HER HEAD	20
INTO THE DEAD CLOCK BURNING THE HOUR	....	175	FIRE RAID	65
INTO THE WINE BURNING LIKE BRANDY,	....	175	FIRE RAID	71
JOY OF THE LONG DEAD CHILD SANG BURNING	....	178	POEM IN OCT	63
OF FIELDS. AND BURNING THEN	....	187	WINTER'S TALE	16
AND HIS NAMELESS NEED BOUND HIM BURNING AND LOST		188	WINTER'S TALE	44
A SHE BIRD ROSE AND RAYED LIKE A BURNING BRIDE.	...	189	WINTER'S TALE	69
THE HEAVENS, THE HEAVEN, THE GRAVE, THE BURNING FONT.		190	WINTER'S TALE	104
BURNING IN THE BRIDE BED OF LOVE, IN THE WHIRL-	...	191	WINTER'S TALE	127
THE MAJESTY AND BURNING OF THE CHILD'S DEATH.	.....	192	REFUSAL MOURN	13
IN THE THROAT, BURNING AND TURNING. ALL NIGHT AFLOAT	194	SLEEP BECALMED	2
BURNING! NIGHT AND THE VEIN OF BIRDS IN THE WINGED,				
SLOE WRIST	....	199	COUNTRY SLEEP	70
AN OLD KIND MAN BRAVE IN HIS BURNING PRIDE.	....	217	ELEGY	24
BURNING ITS SWEET PATH CLEARER THAN BEFORE.	....	232	FURIOUS MOTION	17
BURNS				
HIS TELLING BURNS.	....	12	SKY'S BRIGHT	19
THE DRY FEVER BURNS UNTIL NO HEART IS LEFT,	....	34	THIRST PARCHES	2
BURNS IN MANY MIRRORS.	....	60	FAIRY TALES	25
THE SUN BURNS THE MORNING	....	74	SUN BURNS	T
THE SUN BURNS THE MORNING, A BUSH IN THE BRAIN;	...	74	SUN BURNS	1
WARMS YOUTH AND SEED AND BURNS THE SEEDS OF AGE;		82	LIGHT BREAKS	8
THAT BURNS ALONG MY EYES.	....	134	NOT FROM ANGER	14
BURNS ME HIS NAME AND HIS FLAME	....	180	VISION, PRAYER	28
CRY. MY VOICE BURNS IN HIS HAND.	....	185	VISION, PRAYER	202
BURROW				
BURROW OUR WAY UPWARDS INTO THE BLUE SKY;	....	231	OUR SANCTITY	35
BURST				
HER FAN BURST IN A MILLION LIGHTS	....	11	CABARET	14
TILL THE BIRD HAS BURST HIS SHELL,	....	22	HIGH ON A HILL	12
TO BURST INTO A HANGING LAND	....	85	SEE, SAYS LIME	19
BURST IN THE ROOTS, PUMPED FROM THE EARTH AND ROCK		94	IN BEGINNING	17
THE BLACK, BURST SEA REJOICE,	....	135	HOW MY ANIMAL	19

	PAGE	TITLE	LINE
BURST (CONTINUED)			
HE DROPPED WHERE HE LOVED ON THE BURST PAVEMENT STONE	172	DAWN RAID	4
BURSTING			
THEN SWIFT FROM A BURSTING SEA WITH BOTTLECORK BOATS	151	BELOW A TIME	13
BURSTS			
OF LOVE AND LIGHT BURSTS IN THEIR THROATS.	92	BOYS OF SUMMER	23
BURY			
WHO DOES NOT BURY GOD IN A DEEP GRAVE	55	NO MAN BELIEVE	19
THAT BURY THE SWEET STREET SLOWLY, SEE	142	SAINT TO FALL	33
(BURY THE DEAD FOR FEAR THAT THEY WALK TO THE GRAVE			
IN LABOUR.)	143	24 YEARS	2
BURY ALL RUBBISH AND LOVE SIGNS	156	RETURN	90
FORGOTTEN DARK, REST THEIR PULSE AND BURY THEIR DEAD			
IN HER FAITHLESS SLEEP.	159	INTO HER HEAD	69
I BURY, I TRAVEL TO FIND PRIDE	240	ADMIT THE SUN	12
BUSH			
THE SUN BURNS THE MORNING, A BUSH IN THE BRAIN; ...	74	SUN BURNS	1
WHALEBED AND BULLDANCE, THE GOLD BUSH OF LIONS, ...	131	I MAKE THIS IN	22
LOPS, AS A BUSH PLUMED WITH FLAMES, THE RANT OF THE			
FIERCE EYE, ...	135	HOW MY ANIMAL	38
MY NOSTRILS SEE HER BREATH BURN LIKE A BUSH.	139	FIVE & COUNTRY	10
OR WITH THEIR ORCHARD MAN IN THE CORE OF THE SUN'S			
BUSH	204	GIANT'S THIGH	24
IN THE COAL BLACK BUSH AND LET THEM GRIEVE.	206	LAMENT	12
BUSHED			
DEEP THE GREAT BUSHED BAIT WITH RAINING LIPS	163	LONG-LEGGED	51
ON THE DEPARTED, SNOW BUSHED GREEN, WANTON IN MOON			
LIGHT	189	WINTER'S TALE	72
BUSHES			
CLOUD AND THE ROADSIDE BUSHES BRIMMING WITH WHISTLING	177	POEM IN OCT	22
GREEN CHICKENS OF THE BAY AND BUSHES CLUCK, 'DILLY			
DILLY, ...	202	SIR JOHNS HILL	31
BUSHES AND OWLS BLOW OUT LIKE CANDLES, ...	215	COUNTRY HEAVEN	18
BUSHILY			
THEN, BUSHILY SWANKED IN BEAR WIG AND TAILS, ...	151	BELOW A TIME	19
BUSHY			
SOME DEAD UNDID THEIR BUSHY JAWS, ...	97	TWILIGHT LOCKS	22
THAT SHAPES EACH BUSHY ITEM OF THE AIR	123	FOSTER LIGHT	5
BUSTLING			
BLESSING AND COUNTING THE BUSTLING	156	RETURN	73
BUSY			
THIS BUSY JARRING ON THE NERVES YET NO OUTBREAK?	36	MIDNIGHT ROAD	4
SALUTING THE BUSY BROTHERHOOD	70	SECRET WIND	11
MY BUSY HEART WHO SHUDDERS AS SHE TALKS	98	OCTOBER WIND	7
BUT (151)			
BUTT			
BUTT OF THE TREE-TAILED WORM THAT MOUNTED EVE, ...	117	ALTARWISE	32
BUTT-ENDS			
BUT NOW THERE ARE THE BUTT-ENDS OF SPENT SQUIBS.	52	OUT OF THE PIT	52
BUTTER			
WOULD LEAVE ME COLD AS BUTTER FOR THE FLIES, ...	95	RUB OF LOVE	26
OR, BUTTER FAT GOOSEGIRLS, BOUNCED IN A GAMBO BED,	204	GIANT'S THIGH	37
BUTTERED			
WILDE WORDS, ALL BUTTERED, BADLY BRED, ...	143	THE MOLLS	10
BUTTERMILK			
YARD OF THE BUTTERMILK RAIN ON THE PAIL! THE SERMON	200	COUNTRY SLEEP	77
ROUGH AS COWS' TONGUES AND THRASHED WITH BRAMBLES			
THEIR BUTTERMILK	204	GIANT'S THIGH	25
BUTTOCK			
AND HAND TO BUTTOCK, MAN TO ENGINE, BATTLING, ...	51	OUT OF THE PIT	36

	PAGE	TITLE	LINE
BUTTON			
BUTTON YOUR BODICE ON A HUMP OF SPLINTERS, ...	118	ALTARWISE	51
AND BUTTON UP. HE MINCES AMONG KNICKERS, ...	179	NEW QUAY	23
BUY			
FIRST BUY A HAT, NO PARIS MODEL	83	LETTER TO AUNT	15
BY (177)			
BYRES			
AND THE DUCK POND GLASS AND THE BLINDING BYRES ALONE	188	WINTER'S TALE	35
PAST THE BLIND BARNS AND BYRES OF THE WINDLESS FARM.	190	WINTER'S TALE	90
BYZANTINE			
ROSE MY BYZANTINE ADAM IN THE NIGHT.	118	ALTARWISE	62
CABARET			
CABARET	11	CABARET	T
CABINNED			
THE SKULL, THE CELLS, THE CABINNED EARS	69	SECRET WIND	5
ALL THE CABINNED FAITHS DENY	71	TAKE NEEDLES	15
CADAVER			
YOU HERO SKULL, CADAVER IN THE HANGAR	100	RUNNING GRAVE	29
CADAVEROUS			
THE CADAVEROUS GRAVELS, FALLS THICK AND STEADILY,	110	I, IN IMAGE	44
CADAVER'S			
OF LOVE AM BARER THAN CADAVER'S TRAP	100	RUNNING GRAVE	8
HEART OF CADAVER'S CANDLE WAXES THIN, ...	100	RUNNING GRAVE	12
STRIDE THROUGH CADAVER'S COUNTRY IN MY FORCE, ...	100	RUNNING GRAVE	21
JOY IS THE KNOCK OF DUST, CADAVER'S SHOOT	101	RUNNING GRAVE	37
HAPPY CADAVER'S HUNGER AS YOU TAKE	101	RUNNING GRAVE	49
MAN WAS CADAVER'S MASKER, THE HARNESSING MANTLE,	112	I, IN IMAGE	103
CADENCE			
FAINT ARROWY MOONSTONE ON A TEAR-CULLED CADENCE,	225	SLENDER WIND	3
CAESARED			
DRIVES OUT THE FATHER FROM THE CAESARED CAMP;	115	A GRIEF AGO	27
CAGE			
THE CAUGHT IN THE CAGE, THE BROKEN WINGED, ...	41	YOUNG ARE OLD	37
AND FASTENING IN ITS CAGE THE FLOWERS' COLOUR?	46	POET: 1935	9
AND THE CAGE FOR THE SCYTHE-EYED RAVEN.	106	ALL ALL AND	21
ASSEMBLING WAITS FOR THE SPADE'S RING ON THE CAGE.	172	DAWN RAID	11
AND TO-MORROW WEEPS IN A BLIND CAGE	209	POEM ON B'DAY	42
SILLY TO CAGE AND THEN SET FREE, ...	237	PILLAR BREAKS	8
ALTHOUGH YOUR CAGE IS STRONG.	239	LET ME ESCAPE	8
CAIRO'S			
DRAW ON THE GLOVE OF PRINTS, DEAD CAIRO'S HENNA ...	120	ALTARWISE	117
CAKE			
IS MR. JONES THE CAKE, THAT WINKING-BIT, ...	179	NEW QUAY	20
CALENDAR			
THE SLUG'S A LIVING CALENDAR OF DAYS;	59	HERE IN SPRING	15
THE CALENDAR OF AGE HANGS IN THE HEART, ...	80	ALMANAC TIME	6
CALF			
DIPPING MOON AND DRUNK AS A NEW DROPPED CALF, ...	206	LAMENT	17
NO FLAILING CALF OR CAT IN A FLAME	207	LAMENT	40
AT A CALF THAT IS PLUMP AND DELICIOUS;	221	SONG OF DOG	14
CALL			
SHUT IN THE MADHOUSE CALL FOR COOL AIR TO BREATHE.	26	THERE'S PLENTY	13
CALL BACK THE CASTAWAYS	107	GRIEF THIEF	7
BUT I, ANN'S BARD ON A RAISED HEARTH, CALL ALL	136	AFTER FUNERAL	21
FRIEND BY ENEMY I CALL YOU OUT.	146	TO OTHERS	1
WITH WATER PRAYING AND CALL OF SEAGULL AND ROOK ...	177	POEM IN OCT	6
CALL FOR CONFESSOR AND WISER MIRROR BUT THERE IS NONE	186	HOLY SPRING	10
WHEN I WAS A MAN YOU COULD CALL A MAN	206	LAMENT	25
CALLED			
CALLED FOR CONFESSOR BUT THERE WAS NONE	42	A WAR OF WITS	5

	PAGE	TITLE	LINE
CALLED (CONTINUED)			
AND, MAD, HE CALLED HIS CURSES UPON GOD, ...	50	OUT OF THE PIT	8
CALLED IN MY EYES THE SOUND OF LIGHT.	78	LOVE'S FEVER	21
ONE WHO CALLED DEEPEST DOWN SHALL HOLD HIS PEACE	160	DEATHS AND ENT	9
AND MISTER THEY CALLED HEY MISTER	171	THE HUNCHBACK	15
VOICES HAVE CALLED, AND THE ANSWERS LEMURAL WHISPERS			
FROM THE SEA;	224	IDYLL UNFORGET	34
CALLIGRAPHER			
THE LAMPED CALLIGRAPHER, THE QUEEN IN SPLINTS, ...	120	ALTARWISE	115
CALLIGRAPHY			
LEAP, AS TO TRUMPETS. CALLIGRAPHY OF THE OLD	189	WINTER'S TALE	77
CALLING			
A CALLING FOR COLOUR CALLS WITH THE WIND	54	WE BY SEASAND	6
CALLS			
IN TUNING IMPULSES TO CALLS;	18	NATURAL DAY	6
SO THAT THE PROCESS CALLS FOR LAUGHS, ...	21	BEWILDERED WAY	18
YOUTH CALLS TO AGE	30	YOUTH CALLS	T
YOUTH CALLS TO AGE ACROSS THE TIRED YEARS:	30	YOUTH CALLS	13
AND THE THUNDER OF CALLS AND NOTES.	44	LONGED TO MOVE	10
A CALLING FOR COLOUR CALLS WITH THE WIND	54	WE BY SEASAND	6
CALLS SOME CONTENT TO TRAVEL WITH THE WINDS, ...	56	WHY EAST WIND	17
AMONG THE GARDEN TREES A PIGEON CALLS, ...	57	GREEK PLAY	29
A PIGEON CALLS AND WOMEN TALK OF DEATH.	57	GREEK PLAY	32
CALLS A GREEN DAY AND NIGHT.	128	MY NEOPHYTE	6
CALLS THE GREEN ROCK OF LIGHT.	128	MY NEOPHYTE	12
CALLS THE STARVED FIRE HERD, IS CAST IN ICE, ...	132	I MAKE THIS IN	27
SHALLOW AND SEDGE, AND 'DILLY DILLY', CALLS THE LOFT			
HAWK, ...	202	SIR JOHNS HILL	21
BENEATH THE DEEP BARK CALLS AND MAKES QUIET MUSIC.	226	THE OAK	6
CALM			
WITH A ONE-COLOURED CALM;	54	WE BY SEASAND	13
SHALL CALM HER SORES.	77	THE FORCE THAT	18
YOUR CALM AND CUDDLED IS A SCYTHE OF HAIRS, ...	99	RUNNING GRAVE	2
CATHEDRAL CALM IN THE PULLED HOUSE;	130	SINNERS' BELL	15
A CALM WIND BLOWS THAT RAISED THE TREES LIKE HAIR	133	I MAKE THIS IN	64
THE GRAVE AND MY CALM BODY ARE SHUT TO YOUR COMING			
AS STONE, ...	146	IF HEAD HURT	29
THERE WAS CALM TO BE DONE IN HIS SAFE UNREST, ...	153	WAS A SAVIOUR	11
IN THE MANTLE AND CALM, ...	190	WINTER'S TALE	86
WILL BE THE SAME GRIEF FLYING. WHOM SHALL THEY CALM?	194	CONVERS PRAYER	11
CALM AND STRANGE IS THIS EVENING HOUR IN THE FOREST,	221	FOREST PICTURE	1
CALVE			
IF THE RED TICKLE AS THE CATTLE CALVE	95	RUB OF LOVE	4
CALVES			
GOING HER GLISTENING CALVES THAT MINUTE.	11	CABARET	4
OH THE BULLS OF BISCAY AND THEIR CALVES	164	LONG-LEGGED	68
AND GREEN AND GOLDEN I WAS HUNTSMAN AND HERDSMAN,			
THE CALVES	195	FERN HILL	15
CAME			
BUT CAME FROM OUT THE MOUTH UNKNOWING	23	THE ONLY DEAD	17
MY BRAIN CAME CRYING INTO THE FRESH LIGHT, ...	42	A WAR OF WITS	4
NOT KNOWING RADIANCE CAME AND PASSED.	43	FACES SHONE	13
AND SHAFTED HAWKS CAME SNARLING DOWN THE SKY;	65	WOMAN SPEAKS	57
AND FAMINE GREW, AND LOCUSTS CAME;	66	HAND SIGNED	10
AND AFTER CAME THE IMPRINTS ON THE WATER, ...	94	IN BEGINNING	9
AND FROM THE WINDY WEST CAME TWO-GUNNED GABRIEL,	118	ALTARWISE	57
I DIED BEFORE BEDTIME CAME	140	TOMBSTONE TOLD	26
LIKE THE PARK BIRDS HE CAME EARLY	171	THE HUNCHBACK	13
THAT CAME FROM THE WOUND WRAPPED IN THE SALT SHEET.	194	SLEEP BECALMED	4
SLUNK POUTING OUT WHEN THE LIMP TIME CAME;	207	LAMENT	44

		PAGE	TITLE	LINE
CAME (CONTINUED)				
ON WHOM A WORLD OF ILLS CAME DOWN LIKE SNOW.	....	217	ELEGY	32
CAMEL'S				
MY CAMEL'S EYES WILL NEEDLE THROUGH THE SHROUD.	...	118	ALTARWISE	52
CAMERAS				
WHEN CAMERAS SHUT THEY HURRY TO THEIR HOLE	....	89	EUNUCH DREAMS	15
CAMP				
DRIVES OUT THE FATHER FROM THE CAESARED CAMP;	.....	115	A GRIEF AGO	27
WITH STALE AND TERRIFYING CAMP	....	143	THE MOLLS	6
CAMPED				
CAMPED IN THE DRUG-WHITE SHOWER OF NERVES AND FOOD,		144	PLEASURE-BIRD	8
CAN				
I CANNOT LIFT, BUT CAN,	....	12	SKY'S BRIGHT	11
WHO HAS COMPLETENESS THAT CAN CUT	....	23	THE ONLY DEAD	7
(GOOD FOR CAN RUN	....	24	LITTLE PROBLEM	13
FOR A SPIRIT, CAN	....	24	LITTLE PROBLEM	18
CAN EVER FURTHER,	....	24	LITTLE PROBLEM	21
FOR IT CAN QUICKEN OR IT CAN KILL.	....	24	THE ONLY DEAD	29
FOR IT CAN QUICKEN OR IT CAN KILL.	....	24	THE ONLY DEAD	29
SENSE CAN BUT MAIM IT, WISDOM MAR IT,	....	25	BEAUTY TO DUST	9
CAN BE BUT VANITY, SUCH AN OLD CRY,	....	27	OBLIVIOUS DARK	24
IF LOVE HE CAN BEING NO WOMAN'S MAN.	....	47	POET: 1935	35
CAN WE FEND OFF ROCK ARRIVAL,	....	54	WE BY SEASAND	22
AND THIS IS TRUE, NO MAN CAN LIVE	....	55	NO MAN BELIEVE	18
THERE CAN BE FEW TEARS LEFT: ELECTRA WEPT	....	57	GREEK PLAY	17
AND THE MAGGOT NO MAN CAN SLAY.'	....	61	MEAT ON BONES	16
'THE MAGGOT THAT NO MAN CAN KILL	....	61	MEAT ON BONES	25
AND THE MAN NO ROPE CAN HANG	....	61	MEAT ON BONES	26
NOR CAN I SMOTHER THE SWEET WAKING.'	....	61	MEAT ON BONES	32
HOLD IN HIS VELVET HAND THE CAN OF BLOOD;	....	73	LORD RED HAIL	2
THESE THINGS REMEMBERED, WHAT CAN STOP	....	84	LETTER TO AUNT	56
MINUS THESE CURSES, YOU CAN BE	....	85	LETTER TO AUNT	61
CAN NEVER RAISE THE MIDNIGHT OF A CHUCKLE,	....	96	RUB OF LOVE	39
CAN TIME UNRIDDLE, AND THE CUPBOARD STONE,	....	113	SERVANT SUN	3
BAY. NO-GOOD IS ABROAD. I UNHARDY CAN	....	179	NEW QUAY	8
THAT I CAN HEAR THE WOMB	....	180	VISION, PRAYER	6
AND A FELLOW WHO JESTS THAT A MARE CAN BUILD NESTS		221	SONG OF DOG	7
NO WEEPING THROUGH THAT DEEP REPOSE CAN BREAK.	....	222	MISSING	9
WHICH CAN COMFORT YOU	....	228	NOT DESPAIR	5
NOR CAN THE SNOW	....	229	MY RIVER	17
YOUR EYES CAN BE THE EYES	....	229	MY RIVER	30
YOUR VOICE CAN BE THE VOICE	....	229	MY RIVER	34
WHERE THE FROST CAN NEVER FALL,	....	232	YOUR VOICE	15
NO THOUGHT CAN TROUBLE MY UNWHOLESOME POSE	....	233	NO THOUGHT	T
NO THOUGHT CAN TROUBLE MY UNWHOLESOME POSE,	....	233	NO THOUGHT	1
YOU DO NOT HURT, NOR CAN YOUR HAND	....	233	NO THOUGHT	3
NO LOVE CAN PENETRATE	....	233	NO THOUGHT	9
I CAN DETECT A TOLERANCE,	....	236	WOMAN TAPESTRY	52
THE ROD CAN LIFT ITS TWINING HEAD	....	240	TWINING HEAD	T
THE ROD CAN LIFT ITS TWINING HEAD	....	240	TWINING HEAD	1
THE SAVIOUR OF THE CROSS WHO CAN	....	240	TWINING HEAD	7
IT IS A WEAPON THAT CAN TURN BACK	....	241	ADMIT THE SUN	20
CANAL				
VOLES AT HIS ARMPITS, DOWN THE SAD CANAL	....	51	OUT OF THE PIT	40
FIRE AND JORDAN AND THE SAD CANAL.	....	53	OUT OF THE PIT	99
CANALS				
LAPPING THE STILL CANALS, THE DRY TIDE-MASTER	.....	54	WE BY SEASAND	10
CANCER				
A RIB OF CANCER ON THE FLUID SKY.	....	25	THERE'S PLENTY	7
WOMEN WITH CANCER AT THEIR SIDES	....	41	YOUNG ARE OLD	28

	PAGE	TITLE	LINE
CANCER (CONTINUED)			
WHOM CANCER CROPS, WHOSE DRINKING RUSTS, THESE DIE;	64	WOMAN SPEAKS	43
THE ROOT OF TONGUES ENDS IN A SPENTOUT CANCER, ...	79	LOVE'S FEVER	37
THE REDHAIRED CANCER STILL ALIVE, ...	97	TWILIGHT LOCKS	20
AND SHARE MY BED WITH CAPRICORN AND CANCER.	117	ALTARWISE	14
CANCEROUS			
AND CANCEROUS SPEAKING DRIPPING FROM THEIR MOUTHS,	41	YOUNG ARE OLD	29
CANCER'S			
THE CANCER'S FUSION, OR THE SUMMER FEATHER	100	RUNNING GRAVE	32
CANDLE			
A CANDLE IN THE THIGHS	82	LIGHT BREAKS	7
WHERE NO WAX IS, THE CANDLE SHOWS ITS HAIRS.	82	LIGHT BREAKS	12
HEART OF CADAVER'S CANDLE WAXES THIN, ...	100	RUNNING GRAVE	12
AND A FIREWIND KILL THE CANDLE.	130	SINNERS' BELL	6
GRIEF WITH DRENCHED BOOK AND CANDLE CHRISTENS THE CHERUB TIME	130	SINNERS' BELL	16
CANDLES			
HE WAS BLIND TO THE EYES OF CANDLES	162	LONG-LEGGED	27
BUSHES AND OWLS BLOW OUT LIKE CANDLES, ...	215	COUNTRY HEAVEN	18
CANDLE'S			
HIS WINY SKY, AND, AS THE CANDLE'S MOON, ...	80	ALL THAT I OWE	14
CANDLEWOODS			
THE SUN-LEAVED HOLY CANDLEWOODS	141	SAINT TO FALL	19
CANKERED			
OR EVIL FROM THE CANKERED HEART.	19	THE NEOPHYTE	4
CANNONS			
NOR THE CANNONS OF HIS KINGDOM	126	SEED-AT-ZERO	47
NOR THE CANNONS OF HIS KINGDOM	127	SEED-AT-ZERO	54
CANNOT			
I CANNOT LIFT, BUT CAN, ...	12	SKY'S BRIGHT	11
TIME CANNOT HEAL NOR RESURRECT;	26	THERE'S PLENTY	15
WHO CANNOT COUNT THE SEEDS HE SOWS, ...	29	NEARLY SUMMER	8
AND CANNOT MOUNT A CLOTHESHORSE WITHOUT BLEEDING.	40	YOUNG ARE OLD	10
IN THOSE HIGH GLOBES I CANNOT COUNT, ...	49	LIGHT, I KNOW	19
I CANNOT MURDER, LIKE A FOOL, ...	61	MEAT ON BONES	30
MORE THE THICK STONE CANNOT TELL.	139	TOMBSTONE TOLD	10
JEALOUSY CANNOT FORGET FOR ALL HER SAKES, ...	158	INTO HER HEAD	34
THAT CANNOT SINK OR CEASE	160	DEATHS AND ENT	10
MYSELVES GRIEVE NOW, AND MIRACLES CANNOT ATONE. ...	173	FIRE RAID	16
CANNOT WEAR YOUR EDGE AWAY, ...	228	MY RIVER	3
YOUR BODY CANNOT GLADDEN ME, ...	228	NOT DESPAIR	9
CANNOT DENT YOUR FLANKS;	229	MY RIVER	14
THE WIND CANNOT BLUNT	229	MY RIVER	15
MY RIVER CANNOT RUB YOUR BRIGHT STONE, ...	230	MY RIVER	41
A RHYTHM I CANNOT BREAK	235	WOMAN TAPESTRY	29
BOAT CANNOT GO.	237	PILLAR BREAKS	6
CANONIZED			
AND THE CANONIZED VALLEY	215	COUNTRY HEAVEN	7
CANS			
FROM GARDEN CANS, OR FREE THE FLOODS?	65	GODS THUMP	7
CAN'T			
BETTER NOR US CAN'T GAINSAY WALKING, ...	28	NO WINGS	9
CAN'T READ SENSE IN THE RAIN THAT WILLYNILLY	137	O CHATTERTON	19
CANVAS			
ON THE CANVAS SKY, AND ALL HOT COLOURS MELT	46	POET: 1935	19
FOR PAINING, ON THEIR CANVAS STRIPS, ...	83	LETTER TO AUNT	21
TIME ON THE CANVAS PATHS.	129	MY NEOPHYTE	24
CANYONS			
YOUNG FROM THE CANYONS OF OBLIVION!	182	VISION, PRAYER	93

	PAGE	TITLE	LINE

CAP
    THE INVOKED, SHROUDING VEIL AT THE CAP OF THE FACE,   134   HOW MY ANIMAL   5
    AND A BLACK CAP OF JACK- 201   SIR JOHNS HILL   14
CAPERS
    BUT HE MAKES THEM DANCE, CUT CAPERS 47   POET: 1935   41
CAPES
    IN YOUR BEAKS, ON THE GABBING CAPES! 4   PROLOGUE   66
    WHALES IN THE WAKE LIKE CAPES AND ALPS 163   LONG-LEGGED   49
CAPPED
    WITH MY CHERRY CAPPED DANGLER GREEN AS SEAWEED 152   BELOW A TIME   45
CAPRICORN
    AND SHARE MY BED WITH CAPRICORN AND CANCER. 117   ALTARWISE   14
CAPS
    POUR LIKE A HALO ON THE CAPS AND SERPENTS. 120   ALTARWISE   118
CAPSIZED
    WITH A CAPSIZED FIELD WHERE A SCHOOL SAT STILL 144   COLOUR OF SAY   3
CAPTOR
    AND I, YOUR CAPTOR, HAVE MY LOVE TO KEEP 10   COOL, OH NO   29
CAPTURE
    YOU CAPTURE MORE THAN MAN OR WOMAN GUESSES; 48   POET: 1935   54
CARBOLIC
    FLICKED FROM THE CARBOLIC CITY PUZZLE IN A BED OF
        SORES 142   SAINT TO FALL   28
CARCASS
    AND CONJURED UP A CARCASS SHAPE 98   TWILIGHT LOCKS   35
CARDBOARD
    ADAM, TIME'S JOKER, ON A WITCH OF CARDBOARD 119   ALTARWISE   81
CARDIGAN
    SHUT. SINISTER DARK OVER CARDIGAN 179   NEW QUAY   7
CARDS
    AND THE PACK OF CARDS. 33   HELD-OUT HAND   11
CARE
    MOISTEN YOUR CARE TO CARELESSNESS, ... 20   THE NEOPHYTE   19
    SOON TO MY CARE, MY LOVE, ... 21   BEWILDERED WAY   5
    BY THESE I WOULD NOT CARE TO DIE, ... 44   LONGED TO MOVE   19
    IN THE FIRE OF HIS CARE HIS LOVE IN THE HIGH ROOM.   194   CONVERS PRAYER   16
    WITH ALL MY USUAL CARE. 234   NO, PIGEON   21
CARED
    AND NOTHING I CARED, AT MY SKY BLUE TRADES, THAT
        TIME ALLOWS 196   FERN HILL   42
    NOTHING I CARED, IN THE LAMB WHITE DAYS, THAT TIME
        WOULD TAKE ME 196   FERN HILL   46
CAREFREE
    AND AS I WAS GREEN AND CAREFREE, FAMOUS AMONG THE
        BARNS 195   FERN HILL   10
CARELESSNESS
    MOISTEN YOUR CARE TO CARELESSNESS, ... 20   THE NEOPHYTE   19
CARESS
    HIS UPTURNED FACE WITH ONE DIVINE CARESS. 222   MISSING   3
CARGOED
    AND DROWN THE CARGOED APPLES IN THEIR TIDES. 91   BOYS OF SUMMER   6
CARING
    THE ONE NOT CARING TO WHOM IN HIS SLEEP HE WILL MOVE   193   CONVERS PRAYER   4
    AND THE CHILD NOT CARING TO WHOM HE CLIMBS HIS PRAYER 194   CONVERS PRAYER   17
CARNAGE
    LET ME NOT THINK, OF GOD OF CARNAGE, ... 63   WOMAN SPEAKS   16
CARNAL
    AND THE CARNAL STEM THAT STOOD 22   HIGH ON A HILL   13
    THE FLIGHT OF THE CARNAL SKULL 111   I, IN IMAGE   75

	PAGE	TITLE	LINE
CAROUSES			
HIS WILD CAROUSES, AND HIS LIPS	29	NEARLY SUMMER	10
CAROUSING			
SPIED MOON-MAD BEASTS CAROUSING ON THE HILL,	50	OUT OF THE PIT	9
CARPETING			
IN THE CARPETING OF THE DUSK, OBSCURELY AND ELUSIVELY,	224	IDYLL UNFORGET	41
CARRIED			
LONG BREATH THAT CARRIED TO MY FATHER	69	BEFORE KNOCKED	41
CARRIES			
NO FAITH TO FIX THE TEETH ON CARRIES	41	YOUNG ARE OLD	18
NO SKY FOR ME THAT CARRIES	234	NO, PIGEON	2
CARRION			
HE LEARNS THE CARRION PICKERS OF THE SKY,	63	WOMAN SPEAKS	21
TO THE ANGUISH AND CARRION, TO THE INFANT FOREVER UNFREE,	146	IF HEAD HURT	22
CARRION, PARADISE, CHIRRUP MY BRIGHT YOLK.	159	INTO HER HEAD	60
THE SWINISH PLAINS OF CARRION	183	VISION, PRAYER	103
CARRY			
FOR MY TALL TURRETS CARRY AS YOUR SIN?	112	NOT FATHER ME	6
CARRYING			
AROUND SOME COFFIN CARRYING	152	BELOW A TIME	30
CARRYING CLOUD, DEATH STRIKES THEIR HOUSE.	161	WEDDING ANNIV	8
CART			
O KEEP HIS BONES AWAY FROM THAT COMMON CART,	173	DAWN RAID	12
CARTOON			
CARTOON OF SLASHES ON THE TIDE-TRACED CRATER,	119	ALTARWISE	71
CARVED			
CARVED BIRDS BLUNT THEIR STRIKING THROATS ON THE SALT GRAVEL,	15	SPIRE CRANES	3
WITH CARVED BIRD, SAINT, AND SUN, THE WRACKSPIKED MAIDEN MOUTH	135	HOW MY ANIMAL	37
IS CARVED FROM HER IN A ROOM WITH A WET WINDOW	136	AFTER FUNERAL	29
SAINT CARVED AND SENSUAL AMONG THE SCUDDING	147	UNLUCKILY FOR	5
I SEE THE WANTING NUN SAINT CARVED IN A GARB	148	UNLUCKILY FOR	34
DEATH IN THE CARVED NUNNERY	148	UNLUCKILY FOR	46
PARISH OF SNOW. THE CARVED MOUTHS IN THE ROCK ARE WIND SWEPT STRINGS.	189	WINTER'S TALE	64
THE CARVED LIMBS IN THE ROCK	189	WINTER'S TALE	76
CARVEN			
WIND CARVEN LINES AROUND THE DROOPING MOUTH;	64	WOMAN SPEAKS	50
CARVEN DOMES OF GREEN ARE THE TREES BY THE PATHWAY,	221	FOREST PICTURE	2
CASANOVA			
THE HARP-WAKED CASANOVA RAKES NO RANGE.	159	TO LEDA	2
CAST			
TO REMEMBER, CAST STRICTURE ON MECHANICS AND MAN.	45	PLOUGHMAN GONE	5
O TIDAL WINDS, CAST UP HER CRY FOR ME;	65	WOMAN SPEAKS	54
AND TIME CAST FORTH MY MORTAL CREATURE	69	BEFORE KNOCKED	31
CAST LIGHT UPON MY WEATHER. I AM HEIR	80	ALL THAT I OWE	15
AND CAST A SHADOW CRAB UPON THE LAND,	98	OCTOBER WIND	4
CAST BACK THE BONE OF YOUTH	107	GRIEF THIEF	11
FOR MY TALL TOWER'S SAKE CAST IN HER STONE?	112	NOT FATHER ME	2
ROSE CAST TO PLAGUE,	115	A GRIEF AGO	14
I TELL HER THIS: BEFORE THE SUNCOCK CAST	115	A GRIEF AGO	35
I MEAN BY TIME THE CAST AND CURFEW RASCAL OF OUR MARRIAGE,	130	SINNERS' BELL	25
CALLS THE STARVED FIRE HERD, IS CAST IN ICE,	132	I MAKE THIS IN	27
CAST HIGH, STUNNED ON GILLED STONE; SLY SCISSORS GROUND IN FROST	135	HOW MY ANIMAL	35
NOW CAST DOWN YOUR ROD, FOR THE WHOLE	162	LONG-LEGGED	31

	PAGE	TITLE	LINE
CAST (CONTINUED)			
GOOD-BYE ALWAYS FOR THE FLESH IS CAST	166	LONG-LEGGED	122
BY LOSING HIM ALL IN LOVE, AND CAST HIS NEED	188	WINTER'S TALE	52
IS CAST BEFORE YOU MOVE, ...	193	SIDE OF TRUTH	33
OR CAST YOUR LOVE ASIDE;	228	NOT DESPAIR	3
CASTAWAYS			
CALL BACK THE CASTAWAYS	107	GRIEF THIEF	7
CASTING			
ON CASTING TIDES, ARE TANGLED IN THE SHELLS, ...	105	WORLD PYRAMID	50
CASTING TO-MORROW LIKE A THORN	180	VISION, PRAYER	25
CASTLE			
HOO, THERE, IN CASTLE KEEP, ...	4	PROLOGUE	53
WITH ITS HORNS THROUGH MIST AND THE CASTLE	177	POEM IN OCT	33
CASTS			
WHEREON THE HOODED HAIR CASTS DOWN ITS GIRDLE, ...	76	LASHED RINGS	5
CASTS TO THE PINE ROOTS, RAISING MAN LIKE A MOUNTAIN	109	I, IN IMAGE	11
CASUALTY			
NIGHTINGALES OF THE CASUALTY STATIONS	154	RETURN	23
CAT			
THE CATTLE STIRRING, THE MOUSING CAT STEPPING SHY,	187	WINTER'S TALE	22
NO FLAILING CALF OR CAT IN A FLAME	207	LAMENT	40
AND A CAT HAS A NUMBER OF LIVES;	221	SONG OF DOG	2
CATARACTED			
THE CATARACTED EYES THAT FILMED THEIR CLOTH;	97	TWILIGHT LOCKS	21
CATASTROPHE			
AND DROWN ALL SORROWS IN THE GROSS CATASTROPHE. ...	34	THIRST PARCHES	15
CATCH			
DAYS' NIGHT WHOSE TOWERS WILL CATCH	3	PROLOGUE	20
TO CATCH HER SAILING DOWN THE STREAM--	14	FOR LEDA	4
CATCH THE ROOKS SLEEPING, AND BREAK NO TWIG, ...	31	BEING BUT MEN	7
TO CATCH THE LOVERS' PALSY, ...	34	THIRST PARCHES	11
CATCH THEIR POOR GUTS.	37	WINDMILLS TURN	26
OR CATCH ALL DEATH THAT'S IN THE AIR.	47	POET: 1935	46
AND CATCH A TURNIP GHOST IN EVERY CRANNY.	48	LIGHT, I KNOW	5
WHY WON'T THE NEWS OF THE OLD WORLD CATCH	149	PAPER & STICKS	2
AND THE LONG-TAILED LIGHTNING LIT HIS CATCH.	166	LONG-LEGGED	128
STRIKE AND SING HIS CATCH OF FIELDS	168	LONG-LEGGED	181
I HAVE COME TO CATCH YOUR VOICE	231	YOUR VOICE	T
I HAVE COME TO CATCH YOUR VOICE, ...	231	YOUR VOICE	1
TO CATCH THE SHAFT	231	YOUR VOICE	4
THEN TO CATCH NIGHT	232	YOUR VOICE	8
AND CATCH THE UPRISING WAVE.	238	PILLAR BREAKS	22
CATCHES			
WORDS ON THE AIR AS THE FIRE CATCHES	149	PAPER & STICKS	17
CATCHING			
HER HEART ALL EARS AND EYES, LIPS CATCHING THE AVALANCHE	170	MARRIAGE VIRG	10
AND EYES HAVE BEEN GROVE-GREEN CATCHING MINE FROM THE DEPTH OF THE SILENCE;	224	IDYLL UNFORGET	33
CATHEDRAL			
CATHEDRAL CALM IN THE PULLED HOUSE;	130	SINNERS' BELL	15
FLOATED THE LOST CATHEDRAL	163	LONG-LEGGED	35
CATHEDRALS			
OF THE LUMINOUS CATHEDRALS, ...	175	FIRE RAID	62
CATHERINE			
QUEEN CATHERINE HOWLING BARE	157	INTO HER HEAD	12
CATLIKE			
CREEPING CATLIKE UNDER THE WATER.	231	OUR SANCTITY	41
CATS			
AND IS FED TO THE CATS, ...	39	GAS FADES	8

	PAGE	TITLE	LINE

CATS (CONTINUED)
LIKE CATS, AND LUSTS LAY HALF HOT IN THE COLD. .... 50 OUT OF THE PIT 5
CATS'
THE GRAFTERS OF CATS' HEADS ON CHICKENS' TRUNKS, 41 YOUNG ARE OLD 42
CATTLE
IF THE RED TICKLE AS THE CATTLE CALVE .... 95 RUB OF LOVE 4
THE CATTLE GRAZE ON THE COVERED FOAM, ... 168 LONG-LEGGED 183
THE PALE BREATH OF CATTLE AT THE STEALTHY SAIL, ... 187 WINTER'S TALE 5
THE CATTLE STIRRING, THE MOUSING CAT STEPPING SHY, 187 WINTER'S TALE 22
CAUGHT
AND I, CAUGHT IN MID-AIR PERHAPS, ... 9 MINUTE'S HOUR 6
CAUGHT IN THE TRAP'S MACHINERY, LIGHTS OUT, ... 39 GAS FADES 35
THE CAUGHT IN THE CAGE, THE BROKEN WINGED, ... 41 YOUNG ARE OLD 37
MOVES, AMONG MEN CAUGHT BY THE SUN, ... 46 POET: 1935 11
CAUGHT BY THE CRABBING SUN I WALK ON FIRE .... 98 OCTOBER WIND 3
CAUGHT IN AN OCTAGON OF UNACCUSTOMED LIGHT, ... 116 LANTERNS SHINE 2
UNDER THE CLOUD AGAINST LOVE IS CAUGHT AND HELD AND
KISSED .... 147 UNLUCKILY FOR 17
CAUGHT AMONG NEVER ENOUGH .... 156 RETURN 67
WHEN THE CAUGHT TONGUE NODDED BLIND, ... 173 FIRE RAID 13
AND DROWN IN THE DRIFTS OF HIS NEED, AND LIE CURLED
CAUGHT .... 188 WINTER'S TALE 47
WILD MEN WHO CAUGHT AND SANG THE SUN IN FLIGHT, ... 208 NOT GO GENTLE 10
AND CAUGHT BETWEEN TWO NIGHTS, BLINDNESS AND DEATH. 217 ELEGY 36
TO THE VOICES OF THE WIND CAUGHT IN THE
CRADLE-PETALS OF THE NIGHT: .... 223 IDYLL UNFORGET 8
AND THE WHISPER CAUGHT IN ITS PAGEANT OF TAWNY PEARL, 224 IDYLL UNFORGET 44
CAUL
FROM THE UNFOLDING TO THE SCISSORED CAUL, ... 78 LOVE'S FEVER 3
ALL THAT SHAPES FROM THE CAUL AND SUCKLE, ... 107 ALL ALL AND 28
THIS STORY'S MONSTER HAS A SERPENT CAUL, ... 124 TODAY, INSECT 10
CAULDRON
IN THE CAULDRON .... 181 VISION, PRAYER 49
CAULDRON'S
THE CAULDRON'S ROOT THROUGH THIS ONCE-RINDLESS HAND 132 I MAKE THIS IN 55
CAUSES
UNTHINKING ACTIONS GIVEN CAUSES .... 38 THE GOSSIPERS 4
AND RUIN AND HIS CAUSES .... 186 HOLY SPRING 5
CAUTIOUSLY
AND WHERE THE LIGHT COMES CAUTIOUSLY .... 240 ADMIT THE SUN 3
CAVE
'NOW TO AWAKE HUSKED OF GESTURES AND MY JOY LIKE A
CAVE .... 146 IF HEAD HURT 21
LIKE A CAVE WITH ONE THREAD. .... 230 OUR SANCTITY 21
WADING THROUGH HER DARK CAVE ON FEROCIOUS WINGS. 232 YOUR VOICE 9
CAVEPOOLS
CURL-LOCKED AND ANIMAL CAVEPOOLS OF SPELLS AND BONE, 135 HOW MY ANIMAL 27
CAVERN
YOU BY THE CAVERN OVER THE BLACK STAIRS, ... 117 ALTARWISE 22
CAVERNOUS
DAY TREADS THE TREES AND SHE THE CAVERNOUS NIGHT. 57 GREEK PLAY 12
WHOSE WIZARD SHAPE I TRACE IN THE CAVERNOUS SKULL, 134 HOW MY ANIMAL 2
MY CAVERNOUS, FEATHERBED SELF. .... 156 RETURN 76
IN A CAVERNOUS, SWUNG .... 209 POEM ON B'DAY 37
CAVERS
GLINT IN THE STAVED AND SIREN-PRINTED CAVERS, ... 131 I MAKE THIS IN 20
CAVES
IN THE WATCHED DARK, QUIVERING THROUGH LOCKS AND
CAVES, ... 161 DEATHS AND ENT 31
CAVES THE CRIES OF THE PARCHS AND THEIR FLOCKS. I 179 NEW QUAY 17

	PAGE	TITLE	LINE
CAWING			
CAWING FROM THEIR BLACK BETHELS SOARING, THE HOLY BOOKS	199	COUNTRY SLEEP	68
CEASE			
THAT CANNOT SINK OR CEASE	160	DEATHS AND ENT	10
CELEBRATED			
IS CELEBRATED THERE, AND COMMUNION BETWEEN SUNS.	148	UNLUCKILY FOR	24
CELEBRATES			
HE CELEBRATES AND SPURNS	208	POEM ON B'DAY	7
CELEBRATING			
CELEBRATING AT HER SIDE	158	INTO HER HEAD	42
CELERY			
I PICK A STICK OF CELERY FROM THE VALLEY	137	O CHATTERTON	14
CELESTIAL			
CELESTIAL,	226	THE ELM	7
CELIBATE			
CELIBATE I SIT AND SEE	138	O CHATTERTON	29
CELL			
CLOSED IN YOUR CELL OF SECRET THOUGHTS,	10	COOL, OH NO	28
WOMEN FIGURES ROUND MY CELL,	138	O CHATTERTON	30
A HILL TOUCHES AN ANGEL. OUT OF A SAINT'S CELL	198	COUNTRY SLEEP	27
CELLAR			
TASSELLED IN CELLAR AND SNIPPING SHOP	151	BELOW A TIME	11
CELLED			
THE BRAIN WAS CELLED AND SOLDERED IN THE THOUGHT	94	IN BEGINNING	26
CELLS			
THE SKULL, THE CELLS, THE CABINNED EARS	69	SECRET WIND	5
SHALL IT BE MALE OR FEMALE? SAY THE CELLS,	95	RUB OF LOVE	8
CELL-STEPPED			
AND THE CELL-STEPPED THIMBLE;	111	I, IN IMAGE	76
CELLULOID			
FLAVOURED OF CELLULOID GIVE LOVE THE LIE.	89	EUNUCH DREAMS	20
CEMENTED			
(GIVE, SUMMER, OVER), THE CEMENTED SKIN,	101	RUNNING GRAVE	44
CEMENTING			
A STEM CEMENTING, WRESTLED UP THE TOWER,	114	A GRIEF AGO	5
CENTAUR			
TO HAVE THE CENTAUR LOVER	11	AIR BREATHE	6
HORSES, CENTAUR DEAD, TURN AND TREAD THE DRENCHED WHITE	189	WINTER'S TALE	74
OF NIGHTINGALE AND CENTAUR DEAD HORSE. THE SPRINGS WITHER	191	WINTER'S TALE	117
CENTAUR'S			
AND YOUR HOME IN A CENTAUR'S STABLE.	138	O CHATTERTON	43
CENTRAL			
THE CENTRAL PLAINS OF ASIA IN HIS GARDEN,	121	INCARNATE DEVL	2
CENTRE			
ERECT A WALKING CENTRE IN THE SHROUD,	114	SERVANT SUN	27
SHOULD HE, FOR CENTRE SAKE, HOP IN THE DUST,	127	NOW, SAY NAY	6
FROM THE CHILL, SILENT CENTRE	151	BELOW A TIME	22
IN THE CENTRE OF DARK I PRAY HIM	183	VISION, PRAYER	135
IN THE ALWAYS DESIRING CENTRE OF THE WHITE	188	WINTER'S TALE	48
POOL AT THE WANTING CENTRE, IN THE FOLDS	191	WINTER'S TALE	128
CENTRED			
YOUR CORKSCREW GRAVE CENTRED IN NAVEL AND NIPPLE,	110	I, IN IMAGE	51
CENTRES			
OUR RODS AND SUBSTANTIAL CENTRES,	230	OUR SANCTITY	3
CENTURIES			
THE CENTURIES THROW BACK THEIR HAIR	167	LONG-LEGGED	151
INTO THE CENTURIES OF THE CHILD	173	FIRE RAID	15

	PAGE	TITLE	LINE
CENTURY			
IN YOUR YOUNG YEARS THE VEGETABLE CENTURY.	123	FOSTER LIGHT	12
CENTURY'S			
THE CENTURY'S TRAP WILL HAVE SNAPPED ROUND YOUR			
MIDDLE, ...	38	GAS FADES	4
THE CENTURY'S TRAP WILL HAVE CLOSED FOR GOOD	39	GAS FADES	30
CERECLOTH			
CERECLOTH OF WEED, AND BUILD AN ORDURED BED.	64	WOMAN SPEAKS	27
CEREMENTS			
THE BIRDS MAKE HIM HIS CEREMENTS OF PLUMES, ...	64	WOMAN SPEAKS	26
CEREMONY			
IS CERTAIN GOD, AND THE CEREMONY OF SOULS	148	UNLUCKILY FOR	23
CEREMONY AFTER A FIRE RAID	173	FIRE RAID	T
CERTAIN			
SO IS THERE MISSED A CERTAIN GODLINESS	23	THE ONLY DEAD	26
WILLING WORDS TO MAKE THE RUMOURS CERTAIN, ...	38	THE GOSSIPERS	2
THE INSECT CERTAIN IS THE PLAGUE OF FABLES.	124	TODAY, INSECT	9
THE INSECT FABLE IS THE CERTAIN PROMISE.	124	TODAY, INSECT	18
NO TELL-TALE LOVER HAS AN END MORE CERTAIN, ...	125	TODAY, INSECT	24
IS CERTAIN GOD, AND THE CEREMONY OF SOULS	148	UNLUCKILY FOR	23
CERTAINLY			
FOR THEN THE WRONG WIND CERTAINLY	37	WINDMILLS TURN	17
CERTAINTY			
AND, IN THE GRIEF OF CERTAINTY, ...	19	THE NEOPHYTE	11
THERE MUST, BE PRAISED, SOME CERTAINTY, ...	32	OUT OF SIGHS	7
CHAIN			
HE PULLS THE CHAIN, THE CISTERN MOVES.	75	MY HERO BARES	20
AND LOVE AND HIS PATIENTS ROAR ON A CHAIN;	161	WEDDING ANNIV	6
CHAIN THE STRONG VOICE	233	FURIOUS MOTION	20
CHAINED			
DRINKING WATER FROM THE CHAINED CUP	171	THE HUNCHBACK	8
BUT NOBODY CHAINED HIM UP.	171	THE HUNCHBACK	12
CHAINS			
ONE VOICE IN CHAINS DECLAIMS	158	INTO HER HEAD	52
DIG NO MORE FOR THE CHAINS OF HIS GREY-HAIRED HEART.	172	DAWN RAID	9
AFTER THE LOCKS AND CHAINS	172	THE HUNCHBACK	36
THOUGH I SANG IN MY CHAINS LIKE THE SEA.	196	FERN HILL	54
BEFORE CHAINS BREAK TO A HAMMER FLAME	210	POEM ON B'DAY	44
CHALK			
CHALK COOLED BY LEAVES IN THE HOT SEASON, ...	29	LONG, SKELETON	3
THE FINGER JOINTS ARE CRAMPED WITH CHALK;	66	HAND SIGNED	6
THAT CHALK THE WALLS WITH GREEN GIRLS AND THEIR MEN.	95	RUB OF LOVE	16
UNDER THE CONCEIVING MOON, ON THE HIGH CHALK HILL,	203	GIANT'S THIGH	2
CHALKED			
STAY, IN A CIRCLE CHALKED UPON THE FLOOR, ...	28	NO WINGS	25
I CHALKED UPON THE BREASTBONE'S SLATE	86	SEE, SAYS LIME	27
CHALLENGE			
CHALLENGE MY METAMORPHOSIS, ...	238	MAKES INTERVALS	15
CHALLENGED			
BUT SEASONS MUST BE CHALLENGED OR THEY TOTTER	92	BOYS OF SUMMER	25
CHAMELEON			
THE CHAMELEON COATS OF THE BIG BUGS AND SHOTS,) ...	39	GAS FADES	13
CHANCE			
BY TRICK OR CHANCE HE FELL ASLEEP	98	TWILIGHT LOCKS	34
CHANGE			
OR (CHANGE THE KEY!) GIVE VENT TO UTTERANCES	33	HELD-OUT HAND	8
AS MEANINGLESS AS THE BELLS (OH CHANGE THE LIFE!),	33	HELD-OUT HAND	9
LIFE, TILL THE CHANGE OF MOOD, FORKS	47	POET: 1935	38
AND MANY YEARS SHOULD SEE SOME CHANGE.	116	LANTERNS SHINE	17
MY DEAR WOULD I CHANGE MY TEARS OR YOUR IRON HEAD.	146	IF HEAD HURT	18

		PAGE	TITLE	LINE
CHANGE (CONTINUED)				
NOT YOUR WINGED LUST BUT HIS MUST NOW CHANGE SUIT.		159	TO LEDA	1
TAKING NO PLUME FOR INDEX IN LOVE'S CHANGE	....	159	TO LEDA	5
NOT YOUR WINGED LUST BUT HIS MUST NOW CHANGE SUIT.		159	TO LEDA	6
LET ME CHANGE TO BLUE,	....	238	MAKES INTERVALS	7
CHANGED				
BUT WAYS HAVE CHANGED, AND MOST WAYS LEAD	....	37	WINDMILLS TURN	20
THE WIND HAS CHANGED, BLOWN INSIDE OUT	....	37	WINDMILLS TURN	27
THE CHANGED WIND BLOWS, AND THERE'S A CHOICE OF SIGNS		37	WINDMILLS TURN	31
AND GODS BE CHANGED AS OFTEN AS THE SHIFT.	....	67	LET A FAITH	8
AND CHANGED WITH THE WIND INTO INDISTINCT PATTERNS				
OF FROLIC,	....	224	IDYLL UNFORGET	29
CHANGES				
THE IMAGE CHANGES, AND THE FLOWERS DROP	....	47	POET: 1935	43
WE RUNG OUR WEATHERING CHANGES ON THE LADDER,	.....	118	ALTARWISE	41
CHANKLEY				
THE LITERARY CHANKLEY BORE,	....	83	LETTER TO AUNT	2
CHANNEL				
TURNING THE RIDERLESS DEAD BY THE CHANNEL WALL.	...	110	I, IN IMAGE	48
WHAT RHUBARB MAN PEELED IN HER FOAM-BLUE CHANNEL		121	ALTARWISE	135
CHANNELS				
COURSING ALONG THE CHANNELS	....	17	IN OBLIVION	10
IN THE BOSOM, OR THE EMPTY CHANNELS.	....	17	IN OBLIVION	21
TO CUT THE CHANNELS AT THEIR SOURCE	....	91	WHERE ONCE THE	11
CHANT				
OVER THE CHOIR MINUTE I HEAR THE HOUR CHANT:	......	130	SINNERS' BELL	7
NEVER SHALL MY SELF CHANT	....	148	UNLUCKILY FOR	25
STREET WE CHANT THE FLYING SEA	....	174	FIRE RAID	29
BE SHIELDED BY CHANT AND FLOWER AND GAY MAY YOU	...	198	COUNTRY SLEEP	42
CHANTER				
GULLED AND CHANTER IN YOUNG HEAVEN'S FOLD	....	210	POEM ON B'DAY	62
CHAOS				
OUT OF THE CHAOS WOULD COME BLISS.	....	31	BEING BUT MEN	13
THEN STIRRED A LITTLE CHAOS IN THE SUN.	....	33	IN GARDENS	6
THAT FALLS ON CHAOS.	....	41	YOUNG ARE OLD	25
CHAPEL				
THAT HER LOVE SING AND SWING THROUGH A BROWN CHAPEL,		136	AFTER FUNERAL	25
HE SNUGGLES DEEP AMONG THE CHAPEL THIGHS,	....	179	NEW QUAY	30
AND THE BLACK SPIT OF THE CHAPEL FOLD,	....	205	LAMENT	2
CHAPELS				
AND THE LEGENDS OF THE GREEN CHAPELS	....	178	POEM IN OCT	50
CHAPTER				
LIKE EXODUS A CHAPTER FROM THE GARDEN,	....	115	A GRIEF AGO	18
CHAPTERED				
THE WORD OF TIME LIES ON THE CHAPTERED BONE,	......	80	ALMANAC TIME	11
CHARABANCS				
RIDE IN THEIR CHARABANCS ON ROADS	....	37	WINDMILLS TURN	13
CHARACTERS				
HEADS OF THE CHARACTERS HAMMER THROUGH DAISIES;	...	50	NO DOMINION	25
FIRST CHARACTERS OF BIRTH AND DEATH.	....	94	IN BEGINNING	24
CHARGE				
MY FUSES TIMED TO CHARGE HIS HEART,	....	97	TWILIGHT LOCKS	13
CHARM				
OF OUR CHARM.	....	230	OUR SANCTITY	10
CHARMED				
CREEP AND HARP ON THE TIDE, SINKING THEIR CHARMED,				
BENT PIN	....	135	HOW MY ANIMAL	24
AND THE SKY OF BIRDS IN THE PLUMED VOICE CHARMED		190	WINTER'S TALE	88

		PAGE	TITLE	LINE
CHARMINGLY				
THAT ALL THE CHARMINGLY DROWNED ARISE TO COCKCROW				
AND KILL.		144	COLOUR OF SAY	6
CHARMS				
OR A NACREOUS SLEEP AMONG SOFT PARTICLES AND CHARMS		146	IF HEAD HURT	17
MADE HER LIMBS BLIND BY LUMINOUS CHARMS,		157	INTO HER HEAD	21
OR THE STRUT AND TRADE OF CHARMS		197	CRAFT OR ART	8
CHARNEL				
BUT ALL THIS LAND GIVES OFF A CHARNEL STENCH,		67	REALM OF FLESH	4
CHARNEL-HOUSE				
RATHER THAN CHARNEL-HOUSE AS SYMBOL		29	LONG, SKELETON	12
CHARRED				
CHARRED ON THE BLACK BREAST OF THE GRAVE		173	FIRE RAID	7
CHARTING				
OF THE CHARTING SLEEPERS PRAYS		184	VISION, PRAYER	167
CHASE				
IF HUNTING MEANS ANYTHING MORE THAN THE CHASE		44	TO FOLLOW FOX	18
NO SILVER WHISTLES CHASE HIM DOWN THE WEEKS'		108	GRIEF THIEF	21
AND LOVE TO CHASE RABBITS AND STONES.		221	SONG OF DOG	12
CHASER				
CHASTE AND THE CHASER, MAN WITH THE COCKSHUT EYE,		100	RUNNING GRAVE	17
CHASES				
THAT CHASES THE GHOSTS OF THE TREES		35	LIFT UP FACE	4
CHASTE				
CHASTE AND THE CHASER, MAN WITH THE COCKSHUT EYE,		100	RUNNING GRAVE	17
CHASTITY				
CHASTITY PRAYS FOR ME, PIETY SINGS,		207	LAMENT	57
CHATTER				
AND FEW YOUNG AUDEN'S CODED CHATTER;		84	LETTER TO AUNT	38
CHATTERBOX				
AN OLD CHATTERBOX, BARENAVELED AT NICE,		58	TO ARCHITECTS	8
CHATTERTON				
O CHATTERTON		137	O CHATTERTON	T
O CHATTERTON AND OTHERS IN THE ATTIC		137	O CHATTERTON	1
CHEAP				
DIRTIER WITH GARAGES AND CHEAP TEA SIGNS.		37	WINDMILLS TURN	15
SHE, IN HER CHEAP FROCK, SAYING SOME CHEAP THING,		43	FACES SHONE	11
SHE, IN HER CHEAP FROCK, SAYING SOME CHEAP THING,		43	FACES SHONE	11
CHEAT				
AN INCH IN FROTH. CHIMES CHEAT THE PRISON SPIRE,				
PELTER		15	SPIRE CRANES	5
CHECK				
TOO PROUD TO CRY, TOO FRAIL TO CHECK THE TEARS,		217	ELEGY	35
CHEEK				
ITS HONEYED CHEEK, SOFT-TALKING MOUTH,		35	LIFT UP FACE	16
AND LAID YOUR CHEEK AGAINST A CLOUD-FORMED SHELL:		153	WAS A SAVIOUR	23
DOWN THE CHEEK BONES AND WHINNYING		215	COUNTRY HEAVEN	14
CHEEKS				
WILL CHILL THE ROUNDNESS OF HIS CHEEKS,		17	IN OBLIVION	6
THAT HIS TEARS BURNED MY CHEEKS AND HIS HEART MOVED				
IN MINE.		178	POEM IN OCT	52
CHEMIC				
OF CHEMIC BLOOD, WARNED OF THE COMING FURY.		99	OCTOBER WIND	31
DESIRE IS PHOSPHORUS: THE CHEMIC BRUIT		159	TO LEDA	7
CHERISH				
FOR I CHERISH A PASSION FOR BONES,		221	SONG OF DOG	10
CHERRY				
WITH MY CHERRY CAPPED DANGLER GREEN AS SEAWEED		152	BELOW A TIME	45
CHERUB				
THE TWELVE TRIANGLES OF THE CHERUB WIND		115	A GRIEF AGO	23

	PAGE	TITLE	LINE
CHERUB (CONTINUED)			
GRIEF WITH DRENCHED BOOK AND CANDLE CHRISTENS THE CHERUB TIME	130	SINNERS' BELL	16
CHESTS			
YOUNG MEN WITH FALLEN CHESTS AND OLD MEN'S BREATH,	41	YOUNG ARE OLD	27
OR SANSKRIT PSALMS ON LEPERS' CHESTS.	83	LETTER TO AUNT	28
CHIC			
DON'T HURT THE CHIC ANATOMY	18	NATURAL DAY	9
CHICKEN			
TO FOLLOW, WILD AS THE CHICKEN STEALER, ...	44	TO FOLLOW FOX	3
CHICKENS			
GREEN CHICKENS OF THE BAY AND BUSHES CLUCK, 'DILLY DILLY, ...	202	SIR JOHNS HILL	31
CHICKENS'			
THE GRAFTERS OF CATS' HEADS ON CHICKENS' TRUNKS,	41	YOUNG ARE OLD	42
CHILD			
AND THEN AGAIN: THERE WAS A CHILD	22	ON QUIET NIGHT	15
I AM A TIMID CHILD WHEN LIGHT IS DEAD.	48	LIGHT, I KNOW	11
THE CHILD SHALL QUESTION ALL HIS DAYS, ...	56	WHY EAST WIND	7
THE CHILD TELLS, WHEN THE TREMBLING CHORD IS CUT,	67	LET A FAITH	14
AND A CHILD MIGHT BE MY SLAYER, ...	71	TAKE NEEDLES	17
A CROSS IS TATOOED ON THE BREAST OF THE CHILD, ...	74	SUN BURNS	12
ONCE FOR THE VIRGIN'S CHILD, ONCE FOR HER OWN.	74	SUN BURNS	15
TURNS GHOST TO GHOST; EACH MOTHERED CHILD	88	A PROCESS IN	20
THE SECRET CHILD, I SHIFT ABOUT THE SEA	105	WORLD PYRAMID	59
THE CHILD THAT SUCKETH LONG IS SHOOTING UP, ...	117	ALTARWISE	16
CHILD OF THE SHORT SPARK IN A SHAPELESS COUNTRY ...	117	ALTARWISE	19
CHILD IN WHITE BLOOD BENT ON ITS KNEES	128	MY NEOPHYTE	2
THAT THE GREEN CHILD SEE LIKE A GRAIL	129	MY NEOPHYTE	22
FOREVER IT IS A WHITE CHILD IN THE DARK-SKINNED SUMMER	130	SINNERS' BELL	19
FROM BLANK AND LEAKING WINTER SAILS THE CHILD IN COLOUR, ...	130	SINNERS' BELL	22
AND, PRIDE IS LAST, IS LIKE A CHILD ALONE	131	I MAKE THIS IN	13
TO THE ROOM OF A SECRET CHILD, ...	139	TOMBSTONE TOLD	15
HURLING INTO BEGINNING LIKE CHRIST THE CHILD.	149	UNLUCKILY FOR	52
A CHILD OF A FEW HOURS	173	FIRE RAID	5
INTO THE CENTURIES OF THE CHILD	173	FIRE RAID	15
CHILD BEYOND COCKCROW, BY THE FIRE-DWARFED	174	FIRE RAID	28
CHILD WHO WAS PRIEST AND SERVANTS, ...	174	FIRE RAID	52
JOY OF THE LONG DEAD CHILD SANG BURNING	178	POEM IN OCT	63
CHILD.	180	VISION, PRAYER	17
A REFUSAL TO MOURN THE DEATH, BY FIRE, OF A CHILD IN LONDON	191	REFUSAL MOURN	T
BY THE CHILD GOING TO BED AND THE MAN ON THE STAIRS	193	CONVERS PRAYER	2
FROM THE MAN ON THE STAIRS AND THE CHILD BY HIS BED.	194	CONVERS PRAYER	8
SHALL THE CHILD SLEEP UNHARMED OR THE MAN BE CRYING?	194	CONVERS PRAYER	12
AND THE CHILD NOT CARING TO WHOM HE CLIMBS HIS PRAYER	194	CONVERS PRAYER	17
CHILDISH			
THE DARTED HAIL, THE CHILDISH SNOW, ...	68	BEFORE KNOCKED	14
AND CHILDISH, SNIVELLING QUEEN.	155	RETURN	51
CHILDLESS			
AND WAKE TO THE FARM FOREVER FLED FROM THE CHILDLESS LAND.	196	FERN HILL	51
CHILDLIKE			
AND HIS RUNAWAY BELOVED CHILDLIKE LAID IN THE ACORNED SAND.	157	INTO HER HEAD	23
CHILDREN			
CHILDREN OF DARKNESS GOT NO WINGS	28	NO WINGS	T
CHILDREN OF DARKNESS GOT NO WINGS, ...	28	NO WINGS	1

	PAGE	TITLE	LINE
CHILDREN (CONTINUED)			
CHILDREN OF DARKNESS GOT NO WINGS, ...	28	NO WINGS	23
IF WE WERE CHILDREN WE MIGHT CLIMB, ...	31	BEING BUT MEN	6
CHILDREN IN WONDER WATCHING THE STARS, ...	31	BEING BUT MEN	15
LET CHILDREN KNOW, AND OLD MEN AT THEIR GATES, ...	36	LET BE KNOWN	3
DECLARE THEIR SOULS, LET CHILDREN KNOW, LIVE AFTER.	36	LET BE KNOWN	6
WHEN COMETH JACK FROST? THE CHILDREN ASK.	56	WHY EAST WIND	10
AND THE FIBS FOR CHILDREN;	59	FAIRY TALES	12
STRANGLE THE LITTLE CHILDREN IN THEIR BEDS;	64	WOMAN SPEAKS	46
OF THE DEAD EYES OF CHILDREN	68	REALM OF FLESH	15
TO CHILDREN WHO WERE SUCKLED ON A PLAGUE, ...	81	ALL THAT I OWE	17
OF CHILDREN GO WHO, FROM THEIR VOIDS, ...	91	WHERE ONCE THE	17
I SEE THE SUMMER CHILDREN IN THEIR MOTHERS	92	BOYS OF SUMMER	13
OF THE STAR-GESTURED CHILDREN IN THE PARK.	98	OCTOBER WIND	12
DRIVE CHILDREN UP LIKE BRUISES TO THE THUMB, ...	100	RUNNING GRAVE	14
SUFFER THE HEAVEN'S CHILDREN THROUGH MY HEARTBEAT.	120	ALTARWISE	112
DRIVES FORTH MY MEN, MY CHILDREN, FROM THE HANGING SOUTH.	122	HOLD HARD	6
HOLD HARD, MY COUNTRY CHILDREN IN THE WORLD OF TALES,	122	HOLD HARD	10
SHOULD HE WHO SPLIT HIS CHILDREN WITH A CURE	127	NOW, SAY NAY	13
CHILDREN FROM HOMES AND CHILDREN'S PARKS	129	MY NEOPHYTE	28
CHILDREN KEPT FROM THE SUN	152	WAS A SAVIOUR	4
THE VOICE OF CHILDREN SAYS	153	WAS A SAVIOUR	9
LEADS THEM AS CHILDREN AND AS AIR	167	LONG-LEGGED	149
THAT THE CHILDREN FILLED WITH GRAVEL	171	THE HUNCHBACK	9
O THE WINGS OF THE CHILDREN!	182	VISION, PRAYER	91
BEFORE THE CHILDREN GREEN AND GOLDEN	196	FERN HILL	44
CHILDREN'S			
IN CHILDREN'S CIRCUSES COULD STAY THEIR TROUBLES?	40	WAS THERE TIME	2
SPRINKLES IN CHILDREN'S EYES A LONG-LAST SLEEP	56	WHY EAST WIND	13
AND DUSK IS CROWDED WITH THE CHILDREN'S GHOSTS, ...	56	WHY EAST WIND	14
NO ANSWER TO THE CHILDREN'S CRY	56	WHY EAST WIND	24
WE HAVE BY HEART THE CHILDREN'S STORIES, ...	59	FAIRY TALES	22
ALL THESE, HE SAID WHO SACKED THE CHILDREN'S TOWN,	112	NOT FATHER ME	18
STALKING MY CHILDREN'S FACES WITH A TAIL OF BLOOD,	122	HOLD HARD	20
WINGED LIKE A SABBATH ASS THIS CHILDREN'S PIECE ...	124	TODAY, INSECT	16
CHILDREN FROM HOMES AND CHILDREN'S PARKS	129	MY NEOPHYTE	28
CHILD'S			
SUMMONING A CHILD'S VOICE FROM A WEBFOOT STONE, ...	152	BELOW A TIME	46
AND I SAW IN THE TURNING SO CLEARLY A CHILD'S	178	POEM IN OCT	46
THE MAJESTY AND BURNING OF THE CHILD'S DEATH.	192	REFUSAL MOURN	13
AND THE SHRILL CHILD'S PLAY	201	SIR JOHNS HILL	5
CHILL			
WILL CHILL THE ROUNDNESS OF HIS CHEEKS, ...	17	IN OBLIVION	6
FROM THE CHILL, SILENT CENTRE	151	BELOW A TIME	22
ROOSTS SLEEPING CHILL TILL THE FLAME OF THE COCK CROW	187	WINTER'S TALE	19
SAYING YOU WOULD LET THE CHILL SEAS PASS, ...	227	SPRING-SPIRIT	7
CHILLS			
WHY EAST WIND CHILLS	55	WHY EAST WIND	T
WHY EAST WIND CHILLS AND SOUTH WIND COOLS	55	WHY EAST WIND	1
CHIME			
FLUNG GRAVEL CHIME? LET THE STONES SPEAK	66	GODS THUMP	13
AS THEY DROWN, THE CHIME TRAVELS, ...	110	I, IN IMAGE	61
ALL BIRDS AND BEASTS OF THE LINKED NIGHT UPROAR AND CHIME	204	GIANT'S THIGH	35
CHIMED			
SAID THE ANTIPODES, AND TWICE SPRING CHIMED.	118	ALTARWISE	42
CHIMES			
EACH SILVER MOMENT CHIMES/ IN STEPS OF SOUND, ...	9	MINUTE'S HOUR	5

		PAGE	TITLE	LINE
CHIMES (CONTINUED)				
AN INCH IN FROTH. CHIMES CHEAT THE PRISON SPIRE,				
PELTER	....	15	SPIRE CRANES	5
CHIMES OF THE ROCKED BUOYS.	....	163	LONG-LEGGED	36
CHIMING				
INTO A CHIMING QUARTER	....	92	BOYS OF SUMMER	26
CHIMNEYS				
GOOD-BYE TO CHIMNEYS AND FUNNELS,	....	162	LONG-LEGGED	25
FIELDS HIGH AS THE HOUSE, THE TUNES FROM THE				
CHIMNEYS, IT WAS AIR	....	195	FERN HILL	20
CHIP				
AND CHIP, IN SILENCE AND IN TEARS,	....	239	MAKES INTERVALS	29
CHIPPED				
HEARD HER SPEAK THROUGH THE CHIPPED BEAK	....	140	TOMBSTONE TOLD	24
CHIRRUP				
TANGLED WITH CHIRRUP AND FRUIT,	....	3	PROLOGUE	6
CARRION, PARADISE, CHIRRUP MY BRIGHT YOLK.	....	159	INTO HER HEAD	60
CHOICE				
THOSE CRANING BIRDS ARE CHOICE FOR YOU, SONGS THAT				
JUMP BACK	....	16	SPIRE CRANES	9
THE CHANGED WIND BLOWS, AND THERE'S A CHOICE OF SIGNS		37	WINDMILLS TURN	31
TO LEAVE IT EMPTY'S LION'S OR LOUSE'S CHOICE;	.....	58	TO ARCHITECTS	16
WE HAVE NO CHOICE, THE CHOICE WAS MADE	....	74	WE MOTHERNAKED	11
WE HAVE NO CHOICE, THE CHOICE WAS MADE	....	74	WE MOTHERNAKED	11
'REST BEYOND CHOICE IN THE DUST-APPOINTED GRAIN,		146	IF HEAD HURT	26
CHOIR				
LEFT ONLY THE VOICE IN THE OLD VILLAGE CHOIR	....	45	PLOUGHMAN GONE	4
OF MORTAL VOICES TO THE NINNIES' CHOIR,	....	123	FOSTER LIGHT	16
OVER THE CHOIR MINUTE I HEAR THE HOUR CHANT:	......	130	SINNERS' BELL	7
TO THE WIND THE CHOIR AND CLOISTER	....	147	UNLUCKILY FOR	11
IN A CHOIR OF WINGS, AS THOUGH SHE SLEPT OR DIED,		191	WINTER'S TALE	122
CHOIRS				
THE LIQUID CHOIRS OF HIS TRIBES.	....	167	LONG-LEGGED	164
CHOKE				
CHOKE THE BLADDER WITH A STONE,	....	71	TAKE NEEDLES	13
TO CHOKE THE DESERTS WITH HER TIDES,	....	93	BOYS OF SUMMER	41
AND I WOULD CHOKE THE HEAVENS WITH MY HYMN	....	96	TWELVE	12
CHOKED				
THE STRINGS OF FIRE CHOKED HIS SEX	....	85	SEE, SAYS LIME	17
CHOKING				
BROKEN BY CHOKING,	....	39	GAS FADES	23
CHOPIN				
WE SHALL PLAY CHOPIN IN OUR SUMMER GARDEN,	....	40	YOUNG ARE OLD	12
CHORD				
PAIR OFF, MAKE HARMONIES, A HARMONIOUS CHORD,	.....	53	OUT OF THE PIT	96
THE CHILD TELLS, WHEN THE TREMBLING CHORD IS CUT,		67	LET A FAITH	14
CHOREOGRAPHED				
CHOREOGRAPHED ON PAPER.	....	47	POET: 1935	42
CHOSEN				
OR THE CHOSEN VIRGIN	....	174	FIRE RAID	36
CHRIST				
CHRIST, LET ME WRITE FROM THE HEART,	....	22	HIGH ON A HILL	7
IN GOD OR GODS, CHRIST OR HIS FATHER,	....	41	YOUNG ARE OLD	47
THE MESSAGE OF HIS DYING CHRIST.	....	69	BEFORE KNOCKED	42
MY JACK OF CHRIST BORN THORNY ON THE TREE?	....	96	RUB OF LOVE	45
THIS WAS THE SKY, JACK CHRIST, EACH MINSTREL ANGLE		120	ALTARWISE	105
WITH IMMORTALITY AT MY SIDE LIKE CHRIST THE SKY.		148	UNLUCKILY FOR	49
HURLING INTO BEGINNING LIKE CHRIST THE CHILD.	.....	149	UNLUCKILY FOR	52
CHRISTBREAD				
CUT CHRISTBREAD SPITTING VINEGAR AND ALL	....	141	SAINT TO FALL	16

	PAGE	TITLE	LINE
CHRIST-CROSS-ROW			
HE HAD BY HEART THE CHRIST-CROSS-ROW OF DEATH.	97	TWILIGHT LOCKS	24
CHRISTENED			
MY WORLD WAS CHRISTENED IN A STREAM OF MILK.	78	LOVE'S FEVER	7
CHRISTENS			
GRIEF WITH DRENCHED BOOK AND CANDLE CHRISTENS THE CHERUB TIME	130	SINNERS' BELL	16
CHRISTENS DOWN	185	VISION, PRAYER	194
CHRISTIAN			
LET THE TALE'S SAILOR FROM A CHRISTIAN VOYAGE	121	ALTARWISE	127
I, THE FIRST NAMED, AM THE GHOST OF THIS SIR AND CHRISTIAN FRIEND	141	I, FIRST NAMED	1
CHRIST'S			
GO SILLY AND BE CHRIST'S GOOD BROTHER, ...	25	BEAUTY TO DUST	17
'NO. NOT FOR CHRIST'S DAZZLING BED	146	IF HEAD HURT	16
CHRISTWARD			
THAT NIGHT OF TIME UNDER THE CHRISTWARD SHELTER:	117	ALTARWISE	12
CHRYSALIS			
A CHRYSALIS UNWRINKLING ON THE IRON, ...	115	A GRIEF AGO	10
A CROCODILE BEFORE THE CHRYSALIS, ...	124	TODAY, INSECT	14
CHRYSOLITH			
CHRYSOLITH THY STEP, ...	225	SLENDER WIND	1
CHUCKED			
THE VANISHING OF THE MUSICAL SHIP-WORK AND THE CHUCKED BELLS, ...	141	SAINT TO FALL	8
CHUCKLE			
CAN NEVER RAISE THE MIDNIGHT OF A CHUCKLE, ...	96	RUB OF LOVE	39
CHURCH			
AVOID CHURCH AS A RAT;	59	FAIRY TALES	5
THE ANCHOR DIVES THROUGH THE FLOORS OF A CHURCH.	169	LONG-LEGGED	212
AND OVER THE SEA WET CHURCH THE SIZE OF A SNAIL ...	177	POEM IN OCT	32
CHURCHES			
OF SHEEP AND CHURCHES NOISE	5	PROLOGUE	88
OF CHURCHES MADE FROM ABSTRACT AND CONCRETE.	51	OUT OF THE PIT	28
IT IS THE SINNERS' DUST-TONGUED BELL CLAPS ME TO CHURCHES	130	SINNERS' BELL	1
IN THE CHURCHES OF HIS TEARS, ...	153	WAS A SAVIOUR	18
CHURN			
TOO STIFF TO CHURN WITH LEAVES, ...	14	RAIN CUTS	27
TURN AND CHURN NIGHTSEED TILL IT CURDLE.	67	LET A FAITH	5
CICADA			
ALCOVE OF WORDS OUT OF CICADA SHADE, ...	54	WE BY SEASAND	4
CIGARETTE			
LEAVES IT AMONG THE CIGARETTE ENDS AND THE GLASSES.	30	NEARLY SUMMER	23
CIGARETTES			
STINK OF CIGARETTES AND ARMPITS, ...	28	NO WINGS	16
CINDER			
SHAPES IN A CINDER DEATH; LOVE FOR HIS TRICK, ...	101	RUNNING GRAVE	48
IN THE CINDER OF THE LITTLE SKULL, ...	174	FIRE RAID	40
IN THE CINDER OF THE LITTLE SKULL, ...	174	FIRE RAID	54
CINDER-NESTING			
HER MOLTEN FLIGHT UP CINDER-NESTING COLUMNS, ...	132	I MAKE THIS IN	26
CIPHER			
DID TWIST INTO A LIVING CIPHER, ...	68	BEFORE KNOCKED	21
CIPHERS			
AND, BURNING CIPHERS ON THE ROUND OF SPACE, ...	93	IN BEGINNING	5
CIRCLE			
TO BE THE CIRCLE NOT THE STAIR OF SOUND.	9	MINUTE'S HOUR	17
STAY, IN A CIRCLE CHALKED UPON THE FLOOR, ...	28	NO WINGS	25
I HAVE DESIRED THE CIRCLE OF THE SUN.	52	OUT OF THE PIT	73

	PAGE	TITLE	LINE
CIRCLE (CONTINUED)			
THE VIRGIN LINES BE MATED WITH A CIRCLE.	66	LET A FAITH	3
A CIRCLE SPINS. LET EACH REVOLVING SPOKE	67	LET A FAITH	4
I EYE THE RING OF EARTH, THE AIRY CIRCLE,	76	LASHED RINGS	2
SQUARE IN THESE WORLDS THE MORTAL CIRCLE.	107	ALL ALL AND	30
AND IN THE PINCERS OF THE BOILING CIRCLE,	111	I, IN IMAGE	91
IN SHAPING-TIME THE CIRCLE STUNG AWAKE,	121	INCARNATE DEVL	3
BUT STRIP THE TWELVE-WINDED MARROW FROM HIS CIRCLE;	123	FOSTER LIGHT	3
A MERRY MANSHAPE OF YOUR WALKING CIRCLE.	124	FOSTER LIGHT	30
THE NATURAL CIRCLE OF THE DISCOVERED SKIES	134	HOW MY ANIMAL	10
CIRCLES			
THE PLANET-DUCTED PELICAN OF CIRCLES	117	ALTARWISE	17
RIPPLING IN TWELVE-WINDED CIRCLES,	175	FIRE RAID	64
CIRCULAR			
THESE ARE YOUR YEARS' RECORDERS. THE CIRCULAR WORLD STANDS STILL.)	110	I, IN IMAGE	72
THE CIRCULAR SMILE TOSSED FROM LOVER TO LOVER	134	NOT FROM ANGER	9
CIRCUMAMBULATE			
TO CIRCUMAMBULATE FOR DECENCY	11	CABARET	8
CIRCUSES			
IN CHILDREN'S CIRCUSES COULD STAY THEIR TROUBLES?	40	WAS THERE TIME	2
CISTERN			
HE PULLS THE CHAIN, THE CISTERN MOVES.	75	MY HERO BARES	20
CITIES			
FROM THE CITIES OF NINE	3	PROLOGUE	19
THE CITIES HAVE NOT ROBBED OUR EYES.	70	SECRET WIND	24
CITIES'			
ESCAPES TO THE FLAT CITIES' SAILS	129	MY NEOPHYTE	16
CITY			
THE HAND THAT SIGNED THE PAPER FELLED A CITY;	66	HAND SIGNED	1
A CITY GODHEAD, TURBINE MOVED, STEEL SCULPTURED,	70	SECRET WIND	13
A CITY SAVIOUR, IN THE ORCHARD	70	SECRET WIND	15
THE CITY GOSPEL SHOUT TO HEAVEN.	70	SECRET WIND	21
NOR CITY TAR AND SUBWAY BORED TO FOSTER	100	RUNNING GRAVE	34
CITY OF SPRING, THE GOVERNED FLOWER,	106	ALL ALL AND	4
TIME AT THE CITY SPECTACLES, AND HALF	124	TODAY, INSECT	3
FLICKED FROM THE CARBOLIC CITY PUZZLE IN A BED OF SORES	142	SAINT TO FALL	28
BECAUSE THERE STANDS, ONE STORY OUT OF THE BUM CITY,	144	PLEASURE-BIRD	13
THE RANKEST OF THE CITY	154	RETURN	8
LIFTING HER SMELL OVER THE CITY BUILDINGS.	240	ADMIT THE SUN	14
CITY'S			
ADORNERS OF THE CITY'S FOREHEAD,	70	SECRET WIND	9
ALL THE HYPNOTISED CITY'S	156	RETURN	62
CIVET			
NUTMEG, CIVET, AND SEA-PARSLEY SERVE THE PLAGUED GROOM AND BRIDE	131	SINNERS' BELL	29
CIVILIZATION			
BEFORE CIVILIZATION RISES OR ROTS,	39	GAS FADES	9
CLACK			
CLACK THROUGH THE THICKET OF STRENGTH, LOVE HEWN IN PILLARS DROPS	135	HOW MY ANIMAL	36
BACK TO CLACK SILENCE MELT AND MOURN	181	VISION, PRAYER	61
CLAD			
MALE SHAPES, GIRL-LIPPED, BUT CLAD LIKE BOYS:	143	THE MOLLS	2
CLAIM			
OUR CLAIM IS STAKED FOR ONCE AND ALL	73	WE MOTHERNAKED	5
CLAMOUR			
AND YOUR CLAMOUR STOPPED,	232	FURIOUS MOTION	2

	PAGE	TITLE	LINE
CLAN			
HO, HULLABALLOING CLAN	4	PROLOGUE	64
CLANGOUR			
CLANGOUR AS I HEW AND SMITE	5	PROLOGUE	70
CLAP			
AND CLAP ITS GREAT BLOOD DOWN;	135	HOW MY ANIMAL	31
CLAPPED			
AND, CLAPPED IN WATER TILL THE TRITON DANGLES,	110	I, IN IMAGE	64
CLAPS			
IT IS THE SINNERS' DUST-TONGUED BELL CLAPS ME TO CHURCHES	130	SINNERS' BELL	1
CLARITY			
HOLDING A VOLUPTUOUS CLARITY	237	WOMAN TAPESTRY	73
CLASH			
(A CLASH OF ANVILS FOR MY	5	PROLOGUE	71
CLASH OUT THE MOUNTING DOLPHIN'S DAY,	164	LONG-LEGGED	75
CLASP			
SHALL THEY CLASP A COMET IN THEIR FISTS?	56	WHY EAST WIND	11
TO CLASP MY FURY ON GROUND	135	HOW MY ANIMAL	30
NOW CLASP ME TO THEIR GRAINS IN THE GIGANTIC GLADE,	204	GIANT'S THIGH	19
PRESS, PRESS, AND CLASP STEADILY;	232	FURIOUS MOTION	18
CLASPED			
WHO HOLDS HER CLASPED INSIDE HIS STRONG, WHITE WINGS;	15	FOR LEDA	31
CLOSES ABOUT YOUR CLASPED FINGERS	229	MY RIVER	25
CLATTER			
KICKED, WITH A CLATTER, ASH-BINS MARKED VERBOTEN,	52	OUT OF THE PIT	57
CLAW			
A CLAW I QUESTION FROM THE MOUSE'S BONE,	114	SERVANT SUN	17
CLAW OF THE CRABBED VEINS SQUEEZE FROM EACH RED PARTICLE	135	HOW MY ANIMAL	21
CLAW FOLD AND HOLE FOR THE ROTTEN	152	BELOW A TIME	33
IN THE CLAW TRACKS OF HAWKS	209	POEM ON B'DAY	21
CLAWED			
NO MAN MORE MAGICAL, CLAWED OUT THE CROCODILE.	111	I, IN IMAGE	96
THE BLIND, CLAWED STARE IS COLD AS SLEET.	165	LONG-LEGGED	101
CLAWS			
OF THE SHARP, ENAMELLED EYES AND THE SPECTACLED CLAWS	133	MAKE ME A MASK	2
IN A HOISTED CLOUD, AT DROP OF DUSK, HE PULLS TO HIS CLAWS	201	SIR JOHNS HILL	3
CLAY			
IN HIS AGE THE LASS'S CLAY.	75	SONG: LOVE ME	3
HOW OF MY CLAY IS MADE THE HANGMAN'S LIME.	77	THE FORCE THAT	15
ONCE IN THIS CLAY FENCED BY THE STICKS	85	SEE, SAYS LIME	5
THAT STARRY FENCE THE CLAY OF LIGHT	85	SEE, SAYS LIME	6
MY CLAY UNSUCKLED AND MY SALT UNBORN,	105	WORLD PYRAMID	58
SIGH LONG, CLAY COLD, LIE SHORN,	135	HOW MY ANIMAL	34
ON THE CLAY COLD MOUTH, ON THE FIRE	147	UNLUCKILY FOR	8
IN COMMON CLAY CLOTHES DISGUISED AS SCALES,	151	BELOW A TIME	15
AND THE COLOUR OF CLAY	185	VISION, PRAYER	184
CLAYFELLOW			
SHAPED MY CLAYFELLOW, AND THE HEAVEN'S ARK	124	FOSTER LIGHT	26
CLAYFELLOWS			
MY MAKER'S FLESH THAT GARMENTS MY CLAYFELLOWS.	76	LASHED RINGS	3
CLEAN			
LEPER AMONG A CLEAN PEOPLE	47	POET: 1935	26
WHEN THEIR BONES ARE PICKED CLEAN AND THE CLEAN BONES GONE,	49	NO DOMINION	4
WHEN THEIR BONES ARE PICKED CLEAN AND THE CLEAN BONES GONE,	49	NO DOMINION	4
I TALK TO HIM AS I CLEAN THE GRATE	149	PAPER & STICKS	10

		PAGE	TITLE	LINE
CLEAN (CONTINUED)				
WHERE SITTING IN CLEAN LINEN	....	156	RETURN	93
LET ME BELIEVE IN THE CLEAN FAITH OF THE BODY,	....	235	WOMAN TAPESTRY	24
LIKE THE ARMS OF A CLEAN WOMAN	....	236	WOMAN TAPESTRY	39
AND A CLEAN SURGE OF LOVE MOVING.	....	236	WOMAN TAPESTRY	63
LET ME BELIEVE IN THE CLEAN FAITH OF THE BODY,	....	237	WOMAN TAPESTRY	79
CLEANEST				
HAVE CLEANEST HANDS, AND, AS THE HEARTLESS GHOST		40	WAS THERE TIME	8
CLEAR				
SANG TO MY HORN, THE FOXES ON THE HILLS BARKED CLEAR				
AND COLD,	....	195	FERN HILL	16
OR SKULKS IN THE DELL MOON BUT MOONSHINE ECHOING				
CLEAR	....	198	COUNTRY SLEEP	25
DEATH CLEAR AS A BUOY'S BELL:	....	202	SIR JOHNS HILL	26
AND LEAVE A CLEAR PRINT,	....	229	MY RIVER	8
NOR BE SO CLEAR.	....	234	NO, PIGEON	10
CLEARER				
BURNING ITS SWEET PATH CLEARER THAN BEFORE.	....	232	FURIOUS MOTION	17
CLEARLY				
AS CLEARLY AS THE LIGHT OF MY OWN BRAIN,	....	49	LIGHT, I KNOW	28
RUNNING WHEN HE HAD HEARD THEM CLEARLY	....	171	THE HUNCHBACK	17
AND I SAW IN THE TURNING SO CLEARLY A CHILD'S	.....	178	POEM IN OCT	46
CLEAVING				
ON MY CLEAVING ARM AS I BLASTED IN A WAVE.	....	152	BELOW A TIME	48
CLEAVING THEIR OWN SEDGES,	....	231	OUR SANCTITY	38
CLEFT				
HIS BEAST HEEL CLEFT IN A SANDAL,	....	130	SINNERS' BELL	3
PILLAR BREAKS, AND MAST IS CLEFT	....	237	PILLAR BREAKS	1
CLENCHED				
HER FIST OF A FACE DIED CLENCHED ON A ROUND PAIN;		137	AFTER FUNERAL	34
CLERICAL-GREY				
OVER A RUMP ON THE CLERICAL-GREY SEASHORE,	....	179	NEW QUAY	25
CLIMATES				
HERE WERE FOND CLIMATES AND SWEET SINGERS SUDDENLY		177	POEM IN OCT	26
CLIMB				
IF WE WERE CHILDREN WE MIGHT CLIMB,	....	31	BEING BUT MEN	6
THEY CLIMB THE COUNTRY PINNACLE,	....	109	I, IN IMAGE	37
DO YOU NOT BROTHER ME, NOR, AS YOU CLIMB,	....	112	NOT FATHER ME	7
THE CLOUD CLIMB OF THE EXHALING TOMB	....	182	VISION, PRAYER	76
I CLIMB TO GREET THE WAR IN WHICH I HAVE NO HEART				
BUT ONLY	....	186	HOLY SPRING	8
TIME LET ME HAIL AND CLIMB	....	195	FERN HILL	4
THEIR BREAST, THE VAULTING DOES ROISTER, THE HORNED				
BUCKS CLIMB	....	204	GIANT'S THIGH	33
CLIMBED				
I FLED THE EARTH AND, NAKED, CLIMBED THE WEATHER,		101	FELLOWED SLEEP	6
BEFORE THE CROWING MORNING CLIMBED;	....	157	INTO HER HEAD	19
AND THE ROOTS OF THE TREES CLIMBED THROUGH THE AIR		235	WOMAN TAPESTRY	31
CLIMBER				
THE CLIMBER OF THE WATER SEX	....	128	MY NEOPHYTE	11
CLIMBING				
RAISED UP A VOICE, AND, CLIMBING ON THE WORDS,	....	102	FELLOWED SLEEP	22
AN OLD, MAD MAN STILL CLIMBING IN HIS GHOST,	......	102	FELLOWED SLEEP	29
MY FATHERS' GHOST IS CLIMBING IN THE RAIN.	....	102	FELLOWED SLEEP	30
AND THREE DEAD SEASONS ON A CLIMBING GRAVE	....	117	ALTARWISE	30
A CLIMBING SEA FROM ASIA HAD ME DOWN	....	118	ALTARWISE	65
CLIMBS				
CLINGS TO HER DRIFTING HAIR, AND CLIMBS;	....	167	LONG-LEGGED	161
WHO CLIMBS TO HIS DYING LOVE IN HER HIGH ROOM,	....	193	CONVERS PRAYER	3
AND THE CHILD NOT CARING TO WHOM HE CLIMBS HIS PRAYER		194	CONVERS PRAYER	17

	PAGE	TITLE	LINE
CLIME			
THE TALL MAUVE IRIS OF A SLEEPING CLIME.	222	IN DREAMS	2
CLING			
OF WATERS CLUCK AND CLING, ...	5	PROLOGUE	80
HIS FATHERS CLING TO THE HAND OF THE GIRL	167	LONG-LEGGED	147
CLINGS			
HERE CLINGS THE MEAT TO SEVER FROM HIS SIDE.	81	HERE LIE BEAST	5
SEE WHAT CLINGS TO HAIR AND SKULL	166	LONG-LEGGED	133
CLINGS TO HER DRIFTING HAIR, AND CLIMBS;	167	LONG-LEGGED	161
CLINICS			
ON GARAGES AND CLINICS IN THE TOWN.	52	OUT OF THE PIT	48
CLIPS			
CLIPS SHORT THE GESTURE OF BREATH.	135	HOW MY ANIMAL	39
CLOAK			
LIKE A LIVING CLOAK OVER ME.	235	WOMAN TAPESTRY	5
CLOAKED			
WHEN BLACK BIRDS DIED LIKE PRIESTS IN THE CLOAKED			
HEDGE ROW	190	WINTER'S TALE	92
CLOCK			
A WORM TELLS SUMMER BETTER THAN THE CLOCK, ...	59	HERE IN SPRING	14
BEHIND A POT OF FERNS THE WAGGING CLOCK	99	OCTOBER WIND	17
THE WOUND-DOWN COUGH OF THE BLOOD-COUNTING CLOCK	141	SAINT TO FALL	9
I SET BACK THE CLOCK FACED TAILORS, ...	151	BELOW A TIME	18
INTO THE DEAD CLOCK BURNING THE HOUR	175	FIRE RAID	65
CLOCKED			
HEAR BY DEATH'S ACCIDENT THE CLOCKED AND DASHED-DOWN			
SPIRE	130	SINNERS' BELL	11
CLOCKING			
INVISIBLE, YOUR CLOCKING TIDES	91	WHERE ONCE THE	13
CLOCKS			
BIRDS AND CLOCKS AND CROSS BELLS	150	WHEN I WOKE	2
NO TIME, SPOKE THE CLOCKS, NO GOD, RANG THE BELLS,	150	WHEN I WOKE	28
EMASCULATE THE SEEDY CLOCKS;	156	RETURN	80
THE DUST OF THEIR KETTLES AND CLOCKS SWINGS TO AND			
FRO	205	GIANT'S THIGH	46
CLOCKWISE			
VOYAGING CLOCKWISE OFF THE SYMBOLED HARBOUR, ...	109	I, IN IMAGE	32
THE WINDER OF THE CLOCKWISE SCENE	129	MY NEOPHYTE	32
CLOGS			
GENTLE IN THEIR CLOGS OVER THE FALLEN SKY, ...	187	WINTER'S TALE	24
AND GONE THAT BARLEY DARK WHERE THEIR CLOGS DANCED			
IN THE SPRING, ...	205	GIANT'S THIGH	40
CLOISTER			
TO THE WIND THE CHOIR AND CLOISTER	147	UNLUCKILY FOR	11
CLOSE			
THE DROOPING AS YOU CLOSE ME IN	20	ENCOMPASSED	12
AND CLOSE HER FIST.	115	A GRIEF AGO	40
CLOSE AND FAR SHE ANNOUNCED THE THEFT OF THE HEART	158	INTO HER HEAD	39
OLD AGE SHOULD BURN AND RAVE AT CLOSE OF DAY;	207	NOT GO GENTLE	2
CLOSED			
CLOSED IN YOUR CELL OF SECRET THOUGHTS, ...	10	COOL, OH NO	28
MY HAND WITH HONEY THAT HAD CLOSED UPON A FLOWER.	15	FOR LEDA	19
THE CENTURY'S TRAP WILL HAVE CLOSED FOR GOOD	39	GAS FADES	30
THE FRANK, CLOSED PEARL, THE SEA-GIRLS' LINEAMENTS	131	I MAKE THIS IN	19
OF THE TOWN CLOSED AS THE TOWN AWOKE.	177	POEM IN OCT	20
CLOSER			
OR SUNDERED IT TO LOOK THE CLOSER, ...	25	BEAUTY TO DUST	4
THAT THE CLOSER I MOVE	211	POEM ON B'DAY	91
AND I DREW CLOSER TO HER	234	WOMAN TAPESTRY	3

		PAGE	TITLE	LINE
CLOSES				
CLOSES ABOUT YOUR CLASPED FINGERS	....	229	MY RIVER	25
CLOSE-UP				
ONCE CLOSE-UP SMILING IN THE WALL OF PICTURES,	....	118	ALTARWISE	55
CLOSING				
AND THE SUN HEALS, CLOSING SORE EYES.	....	42	A WAR OF WITS	19
CLOTH				
UNDER HER CLOTH OF TREES NO SORROW,	....	15	FOR LEDA	22
BY WEIGHT OF CLOTH AND FACT,	....	28	NO WINGS	4
THE CATARACTED EYES THAT FILMED THEIR CLOTH;	....	97	TWILIGHT LOCKS	21
BUCKLE TO LINT AND CLOTH THEIR NATRON FOOTSTEPS,		120	ALTARWISE	116
AND ALL LOVE'S SINNERS IN SWEET CLOTH KNEEL TO A				
HYLEG IMAGE,	....	130	SINNERS' BELL	28
TRAILING THE FROST BITTEN CLOTH,	....	151	BELOW A TIME	23
AND OVER THE CLOTH OF COUNTIES THE FAR HILLS RODE				
NEAR,	....	190	WINTER'S TALE	93
SO, THEN, WILL THE DARK CLOTH OF YOUR HAIR	....	232	FURIOUS MOTION	7
CLOTHES				
WAX CLOTHES THAT WAX UPON THE AGEING RIBS;	....	81	ALL THAT I OWE	26
IN COMMON CLAY CLOTHES DISGUISED AS SCALES,	....	151	BELOW A TIME	15
HE PUT ON HIS CLOTHES AND STEPPED OUT AND HE DIED,		172	DAWN RAID	2
CLOTHESHORSE				
AND CANNOT MOUNT A CLOTHESHORSE WITHOUT BLEEDING.		40	YOUNG ARE OLD	10
CLOTHS				
THE MUMMY CLOTHS EXPOSE AN ANCIENT BREAST.	....	116	LANTERNS SHINE	8
CLOTTED				
IN THE STITCHED WOUND AND CLOTTED WIND, MUZZLED	...	103	I DREAMED MY	15
CLOUD				
FIND HARD TO DART AGAINST A CLOUD,	....	37	WINDMILLS TURN	8
WHO ON HIS CLOUD HEARS ALL MY WISHES,	....	48	LIGHT, I KNOW	15
OUT OF A BIRD'S WING WRITING ON A CLOUD	....	48	POET: 1935	53
I HAVE RIDDEN ON GUTTER DUNG AND CLOUD.	....	52	OUT OF THE PIT	67
TOUCHED THE FIRST CLOUD AND LEFT A SIGN.	....	94	IN BEGINNING	12
ON THAT CLOUD COAST TO EACH GRAVE-GABBING SHADE;		102	FELLOWED SLEEP	18
OR SPIRIT UP A CLOUD,	....	114	SERVANT SUN	26
TIME TRACKS THE SOUND OF SHAPE ON MAN AND CLOUD,		120	ALTARWISE	97
A HANDMADE MOON HALF HOLY IN A CLOUD,	....	121	INCARNATE DEVL	8
HIGH LORD ESQUIRE, SPEAK UP THE SINGING CLOUD,	....	123	FOSTER LIGHT	17
THE TWO-A-VEIN, THE FORESKIN, AND THE CLOUD.	......	128	NOW, SAY NAY	35
AND, MILD AS PARDON FROM A CLOUD OF PRIDE,	....	133	I MAKE THIS IN	59
UNDER THE CLOUD AGAINST LOVE IS CAUGHT AND HELD AND				
KISSED	....	147	UNLUCKILY FOR	17
WITH THEIR HEADS IN A CUNNING CLOUD.	....	147	TO OTHERS	21
OR DECKED ON A CLOUD SWALLOWER,	....	151	BELOW A TIME	12
THE CLOUD PERCHED TAILORS' MASTER WITH NERVES FOR				
COTTON.	....	152	BELOW A TIME	35
SWEEP AWAY LIKE A CREAM CLOUD;	....	156	RETURN	89
CARRYING CLOUD, DEATH STRIKES THEIR HOUSE.	....	161	WEDDING ANNIV	8
A CLOUD BLEW THE RAIN FROM ITS THROAT;	....	163	LONG-LEGGED	40
SLEEPS TILL SILENCE BLOWS ON A CLOUD	....	165	LONG-LEGGED	111
AND STEEPLES PIERCE THE CLOUD ON HER SHOULDER	.....	168	LONG-LEGGED	193
CLOUD AND THE ROADSIDE BUSHES BRIMMING WITH WHISTLING		177	POEM IN OCT	22
BEYOND THE BORDER AND UNDER THE LARK FULL CLOUD.		177	POEM IN OCT	37
A CLOUD AGAINST THE GLASSY SUN FLUTTERS HIS	....	179	NEW QUAY	5
THE CLOUD CLIMB OF THE EXHALING TOMB	....	182	VISION, PRAYER	76
AND FIRES WHERE HE SHOULD PROWL DOWN THE CLOUD	....	188	WINTER'S TALE	37
THE CLOUD, THE NEED, THE PLANTED STARS, THE JOY				
BEYOND	....	190	WINTER'S TALE	102
IN A HOISTED CLOUD, AT DROP OF DUSK, HE PULLS TO HIS				
CLAWS	....	201	SIR JOHNS HILL	3

	PAGE	TITLE	LINE
CLOUD (CONTINUED)			
UNDER A SERPENT CLOUD, ...	209	POEM ON B'DAY	32
BE AT CLOUD QUAKING PEACE, ...	210	POEM ON B'DAY	63
THE SHOOTING STAR HAWK STATUED BLIND IN A CLOUD ...	215	COUNTRY HEAVEN	23
OPENING IN THE BLIND CLOUD OVER OUR HEADS;	231	OUR SANCTITY	44
MY LOVE FOR HER IS LIKE THE MOVING OF A CLOUD	235	WOMAN TAPESTRY	13
I'LL CUT THROUGH YOUR DARK CLOUD	239	LET ME ESCAPE	10
CLOUD-FORMED			
AND LAID YOUR CHEEK AGAINST A CLOUD-FORMED SHELL:	153	WAS A SAVIOUR	23
CLOUD-LIKE			
AND CLOUD-LIKE.	225	OF ANY FLOWER	3
CLOUDS			
TACKLED WITH CLOUDS, WHO KNEEL	3	PROLOGUE	13
OR HAS TOO MANY CLOUDS OR BIRDS, ...	12	SKY'S BRIGHT	2
THE WATER FROM A STREET OF CLOUDS.	13	RAIN CUTS	5
STEPPING ON CLOUDS ACROSS THE GOLDEN SKY, ...	30	YOUTH CALLS	2
COMFORT COME THROUGH THE DEVIL'S CLOUDS, ...	35	LIFT UP FACE	11
ABOVE THEM POISE THE SWOLLEN CLOUDS	36	MIDNIGHT ROAD	12
SHALL GODS BE SAID TO THUMP THE CLOUDS	65	GODS THUMP	T
SHALL GODS BE SAID TO THUMP THE CLOUDS	65	GODS THUMP	1
WHEN CLOUDS ARE CURSED BY THUNDER, ...	65	GODS THUMP	2
HOW DEEP THE WAKING IN THE WORLDED CLOUDS.	102	FELLOWED SLEEP	25
THE LOFTY ROOTS OF THE CLOUDS.	142	SAINT TO FALL	30
SHE IS BREAKING WITH SEASONS AND CLOUDS;	168	LONG-LEGGED	176
SHE DELUDES THE HEAVEN-PROOF HOUSE WITH ENTERING CLOUDS	169	LOVE IN ASYLUM	6
UNDER THE NEW MADE CLOUDS AND HAPPY AS THE HEART WAS LONG, ...	196	FERN HILL	38
NIGHT AND THE REINDEER ON THE CLOUDS ABOVE THE HAYCOCKS	199	COUNTRY SLEEP	64
AND SURELY HE SAILS LIKE THE SHIP SHAPE CLOUDS. OH HE	200	COUNTRY SLEEP	99
CLUNG TO THE PITCHING CLOUDS, OR GAY WITH ANY ONE	204	GIANT'S THIGH	15
BEAUTIFULLY LITTLE LIKE CLOUDS:	226	THE ELM	9
ITS SHINING CLOUDS FOR YOU;	234	NO, PIGEON	3
TOUCHING THE SILVER CLOUDS, ...	235	WOMAN TAPESTRY	32
CLOUDS'			
I STAND BENEATH THE CLOUDS' CONFESSIONAL, ...	42	A WAR OF WITS	13
CLOUD'S			
NOW IN THE CLOUD'S BIG BREAST LIE QUIET COUNTRIES,	133	I MAKE THIS IN	61
CLOUD-SOPPED			
THESE CLOUD-SOPPED, MARBLE HANDS, THIS MONUMENTAL	137	AFTER FUNERAL	36
CLOUD-TRACKING			
BLINDS THEIR CLOUD-TRACKING EYE.	104	WORLD PYRAMID	30
CLOUDY			
AND FROM THE CLOUDY BASES OF THE BREATH	94	IN BEGINNING	22
DOWN THE LONG BAYS OF BLUE THAT THOSE CLOUDY HEADLANDS	222	FOREST PICTURE	6
CLOUT			
THAT BREAKS ONE BONE TO LIGHT WITH A JUDGMENT CLOUT,	136	AFTER FUNERAL	9
CLOUTED			
THAN BULLY ILL LOVE IN THE CLOUTED SCENE.	145	IF HEAD HURT	5
DAWN SHIPS CLOUTED AGROUND, ...	211	POEM ON B'DAY	79
CLOUTS			
THAT CLOUTS THE SPITTLE LIKE BUBBLES WITH BROKEN ROOMS, ...	144	PLEASURE-BIRD	6
CLOVE			
WISDOM IS STORED WITH THE CLOVE	240	ADMIT THE SUN	10
CLOVEN			
THE PATCHWORK HALVES WERE CLOVEN AS THEY SCUDDED	104	WORLD PYRAMID	19
THE FELLOW HALVES THAT, CLOVEN AS THEY SWIVEL	105	WORLD PYRAMID	49

	PAGE	TITLE	LINE

CLOVEN (CONTINUED)

HELL IN A HORN OF SULPHUR AND THE CLOVEN MYTH, ... 122 INCARNATE DEVL 16

CLOVER

WHEREVER I RAMPED IN THE CLOVER QUILTS, ... 206 LAMENT 22

CLOVES

AND THIS IS PLENTY, THEN, CLOVES AND SWEET OILS, THE
    BEES' HONEY, ... 36 MIDNIGHT ROAD 5

CLOWN

CLOWN IN THE MOON .... 225 CLOWN IN MOON T

CLUB

TOMORROW'S DRUNK CLUB MAJORS .... 154 RETURN 12

CLUCK

OF WATERS CLUCK AND CLING, ... 5 PROLOGUE 80

GREEN CHICKENS OF THE BAY AND BUSHES CLUCK, 'DILLY
    DILLY, ... 202 SIR JOHNS HILL 31

CLUNG

CLUNG TO THE PITCHING CLOUDS, OR GAY WITH ANY ONE 204 GIANT'S THIGH 15

CLUSTERED

THAT CLUSTERED ROUND HER SHOULDERS, ... 15 FOR LEDA 26

CLUTCHES

SCENT THROUGH THE CLUTCHES OF THE HEATHER, ... 44 TO FOLLOW FOX 4

COAL

IN THE COAL BLACK BUSH AND LET THEM GRIEVE. .... 206 LAMENT 12

FOR MY SULKING, SKULKING, COAL BLACK SOUL! .... 206 LAMENT 36

AND I SHOVED IT INTO THE COAL BLACK SKY .... 207 LAMENT 47

IN THE COAL BLACK SKY AND SHE BORE ANGELS! .... 207 LAMENT 55

COAL-

WHATSOEVER I DID IN THE COAL- .... 206 LAMENT 23

COAST

AND A BONE COAST, ... 62 EARS IN TURRET 12

ON THAT CLOUD COAST TO EACH GRAVE-GABBING SHADE; 102 FELLOWED SLEEP 18

THE BOWS GLIDED DOWN, AND THE COAST .... 161 LONG-LEGGED 1

COASTS

SLOW ROUNDING OF FOUR SEASONS' COASTS, ... 58 HERE IN SPRING 6

COAT

I, THAT TIME'S JACKET OR THE COAT OF ICE .... 100 RUNNING GRAVE 18

COATS

THE CHAMELEON COATS OF THE BIG BUGS AND SHOTS,) ... 39 GAS FADES 13

COBBLED

THE COUNTRY TIDE IS COBBLED WITH TOWNS, ... 168 LONG-LEGGED 192

COBBLES

THE TRODDEN TOWN RANG ITS COBBLES FOR LUCK. .... 161 LONG-LEGGED 4

WHERE THE SEA COBBLES SAIL, ... 202 SIR JOHNS HILL 38

HEARS THE BELFRIES AND THE COBBLES .... 215 COUNTRY HEAVEN 25

COBWEB

WITH LOUD, TORN TOOTH AND TAIL AND COBWEB DRUM .... 133 I MAKE THIS IN 57

AND COBWEB DRUM, ... 176 BREATH SHED 8

COCK

FOR WE SHALL BE A SHOUTER LIKE THE COCK, ... 90 EUNUCH DREAMS 37

AND TELLS THE WINDY WEATHER IN THE COCK. .... 99 OCTOBER WIND 20

OLD COCK FROM NOWHERES AND THE HEAVEN'S EGG, ... 117 ALTARWISE 8

PLUCK, COCK, MY SEA EYE, SAID MEDUSA'S SCRIPTURE, 119 ALTARWISE 75

OLD COCK FROM NOWHERES LOPPED THE MINSTREL TONGUE 119 ALTARWISE 78

ROOSTS SLEEPING CHILL TILL THE FLAME OF THE COCK CROW 187 WINTER'S TALE 19

WITH THE DEW, COME BACK, THE COCK ON HIS SHOULDER:
    IT WAS ALL .... 195 FERN HILL 29

COCKCROW

AND BARNROOFS COCKCROW WAR! .... 5 PROLOGUE 81

THAT ALL THE CHARMINGLY DROWNED ARISE TO COCKCROW
    AND KILL. .... 144 COLOUR OF SAY 6

	PAGE	TITLE	LINE
COCKCROW (CONTINUED)			
CHILD BEYOND COCKCROW, BY THE FIRE-DWARFED	174	FIRE RAID	28
COCKERELS			
PROWLS FLAMING AMONG THE COCKERELS	216	COUNTRY HEAVEN	28
COCKEREL'S			
MURMUR OF SPRING NOR CRUSH THE COCKEREL'S EGGS, ...	123	FOSTER LIGHT	7
THE COCKEREL'S TIDE UPCASTING FROM THE FIRE.	127	NOW, SAY NAY	21
COCKFIGHT			
'ALL GAME PHRASES FIT YOUR RING OF A COCKFIGHT: ...	145	IF HEAD HURT	6
COCKLED			
AND PERRINS ON THE COCKLED TABLECLOTH	179	NEW QUAY	3
COCKLES			
GULLS, PIPERS, COCKLES, AND SAILS, ...	3	PROLOGUE	11
COCK-ON-A-DUNGHILL			
A COCK-ON-A-DUNGHILL	110	I, IN IMAGE	58
COCKS			
OF BIRDS! AMONG THE COCKS LIKE FIRE THE RED FOX ...	199	COUNTRY SLEEP	69
AND NO GREEN COCKS OR HENS	203	SIR JOHNS HILL	53
COCKSHUT			
CHASTE AND THE CHASER, MAN WITH THE COCKSHUT EYE,	100	RUNNING GRAVE	17
COCKWISE			
SHALL YOU TURN COCKWISE ON A TUFTED AXLE.	123	FOSTER LIGHT	24
CODE			
THE CODE OF STARS TRANSLATE IN HEAVEN.	69	SECRET WIND	3
THE CODE OF NIGHT TAPPED ON MY TONGUE;	79	LOVE'S FEVER	40
CODED			
AND FEW YOUNG AUDEN'S CODED CHATTER;	84	LETTER TO AUNT	38
COFFIN			
IN THE DARK OF THE COFFIN AND SHEDS DRY LEAVES, ...	136	AFTER FUNERAL	8
AROUND SOME COFFIN CARRYING	152	BELOW A TIME	30
COGITATIONS			
OUT OF UNSLEEPING COGITATIONS, ...	35	LIFT UP FACE	18
COIL			
TRAP I WITH COIL AND SHEET, ...	114	SERVANT SUN	19
BLIND IN THE COIL SCRAMS ROUND THE BLAZING OUTLINE,	124	TODAY, INSECT	11
THROUGH VEIL AND FIN AND FIRE AND COIL	129	MY NEOPHYTE	23
IN THE GROIN'S ENDLESS COIL A MAN IS TANGLED.'	132	I MAKE THIS IN	53
COIL FROM THE THOROUGHFARES OF HER HAIR	168	LONG-LEGGED	197
COILED			
COILED INTO THEIR BODIES LIKE SNAKES, ...	237	WOMAN TAPESTRY	76
COILING			
DINNED ASIDE THE COILING CROWD, ...	150	WHEN I WOKE	3
COILS			
AND THE HEWN COILS OF HIS TRADE PERCEIVES	209	POEM ON B'DAY	26
COIN			
YOU WITH A BAD COIN IN YOUR SOCKET, ...	146	TO OTHERS	2
COINS			
AND THE COINS ON MY EYELIDS SANG LIKE SHELLS.	150	WHEN I WOKE	30
COITUS			
GIBED THE COITUS OF THE STARS. NO GOD	53	OUT OF THE PIT	78
COLD			
LIE COLD, WITH THEIR HORSES, FOR RAVEN AND KITE.	45	PLOUGHMAN GONE	23
LIKE CATS, AND LUSTS LAY HALF HOT IN THE COLD.	50	OUT OF THE PIT	5
BUT WHEN THE LADIES ARE COLD AS STONE	60	MEAT ON BONES	7
ONE DAY MY WOMAN'S BODY WILL BE COLD.	64	WOMAN SPEAKS	47
AND YOU, BEFORE THE BREATH IS COLD	74	WE MOTHERNAKED	14
WHERE NO COLD IS, THE SKINNING GALES UNPIN	82	LIGHT BREAKS	22
WOULD LEAVE ME COLD AS BUTTER FOR THE FLIES, ...	95	RUB OF LOVE	26
WHO SCALES A HAILING HILL IN HER COLD FLINTSTEPS	132	I MAKE THIS IN	29
SIGH LONG, CLAY COLD, LIE SHORN, ...	135	HOW MY ANIMAL	34

	PAGE	TITLE	LINE
COLD (CONTINUED)			
THE RAIN THROUGH HER COLD HEART SPEAK	139	TOMBSTONE TOLD	8
WHERE AT NIGHT WE STONED THE COLD AND CUCKOO	144	COLOUR OF SAY	8
ON THE CLAY COLD MOUTH, ON THE FIRE	147	UNLUCKILY FOR	8
COLD NANSEN'S BEAK ON A BOAT FULL OF GONGS, ...	152	BELOW A TIME	40
THE BLIND, CLAWED STARE IS COLD AS SLEET.	165	LONG-LEGGED	101
WIND BLOW COLD	177	POEM IN OCT	29
AND THE STARS FALLING COLD, ...	187	WINTER'S TALE	6
HE KNELT ON THE COLD STONES, ...	188	WINTER'S TALE	31
WHEN COLD AS SNOW HE SHOULD RUN THE WENDED VALES			
AMONG	188	WINTER'S TALE	45
SANG TO MY HORN, THE FOXES ON THE HILLS BARKED CLEAR			
AND COLD, ...	195	FERN HILL	16
OH, TIME ENOUGH WHEN THE BLOOD CREEPS COLD, ...	206	LAMENT	34
FLOUNDERS, GULLS, ON THEIR COLD, DYING TRAILS, ...	209	POEM ON B'DAY	11
A COLD KIND MAN BRAVE IN HIS NARROW PRIDE	216	ELEGY	3
AND MAKE YOU BITTER WITH MY COLD, ...	233	NO THOUGHT	6
I SAW THE COLD, GREEN TREES, ...	235	WOMAN TAPESTRY	6
COLDNESS			
WHO FEELS NOT COLDNESS IN THE HEAT, ...	55	NO MAN BELIEVE	8
COLIC			
BRIGHT AS HER SPINNING-WHEELS, THE COLIC SEASON ...	108	I, IN IMAGE	8
COLLAR			
IN LOVE'S LAST COLLAR.	86	SEE, SAYS LIME	24
SPIKED WITH A MASTIFF COLLAR, ...	151	BELOW A TIME	10
COLLECTED			
AGAIN, A COLLECTED POET	155	RETURN	30
COLLECTION			
AND WHEN THE MOIST COLLECTION PLATE IS PASSED	179	NEW QUAY	31
COLOSSAL			
THE COLOSSAL INTIMACIES OF SILENT	157	INTO HER HEAD	14
COLOUR			
THEIR GOLDEN AND THEIR OTHER COLOUR.	11	CABARET	9
LEAVING A CORRUPTED VEIN OF COLOUR, ...	27	OBLIVIOUS DARK	16
AND FASTENING IN ITS CAGE THE FLOWERS' COLOUR?	46	POET: 1935	9
A CALLING FOR COLOUR CALLS WITH THE WIND	54	WE BY SEASAND	6
STAINED A BLOOD COLOUR;	59	FAIRY TALES	19
SHALL RAINBOWS BE THEIR TUNICS' COLOUR?	65	GODS THUMP	4
WHAT COLOUR IS GLORY? DEATH'S FEATHER? TREMBLE	104	WORLD PYRAMID	25
WHO BLOWS DEATH'S FEATHER? WHAT GLORY IS COLOUR? ..	105	WORLD PYRAMID	55
WHO GAVE THESE SEAS THEIR COLOUR IN A SHAPE, ...	123	FOSTER LIGHT	25
FROM BLANK AND LEAKING WINTER SAILS THE CHILD IN			
COLOUR, ...	130	SINNERS' BELL	22
ONCE IT WAS THE COLOUR OF SAYING	144	COLOUR OF SAY	T
ONCE IT WAS THE COLOUR OF SAYING	144	COLOUR OF SAY	1
AND THE COLOUR OF CLAY	185	VISION, PRAYER	184
TO THAT STRANGE COLOUR, SIGHING GENTLY, GRIEVES ...	223	IN DREAMS	6
THE YELLOW BIRD TO SHOW HIS COLOUR.	238	MAKES INTERVALS	5
AND SEE YOUR COLOUR SNAP, ...	239	MAKES INTERVALS	18
COLOURED			
DRY AS A TOMB, YOUR COLOURED LIDS	91	WHERE ONCE THE	19
IN TIME AT FLOOD FILLED WITH HIS COLOURED DOUBLES;	124	FOSTER LIGHT	27
'LINGER NOT DEEPER IN THE COLOURED TREES, ...	227	SPRING-SPIRIT	2
COLOURS			
ON THE CANVAS SKY, AND ALL HOT COLOURS MELT	46	POET: 1935	19
AND I HAVE REFLECTED ITS COLOURS IN THE PEACE OF MY			
EYES;	224	IDYLL UNFORGET	24
FIERCE COLOURS FLED ABOUT THE BRANCHES, ...	226	THE OAK	1
COLTS			
WITH SALTY COLTS AND GALES IN THEIR LIMBS	168	LONG-LEGGED	186

	PAGE	TITLE	LINE
COLUMBUS			
COMBING WITH ANTLERS, COLUMBUS ON FIRE, ...	152	BELOW A TIME	37
COLUMN-MEMBERED			
A FURNACE-NOSTRILLED COLUMN-MEMBERED	158	INTO HER HEAD	28
COLUMNS			
HER MOLTEN FLIGHT UP CINDER-NESTING COLUMNS, ...	132	I MAKE THIS IN	26
COMB			
AND COMB THE COUNTY GARDENS FOR A WREATH.	93	BOYS OF SUMMER	42
I'LL COMB THE SNARED WOODS WITH A GLOVE ON A LAMP,	145	IF HEAD HURT	7
NO WAVE COMB THE SEA, ...	233	NO THOUGHT	14
COMBED			
AND THE STREETS THAT THE FISHERMAN COMBED	168	LONG-LEGGED	194
COMBING			
COMBING WITH ANTLERS, COLUMBUS ON FIRE, ...	152	BELOW A TIME	37
COMBS			
COMBS THROUGH THE MANTLED YARDS AND THE MORNING MEN	187	WINTER'S TALE	20
COME			
WHERE TEARS HAVE COME TO DRY.	12	SKY'S BRIGHT	17
AGE COME TO YOU--YOU'RE BRIGHT AND USELESS, ...	21	BEWILDERED WAY	4
COME WISE IN FOOLISHNESS, ...	25	BEAUTY TO DUST	16
WHEN SPRING IS COME, ...	27	OBLIVIOUS DARK	30
OUT OF THE CHAOS WOULD COME BLISS.	31	BEING BUT MEN	13
COMFORT COME THROUGH THE DEVIL'S CLOUDS, ...	35	LIFT UP FACE	11
LET COMFORT COME SLOWLY, LIFT	35	LIFT UP FACE	14
MUST COME CONTENT.	35	LIFT UP FACE	23
CONTENT SHALL COME AFTER A TWISTED NIGHT	35	LIFT UP FACE	25
SO I HAVE COME TO KNOW, BUT KNOWLEDGE ACHES;	64	WOMAN SPEAKS	48
INTANGIBLE MY WORLD SHALL COME TO NAUGHT, ...	73	LORD RED HAIL	16
COME UNTO SEA-STUCK TOWERS, AT THE FIBRE SCALING,	111	I, IN IMAGE	74
ARE FORMED OF FLESH, BUT LET THE FALSE DAY COME ...	116	LANTERNS SHINE	6
OVER THE WATER COME	129	MY NEOPHYTE	27
THEY COME TOGETHER WHOM THEIR LOVE PARTED:	161	WEDDING ANNIV	10
A STRANGER HAS COME	169	LOVE IN ASYLUM	1
SHE HAS COME POSSESSED	170	LOVE IN ASYLUM	10
COME IN THE MORNING WHERE I WANDERED AND LISTENED	177	POEM IN OCT	27
SWARMS ON THE KINGDOM COME	181	VISION, PRAYER	40
FOR I WAS LOST WHO HAVE COME	181	VISION, PRAYER	62
AND WE HAVE COME	184	VISION, PRAYER	158
VALES WHERE HE PRAYED TO COME TO THE LAST HARM	190	WINTER'S TALE	109
IS COME OF THE SEA TUMBLING IN HARNESS	191	REFUSAL MOURN	6
WITH THE DEW, COME BACK, THE COCK ON HIS SHOULDER:			
IT WAS ALL	195	FERN HILL	29
NAKED AND FORSAKEN TO GRIEVE HE WILL NOT COME.	201	COUNTRY SLEEP	106
'COME AND BE KILLED,'	202	SIR JOHNS HILL	22
COME LET US DIE.'	202	SIR JOHNS HILL	32
OF SUMMER COME IN HIS GREAT GOOD TIME	206	LAMENT	32
TO HIS NIMBUS BELL COOL KINGDOM COME	211	POEM ON B'DAY	85
I HAVE COME TO CATCH YOUR VOICE	231	YOUR VOICE	T
I HAVE COME TO CATCH YOUR VOICE, ...	231	YOUR VOICE	1
'I HAVE COME TO ELEVATE YOU, ...	231	OUR SANCTITY	29
THE LIGHT WILL COME IN AN UNWAVERING LINE.	232	YOUR VOICE	7
I HAVE COME TO PLUCK YOU, ...	232	YOUR VOICE	11
COME, YOU ARE TO LOSE YOUR FRESHNESS.	233	NO THOUGHT	20
COME-A-CROPPER			
THE COME-A-CROPPER RIDER OF THE FLOWER.	128	NOW, SAY NAY	28
COMERS			
AND THE SECOND COMERS, THE SEVERERS, THE ENEMIES			
FROM THE DEEP	159	INTO HER HEAD	68
COMES			
THE BLACK SHADOW COMES DOWN, ...	18	NATURAL DAY	21

	PAGE	TITLE	LINE
COMES (CONTINUED)			
STILL COMES VISITING HIS POOR RELATIONS, ...	29	NEARLY SUMMER	2
THE WELCOME DEVIL COMES AS GUEST, ...	30	NEARLY SUMMER	14
THE WELCOME DEVIL COMES INVITED, ...	30	NEARLY SUMMER	19
OUT OF THE SIGHS A LITTLE COMES, ...	31	OUT OF SIGHS	1
A LITTLE COMES, IS TASTED AND FOUND GOOD;	31	OUT OF SIGHS	5
COMES FROM MY EVIL OR MY GOOD. MAD, MAD, ...	53	OUT OF THE PIT	79
THE MESSAGE COMES FROM NEGRO MYSTICS, ...	58	TO ARCHITECTS	7
COMES, LIKE A SCISSORS STALKING, TAILOR AGE, ...	100	RUNNING GRAVE	6
COMES LOVE'S ANATOMIST WITH SUN-GLOVED HAND	132	I MAKE THIS IN	44
WHO COMES AS RED AS THE FOX AND SLY AS THE HEELED			
WIND.	200	COUNTRY SLEEP	81
ROUND THE SUN, HE COMES TO MY LOVE LIKE THE DESIGNED			
SNOW, ...	200	COUNTRY SLEEP	96
COMES DESIGNED TO MY LOVE TO STEAL NOT HER TIDE			
RAKING	200	COUNTRY SLEEP	100
HE COMES TO TAKE	201	COUNTRY SLEEP	103
HE COMES TO LEAVE HER IN THE LAWLESS SUN AWAKING	201	COUNTRY SLEEP	105
MY DEAR THIS NIGHT HE COMES AND NIGHT WITHOUT END MY			
DEAR	201	COUNTRY SLEEP	108
WHEN THE TIME COMES, ...	230	OUR SANCTITY	16
THE KINGFISHER COMES	230	OUR SANCTITY	23
HERE IS THE THOUGHT THAT COMES	233	NO THOUGHT	16
DEATH COMES TO THE BEAUTIFUL.	236	WOMAN TAPESTRY	41
AND WHERE THE LIGHT COMES CAUTIOUSLY	240	ADMIT THE SUN	3
COMET			
SHALL THEY CLASP A COMET IN THEIR FISTS?	56	WHY EAST WIND	11
COMETH			
WHEN COMETH JACK FROST? THE CHILDREN ASK.	56	WHY EAST WIND	10
COMETS			
AND GHOSTLY COMETS OVER THE RAISED FISTS.	56	WHY EAST WIND	26
COMFORT			
COMFORT COME THROUGH THE DEVIL'S CLOUDS, ...	35	LIFT UP FACE	11
LET COMFORT COME SLOWLY, LIFT	35	LIFT UP FACE	14
WHICH CAN COMFORT YOU	228	NOT DESPAIR	5
YOU SHALL COMFORT ME	236	WOMAN TAPESTRY	47
COMIC			
A COMIC HOUR TO AN END THROUGH WANT OF WOMAN	23	THE ONLY DEAD	8
COMING			
UP TO THE SECOND OF THE DARK COMING, ...	25	THERE'S PLENTY	5
FOR FEAR OF COMING	31	BEING BUT MEN	4
THE SNAIL TELLS OF COMING RAIN.	48	POET: 1935	65
OF CHEMIC BLOOD, WARNED OF THE COMING FURY.	99	OCTOBER WIND	31
'IF MY BUNCHED, MONKEY COMING IS CRUEL	145	IF HEAD HURT	11
THE GRAVE AND MY CALM BODY ARE SHUT TO YOUR COMING			
AS STONE, ...	146	IF HEAD HURT	29
BENEATH MY LIFE, THAT SIGHS FOR THE SEDUCER'S COMING	147	UNLUCKILY FOR	13
AND HEARD THE LEWD, WOOED FIELD FLOW TO THE COMING			
FROST, ...	204	GIANT'S THIGH	30
COMMAS			
AND COMMAS ARE THE WORST OF CRIMES;	84	LETTER TO AUNT	35
COMMIT			
IN SEIZURE OF SILENCE COMMIT THE DEAD NUISANCE: ...	109	I, IN IMAGE	23
COMMON			
BY TOE OR HAIR TO COMMON GOOD, ...	24	LITTLE PROBLEM	12
IN COMMON CLAY CLOTHES DISGUISED AS SCALES, ...	151	BELOW A TIME	15
TO THE BOY OF COMMON THREAD, ...	152	BELOW A TIME	41
O KEEP HIS BONES AWAY FROM THAT COMMON CART, ...	173	DAWN RAID	12
NOW COMMON LAZARUS	184	VISION, PRAYER	166
BUT FOR THE COMMON WAGES	197	CRAFT OR ART	10

	PAGE	TITLE	LINE
COMMON (CONTINUED)			
NINEPIN DOWN ON THE DONKEYS' COMMON, ...	206	LAMENT	7
COMMONER			
COMMONER THAN WATER, CRUELLER THAN TRUTH;	152	WAS A SAVIOUR	3
COMMOTION			
WHERE, WHAT? THERE WAS COMMOTION IN THE SKIES, ...	52	OUT OF THE PIT	76
COMMUNAL			
IN COMMUNAL CRAB FLATS	154	RETURN	17
COMMUNION			
IS CELEBRATED THERE, AND COMMUNION BETWEEN SUNS.	148	UNLUCKILY FOR	24
COMPANION			
AND HAVE THE RAVEN FOR COMPANION.	45	PLOUGHMAN GONE	18
AND HAVE THE RAVEN FOR COMPANION.	46	PLOUGHMAN GONE	32
IT IS THE ENGINE FOR COMPANION.	46	PLOUGHMAN GONE	35
BUT ONE COMPANION.	61	MEAT ON BONES	37
COMPANY			
WALKS WITH THE HILLS FOR COMPANY, ...	47	POET: 1935	27
COMPASSION			
A COMPASSION SPRINGING FROM THE DEEP BODY, ...	236	WOMAN TAPESTRY	53
COMPEL			
COMPEL ETERNITY.	240	TWINING HEAD	8
COMPELS			
LIGHT THAT COMPELS	238	MAKES INTERVALS	4
COMPLAIN			
AND SO COMPLAIN, IN A VAIN VOICE, TO THE STARS. ...	47	POET: 1935	21
I AM ALONE, ALONE COMPLAIN TO THE STARS.	48	POET: 1935	62
COMPLETENESS			
WHO HAS COMPLETENESS THAT CAN CUT	23	THE ONLY DEAD	7
COMPOSURE			
INTO MY EXOTIC COMPOSURE?	233	NO THOUGHT	23
COMPRESSED			
FOOT-HEAD COMPRESSED, ...	24	LITTLE PROBLEM	10
CONCEAL			
FEATHERS TO CONCEAL THE VIEW;	83	LETTER TO AUNT	18
CONCEIVE			
CONCEIVE THESE IMAGES IN AIR	19	IMAGES IN AIR	T
CONCEIVE THESE IMAGES IN AIR, ...	19	IMAGES IN AIR	1
CONCEIVING			
UNDER THE CONCEIVING MOON, ON THE HIGH CHALK HILL,	203	GIANT'S THIGH	2
CONCERN			
BUT WE DO NOT CONCERN OURSELVES, ...	231	OUR SANCTITY	26
CONCRETE			
OF CHURCHES MADE FROM ABSTRACT AND CONCRETE.	51	OUT OF THE PIT	28
CONDEMN			
CONDEMN ME TO AN EVERLASTING FACING	68	REALM OF FLESH	14
CONDENSE			
YOUTH DID CONDENSE; THE TEARS OF SPRING	79	LOVE'S FEVER	48
CONFECTION			
AND RAVENS FED CONFECTION TO THEIR YOUNG.	65	WOMAN SPEAKS	59
CONFESSIONAL			
I STAND BENEATH THE CLOUDS' CONFESSIONAL, ...	42	A WAR OF WITS	13
CONFESSOR			
CALLED FOR CONFESSOR BUT THERE WAS NONE	42	A WAR OF WITS	5
CALL FOR CONFESSOR AND WISER MIRROR BUT THERE IS NONE	186	HOLY SPRING	10
CONFUSED			
WHERE WHEELS, CONFUSING MUSIC, CONFUSED DOUBTS, ...	50	OUT OF THE PIT	2
CONFUSING			
WHERE WHEELS, CONFUSING MUSIC, CONFUSED DOUBTS, ...	50	OUT OF THE PIT	2
CONFUSION			
OUT OF CONFUSION, AS THE WAY IS, ...	31	BEING BUT MEN	11

	PAGE	TITLE	LINE
CONFUSION (CONTINUED)			
A SENSITIVE CONFUSION IN THE BLOOD, ...	235	WOMAN TAPESTRY	28
CONGERED			
CURLEWS ALOUD IN THE CONGERED WAVES	209	POEM ON B'DAY	13
CONJURE			
WHOM NOW I CONJURE TO STAND AS THIEF	146	TO OTHERS	9
CONJURED			
AND CONJURED UP A CARCASS SHAPE	98	TWILIGHT LOCKS	35
DUST BE YOUR SAVIOUR UNDER THE CONJURED SOIL.)	110	I, IN IMAGE	60
CONJURED ME TO RESEMBLE	156	RETURN	68
CONSCIENCE			
OUT OF THE BITTER CONSCIENCE AND THE NERVES, ...	20	THE NEOPHYTE	15
CONSCIOUS			
WE WILL BE CONSCIOUS OF OUR SANCTITY	230	OUR SANCTITY	T
WE WILL BE CONSCIOUS OF OUR SANCTITY	230	OUR SANCTITY	1
WE WILL BE CONSCIOUS OF OUR DIVINITY	230	OUR SANCTITY	15
WE WILL BE CONSCIOUS	231	OUR SANCTITY	42
WE WILL BE CONSCIOUS OF A GREAT DIVINITY	231	OUR SANCTITY	45
CONSECRATED			
IMMUTABLE, AND ARDOUROUSLY CONSECRATED;	223	IDYLL UNFORGET	2
CONSOLING			
CONSOLING FOR NIGHT BY DAY	35	LIFT UP FACE	3
CONSTANT			
HER CONSTANT, NOR THE WINDS OF LOVE BROKEN WIDE ...	147	UNLUCKILY FOR	10
CONSTRUCTED			
YOUR CONSTRUCTED NOTES GOING OUT OF THE THROAT	231	YOUR VOICE	2
CONSUMED			
THOUGH WE'RE CONSUMED BY LOVES AND DOUBTS.	27	OBLIVIOUS DARK	26
CONSUMPTIVES'			
ON THE CONSUMPTIVES' TERRACE TAKING THEIR TWO			
FAREWELLS, ...	109	I, IN IMAGE	34
CONTACT			
THE HEMMING CONTACT THAT'S SO TRAMMELLED	20	ENCOMPASSED	6
AND THE CONTACT WITH HER BREASTS	236	WOMAN TAPESTRY	65
CONTAGES			
WITH WHISTLER'S COUGH CONTAGES, TIME ON TRACK	101	RUNNING GRAVE	47
CONTAGION			
AND SWEET SHALL FALL CONTAGION FROM HIS SIDE, ...	73	LORD RED HAIL	5
AND, FOR THAT MURDER'S SAKE, DARK WITH CONTAGION	132	I MAKE THIS IN	37
CONTAGIOUS			
AND POWER WAS CONTAGIOUS IN MY BIRTH, SECOND	103	I DREAMED MY	21
GHOST WITH HER GHOST, CONTAGIOUS MAN	107	ALL ALL AND	26
CONTEMPLATE			
I, POOR ROMANTIC, CONTEMPLATE	12	CABARET	22
CONTEMPLATED			
BIRD ON THE MAST, (HE CONTEMPLATED), ...	238	PILLAR BREAKS	18
CONTENT			
TAKE NOW CONTENT, NO LONGER POSTURING	29	LONG, SKELETON	7
MUST COME CONTENT.	35	LIFT UP FACE	23
CONTENT SHALL COME AFTER A TWISTED NIGHT	35	LIFT UP FACE	25
CALLS SOME CONTENT TO TRAVEL WITH THE WINDS, ...	56	WHY EAST WIND	17
I HEAR CONTENT, AND 'BE CONTENT'	56	WHY EAST WIND	21
I HEAR CONTENT, AND 'BE CONTENT'	56	WHY EAST WIND	21
CONTINENCE			
CONTINENCE. I SEE THE UNFIRED PHOENIX, HERALD	148	UNLUCKILY FOR	37
CONTINENT			
OF ALL ORESTES' CONTINENT OF PRIDE	56	GREEK PLAY	5
AND A CONTINENT DENY?	126	SEED-AT-ZERO	30
AND A CONTINENT DENY?	126	SEED-AT-ZERO	37
IN THE CONTINENT OF A FOSSIL	166	LONG-LEGGED	144

	PAGE	TITLE	LINE
CONTINUAL			
AND THE OLD TERRORS' CONTINUAL CRY	43	LONGED TO MOVE	3
HER LOVE FOR ME IS FIERCE AND CONTINUAL, ...	235	WOMAN TAPESTRY	11
CONTRARIES			
THESE ARE HER CONTRARIES: THE BEAST WHO FOLLOWS ...	131	I MAKE THIS IN	24
CONVENIENT			
CONVENIENT BIRD AND BEAST LIE LODGED TO SUFFER	144	PLEASURE-BIRD	3
CONVENTION			
HALF CONVENTION AND HALF LIE.	44	LONGED TO MOVE	20
CONVERSATION			
THE CONVERSATION OF PRAYER	193	CONVERS PRAYER	T
THE CONVERSATION OF PRAYERS ABOUT TO BE SAID	193	CONVERS PRAYER	1
THE CONVERSATION OF PRAYERS ABOUT TO BE SAID	194	CONVERS PRAYER	13
CONVULSIONS			
THE CONVULSIONS OF YOUR ART, ...	84	LETTER TO AUNT	59
COO			
COO ROOING THE WOODS' PRAISE, ...	4	PROLOGUE	61
COOED			
TIDY AND CURSED IN MY DOVE COOED ROOM	207	LAMENT	52
COOL			
COOL, OH NO COOL	10	COOL, OH NO	T
COOL, OH NO COOL	10	COOL, OH NO	T
COOL, OH NO COOL, ...	10	COOL, OH NO	1
COOL, OH NO COOL, ...	10	COOL, OH NO	1
SHUT IN THE MADHOUSE CALL FOR COOL AIR TO BREATHE.	26	THERE'S PLENTY	13
FEELING THE WIND ABOUT OUR HEADS THAT DOES NOT COOL,	26	THERE'S PLENTY	18
STOPPED NON-STOP DANCING TO LET HOT FEET COOL, ...	51	OUT OF THE PIT	30
AND NO AEGEAN WIND COOL HER CRACKED HEART;	57	GREEK PLAY	10
COOL AS THE WAX-RED FOUNTAINS OF THE VEINS;	63	WOMAN SPEAKS	5
WALKING IN THE EVENING'S COOL	71	TAKE NEEDLES	31
A BRUTE LAND IN THE COOL TOP OF THE COUNTRY DAYS	135	HOW MY ANIMAL	15
NOR WALK IN THE COOL OF YOUR MORTAL GARDEN	148	UNLUCKILY FOR	48
TREES COOL AND DRY IN THE WHIRLPOOL OF SHIPS	167	LONG-LEGGED	170
AND THE MULTITUDE'S SULTRY TEAR TURNS COOL ON THE WEEPING WALL, ...	186	HOLY SPRING	17
COOL IN YOUR VOWS.	199	COUNTRY SLEEP	47
TO HIS NIMBUS BELL COOL KINGDOM COME	211	POEM ON B'DAY	85
COOLED			
CHALK COOLED BY LEAVES IN THE HOT SEASON, ...	29	LONG, SKELETON	3
COOLER			
BUT COOLER WHEN I TAKE IT BACK, ...	10	COOL, OH NO	5
COOLS			
COOLS ANY ARDOUR THEY MAY HAVE	47	POET: 1935	33
WHY EAST WIND CHILLS AND SOUTH WIND COOLS	55	WHY EAST WIND	1
COPPERS			
AND THE HUNT IN THE HATSTAND DISCOVERS NO COPPERS,	38	GAS FADES	2
CORAL			
UNDER A HIDEOUS SEA WHERE CORAL MEN	52	OUT OF THE PIT	68
AND THE FIVE-FATHOMED HAMLET ON HIS FATHER'S CORAL,	111	I, IN IMAGE	83
TIME'S CORAL SAINT AND THE SALT GRIEF DROWN A FOUL SEPULCHRE	130	SINNERS' BELL	8
THE VOICE OF BIRD ON CORAL PRAYS.	130	SINNERS' BELL	18
CORALS			
THERE SHALL BE CORALS IN YOUR BEDS, ...	91	WHERE ONCE THE	22
CORD			
INTO THE TIDED CORD, THERE GOES	91	WHERE ONCE THE	8
CORE			
OR WITH THEIR ORCHARD MAN IN THE CORE OF THE SUN'S BUSH	204	GIANT'S THIGH	24

	PAGE	TITLE	LINE
CORKSCREW			
YOUR CORKSCREW GRAVE CENTRED IN NAVEL AND NIPPLE,	110	I, IN IMAGE	51
CORMORANTS			
WHERE THE CORMORANTS SCUD,	208	POEM ON B'DAY	3
CORN			
THROUGH THE ATLANTIC CORN.	105	WORLD PYRAMID	48
IN HIGH CORN AND THE HARVEST MELTING ON THEIR TONGUES.	188	WINTER'S TALE	43
AND THE SYNAGOGUE OF THE EAR OF CORN	191	REFUSAL MOURN	9
CORNER			
CORNER THE MOUNTED MEADOWS IN THE HILL CORRAL;	109	I, IN IMAGE	39
I TURN THE CORNER OF PRAYER AND BURN	185	VISION, PRAYER	188
CORNER-CAST			
IS CORNER-CAST, BREATH'S RAG, SCRAWLED WEED, A VAIN	131	I MAKE THIS IN	9
CORNERS			
MAKE BRIGHT ITS CORNERS WHERE A SKELETON	49	LIGHT, I KNOW	23
CORPSE			
IS WITH THE CORPSE OF PEACE,	35	LIFT UP FACE	20
SITS BACK AND SMILES, A TINY CORPSE	49	LIGHT, I KNOW	24
SINCE THE FIRST WOMB SPAT FORTH A BABY'S CORPSE,	64	WOMAN SPEAKS	52
CORPSES			
THEN ONLY OVER CORPSES SHALL THE FEET TREAD,	45	TO FOLLOW FOX	20
CORPSE'S			
ALL ALL AND ALL, THE CORPSE'S LOVER,	106	ALL ALL AND	10
CORRAL			
CORNER THE MOUNTED MEADOWS IN THE HILL CORRAL;	109	I, IN IMAGE	39
CORRECT			
A LETTER TO MY AUNT DISCUSSING THE CORRECT APPROACH TO MODERN POETRY	83	LETTER TO AUNT	T
CORRIDOR			
MY HALF GHOST IN ARMOUR HOLD HARD IN DEATH'S CORRIDOR,	108	I, IN IMAGE	5
CORRIDORS			
RING LIKE A HANDBELL THROUGH THE CORRIDORS,	56	WHY EAST WIND	22
CORROSIVE			
CORROSIVE SPRING OUT OF THE ICEBERG'S CROP,	104	WORLD PYRAMID	8
CORRUPTED			
LEAVING A CORRUPTED VEIN OF COLOUR,	27	OBLIVIOUS DARK	16
CORRUPTING			
AND MY CORRUPTING KNOWLEDGE--	18	NATURAL DAY	30
CORSET			
CORSET THE BONEYARDS FOR A CROOKED BOY?	118	ALTARWISE	50
COST			
FOR WHEN I BOUGHT YOU FOR A THOUGHT, (YOU COST NO MORE)	10	COOL, OH NO	8
COSTLY			
INTO A COSTLY COUNTRY, THE GRAVES	43	FACES SHONE	5
HEIR TO THE SCALDING VEINS THAT HOLD LOVE'S DROP, COSTLY	103	I DREAMED MY	9
COTTON			
AT COTTON WORLDS REVOLVING ON A HIP,	51	OUT OF THE PIT	46
THE CLOUD PERCHED TAILORS' MASTER WITH NERVES FOR COTTON.	152	BELOW A TIME	35
COUCH			
HAS A VOICE AND A HOUSE, AND THERE AND HERE YOU MUST COUCH AND CRY.	146	IF HEAD HURT	25
TO A HAYCOCK COUCH AND THE SCYTHES OF HIS ARMS	157	INTO HER HEAD	17
COUGH			
HEARING THE RAVEN COUGH IN WINTER STICKS,	98	OCTOBER WIND	6
WITH WHISTLER'S COUGH CONTAGES, TIME ON TRACK	101	RUNNING GRAVE	47

	PAGE	TITLE	LINE
COUGH (CONTINUED)			
HACK OF THE COUGH, THE HANGING ALBATROSS, ...	107	GRIEF THIEF	10
THE WOUND-DOWN COUGH OF THE BLOOD-COUNTING CLOCK	141	SAINT TO FALL	9
COULD			
I COULD DEVOTE TO OTHER THINGS.	9	MINUTE'S HOUR	22
HOW COULD I SMOOTH THAT SKIN	10	COOL, OH NO	9
KNOWING A DREAM COULD DARKEN IT, ...	10	COOL, OH NO	10
HOW KISS, WHEN DOLL COULD SAY	10	COOL, OH NO	13
FOR, IF I COULD, I'D FLY AWAY, ...	21	BEWILDERED WAY	22
FOR IF I COULD, I'D FLY AWAY	21	BEWILDERED WAY	23
ALL COULD NOT DISAPPOINT;	32	OUT OF SIGHS	6
THE HOLLOW WORDS COULD BEAR ALL SUFFERING	32	OUT OF SIGHS	22
IN CHILDREN'S CIRCUSES COULD STAY THEIR TROUBLES?	40	WAS THERE TIME	2
THERE WAS A TIME THEY COULD CRY OVER BOOKS, ...	40	WAS THERE TIME	3
WE HAVE GROWN WEAK BEFORE WE COULD GROW STRONG, ...	40	YOUNG ARE OLD	7
HE, TOO, COULD TOUCH THE SEASON'S LIPS AND SMILE,	46	POET: 1935	14
HE COULD HEAR WOMEN BREATHING IN THE DARK, ...	51	OUT OF THE PIT	20
COULD IN A DAY BE SICK WITH SO MUCH BLOOD;	63	WOMAN SPEAKS	13
FOR YOU COULD THEN WRITE WHAT YOU PLEASE, ...	84	LETTER TO AUNT	31
THE SEA OF SCUMS COULD DROWN ME AS IT BROKE	95	RUB OF LOVE	27
IN SACRED WATERS THAT NO FROST COULD HARDEN, ...	122	INCARNATE DEVL	14
'WHO COULD SNAP OFF THE SHAPELESS PRINT	129	MY NEOPHYTE	40
WHO COULD HACK OUT YOUR UNSUCKED HEART, ...	129	MY NEOPHYTE	46
THAN ONE COULD PROBE OUT OF A SERPENT'S GUTS;	137	O CHATTERTON	7
BRANDED FOREHEAD, THAT COULD BIND	147	UNLUCKILY FOR	9
ALL I COULD SEE WERE HIS BROWN EYES BURNING	149	PAPER & STICKS	8
O YOU WHO COULD NOT CRY	153	WAS A SAVIOUR	20
O WE WHO COULD NOT STIR	153	WAS A SAVIOUR	28
NOR COULD SHARE, FOR HIS PRIDE, TO THE LEAST	158	INTO HER HEAD	44
THERE COULD I MARVEL	178	POEM IN OCT	38
AND THERE COULD I MARVEL MY BIRTHDAY	178	POEM IN OCT	61
THE WHOLE OF THE MOON I COULD LOVE AND LEAVE	206	LAMENT	10
WHEN I WAS A MAN YOU COULD CALL A MAN	206	LAMENT	25
BLIND EYES COULD BLAZE LIKE METEORS AND BE GAY, ...	208	NOT GO GENTLE	14
ON THAT DARKEST DAY. OH, HE COULD HIDE	217	ELEGY	38
UNTIL YOU COULD BEAR IT NO LONGER	232	FURIOUS MOTION	12
COULD NEVER TOUCH YOUR SPINNING NOTES, ...	234	NO, PIGEON	9
TO TELL WHAT NOTE I COULD REACH IF I TRIED, ...	234	NO, PIGEON	12
COUNT			
WHO CANNOT COUNT THE SEEDS HE SOWS, ...	29	NEARLY SUMMER	8
COUNT THE ENDLESS DAYS UNTIL THEY END, ...	32	HELD-OUT HAND	2
WHY COUNT SO SADLY?	33	HELD-OUT HAND	6
I'VE SAID MY PIECE: COUNT OR GO MAD.	33	HELD-OUT HAND	17
TO KEEP COUNT OF THE STILES	33	HELD-OUT HAND	21
IN THOSE HIGH GLOBES I CANNOT COUNT, ...	49	LIGHT, I KNOW	19
WHAT SHALL DESTRUCTION COUNT IF THESE ARE FIXTURES?	60	FAIRY TALES	27
THE FIVE KINGS COUNT THE DEAD BUT DO NOT SOFTEN ...	66	HAND SIGNED	13
AND COUNT THE TAKEN, FORSAKEN MYSTERIES IN A BAD			
DARK.	140	NO WORK WORDS	9
AND COUNT BY BIRDS' EGGS AND LEAVES	157	RETURN	97
COUNT MY BLESSINGS ALOUD:	211	POEM ON B'DAY	81
COUNTED			
WHEN I WAS SEVEN I COUNTED FOUR AND FORTY TREES ...	33	HELD-OUT HAND	12
WHO'D RAISE THE ORGANS OF THE COUNTED DUST	160	DEATHS AND ENT	7
THE CURELESS COUNTED BODY, ...	186	HOLY SPRING	4
COUNTENANCE			
SHAPED IN OLD ARMOUR AND OAK THE COUNTENANCE OF A			
DUNCE	133	MAKE ME A MASK	7

	PAGE	TITLE	LINE
COUNTIES			
AND OVER THE CLOTH OF COUNTIES THE FAR HILLS RODE NEAR, ...	190	WINTER'S TALE	93
COUNTING			
BLESSING AND COUNTING THE BUSTLING	156	RETURN	73
COUNTING THE DENIALS OF THE GRAINS	167	LONG-LEGGED	160
COUNTRIES			
NOW IN THE CLOUD'S BIG BREAST LIE QUIET COUNTRIES,	133	I MAKE THIS IN	61
IN ALL LOVE'S COUNTRIES, THAT WILL GROPE AWAKE; ...	139	FIVE & COUNTRY	12
WHO ONCE, GREEN COUNTRIES SINCE, WERE A HEDGEROW OF JOYS.	204	GIANT'S THIGH	20
TO HAVE SEEN COUNTRIES WHICH WERE GLORIOUS, ...	223	IDYLL UNFORGET	1
THESE COUNTRIES I HAVE NOT VISIONED, ...	223	IDYLL UNFORGET	13
COUNTRY			
INTO A COSTLY COUNTRY, THE GRAVES	43	FACES SHONE	5
DUST IN THE LITTLE COUNTRY OF AN URN, ...	56	GREEK PLAY	6
DOUBLED THE GLOBE OF DEAD AND HALVED A COUNTRY; ...	66	HAND SIGNED	3
IN THE COUNTRY OF THE DEAD	72	TAKE NEEDLES	46
STRIDE THROUGH CADAVER'S COUNTRY IN MY FORCE, ...	100	RUNNING GRAVE	21
THEY CLIMB THE COUNTRY PINNACLE, ...	109	I, IN IMAGE	37
CHILD OF THE SHORT SPARK IN A SHAPELESS COUNTRY ...	117	ALTARWISE	19
COUNTRY, YOUR SPORT IS SUMMER, AND DECEMBER'S POOLS	122	HOLD HARD	7
HOLD HARD, MY COUNTRY CHILDREN IN THE WORLD OF TALES,	122	HOLD HARD	10
BUT GRAFT THESE FOUR-FRUITED RIDINGS ON YOUR COUNTRY;	123	FOSTER LIGHT	9
A BRUTE LAND IN THE COOL TOP OF THE COUNTRY DAYS	135	HOW MY ANIMAL	15
WHEN ALL MY FIVE AND COUNTRY SENSES SEE	138	FIVE & COUNTRY	T
WHEN ALL MY FIVE AND COUNTRY SENSES SEE, ...	138	FIVE & COUNTRY	1
A COUNTRY POT, HIS HUTCH IN	154	RETURN	3
THE COUNTRY TIDE IS COBBLED WITH TOWNS, ...	168	LONG-LEGGED	192
OF THE DEATH IN A BED IN ANOTHER COUNTRY.	176	MY BEGGAR ARM	8
IT TURNED AWAY FROM THE BLITHE COUNTRY	178	POEM IN OCT	41
STAR AND COUNTRY TO THE LEGION	184	VISION, PRAYER	154
FOR THE COUNTRY OF DEATH IS THE HEART'S SIZE	184	VISION, PRAYER	169
IN THE BLINDING COUNTRY OF YOUTH, ...	192	SIDE OF TRUTH	4
IN COUNTRY SLEEP	197	COUNTRY SLEEP	T
AND FLOWER OF COUNTRY SLEEP AND THE GREENWOOD KEEP.	198	COUNTRY SLEEP	18
THE COUNTRY IS HOLY: O BIDE IN THAT COUNTRY KIND,	198	COUNTRY SLEEP	39
THE COUNTRY IS HOLY: O BIDE IN THAT COUNTRY KIND,	198	COUNTRY SLEEP	39
AND YOU SHALL WAKE, FROM COUNTRY SLEEP, THIS DAWN AND EACH FIRST DAWN, ...	201	COUNTRY SLEEP	110
IN COUNTRY HEAVEN	215	COUNTRY HEAVEN	T
ALWAYS WHEN HE, IN COUNTRY HEAVEN, ...	215	COUNTRY HEAVEN	1
FROM THE COUNTRY EYES, SALT AND SUN, STAR AND WOE	215	COUNTRY HEAVEN	13
OF A NEW COUNTRY	231	OUR SANCTITY	43
COUNTRY-HANDED			
THE COUNTRY-HANDED GRAVE BOXED INTO LOVE, ...	115	A GRIEF AGO	31
COUNTRYMAN'S			
THE COUNTRYMAN'S RETURN	154	RETURN	T
THE COUNTRYMAN'S RETURN	157	RETURN	96
COUNTRY'S			
A COUNTRY'S TEARS AND VOICED A WORLD'S DESPAIR	57	GREEK PLAY	18
COUNTS			
COUNTS ON HIS FIST	30	NEARLY SUMMER	17
COUNTY			
AND COMB THE COUNTY GARDENS FOR A WREATH.	93	BOYS OF SUMMER	42
TIME, IN A FOLLY'S RIDER, LIKE A COUNTY MAN	122	HOLD HARD	4
HOLD HARD, MY COUNTY DARLINGS, FOR A HAWK DESCENDS,	123	HOLD HARD	22
COUPLE			
ALL ALL AND ALL THE DRY WORLDS COUPLE, ...	107	ALL ALL AND	25

	PAGE	TITLE	LINE
COUPLED			
O LIGHT IN ZENITH, THE COUPLED BUD,	107	ALL ALL AND	32
COURAGE			
TAKE COURAGE, AUNT, AND SEND YOUR STUFF	85	LETTER TO AUNT	63
COURSE			
LOST IN THE SHADES, NO COURSE, NO USE	41	YOUNG ARE OLD	22
PLUNGING AND PIERCING IN HIS COURSE	163	LONG-LEGGED	46
THERE ARE FEWER, OF COURSE, WHO INSIST THAT A HORSE	221	SONG OF DOG	5
COURSING			
COURSING ALONG THE CHANNELS	17	IN OBLIVION	10
THAT OTHER SUN, THE JEALOUS COURSING OF THE UNRIVALLED BLOOD.	170	MARRIAGE VIRG	14
COURT			
TO COURT THE HONEYED HEART FROM YOUR SIDE BEFORE SUNRISE	198	COUNTRY SLEEP	13
COURTERS'			
IN THE COURTERS' LANES, OR TWINED IN THE OX ROASTING SUN	203	GIANT'S THIGH	13
LOVE FOR EVER MERIDIAN THROUGH THE COURTERS' TREES	205	GIANT'S THIGH	59
COVER			
RAIN SHALL DEFILE AND COVER, WIND BEAR AWAY	64	WOMAN SPEAKS	40
COVERED			
THE CATTLE GRAZE ON THE COVERED FOAM,	168	LONG-LEGGED	183
COVERING			
THE COVERING SEA THEIR NIGHTFALL WITH NO NAMES;	158	INTO HER HEAD	50
AND COVERING ALL HAS BEEN A QUIETUDE, AND A SINGING FROM FLAKE-BARE THROATS.	224	IDYLL UNFORGET	35
THE THICK HIDE COVERING,	233	NO THOUGHT	10
COVERINGS			
THE COVERINGS OF DARK AND LIGHT,	37	WINDMILLS TURN	28
COVERS			
THE GRASS HE COVERS IS A PRETTY GREEN;	63	WOMAN SPEAKS	19
COWARDS			
TORN OUT MAGIC FROM THE HEARTS OF COWARDS	60	FAIRY TALES	32
COWL			
FLOCKED WITH THE SHEEP WHITE SMOKE OF THE FARM HOUSE COWL	187	WINTER'S TALE	9
COWPATCHED			
IN A HUTCH IN A COWPATCHED GLEN	156	RETURN	94
COWS'			
ROUGH AS COWS' TONGUES AND THRASHED WITH BRAMBLES THEIR BUTTERMILK	204	GIANT'S THIGH	25
CRAB			
AND CAST A SHADOW CRAB UPON THE LAND,	98	OCTOBER WIND	4
IN COMMUNAL CRAB FLATS	154	RETURN	17
CRAB-BACKED			
FOR THE CRAB-BACKED DEAD ON THE SEA-BED ROSE	165	LONG-LEGGED	99
CRABBED			
SHAKES, IN CRABBED BURIAL SHAWL, BY SORCERER'S INSECT WOKEN,	130	SINNERS' BELL	23
CLAW OF THE CRABBED VEINS SQUEEZE FROM EACH RED PARTICLE	135	HOW MY ANIMAL	21
CRABBING			
CAUGHT BY THE CRABBING SUN I WALK ON FIRE	98	OCTOBER WIND	3
CRABS			
TIME AND THE CRABS AND THE SWEETHEARTING CRIB	95	RUB OF LOVE	25
CRACK			
BUT THE STONES CRACK IT	18	NATURAL DAY	15
SPLIT ALL ENDS UP THEY SHAN'T CRACK;	50	NO DOMINION	17
BULL'S-EYE THE OUTLAW THROUGH A EUNUCH CRACK	108	GRIEF THIEF	19

	PAGE	TITLE	LINE
CRACK (CONTINUED)			
CRACK LIKE A SPRING IN A VICE, BONE BREAKING APRIL,	122	HOLD HARD	17
FLASH, AND THE PLUMES CRACK,	201	SIR JOHNS HILL	13
CRACKED			
AND NO AEGEAN WIND COOL HER CRACKED HEART;	57	GREEK PLAY	10
AND MY HEART IS CRACKED ACROSS;	61	MEAT ON BONES	18
ABADDON IN THE HANGNAIL CRACKED FROM ADAM,	116	ALTARWISE	3
GLORY CRACKED LIKE A FLEA.	141	SAINT TO FALL	18
CRACKLING			
AND, CRACKLING INTO THE AIR, LEAVE ME HALF-BLIND.	44	LONGED TO MOVE	14
CRACKS			
BUT THE SUN CRACKS IT	18	NATURAL DAY	14
UP THROUGH THE FINGERS' CRACKS;	86	SEE, SAYS LIME	29
CRADLE			
I, IN A WIND ON FIRE, FROM GREEN ADAM'S CRADLE,	111	I, IN IMAGE	95
SCRAPED AT MY CRADLE IN A WALKING WORD	117	ALTARWISE	11
SOON SETS ALIGHT A LONG STICK FROM THE CRADLE;	117	ALTARWISE	20
AND, RIP VAN WINKLE FROM A TIMELESS CRADLE,	118	ALTARWISE	37
INHUMAN CRADLE AND THE BRIDE BED FOREVER SOUGHT	188	WINTER'S TALE	49
CRADLE-PETALS			
TO THE VOICES OF THE WIND CAUGHT IN THE CRADLE-PETALS OF THE NIGHT:	223	IDYLL UNFORGET	8
CRADLE'S			
NO CRADLE'S WARMER THAN THIS PERISHED BREAST,	63	WOMAN SPEAKS	6
CRAFT			
I BITTERLY TAKE TO TASK MY POVERTY AND CRAFT:	140	NO WORK WORDS	3
IN MY CRAFT OR SULLEN ART	196	CRAFT OR ART	T
IN MY CRAFT OR SULLEN ART	196	CRAFT OR ART	1
NOR HEED MY CRAFT OR ART.	197	CRAFT OR ART	20
CRAGS			
AND DRINK IN THE TWO MILKED CRAGS,	60	MEAT ON BONES	2
CRAMP			
A MUSCLING LIFE FROM LOVERS IN THEIR CRAMP,	92	BOYS OF SUMMER	33
LIE WITH RELIGION IN THEIR CRAMP, HER THREADBARE	137	AFTER FUNERAL	32
A CRUDE, UNHAPPY, ANAL CRAMP.	143	THE MOLLS	8
CRAMPED			
THE FINGER JOINTS ARE CRAMPED WITH CHALK;	66	HAND SIGNED	6
CRANE			
BY CRANE AND WATER-TOWER BY THE SEEDY TREES	122	HOLD HARD	8
CRANES			
THE SPIRE CRANES	15	SPIRE CRANES	T
THE SPIRE CRANES. ITS STATUE IS AN AVIARY.	15	SPIRE CRANES	1
AND WHARVES OF WATER WHERE THE WALLS DANCE AND THE WHITE CRANES STILT.	202	SIR JOHNS HILL	39
CRANING			
ALIVE WITHIN HIS CRANING THROAT--	14	FOR LEDA	7
THOSE CRANING BIRDS ARE CHOICE FOR YOU, SONGS THAT JUMP BACK	16	SPIRE CRANES	9
CRANNIES			
DUMB DEAD THE CRANNIES HOUSE AND HIDE.	67	REALM OF FLESH	6
CRANNY			
AND CATCH A TURNIP GHOST IN EVERY CRANNY.	48	LIGHT, I KNOW	5
CRASHES			
CRASHES, AND SLOWLY THE FISHING HOLY STALKING HERON	201	SIR JOHNS HILL	11
CRATER			
CARTOON OF SLASHES ON THE TIDE-TRACED CRATER,	119	ALTARWISE	71
FROM EVERY TRUE OR CRATER	161	WEDDING ANNIV	7
CRATERS			
AND THE CRATERS OF HIS EYES GREW SPRINGSHOOTS AND FIRE	172	DAWN RAID	7

	PAGE	TITLE	LINE
CRAWLING			
THIS LILY CRAWLING ROUND THE LOCAL PUBS?	52	OUT OF THE PIT	50
ROARING, CRAWLING, QUARREL	134	HOW MY ANIMAL	8
CRAWLS			
GRIEF THIEF OF TIME CRAWLS OFF,	107	GRIEF THIEF	1
AND THROUGH THE SUNDERED WATER CRAWLS	167	LONG-LEGGED	166
CRAZY			
ACROSS THE SUN WAS SPREAD A CRAZY SMILE.	50	OUT OF THE PIT	11
WHERE, WHAT'S MY GOD AMONG THIS CRAZY RATTLING	51	OUT OF THE PIT	33
CREAM			
SWEEP AWAY LIKE A CREAM CLOUD;	156	RETURN	89
CREASING			
OFF FROM THE CREASING FLESH, FILED	102	I DREAMED MY	6
CREATE			
FOR A LAZY SAKE THAT WON'T CREATE	24	LITTLE PROBLEM	23
CREATE THIS TWIN MIRACLE.	109	I, IN IMAGE	18
CREATED			
CREATED SOMETHING VERY NEW,	83	LETTER TO AUNT	24
CREATION			
BUT YOU SHALL NOT GO FROM ME, CREATION;	10	COOL, OH NO	19
CREATURE			
THE CREATURE WITH THE ANGEL'S FACE	12	SKY'S BRIGHT	12
AND TIME CAST FORTH MY MORTAL CREATURE	69	BEFORE KNOCKED	31
I SENT MY CREATURE SCOUTING ON THE GLOBE,	97	TWILIGHT LOCKS	9
A CREATURE IN MY BONES I	103	I DREAMED MY	10
WERE ONCE SUCH A CREATURE, SO GAY AND FRANK	147	TO OTHERS	14
CREATURES			
OF MEN AND CREATURES HORRIBLY	35	LIFT UP FACE	8
CREDULITY			
SEWING A LIE TO A CREDULITY,	18	NATURAL DAY	11
CREEP			
CREEP AND HARP ON THE TIDE, SINKING THEIR CHARMED, BENT PIN	135	HOW MY ANIMAL	24
CREEPING			
CREEPING CATLIKE UNDER THE WATER.	231	OUR SANCTITY	41
CREEPS			
OH, TIME ENOUGH WHEN THE BLOOD CREEPS COLD,	206	LAMENT	34
CREST			
MOUNTAINS AND GALLERIES TO THE CREST!	166	LONG-LEGGED	132
HE WEPT FROM THE CREST OF GRIEF, HE PRAYED TO THE VEILED SKY	188	WINTER'S TALE	32
CRESTED			
IS A BURNING AND CRESTED ACT,	3	PROLOGUE	25
CREVICES			
INTO THE PLACES AND THE CREVICES	34	THIRST PARCHES	9
CRIB			
TIME AND THE CRABS AND THE SWEETHEARTING CRIB	95	RUB OF LOVE	25
CRIED			
OF KNIVES ON FORKS, HE CRIED, OF NERVE ON NERVE,	51	OUT OF THE PIT	34
GRIEF, LIKE AN OPEN WOUND, HAS CRIED TO HEAVEN.	64	WOMAN SPEAKS	32
THE LOINS CRIED MURDER.	85	SEE, SAYS LIME	16
CRIED THE TOPLESS, INCHTAPED LIPS FROM HANK AND HOOD	132	I MAKE THIS IN	47
SHE CRIED HER WHITE-DRESSED LIMBS WERE BARE	139	TOMBSTONE TOLD	17
ALWAYS GOOD-BYE, CRIED THE VOICES THROUGH THE SHELL,	166	LONG-LEGGED	121
DELIVER HIM, HE CRIED,	188	WINTER'S TALE	51
THE RUDE OWL CRIED LIKE A TELLTALE TIT,	206	LAMENT	5
AND THE SIZZLING BEDS OF THE TOWN CRIED, QUICK!--	206	LAMENT	20
EVEN AS A BABY HE HAD NEVER CRIED;	217	ELEGY	26
HE CRIED AS HE DIED, FEARING AT LAST THE SPHERES'	217	ELEGY	33

	PAGE	TITLE	LINE
CRIER			
AND HEAVEN CRIER, ARROW NOW OF ASPIRING	148	UNLUCKILY FOR	38
CRIERS			
THE CRIERS OF SHABBY AND SHORTEN,	151	BELOW A TIME	27
CRIES			
THE SEASONS' CRIES, FULL OF HIS INTIMATIONS.	29	NEARLY SUMMER	6
'WHAT HAVE YOU FOUND,' HE CRIES, 'WHAT HAVE YOU SOUGHT?'	30	YOUTH CALLS	14
FORGETS, AND CRIES;	31	OUT OF SIGHS	4
NOISELESSLY INTO A WORLD OF WINGS AND CRIES.	31	BEING BUT MEN	5
CRIES NOT ALOUD BLIND AS A BAT,	54	NO MAN BELIEVE	2
CRIES NOT IN TERROR WHEN A BIRD IS DRAWN	54	NO MAN BELIEVE	3
NO MAN BELIEVES WHO CRIES NOT, GOD IS NOT,	55	NO MAN BELIEVE	7
THAT CRIES ALONG HER VEINS. NO SUN OR MOON	56	GREEK PLAY	8
I WOULD ENFORCE THE BLACK APPARELLED CRIES,	96	TWELVE	5
THE OLD FORGET THE CRIES,	107	GRIEF THIEF	5
THE WOMB-EYED, CRIES,	114	SERVANT SUN	32
CAVES THE CRIES OF THE PARCHS AND THEIR FLOCKS. I	179	NEW QUAY	17
CRIME			
WHOSE LOVING CRIME	26	PERSONAL EPIT	8
DO YOU NOT SISTER ME, NOR THE ERECTED CRIME	112	NOT FATHER ME	5
CRIMES			
AND COMMAS ARE THE WORST OF CRIMES;	84	LETTER TO AUNT	35
CRIMSON			
MAY THE CRIMSON	185	VISION, PRAYER	182
CRIPPLE			
THE BROKEN HALVES ARE FELLOWED IN A CRIPPLE,	104	WORLD PYRAMID	13
CRIPPLED			
THE WHOLE, THE CRIPPLED, THE WEAK AND STRONG,	41	YOUNG ARE OLD	43
AND WORDS FALL CRIPPLED FROM THE SLAVING LIPS,	96	TWELVE	2
CRISS-CROSS			
LEAP OVER TO MY CRISS-CROSS RHYTHMS.	33	HELD-OUT HAND	23
CROCKED			
HEAVEN FELL WITH HIS FALL AND ONE CROCKED BELL BEAT THE LEFT AIR.	142	SAINT TO FALL	25
CROCODILE			
NO MAN MORE MAGICAL, CLAWED OUT THE CROCODILE.	111	I, IN IMAGE	96
A CROCODILE BEFORE THE CHRYSALIS,	124	TODAY, INSECT	14
CROCUS			
AN IMAGE OF DECAY DISTURBS THE CROCUS	47	POET: 1935	29
CROOK			
NOW JACK MY FATHERS LET THE TIME-FACED CROOK,	108	GRIEF THIEF	15
CROOKED			
AND I AM DUMB TO TELL THE CROOKED ROSE	77	THE FORCE THAT	4
HOW AT MY SHEET GOES THE SAME CROOKED WORM.	77	THE FORCE THAT	22
CORSET THE BONEYARDS FOR A CROOKED BOY?	118	ALTARWISE	50
IN A FIERCELY MOURNING HOUSE IN A CROOKED YEAR.	136	AFTER FUNERAL	30
STRAIGHT AND TALL FROM HIS CROOKED BONES	172	THE HUNCHBACK	34
CROP			
CORROSIVE SPRING OUT OF THE ICEBERG'S CROP,	104	WORLD PYRAMID	8
CROPS			
WHOM CANCER CROPS, WHOSE DRINKING RUSTS, THESE DIE;	64	WOMAN SPEAKS	43
LAID THE CROPS LOW, BROKE THE GRAPE'S JOY.	86	BREAD I BREAK	5
CROSS			
WITH THEIR FISHWIFE CROSS	3	PROLOGUE	10
CROSS ALL DIRECTIONS, BRACKEN POINTS TO THE SKIES,	44	TO FOLLOW FOX	9
AND FLESH WAS SNIPPED TO CROSS THE LINES	68	BEFORE KNOCKED	22
YOU WHO BOW DOWN AT CROSS AND ALTAR,	69	BEFORE KNOCKED	43
A CROSS IS TATOOED ON THE BREAST OF THE CHILD,	74	SUN BURNS	12
IN SPRING WE CROSS OUR FOREHEADS WITH THE HOLLY,	93	BOYS OF SUMMER	43

		PAGE	TITLE	LINE
CROSS (CONTINUED)				
O SEE THE POLES ARE KISSING AS THEY CROSS.	....	93	BOYS OF SUMMER	54
ADD ONE MORE NAIL OF PRAISE ON TO THE CROSS,	....	96	TWELVE	7
LIT ON THE CUDDLED TREE, THE CROSS OF FEVER,	....	100	RUNNING GRAVE	33
SO CROSS HER HAND WITH THEIR GRAVE GIPSY EYES,	....	115	A GRIEF AGO	39
BLACK AS THE BEAST AND PALER THAN THE CROSS.	....	121	INCARNATE DEVL	12
MY CROSS OF TALES BEHIND THE FABULOUS CURTAIN.'	...	125	TODAY, INSECT	26
WHEN YOU SEW THE DEEP DOOR. THE BED IS A CROSS PLACE.		145	IF HEAD HURT	13
BIRDS AND CLOCKS AND CROSS BELLS	....	150	WHEN I WOKE	2
MIGHT CROSS ITS PLANETS, THE BELL WEEP, NIGHT GATHER HER EYES,	....	200	COUNTRY SLEEP	92
GRAVE, AFTER BELOVED ON THE GRASS GULFED CROSS IS SCRUBBED	....	205	GIANT'S THIGH	54
AND THE BLACK CROSS OF THE HOLY HOUSE,	....	206	LAMENT	26
THE SAVIOUR OF THE CROSS WHO CAN	....	240	TWINING HEAD	7
CROSS-BONED				
NOR WHEN MY LOVE LIES IN THE CROSS-BONED DRIFT	....	123	FOSTER LIGHT	22
CROSS-BONES				
THE HORIZONTAL CROSS-BONES OF ABADDON,	....	117	ALTARWISE	21
CROSSED				
NOR THE CROSSED STICKS OF WAR.	....	95	RUB OF LOVE	14
OF DAY, IN THE THISTLE AISLES, TILL THE WHITE OWL CROSSED	....	204	GIANT'S THIGH	32
HE LIE LIGHTLY, AT LAST, ON THE LAST, CROSSED	.....	216	ELEGY	5
CROSSES				
OF GALLOW CROSSES ON THE LIVER	....	68	BEFORE KNOCKED	23
CROSSES THE BREAST OF THE PRAISING EAST, AND KNEELS,		215	COUNTRY HEAVEN	3
CROSSING				
MY GRAVE IS WATERED BY THE CROSSING JORDAN.	....	105	WORLD PYRAMID	43
BLESS HER BENT SPIRIT WITH FOUR, CROSSING BIRDS.		136	AFTER FUNERAL	26
CROSSLY				
CROSSLY OUT OF THE TOWN NOISES	....	150	WHEN I WOKE	24
CROSS-STROKED				
CROSS-STROKED SALT ADAM TO THE FROZEN ANGEL	....	119	ALTARWISE	67
CROSSTREE				
THE BLOOD THAT TOUCHED THE CROSSTREE AND THE GRAIL		94	IN BEGINNING	11
CROTCH				
OF THE CROTCH OF THE SQUAWKING SHORES,	....	142	SAINT TO FALL	27
AND GUILTS, GREAT CROTCH AND GIANT	....	148	UNLUCKILY FOR	36
CROUCH				
BEFORE I RUSH IN A CROUCH THE GHOST WITH A HAMMER, AIR,	....	145	IF HEAD HURT	9
CROUCHED				
IN THE GROIN OF THE NATURAL DOORWAY I CROUCHED LIKE A TAILOR	....	143	24 YEARS	3
CROUCHED BARE	....	182	VISION, PRAYER	70
WHO SLAVES TO HIS CROUCHED, ETERNAL END	....	209	POEM ON B'DAY	31
CROUCHING				
I PRAYED IN THE CROUCHING ROOM, BY HIS BLIND BED,		216	ELEGY	13
CROW				
OUT THERE, CROW BLACK, MEN	....	3	PROLOGUE	12
AND THE TRIUMPHANT CROW OF LAUGHTER.	....	48	POET: 1935	52
AND THIS, NOR THIS, IS SHADE, THE LANDED CROW,	....	127	NOW, SAY NAY	19
AND OPIUM HEAD, CROW STALK, PUFFED, CUT, AND BLOWN,		131	I MAKE THIS IN	10
ROOSTS SLEEPING CHILL TILL THE FLAME OF THE COCK CROW		187	WINTER'S TALE	19
CROWD				
NOBLE AMONG A CROWD OF LIGHTS.	....	21	BEWILDERED WAY	12
DINNED ASIDE THE COILING CROWD,	....	150	WHEN I WOKE	3
CROWDED				
AND DUSK IS CROWDED WITH THE CHILDREN'S GHOSTS,	...	56	WHY EAST WIND	14

		PAGE	TITLE	LINE
CROWDS				
CRYING SUCH WORDS, HE LEFT THE CRYING CROWDS,	.....	53	OUT OF THE PIT	82
I SEE HIM IN THE CROWDS, NOT SHUT	....	53	OUT OF THE PIT	102
CROWED				
ROSE AND CROWED AND FELL!	....	163	LONG-LEGGED	60
CROWING				
CROWING TO LAZARUS THE MORNING IS VANITY,	....	110	I, IN IMAGE	59
BEFORE THE CROWING MORNING CLIMBED;	....	157	INTO HER HEAD	19
CROWN				
BY HIS TORRID CROWN	....	180	VISION, PRAYER	30
ON THE MOUNTAIN CROWN	....	184	VISION, PRAYER	148
CROW'S-FOOT				
THAT WIPES AWAY NOT CROW'S-FOOT NOR THE LOCK	......	95	RUB OF LOVE	23
CRUCIFIXION				
THIS WAS THE CRUCIFIXION ON THE MOUNTAIN,	....	120	ALTARWISE	99
CRUDE				
A CRUDE, UNHAPPY, ANAL CRAMP.	....	143	THE MOLLS	8
CRUEL				
IN QUICK, SWEET, CRUEL LIGHT TILL THE LOCKED GROUND				
SPROUT OUT,	....	135	HOW MY ANIMAL	18
'IF MY BUNCHED, MONKEY COMING IS CRUEL	....	145	IF HEAD HURT	11
OLD IN HER CRUEL BED.	....	164	LONG-LEGGED	84
CRUELLER				
COMMONER THAN WATER, CRUELLER THAN TRUTH;	....	152	WAS A SAVIOUR	3
CRUELTY				
AND THE CRUELTY OF MY SUBTLE EYES,	....	236	WOMAN TAPESTRY	37
CRUMB				
THAT MEN MIGHT SEE THE DEVIL IN THE CRUMB	....	96	TWELVE	13
WIPE IT AWAY, WIPE A CRUMB	....	138	O CHATTERTON	38
CRUMBLE				
CRUMBLE AND UNDIE	....	3	PROLOGUE	32
IT WOULD CRUMBLE;	....	225	CLOWN IN MOON	6
CRUMBLED				
BEGINNING CRUMBLED BACK TO DARKNESS	....	175	FIRE RAID	58
STREETS OR HUNGERING IN THE CRUMBLED WOOD: TO THESE		205	GIANT'S THIGH	57
CRUMBS				
CRUMBS, BARN, AND HALTER.	....	32	OUT OF SIGHS	29
AND TOOK TO FEEDING BIRDS WITH BROKEN CRUMBS	......	53	OUT OF THE PIT	84
CRUMPLED				
THE CRUMPLED PACKS FLED PAST THIS GHOST IN BLOOM,		133	I MAKE THIS IN	58
BUT A BLACK SHEEP WITH A CRUMPLED HORN,	....	207	LAMENT	42
CRUNCHING				
CRUNCHING THE ALREADY BROKEN,	....	45	TO FOLLOW FOX	21
CRUSH				
MURMUR OF SPRING NOR CRUSH THE COCKEREL'S EGGS,	...	123	FOSTER LIGHT	7
OR CRUSH THEIR VIPER HEADS BENEATH MY FOOT.	....	239	LET ME ESCAPE	5
CRUSH YOUR SHARP LIGHT,	....	239	MAKES INTERVALS	28
CRUSHED				
CUT. CUT THE CRUSHED STREETS, LEAVING	....	156	RETURN	77
TILL EVERY TURTLE CRUSHED FROM HIS SHELL	....	163	LONG-LEGGED	58
CRUST				
WHERE LOVE IS THERE'S A CRUST OF JOY	....	19	THE NEOPHYTE	5
UP THROUGH THE LUBBER CRUST OF WALES	....	151	BELOW A TIME	24
THE STRONG, UNTURNING CRUST THAT HIDES	....	233	NO THOUGHT	11
CRUSTED				
PUFFED, OLD WITH VENOM, FROM A CRUSTED MOUTH.	.....	37	WINDMILLS TURN	30
THE CRUSTED WOUND NOR STROKE THE BROW;	....	66	HAND SIGNED	14
CRUTCH				
THE CRUTCH THAT MARROW TAPS UPON THEIR SLEEP,	.....	104	WORLD PYRAMID	14

		PAGE	TITLE	LINE
CRY				
CRY, MULTITUDES OF ARKS! ACROSS	....	5	PROLOGUE	93
BUT SHE DID NOT CRY, 'I SEE;	....	11	CABARET	12
THOUGH WE CRY DOWN THE FUNNEL,	....	17	IN OBLIVION	16
AND, STANDING OVER THE SEA, SHE'D CRY	....	22	ON QUIET NIGHT	9
CAN BE BUT VANITY, SUCH AN OLD CRY,	....	27	OBLIVIOUS DARK	24
THEY CRY TO BE TAKEN, AND THE DEVIL BREAKS	....	30	NEARLY SUMMER	21
'WE WHO ARE YOUNG ARE OLD. IT IS THE OLDEST CRY.		40	YOUNG ARE OLD	1
THERE WAS A TIME THEY COULD CRY OVER BOOKS,	....	40	WAS THERE TIME	3
WE WHO ARE STILL YOUNG ARE OLD. IT IS A DEAD CRY,		40	YOUNG ARE OLD	5
BELIEVE, BELIEVE AND BE SAVED, WE CRY, WHO HAVE NO				
FAITH.	....	42	YOUNG ARE OLD	57
AND THE OLD TERRORS' CONTINUAL CRY	....	43	LONGED TO MOVE	3
NO MORE MAY GULLS CRY AT THEIR EARS	....	50	NO DOMINION	20
AND THUS, BETWEEN THE SEASONS, HEARD HIM CRY:	.....	52	OUT OF THE PIT	62
NO ANSWER TO THE CHILDREN'S CRY	....	56	WHY EAST WIND	24
THE MOTHER'S CRY HAS FUMED ABOUT THE WINDS;	....	64	WOMAN SPEAKS	53
O TIDAL WINDS, CAST UP HER CRY FOR ME;	....	65	WOMAN SPEAKS	54
THE SECRET VOICE CRY IN OUR EARS,	....	70	SECRET WIND	20
MURDER WITH A CRY OF PAIN;	....	71	TAKE NEEDLES	19
CRY TO THE DOLPHINED SEA.	....	91	WHERE ONCE THE	18
CRY ELOI TO THE GUNS.	....	105	WORLD PYRAMID	42
THE STUFFED LUNG OF THE FOX TWITCH AND CRY LOVE	...	137	AFTER FUNERAL	39
AND, LASHED TO SYLLABLES, THE LYNX TONGUE CRY	.....	139	FIVE & COUNTRY	8
CRY JOY THAT THIS WITCHILIKE MIDWIFE SECOND	....	142	SAINT TO FALL	48
HAS A VOICE AND A HOUSE, AND THERE AND HERE YOU MUST				
COUCH AND CRY.	....	146	IF HEAD HURT	25
CRY MY SEA TOWN WAS BREAKING.	....	150	WHEN I WOKE	27
O YOU WHO COULD NOT CRY	....	153	WAS A SAVIOUR	20
TWO PROUD, BLACKED BROTHERS CRY,	....	153	WAS A SAVIOUR	25
WITH EVERY CRY SINCE LIGHT	....	160	DEATHS AND ENT	23
CRY,	....	174	FIRE RAID	27
CRY.	....	181	VISION, PRAYER	68
CRY. MY VOICE BURNS IN HIS HAND.	....	185	VISION, PRAYER	202
THROUGH THROATS WHERE MANY RIVERS MEET, THE CURLEWS				
CRY,	....	203	GIANT'S THIGH	1
NOW CURLEW CRY ME DOWN TO KISS THE MOUTHS OF THEIR				
DUST.	....	205	GIANT'S THIGH	45
YET, THOUGH I CRY WITH TUMBLEDOWN TONGUE,	....	211	POEM ON B'DAY	80
I AM NOT TOO PROUD TO CRY THAT HE AND HE	....	217	ELEGY	19
TOO PROUD TO CRY, TOO FRAIL TO CHECK THE TEARS,	...	217	ELEGY	35
THE TEARS OUT OF HIS EYES, TOO PROUD TO CRY.	......	217	ELEGY	39
CRYING				
CRYING ALOUD IN PAIN,	....	18	NATURAL DAY	32
OF CRYING OFF THIS UNSHAPED EVIL,	....	21	BEWILDERED WAY	2
CRYING WITH HUNGRY VOICES IN OUR NEST.	....	28	NO WINGS	22
MY BRAIN CAME CRYING INTO THE FRESH LIGHT,	....	42	A WAR OF WITS	4
SO CRYING, HE WAS DRAGGED INTO THE SEWER,	....	51	OUT OF THE PIT	39
SO CRYING, HE WAS PUSHED INTO THE JORDAN.	....	52	OUT OF THE PIT	53
CRYING SUCH WORDS, HE LEFT THE CRYING CROWDS,	.....	53	OUT OF THE PIT	82
CRYING SUCH WORDS, HE LEFT THE CRYING CROWDS,	.....	53	OUT OF THE PIT	82
WAS MUSCLED, MATTED, WISE TO THE CRYING THIGH	.....	78	LOVE'S FEVER	28
CRYING, WHITE GOWNED, FROM THE MIDDLE MOONLIT STAGES		158	INTO HER HEAD	37
IS CRYING FROM NETS TO KNIVES,	....	164	LONG-LEGGED	66
CRYING	....	174	FIRE RAID	25
CRYING IN VAIN	....	181	VISION, PRAYER	48
CRYING AT THE MAN DRENCHED THRONE	....	181	VISION, PRAYER	58
GO CRYING THROUGH YOU AND ME	....	193	SIDE OF TRUTH	18
SHALL THE CHILD SLEEP UNHARMED OR THE MAN BE CRYING?		194	CONVERS PRAYER	12
GOOD MEN, THE LAST WAVE BY, CRYING HOW BRIGHT	.....	208	NOT GO GENTLE	7

	PAGE	TITLE	LINE
CRYING (CONTINUED)			
ALL HIS BONES CRYING, AND POOR IN ALL BUT PAIN, ...	217	ELEGY	21
CRYPT			
PARADED UP THE AISLES AND IN THE CRYPT	51	OUT OF THE PIT	27
CRYSTAL			
CRYSTAL OR FUNERAL, GOT NO HOPE	28	NO WINGS	5
CRYSTAL HARBOUR VALE	202	SIR JOHNS HILL	37
CUBBED			
SAVE BY THEIR LONG DESIRERS IN THE FOX CUBBED	205	GIANT'S THIGH	56
CUCKOO			
WHERE AT NIGHT WE STONED THE COLD AND CUCKOO	144	COLOUR OF SAY	8
CUCKOOING			
I SHOULD LEARN SPRING BY THE CUCKOOING, ...	58	HERE IN SPRING	12
CUCKOO'S			
HOLD HARD, THESE ANCIENT MINUTES IN THE CUCKOO'S MONTH	122	HOLD HARD	T
HOLD HARD, THESE ANCIENT MINUTES IN THE CUCKOO'S MONTH, ...	122	HOLD HARD	1
CUDDLED			
YOUR CALM AND CUDDLED IS A SCYTHE OF HAIRS, ...	99	RUNNING GRAVE	2
LIT ON THE CUDDLED TREE, THE CROSS OF FEVER, ...	100	RUNNING GRAVE	33
CUDGEL			
CUDGEL GREAT AIR, WRECK EAST, AND TOPPLE SUNDOWN,	132	I MAKE THIS IN	33
CUDGELLING			
AND IMMEMORIAL SONS OF THE CUDGELLING, HACKED	203	GIANT'S THIGH	11
CULLED			
WITH ZEST CULLED FROM THEIR LADYLIKE HEAT, ...	18	NATURAL DAY	12
CULTURED			
BUT JUST A KIND AND CULTURED DAME	83	LETTER TO AUNT	5
CUMMINGS			
FEW UNDERSTAND THE WORKS OF CUMMINGS, ...	84	LETTER TO AUNT	36
CUNNING			
WITH THEIR HEADS IN A CUNNING CLOUD.	147	TO OTHERS	21
CUP			
DRINKING WATER FROM THE CHAINED CUP	171	THE HUNCHBACK	8
AND FLOATING FIELDS FROM THE FARM IN THE CUP OF THE VALES, ...	187	WINTER'S TALE	3
AND THE CUP AND THE CUT BREAD IN THE DANCING SHADE,	188	WINTER'S TALE	28
THAT A MAN KNELT ALONE IN THE CUP OF THE VALES, ...	189	WINTER'S TALE	85
CUPBOARD			
STIR THEIR OLD BONES BEHIND CUPBOARD AND CURTAIN.	38	THE GOSSIPERS	5
A CUPBOARD SKELETON	59	FAIRY TALES	15
CAN TIME UNRIDDLE, AND THE CUPBOARD STONE, ...	113	SERVANT SUN	3
CUPIDS			
A MEASURE ON THE LAWN WHERE CUPIDS BLEW	51	OUT OF THE PIT	25
CUPPED			
ON A BREAD WHITE HILL OVER THE CUPPED FARM	190	WINTER'S TALE	107
HOLLOWS, A GRASSBLADE BLOWN IN CUPPED HANDS, IN THE LOOTED ELMS	203	SIR JOHNS HILL	52
CURDLE			
TURN AND CHURN NIGHTSEED TILL IT CURDLE.	67	LET A FAITH	5
CURDLERS			
THESE BOYS OF LIGHT ARE CURDLERS IN THEIR FOLLY,	92	BOYS OF SUMMER	7
CURE			
AND CURE ME OF ILLS.	32	OUT OF SIGHS	23
SHOULD CURE OUR ILLS OF THE WATER	54	WE BY SEASAND	12
SHOULD HE WHO SPLIT HIS CHILDREN WITH A CURE	127	NOW, SAY NAY	13
CURED			
MAN SHOULD BE CURED OF DISTEMPER.	32	OUT OF SIGHS	27

	PAGE	TITLE	LINE
CURELESS			
THE CURELESS COUNTED BODY, ...	186	HOLY SPRING	4
CURES			
SHALL FALL AWAKE WHEN CURES AND THEIR ITCH	89	EUNUCH DREAMS	22
CURFEW			
I MEAN BY TIME THE CAST AND CURFEW RASCAL OF OUR MARRIAGE, ...	130	SINNERS' BELL	25
CURIOUS			
BUT TROUBLED BY THEIR CURIOUS SPEECH	22	ON QUIET NIGHT	6
CURLED			
WHERE HALF DEAD VANITIES WERE SLEEPING CURLED	50	OUT OF THE PIT	4
AND DROWN IN THE DRIFTS OF HIS NEED, AND LIE CURLED CAUGHT	188	WINTER'S TALE	47
CURLEW			
DOWN TO THE CURLEW HERD!	4	PROLOGUE	63
NOW CURLEW CRY ME DOWN TO KISS THE MOUTHS OF THEIR DUST.	205	GIANT'S THIGH	45
CURLEWS			
THROUGH THROATS WHERE MANY RIVERS MEET, THE CURLEWS CRY, ...	203	GIANT'S THIGH	1
THEY YEARN WITH TONGUES OF CURLEWS FOR THE UNCONCEIVED	203	GIANT'S THIGH	10
CURLEWS ALOUD IN THE CONGERED WAVES	209	POEM ON B'DAY	13
CURLING			
AND CURLING ROUND THE BUD THAT FORKS HER EYE.	95	RUB OF LOVE	31
CURL-LOCKED			
CURL-LOCKED AND ANIMAL CAVEPOOLS OF SPELLS AND BONE,	135	HOW MY ANIMAL	27
CURRANTS			
PEARS AND RED CURRANTS	178	POEM IN OCT	45
CURRENCIES			
THAT WILL RAKE AT LAST ALL CURRENCIES OF THE MARKED BREATH	140	NO WORK WORDS	8
CURSE			
NO FAITH TO FOLLOW IS THE WORLD'S CURSE	41	YOUNG ARE OLD	24
CURSE, BLESS, ME NOW WITH YOUR FIERCE TEARS, I PRAY.	208	NOT GO GENTLE	17
CURSED			
WHEN CLOUDS ARE CURSED BY THUNDER, ...	65	GODS THUMP	2
TIDY AND CURSED IN MY DOVE COOED ROOM	207	LAMENT	52
CURSES			
AND, MAD, HE CALLED HIS CURSES UPON GOD, ...	50	OUT OF THE PIT	8
WHO CURSES NOT WHAT MAKES AND SAVES, ...	55	NO MAN BELIEVE	14
MINUS THESE CURSES, YOU CAN BE	85	LETTER TO AUNT	61
CURTAIN			
STIR THEIR OLD BONES BEHIND CUPBOARD AND CURTAIN.	38	THE GOSSIPERS	5
MY CROSS OF TALES BEHIND THE FABULOUS CURTAIN.' ...	125	TODAY, INSECT	26
CURTAINED			
AND THE BREATH-WHITE, CURTAINED MOUTH OF SEED.' ...	132	I MAKE THIS IN	51
CURTAINS			
PULLS DOWN THE SHABBY CURTAINS OF THE SKIN;	88	A PROCESS IN	23
CURVE			
MAN'S RIB ON WOMAN'S, STRAIGHT LINE ON A CURVE, ...	51	OUT OF THE PIT	35
BY THE CURVE OF THE NUDE MOUTH OR THE LAUGH UP THE SLEEVE.	133	MAKE ME A MASK	12
CURVES			
ON GIDDY NIGHTS I SLAP A FEW DRUNK CURVES	138	O CHATTERTON	24
CURVING			
THE LINES OF EARTH, THE CURVING OF THE HEART, ...	73	LORD RED HAIL	14
THE SALTY SCENE AND MY PLAYERED GOB CURVING	179	NEW QUAY	14
AND ALONE IN THE NIGHT'S ETERNAL, CURVING ACT	203	GIANT'S THIGH	9

		PAGE	TITLE	LINE
CUSS				
MEANING IN HOT SOCK SOIL? A LITTLE CUSS	....	137	O CHATTERTON	18
CUT				
TO CUT IN FRONT OF ME	....	12	SKY'S BRIGHT	6
CUT THEM IN ROCK,	....	19	IMAGES IN AIR	9
WHO HAS COMPLETENESS THAT CAN CUT	....	23	THE ONLY DEAD	7
CUT OUR FIGURES, AND RETREAT AT NIGHT	....	28	NO WINGS	17
BUT HE MAKES THEM DANCE, CUT CAPERS	....	47	POET: 1935	41
THE CHILD TELLS, WHEN THE TREMBLING CHORD IS CUT,		67	LET A FAITH	14
CUT MY FINGERS ON A ROSE,	....	70	TAKE NEEDLES	6
TO CUT THE CHANNELS AT THEIR SOURCE	....	91	WHERE ONCE THE	11
THE NURSE OF GIANTS BY THE CUT SEA BASIN,	....	113	SERVANT SUN	10
AND OPIUM HEAD, CROW STALK, PUFFED, CUT, AND BLOWN,		131	I MAKE THIS IN	10
DIE IN RED FEATHERS WHEN THE FLYING HEAVEN'S CUT,		135	HOW MY ANIMAL	40
CUT CHRISTBREAD SPITTING VINEGAR AND ALL	....	141	SAINT TO FALL	16
CUT TO THE STILL STAR IN THE ORDER OF THE QUICK	...	148	UNLUCKILY FOR	20
CUT. CUT THE CRUSHED STREETS, LEAVING	....	156	RETURN	77
CUT. CUT THE CRUSHED STREETS, LEAVING	....	156	RETURN	77
AND O TO CUT THE GREEN FIELD, LEAVING	....	157	RETURN	100
AND THE CUP AND THE CUT BREAD IN THE DANCING SHADE,		188	WINTER'S TALE	28
THAT ONCE CUT THE FIGURES OF BIRDS ON THE DEEP BREAD		190	WINTER'S TALE	114
AND CUT THE BIRDS' BOUGHS THAT THE MINSTREL SAP RAN				
RED.	....	205	GIANT'S THIGH	49
AND ITS EDGE CUT THE SURFACE,	....	232	FURIOUS MOTION	6
I'LL CUT THROUGH YOUR DARK CLOUD	....	239	LET ME ESCAPE	10
CUTS				
RAIN CUTS THE PLACE WE TREAD	....	13	RAIN CUTS	T
RAIN CUTS THE PLACE WE TREAD,	....	13	RAIN CUTS	1
THAT, LIKE A RAZOR, SKIMS, CUTS, AND TURNS,	....	47	POET: 1935	49
HE CUTS HIMSELF ON AN ELDER'S RAZOR LEG.	....	179	NEW QUAY	28
WHICH CUTS INTO THE STRENGTH	....	230	MY RIVER	42
CUTTING				
ARC-LAMPED THROWN BACK UPON THE CUTTING FLOOD.	....	118	ALTARWISE	56
CUTTING THE MORNING OFF,	....	150	WHEN I WOKE	10
CUT-TO-MEASURE				
CUT-TO-MEASURE FLESH BIT,	....	151	BELOW A TIME	3
CYANIDE				
SUCKING THE DARK, KISSED ON THE CYANIDE,	....	104	WORLD PYRAMID	21
CYCLONE				
CYCLONE OF HIS WING	....	181	VISION, PRAYER	56
AS THE WORLD FALLS, SILENT AS THE CYCLONE OF SILENCE.		199	COUNTRY SLEEP	63
CYPRESS				
MY FALLING LUNGS, NOR AS THE CYPRESS	....	75	SONG: LOVE ME	2
MY WORLD IS CYPRESS, AND AN ENGLISH VALLEY.	....	105	WORLD PYRAMID	37
SO THE ILEX AND THE CYPRESS	....	236	WOMAN TAPESTRY	56
CYPRESSES				
HILL OF CYPRESSES! THE DIN AND TALE IN THE SKIMMED		200	COUNTRY SLEEP	76
CYST				
NO MAN UPON THIS CYST OF EARTH	....	55	NO MAN BELIEVE	15
DABBED				
MY DABBED BAY'S DUSK, AS I HACK	....	4	PROLOGUE	36
DABBLES				
HALF OF THE FELLOW MOTHER AS SHE DABBLES	....	103	WORLD PYRAMID	3
DAB-FILLED				
IN THE PEBBLY DAB-FILLED	....	202	SIR JOHNS HILL	20
DAFT				
DAFT WITH THE DRUG THAT'S SMOKING IN A GIRL	....	95	RUB OF LOVE	30
THE DEAR, DAFT TIME I TAKE TO NUDGE THE SENTENCE,		124	TODAY, INSECT	4
DAI				
TOM TIT AND DAI MOUSE!	....	5	PROLOGUE	99

	PAGE	TITLE	LINE
DAISIES			
HEADS OF THE CHARACTERS HAMMER THROUGH DAISIES; ...	50	NO DOMINION	25
TRAIL WITH DAISIES AND BARLEY	195	FERN HILL	8
DAM			
FLESH AND SPIRIT, BABE AND DAM, ...	71	TAKE NEEDLES	30
IN THE DARKNESS DAM AND BABE	71	TAKE NEEDLES	33
DARKNESS IS THE DAM OF PAIN.	71	TAKE NEEDLES	36
DAM AND SIRE, LIVING, LO, ...	72	TAKE NEEDLES	47
THE SALT SUCKED DAM AND DARLINGS OF THE LAND	113	NOT FATHER ME	27
DAME			
BUT JUST A KIND AND CULTURED DAME	83	LETTER TO AUNT	5
DAMNED			
THE SQUEAL OF THE DAMNED OUT OF THE OLD PIT.	40	YOUNG ARE OLD	6
NOR DAMNED THE SEA THAT SPED ABOUT MY FIST, ...	97	TWILIGHT LOCKS	3
SUN. IN THE NAME OF THE DAMNED	185	VISION, PRAYER	190
DAMP			
TURNS DAMP TO DRY; THE GOLDEN SHOT	88	A PROCESS IN	2
IS DAMP AND DRY; THE QUICK AND DEAD	88	A PROCESS IN	17
HERE LOVE'S DAMP MUSCLE DRIES AND DIES, ...	93	BOYS OF SUMMER	46
FROM DAMP LOVE-DARKNESS AND THE NURSE'S TWIST	96	RUB OF LOVE	38
I DAMP THE WAXLIGHTS IN YOUR TOWER DOME.	101	RUNNING GRAVE	36
SHAMES AND THE DAMP DISHONOURS, THE RELIC SCRAPING.	110	I, IN IMAGE	71
WHISPER IN A DAMP WORD, HER WITS DRILLED HOLLOW,	137	AFTER FUNERAL	33
DAMS			
OF SUN AND MOON THEY PAINT THEIR DAMS	92	BOYS OF SUMMER	17
DANCE			
THE OLD FLOWERS' LEGS TOO TAUT TO DANCE, ...	47	POET: 1935	40
BUT HE MAKES THEM DANCE, CUT CAPERS	47	POET: 1935	41
THEY DANCE BETWEEN THEIR ARCLAMPS AND OUR SKULL,	89	EUNUCH DREAMS	17
PECK, SPRINT, DANCE ON FOUNTAINS AND DUCK TIME	145	IF HEAD HURT	8
AND WHARVES OF WATER WHERE THE WALLS DANCE AND THE WHITE CRANES STILT.	202	SIR JOHNS HILL	39
DANCED			
AND GONE THAT BARLEY DARK WHERE THEIR CLOGS DANCED IN THE SPRING, ...	205	GIANT'S THIGH	40
THEIR FRAIL DEEDS MIGHT HAVE DANCED IN A GREEN BAY,	208	NOT GO GENTLE	8
DANCER			
SHE BECAME LIKE A DANCER OR A PRETTY ANIMAL	235	WOMAN TAPESTRY	20
DANCERS			
WAS THERE A TIME WHEN DANCERS WITH THEIR FIDDLES	40	WAS THERE TIME	1
LOOK. AND THE DANCERS MOVE	189	WINTER'S TALE	71
DANCES			
DANCES A MEASURE WITH THE SWAN	15	FOR LEDA	30
DANCING			
AT A WOOD'S DANCING HOOF, ...	3	PROLOGUE	8
SHE IS ON DANCING TOES AGAIN, ...	12	CABARET	18
STOPPED NON-STOP DANCING TO LET HOT FEET COOL, ...	51	OUT OF THE PIT	30
AND THE CUP AND THE CUT BREAD IN THE DANCING SHADE,	188	WINTER'S TALE	28
LEAVES IS DANCING. LINES OF AGE ON THE STONES WEAVE IN A FLOCK.	189	WINTER'S TALE	78
THE DANCING PERISHES	190	WINTER'S TALE	111
DANDY			
THE BRIGHT PRETENDER, THE RIDICULOUS SEA DANDY	152	BELOW A TIME	42
DANES			
AND EVENINGS WITH GREAT DANES, ...	155	RETURN	57
DANGLER			
WITH MY CHERRY CAPPED DANGLER GREEN AS SEAWEED	152	BELOW A TIME	45
DANGLES			
AND, CLAPPED IN WATER TILL THE TRITON DANGLES, ...	110	I, IN IMAGE	64

DARK

	PAGE	TITLE	LINE
IN THE HOOTING, NEARLY DARK	4	PROLOGUE	59
AND DARK SHOALS EVERY HOLY FIELD.	5	PROLOGUE	90
AND BREAK THROUGH DARK;	16	TIME TO ROT	9
OR, WHITE AS MILK, OUT OF THE SEEPING DARK, ...	20	ENCOMPASSED	11
UP TO THE SECOND OF THE DARK COMING, ...	25	THERE'S PLENTY	5
NEVER TO REACH THE OBLIVIOUS DARK	27	OBLIVIOUS DARK	T
NEVER TO REACH THE OBLIVIOUS DARK	27	OBLIVIOUS DARK	1
BRED IN THE DARK BEHIND THE SKIRTING-BOARD, ...	28	NO WINGS	21
THE COVERINGS OF DARK AND LIGHT, ...	37	WINDMILLS TURN	28
BEFORE EVIL OR GOOD, LIGHT OR DARK, ...	39	GAS FADES	16
PLAY PATIENCE IN THE PARLOUR AFTER DARK.	40	YOUNG ARE OLD	14
MEN OLD BEFORE THEIR TIME INTO DARK VALLEYS	41	YOUNG ARE OLD	19
I HAVE BEEN FRIGHTENED OF THE DARK FOR YEARS.	48	LIGHT, I KNOW	6
HE COULD HEAR WOMEN BREATHING IN THE DARK, ...	51	OUT OF THE PIT	20
LIGHT AND DARK ARE NO ENEMIES	61	MEAT ON BONES	36
GROOM THE DARK BRIDES, THE WIDOWS OF THE NIGHT	89	EUNUCH DREAMS	5
OF DOUBT AND DARK THEY FEED THEIR NERVES;	92	BOYS OF SUMMER	11
WE ARE THE DARK DENIERS, LET US SUMMON	92	BOYS OF SUMMER	31
SUCKING THE DARK, KISSED ON THE CYANIDE, ...	104	WORLD PYRAMID	21
RISE BEFORE DARK.	115	A GRIEF AGO	32
THE FEATURES IN THEIR PRIVATE DARK	116	LANTERNS SHINE	5
THERE IS LOUD AND DARK DIRECTLY UNDER THE DUMB FLAME,	130	SINNERS' BELL	13
AND, FOR THAT MURDER'S SAKE, DARK WITH CONTAGION	132	I MAKE THIS IN	37
YOU HAVE KICKED FROM A DARK DEN, LEAPED UP THE			
WHINNYING LIGHT, ...	135	HOW MY ANIMAL	43
IN THE DARK OF THE COFFIN AND SHEDS DRY LEAVES, ...	136	AFTER FUNERAL	8
NOT IN THE SUN BUT IN THE DARK;	138	O CHATTERTON	34
AND COUNT THE TAKEN, FORSAKEN MYSTERIES IN A BAD			
DARK.	140	NO WORK WORDS	9
THROUGH THE DARK ASYLUM, ...	142	SAINT TO FALL	38
AND A LAMP OF LIGHTNING FOR THE POOR IN THE DARK;	144	COLOUR OF SAY	11
OF THE DESCENDING DAY, THE DARK OUR FOLLY	148	UNLUCKILY FOR	19
IN THE ANDROGYNOUS DARK, ...	148	UNLUCKILY FOR	30
NOW IN THE DARK THERE IS ONLY YOURSELF AND MYSELF.	153	WAS A SAVIOUR	24
DARK INVITERS TO KEYHOLES	155	RETURN	56
THERE THE DARK BLADE AND WANTON SIGHING HER DOWN	157	INTO HER HEAD	16
FORGOTTEN DARK, REST THEIR PULSE AND BURY THEIR DEAD			
IN HER FAITHLESS SLEEP.	159	INTO HER HEAD	69
IN THE WATCHED DARK, QUIVERING THROUGH LOCKS AND			
CAVES, ...	161	DEATHS AND ENT	31
HE SPED INTO THE DRINKING DARK;	162	LONG-LEGGED	14
WHITE SPRINGS IN THE DARK.	166	LONG-LEGGED	120
BIRD AFTER DARK AND THE LAUGHING FISH	166	LONG-LEGGED	126
UNTIL THE SUNDAY SOMBRE BELL AT DARK	171	THE HUNCHBACK	6
TO HIS KENNEL IN THE DARK.	172	THE HUNCHBACK	42
A DARK AS DEEP	176	BREATH SHED	9
SHUT. SINISTER DARK OVER CARDIGAN	179	NEW QUAY	7
OPENING AND THE DARK RUN	180	VISION, PRAYER	7
BUT DARK ALONE	180	VISION, PRAYER	14
AND THE DARK THROWN	180	VISION, PRAYER	31
IN THE CENTRE OF DARK I PRAY HIM	183	VISION, PRAYER	135
IN THE DARK	184	VISION, PRAYER	142
AND THE KNOWN DARK OF THE EARTH AMEN.	185	VISION, PRAYER	187
THAT ONE DARK I OWE MY LIGHT, ...	186	HOLY SPRING	9
IN THE LONG AGO LAND THAT GLIDED THE DARK DOOR WIDE	189	WINTER'S TALE	67
INTO THE WINDING DARK	192	SIDE OF TRUTH	11
THE GRAINS BEYOND AGE, THE DARK VEINS OF HER MOTHER,	192	REFUSAL MOURN	21
TURNS IN THE DARK ON THE SOUND THEY KNOW WILL ARISE	193	CONVERS PRAYER	6
DARK, AND THE GUILTY DARK, AND GOOD	193	SIDE OF TRUTH	21

	PAGE	TITLE	LINE
DARK (CONTINUED)			
DARK, AND THE GUILTY DARK, AND GOOD	193	SIDE OF TRUTH	21
AND MARK THE DARK EYED WAVE, THROUGH THE EYES OF SLEEP,	194	CONVERS PRAYER	19
FLASHING INTO THE DARK.	195	FERN HILL	27
YET OUT OF THE BEAKED, WEB DARK AND THE POUNCING BOUGHS	199	COUNTRY SLEEP	48
AND GONE THAT BARLEY DARK WHERE THEIR CLOGS DANCED IN THE SPRING,	205	GIANT'S THIGH	40
THOUGH WISE MEN AT THEIR END KNOW DARK IS RIGHT,	208	NOT GO GENTLE	4
AND LOVE UNBOLTS THE DARK	210	POEM ON B'DAY	45
DARK IS A WAY AND LIGHT IS A PLACE,	210	POEM ON B'DAY	49
BUT DARK IS A LONG WAY.	210	POEM ON B'DAY	64
DOWNS INTO THE LOW BROWSING DARK.	215	COUNTRY HEAVEN	15
LIGHTLY, THOU WIND, OVER HIS DEAR, DARK HEAD,	222	MISSING	4
NOR THE SPLENDOUR OF YOUR DARK HAIR,	228	NOT DESPAIR	10
SO, THEN, WILL THE DARK CLOTH OF YOUR HAIR	232	FURIOUS MOTION	7
WADING THROUGH HER DARK CAVE ON FEROCIOUS WINGS.	232	YOUR VOICE	9
ON THE BALANCE OF HER DARK FOOT,	235	WOMAN TAPESTRY	22
AND SHOWS THEM FAIR AGAINST THE DARK,	238	MAKES INTERVALS	3
I'LL CUT THROUGH YOUR DARK CLOUD	239	LET ME ESCAPE	10
DARKEN			
KNOWING A DREAM COULD DARKEN IT,	10	COOL, OH NO	10
DARKENED			
TO SHUT THE SUN, PLUNGE, MOUNT YOUR DARKENED KEYS	161	DEATHS AND ENT	33
DARKENING			
BORROW MY EYES. THE DARKENING SEA FLINGS LEA	179	NEW QUAY	2
DARKER			
DARKER THAN EVER,	9	MINUTE'S HOUR	11
FADE, THE GREEN GLOOM GROWS DARKER, AND DEEPER THE DUSK:	222	FOREST PICTURE	10
DARKEST			
THE DARKEST WAY, AND DID NOT TURN AWAY,	216	ELEGY	2
ON THAT DARKEST DAY. OH, FOREVER MAY	216	ELEGY	4
THE DARKEST JUSTICE OF DEATH, BLIND AND UNBLESSED.	216	ELEGY	11
ON THAT DARKEST DAY. OH, HE COULD HIDE	217	ELEGY	38
DARKNESS			
AND DARKNESS, HAND IN HAND WITH LIGHT,	15	FOR LEDA	32
I HEAR THEM SAY OUT OF THE DARKNESS	23	ON QUIET NIGHT	21
EMPTY OF LIGHT AND FIND THE DARKNESS LIT--	27	OBLIVIOUS DARK	5
CHILDREN OF DARKNESS GOT NO WINGS	28	NO WINGS	T
CHILDREN OF DARKNESS GOT NO WINGS,	28	NO WINGS	1
CHILDREN OF DARKNESS GOT NO WINGS,	28	NO WINGS	23
DRIPS FROM THE HUMMING DARKNESS OF THE HIVE.	48	LIGHT, I KNOW	10
THE GLOW-WORM LIGHTS HIS DARKNESS, AND	48	POET: 1935	64
SHALL LAMP THE RAVEN DARKNESS OF HER FACE,	57	GREEK PLAY	9
IN THE DARKNESS DAM AND BABE	71	TAKE NEEDLES	33
DARKNESS IS THE DAM OF PAIN.	71	TAKE NEEDLES	36
AND FROM THIS DARKNESS SPIN THE GOLDEN SOUL.	73	LORD RED HAIL	15
LOVE ME, AS LOVES THE MOLE HIS DARKNESS	76	SONG: LOVE ME	13
THE BOY SHE DROPPED FROM DARKNESS AT HER SIDE	78	LOVE'S FEVER	26
A DARKNESS IN THE WEATHER OF THE EYE	88	A PROCESS IN	10
MISTER AND MASTER, DARKNESS FOR HIS EYES,	114	SERVANT SUN	31
AND DARKNESS HUNG THE WALLS WITH BASKETS OF SNAKES,	158	INTO HER HEAD	27
DARKNESS KINDLED BACK INTO BEGINNING	173	FIRE RAID	12
BEGINNING CRUMBLED BACK TO DARKNESS	175	FIRE RAID	58
FATHERING AND ALL HUMBLING DARKNESS	191	REFUSAL MOURN	3
AND THE DAUGHTERS OF DARKNESS FLAME LIKE FAWKES FIRES STILL.	205	GIANT'S THIGH	60
THE DARKNESS IS ILLIMITABLE, GREEN SHADOW,	224	IDYLL UNFORGET	43

	PAGE	TITLE	LINE
DARKNESS (CONTINUED)			
THEY ARE DEEPER IN DARKNESS	226	THE ELM	5
DARK-SKINNED			
FOREVER IT IS A WHITE CHILD IN THE DARK-SKINNED SUMMER	130	SINNERS' BELL	19
DARK-VOWELLED			
BY THE SEA'S SIDE HEAR THE DARK-VOWELLED BIRDS.	99	OCTOBER WIND	32
DARLINGS			
THE SALT SUCKED DAM AND DARLINGS OF THE LAND	113	NOT FATHER ME	27
HOLD HARD, MY COUNTY DARLINGS, FOR A HAWK DESCENDS,	123	HOLD HARD	22
DART			
FIND HARD TO DART AGAINST A CLOUD,	37	WINDMILLS TURN	8
DARTED			
THE DARTED HAIL, THE CHILDISH SNOW,	68	BEFORE KNOCKED	14
DARTING			
LIGHTNING OR THE DARTING VIPER,	71	TAKE NEEDLES	22
'A LIZARD DARTING WITH BLACK VENOM'S THREAD	132	I MAKE THIS IN	49
DASH			
ANCIENT WOODS OF MY BLOOD, DASH DOWN TO THE NUT OF THE SEAS	140	NO WORK WORDS	11
DASHED-DOWN			
HEAR BY DEATH'S ACCIDENT THE CLOCKED AND DASHED-DOWN SPIRE	130	SINNERS' BELL	11
DATED			
A LOVER'S THOUGHT TEARS DOWN THE DATED SHEET,	80	ALMANAC TIME	7
DAUB			
AND DAUB THE UNRISEN SUN WITH LONGING.	15	FOR LEDA	13
DAUBING			
TO KILL AND THEIR OWN TIDE DAUBING BLOOD	209	POEM ON B'DAY	35
DAUGHTER			
WAS BROTHER TO MNETHA'S DAUGHTER	68	BEFORE KNOCKED	5
THRUST, MY DAUGHTER OR SON, TO ESCAPE, THERE IS NONE, NONE, NONE,	146	IF HEAD HURT	19
DEEP WITH THE FIRST DEAD LIES LONDON'S DAUGHTER,	192	REFUSAL MOURN	19
DAUGHTERS			
AND THE GRAVE ITS DAUGHTERS.	148	UNLUCKILY FOR	42
OFF BY THE SUN AND DAUGHTERS NO LONGER GRIEVED	205	GIANT'S THIGH	55
AND THE DAUGHTERS OF DARKNESS FLAME LIKE FAWKES FIRES STILL.	205	GIANT'S THIGH	60
DAVID			
NO GENIUS IN DAVID G.,	83	LETTER TO AUNT	8
A GENIUS LIKE DAVID G.	85	LETTER TO AUNT	62
DAVY'S			
THE BRIGHT-EYED WORM ON DAVY'S LAMP,	92	BOYS OF SUMMER	35
DAWN			
DAWN BREAKS BEHIND THE EYES;	82	LIGHT BREAKS	13
ABOVE THE WASTE ALLOTMENTS THE DAWN HALTS.	82	LIGHT BREAKS	30
AMONG THOSE KILLED IN THE DAWN RAID WAS A MAN AGED A HUNDRED	172	DAWN RAID	T
AND THE FIRST DAWN	181	VISION, PRAYER	38
BACK. LINES OF AGE SLEEP ON THE STONES TILL TRUMPETING DAWN.	191	WINTER'S TALE	118
AND YOU SHALL WAKE, FROM COUNTRY SLEEP, THIS DAWN AND EACH FIRST DAWN,	201	COUNTRY SLEEP	110
AND YOU SHALL WAKE, FROM COUNTRY SLEEP, THIS DAWN AND EACH FIRST DAWN,	201	COUNTRY SLEEP	110
DAWN SHIPS CLOUTED AGROUND,	211	POEM ON B'DAY	79
DAWNED			
A SHE BIRD DAWNED, AND HER BREAST WITH SNOW AND SCARLET DOWNED.	189	WINTER'S TALE	70

	PAGE	TITLE	LINE
DAWS			
DAWS SIR JOHN'S JUST HILL DONS, AND AGAIN THE GULLED BIRDS HARE	201	SIR JOHNS HILL	15
DAY			
THIS DAY WINDING DOWN NOW	3	PROLOGUE	1
THE NATURAL DAY AND NIGHT	17	NATURAL DAY	T
THE NATURAL DAY AND NIGHT	17	NATURAL DAY	1
BUT WHILE DAY IS THERE'S NIGHT TO IT,	18	NATURAL DAY	19
CONSOLING FOR NIGHT BY DAY	35	LIFT UP FACE	3
GROWING MORE TERRIBLE AS THE DAY	43	LONGED TO MOVE	4
OR PRAY FOR DAY TO SOME ATTENTIVE GOD	48	LIGHT, I KNOW	14
AND THERE IS ALWAYS DAY, THE SHINING OF SOME SUN,	49	LIGHT, I KNOW	18
OUT OF THE BUILDINGS OF THE DAY I'VE STEPPED	53	OUT OF THE PIT	90
DAY TREADS THE TREES AND SHE THE CAVERNOUS NIGHT.	57	GREEK PLAY	12
AUTOCRACY OF NIGHT AND DAY,	61	MEAT ON BONES	12
ALONE TILL THE DAY I DIE	62	EARS IN TURRET	6
OR STAY TILL THE DAY I DIE	62	EARS IN TURRET	23
COULD IN A DAY BE SICK WITH SO MUCH BLOOD;	63	WOMAN SPEAKS	13
OR STAY TILL THE DAY I DIE?	63	EARS IN TURRET	31
ONE DAY MY WOMAN'S BODY WILL BE COLD.	64	WOMAN SPEAKS	47
UNGOTTEN I KNEW NIGHT AND DAY.	68	BEFORE KNOCKED	18
THREAD AND TORTURE ALL THE DAY;	72	TAKE NEEDLES	53
AGEING BOTH DAY AND NIGHT.	80	ALMANAC TIME	10
ALL NIGHT AND DAY I EYE THE RAGGED GLOBE	81	ALL THAT I OWE	23
ALL NIGHT AND DAY I WANDER IN THESE SAME	81	ALL THAT I OWE	25
DAY LIGHTS THE BONE;	82	LIGHT BREAKS	21
MAN IN THE DAY OR WIND AT NIGHT	86	BREAD I BREAK	4
TURNS NIGHT TO DAY; BLOOD IN THEIR SUNS	88	A PROCESS IN	5
DOWN IN THE YARD OF DAY.	89	EUNUCH DREAMS	16
DIVIDE THE NIGHT AND DAY WITH FAIRY THUMBS;	92	BOYS OF SUMMER	15
DAYED PEAKS TO DAY TO DEATH,	108	GRIEF THIEF	22
ARE FORMED OF FLESH, BUT LET THE FALSE DAY COME	116	LANTERNS SHINE	6
SOAR, WITH ITS TWO BARK TOWERS, TO THAT DAY	121	ALTARWISE	138
CALLS A GREEN DAY AND NIGHT.	128	MY NEOPHYTE	6
OR POISE THE DAY ON A HORN.	135	HOW MY ANIMAL	33
THAT I STRUCK ONE DAY BY LUCK,	139	TOMBSTONE TOLD	5
OF THE DESCENDING DAY, THE DARK OUR FOLLY	148	UNLUCKILY FOR	19
CLASH OUT THE MOUNTING DOLPHIN'S DAY,	164	LONG-LEGGED	75
MADE ALL DAY UNTIL BELL TIME	172	THE HUNCHBACK	31
AND THE SUN GREW ROUND THAT VERY DAY.	196	FERN HILL	32
OF DAY, IN THE THISTLE AISLES, TILL THE WHITE OWL CROSSED	204	GIANT'S THIGH	32
OLD AGE SHOULD BURN AND RAVE AT CLOSE OF DAY;	207	NOT GO GENTLE	2
THIS SANDGRAIN DAY IN THE BENT BAY'S GRAVE	208	POEM ON B'DAY	6
ON THAT DARKEST DAY. OH, FOREVER MAY	216	ELEGY	4
ON THAT DARKEST DAY. OH, HE COULD HIDE	217	ELEGY	38
THERE ARE MANY WHO SAY THAT A DOG HAS ITS DAY,	221	SONG OF DOG	1
THE BEES ARE GLAD THE LIVELONG DAY,	227	TRIOLET	1
THE BEES ARE GLAD THE LIVELONG DAY,	228	TRIOLET	4
THE BEES ARE GLAD THE LIVELONG DAY,	228	TRIOLET	7
ONE DAY THEY HAD TO FLY,	237	PILLAR BREAKS	14
DAYBREAK			
OVER THE WHIRLING DITCH OF DAYBREAK	175	FIRE RAID	67
DAYED			
DAYED PEAKS TO DAY TO DEATH,	108	GRIEF THIEF	22
DAYLIGHT			
PACK OFF THE SHAPES OF DAYLIGHT AND THEIR STARCH,	90	EUNUCH DREAMS	24
DAYS			
COUNT THE ENDLESS DAYS UNTIL THEY END,	32	HELD-OUT HAND	2
THE CHILD SHALL QUESTION ALL HIS DAYS,	56	WHY EAST WIND	7

	PAGE	TITLE	LINE
DAYS (CONTINUED)			
THE SLUG'S A LIVING CALENDAR OF DAYS;	59	HERE IN SPRING	15
BY SIPPING AT THE VINE OF DAYS.	69	BEFORE KNOCKED	36
YOU BUT WOUND THE LORD OF DAYS;	72	TAKE NEEDLES	54
TUGGED THROUGH THE DAYS	115	A GRIEF AGO	20
A BRUTE LAND IN THE COOL TOP OF THE COUNTRY DAYS	135	HOW MY ANIMAL	15
THE PYRE YET TO BE LIGHTED OF MY SINS AND DAYS,	147	UNLUCKILY FOR	3
DAYS DEEP IN HER BREAST THAT WORE NO HEART	175	MY BEGGAR ARM	2
AND WALKED ABROAD IN A SHOWER OF ALL MY DAYS.	177	POEM IN OCT	16
KING OF YOUR HEART IN THE BLIND DAYS,	193	SIDE OF TRUTH	16
NOTHING I CARED, IN THE LAMB WHITE DAYS, THAT TIME WOULD TAKE ME	196	FERN HILL	46
OR STILL ALL THE NUMBERLESS DAYS OF HIS DEATH, THOUGH	216	ELEGY	8
THAT IN HER GARDEN, RATHER THAN THE DAYS,	223	IN DREAMS	9
DAYS'			
DAYS' NIGHT WHOSE TOWERS WILL CATCH	3	PROLOGUE	20
DAY'S			
UNTIL THE DAY'S BROKEN--	22	HIGH ON A HILL	6
AND THIS DAY'S SUN LEAPT UP THE SKY OUT OF HER THIGHS	170	MARRIAGE VIRG	4
DAZZLE			
DAZZLE THIS FACE OF VOICES ON THE MOON-TURNED TABLE,	110	I, IN IMAGE	69
DAZZLED			
AND THE BULWARKS OF THE DAZZLED QUAY.	162	LONG-LEGGED	10
DAZZLER			
OF THE DAZZLER OF HEAVEN	181	VISION, PRAYER	41
DAZZLING			
SAILED AND SET DAZZLING BY THE HANDSHAPED OCEAN,	131	I MAKE THIS IN	5
'NO. NOT FOR CHRIST'S DAZZLING BED	146	IF HEAD HURT	16
THE DAZZLING PRISON	183	VISION, PRAYER	131
DE			
AND IN HER GARDEN GROW THE FLEUR DE LYS,	222	IN DREAMS	1
DEAD			
THE DINGLE FURRED DEER DEAD!	4	PROLOGUE	56
HE'S DEAD, HOME, HAS NO LOVER,	17	IN OBLIVION	19
THEY ARE THE ONLY DEAD WHO DID NOT LOVE	23	THE ONLY DEAD	T
THEY ARE THE ONLY DEAD WHO DID NOT LOVE,	23	THE ONLY DEAD	1
THERE IS NO DEAD BUT IS NOT LOVED	23	THE ONLY DEAD	19
LOOK, THERE'S THE DEAD WHO DID NOT LOVE,	24	THE ONLY DEAD	30
DEAD LIMB AND MIND,	26	PERSONAL EPIT	14
FOR DEAD OR LIVE,	27	OBLIVIOUS DARK	19
OF THE MOMENT AND THE DEAD HOUR.	29	LONG, SKELETON	13
WE WHO ARE STILL YOUNG ARE OLD. IT IS A DEAD CRY,	40	YOUNG ARE OLD	5
WHERE DEATH LIES DEAD ASLEEP, ONE BRIGHT EYE OPEN,	41	YOUNG ARE OLD	20
THE LIVING DEAD LEFT OVER FROM THE WAR,	41	YOUNG ARE OLD	35
I AM A TIMID CHILD WHEN LIGHT IS DEAD.	48	LIGHT, I KNOW	11
DEAD MEN NAKED THEY SHALL BE ONE	49	NO DOMINION	2
WHERE HALF DEAD VANITIES WERE SLEEPING CURLED	50	OUT OF THE PIT	4
THOUGH THEY BE MAD AND DEAD AS NAILS,	50	NO DOMINION	24
WHERE FLOATED A DEAD DOG WHO MADE HIM ILL,	51	OUT OF THE PIT	41
A WOMAN WAILS HER DEAD AMONG THE TREES,	56	GREEK PLAY	1
AMONG THE TREES THE LANGUAGE OF THE DEAD	57	GREEK PLAY	13
THE DEAD IN HADES HAVE THEIR HOST OF FRIENDS,	57	GREEK PLAY	22
THE DEAD QUEEN WALKETH WITH MYCENAE'S KING	57	GREEK PLAY	23
IF DEAD MEN WALKED THEY, TOO, WOULD HOLLER	59	FAIRY TALES	17
WOULD TURN THE DEAD YELLOW.	59	FAIRY TALES	21
YET HE IS DEAD, AND STILL BY WOMAN'S WOMB	64	WOMAN SPEAKS	35
DOUBLED THE GLOBE OF DEAD AND HALVED A COUNTRY;	66	HAND SIGNED	3
THE FIVE KINGS COUNT THE DEAD BUT DO NOT SOFTEN	66	HAND SIGNED	13
DUMB DEAD THE CRANNIES HOUSE AND HIDE.	67	REALM OF FLESH	6
THE BRAIN ACTS TO THE LEGAL DEAD.	67	REALM OF FLESH	9

DEAD

		PAGE	TITLE	LINE
DEAD (CONTINUED)				
OF THE DEAD EYES OF CHILDREN		68	REALM OF FLESH	15
HOLDING FOR EVER THE DEAD MOON.		69	SECRET WIND	6
OF ROD AND WHEEL THAT WAKE THE DEAD.		70	SECRET WIND	12
IN THE COUNTRY OF THE DEAD		72	TAKE NEEDLES	46
MOON WALKS THE RIVER AND RAISES THE DEAD;		74	SUN BURNS	2
LEFT BY THE DEAD WHO, IN THEIR MOONLESS ACRE,		79	LOVE'S FEVER	35
AND ALL THE DEAD BEQUEATH FROM PALE ESTATES		80	ALL THAT I OWE	2
THE DEAD MAN SAID,		81	HERE LIE BEAST	2
THE DEAD MAN SAID,		81	HERE LIE BEAST	8
AND BROWSE UPON THE POSTURES OF THE DEAD;		81	ALL THAT I OWE	22
IS DAMP AND DRY; THE QUICK AND DEAD		88	A PROCESS IN	17
AND THE HEART GIVES UP ITS DEAD.		88	A PROCESS IN	24
THE DEAD TURNS UP ITS EYE;		90	WHERE ONCE THE	3
BLOWING THE OLD DEAD BACK; OUR SHOTS SHALL SMACK		90	EUNUCH DREAMS	38
FROM THE FAIR DEAD WHO FLUSH THE SEA		92	BOYS OF SUMMER	34
DEAD ON THE SWEETHEARTS' TOES.		95	RUB OF LOVE	28
SOME DEAD UNDID THEIR BUSHY JAWS,		97	TWILIGHT LOCKS	22
GIVES UP ITS DEAD TO SUCH A WORKING SEA;		97	TWILIGHT LOCKS	27
MY BLOOD UPON THE TEMPERED DEAD, FORCING		103	I DREAMED MY	19
I HEAR, THROUGH DEAD MEN'S DRUMS, THE RIDDLED LADS,		105	WORLD PYRAMID	40
DRIP ON MY DEAD HOUSE GARDEN.		105	WORLD PYRAMID	45
IN SEIZURE OF SILENCE COMMIT THE DEAD NUISANCE:		109	I, IN IMAGE	23
TURNING THE RIDERLESS DEAD BY THE CHANNEL WALL.		110	I, IN IMAGE	48
RINGS OUT THE DEAD SEA SCALE;		110	I, IN IMAGE	63
AND THE VELVET DEAD INCH OUT.		114	SERVANT SUN	21
LET HER INHALE HER DEAD, THROUGH SEED AND SOLID		115	A GRIEF AGO	37
AND THREE DEAD SEASONS ON A CLIMBING GRAVE		117	ALTARWISE	30
DRAW ON THE GLOVE OF PRINTS, DEAD CAIRO'S HENNA		120	ALTARWISE	117
AND RIVERS OF THE DEAD AROUND MY NECK.		120	ALTARWISE	126
YEA THE DEAD STIR,		127	NOW, SAY NAY	18
AND WALK THE WARRING SANDS BY THE DEAD TOWN,		132	I MAKE THIS IN	32
'SEE,' DRUMMED THE TAUT MASKS, 'HOW THE DEAD ASCEND:		132	I MAKE THIS IN	52
IN THE SNIVELLING HOURS WITH DEAD, HUMPED ANN		136	AFTER FUNERAL	13
(BURY THE DEAD FOR FEAR THAT THEY WALK TO THE GRAVE IN LABOUR.)		143	24 YEARS	2
IF THE DEAD STARVE, THEIR STOMACHS TURN TO TUMBLE		145	PLEASURE-BIRD	22
DEAD AND GONE, DEDICATE FOREVER TO MY SELF		147	UNLUCKILY FOR	6
UNCLAIMED DEAD, GIRLS FROM GOOD HOMES		154	RETURN	15
FORGOTTEN DARK, REST THEIR PULSE AND BURY THEIR DEAD IN HER FAITHLESS SLEEP.		159	INTO HER HEAD	69
WHO STRODE FOR YOUR OWN DEAD		160	DEATHS AND ENT	20
SING HOW THE SEAL HAS KISSED HER DEAD!		164	LONG-LEGGED	82
FOR THE CRAB-BACKED DEAD ON THE SEA-BED ROSE		165	LONG-LEGGED	99
OH MIRACLE OF FISHES! THE LONG DEAD BITE!		166	LONG-LEGGED	140
AND THE DEAD HAND LEADS THE PAST,		167	LONG-LEGGED	148
AT LARGE AS THE DEAD,		169	LOVE IN ASYLUM	8
OVER THE DEAD INFANTS		174	FIRE RAID	50
INTO THE DEAD CLOCK BURNING THE HOUR		175	FIRE RAID	65
SUMMERTIME OF THE DEAD WHISPERED THE TRUTH OF HIS JOY		178	POEM IN OCT	56
JOY OF THE LONG DEAD CHILD SANG BURNING		178	POEM IN OCT	63
THAT HE LET THE DEAD LIE THOUGH THEY MOAN		184	VISION, PRAYER	136
AND SPELLS ON THE WINDS OF THE DEAD HIS WINTER'S TALE.		189	WINTER'S TALE	59
TIME SINGS THROUGH THE INTRICATELY DEAD SNOW DROP. LISTEN.		189	WINTER'S TALE	65
HORSES, CENTAUR DEAD, TURN AND TREAD THE DRENCHED WHITE		189	WINTER'S TALE	74
PADDOCKS IN THE FARMS OF BIRDS. THE DEAD OAK WALKS FOR LOVE.		189	WINTER'S TALE	75

	PAGE	TITLE	LINE
DEAD (CONTINUED)			
ON THE WHITE, NO LONGER GROWING GREEN, AND, MINSTREL DEAD,	190	WINTER'S TALE	112
OF NIGHTINGALE AND CENTAUR DEAD HORSE. THE SPRINGS WITHER	191	WINTER'S TALE	117
LIKE THE DUST OF THE DEAD.	192	SIDE OF TRUTH	12
DEEP WITH THE FIRST DEAD LIES LONDON'S DAUGHTER,	192	REFUSAL MOURN	19
AND THE OTHER FULL OF TEARS THAT SHE WILL BE DEAD,	193	CONVERS PRAYER	5
TURNS ON THE QUICK AND THE DEAD, AND THE MAN ON THE STAIRS	194	CONVERS PRAYER	14
DRAGGING HIM UP THE STAIRS TO ONE WHO LIES DEAD.	194	CONVERS PRAYER	20
NOR FOR THE TOWERING DEAD	197	CRAFT OR ART	15
THE THIEF FALL ON THE DEAD LIKE THE WILLY NILLY DEW,	200	COUNTRY SLEEP	93
TROUNCED BY HIS WINGS IN THE HISSING SHIPPEN, LONG DEAD	205	GIANT'S THIGH	39
WHO HEARD THE TALL BELL SAIL DOWN THE SUNDAYS OF THE DEAD	205	GIANT'S THIGH	51
HALE DEAD AND DEATHLESS DO THE WOMEN OF THE HILL	205	GIANT'S THIGH	58
THE DEAD GROW FOR HIS JOY.	210	POEM ON B'DAY	54
OR THE STARS' SEASHORE DEAD,	210	POEM ON B'DAY	57
NOON, AND NIGHT, AND LIGHT. THE RIVERS OF THE DEAD	216	ELEGY	15
WHISPER A BENEDICTION FOR THE DEAD.	222	MISSING	6
TEMPLE'S BROKEN AND POOR RAVEN'S DEAD;	238	PILLAR BREAKS	24
BUT IF IT STINGS MY BODY DEAD	240	TWINING HEAD	3
DEADLY			
NONE, AND HIS DEADLY WELCOME	23	THE ONLY DEAD	13
MAKE DEADLY WHOOPEE IN THE BLUE.	84	LETTER TO AUNT	55
SAVOURS THE LICK OF THE TIMES THROUGH A DEADLY WOOD OF HAIR	144	PLEASURE-BIRD	9
THE FEMALE, DEADLY, AND MALE	158	INTO HER HEAD	53
AND ALL THE DEADLY VIRTUES PLAGUE MY DEATH!	207	LAMENT	60
DEADROCK			
THE DEADROCK BASE THE BLOW THE FLOWERED ANCHOR,	127	NOW, SAY NAY	5
DEADWEED			
THE BAGPIPE-BREASTED LADIES IN THE DEADWEED	119	ALTARWISE	83
DEAF			
I WHO WAS DEAF TO SPRING AND SUMMER,	68	BEFORE KNOCKED	7
AND ALL SWEET HELL, DEAF AS AN HOUR'S EAR,	114	SERVANT SUN	33
DEAN			
BEARDLESSLY WAGGING IN DEAN STREET,	156	RETURN	72
DEAR			
THE DEAR, DAFT TIME I TAKE TO NUDGE THE SENTENCE,	124	TODAY, INSECT	4
AND THE DEAR FLOODS OF HIS HAIR.	140	TOMBSTONE TOLD	30
MY DEAR WOULD I CHANGE MY TEARS OR YOUR IRON HEAD.	146	IF HEAD HURT	18
O MY DEAR IT'S NEVER TOO LATE	149	PAPER & STICKS	11
AND TAKEN BY LIGHT IN HER ARMS AT LONG AND DEAR LAST	170	LOVE IN ASYLUM	16
DEAR TOMMY, PLEASE, FROM FAR, SCIATIC KINGSLEY	179	NEW QUAY	1
MY DEAR, MY DEAR,	197	COUNTRY SLEEP	5
MY DEAR, MY DEAR,	197	COUNTRY SLEEP	5
MY DEAR THIS NIGHT HE COMES AND NIGHT WITHOUT END MY DEAR	201	COUNTRY SLEEP	108
MY DEAR THIS NIGHT HE COMES AND NIGHT WITHOUT END MY DEAR	201	COUNTRY SLEEP	108
AND FABULOUS, DEAR GOD.	210	POEM ON B'DAY	48
LIGHTLY, THOU WIND, OVER HIS DEAR, DARK HEAD,	222	MISSING	4
DEATH			
IN DEATH OR OUT OF DEATH,	20	ENCOMPASSED	8
IN DEATH OR OUT OF DEATH,	20	ENCOMPASSED	8
DEATH TO THE MAGICAL WHEN ALL IS DONE,	21	BEWILDERED WAY	3
AND ALL THE MASTERY THERE IS IN DEATH,	22	ON QUIET NIGHT	4

	PAGE	TITLE	LINE
DEATH (CONTINUED)			
WHO HAVE NO TALK BUT THAT OF DEATH.	23	ON QUIET NIGHT	22
DEATH SIGHTS AND SEES WITH GREAT MISGIVING	25	THERE'S PLENTY	6
STILL'S VAIN TO ARGUE AFTER DEATH;	27	OBLIVIOUS DARK	10
WHERE DEATH LIES DEAD ASLEEP, ONE BRIGHT EYE OPEN,	41	YOUNG ARE OLD	20
OR CATCH ALL DEATH THAT'S IN THE AIR.	47	POET: 1935	46
AND DEATH SHALL HAVE NO DOMINION	49	NO DOMINION	T
AND DEATH SHALL HAVE NO DOMINION.	49	NO DOMINION	1
AND DEATH SHALL HAVE NO DOMINION.	49	NO DOMINION	9
AND DEATH SHALL HAVE NO DOMINION.	49	NO DOMINION	10
WILL ONLY DIM LIFE, AND LIGHT DEATH.	49	LIGHT, I KNOW	29
AND DEATH SHALL HAVE NO DOMINION.	50	NO DOMINION	18
AND DEATH SHALL HAVE NO DOMINION.	50	NO DOMINION	19
AND DEATH SHALL HAVE NO DOMINION.	50	NO DOMINION	27
WHEN ANY LIGHT GOES OUT, AND LIFE IS DEATH.	55	NO MAN BELIEVE	6
A PIGEON CALLS AND WOMEN TALK OF DEATH.	57	GREEK PLAY	32
AT SIGHT OF DEATH, THE LAST TWO FISTED KILLER	59	FAIRY TALES	18
DEATH AND EVIL ARE TWIN SPECTRES.	60	FAIRY TALES	26
DEATH AND EVIL, TOO SLOW IN HEEDING WORDS.	60	FAIRY TALES	35
FEAR DEATH AS LITTLE AS THE THUNDER'S SHOT,	60	FAIRY TALES	40
BEFORE DEATH TAKES YOU, O TAKE BACK THIS.	61	MEAT ON BONES	41
NO FOOD SUFFICES BUT THE FOOD OF DEATH;	63	WOMAN SPEAKS	2
NO FOOD SUFFICES BUT THE FOOD OF DEATH;	64	WOMAN SPEAKS	33
THESE FIVE KINGS DID A KING TO DEATH.	66	HAND SIGNED	4
WHY SHOULD I THINK ON DEATH WHEN YOU ARE RULER?	67	REALM OF FLESH	10
HOUSING DEATH IN YOUR KINGDOM,	67	REALM OF FLESH	12
GOD SHALL BE GODS AND MANY DEATHS BE DEATH.	67	LET A FAITH	15
WHEN I YIELD THE TREE TO DEATH,	72	TAKE NEEDLES	45
OF BIRTH AND DEATH, THE TWO SAD KNAVES OF THIEVES,	75	MY HERO BARES	18
MY FALLEN FILLED, THAT HAD THE HINT OF DEATH,	80	ALL THAT I OWE	10
THE BRAINS OF DEATH UNDID THE KNOT	86	SEE, SAYS LIME	22
THE MILK OF DEATH, I FILLED THE HAND	86	SEE, SAYS LIME	30
DRIVES IN A DEATH AS LIFE LEAKS OUT.	88	A PROCESS IN	9
WHERE, PUNCTUAL AS DEATH, WE RING THE STARS;	92	BOYS OF SUMMER	27
DEATH FROM A SUMMER WOMAN,	92	BOYS OF SUMMER	32
FIRST CHARACTERS OF BIRTH AND DEATH.	94	IN BEGINNING	24
AND THE DEATH IN A STARVING IMAGE.	96	TWELVE	14
THE WORDS OF DEATH ARE DRYER THAN HIS STIFF,	96	RUB OF LOVE	46
HE HAD BY HEART THE CHRIST-CROSS-ROW OF DEATH.	97	TWILIGHT LOCKS	24
SHAPES IN A CINDER DEATH; LOVE FOR HIS TRICK,	101	RUNNING GRAVE	48
DEATH ON THE MOUTH THAT ATE THE GAS.	103	I DREAMED MY	16
SHARP IN MY SECOND DEATH I MARKED THE HILLS, HARVEST	103	I DREAMED MY	17
I DREAMED MY GENESIS IN SWEAT OF DEATH, FALLEN	103	I DREAMED MY	25
DEATH FLASHING FROM HIS SLEEVE,	108	GRIEF THIEF	16
DAYED PEAKS TO DAY TO DEATH,	108	GRIEF THIEF	22
NO DEATH MORE NATURAL;	109	I, IN IMAGE	21
(DEATH INSTRUMENTAL,	110	I, IN IMAGE	49
MAN WAS THE SCALES, THE DEATH BIRDS ON ENAMEL,	111	I, IN IMAGE	97
LOVE'S HOUSE, THEY ANSWER, AND THE TOWER DEATH	113	NOT FATHER ME	31
DEATH IS ALL METAPHORS, SHAPE IN ONE HISTORY;	117	ALTARWISE	15
DEATH FROM A BANDAGE, RANTS THE MASK OF SCHOLARS	120	ALTARWISE	120
DEATH: DEATH OF HAMLET AND THE NIGHTMARE MADMEN,	124	TODAY, INSECT	19
DEATH: DEATH OF HAMLET AND THE NIGHTMARE MADMEN,	124	TODAY, INSECT	19
DEATH TO THE YES,	127	NOW, SAY NAY	11
THE YES TO DEATH, THE YESMAN AND THE ANSWER,	127	NOW, SAY NAY	12
DEATH HAIRY-HEELED, AND THE TAPPED GHOST IN WOOD,	128	NOW, SAY NAY	33
MAGNIFIED OUT OF PRAISE; HER DEATH WAS A STILL DROP;	136	AFTER FUNERAL	17
TO LIFT TO LEAVE FROM THE TREASURES OF MAN IS			
PLEASING DEATH	140	NO WORK WORDS	7
DEATH AND THIS MAD HEROINE	140	TOMBSTONE TOLD	22

	PAGE	TITLE	LINE
DEATH (CONTINUED)			
UNLUCKILY FOR A DEATH	147	UNLUCKILY FOR	T
UNLUCKILY FOR A DEATH	147	UNLUCKILY FOR	1
THE DEATH BIDING TWO LIE LONELY.	148	UNLUCKILY FOR	28
DEATH IN THE CARVED NUNNERY	148	UNLUCKILY FOR	46
CARRYING CLOUD, DEATH STRIKES THEIR HOUSE.	161	WEDDING ANNIV	8
REJOICING FOR THAT DRIFTING DEATH	164	LONG-LEGGED	88
AMONG THE STREET BURNED TO TIRELESS DEATH	173	FIRE RAID	4
YOUR DEATH THAT MYSELVES THE BELIEVERS	173	FIRE RAID	20
AS THE GRAINS BLOW, AS YOUR DEATH GROWS, THROUGH OUR			
HEART.	173	FIRE RAID	24
OF THE DEATH IN A BED IN ANOTHER COUNTRY.	176	MY BEGGAR ARM	8
FOR THE COUNTRY OF DEATH IS THE HEART'S SIZE	184	VISION, PRAYER	169
IN THE FAR AGO LAND THE DOOR OF HIS DEATH GLIDED WIDE	190	WINTER'S TALE	105
A REFUSAL TO MOURN THE DEATH, BY FIRE, OF A CHILD IN			
LONDON	191	REFUSAL MOURN	T
THE MAJESTY AND BURNING OF THE CHILD'S DEATH.	192	REFUSAL MOURN	13
OF MOVING ABOUT YOUR DEATH	192	SIDE OF TRUTH	14
AFTER THE FIRST DEATH, THERE IS NO OTHER.	192	REFUSAL MOURN	24
DEATH, AND BAD DEATH, AND THEN	193	SIDE OF TRUTH	22
DEATH, AND BAD DEATH, AND THEN	193	SIDE OF TRUTH	22
DEATH CLEAR AS A BUOY'S BELL:	202	SIR JOHNS HILL	26
AND ALL THE DEADLY VIRTUES PLAGUE MY DEATH!	207	LAMENT	60
GRAVE MEN, NEAR DEATH, WHO SEE WITH BLINDING SIGHT	208	NOT GO GENTLE	13
WORK AT THEIR WAYS TO DEATH, ...	209	POEM ON B'DAY	14
TO DEATH, ONE MAN THROUGH HIS SUNDERED HULKS, ...	211	POEM ON B'DAY	92
OR STILL ALL THE NUMBERLESS DAYS OF HIS DEATH, THOUGH	216	ELEGY	8
THE DARKEST JUSTICE OF DEATH, BLIND AND UNBLESSED.	216	ELEGY	11
(PITY FOR DEATH)	216	COUNTRY HEAVEN	32
AND CAUGHT BETWEEN TWO NIGHTS, BLINDNESS AND DEATH.	217	ELEGY	36
DEATH COMES TO THE BEAUTIFUL.	236	WOMAN TAPESTRY	41
FOR DEATH IS FRIENDLY TO THE MAN	240	TWINING HEAD	5
DEATHBEDS			
IN DEATHBEDS OF ORCHARDS THE BOAT DIES DOWN	169	LONG-LEGGED	207
DEATHLESS			
YOUR FAITH AS DEATHLESS AS THE OUTCRY OF THE RULED			
SUN.	201	COUNTRY SLEEP	111
HALE DEAD AND DEATHLESS DO THE WOMEN OF THE HILL	205	GIANT'S THIGH	58
DEATH'LL			
AT WHOSE BALL-PRYING EVEN DEATH'LL SQUIRM	179	NEW QUAY	22
DEATHS			
GOD SHALL BE GODS AND MANY DEATHS BE DEATH.	67	LET A FAITH	15
THROUGH THE DEVILISH YEARS AND INNOCENT DEATHS	139	TOMBSTONE TOLD	14
BRAVE DEATHS OF ONLY ONES BUT NEVER FOUND, ...	153	WAS A SAVIOUR	35
DEATHS AND ENTRANCES	160	DEATHS AND ENT	T
OF SEVERAL NEAR DEATHS, ...	160	DEATHS AND ENT	2
OF DEATHS AND ENTRANCES, ...	160	DEATHS AND ENT	26
DEATH'S			
TOO LONG, SKELETON, DEATH'S RISEN	29	LONG, SKELETON	1
TOO LONG, SKELETON, DEATH'S ALL ALIVE	29	LONG, SKELETON	4
SHALL I FALL TO DEATH'S FEATHER.	44	LONGED TO MOVE	18
DEATH'S APPETITE IS SHARPENED BY THE BULLET'S THUMB;	64	WOMAN SPEAKS	34
THE HEART STEPS TO DEATH'S FINGER, ...	67	REALM OF FLESH	8
AND I WAS STRUCK DOWN BY DEATH'S FEATHER.	69	BEFORE KNOCKED	39
OF DEATH'S UNDOER.	85	SEE, SAYS LIME	8
DEATH'S DEATH'S UNDOER.	86	SEE, SAYS LIME	32
DEATH'S DEATH'S UNDOER.	86	SEE, SAYS LIME	32
AND WHAT'S THE RUB? DEATH'S FEATHER ON THE NERVE?	96	RUB OF LOVE	43
WHAT COLOUR IS GLORY? DEATH'S FEATHER? TREMBLE	104	WORLD PYRAMID	25
WHO BLOWS DEATH'S FEATHER? WHAT GLORY IS COLOUR?	105	WORLD PYRAMID	55

	PAGE	TITLE	LINE
DEATH'S (CONTINUED)			
MY HALF GHOST IN ARMOUR HOLD HARD IN DEATH'S CORRIDOR,	108	I, IN IMAGE	5
HEAR BY DEATH'S ACCIDENT THE CLOCKED AND DASHED-DOWN SPIRE	130	SINNERS' BELL	11
DEATH-STAGGED			
THE DEATH-STAGGED SCATTER-BREATH	150	WHEN I WOKE	19
DECADENT			
(FOR THOUGHT, WE KNOW, IS DECADENT);	84	LETTER TO AUNT	43
DECAY			
NOW IS DECAY IN BONE AND SINEW,	34	THIRST PARCHES	3
AN IMAGE OF DECAY DISTURBS THE CROCUS	47	POET: 1935	29
AND THE HERALDS OF DECAY,	71	TAKE NEEDLES	11
DECAYED			
PALE AND DECAYED, AN UGLY GROWTH.	239	LET ME ESCAPE	12
DECAYING			
YOUR MONSTROUS OFFICERS AND THE DECAYING ARMY,	110	I, IN IMAGE	56
DECEIVED			
HEAD, DECEIVED, I BELIEVED, MY MAKER,	152	BELOW A TIME	34
DECEMBER'S			
DECEMBER'S THORN SCREWED IN A BROW OF HOLLY.	121	ALTARWISE	132
COUNTRY, YOUR SPORT IS SUMMER, AND DECEMBER'S POOLS	122	HOLD HARD	7
DECENCY			
TO CIRCUMAMBULATE FOR DECENCY	11	CABARET	8
DECISION			
LOVE'S A DECISION OF 3 NERVES	138	O CHATTERTON	22
DECK			
GOOD-BYE TO THE MAN ON THE SEA-LEGGED DECK	162	LONG-LEGGED	18
DECKED			
KNOCKED IN THE FLESH THAT DECKED THE VINE,	86	BREAD I BREAK	7
OR DECKED ON A CLOUD SWALLOWER,	151	BELOW A TIME	12
DECKS			
FILE THROUGH THE FLESH WHERE NO FLESH DECKS THE BONES.	82	LIGHT BREAKS	6
THAT BURN THE BITTEN DECKS,	128	MY NEOPHYTE	9
STRIKE AND SMOOTHE, FOR MY DECKS ARE DRUMS,	164	LONG-LEGGED	77
HIS DECKS ARE DRENCHED WITH MIRACLES.	166	LONG-LEGGED	139
DECLAIMS			
FLIES ON THE SHAFTED DISK, DECLAIMS THE MORNING	99	OCTOBER WIND	19
ONE VOICE IN CHAINS DECLAIMS	158	INTO HER HEAD	52
DECLARE			
DECLARE THEIR SOULS, LET CHILDREN KNOW, LIVE AFTER.	36	LET BE KNOWN	6
DECLENSION			
AND FROM THE FIRST DECLENSION OF THE FLESH	79	LOVE'S FEVER	31
DEDICATE			
DEAD AND GONE, DEDICATE FOREVER TO MY SELF	147	UNLUCKILY FOR	6
DEEDS			
AND ALL YOUR DEEDS AND WORDS,	193	SIDE OF TRUTH	34
THEIR FRAIL DEEDS MIGHT HAVE DANCED IN A GREEN BAY,	208	NOT GO GENTLE	8
DEEP			
ONLY THE DROWNED DEEP BELLS	5	PROLOGUE	87
THIS PUS RUNS DEEP.	27	OBLIVIOUS DARK	13
GOES OVER THE HILL INTO THE DEEP SEA;	43	LONGED TO MOVE	5
WHO DOES NOT BURY GOD IN A DEEP GRAVE	55	NO MAN BELIEVE	19
THROUGH THESE LASHED RINGS SET DEEP INSIDE THEIR HOLLOWS	76	LASHED RINGS	1
THERE IN THE DEEP WITH QUARTERED SHADES	92	BOYS OF SUMMER	16
HOW DEEP THE WAKING IN THE WORLDED CLOUDS.	102	FELLOWED SLEEP	25
OF TIDE-TONGUED HEADS AND BLADDERS IN THE DEEP,	104	WORLD PYRAMID	16

	PAGE	TITLE	LINE
DEEP (CONTINUED)			
FLOOD OF HER HEART'S FAME; SHE WOULD LIE DUMB AND DEEP	136	AFTER FUNERAL	19
WHEN YOU SEW THE DEEP DOOR. THE BED IS A CROSS PLACE.	145	IF HEAD HURT	13
AND THE SECOND COMERS, THE SEVERERS, THE ENEMIES FROM THE DEEP	159	INTO HER HEAD	68
QUAKED THE SICK SEA AND SNOUTED DEEP, ...	163	LONG-LEGGED	50
DEEP THE GREAT BUSHED BAIT WITH RAINING LIPS	163	LONG-LEGGED	51
DAYS DEEP IN HER BREAST THAT WORE NO HEART	175	MY BEGGAR ARM	2
A DARK AS DEEP	176	BREATH SHED	9
HE SNUGGLES DEEP AMONG THE CHAPEL THIGHS, ...	179	NEW QUAY	30
AND DEEP	184	VISION, PRAYER	143
DEEP HILLOCKS AND LOUD ON THE NUMBED LAKES, ...	190	WINTER'S TALE	97
THAT ONCE CUT THE FIGURES OF BIRDS ON THE DEEP BREAD	190	WINTER'S TALE	114
DEEP WITH THE FIRST DEAD LIES LONDON'S DAUGHTER,	192	REFUSAL MOURN	19
SHALL DROWN IN A GRIEF AS DEEP AS HIS MADE GRAVE,	194	CONVERS PRAYER	18
SLEEP, GOOD, FOR EVER, SLOW AND DEEP, SPELLED RARE AND WISE, ...	197	COUNTRY SLEEP	8
DEEP IN ITS BLACK, BASE BONES, ...	211	POEM ON B'DAY	88
NO WEEPING THROUGH THAT DEEP REPOSE CAN BREAK.	222	MISSING	9
BENEATH THE DEEP BARK CALLS AND MAKES QUIET MUSIC.	226	THE OAK	6
AND THE DEEP SKY OVER THEM	235	WOMAN TAPESTRY	9
A COMPASSION SPRINGING FROM THE DEEP BODY, ...	236	WOMAN TAPESTRY	53
DEEPER			
THERE ARE NO SEACAVES DEEPER THAN HER EYES;	57	GREEK PLAY	11
FADE, THE GREEN GLOOM GROWS DARKER, AND DEEPER THE DUSK:	222	FOREST PICTURE	10
THEY ARE DEEPER IN DARKNESS	226	THE ELM	5
'LINGER NOT DEEPER IN THE COLOURED TREES, ...	227	SPRING-SPIRIT	2
DEEPEST			
ONE WHO CALLED DEEPEST DOWN SHALL HOLD HIS PEACE	160	DEATHS AND ENT	9
O DEEPEST WOUND OF ALL THAT HE SHOULD DIE	217	ELEGY	37
DEEPSEA			
HER DEEPSEA PILLOW WHERE ONCE SHE MARRIED ALONE,	170	MARRIAGE VIRG	9
DEER			
THE DINGLE FURRED DEER DEAD!	4	PROLOGUE	56
AND THE TIMID DEER THE TIGRESS:	76	SONG: LOVE ME	14
THE GREENWOOD DYING AS THE DEER FALL IN THEIR TRACKS,	122	HOLD HARD	11
AND FAST THROUGH THE DRIFTS OF THE THICKETS ANTLERED LIKE DEER, ...	190	WINTER'S TALE	95
DEFACED			
SO, NOT TO BE DEFACED, ...	19	IMAGES IN AIR	10
DEFEAT			
AND THAT IS TRUE AFTER PERPETUAL DEFEAT.	32	OUT OF SIGHS	9
DEFILE			
RAIN SHALL DEFILE AND COVER, WIND BEAR AWAY	64	WOMAN SPEAKS	40
DEFT			
AT THE DEFT MOVEMENTS OF THE IRISES	48	POET: 1935	56
DEFYING			
SO FAST I MOVE DEFYING TIME, THE QUIET GENTLEMAN	116	LANTERNS SHINE	14
DELIBERATE			
THE ICICLE OF EACH DELIBERATE FANCY.	10	COOL, OH NO	7
DELICATE			
THE FRAIL AND DELICATE BREATH OF EVEN-TIME.	222	IN DREAMS	4
HIDDEN IN DELICATE DRIFTS OF MIST ARE THEY THAT BECKON, ...	224	IDYLL UNFORGET	37
OF THE PALE-GREEN, DELICATE FISHES, SILVER AS SIGHS;	224	IDYLL UNFORGET	39
THEY ARE FURTHER AND MORE DELICATE	226	THE ELM	3
IS A PETAL THAT HAS DELICATE BREATH	226	SLENDER WIND	7
THEIR DELICATE, SILKEN LEAVES FOLDED, ...	235	WOMAN TAPESTRY	8

		PAGE	TITLE	LINE

DELICATE (CONTINUED)
GROW INTO YOUR DELICATE SKIN, ... 238 MAKES INTERVALS 11
DELICIOUS
AT A CALF THAT IS PLUMP AND DELICIOUS; .... 221 SONG OF DOG 14
YOU LOOSE, DELICIOUS WILL .... 237 PILLAR BREAKS 9
DELIGHT
RARER DELIGHT SHOOTS IN THE BLOOD .... 48 POET: 1935 55
AND OFFER AS THE LAST DELIGHT .... 143 THE MOLLS 7
NOW I DELIGHT, I SUPPOSE, IN .... 156 RETURN 95
THEN IN THE DELIGHT AND GROVE OF BEASTS AND BIRDS 215 COUNTRY HEAVEN 6
BUT MY GREATEST DELIGHT IS TO TAKE A GOOD BITE .... 221 SONG OF DOG 13
UNASHAMED BUT NOT WITH DELIGHT, ... 230 OUR SANCTITY 17
STIRRING ITS POLE STEM IN DELIGHT, ... 235 WOMAN TAPESTRY 16
DELIVER
DELIVER ME WHO, TIMID IN MY TRIBE, ... 100 RUNNING GRAVE 7
DELIVER ME, MY MASTERS, HEAD AND HEART, ... 100 RUNNING GRAVE 11
DELIVER HIM, HE CRIED, ... 188 WINTER'S TALE 51
DELIVERED
DELIVERED SEAS MY LOVE FROM HER PROUD PLACE .... 133 I MAKE THIS IN 62
DELL
FOLLOWING THE NOSE DOWN DELL, UP RISE .... 44 TO FOLLOW FOX 7
OR SKULKS IN THE DELL MOON BUT MOONSHINE ECHOING
CLEAR .... 198 COUNTRY SLEEP 25
DELUDES
SHE DELUDES THE HEAVEN-PROOF HOUSE WITH ENTERING
CLOUDS .... 169 LOVE IN ASYLUM 6
YET SHE DELUDES WITH WALKING THE NIGHTMARISH ROOM, 169 LOVE IN ASYLUM 7
DELUGING
TO MOURN HIS DELUGING .... 184 VISION, PRAYER 156
DELUSIVE
WHO ADMITS THE DELUSIVE LIGHT THROUGH THE BOUNCING
WALL, ... 170 LOVE IN ASYLUM 11
DEN
YOU HAVE KICKED FROM A DARK DEN, LEAPED UP THE
WHINNYING LIGHT, ... 135 HOW MY ANIMAL 43
DENIALS
COUNTING THE DENIALS OF THE GRAINS .... 167 LONG-LEGGED 160
DENIERS
WE ARE THE DARK DENIERS, LET US SUMMON .... 92 BOYS OF SUMMER 31
DOOM ON DENIERS AT THE WIND-TURNED STATEMENT. ..... 119 ALTARWISE 90
DENIES
ANSWER: WHEN HER BABE DENIES HER. .... 72 TAKE NEEDLES 62
DENS
THE DENS OF SHAPE .... 115 A GRIEF AGO 28
DENT
CANNOT DENT YOUR FLANKS; .... 229 MY RIVER 14
DENY
ALL THE CABINNED FAITHS DENY .... 71 TAKE NEEDLES 15
AND A CONTINENT DENY? .... 126 SEED-AT-ZERO 30
AND A CONTINENT DENY? .... 126 SEED-AT-ZERO 37
DEPARTED
HE HAS THE WHOLE FIELD NOW, THE GODS DEPARTED ..... 29 NEARLY SUMMER 7
IN THE DEPARTED VILLAGES. THE NIGHTINGALE, ... 189 WINTER'S TALE 57
ON THE DEPARTED, SNOW BUSHED GREEN, WANTON IN MOON
LIGHT .... 189 WINTER'S TALE 72
DEPARTING
SAIL ON THE LEVEL, THE DEPARTING ADVENTURE, ... 109 I, IN IMAGE 35
DEPARTURE
THAT THIS IS LIES THAT MOANS DEPARTURE, ... 36 LET BE KNOWN 4

	PAGE	TITLE	LINE
DEPENDING			
BALL OF THE FOOT DEPENDING FROM THE SUN, ...	101	RUNNING GRAVE	43
DEPENDS			
REMEMBER THIS: THAT LOVE DEPENDS	84	LETTER TO AUNT	50
DEPTH			
AND EYES HAVE BEEN GROVE-GREEN CATCHING MINE FROM			
THE DEPTH OF THE SILENCE;	224	IDYLL UNFORGET	33
DEPTHS			
BUT ONLY PLUMB SUCH DEPTHS	24	LITTLE PROBLEM	24
AND YOU AROSE FROM DEPTHS OF GRASS	227	SPRING-SPIRIT	5
DERIDE			
AND THE GRAVE SEA, MOCK WHO DERIDE	54	WE BY SEASAND	2
DERIVE			
AS YOU, ORIGINAL, DERIVE.	24	LITTLE PROBLEM	25
DERRY			
PENUMBRA DERRY, ...	18	NATURAL DAY	36
DO, DOWN A DERRY.	18	NATURAL DAY	38
DESCENDED			
POLE-SITTING GIRLS DESCENDED FOR A MEAL, ...	51	OUT OF THE PIT	29
DIPPED ME BREAST-DEEP IN THE DESCENDED BONE;	118	ALTARWISE	38
AND THE BIRD DESCENDED.	190	WINTER'S TALE	106
DESCENDING			
NO, NO, YOU LOVER SKULL, DESCENDING HAMMER	100	RUNNING GRAVE	27
OF THE DESCENDING DAY, THE DARK OUR FOLLY	148	UNLUCKILY FOR	19
DESCENDS			
A SECRET NIGHT DESCENDS BETWEEN	69	SECRET WIND	4
DESCENDS, MY MASTERS, ON THE ENTERED HONOUR.	100	RUNNING GRAVE	28
HOLD HARD, MY COUNTY DARLINGS, FOR A HAWK DESCENDS,	123	HOLD HARD	22
DESERT			
RIBBED BETWEEN DESERT AND WATER STORM, ...	54	WE BY SEASAND	11
WEEPS ON THE DESERT OCHRE AND THE SALT	104	WORLD PYRAMID	32
THIS WAS THE RESURRECTION IN THE DESERT, ...	120	ALTARWISE	119
DESERTS			
TO CHOKE THE DESERTS WITH HER TIDES, ...	93	BOYS OF SUMMER	41
DESERVES			
DESERVES NO BRUSH, BUT A FOOL'S AMBUSH.	44	TO FOLLOW FOX	6
DESIGNED			
ROUND THE SUN, HE COMES TO MY LOVE LIKE THE DESIGNED			
SNOW, ...	200	COUNTRY SLEEP	96
COMES DESIGNED TO MY LOVE TO STEAL NOT HER TIDE			
RAKING	200	COUNTRY SLEEP	100
DESIRE			
HAVE KNOWN MAN'S ENVY AND HIS WEAK DESIRE, ...	30	YOUTH CALLS	3
OF SHADES, SYMBOL OF DESIRE BEYOND MY HOURS	148	UNLUCKILY FOR	35
THAT THE PHOENIX' BID FOR HEAVEN AND THE DESIRE AFTER	148	UNLUCKILY FOR	45
DESIRE IS PHOSPHORUS: THE CHEMIC BRUIT	159	TO LEDA	7
WITH NO MORE DESIRE THAN A GHOST.	166	LONG-LEGGED	124
NO LONGER WILL THE VIBRATIONS OF THE SUN DESIRE ON	170	MARRIAGE VIRG	8
RECALL MY OLD DESIRE	237	WOMAN TAPESTRY	70
DESIRED			
I HAVE DESIRED THE CIRCLE OF THE SUN.	52	OUT OF THE PIT	73
DESIRELESS			
A DESIRELESS FAMILIAR	147	TO OTHERS	15
DESIRERS			
SAVE BY THEIR LONG DESIRERS IN THE FOX CUBBED	205	GIANT'S THIGH	56
DESIRES			
KNEW ALL HIS HORRIBLE DESIRES	128	MY NEOPHYTE	10
THESE WERE MY DESIRES, ETERNAL AS MOUNTAINS, ...	223	IDYLL UNFORGET	9
DESIRING			
IN THE ALWAYS DESIRING CENTRE OF THE WHITE	188	WINTER'S TALE	48

		PAGE	TITLE	LINE
DESOLATE				
SHAKES A DESOLATE BOY WHO SLITS HIS THROAT	....	136	AFTER FUNERAL	7
DESOLATION				
MAKE DESOLATION IN THE VEIN,	....	86	BREAD I BREAK	12
DESPAIR				
A COUNTRY'S TEARS AND VOICED A WORLD'S DESPAIR	....	57	GREEK PLAY	18
LET THE MAGGOT OF DESPAIR	....	70	TAKE NEEDLES	7
DESPAIR OF BLOOD, FAITH IN THE MAIDEN'S SLIME,	....	100	RUNNING GRAVE	23
YOU SHALL NOT DESPAIR	....	228	NOT DESPAIR	T
YOU SHALL NOT DESPAIR	....	228	NOT DESPAIR	1
DESTINATION				
HIS AIM AND DESTINATION.	....	26	PERSONAL EPIT	18
DESTINY				
WAR ON THE DESTINY OF MAN!	....	61	MEAT ON BONES	39
DESTROY				
OH, LET ME DESTROY FOR ONCE,	....	239	MAKES INTERVALS	22
DESTROYER				
IS MY DESTROYER.	....	77	THE FORCE THAT	3
DESTROYING				
DESTROYING SOULS AND LAYING WASTE,	....	33	IN GARDENS	8
DO YOU NOT FATHER ME ON THE DESTROYING SAND?	......	113	NOT FATHER ME	25
DESTROYS				
AND HE DESTROYS, THOUGH FLOWERS ARE HIS LOVES,	....	47	POET: 1935	34
DESTRUCTION				
TOWARDS DESTRUCTION AND REDEMPTION,	....	37	WINDMILLS TURN	3
AND THE SLUG SHOULD TEACH ME DESTRUCTION.	....	58	HERE IN SPRING	13
WHAT SHALL DESTRUCTION COUNT IF THESE ARE FIXTURES?		60	FAIRY TALES	27
DESTRUCTION, PICKED BY BIRDS, BRAYS THROUGH THE JAW-BONE,	....	132	I MAKE THIS IN	36
DETECT				
I CAN DETECT A TOLERANCE,	....	236	WOMAN TAPESTRY	52
DEVELOP				
THAT RIPENS AS WE DEVELOP	....	230	OUR SANCTITY	2
DEVIL				
NEARLY SUMMER, AND THE DEVIL	....	29	NEARLY SUMMER	1
THE WELCOME DEVIL COMES AS GUEST,	....	30	NEARLY SUMMER	14
THE WELCOME DEVIL COMES INVITED,	....	30	NEARLY SUMMER	19
THEY CRY TO BE TAKEN, AND THE DEVIL BREAKS	....	30	NEARLY SUMMER	21
BEFORE THE ARRIVAL OF ANGEL OR DEVIL,	....	39	GAS FADES	15
A SMILE LET LOOSE A DEVIL, A BELL STRUCK.	....	51	OUT OF THE PIT	19
I WOULD NOT FEAR THE DEVIL IN THE LOIN	....	95	RUB OF LOVE	20
THAT MEN MIGHT SEE THE DEVIL IN THE CRUMB	....	96	TWELVE	13
BEARDING THE UNBORN DEVIL,	....	105	WORLD PYRAMID	51
THUS THE SHADOWLESS MAN OR OX, AND THE PICTURED DEVIL,	....	109	I, IN IMAGE	22
INCARNATE DEVIL	....	121	INCARNATE DEVL	T
INCARNATE DEVIL IN A TALKING SNAKE,	....	121	INCARNATE DEVL	1
DEVILDOM				
THE TROUBLE, DEVILDOM, AND HEARTBREAK,	....	38	THE GOSSIPERS	15
DEVILISH				
THROUGH THE DEVILISH YEARS AND INNOCENT DEATHS	....	139	TOMBSTONE TOLD	14
DEVIL'S				
SPELLING ACROSS THE SKY HIS DEVIL'S NEWS,	....	29	NEARLY SUMMER	5
COMFORT COME THROUGH THE DEVIL'S CLOUDS,	....	35	LIFT UP FACE	11
SUSPENDED FROM THE DEVIL'S PRECIPICE,	....	35	LIFT UP FACE	13
WOULD BE THE DEVIL'S WIND, AND THE HIGH TRINITY	...	37	WINDMILLS TURN	18
LET ME IN THE DEVIL'S GROVES	....	70	TAKE NEEDLES	5
AND SILENTLY I MILK THE DEVIL'S BREAST.	....	81	HERE LIE BEAST	3
THIS WORLD IS HALF THE DEVIL'S AND MY OWN,	....	95	RUB OF LOVE	29

		PAGE	TITLE	LINE
DEVOTE				
I COULD DEVOTE TO OTHER THINGS.	....	9	MINUTE'S HOUR	22
DEVOTION				
WITH YOUR SYMMETRICAL DEVOTION	....	236	WOMAN TAPESTRY	48
DEW				
WIND IN ME LEAPED, THE HELLBORN DEW;	....	68	BEFORE KNOCKED	16
PUFFING THE POUNDS OF MANNA UP THROUGH THE DEW TO				
HEAVEN,	....	140	NO WORK WORDS	5
STREAM WITH BELLS AND BAYING WATER BOUNDS. THE DEW				
RINGS	....	189	WINTER'S TALE	62
THAT BELLED AND BOUNDED WITH THE FOSSIL AND THE DEW				
REBORN.	....	191	WINTER'S TALE	120
WITH THE DEW, COME BACK, THE COCK ON HIS SHOULDER:				
IT WAS ALL	....	195	FERN HILL	29
OUT OF A LAIR IN THE FLOCKED LEAVES IN THE DEW				
DIPPED YEAR	....	197	COUNTRY SLEEP	6
AND MIRE OF LOVE, BUT THE THIEF AS MEEK AS THE DEW.		198	COUNTRY SLEEP	38
AND SLY AS SNOW AND MEEK AS DEW BLOWN TO THE THORN,		199	COUNTRY SLEEP	50
THROUGH THE HAYGOLD STALLS, AS THE DEW FALLS ON THE				
WIND-	....	199	COUNTRY SLEEP	58
THE THIEF FALL ON THE DEAD LIKE THE WILLY NILLY DEW,		200	COUNTRY SLEEP	93
FALL AND THE DEW LARKS SING	....	211	POEM ON B'DAY	102
DEWFALL				
WHERE THE DEWFALL STARS SING GRAZING STILL	....	215	COUNTRY HEAVEN	8
DEW'S				
FLOWS TO THE STRAND OF FLOWERS LIKE THE DEW'S RULY				
SEA,	....	200	COUNTRY SLEEP	98
DIAMOND				
WHO PICKS THE LIVE HEART ON A DIAMOND.	....	132	I MAKE THIS IN	45
DIAPHRAGM				
THAT'LL MAKE, IT'S BRITTLE, DIAPHRAGM	....	24	LITTLE PROBLEM	8
DICTATORSHIP				
DICTATORSHIP OF SUN.	....	61	MEAT ON BONES	13
DICTIONARY				
WHAT IS THE METRE OF THE DICTIONARY?	....	118	ALTARWISE	43
DID				
BUT SHE DID NOT CRY, 'I SEE;	....	11	CABARET	12
THEY ARE THE ONLY DEAD WHO DID NOT LOVE	....	23	THE ONLY DEAD	T
THEY ARE THE ONLY DEAD WHO DID NOT LOVE,	....	23	THE ONLY DEAD	1
THEY ARE THE ONLY LIVING THING WHO DID LOVE,	......	23	THE ONLY DEAD	4
LOOK, THERE'S THE DEAD WHO DID NOT LOVE,	....	24	THE ONLY DEAD	30
AND THERE'S THE LIVING WHO DID LOVE,	....	24	THE ONLY DEAD	31
NOW DID THE SOFTEST SOUND OF FOOT OR VOICE	....	50	OUT OF THE PIT	13
THESE FIVE KINGS DID A KING TO DEATH.	....	66	HAND SIGNED	4
AS YET UNGOTTEN, I DID SUFFER;	....	68	BEFORE KNOCKED	19
DID TWIST INTO A LIVING CIPHER,	....	68	BEFORE KNOCKED	21
YOUTH DID CONDENSE; THE TEARS OF SPRING	....	79	LOVE'S FEVER	48
YOU NEVER DID AND HE NEVER DID.	....	149	PAPER & STICKS	18
YOU NEVER DID AND HE NEVER DID.	....	149	PAPER & STICKS	18
THAT DID NOT NURSE OUR BONES,	....	153	WAS A SAVIOUR	34
WHATSOEVER I DID IN THE COAL-	....	206	LAMENT	23
THE DARKEST WAY, AND DID NOT TURN AWAY,	....	216	ELEGY	2
NOR DID HE NOW, SAVE TO HIS SECRET WOUND.	....	217	ELEGY	27
AND IF IT DID, WHO SHOULD I HAVE	....	234	NO, PIGEON	5
DIE				
STOP HAS NO MINUTES,/ BUT I GO OR DIE.	....	9	MINUTE'S HOUR	23
BUT SOON TO DIE	....	21	BEWILDERED WAY	6
THERE'S PLENTY IN THE WORLD THAT DOTH NOT DIE,	....	25	THERE'S PLENTY	1
THERE'S PLENTY THAT DOTH DIE;	....	26	THERE'S PLENTY	14
LOVING AND DOUBTING LIKE ONE WHO IS TO DIE	....	27	OBLIVIOUS DARK	28

	PAGE	TITLE	LINE
DIE (CONTINUED)			
ALL THAT IS BEAUTIFUL BUT BORN TO DIE, ...	30	YOUTH CALLS	6
AND THAT IS LIES THAT, AFTER THE OLD MEN DIE, ...	36	LET BE KNOWN	5
BY THESE I WOULD NOT CARE TO DIE, ...	44	LONGED TO MOVE	19
THEY LYING LONG SHALL NOT DIE WINDILY;	49	NO DOMINION	12
ALONE TILL THE DAY I DIE	62	EARS IN TURRET	6
OR STAY TILL THE DAY I DIE	62	EARS IN TURRET	23
OR STAY TILL THE DAY I DIE?	63	EARS IN TURRET	31
WHOM CANCER CROPS, WHOSE DRINKING RUSTS, THESE DIE;	64	WOMAN SPEAKS	43
THESE DIE WHO SHOVEL THE LAST HOME OF MAN;	64	WOMAN SPEAKS	44
MOTHERS ME UNTIL I DIE, ...	72	TAKE NEEDLES	43
QUESTION: WHEN SHALL ROOT-DAM DIE?	72	TAKE NEEDLES	61
WHEN LOGICS DIE, ...	82	LIGHT BREAKS	27
TILL ALL OUR SEA-FAITHS DIE.	91	WHERE ONCE THE	24
DIE IN RED FEATHERS WHEN THE FLYING HEAVEN'S CUT,	135	HOW MY ANIMAL	40
DRESSED TO DIE, THE SENSUAL STRUT BEGUN, ...	143	24 YEARS	6
WAS THE FIRST TO DIE	174	FIRE RAID	39
DIE.	182	VISION, PRAYER	101
DIE IN UNJUDGING LOVE.	193	SIDE OF TRUTH	36
COME LET US DIE.'	202	SIR JOHNS HILL	32
AS I SAIL OUT TO DIE.	211	POEM ON B'DAY	108
TOO PROUD TO DIE, BROKEN AND BLIND HE DIED	216	ELEGY	1
O DEEPEST WOUND OF ALL THAT HE SHOULD DIE	217	ELEGY	37
UNTIL I DIE HE WILL NOT LEAVE MY SIDE.	217	ELEGY	40
FLOWERLY I DIE, ...	225	OF ANY FLOWER	4
DIED			
IT WAS A HAGGARD NIGHT THE FIRST FLESH DIED, ...	65	WOMAN SPEAKS	56
I DREAMED MY GENESIS AND DIED AGAIN, SHRAPNEL	103	I DREAMED MY	13
HER FIST OF A FACE DIED CLENCHED ON A ROUND PAIN;	137	AFTER FUNERAL	34
THE TOMBSTONE TOLD WHEN SHE DIED	139	TOMBSTONE TOLD	T
THE TOMBSTONE TOLD WHEN SHE DIED.	139	TOMBSTONE TOLD	1
I DIED BEFORE BEDTIME CAME	140	TOMBSTONE TOLD	26
ON TO THE GROUND WHEN A MAN DIED	153	WAS A SAVIOUR	21
AND DIED ON A HISS OF FLAMES	167	LONG-LEGGED	158
HE PUT ON HIS CLOTHES AND STEPPED OUT AND HE DIED,	172	DAWN RAID	2
WHEN BLACK BIRDS DIED LIKE PRIESTS IN THE CLOAKED			
HEDGE ROW	190	WINTER'S TALE	92
IN A CHOIR OF WINGS, AS THOUGH SHE SLEPT OR DIED,	191	WINTER'S TALE	122
TOO PROUD TO DIE, BROKEN AND BLIND HE DIED	216	ELEGY	1
BEING INNOCENT, HE DREADED THAT HE DIED	217	ELEGY	22
HE CRIED AS HE DIED, FEARING AT LAST THE SPHERES'	217	ELEGY	33
DIES			
THE SNIPER DIES; THE FINGERS FROM THE SKY	64	WOMAN SPEAKS	45
TOIL AWAY TILL MUSIC DIES.	70	TAKE NEEDLES	4
HERE LOVE'S DAMP MUSCLE DRIES AND DIES, ...	93	BOYS OF SUMMER	46
IN DEATHBEDS OF ORCHARDS THE BOAT DIES DOWN	169	LONG-LEGGED	207
FOR THE SLEEP IN A SAFE LAND AND THE LOVE WHO DIES	194	CONVERS PRAYER	10
DIFFERENT			
TO DIFFERENT PLACES THAN WERE SAID	37	WINDMILLS TURN	21
DIG			
DIG NO MORE FOR THE CHAINS OF HIS GREY-HAIRED HEART.	172	DAWN RAID	9
DILLY			
SHALLOW AND SEDGE, AND 'DILLY DILLY', CALLS THE LOFT			
HAWK, ...	202	SIR JOHNS HILL	21
SHALLOW AND SEDGE, AND 'DILLY DILLY', CALLS THE LOFT			
HAWK, ...	202	SIR JOHNS HILL	21
GREEN CHICKENS OF THE BAY AND BUSHES CLUCK, 'DILLY			
DILLY, ...	202	SIR JOHNS HILL	31
GREEN CHICKENS OF THE BAY AND BUSHES CLUCK, 'DILLY			
DILLY, ...	202	SIR JOHNS HILL	31

	PAGE	TITLE	LINE
DIM			
WILL ONLY DIM LIFE, AND LIGHT DEATH.	49	LIGHT, I KNOW	29
TOO FULL TO BOW TO THE DIM	155	RETURN	46
THEIR VOICES ARE DIM; THEY HAVE PASSED, ...	224	IDYLL UNFORGET	40
DIN			
HARDLY BEAR THE DIN OF NO-GOOD WRACKED DRY ON	179	NEW QUAY	9
OF THE NIGHTINGALE'S DIN AND TALE! THE UPGIVEN GHOST	200	COUNTRY SLEEP	74
HILL OF CYPRESSES! THE DIN AND TALE IN THE SKIMMED	200	COUNTRY SLEEP	76
DING			
DING DONG FROM THE MUTE TURRETS.	130	SINNERS' BELL	24
DINGLE			
THE DINGLE FURRED DEER DEAD!	4	PROLOGUE	56
THE NIGHT ABOVE THE DINGLE STARRY, ...	195	FERN HILL	3
NOR THE INNOCENT LIE IN THE ROOTING DINGLE WOOED	198	COUNTRY SLEEP	15
OF THE DINGLE TORN TO SINGING AND THE SURPLICED ...	200	COUNTRY SLEEP	75
I YOUNG AESOP FABLING TO THE NEAR NIGHT BY THE DINGLE	202	SIR JOHNS HILL	35
DINNED			
DINNED ASIDE THE COILING CROWD, ...	150	WHEN I WOKE	3
DIP			
AND FLED THEIR LOVE IN A WEAVING DIP.	163	LONG-LEGGED	53
DIPPED			
DIPPED ME BREAST-DEEP IN THE DESCENDED BONE;	118	ALTARWISE	38
OUT OF A LAIR IN THE FLOCKED LEAVES IN THE DEW DIPPED YEAR	197	COUNTRY SLEEP	6
AND HOURS MADE LITTLE I HAVE DIPPED MY ARMS IN THEIR RAPTURE;	224	IDYLL UNFORGET	31
HAZARDOUS REFLECTIONS DIPPED IN EVENING	226	THE OAK	3
DIPPING			
DIPPING MOON AND DRUNK AS A NEW DROPPED CALF, ...	206	LAMENT	17
DIRECTED			
AM I NOT ALL OF YOU BY THE DIRECTED SEA	112	NOT FATHER ME	13
DIRECTION			
AND NOW, MISTAKING THE DIRECTION, ...	37	WINDMILLS TURN	23
IN THE FINAL DIRECTION OF THE ELEMENTARY TOWN	143	24 YEARS	8
BEND, IF MY JOURNEY ACHE, DIRECTION LIKE AN ARC OR MAKE	145	IF HEAD HURT	14
MOVING IN ONE DIRECTION, ...	229	MY RIVER	38
DIRECTIONS			
WITH WINDMILLS TURNING WRONG DIRECTIONS	36	WINDMILLS TURN	T
WITH WINDMILLS TURNING WRONG DIRECTIONS, ...	36	WINDMILLS TURN	1
CROSS ALL DIRECTIONS, BRACKEN POINTS TO THE SKIES,	44	TO FOLLOW FOX	9
DIRECTLY			
THERE IS LOUD AND DARK DIRECTLY UNDER THE DUMB FLAME,	130	SINNERS' BELL	13
DIRT			
LOVERS IN THE DIRT OF THEIR LEAFY BEDS, ...	144	COLOUR OF SAY	9
DIRTBOX			
OF MY WEEK IN THE DIRTBOX	156	RETURN	91
DIRTIER			
DIRTIER WITH GARAGES AND CHEAP TEA SIGNS.	37	WINDMILLS TURN	15
DIRTY			
THAT LEAD AWAY TO DIRTY TOWNS	37	WINDMILLS TURN	14
A DIRTY NOVEL DONE IN ERSE	83	LETTER TO AUNT	25
DISAPPOINT			
ALL COULD NOT DISAPPOINT;	32	OUT OF SIGHS	6
DISCIPLE			
DUCKED IN THE TWELVE, DISCIPLE SEAS	128	MY NEOPHYTE	4
DISCORD			
(NOTES NOT IN SYMPATHY, DISCORD, UNEASE), ...	35	LIFT UP FACE	21
MAKE DISCORD WITH THE VOICE WITHIN HIS RIBS	46	POET: 1935	5

	PAGE	TITLE	LINE
DISCORDANT			
DOWN BREEZE AND SHELL TO A DISCORDANT BEACH, ...	138	FIVE & COUNTRY	7
DISCOVERED			
THE NATURAL CIRCLE OF THE DISCOVERED SKIES	134	HOW MY ANIMAL	10
DISCOVERS			
AND THE HUNT IN THE HATSTAND DISCOVERS NO COPPERS,	38	GAS FADES	2
DISCUSSING			
A LETTER TO MY AUNT DISCUSSING THE CORRECT APPROACH			
TO MODERN POETRY	83	LETTER TO AUNT	T
DISEASE			
ALL SUCH DISEASE I DOCTOR IN MY BLOOD, ...	81	ALL THAT I OWE	19
DISEASES			
OF FAULTY MEN AND THEIR DISEASES, ...	34	IN GARDENS	10
DISGUISED			
IN COMMON CLAY CLOTHES DISGUISED AS SCALES, ...	151	BELOW A TIME	15
DISHEVELLED			
GRIEF WITH DISHEVELLED HANDS TEAR OUT THE ALTAR GHOST	130	SINNERS' BELL	5
DISHONOURS			
SHAMES AND THE DAMP DISHONOURS, THE RELIC SCRAPING.	110	I, IN IMAGE	71
DISHRAG			
WOE DRIP FROM THE DISHRAG HANDS AND THE PRESSED			
SPONGE OF THE FOREHEAD, ...	142	SAINT TO FALL	45
DISK			
FLIES ON THE SHAFTED DISK, DECLAIMS THE MORNING ...	99	OCTOBER WIND	19
LET THE WAX DISK BABBLE	110	I, IN IMAGE	70
DISMANTLED			
AND SOME DISMANTLED WOMEN, ...	155	RETURN	31
DISPELLED			
THE NEXT-DOOR SEA DISPELLED	150	WHEN I WOKE	6
DISPLACED			
WHILE YOU DISPLACED A TRUTH IN THE AIR, ...	147	TO OTHERS	17
DISSECT			
DISSECT THAT STATEMENT, VOICES, ON THE SLABS.	137	O CHATTERTON	21
DISSOLUTION			
OF DISSOLUTION AND THE EMPTY FALL, ...	17	IN OBLIVION	23
DISSOLVED			
DISSOLVED IN SUMMER AND THE HUNDRED SEASONS;	79	LOVE'S FEVER	49
DISSOLVING			
GOLDEN DISSOLVING UNDER THE WATER VEIL.	159	INTO HER HEAD	55
DISTANT			
OF EELS, SAINT HERON HYMNING IN THE SHELL-HUNG			
DISTANT	202	SIR JOHNS HILL	36
DISTEMPER			
MAN SHOULD BE CURED OF DISTEMPER.	32	OUT OF SIGHS	27
DISTURB			
DISTURB NO WINDING-SHEETS, MY SON, ...	60	MEAT ON BONES	6
DISTURB THIS ISLAND'S REST.	62	EARS IN TURRET	16
DISTURBS			
AN IMAGE OF DECAY DISTURBS THE CROCUS	47	POET: 1935	29
DITCH			
OVER THE WHIRLING DITCH OF DAYBREAK	175	FIRE RAID	67
DITCHES			
MIDWIVES GREW IN THE MIDNIGHT DITCHES, ...	206	LAMENT	19
DIVE			
THE FLICKERING RUNS AND DIVE	4	PROLOGUE	55
AS THEY DIVE, THE DUST SETTLES, ...	110	I, IN IMAGE	43
WILL DIVE UP TO HIS TEARS.	160	DEATHS AND ENT	18
DOLPHINS DIVE IN THEIR TURNTURTLE DUST, ...	209	POEM ON B'DAY	33
DIVED			
SHE NIPPED AND DIVED IN THE NICK OF LOVE, ...	163	LONG-LEGGED	55

	PAGE	TITLE	LINE
DIVED (CONTINUED)			
LAST NIGHT I DIVED MY BEGGAR ARM	175	MY BEGGAR ARM	T
LAST NIGHT I DIVED MY BEGGAR ARM	175	MY BEGGAR ARM	1
HIGH TIDE AND THE HERON DIVED WHEN I TOOK THE ROAD	177	POEM IN OCT	17
DIVER			
TO-MORROW'S DIVER IN HER HORNY MILK, ...	103	WORLD PYRAMID	4
DIVER'S			
SWEETLY THE DIVER'S BELL IN THE STEEPLE OF SPINDRIFT	110	I, IN IMAGE	62
DIVES			
THE ANCHOR DIVES THROUGH THE FLOORS OF A CHURCH.	169	LONG-LEGGED	212
DIVIDE			
AS FIRE FALLS, TWO HEMISPHERES DIVIDE, ...	73	LORD RED HAIL	7
DIVIDE THE NIGHT AND DAY WITH FAIRY THUMBS;	92	BOYS OF SUMMER	15
DIVIDED			
IN TRUST AND TALE HAVE I DIVIDED SENSE, ...	124	TODAY, INSECT	5
DIVINE			
HIS UPTURNED FACE WITH ONE DIVINE CARESS.	222	MISSING	3
DIVINELY			
DUMBLY AND DIVINELY STUMBLING	125	SEED-AT-ZERO	6
DUMBLY AND DIVINELY LEAPING	125	SEED-AT-ZERO	13
DIVING			
PIERCE THE SPILT SKY WITH DIVING WING IN WEED AND HEEL	15	SPIRE CRANES	4
GREEN AS BEGINNING, LET THE GARDEN DIVING	121	ALTARWISE	137
DIVINING			
DIVINING IN A SMILE THE OIL OF TEARS.	82	LIGHT BREAKS	18
THE ROD BENDS LOW, DIVINING LAND, ...	167	LONG-LEGGED	165
DIVINITIES			
OF OLD DIVINITIES, SPLIT BITS OF NAMES.	53	OUT OF THE PIT	85
DIVINITY			
AND NOT WITHOUT DIVINITY, ...	24	THE ONLY DEAD	28
A NEW DIVINITY, A GOD OF WHEELS	33	IN GARDENS	7
THERE WAS NO NEED OF A NEW DIVINITY, ...	34	IN GARDENS	18
FAITH IN DIVINITY WOULD SOLVE MOST THINGS, ...	37	WINDMILLS TURN	16
ACQUAINTING ME WITH MY DIVINITY;	77	LASHED RINGS	15
WE WILL BE CONSCIOUS OF OUR DIVINITY	230	OUR SANCTITY	15
WE WILL BE CONSCIOUS OF A GREAT DIVINITY	231	OUR SANCTITY	45
DIVORCING			
FROM THE DIVORCING SKY I LEARNT THE DOUBLE, ...	79	LOVE'S FEVER	44
DO			
BUT DO NOT FOLLOW IT, ...	13	SKY'S BRIGHT	28
BUT DO NOT ACHE.	13	SKY'S BRIGHT	30
WE STRIKE BUT DO NOT STIR IT.	14	RAIN CUTS	31
BUT DO NOT TRAVEL DOWN DUMB WIND LIKE PRODIGALS.	16	SPIRE CRANES	11
DO THE RIGHT THING TO DO THE RIGHT;	18	NATURAL DAY	37
DO THE RIGHT THING TO DO THE RIGHT;	18	NATURAL DAY	37
DO, DOWN A DERRY.	18	NATURAL DAY	38
WHO DO I BLAME	26	PERSONAL EPIT	2
WHO DO I BLAME?	26	PERSONAL EPIT	6
WITH SIGHTLESS EYES AND HEARTS THAT DO NOT BEAT,	39	GAS FADES	36
THE FIVE KINGS COUNT THE DEAD BUT DO NOT SOFTEN ...	66	HAND SIGNED	13
DO NOT FORGET THAT 'LIMPET' RHYMES	84	LETTER TO AUNT	33
DO YOU NOT FATHER ME	112	NOT FATHER ME	T
DO YOU NOT FATHER ME, NOR THE ERECTED ARM	112	NOT FATHER ME	1
DO YOU NOT MOTHER ME, NOR, AS I AM, ...	112	NOT FATHER ME	3
DO YOU NOT SISTER ME, NOR THE ERECTED CRIME	112	NOT FATHER ME	5
DO YOU NOT BROTHER ME, NOR, AS YOU CLIMB, ...	112	NOT FATHER ME	7
DO YOU NOT FATHER ME ON THE DESTROYING SAND?	113	NOT FATHER ME	25
SILENCE, SILENCE TO DO, WHEN EARTH GREW LOUD, ...	153	WAS A SAVIOUR	15
HALE DEAD AND DEATHLESS DO THE WOMEN OF THE HILL	205	GIANT'S THIGH	58

		PAGE	TITLE	LINE
DO (CONTINUED)				
DO NOT GO GENTLE INTO THAT GOOD NIGHT	....	207	NOT GO GENTLE	T
DO NOT GO GENTLE INTO THAT GOOD NIGHT,	....	207	NOT GO GENTLE	1
DO NOT GO GENTLE INTO THAT GOOD NIGHT.	....	208	NOT GO GENTLE	6
DO NOT GO GENTLE INTO THAT GOOD NIGHT.	....	208	NOT GO GENTLE	12
DO NOT GO GENTLE INTO THAT GOOD NIGHT.	....	208	NOT GO GENTLE	18
BUT I DO NOT HUMILIATE YOU;	....	228	NOT DESPAIR	11
SEA, DO NOT FLOW	....	229	MY RIVER	19
BUT WE DO NOT CONCERN OURSELVES,	....	231	OUR SANCTITY	26
YOU DO NOT HURT, NOR CAN YOUR HAND	....	233	NO THOUGHT	3
WHO DO NOT BREAK?	....	241	ADMIT THE SUN	18
DOCTOR				
ALL SUCH DISEASE I DOCTOR IN MY BLOOD,	....	81	ALL THAT I OWE	19
DODGING				
BROTHERS DODGING THROUGH THE FOG	....	155	RETURN	49
DODGING THE PARK KEEPER	....	171	THE HUNCHBACK	23
DOES				
FROM THE STONE NEST IT DOES NOT LET THE FEATHERY		15	SPIRE CRANES	2
BUT OUR SPEAKING DOES NOT THRIVE	....	17	IN OBLIVION	20
FEELING THE WIND ABOUT OUR HEADS THAT DOES NOT COOL,		26	THERE'S PLENTY	18
WHO DOES NOT MAKE A WOUND IN FAITH	....	55	NO MAN BELIEVE	5
NO MAN BELIEVES WHO DOES NOT WONDER WHY.	....	55	NO MAN BELIEVE	12
BELIEVES WHO DOES NOT LANCE HIS FAITH,	....	55	NO MAN BELIEVE	16
WHO DOES NOT BURY GOD IN A DEEP GRAVE	....	55	NO MAN BELIEVE	19
NO MAN WHO DOES NOT BREAK AND MAKE,	....	55	NO MAN BELIEVE	21
WHO DOES NOT BREAK AND MAKE HIS FINAL FAITH.	.....	55	NO MAN BELIEVE	24
THEIR BREAST, THE VAULTING DOES ROISTER, THE HORNED				
BUCKS CLIMB	....	204	GIANT'S THIGH	33
OR THE YELLOW LINNET WHO DOES NOT MERIT IT.	......	230	OUR SANCTITY	14
AND DOES NOT SHOW THE FRUIT TO TASTE;	....	233	NO THOUGHT	13
DOG				
WHERE FLOATED A DEAD DOG WHO MADE HIM ILL,	....	51	OUT OF THE PIT	41
AND, FROM HIS FORK, A DOG AMONG THE FAIRIES,	.....	117	ALTARWISE	4
SLEPT AT NIGHT IN A DOG KENNEL	....	171	THE HUNCHBACK	11
AND THE OLD DOG SLEEPER	....	171	THE HUNCHBACK	25
THE SONG OF THE MISCHIEVOUS DOG	....	221	SONG OF DOG	T
THERE ARE MANY WHO SAY THAT A DOG HAS ITS DAY,	....	221	SONG OF DOG	1
DOGDAYED				
INTO THE DOGDAYED NIGHT.	....	3	PROLOGUE	33
THERE FROM THEIR HEARTS THE DOGDAYED PULSE	....	92	BOYS OF SUMMER	22
DOGS				
LAIN WITH PARCHED THINGS; LOVED DOGS AND WOMEN;	...	52	OUT OF THE PIT	72
DOGS'				
WISELY AT THE DOGS' TAILS, LEADS	....	44	TO FOLLOW FOX	15
DOG'S				
GROPING FOR MATTER UNDER THE DOG'S PLATE,	....	32	OUT OF SIGHS	26
DOING				
SHALL PROVE UNWORTHY FOR HIS DOING,	....	23	THE ONLY DEAD	15
DOING WHAT THEY ARE TOLD,	....	209	POEM ON B'DAY	12
DOING MY LITTLE TRICKS OF SPEECH AGAIN	....	234	NO, PIGEON	20
DOLL				
AND, THE STRING PULLED, SOME MENTAL DOLL	....	10	COOL, OH NO	11
HOW KISS, WHEN DOLL COULD SAY	....	10	COOL, OH NO	13
DOLPHINED				
CRY TO THE DOLPHINED SEA.	....	91	WHERE ONCE THE	18
DOLPHINS				
DOLPHINS DIVE IN THEIR TURNTURTLE DUST,	....	209	POEM ON B'DAY	33
DOLPHIN'S				
CLASH OUT THE MOUNTING DOLPHIN'S DAY,	....	164	LONG-LEGGED	75

		PAGE	TITLE	LINE
DOME				
SWUNG BY MY FATHER FROM HIS DOME.		68	BEFORE KNOCKED	12
HAULED TO THE DOME, ...		99	RUNNING GRAVE	5
I DAMP THE WAXLIGHTS IN YOUR TOWER DOME.		101	RUNNING GRAVE	36
DOMED				
AND OUT OF EVERY DOMED AND SOIL-BASED SHELL		158	INTO HER HEAD	51
DOMES				
THE NIGHTBIRD LAUDS THROUGH NUNNERIES AND DOMES OF LEAVES		198	COUNTRY SLEEP	28
AND THE MOLE SNOUT BLUNT UNDER HIS PILGRIMAGE OF DOMES, ...		204	GIANT'S THIGH	36
AND THE LOST, MOONSHINE DOMES, ...		211	POEM ON B'DAY	86
CARVEN DOMES OF GREEN ARE THE TREES BY THE PATHWAY,		221	FOREST PICTURE	2
DOMINIES				
SOAKS TO THE VEST OLD DOMINIES AND DRUNKS.		137	O CHATTERTON	20
DOMINION				
AND DEATH SHALL HAVE NO DOMINION		49	NO DOMINION	T
AND DEATH SHALL HAVE NO DOMINION.		49	NO DOMINION	1
AND DEATH SHALL HAVE NO DOMINION.		49	NO DOMINION	9
AND DEATH SHALL HAVE NO DOMINION.		49	NO DOMINION	10
AND DEATH SHALL HAVE NO DOMINION.		50	NO DOMINION	18
AND DEATH SHALL HAVE NO DOMINION.		50	NO DOMINION	19
AND DEATH SHALL HAVE NO DOMINION.		50	NO DOMINION	27
GREAT IS THE HAND THAT HOLDS DOMINION OVER		66	HAND SIGNED	11
DONE				
DEATH TO THE MAGICAL WHEN ALL IS DONE, ...		21	BEWILDERED WAY	3
THOUGH, AFTER'S DONE, I		24	LITTLE PROBLEM	15
A DIRTY NOVEL DONE IN ERSE		83	LETTER TO AUNT	25
AND MODERN VERSE IS DONE WITH EASE.		84	LETTER TO AUNT	32
THERE WAS CALM TO BE DONE IN HIS SAFE UNREST, ...		153	WAS A SAVIOUR	11
DONG				
DING DONG FROM THE MUTE TURRETS.		130	SINNERS' BELL	24
DONKEY				
IS AS RARE AS A DONKEY THAT'S RED.		221	SONG OF DOG	8
DONKEYS'				
NINEPIN DOWN ON THE DONKEYS' COMMON, ...		206	LAMENT	7
DONS				
DAWS SIR JOHN'S JUST HILL DONS, AND AGAIN THE GULLED BIRDS HARE		201	SIR JOHNS HILL	15
DON'T				
DON'T HURT THE CHIC ANATOMY		18	NATURAL DAY	9
DOOM				
DOOM ON THE SUN!'		61	MEAT ON BONES	40
AND VEINS ARE SPILLED AND DOOM IS TURNED, ...		74	WE MOTHERNAKED	15
SIR, IS YOUR DOOM.		101	RUNNING GRAVE	40
BEGINNING WITH DOOM IN THE BULB, THE SPRING UNRAVELS,		108	I, IN IMAGE	7
BEGINNING WITH DOOM IN THE GHOST, AND THE SPRINGING MARVELS, ...		109	I, IN IMAGE	13
DOOM ON DENIERS AT THE WIND-TURNED STATEMENT.		119	ALTARWISE	90
DOOR				
HANDS GRUMBLE ON THE DOOR, ...		62	EARS IN TURRET	2
HANDS GRUMBLE ON THE DOOR, ...		62	EARS IN TURRET	26
WHEN YOU SEW THE DEEP DOOR. THE BED IS A CROSS PLACE.		145	IF HEAD HURT	13
BOLTING THE NIGHT OF THE DOOR WITH HER ARM HER PLUME.		169	LOVE IN ASYLUM	4
HE STANDS ALONE AT THE DOOR OF HIS HOME, ...		169	LONG-LEGGED	215
IN THE LONG AGO LAND THAT GLIDED THE DARK DOOR WIDE		189	WINTER'S TALE	67
IN THE FAR AGO LAND THE DOOR OF HIS DEATH GLIDED WIDE		190	WINTER'S TALE	105
DOORS				
RIDE THROUGH THE DOORS OF OUR UNENTERED HOUSE.		154	WAS A SAVIOUR	38
AND THE DOORS BURN IN THEIR BRAIN.		161	WEDDING ANNIV	12

	PAGE	TITLE	LINE
DOORWAY			
IN THE GROIN OF THE NATURAL DOORWAY I CROUCHED LIKE A TAILOR	143	24 YEARS	3
DOORWAYS			
OCTOPUSES IN DOORWAYS,	155	RETURN	55
DOTH			
THERE'S PLENTY IN THE WORLD THAT DOTH NOT DIE,	25	THERE'S PLENTY	1
THERE'S PLENTY THAT DOTH DIE;	26	THERE'S PLENTY	14
DOUBLE			
INTO A DOUBLE OR A SINGLE BED,	28	NO WINGS	18
TESTED BY FIRE, DOUBLE THUMB TO NOSE,	52	OUT OF THE PIT	74
FROM THE DIVORCING SKY I LEARNT THE DOUBLE,	79	LOVE'S FEVER	44
SITS IN THEIR DOUBLE SHADE.	88	A PROCESS IN	21
THE SCALES OF THIS TWIN WORLD TREAD ON THE DOUBLE,	108	I, IN IMAGE	4
SUFFER, MY TOPSY-TURVIES, THAT A DOUBLE ANGEL	111	I, IN IMAGE	77
SLAPPED DOWN THE GUILLOTINE, THE BLOOD-RED DOUBLE	124	TODAY, INSECT	6
THE WARM-VEINED DOUBLE OF TIME	150	WHEN I WOKE	11
GLASS TO MY HANDS ENDOWED WITH DOUBLE STRENGTH.	239	MAKES INTERVALS	19
DOUBLECROSSED			
AND DOUBLECROSSED MY MOTHER'S WOMB.	69	BEFORE KNOCKED	46
DOUBLED			
DOUBLED THE GLOBE OF DEAD AND HALVED A COUNTRY;	66	HAND SIGNED	3
DOUBLED, TO FORK HIM BACK, THROUGH THE LOCKJAW BED	132	I MAKE THIS IN	50
DOUBLES			
HALF OF THE FELLOW FATHER AS HE DOUBLES	103	WORLD PYRAMID	1
IN TIME AT FLOOD FILLED WITH HIS COLOURED DOUBLES;	124	FOSTER LIGHT	27
DOUBLING			
SEE THE REASON FOR UNDOUBLING DOUBLING NOT,	24	LITTLE PROBLEM	16
DOUBT			
I LOVE AND DOUBT, IT'S VAIN, IT'S VAIN,	27	OBLIVIOUS DARK	27
NO DOUBT THE WIND ON WHICH THE ROOKS	37	WINDMILLS TURN	4
THE LOST IN DOUBT, THE NEARLY MAD, THE YOUNG	41	YOUNG ARE OLD	33
OF DOUBT AND DARK THEY FEED THEIR NERVES;	92	BOYS OF SUMMER	11
DOUBTFUL			
AND THOUGH DOUBTFUL OF BISCUIT, I'M WILLING TO RISK IT,	221	SONG OF DOG	11
DOUBTING			
LOVING AND DOUBTING LIKE ONE WHO IS TO DIE	27	OBLIVIOUS DARK	28
DOUBTS			
THOUGH WE'RE CONSUMED BY LOVES AND DOUBTS.	27	OBLIVIOUS DARK	26
WHERE WHEELS, CONFUSING MUSIC, CONFUSED DOUBTS,	50	OUT OF THE PIT	2
DOUSING			
WINDS, FROM THE DOUSING SHADE AND THE ROARER AT THE LATCH,	199	COUNTRY SLEEP	46
DOVE			
O MY RUFFLED RING DOVE	4	PROLOGUE	58
HULOO, MY PROUD DOVE WITH A FLUTE!	5	PROLOGUE	97
AND NOAH'S REKINDLED NOW UNKIND DOVE	157	INTO HER HEAD	5
WHENEVER I DOVE IN A BREAST HIGH SHOAL,	206	LAMENT	21
TIDY AND CURSED IN MY DOVE COOED ROOM	207	LAMENT	52
DOVES			
AND THE SHIPYARDS OF GALILEE'S FOOTPRINTS HIDE A NAVY OF DOVES.	170	MARRIAGE VIRG	7
DOWN			
THIS DAY WINDING DOWN NOW	3	PROLOGUE	1
DOWN TO THE CURLEW HERD!	4	PROLOGUE	63
DOWN INTO MISERY?	12	SKY'S BRIGHT	15
DOWN AN ECSTATIC LINE OF LIGHT,	13	RAIN CUTS	8
TO CATCH HER SAILING DOWN THE STREAM--	14	FOR LEDA	4
WHEN LEDA, ON A TOE OF DOWN,	15	FOR LEDA	29

		PAGE	TITLE	LINE
DOWN (CONTINUED)				
BUT DO NOT TRAVEL DOWN DUMB WIND LIKE PRODIGALS.		16	SPIRE CRANES	11
HE'LL LIE DOWN, AND OUR BREATH	....	17	IN OBLIVION	5
FOR WE MUST WHISPER DOWN THE FUNNEL	....	17	IN OBLIVION	8
THOUGH WE CRY DOWN THE FUNNEL,	....	17	IN OBLIVION	16
THE BLACK SHADOW COMES DOWN,	....	18	NATURAL DAY	21
DO, DOWN A DERRY.	....	18	NATURAL DAY	38
AS SIGNS I'VE NOT BROUGHT DOWN	....	19	IMAGES IN AIR	12
IS FALLEN DOWN	....	22	HIGH ON A HILL	15
WHEN YOU HAVE GROUND SUCH BEAUTY DOWN TO DUST	.....	25	BEAUTY TO DUST	T
WHEN YOU HAVE GROUND SUCH BEAUTY DOWN TO DUST	.....	25	BEAUTY TO DUST	1
BECAUSE LAID DOWN	....	26	PERSONAL EPIT	3
WHICH SPREADS DOWN TO THE DREGS	....	27	OBLIVIOUS DARK	15
STAY, DRAMATIC FIGURES, TETHERED DOWN	....	28	NO WINGS	3
BUT NOT OF GRIEF, FOR I HAVE KNOCKED DOWN THAT	....	31	OUT OF SIGHS	2
LEERS DOWN THE VALLEY LIKE A FOOL	....	33	HELD-OUT HAND	19
AND SIGNPOSTS POINTING UP AND DOWN	....	36	WINDMILLS TURN	2
RUN DOWN THE WORLD'S GUTTERS,	....	39	GAS FADES	32
FOLLOWING THE NOSE DOWN DELL, UP RISE	....	44	TO FOLLOW FOX	7
ROLLED DOWN ALL IMAGES INTO THE PITS	....	50	OUT OF THE PIT	3
THE MOON LEERED DOWN THE VALLEY LIKE A FOOL.	......	50	OUT OF THE PIT	12
BREAK IN THE SUN TILL THE SUN BREAKS DOWN,	....	50	NO DOMINION	26
THE MOON LEERED DOWN THE VALLEY LIKE A FOOL.	......	51	OUT OF THE PIT	32
VOLES AT HIS ARMPITS, DOWN THE SAD CANAL	....	51	OUT OF THE PIT	40
AND SWIMMING DOWN THE GUTTERS HE LOOKS UP	....	51	OUT OF THE PIT	45
RIDING ON GIRDERS OF THE AIR, LOOKS DOWN	....	52	OUT OF THE PIT	47
THE MOON PEERS DOWN THE VALLEY LIKE A SAINT.	......	53	OUT OF THE PIT	94
INTO THE QUICKSAND FEATHERS DOWN,	....	55	NO MAN BELIEVE	4
AND LOVE THAT GOES DOWN LIKE A FLOWER.	....	57	GREEK PLAY	20
DOWN PELTS THE NAKED WEATHER;	....	58	HERE IN SPRING	3
I LAID HER DOWN AND TOLD HER SIN,	....	61	MEAT ON BONES	23
AND THE SKY LAYS DOWN HER LAWS,	....	61	MEAT ON BONES	34
AND SHAFTED HAWKS CAME SNARLING DOWN THE SKY;	.....	65	WOMAN SPEAKS	57
AND I WAS STRUCK DOWN BY DEATH'S FEATHER.	....	69	BEFORE KNOCKED	39
YOU WHO BOW DOWN AT CROSS AND ALTAR,	....	69	BEFORE KNOCKED	43
WHEREON THE HOODED HAIR CASTS DOWN ITS GIRDLE,	....	76	LASHED RINGS	5
A LOVER'S THOUGHT TEARS DOWN THE DATED SHEET,	.....	80	ALMANAC TIME	7
MAN BROKE THE SUN, PULLED THE WIND DOWN.	....	86	BREAD I BREAK	10
FORKS HALF ITS FRUIT; AND HALF DROPS DOWN,	....	88	A PROCESS IN	14
PULLS DOWN THE SHABBY CURTAINS OF THE SKIN;	....	88	A PROCESS IN	23
DOWN IN THE YARD OF DAY.	....	89	EUNUCH DREAMS	16
THE FENCES OF THE LIGHT ARE DOWN,	....	98	TWILIGHT LOCKS	40
WHEN, LIKE A RUNNING GRAVE, TIME TRACKS YOU DOWN,		99	RUNNING GRAVE	1
SNEAK DOWN THE STALLION GRAVE,	....	108	GRIEF THIEF	18
NO SILVER WHISTLES CHASE HIM DOWN THE WEEKS'	......	108	GRIEF THIEF	21
HORNED DOWN WITH SKULLFOOT AND THE SKULL OF TOES		117	ALTARWISE	33
A CLIMBING SEA FROM ASIA HAD ME DOWN	....	118	ALTARWISE	65
AND PLAYED DOWN PARDON FROM THE HEAVENS' HILL.	....	121	INCARNATE DEVL	6
DOWN FALL FOUR PADDING WEATHERS ON THE SCARLET LANDS,		122	HOLD HARD	19
NOR WEATHER WINDS THAT BLOW NOT DOWN THE BONE,	....	123	FOSTER LIGHT	2
SLAPPED DOWN THE GUILLOTINE, THE BLOOD-RED DOUBLE		124	TODAY, INSECT	6
NO GOD-IN-HERO TUMBLE DOWN	....	125	SEED-AT-ZERO	4
NO GOD-IN-HERO TUMBLE DOWN	....	125	SEED-AT-ZERO	11
DOWN THE STACKED SEA AND WATER-PILLARED SHADE,	....	132	I MAKE THIS IN	40
DRAW DOWN TO ITS WEIRD EYES?	....	134	HOW MY ANIMAL	11
AND CLAP ITS GREAT BLOOD DOWN;	....	135	HOW MY ANIMAL	31
GRAVE'S FOOT, BLINDS DOWN THE LIDS, THE TEETH IN BLACK,	....	136	AFTER FUNERAL	4
BOW DOWN THE WALLS OF THE FERNED AND FOXY WOODS	...	136	AFTER FUNERAL	24
DOWN BREEZE AND SHELL TO A DISCORDANT BEACH,	......	138	FIVE & COUNTRY	7

	PAGE	TITLE	LINE
DOWN (CONTINUED)			
AND UP AND DOWN LOVE'S QUESTIONS ASK;	138	O CHATTERTON	23
ANCIENT WOODS OF MY BLOOD, DASH DOWN TO THE NUT OF			
THE SEAS	140	NO WORK WORDS	11
DRIVELLED DOWN TO ONE SINGEING TREE	142	SAINT TO FALL	20
SLASHED DOWN THE LAST SNAKE AS THOUGH	150	WHEN I WOKE	13
NOW SHOWN AND MOSTLY BARE I WOULD LIE DOWN, ...	152	BELOW A TIME	49
LIE DOWN, LIE DOWN AND LIVE	152	BELOW A TIME	50
LIE DOWN, LIE DOWN AND LIVE	152	BELOW A TIME	50
ON STOOLS TO A ONE MAN SHOW DOWN, ...	154	RETURN	20
INTO HER LYING DOWN HEAD	157	INTO HER HEAD	T
INTO HER LYING DOWN HEAD	157	INTO HER HEAD	1
THERE THE DARK BLADE AND WANTON SIGHING HER DOWN	157	INTO HER HEAD	16
ONE WHO CALLED DEEPEST DOWN SHALL HOLD HIS PEACE	160	DEATHS AND ENT	9
THE BOWS GLIDED DOWN, AND THE COAST	161	LONG-LEGGED	1
DOWN THE LONG WALKS OF THEIR VOWS.	161	WEDDING ANNIV	4
NOW CAST DOWN YOUR ROD, FOR THE WHOLE	162	LONG-LEGGED	31
TILL EVERY BEAST BLARED DOWN IN A SWERVE	163	LONG-LEGGED	57
UP AND DOWN THE GREATER WAVES	168	LONG-LEGGED	179
DOWN, DOWN, DOWN, UNDER THE GROUND, ...	169	LONG-LEGGED	201
DOWN, DOWN, DOWN, UNDER THE GROUND, ...	169	LONG-LEGGED	201
DOWN, DOWN, DOWN, UNDER THE GROUND, ...	169	LONG-LEGGED	201
IN DEATHBEDS OF ORCHARDS THE BOAT DIES DOWN	169	LONG-LEGGED	207
FOR A MAN SLEEPS WHERE FIRE LEAPT DOWN AND SHE			
LEARNS THROUGH HIS ARM	170	MARRIAGE VIRG	13
LIKE THE WATER HE SAT DOWN	171	THE HUNCHBACK	14
AND DOWN THE OTHER AIR AND THE BLUE ALTERED SKY ...	178	POEM IN OCT	42
DOWN TO THE WILD, UMBRELLA'D, AND FRENCH LETTERED	179	NEW QUAY	15
BONE WRITHES DOWN	181	VISION, PRAYER	37
DOWN TO THE RIVER ROOTING PLAIN	184	VISION, PRAYER	151
CHRISTENS DOWN	185	VISION, PRAYER	194
AND FIRES WHERE HE SHOULD PROWL DOWN THE CLOUD	188	WINTER'S TALE	37
THOUGH NO SOUND FLOWED DOWN THE HAND FOLDED AIR ...	188	WINTER'S TALE	40
RAGS AND PRAYERS DOWN THE KNEE-	190	WINTER'S TALE	96
EXULTATION LIES DOWN. TIME BURIES THE SPRING WEATHER	191	WINTER'S TALE	119
NOR BLASPHEME DOWN THE STATIONS OF THE BREATH	192	REFUSAL MOURN	16
DOWN THE BEGINNING OF PLANTS	193	SIDE OF TRUTH	30
DOWN THE RIVERS OF THE WINDFALL LIGHT.	195	FERN HILL	9
TO LABOUR AND LOVE THOUGH THEY LAY DOWN LONG AGO.	203	GIANT'S THIGH	5
NOW CURLEW CRY ME DOWN TO KISS THE MOUTHS OF THEIR			
DUST.	205	GIANT'S THIGH	45
WHO HEARD THE TALL BELL SAIL DOWN THE SUNDAYS OF THE			
DEAD	205	GIANT'S THIGH	51
NINEPIN DOWN ON THE DONKEYS' COMMON, ...	206	LAMENT	7
AND I LIE DOWN BUT TO SLEEP IN BED, ...	206	LAMENT	35
I LIE DOWN THIN AND HEAR THE GOOD BELLS JAW--	207	LAMENT	53
THE RIPPLED SEALS STREAK DOWN	209	POEM ON B'DAY	34
LIGHT AND HIS TEARS GLIDE DOWN TOGETHER	215	COUNTRY HEAVEN	11
DOWN THE CHEEK BONES AND WHINNYING	215	COUNTRY HEAVEN	14
ON WHOM A WORLD OF ILLS CAME DOWN LIKE SNOW.	217	ELEGY	32
DOWN THE LONG BAYS OF BLUE THAT THOSE CLOUDY			
HEADLANDS	222	FOREST PICTURE	6
DOWN THESE FANTASTIC AVENUES PASS LIKE SHADOWS. ...	222	FOREST PICTURE	12
WE WILL TIE YOU DOWN	230	OUR SANCTITY	19
WEIGHED STRANGELY DOWN UPON YOU	232	FURIOUS MOTION	11
OR SHALL I DRAG YOU DOWN	233	NO THOUGHT	22
STEPPING DOWN.	235	WOMAN TAPESTRY	23
DOWNED			
PACK BACK THE DOWNED BONE. IF THE UNPRICKED BALL OF			
MY BREATH	145	IF HEAD HURT	2

	PAGE	TITLE	LINE
DOWNED (CONTINUED)			
A SHE BIRD DAWNED, AND HER BREAST WITH SNOW AND			
SCARLET DOWNED.	189	WINTER'S TALE	70
DOWNFALL			
(SIGHED THE OLD RAM ROD, DYING OF DOWNFALL),	207	LAMENT	39
DOWNS			
DOWNS INTO THE LOW BROWSING DARK.	215	COUNTRY HEAVEN	15
DOWNWARD			
THE STOVED BONES' VOYAGE DOWNWARD	111	I, IN IMAGE	87
DOWNY			
UNDER HIS DOWNY ARM YOU SIGHED AS HE STRUCK,	153	WAS A SAVIOUR	19
DOWRY			
A HOME AND A DOWRY:	138	O CHATTERTON	41
3 LITTLE LUSTS SHALL YOUR DOWRY BE,	138	O CHATTERTON	42
DOWSE			
THE SCURRYING, FURRED SMALL FRIARS SQUEAL, IN THE			
DOWSE	204	GIANT'S THIGH	31
DOYEN			
THAT PRINCE OF PIMPS, THAT DOYEN OF DUNG-LICKERS.	179	NEW QUAY	24
DRAG			
AND YOUR MAIEUTIC SLUMBER DRAG IT FORTH.	67	LET A FAITH	13
EYED, WHILE THE TEARS DRAG ON THE TAIL,	155	RETURN	42
OR SHALL I DRAG YOU DOWN	233	NO THOUGHT	22
DRAGGED			
SO CRYING, HE WAS DRAGGED INTO THE SEWER,	51	OUT OF THE PIT	39
DRAGGING			
DRAGGING HIM UP THE STAIRS TO ONE WHO LIES DEAD.	194	CONVERS PRAYER	20
DRAGONFLY			
HAS THE DRAGONFLY AND THE SWORDFISH	231	OUR SANCTITY	37
DRAGS			
TO HIDE WHAT DRAGS ITS BELLY FROM THE EGG,	19	THE NEOPHYTE	6
SEE WHAT THE GOLD GUT DRAGS FROM UNDER	166	LONG-LEGGED	131
DRAIN			
THIS IS A DRAIN OF IRON PLANTS,	14	RAIN CUTS	29
DRAIN THE SPRING WHERE PROMISE GOES.	70	TAKE NEEDLES	8
DRAINED			
THE HEART IS DRAINED THAT, SPELLING IN THE SCURRY	99	OCTOBER WIND	30
DRAINS			
SHEDS THE SYLLABIC BLOOD AND DRAINS HER WORDS.	98	OCTOBER WIND	8
VOICES FROM MANHOLES AND DRAINS,	155	RETURN	53
DRAKED			
AND DUCKED AND DRAKED WHITE LAKE THAT HARPS TO A			
HAIL STONE.	204	GIANT'S THIGH	28
DRAMATIC			
STAY, DRAMATIC FIGURES, TETHERED DOWN	28	NO WINGS	3
DRAMATIC GESTURES IN THE AIR.	34	IN GARDENS	13
DRAMATIC SHADOWS IN A TIN BOX;	57	TO ARCHITECTS	2
BY A DRAMATIC SEA.	129	MY NEOPHYTE	36
DRANK			
SAILS DRANK THE WIND, AND WHITE AS MILK	162	LONG-LEGGED	13
AS THE SAILS DRANK UP THE HAIL OF THUNDER	166	LONG-LEGGED	127
DRAW			
THE WATERS OF HIS MIND DRAW IN.	16	TIME TO ROT	16
DRAW IN THEIR SEAS,	115	A GRIEF AGO	38
DRAW ON THE GLOVE OF PRINTS, DEAD CAIRO'S HENNA	120	ALTARWISE	117
DRAW DOWN TO ITS WEIRD EYES?	134	HOW MY ANIMAL	11
THE BREATH DRAW BACK LIKE A BOLT THROUGH WHITE OIL	142	SAINT TO FALL	46
DRAWING			
NOT DRAWING IN YOUR SUCTION'S KISS.	16	TIME TO ROT	6
AND HEARD THE TEETH OF WEASELS DRAWING BLOOD.	52	OUT OF THE PIT	58

	PAGE	TITLE	LINE
DRAWING (CONTINUED)			
DRAWING THE ENERGY FROM THE LOVE, ...	236	WOMAN TAPESTRY	45
DRAWN			
CRIES NOT IN TERROR WHEN A BIRD IS DRAWN	54	NO MAN BELIEVE	3
BY MAGNET WINDS TO HER BLIND MOTHER DRAWN, ...	131	I MAKE THIS IN	14
THE HEAVENLY AMBULANCE DRAWN BY A WOUND	172	DAWN RAID	10
DRAWS			
AND FROM THESE TONGUE-PLUCKED SENSES DRAWS HIS TUNE;	76	LASHED RINGS	13
DREAD			
SEEK HIM, THOU SUN, IN THE DREAD WILDERNESS, ...	222	MISSING	1
DREADED			
BEING INNOCENT, HE DREADED THAT HE DIED	217	ELEGY	22
DREAM			
KNOWING A DREAM COULD DARKEN IT, ...	10	COOL, OH NO	10
REBEL AGAINST MY FATHER'S DREAM	61	MEAT ON BONES	27
THE DREAM HAS SUCKED THE SLEEPER OF HIS FAITH	90	EUNUCH DREAMS	29
THE DREAM THAT KICKS THE BURIED FROM THEIR SACK ...	90	EUNUCH DREAMS	34
HE DROWNED HIS FATHER'S MAGICS IN A DREAM.	97	TWILIGHT LOCKS	18
AND WHEN I DREAM OF THEM I FIND	143	THE MOLLS	11
SO TREMULOUSLY LIKE A DREAM.	225	CLOWN IN MOON	8
DREAMED			
I DREAMED MY GENESIS	102	I DREAMED MY	T
I DREAMED MY GENESIS IN SWEAT OF SLEEP, BREAKING	102	I DREAMED MY	1
I DREAMED MY GENESIS AND DIED AGAIN, SHRAPNEL	103	I DREAMED MY	13
I DREAMED MY GENESIS IN SWEAT OF DEATH, FALLEN	103	I DREAMED MY	25
DREAMING			
LOVE ME, NOT AS THE DREAMING NURSES	75	SONG: LOVE ME	1
AND DROPPED ON DREAMING AND THE UPWARD SKY.	101	FELLOWED SLEEP	5
'THESE ARE BUT DREAMING MEN. BREATHE, AND THEY FADE.'	102	FELLOWED SLEEP	15
I BLEW THE DREAMING FELLOWS TO THEIR BED	102	FELLOWED SLEEP	19
DREAMLESS			
WHERE NOW THE WINGS OF DREAMLESS SLEEP ARE SPREAD,	222	MISSING	5
DREAMS			
SLEEP PUNCTURED BY WAKING, DREAMS	39	GAS FADES	22
THE RACK OF DREAMS MY LILY BONES	68	BEFORE KNOCKED	20
OUR EUNUCH DREAMS	89	EUNUCH DREAMS	T
OUR EUNUCH DREAMS, ALL SEEDLESS IN THE LIGHT, ...	89	EUNUCH DREAMS	1
IN DREAMS	222	IN DREAMS	T
THE MOONS ARE WHITE FLAMES, LIKE THE MOONS IN DREAMS.	223	IN DREAMS	14
DREAMS'			
STRIP THE DREAMS' LIVERY, ...	67	LET A FAITH	7
DREGS			
WHICH SPREADS DOWN TO THE DREGS	27	OBLIVIOUS DARK	15
THE MERRIEST MARROW AND THE DREGS	60	MEAT ON BONES	3
DRENCHED			
GRIEF WITH DRENCHED BOOK AND CANDLE CHRISTENS THE			
CHERUB TIME	130	SINNERS' BELL	16
HIS DECKS ARE DRENCHED WITH MIRACLES.	166	LONG-LEGGED	139
CRYING AT THE MAN DRENCHED THRONE	181	VISION, PRAYER	58
HORSES, CENTAUR DEAD, TURN AND TREAD THE DRENCHED			
WHITE	189	WINTER'S TALE	74
DRESS			
UNDER HER GRASSY DRESS NO LIMBS--	15	FOR LEDA	23
DRESSED			
DRESSED TO DIE, THE SENSUAL STRUT BEGUN, ...	143	24 YEARS	6
DREW			
AND DREW MY SPIRAL BREATH	11	CABARET	7
DREW IN HIS EYES THE STRAWS OF SLEEP, ...	97	TWILIGHT LOCKS	17
I DREW THE WHITE SHEET OVER THE ISLANDS	150	WHEN I WOKE	29
AND I DREW CLOSER TO HER	234	WOMAN TAPESTRY	3

		PAGE	TITLE	LINE
DRIED				
UNTIL THE SPOUT DRIED UP	....	17	IN OBLIVION	11
DRIES				
SHALL NOT BE KNOWN TILL WINDWELL DRIES	....	55	WHY EAST WIND	2
DRIVES MY RED BLOOD; THAT DRIES THE MOUTHING STREAMS		77	THE FORCE THAT	7
HERE LOVE'S DAMP MUSCLE DRIES AND DIES,	....	93	BOYS OF SUMMER	46
DRIFT				
TO DRIFT OR DROWN UPON THE SEAS	....	69	BEFORE KNOCKED	32
NOR WHEN MY LOVE LIES IN THE CROSS-BONED DRIFT	....	123	FOSTER LIGHT	22
THAT FROZEN WIFE WHOSE JUICES DRIFT LIKE A FIXED SEA		145	PLEASURE-BIRD	14
MY TEARS ARE LIKE THE QUIET DRIFT	....	225	CLOWN IN MOON	1
AND IS MORE BEAUTIFUL THAN THE DRIFT OF LEAVES.	...	226	SLENDER WIND	9
WILL YOU DRIFT INTO THE NET WILLINGLY,	....	233	NO THOUGHT	21
DRIFTING				
DRIFTING IN EASY TIME;	....	13	RAIN CUTS	14
REJOICING FOR THAT DRIFTING DEATH	....	164	LONG-LEGGED	88
CLINGS TO HER DRIFTING HAIR, AND CLIMBS;	....	167	LONG-LEGGED	161
ON A STAR OF FAITH PURE AS THE DRIFTING BREAD,	....	187	WINTER'S TALE	12
DRIFTLESS				
AND I FORGOT THE DRIFTLESS FOAM, AND SAND,	....	227	SPRING-SPIRIT	9
DRIFTS				
THE LONG, LAID MINUTE'S BRIDE DRIFTS ON	....	164	LONG-LEGGED	83
AND DROWN IN THE DRIFTS OF HIS NEED, AND LIE CURLED				
CAUGHT	....	188	WINTER'S TALE	47
AND FAST THROUGH THE DRIFTS OF THE THICKETS ANTLERED				
LIKE DEER,	....	190	WINTER'S TALE	95
HIDDEN IN DELICATE DRIFTS OF MIST ARE THEY THAT				
BECKON,	....	224	IDYLL UNFORGET	37
DRIFTWOOD				
HIS DRIFTWOOD THIRTY-FIFTH WIND TURNED AGE;	....	208	POEM ON B'DAY	8
LEAF DRIFTWOOD THAT HAS BLOWN.	....	226	THE ELM	10
DRILL				
AS MOTOR MUSCLE ON THE DRILL, DRIVING	....	102	I DREAMED MY	3
ROTATING HALVES ARE HORNING AS THEY DRILL	....	104	WORLD PYRAMID	23
DRILLED				
WHISPER IN A DAMP WORD, HER WITS DRILLED HOLLOW,		137	AFTER FUNERAL	33
DRINK				
HAVE FOOD AND DRINK, UNLOVING?	....	23	THE ONLY DEAD	12
WE SPOKE OF DRINK AND GIRLS, FOR HOURS	....	33	IN GARDENS	4
AND DRINK IN THE TWO MILKED CRAGS,	....	60	MEAT ON BONES	2
MY WINE YOU DRINK, MY BREAD YOU SNAP.	....	86	BREAD I BREAK	15
DRINK FROM THE EARTH'S TEATS,	....	137	O CHATTERTON	4
DRINKER				
THERE'S POISON IN YOUR RED WINE, DRINKER,	....	27	OBLIVIOUS DARK	14
DRINKING				
DRINKING NOAH OF THE BAY,	....	5	PROLOGUE	85
WHOM CANCER CROPS, WHOSE DRINKING RUSTS, THESE DIE;		64	WOMAN SPEAKS	43
HE SPED INTO THE DRINKING DARK;	....	162	LONG-LEGGED	14
AS THE BOAT SKIMS ON WITH DRINKING WINGS!	....	166	LONG-LEGGED	134
DRINKING WATER FROM THE CHAINED CUP	....	171	THE HUNCHBACK	8
DRINKS				
WHO ONLY DRINKS HIS PROFITS	....	138	O CHATTERTON	27
DRIP				
DRIP FROM MY OPEN EYES AS HONEY	....	48	LIGHT, I KNOW	9
THE QUEEN IS SLAIN; ORESTES' HANDS DRIP BLOOD;	....	57	GREEK PLAY	15
DRIP ON MY DEAD HOUSE GARDEN.	....	105	WORLD PYRAMID	45
WOE DRIP FROM THE DISHRAG HANDS AND THE PRESSED				
SPONGE OF THE FOREHEAD,	....	142	SAINT TO FALL	45
DRIPPER				
THAT SIN-EMBRACING DRIPPER OF FUN	....	156	RETURN	88

		PAGE	TITLE	LINE
DRIPPING				
AND CANCEROUS SPEAKING DRIPPING FROM THEIR MOUTHS,		41	YOUNG ARE OLD	29
DRIPS				
THE ACID POURS AWAY, THE ACID DRIPS	....	34	THIRST PARCHES	8
DRIPS FROM THE HUMMING DARKNESS OF THE HIVE.	....	48	LIGHT, I KNOW	10
LOVE DRIPS AND GATHERS, BUT THE FALLEN BLOOD	....	77	THE FORCE THAT	17
HERE DRIPS A SILENT HONEY IN MY SHROUD,	....	81	HERE LIE BEAST	10
DRIVE				
OUT OF THE SOIL AND SEED INTO THE DRIVE,	....	29	LONG, SKELETON	2
OR DRIVE THE NIGHT-GEARED FORTH.	....	90	EUNUCH DREAMS	26
THE SECRET OILS THAT DRIVE THE GRASS.	....	94	IN BEGINNING	18
DRIVE CHILDREN UP LIKE BRUISES TO THE THUMB,	....	100	RUNNING GRAVE	14
OUT OF THE SEA, THE DRIVE OF OIL,	....	107	ALL ALL AND	34
AS THE GREEN BLOOMS RIDE UPWARD, TO THE DRIVE OF TIME;	....	122	HOLD HARD	3
DRIVELLED				
DRIVELLED DOWN TO ONE SINGEING TREE	....	142	SAINT TO FALL	20
DRIVEN				
MAN WHO ONCE DROVE IS DRIVEN IN SUN AND RAIN.	.....	46	PLOUGHMAN GONE	34
AND THE FACE TO THE DRIVEN LOVER.	....	106	ALL ALL AND	24
IN THAT PROUD SAILING TREE WITH BRANCHES DRIVEN	...	131	I MAKE THIS IN	6
DRIVER				
THE PLOUGHMAN'S GONE, THE HANSOM DRIVER,	....	45	PLOUGHMAN GONE	1
THE PLOUGHMAN'S GONE, THE HANSOM DRIVER,	....	45	PLOUGHMAN GONE	19
DRIVES				
THE FORCE THAT THROUGH THE GREEN FUSE DRIVES THE FLOWER	....	77	THE FORCE THAT	T
THE FORCE THAT THROUGH THE GREEN FUSE DRIVES THE FLOWER	....	77	THE FORCE THAT	1
DRIVES MY GREEN AGE; THAT BLASTS THE ROOTS OF TREES		77	THE FORCE THAT	2
THE FORCE THAT DRIVES THE WATER THROUGH THE ROCKS		77	THE FORCE THAT	6
DRIVES MY RED BLOOD; THAT DRIES THE MOUTHING STREAMS		77	THE FORCE THAT	7
DRIVES IN A DEATH AS LIFE LEAKS OUT.	....	88	A PROCESS IN	9
SHE HOLDING ME? THE PEOPLE'S SEA DRIVES ON HER,	...	115	A GRIEF AGO	26
DRIVES OUT THE FATHER FROM THE CAESARED CAMP;	......	115	A GRIEF AGO	27
DRIVES FORTH MY MEN, MY CHILDREN, FROM THE HANGING SOUTH.	....	122	HOLD HARD	6
AND A WHIRLPOOL DRIVES THE PRAYERWHEEL;	....	130	SINNERS' BELL	9
DRIVING				
AS MOTOR MUSCLE ON THE DRILL, DRIVING	....	102	I DREAMED MY	3
DROOPED				
AND A TEAR-STAINED WIDOWER GRIEF DROOPED FROM THE LASHES	....	133	MAKE ME A MASK	9
DROOPING				
THE DROOPING AS YOU CLOSE ME IN	....	20	ENCOMPASSED	12
WIND CARVEN LINES AROUND THE DROOPING MOUTH;	....	64	WOMAN SPEAKS	50
FOR THE DROOPING OF HOMES	....	153	WAS A SAVIOUR	33
DROP				
THE IMAGE CHANGES, AND THE FLOWERS DROP	....	47	POET: 1935	43
HEIR TO THE SCALDING VEINS THAT HOLD LOVE'S DROP,		80	ALL THAT I OWE	9
HOLD UP THE NOISY SEA AND DROP HER BIRDS,	....	93	BOYS OF SUMMER	39
AND DROP THE PLUM LIKE FIRE FROM THE FLESH.	....	95	RUB OF LOVE	9
HEIR TO THE SCALDING VEINS THAT HOLD LOVE'S DROP, COSTLY	....	103	I DREAMED MY	9
MAGNIFIED OUT OF PRAISE; HER DEATH WAS A STILL DROP;	136	AFTER FUNERAL	17
SOONER DROP WITH THE WORM OF THE ROPES ROUND MY THROAT	....	145	IF HEAD HURT	4
TIME SINGS THROUGH THE INTRICATELY DEAD SNOW DROP. LISTEN.	....	189	WINTER'S TALE	65

	PAGE	TITLE	LINE
DROP (CONTINUED)			
IN A HOISTED CLOUD, AT DROP OF DUSK, HE PULLS TO HIS CLAWS	201	SIR JOHNS HILL	3
NOR THE PETALS OF ANY FLOWER DROP.	232	YOUR VOICE	16
FLEW FOR A TIME IN VAIN, TO DROP AT LAST	238	PILLAR BREAKS	21
DROP ONTO YOUR WINGS,	240	ADMIT THE SUN	7
DROPPED			
SHALL A DROPPED STONE DRUM ON THE GROUND,	65	GODS THUMP	12
THE BOY SHE DROPPED FROM DARKNESS AT HER SIDE	78	LOVE'S FEVER	26
AND DROPPED ON DREAMING AND THE UPWARD SKY.	101	FELLOWED SLEEP	5
RUIN, THE ROOM OF ERRORS, ONE ROOD DROPPED	132	I MAKE THIS IN	39
HE DROPPED WHERE HE LOVED ON THE BURST PAVEMENT STONE	172	DAWN RAID	4
OVER THE GHOST AND THE DROPPED SON	180	VISION, PRAYER	8
DIPPING MOON AND DRUNK AS A NEW DROPPED CALF,	206	LAMENT	17
DROPPERS			
THE FAMOUS STITCH DROPPERS.	151	BELOW A TIME	28
DROPPING			
LUCIFER THAT BIRD'S DROPPING	165	LONG-LEGGED	113
DROPS			
THAT DROPS TO MAKE A MUSIC IN YOUR BLOOD	87	PAIN BE MUSIC	20
FORKS HALF ITS FRUIT; AND HALF DROPS DOWN,	88	A PROCESS IN	14
CLACK THROUGH THE THICKET OF STRENGTH, LOVE HEWN IN PILLARS DROPS	135	HOW MY ANIMAL	36
AND WHEN BLIND SLEEP DROPS ON THE SPYING SENSES,	139	FIVE & COUNTRY	13
DROP'S			
AND THE BLOOD DROP'S GARDEN	184	VISION, PRAYER	139
DROVE			
MAN WHO ONCE DROVE IS DRIVEN IN SUN AND RAIN.	46	PLOUGHMAN GONE	34
THAT DROVE MY STUFF THROUGH SKIN AND GUT;	86	SEE, SAYS LIME	31
DROVE IN THE HEAVEN-DRIVEN OF THE NAILS	120	ALTARWISE	106
DROWN			
YOU I SHALL DROWN UNREASONABLY,	9	MINUTE'S HOUR	9
ARE FULL ENOUGH TO DROWN MY MELANCHOLY	17	NATURAL DAY	2
AS DROWN, OVER AND OVER, THIS FEVER.	17	IN OBLIVION	18
AND DROWN ALL SORROWS IN THE GROSS CATASTROPHE.	34	THIRST PARCHES	15
THE STRATA OF THE SHORE AND DROWN RED ROCK;	54	WE BY SEASAND	20
THAT I MAY DROWN, LET LOOSE HER FLOOD OF TEARS.	65	WOMAN SPEAKS	55
TO DRIFT OR DROWN UPON THE SEAS	69	BEFORE KNOCKED	32
SHALL DROWN THE BOYS OF BATTLE IN THEIR SWILL,	73	LORD RED HAIL	8
AND DROWN THE CARGOED APPLES IN THEIR TIDES.	91	BOYS OF SUMMER	6
THE SEA OF SCUMS COULD DROWN ME AS IT BROKE	95	RUB OF LOVE	27
AS THEY DROWN, THE CHIME TRAVELS,	110	I, IN IMAGE	61
TIME'S CORAL SAINT AND THE SALT GRIEF DROWN A FOUL SEPULCHRE	130	SINNERS' BELL	8
IT WAS SWEET TO DROWN IN THE READYMADE HANDY WATER	152	BELOW A TIME	44
SCALD ME AND DROWN	185	VISION, PRAYER	199
AND DROWN IN THE DRIFTS OF HIS NEED, AND LIE CURLED CAUGHT	188	WINTER'S TALE	47
SHALL DROWN IN A GRIEF AS DEEP AS HIS MADE GRAVE,	194	CONVERS PRAYER	18
AND DROWN THE GODS IN ME,	239	LET ME ESCAPE	4
DROWNED			
ONLY THE DROWNED DEEP BELLS	5	PROLOGUE	87
FEED IN THE ARMPITS OF DROWNED GIRLS, I'VE SWUM	52	OUT OF THE PIT	69
AND WEST'S NO LONGER DROWNED	55	WHY EAST WIND	3
DROWNS AND IS DROWNED, WHO UTTERS TO THE STARS	57	GREEK PLAY	26
HE DROWNED HIS FATHER'S MAGICS IN A DREAM.	97	TWILIGHT LOCKS	18
ROUND THE PARCHED WORLDS OF WALES AND DROWNED EACH SUN	136	AFTER FUNERAL	15
THAT ALL THE CHARMINGLY DROWNED ARISE TO COCKCROW AND KILL.	144	COLOUR OF SAY	6

	PAGE	TITLE	LINE
DROWNED (CONTINUED)			
AND SAMSON DROWNED IN HIS HAIR, ...	157	INTO HER HEAD	13
SUSANNAH'S DROWNED IN THE BEARDED STREAM	165	LONG-LEGGED	107
AND THE BAIT IS DROWNED AMONG HAYRICKS, ...	169	LONG-LEGGED	208
HEAVY WITH THE DROWNED	183	VISION, PRAYER	106
THE VOICES OF ALL THE DROWNED SWAM ON THE WIND. ...	194	SLEEP BECALMED	8
OR WE SHALL OBEY, AND RIDE WITH YOU THROUGH THE			
DROWNED.	194	SLEEP BECALMED	14
THROUGH WYNDS AND SHELLS OF DROWNED	209	POEM ON B'DAY	23
DROWNS			
DROWNS AND IS DROWNED, WHO UTTERS TO THE STARS	57	GREEK PLAY	26
DRUB			
AND THE DUMB SWANS DRUB BLUE	4	PROLOGUE	35
DRUG			
DAFT WITH THE DRUG THAT'S SMOKING IN A GIRL	95	RUB OF LOVE	30
DRUG-WHITE			
CAMPED IN THE DRUG-WHITE SHOWER OF NERVES AND FOOD,	144	PLEASURE-BIRD	8
DRUID			
AND NEED NO DRUID OF HER BROKEN BODY).	136	AFTER FUNERAL	20
AND DRUID HERONS' VOWS	211	POEM ON B'DAY	77
DRUM			
DRUM HARSHLY ON THE AIR, THE LIGHTNING SWORDS	51	OUT OF THE PIT	15
AND SUNK; WAVED FLAGS TO EVERY FIFE AND DRUM;	52	OUT OF THE PIT	70
SHALL A DROPPED STONE DRUM ON THE GROUND, ...	65	GODS THUMP	12
WITH LOUD, TORN TOOTH AND TAIL AND COBWEB DRUM	133	I MAKE THIS IN	57
THROUGH THE RIPPLED DRUM OF THE HAIR-BURIED EAR; ..	157	INTO HER HEAD	4
FOR ME ALONE BUT ONLY A ROCKED DRUM	175	MY BEGGAR ARM	3
AND COBWEB DRUM, ...	176	BREATH SHED	8
DRUMMED			
'SEE,' DRUMMED THE TAUT MASKS, 'HOW THE DEAD ASCEND:	132	I MAKE THIS IN	52
THE WHISPERING EARS WILL WATCH LOVE DRUMMED AWAY	138	FIVE & COUNTRY	6
DRUMS			
I HEAR, THROUGH DEAD MEN'S DRUMS, THE RIDDLED LADS,	105	WORLD PYRAMID	40
STRIKE AND SMOOTHE, FOR MY DECKS ARE DRUMS, ...	164	LONG-LEGGED	77
DRUNK			
DRUNK AS A VINEYARD SNAIL, FLAILED LIKE AN OCTOPUS,	134	HOW MY ANIMAL	7
ON GIDDY NIGHTS I SLAP A FEW DRUNK CURVES	138	O CHATTERTON	24
SLAP ON THE DRUNK MOON'S MASK.	138	O CHATTERTON	25
TOMORROW'S DRUNK CLUB MAJORS	154	RETURN	12
DIPPING MOON AND DRUNK AS A NEW DROPPED CALF, ...	206	LAMENT	17
DRUNKEN			
SEAPORTS BY A DRUNKEN SHORE	126	SEED-AT-ZERO	34
HAVE THEIR DRUNKEN SAILORS HIDE HIM.	126	SEED-AT-ZERO	42
DRUNKS			
THE PICCADILLY MEN, THE BACK STREET DRUNKS, ...	41	YOUNG ARE OLD	41
SOAKS TO THE VEST OLD DOMINIES AND DRUNKS.	137	O CHATTERTON	20
DRY			
LIKE STALKS OF TALL, DRY STRAW, ...	3	PROLOGUE	22
WHERE TEARS HAVE COME TO DRY.	12	SKY'S BRIGHT	17
AND ON OUR LIPS THE DRY MOUTH OF THE RAIN.	26	THERE'S PLENTY	19
WITH WIDE, DRY MOUTHS AND EYES, ...	28	NO WINGS	14
THE DRY FEVER BURNS UNTIL NO HEART IS LEFT, ...	34	THIRST PARCHES	2
WARMING DRY HANDS AND LISTENING TO THE WIND.	42	YOUNG ARE OLD	55
IN SUN AND RAIN OVER THE DRY SHIRES, ...	45	PLOUGHMAN GONE	25
LAPPING THE STILL CANALS, THE DRY TIDE-MASTER	54	WE BY SEASAND	10
AND YOUNG GUTS DRY BENEATH THE SICKENED SUN.	63	WOMAN SPEAKS	15
TURNS DAMP TO DRY; THE GOLDEN SHOT	88	A PROCESS IN	2
IS DAMP AND DRY; THE QUICK AND DEAD	88	A PROCESS IN	17
SPUN TO MY SCREWS, YOUR DRY GHOST BLOWS, ...	90	WHERE ONCE THE	2
PUSHED UP THEIR HAIR, THE DRY WIND STEERS	90	WHERE ONCE THE	5

	PAGE	TITLE	LINE
DRY (CONTINUED)			
THE WEED OF LOVE'S LEFT DRY;	91	WHERE ONCE THE	15
DRY AS A TOMB, YOUR COLOURED LIDS	91	WHERE ONCE THE	19
AND SWALLOWED DRY THE WATERS OF THE BREAST.	97	TWILIGHT LOCKS	6
AND ALL THE DRY SEABED UNLOCKED,	97	TWILIGHT LOCKS	8
THE DRY SARGASSO OF THE TOMB	97	TWILIGHT LOCKS	26
DRY IN THE HALF-TRACKED THIGH.	105	WORLD PYRAMID	60
ALL ALL AND ALL THE DRY WORLDS LEVER	106	ALL ALL AND	T
ALL ALL AND ALL THE DRY WORLDS LEVER,	106	ALL ALL AND	1
ALL OF THE FLESH, THE DRY WORLDS LEVER.	106	ALL ALL AND	12
ALL ALL AND ALL THE DRY WORLDS COUPLE,	107	ALL ALL AND	25
MAN DRY MAN,	127	NOW, SAY NAY	3
DRY LOVER MINE	127	NOW, SAY NAY	4
TO VEIL BELLADONNA AND LET THE DRY EYES PERCEIVE	133	MAKE ME A MASK	10
LIE DRY, REST ROBBED, MY BEAST.	135	HOW MY ANIMAL	42
IN THE DARK OF THE COFFIN AND SHEDS DRY LEAVES,	136	AFTER FUNERAL	8
TILL THE SWEET TOOTH OF MY LOVE BIT DRY,	146	TO OTHERS	7
WITH DRY FLESH AND EARTH FOR ADORNING AND BED.	152	BELOW A TIME	43
HIGH AND DRY BY THE TOP OF THE MAST,	162	LONG-LEGGED	8
DRY AS ECHOES AND INSECT-FACED,	167	LONG-LEGGED	146
TREES COOL AND DRY IN THE WHIRLPOOL OF SHIPS	167	LONG-LEGGED	170
HARDLY BEAR THE DIN OF NO-GOOD WRACKED DRY ON	179	NEW QUAY	9
WITH DRY, MECHANICAL GESTURES,	231	YOUR VOICE	3
UNHEALTHILY WITH DRY VEINS.	236	WOMAN TAPESTRY	60
DRY-AS-PASTE			
FOR MAN-BEGETTERS IN THE DRY-AS-PASTE,	113	NOT FATHER ME	23
DRYER			
THE WORDS OF DEATH ARE DRYER THAN HIS STIFF,	96	RUB OF LOVE	46
DUALIZING			
NOT FROM THE SENSES' DUALIZING TIP	20	THE NEOPHYTE	16
DUCK			
PECK, SPRINT, DANCE ON FOUNTAINS AND DUCK TIME	145	IF HEAD HURT	8
AND THE DUCK POND GLASS AND THE BLINDING BYRES ALONE	188	WINTER'S TALE	35
DUCK-BILLED			
THE DUCK-BILLED PLATYPUS BROODY IN A MILK OF BIRDS.	148	UNLUCKILY FOR	33
DUCKED			
DUCKED IN THE TWELVE, DISCIPLE SEAS	128	MY NEOPHYTE	4
AND DUCKED AND DRAKED WHITE LAKE THAT HARPS TO A HAIL STONE.	204	GIANT'S THIGH	28
DUCKS			
WHERE BIRDS RIDE LIKE LEAVES AND BOATS LIKE DUCKS	150	WHEN I WOKE	22
DUG			
DUG OF THE SEA, THE GLANDED MORROW,	106	ALL ALL AND	8
AND DUG YOUR GRAVE IN MY BREAST.	135	HOW MY ANIMAL	44
THE MOTHER DUG, AND ITS ARMS FULL OF FIRES.	173	FIRE RAID	8
DUGS			
AN OLD GOD'S DUGS ARE PRESSED AND PRICKED,	65	GODS THUMP	9
DULL			
LET THE TWO DULL STONES BE GREY,	19	IMAGES IN AIR	4
DULLED			
RESEMBLING TO HER DULLED SENSE	158	INTO HER HEAD	30
DUMB			
AND THE DUMB SWANS DRUB BLUE	4	PROLOGUE	35
BUT DO NOT TRAVEL DOWN DUMB WIND LIKE PRODIGALS.	16	SPIRE CRANES	11
AND I WAS STRUCK DUMB BY THE SUN.	42	A WAR OF WITS	7
AND BE STRUCK DUMB, IF ONLY FOR A TIME.	43	A WAR OF WITS	25
DUMB DEAD THE CRANNIES HOUSE AND HIDE.	67	REALM OF FLESH	6
AND I AM DUMB TO TELL THE CROOKED ROSE	77	THE FORCE THAT	4
AND I AM DUMB TO MOUTH UNTO MY VEINS	77	THE FORCE THAT	9
AND I AM DUMB TO TELL THE HANGING MAN	77	THE FORCE THAT	14

		PAGE	TITLE	LINE
DUMB (CONTINUED)				
AND I AM DUMB TO TELL A WEATHER'S WIND	....	77	THE FORCE THAT	19
AND I AM DUMB TO TELL THE LOVER'S TOMB	....	77	THE FORCE THAT	21
AND TO THE FIRST DUMB WONDER AT THE FLESH,	....	78	LOVE'S FEVER	13
THE GHOST IS DUMB THAT STAMMERED IN THE STRAW,	....	104	WORLD PYRAMID	28
THERE IS LOUD AND DARK DIRECTLY UNDER THE DUMB FLAME,		130	SINNERS' BELL	13
FLOOD OF HER HEART'S FAME; SHE WOULD LIE DUMB AND DEEP	....	136	AFTER FUNERAL	19
IS DUMB AND GONE WITH HIS FLAME OF BRIDES.	....	165	LONG-LEGGED	106
BONE AND BE DUMB	....	183	VISION, PRAYER	124
DUMBFOUNDING				
TO DUMBFOUNDING HAVEN	....	181	VISION, PRAYER	63
DUMBLY				
DUMBLY AND DIVINELY STUMBLING	....	125	SEED-AT-ZERO	6
DUMBLY AND DIVINELY LEAPING	....	125	SEED-AT-ZERO	13
DUMBSTRUCK				
GAG OF A DUMBSTRUCK TREE TO BLOCK FROM BARE ENEMIES		133	MAKE ME A MASK	4
DUMMY				
ATLASWISE HOLD HALF-WAY OFF THE DUMMY BAY	....	121	ALTARWISE	128
DUNCE				
SHAPED IN OLD ARMOUR AND OAK THE COUNTENANCE OF A DUNCE	....	133	MAKE ME A MASK	7
DUNES				
AND PROPHETS LOUD ON THE BURNED DUNES;	....	168	LONG-LEGGED	173
DUNG				
I HAVE RIDDEN ON GUTTER DUNG AND CLOUD.	....	52	OUT OF THE PIT	67
AND THE DUNG HILLS WHITE AS WOOL AND THE HEN	......	187	WINTER'S TALE	18
DUNGHILL				
LIGHT OF HIS THIGHS, SPREADEAGLE TO THE DUNGHILL SKY,		204	GIANT'S THIGH	23
DUNG-LICKERS				
THAT PRINCE OF PIMPS, THAT DOYEN OF DUNG-LICKERS.		179	NEW QUAY	24
DUNGS				
HUNGER FOR HIM WHO DUNGS THE VALLEY FIELDS.	....	64	WOMAN SPEAKS	37
DUSK				
MY DABBED BAY'S DUSK, AS I HACK	....	4	PROLOGUE	36
AND DUSK IS CROWDED WITH THE CHILDREN'S GHOSTS,	...	56	WHY EAST WIND	14
AND WOMEN TALK OF HORROR TO THE DUSK.	....	57	GREEK PLAY	16
IN A HOISTED CLOUD, AT DROP OF DUSK, HE PULLS TO HIS CLAWS	....	201	SIR JOHNS HILL	3
OF THE SPARROWS AND SUCH WHO SWANSING, DUSK, IN WRANGLING HEDGES.	....	201	SIR JOHNS HILL	7
ALL PRAISE OF THE HAWK ON FIRE IN HAWK-EYED DUSK BE SUNG,	....	202	SIR JOHNS HILL	27
OF DUSK AND WATER I SEE THE TILTING WHISPERING	....	202	SIR JOHNS HILL	48
FADE, THE GREEN GLOOM GROWS DARKER, AND DEEPER THE DUSK:	....	222	FOREST PICTURE	10
THESE WERE THE WHISPERINGS THAT SIGHED ON MY LIPS AT DUSK,	....	223	IDYLL UNFORGET	10
IN THE CARPETING OF THE DUSK, OBSCURELY AND ELUSIVELY,	....	224	IDYLL UNFORGET	41
VIRGATE AND SPRUNG OF THE DUSK,	....	227	THE PINE	1
DUSKY				
EACH NOTE OF THY DUSKY SONG	....	226	SLENDER WIND	6
DUST				
YOUR MOUTH'S FINE DUST	....	16	TIME TO ROT	7
TOUCHED, BY A FINGER'S NAIL, TO DUST.	....	20	THE NEOPHYTE	25
WHEN YOU HAVE GROUND SUCH BEAUTY DOWN TO DUST	.....	25	BEAUTY TO DUST	T
WHEN YOU HAVE GROUND SUCH BEAUTY DOWN TO DUST	.....	25	BEAUTY TO DUST	1
TRAMPLING TO DUST THE BITS AND PIECES	....	34	IN GARDENS	9
DUST IN THE LITTLE COUNTRY OF AN URN,	....	56	GREEK PLAY	6

		PAGE	TITLE	LINE
DUST (CONTINUED)				
NOT TILL, FROM HIGH AND LOW, THEIR DUST	....	56	WHY EAST WIND	12
THE SADDEST DUST IN ALL THIS HOLLOW WORLD.	....	64	WOMAN SPEAKS	41
THAT DUST YOU HOLD, O STREW THAT LITTLE LEFT;	.....	65	WOMAN SPEAKS	61
THE MORTAL MIRACLE, LET THAT FIRST DUST	....	65	WOMAN SPEAKS	64
HELL'S IN THE DUST.	....	81	HERE LIE BEAST	6
FEET IN THE RUBBING DUST.	....	96	RUB OF LOVE	42
JOY IS THE KNOCK OF DUST, CADAVER'S SHOOT	....	101	RUNNING GRAVE	37
AS THEY DIVE, THE DUST SETTLES.	....	110	I, IN IMAGE	43
DUST BE YOUR SAVIOUR UNDER THE CONJURED SOIL.)	....	110	I, IN IMAGE	60
SHOULD HE, FOR CENTRE SAKE, HOP IN THE DUST,	......	127	NOW, SAY NAY	6
OUR OWN TRUE STRANGERS' DUST	....	153	WAS A SAVIOUR	37
WHO'D RAISE THE ORGANS OF THE COUNTED DUST	....	160	DEATHS AND ENT	7
ONE BY ONE IN DUST AND SHAWL,	....	167	LONG-LEGGED	145
SHE SLEEPS IN THE NARROW TROUGH YET SHE WALKS THE DUST	....	170	LOVE IN ASYLUM	13
AND THE DUST SHALL SING LIKE A BIRD	....	173	FIRE RAID	23
AND THE BIDDEN DUST UPSAILING	....	182	VISION, PRAYER	77
AND THE GREEN DUST	....	183	VISION, PRAYER	107
AND THE BEATING DUST BE BLOWN	....	184	VISION, PRAYER	150
DUST IN THE BURIED WOOD, FLIES ON THE GRAINS OF HER WINGS	....	189	WINTER'S TALE	58
THE VOICE OF THE DUST OF WATER FROM THE WITHERED SPRING	....	189	WINTER'S TALE	60
AS A DUST OF PIGEONS. EXULTING, THE GRAVE HOOVED	189	WINTER'S TALE	73	
AND THE HARP SHAPED VOICE OF THE WATER'S DUST PLUCKS IN A FOLD	....	189	WINTER'S TALE	79
LIKE THE DUST OF THE DEAD.	....	192	SIDE OF TRUTH	12
MILLED DUST OF THE APPLE TREE AND THE POUNDED ISLANDS	199	COUNTRY SLEEP	59	
TIME BY, THEIR DUST WAS FLESH THE SWINEHERD ROOTED SLY,	....	204	GIANT'S THIGH	21
NOW CURLEW CRY ME DOWN TO KISS THE MOUTHS OF THEIR DUST.	....	205	GIANT'S THIGH	45
THE DUST OF THEIR KETTLES AND CLOCKS SWINGS TO AND FRO	....	205	GIANT'S THIGH	46
DOLPHINS DIVE IN THEIR TURNTURTLE DUST,	....	209	POEM ON B'DAY	33
WHICH WAS REST AND DUST, AND IN THE KIND GROUND	...	216	ELEGY	10
DUST-APPOINTED				
'REST BEYOND CHOICE IN THE DUST-APPOINTED GRAIN,	146	IF HEAD HURT	26	
DUSTERS				
FOR, SUNDAY FACED, WITH DUSTERS IN MY GLOVE,	......	100	RUNNING GRAVE	16
DUSTS				
WEDS MY LONG GENTLEMAN TO DUSTS AND FURIES;	....	120	ALTARWISE	122
DUST-TONGUED				
IT IS THE SINNERS' DUST-TONGUED BELL	....	130	SINNERS' BELL	T
IT IS THE SINNERS' DUST-TONGUED BELL CLAPS ME TO CHURCHES	....	130	SINNERS' BELL	1
DWINDLE				
THAN THE YEARS THAT DWINDLE;	....	226	THE ELM	4
DWINDLING				
SAID THE DWINDLING SHIPS.	....	162	LONG-LEGGED	24
PALE RAIN OVER THE DWINDLING HARBOUR	....	177	POEM IN OCT	31
DYING				
THERE'S MORE THAN DYING;	....	32	OUT OF SIGHS	11
THE SUICIDES PARADE AGAIN, NOW RIPE FOR DYING.	....	43	FACES SHONE	14
HEARING THE ENGINES, AND THE WHEAT DYING.	....	46	PLOUGHMAN GONE	26
THE LIVING SUN LAMENTS THE DYING SKIES,	....	56	GREEK PLAY	3
THE MESSAGE OF HIS DYING CHRIST.	....	69	BEFORE KNOCKED	42
TO YOUNG ADORERS DYING ON A KISS.	....	81	ALL THAT I OWE	18
THE GREENWOOD DYING AS THE DEER FALL IN THEIR TRACKS,	122	HOLD HARD	11	

	PAGE	TITLE	LINE
DYING (CONTINUED)			
YOUR DYING	174	FIRE RAID	26
OR FLOWER UNDER THE TIME DYING FLESH ASTRIDE.	188	WINTER'S TALE	55
THE FIELDS OF SEED AND THE TIME DYING FLESH ASTRIDE,	190	WINTER'S TALE	103
WHO CLIMBS TO HIS DYING LOVE IN HER HIGH ROOM,	193	CONVERS PRAYER	3
TO-NIGHT SHALL FIND NO DYING BUT ALIVE AND WARM	194	CONVERS PRAYER	15
TIME HELD ME GREEN AND DYING	196	FERN HILL	53
(SIGHED THE OLD RAM ROD, DYING OF WOMEN),	206	LAMENT	3
(SIGHED THE OLD RAM ROD, DYING OF BITCHES),	206	LAMENT	15
(SIGHED THE OLD RAM ROD, DYING OF WELCOME),	206	LAMENT	27
RAGE, RAGE AGAINST THE DYING OF THE LIGHT.	207	NOT GO GENTLE	3
(SIGHED THE OLD RAM ROD, DYING OF DOWNFALL),	207	LAMENT	39
(SIGHED THE OLD RAM ROD, DYING OF STRANGERS),	207	LAMENT	51
RAGE, RAGE AGAINST THE DYING OF THE LIGHT.	208	NOT GO GENTLE	9
RAGE, RAGE AGAINST THE DYING OF THE LIGHT.	208	NOT GO GENTLE	15
RAGE, RAGE AGAINST THE DYING OF THE LIGHT.	208	NOT GO GENTLE	19
FLOUNDERS, GULLS, ON THEIR COLD, DYING TRAILS,	209	POEM ON B'DAY	11
E.			
IN T. S. E. AND EZRA POUND.	83	LETTER TO AUNT	10
EACH			
EACH SILVER MOMENT CHIMES/ IN STEPS OF SOUND,	9	MINUTE'S HOUR	5
THE ICICLE OF EACH DELIBERATE FANCY.	10	COOL, OH NO	7
IT'S EASY TRACING WHAT EACH GIVES THE OTHER	24	LITTLE PROBLEM	11
BROOD ON EACH HOTHOUSE PLANT	26	THERE'S PLENTY	9
A CIRCLE SPINS. LET EACH REVOLVING SPOKE	67	LET A FAITH	4
EACH GOLDEN GRAIN SPAT LIFE INTO ITS FELLOW,	78	LOVE'S FEVER	23
REMEMBER THIS: EACH ROSE IS WORMY,	84	LETTER TO AUNT	48
TURNS GHOST TO GHOST; EACH MOTHERED CHILD	88	A PROCESS IN	20
THE MILKY ACID ON EACH HINGE,	97	TWILIGHT LOCKS	5
ON THAT CLOUD COAST TO EACH GRAVE-GABBING SHADE;	102	FELLOWED SLEEP	18
EACH RUNG A LOVE OR LOSING TO THE LAST,	102	FELLOWED SLEEP	27
THIS WAS THE SKY, JACK CHRIST, EACH MINSTREL ANGLE	120	ALTARWISE	105
THAT SHAPES EACH BUSHY ITEM OF THE AIR	123	FOSTER LIGHT	5
EACH ANCIENT, STONE-NECKED MINUTE OF LOVE'S SEASON	131	I MAKE THIS IN	2
CLAW OF THE CRABBED VEINS SQUEEZE FROM EACH RED PARTICLE	135	HOW MY ANIMAL	21
ROUND THE PARCHED WORLDS OF WALES AND DROWNED EACH SUN	136	AFTER FUNERAL	15
EACH NEW SENSATION EMITS	137	O CHATTERTON	8
IF I TAKE TO BURN OR RETURN THIS WORLD WHICH IS EACH MAN'S WORK.	140	NO WORK WORDS	12
ON THE FIRST OF EACH HARDSHIP,	151	BELOW A TIME	5
EACH TRUTH, EACH LIE,	193	SIDE OF TRUTH	35
EACH TRUTH, EACH LIE,	193	SIDE OF TRUTH	35
THIS NIGHT AND EACH VAST NIGHT UNTIL THE STERN BELL TALKS	199	COUNTRY SLEEP	51
THIS NIGHT AND EACH NIGHT SINCE THE FALLING STAR YOU WERE BORN,	199	COUNTRY SLEEP	55
BUT HER FAITH THAT EACH VAST NIGHT AND THE SAGA OF PRAYER	201	COUNTRY SLEEP	102
AND YOU SHALL WAKE, FROM COUNTRY SLEEP, THIS DAWN AND EACH FIRST DAWN,	201	COUNTRY SLEEP	110
THEIR GRASSES, EACH A TINY ECSTASY,	223	IDYLL UNFORGET	15
EACH NOTE OF THY DUSKY SONG	226	SLENDER WIND	6
ON THE SAIL OF EACH SLIGHT WING	233	NO THOUGHT	18
EAGLE			
THE POLAR EAGLE WITH HIS TREAD OF SNOW.	164	LONG-LEGGED	80
OR THE EYES OF THE EAGLE	229	MY RIVER	32
WHERE THE EAGLE IS A STRONG BIRD	240	ADMIT THE SUN	2
THAN IN THE GULL AND THE FIERCE EAGLE	241	ADMIT THE SUN	17

		PAGE	TITLE	LINE
EAGLE-MOUTHED				
OH, EAGLE-MOUTHED,	....	232	YOUR VOICE	10
EAGLES				
MARROW OF EAGLES, THE ROOTS OF WHALES	....	210	POEM ON B'DAY	58
EAR				
POISED AT THE READY EAR	....	29	NEARLY SUMMER	11
SOMETIMES AT HIS EAR THE ENGINE'S VOICE	....	46	PLOUGHMAN GONE	27
LET A MAGGOT AT THE EAR	....	70	TAKE NEEDLES	3
AND ALL SWEET HELL, DEAF AS AN HOUR'S EAR,	....	114	SERVANT SUN	33
HE LYING LOW WITH RUIN IN HIS EAR,	....	127	NOW, SAY NAY	20
TONGUE AND EAR IN THE THREAD, ANGLE THE TEMPLE-BOUND		135	HOW MY ANIMAL	26
THROUGH THE RIPPLED DRUM OF THE HAIR-BURIED EAR;		157	INTO HER HEAD	4
AND THE SYNAGOGUE OF THE EAR OF CORN	....	191	REFUSAL MOURN	9
EARDRUM				
RAISE THE LIVE RAFTERS OF THE EARDRUM,	....	142	SAINT TO FALL	36
EARLY				
EARLY IMAGINARY HALF REMEMBERED	....	158	INTO HER HEAD	32
LIKE THE PARK BIRDS HE CAME EARLY	....	171	THE HUNCHBACK	13
EARS				
MY EARS, MY NOSE, MY EYES,	....	18	NATURAL DAY	17
STEALING SO SOFTLY INTO THE EARS.	....	22	ON QUIET NIGHT	7
NO MORE MAY GULLS CRY AT THEIR EARS	....	50	NO DOMINION	20
EARS IN THE TURRETS HEAR	....	62	EARS IN TURRET	T
EARS IN THE TURRETS HEAR	....	62	EARS IN TURRET	1
EARS IN THIS ISLAND HEAR	....	62	EARS IN TURRET	17
AND ON HIS EARS HOSANNAS OF THE GRAVE.	....	63	WOMAN SPEAKS	23
THE SKULL, THE CELLS, THE CABINNED EARS	....	69	SECRET WIND	5
THE SECRET VOICE CRY IN OUR EARS,	....	70	SECRET WIND	20
AND THROUGH THESE EARS HE HARKS MY FIRE BURN	......	77	LASHED RINGS	16
SHONE IN MY EARS THE LIGHT OF SOUND,	....	78	LOVE'S FEVER	20
WINDSHAKE OF SAILSHAPED EARS, MUFFLE-TOED TAP	.....	136	AFTER FUNERAL	2
THE WHISPERING EARS WILL WATCH LOVE DRUMMED AWAY		138	FIVE & COUNTRY	6
HER HEART ALL EARS AND EYES, LIPS CATCHING THE				
AVALANCHE	....	170	MARRIAGE VIRG	10
EARTH				
TO BE ENCOMPASSED BY THE BRILLIANT EARTH	....	20	ENCOMPASSED	T
TO BE ENCOMPASSED BY THE BRILLIANT EARTH	....	20	ENCOMPASSED	1
UPON THE EARTH WHO KNEW NO JOY,	....	22	ON QUIET NIGHT	16
LIPLESS AND TONGUELESS IN THE SOUR EARTH	....	23	THE ONLY DEAD	2
HERE UNDER THE EARTH WITH GIRL AND THIEF,	....	26	PERSONAL EPIT	5
THERE IS BUT ONE MESSAGE FOR THE EARTH,	....	41	YOUNG ARE OLD	26
IT IS GOOD TO STEP ONTO THE EARTH, ALONE,	....	43	A WAR OF WITS	24
WITH HEART UNLOCKED UPON THE GIGANTIC EARTH.	......	46	POET: 1935	12
NO MAN UPON THIS CYST OF EARTH	....	55	NO MAN BELIEVE	15
THERE IS NO FOUNTAIN SPRINGING FROM THE EARTH	.....	63	WOMAN SPEAKS	4
PALM OF THE EARTH, O SPRINKLE ON MY HEAD	....	65	WOMAN SPEAKS	60
THE LINES OF EARTH, THE CURVING OF THE HEART,	.....	73	LORD RED HAIL	14
I EYE THE RING OF EARTH, THE AIRY CIRCLE,	....	76	LASHED RINGS	2
AND EARTH AND SKY WERE AS ONE AIRY HILL,	....	78	LOVE'S FEVER	8
THE EARTH AND SKY WERE AS TWO MOUNTAINS MEETING.		78	LOVE'S FEVER	15
RAISE UP THIS RED-EYED EARTH?	....	89	EUNUCH DREAMS	23
SAGE ON THE EARTH AND SKY;	....	91	WHERE ONCE THE	21
BURST IN THE ROOTS, PUMPED FROM THE EARTH AND ROCK		94	IN BEGINNING	17
I FLED THE EARTH AND, NAKED, CLIMBED THE WEATHER,		101	FELLOWED SLEEP	6
TURNS IN THE EARTH THAT TURNS THE ASHEN	....	106	ALL ALL AND	5
SHALL I STILL BE LOVE'S HOUSE ON THE WIDDERSHIN				
EARTH,	....	113	NOT FATHER ME	29
AND IN THE MIGHTY MORNINGS OF THE EARTH;	....	122	INCARNATE DEVL	15
AND ROLL WITH THE KNOCKED EARTH:	....	135	HOW MY ANIMAL	41

		PAGE	TITLE	LINE
EARTH (CONTINUED)				
THE SKULL OF THE EARTH IS BARBED WITH A WAR OF				
BURNING BRAINS AND HAIR.	....	142	SAINT TO FALL	34
AND THE LIVING EARTH YOUR SONS.	....	149	UNLUCKILY FOR	56
EVERYBODY'S EARTH.	....	150	WHEN I WOKE	21
FROM THE KANGAROO FOOT OF THE EARTH,	....	151	BELOW A TIME	21
WITH DRY FLESH AND EARTH FOR ADORNING AND BED.	....	152	BELOW A TIME	43
SILENCE, SILENCE TO DO, WHEN EARTH GREW LOUD,	.....	153	WAS A SAVIOUR	15
OR WALKED ON THE EARTH IN THE EVENING	....	167	LONG-LEGGED	159
UNDER THE EARTH THE LOUD SEA WALKS,	....	169	LONG-LEGGED	206
AND THE KNOWN DARK OF THE EARTH AMEN.	....	185	VISION, PRAYER	187
WATER AND LIGHT, THE EARTH AND SKY,	....	193	SIDE OF TRUTH	32
EARTH, AIR, WATER, FIRE, SINGING INTO THE WHITE ACT,		200	COUNTRY SLEEP	87
ONLY FOR THE TURNING OF THE EARTH IN HER HOLY	.....	200	COUNTRY SLEEP	94
HE, ON THE EARTH OF THE NIGHT, ALONE	....	210	POEM ON B'DAY	65
I THINK, THAT IF I TOUCHED THE EARTH,	....	225	CLOWN IN MOON	5
TO THRUST YOUR ARM INTO THE EARTH	....	229	MY RIVER	10
IN THE BARBED EARTH,	....	237	WOMAN TAPESTRY	72
EARTH'S				
WHO, UNDESERVING, HAVE SUFFERED THE EARTH'S WRONG,		41	YOUNG ARE OLD	34
DRINK FROM THE EARTH'S TEATS,	....	137	O CHATTERTON	4
EASE				
WERE THAT ENOUGH, ENOUGH TO EASE THE PAIN,	....	32	OUT OF SIGHS	17
AND MODERN VERSE IS DONE WITH EASE.	....	84	LETTER TO AUNT	32
EASIER				
EASIER THAN HE UPON THE ICE.	....	28	NO WINGS	11
THROUGH EASIER HEATHER TO THE FOUL LAIR	....	44	TO FOLLOW FOX	16
EASILY				
AND, ON THE GROUND, GYRATES AS EASILY	....	19	THE NEOPHYTE	7
WHICH GOES AROUND ME EASILY	....	236	WOMAN TAPESTRY	54
EAST				
WHY EAST WIND CHILLS	....	55	WHY EAST WIND	T
WHY EAST WIND CHILLS AND SOUTH WIND COOLS	....	55	WHY EAST WIND	1
ASK THE TALL FISH SWEPT FROM THE BIBLE EAST,	......	121	ALTARWISE	134
CUDGEL GREAT AIR, WRECK EAST, AND TOPPLE SUNDOWN,		132	I MAKE THIS IN	33
CROSSES THE BREAST OF THE PRAISING EAST, AND KNEELS,		215	COUNTRY HEAVEN	3
EASTERN				
MY VEINS FLOWED WITH THE EASTERN WEATHER;	....	68	BEFORE KNOCKED	17
TWINED GOOD AND EVIL ON AN EASTERN TREE;	....	121	INCARNATE DEVL	10
EASY				
DRIFTING IN EASY TIME;	....	13	RAIN CUTS	14
READY TO RISE, EASY TO SLEEP.	....	23	THE ONLY DEAD	6
IT'S EASY TRACING WHAT EACH GIVES THE OTHER	....	24	LITTLE PROBLEM	11
NOW AS I WAS YOUNG AND EASY UNDER THE APPLE BOUGHS		195	FERN HILL	1
OH AS I WAS YOUNG AND EASY IN THE MERCY OF HIS MEANS,		196	FERN HILL	52
EAT				
SLEEP, WAKE, AND SLEEP, EAT, LOVE, AND LAUGH,	.....	28	NO WINGS	13
TO EAT YOUR HEART IN THE HOUSE IN THE ROSY WOOD.		197	COUNTRY SLEEP	7
EATING				
EATING BREAD FROM A NEWSPAPER	....	171	THE HUNCHBACK	7
EAVES				
FOR WHO UNMANNINGLY HAUNTS THE MOUNTAIN RAVENED EAVES		198	COUNTRY SLEEP	24
EBB				
BLOWING WITH THE BLOOD'S EBB,	....	22	HIGH ON A HILL	14
ECHO				
AND WINTER FOLLOW LIKE AN ECHO	....	15	FOR LEDA	24
ECHO A HUNDRED TIMES, THE FLIGHT OF BIRDS	....	50	OUT OF THE PIT	14
SHALL A WHITE ANSWER ECHO FROM THE ROOFTOPS.	......	56	WHY EAST WIND	15
SHADE WITHOUT SHAPE? THE SHAPE OF PHARAOH'S ECHO?		118	ALTARWISE	45
WITH LITTLE, ODD MISTS WAVED IN THE PATH OF ITS ECHO,		224	IDYLL UNFORGET	26

		PAGE	TITLE	LINE
ECHOES				
AND GHOSTLY ECHOES ON PAPER,	....	44	LONGED TO MOVE	9
DRY AS ECHOES AND INSECT-FACED,	....	167	LONG-LEGGED	146
ECHOING				
OR SKULKS IN THE DELL MOON BUT MOONSHINE ECHOING CLEAR	....	198	COUNTRY SLEEP	25
ECHO'S				
OF ECHO'S ANSWER AND THE MAN OF FROST	....	56	WHY EAST WIND	25
ECSTASY				
THEIR GRASSES, EACH A TINY ECSTASY,	....	223	IDYLL UNFORGET	15
ECSTATIC				
DOWN AN ECSTATIC LINE OF LIGHT,	....	13	RAIN CUTS	8
EDEN				
WE KNOW OUR MOTHER GOOSE AND EDEN,	....	59	FAIRY TALES	10
WE IN OUR EDEN KNEW THE SECRET GUARDIAN	....	122	INCARNATE DEVL	13
MURDER OF EDEN AND GREEN GENESIS.	....	124	TODAY, INSECT	8
UNCREDITED BLOWS JERICHO ON EDEN.	....	124	TODAY, INSECT	17
OF THE GARDEN OF EDEN.	....	174	FIRE RAID	46
EDGE				
CANNOT WEAR YOUR EDGE AWAY,	....	228	MY RIVER	3
ON THE EDGE BEYOND YOUR REACH;	....	230	OUR SANCTITY	5
AND ITS EDGE CUT THE SURFACE,	....	232	FURIOUS MOTION	6
EDGES				
AS EDGES OFF YOUR NERVES TO MINE,	....	20	ENCOMPASSED	5
STEPPING IN NIGHTMARE ON A NIGHTMARE'S EDGES.	.....	36	MIDNIGHT ROAD	11
TRAILING THEIR FINGERS ON THE HARD EDGES	....	235	WOMAN TAPESTRY	33
EEL				
IS OLD AS WATER AND PLAIN AS AN EEL;	....	165	LONG-LEGGED	93
EELS				
LOVE LIKE A MIST OR FIRE THROUGH THE BED OF EELS.		111	I, IN IMAGE	90
OF EELS, SAINT HERON HYMNING IN THE SHELL-HUNG DISTANT	....	202	SIR JOHNS HILL	36
EGG				
TO HIDE WHAT DRAGS ITS BELLY FROM THE EGG,	....	19	THE NEOPHYTE	6
AND THE NAKED EGG STAND STRAIGHT,	....	113	SERVANT SUN	7
OLD COCK FROM NOWHERES AND THE HEAVEN'S EGG,	......	117	ALTARWISE	8
AND THE HAWK IN THE EGG KILLS THE WREN.	....	167	LONG-LEGGED	156
HIS HEAD'S IN A NEST WHERE NO BIRD LAYS HER EGG.		179	NEW QUAY	27
EGGS				
MURMUR OF SPRING NOR CRUSH THE COCKEREL'S EGGS,	...	123	FOSTER LIGHT	7
AND COUNT BY BIRDS' EGGS AND LEAVES	....	157	RETURN	97
EGYPTIAN				
WHOSE BEARD WAGS IN EGYPTIAN WIND.	....	116	LANTERNS SHINE	15
EGYPT'S				
MY EGYPT'S ARMOUR BUCKLING IN ITS SHEET,	....	104	WORLD PYRAMID	34
EITHER				
THE VEINS AT EITHER TEMPLE WHIPPED HIM MAD,	....	50	OUT OF THE PIT	7
SLEEPING ON EITHER HAND.	....	54	WE BY SEASAND	8
ELBOW				
THEY SHALL HAVE STARS AT ELBOW AND FOOT;	....	49	NO DOMINION	5
FADED MY ELBOW GHOST, THE MOTHERS-EYED,	....	102	FELLOWED SLEEP	16
ELBOWED				
AND ELBOWED VEINS THAT, NUDGING BLOOD,	....	85	SEE, SAYS LIME	3
ELDER'S				
HE CUTS HIMSELF ON AN ELDER'S RAZOR LEG.	....	179	NEW QUAY	28
ELECTRA				
THERE CAN BE FEW TEARS LEFT: ELECTRA WEPT	....	57	GREEK PLAY	17
PITY ELECTRA LOVELESS, SHE WHOSE GRIEF	....	57	GREEK PLAY	25
ELECTRA'S				
LAMENTING FALLS. PITY ELECTRA'S LOVING	....	56	GREEK PLAY	4

	PAGE	TITLE	LINE
ELECTRIC			
GLITTERS IN THE ELECTRIC STREETS;	70	SECRET WIND	14
OVER THE ELECTRIC GODHEAD GROWS	70	SECRET WIND	22
ELEGIAC			
WHERE THE ELEGIAC FISHERBIRD STABS AND PADDLES	202	SIR JOHNS HILL	19
ELEGY			
ELEGY OF INNOCENCE AND YOUTH.	192	REFUSAL MOURN	18
ELEGY	216	ELEGY	T
ELEMENT			
IN THE LAST ELEMENT	193	SIDE OF TRUTH	23
FOR THE FIFTH ELEMENT IS PITY,	216	COUNTRY HEAVEN	31
ELEMENTAL			
NO ELEMENTAL FORM AND SOUND	83	LETTER TO AUNT	9
ELEMENTARY			
IN THE FINAL DIRECTION OF THE ELEMENTARY TOWN	143	24 YEARS	8
ELEMENTS			
AND ALL THE ELEMENTS OF THE SNOW FALL REJOICED	189	WINTER'S TALE	84
MUSIC OF ELEMENTS, THAT A MIRACLE MAKES!	200	COUNTRY SLEEP	86
FOUR ELEMENTS AND FIVE	211	POEM ON B'DAY	82
ELEVATE			
TO ELEVATE YOUR MIDDLE BROW,	83	LETTER TO AUNT	12
'I HAVE COME TO ELEVATE YOU,	231	OUR SANCTITY	29
ELIOT			
WHO KNOWS NOT ELIOT (TO HER SHAME).	83	LETTER TO AUNT	6
ELM			
STRAIGHT AS A YOUNG ELM	172	THE HUNCHBACK	33
WE GRIEVE AS THE BLITHE BIRDS, NEVER AGAIN, LEAVE SHINGLE AND ELM,	202	SIR JOHNS HILL	33
THE ELM	226	THE ELM	T
ELMED			
IT IS THE HERON AND I, UNDER JUDGING SIR JOHN'S ELMED	202	SIR JOHNS HILL	40
ELMS			
TO FIERY TYBURN OVER THE WRESTLE OF ELMS UNTIL	201	SIR JOHNS HILL	9
HOLLOWS, A GRASSBLADE BLOWN IN CUPPED HANDS, IN THE LOOTED ELMS	203	SIR JOHNS HILL	52
ELOI			
CRY ELOI TO THE GUNS.	105	WORLD PYRAMID	42
ELUSIVELY			
IN THE CARPETING OF THE DUSK, OBSCURELY AND ELUSIVELY,	224	IDYLL UNFORGET	41
ELVES			
OF ELVES AND SATYRS	60	FAIRY TALES	29
EMASCULATE			
EMASCULATE THE SEEDY CLOCKS;	156	RETURN	80
EMBLEM			
AS RAPED AND REAPED, THE FINAL EMBLEM.	29	LONG, SKELETON	8
EMBRACE			
INTO THE RAINBOW'S SHY EMBRACE.	14	RAIN CUTS	35
EMBRACING			
EMBRACING LOW-FALUTIN	154	RETURN	1
EMERALD			
THE EMERALD KISS,	14	RAIN CUTS	38
FROM THE EMERALD, STILL BELL; AND FROM THE PACING WEATHER-COCK	130	SINNERS' BELL	17
WHERE, WOUND IN EMERALD LINEN AND SHARP WIND,	132	I MAKE THIS IN	42
EMETIC			
EMETIC PERCIES FOR THEIR JOYS.	143	THE MOLLS	4
EMITS			
EACH NEW SENSATION EMITS	137	O CHATTERTON	8

		PAGE	TITLE	LINE
EMPEROR				
AND THE HUNGER'S EMPEROR;	....	75	MY HERO BARES	19
MOONFALL AND SAILING EMPEROR, PALE AS THEIR				
TIDE-PRINT,	....	130	SINNERS' BELL	10
EMPTY				
IN THE BOSOM, OR THE EMPTY CHANNELS.	....	17	IN OBLIVION	21
OF DISSOLUTION AND THE EMPTY FALL,	....	17	IN OBLIVION	23
HER LONELINESS ACROSS THE EMPTY WAVES	....	22	ON QUIET NIGHT	10
EMPTY OF LIGHT AND FIND THE DARKNESS LIT--	....	27	OBLIVIOUS DARK	5
IS EMPTY IN SPRINGTIME, AND NO OTHER TIME LESSENS		39	GAS FADES	20
WHEN THE PURSE IS EMPTY	....	39	GAS FADES	27
AND THE BELLY IS EMPTY,	....	39	GAS FADES	28
THAT TURNED THE EMPTY KISSES INTO MEANING,	....	43	FACES SHONE	3
EMPTY, TO LET, ARE SIGNS ON THIS NEW HOUSE;	....	58	TO ARCHITECTS	15
AND TELLS THE PAGE THE EMPTY ILL.	....	75	MY HERO BARES	10
ONE SMILE OF LIGHT ACROSS THE EMPTY FACE;	....	93	IN BEGINNING	2
EMPTY'S				
TO LEAVE IT EMPTY'S LION'S OR LOUSE'S CHOICE;	.....	58	TO ARCHITECTS	16
ENAMEL				
MAN WAS THE SCALES, THE DEATH BIRDS ON ENAMEL,	....	111	I, IN IMAGE	97
ENAMELLED				
OF THE SHARP, ENAMELLED EYES AND THE SPECTACLED CLAWS		133	MAKE ME A MASK	2
ENAMOURED				
AN ENAMOURED MAN ALONE BY THE TWIGS OF HIS EYES, TWO				
FIRES,	....	144	PLEASURE-BIRD	7
ENAMOURING				
MAN WAS THE BURNING ENGLAND SHE WAS SLEEP-WALKING,				
AND THE ENAMOURING ISLAND	....	157	INTO HER HEAD	20
ENCOMPASSED				
TO BE ENCOMPASSED BY THE BRILLIANT EARTH	....	20	ENCOMPASSED	T
TO BE ENCOMPASSED BY THE BRILLIANT EARTH	....	20	ENCOMPASSED	1
ENCOUNTER				
TWELVE WINDS ENCOUNTER BY THE WHITE HOST AT PASTURE,		109	I, IN IMAGE	38
ENCROACHES				
THE AIR YOU BREATHE ENCROACHES	....	11	AIR BREATHE	1
ENCROACHMENT				
MUST FEEL LIKE SUCH ENCROACHMENT	....	20	ENCOMPASSED	4
ENCUMBERED				
UNDER THE ENCUMBERED EYELID,	....	157	INTO HER HEAD	3
END				
AT GOD SPEEDED SUMMER'S END	....	3	PROLOGUE	2
AT GOD SPEEDED SUMMER'S END	....	5	PROLOGUE	101
A COMIC HOUR TO AN END THROUGH WANT OF WOMAN	......	23	THE ONLY DEAD	8
AT THE HOUR'S END	....	23	THE ONLY DEAD	14
HERE IS HER LABOUR'S END,	....	26	PERSONAL EPIT	13
IS THE AIM AND THE END.	....	31	BEING BUT MEN	16
COUNT THE ENDLESS DAYS UNTIL THEY END,	....	32	HELD-OUT HAND	2
YIELDS PEACE AND PLENTY AT THE END. OR IS IT PEACE,		36	MIDNIGHT ROAD	3
A GOOSE'S QUILL HAS PUT AN END TO MURDER	....	66	HAND SIGNED	7
THAT PUT AN END TO TALK.	....	66	HAND SIGNED	8
THE ACTIONS' END.	....	101	RUNNING GRAVE	45
NO TELL-TALE LOVER HAS AN END MORE CERTAIN,	....	125	TODAY, INSECT	24
OF A LACK-A-HEAD GHOST I FEAR TO THE ANONYMOUS END.		141	I, FIRST NAMED	4
ONE. THE SUN ROARS AT THE PRAYER'S END.	....	185	VISION, PRAYER	204
FOR MY VOYAGE TO BEGIN TO THE END OF MY WOUND,	....	194	SLEEP BECALMED	11
MY DEAR THIS NIGHT HE COMES AND NIGHT WITHOUT END MY				
DEAR	....	201	COUNTRY SLEEP	108
THOUGH WISE MEN AT THEIR END KNOW DARK IS RIGHT,		208	NOT GO GENTLE	4
WHO SLAVES TO HIS CROUCHED, ETERNAL END	....	209	POEM ON B'DAY	31

	PAGE	TITLE	LINE
ENDED			
AND THE HOME OF PRAYERS AND FIRES, THE TALE ENDED.	190	WINTER'S TALE	110
ENDING			
EVERYTHING ENDS, THE TOWER ENDING AND, ...	101	RUNNING GRAVE	41
INTRICATE MANHOOD OF ENDING, THE INVALID RIVALS,	109	I, IN IMAGE	31
ENDLESS			
COUNT THE ENDLESS DAYS UNTIL THEY END, ...	32	HELD-OUT HAND	2
'ADAM I LOVE, MY MADMEN'S LOVE IS ENDLESS, ...	125	TODAY, INSECT	23
IN THE GROIN'S ENDLESS COIL A MAN IS TANGLED.'	132	I MAKE THIS IN	53
AND THE ENDLESS BEGINNING OF PRODIGIES SUFFERS OPEN.'	146	IF HEAD HURT	30
ABOUT THE SAINT IN SHADES WHILE THE ENDLESS BREVIARY	148	UNLUCKILY FOR	26
OF THE ENDLESS FALL.	184	VISION, PRAYER	165
ENDLESSLY			
ENDLESSLY TO HIS WOUND	160	DEATHS AND ENT	11
ENDOWED			
GLASS TO MY HANDS ENDOWED WITH DOUBLE STRENGTH. ...	239	MAKES INTERVALS	19
ENDS			
LEAVES IT AMONG THE CIGARETTE ENDS AND THE GLASSES.	30	NEARLY SUMMER	23
TO MAKE ENDS MEET, ...	38	THE GOSSIPERS	10
SPLIT ALL ENDS UP THEY SHAN'T CRACK;	50	NO DOMINION	17
THE ROOT OF TONGUES ENDS IN A SPENTOUT CANCER, ...	79	LOVE'S FEVER	37
EVERYTHING ENDS, THE TOWER ENDING AND, ...	101	RUNNING GRAVE	41
ONLY TO MAKE TWO ENDS MEET, ...	155	RETURN	61
ENDURE			
ENDURE BURIAL UNDER THE SPELLING WALL, ...	134	HOW MY ANIMAL	4
ENDURE THE STONE	184	VISION, PRAYER	140
ENEMIES			
LIGHT AND DARK ARE NO ENEMIES	61	MEAT ON BONES	36
GAG OF A DUMBSTRUCK TREE TO BLOCK FROM BARE ENEMIES	133	MAKE ME A MASK	4
MY FRIENDS WERE ENEMIES ON STILTS	147	TO OTHERS	20
HIS ENEMIES ENTERED BED, ...	157	INTO HER HEAD	2
AND THE SECOND COMERS, THE SEVERERS, THE ENEMIES			
FROM THE DEEP	159	INTO HER HEAD	68
ENEMY			
WIND IS MY ENEMY YOUR HAIR SHANT STIR	11	AIR BREATHE	3
THANK GOD, BUT THE ENEMY STAYS PUT.	59	FAIRY TALES	9
TURNING A PETROL FACE BLIND TO THE ENEMY	110	I, IN IMAGE	47
FRIEND BY ENEMY I CALL YOU OUT.	146	TO OTHERS	1
ONE ENEMY, OF MANY, WHO KNOWNS WELL	160	DEATHS AND ENT	29
OH ALL THE WANTING FLESH HIS ENEMY	165	LONG-LEGGED	91
ENERGY			
SUCH ENERGY MAY GAIN	10	COOL, OH NO	25
DRAWING THE ENERGY FROM THE LOVE, ...	236	WOMAN TAPESTRY	45
ENFORCE			
I WOULD ENFORCE THE BLACK APPARELLED CRIES, ...	96	TWELVE	5
ENGINE			
IT IS THE ENGINE AND NOT THE RAVEN.	46	PLOUGHMAN GONE	33
IT IS THE ENGINE FOR COMPANION.	46	PLOUGHMAN GONE	35
IT IS THE ENGINE UNDER THE UNALTERED SUN.	46	PLOUGHMAN GONE	36
AND HAND TO BUTTOCK, MAN TO ENGINE, BATTLING, ...	51	OUT OF THE PIT	36
ENGINES			
HEARING THE ENGINES, AND THE WHEAT DYING.	46	PLOUGHMAN GONE	26
WITHIN HIS HEAD THE ENGINES MADE THEIR HELL, ...	50	OUT OF THE PIT	6
ENGINE'S			
SOMETIMES AT HIS EAR THE ENGINE'S VOICE	46	PLOUGHMAN GONE	27
ENGLAND			
AND NOW THE HORNS OF ENGLAND, IN THE SOUND OF SHAPE,	122	HOLD HARD	13
MAN WAS THE BURNING ENGLAND SHE WAS SLEEP-WALKING,			
AND THE ENAMOURING ISLAND	157	INTO HER HEAD	20

		PAGE	TITLE	LINE
ENGLISH				
MY WORLD IS CYPRESS, AND AN ENGLISH VALLEY.	....	105	WORLD PYRAMID	37
ENGRAVING				
ENGRAVING GOING.	....	115	A GRIEF AGO	24
ENGULFING				
ALONE AND NAKED IN THE ENGULFING BRIDE,	....	188	WINTER'S TALE	53
AND THROUGH THE THIGHS OF THE ENGULFING BRIDE,	....	191	WINTER'S TALE	124
ENJOYED				
NIGHT, AND ENJOYED AS HE WOULD.	....	158	INTO HER HEAD	36
ENOUGH				
TIME ENOUGH TO ROT	....	16	TIME TO ROT	T
TIME ENOUGH TO ROT;	....	16	TIME TO ROT	1
ARE FULL ENOUGH TO DROWN MY MELANCHOLY	....	17	NATURAL DAY	2
TROUBLE ENOUGH FOR THE WORLD	....	18	NATURAL DAY	28
WERE THAT ENOUGH, ENOUGH TO EASE THE PAIN,	....	32	OUT OF SIGHS	17
WERE THAT ENOUGH, ENOUGH TO EASE THE PAIN,	....	32	OUT OF SIGHS	17
WERE VAGUENESS ENOUGH AND THE SWEET LIES PLENTY,	...	32	OUT OF SIGHS	21
WERE THAT ENOUGH, BONE, BLOOD, AND SINEW,	....	32	OUT OF SIGHS	24
ENOUGH KIND FOOD, ENOUGH KIND SPEAKING,	....	36	MIDNIGHT ROAD	6
ENOUGH KIND FOOD, ENOUGH KIND SPEAKING,	....	36	MIDNIGHT ROAD	6
CAUGHT AMONG NEVER ENOUGH	....	156	RETURN	67
OH, TIME ENOUGH WHEN THE BLOOD CREEPS COLD,	....	206	LAMENT	34
YOU SHALL BE LOVED ENOUGH.	....	228	NOT DESPAIR	14
STRONG ENOUGH TO TREAD ON THE SAND	....	229	MY RIVER	7
STRONG AND BEAUTIFUL ENOUGH	....	229	MY RIVER	9
I'M NOT SECURE ENOUGH	....	234	NO, PIGEON	11
PITY IS NOT ENOUGH:	....	238	PILLAR BREAKS	23
ENTER				
AND FELT A SKEWER ENTER AT HIS SIDE.	....	52	OUT OF THE PIT	55
BEFORE I KNOCKED AND FLESH LET ENTER,	....	68	BEFORE KNOCKED	1
AND A STRANGER ENTER LIKE IRON.	....	142	SAINT TO FALL	47
THAT LETS THE TREES AND WATER ENTER	....	171	THE HUNCHBACK	5
ERUPT, FOUNTAIN, AND ENTER TO UTTER FOR EVER	......	175	FIRE RAID	75
AND I MUST ENTER AGAIN THE ROUND	....	191	REFUSAL MOURN	7
ENTERED				
DESCENDS, MY MASTERS, ON THE ENTERED HONOUR.	....	100	RUNNING GRAVE	28
HIS ENEMIES ENTERED BED,	....	157	INTO HER HEAD	2
ENTERING				
SHE DELUDES THE HEAVEN-PROOF HOUSE WITH ENTERING				
CLOUDS	....	169	LOVE IN ASYLUM	6
ENTERTAINING				
SO THAT SHE APPEARS ENTERTAINING	....	236	WOMAN TAPESTRY	38
ENTICED				
ENTICED WITH TWINKLING BITS OF THE EYE	....	146	TO OTHERS	6
ENTRAIL				
OUT OF THE NAKED ENTRAIL.	....	109	I, IN IMAGE	12
ENTRANCES				
DEATHS AND ENTRANCES	....	160	DEATHS AND ENT	T
OF DEATHS AND ENTRANCES,	....	160	DEATHS AND ENT	26
ENVELOPING				
ENVELOPING THEMSELVES IN THE LADEN EVE;	....	224	IDYLL UNFORGET	42
GREEN-SHADOWED PANOPLY ENVELOPING ALL ITS				
STRANGENESS AND SOFTNESS OF STEALTH.	....	224	IDYLL UNFORGET	45
ENVELOPING THE RAGGED LEAVES UNSEEN AND STREWN.	...	226	THE OAK	2
ENVIOUS				
THE MAZES OF HIS PRAISE AND ENVIOUS TONGUE WERE				
WORKED IN FLAMES AND SHELLS.	....	141	SAINT TO FALL	17
ENVY				
HAVE KNOWN MAN'S ENVY AND HIS WEAK DESIRE,	....	30	YOUTH CALLS	3
IS TREASON'S TIME AND THE TIME OF ENVY.	....	34	THIRST PARCHES	7

		PAGE	TITLE	LINE
EPITAPH				
WRITTEN FOR A PERSONAL EPITAPH	....	26	PERSONAL EPIT	T
EQUABILITY				
BUT I HAVE KNOWN THE STILL ARDOUR OF EQUABILITY;		223	IDYLL UNFORGET	17
ERECT				
ERECT A WALKING CENTRE IN THE SHROUD,	....	114	SERVANT SUN	27
ERECTED				
DO YOU NOT FATHER ME, NOR THE ERECTED ARM	....	112	NOT FATHER ME	1
DO YOU NOT SISTER ME, NOR THE ERECTED CRIME	....	112	NOT FATHER ME	5
A VOICE IN THE ERECTED AIR,	....	150	WHEN I WOKE	25
ERRANDS				
A HOLE OF ERRANDS AND SHADES;	....	156	RETURN	78
ERROR				
PRAISING THE MORTAL ERROR	....	75	MY HERO BARES	17
ERRORS				
RUIN, THE ROOM OF ERRORS, ONE ROOD DROPPED	....	132	I MAKE THIS IN	39
ERSE				
A DIRTY NOVEL DONE IN ERSE	....	83	LETTER TO AUNT	25
ERUPT				
ERUPT, FOUNTAIN, AND ENTER TO UTTER FOR EVER	......	175	FIRE RAID	75
ESCAPE				
THRUST, MY DAUGHTER OR SON, TO ESCAPE, THERE IS				
NONE, NONE, NONE,	....	146	IF HEAD HURT	19
LET ME ESCAPE	....	239	LET ME ESCAPE	T
LET ME ESCAPE,	....	239	LET ME ESCAPE	1
ESCAPES				
ESCAPES TO THE FLAT CITIES' SAILS	....	129	MY NEOPHYTE	16
ESPECIALLY				
ESPECIALLY WHEN THE OCTOBER WIND	....	98	OCTOBER WIND	T
ESPECIALLY WHEN THE OCTOBER WIND	....	98	OCTOBER WIND	1
ESPECIALLY WHEN THE OCTOBER WIND	....	99	OCTOBER WIND	25
ESQUIRE				
HIGH LORD ESQUIRE, SPEAK UP THE SINGING CLOUD,	....	123	FOSTER LIGHT	17
ESTATES				
AND ALL THE DEAD BEQUEATH FROM PALE ESTATES	....	80	ALL THAT I OWE	2
ESTRANGING				
IN MANY MARRIED LONDON'S ESTRANGING GRIEF.	....	160	DEATHS AND ENT	12
ETERNAL				
ETERNAL WATERS AWAY	....	3	PROLOGUE	18
THROUGH HADES' GROVES AND THE ETERNAL LANDS.	......	57	GREEK PLAY	24
AND ALONE IN THE NIGHT'S ETERNAL, CURVING ACT	.....	203	GIANT'S THIGH	9
WHO SLAVES TO HIS CROUCHED, ETERNAL END	....	209	POEM ON B'DAY	31
THESE WERE MY DESIRES, ETERNAL AS MOUNTAINS,	......	223	IDYLL UNFORGET	9
ETERNITY				
COMPEL ETERNITY.	....	240	TWINING HEAD	8
ETHER				
UNDER THE MASK AND THE ETHER, THEY, MAKING BLOODY		110	I, IN IMAGE	53
ETHEREAL				
THEIR PALE, ETHEREAL BEAUTY SEEMS TO BE	....	222	IN DREAMS	3
ETNA				
ON THE ANGELIC ETNA OF THE LAST WHIRRING				
FEATHERLANDS,	....	141	SAINT TO FALL	11
EUNUCH				
OUR EUNUCH DREAMS	....	89	EUNUCH DREAMS	T
OUR EUNUCH DREAMS, ALL SEEDLESS IN THE LIGHT,	.....	89	EUNUCH DREAMS	1
BULL'S-EYE THE OUTLAW THROUGH A EUNUCH CRACK	......	108	GRIEF THIEF	19
EUNUCHS				
HALT AMONG EUNUCHS, AND THE NITRIC STAIN	....	100	RUNNING GRAVE	24
EVE				
BUTT OF THE TREE-TAILED WORM THAT MOUNTED EVE,	....	117	ALTARWISE	32

		PAGE	TITLE	LINE
EVE (CONTINUED)				
ON ALMOST THE INCENDIARY EVE	....	160	DEATHS AND ENT	1
ON ALMOST THE INCENDIARY EVE	....	160	DEATHS AND ENT	13
ON ALMOST THE INCENDIARY EVE	....	160	DEATHS AND ENT	25
ADAM OR EVE, THE ADORNED HOLY BULLOCK	....	174	FIRE RAID	34
O ADAM AND EVE TOGETHER	....	174	FIRE RAID	42
OF ADAM AND EVE IS NEVER FOR A SECOND	....	174	FIRE RAID	48
ENVELOPING THEMSELVES IN THE LADEN EVE;	....	224	IDYLL UNFORGET	42
EVEN				
HEDGEROW, LABORATORY, AND EVEN GLASSHOUSE,	....	18	NATURAL DAY	13
EVEN THE WORDS ARE NOTHING	....	27	OBLIVIOUS DARK	22
EVEN AMONG HIS OWN KIN IS HE LOST,	....	47	POET: 1935	22
AND EVEN HEAVEN HAS A SMELL	....	84	LETTER TO AUNT	53
AT WHOSE BALL-PRYING EVEN DEATH'LL SQUIRM	....	179	NEW QUAY	22
EVEN AS A BABY HE HAD NEVER CRIED;	....	217	ELEGY	26
MY RIVER, EVEN THOUGH IT LIFTS	....	228	MY RIVER	1
EVENING				
SIT AT OUR HEARTHS FROM MORNING UNTIL EVENING,	....	42	YOUNG ARE OLD	54
OR WALKED ON THE EARTH IN THE EVENING	....	167	LONG-LEGGED	159
IN THE INTERPRETED EVENING	....	185	VISION, PRAYER	186
CALM AND STRANGE IS THIS EVENING HOUR IN THE FOREST,		221	FOREST PICTURE	1
SOMEHOW IT SEEMS, AMID THE EVENING HAZE,	....	223	IN DREAMS	8
HAZARDOUS REFLECTIONS DIPPED IN EVENING	....	226	THE OAK	3
EVENINGS				
AND EVENINGS WITH GREAT DANES,	....	155	RETURN	57
EVENING'S				
WALKING IN THE EVENING'S COOL	....	71	TAKE NEEDLES	31
EVEN-TIME				
THE FRAIL AND DELICATE BREATH OF EVEN-TIME.	......	222	IN DREAMS	4
EVER				
DARKER THAN EVER,	....	9	MINUTE'S HOUR	11
CAN EVER FURTHER,	....	24	LITTLE PROBLEM	21
HOLDING FOR EVER THE DEAD MOON.	....	69	SECRET WIND	6
NOR EVER, AS THE WILD TONGUE BREAKS ITS TOMBS,	....	144	PLEASURE-BIRD	11
ERUPT, FOUNTAIN, AND ENTER TO UTTER FOR EVER	......	175	FIRE RAID	75
SLEEP, GOOD, FOR EVER, SLOW AND DEEP, SPELLED RARE AND WISE,	....	197	COUNTRY SLEEP	8
FOR EVER OF ALL NOT THE WOLF IN HIS BAAING HOOD	...	198	COUNTRY SLEEP	36
EVER AND EVER HE FINDS A WAY, AS THE SNOW FALLS,		199	COUNTRY SLEEP	56
EVER AND EVER HE FINDS A WAY, AS THE SNOW FALLS,		199	COUNTRY SLEEP	56
EVER AND EVER BY ALL YOUR VOWS BELIEVE AND FEAR	...	201	COUNTRY SLEEP	107
EVER AND EVER BY ALL YOUR VOWS BELIEVE AND FEAR	...	201	COUNTRY SLEEP	107
LOVE FOR EVER MERIDIAN THROUGH THE COURTERS' TREES		205	GIANT'S THIGH	59
NOR WILL BE EVER IS ALWAYS TRUE,	....	210	POEM ON B'DAY	51
THAN EVER WAS SINCE THE WORLD WAS SAID,	....	211	POEM ON B'DAY	98
THERE SHOULD BE NIGHT FOR EVER, AND NO ROSE,	......	223	IN DREAMS	10
EVERGREEN				
TEACH ME THE LOVE THAT IS EVERGREEN AFTER THE FALL LEAVED	....	205	GIANT'S THIGH	53
EVERLASTING				
CONDEMN ME TO AN EVERLASTING FACING	....	68	REALM OF FLESH	14
EVERY				
AND DARK SHOALS EVERY HOLY FIELD.	....	5	PROLOGUE	90
AND EVERY VOICE:	....	22	ON QUIET NIGHT	12
I AM MAN'S REPLY TO EVERY QUESTION,	....	26	PERSONAL EPIT	17
ON EVERY HAND THE EVIL'S POSITIVE	....	27	OBLIVIOUS DARK	18
AND CATCH A TURNIP GHOST IN EVERY CRANNY.	....	48	LIGHT, I KNOW	5
AND SUNK; WAVED FLAGS TO EVERY FIFE AND DRUM;	.....	52	OUT OF THE PIT	70
AND EVERY LOVELY WOMAN'S GERMY;	....	84	LETTER TO AUNT	49
THE HERO'S HEAD LIES SCRAPED OF EVERY LEGEND,	.....	132	I MAKE THIS IN	43

	PAGE	TITLE	LINE
EVERY (CONTINUED)			
AND EVERY STONE I WIND OFF LIKE A REEL.	144	COLOUR OF SAY	13
BUT BLESSED BY SUCH HEROIC HOSTS IN YOUR EVERY	148	UNLUCKILY FOR	21
IN YOUR EVERY INCH AND GLANCE IS THE GLOBE OF GENESIS SPUN,	149	UNLUCKILY FOR	55
EVERY MORNING I MAKE,	150	WHEN I WOKE	16
AND OUT OF EVERY DOMED AND SOIL-BASED SHELL	158	INTO HER HEAD	51
WITH EVERY CRY SINCE LIGHT	160	DEATHS AND ENT	23
FROM EVERY TRUE OR CRATER	161	WEDDING ANNIV	7
TILL EVERY BEAST BLARED DOWN IN A SWERVE	163	LONG-LEGGED	57
TILL EVERY TURTLE CRUSHED FROM HIS SHELL	163	LONG-LEGGED	58
TILL EVERY BONE IN THE RUSHING GRAVE	163	LONG-LEGGED	59
WITH HIS FLAME IN EVERY GRAIN.	182	VISION, PRAYER	78
WITH EVERY SIMMERING WOMAN HIS MOUSE	206	LAMENT	30
AND EVERY SOUL HIS PRIEST,	210	POEM ON B'DAY	61
AND EVERY WAVE OF THE WAY	211	POEM ON B'DAY	95
AND EVERY NIGHTINGALE A SWAN	234	NO, PIGEON	15
EVERYBODY'S			
EVERYBODY'S EARTH.	150	WHEN I WOKE	21
EVERYTHING			
EVERYTHING ENDS, THE TOWER ENDING AND,	101	RUNNING GRAVE	41
WHEN EVERYTHING SLEPT AND THE SMELL OF THE WAVES WAS STRANGE;	224	IDYLL UNFORGET	27
EVIL			
OUR EVIL, WHEN WE BREATHE IT,	17	IN OBLIVION	22
OR EVIL FROM THE CANKERED HEART.	19	THE NEOPHYTE	4
OF CRYING OFF THIS UNSHAPED EVIL,	21	BEWILDERED WAY	2
IF NOT IN PERSON SENDS HIS UNENDING EVIL	29	NEARLY SUMMER	3
BEFORE EVIL OR GOOD, LIGHT OR DARK,	39	GAS FADES	16
COMES FROM MY EVIL OR MY GOOD. MAD, MAD,	53	OUT OF THE PIT	79
OF EVIL ORACLES AND FUNERAL ILLS;	57	GREEK PLAY	31
DEATH AND EVIL ARE TWIN SPECTRES.	60	FAIRY TALES	26
DEATH AND EVIL, TOO SLOW IN HEEDING WORDS.	60	FAIRY TALES	35
SPELT OUT THE SEVEN SEAS, AND EVIL INDEX,	119	ALTARWISE	82
TWINED GOOD AND EVIL ON AN EASTERN TREE;	121	INCARNATE DEVL	10
EVILS			
AND THE UNICORN EVILS RUN THEM THROUGH;	50	NO DOMINION	16
EVIL'S			
ON EVERY HAND THE EVIL'S POSITIVE	27	OBLIVIOUS DARK	18
EWE			
OR THE WHITE EWE LAMB	174	FIRE RAID	35
EXALTATION			
EXALTATION OF THE BLIND,	156	RETURN	87
EXAMINERS			
TO SHIELD THE GLISTENING BRAIN AND BLUNT THE EXAMINERS,	133	MAKE ME A MASK	8
EXCEEDING			
KNOWING EXCEEDING GRIEF AND THE GODS' SORROW	47	POET: 1935	48
YOU, TOO, KNOW THE EXCEEDING JOY	47	POET: 1935	51
EXERCISED			
EXERCISED IN THE STILL NIGHT	196	CRAFT OR ART	2
EXHALING			
THE CLOUD CLIMB OF THE EXHALING TOMB	182	VISION, PRAYER	76
EXILED			
EXILED IN US WE AROUSE THE SOFT,	154	WAS A SAVIOUR	39
EXODUS			
LIKE EXODUS A CHAPTER FROM THE GARDEN,	115	A GRIEF AGO	18
EXOTIC			
AND TAKE AWAY YOUR EXOTIC PLUMAGE,	232	YOUR VOICE	12
INTO MY EXOTIC COMPOSURE?	233	NO THOUGHT	23

		PAGE	TITLE	LINE
EXPENSIVE				
TO SURRENDER NOW IS TO PAY THE EXPENSIVE OGRE TWICE.		140	NO WORK WORDS	10
EXPLODE				
SOME LIFE, YET UNSPENT, MIGHT EXPLODE		44	LONGED TO MOVE	12
EXPLORE				
TO YOU, MY AUNT, WHO WOULD EXPLORE		83	LETTER TO AUNT	1
EXPOSE				
THE MUMMY CLOTHS EXPOSE AN ANCIENT BREAST.		116	LANTERNS SHINE	8
EX-SOLDIERS				
EX-SOLDIERS WITH HORRORS FOR A FACE, ...		41	YOUNG ARE OLD	31
EXULTATION				
EXULTATION LIES DOWN. TIME BURIES THE SPRING WEATHER		191	WINTER'S TALE	119
EXULTATION'S				
VESSEL OF ABSCESSES AND EXULTATION'S SHELL, ...		134	HOW MY ANIMAL	3
EXULTING				
AS A DUST OF PIGEONS. EXULTING, THE GRAVE HOOVED		189	WINTER'S TALE	73
EXULTS				
AND THE TUSKED, RAMSHACKLING SEA EXULTS;		211	POEM ON B'DAY	94
EYE				
THE PRISM OF THE EYE NOW VOID BY SUCTION, ...		29	LONG, SKELETON	10
WHERE DEATH LIES DEAD ASLEEP, ONE BRIGHT EYE OPEN,		41	YOUNG ARE OLD	20
I EYE THE RING OF EARTH, THE AIRY CIRCLE, ...		76	LASHED RINGS	2
AS FORKS MY EYE;		79	LOVE'S FEVER	47
ALL NIGHT AND DAY I EYE THE RAGGED GLOBE		81	ALL THAT I OWE	23
THE SECRET OF THE SOIL GROWS THROUGH THE EYE, ...		82	LIGHT BREAKS	28
A PROCESS IN THE EYE FOREWARNS		88	A PROCESS IN	7
A DARKNESS IN THE WEATHER OF THE EYE		88	A PROCESS IN	10
MOVE LIKE TWO GHOSTS BEFORE THE EYE.		88	A PROCESS IN	18
STRANGE TO OUR SOLID EYE, ...		89	EUNUCH DREAMS	13
THE DEAD TURNS UP ITS EYE;		90	WHERE ONCE THE	3
THE PHOTOGRAPH IS MARRIED TO THE EYE, ...		90	EUNUCH DREAMS	27
AND CURLING ROUND THE BUD THAT FORKS HER EYE.		95	RUB OF LOVE	31
BREAKS WITH THE WORMY WINTER THROUGH THE EYE.		99	OCTOBER WIND	23
CHASTE AND THE CHASER, MAN WITH THE COCKSHUT EYE,		100	RUNNING GRAVE	17
LET FALL THE TEAR OF TIME; THE SLEEPER'S EYE, ...		101	FELLOWED SLEEP	2
BLINDS THEIR CLOUD-TRACKING EYE.		104	WORLD PYRAMID	30
NO THIRD EYE PROBE INTO A RAINBOW'S SEX		108	GRIEF THIEF	25
SPLITTING THE LONG EYE OPEN, AND THE SPIRAL TURNKEY,		110	I, IN IMAGE	50
PLUCK, COCK, MY SEA EYE, SAID MEDUSA'S SCRIPTURE,		119	ALTARWISE	75
AND LOVE PLUCKED OUT THE STINGING SIREN'S EYE, ...		119	ALTARWISE	77
WITH ORACLE FOR EYE?'		129	MY NEOPHYTE	42
NAILED WITH AN OPEN EYE, IN THE BOWL OF WOUNDS AND WEED		135	HOW MY ANIMAL	29
LOPS, AS A BUSH PLUMED WITH FLAMES, THE RANT OF THE FIERCE EYE, ...		135	HOW MY ANIMAL	38
HOW, THROUGH THE HALFMOON'S VEGETABLE EYE, ...		138	FIVE & COUNTRY	3
ENTICED WITH TWINKLING BITS OF THE EYE		146	TO OTHERS	6
AT HIS THRASHING HAIR AND WHALE-BLUE EYE;		161	LONG-LEGGED	3
SANCTUM SANCTORUM THE ANIMAL EYE OF THE WOOD		198	COUNTRY SLEEP	30
AND I GAVE MY SOUL A BLIND, SLASHED EYE, ...		207	LAMENT	45
WALKING IN THE MEADOWS OF HIS SON'S EYE		217	ELEGY	31
EYED				
THE FLYING LOOSE, ALBINO EYED, WING SINGED, ...		41	YOUNG ARE OLD	38
EYED, WHILE THE TEARS DRAG ON THE TAIL, ...		155	RETURN	42
AND MARK THE DARK EYED WAVE, THROUGH THE EYES OF SLEEP, ...		194	CONVERS PRAYER	19
EYED, IN THE HALOED HOUSE, IN HER RARENESS AND HILLY		200	COUNTRY SLEEP	89
EYEING				
EYEING FROM THE WAX'S TOWER, ...		20	ENCOMPASSED	10

		PAGE	TITLE	LINE
EYELID				
UNDER THE ENCUMBERED EYELID,	....	157	INTO HER HEAD	3
THE TEMPTER UNDER THE EYELID	....	165	LONG-LEGGED	102
EYELIDS				
ITS WRINGING SHELL, AND LET HER EYELIDS FASTEN.	...	132	I MAKE THIS IN	35
AND THE COINS ON MY EYELIDS SANG LIKE SHELLS.	.....	150	WHEN I WOKE	30
EYES				
THEYD SEE WITH EYES LIKE MINE	....	11	AIR BREATHE	10
MY EARS, MY NOSE, MY EYES,	....	18	NATURAL DAY	17
OUT OF MY FILTHY EYES	....	18	NATURAL DAY	29
OUT OF THE WAY OF THE EYES OF MEN,	....	21	HIGH ON A HILL	3
FOR THERE WAS NO LIGHT IN HIS EYES,	....	22	ON QUIET NIGHT	17
WITH WIDE, DRY MOUTHS AND EYES,	....	28	NO WINGS	14
LIFT UP THE BLINDS OVER THE BLIND EYES.	....	35	LIFT UP FACE	17
WITH SIGHTLESS EYES AND HEARTS THAT DO NOT BEAT,	....	39	GAS FADES	36
AND THE SUN HEALS, CLOSING SORE EYES.	....	42	A WAR OF WITS	19
DRIP FROM MY OPEN EYES AS HONEY	....	48	LIGHT, I KNOW	9
WHERE EYES SHOULD BE, AND NOSTRILS FULL OF TOADS.		51	OUT OF THE PIT	23
SPRINKLES IN CHILDREN'S EYES A LONG-LAST SLEEP	....	56	WHY EAST WIND	13
THERE ARE NO SEACAVES DEEPER THAN HER EYES;	....	57	GREEK PLAY	11
EYES IN THE GABLES SEE	....	62	EARS IN TURRET	3
EYES IN THIS ISLAND SEE	....	62	EARS IN TURRET	19
THE EYES REMARK THE ANTICS OF THE HAWK.	....	63	WOMAN SPEAKS	10
OF THE DEAD EYES OF CHILDREN	....	68	REALM OF FLESH	15
THE SPHINX OF LIGHT SIT ON THE EYES,	....	69	SECRET WIND	2
PUT AN IRON AT THE EYES,	....	70	TAKE NEEDLES	2
THE CITIES HAVE NOT ROBBED OUR EYES.	....	70	SECRET WIND	24
AND THROUGH THESE EYES GOD MARKS MYSELF REVOLVING,		76	LASHED RINGS	12
CALLED IN MY EYES THE SOUND OF LIGHT.	....	78	LOVE'S FEVER	21
THEN LOOK, MY EYES, UPON THIS BONEBOUND FORTUNE	...	81	ALL THAT I OWE	21
DAWN BREAKS BEHIND THE EYES;	....	82	LIGHT BREAKS	13
DREW IN HIS EYES THE STRAWS OF SLEEP,	....	97	TWILIGHT LOCKS	17
THE CATARACTED EYES THAT FILMED THEIR CLOTH;	......	97	TWILIGHT LOCKS	21
MISTER AND MASTER, DARKNESS FOR HIS EYES,	....	114	SERVANT SUN	31
SO CROSS HER HAND WITH THEIR GRAVE GIPSY EYES,	....	115	A GRIEF AGO	39
MY CAMEL'S EYES WILL NEEDLE THROUGH THE SHROUD.	...	118	ALTARWISE	52
SO SHALL WINGED HARBOURS THROUGH THE ROCKBIRDS' EYES		121	ALTARWISE	130
THESE ONCE-BLIND EYES HAVE BREATHED A WIND OF VISIONS,	....	132	I MAKE THIS IN	54
OF THE SHARP, ENAMELLED EYES AND THE SPECTACLED CLAWS		133	MAKE ME A MASK	2
TO VEIL BELLADONNA AND LET THE DRY EYES PERCEIVE		133	MAKE ME A MASK	10
PRIDES OF TOMORROW SUCKLING IN HER EYES,	....	133	I MAKE THIS IN	67
DRAW DOWN TO ITS WEIRD EYES?	....	134	HOW MY ANIMAL	11
THAT BURNS ALONG MY EYES.	....	134	NOT FROM ANGER	14
THE SPITTLED EYES, THE SALT PONDS IN THE SLEEVES,		136	AFTER FUNERAL	5
THE HEART IS SENSUAL, THOUGH FIVE EYES BREAK.	......	139	FIVE & COUNTRY	14
TALKED AND TORE THOUGH HER EYES SMILED.	....	139	TOMBSTONE TOLD	20
I AM THE GHOST IN THIS HOUSE THAT IS FILLED WITH THE TONGUE AND EYES		141	I, FIRST NAMED	3
THAT THE EYES ARE ALREADY MURDERED,	....	142	SAINT TO FALL	41
TWENTY-FOUR YEARS REMIND THE TEARS OF MY EYES.	....	143	24 YEARS	1
AN ENAMOURED MAN ALONE BY THE TWIGS OF HIS EYES, TWO FIRES,	....	144	PLEASURE-BIRD	7
TONGUE OF YOUR TRANSLATING EYES. THE YOUNG STARS TOLD ME,	....	148	UNLUCKILY FOR	51
ALL I COULD SEE WERE HIS BROWN EYES BURNING	....	149	PAPER & STICKS	8
I WAS PIERCED BY THE IDOL TAILOR'S EYES,	....	152	BELOW A TIME	38
PRISONERS OF WISHES LOCKED THEIR EYES	....	153	WAS A SAVIOUR	7
WITH HIS GOODS UNDER HIS EYES,	....	155	RETURN	38
FLASHED FIRST ACROSS HIS THUNDERCLAPPING EYES.	....	160	DEATHS AND ENT	24

	PAGE	TITLE	LINE
EYES (CONTINUED)			
HE WAS BLIND TO THE EYES OF CANDLES	162	LONG-LEGGED	27
AND SCUTTLED OVER HER EYES, ...	165	LONG-LEGGED	100
SURPRISED IN THE OPENING OF HER NIGHTLONG EYES	170	MARRIAGE VIRG	2
HER HEART ALL EARS AND EYES, LIPS CATCHING THE AVALANCHE	170	MARRIAGE VIRG	10
AND THE CRATERS OF HIS EYES GREW SPRINGSHOOTS AND FIRE	172	DAWN RAID	7
MADE THE TIGERS JUMP OUT OF THEIR EYES	172	THE HUNCHBACK	28
BORROW MY EYES. THE DARKENING SEA FLINGS LEA	179	NEW QUAY	2
AND THE STAR OF THE LOST THE SHAPE OF THE EYES. ...	185	VISION, PRAYER	170
KING OF YOUR BLUE EYES	192	SIDE OF TRUTH	3
AND MARK THE DARK EYED WAVE, THROUGH THE EYES OF SLEEP, ...	194	CONVERS PRAYER	19
GOLDEN IN THE HEYDAYS OF HIS EYES, ...	195	FERN HILL	5
GULL, ON THE WAVE WITH SAND IN ITS EYES! AND THE FOAL MOVES	200	COUNTRY SLEEP	83
MIGHT CROSS ITS PLANETS, THE BELL WEEP, NIGHT GATHER HER EYES, ...	200	COUNTRY SLEEP	92
AND GALLOWS, UP THE RAYS OF HIS EYES THE SMALL BIRDS OF THE BAY	201	SIR JOHNS HILL	4
WOUND, NOR HER RIDING HIGH, NOR HER EYES, NOR KINDLED HAIR, ...	201	COUNTRY SLEEP	101
WHOEVER I WOULD WITH MY WICKED EYES, ...	206	LAMENT	9
BLIND EYES COULD BLAZE LIKE METEORS AND BE GAY, ...	208	NOT GO GENTLE	14
HOLIER THEN THEIR EYES, ...	211	POEM ON B'DAY	106
FROM THE COUNTRY EYES, SALT AND SUN, STAR AND WOE	215	COUNTRY HEAVEN	13
THROUGH HIS UNSEEING EYES TO THE ROOTS OF THE SEA.	217	ELEGY	17
OUT OF HIS EYES I SAW THE LAST LIGHT GLIDE.	217	ELEGY	28
THE TEARS OUT OF HIS EYES, TOO PROUD TO CRY.	217	ELEGY	39
AND I HAVE REFLECTED ITS COLOURS IN THE PEACE OF MY EYES;	224	IDYLL UNFORGET	24
AND EYES HAVE BEEN GROVE-GREEN CATCHING MINE FROM THE DEPTH OF THE SILENCE;	224	IDYLL UNFORGET	33
YOUR EYES CAN BE THE EYES	229	MY RIVER	30
YOUR EYES CAN BE THE EYES	229	MY RIVER	30
OR THE EYES OF THE EAGLE	229	MY RIVER	32
AND HER EYES PIERCED THEIR INTENSE LOVE INTO ME,	234	WOMAN TAPESTRY	2
AND THE CRUELTY OF MY SUBTLE EYES, ...	236	WOMAN TAPESTRY	37
EYE-TEETH			
AND THE UNDEAD EYE-TEETH, ...	108	GRIEF THIEF	24
EZRA			
IN T. S. E. AND EZRA POUND.	83	LETTER TO AUNT	10
FABLE			
THE INSECT FABLE IS THE CERTAIN PROMISE.	124	TODAY, INSECT	18
I FURNISH WITH THE MEAT OF A FABLE;	145	PLEASURE-BIRD	21
FABLES			
THE INSECT CERTAIN IS THE PLAGUE OF FABLES.	124	TODAY, INSECT	9
THE STAR RISE AT PASTURE AND NIGHTLONG THE FABLES GRAZE	198	COUNTRY SLEEP	34
FABLING			
I YOUNG AESOP FABLING TO THE NEAR NIGHT BY THE DINGLE	202	SIR JOHNS HILL	35
FABULOUS			
MY CROSS OF TALES BEHIND THE FABULOUS CURTAIN.' ...	125	TODAY, INSECT	26
AND FABULOUS, DEAR GOD.	210	POEM ON B'DAY	48
FACE			
AND SAW TOWARDS HER TINY FACE	11	CABARET	3
THE CREATURE WITH THE ANGEL'S FACE	12	SKY'S BRIGHT	12
LIFT UP YOUR FACE	35	LIFT UP FACE	T
LIFT UP YOUR FACE, LIGHT	35	LIFT UP FACE	1

	PAGE	TITLE	LINE
FACE (CONTINUED)			
EX-SOLDIERS WITH HORRORS FOR A FACE,	41	YOUNG ARE OLD	31
SHALL LAMP THE RAVEN DARKNESS OF HER FACE,	57	GREEK PLAY	9
MY FACE IS HAGGARD IN THE GLASS,	61	MEAT ON BONES	19
AND LUSTRELESS WITHIN THE RUINED FACE	63	WOMAN SPEAKS	9
IN THE FACE OF SEED AND FRUIT?	72	TAKE NEEDLES	60
WHERE ONCE THE WATERS OF YOUR FACE	90	WHERE ONCE THE	T
WHERE ONCE THE WATERS OF YOUR FACE	90	WHERE ONCE THE	1
ONE SMILE OF LIGHT ACROSS THE EMPTY FACE;	93	IN BEGINNING	2
STAMP OF THE MINTED FACE UPON THE MOON;	94	IN BEGINNING	10
ON FORK AND FACE.	100	RUNNING GRAVE	25
AND THE FACE TO THE DRIVEN LOVER.	106	ALL ALL AND	24
TURNING A PETROL FACE BLIND TO THE ENEMY	110	I, IN IMAGE	47
DAZZLE THIS FACE OF VOICES ON THE MOON-TURNED TABLE,	110	I, IN IMAGE	69
SHOULD LANTERNS SHINE, THE HOLY FACE,	116	LANTERNS SHINE	1
RAPE AND REBELLION IN THE NURSERIES OF MY FACE,	133	MAKE ME A MASK	3
WALKS WITH NO WOUND, NOR LIGHTNING IN HER FACE,	133	I MAKE THIS IN	63
THE INVOKED, SHROUDING VEIL AT THE CAP OF THE FACE,	134	HOW MY ANIMAL	5
A MADMAN WITH A BRUSH HAS SLAPPED A FACE	137	O CHATTERTON	13
HER FIST OF A FACE DIED CLENCHED ON A ROUND PAIN;	137	AFTER FUNERAL	34
AND THE SUN KILLED IN HER FACE.	139	TOMBSTONE TOLD	9
BEHIND A FACE OF HANDS,	141	SAINT TO FALL	10
MOON WITH A RELATION'S FACE	155	RETURN	47
AND NOTHING SHONE ON THE WATER'S FACE	163	LONG-LEGGED	44
ALWAYS GOOD-BYE TO THE FIRES OF THE FACE,	165	LONG-LEGGED	98
HIS UPTURNED FACE WITH ONE DIVINE CARESS.	222	MISSING	3
FACED			
FOR, SUNDAY FACED, WITH DUSTERS IN MY GLOVE,	100	RUNNING GRAVE	16
I SET BACK THE CLOCK FACED TAILORS,	151	BELOW A TIME	18
FACES			
THE LIVING SKY, THE FACES OF THE STARS.	36	MIDNIGHT ROAD	14
THEIR FACES SHONE UNDER SOME RADIANCE	43	FACES SHONE	T
THEIR FACES SHONE UNDER SOME RADIANCE	43	FACES SHONE	1
THEIR FACES SHONE; THE MIDNIGHT RAIN	43	FACES SHONE	8
SEE WOMEN'S FACES UNDER LIVING SNOODS,	51	OUT OF THE PIT	21
SWEET ARE THEIR FATHERED FACES IN THEIR WINGS.'	102	FELLOWED SLEEP	14
STALKING MY CHILDREN'S FACES WITH A TAIL OF BLOOD,	122	HOLD HARD	20
FACES OF MELTING VISIONS,	156	RETURN	84
LITTLE WHITE-LIPPED FACES HAVE PEERED UP AT ME,	224	IDYLL UNFORGET	32
FACING			
CONDEMN ME TO AN EVERLASTING FACING	68	REALM OF FLESH	14
FACT			
BY WEIGHT OF CLOTH AND FACT,	28	NO WINGS	4
FACTORS			
AND SYMBOLISE THE MADDENING FACTORS	33	HELD-OUT HAND	15
FACULTY			
OUTDO YOUR PRUDE'S GENETIC FACULTY	20	THE NEOPHYTE	13
FADE			
'THESE ARE BUT DREAMING MEN. BREATHE, AND THEY FADE.'	102	FELLOWED SLEEP	15
FADE WITH THEIR ROSE-	215	COUNTRY HEAVEN	20
FADE, THE GREEN GLOOM GROWS DARKER, AND DEEPER THE DUSK:	222	FOREST PICTURE	10
FADED			
WHIRLED IN OUR WORDS, THEN FADED.	34	IN GARDENS	15
FADED MY ELBOW GHOST, THE MOTHERS-EYED,	102	FELLOWED SLEEP	16
AND FROM HER LIPS THE FADED PIGMENTS FALL,	116	LANTERNS SHINE	7
AND THE RAIN WRING OUT ITS TONGUES ON THE FADED YARD,	205	GIANT'S THIGH	52
FADES			
BEFORE THE GAS FADES	38	GAS FADES	T
BEFORE THE GAS FADES WITH A HARSH LAST BUBBLE,	38	GAS FADES	1

	PAGE	TITLE	LINE
FADING			
SLEEP ABOVE IN THE GLOW OF A FADING SUNSET;	222	FOREST PICTURE	7
FAG			
BEFORE THE LAST FAG AND THE SHIRT SLEEVES AND SLIPPERS, ...	38	GAS FADES	3
FAGGOTS			
WHAT WERE YOUNG LIMBS ARE FAGGOTS ON THE LAND, ...	63	WOMAN SPEAKS	14
FAIL			
BUT THE VEINS MUST FAIL.	17	IN OBLIVION	14
ONLY AS WRONG; BUT SHAN'T THE GENIUS FAIL, ...	28	NO WINGS	7
WAITING AND WATCHING FOR YOUR FINGERS TO FAIL	33	HELD-OUT HAND	20
MAY FAIL TO FASTEN WITH A VIRGIN O	100	RUNNING GRAVE	19
TELLS THE STICK, 'FAIL'.	100	RUNNING GRAVE	30
AND FATHER ALL NOR FAIL THE FLY-LORD'S ACRE, ...	123	FOSTER LIGHT	13
SO THE BALL FAIL, ...	128	NOW, SAY NAY	25
BOTH SHALL FAIL IF I BOW NOT TO YOUR BLESSING	148	UNLUCKILY FOR	47
I MAY WITHOUT FAIL	170	LOVE IN ASYLUM	17
FAILING			
TRYING HIS HAND AT FAILING	155	RETURN	29
FAINT			
FAINT ARROWY MOONSTONE ON A TEAR-CULLED CADENCE,	225	SLENDER WIND	3
FAIR			
FROM THE FAIR DEAD WHO FLUSH THE SEA	92	BOYS OF SUMMER	34
AND THE WINGS OF THE GREAT ROC RIBBONED FOR THE FAIR!	199	COUNTRY SLEEP	65
AND SHOWS THEM FAIR AGAINST THE DARK, ...	238	MAKES INTERVALS	3
FAIR-FORMED			
THE TWISTED BRAIN, THE FAIR-FORMED LOIN, ...	32	OUT OF SIGHS	25
FAIRIES			
HAVE BLOWN SKY HIGH THE NURSERY OF FAIRIES;	59	FAIRY TALES	23
AND, FROM HIS FORK, A DOG AMONG THE FAIRIES, ...	117	ALTARWISE	4
FAIRY			
WE HAVE THE FAIRY TALES BY HEART	59	FAIRY TALES	T
WE HAVE THE FAIRY TALES BY HEART, ...	59	FAIRY TALES	1
SHALL WE LEARN FAIRY TALES OFF PAT, ...	60	FAIRY TALES	37
DIVIDE THE NIGHT AND DAY WITH FAIRY THUMBS;	92	BOYS OF SUMMER	15
FAITH			
FAITH IN DIVINITY WOULD SOLVE MOST THINGS, ...	37	WINDMILLS TURN	16
NO FAITH TO FIX THE TEETH ON CARRIES	41	YOUNG ARE OLD	18
NO FAITH TO SHARPEN THE OLD WITS LEAVES US	41	YOUNG ARE OLD	21
NO FAITH TO FOLLOW IS THE WORLD'S CURSE	41	YOUNG ARE OLD	24
FAITH FIXED BEYOND THE SPINNING STARS, ...	41	YOUNG ARE OLD	45
FIXED FAITH, BELIEVING AND WORSHIPPING TOGETHER ...	41	YOUNG ARE OLD	46
FAITH. FAITH. FIRM FAITH IN MANY OR ONE, ...	41	YOUNG ARE OLD	49
FAITH. FAITH. FIRM FAITH IN MANY OR ONE, ...	41	YOUNG ARE OLD	49
FAITH. FAITH. FIRM FAITH IN MANY OR ONE, ...	41	YOUNG ARE OLD	49
FAITH FIXED LIKE A STAR BEYOND THE STARS, ...	42	YOUNG ARE OLD	50
WE HAVE NO FAITH TO SET BETWEEN OUR TEETH.	42	YOUNG ARE OLD	56
BELIEVE, BELIEVE AND BE SAVED, WE CRY, WHO HAVE NO FAITH.	42	YOUNG ARE OLD	57
FAITH IN THEIR HANDS SHALL SNAP IN TWO, ...	50	NO DOMINION	15
WHO DOES NOT MAKE A WOUND IN FAITH	55	NO MAN BELIEVE	5
BELIEVES WHO DOES NOT LANCE HIS FAITH, ...	55	NO MAN BELIEVE	16
WHO IN THE BONES FINDS NOT NEW FAITH, ...	55	NO MAN BELIEVE	22
WHO DOES NOT BREAK AND MAKE HIS FINAL FAITH.	55	NO MAN BELIEVE	24
LET FOR ONE MOMENT A FAITH STATEMENT	66	LET A FAITH	T
LET FOR ONE MOMENT A FAITH STATEMENT	66	LET A FAITH	1
LET FOR ONE MOMENT A FAITH STATEMENT	67	LET A FAITH	6
LET FOR ONE MOMENT A FAITH STATEMENT	67	LET A FAITH	11
THE DREAM HAS SUCKED THE SLEEPER OF HIS FAITH	90	EUNUCH DREAMS	29
THIS IS THE WORLD. HAVE FAITH.	90	EUNUCH DREAMS	36

	PAGE	TITLE	LINE
FAITH (CONTINUED)			
DESPAIR OF BLOOD, FAITH IN THE MAIDEN'S SLIME, ...	100	RUNNING GRAVE	23
THE SEA-HALVED FAITH THAT BLEW TIME TO HIS KNEES,	107	GRIEF THIEF	4
HIS FAITH AROUND HER FLEW UNDONE	158	INTO HER HEAD	26
ON A STAR OF FAITH PURE AS THE DRIFTING BREAD, ...	187	WINTER'S TALE	12
BUT HER FAITH THAT EACH VAST NIGHT AND THE SAGA OF PRAYER	201	COUNTRY SLEEP	102
HER FAITH THAT THIS LAST NIGHT FOR HIS UNSACRED SAKE	201	COUNTRY SLEEP	104
YOUR FAITH AS DEATHLESS AS THE OUTCRY OF THE RULED SUN.	201	COUNTRY SLEEP	111
UNDER THE LIGHTED SHAPES OF FAITH AND THEIR MOONSHADE	204	GIANT'S THIGH	17
WITH MORE TRIUMPHANT FAITH	211	POEM ON B'DAY	97
LET ME BELIEVE IN THE CLEAN FAITH OF THE BODY, ...	235	WOMAN TAPESTRY	24
LET ME BELIEVE IN THE CLEAN FAITH OF THE BODY, ...	237	WOMAN TAPESTRY	79
FAITHLESS			
FORGOTTEN DARK, REST THEIR PULSE AND BURY THEIR DEAD IN HER FAITHLESS SLEEP.	159	INTO HER HEAD	69
FAITHLESSLY			
FAITHLESSLY UNTO HIM	210	POEM ON B'DAY	72
FAITHS			
ALL THE CABINNED FAITHS DENY	71	TAKE NEEDLES	15
FAKE			
SAID THE FAKE GENTLEMAN IN SUIT OF SPADES, ...	118	ALTARWISE	60
FALL			
THAT WILL FLY AND FALL	3	PROLOGUE	30
OF DISSOLUTION AND THE EMPTY FALL, ...	17	IN OBLIVION	23
SEARING THE SKY FOR THUNDERBOLTS TO FALL	34	THIRST PARCHES	5
LEADS, TOO, TO A LEAD PIT, WHINNY AND FALL, ...	44	TO FOLLOW FOX	10
SHALL I FALL TO DEATH'S FEATHER.	44	LONGED TO MOVE	18
AND ON HIS SHOULDERS FALL THEIR WORLD OF WINGS, ...	63	WOMAN SPEAKS	22
BEFORE WE MOTHERNAKED FALL	73	WE MOTHERNAKED	T
BEFORE WE MOTHERNAKED FALL	73	WE MOTHERNAKED	1
AND SWEET SHALL FALL CONTAGION FROM HIS SIDE, ...	73	LORD RED HAIL	5
SHALL FALL AWAY, AND LEAVE ONE SINGING SHELL.	73	LORD RED HAIL	12
SHALL FALL AWAKE WHEN CURES AND THEIR ITCH	89	EUNUCH DREAMS	22
AND WORDS FALL CRIPPLED FROM THE SLAVING LIPS, ...	96	TWELVE	2
MY HOUSE WOULD FALL LIKE BREAD ABOUT MY HOMAGE; ...	96	TWELVE	11
LET FALL THE TEAR OF TIME; THE SLEEPER'S EYE, ...	101	FELLOWED SLEEP	2
HEARING THE WEATHER FALL.	109	I, IN IMAGE	30
AND FROM HER LIPS THE FADED PIGMENTS FALL, ...	116	LANTERNS SHINE	7
THE GREENWOOD DYING AS THE DEER FALL IN THEIR TRACKS,	122	HOLD HARD	11
DOWN FALL FOUR PADDING WEATHERS ON THE SCARLET LANDS,	122	HOLD HARD	19
BEFORE THE FALL FROM LOVE THE FLYING HEARTBONE, ...	124	TODAY, INSECT	15
SO STAR FALL, ...	128	NOW, SAY NAY	24
AND I FELT WITH MY BARE FALL	140	TOMBSTONE TOLD	28
A SAINT ABOUT TO FALL	141	SAINT TO FALL	T
A SAINT ABOUT TO FALL, ...	141	SAINT TO FALL	1
HEAVEN FELL WITH HIS FALL AND ONE CROCKED BELL BEAT THE LEFT AIR.	142	SAINT TO FALL	25
O WAKE TO SEE, AFTER A NOBLE FALL, ...	142	SAINT TO FALL	43
NOW BREAK A GIANT TEAR FOR THE LITTLE KNOWN FALL,	153	WAS A SAVIOUR	32
AND THE FLAKES FALL LIKE HILLS.	166	LONG-LEGGED	136
NIGHT FALL AND THE FRUIT LIKE A SUN, ...	174	FIRE RAID	56
OF THE ENDLESS FALL.	184	VISION, PRAYER	165
AND ALL THE ELEMENTS OF THE SNOW FALL REJOICED	189	WINTER'S TALE	84
THE THIEF FALL ON THE DEAD LIKE THE WILLY NILLY DEW,	200	COUNTRY SLEEP	93
TEACH ME THE LOVE THAT IS EVERGREEN AFTER THE FALL LEAVED	205	GIANT'S THIGH	53
IN THE THISTLEDOWN FALL, ...	209	POEM ON B'DAY	19
FALL AND THE DEW LARKS SING	211	POEM ON B'DAY	102

	PAGE	TITLE	LINE
FALL (CONTINUED)			
YOUR STEP WILL REMAIN ABOUT TO FALL.	232	FURIOUS MOTION	4
WHERE THE FROST CAN NEVER FALL,	232	YOUR VOICE	15
FALLEN			
IS FALLEN DOWN	22	HIGH ON A HILL	15
YOUNG MEN WITH FALLEN CHESTS AND OLD MEN'S BREATH,	41	YOUNG ARE OLD	27
LOVE DRIPS AND GATHERS, BUT THE FALLEN BLOOD	77	THE FORCE THAT	17
MY FALLEN FILLED, THAT HAD THE HINT OF DEATH,	80	ALL THAT I OWE	10
OF SICK OLD MANHOOD ON THE FALLEN JAWS,	95	RUB OF LOVE	24
I DREAMED MY GENESIS IN SWEAT OF DEATH, FALLEN	103	I DREAMED MY	25
GENTLE IN THEIR CLOGS OVER THE FALLEN SKY,	187	WINTER'S TALE	24
THE RAVEN'S FALLEN AND THE MAGPIE'S STILL.	237	PILLAR BREAKS	7
FALLING			
BETWEEN THE RISING AND THE FALLING	15	FOR LEDA	20
SNAPPED IN A RAIN OF PIECES FALLING	21	BEWILDERED WAY	20
YOU WILL NOT SEE THE STEADYING OR FALLING,	39	GAS FADES	37
SWEET IS THE WAXEN BLOOD, HONEY THE FALLING FLESH;	63	WOMAN SPEAKS	3
MY FALLING LUNGS, NOR AS THE CYPRESS	75	SONG: LOVE ME	2
AND LOOK, MY GRAIN, UPON THE FALLING WHEAT;	81	ALL THAT I OWE	29
GOLDEN GLAMORGAN STRAIGHTENS, TO THE FALLING BIRDS.	123	HOLD HARD	23
LONDON'S ARCHES ARE FALLING	154	RETURN	26
OH, JERICHO WAS FALLING IN THEIR LUNGS!	163	LONG-LEGGED	54
UNDER THE NIGHT FOREVER FALLING.	184	VISION, PRAYER	152
FOREVER FALLING NIGHT IS A KNOWN	184	VISION, PRAYER	153
AND THE STARS FALLING COLD,	187	WINTER'S TALE	6
THIS NIGHT AND EACH NIGHT SINCE THE FALLING STAR YOU WERE BORN,	199	COUNTRY SLEEP	55
STEERED BY THE FALLING STARS.	209	POEM ON B'DAY	41
FALLOW			
WORM IN THE SCALP, THE STAKED AND FALLOW.	106	ALL ALL AND	9
FALLS			
THAT RISES AND THEN FALLS, BUDS BUT TO WITHER;	25	THERE'S PLENTY	3
AND THE STATE FALLS TO BITS,	39	GAS FADES	7
THAT FALLS ON CHAOS.	41	YOUNG ARE OLD	25
WHEN THE SUN FALLS AND THE MOON STARES,	48	LIGHT, I KNOW	7
NO MAN BELIEVES WHO, WHEN A STAR FALLS SHOT,	54	NO MAN BELIEVE	1
OF MANY A HUNDRED FALLS;	55	WHY EAST WIND	5
LAMENTING FALLS. PITY ELECTRA'S LOVING	56	GREEK PLAY	4
AS FIRE FALLS, TWO HEMISPHERES DIVIDE,	73	LORD RED HAIL	7
THE CADAVEROUS GRAVELS, FALLS THICK AND STEADILY,	110	I, IN IMAGE	44
NOR FALLS TO HIS GREEN MYTHS?	129	MY NEOPHYTE	18
FALLS ON A RING OF SUMMERS AND LOCKED NOONS.	132	I MAKE THIS IN	30
EVER AND EVER HE FINDS A WAY, AS THE SNOW FALLS,	199	COUNTRY SLEEP	56
AS THE RAIN FALLS, HAIL ON THE FLEECE, AS THE VALE MIST RIDES	199	COUNTRY SLEEP	57
THROUGH THE HAYGOLD STALLS, AS THE DEW FALLS ON THE WIND-	199	COUNTRY SLEEP	58
OF THE MORNING LEAVES, AS THE STAR FALLS, AS THE WINGED	199	COUNTRY SLEEP	60
AND FALLS, AND FLOWERS IN THE YAWNING WOUND AT OUR SIDES,	199	COUNTRY SLEEP	62
AS THE WORLD FALLS, SILENT AS THE CYCLONE OF SILENCE.	199	COUNTRY SLEEP	63
FALSE			
TUMBLE, NOT FLYING, IS FALSE,	37	WINDMILLS TURN	5
ARE FORMED OF FLESH, BUT LET THE FALSE DAY COME	116	LANTERNS SHINE	6
FALSITY			
IN A GAY MOMENT'S FALSITY--	21	BEWILDERED WAY	8
FAME			
FLOOD OF HER HEART'S FAME; SHE WOULD LIE DUMB AND DEEP	136	AFTER FUNERAL	19

	PAGE	TITLE	LINE
FAMILIAR			
THE SCUDDING BASE OF THE FAMILIAR SKY,	142	SAINT TO FALL	29
A DESIRELESS FAMILIAR	147	TO OTHERS	15
FAMINE			
AND FAMINE GREW, AND LOCUSTS CAME;	66	HAND SIGNED	10
WHEN NO MOUTH STIRRED ABOUT THE HANGING FAMINE,	78	LOVE'S FEVER	5
FAMOUS			
INTENT ON VISITING THE FAMOUS SPOTS,	37	WINDMILLS TURN	12
THE FAMOUS STITCH DROPPERS.	151	BELOW A TIME	28
OF THE PACING, FAMOUS SEA BUT ITS SPEECH,	169	LONG-LEGGED	210
AND AS I WAS GREEN AND CAREFREE, FAMOUS AMONG THE BARNS	195	FERN HILL	10
IN THE UNKNOWN, FAMOUS LIGHT OF GREAT	210	POEM ON B'DAY	47
FAN			
HER FAN BURST IN A MILLION LIGHTS	11	CABARET	14
FANCY			
THE ICICLE OF EACH DELIBERATE FANCY.	10	COOL, OH NO	7
GLIDING, ROPE-DANCING, IS HIS FANCY,	28	NO WINGS	8
TIME IS A FOOLISH FANCY, TIME AND FOOL.	100	RUNNING GRAVE	26
FANTASTIC			
DOWN THESE FANTASTIC AVENUES PASS LIKE SHADOWS.	222	FOREST PICTURE	12
FANTASTICALLY			
THE STREAM'S FANTASTICALLY HARD,	14	RAIN CUTS	26
FAR			
AND FAR AWAY'S TOO SHARP A SUN	12	SKY'S BRIGHT	3
REACHING A SECOND GROUND FAR FROM THE STARS;	101	FELLOWED SLEEP	7
CLOSE AND FAR SHE ANNOUNCED THE THEFT OF THE HEART	158	INTO HER HEAD	39
DEAR TOMMY, PLEASE, FROM FAR, SCIATIC KINGSLEY	179	NEW QUAY	1
AND THE SMELL OF HAY IN THE SNOW, AND THE FAR OWL	187	WINTER'S TALE	7
AND OVER THE CLOTH OF COUNTIES THE FAR HILLS RODE NEAR,	190	WINTER'S TALE	93
IN THE FAR AGO LAND THE DOOR OF HIS DEATH GLIDED WIDE	190	WINTER'S TALE	105
NEVER AND NEVER, MY GIRL RIDING FAR AND NEAR	197	COUNTRY SLEEP	1
AND FAR AT SEA HE KNOWS,	209	POEM ON B'DAY	30
FARAWAY			
IN THE WOOD FARAWAY UNDER ME.	177	POEM IN OCT	30
FAREWELLS			
ON THE CONSUMPTIVES' TERRACE TAKING THEIR TWO FAREWELLS,	109	I, IN IMAGE	34
FARING			
PRAISE TO OUR FARING HEARTS.	90	EUNUCH DREAMS	42
FARM			
AND FLOATING FIELDS FROM THE FARM IN THE CUP OF THE VALES,	187	WINTER'S TALE	3
FLOCKED WITH THE SHEEP WHITE SMOKE OF THE FARM HOUSE COWL	187	WINTER'S TALE	9
TORN AND ALONE IN A FARM HOUSE IN A FOLD	187	WINTER'S TALE	15
AND ALL THE WOKEN FARM AT ITS WHITE TRADES,	187	WINTER'S TALE	25
PAST THE BLIND BARNS AND BYRES OF THE WINDLESS FARM.	190	WINTER'S TALE	90
ON A BREAD WHITE HILL OVER THE CUPPED FARM	190	WINTER'S TALE	107
ABOUT THE HAPPY YARD AND SINGING AS THE FARM WAS HOME,	195	FERN HILL	11
AS I RODE TO SLEEP THE OWLS WERE BEARING THE FARM AWAY,	195	FERN HILL	24
AND THEN TO AWAKE, AND THE FARM, LIKE A WANDERER WHITE	195	FERN HILL	28
AND WAKE TO THE FARM FOREVER FLED FROM THE CHILDLESS LAND.	196	FERN HILL	51
NOR THE TUSKED PRINCE, IN THE RUTTISH FARM, AT THE RIND	198	COUNTRY SLEEP	37

	PAGE	TITLE	LINE
FARMER			
FARMER IN TIME OF FROST THE BURNING LEAGUES, ...	123	FOSTER LIGHT	10
WITH A SILVERFOX FARMER	155	RETURN	28
FARMS			
SHEEP WHITE HOLLOW FARMS	4	PROLOGUE	51
HOLLOW FARMS IN A THRONG	5	PROLOGUE	79
GALLOP THROUGH THE ARCHED, GREEN FARMS, ...	168	LONG-LEGGED	188
ABOVE THE FARMS AND THE WHITE HORSES	177	POEM IN OCT	13
PADDOCKS IN THE FARMS OF BIRDS. THE DEAD OAK WALKS			
FOR LOVE.	189	WINTER'S TALE	75
IN THE FARMS OF HEAVEN'S KEEPING, ...	216	COUNTRY HEAVEN	29
FAST			
MADE FAST BY ME.	87	PAIN BE MUSIC	6
SO FAST I MOVE DEFYING TIME, THE QUIET GENTLEMAN	116	LANTERNS SHINE	14
BOAT WITH ITS ANCHOR FREE AND FAST	162	LONG-LEGGED	6
A WIND THROWS A SHADOW AND IT FREEZES FAST.	166	LONG-LEGGED	130
AND FAST THROUGH THE DRIFTS OF THE THICKETS ANTLERED			
LIKE DEER, ...	190	WINTER'S TALE	95
LIE FAST AND SOOTHED, ...	198	COUNTRY SLEEP	19
MAKING OUR AFFECTIONS FAST;	230	OUR SANCTITY	18
FASTEN			
MAY FAIL TO FASTEN WITH A VIRGIN O	100	RUNNING GRAVE	19
ITS WRINGING SHELL, AND LET HER EYELIDS FASTEN. ...	132	I MAKE THIS IN	35
FASTENING			
AND FASTENING IN ITS CAGE THE FLOWERS' COLOUR?	46	POET: 1935	9
FAT			
AT NIGHTBREAK BORN IN THE FAT SIDE, FROM AN ANIMAL			
BED	130	SINNERS' BELL	26
THROUGH THE WAVES OF THE FAT STREETS NOR THE			
SKELETON'S THIN WAYS.	146	IF HEAD HURT	28
OR, BUTTER FAT GOOSEGIRLS, BOUNCED IN A GAMBO BED,	204	GIANT'S THIGH	37
FATE			
LOVE, MY FATE GOT LUCKILY, ...	148	UNLUCKILY FOR	43
FATHER			
IN GOD OR GODS, CHRIST OR HIS FATHER, ...	41	YOUNG ARE OLD	47
SWUNG BY MY FATHER FROM HIS DOME.	68	BEFORE KNOCKED	12
LONG BREATH THAT CARRIED TO MY FATHER	69	BEFORE KNOCKED	41
AND MY FATHER WAS THE LORD.	72	TAKE NEEDLES	44
I AM THE MAN YOUR FATHER WAS.	93	BOYS OF SUMMER	52
HALF OF THE FELLOW FATHER AS HE DOUBLES	103	WORLD PYRAMID	1
DO YOU NOT FATHER ME	112	NOT FATHER ME	T
DO YOU NOT FATHER ME, NOR THE ERECTED ARM	112	NOT FATHER ME	1
AM I NOT FATHER, TOO, AND THE ASCENDING BOY, ...	112	NOT FATHER ME	9
DO YOU NOT FATHER ME ON THE DESTROYING SAND?	113	NOT FATHER ME	25
DRIVES OUT THE FATHER FROM THE CAESARED CAMP;	115	A GRIEF AGO	27
AND FATHER ALL NOR FAIL THE FLY-LORD'S ACRE, ...	123	FOSTER LIGHT	13
SUN THE FATHER HIS QUIVER FULL OF THE INFANTS OF			
PURE FIRE, ...	186	HOLY SPRING	19
AND YOU, MY FATHER, THERE ON THE SAD HEIGHT, ...	208	NOT GO GENTLE	16
FATHERED			
SWEET ARE THEIR FATHERED FACES IN THEIR WINGS.' ...	102	FELLOWED SLEEP	14
LET HIM FIND NO REST BUT THE FATHERED AND FOUND,	216	ELEGY	12
FATHERING			
AND SISTER TO THE FATHERING WORM.	68	BEFORE KNOCKED	6
FATHERING AND ALL HUMBLING DARKNESS	191	REFUSAL MOURN	3
FATHERLESS			
IN THE NAME OF THE FATHERLESS	185	VISION, PRAYER	171
FATHERS			
AND OTHER VIRGINS IN OFFICIAL FATHERS.	38	THE GOSSIPERS	13
NOW JACK MY FATHERS LET THE TIME-FACED CROOK, ...	108	GRIEF THIEF	15

	PAGE	TITLE	LINE
FATHERS (CONTINUED)			
HIS FATHERS CLING TO THE HAND OF THE GIRL	167	LONG-LEGGED	147
FATHERS'			
MY FATHERS' LOVES THAT PULL UPON MY NERVES, ...	80	ALL THAT I OWE	6
'MY FATHERS' GLOBE KNOCKS ON ITS NAVE AND SINGS.'	101	FELLOWED SLEEP	11
'THIS THAT WE TREAD WAS, TOO, YOUR FATHERS' LAND.'	101	FELLOWED SLEEP	12
MY FATHERS' GHOST IS CLIMBING IN THE RAIN.	102	FELLOWED SLEEP	30
SHAPE WITH MY FATHERS' THIEVES.	108	GRIEF THIEF	28
FATHER'S			
AS THE HANDS THAT HELD THEM IN MY FATHER'S TIME.	45	PLOUGHMAN GONE	11
THE SAME TUNE AS IN MY FATHER'S TIME:	46	PLOUGHMAN GONE	29
REBEL AGAINST MY FATHER'S DREAM	61	MEAT ON BONES	27
HE DROWNED HIS FATHER'S MAGICS IN A DREAM.	97	TWILIGHT LOCKS	18
AND THE FIVE-FATHOMED HAMLET ON HIS FATHER'S CORAL,	111	I, IN IMAGE	83
OF HIS FATHER'S HOUSE IN THE SANDS, ...	141	SAINT TO FALL	7
FATHOM			
WINDILY MASTER OF MAN WAS THE ROTTEN FATHOM, ...	112	I, IN IMAGE	104
FATHOMED			
IS HALF ITS LIGHT; THE FATHOMED SEA	88	A PROCESS IN	11
FATS			
SHE WHO WAS WHO I HOLD, THE FATS AND FLOWER, ...	114	A GRIEF AGO	2
THE FATS OF MIDNIGHT WHEN THE SALT WAS SINGING; ...	119	ALTARWISE	80
FAULT			
A WOMAN FIGURE WITHOUT FAULT	172	THE HUNCHBACK	32
FAULTS			
THAT THOUGH I LOVED THEM FOR THEIR FAULTS	147	TO OTHERS	18
FAULTY			
OF FAULTY MEN AND THEIR DISEASES, ...	34	IN GARDENS	10
FAWKES			
AND THE DAUGHTERS OF DARKNESS FLAME LIKE FAWKES			
FIRES STILL.	205	GIANT'S THIGH	60
FEAR			
OF FEAR, RAGE RED, MANALIVE, ...	4	PROLOGUE	48
FOR FEAR OF WAKING THE ROOKS, ...	31	BEING BUT MEN	3
FOR FEAR OF COMING	31	BEING BUT MEN	4
THE LIVING AFTER, THE FILLED WITH FEAR, ...	41	YOUNG ARE OLD	36
NEITHER BY NIGHT'S ANCIENT FEAR, ...	44	LONGED TO MOVE	15
NO LONGER FEAR THE WALKER IN THE GARDEN, ...	59	FAIRY TALES	11
FEAR DEATH AS LITTLE AS THE THUNDER'S SHOT, ...	60	FAIRY TALES	40
HATE AND FEAR BE YOUR TWO LOVES.	76	SONG: LOVE ME	15
I WOULD NOT FEAR THE APPLE NOR THE FLOOD	95	RUB OF LOVE	6
I WOULD NOT FEAR THE GALLOWS NOR THE AXE	95	RUB OF LOVE	13
I WOULD NOT FEAR THE MUSCLING-IN OF LOVE	95	RUB OF LOVE	17
I WOULD NOT FEAR THE DEVIL IN THE LOIN	95	RUB OF LOVE	20
FEAR NOT THE WORKING WORLD, MY MORTAL, ...	106	ALL ALL AND	13
FEAR NOT THE FLAT, SYNTHETIC BLOOD, ...	106	ALL ALL AND	14
FEAR NOT THE TREAD, THE SEEDED MILLING, ...	106	ALL ALL AND	16
FEAR NOT THE SCREWS THAT TURN THE VOICE, ...	106	ALL ALL AND	23
OF A LACK-A-HEAD GHOST I FEAR TO THE ANONYMOUS END.	141	I, FIRST NAMED	4
THROW YOUR FEAR A PARCEL OF STONE	142	SAINT TO FALL	37
(BURY THE DEAD FOR FEAR THAT THEY WALK TO THE GRAVE			
IN LABOUR.)	143	24 YEARS	2
FEAR OR BELIEVE THAT THE WOLF IN A SHEEPWHITE HOOD	197	COUNTRY SLEEP	3
BELL BELIEVE OR FEAR THAT THE RUSTIC SHADE OR SPELL	198	COUNTRY SLEEP	22
ON THE LORD'S-TABLE OF THE BOWING GRASS. FEAR MOST	198	COUNTRY SLEEP	35
EVER AND EVER BY ALL YOUR VOWS BELIEVE AND FEAR ...	201	COUNTRY SLEEP	107
FEAR-BEGGARED			
AND WITH NOT ONE FEAR-BEGGARED SYLLABLE	76	LASHED RINGS	10
FEARING			
HE CRIED AS HE DIED, FEARING AT LAST THE SPHERES'	217	ELEGY	33

	PAGE	TITLE	LINE
FEARS			
SUCH LIGHT SHALL NOT ILLUMINATE MY FEARS	48	LIGHT, I KNOW	4
WE HID OUR FEARS IN THAT MURDERING BREATH, ...	153	WAS A SAVIOUR	14
FEAST			
A PINCH OF AUDEN IS THE LION'S FEAST;	58	TO ARCHITECTS	13
AND RAVEN YOUTH WILL FEAST BUT WHERE HE WILL.	64	WOMAN SPEAKS	51
HERE LIE THE BEASTS OF MAN AND HERE I FEAST, ...	81	HERE LIE BEAST	1
AFTER THE FEAST OF TEAR-STUFFED TIME AND THISTLES	136	AFTER FUNERAL	10
FEATHER			
A LEGENDARY HORSE WITH HOOF AND FEATHER, ...	13	RAIN CUTS	17
SHALL I FALL TO DEATH'S FEATHER.	44	LONGED TO MOVE	18
AND I WAS STRUCK DOWN BY DEATH'S FEATHER.	69	BEFORE KNOCKED	39
AND WHAT'S THE RUB? DEATH'S FEATHER ON THE NERVE?	96	RUB OF LOVE	43
THE CANCER'S FUSION, OR THE SUMMER FEATHER	100	RUNNING GRAVE	32
I FLED THAT GROUND AS LIGHTLY AS A FEATHER.	101	FELLOWED SLEEP	10
WHAT COLOUR IS GLORY? DEATH'S FEATHER? TREMBLE	104	WORLD PYRAMID	25
WHO BLOWS DEATH'S FEATHER? WHAT GLORY IS COLOUR?	105	WORLD PYRAMID	55
I BLOW THE STAMMEL FEATHER IN THE VEIN.	105	WORLD PYRAMID	56
ALWAYS GOOD LUCK, PRAISED THE FINNED IN THE FEATHER	166	LONG-LEGGED	125
FEATHERBED			
MY CAVERNOUS, FEATHERBED SELF.	156	RETURN	76
FEATHERED			
HOPPING HOT LEAVED AND FEATHERED	151	BELOW A TIME	20
ABOVE HER FOLDED HEAD, AND THE SOFT FEATHERED VOICE	189	WINTER'S TALE	82
FEATHERING			
WHITE FEATHERING THE LIVING.	154	RETURN	25
FEATHERLANDS			
ON THE ANGELIC ETNA OF THE LAST WHIRRING			
FEATHERLANDS, ...	141	SAINT TO FALL	11
FEATHERS			
INTO THE QUICKSAND FEATHERS DOWN, ...	55	NO MAN BELIEVE	4
FEATHERS TO CONCEAL THE VIEW;	83	LETTER TO AUNT	18
ARE BUT THE ROOTS OF NETTLES AND OF FEATHERS	117	ALTARWISE	26
DIE IN RED FEATHERS WHEN THE FLYING HEAVEN'S CUT,	135	HOW MY ANIMAL	40
AS THE SNAPT FEATHERS SNOW, ...	203	SIR JOHNS HILL	50
BRUISING THE TIRED FEATHERS.	240	ADMIT THE SUN	8
FEATHERY			
FROM THE STONE NEST IT DOES NOT LET THE FEATHERY	15	SPIRE CRANES	2
WE STRANGELY SANG AMONG THE FEATHERY FLOWERS.	227	SPRING-SPIRIT	12
FEATURES			
THE FEATURES IN THEIR PRIVATE DARK	116	LANTERNS SHINE	5
LOVE'S REFLECTION OF THE MUSHROOM FEATURES, ...	118	ALTARWISE	53
GOLD ON SUCH FEATURES, AND THE LINEN SPIRIT	120	ALTARWISE	121
FED			
AND IS FED TO THE CATS, ...	39	GAS FADES	8
AND RAVENS FED CONFECTION TO THEIR YOUNG.	65	WOMAN SPEAKS	59
ONE SUN, ONE MANNA, WARMED AND FED.	79	LOVE'S FEVER	50
WHERE FISHES' FOOD IS FED THE SHADES	98	TWILIGHT LOCKS	29
FOR THE SALTY BIRDS FLUTTERED AND FED	165	LONG-LEGGED	96
FEEBLE			
AND THE FEEBLE HOUSE OF HOPE.	71	TAKE NEEDLES	16
FEED			
FEED IN THE ARMPITS OF DROWNED GIRLS, I'VE SWUM ...	52	OUT OF THE PIT	69
OF DOUBT AND DARK THEY FEED THEIR NERVES;	92	BOYS OF SUMMER	11
THE STOCKED HEART IS FORCED, AND AGONY HAS ANOTHER			
MOUTH TO FEED.	142	SAINT TO FALL	42
I'D RATHER HAVE THE WORM TO FEED	240	TWINING HEAD	9
FEEDING			
FEEDING THE WORM	26	PERSONAL EPIT	1
AND TOOK TO FEEDING BIRDS WITH BROKEN CRUMBS	53	OUT OF THE PIT	84

	PAGE	TITLE	LINE
FEEDING (CONTINUED)			
TWICE IN THE FEEDING SEA, GROWN	103	I DREAMED MY	26
FEEDS			
TELL ME OF HIM WHO FEEDS THE RAGING BIRDS.	65	WOMAN SPEAKS	65
FEEL			
AND FEEL THE PAIN IT GIVES,	13	SKY'S BRIGHT	29
MUST FEEL LIKE SUCH ENCROACHMENT	20	ENCOMPASSED	4
FEEL THE SAME SOFT BLOOD FLOW THOROUGHLY,	23	THE ONLY DEAD	11
FEEL, AS THE PULSE GROWS TIRED,	32	HELD-OUT HAND	3
INSIDE THIS MOUTH I FEEL HIS MESSAGE MOVING	76	LASHED RINGS	14
FEEL YOUR WOMAN'S BREASTS RISE UP LIKE FLOWERS	238	MAKES INTERVALS	12
I NEVER BREAK BUT FEEL THE SUDDEN PAIN,	239	MAKES INTERVALS	25
FEELING			
FEELING THE WIND ABOUT OUR HEADS THAT DOES NOT COOL,	26	THERE'S PLENTY	18
FEELING REGRET WHEN THIS IS WASTED	32	OUT OF SIGHS	18
FEELING THE SUMMER WIND, HEARING THE SWANS,	48	POET: 1935	59
FEELING THE PINPRICKS OF THE BLOOD, I'VE SAID	53	OUT OF THE PIT	80
FEELS			
WHO FEELS NOT COLDNESS IN THE HEAT,	55	NO MAN BELIEVE	8
FEET			
THEN ONLY OVER CORPSES SHALL THE FEET TREAD,	45	TO FOLLOW FOX	20
STOPPED NON-STOP DANCING TO LET HOT FEET COOL,	51	OUT OF THE PIT	30
(ALL MODERN PAINTERS USE THEIR FEET	83	LETTER TO AUNT	20
FEET IN THE RUBBING DUST.	96	RUB OF LOVE	42
TO WING MY SHOULDERS AND MY FEET?	234	NO, PIGEON	6
YOU BATTER BACK MY FEET),	237	PILLAR BREAKS	5
FELL			
FELL HARD AS WHIPS ON AN OLD WOUND,	42	A WAR OF WITS	3
BY TRICK OR CHANCE HE FELL ASLEEP	98	TWILIGHT LOCKS	34
LOOK TWICE BEFORE HE FELL FROM GRACE.	116	LANTERNS SHINE	4
FOR LOSS OF BLOOD I FELL ON ISHMAEL'S PLAIN,	118	ALTARWISE	63
WHOSE HOODED, FOUNTAIN HEART ONCE FELL IN PUDDLES	136	AFTER FUNERAL	14
HEAVEN FELL WITH HIS FALL AND ONE CROCKED BELL BEAT			
THE LEFT AIR.	142	SAINT TO FALL	25
A SQUALL OF BIRDS BELLOWED AND FELL,	163	LONG-LEGGED	39
ROSE AND CROWED AND FELL!	163	LONG-LEGGED	60
FELLED			
FELLED AND QUILLED, FLASH TO MY PATCH	5	PROLOGUE	83
THE HAND THAT SIGNED THE PAPER FELLED A CITY;	66	HAND SIGNED	1
REMAINS THOUGH GODS BE FELLED TILL NONE ARE LEFT.	67	LET A FAITH	10
I AM, THE TOWER TOLD, FELLED BY A TIMELESS STROKE,	113	NOT FATHER ME	21
THE OAK IS FELLED IN THE ACORN	167	LONG-LEGGED	155
FELLOW			
EACH GOLDEN GRAIN SPAT LIFE INTO ITS FELLOW,	78	LOVE'S FEVER	23
HALF OF THE FELLOW FATHER AS HE DOUBLES	103	WORLD PYRAMID	1
HALF OF THE FELLOW MOTHER AS SHE DABBLES	103	WORLD PYRAMID	3
THE FELLOW HALF WAS FROZEN AS IT BUBBLED	104	WORLD PYRAMID	7
THE FELLOW SEED AND SHADOW AS IT BABBLED	104	WORLD PYRAMID	9
THE FELLOW HALVES THAT, CLOVEN AS THEY SWIVEL	105	WORLD PYRAMID	49
HOW NOW MY FLESH, MY NAKED FELLOW,	106	ALL ALL AND	7
FELLOW WITH SAW AT THE JUGULAR.	137	O CHATTERTON	11
AND A FELLOW WHO JESTS THAT A MARE CAN BUILD NESTS	221	SONG OF DOG	7
FELLOWED			
I FELLOWED SLEEP	101	FELLOWED SLEEP	T
I FELLOWED SLEEP WHO KISSED ME IN THE BRAIN,	101	FELLOWED SLEEP	1
THE BROKEN HALVES ARE FELLOWED IN A CRIPPLE,	104	WORLD PYRAMID	13
FELLOWS			
ALL THAT I OWE THE FELLOWS OF THE GRAVE	80	ALL THAT I OWE	T
ALL THAT I OWE THE FELLOWS OF THE GRAVE	80	ALL THAT I OWE	1
AND WE SHALL BE FIT FELLOWS FOR A LIFE,	90	EUNUCH DREAMS	40

	PAGE	TITLE	LINE
FELLOWS (CONTINUED)			
I BLEW THE DREAMING FELLOWS TO THEIR BED	102	FELLOWED SLEEP	19
FELT			
AND FELT A SKEWER ENTER AT HIS SIDE.	52	OUT OF THE PIT	55
FELT THUD BENEATH MY FLESH'S ARMOUR, ...	68	BEFORE KNOCKED	9
AND I FELT WITH MY BARE FALL	140	TOMBSTONE TOLD	28
FELT THEIR SERENITY OF RIPPLE-WOVEN LOVELINESS; ...	223	IDYLL UNFORGET	4
I HAVE FELT THE SILK WIND BRUSH MY LIPS;	224	IDYLL UNFORGET	19
UNTIL I FELT THE RHYTHM OF HER BODY	234	WOMAN TAPESTRY	4
FEMALE			
SHALL IT BE MALE OR FEMALE? SAY THE CELLS, ...	95	RUB OF LOVE	8
SHALL IT BE MALE OR FEMALE? SAY THE FINGERS	95	RUB OF LOVE	15
THE FEMALE, DEADLY, AND MALE	158	INTO HER HEAD	53
FEMININE			
AND SMALL, FEMININE SHOULDERS, ...	236	WOMAN TAPESTRY	43
FENCE			
THAT STARRY FENCE THE CLAY OF LIGHT	85	SEE, SAYS LIME	6
FENCED			
NOR FENCED, NOR STAKED, THE GUSHERS OF THE SKY	82	LIGHT BREAKS	16
ONCE IN THIS CLAY FENCED BY THE STICKS	85	SEE, SAYS LIME	5
FENCES			
THE FENCES OF THE LIGHT ARE DOWN, ...	98	TWILIGHT LOCKS	40
FEND			
CAN WE FEND OFF ROCK ARRIVAL, ...	54	WE BY SEASAND	22
FERN			
IN A ROOM WITH A STUFFED FOX AND A STALE FERN, ...	136	AFTER FUNERAL	11
AND THE STRUTTING FERN LAY SEEDS ON THE BLACK SILL.	137	AFTER FUNERAL	40
FERN HILL	195	FERN HILL	T
FROM THE BROOMED WITCH'S SPUME YOU ARE SHIELDED BY			
FERN	198	COUNTRY SLEEP	17
FERNED			
BOW DOWN THE WALLS OF THE FERNED AND FOXY WOODS ...	136	AFTER FUNERAL	24
FERNS			
THE SIDEBOARD FRUIT, THE FERNS, THE PICTURE HOUSES	33	HELD-OUT HAND	10
BEHIND A POT OF FERNS THE WAGGING CLOCK	99	OCTOBER WIND	17
FEROCIOUS			
WADING THROUGH HER DARK CAVE ON FEROCIOUS WINGS.	232	YOUR VOICE	9
FERRIES			
THAT THE SNOW BLIND TWILIGHT FERRIES OVER THE LAKES	187	WINTER'S TALE	2
FERRULE			
BE BY YOUR ONE GHOST PIERCED, HIS POINTED FERRULE,	111	I, IN IMAGE	79
FETCH			
OF FROZEN LOVES THEY FETCH THEIR GIRLS, ...	91	BOYS OF SUMMER	5
FEVER			
AS DROWN, OVER AND OVER, THIS FEVER.	17	IN OBLIVION	18
AND, AT THE TOUCH, TREMBLES WITH LOVER'S FEVER, ...	25	BEAUTY TO DUST	3
THE DRY FEVER BURNS UNTIL NO HEART IS LEFT, ...	34	THIRST PARCHES	2
THE HAND THAT SIGNED THE TREATY BRED A FEVER, ...	66	HAND SIGNED	9
MY YOUTH IS BENT BY THE SAME WINTRY FEVER.	77	THE FORCE THAT	5
FROM LOVE'S FIRST FEVER TO HER PLAGUE	78	LOVE'S FEVER	T
FROM LOVE'S FIRST FEVER TO HER PLAGUE, FROM THE SOFT			
SECOND	78	LOVE'S FEVER	1
WHERE FLESH'S FEVER	85	SEE, SAYS LIME	20
LIT ON THE CUDDLED TREE, THE CROSS OF FEVER, ...	100	RUNNING GRAVE	33
FEVERS			
FILL THE VEINS THE FEVERS BROKE, ...	71	TAKE NEEDLES	14
FEVER'S			
ONE BREAST GAVE SUCK THE FEVER'S ISSUE;	79	LOVE'S FEVER	43
FEW			
THERE CAN BE FEW TEARS LEFT: ELECTRA WEPT	57	GREEK PLAY	17

		PAGE	TITLE	LINE
FEW (CONTINUED)				
FEW UNDERSTAND THE WORKS OF CUMMINGS,	....	84	LETTER TO AUNT	36
AND FEW JAMES JOYCE'S MENTAL SLUMMINGS,	....	84	LETTER TO AUNT	37
AND FEW YOUNG AUDEN'S CODED CHATTER;	....	84	LETTER TO AUNT	38
BUT THEN IT IS THE FEW THAT MATTER.	....	84	LETTER TO AUNT	39
NEVER SHALL BEAST BE BORN TO ATLAS THE FEW SEAS	...	135	HOW MY ANIMAL	32
ON GIDDY NIGHTS I SLAP A FEW DRUNK CURVES	....	138	O CHATTERTON	24
A CHILD OF A FEW HOURS	....	173	FIRE RAID	5
IN ALL HIS TUNEFUL TURNING SO FEW AND SUCH MORNING SONGS	....	196	FERN HILL	43
FEWER				
THERE ARE FEWER, OF COURSE, WHO INSIST THAT A HORSE		221	SONG OF DOG	5
FIBRE				
COME UNTO SEA-STUCK TOWERS, AT THE FIBRE SCALING,		111	I, IN IMAGE	74
PROPHETS AND FIBRE KINGS IN OIL AND LETTER,	....	120	ALTARWISE	114
FIBRES				
THE FIBRES, OR THE SENSES' THREAD.	....	233	NO THOUGHT	8
FIBS				
AND THE FIBS FOR CHILDREN;	....	59	FAIRY TALES	12
JOHN'S BEAST, JOB'S PATIENCE, AND THE FIBS OF VISION,		125	TODAY, INSECT	21
FIDDLE				
HUBBUB AND FIDDLE, THIS TUNE	....	5	PROLOGUE	72
FIDDLED				
A SERPENT FIDDLED IN THE SHAPING-TIME.	....	122	INCARNATE DEVL	18
FIDDLES				
WAS THERE A TIME WHEN DANCERS WITH THEIR FIDDLES		40	WAS THERE TIME	1
FIDDLING				
AND GOD WALKED THERE WHO WAS A FIDDLING WARDEN	....	121	INCARNATE DEVL	5
FIE				
FIE ON YOU, AUNT, THAT YOU SHOULD SEE	....	83	LETTER TO AUNT	7
FIE ON YOU, AUNT! I'LL SHOW YOU HOW	....	83	LETTER TO AUNT	11
FIELD				
AND DARK SHOALS EVERY HOLY FIELD.	....	5	PROLOGUE	90
HE HAS THE WHOLE FIELD NOW, THE GODS DEPARTED	.....	29	NEARLY SUMMER	7
STREETS' STOCK, OF THE MOON LIT, ILL LIT, FIELD AND TOWN,	....	45	PLOUGHMAN GONE	22
THEN TAKE THE GUSHER OR THE FIELD	....	74	WE MOTHERNAKED	9
ON FIELD AND SAND	....	115	A GRIEF AGO	22
TILL FIELD AND ROOF LIE LEVEL AND THE SAME	....	116	LANTERNS SHINE	13
STILLS SNAPPED BY NIGHT IN THE BREAD-SIDED FIELD,		118	ALTARWISE	54
WITH A CAPSIZED FIELD WHERE A SCHOOL SAT STILL	....	144	COLOUR OF SAY	3
AND O TO CUT THE GREEN FIELD, LEAVING	....	157	RETURN	100
AND HEARD THE LEWD, WOOED FIELD FLOW TO THE COMING FROST,	....	204	GIANT'S THIGH	30
FIELDS				
NO MORE TOILS OVER THE FIELDS	....	45	PLOUGHMAN GONE	13
AND THUS I SAW HIM IN A SQUARE OF FIELDS,	....	53	OUT OF THE PIT	87
HUNGER FOR HIM WHO DUNGS THE VALLEY FIELDS.	....	64	WOMAN SPEAKS	37
THE FIELDS YET UNDIVIDED BEHIND THE SKULL.	....	73	LORD RED HAIL	10
FROM THE FOREIGN FIELDS OF SPACE,	....	126	SEED-AT-ZERO	44
FROM THE STAR-FLANKED FIELDS OF SPACE,	....	127	SEED-AT-ZERO	51
THE FIELDS, BY A MOTHERLIKE HENRUN)	....	154	RETURN	4
STRIKE AND SING HIS CATCH OF FIELDS	....	168	LONG-LEGGED	181
AND THE TWICE TOLD FIELDS OF INFANCY	....	178	POEM IN OCT	51
AND FLOATING FIELDS FROM THE FARM IN THE CUP OF THE VALES,	....	187	WINTER'S TALE	3
OF FIELDS. AND BURNING THEN	....	187	WINTER'S TALE	16
HUNGER OF BIRDS IN THE FIELDS OF THE BREAD OF WATER, TOSSED	....	188	WINTER'S TALE	42
NEVER TO FLOURISH IN THE FIELDS OF THE WHITE SEED		188	WINTER'S TALE	54

                                                        PAGE   TITLE   LINE
FIELDS (CONTINUED)
     OF FIELDS. FOR LOVE, THE LONG AGO SHE BIRD RISES.
        LOOK. 189   WINTER'S TALE   80
     THE FIELDS OF SEED AND THE TIME DYING FLESH ASTRIDE,   190   WINTER'S TALE   103
     AND THE LAKES AND FLOATING FIELDS AND THE RIVER
        WENDED 190   WINTER'S TALE   108
     FIELDS HIGH AS THE HOUSE, THE TUNES FROM THE
        CHIMNEYS, IT WAS AIR 195   FERN HILL   20
     ON TO THE FIELDS OF PRAISE. 196   FERN HILL   36
     I SHOULD HEAR HIM FLY WITH THE HIGH FIELDS 196   FERN HILL   50
     AND SERAPHIC FIELDS OF SHEPHERDS 215   COUNTRY HEAVEN   19
FIEND
     HOWLS THE FOUL FIEND TO HEEL.   61   MEAT ON BONES   29
FIERCE
     LOPS, AS A BUSH PLUMED WITH FLAMES, THE RANT OF THE
        FIERCE EYE, ... 135   HOW MY ANIMAL   38
     CURSE, BLESS, ME NOW WITH YOUR FIERCE TEARS, I PRAY. 208   NOT GO GENTLE   17
     FIERCE COLOURS FLED ABOUT THE BRANCHES, ... 226   THE OAK   1
     HER LOVE FOR ME IS FIERCE AND CONTINUAL, ... 235   WOMAN TAPESTRY   11
     THAN IN THE GULL AND THE FIERCE EAGLE 241   ADMIT THE SUN   17
FIERCELY
     IN A FIERCELY MOURNING HOUSE IN A CROOKED YEAR. ... 136   AFTER FUNERAL   30
FIERY
     HIS FIERY REEL SINGS OFF ITS FLAMES, ... 164   LONG-LEGGED   64
     TO FIERY TYBURN OVER THE WRESTLE OF ELMS UNTIL 201   SIR JOHNS HILL   9
     THE MANSOULED FIERY ISLANDS! OH, ... 211   POEM ON B'DAY   105
FIFE
     AND SUNK; WAVED FLAGS TO EVERY FIFE AND DRUM;   52   OUT OF THE PIT   70
FIFTH
     LIE THIS FIFTH MONTH UNSKATED, AND THE BIRDS HAVE
        FLOWN; 122   HOLD HARD   9
     FOR THE FIFTH ELEMENT IS PITY, ... 216   COUNTRY HEAVEN   31
FIFTY
     WHERE FIFTY FLOWERS BREED IN A FRUIT BOX, ...   47   POET: 1935   31
FIG
     BRIGHT AS A FIG;   82   LIGHT BREAKS   11
     A FIG FOR 128   NOW, SAY NAY   31
FIGHT
     TO FIGHT THROUGH THE INVISIBLE WEEDS, ...   41   YOUNG ARE OLD   23
     TO PURGE AFTER THE WITS' FIGHT, ...   42   A WAR OF WITS   6
     PRAISE THAT ONLY THE WITS ARE HURT AFTER THE WITS'
        FIGHT.   42   A WAR OF WITS   11
FIGHTING
     AFTER SUCH FIGHTING AS THE WEAKEST KNOW, ...   32   OUT OF SIGHS   10
FIGS
     NOR HAMMER BACK A SEASON IN THE FIGS, ... 123   FOSTER LIGHT   8
FIGURE
     A WOMAN FIGURE WITHOUT FAULT 172   THE HUNCHBACK   32
FIGURES
     STAY, DRAMATIC FIGURES, TETHERED DOWN   28   NO WINGS   3
     CUT OUR FIGURES, AND RETREAT AT NIGHT   28   NO WINGS   17
     THE MIDNIGHT FIGURES OF A SULPHUROUS BROOD   36   MIDNIGHT ROAD   10
     WOMEN FIGURES ROUND MY CELL, ... 138   O CHATTERTON   30
     WOMEN FIGURES ON THE WALL 138   O CHATTERTON   31
     THAT ONCE CUT THE FIGURES OF BIRDS ON THE DEEP BREAD 190   WINTER'S TALE   114
FILE
     FILE THROUGH THE FLESH WHERE NO FLESH DECKS THE
        BONES.   82   LIGHT BREAKS   6
FILED
     OFF FROM THE CREASING FLESH, FILED 102   I DREAMED MY   6

	PAGE	TITLE	LINE
FILL			
FILL THE VEINS THE FEVERS BROKE,	71	TAKE NEEDLES	14
AND FILL THE MOUTHS OF HEAVEN WITH YOUR TONGUE	87	PAIN BE MUSIC	2
FILLED			
THY PLACE IS FILLED, BONES BID FOR AUCTION,	29	LONG, SKELETON	9
THE LIVING AFTER, THE FILLED WITH FEAR,	41	YOUNG ARE OLD	36
MY FALLEN FILLED, THAT HAD THE HINT OF DEATH,	80	ALL THAT I OWE	10
THE MILK OF DEATH, I FILLED THE HAND	86	SEE, SAYS LIME	30
IN TIME AT FLOOD FILLED WITH HIS COLOURED DOUBLES;	124	FOSTER LIGHT	27
I AM THE GHOST IN THIS HOUSE THAT IS FILLED WITH THE TONGUE AND EYES	141	I, FIRST NAMED	3
THAT THE CHILDREN FILLED WITH GRAVEL	171	THE HUNCHBACK	9
TEMPLE SHOULD NEVER HAVE BEEN FILLED	237	PILLAR BREAKS	12
FILLIES			
WITH WILD SEA FILLIES AND SOAKING BRIDLES	168	LONG-LEGGED	185
FILLS			
PRAISE HIM WHO SPRINGS AND FILLS THE TIDAL WELL.	76	LASHED RINGS	11
FILM			
A FILM OF PEOPLE MOVING,	36	MIDNIGHT ROAD	7
THE FILM OF SPRING IS HANGING FROM THE LIDS.	82	LIGHT BREAKS	24
I WHO SAW IN A HURRIED FILM	140	TOMBSTONE TOLD	21
FILMED			
THE CATARACTED EYES THAT FILMED THEIR CLOTH;	97	TWILIGHT LOCKS	21
FILMS			
HE FILMS MY VANITY.	129	MY NEOPHYTE	25
FILTHY			
OUT OF MY FILTHY EYES	18	NATURAL DAY	29
FIN			
FROTH, FLUTE, FIN AND QUILL	3	PROLOGUE	7
THROUGH VEIL AND FIN AND FIRE AND COIL	129	MY NEOPHYTE	23
FINAL			
AS RAPED AND REAPED, THE FINAL EMBLEM.	29	LONG, SKELETON	8
WHO DOES NOT BREAK AND MAKE HIS FINAL FAITH.	55	NO MAN BELIEVE	24
A FINAL WORD: BEFORE YOU START	84	LETTER TO AUNT	58
FINDING THE WATER FINAL,	109	I, IN IMAGE	33
IN THE FINAL DIRECTION OF THE ELEMENTARY TOWN	143	24 YEARS	8
FINALITY			
TO ONE SENSE OF FINALITY	230	OUR SANCTITY	20
FINCHES			
HE SINGS TOWARDS ANGUISH; FINCHES FLY	209	POEM ON B'DAY	20
FIND			
WILL FIND SUCH LOVE AGAINST THE GRAIN,	16	TIME TO ROT	8
EMPTY OF LIGHT AND FIND THE DARKNESS LIT--	27	OBLIVIOUS DARK	5
TO FIND A SWEET BLANKNESS IN THE BLOOD AND SHELL,	27	OBLIVIOUS DARK	12
FIND HARD TO DART AGAINST A CLOUD,	37	WINDMILLS TURN	8
'FIND MEAT ON BONES'	60	MEAT ON BONES	T
'FIND MEAT ON BONES THAT SOON HAVE NONE,	60	MEAT ON BONES	1
LET THE HERO SEED FIND HARBOUR,	126	SEED-AT-ZERO	33
LET THE HERO SEED FIND HARBOUR,	126	SEED-AT-ZERO	40
I FIND A TRIPPER'S KNICKER IN THE GULLY	137	O CHATTERTON	15
AND WHEN I DREAM OF THEM I FIND	143	THE MOLLS	11
TO-NIGHT SHALL FIND NO DYING BUT ALIVE AND WARM	194	CONVERS PRAYER	15
TO FIND A WOMAN'S SOUL FOR A WIFE.	207	LAMENT	48
LET HIM FIND NO REST BUT THE FATHERED AND FOUND,	216	ELEGY	12
TO FIND AND THEN TO STRIKE;	240	ADMIT THE SUN	4
I BURY, I TRAVEL TO FIND PRIDE	240	ADMIT THE SUN	12
FINDING			
FINDING THE WATER FINAL,	109	I, IN IMAGE	33
AND THE FINDING ONE	181	VISION, PRAYER	64
THE FINDING ONE	182	VISION, PRAYER	88

	PAGE	TITLE	LINE
FINDS			
WHO IN THE BONES FINDS NOT NEW FAITH, ...	55	NO MAN BELIEVE	22
NOR WHEN HE FINDS A BEAUTY IN THE BREAST	96	RUB OF LOVE	40
EVER AND EVER HE FINDS A WAY, AS THE SNOW FALLS,	199	COUNTRY SLEEP	56
FINE			
YOUR MOUTH'S FINE DUST	16	TIME TO ROT	7
AND THE GLITTER FROM THE FINE TEETH.	236	WOMAN TAPESTRY	46
FINGER			
THE FINGER JOINTS ARE CRAMPED WITH CHALK;	66	HAND SIGNED	6
THE HEART STEPS TO DEATH'S FINGER, ...	67	REALM OF FLESH	8
THE JACKS OF FROST THEY FINGER IN THE HIVES;	92	BOYS OF SUMMER	9
LOCKED IN THE LONG WORM OF MY FINGER	97	TWILIGHT LOCKS	2
WHO SPEAK ON A FINGER AND THUMB, ...	129	MY NEOPHYTE	29
FINGERMAN			
WRENCHED BY MY FINGERMAN, THE LEADEN BUD	115	A GRIEF AGO	11
FINGERS			
WAITING AND WATCHING FOR YOUR FINGERS TO FAIL	33	HELD-OUT HAND	20
THE FINGERS AT THE LOCKS.	62	EARS IN TURRET	4
THE SNIPER DIES; THE FINGERS FROM THE SKY	64	WOMAN SPEAKS	45
FIVE SOVEREIGN FINGERS TAXED THE BREATH, ...	66	HAND SIGNED	2
CUT MY FINGERS ON A ROSE, ...	70	TAKE NEEDLES	6
SHALL IT BE MALE OR FEMALE? SAY THE FINGERS	95	RUB OF LOVE	15
WITH FROSTY FINGERS PUNISHES MY HAIR, ...	98	OCTOBER WIND	2
THE FINGERS WILL FORGET GREEN THUMBS AND MARK	138	FIVE & COUNTRY	2
AND MY FINGERS HAVE TOUCHED THE GLASS OF THE WATERS,	224	IDYLL UNFORGET	30
CLOSES ABOUT YOUR CLASPED FINGERS	229	MY RIVER	25
WITH SLENDER FINGERS	229	MY RIVER	28
TRAILING THEIR FINGERS ON THE HARD EDGES	235	WOMAN TAPESTRY	33
FINGERS'			
UP THROUGH THE FINGERS' CRACKS;	86	SEE, SAYS LIME	29
FINGER'S			
TOUCHED, BY A FINGER'S NAIL, TO DUST.	20	THE NEOPHYTE	25
FIN-GREEN			
SUFFER THE SLASH OF VISION BY THE FIN-GREEN STUBBLE,	111	I, IN IMAGE	85
FINNED			
O KINGDOM OF NEIGHBOURS, FINNED	5	PROLOGUE	82
ALWAYS GOOD LUCK, PRAISED THE FINNED IN THE FEATHER	166	LONG-LEGGED	125
FINS			
SLIPPED THE FINS OF THOSE HUMPBACKED TONS	163	LONG-LEGGED	52
TO THE HAWK ON FIRE, THE HALTER HEIGHT, OVER TOWY'S FINS, ...	202	SIR JOHNS HILL	16
FIRE			
THE FIRE OF BIRDS IN	3	PROLOGUE	26
YOU TOO HAVE SEEN THE SUN A BIRD OF FIRE	30	YOUTH CALLS	1
PLUNGED IN BLACK WATERS, UNDER HAIL AND FIRE, ...	51	OUT OF THE PIT	42
TESTED BY FIRE, DOUBLE THUMB TO NOSE, ...	52	OUT OF THE PIT	74
FIRE AND JORDAN AND THE SAD CANAL.	53	OUT OF THE PIT	99
THE WIND PASS LIKE A FIRE, ...	62	EARS IN TURRET	18
LET IT BE A SWORD OF FIRE, ...	71	TAKE NEEDLES	21
AS FIRE FALLS, TWO HEMISPHERES DIVIDE, ...	73	LORD RED HAIL	7
AND THROUGH THESE EARS HE HARKS MY FIRE BURN	77	LASHED RINGS	16
ROUSED IT TO FIRE;	85	SEE, SAYS LIME	4
THE STRINGS OF FIRE CHOKED HIS SEX	85	SEE, SAYS LIME	17
HOW WELL YOUR POEMS LIGHT THE FIRE.	85	LETTER TO AUNT	66
IN THE BEGINNING WAS THE MOUNTING FIRE	94	IN BEGINNING	13
AND DROP THE PLUM LIKE FIRE FROM THE FLESH.	95	RUB OF LOVE	9
CAUGHT BY THE CRABBING SUN I WALK ON FIRE	98	OCTOBER WIND	3
TOWNS AROUND ON A WHEEL OF FIRE.	106	ALL ALL AND	6
LOVE LIKE A MIST OR FIRE THROUGH THE BED OF EELS.	111	I, IN IMAGE	90
I, IN A WIND ON FIRE, FROM GREEN ADAM'S CRADLE, ...	111	I, IN IMAGE	95

	PAGE	TITLE	LINE
FIRE (CONTINUED)			
HER BONE TO FIRE,	115	A GRIEF AGO	36
THE COCKEREL'S TIDE UPCASTING FROM THE FIRE.	127	NOW, SAY NAY	21
THE SEAL OF FIRE,	128	NOW, SAY NAY	32
THROUGH VEIL AND FIN AND FIRE AND COIL	129	MY NEOPHYTE	23
CALLS THE STARVED FIRE HERD, IS CAST IN ICE,	132	I MAKE THIS IN	27
ON THE CLAY COLD MOUTH, ON THE FIRE	147	UNLUCKILY FOR	8
AND THE FIRE IN A TEMPER START	149	PAPER & STICKS	3
WORDS ON THE AIR AS THE FIRE CATCHES	149	PAPER & STICKS	17
COMBING WITH ANTLERS, COLUMBUS ON FIRE,	152	BELOW A TIME	37
GREED ON MAN BEATING NEAR THE FIRE NEIGHBOUR	153	WAS A SAVIOUR	30
FIRE ON STARLIGHT, RAKE JESU'S STREAM;	163	LONG-LEGGED	43
HE WHO BLEW THE GREAT FIRE IN	167	LONG-LEGGED	157
WHEN HIS LONG-LEGGED FLESH WAS A WIND ON FIRE	168	LONG-LEGGED	195
FOR A MAN SLEEPS WHERE FIRE LEAPT DOWN AND SHE LEARNS THROUGH HIS ARM	170	MARRIAGE VIRG	13
SUFFER THE FIRST VISION THAT SET FIRE TO THE STARS.	170	LOVE IN ASYLUM	18
AND THE CRATERS OF HIS EYES GREW SPRINGSHOOTS AND FIRE	172	DAWN RAID	7
CEREMONY AFTER A FIRE RAID	173	FIRE RAID	T
OVER THE SUN'S HOVEL AND THE SLUM OF FIRE	175	FIRE RAID	68
SUN THE FATHER HIS QUIVER FULL OF THE INFANTS OF PURE FIRE,	186	HOLY SPRING	19
THE SCROLLS OF FIRE THAT BURNED IN HIS HEART AND HEAD,	187	WINTER'S TALE	14
A REFUSAL TO MOURN THE DEATH, BY FIRE, OF A CHILD IN LONDON	191	REFUSAL MOURN	T
AND FIRE, THE FLYING RANT	193	SIDE OF TRUTH	27
IN THE FIRE OF HIS CARE HIS LOVE IN THE HIGH ROOM.	194	CONVERS PRAYER	16
AND FIRE GREEN AS GRASS.	195	FERN HILL	22
INTO A HOMESTALL KING OR HAMLET OF FIRE	198	COUNTRY SLEEP	11
OF BIRDS! AMONG THE COCKS LIKE FIRE THE RED FOX	199	COUNTRY SLEEP	69
EARTH, AIR, WATER, FIRE, SINGING INTO THE WHITE ACT,	200	COUNTRY SLEEP	87
THE HAWK ON FIRE HANGS STILL;	201	SIR JOHNS HILL	2
TO THE HAWK ON FIRE, THE HALTER HEIGHT, OVER TOWY'S FINS,	202	SIR JOHNS HILL	16
ALL PRAISE OF THE HAWK ON FIRE IN HAWK-EYED DUSK BE SUNG,	202	SIR JOHNS HILL	27
AND THE LONG FOX LIKE FIRE	216	COUNTRY HEAVEN	27
AND THE SUN HAS SMOOTHED IT WITH QUIET FIRE,	224	IDYLL UNFORGET	23
FIREBALL			
WIND-HEELED FOOT IN THE HOLE OF A FIREBALL,	141	SAINT TO FALL	12
FIRE-DWARFED			
CHILD BEYOND COCKCROW, BY THE FIRE-DWARFED	174	FIRE RAID	28
FIREFLY			
AND THEIR FIREFLY HAIRPINS FLEW, AND THE RICKS RAN ROUND--	205	GIANT'S THIGH	41
FIRELIT			
IN HIS FIRELIT ISLAND RINGED BY THE WINGED SNOW	187	WINTER'S TALE	17
FIRES			
IN AUTUMN TEACH THREE SEASONS' FIRES	58	HERE IN SPRING	7
SNAIL OF MAN IN HIS SHIP OF FIRES	128	MY NEOPHYTE	8
AN ENAMOURED MAN ALONE BY THE TWIGS OF HIS EYES, TWO FIRES,	144	PLEASURE-BIRD	7
LIONS AND FIRES OF HIS FLYING BREATH,	160	DEATHS AND ENT	5
ALWAYS GOOD-BYE TO THE FIRES OF THE FACE,	165	LONG-LEGGED	98
THE MOTHER DUG, AND ITS ARMS FULL OF FIRES.	173	FIRE RAID	8
AND FIRES WHERE HE SHOULD PROWL DOWN THE CLOUD	188	WINTER'S TALE	37
AND THE HOME OF PRAYERS AND FIRES, THE TALE ENDED.	190	WINTER'S TALE	110

	PAGE	TITLE	LINE
FIRES (CONTINUED)			
AND THE DAUGHTERS OF DARKNESS FLAME LIKE FAWKES			
FIRES STILL.	205	GIANT'S THIGH	60
FIREWIND			
AND A FIREWIND KILL THE CANDLE.	130	SINNERS' BELL	6
FIREWORKS			
STORM, SNOW, AND FOUNTAIN IN THE WEATHER OF			
FIREWORKS, ...	130	SINNERS' BELL	14
FIRM			
FAITH. FAITH. FIRM FAITH IN MANY OR ONE, ...	41	YOUNG ARE OLD	49
FIRMAMENT			
FIRMAMENT OF FLESH AND BONE	72	TAKE NEEDLES	38
FIRST			
AND THE THUNDER'S FIRST NOTE;	59	FAIRY TALES	3
SINCE THE FIRST FLESH OF MAN WAS RIVEN	64	WOMAN SPEAKS	28
SINCE THE FIRST WOMB SPAT FORTH A BABY'S CORPSE, ..	64	WOMAN SPEAKS	52
IT WAS A HAGGARD NIGHT THE FIRST FLESH DIED, ...	65	WOMAN SPEAKS	56
LET WHAT REMAINS OF THAT FIRST MIRACLE	65	WOMAN SPEAKS	62
THE MORTAL MIRACLE, LET THAT FIRST DUST	65	WOMAN SPEAKS	64
SEE THE FIRST LIVING LIGHT, ...	67	LET A FAITH	12
HERE A MILD BABY SPEAKS HIS FIRST WORD	74	SUN BURNS	9
FROM LOVE'S FIRST FEVER TO HER PLAGUE	78	LOVE'S FEVER	T
FROM LOVE'S FIRST FEVER TO HER PLAGUE, FROM THE SOFT			
SECOND	78	LOVE'S FEVER	1
FROM THE FIRST PRINT OF THE UNSHODDEN FOOT, THE			
LIFTING	78	LOVE'S FEVER	10
FROM THE FIRST SECRET OF THE HEART, THE WARNING			
GHOST, ...	78	LOVE'S FEVER	12
AND TO THE FIRST DUMB WONDER AT THE FLESH, ...	78	LOVE'S FEVER	13
AND FROM THE FIRST DECLENSION OF THE FLESH	79	LOVE'S FEVER	31
FIRST BUY A HAT, NO PARIS MODEL	83	LETTER TO AUNT	15
THE SUBSTANCE FORKED THAT MARROWED THE FIRST SUN; .	93	IN BEGINNING	4
TOUCHED THE FIRST CLOUD AND LEFT A SIGN.	94	IN BEGINNING	12
FIRST CHARACTERS OF BIRTH AND DEATH.	94	IN BEGINNING	24
FIRST THERE WAS THE LAMB ON KNOCKING KNEES	117	ALTARWISE	29
LET THE FIRST PETER FROM A RAINBOW'S QUAYRAIL	121	ALTARWISE	133
THIS FIRST AND STEEPLED SEASON, TO THE SUMMER'S GAME.	122	HOLD HARD	12
I, THE FIRST NAMED	141	I, FIRST NAMED	T
I, THE FIRST NAMED, AM THE GHOST OF THIS SIR AND			
CHRISTIAN FRIEND	141	I, FIRST NAMED	1
ON THE FIRST OF EACH HARDSHIP, ...	151	BELOW A TIME	5
FLASHED FIRST ACROSS HIS THUNDERCLAPPING EYES.	160	DEATHS AND ENT	24
SUFFER THE FIRST VISION THAT SET FIRE TO THE STARS.	170	LOVE IN ASYLUM	18
WAS THE FIRST TO DIE	174	FIRE RAID	39
AND THE FIRST DAWN	181	VISION, PRAYER	38
IN THE FIRST FURY OF HIS STREAM	181	VISION, PRAYER	59
DEEP WITH THE FIRST DEAD LIES LONDON'S DAUGHTER, ..	192	REFUSAL MOURN	19
AFTER THE FIRST DEATH, THERE IS NO OTHER.	192	REFUSAL MOURN	24
IN THE FIRST, SPINNING PLACE, THE SPELLBOUND HORSES			
WALKING WARM	196	FERN HILL	34
AND YOU SHALL WAKE, FROM COUNTRY SLEEP, THIS DAWN			
AND EACH FIRST DAWN, ...	201	COUNTRY SLEEP	110
FISH			
FROM FISH TO JUMPING HILL! LOOK:	4	PROLOGUE	43
MAD BIRDS IN TREES, AND MAD FISH IN A POOL.	50	OUT OF THE PIT	10
NO BIRDS OR FLYING FISH	62	EARS IN TURRET	15
ASK THE TALL FISH SWEPT FROM THE BIBLE EAST, ...	121	ALTARWISE	134
THE LURED FISH UNDER THE FOAM	163	LONG-LEGGED	47
BIRD AFTER DARK AND THE LAUGHING FISH	166	LONG-LEGGED	126
WITH MOVING FISH AND ROUNDED STONES	168	LONG-LEGGED	178

```
                                                  PAGE      TITLE       LINE
FISH  (CONTINUED)
     TO THE TREES AND THE STONES AND THE FISH IN THE TIDE.  178   POEM IN OCT      57
FISHERBIRD
     WHERE THE ELEGIAC FISHERBIRD STABS AND PADDLES   ....  202   SIR JOHNS HILL   19
FISHERMAN
     AND THE FISHERMAN WINDS HIS REEL    ..............     166   LONG-LEGGED     123
     AND THE STREETS THAT THE FISHERMAN COMBED   ........   168   LONG-LEGGED     194
     TO THE FISHERMAN LOST ON THE LAND.   ...............   169   LONG-LEGGED     214
FISHERMANNED
     THEN GOOD-BYE TO THE FISHERMANNED    ..............    162   LONG-LEGGED       5
FISHERMEN
     FISHERMEN OF MERMEN   ..............................   135   HOW MY ANIMAL    23
FISHES
     ALL THE FISHES WERE RAYED IN BLOOD,   ..............   162   LONG-LEGGED      23
     OH MIRACLE OF FISHES! THE LONG DEAD BITE!   ........   166   LONG-LEGGED     140
     METROPOLIS OF FISHES,   ............................   169   LONG-LEGGED     204
     WAS MIRACULOUS VIRGINITY OLD AS LOAVES AND FISHES,    170   MARRIAGE VIRG     5
     AND OVER THE GLAZED LAKES SKATED THE SHAPES OF FISHES  190   WINTER'S TALE   115
     ON A SEIZING SKY; SMALL FISHES GLIDE   .............   209   POEM ON B'DAY    22
     MASTS AND FISHES TO THE STILL QUICK STARS,   .......   210   POEM ON B'DAY    71
     OF THE PALE-GREEN, DELICATE FISHES, SILVER AS SIGHS;   224   IDYLL UNFORGET   39
FISHES'
     WHERE FISHES' FOOD IS FED THE SHADES   .............    98   TWILIGHT LOCKS   29
     FURLED ON THE FISHES' HOUSE AND HELL,   ............   129   MY NEOPHYTE      17
FISH-GILLED
     THE SWEET, FISH-GILLED BOATS BRINGING BLOOD   .......  142   SAINT TO FALL    22
FISHING
     A FISHING BIRD HAS NOTES OF IVORY   ................    14   FOR LEDA          6
     CRASHES, AND SLOWLY THE FISHING HOLY STALKING HERON   201   SIR JOHNS HILL   11
     FISHING IN THE TEAR OF THE TOWY. ONLY A HOOT OWL     203   SIR JOHNS HILL   51
FISHTAIL
     WITH MY FISHTAIL HANDS AND GENTLY   ................   154   RETURN            5
FISHWIFE
     WITH THEIR FISHWIFE CROSS   ........................     3   PROLOGUE         10
FIST
     COUNTS ON HIS FIST   ...............................    30   NEARLY SUMMER    17
     NOR DAMNED THE SEA THAT SPED ABOUT MY FIST,   ......    97   TWILIGHT LOCKS    3
     AND CLOSE HER FIST.   ..............................   115   A GRIEF AGO      40
     HER FIST OF A FACE DIED CLENCHED ON A ROUND PAIN;    137   AFTER FUNERAL    34
FISTED
     AT SIGHT OF DEATH, THE LAST TWO FISTED KILLER   .....   59   FAIRY TALES      18
FISTS
     SHALL THEY CLASP A COMET IN THEIR FISTS?   ..........   56   WHY EAST WIND    11
     AND GHOSTLY COMETS OVER THE RAISED FISTS.   .........   56   WHY EAST WIND    26
     WITH FISTS OF TURNIPS PUNISHES THE LAND,   .........    99   OCTOBER WIND     28
FIT
     MOST FIT FOR LOVERS TO MAKE HARMONY,   .............    34   THIRST PARCHES   10
     AND WE SHALL BE FIT FELLOWS FOR A LIFE,   ..........    90   EUNUCH DREAMS    40
     'ALL GAME PHRASES FIT YOUR RING OF A COCKFIGHT:   ...  145   IF HEAD HURT      6
FIVE
     FIVE SOVEREIGN FINGERS TAXED THE BREATH,   ..........   66   HAND SIGNED       2
     THESE FIVE KINGS DID A KING TO DEATH.   .............   66   HAND SIGNED       4
     THE FIVE KINGS COUNT THE DEAD BUT DO NOT SOFTEN   ...   66   HAND SIGNED      13
     WITH PRIEST'S GRAVE FOOT AND HAND OF FIVE ASSASSINS   131   I MAKE THIS IN   25
     WHEN ALL MY FIVE AND COUNTRY SENSES SEE   ..........   138   FIVE & COUNTRY    T
     WHEN ALL MY FIVE AND COUNTRY SENSES SEE,   .........   138   FIVE & COUNTRY    1
     THE HEART IS SENSUAL, THOUGH FIVE EYES BREAK.   .....  139   FIVE & COUNTRY   14
     FOUR ELEMENTS AND FIVE   ...........................   211   POEM ON B'DAY    82
FIVE-FATHOMED
     AND THE FIVE-FATHOMED HAMLET ON HIS FATHER'S CORAL,   111   I, IN IMAGE      83
```

		PAGE	TITLE	LINE
FIX				
NO FAITH TO FIX THE TEETH ON CARRIES	....	41	YOUNG ARE OLD	18
THE SCALED SEA-SAWERS, FIX IN A NAKED SPONGE	......	119	ALTARWISE	92
FIXED				
FAITH FIXED BEYOND THE SPINNING STARS,	....	41	YOUNG ARE OLD	45
FIXED FAITH, BELIEVING AND WORSHIPPING TOGETHER	...	41	YOUNG ARE OLD	46
FAITH FIXED LIKE A STAR BEYOND THE STARS,	....	42	YOUNG ARE OLD	50
THAT FROZEN WIFE WHOSE JUICES DRIFT LIKE A FIXED SEA		145	PLEASURE-BIRD	14
FIXERS				
WHEEL-WINDERS AND FIXERS OF BOLTS.	....	70	SECRET WIND	18
FIXTURES				
WHAT SHALL DESTRUCTION COUNT IF THESE ARE FIXTURES?		60	FAIRY TALES	27
FLAGS				
AND SUNK; WAVED FLAGS TO EVERY FIFE AND DRUM;	.....	52	OUT OF THE PIT	70
FLAILED				
DRUNK AS A VINEYARD SNAIL, FLAILED LIKE AN OCTOPUS,		134	HOW MY ANIMAL	7
FLAILING				
NO FLAILING CALF OR CAT IN A FLAME	....	207	LAMENT	40
FLAKE				
BUT BEAUTIFULLY FLAKE YOUR HEAD	....	227	SPRING-SPIRIT	3
FLAKE-BARE				
AND COVERING ALL HAS BEEN A QUIETUDE, AND A SINGING				
FROM FLAKE-BARE THROATS.	....	224	IDYLL UNFORGET	35
FLAKES				
AND THE FLAKES FALL LIKE HILLS.	....	166	LONG-LEGGED	136
GLIDING WINDLESS THROUGH THE HAND FOLDED FLAKES,		187	WINTER'S TALE	4
BIRD THROUGH THE TIMES AND LANDS AND TRIBES OF THE				
SLOW FLAKES.	....	190	WINTER'S TALE	99
FLAME				
PUFFING THE LIGHT'S FLAME TO AND FRO,	....	16	TIME TO ROT	5
WRAP THEM IN FLAME, THEY'RE MINE;	....	19	IMAGES IN AIR	2
OF WATER, FLAME, OR AIR.	....	20	THE NEOPHYTE	17
BEFORE THE BLOOD AND FLAME WERE TWINED	....	86	SEE, SAYS LIME	23
AND THE FLAME IN THE FLESH'S VISION.	....	107	ALL ALL AND	33
THERE IS LOUD AND DARK DIRECTLY UNDER THE DUMB FLAME,		130	SINNERS' BELL	13
THE REPTILE PROFLIGATES IN A FLAME,	....	150	WHEN I WOKE	4
IS DUMB AND GONE WITH HIS FLAME OF BRIDES.	....	165	LONG-LEGGED	106
AND HIS LOIN WAS A HUNTING FLAME	....	168	LONG-LEGGED	196
BURNS ME HIS NAME AND HIS FLAME	....	180	VISION, PRAYER	28
WITH HIS FLAME IN EVERY GRAIN.	....	182	VISION, PRAYER	78
ROOSTS SLEEPING CHILL TILL THE FLAME OF THE COCK CROW		187	WINTER'S TALE	19
AND THE DAUGHTERS OF DARKNESS FLAME LIKE FAWKES				
FIRES STILL.	....	205	GIANT'S THIGH	60
NO FLAILING CALF OR CAT IN A FLAME	....	207	LAMENT	40
BEFORE CHAINS BREAK TO A HAMMER FLAME	....	210	POEM ON B'DAY	44
FLAMES				
LOPS, AS A BUSH PLUMED WITH FLAMES, THE RANT OF THE				
FIERCE EYE,	....	135	HOW MY ANIMAL	38
THE MAZES OF HIS PRAISE AND ENVIOUS TONGUE WERE				
WORKED IN FLAMES AND SHELLS.	....	141	SAINT TO FALL	17
HIS FIERY REEL SINGS OFF ITS FLAMES,	....	164	LONG-LEGGED	64
AND DIED ON A HISS OF FLAMES	....	167	LONG-LEGGED	158
INTO THE BREAD IN A WHEATFIELD OF FLAMES,	....	175	FIRE RAID	70
AS THE FOOD AND FLAMES OF THE SNOW, A MAN UNROLLED		187	WINTER'S TALE	13
WHEN HIS VIPERISH FUSE HANGS LOOPED WITH FLAMES				
UNDER THE BRAND	....	202	SIR JOHNS HILL	28
THE MOONS ARE WHITE FLAMES, LIKE THE MOONS IN DREAMS.		223	IN DREAMS	14
FLAMING				
WHOSE FLAMING BLOOD SHALL RUB IT AT THE RIMS	......	87	PAIN BE MUSIC	8
PROWLS FLAMING AMONG THE COCKERELS	....	216	COUNTRY HEAVEN	28

	PAGE	TITLE	LINE
FLANKS			
CANNOT DENT YOUR FLANKS;	229	MY RIVER	14
FLANNEL			
OF MEN WITH FLANNEL SHIRTS	37	WINDMILLS TURN	10
FLARED			
FLARED IN THE REEK OF THE WIVING STY WITH THE RUSH	204	GIANT'S THIGH	22
FLASH			
FELLED AND QUILLED, FLASH TO MY PATCH	5	PROLOGUE	83
FLASH, AND THE PLUMES CRACK, ...	201	SIR JOHNS HILL	13
FLASHED			
FLASHED FIRST ACROSS HIS THUNDERCLAPPING EYES.	160	DEATHS AND ENT	24
THE FLASHED THE NOOSED HAWK	201	SIR JOHNS HILL	10
AS THE ARC OF THE BILLHOOKS THAT FLASHED THE HEDGES LOW	205	GIANT'S THIGH	48
FLASHING			
DEATH FLASHING FROM HIS SLEEVE, ...	108	GRIEF THIEF	16
THE FLASHING NEEDLE ROCK OF SQUATTERS, ...	151	BELOW A TIME	26
FLASHING INTO THE DARK.	195	FERN HILL	27
FLASK			
LIES IN THE FORTUNED BONE, THE FLASK OF BLOOD, ...	80	ALL THAT I OWE	3
HAD STRINGED MY FLASK OF MATTER TO HIS RIB.	97	TWILIGHT LOCKS	12
AND TAKE ANOTHER NIBBLE AT MY FLASK.	137	O CHATTERTON	16
FLAT			
FEAR NOT THE FLAT, SYNTHETIC BLOOD, ...	106	ALL ALL AND	14
ESCAPES TO THE FLAT CITIES' SAILS	129	MY NEOPHYTE	16
FLATS			
THE STAINED FLATS OF HEAVEN HIT AND RAZED	141	SAINT TO FALL	2
IN COMMUNAL CRAB FLATS	154	RETURN	17
FLAVOURED			
THE SHADES OF GIRLS, ALL FLAVOURED FROM THEIR SHROUDS, ...	89	EUNUCH DREAMS	7
FLAVOURED OF CELLULOID GIVE LOVE THE LIE.	89	EUNUCH DREAMS	20
FLAXEN			
STRUNG BY THE FLAXEN WHALE-WEED, FROM THE HANGMAN'S RAFT, ...	110	I, IN IMAGE	65
FLEA			
GLORY CRACKED LIKE A FLEA.	141	SAINT TO FALL	18
FLEAS			
SLY AS AN ADDER, RID OF FLEAS.	29	LONG, SKELETON	6
BONY AND SPAVINED, RICH WITH FLEAS.	45	PLOUGHMAN GONE	9
FLEA-SPECKED			
SWELLING IN FLEA-SPECKED LINEN	154	RETURN	7
FLED			
I FLED THE EARTH AND, NAKED, CLIMBED THE WEATHER,	101	FELLOWED SLEEP	6
I FLED THAT GROUND AS LIGHTLY AS A FEATHER.	101	FELLOWED SLEEP	10
THE CRUMPLED PACKS FLED PAST THIS GHOST IN BLOOM,	133	I MAKE THIS IN	58
AND FLED THEIR LOVE IN A WEAVING DIP.	163	LONG-LEGGED	53
AND WAKE TO THE FARM FOREVER FLED FROM THE CHILDLESS LAND.	196	FERN HILL	51
FIERCE COLOURS FLED ABOUT THE BRANCHES, ...	226	THE OAK	1
FLEECE			
WITH PELT, AND SCALE, AND FLEECE:	5	PROLOGUE	86
AS THE RAIN FALLS, HAIL ON THE FLEECE, AS THE VALE MIST RIDES	199	COUNTRY SLEEP	57
FLEECED			
AS FLEECED AS THEY BOW LOWLY WITH THE SHEEP, ...	96	TWELVE	10
FLESH			
ABOUT YOU, FLESH WILL PERISH, AND BLOOD	39	GAS FADES	31
LENDS NOT FLESH TO RIBS AND NECK, ...	55	NO MAN BELIEVE	23
AT FLESH THAT PERISHES AND BLOOD THAT'S SPILT	57	GREEK PLAY	19

	PAGE	TITLE	LINE
FLESH (CONTINUED)			
REBEL AGAINST THE FLESH AND BONE, ...	61	MEAT ON BONES	14
BY A THIN SEA OF FLESH	62	EARS IN TURRET	11
SWEET IS THE WAXEN BLOOD, HONEY THE FALLING FLESH;	63	WOMAN SPEAKS	3
SINCE THE FIRST FLESH OF MAN WAS RIVEN	64	WOMAN SPEAKS	28
IT WAS A HAGGARD NIGHT THE FIRST FLESH DIED, ...	65	WOMAN SPEAKS	56
YOU ARE THE RULER OF THIS REALM OF FLESH	67	REALM OF FLESH	T
YOU ARE THE RULER OF THIS REALM OF FLESH, ...	67	REALM OF FLESH	1
BEFORE I KNOCKED AND FLESH LET ENTER, ...	68	BEFORE KNOCKED	1
AND FLESH WAS SNIPPED TO CROSS THE LINES	68	BEFORE KNOCKED	22
I, BORN OF FLESH AND GHOST, WAS NEITHER	69	BEFORE KNOCKED	37
WHO TOOK MY FLESH AND BONE FOR ARMOUR	69	BEFORE KNOCKED	45
FLESH IS SUFFERED, IS LAID LOW, ...	71	TAKE NEEDLES	25
FLESH AND SPIRIT, BABE AND DAM, ...	71	TAKE NEEDLES	30
FIRMAMENT OF FLESH AND BONE	72	TAKE NEEDLES	38
OF FLESH AND BONES, ...	73	WE MOTHERNAKED	4
THE BEACH OF FLESH, AND WIND HER BLOODRED PLAIT;	75	MY HERO BARES	13
MY MAKER'S FLESH THAT GARMENTS MY CLAYFELLOWS.	76	LASHED RINGS	3
AND TO THE FIRST DUMB WONDER AT THE FLESH, ...	78	LOVE'S FEVER	13
AND FROM THE FIRST DECLENSION OF THE FLESH	79	LOVE'S FEVER	31
O ALL I OWE IS ALL THE FLESH INHERITS, ...	80	ALL THAT I OWE	5
ACQUAINT THE FLESH WITH A REMEMBERED ITCH, ...	80	ALL THAT I OWE	12
FILE THROUGH THE FLESH WHERE NO FLESH DECKS THE BONES.	82	LIGHT BREAKS	6
FILE THROUGH THE FLESH WHERE NO FLESH DECKS THE BONES.	82	LIGHT BREAKS	6
KNOCKED IN THE FLESH THAT DECKED THE VINE, ...	86	BREAD I BREAK	7
THIS FLESH YOU BREAK, THIS BLOOD YOU LET	86	BREAD I BREAK	11
FLESH BLOOD AND BONE	87	PAIN BE MUSIC	23
A WEATHER IN THE FLESH AND BONE	88	A PROCESS IN	16
AND DROP THE PLUM LIKE FIRE FROM THE FLESH.	95	RUB OF LOVE	9
OFF FROM THE CREASING FLESH, FILED	102	I DREAMED MY	6
I PIECE MY FLESH THAT RATTLED ON THE YARDS	105	WORLD PYRAMID	38
HOW NOW MY FLESH, MY NAKED FELLOW, ...	106	ALL ALL AND	7
ALL OF THE FLESH, THE DRY WORLDS LEVER.	106	ALL ALL AND	12
MAN OF MY FLESH, THE JAWBONE RIVEN, ...	106	ALL ALL AND	19
STROKE OF MECHANICAL FLESH ON MINE, ...	107	ALL ALL AND	29
MARKING THE FLESH AND SUMMER IN THE BAY?	112	NOT FATHER ME	11
ARE FORMED OF FLESH, BUT LET THE FALSE DAY COME ...	116	LANTERNS SHINE	6
HER FLESH WAS MEEK AS MILK, BUT THIS SKYWARD STATUE	136	AFTER FUNERAL	27
TURNS OF YOUR PRAYED FLESH, NOR SHALL I SHOO THE BIRD BELOW ME:	148	UNLUCKILY FOR	27
OF THE LIVING FLESH IS MONSTROUS OR IMMORTAL, ...	148	UNLUCKILY FOR	41
CUT-TO-MEASURE FLESH BIT, ...	151	BELOW A TIME	3
WITH DRY FLESH AND EARTH FOR ADORNING AND BED.	152	BELOW A TIME	43
OH ALL THE WANTING FLESH HIS ENEMY	165	LONG-LEGGED	91
GOOD-BYE ALWAYS FOR THE FLESH IS CAST	166	LONG-LEGGED	122
WHEN HIS LONG-LEGGED FLESH WAS A WIND ON FIRE	168	LONG-LEGGED	195
OR FLOWER UNDER THE TIME DYING FLESH ASTRIDE.	188	WINTER'S TALE	55
THE FIELDS OF SEED AND THE TIME DYING FLESH ASTRIDE,	190	WINTER'S TALE	103
TIME BY, THEIR DUST WAS FLESH THE SWINEHERD ROOTED SLY, ...	204	GIANT'S THIGH	21
LULLING OF SPHERES IN THE SEASHELL FLESH, ...	211	POEM ON B'DAY	89
REND THE BRIGHT FLESH AWAY, ...	239	MAKES INTERVALS	23
UPON MY FLESH AND SKIN, ...	240	TWINING HEAD	10
FLESH'S			
YOU ARE MY FLESH'S RULER WHOM I TREASON, ...	67	REALM OF FLESH	11
FELT THUD BENEATH MY FLESH'S ARMOUR, ...	68	BEFORE KNOCKED	9
WHERE FLESH'S FEVER	85	SEE, SAYS LIME	20
KNOW NOW THE FLESH'S LOCK AND VICE, ...	106	ALL ALL AND	20

	PAGE	TITLE	LINE
FLESH'S (CONTINUED)			
AND THE FLAME IN THE FLESH'S VISION.	107	ALL ALL AND	33
FLEUR			
AND IN HER GARDEN GROW THE FLEUR DE LYS, ...	222	IN DREAMS	1
FLEW			
SO, PLANING-HEELED, I FLEW ALONG MY MAN	101	FELLOWED SLEEP	4
THE GHOST THAT HATCHED HIS HAVOC AS HE FLEW	104	WORLD PYRAMID	29
FLEW MAN-BEARING THERE.	157	INTO HER HEAD	6
HIS FAITH AROUND HER FLEW UNDONE	158	INTO HER HEAD	26
AND THEIR FIREFLY HAIRPINS FLEW, AND THE RICKS RAN			
ROUND--	205	GIANT'S THIGH	41
WHO FLEW HIMSELF BECAUSE THE BOAT REMAINED	238	PILLAR BREAKS	19
FLEW FOR A TIME IN VAIN, TO DROP AT LAST	238	PILLAR BREAKS	21
FLICK			
AND MAKES WITH A FLICK OF THE THUMB AND SUN	142	SAINT TO FALL	50
FLICKED			
FLICKED FROM THE CARBOLIC CITY PUZZLE IN A BED OF			
SORES	142	SAINT TO FALL	28
FLICKERING			
THE FLICKERING RUNS AND DIVE	4	PROLOGUE	55
FLIES			
FLIES FROM THE GUTTER.	16	TIME TO ROT	12
AS FLIES BEFORE THE BREATH	25	BEAUTY TO DUST	2
WOULD LEAVE ME COLD AS BUTTER FOR THE FLIES, ...	95	RUB OF LOVE	26
AND BAGS OF BLOOD LET OUT THEIR FLIES;	97	TWILIGHT LOCKS	23
FLIES ON THE SHAFTED DISK, DECLAIMS THE MORNING ...	99	OCTOBER WIND	19
DUST IN THE BURIED WOOD, FLIES ON THE GRAINS OF HER			
WINGS	189	WINTER'S TALE	58
HE FLIES TOO HIGH.	234	NO, PIGEON	23
FLIGHT			
BY MESSENGERS, THE FLIGHT OF BIRDS	29	NEARLY SUMMER	4
WHEN HEAVEN--OPEN WIDE THE GATES--HAS TAKEN FLIGHT,	34	THIRST PARCHES	4
ECHO A HUNDRED TIMES, THE FLIGHT OF BIRDS	50	OUT OF THE PIT	14
THE FLIGHT OF THE CARNAL SKULL	111	I, IN IMAGE	75
HER MOLTEN FLIGHT UP CINDER-NESTING COLUMNS, ...	132	I MAKE THIS IN	26
HER LOVER'S WINGS THAT FOLD TO-MORROW'S FLIGHT, ...	159	INTO HER HEAD	57
THE WOUNDWARD FLIGHT OF THE ANCIENT	182	VISION, PRAYER	92
HIM UP AND HE RAN LIKE A WIND AFTER THE KINDLING			
FLIGHT	190	WINTER'S TALE	89
WILD MEN WHO CAUGHT AND SANG THE SUN IN FLIGHT, ...	208	NOT GO GENTLE	10
FLINGS			
BORROW MY EYES. THE DARKENING SEA FLINGS LEA	179	NEW QUAY	2
FLINT			
WE ARE THE SONS OF FLINT AND PITCH.	93	BOYS OF SUMMER	53
NOR THE FLINT IN THE LOVER'S MAULING.	106	ALL ALL AND	18
THE YEAR-HEDGED ROW IS LAME WITH FLINT, ...	129	MY NEOPHYTE	38
FLINTSTEPS			
WHO SCALES A HAILING HILL IN HER COLD FLINTSTEPS	132	I MAKE THIS IN	29
FLOAT			
HERE IN THIS SPRING, STARS FLOAT ALONG THE VOID;	58	HERE IN SPRING	1
AND LET YOU FLOAT.'	231	OUR SANCTITY	31
FLOATED			
WHERE FLOATED A DEAD DOG WHO MADE HIM ILL, ...	51	OUT OF THE PIT	41
FLOATED THE LOST CATHEDRAL	163	LONG-LEGGED	35
FLOATING			
UNDER THE FLOATING VILLAGES, ...	169	LONG-LEGGED	202
AND FLOATING FIELDS FROM THE FARM IN THE CUP OF THE			
VALES, ...	187	WINTER'S TALE	3
AND THE LAKES AND FLOATING FIELDS AND THE RIVER			
WENDED	190	WINTER'S TALE	108

	PAGE	TITLE	LINE
FLOCK			
THAT ADAM'S WETHER IN THE FLOCK OF HORNS, ...	117	ALTARWISE	31
HYMNED HIS SHRIVELLING FLOCK, ...	141	SAINT TO FALL	13
LEAVES IS DANCING. LINES OF AGE ON THE STONES WEAVE			
IN A FLOCK.	189	WINTER'S TALE	78
FLOCKED			
FLOCKED WITH THE SHEEP WHITE SMOKE OF THE FARM HOUSE			
COWL	187	WINTER'S TALE	9
OUT OF A LAIR IN THE FLOCKED LEAVES IN THE DEW			
DIPPED YEAR	197	COUNTRY SLEEP	6
FLOCKS			
CAVES THE CRIES OF THE PARCHS AND THEIR FLOCKS. I	179	NEW QUAY	17
WHITE, GOD'S BRIGHT, FLOCKS, THE BELLED LAMBS			
LEAPING, ...	215	COUNTRY HEAVEN	21
YOUNG AMONG THE LONG FLOCKS, AND NEVER LIE LOST ...	216	ELEGY	7
FLOGGING			
FLOGGING INTO THE PORCHES	156	RETURN	75
FLOOD			
AS THE FLOOD BEGINS, ...	4	PROLOGUE	46
HEARS, THERE, THIS FOX LIGHT, MY FLOOD SHIP'S	4	PROLOGUE	69
AND THE FLOOD FLOWERS NOW.	5	PROLOGUE	102
THAT I MAY DROWN, LET LOOSE HER FLOOD OF TEARS. ...	65	WOMAN SPEAKS	55
I WOULD NOT FEAR THE APPLE NOR THE FLOOD	95	RUB OF LOVE	6
ARC-LAMPED THROWN BACK UPON THE CUTTING FLOOD.	118	ALTARWISE	56
IN TIME AT FLOOD FILLED WITH HIS COLOURED DOUBLES;	124	FOSTER LIGHT	27
FLOOD OF HER HEART'S FAME; SHE WOULD LIE DUMB AND			
DEEP	136	AFTER FUNERAL	19
PUT A TEAR FOR JOY IN THE UNEARTHLY FLOOD	153	WAS A SAVIOUR	22
FOR WE SAW HIM THROW TO THE SWIFT FLOOD	162	LONG-LEGGED	21
MAY HOLD IT IN A GREAT FLOOD	173	FIRE RAID	21
FLOODS			
FROM GARDEN CANS, OR FREE THE FLOODS?	65	GODS THUMP	7
THERE IN THEIR HEAT THE WINTER FLOODS	91	BOYS OF SUMMER	4
BENT LIKE A BEAST TO LAP THE SINGULAR FLOODS	134	NOT FROM ANGER	3
AND THE DEAR FLOODS OF HIS HAIR.	140	TOMBSTONE TOLD	30
MILK IN YOUR MOUTH, AT THE SOUR FLOODS	142	SAINT TO FALL	32
FLOOR			
STAY, IN A CIRCLE CHALKED UPON THE FLOOR, ...	28	NO WINGS	25
TWO HEELS OF WATER ON THE FLOOR OF SEED), ...	114	SERVANT SUN	24
I FOUND THEM LYING ON THE FLOOR, ...	143	THE MOLLS	1
OVER THE GARDENS OF THE FLOOR	164	LONG-LEGGED	74
AND THE FUNERAL GRAINS OF THE SLAUGHTERED FLOOR.	172	DAWN RAID	5
FLOORS			
THE ANCHOR DIVES THROUGH THE FLOORS OF A CHURCH.	169	LONG-LEGGED	212
FLOUNDERS			
FLOUNDERS, GULLS, ON THEIR COLD, DYING TRAILS, ...	209	POEM ON B'DAY	11
FLOURISH			
NEVER TO FLOURISH IN THE FIELDS OF THE WHITE SEED	188	WINTER'S TALE	54
FLOW			
TOO FULL WITH BLOOD TO LET MY LOVE FLOW IN.	9	MINUTE'S HOUR	12
AND MY THOUGHTS FLOW SO UNEASILY	10	COOL, OH NO	22
FEEL THE SAME SOFT BLOOD FLOW THOROUGHLY, ...	23	THE ONLY DEAD	11
HANDS HAVE NO TEARS TO FLOW.	66	HAND SIGNED	16
PLEADING IN THE WADED BAY FOR THE SEED TO FLOW	203	GIANT'S THIGH	7
AND HEARD THE LEWD, WOOED FIELD FLOW TO THE COMING			
FROST, ...	204	GIANT'S THIGH	30
SEA, DO NOT FLOW	229	MY RIVER	19
FLOW UNEASILY BEHIND YOU.	232	FURIOUS MOTION	8
FLOWED			
THAT FLOWED OUT OF THE SOIL	17	IN OBLIVION	12

	PAGE	TITLE	LINE
FLOWED (CONTINUED)			
MY VEINS FLOWED WITH THE EASTERN WEATHER;	68	BEFORE KNOCKED	17
THE WORD FLOWED UP, TRANSLATING TO THE HEART	94	IN BEGINNING	23
THOUGH NO SOUND FLOWED DOWN THE HAND FOLDED AIR	188	WINTER'S TALE	40
FLOWER			
FOR WHEN WE TOUCH A FLOWER WITH OUR OAR	14	RAIN CUTS	30
MY HAND WITH HONEY THAT HAD CLOSED UPON A FLOWER.	15	FOR LEDA	19
NO TIDY FLOWER MOVED, NO BATHER GRACEFULLY	34	IN GARDENS	19
WHERE BLEW A FLOWER MAY A FLOWER NO MORE	50	NO DOMINION	22
WHERE BLEW A FLOWER MAY A FLOWER NO MORE	50	NO DOMINION	22
AND LOVE THAT GOES DOWN LIKE A FLOWER.	57	GREEK PLAY	20
THE FORCE THAT THROUGH THE GREEN FUSE DRIVES THE FLOWER	77	THE FORCE THAT	T
THE FORCE THAT THROUGH THE GREEN FUSE DRIVES THE FLOWER	77	THE FORCE THAT	1
AND WHO REMAIN SHALL FLOWER AS THEY LOVE,	90	EUNUCH DREAMS	41
A THREE-EYED, RED-EYED SPARK, BLUNT AS A FLOWER;	94	IN BEGINNING	15
CITY OF SPRING, THE GOVERNED FLOWER,	106	ALL ALL AND	4
FLOWER, FLOWER THE PEOPLE'S FUSION,	107	ALL ALL AND	31
FLOWER, FLOWER THE PEOPLE'S FUSION,	107	ALL ALL AND	31
FLOWER, FLOWER, ALL ALL AND ALL.	107	ALL ALL AND	36
FLOWER, FLOWER, ALL ALL AND ALL.	107	ALL ALL AND	36
IN THE GLASS BED OF GRAPES WITH SNAIL AND FLOWER,	109	I, IN IMAGE	29
THE HARING SNAIL GO GIDDILY ROUND THE FLOWER,	109	I, IN IMAGE	41
SHE WHO WAS WHO I HOLD, THE FATS AND FLOWER,	114	A GRIEF AGO	2
THE COME-A-CROPPER RIDER OF THE FLOWER.	128	NOW, SAY NAY	28
REFUSAL STRUCK HER LOIN AND THE LAME FLOWER	134	NOT FROM ANGER	2
ALL LOVE BUT FOR THE FULL ASSEMBLAGE IN FLOWER	148	UNLUCKILY FOR	40
OR FLOWER UNDER THE TIME DYING FLESH ASTRIDE.	188	WINTER'S TALE	55
BIRD BEAST AND FLOWER	191	REFUSAL MOURN	2
AND FLOWER OF COUNTRY SLEEP AND THE GREENWOOD KEEP.	198	COUNTRY SLEEP	18
BE SHIELDED BY CHANT AND FLOWER AND GAY MAY YOU	198	COUNTRY SLEEP	42
OF ANY FLOWER	225	OF ANY FLOWER	T
THIS PONDEROUS FLOWER	232	FURIOUS MOTION	9
NOR THE PETALS OF ANY FLOWER DROP.	232	YOUR VOICE	16
THE SCENT OF THE GREAT FLOWER WILL STAY,	232	FURIOUS MOTION	16
THE FLOWER FROM THE SMELL,	233	NO THOUGHT	12
OR THE LOTION OF A FLOWER	235	WOMAN TAPESTRY	15
BE FREE, (WIND FOR MY TREE AND WATER FOR MY FLOWER),	239	LET ME ESCAPE	2
FLOWERED			
AND GIRLS WITH FLOWERED HATS	37	WINDMILLS TURN	11
THE DEADROCK BASE THE BLOW THE FLOWERED ANCHOR,	127	NOW, SAY NAY	5
FLOWERING			
AND SHE ROSE WITH HIM FLOWERING IN HER MELTING SNOW.	191	WINTER'S TALE	130
NOW THE SEA HAS A FLOWERING OF FOAM;	224	IDYLL UNFORGET	36
WITH FOAM FLUNG BY THE FLOWERING SEAS.'	227	SPRING-SPIRIT	4
FLOWERLY			
FLOWERLY I DIE,	225	OF ANY FLOWER	4
FLOWERS			
AND THE FLOOD FLOWERS NOW.	5	PROLOGUE	102
SKIRTING THE ORDERED BEDS OF PAINT-BOX FLOWERS,	33	IN GARDENS	3
WHERE FIFTY FLOWERS BREED IN A FRUIT BOX,	47	POET: 1935	31
AND HE DESTROYS, THOUGH FLOWERS ARE HIS LOVES,	47	POET: 1935	34
THE IMAGE CHANGES, AND THE FLOWERS DROP	47	POET: 1935	43
AND SILENTLY I MILK THE BURIED FLOWERS.	81	HERE LIE BEAST	9
WHO PERISCOPE THROUGH FLOWERS TO THE SKY.	98	TWILIGHT LOCKS	30
AND FALLS, AND FLOWERS IN THE YAWNING WOUND AT OUR SIDES,	199	COUNTRY SLEEP	62
FLOWS TO THE STRAND OF FLOWERS LIKE THE DEW'S RULY SEA,	200	COUNTRY SLEEP	98

	PAGE	TITLE	LINE
FLOWERS (CONTINUED)			
THE FOAM HAS LINGERED INTO WHITE, LITTLE FLOWERS,	224	IDYLL UNFORGET	28
NODDING LIKE FLOWERS,	226	THE ELM	2
WE STRANGELY SANG AMONG THE FEATHERY FLOWERS.	227	SPRING-SPIRIT	12
AND HONEY STEAL FROM FLOWERS AGLOW.	228	TRIOLET	6
FEEL YOUR WOMAN'S BREASTS RISE UP LIKE FLOWERS	238	MAKES INTERVALS	12
I BUILD A FORTRESS FROM A HEAP OF FLOWERS;	240	ADMIT THE SUN	9
FLOWERS'			
AND FASTENING IN ITS CAGE THE FLOWERS' COLOUR?	46	POET: 1935	9
THE OLD FLOWERS' LEGS TOO TAUT TO DANCE,	47	POET: 1935	40
FLOWING			
FLOWING FROM HER BUT MINE,	13	SKY'S BRIGHT	24
FLOWING AND MELTING UNDER LIME.	19	IMAGES IN AIR	8
TO THE SEA SOUND FLOWING LIKE BLOOD FROM THE LOUD WOUND	194	SLEEP BECALMED	6
FLOWN			
LIE THIS FIFTH MONTH UNSKATED, AND THE BIRDS HAVE FLOWN;	122	HOLD HARD	9
FLOWS			
NEVER FLOWS OUT FROM THE WOUND OF SLEEP	27	OBLIVIOUS DARK	7
FLOWS OPEN	182	VISION, PRAYER	99
FLOWS TO THE STRAND OF FLOWERS LIKE THE DEW'S RULY SEA,	200	COUNTRY SLEEP	98
AND ALL MY GRIEF FLOWS FROM THE RIFT	225	CLOWN IN MOON	3
FLUCTUANTLY			
HOVER, MAKING THE FOREST FLUCTUANTLY VAGUE.	226	THE OAK	4
FLUES			
I WHISTLED ALL NIGHT IN THE TWISTED FLUES,	206	LAMENT	18
FLUID			
A RIB OF CANCER ON THE FLUID SKY.	25	THERE'S PLENTY	7
TAKING JEYES' FLUID AS NARCOTIC;	137	O CHATTERTON	3
FLUIDS			
TO ROB ME OF MY FLUIDS IN HIS HEART.	98	TWILIGHT LOCKS	36
FLUNG			
FLUNG GRAVEL CHIME? LET THE STONES SPEAK	66	GODS THUMP	13
WITH FOAM FLUNG BY THE FLOWERING SEAS.'	227	SPRING-SPIRIT	4
FLUSH			
FROM THE FAIR DEAD WHO FLUSH THE SEA	92	BOYS OF SUMMER	34
FLUTE			
FROTH, FLUTE, FIN AND QUILL	3	PROLOGUE	7
HULOO, MY PROUD DOVE WITH A FLUTE!	5	PROLOGUE	97
FLUTTERED			
FOR THE SALTY BIRDS FLUTTERED AND FED	165	LONG-LEGGED	96
FLUTTERS			
A CLOUD AGAINST THE GLASSY SUN FLUTTERS HIS	179	NEW QUAY	5
FLY			
THAT WILL FLY AND FALL	3	PROLOGUE	30
FROM WHICH YOU MAY NOT FLY.	10	COOL, OH NO	30
TO THE BUILT VOICE, OR FLY WITH WINTER TO THE BELLS,	16	SPIRE CRANES	10
FOR, IF I COULD, I'D FLY AWAY,	21	BEWILDERED WAY	22
FOR IF I COULD, I'D FLY AWAY	21	BEWILDERED WAY	23
THAT SHROUDED MEN MIGHT MARROW AS THEY FLY.	90	EUNUCH DREAMS	30
FLY LIKE THE STARS' BLOOD,	193	SIDE OF TRUTH	24
I SHOULD HEAR HIM FLY WITH THE HIGH FIELDS	196	FERN HILL	50
HE SINGS TOWARDS ANGUISH; FINCHES FLY	209	POEM ON B'DAY	20
ONE DAY THEY HAD TO FLY,	237	PILLAR BREAKS	14
FLYING			
THE MARK HIS FLYING TAIL HAS LEFT	14	RAIN CUTS	21
TUMBLE, NOT FLYING, IS FALSE,	37	WINDMILLS TURN	5
THE FLYING LOOSE, ALBINO EYED, WING SINGED,	41	YOUNG ARE OLD	38

	PAGE	TITLE	LINE
FLYING (CONTINUED)			
NO BIRDS OR FLYING FISH	62	EARS IN TURRET	15
AND, AS FOR OILS AND OINTMENTS ON THE FLYING GRAIL,	111	I, IN IMAGE	101
HAS SOWN A FLYING GARDEN ROUND THAT SEA-GHOST?	121	ALTARWISE	136
BEFORE THE FALL FROM LOVE THE FLYING HEARTBONE,	124	TODAY, INSECT	15
DIE IN RED FEATHERS WHEN THE FLYING HEAVEN'S CUT,	135	HOW MY ANIMAL	40
LIONS AND FIRES OF HIS FLYING BREATH,	160	DEATHS AND ENT	5
THE MORNING IS FLYING ON THE WINGS OF HIS AGE	173	DAWN RAID	13
STREET WE CHANT THE FLYING SEA	174	FIRE RAID	29
BIRDS AND THE BIRDS OF THE WINGED TREES FLYING MY NAME	177	POEM IN OCT	12
WAS FLYING THROUGH THE HOUSE AS THOUGH THE SHE BIRD PRAISED	189	WINTER'S TALE	83
FLYING. THE RITE IS SHORN	191	WINTER'S TALE	116
AND FIRE, THE FLYING RANT	193	SIDE OF TRUTH	27
WILL BE THE SAME GRIEF FLYING. WHOM SHALL THEY CALM?	194	CONVERS PRAYER	11
FLYING WITH THE RICKS, AND THE HORSES	195	FERN HILL	26
FLY-LORD'S			
AND FATHER ALL NOR FAIL THE FLY-LORD'S ACRE,	123	FOSTER LIGHT	13
FOAL			
GULL, ON THE WAVE WITH SAND IN ITS EYES! AND THE FOAL MOVES	200	COUNTRY SLEEP	83
FOAM			
THE LURED FISH UNDER THE FOAM	163	LONG-LEGGED	47
THE CATTLE GRAZE ON THE COVERED FOAM,	168	LONG-LEGGED	183
AS HORSES IN THE FOAM:	210	POEM ON B'DAY	75
THE FOAM HAS LINGERED INTO WHITE, LITTLE FLOWERS,	224	IDYLL UNFORGET	28
NOW THE SEA HAS A FLOWERING OF FOAM;	224	IDYLL UNFORGET	36
WITH FOAM FLUNG BY THE FLOWERING SEAS.'	227	SPRING-SPIRIT	4
AND I FORGOT THE DRIFTLESS FOAM, AND SAND,	227	SPRING-SPIRIT	9
FOAM-BLUE			
WHAT RHUBARB MAN PEELED IN HER FOAM-BLUE CHANNEL	121	ALTARWISE	135
FOAMED			
AND THE TALL GRAINS FOAMED IN THEIR BILLS;	165	LONG-LEGGED	97
FOAMING			
SKINNY AS SIN, THE FOAMING MARROW,	106	ALL ALL AND	11
FOAMS			
QUICK IN THE WOOD AT LOVE, WHERE A TORCH OF FOXES FOAMS,	204	GIANT'S THIGH	34
FOG			
(FOG HAS A BONE	113	SERVANT SUN	4
(FOG BY HIS SPRING	113	SERVANT SUN	11
BROTHERS DODGING THROUGH THE FOG	155	RETURN	49
FOLD			
FOLD IN THEIR ARMS.	89	EUNUCH DREAMS	6
ALONE ALIVE AMONG HIS MUTTON FOLD,	118	ALTARWISE	40
CLAW FOLD AND HOLE FOR THE ROTTEN	152	BELOW A TIME	33
HER LOVER'S WINGS THAT FOLD TO-MORROW'S FLIGHT,	159	INTO HER HEAD	57
TORN AND ALONE IN A FARM HOUSE IN A FOLD	187	WINTER'S TALE	15
AND THE HARP SHAPED VOICE OF THE WATER'S DUST PLUCKS IN A FOLD	189	WINTER'S TALE	79
AND THE BLACK SPIT OF THE CHAPEL FOLD,	205	LAMENT	2
GULLED AND CHANTER IN YOUNG HEAVEN'S FOLD	210	POEM ON B'DAY	62
IN THE FOLD OF HER ARMS	236	WOMAN TAPESTRY	64
FOLDED			
WAS WHO WAS FOLDED ON THE ROD THE AARON	115	A GRIEF AGO	13
GLIDING WINDLESS THROUGH THE HAND FOLDED FLAKES,	187	WINTER'S TALE	4
THOUGH NO SOUND FLOWED DOWN THE HAND FOLDED AIR	188	WINTER'S TALE	40
ABOVE HER FOLDED HEAD, AND THE SOFT FEATHERED VOICE	189	WINTER'S TALE	82
THEIR DELICATE, SILKEN LEAVES FOLDED,	235	WOMAN TAPESTRY	8

	PAGE	TITLE	LINE
FOLDS			
WARNING AMONG THE FOLDS, AND THE FROZEN HOLD	187	WINTER'S TALE	8
POOL AT THE WANTING CENTRE, IN THE FOLDS	191	WINTER'S TALE	128
FOLLOW			
BUT DO NOT FOLLOW IT,	13	SKY'S BRIGHT	28
AND WINTER FOLLOW LIKE AN ECHO	15	FOR LEDA	24
NO FAITH TO FOLLOW IS THE WORLD'S CURSE	41	YOUNG ARE OLD	24
TO FOLLOW THE FOX	44	TO FOLLOW FOX	T
TO FOLLOW THE FOX AT THE HOUNDS' TAILS	44	TO FOLLOW FOX	1
TO FOLLOW, WILD AS THE CHICKEN STEALER,	44	TO FOLLOW FOX	3
TO FOLLOW THE NOSE IF THE NOSE GOES	44	TO FOLLOW FOX	14
WHO FOLLOW THE RED RIVERS, HOLLOW	54	WE BY SEASAND	3
FOLLOW HIM OUT OF GRACE,	196	FERN HILL	45
FOLLOWED			
HAD FOLLOWED THE HUNCHBACK	172	THE HUNCHBACK	41
FOLLOWING			
FOLLOWING THE NOSE DOWN DELL, UP RISE	44	TO FOLLOW FOX	7
FOLLOWS			
THESE ARE HER CONTRARIES: THE BEAST WHO FOLLOWS	131	I MAKE THIS IN	24
FOLLY			
WISDOM IS FOLLY, LOVE IS NOT,	25	BEAUTY TO DUST	8
FOLLY PURIFY AND MAKE IT TRUE.	25	BEAUTY TO DUST	10
FOR FOLLY WAS	25	BEAUTY TO DUST	11
WHEN FOLLY STIRRED, WARM IN THE FOOLISH HEART.	25	BEAUTY TO DUST	19
OUT OF A WAR OF WITS, WHEN FOLLY OF WORDS	42	A WAR OF WITS	1
THESE BOYS OF LIGHT ARE CURDLERS IN THEIR FOLLY,	92	BOYS OF SUMMER	7
BRASS AND THE BODILESS IMAGE, ON A STICK OF FOLLY	111	I, IN IMAGE	80
WHO RAZED MY WOODEN FOLLY STANDS AGHAST,	113	NOT FATHER ME	22
UNDER THE LANK, FOURTH FOLLY ON GLAMORGAN'S HILL,	122	HOLD HARD	2
OF THE DESCENDING DAY, THE DARK OUR FOLLY	148	UNLUCKILY FOR	19
FOLLY'S			
TIME, IN A FOLLY'S RIDER, LIKE A COUNTY MAN	122	HOLD HARD	4
SPILL THE LANK FOLLY'S HUNTER AND THE HARD-HELD HOPE.	122	HOLD HARD	18
FOND			
THAT HER FOND WOUNDS ARE MENDED BITTERLY.	139	FIVE & COUNTRY	9
HERE WERE FOND CLIMATES AND SWEET SINGERS SUDDENLY	177	POEM IN OCT	26
FONT			
OUT OF THE FONT OF BONE AND PLANTS AT THAT STONE TOCSIN	130	SINNERS' BELL	20
THE HEAVENS, THE HEAVEN, THE GRAVE, THE BURNING FONT.	190	WINTER'S TALE	104
FOOD			
HAVE FOOD AND DRINK, UNLOVING?	23	THE ONLY DEAD	12
ENOUGH KIND FOOD, ENOUGH KIND SPEAKING,	36	MIDNIGHT ROAD	6
NO FOOD SUFFICES BUT THE FOOD OF DEATH;	63	WOMAN SPEAKS	2
NO FOOD SUFFICES BUT THE FOOD OF DEATH;	63	WOMAN SPEAKS	2
ALL THAT WAS LOVED AND LOVED MADE THE FOWLS' FOOD,	64	WOMAN SPEAKS	31
NO FOOD SUFFICES BUT THE FOOD OF DEATH;	64	WOMAN SPEAKS	33
NO FOOD SUFFICES BUT THE FOOD OF DEATH;	64	WOMAN SPEAKS	33
YOUR PAIN SHALL NOT UNMILK YOU OF THE FOOD	87	PAIN BE MUSIC	19
WHERE FISHES' FOOD IS FED THE SHADES	98	TWILIGHT LOCKS	29
MAN MORROW BLOWS THROUGH FOOD.	113	SERVANT SUN	14
CAMPED IN THE DRUG-WHITE SHOWER OF NERVES AND FOOD,	144	PLEASURE-BIRD	8
AS THE FOOD AND FLAMES OF THE SNOW, A MAN UNROLLED	187	WINTER'S TALE	13
FOOL			
LEERS DOWN THE VALLEY LIKE A FOOL	33	HELD-OUT HAND	19
THE MOON LEERED DOWN THE VALLEY LIKE A FOOL.	50	OUT OF THE PIT	12
THE MOON LEERED DOWN THE VALLEY LIKE A FOOL.	51	OUT OF THE PIT	32
I CANNOT MURDER, LIKE A FOOL,	61	MEAT ON BONES	30
TIME IS A FOOLISH FANCY, TIME AND FOOL.	100	RUNNING GRAVE	26
FORSAKE, THE FOOL, THE HARDINESS OF ANGER.	127	NOW, SAY NAY	7

	PAGE	TITLE	LINE
FOOLISH			
WHEN FOLLY STIRRED, WARM IN THE FOOLISH HEART.	25	BEAUTY TO DUST	19
TIME IS A FOOLISH FANCY, TIME AND FOOL.	100	RUNNING GRAVE	26
FOOLISHNESS			
COME WISE IN FOOLISHNESS, ...	25	BEAUTY TO DUST	16
FOOL'S			
LEADS TO FOOL'S PARADISE WHERE THE REDCOATED KILLER	44	TO FOLLOW FOX	5
DESERVES NO BRUSH, BUT A FOOL'S AMBUSH.	44	TO FOLLOW FOX	6
NO FOX, NO GOOD, FOOL'S, NOT A FOX'S, HOLE, ...	44	TO FOLLOW FOX	11
FOOT			
THERE WAS A PURPOSE IN HER POINTED FOOT;	11	CABARET	5
THE RAINBOW'S FOOT IS NOT MORE APT	11	AIR BREATHE	5
AND, AS WE WATCH, THE RAINBOW'S FOOT	13	RAIN CUTS	15
TO STIR THE WATER WITH A BUOYANT FOOT, ...	14	FOR LEDA	2
ON HEAD AND RUNNING FOOT, ...	21	BEWILDERED WAY	21
FOOT, HEAD, OR TRACES	24	LITTLE PROBLEM	1
OF FOOT ON HEAD WE'LL BE THE TIME	24	LITTLE PROBLEM	4
FOR A PURPOSE (HEAD TO FOOT IS HEAD AND FOOT, ...	24	LITTLE PROBLEM	6
FOR A PURPOSE (HEAD TO FOOT IS HEAD AND FOOT, ...	24	LITTLE PROBLEM	6
FOOT HEAD COMPRESSED, ...	24	LITTLE PROBLEM	10
LIFTED HER MARBLE FOOT, OR LOWERED HER HAND	34	IN GARDENS	20
THEY SHALL HAVE STARS AT ELBOW AND FOOT;	49	NO DOMINION	5
NOW DID THE SOFTEST SOUND OF FOOT OR VOICE	50	OUT OF THE PIT	13
FROM THE FIRST PRINT OF THE UNSHODDEN FOOT, THE LIFTING	78	LOVE'S FEVER	10
THE INCH OF TIME'S PROTRACTED TO A FOOT	80	ALMANAC TIME	8
BALL OF THE FOOT DEPENDING FROM THE SUN, ...	101	RUNNING GRAVE	43
WITH PRIEST'S GRAVE FOOT AND HAND OF FIVE ASSASSINS	131	I MAKE THIS IN	25
GRAVE'S FOOT, BLINDS DOWN THE LIDS, THE TEETH IN BLACK, ...	136	AFTER FUNERAL	4
WIND-HEELED FOOT IN THE HOLE OF A FIREBALL, ...	141	SAINT TO FALL	12
'IF MY HEAD HURT A HAIR'S FOOT'	145	IF HEAD HURT	T
'IF MY HEAD HURT A HAIR'S FOOT	145	IF HEAD HURT	1
FROM THE KANGAROO FOOT OF THE EARTH, ...	151	BELOW A TIME	21
MYSELF TO SET FOOT	177	POEM IN OCT	8
THE BLADE OF YOUR LONG FOOT, ...	229	MY RIVER	16
ON THE BALANCE OF HER DARK FOOT, ...	235	WOMAN TAPESTRY	22
OR CRUSH THEIR VIPER HEADS BENEATH MY FOOT.	239	LET ME ESCAPE	5
FOOTED			
ROBBED OF THE FOXY TONGUE, HIS FOOTED TAPE	100	RUNNING GRAVE	9
THE HILLS HAVE FOOTED THE WAVES AWAY, ...	168	LONG-LEGGED	184
FOOTFALL			
MOUNT ON MAN'S FOOTFALL, ...	109	I, IN IMAGE	27
FOOTPRINTS			
AND THE SHIPYARDS OF GALILEE'S FOOTPRINTS HIDE A NAVY OF DOVES.	170	MARRIAGE VIRG	7
FOOTSTEPS			
BUCKLE TO LINT AND CLOTH THEIR NATRON FOOTSTEPS,	120	ALTARWISE	116
FOR (279)			
FORCE			
THE FORCE THAT THROUGH THE GREEN FUSE DRIVES THE FLOWER	77	THE FORCE THAT	T
THE FORCE THAT THROUGH THE GREEN FUSE DRIVES THE FLOWER	77	THE FORCE THAT	1
THE FORCE THAT DRIVES THE WATER THROUGH THE ROCKS	77	THE FORCE THAT	6
STRIDE THROUGH CADAVER'S COUNTRY IN MY FORCE, ...	100	RUNNING GRAVE	21
FORCED			
THE STOCKED HEART IS FORCED, AND AGONY HAS ANOTHER MOUTH TO FEED.	142	SAINT TO FALL	42

	PAGE	TITLE	LINE
FORCING			
MY BLOOD UPON THE TEMPERED DEAD, FORCING	103	I DREAMED MY	19
FORCING FORTH THROUGH THE HAREBELL, ...	109	I, IN IMAGE	15
FOREHEAD			
ADORNERS OF THE CITY'S FOREHEAD, ...	70	SECRET WIND	9
WOE DRIP FROM THE DISHRAG HANDS AND THE PRESSED			
SPONGE OF THE FOREHEAD, ...	142	SAINT TO FALL	45
BRANDED FOREHEAD, THAT COULD BIND	147	UNLUCKILY FOR	9
FOREHEADS			
IN SPRING WE CROSS OUR FOREHEADS WITH THE HOLLY,	93	BOYS OF SUMMER	43
FOREIGN			
THIS WINE UPON A FOREIGN TREE	86	BREAD I BREAK	2
AND BOYS ARE FULL AND FOREIGN IN THE POUCH.	93	BOYS OF SUMMER	51
FROM THE FOREIGN FIELDS OF SPACE, ...	126	SEED-AT-ZERO	44
THUNDERS ON THE FOREIGN TOWN	127	SEED-AT-ZERO	52
FORESKIN			
THE TWO-A-VEIN, THE FORESKIN, AND THE CLOUD.	128	NOW, SAY NAY	35
FOREST			
THE SEED THAT MAKES A FOREST OF THE LOIN	88	A PROCESS IN	13
FOREST PICTURE	221	FOREST PICTURE	T
CALM AND STRANGE IS THIS EVENING HOUR IN THE FOREST,	221	FOREST PICTURE	1
HOVER, MAKING THE FOREST FLUCTUANTLY VAGUE.	226	THE OAK	4
FOREVER			
NOT FOREVER SHALL THE LORD OF THE RED HAIL	73	LORD RED HAIL	T
NOT FOREVER SHALL THE LORD OF THE RED HAIL	73	LORD RED HAIL	1
FOREVER IT IS A WHITE CHILD IN THE DARK-SKINNED			
SUMMER	130	SINNERS' BELL	19
STORM ME FOREVER OVER HER GRAVE UNTIL	137	AFTER FUNERAL	38
I ADVANCE FOR AS LONG AS FOREVER IS.	143	24 YEARS	9
TO THE ANGUISH AND CARRION, TO THE INFANT FOREVER			
UNFREE, ...	146	IF HEAD HURT	22
DEAD AND GONE, DEDICATE FOREVER TO MY SELF	147	UNLUCKILY FOR	6
UNDER THE NIGHT FOREVER FALLING.	184	VISION, PRAYER	152
FOREVER FALLING NIGHT IS A KNOWN	184	VISION, PRAYER	153
INHUMAN CRADLE AND THE BRIDE BED FOREVER SOUGHT ...	188	WINTER'S TALE	49
AND WAKE TO THE FARM FOREVER FLED FROM THE CHILDLESS			
LAND.	196	FERN HILL	51
ON THAT DARKEST DAY. OH, FOREVER MAY	216	ELEGY	4
FOREWARNS			
A PROCESS IN THE EYE FOREWARNS	88	A PROCESS IN	7
FORGED			
FORGED IN MAN'S MINERALS, THE BRASSY ORATOR	108	I, IN IMAGE	2
FORGED IN MAN'S MINERAL.	112	I, IN IMAGE	106
FORGET			
DO NOT FORGET THAT 'LIMPET' RHYMES	84	LETTER TO AUNT	33
THE OLD FORGET THE CRIES, ...	107	GRIEF THIEF	5
THE OLD FORGET THE GRIEF, ...	107	GRIEF THIEF	9
THE FINGERS WILL FORGET GREEN THUMBS AND MARK	138	FIVE & COUNTRY	2
JEALOUSY CANNOT FORGET FOR ALL HER SAKES, ...	158	INTO HER HEAD	34
FORGETS			
FORGETS, AND CRIES;	31	OUT OF SIGHS	4
FORGIVE			
FORGIVE	173	FIRE RAID	17
US FORGIVE	173	FIRE RAID	18
FORGIVING			
YET THIS I MAKE IN A FORGIVING PRESENCE.	133	I MAKE THIS IN	68
FORGOT			
AND I FORGOT THE DRIFTLESS FOAM, AND SAND, ...	227	SPRING-SPIRIT	9

                                              PAGE   TITLE   LINE
FORGOTTEN
    FORGOTTEN DARK, REST THEIR PULSE AND BURY THEIR DEAD
        IN HER FAITHLESS SLEEP.   159   INTO HER HEAD   69
    FORGOTTEN MORNINGS WHEN HE WALKED WITH HIS MOTHER   178   POEM IN OCT   47
    I HAVE MADE MY THROAT AN ARBOUR FOR FORGOTTEN SONGS. 224   IDYLL UNFORGET   20
FORK
    ON FORK AND FACE.   100   RUNNING GRAVE   25
    BLEED FROM MY BURNING FORK AND SMELL MY HEELS. 105   WORLD PYRAMID   52
    AND, FROM HIS FORK, A DOG AMONG THE FAIRIES, ... 117   ALTARWISE   4
    LOP, LOVE, MY FORK TONGUE, SAID THE PIN-HILLED
        NETTLE;   119   ALTARWISE   76
    DOUBLED, TO FORK HIM BACK, THROUGH THE LOCKJAW BED   132   I MAKE THIS IN   50
FORKED
    THE SUBSTANCE FORKED THAT MARROWED THE FIRST SUN;   93   IN BEGINNING   4
    IN SHAPES OF SIN FORKED OUT THE BEARDED APPLE, ... 121   INCARNATE DEVL   4
    BECAUSE THEIR WORDS HAD FORKED NO LIGHTNING THEY   208   NOT GO GENTLE   5
FORKING
    BEFORE THE PITCH WAS FORKING TO A SUN;   94   IN BEGINNING   27
FORKS
    LIFE, TILL THE CHANGE OF MOOD, FORKS   47   POET: 1935   38
    OF KNIVES ON FORKS, HE CRIED, OF NERVE ON NERVE,   51   OUT OF THE PIT   34
    AS FORKS MY EYE;   79   LOVE'S FEVER   47
    FORKS HALF ITS FRUIT; AND HALF DROPS DOWN, ... 88   A PROCESS IN   14
    AND CURLING ROUND THE BUD THAT FORKS HER EYE. 95   RUB OF LOVE   31
FORM
    MOULDED MY FORM   26   PERSONAL EPIT   9
    AS YET WAS IN A MOLTEN FORM, ...   68   BEFORE KNOCKED   10
    NO ELEMENTAL FORM AND SOUND   83   LETTER TO AUNT   9
FORMED
    OR, FORMED OF SAND, ...   19   IMAGES IN AIR   5
    ARE FORMED OF FLESH, BUT LET THE FALSE DAY COME ... 116   LANTERNS SHINE   6
FORSAKE
    FORSAKE, THE FOOL, THE HARDINESS OF ANGER. 127   NOW, SAY NAY   7
FORSAKEN
    AND COUNT THE TAKEN, FORSAKEN MYSTERIES IN A BAD
        DARK.   140   NO WORK WORDS   9
    AT THE POINT OF LOVE, FORSAKEN AND AFRAID. 188   WINTER'S TALE   30
    NAKED AND FORSAKEN TO GRIEVE HE WILL NOT COME. 201   COUNTRY SLEEP   106
    BECAUSE I HAVE FORSAKEN YOU 228   NOT DESPAIR   2
FORTH
    SINCE THE FIRST WOMB SPAT FORTH A BABY'S CORPSE,   64   WOMAN SPEAKS   52
    AND YOUR MAIEUTIC SLUMBER DRAG IT FORTH. 67   LET A FAITH   13
    AND TIME CAST FORTH MY MORTAL CREATURE   69   BEFORE KNOCKED   31
    MOTHER ROOT THAT SHOT ME FORTH, ...   72   TAKE NEEDLES   41
    OR DRIVE THE NIGHT-GEARED FORTH.   90   EUNUCH DREAMS   26
    FORCING FORTH THROUGH THE HAREBELL, ... 109   I, IN IMAGE   15
    DRIVES FORTH MY MEN, MY CHILDREN, FROM THE HANGING
        SOUTH.   122   HOLD HARD   6
    WHO HAVE BROUGHT FORTH THE URCHIN GRIEF. 131   SINNERS' BELL   30
    IN THE STILL SLEEPING TOWN AND SET FORTH. 177   POEM IN OCT   10
FORTRESS
    AND HID BEHIND THE FORTRESS OF THE RIBS   63   WOMAN SPEAKS   7
    I BUILD A FORTRESS FROM A HEAP OF FLOWERS; 240   ADMIT THE SUN   9
FORTUNATE
    THAT, THEN IS FORTUNATE, ... 23   THE ONLY DEAD   23
FORTUNE
    THEN LOOK, MY EYES, UPON THIS BONEBOUND FORTUNE ... 81   ALL THAT I OWE   21
    ALL NIGHT MY FORTUNE SLUMBERS IN ITS SHEET. 81   ALL THAT I OWE   27
    ALL NIGHT MY FORTUNE SLUMBERS IN ITS SHEET. 81   ALL THAT I OWE   30
    THIS IS THE FORTUNE OF MANHOOD: THE NATURAL PERIL, 109   I, IN IMAGE   19

	PAGE	TITLE	LINE
FORTUNED			
LIES IN THE FORTUNED BONE, THE FLASK OF BLOOD, ...	80	ALL THAT I OWE	3
FORTY			
WHEN I WAS SEVEN I COUNTED FOUR AND FORTY TREES ...	33	HELD-OUT HAND	12
FOSSIL			
IN THE CONTINENT OF A FOSSIL	166	LONG-LEGGED	144
THAT BELLED AND BOUNDED WITH THE FOSSIL AND THE DEW			
REBORN.	191	WINTER'S TALE	120
FOSTER			
NOR CITY TAR AND SUBWAY BORED TO FOSTER	100	RUNNING GRAVE	34
FOSTER THE LIGHT	123	FOSTER LIGHT	T
FOSTER THE LIGHT NOR VEIL THE MANSHAPED MOON, ...	123	FOSTER LIGHT	1
FOUL			
THROUGH EASIER HEATHER TO THE FOUL LAIR	44	TO FOLLOW FOX	16
HOWLS THE FOUL FIEND TO HEEL.	61	MEAT ON BONES	29
UNFAILING TILL THE BLOOD RUNS FOUL;	69	BEFORE KNOCKED	28
TIME'S CORAL SAINT AND THE SALT GRIEF DROWN A FOUL			
SEPULCHRE	130	SINNERS' BELL	8
MUTTER AND FOUL WINGBEAT OF THE SOLEMNIZING			
NIGHTPRIEST	158	INTO HER HEAD	45
AT LAST THE SOUL FROM ITS FOUL MOUSEHOLE	207	LAMENT	43
FOUND			
LEAVE YOU IN ME TO BE FOUND	9	MINUTE'S HOUR	10
WAS WHEN SENSE FOUND A WAY TO THEM	25	BEAUTY TO DUST	14
'WHAT HAVE YOU FOUND,' HE CRIES, 'WHAT HAVE YOU			
SOUGHT?'	30	YOUTH CALLS	14
'WHAT YOU HAVE FOUND,' AGE ANSWERS THROUGH HIS TEARS,	30	YOUTH CALLS	15
A LITTLE COMES, IS TASTED AND FOUND GOOD;	31	OUT OF SIGHS	5
FOUND MANAGERS AND WIDOWS WANTING	38	THE GOSSIPERS	11
FOR HE HAS FOUND HIS SOUL IN LONELINESS, ...	53	OUT OF THE PIT	97
I FOUND THEM LYING ON THE FLOOR, ...	143	THE MOLLS	1
BRAVE DEATHS OF ONLY ONES BUT NEVER FOUND, ...	153	WAS A SAVIOUR	35
AM FOUND.	185	VISION, PRAYER	197
FOR, OH, MY SOUL FOUND A SUNDAY WIFE	207	LAMENT	54
LET HIM FIND NO REST BUT THE FATHERED AND FOUND,	216	ELEGY	12
FOUNTAIN			
A SPARKLING FOUNTAIN FOR US	13	RAIN CUTS	2
WITH NO FOUNTAIN BOY BUT ME	13	RAIN CUTS	3
THERE IS NO FOUNTAIN SPRINGING FROM THE EARTH	63	WOMAN SPEAKS	4
THE LIPS OF TIME LEECH TO THE FOUNTAIN HEAD;	77	THE FORCE THAT	16
STORM, SNOW, AND FOUNTAIN IN THE WEATHER OF			
FIREWORKS, ...	130	SINNERS' BELL	14
WHEN, PRAISE IS BLESSED, HER PRIDE IN MAST AND			
FOUNTAIN	131	I MAKE THIS IN	4
WHOSE HOODED, FOUNTAIN HEART ONCE FELL IN PUDDLES	136	AFTER FUNERAL	14
IN THE FOUNTAIN BASIN WHERE I SAILED MY SHIP	171	THE HUNCHBACK	10
ERUPT, FOUNTAIN, AND ENTER TO UTTER FOR EVER	175	FIRE RAID	75
FOUNTAINHEAD			
OUT OF THE FOUNTAINHEAD	4	PROLOGUE	47
FOUNTAINS			
COOL AS THE WAX-RED FOUNTAINS OF THE VEINS;	63	WOMAN SPEAKS	5
PECK, SPRINT, DANCE ON FOUNTAINS AND DUCK TIME	145	IF HEAD HURT	8
IN FOUNTAINS OF ORIGIN GAVE UP THEIR LOVE, ...	157	INTO HER HEAD	9
FOUR			
WHEN I WAS SEVEN I COUNTED FOUR AND FORTY TREES ...	33	HELD-OUT HAND	12
MAN'S MANMADE SPARETIME LASTS THE FOUR SEASONS, ...	39	GAS FADES	19
SLOW ROUNDING OF FOUR SEASONS' COASTS, ...	58	HERE IN SPRING	6
AND FOUR BIRDS' NOTES.	58	HERE IN SPRING	8
AND THE FOUR WINDS, THAT HAD LONG BLOWN AS ONE, ...	78	LOVE'S FEVER	19
DOWN FALL FOUR PADDING WEATHERS ON THE SCARLET LANDS,	122	HOLD HARD	19

	PAGE	TITLE	LINE
FOUR (CONTINUED)			
BLESS HER BENT SPIRIT WITH FOUR, CROSSING BIRDS.	136	AFTER FUNERAL	26
AND STAR: HELD AND BLESSED, THOUGH YOU SCOUR THE HIGH FOUR	199	COUNTRY SLEEP	45
FOUR ELEMENTS AND FIVE	211	POEM ON B'DAY	82
FOUR-FRUITED			
BUT GRAFT THESE FOUR-FRUITED RIDINGS ON YOUR COUNTRY;	123	FOSTER LIGHT	9
FOUR-STRINGED			
SUMMON YOUR SNOWY HORSEMEN, AND THE FOUR-STRINGED HILL,	122	HOLD HARD	14
FOURTH			
UNDER THE LANK, FOURTH FOLLY ON GLAMORGAN'S HILL,	122	HOLD HARD	2
FOUR-WINDED			
WE SUMMER BOYS IN THIS FOUR-WINDED SPINNING,	93	BOYS OF SUMMER	37
FOWLS'			
ALL THAT WAS LOVED AND LOVED MADE THE FOWLS' FOOD,	64	WOMAN SPEAKS	31
FOX			
HEARS, THERE, THIS FOX LIGHT, MY FLOOD SHIP'S	4	PROLOGUE	69
AHOY, OLD, SEA-LEGGED FOX,	5	PROLOGUE	98
TO FOLLOW THE FOX	44	TO FOLLOW FOX	T
TO FOLLOW THE FOX AT THE HOUNDS' TAILS	44	TO FOLLOW FOX	1
NO FOX, NO GOOD, FOOL'S, NOT A FOX'S, HOLE,	44	TO FOLLOW FOX	11
IN A ROOM WITH A STUFFED FOX AND A STALE FERN,	136	AFTER FUNERAL	11
THE STUFFED LUNG OF THE FOX TWITCH AND CRY LOVE	137	AFTER FUNERAL	39
THE OWL AT ITS KNELLING. FOX AND HOLT KNEEL BEFORE BLOOD.	198	COUNTRY SLEEP	32
OF BIRDS! AMONG THE COCKS LIKE FIRE THE RED FOX	199	COUNTRY SLEEP	69
WHO COMES AS RED AS THE FOX AND SLY AS THE HEELED WIND.	200	COUNTRY SLEEP	81
SAVE BY THEIR LONG DESIRERS IN THE FOX CUBBED	205	GIANT'S THIGH	56
AND THE LONG FOX LIKE FIRE	216	COUNTRY HEAVEN	27
FOXES			
SANG TO MY HORN, THE FOXES ON THE HILLS BARKED CLEAR AND COLD,	195	FERN HILL	16
AND HONOURED AMONG FOXES AND PHEASANTS BY THE GAY HOUSE	196	FERN HILL	37
QUICK IN THE WOOD AT LOVE, WHERE A TORCH OF FOXES FOAMS,	204	GIANT'S THIGH	34
FOX'S			
NO FOX, NO GOOD, FOOL'S, NOT A FOX'S, HOLE,	44	TO FOLLOW FOX	11
FOXY			
ROBBED OF THE FOXY TONGUE, HIS FOOTED TAPE	100	RUNNING GRAVE	9
BOW DOWN THE WALLS OF THE FERNED AND FOXY WOODS	136	AFTER FUNERAL	24
FRAGMENTARY			
LIKE FRAGMENTARY RAIN	226	SLENDER WIND	4
FRAIL			
IS BLIND WITH TEARS TOO FRAIL TO TASTE.	15	FOR LEDA	33
THEIR FRAIL DEEDS MIGHT HAVE DANCED IN A GREEN BAY,	208	NOT GO GENTLE	8
TOO PROUD TO CRY, TOO FRAIL TO CHECK THE TEARS,	217	ELEGY	35
THE FRAIL AND DELICATE BREATH OF EVEN-TIME.	222	IN DREAMS	4
FRANK			
THE FRANK, CLOSED PEARL, THE SEA-GIRLS' LINEAMENTS	131	I MAKE THIS IN	19
WERE ONCE SUCH A CREATURE, SO GAY AND FRANK	147	TO OTHERS	14
FRANKINCENSE			
IN THE AGE OF LADY FRANKINCENSE	240	ADMIT THE SUN	13
FREE			
HE ALONE IS FREE, AND, FREE, MOANS TO THE SKY.	46	POET: 1935	13
HE ALONE IS FREE, AND, FREE, MOANS TO THE SKY.	46	POET: 1935	13
FROM GARDEN CANS, OR FREE THE FLOODS?	65	GODS THUMP	7
FREE FROM THEIR BURNING NESTS THE ARROWS' BROOD.	73	LORD RED HAIL	4

	PAGE	TITLE	LINE
FREE (CONTINUED)			
AND FREE THE TWIN-BOXED GRIEF,	108	GRIEF THIEF	20
BOAT WITH ITS ANCHOR FREE AND FAST	162	LONG-LEGGED	6
SILLY TO CAGE AND THEN SET FREE,	237	PILLAR BREAKS	8
BE FREE, (WIND FOR MY TREE AND WATER FOR MY FLOWER),	239	LET ME ESCAPE	2
FREELY			
AND FREELY HE GOES LOST	210	POEM ON B'DAY	46
FREEZE			
SETTING NO STORE BY HARVEST, FREEZE THE SOILS;	91	BOYS OF SUMMER	3
FREEZES			
A WIND THROWS A SHADOW AND IT FREEZES FAST.	166	LONG-LEGGED	130
FREEZING			
STORMS IN THE FREEZING TOMB.	88	A PROCESS IN	3
FRENCH			
DOWN TO THE WILD, UMBRELLA'D, AND FRENCH LETTERED	179	NEW QUAY	15
FRESH			
MAKING FRESH WHAT WAS STALE	35	LIFT UP FACE	6
MY BRAIN CAME CRYING INTO THE FRESH LIGHT,	42	A WAR OF WITS	4
FRESH IMAGES SURROUND THE TREMENDOUS MOON,	47	POET: 1935	45
ROUND HER TRAILED WRIST FRESH WATER WEAVES,	168	LONG-LEGGED	177
STRONG, FRESH, AND OVERPOWERING.	235	WOMAN TAPESTRY	12
HE IS A FRIEND WITH FRESH BREATH	236	WOMAN TAPESTRY	42
FRESHNESS			
COME, YOU ARE TO LOSE YOUR FRESHNESS.	233	NO THOUGHT	20
FRESH-WATER			
AND THE FRESH-WATER BIRD	231	OUR SANCTITY	24
FRIARS			
THE SCURRYING, FURRED SMALL FRIARS SQUEAL, IN THE DOWSE	204	GIANT'S THIGH	31
FRIEND			
ONE SAYS: THERE WAS A WOMAN WITH NO FRIEND,	22	ON QUIET NIGHT	8
WHO ARE HIS FRIENDS? THE WIND IS HIS FRIEND,	48	POET: 1935	63
I, THE FIRST NAMED, AM THE GHOST OF THIS SIR AND CHRISTIAN FRIEND	141	I, FIRST NAMED	1
FRIEND BY ENEMY I CALL YOU OUT.	146	TO OTHERS	1
YOU MY FRIEND THERE WITH A WINNING AIR	146	TO OTHERS	3
HE IS A FRIEND WITH FRESH BREATH	236	WOMAN TAPESTRY	42
FRIENDLY			
FRIENDLY AND BEAUTIFUL TO YOU;	228	NOT DESPAIR	8
FOR DEATH IS FRIENDLY TO THE MAN	240	TWINING HEAD	5
FRIENDS			
WHEN MORE THAN SNAILS ARE FRIENDS.	45	TO FOLLOW FOX	23
WHO ARE HIS FRIENDS? THE WIND IS HIS FRIEND,	48	POET: 1935	63
KNOCKING OFF TURNIP TOPS, WITH TREES FOR FRIENDS,	53	OUT OF THE PIT	88
THE DEAD IN HADES HAVE THEIR HOST OF FRIENDS,	57	GREEK PLAY	22
MY FRIENDS WERE ENEMIES ON STILTS	147	TO OTHERS	20
OF YOUR IMMORTAL FRIENDS	160	DEATHS AND ENT	6
ROBED IN THE LONG FRIENDS,	192	REFUSAL MOURN	20
FRIENDS'			
AFTER THE PERILS OF FRIENDS' TALK	42	A WAR OF WITS	15
FRIGHTENED			
I HAVE BEEN FRIGHTENED OF THE DARK FOR YEARS.	48	LIGHT, I KNOW	6
FRIGID			
THERE IN THE SUN THE FRIGID THREADS	92	BOYS OF SUMMER	10
FRO			
PUFFING THE LIGHT'S FLAME TO AND FRO,	16	TIME TO ROT	5
THE DUST OF THEIR KETTLES AND CLOCKS SWINGS TO AND FRO	205	GIANT'S THIGH	46
FROCK			
SHE, IN HER CHEAP FROCK, SAYING SOME CHEAP THING,	43	FACES SHONE	11

	PAGE	TITLE	LINE
FROG			
THE HORN AND BALL OF WATER ON THE FROG	115	A GRIEF AGO	15
FROGS			
FROGS AND SATANS AND WOMAN-LUCK,	150	WHEN I WOKE	7
FROLIC			
THAT PLAYED IN VOICELESS FROLIC AT THE THRESHOLD OF MY HEART.	223	IDYLL UNFORGET	12
AND CHANGED WITH THE WIND INTO INDISTINCT PATTERNS OF FROLIC,	224	IDYLL UNFORGET	29
FROM (274)			
FRONT			
TO CUT IN FRONT OF ME	12	SKY'S BRIGHT	6
AM I NOT YOU WHO FRONT THE TIDY SHORE,	112	NOT FATHER ME	15
FROST			
HAVE TRACED YOUR PATTERNS IN THE HASTENING FROST.	30	YOUTH CALLS	7
WHEN COMETH JACK FROST? THE CHILDREN ASK.	56	WHY EAST WIND	10
OF ECHO'S ANSWER AND THE MAN OF FROST	56	WHY EAST WIND	25
THE JACKS OF FROST THEY FINGER IN THE HIVES;	92	BOYS OF SUMMER	9
IN SACRED WATERS THAT NO FROST COULD HARDEN,	122	INCARNATE DEVL	14
FARMER IN TIME OF FROST THE BURNING LEAGUES,	123	FOSTER LIGHT	10
CAST HIGH, STUNNED ON GILLED STONE; SLY SCISSORS GROUND IN FROST	135	HOW MY ANIMAL	35
LOVE IN THE FROST IS PARED AND WINTERED BY,	138	FIVE & COUNTRY	5
TRAILING THE FROST BITTEN CLOTH,	151	BELOW A TIME	23
OF THISTLING FROST	200	COUNTRY SLEEP	73
AND HEARD THE LEWD, WOOED FIELD FLOW TO THE COMING FROST,	204	GIANT'S THIGH	30
WHERE THE FROST CAN NEVER FALL,	232	YOUR VOICE	15
LET THE FROST HARDEN	240	ADMIT THE SUN	5
FROSTY			
NO FROSTY GALLOPS THROUGH THE WINTER PARK.	41	YOUNG ARE OLD	16
WITH FROSTY FINGERS PUNISHES MY HAIR,	98	OCTOBER WIND	2
FROTH			
FROTH, FLUTE, FIN AND QUILL	3	PROLOGUE	7
AN INCH IN FROTH. CHIMES CHEAT THE PRISON SPIRE, PELTER	15	SPIRE CRANES	5
FROTH OR A MOMENT'S MOVEMENT	27	OBLIVIOUS DARK	20
PICK THE WORLD'S BALL OF WAVE AND FROTH	93	BOYS OF SUMMER	40
FROZE			
AS KISSES FROZE THE WAXING THOUGHT,	85	SEE, SAYS LIME	14
FROZEN			
OF FROZEN LOVES THEY FETCH THEIR GIRLS,	91	BOYS OF SUMMER	5
THE FELLOW HALF WAS FROZEN AS IT BUBBLED	104	WORLD PYRAMID	7
CROSS-STROKED SALT ADAM TO THE FROZEN ANGEL	119	ALTARWISE	67
THAT FROZEN WIFE WHOSE JUICES DRIFT LIKE A FIXED SEA	145	PLEASURE-BIRD	14
WARNING AMONG THE FOLDS, AND THE FROZEN HOLD	187	WINTER'S TALE	8
FRUCTIFY			
THE MOVING FRUCTIFY;	16	TIME TO ROT	14
FRUIT			
TANGLED WITH CHIRRUP AND FRUIT,	3	PROLOGUE	6
THE SUMMER VOICE SO WARM FROM FRUIT	15	FOR LEDA	25
THE SIDEBOARD FRUIT, THE FERNS, THE PICTURE HOUSES	33	HELD-OUT HAND	10
WHERE FIFTY FLOWERS BREED IN A FRUIT BOX,	47	POET: 1935	31
IN WINDS THAT BRING THE FRUIT AND RIND	55	WHY EAST WIND	4
IN THE FACE OF SEED AND FRUIT?	72	TAKE NEEDLES	60
THE FRUIT OF MAN UNWRINKLES IN THE STARS,	82	LIGHT BREAKS	10
PLUNGED IN ITS FRUIT;	86	BREAD I BREAK	3
FORKS HALF ITS FRUIT; AND HALF DROPS DOWN,	88	A PROCESS IN	14
AGAINST THE FRUIT MACHINE,	155	RETURN	34
THE WORM IS (PIN-POINT) RATIONAL IN THE FRUIT.	159	TO LEDA	3

	PAGE	TITLE	LINE
FRUIT (CONTINUED)			
THE WORM IS (PIN-POINT) RATIONAL IN THE FRUIT.	159	TO LEDA	9
NIGHT FALL AND THE FRUIT LIKE A SUN, ...	174	FIRE RAID	56
AND DOES NOT SHOW THE FRUIT TO TASTE;	233	NO THOUGHT	13
FRUITS			
OF LAMP-POSTS AND HIGH-VOLTED FRUITS, ...	70	SECRET WIND	16
AND LAY THE WET FRUITS LOW.	91	WHERE ONCE THE	12
FULFILL			
BEFORE THE PROMISES FULFILL	74	WE MOTHERNAKED	7
FULL			
TOO FULL WITH BLOOD TO LET MY LOVE FLOW IN.	9	MINUTE'S HOUR	12
ARE FULL ENOUGH TO DROWN MY MELANCHOLY	17	NATURAL DAY	2
SO ARE WE FULL WITH STRENGTH, ...	23	THE ONLY DEAD	5
THE SEASONS' CRIES, FULL OF HIS INTIMATIONS.	29	NEARLY SUMMER	6
IN MORALS AND FULL MARRIAGE BUNTING, ...	38	THE GOSSIPERS	12
WHERE EYES SHOULD BE, AND NOSTRILS FULL OF TOADS.	51	OUT OF THE PIT	23
AND BOYS ARE FULL AND FOREIGN IN THE POUCH.	93	BOYS OF SUMMER	51
WITH MY RED VEINS FULL OF MONEY, ...	143	24 YEARS	7
ALL LOVE BUT FOR THE FULL ASSEMBLAGE IN FLOWER	148	UNLUCKILY FOR	40
COLD NANSEN'S BEAK ON A BOAT FULL OF GONGS, ...	152	BELOW A TIME	40
TOO FULL TO BOW TO THE DIM	155	RETURN	46
THE MOTHER DUG, AND ITS ARMS FULL OF FIRES.	173	FIRE RAID	8
BEYOND THE BORDER AND UNDER THE LARK FULL CLOUD.	177	POEM IN OCT	37
SUN THE FATHER HIS QUIVER FULL OF THE INFANTS OF PURE FIRE, ...	186	HOLY SPRING	19
AND THE OTHER FULL OF TEARS THAT SHE WILL BE DEAD,	193	CONVERS PRAYER	5
THEIR BREASTS FULL OF HONEY, UNDER THEIR GANDER KING	205	GIANT'S THIGH	38
BY FULL TILT RIVER AND SWITCHBACK SEA	208	POEM ON B'DAY	2
FULLNESS			
OUT OF THE FULLNESS OF ANOTHER'S HEART	23	THE ONLY DEAD	21
FUMED			
THE MOTHER'S CRY HAS FUMED ABOUT THE WINDS;	64	WOMAN SPEAKS	53
FUMED LIKE A TREE, AND TOSSED A BURNING BIRD;	133	I MAKE THIS IN	56
FUMING			
WITH FUMING BOWS AND RAM OF ICE, ...	163	LONG-LEGGED	42
FUN			
THAT SIN-EMBRACING DRIPPER OF FUN	156	RETURN	88
FUNERAL			
CRYSTAL OR FUNERAL, GOT NO HOPE	28	NO WINGS	5
OF EVIL ORACLES AND FUNERAL ILLS;	57	GREEK PLAY	31
OR THE FUNERAL OF THE SUN;	58	HERE IN SPRING	11
THE TRAY OF KNIVES, THE ANTISEPTIC FUNERAL, ...	110	I, IN IMAGE	54
AFTER THE FUNERAL	136	AFTER FUNERAL	T
AFTER THE FUNERAL, MULE PRAISES, BRAYS, ...	136	AFTER FUNERAL	1
AND THE FUNERAL GRAINS OF THE SLAUGHTERED FLOOR.	172	DAWN RAID	5
FUNNEL			
FOR WE MUST WHISPER DOWN THE FUNNEL	17	IN OBLIVION	8
THOUGH WE CRY DOWN THE FUNNEL, ...	17	IN OBLIVION	16
FUNNELS			
FUNNELS AND MASTS WENT BY IN A WHIRL.	162	LONG-LEGGED	17
GOOD-BYE TO CHIMNEYS AND FUNNELS, ...	162	LONG-LEGGED	25
FURIED			
FURIED BY HIS STREAM	181	VISION, PRAYER	39
FURIES			
STILL A WORLD OF FURIES	60	FAIRY TALES	24
THE GENTLEMAN LAY GRAVEWARD WITH HIS FURIES;	116	ALTARWISE	2
WEDS MY LONG GENTLEMAN TO DUSTS AND FURIES;	120	ALTARWISE	122
FURIOUS			
WHO SHOULD BE FURIOUS, ...	134	HOW MY ANIMAL	6
THE FURIOUS OX-KILLING HOUSE OF LOVE.	168	LONG-LEGGED	200

	PAGE	TITLE	LINE
FURIOUS (CONTINUED)			
WHEN YOUR FURIOUS MOTION	232	FURIOUS MOTION	T
WHEN YOUR FURIOUS MOTION IS STEADIED,	232	FURIOUS MOTION	1
FURLED			
FURLED ON THE FISHES' HOUSE AND HELL,	129	MY NEOPHYTE	17
FURNACE-NOSTRILLED			
A FURNACE-NOSTRILLED COLUMN-MEMBERED	158	INTO HER HEAD	28
FURNISH			
I FURNISH WITH THE MEAT OF A FABLE;	145	PLEASURE-BIRD	21
FURRED			
THE DINGLE FURRED DEER DEAD!	4	PROLOGUE	56
THE SCURRYING, FURRED SMALL FRIARS SQUEAL, IN THE DOWSE	204	GIANT'S THIGH	31
FURTHER			
CAN EVER FURTHER,	24	LITTLE PROBLEM	21
WITH ANY FURTHER	192	REFUSAL MOURN	17
THEY ARE FURTHER AND MORE DELICATE	226	THE ELM	3
SEEKING NO FURTHER THAN YOUR PETALS THAT STILL SLEPT.	227	SPRING-SPIRIT	8
FURY			
OF CHEMIC BLOOD, WARNED OF THE COMING FURY.	99	OCTOBER WIND	31
TO CLASP MY FURY ON GROUND	135	HOW MY ANIMAL	30
IN THE FIRST FURY OF HIS STREAM	181	VISION, PRAYER	59
FUSE			
THE FORCE THAT THROUGH THE GREEN FUSE DRIVES THE FLOWER	77	THE FORCE THAT	T
THE FORCE THAT THROUGH THE GREEN FUSE DRIVES THE FLOWER	77	THE FORCE THAT	1
WHEN HIS VIPERISH FUSE HANGS LOOPED WITH FLAMES UNDER THE BRAND	202	SIR JOHNS HILL	28
FUSES			
MY FUSES TIMED TO CHARGE HIS HEART,	97	TWILIGHT LOCKS	13
FUSION			
THE CANCER'S FUSION, OR THE SUMMER FEATHER	100	RUNNING GRAVE	32
FLOWER, FLOWER THE PEOPLE'S FUSION,	107	ALL ALL AND	31
I, IN MY FUSION OF ROSE AND MALE MOTION,	109	I, IN IMAGE	17
FUTILITY			
THESE THE IMAGININGS, TENDER AND BLOSSOMED WITH FUTILITY,	223	IDYLL UNFORGET	11
G.			
NO GENIUS IN DAVID G.,	83	LETTER TO AUNT	8
A GENIUS LIKE DAVID G.	85	LETTER TO AUNT	62
GAB			
THE LOVELY GIFT OF THE GAB BANGS BACK ON A BLIND SHAFT.	140	NO WORK WORDS	6
GABBING			
IN YOUR BEAKS, ON THE GABBING CAPES!	4	PROLOGUE	66
GABLES			
EYES IN THE GABLES SEE	62	EARS IN TURRET	3
GABRIEL			
AND FROM THE WINDY WEST CAME TWO-GUNNED GABRIEL,	118	ALTARWISE	57
GABRIEL AND RADIANT SHRUBBERY AS THE MORNING GROWS JOYFUL	186	HOLY SPRING	15
GAG			
GAG OF A DUMBSTRUCK TREE TO BLOCK FROM BARE ENEMIES	133	MAKE ME A MASK	4
GAIETY			
BY US IN SIN OR US IN GAIETY.	17	IN OBLIVION	26
OH GAIETY!	18	NATURAL DAY	34
OH GAIETY!	18	NATURAL DAY	35
AND THE TRIUMPH OF HER PITILESS GAIETY	235	WOMAN TAPESTRY	19
INVOLVE ME IN A GAIETY,	236	WOMAN TAPESTRY	69

	PAGE	TITLE	LINE
GAIN			
SUCH ENERGY MAY GAIN	10	COOL, OH NO	25
IN SUN AND RAIN WORKING FOR GOOD AND GAIN, ...	45	PLOUGHMAN GONE	3
GAINSAY			
BETTER NOR US CAN'T GAINSAY WALKING, ...	28	NO WINGS	9
GALACTIC			
WHEN THE GALACTIC SEA WAS SUCKED	97	TWILIGHT LOCKS	7
GALE			
AND GALE I TACKLE, THE WHOLE WORLD THEN, ...	211	POEM ON B'DAY	96
GALED			
PETTICOATS GALED HIGH, OR SHY WITH THE ROUGH RIDING			
BOYS, ...	204	GIANT'S THIGH	18
GALES			
WHERE NO COLD IS, THE SKINNING GALES UNPIN	82	LIGHT BREAKS	22
WITH SALTY COLTS AND GALES IN THEIR LIMBS	168	LONG-LEGGED	186
GALILEE'S			
AND THE SHIPYARDS OF GALILEE'S FOOTPRINTS HIDE A			
NAVY OF DOVES.	170	MARRIAGE VIRG	7
GALLANTLY			
AND GALLANTLY (WATER, YOU'RE STRONG--	237	PILLAR BREAKS	4
GALLERIES			
TOPPLING AND BURNING IN THE MUDDLE OF TOWERS AND			
GALLERIES	145	PLEASURE-BIRD	18
MOUNTAINS AND GALLERIES BENEATH	164	LONG-LEGGED	86
MOUNTAINS AND GALLERIES TO THE CREST!	166	LONG-LEGGED	132
GALLIC			
ON HOW THE GALLIC LETTER BENDS;	84	LETTER TO AUNT	51
GALLOP			
GALLOP THROUGH THE ARCHED, GREEN FARMS, ...	168	LONG-LEGGED	188
TROT AND GALLOP WITH GULLS UPON THEM	168	LONG-LEGGED	189
GALLOPS			
NO FROSTY GALLOPS THROUGH THE WINTER PARK.	41	YOUNG ARE OLD	16
GALLOW			
OF GALLOW CROSSES ON THE LIVER	68	BEFORE KNOCKED	23
TIME'S NERVE IN VINEGAR, THE GALLOW GRAVE	120	ALTARWISE	100
GALLOWS			
I WOULD NOT FEAR THE GALLOWS NOR THE AXE	95	RUB OF LOVE	13
AND GALLOWS, UP THE RAYS OF HIS EYES THE SMALL BIRDS			
OF THE BAY	201	SIR JOHNS HILL	4
GAMBO			
OR, BUTTER FAT GOOSEGIRLS, BOUNCED IN A GAMBO BED,	204	GIANT'S THIGH	37
GAME			
THIS FIRST AND STEEPLED SEASON, TO THE SUMMER'S GAME.	122	HOLD HARD	12
'ALL GAME PHRASES FIT YOUR RING OF A COCKFIGHT: ...	145	IF HEAD HURT	6
GANDER			
THEIR BREASTS FULL OF HONEY, UNDER THEIR GANDER KING	205	GIANT'S THIGH	38
GANDERS			
IN A SPINNEY OF RINGED BOYS AND GANDERS, SPIKE AND			
BURN, ...	198	COUNTRY SLEEP	14
GANGS			
'BUT THIS WE TREAD BEARS THE ANGELIC GANGS, ...	102	FELLOWED SLEEP	13
GANG'S			
HALF OF THE OLD GANG'S SHOT, ...	59	FAIRY TALES	8
GARAGES			
DIRTIER WITH GARAGES AND CHEAP TEA SIGNS.	37	WINDMILLS TURN	15
ON GARAGES AND CLINICS IN THE TOWN.	52	OUT OF THE PIT	48
GARB			
I SEE THE WANTING NUN SAINT CARVED IN A GARB	148	UNLUCKILY FOR	34
GARDEN			
THE LIVING VESSELS OF THE GARDEN	13	RAIN CUTS	13

	PAGE	TITLE	LINE
GARDEN (CONTINUED)			
OF MARBLE BATHERS TOEING THE GARDEN PONDS,	33	IN GARDENS	2
OVER AND ROUND THE ORDERED GARDEN HUMMED,	34	IN GARDENS	17
WE SHALL PLAY CHOPIN IN OUR SUMMER GARDEN,	40	YOUNG ARE OLD	12
HE, TOO, HAS KNOWN THE AGONY IN THE GARDEN,	52	OUT OF THE PIT	54
GREEK PLAY IN A GARDEN	56	GREEK PLAY	T
AMONG THE GARDEN TREES A PIGEON CALLS,	57	GREEK PLAY	29
NO LONGER FEAR THE WALKER IN THE GARDEN,	59	FAIRY TALES	11
FROM GARDEN CANS, OR FREE THE FLOODS?	65	GODS THUMP	7
DRIP ON MY DEAD HOUSE GARDEN.	105	WORLD PYRAMID	45
LIKE EXODUS A CHAPTER FROM THE GARDEN,	115	A GRIEF AGO	18
ON THUNDEROUS PAVEMENTS IN THE GARDEN TIME;	117	ALTARWISE	34
THE CENTRAL PLAINS OF ASIA IN HIS GARDEN,	121	INCARNATE DEVL	2
THE WISEMEN TELL ME THAT THE GARDEN GODS	121	INCARNATE DEVL	9
HAS SOWN A FLYING GARDEN ROUND THAT SEA-GHOST?	121	ALTARWISE	136
GREEN AS BEGINNING, LET THE GARDEN DIVING	121	ALTARWISE	137
MEASURES HIS OWN LENGTH ON THE GARDEN WALL	124	TODAY, INSECT	12
NOR WALK IN THE COOL OF YOUR MORTAL GARDEN	148	UNLUCKILY FOR	48
A GARDEN HOLDING TO HER HAND	167	LONG-LEGGED	167
FROM THE OPENING OF THE GARDEN LOCK	171	THE HUNCHBACK	4
OF THE GARDEN OF EDEN.	174	FIRE RAID	46
OF THE GARDEN OF WILDERNESS.	175	FIRE RAID	60
AND THE BLOOD DROP'S GARDEN	184	VISION, PRAYER	139
AND IN HER GARDEN GROW THE FLEUR DE LYS,	222	IN DREAMS	1
THAT IN HER GARDEN, RATHER THAN THE DAYS,	223	IN DREAMS	9
HER GARDEN BLOOMS WITH IRIS, AND IT SEEMS	223	IN DREAMS	13
AND MAKE MY GARDEN GLAD AND GAY.	227	TRIOLET	3
GARDEN-CLOSE			
FOR HER WHO WALKS WITHIN HER GARDEN-CLOSE.	223	IN DREAMS	7
GARDENS			
WALKING IN GARDENS	33	IN GARDENS	T
WALKING IN GARDENS BY THE SIDES	33	IN GARDENS	1
AND COMB THE COUNTY GARDENS FOR A WREATH.	93	BOYS OF SUMMER	42
OVER THE GARDENS OF THE FLOOR	164	LONG-LEGGED	74
BUT ALL THE GARDENS	177	POEM IN OCT	35
GARDEN-WALKS			
ALONG THE BORDERS OF THE GARDEN-WALKS.	223	IN DREAMS	12
GARLAND			
WITH STONES OF ODYSSEY FOR ASH AND GARLAND	120	ALTARWISE	125
GARMENTS			
MY MAKER'S FLESH THAT GARMENTS MY CLAYFELLOWS.	76	LASHED RINGS	3
GARRISON			
WITH A STAR-FLANKED GARRISON,	126	SEED-AT-ZERO	46
WITH A SAND-BAGGED GARRISON,	127	SEED-AT-ZERO	53
GARRISONED			
THE SEXTON SENTINEL, GARRISONED UNDER THISTLES,	110	I, IN IMAGE	57
GAS			
BEFORE THE GAS FADES	38	GAS FADES	T
BEFORE THE GAS FADES WITH A HARSH LAST BUBBLE,	38	GAS FADES	1
AND LOVERS TURNING ON THE GAS,	41	YOUNG ARE OLD	30
WHO STEPS ON THE GAS;	58	TO ARCHITECTS	9
DEATH ON THE MOUTH THAT ATE THE GAS.	103	I DREAMED MY	16
LINKED IN ONE GAS BRACKET	137	O CHATTERTON	2
GASKETTED			
GASKETTED AND SIRENSUITED	154	RETURN	21
GATES			
WHEN HEAVEN--OPEN WIDE THE GATES--HAS TAKEN FLIGHT,	34	THIRST PARCHES	4
LET CHILDREN KNOW, AND OLD MEN AT THEIR GATES,	36	LET BE KNOWN	3
AND THE GATES	177	POEM IN OCT	19

	PAGE	TITLE	LINE
GATES (CONTINUED)			
THROW WIDE TO THE WIND THE GATES OF THE WANDERING			
BOAT	194	SLEEP BECALMED	10
GATHER			
MIGHT CROSS ITS PLANETS, THE BELL WEEP, NIGHT GATHER			
HER EYES, ...	200	COUNTRY SLEEP	92
GATHERED			
IS GATHERED AND SPILT	192	SIDE OF TRUTH	10
THE SKY GATHERED AGAIN	196	FERN HILL	31
GATHERS			
LOVE DRIPS AND GATHERS, BUT THE FALLEN BLOOD	77	THE FORCE THAT	17
GAUZE			
BLEW OUT THE BLOOD GAUZE THROUGH THE WOUND OF MANWAX.	119	ALTARWISE	84
GAVE			
WHO GAVE ME LIFE AND THEN THE GRAVE, ...	26	PERSONAL EPIT	11
ONE BREAST GAVE SUCK THE FEVER'S ISSUE;	79	LOVE'S FEVER	43
A MILLION MINDS GAVE SUCK TO SUCH A BUD	79	LOVE'S FEVER	46
YOU ARE ALL THESE, SAID SHE WHO GAVE ME THE LONG			
SUCK, ...	112	NOT FATHER ME	17
WHO GAVE THESE SEAS THEIR COLOUR IN A SHAPE, ...	123	FOSTER LIGHT	25
IN FOUNTAINS OF ORIGIN GAVE UP THEIR LOVE, ...	157	INTO HER HEAD	9
AND I GAVE MY SOUL A BLIND, SLASHED EYE, ...	207	LAMENT	45
GAY			
A GAY PARABOLA	14	RAIN CUTS	23
IN A GAY MOMENT'S FALSITY--	21	BEWILDERED WAY	8
THAT'S GRAVE AND GAY AS GRAVE AND SEA	54	WE BY SEASAND	7
OF THE GRAVE, GAY, SEASIDE LAND.	54	WE BY SEASAND	17
WERE ONCE SUCH A CREATURE, SO GAY AND FRANK	147	TO OTHERS	14
AND HONOURED AMONG FOXES AND PHEASANTS BY THE GAY			
HOUSE	196	FERN HILL	37
BE SHIELDED BY CHANT AND FLOWER AND GAY MAY YOU ...	198	COUNTRY SLEEP	42
CLUNG TO THE PITCHING CLOUDS, OR GAY WITH ANY ONE	204	GIANT'S THIGH	15
BLIND EYES COULD BLAZE LIKE METEORS AND BE GAY, ...	208	NOT GO GENTLE	14
AND MAKE MY GARDEN GLAD AND GAY.	227	TRIOLET	3
GEAR			
LOVE IN HER GEAR IS SLOWLY THROUGH THE HOUSE, ...	99	RUNNING GRAVE	3
IN BOTTOM GEAR THROUGH NIGHT-GEARED MAN.	103	I DREAMED MY	12
GEESE			
GEESE NEARLY IN HEAVEN, BOYS	3	PROLOGUE	15
AND WISHBONES OF WILD GEESE, ...	210	POEM ON B'DAY	59
GENDER			
THE SIZE OF GENESIS? THE SHORT SPARK'S GENDER?	118	ALTARWISE	44
GENDER'S			
WEANS ON AN ARTERY THE GENDER'S STRIP;	117	ALTARWISE	18
GENEROUS			
PUTS IN HIS PENNY, GENEROUS AT LAST.	179	NEW QUAY	32
GENESIS			
I DREAMED MY GENESIS	102	I DREAMED MY	T
I DREAMED MY GENESIS IN SWEAT OF SLEEP, BREAKING	102	I DREAMED MY	1
I DREAMED MY GENESIS AND DIED AGAIN, SHRAPNEL	103	I DREAMED MY	13
I DREAMED MY GENESIS IN SWEAT OF DEATH, FALLEN	103	I DREAMED MY	25
THE SIZE OF GENESIS? THE SHORT SPARK'S GENDER?	118	ALTARWISE	44
GENESIS IN THE ROOT, THE SCARECROW WORD, ...	119	ALTARWISE	88
MURDER OF EDEN AND GREEN GENESIS.	124	TODAY, INSECT	8
IN YOUR EVERY INCH AND GLANCE IS THE GLOBE OF			
GENESIS SPUN, ...	149	UNLUCKILY FOR	55
GENESIS'			
THE SUNDERING ULTIMATE KINGDOM OF GENESIS' THUNDER.	175	FIRE RAID	77
GENETIC			
OUTDO YOUR PRUDE'S GENETIC FACULTY	20	THE NEOPHYTE	13

	PAGE	TITLE	LINE
GENITALS			
AS BELLY, GENITALS, AND ----, ...	84	LETTER TO AUNT	45
GENIUS			
ONLY AS WRONG; BUT SHAN'T THE GENIUS FAIL, ...	28	NO WINGS	7
NO GENIUS IN DAVID G., ...	83	LETTER TO AUNT	8
A GENIUS LIKE DAVID G.	85	LETTER TO AUNT	62
GENTLE			
WITH PRIEST AND PHARAOH BED MY GENTLE WOUND, ...	120	ALTARWISE	123
BULLIES INTO ROUGH SEAS YOU SO GENTLE	142	SAINT TO FALL	49
THE GENTLE SEASLIDES OF SAYING I MUST UNDO	144	COLOUR OF SAY	5
GENTLE IN THEIR CLOGS OVER THE FALLEN SKY, ...	187	WINTER'S TALE	24
DO NOT GO GENTLE INTO THAT GOOD NIGHT	207	NOT GO GENTLE	T
DO NOT GO GENTLE INTO THAT GOOD NIGHT, ...	207	NOT GO GENTLE	1
DO NOT GO GENTLE INTO THAT GOOD NIGHT.	208	NOT GO GENTLE	6
DO NOT GO GENTLE INTO THAT GOOD NIGHT.	208	NOT GO GENTLE	12
DO NOT GO GENTLE INTO THAT GOOD NIGHT.	208	NOT GO GENTLE	18
(HIS GENTLE KIND);	215	COUNTRY HEAVEN	22
GENTLEMAN			
WHO PLAY THE PROPER GENTLEMAN AND LADY.	113	NOT FATHER ME	28
THE GENTLEMAN LAY GRAVEWARD WITH HIS FURIES;	116	ALTARWISE	2
SO FAST I MOVE DEFYING TIME, THE QUIET GENTLEMAN	116	LANTERNS SHINE	14
THEN, PENNY-EYED, THAT GENTLEMAN OF WOUNDS, ...	117	ALTARWISE	7
I AM THE LONG WORLD'S GENTLEMAN, HE SAID, ...	117	ALTARWISE	13
SAID THE FAKE GENTLEMAN IN SUIT OF SPADES, ...	118	ALTARWISE	60
WEDS MY LONG GENTLEMAN TO DUSTS AND FURIES;	120	ALTARWISE	122
GENTLEMEN			
THE SUNNY GENTLEMEN, THE WELSHING RICH, ...	90	EUNUCH DREAMS	25
GENTLY			
GENTLY THEY SIGH TO MY BEHIND	143	THE MOLLS	9
WITH MY FISHTAIL HANDS AND GENTLY	154	RETURN	5
TO THAT STRANGE COLOUR, SIGHING GENTLY, GRIEVES ...	223	IN DREAMS	6
GENTRY			
WHICH SIXTH OF WIND BLEW OUT THE BURNING GENTRY?	118	ALTARWISE	47
GEOFFREY			
TO GEOFFREY GRIGSON WITH MY LUFF, ...	85	LETTER TO AUNT	64
GERANIUM			
HASTENS THE TIME OF THE GERANIUM TO BREATHE;	47	POET: 1935	37
GERMY			
AND EVERY LOVELY WOMAN'S GERMY;	84	LETTER TO AUNT	49
GESTURE			
CLIPS SHORT THE GESTURE OF BREATH.	135	HOW MY ANIMAL	39
ARGUMENT OF THE HEWN VOICE, GESTURE AND PSALM, ...	137	AFTER FUNERAL	37
ONE GESTURE OF THE HEART OR HEAD, ...	192	SIDE OF TRUTH	9
GESTURES			
DRAMATIC GESTURES IN THE AIR.	34	IN GARDENS	13
'NOW TO AWAKE HUSKED OF GESTURES AND MY JOY LIKE A			
CAVE	146	IF HEAD HURT	21
WITH DRY, MECHANICAL GESTURES, ...	231	YOUR VOICE	3
AND THE GESTURES OF UNAGEING LOVE.	235	WOMAN TAPESTRY	26
THE GESTURES OF MY LOVE	236	WOMAN TAPESTRY	68
AND THE GESTURES OF UNAGEING LOVE.	237	WOMAN TAPESTRY	81
GHETTO			
FROM HARLEM, BEDLAM, BABEL, AND THE GHETTO, ...	41	YOUNG ARE OLD	40
GHOST			
HAVE CLEANEST HANDS, AND, AS THE HEARTLESS GHOST	40	WAS THERE TIME	8
AMONG ALL LIVING MEN IS A SAD GHOST.	47	POET: 1935	24
AND CATCH A TURNIP GHOST IN EVERY CRANNY.	48	LIGHT, I KNOW	5
I, BORN OF FLESH AND GHOST, WAS NEITHER	69	BEFORE KNOCKED	37
A GHOST NOR MAN, BUT MORTAL GHOST.	69	BEFORE KNOCKED	38
A GHOST NOR MAN, BUT MORTAL GHOST.	69	BEFORE KNOCKED	38

	PAGE	TITLE	LINE
GHOST (CONTINUED)			
UNPACKS THE HEAD THAT, LIKE A SLEEPY GHOST, ...	75	MY HERO BARES	3
FROM THE FIRST SECRET OF THE HEART, THE WARNING			
GHOST, ...	78	LOVE'S FEVER	12
HERE SLIPS THE GHOST WHO MADE OF MY PALE BED	81	HERE LIE BEAST	11
TURNS GHOST TO GHOST; EACH MOTHERED CHILD	88	A PROCESS IN	20
TURNS GHOST TO GHOST; EACH MOTHERED CHILD	88	A PROCESS IN	20
SPUN TO MY SCREWS, YOUR DRY GHOST BLOWS, ...	90	WHERE ONCE THE	2
FADED MY ELBOW GHOST, THE MOTHERS-EYED, ...	102	FELLOWED SLEEP	16
WHERE STILL THEY SLEEP UNKNOWING OF THEIR GHOST.	102	FELLOWED SLEEP	20
AN OLD, MAD MAN STILL CLIMBING IN HIS GHOST, ...	102	FELLOWED SLEEP	29
MY FATHERS' GHOST IS CLIMBING IN THE RAIN.	102	FELLOWED SLEEP	30
REROBING OF THE NAKED GHOST. MANHOOD	103	I DREAMED MY	23
AND THE UNPLANTED GHOST.	104	WORLD PYRAMID	12
THE GHOST IS DUMB THAT STAMMERED IN THE STRAW, ...	104	WORLD PYRAMID	28
THE GHOST THAT HATCHED HIS HAVOC AS HE FLEW	104	WORLD PYRAMID	29
GHOST WITH HER GHOST, CONTAGIOUS MAN	107	ALL ALL AND	26
GHOST WITH HER GHOST, CONTAGIOUS MAN	107	ALL ALL AND	26
LAYING MY GHOST IN METAL, ...	108	I, IN IMAGE	3
MY HALF GHOST IN ARMOUR HOLD HARD IN DEATH'S			
CORRIDOR, ...	108	I, IN IMAGE	5
BEGINNING WITH DOOM IN THE GHOST, AND THE SPRINGING			
MARVELS, ...	109	I, IN IMAGE	13
BE BY YOUR ONE GHOST PIERCED, HIS POINTED FERRULE,	111	I, IN IMAGE	79
MY GHOST IN HIS METAL NEPTUNE	112	I, IN IMAGE	105
THE RINGED-SEA GHOST, RISE GRIMLY FROM THE WRACK.	113	NOT FATHER ME	24
DEATH HAIRY-HEELED, AND THE TAPPED GHOST IN WOOD,	128	NOW, SAY NAY	33
GRIEF WITH DISHEVELLED HANDS TEAR OUT THE ALTAR GHOST	130	SINNERS' BELL	5
THE CRUMPLED PACKS FLED PAST THIS GHOST IN BLOOM,	133	I MAKE THIS IN	58
I, THE FIRST NAMED, AM THE GHOST OF THIS SIR AND			
CHRISTIAN FRIEND	141	I, FIRST NAMED	1
I AM THE GHOST IN THIS HOUSE THAT IS FILLED WITH THE			
TONGUE AND EYES	141	I, FIRST NAMED	3
OF A LACK-A-HEAD GHOST I FEAR TO THE ANONYMOUS END.	141	I, FIRST NAMED	4
BEFORE I RUSH IN A CROUCH THE GHOST WITH A HAMMER,			
AIR, ...	145	IF HEAD HURT	9
BIRDMAN OR TOLD GHOST I HUNG.	152	BELOW A TIME	31
WITH NO MORE DESIRE THAN A GHOST.	166	LONG-LEGGED	124
OF THE GOLDEN GHOST WHO RINGED WITH HIS STREAMS HER			
MERCURY BONE, ...	170	MARRIAGE VIRG	11
OVER THE GHOST AND THE DROPPED SON	180	VISION, PRAYER	8
THE GHOST	183	VISION, PRAYER	109
IN THE RAIN TELLING ITS BEADS, AND THE GRAVEST GHOST	198	COUNTRY SLEEP	31
OF THE NIGHTINGALE'S DIN AND TALE! THE UPGIVEN GHOST	200	COUNTRY SLEEP	74
WITH BLESSED, UNBORN GOD AND HIS GHOST, ...	210	POEM ON B'DAY	60
GHOSTLY			
AND GHOSTLY ECHOES ON PAPER, ...	44	LONGED TO MOVE	9
AND GHOSTLY COMETS OVER THE RAISED FISTS.	56	WHY EAST WIND	26
AND THERE WE WEPT, I AND THE GHOSTLY OTHER, ...	101	FELLOWED SLEEP	8
GHOSTS			
THAT CHASES THE GHOSTS OF THE TREES	35	LIFT UP FACE	4
AND THE GHOSTS OF THE BRAIN, ...	35	LIFT UP FACE	5
PRESS THE OLD LIES AND THE OLD GHOSTS.	38	THE GOSSIPERS	18
FROM THERE ARE GHOSTS IN THE AIR	43	LONGED TO MOVE	8
AND DUSK IS CROWDED WITH THE CHILDREN'S GHOSTS, ...	56	WHY EAST WIND	14
BUT STILL GHOSTS MADDEN, ...	59	FAIRY TALES	14
AND, BROKEN GHOSTS WITH GLOW-WORMS IN THEIR HEADS,	82	LIGHT BREAKS	4
MOVE LIKE TWO GHOSTS BEFORE THE EYE.	88	A PROCESS IN	18
TWO ONE-DIMENSIONED GHOSTS, LOVE ON A REEL, ...	89	EUNUCH DREAMS	12
THAT TOWN OF GHOSTS, THE TRODDEN WOMB	125	SEED-AT-ZERO	2

		PAGE	TITLE	LINE
GHOSTS (CONTINUED)				
THAT TOWN OF GHOSTS, THE MANWAGED WOMB	....	125	SEED-AT-ZERO	9
GIANT				
WITH THE WILD BREAST AND BLESSED AND GIANT SKULL		136	AFTER FUNERAL	28
AND GUILTS, GREAT CROTCH AND GIANT	....	148	UNLUCKILY FOR	36
NOW BREAK A GIANT TEAR FOR THE LITTLE KNOWN FALL,		153	WAS A SAVIOUR	32
GIANTS				
THE NURSE OF GIANTS BY THE CUT SEA BASIN,	....	113	SERVANT SUN	10
GIANT'S				
IN THE WHITE GIANT'S THIGH	....	203	GIANT'S THIGH	T
AND THERE THIS NIGHT I WALK IN THE WHITE GIANT'S				
THIGH	....	203	GIANT'S THIGH	3
GIBED				
GIBED THE COITUS OF THE STARS. NO GOD	....	53	OUT OF THE PIT	78
GIDDILY				
THE HARING SNAIL GO GIDDILY ROUND THE FLOWER,	.....	109	I, IN IMAGE	41
GIDDY				
ON GIDDY NIGHTS WHEN SLAP ON THE MOON'S MASK	......	137	O CHATTERTON	12
ON GIDDY NIGHTS I SLAP A FEW DRUNK CURVES	....	138	O CHATTERTON	24
GIFT				
THE LOVELY GIFT OF THE GAB BANGS BACK ON A BLIND				
SHAFT.	....	140	NO WORK WORDS	6
GIGANTIC				
WITH HEART UNLOCKED UPON THE GIGANTIC EARTH.	......	46	POET: 1935	12
NOW CLASP ME TO THEIR GRAINS IN THE GIGANTIC GLADE,		204	GIANT'S THIGH	19
GILDERS				
GILDERS OF STREETS, THE RABBLE HAND	....	70	SECRET WIND	10
GILLED				
CAST HIGH, STUNNED ON GILLED STONE; SLY SCISSORS				
GROUND IN FROST	....	135	HOW MY ANIMAL	35
GIPSY				
SO CROSS HER HAND WITH THEIR GRAVE GIPSY EYES,	....	115	A GRIEF AGO	39
GIRDERED				
THROUGH VISION AND THE GIRDERED NERVE,	....	102	I DREAMED MY	4
GIRDERS				
RIDING ON GIRDERS OF THE AIR, LOOKS DOWN	....	52	OUT OF THE PIT	47
GIRDLE				
WHEREON THE HOODED HAIR CASTS DOWN ITS GIRDLE,	....	76	LASHED RINGS	5
GIRL				
HERE UNDER THE EARTH WITH GIRL AND THIEF,	....	26	PERSONAL EPIT	5
A GIRL WHOSE SINGLE BED HELD TWO	....	38	THE GOSSIPERS	9
NO BREASTED GIRL, NO MAN WHO, YOUNG	....	55	NO MAN BELIEVE	10
A MERRY GIRL TOOK ME FOR MAN,	....	61	MEAT ON BONES	22
SEASON AND SUNSHINE, GRACE AND GIRL,	....	61	MEAT ON BONES	31
A ROOKING GIRL WHO STOLE ME FOR HER SIDE,	....	94	RUB OF LOVE	2
DAFT WITH THE DRUG THAT'S SMOKING IN A GIRL	....	95	RUB OF LOVE	30
NOT GIRL FOR BIRD (GOURD BEING MAN) BREAKS ROOT.		159	TO LEDA	4
A GIRL ALIVE WITH HIS HOOKS THROUGH HER LIPS;	.....	162	LONG-LEGGED	22
THROWN TO THE SEA IN THE SHELL OF A GIRL	....	165	LONG-LEGGED	92
HIS FATHERS CLING TO THE HAND OF THE GIRL	....	167	LONG-LEGGED	147
A GIRL MAD AS BIRDS	....	169	LOVE IN ASYLUM	3
NEVER AND NEVER, MY GIRL RIDING FAR AND NEAR	......	197	COUNTRY SLEEP	1
MY GIRL RANGING THE NIGHT IN THE ROSE AND SHIRE	...	197	COUNTRY SLEEP	9
NEVER, MY GIRL, UNTIL TOLLED TO SLEEP BY THE STERN		198	COUNTRY SLEEP	21
LIKE THE BODY OF A GIRL.	....	236	WOMAN TAPESTRY	55
GIRL-CIRCLED				
A THUNDERING BULLRING OF YOUR SILENT AND				
GIRL-CIRCLED ISLAND.	....	142	SAINT TO FALL	51
GIRL-LIPPED				
MALE SHAPES, GIRL-LIPPED, BUT CLAD LIKE BOYS:	.....	143	THE MOLLS	2

		PAGE	TITLE	LINE
GIRLS				
WE SPOKE OF DRINK AND GIRLS, FOR HOURS	....	33	IN GARDENS	4
AND GIRLS WITH FLOWERED HATS	....	37	WINDMILLS TURN	11
POLE-SITTING GIRLS DESCENDED FOR A MEAL,	....	51	OUT OF THE PIT	29
FEED IN THE ARMPITS OF DROWNED GIRLS, I'VE SWUM	...	52	OUT OF THE PIT	69
LOVE ME, NOT AS THE GIRLS OF HEAVEN	....	76	SONG: LOVE ME	5
THE SHADES OF GIRLS, ALL FLAVOURED FROM THEIR				
SHROUDS,	....	89	EUNUCH DREAMS	7
OF FROZEN LOVES THEY FETCH THEIR GIRLS,	....	91	BOYS OF SUMMER	5
THAT CHALK THE WALLS WITH GREEN GIRLS AND THEIR MEN.		95	RUB OF LOVE	16
GIRLS TAKE TO BROOMSTICKS WHEN THE THIEF OF NIGHT		96	TWELVE	3
AND A BLACK AND WHITE PATCH OF GIRLS GREW PLAYING;		144	COLOUR OF SAY	4
UNCLAIMED DEAD, GIRLS FROM GOOD HOMES	....	154	RETURN	15
BEDSITTING GIRLS ON THE BEAT	....	155	RETURN	58
I SKIPPED IN A BLUSH AS THE BIG GIRLS ROLLED	....	206	LAMENT	6
GIVE				
FOR ALL THERE IS TO GIVE I OFFER:	....	32	OUT OF SIGHS	28
OR (CHANGE THE KEY!) GIVE VENT TO UTTERANCES	......	33	HELD-OUT HAND	8
THEIR HANDS OUTSTRETCHED, TO GIVE AND GIVE?	....	36	MIDNIGHT ROAD	8
THEIR HANDS OUTSTRETCHED, TO GIVE AND GIVE?	....	36	MIDNIGHT ROAD	8
TWISTING ON RACKS WHEN SINEWS GIVE WAY,	....	49	NO DOMINION	13
FLAVOURED OF CELLULOID GIVE LOVE THE LIE.	....	89	EUNUCH DREAMS	20
(GIVE, SUMMER, OVER), THE CEMENTED SKIN,	....	101	RUNNING GRAVE	44
GIVE OVER, LOVERS, LOCKING, AND THE SEAWAX STRUGGLE,		111	I, IN IMAGE	89
TO TAKE TO GIVE IS ALL, RETURN WHAT IS HUNGRILY GIVEN		140	NO WORK WORDS	4
GIVE US THE PLEASURE OF REGRET;	....	230	OUR SANCTITY	11
GIVEN				
UNTHINKING ACTIONS GIVEN CAUSES	....	38	THE GOSSIPERS	4
TO TAKE TO GIVE IS ALL, RETURN WHAT IS HUNGRILY GIVEN		140	NO WORK WORDS	4
GIVES				
AND FEEL THE PAIN IT GIVES,	....	13	SKY'S BRIGHT	29
AND THE WARMTH SHE GIVES,	....	23	THE ONLY DEAD	9
IT'S EASY TRACING WHAT EACH GIVES THE OTHER	....	24	LITTLE PROBLEM	11
BUT ALL THIS LAND GIVES OFF A CHARNEL STENCH,	.....	67	REALM OF FLESH	4
AND THE HEART GIVES UP ITS DEAD.	....	88	A PROCESS IN	24
GIVES UP ITS DEAD TO SUCH A WORKING SEA;	....	97	TWILIGHT LOCKS	27
GIZZARDS				
BY NAPE AND GIZZARDS;	....	60	FAIRY TALES	33
GLAD				
THE BEES ARE GLAD THE LIVELONG DAY,	....	227	TRIOLET	1
AND MAKE MY GARDEN GLAD AND GAY.	....	227	TRIOLET	3
THE BEES ARE GLAD THE LIVELONG DAY,	....	228	TRIOLET	4
THE BEES ARE GLAD THE LIVELONG DAY,	....	228	TRIOLET	7
GLADDEN				
YOUR BODY CANNOT GLADDEN ME,	....	228	NOT DESPAIR	9
GLADE				
NOW CLASP ME TO THEIR GRAINS IN THE GIGANTIC GLADE,		204	GIANT'S THIGH	19
GLADNESS				
IN THE VICTORY OF HER GLADNESS	....	235	WOMAN TAPESTRY	18
GLAMORGAN				
GOLDEN GLAMORGAN STRAIGHTENS, TO THE FALLING BIRDS.		123	HOLD HARD	23
GLAMORGAN'S				
UNDER THE LANK, FOURTH FOLLY ON GLAMORGAN'S HILL,		122	HOLD HARD	2
GLAMOUR				
GLAMOUR OF THE BLOODILY BOWED,	....	156	RETURN	86
GLANCE				
TURN INSIDE OUT, AND SEE AT GLANCE	....	25	BEAUTY TO DUST	7
INCH AND GLANCE THAT THE WOUND	....	148	UNLUCKILY FOR	22
IN YOUR EVERY INCH AND GLANCE IS THE GLOBE OF				
GENESIS SPUN,	....	149	UNLUCKILY FOR	55

	PAGE	TITLE	LINE
GLANCING			
GLANCING FROM THE YELLOW NUT, ...	20	ENCOMPASSED	9
GLAND			
WITHIN THE HALLOWED GLAND, BLOOD BLESSED THE HEART,	78	LOVE'S FEVER	18
GLANDED			
DUG OF THE SEA, THE GLANDED MORROW, ...	106	ALL ALL AND	8
GLARED			
GLARED THROUGH SHARK MASK AND NAVIGATING HEAD, ...	152	BELOW A TIME	39
GLASS			
MY FACE IS HAGGARD IN THE GLASS, ...	61	MEAT ON BONES	19
IN THE GLASS BED OF GRAPES WITH SNAIL AND FLOWER,	109	I, IN IMAGE	29
HEAR THEY THE SALT GLASS BREAKERS AND THE TONGUES OF			
BURIAL.	110	I, IN IMAGE	66
AND THE DUCK POND GLASS AND THE BLINDING BYRES ALONE	188	WINTER'S TALE	35
AND MY FINGERS HAVE TOUCHED THE GLASS OF THE WATERS,	224	IDYLL UNFORGET	30
GLASS TO MY HANDS ENDOWED WITH DOUBLE STRENGTH. ...	239	MAKES INTERVALS	19
GLASSES			
LEAVES IT AMONG THE CIGARETTE ENDS AND THE GLASSES.	30	NEARLY SUMMER	23
GLASSHOUSE			
HEDGEROW, LABORATORY, AND EVEN GLASSHOUSE, ...	18	NATURAL DAY	13
GLASSY			
THE SHADOWS FROM THE GLASSY SEA	15	FOR LEDA	11
A CLOUD AGAINST THE GLASSY SUN FLUTTERS HIS	179	NEW QUAY	5
GLAZED			
AND OVER THE GLAZED LAKES SKATED THE SHAPES OF FISHES	190	WINTER'S TALE	115
GLEN			
IN A HUTCH IN A COWPATCHED GLEN	156	RETURN	94
GLIDE			
THE TONGUES OF HEAVEN GOSSIP AS I GLIDE	105	WORLD PYRAMID	53
ON A SEIZING SKY; SMALL FISHES GLIDE	209	POEM ON B'DAY	22
LIGHT AND HIS TEARS GLIDE DOWN TOGETHER	215	COUNTRY HEAVEN	11
OUT OF HIS EYES I SAW THE LAST LIGHT GLIDE.	217	ELEGY	28
GLIDED			
ALONG HER INNOCENCE GLIDED	157	INTO HER HEAD	10
THE BOWS GLIDED DOWN, AND THE COAST	161	LONG-LEGGED	1
IN THE LONG AGO LAND THAT GLIDED THE DARK DOOR WIDE	189	WINTER'S TALE	67
IN THE FAR AGO LAND THE DOOR OF HIS DEATH GLIDED WIDE	190	WINTER'S TALE	105
AND THE WINGS GLIDED WIDE AND HE WAS HYMNED AND			
WEDDED, ...	191	WINTER'S TALE	123
GLIDES			
SHALL NOT BE LATCHED WHILE MAGIC GLIDES	91	WHERE ONCE THE	20
APPLE SEED GLIDES, ...	199	COUNTRY SLEEP	61
GLIDING			
GLIDING, ROPE-DANCING, IS HIS FANCY, ...	28	NO WINGS	8
GLIDING WINDLESS THROUGH THE HAND FOLDED FLAKES,	187	WINTER'S TALE	4
GLINT			
GLINT IN THE STAVED AND SIREN-PRINTED CAVERS, ...	131	I MAKE THIS IN	20
GLISTENING			
GOING HER GLISTENING CALVES THAT MINUTE.	11	CABARET	4
TO SHIELD THE GLISTENING BRAIN AND BLUNT THE			
EXAMINERS, ...	133	MAKE ME A MASK	8
ON THE GRISTED LEAVES AND THE LONG GONE GLISTENING	189	WINTER'S TALE	63
GLITTER			
AND THE GLITTER FROM THE FINE TEETH.	236	WOMAN TAPESTRY	46
GLITTERS			
GLITTERS IN THE ELECTRIC STREETS;	70	SECRET WIND	14
GLOBE			
DOUBLED THE GLOBE OF DEAD AND HALVED A COUNTRY; ...	66	HAND SIGNED	3
TAKE THE SCISSORS TO THIS GLOBE, ...	72	TAKE NEEDLES	37
THE TWO-FRAMED GLOBE THAT SPUN INTO A SCORE;	79	LOVE'S FEVER	45

	PAGE	TITLE	LINE
GLOBE (CONTINUED)			
ALL NIGHT AND DAY I EYE THE RAGGED GLOBE	81	ALL THAT I OWE	23
I SENT MY CREATURE SCOUTING ON THE GLOBE, ...	97	TWILIGHT LOCKS	9
THAT GLOBE ITSELF OF HAIR AND BONE	97	TWILIGHT LOCKS	10
'MY FATHERS' GLOBE KNOCKS ON ITS NAVE AND SINGS.'	101	FELLOWED SLEEP	11
ROUNDED MY GLOBE OF HERITAGE, JOURNEY	103	I DREAMED MY	11
TIME'S SHIP-RACKED GOSPEL ON THE GLOBE I BALANCE:	121	ALTARWISE	129
IN YOUR EVERY INCH AND GLANCE IS THE GLOBE OF			
GENESIS SPUN, ...	149	UNLUCKILY FOR	55
AND WIND HIS GLOBE OUT OF YOUR WATER THREAD	160	DEATHS AND ENT	21
GLOBES			
IN THOSE HIGH GLOBES I CANNOT COUNT, ...	49	LIGHT, I KNOW	19
LIKE SOME PITCH MOON, THE LIMIT OF THE GLOBES;	82	LIGHT BREAKS	20
GLOOM			
FADE, THE GREEN GLOOM GROWS DARKER, AND DEEPER THE			
DUSK:	222	FOREST PICTURE	10
GLORIOUS			
TO HAVE SEEN COUNTRIES WHICH WERE GLORIOUS, ...	223	IDYLL UNFORGET	1
GLORY			
GLORY ALSO THIS STAR, BIRD	4	PROLOGUE	40
THE LOVE WE HAD AND GLORY IN HIS BLOOD	17	IN OBLIVION	9
A HOLY VOICE ACQUAINTS ME WITH HIS GLORY.	76	LASHED RINGS	6
WHAT COLOUR IS GLORY? DEATH'S FEATHER? TREMBLE	104	WORLD PYRAMID	25
WHO BLOWS DEATH'S FEATHER? WHAT GLORY IS COLOUR?	105	WORLD PYRAMID	55
THE LOIN IS GLORY IN A WORKING PALLOR.	105	WORLD PYRAMID	57
O WHO IS GLORY IN THE SHAPELESS MAPS, ...	124	FOSTER LIGHT	28
GLORY CRACKED LIKE A FLEA.	141	SAINT TO FALL	18
THERE WAS GLORY TO HEAR	153	WAS A SAVIOUR	17
GLORY GLORY GLORY	175	FIRE RAID	76
GLORY GLORY GLORY	175	FIRE RAID	76
GLORY GLORY GLORY	175	FIRE RAID	76
IN THE NAME OF THE LOST WHO GLORY IN	183	VISION, PRAYER	102
GLORY'S			
I BY THE TREE OF THIEVES, ALL GLORY'S SAWBONES, ...	120	ALTARWISE	109
GLOVE			
FOR, SUNDAY FACED, WITH DUSTERS IN MY GLOVE, ...	100	RUNNING GRAVE	16
DRAW ON THE GLOVE OF PRINTS, DEAD CAIRO'S HENNA ...	120	ALTARWISE	117
I'LL COMB THE SNARED WOODS WITH A GLOVE ON A LAMP,	145	IF HEAD HURT	7
QUICKNESS OF HAND IN THE VELVET GLOVE	147	TO OTHERS	12
GLOW			
BUT LUNAR NIGHT WILL NOT GLOW IN MY BLACKNESS, ...	49	LIGHT, I KNOW	22
TO GLOW AFTER THE GOD STONING NIGHT	186	HOLY SPRING	11
SLEEP ABOVE IN THE GLOW OF A FADING SUNSET;	222	FOREST PICTURE	7
GLOWING			
THE SWEET, GLOWING VIGOUR	235	WOMAN TAPESTRY	25
THE SWEET, GLOWING VIGOUR, ...	237	WOMAN TAPESTRY	80
GLOW-WORM			
THE GLOW-WORM LIGHTS HIS DARKNESS, AND	48	POET: 1935	64
GLOW-WORMS			
AND, BROKEN GHOSTS WITH GLOW-WORMS IN THEIR HEADS,	82	LIGHT BREAKS	4
GNOMES			
IF THESE TWO GNOMES REMAIN UNMOVED BY STRICTURES?	60	FAIRY TALES	30
GO			
GO IS MY WISH;	9	MINUTE'S HOUR	18
THEN SHALL I GO, ...	9	MINUTE'S HOUR	19
STOP HAS NO MINUTES,/ BUT I GO OR DIE.	9	MINUTE'S HOUR	23
BUT YOU SHALL NOT GO FROM ME, CREATION;	10	COOL, OH NO	19
YOU SHALL NOT GO UNLESS I WILL IT	10	COOL, OH NO	21
AND SEES MY BODY GO	12	SKY'S BRIGHT	14
THE STILL GO HARD, ...	16	TIME TO ROT	13

	PAGE	TITLE	LINE
GO (CONTINUED)			
GO SILLY AND BE CHRIST'S GOOD BROTHER, ...	25	BEAUTY TO DUST	17
I'VE SAID MY PIECE: COUNT OR GO MAD.	33	HELD-OUT HAND	17
YOU SHALL GO AS THE OTHERS HAVE GONE, ...	45	PLOUGHMAN GONE	16
YOU SHALL GO AS THE OTHERS HAVE GONE, ...	46	PLOUGHMAN GONE	30
UNLESS I LEARN THE NIGHT I SHALL GO MAD.	48	LIGHT, I KNOW	12
THOUGH THEY GO MAD THEY SHALL BE SANE, ...	49	NO DOMINION	6
I MUST LEARN NIGHT'S LIGHT OR GO MAD.	49	LIGHT, I KNOW	30
IS HEARD BUT LITTLE TILL THE STARS GO OUT.	56	WHY EAST WIND	20
IN THE WILDERNESS THEY GO, ...	71	TAKE NEEDLES	29
OF CHILDREN GO WHO, FROM THEIR VOIDS, ...	91	WHERE ONCE THE	17
THE HARING SNAIL GO GIDDILY ROUND THE FLOWER, ...	109	I, IN IMAGE	41
AND WOULD A-WOOING GO AROUND THE GRAVES.	138	O CHATTERTON	28
MAY HIS HUNGER GO HOWLING ON BARE WHITE BONES	188	WINTER'S TALE	33
GO CRYING THROUGH YOU AND ME	193	SIDE OF TRUTH	18
HEART! SLYLY, SLOWLY, HEARING THE WOUND IN HER SIDE GO	200	COUNTRY SLEEP	95
HERON, MIRRORED, GO, ...	203	SIR JOHNS HILL	49
DO NOT GO GENTLE INTO THAT GOOD NIGHT	207	NOT GO GENTLE	T
DO NOT GO GENTLE INTO THAT GOOD NIGHT, ...	207	NOT GO GENTLE	1
DO NOT GO GENTLE INTO THAT GOOD NIGHT.	208	NOT GO GENTLE	6
DO NOT GO GENTLE INTO THAT GOOD NIGHT.	208	NOT GO GENTLE	12
DO NOT GO GENTLE INTO THAT GOOD NIGHT.	208	NOT GO GENTLE	18
UNDER AND ROUND HIM GO	209	POEM ON B'DAY	10
WILL NEVER NEVER GO OUT OF MY MIND.	217	ELEGY	20
AN OLD MAN IS WITH ME WHERE I GO	217	ELEGY	30
AND GO INTO THE AIR, ...	231	OUR SANCTITY	34
YOU SHALL NOT LET GO;	233	FURIOUS MOTION	19
BOAT CANNOT GO.	237	PILLAR BREAKS	6
THERE'LL BE MY BONE TO GO:	239	MAKES INTERVALS	21
GOAT-LEGGED			
SO STEAL HER NOT O GOAT-LEGGED WIND	11	AIR BREATHE	7
GOB			
THE SALTY SCENE AND MY PLAYERED GOB CURVING	179	NEW QUAY	14
GOBLIN-SUCKER			
NOR SPROUT ON OWL-SEED LIKE A GOBLIN-SUCKER, ...	123	FOSTER LIGHT	14
GOD			
AT GOD SPEEDED SUMMER'S END	3	PROLOGUE	2
AT GOD SPEEDED SUMMER'S END	5	PROLOGUE	101
A NEW DIVINITY, A GOD OF WHEELS	33	IN GARDENS	7
IN GOD OR GODS, CHRIST OR HIS FATHER, ...	41	YOUNG ARE OLD	47
OR PRAY FOR DAY TO SOME ATTENTIVE GOD	48	LIGHT, I KNOW	14
AND, MAD, HE CALLED HIS CURSES UPON GOD, ...	50	OUT OF THE PIT	8
WHERE, WHAT'S MY GOD AMONG THIS CRAZY RATTLING	51	OUT OF THE PIT	33
BRUISING, WHERE'S GOD'S MY SHEPHERD, GOD IS LOVE? .	51	OUT OF THE PIT	37
WHERE, WHAT'S MY GOD AMONG THIS TAXI STEPPING, ...	52	OUT OF THE PIT	49
WHERE, WHAT'S MY GOD? I HAVE BEEN MAD, AM MAD, ...	52	OUT OF THE PIT	63
BUT NO GOD ROSE. I HAVE SEEN BAD AND WORSE, ...	52	OUT OF THE PIT	77
GIBED THE COITUS OF THE STARS. NO GOD	53	OUT OF THE PIT	78
NO MAN BELIEVES WHO CRIES NOT, GOD IS NOT, ...	55	NO MAN BELIEVE	7
WHO DOES NOT BURY GOD IN A DEEP GRAVE	55	NO MAN BELIEVE	19
THANK GOD, BUT THE ENEMY STAYS PUT.	59	FAIRY TALES	9
LET ME NOT THINK, OF GOD OF CARNAGE, ...	63	WOMAN SPEAKS	16
GOD IS THE SAME THOUGH HE BE PRAISED AS MANY, ...	67	LET A FAITH	9
GOD SHALL BE GODS AND MANY DEATHS BE DEATH.	67	LET A FAITH	15
ONE GOD, MORE MIGHTY THAN THE SUN.	70	SECRET WIND	23
GOD AND I WILL PAY THE SNIPER.	71	TAKE NEEDLES	24
SLAY ME, SLAY THE GOD OF LOVE;	72	TAKE NEEDLES	55
GOD IS SLAIN IN MANY WAYS.	72	TAKE NEEDLES	56
AND THROUGH THESE EYES GOD MARKS MYSELF REVOLVING,	76	LASHED RINGS	12

	PAGE	TITLE	LINE
GOD (CONTINUED)			
THE HOWLING SPIRIT SHAPED A GOD	85	SEE, SAYS LIME	7
THIS WAS THE GOD OF BEGINNING IN THE INTRICATE SEAWHIRL,	112	I, IN IMAGE	107
AND GOD WALKED THERE WHO WAS A FIDDLING WARDEN	121	INCARNATE DEVL	5
IS CERTAIN GOD, AND THE CEREMONY OF SOULS	148	UNLUCKILY FOR	23
GOD IN BED, GOOD AND BAD,	150	WHEN I WOKE	17
NO TIME, SPOKE THE CLOCKS, NO GOD, RANG THE BELLS,	150	WHEN I WOKE	28
TO GLOW AFTER THE GOD STONING NIGHT	186	HOLY SPRING	11
OF THE LED-ASTRAY BIRDS WHOM GOD, FOR THEIR BREAST OF WHISTLES,	202	SIR JOHNS HILL	43
GOD IN HIS WHIRLWIND SILENCE SAVE, WHO MARKS THE SPARROWS HAIL,	202	SIR JOHNS HILL	45
AND FABULOUS, DEAR GOD.	210	POEM ON B'DAY	48
WITH BLESSED, UNBORN GOD AND HIS GHOST,	210	POEM ON B'DAY	60
HATING HIS GOD, BUT WHAT HE WAS WAS PLAIN:	217	ELEGY	23
GODDESSES			
THEY ARE ALL GODDESSES;	226	THE ELM	1
GODHEAD			
A CITY GODHEAD, TURBINE MOVED, STEEL SCULPTURED,	70	SECRET WIND	13
OVER THE ELECTRIC GODHEAD GROWS	70	SECRET WIND	22
BY A GODHEAD OF MY OWN.	72	TAKE NEEDLES	40
GOD-IN-HERO			
NO GOD-IN-HERO TUMBLE DOWN	125	SEED-AT-ZERO	4
NO GOD-IN-HERO TUMBLE DOWN	125	SEED-AT-ZERO	11
GOD-LIES			
LOVE-LIES, AND GOD-LIES, AND LIES-TO-PLEASE,	36	LET BE KNOWN	2
GODLINESS			
SO IS THERE MISSED A CERTAIN GODLINESS	23	THE ONLY DEAD	26
GODS			
FOR IF THE GODS WOULD LOVE	11	AIR BREATHE	9
HE HAS THE WHOLE FIELD NOW, THE GODS DEPARTED	29	NEARLY SUMMER	7
IN GOD OR GODS, CHRIST OR HIS FATHER,	41	YOUNG ARE OLD	47
HER SYLLABLES, AND TO THE GODS HER LOVE;	57	GREEK PLAY	27
SHALL GODS BE SAID TO THUMP THE CLOUDS	65	GODS THUMP	T
SHALL GODS BE SAID TO THUMP THE CLOUDS	65	GODS THUMP	1
WHEN IT IS RAIN WHERE ARE THE GODS?	65	GODS THUMP	5
IT SHALL BE SAID THAT GODS ARE STONE.	65	GODS THUMP	11
AND GODS BE CHANGED AS OFTEN AS THE SHIFT.	67	LET A FAITH	8
REMAINS THOUGH GODS BE FELLED TILL NONE ARE LEFT.	67	LET A FAITH	10
GOD SHALL BE GODS AND MANY DEATHS BE DEATH.	67	LET A FAITH	15
THE WISEMEN TELL ME THAT THE GARDEN GODS	121	INCARNATE DEVL	9
AND DROWN THE GODS IN ME,	239	LET ME ESCAPE	4
GODS'			
O LONELY AMONG MANY, THE GODS' MAN,	47	POET: 1935	47
KNOWING EXCEEDING GRIEF AND THE GODS' SORROW	47	POET: 1935	48
GOD'S			
ON GOD'S ROUGH TUMBLING GROUNDS	5	PROLOGUE	75
BRUISING, WHERE'S GOD'S MY SHEPHERD, GOD IS LOVE?	51	OUT OF THE PIT	37
MY GOD'S A SHEPHERD, GOD'S THE LOVE I HOPED.	53	OUT OF THE PIT	93
MY GOD'S A SHEPHERD, GOD'S THE LOVE I HOPED.	53	OUT OF THE PIT	93
AN OLD GOD'S DUGS ARE PRESSED AND PRICKED,	65	GODS THUMP	9
THE WORLD'S MY WOUND, GOD'S MARY IN HER GRIEF,	120	ALTARWISE	102
WHITE, GOD'S BRIGHT, FLOCKS, THE BELLED LAMBS LEAPING,	215	COUNTRY HEAVEN	21
GOES			
HE GOES ACROSS THE SKY,	13	RAIN CUTS	19
GOES OVER THE HILL INTO THE DEEP SEA;	43	LONGED TO MOVE	5
TO FOLLOW THE NOSE IF THE NOSE GOES	44	TO FOLLOW FOX	14
WHEN ANY LIGHT GOES OUT, AND LIFE IS DEATH.	55	NO MAN BELIEVE	6

		PAGE	TITLE	LINE
GOES (CONTINUED)				
AND LOVE THAT GOES DOWN LIKE A FLOWER.	....	57	GREEK PLAY	20
DRAIN THE SPRING WHERE PROMISE GOES.	....	70	TAKE NEEDLES	8
HOW AT MY SHEET GOES THE SAME CROOKED WORM.	....	77	THE FORCE THAT	22
WHEN SUNLIGHT GOES ARE SUNDERED FROM THE WORM,	....	89	EUNUCH DREAMS	8
INTO THE TIDED CORD, THERE GOES	....	91	WHERE ONCE THE	8
AND FREELY HE GOES LOST	....	210	POEM ON B'DAY	46
WHICH GOES AROUND ME EASILY	....	236	WOMAN TAPESTRY	54
GOING				
BUT IN THE LIGHT OF GOING	....	9	MINUTE'S HOUR	20
GOING HER GLISTENING CALVES THAT MINUTE.	....	11	CABARET	4
A POET GOING TO THE TOP?	....	84	LETTER TO AUNT	57
ENGRAVING GOING.	....	115	A GRIEF AGO	24
THE MANKIND OF HER GOING WITH A GRAVE TRUTH	....	192	REFUSAL MOURN	15
BY THE CHILD GOING TO BED AND THE MAN ON THE STAIRS		193	CONVERS PRAYER	2
LAST SOUND, THE WORLD GOING OUT WITHOUT A BREATH:		217	ELEGY	34
YOUR CONSTRUCTED NOTES GOING OUT OF THE THROAT	....	231	YOUR VOICE	2
GOLD				
UPON THE LAND OF GOLD OR OIL,	....	73	WE MOTHERNAKED	2
WHERE ALL THE HIDDEN STONES ARE GOLD,	....	74	WE MOTHERNAKED	10
LAY THE GOLD TITHINGS BARREN,	....	91	BOYS OF SUMMER	2
GOLD ON SUCH FEATURES, AND THE LINEN SPIRIT	....	120	ALTARWISE	121
WHEN THE WORM BUILDS WITH THE GOLD STRAWS OF VENOM		121	ALTARWISE	139
WHALEBED AND BULLDANCE, THE GOLD BUSH OF LIONS,	...	131	I MAKE THIS IN	22
WITH BRIDEBAIT OF GOLD BREAD, I WITH A LIVING SKEIN,		135	HOW MY ANIMAL	25
TO THE GOLD GUT THAT SINGS ON HIS REEL	....	162	LONG-LEGGED	19
GOLD GUT IS A LIGHTNING THREAD,	....	164	LONG-LEGGED	63
SEE WHAT THE GOLD GUT DRAGS FROM UNDER	....	166	LONG-LEGGED	131
MANES, UNDER HIS QUENCHLESS SUMMER BARBED GOLD TO				
THE BONE,	....	204	GIANT'S THIGH	26
GOLDEN				
THEIR GOLDEN AND THEIR OTHER COLOUR.	....	11	CABARET	9
YOUR GOLDEN BALL OF BLOOD;	....	16	TIME TO ROT	3
STEPPING ON CLOUDS ACROSS THE GOLDEN SKY,	....	30	YOUTH CALLS	2
AND LEANT ON STILES AND ON THE GOLDEN BAR,	....	52	OUT OF THE PIT	66
HIDING THE GOLDEN MOUNTAINS AND MANSIONS	....	54	WE BY SEASAND	16
LIE WATCHING YELLOW UNTIL THE GOLDEN WEATHER	......	54	WE BY SEASAND	23
AND FROM THIS DARKNESS SPIN THE GOLDEN SOUL.	......	73	LORD RED HAIL	15
EACH GOLDEN GRAIN SPAT LIFE INTO ITS FELLOW,	......	78	LOVE'S FEVER	23
TURNS DAMP TO DRY; THE GOLDEN SHOT	....	88	A PROCESS IN	2
GOLDEN GLAMORGAN STRAIGHTENS, TO THE FALLING BIRDS.		123	HOLD HARD	23
AND THE GOLDEN BALL SPINS OUT OF THE SKIES;	....	134	NOT FROM ANGER	10
TO HEAR THE GOLDEN NOTE TURN IN A GROOVE,	....	153	WAS A SAVIOUR	6
GOLDEN DISSOLVING UNDER THE WATER VEIL.	....	159	INTO HER HEAD	55
HIS GOLDEN YESTERDAY ASLEEP UPON THE IRIS	....	170	MARRIAGE VIRG	3
OF THE GOLDEN GHOST WHO RINGED WITH HIS STREAMS HER				
MERCURY BONE,	....	170	MARRIAGE VIRG	11
WHO UNDER THE LIDS OF HER WINDOWS HOISTED HIS GOLDEN				
LUGGAGE,	....	170	MARRIAGE VIRG	12
AND THE GOLDEN PAVEMENTS LAID IN REQUIEMS,	....	175	FIRE RAID	69
GOLDEN IN THE HEYDAYS OF HIS EYES,	....	195	FERN HILL	5
GOLDEN IN THE MERCY OF HIS MEANS,	....	195	FERN HILL	14
AND GREEN AND GOLDEN I WAS HUNTSMAN AND HERDSMAN,				
THE CALVES	....	195	FERN HILL	15
BEFORE THE CHILDREN GREEN AND GOLDEN	....	196	FERN HILL	44
GONE				
GONE FROM MY PALM TO LEAVE IT MARKED	....	12	CABARET	16
GONE NOW TO ROT.	....	26	PERSONAL EPIT	16
THE WESTERN MAN WITH ONE LUNG GONE--	....	41	YOUNG ARE OLD	44
THE PLOUGHMAN'S GONE	....	45	PLOUGHMAN GONE	T

	PAGE	TITLE	LINE
GONE (CONTINUED)			
THE PLOUGHMAN'S GONE, THE HANSOM DRIVER, ...	45	PLOUGHMAN GONE	1
BUT THE HORSES ARE GONE AND THE REINS ARE GREEN ...	45	PLOUGHMAN GONE	10
YOU SHALL GO AS THE OTHERS HAVE GONE, ...	45	PLOUGHMAN GONE	16
THE PLOUGHMAN'S GONE, THE HANSOM DRIVER, ...	45	PLOUGHMAN GONE	19
YOU SHALL GO AS THE OTHERS HAVE GONE, ...	46	PLOUGHMAN GONE	30
WHEN THEIR BONES ARE PICKED CLEAN AND THE CLEAN			
BONES GONE, ...	49	NO DOMINION	4
AND SOME SHINE FOR A SECOND AND ARE GONE, ...	49	LIGHT, I KNOW	20
'THE THIRST IS QUENCHED, THE HUNGER GONE, ...	61	MEAT ON BONES	17
DEAD AND GONE, DEDICATE FOREVER TO MY SELF	147	UNLUCKILY FOR	6
IS DUMB AND GONE WITH HIS FLAME OF BRIDES.	165	LONG-LEGGED	106
ON THE GRISTED LEAVES AND THE LONG GONE GLISTENING	189	WINTER'S TALE	63
AND GONE THAT BARLEY DARK WHERE THEIR CLOGS DANCED			
IN THE SPRING, ...	205	GIANT'S THIGH	40
WHEN YOU ARE GONE	232	FURIOUS MOTION	15
GONGS			
COLD NANSEN'S BEAK ON A BOAT FULL OF GONGS, ...	152	BELOW A TIME	40
GONOCOCCI			
HEAR THEIR LAUGHTER SLY AS GONOCOCCI.	179	NEW QUAY	18
GOOD			
BEASTS WHO SLEEP GOOD AND THIN, ...	5	PROLOGUE	77
THAT GREW FOR GOOD	20	THE NEOPHYTE	14
WHICH WAS GOOD AT WORD, ...	23	THE ONLY DEAD	16
BY TOE OR HAIR TO COMMON GOOD, ...	24	LITTLE PROBLEM	12
(GOOD FOR CAN RUN	24	LITTLE PROBLEM	13
GO SILLY AND BE CHRIST'S GOOD BROTHER, ...	25	BEAUTY TO DUST	17
PLANNING WHAT'S GOOD, THOUGH IT'S BUT WINTER, ...	27	OBLIVIOUS DARK	29
A LITTLE COMES, IS TASTED AND FOUND GOOD;	31	OUT OF SIGHS	5
BEFORE EVIL OR GOOD, LIGHT OR DARK, ...	39	GAS FADES	16
BEFORE GOOD OR BAD LUCK.	39	GAS FADES	18
THE CENTURY'S TRAP WILL HAVE CLOSED FOR GOOD	39	GAS FADES	30
IT IS GOOD THAT THE SUN SHINE, ...	42	A WAR OF WITS	20
IT IS GOOD TO STEP ONTO THE EARTH, ALONE, ...	43	A WAR OF WITS	24
NO FOX, NO GOOD, FOOL'S, NOT A FOX'S, HOLE, ...	44	TO FOLLOW FOX	11
IN SUN AND RAIN WORKING FOR GOOD AND GAIN, ...	45	PLOUGHMAN GONE	3
AND THIS WAY LEADS TO GOOD AND BAD, ...	45	TO FOLLOW FOX	22
COMES FROM MY EVIL OR MY GOOD. MAD, MAD, ...	53	OUT OF THE PIT	79
THE NOVEL THINGS. BUT IT HAS BEEN NO GOOD.	53	OUT OF THE PIT	81
KEATINGS IS GOOD FOR LICE, ...	58	TO ARCHITECTS	12
(AND WHAT A PART) IN ALL GOOD ART.	84	LETTER TO AUNT	47
TWINED GOOD AND EVIL ON AN EASTERN TREE;	121	INCARNATE DEVL	10
O MY LOST LOVE BOUNCED FROM A GOOD HOME;	146	IF HEAD HURT	23
AS MUCH AS FOR THEIR GOOD, ...	147	TO OTHERS	19
GOD IN BED, GOOD AND BAD, ...	150	WHEN I WOKE	17
UNCLAIMED DEAD, GIRLS FROM GOOD HOMES	154	RETURN	15
MADE HIS BAD BED IN HER GOOD	158	INTO HER HEAD	35
GOOD LUCK TO THE HAND ON THE ROD, ...	164	LONG-LEGGED	61
ALWAYS GOOD LUCK, PRAISED THE FINNED IN THE FEATHER	166	LONG-LEGGED	125
GOOD-BYE, GOOD LUCK, STRUCK THE SUN AND THE MOON,	169	LONG-LEGGED	213
TELLING THE HEART I BROKE OF A GOOD HABIT	175	MY BEGGAR ARM	4
GOOD AND BAD, TWO WAYS	192	SIDE OF TRUTH	13
DARK, AND THE GUILTY DARK, AND GOOD	193	SIDE OF TRUTH	21
SLEEP, GOOD, FOR EVER, SLOW AND DEEP, SPELLED RARE			
AND WISE, ...	197	COUNTRY SLEEP	8
KNOW THE GREEN GOOD, ...	198	COUNTRY SLEEP	40
OF SUMMER COME IN HIS GREAT GOOD TIME	206	LAMENT	32
DO NOT GO GENTLE INTO THAT GOOD NIGHT	207	NOT GO GENTLE	T
DO NOT GO GENTLE INTO THAT GOOD NIGHT, ...	207	NOT GO GENTLE	1
I LIE DOWN THIN AND HEAR THE GOOD BELLS JAW--	207	LAMENT	53

		PAGE	TITLE	LINE
GOOD (CONTINUED)				
DO NOT GO GENTLE INTO THAT GOOD NIGHT.	....	208	NOT GO GENTLE	6
GOOD MEN, THE LAST WAVE BY, CRYING HOW BRIGHT	.....	208	NOT GO GENTLE	7
DO NOT GO GENTLE INTO THAT GOOD NIGHT.	....	208	NOT GO GENTLE	12
DO NOT GO GENTLE INTO THAT GOOD NIGHT.	....	208	NOT GO GENTLE	18
SLIDES GOOD IN THE SLEEK MOUTH.	....	209	POEM ON B'DAY	36
BUT MY GREATEST DELIGHT IS TO TAKE A GOOD BITE	....	221	SONG OF DOG	13
GOOD-BYE				
THEN GOOD-BYE TO THE FISHERMANNED	....	162	LONG-LEGGED	5
GOOD-BYE TO THE MAN ON THE SEA-LEGGED DECK	....	162	LONG-LEGGED	18
GOOD-BYE TO CHIMNEYS AND FUNNELS,	....	162	LONG-LEGGED	25
ALWAYS GOOD-BYE TO THE LONG-LEGGED BREAD	....	165	LONG-LEGGED	94
ALWAYS GOOD-BYE TO THE FIRES OF THE FACE,	....	165	LONG-LEGGED	98
ALWAYS GOOD-BYE, CRIED THE VOICES THROUGH THE SHELL,		166	LONG-LEGGED	121
GOOD-BYE ALWAYS FOR THE FLESH IS CAST	....	166	LONG-LEGGED	122
GOOD-BYE, GOOD LUCK, STRUCK THE SUN AND THE MOON,		169	LONG-LEGGED	213
GOODNESS				
OF SUCH GREAT GOODNESS AS IS OURS.	....	23	THE ONLY DEAD	18
GOODS				
WITH HIS GOODS UNDER HIS EYES,	....	155	RETURN	38
GOOSE				
ON A MARE'S BACK OF A MARE'S NEST OR A GOOSE,	.....	45	TO FOLLOW FOX	19
WE KNOW OUR MOTHER GOOSE AND EDEN,	....	59	FAIRY TALES	10
IN A WIND THAT PLUCKED A GOOSE,	....	144	PLEASURE-BIRD	10
LISTEN AND LOOK WHERE SHE SAILS THE GOOSE PLUCKED SEA,	....	190	WINTER'S TALE	100
GOOSEBERRY				
THAT HYMNING GOOSEBERRY, THAT BETHEL-WORM	....	179	NEW QUAY	21
I TIPTOED SHY IN THE GOOSEBERRY WOOD,	....	206	LAMENT	4
GOOSEGIRLS				
OR, BUTTER FAT GOOSEGIRLS, BOUNCED IN A GAMBO BED,		204	GIANT'S THIGH	37
GOOSEHERD				
OF THE HOBNAIL TALES: NO GOOSEHERD OR SWINE WILL TURN		197	COUNTRY SLEEP	10
GOOSE'S				
A GOOSE'S QUILL HAS PUT AN END TO MURDER	....	66	HAND SIGNED	7
HUGGED, AND BARREN AND BARE ON MOTHER GOOSE'S GROUND		205	GIANT'S THIGH	43
GOOSESKIN				
HILL. WHO ONCE IN GOOSESKIN WINTER LOVED ALL ICE LEAVED	....	203	GIANT'S THIGH	12
GOSPEL				
SPEAKS A STEEL GOSPEL TO THE WRETCHED	....	70	SECRET WIND	17
THE CITY GOSPEL SHOUT TO HEAVEN.	....	70	SECRET WIND	21
TIME'S SHIP-RACKED GOSPEL ON THE GLOBE I BALANCE:		121	ALTARWISE	129
LEAPING! THE GOSPEL ROOKS! ALL TELL, THIS NIGHT, OF HIM	....	200	COUNTRY SLEEP	80
GOSSIP				
THE TONGUES OF HEAVEN GOSSIP AS I GLIDE	....	105	WORLD PYRAMID	53
GOSSIPERS				
THE GOSSIPERS	....	38	THE GOSSIPERS	T
THE GOSSIPERS HAVE LOWERED THEIR VOICES,	....	38	THE GOSSIPERS	1
GOT				
CHILDREN OF DARKNESS GOT NO WINGS	....	28	NO WINGS	T
CHILDREN OF DARKNESS GOT NO WINGS,	....	28	NO WINGS	1
THIS WE KNOW WE GOT NO WINGS,	....	28	NO WINGS	2
CRYSTAL OR FUNERAL, GOT NO HOPE	....	28	NO WINGS	5
CHILDREN OF DARKNESS GOT NO WINGS,	....	28	NO WINGS	23
THIS WE KNOW, WE GOT NO WINGS,	....	28	NO WINGS	24
THE BLOOD GOT UP AS RED AS WAX	....	85	SEE, SAYS LIME	13
LOVE, MY FATE GOT LUCKILY,	....	148	UNLUCKILY FOR	43

		PAGE	TITLE	LINE
GOURD				
NOT GIRL FOR BIRD (GOURD BEING MAN) BREAKS ROOT.		159	TO LEDA	4
GOVERNED				
CITY OF SPRING, THE GOVERNED FLOWER, ...		106	ALL ALL AND	4
GOWN				
UNSHELVE THAT ALL MY GRISTLES HAVE A GOWN		113	SERVANT SUN	6
GOWNED				
CRYING, WHITE GOWNED, FROM THE MIDDLE MOONLIT STAGES		158	INTO HER HEAD	37
GRACE				
SEASON AND SUNSHINE, GRACE AND GIRL, ...		61	MEAT ON BONES	31
LOOK TWICE BEFORE HE FELL FROM GRACE.		116	LANTERNS SHINE	4
OVER THE PAST TABLE I REPEAT THIS PRESENT GRACE.		145	PLEASURE-BIRD	25
FOLLOW HIM OUT OF GRACE, ...		196	FERN HILL	45
LIE IN GRACE. SLEEP SPELLED AT REST IN THE LOWLY HOUSE		199	COUNTRY SLEEP	43
GRACEFUL				
OR THE GRACEFUL SOUND OF LAUGHTER.		235	WOMAN TAPESTRY	17
GRACEFULLY				
NO TIDY FLOWER MOVED, NO BATHER GRACEFULLY		34	IN GARDENS	19
GRAFT				
GRAFT, POISON, AND BLUFF, ...		39	GAS FADES	11
BUT GRAFT THESE FOUR-FRUITED RIDINGS ON YOUR COUNTRY;		123	FOSTER LIGHT	9
GRAFTERS				
THE GRAFTERS OF CATS' HEADS ON CHICKENS' TRUNKS,		41	YOUNG ARE OLD	42
GRAFTS				
GRAFTS ON ITS BRIDE ONE-SIDED SKINS OF TRUTH;		90	EUNUCH DREAMS	28
GRAIL				
THE BLOOD THAT TOUCHED THE CROSSTREE AND THE GRAIL		94	IN BEGINNING	11
AND, AS FOR OILS AND OINTMENTS ON THE FLYING GRAIL,		111	I, IN IMAGE	101
THAT THE GREEN CHILD SEE LIKE A GRAIL		129	MY NEOPHYTE	22
GRAIN				
WILL FIND SUCH LOVE AGAINST THE GRAIN, ...		16	TIME TO ROT	8
EACH GOLDEN GRAIN SPAT LIFE INTO ITS FELLOW, ...		78	LOVE'S FEVER	23
AND LOOK, MY GRAIN, UPON THE FALLING WHEAT;		81	ALL THAT I OWE	29
NOW STAMP THE LORD'S PRAYER ON A GRAIN OF RICE, ...		119	ALTARWISE	85
THE GRAIN THAT HURRIES THIS WAY FROM THE RIM OF THE GRAVE		146	IF HEAD HURT	24
'REST BEYOND CHOICE IN THE DUST-APPOINTED GRAIN,		146	IF HEAD HURT	26
WITH HIS FLAME IN EVERY GRAIN.		182	VISION, PRAYER	78
GRAINS				
SOUNDS WITH THE GRAINS AS THEY HURRY		54	WE BY SEASAND	15
THE GRAINS OF LIFE MUST SEETHE BENEATH THE SUN, ...		80	ALMANAC TIME	13
TWO SAND GRAINS TOGETHER IN BED, ...		158	INTO HER HEAD	47
AND THE TALL GRAINS FOAMED IN THEIR BILLS;		165	LONG-LEGGED	97
COUNTING THE DENIALS OF THE GRAINS		167	LONG-LEGGED	160
AND THE FUNERAL GRAINS OF THE SLAUGHTERED FLOOR.		172	DAWN RAID	5
AS THE GRAINS BLOW, AS YOUR DEATH GROWS, THROUGH OUR HEART.		173	FIRE RAID	24
DUST IN THE BURIED WOOD, FLIES ON THE GRAINS OF HER WINGS		189	WINTER'S TALE	58
THE GRAINS BEYOND AGE, THE DARK VEINS OF HER MOTHER,		192	REFUSAL MOURN	21
NOW CLASP ME TO THEIR GRAINS IN THE GIGANTIC GLADE,		204	GIANT'S THIGH	19
GRANITE				
SET AGAINST GRANITE, ...		19	IMAGES IN AIR	3
GRAPE				
WERE OAT AND GRAPE		86	BREAD I BREAK	13
GRAPES				
HANDS, HOLD YOU POISON OR GRAPES?		62	EARS IN TURRET	9
SHIPS, HOLD YOU POISON OR GRAPES?		62	EARS IN TURRET	25
HOLD YOU POISON OR GRAPES?		63	EARS IN TURRET	33

	PAGE	TITLE	LINE
GRAPES (CONTINUED)			
IN THE GLASS BED OF GRAPES WITH SNAIL AND FLOWER,	109	I, IN IMAGE	29
GRAPE'S			
LAID THE CROPS LOW, BROKE THE GRAPE'S JOY.	86	BREAD I BREAK	5
GRAPH			
HIS GRAPH IS MEASURED AS THE PAGE OF PAIN	80	ALMANAC TIME	4
GRAPPLE			
HE SHALL GRAPPLE WITH THE GUARD	126	SEED-AT-ZERO	20
HE SHALL GRAPPLE WITH THE GUARD	126	SEED-AT-ZERO	27
SNIFF, HERE IS SIN! NOW HE MUST GRAPPLE, RISE:	179	NEW QUAY	29
GRASS			
THE GRASS HE COVERS IS A PRETTY GREEN;	63	WOMAN SPEAKS	19
HIS NARROW HOUSE IS WALLED WITH BLADES OF GRASS,	64	WOMAN SPEAKS	24
THE SECRET OILS THAT DRIVE THE GRASS.	94	IN BEGINNING	18
THE SIGNAL GRASS THAT TELLS ME ALL I KNOW	99	OCTOBER WIND	22
THROUGH ALL THE IRONS IN THE GRASS, METAL	102	I DREAMED MY	7
MY SECOND STRUGGLING FROM THE GRASS.	103	I DREAMED MY	20
WHAT MEANING, VOICES, IN THE STRAIGHT-RULED GRASS,	137	O CHATTERTON	17
A BLADE OF GRASS LONGS WITH THE MEADOW, ...	159	INTO HER HEAD	61
THE BIRDS THE GRASS THE TREES THE LAKE	172	THE HUNCHBACK	39
ABOUT THE LILTING HOUSE AND HAPPY AS THE GRASS WAS			
GREEN, ...	195	FERN HILL	2
AND FIRE GREEN AS GRASS.	195	FERN HILL	22
ON THE LORD'S-TABLE OF THE BOWING GRASS. FEAR MOST	198	COUNTRY SLEEP	35
GRAVE, AFTER BELOVED ON THE GRASS GULFED CROSS IS			
SCRUBBED	205	GIANT'S THIGH	54
OR HICKORY BULL IN MILKY GRASS	207	LAMENT	41
HILL, UNDER THE GRASS, IN LOVE, AND THERE GROW	216	ELEGY	6
AND YOU AROSE FROM DEPTHS OF GRASS	227	SPRING-SPIRIT	5
GRASSBLADE			
HOLLOWS, A GRASSBLADE BLOWN IN CUPPED HANDS, IN THE			
LOOTED ELMS	203	SIR JOHNS HILL	52
GRASSES			
THEIR GRASSES, EACH A TINY ECSTASY, ...	223	IDYLL UNFORGET	15
GRASSY			
UNDER HER GRASSY DRESS NO LIMBS--	15	FOR LEDA	23
GRATE			
I TALK TO HIM AS I CLEAN THE GRATE	149	PAPER & STICKS	10
GRAVE			
HE'S NOT AWAKE TO THE GRAVE	17	IN OBLIVION	15
WHO GAVE ME LIFE AND THEN THE GRAVE, ...	26	PERSONAL EPIT	11
AND THE GRAVE SEA, MOCK WHO DERIDE	54	WE BY SEASAND	2
FOR IN THIS YELLOW GRAVE OF SAND AND SEA	54	WE BY SEASAND	5
THAT'S GRAVE AND GAY AS GRAVE AND SEA	54	WE BY SEASAND	7
THAT'S GRAVE AND GAY AS GRAVE AND SEA	54	WE BY SEASAND	7
OF THE GRAVE, GAY, SEASIDE LAND.	54	WE BY SEASAND	17
WHO DOES NOT BURY GOD IN A DEEP GRAVE	55	NO MAN BELIEVE	19
AND ON HIS EARS HOSANNAS OF THE GRAVE.	63	WOMAN SPEAKS	23
ALL THAT I OWE THE FELLOWS OF THE GRAVE	80	ALL THAT I OWE	T
ALL THAT I OWE THE FELLOWS OF THE GRAVE	80	ALL THAT I OWE	1
THROUGH PERISCOPES RIGHTSIGHTED FROM THE GRAVE; ...	81	ALL THAT I OWE	24
NOR THE OUTSPOKEN GRAVE.	95	RUB OF LOVE	21
ALL ISSUE ARMOURED, OF THE GRAVE, ...	97	TWILIGHT LOCKS	19
WHEN, LIKE A RUNNING GRAVE	99	RUNNING GRAVE	T
WHEN, LIKE A RUNNING GRAVE, TIME TRACKS YOU DOWN,	99	RUNNING GRAVE	1
IN THE STRAIGHT GRAVE, ...	100	RUNNING GRAVE	20
AND STAKE THE SLEEPERS IN THE SAVAGE GRAVE	104	WORLD PYRAMID	17
MY GRAVE IS WATERED BY THE CROSSING JORDAN.	105	WORLD PYRAMID	43
THE MOON-DRAWN GRAVE, WITH THE SEAFARING YEARS, ...	107	GRIEF THIEF	2
SOCKET AND GRAVE, THE BRASSY BLOOD, ...	107	ALL ALL AND	35

	PAGE	TITLE	LINE
GRAVE (CONTINUED)			
SNEAK DOWN THE STALLION GRAVE,	108	GRIEF THIEF	18
YOUR CORKSCREW GRAVE CENTRED IN NAVEL AND NIPPLE,	110	I, IN IMAGE	51
LIE ALL UNKNOWING OF THE GRAVE SIN-EATER.	113	NOT FATHER ME	32
THE COUNTRY-HANDED GRAVE BOXED INTO LOVE,	115	A GRIEF AGO	31
SO CROSS HER HAND WITH THEIR GRAVE GIPSY EYES,	115	A GRIEF AGO	39
AND THREE DEAD SEASONS ON A CLIMBING GRAVE	117	ALTARWISE	30
TIME'S NERVE IN VINEGAR, THE GALLOW GRAVE	120	ALTARWISE	100
WITH PRIEST'S GRAVE FOOT AND HAND OF FIVE ASSASSINS	131	I MAKE THIS IN	25
AND DUG YOUR GRAVE IN MY BREAST.	135	HOW MY ANIMAL	44
STORM ME FOREVER OVER HER GRAVE UNTIL	137	AFTER FUNERAL	38
(BURY THE DEAD FOR FEAR THAT THEY WALK TO THE GRAVE IN LABOUR.)	143	24 YEARS	2
THE GRAIN THAT HURRIES THIS WAY FROM THE RIM OF THE GRAVE	146	IF HEAD HURT	24
THE GRAVE AND MY CALM BODY ARE SHUT TO YOUR COMING AS STONE,	146	IF HEAD HURT	29
AND THE GRAVE ITS DAUGHTERS.	148	UNLUCKILY FOR	42
WHALES UNREINED FROM THE GREEN GRAVE	157	INTO HER HEAD	8
HAVE SOUGHT YOUR SINGLE GRAVE,	160	DEATHS AND ENT	28
TILL EVERY BONE IN THE RUSHING GRAVE	163	LONG-LEGGED	59
CHARRED ON THE BLACK BREAST OF THE GRAVE	173	FIRE RAID	7
AND MASK THE GRAVE.	176	BREATH SHED	12
SUN SPIN A GRAVE GREY	185	VISION, PRAYER	183
AS A DUST OF PIGEONS. EXULTING, THE GRAVE HOOVED	189	WINTER'S TALE	73
THE HEAVENS, THE HEAVEN, THE GRAVE, THE BURNING FONT.	190	WINTER'S TALE	104
THE MANKIND OF HER GOING WITH A GRAVE TRUTH	192	REFUSAL MOURN	15
SHALL DROWN IN A GRIEF AS DEEP AS HIS MADE GRAVE,	194	CONVERS PRAYER	18
WEAR-WILLOW RIVER, GRAVE,	203	SIR JOHNS HILL	58
GRAVE, AFTER BELOVED ON THE GRASS GULFED CROSS IS SCRUBBED	205	GIANT'S THIGH	54
THIS SANDGRAIN DAY IN THE BENT BAY'S GRAVE	208	POEM ON B'DAY	6
GRAVE MEN, NEAR DEATH, WHO SEE WITH BLINDING SIGHT	208	NOT GO GENTLE	13
GRAVE-GABBING			
ON THAT CLOUD COAST TO EACH GRAVE-GABBING SHADE;	102	FELLOWED SLEEP	18
GRAVE-GROPING			
RANGE FROM THE GRAVE-GROPING PLACE.	127	SEED-AT-ZERO	56
GRAVEL			
SO STARRED WITH GRAVEL,	13	RAIN CUTS	12
CARVED BIRDS BLUNT THEIR STRIKING THROATS ON THE SALT GRAVEL,	15	SPIRE CRANES	3
SEE, ON GRAVEL PATHS UNDER THE HARPSTRUNG TREES	46	POET: 1935	1
SEE, ON GRAVEL PATHS UNDER THE HARPSTRUNG TREES,	48	POET: 1935	58
FLUNG GRAVEL CHIME? LET THE STONES SPEAK	66	GODS THUMP	13
THAT THE CHILDREN FILLED WITH GRAVEL	171	THE HUNCHBACK	9
GRAVELS			
THE CADAVEROUS GRAVELS, FALLS THICK AND STEADILY,	110	I, IN IMAGE	44
GRAVES			
INTO A COSTLY COUNTRY, THE GRAVES	43	FACES SHONE	5
AND WOULD A-WOOING GO AROUND THE GRAVES.	138	O CHATTERTON	28
QUARTERS AND GRAVES	184	VISION, PRAYER	164
GRAVE'S			
GRAVE'S FOOT, BLINDS DOWN THE LIDS, THE TEETH IN BLACK,	136	AFTER FUNERAL	4
GRAVEST			
IN THE RAIN TELLING ITS BEADS, AND THE GRAVEST GHOST	198	COUNTRY SLEEP	31
GRAVEWARD			
ALL SHALL REMAIN AND ON THE GRAVEWARD GULF	108	GRIEF THIEF	27
THE GENTLEMAN LAY GRAVEWARD WITH HIS FURIES;	116	ALTARWISE	2

	PAGE	TITLE	LINE
GRAVEYARD			
OVER THE GRAVEYARD IN THE WATER	164	LONG-LEGGED	85
GRAZE			
THE CATTLE GRAZE ON THE COVERED FOAM,	168	LONG-LEGGED	183
THE STAR RISE AT PASTURE AND NIGHTLONG THE FABLES			
GRAZE	198	COUNTRY SLEEP	34
GRAZING			
WHERE THE DEWFALL STARS SING GRAZING STILL	215	COUNTRY HEAVEN	8
GREAT			
OF SUCH GREAT GOODNESS AS IS OURS.	23	THE ONLY DEAD	18
DEATH SIGHTS AND SEES WITH GREAT MISGIVING	25	THERE'S PLENTY	6
LOSE THE GREAT PAINS OR STUFF THE WOUND,	32	OUT OF SIGHS	12
TEAR WITH A GREAT SOUND THROUGH THE SKIES,	51	OUT OF THE PIT	16
AND THE GREAT WHEELS' RUT;	59	FAIRY TALES	7
GREAT IS THE HAND THAT HOLDS DOMINION OVER	66	HAND SIGNED	11
IF YOU WOULD BE REGARDED GREAT,	84	LETTER TO AUNT	41
MY GREAT BLOOD'S IRON SINGLE	111	I, IN IMAGE	93
CUDGEL GREAT AIR, WRECK EAST, AND TOPPLE SUNDOWN,	132	I MAKE THIS IN	33
AND CLAP ITS GREAT BLOOD DOWN;	135	HOW MY ANIMAL	31
AND GUILTS, GREAT CROTCH AND GIANT	148	UNLUCKILY FOR	36
AND EVENINGS WITH GREAT DANES,	155	RETURN	57
WHEN ONE AT THE GREAT LEAST OF YOUR BEST LOVED	160	DEATHS AND ENT	3
DEEP THE GREAT BUSHED BAIT WITH RAINING LIPS	163	LONG-LEGGED	51
THE STATUES OF GREAT RAIN STAND STILL,	166	LONG-LEGGED	135
HE WHO BLEW THE GREAT FIRE IN	167	LONG-LEGGED	157
MAY HOLD IT IN A GREAT FLOOD	173	FIRE RAID	21
AND THE WINGS OF THE GREAT ROC RIBBONED FOR THE FAIR!	199	COUNTRY SLEEP	65
OF SUMMER COME IN HIS GREAT GOOD TIME	206	LAMENT	32
IN THE UNKNOWN, FAMOUS LIGHT OF GREAT	210	POEM ON B'DAY	47
WE WILL BE CONSCIOUS OF A GREAT DIVINITY	231	OUR SANCTITY	45
THE SCENT OF THE GREAT FLOWER WILL STAY,	232	FURIOUS MOTION	16
GREATER			
UP AND DOWN THE GREATER WAVES	168	LONG-LEGGED	179
THERE IS A GREATER LOVE THAN MINE	228	NOT DESPAIR	4
WHERE IS THERE GREATER LOVE	241	ADMIT THE SUN	15
GREATEST			
BUT MY GREATEST DELIGHT IS TO TAKE A GOOD BITE	221	SONG OF DOG	13
GREED			
GREED ON MAN BEATING NEAR THE FIRE NEIGHBOUR	153	WAS A SAVIOUR	30
GREEK			
GREEK PLAY IN A GARDEN	56	GREEK PLAY	T
GREEK IN THE IRISH SEA THE AGELESS VOICE:	125	TODAY, INSECT	22
GREEN			
SPRING MAY BE GREEN--	15	FOR LEDA	21
AND THE OAKUM IS PICKED, AND THE SPRING TREES HAVE			
GROWN GREEN,	39	GAS FADES	6
WHERE MEN WOULD ARGUE TILL THE STARS BE GREEN,	43	A WAR OF WITS	23
BUT THE HORSES ARE GONE AND THE REINS ARE GREEN	45	PLOUGHMAN GONE	10
AND GREEN, SNEERS NOT AT THE OLD SKY.	55	NO MAN BELIEVE	11
UNDER THE GREEN ROOF GRIEVES THE LIVING;	56	GREEK PLAY	2
THE GRASS HE COVERS IS A PRETTY GREEN;	63	WOMAN SPEAKS	19
LIKE A GREEN TREE THROUGH THE SWARD,	72	TAKE NEEDLES	42
AND THE GREEN TREE TRUST THE ROOT?	72	TAKE NEEDLES	58
ANSWER: WHEN THE GREEN LEAVES PRIZE HER.	72	TAKE NEEDLES	64
THE FORCE THAT THROUGH THE GREEN FUSE DRIVES THE			
FLOWER	77	THE FORCE THAT	T
THE FORCE THAT THROUGH THE GREEN FUSE DRIVES THE			
FLOWER	77	THE FORCE THAT	1
DRIVES MY GREEN AGE; THAT BLASTS THE ROOTS OF TREES	77	THE FORCE THAT	2
THE TIME FOR BREAST AND THE GREEN APRON AGE	78	LOVE'S FEVER	4

	PAGE	TITLE	LINE
GREEN (CONTINUED)			
GREEN WAS THE SINGING HOUSE.	78	LOVE'S FEVER	24
WHERE ONCE YOUR GREEN KNOTS SANK THEIR SPLICE	91	WHERE ONCE THE	7
THE GREEN UNRAVELLER,	91	WHERE ONCE THE	9
GREEN OF THE SEAWEEDS' IRON,	93	BOYS OF SUMMER	38
THAT CHALK THE WALLS WITH GREEN GIRLS AND THEIR MEN.	95	RUB OF LOVE	16
NO TREAD MORE PERILOUS, THE GREEN STEPS AND SPIRE	109	I, IN IMAGE	26
I, IN A WIND ON FIRE, FROM GREEN ADAM'S CRADLE,	111	I, IN IMAGE	95
GREEN AS BEGINNING, LET THE GARDEN DIVING	121	ALTARWISE	137
AS THE GREEN BLOOMS RIDE UPWARD, TO THE DRIVE OF TIME;	122	HOLD HARD	3
MURDER OF EDEN AND GREEN GENESIS.	124	TODAY, INSECT	8
AND A GREEN INCH BE HIS BEARER;	126	SEED-AT-ZERO	32
A VILLAGE GREEN MAY SCOLD HIM	126	SEED-AT-ZERO	38
CALLS A GREEN DAY AND NIGHT.	128	MY NEOPHYTE	6
CALLS THE GREEN ROCK OF LIGHT.	128	MY NEOPHYTE	12
NOR FALLS TO HIS GREEN MYTHS?	129	MY NEOPHYTE	18
THAT THE GREEN CHILD SEE LIKE A GRAIL	129	MY NEOPHYTE	22
'NOR THE GREEN NOUGHT BE HURT;	129	MY NEOPHYTE	45
O GREEN AND UNBORN AND UNDEAD?'	129	MY NEOPHYTE	47
THE FINGERS WILL FORGET GREEN THUMBS AND MARK	138	FIVE & COUNTRY	2
BY THE GREEN OF A ONE POUND NOTE	149	PAPER & STICKS	9
WITH MY CHERRY CAPPED DANGLER GREEN AS SEAWEED	152	BELOW A TIME	45
WHALES UNREINED FROM THE GREEN GRAVE	157	INTO HER HEAD	8
AND O TO CUT THE GREEN FIELD, LEAVING	157	RETURN	100
ARE MAKING UNDER THE GREEN, LAID VEIL	164	LONG-LEGGED	69
AND STUNNED AND STILL ON THE GREEN, LAID VEIL	167	LONG-LEGGED	171
GALLOP THROUGH THE ARCHED, GREEN FARMS,	168	LONG-LEGGED	188
AND THE LEGENDS OF THE GREEN CHAPELS	178	POEM IN OCT	50
AND THE GREEN DUST	183	VISION, PRAYER	107
ON THE DEPARTED, SNOW BUSHED GREEN, WANTON IN MOON LIGHT	189	WINTER'S TALE	72
ON THE WHITE, NO LONGER GROWING GREEN, AND, MINSTREL DEAD,	190	WINTER'S TALE	112
INTO THE ANSWERING SKIES FROM THE GREEN GROUND,	193	CONVERS PRAYER	7
ABOUT THE LILTING HOUSE AND HAPPY AS THE GRASS WAS GREEN,	195	FERN HILL	2
AND AS I WAS GREEN AND CAREFREE, FAMOUS AMONG THE BARNS	195	FERN HILL	10
AND GREEN AND GOLDEN I WAS HUNTSMAN AND HERDSMAN, THE CALVES	195	FERN HILL	15
AND FIRE GREEN AS GRASS.	195	FERN HILL	22
OUT OF THE WHINNYING GREEN STABLE	196	FERN HILL	35
BEFORE THE CHILDREN GREEN AND GOLDEN	196	FERN HILL	44
TIME HELD ME GREEN AND DYING	196	FERN HILL	53
KNOW THE GREEN GOOD,	198	COUNTRY SLEEP	40
GREEN CHICKENS OF THE BAY AND BUSHES CLUCK, 'DILLY DILLY,	202	SIR JOHNS HILL	31
AND NO GREEN COCKS OR HENS	203	SIR JOHNS HILL	53
WHO ONCE, GREEN COUNTRIES SINCE, WERE A HEDGEROW OF JOYS.	204	GIANT'S THIGH	20
ALL THE GREEN LEAVED LITTLE WEDDINGS' WIVES	206	LAMENT	11
THEIR FRAIL DEEDS MIGHT HAVE DANCED IN A GREEN BAY,	208	NOT GO GENTLE	8
CARVEN DOMES OF GREEN ARE THE TREES BY THE PATHWAY,	221	FOREST PICTURE	2
FADE, THE GREEN GLOOM GROWS DARKER, AND DEEPER THE DUSK:	222	FOREST PICTURE	10
THE DARKNESS IS ILLIMITABLE, GREEN SHADOW,	224	IDYLL UNFORGET	43
I SAW THE COLD, GREEN TREES,	235	WOMAN TAPESTRY	6
OR THE BRANCHES OF A GREEN TREE.	236	WOMAN TAPESTRY	40

		PAGE	TITLE	LINE
GREENER				
GROW LARKED AND GREENER AT BERRY BROWN	....	211	POEM ON B'DAY	101
GREENNESS				
ONE WOULD NOT THINK THE GREENNESS OF THIS VALLEY		63	WOMAN SPEAKS	12
GREEN-SHADOWED				
GREEN-SHADOWED PANOPLY ENVELOPING ALL ITS				
STRANGENESS AND SOFTNESS OF STEALTH.	....	224	IDYLL UNFORGET	45
GREENSWARD				
THROUGH THE SHAKEN GREENSWARD LAKE, SILENT, ON				
MOONSHOD HOOVES,	....	200	COUNTRY SLEEP	84
GREENWOOD				
THE GREENWOOD DYING AS THE DEER FALL IN THEIR TRACKS,		122	HOLD HARD	11
AND FLOWER OF COUNTRY SLEEP AND THE GREENWOOD KEEP.		198	COUNTRY SLEEP	18
GREET				
I CLIMB TO GREET THE WAR IN WHICH I HAVE NO HEART				
BUT ONLY	....	186	HOLY SPRING	8
GREW				
THAT GREW FOR GOOD	....	20	THE NEOPHYTE	14
AND FAMINE GREW, AND LOCUSTS CAME;	....	66	HAND SIGNED	10
INTO THE SIDED LAP OF LIGHT GREW STRONG,	....	78	LOVE'S FEVER	27
AND A BLACK AND WHITE PATCH OF GIRLS GREW PLAYING;		144	COLOUR OF SAY	4
SILENCE, SILENCE TO DO, WHEN EARTH GREW LOUD,	.....	153	WAS A SAVIOUR	15
AND THE CRATERS OF HIS EYES GREW SPRINGSHOOTS AND				
FIRE	....	172	DAWN RAID	7
AND THE SUN GREW ROUND THAT VERY DAY.	....	196	FERN HILL	32
MIDWIVES GREW IN THE MIDNIGHT DITCHES,	....	206	LAMENT	19
GREY				
LET THE TWO DULL STONES BE GREY,	....	19	IMAGES IN AIR	4
THE SUN WAS RED, THE MOON WAS GREY,	....	78	LOVE'S FEVER	14
SUN SPIN A GRAVE GREY	....	185	VISION, PRAYER	183
GREY-HAIRED				
DIG NO MORE FOR THE CHAINS OF HIS GREY-HAIRED HEART.		172	DAWN RAID	9
GRIEF				
AND, IN THE GRIEF OF CERTAINTY,	....	19	THE NEOPHYTE	11
BUT NOT OF GRIEF, FOR I HAVE KNOCKED DOWN THAT	....	31	OUT OF SIGHS	2
KNOWING EXCEEDING GRIEF AND THE GODS' SORROW	....	47	POET: 1935	48
PITY ELECTRA LOVELESS, SHE WHOSE GRIEF	....	57	GREEK PLAY	25
GRIEF, LIKE AN OPEN WOUND, HAS CRIED TO HEAVEN.	...	64	WOMAN SPEAKS	32
GRIEF THIEF OF TIME	....	107	GRIEF THIEF	T
GRIEF THIEF OF TIME CRAWLS OFF,	....	107	GRIEF THIEF	1
THE OLD FORGET THE GRIEF,	....	107	GRIEF THIEF	9
AND FREE THE TWIN-BOXED GRIEF,	....	108	GRIEF THIEF	20
A GRIEF AGO	....	114	A GRIEF AGO	T
A GRIEF AGO,	....	114	A GRIEF AGO	1
WHO IS MY GRIEF,	....	115	A GRIEF AGO	9
THE WORLD'S MY WOUND, GOD'S MARY IN HER GRIEF,	....	120	ALTARWISE	102
THE LANDSCAPE GRIEF, LOVE IN HIS OILS	....	129	MY NEOPHYTE	20
GRIEF WITH DISHEVELLED HANDS TEAR OUT THE ALTAR GHOST		130	SINNERS' BELL	5
TIME'S CORAL SAINT AND THE SALT GRIEF DROWN A FOUL				
SEPULCHRE	....	130	SINNERS' BELL	8
GRIEF WITH DRENCHED BOOK AND CANDLE CHRISTENS THE				
CHERUB TIME	....	130	SINNERS' BELL	16
WHO HAVE BROUGHT FORTH THE URCHIN GRIEF.	....	131	SINNERS' BELL	30
AND A TEAR-STAINED WIDOWER GRIEF DROOPED FROM THE				
LASHES	....	133	MAKE ME A MASK	9
IN MANY MARRIED LONDON'S ESTRANGING GRIEF.	....	160	DEATHS AND ENT	12
HE WEPT FROM THE CREST OF GRIEF, HE PRAYED TO THE				
VEILED SKY	....	188	WINTER'S TALE	32
WILL BE THE SAME GRIEF FLYING. WHOM SHALL THEY CALM?		194	CONVERS PRAYER	11
SHALL DROWN IN A GRIEF AS DEEP AS HIS MADE GRAVE,		194	CONVERS PRAYER	18

	PAGE	TITLE	LINE
GRIEF (CONTINUED)			
AND ALL MY GRIEF FLOWS FROM THE RIFT	225	CLOWN IN MOON	3
GRIEF-LIKE			
FOR ALL THINGS ARE GRIEF-LIKE	225	OF ANY FLOWER	5
GRIEFS			
WITH ALL THEIR GRIEFS IN THEIR ARMS, ...	197	CRAFT OR ART	5
ROUND THE GRIEFS OF THE AGES, ...	197	CRAFT OR ART	18
GRIEVE			
GRIEVE	173	FIRE RAID	3
MYSELVES GRIEVE NOW, AND MIRACLES CANNOT ATONE. ...	173	FIRE RAID	16
NAKED AND FORSAKEN TO GRIEVE HE WILL NOT COME.	201	COUNTRY SLEEP	106
WE GRIEVE AS THE BLITHE BIRDS, NEVER AGAIN, LEAVE			
SHINGLE AND ELM, ...	202	SIR JOHNS HILL	33
IN THE COAL BLACK BUSH AND LET THEM GRIEVE.	206	LAMENT	12
GRIEVED			
OFF BY THE SUN AND DAUGHTERS NO LONGER GRIEVED	205	GIANT'S THIGH	55
AND LEARN, TOO LATE, THEY GRIEVED IT ON ITS WAY,	208	NOT GO GENTLE	11
GRIEVERS			
THE GRIEVERS	173	FIRE RAID	2
GRIEVES			
UNDER THE GREEN ROOF GRIEVES THE LIVING;	56	GREEK PLAY	2
NOW THE HERON GRIEVES IN THE WEEDED VERGE. THROUGH			
WINDOWS	202	SIR JOHNS HILL	47
TO THAT STRANGE COLOUR, SIGHING GENTLY, GRIEVES ...	223	IN DREAMS	6
GRIGSON			
TO GEOFFREY GRIGSON WITH MY LUFF, ...	85	LETTER TO AUNT	64
GRIMACE			
TURNS TO THE ROOF A HIDEOUS GRIMACE, ...	49	LIGHT, I KNOW	25
GRIMLY			
THE RINGED-SEA GHOST, RISE GRIMLY FROM THE WRACK.	113	NOT FATHER ME	24
GRIN			
AND ON THE SWEETHEARTS' BED TO LIE AND GRIN, ...	34	THIRST PARCHES	12
GRINDING			
BY THE GRINDING SEA, ...	192	SIDE OF TRUTH	15
GRIP			
TIME AND PLACES GRIP HER BREAST BONE, ...	168	LONG-LEGGED	175
AND GRIP THE INEXORABLE SONG, ...	233	FURIOUS MOTION	21
GRISTED			
ON THE GRISTED LEAVES AND THE LONG GONE GLISTENING	189	WINTER'S TALE	63
GRISTLE			
GRISTLE AND RIND, AND A ROARER'S LIFE, ...	207	LAMENT	46
GRISTLES			
UNSHELVE THAT ALL MY GRISTLES HAVE A GOWN	113	SERVANT SUN	6
GROIN			
IN THE GROIN OF THE NATURAL DOORWAY I CROUCHED LIKE			
A TAILOR	143	24 YEARS	3
GROIN'S			
IN THE GROIN'S ENDLESS COIL A MAN IS TANGLED.'	132	I MAKE THIS IN	53
GROOM			
GROOM THE DARK BRIDES, THE WIDOWS OF THE NIGHT	89	EUNUCH DREAMS	5
NUTMEG, CIVET, AND SEA-PARSLEY SERVE THE PLAGUED			
GROOM AND BRIDE	131	SINNERS' BELL	29
O BRIDE AND BRIDE GROOM	174	FIRE RAID	41
GROOVE			
TO HEAR THE GOLDEN NOTE TURN IN A GROOVE, ...	153	WAS A SAVIOUR	6
GROOVED			
THE GROOVED LAND ROTATING, THAT THE STYLUS OF			
LIGHTNING	110	I, IN IMAGE	68
GROPE			
IN ALL LOVE'S COUNTRIES, THAT WILL GROPE AWAKE; ...	139	FIVE & COUNTRY	12

	PAGE	TITLE	LINE
GROPING			
GROPING FOR MATTER UNDER THE DOG'S PLATE, ...	32	OUT OF SIGHS	26
GROSS			
AND DROWN ALL SORROWS IN THE GROSS CATASTROPHE. ...	34	THIRST PARCHES	15
GROTTOES			
IN GROTTOES I WORKED WITH BIRDS, ...	151	BELOW A TIME	9
GROUND			
STAMPS ON THE GROUND, ...	13	RAIN CUTS	16
AND, ON THE GROUND, GYRATES AS EASILY	19	THE NEOPHYTE	7
TO THE GROUND.	22	HIGH ON A HILL	16
WHEN YOU HAVE GROUND SUCH BEAUTY DOWN TO DUST	25	BEAUTY TO DUST	T
WHEN YOU HAVE GROUND SUCH BEAUTY DOWN TO DUST	25	BEAUTY TO DUST	1
OUT OF THE OLD LIE BURNING ON THE GROUND, ...	44	LONGED TO MOVE	13
SHALL A DROPPED STONE DRUM ON THE GROUND, ...	65	GODS THUMP	12
REACHING A SECOND GROUND FAR FROM THE STARS;	101	FELLOWED SLEEP	7
I FLED THAT GROUND AS LIGHTLY AS A FEATHER.	101	FELLOWED SLEEP	10
HAS NOT YET REACHED THE GROUND.	116	LANTERNS SHINE	19
MANNA FOR THE RUMBLING GROUND, ...	125	SEED-AT-ZERO	17
MANNA FOR THE GUARDED GROUND, ...	126	SEED-AT-ZERO	24
IN QUICK, SWEET, CRUEL LIGHT TILL THE LOCKED GROUND			
SPROUT OUT, ...	135	HOW MY ANIMAL	18
TO CLASP MY FURY ON GROUND	135	HOW MY ANIMAL	30
CAST HIGH, STUNNED ON GILLED STONE; SLY SCISSORS			
GROUND IN FROST	135	HOW MY ANIMAL	35
ON TO THE GROUND WHEN A MAN DIED	153	WAS A SAVIOUR	21
DOWN, DOWN, DOWN, UNDER THE GROUND, ...	169	LONG-LEGGED	201
THE GROUND	183	VISION, PRAYER	111
AND THERE OUTSIDE ON THE BREAD OF THE GROUND	189	WINTER'S TALE	68
INTO THE ANSWERING SKIES FROM THE GREEN GROUND, ...	193	CONVERS PRAYER	7
HUGGED, AND BARREN AND BARE ON MOTHER GOOSE'S GROUND	205	GIANT'S THIGH	43
WHICH WAS REST AND DUST, AND IN THE KIND GROUND ...	216	ELEGY	10
I'M ALL FOR GROUND, ...	234	NO, PIGEON	17
GROUNDS			
ON GOD'S ROUGH TUMBLING GROUNDS	5	PROLOGUE	75
GROUNDWORKS			
OVER THESE GROUNDWORKS THRUSTING THROUGH A PAVEMENT	117	ALTARWISE	27
GROVE			
IN THE SQUIRREL NIMBLE GROVE, UNDER LINEN AND THATCH	199	COUNTRY SLEEP	44
THEN IN THE DELIGHT AND GROVE OF BEASTS AND BIRDS	215	COUNTRY HEAVEN	6
GROVE-GREEN			
AND EYES HAVE BEEN GROVE-GREEN CATCHING MINE FROM			
THE DEPTH OF THE SILENCE;	224	IDYLL UNFORGET	33
GROVES			
THROUGH HADES' GROVES AND THE ETERNAL LANDS.	57	GREEK PLAY	24
LET ME IN THE DEVIL'S GROVES	70	TAKE NEEDLES	5
THROUGH THE LOUD ZOO OF THE WILLOW GROVES	171	THE HUNCHBACK	22
AND THE GROVES WERE BLUE WITH SAILORS	172	THE HUNCHBACK	30
GROW			
BY WAVES WHICH GROW AGAIN	14	RAIN CUTS	33
WE HAVE GROWN WEAK BEFORE WE COULD GROW STRONG, ...	40	YOUNG ARE OLD	7
QUESTION: WHEN SHALL ROOT-DAM GROW?	72	TAKE NEEDLES	63
THE DEAD GROW FOR HIS JOY.	210	POEM ON B'DAY	54
AND AIR SHAPED HEAVEN WHERE SOULS GROW WILD	210	POEM ON B'DAY	74
GROW LARKED AND GREENER AT BERRY BROWN	211	POEM ON B'DAY	101
HILL, UNDER THE GRASS, IN LOVE, AND THERE GROW	216	ELEGY	6
AND IN HER GARDEN GROW THE FLEUR DE LYS, ...	222	IN DREAMS	1
GROW INTO YOUR DELICATE SKIN, ...	238	MAKES INTERVALS	11
GROWING			
GROWING ON HILLS OR SHINING UNDER WATER.	25	BEAUTY TO DUST	15
GROWING MORE TERRIBLE AS THE DAY	43	LONGED TO MOVE	4

	PAGE	TITLE	LINE
GROWING (CONTINUED)			
GROWING IN PUBLIC PLACES THAN MAN KNOWS.	48	POET: 1935	57
THE GROWING BONES, THE RUMOUR OF MANSEED	78	LOVE'S FEVER	17
OF GROWING BONES THE MUSCLES SLID;	86	SEE, SAYS LIME	26
GROWING THEIR WOUNDS ALREADY, ...	154	RETURN	13
ON THE WHITE, NO LONGER GROWING GREEN, AND, MINSTREL			
DEAD, ...	190	WINTER'S TALE	112
GROWING LIKE A POWERFUL ROOT INSIDE ME.	236	WOMAN TAPESTRY	67
GROWN			
AND THE OAKUM IS PICKED, AND THE SPRING TREES HAVE			
GROWN GREEN, ...	39	GAS FADES	6
WE HAVE GROWN WEAK BEFORE WE COULD GROW STRONG, ...	40	YOUNG ARE OLD	7
TWICE IN THE FEEDING SEA, GROWN	103	I DREAMED MY	26
THOUGH THE NAMES ON THEIR WEED GROWN STONES ARE			
RAINED AWAY, ...	203	GIANT'S THIGH	8
GROWS			
BEFORE THE AGONY; THE SPIRIT GROWS, ...	31	OUT OF SIGHS	3
FEEL, AS THE PULSE GROWS TIRED, ...	32	HELD-OUT HAND	3
OVER THE ELECTRIC GODHEAD GROWS	70	SECRET WIND	22
THE SECRET OF THE SOIL GROWS THROUGH THE EYE, ...	82	LIGHT BREAKS	28
THERE GROWS THE HOURS' LADDER TO THE SUN, ...	102	FELLOWED SLEEP	26
AS THE GRAINS BLOW, AS YOUR DEATH GROWS, THROUGH OUR			
HEART.	173	FIRE RAID	24
GABRIEL AND RADIANT SHRUBBERY AS THE MORNING GROWS			
JOYFUL	186	HOLY SPRING	15
FADE, THE GREEN GLOOM GROWS DARKER, AND DEEPER THE			
DUSK:	222	FOREST PICTURE	10
GROWTH			
PALE AND DECAYED, AN UGLY GROWTH.	239	LET ME ESCAPE	12
GROWTHS			
TEAR BY THE ROOTS THESE TWIN GROWTHS IN YOUR GUT;	60	FAIRY TALES	36
GROYNE			
THROUGH THE LAST VAULT AND VEGETABLE GROYNE, ...	131	I MAKE THIS IN	7
GRUMBLE			
HANDS GRUMBLE ON THE DOOR, ...	62	EARS IN TURRET	2
HANDS GRUMBLE ON THE DOOR, ...	62	EARS IN TURRET	26
GUARD			
HE SHALL GRAPPLE WITH THE GUARD	126	SEED-AT-ZERO	20
HE SHALL GRAPPLE WITH THE GUARD	126	SEED-AT-ZERO	27
GUARDED			
MANNA FOR THE GUARDED GROUND, ...	126	SEED-AT-ZERO	24
GUARDIAN			
WE IN OUR EDEN KNEW THE SECRET GUARDIAN	122	INCARNATE DEVL	13
GUARDING			
OF THE STONE BIRD GUARDING HER:	140	TOMBSTONE TOLD	25
GUESSES			
YOU CAPTURE MORE THAN MAN OR WOMAN GUESSES;	48	POET: 1935	54
GUEST			
THE WELCOME DEVIL COMES AS GUEST, ...	30	NEARLY SUMMER	14
GUIDED			
WHEN WE WERE STRANGERS TO THE GUIDED SEAS, ...	121	INCARNATE DEVL	7
GUIDES			
GUIDES AND BLOWS WICKEDLY, FOR LARKS	37	WINDMILLS TURN	7
GUILLOTINE			
SLAPPED DOWN THE GUILLOTINE, THE BLOOD-RED DOUBLE	124	TODAY, INSECT	6
GUILT			
AND A SILK PIGEON'S GUILT IN HER PROUD ABSENCE, ...	131	I MAKE THIS IN	17
LOVING ON THIS SEA BANGED GUILT	147	UNLUCKILY FOR	15
OF INNOCENCE AND GUILT	192	SIDE OF TRUTH	7
GUILT	202	SIR JOHNS HILL	42

	PAGE	TITLE	LINE
GUILTLESS			
BE GUILTLESS OF THE WINDY WRONGS.	37	WINDMILLS TURN	19
GUILTS			
AND GUILTS, GREAT CROTCH AND GIANT	148	UNLUCKILY FOR	36
GUILTY			
DARK, AND THE GUILTY DARK, AND GOOD	193	SIDE OF TRUTH	21
GULF			
ALL SHALL REMAIN AND ON THE GRAVEWARD GULF	108	GRIEF THIEF	27
GULFED			
GRAVE, AFTER BELOVED ON THE GRASS GULFED CROSS IS			
SCRUBBED	205	GIANT'S THIGH	54
GULL			
WHERE THE ANCHOR RODE LIKE A GULL	163	LONG-LEGGED	37
GULL, ON THE WAVE WITH SAND IN ITS EYES! AND THE			
FOAL MOVES	200	COUNTRY SLEEP	83
THAN IN THE GULL AND THE FIERCE EAGLE	241	ADMIT THE SUN	17
GULLED			
DAWS SIR JOHN'S JUST HILL DONS, AND AGAIN THE GULLED			
BIRDS HARE	201	SIR JOHNS HILL	15
GULLED AND CHANTER IN YOUNG HEAVEN'S FOLD	210	POEM ON B'DAY	62
GULLS			
GULLS, PIPERS, COCKLES, AND SAILS, ...	3	PROLOGUE	11
NO MORE MAY GULLS CRY AT THEIR EARS	50	NO DOMINION	20
OF THE GULLS THE LIP OF WAVES.	76	SONG: LOVE ME	11
TROT AND GALLOP WITH GULLS UPON THEM	168	LONG-LEGGED	189
FLOUNDERS, GULLS, ON THEIR COLD, DYING TRAILS, ...	209	POEM ON B'DAY	11
GULLY			
YOUR STRING SHALL STRETCH A GULLY TWIXT THE THUMBS	87	PAIN BE MUSIC	7
I FIND A TRIPPER'S KNICKER IN THE GULLY	137	O CHATTERTON	15
GULP			
RAPE GULP AND BE MARRY, HE ALSO SERVES	138	O CHATTERTON	26
GUMS			
THE BODY PROSPERED, TEETH IN THE MARROWED GUMS, ...	78	LOVE'S FEVER	16
GUN			
THE HUNGER OF LIVING, THE OVEN AND GUN	39	GAS FADES	24
GUNMAN			
IN THIS OUR AGE THE GUNMAN AND HIS MOLL, ...	89	EUNUCH DREAMS	11
GUNS			
CRY ELOI TO THE GUNS.	105	WORLD PYRAMID	42
HURDLES AND GUNS AND RAILINGS, AS THE BOULDERS HEAVE,	122	HOLD HARD	16
GUSHER			
THEN TAKE THE GUSHER OR THE FIELD	74	WE MOTHERNAKED	9
GUSHERS			
NOR FENCED, NOR STAKED, THE GUSHERS OF THE SKY	82	LIGHT BREAKS	16
GUSTY			
WHEN I WAS A GUSTY MAN AND A HALF	206	LAMENT	13
GUT			
TEAR BY THE ROOTS THESE TWIN GROWTHS IN YOUR GUT;	60	FAIRY TALES	36
THAT DROVE MY STUFF THROUGH SKIN AND GUT;	86	SEE, SAYS LIME	31
TO THE GOLD GUT THAT SINGS ON HIS REEL	162	LONG-LEGGED	19
GOLD GUT IS A LIGHTNING THREAD, ...	164	LONG-LEGGED	63
SEE WHAT THE GOLD GUT DRAGS FROM UNDER	166	LONG-LEGGED	131
GUTS			
CATCH THEIR POOR GUTS.	37	WINDMILLS TURN	26
(IT'S A MATTER OF GUTS, ...	39	GAS FADES	10
AND YOUNG GUTS DRY BENEATH THE SICKENED SUN.	63	WOMAN SPEAKS	15
THAN ONE COULD PROBE OUT OF A SERPENT'S GUTS;	137	O CHATTERTON	7
GUTTER			
FLIES FROM THE GUTTER.	16	TIME TO ROT	12
I HAVE RIDDEN ON GUTTER DUNG AND CLOUD.	52	OUT OF THE PIT	67

	PAGE	TITLE	LINE
GUTTERS			
RUN DOWN THE WORLD'S GUTTERS,	39	GAS FADES	32
AND SWIMMING DOWN THE GUTTERS HE LOOKS UP	51	OUT OF THE PIT	45
GYRATES			
AND, ON THE GROUND, GYRATES AS EASILY	19	THE NEOPHYTE	7
HABIT			
BUT, BY YOUR HABIT UNRETURNED,	23	THE ONLY DEAD	24
AND BY YOUR HABIT UNRETURNABLE.	23	THE ONLY DEAD	25
TELLING THE HEART I BROKE OF A GOOD HABIT	175	MY BEGGAR ARM	4
HACK			
MY DABBED BAY'S DUSK, AS I HACK	4	PROLOGUE	36
HACK OF THE COUGH, THE HANGING ALBATROSS,	107	GRIEF THIEF	10
WHO COULD HACK OUT YOUR UNSUCKED HEART,	129	MY NEOPHYTE	46
HACKED			
THEY SAID, WHO HACKED AND HUMOURED, THEY WERE MINE.	112	NOT FATHER ME	20
AND IMMEMORIAL SONS OF THE CUDGELLING, HACKED	203	GIANT'S THIGH	11
HAD (23)			
HADES			
THE DEAD IN HADES HAVE THEIR HOST OF FRIENDS,	57	GREEK PLAY	22
HADES'			
THROUGH HADES' GROVES AND THE ETERNAL LANDS.	57	GREEK PLAY	24
HAGGARD			
MY FACE IS HAGGARD IN THE GLASS,	61	MEAT ON BONES	19
IT WAS A HAGGARD NIGHT THE FIRST FLESH DIED,	65	WOMAN SPEAKS	56
HAGS			
BEFORE THE LADIES' BREASTS ARE HAGS	60	MEAT ON BONES	4
HAIL			
(HAIL TO HIS BEASTHOOD).	5	PROLOGUE	76
PLUNGED IN BLACK WATERS, UNDER HAIL AND FIRE,	51	OUT OF THE PIT	42
THE DARTED HAIL, THE CHILDISH SNOW,	68	BEFORE KNOCKED	14
NOT FOREVER SHALL THE LORD OF THE RED HAIL	73	LORD RED HAIL	T
NOT FOREVER SHALL THE LORD OF THE RED HAIL	73	LORD RED HAIL	1
HOW SOON, HOW SOON, O LORD OF THE RED HAIL!	73	LORD RED HAIL	18
AS THE SAILS DRANK UP THE HAIL OF THUNDER	166	LONG-LEGGED	127
BUT BLESSED BE HAIL AND UPHEAVAL	186	HOLY SPRING	20
TIME LET ME HAIL AND CLIMB	195	FERN HILL	4
AS THE RAIN FALLS, HAIL ON THE FLEECE, AS THE VALE MIST RIDES	199	COUNTRY SLEEP	57
GOD IN HIS WHIRLWIND SILENCE SAVE, WHO MARKS THE SPARROWS HAIL,	202	SIR JOHNS HILL	45
AND DUCKED AND DRAKED WHITE LAKE THAT HARPS TO A HAIL STONE.	204	GIANT'S THIGH	28
HAILING			
WHO SCALES A HAILING HILL IN HER COLD FLINTSTEPS	132	I MAKE THIS IN	29
HAIR			
WIND IS MY ENEMY YOUR HAIR SHANT STIR	11	AIR BREATHE	3
AND RAVEN HAIR.	11	AIR BREATHE	13
BY TOE OR HAIR TO COMMON GOOD,	24	LITTLE PROBLEM	12
THE PARTING OF HAT FROM HAIR,	44	LONGED TO MOVE	16
STUCK STRAW AND SEVEN STARS UPON MY HAIR,	52	OUT OF THE PIT	65
WITH THE WIND IN MY HAIR,	62	EARS IN TURRET	22
I KNOW THAT AGE IS SNOW UPON THE HAIR,	64	WOMAN SPEAKS	49
BE SOUR IN MY HAIR. THAT I MAY LEARN	65	WOMAN SPEAKS	63
AND THIS HILL OF BONE AND HAIR	67	REALM OF FLESH	2
WHEREON THE HOODED HAIR CASTS DOWN ITS GIRDLE,	76	LASHED RINGS	5
HAND, THE BREAKING OF THE HAIR,	78	LOVE'S FEVER	11
PUSHED UP THEIR HAIR, THE DRY WIND STEERS	90	WHERE ONCE THE	5
IF I WERE TICKLED BY THE HATCHING HAIR,	95	RUB OF LOVE	10
MY WORDY WOUNDS ARE PRINTED WITH YOUR HAIR.	96	RUB OF LOVE	47
THAT GLOBE ITSELF OF HAIR AND BONE	97	TWILIGHT LOCKS	10

	PAGE	TITLE	LINE
HAIR (CONTINUED)			
WITH FROSTY FINGERS PUNISHES MY HAIR,	98	OCTOBER WIND	2
I SPELT MY VISION WITH A HAND AND HAIR,	102	FELLOWED SLEEP	23
AND JONAH'S MOBY SNATCHED ME BY THE HAIR,	119	ALTARWISE	66
A CALM WIND BLOWS THAT RAISED THE TREES LIKE HAIR	133	I MAKE THIS IN	64
WITH A HAND PLUNGED THROUGH HER HAIR,	139	TOMBSTONE TOLD	12
AND THE DEAR FLOODS OF HIS HAIR.	140	TOMBSTONE TOLD	30
THE SKULL OF THE EARTH IS BARBED WITH A WAR OF BURNING BRAINS AND HAIR.	142	SAINT TO FALL	34
SAVOURS THE LICK OF THE TIMES THROUGH A DEADLY WOOD OF HAIR	144	PLEASURE-BIRD	9
AND SAMSON DROWNED IN HIS HAIR,	157	INTO HER HEAD	13
AT HIS THRASHING HAIR AND WHALE-BLUE EYE;	161	LONG-LEGGED	3
SEE WHAT CLINGS TO HAIR AND SKULL	166	LONG-LEGGED	133
THE CENTURIES THROW BACK THEIR HAIR	167	LONG-LEGGED	151
CLINGS TO HER DRIFTING HAIR, AND CLIMBS;	167	LONG-LEGGED	161
COIL FROM THE THOROUGHFARES OF HER HAIR	168	LONG-LEGGED	197
WOUND, NOR HER RIDING HIGH, NOR HER EYES, NOR KINDLED HAIR,	201	COUNTRY SLEEP	101
NOR THE SPLENDOUR OF YOUR DARK HAIR,	228	NOT DESPAIR	10
SO, THEN, WILL THE DARK CLOTH OF YOUR HAIR	232	FURIOUS MOTION	7
HAIR-BURIED			
THROUGH THE RIPPLED DRUM OF THE HAIR-BURIED EAR;	157	INTO HER HEAD	4
HAIRED			
THE HAYGOLD HAIRED, MY LOVE ASLEEP, AND THE RIFT BLUE	200	COUNTRY SLEEP	88
HAIRPINS			
AND THEIR FIREFLY HAIRPINS FLEW, AND THE RICKS RAN ROUND--	205	GIANT'S THIGH	41
HAIRS			
RAISES THE HAIRS OF LAD AND MAIDEN.	59	FAIRY TALES	16
WHERE NO WAX IS, THE CANDLE SHOWS ITS HAIRS.	82	LIGHT BREAKS	12
YOUR CALM AND CUDDLED IS A SCYTHE OF HAIRS,	99	RUNNING GRAVE	2
AND LOOSED THE BRAIDING ADDERS FROM THEIR HAIRS;	104	WORLD PYRAMID	22
HAIRS OF YOUR HEAD, THEN SAID THE HOLLOW AGENT,	117	ALTARWISE	25
HAIR'S			
'IF MY HEAD HURT A HAIR'S FOOT'	145	IF HEAD HURT	T
'IF MY HEAD HURT A HAIR'S FOOT	145	IF HEAD HURT	1
HAIRY-HEELED			
DEATH HAIRY-HEELED, AND THE TAPPED GHOST IN WOOD,	128	NOW, SAY NAY	33
HALE			
HALE DEAD AND DEATHLESS DO THE WOMEN OF THE HILL	205	GIANT'S THIGH	58
HALF			
HALF CONVENTION AND HALF LIE.	44	LONGED TO MOVE	20
HALF CONVENTION AND HALF LIE.	44	LONGED TO MOVE	20
WHERE HALF DEAD VANITIES WERE SLEEPING CURLED	50	OUT OF THE PIT	4
LIKE CATS, AND LUSTS LAY HALF HOT IN THE COLD.	50	OUT OF THE PIT	5
HALF OF THE OLD GANG'S SHOT,	59	FAIRY TALES	8
HALF A SMILE MIGHT BE HER SABRE.	71	TAKE NEEDLES	20
IS HALF ITS LIGHT; THE FATHOMED SEA	88	A PROCESS IN	11
FORKS HALF ITS FRUIT; AND HALF DROPS DOWN,	88	A PROCESS IN	14
FORKS HALF ITS FRUIT; AND HALF DROPS DOWN,	88	A PROCESS IN	14
THIS WORLD IS HALF THE DEVIL'S AND MY OWN,	95	RUB OF LOVE	29
HALF OF THE FELLOW FATHER AS HE DOUBLES	103	WORLD PYRAMID	1
HALF OF THE FELLOW MOTHER AS SHE DABBLES	103	WORLD PYRAMID	3
THE FELLOW HALF WAS FROZEN AS IT BUBBLED	104	WORLD PYRAMID	7
FOR HALF OF LOVE WAS PLANTED IN THE LOST,	104	WORLD PYRAMID	11
MY HALF GHOST IN ARMOUR HOLD HARD IN DEATH'S CORRIDOR,	108	I, IN IMAGE	5
A HANDMADE MOON HALF HOLY IN A CLOUD,	121	INCARNATE DEVL	8
TIME AT THE CITY SPECTACLES, AND HALF	124	TODAY, INSECT	3

		PAGE	TITLE	LINE
HALF (CONTINUED)				
OF THE UPPER OF THE LOWER HALF,	....	156	RETURN	71
EARLY IMAGINARY HALF REMEMBERED	....	158	INTO HER HEAD	32
WHEN I WAS A GUSTY MAN AND A HALF	....	206	LAMENT	13
WHEN I WAS A HALF OF THE MAN I WAS	....	207	LAMENT	37
HALF-AVERTED				
WITH HALF-AVERTED HEADS, AS IF TO LISTEN,	....	40	YOUNG ARE OLD	13
HALF-BLIND				
AND, CRACKLING INTO THE AIR, LEAVE ME HALF-BLIND.		44	LONGED TO MOVE	14
HALFMOON'S				
HOW, THROUGH THE HALFMOON'S VEGETABLE EYE,	....	138	FIVE & COUNTRY	3
HALF-MOULDED				
WITH THAT HALF-MOULDED MIND I SAID WAS YOURS,	.....	10	COOL, OH NO	4
HALF-TRACKED				
DRY IN THE HALF-TRACKED THIGH.	....	105	WORLD PYRAMID	60
HALF-WAY				
ALTARWISE BY OWL-LIGHT IN THE HALF-WAY HOUSE	......	116	ALTARWISE	1
WITH BONES UNBUTTONED TO THE HALF-WAY WINDS,	......	117	ALTARWISE	9
ATLASWISE HOLD HALF-WAY OFF THE DUMMY BAY	....	121	ALTARWISE	128
HALLELUJAH				
SEE HOW HE STUMBLES. HALLELUJAH HEE-HAW!	....	179	NEW QUAY	26
HALLOWED				
WITHIN THE HALLOWED GLAND, BLOOD BLESSED THE HEART,		78	LOVE'S FEVER	18
HALO				
POUR LIKE A HALO ON THE CAPS AND SERPENTS.	....	120	ALTARWISE	118
HALOED				
EYED, IN THE HALOED HOUSE, IN HER RARENESS AND HILLY		200	COUNTRY SLEEP	89
HALT				
HALT AMONG EUNUCHS, AND THE NITRIC STAIN	....	100	RUNNING GRAVE	24
HALTER				
CRUMBS, BARN, AND HALTER.	....	32	OUT OF SIGHS	29
TO THE HAWK ON FIRE, THE HALTER HEIGHT, OVER TOWY'S				
FINS,	....	202	SIR JOHNS HILL	16
HALTS				
ABOVE THE WASTE ALLOTMENTS THE DAWN HALTS.	....	82	LIGHT BREAKS	30
HALVED				
DOUBLED THE GLOBE OF DEAD AND HALVED A COUNTRY;	...	66	HAND SIGNED	3
HALVES				
THE BROKEN HALVES ARE FELLOWED IN A CRIPPLE,	......	104	WORLD PYRAMID	13
THE PATCHWORK HALVES WERE CLOVEN AS THEY SCUDDED		104	WORLD PYRAMID	19
ROTATING HALVES ARE HORNING AS THEY DRILL	....	104	WORLD PYRAMID	23
THE HALVES THAT PIERCE THE PIN'S POINT IN THE AIR,		104	WORLD PYRAMID	26
THE FELLOW HALVES THAT, CLOVEN AS THEY SWIVEL	.....	105	WORLD PYRAMID	49
THAT BRIDGED THE HUMAN HALVES,	....	108	GRIEF THIEF	26
HAMLET				
AND THE FIVE-FATHOMED HAMLET ON HIS FATHER'S CORAL,		111	I, IN IMAGE	83
DEATH: DEATH OF HAMLET AND THE NIGHTMARE MADMEN,		124	TODAY, INSECT	19
INTO A HOMESTALL KING OR HAMLET OF FIRE	....	198	COUNTRY SLEEP	11
HAMLETS				
HOUSED IN HAMLETS OF HEAVEN SWING THE LOFT LAMPS,		215	COUNTRY HEAVEN	16
HAMMER				
HEADS OF THE CHARACTERS HAMMER THROUGH DAISIES;	...	50	NO DOMINION	25
THE LEADEN STARS, THE RAINY HAMMER	....	68	BEFORE KNOCKED	11
NO, NO, YOU LOVER SKULL, DESCENDING HAMMER	....	100	RUNNING GRAVE	27
NOR HAMMER BACK A SEASON IN THE FIGS,	....	123	FOSTER LIGHT	8
BEFORE I RUSH IN A CROUCH THE GHOST WITH A HAMMER,				
AIR,	....	145	IF HEAD HURT	9
AND MY WHOLE HEART UNDER YOUR HAMMER,	....	147	TO OTHERS	13
BEFORE CHAINS BREAK TO A HAMMER FLAME	....	210	POEM ON B'DAY	44

HAND

	PAGE	TITLE	LINE
ONE LADY'S HAND WAS LIFTED,	11	CABARET	11
WHY IS MY HAND TOO BLUNT	12	SKY'S BRIGHT	5
AND WATCH MY HAND,	13	SKY'S BRIGHT	27
MY HAND WITH HONEY THAT HAD CLOSED UPON A FLOWER.	15	FOR LEDA	19
AND DARKNESS, HAND IN HAND WITH LIGHT,	15	FOR LEDA	32
AND DARKNESS, HAND IN HAND WITH LIGHT,	15	FOR LEDA	32
OUT OF MY HAND IN STOPPING UP MY MOUTH,	18	NATURAL DAY	16
AND WATCH THE HAND OF TIME UNCEASINGLY	26	THERE'S PLENTY	11
ON EVERY HAND THE EVIL'S POSITIVE	27	OBLIVIOUS DARK	18
UPON YOUR HELD-OUT HAND	32	HELD-OUT HAND	T
UPON YOUR HELD-OUT HAND	32	HELD-OUT HAND	1
LIFTED HER MARBLE FOOT, OR LOWERED HER HAND	34	IN GARDENS	20
UP YOUR HAND TO STROKE THE LIGHT,	35	LIFT UP FACE	15
AND HAND TO BUTTOCK, MAN TO ENGINE, BATTLING,	51	OUT OF THE PIT	36
ONE HAND AT HEAD, THE OTHER AT A LOSS,	52	OUT OF THE PIT	60
SLEEPING ON EITHER HAND.	54	WE BY SEASAND	8
THE HAND THAT SIGNED THE PAPER	66	HAND SIGNED	T
THE HAND THAT SIGNED THE PAPER FELLED A CITY;	66	HAND SIGNED	1
THE MIGHTY HAND LEADS TO A SLOPING SHOULDER,	66	HAND SIGNED	5
THE HAND THAT SIGNED THE TREATY BRED A FEVER,	66	HAND SIGNED	9
GREAT IS THE HAND THAT HOLDS DOMINION OVER	66	HAND SIGNED	11
A HAND RULES PITY AS A HAND RULES HEAVEN;	66	HAND SIGNED	15
A HAND RULES PITY AS A HAND RULES HEAVEN;	66	HAND SIGNED	15
MOVES TO THE MAHOMET OF YOUR HAND.	67	REALM OF FLESH	3
GILDERS OF STREETS, THE RABBLE HAND	70	SECRET WIND	10
HOLD IN HIS VELVET HAND THE CAN OF BLOOD;	73	LORD RED HAIL	2
THE HAND THAT WHIRLS THE WATER IN THE POOL	77	THE FORCE THAT	11
HAND, THE BREAKING OF THE HAIR,	78	LOVE'S FEVER	11
THE MILK OF DEATH, I FILLED THE HAND	86	SEE, SAYS LIME	30
I SPELT MY VISION WITH A HAND AND HAIR,	102	FELLOWED SLEEP	23
SO CROSS HER HAND WITH THEIR GRAVE GIPSY EYES,	115	A GRIEF AGO	39
WITH PRIEST'S GRAVE FOOT AND HAND OF FIVE ASSASSINS	131	I MAKE THIS IN	25
COMES LOVE'S ANATOMIST WITH SUN-GLOVED HAND	132	I MAKE THIS IN	44
THE CAULDRON'S ROOT THROUGH THIS ONCE-RINDLESS HAND	132	I MAKE THIS IN	55
WITH A HAND PLUNGED THROUGH HER HAIR,	139	TOMBSTONE TOLD	12
RAGE ME BACK TO THE MAKING HOUSE. MY HAND UNRAVEL	145	IF HEAD HURT	12
QUICKNESS OF HAND IN THE VELVET GLOVE	147	TO OTHERS	12
TRYING HIS HAND AT FAILING	155	RETURN	29
THE WEIGHING-SCALES, OF MY HAND.	155	RETURN	43
GOOD LUCK TO THE HAND ON THE ROD,	164	LONG-LEGGED	61
HIS FATHERS CLING TO THE HAND OF THE GIRL	167	LONG-LEGGED	147
AND THE DEAD HAND LEADS THE PAST,	167	LONG-LEGGED	148
A GARDEN HOLDING TO HER HAND	167	LONG-LEGGED	167
WITH HIS LONG-LEGGED HEART IN HIS HAND.	169	LONG-LEGGED	216
AND A HUNDRED STORKS PERCH ON THE SUN'S RIGHT HAND.	173	DAWN RAID	14
CRY. MY VOICE BURNS IN HIS HAND.	185	VISION, PRAYER	202
GLIDING WINDLESS THROUGH THE HAND FOLDED FLAKES,	187	WINTER'S TALE	4
THOUGH NO SOUND FLOWED DOWN THE HAND FOLDED AIR	188	WINTER'S TALE	40
IT WAS A HAND OR SOUND	189	WINTER'S TALE	66
UP TO THE SWALLOW THRONGED LOFT BY THE SHADOW OF MY HAND,	196	FERN HILL	47
(O HAND IN HAND)	215	COUNTRY HEAVEN	12
(O HAND IN HAND)	215	COUNTRY HEAVEN	12
VEINED HIS POOR HAND I HELD, AND I SAW	217	ELEGY	16
AMONG THE QUIET TREES. AND HAND IN HAND	227	SPRING-SPIRIT	11
AMONG THE QUIET TREES. AND HAND IN HAND	227	SPRING-SPIRIT	11
HAND IN HAND WITH THE MERMAID	231	OUR SANCTITY	40
HAND IN HAND WITH THE MERMAID	231	OUR SANCTITY	40
YOU DO NOT HURT, NOR CAN YOUR HAND	233	NO THOUGHT	3

		PAGE	TITLE	LINE
HAND (CONTINUED)				
FROM THE WELL-MADE HAND	••••••••••••••••••••••••	241	ADMIT THE SUN	21
HANDBAGGED				
TWOLEGGED HANDBAGGED SPARROWS,	•••••••••••••••••	156	RETURN	74
HANDBELL				
RING LIKE A HANDBELL THROUGH THE CORRIDORS,	•••••••	56	WHY EAST WIND	22
HANDFULL				
HUSK OF YOUNG STARS AND HANDFULL ZODIAC,	••••••••••	138	FIVE & COUNTRY	4
HANDMADE				
A HANDMADE MOON HALF HOLY IN A CLOUD,	•••••••••••••	121	INCARNATE DEVL	8
HANDPRINT				
ON ROSE AND ICICLE THE RINGING HANDPRINT.	•••••••••	120	ALTARWISE	98
HANDS				
TIME FOR THE SWIMMERS' HANDS, MUSIC FOR SILVER LOCK		15	SPIRE CRANES	7
THEIR HANDS OUTSTRETCHED, TO GIVE AND GIVE?	•••••••	36	MIDNIGHT ROAD	8
SUSPICIOUS HANDS TUG AT THE NEIGHBOURING VICES,	•••	38	THE GOSSIPERS	3
HAVE CLEANEST HANDS, AND, AS THE HEARTLESS GHOST		40	WAS THERE TIME	8
WE WHO ARE YOUNG SIT HOLDING YELLOW HANDS.	•••••••••	41	YOUNG ARE OLD	17
WARMING DRY HANDS AND LISTENING TO THE WIND.	•••••••	42	YOUNG ARE OLD	55
AS THE HANDS THAT HELD THEM IN MY FATHER'S TIME.		45	PLOUGHMAN GONE	11
WITH RAIN-BEATEN HANDS HOLDING THE WHIP,	•••••••••••	45	PLOUGHMAN GONE	20
FAITH IN THEIR HANDS SHALL SNAP IN TWO,	•••••••••••	50	NO DOMINION	15
THE QUEEN IS SLAIN; ORESTES' HANDS DRIP BLOOD;	••••	57	GREEK PLAY	15
HANDS GRUMBLE ON THE DOOR,	••••••••••••••••••••••••	62	EARS IN TURRET	2
HANDS, HOLD YOU POISON OR GRAPES?	•••••••••••••••••	62	EARS IN TURRET	9
HANDS GRUMBLE ON THE DOOR,	••••••••••••••••••••••••	62	EARS IN TURRET	26
HANDS OF THE STRANGER AND HOLDS OF THE SHIPS,	••••••	63	EARS IN TURRET	32
HANDS HAVE NO TEARS TO FLOW.	••••••••••••••••••••••	66	HAND SIGNED	16
WITH LIQUID HANDS TAPPED ON THE WOMB,	•••••••••••••	68	BEFORE KNOCKED	2
GRIEF WITH DISHEVELLED HANDS TEAR OUT THE ALTAR GHOST		130	SINNERS' BELL	5
AND BEAR THOSE TENDRIL HANDS I TOUCH ACROSS	•••••••	134	NOT FROM ANGER	6
I KNOW HER SCRUBBED AND SOUR HUMBLE HANDS	••••••••	136	AFTER FUNERAL	31
THESE CLOUD-SOPPED, MARBLE HANDS, THIS MONUMENTAL		137	AFTER FUNERAL	36
BEHIND A FACE OF HANDS,	•••••••••••••••••••••••••••	141	SAINT TO FALL	10
WOE DRIP FROM THE DISHRAG HANDS AND THE PRESSED				
SPONGE OF THE FOREHEAD,	•••••••••••••••••••••••	142	SAINT TO FALL	45
NIGHT AFTER NIGHT THEIR HANDS IMPLORE	••••••••••••	143	THE MOLLS	3
WITH MY FISHTAIL HANDS AND GENTLY	•••••••••••••••••	154	RETURN	5
FOR HIS BRIARED HANDS TO HOIST THEM	•••••••••••••••	184	VISION, PRAYER	137
HANDS OR INSTRUMENTS	••••••••••••••••••••••••••••••	185	VISION, PRAYER	175
HOLLOWS, A GRASSBLADE BLOWN IN CUPPED HANDS, IN THE				
LOOTED ELMS	••••••••••••••••••••••••••••••••••	203	SIR JOHNS HILL	52
AND TOUCH YOU WITH SOFTER HANDS.	••••••••••••••••••	228	NOT DESPAIR	6
YOU STRETCH OUT YOUR HANDS	••••••••••••••••••••••••	229	MY RIVER	21
YOUR HANDS ARE BEAUTIFUL HANDS	••••••••••••••••••••	229	MY RIVER	27
YOUR HANDS ARE BEAUTIFUL HANDS	••••••••••••••••••••	229	MY RIVER	27
HER WOVEN HANDS BECKONED ME,	••••••••••••••••••••••	234	WOMAN TAPESTRY	1
WITH THE POWER OF MY HANDS	••••••••••••••••••••••••	235	WOMAN TAPESTRY	36
GLASS TO MY HANDS ENDOWED WITH DOUBLE STRENGTH.	•••	239	MAKES INTERVALS	19
AND TWINE THE LIMBS AROUND MY HANDS.	••••••••••••••	239	MAKES INTERVALS	24
HAND'S				
BY LOVE-TIP OR MY HAND'S RED HEAT.	••••••••••••••••	19	IMAGES IN AIR	14
HANDSAW				
HAVE BROTHERLESS HIS SISTER ON THE HANDSAW.	•••••••	127	NOW, SAY NAY	14
HANDSHAPED				
SAILED AND SET DAZZLING BY THE HANDSHAPED OCEAN,		131	I MAKE THIS IN	5
HANDSOME				
I HAD A HANDSOME AND WELL-OFF BOY	••••••••••••••••	149	PAPER & STICKS	13
HANDY				
IT WAS SWEET TO DROWN IN THE READYMADE HANDY WATER		152	BELOW A TIME	44

		PAGE	TITLE	LINE
HANG				
THEN HANG A RAM ROSE OVER THE RAGS.	....	60	MEAT ON BONES	8
AND THE MAN NO ROPE CAN HANG	....	61	MEAT ON BONES	26
AND WORLDS HANG ON THE TREES.	....	98	TWILIGHT LOCKS	42
STORM HER SPED HEART, HANG WITH BEHEADED VEINS	....	132	I MAKE THIS IN	34
HANGAR				
YOU HERO SKULL, CADAVER IN THE HANGAR	....	100	RUNNING GRAVE	29
HANGING				
UNDER THE HANGING BRANCHES HEAR THE WINDS' HARPS.		46	POET: 1935	15
AND I AM DUMB TO TELL THE HANGING MAN	....	77	THE FORCE THAT	14
WHEN NO MOUTH STIRRED ABOUT THE HANGING FAMINE,	...	78	LOVE'S FEVER	5
THE FILM OF SPRING IS HANGING FROM THE LIDS.	......	82	LIGHT BREAKS	24
TO BURST INTO A HANGING LAND	....	85	SEE, SAYS LIME	19
HACK OF THE COUGH, THE HANGING ALBATROSS,	....	107	GRIEF THIEF	10
DRIVES FORTH MY MEN, MY CHILDREN, FROM THE HANGING SOUTH.	....	122	HOLD HARD	6
HANGMAN'S				
HOW OF MY CLAY IS MADE THE HANGMAN'S LIME.	....	77	THE FORCE THAT	15
ITCHED ON THE HANGMAN'S SILKS;	....	85	SEE, SAYS LIME	21
STRUNG BY THE FLAXEN WHALE-WEED, FROM THE HANGMAN'S RAFT,	....	110	I, IN IMAGE	65
HANGNAIL				
ABADDON IN THE HANGNAIL CRACKED FROM ADAM,	....	116	ALTARWISE	3
HANGS				
THE ALMANAC OF TIME HANGS IN THE BRAIN;	....	79	ALMANAC TIME	1
THE CALENDAR OF AGE HANGS IN THE HEART,	....	80	ALMANAC TIME	6
THE HAWK ON FIRE HANGS STILL;	....	201	SIR JOHNS HILL	2
WHEN HIS VIPERISH FUSE HANGS LOOPED WITH FLAMES UNDER THE BRAND	....	202	SIR JOHNS HILL	28
HANK				
CRIED THE TOPLESS, INCHTAPED LIPS FROM HANK AND HOOD		132	I MAKE THIS IN	47
HANSOM				
THE PLOUGHMAN'S GONE, THE HANSOM DRIVER,	....	45	PLOUGHMAN GONE	1
THE PLOUGHMAN'S GONE, THE HANSOM DRIVER,	....	45	PLOUGHMAN GONE	19
HAPPENING				
IN BATTLE! THE HAPPENING	....	182	VISION, PRAYER	95
HAPPILY				
TAP HAPPILY OF ONE PEG IN THE THICK	....	136	AFTER FUNERAL	3
HAPPY				
THAT MADE ME HAPPY IN THE SUN,	....	32	OUT OF SIGHS	19
HOW MUCH WAS HAPPY WHILE IT LASTED,	....	32	OUT OF SIGHS	20
NOW HE HAS HEARD AND READ THE HAPPY WORD.	....	53	OUT OF THE PIT	100
HAPPY CADAVER'S HUNGER AS YOU TAKE	....	101	RUNNING GRAVE	49
ABOUT THE LILTING HOUSE AND HAPPY AS THE GRASS WAS GREEN,	....	195	FERN HILL	2
ABOUT THE HAPPY YARD AND SINGING AS THE FARM WAS HOME,	....	195	FERN HILL	11
UNDER THE NEW MADE CLOUDS AND HAPPY AS THE HEART WAS LONG,	....	196	FERN HILL	38
HARBOUR				
VOYAGING CLOCKWISE OFF THE SYMBOLED HARBOUR,	....	109	I, IN IMAGE	32
LET THE HERO SEED FIND HARBOUR,	....	126	SEED-AT-ZERO	33
LET THE HERO SEED FIND HARBOUR,	....	126	SEED-AT-ZERO	40
WOKE TO MY HEARING FROM HARBOUR AND NEIGHBOUR WOOD		176	POEM IN OCT	2
PALE RAIN OVER THE DWINDLING HARBOUR	....	177	POEM IN OCT	31
CRYSTAL HARBOUR VALE	....	202	SIR JOHNS HILL	37
HARBOURING				
HARBOURING SOME THOUGHT OF HEAVEN, OR HAVEN HOPING,		36	MIDNIGHT ROAD	2
HARBOURS				
SO SHALL WINGED HARBOURS THROUGH THE ROCKBIRDS' EYES		121	ALTARWISE	130

	PAGE	TITLE	LINE
HARBOURS (CONTINUED)			
HARBOURS MY ANCHORED TONGUE, SLIPS THE QUAYSTONE,	131	I MAKE THIS IN	3
HARD			
THE STREAM'S FANTASTICALLY HARD,	14	RAIN CUTS	26
THE STILL GO HARD,	16	TIME TO ROT	13
FIND HARD TO DART AGAINST A CLOUD,	37	WINDMILLS TURN	8
FELL HARD AS WHIPS ON AN OLD WOUND,	42	A WAR OF WITS	3
LAY YOUR HEAD ON A HARD BED OF STONE,	45	PLOUGHMAN GONE	17
LAY YOUR HEAD ON A HARD BED OF STONE,	46	PLOUGHMAN GONE	31
THE PATHS ARE HARD, FOR YOU ARE NOT	83	LETTER TO AUNT	3
MY HALF GHOST IN ARMOUR HOLD HARD IN DEATH'S CORRIDOR,	108	I, IN IMAGE	5
HOLD HARD, THESE ANCIENT MINUTES IN THE CUCKOO'S MONTH	122	HOLD HARD	T
HOLD HARD, THESE ANCIENT MINUTES IN THE CUCKOO'S MONTH,	122	HOLD HARD	1
HOLD HARD, MY COUNTRY CHILDREN IN THE WORLD OF TALES,	122	HOLD HARD	10
HOLD HARD, MY COUNTY DARLINGS, FOR A HAWK DESCENDS,	123	HOLD HARD	22
INSECTS AND VALLEYS HOLD HER THIGHS HARD,	168	LONG-LEGGED	174
THEY FROM HOUSES WHERE THE HARVEST KNEELS, HOLD ME HARD,	205	GIANT'S THIGH	50
OF THE SEA UNDER THE HARD SUN,	229	MY RIVER	35
TRAILING THEIR FINGERS ON THE HARD EDGES	235	WOMAN TAPESTRY	33
HARDEN			
THEY HARDEN AND TAKE SHAPE AGAIN	19	IMAGES IN AIR	11
IN SACRED WATERS THAT NO FROST COULD HARDEN,	122	INCARNATE DEVL	14
LET THE FROST HARDEN	240	ADMIT THE SUN	5
HARDER			
THE HARDER TO BEAR AND THE STRONGER.	39	GAS FADES	29
HARD-HELD			
SPILL THE LANK FOLLY'S HUNTER AND THE HARD-HELD HOPE.	122	HOLD HARD	18
HARDINESS			
FORSAKE, THE FOOL, THE HARDINESS OF ANGER.	127	NOW, SAY NAY	7
HARDLY			
MY SILLY SUIT, HARDLY YET SUFFERED FOR,	152	BELOW A TIME	29
AMONG THE HARDLY POSSESSED.	156	RETURN	65
HARDLY BEAR THE DIN OF NO-GOOD WRACKED DRY ON	179	NEW QUAY	9
HARDSHIP			
ON THE FIRST OF EACH HARDSHIP,	151	BELOW A TIME	5
HARE			
WHISKING HARE! WHO	4	PROLOGUE	68
DAWS SIR JOHN'S JUST HILL DONS, AND AGAIN THE GULLED BIRDS HARE	201	SIR JOHNS HILL	15
HARE-			
THE LEAPING SAGA OF PRAYER! AND HIGH, THERE, ON THE HARE-	199	COUNTRY SLEEP	66
HAREBELL			
FORCING FORTH THROUGH THE HAREBELL,	109	I, IN IMAGE	15
HARING			
THE HARING SNAIL GO GIDDILY ROUND THE FLOWER,	109	I, IN IMAGE	41
HARK			
HARK: I TRUMPET THE PLACE,	4	PROLOGUE	42
HARK! A VOICE AND LAUGHTER--THE LIVING AND LOVING	222	FOREST PICTURE	11
HARKS			
AND THROUGH THESE EARS HE HARKS MY FIRE BURN	77	LASHED RINGS	16
HARLEM			
FROM HARLEM, BEDLAM, BABEL, AND THE GHETTO,	41	YOUNG ARE OLD	40
HARM			
WON'T HARM THE TENT AROUND HIM,	17	IN OBLIVION	24
VALES WHERE HE PRAYED TO COME TO THE LAST HARM	190	WINTER'S TALE	109

	PAGE	TITLE	LINE
HARM (CONTINUED)			
I'LL KNOW I'M OUT OF HARM, ...	240	TWINING HEAD	4
HARMONIES			
PAIR OFF, MAKE HARMONIES, A HARMONIOUS CHORD, ...	53	OUT OF THE PIT	96
HARMONIOUS			
PAIR OFF, MAKE HARMONIES, A HARMONIOUS CHORD, ...	53	OUT OF THE PIT	96
HARMONY			
VIGOUR AND HARMONY IN LIGHT TO NONE, ...	17	NATURAL DAY	4
MOST FIT FOR LOVERS TO MAKE HARMONY, ...	34	THIRST PARCHES	10
HARNESS			
IS COME OF THE SEA TUMBLING IN HARNESS	191	REFUSAL MOURN	6
HARNESSED			
TIME, IN A RIDER RISING, FROM THE HARNESSED VALLEY;	122	HOLD HARD	21
HARNESSING			
MAN WAS CADAVER'S MASKER, THE HARNESSING MANTLE,	112	I, IN IMAGE	103
HARP			
THERE'S TIME TO PLUCK A TUNE UPON THE HARP, ...	15	FOR LEDA	16
CREEP AND HARP ON THE TIDE, SINKING THEIR CHARMED,			
BENT PIN	135	HOW MY ANIMAL	24
AND THE HARP SHAPED VOICE OF THE WATER'S DUST PLUCKS			
IN A FOLD	189	WINTER'S TALE	79
HARPIES			
HARPIES AROUND ME OUT OF HER WOMB!	207	LAMENT	56
HARPS			
UNDER THE HANGING BRANCHES HEAR THE WINDS' HARPS.	46	POET: 1935	15
AND DUCKED AND DRAKED WHITE LAKE THAT HARPS TO A			
HAIL STONE.	204	GIANT'S THIGH	28
HARPSTRUNG			
SEE, ON GRAVEL PATHS UNDER THE HARPSTRUNG TREES ...	46	POET: 1935	1
SEE, ON GRAVEL PATHS UNDER THE HARPSTRUNG TREES,	48	POET: 1935	58
HARP-WAKED			
THE HARP-WAKED CASANOVA RAKES NO RANGE.	159	TO LEDA	2
HARROW			
SHALL HARROW AND SNOW THE BLOOD WHILE YOU RIDE WIDE			
AND NEAR, ...	198	COUNTRY SLEEP	23
HARSH			
BEFORE THE GAS FADES WITH A HARSH LAST BUBBLE, ...	38	GAS FADES	1
A BLAZING RED HARSH HEAD TEAR UP	140	TOMBSTONE TOLD	29
HARSHLY			
DRUM HARSHLY ON THE AIR, THE LIGHTNING SWORDS	51	OUT OF THE PIT	15
HARVEST			
SETTING NO STORE BY HARVEST, FREEZE THE SOILS;	91	BOYS OF SUMMER	3
SHARP IN MY SECOND DEATH I MARKED THE HILLS, HARVEST	103	I DREAMED MY	17
IN HIGH CORN AND THE HARVEST MELTING ON THEIR			
TONGUES.	188	WINTER'S TALE	43
THEY FROM HOUSES WHERE THE HARVEST KNEELS, HOLD ME			
HARD, ...	205	GIANT'S THIGH	50
HAS (61)			
HASTENING			
HAVE TRACED YOUR PATTERNS IN THE HASTENING FROST.	30	YOUTH CALLS	7
HASTENS			
HASTENS THE TIME OF THE GERANIUM TO BREATHE;	47	POET: 1935	37
HAT			
THE PARTING OF HAT FROM HAIR, ...	44	LONGED TO MOVE	16
NO LONGER TREMBLE AT A BISHOP'S HAT, ...	59	FAIRY TALES	2
THE HOLY HAT.	60	FAIRY TALES	41
FIRST BUY A HAT, NO PARIS MODEL	83	LETTER TO AUNT	15
OR LIFT MY HAT TO UNSEEN	155	RETURN	48
HATCH			
THE OLD MUD HATCH AGAIN, THE HORRID	142	SAINT TO FALL	44

		PAGE	TITLE	LINE
HATCHED				
THE GHOST THAT HATCHED HIS HAVOC AS HE FLEW		104	WORLD PYRAMID	29
HATCHED FROM THE WINDY SALVAGE ON ONE LEG, ...		117	ALTARWISE	10
HATCHING				
IF I WERE TICKLED BY THE HATCHING HAIR, ...		95	RUB OF LOVE	10
HATE				
HATE AND FEAR BE YOUR TWO LOVES.		76	SONG: LOVE ME	15
HATING				
HATING HIS GOD, BUT WHAT HE WAS WAS PLAIN:		217	ELEGY	23
HATS				
AND GIRLS WITH FLOWERED HATS		37	WINDMILLS TURN	11
HATSTAND				
AND THE HUNT IN THE HATSTAND DISCOVERS NO COPPERS,		38	GAS FADES	2
HAUL				
SING AND STRIKE HIS HEAVY HAUL		166	LONG-LEGGED	137
ALL THE HORSES OF HIS HAUL OF MIRACLES		168	LONG-LEGGED	187
HAULED				
HAULED TO THE DOME, ...		99	RUNNING GRAVE	5
HAULS				
HAULS MY SHROUD SAIL.		77	THE FORCE THAT	13
HAUNTS				
FOR WHO UNMANNINGLY HAUNTS THE MOUNTAIN RAVENED EAVES	198	COUNTRY SLEEP	24
HAVE (131)				
HAVEN				
HARBOURING SOME THOUGHT OF HEAVEN, OR HAVEN HOPING,		36	MIDNIGHT ROAD	2
TO DUMBFOUNDING HAVEN		181	VISION, PRAYER	63
HAVING				
HAVING SO MUCH TO SPARE.		23	THE ONLY DEAD	22
HAVOC				
THE GHOST THAT HATCHED HIS HAVOC AS HE FLEW		104	WORLD PYRAMID	29
HAWED				
WHO ONCE WERE A BLOOM OF WAYSIDE BRIDES IN THE HAWED HOUSE		204	GIANT'S THIGH	29
HAWK				
THE EYES REMARK THE ANTICS OF THE HAWK.		63	WOMAN SPEAKS	10
HOLD HARD, MY COUNTY DARLINGS, FOR A HAWK DESCENDS,		123	HOLD HARD	22
SINGS TO THE TREADING HAWK		159	INTO HER HEAD	59
AND THE HAWK IN THE EGG KILLS THE WREN.		167	LONG-LEGGED	156
THE HAWK ON FIRE HANGS STILL;		201	SIR JOHNS HILL	2
THE FLASHED THE NOOSED HAWK		201	SIR JOHNS HILL	10
TO THE HAWK ON FIRE, THE HALTER HEIGHT, OVER TOWY'S FINS, ...		202	SIR JOHNS HILL	16
SHALLOW AND SEDGE, AND 'DILLY DILLY', CALLS THE LOFT HAWK, ...		202	SIR JOHNS HILL	21
ALL PRAISE OF THE HAWK ON FIRE IN HAWK-EYED DUSK BE SUNG, ...		202	SIR JOHNS HILL	27
THE SHOOTING STAR HAWK STATUED BLIND IN A CLOUD ...		215	COUNTRY HEAVEN	23
HAWK-EYED				
ALL PRAISE OF THE HAWK ON FIRE IN HAWK-EYED DUSK BE SUNG, ...		202	SIR JOHNS HILL	27
HAWKING				
HAWKING FOR MONEY AND PITY		156	RETURN	64
HAWKS				
AND SHAFTED HAWKS CAME SNARLING DOWN THE SKY;		65	WOMAN SPEAKS	57
IN THE CLAW TRACKS OF HAWKS		209	POEM ON B'DAY	21
HAY				
AND THE SMELL OF HAY IN THE SNOW, AND THE FAR OWL		187	WINTER'S TALE	7
ALL THE SUN LONG IT WAS RUNNING, IT WAS LOVELY, THE HAY		195	FERN HILL	19
MY WISHES RACED THROUGH THE HOUSE HIGH HAY		196	FERN HILL	41

	PAGE	TITLE	LINE
HAY (CONTINUED)			
IN THE WAINS TONNED SO HIGH THAT THE WISPS OF THE HAY	204	GIANT'S THIGH	14
WHERE THE HAY RIDES NOW OR THE BRACKEN KITCHENS RUST	205	GIANT'S THIGH	47
HAYBEDS			
TO TROT WITH A LOUD MATE THE HAYBEDS OF A MILE, ...	135	HOW MY ANIMAL	16
HAYCOCK			
TO A HAYCOCK COUCH AND THE SCYTHES OF HIS ARMS	157	INTO HER HEAD	17
HAYCOCKS			
NIGHT AND THE REINDEER ON THE CLOUDS ABOVE THE HAYCOCKS	199	COUNTRY SLEEP	64
HAYGOLD			
THROUGH THE HAYGOLD STALLS, AS THE DEW FALLS ON THE WIND-	199	COUNTRY SLEEP	58
THE HAYGOLD HAIRED, MY LOVE ASLEEP, AND THE RIFT BLUE	200	COUNTRY SLEEP	88
HAYRICKS			
AND THE BAIT IS DROWNED AMONG HAYRICKS, ...	169	LONG-LEGGED	208
HAYSTACKED			
HIST, IN HOGSBACK WOODS! THE HAYSTACKED	5	PROLOGUE	78
HAZARDOUS			
HAZARDOUS REFLECTIONS DIPPED IN EVENING	226	THE OAK	3
HAZE			
SOMEHOW IT SEEMS, AMID THE EVENING HAZE, ...	223	IN DREAMS	8
HE (147)			
HEAD			
BRIGHT, WELL-HELD HEAD, ...	14	FOR LEDA	9
THEN SWIM YOUR HEAD, ...	16	TIME TO ROT	17
ON HEAD AND RUNNING FOOT, ...	21	BEWILDERED WAY	21
FOOT, HEAD, OR TRACES	24	LITTLE PROBLEM	1
OF FOOT ON HEAD WE'LL BE THE TIME	24	LITTLE PROBLEM	4
FOR A PURPOSE (HEAD TO FOOT IS HEAD AND FOOT, ...	24	LITTLE PROBLEM	6
FOR A PURPOSE (HEAD TO FOOT IS HEAD AND FOOT, ...	24	LITTLE PROBLEM	6
FOOT HEAD COMPRESSED, ...	24	LITTLE PROBLEM	10
NO USE TO RUN YOUR HEAD AGAINST THE WALL	27	OBLIVIOUS DARK	11
THE SAME THOUGHTS IN OUR HEAD.	28	NO WINGS	19
AND BARED YOUR HEAD BENEATH THE LIVING SKY, ...	30	YOUTH CALLS	9
THE ANGELS' WINGS BEATING ABOUT YOUR HEAD	33	HELD-OUT HAND	4
LIFT UP YOUR HEAD, LET	35	LIFT UP FACE	10
LIFT WIT-HURT HEAD FOR SUN TO SYMPATHIZE, ...	42	A WAR OF WITS	18
LAY YOUR HEAD ON A HARD BED OF STONE, ...	45	PLOUGHMAN GONE	17
LAY YOUR HEAD ON A HARD BED OF STONE, ...	46	PLOUGHMAN GONE	31
WITHIN HIS HEAD REVOLVED A LITTLE WORLD	50	OUT OF THE PIT	1
WITHIN HIS HEAD THE ENGINES MADE THEIR HELL, ...	50	OUT OF THE PIT	6
LIFT ITS HEAD TO THE BLOWS OF THE RAIN;	50	NO DOMINION	23
ONE HAND AT HEAD, THE OTHER AT A LOSS, ...	52	OUT OF THE PIT	60
PALM OF THE EARTH, O SPRINKLE ON MY HEAD	65	WOMAN SPEAKS	60
UNPACKS THE HEAD THAT, LIKE A SLEEPY GHOST, ...	75	MY HERO BARES	3
THE LIPS OF TIME LEECH TO THE FOUNTAIN HEAD;	77	THE FORCE THAT	16
MY SISTERS' TEARS THAT SING UPON MY HEAD, ...	80	ALL THAT I OWE	7
DELIVER ME, MY MASTERS, HEAD AND HEART, ...	100	RUNNING GRAVE	11
FROM MAID AND HEAD, ...	100	RUNNING GRAVE	15
BUT HEART, LIKE HEAD, LEADS HELPLESSLY;	116	LANTERNS SHINE	10
HAIRS OF YOUR HEAD, THEN SAID THE HOLLOW AGENT, ...	117	ALTARWISE	25
OF HEAD AND TAIL MADE WITNESSES TO THIS	124	TODAY, INSECT	7
AND OPIUM HEAD, CROW STALK, PUFFED, CUT, AND BLOWN,	131	I MAKE THIS IN	10
THE HERO'S HEAD LIES SCRAPED OF EVERY LEGEND, ...	132	I MAKE THIS IN	43
BEHIND MY HEAD A SQUARE OF SKY SAGS OVER	134	NOT FROM ANGER	8
A BLAZING RED HARSH HEAD TEAR UP	140	TOMBSTONE TOLD	29
'IF MY HEAD HURT A HAIR'S FOOT'	145	IF HEAD HURT	T
'IF MY HEAD HURT A HAIR'S FOOT	145	IF HEAD HURT	1
MY DEAR WOULD I CHANGE MY TEARS OR YOUR IRON HEAD.	146	IF HEAD HURT	18

	PAGE	TITLE	LINE
HEAD (CONTINUED)			
UP TO HIS HEAD IN HIS BLOOD,	150	WHEN I WOKE	9
HEAD, DECEIVED, I BELIEVED, MY MAKER,	152	BELOW A TIME	34
GLARED THROUGH SHARK MASK AND NAVIGATING HEAD,	152	BELOW A TIME	39
INTO HER LYING DOWN HEAD	157	INTO HER HEAD	T
INTO HER LYING DOWN HEAD	157	INTO HER HEAD	1
HEAD TO HEAVEN-CIRCLING HEAD,	158	INTO HER HEAD	48
HEAD TO HEAVEN-CIRCLING HEAD,	158	INTO HER HEAD	48
TO SHARE MY ROOM IN THE HOUSE NOT RIGHT IN THE HEAD,	169	LOVE IN ASYLUM	2
UNDER THE SAD BREAST OF THE HEAD STONE	174	FIRE RAID	44
AND THE SHADOWED HEAD OF PAIN	180	VISION, PRAYER	24
THE SCROLLS OF FIRE THAT BURNED IN HIS HEART AND HEAD,	187	WINTER'S TALE	14
ABOVE HER FOLDED HEAD, AND THE SOFT FEATHERED VOICE	189	WINTER'S TALE	82
ONE GESTURE OF THE HEART OR HEAD,	192	SIDE OF TRUTH	9
HAS A HORN AND TWO HUMPS ON ITS HEAD,	221	SONG OF DOG	6
LIGHTLY, THOU WIND, OVER HIS DEAR, DARK HEAD,	222	MISSING	4
BUT BEAUTIFULLY FLAKE YOUR HEAD	227	SPRING-SPIRIT	3
LEDGES OF WAVES HIGH OVER YOUR HEAD,	228	MY RIVER	2
THE ROD CAN LIFT ITS TWINING HEAD	240	TWINING HEAD	T
THE ROD CAN LIFT ITS TWINING HEAD	240	TWINING HEAD	1
AND THE HEAD OF THE BRIGHT POPPY.	240	ADMIT THE SUN	11
HEADED			
THE WOMAN BREASTED AND THE HEAVEN HEADED	191	WINTER'S TALE	125
HEADLANDS			
DOWN THE LONG BAYS OF BLUE THAT THOSE CLOUDY HEADLANDS	222	FOREST PICTURE	6
HEADLESS			
AND THE MASKED, HEADLESS BOY.	129	MY NEOPHYTE	30
HEADS			
FEELING THE WIND ABOUT OUR HEADS THAT DOES NOT COOL,	26	THERE'S PLENTY	18
THRUST OUT OUR HEADS ABOVE THE BRANCHES	31	BEING BUT MEN	9
WITH HALF-AVERTED HEADS, AS IF TO LISTEN,	40	YOUNG ARE OLD	13
THE GRAFTERS OF CATS' HEADS ON CHICKENS' TRUNKS,	41	YOUNG ARE OLD	42
HEADS OF THE CHARACTERS HAMMER THROUGH DAISIES;	50	NO DOMINION	25
AND, BROKEN GHOSTS WITH GLOW-WORMS IN THEIR HEADS,	82	LIGHT BREAKS	4
AS SUNLIGHT PAINTS THE SHELLING OF THEIR HEADS.	92	BOYS OF SUMMER	18
OF TIDE-TONGUED HEADS AND BLADDERS IN THE DEEP,	104	WORLD PYRAMID	16
BABBLE LIKE A BELLBUOY OVER THE HYMNING HEADS,	136	AFTER FUNERAL	23
WITH THEIR HEADS IN A CUNNING CLOUD.	147	TO OTHERS	21
OPENING IN THE BLIND CLOUD OVER OUR HEADS;	231	OUR SANCTITY	44
OR CRUSH THEIR VIPER HEADS BENEATH MY FOOT.	239	LET ME ESCAPE	5
HEAD'S			
HIS HEAD'S IN A NEST WHERE NO BIRD LAYS HER EGG.	179	NEW QUAY	27
HEADSTONE			
IN THE RIVER TOWY BELOW BOWS HIS TILTED HEADSTONE.	201	SIR JOHNS HILL	12
HEAL			
TIME CANNOT HEAL NOR RESURRECT;	26	THERE'S PLENTY	15
OR ALL-IN WRESTLING FOR TORN LIMBS TO HEAL,	51	OUT OF THE PIT	31
HEALS			
AND THE SUN HEALS, CLOSING SORE EYES.	42	A WAR OF WITS	19
HEAP			
I BUILD A FORTRESS FROM A HEAP OF FLOWERS;	240	ADMIT THE SUN	9
HEAR			
HEAR AND AM STILL THE LITTLE BIRD.	9	MINUTE'S HOUR	7
I HEAR THEM SAY OUT OF THE DARKNESS	23	ON QUIET NIGHT	21
UNDER THE HANGING BRANCHES HEAR THE WINDS' HARPS.	46	POET: 1935	15
HE COULD HEAR WOMEN BREATHING IN THE DARK,	51	OUT OF THE PIT	20
I HEAR CONTENT, AND 'BE CONTENT'	56	WHY EAST WIND	21
EARS IN THE TURRETS HEAR	62	EARS IN TURRET	T

	PAGE	TITLE	LINE
HEAR (CONTINUED)			
EARS IN THE TURRETS HEAR	62	EARS IN TURRET	1
EARS IN THIS ISLAND HEAR	62	EARS IN TURRET	17
WE HEAR RISE THE SECRET WIND BEHIND THE BRAIN,	70	SECRET WIND	19
BY THE SEA'S SIDE HEAR THE DARK-VOWELLED BIRDS.	99	OCTOBER WIND	32
I HEAR, THROUGH DEAD MEN'S DRUMS, THE RIDDLED LADS,	105	WORLD PYRAMID	40
HEAR THEY THE SALT GLASS BREAKERS AND THE TONGUES OF BURIAL.	110	I, IN IMAGE	66
OVER THE CHOIR MINUTE I HEAR THE HOUR CHANT:	130	SINNERS' BELL	7
HEAR BY DEATH'S ACCIDENT THE CLOCKED AND DASHED-DOWN SPIRE	130	SINNERS' BELL	11
TO HEAR THE GOLDEN NOTE TURN IN A GROOVE,	153	WAS A SAVIOUR	6
THERE WAS GLORY TO HEAR	153	WAS A SAVIOUR	17
HEAR THEIR LAUGHTER SLY AS GONOCOCCI.	179	NEW QUAY	18
THAT I CAN HEAR THE WOMB	180	VISION, PRAYER	6
I SHOULD HEAR HIM FLY WITH THE HIGH FIELDS	196	FERN HILL	50
MAKES ALL THE MUSIC; AND I WHO HEAR THE TUNE OF THE SLOW,	203	SIR JOHNS HILL	57
I LIE DOWN THIN AND HEAR THE GOOD BELLS JAW--	207	LAMENT	53
I HEAR THE BOUNCING HILLS	211	POEM ON B'DAY	100
HEARD			
SINCE, ON A QUIET NIGHT, I HEARD THEM TALK	22	ON QUIET NIGHT	1
AND HEARD THE TEETH OF WEASELS DRAWING BLOOD.	52	OUT OF THE PIT	58
AND THUS, BETWEEN THE SEASONS, HEARD HIM CRY:	52	OUT OF THE PIT	62
AND THUS, SOME TIME LATER, I HEARD HIM SAY:	53	OUT OF THE PIT	89
NOW HE HAS HEARD AND READ THE HAPPY WORD.	53	OUT OF THE PIT	100
IS HEARD BUT LITTLE TILL THE STARS GO OUT.	56	WHY EAST WIND	20
I HAVE HEARD MANY YEARS OF TELLING,	116	LANTERNS SHINE	16
BEFORE I HEARD IN MY MOTHER'S SIDE	139	TOMBSTONE TOLD	6
AMONG MEN LATER I HEARD IT SAID	139	TOMBSTONE TOLD	16
HEARD HER SPEAK THROUGH THE CHIPPED BEAK	140	TOMBSTONE TOLD	24
I HEARD, THIS MORNING, WAKING,	150	WHEN I WOKE	23
ONE LEAN SIGH WHEN WE HEARD	153	WAS A SAVIOUR	29
BUT HEARD HIS BAIT BUCK IN THE WAKE	162	LONG-LEGGED	29
RUNNING WHEN HE HAD HEARD THEM CLEARLY	171	THE HUNCHBACK	17
ON THE SILENT SEA WE HAVE HEARD THE SOUND	194	SLEEP BECALMED	3
WE HEARD THE SEA SOUND SING, WE SAW THE SALT SHEET TELL.	194	SLEEP BECALMED	12
ALL THE MOON LONG I HEARD, BLESSED AMONG STABLES, THE NIGHTJARS	195	FERN HILL	25
AND HEARD THE LEWD, WOOED FIELD FLOW TO THE COMING FROST,	204	GIANT'S THIGH	30
WHO HEARD THE TALL BELL SAIL DOWN THE SUNDAYS OF THE DEAD	205	GIANT'S THIGH	51
TO HAVE HEARD THEIR VAGUE, RHAPSODIC SINGINGS,	223	IDYLL UNFORGET	5
HEARING			
HEARING THE ENGINES, AND THE WHEAT DYING.	46	PLOUGHMAN GONE	26
FEELING THE SUMMER WIND, HEARING THE SWANS,	48	POET: 1935	59
BY THE SEA'S SIDE, HEARING THE NOISE OF BIRDS,	98	OCTOBER WIND	5
HEARING THE RAVEN COUGH IN WINTER STICKS,	98	OCTOBER WIND	6
HEARING THE WEATHER FALL.	109	I, IN IMAGE	30
OUT TO THE TIERED AND HEARING TIDE,	158	INTO HER HEAD	38
WOKE TO MY HEARING FROM HARBOUR AND NEIGHBOUR WOOD	176	POEM IN OCT	2
BEACH, HEARING RISE SLIMY FROM THE WELSH LECHERED	179	NEW QUAY	16
WALL HEARING THE MOAN	180	VISION, PRAYER	22
HEART! SLYLY, SLOWLY, HEARING THE WOUND IN HER SIDE GO	200	COUNTRY SLEEP	95
HEARS			
HEARS, THERE, THIS FOX LIGHT, .. FLOOD SHIP'S	4	PROLOGUE	69
WHO ON HIS CLOUD HEARS ALL MY WISHES,	48	LIGHT, I KNOW	15

	PAGE	TITLE	LINE
HEARS (CONTINUED)			
HEARS AND REFUSES. ••••••••••••••••••••••••••••••••••	49	LIGHT, I KNOW	16
(WHOM MY HEART HEARS), ••••••••••••••••••••••••••••	215	COUNTRY HEAVEN	2
HEARS THE BELFRIES AND THE COBBLES •••••••••••••••	215	COUNTRY HEAVEN	25
HEARSE			
UP NAKED STAIRS, A TURTLE IN A HEARSE, ••••••••••••	99	RUNNING GRAVE	4
HEART			
YOU HAVE OFFENDED, PERIODIC HEART; ••••••••••••••••	9	MINUTE'S HOUR	8
WITH QUITE A KIND OF HEART. •••••••••••••••••••••••	12	CABARET	17
SOMETIMES A WOMAN'S HEART HAS SALT, ••••••••••••••	13	SKY'S BRIGHT	20
OR EVIL FROM THE CANKERED HEART. ••••••••••••••••	19	THE NEOPHYTE	4
OUT OF THE HEART FOR ME, •••••••••••••••••••••••••	21	BEWILDERED WAY	16
CHRIST, LET ME WRITE FROM THE HEART, ••••••••••••	22	HIGH ON A HILL	7
WAR ON THE HEART-- ••••••••••••••••••••••••••••••	22	HIGH ON A HILL	8
OUT OF THE FULLNESS OF ANOTHER'S HEART ••••••••••	23	THE ONLY DEAD	21
WHEN FOLLY STIRRED, WARM IN THE FOOLISH HEART. ••••	25	BEAUTY TO DUST	19
THE DRY FEVER BURNS UNTIL NO HEART IS LEFT, ••••••••	34	THIRST PARCHES	2
THAT THUNDERS AS HEART THUNDERS, SLOWS AS HEART			
SLOWS. ••	46	POET: 1935	6
THAT THUNDERS AS HEART THUNDERS, SLOWS AS HEART			
SLOWS. ••	46	POET: 1935	6
IS NOT HIS HEART IMPRISONED BY THE SUMMER ••••••••	46	POET: 1935	7
WITH HEART UNLOCKED UPON THE GIGANTIC EARTH. ••••••	46	POET: 1935	12
AND HAS THE MAD TREES' TALK BY HEART. ••••••••••••	47	POET: 1935	28
MY HEART HURLS FROM MY SIDE AND TEARS ••••••••••••	48	LIGHT, I KNOW	8
BREAKS, O MY HEART'S BLOOD, LIKE A HEART AND HILL.	54	WE BY SEASAND	24
AND NO AEGEAN WIND COOL HER CRACKED HEART; ••••••••	57	GREEK PLAY	10
WE HAVE THE FAIRY TALES BY HEART •••••••••••••••••	59	FAIRY TALES	T
WE HAVE THE FAIRY TALES BY HEART, •••••••••••••••••	59	FAIRY TALES	1
WE HAVE BY HEART THE CHILDREN'S STORIES, ••••••••••	59	FAIRY TALES	22
AND MY HEART IS CRACKED ACROSS; ••••••••••••••••••	61	MEAT ON BONES	18
THE HEART LIES READY FOR THE RAVEN'S MOUTH, •••••••	63	WOMAN SPEAKS	8
YOU RULE THE THUDDING HEART THAT BITES THE SIDE;	67	REALM OF FLESH	7
THE HEART STEPS TO DEATH'S FINGER, ••••••••••••••••	67	REALM OF FLESH	8
MY HEART KNEW LOVE, MY BELLY HUNGER; ••••••••••••••	69	BEFORE KNOCKED	29
THE LINES OF EARTH, THE CURVING OF THE HEART, ••••••	73	LORD RED HAIL	14
MY HERO BARES MY SIDE AND SEES HIS HEART ••••••••••	75	MY HERO BARES	11
HIS AWKWARD HEART INTO SOME SYMMETRY. •••••••••••••	77	LASHED RINGS	17
FROM THE FIRST SECRET OF THE HEART, THE WARNING			
GHOST, ••	78	LOVE'S FEVER	12
WITHIN THE HALLOWED GLAND, BLOOD BLESSED THE HEART,	78	LOVE'S FEVER	18
THE CALENDAR OF AGE HANGS IN THE HEART, ••••••••••	80	ALMANAC TIME	6
THEN LOOK, MY HEART, UPON THE SCARLET TROVE, ••••••	81	ALL THAT I OWE	28
WHERE NO SEA RUNS, THE WATERS OF THE HEART ••••••••	82	LIGHT BREAKS	2
REMOVE YOUR BRAINS, TAKE OUT YOUR HEART; ••••••••••	84	LETTER TO AUNT	60
I PUT ROUND RIBS THAT PACKED THEIR HEART, ••••••••••	85	SEE, SAYS LIME	2
A PROCESS IN THE WEATHER OF THE HEART •••••••••••••	88	A PROCESS IN	T
A PROCESS IN THE WEATHER OF THE HEART •••••••••••••	88	A PROCESS IN	1
AND THE HEART GIVES UP ITS DEAD. •••••••••••••••••	88	A PROCESS IN	24
OF LIGHT AND LOVE, THE TEMPERS OF THE HEART, ••••••	89	EUNUCH DREAMS	2
THE WORD FLOWED UP, TRANSLATING TO THE HEART ••••••	94	IN BEGINNING	23
MY FUSES TIMED TO CHARGE HIS HEART, •••••••••••••••	97	TWILIGHT LOCKS	13
HE HAD BY HEART THE CHRIST-CROSS-ROW OF DEATH. ••••	97	TWILIGHT LOCKS	24
MY BUSY HEART WHO SHUDDERS AS SHE TALKS •••••••••••	98	OCTOBER WIND	7
TO ROB ME OF MY FLUIDS IN HIS HEART. •••••••••••••	98	TWILIGHT LOCKS	36
THE HEART IS DRAINED THAT, SPELLING IN THE SCURRY	99	OCTOBER WIND	30
DELIVER ME, MY MASTERS, HEAD AND HEART, ••••••••••	100	RUNNING GRAVE	11
HEART OF CADAVER'S CANDLE WAXES THIN, •••••••••••••	100	RUNNING GRAVE	12
RAMMED IN THE MARCHING HEART, HOLE •••••••••••••••	103	I DREAMED MY	14
NOR THE HEART IN THE RIBBING METAL. •••••••••••••••	106	ALL ALL AND	15

	PAGE	TITLE	LINE

HEART (CONTINUED)

I HAVE BEEN TOLD TO REASON BY THE HEART, ...	116	LANTERNS SHINE	9
BUT HEART, LIKE HEAD, LEADS HELPLESSLY;	116	LANTERNS SHINE	10
THE SHEATH-DECKED JACKS, QUEEN WITH A SHUFFLED HEART;	118	ALTARWISE	59
WHO COULD HACK OUT YOUR UNSUCKED HEART,	129	MY NEOPHYTE	46
STORM HER SPED HEART, HANG WITH BEHEADED VEINS	132	I MAKE THIS IN	34
WHO PICKS THE LIVE HEART ON A DIAMOND.	132	I MAKE THIS IN	45
THAT MELTS THE LIONHEAD'S HEEL AND HORSESHOE OF THE HEART, ...	135	HOW MY ANIMAL	14
WHOSE HOODED, FOUNTAIN HEART ONCE FELL IN PUDDLES	136	AFTER FUNERAL	14
THE RAIN THROUGH HER COLD HEART SPEAK	139	TOMBSTONE TOLD	8
MY ONE AND NOBLE HEART HAS WITNESSES	139	FIVE & COUNTRY	11
THE HEART IS SENSUAL, THOUGH FIVE EYES BREAK.	139	FIVE & COUNTRY	14
THE STOCKED HEART IS FORCED, AND AGONY HAS ANOTHER MOUTH TO FEED.	142	SAINT TO FALL	42
AND MY WHOLE HEART UNDER YOUR HAMMER, ...	147	TO OTHERS	13
AND I LIVED IN HIS PURSE AND HIS HEART	149	PAPER & STICKS	6
CLOSE AND FAR SHE ANNOUNCED THE THEFT OF THE HEART	158	INTO HER HEAD	39
YOUR HEART IS LUMINOUS	160	DEATHS AND ENT	30
THE WINDOWS POUR INTO THEIR HEART	161	WEDDING ANNIV	11
WITH HIS LONG-LEGGED HEART IN HIS HAND.	169	LONG-LEGGED	216
HER HEART ALL EARS AND EYES, LIPS CATCHING THE AVALANCHE	170	MARRIAGE VIRG	10
DIG NO MORE FOR THE CHAINS OF HIS GREY-HAIRED HEART.	172	DAWN RAID	9
AS THE GRAINS BLOW, AS YOUR DEATH GROWS, THROUGH OUR HEART.	173	FIRE RAID	24
DAYS DEEP IN HER BREAST THAT WORE NO HEART	175	MY BEGGAR ARM	2
TELLING THE HEART I BROKE OF A GOOD HABIT	175	MY BEGGAR ARM	4
THAT HIS TEARS BURNED MY CHEEKS AND HIS HEART MOVED IN MINE.	178	POEM IN OCT	52
AND THE HEART PRINT OF MAN	180	VISION, PRAYER	12
THE INMOST MARROW OF MY HEART BONE	183	VISION, PRAYER	118
NO HEART BONE	184	VISION, PRAYER	146
I CLIMB TO GREET THE WAR IN WHICH I HAVE NO HEART BUT ONLY	186	HOLY SPRING	8
THE SCROLLS OF FIRE THAT BURNED IN HIS HEART AND HEAD, ...	187	WINTER'S TALE	14
ONE GESTURE OF THE HEART OR HEAD, ...	192	SIDE OF TRUTH	9
KING OF YOUR HEART IN THE BLIND DAYS, ...	193	SIDE OF TRUTH	16
UNDER THE NEW MADE CLOUDS AND HAPPY AS THE HEART WAS LONG, ...	196	FERN HILL	38
TO EAT YOUR HEART IN THE HOUSE IN THE ROSY WOOD.	197	COUNTRY SLEEP	7
OF THEIR MOST SECRET HEART.	197	CRAFT OR ART	11
TO COURT THE HONEYED HEART FROM YOUR SIDE BEFORE SUNRISE	198	COUNTRY SLEEP	13
HEART! SLYLY, SLOWLY, HEARING THE WOUND IN HER SIDE GO	200	COUNTRY SLEEP	95
(WHOM MY HEART HEARS), ...	215	COUNTRY HEAVEN	2
THAT PLAYED IN VOICELESS FROLIC AT THE THRESHOLD OF MY HEART.	223	IDYLL UNFORGET	12

HEARTBEAT

SUFFER THE HEAVEN'S CHILDREN THROUGH MY HEARTBEAT.	120	ALTARWISE	112

HEARTBONE

BEFORE THE FALL FROM LOVE THE FLYING HEARTBONE, ...	124	TODAY, INSECT	15
LOVE'S IMAGE TILL MY HEARTBONE BREAKS	129	MY NEOPHYTE	35

HEARTBREAK

THE TROUBLE, DEVILDOM, AND HEARTBREAK, ...	38	THE GOSSIPERS	15
TIME IS THE TUNE MY LADIES LEND THEIR HEARTBREAK,	119	ALTARWISE	95

HEARTH

THE WIRELESS SNARLS ON THE HEARTH.	45	PLOUGHMAN GONE	12

	PAGE	TITLE	LINE
HEARTH (CONTINUED)			
BUT I, ANN'S BARD ON A RAISED HEARTH, CALL ALL	136	AFTER FUNERAL	21
HEARTHS			
SIT AT OUR HEARTHS FROM MORNING UNTIL EVENING, ...	42	YOUNG ARE OLD	54
HEARTHSTONE			
IN THE LAND OF THE HEARTHSTONE TALES, AND SPELLED ASLEEP, ...	197	COUNTRY SLEEP	2
OF THE HEARTHSTONE TALES MY OWN, LOST LOVE; AND THE SOUL WALKS	199	COUNTRY SLEEP	53
HEARTLESS			
HAVE CLEANEST HANDS, AND, AS THE HEARTLESS GHOST	40	WAS THERE TIME	8
SOME LET ME MAKE YOU OF THE HEARTLESS WORDS.	99	OCTOBER WIND	29
HEARTS			
WITH SIGHTLESS EYES AND HEARTS THAT DO NOT BEAT,	39	GAS FADES	36
TORN OUT MAGIC FROM THE HEARTS OF COWARDS	60	FAIRY TALES	32
PRAISE TO OUR FARING HEARTS.	90	EUNUCH DREAMS	42
THERE FROM THEIR HEARTS THE DOGDAYED PULSE	92	BOYS OF SUMMER	22
HEART'S			
BREAKS, O MY HEART'S BLOOD, LIKE A HEART AND HILL.	54	WE BY SEASAND	24
AND THE WAILING HEART'S NAILED TO THE SIDE.	74	SUN BURNS	5
FLOOD OF HER HEART'S FAME; SHE WOULD LIE DUMB AND DEEP	136	AFTER FUNERAL	19
O MAY MY HEART'S TRUTH	178	POEM IN OCT	68
FOR THE COUNTRY OF DEATH IS THE HEART'S SIZE	184	VISION, PRAYER	169
HEART-SHAPED			
BUT RAIL WITH YOUR WIZARD'S RIBS THE HEART-SHAPED PLANET;	123	FOSTER LIGHT	15
HEAT			
WITH ZEST CULLED FROM THEIR LADYLIKE HEAT, ...	18	NATURAL DAY	12
BY LOVE-TIP OR MY HAND'S RED HEAT.	19	IMAGES IN AIR	14
WHO FEELS NOT COLDNESS IN THE HEAT, ...	55	NO MAN BELIEVE	8
THE SOLID WORLD SHALL WITHER IN THE HEAT, ...	73	LORD RED HAIL	17
HE PROMISES A SECRET HEAT.	75	MY HERO BARES	15
THERE IN THEIR HEAT THE WINTER FLOODS	91	BOYS OF SUMMER	4
REHEARSING HEAT UPON A RAW-EDGED NERVE.	95	RUB OF LOVE	19
AND TAKES THE HEAT AWAY.	230	MY RIVER	43
HEATH			
THROUGH HEATH AND HEATHER AT THE MIND'S WILL.	44	TO FOLLOW FOX	13
HEATHER			
SCENT THROUGH THE CLUTCHES OF THE HEATHER, ...	44	TO FOLLOW FOX	4
THROUGH HEATH AND HEATHER AT THE MIND'S WILL.	44	TO FOLLOW FOX	13
THROUGH EASIER HEATHER TO THE FOUL LAIR	44	TO FOLLOW FOX	16
HEATS			
OR LAME THE AIR WITH LEAPING FROM ITS HEATS;	92	BOYS OF SUMMER	21
HEAVE			
HURDLES AND GUNS AND RAILINGS, AS THE BOULDERS HEAVE,	122	HOLD HARD	16
HEAVEN			
GEESE NEARLY IN HEAVEN, BOYS	3	PROLOGUE	15
WHEN HEAVEN--OPEN WIDE THE GATES--HAS TAKEN FLIGHT,	34	THIRST PARCHES	4
HARBOURING SOME THOUGHT OF HEAVEN, OR HAVEN HOPING,	36	MIDNIGHT ROAD	2
GRIEF, LIKE AN OPEN WOUND, HAS CRIED TO HEAVEN. ...	64	WOMAN SPEAKS	32
A HAND RULES PITY AS A HAND RULES HEAVEN;	66	HAND SIGNED	15
THE CODE OF STARS TRANSLATE IN HEAVEN.	69	SECRET WIND	3
A SHOUT WENT UP TO HEAVEN LIKE A ROCKET, ...	70	SECRET WIND	7
THE CITY GOSPEL SHOUT TO HEAVEN.	70	SECRET WIND	21
LOVE ME, NOT AS THE GIRLS OF HEAVEN	76	SONG: LOVE ME	5
HOW TIME HAS TICKED A HEAVEN ROUND THE STARS.	77	THE FORCE THAT	20
AND EVEN HEAVEN HAS A SMELL	84	LETTER TO AUNT	53
AND FILL THE MOUTHS OF HEAVEN WITH YOUR TONGUE	87	PAIN BE MUSIC	2
HEAVEN AND HELL MIXED AS THEY SPUN.	93	IN BEGINNING	6

                                                        PAGE   TITLE   LINE

HEAVEN (CONTINUED)
    AND PRICK THE THUMB-STAINED HEAVEN THROUGH THE
        THIMBLE. 104   WORLD PYRAMID   27
    THE TONGUES OF HEAVEN GOSSIP AS I GLIDE 105   WORLD PYRAMID   53
    ALL HEAVEN IN A MIDNIGHT OF THE SUN, ... 122   INCARNATE DEVL   17
    AND THIS WEAK HOUSE TO MARROW-COLUMNED HEAVEN, ... 131   I MAKE THIS IN   8
    PUFFING THE POUNDS OF MANNA UP THROUGH THE DEW TO
        HEAVEN, ... 140   NO WORK WORDS   5
    THE STAINED FLATS OF HEAVEN HIT AND RAZED 141   SAINT TO FALL   2
    SANG HEAVEN HUNGRY AND THE QUICK 141   SAINT TO FALL   15
    HEAVEN FELL WITH HIS FALL AND ONE CROCKED BELL BEAT
        THE LEFT AIR. 142   SAINT TO FALL   25
    AND HEAVEN CRIER, ARROW NOW OF ASPIRING 148   UNLUCKILY FOR   38
    THAT THE PHOENIX' BID FOR HEAVEN AND THE DESIRE AFTER 148   UNLUCKILY FOR   45
    IT WAS MY THIRTIETH YEAR TO HEAVEN 176   POEM IN OCT   1
    YEAR TO HEAVEN STOOD THERE THEN IN THE SUMMER NOON   178   POEM IN OCT   66
    OF THE DAZZLER OF HEAVEN 181   VISION, PRAYER   41
    THE HEAVENS, THE HEAVEN, THE GRAVE, THE BURNING FONT. 190   WINTER'S TALE   104
    THE WOMAN BREASTED AND THE HEAVEN HEADED 191   WINTER'S TALE   125
    HEAVEN THAT NEVER WAS 210   POEM ON B'DAY   50
    AND AIR SHAPED HEAVEN WHERE SOULS GROW WILD 210   POEM ON B'DAY   74
    IN COUNTRY HEAVEN 215   COUNTRY HEAVEN   T
    ALWAYS WHEN HE, IN COUNTRY HEAVEN, ... 215   COUNTRY HEAVEN   1
    HOUSED IN HAMLETS OF HEAVEN SWING THE LOFT LAMPS,   215   COUNTRY HEAVEN   16
HEAVEN-CIRCLING
    HEAD TO HEAVEN-CIRCLING HEAD, ... 158   INTO HER HEAD   48
HEAVEN-DRIVEN
    DROVE IN THE HEAVEN-DRIVEN OF THE NAILS 120   ALTARWISE   106
HEAVENLY
    OUT OF THE HEAVENLY SEA ONTO THE MOON'S SHORES. ...   48   LIGHT, I KNOW   3
    THE HEAVENLY MUSIC OVER THE SAND   54   WE BY SEASAND   14
    THE HEAVENLY AMBULANCE DRAWN BY A WOUND 172   DAWN RAID   10
HEAVEN-PROOF
    SHE DELUDES THE HEAVEN-PROOF HOUSE WITH ENTERING
        CLOUDS 169   LOVE IN ASYLUM   6
HEAVENS
    AND I WOULD CHOKE THE HEAVENS WITH MY HYMN   96   TWELVE   12
    THE HEAVENS, THE HEAVEN, THE GRAVE, THE BURNING FONT. 190   WINTER'S TALE   104
HEAVENS'
    AND PLAYED DOWN PARDON FROM THE HEAVENS' HILL. 121   INCARNATE DEVL   6
HEAVEN'S
    TO HEAVEN'S TURNED, AND PIOUS LOADS   37   WINDMILLS TURN   32
    THE HEAVEN'S HOUSE.   81   HERE LIE BEAST   12
    AND MY IMAGES ROARED AND ROSE ON HEAVEN'S HILL. ... 112   I, IN IMAGE   108
    OLD COCK FROM NOWHERES AND THE HEAVEN'S EGG, ... 117   ALTARWISE   8
    SUFFER THE HEAVEN'S CHILDREN THROUGH MY HEARTBEAT.   120   ALTARWISE   112
    SHAPED MY CLAYFELLOW, AND THE HEAVEN'S ARK 124   FOSTER LIGHT   26
    DIE IN RED FEATHERS WHEN THE FLYING HEAVEN'S CUT,   135   HOW MY ANIMAL   40
    NOR WHEN ALL PONDEROUS HEAVEN'S HOST OF WATERS
        BREAKS. 146   IF HEAD HURT   20
    GULLED AND CHANTER IN YOUNG HEAVEN'S FOLD 210   POEM ON B'DAY   62
    IN THE FARMS OF HEAVEN'S KEEPING, ... 216   COUNTRY HEAVEN   29
HEAVY
    UNDER THE HEAVY LAYERS OF THE NIGHT   39   GAS FADES   38
    SING AND STRIKE HIS HEAVY HAUL 166   LONG-LEGGED   137
    HEAVY WITH THE DROWNED 183   VISION, PRAYER 106
    SUMMER IS HEAVY WITH AGE, AND LEANS UPON AUTUMN.   221   FOREST PICTURE   4
HEDGE
    WHEN BLACK BIRDS DIED LIKE PRIESTS IN THE CLOAKED
        HEDGE ROW 190   WINTER'S TALE   92

		PAGE	TITLE	LINE
HEDGEROW				
HEDGEROW, LABORATORY, AND EVEN GLASSHOUSE, ...		18	NATURAL DAY	13
WHO ONCE, GREEN COUNTRIES SINCE, WERE A HEDGEROW OF JOYS.		204	GIANT'S THIGH	20
HEDGES				
OF THE SPARROWS AND SUCH WHO SWANSING, DUSK, IN WRANGLING HEDGES.		201	SIR JOHNS HILL	7
AS THE ARC OF THE BILLHOOKS THAT FLASHED THE HEDGES LOW		205	GIANT'S THIGH	48
HEED				
PAYING HEED TO THE THIRSTY VOICE.		67	REALM OF FLESH	13
NOR HEED MY CRAFT OR ART.		197	CRAFT OR ART	20
TAKE HEED OF STRENGTH!		241	ADMIT THE SUN	19
HEEDING				
DEATH AND EVIL, TOO SLOW IN HEEDING WORDS.		60	FAIRY TALES	35
HEEDLESS				
I RAN MY HEEDLESS WAYS, ...		196	FERN HILL	40
HEE-HAW				
SEE HOW HE STUMBLES. HALLELUJAH HEE-HAW!		179	NEW QUAY	26
HEEL				
I, POOR ROMANTIC, HELD HER HEEL		11	CABARET	1
AS THAT HER HEEL WAS LIFTED, ...		12	CABARET	15
OVER HER HEEL AND ME.		12	CABARET	21
PIERCE THE SPILT SKY WITH DIVING WING IN WEED AND HEEL		15	SPIRE CRANES	4
HOWLS THE FOUL FIEND TO HEEL.		61	MEAT ON BONES	29
OVER THE VAULT OF RIDINGS WITH HIS HOUND AT HEEL,		122	HOLD HARD	5
HIS BEAST HEEL CLEFT IN A SANDAL, ...		130	SINNERS' BELL	3
THAT MELTS THE LIONHEAD'S HEEL AND HORSESHOE OF THE HEART, ...		135	HOW MY ANIMAL	14
AND THE OWL HOOD, THE HEEL HIDER, ...		152	BELOW A TIME	32
HEELED				
HEELED WINDS THE ROOKS		199	COUNTRY SLEEP	67
WHO COMES AS RED AS THE FOX AND SLY AS THE HEELED WIND.		200	COUNTRY SLEEP	81
HEELS				
THE WINGING BONE THAT SPROUTED IN THE HEELS, ...		95	RUB OF LOVE	11
BLEED FROM MY BURNING FORK AND SMELL MY HEELS.		105	WORLD PYRAMID	52
TWO HEELS OF WATER ON THE FLOOR OF SEED), ...		114	SERVANT SUN	24
SCATTERED IN THE PATHS OF HIS HEELS		165	LONG-LEGGED	95
HE-GOD'S				
AS A HE-GOD'S PADDLING WATER SKIRTS, ...		151	BELOW A TIME	16
HEIGH				
HEIGH, ON HORSEBACK HILL, JACK		4	PROLOGUE	67
HEIGH HO THE BLOOD AND BERRY, ...		93	BOYS OF SUMMER	44
HEIGHT				
THEIR OWN MELODIOUS HEIGHT, ...		14	RAIN CUTS	34
TO THE HAWK ON FIRE, THE HALTER HEIGHT, OVER TOWY'S FINS, ...		202	SIR JOHNS HILL	16
AND YOU, MY FATHER, THERE ON THE SAD HEIGHT, ...		208	NOT GO GENTLE	16
HEIGHTS				
FROM MODERNIST PARNASSIAN HEIGHTS.		83	LETTER TO AUNT	14
HEIR				
HEIR TO THE SCALDING VEINS THAT HOLD LOVE'S DROP,		80	ALL THAT I OWE	9
HEIR TO THE TELLING SENSES THAT ALONE		80	ALL THAT I OWE	11
CAST LIGHT UPON MY WEATHER. I AM HEIR		80	ALL THAT I OWE	15
HEIR TO THE SCALDING VEINS THAT HOLD LOVE'S DROP, COSTLY		103	I DREAMED MY	9
HELD				
I, POOR ROMANTIC, HELD HER HEEL		11	CABARET	1

		PAGE	TITLE	LINE
HELD (CONTINUED)				
A GIRL WHOSE SINGLE BED HELD TWO	....	38	THE GOSSIPERS	9
AS THE HANDS THAT HELD THEM IN MY FATHER'S TIME.		45	PLOUGHMAN GONE	11
AND HELD A LITTLE SABBATH WITH THE SUN,	....	97	TWILIGHT LOCKS	15
UNDER THE CLOUD AGAINST LOVE IS CAUGHT AND HELD AND				
KISSED	....	147	UNLUCKILY FOR	17
TIME HELD ME GREEN AND DYING	....	196	FERN HILL	53
AND STAR: HELD AND BLESSED, THOUGH YOU SCOUR THE				
HIGH FOUR	....	199	COUNTRY SLEEP	45
HIGH RIDING, HELD AND BLESSED AND TRUE, AND SO STILLY		200	COUNTRY SLEEP	90
VEINED HIS POOR HAND I HELD, AND I SAW	....	217	ELEGY	16
HELD-OUT				
UPON YOUR HELD-OUT HAND	....	32	HELD-OUT HAND	T
UPON YOUR HELD-OUT HAND	....	32	HELD-OUT HAND	1
HELL				
WITHIN HIS HEAD THE ENGINES MADE THEIR HELL,	......	50	OUT OF THE PIT	6
REMEMBER, TOO, THAT LIFE IS HELL	....	84	LETTER TO AUNT	52
HEAVEN AND HELL MIXED AS THEY SPUN.	....	93	IN BEGINNING	6
HELL WIND AND SEA,	....	114	A GRIEF AGO	4
AND ALL SWEET HELL, DEAF AS AN HOUR'S EAR,	....	114	SERVANT SUN	33
HELL IN A HORN OF SULPHUR AND THE CLOVEN MYTH,	....	122	INCARNATE DEVL	16
FURLED ON THE FISHES' HOUSE AND HELL,	....	129	MY NEOPHYTE	17
HE'LL				
HE'LL LIE DOWN, AND OUR BREATH	....	17	IN OBLIVION	5
HE'LL ACHE TOO LONG	....	32	OUT OF SIGHS	13
BOTH QUENCH HIS THIRST HE'LL HAVE A BLACK REPLY.		56	WHY EAST WIND	9
HE'LL TRUMPET INTO MEAT),	....	113	SERVANT SUN	5
HE'LL BATHE HIS RAINING BLOOD IN THE MALE SEA	.....	160	DEATHS AND ENT	19
HELLBORN				
WIND IN ME LEAPED, THE HELLBORN DEW;	....	68	BEFORE KNOCKED	16
HELL'S				
HELL'S IN THE DUST.	....	81	HERE LIE BEAST	6
HELPLESSLY				
BUT HEART, LIKE HEAD, LEADS HELPLESSLY;	....	116	LANTERNS SHINE	10
HEMISPHERE				
A HEMISPHERE MAY SCOLD HIM	....	126	SEED-AT-ZERO	31
HEMISPHERES				
AS FIRE FALLS, TWO HEMISPHERES DIVIDE,	....	73	LORD RED HAIL	7
HEMLOCK				
OF HEMLOCK AND THE BLADES, RUST	....	103	I DREAMED MY	18
HEMLOCK-HEADED				
AND HEMLOCK-HEADED IN THE WOOD OF WEATHERS.	....	117	ALTARWISE	28
HEMMING				
THE HEMMING CONTACT THAT'S SO TRAMMELLED	....	20	ENCOMPASSED	6
HEMS				
TO THE KISSED KITE HEMS OF HIS SHAWL,	....	141	SAINT TO FALL	3
HEN				
AND THE DUNG HILLS WHITE AS WOOL AND THE HEN	......	187	WINTER'S TALE	18
HENNA				
DRAW ON THE GLOVE OF PRINTS, DEAD CAIRO'S HENNA	...	120	ALTARWISE	117
HENRUN				
THE FIELDS, BY A MOTHERLIKE HENRUN)	....	154	RETURN	4
HENS				
AND NO GREEN COCKS OR HENS	....	203	SIR JOHNS HILL	53
HER (215)				
HERALD				
CONTINENCE. I SEE THE UNFIRED PHOENIX, HERALD	.....	148	UNLUCKILY FOR	37
HERALDS				
AND THE HERALDS OF DECAY,	....	71	TAKE NEEDLES	11

	PAGE	TITLE	LINE
HERD			
DOWN TO THE CURLEW HERD!	4	PROLOGUE	63
CALLS THE STARVED FIRE HERD, IS CAST IN ICE,	132	I MAKE THIS IN	27
HERDS			
TO THE SULTRY, BIDING HERDS, I SAID,	206	LAMENT	33
HERDSMAN			
AND GREEN AND GOLDEN I WAS HUNTSMAN AND HERDSMAN, THE CALVES	195	FERN HILL	15
HERE			
HERE UNDER THE EARTH WITH GIRL AND THIEF,	26	PERSONAL EPIT	5
HERE IS HER LABOUR'S END,	26	PERSONAL EPIT	13
HERE IN THIS SPRING	58	HERE IN SPRING	T
HERE IN THIS SPRING, STARS FLOAT ALONG THE VOID;	58	HERE IN SPRING	1
HERE IN THIS ORNAMENTAL WINTER	58	HERE IN SPRING	2
HERE IN MY WILDERNESS WANDERS THE BLOOD;	74	SUN BURNS	3
HERE IS A UNIVERSE BRED IN THE BONE,	74	SUN BURNS	6
HERE IS A SAVIOUR WHO SINGS LIKE A BIRD,	74	SUN BURNS	7
HERE THE NIGHT SHELTERS AND HERE THE STARS SHINE,	74	SUN BURNS	8
HERE THE NIGHT SHELTERS AND HERE THE STARS SHINE,	74	SUN BURNS	8
HERE A MILD BABY SPEAKS HIS FIRST WORD	74	SUN BURNS	9
HERE LIE THE BEASTS	81	HERE LIE BEAST	T
HERE LIE THE BEASTS OF MAN AND HERE I FEAST,	81	HERE LIE BEAST	1
HERE LIE THE BEASTS OF MAN AND HERE I FEAST,	81	HERE LIE BEAST	1
HERE SPRING THE SILENT VENOMS OF HIS BLOOD,	81	HERE LIE BEAST	4
HERE CLINGS THE MEAT TO SEVER FROM HIS SIDE.	81	HERE LIE BEAST	5
HERE LIES THE BEAST OF MAN AND HERE HIS ANGELS,	81	HERE LIE BEAST	7
HERE LIES THE BEAST OF MAN AND HERE HIS ANGELS,	81	HERE LIE BEAST	7
HERE DRIPS A SILENT HONEY IN MY SHROUD,	81	HERE LIE BEAST	10
HERE SLIPS THE GHOST WHO MADE OF MY PALE BED	81	HERE LIE BEAST	11
HERE LOVE'S DAMP MUSCLE DRIES AND DIES,	93	BOYS OF SUMMER	46
HERE BREAK A KISS IN NO LOVE'S QUARRY.	93	BOYS OF SUMMER	47
HAS A VOICE AND A HOUSE, AND THERE AND HERE YOU MUST COUCH AND CRY.	146	IF HEAD HURT	25
HERE WERE FOND CLIMATES AND SWEET SINGERS SUDDENLY	177	POEM IN OCT	26
SNIFF, HERE IS SIN! NOW HE MUST GRAPPLE, RISE:	179	NEW QUAY	29
HERE AMONG THE LIGHT OF THE LORDING SKY	217	ELEGY	29
HERE IS THE THOUGHT THAT COMES	233	NO THOUGHT	16
THAN SIT HERE WASTING, WHILE I BLEED,	240	TWINING HEAD	11
HERITAGE			
I ROUND THIS HERITAGE AS ROUNDS THE SUN	80	ALL THAT I OWE	13
ROUNDED MY GLOBE OF HERITAGE, JOURNEY	103	I DREAMED MY	11
HER ROPES OF HERITAGE, THE WARS OF PARDON,	115	A GRIEF AGO	21
HERMAPHRODITE			
MY SEA HERMAPHRODITE,	128	MY NEOPHYTE	7
HERMITS'			
TO HERMITS' HUTS, AND TALKED TO ANCIENT MEN.	53	OUT OF THE PIT	91
HERO			
MY HERO BARES HIS NERVES	75	MY HERO BARES	T
MY HERO BARES HIS NERVES ALONG MY WRIST	75	MY HERO BARES	1
MY HERO BARES MY SIDE AND SEES HIS HEART	75	MY HERO BARES	11
YOU HERO SKULL, CADAVER IN THE HANGAR	100	RUNNING GRAVE	29
LET THE HERO SEED FIND HARBOUR,	126	SEED-AT-ZERO	33
LET THE HERO SEED FIND HARBOUR,	126	SEED-AT-ZERO	40
HERODS			
LAPPED AMONG HERODS WAIL	142	SAINT TO FALL	39
HEROIC			
BUT BLESSED BY SUCH HEROIC HOSTS IN YOUR EVERY	148	UNLUCKILY FOR	21
HEROINE			
DEATH AND THIS MAD HEROINE	140	TOMBSTONE TOLD	22

	PAGE	TITLE	LINE
HERO-IN-TOMORROW			
SHALL THE HERO-IN-TOMORROW	126	SEED-AT-ZERO	48
SHALL THE HERO-IN-TOMORROW	127	SEED-AT-ZERO	55
HERON			
AND THE MUSSEL POOLED AND THE HERON	176	POEM IN OCT	3
HIGH TIDE AND THE HERON DIVED WHEN I TOOK THE ROAD	177	POEM IN OCT	17
CRASHES, AND SLOWLY THE FISHING HOLY STALKING HERON	201	SIR JOHNS HILL	11
THE HERON AND I, ...	202	SIR JOHNS HILL	34
OF EELS, SAINT HERON HYMNING IN THE SHELL-HUNG			
DISTANT	202	SIR JOHNS HILL	36
IT IS THE HERON AND I, UNDER JUDGING SIR JOHN'S ELMED	202	SIR JOHNS HILL	40
NOW THE HERON GRIEVES IN THE WEEDED VERGE. THROUGH			
WINDOWS	202	SIR JOHNS HILL	47
HERON, MIRRORED, GO, ...	203	SIR JOHNS HILL	49
NOW ON SIR JOHN'S HILL. THE HERON, ANKLING THE SCALY	203	SIR JOHNS HILL	55
HERONS			
STABBING, AND HERONS, AND SHELLS	3	PROLOGUE	16
HERONS SPIRE AND SPEAR.	208	POEM ON B'DAY	9
HERONS, STEEPLE STEMMED, BLESS.	209	POEM ON B'DAY	18
HERONS WALK IN THEIR SHROUD, ...	209	POEM ON B'DAY	27
HERONS'			
AND DRUID HERONS' VOWS	211	POEM ON B'DAY	77
HERO'S			
OF RAVENS AT THE HERO'S MEAT AND NERVES	63	WOMAN SPEAKS	17
THE HERO'S HEAD LIES SCRAPED OF EVERY LEGEND, ...	132	I MAKE THIS IN	43
HERRINGS			
AND ALL THE HERRINGS SMELLING IN THE SEA, ...	95	RUB OF LOVE	33
HERS			
THE PHRASES ON THE WOOD AREN'T HERS;	14	FOR LEDA	5
ANOTHER WITH HERS UNDER HER BELT, ...	155	RETURN	39
HE'S			
BUT, WHEN HE'S OUT OF SIGHT, ...	14	RAIN CUTS	20
HE'S NOT AWAKE TO THE GRAVE	17	IN OBLIVION	15
HE'S DEAD, HOME, HAS NO LOVER, ...	17	IN OBLIVION	19
NO, HE'S A STRANGER, OUTSIDE THE SEASON'S HUMOUR,	46	POET: 1935	10
HESPERIDES			
AND BLOOMS IN THE HESPERIDES. LIGHT STIRS	48	LIGHT, I KNOW	2
HEW			
CLANGOUR AS I HEW AND SMITE	5	PROLOGUE	70
HEWN			
CLACK THROUGH THE THICKET OF STRENGTH, LOVE HEWN IN			
PILLARS DROPS	135	HOW MY ANIMAL	36
ARGUMENT OF THE HEWN VOICE, GESTURE AND PSALM, ...	137	AFTER FUNERAL	37
AND THE HEWN COILS OF HIS TRADE PERCEIVES	209	POEM ON B'DAY	26
HEY			
AND MISTER THEY CALLED HEY MISTER	171	THE HUNCHBACK	15
HEYDAYS			
GOLDEN IN THE HEYDAYS OF HIS EYES, ...	195	FERN HILL	5
HICKORY			
OR HICKORY BULL IN MILKY GRASS	207	LAMENT	41
HID			
AND HID HER UNCOVERED BREAST.	15	FOR LEDA	27
AND HID BEHIND THE FORTRESS OF THE RIBS	63	WOMAN SPEAKS	7
WE HID OUR FEARS IN THAT MURDERING BREATH, ...	153	WAS A SAVIOUR	14
HIDDEN			
WHERE ALL THE HIDDEN STONES ARE GOLD, ...	74	WE MOTHERNAKED	10
THE WATER-SPIRIT MOVES AS IT IS HIDDEN, ...	76	LASHED RINGS	9
OF THE MOTHER HIDDEN	180	VISION, PRAYER	23
TO THE HIDDEN LAND	185	VISION, PRAYER	192

	PAGE	TITLE	LINE
HIDDEN (CONTINUED)			
HIDDEN IN DELICATE DRIFTS OF MIST ARE THEY THAT BECKON,	224	IDYLL UNFORGET	37
HIDE			
TO HIDE WHAT DRAGS ITS BELLY FROM THE EGG,	19	THE NEOPHYTE	6
DUMB DEAD THE CRANNIES HOUSE AND HIDE.	67	REALM OF FLESH	6
HAVE THEIR THIRSTY SAILORS HIDE HIM.	126	SEED-AT-ZERO	35
HAVE THEIR DRUNKEN SAILORS HIDE HIM.	126	SEED-AT-ZERO	42
AND THE SHIPYARDS OF GALILEE'S FOOTPRINTS HIDE A NAVY OF DOVES.	170	MARRIAGE VIRG	7
TO HIDE THE WOLVES OF SLEEP	176	BREATH SHED	11
LIE STILL, SLEEP BECALMED, HIDE THE MOUTH IN THE THROAT,	194	SLEEP BECALMED	13
ON THAT DARKEST DAY. OH, HE COULD HIDE	217	ELEGY	38
THE THICK HIDE COVERING,	233	NO THOUGHT	10
HIDEOUS			
SPLITTING A THOUGHT INTO SUCH HIDEOUS MOMENTS	17	IN OBLIVION	17
TURNS TO THE ROOF A HIDEOUS GRIMACE,	49	LIGHT, I KNOW	25
UNDER A HIDEOUS SEA WHERE CORAL MEN	52	OUT OF THE PIT	68
HIDER			
AND THE OWL HOOD, THE HEEL HIDER,	152	BELOW A TIME	32
HIDES			
MODESTY HIDES MY THIGHS IN HER WINGS,	207	LAMENT	59
AND THE SEA THAT HIDES HIS SECRET SELVES	211	POEM ON B'DAY	87
SOMETHING AUSTERE HIDES, SOMETHING UNCERTAIN	226	THE OAK	5
THE STRONG, UNTURNING CRUST THAT HIDES	233	NO THOUGHT	11
HIDING			
HIDING THE GOLDEN MOUNTAINS AND MANSIONS	54	WE BY SEASAND	16
HIGH			
HIGH ON A HILL	21	HIGH ON A HILL	T
HIGH ON A HILL,	21	HIGH ON A HILL	1
WOULD BE THE DEVIL'S WIND, AND THE HIGH TRINITY	37	WINDMILLS TURN	18
IN THOSE HIGH GLOBES I CANNOT COUNT,	49	LIGHT, I KNOW	19
NOT TILL, FROM HIGH AND LOW, THEIR DUST	56	WHY EAST WIND	12
HAVE BLOWN SKY HIGH THE NURSERY OF FAIRIES;	59	FAIRY TALES	23
LAWED AND ORDERED FROM ON HIGH	72	TAKE NEEDLES	39
WHO TOSSED THE HIGH TIDE IN A TIME OF STORIES	108	GRIEF THIEF	13
HIGH LORD ESQUIRE, SPEAK UP THE SINGING CLOUD,	123	FOSTER LIGHT	17
AND A HIGH SPHERE BE HIS BEARER;	126	SEED-AT-ZERO	39
CAST HIGH, STUNNED ON GILLED STONE; SLY SCISSORS GROUND IN FROST	135	HOW MY ANIMAL	35
HIGH AND DRY BY THE TOP OF THE MAST,	162	LONG-LEGGED	8
HIGH TIDE AND THE HERON DIVED WHEN I TOOK THE ROAD	177	POEM IN OCT	17
ON THIS HIGH HILL IN A YEAR'S TURNING.	178	POEM IN OCT	70
AND THE HIGH NOON	181	VISION, PRAYER	65
IN HIGH CORN AND THE HARVEST MELTING ON THEIR TONGUES.	188	WINTER'S TALE	43
WHO CLIMBS TO HIS DYING LOVE IN HER HIGH ROOM,	193	CONVERS PRAYER	3
IN THE FIRE OF HIS CARE HIS LOVE IN THE HIGH ROOM.	194	CONVERS PRAYER	16
FIELDS HIGH AS THE HOUSE, THE TUNES FROM THE CHIMNEYS, IT WAS AIR	195	FERN HILL	20
MY WISHES RACED THROUGH THE HOUSE HIGH HAY	196	FERN HILL	41
I SHOULD HEAR HIM FLY WITH THE HIGH FIELDS	196	FERN HILL	50
AND STAR: HELD AND BLESSED, THOUGH YOU SCOUR THE HIGH FOUR	199	COUNTRY SLEEP	45
THE LEAPING SAGA OF PRAYER! AND HIGH, THERE, ON THE HARE-	199	COUNTRY SLEEP	66
HIGH RIDING, HELD AND BLESSED AND TRUE, AND SO STILLY	200	COUNTRY SLEEP	90
WOUND, NOR HER RIDING HIGH, NOR HER EYES, NOR KINDLED HAIR,	201	COUNTRY SLEEP	101

	PAGE	TITLE	LINE
HIGH (CONTINUED)			
UNDER THE CONCEIVING MOON, ON THE HIGH CHALK HILL,	203	GIANT'S THIGH	2
IN THE WAINS TONNED SO HIGH THAT THE WISPS OF THE HAY	204	GIANT'S THIGH	14
PETTICOATS GALED HIGH, OR SHY WITH THE ROUGH RIDING BOYS,	204	GIANT'S THIGH	18
WHENEVER I DOVE IN A BREAST HIGH SHOAL,	206	LAMENT	21
IN HIS HOUSE ON STILTS HIGH AMONG BEAKS	208	POEM ON B'DAY	4
LEDGES OF WAVES HIGH OVER YOUR HEAD,	228	MY RIVER	2
MY RIVER HAS HIGH WAVES,	230	MY RIVER	44
BUT NO HIGH TREE FOR ME	234	NO, PIGEON	13
HE FLIES TOO HIGH.	234	NO, PIGEON	23
ADMIT THE SUN INTO YOUR HIGH NEST	240	ADMIT THE SUN	1
HIGHROAD			
THE HIGHROAD OF WATER WHERE THE SEABEAR AND MACKEREL	110	I, IN IMAGE	45
HIGH-VOLTED			
OF LAMP-POSTS AND HIGH-VOLTED FRUITS,	70	SECRET WIND	16
HILL			
FROM FISH TO JUMPING HILL! LOOK:	4	PROLOGUE	43
HEIGH, ON HORSEBACK HILL, JACK	4	PROLOGUE	67
LIKE WOODEN ISLANDS, HILL TO HILL.	5	PROLOGUE	96
LIKE WOODEN ISLANDS, HILL TO HILL.	5	PROLOGUE	96
HIGH ON A HILL	21	HIGH ON A HILL	T
HIGH ON A HILL,	21	HIGH ON A HILL	1
THE NEW ASYLUM ON THE HILL	33	HELD-OUT HAND	18
GOES OVER THE HILL INTO THE DEEP SEA;	43	LONGED TO MOVE	5
SPIED MOON-MAD BEASTS CAROUSING ON THE HILL,	50	OUT OF THE PIT	9
BREAKS, O MY HEART'S BLOOD, LIKE A HEART AND HILL.	54	WE BY SEASAND	24
AND THIS HILL OF BONE AND HAIR	67	REALM OF FLESH	2
AND LOUD HIS ANGER STAMP UPON THE HILL.	73	LORD RED HAIL	6
AND EARTH AND SKY WERE AS ONE AIRY HILL,	78	LOVE'S FEVER	8
THE SPIDER-TONGUED, AND THE LOUD HILL OF WALES)	99	OCTOBER WIND	27
STREWING THEIR VOWELS FROM A HILL OF BONES,	105	WORLD PYRAMID	41
CORNER THE MOUNTED MEADOWS IN THE HILL CORRAL;	109	I, IN IMAGE	39
SMOKE HILL AND HOPHEAD'S VALLEY,	111	I, IN IMAGE	82
AND MY IMAGES ROARED AND ROSE ON HEAVEN'S HILL.	112	I, IN IMAGE	108
AND PLAYED DOWN PARDON FROM THE HEAVENS' HILL.	121	INCARNATE DEVL	6
UNDER THE LANK, FOURTH FOLLY ON GLAMORGAN'S HILL,	122	HOLD HARD	2
SUMMON YOUR SNOWY HORSEMEN, AND THE FOUR-STRINGED HILL,	122	HOLD HARD	14
WHO SCALES A HAILING HILL IN HER COLD FLINTSTEPS	132	I MAKE THIS IN	29
SOAKED MY TABLE THE UGLIER SIDE OF A HILL	144	COLOUR OF SAY	2
A STONE LIES LOST AND LOCKED IN THE LARK-HIGH HILL.	159	INTO HER HEAD	62
ON THIS HIGH HILL IN A YEAR'S TURNING.	178	POEM IN OCT	70
ON A BREAD WHITE HILL OVER THE CUPPED FARM	190	WINTER'S TALE	107
FERN HILL	195	FERN HILL	T
A HILL TOUCHES AN ANGEL. OUT OF A SAINT'S CELL	198	COUNTRY SLEEP	27
HILL OF CYPRESSES! THE DIN AND TALE IN THE SKIMMED	200	COUNTRY SLEEP	76
OVER SIR JOHN'S HILL	201	SIR JOHNS HILL	T
OVER SIR JOHN'S HILL,	201	SIR JOHNS HILL	1
DAWS SIR JOHN'S JUST HILL DONS, AND AGAIN THE GULLED BIRDS HARE	201	SIR JOHNS HILL	15
HILL, TELL-TALE THE KNELLED	202	SIR JOHNS HILL	41
UNDER THE CONCEIVING MOON, ON THE HIGH CHALK HILL,	203	GIANT'S THIGH	2
HILL. WHO ONCE IN GOOSESKIN WINTER LOVED ALL ICE LEAVED	203	GIANT'S THIGH	12
NOW ON SIR JOHN'S HILL. THE HERON, ANKLING THE SCALY	203	SIR JOHNS HILL	55
HALE DEAD AND DEATHLESS DO THE WOMEN OF THE HILL	205	GIANT'S THIGH	58
AND WEEPS ON THE ABASING HILL,	215	COUNTRY HEAVEN	5
HILL, UNDER THE GRASS, IN LOVE, AND THERE GROW	216	ELEGY	6

		PAGE	TITLE	LINE
HILLOCK				
THE HILLOCK OF THE THOUGHTS YOU THINK		10	COOL, OH NO	3
HILLOCKS				
DEEP HILLOCKS AND LOUD ON THE NUMBED LAKES, ...		190	WINTER'S TALE	97
HILLOCKY				
BUT A HILLOCKY BULL IN THE SWELTER		206	LAMENT	31
HILLS				
GROWING ON HILLS OR SHINING UNDER WATER.		25	BEAUTY TO DUST	15
AND YOU HAVE WALKED UPON THE HILLS AT NIGHT, ...		30	YOUTH CALLS	8
INTO THE MAP-BACKED HILLS WHERE PATHS		44	TO FOLLOW FOX	8
WALKS WITH THE HILLS FOR COMPANY, ...		47	POET: 1935	27
ON TUMBLING HILLS ADMIRING THE SEA, ...		48	POET: 1935	61
AND THE HILLS OUT OF MIND.		62	EARS IN TURRET	14
SHARP IN MY SECOND DEATH I MARKED THE HILLS, HARVEST		103	I DREAMED MY	17
AND THE FLAKES FALL LIKE HILLS.		166	LONG-LEGGED	136
THE HILLS HAVE FOOTED THE WAVES AWAY, ...		168	LONG-LEGGED	184
AND THE DUNG HILLS WHITE AS WOOL AND THE HEN		187	WINTER'S TALE	18
AND OVER THE CLOTH OF COUNTIES THE FAR HILLS RODE				
NEAR, ...		190	WINTER'S TALE	93
SANG TO MY HORN, THE FOXES ON THE HILLS BARKED CLEAR				
AND COLD, ...		195	FERN HILL	16
THE BONES OUT OF THE HILLS, ...		210	POEM ON B'DAY	68
I HEAR THE BOUNCING HILLS		211	POEM ON B'DAY	100
SO THE HILLS		237	WOMAN TAPESTRY	75
HILL'S				
ON THE HILL'S SHOULDER, ...		177	POEM IN OCT	25
HILLY				
OF THE SEA IS HILLY WITH WHALES, ...		162	LONG-LEGGED	32
EYED, IN THE HALOED HOUSE, IN HER RARENESS AND HILLY		200	COUNTRY SLEEP	89
HIM (48)				
HIMSELF				
HE CUTS HIMSELF ON AN ELDER'S RAZOR LEG.		179	NEW QUAY	28
WHO FLEW HIMSELF BECAUSE THE BOAT REMAINED		238	PILLAR BREAKS	19
HINDERED				
OLD MEN WHOSE BLOOD IS HINDERED IN THEIR VEINS, ...		64	WOMAN SPEAKS	42
HINDERING				
WHEN HINDERING MAN HURT		153	WAS A SAVIOUR	12
HINGE				
THE MILKY ACID ON EACH HINGE, ...		97	TWILIGHT LOCKS	5
HINT				
MY FALLEN FILLED, THAT HAD THE HINT OF DEATH, ...		80	ALL THAT I OWE	10
HIP				
AT COTTON WORLDS REVOLVING ON A HIP, ...		51	OUT OF THE PIT	46
HIPS				
THEIR WIVES OR MOTHERS MINUS HIPS).		83	LETTER TO AUNT	22
HIS (333)				
HISS				
AND DIED ON A HISS OF FLAMES		167	LONG-LEGGED	158
HISSING				
FROM THE HISSING OF THE SPENT LIE		43	LONGED TO MOVE	2
TROUNCED BY HIS WINGS IN THE HISSING SHIPPEN, LONG				
DEAD		205	GIANT'S THIGH	39
HIST				
HIST, IN HOGSBACK WOODS! THE HAYSTACKED		5	PROLOGUE	78
HISTORY				
DEATH IS ALL METAPHORS, SHAPE IN ONE HISTORY;		117	ALTARWISE	15
WHO KILLS MY HISTORY?		129	MY NEOPHYTE	37
HIT				
THE STAINED FLATS OF HEAVEN HIT AND RAZED		141	SAINT TO FALL	2

		PAGE	TITLE	LINE
HIVE				
DRIPS FROM THE HUMMING DARKNESS OF THE HIVE.		48	LIGHT, I KNOW	10
HIVES				
THE JACKS OF FROST THEY FINGER IN THE HIVES;		92	BOYS OF SUMMER	9
(BUT NOTHING BORE, NO MOUTHING BABE TO THE VEINED HIVES		205	GIANT'S THIGH	42
AND THAT BEES NEVER WORK IN THEIR HIVES.		221	SONG OF DOG	4
HO				
HO, HULLABALLOING CLAN		4	PROLOGUE	64
HEIGH HO THE BLOOD AND BERRY, ...		93	BOYS OF SUMMER	44
HOBNAIL				
OF THE HOBNAIL TALES: NO GOOSEHERD OR SWINE WILL TURN		197	COUNTRY SLEEP	10
HOGSBACK				
HIST, IN HOGSBACK WOODS! THE HAYSTACKED		5	PROLOGUE	78
HOIST				
FOR HIS BRIARED HANDS TO HOIST THEM		184	VISION, PRAYER	137
HOISTED				
WHO UNDER THE LIDS OF HER WINDOWS HOISTED HIS GOLDEN LUGGAGE, ...		170	MARRIAGE VIRG	12
IN A HOISTED CLOUD, AT DROP OF DUSK, HE PULLS TO HIS CLAWS		201	SIR JOHNS HILL	3
HOLD				
I WANT REALITY TO HOLD/ WITHIN MY PALM, ...		9	MINUTE'S HOUR	14
ALL HOLD THE SUM, NOTHING TO NOTHING, ...		27	OBLIVIOUS DARK	21
SO SHALL HE STEP TILL SUMMER LOOSENS ITS HOLD		46	POET: 1935	18
HANDS, HOLD YOU POISON OR GRAPES?		62	EARS IN TURRET	9
SHIPS, HOLD YOU POISON OR GRAPES?		62	EARS IN TURRET	25
HOLD YOU POISON OR GRAPES?		63	EARS IN TURRET	33
THAT DUST YOU HOLD, O STREW THAT LITTLE LEFT;		65	WOMAN SPEAKS	61
HOLD IN HIS VELVET HAND THE CAN OF BLOOD;		73	LORD RED HAIL	2
HEIR TO THE SCALDING VEINS THAT HOLD LOVE'S DROP,		80	ALL THAT I OWE	9
HOLD UP THE NOISY SEA AND DROP HER BIRDS, ...		93	BOYS OF SUMMER	39
HEIR TO THE SCALDING VEINS THAT HOLD LOVE'S DROP, COSTLY		103	I DREAMED MY	9
MY HALF GHOST IN ARMOUR HOLD HARD IN DEATH'S CORRIDOR, ...		108	I, IN IMAGE	5
SHE WHO WAS WHO I HOLD, THE FATS AND FLOWER, ...		114	A GRIEF AGO	2
ATLASWISE HOLD HALF-WAY OFF THE DUMMY BAY		121	ALTARWISE	128
HOLD HARD, THESE ANCIENT MINUTES IN THE CUCKOO'S MONTH		122	HOLD HARD	T
HOLD HARD, THESE ANCIENT MINUTES IN THE CUCKOO'S MONTH, ...		122	HOLD HARD	1
HOLD HARD, MY COUNTRY CHILDREN IN THE WORLD OF TALES,		122	HOLD HARD	10
HOLD HARD, MY COUNTY DARLINGS, FOR A HAWK DESCENDS,		123	HOLD HARD	22
WITH A HOLD OF LEECHES AND STRAWS, ...		142	SAINT TO FALL	24
AND THE VAULTING BIRD BE STILL. O MY TRUE LOVE, HOLD ME.		149	UNLUCKILY FOR	54
OTHERS WHOSE SINGLE BEDS HOLD TWO		155	RETURN	60
ONE WHO CALLED DEEPEST DOWN SHALL HOLD HIS PEACE		160	DEATHS AND ENT	9
INSECTS AND VALLEYS HOLD HER THIGHS HARD, ...		168	LONG-LEGGED	174
MAY HOLD IT IN A GREAT FLOOD		173	FIRE RAID	21
WARNING AMONG THE FOLDS, AND THE FROZEN HOLD		187	WINTER'S TALE	8
THEY FROM HOUSES WHERE THE HARVEST KNEELS, HOLD ME HARD, ...		205	GIANT'S THIGH	50
HOLDING				
WE WHO ARE YOUNG SIT HOLDING YELLOW HANDS.		41	YOUNG ARE OLD	17
WITH RAIN-BEATEN HANDS HOLDING THE WHIP, ...		45	PLOUGHMAN GONE	20
HOLDING FOR EVER THE DEAD MOON.		69	SECRET WIND	6
SHE HOLDING ME? THE PEOPLE'S SEA DRIVES ON HER, ...		115	A GRIEF AGO	26
A GARDEN HOLDING TO HER HAND		167	LONG-LEGGED	167

	PAGE	TITLE	LINE
HOLDING (CONTINUED)			
STROKING THE AIR AND HOLDING LIGHT.	235	WOMAN TAPESTRY	30
HOLDING A VOLUPTUOUS CLARITY	237	WOMAN TAPESTRY	73
HOLDS			
WHO HOLDS HER CLASPED INSIDE HIS STRONG, WHITE WINGS;	15	FOR LEDA	31
HANDS OF THE STRANGER AND HOLDS OF THE SHIPS,	63	EARS IN TURRET	32
GREAT IS THE HAND THAT HOLDS DOMINION OVER	66	HAND SIGNED	11
HE HOLDS THE WIRE FROM THIS BOX OF NERVES	75	MY HERO BARES	16
OUT OF THE HOUSE THAT HOLDS A TOWN	166	LONG-LEGGED	143
HOLE			
NO FOX, NO GOOD, FOOL'S, NOT A FOX'S, HOLE,	44	TO FOLLOW FOX	11
A HOLE IN SPACE SHALL KEEP THE SHAPE OF THOUGHT,	73	LORD RED HAIL	13
WHEN CAMERAS SHUT THEY HURRY TO THEIR HOLE	89	EUNUCH DREAMS	15
RAMMED IN THE MARCHING HEART, HOLE	103	I DREAMED MY	14
WIND-HEELED FOOT IN THE HOLE OF A FIREBALL,	141	SAINT TO FALL	12
CLAW FOLD AND HOLE FOR THE ROTTEN	152	BELOW A TIME	33
A HOLE OF ERRANDS AND SHADES;	156	RETURN	78
HOLIER			
HOLIER THEN THEIR EYES,	211	POEM ON B'DAY	106
HOLLER			
IF DEAD MEN WALKED THEY, TOO, WOULD HOLLER	59	FAIRY TALES	17
HOLLOW			
SHEEP WHITE HOLLOW FARMS	4	PROLOGUE	51
HOLLOW FARMS IN A THRONG	5	PROLOGUE	79
THE HOLLOW WORDS COULD BEAR ALL SUFFERING	32	OUT OF SIGHS	22
WHO FOLLOW THE RED RIVERS, HOLLOW	54	WE BY SEASAND	3
THE SADDEST DUST IN ALL THIS HOLLOW WORLD.	64	WOMAN SPEAKS	41
AND TO THE HOLLOW MINUTE OF THE WOMB,	78	LOVE'S FEVER	2
HIS SEA-SUCKED ADAM IN THE HOLLOW HULK,	103	WORLD PYRAMID	2
HAIRS OF YOUR HEAD, THEN SAID THE HOLLOW AGENT,	117	ALTARWISE	25
WHISPER IN A DAMP WORD, HER WITS DRILLED HOLLOW,	137	AFTER FUNERAL	33
TO THIS INHOSPITABLE HOLLOW YEAR,	153	WAS A SAVIOUR	27
HOLLOWS			
THROUGH THESE LASHED RINGS SET DEEP INSIDE THEIR HOLLOWS	76	LASHED RINGS	1
HOLLOWS, A GRASSBLADE BLOWN IN CUPPED HANDS, IN THE LOOTED ELMS	203	SIR JOHNS HILL	52
HOLLY			
IN SPRING WE CROSS OUR FOREHEADS WITH THE HOLLY,	93	BOYS OF SUMMER	43
DECEMBER'S THORN SCREWED IN A BROW OF HOLLY.	121	ALTARWISE	132
HOLOCAUST			
HIS STRIPED AND NOON MANED TRIBE STRIDING TO HOLOCAUST,	148	UNLUCKILY FOR	31
HOLT			
THE OWL AT ITS KNELLING. FOX AND HOLT KNEEL BEFORE BLOOD.	198	COUNTRY SLEEP	32
HOLY			
AND DARK SHOALS EVERY HOLY FIELD.	5	PROLOGUE	90
THE HOLY HAT.	60	FAIRY TALES	41
A HOLY VOICE ACQUAINTS ME WITH HIS GLORY.	76	LASHED RINGS	6
SHOULD LANTERNS SHINE, THE HOLY FACE,	116	LANTERNS SHINE	1
A HANDMADE MOON HALF HOLY IN A CLOUD,	121	INCARNATE DEVL	8
IN A HOLY ROOM IN A WAVE;	130	SINNERS' BELL	27
SHE WOULD NOT HAVE ME SINKING IN THE HOLY	136	AFTER FUNERAL	18
THE SUN-LEAVED HOLY CANDLEWOODS	141	SAINT TO FALL	19
MY HOLY LUCKY BODY	147	UNLUCKILY FOR	16
HER HOLY UNHOLY HOURS WITH THE ALWAYS ANONYMOUS BEAST.	158	INTO HER HEAD	46
ADAM OR EVE, THE ADORNED HOLY BULLOCK	174	FIRE RAID	34
HOLY SPRING	186	HOLY SPRING	T

	PAGE	TITLE	LINE
HOLY (CONTINUED)			
AND I AM STRUCK AS LONELY AS A HOLY MAKER BY THE SUN.	186	HOLY SPRING	12
AND THE MOTHER AND TOPPLING HOUSE OF THE HOLY SPRING,	186	HOLY SPRING	23
IN THE PEBBLES OF THE HOLY STREAMS.	195	FERN HILL	18
THE COUNTRY IS HOLY: O BIDE IN THAT COUNTRY KIND,	198	COUNTRY SLEEP	39
CAWING FROM THEIR BLACK BETHELS SOARING, THE HOLY BOOKS	199	COUNTRY SLEEP	68
ONLY FOR THE TURNING OF THE EARTH IN HER HOLY	200	COUNTRY SLEEP	94
CRASHES, AND SLOWLY THE FISHING HOLY STALKING HERON	201	SIR JOHNS HILL	11
AND THE BLACK CROSS OF THE HOLY HOUSE,	206	LAMENT	26
OUR BRANCHES AND HOLY LEAVES	230	OUR SANCTITY	4
HOMAGE			
MY HOUSE WOULD FALL LIKE BREAD ABOUT MY HOMAGE;	96	TWELVE	11
HOME			
AND MAKE HIS WIDE MOUTH HOME.	17	IN OBLIVION	7
HE'S DEAD, HOME, HAS NO LOVER,	17	IN OBLIVION	19
BREATHE TILL THE SNAKE IS HOME,	22	HIGH ON A HILL	10
THESE DIE WHO SHOVEL THE LAST HOME OF MAN;	64	WOMAN SPEAKS	44
THAT SHAPED THE JORDAN NEAR MY HOME	68	BEFORE KNOCKED	4
IN ITS LABYRINTHINE HOME.	71	TAKE NEEDLES	28
A HOME AND A DOWRY:	138	O CHATTERTON	41
AND YOUR HOME IN A CENTAUR'S STABLE.	138	O CHATTERTON	43
O MY LOST LOVE BOUNCED FROM A GOOD HOME;	146	IF HEAD HURT	23
AND TERRIBLY LEAD HIM HOME ALIVE	168	LONG-LEGGED	198
LEAD HER PRODIGAL HOME TO HIS TERROR,	168	LONG-LEGGED	199
HE STANDS ALONE AT THE DOOR OF HIS HOME,	169	LONG-LEGGED	215
THE WORLD WINDING HOME!	182	VISION, PRAYER	97
ALONE IN THE HUSK OF MAN'S HOME	186	HOLY SPRING	22
INTO THE HOME OF PRAYERS	188	WINTER'S TALE	36
AND THE HOME OF PRAYERS AND FIRES, THE TALE ENDED.	190	WINTER'S TALE	110
ABOUT THE HAPPY YARD AND SINGING AS THE FARM WAS HOME,	195	FERN HILL	11
THEY OF THE PALE, SEA-WAN BEAUTY, THEY OF THE HOME	224	IDYLL UNFORGET	38
HOMES			
CHILDREN FROM HOMES AND CHILDREN'S PARKS	129	MY NEOPHYTE	28
FOR THE DROOPING OF HOMES	153	WAS A SAVIOUR	33
UNCLAIMED DEAD, GIRLS FROM GOOD HOMES	154	RETURN	15
HOMESTALL			
INTO A HOMESTALL KING OR HAMLET OF FIRE	198	COUNTRY SLEEP	11
HONEY			
MY HAND WITH HONEY THAT HAD CLOSED UPON A FLOWER.	15	FOR LEDA	19
AND THIS IS PLENTY, THEN, CLOVES AND SWEET OILS, THE BEES' HONEY,	36	MIDNIGHT ROAD	5
DRIP FROM MY OPEN EYES AS HONEY	48	LIGHT, I KNOW	9
SWEET IS THE WAXEN BLOOD, HONEY THE FALLING FLESH;	63	WOMAN SPEAKS	3
HERE DRIPS A SILENT HONEY IN MY SHROUD,	81	HERE LIE BEAST	10
SOUR THE BOILING HONEY;	92	BOYS OF SUMMER	8
THEIR BREASTS FULL OF HONEY, UNDER THEIR GANDER KING	205	GIANT'S THIGH	38
AND HONEY STEAL FROM FLOWERS AGLOW.	228	TRIOLET	6
HONEYED			
ITS HONEYED CHEEK, SOFT-TALKING MOUTH,	35	LIFT UP FACE	16
TO COURT THE HONEYED HEART FROM YOUR SIDE BEFORE SUNRISE	198	COUNTRY SLEEP	13
HONOUR			
DESCENDS, MY MASTERS, ON THE ENTERED HONOUR.	100	RUNNING GRAVE	28
HONOURED			
AND LETS THEIR TRASH BE HONOURED AS THE QUICK.	90	EUNUCH DREAMS	35
AND HONOURED AMONG WAGONS I WAS PRINCE OF THE APPLE TOWNS	195	FERN HILL	6

	PAGE	TITLE	LINE
HONOURED (CONTINUED)			
AND HONOURED AMONG FOXES AND PHEASANTS BY THE GAY HOUSE	196	FERN HILL	37
HOO			
HOO, THERE, IN CASTLE KEEP,	4	PROLOGUE	53
HOOD			
BINDING MY ANGEL'S HOOD.	105	WORLD PYRAMID	54
CRIED THE TOPLESS, INCHTAPED LIPS FROM HANK AND HOOD	132	I MAKE THIS IN	47
AND THE OWL HOOD, THE HEEL HIDER,	152	BELOW A TIME	32
FEAR OR BELIEVE THAT THE WOLF IN A SHEEPWHITE HOOD	197	COUNTRY SLEEP	3
FOR EVER OF ALL NOT THE WOLF IN HIS BAAING HOOD	198	COUNTRY SLEEP	36
HOODED			
WHEREON THE HOODED HAIR CASTS DOWN ITS GIRDLE,	76	LASHED RINGS	5
WHOSE HOODED, FOUNTAIN HEART ONCE FELL IN PUDDLES	136	AFTER FUNERAL	14
THE ONCE HOODED ROOM	181	VISION, PRAYER	47
HOOF			
AT A WOOD'S DANCING HOOF,	3	PROLOGUE	8
A LEGENDARY HORSE WITH HOOF AND FEATHER,	13	RAIN CUTS	17
HOOK			
AND MOUTH. BOTH NOTE AND PLUME PLUNGE FROM THE SPIRE'S HOOK.	16	SPIRE CRANES	8
HOOKING			
AS A BIRD HOOKING OVER THE SEA,	162	LONG-LEGGED	7
HOOKS			
A GIRL ALIVE WITH HIS HOOKS THROUGH HER LIPS;	162	LONG-LEGGED	22
HOOT			
FISHING IN THE TEAR OF THE TOWY. ONLY A HOOT OWL	203	SIR JOHNS HILL	51
HOOTING			
IN THE HOOTING, NEARLY DARK	4	PROLOGUE	59
HOOVED			
AS A DUST OF PIGEONS. EXULTING, THE GRAVE HOOVED	189	WINTER'S TALE	73
HOOVES			
THROUGH THE SHAKEN GREENSWARD LAKE, SILENT, ON MOONSHOD HOOVES,	200	COUNTRY SLEEP	84
HOP			
SHOULD HE, FOR CENTRE SAKE, HOP IN THE DUST,	127	NOW, SAY NAY	6
HOPE			
THERE IS NO NEED OF HOPE FOR HOPE,	21	BEWILDERED WAY	9
THERE IS NO NEED OF HOPE FOR HOPE,	21	BEWILDERED WAY	9
CRYSTAL OR FUNERAL, GOT NO HOPE	28	NO WINGS	5
AND THE FEEBLE HOUSE OF HOPE.	71	TAKE NEEDLES	16
SPILL THE LANK FOLLY'S HUNTER AND THE HARD-HELD HOPE.	122	HOLD HARD	18
LET'S HOPE YOU WON'T THINK ME TOO VICIOUS.	221	SONG OF DOG	16
HOPED			
MY GOD'S A SHEPHERD, GOD'S THE LOVE I HOPED.	53	OUT OF THE PIT	93
HOPHEAD'S			
SMOKE HILL AND HOPHEAD'S VALLEY,	111	I, IN IMAGE	82
HOPING			
HARBOURING SOME THOUGHT OF HEAVEN, OR HAVEN HOPING,	36	MIDNIGHT ROAD	2
HOPPING			
IT WAS NOVEMBER THERE WERE WHIZZBANGS HOPPING,	52	OUT OF THE PIT	51
HOPPING HOT LEAVED AND FEATHERED	151	BELOW A TIME	20
THE PUFFED BIRDS HOPPING AND HUNTING, THE MILKMAIDS	187	WINTER'S TALE	23
HORIZON			
ON THE HORIZON WALKING LIKE THE TREES	98	OCTOBER WIND	10
HORIZONTAL			
ON MILES OF HORIZONTAL MILESTONES,	37	WINDMILLS TURN	24
THE HORIZONTAL CROSS-BONES OF ABADDON,	117	ALTARWISE	21
HORN			
THE HORN AND BALL OF WATER ON THE FROG	115	A GRIEF AGO	15

	PAGE	TITLE	LINE
HORN (CONTINUED)			
HELL IN A HORN OF SULPHUR AND THE CLOVEN MYTH, ...	122	INCARNATE DEVL	16
OR POISE THE DAY ON A HORN.	135	HOW MY ANIMAL	33
SANG TO MY HORN, THE FOXES ON THE HILLS BARKED CLEAR			
AND COLD, ...	195	FERN HILL	16
BUT A BLACK SHEEP WITH A CRUMPLED HORN, ...	207	LAMENT	42
HAS A HORN AND TWO HUMPS ON ITS HEAD, ...	221	SONG OF DOG	6
HORNED			
HORNED DOWN WITH SKULLFOOT AND THE SKULL OF TOES	117	ALTARWISE	33
THEIR BREAST, THE VAULTING DOES ROISTER, THE HORNED			
BUCKS CLIMB	204	GIANT'S THIGH	33
HORNING			
ROTATING HALVES ARE HORNING AS THEY DRILL	104	WORLD PYRAMID	23
HORNS			
THAT ADAM'S WETHER IN THE FLOCK OF HORNS, ...	117	ALTARWISE	31
AND NOW THE HORNS OF ENGLAND, IN THE SOUND OF SHAPE,	122	HOLD HARD	13
WITH ITS HORNS THROUGH MIST AND THE CASTLE	177	POEM IN OCT	33
HORNY			
TO-MORROW'S DIVER IN HER HORNY MILK, ...	103	WORLD PYRAMID	4
HORRIBLE			
KNEW ALL HIS HORRIBLE DESIRES	128	MY NEOPHYTE	10
HORRIBLY			
OF MEN AND CREATURES HORRIBLY	35	LIFT UP FACE	8
HORRID			
MY HORRID IMAGES FOR ME, ...	12	SKY'S BRIGHT	7
THE OLD MUD HATCH AGAIN, THE HORRID	142	SAINT TO FALL	44
HORROR			
ALL REASON BROKE, AND HORROR WALKED THE ROADS.	51	OUT OF THE PIT	18
AND WOMEN TALK OF HORROR TO THE DUSK.	57	GREEK PLAY	16
HORRORS			
EX-SOLDIERS WITH HORRORS FOR A FACE, ...	41	YOUNG ARE OLD	31
HORSE			
A LEGENDARY HORSE WITH HOOF AND FEATHER, ...	13	RAIN CUTS	17
AGAINST THE RUSTY SWORD AND THE OLD HORSE	45	PLOUGHMAN GONE	8
THE RAWBONED HORSE TO A MAN'S VOICE	45	PLOUGHMAN GONE	14
AN AIR-DRAWN WINDMILL ON A WOODEN HORSE, ...	124	TODAY, INSECT	20
SHALL THE BLIND HORSE SING SWEETER?	144	PLEASURE-BIRD	2
OF NIGHTINGALE AND CENTAUR DEAD HORSE. THE SPRINGS			
WITHER	191	WINTER'S TALE	117
THERE ARE FEWER, OF COURSE, WHO INSIST THAT A HORSE	221	SONG OF DOG	5
HORSEBACK			
HEIGH, ON HORSEBACK HILL, JACK	4	PROLOGUE	67
HORSEMEN			
SUMMON YOUR SNOWY HORSEMEN, AND THE FOUR-STRINGED			
HILL, ...	122	HOLD HARD	14
HORSES			
BUT THE HORSES ARE GONE AND THE REINS ARE GREEN ...	45	PLOUGHMAN GONE	10
LIE COLD, WITH THEIR HORSES, FOR RAVEN AND KITE.	45	PLOUGHMAN GONE	23
SHE LONGS AMONG HORSES AND ANGELS, ...	163	LONG-LEGGED	33
ALL THE HORSES OF HIS HAUL OF MIRACLES	168	LONG-LEGGED	187
ABOVE THE FARMS AND THE WHITE HORSES	177	POEM IN OCT	13
HORSES, CENTAUR DEAD, TURN AND TREAD THE DRENCHED			
WHITE	189	WINTER'S TALE	74
FLYING WITH THE RICKS, AND THE HORSES	195	FERN HILL	26
IN THE FIRST, SPINNING PLACE, THE SPELLBOUND HORSES			
WALKING WARM	196	FERN HILL	34
AS HORSES IN THE FOAM:	210	POEM ON B'DAY	75
HORSESHOE			
THAT MELTS THE LIONHEAD'S HEEL AND HORSESHOE OF THE			
HEART, ...	135	HOW MY ANIMAL	14

	PAGE	TITLE	LINE
HORSESHOE (CONTINUED)			
WITH THE SPIRITS OF THE HORSESHOE BAY	210	POEM ON B'DAY	56
HOSANNAS			
AND ON HIS EARS HOSANNAS OF THE GRAVE.	63	WOMAN SPEAKS	23
HOSPITAL			
WHEN THAT IMMORTAL HOSPITAL MADE ONE MORE MOVE TO			
SOOTHE	186	HOLY SPRING	3
HOST			
THE DEAD IN HADES HAVE THEIR HOST OF FRIENDS, ...	57	GREEK PLAY	22
TWELVE WINDS ENCOUNTER BY THE WHITE HOST AT PASTURE,	109	I, IN IMAGE	38
NOR WHEN ALL PONDEROUS HEAVEN'S HOST OF WATERS			
BREAKS.	146	IF HEAD HURT	20
BLIND HOST TO SLEEP	184	VISION, PRAYER	141
HOSTS			
BUT BLESSED BY SUCH HEROIC HOSTS IN YOUR EVERY	148	UNLUCKILY FOR	21
HOT			
CHALK COOLED BY LEAVES IN THE HOT SEASON, ...	29	LONG, SKELETON	3
BUT THE HOT BEAMS ROB ME OF SPEECH, ...	42	A WAR OF WITS	14
ON THE CANVAS SKY, AND ALL HOT COLOURS MELT	46	POET: 1935	19
LIKE CATS, AND LUSTS LAY HALF HOT IN THE COLD.	50	OUT OF THE PIT	5
STOPPED NON-STOP DANCING TO LET HOT FEET COOL, ...	51	OUT OF THE PIT	30
MEANING IN HOT SOCK SOIL? A LITTLE CUSS	137	O CHATTERTON	18
BECAUSE THE PLEASURE-BIRD WHISTLES AFTER THE HOT			
WIRES, ...	144	PLEASURE-BIRD	1
SHALL I, STRUCK ON THE HOT AND ROCKING STREET, ...	145	PLEASURE-BIRD	16
HOPPING HOT LEAVED AND FEATHERED	151	BELOW A TIME	20
NO SPRINGTAILED TOM IN THE RED HOT TOWN	206	LAMENT	29
HOTHOUSE			
BROOD ON EACH HOTHOUSE PLANT	26	THERE'S PLENTY	9
HOTTENTOT			
A LITERARY HOTTENTOT	83	LETTER TO AUNT	4
HOUND			
OVER THE VAULT OF RIDINGS WITH HIS HOUND AT HEEL,	122	HOLD HARD	5
HOUNDS'			
TO FOLLOW THE FOX AT THE HOUNDS' TAILS	44	TO FOLLOW FOX	1
HOUR			
I KNOW THIS VICIOUS MINUTE'S HOUR	9	MINUTE'S HOUR	T
I KNOW THIS VICIOUS MINUTE'S HOUR;	9	MINUTE'S HOUR	1
ONE HOUR SPEND MY TIME FOR ME	18	NATURAL DAY	5
I HAVE NOT LAIN AN HOUR ASLEEP	22	ON QUIET NIGHT	5
A COMIC HOUR TO AN END THROUGH WANT OF WOMAN	23	THE ONLY DEAD	8
OF THE MOMENT AND THE DEAD HOUR.	29	LONG, SKELETON	13
NOT STUMPS, AFTER THE HOUR OF BATTLE, ...	42	A WAR OF WITS	9
OVER THE CHOIR MINUTE I HEAR THE HOUR CHANT:	130	SINNERS' BELL	7
STRIKE THE SEA HOUR THROUGH BELLMETAL.	130	SINNERS' BELL	12
INTO THE DEAD CLOCK BURNING THE HOUR	175	FIRE RAID	65
AND THE STILL HOUR	191	REFUSAL MOURN	5
CALM AND STRANGE IS THIS EVENING HOUR IN THE FOREST,	221	FOREST PICTURE	1
WHOSE MINUTE KINDLES MORE THAN THE WISE HOUR.	237	PILLAR BREAKS	11
HOURGLASS			
WHEN, WITH HIS TORCH AND HOURGLASS, LIKE A SULPHUR			
PRIEST, ...	130	SINNERS' BELL	2
HOURLESS			
TIME IN THE HOURLESS HOUSES	111	I, IN IMAGE	99
HOURLY			
HOURLY I SIGH, ...	225	OF ANY FLOWER	1
HOURS			
WE SPOKE OF DRINK AND GIRLS, FOR HOURS	33	IN GARDENS	4
IN THE SNIVELLING HOURS WITH DEAD, HUMPED ANN	136	AFTER FUNERAL	13
OF SHADES, SYMBOL OF DESIRE BEYOND MY HOURS	148	UNLUCKILY FOR	35

	PAGE	TITLE	LINE
HOURS (CONTINUED)			
HER HOLY UNHOLY HOURS WITH THE ALWAYS ANONYMOUS BEAST.	158	INTO HER HEAD	46
A CHILD OF A FEW HOURS	173	FIRE RAID	5
AND HOURS MADE LITTLE I HAVE DIPPED MY ARMS IN THEIR RAPTURE;	224	IDYLL UNFORGET	31
THAN THE HOURS.	226	THE ELM	6
IDLING WITH THE RADIANCE OF THE HOURS	227	SPRING-SPIRIT	10
HOURS'			
THERE GROWS THE HOURS' LADDER TO THE SUN,	102	FELLOWED SLEEP	26
HOUR'S			
AT THE HOUR'S END	23	THE ONLY DEAD	14
TELLS ME THE HOUR'S WORD, THE NEURAL MEANING	99	OCTOBER WIND	18
AND ALL SWEET HELL, DEAF AS AN HOUR'S EAR,	114	SERVANT SUN	33
HOUSE			
IN MY SEASHAKEN HOUSE	3	PROLOGUE	4
FOR OUT OF A HOUSE OF MATCHBOARD AND STONE	43	A WAR OF WITS	22
EMPTY, TO LET, ARE SIGNS ON THIS NEW HOUSE;	58	TO ARCHITECTS	15
IN THIS WHITE HOUSE?	62	EARS IN TURRET	8
HIS NARROW HOUSE IS WALLED WITH BLADES OF GRASS,	64	WOMAN SPEAKS	24
DUMB DEAD THE CRANNIES HOUSE AND HIDE.	67	REALM OF FLESH	6
AND THE FEEBLE HOUSE OF HOPE.	71	TAKE NEEDLES	16
GREEN WAS THE SINGING HOUSE.	78	LOVE'S FEVER	24
THE HEAVEN'S HOUSE.	81	HERE LIE BEAST	12
MY HOUSE WOULD FALL LIKE BREAD ABOUT MY HOMAGE;	96	TWELVE	11
LOVE IN HER GEAR IS SLOWLY THROUGH THE HOUSE,	99	RUNNING GRAVE	3
(HAVE WITH THE HOUSE OF WIND), THE LEANING SCENE,	101	RUNNING GRAVE	42
DRIP ON MY DEAD HOUSE GARDEN.	105	WORLD PYRAMID	45
THE LOVERS' HOUSE, LIE SUFFERING MY STAIN?	112	NOT FATHER ME	4
SHALL I STILL BE LOVE'S HOUSE ON THE WIDDERSHIN EARTH,	113	NOT FATHER ME	29
LOVE'S HOUSE, THEY ANSWER, AND THE TOWER DEATH	113	NOT FATHER ME	31
ALTARWISE BY OWL-LIGHT IN THE HALF-WAY HOUSE	116	ALTARWISE	1
FROM BALD PAVILIONS AND THE HOUSE OF BREAD	120	ALTARWISE	96
FURLED ON THE FISHES' HOUSE AND HELL,	129	MY NEOPHYTE	17
CATHEDRAL CALM IN THE PULLED HOUSE;	130	SINNERS' BELL	15
AND THIS WEAK HOUSE TO MARROW-COLUMNED HEAVEN,	131	I MAKE THIS IN	8
IN A FIERCELY MOURNING HOUSE IN A CROOKED YEAR.	136	AFTER FUNERAL	30
WHO WRITES THESE WORDS I WRITE IN A STILL ROOM IN A SPELLSOAKED HOUSE:	141	I, FIRST NAMED	2
I AM THE GHOST IN THIS HOUSE THAT IS FILLED WITH THE TONGUE AND EYES	141	I, FIRST NAMED	3
OF HIS FATHER'S HOUSE IN THE SANDS,	141	SAINT TO FALL	7
O WAKE IN ME IN MY HOUSE IN THE MUD	142	SAINT TO FALL	26
FROM AN ODD ROOM IN A SPLIT HOUSE STARE,	142	SAINT TO FALL	31
RAGE ME BACK TO THE MAKING HOUSE. MY HAND UNRAVEL	145	IF HEAD HURT	12
HAS A VOICE AND A HOUSE, AND THERE AND HERE YOU MUST COUCH AND CRY.	146	IF HEAD HURT	25
RIDE THROUGH THE DOORS OF OUR UNENTERED HOUSE.	154	WAS A SAVIOUR	38
CARRYING CLOUD, DEATH STRIKES THEIR HOUSE.	161	WEDDING ANNIV	8
OUT OF THE HOUSE THAT HOLDS A TOWN	166	LONG-LEGGED	143
THE FURIOUS OX-KILLING HOUSE OF LOVE.	168	LONG-LEGGED	200
TO SHARE MY ROOM IN THE HOUSE NOT RIGHT IN THE HEAD,	169	LOVE IN ASYLUM	2
SHE DELUDES THE HEAVEN-PROOF HOUSE WITH ENTERING CLOUDS	169	LOVE IN ASYLUM	6
AND THE MOTHER AND TOPPLING HOUSE OF THE HOLY SPRING,	186	HOLY SPRING	23
FLOCKED WITH THE SHEEP WHITE SMOKE OF THE FARM HOUSE COWL	187	WINTER'S TALE	9
TORN AND ALONE IN A FARM HOUSE IN A FOLD	187	WINTER'S TALE	15
IN THE MUFFLED HOUSE, IN THE QUICK OF NIGHT,	188	WINTER'S TALE	29

		PAGE	TITLE	LINE
HOUSE (CONTINUED)				
WAS FLYING THROUGH THE HOUSE AS THOUGH THE SHE BIRD				
PRAISED	....	189	WINTER'S TALE	83
ABOUT THE LILTING HOUSE AND HAPPY AS THE GRASS WAS				
GREEN,	....	195	FERN HILL	2
FIELDS HIGH AS THE HOUSE, THE TUNES FROM THE				
CHIMNEYS, IT WAS AIR	....	195	FERN HILL	20
AND HONOURED AMONG FOXES AND PHEASANTS BY THE GAY				
HOUSE	....	196	FERN HILL	37
MY WISHES RACED THROUGH THE HOUSE HIGH HAY	....	196	FERN HILL	41
TO EAT YOUR HEART IN THE HOUSE IN THE ROSY WOOD.		197	COUNTRY SLEEP	7
LIE IN GRACE. SLEEP SPELLED AT REST IN THE LOWLY				
HOUSE	....	199	COUNTRY SLEEP	43
EYED, IN THE HALOED HOUSE, IN HER RARENESS AND HILLY		200	COUNTRY SLEEP	89
WHO ONCE WERE A BLOOM OF WAYSIDE BRIDES IN THE HAWED				
HOUSE	....	204	GIANT'S THIGH	29
AND THE BLACK CROSS OF THE HOLY HOUSE,	....	206	LAMENT	26
IN HIS HOUSE ON STILTS HIGH AMONG BEAKS	....	208	POEM ON B'DAY	4
IN HIS SLANT, RACKING HOUSE	....	209	POEM ON B'DAY	25
IN THE MUTED HOUSE, ONE MINUTE BEFORE	....	216	ELEGY	14
THE STICKS OF THE HOUSE WERE HIS; HIS BOOKS HE OWNED.		217	ELEGY	25
HOUSED				
HOUSED IN THE SIDE.	....	115	A GRIEF AGO	16
HOUSED IN HAMLETS OF HEAVEN SWING THE LOFT LAMPS,		215	COUNTRY HEAVEN	16
HOUSES				
BUT WE, SHUT IN THE HOUSES OF THE BRAIN,	....	26	THERE'S PLENTY	8
THE SIDEBOARD FRUIT, THE FERNS, THE PICTURE HOUSES		33	HELD-OUT HAND	10
TIME IN THE HOURLESS HOUSES	....	111	I, IN IMAGE	99
AND SWEPT INTO OUR WOUNDS AND HOUSES,	....	186	HOLY SPRING	7
THEY FROM HOUSES WHERE THE HARVEST KNEELS, HOLD ME				
HARD,	....	205	GIANT'S THIGH	50
HOUSING				
HOUSING DEATH IN YOUR KINGDOM,	....	67	REALM OF FLESH	12
HOVEL				
OVER THE SUN'S HOVEL AND THE SLUM OF FIRE	....	175	FIRE RAID	68
HOVER				
HOVER, MAKING THE FOREST FLUCTUANTLY VAGUE.	....	226	THE OAK	4
HOW				
HOW I, A SPINNING MAN,	....	4	PROLOGUE	39
HOW COULD I SMOOTH THAT SKIN	....	10	COOL, OH NO	9
HOW KISS, WHEN DOLL COULD SAY	....	10	COOL, OH NO	13
HOW MUCH WAS HAPPY WHILE IT LASTED,	....	32	OUT OF SIGHS	20
HOW SOON, HOW SOON, O LORD OF THE RED HAIL!	....	73	LORD RED HAIL	18
HOW SOON, HOW SOON, O LORD OF THE RED HAIL!	....	73	LORD RED HAIL	18
HOW AT THE MOUNTAIN SPRING THE SAME MOUTH SUCKS.		77	THE FORCE THAT	10
HOW OF MY CLAY IS MADE THE HANGMAN'S LIME.	....	77	THE FORCE THAT	15
HOW TIME HAS TICKED A HEAVEN ROUND THE STARS.	.....	77	THE FORCE THAT	20
HOW AT MY SHEET GOES THE SAME CROOKED WORM.	....	77	THE FORCE THAT	22
FIE ON YOU, AUNT! I'LL SHOW YOU HOW	....	83	LETTER TO AUNT	11
AND HOW TO SCALE AND SEE THE SIGHTS	....	83	LETTER TO AUNT	13
ON HOW THE GALLIC LETTER BENDS;	....	84	LETTER TO AUNT	51
HOW WELL YOUR POEMS LIGHT THE FIRE.	....	85	LETTER TO AUNT	66
HOW LIGHT THE SLEEPING ON THIS SOILY STAR,	....	102	FELLOWED SLEEP	24
HOW DEEP THE WAKING IN THE WORLDED CLOUDS.	....	102	FELLOWED SLEEP	25
HOW NOW MY FLESH, MY NAKED FELLOW,	....	106	ALL ALL AND	7
HOW SOON THE SERVANT SUN	....	113	SERVANT SUN	T
HOW SOON THE SERVANT SUN,	....	113	SERVANT SUN	1
HOW SOON MY LEVEL, LORD,	....	114	SERVANT SUN	22
'SEE,' DRUMMED THE TAUT MASKS, 'HOW THE DEAD ASCEND:		132	I MAKE THIS IN	52
HOW SHALL MY ANIMAL	....	134	HOW MY ANIMAL	T

	PAGE	TITLE	LINE
HOW (CONTINUED)			
HOW SHALL MY ANIMAL	134	HOW MY ANIMAL	1
HOW SHALL IT MAGNETIZE,	135	HOW MY ANIMAL	12
HOW, THROUGH THE HALFMOON'S VEGETABLE EYE,	138	FIVE & COUNTRY	3
SING HOW THE SEAL HAS KISSED HER DEAD!	164	LONG-LEGGED	82
SEE HOW HE STUMBLES. HALLELUJAH HEE-HAW!	179	NEW QUAY	26
GOOD MEN, THE LAST WAVE BY, CRYING HOW BRIGHT	208	NOT GO GENTLE	7
TALLER THIS THUNDERCLAP SPRING, AND HOW	211	POEM ON B'DAY	103
HOWL			
SING AND HOWL THROUGH SAND AND ANEMONE	165	LONG-LEGGED	89
HOWLING			
THE HOWLING SPIRIT SHAPED A GOD	85	SEE, SAYS LIME	7
QUEEN CATHERINE HOWLING BARE	157	INTO HER HEAD	12
MAY HIS HUNGER GO HOWLING ON BARE WHITE BONES	188	WINTER'S TALE	33
HIS NAKED NEED STRUCK HIM HOWLING AND BOWED	188	WINTER'S TALE	39
HOWLS			
HOWLS THE FOUL FIEND TO HEEL.	61	MEAT ON BONES	29
BE SAID TO WEEP WHEN WEATHER HOWLS?	65	GODS THUMP	3
HUBBUB			
HUBBUB AND FIDDLE, THIS TUNE	5	PROLOGUE	72
HUG			
I HUG TO LOVE WITH MY UNRULY SCRAWL	75	MY HERO BARES	8
HUGE			
PROUD AS A SUCKED STONE AND HUGE AS SANDGRAINS.	131	I MAKE THIS IN	23
HUGE WEDDINGS IN THE WAVES,	164	LONG-LEGGED	72
HUGGED			
HUGGED, AND BARREN AND BARE ON MOTHER GOOSE'S GROUND	205	GIANT'S THIGH	43
HULK			
HIS SEA-SUCKED ADAM IN THE HOLLOW HULK,	103	WORLD PYRAMID	2
AND THE MOON SWAM OUT OF ITS HULK.	162	LONG-LEGGED	16
HULKS			
TO DEATH, ONE MAN THROUGH HIS SUNDERED HULKS,	211	POEM ON B'DAY	92
HULLABALLOING			
HO, HULLABALLOING CLAN	4	PROLOGUE	64
HULOO			
HULOO, ON PLUMBED BRYNS,	4	PROLOGUE	57
HULOO, MY PROUD DOVE WITH A FLUTE!	5	PROLOGUE	97
HUMAN			
AND YET BE HUMAN,	23	THE ONLY DEAD	10
THAT BRIDGED THE HUMAN HALVES,	108	GRIEF THIEF	26
HUMANITY'S			
I PROPPED HUMANITY'S WEIGHT	155	RETURN	33
HUMBLE			
MAY A HUMBLE VILLAGE LABOUR	126	SEED-AT-ZERO	29
MAY A HUMBLE PLANET LABOUR	126	SEED-AT-ZERO	36
I KNOW HER SCRUBBED AND SOUR HUMBLE HANDS	136	AFTER FUNERAL	31
HUMBLE IN ALL HIS PLANETS,	215	COUNTRY HEAVEN	4
HUMBLING			
FATHERING AND ALL HUMBLING DARKNESS	191	REFUSAL MOURN	3
HUMILIATE			
BUT I DO NOT HUMILIATE YOU;	228	NOT DESPAIR	11
HUMMED			
OVER AND ROUND THE ORDERED GARDEN HUMMED,	34	IN GARDENS	17
HUMMING			
DRIPS FROM THE HUMMING DARKNESS OF THE HIVE.	48	LIGHT, I KNOW	10
HUMOUR			
NO, HE'S A STRANGER, OUTSIDE THE SEASON'S HUMOUR,	46	POET: 1935	10
HUMOURED			
THEY SAID, WHO HACKED AND HUMOURED, THEY WERE MINE.	112	NOT FATHER ME	20

	PAGE	TITLE	LINE
HUMP			
BUTTON YOUR BODICE ON A HUMP OF SPLINTERS, ...	118	ALTARWISE	51
HUMPBACKED			
SLIPPED THE FINS OF THOSE HUMPBACKED TONS	163	LONG-LEGGED	52
HUMPED			
IN THE SNIVELLING HOURS WITH DEAD, HUMPED ANN	136	AFTER FUNERAL	13
HUMPS			
HAS A HORN AND TWO HUMPS ON ITS HEAD, ...	221	SONG OF DOG	6
HUNCHBACK			
THE HUNCHBACK IN THE PARK	171	THE HUNCHBACK	T
THE HUNCHBACK IN THE PARK	171	THE HUNCHBACK	1
HAD FOLLOWED THE HUNCHBACK	172	THE HUNCHBACK	41
HUNCHBACKED			
HUNCHBACKED IN MOCKERY	171	THE HUNCHBACK	21
HUNCHBACKS			
(QUESTIONS ARE HUNCHBACKS TO THE POKER MARROW.) ...	118	ALTARWISE	48
HUNDRED			
ECHO A HUNDRED TIMES, THE FLIGHT OF BIRDS	50	OUT OF THE PIT	14
OF MANY A HUNDRED FALLS;	55	WHY EAST WIND	5
HE HAS THE STILL MOON AND THE HUNDRED STARS;	63	WOMAN SPEAKS	20
DISSOLVED IN SUMMER AND THE HUNDRED SEASONS;	79	LOVE'S FEVER	49
RODE AND WHISTLED A HUNDRED TIMES	157	INTO HER HEAD	18
AMONG THOSE KILLED IN THE DAWN RAID WAS A MAN AGED A			
HUNDRED	172	DAWN RAID	T
AND A HUNDRED STORKS PERCH ON THE SUN'S RIGHT HAND.	173	DAWN RAID	14
HUNG			
HUNG POINTED IN THE WIND, ...	43	FACES SHONE	9
HIS SCISSORS OILED, HIS KNIFE HUNG LOOSE	91	WHERE ONCE THE	10
BIRDMAN OR TOLD GHOST I HUNG.	152	BELOW A TIME	31
AND DARKNESS HUNG THE WALLS WITH BASKETS OF SNAKES,	158	INTO HER HEAD	27
HUNGER			
THE HUNGER OF LIVING, THE OVEN AND GUN	39	GAS FADES	24
MAKE THE HUNGER FOR LIVING	39	GAS FADES	26
'THE THIRST IS QUENCHED, THE HUNGER GONE, ...	61	MEAT ON BONES	17
HUNGER FOR HIM WHO DUNGS THE VALLEY FIELDS.	64	WOMAN SPEAKS	37
MY HEART KNEW LOVE, MY BELLY HUNGER;	69	BEFORE KNOCKED	29
THAT UTTERS ALL LOVE HUNGER	75	MY HERO BARES	9
AND TO THE VOICE THAT, LIKE A VOICE OF HUNGER, ...	79	LOVE'S FEVER	29
HAPPY CADAVER'S HUNGER AS YOU TAKE	101	RUNNING GRAVE	49
UNDER THE MILKY MUSHROOMS SLEW MY HUNGER, ...	118	ALTARWISE	64
IN A LAND STRAPPED BY HUNGER	134	NOT FROM ANGER	4
ONE RICH STREET WITH HUNGER IN IT.	157	RETURN	101
MAY HIS HUNGER GO HOWLING ON BARE WHITE BONES	188	WINTER'S TALE	33
HUNGER OF BIRDS IN THE FIELDS OF THE BREAD OF WATER,			
TOSSED	188	WINTER'S TALE	42
HUNGERING			
STREETS OR HUNGERING IN THE CRUMBLED WOOD: TO THESE	205	GIANT'S THIGH	57
HUNGERS			
HUNGERS FOR QUICKENING, AND MY LONELY LIPS	64	WOMAN SPEAKS	36
IF I WERE TICKLED BY THE URCHIN HUNGERS	95	RUB OF LOVE	18
HUNGER'S			
AND THE HUNGER'S EMPEROR;	75	MY HERO BARES	19
HUNGRILY			
TO TAKE TO GIVE IS ALL, RETURN WHAT IS HUNGRILY GIVEN	140	NO WORK WORDS	4
HUNGRY			
CRYING WITH HUNGRY VOICES IN OUR NEST.	28	NO WINGS	22
SPEAK LIKE A HUNGRY PARSON OF THE MANNA, ...	96	TWELVE	6
SANG HEAVEN HUNGRY AND THE QUICK	141	SAINT TO FALL	15
BUT THE HUNGRY KINGS OF THE TIDES;	165	LONG-LEGGED	109

	PAGE	TITLE	LINE
HUNT			
AND THE HUNT IN THE HATSTAND DISCOVERS NO COPPERS,	38	GAS FADES	2
HUNTER			
SPILL THE LANK FOLLY'S HUNTER AND THE HARD-HELD HOPE.	122	HOLD HARD	18
HUNTING			
IF HUNTING MEANS ANYTHING MORE THAN THE CHASE	44	TO FOLLOW FOX	18
AND HIS LOIN WAS A HUNTING FLAME	168	LONG-LEGGED	196
THE PUFFED BIRDS HOPPING AND HUNTING, THE MILKMAIDS	187	WINTER'S TALE	23
HUNTSMAN			
AND GREEN AND GOLDEN I WAS HUNTSMAN AND HERDSMAN,			
THE CALVES	195	FERN HILL	15
HURDLES			
HURDLES AND GUNS AND RAILINGS, AS THE BOULDERS HEAVE,	122	HOLD HARD	16
HURLED			
BY THE BELIEVER LOST AND THE HURLED OUTCAST OF LIGHT.	188	WINTER'S TALE	50
HURLING			
HURLING INTO BEGINNING LIKE CHRIST THE CHILD.	149	UNLUCKILY FOR	52
HURLS			
MY HEART HURLS FROM MY SIDE AND TEARS	48	LIGHT, I KNOW	8
HURRIED			
I WHO SAW IN A HURRIED FILM	140	TOMBSTONE TOLD	21
HURRIES			
THE GRAIN THAT HURRIES THIS WAY FROM THE RIM OF THE			
GRAVE	146	IF HEAD HURT	24
HURRY			
SOUNDS WITH THE GRAINS AS THEY HURRY	54	WE BY SEASAND	15
WHEN CAMERAS SHUT THEY HURRY TO THEIR HOLE	89	EUNUCH DREAMS	15
HURT			
WHO TELLS ME HURT, ...	12	SKY'S BRIGHT	13
THE ANGEL'S HURT IS LEFT;	12	SKY'S BRIGHT	18
DON'T HURT THE CHIC ANATOMY	18	NATURAL DAY	9
FOR USE OF SENSE, (NO HURT NO SENSE).	24	LITTLE PROBLEM	9
PRAISE THAT ONLY THE WITS ARE HURT AFTER THE WITS'			
FIGHT.	42	A WAR OF WITS	11
'NOR THE GREEN NOUGHT BE HURT;	129	MY NEOPHYTE	45
'IF MY HEAD HURT A HAIR'S FOOT'	145	IF HEAD HURT	T
'IF MY HEAD HURT A HAIR'S FOOT	145	IF HEAD HURT	1
WHEN HINDERING MAN HURT	153	WAS A SAVIOUR	12
YOU DO NOT HURT, NOR CAN YOUR HAND	233	NO THOUGHT	3
HUSHES			
THE WASTEFUL HUSHES AMONG TREES.	157	RETURN	99
HUSK			
HUSK OF YOUNG STARS AND HANDFULL ZODIAC, ...	138	FIVE & COUNTRY	4
SEED OF SONS IN THE LOIN OF THE BLACK HUSK LEFT.	174	FIRE RAID	32
ALONE IN THE HUSK OF MAN'S HOME	186	HOLY SPRING	22
HUSKED			
'NOW TO AWAKE HUSKED OF GESTURES AND MY JOY LIKE A			
CAVE	146	IF HEAD HURT	21
HUT			
STILL, IN HIS HUT, HE BROODS AMONG HIS BIRDS.	53	OUT OF THE PIT	101
HUTCH			
A COUNTRY POT, HIS HUTCH IN	154	RETURN	3
IN A HUTCH IN A COWPATCHED GLEN	156	RETURN	94
HUTS			
TO HERMITS' HUTS, AND TALKED TO ANCIENT MEN.	53	OUT OF THE PIT	91
HYDRANGEAS			
TO TOUCH THE HYDRANGEAS, ...	229	MY RIVER	22
HYENA			
NIGHTINGALE AND HYENA	164	LONG-LEGGED	87

	PAGE	TITLE	LINE
HYLEG			
AND ALL LOVE'S SINNERS IN SWEET CLOTH KNEEL TO A			
HYLEG IMAGE, ...	130	SINNERS' BELL	28
HYMN			
AND I WOULD CHOKE THE HEAVENS WITH MY HYMN	96	TWELVE	12
HYMNED			
HYMNED HIS SHRIVELLING FLOCK, ...	141	SAINT TO FALL	13
AND THE WINGS GLIDED WIDE AND HE WAS HYMNED AND			
WEDDED, ...	191	WINTER'S TALE	123
HYMNING			
BABBLE LIKE A BELLBUOY OVER THE HYMNING HEADS, ...	136	AFTER FUNERAL	23
THAT HYMNING GOOSEBERRY, THAT BETHEL-WORM	179	NEW QUAY	21
OF EELS, SAINT HERON HYMNING IN THE SHELL-HUNG			
DISTANT	202	SIR JOHNS HILL	36
HYPNOTISED			
ALL THE HYPNOTISED CITY'S	156	RETURN	62
I			
AT POOR PEACE I SING	3	PROLOGUE	23
MY DABBED BAY'S DUSK, AS I HACK	4	PROLOGUE	36
HOW I, A SPINNING MAN, ...	4	PROLOGUE	39
HARK: I TRUMPET THE PLACE, ...	4	PROLOGUE	42
I BUILD MY BELLOWING ARK	4	PROLOGUE	44
CLANGOUR AS I HEW AND SMITE	5	PROLOGUE	70
I KNOW THIS VICIOUS MINUTE'S HOUR	9	MINUTE'S HOUR	T
I KNOW THIS VICIOUS MINUTE'S HOUR;	9	MINUTE'S HOUR	1
AND I, CAUGHT IN MID-AIR PERHAPS, ...	9	MINUTE'S HOUR	6
YOU I SHALL DROWN UNREASONABLY, ...	9	MINUTE'S HOUR	9
I WANT REALITY TO HOLD/ WITHIN MY PALM, ...	9	MINUTE'S HOUR	14
BUT IT, REALITY, WHOSE VOICE I KNOW	9	MINUTE'S HOUR	16
THEN SHALL I GO, ...	9	MINUTE'S HOUR	19
I COULD DEVOTE TO OTHER THINGS.	9	MINUTE'S HOUR	22
STOP HAS NO MINUTES,/ BUT I GO OR DIE.	9	MINUTE'S HOUR	23
WITH THAT HALF-MOULDED MIND I SAID WAS YOURS, ...	10	COOL, OH NO	4
BUT COOLER WHEN I TAKE IT BACK, ...	10	COOL, OH NO	5
AND SHARPER IF I BREAK ASUNDER	10	COOL, OH NO	6
FOR WHEN I BOUGHT YOU FOR A THOUGHT, (YOU COST NO			
MORE)	10	COOL, OH NO	8
HOW COULD I SMOOTH THAT SKIN	10	COOL, OH NO	9
YOU SHALL NOT GO UNLESS I WILL IT	10	COOL, OH NO	21
AND I, YOUR CAPTOR, HAVE MY LOVE TO KEEP	10	COOL, OH NO	29
I, POOR ROMANTIC, HELD HER HEEL	11	CABARET	1
THE THROAT IS MINE I KNOW THE NECK	11	AIR BREATHE	2
BUT SHOULD NOT TOUCH LIKE I	11	AIR BREATHE	11
BUT SHE DID NOT CRY, 'I SEE;	11	CABARET	12
I SEE THE MAN IS MAD WITH LOVE.'	11	CABARET	13
I WISH TO KNOW	12	SKY'S BRIGHT	10
I CANNOT LIFT, BUT CAN, ...	12	SKY'S BRIGHT	11
I, POOR ROMANTIC, CONTEMPLATE	12	CABARET	22
I TEAR HER BREAST, ...	13	SKY'S BRIGHT	22
AND THEN I THINK	13	SKY'S BRIGHT	25
I, SAID THE BEETLE, OUT OF MY THIN BLACK WOMB, ...	18	NATURAL DAY	26
I TOUCH AND BREAK, ...	20	ENCOMPASSED	14
I TOUCH AND BREAK.	20	ENCOMPASSED	15
FOR, IF I COULD, I'D FLY AWAY, ...	21	BEWILDERED WAY	22
FOR IF I COULD, I'D FLY AWAY	21	BEWILDERED WAY	23
SINCE, ON A QUIET NIGHT, I HEARD THEM TALK	22	ON QUIET NIGHT	1
I HAVE NOT LAIN AN HOUR ASLEEP	22	ON QUIET NIGHT	5
I HEAR THEM SAY OUT OF THE DARKNESS	23	ON QUIET NIGHT	21
THOUGH, AFTER'S DONE, I	24	LITTLE PROBLEM	15
WHO DO I BLAME	26	PERSONAL EPIT	2

		PAGE	TITLE	LINE
I (CONTINUED)				
WHO DO I BLAME?	....	26	PERSONAL EPIT	6
MOTHER I BLAME	....	26	PERSONAL EPIT	7
MOTHER I BLAME.	....	26	PERSONAL EPIT	12
I AM MAN'S REPLY TO EVERY QUESTION,	....	26	PERSONAL EPIT	17
I LOVE AND DOUBT, IT'S VAIN, IT'S VAIN,	....	27	OBLIVIOUS DARK	27
YOU, WHO ARE OLD, HAVE LOVED AND LOST AS I	....	30	YOUTH CALLS	5
KNOWING SUCH JOY AS I.	....	30	YOUTH CALLS	11
BUT NOT OF GRIEF, FOR I HAVE KNOCKED DOWN THAT	....	31	OUT OF SIGHS	2
FOR ALL THERE IS TO GIVE I OFFER:	....	32	OUT OF SIGHS	28
WHEN I WAS SEVEN I COUNTED FOUR AND FORTY TREES	...	33	HELD-OUT HAND	12
WHEN I WAS SEVEN I COUNTED FOUR AND FORTY TREES	...	33	HELD-OUT HAND	12
AND I WAS STRUCK DUMB BY THE SUN.	....	42	A WAR OF WITS	7
I STAND BENEATH THE CLOUDS' CONFESSIONAL,	....	42	A WAR OF WITS	13
I HAVE LONGED TO MOVE AWAY	....	43	LONGED TO MOVE	T
I HAVE LONGED TO MOVE AWAY	....	43	LONGED TO MOVE	1
I HAVE LONGED TO MOVE AWAY	....	43	LONGED TO MOVE	6
I HAVE LONGED TO MOVE AWAY BUT AM AFRAID;	....	44	LONGED TO MOVE	11
SHALL I FALL TO DEATH'S FEATHER.	....	44	LONGED TO MOVE	18
BY THESE I WOULD NOT CARE TO DIE,	....	44	LONGED TO MOVE	19
LIGHT, I KNOW, TREADS THE TEN MILLION STARS	....	48	LIGHT, I KNOW	T
LIGHT, I KNOW, TREADS THE TEN MILLION STARS,	......	48	LIGHT, I KNOW	1
I HAVE BEEN FRIGHTENED OF THE DARK FOR YEARS.	.....	48	LIGHT, I KNOW	6
I AM A TIMID CHILD WHEN LIGHT IS DEAD.	....	48	LIGHT, I KNOW	11
UNLESS I LEARN THE NIGHT I SHALL GO MAD.	....	48	LIGHT, I KNOW	12
UNLESS I LEARN THE NIGHT I SHALL GO MAD.	....	48	LIGHT, I KNOW	12
IT IS NIGHT'S TERRORS I MUST LEARN TO LOVE,	....	48	LIGHT, I KNOW	13
I AM ALONE, ALONE COMPLAIN TO THE STARS.	....	48	POET: 1935	62
IN THOSE HIGH GLOBES I CANNOT COUNT,	....	49	LIGHT, I KNOW	19
I MUST LEARN NIGHT'S LIGHT OR GO MAD.	....	49	LIGHT, I KNOW	30
KNEE-DEEP IN VOMIT. I SAW HIM THERE,	....	51	OUT OF THE PIT	43
AND THUS I SAW HIM SEARCHING FOR HIS SOUL.	....	51	OUT OF THE PIT	44
AND THUS I SAW HIM. HE WAS POISED LIKE THIS,	......	52	OUT OF THE PIT	59
WHERE, WHAT'S MY GOD? I HAVE BEEN MAD, AM MAD,	....	52	OUT OF THE PIT	63
I HAVE RIDDEN ON GUTTER DUNG AND CLOUD.	....	52	OUT OF THE PIT	67
I HAVE DESIRED THE CIRCLE OF THE SUN.	....	52	OUT OF THE PIT	73
BUT NO GOD ROSE. I HAVE SEEN BAD AND WORSE,	....	52	OUT OF THE PIT	77
AND THUS I SAW HIM IN A SQUARE OF FIELDS,	....	53	OUT OF THE PIT	87
AND THUS, SOME TIME LATER, I HEARD HIM SAY:	....	53	OUT OF THE PIT	89
OUT OF THE NOISE INTO QUIET I RAN.	....	53	OUT OF THE PIT	92
MY GOD'S A SHEPHERD, GOD'S THE LOVE I HOPED.	......	53	OUT OF THE PIT	93
I SEE HIM IN THE CROWDS, NOT SHUT	....	53	OUT OF THE PIT	102
I HEAR CONTENT, AND 'BE CONTENT'	....	56	WHY EAST WIND	21
AND 'KNOW NO ANSWER', AND I KNOW	....	56	WHY EAST WIND	23
I SHOULD TELL SUMMER FROM THE TREES, THE WORMS	....	58	HERE IN SPRING	9
I SHOULD LEARN SPRING BY THE CUCKOOING,	....	58	HERE IN SPRING	12
I LAID HER DOWN AND TOLD HER SIN,	....	61	MEAT ON BONES	23
I CANNOT MURDER, LIKE A FOOL,	....	61	MEAT ON BONES	30
NOR CAN I SMOTHER THE SWEET WAKING.'	....	61	MEAT ON BONES	32
SHALL I UNBOLT OR STAY	....	62	EARS IN TURRET	5
ALONE TILL THE DAY I DIE	....	62	EARS IN TURRET	6
SHALL I RUN TO THE SHIPS	....	62	EARS IN TURRET	21
OR STAY TILL THE DAY I DIE	....	62	EARS IN TURRET	23
SHALL I LET IN THE STRANGER,	....	63	EARS IN TURRET	29
SHALL I WELCOME THE SAILOR,	....	63	EARS IN TURRET	30
OR STAY TILL THE DAY I DIE?	....	63	EARS IN TURRET	31
SO I HAVE COME TO KNOW, BUT KNOWLEDGE ACHES;	......	64	WOMAN SPEAKS	48
I KNOW THAT AGE IS SNOW UPON THE HAIR,	....	64	WOMAN SPEAKS	49
THAT I MAY DROWN, LET LOOSE HER FLOOD OF TEARS.	...	65	WOMAN SPEAKS	55
BE SOUR IN MY HAIR. THAT I MAY LEARN	....	65	WOMAN SPEAKS	63

		PAGE	TITLE	LINE
I (CONTINUED)				
WHY SHOULD I THINK ON DEATH WHEN YOU ARE RULER?	...	67	REALM OF FLESH	10
YOU ARE MY FLESH'S RULER WHOM I TREASON,	....	67	REALM OF FLESH	11
BEFORE I KNOCKED	....	68	BEFORE KNOCKED	T
BEFORE I KNOCKED AND FLESH LET ENTER,	....	68	BEFORE KNOCKED	1
I WHO WAS SHAPELESS AS THE WATER	....	68	BEFORE KNOCKED	3
I WHO WAS DEAF TO SPRING AND SUMMER,	....	68	BEFORE KNOCKED	7
I KNEW THE MESSAGE OF THE WINTER,	....	68	BEFORE KNOCKED	13
UNGOTTEN I KNEW NIGHT AND DAY.	....	68	BEFORE KNOCKED	18
AS YET UNGOTTEN, I DID SUFFER;	....	68	BEFORE KNOCKED	19
I SMELT THE MAGGOT IN MY STOOL.	....	69	BEFORE KNOCKED	30
I WHO WAS RICH WAS MADE THE RICHER	....	69	BEFORE KNOCKED	35
I, BORN OF FLESH AND GHOST, WAS NEITHER	....	69	BEFORE KNOCKED	37
AND I WAS STRUCK DOWN BY DEATH'S FEATHER.	....	69	BEFORE KNOCKED	39
I WAS A MORTAL TO THE LAST	....	69	BEFORE KNOCKED	40
GOD AND I WILL PAY THE SNIPER.	....	71	TAKE NEEDLES	24
MOTHERS ME UNTIL I DIE,	....	72	TAKE NEEDLES	43
WHEN I YIELD THE TREE TO DEATH,	....	72	TAKE NEEDLES	45
AND I WILL BUILD MY LIQUID WORLD,	....	74	WE MOTHERNAKED	13
I HUG TO LOVE WITH MY UNRULY SCRAWL	....	75	MY HERO BARES	8
I EYE THE RING OF EARTH, THE AIRY CIRCLE,	....	76	LASHED RINGS	2
THROUGH, I TELL YOU, YOUR TWO MIDNIGHT LIPS I PRAY		76	LASHED RINGS	7
THROUGH, I TELL YOU, YOUR TWO MIDNIGHT LIPS I PRAY		76	LASHED RINGS	7
INSIDE THIS MOUTH I FEEL HIS MESSAGE MOVING	....	76	LASHED RINGS	14
AND I AM DUMB TO TELL THE CROOKED ROSE	....	77	THE FORCE THAT	4
AND I AM DUMB TO MOUTH UNTO MY VEINS	....	77	THE FORCE THAT	9
AND I AM DUMB TO TELL THE HANGING MAN	....	77	THE FORCE THAT	14
AND I AM DUMB TO TELL A WEATHER'S WIND	....	77	THE FORCE THAT	19
AND I AM DUMB TO TELL THE LOVER'S TOMB	....	77	THE FORCE THAT	21
I LEARNT MAN'S TONGUE, TO TWIST THE SHAPES OF THOUGHTS	....	79	LOVE'S FEVER	32
I LEARNT THE VERBS OF WILL, AND HAD MY SECRET;	....	79	LOVE'S FEVER	39
FROM THE DIVORCING SKY I LEARNT THE DOUBLE,	....	79	LOVE'S FEVER	44
ALL THAT I OWE THE FELLOWS OF THE GRAVE	....	80	ALL THAT I OWE	T
ALL THAT I OWE THE FELLOWS OF THE GRAVE	....	80	ALL THAT I OWE	1
O ALL I OWE IS ALL THE FLESH INHERITS,	....	80	ALL THAT I OWE	5
I ROUND THIS HERITAGE AS ROUNDS THE SUN	....	80	ALL THAT I OWE	13
CAST LIGHT UPON MY WEATHER. I AM HEIR	....	80	ALL THAT I OWE	15
HERE LIE THE BEASTS OF MAN AND HERE I FEAST,	......	81	HERE LIE BEAST	1
AND SILENTLY I MILK THE DEVIL'S BREAST.	....	81	HERE LIE BEAST	3
AND SILENTLY I MILK THE BURIED FLOWERS.	....	81	HERE LIE BEAST	9
ALL SUCH DISEASE I DOCTOR IN MY BLOOD,	....	81	ALL THAT I OWE	19
ALL NIGHT AND DAY I EYE THE RAGGED GLOBE	....	81	ALL THAT I OWE	23
ALL NIGHT AND DAY I WANDER IN THESE SAME	....	81	ALL THAT I OWE	25
I PUT ROUND RIBS THAT PACKED THEIR HEART,	....	85	SEE, SAYS LIME	2
AND MAY I YET LIVE TO ADMIRE	....	85	LETTER TO AUNT	65
THIS BREAD I BREAK	....	86	BREAD I BREAK	T
THIS BREAD I BREAK WAS ONCE THE OAT,	....	86	BREAD I BREAK	1
I CHALKED UPON THE BREASTBONE'S SLATE	....	86	SEE, SAYS LIME	27
THE MILK OF DEATH, I FILLED THE HAND	....	86	SEE, SAYS LIME	30
I SEE THE BOYS OF SUMMER	....	91	BOYS OF SUMMER	T
I SEE THE BOYS OF SUMMER IN THEIR RUIN	....	91	BOYS OF SUMMER	1
I SEE THE SUMMER CHILDREN IN THEIR MOTHERS	....	92	BOYS OF SUMMER	13
I SEE THAT FROM THESE BOYS SHALL MEN OF NOTHING	...	92	BOYS OF SUMMER	19
I SEE YOU BOYS OF SUMMER IN YOUR RUIN.	....	93	BOYS OF SUMMER	49
I AM THE MAN YOUR FATHER WAS.	....	93	BOYS OF SUMMER	52
IF I WERE TICKLED BY THE RUB OF LOVE	....	94	RUB OF LOVE	T
IF I WERE TICKLED BY THE RUB OF LOVE,	....	94	RUB OF LOVE	1
I WOULD NOT FEAR THE APPLE NOR THE FLOOD	....	95	RUB OF LOVE	6
IF I WERE TICKLED BY THE HATCHING HAIR,	....	95	RUB OF LOVE	10

I

I (CONTINUED)

	PAGE	TITLE	LINE
I WOULD NOT FEAR THE GALLOWS NOR THE AXE	95	RUB OF LOVE	13
I WOULD NOT FEAR THE MUSCLING-IN OF LOVE	95	RUB OF LOVE	17
IF I WERE TICKLED BY THE URCHIN HUNGERS	95	RUB OF LOVE	18
I WOULD NOT FEAR THE DEVIL IN THE LOIN	95	RUB OF LOVE	20
IF I WERE TICKLED BY THE LOVERS' RUB	95	RUB OF LOVE	22
I SIT AND WATCH THE WORM BENEATH MY NAIL	95	RUB OF LOVE	34
I WOULD ENFORCE THE BLACK APPARELLED CRIES,	96	TWELVE	5
I WOULD BE WOVEN A RELIGIOUS SHAPE;	96	TWELVE	9
AND I WOULD CHOKE THE HEAVENS WITH MY HYMN	96	TWELVE	12
I WOULD BE TICKLED BY THE RUB THAT IS:	96	RUB OF LOVE	48
I SENT MY CREATURE SCOUTING ON THE GLOBE,	97	TWILIGHT LOCKS	9
CAUGHT BY THE CRABBING SUN I WALK ON FIRE	98	OCTOBER WIND	3
SHUT, TOO, IN A TOWER OF WORDS, I MARK	98	OCTOBER WIND	9
I SENT MY OWN AMBASSADOR TO LIGHT;	98	TWILIGHT LOCKS	33
THE SIGNAL GRASS THAT TELLS ME ALL I KNOW	99	OCTOBER WIND	22
I, THAT TIME'S JACKET OR THE COAT OF ICE	100	RUNNING GRAVE	18
I FELLOWED SLEEP	101	FELLOWED SLEEP	T
I FELLOWED SLEEP WHO KISSED ME IN THE BRAIN,	101	FELLOWED SLEEP	1
SO, PLANING-HEELED, I FLEW ALONG MY MAN	101	FELLOWED SLEEP	4
I FLED THE EARTH AND, NAKED, CLIMBED THE WEATHER,	101	FELLOWED SLEEP	6
AND THERE WE WEPT, I AND THE GHOSTLY OTHER,	101	FELLOWED SLEEP	8
I FLED THAT GROUND AS LIGHTLY AS A FEATHER.	101	FELLOWED SLEEP	10
I DAMP THE WAXLIGHTS IN YOUR TOWER DOME.	101	RUNNING GRAVE	36
I DREAMED MY GENESIS	102	I DREAMED MY	T
I DREAMED MY GENESIS IN SWEAT OF SLEEP, BREAKING	102	I DREAMED MY	1
AS, BLOWING ON THE ANGELS, I WAS LOST	102	FELLOWED SLEEP	17
I BLEW THE DREAMING FELLOWS TO THEIR BED	102	FELLOWED SLEEP	19
I SPELT MY VISION WITH A HAND AND HAIR,	102	FELLOWED SLEEP	23
A CREATURE IN MY BONES I	103	I DREAMED MY	10
I DREAMED MY GENESIS AND DIED AGAIN, SHRAPNEL	103	I DREAMED MY	13
SHARP IN MY SECOND DEATH I MARKED THE HILLS, HARVEST	103	I DREAMED MY	17
I DREAMED MY GENESIS IN SWEAT OF DEATH, FALLEN	103	I DREAMED MY	25
OF NEW MAN STRENGTH, I SEEK THE SUN.	103	I DREAMED MY	28
I SCRAPE THROUGH RESIN TO A STARRY BONE	104	WORLD PYRAMID	35
I PIECE MY FLESH THAT RATTLED ON THE YARDS	105	WORLD PYRAMID	38
I HEAR, THROUGH DEAD MEN'S DRUMS, THE RIDDLED LADS,	105	WORLD PYRAMID	40
THE STRAWS OF ASIA, LOSE ME AS I TURN	105	WORLD PYRAMID	47
THE TONGUES OF HEAVEN GOSSIP AS I GLIDE	105	WORLD PYRAMID	53
I BLOW THE STAMMEL FEATHER IN THE VEIN.	105	WORLD PYRAMID	56
THE SECRET CHILD, I SHIFT ABOUT THE SEA	105	WORLD PYRAMID	59
I, IN MY INTRICATE IMAGE	108	I, IN IMAGE	T
I, IN MY INTRICATE IMAGE, STRIDE ON TWO LEVELS,	108	I, IN IMAGE	1
I, IN MY FUSION OF ROSE AND MALE MOTION,	109	I, IN IMAGE	17
I WITH THE WOODEN INSECT IN THE TREE OF NETTLES,	109	I, IN IMAGE	28
I, IN A WIND ON FIRE, FROM GREEN ADAM'S CRADLE,	111	I, IN IMAGE	95
DO YOU NOT MOTHER ME, NOR, AS I AM,	112	NOT FATHER ME	3
AM I NOT FATHER, TOO, AND THE ASCENDING BOY,	112	NOT FATHER ME	9
AM I NOT SISTER, TOO, WHO IS MY SAVIOUR?	112	NOT FATHER ME	12
AM I NOT ALL OF YOU BY THE DIRECTED SEA	112	NOT FATHER ME	13
AM I NOT YOU WHO FRONT THE TIDY SHORE,	112	NOT FATHER ME	15
I AM, THE TOWER TOLD, FELLED BY A TIMELESS STROKE,	113	NOT FATHER ME	21
SHALL I STILL BE LOVE'S HOUSE ON THE WIDDERSHIN EARTH,	113	NOT FATHER ME	29
SHE WHO WAS WHO I HOLD, THE FATS AND FLOWER,	114	A GRIEF AGO	2
A CLAW I QUESTION FROM THE MOUSE'S BONE,	114	SERVANT SUN	17
TRAP I WITH COIL AND SHEET,	114	SERVANT SUN	19
LET THE SOIL SQUEAL I AM THE BITING MAN	114	SERVANT SUN	20
THAT SHE I HAVE,	115	A GRIEF AGO	30
I TELL HER THIS: BEFORE THE SUNCOCK CAST	115	A GRIEF AGO	35

I

		PAGE	TITLE	LINE
I (CONTINUED)				
I HAVE BEEN TOLD TO REASON BY THE HEART,	....	116	LANTERNS SHINE	9
I HAVE BEEN TOLD TO REASON BY THE PULSE,	....	116	LANTERNS SHINE	11
SO FAST I MOVE DEFYING TIME, THE QUIET GENTLEMAN		116	LANTERNS SHINE	14
I HAVE HEARD MANY YEARS OF TELLING,	....	116	LANTERNS SHINE	16
THE BALL I THREW WHILE PLAYING IN THE PARK	....	116	LANTERNS SHINE	18
I AM THE LONG WORLD'S GENTLEMAN, HE SAID,	....	117	ALTARWISE	13
RIP OF THE VAULTS, I TOOK MY MARROW-LADLE	....	118	ALTARWISE	35
FOR LOSS OF BLOOD I FELL ON ISHMAEL'S PLAIN,	......	118	ALTARWISE	63
TILL TALLOW I BLEW FROM THE WAX'S TOWER	....	119	ALTARWISE	79
AS TARRED WITH BLOOD AS THE BRIGHT THORNS I WEPT;		120	ALTARWISE	101
I BY THE TREE OF THIEVES, ALL GLORY'S SAWBONES,	...	120	ALTARWISE	109
TIME'S SHIP-RACKED GOSPEL ON THE GLOBE I BALANCE:		121	ALTARWISE	129
SPOT THE BLOWN WORD, AND ON THE SEAS I IMAGE	......	121	ALTARWISE	131
O RING OF SEAS, NOR SORROW AS I SHIFT	....	123	FOSTER LIGHT	20
TODAY, THIS INSECT, AND THE WORLD I BREATHE,	......	124	TODAY, INSECT	1
THE DEAR, DAFT TIME I TAKE TO NUDGE THE SENTENCE,		124	TODAY, INSECT	4
IN TRUST AND TALE HAVE I DIVIDED SENSE,	....	124	TODAY, INSECT	5
NOW MAKE THE WORLD OF ME AS I HAVE MADE	....	124	FOSTER LIGHT	29
'ADAM I LOVE, MY MADMEN'S LOVE IS ENDLESS,	....	125	TODAY, INSECT	23
I SAW TIME MURDER ME.	....	129	MY NEOPHYTE	48
OVER THE CHOIR MINUTE I HEAR THE HOUR CHANT:	......	130	SINNERS' BELL	7
I MEAN BY TIME THE CAST AND CURFEW RASCAL OF OUR				
MARRIAGE,	....	130	SINNERS' BELL	25
I MAKE THIS IN A WARRING ABSENCE	....	131	I MAKE THIS IN	T
I MAKE THIS IN A WARRING ABSENCE WHEN	....	131	I MAKE THIS IN	1
I MAKE A WEAPON OF AN ASS'S SKELETON	....	132	I MAKE THIS IN	31
LIKE AN APPROACHING WAVE I SPRAWL TO RUIN.	....	132	I MAKE THIS IN	38
IN THAT BRIGHT ANCHORGROUND WHERE I LAY LINENED,		132	I MAKE THIS IN	48
YET THIS I MAKE IN A FORGIVING PRESENCE.	....	133	I MAKE THIS IN	68
WHOSE WIZARD SHAPE I TRACE IN THE CAVERNOUS SKULL,		134	HOW MY ANIMAL	2
AND BEAR THOSE TENDRIL HANDS I TOUCH ACROSS	....	134	NOT FROM ANGER	6
WITH BRIDEBAIT OF GOLD BREAD, I WITH A LIVING SKEIN,		135	HOW MY ANIMAL	25
I STAND, FOR THIS MEMORIAL'S SAKE, ALONE	....	136	AFTER FUNERAL	12
BUT I, ANN'S BARD ON A RAISED HEARTH, CALL ALL	....	136	AFTER FUNERAL	21
I KNOW HER SCRUBBED AND SOUR HUMBLE HANDS	....	136	AFTER FUNERAL	31
I PICK A STICK OF CELERY FROM THE VALLEY	....	137	O CHATTERTON	14
I FIND A TRIPPER'S KNICKER IN THE GULLY	....	137	O CHATTERTON	15
ON GIDDY NIGHTS I SLAP A FEW DRUNK CURVES	....	138	O CHATTERTON	24
CELIBATE I SIT AND SEE	....	138	O CHATTERTON	29
I MUST WAIT FOR A WOMAN'S SMILE	....	138	O CHATTERTON	33
I OFFER YOU WOMEN, NOT WOMAN,	....	138	O CHATTERTON	40
THAT I STRUCK ONE DAY BY LUCK,	....	139	TOMBSTONE TOLD	5
BEFORE I HEARD IN MY MOTHER'S SIDE	....	139	TOMBSTONE TOLD	6
AMONG MEN LATER I HEARD IT SAID	....	139	TOMBSTONE TOLD	16
I BITTERLY TAKE TO TASK MY POVERTY AND CRAFT:	.....	140	NO WORK WORDS	3
IF I TAKE TO BURN OR RETURN THIS WORLD WHICH IS EACH				
MAN'S WORK.	....	140	NO WORK WORDS	12
I WHO SAW IN A HURRIED FILM	....	140	TOMBSTONE TOLD	21
I DIED BEFORE BEDTIME CAME	....	140	TOMBSTONE TOLD	26
AND I FELT WITH MY BARE FALL	....	140	TOMBSTONE TOLD	28
I, THE FIRST NAMED	....	141	I, FIRST NAMED	T
I, THE FIRST NAMED, AM THE GHOST OF THIS SIR AND				
CHRISTIAN FRIEND	....	141	I, FIRST NAMED	1
WHO WRITES THESE WORDS I WRITE IN A STILL ROOM IN A				
SPELLSOAKED HOUSE:	....	141	I, FIRST NAMED	2
I AM THE GHOST IN THIS HOUSE THAT IS FILLED WITH THE				
TONGUE AND EYES	....	141	I, FIRST NAMED	3
OF A LACK-A-HEAD GHOST I FEAR TO THE ANONYMOUS END.		141	I, FIRST NAMED	4
I FOUND THEM LYING ON THE FLOOR,	....	143	THE MOLLS	1

I

	PAGE	TITLE	LINE

I (CONTINUED)

IN THE GROIN OF THE NATURAL DOORWAY I CROUCHED LIKE A TAILOR .... 143 24 YEARS 3
I ADVANCE FOR AS LONG AS FOREVER IS. .... 143 24 YEARS 9
AND WHEN I DREAM OF THEM I FIND .... 143 THE MOLLS 11
AND WHEN I DREAM OF THEM I FIND .... 143 THE MOLLS 11
THE GENTLE SEASLIDES OF SAYING I MUST UNDO .... 144 COLOUR OF SAY 5
WHEN I WHISTLED WITH MITCHING BOYS THROUGH A RESERVOIR PARK .... 144 COLOUR OF SAY 7
AND EVERY STONE I WIND OFF LIKE A REEL. .... 144 COLOUR OF SAY 13
BEFORE I RUSH IN A CROUCH THE GHOST WITH A HAMMER, AIR, ... 145 IF HEAD HURT 9
SHALL I, STRUCK ON THE HOT AND ROCKING STREET, ... 145 PLEASURE-BIRD 16
I FURNISH WITH THE MEAT OF A FABLE; .... 145 PLEASURE-BIRD 21
OVER THE PAST TABLE I REPEAT THIS PRESENT GRACE. .... 145 PLEASURE-BIRD 25
FRIEND BY ENEMY I CALL YOU OUT. .... 146 TO OTHERS 1
RASPED AT LAST, AND I STUMBLED AND SUCKED, ... 146 TO OTHERS 8
WHOM NOW I CONJURE TO STAND AS THIEF .... 146 TO OTHERS 9
MY DEAR WOULD I CHANGE MY TEARS OR YOUR IRON HEAD. .... 146 IF HEAD HURT 18
I NEVER THOUGHT TO UTTER OR THINK .... 147 TO OTHERS 16
THAT THOUGH I LOVED THEM FOR THEIR FAULTS .... 147 TO OTHERS 18
TURNS OF YOUR PRAYED FLESH, NOR SHALL I SHOO THE BIRD BELOW ME: .... 148 UNLUCKILY FOR 27
I SEE THE TIGRON IN TEARS .... 148 UNLUCKILY FOR 29
I SEE THE WANTING NUN SAINT CARVED IN A GARB .... 148 UNLUCKILY FOR 34
CONTINENCE. I SEE THE UNFIRED PHOENIX, HERALD .... 148 UNLUCKILY FOR 37
BOTH SHALL FAIL IF I BOW NOT TO YOUR BLESSING .... 148 UNLUCKILY FOR 47
THIS I KNOW FROM THE NATIVE .... 148 UNLUCKILY FOR 50
ONCE I HAD A RICH BOY FOR MYSELF .... 149 PAPER & STICKS 4
I LOVED HIS BODY AND HIS NAVY BLUE WEALTH .... 149 PAPER & STICKS 5
AND I LIVED IN HIS PURSE AND HIS HEART .... 149 PAPER & STICKS 6
WHEN IN OUR BED I WAS TOSSING AND TURNING .... 149 PAPER & STICKS 7
ALL I COULD SEE WERE HIS BROWN EYES BURNING .... 149 PAPER & STICKS 8
I TALK TO HIM AS I CLEAN THE GRATE .... 149 PAPER & STICKS 10
I TALK TO HIM AS I CLEAN THE GRATE .... 149 PAPER & STICKS 10
I HAD A HANDSOME AND WELL-OFF BOY .... 149 PAPER & STICKS 13
WHEN I WOKE .... 150 WHEN I WOKE T
WHEN I WOKE, THE TOWN SPOKE. .... 150 WHEN I WOKE 1
EVERY MORNING I MAKE, ... 150 WHEN I WOKE 16
I HEARD, THIS MORNING, WAKING, ... 150 WHEN I WOKE 23
I DREW THE WHITE SHEET OVER THE ISLANDS .... 150 WHEN I WOKE 29
IN GROTTOES I WORKED WITH BIRDS, ... 151 BELOW A TIME 9
I ASTOUNDED THE SITTING TAILORS, ... 151 BELOW A TIME 17
I SET BACK THE CLOCK FACED TAILORS, ... 151 BELOW A TIME 18
I ROCKETED TO ASTONISH .... 151 BELOW A TIME 25
BIRDMAN OR TOLD GHOST I HUNG. .... 152 BELOW A TIME 31
HEAD, DECEIVED, I BELIEVED, MY MAKER, ... 152 BELOW A TIME 34
I WAS PIERCED BY THE IDOL TAILOR'S EYES, ... 152 BELOW A TIME 38
NEVER NEVER OH NEVER TO REGRET THE BUGLE I WORE .... 152 BELOW A TIME 47
ON MY CLEAVING ARM AS I BLASTED IN A WAVE. .... 152 BELOW A TIME 48
NOW SHOWN AND MOSTLY BARE I WOULD LIE DOWN, ... 152 BELOW A TIME 49
I SPENT MY UNWASTEABLE .... 154 RETURN 9
I PROPPED HUMANITY'S WEIGHT .... 155 RETURN 33
THEN INTO BLIND STREETS I SWAM .... 155 RETURN 44
AND I IN THE WANTING SWAY .... 156 RETURN 66
NOW I DELIGHT, I SUPPOSE, IN .... 156 RETURN 95
NOW I DELIGHT, I SUPPOSE, IN .... 156 RETURN 95
I MAY WITHOUT FAIL .... 170 LOVE IN ASYLUM 17
IN THE FOUNTAIN BASIN WHERE I SAILED MY SHIP .... 171 THE HUNCHBACK 10
I KNOW NOT WHETHER .... 174 FIRE RAID 33

		PAGE	TITLE	LINE
I (CONTINUED)				
I KNOW THE LEGEND	....	174	FIRE RAID	47
LAST NIGHT I DIVED MY BEGGAR ARM	....	175	MY BEGGAR ARM	T
LAST NIGHT I DIVED MY BEGGAR ARM	....	175	MY BEGGAR ARM	1
TELLING THE HEART I BROKE OF A GOOD HABIT	....	175	MY BEGGAR ARM	4
AND I ROSE	....	177	POEM IN OCT	14
HIGH TIDE AND THE HERON DIVED WHEN I TOOK THE ROAD		177	POEM IN OCT	17
COME IN THE MORNING WHERE I WANDERED AND LISTENED		177	POEM IN OCT	27
THERE COULD I MARVEL	....	178	POEM IN OCT	38
AND I SAW IN THE TURNING SO CLEARLY A CHILD'S	.....	178	POEM IN OCT	46
AND THERE COULD I MARVEL MY BIRTHDAY	....	178	POEM IN OCT	61
BAY. NO-GOOD IS ABROAD. I UNHARDY CAN	....	179	NEW QUAY	8
I SIT AT THE OPEN WINDOW, OBSERVING	....	179	NEW QUAY	13
CAVES THE CRIES OF THE PARCHS AND THEIR FLOCKS. I		179	NEW QUAY	17
THAT I CAN HEAR THE WOMB	....	180	VISION, PRAYER	6
I	....	180	VISION, PRAYER	18
I SHALL RUN LOST IN SUDDEN	....	181	VISION, PRAYER	45
FOR I WAS LOST WHO AM	....	181	VISION, PRAYER	57
FOR I WAS LOST WHO HAVE COME	....	181	VISION, PRAYER	62
BREAST I SHALL WAKEN	....	182	VISION, PRAYER	73
AND I	....	182	VISION, PRAYER	100
I PRAY THOUGH I BELONG	....	183	VISION, PRAYER	115
I PRAY THOUGH I BELONG	....	183	VISION, PRAYER	115
IN THE CENTRE OF DARK I PRAY HIM	....	183	VISION, PRAYER	135
OF SLEEPERS WHOSE TONGUE I TOLL	....	184	VISION, PRAYER	155
BE I PRAY	....	185	VISION, PRAYER	181
I TURN THE CORNER OF PRAYER AND BURN	....	185	VISION, PRAYER	188
I WOULD TURN BACK AND RUN	....	185	VISION, PRAYER	191
I	....	185	VISION, PRAYER	196
NOW I AM LOST IN THE BLINDING	....	185	VISION, PRAYER	203
I CLIMB TO GREET THE WAR IN WHICH I HAVE NO HEART BUT ONLY	....	186	HOLY SPRING	8
I CLIMB TO GREET THE WAR IN WHICH I HAVE NO HEART BUT ONLY	....	186	HOLY SPRING	8
THAT ONE DARK I OWE MY LIGHT,	....	186	HOLY SPRING	9
AND I AM STRUCK AS LONELY AS A HOLY MAKER BY THE SUN.		186	HOLY SPRING	12
AND I MUST ENTER AGAIN THE ROUND	....	191	REFUSAL MOURN	7
SHALL I LET PRAY THE SHADOW OF A SOUND	....	191	REFUSAL MOURN	10
I SHALL NOT MURDER	....	192	REFUSAL MOURN	14
NOW AS I WAS YOUNG AND EASY UNDER THE APPLE BOUGHS		195	FERN HILL	1
AND HONOURED AMONG WAGONS I WAS PRINCE OF THE APPLE TOWNS	....	195	FERN HILL	6
AND ONCE BELOW A TIME I LORDLY HAD THE TREES AND LEAVES	....	195	FERN HILL	7
AND AS I WAS GREEN AND CAREFREE, FAMOUS AMONG THE BARNS	....	195	FERN HILL	10
AND GREEN AND GOLDEN I WAS HUNTSMAN AND HERDSMAN, THE CALVES	....	195	FERN HILL	15
AS I RODE TO SLEEP THE OWLS WERE BEARING THE FARM AWAY,	....	195	FERN HILL	24
ALL THE MOON LONG I HEARD, BLESSED AMONG STABLES, THE NIGHTJARS	....	195	FERN HILL	25
I RAN MY HEEDLESS WAYS,	....	196	FERN HILL	40
AND NOTHING I CARED, AT MY SKY BLUE TRADES, THAT TIME ALLOWS	....	196	FERN HILL	42
NOTHING I CARED, IN THE LAMB WHITE DAYS, THAT TIME WOULD TAKE ME	....	196	FERN HILL	46
I SHOULD HEAR HIM FLY WITH THE HIGH FIELDS	....	196	FERN HILL	50
OH AS I WAS YOUNG AND EASY IN THE MERCY OF HIS MEANS,		196	FERN HILL	52
THOUGH I SANG IN MY CHAINS LIKE THE SEA.	....	196	FERN HILL	54

	PAGE	TITLE	LINE
I (CONTINUED)			
I LABOUR BY SINGING LIGHT	197	CRAFT OR ART	6
FROM THE RAGING MOON I WRITE	197	CRAFT OR ART	13
I OPEN THE LEAVES OF THE WATER AT A PASSAGE	202	SIR JOHNS HILL	23
THE HERON AND I, ...	202	SIR JOHNS HILL	34
I YOUNG AESOP FABLING TO THE NEAR NIGHT BY THE DINGLE	202	SIR JOHNS HILL	35
IT IS THE HERON AND I, UNDER JUDGING SIR JOHN'S ELMED	202	SIR JOHNS HILL	40
OF DUSK AND WATER I SEE THE TILTING WHISPERING	202	SIR JOHNS HILL	48
AND THERE THIS NIGHT I WALK IN THE WHITE GIANT'S THIGH	203	GIANT'S THIGH	3
MAKES ALL THE MUSIC; AND I WHO HEAR THE TUNE OF THE SLOW, ...	203	SIR JOHNS HILL	57
WHEN I WAS A WINDY BOY AND A BIT	205	LAMENT	1
I TIPTOED SHY IN THE GOOSEBERRY WOOD, ...	206	LAMENT	4
I SKIPPED IN A BLUSH AS THE BIG GIRLS ROLLED	206	LAMENT	6
AND ON SEESAW SUNDAY NIGHTS I WOOED	206	LAMENT	8
WHOEVER I WOULD WITH MY WICKED EYES, ...	206	LAMENT	9
THE WHOLE OF THE MOON I COULD LOVE AND LEAVE	206	LAMENT	10
WHEN I WAS A GUSTY MAN AND A HALF	206	LAMENT	13
I WHISTLED ALL NIGHT IN THE TWISTED FLUES, ...	206	LAMENT	18
WHENEVER I DOVE IN A BREAST HIGH SHOAL, ...	206	LAMENT	21
WHEREVER I RAMPED IN THE CLOVER QUILTS, ...	206	LAMENT	22
WHATSOEVER I DID IN THE COAL-	206	LAMENT	23
BLACK NIGHT, I LEFT MY QUIVERING PRINTS.	206	LAMENT	24
WHEN I WAS A MAN YOU COULD CALL A MAN	206	LAMENT	25
TO THE SULTRY, BIDING HERDS, I SAID, ...	206	LAMENT	33
AND I LIE DOWN BUT TO SLEEP IN BED, ...	206	LAMENT	35
WHEN I WAS A HALF OF THE MAN I WAS	207	LAMENT	37
WHEN I WAS A HALF OF THE MAN I WAS	207	LAMENT	37
AND I GAVE MY SOUL A BLIND, SLASHED EYE, ...	207	LAMENT	45
AND I SHOVED IT INTO THE COAL BLACK SKY	207	LAMENT	47
NOW I AM A MAN NO MORE NO MORE	207	LAMENT	49
I LIE DOWN THIN AND HEAR THE GOOD BELLS JAW--	207	LAMENT	53
CURSE, BLESS, ME NOW WITH YOUR FIERCE TEARS, I PRAY.	208	NOT GO GENTLE	17
THE VOYAGE TO RUIN I MUST RUN, ...	211	POEM ON B'DAY	78
YET, THOUGH I CRY WITH TUMBLEDOWN TONGUE, ...	211	POEM ON B'DAY	80
THAT THE CLOSER I MOVE	211	POEM ON B'DAY	91
AND GALE I TACKLE, THE WHOLE WORLD THEN, ...	211	POEM ON B'DAY	96
I HEAR THE BOUNCING HILLS	211	POEM ON B'DAY	100
AS I SAIL OUT TO DIE.	211	POEM ON B'DAY	108
I PRAYED IN THE CROUCHING ROOM, BY HIS BLIND BED,	216	ELEGY	13
VEINED HIS POOR HAND I HELD, AND I SAW	217	ELEGY	16
VEINED HIS POOR HAND I HELD, AND I SAW	217	ELEGY	16
I AM NOT TOO PROUD TO CRY THAT HE AND HE	217	ELEGY	19
OUT OF HIS EYES I SAW THE LAST LIGHT GLIDE.	217	ELEGY	28
AN OLD MAN IS WITH ME WHERE I GO	217	ELEGY	30
UNTIL I DIE HE WILL NOT LEAVE MY SIDE.	217	ELEGY	40
YET IN SPITE OF ALL THIS, I HAVE MOMENTS OF BLISS,	221	SONG OF DOG	9
FOR I CHERISH A PASSION FOR BONES, ...	221	SONG OF DOG	10
AND IF I INDULGE IN A BITE AT A BULGE, ...	221	SONG OF DOG	15
THESE COUNTRIES I HAVE NOT VISIONED, ...	223	IDYLL UNFORGET	13
BUT I HAVE KNOWN THE STILL ARDOUR OF EQUABILITY;	223	IDYLL UNFORGET	17
I HAVE KNOWN THE MYSTERY OF THE SEA TO BE MANTLED ABOUT ME;	223	IDYLL UNFORGET	18
I HAVE FELT THE SILK WIND BRUSH MY LIPS;	224	IDYLL UNFORGET	19
I HAVE MADE MY THROAT AN ARBOUR FOR FORGOTTEN SONGS.	224	IDYLL UNFORGET	20
AND I HAVE REFLECTED ITS COLOURS IN THE PEACE OF MY EYES;	224	IDYLL UNFORGET	24
AND HOURS MADE LITTLE I HAVE DIPPED MY ARMS IN THEIR RAPTURE;	224	IDYLL UNFORGET	31

		PAGE	TITLE	LINE
I (CONTINUED)				
HOURLY I SIGH,	••••••••••••••••••••••••••••••••••••••	225	OF ANY FLOWER	1
FLOWERLY I DIE,	••••••••••••••••••••••••••••••••••••••	225	OF ANY FLOWER	4
I THINK, THAT IF I TOUCHED THE EARTH,	••••••••••••	225	CLOWN IN MOON	5
I THINK, THAT IF I TOUCHED THE EARTH,	••••••••••••	225	CLOWN IN MOON	5
AND WHEN IT WAS SPRING I SAID,	••••••••••••••••••	227	SPRING-SPIRIT	1
AND I FORGOT THE DRIFTLESS FOAM, AND SAND,	••••••••	227	SPRING-SPIRIT	9
BECAUSE I HAVE FORSAKEN YOU	••••••••••••••••••••	228	NOT DESPAIR	2
I AM NO LONGER	••••••••••••••••••••••••••••••••	228	NOT DESPAIR	7
BUT I DO NOT HUMILIATE YOU;	••••••••••••••••••••	228	NOT DESPAIR	11
I HAVE COME TO CATCH YOUR VOICE	••••••••••••••••	231	YOUR VOICE	T
I HAVE COME TO CATCH YOUR VOICE,	••••••••••••••••	231	YOUR VOICE	1
THEN, WHEN I OPEN MY MOUTH,	••••••••••••••••••••	231	YOUR VOICE	6
'I HAVE COME TO ELEVATE YOU,	••••••••••••••••••••	231	OUR SANCTITY	29
I HAVE COME TO PLUCK YOU,	••••••••••••••••••••••	232	YOUR VOICE	11
I TAKE YOU TO MYSELF, SWEET PAIN,	•••••••••••••••	233	NO THOUGHT	5
OR SHALL I DRAG YOU DOWN	••••••••••••••••••••••••	233	NO THOUGHT	22
AND I DREW CLOSER TO HER	••••••••••••••••••••••••	234	WOMAN TAPESTRY	3
UNTIL I FELT THE RHYTHM OF HER BODY	••••••••••••••	234	WOMAN TAPESTRY	4
AND IF IT DID, WHO SHOULD I HAVE	••••••••••••••••	234	NO, PIGEON	5
TO TELL WHAT NOTE I COULD REACH IF I TRIED,	•••••••	234	NO, PIGEON	12
TO TELL WHAT NOTE I COULD REACH IF I TRIED,	•••••••	234	NO, PIGEON	12
I SAW THE COLD, GREEN TREES,	••••••••••••••••••••	235	WOMAN TAPESTRY	6
A RHYTHM I CANNOT BREAK	•••••••••••••••••••••••••	235	WOMAN TAPESTRY	29
I HAVE MADE AN IMAGE OF HER	••••••••••••••••••••	235	WOMAN TAPESTRY	35
I CAN DETECT A TOLERANCE,	••••••••••••••••••••••	236	WOMAN TAPESTRY	52
OR THROW A VIOLET SHADOW WHEN I WILL.	••••••••••••	238	MAKES INTERVALS	8
AND I WILL BREAK YOUR PACING LIGHT.	••••••••••••••	239	MAKES INTERVALS	16
BUT IF YOU BREAK I SUFFER,	••••••••••••••••••••••	239	MAKES INTERVALS	20
I NEVER BREAK BUT FEEL THE SUDDEN PAIN,	•••••••••••	239	MAKES INTERVALS	25
I BUILD A FORTRESS FROM A HEAP OF FLOWERS;	••••••••	240	ADMIT THE SUN	9
THAN SIT HERE WASTING, WHILE I BLEED,	•••••••••••••	240	TWINING HEAD	11
I BURY, I TRAVEL TO FIND PRIDE	••••••••••••••••••	240	ADMIT THE SUN	12
I BURY, I TRAVEL TO FIND PRIDE	••••••••••••••••••	240	ADMIT THE SUN	12
ICE				
EASIER THAN HE UPON THE ICE.	••••••••••••••••••••	28	NO WINGS	11
AND THEIR RIVERS OF BLOOD TURNED TO ICE.	••••••••••	68	REALM OF FLESH	16
WHERE ONCE THE MERMEN THROUGH YOUR ICE	••••••••••••	90	WHERE ONCE THE	4
O SEE THE PULSE OF SUMMER IN THE ICE.	•••••••••••••	92	BOYS OF SUMMER	24
I, THAT TIME'S JACKET OR THE COAT OF ICE	••••••••••	100	RUNNING GRAVE	18
STAGE OF THE ICE, THE SOLID OCEAN,	•••••••••••••••	106	ALL ALL AND	2
CALLS THE STARVED FIRE HERD, IS CAST IN ICE,	••••••	132	I MAKE THIS IN	27
ONCE WHERE THE SOFT SNOW'S BLOOD WAS TURNED TO ICE.	133	I MAKE THIS IN	65
WITH FUMING BOWS AND RAM OF ICE,	••••••••••••••••	163	LONG-LEGGED	42
AND PRINCE OF ICE	•••••••••••••••••••••••••••••••	198	COUNTRY SLEEP	12
HILL, WHO ONCE IN GOOSESKIN WINTER LOVED ALL ICE				
LEAVED	•••	203	GIANT'S THIGH	12
ICEBERG'S				
CORROSIVE SPRING OUT OF THE ICEBERG'S CROP,	••••••••	104	WORLD PYRAMID	8
ICICLE				
THE ICICLE OF EACH DELIBERATE FANCY.	•••••••••••••	10	COOL, OH NO	7
ON ROSE AND ICICLE THE RINGING HANDPRINT.	••••••••••	120	ALTARWISE	98
INTO A POLESTAR POINTED ON AN ICICLE.	•••••••••••••	123	FOSTER LIGHT	6
I'D				
FOR, IF I COULD, I'D FLY AWAY,	••••••••••••••••••	21	BEWILDERED WAY	22
FOR IF I COULD, I'D FLY AWAY	••••••••••••••••••••	21	BEWILDERED WAY	23
I'D RATHER HAVE THE WORM TO FEED	••••••••••••••••	240	TWINING HEAD	9
IDIOM				
INTO THE STONY IDIOM OF THE BRAIN,	•••••••••••••••	79	LOVE'S FEVER	33

	PAGE	TITLE	LINE
IDLING			
IDLING WITH THE RADIANCE OF THE HOURS	227	SPRING-SPIRIT	10
IDOL			
I WAS PIERCED BY THE IDOL TAILOR'S EYES, ...	152	BELOW A TIME	38
IDYLL			
IDYLL OF UNFORGETFULNESS	223	IDYLL UNFORGET	T
IF			
AND SHARPER IF I BREAK ASUNDER	10	COOL, OH NO	6
FOR IF THE GODS WOULD LOVE	11	AIR BREATHE	9
FOR, IF I COULD, I'D FLY AWAY, ...	21	BEWILDERED WAY	22
FOR IF I COULD, I'D FLY AWAY	21	BEWILDERED WAY	23
UNLESS FOR POETRY, WHICH, IF IT ASKS ME	24	LITTLE PROBLEM	17
IF NOT IN PERSON SENDS HIS UNENDING EVIL	29	NEARLY SUMMER	3
IF WE WERE CHILDREN WE MIGHT CLIMB, ...	31	BEING BUT MEN	6
IF NOT OF LOVING WELL, THEN NOT, ...	32	OUT OF SIGHS	8
IF ONLY WITH SUNLIGHT.	35	LIFT UP FACE	26
WITH HALF-AVERTED HEADS, AS IF TO LISTEN, ...	40	YOUNG ARE OLD	13
AND BE STRUCK DUMB, IF ONLY FOR A TIME.	43	A WAR OF WITS	25
TO FOLLOW THE NOSE IF THE NOSE GOES	44	TO FOLLOW FOX	14
IF HUNTING MEANS ANYTHING MORE THAN THE CHASE	44	TO FOLLOW FOX	18
IF LOVE HE CAN BEING NO WOMAN'S MAN.	47	POET: 1935	35
TELL, IF AT ALL, THE WINTER'S STORMS	58	HERE IN SPRING	10
WHAT SHALL IT TELL ME IF A TIMELESS INSECT	59	HERE IN SPRING	16
IF DEAD MEN WALKED THEY, TOO, WOULD HOLLER	59	FAIRY TALES	17
WHAT SHALL DESTRUCTION COUNT IF THESE ARE FIXTURES?	60	FAIRY TALES	27
IF THESE TWO GNOMES REMAIN UNMOVED BY STRICTURES?	60	FAIRY TALES	30
PERHAPS IT WOULD BE BEST IF YOU	83	LETTER TO AUNT	23
BUT IF THIS PROVED IMPOSS-I-BLE	84	LETTER TO AUNT	29
IF YOU WOULD BE REGARDED GREAT, ...	84	LETTER TO AUNT	41
IF I WERE TICKLED BY THE RUB OF LOVE	94	RUB OF LOVE	T
IF I WERE TICKLED BY THE RUB OF LOVE, ...	94	RUB OF LOVE	1
IF THE RED TICKLE AS THE CATTLE CALVE	95	RUB OF LOVE	4
IF I WERE TICKLED BY THE HATCHING HAIR, ...	95	RUB OF LOVE	10
IF I WERE TICKLED BY THE URCHIN HUNGERS	95	RUB OF LOVE	18
IF I WERE TICKLED BY THE LOVERS' RUB	95	RUB OF LOVE	22
IF I TAKE TO BURN OR RETURN THIS WORLD WHICH IS EACH MAN'S WORK.	140	NO WORK WORDS	12
'IF MY HEAD HURT A HAIR'S FOOT'	145	IF HEAD HURT	T
'IF MY HEAD HURT A HAIR'S FOOT	145	IF HEAD HURT	1
PACK BACK THE DOWNED BONE. IF THE UNPRICKED BALL OF MY BREATH	145	IF HEAD HURT	2
'IF MY BUNCHED, MONKEY COMING IS CRUEL	145	IF HEAD HURT	11
BEND, IF MY JOURNEY ACHE, DIRECTION LIKE AN ARC OR MAKE	145	IF HEAD HURT	14
IF THE DEAD STARVE, THEIR STOMACHS TURN TO TUMBLE	145	PLEASURE-BIRD	22
BOTH SHALL FAIL IF I BOW NOT TO YOUR BLESSING	148	UNLUCKILY FOR	47
WINGS. IT WOULD BE BETTER IF THE SHUTTERS IS	179	NEW QUAY	6
IF ONLY FOR A LAST TIME.	186	HOLY SPRING	24
AND IF I INDULGE IN A BITE AT A BULGE, ...	221	SONG OF DOG	15
I THINK, THAT IF I TOUCHED THE EARTH, ...	225	CLOWN IN MOON	5
AND IF IT DID, WHO SHOULD I HAVE	234	NO, PIGEON	5
TO TELL WHAT NOTE I COULD REACH IF I TRIED, ...	234	NO, PIGEON	12
TO-DAY, IF ALL MY SENSES ACT, ...	238	MAKES INTERVALS	9
BUT IF YOU BREAK I SUFFER, ...	239	MAKES INTERVALS	20
BUT IF IT STINGS MY BODY DEAD	240	TWINING HEAD	3
ILEX			
SO THE ILEX AND THE CYPRESS	236	WOMAN TAPESTRY	56
ILL			
STREETS' STOCK, OF THE MOON LIT, ILL LIT, FIELD AND TOWN, ...	45	PLOUGHMAN GONE	22

	PAGE	TITLE	LINE
ILL (CONTINUED)			
WHERE FLOATED A DEAD DOG WHO MADE HIM ILL, ...	51	OUT OF THE PIT	41
AND TELLS THE PAGE THE EMPTY ILL.	75	MY HERO BARES	10
THAN BULLY ILL LOVE IN THE CLOUTED SCENE.	145	IF HEAD HURT	5
I'LL			
FIE ON YOU, AUNT! I'LL SHOW YOU HOW	83	LETTER TO AUNT	11
I'LL COMB THE SNARED WOODS WITH A GLOVE ON A LAMP,	145	IF HEAD HURT	7
I'LL SHARE MY MONEY AND WE'LL RUN FOR JOY	149	PAPER & STICKS	14
I'LL MAKE YOUR SHAPE MY OWN, ...	238	MAKES INTERVALS	10
I'LL CUT THROUGH YOUR DARK CLOUD	239	LET ME ESCAPE	10
I'LL HAVE TO BREAK IN THOUGHT AGAIN, ...	239	MAKES INTERVALS	27
I'LL KNOW I'M OUT OF HARM, ...	240	TWINING HEAD	4
ILLIMITABLE			
THE DARKNESS IS ILLIMITABLE, GREEN SHADOW, ...	224	IDYLL UNFORGET	43
ILL-LIT			
BETWEEN THE STREET-LAMPS AND THE ILL-LIT SKY, ...	52	OUT OF THE PIT	61
ILLS			
AND CURE ME OF ILLS.	32	OUT OF SIGHS	23
SHOULD CURE OUR ILLS OF THE WATER	54	WE BY SEASAND	12
OF EVIL ORACLES AND FUNERAL ILLS;	57	GREEK PLAY	31
ON WHOM A WORLD OF ILLS CAME DOWN LIKE SNOW.	217	ELEGY	32
ILLUMINATE			
SUCH LIGHT SHALL NOT ILLUMINATE MY FEARS	48	LIGHT, I KNOW	4
ILLUMINATION			
ILLUMINATION OF MUSIC! THE LULLED BLACK-BACKED	200	COUNTRY SLEEP	82
ILLUSIONS			
OLD IN ILLUSIONS TURNED TO ACRITUDES, ...	20	THE NEOPHYTE	23
I'M			
THERE STINKS A SNOOP IN BLACK. I'M THINKING IT	179	NEW QUAY	19
AND THOUGH DOUBTFUL OF BISCUIT, I'M WILLING TO RISK IT, ...	221	SONG OF DOG	11
NO, PIGEON, I'M TOO WISE	234	NO, PIGEON	T
NO, PIGEON, I'M TOO WISE;	234	NO, PIGEON	1
I'M NOT SECURE ENOUGH	234	NO, PIGEON	11
I'M ALL FOR GROUND, ...	234	NO, PIGEON	17
I'LL KNOW I'M OUT OF HARM, ...	240	TWINING HEAD	4
IMAGE			
AN IMAGE OF DECAY DISTURBS THE CROCUS	47	POET: 1935	29
AN IMAGE BORN OUT OF THE UPROARIOUS SPRING	47	POET: 1935	36
THE IMAGE CHANGES, AND THE FLOWERS DROP	47	POET: 1935	43
THE IMAGE FROM THE PLATES;	90	EUNUCH DREAMS	39
AND THE DEATH IN A STARVING IMAGE.	96	TWELVE	14
I, IN MY INTRICATE IMAGE	108	I, IN IMAGE	T
I, IN MY INTRICATE IMAGE, STRIDE ON TWO LEVELS, ...	108	I, IN IMAGE	1
IMAGE OF IMAGES, MY METAL PHANTOM	109	I, IN IMAGE	14
BRASS AND THE BODILESS IMAGE, ON A STICK OF FOLLY	111	I, IN IMAGE	80
SPOT THE BLOWN WORD, AND ON THE SEAS I IMAGE	121	ALTARWISE	131
LOVE'S IMAGE TILL MY HEARTBONE BREAKS	129	MY NEOPHYTE	35
AND ALL LOVE'S SINNERS IN SWEET CLOTH KNEEL TO A HYLEG IMAGE, ...	130	SINNERS' BELL	28
(THOUGH THIS FOR HER IS A MONSTROUS IMAGE BLINDLY	136	AFTER FUNERAL	16
I HAVE MADE AN IMAGE OF HER	235	WOMAN TAPESTRY	35
IMAGES			
MY HORRID IMAGES FOR ME, ...	12	SKY'S BRIGHT	7
CONCEIVE THESE IMAGES IN AIR	19	IMAGES IN AIR	T
CONCEIVE THESE IMAGES IN AIR, ...	19	IMAGES IN AIR	1
FRESH IMAGES SURROUND THE TREMENDOUS MOON, ...	47	POET: 1935	45
ROLLED DOWN ALL IMAGES INTO THE PITS	50	OUT OF THE PIT	3
IMAGE OF IMAGES, MY METAL PHANTOM	109	I, IN IMAGE	14
MY IMAGES STALK THE TREES AND THE SLANT SAP'S TUNNEL,	109	I, IN IMAGE	25

	PAGE	TITLE	LINE
IMAGES (CONTINUED)			
AND MY IMAGES ROARED AND ROSE ON HEAVEN'S HILL. ...	112	I, IN IMAGE	108
IMAGINARY			
EARLY IMAGINARY HALF REMEMBERED	158	INTO HER HEAD	32
IMAGINED			
OR RIDES THE IMAGINED OCEANS OF THE MALE WARDS. ...	169	LOVE IN ASYLUM	9
IMAGININGS			
THESE THE IMAGININGS, TENDER AND BLOSSOMED WITH FUTILITY, ...	223	IDYLL UNFORGET	11
IMITATE			
TO IMITATE MYSELF MECHANICALLY, ...	234	NO, PIGEON	19
IMMEASURABLE			
WITH IMMEASURABLE SADNESS.	235	WOMAN TAPESTRY	10
IMMEMORIAL			
AND IMMEMORIAL SONS OF THE CUDGELLING, HACKED	203	GIANT'S THIGH	11
IMMENSE			
MAGNIFIED AND MADE IMMENSE	25	BEAUTY TO DUST	5
IMMENSITY			
OUTLINES MELTING INTO A VAGUE IMMENSITY	222	FOREST PICTURE	9
IMMORTAL			
OF THE LIVING FLESH IS MONSTROUS OR IMMORTAL, ...	148	UNLUCKILY FOR	41
OF YOUR IMMORTAL FRIENDS	160	DEATHS AND ENT	6
WHEN THAT IMMORTAL HOSPITAL MADE ONE MORE MOVE TO SOOTHE	186	HOLY SPRING	3
IMMORTALITY			
WITH IMMORTALITY AT MY SIDE LIKE CHRIST THE SKY.	148	UNLUCKILY FOR	49
IMMUTABLE			
IMMUTABLE, AND ARDOUROUSLY CONSECRATED;	223	IDYLL UNFORGET	2
IMPATIENT			
IMPATIENT TO BE OFF.	13	RAIN CUTS	18
IMPLORE			
NIGHT AFTER NIGHT THEIR HANDS IMPLORE	143	THE MOLLS	3
IMPOSE			
IMPOSE THEIR SHOTS, SHOWING THE NIGHTS AWAY;	89	EUNUCH DREAMS	18
IMPOSS-I-BLE			
BUT IF THIS PROVED IMPOSS-I-BLE	84	LETTER TO AUNT	29
IMPRESS			
NEGATIVES IMPRESS NEGATION, ...	27	OBLIVIOUS DARK	4
IMPRINTS			
AND AFTER CAME THE IMPRINTS ON THE WATER, ...	94	IN BEGINNING	9
IMPRISONED			
IS NOT HIS HEART IMPRISONED BY THE SUMMER	46	POET: 1935	7
IMPULSES			
IN TUNING IMPULSES TO CALLS;	18	NATURAL DAY	6
IMPULSIVE			
UNDER HIS STRONG IMPULSIVE KISS	11	AIR BREATHE	4
IN (1086)			
INCARNATE			
INCARNATE DEVIL	121	INCARNATE DEVL	T
INCARNATE DEVIL IN A TALKING SNAKE, ...	121	INCARNATE DEVL	1
INCENDIARY			
ON ALMOST THE INCENDIARY EVE	160	DEATHS AND ENT	1
ON ALMOST THE INCENDIARY EVE	160	DEATHS AND ENT	13
ON ALMOST THE INCENDIARY EVE	160	DEATHS AND ENT	25
INCESTUOUS			
WITH THE INCESTUOUS SECRET BROTHER IN THE SECONDS TO PERPETUATE THE STARS, ...	159	INTO HER HEAD	66
INCH			
AN INCH IN FROTH. CHIMES CHEAT THE PRISON SPIRE, PELTER	15	SPIRE CRANES	5

		PAGE	TITLE	LINE
INCH (CONTINUED)				
INCH ON THE OLD THIGH	....	22	HIGH ON A HILL	11
AND AT THEIR BAYING MOVE A TAILOR'S INCH	....	44	TO FOLLOW FOX	2
THE INCH OF TIME'S PROTRACTED TO A FOOT	....	80	ALMANAC TIME	8
OF THE BONE INCH,	....	100	RUNNING GRAVE	10
AND THE VELVET DEAD INCH OUT.	....	114	SERVANT SUN	21
AND A GREEN INCH BE HIS BEARER;	....	126	SEED-AT-ZERO	32
INCH AND GLANCE THAT THE WOUND	....	148	UNLUCKILY FOR	22
IN YOUR EVERY INCH AND GLANCE IS THE GLOBE OF GENESIS SPUN,	....	149	UNLUCKILY FOR	55
INCHES				
THE INCHES MONKEYED BY THE BLOOD OF MAN.	....	102	FELLOWED SLEEP	28
INCHTAPED				
CRIED THE TOPLESS, INCHTAPED LIPS FROM HANK AND HOOD	132	I MAKE THIS IN	47
INCISING				
INCISING SUMMER.	....	104	WORLD PYRAMID	33
INCONVENIENCE				
FOR ALL THE INCONVENIENCE THEY MAKE,	....	38	THE GOSSIPERS	14
INDEX				
SPELT OUT THE SEVEN SEAS, AND EVIL INDEX,	....	119	ALTARWISE	82
TAKING NO PLUME FOR INDEX IN LOVE'S CHANGE	....	159	TO LEDA	5
INDIGO				
AND BREATH ON BREATH OF INDIGO.	....	14	RAIN CUTS	39
INDISTINCT				
AND CHANGED WITH THE WIND INTO INDISTINCT PATTERNS OF FROLIC,	....	224	IDYLL UNFORGET	29
INDUCIVE				
YOUR SWEET INDUCIVE THIGHS	....	11	AIR BREATHE	12
INDULGE				
AND IF I INDULGE IN A BITE AT A BULGE,	....	221	SONG OF DOG	15
INEXORABLE				
AND GRIP THE INEXORABLE SONG,	....	233	FURIOUS MOTION	21
INFANCY				
AND THE TWICE TOLD FIELDS OF INFANCY	....	178	POEM IN OCT	51
INFANT				
TO THE ANGUISH AND CARRION, TO THE INFANT FOREVER UNFREE,	....	146	IF HEAD HURT	22
INFANT LIGHT OR	....	183	VISION, PRAYER	130
INFANT-BEARING				
THE MASSES OF THE INFANT-BEARING SEA	....	175	FIRE RAID	74
INFANTS				
OVER THE DEAD INFANTS	....	174	FIRE RAID	50
SUN THE FATHER HIS QUIVER FULL OF THE INFANTS OF PURE FIRE,	....	186	HOLY SPRING	19
INFINITE				
INFINITE SHADOWY ISLES LIE SILENT BEFORE ME,	....	221	FOREST PICTURE	3
INFORMED				
INFORMED BY RUMOUR AND THE REGISTER,	....	38	THE GOSSIPERS	7
INHALE				
LET HER INHALE HER DEAD, THROUGH SEED AND SOLID	...	115	A GRIEF AGO	37
INHERITS				
O ALL I OWE IS ALL THE FLESH INHERITS,	....	80	ALL THAT I OWE	5
INHOSPITABLE				
TO THIS INHOSPITABLE HOLLOW YEAR,	....	153	WAS A SAVIOUR	27
INHUMAN				
INHUMAN CRADLE AND THE BRIDE BED FOREVER SOUGHT	...	188	WINTER'S TALE	49
INMOST				
THE INMOST MARROW OF MY HEART BONE	....	183	VISION, PRAYER	118
INNOCENCE				
SHE MAKES FOR ME A NETTLE'S INNOCENCE	....	131	I MAKE THIS IN	16

		PAGE	TITLE	LINE
INNOCENCE (CONTINUED)				
ALONG HER INNOCENCE GLIDED	....	157	INTO HER HEAD	10
OF INNOCENCE AND GUILT	....	192	SIDE OF TRUTH	7
ELEGY OF INNOCENCE AND YOUTH.	....	192	REFUSAL MOURN	18
INNOCENCE SWEETENS MY LAST BLACK BREATH,	....	207	LAMENT	58
INNOCENT				
THROUGH THE DEVILISH YEARS AND INNOCENT DEATHS	....	139	TOMBSTONE TOLD	14
INNOCENT BETWEEN TWO WARS,	....	159	INTO HER HEAD	65
AND THE WILD BOYS INNOCENT AS STRAWBERRIES	....	172	THE HUNCHBACK	40
INTO THE INNOCENT	....	193	SIDE OF TRUTH	20
NOR THE INNOCENT LIE IN THE ROOTING DINGLE WOOED		198	COUNTRY SLEEP	15
BEING INNOCENT, HE DREADED THAT HE DIED	....	217	ELEGY	22
INSANITY				
INTO THE VOID AGAIN OF THIS BEWILDERMENT AND THAT				
INSANITY	....	21	BEWILDERED WAY	25
INSECT				
THE INSECT ON THIS PAINTED TREE.	....	12	CABARET	23
WHAT SHALL IT TELL ME IF A TIMELESS INSECT	....	59	HERE IN SPRING	16
I WITH THE WOODEN INSECT IN THE TREE OF NETTLES,		109	I, IN IMAGE	28
TODAY, THIS INSECT	....	124	TODAY, INSECT	T
TODAY, THIS INSECT, AND THE WORLD I BREATHE,	......	124	TODAY, INSECT	1
THE INSECT CERTAIN IS THE PLAGUE OF FABLES.	....	124	TODAY, INSECT	9
THE INSECT FABLE IS THE CERTAIN PROMISE.	....	124	TODAY, INSECT	18
SHAKES, IN CRABBED BURIAL SHAWL, BY SORCERER'S				
INSECT WOKEN,	....	130	SINNERS' BELL	23
INSECT-FACED				
DRY AS ECHOES AND INSECT-FACED,	....	167	LONG-LEGGED	146
INSECTS				
INSECTS AND VALLEYS HOLD HER THIGHS HARD,	....	168	LONG-LEGGED	174
INSIDE				
WHO HOLDS HER CLASPED INSIDE HIS STRONG, WHITE WINGS;		15	FOR LEDA	31
TURN INSIDE OUT, AND SEE AT GLANCE	....	25	BEAUTY TO DUST	7
THE WIND HAS CHANGED, BLOWN INSIDE OUT	....	37	WINDMILLS TURN	27
THROUGH THESE LASHED RINGS SET DEEP INSIDE THEIR				
HOLLOWS	....	76	LASHED RINGS	1
INSIDE THIS MOUTH I FEEL HIS MESSAGE MOVING	....	76	LASHED RINGS	14
GROWING LIKE A POWERFUL ROOT INSIDE ME.	....	236	WOMAN TAPESTRY	67
INSIDIOUS				
INSIDIOUS PROCESSION	....	156	RETURN	63
INSIST				
THERE ARE FEWER, OF COURSE, WHO INSIST THAT A HORSE		221	SONG OF DOG	5
INSTRUMENT				
THE SEA AND INSTRUMENT, NICKED IN THE LOCKS OF TIME,		111	I, IN IMAGE	92
INSTRUMENTAL				
(DEATH INSTRUMENTAL,	....	110	I, IN IMAGE	49
INSTRUMENTS				
HANDS OR INSTRUMENTS	....	185	VISION, PRAYER	175
INTANGIBLE				
INTANGIBLE MY WORLD SHALL COME TO NAUGHT,	....	73	LORD RED HAIL	16
INTANGIBLE TO THEM	....	176	BREATH SHED	6
INTENSE				
AND HER EYES PIERCED THEIR INTENSE LOVE INTO ME,		234	WOMAN TAPESTRY	2
INTENT				
INTENT ON VISITING THE FAMOUS SPOTS,	....	37	WINDMILLS TURN	12
INTENTIONS				
PLAYS SCURVY TRICKS WITH VALUES AND INTENTIONS,	...	37	WINDMILLS TURN	6
INTERLUDE				
AND INTERLUDE FOR VIOLINS	....	14	FOR LEDA	3
INTERPRETED				
IN THE INTERPRETED EVENING	....	185	VISION, PRAYER	186

	PAGE	TITLE	LINE
INTERVALS			
IT'S LIGHT THAT MAKES THE INTERVALS	238	MAKES INTERVALS	T
IT'S LIGHT THAT MAKES THE INTERVALS	238	MAKES INTERVALS	1
INTIMACIES			
THE COLOSSAL INTIMACIES OF SILENT	157	INTO HER HEAD	14
INTIMATIONS			
THE SEASONS' CRIES, FULL OF HIS INTIMATIONS.	29	NEARLY SUMMER	6
INTO			
INTO THE DOGDAYED NIGHT.	3	PROLOGUE	33
DOWN INTO MISERY?	12	SKY'S BRIGHT	15
INTO THE RAINBOW'S SHY EMBRACE.	14	RAIN CUTS	35
SPLITTING A THOUGHT INTO SUCH HIDEOUS MOMENTS	17	IN OBLIVION	17
INTO HER VEGETATION'S LAPPING MOUTHS	20	ENCOMPASSED	3
INTO THE VOID AGAIN OF THIS BEWILDERMENT AND THAT			
INSANITY	21	BEWILDERED WAY	25
STEALING SO SOFTLY INTO THE EARS.	22	ON QUIET NIGHT	7
INTO A DOUBLE OR A SINGLE BED, ...	28	NO WINGS	18
OUT OF THE SOIL AND SEED INTO THE DRIVE, ...	29	LONG, SKELETON	2
WHEN IT WAS NOON HAVE WALKED INTO THE LIGHT, ...	30	YOUTH CALLS	10
BEING BUT MEN, WE WALKED INTO THE TREES	31	BEING BUT MEN	1
NOISELESSLY INTO A WORLD OF WINGS AND CRIES.	31	BEING BUT MEN	5
BEING BUT MEN, WE WALKED INTO THE TREES.	31	BEING BUT MEN	17
INTO THE PLACES AND THE CREVICES	34	THIRST PARCHES	9
MEN OLD BEFORE THEIR TIME INTO DARK VALLEYS	41	YOUNG ARE OLD	19
MY BRAIN CAME CRYING INTO THE FRESH LIGHT, ...	42	A WAR OF WITS	4
THAT TURNED THE EMPTY KISSES INTO MEANING, ...	43	FACES SHONE	3
INTO A COSTLY COUNTRY, THE GRAVES	43	FACES SHONE	5
GOES OVER THE HILL INTO THE DEEP SEA;	43	LONGED TO MOVE	5
INTO THE MAP-BACKED HILLS WHERE PATHS	44	TO FOLLOW FOX	8
AND, CRACKLING INTO THE AIR, LEAVE ME HALF-BLIND.	44	LONGED TO MOVE	14
INTO THE BROWNS OF AUTUMN AND THE SHARP WHITES OF			
WINTER, ...	47	POET: 1935	20
INTO THEIR PRISON WITH A SLACK SOUND, ...	47	POET: 1935	44
ROLLED DOWN ALL IMAGES INTO THE PITS	50	OUT OF THE PIT	3
SO CRYING, HE WAS DRAGGED INTO THE SEWER, ...	51	OUT OF THE PIT	39
SO CRYING, HE WAS PUSHED INTO THE JORDAN.	52	OUT OF THE PIT	53
OUT OF THE NOISE INTO QUIET I RAN.	53	OUT OF THE PIT	92
INTO THE QUICKSAND FEATHERS DOWN, ...	55	NO MAN BELIEVE	4
DID TWIST INTO A LIVING CIPHER, ...	68	BEFORE KNOCKED	21
HIS AWKWARD HEART INTO SOME SYMMETRY.	77	LASHED RINGS	17
EACH GOLDEN GRAIN SPAT LIFE INTO ITS FELLOW, ...	78	LOVE'S FEVER	23
INTO THE SIDED LAP OF LIGHT GREW STRONG, ...	78	LOVE'S FEVER	27
INTO THE STONY IDIOM OF THE BRAIN, ...	79	LOVE'S FEVER	33
THE TWO-FRAMED GLOBE THAT SPUN INTO A SCORE;	79	LOVE'S FEVER	45
TO BURST INTO A HANGING LAND	85	SEE, SAYS LIME	19
A PROCESS BLOWS THE MOON INTO THE SUN, ...	88	A PROCESS IN	22
INTO THE TIDED CORD, THERE GOES	91	WHERE ONCE THE	8
INTO A CHIMING QUARTER	92	BOYS OF SUMMER	26
NO THIRD EYE PROBE INTO A RAINBOW'S SEX	108	GRIEF THIEF	25
HE'LL TRUMPET INTO MEAT), ...	113	SERVANT SUN	5
THE COUNTRY-HANDED GRAVE BOXED INTO LOVE, ...	115	A GRIEF AGO	31
INTO A POLESTAR POINTED ON AN ICICLE.	123	FOSTER LIGHT	6
BULLIES INTO ROUGH SEAS YOU SO GENTLE	142	SAINT TO FALL	49
THEY RETCH INTO MY SECRET NIGHT	143	THE MOLLS	5
HURLING INTO BEGINNING LIKE CHRIST THE CHILD.	149	UNLUCKILY FOR	52
OPENED MY BREAST AND INTO	155	RETURN	35
THEN INTO BLIND STREETS I SWAM	155	RETURN	44
FLOGGING INTO THE PORCHES	156	RETURN	75
INTO HER LYING DOWN HEAD	157	INTO HER HEAD	T
INTO HER LYING DOWN HEAD	157	INTO HER HEAD	1

	PAGE	TITLE	LINE
INTO (CONTINUED)			
THE WINDOWS POUR INTO THEIR HEART	161	WEDDING ANNIV	11
HE SPED INTO THE DRINKING DARK;	162	LONG-LEGGED	14
THE OCTOPUS WALKING INTO HER LIMBS	164	LONG-LEGGED	79
THE BOAT SWIMS INTO THE SIX-YEAR WEATHER,	166	LONG-LEGGED	129
AND INTO ITS TALKATIVE SEVEN TOMBS	169	LONG-LEGGED	211
DARKNESS KINDLED BACK INTO BEGINNING	173	FIRE RAID	12
INTO THE CENTURIES OF THE CHILD	173	FIRE RAID	15
INTO THE ORGANPIPES AND STEEPLES	175	FIRE RAID	61
INTO THE WEATHERCOCKS' MOLTEN MOUTHS	175	FIRE RAID	63
INTO THE DEAD CLOCK BURNING THE HOUR	175	FIRE RAID	65
INTO THE BREAD IN A WHEATFIELD OF FLAMES,	175	FIRE RAID	70
INTO THE WINE BURNING LIKE BRANDY,	175	FIRE RAID	71
AND SWEPT INTO OUR WOUNDS AND HOUSES,	186	HOLY SPRING	7
INTO THE HOME OF PRAYERS	188	WINTER'S TALE	36
INTO THE WINDING DARK	192	SIDE OF TRUTH	11
INTO THE ANSWERING SKIES FROM THE GREEN GROUND,	193	CONVERS PRAYER	7
INTO THE INNOCENT	193	SIDE OF TRUTH	20
FLASHING INTO THE DARK.	195	FERN HILL	27
INTO A HOMESTALL KING OR HAMLET OF FIRE	198	COUNTRY SLEEP	11
EARTH, AIR, WATER, FIRE, SINGING INTO THE WHITE ACT,	200	COUNTRY SLEEP	87
DO NOT GO GENTLE INTO THAT GOOD NIGHT	207	NOT GO GENTLE	T
DO NOT GO GENTLE INTO THAT GOOD NIGHT,	207	NOT GO GENTLE	1
AND I SHOVED IT INTO THE COAL BLACK SKY	207	LAMENT	47
DO NOT GO GENTLE INTO THAT GOOD NIGHT.	208	NOT GO GENTLE	6
DO NOT GO GENTLE INTO THAT GOOD NIGHT.	208	NOT GO GENTLE	12
DO NOT GO GENTLE INTO THAT GOOD NIGHT.	208	NOT GO GENTLE	18
DOWNS INTO THE LOW BROWSING DARK.	215	COUNTRY HEAVEN	15
OUTLINES MELTING INTO A VAGUE IMMENSITY	222	FOREST PICTURE	9
THE FOAM HAS LINGERED INTO WHITE, LITTLE FLOWERS,	224	IDYLL UNFORGET	28
AND CHANGED WITH THE WIND INTO INDISTINCT PATTERNS OF FROLIC,	224	IDYLL UNFORGET	29
TO THRUST YOUR ARM INTO THE EARTH	229	MY RIVER	10
WHICH CUTS INTO THE STRENGTH	230	MY RIVER	42
AND GO INTO THE AIR,	231	OUR SANCTITY	34
BURROW OUR WAY UPWARDS INTO THE BLUE SKY;	231	OUR SANCTITY	35
TAKE YOU INTO MY OWN PLACE	232	YOUR VOICE	14
WILL YOU DRIFT INTO THE NET WILLINGLY,	233	NO THOUGHT	21
INTO MY EXOTIC COMPOSURE?	233	NO THOUGHT	23
INTO THE SKY.	233	FURIOUS MOTION	23
AND HER EYES PIERCED THEIR INTENSE LOVE INTO ME,	234	WOMAN TAPESTRY	2
COILED INTO THEIR BODIES LIKE SNAKES,	237	WOMAN TAPESTRY	76
GROW INTO YOUR DELICATE SKIN,	238	MAKES INTERVALS	11
ADMIT THE SUN INTO YOUR HIGH NEST	240	ADMIT THE SUN	1
INTRICATE			
I, IN MY INTRICATE IMAGE	108	I, IN IMAGE	T
I, IN MY INTRICATE IMAGE, STRIDE ON TWO LEVELS,	108	I, IN IMAGE	1
INTRICATE MANHOOD OF ENDING, THE INVALID RIVALS,	109	I, IN IMAGE	31
THIS WAS THE GOD OF BEGINNING IN THE INTRICATE SEAWHIRL,	112	I, IN IMAGE	107
INTRICATELY			
TIME SINGS THROUGH THE INTRICATELY DEAD SNOW DROP. LISTEN.	189	WINTER'S TALE	65
INVALID			
INTRICATE MANHOOD OF ENDING, THE INVALID RIVALS,	109	I, IN IMAGE	31
INVEIGLERS			
BEGGARS, ROBBERS, INVEIGLERS,	155	RETURN	52
INVISIBLE			
TO FIGHT THROUGH THE INVISIBLE WEEDS,	41	YOUNG ARE OLD	23
INVISIBLE, YOUR CLOCKING TIDES	91	WHERE ONCE THE	13

	PAGE	TITLE	LINE
INVISIBLE (CONTINUED)			
INVISIBLE ON THE STUMP	114	SERVANT SUN	28
INVISIBLE TO MAKE	176	BREATH SHED	2
INVITED			
THE WELCOME DEVIL COMES INVITED, ...	30	NEARLY SUMMER	19
INVITERS			
DARK INVITERS TO KEYHOLES	155	RETURN	56
INVOKED			
THE INVOKED, SHROUDING VEIL AT THE CAP OF THE FACE,	134	HOW MY ANIMAL	5
INVOLVE			
INVOLVE ME IN A GAIETY, ...	236	WOMAN TAPESTRY	69
INWARD			
THE SEASONS NUMBERED BY THE INWARD SUN, ...	79	ALMANAC TIME	2
THIS INWARD SIR, ...	114	SERVANT SUN	30
IRIS			
OPENING ITS IRIS MOUTH UPON THE SILL	47	POET: 1935	30
AND TIED AN IRIS IN HIS THROAT	85	SEE, SAYS LIME	18
HIS GOLDEN YESTERDAY ASLEEP UPON THE IRIS	170	MARRIAGE VIRG	3
THE TALL MAUVE IRIS OF A SLEEPING CLIME.	222	IN DREAMS	2
BUT ONLY IRIS ON THEIR SLENDER STALKS	223	IN DREAMS	11
HER GARDEN BLOOMS WITH IRIS, AND IT SEEMS	223	IN DREAMS	13
IRISES			
AT THE DEFT MOVEMENTS OF THE IRISES	48	POET: 1935	56
IRISH			
GREEK IN THE IRISH SEA THE AGELESS VOICE:	125	TODAY, INSECT	22
IRON			
THIS IS A DRAIN OF IRON PLANTS, ...	14	RAIN CUTS	29
MAN TOILS NOW ON AN IRON SADDLE, RIDING	45	PLOUGHMAN GONE	24
PUT AN IRON AT THE EYES, ...	70	TAKE NEEDLES	2
GREEN OF THE SEAWEEDS' IRON, ...	93	BOYS OF SUMMER	38
THRUSTING THE TOM-THUMB VISION UP THE IRON MILE.	111	I, IN IMAGE	84
MY GREAT BLOOD'S IRON SINGLE	111	I, IN IMAGE	93
A CHRYSALIS UNWRINKLING ON THE IRON, ...	115	A GRIEF AGO	10
AND A STRANGER ENTER LIKE IRON.	142	SAINT TO FALL	47
MY DEAR WOULD I CHANGE MY TEARS OR YOUR IRON HEAD.	146	IF HEAD HURT	18
IRONS			
THROUGH ALL THE IRONS IN THE GRASS, METAL	102	I DREAMED MY	7
IS (345)			
ISHMAEL'S			
FOR LOSS OF BLOOD I FELL ON ISHMAEL'S PLAIN, ...	118	ALTARWISE	63
ISLAND			
UPON THE ISLAND OF MY PALM, ...	11	CABARET	2
THE ISLAND OF SUCH PENNY LOVE	43	FACES SHONE	4
BEYOND THIS ISLAND BOUND	62	EARS IN TURRET	10
EARS IN THIS ISLAND HEAR	62	EARS IN TURRET	17
EYES IN THIS ISLAND SEE	62	EARS IN TURRET	19
TO THAT UNENDING SEA AROUND MY ISLAND	76	LASHED RINGS	8
A THUNDERING BULLRING OF YOUR SILENT AND			
GIRL-CIRCLED ISLAND.	142	SAINT TO FALL	51
MAN WAS THE BURNING ENGLAND SHE WAS SLEEP-WALKING,			
AND THE ENAMOURING ISLAND	157	INTO HER HEAD	20
IN HIS FIRELIT ISLAND RINGED BY THE WINGED SNOW ...	187	WINTER'S TALE	17
ISLANDS			
LIKE WOODEN ISLANDS, HILL TO HILL.	5	PROLOGUE	96
AND THE RENOUNCING OF ISLANDS.	148	UNLUCKILY FOR	39
I DREW THE WHITE SHEET OVER THE ISLANDS	150	WHEN I WOKE	29
MILLED DUST OF THE APPLE TREE AND THE POUNDED ISLANDS	199	COUNTRY SLEEP	59
THE MANSOULED FIERY ISLANDS! OH, ...	211	POEM ON B'DAY	105
ISLAND'S			
DISTURB THIS ISLAND'S REST.	62	EARS IN TURRET	16

		PAGE	TITLE	LINE
ISLES				
INFINITE SHADOWY ISLES LIE SILENT BEFORE ME,	....	221	FOREST PICTURE	3
ISSUE				
ONE BREAST GAVE SUCK THE FEVER'S ISSUE;	....	79	LOVE'S FEVER	43
ALL ISSUE ARMOURED, OF THE GRAVE,	....	97	TWILIGHT LOCKS	19
IT (122)				
ITCH				
ACQUAINT THE FLESH WITH A REMEMBERED ITCH,	....	80	ALL THAT I OWE	12
SHALL FALL AWAKE WHEN CURES AND THEIR ITCH	....	89	EUNUCH DREAMS	22
THE ITCH OF MAN UPON THE BABY'S THIGH,	....	95	RUB OF LOVE	12
ITCHED				
ITCHED IN THE NOISE OF WIND AND SUN.	....	79	LOVE'S FEVER	30
ITCHED ON THE HANGMAN'S SILKS;	....	85	SEE, SAYS LIME	21
ITEM				
THAT SHAPES EACH BUSHY ITEM OF THE AIR	....	123	FOSTER LIGHT	5
ITS (78)				
IT'S				
IT'S NOT IN MISERY BUT IN OBLIVION	....	16	IN OBLIVION	T
IT'S NOT IN MISERY BUT IN OBLIVION,	....	16	IN OBLIVION	1
IT'S ACRID IN THE STREETS;	....	16	TIME TO ROT	10
THAT'LL MAKE, IT'S BRITTLE, DIAPHRAGM	....	24	LITTLE PROBLEM	8
IT'S EASY TRACING WHAT EACH GIVES THE OTHER	......	24	LITTLE PROBLEM	11
I LOVE AND DOUBT, IT'S VAIN, IT'S VAIN,	....	27	OBLIVIOUS DARK	27
I LOVE AND DOUBT, IT'S VAIN, IT'S VAIN,	....	27	OBLIVIOUS DARK	27
PLANNING WHAT'S GOOD, THOUGH IT'S BUT WINTER,	.....	27	OBLIVIOUS DARK	29
(IT'S A MATTER OF GUTS,	....	39	GAS FADES	10
O MY DEAR IT'S NEVER TOO LATE	....	149	PAPER & STICKS	11
IT'S LIGHT THAT MAKES THE INTERVALS	....	238	MAKES INTERVALS	T
IT'S LIGHT THAT MAKES THE INTERVALS	....	238	MAKES INTERVALS	1
ITSELF				
THAT GLOBE ITSELF OF HAIR AND BONE	....	97	TWILIGHT LOCKS	10
I'VE				
AS SIGNS I'VE NOT BROUGHT DOWN	....	19	IMAGES IN AIR	12
I'VE SAID MY PIECE: COUNT OR GO MAD.	....	33	HELD-OUT HAND	17
I'VE SAID MY PIECE.	....	33	HELD-OUT HAND	24
PRAISE THAT MY BODY BE WHOLE, I'VE LIMBS,	....	42	A WAR OF WITS	8
FEED IN THE ARMPITS OF DROWNED GIRLS, I'VE SWUM	...	52	OUT OF THE PIT	69
I'VE MOCKED THE MOVING OF THE UNIVERSE.	....	52	OUT OF THE PIT	75
FEELING THE PINPRICKS OF THE BLOOD, I'VE SAID	.....	53	OUT OF THE PIT	80
OUT OF THE BUILDINGS OF THE DAY I'VE STEPPED	......	53	OUT OF THE PIT	90
IVORY				
A FISHING BIRD HAS NOTES OF IVORY	....	14	FOR LEDA	6
OR MICE PLAY WITH AN IVORY TOOTH.	....	49	LIGHT, I KNOW	26
A MOUSE IT WAS PLAYED WITH AN IVORY TOOTH,	....	65	WOMAN SPEAKS	58
ON THE IVORY STAGES	....	197	CRAFT OR ART	9
JACK				
HEIGH, ON HORSEBACK HILL, JACK	....	4	PROLOGUE	67
WHEN COMETH JACK FROST? THE CHILDREN ASK.	....	56	WHY EAST WIND	10
MY JACK OF CHRIST BORN THORNY ON THE TREE?	....	96	RUB OF LOVE	45
NOW JACK MY FATHERS LET THE TIME-FACED CROOK,	.....	108	GRIEF THIEF	15
THIS WAS THE SKY, JACK CHRIST, EACH MINSTREL ANGLE		120	ALTARWISE	105
JACK-				
AND A BLACK CAP OF JACK-	....	201	SIR JOHNS HILL	14
JACKET				
I, THAT TIME'S JACKET OR THE COAT OF ICE	....	100	RUNNING GRAVE	18
IN LOVE TORN BREECHES AND BLISTERED JACKET	....	151	BELOW A TIME	7
JACKS				
THE JACKS OF FROST THEY FINGER IN THE HIVES;	......	92	BOYS OF SUMMER	9
THE SHEATH-DECKED JACKS, QUEEN WITH A SHUFFLED HEART;		118	ALTARWISE	59
THEY WITH THE SIMPLE JACKS WERE A BOULDER OF WIVES)--		205	GIANT'S THIGH	44

	PAGE	TITLE	LINE
JACOB			
AND, MANNED BY MIDNIGHT, JACOB TO THE STARS.	117	ALTARWISE	24
JACOB'S			
STAR-SET AT JACOB'S ANGLE, ...	111	I, IN IMAGE	81
JAILS			
IN THE JAILS AND STUDIES OF HIS KEYLESS SMILES. ...	153	WAS A SAVIOUR	8
JAMES			
AND FEW JAMES JOYCE'S MENTAL SLUMMINGS, ...	84	LETTER TO AUNT	37
JARRING			
THIS BUSY JARRING ON THE NERVES YET NO OUTBREAK?	36	MIDNIGHT ROAD	4
JAW			
THE ATLAS-EATER WITH A JAW FOR NEWS, ...	117	ALTARWISE	5
I LIE DOWN THIN AND HEAR THE GOOD BELLS JAW--	207	LAMENT	53
JAWBONE			
MAN OF MY FLESH, THE JAWBONE RIVEN, ...	106	ALL ALL AND	19
JAW-BONE			
DESTRUCTION, PICKED BY BIRDS, BRAYS THROUGH THE			
JAW-BONE, ...	132	I MAKE THIS IN	36
JAWS			
THE JAWS WILL HAVE SHUT, AND LIFE BE SWITCHED OUT.	39	GAS FADES	14
OF SICK OLD MANHOOD ON THE FALLEN JAWS, ...	95	RUB OF LOVE	24
SOME DEAD UNDID THEIR BUSHY JAWS, ...	97	TWILIGHT LOCKS	22
JEALOUS			
THAT OTHER SUN, THE JEALOUS COURSING OF THE			
UNRIVALLED BLOOD.	170	MARRIAGE VIRG	14
JEALOUSY			
JEALOUSY CANNOT FORGET FOR ALL HER SAKES, ...	158	INTO HER HEAD	34
JERICHO			
UNCREDITED BLOWS JERICHO ON EDEN.	124	TODAY, INSECT	17
OH, JERICHO WAS FALLING IN THEIR LUNGS!	163	LONG-LEGGED	54
JERRYSTONE			
AND JERRYSTONE TRIM VILLAS	156	RETURN	70
JESTS			
AND A FELLOW WHO JESTS THAT A MARE CAN BUILD NESTS	221	SONG OF DOG	7
JESU'S			
FROM JESU'S SLEEVE TRUMPED UP THE KING OF SPOTS,	118	ALTARWISE	58
FIRE ON STARLIGHT, RAKE JESU'S STREAM;	163	LONG-LEGGED	43
JEWELLED			
AND ON A JEWELLED POOL	225	SLENDER WIND	2
JEYES'			
TAKING JEYES' FLUID AS NARCOTIC;	137	O CHATTERTON	3
JOB'S			
JOHN'S BEAST, JOB'S PATIENCE, AND THE FIBS OF VISION,	125	TODAY, INSECT	21
JOHN'S			
JOHN'S BEAST, JOB'S PATIENCE, AND THE FIBS OF VISION,	125	TODAY, INSECT	21
OVER SIR JOHN'S HILL	201	SIR JOHNS HILL	T
OVER SIR JOHN'S HILL, ...	201	SIR JOHNS HILL	1
DAWS SIR JOHN'S JUST HILL DONS, AND AGAIN THE GULLED			
BIRDS HARE	201	SIR JOHNS HILL	15
IT IS THE HERON AND I, UNDER JUDGING SIR JOHN'S ELMED	202	SIR JOHNS HILL	40
NOW ON SIR JOHN'S HILL. THE HERON, ANKLING THE SCALY	203	SIR JOHNS HILL	55
JOINTED			
KNOW, O MY BONE, THE JOINTED LEVER, ...	106	ALL ALL AND	22
JOINTS			
THE FINGER JOINTS ARE CRAMPED WITH CHALK;	66	HAND SIGNED	6
JOKER			
ADAM, TIME'S JOKER, ON A WITCH OF CARDBOARD	119	ALTARWISE	81
JONAH'S			
AND JONAH'S MOBY SNATCHED ME BY THE HAIR, ...	119	ALTARWISE	66

		PAGE	TITLE	LINE
JONES				
	IS MR. JONES THE CAKE, THAT WINKING-BIT, ...	179	NEW QUAY	20
JONQUIL				
	THE JONQUIL AND THE TRUMPET.	27	OBLIVIOUS DARK	31
JORDAN				
	SO CRYING, HE WAS PUSHED INTO THE JORDAN.	52	OUT OF THE PIT	53
	FIRE AND JORDAN AND THE SAD CANAL.	53	OUT OF THE PIT	99
	THAT SHAPED THE JORDAN NEAR MY HOME	68	BEFORE KNOCKED	4
	MY GRAVE IS WATERED BY THE CROSSING JORDAN.	105	WORLD PYRAMID	43
JOURNEY				
	ROUNDED MY GLOBE OF HERITAGE, JOURNEY	103	I DREAMED MY	11
	SEWING A SHROUD FOR A JOURNEY	143	24 YEARS	4
	BEND, IF MY JOURNEY ACHE, DIRECTION LIKE AN ARC OR			
	MAKE	145	IF HEAD HURT	14
JOY				
	NOT VERTICALLY IN A MOOD OF JOY	16	IN OBLIVION	2
	WHERE LOVE IS THERE'S A CRUST OF JOY	19	THE NEOPHYTE	5
	THEN SHALL YOUR SENSES, OUT OF JOY, ...	21	BEWILDERED WAY	13
	UPON THE EARTH WHO KNEW NO JOY, ...	22	ON QUIET NIGHT	16
	KNOWING SUCH JOY AS I.	30	YOUTH CALLS	11
	YOU, TOO, KNOW THE EXCEEDING JOY	47	POET: 1935	51
	LAID THE CROPS LOW, BROKE THE GRAPE'S JOY.	86	BREAD I BREAK	5
	JOY IS NO KNOCKING NATION, SIR AND MADAM, ...	100	RUNNING GRAVE	31
	JOY IS THE KNOCK OF DUST, CADAVER'S SHOOT	101	RUNNING GRAVE	37
	CRY JOY THAT THIS WITCHLIKE MIDWIFE SECOND	142	SAINT TO FALL	48
	'NOW TO AWAKE HUSKED OF GESTURES AND MY JOY LIKE A			
	CAVE	146	IF HEAD HURT	21
	I'LL SHARE MY MONEY AND WE'LL RUN FOR JOY	149	PAPER & STICKS	14
	PUT A TEAR FOR JOY IN THE UNEARTHLY FLOOD	153	WAS A SAVIOUR	22
	SUMMERTIME OF THE DEAD WHISPERED THE TRUTH OF HIS JOY	178	POEM IN OCT	56
	JOY OF THE LONG DEAD CHILD SANG BURNING	178	POEM IN OCT	63
	BRETHREN FOR JOY HAS MOVED WITHIN	183	VISION, PRAYER	117
	THE CLOUD, THE NEED, THE PLANTED STARS, THE JOY			
	BEYOND	190	WINTER'S TALE	102
	THE DEAD GROW FOR HIS JOY.	210	POEM ON B'DAY	54
JOYCE'S				
	AND FEW JAMES JOYCE'S MENTAL SLUMMINGS, ...	84	LETTER TO AUNT	37
JOYFUL				
	GABRIEL AND RADIANT SHRUBBERY AS THE MORNING GROWS			
	JOYFUL	186	HOLY SPRING	15
JOYS				
	AND JOYS ARE PAINS.	74	WE MOTHERNAKED	8
	EMETIC PERCIES FOR THEIR JOYS.	143	THE MOLLS	4
	THE RAINBOW-FISH BEND IN HER JOYS, ...	163	LONG-LEGGED	34
	WHO ONCE, GREEN COUNTRIES SINCE, WERE A HEDGEROW OF			
	JOYS.	204	GIANT'S THIGH	20
JUAN				
	JUAN AFLAME AND SAVAGELY YOUNG KING LEAR, ...	157	INTO HER HEAD	11
JUDGE				
	TO THE JUDGE BLOWN BEDLAM	182	VISION, PRAYER	74
JUDGING				
	IT IS THE HERON AND I, UNDER JUDGING SIR JOHN'S ELMED	202	SIR JOHNS HILL	40
JUDGMENT				
	THAT BREAKS ONE BONE TO LIGHT WITH A JUDGMENT CLOUT,	136	AFTER FUNERAL	9
JUGGERNAUT				
	WE SCORN THE JUGGERNAUT, ...	59	FAIRY TALES	6
JUGULAR				
	FELLOW WITH SAW AT THE JUGULAR.	137	O CHATTERTON	11
JUICES				
	THAT FROZEN WIFE WHOSE JUICES DRIFT LIKE A FIXED SEA	145	PLEASURE-BIRD	14

	PAGE	TITLE	LINE
JUMP			
THOSE CRANING BIRDS ARE CHOICE FOR YOU, SONGS THAT JUMP BACK	16	SPIRE CRANES	9
BUMP ON A SPOUT LET THE BUBBLES JUMP OUT.	145	IF HEAD HURT	3
MADE THE TIGERS JUMP OUT OF THEIR EYES	172	THE HUNCHBACK	28
JUMPING			
FROM FISH TO JUMPING HILL! LOOK:	4	PROLOGUE	43
JUMPS			
AND BLOOD JUMPS IN THE SUN;	82	LIGHT BREAKS	29
JUST			
BUT JUST A KIND AND CULTURED DAME	83	LETTER TO AUNT	5
PERHAPS IT WOULD BE JUST AS WELL,	84	LETTER TO AUNT	30
AND SEAR JUST RIDERS BACK,	161	DEATHS AND ENT	34
DAWS SIR JOHN'S JUST HILL DONS, AND AGAIN THE GULLED BIRDS HARE	201	SIR JOHNS HILL	15
JUSTICE			
THE DARKEST JUSTICE OF DEATH, BLIND AND UNBLESSED.	216	ELEGY	11
KANGAROO			
FROM THE KANGAROO FOOT OF THE EARTH,	151	BELOW A TIME	21
KEATINGS			
KEATINGS IS GOOD FOR LICE,	58	TO ARCHITECTS	12
KEENLY			
THE SEA SPEAKING KEENLY,	229	MY RIVER	36
KEEP			
HOO, THERE, IN CASTLE KEEP,	4	PROLOGUE	53
AND I, YOUR CAPTOR, HAVE MY LOVE TO KEEP	10	COOL, OH NO	29
TO KEEP COUNT OF THE STILES	33	HELD-OUT HAND	21
A HOLE IN SPACE SHALL KEEP THE SHAPE OF THOUGHT,	73	LORD RED HAIL	13
O KEEP HIS BONES AWAY FROM THAT COMMON CART,	173	DAWN RAID	12
AND FLOWER OF COUNTRY SLEEP AND THE GREENWOOD KEEP.	198	COUNTRY SLEEP	18
BUT YOU'LL NOT KEEP ME IN	239	LET ME ESCAPE	7
KEEPER			
AND THE KEEPER OF THE KEY.	126	SEED-AT-ZERO	21
DODGING THE PARK KEEPER	171	THE HUNCHBACK	23
KEEPING			
IN THE FARMS OF HEAVEN'S KEEPING,	216	COUNTRY HEAVEN	29
KENNEL			
SLEPT AT NIGHT IN A DOG KENNEL	171	THE HUNCHBACK	11
TO HIS KENNEL IN THE DARK.	172	THE HUNCHBACK	42
KEPT			
CHILDREN KEPT FROM THE SUN	152	WAS A SAVIOUR	4
KETTLES			
THE DUST OF THEIR KETTLES AND CLOCKS SWINGS TO AND FRO	205	GIANT'S THIGH	46
KEY			
OR (CHANGE THE KEY!) GIVE VENT TO UTTERANCES	33	HELD-OUT HAND	8
AND THE KEEPER OF THE KEY.	126	SEED-AT-ZERO	21
AND THE LOSER OF THE KEY.	126	SEED-AT-ZERO	28
KEYHOLES			
DARK INVITERS TO KEYHOLES	155	RETURN	56
KEYLESS			
IN THE JAILS AND STUDIES OF HIS KEYLESS SMILES.	153	WAS A SAVIOUR	8
KEYS			
WHEN AT YOUR LIPS AND KEYS,	160	DEATHS AND ENT	14
TO SHUT THE SUN, PLUNGE, MOUNT YOUR DARKENED KEYS	161	DEATHS AND ENT	33
WHEN ALL THE KEYS SHOT FROM THE LOCKS, AND RANG.	172	DAWN RAID	8
KICK			
FROM SALT-LIPPED BEAK TO THE KICK OF THE STERN	164	LONG-LEGGED	81
RAGE SHATTERED WATERS KICK	210	POEM ON B'DAY	70

	PAGE	TITLE	LINE
KICKED			
KICKED, WITH A CLATTER, ASH-BINS MARKED VERBOTEN,	52	OUT OF THE PIT	57
YOU HAVE KICKED FROM A DARK DEN, LEAPED UP THE WHINNYING LIGHT,	135	HOW MY ANIMAL	43
KICKS			
THE DREAM THAT KICKS THE BURIED FROM THEIR SACK	90	EUNUCH DREAMS	34
KID			
WITH A BOUNCING AND SILVER SPOONED KID	149	PAPER & STICKS	15
KILL			
FOR IT CAN QUICKEN OR IT CAN KILL.	24	THE ONLY DEAD	29
*THE MAGGOT THAT NO MAN CAN KILL	61	MEAT ON BONES	25
WE WATCH THE SHOW OF SHADOWS KISS OR KILL,	89	EUNUCH DREAMS	19
AND A FIREWIND KILL THE CANDLE.	130	SINNERS' BELL	6
LOVE AND LABOUR AND KILL	135	HOW MY ANIMAL	17
THAT ALL THE CHARMINGLY DROWNED ARISE TO COCKCROW AND KILL.	144	COLOUR OF SAY	6
HE SAW THE STORM SMOKE OUT TO KILL	163	LONG-LEGGED	41
KILL TIME! SHE TURNS IN HER PAIN!	167	LONG-LEGGED	154
TO KILL AND THEIR OWN TIDE DAUBING BLOOD	209	POEM ON B'DAY	35
KILLED			
AND THE SUN KILLED IN HER FACE.	139	TOMBSTONE TOLD	9
AMONG THOSE KILLED IN THE DAWN RAID WAS A MAN AGED A HUNDRED	172	DAWN RAID	T
COME AND BE KILLED,	202	SIR JOHNS HILL	22
KILLER			
LEADS TO FOOL'S PARADISE WHERE THE REDCOATED KILLER	44	TO FOLLOW FOX	5
AT SIGHT OF DEATH, THE LAST TWO FISTED KILLER	59	FAIRY TALES	18
KILLS			
WHO KILLS MY HISTORY?	129	MY NEOPHYTE	37
TIME KILLS ME TERRIBLY.	129	MY NEOPHYTE	43
AND THE HAWK IN THE EGG KILLS THE WREN.	167	LONG-LEGGED	156
KIN			
EVEN AMONG HIS OWN KIN IS HE LOST,	47	POET: 1935	22
KIND			
WITH QUITE A KIND OF HEART.	12	CABARET	17
AND THOUGHTS, BE THEY SO KIND,	20	THE NEOPHYTE	24
ENOUGH KIND FOOD, ENOUGH KIND SPEAKING,	36	MIDNIGHT ROAD	6
ENOUGH KIND FOOD, ENOUGH KIND SPEAKING,	36	MIDNIGHT ROAD	6
BUT JUST A KIND AND CULTURED DAME	83	LETTER TO AUNT	5
THE COUNTRY IS HOLY: O BIDE IN THAT COUNTRY KIND,	198	COUNTRY SLEEP	39
(HIS GENTLE KIND);	215	COUNTRY HEAVEN	22
A COLD KIND MAN BRAVE IN HIS NARROW PRIDE	216	ELEGY	3
WHICH WAS REST AND DUST, AND IN THE KIND GROUND	216	ELEGY	10
AN OLD KIND MAN BRAVE IN HIS BURNING PRIDE.	217	ELEGY	24
PACING IN KIND PRAISE.	235	WOMAN TAPESTRY	34
KINDER			
KINDER;	18	NATURAL DAY	7
KINDLE			
TIME MARKS A BLACK AISLE KINDLE FROM THE BRAND OF ASHES,	130	SINNERS' BELL	4
KINDLED			
DARKNESS KINDLED BACK INTO BEGINNING	173	FIRE RAID	12
WOUND, NOR HER RIDING HIGH, NOR HER EYES, NOR KINDLED HAIR,	201	COUNTRY SLEEP	101
KINDLES			
WHOSE MINUTE KINDLES MORE THAN THE WISE HOUR.	237	PILLAR BREAKS	11
KINDLING			
HIM UP AND HE RAN LIKE A WIND AFTER THE KINDLING FLIGHT	190	WINTER'S TALE	89

```
                                                  PAGE      TITLE        LINE
KING
     YOU KING SINGSONG OWLS, WHO MOONBEAM  ..............    4    PROLOGUE         54
     THE DEAD QUEEN WALKETH WITH MYCENAE'S KING  ........   57    GREEK PLAY       23
     THESE FIVE KINGS DID A KING TO DEATH.  ..............  66    HAND SIGNED       4
     FROM JESU'S SLEEVE TRUMPED UP THE KING OF SPOTS,     118    ALTARWISE        58
     RAZOR MAN AND BELLY KING,  .........................  155    RETURN           32
     JUAN AFLAME AND SAVAGELY YOUNG KING LEAR,  .........  157    INTO HER HEAD    11
     KING OF YOUR BLUE EYES  ............................  192    SIDE OF TRUTH     3
     KING OF YOUR HEART IN THE BLIND DAYS,  .............  193    SIDE OF TRUTH    16
     OF THE SKY, KING OF YOUR SIX YEARS.  ...............  193    SIDE OF TRUTH    28
     INTO A HOMESTALL KING OR HAMLET OF FIRE  ...........  198    COUNTRY SLEEP    11
     THEIR BREASTS FULL OF HONEY, UNDER THEIR GANDER KING  205    GIANT'S THIGH    38
KINGCRAFTS
     THE KINGCRAFTS OF THE WICKED SEA,  .................   61    MEAT ON BONES    11
KINGDOM
     O KINGDOM OF NEIGHBOURS, FINNED  ...................    5    PROLOGUE         82
     HOUSING DEATH IN YOUR KINGDOM,  ....................   67    REALM OF FLESH   12
     NOR THE CANNONS OF HIS KINGDOM  ....................  126    SEED-AT-ZERO     47
     NOR THE CANNONS OF HIS KINGDOM  ....................  127    SEED-AT-ZERO     54
     THE SUNDERING ULTIMATE KINGDOM OF GENESIS' THUNDER.  175    FIRE RAID        77
     SWARMS ON THE KINGDOM COME  ........................  181    VISION, PRAYER   40
     TO HIS NIMBUS BELL COOL KINGDOM COME  ..............  211    POEM ON B'DAY    85
KINGFISHER
     THE KINGFISHER COMES  ..............................  230    OUR SANCTITY     23
KINGLY
     OF AGAMEMNON AND HIS KINGLY BLOOD  .................   56    GREEK PLAY        7
     THE SEA SPEAKS IN A KINGLY VOICE,  .................   61    MEAT ON BONES    35
KINGS
     THESE FIVE KINGS DID A KING TO DEATH.  .............   66    HAND SIGNED       4
     THE FIVE KINGS COUNT THE DEAD BUT DO NOT SOFTEN  ...   66    HAND SIGNED      13
     PROPHETS AND FIBRE KINGS IN OIL AND LETTER,  .......  120    ALTARWISE       114
     BUT THE HUNGRY KINGS OF THE TIDES;  ................  165    LONG-LEGGED     109
KINGSLEY
     DEAR TOMMY, PLEASE, FROM FAR, SCIATIC KINGSLEY  ....  179    NEW QUAY          1
KISS
     HOW KISS, WHEN DOLL COULD SAY  .....................   10    COOL, OH NO      13
     UNDER HIS STRONG IMPULSIVE KISS  ...................   11    AIR BREATHE       4
     THE EMERALD KISS,  .................................   14    RAIN CUTS        38
     TO KISS AWAKE  .....................................   15    FOR LEDA         18
     NOT DRAWING IN YOUR SUCTION'S KISS.  ...............   16    TIME TO ROT       6
     MY LIPS ARE WITHERED WITH A KISS,  .................   61    MEAT ON BONES    20
     TO YOUNG ADORERS DYING ON A KISS.  .................   81    ALL THAT I OWE   18
     WE WATCH THE SHOW OF SHADOWS KISS OR KILL,  ........   89    EUNUCH DREAMS    19
     HERE BREAK A KISS IN NO LOVE'S QUARRY.  ............   93    BOYS OF SUMMER   47
     YOUR MOUTH, MY LOVE, THE THISTLE IN THE KISS?  .....   96    RUB OF LOVE      44
     THOUGH THE BRAWL OF THE KISS HAS NOT OCCURRED  .....  147    UNLUCKILY FOR     7
     WITNESSED WITH A KISS.  ............................  163    LONG-LEGGED      48
     KISS  ..............................................  181    VISION, PRAYER   51
     NOW CURLEW CRY ME DOWN TO KISS THE MOUTHS OF THEIR
        DUST.  ..........................................  205    GIANT'S THIGH    45
     AND NIGHT, WHO STOOPED TO KISS THE PALLID LEAVES     223    IN DREAMS         5
KISSED
     I FELLOWED SLEEP WHO KISSED ME IN THE BRAIN,  ......  101    FELLOWED SLEEP    1
     SUCKING THE DARK, KISSED ON THE CYANIDE,  ..........  104    WORLD PYRAMID    21
     AND HER RED LIPS WERE KISSED BLACK,  ...............  139    TOMBSTONE TOLD   18
     TO THE KISSED KITE HEMS OF HIS SHAWL,  .............  141    SAINT TO FALL     3
     UNDER THE CLOUD AGAINST LOVE IS CAUGHT AND HELD AND
        KISSED  .........................................  147    UNLUCKILY FOR    17
     SING HOW THE SEAL HAS KISSED HER DEAD!  ............  164    LONG-LEGGED      82
```

	PAGE	TITLE	LINE
KISSES			
THAT TURNED THE EMPTY KISSES INTO MEANING, ...	43	FACES SHONE	3
THE WIND OF KISSES SEALED A PACT	85	SEE, SAYS LIME	10
AS KISSES FROZE THE WAXING THOUGHT, ...	85	SEE, SAYS LIME	14
KISSING			
O SEE THE POLES ARE KISSING AS THEY CROSS.	93	BOYS OF SUMMER	54
KISSPROOF			
THE KISSPROOF WORLD.	101	RUNNING GRAVE	50
KITCHENS			
WHERE THE HAY RIDES NOW OR THE BRACKEN KITCHENS RUST	205	GIANT'S THIGH	47
KITE			
LIE COLD, WITH THEIR HORSES, FOR RAVEN AND KITE.	45	PLOUGHMAN GONE	23
TO THE KISSED KITE HEMS OF HIS SHAWL, ...	141	SAINT TO FALL	3
KNAVE			
THE KNAVE OF PAIN STEALS OFF	107	GRIEF THIEF	3
KNAVES			
OF BIRTH AND DEATH, THE TWO SAD KNAVES OF THIEVES,	75	MY HERO BARES	18
KNEADING			
WITH ITS KNEADING MOUTH	173	FIRE RAID	6
KNEE-			
RAGS AND PRAYERS DOWN THE KNEE-	190	WINTER'S TALE	96
KNEE-DEEP			
KNEE-DEEP IN VOMIT. I SAW HIM THERE, ...	51	OUT OF THE PIT	43
KNEEL			
TACKLED WITH CLOUDS, WHO KNEEL	3	PROLOGUE	13
AND ALL LOVE'S SINNERS IN SWEET CLOTH KNEEL TO A HYLEG IMAGE, ...	130	SINNERS' BELL	28
THE OWL AT ITS KNELLING. FOX AND HOLT KNEEL BEFORE BLOOD.	198	COUNTRY SLEEP	32
KNEELS			
THEY FROM HOUSES WHERE THE HARVEST KNEELS, HOLD ME HARD, ...	205	GIANT'S THIGH	50
CROSSES THE BREAST OF THE PRAISING EAST, AND KNEELS,	215	COUNTRY HEAVEN	3
KNEES			
STRADDLE HER WRINKLED KNEES	22	HIGH ON A HILL	5
BOWING ON ITS MOSSY KNEES, ...	72	TAKE NEEDLES	50
THE SEA-HALVED FAITH THAT BLEW TIME TO HIS KNEES,	107	GRIEF THIEF	4
FIRST THERE WAS THE LAMB ON KNOCKING KNEES	117	ALTARWISE	29
CHILD IN WHITE BLOOD BENT ON ITS KNEES	128	MY NEOPHYTE	2
KNELLED			
HILL, TELL-TALE THE KNELLED	202	SIR JOHNS HILL	41
KNELLING			
THE OWL AT ITS KNELLING. FOX AND HOLT KNEEL BEFORE BLOOD.	198	COUNTRY SLEEP	32
KNELLS			
WAVE'S SILENCE, WEPT WHITE ANGELUS KNELLS.	209	POEM ON B'DAY	38
KNELT			
HE KNELT, HE WEPT, HE PRAYED, ...	188	WINTER'S TALE	26
HE KNELT ON THE COLD STONES, ...	188	WINTER'S TALE	31
THAT A MAN KNELT ALONE IN THE CUP OF THE VALES, ...	189	WINTER'S TALE	85
KNEW			
UPON THE EARTH WHO KNEW NO JOY, ...	22	ON QUIET NIGHT	16
WHO KNEW NOT SUN NOR MOON BY NAME, ...	68	BEFORE KNOCKED	8
I KNEW THE MESSAGE OF THE WINTER, ...	68	BEFORE KNOCKED	13
UNGOTTEN I KNEW NIGHT AND DAY.	68	BEFORE KNOCKED	18
MY THROAT KNEW THIRST BEFORE THE STRUCTURE	69	BEFORE KNOCKED	25
MY HEART KNEW LOVE, MY BELLY HUNGER;	69	BEFORE KNOCKED	29
WE IN OUR EDEN KNEW THE SECRET GUARDIAN	122	INCARNATE DEVL	13
KNEW ALL HIS HORRIBLE DESIRES	128	MY NEOPHYTE	10

	PAGE	TITLE	LINE

KNICKER
      I FIND A TRIPPER'S KNICKER IN THE GULLY   137   O CHATTERTON   15
KNICKERS
      AND BUTTON UP. HE MINCES AMONG KNICKERS, ...   179   NEW QUAY   23
KNIFE
      HIS SCISSORS OILED, HIS KNIFE HUNG LOOSE   91   WHERE ONCE THE   10
KNIT
      TO SHADE AND KNIT ANEW THE PATCH OF WORDS   79   LOVE'S FEVER   34
KNIVES
      OF KNIVES ON FORKS, HE CRIED, OF NERVE ON NERVE,   51   OUT OF THE PIT   34
      TAKE THE NEEDLES AND THE KNIVES   70   TAKE NEEDLES   T
      TAKE THE NEEDLES AND THE KNIVES, ...   70   TAKE NEEDLES   1
      THE TRAY OF KNIVES, THE ANTISEPTIC FUNERAL, ...   110   I, IN IMAGE   54
      THE SUPPER AND KNIVES OF A MOOD.   144   PLEASURE-BIRD   4
      IS CRYING FROM NETS TO KNIVES, ...   164   LONG-LEGGED   66
KNOBBLY
      THE KNOBBLY APE THAT SWINGS ALONG HIS SEX   96   RUB OF LOVE   37
KNOCK
      JOY IS THE KNOCK OF DUST, CADAVER'S SHOOT   101   RUNNING GRAVE   37
      AND THE KNOCK OF SAILING BOATS ON THE NET WEBBED WALL   177   POEM IN OCT   7
KNOCKED
      BUT NOT OF GRIEF, FOR I HAVE KNOCKED DOWN THAT   31   OUT OF SIGHS   2
      BEFORE I KNOCKED   68   BEFORE KNOCKED   T
      BEFORE I KNOCKED AND FLESH LET ENTER, ...   68   BEFORE KNOCKED   1
      KNOCKED IN THE FLESH THAT DECKED THE VINE, ...   86   BREAD I BREAK   7
      AND ROLL WITH THE KNOCKED EARTH: 135   HOW MY ANIMAL   41
KNOCKING
      KNOCKING OFF TURNIP TOPS, WITH TREES FOR FRIENDS,   53   OUT OF THE PIT   88
      JOY IS NO KNOCKING NATION, SIR AND MADAM, ...   100   RUNNING GRAVE   31
      FIRST THERE WAS THE LAMB ON KNOCKING KNEES   117   ALTARWISE   29
KNOCKS
      'MY FATHERS' GLOBE KNOCKS ON ITS NAVE AND SINGS.'   101   FELLOWED SLEEP   11
KNOT
      THE BRAINS OF DEATH UNDID THE KNOT   86   SEE, SAYS LIME   22
KNOTS
      WHERE ONCE YOUR GREEN KNOTS SANK THEIR SPLICE   91   WHERE ONCE THE   7
KNOW
      FOR YOU TO KNOW   4   PROLOGUE   38
      I KNOW THIS VICIOUS MINUTE'S HOUR   9   MINUTE'S HOUR   T
      I KNOW THIS VICIOUS MINUTE'S HOUR;   9   MINUTE'S HOUR   1
      BUT IT, REALITY, WHOSE VOICE I KNOW   9   MINUTE'S HOUR   16
      THE THROAT IS MINE I KNOW THE NECK   11   AIR BREATHE   2
      I WISH TO KNOW   12   SKY'S BRIGHT   10
      AND KNOW WHY RUN), ...   24   LITTLE PROBLEM   14
      RUN AND KNOW WHY   24   LITTLE PROBLEM   19
      AND KNOW WHY KNOW, NO WIT, ...   24   LITTLE PROBLEM   20
      AND KNOW WHY KNOW, NO WIT, ...   24   LITTLE PROBLEM   20
      THE SEASON'S SUN, THOUGH HE SHOULD KNOW HIS SETTING   25   THERE'S PLENTY   4
      AND NOT TO KNOW   27   OBLIVIOUS DARK   2
      THIS WE KNOW WE GOT NO WINGS, ...   28   NO WINGS   2
      THIS WE KNOW, WE GOT NO WINGS, ...   28   NO WINGS   24
      WAITING ALL VAINLY THIS WE KNOW.   28   NO WINGS   26
      AFTER SUCH FIGHTING AS THE WEAKEST KNOW, ...   32   OUT OF SIGHS   10
      LET CHILDREN KNOW, AND OLD MEN AT THEIR GATES, ...   36   LET BE KNOWN   3
      DECLARE THEIR SOULS, LET CHILDREN KNOW, LIVE AFTER.   36   LET BE KNOWN   6
      YOU, TOO, KNOW THE EXCEEDING JOY   47   POET: 1935   51
      LIGHT, I KNOW, TREADS THE TEN MILLION STARS   48   LIGHT, I KNOW   T
      LIGHT, I KNOW, TREADS THE TEN MILLION STARS, ...   48   LIGHT, I KNOW   1
      AND 'KNOW NO ANSWER', AND I KNOW   56   WHY EAST WIND   23
      AND 'KNOW NO ANSWER', AND I KNOW   56   WHY EAST WIND   23

		PAGE	TITLE	LINE
KNOW (CONTINUED)				
WE KNOW OUR MOTHER GOOSE AND EDEN,	....	59	FAIRY TALES	10
SO I HAVE COME TO KNOW, BUT KNOWLEDGE ACHES;	....	64	WOMAN SPEAKS	48
I KNOW THAT AGE IS SNOW UPON THE HAIR,	....	64	WOMAN SPEAKS	49
(FOR THOUGHT, WE KNOW, IS DECADENT);	....	84	LETTER TO AUNT	43
THE SIGNAL GRASS THAT TELLS ME ALL I KNOW	....	99	OCTOBER WIND	22
KNOW NOW THE FLESH'S LOCK AND VICE,	....	106	ALL ALL AND	20
KNOW, O MY BONE, THE JOINTED LEVER,	....	106	ALL ALL AND	22
I KNOW HER SCRUBBED AND SOUR HUMBLE HANDS	....	136	AFTER FUNERAL	31
THIS I KNOW FROM THE NATIVE	....	148	UNLUCKILY FOR	50
I KNOW NOT WHETHER	....	174	FIRE RAID	33
I KNOW THE LEGEND	....	174	FIRE RAID	47
TO KNOW ALL	....	184	VISION, PRAYER	159
TURNS IN THE DARK ON THE SOUND THEY KNOW WILL ARISE		193	CONVERS PRAYER	6
KNOW THE GREEN GOOD,	....	198	COUNTRY SLEEP	40
THOUGH WISE MEN AT THEIR END KNOW DARK IS RIGHT,		208	NOT GO GENTLE	4
I'LL KNOW I'M OUT OF HARM,	....	240	TWINING HEAD	4
KNOWING				
KNOWING A DREAM COULD DARKEN IT,	....	10	COOL, OH NO	10
KNOWING SUCH JOY AS I.	....	30	YOUTH CALLS	11
NOT KNOWING RADIANCE CAME AND PASSED.	....	43	FACES SHONE	13
KNOWING EXCEEDING GRIEF AND THE GODS' SORROW	....	47	POET: 1935	48
KNOWLEDGE				
AND MY CORRUPTING KNOWLEDGE--	....	18	NATURAL DAY	30
WITH KNOWLEDGE THAT NO USE AND NOTHING WORTH	......	27	OBLIVIOUS DARK	9
SO I HAVE COME TO KNOW, BUT KNOWLEDGE ACHES;	......	64	WOMAN SPEAKS	48
KNOWN				
HAVE KNOWN MAN'S ENVY AND HIS WEAK DESIRE,	....	30	YOUTH CALLS	3
LET IT BE KNOWN	....	36	LET BE KNOWN	T
LET IT BE KNOWN THAT LITTLE LIVE BUT LIES,	....	36	LET BE KNOWN	1
WHAT'S NEVER KNOWN IS SAFEST IN THIS LIFE.	....	40	WAS THERE TIME	6
HE, TOO, HAS KNOWN THE AGONY IN THE GARDEN,	....	52	OUT OF THE PIT	54
SHALL NOT BE KNOWN TILL WINDWELL DRIES	....	55	WHY EAST WIND	2
ALL THINGS ARE KNOWN: THE STARS' ADVICE	....	56	WHY EAST WIND	16
NOW BREAK A GIANT TEAR FOR THE LITTLE KNOWN FALL,		153	WAS A SAVIOUR	32
AND ALWAYS KNOWN MUST LEAVE	....	160	DEATHS AND ENT	4
FOREVER FALLING NIGHT IS A KNOWN	....	184	VISION, PRAYER	153
AND THE KNOWN DARK OF THE EARTH AMEN.	....	185	VISION, PRAYER	187
TO HAVE KNOWN THEM IN THEIR BLUE-HUED VALIANCE,	...	223	IDYLL UNFORGET	3
BUT I HAVE KNOWN THE STILL ARDOUR OF EQUABILITY;		223	IDYLL UNFORGET	17
I HAVE KNOWN THE MYSTERY OF THE SEA TO BE MANTLED				
ABOUT ME;	....	223	IDYLL UNFORGET	18
KNOWNS				
ONE ENEMY, OF MANY, WHO KNOWNS WELL	....	160	DEATHS AND ENT	29
KNOWS				
SWEET, AUTOMATIC ME KNOWS BEST.	....	10	COOL, OH NO	18
KNOWS HIS LOVE ROTS.	....	20	THE NEOPHYTE	12
FOR US THAT KNOWS MISVENTURE	....	28	NO WINGS	6
AND THE WONDER THAT MAN KNOWS,	....	31	BEING BUT MEN	12
GROWING IN PUBLIC PLACES THAN MAN KNOWS.	....	48	POET: 1935	57
AND KNOWS NO WOE THAT THESE SAD PLAYERS MOUTH	.....	57	GREEK PLAY	30
WHO KNOWS NOT ELIOT (TO HER SHAME).	....	83	LETTER TO AUNT	6
AND FAR AT SEA HE KNOWS,	....	209	POEM ON B'DAY	30
WHO KNOWS THE ROCKETING WIND WILL BLOW	....	210	POEM ON B'DAY	67
LABORATORY				
HEDGEROW, LABORATORY, AND EVEN GLASSHOUSE,	....	18	NATURAL DAY	13
LABOUR				
AND THAT IS THE REWARD OF LABOUR	....	44	TO FOLLOW FOX	12
AND A MOTHER IN HER LABOUR	....	71	TAKE NEEDLES	18
A MOTHER IN LABOUR PAYS TWICE HER PAIN,	....	74	SUN BURNS	14

	PAGE	TITLE	LINE
LABOUR (CONTINUED)			
MAY A HUMBLE VILLAGE LABOUR	126	SEED-AT-ZERO	29
MAY A HUMBLE PLANET LABOUR	126	SEED-AT-ZERO	36
LOVE AND LABOUR AND KILL	135	HOW MY ANIMAL	17
(BURY THE DEAD FOR FEAR THAT THEY WALK TO THE GRAVE			
IN LABOUR.)	143	24 YEARS	2
I LABOUR BY SINGING LIGHT	197	CRAFT OR ART	6
TO LABOUR AND LOVE THOUGH THEY LAY DOWN LONG AGO.	203	GIANT'S THIGH	5
LABOUR'S			
HERE IS HER LABOUR'S END,	26	PERSONAL EPIT	13
LABYRINTHINE			
AT THE LABYRINTHINE PAP.	71	TAKE NEEDLES	12
IN ITS LABYRINTHINE HOME.	71	TAKE NEEDLES	28
LABYRINTHS			
WHO IN THESE LABYRINTHS,	128	MY NEOPHYTE	13
LACED			
OF THE WOOD! PASTORAL BEAT OF BLOOD THROUGH THE			
LACED LEAVES!	199	COUNTRY SLEEP	71
LACK-A-HEAD			
OF A LACK-A-HEAD GHOST I FEAR TO THE ANONYMOUS END.	141	I, FIRST NAMED	4
LAD			
RAISES THE HAIRS OF LAD AND MAIDEN.	59	FAIRY TALES	16
LADDER			
THERE GROWS THE HOURS' LADDER TO THE SUN,	102	FELLOWED SLEEP	26
WE RUNG OUR WEATHERING CHANGES ON THE LADDER,	118	ALTARWISE	41
LADEN			
ENVELOPING THEMSELVES IN THE LADEN EVE;	224	IDYLL UNFORGET	42
LADIES			
BUT WHEN THE LADIES ARE COLD AS STONE	60	MEAT ON BONES	7
THE BAGPIPE-BREASTED LADIES IN THE DEADWEED	119	ALTARWISE	83
TIME'S TUNE MY LADIES WITH THE TEATS OF MUSIC,	119	ALTARWISE	91
TIME IS THE TUNE MY LADIES LEND THEIR HEARTBREAK,	119	ALTARWISE	95
LADIES'			
OF LADIES' NEEDLES WORN TO BREAKING POINT	18	NATURAL DAY	10
BEFORE THE LADIES' BREASTS ARE HAGS	60	MEAT ON BONES	4
LADS			
I HEAR, THROUGH DEAD MEN'S DRUMS, THE RIDDLED LADS,	105	WORLD PYRAMID	40
LADY			
WHO PLAY THE PROPER GENTLEMAN AND LADY.	113	NOT FATHER ME	28
IN THE AGE OF LADY FRANKINCENSE	240	ADMIT THE SUN	13
LADYLIKE			
WITH ZEST CULLED FROM THEIR LADYLIKE HEAT,	18	NATURAL DAY	12
LADY'S			
ONE LADY'S HAND WAS LIFTED,	11	CABARET	11
AND SIRENS SINGING FROM OUR LADY'S SEA-STRAW.	119	ALTARWISE	70
LAGGARDS			
THERE ARE TWO LAGGARDS,	60	FAIRY TALES	34
LAID			
BECAUSE LAID DOWN	26	PERSONAL EPIT	3
I LAID HER DOWN AND TOLD HER SIN,	61	MEAT ON BONES	23
THE SNIPER LAID HIM LOW AND STREWED HIS BRAINS;	63	WOMAN SPEAKS	11
FLESH IS SUFFERED, IS LAID LOW,	71	TAKE NEEDLES	25
LAID THE CROPS LOW, BROKE THE GRAPE'S JOY.	86	BREAD I BREAK	5
AND LAID YOUR CHEEK AGAINST A CLOUD-FORMED SHELL:	153	WAS A SAVIOUR	23
WITH THE SUNFLOWERS LAID ON,	154	RETURN	18
AND HIS RUNAWAY BELOVED CHILDLIKE LAID IN THE			
ACORNED SAND.	157	INTO HER HEAD	23
ARE MAKING UNDER THE GREEN, LAID VEIL	164	LONG-LEGGED	69
THE LONG, LAID MINUTE'S BRIDE DRIFTS ON	164	LONG-LEGGED	83
AND STUNNED AND STILL ON THE GREEN, LAID VEIL	167	LONG-LEGGED	171

		PAGE	TITLE	LINE
LAID (CONTINUED)				
LAID IN HER SNOW	....	174	FIRE RAID	37
AND THE GOLDEN PAVEMENTS LAID IN REQUIEMS,	....	175	FIRE RAID	69
LAIN				
I HAVE NOT LAIN AN HOUR ASLEEP	....	22	ON QUIET NIGHT	5
LAIN WITH PARCHED THINGS; LOVED DOGS AND WOMEN;	...	52	OUT OF THE PIT	72
LAIR				
THROUGH EASIER HEATHER TO THE FOUL LAIR	....	44	TO FOLLOW FOX	16
OUT OF A LAIR IN THE FLOCKED LEAVES IN THE DEW DIPPED YEAR	....	197	COUNTRY SLEEP	6
LAIRS				
IN LAIRS AND ASYLUMS OF THE TREMENDOUS SHOUT.	.....	153	WAS A SAVIOUR	16
OF HIS SNOW BLIND LOVE AND RUSH IN THE WHITE LAIRS.		188	WINTER'S TALE	38
LAKE				
PAST LAKE AND ROCKERY	....	171	THE HUNCHBACK	19
THE BIRDS THE GRASS THE TREES THE LAKE	....	172	THE HUNCHBACK	39
THROUGH THE SHAKEN GREENSWARD LAKE, SILENT, ON MOONSHOD HOOVES,	....	200	COUNTRY SLEEP	84
AND DUCKED AND DRAKED WHITE LAKE THAT HARPS TO A HAIL STONE.	....	204	GIANT'S THIGH	28
LAKES				
WOUND LIKE A BALL OF LAKES	....	129	MY NEOPHYTE	33
THAT THE SNOW BLIND TWILIGHT FERRIES OVER THE LAKES		187	WINTER'S TALE	2
DEEP HILLOCKS AND LOUD ON THE NUMBED LAKES,	....	190	WINTER'S TALE	97
AND THE LAKES AND FLOATING FIELDS AND THE RIVER WENDED	....	190	WINTER'S TALE	108
AND OVER THE GLAZED LAKES SKATED THE SHAPES OF FISHES		190	WINTER'S TALE	115
LAKE'S				
THE LAKE'S VOICE AND THE ROLLING OF MOCK WAVES	....	46	POET: 1935	4
LAMB				
WITH THE LEPER AND THE LAMB.	....	71	TAKE NEEDLES	32
FIRST THERE WAS THE LAMB ON KNOCKING KNEES	....	117	ALTARWISE	29
OR THE WHITE EWE LAMB	....	174	FIRE RAID	35
NOTHING I CARED, IN THE LAMB WHITE DAYS, THAT TIME WOULD TAKE ME	....	196	FERN HILL	46
LAMBS				
WHITE, GOD'S BRIGHT, FLOCKS, THE BELLED LAMBS LEAPING,	....	215	COUNTRY HEAVEN	21
LAME				
OR LAME THE AIR WITH LEAPING FROM ITS HEATS;	......	92	BOYS OF SUMMER	21
THE YEAR-HEDGED ROW IS LAME WITH FLINT,	....	129	MY NEOPHYTE	38
REFUSAL STRUCK HER LOIN AND THE LAME FLOWER	....	134	NOT FROM ANGER	2
LAMENT				
LAMENT	....	205	LAMENT	T
LAMENTING				
LAMENTING FALLS. PITY ELECTRA'S LOVING	....	56	GREEK PLAY	4
OTHERS BETRAY THE LAMENTING LIES OF THEIR LOSSES		133	MAKE ME A MASK	11
NOT WHOLLY TO THAT LAMENTING	....	183	VISION, PRAYER	116
LAMENTS				
THE LIVING SUN LAMENTS THE DYING SKIES,	....	56	GREEK PLAY	3
LAMP				
SHALL LAMP THE RAVEN DARKNESS OF HER FACE,	....	57	GREEK PLAY	9
THE BRIGHT-EYED WORM ON DAVY'S LAMP,	....	92	BOYS OF SUMMER	35
SHALL RAISE A LAMP	....	114	SERVANT SUN	25
AND A LAMP OF LIGHTNING FOR THE POOR IN THE DARK;		144	COLOUR OF SAY	11
I'LL COMB THE SNARED WOODS WITH A GLOVE ON A LAMP,		145	IF HEAD HURT	7
LAMPED				
THE LAMPED CALLIGRAPHER, THE QUEEN IN SPLINTS,	....	120	ALTARWISE	115
LAMPLIGHT				
OF MINGLED MOONLIGHT AND LAMPLIGHT	....	43	FACES SHONE	2

		PAGE	TITLE	LINE
LAMP-POSTS				
OF LAMP-POSTS AND HIGH-VOLTED FRUITS,	....	70	SECRET WIND	16
LAMPS				
HOUSED IN HAMLETS OF HEAVEN SWING THE LOFT LAMPS,		215	COUNTRY HEAVEN	16
LANCE				
BELIEVES WHO DOES NOT LANCE HIS FAITH,	....	55	NO MAN BELIEVE	16
LAND				
OF THE GRAVE, GAY, SEASIDE LAND.	....	54	WE BY SEASAND	17
THE LAND LIES OUT OF SOUND	....	62	EARS IN TURRET	13
WHAT WERE YOUNG LIMBS ARE FAGGOTS ON THE LAND,	....	63	WOMAN SPEAKS	14
BUT ALL THIS LAND GIVES OFF A CHARNEL STENCH,	.....	67	REALM OF FLESH	4
UPON THE LAND OF GOLD OR OIL,	....	73	WE MOTHERNAKED	2
YOUR SOLID LAND.	....	74	WE MOTHERNAKED	16
TO BURST INTO A HANGING LAND	....	85	SEE, SAYS LIME	19
BREAKS ON UNANGLED LAND.	....	88	A PROCESS IN	12
AND CAST A SHADOW CRAB UPON THE LAND,	....	98	OCTOBER WIND	4
WITH FISTS OF TURNIPS PUNISHES THE LAND,	....	99	OCTOBER WIND	28
'THIS THAT WE TREAD WAS, TOO, YOUR FATHERS' LAND.'		101	FELLOWED SLEEP	12
THE GROOVED LAND ROTATING, THAT THE STYLUS OF				
LIGHTNING	....	110	I, IN IMAGE	68
THE SALT SUCKED DAM AND DARLINGS OF THE LAND	......	113	NOT FATHER ME	27
IN A LAND STRAPPED BY HUNGER	....	134	NOT FROM ANGER	4
A BRUTE LAND IN THE COOL TOP OF THE COUNTRY DAYS		135	HOW MY ANIMAL	15
SAID THE LOOKING LAND.	....	162	LONG-LEGGED	12
THE ROD BENDS LOW, DIVINING LAND,	....	167	LONG-LEGGED	165
LAND, LAND, LAND, NOTHING REMAINS	....	169	LONG-LEGGED	209
LAND, LAND, LAND, NOTHING REMAINS	....	169	LONG-LEGGED	209
LAND, LAND, LAND, NOTHING REMAINS	....	169	LONG-LEGGED	209
TO THE FISHERMAN LOST ON THE LAND.	....	169	LONG-LEGGED	214
THE LAND	....	182	VISION, PRAYER	83
TO THE HIDDEN LAND	....	185	VISION, PRAYER	192
IN THE LONG AGO LAND THAT GLIDED THE DARK DOOR WIDE		189	WINTER'S TALE	67
IN THE FAR AGO LAND THE DOOR OF HIS DEATH GLIDED WIDE		190	WINTER'S TALE	105
FOR THE SLEEP IN A SAFE LAND AND THE LOVE WHO DIES		194	CONVERS PRAYER	10
AND WAKE TO THE FARM FOREVER FLED FROM THE CHILDLESS				
LAND.	....	196	FERN HILL	51
IN THE LAND OF THE HEARTHSTONE TALES, AND SPELLED				
ASLEEP,	....	197	COUNTRY SLEEP	2
ALL THE LAND IS RIPE. THERE IS NO MOTION	....	222	FOREST PICTURE	5
LANDED				
AND THIS, NOR THIS, IS SHADE, THE LANDED CROW,	....	127	NOW, SAY NAY	19
LANDS				
THE WATER LIDDED LANDS,	....	5	PROLOGUE	94
THROUGH HADES' GROVES AND THE ETERNAL LANDS.	......	57	GREEK PLAY	24
DOWN FALL FOUR PADDING WEATHERS ON THE SCARLET LANDS,		122	HOLD HARD	19
BIRD THROUGH THE TIMES AND LANDS AND TRIBES OF THE				
SLOW FLAKES.	....	190	WINTER'S TALE	99
LANDSCAPE				
WORLD IN THE SAND, ON THE TRIANGLE LANDSCAPE,	.....	120	ALTARWISE	124
THE LANDSCAPE GRIEF, LOVE IN HIS OILS	....	129	MY NEOPHYTE	20
LANDWARD				
WHO SEEK ME LANDWARD, MARKING IN MY MOUTH	....	105	WORLD PYRAMID	46
LANE				
THIS TIDETHREAD AND THE LANE OF SCALES,	....	128	MY NEOPHYTE	14
LANES				
IN THE COURTERS' LANES, OR TWINED IN THE OX ROASTING				
SUN	....	203	GIANT'S THIGH	13
LANGUAGE				
AMONG THE TREES THE LANGUAGE OF THE DEAD	....	57	GREEK PLAY	13
AND ONE LIGHT'S LANGUAGE IN THE BOOK OF TREES.	....	119	ALTARWISE	89

	PAGE	TITLE	LINE
LANK			
MIGHT PLAY UPON HIS LANK LOCKS WITH ITS WIND, ...	46	POET: 1935	3
UNDER THE LANK, FOURTH FOLLY ON GLAMORGAN'S HILL,	122	HOLD HARD	2
SPILL THE LANK FOLLY'S HUNTER AND THE HARD-HELD HOPE.	122	HOLD HARD	18
LANTERNS			
SHOULD LANTERNS SHINE	116	LANTERNS SHINE	T
SHOULD LANTERNS SHINE, THE HOLY FACE, ...	116	LANTERNS SHINE	1
LAP			
LET THE TINY ARMIES LAP, ...	71	TAKE NEEDLES	10
INTO THE SIDED LAP OF LIGHT GREW STRONG, ...	78	LOVE'S FEVER	27
BENT LIKE A BEAST TO LAP THE SINGULAR FLOODS	134	NOT FROM ANGER	3
LAPPED			
'HIS MOTHER'S WOMB HAD A TONGUE THAT LAPPED UP MUD,'	132	I MAKE THIS IN	46
LAPPED AMONG HERODS WAIL	142	SAINT TO FALL	39
LAPPING			
INTO HER VEGETATION'S LAPPING MOUTHS	20	ENCOMPASSED	3
LAPPING THE STILL CANALS, THE DRY TIDE-MASTER	54	WE BY SEASAND	10
LAPS			
HAS STOLEN THE STARVED BABIES FROM THEIR LAPS, ...	96	TWELVE	4
SAND WITH LEGENDS IN ITS VIRGIN LAPS	167	LONG-LEGGED	172
LARGE			
AT LARGE AS THE DEAD, ...	169	LOVE IN ASYLUM	8
BETWEEN THE PYRAMIDS SO LARGE, ...	238	MAKES INTERVALS	2
LARK			
BEYOND THE BORDER AND UNDER THE LARK FULL CLOUD.	177	POEM IN OCT	37
LARKED			
GROW LARKED AND GREENER AT BERRY BROWN	211	POEM ON B'DAY	101
LARK-HIGH			
A STONE LIES LOST AND LOCKED IN THE LARK-HIGH HILL.	159	INTO HER HEAD	62
LARKS			
GUIDES AND BLOWS WICKEDLY, FOR LARKS	37	WINDMILLS TURN	7
A SPRINGFUL OF LARKS IN A ROLLING	177	POEM IN OCT	21
FALL AND THE DEW LARKS SING	211	POEM ON B'DAY	102
LASHED			
THROUGH THESE LASHED RINGS	76	LASHED RINGS	T
THROUGH THESE LASHED RINGS SET DEEP INSIDE THEIR HOLLOWS	76	LASHED RINGS	1
AND, LASHED TO SYLLABLES, THE LYNX TONGUE CRY	139	FIVE & COUNTRY	8
LASHES			
AND A TEAR-STAINED WIDOWER GRIEF DROOPED FROM THE LASHES	133	MAKE ME A MASK	9
LASS'S			
IN HIS AGE THE LASS'S CLAY.	75	SONG: LOVE ME	3
LAST			
BEFORE THE LAST LIGHT IS BLOWN	21	BEWILDERED WAY	24
AT LAST BY TIME, ...	26	PERSONAL EPIT	4
BEFORE THE GAS FADES WITH A HARSH LAST BUBBLE, ...	38	GAS FADES	1
BEFORE THE LAST FAG AND THE SHIRT SLEEVES AND SLIPPERS, ...	38	GAS FADES	3
UNTIL THE WHISPER OF THE LAST TRUMP LOUDEN	40	YOUNG ARE OLD	11
AND THE SHORES OF THE LAST SUN.	42	YOUNG ARE OLD	52
AT SIGHT OF DEATH, THE LAST TWO FISTED KILLER	59	FAIRY TALES	18
THESE DIE WHO SHOVEL THE LAST HOME OF MAN;	64	WOMAN SPEAKS	44
I WAS A MORTAL TO THE LAST	69	BEFORE KNOCKED	40
TO WOMEN WHO HAVE TWISTED THEIR LAST SMILE, ...	81	ALL THAT I OWE	16
IN LOVE'S LAST COLLAR.	86	SEE, SAYS LIME	24
EACH RUNG A LOVE OR LOSING TO THE LAST, ...	102	FELLOWED SLEEP	27
AND BREAKS HIS SHELL IN THE LAST SHOCKED BEGINNING;	124	TODAY, INSECT	13
THROUGH THE LAST VAULT AND VEGETABLE GROYNE, ...	131	I MAKE THIS IN	7
AND, PRIDE IS LAST, IS LIKE A CHILD ALONE	131	I MAKE THIS IN	13

	PAGE	TITLE	LINE
LAST (CONTINUED)			
THAT WILL RAKE AT LAST ALL CURRENCIES OF THE MARKED BREATH	140	NO WORK WORDS	8
ON THE LAST STREET WAVE PRAISED	141	SAINT TO FALL	4
ON THE ANGELIC ETNA OF THE LAST WHIRRING FEATHERLANDS,	141	SAINT TO FALL	11
ON THE LAST RICK'S TIP BY SPILLED WINE-WELLS	141	SAINT TO FALL	14
AND OFFER AS THE LAST DELIGHT	143	THE MOLLS	7
RASPED AT LAST, AND I STUMBLED AND SUCKED,	146	TO OTHERS	8
SLASHED DOWN THE LAST SNAKE AS THOUGH	150	WHEN I WOKE	13
THE LAST WAR'S PROFESSIONAL	154	RETURN	14
LAST NIGHT IN A RAPING WAVE	157	INTO HER HEAD	7
BLACKENED WITH BIRDS TOOK A LAST LOOK	161	LONG-LEGGED	2
LOOMS THE LAST SAMSON OF YOUR ZODIAC.	161	DEATHS AND ENT	36
AND TAKEN BY LIGHT IN HER ARMS AT LONG AND DEAR LAST	170	LOVE IN ASYLUM	16
LOVE IS THE LAST LIGHT SPOKEN. OH	174	FIRE RAID	31
LAST NIGHT I DIVED MY BEGGAR ARM	175	MY BEGGAR ARM	T
LAST NIGHT I DIVED MY BEGGAR ARM	175	MY BEGGAR ARM	1
PUTS IN HIS PENNY, GENEROUS AT LAST.	179	NEW QUAY	32
IF ONLY FOR A LAST TIME.	186	HOLY SPRING	24
VALES WHERE HE PRAYED TO COME TO THE LAST HARM	190	WINTER'S TALE	109
TELLS WITH SILENCE THE LAST LIGHT BREAKING	191	REFUSAL MOURN	4
IN THE LAST ELEMENT	193	SIDE OF TRUTH	23
HER FAITH THAT THIS LAST NIGHT FOR HIS UNSACRED SAKE	201	COUNTRY SLEEP	104
AT LAST THE SOUL FROM ITS FOUL MOUSEHOLE	207	LAMENT	43
INNOCENCE SWEETENS MY LAST BLACK BREATH,	207	LAMENT	58
GOOD MEN, THE LAST WAVE BY, CRYING HOW BRIGHT	208	NOT GO GENTLE	7
AND THE SCYTHED BOULDERS BLEED, AND THE LAST	210	POEM ON B'DAY	69
AND THIS LAST BLESSING MOST,	211	POEM ON B'DAY	90
HE LIE LIGHTLY, AT LAST, ON THE LAST, CROSSED	216	ELEGY	5
HE LIE LIGHTLY, AT LAST, ON THE LAST, CROSSED	216	ELEGY	5
OUT OF HIS EYES I SAW THE LAST LIGHT GLIDE.	217	ELEGY	28
HE CRIED AS HE DIED, FEARING AT LAST THE SPHERES'	217	ELEGY	33
LAST SOUND, THE WORLD GOING OUT WITHOUT A BREATH:	217	ELEGY	34
FLEW FOR A TIME IN VAIN, TO DROP AT LAST	238	PILLAR BREAKS	21
LASTED			
HOW MUCH WAS HAPPY WHILE IT LASTED,	32	OUT OF SIGHS	20
LASTING			
BURN OUT THE LASTING ROT,	60	FAIRY TALES	39
LASTS			
MAN'S MANMADE SPARETIME LASTS THE FOUR SEASONS,	39	GAS FADES	19
LATCH			
WINDS, FROM THE DOUSING SHADE AND THE ROARER AT THE LATCH,	199	COUNTRY SLEEP	46
LATCHED			
SHALL NOT BE LATCHED WHILE MAGIC GLIDES	91	WHERE ONCE THE	20
LATE			
O MY DEAR IT'S NEVER TOO LATE	149	PAPER & STICKS	11
MY PAID-FOR SLAVED-FOR OWN TOO LATE	151	BELOW A TIME	6
TOO LATE IN THE WRONG RAIN	161	WEDDING ANNIV	9
AND LEARN, TOO LATE, THEY GRIEVED IT ON ITS WAY,	208	NOT GO GENTLE	11
LATER			
AND THUS, SOME TIME LATER, I HEARD HIM SAY:	53	OUT OF THE PIT	89
AMONG MEN LATER I HEARD IT SAID	139	TOMBSTONE TOLD	16
LATERAL			
(TURN THE SEA-SPINDLE LATERAL,	110	I, IN IMAGE	67
LAUDS			
THE NIGHTBIRD LAUDS THROUGH NUNNERIES AND DOMES OF LEAVES	198	COUNTRY SLEEP	28

	PAGE	TITLE	LINE
LAUGH			
SLEEP, WAKE, AND SLEEP, EAT, LOVE, AND LAUGH, ...	28	NO WINGS	13
THAT THE VAMPIRE LAUGH.	104	WORLD PYRAMID	18
BY THE CURVE OF THE NUDE MOUTH OR THE LAUGH UP THE SLEEVE.	133	MAKE ME A MASK	12
LAUGHING			
IS LAUGHING BOY BENEATH HIS OATH, ...	19	THE NEOPHYTE	2
BIRD AFTER DARK AND THE LAUGHING FISH	166	LONG-LEGGED	126
LAUGHING WHEN HE SHOOK HIS PAPER	171	THE HUNCHBACK	20
LAUGHS			
SO THAT THE PROCESS CALLS FOR LAUGHS, ...	21	BEWILDERED WAY	18
LAUGHTER			
AND THE TRIUMPHANT CROW OF LAUGHTER.	48	POET: 1935	52
STILL SET TO SCRATCH A LAUGHTER FROM MY LUNG, ...	95	RUB OF LOVE	5
HEAR THEIR LAUGHTER SLY AS GONOCOCCI.	179	NEW QUAY	18
HARK! A VOICE AND LAUGHTER--THE LIVING AND LOVING	222	FOREST PICTURE	11
THAN OUR LAUGHTER AT THE AIR	230	OUR SANCTITY	13
OR THE GRACEFUL SOUND OF LAUGHTER.	235	WOMAN TAPESTRY	17
LAVA			
ALL FROM THE OIL, THE POUND OF LAVA.	106	ALL ALL AND	3
LAVA'S			
BY LAVA'S LIGHT SPLIT THROUGH THE OYSTER VOWELS ...	119	ALTARWISE	73
LAW			
THE LAW ALLOWS	29	NEARLY SUMMER	9
LAWED			
LAWED AND ORDERED FROM ON HIGH	72	TAKE NEEDLES	39
LAWLESS			
HE COMES TO LEAVE HER IN THE LAWLESS SUN AWAKING	201	COUNTRY SLEEP	105
LAWN			
A MEASURE ON THE LAWN WHERE CUPIDS BLEW	51	OUT OF THE PIT	25
LAWNS			
LEANING FROM WINDOWS OVER A LENGTH OF LAWNS, ...	48	POET: 1935	60
LAWS			
AND THE SKY LAYS DOWN HER LAWS, ...	61	MEAT ON BONES	34
LAY			
WHEN WISDOM LAY NOT IN THE SOUL	25	BEAUTY TO DUST	12
OR LAY THE SENSES' RUMOUR.	30	NEARLY SUMMER	13
LAY YOUR HEAD ON A HARD BED OF STONE, ...	45	PLOUGHMAN GONE	17
LAY YOUR HEAD ON A HARD BED OF STONE, ...	46	PLOUGHMAN GONE	31
LIKE CATS, AND LUSTS LAY HALF HOT IN THE COLD.	50	OUT OF THE PIT	5
LAY THE GOLD TITHINGS BARREN, ...	91	BOYS OF SUMMER	2
AND LAY THE WET FRUITS LOW.	91	WHERE ONCE THE	12
THE GENTLEMAN LAY GRAVEWARD WITH HIS FURIES;	116	ALTARWISE	2
IN THAT BRIGHT ANCHORGROUND WHERE I LAY LINENED,	132	I MAKE THIS IN	48
AND THE STRUTTING FERN LAY SEEDS ON THE BLACK SILL.	137	AFTER FUNERAL	40
BEFORE SHE LAY ON A STRANGER'S BED	139	TOMBSTONE TOLD	11
THOUGH THE TOWN BELOW LAY LEAVED WITH OCTOBER BLOOD.	178	POEM IN OCT	67
FOR THE BIRD LAY BEDDED	191	WINTER'S TALE	121
TO LABOUR AND LOVE THOUGH THEY LAY DOWN LONG AGO.	203	GIANT'S THIGH	5
YOUNG AS THEY IN THE AFTER MILKING MOONLIGHT LAY	204	GIANT'S THIGH	16
LAYERS			
UNDER THE HEAVY LAYERS OF THE NIGHT	39	GAS FADES	38
LAYING			
DESTROYING SOULS AND LAYING WASTE, ...	33	IN GARDENS	8
LAYING MY GHOST IN METAL, ...	108	I, IN IMAGE	3
LAYS			
AND THE SKY LAYS DOWN HER LAWS, ...	61	MEAT ON BONES	34
HIS HEAD'S IN A NEST WHERE NO BIRD LAYS HER EGG.	179	NEW QUAY	27
LAZARUS			
CROWING TO LAZARUS THE MORNING IS VANITY, ...	110	I, IN IMAGE	59

	PAGE	TITLE	LINE
LAZARUS (CONTINUED)			
NOW COMMON LAZARUS	184	VISION, PRAYER	166
LAZY			
FOR A LAZY SAKE THAT WON'T CREATE	24	LITTLE PROBLEM	23
LEA			
BORROW MY EYES. THE DARKENING SEA FLINGS LEA	179	NEW QUAY	2
LEAD			
THAT LEAD AWAY TO DIRTY TOWNS	37	WINDMILLS TURN	14
BUT WAYS HAVE CHANGED, AND MOST WAYS LEAD	37	WINDMILLS TURN	20
LEADS, TOO, TO A LEAD PIT, WHINNY AND FALL,	44	TO FOLLOW FOX	10
AND TERRIBLY LEAD HIM HOME ALIVE	168	LONG-LEGGED	198
LEAD HER PRODIGAL HOME TO HIS TERROR,	168	LONG-LEGGED	199
LEADEN			
THE LEADEN STARS, THE RAINY HAMMER	68	BEFORE KNOCKED	11
WRENCHED BY MY FINGERMAN, THE LEADEN BUD	115	A GRIEF AGO	11
LEADS			
LEADS TO FOOL'S PARADISE WHERE THE REDCOATED KILLER	44	TO FOLLOW FOX	5
LEADS, TOO, TO A LEAD PIT, WHINNY AND FALL,	44	TO FOLLOW FOX	10
WISELY AT THE DOGS' TAILS, LEADS	44	TO FOLLOW FOX	15
AND THIS WAY LEADS TO GOOD AND BAD,	45	TO FOLLOW FOX	22
THE MIGHTY HAND LEADS TO A SLOPING SHOULDER,	66	HAND SIGNED	5
BUT HEART, LIKE HEAD, LEADS HELPLESSLY;	116	LANTERNS SHINE	10
AND THE DEAD HAND LEADS THE PAST,	167	LONG-LEGGED	148
LEADS THEM AS CHILDREN AND AS AIR	167	LONG-LEGGED	149
LEAF			
STITCH THE STEM ON TO THE LEAF,	72	TAKE NEEDLES	51
SHOT THROUGH THE LEAF,	115	A GRIEF AGO	12
ITS TONGUE PEELED IN THE WRAP OF A LEAF.	150	WHEN I WOKE	15
BRANCH AND LEAF THE BIRDLESS ROOFS;	156	RETURN	83
LEAF DRIFTWOOD THAT HAS BLOWN.	226	THE ELM	10
LEAF-LIKE			
FOR ALL THINGS ARE LEAF-LIKE	225	OF ANY FLOWER	2
LEAFY			
LOVERS IN THE DIRT OF THEIR LEAFY BEDS,	144	COLOUR OF SAY	9
LEAGUES			
FARMER IN TIME OF FROST THE BURNING LEAGUES,	123	FOSTER LIGHT	10
LEAK			
LET THE SAP LEAK IN THE BREEZE.	72	TAKE NEEDLES	52
LEAKING			
FROM BLANK AND LEAKING WINTER SAILS THE CHILD IN COLOUR,	130	SINNERS' BELL	22
LEAKS			
DRIVES IN A DEATH AS LIFE LEAKS OUT.	88	A PROCESS IN	9
LEAN			
LEAN TIME ON TIDE AND TIMES THE WIND STOOD ROUGH,	107	GRIEF THIEF	6
ON NO WORK OF WORDS NOW FOR THREE LEAN MONTHS IN THE BLOODY	140	NO WORK WORDS	1
ONE LEAN SIGH WHEN WE HEARD	153	WAS A SAVIOUR	29
LEANING			
LEANING FROM WINDOWS OVER A LENGTH OF LAWNS,	48	POET: 1935	60
(HAVE WITH THE HOUSE OF WIND), THE LEANING SCENE,	101	RUNNING GRAVE	42
LEANS			
LEANS ON MY MORTAL RULER,	75	MY HERO BARES	4
SUMMER IS HEAVY WITH AGE, AND LEANS UPON AUTUMN.	221	FOREST PICTURE	4
WHICH LEANS ONE WAY,	232	FURIOUS MOTION	10
LEANT			
AND LEANT ON STILES AND ON THE GOLDEN BAR,	52	OUT OF THE PIT	66
LEAP			
LEAP OVER TO MY CRISS-CROSS RHYTHMS.	33	HELD-OUT HAND	23

	PAGE	TITLE	LINE
LEAP (CONTINUED)			
A LIMP AND RIDERLESS SHAPE TO LEAP NINE THINNING MONTHS.'	145	IF HEAD HURT	15
AND ALL THE LIFTED WATERS WALK AND LEAP.	165	LONG-LEGGED	112
LEAP, AS TO TRUMPETS. CALLIGRAPHY OF THE OLD	189	WINTER'S TALE	77
LOPING AND BLEATING ROUGHLY AND BLITHELY SHALL LEAP,	197	COUNTRY SLEEP	4
LEAPED			
WIND IN ME LEAPED, THE HELLBORN DEW;	68	BEFORE KNOCKED	16
YOU HAVE KICKED FROM A DARK DEN, LEAPED UP THE WHINNYING LIGHT,	135	HOW MY ANIMAL	43
LEAPING			
THAT LEAPING VEINS THREW TO THE WIND	85	SEE, SAYS LIME	11
OR LAME THE AIR WITH LEAPING FROM ITS HEATS;	92	BOYS OF SUMMER	21
DUMBLY AND DIVINELY LEAPING	125	SEED-AT-ZERO	13
THE LEAPING SAGA OF PRAYER! AND HIGH, THERE, ON THE HARE-	199	COUNTRY SLEEP	66
LEAPING! THE GOSPEL ROOKS! ALL TELL, THIS NIGHT, OF HIM	200	COUNTRY SLEEP	80
WHITE, GOD'S BRIGHT, FLOCKS, THE BELLED LAMBS LEAPING,	215	COUNTRY HEAVEN	21
LEAPS			
A NITRIC SHAPE THAT LEAPS HER, TIME AND ACID;	115	A GRIEF AGO	34
THE SUN THAT LEAPS ON PETALS THROUGH A NOUGHT,	128	NOW, SAY NAY	27
LEAPT			
FROM POLE TO POLE LEAPT ROUND THE SNAIL-WAKED WORLD.	120	ALTARWISE	108
AND THIS DAY'S SUN LEAPT UP THE SKY OUT OF HER THIGHS	170	MARRIAGE VIRG	4
FOR A MAN SLEEPS WHERE FIRE LEAPT DOWN AND SHE LEARNS THROUGH HIS ARM	170	MARRIAGE VIRG	13
LEAR			
JUAN AFLAME AND SAVAGELY YOUNG KING LEAR,	157	INTO HER HEAD	11
LEARN			
LEARN TO BE MERRY WITH THE MERRIEST,	33	HELD-OUT HAND	7
UNLESS I LEARN THE NIGHT I SHALL GO MAD.	48	LIGHT, I KNOW	12
IT IS NIGHT'S TERRORS I MUST LEARN TO LOVE,	48	LIGHT, I KNOW	13
I MUST LEARN NIGHT'S LIGHT OR GO MAD.	49	LIGHT, I KNOW	30
I SHOULD LEARN SPRING BY THE CUCKOOING,	58	HERE IN SPRING	12
SHALL WE LEARN FAIRY TALES OFF PAT,	60	FAIRY TALES	37
BE SOUR IN MY HAIR. THAT I MAY LEARN	65	WOMAN SPEAKS	63
SO THE BETRAYED MIGHT LEARN IN THE SUN BEAMS	176	MY BEGGAR ARM	7
AND LEARN, TOO LATE, THEY GRIEVED IT ON ITS WAY,	208	NOT GO GENTLE	11
LEARNS			
HE LEARNS THE CARRION PICKERS OF THE SKY,	63	WOMAN SPEAKS	21
FOR A MAN SLEEPS WHERE FIRE LEAPT DOWN AND SHE LEARNS THROUGH HIS ARM	170	MARRIAGE VIRG	13
THAT HE WHO LEARNS NOW THE SUN AND MOON	183	VISION, PRAYER	119
LEARNT			
I LEARNT MAN'S TONGUE, TO TWIST THE SHAPES OF THOUGHTS	79	LOVE'S FEVER	32
I LEARNT THE VERBS OF WILL, AND HAD MY SECRET;	79	LOVE'S FEVER	39
FROM THE DIVORCING SKY I LEARNT THE DOUBLE,	79	LOVE'S FEVER	44
LEAST			
NOR COULD SHARE, FOR HIS PRIDE, TO THE LEAST	158	INTO HER HEAD	44
WHEN ONE AT THE GREAT LEAST OF YOUR BEST LOVED	160	DEATHS AND ENT	3
UNTIL THAT ONE LOVED LEAST	161	DEATHS AND ENT	35
IN THE LEAST VALLEY OF SACKCLOTH TO MOURN	191	REFUSAL MOURN	12
LEAVE			
LEAVE YOU IN ME TO BE FOUND	9	MINUTE'S HOUR	10
BUT LEAVE BUT STILL ADORE	11	AIR BREATHE	8
GONE FROM MY PALM TO LEAVE IT MARKED	12	CABARET	16
AND, CRACKLING INTO THE AIR, LEAVE ME HALF-BLIND.	44	LONGED TO MOVE	14

		PAGE	TITLE	LINE
LEAVE (CONTINUED)				
TO LEAVE IT EMPTY'S LION'S OR LOUSE'S CHOICE;	.....	58	TO ARCHITECTS	16
SHALL FALL AWAY, AND LEAVE ONE SINGING SHELL.	.....	73	LORD RED HAIL	12
WOULD LEAVE ME COLD AS BUTTER FOR THE FLIES,	......	95	RUB OF LOVE	26
AND LEAVE THE POPPIED PICKTHANK WHERE HE LIES;	....	98	TWILIGHT LOCKS	39
TO LIFT TO LEAVE FROM THE TREASURES OF MAN IS PLEASING DEATH	....	140	NO WORK WORDS	7
AND ALWAYS KNOWN MUST LEAVE	....	160	DEATHS AND ENT	4
HE COMES TO LEAVE HER IN THE LAWLESS SUN AWAKING		201	COUNTRY SLEEP	105
WE GRIEVE AS THE BLITHE BIRDS, NEVER AGAIN, LEAVE SHINGLE AND ELM,	....	202	SIR JOHNS HILL	33
THE WHOLE OF THE MOON I COULD LOVE AND LEAVE	......	206	LAMENT	10
UNTIL I DIE HE WILL NOT LEAVE MY SIDE.	....	217	ELEGY	40
AND LEAVE A CLEAR PRINT,	....	229	MY RIVER	8
AND LEAVE A TUNNEL	....	229	MY RIVER	11
LEAVED				
HOPPING HOT LEAVED AND FEATHERED	....	151	BELOW A TIME	20
THOUGH THE TOWN BELOW LAY LEAVED WITH OCTOBER BLOOD.		178	POEM IN OCT	67
UNDER THE ONE LEAVED TREES RAN A SCARECROW OF SNOW		190	WINTER'S TALE	94
HILL. WHO ONCE IN GOOSESKIN WINTER LOVED ALL ICE LEAVED	....	203	GIANT'S THIGH	12
TEACH ME THE LOVE THAT IS EVERGREEN AFTER THE FALL LEAVED	....	205	GIANT'S THIGH	53
ALL THE GREEN LEAVED LITTLE WEDDINGS' WIVES	....	206	LAMENT	11
LEAVES				
OUT OF THESE SEATHUMBED LEAVES	....	3	PROLOGUE	29
LIKE LEAVES OF TREES AND AS SOON	....	3	PROLOGUE	31
PADDLE WITH LEAVES	....	13	RAIN CUTS	7
ABOVE A BOAT OF LEAVES AND WEEDS.	....	14	RAIN CUTS	24
TOO STIFF TO CHURN WITH LEAVES,	....	14	RAIN CUTS	27
SPEWING ITS SAPLESS LEAVES AROUND,	....	26	THERE'S PLENTY	10
CHALK COOLED BY LEAVES IN THE HOT SEASON,	....	29	LONG, SKELETON	3
RAPES, LEAVES FOR LOST (THE AMORIST!),	....	30	NEARLY SUMMER	16
LEAVES IT AMONG THE CIGARETTE ENDS AND THE GLASSES.		30	NEARLY SUMMER	23
NO FAITH TO SHARPEN THE OLD WITS LEAVES US	....	41	YOUNG ARE OLD	21
FROM THE UNWATERED LEAVES AND THE STIFF STALKS,	...	47	POET: 1935	39
ANSWER: WHEN THE GREEN LEAVES PRIZE HER.	....	72	TAKE NEEDLES	64
MY MAN OF LEAVES AND THE BRONZE ROOT, MORTAL, UNMORTAL,	....	109	I, IN IMAGE	16
IN THE DARK OF THE COFFIN AND SHEDS DRY LEAVES,	...	136	AFTER FUNERAL	8
WHERE BIRDS RIDE LIKE LEAVES AND BOATS LIKE DUCKS		150	WHEN I WOKE	22
AND COUNT BY BIRDS' EGGS AND LEAVES	....	157	RETURN	97
WITH HIS STICK THAT PICKED UP LEAVES.	....	171	THE HUNCHBACK	24
ON THE GRISTED LEAVES AND THE LONG GONE GLISTENING		189	WINTER'S TALE	63
LEAVES IS DANCING. LINES OF AGE ON THE STONES WEAVE IN A FLOCK.	....	189	WINTER'S TALE	78
AND ONCE BELOW A TIME I LORDLY HAD THE TREES AND LEAVES	....	195	FERN HILL	7
OUT OF A LAIR IN THE FLOCKED LEAVES IN THE DEW DIPPED YEAR	....	197	COUNTRY SLEEP	6
THE NIGHTBIRD LAUDS THROUGH NUNNERIES AND DOMES OF LEAVES	....	198	COUNTRY SLEEP	28
OF THE MORNING LEAVES, AS THE STAR FALLS, AS THE WINGED	....	199	COUNTRY SLEEP	60
OF THE WOOD! PASTORAL BEAT OF BLOOD THROUGH THE LACED LEAVES!	....	199	COUNTRY SLEEP	71
I OPEN THE LEAVES OF THE WATER AT A PASSAGE	....	202	SIR JOHNS HILL	23
THROUGH NAVES OF LEAVES,	....	215	COUNTRY HEAVEN	10
AND NIGHT, WHO STOOPED TO KISS THE PALLID LEAVES		223	IN DREAMS	5
ENVELOPING THE RAGGED LEAVES UNSEEN AND STREWN.	...	226	THE OAK	2

	PAGE	TITLE	LINE
LEAVES (CONTINUED)			
AND IS MORE BEAUTIFUL THAN THE DRIFT OF LEAVES. ...	226	SLENDER WIND	9
OUR BRANCHES AND HOLY LEAVES	230	OUR SANCTITY	4
WHO SAILS ON TIDES OF LEAVES AND SOUND.	234	NO, PIGEON	16
THEIR DELICATE, SILKEN LEAVES FOLDED, ...	235	WOMAN TAPESTRY	8
LEAVING			
LEAVING A CORRUPTED VEIN OF COLOUR, ...	27	OBLIVIOUS DARK	16
THROUGH NO REGRET OF LEAVING WOMAN WAITING	32	OUT OF SIGHS	14
LIGHT WALKS THE SKY, LEAVING NO PRINT, ...	49	LIGHT, I KNOW	17
LEAVING NO PRINT.	49	LIGHT, I KNOW	21
CUT. CUT THE CRUSHED STREETS, LEAVING	156	RETURN	77
AND O TO CUT THE GREEN FIELD, LEAVING	157	RETURN	100
LECHERED			
BEACH, HEARING RISE SLIMY FROM THE WELSH LECHERED	179	NEW QUAY	16
LEDA			
THE MORNING, SPACE FOR LEDA	14	FOR LEDA	T
THE MORNING, SPACE FOR LEDA	14	FOR LEDA	1
WHEN LEDA, ON A TOE OF DOWN, ...	15	FOR LEDA	29
REQUEST TO LEDA	159	TO LEDA	T
LED-ASTRAY			
OF THE LED-ASTRAY BIRDS WHOM GOD, FOR THEIR BREAST			
OF WHISTLES, ...	202	SIR JOHNS HILL	43
LEDGES			
LEDGES OF WAVES HIGH OVER YOUR HEAD, ...	228	MY RIVER	2
LEECH			
THE LIPS OF TIME LEECH TO THE FOUNTAIN HEAD;	77	THE FORCE THAT	16
LEECHES			
WITH A HOLD OF LEECHES AND STRAWS, ...	142	SAINT TO FALL	24
LEERED			
THE MOON LEERED DOWN THE VALLEY LIKE A FOOL.	50	OUT OF THE PIT	12
THE MOON LEERED DOWN THE VALLEY LIKE A FOOL.	51	OUT OF THE PIT	32
LEERS			
LEERS DOWN THE VALLEY LIKE A FOOL	33	HELD-OUT HAND	19
LEFT			
THE ANGEL'S HURT IS LEFT;	12	SKY'S BRIGHT	18
THE MARK HIS FLYING TAIL HAS LEFT	14	RAIN CUTS	21
THE DRY FEVER BURNS UNTIL NO HEART IS LEFT, ...	34	THIRST PARCHES	2
BEFORE WHITE OR BLACK, THE RIGHT OR LEFT SOCK, ...	39	GAS FADES	17
NOT BLACK OR WHITE OR LEFT OR RIGHT.	39	GAS FADES	39
THE LIVING DEAD LEFT OVER FROM THE WAR, ...	41	YOUNG ARE OLD	35
LEFT IN THE RECORDS OF LIVING A NOT-TO-BE-BROKEN			
PICTURE, ...	45	PLOUGHMAN GONE	2
LEFT ONLY THE VOICE IN THE OLD VILLAGE CHOIR	45	PLOUGHMAN GONE	4
BUT HE IS LEFT. SUMMER TO HIM	46	POET: 1935	16
CRYING SUCH WORDS, HE LEFT THE CRYING CROWDS, ...	53	OUT OF THE PIT	82
THERE CAN BE FEW TEARS LEFT: ELECTRA WEPT	57	GREEK PLAY	17
THAT DUST YOU HOLD, O STREW THAT LITTLE LEFT;	65	WOMAN SPEAKS	61
REMAINS THOUGH GODS BE FELLED TILL NONE ARE LEFT.	67	LET A FAITH	10
LEFT BY THE DEAD WHO, IN THEIR MOONLESS ACRE, ...	79	LOVE'S FEVER	35
THE WEED OF LOVE'S LEFT DRY;	91	WHERE ONCE THE	15
TOUCHED THE FIRST CLOUD AND LEFT A SIGN.	94	IN BEGINNING	12
HEAVEN FELL WITH HIS FALL AND ONE CROCKED BELL BEAT			
THE LEFT AIR.	142	SAINT TO FALL	25
THERE IS NOTHING LEFT OF THE SEA BUT ITS SOUND, ...	169	LONG-LEGGED	205
SEED OF SONS IN THE LOIN OF THE BLACK HUSK LEFT.	174	FIRE RAID	32
BLACK NIGHT, I LEFT MY QUIVERING PRINTS.	206	LAMENT	24
LEG			
A LEG AS LONG AS TREES, ...	114	SERVANT SUN	29
HATCHED FROM THE WINDY SALVAGE ON ONE LEG, ...	117	ALTARWISE	10
HE CUTS HIMSELF ON AN ELDER'S RAZOR LEG.	179	NEW QUAY	28

	PAGE	TITLE	LINE
LEGAL			
THE BRAIN ACTS TO THE LEGAL DEAD.	67	REALM OF FLESH	9
LEGEND			
THE HERO'S HEAD LIES SCRAPED OF EVERY LEGEND, ...	132	I MAKE THIS IN	43
I KNOW THE LEGEND	174	FIRE RAID	47
LEGENDARY			
A LEGENDARY HORSE WITH HOOF AND FEATHER, ...	13	RAIN CUTS	17
LEGENDS			
SAND WITH LEGENDS IN ITS VIRGIN LAPS	167	LONG-LEGGED	172
AND THE LEGENDS OF THE GREEN CHAPELS	178	POEM IN OCT	50
LEGENDS'			
ALL LEGENDS' SWEETHEARTS ON A TREE OF STORIES, ...	125	TODAY, INSECT	25
LEGION			
THE TOPS OF TREES, NOR AS THE LEGION	76	SONG: LOVE ME	10
STAR AND COUNTRY TO THE LEGION	184	VISION, PRAYER	154
LEGS			
THE OLD FLOWERS' LEGS TOO TAUT TO DANCE, ...	47	POET: 1935	40
LEISURE			
THE BITTER, THE WICKED, THE LONGLYING LEISURE, ...	39	GAS FADES	21
LEMURAL			
VOICES HAVE CALLED, AND THE ANSWERS LEMURAL WHISPERS			
FROM THE SEA;	224	IDYLL UNFORGET	34
LEND			
TIME IS THE TUNE MY LADIES LEND THEIR HEARTBREAK,	119	ALTARWISE	95
LENDS			
LENDS NOT FLESH TO RIBS AND NECK, ...	55	NO MAN BELIEVE	23
LENGTH			
THEIR LEVEL IS THE LENGTH	24	LITTLE PROBLEM	3
LEANING FROM WINDOWS OVER A LENGTH OF LAWNS, ...	48	POET: 1935	60
MEASURES HIS OWN LENGTH ON THE GARDEN WALL	124	TODAY, INSECT	12
LEPER			
LEPER AMONG A CLEAN PEOPLE	47	POET: 1935	26
WITH THE LEPER AND THE LAMB.	71	TAKE NEEDLES	32
LEPERS'			
OR SANSKRIT PSALMS ON LEPERS' CHESTS.	83	LETTER TO AUNT	28
LESSENS			
IS EMPTY IN SPRINGTIME, AND NO OTHER TIME LESSENS	39	GAS FADES	20
LET			
TOO FULL WITH BLOOD TO LET MY LOVE FLOW IN.	9	MINUTE'S HOUR	12
FROM THE STONE NEST IT DOES NOT LET THE FEATHERY	15	SPIRE CRANES	2
LET THE TWO DULL STONES BE GREY, ...	19	IMAGES IN AIR	4
CHRIST, LET ME WRITE FROM THE HEART, ...	22	HIGH ON A HILL	7
LIFT UP YOUR HEAD, LET	35	LIFT UP FACE	10
LET COMFORT COME SLOWLY, LIFT	35	LIFT UP FACE	14
LET IT BE KNOWN	36	LET BE KNOWN	T
LET IT BE KNOWN THAT LITTLE LIVE BUT LIES, ...	36	LET BE KNOWN	1
LET CHILDREN KNOW, AND OLD MEN AT THEIR GATES, ...	36	LET BE KNOWN	3
DECLARE THEIR SOULS, LET CHILDREN KNOW, LIVE AFTER.	36	LET BE KNOWN	6
A SMILE LET LOOSE A DEVIL, A BELL STRUCK.	51	OUT OF THE PIT	19
STOPPED NON-STOP DANCING TO LET HOT FEET COOL, ...	51	OUT OF THE PIT	30
EMPTY, TO LET, ARE SIGNS ON THIS NEW HOUSE;	58	TO ARCHITECTS	15
LET ME NOT THINK, OF GOD OF CARNAGE, ...	63	WOMAN SPEAKS	16
SHALL I LET IN THE STRANGER, ...	63	EARS IN TURRET	29
THAT I MAY DROWN, LET LOOSE HER FLOOD OF TEARS. ...	65	WOMAN SPEAKS	55
LET WHAT REMAINS OF THAT FIRST MIRACLE	65	WOMAN SPEAKS	62
THE MORTAL MIRACLE, LET THAT FIRST DUST	65	WOMAN SPEAKS	64
LET FOR ONE MOMENT A FAITH STATEMENT	66	LET A FAITH	T
LET FOR ONE MOMENT A FAITH STATEMENT	66	LET A FAITH	1
FLUNG GRAVEL CHIME? LET THE STONES SPEAK	66	GODS THUMP	13
A CIRCLE SPINS. LET EACH REVOLVING SPOKE	67	LET A FAITH	4

	PAGE	TITLE	LINE
LET (CONTINUED)			
LET FOR ONE MOMENT A FAITH STATEMENT	67	LET A FAITH	6
LET FOR ONE MOMENT A FAITH STATEMENT	67	LET A FAITH	11
BEFORE I KNOCKED AND FLESH LET ENTER, ...	68	BEFORE KNOCKED	1
LET A MAGGOT AT THE EAR	70	TAKE NEEDLES	3
LET ME IN THE DEVIL'S GROVES	70	TAKE NEEDLES	5
LET THE MAGGOT OF DESPAIR	70	TAKE NEEDLES	7
LET THE TINY ARMIES LAP, ...	71	TAKE NEEDLES	10
LET IT BE A SWORD OF FIRE, ...	71	TAKE NEEDLES	21
LET THE SAP LEAK IN THE BREEZE.	72	TAKE NEEDLES	52
HE SHALL BE WISE AND LET HIS BRIMSTONE SPILL, ...	73	LORD RED HAIL	3
THIS FLESH YOU BREAK, THIS BLOOD YOU LET	86	BREAD I BREAK	11
WE ARE THE DARK DENIERS, LET US SUMMON	92	BOYS OF SUMMER	31
AND BAGS OF BLOOD LET OUT THEIR FLIES;	97	TWILIGHT LOCKS	23
SOME LET ME MAKE YOU OF THE VOWELLED BEECHES, ...	99	OCTOBER WIND	13
SOME LET ME MAKE YOU OF THE WATER'S SPEECHES.	99	OCTOBER WIND	16
SOME LET ME MAKE YOU OF THE MEADOW'S SIGNS;	99	OCTOBER WIND	21
SOME LET ME TELL YOU OF THE RAVEN'S SINS.	99	OCTOBER WIND	24
(SOME LET ME MAKE YOU OF AUTUMNAL SPELLS, ...	99	OCTOBER WIND	26
SOME LET ME MAKE YOU OF THE HEARTLESS WORDS.	99	OCTOBER WIND	29
LET FALL THE TEAR OF TIME; THE SLEEPER'S EYE, ...	101	FELLOWED SLEEP	2
NOW JACK MY FATHERS LET THE TIME-FACED CROOK, ...	108	GRIEF THIEF	15
LET THE WAX DISK BABBLE	110	I, IN IMAGE	70
LET THE SOIL SQUEAL I AM THE BITING MAN	114	SERVANT SUN	20
LET HER INHALE HER DEAD, THROUGH SEED AND SOLID ...	115	A GRIEF AGO	37
ARE FORMED OF FLESH, BUT LET THE FALSE DAY COME ...	116	LANTERNS SHINE	6
LET THE TALE'S SAILOR FROM A CHRISTIAN VOYAGE	121	ALTARWISE	127
LET THE FIRST PETER FROM A RAINBOW'S QUAYRAIL	121	ALTARWISE	133
GREEN AS BEGINNING, LET THE GARDEN DIVING	121	ALTARWISE	137
LET THE HERO SEED FIND HARBOUR, ...	126	SEED-AT-ZERO	33
LET THE HERO SEED FIND HARBOUR, ...	126	SEED-AT-ZERO	40
ITS WRINGING SHELL, AND LET HER EYELIDS FASTEN. ...	132	I MAKE THIS IN	35
TO VEIL BELLADONNA AND LET THE DRY EYES PERCEIVE	133	MAKE ME A MASK	10
BUMP ON A SPOUT LET THE BUBBLES JUMP OUT.	145	IF HEAD HURT	3
THE SPONGEBAG LET THEM ALL MELT.	155	RETURN	36
THAT HE LET THE DEAD LIE THOUGH THEY MOAN	184	VISION, PRAYER	136
BUT LET IT BREAK	184	VISION, PRAYER	147
O LET HIM	185	VISION, PRAYER	198
SHALL I LET PRAY THE SHADOW OF A SOUND	191	REFUSAL MOURN	10
TIME LET ME HAIL AND CLIMB	195	FERN HILL	4
TIME LET ME PLAY AND BE	195	FERN HILL	13
COME LET US DIE.'	202	SIR JOHNS HILL	32
IN THE COAL BLACK BUSH AND LET THEM GRIEVE.	206	LAMENT	12
OH, LET ME MIDLIFE MOURN BY THE SHRINED	211	POEM ON B'DAY	76
LET HIM FIND NO REST BUT THE FATHERED AND FOUND,	216	ELEGY	12
SAYING YOU WOULD LET THE CHILL SEAS PASS, ...	227	SPRING-SPIRIT	7
AND LET YOU FLOAT.'	231	OUR SANCTITY	31
YOU SHALL NOT LET GO;	233	FURIOUS MOTION	19
LET ME BELIEVE IN THE CLEAN FAITH OF THE BODY, ...	235	WOMAN TAPESTRY	24
LET ME BELIEVE IN THE CLEAN FAITH OF THE BODY, ...	237	WOMAN TAPESTRY	79
LET ME CHANGE TO BLUE, ...	238	MAKES INTERVALS	7
LET ME ESCAPE	239	LET ME ESCAPE	T
LET ME ESCAPE, ...	239	LET ME ESCAPE	1
OH, LET ME DESTROY FOR ONCE, ...	239	MAKES INTERVALS	22
LET THE FROST HARDEN	240	ADMIT THE SUN	5
LETHAL			
SLENDERLY LETHAL THINGS, ...	226	THE ELM	8
LETS			
AND LETS THEIR TRASH BE HONOURED AS THE QUICK.	90	EUNUCH DREAMS	35
THAT LETS THE TREES AND WATER ENTER	171	THE HUNCHBACK	5

	PAGE	TITLE	LINE
LETS (CONTINUED)			
WHO LETS HIS OWN ROD BE	240	TWINING HEAD	6
LET'S			
LET'S HOPE YOU WON'T THINK ME TOO VICIOUS.	221	SONG OF DOG	16
LETTER			
A LETTER TO MY AUNT DISCUSSING THE CORRECT APPROACH TO MODERN POETRY	83	LETTER TO AUNT	T
ON HOW THE GALLIC LETTER BENDS;	84	LETTER TO AUNT	51
PROPHETS AND FIBRE KINGS IN OIL AND LETTER,	120	ALTARWISE	114
LETTERED			
DOWN TO THE WILD, UMBRELLA'D, AND FRENCH LETTERED	179	NEW QUAY	15
LETTERS			
ABSTRACTED ALL THE LETTERS OF THE VOID;	94	IN BEGINNING	21
LETTING			
AFRAID, LETTING OUR SYLLABLES BE SOFT	31	BEING BUT MEN	2
LEVEL			
ARE ON SANDY SOIL THEIR SPIRIT LEVEL;	24	LITTLE PROBLEM	2
THEIR LEVEL IS THE LENGTH	24	LITTLE PROBLEM	3
SAIL ON THE LEVEL, THE DEPARTING ADVENTURE,	109	I, IN IMAGE	35
HOW SOON MY LEVEL, LORD,	114	SERVANT SUN	22
TILL FIELD AND ROOF LIE LEVEL AND THE SAME	116	LANTERNS SHINE	13
LEVELS			
I, IN MY INTRICATE IMAGE, STRIDE ON TWO LEVELS,	108	I, IN IMAGE	1
LEVER			
ALL ALL AND ALL THE DRY WORLDS LEVER	106	ALL ALL AND	T
ALL ALL AND ALL THE DRY WORLDS LEVER,	106	ALL ALL AND	1
ALL OF THE FLESH, THE DRY WORLDS LEVER.	106	ALL ALL AND	12
KNOW, O MY BONE, THE JOINTED LEVER,	106	ALL ALL AND	22
LEWD			
AND HEARD THE LEWD, WOOED FIELD FLOW TO THE COMING FROST,	204	GIANT'S THIGH	30
LIBIDINOUS			
LIBIDINOUS BETRAYAL,	158	INTO HER HEAD	54
LICE			
KEATINGS IS GOOD FOR LICE,	58	TO ARCHITECTS	12
LICK			
SAVOURS THE LICK OF THE TIMES THROUGH A DEADLY WOOD OF HAIR	144	PLEASURE-BIRD	9
LIDDED			
THE WATER LIDDED LANDS,	5	PROLOGUE	94
LIDS			
THE FILM OF SPRING IS HANGING FROM THE LIDS.	82	LIGHT BREAKS	24
DRY AS A TOMB, YOUR COLOURED LIDS	91	WHERE ONCE THE	19
GRAVE'S FOOT, BLINDS DOWN THE LIDS, THE TEETH IN BLACK,	136	AFTER FUNERAL	4
WHO UNDER THE LIDS OF HER WINDOWS HOISTED HIS GOLDEN LUGGAGE,	170	MARRIAGE VIRG	12
LIE			
FOR YOU'VE A SEA TO LIE.	16	TIME TO ROT	18
HE'LL LIE DOWN, AND OUR BREATH	17	IN OBLIVION	5
SEWING A LIE TO A CREDULITY,	18	NATURAL DAY	11
YOU'RE THE PERVERSE TO LIE ACROSS,	21	BEWILDERED WAY	15
AND ON THE SWEETHEARTS' BED TO LIE AND GRIN,	34	THIRST PARCHES	12
FROM THE HISSING OF THE SPENT LIE	43	LONGED TO MOVE	2
OUT OF THE OLD LIE BURNING ON THE GROUND,	44	LONGED TO MOVE	13
HALF CONVENTION AND HALF LIE.	44	LONGED TO MOVE	20
LIE COLD, WITH THEIR HORSES, FOR RAVEN AND KITE.	45	PLOUGHMAN GONE	23
BOUND BY A SOVEREIGN STRIP, WE LIE,	54	WE BY SEASAND	18
LIE WATCHING YELLOW UNTIL THE GOLDEN WEATHER	54	WE BY SEASAND	23
ANSWER: SHALL A MOTHER LIE	72	TAKE NEEDLES	59

	PAGE	TITLE	LINE
LIE (CONTINUED)			
HERE LIE THE BEASTS	81	HERE LIE BEAST	T
HERE LIE THE BEASTS OF MAN AND HERE I FEAST, ...	81	HERE LIE BEAST	1
FLAVOURED OF CELLULOID GIVE LOVE THE LIE.	89	EUNUCH DREAMS	20
THE LOVERS' HOUSE, LIE SUFFERING MY STAIN?	112	NOT FATHER ME	4
LIE ALL UNKNOWING OF THE GRAVE SIN-EATER.	113	NOT FATHER ME	32
TILL FIELD AND ROOF LIE LEVEL AND THE SAME	116	LANTERNS SHINE	13
LIE THIS FIFTH MONTH UNSKATED, AND THE BIRDS HAVE FLOWN;	122	HOLD HARD	9
NOW IN THE CLOUD'S BIG BREAST LIE QUIET COUNTRIES,	133	I MAKE THIS IN	61
SIGH LONG, CLAY COLD, LIE SHORN, ...	135	HOW MY ANIMAL	34
LIE DRY, REST ROBBED, MY BEAST.	135	HOW MY ANIMAL	42
FLOOD OF HER HEART'S FAME; SHE WOULD LIE DUMB AND DEEP	136	AFTER FUNERAL	19
LIE WITH RELIGION IN THEIR CRAMP, HER THREADBARE	137	AFTER FUNERAL	32
CONVENIENT BIRD AND BEAST LIE LODGED TO SUFFER	144	PLEASURE-BIRD	3
WHO PALMED THE LIE ON ME WHEN YOU LOOKED	146	TO OTHERS	4
THE DEATH BIDING TWO LIE LONELY.	148	UNLUCKILY FOR	28
LUCKLESSLY SHE MUST LIE PATIENT	149	UNLUCKILY FOR	53
NOW SHOWN AND MOSTLY BARE I WOULD LIE DOWN, ...	152	BELOW A TIME	49
LIE DOWN, LIE DOWN AND LIVE	152	BELOW A TIME	50
LIE DOWN, LIE DOWN AND LIVE	152	BELOW A TIME	50
SINGLY LIE WITH THE WHOLE WIDE SHORE, ...	158	INTO HER HEAD	49
MUST LIE	180	VISION, PRAYER	19
THAT HE LET THE DEAD LIE THOUGH THEY MOAN	184	VISION, PRAYER	136
AND DROWN IN THE DRIFTS OF HIS NEED, AND LIE CURLED CAUGHT	188	WINTER'S TALE	47
EACH TRUTH, EACH LIE, ...	193	SIDE OF TRUTH	35
LIE STILL, SLEEP BECALMED	194	SLEEP BECALMED	T
LIE STILL, SLEEP BECALMED, SUFFERER WITH THE WOUND	194	SLEEP BECALMED	1
LIE STILL, SLEEP BECALMED, HIDE THE MOUTH IN THE THROAT, ...	194	SLEEP BECALMED	13
AND THE LOVERS LIE ABED	197	CRAFT OR ART	4
NOR THE INNOCENT LIE IN THE ROOTING DINGLE WOOED	198	COUNTRY SLEEP	15
LIE FAST AND SOOTHED, ...	198	COUNTRY SLEEP	19
LIE IN GRACE. SLEEP SPELLED AT REST IN THE LOWLY HOUSE	199	COUNTRY SLEEP	43
WHERE BARREN AS BOULDERS WOMEN LIE LONGING STILL	203	GIANT'S THIGH	4
AND I LIE DOWN BUT TO SLEEP IN BED, ...	206	LAMENT	35
I LIE DOWN THIN AND HEAR THE GOOD BELLS JAW--	207	LAMENT	53
ON SKULL AND SCAR WHERE HIS LOVES LIE WRECKED, ...	209	POEM ON B'DAY	40
HE LIE LIGHTLY, AT LAST, ON THE LAST, CROSSED	216	ELEGY	5
YOUNG AMONG THE LONG FLOCKS, AND NEVER LIE LOST ...	216	ELEGY	7
INFINITE SHADOWY ISLES LIE SILENT BEFORE ME, ...	221	FOREST PICTURE	3
LIES			
WERE VAGUENESS ENOUGH AND THE SWEET LIES PLENTY,	32	OUT OF SIGHS	21
LET IT BE KNOWN THAT LITTLE LIVE BUT LIES, ...	36	LET BE KNOWN	1
THAT THIS IS LIES THAT MOANS DEPARTURE, ...	36	LET BE KNOWN	4
AND THAT IS LIES THAT, AFTER THE OLD MEN DIE, ...	36	LET BE KNOWN	5
PRESS THE OLD LIES AND THE OLD GHOSTS.	38	THE GOSSIPERS	18
WHERE DEATH LIES DEAD ASLEEP, ONE BRIGHT EYE OPEN,	41	YOUNG ARE OLD	20
THE LAND LIES OUT OF SOUND	62	EARS IN TURRET	13
THE HEART LIES READY FOR THE RAVEN'S MOUTH, ...	63	WOMAN SPEAKS	8
LIES IN THE FORTUNED BONE, THE FLASK OF BLOOD, ...	80	ALL THAT I OWE	3
THE WORD OF TIME LIES ON THE CHAPTERED BONE, ...	80	ALMANAC TIME	11
HERE LIES THE BEAST OF MAN AND HERE HIS ANGELS, ...	81	HERE LIE BEAST	7
AND LEAVE THE POPPIED PICKTHANK WHERE HE LIES;	98	TWILIGHT LOCKS	39
AND SALT-EYED STUMBLE BEDWARD WHERE SHE LIES	107	GRIEF THIEF	12
AND TIMELESSLY LIES LOVING WITH THE THIEF.	108	GRIEF THIEF	14
AND SHE WHO LIES, ...	115	A GRIEF AGO	17

	PAGE	TITLE	LINE
LIES (CONTINUED)			
NOR WHEN MY LOVE LIES IN THE CROSS-BONED DRIFT	123	FOSTER LIGHT	22
THE HERO'S HEAD LIES SCRAPED OF EVERY LEGEND, ...	132	I MAKE THIS IN	43
THE PRESENT MOUTH, AND THE SWEETLY BLOWN TRUMPET OF			
LIES, ...	133	MAKE ME A MASK	6
OTHERS BETRAY THE LAMENTING LIES OF THEIR LOSSES	133	MAKE ME A MASK	11
A STONE LIES LOST AND LOCKED IN THE LARK-HIGH HILL.	159	INTO HER HEAD	62
O SHE LIES ALONE AND STILL, ...	159	INTO HER HEAD	64
NOW THEIR LOVE LIES A LOSS	161	WEDDING ANNIV	5
VENUS LIES STAR-STRUCK IN HER WOUND	166	LONG-LEGGED	117
EXULTATION LIES DOWN. TIME BURIES THE SPRING WEATHER	191	WINTER'S TALE	119
DEEP WITH THE FIRST DEAD LIES LONDON'S DAUGHTER,	192	REFUSAL MOURN	19
DRAGGING HIM UP THE STAIRS TO ONE WHO LIES DEAD.	194	CONVERS PRAYER	20
LIES-TO-PLEASE			
LOVE-LIES, AND GOD-LIES, AND LIES-TO-PLEASE, ...	36	LET BE KNOWN	2
LIFE			
OF ALL THE MYSTERY THERE IS IN LIFE	22	ON QUIET NIGHT	3
WHO GAVE ME LIFE AND THEN THE GRAVE, ...	26	PERSONAL EPIT	11
AS MEANINGLESS AS THE BELLS (OH CHANGE THE LIFE!),	33	HELD-OUT HAND	9
THE JAWS WILL HAVE SHUT, AND LIFE BE SWITCHED OUT.	39	GAS FADES	14
WHAT'S NEVER KNOWN IS SAFEST IN THIS LIFE.	40	WAS THERE TIME	6
SOME LIFE, YET UNSPENT, MIGHT EXPLODE	44	LONGED TO MOVE	12
LIFE, TILL THE CHANGE OF MOOD, FORKS	47	POET: 1935	38
WILL ONLY DIM LIFE, AND LIGHT DEATH.	49	LIGHT, I KNOW	29
NO LOVING SHEPHERD IN THIS UPSIDE LIFE.	51	OUT OF THE PIT	38
WHEN ANY LIGHT GOES OUT, AND LIFE IS DEATH.	55	NO MAN BELIEVE	6
SOUNDS, RICH WITH LIFE, OUT OF A PAINTED MASK;	57	GREEK PLAY	14
EACH GOLDEN GRAIN SPAT LIFE INTO ITS FELLOW, ...	78	LOVE'S FEVER	23
THE GRAINS OF LIFE MUST SEETHE BENEATH THE SUN, ...	80	ALMANAC TIME	13
REMEMBER, TOO, THAT LIFE IS HELL	84	LETTER TO AUNT	52
DRIVES IN A DEATH AS LIFE LEAKS OUT.	88	A PROCESS IN	9
AND WE SHALL BE FIT FELLOWS FOR A LIFE, ...	90	EUNUCH DREAMS	40
A MUSCLING LIFE FROM LOVERS IN THEIR CRAMP, ...	92	BOYS OF SUMMER	33
LIFE ROSE AND SPOUTED FROM THE ROLLING SEAS, ...	94	IN BEGINNING	16
LIFE NEAT'S A BETTER POISON THAN IN BOTTLE, ...	137	O CHATTERTON	5
BENEATH MY LIFE, THAT SIGHS FOR THE SEDUCER'S COMING	147	UNLUCKILY FOR	13
GRISTLE AND RIND, AND A ROARER'S LIFE, ...	207	LAMENT	46
AND A BLACK REWARD FOR A ROARING LIFE, ...	207	LAMENT	50
THERE WILL BE A NEW LIFE	236	WOMAN TAPESTRY	66
LIFT			
I CANNOT LIFT, BUT CAN, ...	12	SKY'S BRIGHT	11
LIFT UP YOUR FACE	35	LIFT UP FACE	T
LIFT UP YOUR FACE, LIGHT	35	LIFT UP FACE	1
LIFT UP YOUR HEAD, LET	35	LIFT UP FACE	10
LET COMFORT COME SLOWLY, LIFT	35	LIFT UP FACE	14
LIFT UP THE BLINDS OVER THE BLIND EYES.	35	LIFT UP FACE	17
THEREFORE LIFT UP, SEE, STROKE THE LIGHT.	35	LIFT UP FACE	24
LIFT WIT-HURT HEAD FOR SUN TO SYMPATHIZE, ...	42	A WAR OF WITS	18
LIFT ITS HEAD TO THE BLOWS OF THE RAIN;	50	NO DOMINION	23
LOVE ME AND LIFT YOUR MASK.	75	SONG: LOVE ME	4
LOVE ME AND LIFT YOUR MASK.	76	SONG: LOVE ME	8
LOVE ME AND LIFT YOUR MASK.	76	SONG: LOVE ME	12
LOVE ME AND LIFT YOUR MASK.	76	SONG: LOVE ME	16
TO LIFT TO LEAVE FROM THE TREASURES OF MAN IS			
PLEASING DEATH	140	NO WORK WORDS	7
OR LIFT MY HAT TO UNSEEN	155	RETURN	48
THE ROD CAN LIFT ITS TWINING HEAD	240	TWINING HEAD	T
THE ROD CAN LIFT ITS TWINING HEAD	240	TWINING HEAD	1
LIFTED			
ONE LADY'S HAND WAS LIFTED, ...	11	CABARET	11

	PAGE	TITLE	LINE
LIFTED (CONTINUED)			
AS THAT HER HEEL WAS LIFTED, ...	12	CABARET	15
LIFTED HER MARBLE FOOT, OR LOWERED HER HAND	34	IN GARDENS	20
THAT TURNED ON AND LIFTED IN ANGER	39	GAS FADES	25
AND ALL THE LIFTED WATERS WALK AND LEAP.	165	LONG-LEGGED	112
LIFTING			
FROM THE FIRST PRINT OF THE UNSHODDEN FOOT, THE LIFTING	78	LOVE'S FEVER	10
LIFTING HER SMELL OVER THE CITY BUILDINGS.	240	ADMIT THE SUN	14
LIFTS			
MY RIVER, EVEN THOUGH IT LIFTS	228	MY RIVER	1
LIGHT			
HEARS, THERE, THIS FOX LIGHT, MY FLOOD SHIP'S	4	PROLOGUE	69
BUT IN THE LIGHT OF GOING	9	MINUTE'S HOUR	20
DOWN AN ECSTATIC LINE OF LIGHT, ...	13	RAIN CUTS	8
AND DARKNESS, HAND IN HAND WITH LIGHT, ...	15	FOR LEDA	32
VIGOUR AND HARMONY IN LIGHT TO NONE, ...	17	NATURAL DAY	4
BEFORE THE LAST LIGHT IS BLOWN	21	BEWILDERED WAY	24
FOR THERE WAS NO LIGHT IN HIS EYES, ...	22	ON QUIET NIGHT	17
AND THERE WAS NO LIGHT IN HIS SOUL.	22	ON QUIET NIGHT	18
EMPTY OF LIGHT AND FIND THE DARKNESS LIT--	27	OBLIVIOUS DARK	5
WHEN IT WAS NOON HAVE WALKED INTO THE LIGHT, ...	30	YOUTH CALLS	10
WE MIGHT HAVE TRIED LIGHT MATCHES IN THE WIND.	34	IN GARDENS	16
LIFT UP YOUR FACE, LIGHT	35	LIFT UP FACE	1
UP YOUR HAND TO STROKE THE LIGHT, ...	35	LIFT UP FACE	15
THEREFORE LIFT UP, SEE, STROKE THE LIGHT.	35	LIFT UP FACE	24
THE COVERINGS OF DARK AND LIGHT, ...	37	WINDMILLS TURN	28
BEFORE EVIL OR GOOD, LIGHT OR DARK, ...	39	GAS FADES	16
MY BRAIN CAME CRYING INTO THE FRESH LIGHT, ...	42	A WAR OF WITS	4
LIGHT, I KNOW, TREADS THE TEN MILLION STARS	48	LIGHT, I KNOW	T
LIGHT, I KNOW, TREADS THE TEN MILLION STARS, ...	48	LIGHT, I KNOW	1
AND BLOOMS IN THE HESPERIDES. LIGHT STIRS	48	LIGHT, I KNOW	2
SUCH LIGHT SHALL NOT ILLUMINATE MY FEARS	48	LIGHT, I KNOW	4
I AM A TIMID CHILD WHEN LIGHT IS DEAD.	48	LIGHT, I KNOW	11
LIGHT WALKS THE SKY, LEAVING NO PRINT, ...	49	LIGHT, I KNOW	17
STARS' LIGHT AND SUN'S LIGHT WILL NOT SHINE	49	LIGHT, I KNOW	27
STARS' LIGHT AND SUN'S LIGHT WILL NOT SHINE	49	LIGHT, I KNOW	27
AS CLEARLY AS THE LIGHT OF MY OWN BRAIN, ...	49	LIGHT, I KNOW	28
WILL ONLY DIM LIFE, AND LIGHT DEATH.	49	LIGHT, I KNOW	29
I MUST LEARN NIGHT'S LIGHT OR GO MAD.	49	LIGHT, I KNOW	30
WHEN ANY LIGHT GOES OUT, AND LIFE IS DEATH.	55	NO MAN BELIEVE	6
LIGHT AND DARK ARE NO ENEMIES	61	MEAT ON BONES	36
SEE THE FIRST LIVING LIGHT, ...	67	LET A FAITH	12
THE SPHINX OF LIGHT SIT ON THE EYES, ...	69	SECRET WIND	2
THE SUN AND MOON SHED ONE WHITE LIGHT.	78	LOVE'S FEVER	9
SHONE IN MY EARS THE LIGHT OF SOUND, ...	78	LOVE'S FEVER	20
CALLED IN MY EYES THE SOUND OF LIGHT.	78	LOVE'S FEVER	21
INTO THE SIDED LAP OF LIGHT GREW STRONG, ...	78	LOVE'S FEVER	27
CAST LIGHT UPON MY WEATHER. I AM HEIR	80	ALL THAT I OWE	15
LIGHT BREAKS WHERE NO SUN SHINES	82	LIGHT BREAKS	T
LIGHT BREAKS WHERE NO SUN SHINES;	82	LIGHT BREAKS	1
THE THINGS OF LIGHT	82	LIGHT BREAKS	5
LIGHT BREAKS ON SECRET LOTS, ...	82	LIGHT BREAKS	25
THAT STARRY FENCE THE CLAY OF LIGHT	85	SEE, SAYS LIME	6
HOW WELL YOUR POEMS LIGHT THE FIRE.	85	LETTER TO AUNT	66
IS HALF ITS LIGHT; THE FATHOMED SEA	88	A PROCESS IN	11
OUR EUNUCH DREAMS, ALL SEEDLESS IN THE LIGHT, ...	89	EUNUCH DREAMS	1
OF LIGHT AND LOVE, THE TEMPERS OF THE HEART, ...	89	EUNUCH DREAMS	2
THESE BOYS OF LIGHT ARE CURDLERS IN THEIR FOLLY,	92	BOYS OF SUMMER	7
OF LOVE AND LIGHT BURSTS IN THEIR THROATS.	92	BOYS OF SUMMER	23

LIGHT (CONTINUED)	PAGE	TITLE	LINE
ONE SMILE OF LIGHT ACROSS THE EMPTY FACE;	93	IN BEGINNING	2
THAT FROM THE SOLID BASES OF THE LIGHT	94	IN BEGINNING	20
BLOOD SHOT AND SCATTERED TO THE WINDS OF LIGHT	94	IN BEGINNING	29
AND TALK OF LIGHT TO A MAD MINER.	96	TWELVE	8
HE BLEW LIKE POWDER TO THE LIGHT	97	TWILIGHT LOCKS	14
I SENT MY OWN AMBASSADOR TO LIGHT;	98	TWILIGHT LOCKS	33
THE FENCES OF THE LIGHT ARE DOWN, ...	98	TWILIGHT LOCKS	40
SHIFTING TO LIGHT, TURNED ON ME LIKE A MOON.	101	FELLOWED SLEEP	3
HOW LIGHT THE SLEEPING ON THIS SOILY STAR, ...	102	FELLOWED SLEEP	24
RIDING THE SEA LIGHT ON A SUNKEN PATH, ...	107	GRIEF THIEF	8
O LIGHT IN ZENITH, THE COUPLED BUD, ...	107	ALL ALL AND	32
THE RITE OF LIGHT, ...	114	SERVANT SUN	16
CAUGHT IN AN OCTAGON OF UNACCUSTOMED LIGHT, ...	116	LANTERNS SHINE	2
BY LAVA'S LIGHT SPLIT THROUGH THE OYSTER VOWELS ...	119	ALTARWISE	73
FOSTER THE LIGHT	123	FOSTER LIGHT	T
FOSTER THE LIGHT NOR VEIL THE MANSHAPED MOON, ...	123	FOSTER LIGHT	1
CALLS THE GREEN ROCK OF LIGHT.	128	MY NEOPHYTE	12
SO SOLVE THE MYSTIC SUN, THE WIFE OF LIGHT, ...	128	NOW, SAY NAY	26
IN QUICK, SWEET, CRUEL LIGHT TILL THE LOCKED GROUND SPROUT OUT, ...	135	HOW MY ANIMAL	18
YOU HAVE KICKED FROM A DARK DEN, LEAPED UP THE WHINNYING LIGHT, ...	135	HOW MY ANIMAL	43
THAT BREAKS ONE BONE TO LIGHT WITH A JUDGMENT CLOUT,	136	AFTER FUNERAL	9
BY THE LIGHT OF THE MEAT-EATING SUN.	143	24 YEARS	5
STRIKE LIGHT, AND BLOODY A LOUD ROOM.	145	IF HEAD HURT	10
WITH EVERY CRY SINCE LIGHT	160	DEATHS AND ENT	23
TOPPLING UP THE BOATSIDE IN A SNOW OF LIGHT!	166	LONG-LEGGED	138
WAKING ALONE IN A MULTITUDE OF LOVES WHEN MORNING'S LIGHT	170	MARRIAGE VIRG	1
WHO ADMITS THE DELUSIVE LIGHT THROUGH THE BOUNCING WALL, ...	170	LOVE IN ASYLUM	11
AND TAKEN BY LIGHT IN HER ARMS AT LONG AND DEAR LAST	170	LOVE IN ASYLUM	16
LOVE IS THE LAST LIGHT SPOKEN. OH	174	FIRE RAID	31
OF SUN LIGHT	178	POEM IN OCT	49
LIGHT.	180	VISION, PRAYER	34
INFANT LIGHT OR	183	VISION, PRAYER	130
LIGHT THROUGH SEA AND SOIL	184	VISION, PRAYER	157
THAT ONE DARK I OWE MY LIGHT, ...	186	HOLY SPRING	9
BY THE SPIT AND THE BLACK POT IN THE LOG BRIGHT LIGHT	188	WINTER'S TALE	27
BY THE BELIEVER LOST AND THE HURLED OUTCAST OF LIGHT.	188	WINTER'S TALE	50
ON THE DEPARTED, SNOW BUSHED GREEN, WANTON IN MOON LIGHT	189	WINTER'S TALE	72
BY THE SPIT AND THE BLACK POT IN THE LOG BRIGHT LIGHT.	190	WINTER'S TALE	87
TELLS WITH SILENCE THE LAST LIGHT BREAKING	191	REFUSAL MOURN	4
WATER AND LIGHT, THE EARTH AND SKY, ...	193	SIDE OF TRUTH	32
DOWN THE RIVERS OF THE WINDFALL LIGHT.	195	FERN HILL	9
SO IT MUST HAVE BEEN AFTER THE BIRTH OF THE SIMPLE LIGHT	196	FERN HILL	33
I LABOUR BY SINGING LIGHT	197	CRAFT OR ART	6
LIGHT OF HIS THIGHS, SPREADEAGLE TO THE DUNGHILL SKY,	204	GIANT'S THIGH	23
RAGE, RAGE AGAINST THE DYING OF THE LIGHT.	207	NOT GO GENTLE	3
RAGE, RAGE AGAINST THE DYING OF THE LIGHT.	208	NOT GO GENTLE	9
RAGE, RAGE AGAINST THE DYING OF THE LIGHT.	208	NOT GO GENTLE	15
RAGE, RAGE AGAINST THE DYING OF THE LIGHT.	208	NOT GO GENTLE	19
IN THE UNKNOWN, FAMOUS LIGHT OF GREAT	210	POEM ON B'DAY	47
DARK IS A WAY AND LIGHT IS A PLACE, ...	210	POEM ON B'DAY	49
WHO IS THE LIGHT OF OLD	210	POEM ON B'DAY	73
LIGHT AND HIS TEARS GLIDE DOWN TOGETHER	215	COUNTRY HEAVEN	11

	PAGE	TITLE	LINE
LIGHT (CONTINUED)			
NOON, AND NIGHT, AND LIGHT. THE RIVERS OF THE DEAD	216	ELEGY	15
OUT OF HIS EYES I SAW THE LAST LIGHT GLIDE.	217	ELEGY	28
HERE AMONG THE LIGHT OF THE LORDING SKY	217	ELEGY	29
AND THE WINDS THAT STREAM THROUGH THE RIBBONED LIGHT	227	THE PINE	3
THE LIGHT WILL COME IN AN UNWAVERING LINE.	232	YOUR VOICE	7
STROKING THE AIR AND HOLDING LIGHT.	235	WOMAN TAPESTRY	30
IT'S LIGHT THAT MAKES THE INTERVALS	238	MAKES INTERVALS	T
IT'S LIGHT THAT MAKES THE INTERVALS	238	MAKES INTERVALS	1
LIGHT THAT COMPELS	238	MAKES INTERVALS	4
LIGHT, NOT SO TO ME;	238	MAKES INTERVALS	6
AND I WILL BREAK YOUR PACING LIGHT.	239	MAKES INTERVALS	16
CRUSH YOUR SHARP LIGHT, ...	239	MAKES INTERVALS	28
AND WHERE THE LIGHT COMES CAUTIOUSLY	240	ADMIT THE SUN	3
LIGHTED			
THE PYRE YET TO BE LIGHTED OF MY SINS AND DAYS, ...	147	UNLUCKILY FOR	3
UNDER THE LIGHTED SHAPES OF FAITH AND THEIR MOONSHADE	204	GIANT'S THIGH	17
LIGHTER			
TO ANY LIGHTER STATE	19	IMAGES IN AIR	13
LIGHTLY			
I FLED THAT GROUND AS LIGHTLY AS A FEATHER.	101	FELLOWED SLEEP	10
HE LIE LIGHTLY, AT LAST, ON THE LAST, CROSSED	216	ELEGY	5
LIGHTLY, THOU WIND, OVER HIS DEAR, DARK HEAD, ...	222	MISSING	4
LIGHTNESS			
LIKE A BIRD IN ITS LIGHTNESS, ...	233	NO THOUGHT	17
LIGHTNING			
DRUM HARSHLY ON THE AIR, THE LIGHTNING SWORDS	51	OUT OF THE PIT	15
BY SCALPEL LIGHTNING FROM THE RIFTED SKY, ...	64	WOMAN SPEAKS	29
LIGHTNING OR THE DARTING VIPER, ...	71	TAKE NEEDLES	22
THE GROOVED LAND ROTATING, THAT THE STYLUS OF			
LIGHTNING	110	I, IN IMAGE	68
WALKS WITH NO WOUND, NOR LIGHTNING IN HER FACE, ...	133	I MAKE THIS IN	63
AND A LAMP OF LIGHTNING FOR THE POOR IN THE DARK;	144	COLOUR OF SAY	11
GOLD GUT IS A LIGHTNING THREAD, ...	164	LONG-LEGGED	63
AND THE LONG-TAILED LIGHTNING LIT HIS CATCH.	166	LONG-LEGGED	128
THOUGH THE MOMENT OF A MIRACLE IS UNENDING LIGHTNING	170	MARRIAGE VIRG	6
HIS LIGHTNING ANSWERS MY	185	VISION, PRAYER	201
BECAUSE THEIR WORDS HAD FORKED NO LIGHTNING THEY	208	NOT GO GENTLE	5
LIGHTNINGS			
AND THE LIGHTNINGS OF ADORATION	181	VISION, PRAYER	60
LIGHTS			
HER FAN BURST IN A MILLION LIGHTS	11	CABARET	14
NOBLE AMONG A CROWD OF LIGHTS.	21	BEWILDERED WAY	12
CAUGHT IN THE TRAP'S MACHINERY, LIGHTS OUT, ...	39	GAS FADES	35
AND THE SKYSIGNS AND THE NIGHT LIGHTS, ...	42	YOUNG ARE OLD	51
THE GLOW-WORM LIGHTS HIS DARKNESS, AND	48	POET: 1935	64
DAY LIGHTS THE BONE;	82	LIGHT BREAKS	21
LIGHTS UP THE LIVING WORM.	88	A PROCESS IN	6
LIGHT'S			
PUFFING THE LIGHT'S FLAME TO AND FRO, ...	16	TIME TO ROT	5
AND ONE LIGHT'S LANGUAGE IN THE BOOK OF TREES.	119	ALTARWISE	89
LIKE			
LIKE STALKS OF TALL, DRY STRAW, ...	3	PROLOGUE	22
LIKE LEAVES OF TREES AND AS SOON	3	PROLOGUE	31
LIKE WOODEN ISLANDS, HILL TO HILL.	5	PROLOGUE	96
THAT, LIKE A TREE, HAS ROOTS IN YOU, ...	9	MINUTE'S HOUR	3
THEYD SEE WITH EYES LIKE MINE	11	AIR BREATHE	10
BUT SHOULD NOT TOUCH LIKE I	11	AIR BREATHE	11
IN TIME LIKE OUTLAW RAINS ON THAT PRIEST, WATER,	15	SPIRE CRANES	6
AND WINTER FOLLOW LIKE AN ECHO	15	FOR LEDA	24

LIKE

		PAGE	TITLE	LINE
LIKE (CONTINUED)				
BUT DO NOT TRAVEL DOWN DUMB WIND LIKE PRODIGALS.		16	SPIRE CRANES	11
MUST FEEL LIKE SUCH ENCROACHMENT		20	ENCOMPASSED	4
IN TIME, LIKE ALL, THROUGH MY UNREASON		21	BEWILDERED WAY	7
LOVING AND DOUBTING LIKE ONE WHO IS TO DIE		27	OBLIVIOUS DARK	28
LEERS DOWN THE VALLEY LIKE A FOOL		33	HELD-OUT HAND	19
FAITH FIXED LIKE A STAR BEYOND THE STARS,		42	YOUNG ARE OLD	50
THAT, LIKE A RAZOR, SKIMS, CUTS, AND TURNS,		47	POET: 1935	49
LIKE CATS, AND LUSTS LAY HALF HOT IN THE COLD.		50	OUT OF THE PIT	5
THE MOON LEERED DOWN THE VALLEY LIKE A FOOL.		50	OUT OF THE PIT	12
THE MOON LEERED DOWN THE VALLEY LIKE A FOOL.		51	OUT OF THE PIT	32
AND THUS I SAW HIM. HE WAS POISED LIKE THIS,		52	OUT OF THE PIT	59
THE MOON PEERS DOWN THE VALLEY LIKE A SAINT.		53	OUT OF THE PIT	94
BREAKS, O MY HEART'S BLOOD, LIKE A HEART AND HILL.		54	WE BY SEASAND	24
RING LIKE A HANDBELL THROUGH THE CORRIDORS,		56	WHY EAST WIND	22
AND LOVE THAT GOES DOWN LIKE A FLOWER.		57	GREEK PLAY	20
I CANNOT MURDER, LIKE A FOOL,		61	MEAT ON BONES	30
THE WIND PASS LIKE A FIRE,		62	EARS IN TURRET	18
GRIEF, LIKE AN OPEN WOUND, HAS CRIED TO HEAVEN.		64	WOMAN SPEAKS	32
THE WET NIGHT SCOLDS ME LIKE A NURSE?		65	GODS THUMP	10
A SHOUT WENT UP TO HEAVEN LIKE A ROCKET,		70	SECRET WIND	7
LIKE A GREEN TREE THROUGH THE SWARD,		72	TAKE NEEDLES	42
HERE IS A SAVIOUR WHO SINGS LIKE A BIRD,		74	SUN BURNS	7
UNPACKS THE HEAD THAT, LIKE A SLEEPY GHOST,		75	MY HERO BARES	3
TREAD, LIKE A NAKED VENUS,		75	MY HERO BARES	12
AND TO THE VOICE THAT, LIKE A VOICE OF HUNGER,		79	LOVE'S FEVER	29
LIKE SENNA STIRS ALONG THE RAVAGED ROOTS.		80	ALL THAT I OWE	4
SLIDES LIKE A SEA;		82	LIGHT BREAKS	15
LIKE SOME PITCH MOON, THE LIMIT OF THE GLOBES;		82	LIGHT BREAKS	20
A GENIUS LIKE DAVID G.		85	LETTER TO AUNT	62
MOVE LIKE TWO GHOSTS BEFORE THE EYE.		88	A PROCESS IN	18
FOR WE SHALL BE A SHOUTER LIKE THE COCK,		90	EUNUCH DREAMS	37
AND DROP THE PLUM LIKE FIRE FROM THE FLESH.		95	RUB OF LOVE	9
SPEAK LIKE A HUNGRY PARSON OF THE MANNA,		96	TWELVE	6
MY HOUSE WOULD FALL LIKE BREAD ABOUT MY HOMAGE;		96	TWELVE	11
THE MOUTH OF TIME SUCKED, LIKE A SPONGE,		97	TWILIGHT LOCKS	4
HE BLEW LIKE POWDER TO THE LIGHT		97	TWILIGHT LOCKS	14
ON THE HORIZON WALKING LIKE THE TREES		98	OCTOBER WIND	10
WHEN, LIKE A RUNNING GRAVE		99	RUNNING GRAVE	T
WHEN, LIKE A RUNNING GRAVE, TIME TRACKS YOU DOWN,		99	RUNNING GRAVE	1
COMES, LIKE A SCISSORS STALKING, TAILOR AGE,		100	RUNNING GRAVE	6
DRIVE CHILDREN UP LIKE BRUISES TO THE THUMB,		100	RUNNING GRAVE	14
SHIFTING TO LIGHT, TURNED ON ME LIKE A MOON.		101	FELLOWED SLEEP	3
CASTS TO THE PINE ROOTS, RAISING MAN LIKE A MOUNTAIN		109	I, IN IMAGE	11
SPROUT FROM THE STONY LOCKERS LIKE A TREE ON ARAN.		111	I, IN IMAGE	78
LOVE LIKE A MIST OR FIRE THROUGH THE BED OF EELS.		111	I, IN IMAGE	90
LIKE EXODUS A CHAPTER FROM THE GARDEN,		115	A GRIEF AGO	18
BUT HEART, LIKE HEAD, LEADS HELPLESSLY;		116	LANTERNS SHINE	10
BENT LIKE THREE TREES AND BIRD-PAPPED THROUGH HER SHIFT,		120	ALTARWISE	103
POUR LIKE A HALO ON THE CAPS AND SERPENTS.		120	ALTARWISE	118
TIME, IN A FOLLY'S RIDER, LIKE A COUNTY MAN		122	HOLD HARD	4
CRACK LIKE A SPRING IN A VICE, BONE BREAKING APRIL,		122	HOLD HARD	17
NOR SPROUT ON OWL-SEED LIKE A GOBLIN-SUCKER,		123	FOSTER LIGHT	14
WINGED LIKE A SABBATH ASS THIS CHILDREN'S PIECE		124	TODAY, INSECT	16
LIKE A TOWER ON THE TOWN		125	SEED-AT-ZERO	5
LIKE A TOWER ON THE TOWN		125	SEED-AT-ZERO	12
THAT THE GREEN CHILD SEE LIKE A GRAIL		129	MY NEOPHYTE	22
WOUND LIKE A BALL OF LAKES		129	MY NEOPHYTE	33

LIKE

		PAGE	TITLE	LINE
LIKE (CONTINUED)

WHEN, WITH HIS TORCH AND HOURGLASS, LIKE A SULPHUR PRIEST, ... 130 SINNERS' BELL 2
OR LIKE THE TIDE-LOOPED BREASTKNOT REEFED AGAIN ... 131 I MAKE THIS IN 11
AND, PRIDE IS LAST, IS LIKE A CHILD ALONE .... 131 I MAKE THIS IN 13
LIKE AN APPROACHING WAVE I SPRAWL TO RUIN. .... 132 I MAKE THIS IN 38
FUMED LIKE A TREE, AND TOSSED A BURNING BIRD; ..... 133 I MAKE THIS IN 56
A CALM WIND BLOWS THAT RAISED THE TREES LIKE HAIR 133 I MAKE THIS IN 64
BENT LIKE A BEAST TO LAP THE SINGULAR FLOODS ...... 134 NOT FROM ANGER 3
DRUNK AS A VINEYARD SNAIL, FLAILED LIKE AN OCTOPUS, 134 HOW MY ANIMAL 7
REFUSAL STRUCK LIKE A BELL UNDER WATER .... 134 NOT FROM ANGER 12
BABBLE LIKE A BELLBUOY OVER THE HYMNING HEADS, ... 136 AFTER FUNERAL 23
MY NOSTRILS SEE HER BREATH BURN LIKE A BUSH. ...... 139 FIVE & COUNTRY 10
GLORY CRACKED LIKE A FLEA. .... 141 SAINT TO FALL 18
THE BREATH DRAW BACK LIKE A BOLT THROUGH WHITE OIL 142 SAINT TO FALL 46
AND A STRANGER ENTER LIKE IRON. .... 142 SAINT TO FALL 47
MALE SHAPES, GIRL-LIPPED, BUT CLAD LIKE BOYS: ..... 143 THE MOLLS 2
IN THE GROIN OF THE NATURAL DOORWAY I CROUCHED LIKE A TAILOR .... 143 24 YEARS 3
THAT CLOUTS THE SPITTLE LIKE BUBBLES WITH BROKEN ROOMS, ... 144 PLEASURE-BIRD 6
AND EVERY STONE I WIND OFF LIKE A REEL. .... 144 COLOUR OF SAY 13
THAT FROZEN WIFE WHOSE JUICES DRIFT LIKE A FIXED SEA 145 PLEASURE-BIRD 14
BEND, IF MY JOURNEY ACHE, DIRECTION LIKE AN ARC OR MAKE .... 145 IF HEAD HURT 14
LIKE THE MAULED PICTURES OF BOYS? .... 145 PLEASURE-BIRD 19
'NOW TO AWAKE HUSKED OF GESTURES AND MY JOY LIKE A CAVE .... 146 IF HEAD HURT 21
WITH IMMORTALITY AT MY SIDE LIKE CHRIST THE SKY. 148 UNLUCKILY FOR 49
HURLING INTO BEGINNING LIKE CHRIST THE CHILD. ..... 149 UNLUCKILY FOR 52
WHERE BIRDS RIDE LIKE LEAVES AND BOATS LIKE DUCKS 150 WHEN I WOKE 22
WHERE BIRDS RIDE LIKE LEAVES AND BOATS LIKE DUCKS 150 WHEN I WOKE 22
AND THE COINS ON MY EYELIDS SANG LIKE SHELLS. ..... 150 WHEN I WOKE 30
SWEEP AWAY LIKE A CREAM CLOUD; .... 156 RETURN 89
LUST BEARS LIKE VOLTS, WHO'LL AMPLIFY, AND STRANGE 159 TO LEDA 8
WHERE THE ANCHOR RODE LIKE A GULL .... 163 LONG-LEGGED 37
WHALES IN THE WAKE LIKE CAPES AND ALPS .... 163 LONG-LEGGED 49
SPUN ON A SPOUT LIKE A LONG-LEGGED BALL .... 163 LONG-LEGGED 56
AND THE FLAKES FALL LIKE HILLS. .... 166 LONG-LEGGED 136
WEEPS LIKE THE RISEN SUN AMONG .... 167 LONG-LEGGED 163
LIKE THE PARK BIRDS HE CAME EARLY .... 171 THE HUNCHBACK 13
LIKE THE WATER HE SAT DOWN .... 171 THE HUNCHBACK 14
AND THE DUST SHALL SING LIKE A BIRD .... 173 FIRE RAID 23
NIGHT FALL AND THE FRUIT LIKE A SUN, ... 174 FIRE RAID 56
INTO THE WINE BURNING LIKE BRANDY, ... 175 FIRE RAID 71
OF MUD AND SAND. AND, LIKE A SABLE MOTH, ... 179 NEW QUAY 4
CASTING TO-MORROW LIKE A THORN .... 180 VISION, PRAYER 25
HIS MOUTH AND ROCKED HIM LIKE A STORM .... 181 VISION, PRAYER 44
LIKE POLLEN .... 183 VISION, PRAYER 112
A SHE BIRD ROSE AND RAYED LIKE A BURNING BRIDE. ... 189 WINTER'S TALE 69
HIM UP AND HE RAN LIKE A WIND AFTER THE KINDLING FLIGHT .... 190 WINTER'S TALE 89
WHEN BLACK BIRDS DIED LIKE PRIESTS IN THE CLOAKED HEDGE ROW .... 190 WINTER'S TALE 92
AND FAST THROUGH THE DRIFTS OF THE THICKETS ANTLERED LIKE DEER, ... 190 WINTER'S TALE 95
LIKE THE DUST OF THE DEAD. .... 192 SIDE OF TRUTH 12
BLOW AWAY LIKE BREATH, ... 193 SIDE OF TRUTH 17
FLY LIKE THE STARS' BLOOD, ... 193 SIDE OF TRUTH 24
LIKE THE SUN'S TEARS, ... 193 SIDE OF TRUTH 25

		PAGE	TITLE	LINE
LIKE (CONTINUED)				
LIKE THE MOON'S SEED, RUBBISH	....	193	SIDE OF TRUTH	26
TO THE SEA SOUND FLOWING LIKE BLOOD FROM THE LOUD				
WOUND	....	194	SLEEP BECALMED	6
AND THEN TO AWAKE, AND THE FARM, LIKE A WANDERER				
WHITE	....	195	FERN HILL	28
THOUGH I SANG IN MY CHAINS LIKE THE SEA.	....	196	FERN HILL	54
OF BIRDS! AMONG THE COCKS LIKE FIRE THE RED FOX	...	199	COUNTRY SLEEP	69
THE THIEF FALL ON THE DEAD LIKE THE WILLY NILLY DEW,		200	COUNTRY SLEEP	93
ROUND THE SUN, HE COMES TO MY LOVE LIKE THE DESIGNED				
SNOW,	....	200	COUNTRY SLEEP	96
FLOWS TO THE STRAND OF FLOWERS LIKE THE DEW'S RULY				
SEA,	....	200	COUNTRY SLEEP	98
AND SURELY HE SAILS LIKE THE SHIP SHAPE CLOUDS. OH HE		200	COUNTRY SLEEP	99
AND THE DAUGHTERS OF DARKNESS FLAME LIKE FAWKES				
FIRES STILL.	....	205	GIANT'S THIGH	60
THE RUDE OWL CRIED LIKE A TELLTALE TIT,	....	206	LAMENT	5
BLIND EYES COULD BLAZE LIKE METEORS AND BE GAY,	...	208	NOT GO GENTLE	14
AND THE ANGELS WHIRR LIKE PHEASANTS	....	215	COUNTRY HEAVEN	9
BUSHES AND OWLS BLOW OUT LIKE CANDLES,	....	215	COUNTRY HEAVEN	18
AND THE LONG FOX LIKE FIRE	....	216	COUNTRY HEAVEN	27
ON WHOM A WORLD OF ILLS CAME DOWN LIKE SNOW.	....	217	ELEGY	32
DOWN THESE FANTASTIC AVENUES PASS LIKE SHADOWS.	...	222	FOREST PICTURE	12
THE MOONS ARE WHITE FLAMES, LIKE THE MOONS IN DREAMS.		223	IN DREAMS	14
MY TEARS ARE LIKE THE QUIET DRIFT	....	225	CLOWN IN MOON	1
SO TREMULOUSLY LIKE A DREAM.	....	225	CLOWN IN MOON	8
NODDING LIKE FLOWERS,	....	226	THE ELM	2
LIKE FRAGMENTARY RAIN	....	226	SLENDER WIND	4
BEAUTIFULLY LITTLE LIKE CLOUDS:	....	226	THE ELM	9
IN A PATTERN LIKE A SHELL	....	229	MY RIVER	39
LIKE A CAVE WITH ONE THREAD.	....	230	OUR SANCTITY	21
LIKE A BIRD IN ITS LIGHTNESS,	....	233	NO THOUGHT	17
LIKE A LIVING CLOAK OVER ME.	....	235	WOMAN TAPESTRY	5
MY LOVE FOR HER IS LIKE THE MOVING OF A CLOUD	.....	235	WOMAN TAPESTRY	13
SHE BECAME LIKE A DANCER OR A PRETTY ANIMAL	....	235	WOMAN TAPESTRY	20
LIKE THE ARMS OF A CLEAN WOMAN	....	236	WOMAN TAPESTRY	39
LIKE THE BODY OF A GIRL.	....	236	WOMAN TAPESTRY	55
GROWING LIKE A POWERFUL ROOT INSIDE ME.	....	236	WOMAN TAPESTRY	67
LIKE A SWEET, SENSITIVE PLANT	....	237	WOMAN TAPESTRY	71
COILED INTO THEIR BODIES LIKE SNAKES,	....	237	WOMAN TAPESTRY	76
FEEL YOUR WOMAN'S BREASTS RISE UP LIKE FLOWERS	....	238	MAKES INTERVALS	12
LIKENESS				
THIS IS THE WORLD: THE LYING LIKENESS OF	....	90	EUNUCH DREAMS	31
LILACS				
FOR LILACS IN THEIR BEAUTY BLOW	....	227	TRIOLET	2
FOR LILACS IN THEIR BEAUTY BLOW.	....	228	TRIOLET	8
LILIES				
TAXIS AND LILIES TO TINNED MUSIC STEPPED	....	51	OUT OF THE PIT	24
TAXIS AND LILIES, NOISE AND NO NOISE,	....	53	OUT OF THE PIT	95
LILTING				
ABOUT THE LILTING HOUSE AND HAPPY AS THE GRASS WAS				
GREEN,	....	195	FERN HILL	2
LILY				
THIS LILY CRAWLING ROUND THE LOCAL PUBS?	....	52	OUT OF THE PIT	50
THE RACK OF DREAMS MY LILY BONES	....	68	BEFORE KNOCKED	20
LILY'S				
BRAND OF THE LILY'S ANGER ON HER RING,	....	115	A GRIEF AGO	19
LIMB				
DEAD LIMB AND MIND,	....	26	PERSONAL EPIT	14

	PAGE	TITLE	LINE
LIMBS			
UNDER HER GRASSY DRESS NO LIMBS--	15	FOR LEDA	23
PRAISE THAT MY BODY BE WHOLE, I'VE LIMBS,	42	A WAR OF WITS	8
OR ALL-IN WRESTLING FOR TORN LIMBS TO HEAL,	51	OUT OF THE PIT	31
UNSHACKLED THE WEIGHTS OF WORDS FROM TIRED LIMBS,	53	OUT OF THE PIT	83
AND THE LIMBS ARE TORN.	60	MEAT ON BONES	5
WHAT WERE YOUNG LIMBS ARE FAGGOTS ON THE LAND,	63	WOMAN SPEAKS	14
WHACK THEIR BOYS' LIMBS,	89	EUNUCH DREAMS	3
FROM LIMBS THAT HAD THE MEASURE OF WORM, SHUFFLED	102	I DREAMED MY	5
SHE CRIED HER WHITE-DRESSED LIMBS WERE BARE	139	TOMBSTONE TOLD	17
MADE HER LIMBS BLIND BY LUMINOUS CHARMS,	157	INTO HER HEAD	21
THE OCTOPUS WALKING INTO HER LIMBS	164	LONG-LEGGED	79
WITH SALTY COLTS AND GALES IN THEIR LIMBS	168	LONG-LEGGED	186
THAT HER LOVING, UNFRIENDLY LIMBS	175	MY BEGGAR ARM	5
THE CARVED LIMBS IN THE ROCK	189	WINTER'S TALE	76
AND TWINE THE LIMBS AROUND MY HANDS.	239	MAKES INTERVALS	24
LIME			
FLOWING AND MELTING UNDER LIME.	19	IMAGES IN AIR	8
HOW OF MY CLAY IS MADE THE HANGMAN'S LIME.	77	THE FORCE THAT	15
SEE, SAYS THE LIME	85	SEE, SAYS LIME	T
SEE, SAYS THE LIME, MY WICKED MILKS	85	SEE, SAYS LIME	1
ON THESE BLUE LIPS, THE LIME REMARKS,	85	SEE, SAYS LIME	9
SEE, SAYS THE LIME, AROUND THESE WRECKS	86	SEE, SAYS LIME	25
LIMIT			
LIKE SOME PITCH MOON, THE LIMIT OF THE GLOBES;	82	LIGHT BREAKS	20
LIMP			
LIMP IN THE STREET OF SEA, AMONG THE RABBLE	104	WORLD PYRAMID	15
A LIMP AND RIDERLESS SHAPE TO LEAP NINE THINNING MONTHS.'	145	IF HEAD HURT	15
SLUNK POUTING OUT WHEN THE LIMP TIME CAME;	207	LAMENT	44
LIMPET			
DO NOT FORGET THAT 'LIMPET' RHYMES	84	LETTER TO AUNT	33
LIMP-TREED			
LOST IN A LIMP-TREED AND UNEATING SILENCE,	132	I MAKE THIS IN	28
LINE			
DOWN AN ECSTATIC LINE OF LIGHT,	13	RAIN CUTS	8
MAN'S RIB ON WOMAN'S, STRAIGHT LINE ON A CURVE,	51	OUT OF THE PIT	35
OVER THE MANWAGING LINE.	125	SEED-AT-ZERO	7
OVER THE WARBEARING LINE.	125	SEED-AT-ZERO	14
THE LIGHT WILL COME IN AN UNWAVERING LINE.	232	YOUR VOICE	7
LINEAMENTS			
THE FRANK, CLOSED PEARL, THE SEA-GIRLS' LINEAMENTS	131	I MAKE THIS IN	19
LINEN			
GOLD ON SUCH FEATURES, AND THE LINEN SPIRIT	120	ALTARWISE	121
WHERE, WOUND IN EMERALD LINEN AND SHARP WIND,	132	I MAKE THIS IN	42
SWELLING IN FLEA-SPECKED LINEN	154	RETURN	7
WHERE SITTING IN CLEAN LINEN	156	RETURN	93
IN THE SQUIRREL NIMBLE GROVE, UNDER LINEN AND THATCH	199	COUNTRY SLEEP	44
LINENED			
IN THAT BRIGHT ANCHORGROUND WHERE I LAY LINENED,	132	I MAKE THIS IN	48
LINES			
ROSE IN OUR OUTWORN BRAINS. WE SPOKE OUR LINES,	34	IN GARDENS	11
WIND CARVEN LINES AROUND THE DROOPING MOUTH;	64	WOMAN SPEAKS	50
THE VIRGIN LINES BE MATED WITH A CIRCLE.	66	LET A FAITH	3
AND FLESH WAS SNIPPED TO CROSS THE LINES	68	BEFORE KNOCKED	22
THE LINES OF EARTH, THE CURVING OF THE HEART,	73	LORD RED HAIL	14
LEAVES IS DANCING. LINES OF AGE ON THE STONES WEAVE IN A FLOCK.	189	WINTER'S TALE	78
BACK. LINES OF AGE SLEEP ON THE STONES TILL TRUMPETING DAWN.	191	WINTER'S TALE	118

	PAGE	TITLE	LINE
LINGER			
'LINGER NOT DEEPER IN THE COLOURED TREES, ...	227	SPRING-SPIRIT	2
LINGERED			
THE FOAM HAS LINGERED INTO WHITE, LITTLE FLOWERS,	224	IDYLL UNFORGET	28
LINKED			
LINKED IN ONE GAS BRACKET	137	O CHATTERTON	2
ALL BIRDS AND BEASTS OF THE LINKED NIGHT UPROAR AND			
CHIME	204	GIANT'S THIGH	35
LINNET			
OR THE YELLOW LINNET WHO DOES NOT MERIT IT.	230	OUR SANCTITY	14
LINT			
BUCKLE TO LINT AND CLOTH THEIR NATRON FOOTSTEPS,	120	ALTARWISE	116
LION			
LION OR LOUSE? TAKE YOUR OWN ADVICE;	58	TO ARCHITECTS	17
THE PEBBLES. IT IS TIME FOR THE BLACK LION	179	NEW QUAY	10
LIONHEAD'S			
THAT MELTS THE LIONHEAD'S HEEL AND HORSESHOE OF THE			
HEART, ...	135	HOW MY ANIMAL	14
LIONS			
WHALEBED AND BULLDANCE, THE GOLD BUSH OF LIONS, ...	131	I MAKE THIS IN	22
LIONS AND FIRES OF HIS FLYING BREATH, ...	160	DEATHS AND ENT	5
LION'S			
A PINCH OF AUDEN IS THE LION'S FEAST;	58	TO ARCHITECTS	13
TO LEAVE IT EMPTY'S LION'S OR LOUSE'S CHOICE;	58	TO ARCHITECTS	16
LIP			
THE WEIGHTLESS TOUCHING OF THE LIP	12	SKY'S BRIGHT	9
WETTEN YOUR TONGUE AND LIP, ...	20	THE NEOPHYTE	18
NOW THE THIRST PARCHES LIP AND TONGUE	34	THIRST PARCHES	T
NOW THE THIRST PARCHES LIP AND TONGUE, ...	34	THIRST PARCHES	1
OF THE GULLS THE LIP OF WAVES.	76	SONG: LOVE ME	11
LIPLESS			
LIPLESS AND TONGUELESS IN THE SOUR EARTH	23	THE ONLY DEAD	2
LIPPED			
MARK, TRUMPET LIPPED AND BLACKHEAD	155	RETURN	41
LIPS			
AND TASTE UPON OUR LIPS, THIS MINUTE, ...	14	RAIN CUTS	37
OUT OF MY THIN BLACK LIPS, ...	18	NATURAL DAY	27
AND ON OUR LIPS THE DRY MOUTH OF THE RAIN.	26	THERE'S PLENTY	19
HIS WILD CAROUSES, AND HIS LIPS	29	NEARLY SUMMER	10
PURSED LIPS AT THE RECEIVER, ...	44	LONGED TO MOVE	17
HE, TOO, COULD TOUCH THE SEASON'S LIPS AND SMILE,	46	POET: 1935	14
MY LIPS ARE WITHERED WITH A KISS, ...	61	MEAT ON BONES	20
HUNGERS FOR QUICKENING, AND MY LONELY LIPS	64	WOMAN SPEAKS	36
THROUGH, I TELL YOU, YOUR TWO MIDNIGHT LIPS I PRAY	76	LASHED RINGS	7
THE LIPS OF TIME LEECH TO THE FOUNTAIN HEAD;	77	THE FORCE THAT	16
ON THESE BLUE LIPS, THE LIME REMARKS, ...	85	SEE, SAYS LIME	9
YOUR PAIN SHALL BE A MEANING IN YOUR LIPS	87	PAIN BE MUSIC	13
AND WORDS FALL CRIPPLED FROM THE SLAVING LIPS, ...	96	TWELVE	2
AND FROM HER LIPS THE FADED PIGMENTS FALL, ...	116	LANTERNS SHINE	7
CRIED THE TOPLESS, INCHTAPED LIPS FROM HANK AND HOOD	132	I MAKE THIS IN	47
AND HER RED LIPS WERE KISSED BLACK, ...	139	TOMBSTONE TOLD	18
WHEN AT YOUR LIPS AND KEYS, ...	160	DEATHS AND ENT	14
A GIRL ALIVE WITH HIS HOOKS THROUGH HER LIPS;	162	LONG-LEGGED	22
DEEP THE GREAT BUSHED BAIT WITH RAINING LIPS	163	LONG-LEGGED	51
AND THE OLD MEN SING FROM NEWBORN LIPS:	167	LONG-LEGGED	152
AND HE WHO TAUGHT THEIR LIPS TO SING	167	LONG-LEGGED	162
HER HEART ALL EARS AND EYES, LIPS CATCHING THE			
AVALANCHE	170	MARRIAGE VIRG	10
BEFORE THE LIPS BLAZE AND BLOOM	183	VISION, PRAYER	121

		PAGE	TITLE	LINE
LIPS (CONTINUED)				
THESE WERE THE WHISPERINGS THAT SIGHED ON MY LIPS AT DUSK,	....	223	IDYLL UNFORGET	10
I HAVE FELT THE SILK WIND BRUSH MY LIPS;	....	224	IDYLL UNFORGET	19
AND WHITE, SYMMETRICAL LIPS	....	236	WOMAN TAPESTRY	44
LIQUID				
WITH LIQUID HANDS TAPPED ON THE WOMB,	....	68	BEFORE KNOCKED	2
AND I WILL BUILD MY LIQUID WORLD,	....	74	WE MOTHERNAKED	13
SEASONS OVER THE LIQUID WORLD,	....	166	LONG-LEGGED	119
THE LIQUID CHOIRS OF HIS TRIBES.	....	167	LONG-LEGGED	164
LISTEN				
WITH HALF-AVERTED HEADS, AS IF TO LISTEN,	....	40	YOUNG ARE OLD	13
LISTEN. THE MINSTRELS SING	....	189	WINTER'S TALE	56
TIME SINGS THROUGH THE INTRICATELY DEAD SNOW DROP. LISTEN.	....	189	WINTER'S TALE	65
LISTEN AND LOOK WHERE SHE SAILS THE GOOSE PLUCKED SEA,	....	190	WINTER'S TALE	100
LISTENED				
COME IN THE MORNING WHERE I WANDERED AND LISTENED		177	POEM IN OCT	27
AND LISTENED WHEN A SLOW, STARRED SLUMBER WRAPT THE MOON,	....	223	IDYLL UNFORGET	7
LISTENING				
WARMING DRY HANDS AND LISTENING TO THE WIND.	....	42	YOUNG ARE OLD	55
IN THE LISTENING	....	178	POEM IN OCT	55
UNDER THE MILE OFF MOON WE TREMBLED LISTENING	.....	194	SLEEP BECALMED	5
LIT				
EMPTY OF LIGHT AND FIND THE DARKNESS LIT--	....	27	OBLIVIOUS DARK	5
STREETS' STOCK, OF THE MOON LIT, ILL LIT, FIELD AND TOWN,	....	45	PLOUGHMAN GONE	22
STREETS' STOCK, OF THE MOON LIT, ILL LIT, FIELD AND TOWN,	....	45	PLOUGHMAN GONE	22
LIT ON THE CUDDLED TREE, THE CROSS OF FEVER,	......	100	RUNNING GRAVE	33
AND THE LONG-TAILED LIGHTNING LIT HIS CATCH.	......	166	LONG-LEGGED	128
LITERARY				
THE LITERARY CHANKLEY BORE,	....	83	LETTER TO AUNT	2
A LITERARY HOTTENTOT	....	83	LETTER TO AUNT	4
LITTLE				
HEAR AND AM STILL THE LITTLE BIRD.	....	9	MINUTE'S HOUR	7
AWHILE, A LITTLE,	....	23	THE ONLY DEAD	20
LITTLE PROBLEM	....	24	LITTLE PROBLEM	T
AROUND OUR LITTLE SELVES	....	24	THE ONLY DEAD	32
OUT OF THE SIGHS A LITTLE COMES,	....	31	OUT OF SIGHS	1
A LITTLE COMES, IS TASTED AND FOUND GOOD;	....	31	OUT OF SIGHS	5
THEN STIRRED A LITTLE CHAOS IN THE SUN.	....	33	IN GARDENS	6
LET IT BE KNOWN THAT LITTLE LIVE BUT LIES,	....	36	LET BE KNOWN	1
WITHIN HIS HEAD REVOLVED A LITTLE WORLD	....	50	OUT OF THE PIT	1
DUST IN THE LITTLE COUNTRY OF AN URN,	....	56	GREEK PLAY	6
IS HEARD BUT LITTLE TILL THE STARS GO OUT.	....	56	WHY EAST WIND	20
WE HAVE THESE LITTLE THINGS OFF PAT,	....	59	FAIRY TALES	4
FEAR DEATH AS LITTLE AS THE THUNDER'S SHOT,	....	60	FAIRY TALES	40
STRANGLE THE LITTLE CHILDREN IN THEIR BEDS;	....	64	WOMAN SPEAKS	46
THAT DUST YOU HOLD, O STREW THAT LITTLE LEFT;	.....	65	WOMAN SPEAKS	61
AND HELD A LITTLE SABBATH WITH THE SUN,	....	97	TWILIGHT LOCKS	15
MEANING IN HOT SOCK SOIL? A LITTLE CUSS	....	137	O CHATTERTON	18
POINT THEIR LITTLE BREASTS AT ME;	....	138	O CHATTERTON	32
3 LITTLE LUSTS SHALL YOUR DOWRY BE,	....	138	O CHATTERTON	42
NOW BREAK A GIANT TEAR FOR THE LITTLE KNOWN FALL,		153	WAS A SAVIOUR	32
IN THE CINDER OF THE LITTLE SKULL,	....	174	FIRE RAID	40
IN THE CINDER OF THE LITTLE SKULL,	....	174	FIRE RAID	54
ALL THE GREEN LEAVED LITTLE WEDDINGS' WIVES	....	206	LAMENT	11

	PAGE	TITLE	LINE
LITTLE (CONTINUED)			
WITH LITTLE, ODD MISTS WAVED IN THE PATH OF ITS ECHO,	224	IDYLL UNFORGET	26
THE FOAM HAS LINGERED INTO WHITE, LITTLE FLOWERS,	224	IDYLL UNFORGET	28
AND HOURS MADE LITTLE I HAVE DIPPED MY ARMS IN THEIR RAPTURE;	224	IDYLL UNFORGET	31
LITTLE WHITE-LIPPED FACES HAVE PEERED UP AT ME,	224	IDYLL UNFORGET	32
BEAUTIFULLY LITTLE LIKE CLOUDS:	226	THE ELM	9
YOU STAND A LITTLE APART,	229	MY RIVER	6
DOING MY LITTLE TRICKS OF SPEECH AGAIN	234	NO, PIGEON	20
LIVE			
FOR DEAD OR LIVE,	27	OBLIVIOUS DARK	19
LET IT BE KNOWN THAT LITTLE LIVE BUT LIES,	36	LET BE KNOWN	1
DECLARE THEIR SOULS, LET CHILDREN KNOW, LIVE AFTER.	36	LET BE KNOWN	6
AND THIS IS TRUE, NO MAN CAN LIVE	55	NO MAN BELIEVE	18
AND MAY I YET LIVE TO ADMIRE	85	LETTER TO AUNT	65
WHO PICKS THE LIVE HEART ON A DIAMOND.	132	I MAKE THIS IN	45
RAISE THE LIVE RAFTERS OF THE EARDRUM,	142	SAINT TO FALL	36
LIE DOWN, LIE DOWN AND LIVE	152	BELOW A TIME	50
LIVE SELF FOR SELF,	239	LET ME ESCAPE	3
LIVED			
AND I LIVED IN HIS PURSE AND HIS HEART	149	PAPER & STICKS	6
LIVELONG			
THE LIVELONG RIVER'S ROBE	209	POEM ON B'DAY	28
THE BEES ARE GLAD THE LIVELONG DAY,	227	TRIOLET	1
THE BEES ARE GLAD THE LIVELONG DAY,	228	TRIOLET	4
THE BEES ARE GLAD THE LIVELONG DAY,	228	TRIOLET	7
LIVER			
OF GALLOW CROSSES ON THE LIVER	68	BEFORE KNOCKED	23
LIVERY			
STRIP THE DREAMS' LIVERY,	67	LET A FAITH	7
LIVES			
AND MUCH THAT LIVES TO PERISH,	25	THERE'S PLENTY	2
AND A CAT HAS A NUMBER OF LIVES;	221	SONG OF DOG	2
LIVING			
THE LIVING VESSELS OF THE GARDEN	13	RAIN CUTS	13
THEY ARE THE ONLY LIVING THING WHO DID LOVE,	23	THE ONLY DEAD	4
AND THERE'S THE LIVING WHO DID LOVE,	24	THE ONLY DEAD	31
AND BARED YOUR HEAD BENEATH THE LIVING SKY,	30	YOUTH CALLS	9
THE LIVING SKY, THE FACES OF THE STARS.	36	MIDNIGHT ROAD	14
THE HUNGER OF LIVING, THE OVEN AND GUN	39	GAS FADES	24
MAKE THE HUNGER FOR LIVING	39	GAS FADES	26
THE LIVING DEAD LEFT OVER FROM THE WAR,	41	YOUNG ARE OLD	35
THE LIVING AFTER, THE FILLED WITH FEAR,	41	YOUNG ARE OLD	36
LEFT IN THE RECORDS OF LIVING A NOT-TO-BE-BROKEN PICTURE,	45	PLOUGHMAN GONE	2
AMONG ALL LIVING MEN IS A SAD GHOST.	47	POET: 1935	24
SEE WOMEN'S FACES UNDER LIVING SNOODS,	51	OUT OF THE PIT	21
UNDER THE GREEN ROOF GRIEVES THE LIVING;	56	GREEK PLAY	2
THE LIVING SUN LAMENTS THE DYING SKIES,	56	GREEK PLAY	3
PITY THE LIVING WHO ARE LOST, ALONE;	57	GREEK PLAY	21
THE SLUG'S A LIVING CALENDAR OF DAYS;	59	HERE IN SPRING	15
SEE THE FIRST LIVING LIGHT,	67	LET A FAITH	12
DID TWIST INTO A LIVING CIPHER,	68	BEFORE KNOCKED	21
DAM AND SIRE, LIVING, LO,	72	TAKE NEEDLES	47
LIGHTS UP THE LIVING WORM.	88	A PROCESS IN	6
THEN ALL THE MATTER OF THE LIVING AIR	102	FELLOWED SLEEP	21
WITH BRIDEBAIT OF GOLD BREAD, I WITH A LIVING SKEIN,	135	HOW MY ANIMAL	25
OF THE LIVING FLESH IS MONSTROUS OR IMMORTAL,	148	UNLUCKILY FOR	41
AND THE LIVING EARTH YOUR SONS.	149	UNLUCKILY FOR	56
WHITE FEATHERING THE LIVING.	154	RETURN	25

	PAGE	TITLE	LINE
LIVING (CONTINUED)			
WITH ALL THE LIVING, PRAYS,	210	POEM ON B'DAY	66
HARK! A VOICE AND LAUGHTER--THE LIVING AND LOVING	222	FOREST PICTURE	11
LIKE A LIVING CLOAK OVER ME.	235	WOMAN TAPESTRY	5
LIZARD			
'A LIZARD DARTING WITH BLACK VENOM'S THREAD	132	I MAKE THIS IN	49
LO			
DAM AND SIRE, LIVING, LO,	72	TAKE NEEDLES	47
LOAD			
AND LOAD THE THROATS OF SHELLS	160	DEATHS AND ENT	22
LOADS			
TO LONDON'S TURNED, AND THIRSTY LOADS	37	WINDMILLS TURN	9
TO HEAVEN'S TURNED, AND PIOUS LOADS	37	WINDMILLS TURN	32
LOAM			
MIXES, RIPENS, IN THE LOAM;	71	TAKE NEEDLES	26
LOAVES			
WAS MIRACULOUS VIRGINITY OLD AS LOAVES AND FISHES,	170	MARRIAGE VIRG	5
LOBSTER			
THERE ARE OTHERS WHO THINK THAT A LOBSTER IS PINK,	221	SONG OF DOG	3
LOCAL			
THIS LILY CRAWLING ROUND THE LOCAL PUBS?	52	OUT OF THE PIT	50
LOCK			
TIME FOR THE SWIMMERS' HANDS, MUSIC FOR SILVER LOCK	15	SPIRE CRANES	7
THAT WIPES AWAY NOT CROW'S-FOOT NOR THE LOCK	95	RUB OF LOVE	23
KNOW NOW THE FLESH'S LOCK AND VICE,	106	ALL ALL AND	20
FROM THE OPENING OF THE GARDEN LOCK	171	THE HUNCHBACK	4
LOCKED			
LOCKED IN THE LONG WORM OF MY FINGER	97	TWILIGHT LOCKS	2
FALLS ON A RING OF SUMMERS AND LOCKED NOONS.	132	I MAKE THIS IN	30
IN QUICK, SWEET, CRUEL LIGHT TILL THE LOCKED GROUND SPROUT OUT,	135	HOW MY ANIMAL	18
PRISONERS OF WISHES LOCKED THEIR EYES	153	WAS A SAVIOUR	7
A STONE LIES LOST AND LOCKED IN THE LARK-HIGH HILL.	159	INTO HER HEAD	62
LOCKERS			
SPROUT FROM THE STONY LOCKERS LIKE A TREE ON ARAN.	111	I, IN IMAGE	78
LOCKING			
GIVE OVER, LOVERS, LOCKING, AND THE SEAWAX STRUGGLE,	111	I, IN IMAGE	89
LOCKING, UNLOCKING, THE MURDERED STRANGERS WEAVE,	160	DEATHS AND ENT	15
LOCKJAW			
DOUBLED, TO FORK HIM BACK, THROUGH THE LOCKJAW BED	132	I MAKE THIS IN	50
LOCKS			
MIGHT PLAY UPON HIS LANK LOCKS WITH ITS WIND,	46	POET: 1935	3
THE FINGERS AT THE LOCKS.	62	EARS IN TURRET	4
WHEN ONCE THE TWILIGHT LOCKS NO LONGER	97	TWILIGHT LOCKS	T
WHEN ONCE THE TWILIGHT LOCKS NO LONGER	97	TWILIGHT LOCKS	1
THE SEA AND INSTRUMENT, NICKED IN THE LOCKS OF TIME,	111	I, IN IMAGE	92
IN THE WATCHED DARK, QUIVERING THROUGH LOCKS AND CAVES,	161	DEATHS AND ENT	31
THE LOCKS YAWNED LOOSE AND A BLAST BLEW THEM WIDE,	172	DAWN RAID	3
WHEN ALL THE KEYS SHOT FROM THE LOCKS, AND RANG.	172	DAWN RAID	8
AFTER THE LOCKS AND CHAINS	172	THE HUNCHBACK	36
LOCUSTS			
AND FAMINE GREW, AND LOCUSTS CAME;	66	HAND SIGNED	10
LODGED			
CONVENIENT BIRD AND BEAST LIE LODGED TO SUFFER	144	PLEASURE-BIRD	3
LOFT			
UP TO THE SWALLOW THRONGED LOFT BY THE SHADOW OF MY HAND,	196	FERN HILL	47
SHALLOW AND SEDGE, AND 'DILLY DILLY', CALLS THE LOFT HAWK,	202	SIR JOHNS HILL	21

		PAGE	TITLE	LINE
LOFT (CONTINUED)				
HOUSED IN HAMLETS OF HEAVEN SWING THE LOFT LAMPS,		215	COUNTRY HEAVEN	16
LOFTY				
THE LOFTY ROOTS OF THE CLOUDS.		142	SAINT TO FALL	30
LOG				
BY THE SPIT AND THE BLACK POT IN THE LOG BRIGHT LIGHT		188	WINTER'S TALE	27
BY THE SPIT AND THE BLACK POT IN THE LOG BRIGHT LIGHT.		190	WINTER'S TALE	87
LOGIC				
WHEN BLOOD, SPADE-HANDED, AND THE LOGIC TIME		100	RUNNING GRAVE	13
LOGICS				
WHEN LOGICS DIE,		82	LIGHT BREAKS	27
LOIN				
THE TWISTED BRAIN, THE FAIR-FORMED LOIN,		32	OUT OF SIGHS	25
STRIPPING MY LOIN OF PROMISE,		75	MY HERO BARES	14
THE SEED OF TIME IS SHELTERED IN THE LOIN:		80	ALMANAC TIME	12
THE SEED THAT MAKES A FOREST OF THE LOIN		88	A PROCESS IN	13
I WOULD NOT FEAR THE DEVIL IN THE LOIN		95	RUB OF LOVE	20
THE LOIN IS GLORY IN A WORKING PALLOR.		105	WORLD PYRAMID	57
REFUSAL STRUCK HER LOIN AND THE LAME FLOWER		134	NOT FROM ANGER	2
AND HIS LOIN WAS A HUNTING FLAME		168	LONG-LEGGED	196
SEED OF SONS IN THE LOIN OF THE BLACK HUSK LEFT.		174	FIRE RAID	32
FROM HIS LOIN		180	VISION, PRAYER	32
LOIN-LEAF				
SLEEP TO A NEWBORN SLEEP IN A SWADDLING LOIN-LEAF STROKED AND SANG		157	INTO HER HEAD	22
LOINS				
THE LOINS CRIED MURDER.		85	SEE, SAYS LIME	16
LONDON				
LONDON (SAID THE ODD MAN IN		154	RETURN	2
O ROME AND SODOM TO-MORROW AND LONDON		168	LONG-LEGGED	191
ON THE ALTAR OF LONDON,		174	FIRE RAID	38
A REFUSAL TO MOURN THE DEATH, BY FIRE, OF A CHILD IN LONDON		191	REFUSAL MOURN	T
LONDON'S				
TO LONDON'S TURNED, AND THIRSTY LOADS		37	WINDMILLS TURN	9
LONDON'S ARCHES ARE FALLING		154	RETURN	26
IN MANY MARRIED LONDON'S ESTRANGING GRIEF.		160	DEATHS AND ENT	12
WHEN NEAR AND STRANGE WOUNDED ON LONDON'S WAVES		160	DEATHS AND ENT	27
DEEP WITH THE FIRST DEAD LIES LONDON'S DAUGHTER,		192	REFUSAL MOURN	19
LONELINESS				
HER LONELINESS ACROSS THE EMPTY WAVES		22	ON QUIET NIGHT	10
FOR HE HAS FOUND HIS SOUL IN LONELINESS,		53	OUT OF THE PIT	97
LONELY				
O LONELY AMONG MANY, THE GODS' MAN,		47	POET: 1935	47
HUNGERS FOR QUICKENING, AND MY LONELY LIPS		64	WOMAN SPEAKS	36
THE DEATH BIDING TWO LIE LONELY.		148	UNLUCKILY FOR	28
AND I AM STRUCK AS LONELY AS A HOLY MAKER BY THE SUN.		186	HOLY SPRING	12
LONG				
TOO LONG, SKELETON		29	LONG, SKELETON	T
TOO LONG, SKELETON, DEATH'S RISEN		29	LONG, SKELETON	1
TOO LONG, SKELETON, DEATH'S ALL ALIVE		29	LONG, SKELETON	4
HE'LL ACHE TOO LONG		32	OUT OF SIGHS	13
THEY LYING LONG SHALL NOT DIE WINDILY;		49	NO DOMINION	12
LONG BREATH THAT CARRIED TO MY FATHER		69	BEFORE KNOCKED	41
AND THE FOUR WINDS, THAT HAD LONG BLOWN AS ONE,		78	LOVE'S FEVER	19
LOCKED IN THE LONG WORM OF MY FINGER		97	TWILIGHT LOCKS	2
TURN THE LONG SEA ARTERIAL		110	I, IN IMAGE	46
SPLITTING THE LONG EYE OPEN, AND THE SPIRAL TURNKEY,		110	I, IN IMAGE	50

		PAGE	TITLE	LINE
LONG (CONTINUED)				
YOU ARE ALL THESE, SAID SHE WHO GAVE ME THE LONG SUCK,		112	NOT FATHER ME	17
A LEG AS LONG AS TREES,		114	SERVANT SUN	29
SHAPE ALL HER WHELPS WITH THE LONG VOICE OF WATER,		115	A GRIEF AGO	29
I AM THE LONG WORLD'S GENTLEMAN, HE SAID,		117	ALTARWISE	13
THE CHILD THAT SUCKETH LONG IS SHOOTING UP,		117	ALTARWISE	16
SOON SETS ALIGHT A LONG STICK FROM THE CRADLE;		117	ALTARWISE	20
WITH PINS FOR TEARDROPS IS THE LONG WOUND'S WOMAN.		120	ALTARWISE	104
WEDS MY LONG GENTLEMAN TO DUSTS AND FURIES;		120	ALTARWISE	122
SIGH LONG, CLAY COLD, LIE SHORN,		135	HOW MY ANIMAL	34
I ADVANCE FOR AS LONG AS FOREVER IS.		143	24 YEARS	9
DOWN THE LONG WALKS OF THEIR VOWS.		161	WEDDING ANNIV	4
THE LONG, LAID MINUTE'S BRIDE DRIFTS ON		164	LONG-LEGGED	83
OH MIRACLE OF FISHES! THE LONG DEAD BITE!		166	LONG-LEGGED	140
AND TAKEN BY LIGHT IN HER ARMS AT LONG AND DEAR LAST		170	LOVE IN ASYLUM	16
JOY OF THE LONG DEAD CHILD SANG BURNING		178	POEM IN OCT	63
ON THE GRISTED LEAVES AND THE LONG GONE GLISTENING		189	WINTER'S TALE	63
IN THE LONG AGO LAND THAT GLIDED THE DARK DOOR WIDE		189	WINTER'S TALE	67
OF FIELDS. FOR LOVE, THE LONG AGO SHE BIRD RISES. LOOK.		189	WINTER'S TALE	80
ALL NIGHT LOST AND LONG WADING IN THE WAKE OF THE SHE-		190	WINTER'S TALE	98
ROBED IN THE LONG FRIENDS,		192	REFUSAL MOURN	20
ALL THE SUN LONG IT WAS RUNNING, IT WAS LOVELY, THE HAY		195	FERN HILL	19
ALL THE MOON LONG I HEARD, BLESSED AMONG STABLES, THE NIGHTJARS		195	FERN HILL	25
UNDER THE NEW MADE CLOUDS AND HAPPY AS THE HEART WAS LONG,		196	FERN HILL	38
TO LABOUR AND LOVE THOUGH THEY LAY DOWN LONG AGO.		203	GIANT'S THIGH	5
TROUNCED BY HIS WINGS IN THE HISSING SHIPPEN, LONG DEAD		205	GIANT'S THIGH	39
SAVE BY THEIR LONG DESIRERS IN THE FOX CUBBED		205	GIANT'S THIGH	56
AND THE RHYMER IN THE LONG TONGUED ROOM,		209	POEM ON B'DAY	15
BUT DARK IS A LONG WAY.		210	POEM ON B'DAY	64
YOUNG AMONG THE LONG FLOCKS, AND NEVER LIE LOST		216	ELEGY	7
AND THE LONG FOX LIKE FIRE		216	COUNTRY HEAVEN	27
DOWN THE LONG BAYS OF BLUE THAT THOSE CLOUDY HEADLANDS		222	FOREST PICTURE	6
THE BLADE OF YOUR LONG FOOT,		229	MY RIVER	16
LONGED				
I HAVE LONGED TO MOVE AWAY		43	LONGED TO MOVE	T
I HAVE LONGED TO MOVE AWAY		43	LONGED TO MOVE	1
I HAVE LONGED TO MOVE AWAY		43	LONGED TO MOVE	6
I HAVE LONGED TO MOVE AWAY BUT AM AFRAID;		44	LONGED TO MOVE	11
ABOVE ALL HE LONGED FOR HIS MOTHER'S BREAST		216	ELEGY	9
LONGER				
TAKE NOW CONTENT, NO LONGER POSTURING		29	LONG, SKELETON	7
AND WEST'S NO LONGER DROWNED		55	WHY EAST WIND	3
NO LONGER TREMBLE AT A BISHOP'S HAT,		59	FAIRY TALES	2
NO LONGER FEAR THE WALKER IN THE GARDEN,		59	FAIRY TALES	11
WHEN ONCE THE TWILIGHT LOCKS NO LONGER		97	TWILIGHT LOCKS	T
WHEN ONCE THE TWILIGHT LOCKS NO LONGER		97	TWILIGHT LOCKS	1
NO LONGER WILL THE VIBRATIONS OF THE SUN DESIRE ON		170	MARRIAGE VIRG	8
ON THE WHITE, NO LONGER GROWING GREEN, AND, MINSTREL DEAD,		190	WINTER'S TALE	112
OFF BY THE SUN AND DAUGHTERS NO LONGER GRIEVED		205	GIANT'S THIGH	55
I AM NO LONGER		228	NOT DESPAIR	7
UNTIL YOU COULD BEAR IT NO LONGER		232	FURIOUS MOTION	12

	PAGE	TITLE	LINE
LONGING			
AND DAUB THE UNRISEN SUN WITH LONGING.	15	FOR LEDA	13
WHERE BARREN AS BOULDERS WOMEN LIE LONGING STILL	203	GIANT'S THIGH	4
LONG-LAST			
SPRINKLES IN CHILDREN'S EYES A LONG-LAST SLEEP	56	WHY EAST WIND	13
LONG-LEGGED			
BALLAD OF THE LONG-LEGGED BAIT	161	LONG-LEGGED	T
SPUN ON A SPOUT LIKE A LONG-LEGGED BALL	163	LONG-LEGGED	56
THE LONG-LEGGED BEAUTIFUL BAIT THEIR WIVES.	164	LONG-LEGGED	70
ALWAYS GOOD-BYE TO THE LONG-LEGGED BREAD	165	LONG-LEGGED	94
WHEN HIS LONG-LEGGED FLESH WAS A WIND ON FIRE	168	LONG-LEGGED	195
WITH HIS LONG-LEGGED HEART IN HIS HAND.	169	LONG-LEGGED	216
LONGLYING			
THE BITTER, THE WICKED, THE LONGLYING LEISURE, ...	39	GAS FADES	21
LONGS			
IN THE BREASTED SUMMER LONGS NOT FOR SPRING, ...	55	NO MAN BELIEVE	9
A BLADE OF GRASS LONGS WITH THE MEADOW, ...	159	INTO HER HEAD	61
SHE LONGS AMONG HORSES AND ANGELS, ...	163	LONG-LEGGED	33
LONG-TAILED			
THE LONG-TAILED STONE	114	SERVANT SUN	18
AND THE LONG-TAILED LIGHTNING LIT HIS CATCH.	166	LONG-LEGGED	128
LOOK			
FROM FISH TO JUMPING HILL! LOOK:	4	PROLOGUE	43
AND HER TONGUE, LOOK, ASH, ...	10	COOL, OH NO	15
BY LOVE OF LOOK, ...	20	ENCOMPASSED	7
LOOK, THERE'S THE DEAD WHO DID NOT LOVE, ...	24	THE ONLY DEAD	30
OR SUNDERED IT TO LOOK THE CLOSER, ...	25	BEAUTY TO DUST	4
THEN LOOK, MY EYES, UPON THIS BONEBOUND FORTUNE ...	81	ALL THAT I OWE	21
THEN LOOK, MY HEART, UPON THE SCARLET TROVE, ...	81	ALL THAT I OWE	28
AND LOOK, MY GRAIN, UPON THE FALLING WHEAT;	81	ALL THAT I OWE	29
LOOK TWICE BEFORE HE FELL FROM GRACE.	116	LANTERNS SHINE	4
ROUNDS TO LOOK AT THE RED, WAGGED ROOT.	144	PLEASURE-BIRD	12
BLACKENED WITH BIRDS TOOK A LAST LOOK	161	LONG-LEGGED	2
FOR MY SAKE SAIL, AND NEVER LOOK BACK, ...	162	LONG-LEGGED	11
LOOK. AND THE DANCERS MOVE	189	WINTER'S TALE	71
OF FIELDS. FOR LOVE, THE LONG AGO SHE BIRD RISES.			
LOOK.	189	WINTER'S TALE	80
LISTEN AND LOOK WHERE SHE SAILS THE GOOSE PLUCKED			
SEA, ...	190	WINTER'S TALE	100
LOOKED			
WHO PALMED THE LIE ON ME WHEN YOU LOOKED	146	TO OTHERS	4
LOOKING			
SAID THE LOOKING LAND.	162	LONG-LEGGED	12
LOOKING UP AT YOU.	229	MY RIVER	12
LOOKING-GLASS			
OR SAW IN THE LOOKING-GLASS SHELL	139	TOMBSTONE TOLD	7
LOOKS			
AND SWIMMING DOWN THE GUTTERS HE LOOKS UP	51	OUT OF THE PIT	45
RIDING ON GIRDERS OF THE AIR, LOOKS DOWN	52	OUT OF THE PIT	47
LOOMS			
LOOMS THE LAST SAMSON OF YOUR ZODIAC.	161	DEATHS AND ENT	36
LOOPED			
WHEN HIS VIPERISH FUSE HANGS LOOPED WITH FLAMES			
UNDER THE BRAND	202	SIR JOHNS HILL	28
LOOSE			
THE FLYING LOOSE, ALBINO EYED, WING SINGED, ...	41	YOUNG ARE OLD	38
A SMILE LET LOOSE A DEVIL, A BELL STRUCK.	51	OUT OF THE PIT	19
THAT I MAY DROWN, LET LOOSE HER FLOOD OF TEARS. ...	65	WOMAN SPEAKS	55
HIS SCISSORS OILED, HIS KNIFE HUNG LOOSE	91	WHERE ONCE THE	10
THE LOCKS YAWNED LOOSE AND A BLAST BLEW THEM WIDE,	172	DAWN RAID	3

	PAGE	TITLE	LINE
LOOSE (CONTINUED)			
YOU LOOSE, DELICIOUS WILL	237	PILLAR BREAKS	9
LOOSED			
AND LOOSED THE BRAIDING ADDERS FROM THEIR HAIRS;	104	WORLD PYRAMID	22
LOOSENS			
SO SHALL HE STEP TILL SUMMER LOOSENS ITS HOLD	46	POET: 1935	18
LOOTED			
HOLLOWS, A GRASSBLADE BLOWN IN CUPPED HANDS, IN THE			
LOOTED ELMS	203	SIR JOHNS HILL	52
LOP			
LOP, LOVE, MY FORK TONGUE, SAID THE PIN-HILLED			
NETTLE;	119	ALTARWISE	76
LOPING			
LOPING AND BLEATING ROUGHLY AND BLITHELY SHALL LEAP,	197	COUNTRY SLEEP	4
LOPPED			
OLD COCK FROM NOWHERES LOPPED THE MINSTREL TONGUE	119	ALTARWISE	78
LOPS			
LOPS, AS A BUSH PLUMED WITH FLAMES, THE RANT OF THE			
FIERCE EYE, ...	135	HOW MY ANIMAL	38
LORD			
AND MY FATHER WAS THE LORD.	72	TAKE NEEDLES	44
YOU BUT WOUND THE LORD OF DAYS;	72	TAKE NEEDLES	54
NOT FOREVER SHALL THE LORD OF THE RED HAIL	73	LORD RED HAIL	T
NOT FOREVER SHALL THE LORD OF THE RED HAIL	73	LORD RED HAIL	1
HOW SOON, HOW SOON, O LORD OF THE RED HAIL!	73	LORD RED HAIL	18
HOW SOON MY LEVEL, LORD, ...	114	SERVANT SUN	22
HIGH LORD ESQUIRE, SPEAK UP THE SINGING CLOUD, ...	123	FOSTER LIGHT	17
LORDING			
HERE AMONG THE LIGHT OF THE LORDING SKY	217	ELEGY	29
LORDLY			
AND ONCE BELOW A TIME I LORDLY HAD THE TREES AND			
LEAVES	195	FERN HILL	7
LORD'S			
NOW STAMP THE LORD'S PRAYER ON A GRAIN OF RICE, ...	119	ALTARWISE	85
LORD'S-TABLE			
ON THE LORD'S-TABLE OF THE BOWING GRASS. FEAR MOST	198	COUNTRY SLEEP	35
LOSE			
LOSE THE GREAT PAINS OR STUFF THE WOUND, ...	32	OUT OF SIGHS	12
THE STRAWS OF ASIA, LOSE ME AS I TURN	105	WORLD PYRAMID	47
COME, YOU ARE TO LOSE YOUR FRESHNESS.	233	NO THOUGHT	20
LOSER			
AND THE LOSER OF THE KEY.	126	SEED-AT-ZERO	28
LOSING			
EACH RUNG A LOVE OR LOSING TO THE LAST, ...	102	FELLOWED SLEEP	27
BY LOSING HIM ALL IN LOVE, AND CAST HIS NEED	188	WINTER'S TALE	52
LOSS			
AT ONE SIDE'S LOSS, ...	25	BEAUTY TO DUST	6
ONE HAND AT HEAD, THE OTHER AT A LOSS, ...	52	OUT OF THE PIT	60
FOR LOSS OF BLOOD I FELL ON ISHMAEL'S PLAIN, ...	118	ALTARWISE	63
NOW THEIR LOVE LIES A LOSS	161	WEDDING ANNIV	5
LOSSES			
OTHERS BETRAY THE LAMENTING LIES OF THEIR LOSSES	133	MAKE ME A MASK	11
LOST			
HAVE LOVED AND LOST.	30	YOUTH CALLS	4
YOU, WHO ARE OLD, HAVE LOVED AND LOST AS I	30	YOUTH CALLS	5
RAPES, LEAVES FOR LOST (THE AMORIST!), ...	30	NEARLY SUMMER	16
THE WESTERN MAN HAS LOST ONE LUNG	40	YOUNG ARE OLD	9
LOST IN THE SHADES, NO COURSE, NO USE	41	YOUNG ARE OLD	22
THE LOST IN DOUBT, THE NEARLY MAD, THE YOUNG	41	YOUNG ARE OLD	33
EVEN AMONG HIS OWN KIN IS HE LOST, ...	47	POET: 1935	22

	PAGE	TITLE	LINE
LOST (CONTINUED)			
THOUGH LOVERS BE LOST LOVE SHALL NOT;	49	NO DOMINION	8
PITY THE LIVING WHO ARE LOST, ALONE;	57	GREEK PLAY	21
AS, BLOWING ON THE ANGELS, I WAS LOST	102	FELLOWED SLEEP	17
FOR HALF OF LOVE WAS PLANTED IN THE LOST, ...	104	WORLD PYRAMID	11
LOST IN A LIMP-TREED AND UNEATING SILENCE, ...	132	I MAKE THIS IN	28
O MY LOST LOVE BOUNCED FROM A GOOD HOME;	146	IF HEAD HURT	23
FROM A LOST WILDERNESS	153	WAS A SAVIOUR	10
A STONE LIES LOST AND LOCKED IN THE LARK-HIGH HILL.	159	INTO HER HEAD	62
FLOATED THE LOST CATHEDRAL	163	LONG-LEGGED	35
HAS MELTED AWAY AND IS LOST	165	LONG-LEGGED	115
IS ALWAYS LOST IN HER VAULTED BREATH, ...	165	LONG-LEGGED	116
TO THE FISHERMAN LOST ON THE LAND.	169	LONG-LEGGED	214
I SHALL RUN LOST IN SUDDEN	181	VISION, PRAYER	45
FOR I WAS LOST WHO AM	181	VISION, PRAYER	57
FOR I WAS LOST WHO HAVE COME	181	VISION, PRAYER	62
IN THE NAME OF THE LOST WHO GLORY IN	183	VISION, PRAYER	102
LOST ON THE UNCHRISTENED MOUNTAIN	183	VISION, PRAYER	134
AND THE STAR OF THE LOST THE SHAPE OF THE EYES. ...	185	VISION, PRAYER	170
NOW I AM LOST IN THE BLINDING	185	VISION, PRAYER	203
AND HIS NAMELESS NEED BOUND HIM BURNING AND LOST	188	WINTER'S TALE	44
BY THE BELIEVER LOST AND THE HURLED OUTCAST OF LIGHT.	188	WINTER'S TALE	50
ALL NIGHT LOST AND LONG WADING IN THE WAKE OF THE			
SHE-	190	WINTER'S TALE	98
OF THE HEARTHSTONE TALES MY OWN, LOST LOVE; AND THE			
SOUL WALKS	199	COUNTRY SLEEP	53
AND FREELY HE GOES LOST	210	POEM ON B'DAY	46
AND THE LOST, MOONSHINE DOMES, ...	211	POEM ON B'DAY	86
YOUNG AMONG THE LONG FLOCKS, AND NEVER LIE LOST ...	216	ELEGY	7
LOTH			
WE STILL ARE LOTH TO PART WITH WHAT REMAINS, ...	26	THERE'S PLENTY	17
LOVING AND BEING LOTH;	90	EUNUCH DREAMS	33
LOTION			
OR THE LOTION OF A FLOWER	235	WOMAN TAPESTRY	15
LOTS			
LIGHT BREAKS ON SECRET LOTS, ...	82	LIGHT BREAKS	25
LOUD			
OR WAVES BREAK LOUD ON THE SEASHORES;	50	NO DOMINION	21
AND LOUD HIS ANGER STAMP UPON THE HILL.	73	LORD RED HAIL	6
THE SPIDER-TONGUED, AND THE LOUD HILL OF WALES) ...	99	OCTOBER WIND	27
THERE IS LOUD AND DARK DIRECTLY UNDER THE DUMB FLAME,	130	SINNERS' BELL	13
WITH LOUD, TORN TOOTH AND TAIL AND COBWEB DRUM	133	I MAKE THIS IN	57
TO TROT WITH A LOUD MATE THE HAYBEDS OF A MILE, ...	135	HOW MY ANIMAL	16
STRIKE LIGHT, AND BLOODY A LOUD ROOM.	145	IF HEAD HURT	10
SILENCE, SILENCE TO DO, WHEN EARTH GREW LOUD, ...	153	WAS A SAVIOUR	15
AND PROPHETS LOUD ON THE BURNED DUNES;	168	LONG-LEGGED	173
UNDER THE EARTH THE LOUD SEA WALKS, ...	169	LONG-LEGGED	206
THROUGH THE LOUD ZOO OF THE WILLOW GROVES	171	THE HUNCHBACK	22
SO LOUD TO MY OWN	180	VISION, PRAYER	5
BUT THE LOUD SUN	185	VISION, PRAYER	193
DEEP HILLOCKS AND LOUD ON THE NUMBED LAKES, ...	190	WINTER'S TALE	97
TO THE SEA SOUND FLOWING LIKE BLOOD FROM THE LOUD			
WOUND	194	SLEEP BECALMED	6
OF BLOOD! THE BIRD LOUD VEIN! THE SAGA FROM MERMEN	200	COUNTRY SLEEP	78
LOUDEN			
UNTIL THE WHISPER OF THE LAST TRUMP LOUDEN	40	YOUNG ARE OLD	11
LOUDENING			
OVER THE SEA-GUT LOUDENING, SETS A ROCK ALIVE;	122	HOLD HARD	15
LOUDER			
THE LOUDER THE SUN BLOOMS	211	POEM ON B'DAY	93

	PAGE	TITLE	LINE
LOUSE			
LION OR LOUSE? TAKE YOUR OWN ADVICE;	58	TO ARCHITECTS	17
LOUSE'S			
TO LEAVE IT EMPTY'S LION'S OR LOUSE'S CHOICE;	58	TO ARCHITECTS	16
LOVE			
TO THE BEST OF MY LOVE	4	PROLOGUE	45
TOO FULL WITH BLOOD TO LET MY LOVE FLOW IN.	9	MINUTE'S HOUR	12
AND I, YOUR CAPTOR, HAVE MY LOVE TO KEEP	10	COOL, OH NO	29
FOR IF THE GODS WOULD LOVE	11	AIR BREATHE	9
I SEE THE MAN IS MAD WITH LOVE.'	11	CABARET	13
THE MORNING, TOO, IS TIME FOR LOVE, ...	15	FOR LEDA	28
WILL FIND SUCH LOVE AGAINST THE GRAIN, ...	16	TIME TO ROT	8
THE LOVE WE HAD AND GLORY IN HIS BLOOD	17	IN OBLIVION	9
WHERE LOVE IS THERE'S A CRUST OF JOY	19	THE NEOPHYTE	5
BY LOVE OF LOOK, ...	20	ENCOMPASSED	7
KNOWS HIS LOVE ROTS.	20	THE NEOPHYTE	12
SOON TO MY CARE, MY LOVE, ...	21	BEWILDERED WAY	5
THEY ARE THE ONLY DEAD WHO DID NOT LOVE	23	THE ONLY DEAD	T
THEY ARE THE ONLY DEAD WHO DID NOT LOVE, ...	23	THE ONLY DEAD	1
THEY ARE THE ONLY LIVING THING WHO DID LOVE, ...	23	THE ONLY DEAD	4
LOOK, THERE'S THE DEAD WHO DID NOT LOVE, ...	24	THE ONLY DEAD	30
AND THERE'S THE LIVING WHO DID LOVE, ...	24	THE ONLY DEAD	31
TOUCHING OUR SEPARATE LOVE WITH BADINAGE	24	THE ONLY DEAD	33
WISDOM IS FOLLY, LOVE IS NOT, ...	25	BEAUTY TO DUST	8
ALL LOVE AND SWEAT	26	PERSONAL EPIT	15
I LOVE AND DOUBT, IT'S VAIN, IT'S VAIN, ...	27	OBLIVIOUS DARK	27
SLEEP, WAKE, AND SLEEP, EAT, LOVE, AND LAUGH, ...	28	NO WINGS	13
THE ISLAND OF SUCH PENNY LOVE	43	FACES SHONE	4
IS LOVE A SHADOW ON THE WALL, ...	47	POET: 1935	23
IF LOVE HE CAN BEING NO WOMAN'S MAN.	47	POET: 1935	35
IT IS NIGHT'S TERRORS I MUST LEARN TO LOVE, ...	48	LIGHT, I KNOW	13
THOUGH LOVERS BE LOST LOVE SHALL NOT;	49	NO DOMINION	8
BRUISING, WHERE'S GOD'S MY SHEPHERD, GOD IS LOVE? .	51	OUT OF THE PIT	37
MY GOD'S A SHEPHERD, GOD'S THE LOVE I HOPED.	53	OUT OF THE PIT	93
AND LOVE THAT GOES DOWN LIKE A FLOWER.	57	GREEK PLAY	20
HER SYLLABLES, AND TO THE GODS HER LOVE;	57	GREEK PLAY	27
MY HEART KNEW LOVE, MY BELLY HUNGER;	69	BEFORE KNOCKED	29
SLAY ME, SLAY THE GOD OF LOVE;	72	TAKE NEEDLES	55
LOVE ME, NOT AS THE DREAMING NURSES	75	SONG: LOVE ME	1
LOVE ME AND LIFT YOUR MASK.	75	SONG: LOVE ME	4
I HUG TO LOVE WITH MY UNRULY SCRAWL	75	MY HERO BARES	8
THAT UTTERS ALL LOVE HUNGER	75	MY HERO BARES	9
LOVE ME, NOT AS THE GIRLS OF HEAVEN	76	SONG: LOVE ME	5
LOVE ME AND LIFT YOUR MASK.	76	SONG: LOVE ME	8
LOVE ME, NOT AS THE RUFFLING PIGEON	76	SONG: LOVE ME	9
LOVE ME AND LIFT YOUR MASK.	76	SONG: LOVE ME	12
LOVE ME, AS LOVES THE MOLE HIS DARKNESS	76	SONG: LOVE ME	13
LOVE ME AND LIFT YOUR MASK.	76	SONG: LOVE ME	16
LOVE DRIPS AND GATHERS, BUT THE FALLEN BLOOD	77	THE FORCE THAT	17
REMEMBER THIS: THAT LOVE DEPENDS	84	LETTER TO AUNT	50
OF LIGHT AND LOVE, THE TEMPERS OF THE HEART, ...	89	EUNUCH DREAMS	2
TWO ONE-DIMENSIONED GHOSTS, LOVE ON A REEL, ...	89	EUNUCH DREAMS	12
FLAVOURED OF CELLULOID GIVE LOVE THE LIE.	89	EUNUCH DREAMS	20
AND WHO REMAIN SHALL FLOWER AS THEY LOVE, ...	90	EUNUCH DREAMS	41
OF LOVE AND LIGHT BURSTS IN THEIR THROATS.	92	BOYS OF SUMMER	23
IF I WERE TICKLED BY THE RUB OF LOVE	94	RUB OF LOVE	T
IF I WERE TICKLED BY THE RUB OF LOVE, ...	94	RUB OF LOVE	1
THE RIBBED ORIGINAL OF LOVE.	94	IN BEGINNING	30
I WOULD NOT FEAR THE MUSCLING-IN OF LOVE	95	RUB OF LOVE	17
YOUR MOUTH, MY LOVE, THE THISTLE IN THE KISS?	96	RUB OF LOVE	44

	PAGE	TITLE	LINE
LOVE (CONTINUED)			
LOVE IN HER GEAR IS SLOWLY THROUGH THE HOUSE, ...	99	RUNNING GRAVE	3
OF LOVE AM BARER THAN CADAVER'S TRAP	100	RUNNING GRAVE	8
SHAPES IN A CINDER DEATH; LOVE FOR HIS TRICK, ...	101	RUNNING GRAVE	48
EACH RUNG A LOVE OR LOSING TO THE LAST, ...	102	FELLOWED SLEEP	27
FOR HALF OF LOVE WAS PLANTED IN THE LOST, ...	104	WORLD PYRAMID	11
LOVE LIKE A MIST OR FIRE THROUGH THE BED OF EELS.	111	I, IN IMAGE	90
THE COUNTRY-HANDED GRAVE BOXED INTO LOVE, ...	115	A GRIEF AGO	31
WOULD WITHER UP, AND ANY BOY OF LOVE	116	LANTERNS SHINE	3
LOP, LOVE, MY FORK TONGUE, SAID THE PIN-HILLED			
NETTLE;	119	ALTARWISE	76
AND LOVE PLUCKED OUT THE STINGING SIREN'S EYE, ...	119	ALTARWISE	77
NOR WHEN MY LOVE LIES IN THE CROSS-BONED DRIFT	123	FOSTER LIGHT	22
BEFORE THE FALL FROM LOVE THE FLYING HEARTBONE, ...	124	TODAY, INSECT	15
'ADAM I LOVE, MY MADMEN'S LOVE IS ENDLESS, ...	125	TODAY, INSECT	23
'ADAM I LOVE, MY MADMEN'S LOVE IS ENDLESS, ...	125	TODAY, INSECT	23
THE LANDSCAPE GRIEF, LOVE IN HIS OILS	129	MY NEOPHYTE	20
DELIVERED SEAS MY LOVE FROM HER PROUD PLACE	133	I MAKE THIS IN	62
AND THOUGH MY LOVE PULLS THE PALE, NIPPLED AIR, ...	133	I MAKE THIS IN	66
LOVE AND LABOUR AND KILL	135	HOW MY ANIMAL	17
CLACK THROUGH THE THICKET OF STRENGTH, LOVE HEWN IN			
PILLARS DROPS	135	HOW MY ANIMAL	36
THAT HER LOVE SING AND SWING THROUGH A BROWN CHAPEL,	136	AFTER FUNERAL	25
THE STUFFED LUNG OF THE FOX TWITCH AND CRY LOVE ...	137	AFTER FUNERAL	39
LOVE IN THE FROST IS PARED AND WINTERED BY, ...	138	FIVE & COUNTRY	5
THE WHISPERING EARS WILL WATCH LOVE DRUMMED AWAY	138	FIVE & COUNTRY	6
THAN BULLY ILL LOVE IN THE CLOUTED SCENE.	145	IF HEAD HURT	5
TILL THE SWEET TOOTH OF MY LOVE BIT DRY, ...	146	TO OTHERS	7
O MY LOST LOVE BOUNCED FROM A GOOD HOME;	146	IF HEAD HURT	23
HER CONSTANT, NOR THE WINDS OF LOVE BROKEN WIDE ...	147	UNLUCKILY FOR	10
UNDER THE CLOUD AGAINST LOVE IS CAUGHT AND HELD AND			
KISSED	147	UNLUCKILY FOR	17
ALL LOVE BUT FOR THE FULL ASSEMBLAGE IN FLOWER	148	UNLUCKILY FOR	40
LOVE, MY FATE GOT LUCKILY, ...	148	UNLUCKILY FOR	43
AND THE VAULTING BIRD BE STILL. O MY TRUE LOVE, HOLD			
ME.	149	UNLUCKILY FOR	54
IN LOVE TORN BREECHES AND BLISTERED JACKET	151	BELOW A TIME	7
UNCLENCHED, ARMLESS, SILK AND ROUGH LOVE THAT BREAKS			
ALL ROCKS.	154	WAS A SAVIOUR	40
BURY ALL RUBBISH AND LOVE SIGNS	156	RETURN	90
IN FOUNTAINS OF ORIGIN GAVE UP THEIR LOVE, ...	157	INTO HER HEAD	9
NOW THEIR LOVE LIES A LOSS	161	WEDDING ANNIV	5
AND LOVE AND HIS PATIENTS ROAR ON A CHAIN;	161	WEDDING ANNIV	6
THEY COME TOGETHER WHOM THEIR LOVE PARTED:	161	WEDDING ANNIV	10
AND FLED THEIR LOVE IN A WEAVING DIP.	163	LONG-LEGGED	53
SHE NIPPED AND DIVED IN THE NICK OF LOVE, ...	163	LONG-LEGGED	55
THE FURIOUS OX-KILLING HOUSE OF LOVE.	168	LONG-LEGGED	200
LOVE IN THE ASYLUM	169	LOVE IN ASYLUM	T
LOVE IS THE LAST LIGHT SPOKEN. OH	174	FIRE RAID	31
MY LOVE AS A ROUND WAVE	176	BREATH SHED	10
OUT OF A BED OF LOVE	186	HOLY SPRING	2
AT THE POINT OF LOVE, FORSAKEN AND AFRAID.	188	WINTER'S TALE	30
OF HIS SNOW BLIND LOVE AND RUSH IN THE WHITE LAIRS.	188	WINTER'S TALE	38
BY LOSING HIM ALL IN LOVE, AND CAST HIS NEED	188	WINTER'S TALE	52
PADDOCKS IN THE FARMS OF BIRDS. THE DEAD OAK WALKS			
FOR LOVE.	189	WINTER'S TALE	75
OF FIELDS. FOR LOVE, THE LONG AGO SHE BIRD RISES.			
LOOK.	189	WINTER'S TALE	80
BURNING IN THE BRIDE BED OF LOVE, IN THE WHIRL- ...	191	WINTER'S TALE	127
WHO CLIMBS TO HIS DYING LOVE IN HER HIGH ROOM, ...	193	CONVERS PRAYER	3

	PAGE	TITLE	LINE
LOVE (CONTINUED)			
DIE IN UNJUDGING LOVE.	193	SIDE OF TRUTH	36
FOR THE SLEEP IN A SAFE LAND AND THE LOVE WHO DIES	194	CONVERS PRAYER	10
IN THE FIRE OF HIS CARE HIS LOVE IN THE HIGH ROOM.	194	CONVERS PRAYER	16
AND MIRE OF LOVE, BUT THE THIEF AS MEEK AS THE DEW.	198	COUNTRY SLEEP	38
OF THE HEARTHSTONE TALES MY OWN, LOST LOVE; AND THE			
SOUL WALKS	199	COUNTRY SLEEP	53
THE HAYGOLD HAIRED, MY LOVE ASLEEP, AND THE RIFT BLUE	200	COUNTRY SLEEP	88
ROUND THE SUN, HE COMES TO MY LOVE LIKE THE DESIGNED			
SNOW, ...	200	COUNTRY SLEEP	96
COMES DESIGNED TO MY LOVE TO STEAL NOT HER TIDE			
RAKING	200	COUNTRY SLEEP	100
TO LABOUR AND LOVE THOUGH THEY LAY DOWN LONG AGO.	203	GIANT'S THIGH	5
QUICK IN THE WOOD AT LOVE, WHERE A TORCH OF FOXES			
FOAMS, ...	204	GIANT'S THIGH	34
TEACH ME THE LOVE THAT IS EVERGREEN AFTER THE FALL			
LEAVED	205	GIANT'S THIGH	53
LOVE FOR EVER MERIDIAN THROUGH THE COURTERS' TREES	205	GIANT'S THIGH	59
THE WHOLE OF THE MOON I COULD LOVE AND LEAVE	206	LAMENT	10
AND LOVE UNBOLTS THE DARK	210	POEM ON B'DAY	45
SENSES, AND MAN A SPIRIT IN LOVE	211	POEM ON B'DAY	83
HILL, UNDER THE GRASS, IN LOVE, AND THERE GROW	216	ELEGY	6
AND LOVE TO CHASE RABBITS AND STONES.	221	SONG OF DOG	12
OR CAST YOUR LOVE ASIDE;	228	NOT DESPAIR	3
THERE IS A GREATER LOVE THAN MINE	228	NOT DESPAIR	4
NO LOVE CAN PENETRATE	233	NO THOUGHT	9
AND HER EYES PIERCED THEIR INTENSE LOVE INTO ME,	234	WOMAN TAPESTRY	2
HER LOVE FOR ME IS FIERCE AND CONTINUAL, ...	235	WOMAN TAPESTRY	11
MY LOVE FOR HER IS LIKE THE MOVING OF A CLOUD	235	WOMAN TAPESTRY	13
AND THE GESTURES OF UNAGEING LOVE.	235	WOMAN TAPESTRY	26
DRAWING THE ENERGY FROM THE LOVE, ...	236	WOMAN TAPESTRY	45
AND A CLEAN SURGE OF LOVE MOVING.	236	WOMAN TAPESTRY	63
THE GESTURES OF MY LOVE	236	WOMAN TAPESTRY	68
AND THE GESTURES OF UNAGEING LOVE.	237	WOMAN TAPESTRY	81
WHERE IS THERE GREATER LOVE	241	ADMIT THE SUN	15
LOVEBEDS			
BREAK ON THE LOVEBEDS OF THE WEEDS;	91	WHERE ONCE THE	14
LOVED			
THERE IS NO DEAD BUT IS NOT LOVED	23	THE ONLY DEAD	19
HAVE LOVED AND LOST.	30	YOUTH CALLS	4
YOU, WHO ARE OLD, HAVE LOVED AND LOST AS I	30	YOUTH CALLS	5
LAIN WITH PARCHED THINGS; LOVED DOGS AND WOMEN; ...	52	OUT OF THE PIT	72
ALL THAT WAS LOVED AND LOVED MADE THE FOWLS' FOOD,	64	WOMAN SPEAKS	31
ALL THAT WAS LOVED AND LOVED MADE THE FOWLS' FOOD,	64	WOMAN SPEAKS	31
THAT THOUGH I LOVED THEM FOR THEIR FAULTS	147	TO OTHERS	18
I LOVED HIS BODY AND HIS NAVY BLUE WEALTH	149	PAPER & STICKS	5
WHEN ONE AT THE GREAT LEAST OF YOUR BEST LOVED	160	DEATHS AND ENT	3
UNTIL THAT ONE LOVED LEAST	161	DEATHS AND ENT	35
HE DROPPED WHERE HE LOVED ON THE BURST PAVEMENT STONE	172	DAWN RAID	4
HILL. WHO ONCE IN GOOSESKIN WINTER LOVED ALL ICE			
LEAVED	203	GIANT'S THIGH	12
FOR THAT HE LOVED THEE, SEEK THOU HIM AND BLESS ...	222	MISSING	2
YOU SHALL BE LOVED ENOUGH.	228	NOT DESPAIR	14
SKY HAS NOT LOVED ME MUCH, ...	234	NO, PIGEON	4
LOVE-DARKNESS			
FROM DAMP LOVE-DARKNESS AND THE NURSE'S TWIST	96	RUB OF LOVE	38
LOVELESS			
PITY ELECTRA LOVELESS, SHE WHOSE GRIEF	57	GREEK PLAY	25
LOVE-LIES			
LOVE-LIES, AND GOD-LIES, AND LIES-TO-PLEASE, ...	36	LET BE KNOWN	2

	PAGE	TITLE	LINE

LOVELINESS
THAT, THEN, IS LOVELINESS, WE SAID, ... 31 BEING BUT MEN 14
FELT THEIR SERENITY OF RIPPLE-WOVEN LOVELINESS; ... 223 IDYLL UNFORGET 4
LOVELORN
ACHE ON THE LOVELORN PAPER .... 75 MY HERO BARES 7
LOVELY
AND EVERY LOVELY WOMAN'S GERMY; .... 84 LETTER TO AUNT 49
THE LOVELY GIFT OF THE GAB BANGS BACK ON A BLIND
   SHAFT. .... 140 NO WORK WORDS 6
ALL BLOOD-SIGNED ASSAILINGS AND VANISHED MARRIAGES
   IN WHICH HE HAD NO LOVELY PART .... 158 INTO HER HEAD 43
WALKING IN WISHES AND LOVELY FOR SHAME .... 165 LONG-LEGGED 105
ALL THE SUN LONG IT WAS RUNNING, IT WAS LOVELY, THE
   HAY .... 195 FERN HILL 19
AND PLAYING, LOVELY AND WATERY .... 195 FERN HILL 21
LOVER
TO HAVE THE CENTAUR LOVER .... 11 AIR BREATHE 6
HE'S DEAD, HOME, HAS NO LOVER, ... 17 IN OBLIVION 19
OF LOVER, MOTHER, LOVERS, OR HIS SIX .... 96 RUB OF LOVE 41
NO, NO, YOU LOVER SKULL, DESCENDING HAMMER ..... 100 RUNNING GRAVE 27
ALL ALL AND ALL, THE CORPSE'S LOVER, ... 106 ALL ALL AND 10
AND THE FACE TO THE DRIVEN LOVER. .... 106 ALL ALL AND 24
NO TELL-TALE LOVER HAS AN END MORE CERTAIN, ... 125 TODAY, INSECT 24
DRY LOVER MINE .... 127 NOW, SAY NAY 4
THE CIRCULAR SMILE TOSSED FROM LOVER TO LOVER ... 134 NOT FROM ANGER 9
THE CIRCULAR SMILE TOSSED FROM LOVER TO LOVER ... 134 NOT FROM ANGER 9
OCEANIC LOVER ALONE .... 158 INTO HER HEAD 33
LOVERLESS
OBLIVION IS SO LOVERLESS. .... 17 IN OBLIVION 28
OBLIVION IS AS LOVERLESS; .... 22 ON QUIET NIGHT 13
OBLIVION IS AS LOVERLESS. .... 22 ON QUIET NIGHT 14
LOVERS
HE WHOSE LOVERS WERE BOTH WISE AND SENSIBLE ..... 25 BEAUTY TO DUST 18
MOST FIT FOR LOVERS TO MAKE HARMONY, ... 34 THIRST PARCHES 10
AND LOVERS TURNING ON THE GAS, ... 41 YOUNG ARE OLD 30
THOUGH LOVERS BE LOST LOVE SHALL NOT; .... 49 NO DOMINION 8
THEIR AIRY LOVERS, NOR THE MERMAIDEN .... 76 SONG: LOVE ME 6
HER SALTY LOVERS IN THE SEA. .... 76 SONG: LOVE ME 7
A MUSCLING LIFE FROM LOVERS IN THEIR CRAMP, ... 92 BOYS OF SUMMER 33
OF LOVER, MOTHER, LOVERS, OR HIS SIX .... 96 RUB OF LOVE 41
GIVE OVER, LOVERS, LOCKING, AND THE SEAWAX STRUGGLE, 111 I, IN IMAGE 89
FROM ALL MY MORTAL LOVERS WITH A STARBOARD SMILE; 123 FOSTER LIGHT 21
LOVERS IN THE DIRT OF THEIR LEAFY BEDS, ... 144 COLOUR OF SAY 9
AND THE LOVERS LIE ABED .... 197 CRAFT OR ART 4
BUT FOR THE LOVERS, THEIR ARMS .... 197 CRAFT OR ART 17
LOVERS'
TO CATCH THE LOVERS' PALSY, ... 34 THIRST PARCHES 11
IF I WERE TICKLED BY THE LOVERS' RUB .... 95 RUB OF LOVE 22
THE LOVERS' HOUSE, LIE SUFFERING MY STAIN? ..... 112 NOT FATHER ME 4
LOVER'S
AND, AT THE TOUCH, TREMBLES WITH LOVER'S FEVER, ... 25 BEAUTY TO DUST 3
AND I AM DUMB TO TELL THE LOVER'S TOMB .... 77 THE FORCE THAT 21
A LOVER'S THOUGHT TEARS DOWN THE DATED SHEET, .. 80 ALMANAC TIME 7
NOR THE FLINT IN THE LOVER'S MAULING. .... 106 ALL ALL AND 18
HER LOVER'S WINGS THAT FOLD TO-MORROW'S FLIGHT, ... 159 INTO HER HEAD 57
LOVES
MANNED WITH THEIR LOVES THEY'LL MOVE, ... 5 PROLOGUE 95
THOUGH WE'RE CONSUMED BY LOVES AND DOUBTS. ..... 27 OBLIVIOUS DARK 26
AND HE DESTROYS, THOUGH FLOWERS ARE HIS LOVES, ... 47 POET: 1935 34
LOVE ME, AS LOVES THE MOLE HIS DARKNESS .... 76 SONG: LOVE ME 13

	PAGE	TITLE	LINE
LOVES (CONTINUED)			
HATE AND FEAR BE YOUR TWO LOVES.	76	SONG: LOVE ME	15
MY FATHERS' LOVES THAT PULL UPON MY NERVES,	80	ALL THAT I OWE	6
OF FROZEN LOVES THEY FETCH THEIR GIRLS,	91	BOYS OF SUMMER	5
AND TUSSLE IN A SHOAL OF LOVES.	162	LONG-LEGGED	30
WAKING ALONE IN A MULTITUDE OF LOVES WHEN MORNING'S LIGHT	170	MARRIAGE VIRG	1
ON SKULL AND SCAR WHERE HIS LOVES LIE WRECKED,	209	POEM ON B'DAY	40
LOVE'S			
TO SMIRK AT LOVE'S UNDRESS,	34	THIRST PARCHES	13
FROM LOVE'S FIRST FEVER TO HER PLAGUE	78	LOVE'S FEVER	T
FROM LOVE'S FIRST FEVER TO HER PLAGUE, FROM THE SOFT SECOND	78	LOVE'S FEVER	1
HEIR TO THE SCALDING VEINS THAT HOLD LOVE'S DROP,	80	ALL THAT I OWE	9
AND ALL SUCH LOVE'S A SHRUB SOWN IN THE BREATH.	81	ALL THAT I OWE	20
IN LOVE'S LAST COLLAR.	86	SEE, SAYS LIME	24
THE WEED OF LOVE'S LEFT DRY;	91	WHERE ONCE THE	15
HERE LOVE'S DAMP MUSCLE DRIES AND DIES,	93	BOYS OF SUMMER	46
HERE BREAK A KISS IN NO LOVE'S QUARRY.	93	BOYS OF SUMMER	47
LOVE'S TWILIT NATION AND THE SKULL OF STATE,	101	RUNNING GRAVE	39
HEIR TO THE SCALDING VEINS THAT HOLD LOVE'S DROP, COSTLY	103	I DREAMED MY	9
SHALL I STILL BE LOVE'S HOUSE ON THE WIDDERSHIN EARTH,	113	NOT FATHER ME	29
LOVE'S HOUSE, THEY ANSWER, AND THE TOWER DEATH	113	NOT FATHER ME	31
LOVE'S REFLECTION OF THE MUSHROOM FEATURES,	118	ALTARWISE	53
LOVE'S IMAGE TILL MY HEARTBONE BREAKS	129	MY NEOPHYTE	35
AND ALL LOVE'S SINNERS IN SWEET CLOTH KNEEL TO A HYLEG IMAGE,	130	SINNERS' BELL	28
EACH ANCIENT, STONE-NECKED MINUTE OF LOVE'S SEASON	131	I MAKE THIS IN	2
COMES LOVE'S ANATOMIST WITH SUN-GLOVED HAND	132	I MAKE THIS IN	44
LOVE'S A DECISION OF 3 NERVES	138	O CHATTERTON	22
AND UP AND DOWN LOVE'S QUESTIONS ASK;	138	O CHATTERTON	23
IN ALL LOVE'S COUNTRIES, THAT WILL GROPE AWAKE;	139	FIVE & COUNTRY	12
TAKING NO PLUME FOR INDEX IN LOVE'S CHANGE	159	TO LEDA	5
LOVE-TIP			
BY LOVE-TIP OR MY HAND'S RED HEAT.	19	IMAGES IN AIR	14
LOVING			
WHOSE LOVING CRIME	26	PERSONAL EPIT	8
LOVING AND DOUBTING LIKE ONE WHO IS TO DIE	27	OBLIVIOUS DARK	28
IF NOT OF LOVING WELL, THEN NOT,	32	OUT OF SIGHS	8
NO LOVING SHEPHERD IN THIS UPSIDE LIFE.	51	OUT OF THE PIT	38
LAMENTING FALLS. PITY ELECTRA'S LOVING	56	GREEK PLAY	4
LOVING AND BEING LOTH;	90	EUNUCH DREAMS	33
AND TIMELESSLY LIES LOVING WITH THE THIEF.	108	GRIEF THIEF	14
LOVING ON THIS SEA BANGED GUILT	147	UNLUCKILY FOR	15
THAT HER LOVING, UNFRIENDLY LIMBS	175	MY BEGGAR ARM	5
HARK! A VOICE AND LAUGHTER--THE LIVING AND LOVING	222	FOREST PICTURE	11
LOW			
NOT TILL, FROM HIGH AND LOW, THEIR DUST	56	WHY EAST WIND	12
THE SNIPER LAID HIM LOW AND STREWED HIS BRAINS;	63	WOMAN SPEAKS	11
FLESH IS SUFFERED, IS LAID LOW,	71	TAKE NEEDLES	25
LAID THE CROPS LOW, BROKE THE GRAPE'S JOY.	86	BREAD I BREAK	5
AND LAY THE WET FRUITS LOW.	91	WHERE ONCE THE	12
HE LYING LOW WITH RUIN IN HIS EAR,	127	NOW, SAY NAY	20
THE ROD BENDS LOW, DIVINING LAND,	167	LONG-LEGGED	165
BIRD, HE WAS BROUGHT LOW,	191	WINTER'S TALE	126
AS THE ARC OF THE BILLHOOKS THAT FLASHED THE HEDGES LOW	205	GIANT'S THIGH	48
DOWNS INTO THE LOW BROWSING DARK.	215	COUNTRY HEAVEN	15

	PAGE	TITLE	LINE
LOWER			
OF THE UPPER OF THE LOWER HALF, ...	156	RETURN	71
LOWERED			
LIFTED HER MARBLE FOOT, OR LOWERED HER HAND	34	IN GARDENS	20
THE GOSSIPERS HAVE LOWERED THEIR VOICES, ...	38	THE GOSSIPERS	1
LOW-FALUTIN			
EMBRACING LOW-FALUTIN	154	RETURN	1
LOWLANDS			
LOWLANDS OF THE WAVES	203	SIR JOHNS HILL	56
LOWLY			
AS FLEECED AS THEY BOW LOWLY WITH THE SHEEP, ...	96	TWELVE	10
LIE IN GRACE. SLEEP SPELLED AT REST IN THE LOWLY			
HOUSE	199	COUNTRY SLEEP	43
LUBBER			
UP THROUGH THE LUBBER CRUST OF WALES	151	BELOW A TIME	24
LUCID			
NEVER BE LUCID, NEVER STATE, ...	84	LETTER TO AUNT	40
LUCIFER			
LUCIFER THAT BIRD'S DROPPING	165	LONG-LEGGED	113
LUCK			
BEFORE GOOD OR BAD LUCK.	39	GAS FADES	18
THAT I STRUCK ONE DAY BY LUCK, ...	139	TOMBSTONE TOLD	5
THE TRODDEN TOWN RANG ITS COBBLES FOR LUCK.	161	LONG-LEGGED	4
GOOD LUCK TO THE HAND ON THE ROD, ...	164	LONG-LEGGED	61
ALWAYS GOOD LUCK, PRAISED THE FINNED IN THE FEATHER	166	LONG-LEGGED	125
GOOD-BYE, GOOD LUCK, STRUCK THE SUN AND THE MOON,	169	LONG-LEGGED	213
LUCKILY			
LOVE, MY FATE GOT LUCKILY, ...	148	UNLUCKILY FOR	43
LUCKLESSLY			
LUCKLESSLY SHE MUST LIE PATIENT	149	UNLUCKILY FOR	53
LUCKY			
MY HOLY LUCKY BODY	147	UNLUCKILY FOR	16
LUFF			
TO GEOFFREY GRIGSON WITH MY LUFF, ...	85	LETTER TO AUNT	64
LUGGAGE			
WHO UNDER THE LIDS OF HER WINDOWS HOISTED HIS GOLDEN			
LUGGAGE, ...	170	MARRIAGE VIRG	12
LULL			
LYING IN THE LULL	174	FIRE RAID	43
LULLED			
ILLUMINATION OF MUSIC! THE LULLED BLACK-BACKED	200	COUNTRY SLEEP	82
LULLING			
LULLING OF SPHERES IN THE SEASHELL FLESH, ...	211	POEM ON B'DAY	89
LUMINOUS			
MADE HER LIMBS BLIND BY LUMINOUS CHARMS, ...	157	INTO HER HEAD	21
YOUR HEART IS LUMINOUS	160	DEATHS AND ENT	30
OF THE LUMINOUS CATHEDRALS, ...	175	FIRE RAID	62
LUNAR			
BUT LUNAR NIGHT WILL NOT GLOW IN MY BLACKNESS, ...	49	LIGHT, I KNOW	22
THE LUNAR SILENCES, THE SILENT TIDE	54	WE BY SEASAND	9
LUNG			
THE WESTERN MAN HAS LOST ONE LUNG	40	YOUNG ARE OLD	9
THE WESTERN MAN WITH ONE LUNG GONE--	41	YOUNG ARE OLD	44
STILL SET TO SCRATCH A LAUGHTER FROM MY LUNG, ...	95	RUB OF LOVE	5
THE STUFFED LUNG OF THE FOX TWITCH AND CRY LOVE ...	137	AFTER FUNERAL	39
LUNGE			
BEFORE THE LUNGE OF THE NIGHT, THE NOTES ON THIS			
TIME-SHAKEN	203	SIR JOHNS HILL	59
LUNGS			
MY FALLING LUNGS, NOR AS THE CYPRESS	75	SONG: LOVE ME	2

	PAGE	TITLE	LINE
LUNGS (CONTINUED)			
OH, JERICHO WAS FALLING IN THEIR LUNGS!	163	LONG-LEGGED	54
LURCHED			
LURCHED THROUGH A SCUTTLED SEA	142	SAINT TO FALL	23
LURED			
THE LURED FISH UNDER THE FOAM	163	LONG-LEGGED	47
LUST			
OF THE WINTRY NUNNERY OF THE ORDER OF LUST	147	UNLUCKILY FOR	12
NOT YOUR WINGED LUST BUT HIS MUST NOW CHANGE SUIT.	159	TO LEDA	1
NOT YOUR WINGED LUST BUT HIS MUST NOW CHANGE SUIT.	159	TO LEDA	6
LUST BEARS LIKE VOLTS, WHO'LL AMPLIFY, AND STRANGE	159	TO LEDA	8
LUSTRELESS			
AND LUSTRELESS WITHIN THE RUINED FACE	63	WOMAN SPEAKS	9
LUSTS			
LIKE CATS, AND LUSTS LAY HALF HOT IN THE COLD.	50	OUT OF THE PIT	5
3 LITTLE LUSTS SHALL YOUR DOWRY BE, ...	138	O CHATTERTON	42
LYING			
THEY LYING LONG SHALL NOT DIE WINDILY;	49	NO DOMINION	12
WE LYING BY SEASAND	54	WE BY SEASAND	T
WE LYING BY SEASAND, WATCHING YELLOW	54	WE BY SEASAND	1
THIS IS THE WORLD: THE LYING LIKENESS OF	90	EUNUCH DREAMS	31
HE LYING LOW WITH RUIN IN HIS EAR, ...	127	NOW, SAY NAY	20
I FOUND THEM LYING ON THE FLOOR, ...	143	THE MOLLS	1
INTO HER LYING DOWN HEAD	157	INTO HER HEAD	T
INTO HER LYING DOWN HEAD	157	INTO HER HEAD	1
LYING IN THE LULL	174	FIRE RAID	43
LYING THE SKY	200	COUNTRY SLEEP	91
LYING UPON THE YELLOW BEACH.	229	MY RIVER	40
LYNX			
AND, LASHED TO SYLLABLES, THE LYNX TONGUE CRY	139	FIVE & COUNTRY	8
LYS			
AND IN HER GARDEN GROW THE FLEUR DE LYS, ...	222	IN DREAMS	1
MACADAM			
MAN THROUGH MACADAM.	100	RUNNING GRAVE	35
MACHINE			
THUNDER'S ROD OR MAN'S MACHINE;	71	TAKE NEEDLES	23
AGAINST THE FRUIT MACHINE, ...	155	RETURN	34
MACHINERY			
CAUGHT IN THE TRAP'S MACHINERY, LIGHTS OUT, ...	39	GAS FADES	35
MACKEREL			
THE HIGHROAD OF WATER WHERE THE SEABEAR AND MACKEREL	110	I, IN IMAGE	45
MAD			
I SEE THE MAN IS MAD WITH LOVE.'	11	CABARET	13
AND YET, MAD WITH YOUNG BLOOD OR STAINED WITH AGE,	26	THERE'S PLENTY	16
I'VE SAID MY PIECE: COUNT OR GO MAD.	33	HELD-OUT HAND	17
THE LOST IN DOUBT, THE NEARLY MAD, THE YOUNG	41	YOUNG ARE OLD	33
AND HAS THE MAD TREES' TALK BY HEART.	47	POET: 1935	28
UNLESS I LEARN THE NIGHT I SHALL GO MAD.	48	LIGHT, I KNOW	12
THOUGH THEY GO MAD THEY SHALL BE SANE, ...	49	NO DOMINION	6
I MUST LEARN NIGHT'S LIGHT OR GO MAD.	49	LIGHT, I KNOW	30
THE VEINS AT EITHER TEMPLE WHIPPED HIM MAD, ...	50	OUT OF THE PIT	7
AND, MAD, HE CALLED HIS CURSES UPON GOD, ...	50	OUT OF THE PIT	8
MAD BIRDS IN TREES, AND MAD FISH IN A POOL.	50	OUT OF THE PIT	10
MAD BIRDS IN TREES, AND MAD FISH IN A POOL.	50	OUT OF THE PIT	10
THOUGH THEY BE MAD AND DEAD AS NAILS, ...	50	NO DOMINION	24
WHERE, WHAT'S MY GOD? I HAVE BEEN MAD, AM MAD, ...	52	OUT OF THE PIT	63
WHERE, WHAT'S MY GOD? I HAVE BEEN MAD, AM MAD, ...	52	OUT OF THE PIT	63
COMES FROM MY EVIL OR MY GOOD. MAD, MAD, ...	53	OUT OF THE PIT	79
COMES FROM MY EVIL OR MY GOOD. MAD, MAD, ...	53	OUT OF THE PIT	79
AND TALK OF LIGHT TO A MAD MINER.	96	TWELVE	8

                                              PAGE   TITLE   LINE

MAD (CONTINUED)
    AN OLD, MAD MAN STILL CLIMBING IN HIS GHOST, ...   102   FELLOWED SLEEP   29
    UP ROSE THE ABRAHAM-MAN, MAD FOR MY SAKE, ...   112   NOT FATHER ME   19
    THE SMILING WOMAN IS A MAD STORY, ...   138   O CHATTERTON   37
    DEATH AND THIS MAD HEROINE   140   TOMBSTONE TOLD   22
    A GIRL MAD AS BIRDS   169   LOVE IN ASYLUM   3
MADAM
    JOY IS NO KNOCKING NATION, SIR AND MADAM, ...   100   RUNNING GRAVE   31
MADDEN
    THAT MADDEN BOTH WATCHERS AND ACTORS.   33   HELD-OUT HAND   16
    BUT STILL GHOSTS MADDEN, ...   59   FAIRY TALES   14
MADDENING
    AND SYMBOLISE THE MADDENING FACTORS   33   HELD-OUT HAND   15
MADE
    OUR BOAT IS MADE TO RISE   14   RAIN CUTS   32
    MAGNIFIED AND MADE IMMENSE   25   BEAUTY TO DUST   5
    THAT MADE ME HAPPY IN THE SUN, ...   32   OUT OF SIGHS   19
    MADE, FOR THE BATHERS TO ADMIRE, ...   34   IN GARDENS   12
    MADE MEANING MEANINGLESS. THE WRONG WIND STIRS,   ...   37   WINDMILLS TURN   29
    WITHIN HIS HEAD THE ENGINES MADE THEIR HELL, ...   50   OUT OF THE PIT   6
    OF CHURCHES MADE FROM ABSTRACT AND CONCRETE.   51   OUT OF THE PIT   28
    WHERE FLOATED A DEAD DOG WHO MADE HIM ILL, ...   51   OUT OF THE PIT   41
    ALL THAT WAS LOVED AND LOVED MADE THE FOWLS' FOOD,   64   WOMAN SPEAKS   31
    I WHO WAS RICH WAS MADE THE RICHER   69   BEFORE KNOCKED   35
    WE HAVE NO CHOICE, THE CHOICE WAS MADE   74   WE MOTHERNAKED   11
    HOW OF MY CLAY IS MADE THE HANGMAN'S LIME.   77   THE FORCE THAT   15
    HERE SLIPS THE GHOST WHO MADE OF MY PALE BED   81   HERE LIE BEAST   11
    MADE FAST BY ME.   87   PAIN BE MUSIC   6
    OF HEAD AND TAIL MADE WITNESSES TO THIS   124   TODAY, INSECT   7
    NOW MAKE THE WORLD OF ME AS I HAVE MADE   124   FOSTER LIGHT   29
    SHE WEPT IN HER PAIN AND MADE MOUTHS, ...   139   TOMBSTONE TOLD   19
    MADE HER LIMBS BLIND BY LUMINOUS CHARMS, ...   157   INTO HER HEAD   21
    MADE HIS BAD BED IN HER GOOD   158   INTO HER HEAD   35
    MADE THE TIGERS JUMP OUT OF THEIR EYES   172   THE HUNCHBACK   28
    MADE ALL DAY UNTIL BELL TIME   172   THE HUNCHBACK   31
    WHEN THAT IMMORTAL HOSPITAL MADE ONE MORE MOVE TO
        SOOTHE   186   HOLY SPRING   3
    SHALL DROWN IN A GRIEF AS DEEP AS HIS MADE GRAVE,   194   CONVERS PRAYER   18
    UNDER THE NEW MADE CLOUDS AND HAPPY AS THE HEART WAS
        LONG, ...   196   FERN HILL   38
    I HAVE MADE MY THROAT AN ARBOUR FOR FORGOTTEN SONGS.   224   IDYLL UNFORGET   20
    IT HAS BEEN VAGUE, AND MADE OF SHADOW, ...   224   IDYLL UNFORGET   25
    AND HOURS MADE LITTLE I HAVE DIPPED MY ARMS IN THEIR
        RAPTURE;   224   IDYLL UNFORGET   31
    I HAVE MADE AN IMAGE OF HER   235   WOMAN TAPESTRY   35
MADHOUSE
    SHUT IN THE MADHOUSE CALL FOR COOL AIR TO BREATHE.   26   THERE'S PLENTY   13
    ON THE MADHOUSE BOARDS WORN THIN BY MY WALKING TEARS. 170   LOVE IN ASYLUM   15
MADMAN
    A MADMAN WITH A BRUSH HAS SLAPPED A FACE   137   O CHATTERTON   13
MADMEN
    ALL, MEN MY MADMEN, THE UNWHOLESOME WIND   101   RUNNING GRAVE   46
    DEATH: DEATH OF HAMLET AND THE NIGHTMARE MADMEN,   124   TODAY, INSECT   19
MADMEN'S
    'ADAM I LOVE, MY MADMEN'S LOVE IS ENDLESS, ...   125   TODAY, INSECT   23
MAGDALENE
    MAGDALENE PROSTITUTION, ...   156   RETURN   85
MAGGOT
    BUT TIME HAS SET ITS MAGGOT ON THEIR TRACK.   40   WAS THERE TIME   4
    AND THE MAGGOT NO MAN CAN SLAY.'   61   MEAT ON BONES   16

	PAGE	TITLE	LINE
MAGGOT (CONTINUED)			
'THE MAGGOT THAT NO MAN CAN KILL	61	MEAT ON BONES	25
I SMELT THE MAGGOT IN MY STOOL.	69	BEFORE KNOCKED	30
LET A MAGGOT AT THE EAR	70	TAKE NEEDLES	3
LET THE MAGGOT OF DESPAIR	70	TAKE NEEDLES	7
MAGGOTS			
THAT BUT A NAME, WHERE MAGGOTS HAVE THEIR X.	79	LOVE'S FEVER	38
MAGGOT'S			
MAN IN HIS MAGGOT'S BARREN.	93	BOYS OF SUMMER	50
MAGIC			
TORN OUT MAGIC FROM THE HEARTS OF COWARDS	60	FAIRY TALES	32
SHALL NOT BE LATCHED WHILE MAGIC GLIDES	91	WHERE ONCE THE	20
WHO SUCKS THE BELL-VOICED ADAM OUT OF MAGIC, ...	119	ALTARWISE	93
TIME, MILK, AND MAGIC, FROM THE WORLD BEGINNING.	119	ALTARWISE	94
OF PETALS FROM SOME MAGIC ROSE;	225	CLOWN IN MOON	2
MAGICAL			
DEATH TO THE MAGICAL WHEN ALL IS DONE, ...	21	BEWILDERED WAY	3
NO MAN MORE MAGICAL, CLAWED OUT THE CROCODILE.	111	I, IN IMAGE	96
MAGICS			
HE DROWNED HIS FATHER'S MAGICS IN A DREAM.	97	TWILIGHT LOCKS	18
MAGNET			
BY MAGNET WINDS TO HER BLIND MOTHER DRAWN, ...	131	I MAKE THIS IN	14
MAGNETIZE			
HOW SHALL IT MAGNETIZE, ...	135	HOW MY ANIMAL	12
MAGNIFIED			
MAGNIFIED AND MADE IMMENSE	25	BEAUTY TO DUST	5
MAGNIFIED OUT OF PRAISE; HER DEATH WAS A STILL DROP;	136	AFTER FUNERAL	17
MAGPIE			
IT WAS THE MAGPIE, AFTER, ...	238	PILLAR BREAKS	17
MAGPIE'S			
THE RAVEN'S FALLEN AND THE MAGPIE'S STILL.	237	PILLAR BREAKS	7
BOAT'S BROKEN, TOO, AND MAGPIE'S STILL;	238	PILLAR BREAKS	26
MAHOMET			
MOVES TO THE MAHOMET OF YOUR HAND.	67	REALM OF FLESH	3
MAID			
FROM MAID AND HEAD, ...	100	RUNNING GRAVE	15
ROSE MAID AND MALE, ...	114	A GRIEF AGO	6
MAIDEN			
RAISES THE HAIRS OF LAD AND MAIDEN.	59	FAIRY TALES	16
IS MAIDEN IN THE SHAMEFUL OAK, OMENS	131	I MAKE THIS IN	21
WITH CARVED BIRD, SAINT, AND SUN, THE WRACKSPIKED			
MAIDEN MOUTH	135	HOW MY ANIMAL	37
AND THE SPLASHED MOTHERING MAIDEN	181	VISION, PRAYER	42
SHINING, IT WAS ADAM AND MAIDEN, ...	196	FERN HILL	30
MAIDEN'S			
DESPAIR OF BLOOD, FAITH IN THE MAIDEN'S SLIME, ...	100	RUNNING GRAVE	23
MAIEUTIC			
AND YOUR MAIEUTIC SLUMBER DRAG IT FORTH.	67	LET A FAITH	13
MAIM			
SENSE CAN BUT MAIM IT, WISDOM MAR IT, ...	25	BEAUTY TO DUST	9
TO MAIM OR STING MY ARM, ...	240	TWINING HEAD	2
MAJESTY			
THE MAJESTY AND BURNING OF THE CHILD'S DEATH.	192	REFUSAL MOURN	13
MAJORS			
TOMORROW'S DRUNK CLUB MAJORS	154	RETURN	12
MAKE			
TO MAKE OUR SENSES TAKE TOO MUCH, ...	13	RAIN CUTS	10
AND MAKE HIS WIDE MOUTH HOME.	17	IN OBLIVION	7
THAT'LL MAKE, IT'S BRITTLE, DIAPHRAGM	24	LITTLE PROBLEM	8
FOLLY PURIFY AND MAKE IT TRUE.	25	BEAUTY TO DUST	10

	PAGE	TITLE	LINE

MAKE (CONTINUED)

	PAGE	TITLE	LINE
MOST FIT FOR LOVERS TO MAKE HARMONY,	34	THIRST PARCHES	10
MAKE MOCK OF WOMAN'S MEAT,	34	THIRST PARCHES	14
WILLING WORDS TO MAKE THE RUMOURS CERTAIN,	38	THE GOSSIPERS	2
TO MAKE ENDS MEET,	38	THE GOSSIPERS	10
FOR ALL THE INCONVENIENCE THEY MAKE,	38	THE GOSSIPERS	14
MAKE THE HUNGER FOR LIVING	39	GAS FADES	26
MAKE DISCORD WITH THE VOICE WITHIN HIS RIBS	46	POET: 1935	5
MAKE BRIGHT ITS CORNERS WHERE A SKELETON	49	LIGHT, I KNOW	23
PAIR OFF, MAKE HARMONIES, A HARMONIOUS CHORD,	53	OUT OF THE PIT	96
WHO DOES NOT MAKE A WOUND IN FAITH	55	NO MAN BELIEVE	5
NO MAN WHO DOES NOT BREAK AND MAKE,	55	NO MAN BELIEVE	21
WHO DOES NOT BREAK AND MAKE HIS FINAL FAITH.	55	NO MAN BELIEVE	24
THE BIRDS MAKE HIM HIS CEREMENTS OF PLUMES,	64	WOMAN SPEAKS	26
WHERE WORDS AND WATER MAKE A MIXTURE	69	BEFORE KNOCKED	27
MAKE DEADLY WHOOPEE IN THE BLUE.	84	LETTER TO AUNT	55
MAKE DESOLATION IN THE VEIN,	86	BREAD I BREAK	12
THAT DROPS TO MAKE A MUSIC IN YOUR BLOOD	87	PAIN BE MUSIC	20
SOME LET ME MAKE YOU OF THE VOWELLED BEECHES,	99	OCTOBER WIND	13
SOME LET ME MAKE YOU OF THE WATER'S SPEECHES.	99	OCTOBER WIND	16
SOME LET ME MAKE YOU OF THE MEADOW'S SIGNS;	99	OCTOBER WIND	21
(SOME LET ME MAKE YOU OF AUTUMNAL SPELLS,	99	OCTOBER WIND	26
SOME LET ME MAKE YOU OF THE HEARTLESS WORDS.	99	OCTOBER WIND	29
NOW MAKE THE WORLD OF ME AS I HAVE MADE	124	FOSTER LIGHT	29
WE MAKE ME MYSTIC AS THE ARM OF AIR,	128	NOW, SAY NAY	34
I MAKE THIS IN A WARRING ABSENCE	131	I MAKE THIS IN	T
I MAKE THIS IN A WARRING ABSENCE WHEN	131	I MAKE THIS IN	1
I MAKE A WEAPON OF AN ASS'S SKELETON	132	I MAKE THIS IN	31
O MAKE ME A MASK	133	MAKE ME A MASK	T
O MAKE ME A MASK AND A WALL TO SHUT FROM YOUR SPIES	133	MAKE ME A MASK	1
YET THIS I MAKE IN A FORGIVING PRESENCE.	133	I MAKE THIS IN	68
BEND, IF MY JOURNEY ACHE, DIRECTION LIKE AN ARC OR MAKE	145	IF HEAD HURT	14
EVERY MORNING I MAKE,	150	WHEN I WOKE	16
ONLY TO MAKE TWO ENDS MEET,	155	RETURN	61
AND THE SENSUAL RUINS MAKE	166	LONG-LEGGED	118
INVISIBLE TO MAKE	176	BREATH SHED	2
BEFORE YOU MOVE TO MAKE	192	SIDE OF TRUTH	8
AND MAKE MY GARDEN GLAD AND GAY.	227	TRIOLET	3
NOR MAKE THE STERN SHELL OF MY SPIRIT MOVE.	233	NO THOUGHT	2
AND MAKE YOU BITTER WITH MY COLD,	233	NO THOUGHT	6
SHE SHALL MAKE FOR ME	235	WOMAN TAPESTRY	27
I'LL MAKE YOUR SHAPE MY OWN,	238	MAKES INTERVALS	10

MAKER

| HEAD, DECEIVED, I BELIEVED, MY MAKER, | 152 | BELOW A TIME | 34 |
| AND I AM STRUCK AS LONELY AS A HOLY MAKER BY THE SUN. | 186 | HOLY SPRING | 12 |

MAKER'S

| MY MAKER'S FLESH THAT GARMENTS MY CLAYFELLOWS. | 76 | LASHED RINGS | 3 |

MAKES

THE SWAN MAKES STRINGS OF WATER IN HER WAKE;	15	FOR LEDA	14
BUT HE MAKES THEM DANCE, CUT CAPERS	47	POET: 1935	41
WHO CURSES NOT WHAT MAKES AND SAVES,	55	NO MAN BELIEVE	14
AND THE SWEAT ON THE BROW MAKES A SIGN,	74	SUN BURNS	4
THE SEED THAT MAKES A FOREST OF THE LOIN	88	A PROCESS IN	13
SHE MAKES FOR ME A NETTLE'S INNOCENCE	131	I MAKE THIS IN	16
AND MAKES WITH A FLICK OF THE THUMB AND SUN	142	SAINT TO FALL	50
MUSIC OF ELEMENTS, THAT A MIRACLE MAKES!	200	COUNTRY SLEEP	86
MAKES ALL THE MUSIC; AND I WHO HEAR THE TUNE OF THE SLOW,	203	SIR JOHNS HILL	57
BENEATH THE DEEP BARK CALLS AND MAKES QUIET MUSIC.	226	THE OAK	6

```
                                                 PAGE      TITLE        LINE
MAKES  (CONTINUED)
     IT'S LIGHT THAT MAKES THE INTERVALS    ................  238   MAKES INTERVALS   T
     IT'S LIGHT THAT MAKES THE INTERVALS    ................  238   MAKES INTERVALS   1
MAKING
     MAKING FRESH WHAT WAS STALE    ......................   35   LIFT UP FACE       6
     UNDER THE MASK AND THE ETHER, THEY, MAKING BLOODY     110   I, IN IMAGE       53
     RAGE ME BACK TO THE MAKING HOUSE. MY HAND UNRAVEL     145   IF HEAD HURT      12
     ARE MAKING UNDER THE GREEN, LAID VEIL    .............  164   LONG-LEGGED       69
     NEVER UNTIL THE MANKIND MAKING    ...................  191   REFUSAL MOURN      1
     HOVER, MAKING THE FOREST FLUCTUANTLY VAGUE.  ........  226   THE OAK            4
     MAKING OUR AFFECTIONS FAST;    ......................  230   OUR SANCTITY      18
MALE
     SHALL IT BE MALE OR FEMALE? SAY THE CELLS,   ........   95   RUB OF LOVE        8
     SHALL IT BE MALE OR FEMALE? SAY THE FINGERS   .......   95   RUB OF LOVE       15
     I, IN MY FUSION OF ROSE AND MALE MOTION,   ..........  109   I, IN IMAGE       17
     ROSE MAID AND MALE,   ..............................  114   A GRIEF AGO        6
     TOWARDS THE STUDDED MALE IN A BENT, MIDNIGHT BLAZE    135   HOW MY ANIMAL     13
     MALE SHAPES, GIRL-LIPPED, BUT CLAD LIKE BOYS:  .....  143   THE MOLLS          2
     WOUND THEIR ROOM WITH A MALE MOAN,   ...............  158   INTO HER HEAD     25
     THE FEMALE, DEADLY, AND MALE   .....................  158   INTO HER HEAD     53
     HE'LL BATHE HIS RAINING BLOOD IN THE MALE SEA  .....  160   DEATHS AND ENT    19
     OR RIDES THE IMAGINED OCEANS OF THE MALE WARDS.  ...  169   LOVE IN ASYLUM     9
MAMMOTH
     MAMMOTH AND SPARROWFALL    .........................  150   WHEN I WOKE       20
MAN
     HOW I, A SPINNING MAN,   ...........................    4   PROLOGUE          39
     ROARED, SEA BORN, MAN TORN, BLOOD BLEST.   .........    4   PROLOGUE          41
     I SEE THE MAN IS MAD WITH LOVE.'   .................   11   CABARET           13
     NEW MAN BEST WHOSE BLOOD RUNS THICK,   .............   29   LONG, SKELETON    11
     AND THE WONDER THAT MAN KNOWS,   ...................   31   BEING BUT MEN     12
     MAN SHOULD BE CURED OF DISTEMPER.   ................   32   OUT OF SIGHS      27
     ON MAN AND MOUNTAIN,   .............................   34   THIRST PARCHES     6
     THE WESTERN MAN HAS LOST ONE LUNG   ................   40   YOUNG ARE OLD      9
     ALONE'S UNHURT, SO THE BLIND MAN SEES BEST.  .......   40   WAS THERE TIME     9
     THE WESTERN MAN WITH ONE LUNG GONE--   .............   41   YOUNG ARE OLD     44
     TO REMEMBER, CAST STRICTURE ON MECHANICS AND MAN.     45   PLOUGHMAN GONE     5
     MAN TOILS NOW ON AN IRON SADDLE, RIDING   ..........   45   PLOUGHMAN GONE    24
     MAN WHO ONCE DROVE IS DRIVEN IN SUN AND RAIN.  .....   46   PLOUGHMAN GONE    34
     HE IS NOT MAN'S NOR WOMAN'S MAN,   .................   47   POET: 1935        25
     IF LOVE HE CAN BEING NO WOMAN'S MAN.   .............   47   POET: 1935        35
     O LONELY AMONG MANY, THE GODS' MAN,   ..............   47   POET: 1935        47
     YOU CAPTURE MORE THAN MAN OR WOMAN GUESSES;  .......   48   POET: 1935        54
     GROWING IN PUBLIC PLACES THAN MAN KNOWS.  ..........   48   POET: 1935        57
     WITH THE MAN IN THE WIND AND THE WEST MOON;  .......   49   NO DOMINION        3
     AND HAND TO BUTTOCK, MAN TO ENGINE, BATTLING,  .....   51   OUT OF THE PIT    36
     NO MAN BELIEVES    .................................   54   NO MAN BELIEVE     T
     NO MAN BELIEVES WHO, WHEN A STAR FALLS SHOT,  ......   54   NO MAN BELIEVE     1
     NO MAN BELIEVES WHO CRIES NOT, GOD IS NOT,  ........   55   NO MAN BELIEVE     7
     NO BREASTED GIRL, NO MAN WHO, YOUNG    .............   55   NO MAN BELIEVE    10
     NO MAN BELIEVES WHO DOES NOT WONDER WHY.  ..........   55   NO MAN BELIEVE    12
     BELIEVE AND BE SAVED. NO MAN BELIEVES   ............   55   NO MAN BELIEVE    13
     NO MAN UPON THIS CYST OF EARTH    ..................   55   NO MAN BELIEVE    15
     NO MAN, NO MAN, NO MAN.   ..........................   55   NO MAN BELIEVE    17
     NO MAN, NO MAN, NO MAN.   ..........................   55   NO MAN BELIEVE    17
     NO MAN, NO MAN, NO MAN.   ..........................   55   NO MAN BELIEVE    17
     AND THIS IS TRUE, NO MAN CAN LIVE   ................   55   NO MAN BELIEVE    18
     NO MAN WHO DOES NOT BREAK AND MAKE,   ..............   55   NO MAN BELIEVE    21
     OF ECHO'S ANSWER AND THE MAN OF FROST   ............   56   WHY EAST WIND     25
     AND THE MAGGOT NO MAN CAN SLAY.'   .................   61   MEAT ON BONES     16
     A MERRY GIRL TOOK ME FOR MAN,    ...................   61   MEAT ON BONES     22
```

MAN

	PAGE	TITLE	LINE
MAN (CONTINUED)			
'THE MAGGOT THAT NO MAN CAN KILL	61	MEAT ON BONES	25
AND THE MAN NO ROPE CAN HANG	61	MEAT ON BONES	26
WAR ON THE DESTINY OF MAN!	61	MEAT ON BONES	39
SINCE THE FIRST FLESH OF MAN WAS RIVEN	64	WOMAN SPEAKS	28
THESE DIE WHO SHOVEL THE LAST HOME OF MAN;	64	WOMAN SPEAKS	44
MAN BY A SCRIBBLED NAME.	66	HAND SIGNED	12
A GHOST NOR MAN, BUT MORTAL GHOST.	69	BEFORE KNOCKED	38
AND I AM DUMB TO TELL THE HANGING MAN	77	THE FORCE THAT	14
THE WINTER YEARS, MOVE IN THE PIT OF MAN;	79	ALMANAC TIME	3
TIME SHALL BELONG TO MAN.	80	ALMANAC TIME	15
HERE LIE THE BEASTS OF MAN AND HERE I FEAST,	81	HERE LIE BEAST	1
THE DEAD MAN SAID,	81	HERE LIE BEAST	2
HERE LIES THE BEAST OF MAN AND HERE HIS ANGELS,	81	HERE LIE BEAST	7
THE DEAD MAN SAID,	81	HERE LIE BEAST	8
THE FRUIT OF MAN UNWRINKLES IN THE STARS,	82	LIGHT BREAKS	10
MAN IN THE DAY OR WIND AT NIGHT	86	BREAD I BREAK	4
MAN BROKE THE SUN, PULLED THE WIND DOWN.	86	BREAD I BREAK	10
THE SLEEPY MAN OF WINTER PULLS,	92	BOYS OF SUMMER	29
AND FROM THE PLANTED WOMB THE MAN OF STRAW.	92	BOYS OF SUMMER	36
MAN IN HIS MAGGOT'S BARREN.	93	BOYS OF SUMMER	50
I AM THE MAN YOUR FATHER WAS.	93	BOYS OF SUMMER	52
THE ITCH OF MAN UPON THE BABY'S THIGH,	95	RUB OF LOVE	12
MAN BE MY METAPHOR.	96	RUB OF LOVE	49
CHASTE AND THE CHASER, MAN WITH THE COCKSHUT EYE,	100	RUNNING GRAVE	17
MAN THROUGH MACADAM.	100	RUNNING GRAVE	35
SO, PLANING-HEELED, I FLEW ALONG MY MAN	101	FELLOWED SLEEP	4
THE INCHES MONKEYED BY THE BLOOD OF MAN.	102	FELLOWED SLEEP	28
AN OLD, MAD MAN STILL CLIMBING IN HIS GHOST,	102	FELLOWED SLEEP	29
IN BOTTOM GEAR THROUGH NIGHT-GEARED MAN.	103	I DREAMED MY	12
OF NEW MAN STRENGTH, I SEEK THE SUN.	103	I DREAMED MY	28
MAN OF MY FLESH, THE JAWBONE RIVEN,	106	ALL ALL AND	19
GHOST WITH HER GHOST, CONTAGIOUS MAN	107	ALL ALL AND	26
CASTS TO THE PINE ROOTS, RAISING MAN LIKE A MOUNTAIN	109	I, IN IMAGE	11
MY MAN OF LEAVES AND THE BRONZE ROOT, MORTAL, UNMORTAL,	109	I, IN IMAGE	16
THUS THE SHADOWLESS MAN OR OX, AND THE PICTURED DEVIL,	109	I, IN IMAGE	22
NO MAN MORE MAGICAL, CLAWED OUT THE CROCODILE.	111	I, IN IMAGE	96
MAN WAS THE SCALES, THE DEATH BIRDS ON ENAMEL,	111	I, IN IMAGE	97
ALL-HOLLOWED MAN WEPT FOR HIS WHITE APPAREL.	111	I, IN IMAGE	102
MAN WAS CADAVER'S MASKER, THE HARNESSING MANTLE,	112	I, IN IMAGE	103
WINDILY MASTER OF MAN WAS THE ROTTEN FATHOM,	112	I, IN IMAGE	104
MAN MORROW BLOWS THROUGH FOOD.	113	SERVANT SUN	14
LET THE SOIL SQUEAL I AM THE BITING MAN	114	SERVANT SUN	20
WHAT OF A BAMBOO MAN AMONG YOUR ACRES?	118	ALTARWISE	49
TIME TRACKS THE SOUND OF SHAPE ON MAN AND CLOUD,	120	ALTARWISE	97
WHAT RHUBARB MAN PEELED IN HER FOAM-BLUE CHANNEL	121	ALTARWISE	135
TIME, IN A FOLLY'S RIDER, LIKE A COUNTY MAN	122	HOLD HARD	4
MAN DRY MAN,	127	NOW, SAY NAY	3
MAN DRY MAN,	127	NOW, SAY NAY	3
SNAIL OF MAN IN HIS SHIP OF FIRES	128	MY NEOPHYTE	8
MIRROR FROM MAN TO WHALE	129	MY NEOPHYTE	21
IN THE GROIN'S ENDLESS COIL A MAN IS TANGLED.'	132	I MAKE THIS IN	53
TO LIFT TO LEAVE FROM THE TREASURES OF MAN IS PLEASING DEATH	140	NO WORK WORDS	7
AN ENAMOURED MAN ALONE BY THE TWIGS OF HIS EYES, TWO FIRES,	144	PLEASURE-BIRD	7
AN UPRIGHT MAN IN THE ANTIPODES	145	PLEASURE-BIRD	23
WHILE A MAN OUTSIDE WITH A BILLHOOK,	150	WHEN I WOKE	8

	PAGE	TITLE	LINE
MAN (CONTINUED)			
WHEN HINDERING MAN HURT	153	WAS A SAVIOUR	12
MAN, ANIMAL, OR BIRD	153	WAS A SAVIOUR	13
ON TO THE GROUND WHEN A MAN DIED	153	WAS A SAVIOUR	21
GREED ON MAN BEATING NEAR THE FIRE NEIGHBOUR	153	WAS A SAVIOUR	30
LONDON (SAID THE ODD MAN IN	154	RETURN	2
ON STOOLS TO A ONE MAN SHOW DOWN,	154	RETURN	20
RAZOR MAN AND BELLY KING,	155	RETURN	32
THE BLACK MAN BLEACHED TO HIS TIDE	155	RETURN	40
MAN WAS THE BURNING ENGLAND SHE WAS SLEEP-WALKING, AND THE ENAMOURING ISLAND	157	INTO HER HEAD	20
SUPER-OR-NEAR MAN	158	INTO HER HEAD	29
NOT GIRL FOR BIRD (GOURD BEING MAN) BREAKS ROOT.	159	TO LEDA	4
A MAN TORN UP MOURNS IN THE SOLE NIGHT.	159	INTO HER HEAD	67
GOOD-BYE TO THE MAN ON THE SEA-LEGGED DECK	162	LONG-LEGGED	18
OUT OF THE URN THE SIZE OF A MAN	166	LONG-LEGGED	141
FOR A MAN SLEEPS WHERE FIRE LEAPT DOWN AND SHE LEARNS THROUGH HIS ARM	170	MARRIAGE VIRG	13
AMONG THOSE KILLED IN THE DAWN RAID WAS A MAN AGED A HUNDRED	172	DAWN RAID	T
MAN AND WOMAN UNDONE,	175	FIRE RAID	57
AND THE HEART PRINT OF MAN	180	VISION, PRAYER	12
CRYING AT THE MAN DRENCHED THRONE	181	VISION, PRAYER	58
OF MAN WHEN	182	VISION, PRAYER	82
AS THE FOOD AND FLAMES OF THE SNOW, A MAN UNROLLED	187	WINTER'S TALE	13
THAT A MAN KNELT ALONE IN THE CUP OF THE VALES,	189	WINTER'S TALE	85
BY THE CHILD GOING TO BED AND THE MAN ON THE STAIRS	193	CONVERS PRAYER	2
FROM THE MAN ON THE STAIRS AND THE CHILD BY HIS BED.	194	CONVERS PRAYER	8
SHALL THE CHILD SLEEP UNHARMED OR THE MAN BE CRYING?	194	CONVERS PRAYER	12
TURNS ON THE QUICK AND THE DEAD, AND THE MAN ON THE STAIRS	194	CONVERS PRAYER	14
NOT FOR THE PROUD MAN APART	197	CRAFT OR ART	12
OR WITH THEIR ORCHARD MAN IN THE CORE OF THE SUN'S BUSH	204	GIANT'S THIGH	24
WHEN I WAS A GUSTY MAN AND A HALF	206	LAMENT	13
WHEN I WAS A MAN YOU COULD CALL A MAN	206	LAMENT	25
WHEN I WAS A MAN YOU COULD CALL A MAN	206	LAMENT	25
WHEN I WAS A HALF OF THE MAN I WAS	207	LAMENT	37
NOW I AM A MAN NO MORE NO MORE	207	LAMENT	49
SENSES, AND MAN A SPIRIT IN LOVE	211	POEM ON B'DAY	83
TO DEATH, ONE MAN THROUGH HIS SUNDERED HULKS,	211	POEM ON B'DAY	92
A COLD KIND MAN BRAVE IN HIS NARROW PRIDE	216	ELEGY	3
AN OLD TORMENTED MAN THREE-QUARTERS BLIND,	217	ELEGY	18
AN OLD KIND MAN BRAVE IN HIS BURNING PRIDE.	217	ELEGY	24
AN OLD MAN IS WITH ME WHERE I GO	217	ELEGY	30
FOR DEATH IS FRIENDLY TO THE MAN	240	TWINING HEAD	5
MANAGERS			
FOUND MANAGERS AND WIDOWS WANTING	38	THE GOSSIPERS	11
MANALIVE			
OF FEAR, RAGE RED, MANALIVE,	4	PROLOGUE	48
MAN-BEARING			
FLEW MAN-BEARING THERE.	157	INTO HER HEAD	6
MAN-BEGETTERS			
FOR MAN-BEGETTERS IN THE DRY-AS-PASTE,	113	NOT FATHER ME	23
MANDRAKE			
BIT OUT THE MANDRAKE WITH TO-MORROW'S SCREAM.	117	ALTARWISE	6
AND PLUCK A MANDRAKE MUSIC FROM THE MARROWROOT.	123	FOSTER LIGHT	18
MANED			
HIS STRIPED AND NOON MANED TRIBE STRIDING TO HOLOCAUST,	148	UNLUCKILY FOR	31

	PAGE	TITLE	LINE
MANES			
AND THUNDERBOLTS IN THEIR MANES.	168	LONG-LEGGED	190
MANES, UNDER HIS QUENCHLESS SUMMER BARBED GOLD TO			
THE BONE, ...	204	GIANT'S THIGH	26
MANHOLES			
VOICES FROM MANHOLES AND DRAINS, ...	155	RETURN	53
MANHOOD			
OF SICK OLD MANHOOD ON THE FALLEN JAWS, ...	95	RUB OF LOVE	24
REROBING OF THE NAKED GHOST. MANHOOD	103	I DREAMED MY	23
THIS IS THE FORTUNE OF MANHOOD: THE NATURAL PERIL,	109	I, IN IMAGE	19
INTRICATE MANHOOD OF ENDING, THE INVALID RIVALS,	109	I, IN IMAGE	31
MAN-IN-SEED			
MAN-IN-SEED, IN SEED-AT-ZERO, ...	126	SEED-AT-ZERO	43
MAN-IN-SEED, IN SEE-AT-ZERO, ...	127	SEED-AT-ZERO	50
MAN-IRON			
TO MY MAN-IRON SIDLE.	108	I, IN IMAGE	6
MANKIND			
NEVER UNTIL THE MANKIND MAKING	191	REFUSAL MOURN	1
THE MANKIND OF HER GOING WITH A GRAVE TRUTH	192	REFUSAL MOURN	15
MANMADE			
MAN'S MANMADE SPARETIME LASTS THE FOUR SEASONS, ...	39	GAS FADES	19
MAN-MELTING			
OF SUNS IN THE MAN-MELTING NIGHT.	102	I DREAMED MY	8
MANNA			
ONE SUN, ONE MANNA, WARMED AND FED.	79	LOVE'S FEVER	50
SPEAK LIKE A HUNGRY PARSON OF THE MANNA, ...	96	TWELVE	6
MANNA FOR THE RUMBLING GROUND, ...	125	SEED-AT-ZERO	17
MANNA FOR THE GUARDED GROUND, ...	126	SEED-AT-ZERO	24
PUFFING THE POUNDS OF MANNA UP THROUGH THE DEW TO			
HEAVEN, ...	140	NO WORK WORDS	5
MANNED			
MANNED WITH THEIR LOVES THEY'LL MOVE, ...	5	PROLOGUE	95
AND, MANNED BY MIDNIGHT, JACOB TO THE STARS.	117	ALTARWISE	24
MAN'S			
I AM MAN'S REPLY TO EVERY QUESTION, ...	26	PERSONAL EPIT	17
ANY MAN'S TROUBLES NOT YOUR OWN--	27	OBLIVIOUS DARK	3
HAVE KNOWN MAN'S ENVY AND HIS WEAK DESIRE, ...	30	YOUTH CALLS	3
MAN'S MANMADE SPARETIME LASTS THE FOUR SEASONS, ...	39	GAS FADES	19
THE RAWBONED HORSE TO A MAN'S VOICE	45	PLOUGHMAN GONE	14
HE IS NOT MAN'S NOR WOMAN'S MAN, ...	47	POET: 1935	25
MAN'S RIB ON WOMAN'S, STRAIGHT LINE ON A CURVE, ...	51	OUT OF THE PIT	35
MAN'S MARROW BARBED, AND BREAST RIPPED WITH A STEEL,	64	WOMAN SPEAKS	30
THUNDER'S ROD OR MAN'S MACHINE;	71	TAKE NEEDLES	23
I LEARNT MAN'S TONGUE, TO TWIST THE SHAPES OF			
THOUGHTS	79	LOVE'S FEVER	32
AN OLD MAN'S SHANK ONE-MARROWED WITH MY BONE, ...	95	RUB OF LOVE	32
FORGED IN MAN'S MINERALS, THE BRASSY ORATOR	108	I, IN IMAGE	2
MOUNT ON MAN'S FOOTFALL, ...	109	I, IN IMAGE	27
FORGED IN MAN'S MINERAL.	112	I, IN IMAGE	106
IF I TAKE TO BURN OR RETURN THIS WORLD WHICH IS EACH			
MAN'S WORK.	140	NO WORK WORDS	12
ALONE IN THE HUSK OF MAN'S HOME	186	HOLY SPRING	22
MANSEED			
THE GROWING BONES, THE RUMOUR OF MANSEED	78	LOVE'S FEVER	17
MANSHAPE			
A MERRY MANSHAPE OF YOUR WALKING CIRCLE.	124	FOSTER LIGHT	30
MANSHAPED			
FOSTER THE LIGHT NOR VEIL THE MANSHAPED MOON, ...	123	FOSTER LIGHT	1
MANSION			
BREAD AND MILK MANSION IN A TOOTHLESS TOWN.	131	I MAKE THIS IN	15

	PAGE	TITLE	LINE
MANSIONS			
HIDING THE GOLDEN MOUNTAINS AND MANSIONS	54	WE BY SEASAND	16
MANSOULED			
THE MANSOULED FIERY ISLANDS! OH, ...	211	POEM ON B'DAY	105
MANSTRING			
BE BY THE SHIPS' SEA BROKEN AT THE MANSTRING ANCHORED	111	I, IN IMAGE	86
MANTLE			
MAN WAS CADAVER'S MASKER, THE HARNESSING MANTLE,	112	I, IN IMAGE	103
IN THE MANTLE AND CALM, ...	190	WINTER'S TALE	86
MANTLED			
COMBS THROUGH THE MANTLED YARDS AND THE MORNING MEN	187	WINTER'S TALE	20
I HAVE KNOWN THE MYSTERY OF THE SEA TO BE MANTLED			
ABOUT ME;	223	IDYLL UNFORGET	18
MANURING			
MANURING POPEYE OR	154	RETURN	6
MANWAGED			
THAT TOWN OF GHOSTS, THE MANWAGED WOMB	125	SEED-AT-ZERO	9
MANWAGING			
OVER THE MANWAGING LINE.	125	SEED-AT-ZERO	7
MANWAX			
BLEW OUT THE BLOOD GAUZE THROUGH THE WOUND OF MANWAX.	119	ALTARWISE	84
MANY			
OR HAS TOO MANY CLOUDS OR BIRDS, ...	12	SKY'S BRIGHT	2
AND MANY ARMS TO RAISE	12	CABARET	20
FAITH. FAITH. FIRM FAITH IN MANY OR ONE, ...	41	YOUNG ARE OLD	49
O LONELY AMONG MANY, THE GODS' MAN, ...	47	POET: 1935	47
NOW HE IS ONE WITH MANY, ONE WITH ALL, ...	53	OUT OF THE PIT	98
OF MANY A HUNDRED FALLS;	55	WHY EAST WIND	5
BURNS IN MANY MIRRORS.	60	FAIRY TALES	25
GOD IS THE SAME THOUGH HE BE PRAISED AS MANY, ...	67	LET A FAITH	9
GOD SHALL BE GODS AND MANY DEATHS BE DEATH.	67	LET A FAITH	15
GOD IS SLAIN IN MANY WAYS.	72	TAKE NEEDLES	56
WHAT HAD BEEN ONE WAS MANY SOUNDING MINDED.	79	LOVE'S FEVER	41
OF MANY A THORNY SHIRE TELL YOU NOTES, ...	99	OCTOBER WIND	15
I HAVE HEARD MANY YEARS OF TELLING, ...	116	LANTERNS SHINE	16
AND MANY YEARS SHOULD SEE SOME CHANGE.	116	LANTERNS SHINE	17
THE SHADE OF THEIR TREES WAS A WORD OF MANY SHADES	144	COLOUR OF SAY	10
IN THE TAKEN BODY AT MANY AGES, ...	158	INTO HER HEAD	40
IN MANY MARRIED LONDON'S ESTRANGING GRIEF.	160	DEATHS AND ENT	12
ONE ENEMY, OF MANY, WHO KNOWNS WELL	160	DEATHS AND ENT	29
THROUGH THROATS WHERE MANY RIVERS MEET, THE CURLEWS			
CRY, ...	203	GIANT'S THIGH	1
THROUGH THROATS WHERE MANY RIVERS MEET, THE WOMEN			
PRAY, ...	203	GIANT'S THIGH	6
THERE ARE MANY WHO SAY THAT A DOG HAS ITS DAY, ...	221	SONG OF DOG	1
BUT YOUR STONE IS MANY POINTED, ...	230	MY RIVER	45
MAP-BACKED			
INTO THE MAP-BACKED HILLS WHERE PATHS	44	TO FOLLOW FOX	8
MAPS			
O WHO IS GLORY IN THE SHAPELESS MAPS, ...	124	FOSTER LIGHT	28
MAR			
SENSE CAN BUT MAIM IT, WISDOM MAR IT, ...	25	BEAUTY TO DUST	9
MARBLE			
OF MARBLE BATHERS TOEING THE GARDEN PONDS, ...	33	IN GARDENS	2
LIFTED HER MARBLE FOOT, OR LOWERED HER HAND	34	IN GARDENS	20
THESE CLOUD-SOPPED, MARBLE HANDS, THIS MONUMENTAL	137	AFTER FUNERAL	36
MARCHES			
AS THEIR BLADE MARCHES IN	142	SAINT TO FALL	40
MARCHING			
RAMMED IN THE MARCHING HEART, HOLE	103	I DREAMED MY	14

	PAGE	TITLE	LINE
MARE			
AND A FELLOW WHO JESTS THAT A MARE CAN BUILD NESTS	221	SONG OF DOG	7
MARE'S			
ON A MARE'S BACK OF A MARE'S NEST OR A GOOSE, ...	45	TO FOLLOW FOX	19
ON A MARE'S BACK OF A MARE'S NEST OR A GOOSE, ...	45	TO FOLLOW FOX	19
MARK			
THE MARK HIS FLYING TAIL HAS LEFT	14	RAIN CUTS	21
SHUT, TOO, IN A TOWER OF WORDS, I MARK	98	OCTOBER WIND	9
(SIR MORROW MARK), ...	113	SERVANT SUN	2
THE FINGERS WILL FORGET GREEN THUMBS AND MARK	138	FIVE & COUNTRY	2
STAND IN A QUESTION MARK.	138	O CHATTERTON	36
MARK, TRUMPET LIPPED AND BLACKHEAD	155	RETURN	41
AND MARK THE DARK EYED WAVE, THROUGH THE EYES OF			
SLEEP, ...	194	CONVERS PRAYER	19
MARKED			
GONE FROM MY PALM TO LEAVE IT MARKED	12	CABARET	16
KICKED, WITH A CLATTER, ASH-BINS MARKED VERBOTEN,	52	OUT OF THE PIT	57
SHARP IN MY SECOND DEATH I MARKED THE HILLS, HARVEST	103	I DREAMED MY	17
THAT WILL RAKE AT LAST ALL CURRENCIES OF THE MARKED			
BREATH	140	NO WORK WORDS	8
MARKING			
WHO SEEK ME LANDWARD, MARKING IN MY MOUTH	105	WORLD PYRAMID	46
MARKING THE FLESH AND SUMMER IN THE BAY?	112	NOT FATHER ME	11
MARKS			
AND THROUGH THESE EYES GOD MARKS MYSELF REVOLVING,	76	LASHED RINGS	12
TIME MARKS A BLACK AISLE KINDLE FROM THE BRAND OF			
ASHES, ...	130	SINNERS' BELL	4
GOD IN HIS WHIRLWIND SILENCE SAVE, WHO MARKS THE			
SPARROWS HAIL, ...	202	SIR JOHNS HILL	45
MARRIAGE			
IN MORALS AND FULL MARRIAGE BUNTING, ...	38	THE GOSSIPERS	12
I MEAN BY TIME THE CAST AND CURFEW RASCAL OF OUR			
MARRIAGE, ...	130	SINNERS' BELL	25
ON THE MARRIAGE OF A VIRGIN	170	MARRIAGE VIRG	T
MARRIAGES			
ALL BLOOD-SIGNED ASSAILINGS AND VANISHED MARRIAGES			
IN WHICH HE HAD NO LOVELY PART	158	INTO HER HEAD	43
MARRIED			
THE PHOTOGRAPH IS MARRIED TO THE EYE, ...	90	EUNUCH DREAMS	27
A VIRGIN MARRIED AT REST.	139	TOMBSTONE TOLD	3
SHE MARRIED IN THIS POURING PLACE, ...	139	TOMBSTONE TOLD	4
IN MANY MARRIED LONDON'S ESTRANGING GRIEF.	160	DEATHS AND ENT	12
HER DEEPSEA PILLOW WHERE ONCE SHE MARRIED ALONE,	170	MARRIAGE VIRG	9
MARROW			
ACHES TILL THE METAL MEETS THE MARROW, ...	47	POET: 1935	50
THE MERRIEST MARROW AND THE DREGS	60	MEAT ON BONES	3
MAN'S MARROW BARBED, AND BREAST RIPPED WITH A STEEL,	64	WOMAN SPEAKS	30
THAT SHROUDED MEN MIGHT MARROW AS THEY FLY.	90	EUNUCH DREAMS	30
THE CRUTCH THAT MARROW TAPS UPON THEIR SLEEP, ...	104	WORLD PYRAMID	14
SKINNY AS SIN, THE FOAMING MARROW, ...	106	ALL ALL AND	11
(QUESTIONS ARE HUNCHBACKS TO THE POKER MARROW.) ...	118	ALTARWISE	48
BUT STRIP THE TWELVE-WINDED MARROW FROM HIS CIRCLE;	123	FOSTER LIGHT	3
THE INMOST MARROW OF MY HEART BONE	183	VISION, PRAYER	118
MARROW OF EAGLES, THE ROOTS OF WHALES	210	POEM ON B'DAY	58
MARROW-COLUMNED			
AND THIS WEAK HOUSE TO MARROW-COLUMNED HEAVEN, ...	131	I MAKE THIS IN	8
MARROWED			
THE BODY PROSPERED, TEETH IN THE MARROWED GUMS, ...	78	LOVE'S FEVER	16
THE SUBSTANCE FORKED THAT MARROWED THE FIRST SUN;	93	IN BEGINNING	4

	PAGE	TITLE	LINE
MARROW-LADLE			
RIP OF THE VAULTS, I TOOK MY MARROW-LADLE	118	ALTARWISE	35
MARROWROOT			
AND PLUCK A MANDRAKE MUSIC FROM THE MARROWROOT. ...	123	FOSTER LIGHT	18
MARRY			
RAPE GULP AND BE MARRY, HE ALSO SERVES	138	O CHATTERTON	26
MARTYRDOM			
STREAM UPON HIS MARTYRDOM	185	VISION, PRAYER	185
MARVEL			
THERE COULD I MARVEL	178	POEM IN OCT	38
AND THERE COULD I MARVEL MY BIRTHDAY	178	POEM IN OCT	61
MARVELS			
BEGINNING WITH DOOM IN THE GHOST, AND THE SPRINGING MARVELS, ...	109	I, IN IMAGE	13
MARY			
MARY, VIRGIN, OR ANY OTHER.	41	YOUNG ARE OLD	48
THE WORLD'S MY WOUND, GOD'S MARY IN HER GRIEF, ...	120	ALTARWISE	102
MARYS			
HER ROBIN BREASTED TREE, THREE MARYS IN THE RAYS.	198	COUNTRY SLEEP	29
MASK			
SOUNDS, RICH WITH LIFE, OUT OF A PAINTED MASK;	57	GREEK PLAY	14
LOVE ME AND LIFT YOUR MASK.	75	SONG: LOVE ME	4
LOVE ME AND LIFT YOUR MASK.	76	SONG: LOVE ME	8
LOVE ME AND LIFT YOUR MASK.	76	SONG: LOVE ME	12
LOVE ME AND LIFT YOUR MASK.	76	SONG: LOVE ME	16
UNDER THE MASK AND THE ETHER, THEY, MAKING BLOODY	110	I, IN IMAGE	53
DEATH FROM A BANDAGE, RANTS THE MASK OF SCHOLARS	120	ALTARWISE	120
O MAKE ME A MASK	133	MAKE ME A MASK	T
O MAKE ME A MASK AND A WALL TO SHUT FROM YOUR SPIES	133	MAKE ME A MASK	1
ON GIDDY NIGHTS WHEN SLAP ON THE MOON'S MASK	137	O CHATTERTON	12
SLAP ON THE DRUNK MOON'S MASK.	138	O CHATTERTON	25
GLARED THROUGH SHARK MASK AND NAVIGATING HEAD, ...	152	BELOW A TIME	39
AND MASK THE GRAVE.	176	BREATH SHED	12
MASKED			
AND THE MASKED, HEADLESS BOY.	129	MY NEOPHYTE	30
YOUR BITTERNESS IS MASKED WITH SMILES, ...	236	WOMAN TAPESTRY	50
MASKER			
MAN WAS CADAVER'S MASKER, THE HARNESSING MANTLE,	112	I, IN IMAGE	103
MASKS			
'SEE,' DRUMMED THE TAUT MASKS, 'HOW THE DEAD ASCEND:	132	I MAKE THIS IN	52
MASONS			
WOE TO THE WINDY MASONS AT MY SHELTER?	113	NOT FATHER ME	30
MASSES			
THE MASSES OF THE SEA	175	FIRE RAID	72
THE MASSES OF THE SEA UNDER	175	FIRE RAID	73
THE MASSES OF THE INFANT-BEARING SEA	175	FIRE RAID	74
MAST			
WHEN, PRAISE IS BLESSED, HER PRIDE IN MAST AND FOUNTAIN	131	I MAKE THIS IN	4
HIGH AND DRY BY THE TOP OF THE MAST, ...	162	LONG-LEGGED	8
MY MAST IS A BELL-SPIRE, ...	164	LONG-LEGGED	76
PILLAR BREAKS, AND MAST IS CLEFT	237	PILLAR BREAKS	1
BIRD ON THE MAST, (HE CONTEMPLATED), ...	238	PILLAR BREAKS	18
MASTED			
OR, MASTED VENUS, THROUGH THE PADDLER'S BOWL	114	A GRIEF AGO	7
MASTER			
MASTER, HER MOUTH IS SAWDUST	10	COOL, OH NO	14
WINDILY MASTER OF MAN WAS THE ROTTEN FATHOM, ...	112	I, IN IMAGE	104
MISTER AND MASTER, DARKNESS FOR HIS EYES, ...	114	SERVANT SUN	31
MASTER THE NIGHT NOR SERVE THE SNOWMAN'S BRAIN	123	FOSTER LIGHT	4

	PAGE	TITLE	LINE

MASTER (CONTINUED)
THE CLOUD PERCHED TAILORS' MASTER WITH NERVES FOR
COTTON. . . . 152 BELOW A TIME 35
MASTERLESS
A STEEPLEJACK TOWER, BONERAILED AND MASTERLESS, ... 109 I, IN IMAGE 20
MASTERS
MASTERS OVER UNMASTERED NATURE, ... 45 PLOUGHMAN GONE 21
DELIVER ME, MY MASTERS, HEAD AND HEART, ... 100 RUNNING GRAVE 11
MY PICKBRAIN MASTERS MORSING ON THE STONE ... 100 RUNNING GRAVE 22
DESCENDS, MY MASTERS, ON THE ENTERED HONOUR. ... 100 RUNNING GRAVE 28
TELLS YOU AND YOU, MY MASTERS, AS HIS STRANGE ... 113 SERVANT SUN 13
MASTERY
AND ALL THE MASTERY THERE IS IN DEATH, ... 22 ON QUIET NIGHT 4
MAST-HIGH
MAST-HIGH MOON-WHITE WOMEN NAKED ... 165 LONG-LEGGED 104
MASTIFF
SPIKED WITH A MASTIFF COLLAR, ... 151 BELOW A TIME 10
MASTS
FUNNELS AND MASTS WENT BY IN A WHIRL. ... 162 LONG-LEGGED 17
MASTS AND FISHES TO THE STILL QUICK STARS, ... 210 POEM ON B'DAY 71
MATCH
PAPER AND STICKS AND SHOVEL AND MATCH ... 149 PAPER & STICKS 1
MATCHBOARD
FOR OUT OF A HOUSE OF MATCHBOARD AND STONE ... 43 A WAR OF WITS 22
MATCHES
WE MIGHT HAVE TRIED LIGHT MATCHES IN THE WIND. ... 34 IN GARDENS 16
MATE
TO TROT WITH A LOUD MATE THE HAYBEDS OF A MILE, ... 135 HOW MY ANIMAL 16
MATED
THE VIRGIN LINES BE MATED WITH A CIRCLE. ... 66 LET A FAITH 3
MATERNAL
MATERNAL SHORT TIME PIECES, ... 155 RETURN 54
MATTED
WAS MUSCLED, MATTED, WISE TO THE CRYING THIGH ... 78 LOVE'S FEVER 28
MATTER
GROPING FOR MATTER UNDER THE DOG'S PLATE, ... 32 OUT OF SIGHS 26
(IT'S A MATTER OF GUTS, ... 39 GAS FADES 10
BOTH MIND AND MATTER AT THE SCALDING WORD ... 73 LORD RED HAIL 11
ONE WOMB, ONE MIND, SPEWED OUT THE MATTER, ... 79 LOVE'S FEVER 42
BUT THEN IT IS THE FEW THAT MATTER. ... 84 LETTER TO AUNT 39
HAD STRINGED MY FLASK OF MATTER TO HIS RIB. ... 97 TWILIGHT LOCKS 12
THEN ALL THE MATTER OF THE LIVING AIR ... 102 FELLOWED SLEEP 21
MATURED
THE PLUM MY MOTHER PICKED MATURED SLOWLY, ... 78 LOVE'S FEVER 25
MAULED
LIKE THE MAULED PICTURES OF BOYS? ... 145 PLEASURE-BIRD 19
MAULING
NOR THE FLINT IN THE LOVER'S MAULING. ... 106 ALL ALL AND 18
MAUVE
THE TALL MAUVE IRIS OF A SLEEPING CLIME. ... 222 IN DREAMS 2
MAY
SUCH ENERGY MAY GAIN ... 10 COOL, OH NO 25
FROM WHICH YOU MAY NOT FLY. ... 10 COOL, OH NO 30
SPRING MAY BE GREEN-- ... 15 FOR LEDA 21
WHICH MAY OR MAY NOT BE RELEVANT ... 33 HELD-OUT HAND 14
WHICH MAY OR MAY NOT BE RELEVANT ... 33 HELD-OUT HAND 14
COOLS ANY ARDOUR THEY MAY HAVE ... 47 POET: 1935 33
NO MORE MAY GULLS CRY AT THEIR EARS ... 50 NO DOMINION 20
WHERE BLEW A FLOWER MAY A FLOWER NO MORE ... 50 NO DOMINION 22
THAT I MAY DROWN, LET LOOSE HER FLOOD OF TEARS. ... 65 WOMAN SPEAKS 55

	PAGE	TITLE	LINE
MAY (CONTINUED)			
BE SOUR IN MY HAIR. THAT I MAY LEARN	65	WOMAN SPEAKS	63
AND MAY I YET LIVE TO ADMIRE	85	LETTER TO AUNT	65
MAY FAIL TO FASTEN WITH A VIRGIN O	100	RUNNING GRAVE	19
MAY A HUMBLE VILLAGE LABOUR	126	SEED-AT-ZERO	29
A HEMISPHERE MAY SCOLD HIM	126	SEED-AT-ZERO	31
MAY A HUMBLE PLANET LABOUR	126	SEED-AT-ZERO	36
A VILLAGE GREEN MAY SCOLD HIM	126	SEED-AT-ZERO	38
I MAY WITHOUT FAIL	170	LOVE IN ASYLUM	17
MAY HOLD IT IN A GREAT FLOOD	173	FIRE RAID	21
O MAY MY HEART'S TRUTH	178	POEM IN OCT	68
OF HIS MOTHER'S MILK MAY RETURN	183	VISION, PRAYER	120
MAY THE CRIMSON	185	VISION, PRAYER	182
MAY HIS HUNGER GO HOWLING ON BARE WHITE BONES	188	WINTER'S TALE	33
YOU MAY NOT SEE, MY SON,	192	SIDE OF TRUTH	2
BE SHIELDED BY CHANT AND FLOWER AND GAY MAY YOU	198	COUNTRY SLEEP	42
ON THAT DARKEST DAY. OH, FOREVER MAY	216	ELEGY	4
MAZED			
STRAIT IN THE MAZED BED	169	LOVE IN ASYLUM	5
MAZES			
THE MAZES OF HIS PRAISE AND ENVIOUS TONGUE WERE			
WORKED IN FLAMES AND SHELLS.	141	SAINT TO FALL	17
MAZES	184	VISION, PRAYER	162
ME			
LEAVE YOU IN ME TO BE FOUND	9	MINUTE'S HOUR	10
SWEET, AUTOMATIC ME KNOWS BEST.	10	COOL, OH NO	18
BUT YOU SHALL NOT GO FROM ME, CREATION;	10	COOL, OH NO	19
TO CUT IN FRONT OF ME	12	SKY'S BRIGHT	6
MY HORRID IMAGES FOR ME,	12	SKY'S BRIGHT	7
WHO TELLS ME HURT,	12	SKY'S BRIGHT	13
OVER HER HEEL AND ME.	12	CABARET	21
WITH NO FOUNTAIN BOY BUT ME	13	RAIN CUTS	3
ONE HOUR SPEND MY TIME FOR ME	18	NATURAL DAY	5
WHO TAUGHT ME TROUBLE?	18	NATURAL DAY	25
THE DROOPING AS YOU CLOSE ME IN	20	ENCOMPASSED	12
YOU'LL BRING THE PLACE TO ME	21	BEWILDERED WAY	10
OUT OF THE HEART FOR ME,	21	BEWILDERED WAY	16
CHRIST, LET ME WRITE FROM THE HEART,	22	HIGH ON A HILL	7
UNLESS FOR POETRY, WHICH, IF IT ASKS ME	24	LITTLE PROBLEM	17
WHO GAVE ME LIFE AND THEN THE GRAVE,	26	PERSONAL EPIT	11
THAT MADE ME HAPPY IN THE SUN,	32	OUT OF SIGHS	19
AND CURE ME OF ILLS.	32	OUT OF SIGHS	23
WAS THE WORLD'S TO ME, AND SYLLABLES	42	A WAR OF WITS	2
BUT THE HOT BEAMS ROB ME OF SPEECH,	42	A WAR OF WITS	14
AND, CRACKLING INTO THE AIR, LEAVE ME HALF-BLIND.	44	LONGED TO MOVE	14
FROM YOU OR ME OR WIND OR RAT	53	OUT OF THE PIT	103
AND THE SLUG SHOULD TEACH ME DESTRUCTION.	58	HERE IN SPRING	13
WHAT SHALL IT TELL ME IF A TIMELESS INSECT	59	HERE IN SPRING	16
A MERRY GIRL TOOK ME FOR MAN,	61	MEAT ON BONES	22
LET ME NOT THINK, OF GOD OF CARNAGE,	63	WOMAN SPEAKS	16
THE WET NIGHT SCOLDS ME LIKE A NURSE?	65	GODS THUMP	10
O TIDAL WINDS, CAST UP HER CRY FOR ME;	65	WOMAN SPEAKS	54
TELL ME OF HIM WHO FEEDS THE RAGING BIRDS.	65	WOMAN SPEAKS	65
CONDEMN ME TO AN EVERLASTING FACING	68	REALM OF FLESH	14
WIND IN ME LEAPED, THE HELLBORN DEW;	68	BEFORE KNOCKED	16
REMEMBER ME AND PITY HIM	69	BEFORE KNOCKED	44
LET ME IN THE DEVIL'S GROVES	70	TAKE NEEDLES	5
MOTHER ROOT THAT SHOT ME FORTH,	72	TAKE NEEDLES	41
MOTHERS ME UNTIL I DIE,	72	TAKE NEEDLES	43
SLAY ME, SLAY THE GOD OF LOVE;	72	TAKE NEEDLES	55

ME

		PAGE	TITLE	LINE
ME	(CONTINUED)			
LOVE ME, NOT AS THE DREAMING NURSES	....	75	SONG: LOVE ME	1
LOVE ME AND LIFT YOUR MASK.	....	75	SONG: LOVE ME	4
LOVE ME, NOT AS THE GIRLS OF HEAVEN	....	76	SONG: LOVE ME	5
A HOLY VOICE ACQUAINTS ME WITH HIS GLORY.	....	76	LASHED RINGS	6
LOVE ME AND LIFT YOUR MASK.	....	76	SONG: LOVE ME	8
LOVE ME, NOT AS THE RUFFLING PIGEON	....	76	SONG: LOVE ME	9
LOVE ME AND LIFT YOUR MASK.	....	76	SONG: LOVE ME	12
LOVE ME, AS LOVES THE MOLE HIS DARKNESS	....	76	SONG: LOVE ME	13
LOVE ME AND LIFT YOUR MASK.	....	76	SONG: LOVE ME	16
ACQUAINTING ME WITH MY DIVINITY;	....	77	LASHED RINGS	15
MADE FAST BY ME.	....	87	PAIN BE MUSIC	6
TWIXT YOU AND ME.	....	87	PAIN BE MUSIC	12
NOT MILKED BY ME.	....	87	PAIN BE MUSIC	18
SURROUNDING ME.	....	87	PAIN BE MUSIC	24
A ROOKING GIRL WHO STOLE ME FOR HER SIDE,	....	94	RUB OF LOVE	2
WOULD LEAVE ME COLD AS BUTTER FOR THE FLIES,	....	95	RUB OF LOVE	26
THE SEA OF SCUMS COULD DROWN ME AS IT BROKE	....	95	RUB OF LOVE	27
THAT, SEWN TO ME BY NERVE AND BRAIN,	....	97	TWILIGHT LOCKS	11
TO ROB ME OF MY FLUIDS IN HIS HEART.	....	98	TWILIGHT LOCKS	36
SOME LET ME MAKE YOU OF THE VOWELLED BEECHES,	......	99	OCTOBER WIND	13
SOME LET ME MAKE YOU OF THE WATER'S SPEECHES.	......	99	OCTOBER WIND	16
TELLS ME THE HOUR'S WORD, THE NEURAL MEANING	....	99	OCTOBER WIND	18
SOME LET ME MAKE YOU OF THE MEADOW'S SIGNS;	....	99	OCTOBER WIND	21
THE SIGNAL GRASS THAT TELLS ME ALL I KNOW	....	99	OCTOBER WIND	22
SOME LET ME TELL YOU OF THE RAVEN'S SINS.	....	99	OCTOBER WIND	24
(SOME LET ME MAKE YOU OF AUTUMNAL SPELLS,	....	99	OCTOBER WIND	26
SOME LET ME MAKE YOU OF THE HEARTLESS WORDS.	......	99	OCTOBER WIND	29
DELIVER ME WHO, TIMID IN MY TRIBE,	....	100	RUNNING GRAVE	7
DELIVER ME, MY MASTERS, HEAD AND HEART,	....	100	RUNNING GRAVE	11
I FELLOWED SLEEP WHO KISSED ME IN THE BRAIN,	....	101	FELLOWED SLEEP	1
SHIFTING TO LIGHT, TURNED ON ME LIKE A MOON.	....	101	FELLOWED SLEEP	3
WHO SEEK ME LANDWARD, MARKING IN MY MOUTH	....	105	WORLD PYRAMID	46
THE STRAWS OF ASIA, LOSE ME AS I TURN	....	105	WORLD PYRAMID	47
DO YOU NOT FATHER ME	....	112	NOT FATHER ME	T
DO YOU NOT FATHER ME, NOR THE ERECTED ARM	....	112	NOT FATHER ME	1
DO YOU NOT MOTHER ME, NOR, AS I AM,	....	112	NOT FATHER ME	3
DO YOU NOT SISTER ME, NOR THE ERECTED CRIME	....	112	NOT FATHER ME	5
DO YOU NOT BROTHER ME, NOR, AS YOU CLIMB,	....	112	NOT FATHER ME	7
YOU ARE ALL THESE, SAID SHE WHO GAVE ME THE LONG SUCK,	....	112	NOT FATHER ME	17
DO YOU NOT FATHER ME ON THE DESTROYING SAND?	......	113	NOT FATHER ME	25
SHE HOLDING ME? THE PEOPLE'S SEA DRIVES ON HER,	...	115	A GRIEF AGO	26
DIPPED ME BREAST-DEEP IN THE DESCENDED BONE;	......	118	ALTARWISE	38
A CLIMBING SEA FROM ASIA HAD ME DOWN	....	118	ALTARWISE	65
AND JONAH'S MOBY SNATCHED ME BY THE HAIR,	....	119	ALTARWISE	66
THE WISEMEN TELL ME THAT THE GARDEN GODS	....	121	INCARNATE DEVL	9
NOW MAKE THE WORLD OF ME AS I HAVE MADE	....	124	FOSTER LIGHT	29
WE MAKE ME MYSTIC AS THE ARM OF AIR,	....	128	NOW, SAY NAY	34
TIME KILLS ME TERRIBLY.	....	129	MY NEOPHYTE	43
I SAW TIME MURDER ME.	....	129	MY NEOPHYTE	48
IT IS THE SINNERS' DUST-TONGUED BELL CLAPS ME TO CHURCHES	....	130	SINNERS' BELL	1
SHE MAKES FOR ME A NETTLE'S INNOCENCE	....	131	I MAKE THIS IN	16
O MAKE ME A MASK	....	133	MAKE ME A MASK	T
O MAKE ME A MASK AND A WALL TO SHUT FROM YOUR SPIES		133	MAKE ME A MASK	1
SHE WOULD NOT HAVE ME SINKING IN THE HOLY	....	136	AFTER FUNERAL	18
STORM ME FOREVER OVER HER GRAVE UNTIL	....	137	AFTER FUNERAL	38
POINT THEIR LITTLE BREASTS AT ME;	....	138	O CHATTERTON	32
HER TWO SURNAMES STOPPED ME STILL.	....	139	TOMBSTONE TOLD	2

		PAGE	TITLE	LINE
ME	(CONTINUED)			
O WAKE IN ME IN MY HOUSE IN THE MUD	················	142	SAINT TO FALL	26
RAGE ME BACK TO THE MAKING HOUSE. MY HAND UNRAVEL		145	IF HEAD HURT	12
WHO PALMED THE LIE ON ME WHEN YOU LOOKED	··········	146	TO OTHERS	4
TURNS OF YOUR PRAYED FLESH, NOR SHALL I SHOO THE				
BIRD BELOW ME:	·······························	148	UNLUCKILY FOR	27
TONGUE OF YOUR TRANSLATING EYES. THE YOUNG STARS				
TOLD ME,	·································	148	UNLUCKILY FOR	51
TO TAKE ME AWAY AS YOU WHISPERED AND WROTE	········	149	PAPER & STICKS	12
AND THE VAULTING BIRD BE STILL. O MY TRUE LOVE, HOLD				
ME.	·································	149	UNLUCKILY FOR	54
CONJURED ME TO RESEMBLE	······················	156	RETURN	68
FOR ME ALONE BUT ONLY A ROCKED DRUM	···············	175	MY BEGGAR ARM	3
IN THE WOOD FARAWAY UNDER ME.	················	177	POEM IN OCT	30
BURNS ME HIS NAME AND HIS FLAME	··················	180	VISION, PRAYER	28
SCALD ME AND DROWN	··························	185	VISION, PRAYER	199
ME IN HIS WORLD'S WOUND.	····················	185	VISION, PRAYER	200
GO CRYING THROUGH YOU AND ME	·····················	193	SIDE OF TRUTH	18
TIME LET ME HAIL AND CLIMB	······················	195	FERN HILL	4
TIME LET ME PLAY AND BE	························	195	FERN HILL	13
NOTHING I CARED, IN THE LAMB WHITE DAYS, THAT TIME				
WOULD TAKE ME	················	196	FERN HILL	46
TIME HELD ME GREEN AND DYING	·················	196	FERN HILL	53
NOW CLASP ME TO THEIR GRAINS IN THE GIGANTIC GLADE,		204	GIANT'S THIGH	19
NOW CURLEW CRY ME DOWN TO KISS THE MOUTHS OF THEIR				
DUST.	·························	205	GIANT'S THIGH	45
THEY FROM HOUSES WHERE THE HARVEST KNEELS, HOLD ME				
HARD,	····················	205	GIANT'S THIGH	50
TEACH ME THE LOVE THAT IS EVERGREEN AFTER THE FALL				
LEAVED	····················	205	GIANT'S THIGH	53
AND SERVE ME RIGHT AS THE PREACHERS WARN,	········	207	LAMENT	38
HARPIES AROUND ME OUT OF HER WOMB!	···············	207	LAMENT	56
CHASTITY PRAYS FOR ME, PIETY SINGS,	··············	207	LAMENT	57
CURSE, BLESS, ME NOW WITH YOUR FIERCE TEARS, I PRAY.		208	NOT GO GENTLE	17
OH, LET ME MIDLIFE MOURN BY THE SHRINED	··········	211	POEM ON B'DAY	76
AN OLD MAN IS WITH ME WHERE I GO	················	217	ELEGY	30
INFINITE SHADOWY ISLES LIE SILENT BEFORE ME,	·······	221	FOREST PICTURE	3
LET'S HOPE YOU WON'T THINK ME TOO VICIOUS.	········	221	SONG OF DOG	16
I HAVE KNOWN THE MYSTERY OF THE SEA TO BE MANTLED				
ABOUT ME;	·························	223	IDYLL UNFORGET	18
LITTLE WHITE-LIPPED FACES HAVE PEERED UP AT ME,	···	224	IDYLL UNFORGET	32
YOUR BODY CANNOT GLADDEN ME,	····················	228	NOT DESPAIR	9
HER WOVEN HANDS BECKONED ME,	····················	234	WOMAN TAPESTRY	1
NO SKY FOR ME THAT CARRIES	·····················	234	NO, PIGEON	2
AND HER EYES PIERCED THEIR INTENSE LOVE INTO ME,		234	WOMAN TAPESTRY	2
SKY HAS NOT LOVED ME MUCH,	·····················	234	NO, PIGEON	4
BUT NO HIGH TREE FOR ME	······················	234	NO, PIGEON	13
NO BIRD FOR ME:	··························	234	NO, PIGEON	22
LIKE A LIVING CLOAK OVER ME.	····················	235	WOMAN TAPESTRY	5
HER LOVE FOR ME IS FIERCE AND CONTINUAL,	··········	235	WOMAN TAPESTRY	11
LET ME BELIEVE IN THE CLEAN FAITH OF THE BODY,	····	235	WOMAN TAPESTRY	24
SHE SHALL MAKE FOR ME	························	235	WOMAN TAPESTRY	27
YOU SHALL COMFORT ME	·························	236	WOMAN TAPESTRY	47
WHICH GOES AROUND ME EASILY	····················	236	WOMAN TAPESTRY	54
BINDING ME WITH PAIN,	························	236	WOMAN TAPESTRY	62
GROWING LIKE A POWERFUL ROOT INSIDE ME.	··········	236	WOMAN TAPESTRY	67
INVOLVE ME IN A GAIETY,	······················	236	WOMAN TAPESTRY	69
THAT TEACHES ME TO WAIT,	······················	237	PILLAR BREAKS	10
LET ME BELIEVE IN THE CLEAN FAITH OF THE BODY,	····	237	WOMAN TAPESTRY	79
LIGHT, NOT SO TO ME;	························	238	MAKES INTERVALS	6

		PAGE	TITLE	LINE
ME (CONTINUED)				
LET ME CHANGE TO BLUE,	....	238	MAKES INTERVALS	7
YOUR WIDE SMILE FOR ME.	....	238	MAKES INTERVALS	14
LET ME ESCAPE	....	239	LET ME ESCAPE	T
LET ME ESCAPE,	....	239	LET ME ESCAPE	1
AND DROWN THE GODS IN ME,	....	239	LET ME ESCAPE	4
BUT YOU'LL NOT KEEP ME IN	....	239	LET ME ESCAPE	7
MOCK ME,	....	239	MAKES INTERVALS	17
OH, LET ME DESTROY FOR ONCE,	....	239	MAKES INTERVALS	22
MEADOW				
A BLADE OF GRASS LONGS WITH THE MEADOW,	....	159	INTO HER HEAD	61
MEADOWS				
CORNER THE MOUNTED MEADOWS IN THE HILL CORRAL;	....	109	I, IN IMAGE	39
WALKING IN THE MEADOWS OF HIS SON'S EYE	....	217	ELEGY	31
MEADOW'S				
SOME LET ME MAKE YOU OF THE MEADOW'S SIGNS;	....	99	OCTOBER WIND	21
MEAL				
POLE-SITTING GIRLS DESCENDED FOR A MEAL,	....	51	OUT OF THE PIT	29
MEAN				
I MEAN BY TIME THE CAST AND CURFEW RASCAL OF OUR				
MARRIAGE,	....	130	SINNERS' BELL	25
MEANING				
MADE MEANING MEANINGLESS. THE WRONG WIND STIRS,	...	37	WINDMILLS TURN	29
THAT TURNED THE EMPTY KISSES INTO MEANING,	....	43	FACES SHONE	3
YOUR PAIN SHALL BE A MEANING IN YOUR LIPS	....	87	PAIN BE MUSIC	13
TELLS ME THE HOUR'S WORD, THE NEURAL MEANING	......	99	OCTOBER WIND	18
WHAT MEANING, VOICES, IN THE STRAIGHT-RULED GRASS,		137	O CHATTERTON	17
MEANING IN HOT SOCK SOIL? A LITTLE CUSS	....	137	O CHATTERTON	18
MEANINGLESS				
AS MEANINGLESS AS THE BELLS (OH CHANGE THE LIFE!),		33	HELD-OUT HAND	9
MADE MEANING MEANINGLESS. THE WRONG WIND STIRS,	...	37	WINDMILLS TURN	29
MEANS				
IF HUNTING MEANS ANYTHING MORE THAN THE CHASE	.....	44	TO FOLLOW FOX	18
GOLDEN IN THE MERCY OF HIS MEANS,	....	195	FERN HILL	14
OH AS I WAS YOUNG AND EASY IN THE MERCY OF HIS MEANS,	196	FERN HILL	52
MEASURE				
DANCES A MEASURE WITH THE SWAN	....	15	FOR LEDA	30
A MEASURE ON THE LAWN WHERE CUPIDS BLEW	....	51	OUT OF THE PIT	25
FROM LIMBS THAT HAD THE MEASURE OF WORM, SHUFFLED		102	I DREAMED MY	5
MEASURED				
THERE IS NO MEASURED SEA FOR THEM,	....	10	COOL, OH NO	23
HIS GRAPH IS MEASURED AS THE PAGE OF PAIN	....	80	ALMANAC TIME	4
MEASURES				
MEASURES HIS OWN LENGTH ON THE GARDEN WALL	....	124	TODAY, INSECT	12
MEAT				
MAKE MOCK OF WOMAN'S MEAT,	....	34	THIRST PARCHES	14
'FIND MEAT ON BONES'	....	60	MEAT ON BONES	T
'FIND MEAT ON BONES THAT SOON HAVE NONE,	....	60	MEAT ON BONES	1
OF RAVENS AT THE HERO'S MEAT AND NERVES	....	63	WOMAN SPEAKS	17
HERE CLINGS THE MEAT TO SEVER FROM HIS SIDE.	.....	81	HERE LIE BEAST	5
HE'LL TRUMPET INTO MEAT),	....	113	SERVANT SUN	5
I FURNISH WITH THE MEAT OF A FABLE;	....	145	PLEASURE-BIRD	21
MEAT-EATING				
BY THE LIGHT OF THE MEAT-EATING SUN.	....	143	24 YEARS	5
MECHANICAL				
STROKE OF MECHANICAL FLESH ON MINE,	....	107	ALL ALL AND	29
WITH DRY, MECHANICAL GESTURES,	....	231	YOUR VOICE	3
MECHANICALLY				
TO IMITATE MYSELF MECHANICALLY,	....	234	NO, PIGEON	19

	PAGE	TITLE	LINE
MECHANICS			
TO REMEMBER, CAST STRICTURE ON MECHANICS AND MAN.	45	PLOUGHMAN GONE	5
MEDUSA			
PIN-LEGGED ON POLE-HILLS WITH A BLACK MEDUSA	119	ALTARWISE	68
MEDUSA'S			
PLUCK, COCK, MY SEA EYE, SAID MEDUSA'S SCRIPTURE,	119	ALTARWISE	75
MEEK			
HER FLESH WAS MEEK AS MILK, BUT THIS SKYWARD STATUE	136	AFTER FUNERAL	27
AND MIRE OF LOVE, BUT THE THIEF AS MEEK AS THE DEW.	198	COUNTRY SLEEP	38
AND SLY AS SNOW AND MEEK AS DEW BLOWN TO THE THORN,	199	COUNTRY SLEEP	50
MEET			
TO MAKE ENDS MEET, ...	38	THE GOSSIPERS	10
MEET ONCE ON A MORTAL WALL, ...	140	TOMBSTONE TOLD	23
ONLY TO MAKE TWO ENDS MEET, ...	155	RETURN	61
THROUGH THROATS WHERE MANY RIVERS MEET, THE CURLEWS			
CRY, ...	203	GIANT'S THIGH	1
THROUGH THROATS WHERE MANY RIVERS MEET, THE WOMEN			
PRAY, ...	203	GIANT'S THIGH	6
MEETING			
THE EARTH AND SKY WERE AS TWO MOUNTAINS MEETING.	78	LOVE'S FEVER	15
MEETS			
ACHES TILL THE METAL MEETS THE MARROW, ...	47	POET: 1935	50
MELANCHOLY			
ARE FULL ENOUGH TO DROWN MY MELANCHOLY	17	NATURAL DAY	2
MELODIOUS			
THEIR OWN MELODIOUS HEIGHT, ...	14	RAIN CUTS	34
MELT			
ON THE CANVAS SKY, AND ALL HOT COLOURS MELT	46	POET: 1935	19
THE SPONGEBAG LET THEM ALL MELT.	155	RETURN	36
BACK TO CLACK SILENCE MELT AND MOURN	181	VISION, PRAYER	61
MELTED			
HAS MELTED AWAY AND IS LOST	165	LONG-LEGGED	115
MELTING			
FLOWING AND MELTING UNDER LIME.	19	IMAGES IN AIR	8
FACES OF MELTING VISIONS, ...	156	RETURN	84
IN HIGH CORN AND THE HARVEST MELTING ON THEIR			
TONGUES.	188	WINTER'S TALE	43
AND SHE ROSE WITH HIM FLOWERING IN HER MELTING SNOW.	191	WINTER'S TALE	130
OUTLINES MELTING INTO A VAGUE IMMENSITY	222	FOREST PICTURE	9
MELTS			
THAT MELTS THE LIONHEAD'S HEEL AND HORSESHOE OF THE			
HEART, ...	135	HOW MY ANIMAL	14
MEMORIAL'S			
I STAND, FOR THIS MEMORIAL'S SAKE, ALONE	136	AFTER FUNERAL	12
MEMORY			
IN THE MEMORY WORKED BY MIRRORS, ...	146	TO OTHERS	10
MEN			
OUT THERE, CROW BLACK, MEN	3	PROLOGUE	12
OUT OF THE WAY OF THE EYES OF MEN, ...	21	HIGH ON A HILL	3
FOR WE ARE ORDINARY MEN, ...	28	NO WINGS	12
WE ARE ORDINARY MEN, ...	28	NO WINGS	20
BEING BUT MEN	31	BEING BUT MEN	T
BEING BUT MEN, WE WALKED INTO THE TREES	31	BEING BUT MEN	1
BEING BUT MEN, WE WALKED INTO THE TREES.	31	BEING BUT MEN	17
OF FAULTY MEN AND THEIR DISEASES, ...	34	IN GARDENS	10
OF MEN AND CREATURES HORRIBLY	35	LIFT UP FACE	8
THE MIDNIGHT ROAD, THOUGH YOUNG MEN TREAD UNKNOWING,	36	MIDNIGHT ROAD	1
LET CHILDREN KNOW, AND OLD MEN AT THEIR GATES, ...	36	LET BE KNOWN	3
AND THAT IS LIES THAT, AFTER THE OLD MEN DIE, ...	36	LET BE KNOWN	5
OF MEN WITH FLANNEL SHIRTS	37	WINDMILLS TURN	10

	PAGE	TITLE	LINE
MEN (CONTINUED)			
MEN OLD BEFORE THEIR TIME INTO DARK VALLEYS	41	YOUNG ARE OLD	19
YOUNG MEN WITH FALLEN CHESTS AND OLD MEN'S BREATH,	41	YOUNG ARE OLD	27
THE PICCADILLY MEN, THE BACK STREET DRUNKS,	41	YOUNG ARE OLD	41
WHERE MEN WOULD ARGUE TILL THE STARS BE GREEN,	43	A WAR OF WITS	23
MOVES, AMONG MEN CAUGHT BY THE SUN,	46	POET: 1935	11
AMONG ALL LIVING MEN IS A SAD GHOST.	47	POET: 1935	24
DEAD MEN NAKED THEY SHALL BE ONE	49	NO DOMINION	2
UNDER A HIDEOUS SEA WHERE CORAL MEN	52	OUT OF THE PIT	68
TO HERMITS' HUTS, AND TALKED TO ANCIENT MEN.	53	OUT OF THE PIT	91
IF DEAD MEN WALKED THEY, TOO, WOULD HOLLER	59	FAIRY TALES	17
OLD MEN WHOSE BLOOD IS HINDERED IN THEIR VEINS,	64	WOMAN SPEAKS	42
THE BONES OF MEN, THE BROKEN IN THEIR BEDS,	89	EUNUCH DREAMS	9
THAT SHROUDED MEN MIGHT MARROW AS THEY FLY.	90	EUNUCH DREAMS	30
I SEE THAT FROM THESE BOYS SHALL MEN OF NOTHING	92	BOYS OF SUMMER	19
THAT CHALK THE WALLS WITH GREEN GIRLS AND THEIR MEN.	95	RUB OF LOVE	16
THAT MEN MIGHT SEE THE DEVIL IN THE CRUMB	96	TWELVE	13
ALL, MEN MY MADMEN, THE UNWHOLESOME WIND	101	RUNNING GRAVE	46
'THESE ARE BUT DREAMING MEN. BREATHE, AND THEY FADE.'	102	FELLOWED SLEEP	15
DRIVES FORTH MY MEN, MY CHILDREN, FROM THE HANGING SOUTH.	122	HOLD HARD	6
AMONG MEN LATER I HEARD IT SAID	139	TOMBSTONE TOLD	16
AND THE OLD MEN SING FROM NEWBORN LIPS:	167	LONG-LEGGED	152
WITH MEN AND WOMEN AND WATERFALLS	167	LONG-LEGGED	169
ALL MEN	183	VISION, PRAYER	128
COMBS THROUGH THE MANTLED YARDS AND THE MORNING MEN	187	WINTER'S TALE	20
AND THE SOULS OF ALL MEN	193	SIDE OF TRUTH	19
THOUGH WISE MEN AT THEIR END KNOW DARK IS RIGHT,	208	NOT GO GENTLE	4
GOOD MEN, THE LAST WAVE BY, CRYING HOW BRIGHT	208	NOT GO GENTLE	7
WILD MEN WHO CAUGHT AND SANG THE SUN IN FLIGHT,	208	NOT GO GENTLE	10
GRAVE MEN, NEAR DEATH, WHO SEE WITH BLINDING SIGHT	208	NOT GO GENTLE	13
AND MY SHINING MEN NO MORE ALONE	211	POEM ON B'DAY	107
MENDED			
THAT HER FOND WOUNDS ARE MENDED BITTERLY.	139	FIVE & COUNTRY	9
MEN'S			
YOUNG MEN WITH FALLEN CHESTS AND OLD MEN'S BREATH,	41	YOUNG ARE OLD	27
I HEAR, THROUGH DEAD MEN'S DRUMS, THE RIDDLED LADS,	105	WORLD PYRAMID	40
MENTAL			
AND, THE STRING PULLED, SOME MENTAL DOLL	10	COOL, OH NO	11
AND FEW JAMES JOYCE'S MENTAL SLUMMINGS,	84	LETTER TO AUNT	37
MERCIES			
MY NEST OF MERCIES IN THE RUDE, RED TREE.	121	ALTARWISE	140
MERCURY			
OF THE GOLDEN GHOST WHO RINGED WITH HIS STREAMS HER MERCURY BONE,	170	MARRIAGE VIRG	11
MERCY			
GOLDEN IN THE MERCY OF HIS MEANS,	195	FERN HILL	14
OH AS I WAS YOUNG AND EASY IN THE MERCY OF HIS MEANS,	196	FERN HILL	52
HAVE MERCY ON,	202	SIR JOHNS HILL	44
MERIDIAN			
LOVE FOR EVER MERIDIAN THROUGH THE COURTERS' TREES	205	GIANT'S THIGH	59
MERIT			
OR THE YELLOW LINNET WHO DOES NOT MERIT IT.	230	OUR SANCTITY	14
MERMAID			
HAND IN HAND WITH THE MERMAID	231	OUR SANCTITY	40
MERMAIDEN			
THEIR AIRY LOVERS, NOR THE MERMAIDEN	76	SONG: LOVE ME	6
MERMEN			
WHERE ONCE THE MERMEN THROUGH YOUR ICE	90	WHERE ONCE THE	4
FISHERMEN OF MERMEN	135	HOW MY ANIMAL	23

	PAGE	TITLE	LINE
MERMEN (CONTINUED)			
OF BLOOD! THE BIRD LOUD VEIN! THE SAGA FROM MERMEN	200	COUNTRY SLEEP	78
MERRIEST			
LEARN TO BE MERRY WITH THE MERRIEST, ...	33	HELD-OUT HAND	7
THE MERRIEST MARROW AND THE DREGS	60	MEAT ON BONES	3
MERRY			
FOR MY MERRY WORDS, ...	18	NATURAL DAY	23
LEARN TO BE MERRY WITH THE MERRIEST, ...	33	HELD-OUT HAND	7
A MERRY GIRL TOOK ME FOR MAN, ...	61	MEAT ON BONES	22
THE OAT WAS MERRY IN THE WIND;	86	BREAD I BREAK	9
AND NAIL THE MERRY SQUIRES TO THE TREES;	93	BOYS OF SUMMER	45
A MERRY MANSHAPE OF YOUR WALKING CIRCLE.	124	FOSTER LIGHT	30
MESSAGE			
THERE IS BUT ONE MESSAGE FOR THE EARTH, ...	41	YOUNG ARE OLD	26
THE MESSAGE COMES FROM NEGRO MYSTICS, ...	58	TO ARCHITECTS	7
I KNEW THE MESSAGE OF THE WINTER, ...	68	BEFORE KNOCKED	13
THE MESSAGE OF HIS DYING CHRIST.	69	BEFORE KNOCKED	42
INSIDE THIS MOUTH I FEEL HIS MESSAGE MOVING	76	LASHED RINGS	14
MESSENGERS			
BY MESSENGERS, THE FLIGHT OF BIRDS	29	NEARLY SUMMER	4
METAL			
WHICH IS THE METAL WING	12	CABARET	24
IN WATER OR IN METAL, ...	19	IMAGES IN AIR	7
ACHES TILL THE METAL MEETS THE MARROW, ...	47	POET: 1935	50
THROUGH ALL THE IRONS IN THE GRASS, METAL	102	I DREAMED MY	7
NOR THE HEART IN THE RIBBING METAL.	106	ALL ALL AND	15
LAYING MY GHOST IN METAL, ...	108	I, IN IMAGE	3
IMAGE OF IMAGES, MY METAL PHANTOM	109	I, IN IMAGE	14
MY GHOST IN HIS METAL NEPTUNE	112	I, IN IMAGE	105
METALLIC			
THE METALLIC RAIN	229	MY RIVER	13
METAMORPHOSIS			
CHALLENGE MY METAMORPHOSIS, ...	238	MAKES INTERVALS	15
METAPHOR			
MAN BE MY METAPHOR.	96	RUB OF LOVE	49
METAPHORS			
DEATH IS ALL METAPHORS, SHAPE IN ONE HISTORY;	117	ALTARWISE	15
METEORS			
BLIND EYES COULD BLAZE LIKE METEORS AND BE GAY, ...	208	NOT GO GENTLE	14
METICULOUS			
ALL SEASONS WITH THE SAME METICULOUS POWER, ...	17	IN OBLIVION	13
METRE			
WHAT IS THE METRE OF THE DICTIONARY?	118	ALTARWISE	43
WITH NOTHING FOR THE METRE, ...	155	RETURN	59
METROPOLIS			
METROPOLIS OF FISHES, ...	169	LONG-LEGGED	204
MICE			
OR MICE PLAY WITH AN IVORY TOOTH.	49	LIGHT, I KNOW	26
MID-AIR			
AND I, CAUGHT IN MID-AIR PERHAPS, ...	9	MINUTE'S HOUR	6
MIDDLE			
THE CENTURY'S TRAP WILL HAVE SNAPPED ROUND YOUR			
MIDDLE, ...	38	GAS FADES	4
TO ELEVATE YOUR MIDDLE BROW, ...	83	LETTER TO AUNT	12
CRYING, WHITE GOWNED, FROM THE MIDDLE MOONLIT STAGES	158	INTO HER HEAD	37
MIDLIFE			
OH, LET ME MIDLIFE MOURN BY THE SHRINED	211	POEM ON B'DAY	76
MIDNIGHT			
THE MIDNIGHT ROAD	36	MIDNIGHT ROAD	T
THE MIDNIGHT ROAD, THOUGH YOUNG MEN TREAD UNKNOWING,	36	MIDNIGHT ROAD	1

	PAGE	TITLE	LINE
MIDNIGHT (CONTINUED)			
THE MIDNIGHT FIGURES OF A SULPHUROUS BROOD	36	MIDNIGHT ROAD	10
THEIR FACES SHONE; THE MIDNIGHT RAIN	43	FACES SHONE	8
THROUGH, I TELL YOU, YOUR TWO MIDNIGHT LIPS I PRAY	76	LASHED RINGS	7
BY MIDNIGHT PULLEYS THAT UNHOUSE THE TOMB.	89	EUNUCH DREAMS	10
AND SPEAK THEIR MIDNIGHT NOTHINGS AS THEY SWELL;	89	EUNUCH DREAMS	14
CAN NEVER RAISE THE MIDNIGHT OF A CHUCKLE,	96	RUB OF LOVE	39
AND, MANNED BY MIDNIGHT, JACOB TO THE STARS.	117	ALTARWISE	24
THE FATS OF MIDNIGHT WHEN THE SALT WAS SINGING;	119	ALTARWISE	80
ALL HEAVEN IN A MIDNIGHT OF THE SUN,	122	INCARNATE DEVL	17
TOWARDS THE STUDDED MALE IN A BENT, MIDNIGHT BLAZE	135	HOW MY ANIMAL	13
MIDWIVES GREW IN THE MIDNIGHT DITCHES,	206	LAMENT	19
MIDST			
IN THE MILL OF THE MIDST	148	UNLUCKILY FOR	18
MIDWIFE			
CRY JOY THAT THIS WITCHILIKE MIDWIFE SECOND	142	SAINT TO FALL	48
MIDWIVES			
AND THE MIDWIVES OF MIRACLE SING	180	VISION, PRAYER	26
MIDWIVES GREW IN THE MIDNIGHT DITCHES,	206	LAMENT	19
MIDWIVING			
OF MIDWIVING MORNING'S	185	VISION, PRAYER	174
MIGHT			
IF WE WERE CHILDREN WE MIGHT CLIMB,	31	BEING BUT MEN	6
WE MIGHT HAVE TRIED LIGHT MATCHES IN THE WIND.	34	IN GARDENS	16
SOME LIFE, YET UNSPENT, MIGHT EXPLODE	44	LONGED TO MOVE	12
MIGHT PLAY UPON HIS LANK LOCKS WITH ITS WIND,	46	POET: 1935	3
AND A CHILD MIGHT BE MY SLAYER,	71	TAKE NEEDLES	17
HALF A SMILE MIGHT BE HER SABRE.	71	TAKE NEEDLES	20
THAT SHROUDED MEN MIGHT MARROW AS THEY FLY.	90	EUNUCH DREAMS	30
THAT THE SUM SANITY MIGHT ADD TO NAUGHT	96	TWELVE	1
THAT MEN MIGHT SEE THE DEVIL IN THE CRUMB	96	TWELVE	13
THAT SHE MIGHT STAND IN THE NIGHT	172	THE HUNCHBACK	35
SO THE BETRAYED MIGHT LEARN IN THE SUN BEAMS	176	MY BEGGAR ARM	7
MIGHT CROSS ITS PLANETS, THE BELL WEEP, NIGHT GATHER HER EYES,	200	COUNTRY SLEEP	92
THEIR FRAIL DEEDS MIGHT HAVE DANCED IN A GREEN BAY,	208	NOT GO GENTLE	8
THERE HE MIGHT WANDER BARE	210	POEM ON B'DAY	55
MIGHTY			
THE MIGHTY HAND LEADS TO A SLOPING SHOULDER,	66	HAND SIGNED	5
ONE GOD, MORE MIGHTY THAN THE SUN.	70	SECRET WIND	23
AND IN THE MIGHTY MORNINGS OF THE EARTH;	122	INCARNATE DEVL	15
MILD			
HERE A MILD BABY SPEAKS HIS FIRST WORD	74	SUN BURNS	9
AND, MILD AS PARDON FROM A CLOUD OF PRIDE,	133	I MAKE THIS IN	59
MILD. TURNED AGAIN, WORTHINGTON. NEVER WHISKY.	179	NEW QUAY	12
MILE			
THRUSTING THE TOM-THUMB VISION UP THE IRON MILE.	111	I, IN IMAGE	84
TO TROT WITH A LOUD MATE THE HAYBEDS OF A MILE,	135	HOW MY ANIMAL	16
UNDER THE MILE OFF MOON WE TREMBLED LISTENING	194	SLEEP BECALMED	5
MILES			
ON MILES OF HORIZONTAL MILESTONES,	37	WINDMILLS TURN	24
MILES OVER THE MOONSTRUCK BOAT	163	LONG-LEGGED	38
MILESTONES			
ON MILES OF HORIZONTAL MILESTONES,	37	WINDMILLS TURN	24
MILK			
OR, WHITE AS MILK, OUT OF THE SEEPING DARK,	20	ENCOMPASSED	11
MY WORLD WAS CHRISTENED IN A STREAM OF MILK.	78	LOVE'S FEVER	7
AND SILENTLY I MILK THE DEVIL'S BREAST.	81	HERE LIE BEAST	3
AND SILENTLY I MILK THE BURIED FLOWERS.	81	HERE LIE BEAST	9
THE MILK OF DEATH, I FILLED THE HAND	86	SEE, SAYS LIME	30

	PAGE	TITLE	LINE
MILK (CONTINUED)			
AS MILK SHALL BE A MUSIC IN THE PAPS	87	PAIN BE MUSIC	14
AND MOTHER MILK WAS STIFF AS SAND, ...	98	TWILIGHT LOCKS	32
TO-MORROW'S DIVER IN HER HORNY MILK, ...	103	WORLD PYRAMID	4
THE SWING OF MILK WAS TUFTED IN THE PAP, ...	104	WORLD PYRAMID	10
TIME, MILK, AND MAGIC, FROM THE WORLD BEGINNING.	119	ALTARWISE	94
BREAD AND MILK MANSION IN A TOOTHLESS TOWN.	131	I MAKE THIS IN	15
HER FLESH WAS MEEK AS MILK, BUT THIS SKYWARD STATUE	136	AFTER FUNERAL	27
MILK IN YOUR MOUTH, AT THE SOUR FLOODS	142	SAINT TO FALL	32
THE DUCK-BILLED PLATYPUS BROODY IN A MILK OF BIRDS.	148	UNLUCKILY FOR	33
SAILS DRANK THE WIND, AND WHITE AS MILK	162	LONG-LEGGED	13
OF HIS MOTHER'S MILK MAY RETURN	183	VISION, PRAYER	120
MILKED			
AND DRINK IN THE TWO MILKED CRAGS, ...	60	MEAT ON BONES	2
NOT MILKED BY ME.	87	PAIN BE MUSIC	18
MILKING			
YOUNG AS THEY IN THE AFTER MILKING MOONLIGHT LAY	204	GIANT'S THIGH	16
MILKMAIDS			
THE PUFFED BIRDS HOPPING AND HUNTING, THE MILKMAIDS	187	WINTER'S TALE	23
MILKS			
SEE, SAYS THE LIME, MY WICKED MILKS	85	SEE, SAYS LIME	1
MILK-WHITE			
AND MILK-WHITE NAILS.	229	MY RIVER	29
MILKY			
REACH ASKING ARMS UP TO THE MILKY SKY, ...	42	A WAR OF WITS	16
THE MILKY ACID ON EACH HINGE, ...	97	TWILIGHT LOCKS	5
UNDER THE MILKY MUSHROOMS SLEW MY HUNGER, ...	118	ALTARWISE	64
OR HICKORY BULL IN MILKY GRASS	207	LAMENT	41
MILL			
IN THE MILL OF THE MIDST	148	UNLUCKILY FOR	18
MILLED			
MILLED DUST OF THE APPLE TREE AND THE POUNDED ISLANDS	199	COUNTRY SLEEP	59
MILLING			
FEAR NOT THE TREAD, THE SEEDED MILLING, ...	106	ALL ALL AND	16
MILLION			
HER FAN BURST IN A MILLION LIGHTS	11	CABARET	14
BRANCHES A MILLION SHADES, ...	14	RAIN CUTS	22
LIGHT, I KNOW, TREADS THE TEN MILLION STARS	48	LIGHT, I KNOW	T
LIGHT, I KNOW, TREADS THE TEN MILLION STARS, ...	48	LIGHT, I KNOW	1
A MILLION MINDS GAVE SUCK TO SUCH A BUD	79	LOVE'S FEVER	46
MINCES			
AND BUTTON UP. HE MINCES AMONG KNICKERS, ...	179	NEW QUAY	23
MIND			
WITH THAT HALF-MOULDED MIND I SAID WAS YOURS, ...	10	COOL, OH NO	4
OH NO, MY MIND IS YOUR PANOPTICON;	10	COOL, OH NO	20
THE WATERS OF HIS MIND DRAW IN.	16	TIME TO ROT	16
DEAD LIMB AND MIND, ...	26	PERSONAL EPIT	14
TOUCHED ON THE OUTSKIRTS OF THE MIND, ...	33	IN GARDENS	5
AND THE HILLS OUT OF MIND.	62	EARS IN TURRET	14
BOTH MIND AND MATTER AT THE SCALDING WORD	73	LORD RED HAIL	11
ONE WOMB, ONE MIND, SPEWED OUT THE MATTER, ...	79	LOVE'S FEVER	42
WILL NEVER NEVER GO OUT OF MY MIND.	217	ELEGY	20
MINDED			
WHAT HAD BEEN ONE WAS MANY SOUNDING MINDED.	79	LOVE'S FEVER	41
MINDS			
A MILLION MINDS GAVE SUCK TO SUCH A BUD	79	LOVE'S FEVER	46
MIND'S			
THROUGH HEATH AND HEATHER AT THE MIND'S WILL.	44	TO FOLLOW FOX	13
MINE			
MINUTES ARE MINE	9	MINUTE'S HOUR	21

	PAGE	TITLE	LINE
MINE (CONTINUED)			
THE THROAT IS MINE I KNOW THE NECK	11	AIR BREATHE	2
THEYD SEE WITH EYES LIKE MINE	11	AIR BREATHE	10
AND SEE THE BLOOD IS MINE, ...	13	SKY'S BRIGHT	23
FLOWING FROM HER BUT MINE, ...	13	SKY'S BRIGHT	24
WRAP THEM IN FLAME, THEY'RE MINE;	19	IMAGES IN AIR	2
AS EDGES OFF YOUR NERVES TO MINE, ...	20	ENCOMPASSED	5
TINGLE ON MINE;	21	BEWILDERED WAY	14
TURNS MINE TO WAX.	77	THE FORCE THAT	8
A VEIN OF MINE	87	PAIN BE MUSIC	5
A STREAM OF MINE	87	PAIN BE MUSIC	17
STROKE OF MECHANICAL FLESH ON MINE, ...	107	ALL ALL AND	29
THEY SAID, WHO HACKED AND HUMOURED, THEY WERE MINE.	112	NOT FATHER ME	20
DRY LOVER MINE	127	NOW, SAY NAY	4
NO PROPHET-PROGENY OF MINE, ...	150	WHEN I WOKE	26
THAT HIS TEARS BURNED MY CHEEKS AND HIS HEART MOVED			
IN MINE.	178	POEM IN OCT	52
AND EYES HAVE BEEN GROVE-GREEN CATCHING MINE FROM			
THE DEPTH OF THE SILENCE;	224	IDYLL UNFORGET	33
THERE IS A GREATER LOVE THAN MINE	228	NOT DESPAIR	4
MINER			
AND TALK OF LIGHT TO A MAD MINER.	96	TWELVE	8
MINERAL			
FORGED IN MAN'S MINERAL.	112	I, IN IMAGE	106
MINERALS			
FORGED IN MAN'S MINERALS, THE BRASSY ORATOR	108	I, IN IMAGE	2
MINGLED			
OF MINGLED MOONLIGHT AND LAMPLIGHT	43	FACES SHONE	2
MINISTERS			
BLACK NIGHT STILL MINISTERS THE MOON, ...	61	MEAT ON BONES	33
MINNOWS			
OF MINNOWS WREATHING AROUND THEIR PRAYER;	209	POEM ON B'DAY	29
MINOTAURS			
THE SHE MULES BEAR THEIR MINOTAURS, ...	148	UNLUCKILY FOR	32
MINSTREL			
OLD COCK FROM NOWHERES LOPPED THE MINSTREL TONGUE	119	ALTARWISE	78
THIS WAS THE SKY, JACK CHRIST, EACH MINSTREL ANGLE	120	ALTARWISE	105
ON THE WHITE, NO LONGER GROWING GREEN, AND, MINSTREL			
DEAD, ...	190	WINTER'S TALE	112
AND CUT THE BIRDS' BOUGHS THAT THE MINSTREL SAP RAN			
RED.	205	GIANT'S THIGH	49
MINSTRELS			
LISTEN. THE MINSTRELS SING	189	WINTER'S TALE	56
MINTED			
STAMP OF THE MINTED FACE UPON THE MOON;	94	IN BEGINNING	10
MINUS			
THEIR WIVES OR MOTHERS MINUS HIPS).	83	LETTER TO AUNT	22
MINUS THESE CURSES, YOU CAN BE	85	LETTER TO AUNT	61
MINUTE			
GOING HER GLISTENING CALVES THAT MINUTE.	11	CABARET	4
AND TASTE UPON OUR LIPS, THIS MINUTE, ...	14	RAIN CUTS	37
(AND SKELETONS HAD SAP). ONE MINUTE	43	FACES SHONE	7
AND TO THE HOLLOW MINUTE OF THE WOMB, ...	78	LOVE'S FEVER	2
UNSEX THE SKELETON THIS MOUNTAIN MINUTE, ...	120	ALTARWISE	110
OVER THE CHOIR MINUTE I HEAR THE HOUR CHANT:	130	SINNERS' BELL	7
EACH ANCIENT, STONE-NECKED MINUTE OF LOVE'S SEASON	131	I MAKE THIS IN	2
IN THE MUTED HOUSE, ONE MINUTE BEFORE	216	ELEGY	14
WHOSE MINUTE KINDLES MORE THAN THE WISE HOUR.	237	PILLAR BREAKS	11
MINUTES			
MINUTES ARE MINE	9	MINUTE'S HOUR	21

	PAGE	TITLE	LINE
MINUTES (CONTINUED)			
STOP HAS NO MINUTES,/ BUT I GO OR DIE.	9	MINUTE'S HOUR	23
HOLD HARD, THESE ANCIENT MINUTES IN THE CUCKOO'S MONTH	122	HOLD HARD	T
HOLD HARD, THESE ANCIENT MINUTES IN THE CUCKOO'S MONTH, ...	122	HOLD HARD	1
THE RUSTICATING MINUTES, ...	157	RETURN	98
MINUTE'S			
I KNOW THIS VICIOUS MINUTE'S HOUR	9	MINUTE'S HOUR	T
I KNOW THIS VICIOUS MINUTE'S HOUR;	9	MINUTE'S HOUR	1
THE LONG, LAID MINUTE'S BRIDE DRIFTS ON	164	LONG-LEGGED	83
MIRACLE			
LET WHAT REMAINS OF THAT FIRST MIRACLE	65	WOMAN SPEAKS	62
THE MORTAL MIRACLE, LET THAT FIRST DUST	65	WOMAN SPEAKS	64
CREATE THIS TWIN MIRACLE.	109	I, IN.IMAGE	18
OH MIRACLE OF FISHES! THE LONG DEAD BITE!	166	LONG-LEGGED	140
THOUGH THE MOMENT OF A MIRACLE IS UNENDING LIGHTNING	170	MARRIAGE VIRG	6
AND THE MIDWIVES OF MIRACLE SING	180	VISION, PRAYER	26
MUSIC OF ELEMENTS, THAT A MIRACLE MAKES!	200	COUNTRY SLEEP	86
MIRACLES			
HIS DECKS ARE DRENCHED WITH MIRACLES.	166	LONG-LEGGED	139
ALL THE HORSES OF HIS HAUL OF MIRACLES	168	LONG-LEGGED	187
MYSELVES GRIEVE NOW, AND MIRACLES CANNOT ATONE. ...	173	FIRE RAID	16
MIRACULOUS			
WAS MIRACULOUS VIRGINITY OLD AS LOAVES AND FISHES,	170	MARRIAGE VIRG	5
MIRE			
AND MIRE OF LOVE, BUT THE THIEF AS MEEK AS THE DEW.	198	COUNTRY SLEEP	38
MIRROR			
MIRROR FROM MAN TO WHALE	129	MY NEOPHYTE	21
SHALL HER SMILE BREED THAT MOUTH, BEHIND THE MIRROR,	134	NOT FROM ANGER	13
CALL FOR CONFESSOR AND WISER MIRROR BUT THERE IS NONE	186	HOLY SPRING	10
MIRRORED			
HERON, MIRRORED, GO, ...	203	SIR JOHNS HILL	49
MIRRORS			
BURNS IN MANY MIRRORS.	60	FAIRY TALES	25
IN THE MEMORY WORKED BY MIRRORS, ...	146	TO OTHERS	10
MISCHIEVOUS			
THE SONG OF THE MISCHIEVOUS DOG	221	SONG OF DOG	T
MISERY			
DOWN INTO MISERY?	12	SKY'S BRIGHT	15
IT'S NOT IN MISERY BUT IN OBLIVION	16	IN OBLIVION	T
IT'S NOT IN MISERY BUT IN OBLIVION, ...	16	IN OBLIVION	1
MISGIVING			
DEATH SIGHTS AND SEES WITH GREAT MISGIVING	25	THERE'S PLENTY	6
MISSED			
SO IS THERE MISSED A CERTAIN GODLINESS	23	THE ONLY DEAD	26
MISSING			
MISSING	222	MISSING	T
MIST			
THE NIGHTMARE'S MIST	35	LIFT UP FACE	12
LOVE LIKE A MIST OR FIRE THROUGH THE BED OF EELS.	111	I, IN IMAGE	90
WITH ITS HORNS THROUGH MIST AND THE CASTLE	177	POEM IN OCT	33
AS THE RAIN FALLS, HAIL ON THE FLEECE, AS THE VALE MIST RIDES	199	COUNTRY SLEEP	57
HIDDEN IN DELICATE DRIFTS OF MIST ARE THEY THAT BECKON, ...	224	IDYLL UNFORGET	37
MISTAKING			
AND NOW, MISTAKING THE DIRECTION, ...	37	WINDMILLS TURN	23
MISTER			
MISTER AND MASTER, DARKNESS FOR HIS EYES, ...	114	SERVANT SUN	31

	PAGE	TITLE	LINE
MISTER (CONTINUED)			
A SOLITARY MISTER	171	THE HUNCHBACK	2
AND MISTER THEY CALLED HEY MISTER	171	THE HUNCHBACK	15
AND MISTER THEY CALLED HEY MISTER	171	THE HUNCHBACK	15
MISTS			
WITH LITTLE, ODD MISTS WAVED IN THE PATH OF ITS ECHO,	224	IDYLL UNFORGET	26
MISVENTURE			
FOR US THAT KNOWS MISVENTURE	28	NO WINGS	6
MITCHING			
WHEN I WHISTLED WITH MITCHING BOYS THROUGH A			
RESERVOIR PARK	144	COLOUR OF SAY	7
MIX			
MIX THEIR WILD BLOOD	236	WOMAN TAPESTRY	57
MIXED			
HEAVEN AND HELL MIXED AS THEY SPUN.	93	IN BEGINNING	6
MIXES			
MIXES, RIPENS, IN THE LOAM;	71	TAKE NEEDLES	26
MIXTURE			
WHERE WORDS AND WATER MAKE A MIXTURE	69	BEFORE KNOCKED	27
MNETHA'S			
WAS BROTHER TO MNETHA'S DAUGHTER	68	BEFORE KNOCKED	5
MOAN			
WOUND THEIR ROOM WITH A MALE MOAN, ...	158	INTO HER HEAD	25
WALL HEARING THE MOAN	180	VISION, PRAYER	22
THAT HE LET THE DEAD LIE THOUGH THEY MOAN	184	VISION, PRAYER	136
MOANS			
THAT THIS IS LIES THAT MOANS DEPARTURE, ...	36	LET BE KNOWN	4
HE ALONE IS FREE, AND, FREE, MOANS TO THE SKY.	46	POET: 1935	13
MOBY			
AND JONAH'S MOBY SNATCHED ME BY THE HAIR, ...	119	ALTARWISE	66
MOCK			
MAKE MOCK OF WOMAN'S MEAT, ...	34	THIRST PARCHES	14
SOBSTUFF, MOCK REASON, ...	39	GAS FADES	12
THE LAKE'S VOICE AND THE ROLLING OF MOCK WAVES	46	POET: 1935	4
AND THE GRAVE SEA, MOCK WHO DERIDE	54	WE BY SEASAND	2
MOCK ME, ...	239	MAKES INTERVALS	17
MOCKED			
I'VE MOCKED THE MOVING OF THE UNIVERSE.	52	OUT OF THE PIT	75
MOCKERY			
HUNCHBACKED IN MOCKERY	171	THE HUNCHBACK	21
MODEL			
FIRST BUY A HAT, NO PARIS MODEL	83	LETTER TO AUNT	15
MODERN			
A LETTER TO MY AUNT DISCUSSING THE CORRECT APPROACH			
TO MODERN POETRY	83	LETTER TO AUNT	T
(ALL MODERN PAINTERS USE THEIR FEET	83	LETTER TO AUNT	20
AND MODERN VERSE IS DONE WITH EASE.	84	LETTER TO AUNT	32
MODERNIST			
FROM MODERNIST PARNASSIAN HEIGHTS.	83	LETTER TO AUNT	14
MODESTY			
MODESTY HIDES MY THIGHS IN HER WINGS, ...	207	LAMENT	59
MOIST			
AND WHEN THE MOIST COLLECTION PLATE IS PASSED	179	NEW QUAY	31
MOISTEN			
MOISTEN THE MOUTH OF SLEEP	15	FOR LEDA	17
MOISTEN YOUR CARE TO CARELESSNESS, ...	20	THE NEOPHYTE	19
MOLE			
LOVE ME, AS LOVES THE MOLE HIS DARKNESS	76	SONG: LOVE ME	13
AND THE MOLE SNOUT BLUNT UNDER HIS PILGRIMAGE OF			
DOMES, ...	204	GIANT'S THIGH	36

	PAGE	TITLE	LINE
MOLESTED			
IN THE MOLESTED ROCKS THE SHELL OF VIRGINS, ...	131	I MAKE THIS IN	18
MOLL			
IN THIS OUR AGE THE GUNMAN AND HIS MOLL, ...	89	EUNUCH DREAMS	11
MOLLS			
THE MOLLS	143	THE MOLLS	T
MOLTEN			
MOLTEN AND MOUNTAINOUS TO STREAM	4	PROLOGUE	49
AS YET WAS IN A MOLTEN FORM, ...	68	BEFORE KNOCKED	10
HER MOLTEN FLIGHT UP CINDER-NESTING COLUMNS, ...	132	I MAKE THIS IN	26
INTO THE WEATHERCOCKS' MOLTEN MOUTHS	175	FIRE RAID	63
MOMENT			
EACH SILVER MOMENT CHIMES/ IN STEPS OF SOUND, ...	9	MINUTE'S HOUR	5
OF THE MOMENT AND THE DEAD HOUR.	29	LONG, SKELETON	13
LET FOR ONE MOMENT A FAITH STATEMENT	66	LET A FAITH	T
LET FOR ONE MOMENT A FAITH STATEMENT	66	LET A FAITH	1
LET FOR ONE MOMENT A FAITH STATEMENT	67	LET A FAITH	6
LET FOR ONE MOMENT A FAITH STATEMENT	67	LET A FAITH	11
THOUGH THE MOMENT OF A MIRACLE IS UNENDING LIGHTNING	170	MARRIAGE VIRG	6
MOMENTS			
SPLITTING A THOUGHT INTO SUCH HIDEOUS MOMENTS	17	IN OBLIVION	17
YET IN SPITE OF ALL THIS, I HAVE MOMENTS OF BLISS,	221	SONG OF DOG	9
MOMENT'S			
IN A GAY MOMENT'S FALSITY--	21	BEWILDERED WAY	8
FROTH OR A MOMENT'S MOVEMENT	27	OBLIVIOUS DARK	20
MONEY			
WITH MY RED VEINS FULL OF MONEY, ...	143	24 YEARS	7
I'LL SHARE MY MONEY AND WE'LL RUN FOR JOY	149	PAPER & STICKS	14
HAWKING FOR MONEY AND PITY	156	RETURN	64
MONKEY			
'IF MY BUNCHED, MONKEY COMING IS CRUEL	145	IF HEAD HURT	11
MONKEYED			
THE INCHES MONKEYED BY THE BLOOD OF MAN.	102	FELLOWED SLEEP	28
MONSTER			
THIS STORY'S MONSTER HAS A SERPENT CAUL, ...	124	TODAY, INSECT	10
MONSTROUS			
YOUR MONSTROUS OFFICERS AND THE DECAYING ARMY, ...	110	I, IN IMAGE	56
(THOUGH THIS FOR HER IS A MONSTROUS IMAGE BLINDLY	136	AFTER FUNERAL	16
OF THE LIVING FLESH IS MONSTROUS OR IMMORTAL, ...	148	UNLUCKILY FOR	41
MONTH			
HOLD HARD, THESE ANCIENT MINUTES IN THE CUCKOO'S MONTH	122	HOLD HARD	T
HOLD HARD, THESE ANCIENT MINUTES IN THE CUCKOO'S MONTH, ...	122	HOLD HARD	1
LIE THIS FIFTH MONTH UNSKATED, AND THE BIRDS HAVE FLOWN;	122	HOLD HARD	9
MONTHS			
ON NO WORK OF WORDS NOW FOR THREE LEAN MONTHS IN THE BLOODY	140	NO WORK WORDS	1
A LIMP AND RIDERLESS SHAPE TO LEAP NINE THINNING MONTHS.'	145	IF HEAD HURT	15
MONUMENTAL			
THESE CLOUD-SOPPED, MARBLE HANDS, THIS MONUMENTAL	137	AFTER FUNERAL	36
MOOD			
NOT VERTICALLY IN A MOOD OF JOY	16	IN OBLIVION	2
LIFE, TILL THE CHANGE OF MOOD, FORKS	47	POET: 1935	38
THE SUPPER AND KNIVES OF A MOOD.	144	PLEASURE-BIRD	4
MOON			
SEES THE MOON STILL UP, ...	14	FOR LEDA	8
BETWEEN THE MOON AND SUN	15	FOR LEDA	15

	PAGE	TITLE	LINE
MOON (CONTINUED)			
AND, AFTER IT HAS SUNK, THE SANE MOON, ...	42	A WAR OF WITS	21
BEFORE THE MOON SHIFTED AND THE SAP RAN OUT, ...	43	FACES SHONE	10
STREETS' STOCK, OF THE MOON LIT, ILL LIT, FIELD AND TOWN, ...	45	PLOUGHMAN GONE	22
FRESH IMAGES SURROUND THE TREMENDOUS MOON, ...	47	POET: 1935	45
WHEN THE SUN FALLS AND THE MOON STARES, ...	48	LIGHT, I KNOW	7
WITH THE MAN IN THE WIND AND THE WEST MOON;	49	NO DOMINION	3
THE MOON LEERED DOWN THE VALLEY LIKE A FOOL.	50	OUT OF THE PIT	12
THE MOON LEERED DOWN THE VALLEY LIKE A FOOL.	51	OUT OF THE PIT	32
THE MOON PEERS DOWN THE VALLEY LIKE A SAINT.	53	OUT OF THE PIT	94
THAT CRIES ALONG HER VEINS. NO SUN OR MOON	56	GREEK PLAY	8
'REBEL AGAINST THE BINDING MOON	61	MEAT ON BONES	9
BLACK NIGHT STILL MINISTERS THE MOON, ...	61	MEAT ON BONES	33
HE HAS THE STILL MOON AND THE HUNDRED STARS;	63	WOMAN SPEAKS	20
WHO KNEW NOT SUN NOR MOON BY NAME, ...	68	BEFORE KNOCKED	8
HOLDING FOR EVER THE DEAD MOON.	69	SECRET WIND	6
MOON WALKS THE RIVER AND RAISES THE DEAD;	74	SUN BURNS	2
UNDER THE RIBS SAIL THE MOON AND THE SUN;	74	SUN BURNS	11
THE SUN AND MOON SHED ONE WHITE LIGHT.	78	LOVE'S FEVER	9
THE SUN WAS RED, THE MOON WAS GREY, ...	78	LOVE'S FEVER	14
HIS WINY SKY, AND, AS THE CANDLE'S MOON, ...	80	ALL THAT I OWE	14
LIKE SOME PITCH MOON, THE LIMIT OF THE GLOBES;	82	LIGHT BREAKS	20
A PROCESS BLOWS THE MOON INTO THE SUN, ...	88	A PROCESS IN	22
THE SIGNAL MOON IS ZERO IN THEIR VOIDS.	92	BOYS OF SUMMER	12
OF SUN AND MOON THEY PAINT THEIR DAMS	92	BOYS OF SUMMER	17
STAMP OF THE MINTED FACE UPON THE MOON;	94	IN BEGINNING	10
SHIFTING TO LIGHT, TURNED ON ME LIKE A MOON.	101	FELLOWED SLEEP	3
A HANDMADE MOON HALF HOLY IN A CLOUD, ...	121	INCARNATE DEVL	8
AND WHEN THE MOON ROSE WINDILY IT WAS	121	INCARNATE DEVL	11
FOSTER THE LIGHT NOR VEIL THE MANSHAPED MOON, ...	123	FOSTER LIGHT	1
MOON WITH A RELATION'S FACE	155	RETURN	47
AND THE MOON SWAM OUT OF ITS HULK.	162	LONG-LEGGED	16
BUT THE OIL AND BUBBLE OF THE MOON, ...	163	LONG-LEGGED	45
GOOD-BYE, GOOD LUCK, STRUCK THE SUN AND THE MOON, .	169	LONG-LEGGED	213
THAT HE WHO LEARNS NOW THE SUN AND MOON	183	VISION, PRAYER	119
ON THE DEPARTED, SNOW BUSHED GREEN, WANTON IN MOON LIGHT	189	WINTER'S TALE	72
UNDER THE MILE OFF MOON WE TREMBLED LISTENING	194	SLEEP BECALMED	5
ALL THE MOON LONG I HEARD, BLESSED AMONG STABLES, THE NIGHTJARS	195	FERN HILL	25
WHEN ONLY THE MOON RAGES	196	CRAFT OR ART	3
IN THE MOON THAT IS ALWAYS RISING, ...	196	FERN HILL	48
FROM THE RAGING MOON I WRITE	197	CRAFT OR ART	13
OR SKULKS IN THE DELL MOON BUT MOONSHINE ECHOING CLEAR	198	COUNTRY SLEEP	25
UNDER THE PRAYER WHEELING MOON IN THE ROSY WOOD ...	198	COUNTRY SLEEP	41
UNDER THE CONCEIVING MOON, ON THE HIGH CHALK HILL,	203	GIANT'S THIGH	2
OR RIPPLING SOFT IN THE SPINNEY MOON AS THE SILK	204	GIANT'S THIGH	27
THE WHOLE OF THE MOON I COULD LOVE AND LEAVE	206	LAMENT	10
DIPPING MOON AND DRUNK AS A NEW DROPPED CALF, ...	206	LAMENT	17
AND LISTENED WHEN A SLOW, STARRED SLUMBER WRAPT THE MOON, ...	223	IDYLL UNFORGET	7
CLOWN IN THE MOON	225	CLOWN IN MOON	T
MOON-AND-MIDNIGHT			
NOR BLOWS BACK MOON-AND-MIDNIGHT AS SHE BLOWS.	92	BOYS OF SUMMER	30
MOONBEAM			
YOU KING SINGSONG OWLS, WHO MOONBEAM	4	PROLOGUE	54
MOON-BLOWN			
TWINE IN A MOON-BLOWN SHELL, ...	129	MY NEOPHYTE	15

	PAGE	TITLE	LINE
MOON-CHAINED			
TURNS THE MOON-CHAINED AND WATER-WOUND	169	LONG-LEGGED	203
MOON-DRAWN			
THE MOON-DRAWN GRAVE, WITH THE SEAFARING YEARS, ...	107	GRIEF THIEF	2
MOONFALL			
MOONFALL AND SAILING EMPEROR, PALE AS THEIR			
TIDE-PRINT, ...	130	SINNERS' BELL	10
MOONLESS			
LEFT BY THE DEAD WHO, IN THEIR MOONLESS ACRE, ...	79	LOVE'S FEVER	35
MOONLIGHT			
OF MINGLED MOONLIGHT AND LAMPLIGHT	43	FACES SHONE	2
YOUNG AS THEY IN THE AFTER MILKING MOONLIGHT LAY	204	GIANT'S THIGH	16
MOONLIT			
CRYING, WHITE GOWNED, FROM THE MIDDLE MOONLIT STAGES	158	INTO HER HEAD	37
MOON-MAD			
SPIED MOON-MAD BEASTS CAROUSING ON THE HILL, ...	50	OUT OF THE PIT	9
MOONS			
WHO MOONS HER BLUE NOTES FROM HER NEST	4	PROLOGUE	62
THE MOONS ARE WHITE FLAMES, LIKE THE MOONS IN DREAMS.	223	IN DREAMS	14
THE MOONS ARE WHITE FLAMES, LIKE THE MOONS IN DREAMS.	223	IN DREAMS	14
MOON'S			
OUT OF THE HEAVENLY SEA ONTO THE MOON'S SHORES. ...	48	LIGHT, I KNOW	3
ON GIDDY NIGHTS WHEN SLAP ON THE MOON'S MASK	137	O CHATTERTON	12
SLAP ON THE DRUNK MOON'S MASK.	138	O CHATTERTON	25
LIKE THE MOON'S SEED, RUBBISH	193	SIDE OF TRUTH	26
MOONSHADE			
UNDER THE LIGHTED SHAPES OF FAITH AND THEIR MOONSHADE	204	GIANT'S THIGH	17
MOONSHINE			
WORK ART AND THE MOONSHINE	5	PROLOGUE	84
OR SKULKS IN THE DELL MOON BUT MOONSHINE ECHOING			
CLEAR	198	COUNTRY SLEEP	25
AND THE LOST, MOONSHINE DOMES, ...	211	POEM ON B'DAY	86
MOONSHOD			
THROUGH THE SHAKEN GREENSWARD LAKE, SILENT, ON			
MOONSHOD HOOVES, ...	200	COUNTRY SLEEP	84
MOONSTONE			
FAINT ARROWY MOONSTONE ON A TEAR-CULLED CADENCE,	225	SLENDER WIND	3
MOONSTRUCK			
MILES OVER THE MOONSTRUCK BOAT	163	LONG-LEGGED	38
MOON-TURNED			
DAZZLE THIS FACE OF VOICES ON THE MOON-TURNED TABLE,	110	I, IN IMAGE	69
MOON-WHITE			
MAST-HIGH MOON-WHITE WOMEN NAKED	165	LONG-LEGGED	104
MORALS			
IN MORALS AND FULL MARRIAGE BUNTING, ...	38	THE GOSSIPERS	12
MORE			
FOR WHEN I BOUGHT YOU FOR A THOUGHT, (YOU COST NO			
MORE)	10	COOL, OH NO	8
THE RAINBOW'S FOOT IS NOT MORE APT	11	AIR BREATHE	5
THERE'S MORE THAN DYING;	32	OUT OF SIGHS	11
GROWING MORE TERRIBLE AS THE DAY	43	LONGED TO MOVE	4
IF HUNTING MEANS ANYTHING MORE THAN THE CHASE	44	TO FOLLOW FOX	18
NO MORE TOILS OVER THE FIELDS	45	PLOUGHMAN GONE	13
WHEN MORE THAN SNAILS ARE FRIENDS.	45	TO FOLLOW FOX	23
YOU CAPTURE MORE THAN MAN OR WOMAN GUESSES;	48	POET: 1935	54
NO MORE MAY GULLS CRY AT THEIR EARS	50	NO DOMINION	20
WHERE BLEW A FLOWER MAY A FLOWER NO MORE	50	NO DOMINION	22
ONE GOD, MORE MIGHTY THAN THE SUN.	70	SECRET WIND	23
ADD ONE MORE NAIL OF PRAISE ON TO THE CROSS, ...	96	TWELVE	7
NO DEATH MORE NATURAL;	109	I, IN IMAGE	21

                                             PAGE   TITLE   LINE
MORE (CONTINUED)
    NO TREAD MORE PERILOUS, THE GREEN STEPS AND SPIRE   109   I, IN IMAGE   26
    NO MAN MORE MAGICAL, CLAWED OUT THE CROCODILE.   111   I, IN IMAGE   96
    NO TELL-TALE LOVER HAS AN END MORE CERTAIN, ...   125   TODAY, INSECT   24
    MORE THE THICK STONE CANNOT TELL.   139   TOMBSTONE TOLD   10
    ZIP ONCE MORE FOR A TRAVELLER   155   RETURN   37
    WITH NO MORE DESIRE THAN A GHOST.   166   LONG-LEGGED   124
    DIG NO MORE FOR THE CHAINS OF HIS GREY-HAIRED HEART.   172   DAWN RAID   9
    WHEN THAT IMMORTAL HOSPITAL MADE ONE MORE MOVE TO
        SOOTHE   186   HOLY SPRING   3
    NOW I AM A MAN NO MORE NO MORE   207   LAMENT   49
    NOW I AM A MAN NO MORE NO MORE   207   LAMENT   49
    WITH MORE TRIUMPHANT FAITH   211   POEM ON B'DAY   97
    MORE SPANNED WITH ANGELS RIDE   211   POEM ON B'DAY   104
    AND MY SHINING MEN NO MORE ALONE   211   POEM ON B'DAY   107
    THEY ARE FURTHER AND MORE DELICATE   226   THE ELM   3
    AND IS MORE BEAUTIFUL THAN THE DRIFT OF LEAVES. ...   226   SLENDER WIND   9
    WHOSE MINUTE KINDLES MORE THAN THE WISE HOUR.   237   PILLAR BREAKS   11
MORNING
    THE MORNING, SPACE FOR LEDA   14   FOR LEDA   T
    THE MORNING, SPACE FOR LEDA   14   FOR LEDA   1
    THE MORNING, TOO, IS TIME FOR LOVE, ...   15   FOR LEDA   28
    SIT AT OUR HEARTHS FROM MORNING UNTIL EVENING, ...   42   YOUNG ARE OLD   54
    THE SUN BURNS THE MORNING   74   SUN BURNS   T
    THE SUN BURNS THE MORNING, A BUSH IN THE BRAIN; ...   74   SUN BURNS   1
    A WORKER IN THE MORNING TOWN, ...   98   TWILIGHT LOCKS   38
    FLIES ON THE SHAFTED DISK, DECLAIMS THE MORNING ...   99   OCTOBER WIND   19
    CROWING TO LAZARUS THE MORNING IS VANITY, ...   110   I, IN IMAGE   59
    MORNING SMACK OF THE SPADE THAT WAKES UP SLEEP, ...   136   AFTER FUNERAL   6
    CUTTING THE MORNING OFF, ...   150   WHEN I WOKE   10
    EVERY MORNING I MAKE, ...   150   WHEN I WOKE   16
    I HEARD, THIS MORNING, WAKING, ...   150   WHEN I WOKE   23
    BEFORE THE CROWING MORNING CLIMBED;   157   INTO HER HEAD   19
    WHEN THE MORNING WAS WAKING OVER THE WAR   172   DAWN RAID   1
    THE MORNING IS FLYING ON THE WINGS OF HIS AGE   173   DAWN RAID   13
    THE MORNING BECKON   176   POEM IN OCT   5
    COME IN THE MORNING WHERE I WANDERED AND LISTENED   177   POEM IN OCT   27
    OF THE MORNING   182   VISION, PRAYER   81
    GABRIEL AND RADIANT SHRUBBERY AS THE MORNING GROWS
        JOYFUL   186   HOLY SPRING   15
    COMBS THROUGH THE MANTLED YARDS AND THE MORNING MEN   187   WINTER'S TALE   20
    IN ALL HIS TUNEFUL TURNING SO FEW AND SUCH MORNING
        SONGS   196   FERN HILL   43
    OF THE MORNING LEAVES, AS THE STAR FALLS, AS THE
        WINGED   199   COUNTRY SLEEP   60
    SPINS ITS MORNING OF PRAISE, ...   211   POEM ON B'DAY   99
MORNINGS
    AND IN THE MIGHTY MORNINGS OF THE EARTH;   122   INCARNATE DEVL   15
    FORGOTTEN MORNINGS WHEN HE WALKED WITH HIS MOTHER   178   POEM IN OCT   47
MORNING'S
    WAKING ALONE IN A MULTITUDE OF LOVES WHEN MORNING'S
        LIGHT   170   MARRIAGE VIRG   1
    OF MIDWIVING MORNING'S   185   VISION, PRAYER 174
MORROW
    DUG OF THE SEA, THE GLANDED MORROW, ...   106   ALL ALL AND   8
    (SIR MORROW MARK), ...   113   SERVANT SUN   2
    SIR MORROW AT HIS SPONGE, ...   113   SERVANT SUN   8
    MAN MORROW BLOWS THROUGH FOOD.   113   SERVANT SUN   14
    (SIR MORROW STAMPS   114   SERVANT SUN   23

	PAGE	TITLE	LINE
MORSING			
MY PICKBRAIN MASTERS MORSING ON THE STONE	100	RUNNING GRAVE	22
MORTAL			
THE MORTAL MIRACLE, LET THAT FIRST DUST	65	WOMAN SPEAKS	64
AND TIME CAST FORTH MY MORTAL CREATURE	69	BEFORE KNOCKED	31
A GHOST NOR MAN, BUT MORTAL GHOST.	69	BEFORE KNOCKED	38
I WAS A MORTAL TO THE LAST	69	BEFORE KNOCKED	40
LEANS ON MY MORTAL RULER, ...	75	MY HERO BARES	4
PRAISING THE MORTAL ERROR	75	MY HERO BARES	17
BY YOUTH AND AGE, THE MORTAL STATE AND THOUGHT	80	ALMANAC TIME	9
FEAR NOT THE WORKING WORLD, MY MORTAL, ...	106	ALL ALL AND	13
SQUARE IN THESE WORLDS THE MORTAL CIRCLE.	107	ALL ALL AND	30
MY MAN OF LEAVES AND THE BRONZE ROOT, MORTAL,			
UNMORTAL, ...	109	I, IN IMAGE	16
OF MORTAL VOICES TO THE NINNIES' CHOIR, ...	123	FOSTER LIGHT	16
FROM ALL MY MORTAL LOVERS WITH A STARBOARD SMILE;	123	FOSTER LIGHT	21
MEET ONCE ON A MORTAL WALL, ...	140	TOMBSTONE TOLD	23
NOR WALK IN THE COOL OF YOUR MORTAL GARDEN	148	UNLUCKILY FOR	48
MOSSY			
BOWING ON ITS MOSSY KNEES, ...	72	TAKE NEEDLES	50
MOST			
MOST FIT FOR LOVERS TO MAKE HARMONY, ...	34	THIRST PARCHES	10
FAITH IN DIVINITY WOULD SOLVE MOST THINGS, ...	37	WINDMILLS TURN	16
BUT WAYS HAVE CHANGED, AND MOST WAYS LEAD	37	WINDMILLS TURN	20
ONE WHO IS MOST UNKNOWN, ...	160	DEATHS AND ENT	16
OF THEIR MOST SECRET HEART.	197	CRAFT OR ART	11
ON THE LORD'S-TABLE OF THE BOWING GRASS. FEAR MOST	198	COUNTRY SLEEP	35
AND THIS LAST BLESSING MOST, ...	211	POEM ON B'DAY	90
MOSTLY			
NOW SHOWN AND MOSTLY BARE I WOULD LIE DOWN, ...	152	BELOW A TIME	49
MOTH			
OF MUD AND SAND. AND, LIKE A SABLE MOTH, ...	179	NEW QUAY	4
MOTHER			
MOTHER I BLAME	26	PERSONAL EPIT	7
MOTHER I BLAME.	26	PERSONAL EPIT	12
WE KNOW OUR MOTHER GOOSE AND EDEN, ...	59	FAIRY TALES	10
AND A MOTHER IN HER LABOUR	71	TAKE NEEDLES	18
MOTHER ROOT THAT SHOT ME FORTH, ...	72	TAKE NEEDLES	41
ANSWER: SHALL A MOTHER LIE	72	TAKE NEEDLES	59
A MOTHER IN LABOUR PAYS TWICE HER PAIN, ...	74	SUN BURNS	14
THE PLUM MY MOTHER PICKED MATURED SLOWLY, ...	78	LOVE'S FEVER	25
OF LOVER, MOTHER, LOVERS, OR HIS SIX	96	RUB OF LOVE	41
AND MOTHER MILK WAS STIFF AS SAND, ...	98	TWILIGHT LOCKS	32
HALF OF THE FELLOW MOTHER AS SHE DABBLES	103	WORLD PYRAMID	3
DO YOU NOT MOTHER ME, NOR, AS I AM, ...	112	NOT FATHER ME	3
BY MAGNET WINDS TO HER BLIND MOTHER DRAWN, ...	131	I MAKE THIS IN	14
THE MOTHER DUG, AND ITS ARMS FULL OF FIRES.	173	FIRE RAID	8
FORGOTTEN MORNINGS WHEN HE WALKED WITH HIS MOTHER	178	POEM IN OCT	47
OF THE MOTHER HIDDEN	180	VISION, PRAYER	23
AND THE MOTHER AND TOPPLING HOUSE OF THE HOLY SPRING,	186	HOLY SPRING	23
THE GRAINS BEYOND AGE, THE DARK VEINS OF HER MOTHER,	192	REFUSAL MOURN	21
HUGGED, AND BARREN AND BARE ON MOTHER GOOSE'S GROUND	205	GIANT'S THIGH	43
MOTHERED			
TURNS GHOST TO GHOST; EACH MOTHERED CHILD	88	A PROCESS IN	20
MOTHERING			
AND THE SPLASHED MOTHERING MAIDEN	181	VISION, PRAYER	42
MOTHERLIKE			
THE FIELDS, BY A MOTHERLIKE HENRUN)	154	RETURN	4
MOTHERNAKED			
BEFORE WE MOTHERNAKED FALL	73	WE MOTHERNAKED	T

	PAGE	TITLE	LINE
MOTHERNAKED (CONTINUED)			
BEFORE WE MOTHERNAKED FALL	73	WE MOTHERNAKED	1
MOTHERS			
MOTHERS ME UNTIL I DIE, ...	72	TAKE NEEDLES	43
THEIR WIVES OR MOTHERS MINUS HIPS).	83	LETTER TO AUNT	22
I SEE THE SUMMER CHILDREN IN THEIR MOTHERS	92	BOYS OF SUMMER	13
MOTHER'S			
THE MOTHER'S CRY HAS FUMED ABOUT THE WINDS;	64	WOMAN SPEAKS	53
AND DOUBLECROSSED MY MOTHER'S WOMB.	69	BEFORE KNOCKED	46
'HIS MOTHER'S WOMB HAD A TONGUE THAT LAPPED UP MUD,'	132	I MAKE THIS IN	46
BEFORE I HEARD IN MY MOTHER'S SIDE	139	TOMBSTONE TOLD	6
OF HIS MOTHER'S MILK MAY RETURN	183	VISION, PRAYER	120
ABOVE ALL HE LONGED FOR HIS MOTHER'S BREAST	216	ELEGY	9
SOFTLY, THOU RAIN--AND FOR HIS MOTHER'S SAKE, ...	222	MISSING	7
MOTHERS-EYED			
MY MOTHERS-EYED, UPON THE TOPS OF TREES;	101	FELLOWED SLEEP	9
FADED MY ELBOW GHOST, THE MOTHERS-EYED, ...	102	FELLOWED SLEEP	16
MOTION			
IT IS A SOUR MOTION IN THE BLOOD, ...	9	MINUTE'S HOUR	2
I, IN MY FUSION OF ROSE AND MALE MOTION, ...	109	I, IN IMAGE	17
ALL THE LAND IS RIPE. THERE IS NO MOTION	222	FOREST PICTURE	5
WHEN YOUR FURIOUS MOTION	232	FURIOUS MOTION	T
WHEN YOUR FURIOUS MOTION IS STEADIED, ...	232	FURIOUS MOTION	1
MOTLEY			
AND THE MOTLEY WINDS FROM THE SEAS.	227	THE PINE	4
MOTOR			
AS MOTOR MUSCLE ON THE DRILL, DRIVING	102	I DREAMED MY	3
MOULDED			
MOULDED MY FORM	26	PERSONAL EPIT	9
MOUNT			
AND CANNOT MOUNT A CLOTHESHORSE WITHOUT BLEEDING.	40	YOUNG ARE OLD	10
MOUNT ON MAN'S FOOTFALL, ...	109	I, IN IMAGE	27
TO SHUT THE SUN, PLUNGE, MOUNT YOUR DARKENED KEYS	161	DEATHS AND ENT	33
MOUNTAIN			
ON MAN AND MOUNTAIN, ...	34	THIRST PARCHES	6
HOW AT THE MOUNTAIN SPRING THE SAME MOUTH SUCKS.	77	THE FORCE THAT	10
CASTS TO THE PINE ROOTS, RAISING MAN LIKE A MOUNTAIN	109	I, IN IMAGE	11
THIS WAS THE CRUCIFIXION ON THE MOUNTAIN, ...	120	ALTARWISE	99
UNSEX THE SKELETON THIS MOUNTAIN MINUTE, ...	120	ALTARWISE	110
LOST ON THE UNCHRISTENED MOUNTAIN	183	VISION, PRAYER	134
ON THE MOUNTAIN CROWN	184	VISION, PRAYER	148
FOR WHO UNMANNINGLY HAUNTS THE MOUNTAIN RAVENED EAVES	198	COUNTRY SLEEP	24
MOUNTAINOUS			
MOLTEN AND MOUNTAINOUS TO STREAM	4	PROLOGUE	49
MOUNTAINS			
HIDING THE GOLDEN MOUNTAINS AND MANSIONS	54	WE BY SEASAND	16
THE EARTH AND SKY WERE AS TWO MOUNTAINS MEETING.	78	LOVE'S FEVER	15
MOUNTAINS AND GALLERIES BENEATH	164	LONG-LEGGED	86
MOUNTAINS AND GALLERIES TO THE CREST!	166	LONG-LEGGED	132
THESE WERE MY DESIRES, ETERNAL AS MOUNTAINS, ...	223	IDYLL UNFORGET	9
MOUNTED			
CORNER THE MOUNTED MEADOWS IN THE HILL CORRAL;	109	I, IN IMAGE	39
BUTT OF THE TREE-TAILED WORM THAT MOUNTED EVE, ...	117	ALTARWISE	32
MOUNTING			
IN THE BEGINNING WAS THE MOUNTING FIRE	94	IN BEGINNING	13
CLASH OUT THE MOUNTING DOLPHIN'S DAY, ...	164	LONG-LEGGED	75
MOURN			
BACK TO CLACK SILENCE MELT AND MOURN	181	VISION, PRAYER	61
TO MOURN HIS DELUGING	184	VISION, PRAYER	156

	PAGE	TITLE	LINE
MOURN (CONTINUED)			
A REFUSAL TO MOURN THE DEATH, BY FIRE, OF A CHILD IN LONDON	191	REFUSAL MOURN	T
IN THE LEAST VALLEY OF SACKCLOTH TO MOURN	191	REFUSAL MOURN	12
OH, LET ME MIDLIFE MOURN BY THE SHRINED	211	POEM ON B'DAY	76
MOURNING			
THERE SHALL BE NO MUTE MOURNING OVER HIS ACRE, ...	64	WOMAN SPEAKS	38
IN A FIERCELY MOURNING HOUSE IN A CROOKED YEAR. ...	136	AFTER FUNERAL	30
MOURNS			
A MAN TORN UP MOURNS IN THE SOLE NIGHT.	159	INTO HER HEAD	67
MOUSE			
TOM TIT AND DAI MOUSE!	5	PROLOGUE	99
A MOUSE IT WAS PLAYED WITH AN IVORY TOOTH, ...	65	WOMAN SPEAKS	58
WITH EVERY SIMMERING WOMAN HIS MOUSE	206	LAMENT	30
MOUSEHOLE			
AT LAST THE SOUL FROM ITS FOUL MOUSEHOLE	207	LAMENT	43
MOUSE'S			
A CLAW I QUESTION FROM THE MOUSE'S BONE, ...	114	SERVANT SUN	17
MOUSING			
THE CATTLE STIRRING, THE MOUSING CAT STEPPING SHY,	187	WINTER'S TALE	22
MOUTH			
MASTER, HER MOUTH IS SAWDUST	10	COOL, OH NO	14
MOISTEN THE MOUTH OF SLEEP	15	FOR LEDA	17
AND MOUTH. BOTH NOTE AND PLUME PLUNGE FROM THE SPIRE'S HOOK.	16	SPIRE CRANES	8
AND MAKE HIS WIDE MOUTH HOME.	17	IN OBLIVION	7
OUT OF MY HAND IN STOPPING UP MY MOUTH, ...	18	NATURAL DAY	16
BREATHING NO POISON FROM THE OVAL MOUTH, ...	19	THE NEOPHYTE	3
BOY SUCKS NO SWEETNESS FROM THE WILLING MOUTH, ...	19	THE NEOPHYTE	9
BUT CAME FROM OUT THE MOUTH UNKNOWING	23	THE ONLY DEAD	17
AND ON OUR LIPS THE DRY MOUTH OF THE RAIN.	26	THERE'S PLENTY	19
ITS HONEYED CHEEK, SOFT-TALKING MOUTH, ...	35	LIFT UP FACE	16
PUFFED, OLD WITH VENOM, FROM A CRUSTED MOUTH.	37	WINDMILLS TURN	30
AGE SOURS BEFORE YOUTH'S TASTED IN THE MOUTH	40	YOUNG ARE OLD	2
OPENING ITS IRIS MOUTH UPON THE SILL	47	POET: 1935	30
AND KNOWS NO WOE THAT THESE SAD PLAYERS MOUTH	57	GREEK PLAY	30
THE HEART LIES READY FOR THE RAVEN'S MOUTH, ...	63	WOMAN SPEAKS	8
WIND CARVEN LINES AROUND THE DROOPING MOUTH;	64	WOMAN SPEAKS	50
INSIDE THIS MOUTH I FEEL HIS MESSAGE MOVING	76	LASHED RINGS	14
AND I AM DUMB TO MOUTH UNTO MY VEINS	77	THE FORCE THAT	9
HOW AT THE MOUNTAIN SPRING THE SAME MOUTH SUCKS. ..	77	THE FORCE THAT	10
WHEN NO MOUTH STIRRED ABOUT THE HANGING FAMINE, ...	78	LOVE'S FEVER	5
YOUR MOUTH, MY LOVE, THE THISTLE IN THE KISS?	96	RUB OF LOVE	44
THE MOUTH OF TIME SUCKED, LIKE A SPONGE, ...	97	TWILIGHT LOCKS	4
DEATH ON THE MOUTH THAT ATE THE GAS.	103	I DREAMED MY	16
WHO SEEK ME LANDWARD, MARKING IN MY MOUTH	105	WORLD PYRAMID	46
AND THE BREATH-WHITE, CURTAINED MOUTH OF SEED.' ...	132	I MAKE THIS IN	51
THE PRESENT MOUTH, AND THE SWEETLY BLOWN TRUMPET OF LIES, ...	133	MAKE ME A MASK	6
BY THE CURVE OF THE NUDE MOUTH OR THE LAUGH UP THE SLEEVE.	133	MAKE ME A MASK	12
SHALL HER SMILE BREED THAT MOUTH, BEHIND THE MIRROR,	134	NOT FROM ANGER	13
WITH CARVED BIRD, SAINT, AND SUN, THE WRACKSPIKED MAIDEN MOUTH	135	HOW MY ANIMAL	37
MILK IN YOUR MOUTH, AT THE SOUR FLOODS	142	SAINT TO FALL	32
THE STOCKED HEART IS FORCED, AND AGONY HAS ANOTHER MOUTH TO FEED.	142	SAINT TO FALL	42
ON THE CLAY COLD MOUTH, ON THE FIRE	147	UNLUCKILY FOR	8
WITH ITS KNEADING MOUTH	173	FIRE RAID	6
HIS MOUTH AND ROCKED HIM LIKE A STORM	181	VISION, PRAYER	44

	PAGE	TITLE	LINE
MOUTH (CONTINUED)			
LIE STILL, SLEEP BECALMED, HIDE THE MOUTH IN THE THROAT,	194	SLEEP BECALMED	13
SLIDES GOOD IN THE SLEEK MOUTH.	209	POEM ON B'DAY	36
AS THE MOUTH OF THE TIGER-LILY	229	MY RIVER	24
THEN, WHEN I OPEN MY MOUTH,	231	YOUR VOICE	6
MOUTHED			
THE RIVERS MOUTHED IN NIGHT,	188	WINTER'S TALE	46
MOUTHING			
DRIVES MY RED BLOOD; THAT DRIES THE MOUTHING STREAMS	77	THE FORCE THAT	7
(BUT NOTHING BORE, NO MOUTHING BABE TO THE VEINED HIVES	205	GIANT'S THIGH	42
MOUTHS			
INTO HER VEGETATION'S LAPPING MOUTHS	20	ENCOMPASSED	3
WITH WIDE, DRY MOUTHS AND EYES,	28	NO WINGS	14
AND CANCEROUS SPEAKING DRIPPING FROM THEIR MOUTHS,	41	YOUNG ARE OLD	29
WITH SERPENTS' MOUTHS AND SCALECOPHIDIAN VOIDS	51	OUT OF THE PIT	22
AND FILL THE MOUTHS OF HEAVEN WITH YOUR TONGUE	87	PAIN BE MUSIC	2
SHE WEPT IN HER PAIN AND MADE MOUTHS,	139	TOMBSTONE TOLD	19
INTO THE WEATHERCOCKS' MOLTEN MOUTHS	175	FIRE RAID	63
PARISH OF SNOW. THE CARVED MOUTHS IN THE ROCK ARE WIND SWEPT STRINGS.	189	WINTER'S TALE	64
NOW CURLEW CRY ME DOWN TO KISS THE MOUTHS OF THEIR DUST.	205	GIANT'S THIGH	45
MOUTH'S			
YOUR MOUTH'S FINE DUST	16	TIME TO ROT	7
MOVE			
MANNED WITH THEIR LOVES THEY'LL MOVE,	5	PROLOGUE	95
I HAVE LONGED TO MOVE AWAY	43	LONGED TO MOVE	T
I HAVE LONGED TO MOVE AWAY	43	LONGED TO MOVE	1
I HAVE LONGED TO MOVE AWAY	43	LONGED TO MOVE	6
AND AT THEIR BAYING MOVE A TAILOR'S INCH	44	TO FOLLOW FOX	2
I HAVE LONGED TO MOVE AWAY BUT AM AFRAID;	44	LONGED TO MOVE	11
THE WINTER YEARS, MOVE IN THE PIT OF MAN;	79	ALMANAC TIME	3
MOVE LIKE TWO GHOSTS BEFORE THE EYE.	88	A PROCESS IN	18
OUR STRIPS OF STUFF THAT TATTER AS WE MOVE	90	EUNUCH DREAMS	32
SO FAST I MOVE DEFYING TIME, THE QUIET GENTLEMAN	116	LANTERNS SHINE	14
WHEN THAT IMMORTAL HOSPITAL MADE ONE MORE MOVE TO SOOTHE	186	HOLY SPRING	3
LOOK. AND THE DANCERS MOVE	189	WINTER'S TALE	71
BEFORE YOU MOVE TO MAKE	192	SIDE OF TRUTH	8
THE ONE NOT CARING TO WHOM IN HIS SLEEP HE WILL MOVE	193	CONVERS PRAYER	4
IS CAST BEFORE YOU MOVE,	193	SIDE OF TRUTH	33
THAT THE CLOSER I MOVE	211	POEM ON B'DAY	91
NOR MAKE THE STERN SHELL OF MY SPIRIT MOVE.	233	NO THOUGHT	2
AND THRILL AND BREATHE AND MOVE	236	WOMAN TAPESTRY	59
MOVED			
NO TIDY FLOWER MOVED, NO BATHER GRACEFULLY	34	IN GARDENS	19
A CITY GODHEAD, TURBINE MOVED, STEEL SCULPTURED,	70	SECRET WIND	13
WHO MOVED FOR THREE YEARS IN TUNE	161	WEDDING ANNIV	3
THAT HIS TEARS BURNED MY CHEEKS AND HIS HEART MOVED IN MINE.	178	POEM IN OCT	52
BRETHREN FOR JOY HAS MOVED WITHIN	183	VISION, PRAYER	117
MOVEMENT			
FROTH OR A MOMENT'S MOVEMENT	27	OBLIVIOUS DARK	20
MOVEMENTS			
AT THE DEFT MOVEMENTS OF THE IRISES	48	POET: 1935	56
SUAVE IN HER MOVEMENTS,	235	WOMAN TAPESTRY	21
MOVES			
MOVES, AMONG MEN CAUGHT BY THE SUN,	46	POET: 1935	11

	PAGE	TITLE	LINE
MOVES (CONTINUED)			
MOVES TO THE MAHOMET OF YOUR HAND.	67	REALM OF FLESH	3
HE PULLS THE CHAIN, THE CISTERN MOVES.	75	MY HERO BARES	20
THE WATER-SPIRIT MOVES AS IT IS HIDDEN,	76	LASHED RINGS	9
GULL, ON THE WAVE WITH SAND IN ITS EYES! AND THE FOAL MOVES	200	COUNTRY SLEEP	83
MOVING			
THE MOVING FRUCTIFY;	16	TIME TO ROT	14
A FILM OF PEOPLE MOVING,	36	MIDNIGHT ROAD	7
I'VE MOCKED THE MOVING OF THE UNIVERSE.	52	OUT OF THE PIT	75
INSIDE THIS MOUTH I FEEL HIS MESSAGE MOVING	76	LASHED RINGS	14
WITH MOVING FISH AND ROUNDED STONES	168	LONG-LEGGED	178
OF MOVING ABOUT YOUR DEATH	192	SIDE OF TRUTH	14
MOVING IN ONE DIRECTION,	229	MY RIVER	38
MY LOVE FOR HER IS LIKE THE MOVING OF A CLOUD	235	WOMAN TAPESTRY	13
AND A CLEAN SURGE OF LOVE MOVING.	236	WOMAN TAPESTRY	63
MOWER			
A SINGING WALT FROM THE MOWER	156	RETURN	69
MR.			
IS MR. JONES THE CAKE, THAT WINKING-BIT,	179	NEW QUAY	20
MUCH			
TO MAKE OUR SENSES TAKE TOO MUCH,	13	RAIN CUTS	10
OR TOO MUCH BLOOD;	13	SKY'S BRIGHT	21
HAVING SO MUCH TO SPARE.	23	THE ONLY DEAD	22
AND MUCH THAT LIVES TO PERISH,	25	THERE'S PLENTY	2
HOW MUCH WAS HAPPY WHILE IT LASTED,	32	OUT OF SIGHS	20
COULD IN A DAY BE SICK WITH SO MUCH BLOOD;	63	WOMAN SPEAKS	13
AS MUCH AS FOR THEIR GOOD,	147	TO OTHERS	19
SKY HAS NOT LOVED ME MUCH,	234	NO, PIGEON	4
MUD			
THE STOCK AND STEEL THAT BAYONET FROM THE MUD,	73	LORD RED HAIL	9
'HIS MOTHER'S WOMB HAD A TONGUE THAT LAPPED UP MUD,'	132	I MAKE THIS IN	46
O WAKE IN ME IN MY HOUSE IN THE MUD	142	SAINT TO FALL	26
THE OLD MUD HATCH AGAIN, THE HORRID	142	SAINT TO FALL	44
OF MUD AND SAND. AND, LIKE A SABLE MOTH,	179	NEW QUAY	4
MUDDLE			
TOPPLING AND BURNING IN THE MUDDLE OF TOWERS AND GALLERIES	145	PLEASURE-BIRD	18
MUFFLED			
IN THE MUFFLED HOUSE, IN THE QUICK OF NIGHT,	188	WINTER'S TALE	29
MUFFLE-TOED			
WINDSHAKE OF SAILSHAPED EARS, MUFFLE-TOED TAP	136	AFTER FUNERAL	2
MULATTO			
THE WHITE, THE BLACK, THE YELLOW AND MULATTO	41	YOUNG ARE OLD	39
MULE			
AFTER THE FUNERAL, MULE PRAISES, BRAYS,	136	AFTER FUNERAL	1
MULES			
THE SHE MULES BEAR THEIR MINOTAURS,	148	UNLUCKILY FOR	32
MULTIPLYING			
AND YELLOW WAS THE MULTIPLYING SAND,	78	LOVE'S FEVER	22
MULTITUDE			
WAKING ALONE IN A MULTITUDE OF LOVES WHEN MORNING'S LIGHT	170	MARRIAGE VIRG	1
MULTITUDES			
CRY, MULTITUDES OF ARKS! ACROSS	5	PROLOGUE	93
MULTITUDE'S			
AND THE MULTITUDE'S SULTRY TEAR TURNS COOL ON THE WEEPING WALL,	186	HOLY SPRING	17
MUMMER			
MY WORLD IS PYRAMID. THE PADDED MUMMER	104	WORLD PYRAMID	31

	PAGE	TITLE	LINE
MUMMERY			
IN THE UNSLEEPING MUMMERY	35	LIFT UP FACE	7
MUMMY			
THE MUMMY CLOTHS EXPOSE AN ANCIENT BREAST.	116	LANTERNS SHINE	8
MURDER			
I CANNOT MURDER, LIKE A FOOL,	61	MEAT ON BONES	30
A GOOSE'S QUILL HAS PUT AN END TO MURDER	66	HAND SIGNED	7
MURDER WITH A CRY OF PAIN;	71	TAKE NEEDLES	19
THE LOINS CRIED MURDER.	85	SEE, SAYS LIME	16
MURDER OF EDEN AND GREEN GENESIS.	124	TODAY, INSECT	8
'TIME SHALL NOT MURDER YOU,' HE SAID,	129	MY NEOPHYTE	44
I SAW TIME MURDER ME.	129	MY NEOPHYTE	48
I SHALL NOT MURDER	192	REFUSAL MOURN	14
MURDERED			
THAT THE EYES ARE ALREADY MURDERED,	142	SAINT TO FALL	41
LOCKING, UNLOCKING, THE MURDERED STRANGERS WEAVE,	160	DEATHS AND ENT	15
MURDERING			
WE HID OUR FEARS IN THAT MURDERING BREATH,	153	WAS A SAVIOUR	14
MURDER'S			
AND, FOR THAT MURDER'S SAKE, DARK WITH CONTAGION	132	I MAKE THIS IN	37
MURMUR			
MURMUR OF SPRING NOR CRUSH THE COCKEREL'S EGGS,	123	FOSTER LIGHT	7
MUSCLE			
HERE LOVE'S DAMP MUSCLE DRIES AND DIES,	93	BOYS OF SUMMER	46
AS MOTOR MUSCLE ON THE DRILL, DRIVING	102	I DREAMED MY	3
IN THE SHIPWRECK OF MUSCLE;	111	I, IN IMAGE	88
MUSCLED			
WAS MUSCLED, MATTED, WISE TO THE CRYING THIGH	78	LOVE'S FEVER	28
MUSCLES			
THE SPIRIT RACKED ITS MUSCLES AND	85	SEE, SAYS LIME	15
OF GROWING BONES THE MUSCLES SLID;	86	SEE, SAYS LIME	26
MUSCLING			
A MUSCLING LIFE FROM LOVERS IN THEIR CRAMP,	92	BOYS OF SUMMER	33
MUSCLING-IN			
I WOULD NOT FEAR THE MUSCLING-IN OF LOVE	95	RUB OF LOVE	17
MUSCULAR			
FOR THE MUSCULAR AND THE VICTORIOUS	241	ADMIT THE SUN	16
MUSHROOM			
LOVE'S REFLECTION OF THE MUSHROOM FEATURES,	118	ALTARWISE	53
MUSHROOMS			
UNDER THE MILKY MUSHROOMS SLEW MY HUNGER,	118	ALTARWISE	64
MUSIC			
TIME FOR THE SWIMMERS' HANDS, MUSIC FOR SILVER LOCK	15	SPIRE CRANES	7
WHERE WHEELS, CONFUSING MUSIC, CONFUSED DOUBTS,	50	OUT OF THE PIT	2
TAXIS AND LILIES TO TINNED MUSIC STEPPED	51	OUT OF THE PIT	24
THE HEAVENLY MUSIC OVER THE SAND	54	WE BY SEASAND	14
TOIL AWAY TILL MUSIC DIES.	70	TAKE NEEDLES	4
YOUR PAIN SHALL BE A MUSIC	87	PAIN BE MUSIC	T
YOUR PAIN SHALL BE A MUSIC IN YOUR STRING	87	PAIN BE MUSIC	1
AS MILK SHALL BE A MUSIC IN THE PAPS	87	PAIN BE MUSIC	14
THAT DROPS TO MAKE A MUSIC IN YOUR BLOOD	87	PAIN BE MUSIC	20
TIME'S TUNE MY LADIES WITH THE TEATS OF MUSIC,	119	ALTARWISE	91
AND PLUCK A MANDRAKE MUSIC FROM THE MARROWROOT.	123	FOSTER LIGHT	18
ILLUMINATION OF MUSIC! THE LULLED BLACK-BACKED	200	COUNTRY SLEEP	82
MUSIC OF ELEMENTS, THAT A MIRACLE MAKES!	200	COUNTRY SLEEP	86
MAKES ALL THE MUSIC; AND I WHO HEAR THE TUNE OF THE SLOW,	203	SIR JOHNS HILL	57
BENEATH THE DEEP BARK CALLS AND MAKES QUIET MUSIC.	226	THE OAK	6

	PAGE	TITLE	LINE
MUSICAL			
THE VANISHING OF THE MUSICAL SHIP-WORK AND THE			
CHUCKED BELLS, ...	141	SAINT TO FALL	8
MUSSEL			
AND THE MUSSEL POOLED AND THE HERON	176	POEM IN OCT	3
MUST			
FOR WE MUST WHISPER DOWN THE FUNNEL	17	IN OBLIVION	8
BUT THE VEINS MUST FAIL.	17	IN OBLIVION	14
MUST FEEL LIKE SUCH ENCROACHMENT	20	ENCOMPASSED	4
THERE MUST, BE PRAISED, SOME CERTAINTY, ...	32	OUT OF SIGHS	7
MUST COME CONTENT.	35	LIFT UP FACE	23
IT IS NIGHT'S TERRORS I MUST LEARN TO LOVE, ...	48	LIGHT, I KNOW	13
I MUST LEARN NIGHT'S LIGHT OR GO MAD.	49	LIGHT, I KNOW	30
THE GRAINS OF LIFE MUST SEETHE BENEATH THE SUN, ...	80	ALMANAC TIME	13
BUT SEASONS MUST BE CHALLENGED OR THEY TOTTER	92	BOYS OF SUMMER	25
I MUST WAIT FOR A WOMAN'S SMILE	138	O CHATTERTON	33
THE GENTLE SEASLIDES OF SAYING I MUST UNDO	144	COLOUR OF SAY	5
HAS A VOICE AND A HOUSE, AND THERE AND HERE YOU MUST			
COUCH AND CRY.	146	IF HEAD HURT	25
LUCKLESSLY SHE MUST LIE PATIENT	149	UNLUCKILY FOR	53
NOT YOUR WINGED LUST BUT HIS MUST NOW CHANGE SUIT.	159	TO LEDA	1
NOT YOUR WINGED LUST BUT HIS MUST NOW CHANGE SUIT.	159	TO LEDA	6
AND ALWAYS KNOWN MUST LEAVE	160	DEATHS AND ENT	4
SNIFF, HERE IS SIN! NOW HE MUST GRAPPLE, RISE:	179	NEW QUAY	29
MUST LIE	180	VISION, PRAYER	19
AND I MUST ENTER AGAIN THE ROUND	191	REFUSAL MOURN	7
SO IT MUST HAVE BEEN AFTER THE BIRTH OF THE SIMPLE			
LIGHT	196	FERN HILL	33
THE VOYAGE TO RUIN I MUST RUN, ...	211	POEM ON B'DAY	78
MUSTARDSEED			
IN THE MUSTARDSEED SUN, ...	208	POEM ON B'DAY	1
MUTE			
THERE SHALL BE NO MUTE MOURNING OVER HIS ACRE, ...	64	WOMAN SPEAKS	38
AND SLEEP ROLLS MUTE ABOVE THE BEDS	98	TWILIGHT LOCKS	28
DING DONG FROM THE MUTE TURRETS.	130	SINNERS' BELL	24
MUTED			
IN THE MUTED HOUSE, ONE MINUTE BEFORE	216	ELEGY	14
MUTTER			
MUTTER AND FOUL WINGBEAT OF THE SOLEMNIZING			
NIGHTPRIEST	158	INTO HER HEAD	45
MUTTON			
ALONE ALIVE AMONG HIS MUTTON FOLD, ...	118	ALTARWISE	40
MUZZLED			
IN THE STITCHED WOUND AND CLOTTED WIND, MUZZLED ...	103	I DREAMED MY	15
MY			
IN MY SEASHAKEN HOUSE	3	PROLOGUE	4
FOR MY SAWN, SPLAY SOUNDS), ...	3	PROLOGUE	28
MY DABBED BAY'S DUSK, AS I HACK	4	PROLOGUE	36
I BUILD MY BELLOWING ARK	4	PROLOGUE	44
TO THE BEST OF MY LOVE	4	PROLOGUE	45
TO WALES IN MY ARMS.	4	PROLOGUE	52
O MY RUFFLED RING DOVE	4	PROLOGUE	58
HEARS, THERE, THIS FOX LIGHT, MY FLOOD SHIP'S	4	PROLOGUE	69
(A CLASH OF ANVILS FOR MY	5	PROLOGUE	71
FELLED AND QUILLED, FLASH TO MY PATCH	5	PROLOGUE	83
HULOO, MY PROUD DOVE WITH A FLUTE!	5	PROLOGUE	97
MY ARK SINGS IN THE SUN	5	PROLOGUE	100
TOO FULL WITH BLOOD TO LET MY LOVE FLOW IN.	9	MINUTE'S HOUR	12
I WANT REALITY TO HOLD/ WITHIN MY PALM, ...	9	MINUTE'S HOUR	14
GO IS MY WISH;	9	MINUTE'S HOUR	18

	PAGE	TITLE	LINE

MY (CONTINUED)

	PAGE	TITLE	LINE
OH NO, MY MIND IS YOUR PANOPTICON;	10	COOL, OH NO	20
AND MY THOUGHTS FLOW SO UNEASILY	10	COOL, OH NO	22
YOU WISH TO STAY MY PRISONER	10	COOL, OH NO	27
AND I, YOUR CAPTOR, HAVE MY LOVE TO KEEP	10	COOL, OH NO	29
UPON THE ISLAND OF MY PALM,	11	CABARET	2
WIND IS MY ENEMY YOUR HAIR SHANT STIR	11	AIR BREATHE	3
AND DREW MY SPIRAL BREATH	11	CABARET	7
WHY IS MY HAND TOO BLUNT	12	SKY'S BRIGHT	5
MY HORRID IMAGES FOR ME,	12	SKY'S BRIGHT	7
AND SEES MY BODY GO	12	SKY'S BRIGHT	14
GONE FROM MY PALM TO LEAVE IT MARKED	12	CABARET	16
TO BALANCE ON MY PALMS	13	RAIN CUTS	4
AND WATCH MY HAND,	13	SKY'S BRIGHT	27
MY HAND WITH HONEY THAT HAD CLOSED UPON A FLOWER.	15	FIT LEDA	19
ARE FULL ENOUGH TO DROWN MY MELANCHOLY	17	NATURAL DAY	2
ONE HOUR SPEND MY TIME FOR ME	18	NATURAL DAY	5
OUT OF MY HAND IN STOPPING UP MY MOUTH,	18	NATURAL DAY	16
OUT OF MY HAND IN STOPPING UP MY MOUTH,	18	NATURAL DAY	16
MY EARS, MY NOSE, MY EYES,	18	NATURAL DAY	17
MY EARS, MY NOSE, MY EYES,	18	NATURAL DAY	17
MY EARS, MY NOSE, MY EYES,	18	NATURAL DAY	17
AND ALL MY THIN PREROGATIVE OF TASTE.	18	NATURAL DAY	18
FOR MY MERRY WORDS,	18	NATURAL DAY	23
I, SAID THE BEETLE, OUT OF MY THIN BLACK WOMB,	18	NATURAL DAY	26
OUT OF MY THIN BLACK LIPS,	18	NATURAL DAY	27
OUT OF MY FILTHY EYES	18	NATURAL DAY	29
AND MY CORRUPTING KNOWLEDGE--	18	NATURAL DAY	30
BY LOVE-TIP OR MY HAND'S RED HEAT.	19	IMAGES IN AIR	14
ALTHOUGH THROUGH MY BEWILDERED WAY	21	BEWILDERED WAY	T
ALTHOUGH THROUGH MY BEWILDERED WAY	21	BEWILDERED WAY	1
SOON TO MY CARE, MY LOVE,	21	BEWILDERED WAY	5
SOON TO MY CARE, MY LOVE,	21	BEWILDERED WAY	5
IN TIME, LIKE ALL, THROUGH MY UNREASON	21	BEWILDERED WAY	7
MOULDED MY FORM	26	PERSONAL EPIT	9
THAT STOOD BEFORE MY WINDOW,	33	HELD-OUT HAND	13
I'VE SAID MY PIECE: COUNT OR GO MAD.	33	HELD-OUT HAND	17
LEAP OVER TO MY CRISS-CROSS RHYTHMS.	33	HELD-OUT HAND	23
I'VE SAID MY PIECE.	33	HELD-OUT HAND	24
MY BRAIN CAME CRYING INTO THE FRESH LIGHT,	42	A WAR OF WITS	4
PRAISE THAT MY BODY BE WHOLE, I'VE LIMBS,	42	A WAR OF WITS	8
AS THE HANDS THAT HELD THEM IN MY FATHER'S TIME.	45	PLOUGHMAN GONE	11
THE SAME TUNE AS IN MY FATHER'S TIME:	46	PLOUGHMAN GONE	29
SUCH LIGHT SHALL NOT ILLUMINATE MY FEARS	48	LIGHT, I KNOW	4
MY HEART HURLS FROM MY SIDE AND TEARS	48	LIGHT, I KNOW	8
MY HEART HURLS FROM MY SIDE AND TEARS	48	LIGHT, I KNOW	8
DRIP FROM MY OPEN EYES AS HONEY	48	LIGHT, I KNOW	9
WHO ON HIS CLOUD HEARS ALL MY WISHES,	48	LIGHT, I KNOW	15
BUT LUNAR NIGHT WILL NOT GLOW IN MY BLACKNESS,	49	LIGHT, I KNOW	22
AS CLEARLY AS THE LIGHT OF MY OWN BRAIN,	49	LIGHT, I KNOW	28
WHERE, WHAT'S MY GOD AMONG THIS CRAZY RATTLING	51	OUT OF THE PIT	33
BRUISING, WHERE'S GOD'S MY SHEPHERD, GOD IS LOVE?	51	OUT OF THE PIT	37
WHERE, WHAT'S MY GOD AMONG THIS TAXI STEPPING,	52	OUT OF THE PIT	49
WHERE, WHAT'S MY GOD? I HAVE BEEN MAD, AM MAD,	52	OUT OF THE PIT	63
STUCK STRAW AND SEVEN STARS UPON MY HAIR,	52	OUT OF THE PIT	65
COMES FROM MY EVIL OR MY GOOD. MAD, MAD,	53	OUT OF THE PIT	79
COMES FROM MY EVIL OR MY GOOD. MAD, MAD,	53	OUT OF THE PIT	79
MY GOD'S A SHEPHERD, GOD'S THE LOVE I HOPED.	53	OUT OF THE PIT	93
BREAKS, O MY HEART'S BLOOD, LIKE A HEART AND HILL.	54	WE BY SEASAND	24
DISTURB NO WINDING-SHEETS, MY SON,	60	MEAT ON BONES	6

MY (CONTINUED)	PAGE	TITLE	LINE
AND MY HEART IS CRACKED ACROSS;	61	MEAT ON BONES	18
MY FACE IS HAGGARD IN THE GLASS,	61	MEAT ON BONES	19
MY LIPS ARE WITHERED WITH A KISS,	61	MEAT ON BONES	20
MY BREASTS ARE THIN.	61	MEAT ON BONES	21
REBEL AGAINST MY FATHER'S DREAM	61	MEAT ON BONES	27
WITH THE WIND IN MY HAIR,	62	EARS IN TURRET	22
HUNGERS FOR QUICKENING, AND MY LONELY LIPS	64	WOMAN SPEAKS	36
ONE DAY MY WOMAN'S BODY WILL BE COLD.	64	WOMAN SPEAKS	47
PALM OF THE EARTH, O SPRINKLE ON MY HEAD	65	WOMAN SPEAKS	60
BE SOUR IN MY HAIR. THAT I MAY LEARN	65	WOMAN SPEAKS	63
YOU ARE MY FLESH'S RULER WHOM I TREASON,	67	REALM OF FLESH	11
THAT SHAPED THE JORDAN NEAR MY HOME	68	BEFORE KNOCKED	4
FELT THUD BENEATH MY FLESH'S ARMOUR,	68	BEFORE KNOCKED	9
SWUNG BY MY FATHER FROM HIS DOME.	68	BEFORE KNOCKED	12
AND THE WIND WAS MY SISTER SUITOR;	68	BEFORE KNOCKED	15
MY VEINS FLOWED WITH THE EASTERN WEATHER;	68	BEFORE KNOCKED	17
THE RACK OF DREAMS MY LILY BONES	68	BEFORE KNOCKED	20
MY THROAT KNEW THIRST BEFORE THE STRUCTURE	69	BEFORE KNOCKED	25
MY HEART KNEW LOVE, MY BELLY HUNGER;	69	BEFORE KNOCKED	29
MY HEART KNEW LOVE, MY BELLY HUNGER;	69	BEFORE KNOCKED	29
I SMELT THE MAGGOT IN MY STOOL.	69	BEFORE KNOCKED	30
AND TIME CAST FORTH MY MORTAL CREATURE	69	BEFORE KNOCKED	31
LONG BREATH THAT CARRIED TO MY FATHER	69	BEFORE KNOCKED	41
WHO TOOK MY FLESH AND BONE FOR ARMOUR	69	BEFORE KNOCKED	45
AND DOUBLECROSSED MY MOTHER'S WOMB.	69	BEFORE KNOCKED	46
CUT MY FINGERS ON A ROSE,	70	TAKE NEEDLES	6
AND A CHILD MIGHT BE MY SLAYER,	71	TAKE NEEDLES	17
BY A GODHEAD OF MY OWN.	72	TAKE NEEDLES	40
AND MY FATHER WAS THE LORD.	72	TAKE NEEDLES	44
WILL BE BREATHING BY MY BED.	72	TAKE NEEDLES	48
INTANGIBLE MY WORLD SHALL COME TO NAUGHT,	73	LORD RED HAIL	16
HERE IN MY WILDERNESS WANDERS THE BLOOD;	74	SUN BURNS	3
AND I WILL BUILD MY LIQUID WORLD,	74	WE MOTHERNAKED	13
MY HERO BARES HIS NERVES	75	MY HERO BARES	T
MY HERO BARES HIS NERVES ALONG MY WRIST	75	MY HERO BARES	1
MY HERO BARES HIS NERVES ALONG MY WRIST	75	MY HERO BARES	1
MY FALLING LUNGS, NOR AS THE CYPRESS	75	SONG: LOVE ME	2
LEANS ON MY MORTAL RULER,	75	MY HERO BARES	4
I HUG TO LOVE WITH MY UNRULY SCRAWL	75	MY HERO BARES	8
MY HERO BARES MY SIDE AND SEES HIS HEART	75	MY HERO BARES	11
MY HERO BARES MY SIDE AND SEES HIS HEART	75	MY HERO BARES	11
STRIPPING MY LOIN OF PROMISE,	75	MY HERO BARES	14
MY MAKER'S FLESH THAT GARMENTS MY CLAYFELLOWS.	76	LASHED RINGS	3
MY MAKER'S FLESH THAT GARMENTS MY CLAYFELLOWS.	76	LASHED RINGS	3
TO THAT UNENDING SEA AROUND MY ISLAND	76	LASHED RINGS	8
DRIVES MY GREEN AGE; THAT BLASTS THE ROOTS OF TREES	77	THE FORCE THAT	2
IS MY DESTROYER.	77	THE FORCE THAT	3
MY YOUTH IS BENT BY THE SAME WINTRY FEVER.	77	THE FORCE THAT	5
DRIVES MY RED BLOOD; THAT DRIES THE MOUTHING STREAMS	77	THE FORCE THAT	7
AND I AM DUMB TO MOUTH UNTO MY VEINS	77	THE FORCE THAT	9
HAULS MY SHROUD SAIL.	77	THE FORCE THAT	13
ACQUAINTING ME WITH MY DIVINITY;	77	LASHED RINGS	15
HOW OF MY CLAY IS MADE THE HANGMAN'S LIME.	77	THE FORCE THAT	15
AND THROUGH THESE EARS HE HARKS MY FIRE BURN	77	LASHED RINGS	16
HOW AT MY SHEET GOES THE SAME CROOKED WORM.	77	THE FORCE THAT	22
MY WORLD WAS CHRISTENED IN A STREAM OF MILK.	78	LOVE'S FEVER	7
SHONE IN MY EARS THE LIGHT OF SOUND,	78	LOVE'S FEVER	20
CALLED IN MY EYES THE SOUND OF LIGHT.	78	LOVE'S FEVER	21
THE PLUM MY MOTHER PICKED MATURED SLOWLY,	78	LOVE'S FEVER	25

	PAGE	TITLE	LINE
MY (CONTINUED)			
I LEARNT THE VERBS OF WILL, AND HAD MY SECRET;	79	LOVE'S FEVER	39
THE CODE OF NIGHT TAPPED ON MY TONGUE;	79	LOVE'S FEVER	40
AS FORKS MY EYE;	79	LOVE'S FEVER	47
MY FATHERS' LOVES THAT PULL UPON MY NERVES, ...	80	ALL THAT I OWE	6
MY FATHERS' LOVES THAT PULL UPON MY NERVES, ...	80	ALL THAT I OWE	6
MY SISTERS' TEARS THAT SING UPON MY HEAD, ...	80	ALL THAT I OWE	7
MY SISTERS' TEARS THAT SING UPON MY HEAD, ...	80	ALL THAT I OWE	7
MY BROTHERS' BLOOD THAT SALTS MY OPEN WOUNDS.	80	ALL THAT I OWE	8
MY BROTHERS' BLOOD THAT SALTS MY OPEN WOUNDS.	80	ALL THAT I OWE	8
MY FALLEN FILLED, THAT HAD THE HINT OF DEATH, ...	80	ALL THAT I OWE	10
CAST LIGHT UPON MY WEATHER. I AM HEIR	80	ALL THAT I OWE	15
HERE DRIPS A SILENT HONEY IN MY SHROUD, ...	81	HERE LIE BEAST	10
HERE SLIPS THE GHOST WHO MADE OF MY PALE BED	81	HERE LIE BEAST	11
ALL SUCH DISEASE I DOCTOR IN MY BLOOD, ...	81	ALL THAT I OWE	19
THEN LOOK, MY EYES, UPON THIS BONEBOUND FORTUNE ...	81	ALL THAT I OWE	21
ALL NIGHT MY FORTUNE SLUMBERS IN ITS SHEET.	81	ALL THAT I OWE	27
THEN LOOK, MY HEART, UPON THE SCARLET TROVE, ...	81	ALL THAT I OWE	28
AND LOOK, MY GRAIN, UPON THE FALLING WHEAT;	81	ALL THAT I OWE	29
ALL NIGHT MY FORTUNE SLUMBERS IN ITS SHEET.	81	ALL THAT I OWE	30
A LETTER TO MY AUNT DISCUSSING THE CORRECT APPROACH			
TO MODERN POETRY	83	LETTER TO AUNT	T
TO YOU, MY AUNT, WHO WOULD EXPLORE	83	LETTER TO AUNT	1
SEE, SAYS THE LIME, MY WICKED MILKS	85	SEE, SAYS LIME	1
TO GEOFFREY GRIGSON WITH MY LUFF, ...	85	LETTER TO AUNT	64
MY WINE YOU DRINK, MY BREAD YOU SNAP.	86	BREAD I BREAK	15
MY WINE YOU DRINK, MY BREAD YOU SNAP.	86	BREAD I BREAK	15
THAT DROVE MY STUFF THROUGH SKIN AND GUT;	86	SEE, SAYS LIME	31
O MY UNBORN	87	PAIN BE MUSIC	4
O MY UNSOWN	87	PAIN BE MUSIC	10
O MY UNKNOWN	87	PAIN BE MUSIC	16
O MY UNDONE	87	PAIN BE MUSIC	22
SPUN TO MY SCREWS, YOUR DRY GHOST BLOWS, ...	90	WHERE ONCE THE	2
BROKE THROUGH HER STRAWS, BREAKING MY BANDAGED			
STRING, ...	94	RUB OF LOVE	3
STILL SET TO SCRATCH A LAUGHTER FROM MY LUNG, ...	95	RUB OF LOVE	5
THIS WORLD IS HALF THE DEVIL'S AND MY OWN, ...	95	RUB OF LOVE	29
AN OLD MAN'S SHANK ONE-MARROWED WITH MY BONE, ...	95	RUB OF LOVE	32
I SIT AND WATCH THE WORM BENEATH MY NAIL	95	RUB OF LOVE	34
MY HOUSE WOULD FALL LIKE BREAD ABOUT MY HOMAGE; ...	96	TWELVE	11
MY HOUSE WOULD FALL LIKE BREAD ABOUT MY HOMAGE; ...	96	TWELVE	11
AND I WOULD CHOKE THE HEAVENS WITH MY HYMN	96	TWELVE	12
YOUR MOUTH, MY LOVE, THE THISTLE IN THE KISS?	96	RUB OF LOVE	44
MY JACK OF CHRIST BORN THORNY ON THE TREE?	96	RUB OF LOVE	45
MY WORDY WOUNDS ARE PRINTED WITH YOUR HAIR.	96	RUB OF LOVE	47
MAN BE MY METAPHOR.	96	RUB OF LOVE	49
LOCKED IN THE LONG WORM OF MY FINGER	97	TWILIGHT LOCKS	2
NOR DAMNED THE SEA THAT SPED ABOUT MY FIST, ...	97	TWILIGHT LOCKS	3
I SENT MY CREATURE SCOUTING ON THE GLOBE, ...	97	TWILIGHT LOCKS	9
HAD STRINGED MY FLASK OF MATTER TO HIS RIB.	97	TWILIGHT LOCKS	12
MY FUSES TIMED TO CHARGE HIS HEART, ...	97	TWILIGHT LOCKS	13
WITH FROSTY FINGERS PUNISHES MY HAIR, ...	98	OCTOBER WIND	2
MY BUSY HEART WHO SHUDDERS AS SHE TALKS	98	OCTOBER WIND	7
I SENT MY OWN AMBASSADOR TO LIGHT;	98	TWILIGHT LOCKS	33
TO ROB ME OF MY FLUIDS IN HIS HEART.	98	TWILIGHT LOCKS	36
AWAKE, MY SLEEPER, TO THE SUN, ...	98	TWILIGHT LOCKS	37
DELIVER ME WHO, TIMID IN MY TRIBE, ...	100	RUNNING GRAVE	7
DELIVER ME, MY MASTERS, HEAD AND HEART, ...	100	RUNNING GRAVE	11
FOR, SUNDAY FACED, WITH DUSTERS IN MY GLOVE, ...	100	RUNNING GRAVE	16
STRIDE THROUGH CADAVER'S COUNTRY IN MY FORCE, ...	100	RUNNING GRAVE	21

		PAGE	TITLE	LINE
MY (CONTINUED)				
MY PICKBRAIN MASTERS MORSING ON THE STONE	....	100	RUNNING GRAVE	22
DESCENDS, MY MASTERS, ON THE ENTERED HONOUR.	....	100	RUNNING GRAVE	28
SO, PLANING-HEELED, I FLEW ALONG MY MAN	....	101	FELLOWED SLEEP	4
MY MOTHERS-EYED, UPON THE TOPS OF TREES;	....	101	FELLOWED SLEEP	9
'MY FATHERS' GLOBE KNOCKS ON ITS NAVE AND SINGS.'		101	FELLOWED SLEEP	11
ALL, MEN MY MADMEN, THE UNWHOLESOME WIND	....	101	RUNNING GRAVE	46
I DREAMED MY GENESIS	....	102	I DREAMED MY	T
I DREAMED MY GENESIS IN SWEAT OF SLEEP, BREAKING		102	I DREAMED MY	1
FADED MY ELBOW GHOST, THE MOTHERS-EYED,	....	102	FELLOWED SLEEP	16
I SPELT MY VISION WITH A HAND AND HAIR,	....	102	FELLOWED SLEEP	23
MY FATHERS' GHOST IS CLIMBING IN THE RAIN.	....	102	FELLOWED SLEEP	30
MY WORLD IS PYRAMID	....	103	WORLD PYRAMID	T
A CREATURE IN MY BONES I	....	103	I DREAMED MY	10
ROUNDED MY GLOBE OF HERITAGE, JOURNEY	....	103	I DREAMED MY	11
I DREAMED MY GENESIS AND DIED AGAIN, SHRAPNEL	.....	103	I DREAMED MY	13
SHARP IN MY SECOND DEATH I MARKED THE HILLS, HARVEST		103	I DREAMED MY	17
MY BLOOD UPON THE TEMPERED DEAD, FORCING	....	103	I DREAMED MY	19
MY SECOND STRUGGLING FROM THE GRASS.	....	103	I DREAMED MY	20
AND POWER WAS CONTAGIOUS IN MY BIRTH, SECOND	......	103	I DREAMED MY	21
I DREAMED MY GENESIS IN SWEAT OF DEATH, FALLEN	....	103	I DREAMED MY	25
MY WORLD IS PYRAMID. THE PADDED MUMMER	....	104	WORLD PYRAMID	31
MY EGYPT'S ARMOUR BUCKLING IN ITS SHEET,	....	104	WORLD PYRAMID	34
MY WORLD IS CYPRESS, AND AN ENGLISH VALLEY.	....	105	WORLD PYRAMID	37
I PIECE MY FLESH THAT RATTLED ON THE YARDS	....	105	WORLD PYRAMID	38
MY GRAVE IS WATERED BY THE CROSSING JORDAN.	......	105	WORLD PYRAMID	43
DRIP ON MY DEAD HOUSE GARDEN.	....	105	WORLD PYRAMID	45
WHO SEEK ME LANDWARD, MARKING IN MY MOUTH	....	105	WORLD PYRAMID	46
BLEED FROM MY BURNING FORK AND SMELL MY HEELS.	....	105	WORLD PYRAMID	52
BLEED FROM MY BURNING FORK AND SMELL MY HEELS.	....	105	WORLD PYRAMID	52
BINDING MY ANGEL'S HOOD.	....	105	WORLD PYRAMID	54
MY CLAY UNSUCKLED AND MY SALT UNBORN,	....	105	WORLD PYRAMID	58
MY CLAY UNSUCKLED AND MY SALT UNBORN,	....	105	WORLD PYRAMID	58
HOW NOW MY FLESH, MY NAKED FELLOW,	....	106	ALL ALL AND	7
HOW NOW MY FLESH, MY NAKED FELLOW,	....	106	ALL ALL AND	7
FEAR NOT THE WORKING WORLD, MY MORTAL,	....	106	ALL ALL AND	13
MAN OF MY FLESH, THE JAWBONE RIVEN,	....	106	ALL ALL AND	19
KNOW, O MY BONE, THE JOINTED LEVER,	....	106	ALL ALL AND	22
I, IN MY INTRICATE IMAGE	....	108	I, IN IMAGE	T
I, IN MY INTRICATE IMAGE, STRIDE ON TWO LEVELS,	...	108	I, IN IMAGE	1
LAYING MY GHOST IN METAL,	....	108	I, IN IMAGE	3
MY HALF GHOST IN ARMOUR HOLD HARD IN DEATH'S CORRIDOR,	....	108	I, IN IMAGE	5
TO MY MAN-IRON SIDLE.	....	108	I, IN IMAGE	6
NOW JACK MY FATHERS LET THE TIME-FACED CROOK,	.....	108	GRIEF THIEF	15
SHAPE WITH MY FATHERS' THIEVES.	....	108	GRIEF THIEF	28
IMAGE OF IMAGES, MY METAL PHANTOM	....	109	I, IN IMAGE	14
MY MAN OF LEAVES AND THE BRONZE ROOT, MORTAL, UNMORTAL,	....	109	I, IN IMAGE	16
I, IN MY FUSION OF ROSE AND MALE MOTION,	....	109	I, IN IMAGE	17
MY IMAGES STALK THE TREES AND THE SLANT SAP'S TUNNEL,		109	I, IN IMAGE	25
SUFFER, MY TOPSY-TURVIES, THAT A DOUBLE ANGEL	.....	111	I, IN IMAGE	77
MY GREAT BLOOD'S IRON SINGLE	....	111	I, IN IMAGE	93
FOR MY TALL TOWER'S SAKE CAST IN HER STONE?	....	112	NOT FATHER ME	2
THE LOVERS' HOUSE, LIE SUFFERING MY STAIN?	....	112	NOT FATHER ME	4
FOR MY TALL TURRETS CARRY AS YOUR SIN?	....	112	NOT FATHER ME	6
ADORE MY WINDOWS FOR THEIR SUMMER SCENE?	....	112	NOT FATHER ME	8
AM I NOT SISTER, TOO, WHO IS MY SAVIOUR?	....	112	NOT FATHER ME	12
WHERE BIRD AND SHELL ARE BABBLING IN MY TOWER?	....	112	NOT FATHER ME	14
UP ROSE THE ABRAHAM-MAN, MAD FOR MY SAKE,	....	112	NOT FATHER ME	19

	PAGE	TITLE	LINE
MY (CONTINUED)			
MY GHOST IN HIS METAL NEPTUNE	112	I, IN IMAGE	105
AND MY IMAGES ROARED AND ROSE ON HEAVEN'S HILL.	112	I, IN IMAGE	108
UNSHELVE THAT ALL MY GRISTLES HAVE A GOWN	113	SERVANT SUN	6
TELLS YOU AND YOU, MY MASTERS, AS HIS STRANGE	113	SERVANT SUN	13
WHO RAZED MY WOODEN FOLLY STANDS AGHAST,	113	NOT FATHER ME	22
WOE TO THE WINDY MASONS AT MY SHELTER?	113	NOT FATHER ME	30
HOW SOON MY LEVEL, LORD,	114	SERVANT SUN	22
WHO IS MY GRIEF,	115	A GRIEF AGO	9
WRENCHED BY MY FINGERMAN, THE LEADEN BUD	115	A GRIEF AGO	11
SCRAPED AT MY CRADLE IN A WALKING WORD	117	ALTARWISE	11
AND SHARE MY BED WITH CAPRICORN AND CANCER.	117	ALTARWISE	14
RIP OF THE VAULTS, I TOOK MY MARROW-LADLE	118	ALTARWISE	35
(MY SHAPE OF AGE NAGGING THE WOUNDED WHISPER.)	118	ALTARWISE	46
MY CAMEL'S EYES WILL NEEDLE THROUGH THE SHROUD.	118	ALTARWISE	52
ROSE MY BYZANTINE ADAM IN THE NIGHT.	118	ALTARWISE	62
UNDER THE MILKY MUSHROOMS SLEW MY HUNGER,	118	ALTARWISE	64
PLUCK, COCK, MY SEA EYE, SAID MEDUSA'S SCRIPTURE,	119	ALTARWISE	75
LOP, LOVE, MY FORK TONGUE, SAID THE PIN-HILLED NETTLE;	119	ALTARWISE	76
TIME'S TUNE MY LADIES WITH THE TEATS OF MUSIC,	119	ALTARWISE	91
TIME IS THE TUNE MY LADIES LEND THEIR HEARTBREAK,	119	ALTARWISE	95
THE WORLD'S MY WOUND, GOD'S MARY IN HER GRIEF,	120	ALTARWISE	102
TILL THE THREE-COLOURED RAINBOW FROM MY NIPPLES	120	ALTARWISE	107
SUFFER THE HEAVEN'S CHILDREN THROUGH MY HEARTBEAT.	120	ALTARWISE	112
WEDS MY LONG GENTLEMAN TO DUSTS AND FURIES;	120	ALTARWISE	122
WITH PRIEST AND PHARAOH BED MY GENTLE WOUND,	120	ALTARWISE	123
AND RIVERS OF THE DEAD AROUND MY NECK.	120	ALTARWISE	126
MY NEST OF MERCIES IN THE RUDE, RED TREE.	121	ALTARWISE	140
DRIVES FORTH MY MEN, MY CHILDREN, FROM THE HANGING SOUTH.	122	HOLD HARD	6
DRIVES FORTH MY MEN, MY CHILDREN, FROM THE HANGING SOUTH.	122	HOLD HARD	6
HOLD HARD, MY COUNTRY CHILDREN IN THE WORLD OF TALES,	122	HOLD HARD	10
STALKING MY CHILDREN'S FACES WITH A TAIL OF BLOOD,	122	HOLD HARD	20
FROM ALL MY MORTAL LOVERS WITH A STARBOARD SMILE;	123	FOSTER LIGHT	21
HOLD HARD, MY COUNTY DARLINGS, FOR A HAWK DESCENDS,	123	HOLD HARD	22
NOR WHEN MY LOVE LIES IN THE CROSS-BONED DRIFT	123	FOSTER LIGHT	22
NOW THAT MY SYMBOLS HAVE OUTELBOWED SPACE,	124	TODAY, INSECT	2
SHAPED MY CLAYFELLOW, AND THE HEAVEN'S ARK	124	FOSTER LIGHT	26
'ADAM I LOVE, MY MADMEN'S LOVE IS ENDLESS,	125	TODAY, INSECT	23
MY CROSS OF TALES BEHIND THE FABULOUS CURTAIN.'	125	TODAY, INSECT	26
THEN WAS MY NEOPHYTE	128	MY NEOPHYTE	T
THEN WAS MY NEOPHYTE,	128	MY NEOPHYTE	1
MY SEA HERMAPHRODITE,	128	MY NEOPHYTE	7
HE FILMS MY VANITY.	129	MY NEOPHYTE	25
LOVE'S IMAGE TILL MY HEARTBONE BREAKS	129	MY NEOPHYTE	35
WHO KILLS MY HISTORY?	129	MY NEOPHYTE	37
HARBOURS MY ANCHORED TONGUE, SLIPS THE QUAYSTONE,	131	I MAKE THIS IN	3
WEIGHED IN ROCK SHROUD, IS MY PROUD PYRAMID;	132	I MAKE THIS IN	41
RAPE AND REBELLION IN THE NURSERIES OF MY FACE,	133	MAKE ME A MASK	3
THE TERRIBLE WORLD MY BROTHER BARES HIS SKIN.	133	I MAKE THIS IN	60
DELIVERED SEAS MY LOVE FROM HER PROUD PLACE	133	I MAKE THIS IN	62
AND THOUGH MY LOVE PULLS THE PALE, NIPPLED AIR,	133	I MAKE THIS IN	66
HOW SHALL MY ANIMAL	134	HOW MY ANIMAL	T
HOW SHALL MY ANIMAL	134	HOW MY ANIMAL	1
BEHIND MY HEAD A SQUARE OF SKY SAGS OVER	134	NOT FROM ANGER	8
THAT BURNS ALONG MY EYES.	134	NOT FROM ANGER	14
TO CLASP MY FURY ON GROUND	135	HOW MY ANIMAL	30
LIE DRY, REST ROBBED, MY BEAST.	135	HOW MY ANIMAL	42

	PAGE	TITLE	LINE
MY (CONTINUED)			
AND DUG YOUR GRAVE IN MY BREAST.	135	HOW MY ANIMAL	44
AND TAKE ANOTHER NIBBLE AT MY FLASK.	137	O CHATTERTON	16
WHEN ALL MY FIVE AND COUNTRY SENSES SEE	138	FIVE & COUNTRY	T
WHEN ALL MY FIVE AND COUNTRY SENSES SEE,	138	FIVE & COUNTRY	1
WOMEN FIGURES ROUND MY CELL,	138	O CHATTERTON	30
BEFORE I HEARD IN MY MOTHER'S SIDE	139	TOMBSTONE TOLD	6
MY NOSTRILS SEE HER BREATH BURN LIKE A BUSH.	139	FIVE & COUNTRY	10
MY ONE AND NOBLE HEART HAS WITNESSES	139	FIVE & COUNTRY	11
BELLY OF THE RICH YEAR AND THE BIG PURSE OF MY BODY	140	NO WORK WORDS	2
I BITTERLY TAKE TO TASK MY POVERTY AND CRAFT:	140	NO WORK WORDS	3
ANCIENT WOODS OF MY BLOOD, DASH DOWN TO THE NUT OF THE SEAS	140	NO WORK WORDS	11
BUT MY WOMB WAS BELLOWING	140	TOMBSTONE TOLD	27
AND I FELT WITH MY BARE FALL	140	TOMBSTONE TOLD	28
O WAKE IN ME IN MY HOUSE IN THE MUD	142	SAINT TO FALL	26
TWENTY-FOUR YEARS REMIND THE TEARS OF MY EYES.	143	24 YEARS	1
THEY RETCH INTO MY SECRET NIGHT	143	THE MOLLS	5
WITH MY RED VEINS FULL OF MONEY,	143	24 YEARS	7
GENTLY THEY SIGH TO MY BEHIND	143	THE MOLLS	9
PEACOCKSTAIN'S POEMS ON MY BED.	143	THE MOLLS	12
SOAKED MY TABLE THE UGLIER SIDE OF A HILL	144	COLOUR OF SAY	2
NOW MY SAYING SHALL BE MY UNDOING,	144	COLOUR OF SAY	12
NOW MY SAYING SHALL BE MY UNDOING,	144	COLOUR OF SAY	12
'IF MY HEAD HURT A HAIR'S FOOT'	145	IF HEAD HURT	T
'IF MY HEAD HURT A HAIR'S FOOT	145	IF HEAD HURT	1
PACK BACK THE DOWNED BONE. IF THE UNPRICKED BALL OF MY BREATH	145	IF HEAD HURT	2
SOONER DROP WITH THE WORM OF THE ROPES ROUND MY THROAT	145	IF HEAD HURT	4
'IF MY BUNCHED, MONKEY COMING IS CRUEL	145	IF HEAD HURT	11
RAGE ME BACK TO THE MAKING HOUSE. MY HAND UNRAVEL	145	IF HEAD HURT	12
BEND, IF MY JOURNEY ACHE, DIRECTION LIKE AN ARC OR MAKE	145	IF HEAD HURT	14
YOU MY FRIEND THERE WITH A WINNING AIR	146	TO OTHERS	3
BRASSILY AT MY SHYEST SECRET,	146	TO OTHERS	5
TILL THE SWEET TOOTH OF MY LOVE BIT DRY,	146	TO OTHERS	7
MY DEAR WOULD I CHANGE MY TEARS OR YOUR IRON HEAD.	146	IF HEAD HURT	18
MY DEAR WOULD I CHANGE MY TEARS OR YOUR IRON HEAD.	146	IF HEAD HURT	18
THRUST, MY DAUGHTER OR SON, TO ESCAPE, THERE IS NONE, NONE, NONE,	146	IF HEAD HURT	19
'NOW TO AWAKE HUSKED OF GESTURES AND MY JOY LIKE A CAVE	146	IF HEAD HURT	21
O MY LOST LOVE BOUNCED FROM A GOOD HOME;	146	IF HEAD HURT	23
THE GRAVE AND MY CALM BODY ARE SHUT TO YOUR COMING AS STONE,	146	IF HEAD HURT	29
THE PYRE YET TO BE LIGHTED OF MY SINS AND DAYS,	147	UNLUCKILY FOR	3
DEAD AND GONE, DEDICATE FOREVER TO MY SELF	147	UNLUCKILY FOR	6
AND MY WHOLE HEART UNDER YOUR HAMMER,	147	TO OTHERS	13
BENEATH MY LIFE, THAT SIGHS FOR THE SEDUCER'S COMING	147	UNLUCKILY FOR	13
MY HOLY LUCKY BODY	147	UNLUCKILY FOR	16
MY FRIENDS WERE ENEMIES ON STILTS	147	TO OTHERS	20
NEVER SHALL MY SELF CHANT	148	UNLUCKILY FOR	25
OF SHADES, SYMBOL OF DESIRE BEYOND MY HOURS	148	UNLUCKILY FOR	35
LOVE, MY FATE GOT LUCKILY,	148	UNLUCKILY FOR	43
WITH IMMORTALITY AT MY SIDE LIKE CHRIST THE SKY.	148	UNLUCKILY FOR	49
O MY DEAR IT'S NEVER TOO LATE	149	PAPER & STICKS	11
I'LL SHARE MY MONEY AND WE'LL RUN FOR JOY	149	PAPER & STICKS	14
SHARP AND SHRILL MY SILLY TONGUE SCRATCHES	149	PAPER & STICKS	16

		PAGE	TITLE	LINE
MY (CONTINUED)				
AND THE VAULTING BIRD BE STILL. O MY TRUE LOVE, HOLD ME.		149	UNLUCKILY FOR	54
CRY MY SEA TOWN WAS BREAKING.		150	WHEN I WOKE	27
AND THE COINS ON MY EYELIDS SANG LIKE SHELLS.		150	WHEN I WOKE	30
WHEN MY PINNED-AROUND-THE-SPIRIT		151	BELOW A TIME	2
MY PAID-FOR SLAVED-FOR OWN TOO LATE		151	BELOW A TIME	6
MY SILLY SUIT, HARDLY YET SUFFERED FOR,		152	BELOW A TIME	29
HEAD, DECEIVED, I BELIEVED, MY MAKER,		152	BELOW A TIME	34
ON THE OLD SEAS FROM STORIES, THRASHING MY WINGS,		152	BELOW A TIME	36
WITH MY CHERRY CAPPED DANGLER GREEN AS SEAWEED		152	BELOW A TIME	45
ON MY CLEAVING ARM AS I BLASTED IN A WAVE.		152	BELOW A TIME	48
WITH MY FISHTAIL HANDS AND GENTLY		154	RETURN	5
I SPENT MY UNWASTEABLE		154	RETURN	9
OPENED MY BREAST AND INTO		155	RETURN	35
THE WEIGHING-SCALES, OF MY HAND.		155	RETURN	43
ALONE WITH MY BOUNCING BAG,		155	RETURN	45
OR LIFT MY HAT TO UNSEEN		155	RETURN	48
MY CAVERNOUS, FEATHERBED SELF.		156	RETURN	76
OF MY WEEK IN THE DIRTBOX		156	RETURN	91
CARRION, PARADISE, CHIRRUP MY BRIGHT YOLK.		159	INTO HER HEAD	60
FOR MY SAKE SAIL, AND NEVER LOOK BACK,		162	LONG-LEGGED	11
MY MAST IS A BELL-SPIRE,		164	LONG-LEGGED	76
STRIKE AND SMOOTHE, FOR MY DECKS ARE DRUMS,		164	LONG-LEGGED	77
TO SHARE MY ROOM IN THE HOUSE NOT RIGHT IN THE HEAD,		169	LOVE IN ASYLUM	2
ON THE MADHOUSE BOARDS WORN THIN BY MY WALKING TEARS.		170	LOVE IN ASYLUM	15
IN THE FOUNTAIN BASIN WHERE I SAILED MY SHIP		171	THE HUNCHBACK	10
SILENT IN MY SERVICE		174	FIRE RAID	49
LAST NIGHT I DIVED MY BEGGAR ARM		175	MY BEGGAR ARM	T
LAST NIGHT I DIVED MY BEGGAR ARM		175	MY BEGGAR ARM	1
WOULD PLUNGE MY BETRAYAL FROM SHEET TO SKY		175	MY BEGGAR ARM	6
IT WAS MY THIRTIETH YEAR TO HEAVEN		176	POEM IN OCT	1
WOKE TO MY HEARING FROM HARBOUR AND NEIGHBOUR WOOD		176	POEM IN OCT	2
NIGHT FOR MY SAKE,		176	BREATH SHED	4
MY LOVE AS A ROUND WAVE		176	BREATH SHED	10
MY BIRTHDAY BEGAN WITH THE WATER-		177	POEM IN OCT	11
BIRDS AND THE BIRDS OF THE WINGED TREES FLYING MY NAME		177	POEM IN OCT	12
AND WALKED ABROAD IN A SHOWER OF ALL MY DAYS.		177	POEM IN OCT	16
MY BIRTHDAY		178	POEM IN OCT	39
THAT HIS TEARS BURNED MY CHEEKS AND HIS HEART MOVED IN MINE.		178	POEM IN OCT	52
AND THERE COULD I MARVEL MY BIRTHDAY		178	POEM IN OCT	61
IT WAS MY THIRTIETH		178	POEM IN OCT	65
O MAY MY HEART'S TRUTH		178	POEM IN OCT	68
BORROW MY EYES. THE DARKENING SEA FLINGS LEA		179	NEW QUAY	2
THE SALTY SCENE AND MY PLAYERED GOB CURVING		179	NEW QUAY	14
SO LOUD TO MY OWN		180	VISION, PRAYER	5
BLINDS MY		181	VISION, PRAYER	67
THE INMOST MARROW OF MY HEART BONE		183	VISION, PRAYER	118
HIS LIGHTNING ANSWERS MY		185	VISION, PRAYER	201
CRY. MY VOICE BURNS IN HIS HAND.		185	VISION, PRAYER	202
THAT ONE DARK I OWE MY LIGHT,		186	HOLY SPRING	9
MY ARISING PRODIGAL		186	HOLY SPRING	18
OR SOW MY SALT SEED		191	REFUSAL MOURN	11
YOU MAY NOT SEE, MY SON,		192	SIDE OF TRUTH	2
FOR MY VOYAGE TO BEGIN TO THE END OF MY WOUND,		194	SLEEP BECALMED	11
FOR MY VOYAGE TO BEGIN TO THE END OF MY WOUND,		194	SLEEP BECALMED	11
SANG TO MY HORN, THE FOXES ON THE HILLS BARKED CLEAR AND COLD,		195	FERN HILL	16

		PAGE	TITLE	LINE
MY (CONTINUED)				
IN MY CRAFT OR SULLEN ART		196	CRAFT OR ART	T
IN MY CRAFT OR SULLEN ART		196	CRAFT OR ART	1
I RAN MY HEEDLESS WAYS,		196	FERN HILL	40
MY WISHES RACED THROUGH THE HOUSE HIGH HAY		196	FERN HILL	41
AND NOTHING I CARED, AT MY SKY BLUE TRADES, THAT TIME ALLOWS		196	FERN HILL	42
UP TO THE SWALLOW THRONGED LOFT BY THE SHADOW OF MY HAND,		196	FERN HILL	47
THOUGH I SANG IN MY CHAINS LIKE THE SEA.		196	FERN HILL	54
NEVER AND NEVER, MY GIRL RIDING FAR AND NEAR		197	COUNTRY SLEEP	1
MY DEAR, MY DEAR,		197	COUNTRY SLEEP	5
MY DEAR, MY DEAR,		197	COUNTRY SLEEP	5
MY GIRL RANGING THE NIGHT IN THE ROSE AND SHIRE		197	COUNTRY SLEEP	9
NOR HEED MY CRAFT OR ART.		197	CRAFT OR ART	20
AND STAVED, AND RIVEN AMONG PLUMES MY RIDER WEEP.		198	COUNTRY SLEEP	16
NEVER, MY GIRL, UNTIL TOLLED TO SLEEP BY THE STERN		198	COUNTRY SLEEP	21
OF THE HEARTHSTONE TALES MY OWN, LOST LOVE; AND THE SOUL WALKS		199	COUNTRY SLEEP	53
THE HAYGOLD HAIRED, MY LOVE ASLEEP, AND THE RIFT BLUE		200	COUNTRY SLEEP	88
ROUND THE SUN, HE COMES TO MY LOVE LIKE THE DESIGNED SNOW,		200	COUNTRY SLEEP	96
COMES DESIGNED TO MY LOVE TO STEAL NOT HER TIDE RAKING		200	COUNTRY SLEEP	100
MY DEAR THIS NIGHT HE COMES AND NIGHT WITHOUT END MY DEAR		201	COUNTRY SLEEP	108
MY DEAR THIS NIGHT HE COMES AND NIGHT WITHOUT END MY DEAR		201	COUNTRY SLEEP	108
WHOEVER I WOULD WITH MY WICKED EYES,		206	LAMENT	9
BLACK NIGHT, I LEFT MY QUIVERING PRINTS.		206	LAMENT	24
BRANDY AND RIPE IN MY BRIGHT, BASS PRIME,		206	LAMENT	28
FOR MY SULKING, SKULKING, COAL BLACK SOUL!		206	LAMENT	36
AND I GAVE MY SOUL A BLIND, SLASHED EYE,		207	LAMENT	45
TIDY AND CURSED IN MY DOVE COOED ROOM		207	LAMENT	52
FOR, OH, MY SOUL FOUND A SUNDAY WIFE		207	LAMENT	54
INNOCENCE SWEETENS MY LAST BLACK BREATH,		207	LAMENT	58
MODESTY HIDES MY THIGHS IN HER WINGS,		207	LAMENT	59
AND ALL THE DEADLY VIRTUES PLAGUE MY DEATH!		207	LAMENT	60
AND YOU, MY FATHER, THERE ON THE SAD HEIGHT,		208	NOT GO GENTLE	16
COUNT MY BLESSINGS ALOUD:		211	POEM ON B'DAY	81
AND MY SHINING MEN NO MORE ALONE		211	POEM ON B'DAY	107
(WHOM MY HEART HEARS),		215	COUNTRY HEAVEN	2
WILL NEVER NEVER GO OUT OF MY MIND.		217	ELEGY	20
UNTIL I DIE HE WILL NOT LEAVE MY SIDE.		217	ELEGY	40
BUT MY GREATEST DELIGHT IS TO TAKE A GOOD BITE		221	SONG OF DOG	13
THESE WERE MY DESIRES, ETERNAL AS MOUNTAINS,		223	IDYLL UNFORGET	9
THESE WERE THE WHISPERINGS THAT SIGHED ON MY LIPS AT DUSK,		223	IDYLL UNFORGET	10
THAT PLAYED IN VOICELESS FROLIC AT THE THRESHOLD OF MY HEART.		223	IDYLL UNFORGET	12
HAVE NOT ADORED MY BODY AS IT SOFTLY SMOOTHED THEIR SKIN.		223	IDYLL UNFORGET	16
I HAVE FELT THE SILK WIND BRUSH MY LIPS;		224	IDYLL UNFORGET	19
I HAVE MADE MY THROAT AN ARBOUR FOR FORGOTTEN SONGS.		224	IDYLL UNFORGET	20
AND I HAVE REFLECTED ITS COLOURS IN THE PEACE OF MY EYES;		224	IDYLL UNFORGET	24
AND MY FINGERS HAVE TOUCHED THE GLASS OF THE WATERS,		224	IDYLL UNFORGET	30
AND HOURS MADE LITTLE I HAVE DIPPED MY ARMS IN THEIR RAPTURE;		224	IDYLL UNFORGET	31
MY TEARS ARE LIKE THE QUIET DRIFT		225	CLOWN IN MOON	1

		PAGE	TITLE	LINE
MY	**(CONTINUED)**			
	AND ALL MY GRIEF FLOWS FROM THE RIFT	225	CLOWN IN MOON	3
	AND MAKE MY GARDEN GLAD AND GAY.	227	TRIOLET	3
	MY RIVER	228	MY RIVER	T
	MY RIVER, EVEN THOUGH IT LIFTS	228	MY RIVER	1
	THEY TO MY BLOSSOMS WING THEIR WAY,	228	TRIOLET	5
	MY RIVER CANNOT RUB YOUR BRIGHT STONE,	230	MY RIVER	41
	MY RIVER HAS HIGH WAVES,	230	MY RIVER	44
	THEN, WHEN I OPEN MY MOUTH,	231	YOUR VOICE	6
	TAKE YOU INTO MY OWN PLACE	232	YOUR VOICE	14
	NO THOUGHT CAN TROUBLE MY UNWHOLESOME POSE	233	NO THOUGHT	T
	NO THOUGHT CAN TROUBLE MY UNWHOLESOME POSE,	233	NO THOUGHT	1
	NOR MAKE THE STERN SHELL OF MY SPIRIT MOVE.	233	NO THOUGHT	2
	AND MAKE YOU BITTER WITH MY COLD,	233	NO THOUGHT	6
	MY NET THAT TAKES TO BREAK	233	NO THOUGHT	7
	INTO MY EXOTIC COMPOSURE?	233	NO THOUGHT	23
	TO WING MY SHOULDERS AND MY FEET?	234	NO, PIGEON	6
	TO WING MY SHOULDERS AND MY FEET?	234	NO, PIGEON	6
	AH, NIGHTINGALE, MY VOICE	234	NO, PIGEON	8
	DOING MY LITTLE TRICKS OF SPEECH AGAIN	234	NO, PIGEON	20
	WITH ALL MY USUAL CARE.	234	NO, PIGEON	21
	MY LOVE FOR HER IS LIKE THE MOVING OF A CLOUD	235	WOMAN TAPESTRY	13
	WITH THE POWER OF MY HANDS	235	WOMAN TAPESTRY	36
	AND THE CRUELTY OF MY SUBTLE EYES,	236	WOMAN TAPESTRY	37
	THE GESTURES OF MY LOVE	236	WOMAN TAPESTRY	68
	YOU BATTER BACK MY FEET),	237	PILLAR BREAKS	5
	RECALL MY OLD DESIRE	237	WOMAN TAPESTRY	70
	TO-DAY, IF ALL MY SENSES ACT,	238	MAKES INTERVALS	9
	I'LL MAKE YOUR SHAPE MY OWN,	238	MAKES INTERVALS	10
	CHALLENGE MY METAMORPHOSIS,	238	MAKES INTERVALS	15
	BE FREE, (WIND FOR MY TREE AND WATER FOR MY FLOWER),	239	LET ME ESCAPE	2
	BE FREE, (WIND FOR MY TREE AND WATER FOR MY FLOWER),	239	LET ME ESCAPE	2
	OR CRUSH THEIR VIPER HEADS BENEATH MY FOOT.	239	LET ME ESCAPE	5
	MY STRENGTH SHALL SAP YOUR OWN;	239	LET ME ESCAPE	9
	GLASS TO MY HANDS ENDOWED WITH DOUBLE STRENGTH.	239	MAKES INTERVALS	19
	THERE'LL BE MY BONE TO GO:	239	MAKES INTERVALS	21
	AND TWINE THE LIMBS AROUND MY HANDS.	239	MAKES INTERVALS	24
	TO MAIM OR STING MY ARM,	240	TWINING HEAD	2
	BUT IF IT STINGS MY BODY DEAD	240	TWINING HEAD	3
	UPON MY FLESH AND SKIN,	240	TWINING HEAD	10
	MY APTITUDE FOR SIN.	240	TWINING HEAD	12
MYCENAE'S				
	THE DEAD QUEEN WALKETH WITH MYCENAE'S KING	57	GREEK PLAY	23
MYSELF				
	AND THROUGH THESE EYES GOD MARKS MYSELF REVOLVING,	76	LASHED RINGS	12
	ONCE I HAD A RICH BOY FOR MYSELF	149	PAPER & STICKS	4
	NOW IN THE DARK THERE IS ONLY YOURSELF AND MYSELF.	153	WAS A SAVIOUR	24
	MYSELF TO SET FOOT	177	POEM IN OCT	8
	I TAKE YOU TO MYSELF, SWEET PAIN,	233	NO THOUGHT	5
	TO IMITATE MYSELF MECHANICALLY,	234	NO, PIGEON	19
	TO SEE THE SUN MYSELF,	239	LET ME ESCAPE	11
MYSELVES				
	MYSELVES	173	FIRE RAID	1
	MYSELVES GRIEVE NOW, AND MIRACLES CANNOT ATONE.	173	FIRE RAID	16
	YOUR DEATH THAT MYSELVES THE BELIEVERS	173	FIRE RAID	20
MYSTERIES				
	AND COUNT THE TAKEN, FORSAKEN MYSTERIES IN A BAD DARK.	140	NO WORK WORDS	9
MYSTERY				
	OF ALL THE MYSTERY THERE IS IN LIFE	22	ON QUIET NIGHT	3

	PAGE	TITLE	LINE
MYSTERY (CONTINUED)			
HIS REELS AND MYSTERY	129	MY NEOPHYTE	31
AND THE MYSTERY	178	POEM IN OCT	58
I HAVE KNOWN THE MYSTERY OF THE SEA TO BE MANTLED			
ABOUT ME;	223	IDYLL UNFORGET	18
MYSTIC			
SO SOLVE THE MYSTIC SUN, THE WIFE OF LIGHT, ...	128	NOW, SAY NAY	26
WE MAKE ME MYSTIC AS THE ARM OF AIR, ...	128	NOW, SAY NAY	34
MYSTICS			
THE MESSAGE COMES FROM NEGRO MYSTICS, ...	58	TO ARCHITECTS	7
MYTH			
HELL IN A HORN OF SULPHUR AND THE CLOVEN MYTH, ...	122	INCARNATE DEVL	16
MYTHS			
NOR FALLS TO HIS GREEN MYTHS?	129	MY NEOPHYTE	18
NACREOUS			
OR A NACREOUS SLEEP AMONG SOFT PARTICLES AND CHARMS	146	IF HEAD HURT	17
NAGGING			
(MY SHAPE OF AGE NAGGING THE WOUNDED WHISPER.)	118	ALTARWISE	46
NAIL			
TOUCHED, BY A FINGER'S NAIL, TO DUST.	20	THE NEOPHYTE	25
AND NAIL THE MERRY SQUIRES TO THE TREES;	93	BOYS OF SUMMER	45
I SIT AND WATCH THE WORM BENEATH MY NAIL	95	RUB OF LOVE	34
ADD ONE MORE NAIL OF PRAISE ON TO THE CROSS, ...	96	TWELVE	7
NAILED			
AND THE WAILING HEART'S NAILED TO THE SIDE.	74	SUN BURNS	5
NAILED WITH AN OPEN EYE, IN THE BOWL OF WOUNDS AND			
WEED	135	HOW MY ANIMAL	29
NAILS			
THOUGH THEY BE MAD AND DEAD AS NAILS, ...	50	NO DOMINION	24
DROVE IN THE HEAVEN-DRIVEN OF THE NAILS	120	ALTARWISE	106
AND MILK-WHITE NAILS.	229	MY RIVER	29
NAKED			
DEAD MEN NAKED THEY SHALL BE ONE	49	NO DOMINION	2
DOWN PELTS THE NAKED WEATHER;	58	HERE IN SPRING	3
TREAD, LIKE A NAKED VENUS, ...	75	MY HERO BARES	12
UP NAKED STAIRS, A TURTLE IN A HEARSE, ...	99	RUNNING GRAVE	4
I FLED THE EARTH AND, NAKED, CLIMBED THE WEATHER, .	101	FELLOWED SLEEP	6
REROBING OF THE NAKED GHOST. MANHOOD	103	I DREAMED MY	23
HOW NOW MY FLESH, MY NAKED FELLOW, ...	106	ALL ALL AND	7
OUT OF THE NAKED ENTRAIL.	109	I, IN IMAGE	12
AND THE NAKED EGG STAND STRAIGHT, ...	113	SERVANT SUN	7
THE SCALED SEA-SAWERS, FIX IN A NAKED SPONGE	119	ALTARWISE	92
NAKED AMONG THE BOW-AND-ARROW BIRDS	123	FOSTER LIGHT	23
OPEN AS TO THE AIR TO THE NAKED SHADOW	159	INTO HER HEAD	63
MAST-HIGH MOON-WHITE WOMEN NAKED	165	LONG-LEGGED	104
HIS NAKED NEED STRUCK HIM HOWLING AND BOWED	188	WINTER'S TALE	39
ALONE AND NAKED IN THE ENGULFING BRIDE, ...	188	WINTER'S TALE	53
NAKED AND FORSAKEN TO GRIEVE HE WILL NOT COME.	201	COUNTRY SLEEP	106
NAME			
MAN BY A SCRIBBLED NAME.	66	HAND SIGNED	12
WHO KNEW NOT SUN NOR MOON BY NAME, ...	68	BEFORE KNOCKED	8
THAT BUT A NAME, WHERE MAGGOTS HAVE THEIR X.	79	LOVE'S FEVER	38
BIRDS AND THE BIRDS OF THE WINGED TREES FLYING MY			
NAME	177	POEM IN OCT	12
BURNS ME HIS NAME AND HIS FLAME	180	VISION, PRAYER	28
IN THE NAME OF THE LOST WHO GLORY IN	183	VISION, PRAYER	102
IN THE NAME OF THE WANTON	183	VISION, PRAYER	133
IN THE NAME OF THE FATHERLESS	185	VISION, PRAYER	171
IN THE NAME OF THE UNBORN	185	VISION, PRAYER	172
O IN THE NAME	185	VISION, PRAYER	176

	PAGE	TITLE	LINE
NAME (CONTINUED)			
SUN. IN THE NAME OF THE DAMNED	185	VISION, PRAYER	190
NAMED			
I, THE FIRST NAMED	141	I, FIRST NAMED	T
I, THE FIRST NAMED, AM THE GHOST OF THIS SIR AND			
CHRISTIAN FRIEND	141	I, FIRST NAMED	1
NAMELESS			
AND HIS NAMELESS NEED BOUND HIM BURNING AND LOST	188	WINTER'S TALE	44
NAMES			
OF OLD DIVINITIES, SPLIT BITS OF NAMES.	53	OUT OF THE PIT	85
THE COVERING SEA THEIR NIGHTFALL WITH NO NAMES; ...	158	INTO HER HEAD	50
THOUGH THE NAMES ON THEIR WEED GROWN STONES ARE			
RAINED AWAY, ...	203	GIANT'S THIGH	8
NANSEN'S			
COLD NANSEN'S BEAK ON A BOAT FULL OF GONGS, ...	152	BELOW A TIME	40
NAPE			
FROM NAPE TO TOE, A SANATORIUM PIECE	29	LONG, SKELETON	5
BY NAPE AND GIZZARDS;	60	FAIRY TALES	33
NARCOTIC			
TAKING JEYES' FLUID AS NARCOTIC;	137	O CHATTERTON	3
NARROW			
HIS NARROW HOUSE IS WALLED WITH BLADES OF GRASS,	64	WOMAN SPEAKS	24
SHE SLEEPS IN THE NARROW TROUGH YET SHE WALKS THE			
DUST	170	LOVE IN ASYLUM	13
A COLD KIND MAN BRAVE IN HIS NARROW PRIDE	216	ELEGY	3
NATION			
JOY IS NO KNOCKING NATION, SIR AND MADAM, ...	100	RUNNING GRAVE	31
LOVE'S TWILIT NATION AND THE SKULL OF STATE, ...	101	RUNNING GRAVE	39
NATIVE			
THIS I KNOW FROM THE NATIVE	148	UNLUCKILY FOR	50
NATRON			
BUCKLE TO LINT AND CLOTH THEIR NATRON FOOTSTEPS,	120	ALTARWISE	116
NATURAL			
THE NATURAL DAY AND NIGHT	17	NATURAL DAY	T
THE NATURAL DAY AND NIGHT	17	NATURAL DAY	1
THIS IS THE FORTUNE OF MANHOOD: THE NATURAL PERIL,	109	I, IN IMAGE	19
NO DEATH MORE NATURAL;	109	I, IN IMAGE	21
THE NATURAL PARALLEL.	109	I, IN IMAGE	24
THE NATURAL CIRCLE OF THE DISCOVERED SKIES	134	HOW MY ANIMAL	10
IN THE GROIN OF THE NATURAL DOORWAY I CROUCHED LIKE			
A TAILOR	143	24 YEARS	3
NATURE			
MASTERS OVER UNMASTERED NATURE, ...	45	PLOUGHMAN GONE	21
NAUGHT			
THOUGH THERE ARE YEARS BETWEEN US, THEY ARE NAUGHT;	30	YOUTH CALLS	12
INTANGIBLE MY WORLD SHALL COME TO NAUGHT, ...	73	LORD RED HAIL	16
THAT THE SUM SANITY MIGHT ADD TO NAUGHT	96	TWELVE	1
NAVE			
'MY FATHERS' GLOBE KNOCKS ON ITS NAVE AND SINGS.'	101	FELLOWED SLEEP	11
NAVEL			
YOUR CORKSCREW GRAVE CENTRED IN NAVEL AND NIPPLE,	110	I, IN IMAGE	51
NAVES			
THROUGH NAVES OF LEAVES, ...	215	COUNTRY HEAVEN	10
NAVIGATES			
SLEEP NAVIGATES THE TIDES OF TIME;	97	TWILIGHT LOCKS	25
NAVIGATING			
GLARED THROUGH SHARK MASK AND NAVIGATING HEAD, ...	152	BELOW A TIME	39
NAVY			
I LOVED HIS BODY AND HIS NAVY BLUE WEALTH	149	PAPER & STICKS	5

	PAGE	TITLE	LINE
NAVY (CONTINUED)			
AND THE SHIPYARDS OF GALILEE'S FOOTPRINTS HIDE A			
NAVY OF DOVES.	170	MARRIAGE VIRG	7
NAY			
SAY NAY, ...	127	NOW, SAY NAY	2
SAY NAY, ...	127	NOW, SAY NAY	9
SAY NAY, ...	127	NOW, SAY NAY	16
SAY NAY, ...	128	NOW, SAY NAY	23
SAY NAY	128	NOW, SAY NAY	30
NEAR			
HE STEPS SO NEAR THE WATER THAT A SWAN'S WING	46	POET: 1935	2
THAT SHAPED THE JORDAN NEAR MY HOME	68	BEFORE KNOCKED	4
NEAR TO THE QUARRY OR THE WELL, ...	74	WE MOTHERNAKED	6
THE NIGHT IS NEAR, ...	115	A GRIEF AGO	33
GREED ON MAN BEATING NEAR THE FIRE NEIGHBOUR	153	WAS A SAVIOUR	30
OF SEVERAL NEAR DEATHS, ...	160	DEATHS AND ENT	2
WHEN NEAR AND STRANGE WOUNDED ON LONDON'S WAVES ...	160	DEATHS AND ENT	27
AND OVER THE CLOTH OF COUNTIES THE FAR HILLS RODE			
NEAR, ...	190	WINTER'S TALE	93
NEVER AND NEVER, MY GIRL RIDING FAR AND NEAR	197	COUNTRY SLEEP	1
SHALL HARROW AND SNOW THE BLOOD WHILE YOU RIDE WIDE			
AND NEAR, ...	198	COUNTRY SLEEP	23
I YOUNG AESOP FABLING TO THE NEAR NIGHT BY THE DINGLE	202	SIR JOHNS HILL	35
GRAVE MEN, NEAR DEATH, WHO SEE WITH BLINDING SIGHT	208	NOT GO GENTLE	13
NEARLY			
GEESE NEARLY IN HEAVEN, BOYS	3	PROLOGUE	15
IN THE HOOTING, NEARLY DARK	4	PROLOGUE	59
NEARLY SUMMER	29	NEARLY SUMMER	T
NEARLY SUMMER, AND THE DEVIL	29	NEARLY SUMMER	1
THE LOST IN DOUBT, THE NEARLY MAD, THE YOUNG	41	YOUNG ARE OLD	33
NEAT'S			
LIFE NEAT'S A BETTER POISON THAN IN BOTTLE, ...	137	O CHATTERTON	5
NECK			
THE THROAT IS MINE I KNOW THE NECK	11	AIR BREATHE	2
LENDS NOT FLESH TO RIBS AND NECK, ...	55	NO MAN BELIEVE	23
THE NECK OF THE NOSTRIL, ...	110	I, IN IMAGE	52
AND RIVERS OF THE DEAD AROUND MY NECK.	120	ALTARWISE	126
NECKS			
WHO'LL BREAK OUR NECKS UPON THE PAVEMENT	28	NO WINGS	10
AND WASHING WATER SPILT UPON THEIR NECKS	47	POET: 1935	32
NEED			
THERE IS NO NEED OF HOPE FOR HOPE, ...	21	BEWILDERED WAY	9
THERE WAS NO NEED OF A NEW DIVINITY, ...	34	IN GARDENS	18
NEED NO WORD'S WARMTH.	79	LOVE'S FEVER	36
AND NEED NO DRUID OF HER BROKEN BODY).	136	AFTER FUNERAL	20
HIS NAKED NEED STRUCK HIM HOWLING AND BOWED	188	WINTER'S TALE	39
AND HIS NAMELESS NEED BOUND HIM BURNING AND LOST	188	WINTER'S TALE	44
AND DROWN IN THE DRIFTS OF HIS NEED, AND LIE CURLED			
CAUGHT	188	WINTER'S TALE	47
BY LOSING HIM ALL IN LOVE, AND CAST HIS NEED	188	WINTER'S TALE	52
THE CLOUD, THE NEED, THE PLANTED STARS, THE JOY			
BEYOND	190	WINTER'S TALE	102
NEEDLE			
MY CAMEL'S EYES WILL NEEDLE THROUGH THE SHROUD. ...	118	ALTARWISE	52
THE FLASHING NEEDLE ROCK OF SQUATTERS, ...	151	BELOW A TIME	26
NEEDLES			
OF LADIES' NEEDLES WORN TO BREAKING POINT	18	NATURAL DAY	10
TAKE THE NEEDLES AND THE KNIVES	70	TAKE NEEDLES	T
TAKE THE NEEDLES AND THE KNIVES, ...	70	TAKE NEEDLES	1
TAKE THE NEEDLES TO THIS TREE	72	TAKE NEEDLES	49

	PAGE	TITLE	LINE
NEEDLES (CONTINUED)			
SHE THREADS OFF THE SAP AND NEEDLES, BLOOD AND BUBBLE	108	I, IN IMAGE	10
NEGATION			
NEGATIVES IMPRESS NEGATION, ...	27	OBLIVIOUS DARK	4
NEGATIVES			
NEGATIVES IMPRESS NEGATION, ...	27	OBLIVIOUS DARK	4
NEGRO			
THE MESSAGE COMES FROM NEGRO MYSTICS, ...	58	TO ARCHITECTS	7
NEIGHBOUR			
GREED ON MAN BEATING NEAR THE FIRE NEIGHBOUR	153	WAS A SAVIOUR	30
YOUR POLESTAR NEIGHBOUR, SUN OF ANOTHER STREET, ...	160	DEATHS AND ENT	17
WOKE TO MY HEARING FROM HARBOUR AND NEIGHBOUR WOOD	176	POEM IN OCT	2
NEIGHBOURED			
THAT NEIGHBOURED THEM TO WELLS OF WARMTH, ...	43	FACES SHONE	6
NEIGHBOURING			
SUSPICIOUS HANDS TUG AT THE NEIGHBOURING VICES, ...	38	THE GOSSIPERS	3
NEIGHBOURS			
O KINGDOM OF NEIGHBOURS, FINNED	5	PROLOGUE	82
NEITHER			
NEITHER BY NIGHT'S ANCIENT FEAR, ...	44	LONGED TO MOVE	15
BUT WISHES BREED NOT, NEITHER	54	WE BY SEASAND	21
I, BORN OF FLESH AND GHOST, WAS NEITHER	69	BEFORE KNOCKED	37
NEOPHYTE			
THE NEOPHYTE, BAPTIZED IN SMILES	19	THE NEOPHYTE	T
THE NEOPHYTE, BAPTIZED IN SMILES, ...	19	THE NEOPHYTE	1
THEN WAS MY NEOPHYTE	128	MY NEOPHYTE	T
THEN WAS MY NEOPHYTE, ...	128	MY NEOPHYTE	1
NEOPHYTES			
OF NEOPHYTES TAKE ALTERED ROADS.	37	WINDMILLS TURN	33
NEPTUNE			
MY GHOST IN HIS METAL NEPTUNE	112	I, IN IMAGE	105
NERVE			
OF KNIVES ON FORKS, HE CRIED, OF NERVE ON NERVE,	51	OUT OF THE PIT	34
OF KNIVES ON FORKS, HE CRIED, OF NERVE ON NERVE,	51	OUT OF THE PIT	34
REHEARSING HEAT UPON A RAW-EDGED NERVE.	95	RUB OF LOVE	19
AND WHAT'S THE RUB? DEATH'S FEATHER ON THE NERVE?	96	RUB OF LOVE	43
THAT, SEWN TO ME BY NERVE AND BRAIN, ...	97	TWILIGHT LOCKS	11
THROUGH VISION AND THE GIRDERED NERVE, ...	102	I DREAMED MY	4
TIME'S NERVE IN VINEGAR, THE GALLOW GRAVE	120	ALTARWISE	100
NERVES			
AS EDGES OFF YOUR NERVES TO MINE, ...	20	ENCOMPASSED	5
OUT OF THE BITTER CONSCIENCE AND THE NERVES, ...	20	THE NEOPHYTE	15
THIS BUSY JARRING ON THE NERVES YET NO OUTBREAK?	36	MIDNIGHT ROAD	4
OF RAVENS AT THE HERO'S MEAT AND NERVES	63	WOMAN SPEAKS	17
MY HERO BARES HIS NERVES	75	MY HERO BARES	T
MY HERO BARES HIS NERVES ALONG MY WRIST	75	MY HERO BARES	1
AND THESE POOR NERVES SO WIRED TO THE SKULL	75	MY HERO BARES	6
HE HOLDS THE WIRE FROM THIS BOX OF NERVES	75	MY HERO BARES	16
MY FATHERS' LOVES THAT PULL UPON MY NERVES, ...	80	ALL THAT I OWE	6
OF DOUBT AND DARK THEY FEED THEIR NERVES;	92	BOYS OF SUMMER	11
ALL NERVES TO SERVE THE SUN, ...	114	SERVANT SUN	15
LOVE'S A DECISION OF 3 NERVES	138	O CHATTERTON	22
CAMPED IN THE DRUG-WHITE SHOWER OF NERVES AND FOOD,	144	PLEASURE-BIRD	8
THE CLOUD PERCHED TAILORS' MASTER WITH NERVES FOR			
COTTON.	152	BELOW A TIME	35
NEST			
WHO MOONS HER BLUE NOTES FROM HER NEST	4	PROLOGUE	62
FROM THE STONE NEST IT DOES NOT LET THE FEATHERY	15	SPIRE CRANES	2
CRYING WITH HUNGRY VOICES IN OUR NEST.	28	NO WINGS	22
ON A MARE'S BACK OF A MARE'S NEST OR A GOOSE, ...	45	TO FOLLOW FOX	19

	PAGE	TITLE	LINE
NEST (CONTINUED)			
MY NEST OF MERCIES IN THE RUDE, RED TREE.	121	ALTARWISE	140
HIS HEAD'S IN A NEST WHERE NO BIRD LAYS HER EGG.	179	NEW QUAY	27
ADMIT THE SUN INTO YOUR HIGH NEST	240	ADMIT THE SUN	1
NESTED			
BUT WAILED AND NESTED IN THE SKY-BLUE WALL	153	WAS A SAVIOUR	31
WITHIN THE NESTED TREEFORK	159	INTO HER HEAD	58
NESTLING			
PECKING AND NESTLING ALL THE TIME OF NIGHT.	63	WOMAN SPEAKS	18
NESTS			
FREE FROM THEIR BURNING NESTS THE ARROWS' BROOD.	73	LORD RED HAIL	4
AND A FELLOW WHO JESTS THAT A MARE CAN BUILD NESTS	221	SONG OF DOG	7
NET			
AND THE KNOCK OF SAILING BOATS ON THE NET WEBBED WALL	177	POEM IN OCT	7
MY NET THAT TAKES TO BREAK	233	NO THOUGHT	7
WILL YOU DRIFT INTO THE NET WILLINGLY, ...	233	NO THOUGHT	21
NETS			
TO THE SUNSET NETS, ...	3	PROLOGUE	14
IS CRYING FROM NETS TO KNIVES, ...	164	LONG-LEGGED	66
NETTLE			
LOP, LOVE, MY FORK TONGUE, SAID THE PIN-HILLED			
NETTLE;	119	ALTARWISE	76
NETTLES			
I WITH THE WOODEN INSECT IN THE TREE OF NETTLES,	109	I, IN IMAGE	28
ARE BUT THE ROOTS OF NETTLES AND OF FEATHERS	117	ALTARWISE	26
NETTLE'S			
SHE MAKES FOR ME A NETTLE'S INNOCENCE	131	I MAKE THIS IN	16
NEURAL			
TELLS ME THE HOUR'S WORD, THE NEURAL MEANING	99	OCTOBER WIND	18
NEVER			
NEVER TO REACH THE OBLIVIOUS DARK	27	OBLIVIOUS DARK	T
NEVER TO REACH THE OBLIVIOUS DARK	27	OBLIVIOUS DARK	1
NEVER IS NIGHTMARE, ...	27	OBLIVIOUS DARK	6
NEVER FLOWS OUT FROM THE WOUND OF SLEEP	27	OBLIVIOUS DARK	7
NOTHING NEVER, NOTHING OLDER	27	OBLIVIOUS DARK	25
THAT WAIT FOR BREAKING AND THAT NEVER BREAK, ...	36	MIDNIGHT ROAD	13
WHAT'S NEVER KNOWN IS SAFEST IN THIS LIFE.	40	WAS THERE TIME	6
OF TIDES THAT NEVER TOUCH THE SHORES.	69	BEFORE KNOCKED	34
NEVER BE LUCID, NEVER STATE, ...	84	LETTER TO AUNT	40
NEVER BE LUCID, NEVER STATE, ...	84	LETTER TO AUNT	40
NEVER OMIT SUCH VITAL WORDS	84	LETTER TO AUNT	44
CAN NEVER RAISE THE MIDNIGHT OF A CHUCKLE, ...	96	RUB OF LOVE	39
NEVER SHALL BEAST BE BORN TO ATLAS THE FEW SEAS ...	135	HOW MY ANIMAL	32
I NEVER THOUGHT TO UTTER OR THINK	147	TO OTHERS	16
NEVER SHALL MY SELF CHANT	148	UNLUCKILY FOR	25
O MY DEAR IT'S NEVER TOO LATE	149	PAPER & STICKS	11
YOU NEVER DID AND HE NEVER DID.	149	PAPER & STICKS	18
YOU NEVER DID AND HE NEVER DID.	149	PAPER & STICKS	18
NEVER NEVER OH NEVER TO REGRET THE BUGLE I WORE ...	152	BELOW A TIME	47
NEVER NEVER OH NEVER TO REGRET THE BUGLE I WORE ...	152	BELOW A TIME	47
NEVER NEVER OH NEVER TO REGRET THE BUGLE I WORE ...	152	BELOW A TIME	47
BRAVE DEATHS OF ONLY ONES BUT NEVER FOUND, ...	153	WAS A SAVIOUR	35
CAUGHT AMONG NEVER ENOUGH	156	RETURN	67
FOR MY SAKE SAIL, AND NEVER LOOK BACK, ...	162	LONG-LEGGED	11
OF ADAM AND EVE IS NEVER FOR A SECOND	174	FIRE RAID	48
MILD. TURNED AGAIN, WORTHINGTON. NEVER WHISKY.	179	NEW QUAY	12
NEVER TO AWAKE AND ARISE	184	VISION, PRAYER	168
NEVER TO FLOURISH IN THE FIELDS OF THE WHITE SEED	188	WINTER'S TALE	54
NEVER UNTIL THE MANKIND MAKING	191	REFUSAL MOURN	1
NEVER AND NEVER, MY GIRL RIDING FAR AND NEAR	197	COUNTRY SLEEP	1

		PAGE	TITLE	LINE
NEVER (CONTINUED)				
NEVER AND NEVER, MY GIRL RIDING FAR AND NEAR	......	197	COUNTRY SLEEP	1
NEVER, MY GIRL, UNTIL TOLLED TO SLEEP BY THE STERN		198	COUNTRY SLEEP	21
WE GRIEVE AS THE BLITHE BIRDS, NEVER AGAIN, LEAVE				
SHINGLE AND ELM,	....	202	SIR JOHNS HILL	33
HEAVEN THAT NEVER WAS	....	210	POEM ON B'DAY	50
YOUNG AMONG THE LONG FLOCKS, AND NEVER LIE LOST	...	216	ELEGY	7
WILL NEVER NEVER GO OUT OF MY MIND.	....	217	ELEGY	20
WILL NEVER NEVER GO OUT OF MY MIND.	....	217	ELEGY	20
EVEN AS A BABY HE HAD NEVER CRIED;	....	217	ELEGY	26
AND THAT BEES NEVER WORK IN THEIR HIVES.	....	221	SONG OF DOG	4
WHERE THE FROST CAN NEVER FALL,	....	232	YOUR VOICE	15
COULD NEVER TOUCH YOUR SPINNING NOTES,	....	234	NO, PIGEON	9
TEMPLE SHOULD NEVER HAVE BEEN FILLED	....	237	PILLAR BREAKS	12
I NEVER BREAK BUT FEEL THE SUDDEN PAIN,	....	239	MAKES INTERVALS	25
NEW				
NEW MAN BEST WHOSE BLOOD RUNS THICK,	....	29	LONG, SKELETON	11
A NEW DIVINITY, A GOD OF WHEELS	....	33	IN GARDENS	7
THE NEW ASYLUM ON THE HILL	....	33	HELD-OUT HAND	18
THERE WAS NO NEED OF A NEW DIVINITY,	....	34	IN GARDENS	18
WHO IN THE BONES FINDS NOT NEW FAITH,	....	55	NO MAN BELIEVE	22
EMPTY, TO LET, ARE SIGNS ON THIS NEW HOUSE;	....	58	TO ARCHITECTS	15
CREATED SOMETHING VERY NEW,	....	83	LETTER TO AUNT	24
OF NEW MAN STRENGTH, I SEEK THE SUN.	....	103	I DREAMED MY	28
EACH NEW SENSATION EMITS	....	137	O CHATTERTON	8
A NEW VINEGAR;	....	137	O CHATTERTON	9
NEW QUAY	....	179	NEW QUAY	T
UNTIL THE TURBULENT NEW BORN	....	180	VISION, PRAYER	27
UNDER THE NEW MADE CLOUDS AND HAPPY AS THE HEART WAS				
LONG,	....	196	FERN HILL	38
DIPPING MOON AND DRUNK AS A NEW DROPPED CALF,	.....	206	LAMENT	17
OF A NEW COUNTRY	....	231	OUR SANCTITY	43
THERE WILL BE A NEW BITTERNESS	....	236	WOMAN TAPESTRY	61
THERE WILL BE A NEW LIFE	....	236	WOMAN TAPESTRY	66
NEWBORN				
SLEEP TO A NEWBORN SLEEP IN A SWADDLING LOIN-LEAF				
STROKED AND SANG	....	157	INTO HER HEAD	22
AND THE OLD MEN SING FROM NEWBORN LIPS:	....	167	LONG-LEGGED	152
NEWS				
SPELLING ACROSS THE SKY HIS DEVIL'S NEWS,	....	29	NEARLY SUMMER	5
THE ATLAS-EATER WITH A JAW FOR NEWS,	....	117	ALTARWISE	5
WHY WON'T THE NEWS OF THE OLD WORLD CATCH	....	149	PAPER & STICKS	2
BREAK THE BLACK NEWS AND PAINT ON A SAIL	....	164	LONG-LEGGED	71
NEWSPAPER				
EATING BREAD FROM A NEWSPAPER	....	171	THE HUNCHBACK	7
NEXT				
IN THE NEXT ROOM	....	180	VISION, PRAYER	4
NEXT-DOOR				
THE NEXT-DOOR SEA DISPELLED	....	150	WHEN I WOKE	6
NIBBLE				
AND TAKE ANOTHER NIBBLE AT MY FLASK.	....	137	O CHATTERTON	16
NIBBLES				
THEY SUFFER THE UNDEAD WATER WHERE THE TURTLE				
NIBBLES,	....	111	I, IN IMAGE	73
NICE				
AN OLD CHATTERBOX, BARENAVELED AT NICE,	....	58	TO ARCHITECTS	8
NICK				
SHE NIPPED AND DIVED IN THE NICK OF LOVE,	....	163	LONG-LEGGED	55
NICKED				
THE SEA AND INSTRUMENT, NICKED IN THE LOCKS OF TIME,		111	I, IN IMAGE	92

	PAGE	TITLE	LINE
NIGHT			
DAYS' NIGHT WHOSE TOWERS WILL CATCH	3	PROLOGUE	20
INTO THE DOGDAYED NIGHT.	3	PROLOGUE	33
THE NATURAL DAY AND NIGHT	17	NATURAL DAY	T
THE NATURAL DAY AND NIGHT	17	NATURAL DAY	1
BUT WHILE DAY IS THERE'S NIGHT TO IT,	18	NATURAL DAY	19
AND NIGHT TO IT.	19	NATURAL DAY	20
SINCE, ON A QUIET NIGHT	22	ON QUIET NIGHT	T
SINCE, ON A QUIET NIGHT, I HEARD THEM TALK	22	ON QUIET NIGHT	1
CUT OUR FIGURES, AND RETREAT AT NIGHT	28	NO WINGS	17
AND YOU HAVE WALKED UPON THE HILLS AT NIGHT,	30	YOUTH CALLS	8
CONSOLING FOR NIGHT BY DAY	35	LIFT UP FACE	3
CONTENT SHALL COME AFTER A TWISTED NIGHT	35	LIFT UP FACE	25
UNDER THE HEAVY LAYERS OF THE NIGHT	39	GAS FADES	38
AND THE SKYSIGNS AND THE NIGHT LIGHTS,	42	YOUNG ARE OLD	51
UNLESS I LEARN THE NIGHT I SHALL GO MAD.	48	LIGHT, I KNOW	12
BUT LUNAR NIGHT WILL NOT GLOW IN MY BLACKNESS,	49	LIGHT, I KNOW	22
DAY TREADS THE TREES AND SHE THE CAVERNOUS NIGHT.	57	GREEK PLAY	12
AUTOCRACY OF NIGHT AND DAY,	61	MEAT ON BONES	12
BLACK NIGHT STILL MINISTERS THE MOON,	61	MEAT ON BONES	33
PECKING AND NESTLING ALL THE TIME OF NIGHT.	63	WOMAN SPEAKS	18
THE WET NIGHT SCOLDS ME LIKE A NURSE?	65	GODS THUMP	10
IT WAS A HAGGARD NIGHT THE FIRST FLESH DIED,	65	WOMAN SPEAKS	56
UNGOTTEN I KNEW NIGHT AND DAY.	68	BEFORE KNOCKED	18
A SECRET NIGHT DESCENDS BETWEEN	69	SECRET WIND	4
HERE THE NIGHT SHELTERS AND HERE THE STARS SHINE,	74	SUN BURNS	8
THE CODE OF NIGHT TAPPED ON MY TONGUE;	79	LOVE'S FEVER	40
AGEING BOTH DAY AND NIGHT.	80	ALMANAC TIME	10
ALL NIGHT AND DAY I EYE THE RAGGED GLOBE	81	ALL THAT I OWE	23
ALL NIGHT AND DAY I WANDER IN THESE SAME	81	ALL THAT I OWE	25
ALL NIGHT MY FORTUNE SLUMBERS IN ITS SHEET.	81	ALL THAT I OWE	27
ALL NIGHT MY FORTUNE SLUMBERS IN ITS SHEET.	81	ALL THAT I OWE	30
NIGHT IN THE SOCKETS ROUNDS,	82	LIGHT BREAKS	19
MAN IN THE DAY OR WIND AT NIGHT	86	BREAD I BREAK	4
TURNS NIGHT TO DAY; BLOOD IN THEIR SUNS	88	A PROCESS IN	5
GROOM THE DARK BRIDES, THE WIDOWS OF THE NIGHT	89	EUNUCH DREAMS	5
DIVIDE THE NIGHT AND DAY WITH FAIRY THUMBS;	92	BOYS OF SUMMER	15
THERE, IN HIS NIGHT, THE BLACK-TONGUED BELLS	92	BOYS OF SUMMER	28
GIRLS TAKE TO BROOMSTICKS WHEN THE THIEF OF NIGHT	96	TWELVE	3
OF SUNS IN THE MAN-MELTING NIGHT.	102	I DREAMED MY	8
THE NIGHT IS NEAR,	115	A GRIEF AGO	33
THAT NIGHT OF TIME UNDER THE CHRISTWARD SHELTER:	117	ALTARWISE	12
STILLS SNAPPED BY NIGHT IN THE BREAD-SIDED FIELD,	118	ALTARWISE	54
ROSE MY BYZANTINE ADAM IN THE NIGHT.	118	ALTARWISE	62
MASTER THE NIGHT NOR SERVE THE SNOWMAN'S BRAIN	123	FOSTER LIGHT	4
CALLS A GREEN DAY AND NIGHT.	128	MY NEOPHYTE	6
NIGHT AFTER NIGHT THEIR HANDS IMPLORE	143	THE MOLLS	3
NIGHT AFTER NIGHT THEIR HANDS IMPLORE	143	THE MOLLS	3
THEY RETCH INTO MY SECRET NIGHT	143	THE MOLLS	5
WHERE AT NIGHT WE STONED THE COLD AND CUCKOO	144	COLOUR OF SAY	8
LAST NIGHT IN A RAPING WAVE	157	INTO HER HEAD	7
NIGHT, AND ENJOYED AS HE WOULD.	158	INTO HER HEAD	36
A MAN TORN UP MOURNS IN THE SOLE NIGHT.	159	INTO HER HEAD	67
BOLTING THE NIGHT OF THE DOOR WITH HER ARM HER PLUME.	169	LOVE IN ASYLUM	4
SLEPT AT NIGHT IN A DOG KENNEL	171	THE HUNCHBACK	11
THAT SHE MIGHT STAND IN THE NIGHT	172	THE HUNCHBACK	35
ALL NIGHT IN THE UNMADE PARK	172	THE HUNCHBACK	37
NIGHT FALL AND THE FRUIT LIKE A SUN,	174	FIRE RAID	56
LAST NIGHT I DIVED MY BEGGAR ARM	175	MY BEGGAR ARM	T
LAST NIGHT I DIVED MY BEGGAR ARM	175	MY BEGGAR ARM	1

	PAGE	TITLE	LINE
NIGHT (CONTINUED)			
NIGHT FOR MY SAKE,	176	BREATH SHED	4
UNDER THE NIGHT FOREVER FALLING.	184	VISION, PRAYER	152
FOREVER FALLING NIGHT IS A KNOWN	184	VISION, PRAYER	153
TO GLOW AFTER THE GOD STONING NIGHT	186	HOLY SPRING	11
IN THE MUFFLED HOUSE, IN THE QUICK OF NIGHT,	188	WINTER'S TALE	29
THE RIVERS MOUTHED IN NIGHT,	188	WINTER'S TALE	46
ALL NIGHT LOST AND LONG WADING IN THE WAKE OF THE SHE-	190	WINTER'S TALE	98
IN THE THROAT, BURNING AND TURNING. ALL NIGHT AFLOAT	194	SLEEP BECALMED	2
THE NIGHT ABOVE THE DINGLE STARRY,	195	FERN HILL	3
EXERCISED IN THE STILL NIGHT	196	CRAFT OR ART	2
MY GIRL RANGING THE NIGHT IN THE ROSE AND SHIRE	197	COUNTRY SLEEP	9
THIS NIGHT AND EACH VAST NIGHT UNTIL THE STERN BELL TALKS	199	COUNTRY SLEEP	51
THIS NIGHT AND EACH VAST NIGHT UNTIL THE STERN BELL TALKS	199	COUNTRY SLEEP	51
THIS NIGHT AND EACH NIGHT SINCE THE FALLING STAR YOU WERE BORN,	199	COUNTRY SLEEP	55
THIS NIGHT AND EACH NIGHT SINCE THE FALLING STAR YOU WERE BORN,	199	COUNTRY SLEEP	55
NIGHT AND THE REINDEER ON THE CLOUDS ABOVE THE HAYCOCKS	199	COUNTRY SLEEP	64
BURNING! NIGHT AND THE VEIN OF BIRDS IN THE WINGED, SLOE WRIST	199	COUNTRY SLEEP	70
LEAPING! THE GOSPEL ROOKS! ALL TELL, THIS NIGHT, OF HIM	200	COUNTRY SLEEP	80
MIGHT CROSS ITS PLANETS, THE BELL WEEP, NIGHT GATHER HER EYES,	200	COUNTRY SLEEP	92
BUT HER FAITH THAT EACH VAST NIGHT AND THE SAGA OF PRAYER	201	COUNTRY SLEEP	102
HER FAITH THAT THIS LAST NIGHT FOR HIS UNSACRED SAKE	201	COUNTRY SLEEP	104
MY DEAR THIS NIGHT HE COMES AND NIGHT WITHOUT END MY DEAR	201	COUNTRY SLEEP	108
MY DEAR THIS NIGHT HE COMES AND NIGHT WITHOUT END MY DEAR	201	COUNTRY SLEEP	108
I YOUNG AESOP FABLING TO THE NEAR NIGHT BY THE DINGLE	202	SIR JOHNS HILL	35
AND THERE THIS NIGHT I WALK IN THE WHITE GIANT'S THIGH	203	GIANT'S THIGH	3
BEFORE THE LUNGE OF THE NIGHT, THE NOTES ON THIS TIME-SHAKEN	203	SIR JOHNS HILL	59
ALL BIRDS AND BEASTS OF THE LINKED NIGHT UPROAR AND CHIME	204	GIANT'S THIGH	35
I WHISTLED ALL NIGHT IN THE TWISTED FLUES,	206	LAMENT	18
BLACK NIGHT, I LEFT MY QUIVERING PRINTS.	206	LAMENT	24
DO NOT GO GENTLE INTO THAT GOOD NIGHT	207	NOT GO GENTLE	T
DO NOT GO GENTLE INTO THAT GOOD NIGHT,	207	NOT GO GENTLE	1
DO NOT GO GENTLE INTO THAT GOOD NIGHT.	208	NOT GO GENTLE	6
DO NOT GO GENTLE INTO THAT GOOD NIGHT.	208	NOT GO GENTLE	12
DO NOT GO GENTLE INTO THAT GOOD NIGHT.	208	NOT GO GENTLE	18
HE, ON THE EARTH OF THE NIGHT, ALONE	210	POEM ON B'DAY	65
NOON, AND NIGHT, AND LIGHT. THE RIVERS OF THE DEAD	216	ELEGY	15
OF THE TWELVE APOSTLES' TOWNS RING IN HIS NIGHT;	216	COUNTRY HEAVEN	26
AND NIGHT, WHO STOOPED TO KISS THE PALLID LEAVES	223	IN DREAMS	5
TO THE VOICES OF THE WIND CAUGHT IN THE CRADLE-PETALS OF THE NIGHT:	223	IDYLL UNFORGET	8
THERE SHOULD BE NIGHT FOR EVER, AND NO ROSE,	223	IN DREAMS	10
THEN TO CATCH NIGHT	232	YOUR VOICE	8

	PAGE	TITLE	LINE
NIGHTBIRD			
THE NIGHTBIRD LAUDS THROUGH NUNNERIES AND DOMES OF LEAVES	198	COUNTRY SLEEP	28
NIGHTBREAK			
AT NIGHTBREAK BORN IN THE FAT SIDE, FROM AN ANIMAL BED	130	SINNERS' BELL	26
NIGHTFALL			
THE COVERING SEA THEIR NIGHTFALL WITH NO NAMES;	158	INTO HER HEAD	50
NIGHT-GEARED			
OR DRIVE THE NIGHT-GEARED FORTH.	90	EUNUCH DREAMS	26
IN BOTTOM GEAR THROUGH NIGHT-GEARED MAN.	103	I DREAMED MY	12
NIGHTINGALE			
NIGHTINGALE AND HYENA	164	LONG-LEGGED	87
IN THE DEPARTED VILLAGES. THE NIGHTINGALE,	189	WINTER'S TALE	57
OF NIGHTINGALE AND CENTAUR DEAD HORSE. THE SPRINGS WITHER	191	WINTER'S TALE	117
OF THE NIGHTINGALE,	229	MY RIVER	31
AH, NIGHTINGALE, MY VOICE	234	NO, PIGEON	8
AND EVERY NIGHTINGALE A SWAN	234	NO, PIGEON	15
NIGHTINGALES			
NIGHTINGALES OF THE CASUALTY STATIONS	154	RETURN	23
WITH THEIR NIGHTINGALES AND PSALMS	197	CRAFT OR ART	16
NIGHTINGALE'S			
OF THE NIGHTINGALE'S DIN AND TALE! THE UPGIVEN GHOST	200	COUNTRY SLEEP	74
NIGHTJARS			
ALL THE MOON LONG I HEARD, BLESSED AMONG STABLES, THE NIGHTJARS	195	FERN HILL	25
NIGHTLONG			
SURPRISED IN THE OPENING OF HER NIGHTLONG EYES	170	MARRIAGE VIRG	2
THE STAR RISE AT PASTURE AND NIGHTLONG THE FABLES GRAZE	198	COUNTRY SLEEP	34
NIGHTLY			
NIGHTLY UPON THEIR WRINKLED BREASTS	38	THE GOSSIPERS	17
AND NIGHTLY UNDER THE SIMPLE STARS	195	FERN HILL	23
NIGHTMARE			
NEVER IS NIGHTMARE,	27	OBLIVIOUS DARK	6
STEPPING IN NIGHTMARE ON A NIGHTMARE'S EDGES.	36	MIDNIGHT ROAD	11
DEATH: DEATH OF HAMLET AND THE NIGHTMARE MADMEN,	124	TODAY, INSECT	19
NIGHTMARE'S			
THE NIGHTMARE'S MIST	35	LIFT UP FACE	12
STEPPING IN NIGHTMARE ON A NIGHTMARE'S EDGES.	36	MIDNIGHT ROAD	11
NIGHTMARISH			
YET SHE DELUDES WITH WALKING THE NIGHTMARISH ROOM,	169	LOVE IN ASYLUM	7
NIGHTPRIEST			
MUTTER AND FOUL WINGBEAT OF THE SOLEMNIZING NIGHTPRIEST	158	INTO HER HEAD	45
NIGHTS			
IMPOSE THEIR SHOTS, SHOWING THE NIGHTS AWAY;	89	EUNUCH DREAMS	18
ON GIDDY NIGHTS WHEN SLAP ON THE MOON'S MASK	137	O CHATTERTON	12
ON GIDDY NIGHTS I SLAP A FEW DRUNK CURVES	138	O CHATTERTON	24
AND ON SEESAW SUNDAY NIGHTS I WOOED	206	LAMENT	8
AND CAUGHT BETWEEN TWO NIGHTS, BLINDNESS AND DEATH.	217	ELEGY	36
NIGHT'S			
NEITHER BY NIGHT'S ANCIENT FEAR,	44	LONGED TO MOVE	15
IT IS NIGHT'S TERRORS I MUST LEARN TO LOVE,	48	LIGHT, I KNOW	13
I MUST LEARN NIGHT'S LIGHT OR GO MAD.	49	LIGHT, I KNOW	30
AND ALONE IN THE NIGHT'S ETERNAL, CURVING ACT	203	GIANT'S THIGH	9
NIGHTSEED			
TURN AND CHURN NIGHTSEED TILL IT CURDLE.	67	LET A FAITH	5

		PAGE	TITLE	LINE
NIGHT-TIME				
WHY NIGHT-TIME RAIN AND THE BREAST'S BLOOD	....	56	WHY EAST WIND	8
NILE				
TAIL, NILE, AND SNOUT, A SADDLER OF THE RUSHES,	...	111	I, IN IMAGE	98
NILLY				
THE THIEF FALL ON THE DEAD LIKE THE WILLY NILLY DEW,		200	COUNTRY SLEEP	93
NIMBLE				
IN THE SQUIRREL NIMBLE GROVE, UNDER LINEN AND THATCH		199	COUNTRY SLEEP	44
NIMBUS				
TO HIS NIMBUS BELL COOL KINGDOM COME	....	211	POEM ON B'DAY	85
NINE				
FROM THE CITIES OF NINE	....	3	PROLOGUE	19
A LIMP AND RIDERLESS SHAPE TO LEAP NINE THINNING				
MONTHS.'	....	145	IF HEAD HURT	15
NINEPIN				
NINEPIN DOWN ON THE DONKEYS' COMMON,	....	206	LAMENT	7
NINNIES'				
OF MORTAL VOICES TO THE NINNIES' CHOIR,	....	123	FOSTER LIGHT	16
NIPPED				
SHE NIPPED AND DIVED IN THE NICK OF LOVE,	....	163	LONG-LEGGED	55
NIPPLE				
YOUR CORKSCREW GRAVE CENTRED IN NAVEL AND NIPPLE,		110	I, IN IMAGE	51
NIPPLED				
AND THOUGH MY LOVE PULLS THE PALE, NIPPLED AIR,	...	133	I MAKE THIS IN	66
NIPPLES				
TILL THE THREE-COLOURED RAINBOW FROM MY NIPPLES	...	120	ALTARWISE	107
NITRIC				
HALT AMONG EUNUCHS, AND THE NITRIC STAIN	....	100	RUNNING GRAVE	24
A NITRIC SHAPE THAT LEAPS HER, TIME AND ACID;	.....	115	A GRIEF AGO	34
NO (210)				
NOAH				
DRINKING NOAH OF THE BAY,	....	5	PROLOGUE	85
NOAH'S				
AND NOAH'S REKINDLED NOW UNKIND DOVE	....	157	INTO HER HEAD	5
NOBLE				
NOBLE AMONG A CROWD OF LIGHTS.	....	21	BEWILDERED WAY	12
MY ONE AND NOBLE HEART HAS WITNESSES	....	139	FIVE & COUNTRY	11
O WAKE TO SEE, AFTER A NOBLE FALL,	....	142	SAINT TO FALL	43
NOBODY				
BUT NOBODY CHAINED HIM UP.	....	171	THE HUNCHBACK	12
NODDED				
WHEN THE CAUGHT TONGUE NODDED BLIND,	....	173	FIRE RAID	13
NODDING				
NODDING LIKE FLOWERS,	....	226	THE ELM	2
NO-GOOD				
BAY. NO-GOOD IS ABROAD. I UNHARDY CAN	....	179	NEW QUAY	8
HARDLY BEAR THE DIN OF NO-GOOD WRACKED DRY ON	.....	179	NEW QUAY	9
NOISE				
OF SHEEP AND CHURCHES NOISE	....	5	PROLOGUE	88
AND THE BEAUTIFUL NOISE IS QUELLED,	....	18	NATURAL DAY	22
OUT OF THE NOISE INTO QUIET I RAN.	....	53	OUT OF THE PIT	92
TAXIS AND LILIES, NOISE AND NO NOISE,	....	53	OUT OF THE PIT	95
TAXIS AND LILIES, NOISE AND NO NOISE,	....	53	OUT OF THE PIT	95
ITCHED IN THE NOISE OF WIND AND SUN.	....	79	LOVE'S FEVER	30
BY THE SEA'S SIDE, HEARING THE NOISE OF BIRDS,	....	98	OCTOBER WIND	5
NOISELESSLY				
NOISELESSLY INTO A WORLD OF WINGS AND CRIES.	......	31	BEING BUT MEN	5
NOISES				
CROSSLY OUT OF THE TOWN NOISES	....	150	WHEN I WOKE	24

	PAGE	TITLE	LINE
NOISY			
HOLD UP THE NOISY SEA AND DROP HER BIRDS, ...	93	BOYS OF SUMMER	39
NONE			
VIGOUR AND HARMONY IN LIGHT TO NONE, ...	17	NATURAL DAY	4
NONE, AND HIS DEADLY WELCOME	23	THE ONLY DEAD	13
CALLED FOR CONFESSOR BUT THERE WAS NONE	42	A WAR OF WITS	5
'FIND MEAT ON BONES THAT SOON HAVE NONE, ...	60	MEAT ON BONES	1
REMAINS THOUGH GODS BE FELLED TILL NONE ARE LEFT.	67	LET A FAITH	10
THRUST, MY DAUGHTER OR SON, TO ESCAPE, THERE IS			
NONE, NONE, NONE, ...	146	IF HEAD HURT	19
THRUST, MY DAUGHTER OR SON, TO ESCAPE, THERE IS			
NONE, NONE, NONE, ...	146	IF HEAD HURT	19
THRUST, MY DAUGHTER OR SON, TO ESCAPE, THERE IS			
NONE, NONE, NONE, ...	146	IF HEAD HURT	19
CALL FOR CONFESSOR AND WISER MIRROR BUT THERE IS NONE	186	HOLY SPRING	10
NONSTOP			
NONSTOP; STOPPRESS; VINEGAR FROM WISECRACKS;	57	TO ARCHITECTS	3
NON-STOP			
STOPPED NON-STOP DANCING TO LET HOT FEET COOL, ...	51	OUT OF THE PIT	30
NOON			
WHEN IT WAS NOON HAVE WALKED INTO THE LIGHT, ...	30	YOUTH CALLS	10
HIS STRIPED AND NOON MANED TRIBE STRIDING TO			
HOLOCAUST, ...	148	UNLUCKILY FOR	31
YEAR TO HEAVEN STOOD THERE THEN IN THE SUMMER NOON	178	POEM IN OCT	66
AND THE HIGH NOON	181	VISION, PRAYER	65
NOON, AND NIGHT, AND LIGHT. THE RIVERS OF THE DEAD	216	ELEGY	15
NO-ONE			
AND NO-ONE STIRS AT SHEBA'S SIDE	165	LONG-LEGGED	108
NOONS			
FALLS ON A RING OF SUMMERS AND LOCKED NOONS.	132	I MAKE THIS IN	30
NOOSED			
THE FLASHED THE NOOSED HAWK	201	SIR JOHNS HILL	10
NOR (69)			
NORTH			
OUT OF THE SIDES OF THE NORTH	165	LONG-LEGGED	114
NOSE			
MY EARS, MY NOSE, MY EYES, ...	18	NATURAL DAY	17
A PIG'S SNOUT FOR A NOSE, ...	41	YOUNG ARE OLD	32
FOLLOWING THE NOSE DOWN DELL, UP RISE	44	TO FOLLOW FOX	7
TO FOLLOW THE NOSE IF THE NOSE GOES	44	TO FOLLOW FOX	14
TO FOLLOW THE NOSE IF THE NOSE GOES	44	TO FOLLOW FOX	14
TELLING IT THIS, PATTING ITS BLACK NOSE:	45	PLOUGHMAN GONE	15
WATER FROM NOSE AND ARSE, A SANGER'S SHOW	51	OUT OF THE PIT	26
TESTED BY FIRE, DOUBLE THUMB TO NOSE, ...	52	OUT OF THE PIT	74
NOSTRIL			
THE NECK OF THE NOSTRIL, ...	110	I, IN IMAGE	52
NOSTRILS			
WHERE EYES SHOULD BE, AND NOSTRILS FULL OF TOADS.	51	OUT OF THE PIT	23
MY NOSTRILS SEE HER BREATH BURN LIKE A BUSH.	139	FIVE & COUNTRY	10
NOT (185)			
NOTE			
AND MOUTH. BOTH NOTE AND PLUME PLUNGE FROM THE			
SPIRE'S HOOK.	16	SPIRE CRANES	8
AND THE THUNDER'S FIRST NOTE;	59	FAIRY TALES	3
BY THE GREEN OF A ONE POUND NOTE	149	PAPER & STICKS	9
TO HEAR THE GOLDEN NOTE TURN IN A GROOVE, ...	153	WAS A SAVIOUR	6
EACH NOTE OF THY DUSKY SONG	226	SLENDER WIND	6
TO TELL WHAT NOTE I COULD REACH IF I TRIED, ...	234	NO, PIGEON	12
NOTES			
WHO MOONS HER BLUE NOTES FROM HER NEST	4	PROLOGUE	62

	PAGE	TITLE	LINE
NOTES (CONTINUED)			
A FISHING BIRD HAS NOTES OF IVORY	14	FOR LEDA	6
(NOTES NOT IN SYMPATHY, DISCORD, UNEASE), ...	35	LIFT UP FACE	21
AND THE THUNDER OF CALLS AND NOTES.	44	LONGED TO MOVE	10
AND FOUR BIRDS' NOTES.	58	HERE IN SPRING	8
OF MANY A THORNY SHIRE TELL YOU NOTES, ...	99	OCTOBER WIND	15
BEFORE THE LUNGE OF THE NIGHT, THE NOTES ON THIS TIME-SHAKEN	203	SIR JOHNS HILL	59
YOUR CONSTRUCTED NOTES GOING OUT OF THE THROAT	231	YOUR VOICE	2
COULD NEVER TOUCH YOUR SPINNING NOTES, ...	234	NO, PIGEON	9
NOTHING			
NOTHING BUT POISON FROM THE BREATH, ...	19	THE NEOPHYTE	10
WITH KNOWLEDGE THAT NO USE AND NOTHING WORTH	27	OBLIVIOUS DARK	9
ALL HOLD THE SUM, NOTHING TO NOTHING, ...	27	OBLIVIOUS DARK	21
ALL HOLD THE SUM, NOTHING TO NOTHING, ...	27	OBLIVIOUS DARK	21
EVEN THE WORDS ARE NOTHING	27	OBLIVIOUS DARK	22
NOTHING NEVER, NOTHING OLDER	27	OBLIVIOUS DARK	25
NOTHING NEVER, NOTHING OLDER	27	OBLIVIOUS DARK	25
ALL WORLD WAS ONE, ONE WINDY NOTHING, ...	78	LOVE'S FEVER	6
I SEE THAT FROM THESE BOYS SHALL MEN OF NOTHING ...	92	BOYS OF SUMMER	19
WITH NOTHING FOR THE METRE, ...	155	RETURN	59
AND NOTHING SHONE ON THE WATER'S FACE	163	LONG-LEGGED	44
THERE IS NOTHING LEFT OF THE SEA BUT ITS SOUND, ...	169	LONG-LEGGED	205
LAND, LAND, LAND, NOTHING REMAINS	169	LONG-LEGGED	209
AND NOTHING I CARED, AT MY SKY BLUE TRADES, THAT TIME ALLOWS	196	FERN HILL	42
NOTHING I CARED, IN THE LAMB WHITE DAYS, THAT TIME WOULD TAKE ME	196	FERN HILL	46
(BUT NOTHING BORE, NO MOUTHING BABE TO THE VEINED HIVES	205	GIANT'S THIGH	42
NOTHINGS			
AND SPEAK THEIR MIDNIGHT NOTHINGS AS THEY SWELL;	89	EUNUCH DREAMS	14
NOT-TO-BE-BROKEN			
LEFT IN THE RECORDS OF LIVING A NOT-TO-BE-BROKEN PICTURE, ...	45	PLOUGHMAN GONE	2
NOUGHT			
THE SUN THAT LEAPS ON PETALS THROUGH A NOUGHT, ...	128	NOW, SAY NAY	27
'NOR THE GREEN NOUGHT BE HURT;	129	MY NEOPHYTE	45
NOURISH			
TO NOURISH THINKING OF HIM.	12	SKY'S BRIGHT	4
NOVEL			
THE NOVEL THINGS. BUT IT HAS BEEN NO GOOD.	53	OUT OF THE PIT	81
A DIRTY NOVEL DONE IN ERSE	83	LETTER TO AUNT	25
NOVEMBER			
IT WAS NOVEMBER THERE WERE WHIZZBANGS HOPPING, ...	52	OUT OF THE PIT	51
NOW			
THIS DAY WINDING DOWN NOW	3	PROLOGUE	1
AND THE FLOOD FLOWERS NOW.	5	PROLOGUE	102
GONE NOW TO ROT.	26	PERSONAL EPIT	16
HE HAS THE WHOLE FIELD NOW, THE GODS DEPARTED	29	NEARLY SUMMER	7
TAKE NOW CONTENT, NO LONGER POSTURING	29	LONG, SKELETON	7
THE PRISM OF THE EYE NOW VOID BY SUCTION, ...	29	LONG, SKELETON	10
NOW THE THIRST PARCHES LIP AND TONGUE	34	THIRST PARCHES	T
NOW THE THIRST PARCHES LIP AND TONGUE, ...	34	THIRST PARCHES	1
NOW IS DECAY IN BONE AND SINEW, ...	34	THIRST PARCHES	3
AND NOW BEHIND THE SCREEN ARE VIXEN VOICES, ...	36	MIDNIGHT ROAD	9
AND NOW, MISTAKING THE DIRECTION, ...	37	WINDMILLS TURN	23
THE SUICIDES PARADE AGAIN, NOW RIPE FOR DYING.	43	FACES SHONE	14
MAN TOILS NOW ON AN IRON SADDLE, RIDING	45	PLOUGHMAN GONE	24
NOW DID THE SOFTEST SOUND OF FOOT OR VOICE	50	OUT OF THE PIT	13

		PAGE	TITLE	LINE
NOW (CONTINUED)				
BUT NOW THERE ARE THE BUTT-ENDS OF SPENT SQUIBS.		52	OUT OF THE PIT	52
NOW HE IS ONE WITH MANY, ONE WITH ALL,	....	53	OUT OF THE PIT	98
NOW HE HAS HEARD AND READ THE HAPPY WORD.	....	53	OUT OF THE PIT	100
HOW NOW MY FLESH, MY NAKED FELLOW,	....	106	ALL ALL AND	7
KNOW NOW THE FLESH'S LOCK AND VICE,	....	106	ALL ALL AND	20
NOW JACK MY FATHERS LET THE TIME-FACED CROOK,	......	108	GRIEF THIEF	15
NOW STAMP THE LORD'S PRAYER ON A GRAIN OF RICE,	...	119	ALTARWISE	85
AND NOW THE HORNS OF ENGLAND, IN THE SOUND OF SHAPE,		122	HOLD HARD	13
NOW THAT MY SYMBOLS HAVE OUTELBOWED SPACE,	....	124	TODAY, INSECT	2
NOW MAKE THE WORLD OF ME AS I HAVE MADE	....	124	FOSTER LIGHT	29
NOW	....	127	NOW, SAY NAY	T
NOW	....	127	NOW, SAY NAY	1
NOW	....	127	NOW, SAY NAY	8
NOW	....	127	NOW, SAY NAY	15
NOW	....	128	NOW, SAY NAY	22
NOW	....	128	NOW, SAY NAY	29
NOW IN THE CLOUD'S BIG BREAST LIE QUIET COUNTRIES,		133	I MAKE THIS IN	61
ON NO WORK OF WORDS NOW FOR THREE LEAN MONTHS IN THE BLOODY	....	140	NO WORK WORDS	1
TO SURRENDER NOW IS TO PAY THE EXPENSIVE OGRE TWICE.		140	NO WORK WORDS	10
NOW MY SAYING SHALL BE MY UNDOING,	....	144	COLOUR OF SAY	12
WHOM NOW I CONJURE TO STAND AS THIEF	....	146	TO OTHERS	9
'NOW TO AWAKE HUSKED OF GESTURES AND MY JOY LIKE A CAVE	....	146	IF HEAD HURT	21
AND HEAVEN CRIER, ARROW NOW OF ASPIRING	....	148	UNLUCKILY FOR	38
NOW SHOWN AND MOSTLY BARE I WOULD LIE DOWN,	....	152	BELOW A TIME	49
NOW IN THE DARK THERE IS ONLY YOURSELF AND MYSELF.		153	WAS A SAVIOUR	24
NOW BREAK A GIANT TEAR FOR THE LITTLE KNOWN FALL,		153	WAS A SAVIOUR	32
NOW SEE, ALONE IN US,	....	153	WAS A SAVIOUR	36
NOW I DELIGHT, I SUPPOSE, IN	....	156	RETURN	95
AND NOAH'S REKINDLED NOW UNKIND DOVE	....	157	INTO HER HEAD	5
NOT YOUR WINGED LUST BUT HIS MUST NOW CHANGE SUIT.		159	TO LEDA	1
NOT YOUR WINGED LUST BUT HIS MUST NOW CHANGE SUIT.		159	TO LEDA	6
NOW THEIR LOVE LIES A LOSS	....	161	WEDDING ANNIV	5
NOW CAST DOWN YOUR ROD, FOR THE WHOLE	....	162	LONG-LEGGED	31
MYSELVES GRIEVE NOW, AND MIRACLES CANNOT ATONE.	...	173	FIRE RAID	16
SNIFF, HERE IS SIN! NOW HE MUST GRAPPLE, RISE:	....	179	NEW QUAY	29
THAT HE WHO LEARNS NOW THE SUN AND MOON	....	183	VISION, PRAYER	119
NOW COMMON LAZARUS	....	184	VISION, PRAYER	166
NOW OR	....	185	VISION, PRAYER	178
NOW I AM LOST IN THE BLINDING	....	185	VISION, PRAYER	203
NOW AS I WAS YOUNG AND EASY UNDER THE APPLE BOUGHS		195	FERN HILL	1
NOW THE TALES PRAISE	....	198	COUNTRY SLEEP	33
NOW THE HERON GRIEVES IN THE WEEDED VERGE. THROUGH WINDOWS	....	202	SIR JOHNS HILL	47
NOW ON SIR JOHN'S HILL. THE HERON, ANKLING THE SCALY		203	SIR JOHNS HILL	55
NOW CLASP ME TO THEIR GRAINS IN THE GIGANTIC GLADE,		204	GIANT'S THIGH	19
NOW CURLEW CRY ME DOWN TO KISS THE MOUTHS OF THEIR DUST.	....	205	GIANT'S THIGH	45
WHERE THE HAY RIDES NOW OR THE BRACKEN KITCHENS RUST		205	GIANT'S THIGH	47
NOW I AM A MAN NO MORE NO MORE	....	207	LAMENT	49
CURSE, BLESS, ME NOW WITH YOUR FIERCE TEARS, I PRAY.		208	NOT GO GENTLE	17
NOR DID HE NOW, SAVE TO HIS SECRET WOUND.	....	217	ELEGY	27
WHERE NOW THE WINGS OF DREAMLESS SLEEP ARE SPREAD,		222	MISSING	5
NOW THE SEA HAS A FLOWERING OF FOAM;	....	224	IDYLL UNFORGET	36
NOW THAT THE TEMPLE'S TRUMPETER	....	237	PILLAR BREAKS	2
NOWHERES				
OLD COCK FROM NOWHERES AND THE HEAVEN'S EGG,	......	117	ALTARWISE	8
OLD COCK FROM NOWHERES LOPPED THE MINSTREL TONGUE		119	ALTARWISE	78

	PAGE	TITLE	LINE
NUDE			
BY THE CURVE OF THE NUDE MOUTH OR THE LAUGH UP THE SLEEVE. ••••••••••••••••••••••••••••••••••••	133	MAKE ME A MASK	12
NUDGE			
THE DEAR, DAFT TIME I TAKE TO NUDGE THE SENTENCE,	124	TODAY, INSECT	4
NUDGING			
AND ELBOWED VEINS THAT, NUDGING BLOOD, ••••••••••	85	SEE, SAYS LIME	3
NUISANCE			
IN SEIZURE OF SILENCE COMMIT THE DEAD NUISANCE: •••	109	I, IN IMAGE	23
NUMBED			
DEEP HILLOCKS AND LOUD ON THE NUMBED LAKES, •••••••	190	WINTER'S TALE	97
NUMBER			
AND A CAT HAS A NUMBER OF LIVES; ••••••••••••••••	221	SONG OF DOG	2
NUMBERED			
THE SEASONS NUMBERED BY THE INWARD SUN, •••••••••••	79	ALMANAC TIME	2
NUMBERLESS			
THERE WHERE A NUMBERLESS TONGUE •••••••••••••••••	158	INTO HER HEAD	24
OR STILL ALL THE NUMBERLESS DAYS OF HIS DEATH, THOUGH	216	ELEGY	8
NUN			
I SEE THE WANTING NUN SAINT CARVED IN A GARB ••••••	148	UNLUCKILY FOR	34
NUNNERIES			
THE NIGHTBIRD LAUDS THROUGH NUNNERIES AND DOMES OF LEAVES •••••••••••••••••••••••••••••••••••••••	198	COUNTRY SLEEP	28
NUNNERY			
OF THE WINTRY NUNNERY OF THE ORDER OF LUST ••••••••	147	UNLUCKILY FOR	12
DEATH IN THE CARVED NUNNERY •••••••••••••••••••••	148	UNLUCKILY FOR	46
NURSE			
THE WET NIGHT SCOLDS ME LIKE A NURSE? ••••••••••••	65	GODS THUMP	10
THE NURSE OF GIANTS BY THE CUT SEA BASIN, ••••••••	113	SERVANT SUN	10
THAT DID NOT NURSE OUR BONES, •••••••••••••••••••	153	WAS A SAVIOUR	34
NURSERIES			
RAPE AND REBELLION IN THE NURSERIES OF MY FACE, •••	133	MAKE ME A MASK	3
BARE AS THE NURSERIES ••••••••••••••••••••••••••	175	FIRE RAID	59
NURSERY			
HAVE BLOWN SKY HIGH THE NURSERY OF FAIRIES; •••••••	59	FAIRY TALES	23
NURSES			
LOVE ME, NOT AS THE DREAMING NURSES ••••••••••••••	75	SONG: LOVE ME	1
ALONE BETWEEN NURSES AND SWANS ••••••••••••••••••	171	THE HUNCHBACK	26
NURSE'S			
FROM DAMP LOVE-DARKNESS AND THE NURSE'S TWIST •••••	96	RUB OF LOVE	38
NUT			
GLANCING FROM THE YELLOW NUT, ••••••••••••••••••••	20	ENCOMPASSED	9
ANCIENT WOODS OF MY BLOOD, DASH DOWN TO THE NUT OF THE SEAS •••••••••••••••••••••••••••••••••••••	140	NO WORK WORDS	11
NUTMEG			
NUTMEG, CIVET, AND SEA-PARSLEY SERVE THE PLAGUED GROOM AND BRIDE •••••••••••••••••••••••••••••••	131	SINNERS' BELL	29
O			
O MY RUFFLED RING DOVE •••••••••••••••••••••••••	4	PROLOGUE	58
O KINGDOM OF NEIGHBOURS, FINNED •••••••••••••••••	5	PROLOGUE	82
SO STEAL HER NOT O GOAT-LEGGED WIND ••••••••••••••	11	AIR BREATHE	7
O LONELY AMONG MANY, THE GODS' MAN, ••••••••••••••	47	POET: 1935	47
BREAKS, O MY HEART'S BLOOD, LIKE A HEART AND HILL.	54	WE BY SEASAND	24
BEFORE DEATH TAKES YOU, O TAKE BACK THIS. ••••••••	61	MEAT ON BONES	41
O TIDAL WINDS, CAST UP HER CRY FOR ME; •••••••••••	65	WOMAN SPEAKS	54
PALM OF THE EARTH, O SPRINKLE ON MY HEAD ••••••••••	65	WOMAN SPEAKS	60
THAT DUST YOU HOLD, O STREW THAT LITTLE LEFT; •••••	65	WOMAN SPEAKS	61
HOW SOON, HOW SOON, O LORD OF THE RED HAIL! •••••••	73	LORD RED HAIL	18
O ALL I OWE IS ALL THE FLESH INHERITS, ••••••••••	80	ALL THAT I OWE	5
O MY UNBORN •••••••••••••••••••••••••••••••••••	87	PAIN BE MUSIC	4

	PAGE	TITLE	LINE
O (CONTINUED)			
O MY UNSOWN	87	PAIN BE MUSIC	10
O MY UNKNOWN	87	PAIN BE MUSIC	16
O MY UNDONE	87	PAIN BE MUSIC	22
O SEE THE PULSE OF SUMMER IN THE ICE.	92	BOYS OF SUMMER	24
O SEE THE POLES OF PROMISE IN THE BOYS.	93	BOYS OF SUMMER	48
O SEE THE POLES ARE KISSING AS THEY CROSS.	93	BOYS OF SUMMER	54
MAY FAIL TO FASTEN WITH A VIRGIN O	100	RUNNING GRAVE	19
KNOW, O MY BONE, THE JOINTED LEVER,	106	ALL ALL AND	22
O LIGHT IN ZENITH, THE COUPLED BUD,	107	ALL ALL AND	32
O RING OF SEAS, NOR SORROW AS I SHIFT	123	FOSTER LIGHT	20
O WHO IS GLORY IN THE SHAPELESS MAPS,	124	FOSTER LIGHT	28
O GREEN AND UNBORN AND UNDEAD?'	129	MY NEOPHYTE	47
O MAKE ME A MASK	133	MAKE ME A MASK	T
O MAKE ME A MASK AND A WALL TO SHUT FROM YOUR SPIES	133	MAKE ME A MASK	1
O CHATTERTON	137	O CHATTERTON	T
O CHATTERTON AND OTHERS IN THE ATTIC	137	O CHATTERTON	1
O WAKE IN ME IN MY HOUSE IN THE MUD	142	SAINT TO FALL	26
O WAKE TO SEE, AFTER A NOBLE FALL,	142	SAINT TO FALL	43
O MY LOST LOVE BOUNCED FROM A GOOD HOME;	146	IF HEAD HURT	23
O MY DEAR IT'S NEVER TOO LATE	149	PAPER & STICKS	11
AND THE VAULTING BIRD BE STILL. O MY TRUE LOVE, HOLD ME.	149	UNLUCKILY FOR	54
O YOU WHO COULD NOT CRY	153	WAS A SAVIOUR	20
O WE WHO COULD NOT STIR	153	WAS A SAVIOUR	28
AND O TO CUT THE GREEN FIELD, LEAVING	157	RETURN	100
O SHE LIES ALONE AND STILL,	159	INTO HER HEAD	64
O ROME AND SODOM TO-MORROW AND LONDON	168	LONG-LEGGED	191
O KEEP HIS BONES AWAY FROM THAT COMMON CART,	173	DAWN RAID	12
O BRIDE AND BRIDE GROOM	174	FIRE RAID	41
O ADAM AND EVE TOGETHER	174	FIRE RAID	42
O MAY MY HEART'S TRUTH	178	POEM IN OCT	68
O SPIRAL OF ASCENSION	182	VISION, PRAYER	79
O THE WINGS OF THE CHILDREN!	182	VISION, PRAYER	91
O IN THE NAME	185	VISION, PRAYER	176
O LET HIM	185	VISION, PRAYER	198
O	186	HOLY SPRING	1
THE COUNTRY IS HOLY: O BIDE IN THAT COUNTRY KIND,	198	COUNTRY SLEEP	39
(O HAND IN HAND)	215	COUNTRY HEAVEN	12
O DEEPEST WOUND OF ALL THAT HE SHOULD DIE	217	ELEGY	37
OAK			
IS MAIDEN IN THE SHAMEFUL OAK, OMENS	131	I MAKE THIS IN	21
SHAPED IN OLD ARMOUR AND OAK THE COUNTENANCE OF A DUNCE	133	MAKE ME A MASK	7
THE OAK IS FELLED IN THE ACORN	167	LONG-LEGGED	155
PADDOCKS IN THE FARMS OF BIRDS. THE DEAD OAK WALKS FOR LOVE.	189	WINTER'S TALE	75
THE OAK	226	THE OAK	T
OAKEN			
SOME OF THE OAKEN VOICES, FROM THE ROOTS	99	OCTOBER WIND	14
OAKUM			
AND THE OAKUM IS PICKED, AND THE SPRING TREES HAVE GROWN GREEN,	39	GAS FADES	6
OAR			
FOR WHEN WE TOUCH A FLOWER WITH OUR OAR	14	RAIN CUTS	30
OAT			
THIS BREAD I BREAK WAS ONCE THE OAT,	86	BREAD I BREAK	1
THE OAT WAS MERRY IN THE WIND;	86	BREAD I BREAK	9
WERE OAT AND GRAPE	86	BREAD I BREAK	13

	PAGE	TITLE	LINE
OATH		
IS LAUGHING BOY BENEATH HIS OATH, ...	19	THE NEOPHYTE	2
OBEY		
OR WE SHALL OBEY, AND RIDE WITH YOU THROUGH THE		
DROWNED.	194	SLEEP BECALMED	14
OBLIVION		
IT'S NOT IN MISERY BUT IN OBLIVION	16	IN OBLIVION	T
IT'S NOT IN MISERY BUT IN OBLIVION, ...	16	IN OBLIVION	1
OBLIVION IS SO LOVERLESS.	17	IN OBLIVION	28
OBLIVION IS AS LOVERLESS;	22	ON QUIET NIGHT	13
OBLIVION IS AS LOVERLESS.	22	ON QUIET NIGHT	14
OBLIVION IS AS BLIND, ...	23	ON QUIET NIGHT	19
OBLIVION IS AS BLIND, ...	23	ON QUIET NIGHT	20
YOUNG FROM THE CANYONS OF OBLIVION!	182	VISION, PRAYER	93
OBLIVIOUS		
NEVER TO REACH THE OBLIVIOUS DARK	27	OBLIVIOUS DARK	T
NEVER TO REACH THE OBLIVIOUS DARK	27	OBLIVIOUS DARK	1
OBSCURELY		
IN THE CARPETING OF THE DUSK, OBSCURELY AND		
ELUSIVELY, ...	224	IDYLL UNFORGET	41
OBSERVING		
I SIT AT THE OPEN WINDOW, OBSERVING	179	NEW QUAY	13
OBVIOUS		
BY THOSE WHO PLANNED THE OBVIOUS ROUTES	37	WINDMILLS TURN	22
OCCURRED		
THOUGH THE BRAWL OF THE KISS HAS NOT OCCURRED	147	UNLUCKILY FOR	7
OCEAN		
STAGE OF THE ICE, THE SOLID OCEAN, ...	106	ALL ALL AND	2
SAILED AND SET DAZZLING BY THE HANDSHAPED OCEAN,	131	I MAKE THIS IN	5
OCEANIC		
OCEANIC LOVER ALONE	158	INTO HER HEAD	33
OCEANS		
OR RIDES THE IMAGINED OCEANS OF THE MALE WARDS. ...	169	LOVE IN ASYLUM	9
OCHRE		
WEEPS ON THE DESERT OCHRE AND THE SALT	104	WORLD PYRAMID	32
OCTAGON		
CAUGHT IN AN OCTAGON OF UNACCUSTOMED LIGHT, ...	116	LANTERNS SHINE	2
OCTOBER		
ESPECIALLY WHEN THE OCTOBER WIND	98	OCTOBER WIND	T
ESPECIALLY WHEN THE OCTOBER WIND	98	OCTOBER WIND	1
ESPECIALLY WHEN THE OCTOBER WIND	99	OCTOBER WIND	25
POEM IN OCTOBER	176	POEM IN OCT	T
BLACKBIRDS AND THE SUN OF OCTOBER	177	POEM IN OCT	23
THOUGH THE TOWN BELOW LAY LEAVED WITH OCTOBER BLOOD.	178	POEM IN OCT	67
OCTOPUS		
DRUNK AS A VINEYARD SNAIL, FLAILED LIKE AN OCTOPUS,	134	HOW MY ANIMAL	7
THE OCTOPUS WALKING INTO HER LIMBS	164	LONG-LEGGED	79
OCTOPUSES		
OCTOPUSES IN DOORWAYS, ...	155	RETURN	55
ODD		
FROM AN ODD ROOM IN A SPLIT HOUSE STARE, ...	142	SAINT TO FALL	31
LONDON (SAID THE ODD MAN IN	154	RETURN	2
WITH LITTLE, ODD MISTS WAVED IN THE PATH OF ITS ECHO,	224	IDYLL UNFORGET	26
ODYSSEY		
WITH STONES OF ODYSSEY FOR ASH AND GARLAND	120	ALTARWISE	125
OF (1479)		
OFF		
IMPATIENT TO BE OFF.	13	RAIN CUTS	18
AS EDGES OFF YOUR NERVES TO MINE, ...	20	ENCOMPASSED	5
OF CRYING OFF THIS UNSHAPED EVIL, ...	21	BEWILDERED WAY	2

	PAGE	TITLE	LINE
OFF (CONTINUED)			
KNOCKING OFF TURNIP TOPS, WITH TREES FOR FRIENDS,	53	OUT OF THE PIT	88
PAIR OFF, MAKE HARMONIES, A HARMONIOUS CHORD,	53	OUT OF THE PIT	96
CAN WE FEND OFF ROCK ARRIVAL,	54	WE BY SEASAND	22
WE HAVE THESE LITTLE THINGS OFF PAT,	59	FAIRY TALES	4
SHALL WE LEARN FAIRY TALES OFF PAT,	60	FAIRY TALES	37
SHIPS ANCHOR OFF THE BAY.	62	EARS IN TURRET	20
SHIPS ANCHOR OFF THE BAY,	62	EARS IN TURRET	27
BUT ALL THIS LAND GIVES OFF A CHARNEL STENCH,	67	REALM OF FLESH	4
PACK OFF THE SHAPES OF DAYLIGHT AND THEIR STARCH,	90	EUNUCH DREAMS	24
OFF FROM THE CREASING FLESH, FILED	102	I DREAMED MY	6
GRIEF THIEF OF TIME CRAWLS OFF,	107	GRIEF THIEF	1
THE KNAVE OF PAIN STEALS OFF	107	GRIEF THIEF	3
SHE THREADS OFF THE SAP AND NEEDLES, BLOOD AND BUBBLE	108	I, IN IMAGE	10
VOYAGING CLOCKWISE OFF THE SYMBOLED HARBOUR,	109	I, IN IMAGE	32
ATLASWISE HOLD HALF-WAY OFF THE DUMMY BAY	121	ALTARWISE	128
'WHO COULD SNAP OFF THE SHAPELESS PRINT	129	MY NEOPHYTE	40
AND EVERY STONE I WIND OFF LIKE A REEL.	144	COLOUR OF SAY	13
CUTTING THE MORNING OFF,	150	WHEN I WOKE	10
RUB OFF THE SCRAWL OF PRINTS ON	156	RETURN	81
HIS FIERY REEL SINGS OFF ITS FLAMES,	164	LONG-LEGGED	64
UNDER THE MILE OFF MOON WE TREMBLED LISTENING	194	SLEEP BECALMED	5
OFF BY THE SUN AND DAUGHTERS NO LONGER GRIEVED	205	GIANT'S THIGH	55
OFFENDED			
YOU HAVE OFFENDED, PERIODIC HEART;	9	MINUTE'S HOUR	8
OFFER			
FOR ALL THERE IS TO GIVE I OFFER:	32	OUT OF SIGHS	28
I OFFER YOU WOMEN, NOT WOMAN,	138	O CHATTERTON	40
AND OFFER AS THE LAST DELIGHT	143	THE MOLLS	7
OFFICERS			
YOUR MONSTROUS OFFICERS AND THE DECAYING ARMY,	110	I, IN IMAGE	56
OFFICIAL			
AND OTHER VIRGINS IN OFFICIAL FATHERS.	38	THE GOSSIPERS	13
OFTEN			
AND GODS BE CHANGED AS OFTEN AS THE SHIFT.	67	LET A FAITH	8
OGRE			
TO SURRENDER NOW IS TO PAY THE EXPENSIVE OGRE TWICE.	140	NO WORK WORDS	10
OH			
COOL, OH NO COOL	10	COOL, OH NO	T
COOL, OH NO COOL,	10	COOL, OH NO	1
SHARP, OH NO SHARP,	10	COOL, OH NO	2
OH NO, MY MIND IS YOUR PANOPTICON;	10	COOL, OH NO	20
OH GAIETY!	18	NATURAL DAY	34
OH GAIETY!	18	NATURAL DAY	35
AS MEANINGLESS AS THE BELLS (OH CHANGE THE LIFE!),	33	HELD-OUT HAND	9
NEVER NEVER OH NEVER TO REGRET THE BUGLE I WORE	152	BELOW A TIME	47
OH, JERICHO WAS FALLING IN THEIR LUNGS!	163	LONG-LEGGED	54
OH THE SHEARWATER BIRDS AND THEIR BOATSIZED BROOD	164	LONG-LEGGED	67
OH THE BULLS OF BISCAY AND THEIR CALVES	164	LONG-LEGGED	68
OH ALL THE WANTING FLESH HIS ENEMY	165	LONG-LEGGED	91
OH MIRACLE OF FISHES! THE LONG DEAD BITE!	166	LONG-LEGGED	140
LOVE IS THE LAST LIGHT SPOKEN. OH	174	FIRE RAID	31
OH AS I WAS YOUNG AND EASY IN THE MERCY OF HIS MEANS,	196	FERN HILL	52
AND SURELY HE SAILS LIKE THE SHIP SHAPE CLOUDS. OH HE	200	COUNTRY SLEEP	99
OH, TIME ENOUGH WHEN THE BLOOD CREEPS COLD,	206	LAMENT	34
FOR, OH, MY SOUL FOUND A SUNDAY WIFE	207	LAMENT	54
OH, LET ME MIDLIFE MOURN BY THE SHRINED	211	POEM ON B'DAY	76
THE MANSOULED FIERY ISLANDS! OH,	211	POEM ON B'DAY	105
ON THAT DARKEST DAY. OH, FOREVER MAY	216	ELEGY	4
ON THAT DARKEST DAY. OH, HE COULD HIDE	217	ELEGY	38

	PAGE	TITLE	LINE
OH (CONTINUED)			
OH, EAGLE-MOUTHED, ...	232	YOUR VOICE	10
OH, LET ME DESTROY FOR ONCE, ...	239	MAKES INTERVALS	22
OIL			
UPON THE LAND OF GOLD OR OIL, ...	73	WE MOTHERNAKED	2
DIVINING IN A SMILE THE OIL OF TEARS.	82	LIGHT BREAKS	18
ALL FROM THE OIL, THE POUND OF LAVA.	106	ALL ALL AND	3
OUT OF THE SEA, THE DRIVE OF OIL, ...	107	ALL ALL AND	34
PROPHETS AND FIBRE KINGS IN OIL AND LETTER, ...	120	ALTARWISE	114
THE BREATH DRAW BACK LIKE A BOLT THROUGH WHITE OIL	142	SAINT TO FALL	46
BUT THE OIL AND BUBBLE OF THE MOON, ...	163	LONG-LEGGED	45
OILED			
HIS SCISSORS OILED, HIS KNIFE HUNG LOOSE	91	WHERE ONCE THE	10
OILS			
AND THIS IS PLENTY, THEN, CLOVES AND SWEET OILS, THE			
BEES' HONEY, ...	36	MIDNIGHT ROAD	5
THE SECRET OILS THAT DRIVE THE GRASS.	94	IN BEGINNING	18
AND, AS FOR OILS AND OINTMENTS ON THE FLYING GRAIL,	111	I, IN IMAGE	101
THE LANDSCAPE GRIEF, LOVE IN HIS OILS	129	MY NEOPHYTE	20
OINTMENTS			
AND, AS FOR OILS AND OINTMENTS ON THE FLYING GRAIL,	111	I, IN IMAGE	101
OLD			
AHOY, OLD, SEA-LEGGED FOX, ...	5	PROLOGUE	98
WAS OLD WHEN YOU WERE YOUNG, ...	20	THE NEOPHYTE	22
OLD IN ILLUSIONS TURNED TO ACRITUDES, ...	20	THE NEOPHYTE	23
INCH ON THE OLD THIGH	22	HIGH ON A HILL	11
CAN BE BUT VANITY, SUCH AN OLD CRY, ...	27	OBLIVIOUS DARK	24
YOU, WHO ARE OLD, HAVE LOVED AND LOST AS I	30	YOUTH CALLS	5
LET CHILDREN KNOW, AND OLD MEN AT THEIR GATES, ...	36	LET BE KNOWN	3
AND THAT IS LIES THAT, AFTER THE OLD MEN DIE, ...	36	LET BE KNOWN	5
PUFFED, OLD WITH VENOM, FROM A CRUSTED MOUTH.	37	WINDMILLS TURN	30
STIR THEIR OLD BONES BEHIND CUPBOARD AND CURTAIN.	38	THE GOSSIPERS	5
PRESS THE OLD LIES AND THE OLD GHOSTS.	38	THE GOSSIPERS	18
PRESS THE OLD LIES AND THE OLD GHOSTS.	38	THE GOSSIPERS	18
'WE WHO ARE YOUNG ARE OLD'	40	YOUNG ARE OLD	T
'WE WHO ARE YOUNG ARE OLD. IT IS THE OLDEST CRY.	40	YOUNG ARE OLD	1
WE WHO ARE STILL YOUNG ARE OLD. IT IS A DEAD CRY,	40	YOUNG ARE OLD	5
THE SQUEAL OF THE DAMNED OUT OF THE OLD PIT.	40	YOUNG ARE OLD	6
MEN OLD BEFORE THEIR TIME INTO DARK VALLEYS	41	YOUNG ARE OLD	19
NO FAITH TO SHARPEN THE OLD WITS LEAVES US	41	YOUNG ARE OLD	21
YOUNG MEN WITH FALLEN CHESTS AND OLD MEN'S BREATH,	41	YOUNG ARE OLD	27
FELL HARD AS WHIPS ON AN OLD WOUND, ...	42	A WAR OF WITS	3
WE WHO ARE YOUNG ARE OLD, AND UNBELIEVING, ...	42	YOUNG ARE OLD	53
AND THE OLD TERRORS' CONTINUAL CRY	43	LONGED TO MOVE	3
OUT OF THE OLD LIE BURNING ON THE GROUND, ...	44	LONGED TO MOVE	13
LEFT ONLY THE VOICE IN THE OLD VILLAGE CHOIR	45	PLOUGHMAN GONE	4
AGAINST THE RUSTY SWORD AND THE OLD HORSE	45	PLOUGHMAN GONE	8
THE OLD FLOWERS' LEGS TOO TAUT TO DANCE, ...	47	POET: 1935	40
OF OLD DIVINITIES, SPLIT BITS OF NAMES.	53	OUT OF THE PIT	85
AND GREEN, SNEERS NOT AT THE OLD SKY.	55	NO MAN BELIEVE	11
AN OLD CHATTERBOX, BARENAVELED AT NICE, ...	58	TO ARCHITECTS	8
HALF OF THE OLD GANG'S SHOT, ...	59	FAIRY TALES	8
THE OLD SPELLS ARE UNDONE.	59	FAIRY TALES	13
OLD MEN WHOSE BLOOD IS HINDERED IN THEIR VEINS, ...	64	WOMAN SPEAKS	42
AN OLD GOD'S DUGS ARE PRESSED AND PRICKED, ...	65	GODS THUMP	9
BLOWING THE OLD DEAD BACK; OUR SHOTS SHALL SMACK	90	EUNUCH DREAMS	38
OF SICK OLD MANHOOD ON THE FALLEN JAWS, ...	95	RUB OF LOVE	24
AN OLD MAN'S SHANK ONE-MARROWED WITH MY BONE, ...	95	RUB OF LOVE	32
AN OLD, MAD MAN STILL CLIMBING IN HIS GHOST, ...	102	FELLOWED SLEEP	29
THE OLD FORGET THE CRIES, ...	107	GRIEF THIEF	5

	PAGE	TITLE	LINE
OLD (CONTINUED)			
THE OLD FORGET THE GRIEF,	107	GRIEF THIEF	9
OLD COCK FROM NOWHERES AND THE HEAVEN'S EGG,	117	ALTARWISE	8
THE BLACK RAM, SHUFFLING OF THE YEAR, OLD WINTER,	118	ALTARWISE	39
OLD COCK FROM NOWHERES LOPPED THE MINSTREL TONGUE	119	ALTARWISE	78
SHAPED IN OLD ARMOUR AND OAK THE COUNTENANCE OF A DUNCE	133	MAKE ME A MASK	7
SOAKS TO THE VEST OLD DOMINIES AND DRUNKS.	137	O CHATTERTON	20
THE OLD MUD HATCH AGAIN, THE HORRID	142	SAINT TO FALL	44
NOT SPIN TO STARE AT AN OLD YEAR	145	PLEASURE-BIRD	17
WHY WON'T THE NEWS OF THE OLD WORLD CATCH	149	PAPER & STICKS	2
ON THE OLD SEAS FROM STORIES, THRASHING MY WINGS,	152	BELOW A TIME	36
OLD PAINT-STAINED TUMBLERS RIDING	154	RETURN	19
OLD WIVES THAT SPIN IN THE SMOKE,	162	LONG-LEGGED	26
OLD IN HER CRUEL BED.	164	LONG-LEGGED	84
IS OLD AS WATER AND PLAIN AS AN EEL;	165	LONG-LEGGED	93
AND THE OLD MEN SING FROM NEWBORN LIPS:	167	LONG-LEGGED	152
WAS MIRACULOUS VIRGINITY OLD AS LOAVES AND FISHES,	170	MARRIAGE VIRG	5
AND THE OLD DOG SLEEPER	171	THE HUNCHBACK	25
ONCE WHEN THE WORLD TURNED OLD	187	WINTER'S TALE	11
LEAP, AS TO TRUMPETS. CALLIGRAPHY OF THE OLD	189	WINTER'S TALE	77
(SIGHED THE OLD RAM ROD, DYING OF WOMEN),	206	LAMENT	3
(SIGHED THE OLD RAM ROD, DYING OF BITCHES),	206	LAMENT	15
(SIGHED THE OLD RAM ROD, DYING OF WELCOME),	206	LAMENT	27
OLD AGE SHOULD BURN AND RAVE AT CLOSE OF DAY;	207	NOT GO GENTLE	2
(SIGHED THE OLD RAM ROD, DYING OF DOWNFALL),	207	LAMENT	39
(SIGHED THE OLD RAM ROD, DYING OF STRANGERS),	207	LAMENT	51
WHO IS THE LIGHT OF OLD	210	POEM ON B'DAY	73
AN OLD TORMENTED MAN THREE-QUARTERS BLIND,	217	ELEGY	18
AN OLD KIND MAN BRAVE IN HIS BURNING PRIDE.	217	ELEGY	24
AN OLD MAN IS WITH ME WHERE I GO	217	ELEGY	30
RECALL MY OLD DESIRE	237	WOMAN TAPESTRY	70
OLDER			
NOTHING NEVER, NOTHING OLDER	27	OBLIVIOUS DARK	25
OLDEST			
'WE WHO ARE YOUNG ARE OLD. IT IS THE OLDEST CRY.	40	YOUNG ARE OLD	1
OMENS			
IS MAIDEN IN THE SHAMEFUL OAK, OMENS	131	I MAKE THIS IN	21
OMIT			
NEVER OMIT SUCH VITAL WORDS	84	LETTER TO AUNT	44
ON (431)			
ONCE			
MAN WHO ONCE DROVE IS DRIVEN IN SUN AND RAIN.	46	PLOUGHMAN GONE	34
OUR CLAIM IS STAKED FOR ONCE AND ALL	73	WE MOTHERNAKED	5
ONCE FOR THE VIRGIN'S CHILD, ONCE FOR HER OWN.	74	SUN BURNS	15
ONCE FOR THE VIRGIN'S CHILD, ONCE FOR HER OWN.	74	SUN BURNS	15
ONCE IN THIS CLAY FENCED BY THE STICKS	85	SEE, SAYS LIME	5
THIS BREAD I BREAK WAS ONCE THE OAT,	86	BREAD I BREAK	1
ONCE IN THIS WINE THE SUMMER BLOOD	86	BREAD I BREAK	6
ONCE IN THIS BREAD	86	BREAD I BREAK	8
WHERE ONCE THE WATERS OF YOUR FACE	90	WHERE ONCE THE	T
WHERE ONCE THE WATERS OF YOUR FACE	90	WHERE ONCE THE	1
WHERE ONCE THE MERMEN THROUGH YOUR ICE	90	WHERE ONCE THE	4
WHERE ONCE YOUR GREEN KNOTS SANK THEIR SPLICE	91	WHERE ONCE THE	7
WHEN ONCE THE TWILIGHT LOCKS NO LONGER	97	TWILIGHT LOCKS	T
WHEN ONCE THE TWILIGHT LOCKS NO LONGER	97	TWILIGHT LOCKS	1
WHEN ONCE THE TWILIGHT SCREWS WERE TURNED,	98	TWILIGHT LOCKS	31
ONCE CLOSE-UP SMILING IN THE WALL OF PICTURES,	118	ALTARWISE	55
ONCE WHERE THE SOFT SNOW'S BLOOD WAS TURNED TO ICE.	133	I MAKE THIS IN	65
WHOSE HOODED, FOUNTAIN HEART ONCE FELL IN PUDDLES	136	AFTER FUNERAL	14

	PAGE	TITLE	LINE
ONCE (CONTINUED)			
MEET ONCE ON A MORTAL WALL,	140	TOMBSTONE TOLD	23
ONCE IT WAS THE COLOUR OF SAYING	144	COLOUR OF SAY	T
ONCE IT WAS THE COLOUR OF SAYING	144	COLOUR OF SAY	1
WERE ONCE SUCH A CREATURE, SO GAY AND FRANK	147	TO OTHERS	14
ONCE I HAD A RICH BOY FOR MYSELF	149	PAPER & STICKS	4
ONCE BELOW A TIME	151	BELOW A TIME	T
ONCE BELOW A TIME	151	BELOW A TIME	1
ZIP ONCE MORE FOR A TRAVELLER	155	RETURN	37
ONCE SEEN STRANGERS OR SHADES ON A STAIR;	157	INTO HER HEAD	15
HER DEEPSEA PILLOW WHERE ONCE SHE MARRIED ALONE,	170	MARRIAGE VIRG	9
THE ONCE HOODED ROOM	181	VISION, PRAYER	47
ONCE WHEN THE WORLD TURNED OLD	187	WINTER'S TALE	11
THAT ONCE CUT THE FIGURES OF BIRDS ON THE DEEP BREAD	190	WINTER'S TALE	114
AND ONCE BELOW A TIME I LORDLY HAD THE TREES AND LEAVES	195	FERN HILL	7
IN THE SUN THAT IS YOUNG ONCE ONLY,	195	FERN HILL	12
HILL. WHO ONCE IN GOOSESKIN WINTER LOVED ALL ICE LEAVED	203	GIANT'S THIGH	12
WHO ONCE, GREEN COUNTRIES SINCE, WERE A HEDGEROW OF JOYS.	204	GIANT'S THIGH	20
WHO ONCE WERE A BLOOM OF WAYSIDE BRIDES IN THE HAWED HOUSE	204	GIANT'S THIGH	29
OH, LET ME DESTROY FOR ONCE,	239	MAKES INTERVALS	22
ONCE-BLIND			
THESE ONCE-BLIND EYES HAVE BREATHED A WIND OF VISIONS,	132	I MAKE THIS IN	54
ONCE-RINDLESS			
THE CAULDRON'S ROOT THROUGH THIS ONCE-RINDLESS HAND	132	I MAKE THIS IN	55
ONE			
ONE LADY'S HAND WAS LIFTED,	11	CABARET	11
ONE HOUR SPEND MY TIME FOR ME	18	NATURAL DAY	5
ONE SAYS: THERE WAS A WOMAN WITH NO FRIEND,	22	ON QUIET NIGHT	8
NO WIT, IS ONE),	24	LITTLE PROBLEM	7
AT ONE SIDE'S LOSS,	25	BEAUTY TO DUST	6
LOVING AND DOUBTING LIKE ONE WHO IS TO DIE	27	OBLIVIOUS DARK	28
THE WESTERN MAN HAS LOST ONE LUNG	40	YOUNG ARE OLD	9
WHERE DEATH LIES DEAD ASLEEP, ONE BRIGHT EYE OPEN,	41	YOUNG ARE OLD	20
THERE IS BUT ONE MESSAGE FOR THE EARTH,	41	YOUNG ARE OLD	26
THE WESTERN MAN WITH ONE LUNG GONE--	41	YOUNG ARE OLD	44
FAITH. FAITH. FIRM FAITH IN MANY OR ONE,	41	YOUNG ARE OLD	49
(AND SKELETONS HAD SAP). ONE MINUTE	43	FACES SHONE	7
DEAD MEN NAKED THEY SHALL BE ONE	49	NO DOMINION	2
ONE HAND AT HEAD, THE OTHER AT A LOSS,	52	OUT OF THE PIT	60
NOW HE IS ONE WITH MANY, ONE WITH ALL,	53	OUT OF THE PIT	98
NOW HE IS ONE WITH MANY, ONE WITH ALL,	53	OUT OF THE PIT	98
BUT ONE COMPANION.	61	MEAT ON BONES	37
ONE WOULD NOT THINK THE GREENNESS OF THIS VALLEY	63	WOMAN SPEAKS	12
ONE DAY MY WOMAN'S BODY WILL BE COLD.	64	WOMAN SPEAKS	47
LET FOR ONE MOMENT A FAITH STATEMENT	66	LET A FAITH	T
LET FOR ONE MOMENT A FAITH STATEMENT	66	LET A FAITH	1
LET FOR ONE MOMENT A FAITH STATEMENT	67	LET A FAITH	6
LET FOR ONE MOMENT A FAITH STATEMENT	67	LET A FAITH	11
ONE GOD, MORE MIGHTY THAN THE SUN.	70	SECRET WIND	23
SHALL FALL AWAY, AND LEAVE ONE SINGING SHELL.	73	LORD RED HAIL	12
AND WITH NOT ONE FEAR-BEGGARED SYLLABLE	76	LASHED RINGS	10
ALL WORLD WAS ONE, ONE WINDY NOTHING,	78	LOVE'S FEVER	6
ALL WORLD WAS ONE, ONE WINDY NOTHING,	78	LOVE'S FEVER	6
AND EARTH AND SKY WERE AS ONE AIRY HILL,	78	LOVE'S FEVER	8
THE SUN AND MOON SHED ONE WHITE LIGHT.	78	LOVE'S FEVER	9

	PAGE	TITLE	LINE

ONE (CONTINUED)

AND THE FOUR WINDS, THAT HAD LONG BLOWN AS ONE, ...	78	LOVE'S FEVER	19
WHAT HAD BEEN ONE WAS MANY SOUNDING MINDED.	79	LOVE'S FEVER	41
ONE WOMB, ONE MIND, SPEWED OUT THE MATTER, ...	79	LOVE'S FEVER	42
ONE WOMB, ONE MIND, SPEWED OUT THE MATTER, ...	79	LOVE'S FEVER	42
ONE BREAST GAVE SUCK THE FEVER'S ISSUE;	79	LOVE'S FEVER	43
ONE SUN, ONE MANNA, WARMED AND FED.	79	LOVE'S FEVER	5C
ONE SUN, ONE MANNA, WARMED AND FED.	79	LOVE'S FEVER	50
BUT ONE THE SWISS WEAR WHEN THEY YODEL, ...	83	LETTER TO AUNT	16
A BOWLER THING WITH ONE OR TWO	83	LETTER TO AUNT	17
ONE SMILE OF LIGHT ACROSS THE EMPTY FACE;	93	IN BEGINNING	2
ONE BOUGH OF BONE ACROSS THE ROOTING AIR, ...	93	IN BEGINNING	3
ADD ONE MORE NAIL OF PRAISE ON TO THE CROSS, ...	96	TWELVE	7
BE BY YOUR ONE GHOST PIERCED, HIS POINTED FERRULE,	111	I, IN IMAGE	79
HATCHED FROM THE WINDY SALVAGE ON ONE LEG, ...	117	ALTARWISE	1C
DEATH IS ALL METAPHORS, SHAPE IN ONE HISTORY;	117	ALTARWISE	15
AND ONE LIGHT'S LANGUAGE IN THE BOOK OF TREES.	119	ALTARWISE	89
RUIN, THE ROOM OF ERRORS, ONE ROOD DROPPED	132	I MAKE THIS IN	39
TAP HAPPILY OF ONE PEG IN THE THICK	136	AFTER FUNERAL	3
THAT BREAKS ONE BONE TO LIGHT WITH A JUDGMENT CLOUT,	136	AFTER FUNERAL	9
LINKED IN ONE GAS BRACKET	137	O CHATTERTON	2
THAN ONE COULD PROBE OUT OF A SERPENT'S GUTS;	137	O CHATTERTON	7
THAT I STRUCK ONE DAY BY LUCK, ...	139	TOMBSTONE TOLD	5
MY ONE AND NOBLE HEART HAS WITNESSES	139	FIVE & COUNTRY	11
DRIVELLED DOWN TO ONE SINGEING TREE	142	SAINT TO FALL	20
HEAVEN FELL WITH HIS FALL AND ONE CROCKED BELL BEAT			
THE LEFT AIR.	142	SAINT TO FALL	25
BECAUSE THERE STANDS, ONE STORY OUT OF THE BUM CITY,	144	PLEASURE-BIRD	13
BY THE GREEN OF A ONE POUND NOTE	149	PAPER & STICKS	9
ONE LEAN SIGH WHEN WE HEARD	153	WAS A SAVIOUR	29
ON STOOLS TO A ONE MAN SHOW DOWN, ...	154	RETURN	20
ONE RICH STREET WITH HUNGER IN IT.	157	RETURN	101
ONE VOICE IN CHAINS DECLAIMS	158	INTO HER HEAD	52
WHEN ONE AT THE GREAT LEAST OF YOUR BEST LOVED	160	DEATHS AND ENT	3
ONE WHO CALLED DEEPEST DOWN SHALL HOLD HIS PEACE	160	DEATHS AND ENT	9
ONE WHO IS MOST UNKNOWN, ...	160	DEATHS AND ENT	16
ONE ENEMY, OF MANY, WHO KNOWNS WELL	160	DEATHS AND ENT	29
UNTIL THAT ONE LOVED LEAST	161	DEATHS AND ENT	35
ONE BY ONE IN DUST AND SHAWL, ...	167	LONG-LEGGED	145
ONE BY ONE IN DUST AND SHAWL, ...	167	LONG-LEGGED	145
OVER THE ONE	174	FIRE RAID	51
AND THE FINDING ONE	181	VISION, PRAYER	64
THE FINDING ONE	182	VISION, PRAYER	88
OF NO ONE	185	VISION, PRAYER	177
ONE TO	185	VISION, PRAYER	180
ONE. THE SUN ROARS AT THE PRAYER'S END.	185	VISION, PRAYER	204
WHEN THAT IMMORTAL HOSPITAL MADE ONE MORE MOVE TO			
SOOTHE	186	HOLY SPRING	3
THAT ONE DARK I OWE MY LIGHT, ...	186	HOLY SPRING	9
UNDER THE ONE LEAVED TREES RAN A SCARECROW OF SNOW	190	WINTER'S TALE	94
ONE GESTURE OF THE HEART OR HEAD, ...	192	SIDE OF TRUTH	9
THE ONE NOT CARING TO WHOM IN HIS SLEEP HE WILL MOVE	193	CONVERS PRAYER	4
DRAGGING HIM UP THE STAIRS TO ONE WHO LIES DEAD.	194	CONVERS PRAYER	20
CLUNG TO THE PITCHING CLOUDS, OR GAY WITH ANY ONE	204	GIANT'S THIGH	15
TO DEATH, ONE MAN THROUGH HIS SUNDERED HULKS, ...	211	POEM ON B'DAY	92
IN THE MUTED HOUSE, ONE MINUTE BEFORE	216	ELEGY	14
HIS UPTURNED FACE WITH ONE DIVINE CARESS.	222	MISSING	3
MOVING IN ONE DIRECTION, ...	229	MY RIVER	38
TO ONE SENSE OF FINALITY	230	OUR SANCTITY	20
LIKE A CAVE WITH ONE THREAD.	23C	OUR SANCTITY	21

	PAGE	TITLE	LINE
ONE (CONTINUED)			
WHICH LEANS ONE WAY,	232	FURIOUS MOTION	10
ONE DAY THEY HAD TO FLY,	237	PILLAR BREAKS	14
ONE-COLOURED			
WITH A ONE-COLOURED CALM;	54	WE BY SEASAND	13
ONE-DIMENSIONED			
TWO ONE-DIMENSIONED GHOSTS, LOVE ON A REEL,	89	EUNUCH DREAMS	12
ONE-MARROWED			
AN OLD MAN'S SHANK ONE-MARROWED WITH MY BONE,	95	RUB OF LOVE	32
ONES			
BRAVE DEATHS OF ONLY ONES BUT NEVER FOUND,	153	WAS A SAVIOUR	35
ONE-SIDED			
GRAFTS ON ITS BRIDE ONE-SIDED SKINS OF TRUTH;	90	EUNUCH DREAMS	28
ONLY			
ONLY THE DROWNED DEEP BELLS	5	PROLOGUE	87
THEY ARE THE ONLY DEAD WHO DID NOT LOVE	23	THE ONLY DEAD	T
THEY ARE THE ONLY DEAD WHO DID NOT LOVE,	23	THE ONLY DEAD	1
THEY ARE THE ONLY LIVING THING WHO DID LOVE,	23	THE ONLY DEAD	4
BUT ONLY PLUMB SUCH DEPTHS	24	LITTLE PROBLEM	24
ONLY AS WRONG; BUT SHAN'T THE GENIUS FAIL,	28	NO WINGS	7
THE ONLY VISITOR,	35	LIFT UP FACE	22
IF ONLY WITH SUNLIGHT.	35	LIFT UP FACE	26
PRAISE THAT ONLY THE WITS ARE HURT AFTER THE WITS' FIGHT.	42	A WAR OF WITS	11
AND BE STRUCK DUMB, IF ONLY FOR A TIME.	43	A WAR OF WITS	25
LEFT ONLY THE VOICE IN THE OLD VILLAGE CHOIR	45	PLOUGHMAN GONE	4
THEN ONLY OVER CORPSES SHALL THE FEET TREAD,	45	TO FOLLOW FOX	20
WILL ONLY DIM LIFE, AND LIGHT DEATH.	49	LIGHT, I KNOW	29
VERY ALONE, HE PLOUGHED THE ONLY WAY.	53	OUT OF THE PIT	86
AND THAT'S THE RUB, THE ONLY RUB THAT TICKLES.	96	RUB OF LOVE	36
WHO ONLY DRINKS HIS PROFITS	138	O CHATTERTON	27
NOW IN THE DARK THERE IS ONLY YOURSELF AND MYSELF.	153	WAS A SAVIOUR	24
BRAVE DEATHS OF ONLY ONES BUT NEVER FOUND,	153	WAS A SAVIOUR	35
ONLY TO MAKE TWO ENDS MEET,	155	RETURN	61
FOR ME ALONE BUT ONLY A ROCKED DRUM	175	MY BEGGAR ARM	3
BUT THERE IS ONLY BUCKLEY'S UNFRISKY	179	NEW QUAY	11
I CLIMB TO GREET THE WAR IN WHICH I HAVE NO HEART BUT ONLY	186	HOLY SPRING	8
IF ONLY FOR A LAST TIME.	186	HOLY SPRING	24
BUT ONLY THE WIND STRUNG	188	WINTER'S TALE	41
IN THE SUN THAT IS YOUNG ONCE ONLY,	195	FERN HILL	12
WHEN ONLY THE MOON RAGES	196	CRAFT OR ART	3
ONLY FOR THE TURNING OF THE EARTH IN HER HOLY	200	COUNTRY SLEEP	94
FISHING IN THE TEAR OF THE TOWY. ONLY A HOOT OWL	203	SIR JOHNS HILL	51
BUT ONLY IRIS ON THEIR SLENDER STALKS	223	IN DREAMS	11
ONTO			
IT IS GOOD TO STEP ONTO THE EARTH, ALONE,	43	A WAR OF WITS	24
OUT OF THE HEAVENLY SEA ONTO THE MOON'S SHORES.	48	LIGHT, I KNOW	3
DROP ONTO YOUR WINGS,	240	ADMIT THE SUN	7
OPEN			
WHEN HEAVEN--OPEN WIDE THE GATES--HAS TAKEN FLIGHT,	34	THIRST PARCHES	4
WHERE DEATH LIES DEAD ASLEEP, ONE BRIGHT EYE OPEN,	41	YOUNG ARE OLD	20
DRIP FROM MY OPEN EYES AS HONEY	48	LIGHT, I KNOW	9
GRIEF, LIKE AN OPEN WOUND, HAS CRIED TO HEAVEN.	64	WOMAN SPEAKS	32
MY BROTHERS' BLOOD THAT SALTS MY OPEN WOUNDS.	80	ALL THAT I OWE	8
SPLITTING THE LONG EYE OPEN, AND THE SPIRAL TURNKEY,	110	I, IN IMAGE	50
NAILED WITH AN OPEN EYE, IN THE BOWL OF WOUNDS AND WEED	135	HOW MY ANIMAL	29
AND THE ENDLESS BEGINNING OF PRODIGIES SUFFERS OPEN.'	146	IF HEAD HURT	30
OPEN AS TO THE AIR TO THE NAKED SHADOW	159	INTO HER HEAD	63

		PAGE	TITLE	LINE
OPEN (CONTINUED)				
I SIT AT THE OPEN WINDOW, OBSERVING	....	179	NEW QUAY	13
FLOWS OPEN	....	182	VISION, PRAYER	99
OPEN A PATHWAY THROUGH THE SLOW SAD SAIL,	....	194	SLEEP BECALMED	9
I OPEN THE LEAVES OF THE WATER AT A PASSAGE	....	202	SIR JOHNS HILL	23
THEN, WHEN I OPEN MY MOUTH,	....	231	YOUR VOICE	6
AND PULSE TO OPEN	....	238	MAKES INTERVALS	13
OPENED				
OPENED MY BREAST AND INTO	....	155	RETURN	35
OPENING				
OPENING ITS IRIS MOUTH UPON THE SILL	....	47	POET: 1935	30
AND THERE WAS THUNDER IN AN OPENING ROSE.	....	51	OUT OF THE PIT	17
SURPRISED IN THE OPENING OF HER NIGHTLONG EYES	....	170	MARRIAGE VIRG	2
FROM THE OPENING OF THE GARDEN LOCK	....	171	THE HUNCHBACK	4
OPENING AND THE DARK RUN	....	180	VISION, PRAYER	7
OPENING IN THE BLIND CLOUD OVER OUR HEADS;	....	231	OUR SANCTITY	44
OPIUM				
AND OPIUM HEAD, CROW STALK, PUFFED, CUT, AND BLOWN,		131	I MAKE THIS IN	10
OR (184)				
ORACLE				
WITH ORACLE FOR EYE?'	....	129	MY NEOPHYTE	42
ORACLES				
OF EVIL ORACLES AND FUNERAL ILLS;	....	57	GREEK PLAY	31
ORACULAR				
FROM THE ORACULAR ARCHIVES AND THE PARCHMENT,	.....	120	ALTARWISE	113
ORATOR				
FORGED IN MAN'S MINERALS, THE BRASSY ORATOR	....	108	I, IN IMAGE	2
ORCHARD				
A CITY SAVIOUR, IN THE ORCHARD	....	70	SECRET WIND	15
OR WITH THEIR ORCHARD MAN IN THE CORE OF THE SUN'S				
BUSH	....	204	GIANT'S THIGH	24
ORCHARDS				
BY RED-EYED ORCHARDS SOW THE SEEDS OF SNOW,	....	123	FOSTER LIGHT	11
IN DEATHBEDS OF ORCHARDS THE BOAT DIES DOWN	....	169	LONG-LEGGED	207
ORDER				
OF THE WINTRY NUNNERY OF THE ORDER OF LUST	....	147	UNLUCKILY FOR	12
CUT TO THE STILL STAR IN THE ORDER OF THE QUICK	...	148	UNLUCKILY FOR	20
ORDERED				
SKIRTING THE ORDERED BEDS OF PAINT-BOX FLOWERS,	...	33	IN GARDENS	3
OVER AND ROUND THE ORDERED GARDEN HUMMED,	....	34	IN GARDENS	17
LAWED AND ORDERED FROM ON HIGH	....	72	TAKE NEEDLES	39
ORDINARY				
FOR WE ARE ORDINARY MEN,	....	28	NO WINGS	12
WE ARE ORDINARY MEN,	....	28	NO WINGS	20
ORDURED				
CERECLOTH OF WEED, AND BUILD AN ORDURED BED.	......	64	WOMAN SPEAKS	27
ORESTES'				
OF ALL ORESTES' CONTINENT OF PRIDE	....	56	GREEK PLAY	5
THE QUEEN IS SLAIN; ORESTES' HANDS DRIP BLOOD;	....	57	GREEK PLAY	15
ORGANPIPES				
INTO THE ORGANPIPES AND STEEPLES	....	175	FIRE RAID	61
ORGANS				
WHO'D RAISE THE ORGANS OF THE COUNTED DUST	....	160	DEATHS AND ENT	7
ORIGIN				
IN FOUNTAINS OF ORIGIN GAVE UP THEIR LOVE,	....	157	INTO HER HEAD	9
SANG UPON ORIGIN!	....	182	VISION, PRAYER	90
ORIGINAL				
AS YOU, ORIGINAL, DERIVE.	....	24	LITTLE PROBLEM	25
THE RIBBED ORIGINAL OF LOVE.	....	94	IN BEGINNING	30

	PAGE	TITLE	LINE
ORNAMENTAL			
HERE IN THIS ORNAMENTAL WINTER	58	HERE IN SPRING	2
OTHER			
I COULD DEVOTE TO OTHER THINGS.	9	MINUTE'S HOUR	22
THEIR GOLDEN AND THEIR OTHER COLOUR.	11	CABARET	9
IT'S EASY TRACING WHAT EACH GIVES THE OTHER	24	LITTLE PROBLEM	11
AND OTHER VIRGINS IN OFFICIAL FATHERS.	38	THE GOSSIPERS	13
IS EMPTY IN SPRINGTIME, AND NO OTHER TIME LESSENS	39	GAS FADES	20
MARY, VIRGIN, OR ANY OTHER.	41	YOUNG ARE OLD	48
ONE HAND AT HEAD, THE OTHER AT A LOSS, ...	52	OUT OF THE PIT	60
AND THERE WE WEPT, I AND THE GHOSTLY OTHER, ...	101	FELLOWED SLEEP	8
THAT OTHER SUN, THE JEALOUS COURSING OF THE			
UNRIVALLED BLOOD.	170	MARRIAGE VIRG	14
AND DOWN THE OTHER AIR AND THE BLUE ALTERED SKY ...	178	POEM IN OCT	42
AFTER THE FIRST DEATH, THERE IS NO OTHER.	192	REFUSAL MOURN	24
AND THE OTHER FULL OF TEARS THAT SHE WILL BE DEAD,	193	CONVERS PRAYER	5
OTHERS			
STARING AT OTHERS, POOR UNLOVERS.	23	THE ONLY DEAD	3
YOU SHALL GO AS THE OTHERS HAVE GONE, ...	45	PLOUGHMAN GONE	16
YOU SHALL GO AS THE OTHERS HAVE GONE, ...	46	PLOUGHMAN GONE	30
OTHERS BETRAY THE LAMENTING LIES OF THEIR LOSSES	133	MAKE ME A MASK	11
O CHATTERTON AND OTHERS IN THE ATTIC	137	O CHATTERTON	1
TO OTHERS THAN YOU	146	TO OTHERS	T
OTHERS WHOSE SINGLE BEDS HOLD TWO	155	RETURN	60
THERE ARE OTHERS WHO THINK THAT A LOBSTER IS PINK,	221	SONG OF DOG	3
OTTER			
THE OTTER	231	OUR SANCTITY	39
OTTERS			
SHIP TOWNS TO PASTURES OF OTTERS. HE	209	POEM ON B'DAY	24
OUR (65)			
OURS			
OF SUCH GREAT GOODNESS AS IS OURS.	23	THE ONLY DEAD	18
OURSELVES			
BUT WE DO NOT CONCERN OURSELVES, ...	231	OUR SANCTITY	26
OUT			
OUT THERE, CROW BLACK, MEN	3	PROLOGUE	12
OUT OF THESE SEATHUMBED LEAVES	3	PROLOGUE	29
OUT OF THE FOUNTAINHEAD	4	PROLOGUE	47
WE WILL RIDE OUT ALONE, AND THEN, ...	5	PROLOGUE	91
BUT, WHEN HE'S OUT OF SIGHT, ...	14	RAIN CUTS	20
THAT FLOWED OUT OF THE SOIL	17	IN OBLIVION	12
OUT OF MY HAND IN STOPPING UP MY MOUTH, ...	18	NATURAL DAY	16
I, SAID THE BEETLE, OUT OF MY THIN BLACK WOMB, ...	18	NATURAL DAY	26
OUT OF MY THIN BLACK LIPS, ...	18	NATURAL DAY	27
OUT OF MY FILTHY EYES	18	NATURAL DAY	29
IN DEATH OR OUT OF DEATH, ...	20	ENCOMPASSED	8
OR, WHITE AS MILK, OUT OF THE SEEPING DARK, ...	20	ENCOMPASSED	11
OUT OF THE BITTER CONSCIENCE AND THE NERVES, ...	20	THE NEOPHYTE	15
OUT OF THE WAY OF THE EYES OF MEN, ...	21	HIGH ON A HILL	3
THEN SHALL YOUR SENSES, OUT OF JOY, ...	21	BEWILDERED WAY	13
OUT OF THE HEART FOR ME, ...	21	BEWILDERED WAY	16
OUT OF THE WAY, ...	22	HIGH ON A HILL	4
BUT CAME FROM OUT THE MOUTH UNKNOWING	23	THE ONLY DEAD	17
I HEAR THEM SAY OUT OF THE DARKNESS	23	ON QUIET NIGHT	21
OUT OF THE FULLNESS OF ANOTHER'S HEART	23	THE ONLY DEAD	21
TURN INSIDE OUT, AND SEE AT GLANCE	25	BEAUTY TO DUST	7
NEVER FLOWS OUT FROM THE WOUND OF SLEEP	27	OBLIVIOUS DARK	7
OUT OF THE SOIL AND SEED INTO THE DRIVE, ...	29	LONG, SKELETON	2
OUT OF THE SIGHS	31	OUT OF SIGHS	T
OUT OF THE SIGHS A LITTLE COMES, ...	31	OUT OF SIGHS	1

	PAGE	TITLE	LINE
OUT (CONTINUED)			
THRUST OUT OUR HEADS ABOVE THE BRANCHES	31	BEING BUT MEN	9
OUT OF CONFUSION, AS THE WAY IS,	31	BEING BUT MEN	11
OUT OF THE CHAOS WOULD COME BLISS.	31	BEING BUT MEN	13
OUT OF UNSLEEPING COGITATIONS,	35	LIFT UP FACE	18
THE WIND HAS CHANGED, BLOWN INSIDE OUT	37	WINDMILLS TURN	27
THE VIRGINS SMELT OUT, THREE STREETS UP,	38	THE GOSSIPERS	8
THE JAWS WILL HAVE SHUT, AND LIFE BE SWITCHED OUT.	39	GAS FADES	14
CAUGHT IN THE TRAP'S MACHINERY, LIGHTS OUT,	39	GAS FADES	35
THE SQUEAL OF THE DAMNED OUT OF THE OLD PIT.	40	YOUNG ARE OLD	6
OUT OF A WAR OF WITS	42	A WAR OF WITS	T
OUT OF A WAR OF WITS, WHEN FOLLY OF WORDS	42	A WAR OF WITS	1
BEFORE THE MOON SHIFTED AND THE SAP RAN OUT,	43	FACES SHONE	10
FOR OUT OF A HOUSE OF MATCHBOARD AND STONE	43	A WAR OF WITS	22
OUT OF THE OLD LIE BURNING ON THE GROUND,	44	LONGED TO MOVE	13
AN IMAGE BORN OUT OF THE UPROARIOUS SPRING	47	POET: 1935	36
OUT OF THE HEAVENLY SEA ONTO THE MOON'S SHORES.	48	LIGHT, I KNOW	3
OUT OF A BIRD'S WING WRITING ON A CLOUD	48	POET: 1935	53
OUT OF THE PIT	50	OUT OF THE PIT	T
OUT OF THE BUILDINGS OF THE DAY I'VE STEPPED	53	OUT OF THE PIT	90
OUT OF THE NOISE INTO QUIET I RAN.	53	OUT OF THE PIT	92
ALCOVE OF WORDS OUT OF CICADA SHADE,	54	WE BY SEASAND	4
WHEN ANY LIGHT GOES OUT, AND LIFE IS DEATH.	55	NO MAN BELIEVE	6
IS HEARD BUT LITTLE TILL THE STARS GO OUT.	56	WHY EAST WIND	20
SOUNDS, RICH WITH LIFE, OUT OF A PAINTED MASK;	57	GREEK PLAY	14
TORN OUT MAGIC FROM THE HEARTS OF COWARDS	60	FAIRY TALES	32
BURN OUT THE LASTING ROT,	60	FAIRY TALES	39
THAT OUT OF A BOWER OF RED SWINE	61	MEAT ON BONES	28
THE LAND LIES OUT OF SOUND	62	EARS IN TURRET	13
AND THE HILLS OUT OF MIND.	62	EARS IN TURRET	14
ONE WOMB, ONE MIND, SPEWED OUT THE MATTER,	79	LOVE'S FEVER	42
REMOVE YOUR BRAINS, TAKE OUT YOUR HEART;	84	LETTER TO AUNT	60
DRIVES IN A DEATH AS LIFE LEAKS OUT.	88	A PROCESS IN	9
AND BAGS OF BLOOD LET OUT THEIR FLIES;	97	TWILIGHT LOCKS	23
CORROSIVE SPRING OUT OF THE ICEBERG'S CROP,	104	WORLD PYRAMID	8
OUT OF THE SEA, THE DRIVE OF OIL,	107	ALL ALL AND	34
OUT OF THE NAKED ENTRAIL.	109	I, IN IMAGE	12
BRING OUT THE BLACK PATROL,	110	I, IN IMAGE	55
RINGS OUT THE DEAD SEA SCALE;	110	I, IN IMAGE	63
NO MAN MORE MAGICAL, CLAWED OUT THE CROCODILE.	111	I, IN IMAGE	96
AND THE VELVET DEAD INCH OUT.	114	SERVANT SUN	21
DRIVES OUT THE FATHER FROM THE CAESARED CAMP;	115	A GRIEF AGO	27
BIT OUT THE MANDRAKE WITH TO-MORROW'S SCREAM.	117	ALTARWISE	6
OUT OF THE WRINKLED UNDERTAKER'S VAN,	118	ALTARWISE	36
WHICH SIXTH OF WIND BLEW OUT THE BURNING GENTRY?	118	ALTARWISE	47
AND LOVE PLUCKED OUT THE STINGING SIREN'S EYE,	119	ALTARWISE	77
SPELT OUT THE SEVEN SEAS, AND EVIL INDEX,	119	ALTARWISE	82
BLEW OUT THE BLOOD GAUZE THROUGH THE WOUND OF MANWAX.	119	ALTARWISE	84
WHO SUCKS THE BELL-VOICED ADAM OUT OF MAGIC,	119	ALTARWISE	93
IN SHAPES OF SIN FORKED OUT THE BEARDED APPLE,	121	INCARNATE DEVL	4
WHO COULD HACK OUT YOUR UNSUCKED HEART,	129	MY NEOPHYTE	46
GRIEF WITH DISHEVELLED HANDS TEAR OUT THE ALTAR GHOST	130	SINNERS' BELL	5
OUT OF THE FONT OF BONE AND PLANTS AT THAT STONE TOCSIN	130	SINNERS' BELL	20
AND THE GOLDEN BALL SPINS OUT OF THE SKIES;	134	NOT FROM ANGER	10
IN QUICK, SWEET, CRUEL LIGHT TILL THE LOCKED GROUND SPROUT OUT,	135	HOW MY ANIMAL	18
TRACE OUT A TENTACLE,	135	HOW MY ANIMAL	28
MAGNIFIED OUT OF PRAISE; HER DEATH WAS A STILL DROP;	136	AFTER FUNERAL	17
THAN ONE COULD PROBE OUT OF A SERPENT'S GUTS;	137	O CHATTERTON	7

		PAGE	TITLE	LINE
OUT (CONTINUED)				
BECAUSE THERE STANDS, ONE STORY OUT OF THE BUM CITY,		144	PLEASURE-BIRD	13
BUMP ON A SPOUT LET THE BUBBLES JUMP OUT.	....	145	IF HEAD HURT	3
FRIEND BY ENEMY I CALL YOU OUT.	....	146	TO OTHERS	1
CROSSLY OUT OF THE TOWN NOISES	....	150	WHEN I WOKE	24
OUT TO THE TIERED AND HEARING TIDE,	....	158	INTO HER HEAD	38
AND OUT OF EVERY DOMED AND SOIL-BASED SHELL	....	158	INTO HER HEAD	51
AND WIND HIS GLOBE OUT OF YOUR WATER THREAD	....	160	DEATHS AND ENT	21
AND THE MOON SWAM OUT OF ITS HULK.	....	162	LONG-LEGGED	16
TO THE BAIT THAT STALKED OUT OF THE SACK,	....	162	LONG-LEGGED	20
HE SAW THE STORM SMOKE OUT TO KILL	....	163	LONG-LEGGED	41
CLASH OUT THE MOUNTING DOLPHIN'S DAY,	....	164	LONG-LEGGED	75
OUT OF THE SIDES OF THE NORTH	....	165	LONG-LEGGED	114
OUT OF THE URN THE SIZE OF A MAN	....	166	LONG-LEGGED	141
OUT OF THE ROOM THE WEIGHT OF HIS TROUBLE	....	166	LONG-LEGGED	142
OUT OF THE HOUSE THAT HOLDS A TOWN	....	166	LONG-LEGGED	143
AND THIS DAY'S SUN LEAPT UP THE SKY OUT OF HER THIGHS		170	MARRIAGE VIRG	4
ON OUT OF SOUND	....	171	THE HUNCHBACK	18
HE PUT ON HIS CLOTHES AND STEPPED OUT AND HE DIED,		172	DAWN RAID	2
MADE THE TIGERS JUMP OUT OF THEIR EYES	....	172	THE HUNCHBACK	28
OUT OF A BED OF LOVE	....	186	HOLY SPRING	2
OUT OF THE WOEBEGONE PYRE	....	186	HOLY SPRING	16
STUMBLE OUT WITH THEIR SPADES,	....	187	WINTER'S TALE	21
OUT OF THE WHINNYING GREEN STABLE	....	196	FERN HILL	35
FOLLOW HIM OUT OF GRACE,	....	196	FERN HILL	45
OUT OF A LAIR IN THE FLOCKED LEAVES IN THE DEW DIPPED YEAR	....	197	COUNTRY SLEEP	6
A HILL TOUCHES AN ANGEL. OUT OF A SAINT'S CELL	....	198	COUNTRY SLEEP	27
YET OUT OF THE BEAKED, WEB DARK AND THE POUNCING BOUGHS	....	199	COUNTRY SLEEP	48
AND THE RAIN WRING OUT ITS TONGUES ON THE FADED YARD,		205	GIANT'S THIGH	52
SLUNK POUTING OUT WHEN THE LIMP TIME CAME;	....	207	LAMENT	44
HARPIES AROUND ME OUT OF HER WOMB!	....	207	LAMENT	56
THE BONES OUT OF THE HILLS,	....	210	POEM ON B'DAY	68
AS I SAIL OUT TO DIE.	....	211	POEM ON B'DAY	108
BUSHES AND OWLS BLOW OUT LIKE CANDLES,	....	215	COUNTRY HEAVEN	18
WILL NEVER NEVER GO OUT OF MY MIND.	....	217	ELEGY	20
OUT OF HIS EYES I SAW THE LAST LIGHT GLIDE.	....	217	ELEGY	28
LAST SOUND, THE WORLD GOING OUT WITHOUT A BREATH:		217	ELEGY	34
THE TEARS OUT OF HIS EYES, TOO PROUD TO CRY.	......	217	ELEGY	39
YOU STRETCH OUT YOUR HANDS	....	229	MY RIVER	21
YOUR CONSTRUCTED NOTES GOING OUT OF THE THROAT	....	231	YOUR VOICE	2
I'LL KNOW I'M OUT OF HARM,	....	240	TWINING HEAD	4
OUT OF THE AIR IT STRIKES.	....	241	ADMIT THE SUN	22
OUTBREAK				
THIS BUSY JARRING ON THE NERVES YET NO OUTBREAK?		36	MIDNIGHT ROAD	4
OUTCAST				
BY THE BELIEVER LOST AND THE HURLED OUTCAST OF LIGHT.		188	WINTER'S TALE	50
OUTCRY				
YOUR FAITH AS DEATHLESS AS THE OUTCRY OF THE RULED SUN.	....	201	COUNTRY SLEEP	111
OUTDO				
OUTDO YOUR PRUDE'S GENETIC FACULTY	....	20	THE NEOPHYTE	13
OUTELBOWED				
NOW THAT MY SYMBOLS HAVE OUTELBOWED SPACE,	....	124	TODAY, INSECT	2
OUTLAW				
IN TIME LIKE OUTLAW RAINS ON THAT PRIEST, WATER,		15	SPIRE CRANES	6
BULL'S-EYE THE OUTLAW THROUGH A EUNUCH CRACK	......	108	GRIEF THIEF	19
OUTLINE				
BLIND IN THE COIL SCRAMS ROUND THE BLAZING OUTLINE,		124	TODAY, INSECT	11

	PAGE	TITLE	LINE
OUTLINES			
OUTLINES MELTING INTO A VAGUE IMMENSITY	222	FOREST PICTURE	9
OUT-OF-PERSPECTIVE			
AND OUT-OF-PERSPECTIVE SAILORS, ...	151	BELOW A TIME	14
OUTSIDE			
NO, HE'S A STRANGER, OUTSIDE THE SEASON'S HUMOUR,	46	POET: 1935	10
WITH THE OUTSIDE WEATHERS, ...	134	HOW MY ANIMAL	9
WHILE A MAN OUTSIDE WITH A BILLHOOK, ...	150	WHEN I WOKE	8
AND THERE OUTSIDE ON THE BREAD OF THE GROUND	189	WINTER'S TALE	68
OUTSKIRTS			
TOUCHED ON THE OUTSKIRTS OF THE MIND, ...	33	IN GARDENS	5
OUTSPOKEN			
NOR THE OUTSPOKEN GRAVE.	95	RUB OF LOVE	21
OUTSTRETCHED			
THEIR HANDS OUTSTRETCHED, TO GIVE AND GIVE?	36	MIDNIGHT ROAD	8
OUTWORN			
ROSE IN OUR OUTWORN BRAINS. WE SPOKE OUR LINES, ...	34	IN GARDENS	11
OVAL			
BREATHING NO POISON FROM THE OVAL MOUTH, ...	19	THE NEOPHYTE	3
OVEN			
THE HUNGER OF LIVING, THE OVEN AND GUN	39	GAS FADES	24
OVER			
OVER THE WOUND ASLEEP	4	PROLOGUE	50
OVER HER HEEL AND ME.	12	CABARET	21
OVER THE ANCIENT WINTER, ...	17	IN OBLIVION	4
AS DROWN, OVER AND OVER, THIS FEVER.	17	IN OBLIVION	18
AS DROWN, OVER AND OVER, THIS FEVER.	17	IN OBLIVION	18
AND, STANDING OVER THE SEA, SHE'D CRY	22	ON QUIET NIGHT	9
LEAP OVER TO MY CRISS-CROSS RHYTHMS.	33	HELD-OUT HAND	23
OVER AND ROUND THE ORDERED GARDEN HUMMED, ...	34	IN GARDENS	17
LIFT UP THE BLINDS OVER THE BLIND EYES.	35	LIFT UP FACE	17
THERE WAS A TIME THEY COULD CRY OVER BOOKS, ...	40	WAS THERE TIME	3
THE LIVING DEAD LEFT OVER FROM THE WAR, ...	41	YOUNG ARE OLD	35
GOES OVER THE HILL INTO THE DEEP SEA;	43	LONGED TO MOVE	5
OVER A ROAD THICK WITH THE BONES OF WORDS.	44	TO FOLLOW FOX	17
NO MORE TOILS OVER THE FIELDS	45	PLOUGHMAN GONE	13
THEN ONLY OVER CORPSES SHALL THE FEET TREAD, ...	45	TO FOLLOW FOX	20
MASTERS OVER UNMASTERED NATURE, ...	45	PLOUGHMAN GONE	21
IN SUN AND RAIN OVER THE DRY SHIRES, ...	45	PLOUGHMAN GONE	25
REVOLVES OVER AND OVER AGAIN	46	PLOUGHMAN GONE	28
REVOLVES OVER AND OVER AGAIN	46	PLOUGHMAN GONE	28
LEANING FROM WINDOWS OVER A LENGTH OF LAWNS, ...	48	POET: 1935	60
SAID ALL THE USUAL THINGS OVER AND AGAIN;	52	OUT OF THE PIT	71
THE HEAVENLY MUSIC OVER THE SAND	54	WE BY SEASAND	14
AND GHOSTLY COMETS OVER THE RAISED FISTS.	56	WHY EAST WIND	26
THEN HANG A RAM ROSE OVER THE RAGS.	60	MEAT ON BONES	8
THERE SHALL BE NO MUTE MOURNING OVER HIS ACRE, ...	64	WOMAN SPEAKS	38
GREAT IS THE HAND THAT HOLDS DOMINION OVER	66	HAND SIGNED	11
OVER THE ELECTRIC GODHEAD GROWS	70	SECRET WIND	22
(GIVE, SUMMER, OVER), THE CEMENTED SKIN, ...	101	RUNNING GRAVE	44
GIVE OVER, LOVERS, LOCKING, AND THE SEAWAX STRUGGLE,	111	I, IN IMAGE	89
YOU BY THE CAVERN OVER THE BLACK STAIRS, ...	117	ALTARWISE	22
OVER THESE GROUNDWORKS THRUSTING THROUGH A PAVEMENT	117	ALTARWISE	27
OVER THE VAULT OF RIDINGS WITH HIS HOUND AT HEEL,	122	HOLD HARD	5
OVER THE SEA-GUT LOUDENING, SETS A ROCK ALIVE;	122	HOLD HARD	15
ROLL UNMANLY OVER THIS TURNING TUFT, ...	123	FOSTER LIGHT	19
OVER THE MANWAGING LINE.	125	SEED-AT-ZERO	7
OVER THE WARBEARING LINE.	125	SEED-AT-ZERO	14
OVER THE WATER COME	129	MY NEOPHYTE	27
OVER THE CHOIR MINUTE I HEAR THE HOUR CHANT:	130	SINNERS' BELL	7

	PAGE	TITLE	LINE
OVER (CONTINUED)			
BEHIND MY HEAD A SQUARE OF SKY SAGS OVER	134	NOT FROM ANGER	8
BABBLE LIKE A BELLBUOY OVER THE HYMNING HEADS, ...	136	AFTER FUNERAL	23
STORM ME FOREVER OVER HER GRAVE UNTIL	137	AFTER FUNERAL	38
OVER THE PAST TABLE I REPEAT THIS PRESENT GRACE.	145	PLEASURE-BIRD	25
I DREW THE WHITE SHEET OVER THE ISLANDS	150	WHEN I WOKE	29
AS A BIRD HOOKING OVER THE SEA, ...	162	LONG-LEGGED	7
MILES OVER THE MOONSTRUCK BOAT	163	LONG-LEGGED	38
OVER THE WAKEWARD-FLASHING SPRAY	164	LONG-LEGGED	73
OVER THE GARDENS OF THE FLOOR	164	LONG-LEGGED	74
OVER THE GRAVEYARD IN THE WATER	164	LONG-LEGGED	85
AND SCUTTLED OVER HER EYES, ...	165	LONG-LEGGED	100
SEASONS OVER THE LIQUID WORLD, ...	166	LONG-LEGGED	119
WHEN THE MORNING WAS WAKING OVER THE WAR	172	DAWN RAID	1
OVER THE DEAD INFANTS	174	FIRE RAID	50
OVER THE ONE	174	FIRE RAID	51
OVER THE URN OF SABBATHS	175	FIRE RAID	66
OVER THE WHIRLING DITCH OF DAYBREAK	175	FIRE RAID	67
OVER THE SUN'S HOVEL AND THE SLUM OF FIRE	175	FIRE RAID	68
OVER THE BORDER	177	POEM IN OCT	18
PALE RAIN OVER THE DWINDLING HARBOUR	177	POEM IN OCT	31
AND OVER THE SEA WET CHURCH THE SIZE OF A SNAIL ...	177	POEM IN OCT	32
SHUT. SINISTER DARK OVER CARDIGAN	179	NEW QUAY	7
OVER A RUMP ON THE CLERICAL-GREY SEASHORE, ...	179	NEW QUAY	25
OVER THE GHOST AND THE DROPPED SON	180	VISION, PRAYER	8
OVER THE BARBED AND SHOOTING SEA ASSUMED AN ARMY	186	HOLY SPRING	6
THAT THE SNOW BLIND TWILIGHT FERRIES OVER THE LAKES	187	WINTER'S TALE	2
GENTLE IN THEIR CLOGS OVER THE FALLEN SKY, ...	187	WINTER'S TALE	24
AND OVER THE CLOTH OF COUNTIES THE FAR HILLS RODE			
NEAR, ...	190	WINTER'S TALE	93
ON A BREAD WHITE HILL OVER THE CUPPED FARM	190	WINTER'S TALE	107
AND OVER THE GLAZED LAKES SKATED THE SHAPES OF FISHES	190	WINTER'S TALE	115
IN THE SUN BORN OVER AND OVER, ...	196	FERN HILL	39
IN THE SUN BORN OVER AND OVER, ...	196	FERN HILL	39
IN THE TOWER AND TOLLS TO SLEEP OVER THE STALLS ...	199	COUNTRY SLEEP	52
OVER SIR JOHN'S HILL	201	SIR JOHNS HILL	T
OVER SIR JOHN'S HILL, ...	201	SIR JOHNS HILL	1
TO FIERY TYBURN OVER THE WRESTLE OF ELMS UNTIL	201	SIR JOHNS HILL	9
TO THE HAWK ON FIRE, THE HALTER HEIGHT, OVER TOWY'S			
FINS, ...	202	SIR JOHNS HILL	16
OVER THE BLACKAMOOR SHIRES	215	COUNTRY HEAVEN	24
LIGHTLY, THOU WIND, OVER HIS DEAR, DARK HEAD, ...	222	MISSING	4
LEDGES OF WAVES HIGH OVER YOUR HEAD, ...	228	MY RIVER	2
OPENING IN THE BLIND CLOUD OVER OUR HEADS;	231	OUR SANCTITY	44
LIKE A LIVING CLOAK OVER ME.	235	WOMAN TAPESTRY	5
AND THE DEEP SKY OVER THEM	235	WOMAN TAPESTRY	9
LIFTING HER SMELL OVER THE CITY BUILDINGS.	240	ADMIT THE SUN	14
OVER-FRUITFUL			
OF OVER-FRUITFUL SMILES, ...	12	SKY'S BRIGHT	8
OVERHEAD			
TOSS OVERHEAD	16	TIME TO ROT	2
OVERPOWERING			
STRONG, FRESH, AND OVERPOWERING.	235	WOMAN TAPESTRY	12
OVERWHELMED			
OVERWHELMED BY THE SUN, WITH A TORN BRAIN	42	A WAR OF WITS	12
OWE			
ALL THAT I OWE THE FELLOWS OF THE GRAVE	80	ALL THAT I OWE	T
ALL THAT I OWE THE FELLOWS OF THE GRAVE	80	ALL THAT I OWE	1
O ALL I OWE IS ALL THE FLESH INHERITS, ...	80	ALL THAT I OWE	5
THAT ONE DARK I OWE MY LIGHT, ...	186	HOLY SPRING	9

	PAGE	TITLE	LINE
OWL			
AND THE OWL HOOD, THE HEEL HIDER,	152	BELOW A TIME	32
AND THE SMELL OF HAY IN THE SNOW, AND THE FAR OWL	187	WINTER'S TALE	7
THE OWL AT ITS KNELLING. FOX AND HOLT KNEEL BEFORE BLOOD.	198	COUNTRY SLEEP	32
FISHING IN THE TEAR OF THE TOWY. ONLY A HOOT OWL	203	SIR JOHNS HILL	51
OF DAY, IN THE THISTLE AISLES, TILL THE WHITE OWL CROSSED	204	GIANT'S THIGH	32
THE RUDE OWL CRIED LIKE A TELLTALE TIT,	206	LAMENT	5
OWL-LIGHT			
ALTARWISE BY OWL-LIGHT	116	ALTARWISE	T
ALTARWISE BY OWL-LIGHT IN THE HALF-WAY HOUSE	116	ALTARWISE	1
OWLS			
YOU KING SINGSONG OWLS, WHO MOONBEAM	4	PROLOGUE	54
BROWN AS OWLS	177	POEM IN OCT	34
AS I RODE TO SLEEP THE OWLS WERE BEARING THE FARM AWAY,	195	FERN HILL	24
BUSHES AND OWLS BLOW OUT LIKE CANDLES,	215	COUNTRY HEAVEN	18
OWL-SEED			
NOR SPROUT ON OWL-SEED LIKE A GOBLIN-SUCKER,	123	FOSTER LIGHT	14
OWN			
THEIR OWN MELODIOUS HEIGHT,	14	RAIN CUTS	34
ANY MAN'S TROUBLES NOT YOUR OWN--	27	OBLIVIOUS DARK	3
EVEN AMONG HIS OWN KIN IS HE LOST,	47	POET: 1935	22
AS CLEARLY AS THE LIGHT OF MY OWN BRAIN,	49	LIGHT, I KNOW	28
LION OR LOUSE? TAKE YOUR OWN ADVICE;	58	TO ARCHITECTS	17
BY A GODHEAD OF MY OWN.	72	TAKE NEEDLES	40
ONCE FOR THE VIRGIN'S CHILD, ONCE FOR HER OWN.	74	SUN BURNS	15
THIS WORLD IS HALF THE DEVIL'S AND MY OWN,	95	RUB OF LOVE	29
I SENT MY OWN AMBASSADOR TO LIGHT;	98	TWILIGHT LOCKS	33
MEASURES HIS OWN LENGTH ON THE GARDEN WALL	124	TODAY, INSECT	12
MY PAID-FOR SLAVED-FOR OWN TOO LATE	151	BELOW A TIME	6
OUR OWN TRUE STRANGERS' DUST	153	WAS A SAVIOUR	37
WHO STRODE FOR YOUR OWN DEAD	160	DEATHS AND ENT	20
SO LOUD TO MY OWN	180	VISION, PRAYER	5
OF THE HEARTHSTONE TALES MY OWN, LOST LOVE; AND THE SOUL WALKS	199	COUNTRY SLEEP	53
TO KILL AND THEIR OWN TIDE DAUBING BLOOD	209	POEM ON B'DAY	35
CLEAVING THEIR OWN SEDGES,	231	OUR SANCTITY	38
TAKE YOU INTO MY OWN PLACE	232	YOUR VOICE	14
I'LL MAKE YOUR SHAPE MY OWN,	238	MAKES INTERVALS	10
MY STRENGTH SHALL SAP YOUR OWN;	239	LET ME ESCAPE	9
WHO LETS HIS OWN ROD BE	240	TWINING HEAD	6
OWNED			
THE STICKS OF THE HOUSE WERE HIS; HIS BOOKS HE OWNED.	217	ELEGY	25
OX			
THUS THE SHADOWLESS MAN OR OX, AND THE PICTURED DEVIL,	109	I, IN IMAGE	22
IN THE COURTERS' LANES, OR TWINED IN THE OX ROASTING SUN	203	GIANT'S THIGH	13
OX-KILLING			
THE FURIOUS OX-KILLING HOUSE OF LOVE.	168	LONG-LEGGED	200
OYSTER			
BY LAVA'S LIGHT SPLIT THROUGH THE OYSTER VOWELS	119	ALTARWISE	73
PACE			
AND, WHEN IT QUICKENS, ALTER THE ACTIONS' PACE	116	LANTERNS SHINE	12
PACING			
FROM THE EMERALD, STILL BELL; AND FROM THE PACING WEATHER-COCK	130	SINNERS' BELL	17
OF THE PACING, FAMOUS SEA BUT ITS SPEECH,	169	LONG-LEGGED	210

	PAGE	TITLE	LINE
PACING (CONTINUED)			
PACING IN KIND PRAISE.	235	WOMAN TAPESTRY	34
AND I WILL BREAK YOUR PACING LIGHT.	239	MAKES INTERVALS	16
PACK			
AND THE PACK OF CARDS.	33	HELD-OUT HAND	11
PACK OFF THE SHAPES OF DAYLIGHT AND THEIR STARCH,	90	EUNUCH DREAMS	24
PACK BACK THE DOWNED BONE. IF THE UNPRICKED BALL OF MY BREATH	145	IF HEAD HURT	2
PACKED			
I PUT ROUND RIBS THAT PACKED THEIR HEART,	85	SEE, SAYS LIME	2
PACKS			
THE CRUMPLED PACKS FLED PAST THIS GHOST IN BLOOM,	133	I MAKE THIS IN	58
PACT			
THE WIND OF KISSES SEALED A PACT	85	SEE, SAYS LIME	10
PADDED			
MY WORLD IS PYRAMID. THE PADDED MUMMER	104	WORLD PYRAMID	31
WITH SPRUNG AND PADDED SHOULDERS,	154	RETURN	11
PADDING			
DOWN FALL FOUR PADDING WEATHERS ON THE SCARLET LANDS,	122	HOLD HARD	19
PADDLE			
PADDLE WITH LEAVES	13	RAIN CUTS	7
PADDLER'S			
OR, MASTED VENUS, THROUGH THE PADDLER'S BOWL	114	A GRIEF AGO	7
PADDLES			
WHERE THE ELEGIAC FISHERBIRD STABS AND PADDLES	202	SIR JOHNS HILL	19
PADDLING			
AS A HE-GOD'S PADDLING WATER SKIRTS,	151	BELOW A TIME	16
PADDOCKS			
PADDOCKS IN THE FARMS OF BIRDS. THE DEAD OAK WALKS FOR LOVE.	189	WINTER'S TALE	75
PAGE			
A POME'S A BUILDING ON A PAGE;	58	TO ARCHITECTS	11
AND TELLS THE PAGE THE EMPTY ILL.	75	MY HERO BARES	10
HIS GRAPH IS MEASURED AS THE PAGE OF PAIN	80	ALMANAC TIME	4
PAGEANT			
AND THE WHISPER CAUGHT IN ITS PAGEANT OF TAWNY PEARL,	224	IDYLL UNFORGET	44
PAGES			
ON THESE SPINDRIFT PAGES	197	CRAFT OR ART	14
PAID-FOR			
MY PAID-FOR SLAVED-FOR OWN TOO LATE	151	BELOW A TIME	6
PAIL			
YARD OF THE BUTTERMILK RAIN ON THE PAIL! THE SERMON	200	COUNTRY SLEEP	77
PAIN			
AND FEEL THE PAIN IT GIVES,	13	SKY'S BRIGHT	29
CRYING ALOUD IN PAIN,	18	NATURAL DAY	32
WERE THAT ENOUGH, ENOUGH TO EASE THE PAIN,	32	OUT OF SIGHS	17
MURDER WITH A CRY OF PAIN;	71	TAKE NEEDLES	19
DARKNESS IS THE DAM OF PAIN.	71	TAKE NEEDLES	36
A MOTHER IN LABOUR PAYS TWICE HER PAIN,	74	SUN BURNS	14
HIS GRAPH IS MEASURED AS THE PAGE OF PAIN	80	ALMANAC TIME	4
YOUR PAIN SHALL BE A MUSIC	87	PAIN BE MUSIC	T
YOUR PAIN SHALL BE A MUSIC IN YOUR STRING	87	PAIN BE MUSIC	1
YOUR PAIN SHALL BE	87	PAIN BE MUSIC	3
YOUR PAIN SHALL BE	87	PAIN BE MUSIC	9
YOUR PAIN SHALL BE A MEANING IN YOUR LIPS	87	PAIN BE MUSIC	13
YOUR PAIN SHALL BE	87	PAIN BE MUSIC	15
YOUR PAIN SHALL NOT UNMILK YOU OF THE FOOD	87	PAIN BE MUSIC	19
YOUR PAIN SHALL BE	87	PAIN BE MUSIC	21
SPAT UP FROM THE RESUFFERED PAIN.	103	I DREAMED MY	24
THE KNAVE OF PAIN STEALS OFF	107	GRIEF THIEF	3

		PAGE	TITLE	LINE
PAIN	(CONTINUED)			
HER FIST OF A FACE DIED CLENCHED ON A ROUND PAIN;		137	AFTER FUNERAL	34
SHE WEPT IN HER PAIN AND MADE MOUTHS,	....	139	TOMBSTONE TOLD	19
KILL TIME! SHE TURNS IN HER PAIN!	....	167	LONG-LEGGED	154
AND THE SHADOWED HEAD OF PAIN	....	180	VISION, PRAYER	24
AND THE WHOLE PAIN	....	182	VISION, PRAYER	98
ALL HIS BONES CRYING, AND POOR IN ALL BUT PAIN,	...	217	ELEGY	21
I TAKE YOU TO MYSELF, SWEET PAIN,	....	233	NO THOUGHT	5
BINDING ME WITH PAIN,	....	236	WOMAN TAPESTRY	62
I NEVER BREAK BUT FEEL THE SUDDEN PAIN,	....	239	MAKES INTERVALS	25
PAINING				
FOR PAINING, ON THEIR CANVAS STRIPS,	....	83	LETTER TO AUNT	21
PAINS				
LOSE THE GREAT PAINS OR STUFF THE WOUND,	....	32	OUT OF SIGHS	12
AND JOYS ARE PAINS.	....	74	WE MOTHERNAKED	8
PAINT				
OF SUN AND MOON THEY PAINT THEIR DAMS	....	92	BOYS OF SUMMER	17
BREAK THE BLACK NEWS AND PAINT ON A SAIL	....	164	LONG-LEGGED	71
PAINT-BOX				
SKIRTING THE ORDERED BEDS OF PAINT-BOX FLOWERS,	...	33	IN GARDENS	3
PAINTED				
THE INSECT ON THIS PAINTED TREE.	....	12	CABARET	23
SOUNDS, RICH WITH LIFE, OUT OF A PAINTED MASK;	....	57	GREEK PLAY	14
PAINTERS				
(ALL MODERN PAINTERS USE THEIR FEET	....	83	LETTER TO AUNT	20
PAINTINGS				
OR PAINTINGS ON THE BACKS OF VESTS,	....	83	LETTER TO AUNT	27
PAINTS				
AS SUNLIGHT PAINTS THE SHELLING OF THEIR HEADS.	...	92	BOYS OF SUMMER	18
PAINT-STAINED				
OLD PAINT-STAINED TUMBLERS RIDING	....	154	RETURN	19
PAIR				
PAIR OFF, MAKE HARMONIES, A HARMONIOUS CHORD,	.....	53	OUT OF THE PIT	96
PALAVERS				
AND PALAVERS OF BIRDS	....	208	POEM ON B'DAY	5
PALE				
SICK, PALE, AND PLAIN,	....	21	BEWILDERED WAY	17
AND ALL THE DEAD BEQUEATH FROM PALE ESTATES	....	80	ALL THAT I OWE	2
HERE SLIPS THE GHOST WHO MADE OF MY PALE BED	......	81	HERE LIE BEAST	11
IN THE BEGINNING WAS THE PALE SIGNATURE,	....	94	IN BEGINNING	7
MOONFALL AND SAILING EMPEROR, PALE AS THEIR				
TIDE-PRINT,	....	130	SINNERS' BELL	10
AND THOUGH MY LOVE PULLS THE PALE, NIPPLED AIR,	...	133	I MAKE THIS IN	66
PALE RAIN OVER THE DWINDLING HARBOUR	....	177	POEM IN OCT	31
THE PALE BREATH OF CATTLE AT THE STEALTHY SAIL,	...	187	WINTER'S TALE	5
THEIR PALE, ETHEREAL BEAUTY SEEMS TO BE	....	222	IN DREAMS	3
THEY OF THE PALE, SEA-WAN BEAUTY, THEY OF THE HOME		224	IDYLL UNFORGET	38
PALE AND DECAYED, AN UGLY GROWTH.	....	239	LET ME ESCAPE	12
PALE-GREEN				
OF THE PALE-GREEN, DELICATE FISHES, SILVER AS SIGHS;		224	IDYLL UNFORGET	39
PALER				
BLACK AS THE BEAST AND PALER THAN THE CROSS.	......	121	INCARNATE DEVL	12
PALLID				
AND NIGHT, WHO STOOPED TO KISS THE PALLID LEAVES		223	IN DREAMS	5
PALLOR				
A PANIC'S PALLOR	....	59	FAIRY TALES	20
THE LOIN IS GLORY IN A WORKING PALLOR.	....	105	WORLD PYRAMID	57
PALM				
I WANT REALITY TO HOLD/ WITHIN MY PALM,	....	9	MINUTE'S HOUR	14
UPON THE ISLAND OF MY PALM,	....	11	CABARET	2

		PAGE	TITLE	LINE
PALM (CONTINUED)				
GONE FROM MY PALM TO LEAVE IT MARKED	....	12	CABARET	16
PALM OF THE EARTH, O SPRINKLE ON MY HEAD	....	65	WOMAN SPEAKS	60
PALMED				
WHO PALMED THE LIE ON ME WHEN YOU LOOKED	....	146	TO OTHERS	4
PALMS				
TO BALANCE ON MY PALMS	....	13	RAIN CUTS	4
PALSY				
TO CATCH THE LOVERS' PALSY,	....	34	THIRST PARCHES	11
PAN				
TAKE THE SCISSORS AND THE PAN,	....	71	TAKE NEEDLES	9
PANIC'S				
A PANIC'S PALLOR	....	59	FAIRY TALES	20
PANOPLY				
GREEN-SHADOWED PANOPLY ENVELOPING ALL ITS STRANGENESS AND SOFTNESS OF STEALTH.	....	224	IDYLL UNFORGET	45
PANOPTICON				
OH NO, MY MIND IS YOUR PANOPTICON;	....	10	COOL, OH NO	20
PAP				
AT THE LABYRINTHINE PAP.	....	71	TAKE NEEDLES	12
THE SWING OF MILK WAS TUFTED IN THE PAP,	....	104	WORLD PYRAMID	10
PAPER				
A PAPER WITCH UPON HER SULPHURED BROOM	....	16	TIME TO ROT	11
AND GHOSTLY ECHOES ON PAPER,	....	44	LONGED TO MOVE	9
CHOREOGRAPHED ON PAPER.	....	47	POET: 1935	42
THE HAND THAT SIGNED THE PAPER	....	66	HAND SIGNED	T
THE HAND THAT SIGNED THE PAPER FELLED A CITY;	.....	66	HAND SIGNED	1
ACHE ON THE LOVELORN PAPER	....	75	MY HERO BARES	7
PAPER AND STICKS	....	149	PAPER & STICKS	T
PAPER AND STICKS AND SHOVEL AND MATCH	....	149	PAPER & STICKS	1
LAUGHING WHEN HE SHOOK HIS PAPER	....	171	THE HUNCHBACK	20
PAPER-BLOWING				
PLUG THE PAPER-BLOWING TUBES;	....	156	RETURN	79
PAPS				
AS MILK SHALL BE A MUSIC IN THE PAPS	....	87	PAIN BE MUSIC	14
PARABLES				
THROUGH THE PARABLES	....	178	POEM IN OCT	48
PARABOLA				
A GAY PARABOLA	....	14	RAIN CUTS	23
PARADE				
THE SUICIDES PARADE AGAIN, NOW RIPE FOR DYING.	....	43	FACES SHONE	14
PARADED				
PARADED UP THE AISLES AND IN THE CRYPT	....	51	OUT OF THE PIT	27
PARADISE				
LEADS TO FOOL'S PARADISE WHERE THE REDCOATED KILLER		44	TO FOLLOW FOX	5
CARRION, PARADISE, CHIRRUP MY BRIGHT YOLK.	....	159	INTO HER HEAD	60
OF PARADISE, IN THE SPUN BUD OF THE WORLD.	....	191	WINTER'S TALE	129
PARALLEL				
THE NATURAL PARALLEL.	....	109	I, IN IMAGE	24
PARCEL				
THROW YOUR FEAR A PARCEL OF STONE	....	142	SAINT TO FALL	37
PARCHED				
LAIN WITH PARCHED THINGS; LOVED DOGS AND WOMEN;	...	52	OUT OF THE PIT	72
THE PARCHED AND RAGING VOICE?	....	135	HOW MY ANIMAL	22
ROUND THE PARCHED WORLDS OF WALES AND DROWNED EACH SUN	....	136	AFTER FUNERAL	15
PARCHES				
NOW THE THIRST PARCHES LIP AND TONGUE	....	34	THIRST PARCHES	T
NOW THE THIRST PARCHES LIP AND TONGUE,	....	34	THIRST PARCHES	1

	PAGE	TITLE	LINE
PARCHMENT			
FROM THE ORACULAR ARCHIVES AND THE PARCHMENT, ...	120	ALTARWISE	113
PARCHS			
CAVES THE CRIES OF THE PARCHS AND THEIR FLOCKS. I	179	NEW QUAY	17
PARDON			
HER ROPES OF HERITAGE, THE WARS OF PARDON, ...	115	A GRIEF AGO	21
AND PLAYED DOWN PARDON FROM THE HEAVENS' HILL.	121	INCARNATE DEVL	6
AND, MILD AS PARDON FROM A CLOUD OF PRIDE, ...	133	I MAKE THIS IN	59
PARED			
LOVE IN THE FROST IS PARED AND WINTERED BY, ...	138	FIVE & COUNTRY	5
PARHELION			
AND A BLOOD PARHELION.	104	WORLD PYRAMID	36
PARIS			
FIRST BUY A HAT, NO PARIS MODEL	83	LETTER TO AUNT	15
PARISH			
PARISH OF SNOW. THE CARVED MOUTHS IN THE ROCK ARE			
WIND SWEPT STRINGS.	189	WINTER'S TALE	64
PARK			
NO FROSTY GALLOPS THROUGH THE WINTER PARK.	41	YOUNG ARE OLD	16
OF THE STAR-GESTURED CHILDREN IN THE PARK.	98	OCTOBER WIND	12
THE BALL I THREW WHILE PLAYING IN THE PARK	116	LANTERNS SHINE	18
WHEN I WHISTLED WITH MITCHING BOYS THROUGH A			
RESERVOIR PARK	144	COLOUR OF SAY	7
THE HUNCHBACK IN THE PARK	171	THE HUNCHBACK	T
THE HUNCHBACK IN THE PARK	171	THE HUNCHBACK	1
LIKE THE PARK BIRDS HE CAME EARLY	171	THE HUNCHBACK	13
DODGING THE PARK KEEPER	171	THE HUNCHBACK	23
ALL NIGHT IN THE UNMADE PARK	172	THE HUNCHBACK	37
PARKS			
CHILDREN FROM HOMES AND CHILDREN'S PARKS	129	MY NEOPHYTE	28
PARLIAMENT			
AND THE PARLIAMENT OF SKY, ...	61	MEAT ON BONES	10
PARLOUR			
PLAY PATIENCE IN THE PARLOUR AFTER DARK.	40	YOUNG ARE OLD	14
PARNASSIAN			
FROM MODERNIST PARNASSIAN HEIGHTS.	83	LETTER TO AUNT	14
PARSON			
SPEAK LIKE A HUNGRY PARSON OF THE MANNA, ...	96	TWELVE	6
PART			
PART FROM HER, ...	10	COOL, OH NO	16
PART FROM HER, ...	10	COOL, OH NO	17
WE STILL ARE LOTH TO PART WITH WHAT REMAINS, ...	26	THERE'S PLENTY	17
FOR THESE ARE THINGS THAT PLAY A PART	84	LETTER TO AUNT	46
(AND WHAT A PART) IN ALL GOOD ART.	84	LETTER TO AUNT	47
ALL BLOOD-SIGNED ASSAILINGS AND VANISHED MARRIAGES			
IN WHICH HE HAD NO LOVELY PART	158	INTO HER HEAD	43
PARTED			
THEY COME TOGETHER WHOM THEIR LOVE PARTED:	161	WEDDING ANNIV	10
WHILE ITS VIOLET SHELLS BROKE AND PARTED.	232	FURIOUS MOTION	14
PARTICLE			
CLAW OF THE CRABBED VEINS SQUEEZE FROM EACH RED			
PARTICLE	135	HOW MY ANIMAL	21
PARTICLES			
OR A NACREOUS SLEEP AMONG SOFT PARTICLES AND CHARMS	146	IF HEAD HURT	17
PARTING			
THE PARTING OF HAT FROM HAIR, ...	44	LONGED TO MOVE	16
PASS			
THE WIND PASS LIKE A FIRE, ...	62	EARS IN TURRET	18
DOWN THESE FANTASTIC AVENUES PASS LIKE SHADOWS. ...	222	FOREST PICTURE	12
SAYING YOU WOULD LET THE CHILL SEAS PASS, ...	227	SPRING-SPIRIT	7

	PAGE	TITLE	LINE
PASSAGE			
I OPEN THE LEAVES OF THE WATER AT A PASSAGE	202	SIR JOHNS HILL	23
PASSAGES			
PASSAGES	184	VISION, PRAYER	163
PASSED			
NOT KNOWING RADIANCE CAME AND PASSED.	43	FACES SHONE	13
AND WHEN THE MOIST COLLECTION PLATE IS PASSED	179	NEW QUAY	31
THEIR VOICES ARE DIM; THEY HAVE PASSED, ...	224	IDYLL UNFORGET	40
PASSES			
SUSPICIOUS BUT THAT SOON PASSES.	30	NEARLY SUMMER	20
PASSION			
FOR I CHERISH A PASSION FOR BONES, ...	221	SONG OF DOG	10
PAST			
THE CRUMPLED PACKS FLED PAST THIS GHOST IN BLOOM,	133	I MAKE THIS IN	58
OVER THE PAST TABLE I REPEAT THIS PRESENT GRACE.	145	PLEASURE-BIRD	25
AND THE DEAD HAND LEADS THE PAST, ...	167	LONG-LEGGED	148
PAST LAKE AND ROCKERY	171	THE HUNCHBACK	19
PAST THE STATUES OF THE STABLES AND THE SKY ROOFED			
STIES	188	WINTER'S TALE	34
PAST THE BLIND BARNS AND BYRES OF THE WINDLESS FARM.	190	WINTER'S TALE	90
PASTORAL			
OF THE WOOD! PASTORAL BEAT OF BLOOD THROUGH THE			
LACED LEAVES!	199	COUNTRY SLEEP	71
PASTURE			
TWELVE WINDS ENCOUNTER BY THE WHITE HOST AT PASTURE,	109	I, IN IMAGE	38
THE STAR RISE AT PASTURE AND NIGHTLONG THE FABLES			
GRAZE	198	COUNTRY SLEEP	34
PASTURES			
SHIP TOWNS TO PASTURES OF OTTERS. HE	209	POEM ON B'DAY	24
PAT			
WE HAVE THESE LITTLE THINGS OFF PAT, ...	59	FAIRY TALES	4
SHALL WE LEARN FAIRY TALES OFF PAT, ...	60	FAIRY TALES	37
PATCH			
FELLED AND QUILLED, FLASH TO MY PATCH	5	PROLOGUE	83
TO SHADE AND KNIT ANEW THE PATCH OF WORDS	79	LOVE'S FEVER	34
AND A BLACK AND WHITE PATCH OF GIRLS GREW PLAYING;	144	COLOUR OF SAY	4
PATCHWORK			
THE PATCHWORK HALVES WERE CLOVEN AS THEY SCUDDED	104	WORLD PYRAMID	19
PATH			
WE SAIL A BOAT UPON THE PATH, ...	13	RAIN CUTS	6
RIDING THE SEA LIGHT ON A SUNKEN PATH, ...	107	GRIEF THIEF	8
WITH LITTLE, ODD MISTS WAVED IN THE PATH OF ITS ECHO,	224	IDYLL UNFORGET	26
BURNING ITS SWEET PATH CLEARER THAN BEFORE.	232	FURIOUS MOTION	17
AND SETTLE IN THE STEADY PATH.	233	NO THOUGHT	15
PATHS			
INTO THE MAP-BACKED HILLS WHERE PATHS	44	TO FOLLOW FOX	8
SEE, ON GRAVEL PATHS UNDER THE HARPSTRUNG TREES ...	46	POET: 1935	1
SEE, ON GRAVEL PATHS UNDER THE HARPSTRUNG TREES,	48	POET: 1935	58
THE PATHS ARE HARD, FOR YOU ARE NOT	83	LETTER TO AUNT	3
TIME ON THE CANVAS PATHS.	129	MY NEOPHYTE	24
SCATTERED IN THE PATHS OF HIS HEELS	165	LONG-LEGGED	95
PATHWAY			
OPEN A PATHWAY THROUGH THE SLOW SAD SAIL, ...	194	SLEEP BECALMED	9
CARVEN DOMES OF GREEN ARE THE TREES BY THE PATHWAY,	221	FOREST PICTURE	2
PATIENCE			
PLAY PATIENCE IN THE PARLOUR AFTER DARK.	40	YOUNG ARE OLD	14
JOHN'S BEAST, JOB'S PATIENCE, AND THE FIBS OF VISION,	125	TODAY, INSECT	21
PATIENT			
LUCKLESSLY SHE MUST LIE PATIENT	149	UNLUCKILY FOR	53

	PAGE	TITLE	LINE
PATIENTS			
AND LOVE AND HIS PATIENTS ROAR ON A CHAIN;	161	WEDDING ANNIV	6
PATROL			
BRING OUT THE BLACK PATROL, ...	110	I, IN IMAGE	55
PATTERN			
IN A PATTERN LIKE A SHELL	229	MY RIVER	39
PATTERNED			
ROOFED WITH THE SKY AND PATTERNED WITH BLOND BONES;	64	WOMAN SPEAKS	25
PATTERNS			
HAVE TRACED YOUR PATTERNS IN THE HASTENING FROST.	30	YOUTH CALLS	7
AND CHANGED WITH THE WIND INTO INDISTINCT PATTERNS OF FROLIC, ...	224	IDYLL UNFORGET	29
PATTING			
TELLING IT THIS, PATTING ITS BLACK NOSE:	45	PLOUGHMAN GONE	15
PAVEMENT			
WHO'LL BREAK OUR NECKS UPON THE PAVEMENT	28	NO WINGS	10
OVER THESE GROUNDWORKS THRUSTING THROUGH A PAVEMENT	117	ALTARWISE	27
HE DROPPED WHERE HE LOVED ON THE BURST PAVEMENT STONE	172	DAWN RAID	4
PAVEMENTS			
ON THUNDEROUS PAVEMENTS IN THE GARDEN TIME;	117	ALTARWISE	34
AND THE GOLDEN PAVEMENTS LAID IN REQUIEMS, ...	175	FIRE RAID	69
PAVILIONS			
FROM BALD PAVILIONS AND THE HOUSE OF BREAD	120	ALTARWISE	96
PAY			
GOD AND I WILL PAY THE SNIPER.	71	TAKE NEEDLES	24
TO SURRENDER NOW IS TO PAY THE EXPENSIVE OGRE TWICE.	140	NO WORK WORDS	10
WHO PAY NO PRAISE OR WAGES	197	CRAFT OR ART	19
PAYING			
PAYING HEED TO THE THIRSTY VOICE.	67	REALM OF FLESH	13
PAYS			
A MOTHER IN LABOUR PAYS TWICE HER PAIN, ...	74	SUN BURNS	14
PEACE			
AT POOR PEACE I SING	3	PROLOGUE	23
POOR PEACE AS THE SUN SETS	5	PROLOGUE	89
SOFT SHINING SYMBOLS OF HER PEACE WITH YOU, ...	20	THE NEOPHYTE	21
IS WITH THE CORPSE OF PEACE, ...	35	LIFT UP FACE	20
YIELDS PEACE AND PLENTY AT THE END. OR IS IT PEACE,	36	MIDNIGHT ROAD	3
YIELDS PEACE AND PLENTY AT THE END. OR IS IT PEACE,	36	MIDNIGHT ROAD	3
ONE WHO CALLED DEEPEST DOWN SHALL HOLD HIS PEACE	160	DEATHS AND ENT	9
BE AT CLOUD QUAKING PEACE, ...	210	POEM ON B'DAY	63
AND I HAVE REFLECTED ITS COLOURS IN THE PEACE OF MY EYES;	224	IDYLL UNFORGET	24
PEACOCKSTAIN'S			
PEACOCKSTAIN'S POEMS ON MY BED.	143	THE MOLLS	12
PEAKS			
DAYED PEAKS TO DAY TO DEATH, ...	108	GRIEF THIEF	22
PEARL			
THE FRANK, CLOSED PEARL, THE SEA-GIRLS' LINEAMENTS	131	I MAKE THIS IN	19
THE SUN SHIPWRECKED WEST ON A PEARL	162	LONG-LEGGED	15
AND THE WHISPER CAUGHT IN ITS PAGEANT OF TAWNY PEARL,	224	IDYLL UNFORGET	44
PEARS			
PEARS AND RED CURRANTS	178	POEM IN OCT	45
PEBBLES			
THE PEBBLES. IT IS TIME FOR THE BLACK LION	179	NEW QUAY	10
IN THE PEBBLES OF THE HOLY STREAMS.	195	FERN HILL	18
PEBBLY			
IN THE PEBBLY DAB-FILLED	202	SIR JOHNS HILL	20
PECK			
PECK, SPRINT, DANCE ON FOUNTAINS AND DUCK TIME	145	IF HEAD HURT	8

		PAGE	TITLE	LINE
PECKING				
	PECKING AND NESTLING ALL THE TIME OF NIGHT.	63	WOMAN SPEAKS	18
PEDRO'S				
	IN, IN PEDRO'S OR WENDY'S	154	RETURN	27
PEELED				
	WHAT RHUBARB MAN PEELED IN HER FOAM-BLUE CHANNEL	121	ALTARWISE	135
	ITS TONGUE PEELED IN THE WRAP OF A LEAF.	150	WHEN I WOKE	15
PEERED				
	LITTLE WHITE-LIPPED FACES HAVE PEERED UP AT ME, ...	224	IDYLL UNFORGET	32
PEERS				
	THE MOON PEERS DOWN THE VALLEY LIKE A SAINT.	53	OUT OF THE PIT	94
PEG				
	TAP HAPPILY OF ONE PEG IN THE THICK	136	AFTER FUNERAL	3
PELICAN				
	THE PLANET-DUCTED PELICAN OF CIRCLES	117	ALTARWISE	17
PELT				
	WITH PELT, AND SCALE, AND FLEECE:	5	PROLOGUE	86
PELTER				
	AN INCH IN FROTH. CHIMES CHEAT THE PRISON SPIRE,			
	PELTER	15	SPIRE CRANES	5
PELTS				
	DOWN PELTS THE NAKED WEATHER;	58	HERE IN SPRING	3
PEN				
	SHIFTS TO THE REDWOMBED PEN.	80	ALMANAC TIME	5
PENETRATE				
	NO LOVE CAN PENETRATE	233	NO THOUGHT	9
PENNY				
	THE ISLAND OF SUCH PENNY LOVE	43	FACES SHONE	4
	PUTS IN HIS PENNY, GENEROUS AT LAST.	179	NEW QUAY	32
PENNY-EYED				
	THEN, PENNY-EYED, THAT GENTLEMAN OF WOUNDS, ...	117	ALTARWISE	7
PENUMBRA				
	PENUMBRA DERRY, ...	18	NATURAL DAY	36
PEOPLE				
	A FILM OF PEOPLE MOVING, ...	36	MIDNIGHT ROAD	7
	LEPER AMONG A CLEAN PEOPLE	47	POET: 1935	26
	WITH THE WOMB OF HIS SHAPELESS PEOPLE.	107	ALL ALL AND	27
PEOPLE'S				
	FLOWER, FLOWER THE PEOPLE'S FUSION, ...	107	ALL ALL AND	31
	SHE HOLDING ME? THE PEOPLE'S SEA DRIVES ON HER, ...	115	A GRIEF AGO	26
PERCEIVE				
	TO VEIL BELLADONNA AND LET THE DRY EYES PERCEIVE	133	MAKE ME A MASK	10
PERCEIVES				
	AND THE HEWN COILS OF HIS TRADE PERCEIVES	209	POEM ON B'DAY	26
PERCH				
	AND A HUNDRED STORKS PERCH ON THE SUN'S RIGHT HAND.	173	DAWN RAID	14
PERCHED				
	NO PLACE IN WHICH, WAVE PERCHED ON WAVE, ...	10	COOL, OH NO	24
	THE CLOUD PERCHED TAILORS' MASTER WITH NERVES FOR			
	COTTON.	152	BELOW A TIME	35
PERCIES				
	EMETIC PERCIES FOR THEIR JOYS.	143	THE MOLLS	4
PERHAPS				
	AND I, CAUGHT IN MID-AIR PERHAPS, ...	9	MINUTE'S HOUR	6
	PERHAPS THE SKY'S TOO BRIGHT;	13	SKY'S BRIGHT	26
	PERHAPS IT WOULD BE BEST IF YOU	83	LETTER TO AUNT	23
	PERHAPS IT WOULD BE JUST AS WELL, ...	84	LETTER TO AUNT	30
PERIL				
	THIS IS THE FORTUNE OF MANHOOD: THE NATURAL PERIL,	109	I, IN IMAGE	19

	PAGE	TITLE	LINE

PERILOUS
    NO TREAD MORE PERILOUS, THE GREEN STEPS AND SPIRE   109   I, IN IMAGE   26
PERILS
    AFTER THE PERILS OF FRIENDS' TALK   42   A WAR OF WITS   15
PERIODIC
    YOU HAVE OFFENDED, PERIODIC HEART;   9   MINUTE'S HOUR   8
PERISCOPE
    WHO PERISCOPE THROUGH FLOWERS TO THE SKY.   98   TWILIGHT LOCKS   30
PERISCOPES
    THROUGH PERISCOPES RIGHTSIGHTED FROM THE GRAVE;   ...   81   ALL THAT I OWE   24
PERISH
    AND MUCH THAT LIVES TO PERISH, ...   25   THERE'S PLENTY   2
    ABOUT YOU, FLESH WILL PERISH, AND BLOOD   39   GAS FADES   31
PERISHED
    NO CRADLE'S WARMER THAN THIS PERISHED BREAST, ...   63   WOMAN SPEAKS   6
PERISHES
    AT FLESH THAT PERISHES AND BLOOD THAT'S SPILT   57   GREEK PLAY   19
    THE DANCING PERISHES   190   WINTER'S TALE   111
PERPETUAL
    AND THAT IS TRUE AFTER PERPETUAL DEFEAT.   32   OUT OF SIGHS   9
PERPETUATE
    WITH THE INCESTUOUS SECRET BROTHER IN THE SECONDS TO
        PERPETUATE THE STARS, ...   159   INTO HER HEAD   66
PERPLEXED
    PERPLEXED BEYOND PERPLEXION, ...   37   WINDMILLS TURN   25
PERPLEXION
    PERPLEXED BEYOND PERPLEXION, ...   37   WINDMILLS TURN   25
PERRINS
    AND PERRINS ON THE COCKLED TABLECLOTH   179   NEW QUAY   3
PERSON
    IF NOT IN PERSON SENDS HIS UNENDING EVIL   29   NEARLY SUMMER   3
    THE SALT PERSON AND BLASTED PLACE   145   PLEASURE-BIRD   20
PERSONAL
    WRITTEN FOR A PERSONAL EPITAPH   26   PERSONAL EPIT   T
PERVERSE
    YOU'RE THE PERVERSE TO LIE ACROSS, ...   21   BEWILDERED WAY   15
PETAL
    IS A PETAL THAT HAS DELICATE BREATH   226   SLENDER WIND   7
PETALS
    WORKED ON A WORLD OF PETALS;   108   I, IN IMAGE   9
    THE SUN THAT LEAPS ON PETALS THROUGH A NOUGHT, ...   128   NOW, SAY NAY   27
    OF PETALS FROM SOME MAGIC ROSE;   225   CLOWN IN MOON   2
    SEEKING NO FURTHER THAN YOUR PETALS THAT STILL SLEPT.   227   SPRING-SPIRIT   8
    NOR THE PETALS OF ANY FLOWER DROP.   232   YOUR VOICE   16
PETER
    LET THE FIRST PETER FROM A RAINBOW'S QUAYRAIL   121   ALTARWISE   133
PETROL
    TURNING A PETROL FACE BLIND TO THE ENEMY   110   I, IN IMAGE   47
PETTICOATS
    PETTICOATS GALED HIGH, OR SHY WITH THE ROUGH RIDING
        BOYS, ...   204   GIANT'S THIGH   18
PETTY
    POOR, PETTY VERMIN, ...   28   NO WINGS   15
PEWS
    AND THE BLACK BEAST OF THE BEETLES' PEWS, ...   206   LAMENT   14
PHANTOM
    IMAGE OF IMAGES, MY METAL PHANTOM   109   I, IN IMAGE   14
PHARAOH
    WITH PRIEST AND PHARAOH BED MY GENTLE WOUND, ...   120   ALTARWISE   123

	PAGE	TITLE	LINE
PHARAOH'S			
SHADE WITHOUT SHAPE? THE SHAPE OF PHARAOH'S ECHO?	118	ALTARWISE	45
PHEASANTS			
AND HONOURED AMONG FOXES AND PHEASANTS BY THE GAY HOUSE	196	FERN HILL	37
AND THE ANGELS WHIRR LIKE PHEASANTS	215	COUNTRY HEAVEN	9
PHOENIX			
WAITING WITH PHOENIX UNDER	147	UNLUCKILY FOR	2
CONTINENCE. I SEE THE UNFIRED PHOENIX, HERALD	148	UNLUCKILY FOR	37
PHOENIX'			
THAT THE PHOENIX' BID FOR HEAVEN AND THE DESIRE AFTER	148	UNLUCKILY FOR	45
PHOSPHORUS			
DESIRE IS PHOSPHORUS: THE CHEMIC BRUIT	159	TO LEDA	7
PHOTOGRAPH			
THE PHOTOGRAPH IS MARRIED TO THE EYE,	90	EUNUCH DREAMS	27
PHOTOGRAPHS			
STRETCH THE SALT PHOTOGRAPHS,	129	MY NEOPHYTE	19
PHRASE			
SO PHRASE;	18	NATURAL DAY	8
PHRASES			
THE PHRASES ON THE WOOD AREN'T HERS;	14	FOR LEDA	5
'ALL GAME PHRASES FIT YOUR RING OF A COCKFIGHT:	145	IF HEAD HURT	6
PICCADILLY			
THE PICCADILLY MEN, THE BACK STREET DRUNKS,	41	YOUNG ARE OLD	41
PICK			
PICK THE WORLD'S BALL OF WAVE AND FROTH	93	BOYS OF SUMMER	40
I PICK A STICK OF CELERY FROM THE VALLEY	137	O CHATTERTON	14
PICKBRAIN			
MY PICKBRAIN MASTERS MORSING ON THE STONE	100	RUNNING GRAVE	22
PICKED			
AND THE OAKUM IS PICKED, AND THE SPRING TREES HAVE GROWN GREEN,	39	GAS FADES	6
WHEN THEIR BONES ARE PICKED CLEAN AND THE CLEAN BONES GONE,	49	NO DOMINION	4
THE PLUM MY MOTHER PICKED MATURED SLOWLY,	78	LOVE'S FEVER	25
DESTRUCTION, PICKED BY BIRDS, BRAYS THROUGH THE JAW-BONE,	132	I MAKE THIS IN	36
WITH HIS STICK THAT PICKED UP LEAVES.	171	THE HUNCHBACK	24
PICKERS			
HE LEARNS THE CARRION PICKERS OF THE SKY,	63	WOMAN SPEAKS	21
PICKPOCKET			
THE AFFECTIONATE PICKPOCKET	155	RETURN	50
PICKS			
WHO PICKS THE LIVE HEART ON A DIAMOND.	132	I MAKE THIS IN	45
PICKTHANK			
AND LEAVE THE POPPIED PICKTHANK WHERE HE LIES;	98	TWILIGHT LOCKS	39
PICTURE			
THE SIDEBOARD FRUIT, THE FERNS, THE PICTURE HOUSES	33	HELD-OUT HAND	10
LEFT IN THE RECORDS OF LIVING A NOT-TO-BE-BROKEN PICTURE,	45	PLOUGHMAN GONE	2
FOREST PICTURE	221	FOREST PICTURE	T
PICTURED			
THUS THE SHADOWLESS MAN OR OX, AND THE PICTURED DEVIL,	109	I, IN IMAGE	22
PICTURES			
WHY BLOT THE PICTURES	60	FAIRY TALES	28
ONCE CLOSE-UP SMILING IN THE WALL OF PICTURES,	118	ALTARWISE	55
LIKE THE MAULED PICTURES OF BOYS?	145	PLEASURE-BIRD	19
PIECE			
FROM NAPE TO TOE, A SANATORIUM PIECE	29	LONG, SKELETON	5

		PAGE	TITLE	LINE
PIECE (CONTINUED)				
I'VE SAID MY PIECE: COUNT OR GO MAD.	....	33	HELD-OUT HAND	17
I'VE SAID MY PIECE.	....	33	HELD-OUT HAND	24
I PIECE MY FLESH THAT RATTLED ON THE YARDS	....	105	WORLD PYRAMID	38
WINGED LIKE A SABBATH ASS THIS CHILDREN'S PIECE	...	124	TODAY, INSECT	16
PIECES				
SNAPPED IN A RAIN OF PIECES FALLING	....	21	BEWILDERED WAY	20
TRAMPLING TO DUST THE BITS AND PIECES	....	34	IN GARDENS	9
MATERNAL SHORT TIME PIECES,	....	155	RETURN	54
PIERCE				
PIERCE THE SPILT SKY WITH DIVING WING IN WEED AND HEEL	....	15	SPIRE CRANES	4
THE HALVES THAT PIERCE THE PIN'S POINT IN THE AIR,		104	WORLD PYRAMID	26
AND STEEPLES PIERCE THE CLOUD ON HER SHOULDER	.....	168	LONG-LEGGED	193
PIERCED				
UNEATEN AND NOT TO BE PIERCED	....	17	IN OBLIVION	25
BE BY YOUR ONE GHOST PIERCED, HIS POINTED FERRULE,		111	I, IN IMAGE	79
I WAS PIERCED BY THE IDOL TAILOR'S EYES,	....	152	BELOW A TIME	38
AND HER EYES PIERCED THEIR INTENSE LOVE INTO ME,		234	WOMAN TAPESTRY	2
PIERCING				
PLUNGING AND PIERCING IN HIS COURSE	....	163	LONG-LEGGED	46
PIETY				
CHASTITY PRAYS FOR ME, PIETY SINGS,	....	207	LAMENT	57
PIGEON				
AMONG THE GARDEN TREES A PIGEON CALLS,	....	57	GREEK PLAY	29
A PIGEON CALLS AND WOMEN TALK OF DEATH.	....	57	GREEK PLAY	32
LOVE ME, NOT AS THE RUFFLING PIGEON	....	76	SONG: LOVE ME	9
NO, PIGEON, I'M TOO WISE	....	234	NO, PIGEON	T
NO, PIGEON, I'M TOO WISE;	....	234	NO, PIGEON	1
PIGEONS				
AS A DUST OF PIGEONS. EXULTING, THE GRAVE HOOVED		189	WINTER'S TALE	73
PIGEON'S				
AND A SILK PIGEON'S GUILT IN HER PROUD ABSENCE,	...	131	I MAKE THIS IN	17
PIGMENTS				
AND FROM HER LIPS THE FADED PIGMENTS FALL,	....	116	LANTERNS SHINE	7
PIGS'				
THE WILD PIGS' WOOD, AND SLIME UPON THE TREES,	....	104	WORLD PYRAMID	20
PIG'S				
A PIG'S SNOUT FOR A NOSE,	....	41	YOUNG ARE OLD	32
PILGRIMAGE				
AND THE MOLE SNOUT BLUNT UNDER HIS PILGRIMAGE OF DOMES,	....	204	GIANT'S THIGH	36
PILLAR				
PILLAR BREAKS	....	237	PILLAR BREAKS	T
PILLAR BREAKS, AND MAST IS CLEFT	....	237	PILLAR BREAKS	1
PILLARS				
CLACK THROUGH THE THICKET OF STRENGTH, LOVE HEWN IN PILLARS DROPS	....	135	HOW MY ANIMAL	36
PILLOW				
HER DEEPSEA PILLOW WHERE ONCE SHE MARRIED ALONE,		170	MARRIAGE VIRG	9
PIMPS				
THAT PRINCE OF PIMPS, THAT DOYEN OF DUNG-LICKERS.		179	NEW QUAY	24
PIN				
CREEP AND HARP ON THE TIDE, SINKING THEIR CHARMED, BENT PIN	....	135	HOW MY ANIMAL	24
PINCERED				
OF PSALMS AND SHADOWS AMONG THE PINCERED SANDCRABS PRANCING	....	202	SIR JOHNS HILL	24
PINCERS				
AND IN THE PINCERS OF THE BOILING CIRCLE,	....	111	I, IN IMAGE	91

		PAGE	TITLE	LINE
PINCH				
A PINCH OF AUDEN IS THE LION'S FEAST;	....	58	TO ARCHITECTS	13
PINE				
CASTS TO THE PINE ROOTS, RAISING MAN LIKE A MOUNTAIN		109	I, IN IMAGE	11
THE PINE	....	227	THE PINE	T
THE PINE IS THE TREE OF THE BREEZE,	....	227	THE PINE	2
PIN-HILLED				
LOP, LOVE, MY FORK TONGUE, SAID THE PIN-HILLED NETTLE;	....	119	ALTARWISE	76
PINK				
THERE ARE OTHERS WHO THINK THAT A LOBSTER IS PINK,		221	SONG OF DOG	3
WITH HIS PINK BEAK,	....	231	OUR SANCTITY	25
PIN-LEGGED				
PIN-LEGGED ON POLE-HILLS WITH A BLACK MEDUSA	......	119	ALTARWISE	68
PINNACLE				
THEY CLIMB THE COUNTRY PINNACLE,	....	109	I, IN IMAGE	37
PINNED-AROUND-THE-SPIRIT				
WHEN MY PINNED-AROUND-THE-SPIRIT	....	151	BELOW A TIME	2
PIN-POINT				
THE WORM IS (PIN-POINT) RATIONAL IN THE FRUIT.	....	159	TO LEDA	3
THE WORM IS (PIN-POINT) RATIONAL IN THE FRUIT.	....	159	TO LEDA	9
PINPRICKS				
FEELING THE PINPRICKS OF THE BLOOD, I'VE SAID	.....	53	OUT OF THE PIT	80
PINS				
WITH PINS FOR TEARDROPS IS THE LONG WOUND'S WOMAN.		120	ALTARWISE	104
PIN'S				
THE HALVES THAT PIERCE THE PIN'S POINT IN THE AIR,		104	WORLD PYRAMID	26
PINTABLES				
TIME AMONG WALKING PINTABLES	....	154	RETURN	10
PIOUS				
TO HEAVEN'S TURNED, AND PIOUS LOADS	....	37	WINDMILLS TURN	32
PIPERS				
GULLS, PIPERS, COCKLES, AND SAILS,	....	3	PROLOGUE	11
PIT				
THE SQUEAL OF THE DAMNED OUT OF THE OLD PIT.	......	40	YOUNG ARE OLD	6
LEADS, TOO, TO A LEAD PIT, WHINNY AND FALL,	....	44	TO FOLLOW FOX	10
OUT OF THE PIT	....	50	OUT OF THE PIT	T
THE WINTER YEARS, MOVE IN THE PIT OF MAN;	....	79	ALMANAC TIME	3
PITCH				
LIKE SOME PITCH MOON, THE LIMIT OF THE GLOBES;	....	82	LIGHT BREAKS	20
WE ARE THE SONS OF FLINT AND PITCH.	....	93	BOYS OF SUMMER	53
BEFORE THE PITCH WAS FORKING TO A SUN;	....	94	IN BEGINNING	27
PITCHING				
CLUNG TO THE PITCHING CLOUDS, OR GAY WITH ANY ONE		204	GIANT'S THIGH	15
PITILESS				
AND THE TRIUMPH OF HER PITILESS GAIETY	....	235	WOMAN TAPESTRY	19
PITS				
ROLLED DOWN ALL IMAGES INTO THE PITS	....	50	OUT OF THE PIT	3
PITY				
LAMENTING FALLS. PITY ELECTRA'S LOVING	....	56	GREEK PLAY	4
PITY THE LIVING WHO ARE LOST, ALONE;	....	57	GREEK PLAY	21
PITY ELECTRA LOVELESS, SHE WHOSE GRIEF	....	57	GREEK PLAY	25
PITY THE POOR UNPITIED WHO ARE STRANGE WITH TEARS.		57	GREEK PLAY	28
A HAND RULES PITY AS A HAND RULES HEAVEN;	....	66	HAND SIGNED	15
REMEMBER ME AND PITY HIM	....	69	BEFORE KNOCKED	44
HAWKING FOR MONEY AND PITY	....	156	RETURN	64
FOR THE FIFTH ELEMENT IS PITY,	....	216	COUNTRY HEAVEN	31
(PITY FOR DEATH)	....	216	COUNTRY HEAVEN	32
AND YOUR SHARP PITY IS UNCHANGEABLE.	....	236	WOMAN TAPESTRY	51
PITY IS NOT ENOUGH:	....	238	PILLAR BREAKS	23

		PAGE	TITLE	LINE
PIVOT				
AND, FOR A PIVOT,	....	14	FOR LEDA	10
PLACE				
HARK: I TRUMPET THE PLACE,	....	4	PROLOGUE	42
NO PLACE IN WHICH, WAVE PERCHED ON WAVE,	....	10	COOL, OH NO	24
RAIN CUTS THE PLACE WE TREAD	....	13	RAIN CUTS	T
RAIN CUTS THE PLACE WE TREAD,	....	13	RAIN CUTS	1
YOU'LL BRING THE PLACE TO ME	....	21	BEWILDERED WAY	10
THY PLACE IS FILLED, BONES BID FOR AUCTION,	....	29	LONG, SKELETON	9
RANGE ON THE SKY-SCRAPING PLACE.	....	126	SEED-AT-ZERO	49
RANGE FROM THE GRAVE-GROPING PLACE.	....	127	SEED-AT-ZERO	56
DELIVERED SEAS MY LOVE FROM HER PROUD PLACE	....	133	I MAKE THIS IN	62
SHE MARRIED IN THIS POURING PLACE,	....	139	TOMBSTONE TOLD	4
WHEN YOU SEW THE DEEP DOOR. THE BED IS A CROSS PLACE.		145	IF HEAD HURT	13
THE SALT PERSON AND BLASTED PLACE	....	145	PLEASURE-BIRD	20
IN THE FIRST, SPINNING PLACE, THE SPELLBOUND HORSES WALKING WARM	....	196	FERN HILL	34
DARK IS A WAY AND LIGHT IS A PLACE,	....	210	POEM ON B'DAY	49
TAKE YOU INTO MY OWN PLACE	....	232	YOUR VOICE	14
WENT AWAY FROM THE BRIGHT PLACE.	....	237	WOMAN TAPESTRY	78
PLACES				
INTO THE PLACES AND THE CREVICES	....	34	THIRST PARCHES	9
TO DIFFERENT PLACES THAN WERE SAID	....	37	WINDMILLS TURN	21
GROWING IN PUBLIC PLACES THAN MAN KNOWS.	....	48	POET: 1935	57
TIME AND PLACES GRIP HER BREAST BONE,	....	168	LONG-LEGGED	175
PLACES	....	184	VISION, PRAYER	160
PLAGUE				
FROM LOVE'S FIRST FEVER TO HER PLAGUE	....	78	LOVE'S FEVER	T
FROM LOVE'S FIRST FEVER TO HER PLAGUE, FROM THE SOFT SECOND	....	78	LOVE'S FEVER	1
TO CHILDREN WHO WERE SUCKLED ON A PLAGUE,	....	81	ALL THAT I OWE	17
ROSE CAST TO PLAGUE,	....	115	A GRIEF AGO	14
THE INSECT CERTAIN IS THE PLAGUE OF FABLES.	....	124	TODAY, INSECT	9
AND ALL THE DEADLY VIRTUES PLAGUE MY DEATH!	....	207	LAMENT	60
PLAGUED				
NUTMEG, CIVET, AND SEA-PARSLEY SERVE THE PLAGUED GROOM AND BRIDE	....	131	SINNERS' BELL	29
PLAIN				
SICK, PALE, AND PLAIN,	....	21	BEWILDERED WAY	17
FOR LOSS OF BLOOD I FELL ON ISHMAEL'S PLAIN,	....	118	ALTARWISE	63
IS OLD AS WATER AND PLAIN AS AN EEL;	....	165	LONG-LEGGED	93
DOWN TO THE RIVER ROOTING PLAIN	....	184	VISION, PRAYER	151
HATING HIS GOD, BUT WHAT HE WAS WAS PLAIN:	....	217	ELEGY	23
PLAINS				
THE CENTRAL PLAINS OF ASIA IN HIS GARDEN,	....	121	INCARNATE DEVL	2
THE SWINISH PLAINS OF CARRION	....	183	VISION, PRAYER	103
PLAIT				
THE BEACH OF FLESH, AND WIND HER BLOODRED PLAIT;		75	MY HERO BARES	13
PLANET				
BUT RAIL WITH YOUR WIZARD'S RIBS THE HEART-SHAPED PLANET;	....	123	FOSTER LIGHT	15
MAY A HUMBLE PLANET LABOUR	....	126	SEED-AT-ZERO	36
PLANET-DUCTED				
THE PLANET-DUCTED PELICAN OF CIRCLES	....	117	ALTARWISE	17
PLANETS				
MIGHT CROSS ITS PLANETS, THE BELL WEEP, NIGHT GATHER HER EYES,	....	200	COUNTRY SLEEP	92
HUMBLE IN ALL HIS PLANETS,	....	215	COUNTRY HEAVEN	4
PLANING-HEELED				
SO, PLANING-HEELED, I FLEW ALONG MY MAN	....	101	FELLOWED SLEEP	4

	PAGE	TITLE	LINE
PLANNED			
BY THOSE WHO PLANNED THE OBVIOUS ROUTES	37	WINDMILLS TURN	22
PLANNING			
PLANNING WHAT'S GOOD, THOUGH IT'S BUT WINTER, ...	27	OBLIVIOUS DARK	29
PLANT			
BROOD ON EACH HOTHOUSE PLANT	26	THERE'S PLENTY	9
LIKE A SWEET, SENSITIVE PLANT	237	WOMAN TAPESTRY	71
PLANTED			
AND FROM THE PLANTED WOMB THE MAN OF STRAW.	92	BOYS OF SUMMER	36
FOR HALF OF LOVE WAS PLANTED IN THE LOST, ...	104	WORLD PYRAMID	11
THE CLOUD, THE NEED, THE PLANTED STARS, THE JOY			
BEYOND	190	WINTER'S TALE	102
PLANTS			
THIS IS A DRAIN OF IRON PLANTS, ...	14	RAIN CUTS	29
OUT OF THE FONT OF BONE AND PLANTS AT THAT STONE			
TOCSIN	130	SINNERS' BELL	20
DOWN THE BEGINNING OF PLANTS	193	SIDE OF TRUTH	30
PLATE			
GROPING FOR MATTER UNDER THE DOG'S PLATE, ...	32	OUT OF SIGHS	26
AND WHEN THE MOIST COLLECTION PLATE IS PASSED	179	NEW QUAY	31
PLATES			
THE IMAGE FROM THE PLATES;	90	EUNUCH DREAMS	39
PLATYPUS			
THE DUCK-BILLED PLATYPUS BROODY IN A MILK OF BIRDS.	148	UNLUCKILY FOR	33
PLAY			
WE SHALL PLAY CHOPIN IN OUR SUMMER GARDEN, ...	40	YOUNG ARE OLD	12
PLAY PATIENCE IN THE PARLOUR AFTER DARK.	40	YOUNG ARE OLD	14
MIGHT PLAY UPON HIS LANK LOCKS WITH ITS WIND, ...	46	POET: 1935	3
OR MICE PLAY WITH AN IVORY TOOTH.	49	LIGHT, I KNOW	26
GREEK PLAY IN A GARDEN	56	GREEK PLAY	T
FOR THESE ARE THINGS THAT PLAY A PART	84	LETTER TO AUNT	46
WHO PLAY THE PROPER GENTLEMAN AND LADY.	113	NOT FATHER ME	28
TIME LET ME PLAY AND BE	195	FERN HILL	13
AND THE SHRILL CHILD'S PLAY	201	SIR JOHNS HILL	5
PLAYED			
A MOUSE IT WAS PLAYED WITH AN IVORY TOOTH, ...	65	WOMAN SPEAKS	58
AND PLAYED DOWN PARDON FROM THE HEAVENS' HILL.	121	INCARNATE DEVL	6
THAT PLAYED IN VOICELESS FROLIC AT THE THRESHOLD OF			
MY HEART.	223	IDYLL UNFORGET	12
PLAYERED			
THE SALTY SCENE AND MY PLAYERED GOB CURVING	179	NEW QUAY	14
PLAYERS			
AND KNOWS NO WOE THAT THESE SAD PLAYERS MOUTH	57	GREEK PLAY	30
PLAYING			
THE BAND WAS PLAYING ON THE BLACONY.	11	CABARET	10
THE BALL I THREW WHILE PLAYING IN THE PARK	116	LANTERNS SHINE	18
AND A BLACK AND WHITE PATCH OF GIRLS GREW PLAYING;	144	COLOUR OF SAY	4
AND PLAYING, LOVELY AND WATERY	195	FERN HILL	21
PLAYS			
PLAYS SCURVY TRICKS WITH VALUES AND INTENTIONS, ...	37	WINDMILLS TURN	6
PLEADING			
PLEADING IN THE WADED BAY FOR THE SEED TO FLOW	203	GIANT'S THIGH	7
PLEASE			
FOR YOU COULD THEN WRITE WHAT YOU PLEASE, ...	84	LETTER TO AUNT	31
DEAR TOMMY, PLEASE, FROM FAR, SCIATIC KINGSLEY	179	NEW QUAY	1
PLEASING			
TO LIFT TO LEAVE FROM THE TREASURES OF MAN IS			
PLEASING DEATH	140	NO WORK WORDS	7
PLEASURE			
GIVE US THE PLEASURE OF REGRET;	230	OUR SANCTITY	11

		PAGE	TITLE	LINE
PLEASURE-BIRD				
	BECAUSE THE PLEASURE-BIRD WHISTLES	144	PLEASURE-BIRD	T
	BECAUSE THE PLEASURE-BIRD WHISTLES AFTER THE HOT			
	WIRES, ...	144	PLEASURE-BIRD	1
PLENTY				
	THERE'S PLENTY IN THE WORLD	25	THERE'S PLENTY	T
	THERE'S PLENTY IN THE WORLD THAT DOTH NOT DIE, ...	25	THERE'S PLENTY	1
	THERE'S PLENTY THAT DOTH DIE;	26	THERE'S PLENTY	14
	WERE VAGUENESS ENOUGH AND THE SWEET LIES PLENTY,	32	OUT OF SIGHS	21
	YIELDS PEACE AND PLENTY AT THE END. OR IS IT PEACE,	36	MIDNIGHT ROAD	3
	AND THIS IS PLENTY, THEN, CLOVES AND SWEET OILS, THE			
	BEES' HONEY, ...	36	MIDNIGHT ROAD	5
	PLENTY AS BLACKBERRIES IN THE WOODS	210	POEM ON B'DAY	53
PLOUGHED				
	VERY ALONE, HE PLOUGHED THE ONLY WAY.	53	OUT OF THE PIT	86
PLOUGHMAN'S				
	THE PLOUGHMAN'S GONE	45	PLOUGHMAN GONE	T
	THE PLOUGHMAN'S GONE, THE HANSOM DRIVER, ...	45	PLOUGHMAN GONE	1
	THE PLOUGHMAN'S GONE, THE HANSOM DRIVER, ...	45	PLOUGHMAN GONE	19
PLUCK				
	THERE'S TIME TO PLUCK A TUNE UPON THE HARP, ...	15	FOR LEDA	16
	PLUCK, COCK, MY SEA EYE, SAID MEDUSA'S SCRIPTURE,	119	ALTARWISE	75
	AND PLUCK A MANDRAKE MUSIC FROM THE MARROWROOT. ...	123	FOSTER LIGHT	18
	I HAVE COME TO PLUCK YOU, ...	232	YOUR VOICE	11
PLUCKED				
	AND LOVE PLUCKED OUT THE STINGING SIREN'S EYE, ...	119	ALTARWISE	77
	IN A WIND THAT PLUCKED A GOOSE, ...	144	PLEASURE-BIRD	10
	LISTEN AND LOOK WHERE SHE SAILS THE GOOSE PLUCKED			
	SEA, ...	190	WINTER'S TALE	100
PLUCKS				
	AND THE HARP SHAPED VOICE OF THE WATER'S DUST PLUCKS			
	IN A FOLD	189	WINTER'S TALE	79
PLUG				
	PLUG THE PAPER-BLOWING TUBES;	156	RETURN	79
PLUM				
	THE PLUM MY MOTHER PICKED MATURED SLOWLY, ...	78	LOVE'S FEVER	25
	AND DROP THE PLUM LIKE FIRE FROM THE FLESH.	95	RUB OF LOVE	9
PLUMAGE				
	AND TAKE AWAY YOUR EXOTIC PLUMAGE, ...	232	YOUR VOICE	12
PLUMB				
	BUT ONLY PLUMB SUCH DEPTHS	24	LITTLE PROBLEM	24
PLUMBED				
	HULOO, ON PLUMBED BRYNS, ...	4	PROLOGUE	57
PLUME				
	AND MOUTH. BOTH NOTE AND PLUME PLUNGE FROM THE			
	SPIRE'S HOOK.	16	SPIRE CRANES	8
	TAKING NO PLUME FOR INDEX IN LOVE'S CHANGE	159	TO LEDA	5
	BOLTING THE NIGHT OF THE DOOR WITH HER ARM HER PLUME.	169	LOVE IN ASYLUM	4
	ON THE BLACK PLUME	183	VISION, PRAYER	113
PLUMED				
	LOPS, AS A BUSH PLUMED WITH FLAMES, THE RANT OF THE			
	FIERCE EYE, ...	135	HOW MY ANIMAL	38
	AND THE SKY OF BIRDS IN THE PLUMED VOICE CHARMED	190	WINTER'S TALE	88
PLUMES				
	THE BIRDS MAKE HIM HIS CEREMENTS OF PLUMES, ...	64	WOMAN SPEAKS	26
	AND STAVED, AND RIVEN AMONG PLUMES MY RIDER WEEP.	198	COUNTRY SLEEP	16
	FLASH, AND THE PLUMES CRACK, ...	201	SIR JOHNS HILL	13
PLUMP				
	AT A CALF THAT IS PLUMP AND DELICIOUS;	221	SONG OF DOG	14

	PAGE	TITLE	LINE
PLUNGE			
AND MOUTH. BOTH NOTE AND PLUME PLUNGE FROM THE SPIRE'S HOOK.	16	SPIRE CRANES	8
TO SHUT THE SUN, PLUNGE, MOUNT YOUR DARKENED KEYS	161	DEATHS AND ENT	33
WOULD PLUNGE MY BETRAYAL FROM SHEET TO SKY	175	MY BEGGAR ARM	6
PLUNGED			
PLUNGED IN BLACK WATERS, UNDER HAIL AND FIRE,	51	OUT OF THE PIT	42
PLUNGED IN ITS FRUIT;	86	BREAD I BREAK	3
WITH A HAND PLUNGED THROUGH HER HAIR,	139	TOMBSTONE TOLD	12
PLUNGING			
PLUNGING AND PIERCING IN HIS COURSE	163	LONG-LEGGED	46
POEM			
POEM	176	BREATH SHED	T
POEM IN OCTOBER	176	POEM IN OCT	T
POEM ON HIS BIRTHDAY	208	POEM ON B'DAY	T
POEMS			
HOW WELL YOUR POEMS LIGHT THE FIRE.	85	LETTER TO AUNT	66
PEACOCKSTAIN'S POEMS ON MY BED.	143	THE MOLLS	12
POET			
POET: 1935	46	POET: 1935	T
A POET GOING TO THE TOP?	84	LETTER TO AUNT	57
AGAIN, A COLLECTED POET	155	RETURN	30
POETRY			
UNLESS FOR POETRY, WHICH, IF IT ASKS ME	24	LITTLE PROBLEM	17
A LETTER TO MY AUNT DISCUSSING THE CORRECT APPROACH TO MODERN POETRY	83	LETTER TO AUNT	T
POINT			
OF LADIES' NEEDLES WORN TO BREAKING POINT	18	NATURAL DAY	10
THE HALVES THAT PIERCE THE PIN'S POINT IN THE AIR,	104	WORLD PYRAMID	26
POINT THEIR LITTLE BREASTS AT ME;	138	O CHATTERTON	32
AT THE POINT OF LOVE, FORSAKEN AND AFRAID.	188	WINTER'S TALE	30
POINTED			
THERE WAS A PURPOSE IN HER POINTED FOOT;	11	CABARET	5
HUNG POINTED IN THE WIND,	43	FACES SHONE	9
BE BY YOUR ONE GHOST PIERCED, HIS POINTED FERRULE,	111	I, IN IMAGE	79
INTO A POLESTAR POINTED ON AN ICICLE.	123	FOSTER LIGHT	6
BUT YOUR STONE IS MANY POINTED,	230	MY RIVER	45
POINTING			
AND SIGNPOSTS POINTING UP AND DOWN	36	WINDMILLS TURN	2
POINTS			
CROSS ALL DIRECTIONS, BRACKEN POINTS TO THE SKIES,	44	TO FOLLOW FOX	9
POISE			
ABOVE THEM POISE THE SWOLLEN CLOUDS	36	MIDNIGHT ROAD	12
OR POISE THE DAY ON A HORN.	135	HOW MY ANIMAL	33
POISED			
POISED AT THE READY EAR	29	NEARLY SUMMER	11
AND THUS I SAW HIM. HE WAS POISED LIKE THIS,	52	OUT OF THE PIT	59
POISON			
BREATHING NO POISON FROM THE OVAL MOUTH,	19	THE NEOPHYTE	3
NOTHING BUT POISON FROM THE BREATH,	19	THE NEOPHYTE	10
THERE'S POISON IN YOUR RED WINE, DRINKER,	27	OBLIVIOUS DARK	14
GRAFT, POISON, AND BLUFF,	39	GAS FADES	11
HANDS, HOLD YOU POISON OR GRAPES?	62	EARS IN TURRET	9
SHIPS, HOLD YOU POISON OR GRAPES?	62	EARS IN TURRET	25
HOLD YOU POISON OR GRAPES?	63	EARS IN TURRET	33
LIFE NEAT'S A BETTER POISON THAN IN BOTTLE,	137	O CHATTERTON	5
POKER			
(QUESTIONS ARE HUNCHBACKS TO THE POKER MARROW.)	118	ALTARWISE	48
POKERS			
SPOILERS AND POKERS OF SLEEP,	150	WHEN I WOKE	5

	PAGE	TITLE	LINE
POLAR			
THE POLAR EAGLE WITH HIS TREAD OF SNOW.	164	LONG-LEGGED	80
POLE			
FROM POLE TO POLE LEAPT ROUND THE SNAIL-WAKED WORLD.	120	ALTARWISE	108
FROM POLE TO POLE LEAPT ROUND THE SNAIL-WAKED WORLD.	120	ALTARWISE	108
STIRRING ITS POLE STEM IN DELIGHT,	235	WOMAN TAPESTRY	16
POLE-HILLS			
PIN-LEGGED ON POLE-HILLS WITH A BLACK MEDUSA	119	ALTARWISE	68
POLES			
FROM POLES OF SKULL AND TOE THE WINDY BLOOD	82	LIGHT BREAKS	14
O SEE THE POLES OF PROMISE IN THE BOYS.	93	BOYS OF SUMMER	48
O SEE THE POLES ARE KISSING AS THEY CROSS.	93	BOYS OF SUMMER	54
IN THE POLES OF THE YEAR	190	WINTER'S TALE	91
POLE-SITTING			
POLE-SITTING GIRLS DESCENDED FOR A MEAL,	51	OUT OF THE PIT	29
POLESTAR			
INTO A POLESTAR POINTED ON AN ICICLE.	123	FOSTER LIGHT	6
YOUR POLESTAR NEIGHBOUR, SUN OF ANOTHER STREET,	160	DEATHS AND ENT	17
POLLEN			
LIKE POLLEN	183	VISION, PRAYER	112
POME'S			
A POME'S A BUILDING ON A PAGE;	58	TO ARCHITECTS	11
POND			
TO BRUSH UPON THE WATERS OF THE POND.	34	IN GARDENS	21
AND THE DUCK POND GLASS AND THE BLINDING BYRES ALONE	188	WINTER'S TALE	35
PONDEROUS			
NOR WHEN ALL PONDEROUS HEAVEN'S HOST OF WATERS BREAKS.	146	IF HEAD HURT	20
THIS PONDEROUS FLOWER	232	FURIOUS MOTION	9
PONDS			
OF MARBLE BATHERS TOEING THE GARDEN PONDS,	33	IN GARDENS	2
THE SPITTLED EYES, THE SALT PONDS IN THE SLEEVES,	136	AFTER FUNERAL	5
POOL			
MAD BIRDS IN TREES, AND MAD FISH IN A POOL.	50	OUT OF THE PIT	10
THE HAND THAT WHIRLS THE WATER IN THE POOL	77	THE FORCE THAT	11
POOL AT THE WANTING CENTRE, IN THE FOLDS	191	WINTER'S TALE	128
AND ON A JEWELLED POOL	225	SLENDER WIND	2
POOLED			
AND THE MUSSEL POOLED AND THE HERON	176	POEM IN OCT	3
POOLS			
COUNTRY, YOUR SPORT IS SUMMER, AND DECEMBER'S POOLS	122	HOLD HARD	7
POOR			
AT POOR PEACE I SING	3	PROLOGUE	23
POOR PEACE AS THE SUN SETS	5	PROLOGUE	89
I, POOR ROMANTIC, HELD HER HEEL	11	CABARET	1
I, POOR ROMANTIC, CONTEMPLATE	12	CABARET	22
STARING AT OTHERS, POOR UNLOVERS.	23	THE ONLY DEAD	3
POOR, PETTY VERMIN,	28	NO WINGS	15
STILL COMES VISITING HIS POOR RELATIONS,	29	NEARLY SUMMER	2
CATCH THEIR POOR GUTS.	37	WINDMILLS TURN	26
PITY THE POOR UNPITIED WHO ARE STRANGE WITH TEARS.	57	GREEK PLAY	28
THE WIND SMACKS OF THE POOR	67	REALM OF FLESH	5
AND THESE POOR NERVES SO WIRED TO THE SKULL	75	MY HERO BARES	6
AND A LAMP OF LIGHTNING FOR THE POOR IN THE DARK;	144	COLOUR OF SAY	11
VEINED HIS POOR HAND I HELD, AND I SAW	217	ELEGY	16
ALL HIS BONES CRYING, AND POOR IN ALL BUT PAIN,	217	ELEGY	21
POOR, BROKEN WEBS TO STRIKE THE SKY!	238	PILLAR BREAKS	16
TEMPLE'S BROKEN AND POOR RAVEN'S DEAD;	238	PILLAR BREAKS	24
POPEYE			
MANURING POPEYE OR	154	RETURN	6

	PAGE	TITLE	LINE
POPPIED			
AND LEAVE THE POPPIED PICKTHANK WHERE HE LIES;	98	TWILIGHT LOCKS	39
POPPY			
AND THE HEAD OF THE BRIGHT POPPY.	240	ADMIT THE SUN	11
PORCHES			
FLOGGING INTO THE PORCHES	156	RETURN	75
POSE			
NO THOUGHT CAN TROUBLE MY UNWHOLESOME POSE	233	NO THOUGHT	T
NO THOUGHT CAN TROUBLE MY UNWHOLESOME POSE, ...	233	NO THOUGHT	1
POSITIVE			
ON EVERY HAND THE EVIL'S POSITIVE	27	OBLIVIOUS DARK	18
POSSESSED			
AMONG THE HARDLY POSSESSED.	156	RETURN	65
SHE HAS COME POSSESSED	170	LOVE IN ASYLUM	10
POSSESSED BY THE SKIES	170	LOVE IN ASYLUM	12
POSTER			
THE POSTER IS TODAY'S TEXT, ...	58	TO ARCHITECTS	6
POSTURES			
AND BROWSE UPON THE POSTURES OF THE DEAD;	81	ALL THAT I OWE	22
POSTURING			
TAKE NOW CONTENT, NO LONGER POSTURING	29	LONG, SKELETON	7
POT			
BEHIND A POT OF FERNS THE WAGGING CLOCK	99	OCTOBER WIND	17
A COUNTRY POT, HIS HUTCH IN	154	RETURN	3
BY THE SPIT AND THE BLACK POT IN THE LOG BRIGHT LIGHT	188	WINTER'S TALE	27
BY THE SPIT AND THE BLACK POT IN THE LOG BRIGHT LIGHT.	190	WINTER'S TALE	87
POUCH			
AND BOYS ARE FULL AND FOREIGN IN THE POUCH.	93	BOYS OF SUMMER	51
POUNCING			
YET OUT OF THE BEAKED, WEB DARK AND THE POUNCING BOUGHS	199	COUNTRY SLEEP	48
POUND			
IN T. S. E. AND EZRA POUND.	83	LETTER TO AUNT	10
ALL FROM THE OIL, THE POUND OF LAVA.	106	ALL ALL AND	3
BY THE GREEN OF A ONE POUND NOTE	149	PAPER & STICKS	9
POUNDED			
MILLED DUST OF THE APPLE TREE AND THE POUNDED ISLANDS	199	COUNTRY SLEEP	59
POUNDS			
PUFFING THE POUNDS OF MANNA UP THROUGH THE DEW TO HEAVEN, ...	140	NO WORK WORDS	5
POUR			
POUR LIKE A HALO ON THE CAPS AND SERPENTS.	120	ALTARWISE	118
THE WINDOWS POUR INTO THEIR HEART	161	WEDDING ANNIV	11
POURED			
IN THE SNIFFED AND POURED SNOW ON THE TIP OF THE TONGUE OF THE YEAR	144	PLEASURE-BIRD	5
POURING			
IN THE POURING TOWN, ...	111	I, IN IMAGE	94
SHE MARRIED IN THIS POURING PLACE, ...	139	TOMBSTONE TOLD	4
POURS			
THE ACID POURS AWAY, THE ACID DRIPS	34	THIRST PARCHES	8
POUTING			
SLUNK POUTING OUT WHEN THE LIMP TIME CAME;	207	LAMENT	44
POVERTY			
I BITTERLY TAKE TO TASK MY POVERTY AND CRAFT:	140	NO WORK WORDS	3
POWDER			
HE BLEW LIKE POWDER TO THE LIGHT	97	TWILIGHT LOCKS	14
POWER			
ALL SEASONS WITH THE SAME METICULOUS POWER, ...	17	IN OBLIVION	13

	PAGE	TITLE	LINE
POWER (CONTINUED)			
AND POWER WAS CONTAGIOUS IN MY BIRTH, SECOND	103	I DREAMED MY	21
WITH THE POWER OF MY HANDS	235	WOMAN TAPESTRY	36
POWERFUL			
GROWING LIKE A POWERFUL ROOT INSIDE ME.	236	WOMAN TAPESTRY	67
PRAISE			
COO ROOING THE WOODS' PRAISE, ...	4	PROLOGUE	61
PRAISE THAT MY BODY BE WHOLE, I'VE LIMBS, ...	42	A WAR OF WITS	8
PRAISE THAT ONLY THE WITS ARE HURT AFTER THE WITS'			
FIGHT.	42	A WAR OF WITS	11
PRAISE TO THE ARCHITECTS	57	TO ARCHITECTS	T
PRAISE TO THE ARCHITECTS;	57	TO ARCHITECTS	1
PRAISE TO THE ARCHITECTS;	58	TO ARCHITECTS	4
PRAISE TO THE ARCHITECTS;	58	TO ARCHITECTS	10
PRAISE TO THE ARCHITECTS;	58	TO ARCHITECTS	14
PRAISE TO THE ARCHITECTS.	58	TO ARCHITECTS	18
PRAISE HIM WHO SPRINGS AND FILLS THE TIDAL WELL.	76	LASHED RINGS	11
PRAISE TO OUR FARING HEARTS.	90	EUNUCH DREAMS	42
ADD ONE MORE NAIL OF PRAISE ON TO THE CROSS, ...	96	TWELVE	7
WHEN, PRAISE IS BLESSED, HER PRIDE IN MAST AND			
FOUNTAIN	131	I MAKE THIS IN	4
MAGNIFIED OUT OF PRAISE; HER DEATH WAS A STILL DROP;	136	AFTER FUNERAL	17
THE MAZES OF HIS PRAISE AND ENVIOUS TONGUE WERE			
WORKED IN FLAMES AND SHELLS.	141	SAINT TO FALL	17
TO SHOOT AND SING YOUR PRAISE, ...	160	DEATHS AND ENT	8
PRAISE THAT THE SPRING TIME IS ALL	186	HOLY SPRING	14
ON TO THE FIELDS OF PRAISE.	196	FERN HILL	36
WHO PAY NO PRAISE OR WAGES	197	CRAFT OR ART	19
NOW THE TALES PRAISE	198	COUNTRY SLEEP	33
ALL PRAISE OF THE HAWK ON FIRE IN HAWK-EYED DUSK BE			
SUNG, ...	202	SIR JOHNS HILL	27
SPINS ITS MORNING OF PRAISE, ...	211	POEM ON B'DAY	99
PACING IN KIND PRAISE.	235	WOMAN TAPESTRY	34
PRAISED			
THERE MUST, BE PRAISED, SOME CERTAINTY, ...	32	OUT OF SIGHS	7
GOD IS THE SAME THOUGH HE BE PRAISED AS MANY, ...	67	LET A FAITH	9
ON THE LAST STREET WAVE PRAISED	141	SAINT TO FALL	4
ALWAYS GOOD LUCK, PRAISED THE FINNED IN THE FEATHER	166	LONG-LEGGED	125
PRAISED THE SUN	182	VISION, PRAYER	87
WAS FLYING THROUGH THE HOUSE AS THOUGH THE SHE BIRD			
PRAISED	189	WINTER'S TALE	83
PRAISES			
AFTER THE FUNERAL, MULE PRAISES, BRAYS, ...	136	AFTER FUNERAL	1
PRAISING			
PRAISING THE MORTAL ERROR	75	MY HERO BARES	17
CROSSES THE BREAST OF THE PRAISING EAST, AND KNEELS,	215	COUNTRY HEAVEN	3
PRANCING			
OF PSALMS AND SHADOWS AMONG THE PINCERED SANDCRABS			
PRANCING	202	SIR JOHNS HILL	24
PRAY			
OR PRAY FOR DAY TO SOME ATTENTIVE GOD	48	LIGHT, I KNOW	14
THROUGH, I TELL YOU, YOUR TWO MIDNIGHT LIPS I PRAY	76	LASHED RINGS	7
I PRAY THOUGH I BELONG	183	VISION, PRAYER	115
IN THE CENTRE OF DARK I PRAY HIM	183	VISION, PRAYER	135
BE I PRAY	185	VISION, PRAYER	181
SHALL I LET PRAY THE SHADOW OF A SOUND	191	REFUSAL MOURN	10
THROUGH THROATS WHERE MANY RIVERS MEET, THE WOMEN			
PRAY, ...	203	GIANT'S THIGH	6
CURSE, BLESS, ME NOW WITH YOUR FIERCE TEARS, I PRAY.	208	NOT GO GENTLE	17

	PAGE	TITLE	LINE
PRAYED			
TURNS OF YOUR PRAYED FLESH, NOR SHALL I SHOO THE BIRD BELOW ME:	148	UNLUCKILY FOR	27
HE KNELT, HE WEPT, HE PRAYED,	188	WINTER'S TALE	26
HE WEPT FROM THE CREST OF GRIEF, HE PRAYED TO THE VEILED SKY	188	WINTER'S TALE	32
VALES WHERE HE PRAYED TO COME TO THE LAST HARM	190	WINTER'S TALE	109
I PRAYED IN THE CROUCHING ROOM, BY HIS BLIND BED,	216	ELEGY	13
PRAYER			
NOW STAMP THE LORD'S PRAYER ON A GRAIN OF RICE,	119	ALTARWISE	85
VISION AND PRAYER	180	VISION, PRAYER	T
I TURN THE CORNER OF PRAYER AND BURN	185	VISION, PRAYER	188
THE CONVERSATION OF PRAYER	193	CONVERS PRAYER	T
AND THE CHILD NOT CARING TO WHOM HE CLIMBS HIS PRAYER	194	CONVERS PRAYER	17
UNDER THE PRAYER WHEELING MOON IN THE ROSY WOOD	198	COUNTRY SLEEP	41
THE LEAPING SAGA OF PRAYER! AND HIGH, THERE, ON THE HARE-	199	COUNTRY SLEEP	66
BUT HER FAITH THAT EACH VAST NIGHT AND THE SAGA OF PRAYER	201	COUNTRY SLEEP	102
OF MINNOWS WREATHING AROUND THEIR PRAYER;	209	POEM ON B'DAY	29
PRAYERPIECE			
THE BAYONET TONGUE IN THIS UNDEFENDED PRAYERPIECE,	133	MAKE ME A MASK	5
PRAYERS			
INTO THE HOME OF PRAYERS	188	WINTER'S TALE	36
RAGS AND PRAYERS DOWN THE KNEE-	190	WINTER'S TALE	96
AND THE HOME OF PRAYERS AND FIRES, THE TALE ENDED.	190	WINTER'S TALE	110
THE CONVERSATION OF PRAYERS ABOUT TO BE SAID	193	CONVERS PRAYER	1
THE SOUND ABOUT TO BE SAID IN THE TWO PRAYERS	194	CONVERS PRAYER	9
THE CONVERSATION OF PRAYERS ABOUT TO BE SAID	194	CONVERS PRAYER	13
PRAYER'S			
ONE. THE SUN ROARS AT THE PRAYER'S END.	185	VISION, PRAYER	204
PRAYERWHEEL			
AND A WHIRLPOOL DRIVES THE PRAYERWHEEL;	130	SINNERS' BELL	9
PRAYING			
IN THE PRAYING WINDOWS OF WAVES	162	LONG-LEGGED	28
WITH WATER PRAYING AND CALL OF SEAGULL AND ROOK	177	POEM IN OCT	6
PRAYS			
THE VOICE OF BIRD ON CORAL PRAYS.	130	SINNERS' BELL	18
OF THE CHARTING SLEEPERS PRAYS	184	VISION, PRAYER	167
CHASTITY PRAYS FOR ME, PIETY SINGS,	207	LAMENT	57
WITH ALL THE LIVING, PRAYS,	210	POEM ON B'DAY	66
PREACHERS			
AND SERVE ME RIGHT AS THE PREACHERS WARN,	207	LAMENT	38
PREACHER'S			
FROM THE PREACHER'S TABLE.	138	O CHATTERTON	39
PRECIPICE			
SUSPENDED FROM THE DEVIL'S PRECIPICE,	35	LIFT UP FACE	13
PREROGATIVE			
AND ALL MY THIN PREROGATIVE OF TASTE.	18	NATURAL DAY	18
PRESENCE			
YET THIS I MAKE IN A FORGIVING PRESENCE.	133	I MAKE THIS IN	68
PRESENT			
THE PRESENT MOUTH, AND THE SWEETLY BLOWN TRUMPET OF LIES,	133	MAKE ME A MASK	6
OVER THE PAST TABLE I REPEAT THIS PRESENT GRACE.	145	PLEASURE-BIRD	25
PRESS			
PRESS THE OLD LIES AND THE OLD GHOSTS.	38	THE GOSSIPERS	18
PRESS, PRESS, AND CLASP STEADILY;	232	FURIOUS MOTION	18
PRESS, PRESS, AND CLASP STEADILY;	232	FURIOUS MOTION	18

	PAGE	TITLE	LINE
PRESSED			
AN OLD GOD'S DUGS ARE PRESSED AND PRICKED, ...	65	GODS THUMP	9
WOE DRIP FROM THE DISHRAG HANDS AND THE PRESSED			
SPONGE OF THE FOREHEAD, ...	142	SAINT TO FALL	45
PRETENDER			
THE BRIGHT PRETENDER, THE RIDICULOUS SEA DANDY	152	BELOW A TIME	42
PRETTY			
THE GRASS HE COVERS IS A PRETTY GREEN;	63	WOMAN SPEAKS	19
SHE BECAME LIKE A DANCER OR A PRETTY ANIMAL	235	WOMAN TAPESTRY	20
PRICK			
AND PRICK THE THUMB-STAINED HEAVEN THROUGH THE			
THIMBLE.	104	WORLD PYRAMID	27
PRICKED			
AN OLD GOD'S DUGS ARE PRESSED AND PRICKED, ...	65	GODS THUMP	9
PRIDE			
OF ALL ORESTES' CONTINENT OF PRIDE	56	GREEK PLAY	5
WHEN, PRAISE IS BLESSED, HER PRIDE IN MAST AND			
FOUNTAIN	131	I MAKE THIS IN	4
AND, PRIDE IS LAST, IS LIKE A CHILD ALONE	131	I MAKE THIS IN	13
AND, MILD AS PARDON FROM A CLOUD OF PRIDE, ...	133	I MAKE THIS IN	59
NOR COULD SHARE, FOR HIS PRIDE, TO THE LEAST	158	INTO HER HEAD	44
A COLD KIND MAN BRAVE IN HIS NARROW PRIDE	216	ELEGY	3
AN OLD KIND MAN BRAVE IN HIS BURNING PRIDE.	217	ELEGY	24
I BURY, I TRAVEL TO FIND PRIDE	240	ADMIT THE SUN	12
PRIDES			
PRIDES OF TOMORROW SUCKLING IN HER EYES, ...	133	I MAKE THIS IN	67
PRIEST			
IN TIME LIKE OUTLAW RAINS ON THAT PRIEST, WATER,	15	SPIRE CRANES	6
WITH PRIEST AND PHARAOH BED MY GENTLE WOUND, ...	120	ALTARWISE	123
WHEN, WITH HIS TORCH AND HOURGLASS, LIKE A SULPHUR			
PRIEST, ...	130	SINNERS' BELL	2
CHILD WHO WAS PRIEST AND SERVANTS, ...	174	FIRE RAID	52
THE STREAM FROM THE PRIEST BLACK WRISTED SPINNEY AND			
SLEEVES	200	COUNTRY SLEEP	72
AND EVERY SOUL HIS PRIEST, ...	210	POEM ON B'DAY	61
PRIESTED			
PRIESTED SHORE	176	POEM IN OCT	4
PRIESTS			
WHEN BLACK BIRDS DIED LIKE PRIESTS IN THE CLOAKED			
HEDGE ROW	190	WINTER'S TALE	92
PRIEST'S			
WITH PRIEST'S GRAVE FOOT AND HAND OF FIVE ASSASSINS	131	I MAKE THIS IN	25
PRIME			
BRANDY AND RIPE IN MY BRIGHT, BASS PRIME, ...	206	LAMENT	28
PRINCE			
THAT PRINCE OF PIMPS, THAT DOYEN OF DUNG-LICKERS.	179	NEW QUAY	24
AND HONOURED AMONG WAGONS I WAS PRINCE OF THE APPLE			
TOWNS	195	FERN HILL	6
AND PRINCE OF ICE	198	COUNTRY SLEEP	12
NOR THE TUSKED PRINCE, IN THE RUTTISH FARM, AT THE			
RIND	198	COUNTRY SLEEP	37
PRINT			
LIGHT WALKS THE SKY, LEAVING NO PRINT, ...	49	LIGHT, I KNOW	17
LEAVING NO PRINT.	49	LIGHT, I KNOW	21
FROM THE FIRST PRINT OF THE UNSHODDEN FOOT, THE			
LIFTING	78	LOVE'S FEVER	10
'WHO COULD SNAP OFF THE SHAPELESS PRINT	129	MY NEOPHYTE	40
AND THE HEART PRINT OF MAN	180	VISION, PRAYER	12
AND LEAVE A CLEAR PRINT, ...	229	MY RIVER	8

	PAGE	TITLE	LINE
PRINTED			
MY WORDY WOUNDS ARE PRINTED WITH YOUR HAIR.	96	RUB OF LOVE	47
PRINTS			
DRAW ON THE GLOVE OF PRINTS, DEAD CAIRO'S HENNA ...	120	ALTARWISE	117
RUB OFF THE SCRAWL OF PRINTS ON	156	RETURN	81
BLACK NIGHT, I LEFT MY QUIVERING PRINTS.	206	LAMENT	24
PRISM			
THE PRISM OF THE EYE NOW VOID BY SUCTION, ...	29	LONG, SKELETON	10
PRISMS			
SMOOTH THE PRISMS OF YOUR BREASTS.	229	MY RIVER	18
PRISON			
AN INCH IN FROTH. CHIMES CHEAT THE PRISON SPIRE, PELTER	15	SPIRE CRANES	5
INTO THEIR PRISON WITH A SLACK SOUND, ...	47	POET: 1935	44
THE DAZZLING PRISON	183	VISION, PRAYER	131
PRISONER			
YOU WISH TO STAY MY PRISONER	10	COOL, OH NO	27
PRISONERS			
PRISONERS OF WISHES LOCKED THEIR EYES	153	WAS A SAVIOUR	7
PRIVATE			
THE FEATURES IN THEIR PRIVATE DARK	116	LANTERNS SHINE	5
PRIZE			
ANSWER: WHEN THE GREEN LEAVES PRIZE HER.	72	TAKE NEEDLES	64
PROBE			
NO THIRD EYE PROBE INTO A RAINBOW'S SEX	108	GRIEF THIEF	25
THAN ONE COULD PROBE OUT OF A SERPENT'S GUTS;	137	O CHATTERTON	7
PROBLEM			
LITTLE PROBLEM	24	LITTLE PROBLEM	T
PROCESS			
SO THAT THE PROCESS CALLS FOR LAUGHS, ...	21	BEWILDERED WAY	18
A PROCESS IN THE WEATHER OF THE HEART	88	A PROCESS IN	T
A PROCESS IN THE WEATHER OF THE HEART	88	A PROCESS IN	1
A PROCESS IN THE EYE FOREWARNS	88	A PROCESS IN	7
A PROCESS IN THE WEATHER OF THE WORLD	88	A PROCESS IN	19
A PROCESS BLOWS THE MOON INTO THE SUN, ...	88	A PROCESS IN	22
PROCESSION			
INSIDIOUS PROCESSION	156	RETURN	63
PRODIGAL			
LEAD HER PRODIGAL HOME TO HIS TERROR, ...	168	LONG-LEGGED	199
MY ARISING PRODIGAL	186	HOLY SPRING	18
PRODIGALS			
BUT DO NOT TRAVEL DOWN DUMB WIND LIKE PRODIGALS.	16	SPIRE CRANES	11
PRODIGIES			
AND THE ENDLESS BEGINNING OF PRODIGIES SUFFERS OPEN.'	146	IF HEAD HURT	30
PROFESSIONAL			
THE LAST WAR'S PROFESSIONAL	154	RETURN	14
PROFITS			
WHO ONLY DRINKS HIS PROFITS	138	O CHATTERTON	27
PROFLIGATES			
THE REPTILE PROFLIGATES IN A FLAME, ...	150	WHEN I WOKE	4
PROLOGUE			
PROLOGUE	3	PROLOGUE	T
PROMISE			
DRAIN THE SPRING WHERE PROMISE GOES.	70	TAKE NEEDLES	8
STRIPPING MY LOIN OF PROMISE, ...	75	MY HERO BARES	14
O SEE THE POLES OF PROMISE IN THE BOYS.	93	BOYS OF SUMMER	48
THE INSECT FABLE IS THE CERTAIN PROMISE.	124	TODAY, INSECT	18
PROMISES			
BEFORE THE PROMISES FULFILL	74	WE MOTHERNAKED	7
HE PROMISES A SECRET HEAT.	75	MY HERO BARES	15

	PAGE	TITLE	LINE
PROPER			
WHO PLAY THE PROPER GENTLEMAN AND LADY.	113	NOT FATHER ME	28
PROPHET-PROGENY			
NO PROPHET-PROGENY OF MINE,	150	WHEN I WOKE	26
PROPHETS			
PROPHETS AND FIBRE KINGS IN OIL AND LETTER,	120	ALTARWISE	114
AND PROPHETS LOUD ON THE BURNED DUNES;	168	LONG-LEGGED	173
PROPPED			
I PROPPED HUMANITY'S WEIGHT	155	RETURN	33
PROPPED BETWEEN TREES AND WATER	171	THE HUNCHBACK	3
PROSPERED			
THE BODY PROSPERED, TEETH IN THE MARROWED GUMS,	78	LOVE'S FEVER	16
PROSTITUTION			
MAGDALENE PROSTITUTION,	156	RETURN	85
PROTRACTED			
THE INCH OF TIME'S PROTRACTED TO A FOOT	80	ALMANAC TIME	8
PROUD			
HULOO, MY PROUD DOVE WITH A FLUTE!	5	PROLOGUE	97
THE PROUD SPINE SPURNING TURN AND TWIST.	75	MY HERO BARES	5
IN THAT PROUD SAILING TREE WITH BRANCHES DRIVEN	131	I MAKE THIS IN	6
AND A SILK PIGEON'S GUILT IN HER PROUD ABSENCE,	131	I MAKE THIS IN	17
PROUD AS A SUCKED STONE AND HUGE AS SANDGRAINS.	131	I MAKE THIS IN	23
WEIGHED IN ROCK SHROUD, IS MY PROUD PYRAMID;	132	I MAKE THIS IN	41
DELIVERED SEAS MY LOVE FROM HER PROUD PLACE	133	I MAKE THIS IN	62
TWO PROUD, BLACKED BROTHERS CRY,	153	WAS A SAVIOUR	25
NOT FOR THE PROUD MAN APART	197	CRAFT OR ART	12
TOO PROUD TO DIE, BROKEN AND BLIND HE DIED	216	ELEGY	1
I AM NOT TOO PROUD TO CRY THAT HE AND HE	217	ELEGY	19
TOO PROUD TO CRY, TOO FRAIL TO CHECK THE TEARS,	217	ELEGY	35
THE TEARS OUT OF HIS EYES, TOO PROUD TO CRY.	217	ELEGY	39
HAS STOPPED, (ANGEL, YOU'RE PROUD),	237	PILLAR BREAKS	3
PROVE			
SHALL PROVE UNWORTHY FOR HIS DOING,	23	THE ONLY DEAD	15
PROVED			
BUT IF THIS PROVED IMPOSS-I-BLE	84	LETTER TO AUNT	29
PROW			
SING THROUGH THE WATER-SPOKEN PROW	164	LONG-LEGGED	78
PROWL			
AND FIRES WHERE HE SHOULD PROWL DOWN THE CLOUD	188	WINTER'S TALE	37
PROWLS			
PROWLS FLAMING AMONG THE COCKERELS	216	COUNTRY HEAVEN	28
PRUDE'S			
OUTDO YOUR PRUDE'S GENETIC FACULTY	20	THE NEOPHYTE	13
PSALM			
ARGUMENT OF THE HEWN VOICE, GESTURE AND PSALM,	137	AFTER FUNERAL	37
PSALMS			
OR SANSKRIT PSALMS ON LEPERS' CHESTS.	83	LETTER TO AUNT	28
WITH THEIR NIGHTINGALES AND PSALMS	197	CRAFT OR ART	16
OF PSALMS AND SHADOWS AMONG THE PINCERED SANDCRABS PRANCING	202	SIR JOHNS HILL	24
PUBLIC			
GROWING IN PUBLIC PLACES THAN MAN KNOWS.	48	POET: 1935	57
PUBS			
THIS LILY CRAWLING ROUND THE LOCAL PUBS?	52	OUT OF THE PIT	50
PUDDLES			
WHOSE HOODED, FOUNTAIN HEART ONCE FELL IN PUDDLES	136	AFTER FUNERAL	14
PUFF			
PUFF TILL THE ADDER IS,	22	HIGH ON A HILL	9
PUFFBALL			
ON A TONGUED PUFFBALL)	5	PROLOGUE	73

	PAGE	TITLE	LINE
PUFFED			
PUFFED, OLD WITH VENOM, FROM A CRUSTED MOUTH.	37	WINDMILLS TURN	30
AND OPIUM HEAD, CROW STALK, PUFFED, CUT, AND BLOWN,	131	I MAKE THIS IN	10
THE PUFFED BIRDS HOPPING AND HUNTING, THE MILKMAIDS	187	WINTER'S TALE	23
PUFFING			
PUFFING THE LIGHT'S FLAME TO AND FRO,	16	TIME TO ROT	5
PUFFING THE POUNDS OF MANNA UP THROUGH THE DEW TO HEAVEN,	140	NO WORK WORDS	5
PULL			
MY FATHERS' LOVES THAT PULL UPON MY NERVES,	80	ALL THAT I OWE	6
WILL PULL THE THUNDERBOLTS	161	DEATHS AND ENT	32
PULLED			
AND, THE STRING PULLED, SOME MENTAL DOLL	10	COOL, OH NO	11
MAN BROKE THE SUN, PULLED THE WIND DOWN.	86	BREAD I BREAK	10
CATHEDRAL CALM IN THE PULLED HOUSE;	130	SINNERS' BELL	15
PULLEYS			
BY MIDNIGHT PULLEYS THAT UNHOUSE THE TOMB.	89	EUNUCH DREAMS	10
PULLS			
HE PULLS THE CHAIN, THE CISTERN MOVES.	75	MY HERO BARES	20
PULLS DOWN THE SHABBY CURTAINS OF THE SKIN;	88	A PROCESS IN	23
THE SLEEPY MAN OF WINTER PULLS,	92	BOYS OF SUMMER	29
AND THOUGH MY LOVE PULLS THE PALE, NIPPLED AIR,	133	I MAKE THIS IN	66
IN A HOISTED CLOUD, AT DROP OF DUSK, HE PULLS TO HIS CLAWS	201	SIR JOHNS HILL	3
PULSE			
FEEL, AS THE PULSE GROWS TIRED,	32	HELD-OUT HAND	3
THERE FROM THEIR HEARTS THE DOGDAYED PULSE	92	BOYS OF SUMMER	22
O SEE THE PULSE OF SUMMER IN THE ICE.	92	BOYS OF SUMMER	24
I HAVE BEEN TOLD TO REASON BY THE PULSE,	116	LANTERNS SHINE	11
FORGOTTEN DARK, REST THEIR PULSE AND BURY THEIR DEAD IN HER FAITHLESS SLEEP.	159	INTO HER HEAD	69
AND PULSE TO OPEN	238	MAKES INTERVALS	13
PUMPED			
BURST IN THE ROOTS, PUMPED FROM THE EARTH AND ROCK	94	IN BEGINNING	17
PUNCTUAL			
WHERE, PUNCTUAL AS DEATH, WE RING THE STARS;	92	BOYS OF SUMMER	27
PUNCTURED			
SLEEP PUNCTURED BY WAKING, DREAMS	39	GAS FADES	22
PUNGENTLY			
BREATHING ON ALL SIDES PUNGENTLY	20	ENCOMPASSED	2
PUNISHES			
WITH FROSTY FINGERS PUNISHES MY HAIR,	98	OCTOBER WIND	2
WITH FISTS OF TURNIPS PUNISHES THE LAND,	99	OCTOBER WIND	28
PURE			
SUN THE FATHER HIS QUIVER FULL OF THE INFANTS OF PURE FIRE,	186	HOLY SPRING	19
ON A STAR OF FAITH PURE AS THE DRIFTING BREAD,	187	WINTER'S TALE	12
PURGE			
TO PURGE AFTER THE WITS' FIGHT,	42	A WAR OF WITS	6
PURIFY			
FOLLY PURIFY AND MAKE IT TRUE.	25	BEAUTY TO DUST	10
PURPOSE			
THERE WAS A PURPOSE IN HER POINTED FOOT;	11	CABARET	5
FOR A PURPOSE (HEAD TO FOOT IS HEAD AND FOOT,	24	LITTLE PROBLEM	6
ALL THINGS REST IN THE WILL OF PURPOSE TRIUMPHANT.	222	FOREST PICTURE	8
PURSE			
WHEN THE PURSE IS EMPTY	39	GAS FADES	27
BELLY OF THE RICH YEAR AND THE BIG PURSE OF MY BODY	140	NO WORK WORDS	2
AND I LIVED IN HIS PURSE AND HIS HEART	149	PAPER & STICKS	6

	PAGE	TITLE	LINE
PURSED			
PURSED LIPS AT THE RECEIVER, ...	44	LONGED TO MOVE	17
PUS			
THIS PUS RUNS DEEP.	27	OBLIVIOUS DARK	13
PUSH			
PUSH IN THEIR TIDES;	82	LIGHT BREAKS	3
PUSHED			
SO CRYING, HE WAS PUSHED INTO THE JORDAN.	52	OUT OF THE PIT	53
PUSHED UP THEIR HAIR, THE DRY WIND STEERS	90	WHERE ONCE THE	5
PUT			
NO STOPPING. PUT THE SMILE	12	SKY'S BRIGHT	16
THANK GOD, BUT THE ENEMY STAYS PUT.	59	FAIRY TALES	9
AND PUT BESIDE HER A RAM ROSE.	61	MEAT ON BONES	24
A GOOSE'S QUILL HAS PUT AN END TO MURDER	66	HAND SIGNED	7
THAT PUT AN END TO TALK.	66	HAND SIGNED	8
PUT AN IRON AT THE EYES, ...	70	TAKE NEEDLES	2
I PUT ROUND RIBS THAT PACKED THEIR HEART, ...	85	SEE, SAYS LIME	2
PUT A TEAR FOR JOY IN THE UNEARTHLY FLOOD	153	WAS A SAVIOUR	22
HE PUT ON HIS CLOTHES AND STEPPED OUT AND HE DIED,	172	DAWN RAID	2
PUTREFYING			
OF PUTREFYING ANGELS WHO	84	LETTER TO AUNT	54
PUTS			
PUTS IN HIS PENNY, GENEROUS AT LAST.	179	NEW QUAY	32
PUTTING			
PUTTING TWO AND TWO TOGETHER, ...	38	THE GOSSIPERS	6
PUZZLE			
FLICKED FROM THE CARBOLIC CITY PUZZLE IN A BED OF			
SORES	142	SAINT TO FALL	28
PYRAMID			
MY WORLD IS PYRAMID	103	WORLD PYRAMID	T
MY WORLD IS PYRAMID. THE PADDED MUMMER	104	WORLD PYRAMID	31
WEIGHED IN ROCK SHROUD, IS MY PROUD PYRAMID;	132	I MAKE THIS IN	41
PYRAMIDS			
BETWEEN THE PYRAMIDS SO LARGE, ...	238	MAKES INTERVALS	2
PYRE			
THE PYRE YET TO BE LIGHTED OF MY SINS AND DAYS, ...	147	UNLUCKILY FOR	3
OUT OF THE WOEBEGONE PYRE	186	HOLY SPRING	16
QUAKED			
QUAKED THE SICK SEA AND SNOUTED DEEP, ...	163	LONG-LEGGED	50
QUAKING			
BE AT CLOUD QUAKING PEACE, ...	210	POEM ON B'DAY	63
QUARREL			
A QUARREL OF WEATHERS AND TREES IN THE WINDY SPIRAL.	110	I, IN IMAGE	42
ROARING, CRAWLING, QUARREL	134	HOW MY ANIMAL	8
QUARRY			
NEAR TO THE QUARRY OR THE WELL, ...	74	WE MOTHERNAKED	6
HERE BREAK A KISS IN NO LOVE'S QUARRY.	93	BOYS OF SUMMER	47
QUARTER			
A WEATHER IN THE QUARTER OF THE VEINS	88	A PROCESS IN	4
INTO A CHIMING QUARTER	92	BOYS OF SUMMER	26
QUARTERED			
THERE IN THE DEEP WITH QUARTERED SHADES	92	BOYS OF SUMMER	16
QUARTERS			
QUARTERS AND GRAVES	184	VISION, PRAYER	164
QUAY			
AND THE BULWARKS OF THE DAZZLED QUAY.	162	LONG-LEGGED	10
NEW QUAY	179	NEW QUAY	T
QUAYRAIL			
LET THE FIRST PETER FROM A RAINBOW'S QUAYRAIL	121	ALTARWISE	133

	PAGE	TITLE	LINE
QUAYSTONE			
HARBOURS MY ANCHORED TONGUE, SLIPS THE QUAYSTONE,	131	I MAKE THIS IN	3
QUEEN			
THE QUEEN IS SLAIN; ORESTES' HANDS DRIP BLOOD;	57	GREEK PLAY	15
THE DEAD QUEEN WALKETH WITH MYCENAE'S KING	57	GREEK PLAY	23
THE SHEATH-DECKED JACKS, QUEEN WITH A SHUFFLED HEART;	118	ALTARWISE	59
THE LAMPED CALLIGRAPHER, THE QUEEN IN SPLINTS, ...	120	ALTARWISE	115
AND CHILDISH, SNIVELLING QUEEN.	155	RETURN	51
QUEEN CATHERINE HOWLING BARE	157	INTO HER HEAD	12
QUELLED			
AND THE BEAUTIFUL NOISE IS QUELLED, ...	18	NATURAL DAY	22
QUENCH			
BOTH QUENCH HIS THIRST HE'LL HAVE A BLACK REPLY.	56	WHY EAST WIND	9
QUENCHED			
'THE THIRST IS QUENCHED, THE HUNGER GONE, ...	61	MEAT ON BONES	17
QUENCHLESS			
MANES, UNDER HIS QUENCHLESS SUMMER BARBED GOLD TO			
THE BONE, ...	204	GIANT'S THIGH	26
QUESTION			
I AM MAN'S REPLY TO EVERY QUESTION, ...	26	PERSONAL EPIT	17
THE CHILD SHALL QUESTION ALL HIS DAYS, ...	56	WHY EAST WIND	7
QUESTION: SHALL THE ROOT BE TRUE	72	TAKE NEEDLES	57
QUESTION: WHEN SHALL ROOT-DAM DIE?	72	TAKE NEEDLES	61
QUESTION: WHEN SHALL ROOT-DAM GROW?	72	TAKE NEEDLES	63
A CLAW I QUESTION FROM THE MOUSE'S BONE, ...	114	SERVANT SUN	17
STAND IN A QUESTION MARK.	138	O CHATTERTON	36
QUESTIONS			
AFTER A VOLLEY OF QUESTIONS AND REPLIES	42	A WAR OF WITS	17
(QUESTIONS ARE HUNCHBACKS TO THE POKER MARROW.) ...	118	ALTARWISE	48
AND UP AND DOWN LOVE'S QUESTIONS ASK;	138	O CHATTERTON	23
QUICK			
IS DAMP AND DRY; THE QUICK AND DEAD	88	A PROCESS IN	17
AND LETS THEIR TRASH BE HONOURED AS THE QUICK.	90	EUNUCH DREAMS	35
WEARING THE QUICK AWAY.	95	RUB OF LOVE	35
IN QUICK, SWEET, CRUEL LIGHT TILL THE LOCKED GROUND			
SPROUT OUT, ...	135	HOW MY ANIMAL	18
SANG HEAVEN HUNGRY AND THE QUICK	141	SAINT TO FALL	15
CUT TO THE STILL STAR IN THE ORDER OF THE QUICK ...	148	UNLUCKILY FOR	20
IN THE MUFFLED HOUSE, IN THE QUICK OF NIGHT, ...	188	WINTER'S TALE	29
TURNS ON THE QUICK AND THE DEAD, AND THE MAN ON THE			
STAIRS	194	CONVERS PRAYER	14
QUICK IN THE WOOD AT LOVE, WHERE A TORCH OF FOXES			
FOAMS, ...	204	GIANT'S THIGH	34
AND THE SIZZLING BEDS OF THE TOWN CRIED, QUICK!--	206	LAMENT	20
MASTS AND FISHES TO THE STILL QUICK STARS, ...	210	POEM ON B'DAY	71
QUICKEN			
FOR IT CAN QUICKEN OR IT CAN KILL.	24	THE ONLY DEAD	29
QUICKENING			
HUNGERS FOR QUICKENING, AND MY LONELY LIPS	64	WOMAN SPEAKS	36
QUICKENING FOR THE RIDDLED SEA;	125	SEED-AT-ZERO	18
QUICKENING FOR THE VIRGIN SEA;	126	SEED-AT-ZERO	25
QUICKENS			
AND, WHEN IT QUICKENS, ALTER THE ACTIONS' PACE	116	LANTERNS SHINE	12
QUICKLY			
THEN TAKE THEM AWAY QUICKLY	229	MY RIVER	23
QUICKNESS			
QUICKNESS OF HAND IN THE VELVET GLOVE	147	TO OTHERS	12
QUICKSAND			
INTO THE QUICKSAND FEATHERS DOWN, ...	55	NO MAN BELIEVE	4
STIRS THE QUICKSAND; THAT ROPES THE BLOWING WIND	77	THE FORCE THAT	12

		PAGE	TITLE	LINE
QUIET				
SINCE, ON A QUIET NIGHT	....	22	ON QUIET NIGHT	T
SINCE, ON A QUIET NIGHT, I HEARD THEM TALK	....	22	ON QUIET NIGHT	1
OUT OF THE NOISE INTO QUIET I RAN.	....	53	OUT OF THE PIT	92
SO FAST I MOVE DEFYING TIME, THE QUIET GENTLEMAN		116	LANTERNS SHINE	14
NOW IN THE CLOUD'S BIG BREAST LIE QUIET COUNTRIES,		133	I MAKE THIS IN	61
AS QUIET AS A BONE.	....	152	BELOW A TIME	51
AND THE SUN HAS SMOOTHED IT WITH QUIET FIRE,	......	224	IDYLL UNFORGET	23
MY TEARS ARE LIKE THE QUIET DRIFT	....	225	CLOWN IN MOON	1
BENEATH THE DEEP BARK CALLS AND MAKES QUIET MUSIC.		226	THE OAK	6
AMONG THE QUIET TREES. AND HAND IN HAND	....	227	SPRING-SPIRIT	11
QUIETNESS				
THEIR SILENCES IN SILVER QUIETNESS OF SLEEP,	....	223	IDYLL UNFORGET	6
QUIETUDE				
AND COVERING ALL HAS BEEN A QUIETUDE, AND A SINGING				
FROM FLAKE-BARE THROATS.	....	224	IDYLL UNFORGET	35
QUILL				
FROTH, FLUTE, FIN AND QUILL	....	3	PROLOGUE	7
A GOOSE'S QUILL HAS PUT AN END TO MURDER	....	66	HAND SIGNED	7
QUILLED				
FELLED AND QUILLED, FLASH TO MY PATCH	....	5	PROLOGUE	83
QUILTS				
WHEREVER I RAMPED IN THE CLOVER QUILTS,	....	206	LAMENT	22
QUITE				
WITH QUITE A KIND OF HEART.	....	12	CABARET	17
QUIVER				
SUN THE FATHER HIS QUIVER FULL OF THE INFANTS OF				
PURE FIRE,	....	186	HOLY SPRING	19
QUIVERING				
IN THE WATCHED DARK, QUIVERING THROUGH LOCKS AND				
CAVES,	....	161	DEATHS AND ENT	31
BLACK NIGHT, I LEFT MY QUIVERING PRINTS.	....	206	LAMENT	24
QUOTED				
BY WASTE SEAS WHERE THE WHITE BEAR QUOTED VIRGIL		119	ALTARWISE	69
RABBITS				
AND LOVE TO CHASE RABBITS AND STONES.	....	221	SONG OF DOG	12
RABBLE				
WOE FROM THE RABBLE OF THE BLIND	....	70	SECRET WIND	8
GILDERS OF STREETS, THE RABBLE HAND	....	70	SECRET WIND	10
LIMP IN THE STREET OF SEA, AMONG THE RABBLE	....	104	WORLD PYRAMID	15
RACED				
MY WISHES RACED THROUGH THE HOUSE HIGH HAY	....	196	FERN HILL	41
RACK				
THE RACK OF DREAMS MY LILY BONES	....	68	BEFORE KNOCKED	20
RACKED				
THE SPIRIT RACKED ITS MUSCLES AND	....	85	SEE, SAYS LIME	15
RACKING				
IN HIS SLANT, RACKING HOUSE	....	209	POEM ON B'DAY	25
RACKS				
TWISTING ON RACKS WHEN SINEWS GIVE WAY,	....	49	NO DOMINION	13
RADIANCE				
THEIR FACES SHONE UNDER SOME RADIANCE	....	43	FACES SHONE	T
THEIR FACES SHONE UNDER SOME RADIANCE	....	43	FACES SHONE	1
NOT KNOWING RADIANCE CAME AND PASSED.	....	43	FACES SHONE	13
IDLING WITH THE RADIANCE OF THE HOURS	....	227	SPRING-SPIRIT	10
RADIANT				
GABRIEL AND RADIANT SHRUBBERY AS THE MORNING GROWS				
JOYFUL	....	186	HOLY SPRING	15
RADIO'S				
RADIO'S A BUILDING IN THE AIR;	....	58	TO ARCHITECTS	5

```
                                           PAGE      TITLE       LINE
RADIUM
    RARER THAN RADIUM,      ..............................  152  WAS A SAVIOUR    2
RAFT
    STRUNG BY THE FLAXEN WHALE-WEED, FROM THE HANGMAN'S
        RAFT,      ........................................  110  I, IN IMAGE     65
RAFTERS
    RAISE THE LIVE RAFTERS OF THE EARDRUM,  ............  142  SAINT TO FALL    36
RAG
    IS CORNER-CAST, BREATH'S RAG, SCRAWLED WEED, A VAIN   131  I MAKE THIS IN    9
RAGE
    OF FEAR, RAGE RED, MANALIVE,   .....................    4  PROLOGUE         48
    RAGE ME BACK TO THE MAKING HOUSE. MY HAND UNRAVEL    145  IF HEAD HURT     12
    RAGE, RAGE AGAINST THE DYING OF THE LIGHT.  ........  207  NOT GO GENTLE     3
    RAGE, RAGE AGAINST THE DYING OF THE LIGHT.  ........  207  NOT GO GENTLE     3
    RAGE, RAGE AGAINST THE DYING OF THE LIGHT.  ........  208  NOT GO GENTLE     9
    RAGE, RAGE AGAINST THE DYING OF THE LIGHT.  ........  208  NOT GO GENTLE     9
    RAGE, RAGE AGAINST THE DYING OF THE LIGHT.  ........  208  NOT GO GENTLE    15
    RAGE, RAGE AGAINST THE DYING OF THE LIGHT.  ........  208  NOT GO GENTLE    15
    RAGE, RAGE AGAINST THE DYING OF THE LIGHT.  ........  208  NOT GO GENTLE    19
    RAGE, RAGE AGAINST THE DYING OF THE LIGHT.  ........  208  NOT GO GENTLE    19
    TERROR WILL RAGE APART   ...........................  210  POEM ON B'DAY    43
    RAGE SHATTERED WATERS KICK   .......................  210  POEM ON B'DAY    70
RAGES
    WHEN ONLY THE MOON RAGES   .........................  196  CRAFT OR ART      3
RAGGED
    ALL NIGHT AND DAY I EYE THE RAGGED GLOBE  ..........   81  ALL THAT I OWE   23
    A RAGGED VEIN   ....................................   87  PAIN BE MUSIC    11
    THIS RAGGED ANNIVERSARY OF TWO   ...................  161  WEDDING ANNIV     2
    ENVELOPING THE RAGGED LEAVES UNSEEN AND STREWN.  ...  226  THE OAK           2
RAGING
    TELL ME OF HIM WHO FEEDS THE RAGING BIRDS.  ........   65  WOMAN SPEAKS     65
    THE PARCHED AND RAGING VOICE?   ....................  135  HOW MY ANIMAL    22
    FROM THE RAGING MOON I WRITE   .....................  197  CRAFT OR ART     13
RAGS
    THEN HANG A RAM ROSE OVER THE RAGS.   ..............   60  MEAT ON BONES     8
    RAGS AND PRAYERS DOWN THE KNEE-   ..................  190  WINTER'S TALE    96
RAID
    BETWEEN THE RAID AND THE RESPONSE   ................   73  WE MOTHERNAKED    3
    AMONG THOSE KILLED IN THE DAWN RAID WAS A MAN AGED A
        HUNDRED   .......................................  172  DAWN RAID         T
    CEREMONY AFTER A FIRE RAID   .......................  173  FIRE RAID         T
RAIL
    BUT RAIL WITH YOUR WIZARD'S RIBS THE HEART-SHAPED
        PLANET;   .......................................  123  FOSTER LIGHT     15
RAILINGS
    HURDLES AND GUNS AND RAILINGS, AS THE BOULDERS HEAVE, 122  HOLD HARD        16
    AFTER THE RAILINGS AND SHRUBBERIES   ...............  172  THE HUNCHBACK    38
RAIN
    RAIN CUTS THE PLACE WE TREAD   .....................   13  RAIN CUTS         T
    RAIN CUTS THE PLACE WE TREAD,   ....................   13  RAIN CUTS         1
    SNAPPED IN A RAIN OF PIECES FALLING   ..............   21  BEWILDERED WAY   20
    AND ON OUR LIPS THE DRY MOUTH OF THE RAIN.   .......   26  THERE'S PLENTY   19
    THEIR FACES SHONE; THE MIDNIGHT RAIN   .............   43  FACES SHONE       8
    IN SUN AND RAIN WORKING FOR GOOD AND GAIN,   .......   45  PLOUGHMAN GONE    3
    IN SUN AND RAIN OVER THE DRY SHIRES,   .............   45  PLOUGHMAN GONE   25
    MAN WHO ONCE DROVE IS DRIVEN IN SUN AND RAIN.   ....   46  PLOUGHMAN GONE   34
    THE SNAIL TELLS OF COMING RAIN.   ..................   48  POET: 1935       65
    LIFT ITS HEAD TO THE BLOWS OF THE RAIN;   ..........   50  NO DOMINION      23
    WHY NIGHT-TIME RAIN AND THE BREAST'S BLOOD   .......   56  WHY EAST WIND     8
    RAIN BEATS THE SAND AND SLATES.   ..................   62  EARS IN TURRET   28
```

		PAGE	TITLE	LINE
RAIN (CONTINUED)				
RAIN SHALL DEFILE AND COVER, WIND BEAR AWAY	....	64	WOMAN SPEAKS	40
WHEN IT IS RAIN WHERE ARE THE GODS?	....	65	GODS THUMP	5
ON TIPS OF THOUGHT WHERE THOUGHTS SMELL IN THE RAIN;		82	LIGHT BREAKS	26
MY FATHERS' GHOST IS CLIMBING IN THE RAIN.	....	102	FELLOWED SLEEP	30
CAN'T READ SENSE IN THE RAIN THAT WILLYNILLY	....	137	O CHATTERTON	19
THE RAIN THROUGH HER COLD HEART SPEAK	....	139	TOMBSTONE TOLD	8
TOO LATE IN THE WRONG RAIN	....	161	WEDDING ANNIV	9
A CLOUD BLEW THE RAIN FROM ITS THROAT;	....	163	LONG-LEGGED	40
THE STATUES OF GREAT RAIN STAND STILL,	....	166	LONG-LEGGED	135
TO THE RAIN WRINGING	....	177	POEM IN OCT	28
PALE RAIN OVER THE DWINDLING HARBOUR	....	177	POEM IN OCT	31
IN THE RAIN TELLING ITS BEADS, AND THE GRAVEST GHOST		198	COUNTRY SLEEP	31
AS THE RAIN FALLS, HAIL ON THE FLEECE, AS THE VALE MIST RIDES	....	199	COUNTRY SLEEP	57
YARD OF THE BUTTERMILK RAIN ON THE PAIL! THE SERMON		200	COUNTRY SLEEP	77
AND THE RAIN WRING OUT ITS TONGUES ON THE FADED YARD,		205	GIANT'S THIGH	52
SOFTLY, THOU RAIN--AND FOR HIS MOTHER'S SAKE,	.....	222	MISSING	7
LIKE FRAGMENTARY RAIN	....	226	SLENDER WIND	4
THE METALLIC RAIN	....	229	MY RIVER	13
AND THE SHINING RAIN	....	240	ADMIT THE SUN	6
RAIN-BEATEN				
WITH RAIN-BEATEN HANDS HOLDING THE WHIP,	....	45	PLOUGHMAN GONE	20
RAINBOW				
TILL THE THREE-COLOURED RAINBOW FROM MY NIPPLES	...	120	ALTARWISE	107
RAINBOW-FISH				
THE RAINBOW-FISH BEND IN HER JOYS,	....	163	LONG-LEGGED	34
RAINBOWS				
SHALL RAINBOWS BE THEIR TUNICS' COLOUR?	....	65	GODS THUMP	4
RAINBOW'S				
THE RAINBOW'S FOOT IS NOT MORE APT	....	11	AIR BREATHE	5
AND, AS WE WATCH, THE RAINBOW'S FOOT	....	13	RAIN CUTS	15
INTO THE RAINBOW'S SHY EMBRACE.	....	14	RAIN CUTS	35
NO THIRD EYE PROBE INTO A RAINBOW'S SEX	....	108	GRIEF THIEF	25
LET THE FIRST PETER FROM A RAINBOW'S QUAYRAIL	.....	121	ALTARWISE	133
RAINED				
THOUGH THE NAMES ON THEIR WEED GROWN STONES ARE RAINED AWAY,	....	203	GIANT'S THIGH	8
RAINING				
HE'LL BATHE HIS RAINING BLOOD IN THE MALE SEA	.....	160	DEATHS AND ENT	19
DEEP THE GREAT BUSHED BAIT WITH RAINING LIPS	......	163	LONG-LEGGED	51
A RAINING TRAIL	....	176	BREATH SHED	5
RAINS				
IN TIME LIKE OUTLAW RAINS ON THAT PRIEST, WATER,		15	SPIRE CRANES	6
RAINY				
THE LEADEN STARS, THE RAINY HAMMER	....	68	BEFORE KNOCKED	11
OR THAT RAINY TONGUE BEAT BACK	....	139	TOMBSTONE TOLD	13
IN RAINY AUTUMN	....	177	POEM IN OCT	15
RAISE				
AND MANY ARMS TO RAISE	....	12	CABARET	20
AND THEN RAISE UP THE SKELETON AGAIN,	....	55	NO MAN BELIEVE	20
RAISE UP THIS RED-EYED EARTH?	....	89	EUNUCH DREAMS	23
CAN NEVER RAISE THE MIDNIGHT OF A CHUCKLE,	....	96	RUB OF LOVE	39
SHALL RAISE A LAMP	....	114	SERVANT SUN	25
RAISE THE LIVE RAFTERS OF THE EARDRUM,	....	142	SAINT TO FALL	36
WHO'D RAISE THE ORGANS OF THE COUNTED DUST	....	160	DEATHS AND ENT	7
RAISED				
AND GHOSTLY COMETS OVER THE RAISED FISTS.	....	56	WHY EAST WIND	26
RAISED UP A VOICE, AND, CLIMBING ON THE WORDS,	....	102	FELLOWED SLEEP	22
A CALM WIND BLOWS THAT RAISED THE TREES LIKE HAIR		133	I MAKE THIS IN	64

	PAGE	TITLE	LINE
RAISED (CONTINUED)			
BUT I, ANN'S BARD ON A RAISED HEARTH, CALL ALL	136	AFTER FUNERAL	21
AND THE WILD WINGS WERE RAISED	189	WINTER'S TALE	81
RAISES			
RAISES THE HAIRS OF LAD AND MAIDEN.	59	FAIRY TALES	16
MOON WALKS THE RIVER AND RAISES THE DEAD;	74	SUN BURNS	2
RAISING			
CASTS TO THE PINE ROOTS, RAISING MAN LIKE A MOUNTAIN	109	I, IN IMAGE	11
RAKE			
THAT WILL RAKE AT LAST ALL CURRENCIES OF THE MARKED			
BREATH	140	NO WORK WORDS	8
FIRE ON STARLIGHT, RAKE JESU'S STREAM;	163	LONG-LEGGED	43
RAKES			
THE HARP-WAKED CASANOVA RAKES NO RANGE.	159	TO LEDA	2
RAKING			
COMES DESIGNED TO MY LOVE TO STEAL NOT HER TIDE			
RAKING	200	COUNTRY SLEEP	100
RAM			
THEN HANG A RAM ROSE OVER THE RAGS.	60	MEAT ON BONES	8
AND PUT BESIDE HER A RAM ROSE.	61	MEAT ON BONES	24
THE BLACK RAM, SHUFFLING OF THE YEAR, OLD WINTER,	118	ALTARWISE	39
WITH FUMING BOWS AND RAM OF ICE, ...	163	LONG-LEGGED	42
(SIGHED THE OLD RAM ROD, DYING OF WOMEN), ...	206	LAMENT	3
(SIGHED THE OLD RAM ROD, DYING OF BITCHES), ...	206	LAMENT	15
(SIGHED THE OLD RAM ROD, DYING OF WELCOME), ...	206	LAMENT	27
(SIGHED THE OLD RAM ROD, DYING OF DOWNFALL), ...	207	LAMENT	39
(SIGHED THE OLD RAM ROD, DYING OF STRANGERS), ...	207	LAMENT	51
RAMMED			
RAMMED IN THE MARCHING HEART, HOLE	103	I DREAMED MY	14
RAMPART			
WITH HER RAMPART TO HIS TAPPING, ...	125	SEED-AT-ZERO	3
WITH HER RAMPART TO HIS TAPPING, ...	125	SEED-AT-ZERO	10
THROUGH THE RAMPART OF THE SKY	125	SEED-AT-ZERO	15
THROUGH THE RAMPART OF THE SKY	126	SEED-AT-ZERO	22
RAMPED			
WHEREVER I RAMPED IN THE CLOVER QUILTS, ...	206	LAMENT	22
RAMSHACKLING			
AND THE TUSKED, RAMSHACKLING SEA EXULTS;	211	POEM ON B'DAY	94
RAN			
BEFORE THE MOON SHIFTED AND THE SAP RAN OUT, ...	43	FACES SHONE	10
OUT OF THE NOISE INTO QUIET I RAN.	53	OUT OF THE PIT	92
AND RAN A RIVER	86	SEE, SAYS LIME	28
HIM UP AND HE RAN LIKE A WIND AFTER THE KINDLING			
FLIGHT	190	WINTER'S TALE	89
UNDER THE ONE LEAVED TREES RAN A SCARECROW OF SNOW	190	WINTER'S TALE	94
I RAN MY HEEDLESS WAYS, ...	196	FERN HILL	40
AND THEIR FIREFLY HAIRPINS FLEW, AND THE RICKS RAN			
ROUND--	205	GIANT'S THIGH	41
AND CUT THE BIRDS' BOUGHS THAT THE MINSTREL SAP RAN			
RED.	205	GIANT'S THIGH	49
RANG			
NO TIME, SPOKE THE CLOCKS, NO GOD, RANG THE BELLS,	150	WHEN I WOKE	28
THE TRODDEN TOWN RANG ITS COBBLES FOR LUCK.	161	LONG-LEGGED	4
WHEN ALL THE KEYS SHOT FROM THE LOCKS, AND RANG.	172	DAWN RAID	8
AND THE SABBATH RANG SLOWLY	195	FERN HILL	17
RANGE			
RANGE ON THE SKY-SCRAPING PLACE.	126	SEED-AT-ZERO	49
RANGE FROM THE GRAVE-GROPING PLACE.	127	SEED-AT-ZERO	56
THE HARP-WAKED CASANOVA RAKES NO RANGE.	159	TO LEDA	2

	PAGE	TITLE	LINE
RANGING			
MY GIRL RANGING THE NIGHT IN THE ROSE AND SHIRE ...	197	COUNTRY SLEEP	9
RANKEST			
THE RANKEST OF THE CITY	154	RETURN	8
RANT			
LOPS, AS A BUSH PLUMED WITH FLAMES, THE RANT OF THE FIERCE EYE, ...	135	HOW MY ANIMAL	38
AND FIRE, THE FLYING RANT	193	SIDE OF TRUTH	27
RANTS			
DEATH FROM A BANDAGE, RANTS THE MASK OF SCHOLARS	120	ALTARWISE	120
RAPE			
RAPE AND REBELLION IN THE NURSERIES OF MY FACE, ...	133	MAKE ME A MASK	3
RAPE GULP AND BE MARRY, HE ALSO SERVES	138	O CHATTERTON	26
RAPED			
AS RAPED AND REAPED, THE FINAL EMBLEM.	29	LONG, SKELETON	8
RAPES			
RAPES, LEAVES FOR LOST (THE AMORIST!), ...	30	NEARLY SUMMER	16
RAPING			
LAST NIGHT IN A RAPING WAVE	157	INTO HER HEAD	7
RAPTURE			
AND HOURS MADE LITTLE I HAVE DIPPED MY ARMS IN THEIR RAPTURE;	224	IDYLL UNFORGET	31
RARE			
SO RARE--	18	NATURAL DAY	24
SLEEP, GOOD, FOR EVER, SLOW AND DEEP, SPELLED RARE AND WISE, ...	197	COUNTRY SLEEP	8
IS AS RARE AS A DONKEY THAT'S RED.	221	SONG OF DOG	8
RARENESS			
EYED, IN THE HALOED HOUSE, IN HER RARENESS AND HILLY	200	COUNTRY SLEEP	89
RARER			
RARER DELIGHT SHOOTS IN THE BLOOD	48	POET: 1935	55
RARER THAN RADIUM, ...	152	WAS A SAVIOUR	2
RASCAL			
I MEAN BY TIME THE CAST AND CURFEW RASCAL OF OUR MARRIAGE, ...	130	SINNERS' BELL	25
RASPED			
RASPED AT LAST, AND I STUMBLED AND SUCKED, ...	146	TO OTHERS	8
RAT			
FROM YOU OR ME OR WIND OR RAT	53	OUT OF THE PIT	103
AVOID CHURCH AS A RAT;	59	FAIRY TALES	5
RATHER			
RATHER THAN CHARNEL-HOUSE AS SYMBOL	29	LONG, SKELETON	12
THAT IN HER GARDEN, RATHER THAN THE DAYS, ...	223	IN DREAMS	9
I'D RATHER HAVE THE WORM TO FEED	240	TWINING HEAD	9
RATIONAL			
THE WORM IS (PIN-POINT) RATIONAL IN THE FRUIT.	159	TO LEDA	3
THE WORM IS (PIN-POINT) RATIONAL IN THE FRUIT.	159	TO LEDA	9
RATTLED			
I PIECE MY FLESH THAT RATTLED ON THE YARDS	105	WORLD PYRAMID	38
RATTLING			
WHERE, WHAT'S MY GOD AMONG THIS CRAZY RATTLING	51	OUT OF THE PIT	33
RAVAGE			
RAVAGE AND BREAK, ...	10	COOL, OH NO	12
RAVAGED			
LIKE SENNA STIRS ALONG THE RAVAGED ROOTS.	80	ALL THAT I OWE	4
RAVE			
OLD AGE SHOULD BURN AND RAVE AT CLOSE OF DAY;	207	NOT GO GENTLE	2
RAVEN			
AND RAVEN HAIR.	11	AIR BREATHE	13
AND HAVE THE RAVEN FOR COMPANION.	45	PLOUGHMAN GONE	18

	PAGE	TITLE	LINE
RAVEN (CONTINUED)			
LIE COLD, WITH THEIR HORSES, FOR RAVEN AND KITE.	45	PLOUGHMAN GONE	23
AND HAVE THE RAVEN FOR COMPANION.	46	PLOUGHMAN GONE	32
IT IS THE ENGINE AND NOT THE RAVEN.	46	PLOUGHMAN GONE	33
SHALL LAMP THE RAVEN DARKNESS OF HER FACE,	57	GREEK PLAY	9
AND RAVEN YOUTH WILL FEAST BUT WHERE HE WILL.	64	WOMAN SPEAKS	51
HEARING THE RAVEN COUGH IN WINTER STICKS,	98	OCTOBER WIND	6
AND THE CAGE FOR THE SCYTHE-EYED RAVEN.	106	ALL ALL AND	21
RAVENED			
FOR WHO UNMANNINGLY HAUNTS THE MOUNTAIN RAVENED EAVES	198	COUNTRY SLEEP	24
RAVENS			
OF RAVENS AT THE HERO'S MEAT AND NERVES	63	WOMAN SPEAKS	17
AND RAVENS FED CONFECTION TO THEIR YOUNG.	65	WOMAN SPEAKS	59
WITH RAVENS BEATING ON THE ROOF:	237	PILLAR BREAKS	13
RAVEN'S			
THE HEART LIES READY FOR THE RAVEN'S MOUTH,	63	WOMAN SPEAKS	8
SOME LET ME TELL YOU OF THE RAVEN'S SINS.	99	OCTOBER WIND	24
THE RAVEN'S FALLEN AND THE MAGPIE'S STILL.	237	PILLAR BREAKS	7
TEMPLE'S BROKEN AND POOR RAVEN'S DEAD;	238	PILLAR BREAKS	24
RAVES			
YET RAVES AT HER WILL	170	LOVE IN ASYLUM	14
RAVISHMENT			
WHICH BATHE THEMSELVES IN A RAVISHMENT OF SNOW;	223	IDYLL UNFORGET	14
RAWBONED			
THE RAWBONED HORSE TO A MAN'S VOICE	45	PLOUGHMAN GONE	14
RAW-EDGED			
REHEARSING HEAT UPON A RAW-EDGED NERVE.	95	RUB OF LOVE	19
RAYED			
ALL THE FISHES WERE RAYED IN BLOOD,	162	LONG-LEGGED	23
A SHE BIRD ROSE AND RAYED LIKE A BURNING BRIDE.	189	WINTER'S TALE	69
RAYS			
HER ROBIN BREASTED TREE, THREE MARYS IN THE RAYS.	198	COUNTRY SLEEP	29
AND GALLOWS, UP THE RAYS OF HIS EYES THE SMALL BIRDS OF THE BAY	201	SIR JOHNS HILL	4
RAZED			
WHO RAZED MY WOODEN FOLLY STANDS AGHAST,	113	NOT FATHER ME	22
THE STAINED FLATS OF HEAVEN HIT AND RAZED	141	SAINT TO FALL	2
RAZOR			
THAT, LIKE A RAZOR, SKIMS, CUTS, AND TURNS,	47	POET: 1935	49
RAZOR MAN AND BELLY KING,	155	RETURN	32
HE CUTS HIMSELF ON AN ELDER'S RAZOR LEG.	179	NEW QUAY	28
REACH			
NEVER TO REACH THE OBLIVIOUS DARK	27	OBLIVIOUS DARK	T
NEVER TO REACH THE OBLIVIOUS DARK	27	OBLIVIOUS DARK	1
REACH ASKING ARMS UP TO THE MILKY SKY,	42	A WAR OF WITS	16
ON THE EDGE BEYOND YOUR REACH;	230	OUR SANCTITY	5
TO TELL WHAT NOTE I COULD REACH IF I TRIED,	234	NO, PIGEON	12
REACHED			
HAS NOT YET REACHED THE GROUND.	116	LANTERNS SHINE	19
REACHING			
REACHING A SECOND GROUND FAR FROM THE STARS;	101	FELLOWED SLEEP	7
READ			
NOW HE HAS HEARD AND READ THE HAPPY WORD.	53	OUT OF THE PIT	100
CAN'T READ SENSE IN THE RAIN THAT WILLYNILLY	137	O CHATTERTON	19
AND READ, IN A SHELL,	202	SIR JOHNS HILL	25
READY			
READY TO RISE, EASY TO SLEEP.	23	THE ONLY DEAD	6
POISED AT THE READY EAR	29	NEARLY SUMMER	11
THE HEART LIES READY FOR THE RAVEN'S MOUTH,	63	WOMAN SPEAKS	8

	PAGE	TITLE	LINE
READYMADE			
IT WAS SWEET TO DROWN IN THE READYMADE HANDY WATER	152	BELOW A TIME	44
REAL			
AND WHICH THE REAL?	12	CABARET	25
REALITY			
I WANT REALITY TO HOLD/ WITHIN MY PALM, ...	9	MINUTE'S HOUR	14
BUT IT, REALITY, WHOSE VOICE I KNOW	9	MINUTE'S HOUR	16
REALM			
YOU ARE THE RULER OF THIS REALM OF FLESH	67	REALM OF FLESH	T
YOU ARE THE RULER OF THIS REALM OF FLESH, ...	67	REALM OF FLESH	1
REAPED			
AS RAPED AND REAPED, THE FINAL EMBLEM.	29	LONG, SKELETON	8
ALL HE HAS REAPED IN WONDER.	30	NEARLY SUMMER	18
REASON			
SEE THE REASON FOR UNDOUBLING DOUBLING NOT, ...	24	LITTLE PROBLEM	16
SOBSTUFF, MOCK REASON, ...	39	GAS FADES	12
ALL REASON BROKE, AND HORROR WALKED THE ROADS.	51	OUT OF THE PIT	18
I HAVE BEEN TOLD TO REASON BY THE HEART, ...	116	LANTERNS SHINE	9
I HAVE BEEN TOLD TO REASON BY THE PULSE, ...	116	LANTERNS SHINE	11
REBEL			
'REBEL AGAINST THE BINDING MOON	61	MEAT ON BONES	9
REBEL AGAINST THE FLESH AND BONE, ...	61	MEAT ON BONES	14
REBEL AGAINST MY FATHER'S DREAM	61	MEAT ON BONES	27
REBELLION			
RAPE AND REBELLION IN THE NURSERIES OF MY FACE, ...	133	MAKE ME A MASK	3
REBORN			
THAT BELLED AND BOUNDED WITH THE FOSSIL AND THE DEW			
REBORN.	191	WINTER'S TALE	120
RECALL			
RECALL MY OLD DESIRE	237	WOMAN TAPESTRY	70
RECEIVE			
SHALL SHE RECEIVE A BELLYFUL OF WEEDS	134	NOT FROM ANGER	5
RECEIVER			
PURSED LIPS AT THE RECEIVER, ...	44	LONGED TO MOVE	17
RECORDERS			
THESE ARE YOUR YEARS' RECORDERS. THE CIRCULAR WORLD			
STANDS STILL.)	110	I, IN IMAGE	72
RECORDS			
LEFT IN THE RECORDS OF LIVING A NOT-TO-BE-BROKEN			
PICTURE, ...	45	PLOUGHMAN GONE	2
(THE WOUND RECORDS), ...	113	SERVANT SUN	9
RED			
OF FEAR, RAGE RED, MANALIVE, ...	4	PROLOGUE	48
BY LOVE-TIP OR MY HAND'S RED HEAT.	19	IMAGES IN AIR	14
THERE'S POISON IN YOUR RED WINE, DRINKER, ...	27	OBLIVIOUS DARK	14
WHO FOLLOW THE RED RIVERS, HOLLOW	54	WE BY SEASAND	3
THE STRATA OF THE SHORE AND DROWN RED ROCK;	54	WE BY SEASAND	20
THAT OUT OF A BOWER OF RED SWINE	61	MEAT ON BONES	28
NOT FOREVER SHALL THE LORD OF THE RED HAIL	73	LORD RED HAIL	T
NOT FOREVER SHALL THE LORD OF THE RED HAIL	73	LORD RED HAIL	1
HOW SOON, HOW SOON, O LORD OF THE RED HAIL!	73	LORD RED HAIL	18
DRIVES MY RED BLOOD; THAT DRIES THE MOUTHING STREAMS	77	THE FORCE THAT	7
THE SUN WAS RED, THE MOON WAS GREY, ...	78	LOVE'S FEVER	14
THE BLOOD GOT UP AS RED AS WAX	85	SEE, SAYS LIME	13
IF THE RED TICKLE AS THE CATTLE CALVE	95	RUB OF LOVE	4
RED IN AN AUSTRIAN VOLLEY.	105	WORLD PYRAMID	39
MY NEST OF MERCIES IN THE RUDE, RED TREE.	121	ALTARWISE	140
CLAW OF THE CRABBED VEINS SQUEEZE FROM EACH RED			
PARTICLE	135	HOW MY ANIMAL	21
DIE IN RED FEATHERS WHEN THE FLYING HEAVEN'S CUT,	135	HOW MY ANIMAL	40

	PAGE	TITLE	LINE
RED (CONTINUED)			
AND HER RED LIPS WERE KISSED BLACK, ...	139	TOMBSTONE TOLD	18
A BLAZING RED HARSH HEAD TEAR UP	140	TOMBSTONE TOLD	29
WITH MY RED VEINS FULL OF MONEY, ...	143	24 YEARS	7
ROUNDS TO LOOK AT THE RED, WAGGED ROOT.	144	PLEASURE-BIRD	12
PEARS AND RED CURRANTS	178	POEM IN OCT	45
OF BIRDS! AMONG THE COCKS LIKE FIRE THE RED FOX ...	199	COUNTRY SLEEP	69
WHO COMES AS RED AS THE FOX AND SLY AS THE HEELED WIND.	200	COUNTRY SLEEP	81
AND CUT THE BIRDS' BOUGHS THAT THE MINSTREL SAP RAN RED.	205	GIANT'S THIGH	49
NO SPRINGTAILED TOM IN THE RED HOT TOWN	206	LAMENT	29
IS AS RARE AS A DONKEY THAT'S RED.	221	SONG OF DOG	8
REDCOATED			
LEADS TO FOOL'S PARADISE WHERE THE REDCOATED KILLER	44	TO FOLLOW FOX	5
REDEMPTION			
TOWARDS DESTRUCTION AND REDEMPTION, ...	37	WINDMILLS TURN	3
RED-EYED			
RAISE UP THIS RED-EYED EARTH?	89	EUNUCH DREAMS	23
A THREE-EYED, RED-EYED SPARK, BLUNT AS A FLOWER;	94	IN BEGINNING	15
BY RED-EYED ORCHARDS SOW THE SEEDS OF SNOW, ...	123	FOSTER LIGHT	11
REDHAIRED			
THE REDHAIRED CANCER STILL ALIVE, ...	97	TWILIGHT LOCKS	20
REDWOMBED			
SHIFTS TO THE REDWOMBED PEN.	80	ALMANAC TIME	5
REEFED			
OR LIKE THE TIDE-LOOPED BREASTKNOT REEFED AGAIN ...	131	I MAKE THIS IN	11
REEK			
FLARED IN THE REEK OF THE WIVING STY WITH THE RUSH	204	GIANT'S THIGH	22
REEL			
TWO ONE-DIMENSIONED GHOSTS, LOVE ON A REEL, ...	89	EUNUCH DREAMS	12
AND EVERY STONE I WIND OFF LIKE A REEL.	144	COLOUR OF SAY	13
TO THE GOLD GUT THAT SINGS ON HIS REEL	162	LONG-LEGGED	19
HIS FIERY REEL SINGS OFF ITS FLAMES, ...	164	LONG-LEGGED	64
AND THE FISHERMAN WINDS HIS REEL	166	LONG-LEGGED	123
REELS			
HIS REELS AND MYSTERY	129	MY NEOPHYTE	31
REFLECTED			
AND I HAVE REFLECTED ITS COLOURS IN THE PEACE OF MY EYES;	224	IDYLL UNFORGET	24
REFLECTION			
LOVE'S REFLECTION OF THE MUSHROOM FEATURES, ...	118	ALTARWISE	53
REFLECTIONS			
HAZARDOUS REFLECTIONS DIPPED IN EVENING	226	THE OAK	3
REFUSAL			
REFUSAL STRUCK HER LOIN AND THE LAME FLOWER	134	NOT FROM ANGER	2
REFUSAL STRUCK LIKE A BELL UNDER WATER	134	NOT FROM ANGER	12
A REFUSAL TO MOURN THE DEATH, BY FIRE, OF A CHILD IN LONDON	191	REFUSAL MOURN	T
REFUSES			
HEARS AND REFUSES.	49	LIGHT, I KNOW	16
REGARDED			
IF YOU WOULD BE REGARDED GREAT, ...	84	LETTER TO AUNT	41
REGISTER			
INFORMED BY RUMOUR AND THE REGISTER, ...	38	THE GOSSIPERS	7
REGRET			
THROUGH NO REGRET OF LEAVING WOMAN WAITING	32	OUT OF SIGHS	14
FEELING REGRET WHEN THIS IS WASTED	32	OUT OF SIGHS	18
NEVER NEVER OH NEVER TO REGRET THE BUGLE I WORE ...	152	BELOW A TIME	47
GIVE US THE PLEASURE OF REGRET;	230	OUR SANCTITY	11

	PAGE	TITLE	LINE
REGULAR			
BE A REGULAR	137	O CHATTERTON	10
REHEARSING			
REHEARSING HEAT UPON A RAW-EDGED NERVE.	95	RUB OF LOVE	19
REINDEER			
NIGHT AND THE REINDEER ON THE CLOUDS ABOVE THE			
HAYCOCKS	199	COUNTRY SLEEP	64
REINS			
BUT THE HORSES ARE GONE AND THE REINS ARE GREEN ...	45	PLOUGHMAN GONE	10
REJOICE			
THE BLACK, BURST SEA REJOICE, ...	135	HOW MY ANIMAL	19
REJOICED			
AND ALL THE ELEMENTS OF THE SNOW FALL REJOICED	189	WINTER'S TALE	84
REJOICING			
REJOICING FOR THAT DRIFTING DEATH	164	LONG-LEGGED	88
REKINDLED			
AND NOAH'S REKINDLED NOW UNKIND DOVE	157	INTO HER HEAD	5
RELATIONS			
STILL COMES VISITING HIS POOR RELATIONS, ...	29	NEARLY SUMMER	2
RELATION'S			
MOON WITH A RELATION'S FACE	155	RETURN	47
RELEVANT			
WHICH MAY OR MAY NOT BE RELEVANT	33	HELD-OUT HAND	14
RELIC			
SHAMES AND THE DAMP DISHONOURS, THE RELIC SCRAPING.	110	I, IN IMAGE	71
RELIGION			
LIE WITH RELIGION IN THEIR CRAMP, HER THREADBARE	137	AFTER FUNERAL	32
RELIGIOUS			
IN THE RELIGIOUS WIND	3	PROLOGUE	21
I WOULD BE WOVEN A RELIGIOUS SHAPE;	96	TWELVE	9
REMAIN			
IF THESE TWO GNOMES REMAIN UNMOVED BY STRICTURES?	60	FAIRY TALES	30
AND WHO REMAIN SHALL FLOWER AS THEY LOVE, ...	90	EUNUCH DREAMS	41
ALL SHALL REMAIN AND ON THE GRAVEWARD GULF	108	GRIEF THIEF	27
YOUR STEP WILL REMAIN ABOUT TO FALL.	232	FURIOUS MOTION	4
REMAINED			
WHO FLEW HIMSELF BECAUSE THE BOAT REMAINED	238	PILLAR BREAKS	19
REMAINS			
WE STILL ARE LOTH TO PART WITH WHAT REMAINS, ...	26	THERE'S PLENTY	17
LET WHAT REMAINS OF THAT FIRST MIRACLE	65	WOMAN SPEAKS	62
REMAINS THOUGH GODS BE FELLED TILL NONE ARE LEFT.	67	LET A FAITH	10
LAND, LAND, LAND, NOTHING REMAINS	169	LONG-LEGGED	209
REMARK			
THE EYES REMARK THE ANTICS OF THE HAWK.	63	WOMAN SPEAKS	10
WE WILL REMARK UPON THE SIZE	230	OUR SANCTITY	6
REMARKS			
ON THESE BLUE LIPS, THE LIME REMARKS, ...	85	SEE, SAYS LIME	9
REMEMBER			
TO REMEMBER, CAST STRICTURE ON MECHANICS AND MAN.	45	PLOUGHMAN GONE	5
REMEMBER ME AND PITY HIM	69	BEFORE KNOCKED	44
REMEMBER THIS: EACH ROSE IS WORMY, ...	84	LETTER TO AUNT	48
REMEMBER THIS: THAT LOVE DEPENDS	84	LETTER TO AUNT	50
REMEMBER, TOO, THAT LIFE IS HELL	84	LETTER TO AUNT	52
TOUCH TO REMEMBER AND BE SAD.	233	NO THOUGHT	4
REMEMBERED			
ACQUAINT THE FLESH WITH A REMEMBERED ITCH, ...	80	ALL THAT I OWE	12
THESE THINGS REMEMBERED, WHAT CAN STOP	84	LETTER TO AUNT	56
EARLY IMAGINARY HALF REMEMBERED	158	INTO HER HEAD	32
REMIND			
TWENTY-FOUR YEARS REMIND THE TEARS OF MY EYES.	143	24 YEARS	1

		PAGE	TITLE	LINE
REMOVE				
REMOVE YOUR BRAINS, TAKE OUT YOUR HEART;	....	84	LETTER TO AUNT	60
REND				
REND THE BRIGHT FLESH AWAY,	....	239	MAKES INTERVALS	23
RENOUNCING				
AND THE RENOUNCING OF ISLANDS.	....	148	UNLUCKILY FOR	39
RENT				
OR RENT ANCESTRALLY THE ROPED SEA-HYMEN,	....	131	I MAKE THIS IN	12
REPEAT				
OVER THE PAST TABLE I REPEAT THIS PRESENT GRACE.		145	PLEASURE-BIRD	25
REPETITION				
FROM THE REPETITION OF SALUTES,	....	43	LONGED TO MOVE	7
REPLIES				
AFTER A VOLLEY OF QUESTIONS AND REPLIES	....	42	A WAR OF WITS	17
REPLY				
I AM MAN'S REPLY TO EVERY QUESTION,	....	26	PERSONAL EPIT	17
BOTH QUENCH HIS THIRST HE'LL HAVE A BLACK REPLY.		56	WHY EAST WIND	9
REPLYING				
AND HE REPLYING,	....	43	FACES SHONE	12
REPOSE				
NO WEEPING THROUGH THAT DEEP REPOSE CAN BREAK.	....	222	MISSING	9
REPTILE				
THE REPTILE PROFLIGATES IN A FLAME,	....	150	WHEN I WOKE	4
REQUEST				
REQUEST TO LEDA	....	159	TO LEDA	T
REQUIEMS				
AND THE GOLDEN PAVEMENTS LAID IN REQUIEMS,	....	175	FIRE RAID	69
REROBING				
REROBING OF THE NAKED GHOST. MANHOOD	....	103	I DREAMED MY	23
RESEMBLE				
CONJURED ME TO RESEMBLE	....	156	RETURN	68
RESEMBLING				
RESEMBLING TO HER DULLED SENSE	....	158	INTO HER HEAD	30
RESERVOIR				
WHEN I WHISTLED WITH MITCHING BOYS THROUGH A				
RESERVOIR PARK	....	144	COLOUR OF SAY	7
RESIN				
I SCRAPE THROUGH RESIN TO A STARRY BONE	....	104	WORLD PYRAMID	35
RESPONSE				
BETWEEN THE RAID AND THE RESPONSE	....	73	WE MOTHERNAKED	3
REST				
DISTURB THIS ISLAND'S REST.	....	62	EARS IN TURRET	16
LIE DRY, REST ROBBED, MY BEAST.	....	135	HOW MY ANIMAL	42
A VIRGIN MARRIED AT REST.	....	139	TOMBSTONE TOLD	3
'REST BEYOND CHOICE IN THE DUST-APPOINTED GRAIN,		146	IF HEAD HURT	26
FORGOTTEN DARK, REST THEIR PULSE AND BURY THEIR DEAD				
IN HER FAITHLESS SLEEP.	....	159	INTO HER HEAD	69
LIE IN GRACE. SLEEP SPELLED AT REST IN THE LOWLY				
HOUSE	....	199	COUNTRY SLEEP	43
WHICH WAS REST AND DUST, AND IN THE KIND GROUND	...	216	ELEGY	10
LET HIM FIND NO REST BUT THE FATHERED AND FOUND,		216	ELEGY	12
ALL THINGS REST IN THE WILL OF PURPOSE TRIUMPHANT.		222	FOREST PICTURE	8
RESUFFERED				
SPAT UP FROM THE RESUFFERED PAIN.	....	103	I DREAMED MY	24
RESURRECT				
TIME CANNOT HEAL NOR RESURRECT;	....	26	THERE'S PLENTY	15
RESURRECTION				
THIS WAS THE RESURRECTION IN THE DESERT,	....	120	ALTARWISE	119
RETCH				
THEY RETCH INTO MY SECRET NIGHT	....	143	THE MOLLS	5

	PAGE	TITLE	LINE
RETREAT			
CUT OUR FIGURES, AND RETREAT AT NIGHT	28	NO WINGS	17
RETURN			
TO TAKE TO GIVE IS ALL, RETURN WHAT IS HUNGRILY GIVEN	140	NO WORK WORDS	4
IF I TAKE TO BURN OR RETURN THIS WORLD WHICH IS EACH			
MAN'S WORK.	140	NO WORK WORDS	12
AT THE BREAST STORED WITH SEAS. NO RETURN	146	IF HEAD HURT	27
THE COUNTRYMAN'S RETURN	154	RETURN	T
THE COUNTRYMAN'S RETURN	157	RETURN	96
OF HIS MOTHER'S MILK MAY RETURN	183	VISION, PRAYER	120
THE ACHE RETURN.	239	MAKES INTERVALS	26
REVERENT			
WITH WELSH AND REVERENT ROOK, ...	4	PROLOGUE	60
REVOLUTION			
RUIN AND REVOLUTION	34	IN GARDENS	14
REVOLVED			
WITHIN HIS HEAD REVOLVED A LITTLE WORLD	50	OUT OF THE PIT	1
REVOLVES			
REVOLVES OVER AND OVER AGAIN	46	PLOUGHMAN GONE	28
REVOLVING			
WITH WOODEN ARMS REVOLVING IN THE WIND	45	PLOUGHMAN GONE	7
AT COTTON WORLDS REVOLVING ON A HIP, ...	51	OUT OF THE PIT	46
A CIRCLE SPINS. LET EACH REVOLVING SPOKE	67	LET A FAITH	4
AND THROUGH THESE EYES GOD MARKS MYSELF REVOLVING,	76	LASHED RINGS	12
REWARD			
AND THAT IS THE REWARD OF LABOUR	44	TO FOLLOW FOX	12
AND A BLACK REWARD FOR A ROARING LIFE, ...	207	LAMENT	50
RHAPSODIC			
TO HAVE HEARD THEIR VAGUE, RHAPSODIC SINGINGS, ...	223	IDYLL UNFORGET	5
RHUBARB			
WHAT RHUBARB MAN PEELED IN HER FOAM-BLUE CHANNEL	121	ALTARWISE	135
RHYMER			
AND THE RHYMER IN THE LONG TONGUED ROOM, ...	209	POEM ON B'DAY	15
RHYMES			
DO NOT FORGET THAT 'LIMPET' RHYMES	84	LETTER TO AUNT	33
RHYTHM			
UNTIL I FELT THE RHYTHM OF HER BODY	234	WOMAN TAPESTRY	4
A RHYTHM I CANNOT BREAK	235	WOMAN TAPESTRY	29
RHYTHMS			
LEAP OVER TO MY CRISS-CROSS RHYTHMS.	33	HELD-OUT HAND	23
RIB			
A RIB OF CANCER ON THE FLUID SKY.	25	THERE'S PLENTY	7
MAN'S RIB ON WOMAN'S, STRAIGHT LINE ON A CURVE, ...	51	OUT OF THE PIT	35
HAD STRINGED MY FLASK OF MATTER TO HIS RIB.	97	TWILIGHT LOCKS	12
RIBBED			
RIBBED BETWEEN DESERT AND WATER STORM, ...	54	WE BY SEASAND	11
THE RIBBED ORIGINAL OF LOVE.	94	IN BEGINNING	30
RIBBING			
NOR THE HEART IN THE RIBBING METAL.	106	ALL ALL AND	15
RIBBONED			
AND THE WINGS OF THE GREAT ROC RIBBONED FOR THE FAIR!	199	COUNTRY SLEEP	65
AND THE WINDS THAT STREAM THROUGH THE RIBBONED LIGHT	227	THE PINE	3
RIBS			
MAKE DISCORD WITH THE VOICE WITHIN HIS RIBS	46	POET: 1935	5
LENDS NOT FLESH TO RIBS AND NECK, ...	55	NO MAN BELIEVE	23
AND HID BEHIND THE FORTRESS OF THE RIBS	63	WOMAN SPEAKS	7
UNDER THE RIBS SAIL THE MOON AND THE SUN;	74	SUN BURNS	11
WAX CLOTHES THAT WAX UPON THE AGEING RIBS;	81	ALL THAT I OWE	26
I PUT ROUND RIBS THAT PACKED THEIR HEART, ...	85	SEE, SAYS LIME	2

	PAGE	TITLE	LINE
RIBS (CONTINUED)			
BUT RAIL WITH YOUR WIZARD'S RIBS THE HEART-SHAPED PLANET;	123	FOSTER LIGHT	15
RICE			
NOW STAMP THE LORD'S PRAYER ON A GRAIN OF RICE,	119	ALTARWISE	85
RICH			
BONY AND SPAVINED, RICH WITH FLEAS.	45	PLOUGHMAN GONE	9
SOUNDS, RICH WITH LIFE, OUT OF A PAINTED MASK;	57	GREEK PLAY	14
I WHO WAS RICH WAS MADE THE RICHER	69	BEFORE KNOCKED	35
THE SUNNY GENTLEMEN, THE WELSHING RICH,	90	EUNUCH DREAMS	25
BELLY OF THE RICH YEAR AND THE BIG PURSE OF MY BODY	140	NO WORK WORDS	2
ONCE I HAD A RICH BOY FOR MYSELF	149	PAPER & STICKS	4
ONE RICH STREET WITH HUNGER IN IT.	157	RETURN	101
RICHER			
I WHO WAS RICH WAS MADE THE RICHER	69	BEFORE KNOCKED	35
RICKS			
FLYING WITH THE RICKS, AND THE HORSES	195	FERN HILL	26
AND THEIR FIREFLY HAIRPINS FLEW, AND THE RICKS RAN ROUND--	205	GIANT'S THIGH	41
RICK'S			
ON THE LAST RICK'S TIP BY SPILLED WINE-WELLS	141	SAINT TO FALL	14
RID			
SLY AS AN ADDER, RID OF FLEAS.	29	LONG, SKELETON	6
RIDDEN			
I HAVE RIDDEN ON GUTTER DUNG AND CLOUD.	52	OUT OF THE PIT	67
RIDDLED			
I HEAR, THROUGH DEAD MEN'S DRUMS, THE RIDDLED LADS,	105	WORLD PYRAMID	40
SHALL THE STAR-FLANKED SEED BE RIDDLED,	125	SEED-AT-ZERO	16
QUICKENING FOR THE RIDDLED SEA;	125	SEED-AT-ZERO	18
SHALL THE STAR-FLANKED SEED BE RIDDLED,	126	SEED-AT-ZERO	23
SETTLING ON A RIDDLED STRONGHOLD	126	SEED-AT-ZERO	26
RIDE			
WE WILL RIDE OUT ALONE, AND THEN,	5	PROLOGUE	91
RIDE IN THEIR CHARABANCS ON ROADS	37	WINDMILLS TURN	13
AS THE GREEN BLOOMS RIDE UPWARD, TO THE DRIVE OF TIME;	122	HOLD HARD	3
WHERE BIRDS RIDE LIKE LEAVES AND BOATS LIKE DUCKS	150	WHEN I WOKE	22
RIDE THROUGH THE DOORS OF OUR UNENTERED HOUSE.	154	WAS A SAVIOUR	38
OR WE SHALL OBEY, AND RIDE WITH YOU THROUGH THE DROWNED.	194	SLEEP BECALMED	14
SHALL HARROW AND SNOW THE BLOOD WHILE YOU RIDE WIDE AND NEAR,	198	COUNTRY SLEEP	23
MORE SPANNED WITH ANGELS RIDE	211	POEM ON B'DAY	104
RIDER			
TIME, IN A FOLLY'S RIDER, LIKE A COUNTY MAN	122	HOLD HARD	4
TIME, IN A RIDER RISING, FROM THE HARNESSED VALLEY;	122	HOLD HARD	21
THE COME-A-CROPPER RIDER OF THE FLOWER.	128	NOW, SAY NAY	28
AND STAVED, AND RIVEN AMONG PLUMES MY RIDER WEEP.	198	COUNTRY SLEEP	16
RIDERLESS			
TURNING THE RIDERLESS DEAD BY THE CHANNEL WALL.	110	I, IN IMAGE	48
A LIMP AND RIDERLESS SHAPE TO LEAP NINE THINNING MONTHS.'	145	IF HEAD HURT	15
RIDERS			
ALL BUT THE BRISKEST RIDERS THROWN,	98	TWILIGHT LOCKS	41
AND SEAR JUST RIDERS BACK,	161	DEATHS AND ENT	34
RIDES			
OR RIDES THE IMAGINED OCEANS OF THE MALE WARDS.	169	LOVE IN ASYLUM	9
AS THE RAIN FALLS, HAIL ON THE FLEECE, AS THE VALE MIST RIDES	199	COUNTRY SLEEP	57
WHERE THE HAY RIDES NOW OR THE BRACKEN KITCHENS RUST	205	GIANT'S THIGH	47

	PAGE	TITLE	LINE
RIDICULOUS			
THE BRIGHT PRETENDER, THE RIDICULOUS SEA DANDY	152	BELOW A TIME	42
RIDING			
FOR US THERE IS NO SHOOTING AND NO RIDING, ...	40	YOUNG ARE OLD	8
FOR US THERE IS NO RIDING AND NO SHOOTING, ...	40	YOUNG ARE OLD	15
MAN TOILS NOW ON AN IRON SADDLE, RIDING	45	PLOUGHMAN GONE	24
RIDING ON GIRDERS OF THE AIR, LOOKS DOWN	52	OUT OF THE PIT	47
RIDING THE SEA LIGHT ON A SUNKEN PATH, ...	107	GRIEF THIEF	8
OLD PAINT-STAINED TUMBLERS RIDING.	154	RETURN	19
OF THE RIDING THAMES.	192	REFUSAL MOURN	23
NOR THAT RIDING TO SLEEP	196	FERN HILL	49
NEVER AND NEVER, MY GIRL RIDING FAR AND NEAR	197	COUNTRY SLEEP	1
HIGH RIDING, HELD AND BLESSED AND TRUE, AND SO STILLY	200	COUNTRY SLEEP	90
WOUND, NOR HER RIDING HIGH, NOR HER EYES, NOR			
KINDLED HAIR, ...	201	COUNTRY SLEEP	101
PETTICOATS GALED HIGH, OR SHY WITH THE ROUGH RIDING			
BOYS, ...	204	GIANT'S THIGH	18
RIDINGS			
OVER THE VAULT OF RIDINGS WITH HIS HOUND AT HEEL,	122	HOLD HARD	5
BUT GRAFT THESE FOUR-FRUITED RIDINGS ON YOUR COUNTRY;	123	FOSTER LIGHT	9
RIFT			
THE HAYGOLD HAIRED, MY LOVE ASLEEP, AND THE RIFT BLUE	200	COUNTRY SLEEP	88
AND ALL MY GRIEF FLOWS FROM THE RIFT	225	CLOWN IN MOON	3
RIFTED			
BY SCALPEL LIGHTNING FROM THE RIFTED SKY, ...	64	WOMAN SPEAKS	29
RIGHT			
DO THE RIGHT THING TO DO THE RIGHT;	18	NATURAL DAY	37
DO THE RIGHT THING TO DO THE RIGHT;	18	NATURAL DAY	37
BEFORE WHITE OR BLACK, THE RIGHT OR LEFT SOCK, ...	39	GAS FADES	17
NOT BLACK OR WHITE OR LEFT OR RIGHT.	39	GAS FADES	39
TO SHARE MY ROOM IN THE HOUSE NOT RIGHT IN THE HEAD,	169	LOVE IN ASYLUM	2
AND A HUNDRED STORKS PERCH ON THE SUN'S RIGHT HAND.	173	DAWN RAID	14
AND SERVE ME RIGHT AS THE PREACHERS WARN, ...	207	LAMENT	38
THOUGH WISE MEN AT THEIR END KNOW DARK IS RIGHT,	208	NOT GO GENTLE	4
RIGHTSIGHTED			
THROUGH PERISCOPES RIGHTSIGHTED FROM THE GRAVE; ...	81	ALL THAT I OWE	24
RIM			
THE GRAIN THAT HURRIES THIS WAY FROM THE RIM OF THE			
GRAVE	146	IF HEAD HURT	24
RIMS			
WHOSE FLAMING BLOOD SHALL RUB IT AT THE RIMS	87	PAIN BE MUSIC	8
ON THE SNAPPING RIMS OF THE ASHPIT, ...	151	BELOW A TIME	8
RIND			
IN WINDS THAT BRING THE FRUIT AND RIND	55	WHY EAST WIND	4
NOR THE TUSKED PRINCE, IN THE RUTTISH FARM, AT THE			
RIND	198	COUNTRY SLEEP	37
GRISTLE AND RIND, AND A ROARER'S LIFE, ...	207	LAMENT	46
RING			
O MY RUFFLED RING DOVE	4	PROLOGUE	58
RING LIKE A HANDBELL THROUGH THE CORRIDORS, ...	56	WHY EAST WIND	22
I EYE THE RING OF EARTH, THE AIRY CIRCLE, ...	76	LASHED RINGS	2
WHERE, PUNCTUAL AS DEATH, WE RING THE STARS;	92	BOYS OF SUMMER	27
BRAND OF THE LILY'S ANGER ON HER RING, ...	115	A GRIEF AGO	19
O RING OF SEAS, NOR SORROW AS I SHIFT	123	FOSTER LIGHT	20
FALLS ON A RING OF SUMMERS AND LOCKED NOONS.	132	I MAKE THIS IN	30
'ALL GAME PHRASES FIT YOUR RING OF A COCKFIGHT: ...	145	IF HEAD HURT	6
ASSEMBLING WAITS FOR THE SPADE'S RING ON THE CAGE.	172	DAWN RAID	11
OF THE TWELVE APOSTLES' TOWNS RING IN HIS NIGHT;	216	COUNTRY HEAVEN	26

		PAGE	TITLE	LINE
RINGED				
OF THE GOLDEN GHOST WHO RINGED WITH HIS STREAMS HER MERCURY BONE,	....	170	MARRIAGE VIRG	11
IN HIS FIRELIT ISLAND RINGED BY THE WINGED SNOW	...	187	WINTER'S TALE	17
IN A SPINNEY OF RINGED BOYS AND GANDERS, SPIKE AND BURN,	....	198	COUNTRY SLEEP	14
RINGED-SEA				
THE RINGED-SEA GHOST, RISE GRIMLY FROM THE WRACK.		113	NOT FATHER ME	24
RINGING				
ON ROSE AND ICICLE THE RINGING HANDPRINT.	....	120	ALTARWISE	98
RINGS				
THROUGH THESE LASHED RINGS	....	76	LASHED RINGS	T
THROUGH THESE LASHED RINGS SET DEEP INSIDE THEIR HOLLOWS	....	76	LASHED RINGS	1
AND THROUGH THESE TREMBLING RINGS SET IN THEIR VALLEY		76	LASHED RINGS	4
RINGS OUT THE DEAD SEA SCALE;	....	110	I, IN IMAGE	63
STREAM WITH BELLS AND BAYING WATER BOUNDS. THE DEW RINGS	....	189	WINTER'S TALE	62
RIP				
RIP OF THE VAULTS, I TOOK MY MARROW-LADLE	....	118	ALTARWISE	35
AND, RIP VAN WINKLE FROM A TIMELESS CRADLE,	....	118	ALTARWISE	37
RIPE				
THE SUICIDES PARADE AGAIN, NOW RIPE FOR DYING.	....	43	FACES SHONE	14
BRANDY AND RIPE IN MY BRIGHT, BASS PRIME,	....	206	LAMENT	28
ALL THE LAND IS RIPE. THERE IS NO MOTION	....	222	FOREST PICTURE	5
RIPENS				
MIXES, RIPENS, IN THE LOAM;	....	71	TAKE NEEDLES	26
THAT RIPENS AS WE DEVELOP	....	230	OUR SANCTITY	2
RIPPED				
MAN'S MARROW BARBED, AND BREAST RIPPED WITH A STEEL,		64	WOMAN SPEAKS	30
RIPPLED				
THROUGH THE RIPPLED DRUM OF THE HAIR-BURIED EAR;		157	INTO HER HEAD	4
THE RIPPLED SEALS STREAK DOWN	....	209	POEM ON B'DAY	34
AND BLUE-TIPPED BIRDS HAVE RIPPLED IT,	....	224	IDYLL UNFORGET	22
RIPPLE-WOVEN				
FELT THEIR SERENITY OF RIPPLE-WOVEN LOVELINESS;	...	223	IDYLL UNFORGET	4
RIPPLING				
RIPPLING IN TWELVE-WINDED CIRCLES,	....	175	FIRE RAID	64
OR RIPPLING SOFT IN THE SPINNEY MOON AS THE SILK		204	GIANT'S THIGH	27
RISE				
OUR BOAT IS MADE TO RISE	....	14	RAIN CUTS	32
READY TO RISE, EASY TO SLEEP.	....	23	THE ONLY DEAD	6
FOLLOWING THE NOSE DOWN DELL, UP RISE	....	44	TO FOLLOW FOX	7
THOUGH THEY SINK THROUGH THE SEA THEY SHALL RISE AGAIN;	....	49	NO DOMINION	7
WE SEE RISE THE SECRET WIND	....	69	SECRET WIND	T
WE SEE RISE THE SECRET WIND BEHIND THE BRAIN,	.....	69	SECRET WIND	1
WE HEAR RISE THE SECRET WIND BEHIND THE BRAIN,	....	70	SECRET WIND	19
RISE OF THE SKELETON AND	....	103	I DREAMED MY	22
THE RINGED-SEA GHOST, RISE GRIMLY FROM THE WRACK.		113	NOT FATHER ME	24
RISE BEFORE DARK.	....	115	A GRIEF AGO	32
BEACH, HEARING RISE SLIMY FROM THE WELSH LECHERED		179	NEW QUAY	16
SNIFF, HERE IS SIN! NOW HE MUST GRAPPLE, RISE:	....	179	NEW QUAY	29
THE STAR RISE AT PASTURE AND NIGHTLONG THE FABLES GRAZE	....	198	COUNTRY SLEEP	34
THEN WILL WE RISE	....	231	OUR SANCTITY	32
FEEL YOUR WOMAN'S BREASTS RISE UP LIKE FLOWERS	....	238	MAKES INTERVALS	12
RISEN				
TOO LONG, SKELETON, DEATH'S RISEN	....	29	LONG, SKELETON	1
WEEPS LIKE THE RISEN SUN AMONG	....	167	LONG-LEGGED	163

	PAGE	TITLE	LINE
RISES			
THAT RISES AND THEN FALLS, BUDS BUT TO WITHER;	25	THERE'S PLENTY	3
BEFORE CIVILIZATION RISES OR ROTS, ...	39	GAS FADES	9
OF FIELDS. FOR LOVE, THE LONG AGO SHE BIRD RISES.			
LOOK.	189	WINTER'S TALE	80
RISING			
BETWEEN THE RISING AND THE FALLING	15	FOR LEDA	20
TIME, IN A RIDER RISING, FROM THE HARNESSED VALLEY;	122	HOLD HARD	21
IN THE MOON THAT IS ALWAYS RISING, ...	196	FERN HILL	48
RISING ON BLACK WINGS.	229	MY RIVER	33
WHITE WITH THE RISING WATER.	233	NO THOUGHT	19
RISK			
AND THOUGH DOUBTFUL OF BISCUIT, I'M WILLING TO RISK			
IT, ...	221	SONG OF DOG	11
RITE			
THE RITE OF LIGHT, ...	114	SERVANT SUN	16
FLYING. THE RITE IS SHORN	191	WINTER'S TALE	116
RIVALS			
INTRICATE MANHOOD OF ENDING, THE INVALID RIVALS,	109	I, IN IMAGE	31
RIVEN			
SINCE THE FIRST FLESH OF MAN WAS RIVEN	64	WOMAN SPEAKS	28
MAN OF MY FLESH, THE JAWBONE RIVEN, ...	106	ALL ALL AND	19
AND STAVED, AND RIVEN AMONG PLUMES MY RIDER WEEP.	198	COUNTRY SLEEP	16
RIVER			
MOON WALKS THE RIVER AND RAISES THE DEAD;	74	SUN BURNS	2
AND RAN A RIVER	86	SEE, SAYS LIME	28
A SEPARATE RIVER BREATHES AND RUNS;	168	LONG-LEGGED	180
THESE WERE THE WOODS THE RIVER AND SEA	178	POEM IN OCT	53
DOWN TO THE RIVER ROOTING PLAIN	184	VISION, PRAYER	151
IN THE RIVER WENDED VALES WHERE THE TALE WAS TOLD.	187	WINTER'S TALE	10
AND THE LAKES AND FLOATING FIELDS AND THE RIVER			
WENDED	190	WINTER'S TALE	108
IN THE RIVER TOWY BELOW BOWS HIS TILTED HEADSTONE.	201	SIR JOHNS HILL	12
WEAR-WILLOW RIVER, GRAVE, ...	203	SIR JOHNS HILL	58
BY FULL TILT RIVER AND SWITCHBACK SEA	208	POEM ON B'DAY	2
MY RIVER	228	MY RIVER	T
MY RIVER, EVEN THOUGH IT LIFTS	228	MY RIVER	1
OR THE VOICE OF THE RIVER	229	MY RIVER	37
MY RIVER CANNOT RUB YOUR BRIGHT STONE, ...	230	MY RIVER	41
MY RIVER HAS HIGH WAVES, ...	230	MY RIVER	44
RIVERS			
WHO FOLLOW THE RED RIVERS, HOLLOW	54	WE BY SEASAND	3
AND THEIR RIVERS OF BLOOD TURNED TO ICE.	68	REALM OF FLESH	16
AND RIVERS OF THE DEAD AROUND MY NECK.	120	ALTARWISE	126
THE RIVERS MOUTHED IN NIGHT, ...	188	WINTER'S TALE	46
DOWN THE RIVERS OF THE WINDFALL LIGHT.	195	FERN HILL	9
THROUGH THROATS WHERE MANY RIVERS MEET, THE CURLEWS			
CRY, ...	203	GIANT'S THIGH	1
THROUGH THROATS WHERE MANY RIVERS MEET, THE WOMEN			
PRAY, ...	203	GIANT'S THIGH	6
NOON, AND NIGHT, AND LIGHT. THE RIVERS OF THE DEAD	216	ELEGY	15
RIVER'S			
THE LIVELONG RIVER'S ROBE	209	POEM ON B'DAY	28
ROAD			
THE MIDNIGHT ROAD	36	MIDNIGHT ROAD	T
THE MIDNIGHT ROAD, THOUGH YOUNG MEN TREAD UNKNOWING,	36	MIDNIGHT ROAD	1
OVER A ROAD THICK WITH THE BONES OF WORDS.	44	TO FOLLOW FOX	17
HIGH TIDE AND THE HERON DIVED WHEN I TOOK THE ROAD	177	POEM IN OCT	17
ROADS			
RIDE IN THEIR CHARABANCS ON ROADS	37	WINDMILLS TURN	13

	PAGE	TITLE	LINE
ROADS (CONTINUED)			
OF NEOPHYTES TAKE ALTERED ROADS.	37	WINDMILLS TURN	33
ALL REASON BROKE, AND HORROR WALKED THE ROADS.	51	OUT OF THE PIT	18
ROADSIDE			
CLOUD AND THE ROADSIDE BUSHES BRIMMING WITH WHISTLING	177	POEM IN OCT	22
ROAR			
AND LOVE AND HIS PATIENTS ROAR ON A CHAIN;	161	WEDDING ANNIV	6
TO ROAR ON THE ROCKERY STONES	172	THE HUNCHBACK	29
ROARED			
ROARED, SEA BORN, MAN TORN, BLOOD BLEST.	4	PROLOGUE	41
AND MY IMAGES ROARED AND ROSE ON HEAVEN'S HILL. ...	112	I, IN IMAGE	108
ROARER			
WINDS, FROM THE DOUSING SHADE AND THE ROARER AT THE			
LATCH, ...	199	COUNTRY SLEEP	46
ROARER'S			
GRISTLE AND RIND, AND A ROARER'S LIFE, ...	207	LAMENT	46
ROARING			
ROARING, CRAWLING, QUARREL	134	HOW MY ANIMAL	8
AND A BLACK REWARD FOR A ROARING LIFE, ...	207	LAMENT	50
ROARS			
ONE. THE SUN ROARS AT THE PRAYER'S END.	185	VISION, PRAYER	204
ROASTING			
IN THE COURTERS' LANES, OR TWINED IN THE OX ROASTING			
SUN	203	GIANT'S THIGH	13
ROB			
BUT THE HOT BEAMS ROB ME OF SPEECH, ...	42	A WAR OF WITS	14
TO ROB ME OF MY FLUIDS IN HIS HEART.	98	TWILIGHT LOCKS	36
ROBBED			
THE CITIES HAVE NOT ROBBED OUR EYES.	70	SECRET WIND	24
ROBBED OF THE FOXY TONGUE, HIS FOOTED TAPE	100	RUNNING GRAVE	9
LIE DRY, REST ROBBED, MY BEAST.	135	HOW MY ANIMAL	42
ROBBERS			
BEGGARS, ROBBERS, INVEIGLERS, ...	155	RETURN	52
ROBE			
THE LIVELONG RIVER'S ROBE	209	POEM ON B'DAY	28
ROBED			
ROBED IN THE LONG FRIENDS, ...	192	REFUSAL MOURN	20
ROBES			
THE WINTER'S ROBES;	82	LIGHT BREAKS	23
ROBIN			
HER ROBIN BREASTED TREE, THREE MARYS IN THE RAYS.	198	COUNTRY SLEEP	29
ROC			
AND THE WINGS OF THE GREAT ROC RIBBONED FOR THE FAIR!	199	COUNTRY SLEEP	65
ROCK			
CUT THEM IN ROCK, ...	19	IMAGES IN AIR	9
THE STRATA OF THE SHORE AND DROWN RED ROCK;	54	WE BY SEASAND	20
CAN WE FEND OFF ROCK ARRIVAL, ...	54	WE BY SEASAND	22
BURST IN THE ROOTS, PUMPED FROM THE EARTH AND ROCK	94	IN BEGINNING	17
OVER THE SEA-GUT LOUDENING, SETS A ROCK ALIVE;	122	HOLD HARD	15
CALLS THE GREEN ROCK OF LIGHT.	128	MY NEOPHYTE	12
WEIGHED IN ROCK SHROUD, IS MY PROUD PYRAMID;	132	I MAKE THIS IN	41
THE UNWINDING, SONG BY ROCK, ...	141	SAINT TO FALL	5
THE FLASHING NEEDLE ROCK OF SQUATTERS, ...	151	BELOW A TIME	26
ROCK	184	VISION, PRAYER	144
PARISH OF SNOW. THE CARVED MOUTHS IN THE ROCK ARE			
WIND SWEPT STRINGS.	189	WINTER'S TALE	64
THE CARVED LIMBS IN THE ROCK	189	WINTER'S TALE	76
YOUR ROCK OF SOUND.	239	MAKES INTERVALS	30
ROCKBIRDS'			
SO SHALL WINGED HARBOURS THROUGH THE ROCKBIRDS' EYES	121	ALTARWISE	130

	PAGE	TITLE	LINE
ROCK-CHESTED			
OR SPRAY-BASED AND ROCK-CHESTED SEA:	145	PLEASURE-BIRD	24
ROCKED			
CHIMES OF THE ROCKED BUOYS.	163	LONG-LEGGED	36
FOR ME ALONE BUT ONLY A ROCKED DRUM	175	MY BEGGAR ARM	3
HIS MOUTH AND ROCKED HIM LIKE A STORM	181	VISION, PRAYER	44
ROCKERY			
PAST LAKE AND ROCKERY	171	THE HUNCHBACK	19
TO ROAR ON THE ROCKERY STONES	172	THE HUNCHBACK	29
ROCKET			
A SHOUT WENT UP TO HEAVEN LIKE A ROCKET,	70	SECRET WIND	7
ROCKETED			
I ROCKETED TO ASTONISH	151	BELOW A TIME	25
ROCKETING			
WHO KNOWS THE ROCKETING WIND WILL BLOW	210	POEM ON B'DAY	67
ROCKING			
BEFORE THE WORLD STEADIES, STOPS ROCKING, IS STEADY,	39	GAS FADES	33
STRIP TO THIS TREE: A ROCKING ALPHABET,	119	ALTARWISE	87
SHALL I, STRUCK ON THE HOT AND ROCKING STREET,	145	PLEASURE-BIRD	16
ROCKS			
ON A BREAKNECK OF ROCKS	3	PROLOGUE	5
OR ROCKS, SWINGS AND ROCKS, BEFORE THE WORLD TOTTERS.	39	GAS FADES	34
OR ROCKS, SWINGS AND ROCKS, BEFORE THE WORLD TOTTERS.	39	GAS FADES	34
THE FORCE THAT DRIVES THE WATER THROUGH THE ROCKS	77	THE FORCE THAT	6
UNDER THE BELL OF ROCKS,	128	MY NEOPHYTE	3
IN THE MOLESTED ROCKS THE SHELL OF VIRGINS,	131	I MAKE THIS IN	18
UNCLENCHED, ARMLESS, SILK AND ROUGH LOVE THAT BREAKS ALL ROCKS.	154	WAS A SAVIOUR	40
ROD			
OF ROD AND WHEEL THAT WAKE THE DEAD.	70	SECRET WIND	12
THUNDER'S ROD OR MAN'S MACHINE;	71	TAKE NEEDLES	23
SPOUT TO THE ROD	82	LIGHT BREAKS	17
WAS WHO WAS FOLDED ON THE ROD THE AARON	115	A GRIEF AGO	13
NOW CAST DOWN YOUR ROD, FOR THE WHOLE	162	LONG-LEGGED	31
GOOD LUCK TO THE HAND ON THE ROD,	164	LONG-LEGGED	61
THE ROD BENDS LOW, DIVINING LAND,	167	LONG-LEGGED	165
(SIGHED THE OLD RAM ROD, DYING OF WOMEN),	206	LAMENT	3
(SIGHED THE OLD RAM ROD, DYING OF BITCHES),	206	LAMENT	15
(SIGHED THE OLD RAM ROD, DYING OF WELCOME),	206	LAMENT	27
(SIGHED THE OLD RAM ROD, DYING OF DOWNFALL),	207	LAMENT	39
(SIGHED THE OLD RAM ROD, DYING OF STRANGERS),	207	LAMENT	51
THE ROD CAN LIFT ITS TWINING HEAD	240	TWINING HEAD	T
THE ROD CAN LIFT ITS TWINING HEAD	240	TWINING HEAD	1
WHO LETS HIS OWN ROD BE	240	TWINING HEAD	6
RODE			
RODE AND WHISTLED A HUNDRED TIMES	157	INTO HER HEAD	18
WHERE THE ANCHOR RODE LIKE A GULL	163	LONG-LEGGED	37
AND OVER THE CLOTH OF COUNTIES THE FAR HILLS RODE NEAR,	190	WINTER'S TALE	93
AS I RODE TO SLEEP THE OWLS WERE BEARING THE FARM AWAY,	195	FERN HILL	24
RODS			
OUR RODS AND SUBSTANTIAL CENTRES,	230	OUR SANCTITY	3
ROE			
THROUGH SALT AND ROOT AND ROE.	90	WHERE ONCE THE	6
ROISTER			
THEIR BREAST, THE VAULTING DOES ROISTER, THE HORNED BUCKS CLIMB	204	GIANT'S THIGH	33
ROLL			
ROLL UNMANLY OVER THIS TURNING TUFT,	123	FOSTER LIGHT	19

	PAGE	TITLE	LINE
ROLL (CONTINUED)			
AND ROLL WITH THE KNOCKED EARTH:	135	HOW MY ANIMAL	41
ROLLED			
ROLLED DOWN ALL IMAGES INTO THE PITS	50	OUT OF THE PIT	3
I SKIPPED IN A BLUSH AS THE BIG GIRLS ROLLED	206	LAMENT	6
ROLLING			
THE LAKE'S VOICE AND THE ROLLING OF MOCK WAVES	46	POET: 1935	4
LIFE ROSE AND SPOUTED FROM THE ROLLING SEAS, ...	94	IN BEGINNING	16
A SPRINGFUL OF LARKS IN A ROLLING	177	POEM IN OCT	21
ROLLS			
AND SLEEP ROLLS MUTE ABOVE THE BEDS	98	TWILIGHT LOCKS	28
ROMANTIC			
I, POOR ROMANTIC, HELD HER HEEL	11	CABARET	1
I, POOR ROMANTIC, CONTEMPLATE	12	CABARET	22
ROME			
O ROME AND SODOM TO-MORROW AND LONDON	168	LONG-LEGGED	191
ROOD			
RUIN, THE ROOM OF ERRORS, ONE ROOD DROPPED	132	I MAKE THIS IN	39
ROOF			
TURNS TO THE ROOF A HIDEOUS GRIMACE, ...	49	LIGHT, I KNOW	25
UNDER THE GREEN ROOF GRIEVES THE LIVING;	56	GREEK PLAY	2
NOR ROOF OF SAND, NOR YET THE TOWERING TILER?	112	NOT FATHER ME	16
TILL FIELD AND ROOF LIE LEVEL AND THE SAME	116	LANTERNS SHINE	13
WITH RAVENS BEATING ON THE ROOF:	237	PILLAR BREAKS	13
ROOFED			
ROOFED WITH THE SKY AND PATTERNED WITH BLOND BONES;	64	WOMAN SPEAKS	25
PAST THE STATUES OF THE STABLES AND THE SKY ROOFED			
STIES	188	WINTER'S TALE	34
ROOFS			
BRANCH AND LEAF THE BIRDLESS ROOFS;	156	RETURN	83
ROOFTOPS			
SHALL A WHITE ANSWER ECHO FROM THE ROOFTOPS.	56	WHY EAST WIND	15
ROOING			
COO ROOING THE WOODS' PRAISE, ...	4	PROLOGUE	61
ROOK			
WITH WELSH AND REVERENT ROOK, ...	4	PROLOGUE	60
WITH WATER PRAYING AND CALL OF SEAGULL AND ROOK ...	177	POEM IN OCT	6
ROOKING			
A ROOKING GIRL WHO STOLE ME FOR HER SIDE, ...	94	RUB OF LOVE	2
ROOKS			
FOR FEAR OF WAKING THE ROOKS, ...	31	BEING BUT MEN	3
CATCH THE ROOKS SLEEPING, AND BREAK NO TWIG, ...	31	BEING BUT MEN	7
NO DOUBT THE WIND ON WHICH THE ROOKS	37	WINDMILLS TURN	4
HEELED WINDS THE ROOKS	199	COUNTRY SLEEP	67
LEAPING! THE GOSPEL ROOKS! ALL TELL, THIS NIGHT, OF			
HIM	200	COUNTRY SLEEP	80
ROOM			
IN A HOLY ROOM IN A WAVE;	130	SINNERS' BELL	27
RUIN, THE ROOM OF ERRORS, ONE ROOD DROPPED	132	I MAKE THIS IN	39
IN A ROOM WITH A STUFFED FOX AND A STALE FERN, ...	136	AFTER FUNERAL	11
IS CARVED FROM HER IN A ROOM WITH A WET WINDOW	136	AFTER FUNERAL	29
TO THE ROOM OF A SECRET CHILD, ...	139	TOMBSTONE TOLD	15
WHO WRITES THESE WORDS I WRITE IN A STILL ROOM IN A			
SPELLSOAKED HOUSE:	141	I, FIRST NAMED	2
FROM AN ODD ROOM IN A SPLIT HOUSE STARE, ...	142	SAINT TO FALL	31
STRIKE LIGHT, AND BLOODY A LOUD ROOM.	145	IF HEAD HURT	10
WOUND THEIR ROOM WITH A MALE MOAN, ...	158	INTO HER HEAD	25
OUT OF THE ROOM THE WEIGHT OF HIS TROUBLE	166	LONG-LEGGED	142
TO SHARE MY ROOM IN THE HOUSE NOT RIGHT IN THE HEAD,	169	LOVE IN ASYLUM	2
YET SHE DELUDES WITH WALKING THE NIGHTMARISH ROOM,	169	LOVE IN ASYLUM	7

	PAGE	TITLE	LINE
ROOM (CONTINUED)			
IN THE NEXT ROOM	180	VISION, PRAYER	4
IN THE BIRTH BLOODY ROOM UNKNOWN	180	VISION, PRAYER	10
THE ONCE HOODED ROOM	181	VISION, PRAYER	47
TO THE BIRTH BLOODY ROOM	183	VISION, PRAYER	122
WHO CLIMBS TO HIS DYING LOVE IN HER HIGH ROOM,	193	CONVERS PRAYER	3
IN THE FIRE OF HIS CARE HIS LOVE IN THE HIGH ROOM.	194	CONVERS PRAYER	16
TIDY AND CURSED IN MY DOVE COOED ROOM	207	LAMENT	52
AND THE RHYMER IN THE LONG TONGUED ROOM,	209	POEM ON B'DAY	15
I PRAYED IN THE CROUCHING ROOM, BY HIS BLIND BED,	216	ELEGY	13
ROOMS			
THAT CLOUTS THE SPITTLE LIKE BUBBLES WITH BROKEN POOMS,	144	PLEASURE-BIRD	6
ROOSTS			
ROOSTS SLEEPING CHILL TILL THE FLAME OF THE COCK CROW	187	WINTER'S TALE	19
ROOT			
MOTHER ROOT THAT SHOT ME FORTH,	72	TAKE NEEDLES	41
QUESTION: SHALL THE ROOT BE TRUE	72	TAKE NEEDLES	57
AND THE GREEN TREE TRUST THE ROOT?	72	TAKE NEEDLES	58
THE ROOT OF TONGUES ENDS IN A SPENTOUT CANCER,	79	LOVE'S FEVER	37
BORN OF THE SENSUAL ROOT AND SAP;	86	BREAD I BREAK	14
THROUGH SALT AND ROOT AND ROE.	90	WHERE ONCE THE	6
MY MAN OF LEAVES AND THE BRONZE ROOT, MORTAL, UNMORTAL,	109	I, IN IMAGE	16
GENESIS IN THE ROOT, THE SCARECROW WORD,	119	ALTARWISE	88
THE CAULDRON'S ROOT THROUGH THIS ONCE-RINDLESS HAND	132	I MAKE THIS IN	55
ROUNDS TO LOOK AT THE RED, WAGGED ROOT.	144	PLEASURE-BIRD	12
NOT GIRL FOR BIRD (GOURD BEING MAN) BREAKS ROOT.	159	TO LEDA	4
GROWING LIKE A POWERFUL ROOT INSIDE ME.	236	WOMAN TAPESTRY	67
ROOT-DAM			
QUESTION: WHEN SHALL ROOT-DAM DIE?	72	TAKE NEEDLES	61
QUESTION: WHEN SHALL ROOT-DAM GROW?	72	TAKE NEEDLES	63
ROOTED			
TIME BY, THEIR DUST WAS FLESH THE SWINEHERD ROOTED SLY,	204	GIANT'S THIGH	21
ROOTING			
ONE BOUGH OF BONE ACROSS THE ROOTING AIR,	93	IN BEGINNING	3
DOWN TO THE RIVER ROOTING PLAIN	184	VISION, PRAYER	151
NOR THE INNOCENT LIE IN THE ROOTING DINGLE WOOED	198	COUNTRY SLEEP	15
ROOTS			
THAT, LIKE A TREE, HAS ROOTS IN YOU,	9	MINUTE'S HOUR	3
TEAR BY THE ROOTS THESE TWIN GROWTHS IN YOUR GUT;	60	FAIRY TALES	36
DRIVES MY GREEN AGE; THAT BLASTS THE ROOTS OF TREES	77	THE FORCE THAT	2
LIKE SENNA STIRS ALONG THE RAVAGED ROOTS.	80	ALL THAT I OWE	4
BURST IN THE ROOTS, PUMPED FROM THE EARTH AND ROCK	94	IN BEGINNING	17
SOME OF THE OAKEN VOICES, FROM THE ROOTS	99	OCTOBER WIND	14
CASTS TO THE PINE ROOTS, RAISING MAN LIKE A MOUNTAIN	109	I, IN IMAGE	11
ARE BUT THE ROOTS OF NETTLES AND OF FEATHERS	117	ALTARWISE	26
THE LOFTY ROOTS OF THE CLOUDS.	142	SAINT TO FALL	30
MARROW OF EAGLES, THE ROOTS OF WHALES	210	POEM ON B'DAY	58
THROUGH HIS UNSEEING EYES TO THE ROOTS OF THE SEA.	217	ELEGY	17
OF OUR ROOTS,	230	OUR SANCTITY	7
BEAUTIFUL ROOTS	230	OUR SANCTITY	8
TO SAW THROUGH YOUR ROOTS	231	OUR SANCTITY	30
AND THE ROOTS OF THE TREES CLIMBED THROUGH THE AIR	235	WOMAN TAPESTRY	31
ROPE			
AND THE MAN NO ROPE CAN HANG	61	MEAT ON BONES	26
ROPED			
OR RENT ANCESTRALLY THE ROPED SEA-HYMEN,	131	I MAKE THIS IN	12

	PAGE	TITLE	LINE
ROPE-DANCING			
GLIDING, ROPE-DANCING, IS HIS FANCY, ...	28	NO WINGS	8
ROPES			
STIRS THE QUICKSAND; THAT ROPES THE BLOWING WIND	77	THE FORCE THAT	12
HER ROPES OF HERITAGE, THE WARS OF PARDON, ...	115	A GRIEF AGO	21
SOONER DROP WITH THE WORM OF THE ROPES ROUND MY			
THROAT	145	IF HEAD HURT	4
ROSE			
ROSE IN OUR OUTWORN BRAINS. WE SPOKE OUR LINES, ...	34	IN GARDENS	11
AND THERE WAS THUNDER IN AN OPENING ROSE.	51	OUT OF THE PIT	17
BUT NO GOD ROSE. I HAVE SEEN BAD AND WORSE, ...	52	OUT OF THE PIT	77
THEN HANG A RAM ROSE OVER THE RAGS.	60	MEAT ON BONES	8
AND PUT BESIDE HER A RAM ROSE.	61	MEAT ON BONES	24
CUT MY FINGERS ON A ROSE, ...	70	TAKE NEEDLES	6
AND I AM DUMB TO TELL THE CROOKED ROSE	77	THE FORCE THAT	4
REMEMBER THIS: EACH ROSE IS WORMY, ...	84	LETTER TO AUNT	48
LIFE ROSE AND SPOUTED FROM THE ROLLING SEAS, ...	94	IN BEGINNING	16
I, IN MY FUSION OF ROSE AND MALE MOTION, ...	109	I, IN IMAGE	17
UP ROSE THE ABRAHAM-MAN, MAD FOR MY SAKE, ...	112	NOT FATHER ME	19
AND MY IMAGES ROARED AND ROSE ON HEAVEN'S HILL. ...	112	I, IN IMAGE	108
ROSE MAID AND MALE, ...	114	A GRIEF AGO	6
ROSE CAST TO PLAGUE, ...	115	A GRIEF AGO	14
ROSE MY BYZANTINE ADAM IN THE NIGHT.	118	ALTARWISE	62
ON ROSE AND ICICLE THE RINGING HANDPRINT.	120	ALTARWISE	98
AND WHEN THE MOON ROSE WINDILY IT WAS	121	INCARNATE DEVL	11
ROSE AND CROWED AND FELL!	163	LONG-LEGGED	60
FOR THE CRAB-BACKED DEAD ON THE SEA-BED ROSE	165	LONG-LEGGED	99
AND I ROSE	177	POEM IN OCT	14
A SHE BIRD ROSE AND RAYED LIKE A BURNING BRIDE. ...	189	WINTER'S TALE	69
AND SHE ROSE WITH HIM FLOWERING IN HER MELTING SNOW.	191	WINTER'S TALE	130
MY GIRL RANGING THE NIGHT IN THE ROSE AND SHIRE ...	197	COUNTRY SLEEP	9
THERE SHOULD BE NIGHT FOR EVER, AND NO ROSE, ...	223	IN DREAMS	10
OF PETALS FROM SOME MAGIC ROSE;	225	CLOWN IN MOON	2
ROSE-			
FADE WITH THEIR ROSE-	215	COUNTRY HEAVEN	20
ROSY			
TO EAT YOUR HEART IN THE HOUSE IN THE ROSY WOOD.	197	COUNTRY SLEEP	7
UNDER THE PRAYER WHEELING MOON IN THE ROSY WOOD ...	198	COUNTRY SLEEP	41
ROT			
TIME ENOUGH TO ROT	16	TIME TO ROT	T
TIME ENOUGH TO ROT;	16	TIME TO ROT	1
GONE NOW TO ROT.	26	PERSONAL EPIT	16
BURN OUT THE LASTING ROT, ...	60	FAIRY TALES	39
ROTATING			
THROUGH THE ROTATING SHELL, STRONG	102	I DREAMED MY	2
ROTATING HALVES ARE HORNING AS THEY DRILL	104	WORLD PYRAMID	23
THE GROOVED LAND ROTATING, THAT THE STYLUS OF			
LIGHTNING	110	I, IN IMAGE	68
ROTS			
KNOWS HIS LOVE ROTS.	20	THE NEOPHYTE	12
BEFORE CIVILIZATION RISES OR ROTS, ...	39	GAS FADES	9
ROTTEN			
HE, TOO, HAS SEEN THE WORLD AS BOTTOM ROTTEN, ...	52	OUT OF THE PIT	56
WINDILY MASTER OF MAN WAS THE ROTTEN FATHOM, ...	112	I, IN IMAGE	104
CLAW FOLD AND HOLE FOR THE ROTTEN	152	BELOW A TIME	33
ROUGH			
ON GOD'S ROUGH TUMBLING GROUNDS	5	PROLOGUE	75
LEAN TIME ON TIDE AND TIMES THE WIND STOOD ROUGH,	107	GRIEF THIEF	6
BULLIES INTO ROUGH SEAS YOU SO GENTLE	142	SAINT TO FALL	49

	PAGE	TITLE	LINE
ROUGH (CONTINUED)			
UNCLENCHED, ARMLESS, SILK AND ROUGH LOVE THAT BREAKS			
ALL ROCKS. ••	154	WAS A SAVIOUR	40
PETTICOATS GALED HIGH, OR SHY WITH THE ROUGH RIDING			
BOYS, •••	204	GIANT'S THIGH	18
ROUGH AS COWS' TONGUES AND THRASHED WITH BRAMBLES			
THEIR BUTTERMILK ••••••••••••••••••••••••••••••	204	GIANT'S THIGH	25
ROUGHLY			
LOPING AND BLEATING ROUGHLY AND BLITHELY SHALL LEAP,	197	COUNTRY SLEEP	4
ROUND			
THAT CLUSTERED ROUND HER SHOULDERS, ••••••••••••••	15	FOR LEDA	26
OVER AND ROUND THE ORDERED GARDEN HUMMED, ••••••••	34	IN GARDENS	17
THE CENTURY'S TRAP WILL HAVE SNAPPED ROUND YOUR			
MIDDLE, •••••••••••••••••••••••••••••••••••••••	38	GAS FADES	4
THIS LILY CRAWLING ROUND THE LOCAL PUBS? •••••••••	52	OUT OF THE PIT	50
THOUGH WHAT THE STARS ASK AS THEY ROUND ••••••••••	56	WHY EAST WIND	18
HOW TIME HAS TICKED A HEAVEN ROUND THE STARS. •••••	77	THE FORCE THAT	20
I ROUND THIS HERITAGE AS ROUNDS THE SUN ••••••••••	80	ALL THAT I OWE	13
I PUT ROUND RIBS THAT PACKED THEIR HEART, ••••••••	85	SEE, SAYS LIME	2
THERE ROUND ABOUT YOUR STONES THE SHADES •••••••••	91	WHERE ONCE THE	16
AND, BURNING CIPHERS ON THE ROUND OF SPACE, •••••••	93	IN BEGINNING	5
AND CURLING ROUND THE BUD THAT FORKS HER EYE. •••••	95	RUB OF LOVE	31
THE HARING SNAIL GO GIDDILY ROUND THE FLOWER, ••••	109	I, IN IMAGE	41
FROM POLE TO POLE LEAPT ROUND THE SNAIL-WAKED WORLD.	120	ALTARWISE	108
HAS SOWN A FLYING GARDEN ROUND THAT SEA-GHOST? ••••	121	ALTARWISE	136
BLIND IN THE COIL SCRAMS ROUND THE BLAZING OUTLINE,	124	TODAY, INSECT	11
ROUND THE PARCHED WORLDS OF WALES AND DROWNED EACH			
SUN •••	136	AFTER FUNERAL	15
HER FIST OF A FACE DIED CLENCHED ON A ROUND PAIN;	137	AFTER FUNERAL	34
WOMEN FIGURES ROUND MY CELL, •••••••••••••••••••••	138	O CHATTERTON	30
SOONER DROP WITH THE WORM OF THE ROPES ROUND MY			
THROAT •••	145	IF HEAD HURT	4
ROUND HER TRAILED WRIST FRESH WATER WEAVES, •••••••	168	LONG-LEGGED	177
MY LOVE AS A ROUND WAVE •••••••••••••••••••••••••	176	BREATH SHED	10
AND I MUST ENTER AGAIN THE ROUND ••••••••••••••••	191	REFUSAL MOURN	7
AND THE SUN GREW ROUND THAT VERY DAY. •••••••••••	196	FERN HILL	32
ROUND THE GRIEFS OF THE AGES, ••••••••••••••••••••	197	CRAFT OR ART	18
ROUND THE SUN, HE COMES TO MY LOVE LIKE THE DESIGNED			
SNOW, •••	200	COUNTRY SLEEP	96
AND THEIR FIREFLY HAIRPINS FLEW, AND THE RICKS RAN			
ROUND-- ••	205	GIANT'S THIGH	41
UNDER AND ROUND HIM GO •••••••••••••••••••••••••••	209	POEM ON B'DAY	10
ROUND IT SO SMOOTHLY, ••••••••••••••••••••••••••••	228	MY RIVER	4
ROUNDED			
ROUNDED MY GLOBE OF HERITAGE, JOURNEY •••••••••••	103	I DREAMED MY	11
WITH MOVING FISH AND ROUNDED STONES ••••••••••••••	168	LONG-LEGGED	178
ROUNDING			
SLOW ROUNDING OF FOUR SEASONS' COASTS, •••••••••••	58	HERE IN SPRING	6
ROUNDNESS			
WILL CHILL THE ROUNDNESS OF HIS CHEEKS, ••••••••••	17	IN OBLIVION	6
ROUNDS			
I ROUND THIS HERITAGE AS ROUNDS THE SUN ••••••••••	80	ALL THAT I OWE	13
NIGHT IN THE SOCKETS ROUNDS, ••••••••••••••••••••	82	LIGHT BREAKS	19
ROUNDS TO LOOK AT THE RED, WAGGED ROOT. •••••••••	144	PLEASURE-BIRD	12
ROUSED			
ROUSED IT TO FIRE; ••••••••••••••••••••••••••••••	85	SEE, SAYS LIME	4
ROUTES			
BY THOSE WHO PLANNED THE OBVIOUS ROUTES ••••••••••	37	WINDMILLS TURN	22
ROW			
THE YEAR-HEDGED ROW IS LAME WITH FLINT, •••••••••	129	MY NEOPHYTE	38

	PAGE	TITLE	LINE
ROW (CONTINUED)			
WHEN BLACK BIRDS DIED LIKE PRIESTS IN THE CLOAKED HEDGE ROW	190	WINTER'S TALE	92
ROWS			
THE WORDY SHAPES OF WOMEN, AND THE ROWS	98	OCTOBER WIND	11
RUB			
WHOSE FLAMING BLOOD SHALL RUB IT AT THE RIMS	87	PAIN BE MUSIC	8
IF I WERE TICKLED BY THE RUB OF LOVE	94	RUB OF LOVE	T
IF I WERE TICKLED BY THE RUB OF LOVE, ...	94	RUB OF LOVE	1
IF I WERE TICKLED BY THE LOVERS' RUB	95	RUB OF LOVE	22
AND THAT'S THE RUB, THE ONLY RUB THAT TICKLES.	96	RUB OF LOVE	36
AND THAT'S THE RUB, THE ONLY RUB THAT TICKLES.	96	RUB OF LOVE	36
AND WHAT'S THE RUB? DEATH'S FEATHER ON THE NERVE?	96	RUB OF LOVE	43
I WOULD BE TICKLED BY THE RUB THAT IS:	96	RUB OF LOVE	48
RUB OFF THE SCRAWL OF PRINTS ON	156	RETURN	81
OR RUB YOUR BRIGHT STONE.	228	MY RIVER	5
MY RIVER CANNOT RUB YOUR BRIGHT STONE, ...	230	MY RIVER	41
RUBBING			
FEET IN THE RUBBING DUST.	96	RUB OF LOVE	42
RUBBISH			
BURY ALL RUBBISH AND LOVE SIGNS	156	RETURN	90
LIKE THE MOON'S SEED, RUBBISH	193	SIDE OF TRUTH	26
RUDE			
MY NEST OF MERCIES IN THE RUDE, RED TREE.	121	ALTARWISE	140
THE RUDE OWL CRIED LIKE A TELLTALE TIT, ...	206	LAMENT	5
RUFFLED			
O MY RUFFLED RING DOVE	4	PROLOGUE	58
RUFFLING			
LOVE ME, NOT AS THE RUFFLING PIGEON	76	SONG: LOVE ME	9
RUIN			
RUIN AND REVOLUTION	34	IN GARDENS	14
AND THE RUIN OF THE SKY;	71	TAKE NEEDLES	35
I SEE THE BOYS OF SUMMER IN THEIR RUIN	91	BOYS OF SUMMER	1
I SEE YOU BOYS OF SUMMER IN YOUR RUIN.	93	BOYS OF SUMMER	49
HE LYING LOW WITH RUIN IN HIS EAR, ...	127	NOW, SAY NAY	20
LIKE AN APPROACHING WAVE I SPRAWL TO RUIN.	132	I MAKE THIS IN	38
RUIN, THE ROOM OF ERRORS, ONE ROOD DROPPED	132	I MAKE THIS IN	39
AND RUIN AND HIS CAUSES	186	HOLY SPRING	5
THE VOYAGE TO RUIN I MUST RUN, ...	211	POEM ON B'DAY	78
RUINED			
AND LUSTRELESS WITHIN THE RUINED FACE	63	WOMAN SPEAKS	9
RUINS			
AND THE SENSUAL RUINS MAKE	166	LONG-LEGGED	118
RULE			
RULE THE BLANK SHEET OF SLEEP, ...	66	LET A FAITH	2
YOU RULE THE THUDDING HEART THAT BITES THE SIDE;	67	REALM OF FLESH	7
RULED			
YOUR FAITH AS DEATHLESS AS THE OUTCRY OF THE RULED SUN.	201	COUNTRY SLEEP	111
RULER			
YOU ARE THE RULER OF THIS REALM OF FLESH	67	REALM OF FLESH	T
YOU ARE THE RULER OF THIS REALM OF FLESH, ...	67	REALM OF FLESH	1
WHY SHOULD I THINK ON DEATH WHEN YOU ARE RULER? ...	67	REALM OF FLESH	10
YOU ARE MY FLESH'S RULER WHOM I TREASON, ...	67	REALM OF FLESH	11
LEANS ON MY MORTAL RULER, ...	75	MY HERO BARES	4
RULES			
A HAND RULES PITY AS A HAND RULES HEAVEN;	66	HAND SIGNED	15
A HAND RULES PITY AS A HAND RULES HEAVEN;	66	HAND SIGNED	15
THAT RULES FROM WRIST TO SHOULDER, ...	75	MY HERO BARES	2

	PAGE	TITLE	LINE
RULY			
FLOWS TO THE STRAND OF FLOWERS LIKE THE DEW'S RULY			
SEA, ...	200	COUNTRY SLEEP	98
RUMBLING			
MANNA FOR THE RUMBLING GROUND, ...	125	SEED-AT-ZERO	17
RUMOUR			
OR LAY THE SENSES' RUMOUR.	30	NEARLY SUMMER	13
INFORMED BY RUMOUR AND THE REGISTER, ...	38	THE GOSSIPERS	7
THE GROWING BONES, THE RUMOUR OF MANSEED	78	LOVE'S FEVER	17
RUMOURS			
WILLING WORDS TO MAKE THE RUMOURS CERTAIN, ...	38	THE GOSSIPERS	2
RUMP			
OVER A RUMP ON THE CLERICAL-GREY SEASHORE, ...	179	NEW QUAY	25
RUMPUS			
THIS RUMPUS OF SHAPES	4	PROLOGUE	37
RUN			
(GOOD FOR CAN RUN	24	LITTLE PROBLEM	13
AND KNOW WHY RUN), ...	24	LITTLE PROBLEM	14
RUN AND KNOW WHY	24	LITTLE PROBLEM	19
NO USE TO RUN YOUR HEAD AGAINST THE WALL	27	OBLIVIOUS DARK	11
RUN DOWN THE WORLD'S GUTTERS, ...	39	GAS FADES	32
AND THE UNICORN EVILS RUN THEM THROUGH;	50	NO DOMINION	16
SHALL I RUN TO THE SHIPS	62	EARS IN TURRET	21
I'LL SHARE MY MONEY AND WE'LL RUN FOR JOY	149	PAPER & STICKS	14
OPENING AND THE DARK RUN	180	VISION, PRAYER	7
I SHALL RUN LOST IN SUDDEN	181	VISION, PRAYER	45
I WOULD TURN BACK AND RUN	185	VISION, PRAYER	191
WHEN COLD AS SNOW HE SHOULD RUN THE WENDED VALES			
AMONG	188	WINTER'S TALE	45
THE VOYAGE TO RUIN I MUST RUN, ...	211	POEM ON B'DAY	78
RUNAWAY			
AND HIS RUNAWAY BELOVED CHILDLIKE LAID IN THE			
ACORNED SAND.	157	INTO HER HEAD	23
RUNG			
EACH RUNG A LOVE OR LOSING TO THE LAST, ...	102	FELLOWED SLEEP	27
RUNG BONE AND BLADE, THE VERTICALS OF ADAM, ...	117	ALTARWISE	23
WE RUNG OUR WEATHERING CHANGES ON THE LADDER, ...	118	ALTARWISE	41
RUNNING			
ON HEAD AND RUNNING FOOT, ...	21	BEWILDERED WAY	21
WHEN, LIKE A RUNNING GRAVE	99	RUNNING GRAVE	T
WHEN, LIKE A RUNNING GRAVE, TIME TRACKS YOU DOWN,	99	RUNNING GRAVE	1
RUNNING WHEN HE HAD HEARD THEM CLEARLY	171	THE HUNCHBACK	17
ALL THE SUN LONG IT WAS RUNNING, IT WAS LOVELY, THE			
HAY	195	FERN HILL	19
RUNS			
THE FLICKERING RUNS AND DIVE	4	PROLOGUE	55
THIS PUS RUNS DEEP.	27	OBLIVIOUS DARK	13
NEW MAN BEST WHOSE BLOOD RUNS THICK, ...	29	LONG, SKELETON	11
UNFAILING TILL THE BLOOD RUNS FOUL;	69	BEFORE KNOCKED	28
WHERE NO SEA RUNS, THE WATERS OF THE HEART	82	LIGHT BREAKS	2
YOUR SPORT IS SUMMER AS THE SPRING RUNS ANGRILY.	123	HOLD HARD	24
A SEPARATE RIVER BREATHES AND RUNS;	168	LONG-LEGGED	180
RUSH			
BEFORE I RUSH IN A CROUCH THE GHOST WITH A HAMMER,			
AIR, ...	145	IF HEAD HURT	9
OF HIS SNOW BLIND LOVE AND RUSH IN THE WHITE LAIRS.	188	WINTER'S TALE	38
FLARED IN THE REEK OF THE WIVING STY WITH THE RUSH	204	GIANT'S THIGH	22
RUSHES			
TAIL, NILE, AND SNOUT, A SADDLER OF THE RUSHES, ...	111	I, IN IMAGE	98

	PAGE	TITLE	LINE
RUSHING			
TILL EVERY BONE IN THE RUSHING GRAVE	163	LONG-LEGGED	59
RUSHY			
SAFE BE AND SMOOTH FROM THE BELLOWS OF THE RUSHY BROOD.	198	COUNTRY SLEEP	20
RUST			
OF HEMLOCK AND THE BLADES, RUST	103	I DREAMED MY	18
WHERE THE HAY RIDES NOW OR THE BRACKEN KITCHENS RUST	205	GIANT'S THIGH	47
RUSTIC			
BELL BELIEVE OR FEAR THAT THE RUSTIC SHADE OR SPELL	198	COUNTRY SLEEP	22
RUSTICATING			
THE RUSTICATING MINUTES, ...	157	RETURN	98
RUSTS			
WHOM CANCER CROPS, WHOSE DRINKING RUSTS, THESE DIE;	64	WOMAN SPEAKS	43
RUSTY			
AGAINST THE RUSTY SWORD AND THE OLD HORSE	45	PLOUGHMAN GONE	8
RUT			
AND THE GREAT WHEELS' RUT;	59	FAIRY TALES	7
RUTTISH			
NOR THE TUSKED PRINCE, IN THE RUTTISH FARM, AT THE RIND	198	COUNTRY SLEEP	37
S.			
IN T. S. E. AND EZRA POUND.	83	LETTER TO AUNT	10
SABBATH			
AND HELD A LITTLE SABBATH WITH THE SUN, ...	97	TWILIGHT LOCKS	15
WINGED LIKE A SABBATH ASS THIS CHILDREN'S PIECE ...	124	TODAY, INSECT	16
AND THE SABBATH RANG SLOWLY	195	FERN HILL	17
SABBATHS			
OVER THE URN OF SABBATHS	175	FIRE RAID	66
SABLE			
OF MUD AND SAND. AND, LIKE A SABLE MOTH, ...	179	NEW QUAY	4
SABRE			
HALF A SMILE MIGHT BE HER SABRE.	71	TAKE NEEDLES	20
SACK			
THE DREAM THAT KICKS THE BURIED FROM THEIR SACK ...	90	EUNUCH DREAMS	34
WITH SWAG OF BUBBLES IN A SEEDY SACK	108	GRIEF THIEF	17
TO THE BAIT THAT STALKED OUT OF THE SACK, ...	162	LONG-LEGGED	20
SACKCLOTH			
IN THE LEAST VALLEY OF SACKCLOTH TO MOURN	191	REFUSAL MOURN	12
SACKED			
ALL THESE, HE SAID WHO SACKED THE CHILDREN'S TOWN,	112	NOT FATHER ME	18
SACRED			
IN SACRED WATERS THAT NO FROST COULD HARDEN, ...	122	INCARNATE DEVL	14
SAD			
AMONG ALL LIVING MEN IS A SAD GHOST.	47	POET: 1935	24
VOLES AT HIS ARMPITS, DOWN THE SAD CANAL	51	OUT OF THE PIT	40
FIRE AND JORDAN AND THE SAD CANAL.	53	OUT OF THE PIT	99
AND KNOWS NO WOE THAT THESE SAD PLAYERS MOUTH	57	GREEK PLAY	30
OF BIRTH AND DEATH, THE TWO SAD KNAVES OF THIEVES,	75	MY HERO BARES	18
UNDER THE SAD BREAST OF THE HEAD STONE	174	FIRE RAID	44
OPEN A PATHWAY THROUGH THE SLOW SAD SAIL, ...	194	SLEEP BECALMED	9
AND YOU, MY FATHER, THERE ON THE SAD HEIGHT, ...	208	NOT GO GENTLE	16
IT IS SO SAD AND BEAUTIFUL, ...	225	CLOWN IN MOON	7
TOUCH TO REMEMBER AND BE SAD.	233	NO THOUGHT	4
SADDEST			
THE SADDEST DUST IN ALL THIS HOLLOW WORLD.	64	WOMAN SPEAKS	41
SADDLE			
MAN TOILS NOW ON AN IRON SADDLE, RIDING	45	PLOUGHMAN GONE	24
SADDLER			
TAIL, NILE, AND SNOUT, A SADDLER OF THE RUSHES, ...	111	I, IN IMAGE	98

	PAGE	TITLE	LINE
SADLY			
WHY COUNT SO SADLY?	33	HELD-OUT HAND	6
SADNESS			
WITH IMMEASURABLE SADNESS.	235	WOMAN TAPESTRY	10
SAFE			
THERE WAS CALM TO BE DONE IN HIS SAFE UNREST,	153	WAS A SAVIOUR	11
FOR THE SLEEP IN A SAFE LAND AND THE LOVE WHO DIES	194	CONVERS PRAYER	10
SAFE BE AND SMOOTH FROM THE BELLOWS OF THE RUSHY BROOD.	198	COUNTRY SLEEP	20
SAFEST			
WHAT'S NEVER KNOWN IS SAFEST IN THIS LIFE.	40	WAS THERE TIME	6
SAGA			
THE LEAPING SAGA OF PRAYER! AND HIGH, THERE, ON THE HARE-	199	COUNTRY SLEEP	66
OF BLOOD! THE BIRD LOUD VEIN! THE SAGA FROM MERMEN	200	COUNTRY SLEEP	78
BUT HER FAITH THAT EACH VAST NIGHT AND THE SAGA OF PRAYER	201	COUNTRY SLEEP	102
SAGE			
SAGE ON THE EARTH AND SKY;	91	WHERE ONCE THE	21
SAGS			
BEHIND MY HEAD A SQUARE OF SKY SAGS OVER	134	NOT FROM ANGER	8
SAHARA			
VALLEY AND SAHARA IN A SHELL,	165	LONG-LEGGED	90
SAID			
WITH THAT HALF-MOULDED MIND I SAID WAS YOURS,	10	COOL, OH NO	4
I, SAID THE BEETLE, OUT OF MY THIN BLACK WOMB,	18	NATURAL DAY	26
THAT, THEN, IS LOVELINESS, WE SAID,	31	BEING BUT MEN	14
I'VE SAID MY PIECE: COUNT OR GO MAD.	33	HELD-OUT HAND	17
I'VE SAID MY PIECE.	33	HELD-OUT HAND	24
TO DIFFERENT PLACES THAN WERE SAID	37	WINDMILLS TURN	21
SAID ALL THE USUAL THINGS OVER AND AGAIN;	52	OUT OF THE PIT	71
FEELING THE PINPRICKS OF THE BLOOD, I'VE SAID	53	OUT OF THE PIT	80
SHALL GODS BE SAID TO THUMP THE CLOUDS	65	GODS THUMP	T
SHALL GODS BE SAID TO THUMP THE CLOUDS	65	GODS THUMP	1
BE SAID TO WEEP WHEN WEATHER HOWLS?	65	GODS THUMP	3
SHALL IT BE SAID THEY SPRINKLE WATER	65	GODS THUMP	6
SHALL IT BE SAID THAT, VENUSWISE,	65	GODS THUMP	8
IT SHALL BE SAID THAT GODS ARE STONE.	65	GODS THUMP	11
THE SYLLABLES BE SAID AND SAID AGAIN:	80	ALMANAC TIME	14
THE SYLLABLES BE SAID AND SAID AGAIN:	80	ALMANAC TIME	14
THE DEAD MAN SAID,	81	HERE LIE BEAST	2
THE DEAD MAN SAID,	81	HERE LIE BEAST	8
YOU ARE ALL THESE, SAID SHE WHO GAVE ME THE LONG SUCK,	112	NOT FATHER ME	17
ALL THESE, HE SAID WHO SACKED THE CHILDREN'S TOWN,	112	NOT FATHER ME	18
THEY SAID, WHO HACKED AND HUMOURED, THEY WERE MINE.	112	NOT FATHER ME	20
YOU ARE YOUR SISTERS' SIRE, SAID SEAWEEDY,	113	NOT FATHER ME	26
I AM THE LONG WORLD'S GENTLEMAN, HE SAID,	117	ALTARWISE	13
HAIRS OF YOUR HEAD, THEN SAID THE HOLLOW AGENT,	117	ALTARWISE	25
SAID THE ANTIPODES, AND TWICE SPRING CHIMED.	118	ALTARWISE	42
SAID THE FAKE GENTLEMAN IN SUIT OF SPADES,	118	ALTARWISE	60
PLUCK, COCK, MY SEA EYE, SAID MEDUSA'S SCRIPTURE,	119	ALTARWISE	75
LOP, LOVE, MY FORK TONGUE, SAID THE PIN-HILLED NETTLE;	119	ALTARWISE	76
'TIME SHALL NOT MURDER YOU,' HE SAID,	129	MY NEOPHYTE	44
AMONG MEN LATER I HEARD IT SAID	139	TOMBSTONE TOLD	16
LONDON (SAID THE ODD MAN IN	154	RETURN	2
SAID THE LOOKING LAND.	162	LONG-LEGGED	12
SAID THE DWINDLING SHIPS.	162	LONG-LEGGED	24
THE CONVERSATION OF PRAYERS ABOUT TO BE SAID	193	CONVERS PRAYER	1

	PAGE	TITLE	LINE
SAID (CONTINUED)			
THE SOUND ABOUT TO BE SAID IN THE TWO PRAYERS	194	CONVERS PRAYER	9
THE CONVERSATION OF PRAYERS ABOUT TO BE SAID	194	CONVERS PRAYER	13
TO THE SULTRY, BIDING HERDS, I SAID, ...	206	LAMENT	33
THAN EVER WAS SINCE THE WORLD WAS SAID, ...	211	POEM ON B'DAY	98
AND WHEN IT WAS SPRING I SAID, ...	227	SPRING-SPIRIT	1
SAIL			
WE SAIL A BOAT UPON THE PATH, ...	13	RAIN CUTS	6
UNDER THE RIBS SAIL THE MOON AND THE SUN;	74	SUN BURNS	11
HAULS MY SHROUD SAIL.	77	THE FORCE THAT	13
SAIL ON THE LEVEL, THE DEPARTING ADVENTURE, ...	109	I, IN IMAGE	35
FOR MY SAKE SAIL, AND NEVER LOOK BACK, ...	162	LONG-LEGGED	11
BREAK THE BLACK NEWS AND PAINT ON A SAIL	164	LONG-LEGGED	71
THE PALE BREATH OF CATTLE AT THE STEALTHY SAIL, ...	187	WINTER'S TALE	5
OPEN A PATHWAY THROUGH THE SLOW SAD SAIL, ...	194	SLEEP BECALMED	9
WHERE THE SEA COBBLES SAIL, ...	202	SIR JOHNS HILL	38
WHO HEARD THE TALL BELL SAIL DOWN THE SUNDAYS OF THE			
DEAD	205	GIANT'S THIGH	51
AS I SAIL OUT TO DIE.	211	POEM ON B'DAY	108
ON THE SAIL OF EACH SLIGHT WING	233	NO THOUGHT	18
SAILED			
SAILED UP THE SUN;	114	A GRIEF AGO	8
SAILED AND SET DAZZLING BY THE HANDSHAPED OCEAN,	131	I MAKE THIS IN	5
IN THE FOUNTAIN BASIN WHERE I SAILED MY SHIP	171	THE HUNCHBACK	10
SAILING			
TO CATCH HER SAILING DOWN THE STREAM--	14	FOR LEDA	4
MOONFALL AND SAILING EMPEROR, PALE AS THEIR			
TIDE-PRINT, ...	130	SINNERS' BELL	10
IN THAT PROUD SAILING TREE WITH BRANCHES DRIVEN ...	131	I MAKE THIS IN	6
AND THE KNOCK OF SAILING BOATS ON THE NET WEBBED WALL	177	POEM IN OCT	7
STONE FOR THE SAKE OF THE SOULS OF THE SLAIN BIRDS			
SAILING.	203	SIR JOHNS HILL	60
SAILOR			
AND WELCOME NO SAILOR?	62	EARS IN TURRET	24
SHALL I WELCOME THE SAILOR, ...	63	EARS IN TURRET	30
LET THE TALE'S SAILOR FROM A CHRISTIAN VOYAGE	121	ALTARWISE	127
SAILORS			
HAVE THEIR THIRSTY SAILORS HIDE HIM.	126	SEED-AT-ZERO	35
HAVE THEIR DRUNKEN SAILORS HIDE HIM.	126	SEED-AT-ZERO	42
AND OUT-OF-PERSPECTIVE SAILORS, ...	151	BELOW A TIME	14
AND THE GROVES WERE BLUE WITH SAILORS	172	THE HUNCHBACK	30
SAILS			
GULLS, PIPERS, COCKLES, AND SAILS, ...	3	PROLOGUE	11
ESCAPES TO THE FLAT CITIES' SAILS	129	MY NEOPHYTE	16
FROM BLANK AND LEAKING WINTER SAILS THE CHILD IN			
COLOUR, ...	130	SINNERS' BELL	22
SAILS DRANK THE WIND, AND WHITE AS MILK	162	LONG-LEGGED	13
AS THE SAILS DRANK UP THE HAIL OF THUNDER	166	LONG-LEGGED	127
LISTEN AND LOOK WHERE SHE SAILS THE GOOSE PLUCKED			
SEA, ...	190	WINTER'S TALE	100
AND SURELY HE SAILS LIKE THE SHIP SHAPE CLOUDS. OH HE	200	COUNTRY SLEEP	99
WHO SAILS ON TIDES OF LEAVES AND SOUND.	234	NO, PIGEON	16
SAILSHAPED			
WINDSHAKE OF SAILSHAPED EARS, MUFFLE-TOED TAP	136	AFTER FUNERAL	2
SAINT			
THE MOON PEERS DOWN THE VALLEY LIKE A SAINT.	53	OUT OF THE PIT	94
TIME'S CORAL SAINT AND THE SALT GRIEF DROWN A FOUL			
SEPULCHRE	130	SINNERS' BELL	8
WITH CARVED BIRD, SAINT, AND SUN, THE WRACKSPIKED			
MAIDEN MOUTH	135	HOW MY ANIMAL	37

		PAGE	TITLE	LINE
SAINT (CONTINUED)				
A SAINT ABOUT TO FALL	....	141	SAINT TO FALL	T
A SAINT ABOUT TO FALL,	....	141	SAINT TO FALL	1
SAINT CARVED AND SENSUAL AMONG THE SCUDDING	....	147	UNLUCKILY FOR	5
ABOUT THE SAINT IN SHADES WHILE THE ENDLESS BREVIARY		148	UNLUCKILY FOR	26
I SEE THE WANTING NUN SAINT CARVED IN A GARB	...»...	148	UNLUCKILY FOR	34
OF EELS, SAINT HERON HYMNING IN THE SHELL-HUNG				
DISTANT	....	202	SIR JOHNS HILL	36
SAINTS				
OF SAINTS TO THEIR VISION!	....	182	VISION, PRAYER	96
SAINT'S				
A HILL TOUCHES AN ANGEL. OUT OF A SAINT'S CELL	....	198	COUNTRY SLEEP	27
SAKE				
FOR A LAZY SAKE THAT WON'T CREATE	....	24	LITTLE PROBLEM	23
FOR MY TALL TOWER'S SAKE CAST IN HER STONE?	....	112	NOT FATHER ME	2
UP ROSE THE ABRAHAM-MAN, MAD FOR MY SAKE,	....	112	NOT FATHER ME	19
SHOULD HE, FOR CENTRE SAKE, HOP IN THE DUST,	......	127	NOW, SAY NAY	6
AND, FOR THAT MURDER'S SAKE, DARK WITH CONTAGION		132	I MAKE THIS IN	37
I STAND, FOR THIS MEMORIAL'S SAKE, ALONE	....	136	AFTER FUNERAL	12
FOR MY SAKE SAIL, AND NEVER LOOK BACK,	....	162	LONG-LEGGED	11
NIGHT FOR MY SAKE,	....	176	BREATH SHED	4
HER FAITH THAT THIS LAST NIGHT FOR HIS UNSACRED SAKE		201	COUNTRY SLEEP	104
STONE FOR THE SAKE OF THE SOULS OF THE SLAIN BIRDS				
SAILING.	....	203	SIR JOHNS HILL	60
SOFTLY, THOU RAIN--AND FOR HIS MOTHER'S SAKE,	.....	222	MISSING	7
SAKES				
JEALOUSY CANNOT FORGET FOR ALL HER SAKES,	....	158	INTO HER HEAD	34
SALMON				
IN THE TORRENT SALMON SUN,	....	3	PROLOGUE	3
SEAWARD THE SALMON, SUCKED SUN SLIPS,	....	3	PROLOGUE	34
SALT				
SOMETIMES A WOMAN'S HEART HAS SALT,	....	13	SKY'S BRIGHT	20
CARVED BIRDS BLUNT THEIR STRIKING THROATS ON THE				
SALT GRAVEL,	....	15	SPIRE CRANES	3
WHILE THE SUN'S TURNED TO SALT,	....	27	OBLIVIOUS DARK	23
ACQUAINTED WITH THE SALT ADVENTURE	....	69	BEFORE KNOCKED	33
THROUGH SALT AND ROOT AND ROE.	....	90	WHERE ONCE THE	6
BOLT FOR THE SALT UNBORN.	....	103	WORLD PYRAMID	6
WEEPS ON THE DESERT OCHRE AND THE SALT	....	104	WORLD PYRAMID	32
MY CLAY UNSUCKLED AND MY SALT UNBORN,	....	105	WORLD PYRAMID	58
HEAR THEY THE SALT GLASS BREAKERS AND THE TONGUES OF				
BURIAL.	....	110	I, IN IMAGE	66
THE SALT SUCKED DAM AND DARLINGS OF THE LAND	......	113	NOT FATHER ME	27
CROSS-STROKED SALT ADAM TO THE FROZEN ANGEL	....	119	ALTARWISE	67
THE FATS OF MIDNIGHT WHEN THE SALT WAS SINGING;	...	119	ALTARWISE	80
STRETCH THE SALT PHOTOGRAPHS,	....	129	MY NEOPHYTE	19
TIME'S CORAL SAINT AND THE SALT GRIEF DROWN A FOUL				
SEPULCHRE	....	130	SINNERS' BELL	8
THE SPITTLED EYES, THE SALT PONDS IN THE SLEEVES,		136	AFTER FUNERAL	5
THE SALT PERSON AND BLASTED PLACE	....	145	PLEASURE-BIRD	20
OR SOW MY SALT SEED	....	191	REFUSAL MOURN	11
THAT CAME FROM THE WOUND WRAPPED IN THE SALT SHEET.		194	SLEEP BECALMED	4
AND WHEN THE SALT SHEET BROKE IN A STORM OF SINGING		194	SLEEP BECALMED	7
WE HEARD THE SEA SOUND SING, WE SAW THE SALT SHEET				
TELL.	....	194	SLEEP BECALMED	12
FROM THE COUNTRY EYES, SALT AND SUN, STAR AND WOE		215	COUNTRY HEAVEN	13
SALT-EYED				
AND SALT-EYED STUMBLE BEDWARD WHERE SHE LIES	......	107	GRIEF THIEF	12
SALT-LIPPED				
FROM SALT-LIPPED BEAK TO THE KICK OF THE STERN	....	164	LONG-LEGGED	81

	PAGE	TITLE	LINE
SALTS			
MY BROTHERS' BLOOD THAT SALTS MY OPEN WOUNDS.	80	ALL THAT I OWE	8
SALTY			
HER SALTY LOVERS IN THE SEA.	76	SONG: LOVE ME	7
FOR THE SALTY BIRDS FLUTTERED AND FED	165	LONG-LEGGED	96
WITH SALTY COLTS AND GALES IN THEIR LIMBS	168	LONG-LEGGED	186
THE SALTY SCENE AND MY PLAYERED GOB CURVING	179	NEW QUAY	14
SALUTES			
FROM THE REPETITION OF SALUTES, ...	43	LONGED TO MOVE	7
SALUTING			
SALUTING THE BUSY BROTHERHOOD	70	SECRET WIND	11
SALVAGE			
HATCHED FROM THE WINDY SALVAGE ON ONE LEG, ...	117	ALTARWISE	10
SALVATION'S			
BLACK-TONGUED AND TIPSY FROM SALVATION'S BOTTLE.	118	ALTARWISE	61
SAME			
ALL SEASONS WITH THE SAME METICULOUS POWER, ...	17	IN OBLIVION	13
FEEL THE SAME SOFT BLOOD FLOW THOROUGHLY, ...	23	THE ONLY DEAD	11
THE SAME THOUGHTS IN OUR HEAD.	28	NO WINGS	19
THE SAME TUNE AS IN MY FATHER'S TIME:	46	PLOUGHMAN GONE	29
GOD IS THE SAME THOUGH HE BE PRAISED AS MANY, ...	67	LET A FAITH	9
MY YOUTH IS BENT BY THE SAME WINTRY FEVER.	77	THE FORCE THAT	5
HOW AT THE MOUNTAIN SPRING THE SAME MOUTH SUCKS.	77	THE FORCE THAT	10
HOW AT MY SHEET GOES THE SAME CROOKED WORM.	77	THE FORCE THAT	22
ALL NIGHT AND DAY I WANDER IN THESE SAME	81	ALL THAT I OWE	25
TILL FIELD AND ROOF LIE LEVEL AND THE SAME	116	LANTERNS SHINE	13
WILL BE THE SAME GRIEF FLYING. WHOM SHALL THEY CALM?	194	CONVERS PRAYER	11
SAMSON			
AND SAMSON DROWNED IN HIS HAIR, ...	157	INTO HER HEAD	13
LOOMS THE LAST SAMSON OF YOUR ZODIAC.	161	DEATHS AND ENT	36
SANATORIUM			
FROM NAPE TO TOE, A SANATORIUM PIECE	29	LONG, SKELETON	5
SANCTITY			
WE WILL BE CONSCIOUS OF OUR SANCTITY	230	OUR SANCTITY	T
WE WILL BE CONSCIOUS OF OUR SANCTITY	230	OUR SANCTITY	1
SANCTORUM			
SANCTUM SANCTORUM THE ANIMAL EYE OF THE WOOD	198	COUNTRY SLEEP	30
SANCTUM			
SANCTUM SANCTORUM THE ANIMAL EYE OF THE WOOD	198	COUNTRY SLEEP	30
SAND			
OR, FORMED OF SAND, ...	19	IMAGES IN AIR	5
FOR IN THIS YELLOW GRAVE OF SAND AND SEA	54	WE BY SEASAND	5
THE HEAVENLY MUSIC OVER THE SAND	54	WE BY SEASAND	14
RAIN BEATS THE SAND AND SLATES.	62	EARS IN TURRET	28
AND YELLOW WAS THE MULTIPLYING SAND, ...	78	LOVE'S FEVER	22
AND MOTHER MILK WAS STIFF AS SAND, ...	98	TWILIGHT LOCKS	32
NOR ROOF OF SAND, NOR YET THE TOWERING TILER?	112	NOT FATHER ME	16
DO YOU NOT FATHER ME ON THE DESTROYING SAND?	113	NOT FATHER ME	25
ON FIELD AND SAND	115	A GRIEF AGO	22
WORLD IN THE SAND, ON THE TRIANGLE LANDSCAPE, ...	120	ALTARWISE	124
AND HIS RUNAWAY BELOVED CHILDLIKE LAID IN THE ACORNED SAND.	157	INTO HER HEAD	23
TWO SAND GRAINS TOGETHER IN BED, ...	158	INTO HER HEAD	47
WHISPERED THE AFFECTIONATE SAND	162	LONG-LEGGED	9
SING AND HOWL THROUGH SAND AND ANEMONE	165	LONG-LEGGED	89
SAND WITH LEGENDS IN ITS VIRGIN LAPS	167	LONG-LEGGED	172
OF MUD AND SAND. AND, LIKE A SABLE MOTH, ...	179	NEW QUAY	4
GULL, ON THE WAVE WITH SAND IN ITS EYES! AND THE FOAL MOVES	200	COUNTRY SLEEP	83
AND I FORGOT THE DRIFTLESS FOAM, AND SAND, ...	227	SPRING-SPIRIT	9

	PAGE	TITLE	LINE
SAND (CONTINUED)			
STRONG ENOUGH TO TREAD ON THE SAND	229	MY RIVER	7
SANDAL			
HIS BEAST HEEL CLEFT IN A SANDAL, ...	130	SINNERS' BELL	3
SANDALS			
AND THEN IN SANDALS WALK THE STREET	83	LETTER TO AUNT	19
SAND-BAGGED			
WITH A SAND-BAGGED GARRISON, ...	127	SEED-AT-ZERO	53
SANDCRABS			
OF PSALMS AND SHADOWS AMONG THE PINCERED SANDCRABS			
PRANCING	202	SIR JOHNS HILL	24
SANDGRAIN			
THIS SANDGRAIN DAY IN THE BENT BAY'S GRAVE	208	POEM ON B'DAY	6
SANDGRAINS			
PROUD AS A SUCKED STONE AND HUGE AS SANDGRAINS. ...	131	I MAKE THIS IN	23
SANDS			
BY SCUMMED, STARFISH SANDS	3	PROLOGUE	9
AND WALK THE WARRING SANDS BY THE DEAD TOWN, ...	132	I MAKE THIS IN	32
OF HIS FATHER'S HOUSE IN THE SANDS, ...	141	SAINT TO FALL	7
SANDY			
ARE ON SANDY SOIL THEIR SPIRIT LEVEL;	24	LITTLE PROBLEM	2
SANE			
AND, AFTER IT HAS SUNK, THE SANE MOON, ...	42	A WAR OF WITS	21
THOUGH THEY GO MAD THEY SHALL BE SANE, ...	49	NO DOMINION	6
SANG			
SANG HEAVEN HUNGRY AND THE QUICK	141	SAINT TO FALL	15
AND THE COINS ON MY EYELIDS SANG LIKE SHELLS.	150	WHEN I WOKE	30
SLEEP TO A NEWBORN SLEEP IN A SWADDLING LOIN-LEAF			
STROKED AND SANG	157	INTO HER HEAD	22
SANG ALIVE	178	POEM IN OCT	59
JOY OF THE LONG DEAD CHILD SANG BURNING	178	POEM IN OCT	63
SANG UPON ORIGIN!	182	VISION, PRAYER	90
SANG TO MY HORN, THE FOXES ON THE HILLS BARKED CLEAR			
AND COLD, ...	195	FERN HILL	16
THOUGH I SANG IN MY CHAINS LIKE THE SEA.	196	FERN HILL	54
WILD MEN WHO CAUGHT AND SANG THE SUN IN FLIGHT, ...	208	NOT GO GENTLE	10
WE STRANGELY SANG AMONG THE FEATHERY FLOWERS.	227	SPRING-SPIRIT	12
SANGER'S			
WATER FROM NOSE AND ARSE, A SANGER'S SHOW	51	OUT OF THE PIT	26
SANITY			
THAT THE SUM SANITY MIGHT ADD TO NAUGHT	96	TWELVE	1
AND A WIDE SANITY	231	OUR SANCTITY	46
SANK			
WHERE ONCE YOUR GREEN KNOTS SANK THEIR SPLICE	91	WHERE ONCE THE	7
SANSKRIT			
OR SANSKRIT PSALMS ON LEPERS' CHESTS.	83	LETTER TO AUNT	28
SAP			
(AND SKELETONS HAD SAP). ONE MINUTE	43	FACES SHONE	7
BEFORE THE MOON SHIFTED AND THE SAP RAN OUT, ...	43	FACES SHONE	10
LET THE SAP LEAK IN THE BREEZE.	72	TAKE NEEDLES	52
BORN OF THE SENSUAL ROOT AND SAP;	86	BREAD I BREAK	14
SHE THREADS OFF THE SAP AND NEEDLES, BLOOD AND BUBBLE	108	I, IN IMAGE	10
AND CUT THE BIRDS' BOUGHS THAT THE MINSTREL SAP RAN			
RED.	205	GIANT'S THIGH	49
MY STRENGTH SHALL SAP YOUR OWN;	239	LET ME ESCAPE	9
SAPLESS			
SPEWING ITS SAPLESS LEAVES AROUND, ...	26	THERE'S PLENTY	10
SAPPHIRE			
THE SEA HAS BEEN BREEZE-SERENE SAPPHIRE, ...	224	IDYLL UNFORGET	21

	PAGE	TITLE	LINE
SAP'S			
MY IMAGES STALK THE TREES AND THE SLANT SAP'S TUNNEL,	109	I, IN IMAGE	25
SARGASSO			
THE DRY SARGASSO OF THE TOMB	97	TWILIGHT LOCKS	26
SAT			
WITH A CAPSIZED FIELD WHERE A SCHOOL SAT STILL	144	COLOUR OF SAY	3
LIKE THE WATER HE SAT DOWN	171	THE HUNCHBACK	14
SATANS			
FROGS AND SATANS AND WOMAN-LUCK, ...	150	WHEN I WOKE	7
SATYRS			
OF ELVES AND SATYRS	60	FAIRY TALES	29
SAVAGE			
AND STAKE THE SLEEPERS IN THE SAVAGE GRAVE	104	WORLD PYRAMID	17
SAVAGELY			
JUAN AFLAME AND SAVAGELY YOUNG KING LEAR, ...	157	INTO HER HEAD	11
SAVE			
GOD IN HIS WHIRLWIND SILENCE SAVE, WHO MARKS THE SPARROWS HAIL, ...	202	SIR JOHNS HILL	45
SAVE BY THEIR LONG DESIRERS IN THE FOX CUBBED	205	GIANT'S THIGH	56
NOR DID HE NOW, SAVE TO HIS SECRET WOUND.	217	ELEGY	27
SAVED			
BELIEVE, BELIEVE AND BE SAVED, WE CRY, WHO HAVE NO FAITH.	42	YOUNG ARE OLD	57
BELIEVE AND BE SAVED. NO MAN BELIEVES	55	NO MAN BELIEVE	13
SAVES			
WHO CURSES NOT WHAT MAKES AND SAVES, ...	55	NO MAN BELIEVE	14
SAVIOUR			
A CITY SAVIOUR, IN THE ORCHARD	70	SECRET WIND	15
HERE IS A SAVIOUR WHO SINGS LIKE A BIRD, ...	74	SUN BURNS	7
DUST BE YOUR SAVIOUR UNDER THE CONJURED SOIL.)	110	I, IN IMAGE	60
AM I NOT SISTER, TOO, WHO IS MY SAVIOUR?	112	NOT FATHER ME	12
THERE WAS A SAVIOUR	152	WAS A SAVIOUR	T
THERE WAS A SAVIOUR	152	WAS A SAVIOUR	1
THE SAVIOUR OF THE CROSS WHO CAN	240	TWINING HEAD	7
SAVOURS			
SAVOURS THE LICK OF THE TIMES THROUGH A DEADLY WOOD OF HAIR	144	PLEASURE-BIRD	9
SAW			
AND SAW TOWARDS HER TINY FACE	11	CABARET	3
KNEE-DEEP IN VOMIT. I SAW HIM THERE, ...	51	OUT OF THE PIT	43
AND THUS I SAW HIM SEARCHING FOR HIS SOUL.	51	OUT OF THE PIT	44
AND THUS I SAW HIM. HE WAS POISED LIKE THIS, ...	52	OUT OF THE PIT	59
AND THUS I SAW HIM IN A SQUARE OF FIELDS, ...	53	OUT OF THE PIT	87
I SAW TIME MURDER ME.	129	MY NEOPHYTE	48
FELLOW WITH SAW AT THE JUGULAR.	137	O CHATTERTON	11
OR SAW IN THE LOOKING-GLASS SHELL	139	TOMBSTONE TOLD	7
I WHO SAW IN A HURRIED FILM	140	TOMBSTONE TOLD	21
FOR WE SAW HIM THROW TO THE SWIFT FLOOD	162	LONG-LEGGED	21
HE SAW THE STORM SMOKE OUT TO KILL	163	LONG-LEGGED	41
AND I SAW IN THE TURNING SO CLEARLY A CHILD'S	178	POEM IN OCT	46
WE HEARD THE SEA SOUND SING, WE SAW THE SALT SHEET TELL.	194	SLEEP BECALMED	12
VEINED HIS POOR HAND I HELD, AND I SAW	217	ELEGY	16
OUT OF HIS EYES I SAW THE LAST LIGHT GLIDE.	217	ELEGY	28
TO SAW THROUGH YOUR ROOTS	231	OUR SANCTITY	30
I SAW THE COLD, GREEN TREES, ...	235	WOMAN TAPESTRY	6
SAWBONES			
I BY THE TREE OF THIEVES, ALL GLORY'S SAWBONES, ...	120	ALTARWISE	109
SAWDUST			
MASTER, HER MOUTH IS SAWDUST	10	COOL, OH NO	14

```
                                              PAGE      TITLE       LINE
SAWDUST  (CONTINUED)
     SAWDUST BENEATH THE SKIRTS;    ....................  27   OBLIVIOUS DARK   17
SAWN
     FOR MY SAWN, SPLAY SOUNDS),    ....................   3   PROLOGUE         28
SAY
     HOW KISS, WHEN DOLL COULD SAY    .................   10   COOL, OH NO      13
     I HEAR THEM SAY OUT OF THE DARKNESS   .............   23   ON QUIET NIGHT   21
     AND THUS, SOME TIME LATER, I HEARD HIM SAY:   .......  53   OUT OF THE PIT   89
     SHALL IT BE MALE OR FEMALE? SAY THE CELLS,   ........  95   RUB OF LOVE       8
     SHALL IT BE MALE OR FEMALE? SAY THE FINGERS   .......  95   RUB OF LOVE      15
     SAY NAY,    ........................................  127   NOW, SAY NAY      2
     SAY NAY,    ........................................  127   NOW, SAY NAY      9
     SIR NO SAY,   ......................................  127   NOW, SAY NAY     10
     SAY NAY,    ........................................  127   NOW, SAY NAY     16
     NO SAY SIR    ......................................  127   NOW, SAY NAY     17
     SAY NAY,    ........................................  128   NOW, SAY NAY     23
     SAY NAY    .........................................  128   NOW, SAY NAY     30
     THERE ARE MANY WHO SAY THAT A DOG HAS ITS DAY,   ....  221   SONG OF DOG       1
     WAITING FOR THE BIRD WHO SHALL SAY,   ..............  231   OUR SANCTITY     28
     NO SPACE, NO SPACE, YOU SAY,    ....................  239   LET ME ESCAPE     6
SAYING
     SHE, IN HER CHEAP FROCK, SAYING SOME CHEAP THING,    43   FACES SHONE      11
     ONCE IT WAS THE COLOUR OF SAYING    ................  144   COLOUR OF SAY     T
     ONCE IT WAS THE COLOUR OF SAYING    ................  144   COLOUR OF SAY     1
     THE GENTLE SEASLIDES OF SAYING I MUST UNDO   .......  144   COLOUR OF SAY     5
     NOW MY SAYING SHALL BE MY UNDOING,    ..............  144   COLOUR OF SAY    12
     SAYING YOU WOULD LET THE CHILL SEAS PASS,   ........  227   SPRING-SPIRIT     7
SAYS
     ONE SAYS: THERE WAS A WOMAN WITH NO FRIEND,   .......  22   ON QUIET NIGHT    8
     SAYS THE WORLD WEARS AWAY?    ......................   59   HERE IN SPRING   17
     SEE, SAYS THE LIME    .............................   85   SEE, SAYS LIME    T
     SEE, SAYS THE LIME, MY WICKED MILKS    .............   85   SEE, SAYS LIME    1
     SEE, SAYS THE LIME, AROUND THESE WRECKS   ..........   86   SEE, SAYS LIME   25
     THE VOICE OF CHILDREN SAYS    ......................  153   WAS A SAVIOUR     9
SCALD
     SCALD ME AND DROWN    ..............................  185   VISION, PRAYER  199
SCALDING
     BOTH MIND AND MATTER AT THE SCALDING WORD   ........   73   LORD RED HAIL    11
     HEIR TO THE SCALDING VEINS THAT HOLD LOVE'S DROP,    80   ALL THAT I OWE    9
     HEIR TO THE SCALDING VEINS THAT HOLD LOVE'S DROP,
         COSTLY   ......................................  103   I DREAMED MY      9
SCALE
     WITH PELT, AND SCALE, AND FLEECE:    ...............   5   PROLOGUE         86
     AND HOW TO SCALE AND SEE THE SIGHTS    .............   83   LETTER TO AUNT   13
     RINGS OUT THE DEAD SEA SCALE;    ...................  110   I, IN IMAGE      63
SCALECOPHIDIAN
     WITH SERPENTS' MOUTHS AND SCALECOPHIDIAN VOIDS   ....  51   OUT OF THE PIT   22
SCALED
     THE SCALED SEA-SAWERS, FIX IN A NAKED SPONGE   .....  119   ALTARWISE        92
SCALES
     THE SCALES OF THIS TWIN WORLD TREAD ON THE DOUBLE,   108   I, IN IMAGE       4
     MAN WAS THE SCALES, THE DEATH BIRDS ON ENAMEL,   ....  111   I, IN IMAGE      97
     THIS TIDETHREAD AND THE LANE OF SCALES,   ..........  128   MY NEOPHYTE      14
     SCALES THE BLUE WALL OF SPIRITS;    ................  130   SINNERS' BELL    21
     WHO SCALES A HAILING HILL IN HER COLD FLINTSTEPS    132   I MAKE THIS IN   29
     IN COMMON CLAY CLOTHES DISGUISED AS SCALES,   ......  151   BELOW A TIME     15
SCALING
     COME UNTO SEA-STUCK TOWERS, AT THE FIBRE SCALING,    111   I, IN IMAGE      74
SCALP
     WORM IN THE SCALP, THE STAKED AND FALLOW.   ........  106   ALL ALL AND       9
```

```
                                               PAGE       TITLE      LINE
SCALPEL
     BY SCALPEL LIGHTNING FROM THE RIFTED SKY,  .........  64   WOMAN SPEAKS     29
SCALY
     NOW ON SIR JOHN'S HILL. THE HERON, ANKLING THE SCALY  203  SIR JOHNS HILL   55
SCAR
     ON SKULL AND SCAR WHERE HIS LOVES LIE WRECKED,  ....  209  POEM ON B'DAY    40
SCARECROW
     GENESIS IN THE ROOT, THE SCARECROW WORD,  ..........  119  ALTARWISE        88
     UNDER THE ONE LEAVED TREES RAN A SCARECROW OF SNOW    190  WINTER'S TALE    94
SCARLET
     AND SEWN ON HIS SKULL A SCARLET THORN;  ............   74  SUN BURNS        13
     THEN LOOK, MY HEART, UPON THE SCARLET TROVE,  ......   81  ALL THAT I OWE   28
     DOWN FALL FOUR PADDING WEATHERS ON THE SCARLET LANDS, 122  HOLD HARD        19
     A SHE BIRD DAWNED, AND HER BREAST WITH SNOW AND
          SCARLET DOWNED.  ..............................  189  WINTER'S TALE    70
SCARVING
     AND HIS SCARVING BEARD FROM A BOOK,  ...............  150  WHEN I WOKE      12
SCATTER-BREATH
     THE DEATH-STAGGED SCATTER-BREATH  .................  150  WHEN I WOKE      19
SCATTERED
     BLOOD SHOT AND SCATTERED TO THE WINDS OF LIGHT  ....   94  IN BEGINNING     29
     SCATTERED IN THE PATHS OF HIS HEELS  ..............  165  LONG-LEGGED      95
SCENE
     (HAVE WITH THE HOUSE OF WIND), THE LEANING SCENE,    101  RUNNING GRAVE    42
     ADORE MY WINDOWS FOR THEIR SUMMER SCENE?  .........  112  NOT FATHER ME     8
     THE WINDER OF THE CLOCKWISE SCENE  ................  129  MY NEOPHYTE      32
     THAN BULLY ILL LOVE IN THE CLOUTED SCENE.  ........  145  IF HEAD HURT      5
     IN THIS ANACHRONISTIC SCENE  ......................  156  RETURN           92
     THE SALTY SCENE AND MY PLAYERED GOB CURVING  ......  179  NEW QUAY         14
SCENT
     SCENT THROUGH THE CLUTCHES OF THE HEATHER,  .......   44  TO FOLLOW FOX     4
     THE SCENT OF THE GREAT FLOWER WILL STAY,  .........  232  FURIOUS MOTION   16
SCHOLARS
     DEATH FROM A BANDAGE, RANTS THE MASK OF SCHOLARS    120  ALTARWISE       120
SCHOOL
     WITH A CAPSIZED FIELD WHERE A SCHOOL SAT STILL  ....  144  COLOUR OF SAY     3
SCIATIC
     DEAR TOMMY, PLEASE, FROM FAR, SCIATIC KINGSLEY  ....  179  NEW QUAY          1
SCISSORED
     FROM THE UNFOLDING TO THE SCISSORED CAUL,  ........   78  LOVE'S FEVER      3
SCISSORS
     TAKE THE SCISSORS AND THE PAN,  ...................   71  TAKE NEEDLES      9
     TAKE THE SCISSORS TO THIS GLOBE,  .................   72  TAKE NEEDLES     37
     HIS SCISSORS OILED, HIS KNIFE HUNG LOOSE  .........   91  WHERE ONCE THE   10
     COMES, LIKE A SCISSORS STALKING, TAILOR AGE,  .....  100  RUNNING GRAVE     6
     CAST HIGH, STUNNED ON GILLED STONE; SLY SCISSORS
          GROUND IN FROST  .............................  135  HOW MY ANIMAL    35
SCOLD
     A HEMISPHERE MAY SCOLD HIM  .......................  126  SEED-AT-ZERO     31
     A VILLAGE GREEN MAY SCOLD HIM  ....................  126  SEED-AT-ZERO     38
SCOLDS
     THE WET NIGHT SCOLDS ME LIKE A NURSE?  ............   65  GODS THUMP       10
SCORE
     THE TWO-FRAMED GLOBE THAT SPUN INTO A SCORE;  .....   79  LOVE'S FEVER     45
SCORN
     WE SCORN THE JUGGERNAUT,  .........................   59  FAIRY TALES       6
SCOUR
     AND STAR: HELD AND BLESSED, THOUGH YOU SCOUR THE
          HIGH FOUR  ...................................  199  COUNTRY SLEEP    45
```

	PAGE	TITLE	LINE
SCOUTING			
I SENT MY CREATURE SCOUTING ON THE GLOBE, ...	97	TWILIGHT LOCKS	9
SCRAMS			
BLIND IN THE COIL SCRAMS ROUND THE BLAZING OUTLINE,	124	TODAY, INSECT	11
SCRAPE			
I SCRAPE THROUGH RESIN TO A STARRY BONE	104	WORLD PYRAMID	35
SCRAPED			
SCRAPED AT MY CRADLE IN A WALKING WORD	117	ALTARWISE	11
THE HERO'S HEAD LIES SCRAPED OF EVERY LEGEND, ...	132	I MAKE THIS IN	43
SCRAPING			
SHAMES AND THE DAMP DISHONOURS, THE RELIC SCRAPING.	110	I, IN IMAGE	71
SCRATCH			
STILL SET TO SCRATCH A LAUGHTER FROM MY LUNG, ...	95	RUB OF LOVE	5
SCRATCHES			
SHARP AND SHRILL MY SILLY TONGUE SCRATCHES	149	PAPER & STICKS	16
SCRAWL			
I HUG TO LOVE WITH MY UNRULY SCRAWL	75	MY HERO BARES	8
RUB OFF THE SCRAWL OF PRINTS ON	156	RETURN	81
SCRAWLED			
IS CORNER-CAST, BREATH'S RAG, SCRAWLED WEED, A VAIN	131	I MAKE THIS IN	9
SCREAM			
BIT OUT THE MANDRAKE WITH TO-MORROW'S SCREAM.	117	ALTARWISE	6
SCREAMING			
SCREAMING THE SPRING	16	IN OBLIVION	3
SCREEN			
AND NOW BEHIND THE SCREEN ARE VIXEN VOICES, ...	36	MIDNIGHT ROAD	9
THEN THREW ON THAT TIDE-HOISTED SCREEN	129	MY NEOPHYTE	34
SCREWED			
DECEMBER'S THORN SCREWED IN A BROW OF HOLLY.	121	ALTARWISE	132
SCREWS			
SPUN TO MY SCREWS, YOUR DRY GHOST BLOWS, ...	90	WHERE ONCE THE	2
WHEN ONCE THE TWILIGHT SCREWS WERE TURNED, ...	98	TWILIGHT LOCKS	31
FEAR NOT THE SCREWS THAT TURN THE VOICE, ...	106	ALL ALL AND	23
SCRIBBLED			
MAN BY A SCRIBBLED NAME.	66	HAND SIGNED	12
SCRIPTURE			
PLUCK, COCK, MY SEA EYE, SAID MEDUSA'S SCRIPTURE,	119	ALTARWISE	75
SCROLLS			
THE SCROLLS OF FIRE THAT BURNED IN HIS HEART AND HEAD, ...	187	WINTER'S TALE	14
SCRUBBED			
I KNOW HER SCRUBBED AND SOUR HUMBLE HANDS	136	AFTER FUNERAL	31
GRAVE, AFTER BELOVED ON THE GRASS GULFED CROSS IS SCRUBBED	205	GIANT'S THIGH	54
SCUD			
WHERE THE CORMORANTS SCUD, ...	208	POEM ON B'DAY	3
SCUDDED			
THE PATCHWORK HALVES WERE CLOVEN AS THEY SCUDDED	104	WORLD PYRAMID	19
SCUDDING			
THE SCUDDING BASE OF THE FAMILIAR SKY, ...	142	SAINT TO FALL	29
SAINT CARVED AND SENSUAL AMONG THE SCUDDING	147	UNLUCKILY FOR	5
SCULPTURED			
A CITY GODHEAD, TURBINE MOVED, STEEL SCULPTURED,	70	SECRET WIND	13
AND SCULPTURED ANN IS SEVENTY YEARS OF STONE.	137	AFTER FUNERAL	35
SCUMMED			
BY SCUMMED, STARFISH SANDS	3	PROLOGUE	9
SCUMS			
THE SEA OF SCUMS COULD DROWN ME AS IT BROKE	95	RUB OF LOVE	27
SCURRY			
THE HEART IS DRAINED THAT, SPELLING IN THE SCURRY	99	OCTOBER WIND	30

	PAGE	TITLE	LINE
SCURRYING			
THE SCURRYING, FURRED SMALL FRIARS SQUEAL, IN THE DOWSE	204	GIANT'S THIGH	31
SCURVY			
PLAYS SCURVY TRICKS WITH VALUES AND INTENTIONS, ...	37	WINDMILLS TURN	6
SCUT			
THE ARCTIC SCUT, AND BASIN OF THE SOUTH, ...	105	WORLD PYRAMID	44
SCUTTLED			
LURCHED THROUGH A SCUTTLED SEA	142	SAINT TO FALL	23
AND SCUTTLED OVER HER EYES, ...	165	LONG-LEGGED	100
SCYTHE			
YOUR CALM AND CUDDLED IS A SCYTHE OF HAIRS, ...	99	RUNNING GRAVE	2
THE TRIGGER AND SCYTHE, THE BRIDAL BLADE, ...	106	ALL ALL AND	17
BLUNT SCYTHE AND WATER BLADE.	129	MY NEOPHYTE	39
SCYTHED			
AND THE SCYTHED BOULDERS BLEED, AND THE LAST	210	POEM ON B'DAY	69
SCYTHE-EYED			
AND THE CAGE FOR THE SCYTHE-EYED RAVEN.	106	ALL ALL AND	21
SCYTHES			
TO A HAYCOCK COUCH AND THE SCYTHES OF HIS ARMS	157	INTO HER HEAD	17
SCYTHE-SIDED			
OR, WATER-LAMMED, FROM THE SCYTHE-SIDED THORN, ...	114	A GRIEF AGO	3
SEA			
ROARED, SEA BORN, MAN TORN, BLOOD BLEST.	4	PROLOGUE	41
THERE IS NO MEASURED SEA FOR THEM, ...	10	COOL, OH NO	23
THE SHADOWS FROM THE GLASSY SEA	15	FOR LEDA	11
FO O ' E A SEA TO LIE.	1	TIM TO ROT	18
FOR YOU'VE A SEA TO LIE.	16	TIME TO ROT	18
AND, STANDING OVER THE SEA, SHE'D CRY	22	ON QUIET NIGHT	9
GOES OVER THE HILL INTO THE DEEP SEA;	43	LONGED TO MOVE	5
OUT OF THE HEAVENLY SEA ONTO THE MOON'S SHORES. ...	48	LIGHT, I KNOW	3
ON TUMBLING HILLS ADMIRING THE SEA, ...	48	POET: 1935	61
THOUGH THEY SINK THROUGH THE SEA THEY SHALL RISE AGAIN;	49	NO DOMINION	7
UNDER THE WINDINGS OF THE SEA	49	NO DOMINION	11
HAVE SEARCHED FOR SHELLS AND SIGNS ON THE SEA SHORE,	52	OUT OF THE PIT	64
UNDER A HIDEOUS SEA WHERE CORAL MEN	52	OUT OF THE PIT	68
AND THE GRAVE SEA, MOCK WHO DERIDE	54	WE BY SEASAND	2
FOR IN THIS YELLOW GRAVE OF SAND AND SEA	54	WE BY SEASAND	5
THAT'S GRAVE AND GAY AS GRAVE AND SEA	54	WE BY SEASAND	7
THE KINGCRAFTS OF THE WICKED SEA, ...	61	MEAT ON BONES	11
THE SEA SPEAKS IN A KINGLY VOICE, ...	61	MEAT ON BONES	35
BY A THIN SEA OF FLESH	62	EARS IN TURRET	11
HER SALTY LOVERS IN THE SEA.	76	SONG: LOVE ME	7
TO THAT UNENDING SEA AROUND MY ISLAND	76	LASHED RINGS	8
WHERE NO SEA RUNS, THE WATERS OF THE HEART	82	LIGHT BREAKS	2
SLIDES LIKE A SEA;	82	LIGHT BREAKS	15
IS HALF ITS LIGHT; THE FATHOMED SEA	88	A PROCESS IN	11
CRY TO THE DOLPHINED SEA.	91	WHERE ONCE THE	18
FROM THE FAIR DEAD WHO FLUSH THE SEA	92	BOYS OF SUMMER	34
HOLD UP THE NOISY SEA AND DROP HER BIRDS, ...	93	BOYS OF SUMMER	39
THE SEA OF SCUMS COULD DROWN ME AS IT BROKE	95	RUB OF LOVE	27
AND ALL THE HERRINGS SMELLING IN THE SEA, ...	95	RUB OF LOVE	33
NOR DAMNED THE SEA THAT SPED ABOUT MY FIST, ...	97	TWILIGHT LOCKS	3
WHEN THE GALACTIC SEA WAS SUCKED	97	TWILIGHT LOCKS	7
GIVES UP ITS DEAD TO SUCH A WORKING SEA;	97	TWILIGHT LOCKS	27
TWICE IN THE FEEDING SEA, GROWN	103	I DREAMED MY	26
LIMP IN THE STREET OF SEA, AMONG THE RABBLE	104	WORLD PYRAMID	15
THE SECRET CHILD, I SHIFT ABOUT THE SEA	105	WORLD PYRAMID	59
DUG OF THE SEA, THE GLANDED MORROW, ...	106	ALL ALL AND	8
RIDING THE SEA LIGHT ON A SUNKEN PATH, ...	107	GRIEF THIEF	8

SEA

	PAGE	TITLE	LINE
SEA (CONTINUED)			
OUT OF THE SEA, THE DRIVE OF OIL,	107	ALL ALL AND	34
TURN THE LONG SEA ARTERIAL	110	I, IN IMAGE	46
RINGS OUT THE DEAD SEA SCALE;	110	I, IN IMAGE	63
BE BY THE SHIPS' SEA BROKEN AT THE MANSTRING ANCHORED	111	I, IN IMAGE	86
THE SEA AND INSTRUMENT, NICKED IN THE LOCKS OF TIME,	111	I, IN IMAGE	92
AM I NOT ALL OF YOU BY THE DIRECTED SEA	112	NOT FATHER ME	13
THE NURSE OF GIANTS BY THE CUT SEA BASIN,	113	SERVANT SUN	10
HELL WIND AND SEA,	114	A GRIEF AGO	4
SHE HOLDING ME? THE PEOPLE'S SEA DRIVES ON HER,	115	A GRIEF AGO	26
A CLIMBING SEA FROM ASIA HAD ME DOWN	118	ALTARWISE	65
AND BURNED SEA SILENCE ON A WICK OF WORLDS.	119	ALTARWISE	74
PLUCK, COCK, MY SEA EYE, SAID MEDUSA'S SCRIPTURE,	119	ALTARWISE	75
QUICKENING FOR THE RIDDLED SEA;	125	SEED-AT-ZERO	18
GREEK IN THE IRISH SEA THE AGELESS VOICE:	125	TODAY, INSECT	22
QUICKENING FOR THE VIRGIN SEA;	126	SEED-AT-ZERO	25
MY SEA HERMAPHRODITE,	128	MY NEOPHYTE	7
BY A DRAMATIC SEA.	129	MY NEOPHYTE	36
STRIKE THE SEA HOUR THROUGH BELLMETAL.	130	SINNERS' BELL	12
DOWN THE STACKED SEA AND WATER-PILLARED SHADE,	132	I MAKE THIS IN	40
THE BLACK, BURST SEA REJOICE,	135	HOW MY ANIMAL	19
LURCHED THROUGH A SCUTTLED SEA	142	SAINT TO FALL	23
THAT FROZEN WIFE WHOSE JUICES DRIFT LIKE A FIXED SEA	145	PLEASURE-BIRD	14
OR SPRAY-BASED AND ROCK-CHESTED SEA:	145	PLEASURE-BIRD	24
LOVING ON THIS SEA BANGED GUILT	147	UNLUCKILY FOR	15
THE NEXT-DOOR SEA DISPELLED	150	WHEN I WOKE	6
CRY MY SEA TOWN WAS BREAKING.	150	WHEN I WOKE	27
THEN SWIFT FROM A BURSTING SEA WITH BOTTLECORK BOATS	151	BELOW A TIME	13
THE BRIGHT PRETENDER, THE RIDICULOUS SEA DANDY	152	BELOW A TIME	42
THE COVERING SEA THEIR NIGHTFALL WITH NO NAMES;	158	INTO HER HEAD	50
HE'LL BATHE HIS RAINING BLOOD IN THE MALE SEA	160	DEATHS AND ENT	19
AS A BIRD HOOKING OVER THE SEA,	162	LONG-LEGGED	7
OF THE SEA IS HILLY WITH WHALES,	162	LONG-LEGGED	32
QUAKED THE SICK SEA AND SNOUTED DEEP,	163	LONG-LEGGED	50
THROWN TO THE SEA IN THE SHELL OF A GIRL	165	LONG-LEGGED	92
WITH WILD SEA FILLIES AND SOAKING BRIDLES	168	LONG-LEGGED	185
THERE IS NOTHING LEFT OF THE SEA BUT ITS SOUND,	169	LONG-LEGGED	205
UNDER THE EARTH THE LOUD SEA WALKS,	169	LONG-LEGGED	206
OF THE PACING, FAMOUS SEA BUT ITS SPEECH,	169	LONG-LEGGED	210
STREET WE CHANT THE FLYING SEA	174	FIRE RAID	29
THE MASSES OF THE SEA	175	FIRE RAID	72
THE MASSES OF THE SEA UNDER	175	FIRE RAID	73
THE MASSES OF THE INFANT-BEARING SEA	175	FIRE RAID	74
AND OVER THE SEA WET CHURCH THE SIZE OF A SNAIL	177	POEM IN OCT	32
THESE WERE THE WOODS THE RIVER AND SEA	178	POEM IN OCT	53
BORROW MY EYES. THE DARKENING SEA FLINGS LEA	179	NEW QUAY	2
OF THE UNCAGED SEA BOTTOM	182	VISION, PRAYER	75
BORN SEA	182	VISION, PRAYER	86
LIGHT THROUGH SEA AND SOIL	184	VISION, PRAYER	157
OVER THE BARBED AND SHOOTING SEA ASSUMED AN ARMY	186	HOLY SPRING	6
LISTEN AND LOOK WHERE SHE SAILS THE GOOSE PLUCKED SEA,	190	WINTER'S TALE	100
IS COME OF THE SEA TUMBLING IN HARNESS	191	REFUSAL MOURN	6
BY THE GRINDING SEA,	192	SIDE OF TRUTH	15
ON THE SILENT SEA WE HAVE HEARD THE SOUND	194	SLEEP BECALMED	3
TO THE SEA SOUND FLOWING LIKE BLOOD FROM THE LOUD WOUND	194	SLEEP BECALMED	6
WE HEARD THE SEA SOUND SING, WE SAW THE SALT SHEET TELL.	194	SLEEP BECALMED	12
THOUGH I SANG IN MY CHAINS LIKE THE SEA.	196	FERN HILL	54

	PAGE	TITLE	LINE
SEA (CONTINUED)			
FLOWS TO THE STRAND OF FLOWERS LIKE THE DEW'S RULY SEA,	200	COUNTRY SLEEP	98
WHERE THE SEA COBBLES SAIL,	202	SIR JOHNS HILL	38
BY FULL TILT RIVER AND SWITCHBACK SEA	208	POEM ON B'DAY	2
AND FAR AT SEA HE KNOWS,	209	POEM ON B'DAY	30
AND THE SEA THAT HIDES HIS SECRET SELVES	211	POEM ON B'DAY	87
AND THE TUSKED, RAMSHACKLING SEA EXULTS;	211	POEM ON B'DAY	94
THROUGH HIS UNSEEING EYES TO THE ROOTS OF THE SEA.	217	ELEGY	17
I HAVE KNOWN THE MYSTERY OF THE SEA TO BE MANTLED ABOUT ME;	223	IDYLL UNFORGET	18
THE SEA HAS BEEN BREEZE-SERENE SAPPHIRE,	224	IDYLL UNFORGET	21
VOICES HAVE CALLED, AND THE ANSWERS LEMURAL WHISPERS FROM THE SEA;	224	IDYLL UNFORGET	34
NOW THE SEA HAS A FLOWERING OF FOAM;	224	IDYLL UNFORGET	36
SEA, DO NOT FLOW	229	MY RIVER	19
OF THE SEA UNDER THE HARD SUN,	229	MY RIVER	35
THE SEA SPEAKING KEENLY,	229	MY RIVER	36
NO WAVE COMB THE SEA,	233	NO THOUGHT	14
UNMOVING IN A SHOULDERING SEA,	238	PILLAR BREAKS	20
SEABEAR			
THE HIGHROAD OF WATER WHERE THE SEABEAR AND MACKEREL	110	I, IN IMAGE	45
SEABED			
AND ALL THE DRY SEABED UNLOCKED,	97	TWILIGHT LOCKS	8
SEA-BED			
FOR THE CRAB-BACKED DEAD ON THE SEA-BED ROSE	165	LONG-LEGGED	99
SEA-BLOWN			
TO THE SEA-BLOWN ARRIVAL.	109	I, IN IMAGE	36
SEACAVES			
THERE ARE NO SEACAVES DEEPER THAN HER EYES;	57	GREEK PLAY	11
SEA-FAITHS			
TILL ALL OUR SEA-FAITHS DIE.	91	WHERE ONCE THE	24
SEAFARING			
THE MOON-DRAWN GRAVE, WITH THE SEAFARING YEARS,	107	GRIEF THIEF	2
SEA-GHOST			
HAS SOWN A FLYING GARDEN ROUND THAT SEA-GHOST?	121	ALTARWISE	136
SEA-GIRLS'			
THE FRANK, CLOSED PEARL, THE SEA-GIRLS' LINEAMENTS	131	I MAKE THIS IN	19
SEAGULL			
WITH WATER PRAYING AND CALL OF SEAGULL AND ROOK	177	POEM IN OCT	6
SEA-GUT			
OVER THE SEA-GUT LOUDENING, SETS A ROCK ALIVE;	122	HOLD HARD	15
SEA-HALVED			
THE SEA-HALVED FAITH THAT BLEW TIME TO HIS KNEES,	107	GRIEF THIEF	4
SEA-HATCHED			
SHAKING THE SEA-HATCHED SKULL,	111	I, IN IMAGE	100
SEA-HYMEN			
OR RENT ANCESTRALLY THE ROPED SEA-HYMEN,	131	I MAKE THIS IN	12
SEAL			
THE SEAL OF FIRE,	128	NOW, SAY NAY	32
SING HOW THE SEAL HAS KISSED HER DEAD!	164	LONG-LEGGED	82
SEALED			
THE WIND OF KISSES SEALED A PACT	85	SEE, SAYS LIME	10
SEA-LEGGED			
AHOY, OLD, SEA-LEGGED FOX,	5	PROLOGUE	98
GOOD-BYE TO THE MAN ON THE SEA-LEGGED DECK	162	LONG-LEGGED	18
SEALS			
THE RIPPLED SEALS STREAK DOWN	209	POEM ON B'DAY	34

	PAGE	TITLE	LINE
SEA-PARSLEY			
NUTMEG, CIVET, AND SEA-PARSLEY SERVE THE PLAGUED			
GROOM AND BRIDE	131	SINNERS' BELL	29
SEAPORTS			
SEAPORTS BY A DRUNKEN SHORE	126	SEED-AT-ZERO	34
SEAPORTS BY A THIRSTY SHORE	126	SEED-AT-ZERO	41
SEAR			
AND SEAR JUST RIDERS BACK, ...	161	DEATHS AND ENT	34
SEARCHED			
HAVE SEARCHED FOR SHELLS AND SIGNS ON THE SEA SHORE,	52	OUT OF THE PIT	64
SEARCHING			
AND THUS I SAW HIM SEARCHING FOR HIS SOUL.	51	OUT OF THE PIT	44
SEARING			
SEARING THE SKY FOR THUNDERBOLTS TO FALL	34	THIRST PARCHES	5
SEAS			
THAT SPEAK SEVEN SEAS, ...	3	PROLOGUE	17
TO DRIFT OR DROWN UPON THE SEAS	69	BEFORE KNOCKED	32
LIFE ROSE AND SPOUTED FROM THE ROLLING SEAS, ...	94	IN BEGINNING	16
DRAW IN THEIR SEAS, ...	115	A GRIEF AGO	38
BY WASTE SEAS WHERE THE WHITE BEAR QUOTED VIRGIL	119	ALTARWISE	69
SPELT OUT THE SEVEN SEAS, AND EVIL INDEX, ...	119	ALTARWISE	82
WHEN WE WERE STRANGERS TO THE GUIDED SEAS, ...	121	INCARNATE DEVL	7
SPOT THE BLOWN WORD, AND ON THE SEAS I IMAGE	121	ALTARWISE	131
O RING OF SEAS, NOR SORROW AS I SHIFT	123	FOSTER LIGHT	20
WHO GAVE THESE SEAS THEIR COLOUR IN A SHAPE, ...	123	FOSTER LIGHT	25
DUCKED IN THE TWELVE, DISCIPLE SEAS	128	MY NEOPHYTE	4
DELIVERED SEAS MY LOVE FROM HER PROUD PLACE	133	I MAKE THIS IN	62
THE AGONIZED, TWO SEAS.	134	NOT FROM ANGER	7
NEVER SHALL BEAST BE BORN TO ATLAS THE FEW SEAS ...	135	HOW MY ANIMAL	32
THE SEAS TO SERVICE THAT HER WOOD-TONGUED VIRTUE	136	AFTER FUNERAL	22
ANCIENT WOODS OF MY BLOOD, DASH DOWN TO THE NUT OF			
THE SEAS	140	NO WORK WORDS	11
BULLIES INTO ROUGH SEAS YOU SO GENTLE	142	SAINT TO FALL	49
AT THE BREAST STORED WITH SEAS. NO RETURN	146	IF HEAD HURT	27
ON THE OLD SEAS FROM STORIES, THRASHING MY WINGS,	152	BELOW A TIME	36
AND THE MOTLEY WINDS FROM THE SEAS.	227	THE PINE	4
WITH FOAM FLUNG BY THE FLOWERING SEAS.'	227	SPRING-SPIRIT	4
SAYING YOU WOULD LET THE CHILL SEAS PASS, ...	227	SPRING-SPIRIT	7
SEA'S			
BY THE SEA'S SIDE, HEARING THE NOISE OF BIRDS, ...	98	OCTOBER WIND	5
BY THE SEA'S SIDE HEAR THE DARK-VOWELLED BIRDS. ...	99	OCTOBER WIND	32
SEASAND			
WE LYING BY SEASAND	54	WE BY SEASAND	T
WE LYING BY SEASAND, WATCHING YELLOW	54	WE BY SEASAND	1
SEA-SAWERS			
THE SCALED SEA-SAWERS, FIX IN A NAKED SPONGE	119	ALTARWISE	92
SEASHAKEN			
IN MY SEASHAKEN HOUSE	3	PROLOGUE	4
SEASHELL			
LULLING OF SPHERES IN THE SEASHELL FLESH, ...	211	POEM ON B'DAY	89
SEASHORE			
OVER A RUMP ON THE CLERICAL-GREY SEASHORE, ...	179	NEW QUAY	25
OR THE STARS' SEASHORE DEAD, ...	210	POEM ON B'DAY	57
SEASHORES			
OR WAVES BREAK LOUD ON THE SEASHORES;	50	NO DOMINION	21
SEASIDE			
OF THE GRAVE, GAY, SEASIDE LAND.	54	WE BY SEASAND	17
SEASLIDES			
THE GENTLE SEASLIDES OF SAYING I MUST UNDO	144	COLOUR OF SAY	5

		PAGE	TITLE	LINE
SEASON				
CHALK COOLED BY LEAVES IN THE HOT SEASON, ...		29	LONG, SKELETON	3
SEASON AND SUNSHINE, GRACE AND GIRL, ...		61	MEAT ON BONES	31
BRIGHT AS HER SPINNING-WHEELS, THE COLIC SEASON ...		108	I, IN IMAGE	8
THIS FIRST AND STEEPLED SEASON, TO THE SUMMER'S GAME.		122	HOLD HARD	12
NOR HAMMER BACK A SEASON IN THE FIGS, ...		123	FOSTER LIGHT	8
EACH ANCIENT, STONE-NECKED MINUTE OF LOVE'S SEASON		131	I MAKE THIS IN	2
SEASONS				
ALL SEASONS WITH THE SAME METICULOUS POWER, ...		17	IN OBLIVION	13
MAN'S MANMADE SPARETIME LASTS THE FOUR SEASONS, ...		39	GAS FADES	19
AND THUS, BETWEEN THE SEASONS, HEARD HIM CRY:		52	OUT OF THE PIT	62
THE SEASONS NUMBERED BY THE INWARD SUN, ...		79	ALMANAC TIME	2
DISSOLVED IN SUMMER AND THE HUNDRED SEASONS;		79	LOVE'S FEVER	49
BUT SEASONS MUST BE CHALLENGED OR THEY TOTTER		92	BOYS OF SUMMER	25
AND THREE DEAD SEASONS ON A CLIMBING GRAVE		117	ALTARWISE	30
SEASONS OVER THE LIQUID WORLD, ...		166	LONG-LEGGED	119
SHE IS BREAKING WITH SEASONS AND CLOUDS;		168	LONG-LEGGED	176
SEASONS'				
THE SEASONS' CRIES, FULL OF HIS INTIMATIONS.		29	NEARLY SUMMER	6
SLOW ROUNDING OF FOUR SEASONS' COASTS, ...		58	HERE IN SPRING	6
IN AUTUMN TEACH THREE SEASONS' FIRES		58	HERE IN SPRING	7
SEASON'S				
THE SEASON'S SUN, THOUGH HE SHOULD KNOW HIS SETTING		25	THERE'S PLENTY	4
NO, HE'S A STRANGER, OUTSIDE THE SEASON'S HUMOUR,		46	POET: 1935	10
HE, TOO, COULD TOUCH THE SEASON'S LIPS AND SMILE,		46	POET: 1935	14
SEA-SPINDLE				
(TURN THE SEA-SPINDLE LATERAL, ...		110	I, IN IMAGE	67
SEA-STRAW				
AND SIRENS SINGING FROM OUR LADY'S SEA-STRAW.		119	ALTARWISE	70
SEA-STUCK				
COME UNTO SEA-STUCK TOWERS, AT THE FIBRE SCALING,		111	I, IN IMAGE	74
SEA-SUCKED				
HIS SEA-SUCKED ADAM IN THE HOLLOW HULK, ...		103	WORLD PYRAMID	2
SEATHUMBED				
OUT OF THESE SEATHUMBED LEAVES		3	PROLOGUE	29
SEA-WAN				
THEY OF THE PALE, SEA-WAN BEAUTY, THEY OF THE HOME		224	IDYLL UNFORGET	38
SEAWARD				
SEAWARD THE SALMON, SUCKED SUN SLIPS, ...		3	PROLOGUE	34
SEAWAX				
GIVE OVER, LOVERS, LOCKING, AND THE SEAWAX STRUGGLE,		111	I, IN IMAGE	89
SEAWEED				
WITH MY CHERRY CAPPED DANGLER GREEN AS SEAWEED		152	BELOW A TIME	45
SEAWEEDS'				
GREEN OF THE SEAWEEDS' IRON, ...		93	BOYS OF SUMMER	38
SEAWEEDY				
YOU ARE YOUR SISTERS' SIRE, SAID SEAWEEDY, ...		113	NOT FATHER ME	26
SEAWHIRL				
THIS WAS THE GOD OF BEGINNING IN THE INTRICATE SEAWHIRL, ...		112	I, IN IMAGE	107
SECOND				
UP TO THE SECOND OF THE DARK COMING, ...		25	THERE'S PLENTY	5
AND SOME SHINE FOR A SECOND AND ARE GONE, ...		49	LIGHT, I KNOW	20
FROM LOVE'S FIRST FEVER TO HER PLAGUE, FROM THE SOFT SECOND		78	LOVE'S FEVER	1
REACHING A SECOND GROUND FAR FROM THE STARS;		101	FELLOWED SLEEP	7
SHARP IN MY SECOND DEATH I MARKED THE HILLS, HARVEST		103	I DREAMED MY	17
MY SECOND STRUGGLING FROM THE GRASS.		103	I DREAMED MY	20
AND POWER WAS CONTAGIOUS IN MY BIRTH, SECOND		103	I DREAMED MY	21
CRY JOY THAT THIS WITCHILIKE MIDWIFE SECOND		142	SAINT TO FALL	48

	PAGE	TITLE	LINE

SECOND (CONTINUED)

AND THE SECOND COMERS, THE SEVERERS, THE ENEMIES
    FROM THE DEEP ••••••••••••••••••••••••••••••••••••••   159   INTO HER HEAD   68
OF ADAM AND EVE IS NEVER FOR A SECOND •••••••••••••   174   FIRE RAID   48
THAT SECOND ••••••••••••••••••••••••••••••••••••   177   POEM IN OCT   9

SECONDS

WITH THE INCESTUOUS SECRET BROTHER IN THE SECONDS TO
    PERPETUATE THE STARS, •••••••••••••••••••••••••••   159   INTO HER HEAD   66

SECRET

CLOSED IN YOUR CELL OF SECRET THOUGHTS, ••••••••••••   10   COOL, OH NO   28
WE SEE RISE THE SECRET WIND ••••••••••••••••••••••   69   SECRET WIND   T
WE SEE RISE THE SECRET WIND BEHIND THE BRAIN, •••••   69   SECRET WIND   1
A SECRET NIGHT DESCENDS BETWEEN ••••••••••••••••••   69   SECRET WIND   4
WE HEAR RISE THE SECRET WIND BEHIND THE BRAIN, ••••   70   SECRET WIND   19
THE SECRET VOICE CRY IN OUR EARS, ••••••••••••••••   70   SECRET WIND   20
HE PROMISES A SECRET HEAT. ••••••••••••••••••••••   75   MY HERO BARES   15
FROM THE FIRST SECRET OF THE HEART, THE WARNING
    GHOST, ••••••••••••••••••••••••••••••••••••••   78   LOVE'S FEVER   12
I LEARNT THE VERBS OF WILL, AND HAD MY SECRET; ••••   79   LOVE'S FEVER   39
LIGHT BREAKS ON SECRET LOTS, •••••••••••••••••••••   82   LIGHT BREAKS   25
THE SECRET OF THE SOIL GROWS THROUGH THE EYE, •••••   82   LIGHT BREAKS   28
THE SECRET OILS THAT DRIVE THE GRASS. •••••••••••••   94   IN BEGINNING   18
IN THE BEGINNING WAS THE SECRET BRAIN. •••••••••••   94   IN BEGINNING   25
THE SECRET CHILD, I SHIFT ABOUT THE SEA •••••••••••   105   WORLD PYRAMID   59
WE IN OUR EDEN KNEW THE SECRET GUARDIAN •••••••••••   122   INCARNATE DEVL   13
TO THE ROOM OF A SECRET CHILD, ••••••••••••••••••   139   TOMBSTONE TOLD   15
THEY RETCH INTO MY SECRET NIGHT ••••••••••••••••••   143   THE MOLLS   5
BRASSILY AT MY SHYEST SECRET, ••••••••••••••••••••   146   TO OTHERS   5
WITH THE INCESTUOUS SECRET BROTHER IN THE SECONDS TO
    PERPETUATE THE STARS, •••••••••••••••••••••••••••   159   INTO HER HEAD   66
SECRET BY THE UNMOURNING WATER ••••••••••••••••••••   192   REFUSAL MOURN   22
OF THEIR MOST SECRET HEART. ••••••••••••••••••••••   197   CRAFT OR ART   11
AND THE SEA THAT HIDES HIS SECRET SELVES •••••••••••   211   POEM ON B'DAY   87
NOR DID HE NOW, SAVE TO HIS SECRET WOUND. •••••••••   217   ELEGY   27

SECRETLY

SECRETLY IN STATUARY, ••••••••••••••••••••••••••••   145   PLEASURE-BIRD   15

SECURE

I'M NOT SECURE ENOUGH •••••••••••••••••••••••••••   234   NO, PIGEON   11

SEDGE

A SEDGE OF BROKEN STALKS AND SHELLS. •••••••••••••   14   RAIN CUTS   28
SHALLOW AND SEDGE, AND 'DILLY DILLY', CALLS THE LOFT
    HAWK, ••   202   SIR JOHNS HILL   21

SEDGES

CLEAVING THEIR OWN SEDGES, ••••••••••••••••••••••   231   OUR SANCTITY   38

SEDUCER'S

BENEATH MY LIFE, THAT SIGHS FOR THE SEDUCER'S COMING   147   UNLUCKILY FOR   13

SEE

THEYD SEE WITH EYES LIKE MINE ••••••••••••••••••••   11   AIR BREATHE   10
BUT SHE DID NOT CRY, 'I SEE; ••••••••••••••••••••   11   CABARET   12
I SEE THE MAN IS MAD WITH LOVE.' •••••••••••••••••   11   CABARET   13
AND SEE THE BLOOD IS MINE, ••••••••••••••••••••••   13   SKY'S BRIGHT   23
SEE THE REASON FOR UNDOUBLING DOUBLING NOT, •••••••   24   LITTLE PROBLEM   16
TURN INSIDE OUT, AND SEE AT GLANCE •••••••••••••••   25   BEAUTY TO DUST   7
THEREFORE LIFT UP, SEE, STROKE THE LIGHT. •••••••••   35   LIFT UP FACE   24
YOU WILL NOT SEE THE STEADYING OR FALLING, ••••••••   39   GAS FADES   37
SEE, ON GRAVEL PATHS UNDER THE HARPSTRUNG TREES •••   46   POET: 1935   1
SEE, ON GRAVEL PATHS UNDER THE HARPSTRUNG TREES, ••   48   POET: 1935   58
SEE WOMEN'S FACES UNDER LIVING SNOODS, •••••••••••   51   OUT OF THE PIT   21
I SEE HIM IN THE CROWDS, NOT SHUT •••••••••••••••   53   OUT OF THE PIT   102
EYES IN THE GABLES SEE •••••••••••••••••••••••••••   62   EARS IN TURRET   3

		PAGE	TITLE	LINE
SEE (CONTINUED)				
EYES IN THIS ISLAND SEE	....	62	EARS IN TURRET	19
SEE THE FIRST LIVING LIGHT,	....	67	LET A FAITH	12
WE SEE RISE THE SECRET WIND	....	69	SECRET WIND	T
WE SEE RISE THE SECRET WIND BEHIND THE BRAIN,	.....	69	SECRET WIND	1
FIE ON YOU, AUNT, THAT YOU SHOULD SEE	....	83	LETTER TO AUNT	7
AND HOW TO SCALE AND SEE THE SIGHTS	....	83	LETTER TO AUNT	13
SEE, SAYS THE LIME	....	85	SEE, SAYS LIME	T
SEE, SAYS THE LIME, MY WICKED MILKS	....	85	SEE, SAYS LIME	1
SEE, SAYS THE LIME, AROUND THESE WRECKS	....	86	SEE, SAYS LIME	25
I SEE THE BOYS OF SUMMER	....	91	BOYS OF SUMMER	T
I SEE THE BOYS OF SUMMER IN THEIR RUIN	....	91	BOYS OF SUMMER	1
I SEE THE SUMMER CHILDREN IN THEIR MOTHERS	....	92	BOYS OF SUMMER	13
I SEE THAT FROM THESE BOYS SHALL MEN OF NOTHING	...	92	BOYS OF SUMMER	19
O SEE THE PULSE OF SUMMER IN THE ICE.	....	92	BOYS OF SUMMER	24
O SEE THE POLES OF PROMISE IN THE BOYS.	....	93	BOYS OF SUMMER	48
I SEE YOU BOYS OF SUMMER IN YOUR RUIN.	....	93	BOYS OF SUMMER	49
O SEE THE POLES ARE KISSING AS THEY CROSS.	....	93	BOYS OF SUMMER	54
THAT MEN MIGHT SEE THE DEVIL IN THE CRUMB	....	96	TWELVE	13
THEY SEE THE SQUIRREL STUMBLE,	....	109	I, IN IMAGE	40
AND MANY YEARS SHOULD SEE SOME CHANGE.	....	116	LANTERNS SHINE	17
THAT THE GREEN CHILD SEE LIKE A GRAIL	....	129	MY NEOPHYTE	22
'SEE,' DRUMMED THE TAUT MASKS, 'HOW THE DEAD ASCEND:		132	I MAKE THIS IN	52
WHEN ALL MY FIVE AND COUNTRY SENSES SEE	....	138	FIVE & COUNTRY	T
WHEN ALL MY FIVE AND COUNTRY SENSES SEE,	....	138	FIVE & COUNTRY	1
CELIBATE I SIT AND SEE	....	138	O CHATTERTON	29
MY NOSTRILS SEE HER BREATH BURN LIKE A BUSH.	......	139	FIVE & COUNTRY	10
THAT BURY THE SWEET STREET SLOWLY, SEE	....	142	SAINT TO FALL	33
O WAKE TO SEE, AFTER A NOBLE FALL,	....	142	SAINT TO FALL	43
I SEE THE TIGRON IN TEARS	....	148	UNLUCKILY FOR	29
I SEE THE WANTING NUN SAINT CARVED IN A GARB	......	148	UNLUCKILY FOR	34
CONTINENCE. I SEE THE UNFIRED PHOENIX, HERALD	.....	148	UNLUCKILY FOR	37
ALL I COULD SEE WERE HIS BROWN EYES BURNING	....	149	PAPER & STICKS	8
NOW SEE, ALONE IN US,	....	153	WAS A SAVIOUR	36
SEE WHAT THE GOLD GUT DRAGS FROM UNDER	....	166	LONG-LEGGED	131
SEE WHAT CLINGS TO HAIR AND SKULL	....	166	LONG-LEGGED	133
SEE HOW HE STUMBLES. HALLELUJAH HEE-HAW!	....	179	NEW QUAY	26
YOU MAY NOT SEE, MY SON,	....	192	SIDE OF TRUTH	2
OF DUSK AND WATER I SEE THE TILTING WHISPERING	....	202	SIR JOHNS HILL	48
GRAVE MEN, NEAR DEATH, WHO SEE WITH BLINDING SIGHT		208	NOT GO GENTLE	13
TO SEE THE SUN MYSELF,	....	239	LET ME ESCAPE	11
AND SEE YOUR COLOUR SNAP,	....	239	MAKES INTERVALS	18
SEE-AT-ZERO				
MAN-IN-SEED, IN SEE-AT-ZERO,	....	127	SEED-AT-ZERO	50
SEED				
OUT OF THE SOIL AND SEED INTO THE DRIVE,	....	29	LONG, SKELETON	2
IN THE FACE OF SEED AND FRUIT?	....	72	TAKE NEEDLES	60
THE SEED OF TIME IS SHELTERED IN THE LOIN:	....	80	ALMANAC TIME	12
WARMS YOUTH AND SEED AND BURNS THE SEEDS OF AGE;		82	LIGHT BREAKS	8
WHERE NO SEED STIRS,	....	82	LIGHT BREAKS	9
THE SEED THAT MAKES A FOREST OF THE LOIN	....	88	A PROCESS IN	13
THE FELLOW SEED AND SHADOW AS IT BABBLED	....	104	WORLD PYRAMID	9
TWO HEELS OF WATER ON THE FLOOR OF SEED),	....	114	SERVANT SUN	24
LET HER INHALE HER DEAD, THROUGH SEED AND SOLID	...	115	A GRIEF AGO	37
SHALL THE STAR-FLANKED SEED BE RIDDLED,	....	125	SEED-AT-ZERO	16
SHALL THE STAR-FLANKED SEED BE RIDDLED,	....	126	SEED-AT-ZERO	23
LET THE HERO SEED FIND HARBOUR,	....	126	SEED-AT-ZERO	33
LET THE HERO SEED FIND HARBOUR,	....	126	SEED-AT-ZERO	40
AND THE BREATH-WHITE, CURTAINED MOUTH OF SEED.'	...	132	I MAKE THIS IN	51
SEED OF SONS IN THE LOIN OF THE BLACK HUSK LEFT.		174	FIRE RAID	32

	PAGE	TITLE	LINE
SEED (CONTINUED)			
NEVER TO FLOURISH IN THE FIELDS OF THE WHITE SEED	188	WINTER'S TALE	54
THE FIELDS OF SEED AND THE TIME DYING FLESH ASTRIDE,	190	WINTER'S TALE	103
OR SOW MY SALT SEED	191	REFUSAL MOURN	11
LIKE THE MOON'S SEED, RUBBISH	193	SIDE OF TRUTH	26
APPLE SEED GLIDES,	199	COUNTRY SLEEP	61
PLEADING IN THE WADED BAY FOR THE SEED TO FLOW	203	GIANT'S THIGH	7
SEED-AT-ZERO			
THE SEED-AT-ZERO	125	SEED-AT-ZERO	T
THE SEED-AT-ZERO SHALL NOT STORM	125	SEED-AT-ZERO	1
THE SEED-AT-ZERO SHALL NOT STORM	125	SEED-AT-ZERO	8
MAN-IN-SEED, IN SEED-AT-ZERO,	126	SEED-AT-ZERO	43
SEEDED			
FEAR NOT THE TREAD, THE SEEDED MILLING,	106	ALL ALL AND	16
SEEDLESS			
OUR EUNUCH DREAMS, ALL SEEDLESS IN THE LIGHT,	89	EUNUCH DREAMS	1
SEEDS			
WHO CANNOT COUNT THE SEEDS HE SOWS,	29	NEARLY SUMMER	8
WARMS YOUTH AND SEED AND BURNS THE SEEDS OF AGE;	82	LIGHT BREAKS	8
BY RED-EYED ORCHARDS SOW THE SEEDS OF SNOW,	123	FOSTER LIGHT	11
AND THE STRUTTING FERN LAY SEEDS ON THE BLACK SILL.	137	AFTER FUNERAL	40
SEEDY			
STATURE BY SEEDY SHIFTING,	92	BOYS OF SUMMER	20
WITH SWAG OF BUBBLES IN A SEEDY SACK	108	GRIEF THIEF	17
BY CRANE AND WATER-TOWER BY THE SEEDY TREES	122	HOLD HARD	8
EMASCULATE THE SEEDY CLOCKS;	156	RETURN	80
SEEK			
OF NEW MAN STRENGTH, I SEEK THE SUN.	103	I DREAMED MY	28
WHO SEEK ME LANDWARD, MARKING IN MY MOUTH	105	WORLD PYRAMID	46
BE YOU SURE THE THIEF WILL SEEK A WAY SLY AND SURE	199	COUNTRY SLEEP	49
SEEK HIM, THOU SUN, IN THE DREAD WILDERNESS,	222	MISSING	1
FOR THAT HE LOVED THEE, SEEK THOU HIM AND BLESS	222	MISSING	2
SEEKING			
SEEKING NO FURTHER THAN YOUR PETALS THAT STILL SLEPT.	227	SPRING-SPIRIT	8
SEEMS			
THEIR PALE, ETHEREAL BEAUTY SEEMS TO BE	222	IN DREAMS	3
SOMEHOW IT SEEMS, AMID THE EVENING HAZE,	223	IN DREAMS	8
HER GARDEN BLOOMS WITH IRIS, AND IT SEEMS	223	IN DREAMS	13
SEEN			
YOU TOO HAVE SEEN THE SUN A BIRD OF FIRE	30	YOUTH CALLS	1
HE, TOO, HAS SEEN THE WORLD AS BOTTOM ROTTEN,	52	OUT OF THE PIT	56
BUT NO GOD ROSE. I HAVE SEEN BAD AND WORSE,	52	OUT OF THE PIT	77
ONCE SEEN STRANGERS OR SHADES ON A STAIR;	157	INTO HER HEAD	15
TO HAVE SEEN COUNTRIES WHICH WERE GLORIOUS,	223	IDYLL UNFORGET	1
SEEPING			
OR, WHITE AS MILK, OUT OF THE SEEPING DARK,	20	ENCOMPASSED	11
SEES			
AND SEES MY BODY GO	12	SKY'S BRIGHT	14
SEES THE MOON STILL UP,	14	FOR LEDA	8
DEATH SIGHTS AND SEES WITH GREAT MISGIVING	25	THERE'S PLENTY	6
ALONE'S UNHURT, SO THE BLIND MAN SEES BEST.	40	WAS THERE TIME	9
MY HERO BARES MY SIDE AND SEES HIS HEART	75	MY HERO BARES	11
SEESAW			
AND ON SEESAW SUNDAY NIGHTS I WOOED	206	LAMENT	8
SEETHE			
THE GRAINS OF LIFE MUST SEETHE BENEATH THE SUN,	80	ALMANAC TIME	13
SEETHES			
A BETTER VENOM SEETHES IN SPITTLE	137	O CHATTERTON	6
SEIZING			
ON A SEIZING SKY; SMALL FISHES GLIDE	209	POEM ON B'DAY	22

	PAGE	TITLE	LINE
SEIZURE			
IN SEIZURE OF SILENCE COMMIT THE DEAD NUISANCE: ...	109	I, IN IMAGE	23
SELECTED			
SYMBOLS ARE SELECTED FROM THE YEARS'	58	HERE IN SPRING	5
SELF			
DEAD AND GONE, DEDICATE FOREVER TO MY SELF	147	UNLUCKILY FOR	6
NEVER SHALL MY SELF CHANT	148	UNLUCKILY FOR	25
MY CAVERNOUS, FEATHERBED SELF.	156	RETURN	76
LIVE SELF FOR SELF, ...	239	LET ME ESCAPE	3
LIVE SELF FOR SELF, ...	239	LET ME ESCAPE	3
SELVES			
AROUND OUR LITTLE SELVES	24	THE ONLY DEAD	32
WHO SHOWS TO THE SELVES ASLEEP	165	LONG-LEGGED	103
AND THE SEA THAT HIDES HIS SECRET SELVES	211	POEM ON B'DAY	87
SEND			
TAKE COURAGE, AUNT, AND SEND YOUR STUFF	85	LETTER TO AUNT	63
SENDS			
IF NOT IN PERSON SENDS HIS UNENDING EVIL	29	NEARLY SUMMER	3
SENNA			
LIKE SENNA STIRS ALONG THE RAVAGED ROOTS.	80	ALL THAT I OWE	4
SENSATION			
EACH NEW SENSATION EMITS	137	O CHATTERTON	8
SENSE			
THE SENSE IT IS TO HAVE.	10	COOL, OH NO	26
FOR USE OF SENSE, (NO HURT NO SENSE).	24	LITTLE PROBLEM	9
FOR USE OF SENSE, (NO HURT NO SENSE).	24	LITTLE PROBLEM	9
SENSE CAN BUT MAIM IT, WISDOM MAR IT, ...	25	BEAUTY TO DUST	9
WAS WHEN SENSE FOUND A WAY TO THEM	25	BEAUTY TO DUST	14
IN TRUST AND TALE HAVE I DIVIDED SENSE, ...	124	TODAY, INSECT	5
CAN'T READ SENSE IN THE RAIN THAT WILLYNILLY	137	O CHATTERTON	19
RESEMBLING TO HER DULLED SENSE	158	INTO HER HEAD	30
TO ONE SENSE OF FINALITY	230	OUR SANCTITY	20
SENSES			
TO MAKE OUR SENSES TAKE TOO MUCH, ...	13	RAIN CUTS	10
THEN SHALL YOUR SENSES, OUT OF JOY, ...	21	BEWILDERED WAY	13
AND FROM THESE TONGUE-PLUCKED SENSES DRAWS HIS TUNE;	76	LASHED RINGS	13
HEIR TO THE TELLING SENSES THAT ALONE	80	ALL THAT I OWE	11
WHEN ALL MY FIVE AND COUNTRY SENSES SEE	138	FIVE & COUNTRY	T
WHEN ALL MY FIVE AND COUNTRY SENSES SEE, ...	138	FIVE & COUNTRY	1
AND WHEN BLIND SLEEP DROPS ON THE SPYING SENSES,	139	FIVE & COUNTRY	13
SENSES, AND MAN A SPIRIT IN LOVE	211	POEM ON B'DAY	83
AND THE WEB OF YOUR STRAIGHT SENSES.	236	WOMAN TAPESTRY	49
TO-DAY, IF ALL MY SENSES ACT, ...	238	MAKES INTERVALS	9
SENSES'			
NOT FROM THE SENSES' DUALIZING TIP	20	THE NEOPHYTE	16
TO WHISPER, WHEN HE WANTS, THE SENSES' WAR	29	NEARLY SUMMER	12
OR LAY THE SENSES' RUMOUR.	30	NEARLY SUMMER	13
THE FIBRES, OR THE SENSES' THREAD.	233	NO THOUGHT	8
SENSIBLE			
HE WHOSE LOVERS WERE BOTH WISE AND SENSIBLE	25	BEAUTY TO DUST	18
SENSITIVE			
A SENSITIVE CONFUSION IN THE BLOOD, ...	235	WOMAN TAPESTRY	28
LIKE A SWEET, SENSITIVE PLANT	237	WOMAN TAPESTRY	71
SENSUAL			
BORN OF THE SENSUAL ROOT AND SAP;	86	BREAD I BREAK	14
THE HEART IS SENSUAL, THOUGH FIVE EYES BREAK.	139	FIVE & COUNTRY	14
DRESSED TO DIE, THE SENSUAL STRUT BEGUN, ...	143	24 YEARS	6
SAINT CARVED AND SENSUAL AMONG THE SCUDDING	147	UNLUCKILY FOR	5
AND THE SENSUAL RUINS MAKE	166	LONG-LEGGED	118

	PAGE	TITLE	LINE
SENT			
I SENT MY CREATURE SCOUTING ON THE GLOBE, ...	97	TWILIGHT LOCKS	9
I SENT MY OWN AMBASSADOR TO LIGHT;	98	TWILIGHT LOCKS	33
SENTENCE			
THE DEAR, DAFT TIME I TAKE TO NUDGE THE SENTENCE,	124	TODAY, INSECT	4
SENTIMENT			
THE SIMPLEST THOUGHT OR SENTIMENT, ...	84	LETTER TO AUNT	42
SENTINEL			
THE SEXTON SENTINEL, GARRISONED UNDER THISTLES, ...	110	I, IN IMAGE	57
SEPARATE			
TOUCHING OUR SEPARATE LOVE WITH BADINAGE	24	THE ONLY DEAD	33
A SEPARATE RIVER BREATHES AND RUNS;	168	LONG-LEGGED	180
SEPULCHRE			
TIME'S CORAL SAINT AND THE SALT GRIEF DROWN A FOUL			
SEPULCHRE	130	SINNERS' BELL	8
SERAPHIC			
AND SERAPHIC FIELDS OF SHEPHERDS	215	COUNTRY HEAVEN	19
SERAPHIM			
TO SERAPHIM	200	COUNTRY SLEEP	79
SERENE			
SERENE AND UNBROKEN, ...	235	WOMAN TAPESTRY	14
SERENITY			
FELT THEIR SERENITY OF RIPPLE-WOVEN LOVELINESS; ...	223	IDYLL UNFORGET	4
SERIAL			
SUIT FOR A SERIAL SUM	151	BELOW A TIME	4
SERMON			
YARD OF THE BUTTERMILK RAIN ON THE PAIL! THE SERMON	200	COUNTRY SLEEP	77
SERPENT			
A SERPENT FIDDLED IN THE SHAPING-TIME.	122	INCARNATE DEVL	18
THIS STORY'S MONSTER HAS A SERPENT CAUL, ...	124	TODAY, INSECT	10
UNDER A SERPENT CLOUD, ...	209	POEM ON B'DAY	32
SERPENTS			
THERE SHALL BE SERPENTS IN YOUR TIDES, ...	91	WHERE ONCE THE	23
POUR LIKE A HALO ON THE CAPS AND SERPENTS.	120	ALTARWISE	118
SERPENTS'			
WITH SERPENTS' MOUTHS AND SCALECOPHIDIAN VOIDS	51	OUT OF THE PIT	22
SERPENT'S			
THAN ONE COULD PROBE OUT OF A SERPENT'S GUTS;	137	O CHATTERTON	7
WHO WAS THE SERPENT'S	174	FIRE RAID	55
SERVANT			
HOW SOON THE SERVANT SUN	113	SERVANT SUN	T
HOW SOON THE SERVANT SUN, ...	113	SERVANT SUN	1
SERVANTS			
CHILD WHO WAS PRIEST AND SERVANTS, ...	174	FIRE RAID	52
SERVE			
ALL NERVES TO SERVE THE SUN, ...	114	SERVANT SUN	15
MASTER THE NIGHT NOR SERVE THE SNOWMAN'S BRAIN	123	FOSTER LIGHT	4
NUTMEG, CIVET, AND SEA-PARSLEY SERVE THE PLAGUED			
GROOM AND BRIDE	131	SINNERS' BELL	29
AND SERVE ME RIGHT AS THE PREACHERS WARN, ...	207	LAMENT	38
SERVES			
RAPE GULP AND BE MARRY, HE ALSO SERVES	138	O CHATTERTON	26
SERVICE			
THE SEAS TO SERVICE THAT HER WOOD-TONGUED VIRTUE	136	AFTER FUNERAL	22
SILENT IN MY SERVICE	174	FIRE RAID	49
SET			
SET AGAINST GRANITE, ...	19	IMAGES IN AIR	3
BUT TIME HAS SET ITS MAGGOT ON THEIR TRACK.	40	WAS THERE TIME	4
WE HAVE NO FAITH TO SET BETWEEN OUR TEETH.	42	YOUNG ARE OLD	56

	PAGE	TITLE	LINE
SET (CONTINUED)			
THROUGH THESE LASHED RINGS SET DEEP INSIDE THEIR			
HOLLOWS	76	LASHED RINGS	1
AND THROUGH THESE TREMBLING RINGS SET IN THEIR VALLEY	76	LASHED RINGS	4
THAT SET ALIGHT THE WEATHERS FROM A SPARK, ...	94	IN BEGINNING	14
STILL SET TO SCRATCH A LAUGHTER FROM MY LUNG, ...	95	RUB OF LOVE	5
SAILED AND SET DAZZLING BY THE HANDSHAPED OCEAN,	131	I MAKE THIS IN	5
I SET BACK THE CLOCK FACED TAILORS, ...	151	BELOW A TIME	18
SUFFER THE FIRST VISION THAT SET FIRE TO THE STARS.	170	LOVE IN ASYLUM	18
MYSELF TO SET FOOT	177	POEM IN OCT	8
IN THE STILL SLEEPING TOWN AND SET FORTH.	177	POEM IN OCT	10
SILLY TO CAGE AND THEN SET FREE, ...	237	PILLAR BREAKS	8
SETS			
POOR PEACE AS THE SUN SETS	5	PROLOGUE	89
SOON SETS ALIGHT A LONG STICK FROM THE CRADLE;	117	ALTARWISE	20
OVER THE SEA-GUT LOUDENING, SETS A ROCK ALIVE;	122	HOLD HARD	15
SETTING			
THE SEASON'S SUN, THOUGH HE SHOULD KNOW HIS SETTING	25	THERE'S PLENTY	4
SETTING NO STORE BY HARVEST, FREEZE THE SOILS;	91	BOYS OF SUMMER	3
SETTLE			
AND SETTLE IN THE STEADY PATH.	233	NO THOUGHT	15
SETTLED			
SETTLED ON A VIRGIN STRONGHOLD	125	SEED-AT-ZERO	19
SETTLES			
AS THEY DIVE, THE DUST SETTLES, ...	110	I, IN IMAGE	43
SETTLING			
SETTLING ON A RIDDLED STRONGHOLD	126	SEED-AT-ZERO	26
SEVEN			
THAT SPEAK SEVEN SEAS, ...	3	PROLOGUE	17
WHEN I WAS SEVEN I COUNTED FOUR AND FORTY TREES ...	33	HELD-OUT HAND	12
STUCK STRAW AND SEVEN STARS UPON MY HAIR, ...	52	OUT OF THE PIT	65
SPELT OUT THE SEVEN SEAS, AND EVIL INDEX, ...	119	ALTARWISE	82
AND INTO ITS TALKATIVE SEVEN TOMBS	169	LONG-LEGGED	211
SEVENTY			
AND SCULPTURED ANN IS SEVENTY YEARS OF STONE.	137	AFTER FUNERAL	35
SEVER			
HERE CLINGS THE MEAT TO SEVER FROM HIS SIDE.	81	HERE LIE BEAST	5
SEVERAL			
OF SEVERAL NEAR DEATHS, ...	160	DEATHS AND ENT	2
SEVERERS			
AND THE SECOND COMERS, THE SEVERERS, THE ENEMIES			
FROM THE DEEP	159	INTO HER HEAD	68
SEW			
WHEN YOU SEW THE DEEP DOOR. THE BED IS A CROSS PLACE.	145	IF HEAD HURT	13
SEWER			
SO CRYING, HE WAS DRAGGED INTO THE SEWER, ...	51	OUT OF THE PIT	39
SEWING			
SEWING A LIE TO A CREDULITY, ...	18	NATURAL DAY	11
SOAKS UP THE SEWING TIDES), ...	113	SERVANT SUN	12
SEWING A SHROUD FOR A JOURNEY	143	24 YEARS	4
SEWN			
AND SEWN ON HIS SKULL A SCARLET THORN;	74	SUN BURNS	13
THAT, SEWN TO ME BY NERVE AND BRAIN, ...	97	TWILIGHT LOCKS	11
SEX			
THE STRINGS OF FIRE CHOKED HIS SEX	85	SEE, SAYS LIME	17
THE KNOBBLY APE THAT SWINGS ALONG HIS SEX	96	RUB OF LOVE	37
NO THIRD EYE PROBE INTO A RAINBOW'S SEX	108	GRIEF THIEF	25
THE CLIMBER OF THE WATER SEX	128	MY NEOPHYTE	11
SEXTON			
THE SEXTON SENTINEL, GARRISONED UNDER THISTLES, ...	110	I, IN IMAGE	57

	PAGE	TITLE	LINE
SHABBY			
PULLS DOWN THE SHABBY CURTAINS OF THE SKIN;	88	A PROCESS IN	23
THE CRIERS OF SHABBY AND SHORTEN, ...	151	BELOW A TIME	27
SHADE			
ALCOVE OF WORDS OUT OF CICADA SHADE, ...	54	WE BY SEASAND	4
TO SHADE AND KNIT ANEW THE PATCH OF WORDS	79	LOVE'S FEVER	34
SITS IN THEIR DOUBLE SHADE.	88	A PROCESS IN	21
ON THAT CLOUD COAST TO EACH GRAVE-GABBING SHADE;	102	FELLOWED SLEEP	18
SHADE WITHOUT SHAPE? THE SHAPE OF PHARAOH'S ECHO?	118	ALTARWISE	45
AND THIS, NOR THIS, IS SHADE, THE LANDED CROW, ...	127	NOW, SAY NAY	19
FROM YOUR TOMORROW-TREADING SHADE	129	MY NEOPHYTE	41
DOWN THE STACKED SEA AND WATER-PILLARED SHADE, ...	132	I MAKE THIS IN	40
THE SHADE OF THEIR TREES WAS A WORD OF MANY SHADES	144	COLOUR OF SAY	10
AND THE CUP AND THE CUT BREAD IN THE DANCING SHADE,	188	WINTER'S TALE	28
BELL BELIEVE OR FEAR THAT THE RUSTIC SHADE OR SPELL	198	COUNTRY SLEEP	22
WINDS, FROM THE DOUSING SHADE AND THE ROARER AT THE LATCH, ...	199	COUNTRY SLEEP	46
UNDER THIS SHADE	230	OUR SANCTITY	22
THIS SHADE	231	OUR SANCTITY	36
SHADES			
BRANCHES A MILLION SHADES, ...	14	RAIN CUTS	22
LOST IN THE SHADES, NO COURSE, NO USE	41	YOUNG ARE OLD	22
THE SHADES OF GIRLS, ALL FLAVOURED FROM THEIR SHROUDS, ...	89	EUNUCH DREAMS	7
THERE ROUND ABOUT YOUR STONES THE SHADES	91	WHERE ONCE THE	16
THERE IN THE DEEP WITH QUARTERED SHADES	92	BOYS OF SUMMER	16
WHERE FISHES' FOOD IS FED THE SHADES	98	TWILIGHT LOCKS	29
THE SHADE OF THEIR TREES WAS A WORD OF MANY SHADES	144	COLOUR OF SAY	10
AND FOR THE WOMAN IN SHADES	147	UNLUCKILY FOR	4
ABOUT THE SAINT IN SHADES WHILE THE ENDLESS BREVIARY	148	UNLUCKILY FOR	26
OF SHADES, SYMBOL OF DESIRE BEYOND MY HOURS	148	UNLUCKILY FOR	35
A HOLE OF ERRANDS AND SHADES;	156	RETURN	78
ONCE SEEN STRANGERS OR SHADES ON A STAIR;	157	INTO HER HEAD	15
SHADOW			
THE BLACK SHADOW COMES DOWN, ...	18	NATURAL DAY	21
IS LOVE A SHADOW ON THE WALL, ...	47	POET: 1935	23
AND CAST A SHADOW CRAB UPON THE LAND, ...	98	OCTOBER WIND	4
THE FELLOW SEED AND SHADOW AS IT BABBLED	104	WORLD PYRAMID	9
OPEN AS TO THE AIR TO THE NAKED SHADOW	159	INTO HER HEAD	63
A WIND THROWS A SHADOW AND IT FREEZES FAST.	166	LONG-LEGGED	130
SHALL I LET PRAY THE SHADOW OF A SOUND	191	REFUSAL MOURN	10
UP TO THE SWALLOW THRONGED LOFT BY THE SHADOW OF MY HAND, ...	196	FERN HILL	47
IT HAS BEEN VAGUE, AND MADE OF SHADOW, ...	224	IDYLL UNFORGET	25
THE DARKNESS IS ILLIMITABLE, GREEN SHADOW, ...	224	IDYLL UNFORGET	43
OR THROW A VIOLET SHADOW WHEN I WILL.	238	MAKES INTERVALS	8
SHADOWED			
AND THE SHADOWED HEAD OF PAIN	180	VISION, PRAYER	24
SHADOWLESS			
THUS THE SHADOWLESS MAN OR OX, AND THE PICTURED DEVIL, ...	109	I, IN IMAGE	22
SHADOWS			
THE SHADOWS FROM THE GLASSY SEA	15	FOR LEDA	11
DRAMATIC SHADOWS IN A TIN BOX;	57	TO ARCHITECTS	2
WE WATCH THE SHOW OF SHADOWS KISS OR KILL, ...	89	EUNUCH DREAMS	19
BISECTED SHADOWS ON THE THUNDER'S BONE	103	WORLD PYRAMID	5
OF PSALMS AND SHADOWS AMONG THE PINCERED SANDCRABS PRANCING	202	SIR JOHNS HILL	24
DOWN THESE FANTASTIC AVENUES PASS LIKE SHADOWS. ...	222	FOREST PICTURE	12

	PAGE	TITLE	LINE
SHADOWY			
INFINITE SHADOWY ISLES LIE SILENT BEFORE ME, ...	221	FOREST PICTURE	3
SHAFT			
THE LOVELY GIFT OF THE GAB BANGS BACK ON A BLIND			
SHAFT.	140	NO WORK WORDS	6
TO CATCH THE SHAFT	231	YOUR VOICE	4
SHAFTED			
AND SHAFTED HAWKS CAME SNARLING DOWN THE SKY;	65	WOMAN SPEAKS	57
FLIES ON THE SHAFTED DISK, DECLAIMS THE MORNING ...	99	OCTOBER WIND	19
SHAKEN			
THROUGH THE SHAKEN GREENSWARD LAKE, SILENT, ON			
MOONSHOD HOOVES, ...	200	COUNTRY SLEEP	84
SHAKEN SILKILY FROM STAR-SCALED BOUGHS.	226	SLENDER WIND	5
SHAKES			
SHAKES, IN CRABBED BURIAL SHAWL, BY SORCERER'S			
INSECT WOKEN, ...	130	SINNERS' BELL	23
SHAKES A DESOLATE BOY WHO SLITS HIS THROAT	136	AFTER FUNERAL	7
SHAKING			
BEFORE THE VEINS WERE SHAKING IN THEIR SIEVE, ...	94	IN BEGINNING	28
SHAKING THE SEA-HATCHED SKULL, ...	111	I, IN IMAGE	100
SHALL			
YOU I SHALL DROWN UNREASONABLY, ...	9	MINUTE'S HOUR	9
THEN SHALL I GO, ...	9	MINUTE'S HOUR	19
BUT YOU SHALL NOT GO FROM ME, CREATION;	10	COOL, OH NO	19
YOU SHALL NOT GO UNLESS I WILL IT	10	COOL, OH NO	21
AND WHO SHALL TELL THE AMORIST	17	IN OBLIVION	27
THEN SHALL YOUR SENSES, OUT OF JOY, ...	21	BEWILDERED WAY	13
SHALL PROVE UNWORTHY FOR HIS DOING, ...	23	THE ONLY DEAD	15
CONTENT SHALL COME AFTER A TWISTED NIGHT	35	LIFT UP FACE	25
WE SHALL PLAY CHOPIN IN OUR SUMMER GARDEN, ...	40	YOUNG ARE OLD	12
SHALL I FALL TO DEATH'S FEATHER.	44	LONGED TO MOVE	18
YOU SHALL GO AS THE OTHERS HAVE GONE, ...	45	PLOUGHMAN GONE	16
THEN ONLY OVER CORPSES SHALL THE FEET TREAD, ...	45	TO FOLLOW FOX	20
SO SHALL HE STEP TILL SUMMER LOOSENS ITS HOLD	46	POET: 1935	18
YOU SHALL GO AS THE OTHERS HAVE GONE, ...	46	PLOUGHMAN GONE	30
SUCH LIGHT SHALL NOT ILLUMINATE MY FEARS	48	LIGHT, I KNOW	4
UNLESS I LEARN THE NIGHT I SHALL GO MAD.	48	LIGHT, I KNOW	12
AND DEATH SHALL HAVE NO DOMINION	49	NO DOMINION	T
AND DEATH SHALL HAVE NO DOMINION.	49	NO DOMINION	1
DEAD MEN NAKED THEY SHALL BE ONE	49	NO DOMINION	2
THEY SHALL HAVE STARS AT ELBOW AND FOOT;	49	NO DOMINION	5
THOUGH THEY GO MAD THEY SHALL BE SANE, ...	49	NO DOMINION	6
THOUGH THEY SINK THROUGH THE SEA THEY SHALL RISE			
AGAIN;	49	NO DOMINION	7
THOUGH LOVERS BE LOST LOVE SHALL NOT;	49	NO DOMINION	8
AND DEATH SHALL HAVE NO DOMINION.	49	NO DOMINION	9
AND DEATH SHALL HAVE NO DOMINION.	49	NO DOMINION	10
THEY LYING LONG SHALL NOT DIE WINDILY;	49	NO DOMINION	12
STRAPPED TO A WHEEL, YET THEY SHALL NOT BREAK;	49	NO DOMINION	14
FAITH IN THEIR HANDS SHALL SNAP IN TWO, ...	50	NO DOMINION	15
AND DEATH SHALL HAVE NO DOMINION.	50	NO DOMINION	18
AND DEATH SHALL HAVE NO DOMINION.	50	NO DOMINION	19
AND DEATH SHALL HAVE NO DOMINION.	50	NO DOMINION	27
SHALL NOT BE KNOWN TILL WINDWELL DRIES	55	WHY EAST WIND	2
THE CHILD SHALL QUESTION ALL HIS DAYS, ...	56	WHY EAST WIND	7
SHALL THEY CLASP A COMET IN THEIR FISTS?	56	WHY EAST WIND	11
SHALL A WHITE ANSWER ECHO FROM THE ROOFTOPS.	56	WHY EAST WIND	15
SHALL LAMP THE RAVEN DARKNESS OF HER FACE, ...	57	GREEK PLAY	9
WHAT SHALL IT TELL ME IF A TIMELESS INSECT	59	HERE IN SPRING	16
WHAT SHALL DESTRUCTION COUNT IF THESE ARE FIXTURES?	60	FAIRY TALES	27

SHALL (CONTINUED)

		PAGE	TITLE	LINE
SHALL WE LEARN FAIRY TALES OFF PAT,	....	60	FAIRY TALES	37
SHALL I UNBOLT OR STAY	....	62	EARS IN TURRET	5
SHALL I RUN TO THE SHIPS	....	62	EARS IN TURRET	21
SHALL I LET IN THE STRANGER,	....	63	EARS IN TURRET	29
SHALL I WELCOME THE SAILOR,	....	63	EARS IN TURRET	30
THERE SHALL BE NO MUTE MOURNING OVER HIS ACRE,	....	64	WOMAN SPEAKS	38
SORROW SHALL HAVE NO WORDS, NO WILLOW WEARING;	....	64	WOMAN SPEAKS	39
RAIN SHALL DEFILE AND COVER, WIND BEAR AWAY	....	64	WOMAN SPEAKS	40
SHALL GODS BE SAID TO THUMP THE CLOUDS	....	65	GODS THUMP	T
SHALL GODS BE SAID TO THUMP THE CLOUDS	....	65	GODS THUMP	1
SHALL RAINBOWS BE THEIR TUNICS' COLOUR?	....	65	GODS THUMP	4
SHALL IT BE SAID THEY SPRINKLE WATER	....	65	GODS THUMP	6
SHALL IT BE SAID THAT, VENUSWISE,	....	65	GODS THUMP	8
IT SHALL BE SAID THAT GODS ARE STONE.	....	65	GODS THUMP	11
SHALL A DROPPED STONE DRUM ON THE GROUND,	....	65	GODS THUMP	12
GOD SHALL BE GODS AND MANY DEATHS BE DEATH.	....	67	LET A FAITH	15
QUESTION: SHALL THE ROOT BE TRUE	....	72	TAKE NEEDLES	57
ANSWER: SHALL A MOTHER LIE	....	72	TAKE NEEDLES	59
QUESTION: WHEN SHALL ROOT-DAM DIE?	....	72	TAKE NEEDLES	61
QUESTION: WHEN SHALL ROOT-DAM GROW?	....	72	TAKE NEEDLES	63
NOT FOREVER SHALL THE LORD OF THE RED HAIL	....	73	LORD RED HAIL	T
NOT FOREVER SHALL THE LORD OF THE RED HAIL	....	73	LORD RED HAIL	1
HE SHALL BE WISE AND LET HIS BRIMSTONE SPILL,	......	73	LORD RED HAIL	3
AND SWEET SHALL FALL CONTAGION FROM HIS SIDE,	......	73	LORD RED HAIL	5
SHALL DROWN THE BOYS OF BATTLE IN THEIR SWILL,	....	73	LORD RED HAIL	8
SHALL FALL AWAY, AND LEAVE ONE SINGING SHELL.	......	73	LORD RED HAIL	12
A HOLE IN SPACE SHALL KEEP THE SHAPE OF THOUGHT,		73	LORD RED HAIL	13
INTANGIBLE MY WORLD SHALL COME TO NAUGHT,	....	73	LORD RED HAIL	16
THE SOLID WORLD SHALL WITHER IN THE HEAT,	....	73	LORD RED HAIL	17
SHALL CALM HER SORES.	....	77	THE FORCE THAT	18
TIME SHALL BELONG TO MAN.	....	80	ALMANAC TIME	15
YOUR PAIN SHALL BE A MUSIC	....	87	PAIN BE MUSIC	T
YOUR PAIN SHALL BE A MUSIC IN YOUR STRING	....	87	PAIN BE MUSIC	1
YOUR PAIN SHALL BE	....	87	PAIN BE MUSIC	3
YOUR STRING SHALL STRETCH A GULLY TWIXT THE THUMBS		87	PAIN BE MUSIC	7
WHOSE FLAMING BLOOD SHALL RUB IT AT THE RIMS	......	87	PAIN BE MUSIC	8
YOUR PAIN SHALL BE	....	87	PAIN BE MUSIC	9
YOUR PAIN SHALL BE A MEANING IN YOUR LIPS	....	87	PAIN BE MUSIC	13
AS MILK SHALL BE A MUSIC IN THE PAPS	....	87	PAIN BE MUSIC	14
YOUR PAIN SHALL BE	....	87	PAIN BE MUSIC	15
YOUR PAIN SHALL NOT UNMILK YOU OF THE FOOD	....	87	PAIN BE MUSIC	19
YOUR PAIN SHALL BE	....	87	PAIN BE MUSIC	21
SHALL FALL AWAKE WHEN CURES AND THEIR ITCH	....	89	EUNUCH DREAMS	22
FOR WE SHALL BE A SHOUTER LIKE THE COCK,	....	90	EUNUCH DREAMS	37
BLOWING THE OLD DEAD BACK; OUR SHOTS SHALL SMACK		90	EUNUCH DREAMS	38
AND WE SHALL BE FIT FELLOWS FOR A LIFE,	....	90	EUNUCH DREAMS	40
AND WHO REMAIN SHALL FLOWER AS THEY LOVE,	....	90	EUNUCH DREAMS	41
SHALL NOT BE LATCHED WHILE MAGIC GLIDES	....	91	WHERE ONCE THE	20
THERE SHALL BE CORALS IN YOUR BEDS,	....	91	WHERE ONCE THE	22
THERE SHALL BE SERPENTS IN YOUR TIDES,	....	91	WHERE ONCE THE	23
I SEE THAT FROM THESE BOYS SHALL MEN OF NOTHING	...	92	BOYS OF SUMMER	19
SHALL IT BE MALE OR FEMALE? SAY THE CELLS,	....	95	RUB OF LOVE	8
SHALL IT BE MALE OR FEMALE? SAY THE FINGERS	....	95	RUB OF LOVE	15
ALL SHALL REMAIN AND ON THE GRAVEWARD GULF	....	108	GRIEF THIEF	27
SHALL I STILL BE LOVE'S HOUSE ON THE WIDDERSHIN EARTH,	....	113	NOT FATHER ME	29
SHALL RAISE A LAMP	....	114	SERVANT SUN	25
SO SHALL WINGED HARBOURS THROUGH THE ROCKBIRDS' EYES		121	ALTARWISE	130
SHALL YOU TURN COCKWISE ON A TUFTED AXLE.	....	123	FOSTER LIGHT	24

		PAGE	TITLE	LINE
SHALL (CONTINUED)				
THE SEED-AT-ZERO SHALL NOT STORM	....	125	SEED-AT-ZERO	1
THE SEED-AT-ZERO SHALL NOT STORM	....	125	SEED-AT-ZERO	8
SHALL THE STAR-FLANKED SEED BE RIDDLED,	....	125	SEED-AT-ZERO	16
HE SHALL GRAPPLE WITH THE GUARD	....	126	SEED-AT-ZERO	20
SHALL THE STAR-FLANKED SEED BE RIDDLED,	....	126	SEED-AT-ZERO	23
HE SHALL GRAPPLE WITH THE GUARD	....	126	SEED-AT-ZERO	27
SHALL NOT THUNDER ON THE TOWN	....	126	SEED-AT-ZERO	45
SHALL THE HERO-IN-TOMORROW	....	126	SEED-AT-ZERO	48
SHALL THE HERO-IN-TOMORROW	....	127	SEED-AT-ZERO	55
'TIME SHALL NOT MURDER YOU,' HE SAID,	....	129	MY NEOPHYTE	44
HOW SHALL MY ANIMAL	....	134	HOW MY ANIMAL	T
HOW SHALL MY ANIMAL	....	134	HOW MY ANIMAL	1
SHALL SHE RECEIVE A BELLYFUL OF WEEDS	....	134	NOT FROM ANGER	5
SHALL HER SMILE BREED THAT MOUTH, BEHIND THE MIRROR,		134	NOT FROM ANGER	13
HOW SHALL IT MAGNETIZE,	....	135	HOW MY ANIMAL	12
NEVER SHALL BEAST BE BORN TO ATLAS THE FEW SEAS	...	135	HOW MY ANIMAL	32
3 LITTLE LUSTS SHALL YOUR DOWRY BE,	....	138	O CHATTERTON	42
SHALL THE BLIND HORSE SING SWEETER?	....	144	PLEASURE-BIRD	2
NOW MY SAYING SHALL BE MY UNDOING,	....	144	COLOUR OF SAY	12
SHALL I, STRUCK ON THE HOT AND ROCKING STREET,	....	145	PLEASURE-BIRD	16
NEVER SHALL MY SELF CHANT	....	148	UNLUCKILY FOR	25
TURNS OF YOUR PRAYED FLESH, NOR SHALL I SHOO THE BIRD BELOW ME:	....	148	UNLUCKILY FOR	27
BOTH SHALL FAIL IF I BOW NOT TO YOUR BLESSING	.....	148	UNLUCKILY FOR	47
ONE WHO CALLED DEEPEST DOWN SHALL HOLD HIS PEACE		160	DEATHS AND ENT	9
TILL THE BLOOD SHALL SPURT,	....	173	FIRE RAID	22
AND THE DUST SHALL SING LIKE A BIRD	....	173	FIRE RAID	23
I SHALL RUN LOST IN SUDDEN	....	181	VISION, PRAYER	45
BREAST I SHALL WAKEN	....	182	VISION, PRAYER	73
SHALL I LET PRAY THE SHADOW OF A SOUND	....	191	REFUSAL MOURN	10
I SHALL NOT MURDER	....	192	REFUSAL MOURN	14
WILL BE THE SAME GRIEF FLYING. WHOM SHALL THEY CALM?		194	CONVERS PRAYER	11
SHALL THE CHILD SLEEP UNHARMED OR THE MAN BE CRYING?		194	CONVERS PRAYER	12
OR WE SHALL OBEY, AND RIDE WITH YOU THROUGH THE DROWNED.	....	194	SLEEP BECALMED	14
TO-NIGHT SHALL FIND NO DYING BUT ALIVE AND WARM	...	194	CONVERS PRAYER	15
SHALL DROWN IN A GRIEF AS DEEP AS HIS MADE GRAVE,		194	CONVERS PRAYER	18
LOPING AND BLEATING ROUGHLY AND BLITHELY SHALL LEAP,		197	COUNTRY SLEEP	4
SHALL HARROW AND SNOW THE BLOOD WHILE YOU RIDE WIDE AND NEAR,	....	198	COUNTRY SLEEP	23
AND YOU SHALL WAKE, FROM COUNTRY SLEEP, THIS DAWN AND EACH FIRST DAWN,	....	201	COUNTRY SLEEP	110
WING, AND BLEST SHALL	....	202	SIR JOHNS HILL	29
YOU SHALL NOT DESPAIR	....	228	NOT DESPAIR	T
YOU SHALL NOT DESPAIR	....	228	NOT DESPAIR	1
YOU SHALL BE TAKEN SWEETLY AGAIN	....	228	NOT DESPAIR	12
YOU SHALL BE LOVED ENOUGH.	....	228	NOT DESPAIR	14
WAITING FOR THE BIRD WHO SHALL SAY,	....	231	OUR SANCTITY	28
YOU SHALL NOT LET GO;	....	233	FURIOUS MOTION	19
OR SHALL I DRAG YOU DOWN	....	233	NO THOUGHT	22
SHE SHALL MAKE FOR ME	....	235	WOMAN TAPESTRY	27
YOU SHALL COMFORT ME	....	236	WOMAN TAPESTRY	47
MY STRENGTH SHALL SAP YOUR OWN;	....	239	LET ME ESCAPE	9
SHALLOW				
SHALLOW AND SEDGE, AND 'DILLY DILLY', CALLS THE LOFT HAWK,	....	202	SIR JOHNS HILL	21
SHAME				
WHO KNOWS NOT ELIOT (TO HER SHAME).	....	83	LETTER TO AUNT	6
WALKING IN WISHES AND LOVELY FOR SHAME	....	165	LONG-LEGGED	105

		PAGE	TITLE	LINE
SHAMEFUL				
IS MAIDEN IN THE SHAMEFUL OAK, OMENS	....	131	I MAKE THIS IN	21
SHAMES				
SHAMES AND THE DAMP DISHONOURS, THE RELIC SCRAPING.		110	I, IN IMAGE	71
SHANK				
AN OLD MAN'S SHANK ONE-MARROWED WITH MY BONE,	.....	95	RUB OF LOVE	32
SHANT				
WIND IS MY ENEMY YOUR HAIR SHANT STIR	....	11	AIR BREATHE	3
SHAN'T				
ONLY AS WRONG; BUT SHAN'T THE GENIUS FAIL,	....	28	NO WINGS	7
SPLIT ALL ENDS UP THEY SHAN'T CRACK;	....	50	NO DOMINION	17
SHAPE				
THEY HARDEN AND TAKE SHAPE AGAIN	....	19	IMAGES IN AIR	11
A HOLE IN SPACE SHALL KEEP THE SHAPE OF THOUGHT,		73	LORD RED HAIL	13
I WOULD BE WOVEN A RELIGIOUS SHAPE;	....	96	TWELVE	9
BUT WHEN THE STARS, ASSUMING SHAPE,	....	97	TWILIGHT LOCKS	16
AND CONJURED UP A CARCASS SHAPE	....	98	TWILIGHT LOCKS	35
SHAPE WITH MY FATHERS' THIEVES.	....	108	GRIEF THIEF	28
THE DENS OF SHAPE	....	115	A GRIEF AGO	28
SHAPE ALL HER WHELPS WITH THE LONG VOICE OF WATER,		115	A GRIEF AGO	29
A NITRIC SHAPE THAT LEAPS HER, TIME AND ACID;	.....	115	A GRIEF AGO	34
DEATH IS ALL METAPHORS, SHAPE IN ONE HISTORY;	.....	117	ALTARWISE	15
SHADE WITHOUT SHAPE? THE SHAPE OF PHARAOH'S ECHO?		118	ALTARWISE	45
SHADE WITHOUT SHAPE? THE SHAPE OF PHARAOH'S ECHO?		118	ALTARWISE	45
(MY SHAPE OF AGE NAGGING THE WOUNDED WHISPER.)	....	118	ALTARWISE	46
TIME TRACKS THE SOUND OF SHAPE ON MAN AND CLOUD,		120	ALTARWISE	97
AND NOW THE HORNS OF ENGLAND, IN THE SOUND OF SHAPE,		122	HOLD HARD	13
WHO GAVE THESE SEAS THEIR COLOUR IN A SHAPE,	.....	123	FOSTER LIGHT	25
WHOSE WIZARD SHAPE I TRACE IN THE CAVERNOUS SKULL,		134	HOW MY ANIMAL	2
A LIMP AND RIDERLESS SHAPE TO LEAP NINE THINNING				
MONTHS.'	....	145	IF HEAD HURT	15
SIN WHO HAD A WOMAN'S SHAPE	....	165	LONG-LEGGED	110
AND THE STAR OF THE LOST THE SHAPE OF THE EYES.	...	185	VISION, PRAYER	170
AND SURELY HE SAILS LIKE THE SHIP SHAPE CLOUDS. OH HE		200	COUNTRY SLEEP	99
I'LL MAKE YOUR SHAPE MY OWN,	....	238	MAKES INTERVALS	10
SHAPED				
THAT SHAPED THE JORDAN NEAR MY HOME	....	68	BEFORE KNOCKED	4
THE HOWLING SPIRIT SHAPED A GOD	....	85	SEE, SAYS LIME	7
SHAPED MY CLAYFELLOW, AND THE HEAVEN'S ARK	....	124	FOSTER LIGHT	26
SHAPED IN OLD ARMOUR AND OAK THE COUNTENANCE OF A				
DUNCE	....	133	MAKE ME A MASK	7
AND THE HARP SHAPED VOICE OF THE WATER'S DUST PLUCKS				
IN A FOLD	....	189	WINTER'S TALE	79
AND AIR SHAPED HEAVEN WHERE SOULS GROW WILD	....	210	POEM ON B'DAY	74
SHAPELESS				
I WHO WAS SHAPELESS AS THE WATER	....	68	BEFORE KNOCKED	3
WITH THE WOMB OF HIS SHAPELESS PEOPLE.	....	107	ALL ALL AND	27
CHILD OF THE SHORT SPARK IN A SHAPELESS COUNTRY	...	117	ALTARWISE	19
O WHO IS GLORY IN THE SHAPELESS MAPS,	....	124	FOSTER LIGHT	28
'WHO COULD SNAP OFF THE SHAPELESS PRINT	....	129	MY NEOPHYTE	40
SHAPES				
THIS RUMPUS OF SHAPES	....	4	PROLOGUE	37
I LEARNT MAN'S TONGUE, TO TWIST THE SHAPES OF				
THOUGHTS	....	79	LOVE'S FEVER	32
PACK OFF THE SHAPES OF DAYLIGHT AND THEIR STARCH,		90	EUNUCH DREAMS	24
THE WORDY SHAPES OF WOMEN, AND THE ROWS	....	98	OCTOBER WIND	11
SHAPES IN A CINDER DEATH; LOVE FOR HIS TRICK,	.....	101	RUNNING GRAVE	48
ALL THAT SHAPES FROM THE CAUL AND SUCKLE,	....	107	ALL ALL AND	28
IN SHAPES OF SIN FORKED OUT THE BEARDED APPLE,	....	121	INCARNATE DEVL	4
THAT SHAPES EACH BUSHY ITEM OF THE AIR	....	123	FOSTER LIGHT	5

	PAGE	TITLE	LINE

SHAPES (CONTINUED)

MALE SHAPES, GIRL-LIPPED, BUT CLAD LIKE BOYS:	143	THE MOLLS	2
AND OVER THE GLAZED LAKES SKATED THE SHAPES OF FISHES	190	WINTER'S TALE	115
UNDER THE LIGHTED SHAPES OF FAITH AND THEIR MOONSHADE	204	GIANT'S THIGH	17

SHAPING-TIME

| IN SHAPING-TIME THE CIRCLE STUNG AWAKE, ... | 121 | INCARNATE DEVL | 3 |
| A SERPENT FIDDLED IN THE SHAPING-TIME. .... | 122 | INCARNATE DEVL | 18 |

SHARE

AND SHARE MY BED WITH CAPRICORN AND CANCER.	117	ALTARWISE	14
I'LL SHARE MY MONEY AND WE'LL RUN FOR JOY	149	PAPER & STICKS	14
NOR COULD SHARE, FOR HIS PRIDE, TO THE LEAST	158	INTO HER HEAD	44
TO SHARE MY ROOM IN THE HOUSE NOT RIGHT IN THE HEAD,	169	LOVE IN ASYLUM	2

SHARK

| GLARED THROUGH SHARK MASK AND NAVIGATING HEAD, ... | 152 | BELOW A TIME | 39 |

SHARP

SHARP, OH NO SHARP, ...	10	COOL, OH NO	2
SHARP, OH NO SHARP, ...	10	COOL, OH NO	2
AND FAR AWAY'S TOO SHARP A SUN	12	SKY'S BRIGHT	3
INTO THE BROWNS OF AUTUMN AND THE SHARP WHITES OF WINTER, ...	47	POET: 1935	20
SHARP IN MY SECOND DEATH I MARKED THE HILLS, HARVEST	103	I DREAMED MY	17
WHERE, WOUND IN EMERALD LINEN AND SHARP WIND, ...	132	I MAKE THIS IN	42
OF THE SHARP, ENAMELLED EYES AND THE SPECTACLED CLAWS	133	MAKE ME A MASK	2
SHARP AND SHRILL MY SILLY TONGUE SCRATCHES	149	PAPER & STICKS	16
AND YOUR SHARP PITY IS UNCHANGEABLE.	236	WOMAN TAPESTRY	51
CRUSH YOUR SHARP LIGHT, ...	239	MAKES INTERVALS	28

SHARPEN

| NO FAITH TO SHARPEN THE OLD WITS LEAVES US .... | 41 | YOUNG ARE OLD | 21 |

SHARPENED

| DEATH'S APPETITE IS SHARPENED BY THE BULLET'S THUMB; | 64 | WOMAN SPEAKS | 34 |

SHARPER

| AND SHARPER IF I BREAK ASUNDER .... | 10 | COOL, OH NO | 6 |

SHATTERED

| RAGE SHATTERED WATERS KICK .... | 210 | POEM ON B'DAY | 70 |

SHAWL

AND, WINDING-FOOTED IN THEIR SHAWL AND SHEET, ...	89	EUNUCH DREAMS	4
SHAKES, IN CRABBED BURIAL SHAWL, BY SORCERER'S INSECT WOKEN, ...	130	SINNERS' BELL	23
TO THE KISSED KITE HEMS OF HIS SHAWL, ...	141	SAINT TO FALL	3
ONE BY ONE IN DUST AND SHAWL, ...	167	LONG-LEGGED	145

SHE (59)

SHE-

| ALL NIGHT LOST AND LONG WADING IN THE WAKE OF THE SHE- .... | 190 | WINTER'S TALE | 98 |

SHEARWATER

| OH THE SHEARWATER BIRDS AND THEIR BOATSIZED BROOD | 164 | LONG-LEGGED | 67 |

SHEATH-DECKED

| THE SHEATH-DECKED JACKS, QUEEN WITH A SHUFFLED HEART; | 118 | ALTARWISE | 59 |

SHEBA'S

| AND NO-ONE STIRS AT SHEBA'S SIDE .... | 165 | LONG-LEGGED | 108 |

SHED

THE SUN AND MOON SHED ONE WHITE LIGHT.	78	LOVE'S FEVER	9
YOUR BREATH WAS SHED	176	BREATH SHED	1
SHED THOU THY TEARS ON HIM; HE WILL NOT WAKE, ...	222	MISSING	8

SHE'D

| AND, STANDING OVER THE SEA, SHE'D CRY .... | 22 | ON QUIET NIGHT | 9 |

SHEDS

| SHEDS THE SYLLABIC BLOOD AND DRAINS HER WORDS. .... | 98 | OCTOBER WIND | 8 |
| IN THE DARK OF THE COFFIN AND SHEDS DRY LEAVES, ... | 136 | AFTER FUNERAL | 8 |

	PAGE	TITLE	LINE
SHEEP			
SHEEP WHITE HOLLOW FARMS	4	PROLOGUE	51
OF SHEEP AND CHURCHES NOISE	5	PROLOGUE	88
THE THOUSAND SHEEP	33	HELD-OUT HAND	22
AS FLEECED AS THEY BOW LOWLY WITH THE SHEEP, ...	96	TWELVE	10
FLOCKED WITH THE SHEEP WHITE SMOKE OF THE FARM HOUSE			
COWL	187	WINTER'S TALE	9
BUT A BLACK SHEEP WITH A CRUMPLED HORN, ...	207	LAMENT	42
SHEEPWHITE			
FEAR OR BELIEVE THAT THE WOLF IN A SHEEPWHITE HOOD	197	COUNTRY SLEEP	3
SHEET			
RULE THE BLANK SHEET OF SLEEP, ...	66	LET A FAITH	2
HOW AT MY SHEET GOES THE SAME CROOKED WORM.	77	THE FORCE THAT	22
A LOVER'S THOUGHT TEARS DOWN THE DATED SHEET, ...	80	ALMANAC TIME	7
ALL NIGHT MY FORTUNE SLUMBERS IN ITS SHEET.	81	ALL THAT I OWE	27
ALL NIGHT MY FORTUNE SLUMBERS IN ITS SHEET.	81	ALL THAT I OWE	30
AND, WINDING-FOOTED IN THEIR SHAWL AND SHEET, ...	89	EUNUCH DREAMS	4
MY EGYPT'S ARMOUR BUCKLING IN ITS SHEET, ...	104	WORLD PYRAMID	34
TRAP I WITH COIL AND SHEET, ...	114	SERVANT SUN	19
I DREW THE WHITE SHEET OVER THE ISLANDS	150	WHEN I WOKE	29
WOULD PLUNGE MY BETRAYAL FROM SHEET TO SKY	175	MY BEGGAR ARM	6
THAT CAME FROM THE WOUND WRAPPED IN THE SALT SHEET.	194	SLEEP BECALMED	4
AND WHEN THE SALT SHEET BROKE IN A STORM OF SINGING	194	SLEEP BECALMED	7
WE HEARD THE SEA SOUND SING, WE SAW THE SALT SHEET			
TELL.	194	SLEEP BECALMED	12
SHELL			
TILL THE BIRD HAS BURST HIS SHELL, ...	22	HIGH ON A HILL	12
TO FIND A SWEET BLANKNESS IN THE BLOOD AND SHELL,	27	OBLIVIOUS DARK	12
SHALL FALL AWAY, AND LEAVE ONE SINGING SHELL.	73	LORD RED HAIL	12
THROUGH THE ROTATING SHELL, STRONG	102	I DREAMED MY	2
WHERE BIRD AND SHELL ARE BABBLING IN MY TOWER?	112	NOT FATHER ME	14
AND BREAKS HIS SHELL IN THE LAST SHOCKED BEGINNING;	124	TODAY, INSECT	13
TWINE IN A MOON-BLOWN SHELL, ...	129	MY NEOPHYTE	15
IN THE MOLESTED ROCKS THE SHELL OF VIRGINS, ...	131	I MAKE THIS IN	18
ITS WRINGING SHELL, AND LET HER EYELIDS FASTEN. ...	132	I MAKE THIS IN	35
VESSEL OF ABSCESSES AND EXULTATION'S SHELL, ...	134	HOW MY ANIMAL	3
DOWN BREEZE AND SHELL TO A DISCORDANT BEACH, ...	138	FIVE & COUNTRY	7
OR SAW IN THE LOOKING-GLASS SHELL	139	TOMBSTONE TOLD	7
AND LAID YOUR CHEEK AGAINST A CLOUD-FORMED SHELL:	153	WAS A SAVIOUR	23
AND OUT OF EVERY DOMED AND SOIL-BASED SHELL	158	INTO HER HEAD	51
TILL EVERY TURTLE CRUSHED FROM HIS SHELL	163	LONG-LEGGED	58
VALLEY AND SAHARA IN A SHELL, ...	165	LONG-LEGGED	90
THROWN TO THE SEA IN THE SHELL OF A GIRL	165	LONG-LEGGED	92
ALWAYS GOOD-BYE, CRIED THE VOICES THROUGH THE SHELL,	166	LONG-LEGGED	121
AND READ, IN A SHELL, ...	202	SIR JOHNS HILL	25
IN A PATTERN LIKE A SHELL	229	MY RIVER	39
NOR MAKE THE STERN SHELL OF MY SPIRIT MOVE.	233	NO THOUGHT	2
SHELL-HUNG			
OF EELS, SAINT HERON HYMNING IN THE SHELL-HUNG			
DISTANT	202	SIR JOHNS HILL	36
SHELLING			
AS SUNLIGHT PAINTS THE SHELLING OF THEIR HEADS. ...	92	BOYS OF SUMMER	18
SHELLS			
STABBING, AND HERONS, AND SHELLS	3	PROLOGUE	16
A SEDGE OF BROKEN STALKS AND SHELLS.	14	RAIN CUTS	28
HAVE SEARCHED FOR SHELLS AND SIGNS ON THE SEA SHORE,	52	OUT OF THE PIT	64
ON CASTING TIDES, ARE TANGLED IN THE SHELLS, ...	105	WORLD PYRAMID	50
THE MAZES OF HIS PRAISE AND ENVIOUS TONGUE WERE			
WORKED IN FLAMES AND SHELLS.	141	SAINT TO FALL	17
AND THE COINS ON MY EYELIDS SANG LIKE SHELLS.	150	WHEN I WOKE	30

	PAGE	TITLE	LINE
SHELLS (CONTINUED)			
AND LOAD THE THROATS OF SHELLS	160	DEATHS AND ENT	22
THROUGH WYNDS AND SHELLS OF DROWNED	209	POEM ON B'DAY	23
WHILE ITS VIOLET SHELLS BROKE AND PARTED.	232	FURIOUS MOTION	14
SHELTER			
WOE TO THE WINDY MASONS AT MY SHELTER?	113	NOT FATHER ME	30
THAT NIGHT OF TIME UNDER THE CHRISTWARD SHELTER:	117	ALTARWISE	12
SHELTERED			
THE SEED OF TIME IS SHELTERED IN THE LOIN:	80	ALMANAC TIME	12
SHELTERS			
HERE THE NIGHT SHELTERS AND HERE THE STARS SHINE,	74	SUN BURNS	8
SHEPHERD			
BRUISING, WHERE'S GOD'S MY SHEPHERD, GOD IS LOVE?	51	OUT OF THE PIT	37
NO LOVING SHEPHERD IN THIS UPSIDE LIFE.	51	OUT OF THE PIT	38
MY GOD'S A SHEPHERD, GOD'S THE LOVE I HOPED.	53	OUT OF THE PIT	93
SHEPHERDS			
AND SERAPHIC FIELDS OF SHEPHERDS	215	COUNTRY HEAVEN	19
SHIELD			
TO SHIELD THE GLISTENING BRAIN AND BLUNT THE EXAMINERS, ...	133	MAKE ME A MASK	8
SHIELDED			
FROM THE BROOMED WITCH'S SPUME YOU ARE SHIELDED BY FERN	198	COUNTRY SLEEP	17
BE SHIELDED BY CHANT AND FLOWER AND GAY MAY YOU ...	198	COUNTRY SLEEP	42
SHIFT			
AND GODS BE CHANGED AS OFTEN AS THE SHIFT.	67	LET A FAITH	8
OF BUD OF ADAM THROUGH HIS BOXY SHIFT, ...	101	RUNNING GRAVE	38
THE SECRET CHILD, I SHIFT ABOUT THE SEA	105	WORLD PYRAMID	59
BENT LIKE THREE TREES AND BIRD-PAPPED THROUGH HER SHIFT, ...	120	ALTARWISE	103
O RING OF SEAS, NOR SORROW AS I SHIFT	123	FOSTER LIGHT	20
SHIFTED			
BEFORE THE MOON SHIFTED AND THE SAP RAN OUT, ...	43	FACES SHONE	10
SHIFTING			
STATURE BY SEEDY SHIFTING, ...	92	BOYS OF SUMMER	20
SHIFTING TO LIGHT, TURNED ON ME LIKE A MOON.	101	FELLOWED SLEEP	3
SHIFTS			
SHIFTS TO THE REDWOMBED PEN.	80	ALMANAC TIME	5
SHINE			
IT IS GOOD THAT THE SUN SHINE, ...	42	A WAR OF WITS	20
AND SOME SHINE FOR A SECOND AND ARE GONE, ...	49	LIGHT, I KNOW	20
STARS' LIGHT AND SUN'S LIGHT WILL NOT SHINE	49	LIGHT, I KNOW	27
HERE THE NIGHT SHELTERS AND HERE THE STARS SHINE,	74	SUN BURNS	8
SHOULD LANTERNS SHINE	116	LANTERNS SHINE	T
SHOULD LANTERNS SHINE, THE HOLY FACE, ...	116	LANTERNS SHINE	1
SHINES			
LIGHT BREAKS WHERE NO SUN SHINES	82	LIGHT BREAKS	T
LIGHT BREAKS WHERE NO SUN SHINES;	82	LIGHT BREAKS	1
SHINGLE			
WE GRIEVE AS THE BLITHE BIRDS, NEVER AGAIN, LEAVE SHINGLE AND ELM, ...	202	SIR JOHNS HILL	33
SHINING			
SOFT SHINING SYMBOLS OF HER PEACE WITH YOU, ...	20	THE NEOPHYTE	21
GROWING ON HILLS OR SHINING UNDER WATER.	25	BEAUTY TO DUST	15
AND THERE IS ALWAYS DAY, THE SHINING OF SOME SUN,	49	LIGHT, I KNOW	18
TERROR AND SHINING FROM	181	VISION, PRAYER	46
SHINING, IT WAS ADAM AND MAIDEN, ...	196	FERN HILL	30
AND MY SHINING MEN NO MORE ALONE	211	POEM ON B'DAY	107
ITS SHINING CLOUDS FOR YOU;	234	NO, PIGEON	3
AND THE SHINING RAIN	240	ADMIT THE SUN	6

	PAGE	TITLE	LINE

SHIP
SNAIL OF MAN IN HIS SHIP OF FIRES .... 128 MY NEOPHYTE 8
IN THE FOUNTAIN BASIN WHERE I SAILED MY SHIP .... 171 THE HUNCHBACK 10
AND SURELY HE SAILS LIKE THE SHIP SHAPE CLOUDS. OH HE 200 COUNTRY SLEEP 99
SHIP TOWNS TO PASTURES OF OTTERS. HE .... 209 POEM ON B'DAY 24
SHIPPEN
TROUNCED BY HIS WINGS IN THE HISSING SHIPPEN, LONG
DEAD .... 205 GIANT'S THIGH 39
SHIP-RACKED
TIME'S SHIP-RACKED GOSPEL ON THE GLOBE I BALANCE: 121 ALTARWISE 129
SHIPS
SHIPS ANCHOR OFF THE BAY. .... 62 EARS IN TURRET 20
SHALL I RUN TO THE SHIPS .... 62 EARS IN TURRET 21
SHIPS, HOLD YOU POISON OR GRAPES? .... 62 EARS IN TURRET 25
SHIPS ANCHOR OFF THE BAY, ... 62 EARS IN TURRET 27
HANDS OF THE STRANGER AND HOLDS OF THE SHIPS, ... 63 EARS IN TURRET 32
SAID THE DWINDLING SHIPS. .... 162 LONG-LEGGED 24
TREES COOL AND DRY IN THE WHIRLPOOL OF SHIPS .... 167 LONG-LEGGED 170
DAWN SHIPS CLOUTED AGROUND, ... 211 POEM ON B'DAY 79
SHIPS'
BE BY THE SHIPS' SEA BROKEN AT THE MANSTRING ANCHORED 111 I, IN IMAGE 86
SHIP'S
HEARS, THERE, THIS FOX LIGHT, MY FLOOD SHIP'S ..... 4 PROLOGUE 69
SHIP-WORK
THE VANISHING OF THE MUSICAL SHIP-WORK AND THE
CHUCKED BELLS, ... 141 SAINT TO FALL 8
SHIPWRECK
IN THE SHIPWRECK OF MUSCLE; .... 111 I, IN IMAGE 88
SHIPWRECKED
THE SUN SHIPWRECKED WEST ON A PEARL .... 162 LONG-LEGGED 15
SHIPYARDS
AND THE SHIPYARDS OF GALILEE'S FOOTPRINTS HIDE A
NAVY OF DOVES. .... 170 MARRIAGE VIRG 7
SHIRE
OF MANY A THORNY SHIRE TELL YOU NOTES, ... 99 OCTOBER WIND 15
MY GIRL RANGING THE NIGHT IN THE ROSE AND SHIRE ... 197 COUNTRY SLEEP 9
SHIRES
IN SUN AND RAIN OVER THE DRY SHIRES, ... 45 PLOUGHMAN GONE 25
OVER THE BLACKAMOOR SHIRES .... 215 COUNTRY HEAVEN 24
SHIRT
BEFORE THE LAST FAG AND THE SHIRT SLEEVES AND
SLIPPERS, ... 38 GAS FADES 3
SHIRTS
OF MEN WITH FLANNEL SHIRTS .... 37 WINDMILLS TURN 10
SHIVER
WE SHIVER UNCOMPLAININGLY, ... 14 RAIN CUTS 36
SHOAL
AND TUSSLE IN A SHOAL OF LOVES. .... 162 LONG-LEGGED 30
WHENEVER I DOVE IN A BREAST HIGH SHOAL, ... 206 LAMENT 21
SHOALS
AND DARK SHOALS EVERY HOLY FIELD. .... 5 PROLOGUE 90
SHOCKED
AND BREAKS HIS SHELL IN THE LAST SHOCKED BEGINNING; 124 TODAY, INSECT 13
SHOED
THE SINGING BREAKS IN THE SNOW SHOED VILLAGES OF
WISHES .... 190 WINTER'S TALE 113
SHONE
THEIR FACES SHONE UNDER SOME RADIANCE .... 43 FACES SHONE T
THEIR FACES SHONE UNDER SOME RADIANCE .... 43 FACES SHONE 1
THEIR FACES SHONE; THE MIDNIGHT RAIN .... 43 FACES SHONE 8

		PAGE	TITLE	LINE
SHONE (CONTINUED)				
SHONE IN MY EARS THE LIGHT OF SOUND,		78	LOVE'S FEVER	20
AND NOTHING SHONE ON THE WATER'S FACE		163	LONG-LEGGED	44
SHOO				
TURNS OF YOUR PRAYED FLESH, NOR SHALL I SHOO THE BIRD BELOW ME:		148	UNLUCKILY FOR	27
SHOOK				
LAUGHING WHEN HE SHOOK HIS PAPER		171	THE HUNCHBACK	20
SHOOT				
JOY IS THE KNOCK OF DUST, CADAVER'S SHOOT		101	RUNNING GRAVE	37
TO SHOOT AND SING YOUR PRAISE,		160	DEATHS AND ENT	8
SHOOTING				
FOR US THERE IS NO SHOOTING AND NO RIDING,		40	YOUNG ARE OLD	8
FOR US THERE IS NO RIDING AND NO SHOOTING,		40	YOUNG ARE OLD	15
THE CHILD THAT SUCKETH LONG IS SHOOTING UP,		117	ALTARWISE	16
OVER THE BARBED AND SHOOTING SEA ASSUMED AN ARMY		186	HOLY SPRING	6
THE SHOOTING STAR HAWK STATUED BLIND IN A CLOUD		215	COUNTRY HEAVEN	23
SHOOTS				
RARER DELIGHT SHOOTS IN THE BLOOD		48	POET: 1935	55
SHOP				
TASSELLED IN CELLAR AND SNIPPING SHOP		151	BELOW A TIME	11
SHORE				
HAVE SEARCHED FOR SHELLS AND SIGNS ON THE SEA SHORE,		52	OUT OF THE PIT	64
THE STRATA OF THE SHORE AND DROWN RED ROCK;		54	WE BY SEASAND	20
AM I NOT YOU WHO FRONT THE TIDY SHORE,		112	NOT FATHER ME	15
SEAPORTS BY A DRUNKEN SHORE		126	SEED-AT-ZERO	34
SEAPORTS BY A THIRSTY SHORE		126	SEED-AT-ZERO	41
SINGLY LIE WITH THE WHOLE WIDE SHORE,		158	INTO HER HEAD	49
PRIESTED SHORE		176	POEM IN OCT	4
SHORES				
AND THE SHORES OF THE LAST SUN.		42	YOUNG ARE OLD	52
OUT OF THE HEAVENLY SEA ONTO THE MOON'S SHORES.		48	LIGHT, I KNOW	3
OF TIDES THAT NEVER TOUCH THE SHORES.		69	BEFORE KNOCKED	34
OF THE CROTCH OF THE SQUAWKING SHORES,		142	SAINT TO FALL	27
SHORN				
SIGH LONG, CLAY COLD, LIE SHORN,		135	HOW MY ANIMAL	34
FLYING. THE RITE IS SHORN		191	WINTER'S TALE	116
THE WATERS SHORN.		199	COUNTRY SLEEP	54
SHORT				
CHILD OF THE SHORT SPARK IN A SHAPELESS COUNTRY		117	ALTARWISE	19
THE SIZE OF GENESIS? THE SHORT SPARK'S GENDER?		118	ALTARWISE	44
CLIPS SHORT THE GESTURE OF BREATH.		135	HOW MY ANIMAL	39
MATERNAL SHORT TIME PIECES,		155	RETURN	54
SHORTEN				
THE CRIERS OF SHABBY AND SHORTEN,		151	BELOW A TIME	27
SHOT				
NO MAN BELIEVES WHO, WHEN A STAR FALLS SHOT,		54	NO MAN BELIEVE	1
HALF OF THE OLD GANG'S SHOT,		59	FAIRY TALES	8
FEAR DEATH AS LITTLE AS THE THUNDER'S SHOT,		60	FAIRY TALES	40
MOTHER ROOT THAT SHOT ME FORTH,		72	TAKE NEEDLES	41
TURNS DAMP TO DRY; THE GOLDEN SHOT		88	A PROCESS IN	2
BLOOD SHOT AND SCATTERED TO THE WINDS OF LIGHT		94	IN BEGINNING	29
SHOT THROUGH THE LEAF,		115	A GRIEF AGO	12
SHOT IN THE WIND, BY TILTED ARCS,		129	MY NEOPHYTE	26
WHEN ALL THE KEYS SHOT FROM THE LOCKS, AND RANG.		172	DAWN RAID	8
SHOTS				
THE CHAMELEON COATS OF THE BIG BUGS AND SHOTS,)		39	GAS FADES	13
IMPOSE THEIR SHOTS, SHOWING THE NIGHTS AWAY;		89	EUNUCH DREAMS	18
BLOWING THE OLD DEAD BACK; OUR SHOTS SHALL SMACK		90	EUNUCH DREAMS	38

	PAGE	TITLE	LINE
SHOULD			
BUT SHOULD NOT TOUCH LIKE I	11	AIR BREATHE	11
THE SEASON'S SUN, THOUGH HE SHOULD KNOW HIS SETTING	25	THERE'S PLENTY	4
MAN SHOULD BE CURED OF DISTEMPER.	32	OUT OF SIGHS	27
WHERE EYES SHOULD BE, AND NOSTRILS FULL OF TOADS.	51	OUT OF THE PIT	23
SHOULD CURE OUR ILLS OF THE WATER	54	WE BY SEASAND	12
I SHOULD TELL SUMMER FROM THE TREES, THE WORMS	58	HERE IN SPRING	9
I SHOULD LEARN SPRING BY THE CUCKOOING,	58	HERE IN SPRING	12
AND THE SLUG SHOULD TEACH ME DESTRUCTION.	58	HERE IN SPRING	13
WHY SHOULD I THINK ON DEATH WHEN YOU ARE RULER?	67	REALM OF FLESH	10
FIE ON YOU, AUNT, THAT YOU SHOULD SEE	83	LETTER TO AUNT	7
SHOULD LANTERNS SHINE	116	LANTERNS SHINE	T
SHOULD LANTERNS SHINE, THE HOLY FACE,	116	LANTERNS SHINE	1
AND MANY YEARS SHOULD SEE SOME CHANGE.	116	LANTERNS SHINE	17
SHOULD HE, FOR CENTRE SAKE, HOP IN THE DUST,	127	NOW, SAY NAY	6
SHOULD HE WHO SPLIT HIS CHILDREN WITH A CURE	127	NOW, SAY NAY	13
WHO SHOULD BE FURIOUS,	134	HOW MY ANIMAL	6
AND FIRES WHERE HE SHOULD PROWL DOWN THE CLOUD	188	WINTER'S TALE	37
WHEN COLD AS SNOW HE SHOULD RUN THE WENDED VALES AMONG	188	WINTER'S TALE	45
I SHOULD HEAR HIM FLY WITH THE HIGH FIELDS	196	FERN HILL	50
OLD AGE SHOULD BURN AND RAVE AT CLOSE OF DAY;	207	NOT GO GENTLE	2
O DEEPEST WOUND OF ALL THAT HE SHOULD DIE	217	ELEGY	37
THERE SHOULD BE NIGHT FOR EVER, AND NO ROSE,	223	IN DREAMS	10
AND IF IT DID, WHO SHOULD I HAVE	234	NO, PIGEON	5
TEMPLE SHOULD NEVER HAVE BEEN FILLED	237	PILLAR BREAKS	12
SHOULDER			
THE MIGHTY HAND LEADS TO A SLOPING SHOULDER,	66	HAND SIGNED	5
THAT RULES FROM WRIST TO SHOULDER,	75	MY HERO BARES	2
AND STEEPLES PIERCE THE CLOUD ON HER SHOULDER	168	LONG-LEGGED	193
ON THE HILL'S SHOULDER,	177	POEM IN OCT	25
WITH THE DEW, COME BACK, THE COCK ON HIS SHOULDER: IT WAS ALL	195	FERN HILL	29
SHOULDERING			
UNMOVING IN A SHOULDERING SEA,	238	PILLAR BREAKS	20
SHOULDERS			
THAT CLUSTERED ROUND HER SHOULDERS,	15	FOR LEDA	26
AND ON HIS SHOULDERS FALL THEIR WORLD OF WINGS,	63	WOMAN SPEAKS	22
WITH SPRUNG AND PADDED SHOULDERS,	154	RETURN	11
TO WING MY SHOULDERS AND MY FEET?	234	NO, PIGEON	6
AND SMALL, FEMININE SHOULDERS,	236	WOMAN TAPESTRY	43
SHOUT			
A SHOUT WENT UP TO HEAVEN LIKE A ROCKET,	70	SECRET WIND	7
THE CITY GOSPEL SHOUT TO HEAVEN.	70	SECRET WIND	21
IN LAIRS AND ASYLUMS OF THE TREMENDOUS SHOUT.	153	WAS A SAVIOUR	16
SHOUT	203	SIR JOHNS HILL	54
SHOUTER			
FOR WE SHALL BE A SHOUTER LIKE THE COCK,	90	EUNUCH DREAMS	37
SHOVED			
AND I SHOVED IT INTO THE COAL BLACK SKY	207	LAMENT	47
SHOVEL			
THESE DIE WHO SHOVEL THE LAST HOME OF MAN;	64	WOMAN SPEAKS	44
PAPER AND STICKS AND SHOVEL AND MATCH	149	PAPER & STICKS	1
SHOW			
WATER FROM NOSE AND ARSE, A SANGER'S SHOW	51	OUT OF THE PIT	26
FIE ON YOU, AUNT! I'LL SHOW YOU HOW	83	LETTER TO AUNT	11
WE WATCH THE SHOW OF SHADOWS KISS OR KILL,	89	EUNUCH DREAMS	19
ON STOOLS TO A ONE MAN SHOW DOWN,	154	RETURN	20
AND DOES NOT SHOW THE FRUIT TO TASTE;	233	NO THOUGHT	13
THE YELLOW BIRD TO SHOW HIS COLOUR.	238	MAKES INTERVALS	5

	PAGE	TITLE	LINE
SHOWER			
CAMPED IN THE DRUG-WHITE SHOWER OF NERVES AND FOOD,	144	PLEASURE-BIRD	8
AND WALKED ABROAD IN A SHOWER OF ALL MY DAYS.	177	POEM IN OCT	16
SHOWING			
IMPOSE THEIR SHOTS, SHOWING THE NIGHTS AWAY;	89	EUNUCH DREAMS	18
SHOWN			
NOW SHOWN AND MOSTLY BARE I WOULD LIE DOWN, ...	152	BELOW A TIME	49
SHOWS			
WHERE NO WAX IS, THE CANDLE SHOWS ITS HAIRS.	82	LIGHT BREAKS	12
WHO SHOWS TO THE SELVES ASLEEP	165	LONG-LEGGED	103
AND SHOWS THEM FAIR AGAINST THE DARK, ...	238	MAKES INTERVALS	3
SHRAPNEL			
I DREAMED MY GENESIS AND DIED AGAIN, SHRAPNEL	103	I DREAMED MY	13
SHRILL			
SHARP AND SHRILL MY SILLY TONGUE SCRATCHES	149	PAPER & STICKS	16
AND THE SHRILL CHILD'S PLAY	201	SIR JOHNS HILL	5
SHRINE			
IN THE SHRINE	182	VISION, PRAYER	71
TO THE SHRINE OF HIS WORLD'S WOUND	184	VISION, PRAYER	138
SHRINED			
OH, LET ME MIDLIFE MOURN BY THE SHRINED	211	POEM ON B'DAY	76
SHRIVELLING			
HYMNED HIS SHRIVELLING FLOCK, ...	141	SAINT TO FALL	13
SHROUD			
HAULS MY SHROUD SAIL.	77	THE FORCE THAT	13
HERE DRIPS A SILENT HONEY IN MY SHROUD, ...	81	HERE LIE BEAST	10
ERECT A WALKING CENTRE IN THE SHROUD, ...	114	SERVANT SUN	27
MY CAMEL'S EYES WILL NEEDLE THROUGH THE SHROUD. ...	118	ALTARWISE	52
WEIGHED IN ROCK SHROUD, IS MY PROUD PYRAMID;	132	I MAKE THIS IN	41
SEWING A SHROUD FOR A JOURNEY	143	24 YEARS	4
HERONS WALK IN THEIR SHROUD, ...	209	POEM ON B'DAY	27
SHROUDED			
THAT SHROUDED MEN MIGHT MARROW AS THEY FLY.	90	EUNUCH DREAMS	30
SHROUDING			
THE INVOKED, SHROUDING VEIL AT THE CAP OF THE FACE,	134	HOW MY ANIMAL	5
SHROUD-LIKE			
AND SHROUD-LIKE.	225	OF ANY FLOWER	6
SHROUDS			
THE SHADES OF GIRLS, ALL FLAVOURED FROM THEIR			
SHROUDS, ...	89	EUNUCH DREAMS	7
SHRUB			
AND ALL SUCH LOVE'S A SHRUB SOWN IN THE BREATH. ...	81	ALL THAT I OWE	20
SHRUBBERIES			
AFTER THE RAILINGS AND SHRUBBERIES	172	THE HUNCHBACK	38
SHRUBBERY			
GABRIEL AND RADIANT SHRUBBERY AS THE MORNING GROWS			
JOYFUL	186	HOLY SPRING	15
SHUDDERS			
MY BUSY HEART WHO SHUDDERS AS SHE TALKS	98	OCTOBER WIND	7
SHUFFLED			
FROM LIMBS THAT HAD THE MEASURE OF WORM, SHUFFLED	102	I DREAMED MY	5
THE SHEATH-DECKED JACKS, QUEEN WITH A SHUFFLED HEART;	118	ALTARWISE	59
SHUFFLING			
THE BLACK RAM, SHUFFLING OF THE YEAR, OLD WINTER,	118	ALTARWISE	39
SHUT			
BUT WE, SHUT IN THE HOUSES OF THE BRAIN, ...	26	THERE'S PLENTY	8
SHUT IN THE MADHOUSE CALL FOR COOL AIR TO BREATHE.	26	THERE'S PLENTY	13
THE JAWS WILL HAVE SHUT, AND LIFE BE SWITCHED OUT.	39	GAS FADES	14
I SEE HIM IN THE CROWDS, NOT SHUT	53	OUT OF THE PIT	102
WHEN CAMERAS SHUT THEY HURRY TO THEIR HOLE	89	EUNUCH DREAMS	15

	PAGE	TITLE	LINE
SHUT (CONTINUED)			
SHUT, TOO, IN A TOWER OF WORDS, I MARK	98	OCTOBER WIND	9
O MAKE ME A MASK AND A WALL TO SHUT FROM YOUR SPIES	133	MAKE ME A MASK	1
THE GRAVE AND MY CALM BODY ARE SHUT TO YOUR COMING			
AS STONE, ...	146	IF HEAD HURT	29
TO SHUT THE SUN, PLUNGE, MOUNT YOUR DARKENED KEYS	161	DEATHS AND ENT	33
SHUT. SINISTER DARK OVER CARDIGAN	179	NEW QUAY	7
SHUTTERS			
WINGS. IT WOULD BE BETTER IF THE SHUTTERS IS	179	NEW QUAY	6
SHY			
INTO THE RAINBOW'S SHY EMBRACE.	14	RAIN CUTS	35
THE CATTLE STIRRING, THE MOUSING CAT STEPPING SHY,	187	WINTER'S TALE	22
PETTICOATS GALED HIGH, OR SHY WITH THE ROUGH RIDING			
BOYS, ...	204	GIANT'S THIGH	18
I TIPTOED SHY IN THE GOOSEBERRY WOOD, ...	206	LAMENT	4
SHYEST			
BRASSILY AT MY SHYEST SECRET, ...	146	TO OTHERS	5
SICK			
SICK, PALE, AND PLAIN, ...	21	BEWILDERED WAY	17
COULD IN A DAY BE SICK WITH SO MUCH BLOOD;	63	WOMAN SPEAKS	13
OF SICK OLD MANHOOD ON THE FALLEN JAWS, ...	95	RUB OF LOVE	24
QUAKED THE SICK SEA AND SNOUTED DEEP, ...	163	LONG-LEGGED	50
SICKENED			
AND YOUNG GUTS DRY BENEATH THE SICKENED SUN.	63	WOMAN SPEAKS	15
SIDE			
MY HEART HURLS FROM MY SIDE AND TEARS	48	LIGHT, I KNOW	8
AND FELT A SKEWER ENTER AT HIS SIDE.	52	OUT OF THE PIT	55
YOU RULE THE THUDDING HEART THAT BITES THE SIDE;	67	REALM OF FLESH	7
AND SWEET SHALL FALL CONTAGION FROM HIS SIDE, ...	73	LORD RED HAIL	5
AND THE WAILING HEART'S NAILED TO THE SIDE.	74	SUN BURNS	5
MY HERO BARES MY SIDE AND SEES HIS HEART	75	MY HERO BARES	11
THE BOY SHE DROPPED FROM DARKNESS AT HER SIDE	78	LOVE'S FEVER	26
HERE CLINGS THE MEAT TO SEVER FROM HIS SIDE.	81	HERE LIE BEAST	5
A ROOKING GIRL WHO STOLE ME FOR HER SIDE, ...	94	RUB OF LOVE	2
BY THE SEA'S SIDE, HEARING THE NOISE OF BIRDS, ...	98	OCTOBER WIND	5
BY THE SEA'S SIDE HEAR THE DARK-VOWELLED BIRDS. ...	99	OCTOBER WIND	32
HOUSED IN THE SIDE.	115	A GRIEF AGO	16
AT NIGHTBREAK BORN IN THE FAT SIDE, FROM AN ANIMAL			
BED	130	SINNERS' BELL	26
BEFORE I HEARD IN MY MOTHER'S SIDE	139	TOMBSTONE TOLD	6
SOAKED MY TABLE THE UGLIER SIDE OF A HILL	144	COLOUR OF SAY	2
WITH IMMORTALITY AT MY SIDE LIKE CHRIST THE SKY.	148	UNLUCKILY FOR	49
WINTER-LOCKED SIDE BY SIDE, ...	153	WAS A SAVIOUR	26
WINTER-LOCKED SIDE BY SIDE, ...	153	WAS A SAVIOUR	26
CELEBRATING AT HER SIDE	158	INTO HER HEAD	42
AND NO-ONE STIRS AT SHEBA'S SIDE	165	LONG-LEGGED	108
THIS SIDE OF THE TRUTH	192	SIDE OF TRUTH	T
THIS SIDE OF THE TRUTH, ...	192	SIDE OF TRUTH	1
TO COURT THE HONEYED HEART FROM YOUR SIDE BEFORE			
SUNRISE	198	COUNTRY SLEEP	13
HEART! SLYLY, SLOWLY, HEARING THE WOUND IN HER SIDE			
GO	200	COUNTRY SLEEP	95
UNTIL I DIE HE WILL NOT LEAVE MY SIDE.	217	ELEGY	40
AGAINST THIS SIDE.	229	MY RIVER	20
AND YOUR SIDE IS STEEP.	230	MY RIVER	46
SIDEBOARD			
THE SIDEBOARD FRUIT, THE FERNS, THE PICTURE HOUSES	33	HELD-OUT HAND	10
SIDED			
INTO THE SIDED LAP OF LIGHT GREW STRONG, ...	78	LOVE'S FEVER	27

		PAGE	TITLE	LINE
SIDES				
BREATHING ON ALL SIDES PUNGENTLY	....	20	ENCOMPASSED	2
WALKING IN GARDENS BY THE SIDES	....	33	IN GARDENS	1
WOMEN WITH CANCER AT THEIR SIDES	....	41	YOUNG ARE OLD	28
OUT OF THE SIDES OF THE NORTH	....	165	LONG-LEGGED	114
AND FALLS, AND FLOWERS IN THE YAWNING WOUND AT OUR SIDES,	....	199	COUNTRY SLEEP	62
SIDE'S				
AT ONE SIDE'S LOSS,	....	25	BEAUTY TO DUST	6
SIDLE				
TO MY MAN-IRON SIDLE.	....	108	I, IN IMAGE	6
SIEVE				
BEFORE THE VEINS WERE SHAKING IN THEIR SIEVE,	.....	94	IN BEGINNING	28
SIGH				
SIGH LONG, CLAY COLD, LIE SHORN,	....	135	HOW MY ANIMAL	34
GENTLY THEY SIGH TO MY BEHIND	....	143	THE MOLLS	9
ONE LEAN SIGH WHEN WE HEARD	....	153	WAS A SAVIOUR	29
HOURLY I SIGH,	....	225	OF ANY FLOWER	1
SIGHED				
UNDER HIS DOWNY ARM YOU SIGHED AS HE STRUCK,	......	153	WAS A SAVIOUR	19
(SIGHED THE OLD RAM ROD, DYING OF WOMEN),	....	206	LAMENT	3
(SIGHED THE OLD RAM ROD, DYING OF BITCHES),	....	206	LAMENT	15
(SIGHED THE OLD RAM ROD, DYING OF WELCOME),	....	206	LAMENT	27
(SIGHED THE OLD RAM ROD, DYING OF DOWNFALL),	......	207	LAMENT	39
(SIGHED THE OLD RAM ROD, DYING OF STRANGERS),	.....	207	LAMENT	51
THESE WERE THE WHISPERINGS THAT SIGHED ON MY LIPS AT DUSK,	....	223	IDYLL UNFORGET	10
SIGHING				
THERE THE DARK BLADE AND WANTON SIGHING HER DOWN		157	INTO HER HEAD	16
TO THAT STRANGE COLOUR, SIGHING GENTLY, GRIEVES	...	223	IN DREAMS	6
SIGHS				
OUT OF THE SIGHS	....	31	OUT OF SIGHS	T
OUT OF THE SIGHS A LITTLE COMES,	....	31	OUT OF SIGHS	1
BENEATH MY LIFE, THAT SIGHS FOR THE SEDUCER'S COMING		147	UNLUCKILY FOR	13
OF THE PALE-GREEN, DELICATE FISHES, SILVER AS SIGHS;		224	IDYLL UNFORGET	39
SIGHT				
BUT, WHEN HE'S OUT OF SIGHT,	....	14	RAIN CUTS	20
OF SOUND AND SIGHT,	....	17	NATURAL DAY	3
AT SIGHT OF DEATH, THE LAST TWO FISTED KILLER	.....	59	FAIRY TALES	18
GRAVE MEN, NEAR DEATH, WHO SEE WITH BLINDING SIGHT		208	NOT GO GENTLE	13
SIGHTLESS				
WITH SIGHTLESS EYES AND HEARTS THAT DO NOT BEAT,		39	GAS FADES	36
SIGHTS				
DEATH SIGHTS AND SEES WITH GREAT MISGIVING	....	25	THERE'S PLENTY	6
AND HOW TO SCALE AND SEE THE SIGHTS	....	83	LETTER TO AUNT	13
SIGN				
AND THE SWEAT ON THE BROW MAKES A SIGN,	....	74	SUN BURNS	4
TOUCHED THE FIRST CLOUD AND LEFT A SIGN.	....	94	IN BEGINNING	12
SIGNAL				
THE SIGNAL MOON IS ZERO IN THEIR VOIDS.	....	92	BOYS OF SUMMER	12
THE SIGNAL GRASS THAT TELLS ME ALL I KNOW	....	99	OCTOBER WIND	22
SIGNATURE				
IN THE BEGINNING WAS THE PALE SIGNATURE,	....	94	IN BEGINNING	7
SIGNED				
THE HAND THAT SIGNED THE PAPER	....	66	HAND SIGNED	T
THE HAND THAT SIGNED THE PAPER FELLED A CITY;	.....	66	HAND SIGNED	1
THE HAND THAT SIGNED THE TREATY BRED A FEVER,	.....	66	HAND SIGNED	9
SIGNPOSTS				
AND SIGNPOSTS POINTING UP AND DOWN	....	36	WINDMILLS TURN	2

	PAGE	TITLE	LINE
SIGNS			
AS SIGNS I'VE NOT BROUGHT DOWN	19	IMAGES IN AIR	12
DIRTIER WITH GARAGES AND CHEAP TEA SIGNS.	37	WINDMILLS TURN	15
THE CHANGED WIND BLOWS, AND THERE'S A CHOICE OF SIGNS	37	WINDMILLS TURN	31
HAVE SEARCHED FOR SHELLS AND SIGNS ON THE SEA SHORE,	52	OUT OF THE PIT	64
EMPTY, TO LET, ARE SIGNS ON THIS NEW HOUSE;	58	TO ARCHITECTS	15
SOME LET ME MAKE YOU OF THE MEADOW'S SIGNS;	99	OCTOBER WIND	21
BURY ALL RUBBISH AND LOVE SIGNS	156	RETURN	90
SILENCE			
IN SEIZURE OF SILENCE COMMIT THE DEAD NUISANCE: ...	109	I, IN IMAGE	23
AND BURNED SEA SILENCE ON A WICK OF WORLDS.	119	ALTARWISE	74
LOST IN A LIMP-TREED AND UNEATING SILENCE, ...	132	I MAKE THIS IN	28
SILENCE, SILENCE TO DO, WHEN EARTH GREW LOUD, ...	153	WAS A SAVIOUR	15
SILENCE, SILENCE TO DO, WHEN EARTH GREW LOUD, ...	153	WAS A SAVIOUR	15
SLEEPS TILL SILENCE BLOWS ON A CLOUD	165	LONG-LEGGED	111
BACK TO CLACK SILENCE MELT AND MOURN, ...	181	VISION, PRAYER	61
TELLS WITH SILENCE THE LAST LIGHT BREAKING	191	REFUSAL MOURN	4
AS THE WORLD FALLS, SILENT AS THE CYCLONE OF SILENCE.	199	COUNTRY SLEEP	63
GOD IN HIS WHIRLWIND SILENCE SAVE, WHO MARKS THE			
SPARROWS HAIL, ...	202	SIR JOHNS HILL	45
WAVE'S SILENCE, WEPT WHITE ANGELUS KNELLS.	209	POEM ON B'DAY	38
AND EYES HAVE BEEN GROVE-GREEN CATCHING MINE FROM			
THE DEPTH OF THE SILENCE;	224	IDYLL UNFORGET	33
AND CHIP, IN SILENCE AND IN TEARS, ...	239	MAKES INTERVALS	29
SILENCES			
THE LUNAR SILENCES, THE SILENT TIDE	54	WE BY SEASAND	9
THEIR SILENCES IN SILVER QUIETNESS OF SLEEP, ...	223	IDYLL UNFORGET	6
SILENT			
THE LUNAR SILENCES, THE SILENT TIDE	54	WE BY SEASAND	9
HERE SPRING THE SILENT VENOMS OF HIS BLOOD, ...	81	HERE LIE BEAST	4
HERE DRIPS A SILENT HONEY IN MY SHROUD, ...	81	HERE LIE BEAST	10
A THUNDERING BULLRING OF YOUR SILENT AND			
GIRL-CIRCLED ISLAND.	142	SAINT TO FALL	51
FROM THE CHILL, SILENT CENTRE	151	BELOW A TIME	22
THE COLOSSAL INTIMACIES OF SILENT	157	INTO HER HEAD	14
SILENT IN MY SERVICE	174	FIRE RAID	49
ON THE SILENT SEA WE HAVE HEARD THE SOUND	194	SLEEP BECALMED	3
AS THE WORLD FALLS, SILENT AS THE CYCLONE OF SILENCE.	199	COUNTRY SLEEP	63
THROUGH THE SHAKEN GREENSWARD LAKE, SILENT, ON			
MOONSHOD HOOVES, ...	200	COUNTRY SLEEP	84
INFINITE SHADOWY ISLES LIE SILENT BEFORE ME, ...	221	FOREST PICTURE	3
SILENTLY			
AND SILENTLY I MILK THE DEVIL'S BREAST.	81	HERE LIE BEAST	3
AND SILENTLY I MILK THE BURIED FLOWERS.	81	HERE LIE BEAST	9
SILK			
WHY SILK IS SOFT AND THE STONE WOUNDS	55	WHY EAST WIND	6
AND A SILK PIGEON'S GUILT IN HER PROUD ABSENCE, ...	131	I MAKE THIS IN	17
UNCLENCHED, ARMLESS, SILK AND ROUGH LOVE THAT BREAKS			
ALL ROCKS.	154	WAS A SAVIOUR	40
OR RIPPLING SOFT IN THE SPINNEY MOON AS THE SILK	204	GIANT'S THIGH	27
I HAVE FELT THE SILK WIND BRUSH MY LIPS;	224	IDYLL UNFORGET	19
SILKEN			
THEIR SILKEN BRANCHES UNMOVING, ...	235	WOMAN TAPESTRY	7
THEIR DELICATE, SILKEN LEAVES FOLDED, ...	235	WOMAN TAPESTRY	8
SILKILY			
SHAKEN SILKILY FROM STAR-SCALED BOUGHS.	226	SLENDER WIND	5
SILKS			
ITCHED ON THE HANGMAN'S SILKS;	85	SEE, SAYS LIME	21
SILL			
OPENING ITS IRIS MOUTH UPON THE SILL	47	POET: 1935	30

	PAGE	TITLE	LINE
SILL (CONTINUED)			
AND THE STRUTTING FERN LAY SEEDS ON THE BLACK SILL.	137	AFTER FUNERAL	40
SILLY			
THE SILLY BINDING	21	BEWILDERED WAY	19
GO SILLY AND BE CHRIST'S GOOD BROTHER,	25	BEAUTY TO DUST	17
SHARP AND SHRILL MY SILLY TONGUE SCRATCHES	149	PAPER & STICKS	16
MY SILLY SUIT, HARDLY YET SUFFERED FOR,	152	BELOW A TIME	29
SILLY TO CAGE AND THEN SET FREE,	237	PILLAR BREAKS	8
SILVER			
EACH SILVER MOMENT CHIMES/ IN STEPS OF SOUND,	9	MINUTE'S HOUR	5
TIME FOR THE SWIMMERS' HANDS, MUSIC FOR SILVER LOCK	15	SPIRE CRANES	7
NO SILVER WHISTLES CHASE HIM DOWN THE WEEKS'	108	GRIEF THIEF	21
WITH A BOUNCING AND SILVER SPOONED KID	149	PAPER & STICKS	15
THEIR SILENCES IN SILVER QUIETNESS OF SLEEP,	223	IDYLL UNFORGET	6
OF THE PALE-GREEN, DELICATE FISHES, SILVER AS SIGHS;	224	IDYLL UNFORGET	39
TOUCHING THE SILVER CLOUDS,	235	WOMAN TAPESTRY	32
SILVERFOX			
WITH A SILVERFOX FARMER	155	RETURN	28
SIMMERING			
WITH EVERY SIMMERING WOMAN HIS MOUSE	206	LAMENT	30
SIMPLE			
AND NIGHTLY UNDER THE SIMPLE STARS	195	FERN HILL	23
SO IT MUST HAVE BEEN AFTER THE BIRTH OF THE SIMPLE LIGHT	196	FERN HILL	33
THEY WITH THE SIMPLE JACKS WERE A BOULDER OF WIVES)--	205	GIANT'S THIGH	44
SIMPLEST			
THE SIMPLEST THOUGHT OR SENTIMENT,	84	LETTER TO AUNT	42
SIN			
THE WALKER'S APPLE'S BLACK AS SIN;	16	TIME TO ROT	15
BY US IN SIN OR US IN GAIETY.	17	IN OBLIVION	26
I LAID HER DOWN AND TOLD HER SIN,	61	MEAT ON BONES	23
SKINNY AS SIN, THE FOAMING MARROW,	106	ALL ALL AND	11
FOR MY TALL TURRETS CARRY AS YOUR SIN?	112	NOT FATHER ME	6
IN SHAPES OF SIN FORKED OUT THE BEARDED APPLE,	121	INCARNATE DEVL	4
SIN WHO HAD A WOMAN'S SHAPE	165	LONG-LEGGED	110
SNIFF, HERE IS SIN! NOW HE MUST GRAPPLE, RISE:	179	NEW QUAY	29
MY APTITUDE FOR SIN.	240	TWINING HEAD	12
SINCE			
SINCE, ON A QUIET NIGHT	22	ON QUIET NIGHT	T
SINCE, ON A QUIET NIGHT, I HEARD THEM TALK	22	ON QUIET NIGHT	1
SINCE THE FIRST FLESH OF MAN WAS RIVEN	64	WOMAN SPEAKS	28
SINCE THE FIRST WOMB SPAT FORTH A BABY'S CORPSE,	64	WOMAN SPEAKS	52
WITH EVERY CRY SINCE LIGHT	160	DEATHS AND ENT	23
THIS NIGHT AND EACH NIGHT SINCE THE FALLING STAR YOU WERE BORN,	199	COUNTRY SLEEP	55
SINCE YOU WERE BORN:	201	COUNTRY SLEEP	109
WHO ONCE, GREEN COUNTRIES SINCE, WERE A HEDGEROW OF JOYS.	204	GIANT'S THIGH	20
THAN EVER WAS SINCE THE WORLD WAS SAID,	211	POEM ON B'DAY	98
SIN-EATER			
LIE ALL UNKNOWING OF THE GRAVE SIN-EATER.	113	NOT FATHER ME	32
SIN-EMBRACING			
THAT SIN-EMBRACING DRIPPER OF FUN	156	RETURN	88
SINEW			
WERE THAT ENOUGH, BONE, BLOOD, AND SINEW,	32	OUT OF SIGHS	24
NOW IS DECAY IN BONE AND SINEW,	34	THIRST PARCHES	3
SINEWS			
TWISTING ON RACKS WHEN SINEWS GIVE WAY,	49	NO DOMINION	13
SING			
AT POOR PEACE I SING	3	PROLOGUE	23

                                          PAGE   TITLE   LINE
SING (CONTINUED)
     MY SISTERS' TEARS THAT SING UPON MY HEAD, ...   80   ALL THAT I OWE   7
     THAT HER LOVE SING AND SWING THROUGH A BROWN CHAPEL,   136   AFTER FUNERAL   25
     SHALL THE BLIND HORSE SING SWEETER?   144   PLEASURE-BIRD   2
     TO SHOOT AND SING YOUR PRAISE, ...   160   DEATHS AND ENT   8
     SING THROUGH THE WATER-SPOKEN PROW   164   LONG-LEGGED   78
     SING HOW THE SEAL HAS KISSED HER DEAD!   164   LONG-LEGGED   82
     SING AND HOWL THROUGH SAND AND ANEMONE   165   LONG-LEGGED   89
     SING AND STRIKE HIS HEAVY HAUL   166   LONG-LEGGED   137
     AND THE OLD MEN SING FROM NEWBORN LIPS: 167   LONG-LEGGED   152
     AND HE WHO TAUGHT THEIR LIPS TO SING   167   LONG-LEGGED   162
     STRIKE AND SING HIS CATCH OF FIELDS   168   LONG-LEGGED   181
     SING   173   FIRE RAID   11
     AND THE DUST SHALL SING LIKE A BIRD   173   FIRE RAID   23
     AND THE MIDWIVES OF MIRACLE SING   180   VISION, PRAYER   26
     THAT UNCALM STILL IT IS SURE ALONE TO STAND AND SING   186   HOLY SPRING   21
     LISTEN. THE MINSTRELS SING   189   WINTER'S TALE   56
     WE HEARD THE SEA SOUND SING, WE SAW THE SALT SHEET
          TELL.   194   SLEEP BECALMED   12
     THIRTY-FIVE BELLS SING STRUCK   209   POEM ON B'DAY   39
     FALL AND THE DEW LARKS SING   211   POEM ON B'DAY   102
     WHERE THE DEWFALL STARS SING GRAZING STILL   215   COUNTRY HEAVEN   8
SINGED
     THE FLYING LOOSE, ALBINO EYED, WING SINGED, ...   41   YOUNG ARE OLD   38
SINGEING
     DRIVELLED DOWN TO ONE SINGEING TREE   142   SAINT TO FALL   20
SINGERS
     WORD, SINGERS, AND TONGUE   174   FIRE RAID   53
     HERE WERE FOND CLIMATES AND SWEET SINGERS SUDDENLY   177   POEM IN OCT   26
SINGING
     SHALL FALL AWAY, AND LEAVE ONE SINGING SHELL.   73   LORD RED HAIL   12
     GREEN WAS THE SINGING HOUSE.   78   LOVE'S FEVER   24
     AND SIRENS SINGING FROM OUR LADY'S SEA-STRAW.   119   ALTARWISE   70
     THE FATS OF MIDNIGHT WHEN THE SALT WAS SINGING;   ...   119   ALTARWISE   80
     HIGH LORD ESQUIRE, SPEAK UP THE SINGING CLOUD, ...   123   FOSTER LIGHT   17
     A SINGING WALL FROM THE MOWER   156   RETURN   69
     WITH SINGING   173   FIRE RAID   10
     THE SINGING BREAKS IN THE SNOW SHOED VILLAGES OF
          WISHES   190   WINTER'S TALE   113
     AND WHEN THE SALT SHEET BROKE IN A STORM OF SINGING   194   SLEEP BECALMED   7
     ABOUT THE HAPPY YARD AND SINGING AS THE FARM WAS
          HOME, ...   195   FERN HILL   11
     I LABOUR BY SINGING LIGHT   197   CRAFT OR ART   6
     OF THE DINGLE TORN TO SINGING AND THE SURPLICED   ...   200   COUNTRY SLEEP   75
     EARTH, AIR, WATER, FIRE, SINGING INTO THE WHITE ACT,   200   COUNTRY SLEEP   87
     AND COVERING ALL HAS BEEN A QUIETUDE, AND A SINGING
          FROM FLAKE-BARE THROATS.   224   IDYLL UNFORGET   35
     WITH BRANCHES WAITING FOR A SINGING BIRD, ...   234   NO, PIGEON   14
SINGINGBIRDS
     STILL IN THE WATER AND SINGINGBIRDS.   178   POEM IN OCT   60
SINGINGS
     TO HAVE HEARD THEIR VAGUE, RHAPSODIC SINGINGS, ...   223   IDYLL UNFORGET   5
SINGLE
     INTO A DOUBLE OR A SINGLE BED, ...   28   NO WINGS   18
     A GIRL WHOSE SINGLE BED HELD TWO   38   THE GOSSIPERS   9
     MY GREAT BLOOD'S IRON SINGLE   111   I, IN IMAGE   93
     OTHERS WHOSE SINGLE BEDS HOLD TWO   155   RETURN   60
     HAVE SOUGHT YOUR SINGLE GRAVE, ...   160   DEATHS AND ENT   28
SINGLY
     SINGLY LIE WITH THE WHOLE WIDE SHORE, ...   158   INTO HER HEAD   49

	PAGE	TITLE	LINE
SINGS			
MY ARK SINGS IN THE SUN	5	PROLOGUE	100
HERE IS A SAVIOUR WHO SINGS LIKE A BIRD,	74	SUN BURNS	7
'MY FATHERS' GLOBE KNOCKS ON ITS NAVE AND SINGS.'	101	FELLOWED SLEEP	11
SINGS TO THE TREADING HAWK	159	INTO HER HEAD	59
TO THE GOLD GUT THAT SINGS ON HIS REEL	162	LONG-LEGGED	19
HIS FIERY REEL SINGS OFF ITS FLAMES,	164	LONG-LEGGED	64
TIME SINGS THROUGH THE INTRICATELY DEAD SNOW DROP.			
LISTEN.	189	WINTER'S TALE	65
CHASTITY PRAYS FOR ME, PIETY SINGS,	207	LAMENT	57
HE SINGS TOWARDS ANGUISH; FINCHES FLY	209	POEM ON B'DAY	20
SINGSONG			
YOU KING SINGSONG OWLS, WHO MOONBEAM	4	PROLOGUE	54
SINGULAR			
BENT LIKE A BEAST TO LAP THE SINGULAR FLOODS	134	NOT FROM ANGER	3
SINISTER			
SHUT. SINISTER DARK OVER CARDIGAN	179	NEW QUAY	7
SINK			
THOUGH THEY SINK THROUGH THE SEA THEY SHALL RISE			
AGAIN;	49	NO DOMINION	7
THAT CANNOT SINK OR CEASE	160	DEATHS AND ENT	10
SINKING			
CREEP AND HARP ON THE TIDE, SINKING THEIR CHARMED,			
BENT PIN	135	HOW MY ANIMAL	24
SHE WOULD NOT HAVE ME SINKING IN THE HOLY	136	AFTER FUNERAL	18
SINNERS			
AND ALL LOVE'S SINNERS IN SWEET CLOTH KNEEL TO A			
HYLEG IMAGE,	130	SINNERS' BELL	28
SINNERS'			
IT IS THE SINNERS' DUST-TONGUED BELL	130	SINNERS' BELL	T
IT IS THE SINNERS' DUST-TONGUED BELL CLAPS ME TO			
CHURCHES	130	SINNERS' BELL	1
SINS			
SOME LET ME TELL YOU OF THE RAVEN'S SINS.	99	OCTOBER WIND	24
THE PYRE YET TO BE LIGHTED OF MY SINS AND DAYS,	147	UNLUCKILY FOR	3
SIPPING			
BY SIPPING AT THE VINE OF DAYS.	69	BEFORE KNOCKED	36
SIR			
JOY IS NO KNOCKING NATION, SIR AND MADAM,	100	RUNNING GRAVE	31
SIR, IS YOUR DOOM.	101	RUNNING GRAVE	40
(SIR MORROW MARK),	113	SERVANT SUN	2
SIR MORROW AT HIS SPONGE,	113	SERVANT SUN	8
(SIR MORROW STAMPS	114	SERVANT SUN	23
THIS INWARD SIR,	114	SERVANT SUN	30
SIR NO SAY,	127	NOW, SAY NAY	10
NO SAY SIR	127	NOW, SAY NAY	17
I, THE FIRST NAMED, AM THE GHOST OF THIS SIR AND			
CHRISTIAN FRIEND	141	I, FIRST NAMED	1
OVER SIR JOHN'S HILL	201	SIR JOHNS HILL	T
OVER SIR JOHN'S HILL,	201	SIR JOHNS HILL	1
DAWS SIR JOHN'S JUST HILL DONS, AND AGAIN THE GULLED			
BIRDS HARE	201	SIR JOHNS HILL	15
IT IS THE HERON AND I, UNDER JUDGING SIR JOHN'S ELMED	202	SIR JOHNS HILL	40
NOW ON SIR JOHN'S HILL. THE HERON, ANKLING THE SCALY	203	SIR JOHNS HILL	55
SIRE			
DAM AND SIRE, LIVING, LO,	72	TAKE NEEDLES	47
YOU ARE YOUR SISTERS' SIRE, SAID SEAWEEDY,	113	NOT FATHER ME	26
SIREN-PRINTED			
GLINT IN THE STAVED AND SIREN-PRINTED CAVERS,	131	I MAKE THIS IN	20

	PAGE	TITLE	LINE
SIRENS			
AND SIRENS SINGING FROM OUR LADY'S SEA-STRAW.	119	ALTARWISE	70
SIREN'S			
AND LOVE PLUCKED OUT THE STINGING SIREN'S EYE, ...	119	ALTARWISE	77
SIRENSUITED			
GASKETTED AND SIRENSUITED	154	RETURN	21
SISTER			
AND SISTER TO THE FATHERING WORM.	68	BEFORE KNOCKED	6
AND THE WIND WAS MY SISTER SUITOR;	68	BEFORE KNOCKED	15
DO YOU NOT SISTER ME, NOR THE ERECTED CRIME	112	NOT FATHER ME	5
AM I NOT SISTER, TOO, WHO IS MY SAVIOUR?	112	NOT FATHER ME	12
HAVE BROTHERLESS HIS SISTER ON THE HANDSAW.	127	NOW, SAY NAY	14
SISTERS'			
MY SISTERS' TEARS THAT SING UPON MY HEAD, ...	80	ALL THAT I OWE	7
YOU ARE YOUR SISTERS' SIRE, SAID SEAWEEDY, ...	113	NOT FATHER ME	26
SIT			
WE WHO ARE YOUNG SIT HOLDING YELLOW HANDS.	41	YOUNG ARE OLD	17
SIT AT OUR HEARTHS FROM MORNING UNTIL EVENING, ...	42	YOUNG ARE OLD	54
THE SPHINX OF LIGHT SIT ON THE EYES, ...	69	SECRET WIND	2
I SIT AND WATCH THE WORM BENEATH MY NAIL	95	RUB OF LOVE	34
CELIBATE I SIT AND SEE	138	O CHATTERTON	29
I SIT AT THE OPEN WINDOW, OBSERVING	179	NEW QUAY	13
THAN SIT HERE WASTING, WHILE I BLEED, ...	240	TWINING HEAD	11
SITS			
SITS BACK AND SMILES, A TINY CORPSE	49	LIGHT, I KNOW	24
SITS IN THEIR DOUBLE SHADE.	88	A PROCESS IN	21
SITTING			
I ASTOUNDED THE SITTING TAILORS, ...	151	BELOW A TIME	17
WHERE SITTING IN CLEAN LINEN	156	RETURN	93
SIX			
OF LOVER, MOTHER, LOVERS, OR HIS SIX	96	RUB OF LOVE	41
OF THE SKY, KING OF YOUR SIX YEARS.	193	SIDE OF TRUTH	28
SIXTH			
WHICH SIXTH OF WIND BLEW OUT THE BURNING GENTRY?	118	ALTARWISE	47
SIX-YEAR			
THE BOAT SWIMS INTO THE SIX-YEAR WEATHER, ...	166	LONG-LEGGED	129
SIZE			
THE SIZE OF GENESIS? THE SHORT SPARK'S GENDER?	118	ALTARWISE	44
OUT OF THE URN THE SIZE OF A MAN	166	LONG-LEGGED	141
AND OVER THE SEA WET CHURCH THE SIZE OF A SNAIL ...	177	POEM IN OCT	32
FOR THE COUNTRY OF DEATH IS THE HEART'S SIZE	184	VISION, PRAYER	169
WE WILL REMARK UPON THE SIZE	230	OUR SANCTITY	6
SIZZLING			
AND THE SIZZLING BEDS OF THE TOWN CRIED, QUICK!--	206	LAMENT	20
SKATED			
AND OVER THE GLAZED LAKES SKATED THE SHAPES OF FISHES	190	WINTER'S TALE	115
SKEIN			
WITH BRIDEBAIT OF GOLD BREAD, I WITH A LIVING SKEIN,	135	HOW MY ANIMAL	25
SKELETON			
TOO LONG, SKELETON	29	LONG, SKELETON	T
TOO LONG, SKELETON, DEATH'S RISEN	29	LONG, SKELETON	1
TOO LONG, SKELETON, DEATH'S ALL ALIVE	29	LONG, SKELETON	4
WHEN THE SKELETON OF WAR	35	LIFT UP FACE	19
MAKE BRIGHT ITS CORNERS WHERE A SKELETON	49	LIGHT, I KNOW	23
AND THEN RAISE UP THE SKELETON AGAIN, ...	55	NO MAN BELIEVE	20
A CUPBOARD SKELETON	59	FAIRY TALES	15
RISE OF THE SKELETON AND	103	I DREAMED MY	22
UNSEX THE SKELETON THIS MOUNTAIN MINUTE, ...	120	ALTARWISE	110
I MAKE A WEAPON OF AN ASS'S SKELETON	132	I MAKE THIS IN	31
WHITE AS THE SKELETON	174	FIRE RAID	45

		PAGE	TITLE	LINE
SKELETONS				
(AND SKELETONS HAD SAP). ONE MINUTE		43	FACES SHONE	7
SKELETON'S				
THROUGH THE WAVES OF THE FAT STREETS NOR THE				
SKELETON'S THIN WAYS.		146	IF HEAD HURT	28
SKEWER				
AND FELT A SKEWER ENTER AT HIS SIDE.		52	OUT OF THE PIT	55
SKIES				
CROSS ALL DIRECTIONS, BRACKEN POINTS TO THE SKIES,		44	TO FOLLOW FOX	9
TEAR WITH A GREAT SOUND THROUGH THE SKIES, ...		51	OUT OF THE PIT	16
WHERE, WHAT? THERE WAS COMMOTION IN THE SKIES, ...		52	OUT OF THE PIT	76
THE LIVING SUN LAMENTS THE DYING SKIES, ...		56	GREEK PLAY	3
TIME UPON TIME THE TOWERS OF THE SKIES		56	WHY EAST WIND	19
AND THE GOLDEN BALL SPINS OUT OF THE SKIES;		134	NOT FROM ANGER	10
THE NATURAL CIRCLE OF THE DISCOVERED SKIES		134	HOW MY ANIMAL	10
POSSESSED BY THE SKIES		170	LOVE IN ASYLUM	12
UNDER THE UNMINDING SKIES, ...		192	SIDE OF TRUTH	6
INTO THE ANSWERING SKIES FROM THE GREEN GROUND, ...		193	CONVERS PRAYER	7
OF UNREMEMBERED SKIES AND SNOWS.		225	CLOWN IN MOON	4
SKIMMED				
HILL OF CYPRESSES! THE DIN AND TALE IN THE SKIMMED		200	COUNTRY SLEEP	76
SKIMS				
THAT, LIKE A RAZOR, SKIMS, CUTS, AND TURNS, ...		47	POET: 1935	49
AS THE BOAT SKIMS ON WITH DRINKING WINGS!		166	LONG-LEGGED	134
SKIN				
HOW COULD I SMOOTH THAT SKIN		10	COOL, OH NO	9
THE WORD OF THE BLOOD, THE WILY SKIN, ...		61	MEAT ON BONES	15
OF SKIN AND VEIN AROUND THE WELL		69	BEFORE KNOCKED	26
IN THE STABLE UNDER THE SKIN.		74	SUN BURNS	10
THAT DROVE MY STUFF THROUGH SKIN AND GUT;		86	SEE, SAYS LIME	31
PULLS DOWN THE SHABBY CURTAINS OF THE SKIN;		88	A PROCESS IN	23
(GIVE, SUMMER, OVER), THE CEMENTED SKIN, ...		101	RUNNING GRAVE	44
THE TERRIBLE WORLD MY BROTHER BARES HIS SKIN.		133	I MAKE THIS IN	60
HAVE NOT ADORED MY BODY AS IT SOFTLY SMOOTHED THEIR				
SKIN.		223	IDYLL UNFORGET	16
GROW INTO YOUR DELICATE SKIN, ...		238	MAKES INTERVALS	11
UPON MY FLESH AND SKIN, ...		240	TWINING HEAD	10
SKINNING				
WHERE NO COLD IS, THE SKINNING GALES UNPIN		82	LIGHT BREAKS	22
SKINNY				
SKINNY AS SIN, THE FOAMING MARROW, ...		106	ALL ALL AND	11
SKINS				
GRAFTS ON ITS BRIDE ONE-SIDED SKINS OF TRUTH;		90	EUNUCH DREAMS	28
SKIN'S				
FOR THE BODY'S BRITTLE AND THE SKIN'S WHITE.		42	A WAR OF WITS	10
SKIPPED				
I SKIPPED IN A BLUSH AS THE BIG GIRLS ROLLED		206	LAMENT	6
SKIRTING				
SKIRTING THE ORDERED BEDS OF PAINT-BOX FLOWERS, ...		33	IN GARDENS	3
SKIRTING-BOARD				
BRED IN THE DARK BEHIND THE SKIRTING-BOARD, ...		28	NO WINGS	21
SKIRTS				
SAWDUST BENEATH THE SKIRTS;		27	OBLIVIOUS DARK	17
AS A HE-GOD'S PADDLING WATER SKIRTS, ...		151	BELOW A TIME	16
SKULKING				
FOR MY SULKING, SKULKING, COAL BLACK SOUL!		206	LAMENT	36
SKULKS				
OR SKULKS IN THE DELL MOON BUT MOONSHINE ECHOING				
CLEAR		198	COUNTRY SLEEP	25

	PAGE	TITLE	LINE
SKULL			
THICK TO THE SKULL,	18	NATURAL DAY	33
THE SKULL, THE CELLS, THE CABINNED EARS	69	SECRET WIND	5
THE FIELDS YET UNDIVIDED BEHIND THE SKULL.	73	LORD RED HAIL	10
AND SEWN ON HIS SKULL A SCARLET THORN;	74	SUN BURNS	13
AND THESE POOR NERVES SO WIRED TO THE SKULL	75	MY HERO BARES	6
FROM POLES OF SKULL AND TOE THE WINDY BLOOD	82	LIGHT BREAKS	14
THEY DANCE BETWEEN THEIR ARCLAMPS AND OUR SKULL,	89	EUNUCH DREAMS	17
NO, NO, YOU LOVER SKULL, DESCENDING HAMMER	100	RUNNING GRAVE	27
YOU HERO SKULL, CADAVER IN THE HANGAR	100	RUNNING GRAVE	29
LOVE'S TWILIT NATION AND THE SKULL OF STATE,	101	RUNNING GRAVE	39
THE FLIGHT OF THE CARNAL SKULL	111	I, IN IMAGE	75
SHAKING THE SEA-HATCHED SKULL,	111	I, IN IMAGE	100
HORNED DOWN WITH SKULLFOOT AND THE SKULL OF TOES	117	ALTARWISE	33
WHOSE WIZARD SHAPE I TRACE IN THE CAVERNOUS SKULL,	134	HOW MY ANIMAL	2
WITH THE WILD BREAST AND BLESSED AND GIANT SKULL	136	AFTER FUNERAL	28
THE SKULL OF THE EARTH IS BARBED WITH A WAR OF BURNING BRAINS AND HAIR.	142	SAINT TO FALL	34
SEE WHAT CLINGS TO HAIR AND SKULL	166	LONG-LEGGED	133
IN THE CINDER OF THE LITTLE SKULL,	174	FIRE RAID	40
IN THE CINDER OF THE LITTLE SKULL,	174	FIRE RAID	54
ON SKULL AND SCAR WHERE HIS LOVES LIE WRECKED,	209	POEM ON B'DAY	40
SKULLFOOT			
HORNED DOWN WITH SKULLFOOT AND THE SKULL OF TOES	117	ALTARWISE	33
SKY			
HE GOES ACROSS THE SKY,	13	RAIN CUTS	19
PIERCE THE SPILT SKY WITH DIVING WING IN WEED AND HEEL	15	SPIRE CRANES	4
TO WET THE SKY WITH TEARS,	15	FOR LEDA	12
A RIB OF CANCER ON THE FLUID SKY.	25	THERE'S PLENTY	7
SPELLING ACROSS THE SKY HIS DEVIL'S NEWS,	29	NEARLY SUMMER	5
STEPPING ON CLOUDS ACROSS THE GOLDEN SKY,	30	YOUTH CALLS	2
AND BARED YOUR HEAD BENEATH THE LIVING SKY,	30	YOUTH CALLS	9
SEARING THE SKY FOR THUNDERBOLTS TO FALL	34	THIRST PARCHES	5
BREAKING, STARE AT THE SKY	35	LIFT UP FACE	2
THE LIVING SKY, THE FACES OF THE STARS.	36	MIDNIGHT ROAD	14
UNDER THE ARC OF THE SKY THEY ARE UNSAFE.	40	WAS THERE TIME	5
REACH ASKING ARMS UP TO THE MILKY SKY,	42	A WAR OF WITS	16
HE ALONE IS FREE, AND, FREE, MOANS TO THE SKY.	46	POET: 1935	13
ON THE CANVAS SKY, AND ALL HOT COLOURS MELT	46	POET: 1935	19
LIGHT WALKS THE SKY, LEAVING NO PRINT,	49	LIGHT, I KNOW	17
BETWEEN THE STREET-LAMPS AND THE ILL-LIT SKY,	52	OUT OF THE PIT	61
AND GREEN, SNEERS NOT AT THE OLD SKY.	55	NO MAN BELIEVE	11
HAVE BLOWN SKY HIGH THE NURSERY OF FAIRIES;	59	FAIRY TALES	23
AND THE PARLIAMENT OF SKY,	61	MEAT ON BONES	10
AND THE SKY LAYS DOWN HER LAWS,	61	MEAT ON BONES	34
HE LEARNS THE CARRION PICKERS OF THE SKY,	63	WOMAN SPEAKS	21
ROOFED WITH THE SKY AND PATTERNED WITH BLOND BONES;	64	WOMAN SPEAKS	25
BY SCALPEL LIGHTNING FROM THE RIFTED SKY,	64	WOMAN SPEAKS	29
THE SNIPER DIES; THE FINGERS FROM THE SKY	64	WOMAN SPEAKS	45
AND SHAFTED HAWKS CAME SNARLING DOWN THE SKY;	65	WOMAN SPEAKS	57
AND THE RUIN OF THE SKY;	71	TAKE NEEDLES	35
AND EARTH AND SKY WERE AS ONE AIRY HILL,	78	LOVE'S FEVER	8
THE EARTH AND SKY WERE AS TWO MOUNTAINS MEETING.	78	LOVE'S FEVER	15
FROM THE DIVORCING SKY I LEARNT THE DOUBLE,	79	LOVE'S FEVER	44
HIS WINY SKY, AND, AS THE CANDLE'S MOON,	80	ALL THAT I OWE	14
NOR FENCED, NOR STAKED, THE GUSHERS OF THE SKY	82	LIGHT BREAKS	16
SAGE ON THE EARTH AND SKY;	91	WHERE ONCE THE	21
WHO PERISCOPE THROUGH FLOWERS TO THE SKY.	98	TWILIGHT LOCKS	30
AND DROPPED ON DREAMING AND THE UPWARD SKY.	101	FELLOWED SLEEP	5

		PAGE	TITLE	LINE
SKY (CONTINUED)				
THIS WAS THE SKY, JACK CHRIST, EACH MINSTREL ANGLE		120	ALTARWISE	105
THROUGH THE RAMPART OF THE SKY	....	125	SEED-AT-ZERO	15
THROUGH THE RAMPART OF THE SKY	....	126	SEED-AT-ZERO	22
BEHIND MY HEAD A SQUARE OF SKY SAGS OVER	....	134	NOT FROM ANGER	8
THE SCUDDING BASE OF THE FAMILIAR SKY,	....	142	SAINT TO FALL	29
WITH IMMORTALITY AT MY SIDE LIKE CHRIST THE SKY.		148	UNLUCKILY FOR	49
THE SKY IS TORN ACROSS	....	161	WEDDING ANNIV	1
AND THIS DAY'S SUN LEAPT UP THE SKY OUT OF HER THIGHS		170	MARRIAGE VIRG	4
WOULD PLUNGE MY BETRAYAL FROM SHEET TO SKY	....	175	MY BEGGAR ARM	6
AND DOWN THE OTHER AIR AND THE BLUE ALTERED SKY	...	178	POEM IN OCT	42
THE SKY STRIDE OF THE ALWAYS SLAIN	....	182	VISION, PRAYER	94
THE SKY.	....	185	VISION, PRAYER	195
GENTLE IN THEIR CLOGS OVER THE FALLEN SKY,	....	187	WINTER'S TALE	24
HE WEPT FROM THE CREST OF GRIEF, HE PRAYED TO THE VEILED SKY	....	188	WINTER'S TALE	32
PAST THE STATUES OF THE STABLES AND THE SKY ROOFED STIES	....	188	WINTER'S TALE	34
AND THE SKY OF BIRDS IN THE PLUMED VOICE CHARMED		190	WINTER'S TALE	88
THE SKY, THE BIRD, THE BRIDE,	....	190	WINTER'S TALE	101
OF THE SKY, KING OF YOUR SIX YEARS.	....	193	SIDE OF TRUTH	28
WATER AND LIGHT, THE EARTH AND SKY,	....	193	SIDE OF TRUTH	32
THE SKY GATHERED AGAIN	....	196	FERN HILL	31
AND NOTHING I CARED, AT MY SKY BLUE TRADES, THAT TIME ALLOWS	....	196	FERN HILL	42
LYING THE SKY	....	200	COUNTRY SLEEP	91
LIGHT OF HIS THIGHS, SPREADEAGLE TO THE DUNGHILL SKY,	204	GIANT'S THIGH	23
AND I SHOVED IT INTO THE COAL BLACK SKY	....	207	LAMENT	47
IN THE COAL BLACK SKY AND SHE BORE ANGELS!	....	207	LAMENT	55
ON A SEIZING SKY; SMALL FISHES GLIDE	....	209	POEM ON B'DAY	22
HERE AMONG THE LIGHT OF THE LORDING SKY	....	217	ELEGY	29
BURROW OUR WAY UPWARDS INTO THE BLUE SKY;	....	231	OUR SANCTITY	35
INTO THE SKY.	....	233	FURIOUS MOTION	23
NO SKY FOR ME THAT CARRIES	....	234	NO, PIGEON	2
SKY HAS NOT LOVED ME MUCH,	....	234	NO, PIGEON	4
AND THE DEEP SKY OVER THEM	....	235	WOMAN TAPESTRY	9
POOR, BROKEN WEBS TO STRIKE THE SKY!	....	238	PILLAR BREAKS	16
SKY-BLUE				
BUT WAILED AND NESTED IN THE SKY-BLUE WALL	....	153	WAS A SAVIOUR	31
SKY'S				
SOMETIMES THE SKY'S TOO BRIGHT	....	12	SKY'S BRIGHT	T
SOMETIMES THE SKY'S TOO BRIGHT,	....	12	SKY'S BRIGHT	1
PERHAPS THE SKY'S TOO BRIGHT;	....	13	SKY'S BRIGHT	26
SKY-SCRAPING				
RANGE ON THE SKY-SCRAPING PLACE.	....	126	SEED-AT-ZERO	49
SKYSIGNS				
UNDER THE SKYSIGNS THEY WHO HAVE NO ARMS	....	40	WAS THERE TIME	7
AND THE SKYSIGNS AND THE NIGHT LIGHTS,	....	42	YOUNG ARE OLD	51
SKYWARD				
HER FLESH WAS MEEK AS MILK, BUT THIS SKYWARD STATUE		136	AFTER FUNERAL	27
SLABS				
DISSECT THAT STATEMENT, VOICES, ON THE SLABS.	.....	137	O CHATTERTON	21
SLACK				
INTO THEIR PRISON WITH A SLACK SOUND,	....	47	POET: 1935	44
SLAIN				
THE QUEEN IS SLAIN; ORESTES' HANDS DRIP BLOOD;	....	57	GREEK PLAY	15
GOD IS SLAIN IN MANY WAYS.	....	72	TAKE NEEDLES	56
THE SKY STRIDE OF THE ALWAYS SLAIN	....	182	VISION, PRAYER	94
STONE FOR THE SAKE OF THE SOULS OF THE SLAIN BIRDS SAILING.	....	203	SIR JOHNS HILL	60

	PAGE	TITLE	LINE
SLANT			
MY IMAGES STALK THE TREES AND THE SLANT SAP'S TUNNEL,	109	I, IN IMAGE	25
IN HIS SLANT, RACKING HOUSE	209	POEM ON B'DAY	25
SLAP			
ON GIDDY NIGHTS WHEN SLAP ON THE MOON'S MASK	137	O CHATTERTON	12
ON GIDDY NIGHTS I SLAP A FEW DRUNK CURVES	138	O CHATTERTON	24
SLAP ON THE DRUNK MOON'S MASK.	138	O CHATTERTON	25
SLAPPED			
SLAPPED DOWN THE GUILLOTINE, THE BLOOD-RED DOUBLE	124	TODAY, INSECT	6
A MADMAN WITH A BRUSH HAS SLAPPED A FACE	137	O CHATTERTON	13
SLASH			
SUFFER THE SLASH OF VISION BY THE FIN-GREEN STUBBLE,	111	I, IN IMAGE	85
SLASHED			
SLASHED DOWN THE LAST SNAKE AS THOUGH	150	WHEN I WOKE	13
AND I GAVE MY SOUL A BLIND, SLASHED EYE, ...	207	LAMENT	45
SLASHES			
CARTOON OF SLASHES ON THE TIDE-TRACED CRATER, ...	119	ALTARWISE	71
SLATE			
I CHALKED UPON THE BREASTBONE'S SLATE	86	SEE, SAYS LIME	27
SLATES			
RAIN BEATS THE SAND AND SLATES.	62	EARS IN TURRET	28
SLAUGHTERED			
AND THE FUNERAL GRAINS OF THE SLAUGHTERED FLOOR.	172	DAWN RAID	5
SLAVED-FOR			
MY PAID-FOR SLAVED-FOR OWN TOO LATE	151	BELOW A TIME	6
SLAVES			
WHO SLAVES TO HIS CROUCHED, ETERNAL END	209	POEM ON B'DAY	31
SLAVING			
AND WORDS FALL CRIPPLED FROM THE SLAVING LIPS, ...	96	TWELVE	2
SLAY			
AND THE MAGGOT NO MAN CAN SLAY.'	61	MEAT ON BONES	16
SLAY ME, SLAY THE GOD OF LOVE;	72	TAKE NEEDLES	55
SLAY ME, SLAY THE GOD OF LOVE;	72	TAKE NEEDLES	55
SLAYER			
AND A CHILD MIGHT BE MY SLAYER, ...	71	TAKE NEEDLES	17
SLEEK			
SLIDES GOOD IN THE SLEEK MOUTH.	209	POEM ON B'DAY	36
SLEEP			
BEASTS WHO SLEEP GOOD AND THIN, ...	5	PROLOGUE	77
MOISTEN THE MOUTH OF SLEEP	15	FOR LEDA	17
READY TO RISE, EASY TO SLEEP.	23	THE ONLY DEAD	6
NEVER FLOWS OUT FROM THE WOUND OF SLEEP	27	OBLIVIOUS DARK	7
SLEEP, WAKE, AND SLEEP, EAT, LOVE, AND LAUGH, ...	28	NO WINGS	13
SLEEP, WAKE, AND SLEEP, EAT, LOVE, AND LAUGH, ...	28	NO WINGS	13
SLEEP PUNCTURED BY WAKING, DREAMS	39	GAS FADES	22
SPRINKLES IN CHILDREN'S EYES A LONG-LAST SLEEP	56	WHY EAST WIND	13
RULE THE BLANK SHEET OF SLEEP, ...	66	LET A FAITH	2
DREW IN HIS EYES THE STRAWS OF SLEEP, ...	97	TWILIGHT LOCKS	17
SLEEP NAVIGATES THE TIDES OF TIME;	97	TWILIGHT LOCKS	25
AND SLEEP ROLLS MUTE ABOVE THE BEDS	98	TWILIGHT LOCKS	28
I FELLOWED SLEEP	101	FELLOWED SLEEP	T
I FELLOWED SLEEP WHO KISSED ME IN THE BRAIN, ...	101	FELLOWED SLEEP	1
I DREAMED MY GENESIS IN SWEAT OF SLEEP, BREAKING	102	I DREAMED MY	1
WHERE STILL THEY SLEEP UNKNOWING OF THEIR GHOST.	102	FELLOWED SLEEP	20
THE CRUTCH THAT MARROW TAPS UPON THEIR SLEEP, ...	104	WORLD PYRAMID	14
MORNING SMACK OF THE SPADE THAT WAKES UP SLEEP, ...	136	AFTER FUNERAL	6
AND WHEN BLIND SLEEP DROPS ON THE SPYING SENSES,	139	FIVE & COUNTRY	13
OR A NACREOUS SLEEP AMONG SOFT PARTICLES AND CHARMS	146	IF HEAD HURT	17
SPOILERS AND POKERS OF SLEEP, ...	150	WHEN I WOKE	5

	PAGE	TITLE	LINE
SLEEP (CONTINUED)			
SLEEP TO A NEWBORN SLEEP IN A SWADDLING LOIN-LEAF STROKED AND SANG	157	INTO HER HEAD	22
SLEEP TO A NEWBORN SLEEP IN A SWADDLING LOIN-LEAF STROKED AND SANG	157	INTO HER HEAD	22
FORGOTTEN DARK, REST THEIR PULSE AND BURY THEIR DEAD IN HER FAITHLESS SLEEP.	159	INTO HER HEAD	69
TO HIDE THE WOLVES OF SLEEP	176	BREATH SHED	11
BLIND HOST TO SLEEP	184	VISION, PRAYER	141
BACK. LINES OF AGE SLEEP ON THE STONES TILL TRUMPETING DAWN.	191	WINTER'S TALE	118
THE ONE NOT CARING TO WHOM IN HIS SLEEP HE WILL MOVE	193	CONVERS PRAYER	4
LIE STILL, SLEEP BECALMED	194	SLEEP BECALMED	T
LIE STILL, SLEEP BECALMED, SUFFERER WITH THE WOUND	194	SLEEP BECALMED	1
FOR THE SLEEP IN A SAFE LAND AND THE LOVE WHO DIES	194	CONVERS PRAYER	10
SHALL THE CHILD SLEEP UNHARMED OR THE MAN BE CRYING?	194	CONVERS PRAYER	12
LIE STILL, SLEEP BECALMED, HIDE THE MOUTH IN THE THROAT,	194	SLEEP BECALMED	13
AND MARK THE DARK EYED WAVE, THROUGH THE EYES OF SLEEP,	194	CONVERS PRAYER	19
AS I RODE TO SLEEP THE OWLS WERE BEARING THE FARM AWAY,	195	FERN HILL	24
NOR THAT RIDING TO SLEEP	196	FERN HILL	49
IN COUNTRY SLEEP	197	COUNTRY SLEEP	T
SLEEP, GOOD, FOR EVER, SLOW AND DEEP, SPELLED RARE AND WISE,	197	COUNTRY SLEEP	8
AND FLOWER OF COUNTRY SLEEP AND THE GREENWOOD KEEP.	198	COUNTRY SLEEP	18
NEVER, MY GIRL, UNTIL TOLLED TO SLEEP BY THE STERN	198	COUNTRY SLEEP	21
LIE IN GRACE. SLEEP SPELLED AT REST IN THE LOWLY HOUSE	199	COUNTRY SLEEP	43
IN THE TOWER AND TOLLS TO SLEEP OVER THE STALLS	199	COUNTRY SLEEP	52
AND YOU SHALL WAKE, FROM COUNTRY SLEEP, THIS DAWN AND EACH FIRST DAWN,	201	COUNTRY SLEEP	110
AND I LIE DOWN BUT TO SLEEP IN BED,	206	LAMENT	35
BUT THEY SLEEP SOUND.	216	COUNTRY HEAVEN	30
WHERE NOW THE WINGS OF DREAMLESS SLEEP ARE SPREAD,	222	MISSING	5
SLEEP ABOVE IN THE GLOW OF A FADING SUNSET;	222	FOREST PICTURE	7
THEIR SILENCES IN SILVER QUIETNESS OF SLEEP,	223	IDYLL UNFORGET	6
SLEEPER			
THE DREAM HAS SUCKED THE SLEEPER OF HIS FAITH	90	EUNUCH DREAMS	29
AWAKE, MY SLEEPER, TO THE SUN,	98	TWILIGHT LOCKS	37
AND THE OLD DOG SLEEPER	171	THE HUNCHBACK	25
SLEEPERS			
AND STAKE THE SLEEPERS IN THE SAVAGE GRAVE	104	WORLD PYRAMID	17
OF SLEEPERS WHOSE TONGUE I TOLL	184	VISION, PRAYER	155
OF THE CHARTING SLEEPERS PRAYS	184	VISION, PRAYER	167
SLEEPER'S			
LET FALL THE TEAR OF TIME; THE SLEEPER'S EYE,	101	FELLOWED SLEEP	2
SLEEPING			
CATCH THE ROOKS SLEEPING, AND BREAK NO TWIG,	31	BEING BUT MEN	7
WHERE HALF DEAD VANITIES WERE SLEEPING CURLED	50	OUT OF THE PIT	4
SLEEPING ON EITHER HAND.	54	WE BY SEASAND	8
SLOW IN A SLEEPING WIND.	88	A PROCESS IN	15
HOW LIGHT THE SLEEPING ON THIS SOILY STAR,	102	FELLOWED SLEEP	24
A SHE BIRD SLEEPING BRITTLE BY	159	INTO HER HEAD	56
IN THE STILL SLEEPING TOWN AND SET FORTH.	177	POEM IN OCT	10
ROOSTS SLEEPING CHILL TILL THE FLAME OF THE COCK CROW	187	WINTER'S TALE	19
THE TALL MAUVE IRIS OF A SLEEPING CLIME.	222	IN DREAMS	2
SLEEPINGS			
WHICH IS THE WORLD? OF OUR TWO SLEEPINGS, WHICH	89	EUNUCH DREAMS	21

	PAGE	TITLE	LINE
SLEEPS			
SLEEPS TILL SILENCE BLOWS ON A CLOUD	165	LONG-LEGGED	111
FOR A MAN SLEEPS WHERE FIRE LEAPT DOWN AND SHE LEARNS THROUGH HIS ARM	170	MARRIAGE VIRG	13
SHE SLEEPS IN THE NARROW TROUGH YET SHE WALKS THE DUST	170	LOVE IN ASYLUM	13
SLEEP-WALKING			
MAN WAS THE BURNING ENGLAND SHE WAS SLEEP-WALKING, AND THE ENAMOURING ISLAND	157	INTO HER HEAD	20
SLEEPY			
UNPACKS THE HEAD THAT, LIKE A SLEEPY GHOST, ...	75	MY HERO BARES	3
THE SLEEPY MAN OF WINTER PULLS, ...	92	BOYS OF SUMMER	29
SLEET			
THE BLIND, CLAWED STARE IS COLD AS SLEET.	165	LONG-LEGGED	101
SLEEVE			
DEATH FLASHING FROM HIS SLEEVE, ...	108	GRIEF THIEF	16
FROM JESU'S SLEEVE TRUMPED UP THE KING OF SPOTS,	118	ALTARWISE	58
BY THE CURVE OF THE NUDE MOUTH OR THE LAUGH UP THE SLEEVE.	133	MAKE ME A MASK	12
SLEEVES			
BEFORE THE LAST FAG AND THE SHIRT SLEEVES AND SLIPPERS, ...	38	GAS FADES	3
THE SPITTLED EYES, THE SALT PONDS IN THE SLEEVES,	136	AFTER FUNERAL	5
THE STREAM FROM THE PRIEST BLACK WRISTED SPINNEY AND SLEEVES	200	COUNTRY SLEEP	72
SLENDER			
BUT ONLY IRIS ON THEIR SLENDER STALKS	223	IN DREAMS	11
TO A SLENDER WIND	225	SLENDER WIND	T
WITH SLENDER FINGERS	229	MY RIVER	28
SLENDERLY			
SLENDERLY LETHAL THINGS, ...	226	THE ELM	8
SLEPT			
SLEPT AT NIGHT IN A DOG KENNEL	171	THE HUNCHBACK	11
IN A CHOIR OF WINGS, AS THOUGH SHE SLEPT OR DIED,	191	WINTER'S TALE	122
WHEN EVERYTHING SLEPT AND THE SMELL OF THE WAVES WAS STRANGE;	224	IDYLL UNFORGET	27
SEEKING NO FURTHER THAN YOUR PETALS THAT STILL SLEPT.	227	SPRING-SPIRIT	8
SLEW			
UNDER THE MILKY MUSHROOMS SLEW MY HUNGER, ...	118	ALTARWISE	64
SLID			
OF GROWING BONES THE MUSCLES SLID;	86	SEE, SAYS LIME	26
SLIDES			
SLIDES LIKE A SEA;	82	LIGHT BREAKS	15
SLIDES GOOD IN THE SLEEK MOUTH.	209	POEM ON B'DAY	36
SLIGHT			
ALTHOUGH YOUR ANGER IS NOT A SLIGHT THING, ...	232	YOUR VOICE	13
ON THE SAIL OF EACH SLIGHT WING	233	NO THOUGHT	18
SLIME			
DESPAIR OF BLOOD, FAITH IN THE MAIDEN'S SLIME, ...	100	RUNNING GRAVE	23
THE WILD PIGS' WOOD, AND SLIME UPON THE TREES, ...	104	WORLD PYRAMID	20
AND THE BEAK OF SLIME	183	VISION, PRAYER	114
TANGLING THOUGH THIS SPUN SLIME	211	POEM ON B'DAY	84
SLIMY			
BEACH, HEARING RISE SLIMY FROM THE WELSH LECHERED	179	NEW QUAY	16
SLIPPED			
SLIPPED THE FINS OF THOSE HUMPBACKED TONS	163	LONG-LEGGED	52
SLIPPERS			
BEFORE THE LAST FAG AND THE SHIRT SLEEVES AND SLIPPERS, ...	38	GAS FADES	3

	PAGE	TITLE	LINE
SLIPS			
SEAWARD THE SALMON, SUCKED SUN SLIPS, ...	3	PROLOGUE	34
HERE SLIPS THE GHOST WHO MADE OF MY PALE BED	81	HERE LIE BEAST	11
HARBOURS MY ANCHORED TONGUE, SLIPS THE QUAYSTONE,	131	I MAKE THIS IN	3
SLITS			
SHAKES A DESOLATE BOY WHO SLITS HIS THROAT	136	AFTER FUNERAL	7
SLOE			
BURNING! NIGHT AND THE VEIN OF BIRDS IN THE WINGED,			
SLOE WRIST •••••••••••••••••••••••••••••••••••••	199	COUNTRY SLEEP	70
SLOPING			
THE MIGHTY HAND LEADS TO A SLOPING SHOULDER, ...	66	HAND SIGNED	5
SLOW			
SLOW ROUNDING OF FOUR SEASONS' COASTS, ...	58	HERE IN SPRING	6
DEATH AND EVIL, TOO SLOW IN HEEDING WORDS.	60	FAIRY TALES	35
SLOW IN A SLEEPING WIND. •••••••••••••••••••••••••••	88	A PROCESS IN	15
BIRD THROUGH THE TIMES AND LANDS AND TRIBES OF THE			
SLOW FLAKES. •••••••••••••••••••••••••••••••••••••	190	WINTER'S TALE	99
OPEN A PATHWAY THROUGH THE SLOW SAD SAIL, ...	194	SLEEP BECALMED	9
SLEEP, GOOD, FOR EVER, SLOW AND DEEP, SPELLED RARE			
AND WISE, •••••••••••••••••••••••••••••••••••••	197	COUNTRY SLEEP	8
MAKES ALL THE MUSIC; AND I WHO HEAR THE TUNE OF THE			
SLOW, •••	203	SIR JOHNS HILL	57
AND LISTENED WHEN A SLOW, STARRED SLUMBER WRAPT THE			
MOON, •••	223	IDYLL UNFORGET	7
AND SOOTHED WITH SLOW TEARS; •••••••••••••••••••••	228	NOT DESPAIR	13
SLOWLY			
LET COMFORT COME SLOWLY, LIFT •••••••••••••••••••••	35	LIFT UP FACE	14
THE PLUM MY MOTHER PICKED MATURED SLOWLY, ...	78	LOVE'S FEVER	25
LOVE IN HER GEAR IS SLOWLY THROUGH THE HOUSE, ...	99	RUNNING GRAVE	3
THAT BURY THE SWEET STREET SLOWLY, SEE	142	SAINT TO FALL	33
AND THE SABBATH RANG SLOWLY •••••••••••••••••••••••	195	FERN HILL	17
HEART! SLYLY, SLOWLY, HEARING THE WOUND IN HER SIDE			
GO •••	200	COUNTRY SLEEP	95
CRASHES, AND SLOWLY THE FISHING HOLY STALKING HERON	201	SIR JOHNS HILL	11
SLOWS			
THAT THUNDERS AS HEART THUNDERS, SLOWS AS HEART			
SLOWS. •••	46	POET: 1935	6
THAT THUNDERS AS HEART THUNDERS, SLOWS AS HEART			
SLOWS. •••	46	POET: 1935	6
SLUG			
AND THE SLUG SHOULD TEACH ME DESTRUCTION.	58	HERE IN SPRING	13
SLUG'S			
THE SLUG'S A LIVING CALENDAR OF DAYS;	59	HERE IN SPRING	15
SLUM			
OVER THE SUN'S HOVEL AND THE SLUM OF FIRE	175	FIRE RAID	68
SLUMBER			
AND YOUR MAIEUTIC SLUMBER DRAG IT FORTH.	67	LET A FAITH	13
AND LISTENED WHEN A SLOW, STARRED SLUMBER WRAPT THE			
MOON, •••	223	IDYLL UNFORGET	7
SLUMBERS			
ALL NIGHT MY FORTUNE SLUMBERS IN ITS SHEET.	81	ALL THAT I OWE	27
ALL NIGHT MY FORTUNE SLUMBERS IN ITS SHEET.	81	ALL THAT I OWE	30
SLUMMINGS			
AND FEW JAMES JOYCE'S MENTAL SLUMMINGS, ...	84	LETTER TO AUNT	37
SLUNK			
SLUNK POUTING OUT WHEN THE LIMP TIME CAME;	207	LAMENT	44
SLY			
SLY AS AN ADDER, RID OF FLEAS.	29	LONG, SKELETON	6
CAST HIGH, STUNNED ON GILLED STONE; SLY SCISSORS			
GROUND IN FROST •••••••••••••••••••••••••••••••••	135	HOW MY ANIMAL	35

	PAGE	TITLE	LINE
SLY (CONTINUED)			
HEAR THEIR LAUGHTER SLY AS GONOCOCCI.	179	NEW QUAY	18
BE YOU SURE THE THIEF WILL SEEK A WAY SLY AND SURE	199	COUNTRY SLEEP	49
AND SLY AS SNOW AND MEEK AS DEW BLOWN TO THE THORN,	199	COUNTRY SLEEP	50
WHO COMES AS RED AS THE FOX AND SLY AS THE HEELED WIND.	200	COUNTRY SLEEP	81
TIME BY, THEIR DUST WAS FLESH THE SWINEHERD ROOTED SLY,	204	GIANT'S THIGH	21
SLYLY			
HEART! SLYLY, SLOWLY, HEARING THE WOUND IN HER SIDE GO	200	COUNTRY SLEEP	95
SMACK			
BLOWING THE OLD DEAD BACK; OUR SHOTS SHALL SMACK	90	EUNUCH DREAMS	38
MORNING SMACK OF THE SPADE THAT WAKES UP SLEEP,	136	AFTER FUNERAL	6
SMACKS			
THE WIND SMACKS OF THE POOR	67	REALM OF FLESH	5
SMALL			
AND GALLOWS, UP THE RAYS OF HIS EYES THE SMALL BIRDS OF THE BAY	201	SIR JOHNS HILL	4
THE SCURRYING, FURRED SMALL FRIARS SQUEAL, IN THE DOWSE	204	GIANT'S THIGH	31
ON A SEIZING SKY; SMALL FISHES GLIDE	209	POEM ON B'DAY	22
AND SMALL, FEMININE SHOULDERS,	236	WOMAN TAPESTRY	43
SMELL			
ON TIPS OF THOUGHT WHERE THOUGHTS SMELL IN THE RAIN;	82	LIGHT BREAKS	26
AND EVEN HEAVEN HAS A SMELL	84	LETTER TO AUNT	53
BLEED FROM MY BURNING FORK AND SMELL MY HEELS.	105	WORLD PYRAMID	52
AND THE SMELL OF HAY IN THE SNOW, AND THE FAR OWL	187	WINTER'S TALE	7
WHEN EVERYTHING SLEPT AND THE SMELL OF THE WAVES WAS STRANGE;	224	IDYLL UNFORGET	27
THE FLOWER FROM THE SMELL,	233	NO THOUGHT	12
LIFTING HER SMELL OVER THE CITY BUILDINGS.	240	ADMIT THE SUN	14
SMELLING			
AND ALL THE HERRINGS SMELLING IN THE SEA,	95	RUB OF LOVE	33
SMELT			
THE VIRGINS SMELT OUT, THREE STREETS UP,	38	THE GOSSIPERS	8
I SMELT THE MAGGOT IN MY STOOL.	69	BEFORE KNOCKED	30
SMILE			
NO STOPPING. PUT THE SMILE	12	SKY'S BRIGHT	16
HE, TOO, COULD TOUCH THE SEASON'S LIPS AND SMILE,	46	POET: 1935	14
ACROSS THE SUN WAS SPREAD A CRAZY SMILE.	50	OUT OF THE PIT	11
A SMILE LET LOOSE A DEVIL, A BELL STRUCK.	51	OUT OF THE PIT	19
HALF A SMILE MIGHT BE HER SABRE.	71	TAKE NEEDLES	20
TO WOMEN WHO HAVE TWISTED THEIR LAST SMILE,	81	ALL THAT I OWE	16
DIVINING IN A SMILE THE OIL OF TEARS.	82	LIGHT BREAKS	18
ONE SMILE OF LIGHT ACROSS THE EMPTY FACE;	93	IN BEGINNING	2
THREE-SYLLABLED AND STARRY AS THE SMILE;	94	IN BEGINNING	8
FROM ALL MY MORTAL LOVERS WITH A STARBOARD SMILE;	123	FOSTER LIGHT	21
THE CIRCULAR SMILE TOSSED FROM LOVER TO LOVER	134	NOT FROM ANGER	9
SHALL HER SMILE BREED THAT MOUTH, BEHIND THE MIRROR,	134	NOT FROM ANGER	13
I MUST WAIT FOR A WOMAN'S SMILE	138	O CHATTERTON	33
YOUR WIDE SMILE FOR ME.	238	MAKES INTERVALS	14
SMILED			
TALKED AND TORE THOUGH HER EYES SMILED.	139	TOMBSTONE TOLD	20
SMILES			
OF OVER-FRUITFUL SMILES,	12	SKY'S BRIGHT	8
THE NEOPHYTE, BAPTIZED IN SMILES	19	THE NEOPHYTE	T
THE NEOPHYTE, BAPTIZED IN SMILES,	19	THE NEOPHYTE	1
SITS BACK AND SMILES, A TINY CORPSE	49	LIGHT, I KNOW	24
IN THE JAILS AND STUDIES OF HIS KEYLESS SMILES.	153	WAS A SAVIOUR	8

	PAGE	TITLE	LINE
SMILES (CONTINUED)			
YOUR BITTERNESS IS MASKED WITH SMILES, ...	236	WOMAN TAPESTRY	50
SMILING			
ONCE CLOSE-UP SMILING IN THE WALL OF PICTURES, ...	118	ALTARWISE	55
THE SMILING WOMAN IS A MAD STORY, ...	138	O CHATTERTON	37
WITH UNFORGETTABLY SMILING ACT, ...	146	TO OTHERS	11
SMIRK			
TO SMIRK AT LOVE'S UNDRESS, ...	34	THIRST PARCHES	13
SMITE			
CLANGOUR AS I HEW AND SMITE	5	PROLOGUE	70
SMOKE			
SMOKE HILL AND HOPHEAD'S VALLEY, ...	111	I, IN IMAGE	82
OLD WIVES THAT SPIN IN THE SMOKE, ...	162	LONG-LEGGED	26
HE SAW THE STORM SMOKE OUT TO KILL	163	LONG-LEGGED	41
FLOCKED WITH THE SHEEP WHITE SMOKE OF THE FARM HOUSE COWL	187	WINTER'S TALE	9
SMOKING			
DAFT WITH THE DRUG THAT'S SMOKING IN A GIRL	95	RUB OF LOVE	30
SMOOTH			
HOW COULD I SMOOTH THAT SKIN	10	COOL, OH NO	9
SAFE BE AND SMOOTH FROM THE BELLOWS OF THE RUSHY BROOD.	198	COUNTRY SLEEP	20
SMOOTH THE PRISMS OF YOUR BREASTS.	229	MY RIVER	18
SMOOTHE			
STRIKE AND SMOOTHE, FOR MY DECKS ARE DRUMS, ...	164	LONG-LEGGED	77
SMOOTHED			
HAVE NOT ADORED MY BODY AS IT SOFTLY SMOOTHED THEIR SKIN.	223	IDYLL UNFORGET	16
AND THE SUN HAS SMOOTHED IT WITH QUIET FIRE, ...	224	IDYLL UNFORGET	23
SMOOTHLY			
ROUND IT SO SMOOTHLY, ...	228	MY RIVER	4
SMOTHER			
NOR CAN I SMOTHER THE SWEET WAKING.'	61	MEAT ON BONES	32
SNAIL			
THE SNAIL TELLS OF COMING RAIN.	48	POET: 1935	65
IN THE GLASS BED OF GRAPES WITH SNAIL AND FLOWER,	109	I, IN IMAGE	29
THE HARING SNAIL GO GIDDILY ROUND THE FLOWER, ...	109	I, IN IMAGE	41
SNAIL OF MAN IN HIS SHIP OF FIRES	128	MY NEOPHYTE	8
DRUNK AS A VINEYARD SNAIL, FLAILED LIKE AN OCTOPUS,	134	HOW MY ANIMAL	7
AND OVER THE SEA WET CHURCH THE SIZE OF A SNAIL ...	177	POEM IN OCT	32
SNAILS			
WHEN MORE THAN SNAILS ARE FRIENDS.	45	TO FOLLOW FOX	23
SNAIL-WAKED			
FROM POLE TO POLE LEAPT ROUND THE SNAIL-WAKED WORLD.	120	ALTARWISE	108
SNAKE			
BREATHE TILL THE SNAKE IS HOME, ...	22	HIGH ON A HILL	10
INCARNATE DEVIL IN A TALKING SNAKE, ...	121	INCARNATE DEVL	1
SLASHED DOWN THE LAST SNAKE AS THOUGH	150	WHEN I WOKE	13
SNAKES			
THESE STOLEN BUBBLES HAVE THE BITES OF SNAKES	108	GRIEF THIEF	23
AND DARKNESS HUNG THE WALLS WITH BASKETS OF SNAKES,	158	INTO HER HEAD	27
COILED INTO THEIR BODIES LIKE SNAKES, ...	237	WOMAN TAPESTRY	76
SNAP			
FAITH IN THEIR HANDS SHALL SNAP IN TWO, ...	50	NO DOMINION	15
MY WINE YOU DRINK, MY BREAD YOU SNAP.	86	BREAD I BREAK	15
'WHO COULD SNAP OFF THE SHAPELESS PRINT	129	MY NEOPHYTE	40
AND SEE YOUR COLOUR SNAP, ...	239	MAKES INTERVALS	18
SNAPPED			
SNAPPED IN A RAIN OF PIECES FALLING	21	BEWILDERED WAY	20

	PAGE	TITLE	LINE
SNAPPED (CONTINUED)			
THE CENTURY'S TRAP WILL HAVE SNAPPED ROUND YOUR MIDDLE,	38	GAS FADES	4
STILLS SNAPPED BY NIGHT IN THE BREAD-SIDED FIELD,	118	ALTARWISE	54
SNAPPING			
ON THE SNAPPING RIMS OF THE ASHPIT,	151	BELOW A TIME	8
SNAPT			
AS THE SNAPT FEATHERS SNOW,	203	SIR JOHNS HILL	50
SNARED			
I'LL COMB THE SNARED WOODS WITH A GLOVE ON A LAMP,	145	IF HEAD HURT	7
SNARING			
SNARING THE WHISTLES OF THE BIRDS	46	POET: 1935	8
SNARLING			
AND SHAFTED HAWKS CAME SNARLING DOWN THE SKY;	65	WOMAN SPEAKS	57
SNARLS			
THE WIRELESS SNARLS ON THE HEARTH.	45	PLOUGHMAN GONE	12
SNATCHED			
AND JONAH'S MOBY SNATCHED ME BY THE HAIR,	119	ALTARWISE	66
SNEAK			
SNEAK DOWN THE STALLION GRAVE,	108	GRIEF THIEF	18
SNEERS			
AND GREEN, SNEERS NOT AT THE OLD SKY.	55	NO MAN BELIEVE	11
SNIFF			
SNIFF, HERE IS SIN! NOW HE MUST GRAPPLE, RISE:	179	NEW QUAY	29
SNIFFED			
IN THE SNIFFED AND POURED SNOW ON THE TIP OF THE TONGUE OF THE YEAR	144	PLEASURE-BIRD	5
SNIPER			
THE SNIPER LAID HIM LOW AND STREWED HIS BRAINS;	63	WOMAN SPEAKS	11
THE SNIPER DIES; THE FINGERS FROM THE SKY	64	WOMAN SPEAKS	45
GOD AND I WILL PAY THE SNIPER.	71	TAKE NEEDLES	24
SNIPPED			
AND FLESH WAS SNIPPED TO CROSS THE LINES	68	BEFORE KNOCKED	22
SNIPPING			
TASSELLED IN CELLAR AND SNIPPING SHOP	151	BELOW A TIME	11
SNIVELLING			
IN THE SNIVELLING HOURS WITH DEAD, HUMPED ANN	136	AFTER FUNERAL	13
AND CHILDISH, SNIVELLING QUEEN.	155	RETURN	51
SNOODS			
SEE WOMEN'S FACES UNDER LIVING SNOODS,	51	OUT OF THE PIT	21
SNOOP			
THERE STINKS A SNOOP IN BLACK. I'M THINKING IT	179	NEW QUAY	19
SNOUT			
A PIG'S SNOUT FOR A NOSE,	41	YOUNG ARE OLD	32
TAIL, NILE, AND SNOUT, A SADDLER OF THE RUSHES,	111	I, IN IMAGE	98
AND THE MOLE SNOUT BLUNT UNDER HIS PILGRIMAGE OF DOMES,	204	GIANT'S THIGH	36
SNOUTED			
QUAKED THE SICK SEA AND SNOUTED DEEP,	163	LONG-LEGGED	50
SNOW			
I KNOW THAT AGE IS SNOW UPON THE HAIR,	64	WOMAN SPEAKS	49
THE DARTED HAIL, THE CHILDISH SNOW,	68	BEFORE KNOCKED	14
BY RED-EYED ORCHARDS SOW THE SEEDS OF SNOW,	123	FOSTER LIGHT	11
STORM, SNOW, AND FOUNTAIN IN THE WEATHER OF FIREWORKS,	130	SINNERS' BELL	14
IN THE SNIFFED AND POURED SNOW ON THE TIP OF THE TONGUE OF THE YEAR	144	PLEASURE-BIRD	5
THE POLAR EAGLE WITH HIS TREAD OF SNOW.	164	LONG-LEGGED	80
TOPPLING UP THE BOATSIDE IN A SNOW OF LIGHT!	166	LONG-LEGGED	138
LAID IN HER SNOW	174	FIRE RAID	37

	PAGE	TITLE	LINE
SNOW (CONTINUED)			
THAT THE SNOW BLIND TWILIGHT FERRIES OVER THE LAKES	187	WINTER'S TALE	2
AND THE SMELL OF HAY IN THE SNOW, AND THE FAR OWL	187	WINTER'S TALE	7
AS THE FOOD AND FLAMES OF THE SNOW, A MAN UNROLLED	187	WINTER'S TALE	13
IN HIS FIRELIT ISLAND RINGED BY THE WINGED SNOW ...	187	WINTER'S TALE	17
OF HIS SNOW BLIND LOVE AND RUSH IN THE WHITE LAIRS.	188	WINTER'S TALE	38
WHEN COLD AS SNOW HE SHOULD RUN THE WENDED VALES AMONG	188	WINTER'S TALE	45
PARISH OF SNOW. THE CARVED MOUTHS IN THE ROCK ARE WIND SWEPT STRINGS.	189	WINTER'S TALE	64
TIME SINGS THROUGH THE INTRICATELY DEAD SNOW DROP. LISTEN.	189	WINTER'S TALE	65
A SHE BIRD DAWNED, AND HER BREAST WITH SNOW AND SCARLET DOWNED.	189	WINTER'S TALE	70
ON THE DEPARTED, SNOW BUSHED GREEN, WANTON IN MOON LIGHT	189	WINTER'S TALE	72
AND ALL THE ELEMENTS OF THE SNOW FALL REJOICED	189	WINTER'S TALE	84
UNDER THE ONE LEAVED TREES RAN A SCARECROW OF SNOW	190	WINTER'S TALE	94
THE SINGING BREAKS IN THE SNOW SHOED VILLAGES OF WISHES	190	WINTER'S TALE	113
AND SHE ROSE WITH HIM FLOWERING IN HER MELTING SNOW.	191	WINTER'S TALE	130
SHALL HARROW AND SNOW THE BLOOD WHILE YOU RIDE WIDE AND NEAR,	198	COUNTRY SLEEP	23
AND SLY AS SNOW AND MEEK AS DEW BLOWN TO THE THORN,	199	COUNTRY SLEEP	50
EVER AND EVER HE FINDS A WAY, AS THE SNOW FALLS,	199	COUNTRY SLEEP	56
ROUND THE SUN, HE COMES TO MY LOVE LIKE THE DESIGNED SNOW,	200	COUNTRY SLEEP	96
AS THE SNAPT FEATHERS SNOW,	203	SIR JOHNS HILL	50
ON WHOM A WORLD OF ILLS CAME DOWN LIKE SNOW.	217	ELEGY	32
WHICH BATHE THEMSELVES IN A RAVISHMENT OF SNOW; ...	223	IDYLL UNFORGET	14
NOR CAN THE SNOW	229	MY RIVER	17
SNOWMAN'S			
MASTER THE NIGHT NOR SERVE THE SNOWMAN'S BRAIN	123	FOSTER LIGHT	4
SNOWS			
OF UNREMEMBERED SKIES AND SNOWS.	225	CLOWN IN MOON	4
SNOW'S			
ONCE WHERE THE SOFT SNOW'S BLOOD WAS TURNED TO ICE.	133	I MAKE THIS IN	65
SNOWY			
SUMMON YOUR SNOWY HORSEMEN, AND THE FOUR-STRINGED HILL,	122	HOLD HARD	14
SNUGGLES			
HE SNUGGLES DEEP AMONG THE CHAPEL THIGHS, ...	179	NEW QUAY	30
SO			
AND MY THOUGHTS FLOW SO UNEASILY	10	COOL, OH NO	22
SO STEAL HER NOT O GOAT-LEGGED WIND	11	AIR BREATHE	7
SO STARRED WITH GRAVEL, ...	13	RAIN CUTS	12
THE SUMMER VOICE SO WARM FROM FRUIT	15	FOR LEDA	25
OBLIVION IS SO LOVERLESS.	17	IN OBLIVION	28
SO PHRASE;	18	NATURAL DAY	8
SO RARE--	18	NATURAL DAY	24
SO, NOT TO BE DEFACED, ...	19	IMAGES IN AIR	10
THE HEMMING CONTACT THAT'S SO TRAMMELLED	20	ENCOMPASSED	6
AND THOUGHTS, BE THEY SO KIND, ...	20	THE NEOPHYTE	24
SO THAT THE PROCESS CALLS FOR LAUGHS, ...	21	BEWILDERED WAY	18
STEALING SO SOFTLY INTO THE EARS.	22	ON QUIET NIGHT	7
SO ARE WE FULL WITH STRENGTH, ...	23	THE ONLY DEAD	5
HAVING SO MUCH TO SPARE.	23	THE ONLY DEAD	22
SO IS THERE MISSED A CERTAIN GODLINESS	23	THE ONLY DEAD	26
UNSOUNDING, THEY BEAT SO SOFT.	33	HELD-OUT HAND	5
WHY COUNT SO SADLY?	33	HELD-OUT HAND	6

	PAGE	TITLE	LINE
SO (CONTINUED)			
ALONE'S UNHURT, SO THE BLIND MAN SEES BEST.	40	WAS THERE TIME	9
HE STEPS SO NEAR THE WATER THAT A SWAN'S WING	46	POET: 1935	2
SO SHALL HE STEP TILL SUMMER LOOSENS ITS HOLD	46	POET: 1935	18
AND SO COMPLAIN, IN A VAIN VOICE, TO THE STARS. ...	47	POET: 1935	21
SO CRYING, HE WAS DRAGGED INTO THE SEWER, ...	51	OUT OF THE PIT	39
SO CRYING, HE WAS PUSHED INTO THE JORDAN.	52	OUT OF THE PIT	53
COULD IN A DAY BE SICK WITH SO MUCH BLOOD;	63	WOMAN SPEAKS	13
SO I HAVE COME TO KNOW, BUT KNOWLEDGE ACHES;	64	WOMAN SPEAKS	48
AND THESE POOR NERVES SO WIRED TO THE SKULL	75	MY HERO BARES	6
SO, PLANING-HEELED, I FLEW ALONG MY MAN	101	FELLOWED SLEEP	4
SO CROSS HER HAND WITH THEIR GRAVE GIPSY EYES, ...	115	A GRIEF AGO	39
SO FAST I MOVE DEFYING TIME, THE QUIET GENTLEMAN	116	LANTERNS SHINE	14
SO SHALL WINGED HARBOURS THROUGH THE ROCKBIRDS' EYES	121	ALTARWISE	130
SO STAR FALL, ...	128	NOW, SAY NAY	24
SO THE BALL FAIL, ...	128	NOW, SAY NAY	25
SO SOLVE THE MYSTIC SUN, THE WIFE OF LIGHT, ...	128	NOW, SAY NAY	26
BULLIES INTO ROUGH SEAS YOU SO GENTLE	142	SAINT TO FALL	49
WERE ONCE SUCH A CREATURE, SO GAY AND FRANK	147	TO OTHERS	14
SO THE BETRAYED MIGHT LEARN IN THE SUN BEAMS	176	MY BEGGAR ARM	7
AND I SAW IN THE TURNING SO CLEARLY A CHILD'S	178	POEM IN OCT	46
SO LOUD TO MY OWN	180	VISION, PRAYER	5
SO IT MUST HAVE BEEN AFTER THE BIRTH OF THE SIMPLE LIGHT	196	FERN HILL	33
IN ALL HIS TUNEFUL TURNING SO FEW AND SUCH MORNING SONGS	196	FERN HILL	43
HIGH RIDING, HELD AND BLESSED AND TRUE, AND SO STILLY	200	COUNTRY SLEEP	90
IN THE WAINS TONNED SO HIGH THAT THE WISPS OF THE HAY	204	GIANT'S THIGH	14
IT IS SO SAD AND BEAUTIFUL, ...	225	CLOWN IN MOON	7
SO TREMULOUSLY LIKE A DREAM.	225	CLOWN IN MOON	8
ROUND IT SO SMOOTHLY, ...	228	MY RIVER	4
ALTHOUGH IT IS SO STRAIGHT AND UNBENDING;	231	YOUR VOICE	5
SO WILL YOUR VOICE VIBRATE	232	FURIOUS MOTION	5
SO, THEN, WILL THE DARK CLOTH OF YOUR HAIR	232	FURIOUS MOTION	7
NOR BE SO CLEAR.	234	NO, PIGEON	10
SO THAT SHE APPEARS ENTERTAINING	236	WOMAN TAPESTRY	38
SO THE ILEX AND THE CYPRESS	236	WOMAN TAPESTRY	56
SO THE HILLS	237	WOMAN TAPESTRY	75
BETWEEN THE PYRAMIDS SO LARGE, ...	238	MAKES INTERVALS	2
LIGHT, NOT SO TO ME;	238	MAKES INTERVALS	6
SOAK			
STRADDLE AND SOAK, ...	21	HIGH ON A HILL	2
SOAKED			
SOAKED MY TABLE THE UGLIER SIDE OF A HILL	144	COLOUR OF SAY	2
SOAKING			
WITH WILD SEA FILLIES AND SOAKING BRIDLES	168	LONG-LEGGED	185
SOAKS			
SOAKS UP THE SEWING TIDES), ...	113	SERVANT SUN	12
SOAKS TO THE VEST OLD DOMINIES AND DRUNKS.	137	O CHATTERTON	20
SOAR			
SOAR, WITH ITS TWO BARK TOWERS, TO THAT DAY	121	ALTARWISE	138
SOARING			
CAWING FROM THEIR BLACK BETHELS SOARING, THE HOLY BOOKS	199	COUNTRY SLEEP	68
SOBSTUFF			
SOBSTUFF, MOCK REASON, ...	39	GAS FADES	12
SOCK			
BEFORE WHITE OR BLACK, THE RIGHT OR LEFT SOCK, ...	39	GAS FADES	17
MEANING IN HOT SOCK SOIL? A LITTLE CUSS	137	O CHATTERTON	18

		PAGE	TITLE	LINE
SOCKET				
SOCKET AND GRAVE, THE BRASSY BLOOD,	....	107	ALL ALL AND	35
YOU WITH A BAD COIN IN YOUR SOCKET,	....	146	TO OTHERS	2
SOCKETS				
NIGHT IN THE SOCKETS ROUNDS,	....	82	LIGHT BREAKS	19
SODOM				
O ROME AND SODOM TO-MORROW AND LONDON	....	168	LONG-LEGGED	191
SOFT				
SOFT SHINING SYMBOLS OF HER PEACE WITH YOU,	....	20	THE NEOPHYTE	21
FEEL THE SAME SOFT BLOOD FLOW THOROUGHLY,	....	23	THE ONLY DEAD	11
AFRAID, LETTING OUR SYLLABLES BE SOFT	....	31	BEING BUT MEN	2
AND, AFTER THE SOFT ASCENT,	....	31	BEING BUT MEN	8
UNSOUNDING, THEY BEAT SO SOFT.	....	33	HELD-OUT HAND	5
WHY SILK IS SOFT AND THE STONE WOUNDS	....	55	WHY EAST WIND	6
FROM LOVE'S FIRST FEVER TO HER PLAGUE, FROM THE SOFT				
SECOND	....	78	LOVE'S FEVER	1
ONCE WHERE THE SOFT SNOW'S BLOOD WAS TURNED TO ICE.		133	I MAKE THIS IN	65
OR A NACREOUS SLEEP AMONG SOFT PARTICLES AND CHARMS		146	IF HEAD HURT	17
EXILED IN US WE AROUSE THE SOFT,	....	154	WAS A SAVIOUR	39
ABOVE HER FOLDED HEAD, AND THE SOFT FEATHERED VOICE		189	WINTER'S TALE	82
OR RIPPLING SOFT IN THE SPINNEY MOON AS THE SILK		204	GIANT'S THIGH	27
SOFTEN				
THE FIVE KINGS COUNT THE DEAD BUT DO NOT SOFTEN	...	66	HAND SIGNED	13
SOFTER				
AND TOUCH YOU WITH SOFTER HANDS.	....	228	NOT DESPAIR	6
SOFTEST				
NOW DID THE SOFTEST SOUND OF FOOT OR VOICE	....	50	OUT OF THE PIT	13
SOFTLY				
STEALING SO SOFTLY INTO THE EARS.	....	22	ON QUIET NIGHT	7
SOFTLY, THOU RAIN--AND FOR HIS MOTHER'S SAKE,	.....	222	MISSING	7
HAVE NOT ADORED MY BODY AS IT SOFTLY SMOOTHED THEIR				
SKIN.	....	223	IDYLL UNFORGET	16
SOFTNESS				
GREEN-SHADOWED PANOPLY ENVELOPING ALL ITS				
STRANGENESS AND SOFTNESS OF STEALTH.	....	224	IDYLL UNFORGET	45
SOFT-TALKING				
ITS HONEYED CHEEK, SOFT-TALKING MOUTH,	....	35	LIFT UP FACE	16
SOIL				
THAT FLOWED OUT OF THE SOIL	....	17	IN OBLIVION	12
ARE ON SANDY SOIL THEIR SPIRIT LEVEL;	....	24	LITTLE PROBLEM	2
OUT OF THE SOIL AND SEED INTO THE DRIVE,	....	29	LONG, SKELETON	2
THE SECRET OF THE SOIL GROWS THROUGH THE EYE,	.....	82	LIGHT BREAKS	28
DUST BE YOUR SAVIOUR UNDER THE CONJURED SOIL.)	....	110	I, IN IMAGE	60
LET THE SOIL SQUEAL I AM THE BITING MAN	....	114	SERVANT SUN	20
MEANING IN HOT SOCK SOIL? A LITTLE CUSS	....	137	O CHATTERTON	18
LIGHT THROUGH SEA AND SOIL	....	184	VISION, PRAYER	157
SOIL-BASED				
AND OUT OF EVERY DOMED AND SOIL-BASED SHELL	....	158	INTO HER HEAD	51
SOILED				
ABOUT THE SOILED UNDEAD	....	176	BREATH SHED	3
SOILS				
SETTING NO STORE BY HARVEST, FREEZE THE SOILS;	....	91	BOYS OF SUMMER	3
SOILY				
HOW LIGHT THE SLEEPING ON THIS SOILY STAR,	....	102	FELLOWED SLEEP	24
SOLDERED				
THE BRAIN WAS CELLED AND SOLDERED IN THE THOUGHT		94	IN BEGINNING	26
SOLDIER				
FOR HER SOLDIER STAINED WITH SPILT WORDS	....	32	OUT OF SIGHS	15
SOLE				
A MAN TORN UP MOURNS IN THE SOLE NIGHT.	....	159	INTO HER HEAD	67

	PAGE	TITLE	LINE

SOLEMNIZING
    MUTTER AND FOUL WINGBEAT OF THE SOLEMNIZING
        NIGHTPRIEST .... 158 INTO HER HEAD 45
SOLID
    THE SOLID WORLD SHALL WITHER IN THE HEAT, ... 73 LORD RED HAIL 17
    YOUR SOLID LAND. .... 74 WE MOTHERNAKED 16
    STRANGE TO OUR SOLID EYE, ... 89 EUNUCH DREAMS 13
    THAT FROM THE SOLID BASES OF THE LIGHT .... 94 IN BEGINNING 20
    STAGE OF THE ICE, THE SOLID OCEAN, ... 106 ALL ALL AND 2
    LET HER INHALE HER DEAD, THROUGH SEED AND SOLID ... 115 A GRIEF AGO 37
SOLITARY
    A SOLITARY MISTER .... 171 THE HUNCHBACK 2
SOLVE
    FAITH IN DIVINITY WOULD SOLVE MOST THINGS, ... 37 WINDMILLS TURN 16
    SO SOLVE THE MYSTIC SUN, THE WIFE OF LIGHT, ... 128 NOW, SAY NAY 26
SOMBRE
    UNTIL THE SUNDAY SOMBRE BELL AT DARK .... 171 THE HUNCHBACK 6
SOME
    AND, THE STRING PULLED, SOME MENTAL DOLL .... 10 COOL, OH NO 11
    THERE MUST, BE PRAISED, SOME CERTAINTY, ... 32 OUT OF SIGHS 7
    HARBOURING SOME THOUGHT OF HEAVEN, OR HAVEN HOPING, 36 MIDNIGHT ROAD 2
    THEIR FACES SHONE UNDER SOME RADIANCE .... 43 FACES SHONE T
    THEIR FACES SHONE UNDER SOME RADIANCE .... 43 FACES SHONE 1
    SHE, IN HER CHEAP FROCK, SAYING SOME CHEAP THING, . 43 FACES SHONE 11
    SOME LIFE, YET UNSPENT, MIGHT EXPLODE .... 44 LONGED TO MOVE 12
    OR PRAY FOR DAY TO SOME ATTENTIVE GOD .... 48 LIGHT, I KNOW 14
    AND THERE IS ALWAYS DAY, THE SHINING OF SOME SUN, . 49 LIGHT, I KNOW 18
    AND SOME SHINE FOR A SECOND AND ARE GONE, ... 49 LIGHT, I KNOW 20
    AND THUS, SOME TIME LATER, I HEARD HIM SAY: .... 53 OUT OF THE PIT 89
    CALLS SOME CONTENT TO TRAVEL WITH THE WINDS, ... 56 WHY EAST WIND 17
    HIS AWKWARD HEART INTO SOME SYMMETRY. .... 77 LASHED RINGS 17
    LIKE SOME PITCH MOON, THE LIMIT OF THE GLOBES; .... 82 LIGHT BREAKS 20
    SOME DEAD UNDID THEIR BUSHY JAWS, ... 97 TWILIGHT LOCKS 22
    SOME LET ME MAKE YOU OF THE VOWELLED BEECHES, ... 99 OCTOBER WIND 13
    SOME OF THE OAKEN VOICES, FROM THE ROOTS .... 99 OCTOBER WIND 14
    SOME LET ME MAKE YOU OF THE WATER'S SPEECHES. ..... 99 OCTOBER WIND 16
    SOME LET ME MAKE YOU OF THE MEADOW'S SIGNS; .... 99 OCTOBER WIND 21
    SOME LET ME TELL YOU OF THE RAVEN'S SINS. .... 99 OCTOBER WIND 24
    (SOME LET ME MAKE YOU OF AUTUMNAL SPELLS, ... 99 OCTOBER WIND 26
    SOME LET ME MAKE YOU OF THE HEARTLESS WORDS. ...... 99 OCTOBER WIND 29
    AND MANY YEARS SHOULD SEE SOME CHANGE. .... 116 LANTERNS SHINE 17
    AROUND SOME COFFIN CARRYING .... 152 BELOW A TIME 30
    AND SOME DISMANTLED WOMEN, ... 155 RETURN 31
    OF PETALS FROM SOME MAGIC ROSE; .... 225 CLOWN IN MOON 2
SOMEHOW
    SOMEHOW IT SEEMS, AMID THE EVENING HAZE, ... 223 IN DREAMS 8
SOMETHING
    CREATED SOMETHING VERY NEW, ... 83 LETTER TO AUNT 24
    SOMETHING AUSTERE HIDES, SOMETHING UNCERTAIN ...... 226 THE OAK 5
    SOMETHING AUSTERE HIDES, SOMETHING UNCERTAIN ...... 226 THE OAK 5
SOMETIMES
    SOMETIMES THE SKY'S TOO BRIGHT .... 12 SKY'S BRIGHT T
    SOMETIMES THE SKY'S TOO BRIGHT, ... 12 SKY'S BRIGHT 1
    SOMETIMES A WOMAN'S HEART HAS SALT, ... 13 SKY'S BRIGHT 20
    SOMETIMES AT HIS EAR THE ENGINE'S VOICE .... 46 PLOUGHMAN GONE 27
SON
    DISTURB NO WINDING-SHEETS, MY SON, ... 60 MEAT ON BONES 6
    THRUST, MY DAUGHTER OR SON, TO ESCAPE, THERE IS
        NONE, NONE, NONE, ... 146 IF HEAD HURT 19
    TIME IS BEARING ANOTHER SON. .... 167 LONG-LEGGED 153

	PAGE	TITLE	LINE
SON (CONTINUED)			
OVER THE GHOST AND THE DROPPED SON	180	VISION, PRAYER	8
YOU MAY NOT SEE, MY SON,	192	SIDE OF TRUTH	2
SONG			
TO YOU STRANGERS (THOUGH SONG	3	PROLOGUE	24
SONG	75	SONG: LOVE ME	T
THE UNWINDING, SONG BY ROCK,	141	SAINT TO FALL	5
UNDER THE BURIAL SONG	183	VISION, PRAYER	104
FOR THEIR SOULS' SONG.	202	SIR JOHNS HILL	46
THE SONG OF THE MISCHIEVOUS DOG	221	SONG OF DOG	T
EACH NOTE OF THY DUSKY SONG	226	SLENDER WIND	6
AND GRIP THE INEXORABLE SONG,	233	FURIOUS MOTION	21
SONGS			
THOSE CRANING BIRDS ARE CHOICE FOR YOU, SONGS THAT JUMP BACK	16	SPIRE CRANES	9
IN ALL HIS TUNEFUL TURNING SO FEW AND SUCH MORNING SONGS	196	FERN HILL	43
I HAVE MADE MY THROAT AN ARBOUR FOR FORGOTTEN SONGS.	224	IDYLL UNFORGET	20
SONS			
WE ARE THE SONS OF FLINT AND PITCH.	93	BOYS OF SUMMER	53
AND THE LIVING EARTH YOUR SONS.	149	UNLUCKILY FOR	56
SEED OF SONS IN THE LOIN OF THE BLACK HUSK LEFT.	174	FIRE RAID	32
AND IMMEMORIAL SONS OF THE CUDGELLING, HACKED	203	GIANT'S THIGH	11
SON'S			
WALKING IN THE MEADOWS OF HIS SON'S EYE	217	ELEGY	31
SOON			
LIKE LEAVES OF TREES AND AS SOON	3	PROLOGUE	31
SOON TO MY CARE, MY LOVE,	21	BEWILDERED WAY	5
BUT SOON TO DIE	21	BEWILDERED WAY	6
SUSPICIOUS BUT THAT SOON PASSES.	30	NEARLY SUMMER	20
'FIND MEAT ON BONES THAT SOON HAVE NONE,	60	MEAT ON BONES	1
HOW SOON, HOW SOON, O LORD OF THE RED HAIL!	73	LORD RED HAIL	18
HOW SOON, HOW SOON, O LORD OF THE RED HAIL!	73	LORD RED HAIL	18
HOW SOON THE SERVANT SUN	113	SERVANT SUN	T
HOW SOON THE SERVANT SUN,	113	SERVANT SUN	1
HOW SOON MY LEVEL, LORD,	114	SERVANT SUN	22
SOON SETS ALIGHT A LONG STICK FROM THE CRADLE;	117	ALTARWISE	20
SOONER			
SOONER DROP WITH THE WORM OF THE ROPES ROUND MY THROAT	145	IF HEAD HURT	4
SOOTHE			
WHEN THAT IMMORTAL HOSPITAL MADE ONE MORE MOVE TO SOOTHE	186	HOLY SPRING	3
SOOTHED			
LIE FAST AND SOOTHED,	198	COUNTRY SLEEP	19
AND SOOTHED WITH SLOW TEARS;	228	NOT DESPAIR	13
SORCERER'S			
SHAKES, IN CRABBED BURIAL SHAWL, BY SORCERER'S INSECT WOKEN,	130	SINNERS' BELL	23
SORE			
AND THE SUN HEALS, CLOSING SORE EYES.	42	A WAR OF WITS	19
SORES			
SHALL CALM HER SORES.	77	THE FORCE THAT	18
FLICKED FROM THE CARBOLIC CITY PUZZLE IN A BED OF SORES	142	SAINT TO FALL	28
SORROW			
UNDER HER CLOTH OF TREES NO SORROW,	15	FOR LEDA	22
KNOWING EXCEEDING GRIEF AND THE GODS' SORROW	47	POET: 1935	48
SORROW SHALL HAVE NO WORDS, NO WILLOW WEARING;	64	WOMAN SPEAKS	39
O RING OF SEAS, NOR SORROW AS I SHIFT	123	FOSTER LIGHT	20

	PAGE	TITLE	LINE
SORROWS			
AND DROWN ALL SORROWS IN THE GROSS CATASTROPHE. ...	34	THIRST PARCHES	15
SOUGHT			
"WHAT HAVE YOU FOUND," HE CRIES, "WHAT HAVE YOU SOUGHT?"	30	YOUTH CALLS	14
"WHAT YOU HAVE SOUGHT."	30	YOUTH CALLS	16
HAVE SOUGHT YOUR SINGLE GRAVE, ...	160	DEATHS AND ENT	28
INHUMAN CRADLE AND THE BRIDE BED FOREVER SOUGHT ...	188	WINTER'S TALE	49
SOUL			
AND THERE WAS NO LIGHT IN HIS SOUL.	22	ON QUIET NIGHT	18
WHEN WISDOM LAY NOT IN THE SOUL	25	BEAUTY TO DUST	12
AND THUS I SAW HIM SEARCHING FOR HIS SOUL.	51	OUT OF THE PIT	44
FOR HE HAS FOUND HIS SOUL IN LONELINESS, ...	53	OUT OF THE PIT	97
AND FROM THIS DARKNESS SPIN THE GOLDEN SOUL.	73	LORD RED HAIL	15
OF THE HEARTHSTONE TALES MY OWN, LOST LOVE; AND THE SOUL WALKS	199	COUNTRY SLEEP	53
FOR MY SULKING, SKULKING, COAL BLACK SOUL!	206	LAMENT	36
AT LAST THE SOUL FROM ITS FOUL MOUSEHOLE	207	LAMENT	43
AND I GAVE MY SOUL A BLIND, SLASHED EYE, ...	207	LAMENT	45
TO FIND A WOMAN'S SOUL FOR A WIFE.	207	LAMENT	48
FOR, OH, MY SOUL FOUND A SUNDAY WIFE	207	LAMENT	54
AND EVERY SOUL HIS PRIEST, ...	210	POEM ON B'DAY	61
SOULS			
DESTROYING SOULS AND LAYING WASTE, ...	33	IN GARDENS	8
DECLARE THEIR SOULS, LET CHILDREN KNOW, LIVE AFTER.	36	LET BE KNOWN	6
IS CERTAIN GOD, AND THE CEREMONY OF SOULS	148	UNLUCKILY FOR	23
AND THE SOULS OF ALL MEN	193	SIDE OF TRUTH	19
STONE FOR THE SAKE OF THE SOULS OF THE SLAIN BIRDS SAILING.	203	SIR JOHNS HILL	60
AND AIR SHAPED HEAVEN WHERE SOULS GROW WILD	210	POEM ON B'DAY	74
SOULS'			
FOR THEIR SOULS' SONG.	202	SIR JOHNS HILL	46
SOUND			
EACH SILVER MOMENT CHIMES/ IN STEPS OF SOUND, ...	9	MINUTE'S HOUR	5
TO BE THE CIRCLE NOT THE STAIR OF SOUND.	9	MINUTE'S HOUR	17
OF SOUND AND SIGHT, ...	17	NATURAL DAY	3
INTO THEIR PRISON WITH A SLACK SOUND, ...	47	POET: 1935	44
NOW DID THE SOFTEST SOUND OF FOOT OR VOICE	50	OUT OF THE PIT	13
TEAR WITH A GREAT SOUND THROUGH THE SKIES, ...	51	OUT OF THE PIT	16
THE LAND LIES OUT OF SOUND	62	EARS IN TURRET	13
SHONE IN MY EARS THE LIGHT OF SOUND, ...	78	LOVE'S FEVER	20
CALLED IN MY EYES THE SOUND OF LIGHT.	78	LOVE'S FEVER	21
NO ELEMENTAL FORM AND SOUND	83	LETTER TO AUNT	9
TIME TRACKS THE SOUND OF SHAPE ON MAN AND CLOUD,	120	ALTARWISE	97
AND NOW THE HORNS OF ENGLAND, IN THE SOUND OF SHAPE,	122	HOLD HARD	13
THERE IS NOTHING LEFT OF THE SEA BUT ITS SOUND, ...	169	LONG-LEGGED	205
ON OUT OF SOUND	171	THE HUNCHBACK	18
THOUGH NO SOUND FLOWED DOWN THE HAND FOLDED AIR ...	188	WINTER'S TALE	40
IT WAS A HAND OR SOUND	189	WINTER'S TALE	66
SHALL I LET PRAY THE SHADOW OF A SOUND	191	REFUSAL MOURN	10
TURNS IN THE DARK ON THE SOUND THEY KNOW WILL ARISE	193	CONVERS PRAYER	6
ON THE SILENT SEA WE HAVE HEARD THE SOUND	194	SLEEP BECALMED	3
TO THE SEA SOUND FLOWING LIKE BLOOD FROM THE LOUD WOUND	194	SLEEP BECALMED	6
THE SOUND ABOUT TO BE SAID IN THE TWO PRAYERS	194	CONVERS PRAYER	9
WE HEARD THE SEA SOUND SING, WE SAW THE SALT SHEET TELL.	194	SLEEP BECALMED	12
BUT THEY SLEEP SOUND.	216	COUNTRY HEAVEN	30
LAST SOUND, THE WORLD GOING OUT WITHOUT A BREATH:	217	ELEGY	34
OUR TEARS SOUND WISER	230	OUR SANCTITY	12

	PAGE	TITLE	LINE
SOUND (CONTINUED)			
WHO SAILS ON TIDES OF LEAVES AND SOUND.	234	NO, PIGEON	16
OR THE GRACEFUL SOUND OF LAUGHTER.	235	WOMAN TAPESTRY	17
YOUR ROCK OF SOUND.	239	MAKES INTERVALS	30
SOUNDING			
WHAT HAD BEEN ONE WAS MANY SOUNDING MINDED.	79	LOVE'S FEVER	41
SOUNDS			
FOR MY SAWN, SPLAY SOUNDS), ...	3	PROLOGUE	28
SOUNDS WITH THE GRAINS AS THEY HURRY	54	WE BY SEASAND	15
SOUNDS, RICH WITH LIFE, OUT OF A PAINTED MASK;	57	GREEK PLAY	14
SOUR			
IT IS A SOUR MOTION IN THE BLOOD, ...	9	MINUTE'S HOUR	2
LIPLESS AND TONGUELESS IN THE SOUR EARTH	23	THE ONLY DEAD	2
BE SOUR IN MY HAIR. THAT I MAY LEARN	65	WOMAN SPEAKS	63
AND BRAINS TURNED SOUR;	85	SEE, SAYS LIME	12
SOUR THE BOILING HONEY;	92	BOYS OF SUMMER	8
I KNOW HER SCRUBBED AND SOUR HUMBLE HANDS	136	AFTER FUNERAL	31
MILK IN YOUR MOUTH, AT THE SOUR FLOODS	142	SAINT TO FALL	32
SOURCE			
TO CUT THE CHANNELS AT THEIR SOURCE	91	WHERE ONCE THE	11
SOURS			
AGE SOURS BEFORE YOUTH'S TASTED IN THE MOUTH	40	YOUNG ARE OLD	2
SOUTH			
WHY EAST WIND CHILLS AND SOUTH WIND COOLS	55	WHY EAST WIND	1
THE ARCTIC SCUT, AND BASIN OF THE SOUTH, ...	105	WORLD PYRAMID	44
DRIVES FORTH MY MEN, MY CHILDREN, FROM THE HANGING			
SOUTH.	122	HOLD HARD	6
SOVEREIGN			
BOUND BY A SOVEREIGN STRIP, WE LIE, ...	54	WE BY SEASAND	18
FIVE SOVEREIGN FINGERS TAXED THE BREATH, ...	66	HAND SIGNED	2
SOW			
BY RED-EYED ORCHARDS SOW THE SEEDS OF SNOW, ...	123	FOSTER LIGHT	11
OR SOW MY SALT SEED	191	REFUSAL MOURN	11
SOWN			
BEFORE THE ALLOTMENT IS WEEDED AND SOWN, ...	38	GAS FADES	5
AND ALL SUCH LOVE'S A SHRUB SOWN IN THE BREATH. ...	81	ALL THAT I OWE	20
HAS SOWN A FLYING GARDEN ROUND THAT SEA-GHOST?	121	ALTARWISE	136
FOR THE SURGE IS SOWN WITH BARLEY, ...	168	LONG-LEGGED	182
SOWS			
WHO CANNOT COUNT THE SEEDS HE SOWS, ...	29	NEARLY SUMMER	8
SPACE			
THE MORNING, SPACE FOR LEDA	14	FOR LEDA	T
THE MORNING, SPACE FOR LEDA	14	FOR LEDA	1
A HOLE IN SPACE SHALL KEEP THE SHAPE OF THOUGHT,	73	LORD RED HAIL	13
AND, BURNING CIPHERS ON THE ROUND OF SPACE, ...	93	IN BEGINNING	5
NOW THAT MY SYMBOLS HAVE OUTELBOWED SPACE, ...	124	TODAY, INSECT	2
FROM THE FOREIGN FIELDS OF SPACE, ...	126	SEED-AT-ZERO	44
FROM THE STAR-FLANKED FIELDS OF SPACE, ...	127	SEED-AT-ZERO	51
NO SPACE, NO SPACE, YOU SAY, ...	239	LET ME ESCAPE	6
NO SPACE, NO SPACE, YOU SAY, ...	239	LET ME ESCAPE	6
SPADE			
MORNING SMACK OF THE SPADE THAT WAKES UP SLEEP, ...	136	AFTER FUNERAL	6
SPADE-HANDED			
WHEN BLOOD, SPADE-HANDED, AND THE LOGIC TIME	100	RUNNING GRAVE	13
SPADES			
SAID THE FAKE GENTLEMAN IN SUIT OF SPADES, ...	118	ALTARWISE	60
STUMBLE OUT WITH THEIR SPADES, ...	187	WINTER'S TALE	21
SPADE'S			
ASSEMBLING WAITS FOR THE SPADE'S RING ON THE CAGE.	172	DAWN RAID	11

	PAGE	TITLE	LINE
SPANNED			
MORE SPANNED WITH ANGELS RIDE	211	POEM ON B'DAY	104
SPARE			
HAVING SO MUCH TO SPARE.	23	THE ONLY DEAD	22
SPARETIME			
MAN'S MANMADE SPARETIME LASTS THE FOUR SEASONS, ...	39	GAS FADES	19
SPARK			
THAT SET ALIGHT THE WEATHERS FROM A SPARK, ...	94	IN BEGINNING	14
A THREE-EYED, RED-EYED SPARK, BLUNT AS A FLOWER;	94	IN BEGINNING	15
CHILD OF THE SHORT SPARK IN A SHAPELESS COUNTRY ...	117	ALTARWISE	19
SPARKLING			
SPARKLING A TWELVE-LEGGED BODY	12	CABARET	19
A SPARKLING FOUNTAIN FOR US	13	RAIN CUTS	2
SPARK'S			
THE SIZE OF GENESIS? THE SHORT SPARK'S GENDER?	118	ALTARWISE	44
SPARROWFALL			
MAMMOTH AND SPARROWFALL	150	WHEN I WOKE	20
SPARROWS			
TWOLEGGED HANDBAGGED SPARROWS, ...	156	RETURN	74
OF THE SPARROWS AND SUCH WHO SWANSING, DUSK, IN			
WRANGLING HEDGES.	201	SIR JOHNS HILL	7
GOD IN HIS WHIRLWIND SILENCE SAVE, WHO MARKS THE			
SPARROWS HAIL, ...	202	SIR JOHNS HILL	45
SPAT			
SINCE THE FIRST WOMB SPAT FORTH A BABY'S CORPSE,	64	WOMAN SPEAKS	52
EACH GOLDEN GRAIN SPAT LIFE INTO ITS FELLOW, ...	78	LOVE'S FEVER	23
SPAT UP FROM THE RESUFFERED PAIN.	103	I DREAMED MY	24
SPAVINED			
BONY AND SPAVINED, RICH WITH FLEAS.	45	PLOUGHMAN GONE	9
SPEAK			
THAT SPEAK SEVEN SEAS, ...	3	PROLOGUE	17
FLUNG GRAVEL CHIME? LET THE STONES SPEAK	66	GODS THUMP	13
AND SPEAK THEIR MIDNIGHT NOTHINGS AS THEY SWELL;	89	EUNUCH DREAMS	14
SPEAK LIKE A HUNGRY PARSON OF THE MANNA, ...	96	TWELVE	6
HIGH LORD ESQUIRE, SPEAK UP THE SINGING CLOUD, ...	123	FOSTER LIGHT	17
WHO SPEAK ON A FINGER AND THUMB, ...	129	MY NEOPHYTE	29
THE RAIN THROUGH HER COLD HEART SPEAK	139	TOMBSTONE TOLD	8
HEARD HER SPEAK THROUGH THE CHIPPED BEAK	140	TOMBSTONE TOLD	24
SPEAKING			
NOT, AS A SYMBOL, STONE/ SPEAKING OR NO, ...	9	MINUTE'S HOUR	15
BUT OUR SPEAKING DOES NOT THRIVE	17	IN OBLIVION	20
ENOUGH KIND FOOD, ENOUGH KIND SPEAKING, ...	36	MIDNIGHT ROAD	6
AND CANCEROUS SPEAKING DRIPPING FROM THEIR MOUTHS,	41	YOUNG ARE OLD	29
THE SEA SPEAKING KEENLY, ...	229	MY RIVER	36
SPEAKS			
THE SEA SPEAKS IN A KINGLY VOICE, ...	61	MEAT ON BONES	35
THE WOMAN SPEAKS	63	WOMAN SPEAKS	T
THE WOMAN SPEAKS:	63	WOMAN SPEAKS	1
SPEAKS A STEEL GOSPEL TO THE WRETCHED	70	SECRET WIND	17
HERE A MILD BABY SPEAKS HIS FIRST WORD	74	SUN BURNS	9
SPEAR			
HERONS SPIRE AND SPEAR.	208	POEM ON B'DAY	9
SPECTACLED			
OF THE SHARP, ENAMELLED EYES AND THE SPECTACLED CLAWS	133	MAKE ME A MASK	2
SPECTACLES			
TIME AT THE CITY SPECTACLES, AND HALF	124	TODAY, INSECT	3
SPECTRES			
DEATH AND EVIL ARE TWIN SPECTRES.	60	FAIRY TALES	26
SPED			
NOR DAMNED THE SEA THAT SPED ABOUT MY FIST, ...	97	TWILIGHT LOCKS	3

		PAGE	TITLE	LINE
SPED (CONTINUED)				
STORM HER SPED HEART, HANG WITH BEHEADED VEINS	....	132	I MAKE THIS IN	34
HE SPED INTO THE DRINKING DARK;	....	162	LONG-LEGGED	14
SPEECH				
BUT TROUBLED BY THEIR CURIOUS SPEECH	....	22	ON QUIET NIGHT	6
BUT THE HOT BEAMS ROB ME OF SPEECH,	....	42	A WAR OF WITS	14
OF THE PACING, FAMOUS SEA BUT ITS SPEECH,	....	169	LONG-LEGGED	210
DOING MY LITTLE TRICKS OF SPEECH AGAIN	....	234	NO, PIGEON	20
SPEECHES				
SOME LET ME MAKE YOU OF THE WATER'S SPEECHES.	.....	99	OCTOBER WIND	16
SPEEDED				
AT GOD SPEEDED SUMMER'S END	....	3	PROLOGUE	2
AT GOD SPEEDED SUMMER'S END	....	5	PROLOGUE	101
SPELL				
BELL BELIEVE OR FEAR THAT THE RUSTIC SHADE OR SPELL		198	COUNTRY SLEEP	22
SPELLBOUND				
IN THE FIRST, SPINNING PLACE, THE SPELLBOUND HORSES WALKING WARM	....	196	FERN HILL	34
SPELLED				
IN THE LAND OF THE HEARTHSTONE TALES, AND SPELLED ASLEEP,	....	197	COUNTRY SLEEP	2
SLEEP, GOOD, FOR EVER, SLOW AND DEEP, SPELLED RARE AND WISE,	....	197	COUNTRY SLEEP	8
LIE IN GRACE. SLEEP SPELLED AT REST IN THE LOWLY HOUSE	....	199	COUNTRY SLEEP	43
SPELLING				
SPELLING ACROSS THE SKY HIS DEVIL'S NEWS,	....	29	NEARLY SUMMER	5
THE HEART IS DRAINED THAT, SPELLING IN THE SCURRY		99	OCTOBER WIND	30
ENDURE BURIAL UNDER THE SPELLING WALL,	....	134	HOW MY ANIMAL	4
SPELLS				
THE OLD SPELLS ARE UNDONE.	....	59	FAIRY TALES	13
(SOME LET ME MAKE YOU OF AUTUMNAL SPELLS,	....	99	OCTOBER WIND	26
CURL-LOCKED AND ANIMAL CAVEPOOLS OF SPELLS AND BONE,		135	HOW MY ANIMAL	27
AND SPELLS ON THE WINDS OF THE DEAD HIS WINTER'S TALE.	....	189	WINTER'S TALE	59
SPELLSOAKED				
WHO WRITES THESE WORDS I WRITE IN A STILL ROOM IN A SPELLSOAKED HOUSE:	....	141	I, FIRST NAMED	2
SPELT				
I SPELT MY VISION WITH A HAND AND HAIR,	....	102	FELLOWED SLEEP	23
SPELT OUT THE SEVEN SEAS, AND EVIL INDEX,	....	119	ALTARWISE	82
SPEND				
ONE HOUR SPEND MY TIME FOR ME	....	18	NATURAL DAY	5
SPENT				
FROM THE HISSING OF THE SPENT LIE	....	43	LONGED TO MOVE	2
BUT NOW THERE ARE THE BUTT-ENDS OF SPENT SQUIBS.		52	OUT OF THE PIT	52
I SPENT MY UNWASTEABLE	....	154	RETURN	9
SPENTOUT				
THE ROOT OF TONGUES ENDS IN A SPENTOUT CANCER,	....	79	LOVE'S FEVER	37
SPEWED				
ONE WOMB, ONE MIND, SPEWED OUT THE MATTER,	....	79	LOVE'S FEVER	42
SPEWING				
SPEWING ITS SAPLESS LEAVES AROUND,	....	26	THERE'S PLENTY	10
SPHERE				
AND A HIGH SPHERE BE HIS BEARER;	....	126	SEED-AT-ZERO	39
SPHERES				
LULLING OF SPHERES IN THE SEASHELL FLESH,	....	211	POEM ON B'DAY	89
SPHERES'				
HE CRIED AS HE DIED, FEARING AT LAST THE SPHERES'		217	ELEGY	33

	PAGE	TITLE	LINE
SPHINX			
THE SPHINX OF LIGHT SIT ON THE EYES, ...	69	SECRET WIND	2
SPIDER			
'WAR ON THE SPIDER AND THE WREN!'	61	MEAT ON BONES	38
SPIDER-TONGUED			
THE SPIDER-TONGUED, AND THE LOUD HILL OF WALES) ...	99	OCTOBER WIND	27
SPIED			
SPIED MOON-MAD BEASTS CAROUSING ON THE HILL, ...	50	OUT OF THE PIT	9
SPIES			
O MAKE ME A MASK AND A WALL TO SHUT FROM YOUR SPIES	133	MAKE ME A MASK	1
SPIKE			
IN A SPINNEY OF RINGED BOYS AND GANDERS, SPIKE AND			
BURN, ...	198	COUNTRY SLEEP	14
SPIKED			
SPIKED WITH A MASTIFF COLLAR, ...	151	BELOW A TIME	10
SPILL			
THAT SPILL SUCH ACRID BLOOD.	32	OUT OF SIGHS	16
HE SHALL BE WISE AND LET HIS BRIMSTONE SPILL, ...	73	LORD RED HAIL	3
SPILL THE LANK FOLLY'S HUNTER AND THE HARD-HELD HOPE.	122	HOLD HARD	18
SPILLED			
AND VEINS ARE SPILLED AND DOOM IS TURNED, ...	74	WE MOTHERNAKED	15
ON THE LAST RICK'S TIP BY SPILLED WINE-WELLS	141	SAINT TO FALL	14
SPILT			
PIERCE THE SPILT SKY WITH DIVING WING IN WEED AND			
HEEL	15	SPIRE CRANES	4
FOR HER SOLDIER STAINED WITH SPILT WORDS	32	OUT OF SIGHS	15
AND WASHING WATER SPILT UPON THEIR NECKS	47	POET: 1935	32
AT FLESH THAT PERISHES AND BLOOD THAT'S SPILT	57	GREEK PLAY	19
IS GATHERED AND SPILT	192	SIDE OF TRUTH	10
SPIN			
AND FROM THIS DARKNESS SPIN THE GOLDEN SOUL.	73	LORD RED HAIL	15
NOT SPIN TO STARE AT AN OLD YEAR	145	PLEASURE-BIRD	17
OLD WIVES THAT SPIN IN THE SMOKE, ...	162	LONG-LEGGED	26
THE SPIN	181	VISION, PRAYER	53
SUN SPIN A GRAVE GREY	185	VISION, PRAYER	183
SPINDRIFT			
SWEETLY THE DIVER'S BELL IN THE STEEPLE OF SPINDRIFT	110	I, IN IMAGE	62
ON THESE SPINDRIFT PAGES	197	CRAFT OR ART	14
SPINE			
THE PROUD SPINE SPURNING TURN AND TWIST.	75	MY HERO BARES	5
SPINNEY			
IN A SPINNEY OF RINGED BOYS AND GANDERS, SPIKE AND			
BURN, ...	198	COUNTRY SLEEP	14
THE STREAM FROM THE PRIEST BLACK WRISTED SPINNEY AND			
SLEEVES	200	COUNTRY SLEEP	72
OR RIPPLING SOFT IN THE SPINNEY MOON AS THE SILK	204	GIANT'S THIGH	27
SPINNEYS			
IN THE BLACK BURIED SPINNEYS	215	COUNTRY HEAVEN	17
SPINNING			
HOW I, A SPINNING MAN, ...	4	PROLOGUE	39
AS THOUGH THE SUN WERE SPINNING UP THROUGH IT.	19	THE NEOPHYTE	8
FAITH FIXED BEYOND THE SPINNING STARS, ...	41	YOUNG ARE OLD	45
WE SUMMER BOYS IN THIS FOUR-WINDED SPINNING, ...	93	BOYS OF SUMMER	37
IN THE FIRST, SPINNING PLACE, THE SPELLBOUND HORSES			
WALKING WARM	196	FERN HILL	34
COULD NEVER TOUCH YOUR SPINNING NOTES, ...	234	NO, PIGEON	9
SPINNING-WHEELS			
BRIGHT AS HER SPINNING-WHEELS, THE COLIC SEASON ...	108	I, IN IMAGE	8
SPINS			
A CIRCLE SPINS. LET EACH REVOLVING SPOKE	67	LET A FAITH	4

	PAGE	TITLE	LINE
SPINS (CONTINUED)			
AND THE GOLDEN BALL SPINS OUT OF THE SKIES;	134	NOT FROM ANGER	10
SPINS ITS MORNING OF PRAISE, ...	211	POEM ON B'DAY	99
SPIRAL			
AND DREW MY SPIRAL BREATH	11	CABARET	7
A QUARREL OF WEATHERS AND TREES IN THE WINDY SPIRAL.	110	I, IN IMAGE	42
SPLITTING THE LONG EYE OPEN, AND THE SPIRAL TURNKEY,	110	I, IN IMAGE	50
O SPIRAL OF ASCENSION	182	VISION, PRAYER	79
WITH UNEVEN, SPIRAL TEETH.	229	MY RIVER	26
SPIRE			
THE SPIRE CRANES	15	SPIRE CRANES	T
THE SPIRE CRANES. ITS STATUE IS AN AVIARY.	15	SPIRE CRANES	1
AN INCH IN FROTH. CHIMES CHEAT THE PRISON SPIRE,			
PELTER	15	SPIRE CRANES	5
NO TREAD MORE PERILOUS, THE GREEN STEPS AND SPIRE	109	I, IN IMAGE	26
HEAR BY DEATH'S ACCIDENT THE CLOCKED AND DASHED-DOWN			
SPIRE	130	SINNERS' BELL	11
HERONS SPIRE AND SPEAR.	208	POEM ON B'DAY	9
SPIRE'S			
AND MOUTH. BOTH NOTE AND PLUME PLUNGE FROM THE			
SPIRE'S HOOK.	16	SPIRE CRANES	8
SPIRIT			
ARE ON SANDY SOIL THEIR SPIRIT LEVEL;	24	LITTLE PROBLEM	2
FOR A SPIRIT, CAN	24	LITTLE PROBLEM	18
BEFORE THE AGONY; THE SPIRIT GROWS, ...	31	OUT OF SIGHS	3
SPIRIT SUFFERS BUT IS STILL	71	TAKE NEEDLES	27
FLESH AND SPIRIT, BABE AND DAM, ...	71	TAKE NEEDLES	30
THE HOWLING SPIRIT SHAPED A GOD	85	SEE, SAYS LIME	7
THE SPIRIT RACKED ITS MUSCLES AND	85	SEE, SAYS LIME	15
OR SPIRIT UP A CLOUD, ...	114	SERVANT SUN	26
GOLD ON SUCH FEATURES, AND THE LINEN SPIRIT	120	ALTARWISE	121
BLESS HER BENT SPIRIT WITH FOUR, CROSSING BIRDS.	136	AFTER FUNERAL	26
SENSES, AND MAN A SPIRIT IN LOVE	211	POEM ON B'DAY	83
NOR MAKE THE STERN SHELL OF MY SPIRIT MOVE.	233	NO THOUGHT	2
SPIRITS			
SCALES THE BLUE WALL OF SPIRITS;	130	SINNERS' BELL	21
WITH THE SPIRITS OF THE HORSESHOE BAY	210	POEM ON B'DAY	56
SPIT			
BY THE SPIT AND THE BLACK POT IN THE LOG BRIGHT LIGHT	188	WINTER'S TALE	27
BY THE SPIT AND THE BLACK POT IN THE LOG BRIGHT			
LIGHT.	190	WINTER'S TALE	87
AND THE BLACK SPIT OF THE CHAPEL FOLD, ...	205	LAMENT	2
SPITE			
YET IN SPITE OF ALL THIS, I HAVE MOMENTS OF BLISS,	221	SONG OF DOG	9
SPITTING			
CUT CHRISTBREAD SPITTING VINEGAR AND ALL	141	SAINT TO FALL	16
SPITTLE			
A BETTER VENOM SEETHES IN SPITTLE	137	O CHATTERTON	6
THAT CLOUTS THE SPITTLE LIKE BUBBLES WITH BROKEN			
ROOMS, ...	144	PLEASURE-BIRD	6
SPITTLED			
THE SPITTLED EYES, THE SALT PONDS IN THE SLEEVES,	136	AFTER FUNERAL	5
SPLASHED			
AND THE SPLASHED MOTHERING MAIDEN	181	VISION, PRAYER	42
SPLAY			
FOR MY SAWN, SPLAY SOUNDS), ...	3	PROLOGUE	28
SPLENDOUR			
STEALS WHAT IS BEST--THE BODY'S SPLENDOUR--	30	NEARLY SUMMER	15
NOR THE SPLENDOUR OF YOUR DARK HAIR, ...	228	NOT DESPAIR	10

	PAGE	TITLE	LINE
SPLICE			
WHERE ONCE YOUR GREEN KNOTS SANK THEIR SPLICE	91	WHERE ONCE THE	7
SPLINTERS			
BUTTON YOUR BODICE ON A HUMP OF SPLINTERS, ...	118	ALTARWISE	51
SPLINTS			
THE LAMPED CALLIGRAPHER, THE QUEEN IN SPLINTS, ...	120	ALTARWISE	115
SPLIT			
SPLIT ALL ENDS UP THEY SHAN'T CRACK;	50	NO DOMINION	17
OF OLD DIVINITIES, SPLIT BITS OF NAMES.	53	OUT OF THE PIT	85
SPLIT UP THE BRAWNED WOMB'S WEATHERS, ...	92	BOYS OF SUMMER	14
BY LAVA'S LIGHT SPLIT THROUGH THE OYSTER VOWELS ...	119	ALTARWISE	73
SHOULD HE WHO SPLIT HIS CHILDREN WITH A CURE	127	NOW, SAY NAY	13
FROM AN ODD ROOM IN A SPLIT HOUSE STARE, ...	142	SAINT TO FALL	31
SPLITTING			
SPLITTING A THOUGHT INTO SUCH HIDEOUS MOMENTS	17	IN OBLIVION	17
SPLITTING THE LONG EYE OPEN, AND THE SPIRAL TURNKEY,	110	I, IN IMAGE	50
SPOILERS			
SPOILERS AND POKERS OF SLEEP, ...	150	WHEN I WOKE	5
SPOKE			
WE SPOKE OF DRINK AND GIRLS, FOR HOURS	33	IN GARDENS	4
ROSE IN OUR OUTWORN BRAINS. WE SPOKE OUR LINES, ...	34	IN GARDENS	11
A CIRCLE SPINS. LET EACH REVOLVING SPOKE	67	LET A FAITH	4
WHEN I WOKE, THE TOWN SPOKE.	150	WHEN I WOKE	1
NO TIME, SPOKE THE CLOCKS, NO GOD, RANG THE BELLS,	150	WHEN I WOKE	28
SPOKEN			
LOVE IS THE LAST LIGHT SPOKEN. OH	174	FIRE RAID	31
SPONGE			
THE MOUTH OF TIME SUCKED, LIKE A SPONGE, ...	97	TWILIGHT LOCKS	4
SIR MORROW AT HIS SPONGE, ...	113	SERVANT SUN	8
THE SCALED SEA-SAWERS, FIX IN A NAKED SPONGE	119	ALTARWISE	92
WOE DRIP FROM THE DISHRAG HANDS AND THE PRESSED SPONGE OF THE FOREHEAD, ...	142	SAINT TO FALL	45
SPONGEBAG			
THE SPONGEBAG LET THEM ALL MELT.	155	RETURN	36
SPOONED			
WITH A BOUNCING AND SILVER SPOONED KID	149	PAPER & STICKS	15
SPORT			
COUNTRY, YOUR SPORT IS SUMMER, AND DECEMBER'S POOLS	122	HOLD HARD	7
YOUR SPORT IS SUMMER AS THE SPRING RUNS ANGRILY.	123	HOLD HARD	24
SPOT			
SPOT THE BLOWN WORD, AND ON THE SEAS I IMAGE	121	ALTARWISE	131
SPOTS			
INTENT ON VISITING THE FAMOUS SPOTS, ...	37	WINDMILLS TURN	12
FROM JESU'S SLEEVE TRUMPED UP THE KING OF SPOTS,	118	ALTARWISE	58
SPOUT			
UNTIL THE SPOUT DRIED UP	17	IN OBLIVION	11
SPOUT TO THE ROD	82	LIGHT BREAKS	17
BUMP ON A SPOUT LET THE BUBBLES JUMP OUT.	145	IF HEAD HURT	3
SPUN ON A SPOUT LIKE A LONG-LEGGED BALL	163	LONG-LEGGED	56
SPOUTED			
LIFE ROSE AND SPOUTED FROM THE ROLLING SEAS, ...	94	IN BEGINNING	16
SPRAWL			
LIKE AN APPROACHING WAVE I SPRAWL TO RUIN.	132	I MAKE THIS IN	38
SPRAY			
OVER THE WAKEWARD-FLASHING SPRAY	164	LONG-LEGGED	73
SPRAY-BASED			
OR SPRAY-BASED AND ROCK-CHESTED SEA:	145	PLEASURE-BIRD	24
SPREAD			
ACROSS THE SUN WAS SPREAD A CRAZY SMILE.	50	OUT OF THE PIT	11
WHERE NOW THE WINGS OF DREAMLESS SLEEP ARE SPREAD,	222	MISSING	5

	PAGE	TITLE	LINE
SPREADEAGLE			
LIGHT OF HIS THIGHS, SPREADEAGLE TO THE DUNGHILL SKY,	204	GIANT'S THIGH	23
SPREADS			
WHICH SPREADS DOWN TO THE DREGS	27	OBLIVIOUS DARK	15
SPRING			
SPRING MAY BE GREEN--	15	FOR LEDA	21
SCREAMING THE SPRING	16	IN OBLIVION	3
WHEN SPRING IS COME, ...	27	OBLIVIOUS DARK	30
AND THE OAKUM IS PICKED, AND THE SPRING TREES HAVE			
GROWN GREEN, ...	39	GAS FADES	6
AN IMAGE BORN OUT OF THE UPROARIOUS SPRING	47	POET: 1935	36
IN THE BREASTED SUMMER LONGS NOT FOR SPRING, ...	55	NO MAN BELIEVE	9
HERE IN THIS SPRING	58	HERE IN SPRING	T
HERE IN THIS SPRING, STARS FLOAT ALONG THE VOID;	58	HERE IN SPRING	1
THIS SUMMER BURIES A SPRING BIRD.	58	HERE IN SPRING	4
I SHOULD LEARN SPRING BY THE CUCKOOING, ...	58	HERE IN SPRING	12
I WHO WAS DEAF TO SPRING AND SUMMER, ...	68	BEFORE KNOCKED	7
DRAIN THE SPRING WHERE PROMISE GOES.	70	TAKE NEEDLES	8
HOW AT THE MOUNTAIN SPRING THE SAME MOUTH SUCKS.	77	THE FORCE THAT	10
YOUTH DID CONDENSE; THE TEARS OF SPRING	79	LOVE'S FEVER	48
HERE SPRING THE SILENT VENOMS OF HIS BLOOD, ...	81	HERE LIE BEAST	4
THE FILM OF SPRING IS HANGING FROM THE LIDS.	82	LIGHT BREAKS	24
IN SPRING WE CROSS OUR FOREHEADS WITH THE HOLLY,	93	BOYS OF SUMMER	43
NOR THE BAD BLOOD OF SPRING.	95	RUB OF LOVE	7
CORROSIVE SPRING OUT OF THE ICEBERG'S CROP, ...	104	WORLD PYRAMID	8
CITY OF SPRING, THE GOVERNED FLOWER, ...	106	ALL ALL AND	4
BEGINNING WITH DOOM IN THE BULB, THE SPRING UNRAVELS,	108	I, IN IMAGE	7
(FOG BY HIS SPRING	113	SERVANT SUN	11
SAID THE ANTIPODES, AND TWICE SPRING CHIMED.	118	ALTARWISE	42
CRACK LIKE A SPRING IN A VICE, BONE BREAKING APRIL,	122	HOLD HARD	17
MURMUR OF SPRING NOR CRUSH THE COCKEREL'S EGGS, ...	123	FOSTER LIGHT	7
YOUR SPORT IS SUMMER AS THE SPRING RUNS ANGRILY.	123	HOLD HARD	24
OF SPRING AND SUMMER WERE BLOOMING IN THE TALL TALES	177	POEM IN OCT	36
HOLY SPRING	186	HOLY SPRING	T
PRAISE THAT THE SPRING TIME IS ALL	186	HOLY SPRING	14
AND THE MOTHER AND TOPPLING HOUSE OF THE HOLY SPRING,	186	HOLY SPRING	23
THE VOICE OF THE DUST OF WATER FROM THE WITHERED			
SPRING	189	WINTER'S TALE	60
EXULTATION LIES DOWN. TIME BURIES THE SPRING WEATHER	191	WINTER'S TALE	119
AND GONE THAT BARLEY DARK WHERE THEIR CLOGS DANCED			
IN THE SPRING, ...	205	GIANT'S THIGH	40
TALLER THIS THUNDERCLAP SPRING, AND HOW	211	POEM ON B'DAY	103
AND WHEN IT WAS SPRING I SAID, ...	227	SPRING-SPIRIT	1
SPRINGFUL			
A SPRINGFUL OF LARKS IN A ROLLING	177	POEM IN OCT	21
SPRINGING			
THERE IS NO FOUNTAIN SPRINGING FROM THE EARTH	63	WOMAN SPEAKS	4
BEGINNING WITH DOOM IN THE GHOST, AND THE SPRINGING			
MARVELS, ...	109	I, IN IMAGE	13
A COMPASSION SPRINGING FROM THE DEEP BODY, ...	236	WOMAN TAPESTRY	53
SPRINGS			
PRAISE HIM WHO SPRINGS AND FILLS THE TIDAL WELL.	76	LASHED RINGS	11
WHITE SPRINGS IN THE DARK.	166	LONG-LEGGED	120
OF NIGHTINGALE AND CENTAUR DEAD HORSE. THE SPRINGS			
WITHER	191	WINTER'S TALE	117
SPRINGSHOOTS			
AND THE CRATERS OF HIS EYES GREW SPRINGSHOOTS AND			
FIRE	172	DAWN RAID	7
SPRING-SPIRIT			
TO THE SPRING-SPIRIT	227	SPRING-SPIRIT	T

	PAGE	TITLE	LINE
SPRINGTAILED			
NO SPRINGTAILED TOM IN THE RED HOT TOWN	206	LAMENT	29
SPRINGTIME			
IS EMPTY IN SPRINGTIME, AND NO OTHER TIME LESSENS	39	GAS FADES	20
SPRINKLE			
SHALL IT BE SAID THEY SPRINKLE WATER	65	GODS THUMP	6
PALM OF THE EARTH, O SPRINKLE ON MY HEAD	65	WOMAN SPEAKS	60
SPRINKLED			
FOR SHE WHO SPRINKLED ON YOUR BROW	20	THE NEOPHYTE	20
SPRINKLES			
SPRINKLES IN CHILDREN'S EYES A LONG-LAST SLEEP	56	WHY EAST WIND	13
SPRINT			
PECK, SPRINT, DANCE ON FOUNTAINS AND DUCK TIME	145	IF HEAD HURT	8
SPROUT			
SPROUT FROM THE STONY LOCKERS LIKE A TREE ON ARAN.	111	I, IN IMAGE	78
NOR SPROUT ON OWL-SEED LIKE A GOBLIN-SUCKER, ...	123	FOSTER LIGHT	14
IN QUICK, SWEET, CRUEL LIGHT TILL THE LOCKED GROUND			
SPROUT OUT, ...	135	HOW MY ANIMAL	18
SPROUTED			
THE WINGING BONE THAT SPROUTED IN THE HEELS, ...	95	RUB OF LOVE	11
SPRUNG			
WITH SPRUNG AND PADDED SHOULDERS, ...	154	RETURN	11
VIRGATE AND SPRUNG OF THE DUSK, ...	227	THE PINE	1
SPUME			
FROM THE BROOMED WITCH'S SPUME YOU ARE SHIELDED BY			
FERN	198	COUNTRY SLEEP	17
SPUMING			
IN THE SPUMING	181	VISION, PRAYER	55
SPUN			
THE TWO-FRAMED GLOBE THAT SPUN INTO A SCORE;	79	LOVE'S FEVER	45
SPUN TO MY SCREWS, YOUR DRY GHOST BLOWS, ...	90	WHERE ONCE THE	2
HEAVEN AND HELL MIXED AS THEY SPUN.	93	IN BEGINNING	6
IN YOUR EVERY INCH AND GLANCE IS THE GLOBE OF			
GENESIS SPUN, ...	149	UNLUCKILY FOR	55
SPUN ON A SPOUT LIKE A LONG-LEGGED BALL	163	LONG-LEGGED	56
OF PARADISE, IN THE SPUN BUD OF THE WORLD.	191	WINTER'S TALE	129
TANGLING THOUGH THIS SPUN SLIME	211	POEM ON B'DAY	84
SPURNING			
THE PROUD SPINE SPURNING TURN AND TWIST.	75	MY HERO BARES	5
SPURNS			
HE CELEBRATES AND SPURNS	208	POEM ON B'DAY	7
SPURT			
TILL THE BLOOD SHALL SPURT, ...	173	FIRE RAID	22
SPYING			
AND WHEN BLIND SLEEP DROPS ON THE SPYING SENSES,	139	FIVE & COUNTRY	13
SQUALL			
A SQUALL OF BIRDS BELLOWED AND FELL, ...	163	LONG-LEGGED	39
SQUARE			
AND THUS I SAW HIM IN A SQUARE OF FIELDS, ...	53	OUT OF THE PIT	87
SQUARE IN THESE WORLDS THE MORTAL CIRCLE.	107	ALL ALL AND	30
BEHIND MY HEAD A SQUARE OF SKY SAGS OVER	134	NOT FROM ANGER	8
SQUATTERS			
THE FLASHING NEEDLE ROCK OF SQUATTERS, ...	151	BELOW A TIME	26
SQUAWK			
AND BLITHELY THEY SQUAWK	201	SIR JOHNS HILL	8
SQUAWKING			
OF THE CROTCH OF THE SQUAWKING SHORES, ...	142	SAINT TO FALL	27
SQUEAL			
THE SQUEAL OF THE DAMNED OUT OF THE OLD PIT.	40	YOUNG ARE OLD	6
LET THE SOIL SQUEAL I AM THE BITING MAN	114	SERVANT SUN	20

		PAGE	TITLE	LINE

SQUEAL (CONTINUED)
THE SCURRYING, FURRED SMALL FRIARS SQUEAL, IN THE
    DOWSE .... 204 GIANT'S THIGH 31
SQUEEZE
CLAW OF THE CRABBED VEINS SQUEEZE FROM EACH RED
    PARTICLE .... 135 HOW MY ANIMAL 21
SQUIBS
BUT NOW THERE ARE THE BUTT-ENDS OF SPENT SQUIBS. 52 OUT OF THE PIT 52
SQUIRES
AND NAIL THE MERRY SQUIRES TO THE TREES; .... 93 BOYS OF SUMMER 45
SQUIRM
AT WHOSE BALL-PRYING EVEN DEATH'LL SQUIRM .... 179 NEW QUAY 22
SQUIRREL
THEY SEE THE SQUIRREL STUMBLE, ... 109 I, IN IMAGE 40
IN THE SQUIRREL NIMBLE GROVE, UNDER LINEN AND THATCH 199 COUNTRY SLEEP 44
STABBING
STABBING, AND HERONS, AND SHELLS .... 3 PROLOGUE 16
STABLE
IN THE STABLE UNDER THE SKIN. .... 74 SUN BURNS 10
AND YOUR HOME IN A CENTAUR'S STABLE. .... 138 O CHATTERTON 43
OUT OF THE WHINNYING GREEN STABLE .... 196 FERN HILL 35
STABLES
PAST THE STATUES OF THE STABLES AND THE SKY ROOFED
    STIES .... 188 WINTER'S TALE 34
ALL THE MOON LONG I HEARD, BLESSED AMONG STABLES,
    THE NIGHTJARS .... 195 FERN HILL 25
STABS
WHERE THE ELEGIAC FISHERBIRD STABS AND PADDLES .... 202 SIR JOHNS HILL 19
STACKED
DOWN THE STACKED SEA AND WATER-PILLARED SHADE, ... 132 I MAKE THIS IN 40
STAGE
STAGE OF THE ICE, THE SOLID OCEAN, ... 106 ALL ALL AND 2
STAGES
CRYING, WHITE GOWNED, FROM THE MIDDLE MOONLIT STAGES 158 INTO HER HEAD 37
ON THE IVORY STAGES .... 197 CRAFT OR ART 9
STAIN
TREMBLE AT THE STARRY STAIN, ... 71 TAKE NEEDLES 34
HALT AMONG EUNUCHS, AND THE NITRIC STAIN .... 100 RUNNING GRAVE 24
THE LOVERS' HOUSE, LIE SUFFERING MY STAIN? .... 112 NOT FATHER ME 4
STAINED
AND YET, MAD WITH YOUNG BLOOD OR STAINED WITH AGE, 26 THERE'S PLENTY 16
FOR HER SOLDIER STAINED WITH SPILT WORDS .... 32 OUT OF SIGHS 15
STAINED A BLOOD COLOUR; .... 59 FAIRY TALES 19
THE STAINED FLATS OF HEAVEN HIT AND RAZED .... 141 SAINT TO FALL 2
STAINING
STAINING THE BROKEN BRAIN .... 27 OBLIVIOUS DARK 8
STAIR
TO BE THE CIRCLE NOT THE STAIR OF SOUND. .... 9 MINUTE'S HOUR 17
ONCE SEEN STRANGERS OR SHADES ON A STAIR; .... 157 INTO HER HEAD 15
STAIRS
UP NAKED STAIRS, A TURTLE IN A HEARSE, ... 99 RUNNING GRAVE 4
YOU BY THE CAVERN OVER THE BLACK STAIRS, ... 117 ALTARWISE 22
BY THE CHILD GOING TO BED AND THE MAN ON THE STAIRS 193 CONVERS PRAYER 2
FROM THE MAN ON THE STAIRS AND THE CHILD BY HIS BED. 194 CONVERS PRAYER 8
TURNS ON THE QUICK AND THE DEAD, AND THE MAN ON THE
    STAIRS .... 194 CONVERS PRAYER 14
DRAGGING HIM UP THE STAIRS TO ONE WHO LIES DEAD. 194 CONVERS PRAYER 20
STAKE
AND STAKE THE SLEEPERS IN THE SAVAGE GRAVE .... 104 WORLD PYRAMID 17

		PAGE	TITLE	LINE
STAKED				
	OUR CLAIM IS STAKED FOR ONCE AND ALL	73	WE MOTHERNAKED	5
	NOR FENCED, NOR STAKED, THE GUSHERS OF THE SKY	82	LIGHT BREAKS	16
	WORM IN THE SCALP, THE STAKED AND FALLOW.	106	ALL ALL AND	9
STALE				
	MAKING FRESH WHAT WAS STALE	35	LIFT UP FACE	6
	STALE OF ADAM'S BRINE UNTIL, VISION	103	I DREAMED MY	27
	IN A ROOM WITH A STUFFED FOX AND A STALE FERN,	136	AFTER FUNERAL	11
	WITH STALE AND TERRIFYING CAMP	143	THE MOLLS	6
STALK				
	MY IMAGES STALK THE TREES AND THE SLANT SAP'S TUNNEL,	109	I, IN IMAGE	25
	AND OPIUM HEAD, CROW STALK, PUFFED, CUT, AND BLOWN,	131	I MAKE THIS IN	10
STALKED				
	TO THE BAIT THAT STALKED OUT OF THE SACK,	162	LONG-LEGGED	20
STALKING				
	COMES, LIKE A SCISSORS STALKING, TAILOR AGE,	100	RUNNING GRAVE	6
	STALKING MY CHILDREN'S FACES WITH A TAIL OF BLOOD,	122	HOLD HARD	20
	CRASHES, AND SLOWLY THE FISHING HOLY STALKING HERON	201	SIR JOHNS HILL	11
STALKS				
	LIKE STALKS OF TALL, DRY STRAW,	3	PROLOGUE	22
	A SEDGE OF BROKEN STALKS AND SHELLS.	14	RAIN CUTS	28
	FROM THE UNWATERED LEAVES AND THE STIFF STALKS,	47	POET: 1935	39
	BUT ONLY IRIS ON THEIR SLENDER STALKS	223	IN DREAMS	11
STALLION				
	SNEAK DOWN THE STALLION GRAVE,	108	GRIEF THIEF	18
	THE TWO WORDS STALLION AND STERILE	138	O CHATTERTON	35
STALLS				
	IN THE TOWER AND TOLLS TO SLEEP OVER THE STALLS	199	COUNTRY SLEEP	52
	THROUGH THE HAYGOLD STALLS, AS THE DEW FALLS ON THE WIND-	199	COUNTRY SLEEP	58
STAMMEL				
	I BLOW THE STAMMEL FEATHER IN THE VEIN.	105	WORLD PYRAMID	56
STAMMERED				
	THE GHOST IS DUMB THAT STAMMERED IN THE STRAW,	104	WORLD PYRAMID	28
STAMP				
	AND LOUD HIS ANGER STAMP UPON THE HILL.	73	LORD RED HAIL	6
	STAMP OF THE MINTED FACE UPON THE MOON;	94	IN BEGINNING	10
	NOW STAMP THE LORD'S PRAYER ON A GRAIN OF RICE,	119	ALTARWISE	85
STAMPS				
	STAMPS ON THE GROUND,	13	RAIN CUTS	16
	(SIR MORROW STAMPS	114	SERVANT SUN	23
STAND				
	I STAND BENEATH THE CLOUDS' CONFESSIONAL,	42	A WAR OF WITS	13
	THE WINDMILLS OF THE WORLD STILL STAND	45	PLOUGHMAN GONE	6
	AND THE NAKED EGG STAND STRAIGHT,	113	SERVANT SUN	7
	I STAND, FOR THIS MEMORIAL'S SAKE, ALONE	136	AFTER FUNERAL	12
	STAND IN A QUESTION MARK.	138	O CHATTERTON	36
	WHOM NOW I CONJURE TO STAND AS THIEF	146	TO OTHERS	9
	THE STATUES OF GREAT RAIN STAND STILL,	166	LONG-LEGGED	135
	THAT SHE MIGHT STAND IN THE NIGHT	172	THE HUNCHBACK	35
	THAT UNCALM STILL IT IS SURE ALONE TO STAND AND SING	186	HOLY SPRING	21
	YOU STAND A LITTLE APART,	229	MY RIVER	6
STANDING				
	AND, STANDING OVER THE SEA, SHE'D CRY	22	ON QUIET NIGHT	9
STANDS				
	THESE ARE YOUR YEARS' RECORDERS. THE CIRCULAR WORLD STANDS STILL.)	110	I, IN IMAGE	72
	WHO RAZED MY WOODEN FOLLY STANDS AGHAST,	113	NOT FATHER ME	22
	BECAUSE THERE STANDS, ONE STORY OUT OF THE BUM CITY,	144	PLEASURE-BIRD	13
	HE STANDS ALONE AT THE DOOR OF HIS HOME,	169	LONG-LEGGED	215

	PAGE	TITLE	LINE
STAR			
GLORY ALSO THIS STAR, BIRD	4	PROLOGUE	40
FAITH FIXED LIKE A STAR BEYOND THE STARS,	42	YOUNG ARE OLD	50
NO MAN BELIEVES WHO, WHEN A STAR FALLS SHOT,	54	NO MAN BELIEVE	1
IN THE BEGINNING WAS THE THREE-POINTED STAR,	93	IN BEGINNING	1
HOW LIGHT THE SLEEPING ON THIS SOILY STAR,	102	FELLOWED SLEEP	24
SO STAR FALL,	128	NOW, SAY NAY	24
CUT TO THE STILL STAR IN THE ORDER OF THE QUICK	148	UNLUCKILY FOR	20
A STAR WAS BROKEN	173	FIRE RAID	14
STAR AND COUNTRY TO THE LEGION	184	VISION, PRAYER	154
AND THE STAR OF THE LOST THE SHAPE OF THE EYES.	185	VISION, PRAYER	170
ON A STAR OF FAITH PURE AS THE DRIFTING BREAD,	187	WINTER'S TALE	12
THE STAR RISE AT PASTURE AND NIGHTLONG THE FABLES GRAZE	198	COUNTRY SLEEP	34
AND STAR: HELD AND BLESSED, THOUGH YOU SCOUR THE HIGH FOUR	199	COUNTRY SLEEP	45
THIS NIGHT AND EACH NIGHT SINCE THE FALLING STAR YOU WERE BORN,	199	COUNTRY SLEEP	55
OF THE MORNING LEAVES, AS THE STAR FALLS, AS THE WINGED	199	COUNTRY SLEEP	60
FROM THE COUNTRY EYES, SALT AND SUN, STAR AND WOE	215	COUNTRY HEAVEN	13
THE SHOOTING STAR HAWK STATUED BLIND IN A CLOUD	215	COUNTRY HEAVEN	23
STARBOARD			
FROM ALL MY MORTAL LOVERS WITH A STARBOARD SMILE;	123	FOSTER LIGHT	21
STARCH			
PACK OFF THE SHAPES OF DAYLIGHT AND THEIR STARCH,	90	EUNUCH DREAMS	24
STARE			
BREAKING, STARE AT THE SKY	35	LIFT UP FACE	2
FROM AN ODD ROOM IN A SPLIT HOUSE STARE,	142	SAINT TO FALL	31
NOT SPIN TO STARE AT AN OLD YEAR	145	PLEASURE-BIRD	17
THE BLIND, CLAWED STARE IS COLD AS SLEET.	165	LONG-LEGGED	101
STARER			
THE BOY OF WOMAN AND THE WANTON STARER	112	NOT FATHER ME	10
STARES			
WHEN THE SUN FALLS AND THE MOON STARES,	48	LIGHT, I KNOW	7
STARFISH			
BY SCUMMED, STARFISH SANDS	3	PROLOGUE	9
STAR-FLANKED			
SHALL THE STAR-FLANKED SEED BE RIDDLED,	125	SEED-AT-ZERO	16
SHALL THE STAR-FLANKED SEED BE RIDDLED,	126	SEED-AT-ZERO	23
WITH A STAR-FLANKED GARRISON,	126	SEED-AT-ZERO	46
FROM THE STAR-FLANKED FIELDS OF SPACE,	127	SEED-AT-ZERO	51
STAR-GESTURED			
OF THE STAR-GESTURED CHILDREN IN THE PARK.	98	OCTOBER WIND	12
STARING			
STARING AT OTHERS, POOR UNLOVERS.	23	THE ONLY DEAD	3
STARING AT STONE WALLS.	35	LIFT UP FACE	9
STARLIGHT			
FIRE ON STARLIGHT, RAKE JESU'S STREAM;	163	LONG-LEGGED	43
STARRED			
SO STARRED WITH GRAVEL,	13	RAIN CUTS	12
FROM THE STARRED WELL?	198	COUNTRY SLEEP	26
AND LISTENED WHEN A SLOW, STARRED SLUMBER WRAPT THE MOON,	223	IDYLL UNFORGET	7
STARRY			
TREMBLE AT THE STARRY STAIN,	71	TAKE NEEDLES	34
THAT STARRY FENCE THE CLAY OF LIGHT	85	SEE, SAYS LIME	6
THREE-SYLLABLED AND STARRY AS THE SMILE;	94	IN BEGINNING	8
I SCRAPE THROUGH RESIN TO A STARRY BONE	104	WORLD PYRAMID	35
THE NIGHT ABOVE THE DINGLE STARRY,	195	FERN HILL	3

	PAGE	TITLE	LINE
STARS			
UNDER THE STARS OF WALES,	5	PROLOGUE	92
TO WONDER AT THE UNFAILING STARS.	31	BEING BUT MEN	10
CHILDREN IN WONDER WATCHING THE STARS,	31	BEING BUT MEN	15
THE LIVING SKY, THE FACES OF THE STARS.	36	MIDNIGHT ROAD	14
FAITH FIXED BEYOND THE SPINNING STARS,	41	YOUNG ARE OLD	45
FAITH FIXED LIKE A STAR BEYOND THE STARS,	42	YOUNG ARE OLD	50
WHERE MEN WOULD ARGUE TILL THE STARS BE GREEN,	43	A WAR OF WITS	23
AND SO COMPLAIN, IN A VAIN VOICE, TO THE STARS.	47	POET: 1935	21
LIGHT, I KNOW, TREADS THE TEN MILLION STARS	48	LIGHT, I KNOW	T
LIGHT, I KNOW, TREADS THE TEN MILLION STARS,	48	LIGHT, I KNOW	1
I AM ALONE, ALONE COMPLAIN TO THE STARS.	48	POET: 1935	62
THEY SHALL HAVE STARS AT ELBOW AND FOOT;	49	NO DOMINION	5
STUCK STRAW AND SEVEN STARS UPON MY HAIR,	52	OUT OF THE PIT	65
GIBED THE COITUS OF THE STARS. NO GOD	53	OUT OF THE PIT	78
THOUGH WHAT THE STARS ASK AS THEY ROUND	56	WHY EAST WIND	18
IS HEARD BUT LITTLE TILL THE STARS GO OUT.	56	WHY EAST WIND	20
DROWNS AND IS DROWNED, WHO UTTERS TO THE STARS	57	GREEK PLAY	26
HERE IN THIS SPRING, STARS FLOAT ALONG THE VOID;	58	HERE IN SPRING	1
HE HAS THE STILL MOON AND THE HUNDRED STARS;	63	WOMAN SPEAKS	20
THE LEADEN STARS, THE RAINY HAMMER	68	BEFORE KNOCKED	11
THE CODE OF STARS TRANSLATE IN HEAVEN.	69	SECRET WIND	3
HERE THE NIGHT SHELTERS AND HERE THE STARS SHINE,	74	SUN BURNS	8
HOW TIME HAS TICKED A HEAVEN ROUND THE STARS.	77	THE FORCE THAT	20
THE FRUIT OF MAN UNWRINKLES IN THE STARS,	82	LIGHT BREAKS	10
WHERE, PUNCTUAL AS DEATH, WE RING THE STARS;	92	BOYS OF SUMMER	27
BUT WHEN THE STARS, ASSUMING SHAPE,	97	TWILIGHT LOCKS	16
REACHING A SECOND GROUND FAR FROM THE STARS;	101	FELLOWED SLEEP	7
AND, MANNED BY MIDNIGHT, JACOB TO THE STARS.	117	ALTARWISE	24
HUSK OF YOUNG STARS AND HANDFULL ZODIAC,	138	FIVE & COUNTRY	4
TONGUE OF YOUR TRANSLATING EYES. THE YOUNG STARS TOLD ME,	148	UNLUCKILY FOR	51
WITH THE INCESTUOUS SECRET BROTHER IN THE SECONDS TO PERPETUATE THE STARS,	159	INTO HER HEAD	66
SUFFER THE FIRST VISION THAT SET FIRE TO THE STARS.	170	LOVE IN ASYLUM	18
AND THE STARS FALLING COLD,	187	WINTER'S TALE	6
THE CLOUD, THE NEED, THE PLANTED STARS, THE JOY BEYOND	190	WINTER'S TALE	102
AND NIGHTLY UNDER THE SIMPLE STARS	195	FERN HILL	23
STEERED BY THE FALLING STARS.	209	POEM ON B'DAY	41
MASTS AND FISHES TO THE STILL QUICK STARS,	210	POEM ON B'DAY	71
WHERE THE DEWFALL STARS SING GRAZING STILL	215	COUNTRY HEAVEN	8
STARS'			
STARS' LIGHT AND SUN'S LIGHT WILL NOT SHINE	49	LIGHT, I KNOW	27
ALL THINGS ARE KNOWN: THE STARS' ADVICE	56	WHY EAST WIND	16
FLY LIKE THE STARS' BLOOD,	193	SIDE OF TRUTH	24
OR THE STARS' SEASHORE DEAD,	210	POEM ON B'DAY	57
STAR-SCALED			
SHAKEN SILKILY FROM STAR-SCALED BOUGHS.	226	SLENDER WIND	5
STAR-SET			
STAR-SET AT JACOB'S ANGLE,	111	I, IN IMAGE	81
STAR-STRUCK			
VENUS LIES STAR-STRUCK IN HER WOUND	166	LONG-LEGGED	117
START			
A FINAL WORD: BEFORE YOU START	84	LETTER TO AUNT	58
AND THE FIRE IN A TEMPER START	149	PAPER & STICKS	3
STARVE			
IF THE DEAD STARVE, THEIR STOMACHS TURN TO TUMBLE	145	PLEASURE-BIRD	22
STARVED			
HAS STOLEN THE STARVED BABIES FROM THEIR LAPS,	96	TWELVE	4

	PAGE	TITLE	LINE
STARVED (CONTINUED)			
CALLS THE STARVED FIRE HERD, IS CAST IN ICE, ...	132	I MAKE THIS IN	27
STARVING			
AND THE DEATH IN A STARVING IMAGE.	96	TWELVE	14
STATE			
TO ANY LIGHTER STATE	19	IMAGES IN AIR	13
AND THE STATE FALLS TO BITS, ...	39	GAS FADES	7
BY YOUTH AND AGE, THE MORTAL STATE AND THOUGHT	80	ALMANAC TIME	9
NEVER BE LUCID, NEVER STATE, ...	84	LETTER TO AUNT	40
LOVE'S TWILIT NATION AND THE SKULL OF STATE, ...	101	RUNNING GRAVE	39
STATEMENT			
LET FOR ONE MOMENT A FAITH STATEMENT	66	LET A FAITH	T
LET FOR ONE MOMENT A FAITH STATEMENT	66	LET A FAITH	1
LET FOR ONE MOMENT A FAITH STATEMENT	67	LET A FAITH	6
LET FOR ONE MOMENT A FAITH STATEMENT	67	LET A FAITH	11
DOOM ON DENIERS AT THE WIND-TURNED STATEMENT.	119	ALTARWISE	90
DISSECT THAT STATEMENT, VOICES, ON THE SLABS.	137	O CHATTERTON	21
STATIONS			
NIGHTINGALES OF THE CASUALTY STATIONS	154	RETURN	23
NOR BLASPHEME DOWN THE STATIONS OF THE BREATH	192	REFUSAL MOURN	16
STATUARY			
SECRETLY IN STATUARY, ...	145	PLEASURE-BIRD	15
STATUE			
THE SPIRE CRANES. ITS STATUE IS AN AVIARY.	15	SPIRE CRANES	1
HER FLESH WAS MEEK AS MILK, BUT THIS SKYWARD STATUE	136	AFTER FUNERAL	27
STATUED			
THE SHOOTING STAR HAWK STATUED BLIND IN A CLOUD ...	215	COUNTRY HEAVEN	23
STATUES			
THE STATUES OF GREAT RAIN STAND STILL, ...	166	LONG-LEGGED	135
PAST THE STATUES OF THE STABLES AND THE SKY ROOFED STIES	188	WINTER'S TALE	34
STATURE			
STATURE BY SEEDY SHIFTING, ...	92	BOYS OF SUMMER	20
STAVED			
GLINT IN THE STAVED AND SIREN-PRINTED CAVERS, ...	131	I MAKE THIS IN	20
AND STAVED, AND RIVEN AMONG PLUMES MY RIDER WEEP.	198	COUNTRY SLEEP	16
STAY			
YOU WISH TO STAY MY PRISONER	10	COOL, OH NO	27
STAY, DRAMATIC FIGURES, TETHERED DOWN	28	NO WINGS	3
STAY, IN A CIRCLE CHALKED UPON THE FLOOR, ...	28	NO WINGS	25
IN CHILDREN'S CIRCUSES COULD STAY THEIR TROUBLES?	40	WAS THERE TIME	2
SHALL I UNBOLT OR STAY	62	EARS IN TURRET	5
OR STAY TILL THE DAY I DIE	62	EARS IN TURRET	23
OR STAY TILL THE DAY I DIE?	63	EARS IN TURRET	31
THE SCENT OF THE GREAT FLOWER WILL STAY, ...	232	FURIOUS MOTION	16
STAYS			
THANK GOD, BUT THE ENEMY STAYS PUT.	59	FAIRY TALES	9
STEADIED			
WHEN YOUR FURIOUS MOTION IS STEADIED, ...	232	FURIOUS MOTION	1
STEADIES			
BEFORE THE WORLD STEADIES, STOPS ROCKING, IS STEADY,	39	GAS FADES	33
STEADILY			
THE CADAVEROUS GRAVELS, FALLS THICK AND STEADILY,	110	I, IN IMAGE	44
PRESS, PRESS, AND CLASP STEADILY;	232	FURIOUS MOTION	18
STEADY			
BEFORE THE WORLD STEADIES, STOPS ROCKING, IS STEADY,	39	GAS FADES	33
AND SETTLE IN THE STEADY PATH.	233	NO THOUGHT	15
STEADYING			
YOU WILL NOT SEE THE STEADYING OR FALLING, ...	39	GAS FADES	37

	PAGE	TITLE	LINE
STEAL			
SO STEAL HER NOT O GOAT-LEGGED WIND	11	AIR BREATHE	7
COMES DESIGNED TO MY LOVE TO STEAL NOT HER TIDE			
RAKING	200	COUNTRY SLEEP	100
AND HONEY STEAL FROM FLOWERS AGLOW.	228	TRIOLET	6
STEALER			
TO FOLLOW, WILD AS THE CHICKEN STEALER, ...	44	TO FOLLOW FOX	3
STEALING			
STEALING SO SOFTLY INTO THE EARS.	22	ON QUIET NIGHT	7
STEALS			
STEALS WHAT IS BEST--THE BODY'S SPLENDOUR--	30	NEARLY SUMMER	15
THE KNAVE OF PAIN STEALS OFF	107	GRIEF THIEF	3
STEALTH			
GREEN-SHADOWED PANOPLY ENVELOPING ALL ITS			
STRANGENESS AND SOFTNESS OF STEALTH.	224	IDYLL UNFORGET	45
STEALTHY			
THE PALE BREATH OF CATTLE AT THE STEALTHY SAIL, ...	187	WINTER'S TALE	5
STEEL			
MAN'S MARROW BARBED, AND BREAST RIPPED WITH A STEEL,	64	WOMAN SPEAKS	30
A CITY GODHEAD, TURBINE MOVED, STEEL SCULPTURED,	70	SECRET WIND	13
SPEAKS A STEEL GOSPEL TO THE WRETCHED	70	SECRET WIND	17
THE STOCK AND STEEL THAT BAYONET FROM THE MUD, ...	73	LORD RED HAIL	9
STEEP			
AND YOUR SIDE IS STEEP.	230	MY RIVER	46
STEEPLE			
SWEETLY THE DIVER'S BELL IN THE STEEPLE OF SPINDRIFT	110	I, IN IMAGE	62
HERONS, STEEPLE STEMMED, BLESS.	209	POEM ON B'DAY	18
STEEPLED			
THIS FIRST AND STEEPLED SEASON, TO THE SUMMER'S GAME.	122	HOLD HARD	12
STEEPLEJACK			
A STEEPLEJACK TOWER, BONERAILED AND MASTERLESS, ...	109	I, IN IMAGE	20
STEEPLES			
AND STEEPLES PIERCE THE CLOUD ON HER SHOULDER	168	LONG-LEGGED	193
INTO THE ORGANPIPES AND STEEPLES	175	FIRE RAID	61
STEER			
WE TRY TO STEER;	14	RAIN CUTS	25
STEERED			
STEERED BY THE FALLING STARS.	209	POEM ON B'DAY	41
STEERS			
PUSHED UP THEIR HAIR, THE DRY WIND STEERS	90	WHERE ONCE THE	5
STEM			
AND THE CARNAL STEM THAT STOOD	22	HIGH ON A HILL	13
STITCH THE STEM ON TO THE LEAF, ...	72	TAKE NEEDLES	51
A STEM CEMENTING, WRESTLED UP THE TOWER, ...	114	A GRIEF AGO	5
STIRRING ITS POLE STEM IN DELIGHT, ...	235	WOMAN TAPESTRY	16
STEMMED			
HERONS, STEEPLE STEMMED, BLESS.	209	POEM ON B'DAY	18
STENCH			
BUT ALL THIS LAND GIVES OFF A CHARNEL STENCH, ...	67	REALM OF FLESH	4
STEP			
IT IS GOOD TO STEP ONTO THE EARTH, ALONE, ...	43	A WAR OF WITS	24
SO SHALL HE STEP TILL SUMMER LOOSENS ITS HOLD	46	POET: 1935	18
CHRYSOLITH THY STEP, ...	225	SLENDER WIND	1
YOUR STEP WILL REMAIN ABOUT TO FALL.	232	FURIOUS MOTION	4
STEPPED			
TAXIS AND LILIES TO TINNED MUSIC STEPPED	51	OUT OF THE PIT	24
OUT OF THE BUILDINGS OF THE DAY I'VE STEPPED	53	OUT OF THE PIT	90
HE PUT ON HIS CLOTHES AND STEPPED OUT AND HE DIED,	172	DAWN RAID	2
STEPPING			
STEPPING ON CLOUDS ACROSS THE GOLDEN SKY, ...	30	YOUTH CALLS	2

		PAGE	TITLE	LINE
STEPPING (CONTINUED)				
STEPPING IN NIGHTMARE ON A NIGHTMARE'S EDGES.	.....	36	MIDNIGHT ROAD	11
WHERE, WHAT'S MY GOD AMONG THIS TAXI STEPPING,	....	52	OUT OF THE PIT	49
THE CATTLE STIRRING, THE MOUSING CAT STEPPING SHY,		187	WINTER'S TALE	22
STEPPING DOWN.	....	235	WOMAN TAPESTRY	23
STEPS				
EACH SILVER MOMENT CHIMES/ IN STEPS OF SOUND,	.....	9	MINUTE'S HOUR	5
HE STEPS SO NEAR THE WATER THAT A SWAN'S WING	.....	46	POET: 1935	2
WHO STEPS ON THE GAS;	....	58	TO ARCHITECTS	9
THE HEART STEPS TO DEATH'S FINGER,	....	67	REALM OF FLESH	8
NO TREAD MORE PERILOUS, THE GREEN STEPS AND SPIRE		109	I, IN IMAGE	26
STERILE				
THE TWO WORDS STALLION AND STERILE	....	138	O CHATTERTON	35
STERN				
FROM SALT-LIPPED BEAK TO THE KICK OF THE STERN	....	164	LONG-LEGGED	81
NEVER, MY GIRL, UNTIL TOLLED TO SLEEP BY THE STERN		198	COUNTRY SLEEP	21
THIS NIGHT AND EACH VAST NIGHT UNTIL THE STERN BELL				
TALKS	....	199	COUNTRY SLEEP	51
NOR MAKE THE STERN SHELL OF MY SPIRIT MOVE.	....	233	NO THOUGHT	2
STICK				
TELLS THE STICK, 'FAIL'.	....	100	RUNNING GRAVE	30
BRASS AND THE BODILESS IMAGE, ON A STICK OF FOLLY		111	I, IN IMAGE	80
SOON SETS ALIGHT A LONG STICK FROM THE CRADLE;	....	117	ALTARWISE	20
I PICK A STICK OF CELERY FROM THE VALLEY	....	137	O CHATTERTON	14
WITH HIS STICK THAT PICKED UP LEAVES.	....	171	THE HUNCHBACK	24
STICKS				
ONCE IN THIS CLAY FENCED BY THE STICKS	....	85	SEE, SAYS LIME	5
NOR THE CROSSED STICKS OF WAR.	....	95	RUB OF LOVE	14
HEARING THE RAVEN COUGH IN WINTER STICKS,	....	98	OCTOBER WIND	6
PAPER AND STICKS	....	149	PAPER & STICKS	T
PAPER AND STICKS AND SHOVEL AND MATCH	....	149	PAPER & STICKS	1
THE STICKS OF THE HOUSE WERE HIS; HIS BOOKS HE OWNED.		217	ELEGY	25
STIES				
PAST THE STATUES OF THE STABLES AND THE SKY ROOFED				
STIES	....	188	WINTER'S TALE	34
STIFF				
TOO STIFF TO CHURN WITH LEAVES,	....	14	RAIN CUTS	27
FROM THE UNWATERED LEAVES AND THE STIFF STALKS,	...	47	POET: 1935	39
THE WORDS OF DEATH ARE DRYER THAN HIS STIFF,	......	96	RUB OF LOVE	46
AND MOTHER MILK WAS STIFF AS SAND,	....	98	TWILIGHT LOCKS	32
STILES				
TO KEEP COUNT OF THE STILES	....	33	HELD-OUT HAND	21
AND LEANT ON STILES AND ON THE GOLDEN BAR,	....	52	OUT OF THE PIT	66
STILL				
HEAR AND AM STILL THE LITTLE BIRD.	....	9	MINUTE'S HOUR	7
BUT LEAVE BUT STILL ADORE	....	11	AIR BREATHE	8
SEES THE MOON STILL UP,	....	14	FOR LEDA	8
THE STILL GO HARD,	....	16	TIME TO ROT	13
WE STILL ARE LOTH TO PART WITH WHAT REMAINS,	......	26	THERE'S PLENTY	17
STILL COMES VISITING HIS POOR RELATIONS,	....	29	NEARLY SUMMER	2
WE WHO ARE STILL YOUNG ARE OLD. IT IS A DEAD CRY,		40	YOUNG ARE OLD	5
THE WINDMILLS OF THE WORLD STILL STAND	....	45	PLOUGHMAN GONE	6
STILL, IN HIS HUT, HE BROODS AMONG HIS BIRDS.	.....	53	OUT OF THE PIT	101
LAPPING THE STILL CANALS, THE DRY TIDE-MASTER	.....	54	WE BY SEASAND	10
BUT STILL GHOSTS MADDEN,	....	59	FAIRY TALES	14
STILL A WORLD OF FURIES	....	60	FAIRY TALES	24
BLACK NIGHT STILL MINISTERS THE MOON,	....	61	MEAT ON BONES	33
HE HAS THE STILL MOON AND THE HUNDRED STARS;	......	63	WOMAN SPEAKS	20
YET HE IS DEAD, AND STILL BY WOMAN'S WOMB	....	64	WOMAN SPEAKS	35
SPIRIT SUFFERS BUT IS STILL	....	71	TAKE NEEDLES	27

		PAGE	TITLE	LINE
STILL (CONTINUED)				
STILL SET TO SCRATCH A LAUGHTER FROM MY LUNG,	.....	95	RUB OF LOVE	5
THE REDHAIRED CANCER STILL ALIVE,	....	97	TWILIGHT LOCKS	20
WHERE STILL THEY SLEEP UNKNOWING OF THEIR GHOST.		102	FELLOWED SLEEP	20
AN OLD, MAD MAN STILL CLIMBING IN HIS GHOST,	......	102	FELLOWED SLEEP	29
THESE ARE YOUR YEARS' RECORDERS. THE CIRCULAR WORLD				
STANDS STILL.)	....	110	I, IN IMAGE	72
SHALL I STILL BE LOVE'S HOUSE ON THE WIDDERSHIN				
EARTH,	....	113	NOT FATHER ME	29
FROM THE EMERALD, STILL BELL; AND FROM THE PACING				
WEATHER-COCK	....	130	SINNERS' BELL	17
MAGNIFIED OUT OF PRAISE; HER DEATH WAS A STILL DROP;		136	AFTER FUNERAL	17
HER TWO SURNAMES STOPPED ME STILL.	....	139	TOMBSTONE TOLD	2
WHO WRITES THESE WORDS I WRITE IN A STILL ROOM IN A				
SPELLSOAKED HOUSE:	....	141	I, FIRST NAMED	2
WITH A CAPSIZED FIELD WHERE A SCHOOL SAT STILL	....	144	COLOUR OF SAY	3
CUT TO THE STILL STAR IN THE ORDER OF THE QUICK	...	148	UNLUCKILY FOR	20
AND THE VAULTING BIRD BE STILL. O MY TRUE LOVE, HOLD				
ME.	....	149	UNLUCKILY FOR	54
O SHE LIES ALONE AND STILL,	....	159	INTO HER HEAD	64
THE STATUES OF GREAT RAIN STAND STILL,	....	166	LONG-LEGGED	135
AND STUNNED AND STILL ON THE GREEN, LAID VEIL	.....	167	LONG-LEGGED	171
IN THE STILL SLEEPING TOWN AND SET FORTH.	....	177	POEM IN OCT	10
STILL IN THE WATER AND SINGINGBIRDS.	....	178	POEM IN OCT	60
STILL BE SUNG	....	178	POEM IN OCT	69
STILL AS STONE	....	180	VISION, PRAYER	20
THAT UNCALM STILL IT IS SURE ALONE TO STAND AND SING		186	HOLY SPRING	21
AND THE STILL HOUR	....	191	REFUSAL MOURN	5
LIE STILL, SLEEP BECALMED	....	194	SLEEP BECALMED	T
LIE STILL, SLEEP BECALMED, SUFFERER WITH THE WOUND		194	SLEEP BECALMED	1
LIE STILL, SLEEP BECALMED, HIDE THE MOUTH IN THE				
THROAT,	....	194	SLEEP BECALMED	13
EXERCISED IN THE STILL NIGHT	....	196	CRAFT OR ART	2
THE HAWK ON FIRE HANGS STILL;	....	201	SIR JOHNS HILL	2
WHERE BARREN AS BOULDERS WOMEN LIE LONGING STILL		203	GIANT'S THIGH	4
AND THE DAUGHTERS OF DARKNESS FLAME LIKE FAWKES				
FIRES STILL.	....	205	GIANT'S THIGH	60
MASTS AND FISHES TO THE STILL QUICK STARS,	....	210	POEM ON B'DAY	71
WHERE THE DEWFALL STARS SING GRAZING STILL	....	215	COUNTRY HEAVEN	8
OR STILL ALL THE NUMBERLESS DAYS OF HIS DEATH, THOUGH	216	ELEGY	8
BUT I HAVE KNOWN THE STILL ARDOUR OF EQUABILITY;		223	IDYLL UNFORGET	17
SEEKING NO FURTHER THAN YOUR PETALS THAT STILL SLEPT.		227	SPRING-SPIRIT	8
THE RAVEN'S FALLEN AND THE MAGPIE'S STILL.	....	237	PILLAR BREAKS	7
BOAT'S BROKEN, TOO, AND MAGPIE'S STILL;	....	238	PILLAR BREAKS	26
STILLED				
AND WHEN THE BRIGHT WHEEL OF YOUR TURNING VOICE IS				
STILLED,	....	232	FURIOUS MOTION	3
STILLS				
STILLS SNAPPED BY NIGHT IN THE BREAD-SIDED FIELD,		118	ALTARWISE	54
STILL'S				
STILL'S VAIN TO ARGUE AFTER DEATH;	....	27	OBLIVIOUS DARK	10
STILLY				
HIGH RIDING, HELD AND BLESSED AND TRUE, AND SO STILLY	200	COUNTRY SLEEP	90
STILT				
AND WHARVES OF WATER WHERE THE WALLS DANCE AND THE				
WHITE CRANES STILT.	....	202	SIR JOHNS HILL	39
STILTS				
MY FRIENDS WERE ENEMIES ON STILTS	....	147	TO OTHERS	20
IN HIS HOUSE ON STILTS HIGH AMONG BEAKS	....	208	POEM ON B'DAY	4

		PAGE	TITLE	LINE
STING				
TO MAIM OR STING MY ARM,	....	240	TWINING HEAD	2
STINGING				
AND LOVE PLUCKED OUT THE STINGING SIREN'S EYE,	....	119	ALTARWISE	77
STINGS				
BUT IF IT STINGS MY BODY DEAD	....	240	TWINING HEAD	3
STINK				
STINK OF CIGARETTES AND ARMPITS,	....	28	NO WINGS	16
STINKS				
THERE STINKS A SNOOP IN BLACK. I'M THINKING IT	....	179	NEW QUAY	19
STIR				
WIND IS MY ENEMY YOUR HAIR SHANT STIR	....	11	AIR BREATHE	3
TO STIR THE WATER WITH A BUOYANT FOOT,	....	14	FOR LEDA	2
WE STRIKE BUT DO NOT STIR IT.	....	14	RAIN CUTS	31
STIR THEIR OLD BONES BEHIND CUPBOARD AND CURTAIN.		38	THE GOSSIPERS	5
YEA THE DEAD STIR,	....	127	NOW, SAY NAY	18
O WE WHO COULD NOT STIR	....	153	WAS A SAVIOUR	28
STIRRED				
WHEN FOLLY STIRRED, WARM IN THE FOOLISH HEART.	....	25	BEAUTY TO DUST	19
THEN STIRRED A LITTLE CHAOS IN THE SUN.	....	33	IN GARDENS	6
WHEN NO MOUTH STIRRED ABOUT THE HANGING FAMINE,	...	78	LOVE'S FEVER	5
STIRRING				
THE CATTLE STIRRING, THE MOUSING CAT STEPPING SHY,		187	WINTER'S TALE	22
STIRRING ITS POLE STEM IN DELIGHT,	....	235	WOMAN TAPESTRY	16
STIRS				
MADE MEANING MEANINGLESS. THE WRONG WIND STIRS,	...	37	WINDMILLS TURN	29
AND BLOOMS IN THE HESPERIDES. LIGHT STIRS	....	48	LIGHT, I KNOW	2
STIRS THE QUICKSAND; THAT ROPES THE BLOWING WIND		77	THE FORCE THAT	12
LIKE SENNA STIRS ALONG THE RAVAGED ROOTS.	....	80	ALL THAT I OWE	4
WHERE NO SEED STIRS,	....	82	LIGHT BREAKS	9
AND NO-ONE STIRS AT SHEBA'S SIDE	....	165	LONG-LEGGED	108
STITCH				
STITCH THE STEM ON TO THE LEAF,	....	72	TAKE NEEDLES	51
THE FAMOUS STITCH DROPPERS.	....	151	BELOW A TIME	28
STITCHED				
IN THE STITCHED WOUND AND CLOTTED WIND, MUZZLED	...	103	I DREAMED MY	15
STOCK				
STREETS' STOCK, OF THE MOON LIT, ILL LIT, FIELD AND				
TOWN,	....	45	PLOUGHMAN GONE	22
THE STOCK AND STEEL THAT BAYONET FROM THE MUD,	....	73	LORD RED HAIL	9
STOCKED				
THE STOCKED HEART IS FORCED, AND AGONY HAS ANOTHER				
MOUTH TO FEED.	....	142	SAINT TO FALL	42
STOLE				
A ROOKING GIRL WHO STOLE ME FOR HER SIDE,	....	94	RUB OF LOVE	2
STOLEN				
HAS STOLEN THE STARVED BABIES FROM THEIR LAPS,	....	96	TWELVE	4
THESE STOLEN BUBBLES HAVE THE BITES OF SNAKES	.....	108	GRIEF THIEF	23
STOMACHS				
IF THE DEAD STARVE, THEIR STOMACHS TURN TO TUMBLE		145	PLEASURE-BIRD	22
STONE				
NOT, AS A SYMBOL, STONE/ SPEAKING OR NO,	....	9	MINUTE'S HOUR	15
FROM THE STONE NEST IT DOES NOT LET THE FEATHERY		15	SPIRE CRANES	2
STARING AT STONE WALLS.	....	35	LIFT UP FACE	9
FOR OUT OF A HOUSE OF MATCHBOARD AND STONE	....	43	A WAR OF WITS	22
LAY YOUR HEAD ON A HARD BED OF STONE,	....	45	PLOUGHMAN GONE	17
LAY YOUR HEAD ON A HARD BED OF STONE,	....	46	PLOUGHMAN GONE	31
WHY SILK IS SOFT AND THE STONE WOUNDS	....	55	WHY EAST WIND	6
BUT WHEN THE LADIES ARE COLD AS STONE	....	60	MEAT ON BONES	7
IT SHALL BE SAID THAT GODS ARE STONE.	....	65	GODS THUMP	11

		PAGE	TITLE	LINE
STONE (CONTINUED)				
SHALL A DROPPED STONE DRUM ON THE GROUND,	....	65	GODS THUMP	12
CHOKE THE BLADDER WITH A STONE,	....	71	TAKE NEEDLES	13
MY PICKBRAIN MASTERS MORSING ON THE STONE	....	100	RUNNING GRAVE	22
FOR MY TALL TOWER'S SAKE CAST IN HER STONE?	....	112	NOT FATHER ME	2
CAN TIME UNRIDDLE, AND THE CUPBOARD STONE,	....	113	SERVANT SUN	3
THE LONG-TAILED STONE	....	114	SERVANT SUN	18
OUT OF THE FONT OF BONE AND PLANTS AT THAT STONE TOCSIN	....	130	SINNERS' BELL	20
PROUD AS A SUCKED STONE AND HUGE AS SANDGRAINS.	...	131	I MAKE THIS IN	23
CAST HIGH, STUNNED ON GILLED STONE; SLY SCISSORS GROUND IN FROST	....	135	HOW MY ANIMAL	35
AND SCULPTURED ANN IS SEVENTY YEARS OF STONE.	.....	137	AFTER FUNERAL	35
MORE THE THICK STONE CANNOT TELL.	....	139	TOMBSTONE TOLD	10
OF THE STONE BIRD GUARDING HER:	....	140	TOMBSTONE TOLD	25
THROW YOUR FEAR A PARCEL OF STONE	....	142	SAINT TO FALL	37
AND EVERY STONE I WIND OFF LIKE A REEL.	....	144	COLOUR OF SAY	13
THE GRAVE AND MY CALM BODY ARE SHUT TO YOUR COMING AS STONE,	....	146	IF HEAD HURT	29
SUMMONING A CHILD'S VOICE FROM A WEBFOOT STONE,	...	152	BELOW A TIME	46
A STONE LIES LOST AND LOCKED IN THE LARK-HIGH HILL.		159	INTO HER HEAD	62
HE DROPPED WHERE HE LOVED ON THE BURST PAVEMENT STONE		172	DAWN RAID	4
UNDER THE SAD BREAST OF THE HEAD STONE	....	174	FIRE RAID	44
STILL AS STONE	....	180	VISION, PRAYER	20
ENDURE THE STONE	....	184	VISION, PRAYER	140
STONE FOR THE SAKE OF THE SOULS OF THE SLAIN BIRDS SAILING.	....	203	SIR JOHNS HILL	60
AND DUCKED AND DRAKED WHITE LAKE THAT HARPS TO A HAIL STONE.	....	204	GIANT'S THIGH	28
OR RUB YOUR BRIGHT STONE.	....	228	MY RIVER	5
MY RIVER CANNOT RUB YOUR BRIGHT STONE,	....	230	MY RIVER	41
BUT YOUR STONE IS MANY POINTED,	....	230	MY RIVER	45
OR THROW IT, STONE BY STONE,	....	233	FURIOUS MOTION	22
OR THROW IT, STONE BY STONE,	....	233	FURIOUS MOTION	22
STONED				
WHERE AT NIGHT WE STONED THE COLD AND CUCKOO	......	144	COLOUR OF SAY	8
STONE-NECKED				
EACH ANCIENT, STONE-NECKED MINUTE OF LOVE'S SEASON		131	I MAKE THIS IN	2
STONES				
BUT THE STONES CRACK IT	....	18	NATURAL DAY	15
LET THE TWO DULL STONES BE GREY,	....	19	IMAGES IN AIR	4
BUT IN THE BODY OF THE TREES AND STONES,	....	25	BEAUTY TO DUST	13
FLUNG GRAVEL CHIME? LET THE STONES SPEAK	....	66	GODS THUMP	13
WHERE ALL THE HIDDEN STONES ARE GOLD,	....	74	WE MOTHERNAKED	10
THERE ROUND ABOUT YOUR STONES THE SHADES	....	91	WHERE ONCE THE	16
WITH STONES OF ODYSSEY FOR ASH AND GARLAND	....	120	ALTARWISE	125
WITH MOVING FISH AND ROUNDED STONES	....	168	LONG-LEGGED	178
TO ROAR ON THE ROCKERY STONES	....	172	THE HUNCHBACK	29
TO THE TREES AND THE STONES AND THE FISH IN THE TIDE.		178	POEM IN OCT	57
HE KNELT ON THE COLD STONES,	....	188	WINTER'S TALE	31
LEAVES IS DANCING. LINES OF AGE ON THE STONES WEAVE IN A FLOCK.	....	189	WINTER'S TALE	78
BACK. LINES OF AGE SLEEP ON THE STONES TILL TRUMPETING DAWN.	....	191	WINTER'S TALE	118
THOUGH THE NAMES ON THEIR WEED GROWN STONES ARE RAINED AWAY,	....	203	GIANT'S THIGH	8
AND LOVE TO CHASE RABBITS AND STONES.	....	221	SONG OF DOG	12
STONING				
TO GLOW AFTER THE GOD STONING NIGHT	....	186	HOLY SPRING	11

		PAGE	TITLE	LINE
STONY				
	INTO THE STONY IDIOM OF THE BRAIN,	79	LOVE'S FEVER	33
	SPROUT FROM THE STONY LOCKERS LIKE A TREE ON ARAN.	111	I, IN IMAGE	78
STOOD				
	AND THE CARNAL STEM THAT STOOD	22	HIGH ON A HILL	13
	THAT STOOD BEFORE MY WINDOW,	33	HELD-OUT HAND	13
	LEAN TIME ON TIDE AND TIMES THE WIND STOOD ROUGH,	107	GRIEF THIEF	6
	YEAR TO HEAVEN STOOD THERE THEN IN THE SUMMER NOON	178	POEM IN OCT	66
STOOL				
	I SMELT THE MAGGOT IN MY STOOL.	69	BEFORE KNOCKED	30
STOOLS				
	ON STOOLS TO A ONE MAN SHOW DOWN,	154	RETURN	20
STOOPED				
	AND NIGHT, WHO STOOPED TO KISS THE PALLID LEAVES	223	IN DREAMS	5
STOP				
	STOP IS UNREAL;	9	MINUTE'S HOUR	13
	STOP HAS NO MINUTES,/ BUT I GO OR DIE.	9	MINUTE'S HOUR	23
	THESE THINGS REMEMBERED, WHAT CAN STOP	84	LETTER TO AUNT	56
STOPPED				
	STOPPED NON-STOP DANCING TO LET HOT FEET COOL,	51	OUT OF THE PIT	30
	HER TWO SURNAMES STOPPED ME STILL.	139	TOMBSTONE TOLD	2
	TELL HIS STREET ON ITS BACK HE STOPPED A SUN	172	DAWN RAID	6
	AND YOUR CLAMOUR STOPPED,	232	FURIOUS MOTION	2
	HAS STOPPED, (ANGEL, YOU'RE PROUD),	237	PILLAR BREAKS	3
STOPPING				
	NO STOPPING. PUT THE SMILE	12	SKY'S BRIGHT	16
	OUT OF MY HAND IN STOPPING UP MY MOUTH,	18	NATURAL DAY	16
STOPPRESS				
	NONSTOP; STOPPRESS; VINEGAR FROM WISECRACKS;	57	TO ARCHITECTS	3
STOPS				
	BEFORE THE WORLD STEADIES, STOPS ROCKING, IS STEADY,	39	GAS FADES	33
STORE				
	SETTING NO STORE BY HARVEST, FREEZE THE SOILS;	91	BOYS OF SUMMER	3
STORED				
	AT THE BREAST STORED WITH SEAS. NO RETURN	146	IF HEAD HURT	27
	WISDOM IS STORED WITH THE CLOVE	240	ADMIT THE SUN	10
STORIES				
	WE HAVE BY HEART THE CHILDREN'S STORIES,	59	FAIRY TALES	22
	WE HAVE THE STORIES BACKWARDS,	60	FAIRY TALES	31
	WHO TOSSED THE HIGH TIDE IN A TIME OF STORIES	108	GRIEF THIEF	13
	ALL LEGENDS' SWEETHEARTS ON A TREE OF STORIES,	125	TODAY, INSECT	25
	ON THE OLD SEAS FROM STORIES, THRASHING MY WINGS,	152	BELOW A TIME	36
STORKS				
	AND A HUNDRED STORKS PERCH ON THE SUN'S RIGHT HAND.	173	DAWN RAID	14
STORM				
	RIBBED BETWEEN DESERT AND WATER STORM,	54	WE BY SEASAND	11
	THE SEED-AT-ZERO SHALL NOT STORM	125	SEED-AT-ZERO	1
	THE SEED-AT-ZERO SHALL NOT STORM	125	SEED-AT-ZERO	8
	STORM, SNOW, AND FOUNTAIN IN THE WEATHER OF FIREWORKS,	130	SINNERS' BELL	14
	STORM HER SPED HEART, HANG WITH BEHEADED VEINS	132	I MAKE THIS IN	34
	STORM ME FOREVER OVER HER GRAVE UNTIL	137	AFTER FUNERAL	38
	HE SAW THE STORM SMOKE OUT TO KILL	163	LONG-LEGGED	41
	HIS MOUTH AND ROCKED HIM LIKE A STORM	181	VISION, PRAYER	44
	AND WHEN THE SALT SHEET BROKE IN A STORM OF SINGING	194	SLEEP BECALMED	7
STORMS				
	TELL, IF AT ALL, THE WINTER'S STORMS	58	HERE IN SPRING	10
	STORMS IN THE FREEZING TOMB.	88	A PROCESS IN	3
STORY				
	THE SMILING WOMAN IS A MAD STORY,	138	O CHATTERTON	37

	PAGE	TITLE	LINE
STORY (CONTINUED)			
BECAUSE THERE STANDS, ONE STORY OUT OF THE BUM CITY,	144	PLEASURE-BIRD	13
STORY'S			
THIS STORY'S MONSTER HAS A SERPENT CAUL, ...	124	TODAY, INSECT	10
STOVED			
THE STOVED BONES' VOYAGE DOWNWARD	111	I, IN IMAGE	87
STRADDLE			
STRADDLE AND SOAK, ...	21	HIGH ON A HILL	2
STRADDLE HER WRINKLED KNEES	22	HIGH ON A HILL	5
STRAIGHT			
MAN'S RIB ON WOMAN'S, STRAIGHT LINE ON A CURVE, ...	51	OUT OF THE PIT	35
IN THE STRAIGHT GRAVE, ...	100	RUNNING GRAVE	20
AND THE NAKED EGG STAND STRAIGHT, ...	113	SERVANT SUN	7
STRAIGHT AS A YOUNG ELM	172	THE HUNCHBACK	33
STRAIGHT AND TALL FROM HIS CROOKED BONES	172	THE HUNCHBACK	34
ALTHOUGH IT IS SO STRAIGHT AND UNBENDING;	231	YOUR VOICE	5
AND THE WEB OF YOUR STRAIGHT SENSES.	236	WOMAN TAPESTRY	49
STRAIGHTENS			
GOLDEN GLAMORGAN STRAIGHTENS, TO THE FALLING BIRDS.	123	HOLD HARD	23
STRAIGHT-RULED			
WHAT MEANING, VOICES, IN THE STRAIGHT-RULED GRASS,	137	O CHATTERTON	17
STRAIT			
STRAIT IN THE MAZED BED	169	LOVE IN ASYLUM	5
STRAND			
FLOWS TO THE STRAND OF FLOWERS LIKE THE DEW'S RULY			
SEA, ...	200	COUNTRY SLEEP	98
STRANGE			
PITY THE POOR UNPITIED WHO ARE STRANGE WITH TEARS.	57	GREEK PLAY	28
STRANGE TO OUR SOLID EYE, ...	89	EUNUCH DREAMS	13
TELLS YOU AND YOU, MY MASTERS, AS HIS STRANGE	113	SERVANT SUN	13
LUST BEARS LIKE VOLTS, WHO'LL AMPLIFY, AND STRANGE	159	TO LEDA	8
WHEN NEAR AND STRANGE WOUNDED ON LONDON'S WAVES ...	160	DEATHS AND ENT	27
CALM AND STRANGE IS THIS EVENING HOUR IN THE FOREST,	221	FOREST PICTURE	1
TO THAT STRANGE COLOUR, SIGHING GENTLY, GRIEVES ...	223	IN DREAMS	6
WHEN EVERYTHING SLEPT AND THE SMELL OF THE WAVES WAS			
STRANGE;	224	IDYLL UNFORGET	27
STRANGELY			
WE STRANGELY SANG AMONG THE FEATHERY FLOWERS.	227	SPRING-SPIRIT	12
WEIGHED STRANGELY DOWN UPON YOU	232	FURIOUS MOTION	11
STRANGENESS			
GREEN-SHADOWED PANOPLY ENVELOPING ALL ITS			
STRANGENESS AND SOFTNESS OF STEALTH.	224	IDYLL UNFORGET	45
STRANGER			
NO, HE'S A STRANGER, OUTSIDE THE SEASON'S HUMOUR,	46	POET: 1935	10
SHALL I LET IN THE STRANGER, ...	63	EARS IN TURRET	29
HANDS OF THE STRANGER AND HOLDS OF THE SHIPS, ...	63	EARS IN TURRET	32
AND A STRANGER ENTER LIKE IRON.	142	SAINT TO FALL	47
A STRANGER HAS COME	169	LOVE IN ASYLUM	1
STRANGER-EYES			
UNSEEN BY STRANGER-EYES	62	EARS IN TURRET	7
STRANGERS			
TO YOU STRANGERS (THOUGH SONG	3	PROLOGUE	24
WHEN WE WERE STRANGERS TO THE GUIDED SEAS, ...	121	INCARNATE DEVL	7
ONCE SEEN STRANGERS OR SHADES ON A STAIR;	157	INTO HER HEAD	15
LOCKING, UNLOCKING, THE MURDERED STRANGERS WEAVE,	160	DEATHS AND ENT	15
(SIGHED THE OLD RAM ROD, DYING OF STRANGERS), ...	207	LAMENT	51
STRANGERS'			
OUR OWN TRUE STRANGERS' DUST	153	WAS A SAVIOUR	37
STRANGER'S			
BEFORE SHE LAY ON A STRANGER'S BED	139	TOMBSTONE TOLD	11

	PAGE	TITLE	LINE
STRANGLE			
STRANGLE THE LITTLE CHILDREN IN THEIR BEDS;	64	WOMAN SPEAKS	46
STRAPPED			
STRAPPED TO A WHEEL, YET THEY SHALL NOT BREAK;	49	NO DOMINION	14
IN A LAND STRAPPED BY HUNGER	134	NOT FROM ANGER	4
STRATA			
THE STRATA OF THE SHORE AND DROWN RED ROCK;	54	WE BY SEASAND	20
STRAW			
LIKE STALKS OF TALL, DRY STRAW, ...	3	PROLOGUE	22
STUCK STRAW AND SEVEN STARS UPON MY HAIR, ...	52	OUT OF THE PIT	65
AND FROM THE PLANTED WOMB THE MAN OF STRAW.	92	BOYS OF SUMMER	36
THE GHOST IS DUMB THAT STAMMERED IN THE STRAW, ...	104	WORLD PYRAMID	28
STRAWBERRIES			
AND THE WILD BOYS INNOCENT AS STRAWBERRIES	172	THE HUNCHBACK	40
STRAWS			
BROKE THROUGH HER STRAWS, BREAKING MY BANDAGED STRING, ...	94	RUB OF LOVE	3
DREW IN HIS EYES THE STRAWS OF SLEEP, ...	97	TWILIGHT LOCKS	17
THE STRAWS OF ASIA, LOSE ME AS I TURN	105	WORLD PYRAMID	47
WHEN THE WORM BUILDS WITH THE GOLD STRAWS OF VENOM	121	ALTARWISE	139
WITH A HOLD OF LEECHES AND STRAWS, ...	142	SAINT TO FALL	24
STREAK			
THE RIPPLED SEALS STREAK DOWN	209	POEM ON B'DAY	34
STREAM			
MOLTEN AND MOUNTAINOUS TO STREAM	4	PROLOGUE	49
TO CATCH HER SAILING DOWN THE STREAM--	14	FOR LEDA	4
MY WORLD WAS CHRISTENED IN A STREAM OF MILK.	78	LOVE'S FEVER	7
A STREAM OF MINE	87	PAIN BE MUSIC	17
FIRE ON STARLIGHT, RAKE JESU'S STREAM;	163	LONG-LEGGED	43
SUSANNAH'S DROWNED IN THE BEARDED STREAM	165	LONG-LEGGED	107
FURIED BY HIS STREAM	181	VISION, PRAYER	39
IN THE FIRST FURY OF HIS STREAM	181	VISION, PRAYER	59
STREAM UPON HIS MARTYRDOM	185	VISION, PRAYER	185
STREAM WITH BELLS AND BAYING WATER BOUNDS. THE DEW RINGS	189	WINTER'S TALE	62
THE STREAM FROM THE PRIEST BLACK WRISTED SPINNEY AND SLEEVES	200	COUNTRY SLEEP	72
AND THE WINDS THAT STREAM THROUGH THE RIBBONED LIGHT	227	THE PINE	3
STREAMED			
STREAMED AGAIN A WONDER OF SUMMER	178	POEM IN OCT	43
STREAMS			
DRIVES MY RED BLOOD; THAT DRIES THE MOUTHING STREAMS	77	THE FORCE THAT	7
OF THE GOLDEN GHOST WHO RINGED WITH HIS STREAMS HER MERCURY BONE, ...	170	MARRIAGE VIRG	11
IN THE PEBBLES OF THE HOLY STREAMS.	195	FERN HILL	18
STREAM'S			
THE STREAM'S FANTASTICALLY HARD, ...	14	RAIN CUTS	26
STREET			
THE WATER FROM A STREET OF CLOUDS.	13	RAIN CUTS	5
THE PICCADILLY MEN, THE BACK STREET DRUNKS, ...	41	YOUNG ARE OLD	41
AND THEN IN SANDALS WALK THE STREET	83	LETTER TO AUNT	19
LIMP IN THE STREET OF SEA, AMONG THE RABBLE	104	WORLD PYRAMID	15
ON THE LAST STREET WAVE PRAISED	141	SAINT TO FALL	4
THAT BURY THE SWEET STREET SLOWLY, SEE	142	SAINT TO FALL	33
SHALL I, STRUCK ON THE HOT AND ROCKING STREET, ...	145	PLEASURE-BIRD	16
BEARDLESSLY WAGGING IN DEAN STREET, ...	156	RETURN	72
ONE RICH STREET WITH HUNGER IN IT.	157	RETURN	101
YOUR POLESTAR NEIGHBOUR, SUN OF ANOTHER STREET, ...	160	DEATHS AND ENT	17
TELL HIS STREET ON ITS BACK HE STOPPED A SUN	172	DAWN RAID	6
AMONG THE STREET BURNED TO TIRELESS DEATH	173	FIRE RAID	4

	PAGE	TITLE	LINE
STREET (CONTINUED)			
STREET WE CHANT THE FLYING SEA	174	FIRE RAID	29
STREET-LAMPS			
BETWEEN THE STREET-LAMPS AND THE ILL-LIT SKY,	52	OUT OF THE PIT	61
STREETS			
IT'S ACRID IN THE STREETS;	16	TIME TO ROT	10
THE VIRGINS SMELT OUT, THREE STREETS UP,	38	THE GOSSIPERS	8
GILDERS OF STREETS, THE RABBLE HAND	70	SECRET WIND	10
GLITTERS IN THE ELECTRIC STREETS;	70	SECRET WIND	14
THROUGH THE WAVES OF THE FAT STREETS NOR THE SKELETON'S THIN WAYS.	146	IF HEAD HURT	28
THEN INTO BLIND STREETS I SWAM	155	RETURN	44
CUT. CUT THE CRUSHED STREETS, LEAVING	156	RETURN	77
AND THE STREETS THAT THE FISHERMAN COMBED	168	LONG-LEGGED	194
STREETS OR HUNGERING IN THE CRUMBLED WOOD: TO THESE	205	GIANT'S THIGH	57
STREETS'			
STREETS' STOCK, OF THE MOON LIT, ILL LIT, FIELD AND TOWN,	45	PLOUGHMAN GONE	22
STRENGTH			
SO ARE WE FULL WITH STRENGTH,	23	THE ONLY DEAD	5
OF NEW MAN STRENGTH, I SEEK THE SUN.	103	I DREAMED MY	28
CLACK THROUGH THE THICKET OF STRENGTH, LOVE HEWN IN PILLARS DROPS	135	HOW MY ANIMAL	36
WHICH CUTS INTO THE STRENGTH	230	MY RIVER	42
MY STRENGTH SHALL SAP YOUR OWN;	239	LET ME ESCAPE	9
GLASS TO MY HANDS ENDOWED WITH DOUBLE STRENGTH.	239	MAKES INTERVALS	19
TAKE HEED OF STRENGTH!	241	ADMIT THE SUN	19
STRETCH			
YOUR STRING SHALL STRETCH A GULLY TWIXT THE THUMBS	87	PAIN BE MUSIC	7
STRETCH THE SALT PHOTOGRAPHS,	129	MY NEOPHYTE	19
YOU STRETCH OUT YOUR HANDS	229	MY RIVER	21
STREW			
THAT DUST YOU HOLD, O STREW THAT LITTLE LEFT;	65	WOMAN SPEAKS	61
STREWED			
THE SNIPER LAID HIM LOW AND STREWED HIS BRAINS;	63	WOMAN SPEAKS	11
STREWING			
STREWING THEIR VOWELS FROM A HILL OF BONES,	105	WORLD PYRAMID	41
STREWN			
ENVELOPING THE RAGGED LEAVES UNSEEN AND STREWN.	226	THE OAK	2
STRICTURE			
TO REMEMBER, CAST STRICTURE ON MECHANICS AND MAN.	45	PLOUGHMAN GONE	5
STRICTURES			
IF THESE TWO GNOMES REMAIN UNMOVED BY STRICTURES?	60	FAIRY TALES	30
STRIDE			
STRIDE THROUGH CADAVER'S COUNTRY IN MY FORCE,	100	RUNNING GRAVE	21
I, IN MY INTRICATE IMAGE, STRIDE ON TWO LEVELS,	108	I, IN IMAGE	1
THE SKY STRIDE OF THE ALWAYS SLAIN	182	VISION, PRAYER	94
STRIDING			
HIS STRIPED AND NOON MANED TRIBE STRIDING TO HOLOCAUST,	148	UNLUCKILY FOR	31
STRIKE			
WE STRIKE BUT DO NOT STIR IT.	14	RAIN CUTS	31
STRIKE THE SEA HOUR THROUGH BELLMETAL.	130	SINNERS' BELL	12
STRIKE IN THE TIME-BOMB TOWN,	142	SAINT TO FALL	35
STRIKE LIGHT, AND BLOODY A LOUD ROOM.	145	IF HEAD HURT	10
STRIKE AND SMOOTHE, FOR MY DECKS ARE DRUMS,	164	LONG-LEGGED	77
SING AND STRIKE HIS HEAVY HAUL	166	LONG-LEGGED	137
STRIKE AND SING HIS CATCH OF FIELDS	168	LONG-LEGGED	181
POOR, BROKEN WEBS TO STRIKE THE SKY!	238	PILLAR BREAKS	16
TO FIND AND THEN TO STRIKE;	240	ADMIT THE SUN	4

	PAGE	TITLE	LINE
STRIKES			
CARRYING CLOUD, DEATH STRIKES THEIR HOUSE.	161	WEDDING ANNIV	8
OUT OF THE AIR IT STRIKES.	241	ADMIT THE SUN	22
STRIKING			
CARVED BIRDS BLUNT THEIR STRIKING THROATS ON THE			
SALT GRAVEL, ...	15	SPIRE CRANES	3
STRING			
AND, THE STRING PULLED, SOME MENTAL DOLL	10	COOL, OH NO	11
YOUR PAIN SHALL BE A MUSIC IN YOUR STRING	87	PAIN BE MUSIC	1
YOUR STRING SHALL STRETCH A GULLY TWIXT THE THUMBS	87	PAIN BE MUSIC	7
BROKE THROUGH HER STRAWS, BREAKING MY BANDAGED			
STRING, ...	94	RUB OF LOVE	3
STRINGED			
HAD STRINGED MY FLASK OF MATTER TO HIS RIB.	97	TWILIGHT LOCKS	12
STRINGS			
THE SWAN MAKES STRINGS OF WATER IN HER WAKE;	15	FOR LEDA	14
THE STRINGS OF FIRE CHOKED HIS SEX	85	SEE, SAYS LIME	17
PARISH OF SNOW. THE CARVED MOUTHS IN THE ROCK ARE			
WIND SWEPT STRINGS.	189	WINTER'S TALE	64
STRIP			
BOUND BY A SOVEREIGN STRIP, WE LIE, ...	54	WE BY SEASAND	18
STRIP THE DREAMS' LIVERY, ...	67	LET A FAITH	7
WEANS ON AN ARTERY THE GENDER'S STRIP;	117	ALTARWISE	18
STRIP TO THIS TREE: A ROCKING ALPHABET, ...	119	ALTARWISE	87
BUT STRIP THE TWELVE-WINDED MARROW FROM HIS CIRCLE;	123	FOSTER LIGHT	3
STRIPED			
HIS STRIPED AND NOON MANED TRIBE STRIDING TO			
HOLOCAUST, ...	148	UNLUCKILY FOR	31
STRIPPING			
STRIPPING MY LOIN OF PROMISE, ...	75	MY HERO BARES	14
STRIPS			
FOR PAINING, ON THEIR CANVAS STRIPS, ...	83	LETTER TO AUNT	21
OUR STRIPS OF STUFF THAT TATTER AS WE MOVE	90	EUNUCH DREAMS	32
STRODE			
WHO STRODE FOR YOUR OWN DEAD	160	DEATHS AND ENT	20
STROKE			
UP YOUR HAND TO STROKE THE LIGHT, ...	35	LIFT UP FACE	15
THEREFORE LIFT UP, SEE, STROKE THE LIGHT.	35	LIFT UP FACE	24
THE CRUSTED WOUND NOR STROKE THE BROW;	66	HAND SIGNED	14
STROKE OF MECHANICAL FLESH ON MINE, ...	107	ALL ALL AND	29
I AM, THE TOWER TOLD, FELLED BY A TIMELESS STROKE,	113	NOT FATHER ME	21
STROKED			
SLEEP TO A NEWBORN SLEEP IN A SWADDLING LOIN-LEAF			
STROKED AND SANG	157	INTO HER HEAD	22
STROKES			
IN THE SUN STROKES OF SUMMER, ...	147	UNLUCKILY FOR	14
STROKING			
STROKING THE AIR AND HOLDING LIGHT.	235	WOMAN TAPESTRY	30
STRONG			
UNDER HIS STRONG IMPULSIVE KISS	11	AIR BREATHE	4
WHO HOLDS HER CLASPED INSIDE HIS STRONG, WHITE WINGS;	15	FOR LEDA	31
WE HAVE GROWN WEAK BEFORE WE COULD GROW STRONG, ...	40	YOUNG ARE OLD	7
THE WHOLE, THE CRIPPLED, THE WEAK AND STRONG, ...	41	YOUNG ARE OLD	43
INTO THE SIDED LAP OF LIGHT GREW STRONG, ...	78	LOVE'S FEVER	27
THROUGH THE ROTATING SHELL, STRONG	102	I DREAMED MY	2
STRONG ENOUGH TO TREAD ON THE SAND	229	MY RIVER	7
STRONG AND BEAUTIFUL ENOUGH	229	MY RIVER	9
THE STRONG, UNTURNING CRUST THAT HIDES	233	NO THOUGHT	11
CHAIN THE STRONG VOICE	233	FURIOUS MOTION	20
STRONG, FRESH, AND OVERPOWERING.	235	WOMAN TAPESTRY	12

	PAGE	TITLE	LINE
STRONG (CONTINUED)			
AND GALLANTLY (WATER, YOU'RE STRONG--	237	PILLAR BREAKS	4
ALTHOUGH YOUR CAGE IS STRONG.	239	LET ME ESCAPE	8
WHERE THE EAGLE IS A STRONG BIRD	240	ADMIT THE SUN	2
STRONGER			
THE HARDER TO BEAR AND THE STRONGER.	39	GAS FADES	29
STRONGHOLD			
SETTLED ON A VIRGIN STRONGHOLD	125	SEED-AT-ZERO	19
SETTLING ON A RIDDLED STRONGHOLD	126	SEED-AT-ZERO	26
STRUCK			
AND I WAS STRUCK DUMB BY THE SUN.	42	A WAR OF WITS	7
AND BE STRUCK DUMB, IF ONLY FOR A TIME.	43	A WAR OF WITS	25
A SMILE LET LOOSE A DEVIL, A BELL STRUCK.	51	OUT OF THE PIT	19
AND I WAS STRUCK DOWN BY DEATH'S FEATHER.	69	BEFORE KNOCKED	39
REFUSAL STRUCK HER LOIN AND THE LAME FLOWER	134	NOT FROM ANGER	2
REFUSAL STRUCK LIKE A BELL UNDER WATER	134	NOT FROM ANGER	12
THAT I STRUCK ONE DAY BY LUCK,	139	TOMBSTONE TOLD	5
SHALL I, STRUCK ON THE HOT AND ROCKING STREET,	145	PLEASURE-BIRD	16
UNDER HIS DOWNY ARM YOU SIGHED AS HE STRUCK,	153	WAS A SAVIOUR	19
GOOD-BYE, GOOD LUCK, STRUCK THE SUN AND THE MOON,	169	LONG-LEGGED	213
AND I AM STRUCK AS LONELY AS A HOLY MAKER BY THE SUN.	186	HOLY SPRING	12
HIS NAKED NEED STRUCK HIM HOWLING AND BOWED	188	WINTER'S TALE	39
THIRTY-FIVE BELLS SING STRUCK	209	POEM ON B'DAY	39
STRUCTURE			
MY THROAT KNEW THIRST BEFORE THE STRUCTURE	69	BEFORE KNOCKED	25
STRUGGLE			
GIVE OVER, LOVERS, LOCKING, AND THE SEAWAX STRUGGLE,	111	I, IN IMAGE	89
STRUGGLING			
MY SECOND STRUGGLING FROM THE GRASS.	103	I DREAMED MY	20
STRUMPET			
WITH 'STRUMPET' IN THESE TROUBLED TIMES,	84	LETTER TO AUNT	34
STRUNG			
STRUNG BY THE FLAXEN WHALE-WEED, FROM THE HANGMAN'S RAFT,	110	I, IN IMAGE	65
BUT ONLY THE WIND STRUNG	188	WINTER'S TALE	41
STRUT			
DRESSED TO DIE, THE SENSUAL STRUT BEGUN,	143	24 YEARS	6
OR THE STRUT AND TRADE OF CHARMS	197	CRAFT OR ART	8
STRUTTING			
AND THE STRUTTING FERN LAY SEEDS ON THE BLACK SILL.	137	AFTER FUNERAL	40
STUB			
WITH A STUB OF BLACK BUDS,	142	SAINT TO FALL	21
STUBBLE			
SUFFER THE SLASH OF VISION BY THE FIN-GREEN STUBBLE,	111	I, IN IMAGE	85
STUCK			
STUCK STRAW AND SEVEN STARS UPON MY HAIR,	52	OUT OF THE PIT	65
STUDDED			
TOWARDS THE STUDDED MALE IN A BENT, MIDNIGHT BLAZE	135	HOW MY ANIMAL	13
STUDIES			
IN THE JAILS AND STUDIES OF HIS KEYLESS SMILES.	153	WAS A SAVIOUR	8
STUDYING			
STUDYING THE TESTICLE	154	RETURN	16
STUFF			
LOSE THE GREAT PAINS OR STUFF THE WOUND,	32	OUT OF SIGHS	12
TAKE COURAGE, AUNT, AND SEND YOUR STUFF	85	LETTER TO AUNT	63
THAT DROVE MY STUFF THROUGH SKIN AND GUT;	86	SEE, SAYS LIME	31
OUR STRIPS OF STUFF THAT TATTER AS WE MOVE	90	EUNUCH DREAMS	32
STUFFED			
IN A ROOM WITH A STUFFED FOX AND A STALE FERN,	136	AFTER FUNERAL	11
THE STUFFED LUNG OF THE FOX TWITCH AND CRY LOVE	137	AFTER FUNERAL	39

	PAGE	TITLE	LINE
STUMBLE			
AND SALT-EYED STUMBLE BEDWARD WHERE SHE LIES	107	GRIEF THIEF	12
THEY SEE THE SQUIRREL STUMBLE,	109	I, IN IMAGE	40
STUMBLE OUT WITH THEIR SPADES,	187	WINTER'S TALE	21
STUMBLED			
RASPED AT LAST, AND I STUMBLED AND SUCKED,	146	TO OTHERS	8
STUMBLES			
SEE HOW HE STUMBLES. HALLELUJAH HEE-HAW!	179	NEW QUAY	26
STUMBLING			
DUMBLY AND DIVINELY STUMBLING	125	SEED-AT-ZERO	6
STUMP			
INVISIBLE ON THE STUMP	114	SERVANT SUN	28
STUMPS			
NOT STUMPS, AFTER THE HOUR OF BATTLE,	42	A WAR OF WITS	9
STUNG			
IN SHAPING-TIME THE CIRCLE STUNG AWAKE,	121	INCARNATE DEVL	3
STUNNED			
CAST HIGH, STUNNED ON GILLED STONE; SLY SCISSORS GROUND IN FROST	135	HOW MY ANIMAL	35
AND STUNNED AND STILL ON THE GREEN, LAID VEIL	167	LONG-LEGGED	171
STY			
FLARED IN THE REEK OF THE WIVING STY WITH THE RUSH	204	GIANT'S THIGH	22
STYLUS			
THE GROOVED LAND ROTATING, THAT THE STYLUS OF LIGHTNING	110	I, IN IMAGE	68
SUAVE			
SUAVE IN HER MOVEMENTS,	235	WOMAN TAPESTRY	21
SUBSTANCE			
THE SUBSTANCE FORKED THAT MARROWED THE FIRST SUN;	93	IN BEGINNING	4
SUBSTANTIAL			
OUR RODS AND SUBSTANTIAL CENTRES,	230	OUR SANCTITY	3
SUBTLE			
IT WERE A WAND OR SUBTLE BOUGH,	150	WHEN I WOKE	14
AND THE CRUELTY OF MY SUBTLE EYES,	236	WOMAN TAPESTRY	37
SUBWAY			
NOR CITY TAR AND SUBWAY BORED TO FOSTER	100	RUNNING GRAVE	34
SUCH			
SUCH ENERGY MAY GAIN	10	COOL, OH NO	25
WILL FIND SUCH LOVE AGAINST THE GRAIN,	16	TIME TO ROT	8
SPLITTING A THOUGHT INTO SUCH HIDEOUS MOMENTS	17	IN OBLIVION	17
MUST FEEL LIKE SUCH ENCROACHMENT	20	ENCOMPASSED	4
OF SUCH GREAT GOODNESS AS IS OURS.	23	THE ONLY DEAD	18
BUT ONLY PLUMB SUCH DEPTHS	24	LITTLE PROBLEM	24
WHEN YOU HAVE GROUND SUCH BEAUTY DOWN TO DUST	25	BEAUTY TO DUST	T
WHEN YOU HAVE GROUND SUCH BEAUTY DOWN TO DUST	25	BEAUTY TO DUST	1
CAN BE BUT VANITY, SUCH AN OLD CRY,	27	OBLIVIOUS DARK	24
KNOWING SUCH JOY AS I.	30	YOUTH CALLS	11
AFTER SUCH FIGHTING AS THE WEAKEST KNOW,	32	OUT OF SIGHS	10
THAT SPILL SUCH ACRID BLOOD.	32	OUT OF SIGHS	16
THE ISLAND OF SUCH PENNY LOVE	43	FACES SHONE	4
SUCH LIGHT SHALL NOT ILLUMINATE MY FEARS	48	LIGHT, I KNOW	4
CRYING SUCH WORDS, HE LEFT THE CRYING CROWDS,	53	OUT OF THE PIT	82
A MILLION MINDS GAVE SUCK TO SUCH A BUD	79	LOVE'S FEVER	46
ALL SUCH DISEASE I DOCTOR IN MY BLOOD,	81	ALL THAT I OWE	19
AND ALL SUCH LOVE'S A SHRUB SOWN IN THE BREATH.	81	ALL THAT I OWE	20
NEVER OMIT SUCH VITAL WORDS	84	LETTER TO AUNT	44
GIVES UP ITS DEAD TO SUCH A WORKING SEA;	97	TWILIGHT LOCKS	27
GOLD ON SUCH FEATURES, AND THE LINEN SPIRIT	120	ALTARWISE	121
WERE ONCE SUCH A CREATURE, SO GAY AND FRANK	147	TO OTHERS	14
BUT BLESSED BY SUCH HEROIC HOSTS IN YOUR EVERY	148	UNLUCKILY FOR	21

	PAGE	TITLE	LINE

SUCH (CONTINUED)

IN ALL HIS TUNEFUL TURNING SO FEW AND SUCH MORNING
SONGS •• 196 FERN HILL 43
OF THE SPARROWS AND SUCH WHO SWANSING, DUSK, IN
WRANGLING HEDGES. •••••••••••••••••••••••••••••••• 201 SIR JOHNS HILL 7

SUCK

ONE BREAST GAVE SUCK THE FEVER'S ISSUE; ••••••••••• 79 LOVE'S FEVER 43
A MILLION MINDS GAVE SUCK TO SUCH A BUD ••••••••••• 79 LOVE'S FEVER 46
YOU ARE ALL THESE, SAID SHE WHO GAVE ME THE LONG
SUCK, •• 112 NOT FATHER ME 17

.SUCKED

SEAWARD THE SALMON, SUCKED SUN SLIPS, ••••••••••••• 3 PROLOGUE 34
IS SUCKED AWAY.' •••••••••••••••••••••••••••••••••• 40 YOUNG ARE OLD 4
THE DREAM HAS SUCKED THE SLEEPER OF HIS FAITH ••••• 90 EUNUCH DREAMS 29
THE MOUTH OF TIME SUCKED, LIKE A SPONGE, •••••••••• 97 TWILIGHT LOCKS 4
WHEN THE GALACTIC SEA WAS SUCKED ••••••••••••••••• 97 TWILIGHT LOCKS 7
THE SALT SUCKED DAM AND DARLINGS OF THE LAND •••••• 113 NOT FATHER ME 27
PROUD AS A SUCKED STONE AND HUGE AS SANDGRAINS. ••• 131 I MAKE THIS IN 23
RASPED AT LAST, AND I STUMBLED AND SUCKED, •••••••• 146 TO OTHERS 8

SUCKETH

THE CHILD THAT SUCKETH LONG IS SHOOTING UP, ••••••• 117 ALTARWISE 16

SUCKING

SUCKING THE DARK, KISSED ON THE CYANIDE, ••••••••• 104 WORLD PYRAMID 21

SUCKLE

ALL THAT SHAPES FROM THE CAUL AND SUCKLE, ••••••••• 107 ALL ALL AND 28

SUCKLED

TO CHILDREN WHO WERE SUCKLED ON A PLAGUE, ••••••••• 81 ALL THAT I OWE 17

SUCKLING

PRIDES OF TOMORROW SUCKLING IN HER EYES, ••••••••• 133 I MAKE THIS IN 67

SUCKS

BOY SUCKS NO SWEETNESS FROM THE WILLING MOUTH, •••• 19 THE NEOPHYTE 9
HOW AT THE MOUNTAIN SPRING THE SAME MOUTH SUCKS. 77 THE FORCE THAT 10
WHO SUCKS THE BELL-VOICED ADAM OUT OF MAGIC, •••••• 119 ALTARWISE 93

SUCTION

THE PRISM OF THE EYE NOW VOID BY SUCTION, ••••••••• 29 LONG, SKELETON 10

SUCTION'S

NOT DRAWING IN YOUR SUCTION'S KISS. •••••••••••••• 16 TIME TO ROT 6

SUDDEN

I SHALL RUN LOST IN SUDDEN •••••••••••••••••••••••• 181 VISION, PRAYER 45
IN A BLESSING OF THE SUDDEN •••••••••••••••••••••• 185 VISION, PRAYER 189
I NEVER BREAK BUT FEEL THE SUDDEN PAIN, ••••••••••• 239 MAKES INTERVALS 25

SUDDENLY

HERE WERE FOND CLIMATES AND SWEET SINGERS SUDDENLY 177 POEM IN OCT 26

SUFFER

AS YET UNGOTTEN, I DID SUFFER; •••••••••••••••••••• 68 BEFORE KNOCKED 19
THEY SUFFER THE UNDEAD WATER WHERE THE TURTLE
NIBBLES, •• 111 I, IN IMAGE 73
SUFFER, MY TOPSY-TURVIES, THAT A DOUBLE ANGEL ••••• 111 I, IN IMAGE 77
SUFFER THE SLASH OF VISION BY THE FIN-GREEN STUBBLE, 111 I, IN IMAGE 85
SUFFER THE HEAVEN'S CHILDREN THROUGH MY HEARTBEAT. 120 ALTARWISE 112
CONVENIENT BIRD AND BEAST LIE LODGED TO SUFFER •••• 144 PLEASURE-BIRD 3
SUFFER THE FIRST VISION THAT SET FIRE TO THE STARS. 170 LOVE IN ASYLUM 18
BUT IF YOU BREAK I SUFFER, •••••••••••••••••••••••• 239 MAKES INTERVALS 20

SUFFERED

WHO, UNDESERVING, HAVE SUFFERED THE EARTH'S WRONG, 41 YOUNG ARE OLD 34
FLESH IS SUFFERED, IS LAID LOW, •••••••••••••••••• 71 TAKE NEEDLES 25
MY SILLY SUIT, HARDLY YET SUFFERED FOR, ••••••••••• 152 BELOW A TIME 29

SUFFERER

LIE STILL, SLEEP BECALMED, SUFFERER WITH THE WOUND 194 SLEEP BECALMED 1

	PAGE	TITLE	LINE
SUFFERING			
THE HOLLOW WORDS COULD BEAR ALL SUFFERING	32	OUT OF SIGHS	22
THE LOVERS' HOUSE, LIE SUFFERING MY STAIN?	112	NOT FATHER ME	4
SUFFERS			
SPIRIT SUFFERS BUT IS STILL	71	TAKE NEEDLES	27
AND THE ENDLESS BEGINNING OF PRODIGIES SUFFERS OPEN.'	146	IF HEAD HURT	30
SUFFICES			
NO FOOD SUFFICES BUT THE FOOD OF DEATH;	63	WOMAN SPEAKS	2
NO FOOD SUFFICES BUT THE FOOD OF DEATH;	64	WOMAN SPEAKS	33
SUICIDES			
THE SUICIDES PARADE AGAIN, NOW RIPE FOR DYING.	43	FACES SHONE	14
SUIT			
SAID THE FAKE GENTLEMAN IN SUIT OF SPADES, ...	118	ALTARWISE	60
SUIT FOR A SERIAL SUM	151	BELOW A TIME	4
MY SILLY SUIT, HARDLY YET SUFFERED FOR, ...	152	BELOW A TIME	29
NOT YOUR WINGED LUST BUT HIS MUST NOW CHANGE SUIT.	159	TO LEDA	1
NOT YOUR WINGED LUST BUT HIS MUST NOW CHANGE SUIT.	159	TO LEDA	6
SUITOR			
AND THE WIND WAS MY SISTER SUITOR;	68	BEFORE KNOCKED	15
SULKING			
FOR MY SULKING, SKULKING, COAL BLACK SOUL!	206	LAMENT	36
SULLEN			
IN MY CRAFT OR SULLEN ART	196	CRAFT OR ART	T
IN MY CRAFT OR SULLEN ART	196	CRAFT OR ART	1
SULPHUR			
HELL IN A HORN OF SULPHUR AND THE CLOVEN MYTH, ...	122	INCARNATE DEVL	16
WHEN, WITH HIS TORCH AND HOURGLASS, LIKE A SULPHUR			
PRIEST, ...	130	SINNERS' BELL	2
SULPHURED			
A PAPER WITCH UPON HER SULPHURED BROOM	16	TIME TO ROT	11
SULPHUROUS			
THE MIDNIGHT FIGURES OF A SULPHUROUS BROOD	36	MIDNIGHT ROAD	10
SULTRY			
AND THE MULTITUDE'S SULTRY TEAR TURNS COOL ON THE			
WEEPING WALL, ...	186	HOLY SPRING	17
TO THE SULTRY, BIDING HERDS, I SAID, ...	206	LAMENT	33
SUM			
ALL HOLD THE SUM, NOTHING TO NOTHING, ...	27	OBLIVIOUS DARK	21
THAT THE SUM SANITY MIGHT ADD TO NAUGHT	96	TWELVE	1
SUIT FOR A SERIAL SUM	151	BELOW A TIME	4
SUMMER			
THE SUMMER VOICE SO WARM FROM FRUIT	15	FOR LEDA	25
NEARLY SUMMER	29	NEARLY SUMMER	T
NEARLY SUMMER, AND THE DEVIL	29	NEARLY SUMMER	1
WE SHALL PLAY CHOPIN IN OUR SUMMER GARDEN, ...	40	YOUNG ARE OLD	12
IS NOT HIS HEART IMPRISONED BY THE SUMMER	46	POET: 1935	7
BUT HE IS LEFT. SUMMER TO HIM	46	POET: 1935	16
SO SHALL HE STEP TILL SUMMER LOOSENS ITS HOLD	46	POET: 1935	18
FEELING THE SUMMER WIND, HEARING THE SWANS, ...	48	POET: 1935	59
IN THE BREASTED SUMMER LONGS NOT FOR SPRING, ...	55	NO MAN BELIEVE	9
THIS SUMMER BURIES A SPRING BIRD.	58	HERE IN SPRING	4
I SHOULD TELL SUMMER FROM THE TREES, THE WORMS	58	HERE IN SPRING	9
A WORM TELLS SUMMER BETTER THAN THE CLOCK, ...	59	HERE IN SPRING	14
I WHO WAS DEAF TO SPRING AND SUMMER, ...	68	BEFORE KNOCKED	7
DISSOLVED IN SUMMER AND THE HUNDRED SEASONS;	79	LOVE'S FEVER	49
ONCE IN THIS WINE THE SUMMER BLOOD	86	BREAD I BREAK	6
I SEE THE BOYS OF SUMMER	91	BOYS OF SUMMER	T
I SEE THE BOYS OF SUMMER IN THEIR RUIN	91	BOYS OF SUMMER	1
I SEE THE SUMMER CHILDREN IN THEIR MOTHERS	92	BOYS OF SUMMER	13
O SEE THE PULSE OF SUMMER IN THE ICE.	92	BOYS OF SUMMER	24

	PAGE	TITLE	LINE
SUMMER (CONTINUED)			
DEATH FROM A SUMMER WOMAN,	92	BOYS OF SUMMER	32
WE SUMMER BOYS IN THIS FOUR-WINDED SPINNING,	93	BOYS OF SUMMER	37
I SEE YOU BOYS OF SUMMER IN YOUR RUIN.	93	BOYS OF SUMMER	49
THE CANCER'S FUSION, OR THE SUMMER FEATHER	100	RUNNING GRAVE	32
(GIVE, SUMMER, OVER), THE CEMENTED SKIN,	101	RUNNING GRAVE	44
INCISING SUMMER.	104	WORLD PYRAMID	33
ADORE MY WINDOWS FOR THEIR SUMMER SCENE?	112	NOT FATHER ME	8
MARKING THE FLESH AND SUMMER IN THE BAY?	112	NOT FATHER ME	11
COUNTRY, YOUR SPORT IS SUMMER, AND DECEMBER'S POOLS	122	HOLD HARD	7
YOUR SPORT IS SUMMER AS THE SPRING RUNS ANGRILY.	123	HOLD HARD	24
FOREVER IT IS A WHITE CHILD IN THE DARK-SKINNED SUMMER	130	SINNERS' BELL	19
IN THE SUN STROKES OF SUMMER,	147	UNLUCKILY FOR	14
OF SPRING AND SUMMER WERE BLOOMING IN THE TALL TALES	177	POEM IN OCT	36
STREAMED AGAIN A WONDER OF SUMMER	178	POEM IN OCT	43
YEAR TO HEAVEN STOOD THERE THEN IN THE SUMMER NOON	178	POEM IN OCT	66
MANES, UNDER HIS QUENCHLESS SUMMER BARBED GOLD TO THE BONE,	204	GIANT'S THIGH	26
OF SUMMER COME IN HIS GREAT GOOD TIME	206	LAMENT	32
SUMMER IS HEAVY WITH AGE, AND LEANS UPON AUTUMN.	221	FOREST PICTURE	4
SUMMERS			
FALLS ON A RING OF SUMMERS AND LOCKED NOONS.	132	I MAKE THIS IN	30
SUMMER'S			
AT GOD SPEEDED SUMMER'S END	3	PROLOGUE	2
AT GOD SPEEDED SUMMER'S END	5	PROLOGUE	101
THIS FIRST AND STEEPLED SEASON, TO THE SUMMER'S GAME.	122	HOLD HARD	12
SUMMERTIME			
SUMMERTIME OF THE DEAD WHISPERED THE TRUTH OF HIS JOY	178	POEM IN OCT	56
SUMMERY			
SUMMERY	177	POEM IN OCT	24
SUMMON			
WE ARE THE DARK DENIERS, LET US SUMMON	92	BOYS OF SUMMER	31
SUMMON YOUR SNOWY HORSEMEN, AND THE FOUR-STRINGED HILL,	122	HOLD HARD	14
SUMMONING			
SUMMONING A CHILD'S VOICE FROM A WEBFOOT STONE,	152	BELOW A TIME	46
SUN			
IN THE TORRENT SALMON SUN,	3	PROLOGUE	3
SEAWARD THE SALMON, SUCKED SUN SLIPS,	3	PROLOGUE	34
POOR PEACE AS THE SUN SETS	5	PROLOGUE	89
MY ARK SINGS IN THE SUN	5	PROLOGUE	100
AND FAR AWAY'S TOO SHARP A SUN	12	SKY'S BRIGHT	3
AND DAUB THE UNRISEN SUN WITH LONGING.	15	FOR LEDA	13
BETWEEN THE MOON AND SUN	15	FOR LEDA	15
BUT THE SUN CRACKS IT	18	NATURAL DAY	14
AS THOUGH THE SUN WERE SPINNING UP THROUGH IT.	19	THE NEOPHYTE	8
THE SEASON'S SUN, THOUGH HE SHOULD KNOW HIS SETTING	25	THERE'S PLENTY	4
YOU TOO HAVE SEEN THE SUN A BIRD OF FIRE	30	YOUTH CALLS	1
THAT MADE ME HAPPY IN THE SUN,	32	OUT OF SIGHS	19
THEN STIRRED A LITTLE CHAOS IN THE SUN.	33	IN GARDENS	6
AND I WAS STRUCK DUMB BY THE SUN.	42	A WAR OF WITS	7
OVERWHELMED BY THE SUN, WITH A TORN BRAIN	42	A WAR OF WITS	12
LIFT WIT-HURT HEAD FOR SUN TO SYMPATHIZE,	42	A WAR OF WITS	18
AND THE SUN HEALS, CLOSING SORE EYES.	42	A WAR OF WITS	19
IT IS GOOD THAT THE SUN SHINE,	42	A WAR OF WITS	20
AND THE SHORES OF THE LAST SUN.	42	YOUNG ARE OLD	52
IN SUN AND RAIN WORKING FOR GOOD AND GAIN,	45	PLOUGHMAN GONE	3
IN SUN AND RAIN OVER THE DRY SHIRES,	45	PLOUGHMAN GONE	25
MOVES, AMONG MEN CAUGHT BY THE SUN,	46	POET: 1935	11

	PAGE	TITLE	LINE
SUN (CONTINUED)			
IS THE UNBOSOMING OF THE SUN.	46	POET: 1935	17
MAN WHO ONCE DROVE IS DRIVEN IN SUN AND RAIN.	46	PLOUGHMAN GONE	34
IT IS THE ENGINE UNDER THE UNALTERED SUN.	46	PLOUGHMAN GONE	36
WHEN THE SUN FALLS AND THE MOON STARES,	48	LIGHT, I KNOW	7
AND THERE IS ALWAYS DAY, THE SHINING OF SOME SUN,	49	LIGHT, I KNOW	18
ACROSS THE SUN WAS SPREAD A CRAZY SMILE.	50	OUT OF THE PIT	11
BREAK IN THE SUN TILL THE SUN BREAKS DOWN,	50	NO DOMINION	26
BREAK IN THE SUN TILL THE SUN BREAKS DOWN,	50	NO DOMINION	26
I HAVE DESIRED THE CIRCLE OF THE SUN.	52	OUT OF THE PIT	73
THE LIVING SUN LAMENTS THE DYING SKIES,	56	GREEK PLAY	3
THAT CRIES ALONG HER VEINS. NO SUN OR MOON	56	GREEK PLAY	8
OR THE FUNERAL OF THE SUN;	58	HERE IN SPRING	11
DICTATORSHIP OF SUN.	61	MEAT ON BONES	13
DOOM ON THE SUN!'	61	MEAT ON BONES	40
AND YOUNG GUTS DRY BENEATH THE SICKENED SUN.	63	WOMAN SPEAKS	15
WHO KNEW NOT SUN NOR MOON BY NAME,	68	BEFORE KNOCKED	8
ONE GOD, MORE MIGHTY THAN THE SUN.	70	SECRET WIND	23
THE SUN BURNS THE MORNING	74	SUN BURNS	T
THE SUN BURNS THE MORNING, A BUSH IN THE BRAIN;	74	SUN BURNS	1
UNDER THE RIBS SAIL THE MOON AND THE SUN;	74	SUN BURNS	11
THE SUN AND MOON SHED ONE WHITE LIGHT.	78	LOVE'S FEVER	9
THE SUN WAS RED, THE MOON WAS GREY,	78	LOVE'S FEVER	14
THE SEASONS NUMBERED BY THE INWARD SUN,	79	ALMANAC TIME	2
ITCHED IN THE NOISE OF WIND AND SUN.	79	LOVE'S FEVER	30
ONE SUN, ONE MANNA, WARMED AND FED.	79	LOVE'S FEVER	50
I ROUND THIS HERITAGE AS ROUNDS THE SUN	80	ALL THAT I OWE	13
THE GRAINS OF LIFE MUST SEETHE BENEATH THE SUN,	80	ALMANAC TIME	13
LIGHT BREAKS WHERE NO SUN SHINES	82	LIGHT BREAKS	T
LIGHT BREAKS WHERE NO SUN SHINES;	82	LIGHT BREAKS	1
AND BLOOD JUMPS IN THE SUN;	82	LIGHT BREAKS	29
MAN BROKE THE SUN, PULLED THE WIND DOWN.	86	BREAD I BREAK	10
A PROCESS BLOWS THE MOON INTO THE SUN,	88	A PROCESS IN	22
THERE IN THE SUN THE FRIGID THREADS	92	BOYS OF SUMMER	10
OF SUN AND MOON THEY PAINT THEIR DAMS	92	BOYS OF SUMMER	17
THE SUBSTANCE FORKED THAT MARROWED THE FIRST SUN;	93	IN BEGINNING	4
BEFORE THE PITCH WAS FORKING TO A SUN;	94	IN BEGINNING	27
AND HELD A LITTLE SABBATH WITH THE SUN,	97	TWILIGHT LOCKS	15
CAUGHT BY THE CRABBING SUN I WALK ON FIRE	98	OCTOBER WIND	3
AWAKE, MY SLEEPER, TO THE SUN,	98	TWILIGHT LOCKS	37
BALL OF THE FOOT DEPENDING FROM THE SUN,	101	RUNNING GRAVE	43
THERE GROWS THE HOURS' LADDER TO THE SUN,	102	FELLOWED SLEEP	26
OF NEW MAN STRENGTH, I SEEK THE SUN.	103	I DREAMED MY	28
HOW SOON THE SERVANT SUN	113	SERVANT SUN	T
HOW SOON THE SERVANT SUN,	113	SERVANT SUN	1
SAILED UP THE SUN;	114	A GRIEF AGO	8
ALL NERVES TO SERVE THE SUN,	114	SERVANT SUN	15
AND BY THIS BLOWCLOCK WITNESS OF THE SUN	120	ALTARWISE	111
ALL HEAVEN IN A MIDNIGHT OF THE SUN,	122	INCARNATE DEVL	17
SO SOLVE THE MYSTIC SUN, THE WIFE OF LIGHT,	128	NOW, SAY NAY	26
THE SUN THAT LEAPS ON PETALS THROUGH A NOUGHT,	128	NOW, SAY NAY	27
WITH CARVED BIRD, SAINT, AND SUN, THE WRACKSPIKED MAIDEN MOUTH	135	HOW MY ANIMAL	37
ROUND THE PARCHED WORLDS OF WALES AND DROWNED EACH SUN	136	AFTER FUNERAL	15
NOT IN THE SUN BUT IN THE DARK;	138	O CHATTERTON	34
AND THE SUN KILLED IN HER FACE.	139	TOMBSTONE TOLD	9
AND MAKES WITH A FLICK OF THE THUMB AND SUN	142	SAINT TO FALL	50
BY THE LIGHT OF THE MEAT-EATING SUN.	143	24 YEARS	5
IN THE SUN STROKES OF SUMMER,	147	UNLUCKILY FOR	14

		PAGE	TITLE	LINE
SUN (CONTINUED)				
CHILDREN KEPT FROM THE SUN	....	152	WAS A SAVIOUR	4
YOUR POLESTAR NEIGHBOUR, SUN OF ANOTHER STREET,	...	160	DEATHS AND ENT	17
TO SHUT THE SUN, PLUNGE, MOUNT YOUR DARKENED KEYS		161	DEATHS AND ENT	33
THE SUN SHIPWRECKED WEST ON A PEARL	....	162	LONG-LEGGED	15
WEEPS LIKE THE RISEN SUN AMONG	....	167	LONG-LEGGED	163
GOOD-BYE, GOOD LUCK, STRUCK THE SUN AND THE MOON,		169	LONG-LEGGED	213
AND THIS DAY'S SUN LEAPT UP THE SKY OUT OF HER THIGHS		170	MARRIAGE VIRG	4
NO LONGER WILL THE VIBRATIONS OF THE SUN DESIRE ON		170	MARRIAGE VIRG	8
THAT OTHER SUN, THE JEALOUS COURSING OF THE				
UNRIVALLED BLOOD.	....	170	MARRIAGE VIRG	14
TELL HIS STREET ON ITS BACK HE STOPPED A SUN	......	172	DAWN RAID	6
NIGHT FALL AND THE FRUIT LIKE A SUN,	....	174	FIRE RAID	56
SO THE BETRAYED MIGHT LEARN IN THE SUN BEAMS	......	176	MY BEGGAR ARM	7
BLACKBIRDS AND THE SUN OF OCTOBER	....	177	POEM IN OCT	23
OF SUN LIGHT	....	178	POEM IN OCT	49
IN THE SUN.	....	178	POEM IN OCT	64
A CLOUD AGAINST THE GLASSY SUN FLUTTERS HIS	....	179	NEW QUAY	5
OF THE SUN	....	181	VISION, PRAYER	54
PRAISED THE SUN	....	182	VISION, PRAYER	87
THAT HE WHO LEARNS NOW THE SUN AND MOON	....	183	VISION, PRAYER	119
UNBIDDEN BY THE SUN	....	184	VISION, PRAYER	149
SUN SPIN A GRAVE GREY	....	185	VISION, PRAYER	183
SUN. IN THE NAME OF THE DAMNED	....	185	VISION, PRAYER	190
BUT THE LOUD SUN	....	185	VISION, PRAYER	193
ONE. THE SUN ROARS AT THE PRAYER'S END.	....	185	VISION, PRAYER	204
AND I AM STRUCK AS LONELY AS A HOLY MAKER BY THE SUN.		186	HOLY SPRING	12
SUN THE FATHER HIS QUIVER FULL OF THE INFANTS OF				
PURE FIRE,	....	186	HOLY SPRING	19
IN THE SUN THAT IS YOUNG ONCE ONLY,	....	195	FERN HILL	12
ALL THE SUN LONG IT WAS RUNNING, IT WAS LOVELY, THE				
HAY	....	195	FERN HILL	19
AND THE SUN GREW ROUND THAT VERY DAY.	....	196	FERN HILL	32
IN THE SUN BORN OVER AND OVER,	....	196	FERN HILL	39
ROUND THE SUN, HE COMES TO MY LOVE LIKE THE DESIGNED				
SNOW,	....	200	COUNTRY SLEEP	96
HE COMES TO LEAVE HER IN THE LAWLESS SUN AWAKING		201	COUNTRY SLEEP	105
YOUR FAITH AS DEATHLESS AS THE OUTCRY OF THE RULED				
SUN.	....	201	COUNTRY SLEEP	111
IN THE COURTERS' LANES, OR TWINED IN THE OX ROASTING				
SUN	....	203	GIANT'S THIGH	13
OFF BY THE SUN AND DAUGHTERS NO LONGER GRIEVED	....	205	GIANT'S THIGH	55
IN THE MUSTARDSEED SUN,	....	208	POEM ON B'DAY	1
WILD MEN WHO CAUGHT AND SANG THE SUN IN FLIGHT,	...	208	NOT GO GENTLE	10
THE LOUDER THE SUN BLOOMS	....	211	POEM ON B'DAY	93
FROM THE COUNTRY EYES, SALT AND SUN, STAR AND WOE		215	COUNTRY HEAVEN	13
SEEK HIM, THOU SUN, IN THE DREAD WILDERNESS,	....	222	MISSING	1
AND THE SUN HAS SMOOTHED IT WITH QUIET FIRE,	......	224	IDYLL UNFORGET	23
OF THE SEA UNDER THE HARD SUN,	....	229	MY RIVER	35
TO SEE THE SUN MYSELF,	....	239	LET ME ESCAPE	11
ADMIT THE SUN	....	240	ADMIT THE SUN	T
ADMIT THE SUN INTO YOUR HIGH NEST	....	240	ADMIT THE SUN	1
SUNCOCK				
I TELL HER THIS: BEFORE THE SUNCOCK CAST	....	115	A GRIEF AGO	35
SUNDAY				
FOR, SUNDAY FACED, WITH DUSTERS IN MY GLOVE,	......	100	RUNNING GRAVE	16
UNTIL THE SUNDAY SOMBRE BELL AT DARK	....	171	THE HUNCHBACK	6
AND ON SEESAW SUNDAY NIGHTS I WOOED	....	206	LAMENT	8
FOR, OH, MY SOUL FOUND A SUNDAY WIFE	....	207	LAMENT	54

	PAGE	TITLE	LINE
SUNDAYS			
WHO HEARD THE TALL BELL SAIL DOWN THE SUNDAYS OF THE DEAD	205	GIANT'S THIGH	51
SUNDERED			
OR SUNDERED IT TO LOOK THE CLOSER,	25	BEAUTY TO DUST	4
WHEN SUNLIGHT GOES ARE SUNDERED FROM THE WORM,	89	EUNUCH DREAMS	8
AND THROUGH THE SUNDERED WATER CRAWLS	167	LONG-LEGGED	166
TO DEATH, ONE MAN THROUGH HIS SUNDERED HULKS,	211	POEM ON B'DAY	92
SUNDERING			
THE SUNDERING ULTIMATE KINGDOM OF GENESIS' THUNDER.	175	FIRE RAID	77
SUNDOWN			
CUDGEL GREAT AIR, WRECK EAST, AND TOPPLE SUNDOWN,	132	I MAKE THIS IN	33
SUNFLOWERS			
WITH THE SUNFLOWERS LAID ON,	154	RETURN	18
SUNG			
STILL BE SUNG	178	POEM IN OCT	69
ALL PRAISE OF THE HAWK ON FIRE IN HAWK-EYED DUSK BE SUNG,	202	SIR JOHNS HILL	27
SUN-GLOVED			
COMES LOVE'S ANATOMIST WITH SUN-GLOVED HAND	132	I MAKE THIS IN	44
SUNK			
AND, AFTER IT HAS SUNK, THE SANE MOON,	42	A WAR OF WITS	21
AND SUNK; WAVED FLAGS TO EVERY FIFE AND DRUM;	52	OUT OF THE PIT	70
SUNKEN			
RIDING THE SEA LIGHT ON A SUNKEN PATH,	107	GRIEF THIEF	8
SUN-LEAVED			
THE SUN-LEAVED HOLY CANDLEWOODS	141	SAINT TO FALL	19
SUNLIGHT			
IF ONLY WITH SUNLIGHT.	35	LIFT UP FACE	26
WHEN SUNLIGHT GOES ARE SUNDERED FROM THE WORM,	89	EUNUCH DREAMS	8
AS SUNLIGHT PAINTS THE SHELLING OF THEIR HEADS.	92	BOYS OF SUMMER	18
SUNNY			
THE SUNNY GENTLEMEN, THE WELSHING RICH,	90	EUNUCH DREAMS	25
SUNRISE			
TO COURT THE HONEYED HEART FROM YOUR SIDE BEFORE SUNRISE	198	COUNTRY SLEEP	13
SUNS			
TURNS NIGHT TO DAY; BLOOD IN THEIR SUNS	88	A PROCESS IN	5
OF SUNS IN THE MAN-MELTING NIGHT.	102	I DREAMED MY	8
IS CELEBRATED THERE, AND COMMUNION BETWEEN SUNS.	148	UNLUCKILY FOR	24
SUN'S			
WHILE THE SUN'S TURNED TO SALT,	27	OBLIVIOUS DARK	23
STARS' LIGHT AND SUN'S LIGHT WILL NOT SHINE	49	LIGHT, I KNOW	27
AND A HUNDRED STORKS PERCH ON THE SUN'S RIGHT HAND.	173	DAWN RAID	14
OVER THE SUN'S HOVEL AND THE SLUM OF FIRE	175	FIRE RAID	68
LIKE THE SUN'S TEARS,	193	SIDE OF TRUTH	25
OR WITH THEIR ORCHARD MAN IN THE CORE OF THE SUN'S BUSH	204	GIANT'S THIGH	24
SUNSET			
TO THE SUNSET NETS,	3	PROLOGUE	14
SLEEP ABOVE IN THE GLOW OF A FADING SUNSET;	222	FOREST PICTURE	7
SUNSHINE			
SEASON AND SUNSHINE, GRACE AND GIRL,	61	MEAT ON BONES	31
SUPER-OR-NEAR			
SUPER-OR-NEAR MAN	158	INTO HER HEAD	29
SUPPER			
THE SUPPER AND KNIVES OF A MOOD.	144	PLEASURE-BIRD	4
SUPPOSE			
NOW I DELIGHT, I SUPPOSE, IN	156	RETURN	95

	PAGE	TITLE	LINE
SURE			
THAT UNCALM STILL IT IS SURE ALONE TO STAND AND SING	186	HOLY SPRING	21
BE YOU SURE THE THIEF WILL SEEK A WAY SLY AND SURE	199	COUNTRY SLEEP	49
BE YOU SURE THE THIEF WILL SEEK A WAY SLY AND SURE	199	COUNTRY SLEEP	49
SURELY			
AND SURELY HE SAILS LIKE THE SHIP SHAPE CLOUDS. OH HE	200	COUNTRY SLEEP	99
SURFACE			
BECAUSE THEY ARE UNDER THE SURFACE	230	OUR SANCTITY	9
AND ITS EDGE CUT THE SURFACE,	232	FURIOUS MOTION	6
SURGE			
FOR THE SURGE IS SOWN WITH BARLEY,	168	LONG-LEGGED	182
AND A CLEAN SURGE OF LOVE MOVING.	236	WOMAN TAPESTRY	63
SURNAMES			
HER TWO SURNAMES STOPPED ME STILL.	139	TOMBSTONE TOLD	2
SURPLICED			
OF THE DINGLE TORN TO SINGING AND THE SURPLICED	200	COUNTRY SLEEP	75
SURPRISED			
SURPRISED IN THE OPENING OF HER NIGHTLONG EYES	170	MARRIAGE VIRG	2
SURRENDER			
TO SURRENDER NOW IS TO PAY THE EXPENSIVE OGRE TWICE.	140	NO WORK WORDS	10
SURROUND			
FRESH IMAGES SURROUND THE TREMENDOUS MOON,	47	POET: 1935	45
SURROUNDING			
SURROUNDING ME.	87	PAIN BE MUSIC	24
SUSANNAH'S			
SUSANNAH'S DROWNED IN THE BEARDED STREAM	165	LONG-LEGGED	107
SUSPENDED			
SUSPENDED FROM THE DEVIL'S PRECIPICE,	35	LIFT UP FACE	13
SUSPICIOUS			
SUSPICIOUS BUT THAT SOON PASSES.	30	NEARLY SUMMER	20
SUSPICIOUS HANDS TUG AT THE NEIGHBOURING VICES,	38	THE GOSSIPERS	3
SWADDLING			
SLEEP TO A NEWBORN SLEEP IN A SWADDLING LOIN-LEAF STROKED AND SANG	157	INTO HER HEAD	22
SWAG			
WITH SWAG OF BUBBLES IN A SEEDY SACK	108	GRIEF THIEF	17
SWALLOW			
UP TO THE SWALLOW THRONGED LOFT BY THE SHADOW OF MY HAND,	196	FERN HILL	47
SWALLOWED			
AND SWALLOWED DRY THE WATERS OF THE BREAST.	97	TWILIGHT LOCKS	6
SWALLOWER			
OR DECKED ON A CLOUD SWALLOWER,	151	BELOW A TIME	12
SWAM			
THEN INTO BLIND STREETS I SWAM	155	RETURN	44
AND THE MOON SWAM OUT OF ITS HULK.	162	LONG-LEGGED	16
THE VOICES OF ALL THE DROWNED SWAM ON THE WIND.	194	SLEEP BECALMED	8
SWAN			
THE SWAN MAKES STRINGS OF WATER IN HER WAKE;	15	FOR LEDA	14
DANCES A MEASURE WITH THE SWAN	15	FOR LEDA	30
AND EVERY NIGHTINGALE A SWAN	234	NO, PIGEON	15
SWANKED			
THEN, BUSHILY SWANKED IN BEAR WIG AND TAILS,	151	BELOW A TIME	19
SWANS			
AND THE DUMB SWANS DRUB BLUE	4	PROLOGUE	35
FEELING THE SUMMER WIND, HEARING THE SWANS,	48	POET: 1935	59
ALONE BETWEEN NURSES AND SWANS	171	THE HUNCHBACK	26
SWAN'S			
HE STEPS SO NEAR THE WATER THAT A SWAN'S WING	46	POET: 1935	2

		PAGE	TITLE	LINE
SWANSING				
OF THE SPARROWS AND SUCH WHO SWANSING, DUSK, IN WRANGLING HEDGES.	....	201	SIR JOHNS HILL	7
SWARD				
LIKE A GREEN TREE THROUGH THE SWARD,	....	72	TAKE NEEDLES	42
SWARMS				
SWARMS ON THE KINGDOM COME	....	181	VISION, PRAYER	40
SWAY				
AND I IN THE WANTING SWAY	....	156	RETURN	66
SWEAT				
ALL LOVE AND SWEAT	....	26	PERSONAL EPIT	15
AND THE SWEAT ON THE BROW MAKES A SIGN,	....	74	SUN BURNS	4
I DREAMED MY GENESIS IN SWEAT OF SLEEP, BREAKING		102	I DREAMED MY	1
I DREAMED MY GENESIS IN SWEAT OF DEATH, FALLEN	....	103	I DREAMED MY	25
SWEEP				
SWEEP AWAY LIKE A CREAM CLOUD;	....	156	RETURN	89
SWEET				
SWEET, AUTOMATIC ME KNOWS BEST.	....	10	COOL, OH NO	18
HER THIGHS AND UNDERCLOTHES WERE SWEET,	....	11	CABARET	6
YOUR SWEET INDUCIVE THIGHS	....	11	AIR BREATHE	12
TO FIND A SWEET BLANKNESS IN THE BLOOD AND SHELL,		27	OBLIVIOUS DARK	12
WERE VAGUENESS ENOUGH AND THE SWEET LIES PLENTY,		32	OUT OF SIGHS	21
AND THIS IS PLENTY, THEN, CLOVES AND SWEET OILS, THE BEES' HONEY,	....	36	MIDNIGHT ROAD	5
NOR CAN I SMOTHER THE SWEET WAKING.'	....	61	MEAT ON BONES	32
SWEET IS THE WAXEN BLOOD, HONEY THE FALLING FLESH;		63	WOMAN SPEAKS	3
AND SWEET SHALL FALL CONTAGION FROM HIS SIDE,	.....	73	LORD RED HAIL	5
SWEET ARE THEIR FATHERED FACES IN THEIR WINGS.'	...	102	FELLOWED SLEEP	14
AND ALL SWEET HELL, DEAF AS AN HOUR'S EAR,	....	114	SERVANT SUN	33
AND ALL LOVE'S SINNERS IN SWEET CLOTH KNEEL TO A HYLEG IMAGE,	....	130	SINNERS' BELL	28
IN QUICK, SWEET, CRUEL LIGHT TILL THE LOCKED GROUND SPROUT OUT,	....	135	HOW MY ANIMAL	18
THE SWEET, FISH-GILLED BOATS BRINGING BLOOD	....	142	SAINT TO FALL	22
THAT BURY THE SWEET STREET SLOWLY, SEE	....	142	SAINT TO FALL	33
TILL THE SWEET TOOTH OF MY LOVE BIT DRY,	....	146	TO OTHERS	7
IT WAS SWEET TO DROWN IN THE READYMADE HANDY WATER		152	BELOW A TIME	44
HERE WERE FOND CLIMATES AND SWEET SINGERS SUDDENLY		177	POEM IN OCT	26
BURNING ITS SWEET PATH CLEARER THAN BEFORE.	....	232	FURIOUS MOTION	17
I TAKE YOU TO MYSELF, SWEET PAIN,	....	233	NO THOUGHT	5
THE SWEET, GLOWING VIGOUR	....	235	WOMAN TAPESTRY	25
LIKE A SWEET, SENSITIVE PLANT	....	237	WOMAN TAPESTRY	71
THE SWEET, GLOWING VIGOUR,	....	237	WOMAN TAPESTRY	80
SWEETENS				
INNOCENCE SWEETENS MY LAST BLACK BREATH,	....	207	LAMENT	58
SWEETER				
SHALL THE BLIND HORSE SING SWEETER?	....	144	PLEASURE-BIRD	2
SWEETHEARTING				
TIME AND THE CRABS AND THE SWEETHEARTING CRIB	.....	95	RUB OF LOVE	25
SWEETHEARTS				
ALL LEGENDS' SWEETHEARTS ON A TREE OF STORIES,	....	125	TODAY, INSECT	25
SWEETHEARTS'				
AND ON THE SWEETHEARTS' BED TO LIE AND GRIN,	....	34	THIRST PARCHES	12
DEAD ON THE SWEETHEARTS' TOES.	....	95	RUB OF LOVE	28
SWEETLY				
SWEETLY THE DIVER'S BELL IN THE STEEPLE OF SPINDRIFT		110	I, IN IMAGE	62
THE PRESENT MOUTH, AND THE SWEETLY BLOWN TRUMPET OF LIES,	....	133	MAKE ME A MASK	6
YOU SHALL BE TAKEN SWEETLY AGAIN	....	228	NOT DESPAIR	12

	PAGE	TITLE	LINE
SWEETNESS			
BOY SUCKS NO SWEETNESS FROM THE WILLING MOUTH, ...	19	THE NEOPHYTE	9
AND ANY SWEETNESS THAT IT HAS	40	YOUNG ARE OLD	3
SWELL			
AND SPEAK THEIR MIDNIGHT NOTHINGS AS THEY SWELL;	89	EUNUCH DREAMS	14
SWELLING			
SWELLING IN FLEA-SPECKED LINEN	154	RETURN	7
SWELTER			
BUT A HILLOCKY BULL IN THE SWELTER	206	LAMENT	31
SWEPT			
ASK THE TALL FISH SWEPT FROM THE BIBLE EAST, ...	121	ALTARWISE	134
AND SWEPT INTO OUR WOUNDS AND HOUSES, ...	186	HOLY SPRING	7
PARISH OF SNOW. THE CARVED MOUTHS IN THE ROCK ARE			
WIND SWEPT STRINGS.	189	WINTER'S TALE	64
SWERVE			
TILL EVERY BEAST BLARED DOWN IN A SWERVE	163	LONG-LEGGED	57
SWIFT			
THEN SWIFT FROM A BURSTING SEA WITH BOTTLECORK BOATS	151	BELOW A TIME	13
FOR WE SAW HIM THROW TO THE SWIFT FLOOD	162	LONG-LEGGED	21
SWILL			
SHALL DROWN THE BOYS OF BATTLE IN THEIR SWILL, ...	73	LORD RED HAIL	8
SWIM			
THEN SWIM YOUR HEAD, ...	16	TIME TO ROT	17
SWIMMERS'			
TIME FOR THE SWIMMERS' HANDS, MUSIC FOR SILVER LOCK	15	SPIRE CRANES	7
SWIMMING			
AND SWIMMING DOWN THE GUTTERS HE LOOKS UP	51	OUT OF THE PIT	45
SWIMS			
THE BOAT SWIMS INTO THE SIX-YEAR WEATHER, ...	166	LONG-LEGGED	129
SWINE			
THAT OUT OF A BOWER OF RED SWINE	61	MEAT ON BONES	28
OF THE HOBNAIL TALES: NO GOOSEHERD OR SWINE WILL TURN	197	COUNTRY SLEEP	10
SWINEHERD			
TIME BY, THEIR DUST WAS FLESH THE SWINEHERD ROOTED			
SLY, ...	204	GIANT'S THIGH	21
SWING			
THE SWING OF MILK WAS TUFTED IN THE PAP, ...	104	WORLD PYRAMID	10
THAT HER LOVE SING AND SWING THROUGH A BROWN CHAPEL,	136	AFTER FUNERAL	25
HOUSED IN HAMLETS OF HEAVEN SWING THE LOFT LAMPS,	215	COUNTRY HEAVEN	16
SWINGS			
OR ROCKS, SWINGS AND ROCKS, BEFORE THE WORLD TOTTERS.	39	GAS FADES	34
THE KNOBBLY APE THAT SWINGS ALONG HIS SEX	96	RUB OF LOVE	37
THE DUST OF THEIR KETTLES AND CLOCKS SWINGS TO AND			
FRO	205	GIANT'S THIGH	46
SWINISH			
THE SWINISH PLAINS OF CARRION	183	VISION, PRAYER	103
SWISS			
BUT ONE THE SWISS WEAR WHEN THEY YODEL, ...	83	LETTER TO AUNT	16
SWITCHBACK			
BY FULL TILT RIVER AND SWITCHBACK SEA	208	POEM ON B'DAY	2
SWITCHED			
THE JAWS WILL HAVE SHUT, AND LIFE BE SWITCHED OUT.	39	GAS FADES	14
SWIVEL			
THE FELLOW HALVES THAT, CLOVEN AS THEY SWIVEL	105	WORLD PYRAMID	49
SWOLLEN			
ABOVE THEM POISE THE SWOLLEN CLOUDS	36	MIDNIGHT ROAD	12
SWORD			
AGAINST THE RUSTY SWORD AND THE OLD HORSE	45	PLOUGHMAN GONE	8
LET IT BE A SWORD OF FIRE, ...	71	TAKE NEEDLES	21

	PAGE	TITLE	LINE
SWORDFISH			
HAS THE DRAGONFLY AND THE SWORDFISH	231	OUR SANCTITY	37
SWORDS			
DRUM HARSHLY ON THE AIR, THE LIGHTNING SWORDS	51	OUT OF THE PIT	15
SWUM			
FEED IN THE ARMPITS OF DROWNED GIRLS, I'VE SWUM ...	52	OUT OF THE PIT	69
SWUNG			
SWUNG BY MY FATHER FROM HIS DOME.	68	BEFORE KNOCKED	12
IN A CAVERNOUS, SWUNG	209	POEM ON B'DAY	37
SYLLABIC			
SHEDS THE SYLLABIC BLOOD AND DRAINS HER WORDS.	98	OCTOBER WIND	8
SYLLABLE			
AND WITH NOT ONE FEAR-BEGGARED SYLLABLE	76	LASHED RINGS	10
SYLLABLES			
AFRAID, LETTING OUR SYLLABLES BE SOFT	31	BEING BUT MEN	2
WAS THE WORLD'S TO ME, AND SYLLABLES	42	A WAR OF WITS	2
HER SYLLABLES, AND TO THE GODS HER LOVE;	57	GREEK PLAY	27
THE SYLLABLES BE SAID AND SAID AGAIN:	80	ALMANAC TIME	14
AND, LASHED TO SYLLABLES, THE LYNX TONGUE CRY	139	FIVE & COUNTRY	8
SYMBOL			
NOT, AS A SYMBOL, STONE/ SPEAKING OR NO, ...	9	MINUTE'S HOUR	15
RATHER THAN CHARNEL-HOUSE AS SYMBOL	29	LONG, SKELETON	12
OF SHADES, SYMBOL OF DESIRE BEYOND MY HOURS	148	UNLUCKILY FOR	35
SYMBOLED			
VOYAGING CLOCKWISE OFF THE SYMBOLED HARBOUR, ...	109	I, IN IMAGE	32
SYMBOLISE			
AND SYMBOLISE THE MADDENING FACTORS	33	HELD-OUT HAND	15
SYMBOLS			
SOFT SHINING SYMBOLS OF HER PEACE WITH YOU, ...	20	THE NEOPHYTE	21
SYMBOLS ARE SELECTED FROM THE YEARS'	58	HERE IN SPRING	5
NOW THAT MY SYMBOLS HAVE OUTELBOWED SPACE, ...	124	TODAY, INSECT	2
SYMMETRICAL			
AND WHITE, SYMMETRICAL LIPS	236	WOMAN TAPESTRY	44
WITH YOUR SYMMETRICAL DEVOTION	236	WOMAN TAPESTRY	48
SYMMETRY			
HIS AWKWARD HEART INTO SOME SYMMETRY.	77	LASHED RINGS	17
SYMPATHIZE			
LIFT WIT-HURT HEAD FOR SUN TO SYMPATHIZE, ...	42	A WAR OF WITS	18
SYMPATHY			
(NOTES NOT IN SYMPATHY, DISCORD, UNEASE), ...	35	LIFT UP FACE	21
SYNAGOGUE			
AND THE SYNAGOGUE OF THE EAR OF CORN	191	REFUSAL MOURN	9
SYNTHETIC			
FEAR NOT THE FLAT, SYNTHETIC BLOOD, ...	106	ALL ALL AND	14
T.			
IN T. S. E. AND EZRA POUND.	83	LETTER TO AUNT	10
TABLE			
DAZZLE THIS FACE OF VOICES ON THE MOON-TURNED TABLE,	110	I, IN IMAGE	69
FROM THE PREACHER'S TABLE.	138	O CHATTERTON	39
SOAKED MY TABLE THE UGLIER SIDE OF A HILL	144	COLOUR OF SAY	2
OVER THE PAST TABLE I REPEAT THIS PRESENT GRACE.	145	PLEASURE-BIRD	25
TABLECLOTH			
AND PERRINS ON THE COCKLED TABLECLOTH	179	NEW QUAY	3
TACKLE			
AND GALE I TACKLE, THE WHOLE WORLD THEN, ...	211	POEM ON B'DAY	96
TACKLED			
TACKLED WITH CLOUDS, WHO KNEEL	3	PROLOGUE	13
TAIL			
THE MARK HIS FLYING TAIL HAS LEFT	14	RAIN CUTS	21
TAIL, NILE, AND SNOUT, A SADDLER OF THE RUSHES, ...	111	I, IN IMAGE	98

	PAGE	TITLE	LINE
TAIL (CONTINUED)			
STALKING MY CHILDREN'S FACES WITH A TAIL OF BLOOD,	122	HOLD HARD	20
OF HEAD AND TAIL MADE WITNESSES TO THIS	124	TODAY, INSECT	7
WITH LOUD, TORN TOOTH AND TAIL AND COBWEB DRUM	133	I MAKE THIS IN	57
EYED, WHILE THE TEARS DRAG ON THE TAIL,	155	RETURN	42
WITH BITER'S TOOTH AND TAIL	176	BREATH SHED	7
TAILOR			
COMES, LIKE A SCISSORS STALKING, TAILOR AGE,	100	RUNNING GRAVE	6
IN THE GROIN OF THE NATURAL DOORWAY I CROUCHED LIKE A TAILOR	143	24 YEARS	3
TAILORS			
I ASTOUNDED THE SITTING TAILORS,	151	BELOW A TIME	17
I SET BACK THE CLOCK FACED TAILORS,	151	BELOW A TIME	18
TAILORS'			
THE CLOUD PERCHED TAILORS' MASTER WITH NERVES FOR COTTON.	152	BELOW A TIME	35
TAILOR'S			
AND AT THEIR BAYING MOVE A TAILOR'S INCH	44	TO FOLLOW FOX	2
I WAS PIERCED BY THE IDOL TAILOR'S EYES,	152	BELOW A TIME	38
TAILS			
TO FOLLOW THE FOX AT THE HOUNDS' TAILS	44	TO FOLLOW FOX	1
WISELY AT THE DOGS' TAILS, LEADS	44	TO FOLLOW FOX	15
THEN, BUSHILY SWANKED IN BEAR WIG AND TAILS,	151	BELOW A TIME	19
TAKE			
BUT COOLER WHEN I TAKE IT BACK,	10	COOL, OH NO	5
TO MAKE OUR SENSES TAKE TOO MUCH,	13	RAIN CUTS	10
THEY HARDEN AND TAKE SHAPE AGAIN	19	IMAGES IN AIR	11
TAKE NOW CONTENT, NO LONGER POSTURING	29	LONG, SKELETON	7
OF NEOPHYTES TAKE ALTERED ROADS.	37	WINDMILLS TURN	33
LION OR LOUSE? TAKE YOUR OWN ADVICE;	58	TO ARCHITECTS	17
BEFORE DEATH TAKES YOU, O TAKE BACK THIS.	61	MEAT ON BONES	41
TAKE THE NEEDLES AND THE KNIVES	70	TAKE NEEDLES	T
TAKE THE NEEDLES AND THE KNIVES,	70	TAKE NEEDLES	1
TAKE THE SCISSORS AND THE PAN,	71	TAKE NEEDLES	9
TAKE THE SCISSORS TO THIS GLOBE,	72	TAKE NEEDLES	37
TAKE THE NEEDLES TO THIS TREE	72	TAKE NEEDLES	49
THEN TAKE THE GUSHER OR THE FIELD	74	WE MOTHERNAKED	9
REMOVE YOUR BRAINS, TAKE OUT YOUR HEART;	84	LETTER TO AUNT	60
TAKE COURAGE, AUNT, AND SEND YOUR STUFF	85	LETTER TO AUNT	63
GIRLS TAKE TO BROOMSTICKS WHEN THE THIEF OF NIGHT	96	TWELVE	3
HAPPY CADAVER'S HUNGER AS YOU TAKE	101	RUNNING GRAVE	49
THE DEAR, DAFT TIME I TAKE TO NUDGE THE SENTENCE,	124	TODAY, INSECT	4
AND TAKE ANOTHER NIBBLE AT MY FLASK.	137	O CHATTERTON	16
I BITTERLY TAKE TO TASK MY POVERTY AND CRAFT:	140	NO WORK WORDS	3
TO TAKE TO GIVE IS ALL, RETURN WHAT IS HUNGRILY GIVEN	140	NO WORK WORDS	4
IF I TAKE TO BURN OR RETURN THIS WORLD WHICH IS EACH MAN'S WORK.	140	NO WORK WORDS	12
TO TAKE ME AWAY AS YOU WHISPERED AND WROTE	149	PAPER & STICKS	12
NOTHING I CARED, IN THE LAMB WHITE DAYS, THAT TIME WOULD TAKE ME	196	FERN HILL	46
HE COMES TO TAKE	201	COUNTRY SLEEP	103
BUT MY GREATEST DELIGHT IS TO TAKE A GOOD BITE	221	SONG OF DOG	13
THEN TAKE THEM AWAY QUICKLY	229	MY RIVER	23
AND TAKE AWAY YOUR EXOTIC PLUMAGE,	232	YOUR VOICE	12
TAKE YOU INTO MY OWN PLACE	232	YOUR VOICE	14
I TAKE YOU TO MYSELF, SWEET PAIN,	233	NO THOUGHT	5
TAKE HEED OF STRENGTH!	241	ADMIT THE SUN	19
TAKEN			
THEY CRY TO BE TAKEN, AND THE DEVIL BREAKS	30	NEARLY SUMMER	21
WHEN HEAVEN--OPEN WIDE THE GATES--HAS TAKEN FLIGHT,	34	THIRST PARCHES	4

	PAGE	TITLE	LINE
TAKEN (CONTINUED)			
AND COUNT THE TAKEN, FORSAKEN MYSTERIES IN A BAD DARK.	140	NO WORK WORDS	9
IN THE TAKEN BODY AT MANY AGES,	158	INTO HER HEAD	40
AND TAKEN BY LIGHT IN HER ARMS AT LONG AND DEAR LAST	170	LOVE IN ASYLUM	16
YOU SHALL BE TAKEN SWEETLY AGAIN	228	NOT DESPAIR	12
TAKES			
BEFORE DEATH TAKES YOU, O TAKE BACK THIS.	61	MEAT ON BONES	41
AND TAKES THE HEAT AWAY.	230	MY RIVER	43
MY NET THAT TAKES TO BREAK	233	NO THOUGHT	7
TAKING			
ON THE CONSUMPTIVES' TERRACE TAKING THEIR TWO FAREWELLS,	109	I, IN IMAGE	34
TAKING JEYES' FLUID AS NARCOTIC;	137	O CHATTERTON	3
TAKING NO PLUME FOR INDEX IN LOVE'S CHANGE	159	TO LEDA	5
TALE			
IN TRUST AND TALE HAVE I DIVIDED SENSE,	124	TODAY, INSECT	5
A WINTER'S TALE	187	WINTER'S TALE	T
IT IS A WINTER'S TALE	187	WINTER'S TALE	1
IN THE RIVER WENDED VALES WHERE THE TALE WAS TOLD.	187	WINTER'S TALE	10
AND SPELLS ON THE WINDS OF THE DEAD HIS WINTER'S TALE.	189	WINTER'S TALE	59
AND THE HOME OF PRAYERS AND FIRES, THE TALE ENDED.	190	WINTER'S TALE	110
OF THE NIGHTINGALE'S DIN AND TALE! THE UPGIVEN GHOST	200	COUNTRY SLEEP	74
HILL OF CYPRESSES! THE DIN AND TALE IN THE SKIMMED	200	COUNTRY SLEEP	76
TALES			
WE HAVE THE FAIRY TALES BY HEART	59	FAIRY TALES	T
WE HAVE THE FAIRY TALES BY HEART,	59	FAIRY TALES	1
SHALL WE LEARN FAIRY TALES OFF PAT,	60	FAIRY TALES	37
HOLD HARD, MY COUNTRY CHILDREN IN THE WORLD OF TALES,	122	HOLD HARD	10
MY CROSS OF TALES BEHIND THE FABULOUS CURTAIN.'	125	TODAY, INSECT	26
OF SPRING AND SUMMER WERE BLOOMING IN THE TALL TALES	177	POEM IN OCT	36
IN THE LAND OF THE HEARTHSTONE TALES, AND SPELLED ASLEEP,	197	COUNTRY SLEEP	2
OF THE HOBNAIL TALES: NO GOOSEHERD OR SWINE WILL TURN	197	COUNTRY SLEEP	10
NOW THE TALES PRAISE	198	COUNTRY SLEEP	33
OF THE HEARTHSTONE TALES MY OWN, LOST LOVE; AND THE SOUL WALKS	199	COUNTRY SLEEP	53
TALE'S			
LET THE TALE'S SAILOR FROM A CHRISTIAN VOYAGE	121	ALTARWISE	127
TALK			
SINCE, ON A QUIET NIGHT, I HEARD THEM TALK	22	ON QUIET NIGHT	1
WHO HAVE NO TALK BUT THAT OF DEATH.	23	ON QUIET NIGHT	22
AFTER THE PERILS OF FRIENDS' TALK	42	A WAR OF WITS	15
AND HAS THE MAD TREES' TALK BY HEART.	47	POET: 1935	28
AND WOMEN TALK OF HORROR TO THE DUSK.	57	GREEK PLAY	16
A PIGEON CALLS AND WOMEN TALK OF DEATH.	57	GREEK PLAY	32
THAT PUT AN END TO TALK.	66	HAND SIGNED	8
WITH TONGUES THAT TALK ALL TONGUES.	66	GODS THUMP	14
AND TALK OF LIGHT TO A MAD MINER.	96	TWELVE	8
I TALK TO HIM AS I CLEAN THE GRATE	149	PAPER & STICKS	10
TALKATIVE			
AND INTO ITS TALKATIVE SEVEN TOMBS	169	LONG-LEGGED	211
TALKED			
TO HERMITS' HUTS, AND TALKED TO ANCIENT MEN.	53	OUT OF THE PIT	91
TALKED AND TORE THOUGH HER EYES SMILED.	139	TOMBSTONE TOLD	20
TALKING			
INCARNATE DEVIL IN A TALKING SNAKE,	121	INCARNATE DEVL	1
TALKS			
MY BUSY HEART WHO SHUDDERS AS SHE TALKS	98	OCTOBER WIND	7

	PAGE	TITLE	LINE
TALKS (CONTINUED)			
THIS NIGHT AND EACH VAST NIGHT UNTIL THE STERN BELL			
TALKS	199	COUNTRY SLEEP	51
TALL			
LIKE STALKS OF TALL, DRY STRAW, ...	3	PROLOGUE	22
FOR MY TALL TOWER'S SAKE CAST IN HER STONE?	112	NOT FATHER ME	2
FOR MY TALL TURRETS CARRY AS YOUR SIN?	112	NOT FATHER ME	6
ASK THE TALL FISH SWEPT FROM THE BIBLE EAST, ...	121	ALTARWISE	134
AND THE TALL GRAINS FOAMED IN THEIR BILLS;	165	LONG-LEGGED	97
STRAIGHT AND TALL FROM HIS CROOKED BONES	172	THE HUNCHBACK	34
OF SPRING AND SUMMER WERE BLOOMING IN THE TALL TALES	177	POEM IN OCT	36
WHO HEARD THE TALL BELL SAIL DOWN THE SUNDAYS OF THE			
DEAD	205	GIANT'S THIGH	51
THE TALL MAUVE IRIS OF A SLEEPING CLIME.	222	IN DREAMS	2
TALLER			
TALLER THIS THUNDERCLAP SPRING, AND HOW	211	POEM ON B'DAY	103
TALLOW			
TILL TALLOW I BLEW FROM THE WAX'S TOWER	119	ALTARWISE	79
TALLOW-EYED			
HE IN A BOOK OF WATER TALLOW-EYED	119	ALTARWISE	72
TANGLED			
TANGLED WITH CHIRRUP AND FRUIT, ...	3	PROLOGUE	6
ON CASTING TIDES, ARE TANGLED IN THE SHELLS, ...	105	WORLD PYRAMID	50
IN THE GROIN'S ENDLESS COIL A MAN IS TANGLED.'	132	I MAKE THIS IN	53
TANGLING			
TANGLING THOUGH THIS SPUN SLIME	211	POEM ON B'DAY	84
TAP			
WINDSHAKE OF SAILSHAPED EARS, MUFFLE-TOED TAP	136	AFTER FUNERAL	2
TAP HAPPILY OF ONE PEG IN THE THICK	136	AFTER FUNERAL	3
TAPE			
ROBBED OF THE FOXY TONGUE, HIS FOOTED TAPE	100	RUNNING GRAVE	9
TAPESTRY			
WOMAN ON TAPESTRY	234	WOMAN TAPESTRY	T
TAPPED			
WITH LIQUID HANDS TAPPED ON THE WOMB, ...	68	BEFORE KNOCKED	2
THE CODE OF NIGHT TAPPED ON MY TONGUE;	79	LOVE'S FEVER	40
DEATH HAIRY-HEELED, AND THE TAPPED GHOST IN WOOD,	128	NOW, SAY NAY	33
TAPPING			
WITH HER RAMPART TO HIS TAPPING, ...	125	SEED-AT-ZERO	3
WITH HER RAMPART TO HIS TAPPING, ...	125	SEED-AT-ZERO	10
TAPS			
THE CRUTCH THAT MARROW TAPS UPON THEIR SLEEP, ...	104	WORLD PYRAMID	14
TAR			
NOR CITY TAR AND SUBWAY BORED TO FOSTER	100	RUNNING GRAVE	34
TARRED			
AS TARRED WITH BLOOD AS THE BRIGHT THORNS I WEPT;	120	ALTARWISE	101
TASK			
I BITTERLY TAKE TO TASK MY POVERTY AND CRAFT:	140	NO WORK WORDS	3
TASSELLED			
TASSELLED IN CELLAR AND SNIPPING SHOP	151	BELOW A TIME	11
TASTE			
AND TASTE UPON OUR LIPS, THIS MINUTE, ...	14	RAIN CUTS	37
IS BLIND WITH TEARS TOO FRAIL TO TASTE.	15	FOR LEDA	33
AND ALL MY THIN PREROGATIVE OF TASTE.	18	NATURAL DAY	18
AND DOES NOT SHOW THE FRUIT TO TASTE;	233	NO THOUGHT	13
TASTED			
A LITTLE COMES, IS TASTED AND FOUND GOOD;	31	OUT OF SIGHS	5
AGE SOURS BEFORE YOUTH'S TASTED IN THE MOUTH	40	YOUNG ARE OLD	2
TATOOED			
A CROSS IS TATOOED ON THE BREAST OF THE CHILD, ...	74	SUN BURNS	12

	PAGE	TITLE	LINE
TATTER			
OUR STRIPS OF STUFF THAT TATTER AS WE MOVE	90	EUNUCH DREAMS	32
TAUGHT			
WHO TAUGHT ME TROUBLE?	18	NATURAL DAY	25
AND HE WHO TAUGHT THEIR LIPS TO SING	167	LONG-LEGGED	162
TAUT			
THE OLD FLOWERS' LEGS TOO TAUT TO DANCE, ...	47	POET: 1935	40
'SEE,' DRUMMED THE TAUT MASKS, 'HOW THE DEAD ASCEND:	132	I MAKE THIS IN	52
TAWNY			
AND THE WHISPER CAUGHT IN ITS PAGEANT OF TAWNY PEARL,	224	IDYLL UNFORGET	44
TAXED			
FIVE SOVEREIGN FINGERS TAXED THE BREATH, ...	66	HAND SIGNED	2
TAXI			
WHERE, WHAT'S MY GOD AMONG THIS TAXI STEPPING, ...	52	OUT OF THE PIT	49
TAXIS			
TAXIS AND LILIES TO TINNED MUSIC STEPPED	51	OUT OF THE PIT	24
TAXIS AND LILIES, NOISE AND NO NOISE, ...	53	OUT OF THE PIT	95
TEA			
DIRTIER WITH GARAGES AND CHEAP TEA SIGNS.	37	WINDMILLS TURN	15
TEACH			
IN AUTUMN TEACH THREE SEASONS' FIRES	58	HERE IN SPRING	7
AND THE SLUG SHOULD TEACH ME DESTRUCTION.	58	HERE IN SPRING	13
TEACH ME THE LOVE THAT IS EVERGREEN AFTER THE FALL			
LEAVED	205	GIANT'S THIGH	53
TEACHES			
TEACHES WITH NO TELLING	148	UNLUCKILY FOR	44
THAT TEACHES ME TO WAIT, ...	237	PILLAR BREAKS	10
TEAR			
I TEAR HER BREAST, ...	13	SKY'S BRIGHT	22
TEAR WITH A GREAT SOUND THROUGH THE SKIES, ...	51	OUT OF THE PIT	16
TEAR BY THE ROOTS THESE TWIN GROWTHS IN YOUR GUT;	60	FAIRY TALES	36
LET FALL THE TEAR OF TIME; THE SLEEPER'S EYE, ...	101	FELLOWED SLEEP	2
GRIEF WITH DISHEVELLED HANDS TEAR OUT THE ALTAR GHOST	130	SINNERS' BELL	5
A BLAZING RED HARSH HEAD TEAR UP	140	TOMBSTONE TOLD	29
PUT A TEAR FOR JOY IN THE UNEARTHLY FLOOD	153	WAS A SAVIOUR	22
NOW BREAK A GIANT TEAR FOR THE LITTLE KNOWN FALL,	153	WAS A SAVIOUR	32
AND THE MULTITUDE'S SULTRY TEAR TURNS COOL ON THE			
WEEPING WALL, ...	186	HOLY SPRING	17
FISHING IN THE TEAR OF THE TOWY. ONLY A HOOT OWL	203	SIR JOHNS HILL	51
TEAR-CULLED			
FAINT ARROWY MOONSTONE ON A TEAR-CULLED CADENCE,	225	SLENDER WIND	3
TEARDROPS			
WITH PINS FOR TEARDROPS IS THE LONG WOUND'S WOMAN.	120	ALTARWISE	104
TEARS			
WHERE TEARS HAVE COME TO DRY.	12	SKY'S BRIGHT	17
TO WET THE SKY WITH TEARS, ...	15	FOR LEDA	12
IS BLIND WITH TEARS TOO FRAIL TO TASTE.	15	FOR LEDA	33
'WHAT YOU HAVE FOUND,' AGE ANSWERS THROUGH HIS TEARS,	30	YOUTH CALLS	15
MY HEART HURLS FROM MY SIDE AND TEARS	48	LIGHT, I KNOW	8
THERE CAN BE FEW TEARS LEFT: ELECTRA WEPT	57	GREEK PLAY	17
A COUNTRY'S TEARS AND VOICED A WORLD'S DESPAIR	57	GREEK PLAY	18
PITY THE POOR UNPITIED WHO ARE STRANGE WITH TEARS.	57	GREEK PLAY	28
THAT I MAY DROWN, LET LOOSE HER FLOOD OF TEARS. ...	65	WOMAN SPEAKS	55
HANDS HAVE NO TEARS TO FLOW.	66	HAND SIGNED	16
YOUTH DID CONDENSE; THE TEARS OF SPRING	79	LOVE'S FEVER	48
MY SISTERS' TEARS THAT SING UPON MY HEAD, ...	80	ALL THAT I OWE	7
A LOVER'S THOUGHT TEARS DOWN THE DATED SHEET, ...	80	ALMANAC TIME	7
DIVINING IN A SMILE THE OIL OF TEARS.	82	LIGHT BREAKS	18
TWENTY-FOUR YEARS REMIND THE TEARS OF MY EYES.	143	24 YEARS	1
MY DEAR WOULD I CHANGE MY TEARS OR YOUR IRON HEAD.	146	IF HEAD HURT	18

	PAGE	TITLE	LINE
TEARS (CONTINUED)			
I SEE THE TIGRON IN TEARS	148	UNLUCKILY FOR	29
IN THE CHURCHES OF HIS TEARS,	153	WAS A SAVIOUR	18
EYED, WHILE THE TEARS DRAG ON THE TAIL,	155	RETURN	42
WILL DIVE UP TO HIS TEARS.	160	DEATHS AND ENT	18
ON THE MADHOUSE BOARDS WORN THIN BY MY WALKING TEARS.	170	LOVE IN ASYLUM	15
THAT HIS TEARS BURNED MY CHEEKS AND HIS HEART MOVED IN MINE.	178	POEM IN OCT	52
AND THE OTHER FULL OF TEARS THAT SHE WILL BE DEAD,	193	CONVERS PRAYER	5
LIKE THE SUN'S TEARS,	193	SIDE OF TRUTH	25
CURSE, BLESS, ME NOW WITH YOUR FIERCE TEARS, I PRAY.	208	NOT GO GENTLE	17
LIGHT AND HIS TEARS GLIDE DOWN TOGETHER	215	COUNTRY HEAVEN	11
TOO PROUD TO CRY, TOO FRAIL TO CHECK THE TEARS,	217	ELEGY	35
THE TEARS OUT OF HIS EYES, TOO PROUD TO CRY.	217	ELEGY	39
SHED THOU THY TEARS ON HIM; HE WILL NOT WAKE,	222	MISSING	8
MY TEARS ARE LIKE THE QUIET DRIFT	225	CLOWN IN MOON	1
AND SOOTHED WITH SLOW TEARS;	228	NOT DESPAIR	13
OUR TEARS SOUND WISER	230	OUR SANCTITY	12
AND CHIP, IN SILENCE AND IN TEARS,	239	MAKES INTERVALS	29
TEAR-STAINED			
AND A TEAR-STAINED WIDOWER GRIEF DROOPED FROM THE LASHES	133	MAKE ME A MASK	9
TEAR-STUFFED			
AFTER THE FEAST OF TEAR-STUFFED TIME AND THISTLES	136	AFTER FUNERAL	10
TEATS			
TIME'S TUNE MY LADIES WITH THE TEATS OF MUSIC,	119	ALTARWISE	91
DRINK FROM THE EARTH'S TEATS,	137	O CHATTERTON	4
TEETH			
NO FAITH TO FIX THE TEETH ON CARRIES	41	YOUNG ARE OLD	18
WE HAVE NO FAITH TO SET BETWEEN OUR TEETH.	42	YOUNG ARE OLD	56
AND HEARD THE TEETH OF WEASELS DRAWING BLOOD.	52	OUT OF THE PIT	58
THE BODY PROSPERED, TEETH IN THE MARROWED GUMS,	78	LOVE'S FEVER	16
GRAVE'S FOOT, BLINDS DOWN THE LIDS, THE TEETH IN BLACK,	136	AFTER FUNERAL	4
WITH UNEVEN, SPIRAL TEETH.	229	MY RIVER	26
AND THE GLITTER FROM THE FINE TEETH.	236	WOMAN TAPESTRY	46
TELL			
AND WHO SHALL TELL THE AMORIST	17	IN OBLIVION	27
I SHOULD TELL SUMMER FROM THE TREES, THE WORMS	58	HERE IN SPRING	9
TELL, IF AT ALL, THE WINTER'S STORMS	58	HERE IN SPRING	10
WHAT SHALL IT TELL ME IF A TIMELESS INSECT	59	HERE IN SPRING	16
TELL ME OF HIM WHO FEEDS THE RAGING BIRDS.	65	WOMAN SPEAKS	65
THROUGH, I TELL YOU, YOUR TWO MIDNIGHT LIPS I PRAY	76	LASHED RINGS	7
AND I AM DUMB TO TELL THE CROOKED ROSE	77	THE FORCE THAT	4
AND I AM DUMB TO TELL THE HANGING MAN	77	THE FORCE THAT	14
AND I AM DUMB TO TELL A WEATHER'S WIND	77	THE FORCE THAT	19
AND I AM DUMB TO TELL THE LOVER'S TOMB	77	THE FORCE THAT	21
OF MANY A THORNY SHIRE TELL YOU NOTES,	99	OCTOBER WIND	15
SOME LET ME TELL YOU OF THE RAVEN'S SINS.	99	OCTOBER WIND	24
I TELL HER THIS: BEFORE THE SUNCOCK CAST	115	A GRIEF AGO	35
THE WISEMEN TELL ME THAT THE GARDEN GODS	121	INCARNATE DEVL	9
MORE THE THICK STONE CANNOT TELL.	139	TOMBSTONE TOLD	10
TELL HIS STREET ON ITS BACK HE STOPPED A SUN	172	DAWN RAID	6
WE HEARD THE SEA SOUND SING, WE SAW THE SALT SHEET TELL.	194	SLEEP BECALMED	12
LEAPING! THE GOSPEL ROOKS! ALL TELL, THIS NIGHT, OF HIM	200	COUNTRY SLEEP	80
TO TELL WHAT NOTE I COULD REACH IF I TRIED,	234	NO, PIGEON	12
TELLING			
HIS TELLING BURNS.	12	SKY'S BRIGHT	19

		PAGE	TITLE	LINE
TELLING (CONTINUED)				
TELLING IT THIS, PATTING ITS BLACK NOSE:	....	45	PLOUGHMAN GONE	15
HEIR TO THE TELLING SENSES THAT ALONE	....	80	ALL THAT I OWE	11
I HAVE HEARD MANY YEARS OF TELLING,	....	116	LANTERNS SHINE	16
TEACHES WITH NO TELLING	....	148	UNLUCKILY FOR	44
TELLING THE HEART I BROKE OF A GOOD HABIT	....	175	MY BEGGAR ARM	4
IS TELLING. THE WIZENED	....	189	WINTER'S TALE	61
IN THE RAIN TELLING ITS BEADS, AND THE GRAVEST GHOST		198	COUNTRY SLEEP	31
TELLS				
WHO TELLS ME HURT,	....	12	SKY'S BRIGHT	13
THE SNAIL TELLS OF COMING RAIN.	....	48	POET: 1935	65
A WORM TELLS SUMMER BETTER THAN THE CLOCK,	....	59	HERE IN SPRING	14
THE CHILD TELLS, WHEN THE TREMBLING CHORD IS CUT,		67	LET A FAITH	14
AND TELLS THE PAGE THE EMPTY ILL.	....	75	MY HERO BARES	10
TELLS ME THE HOUR'S WORD, THE NEURAL MEANING	......	99	OCTOBER WIND	18
AND TELLS THE WINDY WEATHER IN THE COCK.	....	99	OCTOBER WIND	20
THE SIGNAL GRASS THAT TELLS ME ALL I KNOW	....	99	OCTOBER WIND	22
TELLS THE STICK, 'FAIL'.	....	100	RUNNING GRAVE	30
TELLS YOU AND YOU, MY MASTERS, AS HIS STRANGE	.....	113	SERVANT SUN	13
TELLS WITH SILENCE THE LAST LIGHT BREAKING	....	191	REFUSAL MOURN	4
TELLTALE				
THE RUDE OWL CRIED LIKE A TELLTALE TIT,	....	206	LAMENT	5
TELL-TALE				
NO TELL-TALE LOVER HAS AN END MORE CERTAIN,	....	125	TODAY, INSECT	24
HILL, TELL-TALE THE KNELLED	....	202	SIR JOHNS HILL	41
TEMPER				
AND THE FIRE IN A TEMPER START	....	149	PAPER & STICKS	3
TEMPERED				
MY BLOOD UPON THE TEMPERED DEAD, FORCING	....	103	I DREAMED MY	19
TEMPERS				
OF LIGHT AND LOVE, THE TEMPERS OF THE HEART,	......	89	EUNUCH DREAMS	2
TEMPLE				
THE VEINS AT EITHER TEMPLE WHIPPED HIM MAD,	....	50	OUT OF THE PIT	7
TEMPLE SHOULD NEVER HAVE BEEN FILLED	....	237	PILLAR BREAKS	12
TEMPLE-BOUND				
TONGUE AND EAR IN THE THREAD, ANGLE THE TEMPLE-BOUND		135	HOW MY ANIMAL	26
TEMPLE'S				
NOW THAT THE TEMPLE'S TRUMPETER	....	237	PILLAR BREAKS	2
TEMPLE'S BROKEN AND POOR RAVEN'S DEAD;	....	238	PILLAR BREAKS	24
TEMPTER				
THE TEMPTER UNDER THE EYELID	....	165	LONG-LEGGED	102
TEN				
LIGHT, I KNOW, TREADS THE TEN MILLION STARS	....	48	LIGHT, I KNOW	T
LIGHT, I KNOW, TREADS THE TEN MILLION STARS,	......	48	LIGHT, I KNOW	1
TENDER				
THESE THE IMAGININGS, TENDER AND BLOSSOMED WITH				
FUTILITY,	....	223	IDYLL UNFORGET	11
TENDRIL				
AND BEAR THOSE TENDRIL HANDS I TOUCH ACROSS	....	134	NOT FROM ANGER	6
TENT				
WON'T HARM THE TENT AROUND HIM,	....	17	IN OBLIVION	24
UNDER THE TENT OF ITS WINGS.	....	237	WOMAN TAPESTRY	74
TENTACLE				
TRACE OUT A TENTACLE,	....	135	HOW MY ANIMAL	28
TERRACE				
ON THE CONSUMPTIVES' TERRACE TAKING THEIR TWO				
FAREWELLS,	....	109	I, IN IMAGE	34
TERRIBLE				
GROWING MORE TERRIBLE AS THE DAY	....	43	LONGED TO MOVE	4
THE TERRIBLE WORLD MY BROTHER BARES HIS SKIN.	.....	133	I MAKE THIS IN	60

	PAGE	TITLE	LINE
TERRIBLY			
TIME KILLS ME TERRIBLY.	129	MY NEOPHYTE	43
AND TERRIBLY LEAD HIM HOME ALIVE	168	LONG-LEGGED	198
TERRIFYING			
WITH STALE AND TERRIFYING CAMP	143	THE MOLLS	6
TERROR			
CRIES NOT IN TERROR WHEN A BIRD IS DRAWN	54	NO MAN BELIEVE	3
LEAD HER PRODIGAL HOME TO HIS TERROR,	168	LONG-LEGGED	199
TERROR AND SHINING FROM	181	VISION, PRAYER	46
TERROR WILL RAGE APART	210	POEM ON B'DAY	43
TERRORS			
IT IS NIGHT'S TERRORS I MUST LEARN TO LOVE,	48	LIGHT, I KNOW	13
TERRORS'			
AND THE OLD TERRORS' CONTINUAL CRY	43	LONGED TO MOVE	3
TESTED			
TESTED BY FIRE, DOUBLE THUMB TO NOSE,	52	OUT OF THE PIT	74
TESTICLE			
STUDYING THE TESTICLE	154	RETURN	16
TETHERED			
STAY, DRAMATIC FIGURES, TETHERED DOWN	28	NO WINGS	3
TEXT			
THE POSTER IS TODAY'S TEXT,	58	TO ARCHITECTS	6
THAMES			
OF THE RIDING THAMES.	192	REFUSAL MOURN	23
THAN			
DARKER THAN EVER,	9	MINUTE'S HOUR	11
EASIER THAN HE UPON THE ICE.	28	NO WINGS	11
RATHER THAN CHARNEL-HOUSE AS SYMBOL	29	LONG, SKELETON	12
THERE'S MORE THAN DYING;	32	OUT OF SIGHS	11
TO DIFFERENT PLACES THAN WERE SAID	37	WINDMILLS TURN	21
IF HUNTING MEANS ANYTHING MORE THAN THE CHASE	44	TO FOLLOW FOX	18
WHEN MORE THAN SNAILS ARE FRIENDS.	45	TO FOLLOW FOX	23
YOU CAPTURE MORE THAN MAN OR WOMAN GUESSES;	48	POET: 1935	54
GROWING IN PUBLIC PLACES THAN MAN KNOWS.	48	POET: 1935	57
THERE ARE NO SEACAVES DEEPER THAN HER EYES;	57	GREEK PLAY	11
A WORM TELLS SUMMER BETTER THAN THE CLOCK,	59	HERE IN SPRING	14
NO CRADLE'S WARMER THAN THIS PERISHED BREAST,	63	WOMAN SPEAKS	6
ONE GOD, MORE MIGHTY THAN THE SUN.	70	SECRET WIND	23
THE WORDS OF DEATH ARE DRYER THAN HIS STIFF,	96	RUB OF LOVE	46
OF LOVE AM BARER THAN CADAVER'S TRAP	100	RUNNING GRAVE	8
BLACK AS THE BEAST AND PALER THAN THE CROSS.	121	INCARNATE DEVL	12
LIFE NEAT'S A BETTER POISON THAN IN BOTTLE,	137	O CHATTERTON	5
THAN ONE COULD PROBE OUT OF A SERPENT'S GUTS;	137	O CHATTERTON	7
THAN BULLY ILL LOVE IN THE CLOUTED SCENE.	145	IF HEAD HURT	5
TO OTHERS THAN YOU	146	TO OTHERS	T
RARER THAN RADIUM,	152	WAS A SAVIOUR	2
COMMONER THAN WATER, CRUELLER THAN TRUTH;	152	WAS A SAVIOUR	3
COMMONER THAN WATER, CRUELLER THAN TRUTH;	152	WAS A SAVIOUR	3
WITH NO MORE DESIRE THAN A GHOST.	166	LONG-LEGGED	124
THAN EVER WAS SINCE THE WORLD WAS SAID,	211	POEM ON B'DAY	98
THAT IN HER GARDEN, RATHER THAN THE DAYS,	223	IN DREAMS	9
THAN THE YEARS THAT DWINDLE;	226	THE ELM	4
THAN THE HOURS.	226	THE ELM	6
AND IS MORE BEAUTIFUL THAN THE DRIFT OF LEAVES.	226	SLENDER WIND	9
SEEKING NO FURTHER THAN YOUR PETALS THAT STILL SLEPT.	227	SPRING-SPIRIT	8
THERE IS A GREATER LOVE THAN MINE	228	NOT DESPAIR	4
THAN OUR LAUGHTER AT THE AIR	230	OUR SANCTITY	13
BURNING ITS SWEET PATH CLEARER THAN BEFORE.	232	FURIOUS MOTION	17
WHOSE MINUTE KINDLES MORE THAN THE WISE HOUR.	237	PILLAR BREAKS	11
THAN SIT HERE WASTING, WHILE I BLEED,	240	TWINING HEAD	11

	PAGE	TITLE	LINE
THAN (CONTINUED)			
THAN IN THE GULL AND THE FIERCE EAGLE	241	ADMIT THE SUN	17
THANK			
THANK GOD, BUT THE ENEMY STAYS PUT.	59	FAIRY TALES	9
THAT (351)			
THATCH			
IN THE SQUIRREL NIMBLE GROVE, UNDER LINEN AND THATCH	199	COUNTRY SLEEP	44
THAT'LL			
THAT'LL MAKE, IT'S BRITTLE, DIAPHRAGM	24	LITTLE PROBLEM	8
THAT'S			
THE HEMMING CONTACT THAT'S SO TRAMMELLED	20	ENCOMPASSED	6
THAT'S NOT WITHOUT ITS WOE, ...	23	THE ONLY DEAD	27
OR CATCH ALL DEATH THAT'S IN THE AIR.	47	POET: 1935	46
THAT'S GRAVE AND GAY AS GRAVE AND SEA	54	WE BY SEASAND	7
AT FLESH THAT PERISHES AND BLOOD THAT'S SPILT	57	GREEK PLAY	19
DAFT WITH THE DRUG THAT'S SMOKING IN A GIRL	95	RUB OF LOVE	30
AND THAT'S THE RUB, THE ONLY RUB THAT TICKLES.	96	RUB OF LOVE	36
IS AS RARE AS A DONKEY THAT'S RED.	221	SONG OF DOG	8
THE (4521)			
THEE			
FOR THAT HE LOVED THEE, SEEK THOU HIM AND BLESS ...	222	MISSING	2
THEFT			
CLOSE AND FAR SHE ANNOUNCED THE THEFT OF THE HEART	158	INTO HER HEAD	39
THEIR (216)			
THEM (27)			
THEMSELVES			
WHICH BATHE THEMSELVES IN A RAVISHMENT OF SNOW; ...	223	IDYLL UNFORGET	14
ENVELOPING THEMSELVES IN THE LADEN EVE;	224	IDYLL UNFORGET	42
THEN			
WE WILL RIDE OUT ALONE, AND THEN, ...	5	PROLOGUE	91
THEN SHALL I GO, ...	9	MINUTE'S HOUR	19
AND THEN I THINK	13	SKY'S BRIGHT	25
THEN SWIM YOUR HEAD, ...	16	TIME TO ROT	17
THEN SHALL YOUR SENSES, OUT OF JOY, ...	21	BEWILDERED WAY	13
AND THEN AGAIN: THERE WAS A CHILD	22	ON QUIET NIGHT	15
THAT, THEN IS FORTUNATE, ...	23	THE ONLY DEAD	23
THAT RISES AND THEN FALLS, BUDS BUT TO WITHER;	25	THERE'S PLENTY	3
WHO GAVE ME LIFE AND THEN THE GRAVE, ...	26	PERSONAL EPIT	11
THAT, THEN, IS LOVELINESS, WE SAID, ...	31	BEING BUT MEN	14
IF NOT OF LOVING WELL, THEN NOT, ...	32	OUT OF SIGHS	8
THEN STIRRED A LITTLE CHAOS IN THE SUN.	33	IN GARDENS	6
WHIRLED IN OUR WORDS, THEN FADED.	34	IN GARDENS	15
AND THIS IS PLENTY, THEN, CLOVES AND SWEET OILS, THE			
BEES' HONEY, ...	36	MIDNIGHT ROAD	5
FOR THEN THE WRONG WIND CERTAINLY	37	WINDMILLS TURN	17
THEN ONLY OVER CORPSES SHALL THE FEET TREAD, ...	45	TO FOLLOW FOX	20
AND THEN RAISE UP THE SKELETON AGAIN, ...	55	NO MAN BELIEVE	20
THEN HANG A RAM ROSE OVER THE RAGS.	60	MEAT ON BONES	8
THEN TAKE THE GUSHER OR THE FIELD	74	WE MOTHERNAKED	9
THEN LOOK, MY EYES, UPON THIS BONEBOUND FORTUNE ...	81	ALL THAT I OWE	21
THEN LOOK, MY HEART, UPON THE SCARLET TROVE, ...	81	ALL THAT I OWE	28
AND THEN IN SANDALS WALK THE STREET	83	LETTER TO AUNT	19
FOR YOU COULD THEN WRITE WHAT YOU PLEASE, ...	84	LETTER TO AUNT	31
BUT THEN IT IS THE FEW THAT MATTER.	84	LETTER TO AUNT	39
THEN ALL THE MATTER OF THE LIVING AIR	102	FELLOWED SLEEP	21
WHO THEN IS SHE, ...	115	A GRIEF AGO	25
THEN, PENNY-EYED, THAT GENTLEMAN OF WOUNDS, ...	117	ALTARWISE	7
HAIRS OF YOUR HEAD, THEN SAID THE HOLLOW AGENT, ...	117	ALTARWISE	25
THEN WAS MY NEOPHYTE	128	MY NEOPHYTE	T
THEN WAS MY NEOPHYTE, ...	128	MY NEOPHYTE	1

	PAGE	TITLE	LINE
THEN (CONTINUED)			
THEN THREW ON THAT TIDE-HOISTED SCREEN	129	MY NEOPHYTE	34
THEN SWIFT FROM A BURSTING SEA WITH BOTTLECORK BOATS	151	BELOW A TIME	13
THEN, BUSHILY SWANKED IN BEAR WIG AND TAILS, ...	151	BELOW A TIME	19
THEN INTO BLIND STREETS I SWAM	155	RETURN	44
THEN GOOD-BYE TO THE FISHERMANNED	162	LONG-LEGGED	5
YEAR TO HEAVEN STOOD THERE THEN IN THE SUMMER NOON	178	POEM IN OCT	66
OF FIELDS. AND BURNING THEN	187	WINTER'S TALE	16
DEATH, AND BAD DEATH, AND THEN	193	SIDE OF TRUTH	22
AND THEN TO AWAKE, AND THE FARM, LIKE A WANDERER WHITE	195	FERN HILL	28
AND GALE I TACKLE, THE WHOLE WORLD THEN, ...	211	POEM ON B'DAY	96
HOLIER THEN THEIR EYES, ...	211	POEM ON B'DAY	106
THEN IN THE DELIGHT AND GROVE OF BEASTS AND BIRDS	215	COUNTRY HEAVEN	6
THEN TAKE THEM AWAY QUICKLY	229	MY RIVER	23
THEN, WHEN I OPEN MY MOUTH, ...	231	YOUR VOICE	6
THEN WILL WE RISE	231	OUR SANCTITY	32
SO, THEN, WILL THE DARK CLOTH OF YOUR HAIR	232	FURIOUS MOTION	7
THEN TO CATCH NIGHT	232	YOUR VOICE	8
SILLY TO CAGE AND THEN SET FREE, ...	237	PILLAR BREAKS	8
TO FIND AND THEN TO STRIKE;	240	ADMIT THE SUN	4
THERE			
OUT THERE, CROW BLACK, MEN	3	PROLOGUE	12
HOO, THERE, IN CASTLE KEEP, ...	4	PROLOGUE	53
HEARS, THERE, THIS FOX LIGHT, MY FLOOD SHIP'S	4	PROLOGUE	69
THERE IS NO MEASURED SEA FOR THEM, ...	10	COOL, OH NO	23
THERE WAS A PURPOSE IN HER POINTED FOOT;	11	CABARET	5
THERE IS NO NEED OF HOPE FOR HOPE, ...	21	BEWILDERED WAY	9
OF ALL THE MYSTERY THERE IS IN LIFE	22	ON QUIET NIGHT	3
AND ALL THE MASTERY THERE IS IN DEATH, ...	22	ON QUIET NIGHT	4
ONE SAYS: THERE WAS A WOMAN WITH NO FRIEND, ...	22	ON QUIET NIGHT	8
AND THEN AGAIN: THERE WAS A CHILD	22	ON QUIET NIGHT	15
FOR THERE WAS NO LIGHT IN HIS EYES, ...	22	ON QUIET NIGHT	17
AND THERE WAS NO LIGHT IN HIS SOUL.	22	ON QUIET NIGHT	18
THERE IS NO DEAD BUT IS NOT LOVED	23	THE ONLY DEAD	19
SO IS THERE MISSED A CERTAIN GODLINESS	23	THE ONLY DEAD	26
THOUGH THERE ARE YEARS BETWEEN US, THEY ARE NAUGHT;	30	YOUTH CALLS	12
THERE MUST, BE PRAISED, SOME CERTAINTY, ...	32	OUT OF SIGHS	7
FOR ALL THERE IS TO GIVE I OFFER:	32	OUT OF SIGHS	28
THERE WAS NO NEED OF A NEW DIVINITY, ...	34	IN GARDENS	18
WAS THERE A TIME	40	WAS THERE TIME	T
WAS THERE A TIME WHEN DANCERS WITH THEIR FIDDLES	40	WAS THERE TIME	1
THERE WAS A TIME THEY COULD CRY OVER BOOKS, ...	40	WAS THERE TIME	3
FOR US THERE IS NO SHOOTING AND NO RIDING, ...	40	YOUNG ARE OLD	8
FOR US THERE IS NO RIDING AND NO SHOOTING, ...	40	YOUNG ARE OLD	15
THERE IS BUT ONE MESSAGE FOR THE EARTH, ...	41	YOUNG ARE OLD	26
CALLED FOR CONFESSOR BUT THERE WAS NONE	42	A WAR OF WITS	5
FROM THERE ARE GHOSTS IN THE AIR	43	LONGED TO MOVE	8
AND THERE IS ALWAYS DAY, THE SHINING OF SOME SUN,	49	LIGHT, I KNOW	18
AND THERE WAS THUNDER IN AN OPENING ROSE.	51	OUT OF THE PIT	17
KNEE-DEEP IN VOMIT. I SAW HIM THERE, ...	51	OUT OF THE PIT	43
IT WAS NOVEMBER THERE WERE WHIZZBANGS HOPPING, ...	52	OUT OF THE PIT	51
BUT NOW THERE ARE THE BUTT-ENDS OF SPENT SQUIBS.	52	OUT OF THE PIT	52
WHERE, WHAT? THERE WAS COMMOTION IN THE SKIES, ...	52	OUT OF THE PIT	76
THERE ARE NO SEACAVES DEEPER THAN HER EYES;	57	GREEK PLAY	11
THERE CAN BE FEW TEARS LEFT: ELECTRA WEPT	57	GREEK PLAY	17
THERE ARE TWO LAGGARDS, ...	60	FAIRY TALES	34
THERE IS NO FOUNTAIN SPRINGING FROM THE EARTH	63	WOMAN SPEAKS	4
THERE SHALL BE NO MUTE MOURNING OVER HIS ACRE, ...	64	WOMAN SPEAKS	38
THERE IN THEIR HEAT THE WINTER FLOODS	91	BOYS OF SUMMER	4

	PAGE	TITLE	LINE
THERE (CONTINUED)			
INTO THE TIDED CORD, THERE GOES	91	WHERE ONCE THE	8
THERE ROUND ABOUT YOUR STONES THE SHADES	91	WHERE ONCE THE	16
THERE SHALL BE CORALS IN YOUR BEDS, ...	91	WHERE ONCE THE	22
THERE SHALL BE SERPENTS IN YOUR TIDES, ...	91	WHERE ONCE THE	23
THERE IN THE SUN THE FRIGID THREADS	92	BOYS OF SUMMER	10
THERE IN THE DEEP WITH QUARTERED SHADES	92	BOYS OF SUMMER	16
THERE FROM THEIR HEARTS THE DOGDAYED PULSE	92	BOYS OF SUMMER	22
THERE, IN HIS NIGHT, THE BLACK-TONGUED BELLS	92	BOYS OF SUMMER	28
AND THERE WE WEPT, I AND THE GHOSTLY OTHER, ...	101	FELLOWED SLEEP	8
THERE GROWS THE HOURS' LADDER TO THE SUN, ...	102	FELLOWED SLEEP	26
FIRST THERE WAS THE LAMB ON KNOCKING KNEES	117	ALTARWISE	29
AND GOD WALKED THERE WHO WAS A FIDDLING WARDEN	121	INCARNATE DEVL	5
THERE IS LOUD AND DARK DIRECTLY UNDER THE DUMB FLAME,	130	SINNERS' BELL	13
BECAUSE THERE STANDS, ONE STORY OUT OF THE BUM CITY,	144	PLEASURE-BIRD	13
YOU MY FRIEND THERE WITH A WINNING AIR	146	TO OTHERS	3
THRUST, MY DAUGHTER OR SON, TO ESCAPE, THERE IS			
NONE, NONE, NONE, ...	146	IF HEAD HURT	19
HAS A VOICE AND A HOUSE, AND THERE AND HERE YOU MUST			
COUCH AND CRY.	146	IF HEAD HURT	25
IS CELEBRATED THERE, AND COMMUNION BETWEEN SUNS.	148	UNLUCKILY FOR	24
THERE WAS A SAVIOUR	152	WAS A SAVIOUR	T
THERE WAS A SAVIOUR	152	WAS A SAVIOUR	1
THERE WAS CALM TO BE DONE IN HIS SAFE UNREST, ...	153	WAS A SAVIOUR	11
THERE WAS GLORY TO HEAR	153	WAS A SAVIOUR	17
NOW IN THE DARK THERE IS ONLY YOURSELF AND MYSELF.	153	WAS A SAVIOUR	24
FLEW MAN-BEARING THERE.	157	INTO HER HEAD	6
THERE THE DARK BLADE AND WANTON SIGHING HER DOWN	157	INTO HER HEAD	16
THERE WHERE A NUMBERLESS TONGUE	158	INTO HER HEAD	24
THERE IS THUNDER UNDER ITS THUMBS;	164	LONG-LEGGED	62
THERE IS NOTHING LEFT OF THE SEA BUT ITS SOUND, ...	169	LONG-LEGGED	205
THERE COULD I MARVEL	178	POEM IN OCT	38
AND THERE COULD I MARVEL MY BIRTHDAY	178	POEM IN OCT	61
YEAR TO HEAVEN STOOD THERE THEN IN THE SUMMER NOON	178	POEM IN OCT	66
BUT THERE IS ONLY BUCKLEY'S UNFRISKY	179	NEW QUAY	11
THERE STINKS A SNOOP IN BLACK. I'M THINKING IT	179	NEW QUAY	19
THERE	182	VISION, PRAYER	69
CALL FOR CONFESSOR AND WISER MIRROR BUT THERE IS NONE	186	HOLY SPRING	10
AND THERE OUTSIDE ON THE BREAD OF THE GROUND	189	WINTER'S TALE	68
AFTER THE FIRST DEATH, THERE IS NO OTHER.	192	REFUSAL MOURN	24
THE LEAPING SAGA OF PRAYER! AND HIGH, THERE, ON THE			
HARE-	199	COUNTRY SLEEP	66
THERE	202	SIR JOHNS HILL	18
AND THERE THIS NIGHT I WALK IN THE WHITE GIANT'S			
THIGH	203	GIANT'S THIGH	3
AND YOU, MY FATHER, THERE ON THE SAD HEIGHT, ...	208	NOT GO GENTLE	16
THERE HE MIGHT WANDER BARE	210	POEM ON B'DAY	55
HILL, UNDER THE GRASS, IN LOVE, AND THERE GROW	216	ELEGY	6
THERE ARE MANY WHO SAY THAT A DOG HAS ITS DAY, ...	221	SONG OF DOG	1
THERE ARE OTHERS WHO THINK THAT A LOBSTER IS PINK,	221	SONG OF DOG	3
THERE ARE FEWER, OF COURSE, WHO INSIST THAT A HORSE	221	SONG OF DOG	5
ALL THE LAND IS RIPE. THERE IS NO MOTION	222	FOREST PICTURE	5
THERE SHOULD BE NIGHT FOR EVER, AND NO ROSE, ...	223	IN DREAMS	10
THERE IS A GREATER LOVE THAN MINE	228	NOT DESPAIR	4
THERE WILL BE A NEW BITTERNESS	236	WOMAN TAPESTRY	61
THERE WILL BE A NEW LIFE	236	WOMAN TAPESTRY	66
AND, THERE, WHAT WINGS THEY HAD, ...	238	PILLAR BREAKS	15
WHERE IS THERE GREATER LOVE	241	ADMIT THE SUN	15
THEREFORE			
THEREFORE LIFT UP, SEE, STROKE THE LIGHT.	35	LIFT UP FACE	24

	PAGE	TITLE	LINE
THERE'LL			
THERE'LL BE MY BONE TO GO:	239	MAKES INTERVALS	21
THERE'S			
THERE'S TIME TO PLUCK A TUNE UPON THE HARP, ...	15	FOR LEDA	16
BUT WHILE DAY IS THERE'S NIGHT TO IT, ...	18	NATURAL DAY	19
WHERE LOVE IS THERE'S A CRUST OF JOY	19	THE NEOPHYTE	5
LOOK, THERE'S THE DEAD WHO DID NOT LOVE, ...	24	THE ONLY DEAD	30
AND THERE'S THE LIVING WHO DID LOVE, ...	24	THE ONLY DEAD	31
THERE'S PLENTY IN THE WORLD	25	THERE'S PLENTY	T
THERE'S PLENTY IN THE WORLD THAT DOTH NOT DIE, ...	25	THERE'S PLENTY	1
THERE'S PLENTY THAT DOTH DIE;	26	THERE'S PLENTY	14
THERE'S POISON IN YOUR RED WINE, DRINKER, ...	27	OBLIVIOUS DARK	14
THERE'S MORE THAN DYING;	32	OUT OF SIGHS	11
THE CHANGED WIND BLOWS, AND THERE'S A CHOICE OF SIGNS	37	WINDMILLS TURN	31
THERE'S NO WAY.	234	NO, PIGEON	7
THESE (52)			
THEY (89)			
THEYD			
THEYD SEE WITH EYES LIKE MINE	11	AIR BREATHE	10
THEY'LL			
MANNED WITH THEIR LOVES THEY'LL MOVE, ...	5	PROLOGUE	95
THEY'RE			
WRAP THEM IN FLAME, THEY'RE MINE;	19	IMAGES IN AIR	2
THICK			
BUT ANIMALS THICK AS THIEVES	5	PROLOGUE	74
THICK TO THE SKULL, ...	18	NATURAL DAY	33
NEW MAN BEST WHOSE BLOOD RUNS THICK, ...	29	LONG, SKELETON	11
OVER A ROAD THICK WITH THE BONES OF WORDS.	44	TO FOLLOW FOX	17
THE CADAVEROUS GRAVELS, FALLS THICK AND STEADILY,	110	I, IN IMAGE	44
TAP HAPPILY OF ONE PEG IN THE THICK	136	AFTER FUNERAL	3
MORE THE THICK STONE CANNOT TELL.	139	TOMBSTONE TOLD	10
THE THICK HIDE COVERING, ...	233	NO THOUGHT	10
THICKET			
CLACK THROUGH THE THICKET OF STRENGTH, LOVE HEWN IN			
PILLARS DROPS	135	HOW MY ANIMAL	36
THICKETS			
AND FAST THROUGH THE DRIFTS OF THE THICKETS ANTLERED			
LIKE DEER, ...	190	WINTER'S TALE	95
THIEF			
HERE UNDER THE EARTH WITH GIRL AND THIEF, ...	26	PERSONAL EPIT	5
GIRLS TAKE TO BROOMSTICKS WHEN THE THIEF OF NIGHT	96	TWELVE	3
GRIEF THIEF OF TIME	107	GRIEF THIEF	T
GRIEF THIEF OF TIME CRAWLS OFF, ...	107	GRIEF THIEF	1
AND TIMELESSLY LIES LOVING WITH THE THIEF.	108	GRIEF THIEF	14
WHOM NOW I CONJURE TO STAND AS THIEF	146	TO OTHERS	9
THE THIEF OF ADOLESCENCE, ...	158	INTO HER HEAD	31
AND MIRE OF LOVE, BUT THE THIEF AS MEEK AS THE DEW.	198	COUNTRY SLEEP	38
BE YOU SURE THE THIEF WILL SEEK A WAY SLY AND SURE	199	COUNTRY SLEEP	49
THE THIEF FALL ON THE DEAD LIKE THE WILLY NILLY DEW,	200	COUNTRY SLEEP	93
THIEVES			
BUT ANIMALS THICK AS THIEVES	5	PROLOGUE	74
OF BIRTH AND DEATH, THE TWO SAD KNAVES OF THIEVES,	75	MY HERO BARES	18
SHAPE WITH MY FATHERS' THIEVES.	108	GRIEF THIEF	28
I BY THE TREE OF THIEVES, ALL GLORY'S SAWBONES, ...	120	ALTARWISE	109
THIGH			
INCH ON THE OLD THIGH	22	HIGH ON A HILL	11
WAS MUSCLED, MATTED, WISE TO THE CRYING THIGH	78	LOVE'S FEVER	28
THE ITCH OF MAN UPON THE BABY'S THIGH, ...	95	RUB OF LOVE	12
DRY IN THE HALF-TRACKED THIGH.	105	WORLD PYRAMID	60
IN THE WHITE GIANT'S THIGH	203	GIANT'S THIGH	T

	PAGE	TITLE	LINE
THIGH (CONTINUED)			
AND THERE THIS NIGHT I WALK IN THE WHITE GIANT'S THIGH	203	GIANT'S THIGH	3
THIGHS			
HER THIGHS AND UNDERCLOTHES WERE SWEET, ...	11	CABARET	6
YOUR SWEET INDUCIVE THIGHS	11	AIR BREATHE	12
A CANDLE IN THE THIGHS	82	LIGHT BREAKS	7
INSECTS AND VALLEYS HOLD HER THIGHS HARD, ...	168	LONG-LEGGED	174
AND THIS DAY'S SUN LEAPT UP THE SKY OUT OF HER THIGHS	170	MARRIAGE VIRG	4
HE SNUGGLES DEEP AMONG THE CHAPEL THIGHS, ...	179	NEW QUAY	30
AND THROUGH THE THIGHS OF THE ENGULFING BRIDE, ...	191	WINTER'S TALE	124
LIGHT OF HIS THIGHS, SPREADEAGLE TO THE DUNGHILL SKY,	204	GIANT'S THIGH	23
MODESTY HIDES MY THIGHS IN HER WINGS, ...	207	LAMENT	59
THIMBLE			
AND PRICK THE THUMB-STAINED HEAVEN THROUGH THE THIMBLE.	104	WORLD PYRAMID	27
AND THE CELL-STEPPED THIMBLE;	111	I, IN IMAGE	76
THIN			
BEASTS WHO SLEEP GOOD AND THIN, ...	5	PROLOGUE	77
AND ALL MY THIN PREROGATIVE OF TASTE.	18	NATURAL DAY	18
I, SAID THE BEETLE, OUT OF MY THIN BLACK WOMB, ...	18	NATURAL DAY	26
OUT OF MY THIN BLACK LIPS, ...	18	NATURAL DAY	27
MY BREASTS ARE THIN.	61	MEAT ON BONES	21
BY A THIN SEA OF FLESH	62	EARS IN TURRET	11
HEART OF CADAVER'S CANDLE WAXES THIN, ...	100	RUNNING GRAVE	12
THROUGH THE WAVES OF THE FAT STREETS NOR THE SKELETON'S THIN WAYS.	146	IF HEAD HURT	28
ON THE MADHOUSE BOARDS WORN THIN BY MY WALKING TEARS.	170	LOVE IN ASYLUM	15
BEHIND THE WALL THIN AS A WREN'S BONE?	180	VISION, PRAYER	9
I LIE DOWN THIN AND HEAR THE GOOD BELLS JAW--	207	LAMENT	53
THING			
DO THE RIGHT THING TO DO THE RIGHT;	18	NATURAL DAY	37
THEY ARE THE ONLY LIVING THING WHO DID LOVE, ...	23	THE ONLY DEAD	4
SHE, IN HER CHEAP FROCK, SAYING SOME CHEAP THING,	43	FACES SHONE	11
A BOWLER THING WITH ONE OR TWO	83	LETTER TO AUNT	17
ALTHOUGH YOUR ANGER IS NOT A SLIGHT THING, ...	232	YOUR VOICE	13
THINGS			
I COULD DEVOTE TO OTHER THINGS.	9	MINUTE'S HOUR	22
FAITH IN DIVINITY WOULD SOLVE MOST THINGS, ...	37	WINDMILLS TURN	16
SAID ALL THE USUAL THINGS OVER AND AGAIN;	52	OUT OF THE PIT	71
LAIN WITH PARCHED THINGS; LOVED DOGS AND WOMEN; ...	52	OUT OF THE PIT	72
THE NOVEL THINGS. BUT IT HAS BEEN NO GOOD.	53	OUT OF THE PIT	81
ALL THINGS ARE KNOWN: THE STARS' ADVICE	56	WHY EAST WIND	16
WE HAVE THESE LITTLE THINGS OFF PAT, ...	59	FAIRY TALES	4
THE THINGS OF LIGHT	82	LIGHT BREAKS	5
FOR THESE ARE THINGS THAT PLAY A PART	84	LETTER TO AUNT	46
THESE THINGS REMEMBERED, WHAT CAN STOP	84	LETTER TO AUNT	56
ALL THINGS REST IN THE WILL OF PURPOSE TRIUMPHANT.	222	FOREST PICTURE	8
FOR ALL THINGS ARE LEAF-LIKE	225	OF ANY FLOWER	2
FOR ALL THINGS ARE GRIEF-LIKE	225	OF ANY FLOWER	5
SLENDERLY LETHAL THINGS, ...	226	THE ELM	8
THINK			
THE HILLOCK OF THE THOUGHTS YOU THINK	10	COOL, OH NO	3
AND THEN I THINK	13	SKY'S BRIGHT	25
ONE WOULD NOT THINK THE GREENNESS OF THIS VALLEY	63	WOMAN SPEAKS	12
LET ME NOT THINK, OF GOD OF CARNAGE, ...	63	WOMAN SPEAKS	16
WHY SHOULD I THINK ON DEATH WHEN YOU ARE RULER? ...	67	REALM OF FLESH	10
I NEVER THOUGHT TO UTTER OR THINK	147	TO OTHERS	16
THERE ARE OTHERS WHO THINK THAT A LOBSTER IS PINK,	221	SONG OF DOG	3
LET'S HOPE YOU WON'T THINK ME TOO VICIOUS.	221	SONG OF DOG	16

	PAGE	TITLE	LINE
THINK (CONTINUED)			
I THINK, THAT IF I TOUCHED THE EARTH, ...	225	CLOWN IN MOON	5
THINKING			
TO NOURISH THINKING OF HIM.	12	SKY'S BRIGHT	4
THERE STINKS A SNOOP IN BLACK. I'M THINKING IT	179	NEW QUAY	19
THINNING			
A LIMP AND RIDERLESS SHAPE TO LEAP NINE THINNING			
MONTHS.'	145	IF HEAD HURT	15
THIRD			
NO THIRD EYE PROBE INTO A RAINBOW'S SEX	108	GRIEF THIEF	25
THIRST			
NOW THE THIRST PARCHES LIP AND TONGUE	34	THIRST PARCHES	T
NOW THE THIRST PARCHES LIP AND TONGUE, ...	34	THIRST PARCHES	1
BOTH QUENCH HIS THIRST HE'LL HAVE A BLACK REPLY.	56	WHY EAST WIND	9
'THE THIRST IS QUENCHED, THE HUNGER GONE, ...	61	MEAT ON BONES	17
MY THROAT KNEW THIRST BEFORE THE STRUCTURE	69	BEFORE KNOCKED	25
THIRSTY			
TO LONDON'S TURNED, AND THIRSTY LOADS	37	WINDMILLS TURN	9
PAYING HEED TO THE THIRSTY VOICE.	67	REALM OF FLESH	13
HAVE THEIR THIRSTY SAILORS HIDE HIM.	126	SEED-AT-ZERO	35
SEAPORTS BY A THIRSTY SHORE	126	SEED-AT-ZERO	41
THIRTIETH			
IT WAS MY THIRTIETH YEAR TO HEAVEN	176	POEM IN OCT	1
IT WAS MY THIRTIETH	178	POEM IN OCT	65
THIRTY-FIFTH			
HIS DRIFTWOOD THIRTY-FIFTH WIND TURNED AGE;	208	POEM ON B'DAY	8
THIRTY-FIVE			
THIRTY-FIVE BELLS SING STRUCK	209	POEM ON B'DAY	39
THIS (152)			
THISTLE			
YOUR MOUTH, MY LOVE, THE THISTLE IN THE KISS?	96	RUB OF LOVE	44
OF DAY, IN THE THISTLE AISLES, TILL THE WHITE OWL			
CROSSED	204	GIANT'S THIGH	32
THISTLEDOWN			
IN THE THISTLEDOWN FALL, ...	209	POEM ON B'DAY	19
THISTLES			
THE SEXTON SENTINEL, GARRISONED UNDER THISTLES, ...	110	I, IN IMAGE	57
AFTER THE FEAST OF TEAR-STUFFED TIME AND THISTLES	136	AFTER FUNERAL	10
THISTLING			
OF THISTLING FROST	200	COUNTRY SLEEP	73
THORN			
AND SEWN ON HIS SKULL A SCARLET THORN;	74	SUN BURNS	13
OR, WATER-LAMMED, FROM THE SCYTHE-SIDED THORN, ...	114	A GRIEF AGO	3
DECEMBER'S THORN SCREWED IN A BROW OF HOLLY.	121	ALTARWISE	132
CASTING TO-MORROW LIKE A THORN	180	VISION, PRAYER	25
AND SLY AS SNOW AND MEEK AS DEW BLOWN TO THE THORN,	199	COUNTRY SLEEP	50
THORNS			
AS TARRED WITH BLOOD AS THE BRIGHT THORNS I WEPT;	120	ALTARWISE	101
THORNY			
MY JACK OF CHRIST BORN THORNY ON THE TREE?	96	RUB OF LOVE	45
OF MANY A THORNY SHIRE TELL YOU NOTES, ...	99	OCTOBER WIND	15
THOROUGHFARES			
COIL FROM THE THOROUGHFARES OF HER HAIR	168	LONG-LEGGED	197
THOROUGHLY			
FEEL THE SAME SOFT BLOOD FLOW THOROUGHLY, ...	23	THE ONLY DEAD	11
THOSE (7)			
THOU			
SEEK HIM, THOU SUN, IN THE DREAD WILDERNESS, ...	222	MISSING	1
FOR THAT HE LOVED THEE, SEEK THOU HIM AND BLESS ...	222	MISSING	2
LIGHTLY, THOU WIND, OVER HIS DEAR, DARK HEAD, ...	222	MISSING	4

	PAGE	TITLE	LINE
THOU (CONTINUED)			
SOFTLY, THOU RAIN--AND FOR HIS MOTHER'S SAKE, ...	222	MISSING	7
SHED THOU THY TEARS ON HIM; HE WILL NOT WAKE, ...	222	MISSING	8
THOUGH			
TO YOU STRANGERS (THOUGH SONG	3	PROLOGUE	24
THOUGH WE CRY DOWN THE FUNNEL, ...	17	IN OBLIVION	16
AS THOUGH THE SUN WERE SPINNING UP THROUGH IT.	19	THE NEOPHYTE	8
THOUGH, AFTER'S DONE, I	24	LITTLE PROBLEM	15
THOUGH NO ASK BRINGS IT	24	LITTLE PROBLEM	22
THE SEASON'S SUN, THOUGH HE SHOULD KNOW HIS SETTING	25	THERE'S PLENTY	4
THOUGH WE'RE CONSUMED BY LOVES AND DOUBTS.	27	OBLIVIOUS DARK	26
PLANNING WHAT'S GOOD, THOUGH IT'S BUT WINTER, ...	27	OBLIVIOUS DARK	29
THOUGH THERE ARE YEARS BETWEEN US, THEY ARE NAUGHT;	30	YOUTH CALLS	12
THE MIDNIGHT ROAD, THOUGH YOUNG MEN TREAD UNKNOWING,	36	MIDNIGHT ROAD	1
AND HE DESTROYS, THOUGH FLOWERS ARE HIS LOVES, ...	47	POET: 1935	34
THOUGH THEY GO MAD THEY SHALL BE SANE, ...	49	NO DOMINION	6
THOUGH THEY SINK THROUGH THE SEA THEY SHALL RISE			
AGAIN;	49	NO DOMINION	7
THOUGH LOVERS BE LOST LOVE SHALL NOT;	49	NO DOMINION	8
THOUGH THEY BE MAD AND DEAD AS NAILS, ...	50	NO DOMINION	24
THOUGH WHAT THE STARS ASK AS THEY ROUND	56	WHY EAST WIND	18
GOD IS THE SAME THOUGH HE BE PRAISED AS MANY, ...	67	LET A FAITH	9
REMAINS THOUGH GODS BE FELLED TILL NONE ARE LEFT.	67	LET A FAITH	10
AND THOUGH MY LOVE PULLS THE PALE, NIPPLED AIR, ...	133	I MAKE THIS IN	66
(THOUGH THIS FOR HER IS A MONSTROUS IMAGE BLINDLY	136	AFTER FUNERAL	16
THE HEART IS SENSUAL, THOUGH FIVE EYES BREAK.	139	FIVE & COUNTRY	14
TALKED AND TORE THOUGH HER EYES SMILED.	139	TOMBSTONE TOLD	20
THOUGH THE BRAWL OF THE KISS HAS NOT OCCURRED	147	UNLUCKILY FOR	7
THAT THOUGH I LOVED THEM FOR THEIR FAULTS	147	TO OTHERS	18
SLASHED DOWN THE LAST SNAKE AS THOUGH	150	WHEN I WOKE	13
THOUGH THE MOMENT OF A MIRACLE IS UNENDING LIGHTNING	170	MARRIAGE VIRG	6
THOUGH THE TOWN BELOW LAY LEAVED WITH OCTOBER BLOOD.	178	POEM IN OCT	67
I PRAY THOUGH I BELONG	183	VISION, PRAYER	115
THAT HE LET THE DEAD LIE THOUGH THEY MOAN	184	VISION, PRAYER	136
THOUGH NO SOUND FLOWED DOWN THE HAND FOLDED AIR ...	188	WINTER'S TALE	40
WAS FLYING THROUGH THE HOUSE AS THOUGH THE SHE BIRD			
PRAISED	189	WINTER'S TALE	83
IN A CHOIR OF WINGS, AS THOUGH SHE SLEPT OR DIED,	191	WINTER'S TALE	122
THOUGH I SANG IN MY CHAINS LIKE THE SEA.	196	FERN HILL	54
AND STAR: HELD AND BLESSED, THOUGH YOU SCOUR THE			
HIGH FOUR	199	COUNTRY SLEEP	45
TO LABOUR AND LOVE THOUGH THEY LAY DOWN LONG AGO.	203	GIANT'S THIGH	5
THOUGH THE NAMES ON THEIR WEED GROWN STONES ARE			
RAINED AWAY, ...	203	GIANT'S THIGH	8
THOUGH WISE MEN AT THEIR END KNOW DARK IS RIGHT,	208	NOT GO GENTLE	4
YET, THOUGH I CRY WITH TUMBLEDOWN TONGUE, ...	211	POEM ON B'DAY	80
TANGLING THOUGH THIS SPUN SLIME	211	POEM ON B'DAY	84
OR STILL ALL THE NUMBERLESS DAYS OF HIS DEATH, THOUGH	216	ELEGY	8
AND THOUGH DOUBTFUL OF BISCUIT, I'M WILLING TO RISK			
IT, ...	221	SONG OF DOG	11
MY RIVER, EVEN THOUGH IT LIFTS	228	MY RIVER	1
THOUGHT			
FOR WHEN I BOUGHT YOU FOR A THOUGHT, (YOU COST NO			
MORE)	10	COOL, OH NO	8
SPLITTING A THOUGHT INTO SUCH HIDEOUS MOMENTS	17	IN OBLIVION	17
TRICKLE AWAY THROUGH THOUGHT, ...	19	IMAGES IN AIR	6
HARBOURING SOME THOUGHT OF HEAVEN, OR HAVEN HOPING,	36	MIDNIGHT ROAD	2
A HOLE IN SPACE SHALL KEEP THE SHAPE OF THOUGHT,	73	LORD RED HAIL	13
A LOVER'S THOUGHT TEARS DOWN THE DATED SHEET, ...	80	ALMANAC TIME	7
BY YOUTH AND AGE, THE MORTAL STATE AND THOUGHT	80	ALMANAC TIME	9

	PAGE	TITLE	LINE
THOUGHT (CONTINUED)			
ON TIPS OF THOUGHT WHERE THOUGHTS SMELL IN THE RAIN;	82	LIGHT BREAKS	26
THE SIMPLEST THOUGHT OR SENTIMENT,	84	LETTER TO AUNT	42
(FOR THOUGHT, WE KNOW, IS DECADENT);	84	LETTER TO AUNT	43
AS KISSES FROZE THE WAXING THOUGHT,	85	SEE, SAYS LIME	14
THE BRAIN WAS CELLED AND SOLDERED IN THE THOUGHT	94	IN BEGINNING	26
I NEVER THOUGHT TO UTTER OR THINK	147	TO OTHERS	16
NO THOUGHT CAN TROUBLE MY UNWHOLESOME POSE	233	NO THOUGHT	T
NO THOUGHT CAN TROUBLE MY UNWHOLESOME POSE,	233	NO THOUGHT	1
HERE IS THE THOUGHT THAT COMES	233	NO THOUGHT	16
I'LL HAVE TO BREAK IN THOUGHT AGAIN,	239	MAKES INTERVALS	27
THOUGHTS			
THE HILLOCK OF THE THOUGHTS YOU THINK	10	COOL, OH NO	3
AND MY THOUGHTS FLOW SO UNEASILY	10	COOL, OH NO	22
CLOSED IN YOUR CELL OF SECRET THOUGHTS,	10	COOL, OH NO	28
AND THOUGHTS, BE THEY SO KIND,	20	THE NEOPHYTE	24
THE SAME THOUGHTS IN OUR HEAD.	28	NO WINGS	19
I LEARNT MAN'S TONGUE, TO TWIST THE SHAPES OF THOUGHTS	79	LOVE'S FEVER	32
ON TIPS OF THOUGHT WHERE THOUGHTS SMELL IN THE RAIN;	82	LIGHT BREAKS	26
THOUSAND			
THE THOUSAND SHEEP	33	HELD-OUT HAND	22
THRASHED			
ROUGH AS COWS' TONGUES AND THRASHED WITH BRAMBLES THEIR BUTTERMILK	204	GIANT'S THIGH	25
THRASHING			
ON THE OLD SEAS FROM STORIES, THRASHING MY WINGS,	152	BELOW A TIME	36
AT HIS THRASHING HAIR AND WHALE-BLUE EYE;	161	LONG-LEGGED	3
THREAD			
THREAD AND TORTURE ALL THE DAY;	72	TAKE NEEDLES	53
'A LIZARD DARTING WITH BLACK VENOM'S THREAD	132	I MAKE THIS IN	49
TONGUE AND EAR IN THE THREAD, ANGLE THE TEMPLE-BOUND	135	HOW MY ANIMAL	26
TO THE BOY OF COMMON THREAD,	152	BELOW A TIME	41
AND WIND HIS GLOBE OUT OF YOUR WATER THREAD	160	DEATHS AND ENT	21
GOLD GUT IS A LIGHTNING THREAD,	164	LONG-LEGGED	63
LIKE A CAVE WITH ONE THREAD.	230	OUR SANCTITY	21
THE FIBRES, OR THE SENSES' THREAD.	233	NO THOUGHT	8
THREADBARE			
LIE WITH RELIGION IN THEIR CRAMP, HER THREADBARE	137	AFTER FUNERAL	32
THREADS			
THERE IN THE SUN THE FRIGID THREADS	92	BOYS OF SUMMER	10
SHE THREADS OFF THE SAP AND NEEDLES, BLOOD AND BUBBLE	108	I, IN IMAGE	10
THREE			
THE VIRGINS SMELT OUT, THREE STREETS UP,	38	THE GOSSIPERS	8
IN AUTUMN TEACH THREE SEASONS' FIRES	58	HERE IN SPRING	7
AND THREE DEAD SEASONS ON A CLIMBING GRAVE	117	ALTARWISE	30
BENT LIKE THREE TREES AND BIRD-PAPPED THROUGH HER SHIFT,	120	ALTARWISE	103
ON NO WORK OF WORDS NOW FOR THREE LEAN MONTHS IN THE BLOODY	140	NO WORK WORDS	1
WHO MOVED FOR THREE YEARS IN TUNE	161	WEDDING ANNIV	3
HER ROBIN BREASTED TREE, THREE MARYS IN THE RAYS.	198	COUNTRY SLEEP	29
THREE-COLOURED			
TILL THE THREE-COLOURED RAINBOW FROM MY NIPPLES	120	ALTARWISE	107
THREE-EYED			
A THREE-EYED, RED-EYED SPARK, BLUNT AS A FLOWER;	94	IN BEGINNING	15
THREE-POINTED			
IN THE BEGINNING WAS THE THREE-POINTED STAR,	93	IN BEGINNING	1
THREE-QUARTERS			
AN OLD TORMENTED MAN THREE-QUARTERS BLIND,	217	ELEGY	18

	PAGE	TITLE	LINE
THREE-SYLLABLED			
THREE-SYLLABLED AND STARRY AS THE SMILE;	94	IN BEGINNING	8
THRESHOLD			
THAT PLAYED IN VOICELESS FROLIC AT THE THRESHOLD OF MY HEART.	223	IDYLL UNFORGET	12
THREW			
THAT LEAPING VEINS THREW TO THE WIND	85	SEE, SAYS LIME	11
THE BALL I THREW WHILE PLAYING IN THE PARK	116	LANTERNS SHINE	18
THEN THREW ON THAT TIDE-HOISTED SCREEN	129	MY NEOPHYTE	34
THRILL			
AND THRILL AND BREATHE AND MOVE	236	WOMAN TAPESTRY	59
THRIVE			
BUT OUR SPEAKING DOES NOT THRIVE	17	IN OBLIVION	20
THROAT			
THE THROAT IS MINE I KNOW THE NECK	11	AIR BREATHE	2
ALIVE WITHIN HIS CRANING THROAT--	14	FOR LEDA	7
MY THROAT KNEW THIRST BEFORE THE STRUCTURE	69	BEFORE KNOCKED	25
AND TIED AN IRIS IN HIS THROAT	85	SEE, SAYS LIME	18
SHAKES A DESOLATE BOY WHO SLITS HIS THROAT	136	AFTER FUNERAL	7
SOONER DROP WITH THE WORM OF THE ROPES ROUND MY THROAT	145	IF HEAD HURT	4
A CLOUD BLEW THE RAIN FROM ITS THROAT;	163	LONG-LEGGED	40
IN THE THROAT, BURNING AND TURNING. ALL NIGHT AFLOAT	194	SLEEP BECALMED	2
LIE STILL, SLEEP BECALMED, HIDE THE MOUTH IN THE THROAT, ...	194	SLEEP BECALMED	13
I HAVE MADE MY THROAT AN ARBOUR FOR FORGOTTEN SONGS.	224	IDYLL UNFORGET	20
YOUR CONSTRUCTED NOTES GOING OUT OF THE THROAT	231	YOUR VOICE	2
THROATS			
CARVED BIRDS BLUNT THEIR STRIKING THROATS ON THE SALT GRAVEL, ...	15	SPIRE CRANES	3
OF LOVE AND LIGHT BURSTS IN THEIR THROATS.	92	BOYS OF SUMMER	23
AND LOAD THE THROATS OF SHELLS	160	DEATHS AND ENT	22
THROUGH THROATS WHERE MANY RIVERS MEET, THE CURLEWS CRY, ...	203	GIANT'S THIGH	1
THROUGH THROATS WHERE MANY RIVERS MEET, THE WOMEN PRAY, ...	203	GIANT'S THIGH	6
AND COVERING ALL HAS BEEN A QUIETUDE, AND A SINGING FROM FLAKE-BARE THROATS.	224	IDYLL UNFORGET	35
THRONE			
CRYING AT THE MAN DRENCHED THRONE	181	VISION, PRAYER	58
THRONG			
HOLLOW FARMS IN A THRONG	5	PROLOGUE	79
THRONGED			
UP TO THE SWALLOW THRONGED LOFT BY THE SHADOW OF MY HAND, ...	196	FERN HILL	47
THROUGH (141)			
THROW			
THROW YOUR FEAR A PARCEL OF STONE	142	SAINT TO FALL	37
FOR WE SAW HIM THROW TO THE SWIFT FLOOD	162	LONG-LEGGED	21
THE CENTURIES THROW BACK THEIR HAIR	167	LONG-LEGGED	151
THROW WIDE TO THE WIND THE GATES OF THE WANDERING BOAT	194	SLEEP BECALMED	10
OR THROW IT, STONE BY STONE, ...	233	FURIOUS MOTION	22
OR THROW A VIOLET SHADOW WHEN I WILL.	238	MAKES INTERVALS	8
THROWN			
ALL BUT THE BRISKEST RIDERS THROWN, ...	98	TWILIGHT LOCKS	41
ARC-LAMPED THROWN BACK UPON THE CUTTING FLOOD.	118	ALTARWISE	56
THROWN TO THE SEA IN THE SHELL OF A GIRL	165	LONG-LEGGED	92
AND THE DARK THROWN	180	VISION, PRAYER	31

		PAGE	TITLE	LINE
THROWS				
	A WIND THROWS A SHADOW AND IT FREEZES FAST.	166	LONG-LEGGED	130
THRUST				
	THRUST OUT OUR HEADS ABOVE THE BRANCHES	31	BEING BUT MEN	9
	THRUST, MY DAUGHTER OR SON, TO ESCAPE, THERE IS			
	NONE, NONE, NONE, ...	146	IF HEAD HURT	19
	TO THRUST YOUR ARM INTO THE EARTH	229	MY RIVER	10
THRUSTING				
	THRUSTING THE TOM-THUMB VISION UP THE IRON MILE.	111	I, IN IMAGE	84
	OVER THESE GROUNDWORKS THRUSTING THROUGH A PAVEMENT	117	ALTARWISE	27
THUD				
	FELT THUD BENEATH MY FLESH'S ARMOUR, ...	68	BEFORE KNOCKED	9
THUDDING				
	YOU RULE THE THUDDING HEART THAT BITES THE SIDE;	67	REALM OF FLESH	7
THUMB				
	TESTED BY FIRE, DOUBLE THUMB TO NOSE, ...	52	OUT OF THE PIT	74
	DEATH'S APPETITE IS SHARPENED BY THE BULLET'S THUMB;	64	WOMAN SPEAKS	34
	DRIVE CHILDREN UP LIKE BRUISES TO THE THUMB, ...	100	RUNNING GRAVE	14
	WHO SPEAK ON A FINGER AND THUMB, ...	129	MY NEOPHYTE	29
	AND MAKES WITH A FLICK OF THE THUMB AND SUN	142	SAINT TO FALL	50
THUMBS				
	YOUR STRING SHALL STRETCH A GULLY TWIXT THE THUMBS	87	PAIN BE MUSIC	7
	DIVIDE THE NIGHT AND DAY WITH FAIRY THUMBS;	92	BOYS OF SUMMER	15
	THE FINGERS WILL FORGET GREEN THUMBS AND MARK	138	FIVE & COUNTRY	2
	THERE IS THUNDER UNDER ITS THUMBS;	164	LONG-LEGGED	62
THUMB-STAINED				
	AND PRICK THE THUMB-STAINED HEAVEN THROUGH THE			
	THIMBLE.	104	WORLD PYRAMID	27
THUMP				
	SHALL GODS BE SAID TO THUMP THE CLOUDS	65	GODS THUMP	T
	SHALL GODS BE SAID TO THUMP THE CLOUDS	65	GODS THUMP	1
THUNDER				
	AND THE THUNDER OF CALLS AND NOTES.	44	LONGED TO MOVE	10
	AND THERE WAS THUNDER IN AN OPENING ROSE.	51	OUT OF THE PIT	17
	WHEN CLOUDS ARE CURSED BY THUNDER, ...	65	GODS THUMP	2
	SHALL NOT THUNDER ON THE TOWN	126	SEED-AT-ZERO	45
	THERE IS THUNDER UNDER ITS THUMBS;	164	LONG-LEGGED	62
	AS THE SAILS DRANK UP THE HAIL OF THUNDER	166	LONG-LEGGED	127
	THE SUNDERING ULTIMATE KINGDOM OF GENESIS' THUNDER.	175	FIRE RAID	77
THUNDERBOLTS				
	SEARING THE SKY FOR THUNDERBOLTS TO FALL	34	THIRST PARCHES	5
	WILL PULL THE THUNDERBOLTS	161	DEATHS AND ENT	32
	AND THUNDERBOLTS IN THEIR MANES.	168	LONG-LEGGED	190
THUNDERCLAP				
	TALLER THIS THUNDERCLAP SPRING, AND HOW	211	POEM ON B'DAY	103
THUNDERCLAPPING				
	FLASHED FIRST ACROSS HIS THUNDERCLAPPING EYES.	160	DEATHS AND ENT	24
THUNDERING				
	A THUNDERING BULLRING OF YOUR SILENT AND			
	GIRL-CIRCLED ISLAND.	142	SAINT TO FALL	51
THUNDEROUS				
	ON THUNDEROUS PAVEMENTS IN THE GARDEN TIME;	117	ALTARWISE	34
THUNDERS				
	THAT THUNDERS AS HEART THUNDERS, SLOWS AS HEART			
	SLOWS.	46	POET: 1935	6
	THAT THUNDERS AS HEART THUNDERS, SLOWS AS HEART			
	SLOWS.	46	POET: 1935	6
	THUNDERS ON THE FOREIGN TOWN	127	SEED-AT-ZERO	52
THUNDER'S				
	AND THE THUNDER'S FIRST NOTE;	59	FAIRY TALES	3

		PAGE	TITLE	LINE
THUNDER'S (CONTINUED)				
FEAR DEATH AS LITTLE AS THE THUNDER'S SHOT,	....	60	FAIRY TALES	40
THUNDER'S ROD OR MAN'S MACHINE;	....	71	TAKE NEEDLES	23
BISECTED SHADOWS ON THE THUNDER'S BONE	....	103	WORLD PYRAMID	5
THUS				
AND THUS I SAW HIM SEARCHING FOR HIS SOUL.	....	51	OUT OF THE PIT	44
AND THUS I SAW HIM. HE WAS POISED LIKE THIS,	....	52	OUT OF THE PIT	59
AND THUS, BETWEEN THE SEASONS, HEARD HIM CRY:	.....	52	OUT OF THE PIT	62
AND THUS I SAW HIM IN A SQUARE OF FIELDS,	....	53	OUT OF THE PIT	87
AND THUS, SOME TIME LATER, I HEARD HIM SAY:	....	53	OUT OF THE PIT	89
THUS THE SHADOWLESS MAN OR OX, AND THE PICTURED				
DEVIL,	....	109	I, IN IMAGE	22
THY				
THY PLACE IS FILLED, BONES BID FOR AUCTION,	....	29	LONG, SKELETON	9
SHED THOU THY TEARS ON HIM; HE WILL NOT WAKE,	.....	222	MISSING	8
CHRYSOLITH THY STEP,	....	225	SLENDER WIND	1
EACH NOTE OF THY DUSKY SONG	....	226	SLENDER WIND	6
TICKED				
HOW TIME HAS TICKED A HEAVEN ROUND THE STARS.	.....	77	THE FORCE THAT	20
TICKING				
TICKING THE WORLD AWAY,	....	26	THERE'S PLENTY	12
TICKLE				
IF THE RED TICKLE AS THE CATTLE CALVE	....	95	RUB OF LOVE	4
TICKLED				
IF I WERE TICKLED BY THE RUB OF LOVE	....	94	RUB OF LOVE	T
IF I WERE TICKLED BY THE RUB OF LOVE,	....	94	RUB OF LOVE	1
IF I WERE TICKLED BY THE HATCHING HAIR,	....	95	RUB OF LOVE	10
IF I WERE TICKLED BY THE URCHIN HUNGERS	....	95	RUB OF LOVE	18
IF I WERE TICKLED BY THE LOVERS' RUB	....	95	RUB OF LOVE	22
I WOULD BE TICKLED BY THE RUB THAT IS:	....	96	RUB OF LOVE	48
TICKLES				
AND THAT'S THE RUB, THE ONLY RUB THAT TICKLES.	....	96	RUB OF LOVE	36
TIDAL				
O TIDAL WINDS, CAST UP HER CRY FOR ME;	....	65	WOMAN SPEAKS	54
PRAISE HIM WHO SPRINGS AND FILLS THE TIDAL WELL.		76	LASHED RINGS	11
TIDE				
THE LUNAR SILENCES, THE SILENT TIDE	....	54	WE BY SEASAND	9
LEAN TIME ON TIDE AND TIMES THE WIND STOOD ROUGH,		107	GRIEF THIEF	6
WHO TOSSED THE HIGH TIDE IN A TIME OF STORIES	.....	108	GRIEF THIEF	13
THE COCKEREL'S TIDE UPCASTING FROM THE FIRE.	......	127	NOW, SAY NAY	21
CREEP AND HARP ON THE TIDE, SINKING THEIR CHARMED,				
BENT PIN	....	135	HOW MY ANIMAL	24
THE BLACK MAN BLEACHED TO HIS TIDE	....	155	RETURN	40
OUT TO THE TIERED AND HEARING TIDE,	....	158	INTO HER HEAD	38
THE COUNTRY TIDE IS COBBLED WITH TOWNS,	....	168	LONG-LEGGED	192
HIGH TIDE AND THE HERON DIVED WHEN I TOOK THE ROAD		177	POEM IN OCT	17
TO THE TREES AND THE STONES AND THE FISH IN THE TIDE.		178	POEM IN OCT	57
COMES DESIGNED TO MY LOVE TO STEAL NOT HER TIDE				
RAKING	....	200	COUNTRY SLEEP	100
TO KILL AND THEIR OWN TIDE DAUBING BLOOD	....	209	POEM ON B'DAY	35
TIDED				
INTO THE TIDED CORD, THERE GOES	....	91	WHERE ONCE THE	8
TIDE-HOISTED				
THEN THREW ON THAT TIDE-HOISTED SCREEN	....	129	MY NEOPHYTE	34
TIDE-LOOPED				
OR LIKE THE TIDE-LOOPED BREASTKNOT REEFED AGAIN	...	131	I MAKE THIS IN	11
TIDE-MASTER				
LAPPING THE STILL CANALS, THE DRY TIDE-MASTER	.....	54	WE BY SEASAND	10

	PAGE	TITLE	LINE
TIDE-PRINT			
MOONFALL AND SAILING EMPEROR, PALE AS THEIR			
TIDE-PRINT, ...	130	SINNERS' BELL	10
TIDES			
OF TIDES THAT NEVER TOUCH THE SHORES.	69	BEFORE KNOCKED	34
PUSH IN THEIR TIDES;	82	LIGHT BREAKS	3
AND DROWN THE CARGOED APPLES IN THEIR TIDES.	91	BOYS OF SUMMER	6
INVISIBLE, YOUR CLOCKING TIDES	91	WHERE ONCE THE	13
THERE SHALL BE SERPENTS IN YOUR TIDES, ...	91	WHERE ONCE THE	23
TO CHOKE THE DESERTS WITH HER TIDES, ...	93	BOYS OF SUMMER	41
SLEEP NAVIGATES THE TIDES OF TIME;	97	TWILIGHT LOCKS	25
ON CASTING TIDES, ARE TANGLED IN THE SHELLS, ...	105	WORLD PYRAMID	50
SOAKS UP THE SEWING TIDES), ...	113	SERVANT SUN	12
BUT THE HUNGRY KINGS OF THE TIDES;	165	LONG-LEGGED	109
WHO SAILS ON TIDES OF LEAVES AND SOUND.	234	NO, PIGEON	16
TIDETHREAD			
THIS TIDETHREAD AND THE LANE OF SCALES, ...	128	MY NEOPHYTE	14
TIDE-TONGUED			
OF TIDE-TONGUED HEADS AND BLADDERS IN THE DEEP, ...	104	WORLD PYRAMID	16
TIDE-TRACED			
CARTOON OF SLASHES ON THE TIDE-TRACED CRATER, ...	119	ALTARWISE	71
TIDY			
NO TIDY FLOWER MOVED, NO BATHER GRACEFULLY	34	IN GARDENS	19
AM I NOT YOU WHO FRONT THE TIDY SHORE, ...	112	NOT FATHER ME	15
TIDY AND CURSED IN MY DOVE COOED ROOM	207	LAMENT	52
TIE			
WE WILL TIE YOU DOWN	230	OUR SANCTITY	19
TIED			
AND TIED AN IRIS IN HIS THROAT	85	SEE, SAYS LIME	18
TIERED			
OUT TO THE TIERED AND HEARING TIDE, ...	158	INTO HER HEAD	38
TIGER-LILY			
AS THE MOUTH OF THE TIGER-LILY	229	MY RIVER	24
TIGERS			
MADE THE TIGERS JUMP OUT OF THEIR EYES	172	THE HUNCHBACK	28
TIGRESS			
AND THE TIMID DEER THE TIGRESS:	76	SONG: LOVE ME	14
TIGRON			
I SEE THE TIGRON IN TEARS	148	UNLUCKILY FOR	29
TILER			
NOR ROOF OF SAND, NOR YET THE TOWERING TILER?	112	NOT FATHER ME	16
TILL			
PUFF TILL THE ADDER IS, ...	22	HIGH ON A HILL	9
BREATHE TILL THE SNAKE IS HOME, ...	22	HIGH ON A HILL	10
TILL THE BIRD HAS BURST HIS SHELL, ...	22	HIGH ON A HILL	12
WHERE MEN WOULD ARGUE TILL THE STARS BE GREEN, ...	43	A WAR OF WITS	23
SO SHALL HE STEP TILL SUMMER LOOSENS ITS HOLD	46	POET: 1935	18
LIFE, TILL THE CHANGE OF MOOD, FORKS	47	POET: 1935	38
ACHES TILL THE METAL MEETS THE MARROW, ...	47	POET: 1935	50
BREAK IN THE SUN TILL THE SUN BREAKS DOWN, ...	50	NO DOMINION	26
SHALL NOT BE KNOWN TILL WINDWELL DRIES	55	WHY EAST WIND	2
NOT TILL, FROM HIGH AND LOW, THEIR DUST	56	WHY EAST WIND	12
IS HEARD BUT LITTLE TILL THE STARS GO OUT.	56	WHY EAST WIND	20
ALONE TILL THE DAY I DIE	62	EARS IN TURRET	6
OR STAY TILL THE DAY I DIE	62	EARS IN TURRET	23
OR STAY TILL THE DAY I DIE?	63	EARS IN TURRET	31
TURN AND CHURN NIGHTSEED TILL IT CURDLE.	67	LET A FAITH	5
REMAINS THOUGH GODS BE FELLED TILL NONE ARE LEFT.	67	LET A FAITH	10
UNFAILING TILL THE BLOOD RUNS FOUL;	69	BEFORE KNOCKED	28
TOIL AWAY TILL MUSIC DIES.	70	TAKE NEEDLES	4

	PAGE	TITLE	LINE
TILL (CONTINUED)			
TILL ALL OUR SEA-FAITHS DIE.	91	WHERE ONCE THE	24
AND, CLAPPED IN WATER TILL THE TRITON DANGLES, ...	110	I, IN IMAGE	64
TILL FIELD AND ROOF LIE LEVEL AND THE SAME	116	LANTERNS SHINE	13
TILL TALLOW I BLEW FROM THE WAX'S TOWER	119	ALTARWISE	79
TILL THE THREE-COLOURED RAINBOW FROM MY NIPPLES ...	120	ALTARWISE	107
LOVE'S IMAGE TILL MY HEARTBONE BREAKS	129	MY NEOPHYTE	35
IN QUICK, SWEET, CRUEL LIGHT TILL THE LOCKED GROUND			
SPROUT OUT, ...	135	HOW MY ANIMAL	18
TILL THE SWEET TOOTH OF MY LOVE BIT DRY, ...	146	TO OTHERS	7
TILL EVERY BEAST BLARED DOWN IN A SWERVE	163	LONG-LEGGED	57
TILL EVERY TURTLE CRUSHED FROM HIS SHELL	163	LONG-LEGGED	58
TILL EVERY BONE IN THE RUSHING GRAVE	163	LONG-LEGGED	59
SLEEPS TILL SILENCE BLOWS ON A CLOUD	165	LONG-LEGGED	111
TILL THE BLOOD SHALL SPURT, ...	173	FIRE RAID	22
ROOSTS SLEEPING CHILL TILL THE FLAME OF THE COCK CROW	187	WINTER'S TALE	19
BACK. LINES OF AGE SLEEP ON THE STONES TILL			
TRUMPETING DAWN.	191	WINTER'S TALE	118
OF DAY, IN THE THISTLE AISLES, TILL THE WHITE OWL			
CROSSED	204	GIANT'S THIGH	32
TILT			
BY FULL TILT RIVER AND SWITCHBACK SEA	208	POEM ON B'DAY	2
TILTED			
SHOT IN THE WIND, BY TILTED ARCS, ...	129	MY NEOPHYTE	26
IN THE RIVER TOWY BELOW BOWS HIS TILTED HEADSTONE.	201	SIR JOHNS HILL	12
TILTING			
OF DUSK AND WATER I SEE THE TILTING WHISPERING	202	SIR JOHNS HILL	48
TIME			
DRIFTING IN EASY TIME;	13	RAIN CUTS	14
IN TIME LIKE OUTLAW RAINS ON THAT PRIEST, WATER,	15	SPIRE CRANES	6
TIME FOR THE SWIMMERS' HANDS, MUSIC FOR SILVER LOCK	15	SPIRE CRANES	7
THERE'S TIME TO PLUCK A TUNE UPON THE HARP, ...	15	FOR LEDA	16
THE MORNING, TOO, IS TIME FOR LOVE, ...	15	FOR LEDA	28
TIME ENOUGH TO ROT	16	TIME TO ROT	T
TIME ENOUGH TO ROT;	16	TIME TO ROT	1
ONE HOUR SPEND MY TIME FOR ME	18	NATURAL DAY	5
IN TIME, LIKE ALL, THROUGH MY UNREASON	21	BEWILDERED WAY	7
TIME AFTER TIME.	22	ON QUIET NIGHT	11
TIME AFTER TIME.	22	ON QUIET NIGHT	11
OF FOOT ON HEAD WE'LL BE THE TIME	24	LITTLE PROBLEM	4
AT LAST BY TIME, ...	26	PERSONAL EPIT	4
AND WATCH THE HAND OF TIME UNCEASINGLY	26	THERE'S PLENTY	11
TIME CANNOT HEAL NOR RESURRECT;	26	THERE'S PLENTY	15
IS TREASON'S TIME AND THE TIME OF ENVY.	34	THIRST PARCHES	7
IS TREASON'S TIME AND THE TIME OF ENVY.	34	THIRST PARCHES	7
IS EMPTY IN SPRINGTIME, AND NO OTHER TIME LESSENS	39	GAS FADES	20
WAS THERE A TIME	40	WAS THERE TIME	T
WAS THERE A TIME WHEN DANCERS WITH THEIR FIDDLES	40	WAS THERE TIME	1
THERE WAS A TIME THEY COULD CRY OVER BOOKS, ...	40	WAS THERE TIME	3
BUT TIME HAS SET ITS MAGGOT ON THEIR TRACK.	40	WAS THERE TIME	4
MEN OLD BEFORE THEIR TIME INTO DARK VALLEYS	41	YOUNG ARE OLD	19
AND BE STRUCK DUMB, IF ONLY FOR A TIME.	43	A WAR OF WITS	25
AS THE HANDS THAT HELD THEM IN MY FATHER'S TIME.	45	PLOUGHMAN GONE	11
THE SAME TUNE AS IN MY FATHER'S TIME:	46	PLOUGHMAN GONE	29
HASTENS THE TIME OF THE GERANIUM TO BREATHE;	47	POET: 1935	37
AND THUS, SOME TIME LATER, I HEARD HIM SAY:	53	OUT OF THE PIT	89
TIME UPON TIME THE TOWERS OF THE SKIES	56	WHY EAST WIND	19
TIME UPON TIME THE TOWERS OF THE SKIES	56	WHY EAST WIND	19
PECKING AND NESTLING ALL THE TIME OF NIGHT.	63	WOMAN SPEAKS	18
AND TIME CAST FORTH MY MORTAL CREATURE	69	BEFORE KNOCKED	31

		PAGE	TITLE	LINE
TIME (CONTINUED)				
THE LIPS OF TIME LEECH TO THE FOUNTAIN HEAD;	......	77	THE FORCE THAT	16
HOW TIME HAS TICKED A HEAVEN ROUND THE STARS.	......	77	THE FORCE THAT	20
THE TIME FOR BREAST AND THE GREEN APRON AGE	....	78	LOVE'S FEVER	4
THE ALMANAC OF TIME	....	79	ALMANAC TIME	T
THE ALMANAC OF TIME HANGS IN THE BRAIN;	....	79	ALMANAC TIME	1
THE WORD OF TIME LIES ON THE CHAPTERED BONE,	....	80	ALMANAC TIME	11
THE SEED OF TIME IS SHELTERED IN THE LOIN:	....	80	ALMANAC TIME	12
TIME SHALL BELONG TO MAN.	....	80	ALMANAC TIME	15
TIME AND THE CRABS AND THE SWEETHEARTING CRIB	......	95	RUB OF LOVE	25
THE MOUTH OF TIME SUCKED, LIKE A SPONGE,	....	97	TWILIGHT LOCKS	4
SLEEP NAVIGATES THE TIDES OF TIME;	....	97	TWILIGHT LOCKS	25
WHEN, LIKE A RUNNING GRAVE, TIME TRACKS YOU DOWN,		99	RUNNING GRAVE	1
WHEN BLOOD, SPADE-HANDED, AND THE LOGIC TIME	......	100	RUNNING GRAVE	13
TIME IS A FOOLISH FANCY, TIME AND FOOL.	....	100	RUNNING GRAVE	26
TIME IS A FOOLISH FANCY, TIME AND FOOL.	....	100	RUNNING GRAVE	26
LET FALL THE TEAR OF TIME; THE SLEEPER'S EYE,	......	101	FELLOWED SLEEP	2
WITH WHISTLER'S COUGH CONTAGES, TIME ON TRACK	......	101	RUNNING GRAVE	47
GRIEF THIEF OF TIME	....	107	GRIEF THIEF	T
GRIEF THIEF OF TIME CRAWLS OFF,	....	107	GRIEF THIEF	1
THE SEA-HALVED FAITH THAT BLEW TIME TO HIS KNEES,		107	GRIEF THIEF	4
LEAN TIME ON TIDE AND TIMES THE WIND STOOD ROUGH,		107	GRIEF THIEF	6
WHO TOSSED THE HIGH TIDE IN A TIME OF STORIES	.....	108	GRIEF THIEF	13
THE SEA AND INSTRUMENT, NICKED IN THE LOCKS OF TIME,		111	I, IN IMAGE	92
TIME IN THE HOURLESS HOUSES	....	111	I, IN IMAGE	99
CAN TIME UNRIDDLE, AND THE CUPBOARD STONE,	....	113	SERVANT SUN	3
A NITRIC SHAPE THAT LEAPS HER, TIME AND ACID;	.....	115	A GRIEF AGO	34
SO FAST I MOVE DEFYING TIME, THE QUIET GENTLEMAN		116	LANTERNS SHINE	14
THAT NIGHT OF TIME UNDER THE CHRISTWARD SHELTER:		117	ALTARWISE	12
ON THUNDEROUS PAVEMENTS IN THE GARDEN TIME;	....	117	ALTARWISE	34
TIME, MILK, AND MAGIC, FROM THE WORLD BEGINNING.		119	ALTARWISE	94
TIME IS THE TUNE MY LADIES LEND THEIR HEARTBREAK,		119	ALTARWISE	95
TIME TRACKS THE SOUND OF SHAPE ON MAN AND CLOUD,		120	ALTARWISE	97
AS THE GREEN BLOOMS RIDE UPWARD, TO THE DRIVE OF TIME;		122	HOLD HARD	3
TIME, IN A FOLLY'S RIDER, LIKE A COUNTY MAN	....	122	HOLD HARD	4
TIME, IN A RIDER RISING, FROM THE HARNESSED VALLEY;		122	HOLD HARD	21
FARMER IN TIME OF FROST THE BURNING LEAGUES,	......	123	FOSTER LIGHT	10
TIME AT THE CITY SPECTACLES, AND HALF	....	124	TODAY, INSECT	3
THE DEAR, DAFT TIME I TAKE TO NUDGE THE SENTENCE,		124	TODAY, INSECT	4
IN TIME AT FLOOD FILLED WITH HIS COLOURED DOUBLES;		124	FOSTER LIGHT	27
TIME ON THE CANVAS PATHS.	....	129	MY NEOPHYTE	24
TIME KILLS ME TERRIBLY.	....	129	MY NEOPHYTE	43
'TIME SHALL NOT MURDER YOU,' HE SAID,	....	129	MY NEOPHYTE	44
I SAW TIME MURDER ME.	....	129	MY NEOPHYTE	48
TIME MARKS A BLACK AISLE KINDLE FROM THE BRAND OF ASHES,	....	130	SINNERS' BELL	4
GRIEF WITH DRENCHED BOOK AND CANDLE CHRISTENS THE CHERUB TIME	....	130	SINNERS' BELL	16
I MEAN BY TIME THE CAST AND CURFEW RASCAL OF OUR MARRIAGE,	....	130	SINNERS' BELL	25
AFTER THE FEAST OF TEAR-STUFFED TIME AND THISTLES		136	AFTER FUNERAL	10
PECK, SPRINT, DANCE ON FOUNTAINS AND DUCK TIME	....	145	IF HEAD HURT	8
THE WARM-VEINED DOUBLE OF TIME	....	150	WHEN I WOKE	11
NO TIME, SPOKE THE CLOCKS, NO GOD, RANG THE BELLS,		150	WHEN I WOKE	28
ONCE BELOW A TIME	....	151	BELOW A TIME	T
ONCE BELOW A TIME	....	151	BELOW A TIME	1
TIME AMONG WALKING PINTABLES	....	154	RETURN	10
MATERNAL SHORT TIME PIECES,	....	155	RETURN	54
TIME IS BEARING ANOTHER SON.	....	167	LONG-LEGGED	153

	PAGE	TITLE	LINE
TIME (CONTINUED)			
KILL TIME! SHE TURNS IN HER PAIN!	167	LONG-LEGGED	154
TIME AND PLACES GRIP HER BREAST BONE,	168	LONG-LEGGED	175
MADE ALL DAY UNTIL BELL TIME	172	THE HUNCHBACK	31
THE PEBBLES. IT IS TIME FOR THE BLACK LION	179	NEW QUAY	10
TO THE BURN AND TURN OF TIME	180	VISION, PRAYER	11
PRAISE THAT THE SPRING TIME IS ALL	186	HOLY SPRING	14
IF ONLY FOR A LAST TIME.	186	HOLY SPRING	24
OR FLOWER UNDER THE TIME DYING FLESH ASTRIDE.	188	WINTER'S TALE	55
TIME SINGS THROUGH THE INTRICATELY DEAD SNOW DROP. LISTEN.	189	WINTER'S TALE	65
THE FIELDS OF SEED AND THE TIME DYING FLESH ASTRIDE,	190	WINTER'S TALE	103
EXULTATION LIES DOWN. TIME BURIES THE SPRING WEATHER	191	WINTER'S TALE	119
TIME LET ME HAIL AND CLIMB	195	FERN HILL	4
AND ONCE BELOW A TIME I LORDLY HAD THE TREES AND LEAVES	195	FERN HILL	7
TIME LET ME PLAY AND BE	195	FERN HILL	13
AND NOTHING I CARED, AT MY SKY BLUE TRADES, THAT TIME ALLOWS	196	FERN HILL	42
NOTHING I CARED, IN THE LAMB WHITE DAYS, THAT TIME WOULD TAKE ME	196	FERN HILL	46
TIME HELD ME GREEN AND DYING	196	FERN HILL	53
TIME BY, THEIR DUST WAS FLESH THE SWINEHERD ROOTED SLY,	204	GIANT'S THIGH	21
OF SUMMER COME IN HIS GREAT GOOD TIME	206	LAMENT	32
OH, TIME ENOUGH WHEN THE BLOOD CREEPS COLD,	206	LAMENT	34
SLUNK POUTING OUT WHEN THE LIMP TIME CAME;	207	LAMENT	44
WHEN THE TIME COMES,	230	OUR SANCTITY	16
FLEW FOR A TIME IN VAIN, TO DROP AT LAST	238	PILLAR BREAKS	21
TIME-BOMB			
STRIKE IN THE TIME-BOMB TOWN,	142	SAINT TO FALL	35
TIMED			
MY FUSES TIMED TO CHARGE HIS HEART,	97	TWILIGHT LOCKS	13
TIME-FACED			
NOW JACK MY FATHERS LET THE TIME-FACED CROOK,	108	GRIEF THIEF	15
TIMELESS			
WHAT SHALL IT TELL ME IF A TIMELESS INSECT	59	HERE IN SPRING	16
I AM, THE TOWER TOLD, FELLED BY A TIMELESS STROKE,	113	NOT FATHER ME	21
AND, RIP VAN WINKLE FROM A TIMELESS CRADLE,	118	ALTARWISE	37
TIMELESSLY			
AND TIMELESSLY LIES LOVING WITH THE THIEF.	108	GRIEF THIEF	14
TIMES			
ECHO A HUNDRED TIMES, THE FLIGHT OF BIRDS	50	OUT OF THE PIT	14
WITH 'STRUMPET' IN THESE TROUBLED TIMES,	84	LETTER TO AUNT	34
LEAN TIME ON TIDE AND TIMES THE WIND STOOD ROUGH,	107	GRIEF THIEF	6
SAVOURS THE LICK OF THE TIMES THROUGH A DEADLY WOOD OF HAIR	144	PLEASURE-BIRD	9
RODE AND WHISTLED A HUNDRED TIMES	157	INTO HER HEAD	18
BIRD THROUGH THE TIMES AND LANDS AND TRIBES OF THE SLOW FLAKES.	190	WINTER'S TALE	99
TIME'S			
THE INCH OF TIME'S PROTRACTED TO A FOOT	80	ALMANAC TIME	8
I, THAT TIME'S JACKET OR THE COAT OF ICE	100	RUNNING GRAVE	18
ADAM, TIME'S JOKER, ON A WITCH OF CARDBOARD	119	ALTARWISE	81
TIME'S TUNE MY LADIES WITH THE TEATS OF MUSIC,	119	ALTARWISE	91
TIME'S NERVE IN VINEGAR, THE GALLOW GRAVE	120	ALTARWISE	100
TIME'S SHIP-RACKED GOSPEL ON THE GLOBE I BALANCE:	121	ALTARWISE	129
TIME'S CORAL SAINT AND THE SALT GRIEF DROWN A FOUL SEPULCHRE	130	SINNERS' BELL	8

	PAGE	TITLE	LINE
TIME-SHAKEN			
BEFORE THE LUNGE OF THE NIGHT, THE NOTES ON THIS TIME-SHAKEN	203	SIR JOHNS HILL	59
TIMID			
I AM A TIMID CHILD WHEN LIGHT IS DEAD.	48	LIGHT, I KNOW	11
AND THE TIMID DEER THE TIGRESS:	76	SONG: LOVE ME	14
DELIVER ME WHO, TIMID IN MY TRIBE, ...	100	RUNNING GRAVE	7
TIN			
DRAMATIC SHADOWS IN A TIN BOX;	57	TO ARCHITECTS	2
TINGLE			
TINGLE ON MINE;	21	BEWILDERED WAY	14
TINNED			
TAXIS AND LILIES TO TINNED MUSIC STEPPED	51	OUT OF THE PIT	24
TINY			
AND SAW TOWARDS HER TINY FACE	11	CABARET	3
SITS BACK AND SMILES, A TINY CORPSE	49	LIGHT, I KNOW	24
LET THE TINY ARMIES LAP, ...	71	TAKE NEEDLES	10
THEIR GRASSES, EACH A TINY ECSTASY, ...	223	IDYLL UNFORGET	15
TIP			
NOT FROM THE SENSES' DUALIZING TIP	20	THE NEOPHYTE	16
ON THE LAST RICK'S TIP BY SPILLED WINE-WELLS	141	SAINT TO FALL	14
IN THE SNIFFED AND POURED SNOW ON THE TIP OF THE TONGUE OF THE YEAR	144	PLEASURE-BIRD	5
TIPS			
ON TIPS OF THOUGHT WHERE THOUGHTS SMELL IN THE RAIN;	82	LIGHT BREAKS	26
TIPSY			
BLACK-TONGUED AND TIPSY FROM SALVATION'S BOTTLE.	118	ALTARWISE	61
TIPTOED			
I TIPTOED SHY IN THE GOOSEBERRY WOOD, ...	206	LAMENT	4
TIRED			
YOUTH CALLS TO AGE ACROSS THE TIRED YEARS:	30	YOUTH CALLS	13
FEEL, AS THE PULSE GROWS TIRED, ...	32	HELD-OUT HAND	3
UNSHACKLED THE WEIGHTS OF WORDS FROM TIRED LIMBS,	53	OUT OF THE PIT	83
BRUISING THE TIRED FEATHERS.	240	ADMIT THE SUN	8
TIRELESS			
AMONG THE STREET BURNED TO TIRELESS DEATH	173	FIRE RAID	4
TIT			
TOM TIT AND DAI MOUSE!	5	PROLOGUE	99
THE RUDE OWL CRIED LIKE A TELLTALE TIT, ...	206	LAMENT	5
TITHINGS			
LAY THE GOLD TITHINGS BARREN, ...	91	BOYS OF SUMMER	2
TO (662)			
TOADS			
WHERE EYES SHOULD BE, AND NOSTRILS FULL OF TOADS.	51	OUT OF THE PIT	23
TOCSIN			
OUT OF THE FONT OF BONE AND PLANTS AT THAT STONE TOCSIN	130	SINNERS' BELL	20
TODAY			
TODAY, THIS INSECT	124	TODAY, INSECT	T
TODAY, THIS INSECT, AND THE WORLD I BREATHE, ...	124	TODAY, INSECT	1
TO-DAY			
TO-DAY, IF ALL MY SENSES ACT, ...	238	MAKES INTERVALS	9
TODAY'S			
THE POSTER IS TODAY'S TEXT, ...	58	TO ARCHITECTS	6
TOE			
WHEN LEDA, ON A TOE OF DOWN, ...	15	FOR LEDA	29
BY TOE OR HAIR TO COMMON GOOD, ...	24	LITTLE PROBLEM	12
FROM NAPE TO TOE, A SANATORIUM PIECE	29	LONG, SKELETON	5
FROM POLES OF SKULL AND TOE THE WINDY BLOOD	82	LIGHT BREAKS	14

```
                                          PAGE      TITLE        LINE
TOEING
    OF MARBLE BATHERS TOEING THE GARDEN PONDS,   ........   33   IN GARDENS         2
TOES
    SHE IS ON DANCING TOES AGAIN,     ...................   12   CABARET           18
    DEAD ON THE SWEETHEARTS' TOES.    ...................   95   RUB OF LOVE       28
    HORNED DOWN WITH SKULLFOOT AND THE SKULL OF TOES      117   ALTARWISE         33
TOGETHER
    PUTTING TWO AND TWO TOGETHER,     ...................   38   THE GOSSIPERS      6
    FIXED FAITH, BELIEVING AND WORSHIPPING TOGETHER  ...   41   YOUNG ARE OLD     46
    TWO SAND GRAINS TOGETHER IN BED,   ..................  158   INTO HER HEAD     47
    THEY COME TOGETHER WHOM THEIR LOVE PARTED:  ........  161   WEDDING ANNIV     10
    O ADAM AND EVE TOGETHER    .........................  174   FIRE RAID         42
    LIGHT AND HIS TEARS GLIDE DOWN TOGETHER   ..........  215   COUNTRY HEAVEN    11
TOIL
    TOIL AWAY TILL MUSIC DIES.    ......................   70   TAKE NEEDLES       4
TOILS
    NO MORE TOILS OVER THE FIELDS    ...................   45   PLOUGHMAN GONE    13
    MAN TOILS NOW ON AN IRON SADDLE, RIDING   ..........   45   PLOUGHMAN GONE    24
    TOILS TOWARDS THE AMBUSH OF HIS WOUNDS;   ..........  209   POEM ON B'DAY     17
TOLD
    I LAID HER DOWN AND TOLD HER SIN,   ................   61   MEAT ON BONES     23
    I AM, THE TOWER TOLD, FELLED BY A TIMELESS STROKE,   113   NOT FATHER ME     21
    I HAVE BEEN TOLD TO REASON BY THE HEART,   .........  116   LANTERNS SHINE     9
    I HAVE BEEN TOLD TO REASON BY THE PULSE,   .........  116   LANTERNS SHINE    11
    THE TOMBSTONE TOLD WHEN SHE DIED    ................  139   TOMBSTONE TOLD     T
    THE TOMBSTONE TOLD WHEN SHE DIED.   ................  139   TOMBSTONE TOLD     1
    TONGUE OF YOUR TRANSLATING EYES. THE YOUNG STARS
        TOLD ME,   ....................................  148   UNLUCKILY FOR     51
    BIRDMAN OR TOLD GHOST I HUNG.   ....................  152   BELOW A TIME      31
    AND THE TWICE TOLD FIELDS OF INFANCY   .............  178   POEM IN OCT       51
    IN THE RIVER WENDED VALES WHERE THE TALE WAS TOLD.   187   WINTER'S TALE     10
    DOING WHAT THEY ARE TOLD,    .......................  209   POEM ON B'DAY     12
TOLERANCE
    I CAN DETECT A TOLERANCE,    .......................  236   WOMAN TAPESTRY    52
TOLL
    OF SLEEPERS WHOSE TONGUE I TOLL    .................  184   VISION, PRAYER   155
TOLLED
    NEVER, MY GIRL, UNTIL TOLLED TO SLEEP BY THE STERN   198   COUNTRY SLEEP     21
TOLLS
    IN THE TOWER AND TOLLS TO SLEEP OVER THE STALLS  ...  199   COUNTRY SLEEP     52
    WHO TOLLS HIS BIRTHDAY BELL,   .....................  209   POEM ON B'DAY     16
TOM
    TOM TIT AND DAI MOUSE!    ..........................    5   PROLOGUE          99
    NO SPRINGTAILED TOM IN THE RED HOT TOWN   ..........  206   LAMENT            29
TOMB
    AND I AM DUMB TO TELL THE LOVER'S TOMB   ...........   77   THE FORCE THAT    21
    STORMS IN THE FREEZING TOMB.    ....................   88   A PROCESS IN       3
    BY MIDNIGHT PULLEYS THAT UNHOUSE THE TOMB.   .......   89   EUNUCH DREAMS     10
    DRY AS A TOMB, YOUR COLOURED LIDS    ...............   91   WHERE ONCE THE    19
    THE DRY SARGASSO OF THE TOMB    ....................   97   TWILIGHT LOCKS    26
    THE CLOUD CLIMB OF THE EXHALING TOMB   .............  182   VISION, PRAYER    76
TOMBS
    NOR EVER, AS THE WILD TONGUE BREAKS ITS TOMBS,  ....  144   PLEASURE-BIRD     11
    AND INTO ITS TALKATIVE SEVEN TOMBS   ...............  169   LONG-LEGGED      211
TOMBSTONE
    THE TOMBSTONE TOLD WHEN SHE DIED    ................  139   TOMBSTONE TOLD     T
    THE TOMBSTONE TOLD WHEN SHE DIED.   ................  139   TOMBSTONE TOLD     1
TOMMY
    DEAR TOMMY, PLEASE, FROM FAR, SCIATIC KINGSLEY  ....  179   NEW QUAY           1
```

	PAGE	TITLE	LINE
TOMORROW			
PRIDES OF TOMORROW SUCKLING IN HER EYES, ...	133	I MAKE THIS IN	67
TO-MORROW			
O ROME AND SODOM TO-MORROW AND LONDON	168	LONG-LEGGED	191
CASTING TO-MORROW LIKE A THORN	180	VISION, PRAYER	25
AND TO-MORROW WEEPS IN A BLIND CAGE	209	POEM ON B'DAY	42
TOMORROW'S			
TOMORROW'S DRUNK CLUB MAJORS	154	RETURN	12
TO-MORROW'S			
TO-MORROW'S DIVER IN HER HORNY MILK, ...	103	WORLD PYRAMID	4
BIT OUT THE MANDRAKE WITH TO-MORROW'S SCREAM.	117	ALTARWISE	6
HER LOVER'S WINGS THAT FOLD TO-MORROW'S FLIGHT, ...	159	INTO HER HEAD	57
TOMORROW-TREADING			
FROM YOUR TOMORROW-TREADING SHADE	129	MY NEOPHYTE	41
TOM-THUMB			
THRUSTING THE TOM-THUMB VISION UP THE IRON MILE.	111	I, IN IMAGE	84
TONGUE			
AND HER TONGUE, LOOK, ASH, ...	10	COOL, OH NO	15
WETTEN YOUR TONGUE AND LIP, ...	20	THE NEOPHYTE	18
NOW THE THIRST PARCHES LIP AND TONGUE	34	THIRST PARCHES	T
NOW THE THIRST PARCHES LIP AND TONGUE, ...	34	THIRST PARCHES	1
I LEARNT MAN'S TONGUE, TO TWIST THE SHAPES OF THOUGHTS	79	LOVE'S FEVER	32
THE CODE OF NIGHT TAPPED ON MY TONGUE;	79	LOVE'S FEVER	40
AND FILL THE MOUTHS OF HEAVEN WITH YOUR TONGUE	87	PAIN BE MUSIC	2
ROBBED OF THE FOXY TONGUE, HIS FOOTED TAPE	100	RUNNING GRAVE	9
LOP, LOVE, MY FORK TONGUE, SAID THE PIN-HILLED NETTLE;	119	ALTARWISE	76
OLD COCK FROM NOWHERES LOPPED THE MINSTREL TONGUE	119	ALTARWISE	78
HARBOURS MY ANCHORED TONGUE, SLIPS THE QUAYSTONE,	131	I MAKE THIS IN	3
'HIS MOTHER'S WOMB HAD A TONGUE THAT LAPPED UP MUD,	132	I MAKE THIS IN	46
THE BAYONET TONGUE IN THIS UNDEFENDED PRAYERPIECE,	133	MAKE ME A MASK	5
TONGUE AND EAR IN THE THREAD, ANGLE THE TEMPLE-BOUND	135	HOW MY ANIMAL	26
AND, LASHED TO SYLLABLES, THE LYNX TONGUE CRY	139	FIVE & COUNTRY	8
OR THAT RAINY TONGUE BEAT BACK	139	TOMBSTONE TOLD	13
I AM THE GHOST IN THIS HOUSE THAT IS FILLED WITH THE TONGUE AND EYES	141	I, FIRST NAMED	3
THE MAZES OF HIS PRAISE AND ENVIOUS TONGUE WERE WORKED IN FLAMES AND SHELLS.	141	SAINT TO FALL	17
IN THE SNIFFED AND POURED SNOW ON THE TIP OF THE TONGUE OF THE YEAR	144	PLEASURE-BIRD	5
NOR EVER, AS THE WILD TONGUE BREAKS ITS TOMBS, ...	144	PLEASURE-BIRD	11
TONGUE OF YOUR TRANSLATING EYES. THE YOUNG STARS TOLD ME, ...	148	UNLUCKILY FOR	51
SHARP AND SHRILL MY SILLY TONGUE SCRATCHES	149	PAPER & STICKS	16
ITS TONGUE PEELED IN THE WRAP OF A LEAF.	150	WHEN I WOKE	15
ASSEMBLED AT HIS TONGUE	152	WAS A SAVIOUR	5
THERE WHERE A NUMBERLESS TONGUE	158	INTO HER HEAD	24
WHEN THE CAUGHT TONGUE NODDED BLIND, ...	173	FIRE RAID	13
WORD, SINGERS, AND TONGUE	174	FIRE RAID	53
OF SLEEPERS WHOSE TONGUE I TOLL	184	VISION, PRAYER	155
YET, THOUGH I CRY WITH TUMBLEDOWN TONGUE, ...	211	POEM ON B'DAY	80
TONGUED			
ON A TONGUED PUFFBALL)	5	PROLOGUE	73
AND THE RHYMER IN THE LONG TONGUED ROOM, ...	209	POEM ON B'DAY	15
TONGUELESS			
LIPLESS AND TONGUELESS IN THE SOUR EARTH	23	THE ONLY DEAD	2
TONGUE-PLUCKED			
AND FROM THESE TONGUE-PLUCKED SENSES DRAWS HIS TUNE;	76	LASHED RINGS	13

		PAGE	TITLE	LINE
TONGUES				
WITH TONGUES THAT TALK ALL TONGUES.		66	GODS THUMP	14
WITH TONGUES THAT TALK ALL TONGUES.		66	GODS THUMP	14
THE ROOT OF TONGUES ENDS IN A SPENTOUT CANCER, ...		79	LOVE'S FEVER	37
THE TONGUES OF HEAVEN GOSSIP AS I GLIDE		105	WORLD PYRAMID	53
HEAR THEY THE SALT GLASS BREAKERS AND THE TONGUES OF BURIAL.		110	I, IN IMAGE	66
IN HIGH CORN AND THE HARVEST MELTING ON THEIR TONGUES.		188	WINTER'S TALE	43
THEY YEARN WITH TONGUES OF CURLEWS FOR THE UNCONCEIVED		203	GIANT'S THIGH	10
ROUGH AS COWS' TONGUES AND THRASHED WITH BRAMBLES THEIR BUTTERMILK		204	GIANT'S THIGH	25
AND THE RAIN WRING OUT ITS TONGUES ON THE FADED YARD,		205	GIANT'S THIGH	52
TO-NIGHT				
TO-NIGHT SHALL FIND NO DYING BUT ALIVE AND WARM ...		194	CONVERS PRAYER	15
TONNED				
IN THE WAINS TONNED SO HIGH THAT THE WISPS OF THE HAY		204	GIANT'S THIGH	14
TONS				
SLIPPED THE FINS OF THOSE HUMPBACKED TONS		163	LONG-LEGGED	52
TOO				
TOO FULL WITH BLOOD TO LET MY LOVE FLOW IN.		9	MINUTE'S HOUR	12
SOMETIMES THE SKY'S TOO BRIGHT		12	SKY'S BRIGHT	T
SOMETIMES THE SKY'S TOO BRIGHT, ...		12	SKY'S BRIGHT	1
OR HAS TOO MANY CLOUDS OR BIRDS, ...		12	SKY'S BRIGHT	2
AND FAR AWAY'S TOO SHARP A SUN		12	SKY'S BRIGHT	3
WHY IS MY HAND TOO BLUNT		12	SKY'S BRIGHT	5
WATCHING, NOT TOO AWARE		13	RAIN CUTS	9
TO MAKE OUR SENSES TAKE TOO MUCH, ...		13	RAIN CUTS	10
OR TOO MUCH BLOOD;		13	SKY'S BRIGHT	21
PERHAPS THE SKY'S TOO BRIGHT;		13	SKY'S BRIGHT	26
TOO STIFF TO CHURN WITH LEAVES, ...		14	RAIN CUTS	27
THE MORNING, TOO, IS TIME FOR LOVE, ...		15	FOR LEDA	28
IS BLIND WITH TEARS TOO FRAIL TO TASTE.		15	FOR LEDA	33
TOO LONG, SKELETON		29	LONG, SKELETON	T
TOO LONG, SKELETON, DEATH'S RISEN		29	LONG, SKELETON	1
TOO LONG, SKELETON, DEATH'S ALL ALIVE		29	LONG, SKELETON	4
YOU TOO HAVE SEEN THE SUN A BIRD OF FIRE		30	YOUTH CALLS	1
HE'LL ACHE TOO LONG		32	OUT OF SIGHS	13
LEADS, TOO, TO A LEAD PIT, WHINNY AND FALL, ...		44	TO FOLLOW FOX	10
HE, TOO, COULD TOUCH THE SEASON'S LIPS AND SMILE,		46	POET: 1935	14
THE OLD FLOWERS' LEGS TOO TAUT TO DANCE, ...		47	POET: 1935	40
YOU, TOO, KNOW THE EXCEEDING JOY		47	POET: 1935	51
HE, TOO, HAS KNOWN THE AGONY IN THE GARDEN, ...		52	OUT OF THE PIT	54
HE, TOO, HAS SEEN THE WORLD AS BOTTOM ROTTEN, ...		52	OUT OF THE PIT	56
IF DEAD MEN WALKED THEY, TOO, WOULD HOLLER		59	FAIRY TALES	17
DEATH AND EVIL, TOO SLOW IN HEEDING WORDS.		60	FAIRY TALES	35
REMEMBER, TOO, THAT LIFE IS HELL		84	LETTER TO AUNT	52
SHUT, TOO, IN A TOWER OF WORDS, I MARK		98	OCTOBER WIND	9
'THIS THAT WE TREAD WAS, TOO, YOUR FATHERS' LAND.'		101	FELLOWED SLEEP	12
AM I NOT FATHER, TOO, AND THE ASCENDING BOY, ...		112	NOT FATHER ME	9
AM I NOT SISTER, TOO, WHO IS MY SAVIOUR?		112	NOT FATHER ME	12
O MY DEAR IT'S NEVER TOO LATE		149	PAPER & STICKS	11
MY PAID-FOR SLAVED-FOR OWN TOO LATE		151	BELOW A TIME	6
TOO FULL TO BOW TO THE DIM		155	RETURN	46
TOO LATE IN THE WRONG RAIN		161	WEDDING ANNIV	9
AND LEARN, TOO LATE, THEY GRIEVED IT ON ITS WAY,		208	NOT GO GENTLE	11
TOO PROUD TO DIE, BROKEN AND BLIND HE DIED		216	ELEGY	1
I AM NOT TOO PROUD TO CRY THAT HE AND HE		217	ELEGY	19
TOO PROUD TO CRY, TOO FRAIL TO CHECK THE TEARS, ...		217	ELEGY	35

	PAGE	TITLE	LINE
TOO (CONTINUED)			
TOO PROUD TO CRY, TOO FRAIL TO CHECK THE TEARS, ...	217	ELEGY	35
THE TEARS OUT OF HIS EYES, TOO PROUD TO CRY.	217	ELEGY	39
LET'S HOPE YOU WON'T THINK ME TOO VICIOUS.	221	SONG OF DOG	16
NO, PIGEON, I'M TOO WISE	234	NO, PIGEON	T
NO, PIGEON, I'M TOO WISE;	234	NO, PIGEON	1
HE FLIES TOO HIGH.	234	NO, PIGEON	23
BOAT'S BROKEN, TOO, AND MAGPIE'S STILL;	238	PILLAR BREAKS	26
TOOK			
AND TOOK TO FEEDING BIRDS WITH BROKEN CRUMBS	53	OUT OF THE PIT	84
A MERRY GIRL TOOK ME FOR MAN, ...	61	MEAT ON BONES	22
WHO TOOK MY FLESH AND BONE FOR ARMOUR	69	BEFORE KNOCKED	45
RIP OF THE VAULTS, I TOOK MY MARROW-LADLE	118	ALTARWISE	35
BLACKENED WITH BIRDS TOOK A LAST LOOK	161	LONG-LEGGED	2
HIGH TIDE AND THE HERON DIVED WHEN I TOOK THE ROAD	177	POEM IN OCT	17
TOOTH			
OR MICE PLAY WITH AN IVORY TOOTH.	49	LIGHT, I KNOW	26
A MOUSE IT WAS PLAYED WITH AN IVORY TOOTH, ...	65	WOMAN SPEAKS	58
WITH LOUD, TORN TOOTH AND TAIL AND COBWEB DRUM	133	I MAKE THIS IN	57
TILL THE SWEET TOOTH OF MY LOVE BIT DRY, ...	146	TO OTHERS	7
WITH BITER'S TOOTH AND TAIL	176	BREATH SHED	7
TOOTHLESS			
BREAD AND MILK MANSION IN A TOOTHLESS TOWN.	131	I MAKE THIS IN	15
TOP			
A POET GOING TO THE TOP?	84	LETTER TO AUNT	57
A BRUTE LAND IN THE COOL TOP OF THE COUNTRY DAYS	135	HOW MY ANIMAL	15
HIGH AND DRY BY THE TOP OF THE MAST, ...	162	LONG-LEGGED	8
TOPLESS			
CRIED THE TOPLESS, INCHTAPED LIPS FROM HANK AND HOOD	132	I MAKE THIS IN	47
TOPPLE			
CUDGEL GREAT AIR, WRECK EAST, AND TOPPLE SUNDOWN,	132	I MAKE THIS IN	33
TOPPLING			
TOPPLING AND BURNING IN THE MUDDLE OF TOWERS AND GALLERIES	145	PLEASURE-BIRD	18
TOPPLING UP THE BOATSIDE IN A SNOW OF LIGHT!	166	LONG-LEGGED	138
AND THE MOTHER AND TOPPLING HOUSE OF THE HOLY SPRING,	186	HOLY SPRING	23
TOPS			
KNOCKING OFF TURNIP TOPS, WITH TREES FOR FRIENDS,	53	OUT OF THE PIT	88
THE TOPS OF TREES, NOR AS THE LEGION	76	SONG: LOVE ME	10
MY MOTHERS-EYED, UPON THE TOPS OF TREES;	101	FELLOWED SLEEP	9
ON TO THE BLINDLY TOSSING TOPS;	167	LONG-LEGGED	150
TOPSY-TURVIES			
SUFFER, MY TOPSY-TURVIES, THAT A DOUBLE ANGEL	111	I, IN IMAGE	77
TORCH			
WHEN, WITH HIS TORCH AND HOURGLASS, LIKE A SULPHUR PRIEST, ...	130	SINNERS' BELL	2
QUICK IN THE WOOD AT LOVE, WHERE A TORCH OF FOXES FOAMS, ...	204	GIANT'S THIGH	34
TORE			
TALKED AND TORE THOUGH HER EYES SMILED.	139	TOMBSTONE TOLD	20
TORMENTED			
AN OLD TORMENTED MAN THREE-QUARTERS BLIND, ...	217	ELEGY	18
TORN			
ROARED, SEA BORN, MAN TORN, BLOOD BLEST.	4	PROLOGUE	41
OVERWHELMED BY THE SUN, WITH A TORN BRAIN	42	A WAR OF WITS	12
OR ALL-IN WRESTLING FOR TORN LIMBS TO HEAL, ...	51	OUT OF THE PIT	31
AND THE LIMBS ARE TORN.	60	MEAT ON BONES	5
TORN OUT MAGIC FROM THE HEARTS OF COWARDS	60	FAIRY TALES	32
WITH LOUD, TORN TOOTH AND TAIL AND COBWEB DRUM	133	I MAKE THIS IN	57
IN LOVE TORN BREECHES AND BLISTERED JACKET	151	BELOW A TIME	7

	PAGE	TITLE	LINE
TORN (CONTINUED)			
A MAN TORN UP MOURNS IN THE SOLE NIGHT.	159	INTO HER HEAD	67
THE SKY IS TORN ACROSS	161	WEDDING ANNIV	1
AND THE WINGED WALL IS TORN	180	VISION, PRAYER	29
TORN AND ALONE IN A FARM HOUSE IN A FOLD	187	WINTER'S TALE	15
OF THE DINGLE TORN TO SINGING AND THE SURPLICED	200	COUNTRY SLEEP	75
TORRENT			
IN THE TORRENT SALMON SUN,	3	PROLOGUE	3
TORRID			
BY HIS TORRID CROWN	180	VISION, PRAYER	30
TORTURE			
THREAD AND TORTURE ALL THE DAY;	72	TAKE NEEDLES	53
TOSS			
TOSS OVERHEAD	16	TIME TO ROT	2
TOSSED			
WHO TOSSED THE HIGH TIDE IN A TIME OF STORIES	108	GRIEF THIEF	13
FUMED LIKE A TREE, AND TOSSED A BURNING BIRD;	133	I MAKE THIS IN	56
THE CIRCULAR SMILE TOSSED FROM LOVER TO LOVER	134	NOT FROM ANGER	9
HUNGER OF BIRDS IN THE FIELDS OF THE BREAD OF WATER, TOSSED	188	WINTER'S TALE	42
TOSSING			
WHEN IN OUR BED I WAS TOSSING AND TURNING	149	PAPER & STICKS	7
ON TO THE BLINDLY TOSSING TOPS;	167	LONG-LEGGED	150
TOTTER			
BUT SEASONS MUST BE CHALLENGED OR THEY TOTTER	92	BOYS OF SUMMER	25
TOTTERS			
OR ROCKS, SWINGS AND ROCKS, BEFORE THE WORLD TOTTERS.	39	GAS FADES	34
TOUCH			
BUT SHOULD NOT TOUCH LIKE I	11	AIR BREATHE	11
FOR WHEN WE TOUCH A FLOWER WITH OUR OAR	14	RAIN CUTS	30
I TOUCH AND BREAK,	20	ENCOMPASSED	14
I TOUCH AND BREAK.	20	ENCOMPASSED	15
AND, AT THE TOUCH, TREMBLES WITH LOVER'S FEVER,	25	BEAUTY TO DUST	3
HE, TOO, COULD TOUCH THE SEASON'S LIPS AND SMILE,	46	POET: 1935	14
OF TIDES THAT NEVER TOUCH THE SHORES.	69	BEFORE KNOCKED	34
AND BEAR THOSE TENDRIL HANDS I TOUCH ACROSS	134	NOT FROM ANGER	6
AND TOUCH YOU WITH SOFTER HANDS.	228	NOT DESPAIR	6
TO TOUCH THE HYDRANGEAS,	229	MY RIVER	22
TOUCH TO REMEMBER AND BE SAD.	233	NO THOUGHT	4
COULD NEVER TOUCH YOUR SPINNING NOTES,	234	NO, PIGEON	9
TO TOUCH WHAT'S TO BE TOUCHED,	234	NO, PIGEON	18
TOUCHED			
TOUCHED, BY A FINGER'S NAIL, TO DUST.	20	THE NEOPHYTE	25
TOUCHED ON THE OUTSKIRTS OF THE MIND,	33	IN GARDENS	5
THE BLOOD THAT TOUCHED THE CROSSTREE AND THE GRAIL	94	IN BEGINNING	11
TOUCHED THE FIRST CLOUD AND LEFT A SIGN.	94	IN BEGINNING	12
AND MY FINGERS HAVE TOUCHED THE GLASS OF THE WATERS,	224	IDYLL UNFORGET	30
I THINK, THAT IF I TOUCHED THE EARTH,	225	CLOWN IN MOON	5
TO TOUCH WHAT'S TO BE TOUCHED,	234	NO, PIGEON	18
TOUCHES			
A HILL TOUCHES AN ANGEL. OUT OF A SAINT'S CELL	198	COUNTRY SLEEP	27
TOUCHING			
THE WEIGHTLESS TOUCHING OF THE LIP	12	SKY'S BRIGHT	9
TOUCHING OUR SEPARATE LOVE WITH BADINAGE	24	THE ONLY DEAD	33
TOUCHING THE SILVER CLOUDS,	235	WOMAN TAPESTRY	32
TOWARDS			
AND SAW TOWARDS HER TINY FACE	11	CABARET	3
TOWARDS DESTRUCTION AND REDEMPTION,	37	WINDMILLS TURN	3
TOWARDS THE STUDDED MALE IN A BENT, MIDNIGHT BLAZE	135	HOW MY ANIMAL	13
TOILS TOWARDS THE AMBUSH OF HIS WOUNDS;	209	POEM ON B'DAY	17

	PAGE	TITLE	LINE
TOWARDS (CONTINUED)			
HE SINGS TOWARDS ANGUISH; FINCHES FLY	209	POEM ON B'DAY	20
TOWER			
EYEING FROM THE WAX'S TOWER,	20	ENCOMPASSED	10
SHUT, TOO, IN A TOWER OF WORDS, I MARK	98	OCTOBER WIND	9
I DAMP THE WAXLIGHTS IN YOUR TOWER DOME.	101	RUNNING GRAVE	36
EVERYTHING ENDS, THE TOWER ENDING AND,	101	RUNNING GRAVE	41
A STEEPLEJACK TOWER, BONERAILED AND MASTERLESS,	109	I, IN IMAGE	20
WHERE BIRD AND SHELL ARE BABBLING IN MY TOWER?	112	NOT FATHER ME	14
I AM, THE TOWER TOLD, FELLED BY A TIMELESS STROKE,	113	NOT FATHER ME	21
LOVE'S HOUSE, THEY ANSWER, AND THE TOWER DEATH	113	NOT FATHER ME	31
A STEM CEMENTING, WRESTLED UP THE TOWER,	114	A GRIEF AGO	5
TILL TALLOW I BLEW FROM THE WAX'S TOWER	119	ALTARWISE	79
LIKE A TOWER ON THE TOWN	125	SEED-AT-ZERO	5
LIKE A TOWER ON THE TOWN	125	SEED-AT-ZERO	12
IN THE TOWER AND TOLLS TO SLEEP OVER THE STALLS	199	COUNTRY SLEEP	52
TOWERING			
NOR ROOF OF SAND, NOR YET THE TOWERING TILER?	112	NOT FATHER ME	16
NOR FOR THE TOWERING DEAD	197	CRAFT OR ART	15
TOWERS			
DAYS' NIGHT WHOSE TOWERS WILL CATCH	3	PROLOGUE	20
TIME UPON TIME THE TOWERS OF THE SKIES	56	WHY EAST WIND	19
COME UNTO SEA-STUCK TOWERS, AT THE FIBRE SCALING,	111	I, IN IMAGE	74
SOAR, WITH ITS TWO BARK TOWERS, TO THAT DAY	121	ALTARWISE	138
TOPPLING AND BURNING IN THE MUDDLE OF TOWERS AND GALLERIES	145	PLEASURE-BIRD	18
TOWER'S			
FOR MY TALL TOWER'S SAKE CAST IN HER STONE?	112	NOT FATHER ME	2
TOWN			
STREETS' STOCK, OF THE MOON LIT, ILL LIT, FIELD AND TOWN,	45	PLOUGHMAN GONE	22
ON GARAGES AND CLINICS IN THE TOWN.	52	OUT OF THE PIT	48
A WORKER IN THE MORNING TOWN,	98	TWILIGHT LOCKS	38
IN THE POURING TOWN,	111	I, IN IMAGE	94
ALL THESE, HE SAID WHO SACKED THE CHILDREN'S TOWN,	112	NOT FATHER ME	18
THAT TOWN OF GHOSTS, THE TRODDEN WOMB	125	SEED-AT-ZERO	2
LIKE A TOWER ON THE TOWN	125	SEED-AT-ZERO	5
THAT TOWN OF GHOSTS, THE MANWAGED WOMB	125	SEED-AT-ZERO	9
LIKE A TOWER ON THE TOWN	125	SEED-AT-ZERO	12
SHALL NOT THUNDER ON THE TOWN	126	SEED-AT-ZERO	45
THUNDERS ON THE FOREIGN TOWN	127	SEED-AT-ZERO	52
BREAD AND MILK MANSION IN A TOOTHLESS TOWN.	131	I MAKE THIS IN	15
AND WALK THE WARRING SANDS BY THE DEAD TOWN,	132	I MAKE THIS IN	32
STRIKE IN THE TIME-BOMB TOWN,	142	SAINT TO FALL	35
IN THE FINAL DIRECTION OF THE ELEMENTARY TOWN	143	24 YEARS	8
WHEN I WOKE, THE TOWN SPOKE.	150	WHEN I WOKE	1
CROSSLY OUT OF THE TOWN NOISES	150	WHEN I WOKE	24
CRY MY SEA TOWN WAS BREAKING.	150	WHEN I WOKE	27
THE TRODDEN TOWN RANG ITS COBBLES FOR LUCK.	161	LONG-LEGGED	4
OUT OF THE HOUSE THAT HOLDS A TOWN	166	LONG-LEGGED	143
THE TRUANT BOYS FROM THE TOWN	171	THE HUNCHBACK	16
IN THE STILL SLEEPING TOWN AND SET FORTH.	177	POEM IN OCT	10
OF THE TOWN CLOSED AS THE TOWN AWOKE.	177	POEM IN OCT	20
OF THE TOWN CLOSED AS THE TOWN AWOKE.	177	POEM IN OCT	20
THOUGH THE TOWN BELOW LAY LEAVED WITH OCTOBER BLOOD.	178	POEM IN OCT	67
AND THE SIZZLING BEDS OF THE TOWN CRIED, QUICK!--	206	LAMENT	20
NO SPRINGTAILED TOM IN THE RED HOT TOWN	206	LAMENT	29
TOWNS			
THAT LEAD AWAY TO DIRTY TOWNS	37	WINDMILLS TURN	14
TOWNS AROUND ON A WHEEL OF FIRE.	106	ALL ALL AND	6

		PAGE	TITLE	LINE
TOWNS (CONTINUED)				
THE COUNTRY TIDE IS COBBLED WITH TOWNS,	....	168	LONG-LEGGED	192
AND HONOURED AMONG WAGONS I WAS PRINCE OF THE APPLE				
TOWNS	....	195	FERN HILL	6
SHIP TOWNS TO PASTURES OF OTTERS. HE	....	209	POEM ON B'DAY	24
OF THE TWELVE APOSTLES' TOWNS RING IN HIS NIGHT;		216	COUNTRY HEAVEN	26
TOWY				
IN THE RIVER TOWY BELOW BOWS HIS TILTED HEADSTONE.		201	SIR JOHNS HILL	12
FISHING IN THE TEAR OF THE TOWY. ONLY A HOOT OWL		203	SIR JOHNS HILL	51
TOWY'S				
TO THE HAWK ON FIRE, THE HALTER HEIGHT, OVER TOWY'S				
FINS,	....	202	SIR JOHNS HILL	16
TRACE				
WHOSE WIZARD SHAPE I TRACE IN THE CAVERNOUS SKULL,		134	HOW MY ANIMAL	2
TRACE OUT A TENTACLE,	....	135	HOW MY ANIMAL	28
TRACED				
HAVE TRACED YOUR PATTERNS IN THE HASTENING FROST.		30	YOUTH CALLS	7
TRACES				
FOOT, HEAD, OR TRACES	....	24	LITTLE PROBLEM	1
TRACING				
IN TRACING	....	24	LITTLE PROBLEM	5
IT'S EASY TRACING WHAT EACH GIVES THE OTHER	....	24	LITTLE PROBLEM	11
TRACK				
BUT TIME HAS SET ITS MAGGOT ON THEIR TRACK.	....	40	WAS THERE TIME	4
WITH WHISTLER'S COUGH CONTAGES, TIME ON TRACK	.....	101	RUNNING GRAVE	47
TRACKS				
WHEN, LIKE A RUNNING GRAVE, TIME TRACKS YOU DOWN,		99	RUNNING GRAVE	1
TIME TRACKS THE SOUND OF SHAPE ON MAN AND CLOUD,		120	ALTARWISE	97
THE GREENWOOD DYING AS THE DEER FALL IN THEIR TRACKS,		122	HOLD HARD	11
IN THE CLAW TRACKS OF HAWKS	....	209	POEM ON B'DAY	21
TRADE				
OR THE STRUT AND TRADE OF CHARMS	....	197	CRAFT OR ART	8
AND THE HEWN COILS OF HIS TRADE PERCEIVES	....	209	POEM ON B'DAY	26
TRADES				
AND ALL THE WOKEN FARM AT ITS WHITE TRADES,	....	187	WINTER'S TALE	25
AND NOTHING I CARED, AT MY SKY BLUE TRADES, THAT				
TIME ALLOWS	....	196	FERN HILL	42
TRAIL				
A RAINING TRAIL	....	176	BREATH SHED	5
TRAIL WITH DAISIES AND BARLEY	....	195	FERN HILL	8
TRAILED				
ROUND HER TRAILED WRIST FRESH WATER WEAVES,	....	168	LONG-LEGGED	177
TRAILING				
TRAILING THE FROST BITTEN CLOTH,	....	151	BELOW A TIME	23
TRAILING THEIR FINGERS ON THE HARD EDGES	....	235	WOMAN TAPESTRY	33
TRAILS				
FLOUNDERS, GULLS, ON THEIR COLD, DYING TRAILS,	....	209	POEM ON B'DAY	11
TRAMMELLED				
THE HEMMING CONTACT THAT'S SO TRAMMELLED	....	20	ENCOMPASSED	6
TRAMPLING				
TRAMPLING TO DUST THE BITS AND PIECES	....	34	IN GARDENS	9
TRANSLATE				
THE CODE OF STARS TRANSLATE IN HEAVEN.	....	69	SECRET WIND	3
TRANSLATING				
THE WORD FLOWED UP, TRANSLATING TO THE HEART	......	94	IN BEGINNING	23
TONGUE OF YOUR TRANSLATING EYES. THE YOUNG STARS				
TOLD ME,	....	148	UNLUCKILY FOR	51
TRAP				
THE CENTURY'S TRAP WILL HAVE SNAPPED ROUND YOUR				
MIDDLE,	....	38	GAS FADES	4

	PAGE	TITLE	LINE
TRAP (CONTINUED)			
THE CENTURY'S TRAP WILL HAVE CLOSED FOR GOOD	39	GAS FADES	30
OF LOVE AM BARER THAN CADAVER'S TRAP	100	RUNNING GRAVE	8
TRAP I WITH COIL AND SHEET, ...	114	SERVANT SUN	19
TRAP'S			
CAUGHT IN THE TRAP'S MACHINERY, LIGHTS OUT, ...	39	GAS FADES	35
TRASH			
AND LETS THEIR TRASH BE HONOURED AS THE QUICK.	90	EUNUCH DREAMS	35
TRAVEL			
BUT DO NOT TRAVEL DOWN DUMB WIND LIKE PRODIGALS.	16	SPIRE CRANES	11
CALLS SOME CONTENT TO TRAVEL WITH THE WINDS, ...	56	WHY EAST WIND	17
I BURY, I TRAVEL TO FIND PRIDE	240	ADMIT THE SUN	12
TRAVELLER			
ZIP ONCE MORE FOR A TRAVELLER	155	RETURN	37
TRAVELS			
AS THEY DROWN, THE CHIME TRAVELS, ...	110	I, IN IMAGE	61
TRAY			
THE TRAY OF KNIVES, THE ANTISEPTIC FUNERAL, ...	110	I, IN IMAGE	54
TREAD			
RAIN CUTS THE PLACE WE TREAD	13	RAIN CUTS	T
RAIN CUTS THE PLACE WE TREAD, ...	13	RAIN CUTS	1
THE MIDNIGHT ROAD, THOUGH YOUNG MEN TREAD UNKNOWING,	36	MIDNIGHT ROAD	1
THEN ONLY OVER CORPSES SHALL THE FEET TREAD, ...	45	TO FOLLOW FOX	20
TREAD, LIKE A NAKED VENUS, ...	75	MY HERO BARES	12
'THIS THAT WE TREAD WAS, TOO, YOUR FATHERS' LAND.'	101	FELLOWED SLEEP	12
'BUT THIS WE TREAD BEARS THE ANGELIC GANGS, ...	102	FELLOWED SLEEP	13
FEAR NOT THE TREAD, THE SEEDED MILLING, ...	106	ALL ALL AND	16
THE SCALES OF THIS TWIN WORLD TREAD ON THE DOUBLE,	108	I, IN IMAGE	4
NO TREAD MORE PERILOUS, THE GREEN STEPS AND SPIRE	109	I, IN IMAGE	26
THE POLAR EAGLE WITH HIS TREAD OF SNOW.	164	LONG-LEGGED	80
HORSES, CENTAUR DEAD, TURN AND TREAD THE DRENCHED WHITE	189	WINTER'S TALE	74
STRONG ENOUGH TO TREAD ON THE SAND	229	MY RIVER	7
TREADING			
SINGS TO THE TREADING HAWK	159	INTO HER HEAD	59
TREADS			
LIGHT, I KNOW, TREADS THE TEN MILLION STARS	48	LIGHT, I KNOW	T
LIGHT, I KNOW, TREADS THE TEN MILLION STARS, ...	48	LIGHT, I KNOW	1
DAY TREADS THE TREES AND SHE THE CAVERNOUS NIGHT.	57	GREEK PLAY	12
TREASON			
YOU ARE MY FLESH'S RULER WHOM I TREASON, ...	67	REALM OF FLESH	11
TREASON'S			
IS TREASON'S TIME AND THE TIME OF ENVY.	34	THIRST PARCHES	7
TREASURES			
TO LIFT TO LEAVE FROM THE TREASURES OF MAN IS PLEASING DEATH	140	NO WORK WORDS	7
TREATY			
THE HAND THAT SIGNED THE TREATY BRED A FEVER, ...	66	HAND SIGNED	9
TREE			
THAT, LIKE A TREE, HAS ROOTS IN YOU, ...	9	MINUTE'S HOUR	3
THE INSECT ON THIS PAINTED TREE.	12	CABARET	23
LIKE A GREEN TREE THROUGH THE SWARD, ...	72	TAKE NEEDLES	42
WHEN I YIELD THE TREE TO DEATH, ...	72	TAKE NEEDLES	45
TAKE THE NEEDLES TO THIS TREE	72	TAKE NEEDLES	49
AND THE GREEN TREE TRUST THE ROOT?	72	TAKE NEEDLES	58
THIS WINE UPON A FOREIGN TREE	86	BREAD I BREAK	2
MY JACK OF CHRIST BORN THORNY ON THE TREE?	96	RUB OF LOVE	45
LIT ON THE CUDDLED TREE, THE CROSS OF FEVER, ...	100	RUNNING GRAVE	33
I WITH THE WOODEN INSECT IN THE TREE OF NETTLES,	109	I, IN IMAGE	28
SPROUT FROM THE STONY LOCKERS LIKE A TREE ON ARAN.	111	I, IN IMAGE	78

	PAGE	TITLE	LINE
TREE (CONTINUED)			
STRIP TO THIS TREE: A ROCKING ALPHABET, ...	119	ALTARWISE	87
I BY THE TREE OF THIEVES, ALL GLORY'S SAWBONES, ...	120	ALTARWISE	109
TWINED GOOD AND EVIL ON AN EASTERN TREE;	121	INCARNATE DEVL	10
MY NEST OF MERCIES IN THE RUDE, RED TREE.	121	ALTARWISE	140
ALL LEGENDS' SWEETHEARTS ON A TREE OF STORIES, ...	125	TODAY, INSECT	25
IN THAT PROUD SAILING TREE WITH BRANCHES DRIVEN ...	131	I MAKE THIS IN	6
GAG OF A DUMBSTRUCK TREE TO BLOCK FROM BARE ENEMIES	133	MAKE ME A MASK	4
FUMED LIKE A TREE, AND TOSSED A BURNING BIRD;	133	I MAKE THIS IN	56
DRIVELLED DOWN TO ONE SINGEING TREE	142	SAINT TO FALL	20
HER ROBIN BREASTED TREE, THREE MARYS IN THE RAYS.	198	COUNTRY SLEEP	29
MILLED DUST OF THE APPLE TREE AND THE POUNDED ISLANDS	199	COUNTRY SLEEP	59
THE PINE IS THE TREE OF THE BREEZE, ...	227	THE PINE	2
BUT NO HIGH TREE FOR ME	234	NO, PIGEON	13
OR THE BRANCHES OF A GREEN TREE.	236	WOMAN TAPESTRY	40
BE FREE, (WIND FOR MY TREE AND WATER FOR MY FLOWER),	239	LET ME ESCAPE	2
TREEFORK			
WITHIN THE NESTED TREEFORK	159	INTO HER HEAD	58
TREES			
LIKE LEAVES OF TREES AND AS SOON	3	PROLOGUE	31
UNDER HER CLOTH OF TREES NO SORROW, ...	15	FOR LEDA	22
BUT IN THE BODY OF THE TREES AND STONES, ...	25	BEAUTY TO DUST	13
BEING BUT MEN, WE WALKED INTO THE TREES	31	BEING BUT MEN	1
BEING BUT MEN, WE WALKED INTO THE TREES.	31	BEING BUT MEN	17
WHEN I WAS SEVEN I COUNTED FOUR AND FORTY TREES ...	33	HELD-OUT HAND	12
THAT CHASES THE GHOSTS OF THE TREES	35	LIFT UP FACE	4
AND THE OAKUM IS PICKED, AND THE SPRING TREES HAVE GROWN GREEN, ...	39	GAS FADES	6
SEE, ON GRAVEL PATHS UNDER THE HARPSTRUNG TREES ...	46	POET: 1935	1
SEE, ON GRAVEL PATHS UNDER THE HARPSTRUNG TREES,	48	POET: 1935	58
MAD BIRDS IN TREES, AND MAD FISH IN A POOL.	50	OUT OF THE PIT	10
KNOCKING OFF TURNIP TOPS, WITH TREES FOR FRIENDS,	53	OUT OF THE PIT	88
A WOMAN WAILS HER DEAD AMONG THE TREES, ...	56	GREEK PLAY	1
DAY TREADS THE TREES AND SHE THE CAVERNOUS NIGHT.	57	GREEK PLAY	12
AMONG THE TREES THE LANGUAGE OF THE DEAD	57	GREEK PLAY	13
AMONG THE GARDEN TREES A PIGEON CALLS, ...	57	GREEK PLAY	29
I SHOULD TELL SUMMER FROM THE TREES, THE WORMS	58	HERE IN SPRING	9
THE TOPS OF TREES, NOR AS THE LEGION	76	SONG: LOVE ME	10
DRIVES MY GREEN AGE; THAT BLASTS THE ROOTS OF TREES	77	THE FORCE THAT	2
AND NAIL THE MERRY SQUIRES TO THE TREES;	93	BOYS OF SUMMER	45
ON THE HORIZON WALKING LIKE THE TREES	98	OCTOBER WIND	10
AND WORLDS HANG ON THE TREES.	98	TWILIGHT LOCKS	42
MY MOTHERS-EYED, UPON THE TOPS OF TREES;	101	FELLOWED SLEEP	9
THE WILD PIGS' WOOD, AND SLIME UPON THE TREES, ...	104	WORLD PYRAMID	20
MY IMAGES STALK THE TREES AND THE SLANT SAP'S TUNNEL,	109	I, IN IMAGE	25
A QUARREL OF WEATHERS AND TREES IN THE WINDY SPIRAL.	110	I, IN IMAGE	42
A LEG AS LONG AS TREES, ...	114	SERVANT SUN	29
AND ONE LIGHT'S LANGUAGE IN THE BOOK OF TREES.	119	ALTARWISE	89
BENT LIKE THREE TREES AND BIRD-PAPPED THROUGH HER SHIFT, ...	120	ALTARWISE	103
BY CRANE AND WATER-TOWER BY THE SEEDY TREES	122	HOLD HARD	8
A CALM WIND BLOWS THAT RAISED THE TREES LIKE HAIR	133	I MAKE THIS IN	64
THE SHADE OF THEIR TREES WAS A WORD OF MANY SHADES	144	COLOUR OF SAY	10
THE WASTEFUL HUSHES AMONG TREES.	157	RETURN	99
TREES COOL AND DRY IN THE WHIRLPOOL OF SHIPS	167	LONG-LEGGED	170
PROPPED BETWEEN TREES AND WATER	171	THE HUNCHBACK	3
THAT LETS THE TREES AND WATER ENTER	171	THE HUNCHBACK	5
THE BIRDS THE GRASS THE TREES THE LAKE	172	THE HUNCHBACK	39
BIRDS AND THE BIRDS OF THE WINGED TREES FLYING MY NAME	177	POEM IN OCT	12

	PAGE	TITLE	LINE
TREES (CONTINUED)			
TO THE TREES AND THE STONES AND THE FISH IN THE TIDE.	178	POEM IN OCT	57
UNDER THE ONE LEAVED TREES RAN A SCARECROW OF SNOW	190	WINTER'S TALE	94
AND ONCE BELOW A TIME I LORDLY HAD THE TREES AND LEAVES	195	FERN HILL	7
LOVE FOR EVER MERIDIAN THROUGH THE COURTERS' TREES	205	GIANT'S THIGH	59
CARVEN DOMES OF GREEN ARE THE TREES BY THE PATHWAY,	221	FOREST PICTURE	2
'LINGER NOT DEEPER IN THE COLOURED TREES,	227	SPRING-SPIRIT	2
AMONG THE QUIET TREES. AND HAND IN HAND	227	SPRING-SPIRIT	11
I SAW THE COLD, GREEN TREES,	235	WOMAN TAPESTRY	6
AND THE ROOTS OF THE TREES CLIMBED THROUGH THE AIR	235	WOMAN TAPESTRY	31
AND THE TREES	237	WOMAN TAPESTRY	77
TREES'			
AND HAS THE MAD TREES' TALK BY HEART.	47	POET: 1935	28
TREE-TAILED			
BUTT OF THE TREE-TAILED WORM THAT MOUNTED EVE,	117	ALTARWISE	32
TREMBLE			
NO LONGER TREMBLE AT A BISHOP'S HAT,	59	FAIRY TALES	2
TREMBLE AT THE STARRY STAIN,	71	TAKE NEEDLES	34
WHAT COLOUR IS GLORY? DEATH'S FEATHER? TREMBLE	104	WORLD PYRAMID	25
TREMBLED			
UNDER THE MILE OFF MOON WE TREMBLED LISTENING	194	SLEEP BECALMED	5
TREMBLES			
AND, AT THE TOUCH, TREMBLES WITH LOVER'S FEVER,	25	BEAUTY TO DUST	3
TREMBLING			
THE CHILD TELLS, WHEN THE TREMBLING CHORD IS CUT,	67	LET A FAITH	14
AND THROUGH THESE TREMBLING RINGS SET IN THEIR VALLEY	76	LASHED RINGS	4
TREMENDOUS			
FRESH IMAGES SURROUND THE TREMENDOUS MOON,	47	POET: 1935	45
IN LAIRS AND ASYLUMS OF THE TREMENDOUS SHOUT.	153	WAS A SAVIOUR	16
TREMULOUSLY			
SO TREMULOUSLY LIKE A DREAM.	225	CLOWN IN MOON	8
TRESPASSER			
TRESPASSER AND BROKEN BRIDE	158	INTO HER HEAD	41
TRIANGLE			
WORLD IN THE SAND, ON THE TRIANGLE LANDSCAPE,	120	ALTARWISE	124
TRIANGLES			
THE TWELVE TRIANGLES OF THE CHERUB WIND	115	A GRIEF AGO	23
TRIBE			
DELIVER ME WHO, TIMID IN MY TRIBE,	100	RUNNING GRAVE	7
HIS STRIPED AND NOON MANED TRIBE STRIDING TO HOLOCAUST,	148	UNLUCKILY FOR	31
TRIBES			
THE LIQUID CHOIRS OF HIS TRIBES.	167	LONG-LEGGED	164
BIRD THROUGH THE TIMES AND LANDS AND TRIBES OF THE SLOW FLAKES.	190	WINTER'S TALE	99
TRICK			
BY TRICK OR CHANCE HE FELL ASLEEP	98	TWILIGHT LOCKS	34
SHAPES IN A CINDER DEATH; LOVE FOR HIS TRICK,	101	RUNNING GRAVE	48
TRICKLE			
TRICKLE AWAY THROUGH THOUGHT,	19	IMAGES IN AIR	6
TRICKS			
PLAYS SCURVY TRICKS WITH VALUES AND INTENTIONS,	37	WINDMILLS TURN	6
DOING MY LITTLE TRICKS OF SPEECH AGAIN	234	NO, PIGEON	20
TRIED			
WE MIGHT HAVE TRIED LIGHT MATCHES IN THE WIND.	34	IN GARDENS	16
TO TELL WHAT NOTE I COULD REACH IF I TRIED,	234	NO, PIGEON	12
TRIGGER			
THE TRIGGER AND SCYTHE, THE BRIDAL BLADE,	106	ALL ALL AND	17

	PAGE	TITLE	LINE
TRIM			
AND JERRYSTONE TRIM VILLAS	156	RETURN	70
TRINITY			
WOULD BE THE DEVIL'S WIND, AND THE HIGH TRINITY ...	37	WINDMILLS TURN	18
TRIOLET			
TRIOLET	227	TRIOLET	T
TRIPPER'S			
I FIND A TRIPPER'S KNICKER IN THE GULLY	137	O CHATTERTON	15
TRITON			
AND, CLAPPED IN WATER TILL THE TRITON DANGLES, ...	110	I, IN IMAGE	64
TRIUMPH			
AND THE TRIUMPH OF HER PITILESS GAIETY	235	WOMAN TAPESTRY	19
TRIUMPHANT			
AND THE TRIUMPHANT CROW OF LAUGHTER.	48	POET: 1935	52
WITH MORE TRIUMPHANT FAITH	211	POEM ON B'DAY	97
ALL THINGS REST IN THE WILL OF PURPOSE TRIUMPHANT.	222	FOREST PICTURE	8
TRODDEN			
THAT TOWN OF GHOSTS, THE TRODDEN WOMB	125	SEED-AT-ZERO	2
THE TRODDEN TOWN RANG ITS COBBLES FOR LUCK.	161	LONG-LEGGED	4
TROT			
TO TROT WITH A LOUD MATE THE HAYBEDS OF A MILE, ...	135	HOW MY ANIMAL	16
TROT AND GALLOP WITH GULLS UPON THEM	168	LONG-LEGGED	189
TROUBLE			
WHO TAUGHT ME TROUBLE?	18	NATURAL DAY	25
TROUBLE ENOUGH FOR THE WORLD	18	NATURAL DAY	28
THE TROUBLE, DEVILDOM, AND HEARTBREAK, ...	38	THE GOSSIPERS	15
OUT OF THE ROOM THE WEIGHT OF HIS TROUBLE	166	LONG-LEGGED	142
NO THOUGHT CAN TROUBLE MY UNWHOLESOME POSE	233	NO THOUGHT	T
NO THOUGHT CAN TROUBLE MY UNWHOLESOME POSE, ...	233	NO THOUGHT	1
TROUBLED			
BUT TROUBLED BY THEIR CURIOUS SPEECH	22	ON QUIET NIGHT	6
WITH 'STRUMPET' IN THESE TROUBLED TIMES, ...	84	LETTER TO AUNT	34
TROUBLES			
ANY MAN'S TROUBLES NOT YOUR OWN--	27	OBLIVIOUS DARK	3
IN CHILDREN'S CIRCUSES COULD STAY THEIR TROUBLES?	40	WAS THERE TIME	2
TROUGH			
SHE SLEEPS IN THE NARROW TROUGH YET SHE WALKS THE			
DUST	170	LOVE IN ASYLUM	13
TROUNCED			
TROUNCED BY HIS WINGS IN THE HISSING SHIPPEN, LONG			
DEAD	205	GIANT'S THIGH	39
TROVE			
THEN LOOK, MY HEART, UPON THE SCARLET TROVE, ...	81	ALL THAT I OWE	28
TRUANT			
THE TRUANT BOYS FROM THE TOWN	171	THE HUNCHBACK	16
TRUE			
FOLLY PURIFY AND MAKE IT TRUE.	25	BEAUTY TO DUST	10
AND THAT IS TRUE AFTER PERPETUAL DEFEAT.	32	OUT OF SIGHS	9
AND THIS IS TRUE, NO MAN CAN LIVE	55	NO MAN BELIEVE	18
QUESTION: SHALL THE ROOT BE TRUE	72	TAKE NEEDLES	57
AND THE VAULTING BIRD BE STILL. O MY TRUE LOVE, HOLD			
ME.	149	UNLUCKILY FOR	54
OUR OWN TRUE STRANGERS' DUST	153	WAS A SAVIOUR	37
FROM EVERY TRUE OR CRATER	161	WEDDING ANNIV	7
AWAY BUT THE WEATHER TURNED AROUND. AND THE TRUE	178	POEM IN OCT	62
HIGH RIDING, HELD AND BLESSED AND TRUE, AND SO STILLY	200	COUNTRY SLEEP	90
NOR WILL BE EVER IS ALWAYS TRUE, ...	210	POEM ON B'DAY	51
TRULY			
AND TRULY HE	200	COUNTRY SLEEP	97

	PAGE	TITLE	LINE
TRUMP			
UNTIL THE WHISPER OF THE LAST TRUMP LOUDEN	40	YOUNG ARE OLD	11
TRUMPED			
FROM JESU'S SLEEVE TRUMPED UP THE KING OF SPOTS,	118	ALTARWISE	58
TRUMPET			
HARK: I TRUMPET THE PLACE, ...	4	PROLOGUE	42
THE JONQUIL AND THE TRUMPET.	27	OBLIVIOUS DARK	31
HE'LL TRUMPET INTO MEAT), ...	113	SERVANT SUN	5
BLASTS BACK THE TRUMPET VOICE.	114	SERVANT SUN	34
THE PRESENT MOUTH, AND THE SWEETLY BLOWN TRUMPET OF			
LIES, ...	133	MAKE ME A MASK	6
MARK, TRUMPET LIPPED AND BLACKHEAD	155	RETURN	41
TRUMPETER			
NOW THAT THE TEMPLE'S TRUMPETER	237	PILLAR BREAKS	2
TRUMPETING			
BACK. LINES OF AGE SLEEP ON THE STONES TILL			
TRUMPETING DAWN.	191	WINTER'S TALE	118
TRUMPETS			
LEAP, AS TO TRUMPETS. CALLIGRAPHY OF THE OLD	189	WINTER'S TALE	77
TRUNKS			
THE GRAFTERS OF CATS' HEADS ON CHICKENS' TRUNKS,	41	YOUNG ARE OLD	42
TRUST			
AND THE GREEN TREE TRUST THE ROOT?	72	TAKE NEEDLES	58
IN TRUST AND TALE HAVE I DIVIDED SENSE, ...	124	TODAY, INSECT	5
TRUTH			
GRAFTS ON ITS BRIDE ONE-SIDED SKINS OF TRUTH;	90	EUNUCH DREAMS	28
WHILE YOU DISPLACED A TRUTH IN THE AIR, ...	147	TO OTHERS	17
COMMONER THAN WATER, CRUELLER THAN TRUTH;	152	WAS A SAVIOUR	3
SUMMERTIME OF THE DEAD WHISPERED THE TRUTH OF HIS JOY	178	POEM IN OCT	56
O MAY MY HEART'S TRUTH	178	POEM IN OCT	68
THIS SIDE OF THE TRUTH	192	SIDE OF TRUTH	T
THIS SIDE OF THE TRUTH, ...	192	SIDE OF TRUTH	1
THE MANKIND OF HER GOING WITH A GRAVE TRUTH	192	REFUSAL MOURN	15
EACH TRUTH, EACH LIE, ...	193	SIDE OF TRUTH	35
TRY			
WE TRY TO STEER;	14	RAIN CUTS	25
TRYING			
TRYING HIS HAND AT FAILING	155	RETURN	29
TUBES			
PLUG THE PAPER-BLOWING TUBES;	156	RETURN	79
TUFT			
ROLL UNMANLY OVER THIS TURNING TUFT, ...	123	FOSTER LIGHT	19
TUFTED			
THE SWING OF MILK WAS TUFTED IN THE PAP, ...	104	WORLD PYRAMID	10
SHALL YOU TURN COCKWISE ON A TUFTED AXLE.	123	FOSTER LIGHT	24
TUG			
SUSPICIOUS HANDS TUG AT THE NEIGHBOURING VICES, ...	38	THE GOSSIPERS	3
TUGGED			
TUGGED THROUGH THE DAYS	115	A GRIEF AGO	20
TUMBLE			
TUMBLE, NOT FLYING, IS FALSE, ...	37	WINDMILLS TURN	5
NO GOD-IN-HERO TUMBLE DOWN	125	SEED-AT-ZERO	4
NO GOD-IN-HERO TUMBLE DOWN	125	SEED-AT-ZERO	11
IF THE DEAD STARVE, THEIR STOMACHS TURN TO TUMBLE	145	PLEASURE-BIRD	22
TUMBLEDOWN			
YET, THOUGH I CRY WITH TUMBLEDOWN TONGUE, ...	211	POEM ON B'DAY	80
TUMBLERS			
OLD PAINT-STAINED TUMBLERS RIDING	154	RETURN	19
TUMBLING			
ON GOD'S ROUGH TUMBLING GROUNDS	5	PROLOGUE	75

	PAGE	TITLE	LINE
TUMBLING (CONTINUED)			
ON TUMBLING HILLS ADMIRING THE SEA, ...	48	POET: 1935	61
IS COME OF THE SEA TUMBLING IN HARNESS	191	REFUSAL MOURN	6
TUNE			
HUBBUB AND FIDDLE, THIS TUNE	5	PROLOGUE	72
THERE'S TIME TO PLUCK A TUNE UPON THE HARP, ...	15	FOR LEDA	16
THE SAME TUNE AS IN MY FATHER'S TIME:	46	PLOUGHMAN GONE	29
AND FROM THESE TONGUE-PLUCKED SENSES DRAWS HIS TUNE;	76	LASHED RINGS	13
TIME'S TUNE MY LADIES WITH THE TEATS OF MUSIC, ...	119	ALTARWISE	91
TIME IS THE TUNE MY LADIES LEND THEIR HEARTBREAK,	119	ALTARWISE	95
WHO MOVED FOR THREE YEARS IN TUNE	161	WEDDING ANNIV	3
MAKES ALL THE MUSIC; AND I WHO HEAR THE TUNE OF THE			
SLOW, ...	203	SIR JOHNS HILL	57
TUNEFUL			
IN ALL HIS TUNEFUL TURNING SO FEW AND SUCH MORNING			
SONGS	196	FERN HILL	43
TUNES			
FIELDS HIGH AS THE HOUSE, THE TUNES FROM THE			
CHIMNEYS, IT WAS AIR	195	FERN HILL	20
TUNICS'			
SHALL RAINBOWS BE THEIR TUNICS' COLOUR?	65	GODS THUMP	4
TUNING			
IN TUNING IMPULSES TO CALLS;	18	NATURAL DAY	6
TUNNEL			
MY IMAGES STALK THE TREES AND THE SLANT SAP'S TUNNEL,	109	I, IN IMAGE	25
AND LEAVE A TUNNEL	229	MY RIVER	11
TURBINE			
A CITY GODHEAD, TURBINE MOVED, STEEL SCULPTURED,	70	SECRET WIND	13
TURBULENT			
UNTIL THE TURBULENT NEW BORN	180	VISION, PRAYER	27
TURN			
TURN INSIDE OUT, AND SEE AT GLANCE	25	BEAUTY TO DUST	7
WOULD TURN THE DEAD YELLOW.	59	FAIRY TALES	21
TURN AND CHURN NIGHTSEED TILL IT CURDLE.	67	LET A FAITH	5
THE PROUD SPINE SPURNING TURN AND TWIST.	75	MY HERO BARES	5
THE STRAWS OF ASIA, LOSE ME AS I TURN	105	WORLD PYRAMID	47
FEAR NOT THE SCREWS THAT TURN THE VOICE, ...	106	ALL ALL AND	23
TURN THE LONG SEA ARTERIAL	110	I, IN IMAGE	46
(TURN THE SEA-SPINDLE LATERAL, ...	110	I, IN IMAGE	67
SHALL YOU TURN COCKWISE ON A TUFTED AXLE.	123	FOSTER LIGHT	24
THE BOWELS TURN TURTLE, ...	135	HOW MY ANIMAL	20
IF THE DEAD STARVE, THEIR STOMACHS TURN TO TUMBLE	145	PLEASURE-BIRD	22
TO HEAR THE GOLDEN NOTE TURN IN A GROOVE, ...	153	WAS A SAVIOUR	6
TO THE BURN AND TURN OF TIME	180	VISION, PRAYER	11
I TURN THE CORNER OF PRAYER AND BURN	185	VISION, PRAYER	188
I WOULD TURN BACK AND RUN	185	VISION, PRAYER	191
HORSES, CENTAUR DEAD, TURN AND TREAD THE DRENCHED			
WHITE	189	WINTER'S TALE	74
OF THE HOBNAIL TALES: NO GOOSEHERD OR SWINE WILL TURN	197	COUNTRY SLEEP	10
THE DARKEST WAY, AND DID NOT TURN AWAY, ...	216	ELEGY	2
IT IS A WEAPON THAT CAN TURN BACK	241	ADMIT THE SUN	20
TURNED			
OLD IN ILLUSIONS TURNED TO ACRITUDES, ...	20	THE NEOPHYTE	23
WHILE THE SUN'S TURNED TO SALT, ...	27	OBLIVIOUS DARK	23
TO LONDON'S TURNED, AND THIRSTY LOADS	37	WINDMILLS TURN	9
TO HEAVEN'S TURNED, AND PIOUS LOADS	37	WINDMILLS TURN	32
THAT TURNED ON AND LIFTED IN ANGER	39	GAS FADES	25
THAT TURNED THE EMPTY KISSES INTO MEANING, ...	43	FACES SHONE	3
AND THEIR RIVERS OF BLOOD TURNED TO ICE.	68	REALM OF FLESH	16
AND VEINS ARE SPILLED AND DOOM IS TURNED, ...	74	WE MOTHERNAKED	15

	PAGE	TITLE	LINE
TURNED (CONTINUED)			
AND BRAINS TURNED SOUR;	85	SEE, SAYS LIME	12
WHEN ONCE THE TWILIGHT SCREWS WERE TURNED, ...	98	TWILIGHT LOCKS	31
SHIFTING TO LIGHT, TURNED ON ME LIKE A MOON.	101	FELLOWED SLEEP	3
ONCE WHERE THE SOFT SNOW'S BLOOD WAS TURNED TO ICE.	133	I MAKE THIS IN	65
AWAY BUT THE WEATHER TURNED AROUND.	178	POEM IN OCT	40
IT TURNED AWAY FROM THE BLITHE COUNTRY	178	POEM IN OCT	41
AWAY BUT THE WEATHER TURNED AROUND. AND THE TRUE	178	POEM IN OCT	62
MILD. TURNED AGAIN, WORTHINGTON. NEVER WHISKY.	179	NEW QUAY	12
ONCE WHEN THE WORLD TURNED OLD	187	WINTER'S TALE	11
HIS DRIFTWOOD THIRTY-FIFTH WIND TURNED AGE;	208	POEM ON B'DAY	8
TURNING			
THE WORLD'S TURNING WOOD, ...	3	PROLOGUE	27
WITH WINDMILLS TURNING WRONG DIRECTIONS	36	WINDMILLS TURN	T
WITH WINDMILLS TURNING WRONG DIRECTIONS, ...	36	WINDMILLS TURN	1
AND LOVERS TURNING ON THE GAS, ...	41	YOUNG ARE OLD	30
TURNING A PETROL FACE BLIND TO THE ENEMY	110	I, IN IMAGE	47
TURNING THE RIDERLESS DEAD BY THE CHANNEL WALL. ...	110	I, IN IMAGE	48
ROLL UNMANLY OVER THIS TURNING TUFT, ...	123	FOSTER LIGHT	19
WHEN IN OUR BED I WAS TOSSING AND TURNING	149	PAPER & STICKS	7
AND I SAW IN THE TURNING SO CLEARLY A CHILD'S	178	POEM IN OCT	46
ON THIS HIGH HILL IN A YEAR'S TURNING.	178	POEM IN OCT	70
IN THE THROAT, BURNING AND TURNING. ALL NIGHT AFLOAT	194	SLEEP BECALMED	2
IN ALL HIS TUNEFUL TURNING SO FEW AND SUCH MORNING			
SONGS	196	FERN HILL	43
ONLY FOR THE TURNING OF THE EARTH IN HER HOLY	200	COUNTRY SLEEP	94
AND WHEN THE BRIGHT WHEEL OF YOUR TURNING VOICE IS			
STILLED, ...	232	FURIOUS MOTION	3
TURNIP			
AND CATCH A TURNIP GHOST IN EVERY CRANNY.	48	LIGHT, I KNOW	5
KNOCKING OFF TURNIP TOPS, WITH TREES FOR FRIENDS,	53	OUT OF THE PIT	88
TURNIPS			
WITH FISTS OF TURNIPS PUNISHES THE LAND, ...	99	OCTOBER WIND	28
TURNKEY			
SPLITTING THE LONG EYE OPEN, AND THE SPIRAL TURNKEY,	110	I, IN IMAGE	50
TURNS			
THAT, LIKE A RAZOR, SKIMS, CUTS, AND TURNS, ...	47	POET: 1935	49
TURNS TO THE ROOF A HIDEOUS GRIMACE, ...	49	LIGHT, I KNOW	25
TURNS MINE TO WAX.	77	THE FORCE THAT	8
TURNS DAMP TO DRY; THE GOLDEN SHOT	88	A PROCESS IN	2
TURNS NIGHT TO DAY; BLOOD IN THEIR SUNS	88	A PROCESS IN	5
TURNS GHOST TO GHOST; EACH MOTHERED CHILD	88	A PROCESS IN	20
THE DEAD TURNS UP ITS EYE;	90	WHERE ONCE THE	3
TURNS IN THE EARTH THAT TURNS THE ASHEN	106	ALL ALL AND	5
TURNS IN THE EARTH THAT TURNS THE ASHEN	106	ALL ALL AND	5
TURNS OF YOUR PRAYED FLESH, NOR SHALL I SHOO THE			
BIRD BELOW ME:	148	UNLUCKILY FOR	27
KILL TIME! SHE TURNS IN HER PAIN!	167	LONG-LEGGED	154
TURNS THE MOON-CHAINED AND WATER-WOUND	169	LONG-LEGGED	203
AND THE MULTITUDE'S SULTRY TEAR TURNS COOL ON THE			
WEEPING WALL, ...	186	HOLY SPRING	17
TURNS IN THE DARK ON THE SOUND THEY KNOW WILL ARISE	193	CONVERS PRAYER	6
TURNS ON THE QUICK AND THE DEAD, AND THE MAN ON THE			
STAIRS	194	CONVERS PRAYER	14
TURNTURTLE			
DOLPHINS DIVE IN THEIR TURNTURTLE DUST, ...	209	POEM ON B'DAY	33
TURRETS			
EARS IN THE TURRETS HEAR	62	EARS IN TURRET	T
EARS IN THE TURRETS HEAR	62	EARS IN TURRET	1
FOR MY TALL TURRETS CARRY AS YOUR SIN?	112	NOT FATHER ME	6

	PAGE	TITLE	LINE
TURRETS (CONTINUED)			
DING DONG FROM THE MUTE TURRETS.	130	SINNERS' BELL	24
TURTLE			
UP NAKED STAIRS, A TURTLE IN A HEARSE,	99	RUNNING GRAVE	4
THEY SUFFER THE UNDEAD WATER WHERE THE TURTLE NIBBLES,	111	I, IN IMAGE	73
THE BOWELS TURN TURTLE,	135	HOW MY ANIMAL	20
TILL EVERY TURTLE CRUSHED FROM HIS SHELL	163	LONG-LEGGED	58
TUSKED			
NOR THE TUSKED PRINCE, IN THE RUTTISH FARM, AT THE RIND	198	COUNTRY SLEEP	37
AND THE TUSKED, RAMSHACKLING SEA EXULTS;	211	POEM ON B'DAY	94
TUSSLE			
AND TUSSLE IN A SHOAL OF LOVES.	162	LONG-LEGGED	30
TWELVE			
TWELVE	96	TWELVE	T
TWELVE WINDS ENCOUNTER BY THE WHITE HOST AT PASTURE,	109	I, IN IMAGE	38
THE TWELVE TRIANGLES OF THE CHERUB WIND	115	A GRIEF AGO	23
DUCKED IN THE TWELVE, DISCIPLE SEAS	128	MY NEOPHYTE	4
OF THE TWELVE APOSTLES' TOWNS RING IN HIS NIGHT;	216	COUNTRY HEAVEN	26
TWELVE-LEGGED			
SPARKLING A TWELVE-LEGGED BODY	12	CABARET	19
TWELVE-WINDED			
BUT STRIP THE TWELVE-WINDED MARROW FROM HIS CIRCLE;	123	FOSTER LIGHT	3
RIPPLING IN TWELVE-WINDED CIRCLES,	175	FIRE RAID	64
TWENTY-FOUR			
TWENTY-FOUR YEARS	143	24 YEARS	T
TWENTY-FOUR YEARS REMIND THE TEARS OF MY EYES.	143	24 YEARS	1
TWICE			
A MOTHER IN LABOUR PAYS TWICE HER PAIN,	74	SUN BURNS	14
TWICE IN THE FEEDING SEA, GROWN	103	I DREAMED MY	26
LOOK TWICE BEFORE HE FELL FROM GRACE.	116	LANTERNS SHINE	4
SAID THE ANTIPODES, AND TWICE SPRING CHIMED.	118	ALTARWISE	42
TO SURRENDER NOW IS TO PAY THE EXPENSIVE OGRE TWICE.	140	NO WORK WORDS	10
AND THE TWICE TOLD FIELDS OF INFANCY	178	POEM IN OCT	51
TWIG			
CATCH THE ROOKS SLEEPING, AND BREAK NO TWIG,	31	BEING BUT MEN	7
TWIGS			
AN ENAMOURED MAN ALONE BY THE TWIGS OF HIS EYES, TWO FIRES,	144	PLEASURE-BIRD	7
TWILIGHT			
WHEN ONCE THE TWILIGHT LOCKS NO LONGER	97	TWILIGHT LOCKS	T
WHEN ONCE THE TWILIGHT LOCKS NO LONGER	97	TWILIGHT LOCKS	1
WHEN ONCE THE TWILIGHT SCREWS WERE TURNED,	98	TWILIGHT LOCKS	31
THAT THE SNOW BLIND TWILIGHT FERRIES OVER THE LAKES	187	WINTER'S TALE	2
TWILIT			
LOVE'S TWILIT NATION AND THE SKULL OF STATE,	101	RUNNING GRAVE	39
TWIN			
DEATH AND EVIL ARE TWIN SPECTRES.	60	FAIRY TALES	26
TEAR BY THE ROOTS THESE TWIN GROWTHS IN YOUR GUT;	60	FAIRY TALES	36
THE SCALES OF THIS TWIN WORLD TREAD ON THE DOUBLE,	108	I, IN IMAGE	4
CREATE THIS TWIN MIRACLE.	109	I, IN IMAGE	18
TWIN-BOXED			
AND FREE THE TWIN-BOXED GRIEF,	108	GRIEF THIEF	20
TWINE			
TWINE IN A MOON-BLOWN SHELL,	129	MY NEOPHYTE	15
AND TWINE THE LIMBS AROUND MY HANDS.	239	MAKES INTERVALS	24
TWINED			
BEFORE THE BLOOD AND FLAME WERE TWINED	86	SEE, SAYS LIME	23
TWINED GOOD AND EVIL ON AN EASTERN TREE;	121	INCARNATE DEVL	10

	PAGE	TITLE	LINE
TWINED (CONTINUED)			
IN THE COURTERS' LANES, OR TWINED IN THE OX ROASTING			
SUN	203	GIANT'S THIGH	13
TWINING			
THE ROD CAN LIFT ITS TWINING HEAD	240	TWINING HEAD	T
THE ROD CAN LIFT ITS TWINING HEAD	240	TWINING HEAD	1
TWINKLING			
ENTICED WITH TWINKLING BITS OF THE EYE	146	TO OTHERS	6
TWIST			
DID TWIST INTO A LIVING CIPHER, ...	68	BEFORE KNOCKED	21
THE PROUD SPINE SPURNING TURN AND TWIST.	75	MY HERO BARES	5
I LEARNT MAN'S TONGUE, TO TWIST THE SHAPES OF			
THOUGHTS	79	LOVE'S FEVER	32
FROM DAMP LOVE-DARKNESS AND THE NURSE'S TWIST	96	RUB OF LOVE	38
TWISTED			
THE TWISTED BRAIN, THE FAIR-FORMED LOIN, ...	32	OUT OF SIGHS	25
CONTENT SHALL COME AFTER A TWISTED NIGHT	35	LIFT UP FACE	25
TO WOMEN WHO HAVE TWISTED THEIR LAST SMILE, ...	81	ALL THAT I OWE	16
I WHISTLED ALL NIGHT IN THE TWISTED FLUES, ...	206	LAMENT	18
TWISTING			
TWISTING ON RACKS WHEN SINEWS GIVE WAY, ...	49	NO DOMINION	13
TWITCH			
THE STUFFED LUNG OF THE FOX TWITCH AND CRY LOVE ...	137	AFTER FUNERAL	39
TWIXT			
YOUR STRING SHALL STRETCH A GULLY TWIXT THE THUMBS	87	PAIN BE MUSIC	7
TWIXT YOU AND ME.	87	PAIN BE MUSIC	12
TWO			
LET THE TWO DULL STONES BE GREY, ...	19	IMAGES IN AIR	4
PUTTING TWO AND TWO TOGETHER, ...	38	THE GOSSIPERS	6
PUTTING TWO AND TWO TOGETHER, ...	38	THE GOSSIPERS	6
A GIRL WHOSE SINGLE BED HELD TWO	38	THE GOSSIPERS	9
FAITH IN THEIR HANDS SHALL SNAP IN TWO, ...	50	NO DOMINION	15
AT SIGHT OF DEATH, THE LAST TWO FISTED KILLER	59	FAIRY TALES	18
AND DRINK IN THE TWO MILKED CRAGS, ...	60	MEAT ON BONES	2
IF THESE TWO GNOMES REMAIN UNMOVED BY STRICTURES?	60	FAIRY TALES	30
THERE ARE TWO LAGGARDS, ...	60	FAIRY TALES	34
AS FIRE FALLS, TWO HEMISPHERES DIVIDE, ...	73	LORD RED HAIL	7
OF BIRTH AND DEATH, THE TWO SAD KNAVES OF THIEVES,	75	MY HERO BARES	18
THROUGH, I TELL YOU, YOUR TWO MIDNIGHT LIPS I PRAY	76	LASHED RINGS	7
HATE AND FEAR BE YOUR TWO LOVES.	76	SONG: LOVE ME	15
THE EARTH AND SKY WERE AS TWO MOUNTAINS MEETING.	78	LOVE'S FEVER	15
A BOWLER THING WITH ONE OR TWO	83	LETTER TO AUNT	17
MOVE LIKE TWO GHOSTS BEFORE THE EYE.	88	A PROCESS IN	18
TWO ONE-DIMENSIONED GHOSTS, LOVE ON A REEL, ...	89	EUNUCH DREAMS	12
WHICH IS THE WORLD? OF OUR TWO SLEEPINGS, WHICH ...	89	EUNUCH DREAMS	21
I, IN MY INTRICATE IMAGE, STRIDE ON TWO LEVELS, ...	108	I, IN IMAGE	1
ON THE CONSUMPTIVES' TERRACE TAKING THEIR TWO			
FAREWELLS, ...	109	I, IN IMAGE	34
TWO HEELS OF WATER ON THE FLOOR OF SEED), ...	114	SERVANT SUN	24
SOAR, WITH ITS TWO BARK TOWERS, TO THAT DAY	121	ALTARWISE	138
THE AGONIZED, TWO SEAS.	134	NOT FROM ANGER	7
THE TWO WORDS STALLION AND STERILE	138	O CHATTERTON	35
HER TWO SURNAMES STOPPED ME STILL.	139	TOMBSTONE TOLD	2
AN ENAMOURED MAN ALONE BY THE TWIGS OF HIS EYES, TWO			
FIRES, ...	144	PLEASURE-BIRD	7
THE DEATH BIDING TWO LIE LONELY.	148	UNLUCKILY FOR	28
TWO PROUD, BLACKED BROTHERS CRY, ...	153	WAS A SAVIOUR	25
OTHERS WHOSE SINGLE BEDS HOLD TWO	155	RETURN	60
ONLY TO MAKE TWO ENDS MEET, ...	155	RETURN	61
TWO SAND GRAINS TOGETHER IN BED, ...	158	INTO HER HEAD	47

		PAGE	TITLE	LINE
TWO (CONTINUED)				
INNOCENT BETWEEN TWO WARS,	....	159	INTO HER HEAD	65
THIS RAGGED ANNIVERSARY OF TWO	....	161	WEDDING ANNIV	2
GOOD AND BAD, TWO WAYS	....	192	SIDE OF TRUTH	13
THE SOUND ABOUT TO BE SAID IN THE TWO PRAYERS	.....	194	CONVERS PRAYER	9
AND CAUGHT BETWEEN TWO NIGHTS, BLINDNESS AND DEATH.		217	ELEGY	36
HAS A HORN AND TWO HUMPS ON ITS HEAD,	....	221	SONG OF DOG	6
TWO-A-VEIN				
THE TWO-A-VEIN, THE FORESKIN, AND THE CLOUD.	......	128	NOW, SAY NAY	35
TWO-FRAMED				
THE TWO-FRAMED GLOBE THAT SPUN INTO A SCORE;	......	79	LOVE'S FEVER	45
TWO-GUNNED				
AND FROM THE WINDY WEST CAME TWO-GUNNED GABRIEL,		118	ALTARWISE	57
TWOLEGGED				
TWOLEGGED HANDBAGGED SPARROWS,	....	156	RETURN	74
TYBURN				
TO FIERY TYBURN OVER THE WRESTLE OF ELMS UNTIL	....	201	SIR JOHNS HILL	9
UGLIER				
SOAKED MY TABLE THE UGLIER SIDE OF A HILL	....	144	COLOUR OF SAY	2
UGLY				
PALE AND DECAYED, AN UGLY GROWTH.	....	239	LET ME ESCAPE	12
ULTIMATE				
THE SUNDERING ULTIMATE KINGDOM OF GENESIS' THUNDER.		175	FIRE RAID	77
UMBRELLA'D				
DOWN TO THE WILD, UMBRELLA'D, AND FRENCH LETTERED		179	NEW QUAY	15
UNACCUSTOMED				
CAUGHT IN AN OCTAGON OF UNACCUSTOMED LIGHT,	....	116	LANTERNS SHINE	2
UNAGEING				
AND THE GESTURES OF UNAGEING LOVE.	....	235	WOMAN TAPESTRY	26
AND THE GESTURES OF UNAGEING LOVE.	....	237	WOMAN TAPESTRY	81
UNALTERED				
IT IS THE ENGINE UNDER THE UNALTERED SUN.	....	46	PLOUGHMAN GONE	36
UNANGLED				
BREAKS ON UNANGLED LAND.	....	88	A PROCESS IN	12
UNASHAMED				
UNASHAMED BUT NOT WITH DELIGHT,	....	230	OUR SANCTITY	17
UNBELIEVING				
WE WHO ARE YOUNG ARE OLD, AND UNBELIEVING,	....	42	YOUNG ARE OLD	53
UNBENDING				
ALTHOUGH IT IS SO STRAIGHT AND UNBENDING;	....	231	YOUR VOICE	5
UNBIDDEN				
UNBIDDEN BY THE SUN	....	184	VISION, PRAYER	149
UNBLESSED				
THE DARKEST JUSTICE OF DEATH, BLIND AND UNBLESSED.		216	ELEGY	11
UNBOLT				
SHALL I UNBOLT OR STAY	....	62	EARS IN TURRET	5
UNBOLTS				
AND LOVE UNBOLTS THE DARK	....	210	POEM ON B'DAY	45
UNBORN				
O MY UNBORN	....	87	PAIN BE MUSIC	4
BOLT FOR THE SALT UNBORN.	....	103	WORLD PYRAMID	6
BEARDING THE UNBORN DEVIL,	....	105	WORLD PYRAMID	51
MY CLAY UNSUCKLED AND MY SALT UNBORN,	....	105	WORLD PYRAMID	58
O GREEN AND UNBORN AND UNDEAD?'	....	129	MY NEOPHYTE	47
IN THE NAME OF THE UNBORN	....	185	VISION, PRAYER	172
WITH BLESSED, UNBORN GOD AND HIS GHOST,	....	210	POEM ON B'DAY	60
UNBOSOMING				
IS THE UNBOSOMING OF THE SUN.	....	46	POET: 1935	17
UNBROKEN				
SERENE AND UNBROKEN,	....	235	WOMAN TAPESTRY	14

	PAGE	TITLE	LINE
UNBUTTONED			
WITH BONES UNBUTTONED TO THE HALF-WAY WINDS, ...	117	ALTARWISE	9
UNCAGED			
OF THE UNCAGED SEA BOTTOM	182	VISION, PRAYER	75
UNCALM			
THAT UNCALM STILL IT IS SURE ALONE TO STAND AND SING	186	HOLY SPRING	21
UNCEASINGLY			
AND WATCH THE HAND OF TIME UNCEASINGLY	26	THERE'S PLENTY	11
UNCERTAIN			
SOMETHING AUSTERE HIDES, SOMETHING UNCERTAIN	226	THE OAK	5
UNCHANGEABLE			
AND YOUR SHARP PITY IS UNCHANGEABLE.	236	WOMAN TAPESTRY	51
UNCHRISTENED			
LOST ON THE UNCHRISTENED MOUNTAIN	183	VISION, PRAYER	134
UNCLAIMED			
UNCLAIMED DEAD, GIRLS FROM GOOD HOMES	154	RETURN	15
UNCLENCHED			
UNCLENCHED, ARMLESS, SILK AND ROUGH LOVE THAT BREAKS			
ALL ROCKS.	154	WAS A SAVIOUR	40
UNCOMPLAININGLY			
WE SHIVER UNCOMPLAININGLY, ...	14	RAIN CUTS	36
UNCONCEIVED			
THEY YEARN WITH TONGUES OF CURLEWS FOR THE			
UNCONCEIVED	203	GIANT'S THIGH	10
UNCOVERED			
AND HID HER UNCOVERED BREAST.	15	FOR LEDA	27
UNCREDITED			
UNCREDITED BLOWS JERICHO ON EDEN.	124	TODAY, INSECT	17
UNDEAD			
AND THE UNDEAD EYE-TEETH, ...	108	GRIEF THIEF	24
THEY SUFFER THE UNDEAD WATER WHERE THE TURTLE			
NIBBLES, ...	111	I, IN IMAGE	73
O GREEN AND UNBORN AND UNDEAD?'	129	MY NEOPHYTE	47
ABOUT THE SOILED UNDEAD	176	BREATH SHED	3
UNDEFENDED			
THE BAYONET TONGUE IN THIS UNDEFENDED PRAYERPIECE,	133	MAKE ME A MASK	5
UNDER			
UNDER THE STARS OF WALES, ...	5	PROLOGUE	92
UNDER HIS STRONG IMPULSIVE KISS	11	AIR BREATHE	4
UNDER HER CLOTH OF TREES NO SORROW, ...	15	FOR LEDA	22
UNDER HER GRASSY DRESS NO LIMBS--	15	FOR LEDA	23
FLOWING AND MELTING UNDER LIME.	19	IMAGES IN AIR	8
GROWING ON HILLS OR SHINING UNDER WATER.	25	BEAUTY TO DUST	15
HERE UNDER THE EARTH WITH GIRL AND THIEF, ...	26	PERSONAL EPIT	5
GROPING FOR MATTER UNDER THE DOG'S PLATE, ...	32	OUT OF SIGHS	26
UNDER THE HEAVY LAYERS OF THE NIGHT	39	GAS FADES	38
UNDER THE ARC OF THE SKY THEY ARE UNSAFE.	40	WAS THERE TIME	5
UNDER THE SKYSIGNS THEY WHO HAVE NO ARMS	40	WAS THERE TIME	7
THEIR FACES SHONE UNDER SOME RADIANCE	43	FACES SHONE	T
THEIR FACES SHONE UNDER SOME RADIANCE	43	FACES SHONE	1
SEE, ON GRAVEL PATHS UNDER THE HARPSTRUNG TREES ...	46	POET: 1935	1
UNDER THE HANGING BRANCHES HEAR THE WINDS' HARPS.	46	POET: 1935	15
IT IS THE ENGINE UNDER THE UNALTERED SUN.	46	PLOUGHMAN GONE	36
SEE, ON GRAVEL PATHS UNDER THE HARPSTRUNG TREES,	48	POET: 1935	58
UNDER THE WINDINGS OF THE SEA	49	NO DOMINION	11
SEE WOMEN'S FACES UNDER LIVING SNOODS, ...	51	OUT OF THE PIT	21
PLUNGED IN BLACK WATERS, UNDER HAIL AND FIRE, ...	51	OUT OF THE PIT	42
UNDER A HIDEOUS SEA WHERE CORAL MEN	52	OUT OF THE PIT	68
UNDER THE GREEN ROOF GRIEVES THE LIVING;	56	GREEK PLAY	2
IN THE STABLE UNDER THE SKIN.	74	SUN BURNS	10

	PAGE	TITLE	LINE
UNDER (CONTINUED)			
UNDER THE RIBS SAIL THE MOON AND THE SUN;	74	SUN BURNS	11
UNDER THE MASK AND THE ETHER, THEY, MAKING BLOODY	110	I, IN IMAGE	53
THE SEXTON SENTINEL, GARRISONED UNDER THISTLES, ...	110	I, IN IMAGE	57
DUST BE YOUR SAVIOUR UNDER THE CONJURED SOIL.)	110	I, IN IMAGE	60
THAT NIGHT OF TIME UNDER THE CHRISTWARD SHELTER:	117	ALTARWISE	12
UNDER THE MILKY MUSHROOMS SLEW MY HUNGER, ...	118	ALTARWISE	64
UNDER THE LANK, FOURTH FOLLY ON GLAMORGAN'S HILL,	122	HOLD HARD	2
UNDER THE BELL OF ROCKS, ...	128	MY NEOPHYTE	3
THERE IS LOUD AND DARK DIRECTLY UNDER THE DUMB FLAME,	130	SINNERS' BELL	13
ENDURE BURIAL UNDER THE SPELLING WALL, ...	134	HOW MY ANIMAL	4
REFUSAL STRUCK LIKE A BELL UNDER WATER	134	NOT FROM ANGER	12
WAITING WITH PHOENIX UNDER	147	UNLUCKILY FOR	2
AND MY WHOLE HEART UNDER YOUR HAMMER, ...	147	TO OTHERS	13
UNDER THE CLOUD AGAINST LOVE IS CAUGHT AND HELD AND			
KISSED	147	UNLUCKILY FOR	17
UNDER HIS DOWNY ARM YOU SIGHED AS HE STRUCK, ...	153	WAS A SAVIOUR	19
WITH HIS GOODS UNDER HIS EYES, ...	155	RETURN	38
ANOTHER WITH HERS UNDER HER BELT, ...	155	RETURN	39
UNDER THE ENCUMBERED EYELID, ...	157	INTO HER HEAD	3
GOLDEN DISSOLVING UNDER THE WATER VEIL.	159	INTO HER HEAD	55
THE LURED FISH UNDER THE FOAM	163	LONG-LEGGED	47
THERE IS THUNDER UNDER ITS THUMBS;	164	LONG-LEGGED	62
ARE MAKING UNDER THE GREEN, LAID VEIL	164	LONG-LEGGED	69
THE TEMPTER UNDER THE EYELID	165	LONG-LEGGED	102
SEE WHAT THE GOLD GUT DRAGS FROM UNDER	166	LONG-LEGGED	131
DOWN, DOWN, DOWN, UNDER THE GROUND, ...	169	LONG-LEGGED	201
UNDER THE FLOATING VILLAGES, ...	169	LONG-LEGGED	202
UNDER THE EARTH THE LOUD SEA WALKS, ...	169	LONG-LEGGED	206
WHO UNDER THE LIDS OF HER WINDOWS HOISTED HIS GOLDEN			
LUGGAGE, ...	170	MARRIAGE VIRG	12
UNDER THE SAD BREAST OF THE HEAD STONE	174	FIRE RAID	44
THE MASSES OF THE SEA UNDER	175	FIRE RAID	73
IN THE WOOD FARAWAY UNDER ME.	177	POEM IN OCT	30
BEYOND THE BORDER AND UNDER THE LARK FULL CLOUD.	177	POEM IN OCT	37
UNDER THE BURIAL SONG	183	VISION, PRAYER	104
UNDER THE NIGHT FOREVER FALLING.	184	VISION, PRAYER	152
OR FLOWER UNDER THE TIME DYING FLESH ASTRIDE.	188	WINTER'S TALE	55
UNDER THE ONE LEAVED TREES RAN A SCARECROW OF SNOW	190	WINTER'S TALE	94
UNDER THE UNMINDING SKIES, ...	192	SIDE OF TRUTH	6
UNDER THE MILE OFF MOON WE TREMBLED LISTENING	194	SLEEP BECALMED	5
NOW AS I WAS YOUNG AND EASY UNDER THE APPLE BOUGHS	195	FERN HILL	1
AND NIGHTLY UNDER THE SIMPLE STARS	195	FERN HILL	23
UNDER THE NEW MADE CLOUDS AND HAPPY AS THE HEART WAS			
LONG, ...	196	FERN HILL	38
UNDER THE PRAYER WHEELING MOON IN THE ROSY WOOD ...	198	COUNTRY SLEEP	41
IN THE SQUIRREL NIMBLE GROVE, UNDER LINEN AND THATCH	199	COUNTRY SLEEP	44
WHEN HIS VIPERISH FUSE HANGS LOOPED WITH FLAMES			
UNDER THE BRAND	202	SIR JOHNS HILL	28
IT IS THE HERON AND I, UNDER JUDGING SIR JOHN'S ELMED	202	SIR JOHNS HILL	40
UNDER THE CONCEIVING MOON, ON THE HIGH CHALK HILL,	203	GIANT'S THIGH	2
UNDER THE LIGHTED SHAPES OF FAITH AND THEIR MOONSHADE	204	GIANT'S THIGH	17
MANES, UNDER HIS QUENCHLESS SUMMER BARBED GOLD TO			
THE BONE, ...	204	GIANT'S THIGH	26
AND THE MOLE SNOUT BLUNT UNDER HIS PILGRIMAGE OF			
DOMES, ...	204	GIANT'S THIGH	36
THEIR BREASTS FULL OF HONEY, UNDER THEIR GANDER KING	205	GIANT'S THIGH	38
UNDER AND ROUND HIM GO	209	POEM ON B'DAY	10
UNDER A SERPENT CLOUD, ...	209	POEM ON B'DAY	32
HILL, UNDER THE GRASS, IN LOVE, AND THERE GROW	216	ELEGY	6

	PAGE	TITLE	LINE
UNDER (CONTINUED)			
OF THE SEA UNDER THE HARD SUN,	229	MY RIVER	35
BECAUSE THEY ARE UNDER THE SURFACE	230	OUR SANCTITY	9
UNDER THIS SHADE	230	OUR SANCTITY	22
CREEPING CATLIKE UNDER THE WATER.	231	OUR SANCTITY	41
AND BENT UNDER IT,	232	FURIOUS MOTION	13
UNDER THE TENT OF ITS WINGS.	237	WOMAN TAPESTRY	74
UNDERCLOTHES			
HER THIGHS AND UNDERCLOTHES WERE SWEET,	11	CABARET	6
UNDERSTAND			
FEW UNDERSTAND THE WORKS OF CUMMINGS,	84	LETTER TO AUNT	36
UNDERTAKER'S			
OUT OF THE WRINKLED UNDERTAKER'S VAN,	118	ALTARWISE	36
UNDESERVING			
WHO, UNDESERVING, HAVE SUFFERED THE EARTH'S WRONG,	41	YOUNG ARE OLD	34
UNDESIRERS			
AND THE UNDESIRERS	185	VISION, PRAYER	173
UNDID			
THE BRAINS OF DEATH UNDID THE KNOT	86	SEE, SAYS LIME	22
SOME DEAD UNDID THEIR BUSHY JAWS,	97	TWILIGHT LOCKS	22
UNDIE			
CRUMBLE AND UNDIE	3	PROLOGUE	32
UNDIVIDED			
THE FIELDS YET UNDIVIDED BEHIND THE SKULL.	73	LORD RED HAIL	10
UNDO			
THE GENTLE SEASLIDES OF SAYING I MUST UNDO	144	COLOUR OF SAY	5
UNDOER			
OF DEATH'S UNDOER.	85	SEE, SAYS LIME	8
DEATH'S DEATH'S UNDOER.	86	SEE, SAYS LIME	32
UNDOING			
NOW MY SAYING SHALL BE MY UNDOING,	144	COLOUR OF SAY	12
UNDONE			
THE OLD SPELLS ARE UNDONE.	59	FAIRY TALES	13
O MY UNDONE	87	PAIN BE MUSIC	22
HIS FAITH AROUND HER FLEW UNDONE	158	INTO HER HEAD	26
MAN AND WOMAN UNDONE,	175	FIRE RAID	57
THAT ALL IS UNDONE,	192	SIDE OF TRUTH	5
UNDOUBLING			
SEE THE REASON FOR UNDOUBLING DOUBLING NOT,	24	LITTLE PROBLEM	16
UNDRESS			
TO SMIRK AT LOVE'S UNDRESS,	34	THIRST PARCHES	13
UNEARTHLY			
PUT A TEAR FOR JOY IN THE UNEARTHLY FLOOD	153	WAS A SAVIOUR	22
UNEASE			
(NOTES NOT IN SYMPATHY, DISCORD, UNEASE),	35	LIFT UP FACE	21
UNEASILY			
AND MY THOUGHTS FLOW SO UNEASILY	10	COOL, OH NO	22
FLOW UNEASILY BEHIND YOU.	232	FURIOUS MOTION	8
UNEATEN			
UNEATEN AND NOT TO BE PIERCED	17	IN OBLIVION	25
UNEATING			
LOST IN A LIMP-TREED AND UNEATING SILENCE,	132	I MAKE THIS IN	28
UNENDING			
IF NOT IN PERSON SENDS HIS UNENDING EVIL	29	NEARLY SUMMER	3
TO THAT UNENDING SEA AROUND MY ISLAND	76	LASHED RINGS	8
THOUGH THE MOMENT OF A MIRACLE IS UNENDING LIGHTNING	170	MARRIAGE VIRG	6
UNENTERED			
RIDE THROUGH THE DOORS OF OUR UNENTERED HOUSE.	154	WAS A SAVIOUR	38
UNEVEN			
WITH UNEVEN, SPIRAL TEETH.	229	MY RIVER	26

		PAGE	TITLE	LINE
UNFAILING				
TO WONDER AT THE UNFAILING STARS.		31	BEING BUT MEN	10
UNFAILING TILL THE BLOOD RUNS FOUL;		69	BEFORE KNOCKED	28
UNFIRED				
CONTINENCE. I SEE THE UNFIRED PHOENIX, HERALD		148	UNLUCKILY FOR	37
UNFOLDING				
FROM THE UNFOLDING TO THE SCISSORED CAUL, ...		78	LOVE'S FEVER	3
UNFORGETFULNESS				
IDYLL OF UNFORGETFULNESS		223	IDYLL UNFORGET	T
UNFORGETTABLY				
WITH UNFORGETTABLY SMILING ACT, ...		146	TO OTHERS	11
UNFREE				
TO THE ANGUISH AND CARRION, TO THE INFANT FOREVER				
UNFREE, ...		146	IF HEAD HURT	22
UNFRIENDLY				
THAT HER LOVING, UNFRIENDLY LIMBS		175	MY BEGGAR ARM	5
UNFRISKY				
BUT THERE IS ONLY BUCKLEY'S UNFRISKY		179	NEW QUAY	11
UNGOTTEN				
UNGOTTEN I KNEW NIGHT AND DAY.		68	BEFORE KNOCKED	18
AS YET UNGOTTEN, I DID SUFFER;		68	BEFORE KNOCKED	19
UNHAPPY				
A CRUDE, UNHAPPY, ANAL CRAMP.		143	THE MOLLS	8
UNHARDY				
BAY. NO-GOOD IS ABROAD. I UNHARDY CAN		179	NEW QUAY	8
UNHARMED				
SHALL THE CHILD SLEEP UNHARMED OR THE MAN BE CRYING?		194	CONVERS PRAYER	12
UNHEALTHILY				
UNHEALTHILY WITH DRY VEINS.		236	WOMAN TAPESTRY	60
UNHOLY				
HER HOLY UNHOLY HOURS WITH THE ALWAYS ANONYMOUS				
BEAST.		158	INTO HER HEAD	46
UNHOUSE				
BY MIDNIGHT PULLEYS THAT UNHOUSE THE TOMB.		89	EUNUCH DREAMS	10
UNHURT				
ALONE'S UNHURT, SO THE BLIND MAN SEES BEST.		40	WAS THERE TIME	9
UNICORN				
AND THE UNICORN EVILS RUN THEM THROUGH;		50	NO DOMINION	16
UNIVERSE				
I'VE MOCKED THE MOVING OF THE UNIVERSE.		52	OUT OF THE PIT	75
HERE IS A UNIVERSE BRED IN THE BONE, ...		74	SUN BURNS	6
UNJUDGING				
DIE IN UNJUDGING LOVE.		193	SIDE OF TRUTH	36
UNKIND				
AND NOAH'S REKINDLED NOW UNKIND DOVE		157	INTO HER HEAD	5
UNKNOWING				
BUT CAME FROM OUT THE MOUTH UNKNOWING		23	THE ONLY DEAD	17
THE MIDNIGHT ROAD, THOUGH YOUNG MEN TREAD UNKNOWING,		36	MIDNIGHT ROAD	1
WHERE STILL THEY SLEEP UNKNOWING OF THEIR GHOST.		102	FELLOWED SLEEP	20
LIE ALL UNKNOWING OF THE GRAVE SIN-EATER.		113	NOT FATHER ME	32
UNKNOWN				
O MY UNKNOWN		87	PAIN BE MUSIC	16
ONE WHO IS MOST UNKNOWN, ...		160	DEATHS AND ENT	16
IN THE BIRTH BLOODY ROOM UNKNOWN		180	VISION, PRAYER	10
IN THE UNKNOWN, FAMOUS LIGHT OF GREAT		210	POEM ON B'DAY	47
UNLESS				
YOU SHALL NOT GO UNLESS I WILL IT		10	COOL, OH NO	21
UNLESS FOR POETRY, WHICH, IF IT ASKS ME		24	LITTLE PROBLEM	17
UNLESS I LEARN THE NIGHT I SHALL GO MAD.		48	LIGHT, I KNOW	12

	PAGE	TITLE	LINE
UNLOCKED			
WITH HEART UNLOCKED UPON THE GIGANTIC EARTH.	46	POET: 1935	12
AND ALL THE DRY SEABED UNLOCKED,	97	TWILIGHT LOCKS	8
UNLOCKING			
LOCKING, UNLOCKING, THE MURDERED STRANGERS WEAVE,	160	DEATHS AND ENT	15
UNLOVERS			
STARING AT OTHERS, POOR UNLOVERS.	23	THE ONLY DEAD	3
UNLOVING			
HAVE FOOD AND DRINK, UNLOVING?	23	THE ONLY DEAD	12
UNLUCKILY			
UNLUCKILY FOR A DEATH	147	UNLUCKILY FOR	T
UNLUCKILY FOR A DEATH	147	UNLUCKILY FOR	1
UNMADE			
ALL NIGHT IN THE UNMADE PARK	172	THE HUNCHBACK	37
UNMANLY			
ROLL UNMANLY OVER THIS TURNING TUFT,	123	FOSTER LIGHT	19
UNMANNINGLY			
FOR WHO UNMANNINGLY HAUNTS THE MOUNTAIN RAVENED EAVES	198	COUNTRY SLEEP	24
UNMASTERED			
MASTERS OVER UNMASTERED NATURE,	45	PLOUGHMAN GONE	21
UNMILK			
YOUR PAIN SHALL NOT UNMILK YOU OF THE FOOD	87	PAIN BE MUSIC	19
UNMINDING			
UNDER THE UNMINDING SKIES,	192	SIDE OF TRUTH	6
UNMORTAL			
MY MAN OF LEAVES AND THE BRONZE ROOT, MORTAL,			
UNMORTAL,	109	I, IN IMAGE	16
UNMOURNING			
SECRET BY THE UNMOURNING WATER	192	REFUSAL MOURN	22
UNMOVED			
IF THESE TWO GNOMES REMAIN UNMOVED BY STRICTURES?	60	FAIRY TALES	30
UNMOVING			
THEIR SILKEN BRANCHES UNMOVING,	235	WOMAN TAPESTRY	7
UNMOVING IN A SHOULDERING SEA,	238	PILLAR BREAKS	20
UNPACKS			
UNPACKS THE HEAD THAT, LIKE A SLEEPY GHOST,	75	MY HERO BARES	3
UNPIN			
WHERE NO COLD IS, THE SKINNING GALES UNPIN	82	LIGHT BREAKS	22
UNPITIED			
PITY THE POOR UNPITIED WHO ARE STRANGE WITH TEARS.	57	GREEK PLAY	28
UNPLANTED			
AND THE UNPLANTED GHOST.	104	WORLD PYRAMID	12
UNPRICKED			
PACK BACK THE DOWNED BONE. IF THE UNPRICKED BALL OF			
MY BREATH	145	IF HEAD HURT	2
UNRAVEL			
RAGE ME BACK TO THE MAKING HOUSE. MY HAND UNRAVEL	145	IF HEAD HURT	12
UNRAVELLER			
THE GREEN UNRAVELLER,	91	WHERE ONCE THE	9
UNRAVELS			
BEGINNING WITH DOOM IN THE BULB, THE SPRING UNRAVELS,	108	I, IN IMAGE	7
UNREAL			
STOP IS UNREAL;	9	MINUTE'S HOUR	13
UNREASON			
IN TIME, LIKE ALL, THROUGH MY UNREASON	21	BEWILDERED WAY	7
UNREASONABLY			
YOU I SHALL DROWN UNREASONABLY,	9	MINUTE'S HOUR	9
UNREINED			
WHALES UNREINED FROM THE GREEN GRAVE	157	INTO HER HEAD	8

	PAGE	TITLE	LINE
UNREMEMBERED			
OF UNREMEMBERED SKIES AND SNOWS.	225	CLOWN IN MOON	4
UNREST			
THERE WAS CALM TO BE DONE IN HIS SAFE UNREST, ...	153	WAS A SAVIOUR	11
UNRETURNABLE			
AND BY YOUR HABIT UNRETURNABLE.	23	THE ONLY DEAD	25
UNRETURNED			
BUT, BY YOUR HABIT UNRETURNED, ...	23	THE ONLY DEAD	24
UNRIDDLE			
CAN TIME UNRIDDLE, AND THE CUPBOARD STONE, ...	113	SERVANT SUN	3
UNRISEN			
AND DAUB THE UNRISEN SUN WITH LONGING.	15	FOR LEDA	13
UNRIVALLED			
THAT OTHER SUN, THE JEALOUS COURSING OF THE			
UNRIVALLED BLOOD.	170	MARRIAGE VIRG	14
UNROLLED			
THE UNROLLED WAVES	13	RAIN CUTS	11
AS THE FOOD AND FLAMES OF THE SNOW, A MAN UNROLLED	187	WINTER'S TALE	13
UNRULY			
I HUG TO LOVE WITH MY UNRULY SCRAWL	75	MY HERO BARES	8
UNSACRED			
HER FAITH THAT THIS LAST NIGHT FOR HIS UNSACRED SAKE	201	COUNTRY SLEEP	104
UNSAFE			
UNDER THE ARC OF THE SKY THEY ARE UNSAFE.	40	WAS THERE TIME	5
UNSEEING			
THROUGH HIS UNSEEING EYES TO THE ROOTS OF THE SEA.	217	ELEGY	17
UNSEEN			
UNSEEN BY STRANGER-EYES	62	EARS IN TURRET	7
OR LIFT MY HAT TO UNSEEN	155	RETURN	48
ENVELOPING THE RAGGED LEAVES UNSEEN AND STREWN. ...	226	THE OAK	2
UNSEX			
UNSEX THE SKELETON THIS MOUNTAIN MINUTE, ...	120	ALTARWISE	110
UNSHACKLED			
UNSHACKLED THE WEIGHTS OF WORDS FROM TIRED LIMBS,	53	OUT OF THE PIT	83
UNSHAPED			
OF CRYING OFF THIS UNSHAPED EVIL, ...	21	BEWILDERED WAY	2
UNSHELVE			
UNSHELVE THAT ALL MY GRISTLES HAVE A GOWN	113	SERVANT SUN	6
UNSHODDEN			
FROM THE FIRST PRINT OF THE UNSHODDEN FOOT, THE			
LIFTING	78	LOVE'S FEVER	10
UNSKATED			
LIE THIS FIFTH MONTH UNSKATED, AND THE BIRDS HAVE			
FLOWN;	122	HOLD HARD	9
UNSLEEPING			
IN THE UNSLEEPING MUMMERY	35	LIFT UP FACE	7
OUT OF UNSLEEPING COGITATIONS, ...	35	LIFT UP FACE	18
UNSOUNDING			
UNSOUNDING, THEY BEAT SO SOFT.	33	HELD-OUT HAND	5
UNSOWN			
O MY UNSOWN	87	PAIN BE MUSIC	10
UNSPENT			
SOME LIFE, YET UNSPENT, MIGHT EXPLODE	44	LONGED TO MOVE	12
UNSUCKED			
WHO COULD HACK OUT YOUR UNSUCKED HEART, ...	129	MY NEOPHYTE	46
UNSUCKLED			
MY CLAY UNSUCKLED AND MY SALT UNBORN, ...	105	WORLD PYRAMID	58
UNTHINKING			
UNTHINKING ACTIONS GIVEN CAUSES	38	THE GOSSIPERS	4

	PAGE	TITLE	LINE
UNTIL			
UNTIL THE SPOUT DRIED UP	17	IN OBLIVION	11
UNTIL THE DAY'S BROKEN--	22	HIGH ON A HILL	6
COUNT THE ENDLESS DAYS UNTIL THEY END, ...	32	HELD-OUT HAND	2
THE DRY FEVER BURNS UNTIL NO HEART IS LEFT, ...	34	THIRST PARCHES	2
UNTIL THE WHISPER OF THE LAST TRUMP LOUDEN	40	YOUNG ARE OLD	11
SIT AT OUR HEARTHS FROM MORNING UNTIL EVENING, ...	42	YOUNG ARE OLD	54
LIE WATCHING YELLOW UNTIL THE GOLDEN WEATHER	54	WE BY SEASAND	23
MOTHERS ME UNTIL I DIE, ...	72	TAKE NEEDLES	43
STALE OF ADAM'S BRINE UNTIL, VISION	103	I DREAMED MY	27
STORM ME FOREVER OVER HER GRAVE UNTIL	137	AFTER FUNERAL	38
UNTIL THAT ONE LOVED LEAST	161	DEATHS AND ENT	35
UNTIL THE SUNDAY SOMBRE BELL AT DARK	171	THE HUNCHBACK	6
MADE ALL DAY UNTIL BELL TIME	172	THE HUNCHBACK	31
UNTIL THE TURBULENT NEW BORN	180	VISION, PRAYER	27
NEVER UNTIL THE MANKIND MAKING	191	REFUSAL MOURN	1
NEVER, MY GIRL, UNTIL TOLLED TO SLEEP BY THE STERN	198	COUNTRY SLEEP	21
THIS NIGHT AND EACH VAST NIGHT UNTIL THE STERN BELL			
TALKS	199	COUNTRY SLEEP	51
TO FIERY TYBURN OVER THE WRESTLE OF ELMS UNTIL	201	SIR JOHNS HILL	9
UNTIL I DIE HE WILL NOT LEAVE MY SIDE.	217	ELEGY	40
UNTIL YOU COULD BEAR IT NO LONGER	232	FURIOUS MOTION	12
UNTIL I FELT THE RHYTHM OF HER BODY	234	WOMAN TAPESTRY	4
UNTO			
AND I AM DUMB TO MOUTH UNTO MY VEINS	77	THE FORCE THAT	9
COME UNTO SEA-STUCK TOWERS, AT THE FIBRE SCALING,	111	I, IN IMAGE	74
FAITHLESSLY UNTO HIM	210	POEM ON B'DAY	72
UNTURNING			
THE STRONG, UNTURNING CRUST THAT HIDES	233	NO THOUGHT	11
UNWASTEABLE			
I SPENT MY UNWASTEABLE	154	RETURN	9
UNWATERED			
FROM THE UNWATERED LEAVES AND THE STIFF STALKS, ...	47	POET: 1935	39
UNWAVERING			
THE LIGHT WILL COME IN AN UNWAVERING LINE.	232	YOUR VOICE	7
UNWHOLESOME			
ALL, MEN MY MADMEN, THE UNWHOLESOME WIND	101	RUNNING GRAVE	46
NO THOUGHT CAN TROUBLE MY UNWHOLESOME POSE	233	NO THOUGHT	T
NO THOUGHT CAN TROUBLE MY UNWHOLESOME POSE, ...	233	NO THOUGHT	1
UNWINDING			
THE UNWINDING, SONG BY ROCK, ...	141	SAINT TO FALL	5
UNWORTHY			
SHALL PROVE UNWORTHY FOR HIS DOING, ...	23	THE ONLY DEAD	15
UNWRINKLES			
THE FRUIT OF MAN UNWRINKLES IN THE STARS, ...	82	LIGHT BREAKS	10
UNWRINKLING			
A CHRYSALIS UNWRINKLING ON THE IRON, ...	115	A GRIEF AGO	10
UP			
SEES THE MOON STILL UP, ...	14	FOR LEDA	8
UNTIL THE SPOUT DRIED UP	17	IN OBLIVION	11
OUT OF MY HAND IN STOPPING UP MY MOUTH, ...	18	NATURAL DAY	16
AS THOUGH THE SUN WERE SPINNING UP THROUGH IT.	19	THE NEOPHYTE	8
UP TO THE SECOND OF THE DARK COMING, ...	25	THERE'S PLENTY	5
LIFT UP YOUR FACE	35	LIFT UP FACE	T
LIFT UP YOUR FACE, LIGHT	35	LIFT UP FACE	1
LIFT UP YOUR HEAD, LET	35	LIFT UP FACE	10
UP YOUR HAND TO STROKE THE LIGHT, ...	35	LIFT UP FACE	15
LIFT UP THE BLINDS OVER THE BLIND EYES.	35	LIFT UP FACE	17
THEREFORE LIFT UP, SEE, STROKE THE LIGHT.	35	LIFT UP FACE	24
AND SIGNPOSTS POINTING UP AND DOWN	36	WINDMILLS TURN	2

		PAGE	TITLE	LINE
UP (CONTINUED)				
THE VIRGINS SMELT OUT, THREE STREETS UP,	....	38	THE GOSSIPERS	8
REACH ASKING ARMS UP TO THE MILKY SKY,	....	42	A WAR OF WITS	16
FOLLOWING THE NOSE DOWN DELL, UP RISE	....	44	TO FOLLOW FOX	7
SPLIT ALL ENDS UP THEY SHAN'T CRACK;	....	50	NO DOMINION	17
PARADED UP THE AISLES AND IN THE CRYPT	....	51	OUT OF THE PIT	27
AND SWIMMING DOWN THE GUTTERS HE LOOKS UP	....	51	OUT OF THE PIT	45
AND THEN RAISE UP THE SKELETON AGAIN,	....	55	NO MAN BELIEVE	20
O TIDAL WINDS, CAST UP HER CRY FOR ME;	....	65	WOMAN SPEAKS	54
A SHOUT WENT UP TO HEAVEN LIKE A ROCKET,	....	70	SECRET WIND	7
THE BLOOD GOT UP AS RED AS WAX	....	85	SEE, SAYS LIME	13
UP THROUGH THE FINGERS' CRACKS;	....	86	SEE, SAYS LIME	29
LIGHTS UP THE LIVING WORM.	....	88	A PROCESS IN	6
AND THE HEART GIVES UP ITS DEAD.	....	88	A PROCESS IN	24
RAISE UP THIS RED-EYED EARTH?	....	89	EUNUCH DREAMS	23
THE DEAD TURNS UP ITS EYE;	....	90	WHERE ONCE THE	3
PUSHED UP THEIR HAIR, THE DRY WIND STEERS	....	90	WHERE ONCE THE	5
SPLIT UP THE BRAWNED WOMB'S WEATHERS,	....	92	BOYS OF SUMMER	14
HOLD UP THE NOISY SEA AND DROP HER BIRDS,	....	93	BOYS OF SUMMER	39
THE WORD FLOWED UP, TRANSLATING TO THE HEART	......	94	IN BEGINNING	23
GIVES UP ITS DEAD TO SUCH A WORKING SEA;	....	97	TWILIGHT LOCKS	27
AND CONJURED UP A CARCASS SHAPE	....	98	TWILIGHT LOCKS	35
UP NAKED STAIRS, A TURTLE IN A HEARSE,	....	99	RUNNING GRAVE	4
DRIVE CHILDREN UP LIKE BRUISES TO THE THUMB,	......	100	RUNNING GRAVE	14
RAISED UP A VOICE, AND, CLIMBING ON THE WORDS,	....	102	FELLOWED SLEEP	22
SPAT UP FROM THE RESUFFERED PAIN.	....	103	I DREAMED MY	24
THRUSTING THE TOM-THUMB VISION UP THE IRON MILE.		111	I, IN IMAGE	84
UP ROSE THE ABRAHAM-MAN, MAD FOR MY SAKE,	....	112	NOT FATHER ME	19
SOAKS UP THE SEWING TIDES),	....	113	SERVANT SUN	12
A STEM CEMENTING, WRESTLED UP THE TOWER,	....	114	A GRIEF AGO	5
SAILED UP THE SUN;	....	114	A GRIEF AGO	8
OR SPIRIT UP A CLOUD,	....	114	SERVANT SUN	26
WOULD WITHER UP, AND ANY BOY OF LOVE	....	116	LANTERNS SHINE	3
THE CHILD THAT SUCKETH LONG IS SHOOTING UP,	....	117	ALTARWISE	16
FROM JESU'S SLEEVE TRUMPED UP THE KING OF SPOTS,		118	ALTARWISE	58
HIGH LORD ESQUIRE, SPEAK UP THE SINGING CLOUD,	....	123	FOSTER LIGHT	17
HER MOLTEN FLIGHT UP CINDER-NESTING COLUMNS,	......	132	I MAKE THIS IN	26
'HIS MOTHER'S WOMB HAD A TONGUE THAT LAPPED UP MUD,'		132	I MAKE THIS IN	46
BY THE CURVE OF THE NUDE MOUTH OR THE LAUGH UP THE SLEEVE.	....	133	MAKE ME A MASK	12
YOU HAVE KICKED FROM A DARK DEN, LEAPED UP THE WHINNYING LIGHT,	....	135	HOW MY ANIMAL	43
MORNING SMACK OF THE SPADE THAT WAKES UP SLEEP,	...	136	AFTER FUNERAL	6
AND UP AND DOWN LOVE'S QUESTIONS ASK;	....	138	O CHATTERTON	23
PUFFING THE POUNDS OF MANNA UP THROUGH THE DEW TO HEAVEN,	....	140	NO WORK WORDS	5
A BLAZING RED HARSH HEAD TEAR UP	....	140	TOMBSTONE TOLD	29
UP TO HIS HEAD IN HIS BLOOD,	....	150	WHEN I WOKE	9
UP THROUGH THE LUBBER CRUST OF WALES	....	151	BELOW A TIME	24
IN FOUNTAINS OF ORIGIN GAVE UP THEIR LOVE,	....	157	INTO HER HEAD	9
A MAN TORN UP MOURNS IN THE SOLE NIGHT.	....	159	INTO HER HEAD	67
WILL DIVE UP TO HIS TEARS.	....	160	DEATHS AND ENT	18
AS THE SAILS DRANK UP THE HAIL OF THUNDER	....	166	LONG-LEGGED	127
TOPPLING UP THE BOATSIDE IN A SNOW OF LIGHT!'	......	166	LONG-LEGGED	138
UP AND DOWN THE GREATER WAVES	....	168	LONG-LEGGED	179
AND THIS DAY'S SUN LEAPT UP THE SKY OUT OF HER THIGHS		170	MARRIAGE VIRG	4
BUT NOBODY CHAINED HIM UP.	....	171	THE HUNCHBACK	12
WITH HIS STICK THAT PICKED UP LEAVES.	....	171	THE HUNCHBACK	24
AND BUTTON UP. HE MINCES AMONG KNICKERS,	....	179	NEW QUAY	23

	PAGE	TITLE	LINE
UP (CONTINUED)			
HIM UP AND HE RAN LIKE A WIND AFTER THE KINDLING FLIGHT	190	WINTER'S TALE	89
DRAGGING HIM UP THE STAIRS TO ONE WHO LIES DEAD.	194	CONVERS PRAYER	20
UP TO THE SWALLOW THRONGED LOFT BY THE SHADOW OF MY HAND,	196	FERN HILL	47
AND GALLOWS, UP THE RAYS OF HIS EYES THE SMALL BIRDS OF THE BAY	201	SIR JOHNS HILL	4
LITTLE WHITE-LIPPED FACES HAVE PEERED UP AT ME,	224	IDYLL UNFORGET	32
LOOKING UP AT YOU.	229	MY RIVER	12
FEEL YOUR WOMAN'S BREASTS RISE UP LIKE FLOWERS	238	MAKES INTERVALS	12
UPCASTING			
THE COCKEREL'S TIDE UPCASTING FROM THE FIRE.	127	NOW, SAY NAY	21
UPCOMING			
YAWN TO HIS UPCOMING.	183	VISION, PRAYER	132
UPGIVEN			
OF THE NIGHTINGALE'S DIN AND TALE! THE UPGIVEN GHOST	200	COUNTRY SLEEP	74
UPHEAVAL			
BUT BLESSED BE HAIL AND UPHEAVAL	186	HOLY SPRING	20
UPON			
UPON THE ISLAND OF MY PALM,	11	CABARET	2
WE SAIL A BOAT UPON THE PATH,	13	RAIN CUTS	6
AND TASTE UPON OUR LIPS, THIS MINUTE,	14	RAIN CUTS	37
THERE'S TIME TO PLUCK A TUNE UPON THE HARP,	15	FOR LEDA	16
MY HAND WITH HONEY THAT HAD CLOSED UPON A FLOWER.	15	FOR LEDA	19
A PAPER WITCH UPON HER SULPHURED BROOM	16	TIME TO ROT	11
UPON THE EARTH WHO KNEW NO JOY,	22	ON QUIET NIGHT	16
WHO'LL BREAK OUR NECKS UPON THE PAVEMENT	28	NO WINGS	10
EASIER THAN HE UPON THE ICE.	28	NO WINGS	11
STAY, IN A CIRCLE CHALKED UPON THE FLOOR,	28	NO WINGS	25
AND YOU HAVE WALKED UPON THE HILLS AT NIGHT,	30	YOUTH CALLS	8
UPON YOUR HELD-OUT HAND	32	HELD-OUT HAND	T
UPON YOUR HELD-OUT HAND	32	HELD-OUT HAND	1
TO BRUSH UPON THE WATERS OF THE POND.	34	IN GARDENS	21
NIGHTLY UPON THEIR WRINKLED BREASTS	38	THE GOSSIPERS	17
MIGHT PLAY UPON HIS LANK LOCKS WITH ITS WIND,	46	POET: 1935	3
WITH HEART UNLOCKED UPON THE GIGANTIC EARTH.	46	POET: 1935	12
OPENING ITS IRIS MOUTH UPON THE SILL	47	POET: 1935	30
AND WASHING WATER SPILT UPON THEIR NECKS	47	POET: 1935	32
AND, MAD, HE CALLED HIS CURSES UPON GOD,	50	OUT OF THE PIT	8
STUCK STRAW AND SEVEN STARS UPON MY HAIR,	52	OUT OF THE PIT	65
NO MAN UPON THIS CYST OF EARTH	55	NO MAN BELIEVE	15
TIME UPON TIME THE TOWERS OF THE SKIES	56	WHY EAST WIND	19
I KNOW THAT AGE IS SNOW UPON THE HAIR,	64	WOMAN SPEAKS	49
TO DRIFT OR DROWN UPON THE SEAS	69	BEFORE KNOCKED	32
UPON THE LAND OF GOLD OR OIL,	73	WE MOTHERNAKED	2
AND LOUD HIS ANGER STAMP UPON THE HILL.	73	LORD RED HAIL	6
MY FATHERS' LOVES THAT PULL UPON MY NERVES,	80	ALL THAT I OWE	6
MY SISTERS' TEARS THAT SING UPON MY HEAD,	80	ALL THAT I OWE	7
CAST LIGHT UPON MY WEATHER. I AM HEIR	80	ALL THAT I OWE	15
THEN LOOK, MY EYES, UPON THIS BONEBOUND FORTUNE	81	ALL THAT I OWE	21
AND BROWSE UPON THE POSTURES OF THE DEAD;	81	ALL THAT I OWE	22
WAX CLOTHES THAT WAX UPON THE AGEING RIBS;	81	ALL THAT I OWE	26
THEN LOOK, MY HEART, UPON THE SCARLET TROVE,	81	ALL THAT I OWE	28
AND LOOK, MY GRAIN, UPON THE FALLING WHEAT;	81	ALL THAT I OWE	29
THIS WINE UPON A FOREIGN TREE	86	BREAD I BREAK	2
I CHALKED UPON THE BREASTBONE'S SLATE	86	SEE, SAYS LIME	27
STAMP OF THE MINTED FACE UPON THE MOON;	94	IN BEGINNING	10
THE ITCH OF MAN UPON THE BABY'S THIGH,	95	RUB OF LOVE	12
REHEARSING HEAT UPON A RAW-EDGED NERVE.	95	RUB OF LOVE	19

	PAGE	TITLE	LINE
UPON (CONTINUED)			
AND CAST A SHADOW CRAB UPON THE LAND, ...	98	OCTOBER WIND	4
MY MOTHERS-EYED, UPON THE TOPS OF TREES;	101	FELLOWED SLEEP	9
MY BLOOD UPON THE TEMPERED DEAD, FORCING	103	I DREAMED MY	19
THE CRUTCH THAT MARROW TAPS UPON THEIR SLEEP, ...	104	WORLD PYRAMID	14
THE WILD PIGS' WOOD, AND SLIME UPON THE TREES, ...	104	WORLD PYRAMID	20
ARC-LAMPED THROWN BACK UPON THE CUTTING FLOOD.	118	ALTARWISE	56
TROT AND GALLOP WITH GULLS UPON THEM	168	LONG-LEGGED	189
HIS GOLDEN YESTERDAY ASLEEP UPON THE IRIS	170	MARRIAGE VIRG	3
SANG UPON ORIGIN!	182	VISION, PRAYER	90
STREAM UPON HIS MARTYRDOM	185	VISION, PRAYER	185
SUMMER IS HEAVY WITH AGE, AND LEANS UPON AUTUMN.	221	FOREST PICTURE	4
LYING UPON THE YELLOW BEACH.	229	MY RIVER	40
WE WILL REMARK UPON THE SIZE	230	OUR SANCTITY	6
UPON BROAD WINGS	231	OUR SANCTITY	33
WEIGHED STRANGELY DOWN UPON YOU	232	FURIOUS MOTION	11
UPON MY FLESH AND SKIN, ...	240	TWINING HEAD	10
UPPER			
OF THE UPPER OF THE LOWER HALF, ...	156	RETURN	71
UPRIGHT			
AN UPRIGHT MAN IN THE ANTIPODES	145	PLEASURE-BIRD	23
AND UPRIGHT ADAM	182	VISION, PRAYER	89
UPRISING			
AND CATCH THE UPRISING WAVE.	238	PILLAR BREAKS	22
UPROAR			
ALL BIRDS AND BEASTS OF THE LINKED NIGHT UPROAR AND			
CHIME	204	GIANT'S THIGH	35
UPROARIOUS			
AN IMAGE BORN OUT OF THE UPROARIOUS SPRING	47	POET: 1935	36
UPSAILING			
AND THE BIDDEN DUST UPSAILING	182	VISION, PRAYER	77
UPSIDE			
NO LOVING SHEPHERD IN THIS UPSIDE LIFE.	51	OUT OF THE PIT	38
UPTURNED			
HIS UPTURNED FACE WITH ONE DIVINE CARESS.	222	MISSING	3
UPWARD			
AND DROPPED ON DREAMING AND THE UPWARD SKY.	101	FELLOWED SLEEP	5
AS THE GREEN BLOOMS RIDE UPWARD, TO THE DRIVE OF			
TIME;	122	HOLD HARD	3
UPWARDS			
BURROW OUR WAY UPWARDS INTO THE BLUE SKY;	231	OUR SANCTITY	35
URCHIN			
IF I WERE TICKLED BY THE URCHIN HUNGERS	95	RUB OF LOVE	18
WHO HAVE BROUGHT FORTH THE URCHIN GRIEF.	131	SINNERS' BELL	30
URN			
DUST IN THE LITTLE COUNTRY OF AN URN, ...	56	GREEK PLAY	6
OUT OF THE URN THE SIZE OF A MAN	166	LONG-LEGGED	141
OVER THE URN OF SABBATHS	175	FIRE RAID	66
FROM THE VULTURED URN	182	VISION, PRAYER	80
US (16)			
USE			
FOR USE OF SENSE, (NO HURT NO SENSE).	24	LITTLE PROBLEM	9
WITH KNOWLEDGE THAT NO USE AND NOTHING WORTH	27	OBLIVIOUS DARK	9
NO USE TO RUN YOUR HEAD AGAINST THE WALL	27	OBLIVIOUS DARK	11
LOST IN THE SHADES, NO COURSE, NO USE	41	YOUNG ARE OLD	22
(ALL MODERN PAINTERS USE THEIR FEET	83	LETTER TO AUNT	20
USELESS			
AGE COME TO YOU--YOU'RE BRIGHT AND USELESS, ...	21	BEWILDERED WAY	4
USUAL			
SAID ALL THE USUAL THINGS OVER AND AGAIN;	52	OUT OF THE PIT	71

	PAGE	TITLE	LINE
USUAL (CONTINUED)			
WITH ALL MY USUAL CARE.	234	NO, PIGEON	21
UTTER			
I NEVER THOUGHT TO UTTER OR THINK	147	TO OTHERS	16
ERUPT, FOUNTAIN, AND ENTER TO UTTER FOR EVER	175	FIRE RAID	75
UTTERANCES			
OR (CHANGE THE KEY!) GIVE VENT TO UTTERANCES	33	HELD-OUT HAND	8
UTTERS			
DROWNS AND IS DROWNED, WHO UTTERS TO THE STARS	57	GREEK PLAY	26
THAT UTTERS ALL LOVE HUNGER	75	MY HERO BARES	9
VAGUE			
OUTLINES MELTING INTO A VAGUE IMMENSITY	222	FOREST PICTURE	9
TO HAVE HEARD THEIR VAGUE, RHAPSODIC SINGINGS, ...	223	IDYLL UNFORGET	5
IT HAS BEEN VAGUE, AND MADE OF SHADOW, ...	224	IDYLL UNFORGET	25
HOVER, MAKING THE FOREST FLUCTUANTLY VAGUE.	226	THE OAK	4
VAGUENESS			
WERE VAGUENESS ENOUGH AND THE SWEET LIES PLENTY,	32	OUT OF SIGHS	21
VAIN			
STILL'S VAIN TO ARGUE AFTER DEATH;	27	OBLIVIOUS DARK	10
I LOVE AND DOUBT, IT'S VAIN, IT'S VAIN, ...	27	OBLIVIOUS DARK	27
I LOVE AND DOUBT, IT'S VAIN, IT'S VAIN, ...	27	OBLIVIOUS DARK	27
AND SO COMPLAIN, IN A VAIN VOICE, TO THE STARS. ...	47	POET: 1935	21
IS CORNER-CAST, BREATH'S RAG, SCRAWLED WEED, A VAIN	131	I MAKE THIS IN	9
CRYING IN VAIN	181	VISION, PRAYER	48
FLEW FOR A TIME IN VAIN, TO DROP AT LAST	238	PILLAR BREAKS	21
VAINLY			
WAITING ALL VAINLY THIS WE KNOW.	28	NO WINGS	26
VALE			
AS THE RAIN FALLS, HAIL ON THE FLEECE, AS THE VALE			
MIST RIDES	199	COUNTRY SLEEP	57
CRYSTAL HARBOUR VALE	202	SIR JOHNS HILL	37
VALES			
AND FLOATING FIELDS FROM THE FARM IN THE CUP OF THE			
VALES, ...	187	WINTER'S TALE	3
IN THE RIVER WENDED VALES WHERE THE TALE WAS TOLD.	187	WINTER'S TALE	10
WHEN COLD AS SNOW HE SHOULD RUN THE WENDED VALES			
AMONG	188	WINTER'S TALE	45
THAT A MAN KNELT ALONE IN THE CUP OF THE VALES, ...	189	WINTER'S TALE	85
VALES WHERE HE PRAYED TO COME TO THE LAST HARM	190	WINTER'S TALE	109
VALIANCE			
TO HAVE KNOWN THEM IN THEIR BLUE-HUED VALIANCE, ...	223	IDYLL UNFORGET	3
VALLEY			
LEERS DOWN THE VALLEY LIKE A FOOL	33	HELD-OUT HAND	19
THE MOON LEERED DOWN THE VALLEY LIKE A FOOL.	50	OUT OF THE PIT	12
THE MOON LEERED DOWN THE VALLEY LIKE A FOOL.	51	OUT OF THE PIT	32
THE MOON PEERS DOWN THE VALLEY LIKE A SAINT.	53	OUT OF THE PIT	94
ONE WOULD NOT THINK THE GREENNESS OF THIS VALLEY	63	WOMAN SPEAKS	12
HUNGER FOR HIM WHO DUNGS THE VALLEY FIELDS.	64	WOMAN SPEAKS	37
AND THROUGH THESE TREMBLING RINGS SET IN THEIR VALLEY	76	LASHED RINGS	4
MY WORLD IS CYPRESS, AND AN ENGLISH VALLEY.	105	WORLD PYRAMID	37
SMOKE HILL AND HOPHEAD'S VALLEY, ...	111	I, IN IMAGE	82
TIME, IN A RIDER RISING, FROM THE HARNESSED VALLEY;	122	HOLD HARD	21
I PICK A STICK OF CELERY FROM THE VALLEY	137	O CHATTERTON	14
VALLEY AND SAHARA IN A SHELL, ...	165	LONG-LEGGED	90
IN THE LEAST VALLEY OF SACKCLOTH TO MOURN	191	REFUSAL MOURN	12
AND THE CANONIZED VALLEY	215	COUNTRY HEAVEN	7
VALLEYS			
MEN OLD BEFORE THEIR TIME INTO DARK VALLEYS	41	YOUNG ARE OLD	19
INSECTS AND VALLEYS HOLD HER THIGHS HARD, ...	168	LONG-LEGGED	174

	PAGE	TITLE	LINE
VALUES			
PLAYS SCURVY TRICKS WITH VALUES AND INTENTIONS, ...	37	WINDMILLS TURN	6
VAMPIRE			
THAT THE VAMPIRE LAUGH.	104	WORLD PYRAMID	18
VAN			
OUT OF THE WRINKLED UNDERTAKER'S VAN, ...	118	ALTARWISE	36
AND, RIP VAN WINKLE FROM A TIMELESS CRADLE, ...	118	ALTARWISE	37
VANISHED			
ALL BLOOD-SIGNED ASSAILINGS AND VANISHED MARRIAGES			
IN WHICH HE HAD NO LOVELY PART	158	INTO HER HEAD	43
VANISHING			
THE VANISHING OF THE MUSICAL SHIP-WORK AND THE			
CHUCKED BELLS, ...	141	SAINT TO FALL	8
VANITIES			
WHERE HALF DEAD VANITIES WERE SLEEPING CURLED	50	OUT OF THE PIT	4
VANITY			
CAN BE BUT VANITY, SUCH AN OLD CRY, ...	27	OBLIVIOUS DARK	24
CROWING TO LAZARUS THE MORNING IS VANITY, ...	110	I, IN IMAGE	59
HE FILMS MY VANITY.	129	MY NEOPHYTE	25
VAST			
THIS NIGHT AND EACH VAST NIGHT UNTIL THE STERN BELL			
TALKS	199	COUNTRY SLEEP	51
BUT HER FAITH THAT EACH VAST NIGHT AND THE SAGA OF			
PRAYER	201	COUNTRY SLEEP	102
VAULT			
OVER THE VAULT OF RIDINGS WITH HIS HOUND AT HEEL,	122	HOLD HARD	5
THROUGH THE LAST VAULT AND VEGETABLE GROYNE, ...	131	I MAKE THIS IN	7
VAULTED			
IS ALWAYS LOST IN HER VAULTED BREATH, ...	165	LONG-LEGGED	116
VAULTING			
AND THE VAULTING BIRD BE STILL. O MY TRUE LOVE, HOLD			
ME.	149	UNLUCKILY FOR	54
THEIR BREAST, THE VAULTING DOES ROISTER, THE HORNED			
BUCKS CLIMB	204	GIANT'S THIGH	33
VAULTS			
RIP OF THE VAULTS, I TOOK MY MARROW-LADLE	118	ALTARWISE	35
VEGETABLE			
IN YOUR YOUNG YEARS THE VEGETABLE CENTURY.	123	FOSTER LIGHT	12
THROUGH THE LAST VAULT AND VEGETABLE GROYNE, ...	131	I MAKE THIS IN	7
HOW, THROUGH THE HALFMOON'S VEGETABLE EYE, ...	138	FIVE & COUNTRY	3
VEGETATION'S			
INTO HER VEGETATION'S LAPPING MOUTHS	20	ENCOMPASSED	3
VEIL			
FOSTER THE LIGHT NOR VEIL THE MANSHAPED MOON, ...	123	FOSTER LIGHT	1
THROUGH VEIL AND FIN AND FIRE AND COIL	129	MY NEOPHYTE	23
TO VEIL BELLADONNA AND LET THE DRY EYES PERCEIVE	133	MAKE ME A MASK	10
THE INVOKED, SHROUDING VEIL AT THE CAP OF THE FACE,	134	HOW MY ANIMAL	5
GOLDEN DISSOLVING UNDER THE WATER VEIL.	159	INTO HER HEAD	55
ARE MAKING UNDER THE GREEN, LAID VEIL	164	LONG-LEGGED	69
AND STUNNED AND STILL ON THE GREEN, LAID VEIL	167	LONG-LEGGED	171
VEILED			
HE WEPT FROM THE CREST OF GRIEF, HE PRAYED TO THE			
VEILED SKY	188	WINTER'S TALE	32
VEIN			
LEAVING A CORRUPTED VEIN OF COLOUR, ...	27	OBLIVIOUS DARK	16
OF SKIN AND VEIN AROUND THE WELL	69	BEFORE KNOCKED	26
MAKE DESOLATION IN THE VEIN, ...	86	BREAD I BREAK	12
A VEIN OF MINE	87	PAIN BE MUSIC	5
A RAGGED VEIN	87	PAIN BE MUSIC	11
I BLOW THE STAMMEL FEATHER IN THE VEIN.	105	WORLD PYRAMID	56

	PAGE	TITLE	LINE
VEIN (CONTINUED)			
BURNING! NIGHT AND THE VEIN OF BIRDS IN THE WINGED, SLOE WRIST	199	COUNTRY SLEEP	70
OF BLOOD! THE BIRD LOUD VEIN! THE SAGA FROM MERMEN	200	COUNTRY SLEEP	78
VEINED			
(BUT NOTHING BORE, NO MOUTHING BABE TO THE VEINED HIVES	205	GIANT'S THIGH	42
VEINED HIS POOR HAND I HELD, AND I SAW	217	ELEGY	16
VEINS			
BUT THE VEINS MUST FAIL.	17	IN OBLIVION	14
THE VEINS AT EITHER TEMPLE WHIPPED HIM MAD,	50	OUT OF THE PIT	7
THAT CRIES ALONG HER VEINS. NO SUN OR MOON	56	GREEK PLAY	8
COOL AS THE WAX-RED FOUNTAINS OF THE VEINS;	63	WOMAN SPEAKS	5
OLD MEN WHOSE BLOOD IS HINDERED IN THEIR VEINS,	64	WOMAN SPEAKS	42
MY VEINS FLOWED WITH THE EASTERN WEATHER;	68	BEFORE KNOCKED	17
FILL THE VEINS THE FEVERS BROKE,	71	TAKE NEEDLES	14
AND VEINS ARE SPILLED AND DOOM IS TURNED,	74	WE MOTHERNAKED	15
AND I AM DUMB TO MOUTH UNTO MY VEINS	77	THE FORCE THAT	9
HEIR TO THE SCALDING VEINS THAT HOLD LOVE'S DROP,	80	ALL THAT I OWE	9
AND ELBOWED VEINS THAT, NUDGING BLOOD,	85	SEE, SAYS LIME	3
THAT LEAPING VEINS THREW TO THE WIND	85	SEE, SAYS LIME	11
A WEATHER IN THE QUARTER OF THE VEINS	88	A PROCESS IN	4
BEFORE THE VEINS WERE SHAKING IN THEIR SIEVE,	94	IN BEGINNING	28
HEIR TO THE SCALDING VEINS THAT HOLD LOVE'S DROP, COSTLY	103	I DREAMED MY	9
STORM HER SPED HEART, HANG WITH BEHEADED VEINS	132	I MAKE THIS IN	34
CLAW OF THE CRABBED VEINS SQUEEZE FROM EACH RED PARTICLE	135	HOW MY ANIMAL	21
WITH MY RED VEINS FULL OF MONEY,	143	24 YEARS	7
THE GRAINS BEYOND AGE, THE DARK VEINS OF HER MOTHER,	192	REFUSAL MOURN	21
UNHEALTHILY WITH DRY VEINS.	236	WOMAN TAPESTRY	60
VELVET			
HOLD IN HIS VELVET HAND THE CAN OF BLOOD;	73	LORD RED HAIL	2
AND THE VELVET DEAD INCH OUT.	114	SERVANT SUN	21
QUICKNESS OF HAND IN THE VELVET GLOVE	147	TO OTHERS	12
VENOM			
PUFFED, OLD WITH VENOM, FROM A CRUSTED MOUTH.	37	WINDMILLS TURN	30
WHEN THE WORM BUILDS WITH THE GOLD STRAWS OF VENOM	121	ALTARWISE	139
A BETTER VENOM SEETHES IN SPITTLE	137	O CHATTERTON	6
VENOMS			
HERE SPRING THE SILENT VENOMS OF HIS BLOOD,	81	HERE LIE BEAST	4
VENOM'S			
'A LIZARD DARTING WITH BLACK VENOM'S THREAD	132	I MAKE THIS IN	49
VENT			
OR (CHANGE THE KEY!) GIVE VENT TO UTTERANCES	33	HELD-OUT HAND	8
VENUS			
TREAD, LIKE A NAKED VENUS,	75	MY HERO BARES	12
OR, MASTED VENUS, THROUGH THE PADDLER'S BOWL	114	A GRIEF AGO	7
VENUS LIES STAR-STRUCK IN HER WOUND	166	LONG-LEGGED	117
VENUSWISE			
SHALL IT BE SAID THAT, VENUSWISE,	65	GODS THUMP	8
VERBOTEN			
KICKED, WITH A CLATTER, ASH-BINS MARKED VERBOTEN,	52	OUT OF THE PIT	57
VERBS			
I LEARNT THE VERBS OF WILL, AND HAD MY SECRET;	79	LOVE'S FEVER	39
VERGE			
NOW THE HERON GRIEVES IN THE WEEDED VERGE. THROUGH WINDOWS	202	SIR JOHNS HILL	47
VERMIN			
POOR, PETTY VERMIN,	28	NO WINGS	15

	PAGE	TITLE	LINE
VERSE			
OR WRITTEN BACKWARDS IN WELSH VERSE, ...	83	LETTER TO AUNT	26
AND MODERN VERSE IS DONE WITH EASE.	84	LETTER TO AUNT	32
VERTICALLY			
NOT VERTICALLY IN A MOOD OF JOY	16	IN OBLIVION	2
VERTICALS			
RUNG BONE AND BLADE, THE VERTICALS OF ADAM, ...	117	ALTARWISE	23
VERY			
VERY ALONE, HE PLOUGHED THE ONLY WAY.	53	OUT OF THE PIT	86
CREATED SOMETHING VERY NEW, ...	83	LETTER TO AUNT	24
AND THE SUN GREW ROUND THAT VERY DAY.	196	FERN HILL	32
VESSEL			
VESSEL OF ABSCESSES AND EXULTATION'S SHELL, ...	134	HOW MY ANIMAL	3
VESSELS			
THE LIVING VESSELS OF THE GARDEN	13	RAIN CUTS	13
VEST			
SOAKS TO THE VEST OLD DOMINIES AND DRUNKS.	137	O CHATTERTON	20
VESTS			
OR PAINTINGS ON THE BACKS OF VESTS, ...	83	LETTER TO AUNT	27
VIBRATE			
SO WILL YOUR VOICE VIBRATE	232	FURIOUS MOTION	5
VIBRATIONS			
NO LONGER WILL THE VIBRATIONS OF THE SUN DESIRE ON	170	MARRIAGE VIRG	8
VICE			
KNOW NOW THE FLESH'S LOCK AND VICE, ...	106	ALL ALL AND	20
CRACK LIKE A SPRING IN A VICE, BONE BREAKING APRIL,	122	HOLD HARD	17
VICES			
SUSPICIOUS HANDS TUG AT THE NEIGHBOURING VICES, ...	38	THE GOSSIPERS	3
VICIOUS			
I KNOW THIS VICIOUS MINUTE'S HOUR	9	MINUTE'S HOUR	T
I KNOW THIS VICIOUS MINUTE'S HOUR;	9	MINUTE'S HOUR	1
LET'S HOPE YOU WON'T THINK ME TOO VICIOUS.	221	SONG OF DOG	16
VICIOUSLY			
BORED AND VICIOUSLY WAITING	154	RETURN	22
VICTORIOUS			
FOR THE MUSCULAR AND THE VICTORIOUS	241	ADMIT THE SUN	16
VICTORY			
IN THE VICTORY OF HER GLADNESS	235	WOMAN TAPESTRY	18
VIEW			
FEATHERS TO CONCEAL THE VIEW;	83	LETTER TO AUNT	18
VIGOUR			
VIGOUR AND HARMONY IN LIGHT TO NONE, ...	17	NATURAL DAY	4
THE SWEET, GLOWING VIGOUR	235	WOMAN TAPESTRY	25
THE SWEET, GLOWING VIGOUR, ...	237	WOMAN TAPESTRY	80
VILLAGE			
LEFT ONLY THE VOICE IN THE OLD VILLAGE CHOIR	45	PLOUGHMAN GONE	4
MAY A HUMBLE VILLAGE LABOUR	126	SEED-AT-ZERO	29
A VILLAGE GREEN MAY SCOLD HIM	126	SEED-AT-ZERO	38
VILLAGES			
UNDER THE FLOATING VILLAGES, ...	169	LONG-LEGGED	202
IN THE DEPARTED VILLAGES. THE NIGHTINGALE, ...	189	WINTER'S TALE	57
THE SINGING BREAKS IN THE SNOW SHOED VILLAGES OF WISHES	190	WINTER'S TALE	113
VILLAS			
AND JERRYSTONE TRIM VILLAS	156	RETURN	70
VINE			
BY SIPPING AT THE VINE OF DAYS.	69	BEFORE KNOCKED	36
KNOCKED IN THE FLESH THAT DECKED THE VINE, ...	86	BREAD I BREAK	7
VINEGAR			
NONSTOP; STOPPRESS; VINEGAR FROM WISECRACKS;	57	TO ARCHITECTS	3

	PAGE	TITLE	LINE
VINEGAR (CONTINUED)			
TIME'S NERVE IN VINEGAR, THE GALLOW GRAVE	120	ALTARWISE	100
A NEW VINEGAR;	137	O CHATTERTON	9
CUT CHRISTBREAD SPITTING VINEGAR AND ALL	141	SAINT TO FALL	16
VINEYARD			
DRUNK AS A VINEYARD SNAIL, FLAILED LIKE AN OCTOPUS,	134	HOW MY ANIMAL	7
VIOLET			
WHILE ITS VIOLET SHELLS BROKE AND PARTED.	232	FURIOUS MOTION	14
OR THROW A VIOLET SHADOW WHEN I WILL.	238	MAKES INTERVALS	8
VIOLINS			
AND INTERLUDE FOR VIOLINS	14	FOR LEDA	3
VIPER			
LIGHTNING OR THE DARTING VIPER, ...	71	TAKE NEEDLES	22
OR CRUSH THEIR VIPER HEADS BENEATH MY FOOT.	239	LET ME ESCAPE	5
VIPERISH			
WHEN HIS VIPERISH FUSE HANGS LOOPED WITH FLAMES UNDER THE BRAND	202	SIR JOHNS HILL	28
VIRGATE			
VIRGATE AND SPRUNG OF THE DUSK, ...	227	THE PINE	1
VIRGIL			
BY WASTE SEAS WHERE THE WHITE BEAR QUOTED VIRGIL	119	ALTARWISE	69
VIRGIN			
MARY, VIRGIN, OR ANY OTHER.	41	YOUNG ARE OLD	48
THE VIRGIN LINES BE MATED WITH A CIRCLE.	66	LET A FAITH	3
MAY FAIL TO FASTEN WITH A VIRGIN O	100	RUNNING GRAVE	19
SETTLED ON A VIRGIN STRONGHOLD	125	SEED-AT-ZERO	19
QUICKENING FOR THE VIRGIN SEA;	126	SEED-AT-ZERO	25
A VIRGIN MARRIED AT REST.	139	TOMBSTONE TOLD	3
SAND WITH LEGENDS IN ITS VIRGIN LAPS	167	LONG-LEGGED	172
ON THE MARRIAGE OF A VIRGIN	170	MARRIAGE VIRG	T
OR THE CHOSEN VIRGIN	174	FIRE RAID	36
VIRGINITY			
WAS MIRACULOUS VIRGINITY OLD AS LOAVES AND FISHES,	170	MARRIAGE VIRG	5
VIRGINS			
THE VIRGINS SMELT OUT, THREE STREETS UP, ...	38	THE GOSSIPERS	8
AND OTHER VIRGINS IN OFFICIAL FATHERS.	38	THE GOSSIPERS	13
IN THE MOLESTED ROCKS THE SHELL OF VIRGINS, ...	131	I MAKE THIS IN	18
VIRGIN'S			
ONCE FOR THE VIRGIN'S CHILD, ONCE FOR HER OWN.	74	SUN BURNS	15
VIRTUE			
THE SEAS TO SERVICE THAT HER WOOD-TONGUED VIRTUE	136	AFTER FUNERAL	22
VIRTUES			
AND ALL THE DEADLY VIRTUES PLAGUE MY DEATH!	207	LAMENT	60
VISION			
THROUGH VISION AND THE GIRDERED NERVE, ...	102	I DREAMED MY	4
I SPELT MY VISION WITH A HAND AND HAIR, ...	102	FELLOWED SLEEP	23
STALE OF ADAM'S BRINE UNTIL, VISION	103	I DREAMED MY	27
AND THE FLAME IN THE FLESH'S VISION.	107	ALL ALL AND	33
THRUSTING THE TOM-THUMB VISION UP THE IRON MILE.	111	I, IN IMAGE	84
SUFFER THE SLASH OF VISION BY THE FIN-GREEN STUBBLE,	111	I, IN IMAGE	85
JOHN'S BEAST, JOB'S PATIENCE, AND THE FIBS OF VISION,	125	TODAY, INSECT	21
SUFFER THE FIRST VISION THAT SET FIRE TO THE STARS.	170	LOVE IN ASYLUM	18
VISION AND PRAYER	180	VISION, PRAYER	T
OF SAINTS TO THEIR VISION!	182	VISION, PRAYER	96
VISIONED			
THESE COUNTRIES I HAVE NOT VISIONED, ...	223	IDYLL UNFORGET	13
VISIONS			
THESE ONCE-BLIND EYES HAVE BREATHED A WIND OF VISIONS, ...	132	I MAKE THIS IN	54
FACES OF MELTING VISIONS, ...	156	RETURN	84

		PAGE	TITLE	LINE
VISITING				
STILL COMES VISITING HIS POOR RELATIONS,	....	29	NEARLY SUMMER	2
INTENT ON VISITING THE FAMOUS SPOTS,	....	37	WINDMILLS TURN	12
VISITOR				
THE ONLY VISITOR,	....	35	LIFT UP FACE	22
VITAL				
NEVER OMIT SUCH VITAL WORDS	....	84	LETTER TO AUNT	44
VIXEN				
AND NOW BEHIND THE SCREEN ARE VIXEN VOICES,	....	36	MIDNIGHT ROAD	9
VOICE				
BUT IT, REALITY, WHOSE VOICE I KNOW	....	9	MINUTE'S HOUR	16
THE SUMMER VOICE SO WARM FROM FRUIT	....	15	FOR LEDA	25
TO THE BUILT VOICE, OR FLY WITH WINTER TO THE BELLS,		16	SPIRE CRANES	10
AND EVERY VOICE:	....	22	ON QUIET NIGHT	12
LEFT ONLY THE VOICE IN THE OLD VILLAGE CHOIR	......	45	PLOUGHMAN GONE	4
THE RAWBONED HORSE TO A MAN'S VOICE	....	45	PLOUGHMAN GONE	14
THE LAKE'S VOICE AND THE ROLLING OF MOCK WAVES	....	46	POET: 1935	4
MAKE DISCORD WITH THE VOICE WITHIN HIS RIBS	....	46	POET: 1935	5
SOMETIMES AT HIS EAR THE ENGINE'S VOICE	....	46	PLOUGHMAN GONE	27
AND SO COMPLAIN, IN A VAIN VOICE, TO THE STARS.	...	47	POET: 1935	21
NOW DID THE SOFTEST SOUND OF FOOT OR VOICE	....	50	OUT OF THE PIT	13
THE SEA SPEAKS IN A KINGLY VOICE,	....	61	MEAT ON BONES	35
PAYING HEED TO THE THIRSTY VOICE.	....	67	REALM OF FLESH	13
THE SECRET VOICE CRY IN OUR EARS,	....	70	SECRET WIND	20
A HOLY VOICE ACQUAINTS ME WITH HIS GLORY.	....	76	LASHED RINGS	6
AND TO THE VOICE THAT, LIKE A VOICE OF HUNGER,	....	79	LOVE'S FEVER	29
AND TO THE VOICE THAT, LIKE A VOICE OF HUNGER,	....	79	LOVE'S FEVER	29
RAISED UP A VOICE, AND, CLIMBING ON THE WORDS,	....	102	FELLOWED SLEEP	22
FEAR NOT THE SCREWS THAT TURN THE VOICE,	....	106	ALL ALL AND	23
BLASTS BACK THE TRUMPET VOICE.	....	114	SERVANT SUN	34
SHAPE ALL HER WHELPS WITH THE LONG VOICE OF WATER,		115	A GRIEF AGO	29
GREEK IN THE IRISH SEA THE AGELESS VOICE:	....	125	TODAY, INSECT	22
THE VOICE OF BIRD ON CORAL PRAYS.	....	130	SINNERS' BELL	18
THE PARCHED AND RAGING VOICE?	....	135	HOW MY ANIMAL	22
ARGUMENT OF THE HEWN VOICE, GESTURE AND PSALM,	....	137	AFTER FUNERAL	37
HAS A VOICE AND A HOUSE, AND THERE AND HERE YOU MUST				
COUCH AND CRY.	....	146	IF HEAD HURT	25
A VOICE IN THE ERECTED AIR,	....	150	WHEN I WOKE	25
SUMMONING A CHILD'S VOICE FROM A WEBFOOT STONE,	...	152	BELOW A TIME	46
THE VOICE OF CHILDREN SAYS	....	153	WAS A SAVIOUR	9
ONE VOICE IN CHAINS DECLAIMS	....	158	INTO HER HEAD	52
CRY. MY VOICE BURNS IN HIS HAND.	....	185	VISION, PRAYER	202
THE VOICE OF THE DUST OF WATER FROM THE WITHERED				
SPRING	....	189	WINTER'S TALE	60
AND THE HARP SHAPED VOICE OF THE WATER'S DUST PLUCKS				
IN A FOLD	....	189	WINTER'S TALE	79
ABOVE HER FOLDED HEAD, AND THE SOFT FEATHERED VOICE		189	WINTER'S TALE	82
AND THE SKY OF BIRDS IN THE PLUMED VOICE CHARMED		190	WINTER'S TALE	88
HARK! A VOICE AND LAUGHTER--THE LIVING AND LOVING		222	FOREST PICTURE	11
YOUR VOICE CAN BE THE VOICE	....	229	MY RIVER	34
YOUR VOICE CAN BE THE VOICE	....	229	MY RIVER	34
OR THE VOICE OF THE RIVER	....	229	MY RIVER	37
I HAVE COME TO CATCH YOUR VOICE	....	231	YOUR VOICE	T
I HAVE COME TO CATCH YOUR VOICE,	....	231	YOUR VOICE	1
AND WHEN THE BRIGHT WHEEL OF YOUR TURNING VOICE IS				
STILLED,	....	232	FURIOUS MOTION	3
SO WILL YOUR VOICE VIBRATE	....	232	FURIOUS MOTION	5
CHAIN THE STRONG VOICE	....	233	FURIOUS MOTION	20
AH, NIGHTINGALE, MY VOICE	....	234	NO, PIGEON	8

		PAGE	TITLE	LINE

VOICED

A COUNTRY'S TEARS AND VOICED A WORLD'S DESPAIR   57   GREEK PLAY   18

VOICELESS

THAT PLAYED IN VOICELESS FROLIC AT THE THRESHOLD OF
    MY HEART.   223   IDYLL UNFORGET   12

VOICES

WHO HAVE NO VOICES BUT THE WINDS'   22   ON QUIET NIGHT   2

CRYING WITH HUNGRY VOICES IN OUR NEST.   28   NO WINGS   22

AND NOW BEHIND THE SCREEN ARE VIXEN VOICES, ...   36   MIDNIGHT ROAD   9

THE GOSSIPERS HAVE LOWERED THEIR VOICES, ...   38   THE GOSSIPERS   1

SOME OF THE OAKEN VOICES, FROM THE ROOTS   99   OCTOBER WIND   14

DAZZLE THIS FACE OF VOICES ON THE MOON-TURNED TABLE,   110   I, IN IMAGE   69

OF MORTAL VOICES TO THE NINNIES' CHOIR, ...   123   FOSTER LIGHT   16

WHAT MEANING, VOICES, IN THE STRAIGHT-RULED GRASS,   137   O CHATTERTON   17

DISSECT THAT STATEMENT, VOICES, ON THE SLABS.   137   O CHATTERTON   21

VOICES FROM MANHOLES AND DRAINS, ...   155   RETURN   53

ALWAYS GOOD-BYE, CRIED THE VOICES THROUGH THE SHELL,   166   LONG-LEGGED   121

THE VOICES OF ALL THE DROWNED SWAM ON THE WIND. ...   194   SLEEP BECALMED   8

TO THE VOICES OF THE WIND CAUGHT IN THE
    CRADLE-PETALS OF THE NIGHT: 223   IDYLL UNFORGET   8

VOICES HAVE CALLED, AND THE ANSWERS LEMURAL WHISPERS
    FROM THE SEA;   224   IDYLL UNFORGET   34

THEIR VOICES ARE DIM; THEY HAVE PASSED, ...   224   IDYLL UNFORGET   40

VOID

INTO THE VOID AGAIN OF THIS BEWILDERMENT AND THAT
    INSANITY   21   BEWILDERED WAY   25

THE PRISM OF THE EYE NOW VOID BY SUCTION, ...   29   LONG, SKELETON   10

HERE IN THIS SPRING, STARS FLOAT ALONG THE VOID;   58   HERE IN SPRING   1

ABSTRACTED ALL THE LETTERS OF THE VOID;   94   IN BEGINNING   21

AND, IN THAT BRAMBLED VOID, ...   210   POEM ON B'DAY   52

VOIDS

WITH SERPENTS' MOUTHS AND SCALECOPHIDIAN VOIDS   51   OUT OF THE PIT   22

OF CHILDREN GO WHO, FROM THEIR VOIDS, ...   91   WHERE ONCE THE   17

THE SIGNAL MOON IS ZERO IN THEIR VOIDS.   92   BOYS OF SUMMER   12

VOLES

VOLES AT HIS ARMPITS, DOWN THE SAD CANAL   51   OUT OF THE PIT   40

VOLLEY

AFTER A VOLLEY OF QUESTIONS AND REPLIES   42   A WAR OF WITS   17

RED IN AN AUSTRIAN VOLLEY.   105   WORLD PYRAMID   39

VOLTS

LUST BEARS LIKE VOLTS, WHO'LL AMPLIFY, AND STRANGE   159   TO LEDA   8

VOLUPTUOUS

HOLDING A VOLUPTUOUS CLARITY   237   WOMAN TAPESTRY   73

VOMIT

KNEE-DEEP IN VOMIT. I SAW HIM THERE, ...   51   OUT OF THE PIT   43

VOWELLED

SOME LET ME MAKE YOU OF THE VOWELLED BEECHES, ...   99   OCTOBER WIND   13

VOWELS

STREWING THEIR VOWELS FROM A HILL OF BONES, ...   105   WORLD PYRAMID   41

BY LAVA'S LIGHT SPLIT THROUGH THE OYSTER VOWELS ...   119   ALTARWISE   73

VOWS

DOWN THE LONG WALKS OF THEIR VOWS.   161   WEDDING ANNIV   4

COOL IN YOUR VOWS.   199   COUNTRY SLEEP   47

EVER AND EVER BY ALL YOUR VOWS BELIEVE AND FEAR ...   201   COUNTRY SLEEP   107

AND DRUID HERONS' VOWS   211   POEM ON B'DAY   77

VOYAGE

THE STOVED BONES' VOYAGE DOWNWARD   111   I, IN IMAGE   87

LET THE TALE'S SAILOR FROM A CHRISTIAN VOYAGE   121   ALTARWISE   127

FOR MY VOYAGE TO BEGIN TO THE END OF MY WOUND, ...   194   SLEEP BECALMED   11

THE VOYAGE TO RUIN I MUST RUN, ...   211   POEM ON B'DAY   78

	PAGE	TITLE	LINE

VOYAGING
      VOYAGING CLOCKWISE OFF THE SYMBOLED HARBOUR, ... 109 I, IN IMAGE 32
VULTURED
      FROM THE VULTURED URN   .... 182 VISION, PRAYER 80
WADED
      PLEADING IN THE WADED BAY FOR THE SEED TO FLOW .... 203 GIANT'S THIGH 7
WADING
      ALL NIGHT LOST AND LONG WADING IN THE WAKE OF THE
          SHE- .... 190 WINTER'S TALE 98
      WADING THROUGH HER DARK CAVE ON FEROCIOUS WINGS. 232 YOUR VOICE 9
WAGES
      BUT FOR THE COMMON WAGES   .... 197 CRAFT OR ART 10
      WHO PAY NO PRAISE OR WAGES   .... 197 CRAFT OR ART 19
WAGGED
      ROUNDS TO LOOK AT THE RED, WAGGED ROOT. .... 144 PLEASURE-BIRD 12
WAGGING
      BEHIND A POT OF FERNS THE WAGGING CLOCK .... 99 OCTOBER WIND 17
      BEARDLESSLY WAGGING IN DEAN STREET, ... 156 RETURN 72
WAGONS
      AND HONOURED AMONG WAGONS I WAS PRINCE OF THE APPLE
          TOWNS .... 195 FERN HILL 6
WAGS
      WHOSE BEARD WAGS IN EGYPTIAN WIND. .... 116 LANTERNS SHINE 15
WAIL
      LAPPED AMONG HERODS WAIL   .... 142 SAINT TO FALL 39
WAILED
      BUT WAILED AND NESTED IN THE SKY-BLUE WALL .... 153 WAS A SAVIOUR 31
WAILING
      AND THE WAILING HEART'S NAILED TO THE SIDE. .... 74 SUN BURNS 5
WAILS
      A WOMAN WAILS HER DEAD AMONG THE TREES, ... 56 GREEK PLAY 1
WAINS
      IN THE WAINS TONNED SO HIGH THAT THE WISPS OF THE HAY 204 GIANT'S THIGH 14
WAIT
      THAT WAIT FOR BREAKING AND THAT NEVER BREAK, ... 36 MIDNIGHT ROAD 13
      I MUST WAIT FOR A WOMAN'S SMILE   .... 138 O CHATTERTON 33
      THAT TEACHES ME TO WAIT, ... 237 PILLAR BREAKS 10
WAITING
      WAITING ALL VAINLY THIS WE KNOW. .... 28 NO WINGS 26
      THROUGH NO REGRET OF LEAVING WOMAN WAITING .... 32 OUT OF SIGHS 14
      WAITING AND WATCHING FOR YOUR FINGERS TO FAIL ..... 33 HELD-OUT HAND 20
      WAITING WITH PHOENIX UNDER   .... 147 UNLUCKILY FOR 2
      BORED AND VICIOUSLY WAITING   .... 154 RETURN 22
      WAITING, WAITING, ... 231 OUR SANCTITY 27
      WAITING, WAITING, ... 231 OUR SANCTITY 27
      WAITING FOR THE BIRD WHO SHALL SAY, ... 231 OUR SANCTITY 28
      WITH BRANCHES WAITING FOR A SINGING BIRD, ... 234 NO, PIGEON 14
WAITS
      ASSEMBLING WAITS FOR THE SPADE'S RING ON THE CAGE. 172 DAWN RAID 11
WAKE
      THE SWAN MAKES STRINGS OF WATER IN HER WAKE; ...... 15 FOR LEDA 14
      SLEEP, WAKE, AND SLEEP, EAT, LOVE, AND LAUGH, ... 28 NO WINGS 13
      OF ROD AND WHEEL THAT WAKE THE DEAD. .... 70 SECRET WIND 12
      O WAKE IN ME IN MY HOUSE IN THE MUD   .... 142 SAINT TO FALL 26
      O WAKE TO SEE, AFTER A NOBLE FALL, ... 142 SAINT TO FALL 43
      BUT HEARD HIS BAIT BUCK IN THE WAKE .... 162 LONG-LEGGED 29
      WHALES IN THE WAKE LIKE CAPES AND ALPS .... 163 LONG-LEGGED 49
      ALL NIGHT LOST AND LONG WADING IN THE WAKE OF THE
          SHE- .... 190 WINTER'S TALE 98

	PAGE	TITLE	LINE
WAKE (CONTINUED)			
AND WAKE TO THE FARM FOREVER FLED FROM THE CHILDLESS LAND.	196	FERN HILL	51
AND YOU SHALL WAKE, FROM COUNTRY SLEEP, THIS DAWN AND EACH FIRST DAWN,	201	COUNTRY SLEEP	110
SHED THOU THY TEARS ON HIM; HE WILL NOT WAKE,	222	MISSING	8
WAKEN			
BREAST I SHALL WAKEN	182	VISION, PRAYER	73
WAKES			
MORNING SMACK OF THE SPADE THAT WAKES UP SLEEP,	136	AFTER FUNERAL	6
IN THE WINDS' WAKES.	200	COUNTRY SLEEP	85
WAKEWARD-FLASHING			
OVER THE WAKEWARD-FLASHING SPRAY	164	LONG-LEGGED	73
WAKING			
FOR FEAR OF WAKING THE ROOKS,	31	BEING BUT MEN	3
SLEEP PUNCTURED BY WAKING, DREAMS	39	GAS FADES	22
NOR CAN I SMOTHER THE SWEET WAKING.	61	MEAT ON BONES	32
HOW DEEP THE WAKING IN THE WORLDED CLOUDS.	102	FELLOWED SLEEP	25
I HEARD, THIS MORNING, WAKING,	150	WHEN I WOKE	23
WAKING ALONE IN A MULTITUDE OF LOVES WHEN MORNING'S LIGHT	170	MARRIAGE VIRG	1
WHEN THE MORNING WAS WAKING OVER THE WAR	172	DAWN RAID	1
WALES			
TO WALES IN MY ARMS.	4	PROLOGUE	52
UNDER THE STARS OF WALES,	5	PROLOGUE	92
THE SPIDER-TONGUED, AND THE LOUD HILL OF WALES)	99	OCTOBER WIND	27
ROUND THE PARCHED WORLDS OF WALES AND DROWNED EACH SUN	136	AFTER FUNERAL	15
UP THROUGH THE LUBBER CRUST OF WALES	151	BELOW A TIME	24
WALK			
AND THEN IN SANDALS WALK THE STREET	83	LETTER TO AUNT	19
CAUGHT BY THE CRABBING SUN I WALK ON FIRE	98	OCTOBER WIND	3
AND WALK THE WARRING SANDS BY THE DEAD TOWN,	132	I MAKE THIS IN	32
(BURY THE DEAD FOR FEAR THAT THEY WALK TO THE GRAVE IN LABOUR.)	143	24 YEARS	2
NOR WALK IN THE COOL OF YOUR MORTAL GARDEN	148	UNLUCKILY FOR	48
AFTER A WATER-FACE WALK,	150	WHEN I WOKE	18
AND ALL THE LIFTED WATERS WALK AND LEAP.	165	LONG-LEGGED	112
AND THERE THIS NIGHT I WALK IN THE WHITE GIANT'S THIGH	203	GIANT'S THIGH	3
HERONS WALK IN THEIR SHROUD,	209	POEM ON B'DAY	27
WALKED			
AND YOU HAVE WALKED UPON THE HILLS AT NIGHT,	30	YOUTH CALLS	8
WHEN IT WAS NOON HAVE WALKED INTO THE LIGHT,	30	YOUTH CALLS	10
BEING BUT MEN, WE WALKED INTO THE TREES	31	BEING BUT MEN	1
BEING BUT MEN, WE WALKED INTO THE TREES.	31	BEING BUT MEN	17
ALL REASON BROKE, AND HORROR WALKED THE ROADS.	51	OUT OF THE PIT	18
IF DEAD MEN WALKED THEY, TOO, WOULD HOLLER	59	FAIRY TALES	17
AND GOD WALKED THERE WHO WAS A FIDDLING WARDEN	121	INCARNATE DEVL	5
OR WALKED ON THE EARTH IN THE EVENING	167	LONG-LEGGED	159
AND WALKED ABROAD IN A SHOWER OF ALL MY DAYS.	177	POEM IN OCT	16
FORGOTTEN MORNINGS WHEN HE WALKED WITH HIS MOTHER	178	POEM IN OCT	47
WALKER			
NO LONGER FEAR THE WALKER IN THE GARDEN,	59	FAIRY TALES	11
WALKER'S			
THE WALKER'S APPLE'S BLACK AS SIN;	16	TIME TO ROT	15
WALKETH			
THE DEAD QUEEN WALKETH WITH MYCENAE'S KING	57	GREEK PLAY	23
WALKING			
BETTER NOR US CAN'T GAINSAY WALKING,	28	NO WINGS	9

		PAGE	TITLE	LINE
WALKING (CONTINUED)				
WALKING IN GARDENS	....	33	IN GARDENS	T
WALKING IN GARDENS BY THE SIDES	....	33	IN GARDENS	1
WALKING IN THE EVENING'S COOL	....	71	TAKE NEEDLES	31
ON THE HORIZON WALKING LIKE THE TREES	....	98	OCTOBER WIND	10
ERECT A WALKING CENTRE IN THE SHROUD,	....	114	SERVANT SUN	27
SCRAPED AT MY CRADLE IN A WALKING WORD	....	117	ALTARWISE	11
A MERRY MANSHAPE OF YOUR WALKING CIRCLE.	....	124	FOSTER LIGHT	30
TIME AMONG WALKING PINTABLES	....	154	RETURN	10
THE OCTOPUS WALKING INTO HER LIMBS	....	164	LONG-LEGGED	79
WALKING IN WISHES AND LOVELY FOR SHAME	....	165	LONG-LEGGED	105
YET SHE DELUDES WITH WALKING THE NIGHTMARISH ROOM,		169	LOVE IN ASYLUM	7
ON THE MADHOUSE BOARDS WORN THIN BY MY WALKING TEARS.		170	LOVE IN ASYLUM	15
IN THE FIRST, SPINNING PLACE, THE SPELLBOUND HORSES WALKING WARM	....	196	FERN HILL	34
WALKING IN THE MEADOWS OF HIS SON'S EYE	....	217	ELEGY	31
WALKS				
WALKS WITH THE HILLS FOR COMPANY,	....	47	POET: 1935	27
LIGHT WALKS THE SKY, LEAVING NO PRINT,	....	49	LIGHT, I KNOW	17
MOON WALKS THE RIVER AND RAISES THE DEAD;	....	74	SUN BURNS	2
WALKS WITH NO WOUND, NOR LIGHTNING IN HER FACE,	...	133	I MAKE THIS IN	63
DOWN THE LONG WALKS OF THEIR VOWS.	....	161	WEDDING ANNIV	4
UNDER THE EARTH THE LOUD SEA WALKS,	....	169	LONG-LEGGED	206
SHE SLEEPS IN THE NARROW TROUGH YET SHE WALKS THE DUST	....	170	LOVE IN ASYLUM	13
PADDOCKS IN THE FARMS OF BIRDS. THE DEAD OAK WALKS FOR LOVE.	....	189	WINTER'S TALE	75
OF THE HEARTHSTONE TALES MY OWN, LOST LOVE; AND THE SOUL WALKS	....	199	COUNTRY SLEEP	53
FOR HER WHO WALKS WITHIN HER GARDEN-CLOSE.	....	223	IN DREAMS	7
WALL				
NO USE TO RUN YOUR HEAD AGAINST THE WALL	....	27	OBLIVIOUS DARK	11
IS LOVE A SHADOW ON THE WALL,	....	47	POET: 1935	23
TURNING THE RIDERLESS DEAD BY THE CHANNEL WALL.	...	110	I, IN IMAGE	48
ONCE CLOSE-UP SMILING IN THE WALL OF PICTURES,	....	118	ALTARWISE	55
MEASURES HIS OWN LENGTH ON THE GARDEN WALL	....	124	TODAY, INSECT	12
SCALES THE BLUE WALL OF SPIRITS;	....	130	SINNERS' BELL	21
O MAKE ME A MASK AND A WALL TO SHUT FROM YOUR SPIES		133	MAKE ME A MASK	1
ENDURE BURIAL UNDER THE SPELLING WALL,	....	134	HOW MY ANIMAL	4
WOMEN FIGURES ON THE WALL	....	138	O CHATTERTON	31
MEET ONCE ON A MORTAL WALL,	....	140	TOMBSTONE TOLD	23
OF THE WOVEN WALL	....	141	SAINT TO FALL	6
BUT WAILED AND NESTED IN THE SKY-BLUE WALL	....	153	WAS A SAVIOUR	31
WHO ADMITS THE DELUSIVE LIGHT THROUGH THE BOUNCING WALL,	....	170	LOVE IN ASYLUM	11
AND THE KNOCK OF SAILING BOATS ON THE NET WEBBED WALL		177	POEM IN OCT	7
BEHIND THE WALL THIN AS A WREN'S BONE?	....	180	VISION, PRAYER	9
WALL HEARING THE MOAN	....	180	VISION, PRAYER	22
AND THE WINGED WALL IS TORN	....	180	VISION, PRAYER	29
AND THE MULTITUDE'S SULTRY TEAR TURNS COOL ON THE WEEPING WALL,	....	186	HOLY SPRING	17
WALLED				
HIS NARROW HOUSE IS WALLED WITH BLADES OF GRASS,		64	WOMAN SPEAKS	24
WALLS				
STARING AT STONE WALLS.	....	35	LIFT UP FACE	9
THAT CHALK THE WALLS WITH GREEN GIRLS AND THEIR MEN.		95	RUB OF LOVE	16
BOW DOWN THE WALLS OF THE FERNED AND FOXY WOODS	...	136	AFTER FUNERAL	24
AND DARKNESS HUNG THE WALLS WITH BASKETS OF SNAKES,		158	INTO HER HEAD	27
AND WHARVES OF WATER WHERE THE WALLS DANCE AND THE WHITE CRANES STILT.	....	202	SIR JOHNS HILL	39

	PAGE	TITLE	LINE
WALL'S			
BEHIND THE WALL'S WREN	183	VISION, PRAYER	123
WALT			
A SINGING WALT FROM THE MOWER	156	RETURN	69
WAND			
IT WERE A WAND OR SUBTLE BOUGH, ...	150	WHEN I WOKE	14
WANDER			
ALL NIGHT AND DAY I WANDER IN THESE SAME	81	ALL THAT I OWE	25
THERE HE MIGHT WANDER BARE	210	POEM ON B'DAY	55
WANDERED			
COME IN THE MORNING WHERE I WANDERED AND LISTENED	177	POEM IN OCT	27
WANDERER			
AND THEN TO AWAKE, AND THE FARM, LIKE A WANDERER			
WHITE	195	FERN HILL	28
WANDERING			
THROW WIDE TO THE WIND THE GATES OF THE WANDERING			
BOAT	194	SLEEP BECALMED	10
WANDERS			
HERE IN MY WILDERNESS WANDERS THE BLOOD;	74	SUN BURNS	3
WANT			
I WANT REALITY TO HOLD/ WITHIN MY PALM, ...	9	MINUTE'S HOUR	14
A COMIC HOUR TO AN END THROUGH WANT OF WOMAN	23	THE ONLY DEAD	8
WANTING			
FOUND MANAGERS AND WIDOWS WANTING	38	THE GOSSIPERS	11
I SEE THE WANTING NUN SAINT CARVED IN A GARB	148	UNLUCKILY FOR	34
AND I IN THE WANTING SWAY	156	RETURN	66
OH ALL THE WANTING FLESH HIS ENEMY	165	LONG-LEGGED	91
POOL AT THE WANTING CENTRE, IN THE FOLDS	191	WINTER'S TALE	128
WANTON			
THE BOY OF WOMAN AND THE WANTON STARER	112	NOT FATHER ME	10
THERE THE DARK BLADE AND WANTON SIGHING HER DOWN	157	INTO HER HEAD	16
IN THE NAME OF THE WANTON	183	VISION, PRAYER	133
ON THE DEPARTED, SNOW BUSHED GREEN, WANTON IN MOON			
LIGHT	189	WINTER'S TALE	72
WANTS			
TO WHISPER, WHEN HE WANTS, THE SENSES' WAR	29	NEARLY SUMMER	12
WAR			
AND BARNROOFS COCKCROW WAR!	5	PROLOGUE	81
WAR ON THE HEART--	22	HIGH ON A HILL	8
TO WHISPER, WHEN HE WANTS, THE SENSES' WAR	29	NEARLY SUMMER	12
WHEN THE SKELETON OF WAR	35	LIFT UP FACE	19
THE LIVING DEAD LEFT OVER FROM THE WAR, ...	41	YOUNG ARE OLD	35
OUT OF A WAR OF WITS	42	A WAR OF WITS	T
OUT OF A WAR OF WITS, WHEN FOLLY OF WORDS	42	A WAR OF WITS	1
'WAR ON THE SPIDER AND THE WREN!	61	MEAT ON BONES	38
WAR ON THE DESTINY OF MAN!	61	MEAT ON BONES	39
NOR THE CROSSED STICKS OF WAR.	95	RUB OF LOVE	14
THE SKULL OF THE EARTH IS BARBED WITH A WAR OF			
BURNING BRAINS AND HAIR.	142	SAINT TO FALL	34
WHEN THE MORNING WAS WAKING OVER THE WAR	172	DAWN RAID	1
I CLIMB TO GREET THE WAR IN WHICH I HAVE NO HEART			
BUT ONLY	186	HOLY SPRING	8
WARBEARING			
OVER THE WARBEARING LINE.	125	SEED-AT-ZERO	14
WARDEN			
AND GOD WALKED THERE WHO WAS A FIDDLING WARDEN	121	INCARNATE DEVL	5
WARDS			
OR RIDES THE IMAGINED OCEANS OF THE MALE WARDS. ...	169	LOVE IN ASYLUM	9
WARM			
THE SUMMER VOICE SO WARM FROM FRUIT	15	FOR LEDA	25

	PAGE	TITLE	LINE
WARM (CONTINUED)			
WHEN FOLLY STIRRED, WARM IN THE FOOLISH HEART.	25	BEAUTY TO DUST	19
TO-NIGHT SHALL FIND NO DYING BUT ALIVE AND WARM ...	194	CONVERS PRAYER	15
IN THE FIRST, SPINNING PLACE, THE SPELLBOUND HORSES			
WALKING WARM	196	FERN HILL	34
WARMED			
ONE SUN, ONE MANNA, WARMED AND FED.	79	LOVE'S FEVER	50
WARMER			
NO CRADLE'S WARMER THAN THIS PERISHED BREAST, ...	63	WOMAN SPEAKS	6
WARMING			
WARMING DRY HANDS AND LISTENING TO THE WIND.	42	YOUNG ARE OLD	55
WARMS			
WARMS YOUTH AND SEED AND BURNS THE SEEDS OF AGE;	82	LIGHT BREAKS	8
WARMTH			
AND THE WARMTH SHE GIVES, ...	23	THE ONLY DEAD	9
THAT NEIGHBOURED THEM TO WELLS OF WARMTH, ...	43	FACES SHONE	6
NEED NO WORD'S WARMTH.	79	LOVE'S FEVER	36
WARM-VEINED			
THE WARM-VEINED DOUBLE OF TIME	150	WHEN I WOKE	11
WARN			
AND SERVE ME RIGHT AS THE PREACHERS WARN, ...	207	LAMENT	38
WARNED			
OF CHEMIC BLOOD, WARNED OF THE COMING FURY.	99	OCTOBER WIND	31
WARNING			
FROM THE FIRST SECRET OF THE HEART, THE WARNING			
GHOST, ...	78	LOVE'S FEVER	12
WARNING AMONG THE FOLDS, AND THE FROZEN HOLD	187	WINTER'S TALE	8
WARRING			
I MAKE THIS IN A WARRING ABSENCE	131	I MAKE THIS IN	T
I MAKE THIS IN A WARRING ABSENCE WHEN	131	I MAKE THIS IN	1
AND WALK THE WARRING SANDS BY THE DEAD TOWN, ...	132	I MAKE THIS IN	32
WARS			
HER ROPES OF HERITAGE, THE WARS OF PARDON, ...	115	A GRIEF AGO	21
INNOCENT BETWEEN TWO WARS, ...	159	INTO HER HEAD	65
WARS	201	SIR JOHNS HILL	6
WAR'S			
THE LAST WAR'S PROFESSIONAL	154	RETURN	14
WAS (156)			
WASHING			
AND WASHING WATER SPILT UPON THEIR NECKS	47	POET: 1935	32
WASTE			
DESTROYING SOULS AND LAYING WASTE, ...	33	IN GARDENS	8
ABOVE THE WASTE ALLOTMENTS THE DAWN HALTS.	82	LIGHT BREAKS	30
BY WASTE SEAS WHERE THE WHITE BEAR QUOTED VIRGIL	119	ALTARWISE	69
WASTED			
FEELING REGRET WHEN THIS IS WASTED	32	OUT OF SIGHS	18
WASTEFUL			
THE WASTEFUL HUSHES AMONG TREES.	157	RETURN	99
WASTERS			
IN THE AFTERNOON WASTERS	154	RETURN	24
WASTING			
THAN SIT HERE WASTING, WHILE I BLEED, ...	240	TWINING HEAD	11
WATCH			
AND, AS WE WATCH, THE RAINBOW'S FOOT	13	RAIN CUTS	15
AND WATCH MY HAND, ...	13	SKY'S BRIGHT	27
AND WATCH THE HAND OF TIME UNCEASINGLY	26	THERE'S PLENTY	11
WATCH YELLOW, WISH FOR WIND TO BLOW AWAY	54	WE BY SEASAND	19
WE WATCH THE SHOW OF SHADOWS KISS OR KILL, ...	89	EUNUCH DREAMS	19
I SIT AND WATCH THE WORM BENEATH MY NAIL	95	RUB OF LOVE	34
THE WHISPERING EARS WILL WATCH LOVE DRUMMED AWAY	138	FIVE & COUNTRY	6

	PAGE	TITLE	LINE
WATCHED			
IN THE WATCHED DARK, QUIVERING THROUGH LOCKS AND			
CAVES, ••••••••••••••••••••••••••••••••••••	161	DEATHS AND ENT	31
WATCHERS			
THAT MADDEN BOTH WATCHERS AND ACTORS. ••••••••••••	33	HELD-OUT HAND	16
WATCHING			
WATCHING, NOT TOO AWARE •••••••••••••••••••••••••	13	RAIN CUTS	9
CHILDREN IN WONDER WATCHING THE STARS, ••••••••••••	31	BEING BUT MEN	15
WAITING AND WATCHING FOR YOUR FINGERS TO FAIL •••••	33	HELD-OUT HAND	20
WE LYING BY SEASAND, WATCHING YELLOW •••••••••••••	54	WE BY SEASAND	1
LIE WATCHING YELLOW UNTIL THE GOLDEN WEATHER •••••••	54	WE BY SEASAND	23
WATER			
THE WATER LIDDED LANDS, ••••••••••••••••••••••••••	5	PROLOGUE	94
THE WATER FROM A STREET OF CLOUDS. •••••••••••••••	13	RAIN CUTS	5
TO STIR THE WATER WITH A BUOYANT FOOT, ••••••••••••	14	FOR LEDA	2
IN TIME LIKE OUTLAW RAINS ON THAT PRIEST, WATER,	15	SPIRE CRANES	6
THE SWAN MAKES STRINGS OF WATER IN HER WAKE; ••••••	15	FOR LEDA	14
IN WATER OR IN METAL, •••••••••••••••••••••••••••	19	IMAGES IN AIR	7
OF WATER, FLAME, OR AIR. •••••••••••••••••••••••••	20	THE NEOPHYTE	17
GROWING ON HILLS OR SHINING UNDER WATER. ••••••••••	25	BEAUTY TO DUST	15
HE STEPS SO NEAR THE WATER THAT A SWAN'S WING •••••	46	POET: 1935	2
AND WASHING WATER SPILT UPON THEIR NECKS ••••••••••	47	POET: 1935	32
WATER FROM NOSE AND ARSE, A SANGER'S SHOW ••••••••••	51	OUT OF THE PIT	26
RIBBED BETWEEN DESERT AND WATER STORM, ••••••••••••	54	WE BY SEASAND	11
SHOULD CURE OUR ILLS OF THE WATER ••••••••••••••••	54	WE BY SEASAND	12
SHALL IT BE SAID THEY SPRINKLE WATER •••••••••••••	65	GODS THUMP	6
I WHO WAS SHAPELESS AS THE WATER •••••••••••••••••	68	BEFORE KNOCKED	3
WHERE WORDS AND WATER MAKE A MIXTURE •••••••••••••	69	BEFORE KNOCKED	27
THE FORCE THAT DRIVES THE WATER THROUGH THE ROCKS	77	THE FORCE THAT	6
THE HAND THAT WHIRLS THE WATER IN THE POOL •••••••	77	THE FORCE THAT	11
AND AFTER CAME THE IMPRINTS ON THE WATER, ••••••••	94	IN BEGINNING	9
FINDING THE WATER FINAL, ••••••••••••••••••••••••	109	I, IN IMAGE	33
THE HIGHROAD OF WATER WHERE THE SEABEAR AND MACKEREL	110	I, IN IMAGE	45
AND, CLAPPED IN WATER TILL THE TRITON DANGLES, ••••	110	I, IN IMAGE	64
THEY SUFFER THE UNDEAD WATER WHERE THE TURTLE			
NIBBLES, ••••••••••••••••••••••••••••••••••••••	111	I, IN IMAGE	73
TWO HEELS OF WATER ON THE FLOOR OF SEED), ••••••••	114	SERVANT SUN	24
THE HORN AND BALL OF WATER ON THE FROG •••••••••••	115	A GRIEF AGO	15
SHAPE ALL HER WHELPS WITH THE LONG VOICE OF WATER,	115	A GRIEF AGO	29
HE IN A BOOK OF WATER TALLOW-EYED ••••••••••••••••	119	ALTARWISE	72
THE CLIMBER OF THE WATER SEX •••••••••••••••••••••	128	MY NEOPHYTE	11
OVER THE WATER COME •••••••••••••••••••••••••••••	129	MY NEOPHYTE	27
BLUNT SCYTHE AND WATER BLADE. ••••••••••••••••••••	129	MY NEOPHYTE	39
REFUSAL STRUCK LIKE A BELL UNDER WATER ••••••••••••	134	NOT FROM ANGER	12
AS A HE-GOD'S PADDLING WATER SKIRTS, •••••••••••••	151	BELOW A TIME	16
COMMONER THAN WATER, CRUELLER THAN TRUTH; ••••••••	152	WAS A SAVIOUR	3
IT WAS SWEET TO DROWN IN THE READYMADE HANDY WATER	152	BELOW A TIME	44
GOLDEN DISSOLVING UNDER THE WATER VEIL. •••••••••••	159	INTO HER HEAD	55
AND WIND HIS GLOBE OUT OF YOUR WATER THREAD ••••••••	160	DEATHS AND ENT	21
OVER THE GRAVEYARD IN THE WATER •••••••••••••••••	164	LONG-LEGGED	85
IS OLD AS WATER AND PLAIN AS AN EEL; •••••••••••••	165	LONG-LEGGED	93
AND THROUGH THE SUNDERED WATER CRAWLS •••••••••••	167	LONG-LEGGED	166
ROUND HER TRAILED WRIST FRESH WATER WEAVES, •••••••	168	LONG-LEGGED	177
PROPPED BETWEEN TREES AND WATER •••••••••••••••••	171	THE HUNCHBACK	3
THAT LETS THE TREES AND WATER ENTER •••••••••••••	171	THE HUNCHBACK	5
DRINKING WATER FROM THE CHAINED CUP ••••••••••••••	171	THE HUNCHBACK	8
LIKE THE WATER HE SAT DOWN •••••••••••••••••••••••	171	THE HUNCHBACK	14
WITH WATER PRAYING AND CALL OF SEAGULL AND ROOK •••	177	POEM IN OCT	6
STILL IN THE WATER AND SINGINGBIRDS. •••••••••••••	178	POEM IN OCT	60

	PAGE	TITLE	LINE
WATER (CONTINUED)			
HUNGER OF BIRDS IN THE FIELDS OF THE BREAD OF WATER,			
TOSSED	188	WINTER'S TALE	42
THE VOICE OF THE DUST OF WATER FROM THE WITHERED			
SPRING	189	WINTER'S TALE	60
STREAM WITH BELLS AND BAYING WATER BOUNDS. THE DEW			
RINGS	189	WINTER'S TALE	62
ZION OF THE WATER BEAD	191	REFUSAL MOURN	8
SECRET BY THE UNMOURNING WATER	192	REFUSAL MOURN	22
WATER AND LIGHT, THE EARTH AND SKY,	193	SIDE OF TRUTH	32
EARTH, AIR, WATER, FIRE, SINGING INTO THE WHITE ACT,	200	COUNTRY SLEEP	87
I OPEN THE LEAVES OF THE WATER AT A PASSAGE	202	SIR JOHNS HILL	23
AND WHARVES OF WATER WHERE THE WALLS DANCE AND THE			
WHITE CRANES STILT.	202	SIR JOHNS HILL	39
OF DUSK AND WATER I SEE THE TILTING WHISPERING	202	SIR JOHNS HILL	48
CREEPING CATLIKE UNDER THE WATER.	231	OUR SANCTITY	41
WHITE WITH THE RISING WATER.	233	NO THOUGHT	19
AND GALLANTLY (WATER, YOU'RE STRONG--	237	PILLAR BREAKS	4
BE FREE, (WIND FOR MY TREE AND WATER FOR MY FLOWER),	239	LET ME ESCAPE	2
WATER-			
MY BIRTHDAY BEGAN WITH THE WATER-	177	POEM IN OCT	11
WATER-CLOCKS			
THE WINDER OF THE WATER-CLOCKS	128	MY NEOPHYTE	5
WATERED			
MY GRAVE IS WATERED BY THE CROSSING JORDAN.	105	WORLD PYRAMID	43
WATER-FACE			
AFTER A WATER-FACE WALK,	150	WHEN I WOKE	18
WATERFALLS			
WITH MEN AND WOMEN AND WATERFALLS	167	LONG-LEGGED	169
WATER-LAMMED			
OR, WATER-LAMMED, FROM THE SCYTHE-SIDED THORN,	114	A GRIEF AGO	3
WATER-PILLARED			
DOWN THE STACKED SEA AND WATER-PILLARED SHADE,	132	I MAKE THIS IN	40
WATERS			
ETERNAL WATERS AWAY	3	PROLOGUE	18
OF WATERS CLUCK AND CLING,	5	PROLOGUE	80
THE WATERS OF HIS MIND DRAW IN.	16	TIME TO ROT	16
TO BRUSH UPON THE WATERS OF THE POND.	34	IN GARDENS	21
PLUNGED IN BLACK WATERS, UNDER HAIL AND FIRE,	51	OUT OF THE PIT	42
WHERE NO SEA RUNS, THE WATERS OF THE HEART	82	LIGHT BREAKS	2
WHERE ONCE THE WATERS OF YOUR FACE	90	WHERE ONCE THE	T
WHERE ONCE THE WATERS OF YOUR FACE	90	WHERE ONCE THE	1
AND SWALLOWED DRY THE WATERS OF THE BREAST.	97	TWILIGHT LOCKS	6
IN SACRED WATERS THAT NO FROST COULD HARDEN,	122	INCARNATE DEVL	14
NOR WHEN ALL PONDEROUS HEAVEN'S HOST OF WATERS			
BREAKS.	146	IF HEAD HURT	20
AND ALL THE LIFTED WATERS WALK AND LEAP.	165	LONG-LEGGED	112
THE WATERS SHORN.	199	COUNTRY SLEEP	54
RAGE SHATTERED WATERS KICK	210	POEM ON B'DAY	70
AND MY FINGERS HAVE TOUCHED THE GLASS OF THE WATERS,	224	IDYLL UNFORGET	30
WATER'S			
SOME LET ME MAKE YOU OF THE WATER'S SPEECHES.	99	OCTOBER WIND	16
AND NOTHING SHONE ON THE WATER'S FACE	163	LONG-LEGGED	44
AND THE HARP SHAPED VOICE OF THE WATER'S DUST PLUCKS			
IN A FOLD	189	WINTER'S TALE	79
WATER-SPIRIT			
THE WATER-SPIRIT MOVES AS IT IS HIDDEN,	76	LASHED RINGS	9
WATER-SPOKEN			
SING THROUGH THE WATER-SPOKEN PROW	164	LONG-LEGGED	78

	PAGE	TITLE	LINE
WATER-TOWER			
BY CRANE AND WATER-TOWER BY THE SEEDY TREES	122	HOLD HARD	8
WATER-WOUND			
TURNS THE MOON-CHAINED AND WATER-WOUND	169	LONG-LEGGED	203
WATERY			
AND PLAYING, LOVELY AND WATERY	195	FERN HILL	21
WAVE			
NO PLACE IN WHICH, WAVE PERCHED ON WAVE, ...	10	COOL, OH NO	24
NO PLACE IN WHICH, WAVE PERCHED ON WAVE, ...	10	COOL, OH NO	24
PICK THE WORLD'S BALL OF WAVE AND FROTH	93	BOYS OF SUMMER	40
IN A HOLY ROOM IN A WAVE;	130	SINNERS' BELL	27
LIKE AN APPROACHING WAVE I SPRAWL TO RUIN.	132	I MAKE THIS IN	38
ON THE LAST STREET WAVE PRAISED	141	SAINT TO FALL	4
ON MY CLEAVING ARM AS I BLASTED IN A WAVE.	152	BELOW A TIME	48
LAST NIGHT IN A RAPING WAVE	157	INTO HER HEAD	7
MY LOVE AS A ROUND WAVE	176	BREATH SHED	10
AND MARK THE DARK EYED WAVE, THROUGH THE EYES OF SLEEP, ...	194	CONVERS PRAYER	19
GULL, ON THE WAVE WITH SAND IN ITS EYES! AND THE FOAL MOVES	200	COUNTRY SLEEP	83
GOOD MEN, THE LAST WAVE BY, CRYING HOW BRIGHT	208	NOT GO GENTLE	7
AND EVERY WAVE OF THE WAY	211	POEM ON B'DAY	95
NO WAVE COMB THE SEA, ...	233	NO THOUGHT	14
AND CATCH THE UPRISING WAVE.	238	PILLAR BREAKS	22
WAVED			
AND SUNK; WAVED FLAGS TO EVERY FIFE AND DRUM;	52	OUT OF THE PIT	70
WITH LITTLE, ODD MISTS WAVED IN THE PATH OF ITS ECHO,	224	IDYLL UNFORGET	26
WAVES			
THE UNROLLED WAVES	13	RAIN CUTS	11
BY WAVES WHICH GROW AGAIN	14	RAIN CUTS	33
HER LONELINESS ACROSS THE EMPTY WAVES	22	ON QUIET NIGHT	10
THE LAKE'S VOICE AND THE ROLLING OF MOCK WAVES	46	POET: 1935	4
OR WAVES BREAK LOUD ON THE SEASHORES;	50	NO DOMINION	21
OF THE GULLS THE LIP OF WAVES.	76	SONG: LOVE ME	11
THROUGH THE WAVES OF THE FAT STREETS NOR THE SKELETON'S THIN WAYS.	146	IF HEAD HURT	28
WHEN NEAR AND STRANGE WOUNDED ON LONDON'S WAVES ...	160	DEATHS AND ENT	27
IN THE PRAYING WINDOWS OF WAVES	162	LONG-LEGGED	28
HUGE WEDDINGS IN THE WAVES, ...	164	LONG-LEGGED	72
UP AND DOWN THE GREATER WAVES	168	LONG-LEGGED	179
THE HILLS HAVE FOOTED THE WAVES AWAY, ...	168	LONG-LEGGED	184
LOWLANDS OF THE WAVES	203	SIR JOHNS HILL	56
CURLEWS ALOUD IN THE CONGERED WAVES	209	POEM ON B'DAY	13
WHEN EVERYTHING SLEPT AND THE SMELL OF THE WAVES WAS STRANGE;	224	IDYLL UNFORGET	27
LEDGES OF WAVES HIGH OVER YOUR HEAD, ...	228	MY RIVER	2
MY RIVER HAS HIGH WAVES, ...	230	MY RIVER	44
WAVE'S			
WAVE'S SILENCE, WEPT WHITE ANGELUS KNELLS.	209	POEM ON B'DAY	38
WAX			
TURNS MINE TO WAX.	77	THE FORCE THAT	8
WAX CLOTHES THAT WAX UPON THE AGEING RIBS;	81	ALL THAT I OWE	26
WAX CLOTHES THAT WAX UPON THE AGEING RIBS;	81	ALL THAT I OWE	26
WHERE NO WAX IS, THE CANDLE SHOWS ITS HAIRS.	82	LIGHT BREAKS	12
THE BLOOD GOT UP AS RED AS WAX	85	SEE, SAYS LIME	13
LET THE WAX DISK BABBLE	110	I, IN IMAGE	70
WAXEN			
SWEET IS THE WAXEN BLOOD, HONEY THE FALLING FLESH;	63	WOMAN SPEAKS	3
WAXES			
HEART OF CADAVER'S CANDLE WAXES THIN, ...	100	RUNNING GRAVE	12

	PAGE	TITLE	LINE
WAXING			
AS KISSES FROZE THE WAXING THOUGHT, ...	85	SEE, SAYS LIME	14
WAXLIGHTS			
I DAMP THE WAXLIGHTS IN YOUR TOWER DOME.	101	RUNNING GRAVE	36
WAX-RED			
COOL AS THE WAX-RED FOUNTAINS OF THE VEINS;	63	WOMAN SPEAKS	5
WAX'S			
EYEING FROM THE WAX'S TOWER, ...	20	ENCOMPASSED	10
TILL TALLOW I BLEW FROM THE WAX'S TOWER	119	ALTARWISE	79
WAY			
ALTHOUGH THROUGH MY BEWILDERED WAY	21	BEWILDERED WAY	T
ALTHOUGH THROUGH MY BEWILDERED WAY	21	BEWILDERED WAY	1
OUT OF THE WAY OF THE EYES OF MEN, ...	21	HIGH ON A HILL	3
OUT OF THE WAY, ...	22	HIGH ON A HILL	4
WAS WHEN SENSE FOUND A WAY TO THEM	25	BEAUTY TO DUST	14
OUT OF CONFUSION, AS THE WAY IS, ...	31	BEING BUT MEN	11
AND THIS WAY LEADS TO GOOD AND BAD, ...	45	TO FOLLOW FOX	22
TWISTING ON RACKS WHEN SINEWS GIVE WAY, ...	49	NO DOMINION	13
VERY ALONE, HE PLOUGHED THE ONLY WAY.	53	OUT OF THE PIT	86
THE GRAIN THAT HURRIES THIS WAY FROM THE RIM OF THE			
GRAVE	146	IF HEAD HURT	24
BE YOU SURE THE THIEF WILL SEEK A WAY SLY AND SURE	199	COUNTRY SLEEP	49
EVER AND EVER HE FINDS A WAY, AS THE SNOW FALLS,	199	COUNTRY SLEEP	56
AND LEARN, TOO LATE, THEY GRIEVED IT ON ITS WAY,	208	NOT GO GENTLE	11
DARK IS A WAY AND LIGHT IS A PLACE, ...	210	POEM ON B'DAY	49
BUT DARK IS A LONG WAY.	210	POEM ON B'DAY	64
AND EVERY WAVE OF THE WAY	211	POEM ON B'DAY	95
THE DARKEST WAY, AND DID NOT TURN AWAY, ...	216	ELEGY	2
THEY TO MY BLOSSOMS WING THEIR WAY, ...	228	TRIOLET	5
BURROW OUR WAY UPWARDS INTO THE BLUE SKY;	231	OUR SANCTITY	35
WHICH LEANS ONE WAY, ...	232	FURIOUS MOTION	10
THERE'S NO WAY.	234	NO, PIGEON	7
WAYS			
BUT WAYS HAVE CHANGED, AND MOST WAYS LEAD	37	WINDMILLS TURN	20
BUT WAYS HAVE CHANGED, AND MOST WAYS LEAD	37	WINDMILLS TURN	20
GOD IS SLAIN IN MANY WAYS.	72	TAKE NEEDLES	56
THROUGH THE WAVES OF THE FAT STREETS NOR THE			
SKELETON'S THIN WAYS.	146	IF HEAD HURT	28
WAYS	184	VISION, PRAYER	161
GOOD AND BAD, TWO WAYS	192	SIDE OF TRUTH	13
I RAN MY HEEDLESS WAYS, ...	196	FERN HILL	40
WORK AT THEIR WAYS TO DEATH, ...	209	POEM ON B'DAY	14
WAYSIDE			
WHO ONCE WERE A BLOOM OF WAYSIDE BRIDES IN THE HAWED			
HOUSE	204	GIANT'S THIGH	29
WE (101)			
WEAK			
HAVE KNOWN MAN'S ENVY AND HIS WEAK DESIRE, ...	30	YOUTH CALLS	3
WE HAVE GROWN WEAK BEFORE WE COULD GROW STRONG, ...	40	YOUNG ARE OLD	7
THE WHOLE, THE CRIPPLED, THE WEAK AND STRONG, ...	41	YOUNG ARE OLD	43
AND THIS WEAK HOUSE TO MARROW-COLUMNED HEAVEN, ...	131	I MAKE THIS IN	8
WEAKEST			
AFTER SUCH FIGHTING AS THE WEAKEST KNOW, ...	32	OUT OF SIGHS	10
WEALTH			
I LOVED HIS BODY AND HIS NAVY BLUE WEALTH	149	PAPER & STICKS	5
WEANS			
WEANS ON AN ARTERY THE GENDER'S STRIP;	117	ALTARWISE	18
WEAPON			
I MAKE A WEAPON OF AN ASS'S SKELETON	132	I MAKE THIS IN	31
IT IS A WEAPON THAT CAN TURN BACK	241	ADMIT THE SUN	20

	PAGE	TITLE	LINE
WEAR			
BUT ONE THE SWISS WEAR WHEN THEY YODEL,	83	LETTER TO AUNT	16
CANNOT WEAR YOUR EDGE AWAY,	228	MY RIVER	3
WEARING			
SORROW SHALL HAVE NO WORDS, NO WILLOW WEARING;	64	WOMAN SPEAKS	39
WEARING THE QUICK AWAY.	95	RUB OF LOVE	35
WEARS			
SAYS THE WORLD WEARS AWAY?	59	HERE IN SPRING	17
WEAR-WILLOW			
WEAR-WILLOW RIVER, GRAVE,	203	SIR JOHNS HILL	58
WEASELS			
AND HEARD THE TEETH OF WEASELS DRAWING BLOOD.	52	OUT OF THE PIT	58
WEATHER			
LIE WATCHING YELLOW UNTIL THE GOLDEN WEATHER	54	WE BY SEASAND	23
DOWN PELTS THE NAKED WEATHER;	58	HERE IN SPRING	3
BE SAID TO WEEP WHEN WEATHER HOWLS?	65	GODS THUMP	3
MY VEINS FLOWED WITH THE EASTERN WEATHER;	68	BEFORE KNOCKED	17
CAST LIGHT UPON MY WEATHER. I AM HEIR	80	ALL THAT I OWE	15
A PROCESS IN THE WEATHER OF THE HEART	88	A PROCESS IN	T
A PROCESS IN THE WEATHER OF THE HEART	88	A PROCESS IN	1
A WEATHER IN THE QUARTER OF THE VEINS	88	A PROCESS IN	4
A DARKNESS IN THE WEATHER OF THE EYE	88	A PROCESS IN	10
A WEATHER IN THE FLESH AND BONE	88	A PROCESS IN	16
A PROCESS IN THE WEATHER OF THE WORLD	88	A PROCESS IN	19
AND TELLS THE WINDY WEATHER IN THE COCK.	99	OCTOBER WIND	20
I FLED THE EARTH AND, NAKED, CLIMBED THE WEATHER,	101	FELLOWED SLEEP	6
HEARING THE WEATHER FALL.	109	I, IN IMAGE	30
NOR WEATHER WINDS THAT BLOW NOT DOWN THE BONE,	123	FOSTER LIGHT	2
STORM, SNOW, AND FOUNTAIN IN THE WEATHER OF FIREWORKS,	130	SINNERS' BELL	14
THE BOAT SWIMS INTO THE SIX-YEAR WEATHER,	166	LONG-LEGGED	129
AWAY BUT THE WEATHER TURNED AROUND.	178	POEM IN OCT	40
AWAY BUT THE WEATHER TURNED AROUND. AND THE TRUE	178	POEM IN OCT	62
EXULTATION LIES DOWN. TIME BURIES THE SPRING WEATHER	191	WINTER'S TALE	119
WEATHER-COCK			
FROM THE EMERALD, STILL BELL; AND FROM THE PACING WEATHER-COCK	130	SINNERS' BELL	17
WEATHERCOCKS'			
INTO THE WEATHERCOCKS' MOLTEN MOUTHS	175	FIRE RAID	63
WEATHERING			
WE RUNG OUR WEATHERING CHANGES ON THE LADDER,	118	ALTARWISE	41
WEATHERS			
SPLIT UP THE BRAWNED WOMB'S WEATHERS,	92	BOYS OF SUMMER	14
THAT SET ALIGHT THE WEATHERS FROM A SPARK,	94	IN BEGINNING	14
A QUARREL OF WEATHERS AND TREES IN THE WINDY SPIRAL.	110	I, IN IMAGE	42
AND HEMLOCK-HEADED IN THE WOOD OF WEATHERS.	117	ALTARWISE	28
DOWN FALL FOUR PADDING WEATHERS ON THE SCARLET LANDS,	122	HOLD HARD	19
WITH THE OUTSIDE WEATHERS,	134	HOW MY ANIMAL	9
WEATHER'S			
AND I AM DUMB TO TELL A WEATHER'S WIND	77	THE FORCE THAT	19
WEAVE			
LOCKING, UNLOCKING, THE MURDERED STRANGERS WEAVE,	160	DEATHS AND ENT	15
LEAVES IS DANCING. LINES OF AGE ON THE STONES WEAVE IN A FLOCK.	189	WINTER'S TALE	78
WEAVES			
ROUND HER TRAILED WRIST FRESH WATER WEAVES,	168	LONG-LEGGED	177
WEAVING			
AND FLED THEIR LOVE IN A WEAVING DIP.	163	LONG-LEGGED	53

	PAGE	TITLE	LINE
WEB			
YET OUT OF THE BEAKED, WEB DARK AND THE POUNCING BOUGHS	199	COUNTRY SLEEP	48
AND THE WEB OF YOUR STRAIGHT SENSES.	236	WOMAN TAPESTRY	49
WEBBED			
AND THE KNOCK OF SAILING BOATS ON THE NET WEBBED WALL	177	POEM IN OCT	7
WEBFOOT			
SUMMONING A CHILD'S VOICE FROM A WEBFOOT STONE,	152	BELOW A TIME	46
WEBS			
A WORLD OF WEBS	20	ENCOMPASSED	13
POOR, BROKEN WEBS TO STRIKE THE SKY!	238	PILLAR BREAKS	16
WEDDED			
AND THE WINGS GLIDED WIDE AND HE WAS HYMNED AND WEDDED,	191	WINTER'S TALE	123
WEDDING			
ON A WEDDING ANNIVERSARY	161	WEDDING ANNIV	T
WEDDINGS			
HUGE WEDDINGS IN THE WAVES,	164	LONG-LEGGED	72
WEDDINGS'			
ALL THE GREEN LEAVED LITTLE WEDDINGS' WIVES	206	LAMENT	11
WEDS			
WEDS MY LONG GENTLEMAN TO DUSTS AND FURIES;	120	ALTARWISE	122
WEED			
PIERCE THE SPILT SKY WITH DIVING WING IN WEED AND HEEL	15	SPIRE CRANES	4
CERECLOTH OF WEED, AND BUILD AN ORDURED BED.	64	WOMAN SPEAKS	27
THE WEED OF LOVE'S LEFT DRY;	91	WHERE ONCE THE	15
IS CORNER-CAST, BREATH'S RAG, SCRAWLED WEED, A VAIN	131	I MAKE THIS IN	9
NAILED WITH AN OPEN EYE, IN THE BOWL OF WOUNDS AND WEED	135	HOW MY ANIMAL	29
THOUGH THE NAMES ON THEIR WEED GROWN STONES ARE RAINED AWAY,	203	GIANT'S THIGH	8
WEEDED			
BEFORE THE ALLOTMENT IS WEEDED AND SOWN,	38	GAS FADES	5
NOW THE HERON GRIEVES IN THE WEEDED VERGE. THROUGH WINDOWS	202	SIR JOHNS HILL	47
WEEDS			
ABOVE A BOAT OF LEAVES AND WEEDS.	14	RAIN CUTS	24
TO FIGHT THROUGH THE INVISIBLE WEEDS,	41	YOUNG ARE OLD	23
BREAK ON THE LOVEBEDS OF THE WEEDS;	91	WHERE ONCE THE	14
SHALL SHE RECEIVE A BELLYFUL OF WEEDS	134	NOT FROM ANGER	5
WEEK			
OF MY WEEK IN THE DIRTBOX	156	RETURN	91
WEEKS'			
NO SILVER WHISTLES CHASE HIM DOWN THE WEEKS'	108	GRIEF THIEF	21
WEEP			
BE SAID TO WEEP WHEN WEATHER HOWLS?	65	GODS THUMP	3
AND STAVED, AND RIVEN AMONG PLUMES MY RIDER WEEP.	198	COUNTRY SLEEP	16
MIGHT CROSS ITS PLANETS, THE BELL WEEP, NIGHT GATHER HER EYES,	200	COUNTRY SLEEP	92
WEEPING			
THEY ARE WORDS FOR WEEPING.	18	NATURAL DAY	31
AND THE MULTITUDE'S SULTRY TEAR TURNS COOL ON THE WEEPING WALL,	186	HOLY SPRING	17
NO WEEPING THROUGH THAT DEEP REPOSE CAN BREAK.	222	MISSING	9
WEEPS			
WEEPS ON THE DESERT OCHRE AND THE SALT	104	WORLD PYRAMID	32
WEEPS LIKE THE RISEN SUN AMONG	167	LONG-LEGGED	163
AND TO-MORROW WEEPS IN A BLIND CAGE	209	POEM ON B'DAY	42
AND WEEPS ON THE ABASING HILL,	215	COUNTRY HEAVEN	5

	PAGE	TITLE	LINE
WEIGHED			
WEIGHED IN ROCK SHROUD, IS MY PROUD PYRAMID;	132	I MAKE THIS IN	41
WEIGHED STRANGELY DOWN UPON YOU	232	FURIOUS MOTION	11
WEIGHING-SCALES			
THE WEIGHING-SCALES, OF MY HAND.	155	RETURN	43
WEIGHT			
BY WEIGHT OF CLOTH AND FACT, ...	28	NO WINGS	4
I PROPPED HUMANITY'S WEIGHT	155	RETURN	33
OUT OF THE ROOM THE WEIGHT OF HIS TROUBLE	166	LONG-LEGGED	142
WEIGHTLESS			
THE WEIGHTLESS TOUCHING OF THE LIP	12	SKY'S BRIGHT	9
WEIGHTS			
UNSHACKLED THE WEIGHTS OF WORDS FROM TIRED LIMBS,	53	OUT OF THE PIT	83
WEIRD			
DRAW DOWN TO ITS WEIRD EYES?	134	HOW MY ANIMAL	11
WELCOME			
NONE, AND HIS DEADLY WELCOME	23	THE ONLY DEAD	13
THE WELCOME DEVIL COMES AS GUEST, ...	30	NEARLY SUMMER	14
THE WELCOME DEVIL COMES INVITED, ...	30	NEARLY SUMMER	19
AND WELCOME NO SAILOR?	62	EARS IN TURRET	24
SHALL I WELCOME THE SAILOR, ...	63	EARS IN TURRET	30
(SIGHED THE OLD RAM ROD, DYING OF WELCOME), ...	206	LAMENT	27
WELL			
WHERE ALL IS WELL, ...	21	BEWILDERED WAY	11
IF NOT OF LOVING WELL, THEN NOT, ...	32	OUT OF SIGHS	8
OF SKIN AND VEIN AROUND THE WELL	69	BEFORE KNOCKED	26
NEAR TO THE QUARRY OR THE WELL, ...	74	WE MOTHERNAKED	6
PRAISE HIM WHO SPRINGS AND FILLS THE TIDAL WELL.	76	LASHED RINGS	11
PERHAPS IT WOULD BE JUST AS WELL, ...	84	LETTER TO AUNT	30
HOW WELL YOUR POEMS LIGHT THE FIRE.	85	LETTER TO AUNT	66
ONE ENEMY, OF MANY, WHO KNOWNS WELL	160	DEATHS AND ENT	29
FROM THE STARRED WELL?	198	COUNTRY SLEEP	26
WE'LL			
OF FOOT ON HEAD WE'LL BE THE TIME	24	LITTLE PROBLEM	4
I'LL SHARE MY MONEY AND WE'LL RUN FOR JOY	149	PAPER & STICKS	14
WELL-HELD			
BRIGHT, WELL-HELD HEAD, ...	14	FOR LEDA	9
WELL-MADE			
FROM THE WELL-MADE HAND	241	ADMIT THE SUN	21
WELL-OFF			
I HAD A HANDSOME AND WELL-OFF BOY	149	PAPER & STICKS	13
WELLS			
THAT NEIGHBOURED THEM TO WELLS OF WARMTH, ...	43	FACES SHONE	6
WELSH			
WITH WELSH AND REVERENT ROOK, ...	4	PROLOGUE	60
OR WRITTEN BACKWARDS IN WELSH VERSE, ...	83	LETTER TO AUNT	26
BEACH, HEARING RISE SLIMY FROM THE WELSH LECHERED	179	NEW QUAY	16
WELSHING			
THE SUNNY GENTLEMEN, THE WELSHING RICH, ...	90	EUNUCH DREAMS	25
WENDED			
IN THE RIVER WENDED VALES WHERE THE TALE WAS TOLD.	187	WINTER'S TALE	10
WHEN COLD AS SNOW HE SHOULD RUN THE WENDED VALES AMONG	188	WINTER'S TALE	45
AND THE LAKES AND FLOATING FIELDS AND THE RIVER WENDED	190	WINTER'S TALE	108
WENDY'S			
IN, IN PEDRO'S OR WENDY'S	154	RETURN	27
WENT			
A SHOUT WENT UP TO HEAVEN LIKE A ROCKET, ...	70	SECRET WIND	7
FUNNELS AND MASTS WENT BY IN A WHIRL.	162	LONG-LEGGED	17

	PAGE	TITLE	LINE
WENT (CONTINUED)			
WENT AWAY FROM THE BRIGHT PLACE.	237	WOMAN TAPESTRY	78
WEPT			
THERE CAN BE FEW TEARS LEFT: ELECTRA WEPT	57	GREEK PLAY	17
AND THERE WE WEPT, I AND THE GHOSTLY OTHER, ...	101	FELLOWED SLEEP	8
ALL-HOLLOWED MAN WEPT FOR HIS WHITE APPAREL.	111	I, IN IMAGE	102
AS TARRED WITH BLOOD AS THE BRIGHT THORNS I WEPT;	120	ALTARWISE	101
SHE WEPT IN HER PAIN AND MADE MOUTHS, ...	139	TOMBSTONE TOLD	19
HE KNELT, HE WEPT, HE PRAYED, ...	188	WINTER'S TALE	26
HE WEPT FROM THE CREST OF GRIEF, HE PRAYED TO THE VEILED SKY	188	WINTER'S TALE	32
WAVE'S SILENCE, WEPT WHITE ANGELUS KNELLS.	209	POEM ON B'DAY	38
THAT WHISPERED WITH THE WIND AND WEPT, ...	227	SPRING-SPIRIT	6
WERE (50)			
WE'RE			
THOUGH WE'RE CONSUMED BY LOVES AND DOUBTS.	27	OBLIVIOUS DARK	26
WEST			
WITH THE MAN IN THE WIND AND THE WEST MOON;	49	NO DOMINION	3
AND FROM THE WINDY WEST CAME TWO-GUNNED GABRIEL,	118	ALTARWISE	57
THE SUN SHIPWRECKED WEST ON A PEARL	162	LONG-LEGGED	15
WESTERN			
THE WESTERN MAN HAS LOST ONE LUNG	40	YOUNG ARE OLD	9
THE WESTERN MAN WITH ONE LUNG GONE--	41	YOUNG ARE OLD	44
WEST'S			
AND WEST'S NO LONGER DROWNED	55	WHY EAST WIND	3
WET			
TO WET THE SKY WITH TEARS, ...	15	FOR LEDA	12
THE WET NIGHT SCOLDS ME LIKE A NURSE?	65	GODS THUMP	10
AND LAY THE WET FRUITS LOW.	91	WHERE ONCE THE	12
IS CARVED FROM HER IN A ROOM WITH A WET WINDOW	136	AFTER FUNERAL	29
AND OVER THE SEA WET CHURCH THE SIZE OF A SNAIL ...	177	POEM IN OCT	32
WETHER			
THAT ADAM'S WETHER IN THE FLOCK OF HORNS, ...	117	ALTARWISE	31
WETTEN			
WETTEN YOUR TONGUE AND LIP, ...	20	THE NEOPHYTE	18
WHACK			
WHACK THEIR BOYS' LIMBS, ...	89	EUNUCH DREAMS	3
IN A WHACK OF WIND.	202	SIR JOHNS HILL	17
WHALE			
MIRROR FROM MAN TO WHALE	129	MY NEOPHYTE	21
WHALEBED			
WHALEBED AND BULLDANCE, THE GOLD BUSH OF LIONS, ...	131	I MAKE THIS IN	22
WHALE-BLUE			
AT HIS THRASHING HAIR AND WHALE-BLUE EYE;	161	LONG-LEGGED	3
WHALES			
WHALES UNREINED FROM THE GREEN GRAVE	157	INTO HER HEAD	8
OF THE SEA IS HILLY WITH WHALES, ...	162	LONG-LEGGED	32
WHALES IN THE WAKE LIKE CAPES AND ALPS	163	LONG-LEGGED	49
MARROW OF EAGLES, THE ROOTS OF WHALES	210	POEM ON B'DAY	58
WHALE-WEED			
STRUNG BY THE FLAXEN WHALE-WEED, FROM THE HANGMAN'S RAFT, ...	110	I, IN IMAGE	65
WHARVES			
AND WHARVES OF WATER WHERE THE WALLS DANCE AND THE WHITE CRANES STILT.	202	SIR JOHNS HILL	39
WHAT			
TO HIDE WHAT DRAGS ITS BELLY FROM THE EGG, ...	19	THE NEOPHYTE	6
IT'S EASY TRACING WHAT EACH GIVES THE OTHER	24	LITTLE PROBLEM	11
WE STILL ARE LOTH TO PART WITH WHAT REMAINS, ...	26	THERE'S PLENTY	17

	PAGE	TITLE	LINE
WHAT (CONTINUED)			
'WHAT HAVE YOU FOUND,' HE CRIES, 'WHAT HAVE YOU SOUGHT?'	30	YOUTH CALLS	14
'WHAT HAVE YOU FOUND,' HE CRIES, 'WHAT HAVE YOU SOUGHT?'	30	YOUTH CALLS	14
'WHAT YOU HAVE FOUND,' AGE ANSWERS THROUGH HIS TEARS,	30	YOUTH CALLS	15
STEALS WHAT IS BEST--THE BODY'S SPLENDOUR--	30	NEARLY SUMMER	15
'WHAT YOU HAVE SOUGHT.'	30	YOUTH CALLS	16
MAKING FRESH WHAT WAS STALE	35	LIFT UP FACE	6
WHERE, WHAT? THERE WAS COMMOTION IN THE SKIES,	52	OUT OF THE PIT	76
WHO CURSES NOT WHAT MAKES AND SAVES,	55	NO MAN BELIEVE	14
THOUGH WHAT THE STARS ASK AS THEY ROUND	56	WHY EAST WIND	18
WHAT SHALL IT TELL ME IF A TIMELESS INSECT	59	HERE IN SPRING	16
WHAT SHALL DESTRUCTION COUNT IF THESE ARE FIXTURES?	60	FAIRY TALES	27
WHAT WERE YOUNG LIMBS ARE FAGGOTS ON THE LAND,	63	WOMAN SPEAKS	14
LET WHAT REMAINS OF THAT FIRST MIRACLE	65	WOMAN SPEAKS	62
WHAT HAD BEEN ONE WAS MANY SOUNDING MINDED.	79	LOVE'S FEVER	41
FOR YOU COULD THEN WRITE WHAT YOU PLEASE,	84	LETTER TO AUNT	31
(AND WHAT A PART) IN ALL GOOD ART.	84	LETTER TO AUNT	47
THESE THINGS REMEMBERED, WHAT CAN STOP	84	LETTER TO AUNT	56
WHAT COLOUR IS GLORY? DEATH'S FEATHER? TREMBLE	104	WORLD PYRAMID	25
WHO BLOWS DEATH'S FEATHER? WHAT GLORY IS COLOUR?	105	WORLD PYRAMID	55
WHAT IS THE METRE OF THE DICTIONARY?	118	ALTARWISE	43
WHAT OF A BAMBOO MAN AMONG YOUR ACRES?	118	ALTARWISE	49
WHAT RHUBARB MAN PEELED IN HER FOAM-BLUE CHANNEL	121	ALTARWISE	135
WHAT MEANING, VOICES, IN THE STRAIGHT-RULED GRASS,	137	O CHATTERTON	17
TO TAKE TO GIVE IS ALL, RETURN WHAT IS HUNGRILY GIVEN	140	NO WORK WORDS	4
SEE WHAT THE GOLD GUT DRAGS FROM UNDER	166	LONG-LEGGED	131
SEE WHAT CLINGS TO HAIR AND SKULL	166	LONG-LEGGED	133
DOING WHAT THEY ARE TOLD,	209	POEM ON B'DAY	12
HATING HIS GOD, BUT WHAT HE WAS WAS PLAIN:	217	ELEGY	23
TO TELL WHAT NOTE I COULD REACH IF I TRIED,	234	NO, PIGEON	12
AND, THERE, WHAT WINGS THEY HAD,	238	PILLAR BREAKS	15
WHAT'S			
PLANNING WHAT'S GOOD, THOUGH IT'S BUT WINTER,	27	OBLIVIOUS DARK	29
WHAT'S NEVER KNOWN IS SAFEST IN THIS LIFE.	40	WAS THERE TIME	6
WHERE, WHAT'S MY GOD AMONG THIS CRAZY RATTLING	51	OUT OF THE PIT	33
WHERE, WHAT'S MY GOD AMONG THIS TAXI STEPPING,	52	OUT OF THE PIT	49
WHERE, WHAT'S MY GOD? I HAVE BEEN MAD, AM MAD,	52	OUT OF THE PIT	63
AND WHAT'S THE RUB? DEATH'S FEATHER ON THE NERVE?	96	RUB OF LOVE	43
TO TOUCH WHAT'S TO BE TOUCHED,	234	NO, PIGEON	18
WHATSOEVER			
WHATSOEVER I DID IN THE COAL-	206	LAMENT	23
WHEAT			
HEARING THE ENGINES, AND THE WHEAT DYING.	46	PLOUGHMAN GONE	26
AND LOOK, MY GRAIN, UPON THE FALLING WHEAT;	81	ALL THAT I OWE	29
WHEATFIELD			
INTO THE BREAD IN A WHEATFIELD OF FLAMES,	175	FIRE RAID	70
WHEEL			
STRAPPED TO A WHEEL, YET THEY SHALL NOT BREAK;	49	NO DOMINION	14
OF ROD AND WHEEL THAT WAKE THE DEAD.	70	SECRET WIND	12
TOWNS AROUND ON A WHEEL OF FIRE.	106	ALL ALL AND	6
AND WHEN THE BRIGHT WHEEL OF YOUR TURNING VOICE IS STILLED,	232	FURIOUS MOTION	3
WHEELING			
UNDER THE PRAYER WHEELING MOON IN THE ROSY WOOD	198	COUNTRY SLEEP	41
WHEELS			
A NEW DIVINITY, A GOD OF WHEELS	33	IN GARDENS	7
WHERE WHEELS, CONFUSING MUSIC, CONFUSED DOUBTS,	50	OUT OF THE PIT	2

	PAGE	TITLE	LINE
WHEELS'			
AND THE GREAT WHEELS' RUT;	59	FAIRY TALES	7
WHEEL-WINDERS			
WHEEL-WINDERS AND FIXERS OF BOLTS.	70	SECRET WIND	18
WHELPS			
SHAPE ALL HER WHELPS WITH THE LONG VOICE OF WATER,	115	A GRIEF AGO	29
WHEN			
BUT COOLER WHEN I TAKE IT BACK, ...	10	COOL, OH NO	5
FOR WHEN I BOUGHT YOU FOR A THOUGHT, (YOU COST NO			
MORE)	10	COOL, OH NO	8
HOW KISS, WHEN DOLL COULD SAY	10	COOL, OH NO	13
BUT, WHEN HE'S OUT OF SIGHT, ...	14	RAIN CUTS	20
FOR WHEN WE TOUCH A FLOWER WITH OUR OAR	14	RAIN CUTS	30
WHEN LEDA, ON A TOE OF DOWN, ...	15	FOR LEDA	29
OUR EVIL, WHEN WE BREATHE IT, ...	17	IN OBLIVION	22
WAS OLD WHEN YOU WERE YOUNG, ...	20	THE NEOPHYTE	22
DEATH TO THE MAGICAL WHEN ALL IS DONE, ...	21	BEWILDERED WAY	3
WHEN YOU HAVE GROUND SUCH BEAUTY DOWN TO DUST	25	BEAUTY TO DUST	T
WHEN YOU HAVE GROUND SUCH BEAUTY DOWN TO DUST	25	BEAUTY TO DUST	1
WHEN WISDOM LAY NOT IN THE SOUL	25	BEAUTY TO DUST	12
WAS WHEN SENSE FOUND A WAY TO THEM	25	BEAUTY TO DUST	14
WHEN FOLLY STIRRED, WARM IN THE FOOLISH HEART.	25	BEAUTY TO DUST	19
WHEN SPRING IS COME, ...	27	OBLIVIOUS DARK	30
TO WHISPER, WHEN HE WANTS, THE SENSES' WAR	29	NEARLY SUMMER	12
WHEN IT WAS NOON HAVE WALKED INTO THE LIGHT, ...	30	YOUTH CALLS	10
FEELING REGRET WHEN THIS IS WASTED	32	OUT OF SIGHS	18
WHEN I WAS SEVEN I COUNTED FOUR AND FORTY TREES ...	33	HELD-OUT HAND	12
WHEN HEAVEN--OPEN WIDE THE GATES--HAS TAKEN FLIGHT,	34	THIRST PARCHES	4
WHEN THE SKELETON OF WAR	35	LIFT UP FACE	19
WHEN THE PURSE IS EMPTY	39	GAS FADES	27
WAS THERE A TIME WHEN DANCERS WITH THEIR FIDDLES	40	WAS THERE TIME	1
OUT OF A WAR OF WITS, WHEN FOLLY OF WORDS	42	A WAR OF WITS	1
WHEN MORE THAN SNAILS ARE FRIENDS.	45	TO FOLLOW FOX	23
WHEN THE SUN FALLS AND THE MOON STARES, ...	48	LIGHT, I KNOW	7
I AM A TIMID CHILD WHEN LIGHT IS DEAD.	48	LIGHT, I KNOW	11
WHEN THEIR BONES ARE PICKED CLEAN AND THE CLEAN			
BONES GONE, ...	49	NO DOMINION	4
TWISTING ON RACKS WHEN SINEWS GIVE WAY, ...	49	NO DOMINION	13
NO MAN BELIEVES WHO, WHEN A STAR FALLS SHOT, ...	54	NO MAN BELIEVE	1
CRIES NOT IN TERROR WHEN A BIRD IS DRAWN	54	NO MAN BELIEVE	3
WHEN ANY LIGHT GOES OUT, AND LIFE IS DEATH.	55	NO MAN BELIEVE	6
WHEN COMETH JACK FROST? THE CHILDREN ASK.	56	WHY EAST WIND	10
BUT WHEN THE LADIES ARE COLD AS STONE	60	MEAT ON BONES	7
WHEN CLOUDS ARE CURSED BY THUNDER, ...	65	GODS THUMP	2
BE SAID TO WEEP WHEN WEATHER HOWLS?	65	GODS THUMP	3
WHEN IT IS RAIN WHERE ARE THE GODS?	65	GODS THUMP	5
WHY SHOULD I THINK ON DEATH WHEN YOU ARE RULER? ...	67	REALM OF FLESH	10
THE CHILD TELLS, WHEN THE TREMBLING CHORD IS CUT,	67	LET A FAITH	14
WHEN I YIELD THE TREE TO DEATH, ...	72	TAKE NEEDLES	45
QUESTION: WHEN SHALL ROOT-DAM DIE?	72	TAKE NEEDLES	61
ANSWER: WHEN HER BABE DENIES HER.	72	TAKE NEEDLES	62
QUESTION: WHEN SHALL ROOT-DAM GROW?	72	TAKE NEEDLES	63
ANSWER: WHEN THE GREEN LEAVES PRIZE HER.	72	TAKE NEEDLES	64
WHEN NO MOUTH STIRRED ABOUT THE HANGING FAMINE, ...	78	LOVE'S FEVER	5
WHEN LOGICS DIE, ...	82	LIGHT BREAKS	27
BUT ONE THE SWISS WEAR WHEN THEY YODEL, ...	83	LETTER TO AUNT	16
WHEN SUNLIGHT GOES ARE SUNDERED FROM THE WORM, ...	89	EUNUCH DREAMS	8
WHEN CAMERAS SHUT THEY HURRY TO THEIR HOLE	89	EUNUCH DREAMS	15
SHALL FALL AWAKE WHEN CURES AND THEIR ITCH	89	EUNUCH DREAMS	22
GIRLS TAKE TO BROOMSTICKS WHEN THE THIEF OF NIGHT	96	TWELVE	3

	PAGE	TITLE	LINE
WHEN (CONTINUED)			
NOR WHEN HE FINDS A BEAUTY IN THE BREAST	96	RUB OF LOVE	40
WHEN ONCE THE TWILIGHT LOCKS NO LONGER	97	TWILIGHT LOCKS	T
WHEN ONCE THE TWILIGHT LOCKS NO LONGER	97	TWILIGHT LOCKS	1
WHEN THE GALACTIC SEA WAS SUCKED	97	TWILIGHT LOCKS	7
BUT WHEN THE STARS, ASSUMING SHAPE, ...	97	TWILIGHT LOCKS	16
ESPECIALLY WHEN THE OCTOBER WIND	98	OCTOBER WIND	T
ESPECIALLY WHEN THE OCTOBER WIND	98	OCTOBER WIND	1
WHEN ONCE THE TWILIGHT SCREWS WERE TURNED, ...	98	TWILIGHT LOCKS	31
WHEN, LIKE A RUNNING GRAVE	99	RUNNING GRAVE	T
WHEN, LIKE A RUNNING GRAVE, TIME TRACKS YOU DOWN,	99	RUNNING GRAVE	1
ESPECIALLY WHEN THE OCTOBER WIND	99	OCTOBER WIND	25
WHEN BLOOD, SPADE-HANDED, AND THE LOGIC TIME	100	RUNNING GRAVE	13
AND, WHEN IT QUICKENS, ALTER THE ACTIONS' PACE	116	LANTERNS SHINE	12
THE FATS OF MIDNIGHT WHEN THE SALT WAS SINGING; ...	119	ALTARWISE	80
WHEN WE WERE STRANGERS TO THE GUIDED SEAS, ...	121	INCARNATE DEVL	7
AND WHEN THE MOON ROSE WINDILY IT WAS	121	INCARNATE DEVL	11
WHEN THE WORM BUILDS WITH THE GOLD STRAWS OF VENOM	121	ALTARWISE	139
NOR WHEN MY LOVE LIES IN THE CROSS-BONED DRIFT	123	FOSTER LIGHT	22
WHEN, WITH HIS TORCH AND HOURGLASS, LIKE A SULPHUR PRIEST, ...	130	SINNERS' BELL	2
I MAKE THIS IN A WARRING ABSENCE WHEN	131	I MAKE THIS IN	1
WHEN, PRAISE IS BLESSED, HER PRIDE IN MAST AND FOUNTAIN	131	I MAKE THIS IN	4
DIE IN RED FEATHERS WHEN THE FLYING HEAVEN'S CUT,	135	HOW MY ANIMAL	40
ON GIDDY NIGHTS WHEN SLAP ON THE MOON'S MASK	137	O CHATTERTON	12
WHEN ALL MY FIVE AND COUNTRY SENSES SEE	138	FIVE & COUNTRY	T
WHEN ALL MY FIVE AND COUNTRY SENSES SEE, ...	138	FIVE & COUNTRY	1
THE TOMBSTONE TOLD WHEN SHE DIED	139	TOMBSTONE TOLD	T
THE TOMBSTONE TOLD WHEN SHE DIED.	139	TOMBSTONE TOLD	1
AND WHEN BLIND SLEEP DROPS ON THE SPYING SENSES,	139	FIVE & COUNTRY	13
AND WHEN I DREAM OF THEM I FIND	143	THE MOLLS	11
WHEN I WHISTLED WITH MITCHING BOYS THROUGH A RESERVOIR PARK	144	COLOUR OF SAY	7
WHEN YOU SEW THE DEEP DOOR. THE BED IS A CROSS PLACE.	145	IF HEAD HURT	13
WHO PALMED THE LIE ON ME WHEN YOU LOOKED	146	TO OTHERS	4
NOR WHEN ALL PONDEROUS HEAVEN'S HOST OF WATERS BREAKS.	146	IF HEAD HURT	20
WHEN IN OUR BED I WAS TOSSING AND TURNING	149	PAPER & STICKS	7
WHEN I WOKE	150	WHEN I WOKE	T
WHEN I WOKE, THE TOWN SPOKE.	150	WHEN I WOKE	1
WHEN MY PINNED-AROUND-THE-SPIRIT	151	BELOW A TIME	2
WHEN HINDERING MAN HURT	153	WAS A SAVIOUR	12
SILENCE, SILENCE TO DO, WHEN EARTH GREW LOUD, ...	153	WAS A SAVIOUR	15
ON TO THE GROUND WHEN A MAN DIED	153	WAS A SAVIOUR	21
ONE LEAN SIGH WHEN WE HEARD	153	WAS A SAVIOUR	29
WHEN ONE AT THE GREAT LEAST OF YOUR BEST LOVED	160	DEATHS AND ENT	3
WHEN AT YOUR LIPS AND KEYS, ...	160	DEATHS AND ENT	14
WHEN NEAR AND STRANGE WOUNDED ON LONDON'S WAVES ...	160	DEATHS AND ENT	27
WHEN HIS LONG-LEGGED FLESH WAS A WIND ON FIRE	168	LONG-LEGGED	195
WAKING ALONE IN A MULTITUDE OF LOVES WHEN MORNING'S LIGHT	170	MARRIAGE VIRG	1
RUNNING WHEN HE HAD HEARD THEM CLEARLY	171	THE HUNCHBACK	17
LAUGHING WHEN HE SHOOK HIS PAPER	171	THE HUNCHBACK	20
WHEN THE MORNING WAS WAKING OVER THE WAR	172	DAWN RAID	1
WHEN ALL THE KEYS SHOT FROM THE LOCKS, AND RANG.	172	DAWN RAID	8
WHEN THE CAUGHT TONGUE NODDED BLIND, ...	173	FIRE RAID	13
HIGH TIDE AND THE HERON DIVED WHEN I TOOK THE ROAD	177	POEM IN OCT	17
FORGOTTEN MORNINGS WHEN HE WALKED WITH HIS MOTHER	178	POEM IN OCT	47
AND WHEN THE MOIST COLLECTION PLATE IS PASSED	179	NEW QUAY	31

	PAGE	TITLE	LINE
WHEN (CONTINUED)			
WHEN	181	VISION, PRAYER	35
OF MAN WHEN	182	VISION, PRAYER	82
WHEN THAT IMMORTAL HOSPITAL MADE ONE MORE MOVE TO SOOTHE	186	HOLY SPRING	3
ONCE WHEN THE WORLD TURNED OLD	187	WINTER'S TALE	11
WHEN COLD AS SNOW HE SHOULD RUN THE WENDED VALES AMONG	188	WINTER'S TALE	45
WHEN BLACK BIRDS DIED LIKE PRIESTS IN THE CLOAKED HEDGE ROW	190	WINTER'S TALE	92
AND WHEN THE SALT SHEET BROKE IN A STORM OF SINGING	194	SLEEP BECALMED	7
WHEN ONLY THE MOON RAGES	196	CRAFT OR ART	3
WHEN HIS VIPERISH FUSE HANGS LOOPED WITH FLAMES UNDER THE BRAND	202	SIR JOHNS HILL	28
WHEN I WAS A WINDY BOY AND A BIT	205	LAMENT	1
WHEN I WAS A GUSTY MAN AND A HALF	206	LAMENT	13
WHEN I WAS A MAN YOU COULD CALL A MAN	206	LAMENT	25
OH, TIME ENOUGH WHEN THE BLOOD CREEPS COLD, ...	206	LAMENT	34
WHEN I WAS A HALF OF THE MAN I WAS	207	LAMENT	37
SLUNK POUTING OUT WHEN THE LIMP TIME CAME;	207	LAMENT	44
ALWAYS WHEN HE, IN COUNTRY HEAVEN, ...	215	COUNTRY HEAVEN	1
AND LISTENED WHEN A SLOW, STARRED SLUMBER WRAPT THE MOON, ...	223	IDYLL UNFORGET	7
WHEN EVERYTHING SLEPT AND THE SMELL OF THE WAVES WAS STRANGE;	224	IDYLL UNFORGET	27
AND WHEN IT WAS SPRING I SAID, ...	227	SPRING-SPIRIT	1
WHEN THE TIME COMES, ...	230	OUR SANCTITY	16
THEN, WHEN I OPEN MY MOUTH, ...	231	YOUR VOICE	6
WHEN YOUR FURIOUS MOTION	232	FURIOUS MOTION	T
WHEN YOUR FURIOUS MOTION IS STEADIED, ...	232	FURIOUS MOTION	1
AND WHEN THE BRIGHT WHEEL OF YOUR TURNING VOICE IS STILLED, ...	232	FURIOUS MOTION	3
WHEN YOU ARE GONE	232	FURIOUS MOTION	15
OR THROW A VIOLET SHADOW WHEN I WILL.	238	MAKES INTERVALS	8
WHENEVER			
WHENEVER I DOVE IN A BREAST HIGH SHOAL, ...	206	LAMENT	21
WHERE			
WHERE TEARS HAVE COME TO DRY.	12	SKY'S BRIGHT	17
WHERE LOVE IS THERE'S A CRUST OF JOY	19	THE NEOPHYTE	5
WHERE ALL IS WELL, ...	21	BEWILDERED WAY	11
WHERE DEATH LIES DEAD ASLEEP, ONE BRIGHT EYE OPEN,	41	YOUNG ARE OLD	20
WHERE MEN WOULD ARGUE TILL THE STARS BE GREEN, ...	43	A WAR OF WITS	23
LEADS TO FOOL'S PARADISE WHERE THE REDCOATED KILLER	44	TO FOLLOW FOX	5
INTO THE MAP-BACKED HILLS WHERE PATHS	44	TO FOLLOW FOX	8
WHERE FIFTY FLOWERS BREED IN A FRUIT BOX, ...	47	POET: 1935	31
MAKE BRIGHT ITS CORNERS WHERE A SKELETON	49	LIGHT, I KNOW	23
WHERE WHEELS, CONFUSING MUSIC, CONFUSED DOUBTS, ...	50	OUT OF THE PIT	2
WHERE HALF DEAD VANITIES WERE SLEEPING CURLED	50	OUT OF THE PIT	4
WHERE BLEW A FLOWER MAY A FLOWER NO MORE	50	NO DOMINION	22
WHERE EYES SHOULD BE, AND NOSTRILS FULL OF TOADS.	51	OUT OF THE PIT	23
A MEASURE ON THE LAWN WHERE CUPIDS BLEW	51	OUT OF THE PIT	25
WHERE, WHAT'S MY GOD AMONG THIS CRAZY RATTLING	51	OUT OF THE PIT	33
WHERE FLOATED A DEAD DOG WHO MADE HIM ILL, ...	51	OUT OF THE PIT	41
WHERE, WHAT'S MY GOD AMONG THIS TAXI STEPPING, ...	52	OUT OF THE PIT	49
WHERE, WHAT'S MY GOD? I HAVE BEEN MAD, AM MAD, ...	52	OUT OF THE PIT	63
UNDER A HIDEOUS SEA WHERE CORAL MEN	52	OUT OF THE PIT	68
WHERE, WHAT? THERE WAS COMMOTION IN THE SKIES, ...	52	OUT OF THE PIT	76
AND RAVEN YOUTH WILL FEAST BUT WHERE HE WILL.	64	WOMAN SPEAKS	51
WHEN IT IS RAIN WHERE ARE THE GODS?	65	GODS THUMP	5
WHERE WORDS AND WATER MAKE A MIXTURE	69	BEFORE KNOCKED	27

	PAGE	TITLE	LINE
WHERE (CONTINUED)			
DRAIN THE SPRING WHERE PROMISE GOES.	70	TAKE NEEDLES	8
WHERE ALL THE HIDDEN STONES ARE GOLD,	74	WE MOTHERNAKED	10
THAT BUT A NAME, WHERE MAGGOTS HAVE THEIR X.	79	LOVE'S FEVER	38
LIGHT BREAKS WHERE NO SUN SHINES	82	LIGHT BREAKS	T
LIGHT BREAKS WHERE NO SUN SHINES;	82	LIGHT BREAKS	1
WHERE NO SEA RUNS, THE WATERS OF THE HEART	82	LIGHT BREAKS	2
FILE THROUGH THE FLESH WHERE NO FLESH DECKS THE			
BONES.	82	LIGHT BREAKS	6
WHERE NO SEED STIRS,	82	LIGHT BREAKS	9
WHERE NO WAX IS, THE CANDLE SHOWS ITS HAIRS.	82	LIGHT BREAKS	12
WHERE NO COLD IS, THE SKINNING GALES UNPIN	82	LIGHT BREAKS	22
ON TIPS OF THOUGHT WHERE THOUGHTS SMELL IN THE RAIN;	82	LIGHT BREAKS	26
WHERE FLESH'S FEVER	85	SEE, SAYS LIME	20
WHERE ONCE THE WATERS OF YOUR FACE	90	WHERE ONCE THE	T
WHERE ONCE THE WATERS OF YOUR FACE	90	WHERE ONCE THE	1
WHERE ONCE THE MERMEN THROUGH YOUR ICE	90	WHERE ONCE THE	4
WHERE ONCE YOUR GREEN KNOTS SANK THEIR SPLICE	91	WHERE ONCE THE	7
WHERE, PUNCTUAL AS DEATH, WE RING THE STARS;	92	BOYS OF SUMMER	27
WHERE FISHES' FOOD IS FED THE SHADES	98	TWILIGHT LOCKS	29
AND LEAVE THE POPPIED PICKTHANK WHERE HE LIES;	98	TWILIGHT LOCKS	39
WHERE STILL THEY SLEEP UNKNOWING OF THEIR GHOST.	102	FELLOWED SLEEP	20
AND SALT-EYED STUMBLE BEDWARD WHERE SHE LIES	107	GRIEF THIEF	12
THE HIGHROAD OF WATER WHERE THE SEABEAR AND MACKEREL	110	I, IN IMAGE	45
THEY SUFFER THE UNDEAD WATER WHERE THE TURTLE			
NIBBLES,	111	I, IN IMAGE	73
WHERE BIRD AND SHELL ARE BABBLING IN MY TOWER?	112	NOT FATHER ME	14
BY WASTE SEAS WHERE THE WHITE BEAR QUOTED VIRGIL	119	ALTARWISE	69
WHERE, WOUND IN EMERALD LINEN AND SHARP WIND,	132	I MAKE THIS IN	42
IN THAT BRIGHT ANCHORGROUND WHERE I LAY LINENED,	132	I MAKE THIS IN	48
ONCE WHERE THE SOFT SNOW'S BLOOD WAS TURNED TO ICE.	133	I MAKE THIS IN	65
WITH A CAPSIZED FIELD WHERE A SCHOOL SAT STILL	144	COLOUR OF SAY	3
WHERE AT NIGHT WE STONED THE COLD AND CUCKOO	144	COLOUR OF SAY	8
WHERE BIRDS RIDE LIKE LEAVES AND BOATS LIKE DUCKS	150	WHEN I WOKE	22
WHERE SITTING IN CLEAN LINEN	156	RETURN	93
THERE WHERE A NUMBERLESS TONGUE	158	INTO HER HEAD	24
WHERE THE ANCHOR RODE LIKE A GULL	163	LONG-LEGGED	37
HER DEEPSEA PILLOW WHERE ONCE SHE MARRIED ALONE,	170	MARRIAGE VIRG	9
FOR A MAN SLEEPS WHERE FIRE LEAPT DOWN AND SHE			
LEARNS THROUGH HIS ARM	170	MARRIAGE VIRG	13
IN THE FOUNTAIN BASIN WHERE I SAILED MY SHIP	171	THE HUNCHBACK	10
HE DROPPED WHERE HE LOVED ON THE BURST PAVEMENT STONE	172	DAWN RAID	4
COME IN THE MORNING WHERE I WANDERED AND LISTENED	177	POEM IN OCT	27
WHERE A BOY	178	POEM IN OCT	54
HIS HEAD'S IN A NEST WHERE NO BIRD LAYS HER EGG.	179	NEW QUAY	27
IN THE RIVER WENDED VALES WHERE THE TALE WAS TOLD.	187	WINTER'S TALE	10
AND FIRES WHERE HE SHOULD PROWL DOWN THE CLOUD	188	WINTER'S TALE	37
LISTEN AND LOOK WHERE SHE SAILS THE GOOSE PLUCKED			
SEA,	190	WINTER'S TALE	100
VALES WHERE HE PRAYED TO COME TO THE LAST HARM	190	WINTER'S TALE	109
WHERE THE ELEGIAC FISHERBIRD STABS AND PADDLES	202	SIR JOHNS HILL	19
WHERE THE SEA COBBLES SAIL,	202	SIR JOHNS HILL	38
AND WHARVES OF WATER WHERE THE WALLS DANCE AND THE			
WHITE CRANES STILT.	202	SIR JOHNS HILL	39
THROUGH THROATS WHERE MANY RIVERS MEET, THE CURLEWS			
CRY,	203	GIANT'S THIGH	1
WHERE BARREN AS BOULDERS WOMEN LIE LONGING STILL	203	GIANT'S THIGH	4
THROUGH THROATS WHERE MANY RIVERS MEET, THE WOMEN			
PRAY,	203	GIANT'S THIGH	6

	PAGE	TITLE	LINE
WHERE (CONTINUED)			
QUICK IN THE WOOD AT LOVE, WHERE A TORCH OF FOXES			
FOAMS, ...	204	GIANT'S THIGH	34
AND GONE THAT BARLEY DARK WHERE THEIR CLOGS DANCED			
IN THE SPRING, ...	205	GIANT'S THIGH	40
WHERE THE HAY RIDES NOW OR THE BRACKEN KITCHENS RUST	205	GIANT'S THIGH	47
THEY FROM HOUSES WHERE THE HARVEST KNEELS, HOLD ME			
HARD, ...	205	GIANT'S THIGH	50
WHERE THE CORMORANTS SCUD, ...	208	POEM ON B'DAY	3
ON SKULL AND SCAR WHERE HIS LOVES LIE WRECKED, ...	209	POEM ON B'DAY	40
AND AIR SHAPED HEAVEN WHERE SOULS GROW WILD	210	POEM ON B'DAY	74
WHERE THE DEWFALL STARS SING GRAZING STILL	215	COUNTRY HEAVEN	8
AN OLD MAN IS WITH ME WHERE I GO	217	ELEGY	30
WHERE NOW THE WINGS OF DREAMLESS SLEEP ARE SPREAD,	222	MISSING	5
WHERE THE FROST CAN NEVER FALL, ...	232	YOUR VOICE	15
WHERE THE EAGLE IS A STRONG BIRD	240	ADMIT THE SUN	2
AND WHERE THE LIGHT COMES CAUTIOUSLY	240	ADMIT THE SUN	3
WHERE IS THERE GREATER LOVE	241	ADMIT THE SUN	15
WHEREON			
WHEREON THE HOODED HAIR CASTS DOWN ITS GIRDLE, ...	76	LASHED RINGS	5
WHERE'S			
BRUISING, WHERE'S GOD'S MY SHEPHERD, GOD IS LOVE?	51	OUT OF THE PIT	37
WHEREVER			
WHEREVER I RAMPED IN THE CLOVER QUILTS, ...	206	LAMENT	22
WHETHER			
I KNOW NOT WHETHER	174	FIRE RAID	33
WHICH			
NO PLACE IN WHICH, WAVE PERCHED ON WAVE, ...	10	COOL, OH NO	24
FROM WHICH YOU MAY NOT FLY.	10	COOL, OH NO	30
WHICH IS THE METAL WING	12	CABARET	24
AND WHICH THE REAL?	12	CABARET	25
BY WAVES WHICH GROW AGAIN	14	RAIN CUTS	33
WHICH WAS GOOD AT WORD, ...	23	THE ONLY DEAD	16
UNLESS FOR POETRY, WHICH, IF IT ASKS ME	24	LITTLE PROBLEM	17
WHICH SPREADS DOWN TO THE DREGS	27	OBLIVIOUS DARK	15
WHICH MAY OR MAY NOT BE RELEVANT	33	HELD-OUT HAND	14
NO DOUBT THE WIND ON WHICH THE ROOKS	37	WINDMILLS TURN	4
WHICH IS THE WORLD? OF OUR TWO SLEEPINGS, WHICH ...	89	EUNUCH DREAMS	21
WHICH IS THE WORLD? OF OUR TWO SLEEPINGS, WHICH ...	89	EUNUCH DREAMS	21
WHICH SIXTH OF WIND BLEW OUT THE BURNING GENTRY?	118	ALTARWISE	47
IF I TAKE TO BURN OR RETURN THIS WORLD WHICH IS EACH			
MAN'S WORK.	140	NO WORK WORDS	12
ALL BLOOD-SIGNED ASSAILINGS AND VANISHED MARRIAGES			
IN WHICH HE HAD NO LOVELY PART	158	INTO HER HEAD	43
I CLIMB TO GREET THE WAR IN WHICH I HAVE NO HEART			
BUT ONLY	186	HOLY SPRING	8
WHICH WAS REST AND DUST, AND IN THE KIND GROUND ...	216	ELEGY	10
TO HAVE SEEN COUNTRIES WHICH WERE GLORIOUS, ...	223	IDYLL UNFORGET	1
WHICH BATHE THEMSELVES IN A RAVISHMENT OF SNOW; ...	223	IDYLL UNFORGET	14
WHICH CAN COMFORT YOU	228	NOT DESPAIR	5
WHICH CUTS INTO THE STRENGTH	230	MY RIVER	42
WHICH LEANS ONE WAY, ...	232	FURIOUS MOTION	10
WHICH GOES AROUND ME EASILY	236	WOMAN TAPESTRY	54
WHILE			
BUT WHILE DAY IS THERE'S NIGHT TO IT, ...	18	NATURAL DAY	19
WHILE THE SUN'S TURNED TO SALT, ...	27	OBLIVIOUS DARK	23
HOW MUCH WAS HAPPY WHILE IT LASTED, ...	32	OUT OF SIGHS	20
SHALL NOT BE LATCHED WHILE MAGIC GLIDES	91	WHERE ONCE THE	20
THE BALL I THREW WHILE PLAYING IN THE PARK	116	LANTERNS SHINE	18
WHILE YOU DISPLACED A TRUTH IN THE AIR, ...	147	TO OTHERS	17

	PAGE	TITLE	LINE
WHILE (CONTINUED)			
ABOUT THE SAINT IN SHADES WHILE THE ENDLESS BREVIARY	148	UNLUCKILY FOR	26
WHILE A MAN OUTSIDE WITH A BILLHOOK, ...	150	WHEN I WOKE	8
EYED, WHILE THE TEARS DRAG ON THE TAIL, ...	155	RETURN	42
WHILE THE BOYS AMONG WILLOWS	171	THE HUNCHBACK	27
SHALL HARROW AND SNOW THE BLOOD WHILE YOU RIDE WIDE			
AND NEAR, ...	198	COUNTRY SLEEP	23
WHILE ITS VIOLET SHELLS BROKE AND PARTED.	232	FURIOUS MOTION	14
THAN SIT HERE WASTING, WHILE I BLEED, ...	240	TWINING HEAD	11
WHINNY			
LEADS, TOO, TO A LEAD PIT, WHINNY AND FALL, ...	44	TO FOLLOW FOX	10
WHINNYING			
YOU HAVE KICKED FROM A DARK DEN, LEAPED UP THE			
WHINNYING LIGHT, ...	135	HOW MY ANIMAL	43
OUT OF THE WHINNYING GREEN STABLE	196	FERN HILL	35
DOWN THE CHEEK BONES AND WHINNYING	215	COUNTRY HEAVEN	14
WHIP			
WITH RAIN-BEATEN HANDS HOLDING THE WHIP, ...	45	PLOUGHMAN GONE	20
WHIPPED			
THE VEINS AT EITHER TEMPLE WHIPPED HIM MAD, ...	50	OUT OF THE PIT	7
WHIPS			
FELL HARD AS WHIPS ON AN OLD WOUND, ...	42	A WAR OF WITS	3
WHIRL			
FUNNELS AND MASTS WENT BY IN A WHIRL.	162	LONG-LEGGED	17
WHIRL-			
BURNING IN THE BRIDE BED OF LOVE, IN THE WHIRL- ...	191	WINTER'S TALE	127
WHIRLED			
WHIRLED IN OUR WORDS, THEN FADED.	34	IN GARDENS	15
THE WHIRLED BOAT IN THE BURN OF HIS BLOOD	164	LONG-LEGGED	65
WHIRLING			
OVER THE WHIRLING DITCH OF DAYBREAK	175	FIRE RAID	67
WHIRLPOOL			
AND A WHIRLPOOL DRIVES THE PRAYERWHEEL;	130	SINNERS' BELL	9
TREES COOL AND DRY IN THE WHIRLPOOL OF SHIPS	167	LONG-LEGGED	170
WHIRLS			
THE HAND THAT WHIRLS THE WATER IN THE POOL	77	THE FORCE THAT	11
WHIRLWIND			
GOD IN HIS WHIRLWIND SILENCE SAVE, WHO MARKS THE			
SPARROWS HAIL, ...	202	SIR JOHNS HILL	45
WHIRR			
AND THE ANGELS WHIRR LIKE PHEASANTS	215	COUNTRY HEAVEN	9
WHIRRING			
ON THE ANGELIC ETNA OF THE LAST WHIRRING			
FEATHERLANDS, ...	141	SAINT TO FALL	11
WHISKING			
WHISKING HARE! WHO	4	PROLOGUE	68
WHISKY			
MILD. TURNED AGAIN, WORTHINGTON. NEVER WHISKY.	179	NEW QUAY	12
WHISPER			
FOR WE MUST WHISPER DOWN THE FUNNEL	17	IN OBLIVION	8
TO WHISPER, WHEN HE WANTS, THE SENSES' WAR	29	NEARLY SUMMER	12
UNTIL THE WHISPER OF THE LAST TRUMP LOUDEN	40	YOUNG ARE OLD	11
(MY SHAPE OF AGE NAGGING THE WOUNDED WHISPER.)	118	ALTARWISE	46
WHISPER IN A DAMP WORD, HER WITS DRILLED HOLLOW,	137	AFTER FUNERAL	33
WHISPER A BENEDICTION FOR THE DEAD.	222	MISSING	6
AND THE WHISPER CAUGHT IN ITS PAGEANT OF TAWNY PEARL,	224	IDYLL UNFORGET	44
WHISPERED			
TO TAKE ME AWAY AS YOU WHISPERED AND WROTE	149	PAPER & STICKS	12
WHISPERED THE AFFECTIONATE SAND	162	LONG-LEGGED	9
SUMMERTIME OF THE DEAD WHISPERED THE TRUTH OF HIS JOY	178	POEM IN OCT	56

	PAGE	TITLE	LINE
WHISPERED (CONTINUED)			
THAT WHISPERED WITH THE WIND AND WEPT, ...	227	SPRING-SPIRIT	6
WHISPERING			
THE WHISPERING EARS WILL WATCH LOVE DRUMMED AWAY	138	FIVE & COUNTRY	6
OF DUSK AND WATER I SEE THE TILTING WHISPERING	202	SIR JOHNS HILL	48
WHISPERINGS			
THESE WERE THE WHISPERINGS THAT SIGHED ON MY LIPS AT			
DUSK, ...	223	IDYLL UNFORGET	10
WHISPERS			
VOICES HAVE CALLED, AND THE ANSWERS LEMURAL WHISPERS			
FROM THE SEA;	224	IDYLL UNFORGET	34
WHISTLED			
WHEN I WHISTLED WITH MITCHING BOYS THROUGH A			
RESERVOIR PARK	144	COLOUR OF SAY	7
RODE AND WHISTLED A HUNDRED TIMES	157	INTO HER HEAD	18
I WHISTLED ALL NIGHT IN THE TWISTED FLUES, ...	206	LAMENT	18
WHISTLER'S			
WITH WHISTLER'S COUGH CONTAGES, TIME ON TRACK	101	RUNNING GRAVE	47
WHISTLES			
SNARING THE WHISTLES OF THE BIRDS	46	POET: 1935	8
NO SILVER WHISTLES CHASE HIM DOWN THE WEEKS'	108	GRIEF THIEF	21
BECAUSE THE PLEASURE-BIRD WHISTLES	144	PLEASURE-BIRD	T
BECAUSE THE PLEASURE-BIRD WHISTLES AFTER THE HOT			
WIRES, ...	144	PLEASURE-BIRD	1
OF THE LED-ASTRAY BIRDS WHOM GOD, FOR THEIR BREAST			
OF WHISTLES, ...	202	SIR JOHNS HILL	43
WHISTLING			
CLOUD AND THE ROADSIDE BUSHES BRIMMING WITH WHISTLING	177	POEM IN OCT	22
WHITE			
SHEEP WHITE HOLLOW FARMS	4	PROLOGUE	51
WHO HOLDS HER CLASPED INSIDE HIS STRONG, WHITE WINGS;	15	FOR LEDA	31
OR, WHITE AS MILK, OUT OF THE SEEPING DARK, ...	20	ENCOMPASSED	11
BEFORE WHITE OR BLACK, THE RIGHT OR LEFT SOCK, ...	39	GAS FADES	17
NOT BLACK OR WHITE OR LEFT OR RIGHT.	39	GAS FADES	39
THE WHITE, THE BLACK, THE YELLOW AND MULATTO	41	YOUNG ARE OLD	39
FOR THE BODY'S BRITTLE AND THE SKIN'S WHITE.	42	A WAR OF WITS	10
SHALL A WHITE ANSWER ECHO FROM THE ROOFTOPS.	56	WHY EAST WIND	15
IN THIS WHITE HOUSE?	62	EARS IN TURRET	8
THE SUN AND MOON SHED ONE WHITE LIGHT.	78	LOVE'S FEVER	9
TWELVE WINDS ENCOUNTER BY THE WHITE HOST AT PASTURE,	109	I, IN IMAGE	38
ALL-HOLLOWED MAN WEPT FOR HIS WHITE APPAREL.	111	I, IN IMAGE	102
BY WASTE SEAS WHERE THE WHITE BEAR QUOTED VIRGIL	119	ALTARWISE	69
CHILD IN WHITE BLOOD BENT ON ITS KNEES	128	MY NEOPHYTE	2
FOREVER IT IS A WHITE CHILD IN THE DARK-SKINNED			
SUMMER	130	SINNERS' BELL	19
THE BREATH DRAW BACK LIKE A BOLT THROUGH WHITE OIL	142	SAINT TO FALL	46
AND A BLACK AND WHITE PATCH OF GIRLS GREW PLAYING;	144	COLOUR OF SAY	4
I DREW THE WHITE SHEET OVER THE ISLANDS	150	WHEN I WOKE	29
WHITE FEATHERING THE LIVING.	154	RETURN	25
CRYING, WHITE GOWNED, FROM THE MIDDLE MOONLIT STAGES	158	INTO HER HEAD	37
SAILS DRANK THE WIND, AND WHITE AS MILK	162	LONG-LEGGED	13
WHITE SPRINGS IN THE DARK.	166	LONG-LEGGED	120
OR THE WHITE EWE LAMB	174	FIRE RAID	35
WHITE AS THE SKELETON	174	FIRE RAID	45
ABOVE THE FARMS AND THE WHITE HORSES	177	POEM IN OCT	13
FLOCKED WITH THE SHEEP WHITE SMOKE OF THE FARM HOUSE			
COWL	187	WINTER'S TALE	9
AND THE DUNG HILLS WHITE AS WOOL AND THE HEN	187	WINTER'S TALE	18
AND ALL THE WOKEN FARM AT ITS WHITE TRADES, ...	187	WINTER'S TALE	25
MAY HIS HUNGER GO HOWLING ON BARE WHITE BONES	188	WINTER'S TALE	33

	PAGE	TITLE	LINE
WHITE (CONTINUED)			
OF HIS SNOW BLIND LOVE AND RUSH IN THE WHITE LAIRS.	188	WINTER'S TALE	38
IN THE ALWAYS DESIRING CENTRE OF THE WHITE	188	WINTER'S TALE	48
NEVER TO FLOURISH IN THE FIELDS OF THE WHITE SEED	188	WINTER'S TALE	54
HORSES, CENTAUR DEAD, TURN AND TREAD THE DRENCHED			
WHITE	189	WINTER'S TALE	74
ON A BREAD WHITE HILL OVER THE CUPPED FARM	190	WINTER'S TALE	107
ON THE WHITE, NO LONGER GROWING GREEN, AND, MINSTREL			
DEAD, ...	190	WINTER'S TALE	112
AND THEN TO AWAKE, AND THE FARM, LIKE A WANDERER			
WHITE	195	FERN HILL	28
NOTHING I CARED, IN THE LAMB WHITE DAYS, THAT TIME			
WOULD TAKE ME	196	FERN HILL	46
EARTH, AIR, WATER, FIRE, SINGING INTO THE WHITE ACT,	200	COUNTRY SLEFP	87
AND WHARVES OF WATER WHERE THE WALLS DANCE AND THE			
WHITE CRANES STILT.	202	SIR JOHNS HILL	39
IN THE WHITE GIANT'S THIGH	203	GIANT'S THIGH	T
AND THERE THIS NIGHT I WALK IN THE WHITE GIANT'S			
THIGH	203	GIANT'S THIGH	3
AND DUCKED AND DRAKED WHITE LAKE THAT HARPS TO A			
HAIL STONE.	204	GIANT'S THIGH	28
OF DAY, IN THE THISTLE AISLES, TILL THE WHITE OWL			
CROSSED	204	GIANT'S THIGH	32
WAVE'S SILENCE, WEPT WHITE ANGELUS KNELLS.	209	POEM ON B'DAY	38
WHITE, GOD'S BRIGHT, FLOCKS, THE BELLED LAMBS			
LEAPING, ...	215	COUNTRY HEAVEN	21
THE MOONS ARE WHITE FLAMES, LIKE THE MOONS IN DREAMS.	223	IN DREAMS	14
THE FOAM HAS LINGERED INTO WHITE, LITTLE FLOWERS,	224	IDYLL UNFORGET	28
WHITE WITH THE RISING WATER.	233	NO THOUGHT	19
AND WHITE, SYMMETRICAL LIPS	236	WOMAN TAPESTRY	44
WHITE-DRESSED			
SHE CRIED HER WHITE-DRESSED LIMBS WERE BARE	139	TOMBSTONE TOLD	17
WHITE-LIPPED			
LITTLE WHITE-LIPPED FACES HAVE PEERED UP AT ME, ...	224	IDYLL UNFORGET	32
WHITES			
INTO THE BROWNS OF AUTUMN AND THE SHARP WHITES OF			
WINTER, ...	47	POET: 1935	20
WHIZZBANGS			
IT WAS NOVEMBER THERE WERE WHIZZBANGS HOPPING, ...	52	OUT OF THE PIT	51
WHO			
TACKLED WITH CLOUDS, WHO KNEEL	3	PROLOGUE	13
YOU KING SINGSONG OWLS, WHO MOONBEAM	4	PROLOGUE	54
WHO MOONS HER BLUE NOTES FROM HER NEST	4	PROLOGUE	62
WHISKING HARE! WHO	4	PROLOGUE	68
BEASTS WHO SLEEP GOOD AND THIN, ...	5	PROLOGUE	77
WHO TELLS ME HURT, ...	12	SKY'S BRIGHT	13
WHO HOLDS HER CLASPED INSIDE HIS STRONG, WHITE WINGS;	15	FOR LEDA	31
AND WHO SHALL TELL THE AMORIST	17	IN OBLIVION	27
WHO TAUGHT ME TROUBLE?	18	NATURAL DAY	25
FOR SHE WHO SPRINKLED ON YOUR BROW	20	THE NEOPHYTE	20
WHO HAVE NO VOICES BUT THE WINDS'	22	ON QUIET NIGHT	2
UPON THE EARTH WHO KNEW NO JOY, ...	22	ON QUIET NIGHT	16
THEY ARE THE ONLY DEAD WHO DID NOT LOVE	23	THE ONLY DEAD	T
THEY ARE THE ONLY DEAD WHO DID NOT LOVE, ...	23	THE ONLY DEAD	1
THEY ARE THE ONLY LIVING THING WHO DID LOVE, ...	23	THE ONLY DEAD	4
WHO HAS COMPLETENESS THAT CAN CUT	23	THE ONLY DEAD	7
WHO HAVE NO TALK BUT THAT OF DEATH.	23	ON QUIET NIGHT	22
LOOK, THERE'S THE DEAD WHO DID NOT LOVE, ...	24	THE ONLY DEAD	30
AND THERE'S THE LIVING WHO DID LOVE, ...	24	THE ONLY DEAD	31
WHO DO I BLAME	26	PERSONAL EPIT	2

	PAGE	TITLE	LINE
WHO (CONTINUED)			
WHO DO I BLAME?	26	PERSONAL EPIT	6
WHO GAVE ME LIFE AND THEN THE GRAVE, ...	26	PERSONAL EPIT	11
LOVING AND DOUBTING LIKE ONE WHO IS TO DIE	27	OBLIVIOUS DARK	28
WHO CANNOT COUNT THE SEEDS HE SOWS, ...	29	NEARLY SUMMER	8
YOU, WHO ARE OLD, HAVE LOVED AND LOST AS I	30	YOUTH CALLS	5
BY THOSE WHO PLANNED THE OBVIOUS ROUTES	37	WINDMILLS TURN	22
'WE WHO ARE YOUNG ARE OLD'	40	YOUNG ARE OLD	T
'WE WHO ARE YOUNG ARE OLD. IT IS THE OLDEST CRY.	40	YOUNG ARE OLD	1
WE WHO ARE STILL YOUNG ARE OLD. IT IS A DEAD CRY,	40	YOUNG ARE OLD	5
UNDER THE SKYSIGNS THEY WHO HAVE NO ARMS	40	WAS THERE TIME	7
WE WHO ARE YOUNG SIT HOLDING YELLOW HANDS.	41	YOUNG ARE OLD	17
WHO, UNDESERVING, HAVE SUFFERED THE EARTH'S WRONG,	41	YOUNG ARE OLD	34
WE WHO ARE YOUNG ARE OLD, AND UNBELIEVING, ...	42	YOUNG ARE OLD	53
BELIEVE, BELIEVE AND BE SAVED, WE CRY, WHO HAVE NO			
FAITH.	42	YOUNG ARE OLD	57
MAN WHO ONCE DROVE IS DRIVEN IN SUN AND RAIN.	46	PLOUGHMAN GONE	34
WHO ON HIS CLOUD HEARS ALL MY WISHES, ...	48	LIGHT, I KNOW	15
WHO ARE HIS FRIENDS? THE WIND IS HIS FRIEND, ...	48	POET: 1935	63
WHERE FLOATED A DEAD DOG WHO MADE HIM ILL, ...	51	OUT OF THE PIT	41
NO MAN BELIEVES WHO, WHEN A STAR FALLS SHOT, ...	54	NO MAN BELIEVE	1
AND THE GRAVE SEA, MOCK WHO DERIDE	54	WE BY SEASAND	2
WHO FOLLOW THE RED RIVERS, HOLLOW	54	WE BY SEASAND	3
WHO DOES NOT MAKE A WOUND IN FAITH	55	NO MAN BELIEVE	5
NO MAN BELIEVES WHO CRIES NOT, GOD IS NOT, ...	55	NO MAN BELIEVE	7
WHO FEELS NOT COLDNESS IN THE HEAT, ...	55	NO MAN BELIEVE	8
NO BREASTED GIRL, NO MAN WHO, YOUNG	55	NO MAN BELIEVE	10
NO MAN BELIEVES WHO DOES NOT WONDER WHY.	55	NO MAN BELIEVE	12
WHO CURSES NOT WHAT MAKES AND SAVES, ...	55	NO MAN BELIEVE	14
BELIEVES WHO DOES NOT LANCE HIS FAITH, ...	55	NO MAN BELIEVE	16
WHO DOES NOT BURY GOD IN A DEEP GRAVE	55	NO MAN BELIEVE	19
NO MAN WHO DOES NOT BREAK AND MAKE, ...	55	NO MAN BELIEVE	21
WHO IN THE BONES FINDS NOT NEW FAITH, ...	55	NO MAN BELIEVE	22
WHO DOES NOT BREAK AND MAKE HIS FINAL FAITH.	55	NO MAN BELIEVE	24
PITY THE LIVING WHO ARE LOST, ALONE;	57	GREEK PLAY	21
DROWNS AND IS DROWNED, WHO UTTERS TO THE STARS	57	GREEK PLAY	26
PITY THE POOR UNPITIED WHO ARE STRANGE WITH TEARS.	57	GREEK PLAY	28
WHO STEPS ON THE GAS;	58	TO ARCHITECTS	9
HUNGER FOR HIM WHO DUNGS THE VALLEY FIELDS.	64	WOMAN SPEAKS	37
THESE DIE WHO SHOVEL THE LAST HOME OF MAN;	64	WOMAN SPEAKS	44
TELL ME OF HIM WHO FEEDS THE RAGING BIRDS.	65	WOMAN SPEAKS	65
I WHO WAS SHAPELESS AS THE WATER	68	BEFORE KNOCKED	3
I WHO WAS DEAF TO SPRING AND SUMMER, ...	68	BEFORE KNOCKED	7
WHO KNEW NOT SUN NOR MOON BY NAME, ...	68	BEFORE KNOCKED	8
I WHO WAS RICH WAS MADE THE RICHER	69	BEFORE KNOCKED	35
YOU WHO BOW DOWN AT CROSS AND ALTAR, ...	69	BEFORE KNOCKED	43
WHO TOOK MY FLESH AND BONE FOR ARMOUR	69	BEFORE KNOCKED	45
HERE IS A SAVIOUR WHO SINGS LIKE A BIRD, ...	74	SUN BURNS	7
PRAISE HIM WHO SPRINGS AND FILLS THE TIDAL WELL.	76	LASHED RINGS	11
LEFT BY THE DEAD WHO, IN THEIR MOONLESS ACRE, ...	79	LOVE'S FEVER	35
HERE SLIPS THE GHOST WHO MADE OF MY PALE BED	81	HERE LIE BEAST	11
TO WOMEN WHO HAVE TWISTED THEIR LAST SMILE, ...	81	ALL THAT I OWE	16
TO CHILDREN WHO WERE SUCKLED ON A PLAGUE, ...	81	ALL THAT I OWE	17
TO YOU, MY AUNT, WHO WOULD EXPLORE	83	LETTER TO AUNT	1
WHO KNOWS NOT ELIOT (TO HER SHAME).	83	LETTER TO AUNT	6
OF PUTREFYING ANGELS WHO	84	LETTER TO AUNT	54
AND WHO REMAIN SHALL FLOWER AS THEY LOVE, ...	90	EUNUCH DREAMS	41
OF CHILDREN GO WHO, FROM THEIR VOIDS, ...	91	WHERE ONCE THE	17
FROM THE FAIR DEAD WHO FLUSH THE SEA	92	BOYS OF SUMMER	34
A ROOKING GIRL WHO STOLE ME FOR HER SIDE, ...	94	RUB OF LOVE	2

	PAGE	TITLE	LINE
WHO (CONTINUED)			
MY BUSY HEART WHO SHUDDERS AS SHE TALKS	98	OCTOBER WIND	7
WHO PERISCOPE THROUGH FLOWERS TO THE SKY.	98	TWILIGHT LOCKS	30
DELIVER ME WHO, TIMID IN MY TRIBE,	100	RUNNING GRAVE	7
I FELLOWED SLEEP WHO KISSED ME IN THE BRAIN,	101	FELLOWED SLEEP	1
WHO SEEK ME LANDWARD, MARKING IN MY MOUTH	105	WORLD PYRAMID	46
WHO BLOWS DEATH'S FEATHER? WHAT GLORY IS COLOUR?	105	WORLD PYRAMID	55
WHO TOSSED THE HIGH TIDE IN A TIME OF STORIES	108	GRIEF THIEF	13
AM I NOT SISTER, TOO, WHO IS MY SAVIOUR?	112	NOT FATHER ME	12
AM I NOT YOU WHO FRONT THE TIDY SHORE,	112	NOT FATHER ME	15
YOU ARE ALL THESE, SAID SHE WHO GAVE ME THE LONG SUCK,	112	NOT FATHER ME	17
ALL THESE, HE SAID WHO SACKED THE CHILDREN'S TOWN,	112	NOT FATHER ME	18
THEY SAID, WHO HACKED AND HUMOURED, THEY WERE MINE.	112	NOT FATHER ME	20
WHO RAZED MY WOODEN FOLLY STANDS AGHAST,	113	NOT FATHER ME	22
WHO PLAY THE PROPER GENTLEMAN AND LADY.	113	NOT FATHER ME	28
SHE WHO WAS WHO I HOLD, THE FATS AND FLOWER,	114	A GRIEF AGO	2
SHE WHO WAS WHO I HOLD, THE FATS AND FLOWER,	114	A GRIEF AGO	2
WHO IS MY GRIEF,	115	A GRIEF AGO	9
WAS WHO WAS FOLDED ON THE ROD THE AARON	115	A GRIEF AGO	13
AND SHE WHO LIES,	115	A GRIEF AGO	17
WHO THEN IS SHE,	115	A GRIEF AGO	25
WHO SUCKS THE BELL-VOICED ADAM OUT OF MAGIC,	119	ALTARWISE	93
AND GOD WALKED THERE WHO WAS A FIDDLING WARDEN	121	INCARNATE DEVL	5
WHO GAVE THESE SEAS THEIR COLOUR IN A SHAPE,	123	FOSTER LIGHT	25
O WHO IS GLORY IN THE SHAPELESS MAPS,	124	FOSTER LIGHT	28
SHOULD HE WHO SPLIT HIS CHILDREN WITH A CURE	127	NOW, SAY NAY	13
WHO IN THESE LABYRINTHS,	128	MY NEOPHYTE	13
WHO SPEAK ON A FINGER AND THUMB,	129	MY NEOPHYTE	29
WHO KILLS MY HISTORY?	129	MY NEOPHYTE	37
'WHO COULD SNAP OFF THE SHAPELESS PRINT	129	MY NEOPHYTE	40
WHO COULD HACK OUT YOUR UNSUCKED HEART,	129	MY NEOPHYTE	46
THESE ARE HER CONTRARIES: THE BEAST WHO FOLLOWS	131	I MAKE THIS IN	24
WHO HAVE BROUGHT FORTH THE URCHIN GRIEF.	131	SINNERS' BELL	30
WHO SCALES A HAILING HILL IN HER COLD FLINTSTEPS	132	I MAKE THIS IN	29
WHO PICKS THE LIVE HEART ON A DIAMOND.	132	I MAKE THIS IN	45
WHO SHOULD BE FURIOUS,	134	HOW MY ANIMAL	6
SHAKES A DESOLATE BOY WHO SLITS HIS THROAT	136	AFTER FUNERAL	7
WHO ONLY DRINKS HIS PROFITS	138	O CHATTERTON	27
I WHO SAW IN A HURRIED FILM	140	TOMBSTONE TOLD	21
WHO WRITES THESE WORDS I WRITE IN A STILL ROOM IN A SPELLSOAKED HOUSE:	141	I, FIRST NAMED	2
WHO PALMED THE LIE ON ME WHEN YOU LOOKED	146	TO OTHERS	4
O YOU WHO COULD NOT CRY	153	WAS A SAVIOUR	20
O WE WHO COULD NOT STIR	153	WAS A SAVIOUR	28
ONE WHO CALLED DEEPEST DOWN SHALL HOLD HIS PEACE	160	DEATHS AND ENT	9
ONE WHO IS MOST UNKNOWN,	160	DEATHS AND ENT	16
WHO STRODE FOR YOUR OWN DEAD	160	DEATHS AND ENT	20
ONE ENEMY, OF MANY, WHO KNOWNS WELL	160	DEATHS AND ENT	29
WHO MOVED FOR THREE YEARS IN TUNE	161	WEDDING ANNIV	3
WHO SHOWS TO THE SELVES ASLEEP	165	LONG-LEGGED	103
SIN WHO HAD A WOMAN'S SHAPE	165	LONG-LEGGED	110
HE WHO BLEW THE GREAT FIRE IN	167	LONG-LEGGED	157
AND HE WHO TAUGHT THEIR LIPS TO SING	167	LONG-LEGGED	162
WHO ADMITS THE DELUSIVE LIGHT THROUGH THE BOUNCING WALL,	170	LOVE IN ASYLUM	11
OF THE GOLDEN GHOST WHO RINGED WITH HIS STREAMS HER MERCURY BONE,	170	MARRIAGE VIRG	11
WHO UNDER THE LIDS OF HER WINDOWS HOISTED HIS GOLDEN LUGGAGE,	170	MARRIAGE VIRG	12

	PAGE	TITLE	LINE
WHO (CONTINUED)			
CHILD WHO WAS PRIEST AND SERVANTS,	174	FIRE RAID	52
WHO WAS THE SERPENT'S	174	FIRE RAID	55
WHO	180	VISION, PRAYER	1
WHO IS BORN	180	VISION, PRAYER	3
WHO BORE HIM WITH A BONFIRE IN	181	VISION, PRAYER	43
FOR I WAS LOST WHO AM	181	VISION, PRAYER	57
FOR I WAS LOST WHO HAVE COME	181	VISION, PRAYER	62
IN THE NAME OF THE LOST WHO GLORY IN	183	VISION, PRAYER	102
THAT HE WHO LEARNS NOW THE SUN AND MOON	183	VISION, PRAYER	119
WHO CLIMBS TO HIS DYING LOVE IN HER HIGH ROOM,	193	CONVERS PRAYER	3
FOR THE SLEEP IN A SAFE LAND AND THE LOVE WHO DIES	194	CONVERS PRAYER	10
DRAGGING HIM UP THE STAIRS TO ONE WHO LIES DEAD.	194	CONVERS PRAYER	20
WHO PAY NO PRAISE OR WAGES	197	CRAFT OR ART	19
FOR WHO UNMANNINGLY HAUNTS THE MOUNTAIN RAVENED EAVES	198	COUNTRY SLEEP	24
WHO COMES AS RED AS THE FOX AND SLY AS THE HEELED WIND.	200	COUNTRY SLEEP	81
OF THE SPARROWS AND SUCH WHO SWANSING, DUSK, IN WRANGLING HEDGES.	201	SIR JOHNS HILL	7
GOD IN HIS WHIRLWIND SILENCE SAVE, WHO MARKS THE SPARROWS HAIL,	202	SIR JOHNS HILL	45
HILL. WHO ONCE IN GOOSESKIN WINTER LOVED ALL ICE LEAVED	203	GIANT'S THIGH	12
MAKES ALL THE MUSIC; AND I WHO HEAR THE TUNE OF THE SLOW,	203	SIR JOHNS HILL	57
WHO ONCE, GREEN COUNTRIES SINCE, WERE A HEDGEROW OF JOYS.	204	GIANT'S THIGH	20
WHO ONCE WERE A BLOOM OF WAYSIDE BRIDES IN THE HAWED HOUSE	204	GIANT'S THIGH	29
WHO HEARD THE TALL BELL SAIL DOWN THE SUNDAYS OF THE DEAD	205	GIANT'S THIGH	51
WILD MEN WHO CAUGHT AND SANG THE SUN IN FLIGHT,	208	NOT GO GENTLE	10
GRAVE MEN, NEAR DEATH, WHO SEE WITH BLINDING SIGHT	208	NOT GO GENTLE	13
WHO TOLLS HIS BIRTHDAY BELL,	209	POEM ON B'DAY	16
WHO SLAVES TO HIS CROUCHED, ETERNAL END	209	POEM ON B'DAY	31
WHO KNOWS THE ROCKETING WIND WILL BLOW	210	POEM ON B'DAY	67
WHO IS THE LIGHT OF OLD	210	POEM ON B'DAY	73
THERE ARE MANY WHO SAY THAT A DOG HAS ITS DAY,	221	SONG OF DOG	1
THERE ARE OTHERS WHO THINK THAT A LOBSTER IS PINK,	221	SONG OF DOG	3
THERE ARE FEWER, OF COURSE, WHO INSIST THAT A HORSE	221	SONG OF DOG	5
AND A FELLOW WHO JESTS THAT A MARE CAN BUILD NESTS	221	SONG OF DOG	7
AND NIGHT, WHO STOOPED TO KISS THE PALLID LEAVES	223	IN DREAMS	5
FOR HER WHO WALKS WITHIN HER GARDEN-CLOSE.	223	IN DREAMS	7
OR THE YELLOW LINNET WHO DOES NOT MERIT IT.	230	OUR SANCTITY	14
WAITING FOR THE BIRD WHO SHALL SAY,	231	OUR SANCTITY	28
AND IF IT DID, WHO SHOULD I HAVE	234	NO, PIGEON	5
WHO SAILS ON TIDES OF LEAVES AND SOUND.	234	NO, PIGEON	16
WHO FLEW HIMSELF BECAUSE THE BOAT REMAINED	238	PILLAR BREAKS	19
WHO LETS HIS OWN ROD BE	240	TWINING HEAD	6
THE SAVIOUR OF THE CROSS WHO CAN	240	TWINING HEAD	7
WHO DO NOT BREAK?	241	ADMIT THE SUN	18
WHO'D			
WHO'D RAISE THE ORGANS OF THE COUNTED DUST	160	DEATHS AND ENT	7
WHOEVER			
WHOEVER I WOULD WITH MY WICKED EYES,	206	LAMENT	9
WHOLE			
HE HAS THE WHOLE FIELD NOW, THE GODS DEPARTED	29	NEARLY SUMMER	7
THE WHOLE, THE CRIPPLED, THE WEAK AND STRONG,	41	YOUNG ARE OLD	43
PRAISE THAT MY BODY BE WHOLE, I'VE LIMBS,	42	A WAR OF WITS	8
AND MY WHOLE HEART UNDER YOUR HAMMER,	147	TO OTHERS	13

		PAGE	TITLE	LINE
WHOLE (CONTINUED)				
SINGLY LIE WITH THE WHOLE WIDE SHORE,	....	158	INTO HER HEAD	49
NOW CAST DOWN YOUR ROD, FOR THE WHOLE	....	162	LONG-LEGGED	31
AND THE WHOLE PAIN	......	182	VISION, PRAYER	98
THE WHOLE OF THE MOON I COULD LOVE AND LEAVE	....	206	LAMENT	10
AND GALE I TACKLE, THE WHOLE WORLD THEN,	....	211	POEM ON B'DAY	96
WHO'LL				
WHO'LL BREAK OUR NECKS UPON THE PAVEMENT	....	28	NO WINGS	10
LUST BEARS LIKE VOLTS, WHO'LL AMPLIFY, AND STRANGE		159	TO LEDA	8
WHOLLY				
NOT WHOLLY TO THAT LAMENTING	....	183	VISION, PRAYER	116
WHOM				
WHOM CANCER CROPS, WHOSE DRINKING RUSTS, THESE DIE;		64	WOMAN SPEAKS	43
YOU ARE MY FLESH'S RULER WHOM I TREASON,	....	67	REALM OF FLESH	11
WHOM NOW I CONJURE TO STAND AS THIEF	....	146	TO OTHERS	9
THEY COME TOGETHER WHOM THEIR LOVE PARTED:	....	161	WEDDING ANNIV	10
THE ONE NOT CARING TO WHOM IN HIS SLEEP HE WILL MOVE		193	CONVERS PRAYER	4
WILL BE THE SAME GRIEF FLYING. WHOM SHALL THEY CALM?		194	CONVERS PRAYER	11
AND THE CHILD NOT CARING TO WHOM HE CLIMBS HIS PRAYER		194	CONVERS PRAYER	17
OF THE LED-ASTRAY BIRDS WHOM GOD, FOR THEIR BREAST				
OF WHISTLES,	....	202	SIR JOHNS HILL	43
(WHOM MY HEART HEARS),	....	215	COUNTRY HEAVEN	2
ON WHOM A WORLD OF ILLS CAME DOWN LIKE SNOW.	....	217	ELEGY	32
WHOOPEE				
MAKE DEADLY WHOOPEE IN THE BLUE.	....	84	LETTER TO AUNT	55
WHOSE				
DAYS' NIGHT WHOSE TOWERS WILL CATCH	....	3	PROLOGUE	20
BUT IT, REALITY, WHOSE VOICE I KNOW	....	9	MINUTE'S HOUR	16
HE WHOSE LOVERS WERE BOTH WISE AND SENSIBLE	....	25	BEAUTY TO DUST	18
WHOSE LOVING CRIME	....	26	PERSONAL EPIT	8
NEW MAN BEST WHOSE BLOOD RUNS THICK,	....	29	LONG, SKELETON	11
A GIRL WHOSE SINGLE BED HELD TWO	....	38	THE GOSSIPERS	9
PITY ELECTRA LOVELESS, SHE WHOSE GRIEF	....	57	GREEK PLAY	25
OLD MEN WHOSE BLOOD IS HINDERED IN THEIR VEINS,	...	64	WOMAN SPEAKS	42
WHOM CANCER CROPS, WHOSE DRINKING RUSTS, THESE DIE;		64	WOMAN SPEAKS	43
WHOSE FLAMING BLOOD SHALL RUB IT AT THE RIMS	......	87	PAIN BE MUSIC	8
WHOSE BEARD WAGS IN EGYPTIAN WIND.	....	116	LANTERNS SHINE	15
WHOSE WIZARD SHAPE I TRACE IN THE CAVERNOUS SKULL,		134	HOW MY ANIMAL	2
WHOSE HOODED, FOUNTAIN HEART ONCE FELL IN PUDDLES		136	AFTER FUNERAL	14
THAT FROZEN WIFE WHOSE JUICES DRIFT LIKE A FIXED SEA		145	PLEASURE-BIRD	14
OTHERS WHOSE SINGLE BEDS HOLD TWO	....	155	RETURN	60
AT WHOSE BALL-PRYING EVEN DEATH'LL SQUIRM	....	179	NEW QUAY	22
OF SLEEPERS WHOSE TONGUE I TOLL	....	184	VISION, PRAYER	155
WHOSE MINUTE KINDLES MORE THAN THE WISE HOUR.	.....	237	PILLAR BREAKS	11
WHY				
WHY IS MY HAND TOO BLUNT	....	12	SKY'S BRIGHT	5
AND KNOW WHY RUN),	....	24	LITTLE PROBLEM	14
RUN AND KNOW WHY	....	24	LITTLE PROBLEM	19
AND KNOW WHY KNOW, NO WIT,	....	24	LITTLE PROBLEM	20
WHY COUNT SO SADLY?	....	33	HELD-OUT HAND	6
WHY EAST WIND CHILLS	....	55	WHY EAST WIND	T
WHY EAST WIND CHILLS AND SOUTH WIND COOLS	....	55	WHY EAST WIND	1
WHY SILK IS SOFT AND THE STONE WOUNDS	....	55	WHY EAST WIND	6
NO MAN BELIEVES WHO DOES NOT WONDER WHY.	....	55	NO MAN BELIEVE	12
WHY NIGHT-TIME RAIN AND THE BREAST'S BLOOD	....	56	WHY EAST WIND	8
WHY BLOT THE PICTURES	....	60	FAIRY TALES	28
WHY SHOULD I THINK ON DEATH WHEN YOU ARE RULER?	...	67	REALM OF FLESH	10
WHY WON'T THE NEWS OF THE OLD WORLD CATCH	....	149	PAPER & STICKS	2
WICK				
AND BURNED SEA SILENCE ON A WICK OF WORLDS.	....	119	ALTARWISE	74

	PAGE	TITLE	LINE
WICK-			
NOT A BOY AND A BIT IN THE WICK-	206	LAMENT	16
WICKED			
THE BITTER, THE WICKED, THE LONGLYING LEISURE, ...	39	GAS FADES	21
THE KINGCRAFTS OF THE WICKED SEA, ...	61	MEAT ON BONES	11
SEE, SAYS THE LIME, MY WICKED MILKS	85	SEE, SAYS LIME	1
AND THE WICKED WISH, ...	193	SIDE OF TRUTH	29
WHOEVER I WOULD WITH MY WICKED EYES, ...	206	LAMENT	9
WICKEDLY			
GUIDES AND BLOWS WICKEDLY, FOR LARKS	37	WINDMILLS TURN	7
WIDDERSHIN			
SHALL I STILL BE LOVE'S HOUSE ON THE WIDDERSHIN			
EARTH, ...	113	NOT FATHER ME	29
WIDE			
AND MAKE HIS WIDE MOUTH HOME.	17	IN OBLIVION	7
WITH WIDE, DRY MOUTHS AND EYES, ...	28	NO WINGS	14
WHEN HEAVEN--OPEN WIDE THE GATES--HAS TAKEN FLIGHT,	34	THIRST PARCHES	4
HER CONSTANT, NOR THE WINDS OF LOVE BROKEN WIDE ...	147	UNLUCKILY FOR	10
SINGLY LIE WITH THE WHOLE WIDE SHORE, ...	158	INTO HER HEAD	49
THE LOCKS YAWNED LOOSE AND A BLAST BLEW THEM WIDE,	172	DAWN RAID	3
IN THE LONG AGO LAND THAT GLIDED THE DARK DOOR WIDE	189	WINTER'S TALE	67
IN THE FAR AGO LAND THE DOOR OF HIS DEATH GLIDED WIDE	190	WINTER'S TALE	105
AND THE WINGS GLIDED WIDE AND HE WAS HYMNED AND			
WEDDED, ...	191	WINTER'S TALE	123
THROW WIDE TO THE WIND THE GATES OF THE WANDERING			
BOAT	194	SLEEP BECALMED	10
SHALL HARROW AND SNOW THE BLOOD WHILE YOU RIDE WIDE			
AND NEAR, ...	198	COUNTRY SLEEP	23
AND A WIDE SANITY	231	OUR SANCTITY	46
YOUR WIDE SMILE FOR ME.	238	MAKES INTERVALS	14
WIDOWER			
AND A TEAR-STAINED WIDOWER GRIEF DROOPED FROM THE			
LASHES	133	MAKE ME A MASK	9
WIDOWS			
FOUND MANAGERS AND WIDOWS WANTING	38	THE GOSSIPERS	11
GROOM THE DARK BRIDES, THE WIDOWS OF THE NIGHT	89	EUNUCH DREAMS	5
WIFE			
SO SOLVE THE MYSTIC SUN, THE WIFE OF LIGHT, ...	128	NOW, SAY NAY	26
THAT FROZEN WIFE WHOSE JUICES DRIFT LIKE A FIXED SEA	145	PLEASURE-BIRD	14
TO FIND A WOMAN'S SOUL FOR A WIFE.	207	LAMENT	48
FOR, OH, MY SOUL FOUND A SUNDAY WIFE	207	LAMENT	54
WIG			
THEN, BUSHILY SWANKED IN BEAR WIG AND TAILS, ...	151	BELOW A TIME	19
WILD			
HIS WILD CAROUSES, AND HIS LIPS	29	NEARLY SUMMER	10
TO FOLLOW, WILD AS THE CHICKEN STEALER, ...	44	TO FOLLOW FOX	3
THE WILD PIGS' WOOD, AND SLIME UPON THE TREES, ...	104	WORLD PYRAMID	20
WITH THE WILD BREAST AND BLESSED AND GIANT SKULL	136	AFTER FUNERAL	28
NOR EVER, AS THE WILD TONGUE BREAKS ITS TOMBS, ...	144	PLEASURE-BIRD	11
WITH WILD SEA FILLIES AND SOAKING BRIDLES	168	LONG-LEGGED	185
AND THE WILD BOYS INNOCENT AS STRAWBERRIES	172	THE HUNCHBACK	40
DOWN TO THE WILD, UMBRELLA'D, AND FRENCH LETTERED	179	NEW QUAY	15
THE WILD	180	VISION, PRAYER	16
AND THE WILD WINGS WERE RAISED	189	WINTER'S TALE	81
WILD MEN WHO CAUGHT AND SANG THE SUN IN FLIGHT, ...	208	NOT GO GENTLE	10
AND WISHBONES OF WILD GEESE, ...	210	POEM ON B'DAY	59
AND AIR SHAPED HEAVEN WHERE SOULS GROW WILD	210	POEM ON B'DAY	74
MIX THEIR WILD BLOOD	236	WOMAN TAPESTRY	57
WILDE			
WILDE WORDS, ALL BUTTERED, BADLY BRED, ...	143	THE MOLLS	10

	PAGE	TITLE	LINE
WILDERNESS			
IN THE WILDERNESS THEY GO,	71	TAKE NEEDLES	29
HERE IN MY WILDERNESS WANDERS THE BLOOD;	74	SUN BURNS	3
FROM A LOST WILDERNESS	153	WAS A SAVIOUR	10
OF THE GARDEN OF WILDERNESS.	175	FIRE RAID	60
SEEK HIM, THOU SUN, IN THE DREAD WILDERNESS,	222	MISSING	1
WILL			
DAYS' NIGHT WHOSE TOWERS WILL CATCH	3	PROLOGUE	20
THAT WILL FLY AND FALL	3	PROLOGUE	30
WE WILL RIDE OUT ALONE, AND THEN,	5	PROLOGUE	91
YOU SHALL NOT GO UNLESS I WILL IT	10	COOL, OH NO	21
WILL FIND SUCH LOVE AGAINST THE GRAIN,	16	TIME TO ROT	8
WILL CHILL THE ROUNDNESS OF HIS CHEEKS,	17	IN OBLIVION	6
THE CENTURY'S TRAP WILL HAVE SNAPPED ROUND YOUR MIDDLE,	38	GAS FADES	4
THE JAWS WILL HAVE SHUT, AND LIFE BE SWITCHED OUT.	39	GAS FADES	14
THE CENTURY'S TRAP WILL HAVE CLOSED FOR GOOD	39	GAS FADES	30
ABOUT YOU, FLESH WILL PERISH, AND BLOOD	39	GAS FADES	31
YOU WILL NOT SEE THE STEADYING OR FALLING,	39	GAS FADES	37
THROUGH HEATH AND HEATHER AT THE MIND'S WILL.	44	TO FOLLOW FOX	13
BUT LUNAR NIGHT WILL NOT GLOW IN MY BLACKNESS,	49	LIGHT, I KNOW	22
STARS' LIGHT AND SUN'S LIGHT WILL NOT SHINE	49	LIGHT, I KNOW	27
WILL ONLY DIM LIFE, AND LIGHT DEATH.	49	LIGHT, I KNOW	29
ONE DAY MY WOMAN'S BODY WILL BE COLD.	64	WOMAN SPEAKS	47
AND RAVEN YOUTH WILL FEAST BUT WHERE HE WILL.	64	WOMAN SPEAKS	51
AND RAVEN YOUTH WILL FEAST BUT WHERE HE WILL.	64	WOMAN SPEAKS	51
GOD AND I WILL PAY THE SNIPER.	71	TAKE NEEDLES	24
WILL BE BREATHING BY MY BED.	72	TAKE NEEDLES	48
AND I WILL BUILD MY LIQUID WORLD,	74	WE MOTHERNAKED	13
I LEARNT THE VERBS OF WILL, AND HAD MY SECRET;	79	LOVE'S FEVER	39
MY CAMEL'S EYES WILL NEEDLE THROUGH THE SHROUD.	118	ALTARWISE	52
THE FINGERS WILL FORGET GREEN THUMBS AND MARK	138	FIVE & COUNTRY	2
THE WHISPERING EARS WILL WATCH LOVE DRUMMED AWAY	138	FIVE & COUNTRY	6
IN ALL LOVE'S COUNTRIES, THAT WILL GROPE AWAKE;	139	FIVE & COUNTRY	12
THAT WILL RAKE AT LAST ALL CURRENCIES OF THE MARKED BREATH	140	NO WORK WORDS	8
WILL DIVE UP TO HIS TEARS.	160	DEATHS AND ENT	18
WILL PULL THE THUNDERBOLTS	161	DEATHS AND ENT	32
NO LONGER WILL THE VIBRATIONS OF THE SUN DESIRE ON	170	MARRIAGE VIRG	8
YET RAVES AT HER WILL	170	LOVE IN ASYLUM	14
THE ONE NOT CARING TO WHOM IN HIS SLEEP HE WILL MOVE	193	CONVERS PRAYER	4
AND THE OTHER FULL OF TEARS THAT SHE WILL BE DEAD,	193	CONVERS PRAYER	5
TURNS IN THE DARK ON THE SOUND THEY KNOW WILL ARISE	193	CONVERS PRAYER	6
WILL BE THE SAME GRIEF FLYING. WHOM SHALL THEY CALM?	194	CONVERS PRAYER	11
OF THE HOBNAIL TALES: NO GOOSEHERD OR SWINE WILL TURN	197	COUNTRY SLEEP	10
BE YOU SURE THE THIEF WILL SEEK A WAY SLY AND SURE	199	COUNTRY SLEEP	49
NAKED AND FORSAKEN TO GRIEVE HE WILL NOT COME.	201	COUNTRY SLEEP	106
TERROR WILL RAGE APART	210	POEM ON B'DAY	43
NOR WILL BE EVER IS ALWAYS TRUE,	210	POEM ON B'DAY	51
WHO KNOWS THE ROCKETING WIND WILL BLOW	210	POEM ON B'DAY	67
WILL NEVER NEVER GO OUT OF MY MIND.	217	ELEGY	20
UNTIL I DIE HE WILL NOT LEAVE MY SIDE.	217	ELEGY	40
SHED THOU THY TEARS ON HIM; HE WILL NOT WAKE,	222	MISSING	8
ALL THINGS REST IN THE WILL OF PURPOSE TRIUMPHANT.	222	FOREST PICTURE	8
WE WILL BE CONSCIOUS OF OUR SANCTITY	230	OUR SANCTITY	T
WE WILL BE CONSCIOUS OF OUR SANCTITY	230	OUR SANCTITY	1
WE WILL REMARK UPON THE SIZE	230	OUR SANCTITY	6
WE WILL BE CONSCIOUS OF OUR DIVINITY	230	OUR SANCTITY	15
WE WILL TIE YOU DOWN	230	OUR SANCTITY	19
THEN WILL WE RISE	231	OUR SANCTITY	32

		PAGE	TITLE	LINE
WILL (CONTINUED)				
WE WILL BE CONSCIOUS	....	231	OUR SANCTITY	42
WE WILL BE CONSCIOUS OF A GREAT DIVINITY	....	231	OUR SANCTITY	45
YOUR STEP WILL REMAIN ABOUT TO FALL.	....	232	FURIOUS MOTION	4
SO WILL YOUR VOICE VIBRATE	....	232	FURIOUS MOTION	5
SO, THEN, WILL THE DARK CLOTH OF YOUR HAIR	....	232	FURIOUS MOTION	7
THE LIGHT WILL COME IN AN UNWAVERING LINE.	....	232	YOUR VOICE	7
THE SCENT OF THE GREAT FLOWER WILL STAY,	....	232	FURIOUS MOTION	16
WILL YOU DRIFT INTO THE NET WILLINGLY,	....	233	NO THOUGHT	21
THERE WILL BE A NEW BITTERNESS	....	236	WOMAN TAPESTRY	61
THERE WILL BE A NEW LIFE	....	236	WOMAN TAPESTRY	66
YOU LOOSE, DELICIOUS WILL	....	237	PILLAR BREAKS	9
OR THROW A VIOLET SHADOW WHEN I WILL.	....	238	MAKES INTERVALS	8
AND I WILL BREAK YOUR PACING LIGHT.	....	239	MAKES INTERVALS	16
WILLING				
BOY SUCKS NO SWEETNESS FROM THE WILLING MOUTH,	....	19	THE NEOPHYTE	9
WILLING WORDS TO MAKE THE RUMOURS CERTAIN,	....	38	THE GOSSIPERS	2
AND THOUGH DOUBTFUL OF BISCUIT, I'M WILLING TO RISK IT,	....	221	SONG OF DOG	11
WILLINGLY				
WILL YOU DRIFT INTO THE NET WILLINGLY,	....	233	NO THOUGHT	21
WILLOW				
SORROW SHALL HAVE NO WORDS, NO WILLOW WEARING;	....	64	WOMAN SPEAKS	39
THROUGH THE LOUD ZOO OF THE WILLOW GROVES	....	171	THE HUNCHBACK	22
WILLOWS				
WHILE THE BOYS AMONG WILLOWS	....	171	THE HUNCHBACK	27
WILLY				
THE THIEF FALL ON THE DEAD LIKE THE WILLY NILLY DEW,		200	COUNTRY SLEEP	93
WILLYNILLY				
CAN'T READ SENSE IN THE RAIN THAT WILLYNILLY	....	137	O CHATTERTON	19
WILY				
THE WORD OF THE BLOOD, THE WILY SKIN,	....	61	MEAT ON BONES	15
WIN				
THE WITHERED WOMEN WIN THEM BEDFELLOWS.	....	38	THE GOSSIPERS	16
WIND				
IN THE RELIGIOUS WIND	....	3	PROLOGUE	21
WIND IS MY ENEMY YOUR HAIR SHANT STIR	....	11	AIR BREATHE	3
SO STEAL HER NOT O GOAT-LEGGED WIND	....	11	AIR BREATHE	7
BUT DO NOT TRAVEL DOWN DUMB WIND LIKE PRODIGALS.		16	SPIRE CRANES	11
FEELING THE WIND ABOUT OUR HEADS THAT DOES NOT COOL,		26	THERE'S PLENTY	18
WE MIGHT HAVE TRIED LIGHT MATCHES IN THE WIND.	....	34	IN GARDENS	16
NO DOUBT THE WIND ON WHICH THE ROOKS	....	37	WINDMILLS TURN	4
FOR THEN THE WRONG WIND CERTAINLY	....	37	WINDMILLS TURN	17
WOULD BE THE DEVIL'S WIND, AND THE HIGH TRINITY	...	37	WINDMILLS TURN	18
THE WIND HAS CHANGED, BLOWN INSIDE OUT	....	37	WINDMILLS TURN	27
MADE MEANING MEANINGLESS. THE WRONG WIND STIRS,	...	37	WINDMILLS TURN	29
THE CHANGED WIND BLOWS, AND THERE'S A CHOICE OF SIGNS		37	WINDMILLS TURN	31
WARMING DRY HANDS AND LISTENING TO THE WIND.	......	42	YOUNG ARE OLD	55
HUNG POINTED IN THE WIND,	....	43	FACES SHONE	9
WITH WOODEN ARMS REVOLVING IN THE WIND	....	45	PLOUGHMAN GONE	7
MIGHT PLAY UPON HIS LANK LOCKS WITH ITS WIND,	.....	46	POET: 1935	3
FEELING THE SUMMER WIND, HEARING THE SWANS,	....	48	POET: 1935	59
WHO ARE HIS FRIENDS? THE WIND IS HIS FRIEND,	......	48	POET: 1935	63
WITH THE MAN IN THE WIND AND THE WEST MOON;	....	49	NO DOMINION	3
FROM YOU OR ME OR WIND OR RAT	....	53	OUT OF THE PIT	103
A CALLING FOR COLOUR CALLS WITH THE WIND	....	54	WE BY SEASAND	6
WATCH YELLOW, WISH FOR WIND TO BLOW AWAY	....	54	WE BY SEASAND	19
WHY EAST WIND CHILLS	....	55	WHY EAST WIND	T
WHY EAST WIND CHILLS AND SOUTH WIND COOLS	....	55	WHY EAST WIND	1
WHY EAST WIND CHILLS AND SOUTH WIND COOLS	....	55	WHY EAST WIND	1

WIND

	PAGE	TITLE	LINE

WIND (CONTINUED)

	PAGE	TITLE	LINE
AND NO AEGEAN WIND COOL HER CRACKED HEART;	57	GREEK PLAY	10
THE WIND PASS LIKE A FIRE,	62	EARS IN TURRET	18
WITH THE WIND IN MY HAIR,	62	EARS IN TURRET	22
RAIN SHALL DEFILE AND COVER, WIND BEAR AWAY	64	WOMAN SPEAKS	40
WIND CARVEN LINES AROUND THE DROOPING MOUTH;	64	WOMAN SPEAKS	50
THE WIND SMACKS OF THE POOR	67	REALM OF FLESH	5
AND THE WIND WAS MY SISTER SUITOR;	68	BEFORE KNOCKED	15
WIND IN ME LEAPED, THE HELLBORN DEW;	68	BEFORE KNOCKED	16
WE SEE RISE THE SECRET WIND	69	SECRET WIND	T
WE SEE RISE THE SECRET WIND BEHIND THE BRAIN,	69	SECRET WIND	1
WE HEAR RISE THE SECRET WIND BEHIND THE BRAIN,	70	SECRET WIND	19
THE BEACH OF FLESH, AND WIND HER BLOODRED PLAIT;	75	MY HERO BARES	13
STIRS THE QUICKSAND; THAT ROPES THE BLOWING WIND	77	THE FORCE THAT	12
AND I AM DUMB TO TELL A WEATHER'S WIND	77	THE FORCE THAT	19
ITCHED IN THE NOISE OF WIND AND SUN.	79	LOVE'S FEVER	30
THE WIND OF KISSES SEALED A PACT	85	SEE, SAYS LIME	10
THAT LEAPING VEINS THREW TO THE WIND	85	SEE, SAYS LIME	11
MAN IN THE DAY OR WIND AT NIGHT	86	BREAD I BREAK	4
THE OAT WAS MERRY IN THE WIND;	86	BREAD I BREAK	9
MAN BROKE THE SUN, PULLED THE WIND DOWN.	86	BREAD I BREAK	10
SLOW IN A SLEEPING WIND.	88	A PROCESS IN	15
PUSHED UP THEIR HAIR, THE DRY WIND STEERS	90	WHERE ONCE THE	5
ESPECIALLY WHEN THE OCTOBER WIND	98	OCTOBER WIND	T
ESPECIALLY WHEN THE OCTOBER WIND	98	OCTOBER WIND	1
ESPECIALLY WHEN THE OCTOBER WIND	99	OCTOBER WIND	25
(HAVE WITH THE HOUSE OF WIND), THE LEANING SCENE,	101	RUNNING GRAVE	42
ALL, MEN MY MADMEN, THE UNWHOLESOME WIND	101	RUNNING GRAVE	46
IN THE STITCHED WOUND AND CLOTTED WIND, MUZZLED	103	I DREAMED MY	15
LEAN TIME ON TIDE AND TIMES THE WIND STOOD ROUGH,	107	GRIEF THIEF	6
I, IN A WIND ON FIRE, FROM GREEN ADAM'S CRADLE,	111	I, IN IMAGE	95
HELL WIND AND SEA,	114	A GRIEF AGO	4
THE TWELVE TRIANGLES OF THE CHERUB WIND	115	A GRIEF AGO	23
WHOSE BEARD WAGS IN EGYPTIAN WIND.	116	LANTERNS SHINE	15
WHICH SIXTH OF WIND BLEW OUT THE BURNING GENTRY?	118	ALTARWISE	47
SHOT IN THE WIND, BY TILTED ARCS,	129	MY NEOPHYTE	26
WHERE, WOUND IN EMERALD LINEN AND SHARP WIND,	132	I MAKE THIS IN	42
THESE ONCE-BLIND EYES HAVE BREATHED A WIND OF VISIONS,	132	I MAKE THIS IN	54
A CALM WIND BLOWS THAT RAISED THE TREES LIKE HAIR	133	I MAKE THIS IN	64
IN A WIND THAT PLUCKED A GOOSE,	144	PLEASURE-BIRD	10
AND EVERY STONE I WIND OFF LIKE A REEL.	144	COLOUR OF SAY	13
TO THE WIND THE CHOIR AND CLOISTER	147	UNLUCKILY FOR	11
AND WIND HIS GLOBE OUT OF YOUR WATER THREAD	160	DEATHS AND ENT	21
SAILS DRANK THE WIND, AND WHITE AS MILK	162	LONG-LEGGED	13
A WIND THROWS A SHADOW AND IT FREEZES FAST.	166	LONG-LEGGED	130
WHEN HIS LONG-LEGGED FLESH WAS A WIND ON FIRE	168	LONG-LEGGED	195
WIND BLOW COLD	177	POEM IN OCT	29
BUT ONLY THE WIND STRUNG	188	WINTER'S TALE	41
PARISH OF SNOW. THE CARVED MOUTHS IN THE ROCK ARE WIND SWEPT STRINGS.	189	WINTER'S TALE	64
HIM UP AND HE RAN LIKE A WIND AFTER THE KINDLING FLIGHT	190	WINTER'S TALE	89
THE VOICES OF ALL THE DROWNED SWAM ON THE WIND.	194	SLEEP BECALMED	8
THROW WIDE TO THE WIND THE GATES OF THE WANDERING BOAT	194	SLEEP BECALMED	10
WHO COMES AS RED AS THE FOX AND SLY AS THE HEELED WIND.	200	COUNTRY SLEEP	81
IN A WHACK OF WIND.	202	SIR JOHNS HILL	17
HIS DRIFTWOOD THIRTY-FIFTH WIND TURNED AGE;	208	POEM ON B'DAY	8

	PAGE	TITLE	LINE
WIND (CONTINUED)			
WHO KNOWS THE ROCKETING WIND WILL BLOW	210	POEM ON B'DAY	67
LIGHTLY, THOU WIND, OVER HIS DEAR, DARK HEAD, ...	222	MISSING	4
TO THE VOICES OF THE WIND CAUGHT IN THE			
CRADLE-PETALS OF THE NIGHT:	223	IDYLL UNFORGET	8
I HAVE FELT THE SILK WIND BRUSH MY LIPS;	224	IDYLL UNFORGET	19
AND CHANGED WITH THE WIND INTO INDISTINCT PATTERNS			
OF FROLIC, ...	224	IDYLL UNFORGET	29
TO A SLENDER WIND	225	SLENDER WIND	T
THAT WHISPERED WITH THE WIND AND WEPT, ...	227	SPRING-SPIRIT	6
THE WIND CANNOT BLUNT	229	MY RIVER	15
BE FREE, (WIND FOR MY TREE AND WATER FOR MY FLOWER),	239	LET ME ESCAPE	2
WIND-			
THROUGH THE HAYGOLD STALLS, AS THE DEW FALLS ON THE			
WIND-	199	COUNTRY SLEEP	58
WINDER			
THE WINDER OF THE WATER-CLOCKS	128	MY NEOPHYTE	5
THE WINDER OF THE CLOCKWISE SCENE	129	MY NEOPHYTE	32
WINDFALL			
DOWN THE RIVERS OF THE WINDFALL LIGHT.	195	FERN HILL	9
WIND-HEELED			
WIND-HEELED FOOT IN THE HOLE OF A FIREBALL, ...	141	SAINT TO FALL	12
WINDILY			
THEY LYING LONG SHALL NOT DIE WINDILY;	49	NO DOMINION	12
WINDILY MASTER OF MAN WAS THE ROTTEN FATHOM, ...	112	I, IN IMAGE	104
AND WHEN THE MOON ROSE WINDILY IT WAS	121	INCARNATE DEVL	11
WINDING			
THIS DAY WINDING DOWN NOW	3	PROLOGUE	1
THE WORLD WINDING HOME!	182	VISION, PRAYER	97
INTO THE WINDING DARK	192	SIDE OF TRUTH	11
WINDING-FOOTED			
AND, WINDING-FOOTED IN THEIR SHAWL AND SHEET, ...	89	EUNUCH DREAMS	4
WINDINGS			
UNDER THE WINDINGS OF THE SEA	49	NO DOMINION	11
WINDING-SHEETS			
DISTURB NO WINDING-SHEETS, MY SON, ...	60	MEAT ON BONES	6
WINDLESS			
GLIDING WINDLESS THROUGH THE HAND FOLDED FLAKES,	187	WINTER'S TALE	4
PAST THE BLIND BARNS AND BYRES OF THE WINDLESS FARM.	190	WINTER'S TALE	90
WINDMILL			
AN AIR-DRAWN WINDMILL ON A WOODEN HORSE, ...	124	TODAY, INSECT	20
WINDMILLS			
WITH WINDMILLS TURNING WRONG DIRECTIONS	36	WINDMILLS TURN	T
WITH WINDMILLS TURNING WRONG DIRECTIONS, ...	36	WINDMILLS TURN	1
THE WINDMILLS OF THE WORLD STILL STAND	45	PLOUGHMAN GONE	6
WINDOW			
THAT STOOD BEFORE MY WINDOW, ...	33	HELD-OUT HAND	13
IS CARVED FROM HER IN A ROOM WITH A WET WINDOW	136	AFTER FUNERAL	29
I SIT AT THE OPEN WINDOW, OBSERVING	179	NEW QUAY	13
WINDOWS			
LEANING FROM WINDOWS OVER A LENGTH OF LAWNS, ...	48	POET: 1935	60
ADORE MY WINDOWS FOR THEIR SUMMER SCENE?	112	NOT FATHER ME	8
THE WINDOWS POUR INTO THEIR HEART	161	WEDDING ANNIV	11
IN THE PRAYING WINDOWS OF WAVES	162	LONG-LEGGED	28
WHO UNDER THE LIDS OF HER WINDOWS HOISTED HIS GOLDEN			
LUGGAGE, ...	170	MARRIAGE VIRG	12
NOW THE HERON GRIEVES IN THE WEEDED VERGE. THROUGH			
WINDOWS	202	SIR JOHNS HILL	47
WINDS			
IN WINDS THAT BRING THE FRUIT AND RIND	55	WHY EAST WIND	4

		PAGE	TITLE	LINE
WINDS (CONTINUED)				
CALLS SOME CONTENT TO TRAVEL WITH THE WINDS,	....	56	WHY EAST WIND	17
THE MOTHER'S CRY HAS FUMED ABOUT THE WINDS;	....	64	WOMAN SPEAKS	53
O TIDAL WINDS, CAST UP HER CRY FOR ME;	....	65	WOMAN SPEAKS	54
AND THE FOUR WINDS, THAT HAD LONG BLOWN AS ONE,	...	78	LOVE'S FEVER	19
BLOOD SHOT AND SCATTERED TO THE WINDS OF LIGHT	....	94	IN BEGINNING	29
TWELVE WINDS ENCOUNTER BY THE WHITE HOST AT PASTURE,		109	I, IN IMAGE	38
WITH BONES UNBUTTONED TO THE HALF-WAY WINDS,	....	117	ALTARWISE	9
NOR WEATHER WINDS THAT BLOW NOT DOWN THE BONE,	....	123	FOSTER LIGHT	2
BY MAGNET WINDS TO HER BLIND MOTHER DRAWN,	....	131	I MAKE THIS IN	14
HER CONSTANT, NOR THE WINDS OF LOVE BROKEN WIDE	...	147	UNLUCKILY FOR	10
AND THE FISHERMAN WINDS HIS REEL	....	166	LONG-LEGGED	123
AND SPELLS ON THE WINDS OF THE DEAD HIS WINTER'S				
TALE.	....	189	WINTER'S TALE	59
WINDS, FROM THE DOUSING SHADE AND THE ROARER AT THE				
LATCH,	....	199	COUNTRY SLEEP	46
HEELED WINDS THE ROOKS	....	199	COUNTRY SLEEP	67
AND THE WINDS THAT STREAM THROUGH THE RIBBONED LIGHT		227	THE PINE	3
AND THE MOTLEY WINDS FROM THE SEAS.	....	227	THE PINE	4
WINDS'				
WHO HAVE NO VOICES BUT THE WINDS'	....	22	ON QUIET NIGHT	2
UNDER THE HANGING BRANCHES HEAR THE WINDS' HARPS.		46	POET: 1935	15
IN THE WINDS' WAKES.	....	200	COUNTRY SLEEP	85
WINDSHAKE				
WINDSHAKE OF SAILSHAPED EARS, MUFFLE-TOED TAP	.....	136	AFTER FUNERAL	2
WIND-TURNED				
DOOM ON DENIERS AT THE WIND-TURNED STATEMENT.	.....	119	ALTARWISE	90
WINDWELL				
SHALL NOT BE KNOWN TILL WINDWELL DRIES	....	55	WHY EAST WIND	2
WINDY				
BE GUILTLESS OF THE WINDY WRONGS.	....	37	WINDMILLS TURN	19
ALL WORLD WAS ONE, ONE WINDY NOTHING,	....	78	LOVE'S FEVER	6
FROM POLES OF SKULL AND TOE THE WINDY BLOOD	....	82	LIGHT BREAKS	14
AND TELLS THE WINDY WEATHER IN THE COCK.	....	99	OCTOBER WIND	20
A QUARREL OF WEATHERS AND TREES IN THE WINDY SPIRAL.		110	I, IN IMAGE	42
WOE TO THE WINDY MASONS AT MY SHELTER?	....	113	NOT FATHER ME	30
HATCHED FROM THE WINDY SALVAGE ON ONE LEG,	....	117	ALTARWISE	10
AND FROM THE WINDY WEST CAME TWO-GUNNED GABRIEL,	...	118	ALTARWISE	57
WHEN I WAS A WINDY BOY AND A BIT	....	205	LAMENT	1
WINE				
THERE'S POISON IN YOUR RED WINE, DRINKER,	....	27	OBLIVIOUS DARK	14
THIS WINE UPON A FOREIGN TREE	....	86	BREAD I BREAK	2
ONCE IN THIS WINE THE SUMMER BLOOD	....	86	BREAD I BREAK	6
MY WINE YOU DRINK, MY BREAD YOU SNAP.	....	86	BREAD I BREAK	15
INTO THE WINE BURNING LIKE BRANDY,	....	175	FIRE RAID	71
WINE-WELLS				
ON THE LAST RICK'S TIP BY SPILLED WINE-WELLS	....	141	SAINT TO FALL	14
WING				
WHICH IS THE METAL WING	....	12	CABARET	24
PIERCE THE SPILT SKY WITH DIVING WING IN WEED AND				
HEEL	....	15	SPIRE CRANES	4
THE FLYING LOOSE, ALBINO EYED, WING SINGED,	....	41	YOUNG ARE OLD	38
HE STEPS SO NEAR THE WATER THAT A SWAN'S WING	.....	46	POET: 1935	2
OUT OF A BIRD'S WING WRITING ON A CLOUD	....	48	POET: 1935	53
CYCLONE OF HIS WING	....	181	VISION, PRAYER	56
WING, AND BLEST SHALL	....	202	SIR JOHNS HILL	29
THEY TO MY BLOSSOMS WING THEIR WAY,	....	228	TRIOLET	5
ON THE SAIL OF EACH SLIGHT WING	....	233	NO THOUGHT	18
TO WING MY SHOULDERS AND MY FEET?	....	234	NO, PIGEON	6

	PAGE	TITLE	LINE
WINGBEAT			
MUTTER AND FOUL WINGBEAT OF THE SOLEMNIZING NIGHTPRIEST	158	INTO HER HEAD	45
WINGED			
THE CAUGHT IN THE CAGE, THE BROKEN WINGED, ...	41	YOUNG ARE OLD	37
SO SHALL WINGED HARBOURS THROUGH THE ROCKBIRDS' EYES	121	ALTARWISE	130
WINGED LIKE A SABBATH ASS THIS CHILDREN'S PIECE ...	124	TODAY, INSECT	16
NOT YOUR WINGED LUST BUT HIS MUST NOW CHANGE SUIT.	159	TO LEDA	1
NOT YOUR WINGED LUST BUT HIS MUST NOW CHANGE SUIT.	159	TO LEDA	6
BIRDS AND THE BIRDS OF THE WINGED TREES FLYING MY NAME	177	POEM IN OCT	12
AND THE WINGED WALL IS TORN	180	VISION, PRAYER	29
IN HIS FIRELIT ISLAND RINGED BY THE WINGED SNOW ...	187	WINTER'S TALE	17
OF THE MORNING LEAVES, AS THE STAR FALLS, AS THE WINGED	199	COUNTRY SLEEP	60
BURNING! NIGHT AND THE VEIN OF BIRDS IN THE WINGED, SLOE WRIST	199	COUNTRY SLEEP	70
WINGING			
THE WINGING BONE THAT SPROUTED IN THE HEELS, ...	95	RUB OF LOVE	11
WINGS			
WHO HOLDS HER CLASPED INSIDE HIS STRONG, WHITE WINGS;	15	FOR LEDA	31
CHILDREN OF DARKNESS GOT NO WINGS	28	NO WINGS	T
CHILDREN OF DARKNESS GOT NO WINGS, ...	28	NO WINGS	1
THIS WE KNOW WE GOT NO WINGS, ...	28	NO WINGS	2
CHILDREN OF DARKNESS GOT NO WINGS, ...	28	NO WINGS	23
THIS WE KNOW, WE GOT NO WINGS, ...	28	NO WINGS	24
NOISELESSLY INTO A WORLD OF WINGS AND CRIES.	31	BEING BUT MEN	5
THE ANGELS' WINGS BEATING ABOUT YOUR HEAD	33	HELD-OUT HAND	4
AND ON HIS SHOULDERS FALL THEIR WORLD OF WINGS, ...	63	WOMAN SPEAKS	22
SWEET ARE THEIR FATHERED FACES IN THEIR WINGS.' ...	102	FELLOWED SLEEP	14
ON THE OLD SEAS FROM STORIES, THRASHING MY WINGS,	152	BELOW A TIME	36
HER LOVER'S WINGS THAT FOLD TO-MORROW'S FLIGHT, ...	159	INTO HER HEAD	57
AS THE BOAT SKIMS ON WITH DRINKING WINGS!	166	LONG-LEGGED	134
THE MORNING IS FLYING ON THE WINGS OF HIS AGE	173	DAWN RAID	13
WINGS. IT WOULD BE BETTER IF THE SHUTTERS IS	179	NEW QUAY	6
O THE WINGS OF THE CHILDREN!	182	VISION, PRAYER	91
DUST IN THE BURIED WOOD, FLIES ON THE GRAINS OF HER WINGS	189	WINTER'S TALE	58
AND THE WILD WINGS WERE RAISED	189	WINTER'S TALE	81
IN A CHOIR OF WINGS, AS THOUGH SHE SLEPT OR DIED,	191	WINTER'S TALE	122
AND THE WINGS GLIDED WIDE AND HE WAS HYMNED AND WEDDED, ...	191	WINTER'S TALE	123
AND THE WINGS OF THE GREAT ROC RIBBONED FOR THE FAIR!	199	COUNTRY SLEEP	65
TROUNCED BY HIS WINGS IN THE HISSING SHIPPEN, LONG DEAD	205	GIANT'S THIGH	39
MODESTY HIDES MY THIGHS IN HER WINGS, ...	207	LAMENT	59
WHERE NOW THE WINGS OF DREAMLESS SLEEP ARE SPREAD,	222	MISSING	5
RISING ON BLACK WINGS.	229	MY RIVER	33
UPON BROAD WINGS	231	OUR SANCTITY	33
WADING THROUGH HER DARK CAVE ON FEROCIOUS WINGS.	232	YOUR VOICE	9
UNDER THE TENT OF ITS WINGS.	237	WOMAN TAPESTRY	74
AND, THERE, WHAT WINGS THEY HAD, ...	238	PILLAR BREAKS	15
DROP ONTO YOUR WINGS, ...	240	ADMIT THE SUN	7
WINKING-BIT			
IS MR. JONES THE CAKE, THAT WINKING-BIT, ...	179	NEW QUAY	20
WINKLE			
AND, RIP VAN WINKLE FROM A TIMELESS-CRADLE, ...	118	ALTARWISE	37
WINNING			
YOU MY FRIEND THERE WITH A WINNING AIR	146	TO OTHERS	3

	PAGE	TITLE	LINE
WINTER			
AND WINTER FOLLOW LIKE AN ECHO	15	FOR LEDA	24
TO THE BUILT VOICE, OR FLY WITH WINTER TO THE BELLS,	16	SPIRE CRANES	10
OVER THE ANCIENT WINTER, ...	17	IN OBLIVION	4
PLANNING WHAT'S GOOD, THOUGH IT'S BUT WINTER, ...	27	OBLIVIOUS DARK	29
NO FROSTY GALLOPS THROUGH THE WINTER PARK.	41	YOUNG ARE OLD	16
INTO THE BROWNS OF AUTUMN AND THE SHARP WHITES OF WINTER, ...	47	POET: 1935	20
HERE IN THIS ORNAMENTAL WINTER	58	HERE IN SPRING	2
I KNEW THE MESSAGE OF THE WINTER, ...	68	BEFORE KNOCKED	13
THE WINTER YEARS, MOVE IN THE PIT OF MAN;	79	ALMANAC TIME	3
THERE IN THEIR HEAT THE WINTER FLOODS	91	BOYS OF SUMMER	4
THE SLEEPY MAN OF WINTER PULLS, ...	92	BOYS OF SUMMER	29
HEARING THE RAVEN COUGH IN WINTER STICKS, ...	98	OCTOBER WIND	6
BREAKS WITH THE WORMY WINTER THROUGH THE EYE.	99	OCTOBER WIND	23
THE BLACK RAM, SHUFFLING OF THE YEAR, OLD WINTER,	118	ALTARWISE	39
FROM BLANK AND LEAKING WINTER SAILS THE CHILD IN COLOUR, ...	130	SINNERS' BELL	22
HILL. WHO ONCE IN GOOSESKIN WINTER LOVED ALL ICE LEAVED	203	GIANT'S THIGH	12
WINTERED			
LOVE IN THE FROST IS PARED AND WINTERED BY, ...	138	FIVE & COUNTRY	5
WINTER-LOCKED			
WINTER-LOCKED SIDE BY SIDE, ...	153	WAS A SAVIOUR	26
WINTER'S			
TELL, IF AT ALL, THE WINTER'S STORMS	58	HERE IN SPRING	10
THE WINTER'S ROBES;	82	LIGHT BREAKS	23
A WINTER'S TALE	187	WINTER'S TALE	T
IT IS A WINTER'S TALE	187	WINTER'S TALE	1
AND SPELLS ON THE WINDS OF THE DEAD HIS WINTER'S TALE.	189	WINTER'S TALE	59
WINTRY			
MY YOUTH IS BENT BY THE SAME WINTRY FEVER.	77	THE FORCE THAT	5
OF THE WINTRY NUNNERY OF THE ORDER OF LUST	147	UNLUCKILY FOR	12
WINY			
HIS WINY SKY, AND, AS THE CANDLE'S MOON, ...	80	ALL THAT I OWE	14
WIPE			
WIPE IT AWAY, WIPE A CRUMB	138	O CHATTERTON	38
WIPE IT AWAY, WIPE A CRUMB	138	O CHATTERTON	38
WIPES			
THAT WIPES AWAY NOT CROW'S-FOOT NOR THE LOCK	95	RUB OF LOVE	23
WIRE			
HE HOLDS THE WIRE FROM THIS BOX OF NERVES	75	MY HERO BARES	16
WIRED			
AND THESE POOR NERVES SO WIRED TO THE SKULL	75	MY HERO BARES	6
WIRELESS			
THE WIRELESS SNARLS ON THE HEARTH.	45	PLOUGHMAN GONE	12
WIRES			
BECAUSE THE PLEASURE-BIRD WHISTLES AFTER THE HOT WIRES, ...	144	PLEASURE-BIRD	1
WISDOM			
WISDOM IS FOLLY, LOVE IS NOT, ...	25	BEAUTY TO DUST	8
SENSE CAN BUT MAIM IT, WISDOM MAR IT, ...	25	BEAUTY TO DUST	9
WHEN WISDOM LAY NOT IN THE SOUL	25	BEAUTY TO DUST	12
WISDOM IS STORED WITH THE CLOVE	240	ADMIT THE SUN	10
WISE			
COME WISE IN FOOLISHNESS, ...	25	BEAUTY TO DUST	16
HE WHOSE LOVERS WERE BOTH WISE AND SENSIBLE	25	BEAUTY TO DUST	18
HE SHALL BE WISE AND LET HIS BRIMSTONE SPILL, ...	73	LORD RED HAIL	3
WAS MUSCLED, MATTED, WISE TO THE CRYING THIGH	78	LOVE'S FEVER	28

	PAGE	TITLE	LINE
WISE (CONTINUED)			
SLEEP, GOOD, FOR EVER, SLOW AND DEEP, SPELLED RARE			
AND WISE,	197	COUNTRY SLEEP	8
THOUGH WISE MEN AT THEIR END KNOW DARK IS RIGHT,	208	NOT GO GENTLE	4
NO, PIGEON, I'M TOO WISE	234	NO, PIGEON	T
NO, PIGEON, I'M TOO WISE;	234	NO, PIGEON	1
WHOSE MINUTE KINDLES MORE THAN THE WISE HOUR.	237	PILLAR BREAKS	11
WISECRACKS			
NONSTOP; STOPPRESS; VINEGAR FROM WISECRACKS;	57	TO ARCHITECTS	3
WISELY			
WISELY AT THE DOGS' TAILS, LEADS	44	TO FOLLOW FOX	15
WISEMEN			
THE WISEMEN TELL ME THAT THE GARDEN GODS	121	INCARNATE DEVL	9
WISER			
CALL FOR CONFESSOR AND WISER MIRROR BUT THERE IS NONE	186	HOLY SPRING	10
OUR TEARS SOUND WISER	230	OUR SANCTITY	12
WISH			
GO IS MY WISH;	9	MINUTE'S HOUR	18
YOU WISH TO STAY MY PRISONER	10	COOL, OH NO	27
I WISH TO KNOW	12	SKY'S BRIGHT	10
WATCH YELLOW, WISH FOR WIND TO BLOW AWAY	54	WE BY SEASAND	19
AND THE WICKED WISH,	193	SIDE OF TRUTH	29
WISHBONES			
AND WISHBONES OF WILD GEESE,	210	POEM ON B'DAY	59
WISHES			
WHO ON HIS CLOUD HEARS ALL MY WISHES,	48	LIGHT, I KNOW	15
BUT WISHES BREED NOT, NEITHER	54	WE BY SEASAND	21
PRISONERS OF WISHES LOCKED THEIR EYES	153	WAS A SAVIOUR	7
WALKING IN WISHES AND LOVELY FOR SHAME	165	LONG-LEGGED	105
THE SINGING BREAKS IN THE SNOW SHOED VILLAGES OF			
WISHES	190	WINTER'S TALE	113
MY WISHES RACED THROUGH THE HOUSE HIGH HAY	196	FERN HILL	41
WISPS			
IN THE WAINS TONNED SO HIGH THAT THE WISPS OF THE HAY	204	GIANT'S THIGH	14
WIT			
NO WIT, IS ONE),	24	LITTLE PROBLEM	7
AND KNOW WHY KNOW, NO WIT,	24	LITTLE PROBLEM	20
WITCH			
A PAPER WITCH UPON HER SULPHURED BROOM	16	TIME TO ROT	11
ADAM, TIME'S JOKER, ON A WITCH OF CARDBOARD	119	ALTARWISE	81
WITCHILIKE			
CRY JOY THAT THIS WITCHILIKE MIDWIFE SECOND	142	SAINT TO FALL	48
WITCH'S			
FROM THE BROOMED WITCH'S SPUME YOU ARE SHIELDED BY			
FERN	198	COUNTRY SLEEP	17
WITH (386)			
WITHER			
THAT RISES AND THEN FALLS, BUDS BUT TO WITHER;	25	THERE'S PLENTY	3
THE SOLID WORLD SHALL WITHER IN THE HEAT,	73	LORD RED HAIL	17
WOULD WITHER UP, AND ANY BOY OF LOVE	116	LANTERNS SHINE	3
OF NIGHTINGALE AND CENTAUR DEAD HORSE. THE SPRINGS			
WITHER	191	WINTER'S TALE	117
WITHERED			
THE WITHERED WOMEN WIN THEM BEDFELLOWS.	38	THE GOSSIPERS	16
MY LIPS ARE WITHERED WITH A KISS,	61	MEAT ON BONES	20
THE VOICE OF THE DUST OF WATER FROM THE WITHERED			
SPRING	189	WINTER'S TALE	60
WITHIN			
I WANT REALITY TO HOLD/ WITHIN MY PALM,	9	MINUTE'S HOUR	14
ALIVE WITHIN HIS CRANING THROAT--	14	FOR LEDA	7

		PAGE	TITLE	LINE
WITHIN (CONTINUED)				
WITHIN HER WOMB,	....	26	PERSONAL EPIT	10
MAKE DISCORD WITH THE VOICE WITHIN HIS RIBS	....	46	POET: 1935	5
WITHIN HIS HEAD REVOLVED A LITTLE WORLD	....	50	OUT OF THE PIT	1
WITHIN HIS HEAD THE ENGINES MADE THEIR HELL,	....	50	OUT OF THE PIT	6
AND LUSTRELESS WITHIN THE RUINED FACE	....	63	WOMAN SPEAKS	9
WITHIN THE HALLOWED GLAND, BLOOD BLESSED THE HEART,		78	LOVE'S FEVER	18
WITHIN THE NESTED TREEFORK	....	159	INTO HER HEAD	58
BRETHREN FOR JOY HAS MOVED WITHIN	....	183	VISION, PRAYER	117
FOR HER WHO WALKS WITHIN HER GARDEN-CLOSE.	....	223	IN DREAMS	7
WITHOUT				
THAT'S NOT WITHOUT ITS WOE,	....	23	THE ONLY DEAD	27
AND NOT WITHOUT DIVINITY,	....	24	THE ONLY DEAD	28
AND CANNOT MOUNT A CLOTHESHORSE WITHOUT BLEEDING.		40	YOUNG ARE OLD	10
SHADE WITHOUT SHAPE? THE SHAPE OF PHARAOH'S ECHO?		118	ALTARWISE	45
I MAY WITHOUT FAIL	....	170	LOVE IN ASYLUM	17
A WOMAN FIGURE WITHOUT FAULT	....	172	THE HUNCHBACK	32
MY DEAR THIS NIGHT HE COMES AND NIGHT WITHOUT END MY DEAR	....	201	COUNTRY SLEEP	108
LAST SOUND, THE WORLD GOING OUT WITHOUT A BREATH:		217	ELEGY	34
WIT-HURT				
LIFT WIT-HURT HEAD FOR SUN TO SYMPATHIZE,	....	42	A WAR OF WITS	18
WITNESS				
AND BY THIS BLOWCLOCK WITNESS OF THE SUN	....	120	ALTARWISE	111
WITNESSED				
WITNESSED WITH A KISS.	....	163	LONG-LEGGED	48
WITNESSES				
OF HEAD AND TAIL MADE WITNESSES TO THIS	....	124	TODAY, INSECT	7
MY ONE AND NOBLE HEART HAS WITNESSES	....	139	FIVE & COUNTRY	11
WITS				
NO FAITH TO SHARPEN THE OLD WITS LEAVES US	....	41	YOUNG ARE OLD	21
OUT OF A WAR OF WITS	....	42	A WAR OF WITS	T
OUT OF A WAR OF WITS, WHEN FOLLY OF WORDS	....	42	A WAR OF WITS	1
PRAISE THAT ONLY THE WITS ARE HURT AFTER THE WITS' FIGHT.	....	42	A WAR OF WITS	11
WHISPER IN A DAMP WORD, HER WITS DRILLED HOLLOW,		137	AFTER FUNERAL	33
WITS'				
TO PURGE AFTER THE WITS' FIGHT,	....	42	A WAR OF WITS	6
PRAISE THAT ONLY THE WITS ARE HURT AFTER THE WITS' FIGHT.	....	42	A WAR OF WITS	11
WIVES				
THEIR WIVES OR MOTHERS MINUS HIPS).	....	83	LETTER TO AUNT	22
OLD WIVES THAT SPIN IN THE SMOKE,	....	162	LONG-LEGGED	26
THE LONG-LEGGED BEAUTIFUL BAIT THEIR WIVES.	....	164	LONG-LEGGED	70
THEY WITH THE SIMPLE JACKS WERE A BOULDER OF WIVES)--		205	GIANT'S THIGH	44
ALL THE GREEN LEAVED LITTLE WEDDINGS' WIVES	....	206	LAMENT	11
WIVING				
FLARED IN THE REEK OF THE WIVING STY WITH THE RUSH		204	GIANT'S THIGH	22
WIZARD				
WHOSE WIZARD SHAPE I TRACE IN THE CAVERNOUS SKULL,		134	HOW MY ANIMAL	2
WIZARD'S				
BUT RAIL WITH YOUR WIZARD'S RIBS THE HEART-SHAPED PLANET;	....	123	FOSTER LIGHT	15
WIZENED				
IS TELLING. THE WIZENED	....	189	WINTER'S TALE	61
WOE				
AGAPE, WITH WOE	....	4	PROLOGUE	65
THAT'S NOT WITHOUT ITS WOE,	....	23	THE ONLY DEAD	27
AND KNOWS NO WOE THAT THESE SAD PLAYERS MOUTH	.....	57	GREEK PLAY	30
WOE FROM THE RABBLE OF THE BLIND	....	70	SECRET WIND	8

	PAGE	TITLE	LINE
WOE (CONTINUED)			
WOE TO THE WINDY MASONS AT MY SHELTER?	113	NOT FATHER ME	30
WOE DRIP FROM THE DISHRAG HANDS AND THE PRESSED			
SPONGE OF THE FOREHEAD, ...	142	SAINT TO FALL	45
FROM THE COUNTRY EYES, SALT AND SUN, STAR AND WOE	215	COUNTRY HEAVEN	13
WOEBEGONE			
OUT OF THE WOEBEGONE PYRE	186	HOLY SPRING	16
WOKE			
WHEN I WOKE	150	WHEN I WOKE	T
WHEN I WOKE, THE TOWN SPOKE.	150	WHEN I WOKE	1
WOKE TO MY HEARING FROM HARBOUR AND NEIGHBOUR WOOD	176	POEM IN OCT	2
WOKEN			
SHAKES, IN CRABBED BURIAL SHAWL, BY SORCERER'S			
INSECT WOKEN, ...	130	SINNERS' BELL	23
AND ALL THE WOKEN FARM AT ITS WHITE TRADES, ...	187	WINTER'S TALE	25
WOLF			
FEAR OR BELIEVE THAT THE WOLF IN A SHEEPWHITE HOOD	197	COUNTRY SLEEP	3
FOR EVER OF ALL NOT THE WOLF IN HIS BAAING HOOD ...	198	COUNTRY SLEEP	36
WOLVES			
TO HIDE THE WOLVES OF SLEEP	176	BREATH SHED	11
WOMAN			
ONE SAYS: THERE WAS A WOMAN WITH NO FRIEND, ...	22	ON QUIET NIGHT	8
A COMIC HOUR TO AN END THROUGH WANT OF WOMAN	23	THE ONLY DEAD	8
THROUGH NO REGRET OF LEAVING WOMAN WAITING	32	OUT OF SIGHS	14
YOU CAPTURE MORE THAN MAN OR WOMAN GUESSES;	48	POET: 1935	54
A WOMAN WAILS HER DEAD AMONG THE TREES, ...	56	GREEK PLAY	1
THE WOMAN SPEAKS	63	WOMAN SPEAKS	T
THE WOMAN SPEAKS:	63	WOMAN SPEAKS	1
DEATH FROM A SUMMER WOMAN, ...	92	BOYS OF SUMMER	32
THE BOY OF WOMAN AND THE WANTON STARER	112	NOT FATHER ME	10
WITH PINS FOR TEARDROPS IS THE LONG WOUND'S WOMAN.	120	ALTARWISE	104
THE SMILING WOMAN IS A MAD STORY, ...	138	O CHATTERTON	37
I OFFER YOU WOMEN, NOT WOMAN, ...	138	O CHATTERTON	40
AND FOR THE WOMAN IN SHADES	147	UNLUCKILY FOR	4
A WOMAN FIGURE WITHOUT FAULT	172	THE HUNCHBACK	32
MAN AND WOMAN UNDONE, ...	175	FIRE RAID	57
THE WOMAN BREASTED AND THE HEAVEN HEADED	191	WINTER'S TALE	125
WITH EVERY SIMMERING WOMAN HIS MOUSE	206	LAMENT	30
WOMAN ON TAPESTRY	234	WOMAN TAPESTRY	T
LIKE THE ARMS OF A CLEAN WOMAN	236	WOMAN TAPESTRY	39
WOMAN-LUCK			
FROGS AND SATANS AND WOMAN-LUCK, ...	150	WHEN I WOKE	7
WOMAN'S			
SOMETIMES A WOMAN'S HEART HAS SALT, ...	13	SKY'S BRIGHT	20
MAKE MOCK OF WOMAN'S MEAT, ...	34	THIRST PARCHES	14
HE IS NOT MAN'S NOR WOMAN'S MAN, ...	47	POET: 1935	25
IF LOVE HE CAN BEING NO WOMAN'S MAN.	47	POET: 1935	35
MAN'S RIB ON WOMAN'S, STRAIGHT LINE ON A CURVE, ...	51	OUT OF THE PIT	35
YET HE IS DEAD, AND STILL BY WOMAN'S WOMB	64	WOMAN SPEAKS	35
ONE DAY MY WOMAN'S BODY WILL BE COLD.	64	WOMAN SPEAKS	47
AND EVERY LOVELY WOMAN'S GERMY;	84	LETTER TO AUNT	49
I MUST WAIT FOR A WOMAN'S SMILE	138	O CHATTERTON	33
SIN WHO HAD A WOMAN'S SHAPE	165	LONG-LEGGED	110
TO FIND A WOMAN'S SOUL FOR A WIFE.	207	LAMENT	48
FEEL YOUR WOMAN'S BREASTS RISE UP LIKE FLOWERS	238	MAKES INTERVALS	12
WOMB			
I, SAID THE BEETLE, OUT OF MY THIN BLACK WOMB, ...	18	NATURAL DAY	26
WITHIN HER WOMB, ...	26	PERSONAL EPIT	10
YET HE IS DEAD, AND STILL BY WOMAN'S WOMB	64	WOMAN SPEAKS	35
SINCE THE FIRST WOMB SPAT FORTH A BABY'S CORPSE,	64	WOMAN SPEAKS	52

	PAGE	TITLE	LINE
WOMB (CONTINUED)			
WITH LIQUID HANDS TAPPED ON THE WOMB,	68	BEFORE KNOCKED	2
AND DOUBLECROSSED MY MOTHER'S WOMB.	69	BEFORE KNOCKED	46
AND TO THE HOLLOW MINUTE OF THE WOMB,	78	LOVE'S FEVER	2
ONE WOMB, ONE MIND, SPEWED OUT THE MATTER,	79	LOVE'S FEVER	42
THE BONES OF BLINDNESS; AND THE WOMB	88	A PROCESS IN	8
AND FROM THE PLANTED WOMB THE MAN OF STRAW.	92	BOYS OF SUMMER	36
WITH THE WOMB OF HIS SHAPELESS PEOPLE.	107	ALL ALL AND	27
THAT TOWN OF GHOSTS, THE TRODDEN WOMB	125	SEED-AT-ZERO	2
THAT TOWN OF GHOSTS, THE MANWAGED WOMB	125	SEED-AT-ZERO	9
'HIS MOTHER'S WOMB HAD A TONGUE THAT LAPPED UP MUD,'	132	I MAKE THIS IN	46
BUT MY WOMB WAS BELLOWING	140	TOMBSTONE TOLD	27
THAT I CAN HEAR THE WOMB	180	VISION, PRAYER	6
AND THE WOMB	183	VISION, PRAYER	125
HARPIES AROUND ME OUT OF HER WOMB!	207	LAMENT	56
WOMB-EYED			
THE WOMB-EYED, CRIES,	114	SERVANT SUN	32
WOMB'S			
SPLIT UP THE BRAWNED WOMB'S WEATHERS,	92	BOYS OF SUMMER	14
WOMEN			
THE WITHERED WOMEN WIN THEM BEDFELLOWS.	38	THE GOSSIPERS	16
WOMEN WITH CANCER AT THEIR SIDES	41	YOUNG ARE OLD	28
HE COULD HEAR WOMEN BREATHING IN THE DARK,	51	OUT OF THE PIT	20
LAIN WITH PARCHED THINGS; LOVED DOGS AND WOMEN;	52	OUT OF THE PIT	72
AND WOMEN TALK OF HORROR TO THE DUSK.	57	GREEK PLAY	16
A PIGEON CALLS AND WOMEN TALK OF DEATH.	57	GREEK PLAY	32
TO WOMEN WHO HAVE TWISTED THEIR LAST SMILE,	81	ALL THAT I OWE	16
THE WORDY SHAPES OF WOMEN, AND THE ROWS	98	OCTOBER WIND	11
WOMEN FIGURES ROUND MY CELL,	138	O CHATTERTON	30
WOMEN FIGURES ON THE WALL	138	O CHATTERTON	31
I OFFER YOU WOMEN, NOT WOMAN,	138	O CHATTERTON	40
AND SOME DISMANTLED WOMEN,	155	RETURN	31
MAST-HIGH MOON-WHITE WOMEN NAKED	165	LONG-LEGGED	104
WITH MEN AND WOMEN AND WATERFALLS	167	LONG-LEGGED	169
WHERE BARREN AS BOULDERS WOMEN LIE LONGING STILL	203	GIANT'S THIGH	4
THROUGH THROATS WHERE MANY RIVERS MEET, THE WOMEN PRAY,	203	GIANT'S THIGH	6
HALE DEAD AND DEATHLESS DO THE WOMEN OF THE HILL	205	GIANT'S THIGH	58
(SIGHED THE OLD RAM ROD, DYING OF WOMEN),	206	LAMENT	3
WOMEN'S			
SEE WOMEN'S FACES UNDER LIVING SNOODS,	51	OUT OF THE PIT	21
WONDER			
ALL HE HAS REAPED IN WONDER.	30	NEARLY SUMMER	18
TO WONDER AT THE UNFAILING STARS.	31	BEING BUT MEN	10
AND THE WONDER THAT MAN KNOWS,	31	BEING BUT MEN	12
CHILDREN IN WONDER WATCHING THE STARS,	31	BEING BUT MEN	15
NO MAN BELIEVES WHO DOES NOT WONDER WHY.	55	NO MAN BELIEVE	12
AND TO THE FIRST DUMB WONDER AT THE FLESH,	78	LOVE'S FEVER	13
STREAMED AGAIN A WONDER OF SUMMER	178	POEM IN OCT	43
WON'T			
WON'T HARM THE TENT AROUND HIM,	17	IN OBLIVION	24
FOR A LAZY SAKE THAT WON'T CREATE	24	LITTLE PROBLEM	23
WHY WON'T THE NEWS OF THE OLD WORLD CATCH	149	PAPER & STICKS	2
LET'S HOPE YOU WON'T THINK ME TOO VICIOUS.	221	SONG OF DOG	16
WOOD			
THE WORLD'S TURNING WOOD,	3	PROLOGUE	27
THE PHRASES ON THE WOOD AREN'T HERS;	14	FOR LEDA	5
THE WILD PIGS' WOOD, AND SLIME UPON THE TREES,	104	WORLD PYRAMID	20
AND HEMLOCK-HEADED IN THE WOOD OF WEATHERS.	117	ALTARWISE	28
DEATH HAIRY-HEELED, AND THE TAPPED GHOST IN WOOD,	128	NOW, SAY NAY	33

	PAGE	TITLE	LINE
WOOD (CONTINUED)			
SAVOURS THE LICK OF THE TIMES THROUGH A DEADLY WOOD OF HAIR	144	PLEASURE-BIRD	9
WOKE TO MY HEARING FROM HARBOUR AND NEIGHBOUR WOOD	176	POEM IN OCT	2
IN THE WOOD FARAWAY UNDER ME.	177	POEM IN OCT	30
DUST IN THE BURIED WOOD, FLIES ON THE GRAINS OF HER WINGS	189	WINTER'S TALE	58
TO EAT YOUR HEART IN THE HOUSE IN THE ROSY WOOD.	197	COUNTRY SLEEP	7
SANCTUM SANCTORUM THE ANIMAL EYE OF THE WOOD	198	COUNTRY SLEEP	30
UNDER THE PRAYER WHEELING MOON IN THE ROSY WOOD	198	COUNTRY SLEEP	41
OF THE WOOD! PASTORAL BEAT OF BLOOD THROUGH THE LACED LEAVES!	199	COUNTRY SLEEP	71
QUICK IN THE WOOD AT LOVE, WHERE A TORCH OF FOXES FOAMS,	204	GIANT'S THIGH	34
STREETS OR HUNGERING IN THE CRUMBLED WOOD: TO THESE	205	GIANT'S THIGH	57
I TIPTOED SHY IN THE GOOSEBERRY WOOD,	206	LAMENT	4
WOODEN			
LIKE WOODEN ISLANDS, HILL TO HILL.	5	PROLOGUE	96
WITH WOODEN ARMS REVOLVING IN THE WIND	45	PLOUGHMAN GONE	7
I WITH THE WOODEN INSECT IN THE TREE OF NETTLES,	109	I, IN IMAGE	28
WHO RAZED MY WOODEN FOLLY STANDS AGHAST,	113	NOT FATHER ME	22
AN AIR-DRAWN WINDMILL ON A WOODEN HORSE,	124	TODAY, INSECT	20
WOODS			
HIST, IN HOGSBACK WOODS! THE HAYSTACKED	5	PROLOGUE	78
A BIBLE-LEAVED OF ALL THE WRITTEN WOODS	119	ALTARWISE	86
BOW DOWN THE WALLS OF THE FERNED AND FOXY WOODS	136	AFTER FUNERAL	24
ANCIENT WOODS OF MY BLOOD, DASH DOWN TO THE NUT OF THE SEAS	140	NO WORK WORDS	11
I'LL COMB THE SNARED WOODS WITH A GLOVE ON A LAMP,	145	IF HEAD HURT	7
THESE WERE THE WOODS THE RIVER AND SEA	178	POEM IN OCT	53
PLENTY AS BLACKBERRIES IN THE WOODS	210	POEM ON B'DAY	53
WOODS'			
COO ROOING THE WOODS' PRAISE,	4	PROLOGUE	61
WOOD'S			
AT A WOOD'S DANCING HOOF,	3	PROLOGUE	8
WOOD-TONGUED			
THE SEAS TO SERVICE THAT HER WOOD-TONGUED VIRTUE	136	AFTER FUNERAL	22
WOOED			
NOR THE INNOCENT LIE IN THE ROOTING DINGLE WOOED	198	COUNTRY SLEEP	15
AND HEARD THE LEWD, WOOED FIELD FLOW TO THE COMING FROST,	204	GIANT'S THIGH	30
AND ON SEESAW SUNDAY NIGHTS I WOOED	206	LAMENT	8
WOOL			
AND THE DUNG HILLS WHITE AS WOOL AND THE HEN	187	WINTER'S TALE	18
WORD			
WHICH WAS GOOD AT WORD,	23	THE ONLY DEAD	16
NOW HE HAS HEARD AND READ THE HAPPY WORD.	53	OUT OF THE PIT	100
THE WORD OF THE BLOOD, THE WILY SKIN,	61	MEAT ON BONES	15
BOTH MIND AND MATTER AT THE SCALDING WORD	73	LORD RED HAIL	11
HERE A MILD BABY SPEAKS HIS FIRST WORD	74	SUN BURNS	9
THE WORD OF TIME LIES ON THE CHAPTERED BONE,	80	ALMANAC TIME	11
A FINAL WORD: BEFORE YOU START	84	LETTER TO AUNT	58
IN THE BEGINNING WAS THE WORD, THE WORD	94	IN BEGINNING	19
IN THE BEGINNING WAS THE WORD, THE WORD	94	IN BEGINNING	19
THE WORD FLOWED UP, TRANSLATING TO THE HEART	94	IN BEGINNING	23
TELLS ME THE HOUR'S WORD, THE NEURAL MEANING	99	OCTOBER WIND	18
SCRAPED AT MY CRADLE IN A WALKING WORD	117	ALTARWISE	11
GENESIS IN THE ROOT, THE SCARECROW WORD,	119	ALTARWISE	88
SPOT THE BLOWN WORD, AND ON THE SEAS I IMAGE	121	ALTARWISE	131
WHISPER IN A DAMP WORD, HER WITS DRILLED HOLLOW,	137	AFTER FUNERAL	33

	PAGE	TITLE	LINE
WORD (CONTINUED)			
THE SHADE OF THEIR TREES WAS A WORD OF MANY SHADES	144	COLOUR OF SAY	10
WORD, SINGERS, AND TONGUE	174	FIRE RAID	53
WORDS			
FOR MY MERRY WORDS,	18	NATURAL DAY	23
THEY ARE WORDS FOR WEEPING.	18	NATURAL DAY	31
EVEN THE WORDS ARE NOTHING	27	OBLIVIOUS DARK	22
FOR HER SOLDIER STAINED WITH SPILT WORDS	32	OUT OF SIGHS	15
THE HOLLOW WORDS COULD BEAR ALL SUFFERING	32	OUT OF SIGHS	22
WHIRLED IN OUR WORDS, THEN FADED.	34	IN GARDENS	15
WILLING WORDS TO MAKE THE RUMOURS CERTAIN,	38	THE GOSSIPERS	2
OUT OF A WAR OF WITS, WHEN FOLLY OF WORDS	42	A WAR OF WITS	1
OVER A ROAD THICK WITH THE BONES OF WORDS.	44	TO FOLLOW FOX	17
CRYING SUCH WORDS, HE LEFT THE CRYING CROWDS,	53	OUT OF THE PIT	82
UNSHACKLED THE WEIGHTS OF WORDS FROM TIRED LIMBS,	53	OUT OF THE PIT	83
ALCOVE OF WORDS OUT OF CICADA SHADE,	54	WE BY SEASAND	4
DEATH AND EVIL, TOO SLOW IN HEEDING WORDS.	60	FAIRY TALES	35
SORROW SHALL HAVE NO WORDS, NO WILLOW WEARING;	64	WOMAN SPEAKS	39
WHERE WORDS AND WATER MAKE A MIXTURE	69	BEFORE KNOCKED	27
TO SHADE AND KNIT ANEW THE PATCH OF WORDS	79	LOVE'S FEVER	34
NEVER OMIT SUCH VITAL WORDS	84	LETTER TO AUNT	44
AND WORDS FALL CRIPPLED FROM THE SLAVING LIPS,	96	TWELVE	2
THE WORDS OF DEATH ARE DRYER THAN HIS STIFF,	96	RUB OF LOVE	46
SHEDS THE SYLLABIC BLOOD AND DRAINS HER WORDS.	98	OCTOBER WIND	8
SHUT, TOO, IN A TOWER OF WORDS, I MARK	98	OCTOBER WIND	9
SOME LET ME MAKE YOU OF THE HEARTLESS WORDS.	99	OCTOBER WIND	29
RAISED UP A VOICE, AND, CLIMBING ON THE WORDS,	102	FELLOWED SLEEP	22
THE TWO WORDS STALLION AND STERILE	138	O CHATTERTON	35
ON NO WORK OF WORDS	140	NO WORK WORDS	T
ON NO WORK OF WORDS NOW FOR THREE LEAN MONTHS IN THE BLOODY	140	NO WORK WORDS	1
WHO WRITES THESE WORDS I WRITE IN A STILL ROOM IN A SPELLSOAKED HOUSE:	141	I, FIRST NAMED	2
WILDE WORDS, ALL BUTTERED, BADLY BRED,	143	THE MOLLS	10
WORDS ON THE AIR AS THE FIRE CATCHES	149	PAPER & STICKS	17
AND ALL YOUR DEEDS AND WORDS,	193	SIDE OF TRUTH	34
BECAUSE THEIR WORDS HAD FORKED NO LIGHTNING THEY	208	NOT GO GENTLE	5
WORD'S			
NEED NO WORD'S WARMTH.	79	LOVE'S FEVER	36
WORDY			
MY WORDY WOUNDS ARE PRINTED WITH YOUR HAIR.	96	RUB OF LOVE	47
THE WORDY SHAPES OF WOMEN, AND THE ROWS	98	OCTOBER WIND	11
WORE			
NEVER NEVER OH NEVER TO REGRET THE BUGLE I WORE	152	BELOW A TIME	47
DAYS DEEP IN HER BREAST THAT WORE NO HEART	175	MY BEGGAR ARM	2
WORK			
WORK ART AND THE MOONSHINE	5	PROLOGUE	84
ON NO WORK OF WORDS	140	NO WORK WORDS	T
ON NO WORK OF WORDS NOW FOR THREE LEAN MONTHS IN THE BLOODY	140	NO WORK WORDS	1
IF I TAKE TO BURN OR RETURN THIS WORLD WHICH IS EACH MAN'S WORK.	140	NO WORK WORDS	12
WORK AT THEIR WAYS TO DEATH,	209	POEM ON B'DAY	14
AND THAT BEES NEVER WORK IN THEIR HIVES.	221	SONG OF DOG	4
WORKED			
WORKED ON A WORLD OF PETALS;	108	I, IN IMAGE	9
THE MAZES OF HIS PRAISE AND ENVIOUS TONGUE WERE WORKED IN FLAMES AND SHELLS.	141	SAINT TO FALL	17
IN THE MEMORY WORKED BY MIRRORS,	146	TO OTHERS	10
IN GROTTOES I WORKED WITH BIRDS,	151	BELOW A TIME	9

	PAGE	TITLE	LINE
WORKER			
A WORKER IN THE MORNING TOWN,	98	TWILIGHT LOCKS	38
WORKING			
IN SUN AND RAIN WORKING FOR GOOD AND GAIN,	45	PLOUGHMAN GONE	3
GIVES UP ITS DEAD TO SUCH A WORKING SEA;	97	TWILIGHT LOCKS	27
THE LOIN IS GLORY IN A WORKING PALLOR.	105	WORLD PYRAMID	57
FEAR NOT THE WORKING WORLD, MY MORTAL,	106	ALL ALL AND	13
WORKS			
FEW UNDERSTAND THE WORKS OF CUMMINGS,	84	LETTER TO AUNT	36
WORLD			
TROUBLE ENOUGH FOR THE WORLD	18	NATURAL DAY	28
A WORLD OF WEBS	20	ENCOMPASSED	13
THERE'S PLENTY IN THE WORLD	25	THERE'S PLENTY	T
THERE'S PLENTY IN THE WORLD THAT DOTH NOT DIE,	25	THERE'S PLENTY	1
TICKING THE WORLD AWAY,	26	THERE'S PLENTY	12
NOISELESSLY INTO A WORLD OF WINGS AND CRIES.	31	BEING BUT MEN	5
BEFORE THE WORLD STEADIES, STOPS ROCKING, IS STEADY,	39	GAS FADES	33
OR ROCKS, SWINGS AND ROCKS, BEFORE THE WORLD TOTTERS.	39	GAS FADES	34
THE WINDMILLS OF THE WORLD STILL STAND	45	PLOUGHMAN GONE	6
WITHIN HIS HEAD REVOLVED A LITTLE WORLD	50	OUT OF THE PIT	1
HE, TOO, HAS SEEN THE WORLD AS BOTTOM ROTTEN,	52	OUT OF THE PIT	56
SAYS THE WORLD WEARS AWAY?	59	HERE IN SPRING	17
STILL A WORLD OF FURIES	60	FAIRY TALES	24
AND ON HIS SHOULDERS FALL THEIR WORLD OF WINGS,	63	WOMAN SPEAKS	22
THE SADDEST DUST IN ALL THIS HOLLOW WORLD.	64	WOMAN SPEAKS	41
INTANGIBLE MY WORLD SHALL COME TO NAUGHT,	73	LORD RED HAIL	16
THE SOLID WORLD SHALL WITHER IN THE HEAT,	73	LORD RED HAIL	17
AND I WILL BUILD MY LIQUID WORLD,	74	WE MOTHERNAKED	13
ALL WORLD WAS ONE, ONE WINDY NOTHING,	78	LOVE'S FEVER	6
MY WORLD WAS CHRISTENED IN A STREAM OF MILK.	78	LOVE'S FEVER	7
A PROCESS IN THE WEATHER OF THE WORLD	88	A PROCESS IN	19
WHICH IS THE WORLD? OF OUR TWO SLEEPINGS, WHICH	89	EUNUCH DREAMS	21
THIS IS THE WORLD: THE LYING LIKENESS OF	90	EUNUCH DREAMS	31
THIS IS THE WORLD. HAVE FAITH.	90	EUNUCH DREAMS	36
THIS WORLD IS HALF THE DEVIL'S AND MY OWN,	95	RUB OF LOVE	29
THE KISSPROOF WORLD.	101	RUNNING GRAVE	50
MY WORLD IS PYRAMID	103	WORLD PYRAMID	T
MY WORLD IS PYRAMID. THE PADDED MUMMER	104	WORLD PYRAMID	31
MY WORLD IS CYPRESS, AND AN ENGLISH VALLEY.	105	WORLD PYRAMID	37
FEAR NOT THE WORKING WORLD, MY MORTAL,	106	ALL ALL AND	13
THE SCALES OF THIS TWIN WORLD TREAD ON THE DOUBLE,	108	I, IN IMAGE	4
WORKED ON A WORLD OF PETALS;	108	I, IN IMAGE	9
THESE ARE YOUR YEARS' RECORDERS. THE CIRCULAR WORLD STANDS STILL.)	110	I, IN IMAGE	72
TIME, MILK, AND MAGIC, FROM THE WORLD BEGINNING.	119	ALTARWISE	94
FROM POLE TO POLE LEAPT ROUND THE SNAIL-WAKED WORLD.	120	ALTARWISE	108
WORLD IN THE SAND, ON THE TRIANGLE LANDSCAPE,	120	ALTARWISE	124
HOLD HARD, MY COUNTRY CHILDREN IN THE WORLD OF TALES,	122	HOLD HARD	10
TODAY, THIS INSECT, AND THE WORLD I BREATHE,	124	TODAY, INSECT	1
NOW MAKE THE WORLD OF ME AS I HAVE MADE	124	FOSTER LIGHT	29
THE TERRIBLE WORLD MY BROTHER BARES HIS SKIN.	133	I MAKE THIS IN	60
IF I TAKE TO BURN OR RETURN THIS WORLD WHICH IS EACH MAN'S WORK.	140	NO WORK WORDS	12
WHY WON'T THE NEWS OF THE OLD WORLD CATCH	149	PAPER & STICKS	2
SEASONS OVER THE LIQUID WORLD,	166	LONG-LEGGED	119
THE WORLD WINDING HOME!	182	VISION, PRAYER	97
ONCE WHEN THE WORLD TURNED OLD	187	WINTER'S TALE	11
OF PARADISE, IN THE SPUN BUD OF THE WORLD.	191	WINTER'S TALE	129
AS THE WORLD FALLS, SILENT AS THE CYCLONE OF SILENCE.	199	COUNTRY SLEEP	63
AND GALE I TACKLE, THE WHOLE WORLD THEN,	211	POEM ON B'DAY	96

	PAGE	TITLE	LINE
WORLD (CONTINUED)			
THAN EVER WAS SINCE THE WORLD WAS SAID,	211	POEM ON B'DAY	98
ON WHOM A WORLD OF ILLS CAME DOWN LIKE SNOW.	217	ELEGY	32
LAST SOUND, THE WORLD GOING OUT WITHOUT A BREATH:	217	ELEGY	34
WORLDED			
HOW DEEP THE WAKING IN THE WORLDED CLOUDS.	102	FELLOWED SLEEP	25
WORLDS			
AT COTTON WORLDS REVOLVING ON A HIP,	51	OUT OF THE PIT	46
AND WORLDS HANG ON THE TREES.	98	TWILIGHT LOCKS	42
ALL ALL AND ALL THE DRY WORLDS LEVER	106	ALL ALL AND	T
ALL ALL AND ALL THE DRY WORLDS LEVER,	106	ALL ALL AND	1
ALL OF THE FLESH, THE DRY WORLDS LEVER.	106	ALL ALL AND	12
ALL ALL AND ALL THE DRY WORLDS COUPLE,	107	ALL ALL AND	25
SQUARE IN THESE WORLDS THE MORTAL CIRCLE.	107	ALL ALL AND	30
AND BURNED SEA SILENCE ON A WICK OF WORLDS.	119	ALTARWISE	74
ROUND THE PARCHED WORLDS OF WALES AND DROWNED EACH SUN	136	AFTER FUNERAL	15
WORLD'S			
THE WORLD'S TURNING WOOD,	3	PROLOGUE	27
RUN DOWN THE WORLD'S GUTTERS,	39	GAS FADES	32
NO FAITH TO FOLLOW IS THE WORLD'S CURSE	41	YOUNG ARE OLD	24
WAS THE WORLD'S TO ME, AND SYLLABLES	42	A WAR OF WITS	2
A COUNTRY'S TEARS AND VOICED A WORLD'S DESPAIR	57	GREEK PLAY	18
PICK THE WORLD'S BALL OF WAVE AND FROTH	93	BOYS OF SUMMER	40
I AM THE LONG WORLD'S GENTLEMAN, HE SAID,	117	ALTARWISE	13
THE WORLD'S MY WOUND, GOD'S MARY IN HER GRIEF,	120	ALTARWISE	102
TO THE SHRINE OF HIS WORLD'S WOUND	184	VISION, PRAYER	138
ME IN HIS WORLD'S WOUND.	185	VISION, PRAYER	200
WORM			
FEEDING THE WORM	26	PERSONAL EPIT	1
A WORM TELLS SUMMER BETTER THAN THE CLOCK,	59	HERE IN SPRING	14
AND SISTER TO THE FATHERING WORM.	68	BEFORE KNOCKED	6
HOW AT MY SHEET GOES THE SAME CROOKED WORM.	77	THE FORCE THAT	22
LIGHTS UP THE LIVING WORM.	88	A PROCESS IN	6
WHEN SUNLIGHT GOES ARE SUNDERED FROM THE WORM,	89	EUNUCH DREAMS	8
THE BRIGHT-EYED WORM ON DAVY'S LAMP,	92	BOYS OF SUMMER	35
I SIT AND WATCH THE WORM BENEATH MY NAIL	95	RUB OF LOVE	34
LOCKED IN THE LONG WORM OF MY FINGER	97	TWILIGHT LOCKS	2
FROM LIMBS THAT HAD THE MEASURE OF WORM, SHUFFLED	102	I DREAMED MY	5
WORM IN THE SCALP, THE STAKED AND FALLOW.	106	ALL ALL AND	9
BUTT OF THE TREE-TAILED WORM THAT MOUNTED EVE,	117	ALTARWISE	32
WHEN THE WORM BUILDS WITH THE GOLD STRAWS OF VENOM	121	ALTARWISE	139
SOONER DROP WITH THE WORM OF THE ROPES ROUND MY THROAT	145	IF HEAD HURT	4
THE WORM IS (PIN-POINT) RATIONAL IN THE FRUIT.	159	TO LEDA	3
THE WORM IS (PIN-POINT) RATIONAL IN THE FRUIT.	159	TO LEDA	9
I'D RATHER HAVE THE WORM TO FEED	240	TWINING HEAD	9
WORMS			
I SHOULD TELL SUMMER FROM THE TREES, THE WORMS	58	HERE IN SPRING	9
WORMY			
REMEMBER THIS: EACH ROSE IS WORMY,	84	LETTER TO AUNT	48
BREAKS WITH THE WORMY WINTER THROUGH THE EYE.	99	OCTOBER WIND	23
WORN			
OF LADIES' NEEDLES WORN TO BREAKING POINT	18	NATURAL DAY	10
ON THE MADHOUSE BOARDS WORN THIN BY MY WALKING TEARS.	170	LOVE IN ASYLUM	15
WORSE			
BUT NO GOD ROSE. I HAVE SEEN BAD AND WORSE,	52	OUT OF THE PIT	77
WORSHIPPING			
FIXED FAITH, BELIEVING AND WORSHIPPING TOGETHER	41	YOUNG ARE OLD	46

	PAGE	TITLE	LINE
WORST			
AND COMMAS ARE THE WORST OF CRIMES;	84	LETTER TO AUNT	35
WORTH			
WITH KNOWLEDGE THAT NO USE AND NOTHING WORTH	27	OBLIVIOUS DARK	9
WORTHINGTON			
MILD. TURNED AGAIN, WORTHINGTON. NEVER WHISKY.	179	NEW QUAY	12
WOULD			
FOR IF THE GODS WOULD LOVE	11	AIR BREATHE	9
OUT OF THE CHAOS WOULD COME BLISS.	31	BEING BUT MEN	13
FAITH IN DIVINITY WOULD SOLVE MOST THINGS, ...	37	WINDMILLS TURN	16
WOULD BE THE DEVIL'S WIND, AND THE HIGH TRINITY ...	37	WINDMILLS TURN	18
WHERE MEN WOULD ARGUE TILL THE STARS BE GREEN, ...	43	A WAR OF WITS	23
BY THESE I WOULD NOT CARE TO DIE, ...	44	LONGED TO MOVE	19
IF DEAD MEN WALKED THEY, TOO, WOULD HOLLER	59	FAIRY TALES	17
WOULD TURN THE DEAD YELLOW.	59	FAIRY TALES	21
ONE WOULD NOT THINK THE GREENNESS OF THIS VALLEY	63	WOMAN SPEAKS	12
TO YOU, MY AUNT, WHO WOULD EXPLORE	83	LETTER TO AUNT	1
PERHAPS IT WOULD BE BEST IF YOU	83	LETTER TO AUNT	23
PERHAPS IT WOULD BE JUST AS WELL, ...	84	LETTER TO AUNT	30
IF YOU WOULD BE REGARDED GREAT, ...	84	LETTER TO AUNT	41
I WOULD NOT FEAR THE APPLE NOR THE FLOOD	95	RUB OF LOVE	6
I WOULD NOT FEAR THE GALLOWS NOR THE AXE	95	RUB OF LOVE	13
I WOULD NOT FEAR THE MUSCLING-IN OF LOVE	95	RUB OF LOVE	17
I WOULD NOT FEAR THE DEVIL IN THE LOIN	95	RUB OF LOVE	20
WOULD LEAVE ME COLD AS BUTTER FOR THE FLIES, ...	95	RUB OF LOVE	26
I WOULD ENFORCE THE BLACK APPARELLED CRIES, ...	96	TWELVE	5
I WOULD BE WOVEN A RELIGIOUS SHAPE;	96	TWELVE	9
MY HOUSE WOULD FALL LIKE BREAD ABOUT MY HOMAGE; ...	96	TWELVE	11
AND I WOULD CHOKE THE HEAVENS WITH MY HYMN	96	TWELVE	12
I WOULD BE TICKLED BY THE RUB THAT IS:	96	RUB OF LOVE	48
WOULD WITHER UP, AND ANY BOY OF LOVE	116	LANTERNS SHINE	3
SHE WOULD NOT HAVE ME SINKING IN THE HOLY	136	AFTER FUNERAL	18
FLOOD OF HER HEART'S FAME; SHE WOULD LIE DUMB AND			
DEEP	136	AFTER FUNERAL	19
AND WOULD A-WOOING GO AROUND THE GRAVES.	138	O CHATTERTON	28
MY DEAR WOULD I CHANGE MY TEARS OR YOUR IRON HEAD.	146	IF HEAD HURT	18
NOW SHOWN AND MOSTLY BARE I WOULD LIE DOWN, ...	152	BELOW A TIME	49
NIGHT, AND ENJOYED AS HE WOULD.	158	INTO HER HEAD	36
WOULD PLUNGE MY BETRAYAL FROM SHEET TO SKY	175	MY BEGGAR ARM	6
WINGS. IT WOULD BE BETTER IF THE SHUTTERS IS	179	NEW QUAY	6
I WOULD TURN BACK AND RUN	185	VISION, PRAYER	191
NOTHING I CARED, IN THE LAMB WHITE DAYS, THAT TIME			
WOULD TAKE ME	196	FERN HILL	46
WHOEVER I WOULD WITH MY WICKED EYES, ...	206	LAMENT	9
IT WOULD CRUMBLE;	225	CLOWN IN MOON	6
SAYING YOU WOULD LET THE CHILL SEAS PASS, ...	227	SPRING-SPIRIT	7
WOUND			
OVER THE WOUND ASLEEP	4	PROLOGUE	50
NEVER FLOWS OUT FROM THE WOUND OF SLEEP	27	OBLIVIOUS DARK	7
LOSE THE GREAT PAINS OR STUFF THE WOUND, ...	32	OUT OF SIGHS	12
FELL HARD AS WHIPS ON AN OLD WOUND, ...	42	A WAR OF WITS	3
WHO DOES NOT MAKE A WOUND IN FAITH	55	NO MAN BELIEVE	5
GRIEF, LIKE AN OPEN WOUND, HAS CRIED TO HEAVEN. ...	64	WOMAN SPEAKS	32
THE CRUSTED WOUND NOR STROKE THE BROW;	66	HAND SIGNED	14
YOU BUT WOUND THE LORD OF DAYS;	72	TAKE NEEDLES	54
IN THE STITCHED WOUND AND CLOTTED WIND, MUZZLED ...	103	I DREAMED MY	15
(THE WOUND RECORDS), ...	113	SERVANT SUN	9
BLEW OUT THE BLOOD GAUZE THROUGH THE WOUND OF MANWAX.	119	ALTARWISE	84
THE WORLD'S MY WOUND, GOD'S MARY IN HER GRIEF, ...	120	ALTARWISE	102
WITH PRIEST AND PHARAOH BED MY GENTLE WOUND, ...	120	ALTARWISE	123

	PAGE	TITLE	LINE
WOUND (CONTINUED)			
WOUND LIKE A BALL OF LAKES	129	MY NEOPHYTE	33
WHERE, WOUND IN EMERALD LINEN AND SHARP WIND,	132	I MAKE THIS IN	42
WALKS WITH NO WOUND, NOR LIGHTNING IN HER FACE,	133	I MAKE THIS IN	63
INCH AND GLANCE THAT THE WOUND	148	UNLUCKILY FOR	22
WOUND THEIR ROOM WITH A MALE MOAN,	158	INTO HER HEAD	25
ENDLESSLY TO HIS WOUND	160	DEATHS AND ENT	11
VENUS LIES STAR-STRUCK IN HER WOUND	166	LONG-LEGGED	117
THE HEAVENLY AMBULANCE DRAWN BY A WOUND	172	DAWN RAID	10
OF HIS WOUND	181	VISION, PRAYER	66
TO THE SHRINE OF HIS WORLD'S WOUND	184	VISION, PRAYER	138
ME IN HIS WORLD'S WOUND.	185	VISION, PRAYER	200
LIE STILL, SLEEP BECALMED, SUFFERER WITH THE WOUND	194	SLEEP BECALMED	1
THAT CAME FROM THE WOUND WRAPPED IN THE SALT SHEET.	194	SLEEP BECALMED	4
TO THE SEA SOUND FLOWING LIKE BLOOD FROM THE LOUD WOUND	194	SLEEP BECALMED	6
FOR MY VOYAGE TO BEGIN TO THE END OF MY WOUND,	194	SLEEP BECALMED	11
AND FALLS, AND FLOWERS IN THE YAWNING WOUND AT OUR SIDES,	199	COUNTRY SLEEP	62
HEART! SLYLY, SLOWLY, HEARING THE WOUND IN HER SIDE GO	200	COUNTRY SLEEP	95
WOUND, NOR HER RIDING HIGH, NOR HER EYES, NOR KINDLED HAIR,	201	COUNTRY SLEEP	101
NOR DID HE NOW, SAVE TO HIS SECRET WOUND.	217	ELEGY	27
O DEEPEST WOUND OF ALL THAT HE SHOULD DIE	217	ELEGY	37
WOUND-DOWN			
THE WOUND-DOWN COUGH OF THE BLOOD-COUNTING CLOCK	141	SAINT TO FALL	9
WOUNDED			
(MY SHAPE OF AGE NAGGING THE WOUNDED WHISPER.)	118	ALTARWISE	46
WHEN NEAR AND STRANGE WOUNDED ON LONDON'S WAVES	160	DEATHS AND ENT	27
WOUNDS			
WHY SILK IS SOFT AND THE STONE WOUNDS	55	WHY EAST WIND	6
MY BROTHERS' BLOOD THAT SALTS MY OPEN WOUNDS.	80	ALL THAT I OWE	8
MY WORDY WOUNDS ARE PRINTED WITH YOUR HAIR.	96	RUB OF LOVE	47
THEN, PENNY-EYED, THAT GENTLEMAN OF WOUNDS,	117	ALTARWISE	7
NAILED WITH AN OPEN EYE, IN THE BOWL OF WOUNDS AND WEED	135	HOW MY ANIMAL	29
THAT HER FOND WOUNDS ARE MENDED BITTERLY.	139	FIVE & COUNTRY	9
GROWING THEIR WOUNDS ALREADY,	154	RETURN	13
AND SWEPT INTO OUR WOUNDS AND HOUSES,	186	HOLY SPRING	7
TOILS TOWARDS THE AMBUSH OF HIS WOUNDS;	209	POEM ON B'DAY	17
WOUND'S			
WITH PINS FOR TEARDROPS IS THE LONG WOUND'S WOMAN.	120	ALTARWISE	104
WOUNDWARD			
THE WOUNDWARD FLIGHT OF THE ANCIENT	182	VISION, PRAYER	92
WOVEN			
I WOULD BE WOVEN A RELIGIOUS SHAPE;	96	TWELVE	9
OF THE WOVEN WALL	141	SAINT TO FALL	6
HER WOVEN HANDS BECKONED ME,	234	WOMAN TAPESTRY	1
WRACK			
THE RINGED-SEA GHOST, RISE GRIMLY FROM THE WRACK.	113	NOT FATHER ME	24
WRACKED			
HARDLY BEAR THE DIN OF NO-GOOD WRACKED DRY ON	179	NEW QUAY	9
WRACKSPIKED			
WITH CARVED BIRD, SAINT, AND SUN, THE WRACKSPIKED MAIDEN MOUTH	135	HOW MY ANIMAL	37
WRANGLING			
OF THE SPARROWS AND SUCH WHO SWANSING, DUSK, IN WRANGLING HEDGES.	201	SIR JOHNS HILL	7

		PAGE	TITLE	LINE
WRAP				
WRAP THEM IN FLAME, THEY'RE MINE;	....	19	IMAGES IN AIR	2
ITS TONGUE PEELED IN THE WRAP OF A LEAF.	....	150	WHEN I WOKE	15
WRAPPED				
THAT CAME FROM THE WOUND WRAPPED IN THE SALT SHEET.		194	SLEEP BECALMED	4
WRAPT				
AND LISTENED WHEN A SLOW, STARRED SLUMBER WRAPT THE				
MOON,	....	223	IDYLL UNFORGET	7
WREATH				
AND COMB THE COUNTY GARDENS FOR A WREATH.	....	93	BOYS OF SUMMER	42
WREATHING				
OF MINNOWS WREATHING AROUND THEIR PRAYER;	....	209	POEM ON B'DAY	29
WRECK				
CUDGEL GREAT AIR, WRECK EAST, AND TOPPLE SUNDOWN,		132	I MAKE THIS IN	33
WRECKED				
ON SKULL AND SCAR WHERE HIS LOVES LIE WRECKED,	....	209	POEM ON B'DAY	40
WRECKS				
SEE, SAYS THE LIME, AROUND THESE WRECKS	....	86	SEE, SAYS LIME	25
WREN				
'WAR ON THE SPIDER AND THE WREN!'	....	61	MEAT ON BONES	38
AND THE HAWK IN THE EGG KILLS THE WREN.	....	167	LONG-LEGGED	156
BY THE WREN BONE	....	180	VISION, PRAYER	21
THE WREN	....	181	VISION, PRAYER	36
BEHIND THE WALL'S WREN	....	183	VISION, PRAYER	123
WRENCHED				
WRENCHED BY MY FINGERMAN, THE LEADEN BUD	....	115	A GRIEF AGO	11
WREN'S				
BEHIND THE WALL THIN AS A WREN'S BONE?	....	180	VISION, PRAYER	9
WRESTLE				
TO FIERY TYBURN OVER THE WRESTLE OF ELMS UNTIL	....	201	SIR JOHNS HILL	9
WRESTLED				
A STEM CEMENTING, WRESTLED UP THE TOWER,	....	114	A GRIEF AGO	5
WRESTLING				
OR ALL-IN WRESTLING FOR TORN LIMBS TO HEAL,	....	51	OUT OF THE PIT	31
WRETCHED				
SPEAKS A STEEL GOSPEL TO THE WRETCHED	....	70	SECRET WIND	17
WRING				
AND THE RAIN WRING OUT ITS TONGUES ON THE FADED YARD,		205	GIANT'S THIGH	52
WRINGING				
AND BRAMBLES IN THE WRINGING BRAINS.	....	68	BEFORE KNOCKED	24
ITS WRINGING SHELL, AND LET HER EYELIDS FASTEN.	...	132	I MAKE THIS IN	35
TO THE RAIN WRINGING	....	177	POEM IN OCT	28
WRINKLED				
STRADDLE HER WRINKLED KNEES	....	22	HIGH ON A HILL	5
NIGHTLY UPON THEIR WRINKLED BREASTS	....	38	THE GOSSIPERS	17
OUT OF THE WRINKLED UNDERTAKER'S VAN,	....	118	ALTARWISE	36
WRIST				
MY HERO BARES HIS NERVES ALONG MY WRIST	....	75	MY HERO BARES	1
THAT RULES FROM WRIST TO SHOULDER,	....	75	MY HERO BARES	2
ROUND HER TRAILED WRIST FRESH WATER WEAVES,	....	168	LONG-LEGGED	177
BURNING! NIGHT AND THE VEIN OF BIRDS IN THE WINGED,				
SLOE WRIST	....	199	COUNTRY SLEEP	70
WRISTED				
THE STREAM FROM THE PRIEST BLACK WRISTED SPINNEY AND				
SLEEVES	....	200	COUNTRY SLEEP	72
WRITE				
CHRIST, LET ME WRITE FROM THE HEART,	....	22	HIGH ON A HILL	7
FOR YOU COULD THEN WRITE WHAT YOU PLEASE,	....	84	LETTER TO AUNT	31
WHO WRITES THESE WORDS I WRITE IN A STILL ROOM IN A				
SPELLSOAKED HOUSE:	....	141	I, FIRST NAMED	2

		PAGE	TITLE	LINE
WRITE (CONTINUED)				
FROM THE RAGING MOON I WRITE	....	197	CRAFT OR ART	13
WRITES				
WHO WRITES THESE WORDS I WRITE IN A STILL ROOM IN A				
SPELLSOAKED HOUSE:	....	141	I, FIRST NAMED	2
WRITHES				
BONE WRITHES DOWN	....	181	VISION, PRAYER	37
WRITING				
OUT OF A BIRD'S WING WRITING ON A CLOUD	....	48	POET: 1935	53
WRITTEN				
WRITTEN FOR A PERSONAL EPITAPH	....	26	PERSONAL EPIT	T
OR WRITTEN BACKWARDS IN WELSH VERSE,	....	83	LETTER TO AUNT	26
A BIBLE-LEAVED OF ALL THE WRITTEN WOODS	....	119	ALTARWISE	86
WRONG				
ONLY AS WRONG; BUT SHAN'T THE GENIUS FAIL,	....	28	NO WINGS	7
WITH WINDMILLS TURNING WRONG DIRECTIONS	....	36	WINDMILLS TURN	T
WITH WINDMILLS TURNING WRONG DIRECTIONS,	....	36	WINDMILLS TURN	1
FOR THEN THE WRONG WIND CERTAINLY	....	37	WINDMILLS TURN	17
MADE MEANING MEANINGLESS. THE WRONG WIND STIRS,	...	37	WINDMILLS TURN	29
WHO, UNDESERVING, HAVE SUFFERED THE EARTH'S WRONG,		41	YOUNG ARE OLD	34
TOO LATE IN THE WRONG RAIN	....	161	WEDDING ANNIV	9
WRONGS				
BE GUILTLESS OF THE WINDY WRONGS.	....	37	WINDMILLS TURN	19
WROTE				
TO TAKE ME AWAY AS YOU WHISPERED AND WROTE	....	149	PAPER & STICKS	12
WYNDS				
THROUGH WYNDS AND SHELLS OF DROWNED	....	209	POEM ON B'DAY	23
X				
THAT BUT A NAME, WHERE MAGGOTS HAVE THEIR X.	......	79	LOVE'S FEVER	38
YARD				
DOWN IN THE YARD OF DAY.	....	89	EUNUCH DREAMS	16
ABOUT THE HAPPY YARD AND SINGING AS THE FARM WAS				
HOME,	....	195	FERN HILL	11
YARD OF THE BUTTERMILK RAIN ON THE PAIL! THE SERMON		200	COUNTRY SLEEP	77
AND THE RAIN WRING OUT ITS TONGUES ON THE FADED YARD,		205	GIANT'S THIGH	52
YARDS				
I PIECE MY FLESH THAT RATTLED ON THE YARDS	....	105	WORLD PYRAMID	38
COMBS THROUGH THE MANTLED YARDS AND THE MORNING MEN		187	WINTER'S TALE	20
YAWN				
YAWN TO HIS UPCOMING.	....	183	VISION, PRAYER	132
YAWNED				
THE LOCKS YAWNED LOOSE AND A BLAST BLEW THEM WIDE,		172	DAWN RAID	3
YAWNING				
AND FALLS, AND FLOWERS IN THE YAWNING WOUND AT OUR				
SIDES,	....	199	COUNTRY SLEEP	62
YEA				
YEA THE DEAD STIR,	....	127	NOW, SAY NAY	18
YEAR				
THE BLACK RAM, SHUFFLING OF THE YEAR, OLD WINTER,		118	ALTARWISE	39
IN A FIERCELY MOURNING HOUSE IN A CROOKED YEAR.	...	136	AFTER FUNERAL	30
BELLY OF THE RICH YEAR AND THE BIG PURSE OF MY BODY		140	NO WORK WORDS	2
IN THE SNIFFED AND POURED SNOW ON THE TIP OF THE				
TONGUE OF THE YEAR	....	144	PLEASURE-BIRD	5
NOT SPIN TO STARE AT AN OLD YEAR	....	145	PLEASURE-BIRD	17
TO THIS INHOSPITABLE HOLLOW YEAR,	....	153	WAS A SAVIOUR	27
IT WAS MY THIRTIETH YEAR TO HEAVEN	....	176	POEM IN OCT	1
YEAR TO HEAVEN STOOD THERE THEN IN THE SUMMER NOON		178	POEM IN OCT	66
IN THE POLES OF THE YEAR	....	190	WINTER'S TALE	91
OUT OF A LAIR IN THE FLOCKED LEAVES IN THE DEW				
DIPPED YEAR	....	197	COUNTRY SLEEP	6

	PAGE	TITLE	LINE
YEAR-HEDGED			
THE YEAR-HEDGED ROW IS LAME WITH FLINT, ...	129	MY NEOPHYTE	38
YEARN			
THEY YEARN WITH TONGUES OF CURLEWS FOR THE UNCONCEIVED	203	GIANT'S THIGH	10
YEARS			
THOUGH THERE ARE YEARS BETWEEN US, THEY ARE NAUGHT;	30	YOUTH CALLS	12
YOUTH CALLS TO AGE ACROSS THE TIRED YEARS:	30	YOUTH CALLS	13
I HAVE BEEN FRIGHTENED OF THE DARK FOR YEARS.	48	LIGHT, I KNOW	6
THE WINTER YEARS, MOVE IN THE PIT OF MAN;	79	ALMANAC TIME	3
THE MOON-DRAWN GRAVE, WITH THE SEAFARING YEARS, ...	107	GRIEF THIEF	2
I HAVE HEARD MANY YEARS OF TELLING, ...	116	LANTERNS SHINE	16
AND MANY YEARS SHOULD SEE SOME CHANGE.	116	LANTERNS SHINE	17
IN YOUR YOUNG YEARS THE VEGETABLE CENTURY.	123	FOSTER LIGHT	12
AND SCULPTURED ANN IS SEVENTY YEARS OF STONE.	137	AFTER FUNERAL	35
THROUGH THE DEVILISH YEARS AND INNOCENT DEATHS	139	TOMBSTONE TOLD	14
TWENTY-FOUR YEARS	143	24 YEARS	T
TWENTY-FOUR YEARS REMIND THE TEARS OF MY EYES.	143	24 YEARS	1
WHO MOVED FOR THREE YEARS IN TUNE	161	WEDDING ANNIV	3
OF THE SKY, KING OF YOUR SIX YEARS.	193	SIDE OF TRUTH	28
THAN THE YEARS THAT DWINDLE;	226	THE ELM	4
YEARS'			
SYMBOLS ARE SELECTED FROM THE YEARS'	58	HERE IN SPRING	5
THESE ARE YOUR YEARS' RECORDERS. THE CIRCULAR WORLD STANDS STILL.)	110	I, IN IMAGE	72
YEAR'S			
ON THIS HIGH HILL IN A YEAR'S TURNING.	178	POEM IN OCT	70
YELLOW			
GLANCING FROM THE YELLOW NUT, ...	20	ENCOMPASSED	9
WE WHO ARE YOUNG SIT HOLDING YELLOW HANDS.	41	YOUNG ARE OLD	17
THE WHITE, THE BLACK, THE YELLOW AND MULATTO	41	YOUNG ARE OLD	39
WE LYING BY SEASAND, WATCHING YELLOW	54	WE BY SEASAND	1
FOR IN THIS YELLOW GRAVE OF SAND AND SEA	54	WE BY SEASAND	5
WATCH YELLOW, WISH FOR WIND TO BLOW AWAY	54	WE BY SEASAND	19
LIE WATCHING YELLOW UNTIL THE GOLDEN WEATHER	54	WE BY SEASAND	23
WOULD TURN THE DEAD YELLOW.	59	FAIRY TALES	21
AND YELLOW WAS THE MULTIPLYING SAND, ...	78	LOVE'S FEVER	22
LYING UPON THE YELLOW BEACH.	229	MY RIVER	40
OR THE YELLOW LINNET WHO DOES NOT MERIT IT.	230	OUR SANCTITY	14
THE YELLOW BIRD TO SHOW HIS COLOUR.	238	MAKES INTERVALS	5
YES			
DEATH TO THE YES, ...	127	NOW, SAY NAY	11
THE YES TO DEATH, THE YESMAN AND THE ANSWER, ...	127	NOW, SAY NAY	12
YESMAN			
THE YES TO DEATH, THE YESMAN AND THE ANSWER, ...	127	NOW, SAY NAY	12
YESTERDAY			
HIS GOLDEN YESTERDAY ASLEEP UPON THE IRIS	170	MARRIAGE VIRG	3
YET			
AND YET BE HUMAN, ...	23	THE ONLY DEAD	10
AND YET, MAD WITH YOUNG BLOOD OR STAINED WITH AGE,	26	THERE'S PLENTY	16
THIS BUSY JARRING ON THE NERVES YET NO OUTBREAK?	36	MIDNIGHT ROAD	4
SOME LIFE, YET UNSPENT, MIGHT EXPLODE	44	LONGED TO MOVE	12
STRAPPED TO A WHEEL, YET THEY SHALL NOT BREAK;	49	NO DOMINION	14
YET HE IS DEAD, AND STILL BY WOMAN'S WOMB	64	WOMAN SPEAKS	35
AS YET WAS IN A MOLTEN FORM, ...	68	BEFORE KNOCKED	10
AS YET UNGOTTEN, I DID SUFFER;	68	BEFORE KNOCKED	19
THE FIELDS YET UNDIVIDED BEHIND THE SKULL.	73	LORD RED HAIL	10
AND MAY I YET LIVE TO ADMIRE	85	LETTER TO AUNT	65
NOR ROOF OF SAND, NOR YET THE TOWERING TILER?	112	NOT FATHER ME	16
HAS NOT YET REACHED THE GROUND.	116	LANTERNS SHINE	19

	PAGE	TITLE	LINE
YET (CONTINUED)			
YET THIS I MAKE IN A FORGIVING PRESENCE.	133	I MAKE THIS IN	68
THE PYRE YET TO BE LIGHTED OF MY SINS AND DAYS, ...	147	UNLUCKILY FOR	3
MY SILLY SUIT, HARDLY YET SUFFERED FOR, ...	152	BELOW A TIME	29
YET SHE DELUDES WITH WALKING THE NIGHTMARISH ROOM,	169	LOVE IN ASYLUM	7
SHE SLEEPS IN THE NARROW TROUGH YET SHE WALKS THE DUST	170	LOVE IN ASYLUM	13
YET RAVES AT HER WILL	170	LOVE IN ASYLUM	14
YET OUT OF THE BEAKED, WEB DARK AND THE POUNCING BOUGHS	199	COUNTRY SLEEP	48
YET, THOUGH I CRY WITH TUMBLEDOWN TONGUE, ...	211	POEM ON B'DAY	80
YET IN SPITE OF ALL THIS, I HAVE MOMENTS OF BLISS,	221	SONG OF DOG	9
YIELD			
WHEN I YIELD THE TREE TO DEATH, ...	72	TAKE NEEDLES	45
YIELDS			
YIELDS PEACE AND PLENTY AT THE END. OR IS IT PEACE,	36	MIDNIGHT ROAD	3
YODEL			
BUT ONE THE SWISS WEAR WHEN THEY YODEL, ...	83	LETTER TO AUNT	16
YOLK			
CARRION, PARADISE, CHIRRUP MY BRIGHT YOLK.	159	INTO HER HEAD	60
YOU (167)			
YOU'LL			
YOU'LL BRING THE PLACE TO ME	21	BEWILDERED WAY	10
BUT YOU'LL NOT KEEP ME IN	239	LET ME ESCAPE	7
YOUNG			
WAS OLD WHEN YOU WERE YOUNG, ...	20	THE NEOPHYTE	22
AND YET, MAD WITH YOUNG BLOOD OR STAINED WITH AGE,	26	THERE'S PLENTY	16
THE MIDNIGHT ROAD, THOUGH YOUNG MEN TREAD UNKNOWING,	36	MIDNIGHT ROAD	1
'WE WHO ARE YOUNG ARE OLD'	40	YOUNG ARE OLD	T
'WE WHO ARE YOUNG ARE OLD. IT IS THE OLDEST CRY.	40	YOUNG ARE OLD	1
WE WHO ARE STILL YOUNG ARE OLD. IT IS A DEAD CRY,	40	YOUNG ARE OLD	5
WE WHO ARE YOUNG SIT HOLDING YELLOW HANDS.	41	YOUNG ARE OLD	17
YOUNG MEN WITH FALLEN CHESTS AND OLD MEN'S BREATH,	41	YOUNG ARE OLD	27
THE LOST IN DOUBT, THE NEARLY MAD, THE YOUNG	41	YOUNG ARE OLD	33
WE WHO ARE YOUNG ARE OLD, AND UNBELIEVING, ...	42	YOUNG ARE OLD	53
NO BREASTED GIRL, NO MAN WHO, YOUNG	55	NO MAN BELIEVE	10
WHAT WERE YOUNG LIMBS ARE FAGGOTS ON THE LAND, ...	63	WOMAN SPEAKS	14
AND YOUNG GUTS DRY BENEATH THE SICKENED SUN.	63	WOMAN SPEAKS	15
AND RAVENS FED CONFECTION TO THEIR YOUNG.	65	WOMAN SPEAKS	59
TO YOUNG ADORERS DYING ON A KISS.	81	ALL THAT I OWE	18
AND FEW YOUNG AUDEN'S CODED CHATTER;	84	LETTER TO AUNT	38
IN YOUR YOUNG YEARS THE VEGETABLE CENTURY.	123	FOSTER LIGHT	12
HUSK OF YOUNG STARS AND HANDFULL ZODIAC, ...	138	FIVE & COUNTRY	4
TONGUE OF YOUR TRANSLATING EYES. THE YOUNG STARS TOLD ME, ...	148	UNLUCKILY FOR	51
JUAN AFLAME AND SAVAGELY YOUNG KING LEAR, ...	157	INTO HER HEAD	11
STRAIGHT AS A YOUNG ELM	172	THE HUNCHBACK	33
YOUNG FROM THE CANYONS OF OBLIVION!	182	VISION, PRAYER	93
NOW AS I WAS YOUNG AND EASY UNDER THE APPLE BOUGHS	195	FERN HILL	1
IN THE SUN THAT IS YOUNG ONCE ONLY, ...	195	FERN HILL	12
OH AS I WAS YOUNG AND EASY IN THE MERCY OF HIS MEANS,	196	FERN HILL	52
YOUNG	202	SIR JOHNS HILL	30
I YOUNG AESOP FABLING TO THE NEAR NIGHT BY THE DINGLE	202	SIR JOHNS HILL	35
YOUNG AS THEY IN THE AFTER MILKING MOONLIGHT LAY	204	GIANT'S THIGH	16
GULLED AND CHANTER IN YOUNG HEAVEN'S FOLD	210	POEM ON B'DAY	62
YOUNG AMONG THE LONG FLOCKS, AND NEVER LIE LOST ...	216	ELEGY	7
YOUR (205)			
YOU'RE			
AGE COME TO YOU--YOU'RE BRIGHT AND USELESS, ...	21	BEWILDERED WAY	4
YOU'RE THE PERVERSE TO LIE ACROSS, ...	21	BEWILDERED WAY	15

	PAGE	TITLE	LINE
YOU'RE (CONTINUED)			
HAS STOPPED, (ANGEL, YOU'RE PROUD),	237	PILLAR BREAKS	3
AND GALLANTLY (WATER, YOU'RE STRONG--	237	PILLAR BREAKS	4
YOURS			
WITH THAT HALF-MOULDED MIND I SAID WAS YOURS,	10	COOL, OH NO	4
WITH YOURS,	236	WOMAN TAPESTRY	58
YOURSELF			
NOW IN THE DARK THERE IS ONLY YOURSELF AND MYSELF.	153	WAS A SAVIOUR	24
YOUTH			
YOUTH CALLS TO AGE	30	YOUTH CALLS	T
YOUTH CALLS TO AGE ACROSS THE TIRED YEARS:	30	YOUTH CALLS	13
AND RAVEN YOUTH WILL FEAST BUT WHERE HE WILL.	64	WOMAN SPEAKS	51
MY YOUTH IS BENT BY THE SAME WINTRY FEVER.	77	THE FORCE THAT	5
YOUTH DID CONDENSE; THE TEARS OF SPRING	79	LOVE'S FEVER	48
BY YOUTH AND AGE, THE MORTAL STATE AND THOUGHT	80	ALMANAC TIME	9
WARMS YOUTH AND SEED AND BURNS THE SEEDS OF AGE;	82	LIGHT BREAKS	8
CAST BACK THE BONE OF YOUTH	107	GRIEF THIEF	11
IN THE BLINDING COUNTRY OF YOUTH,	192	SIDE OF TRUTH	4
ELEGY OF INNOCENCE AND YOUTH.	192	REFUSAL MOURN	18
YOUTH'S			
AGE SOURS BEFORE YOUTH'S TASTED IN THE MOUTH	40	YOUNG ARE OLD	2
YOU'VE			
FOR YOU'VE A SEA TO LIE.	16	TIME TO ROT	18
ZENITH			
O LIGHT IN ZENITH, THE COUPLED BUD,	107	ALL ALL AND	32
ZERO			
THE SIGNAL MOON IS ZERO IN THEIR VOIDS.	92	BOYS OF SUMMER	12
ZEST			
WITH ZEST CULLED FROM THEIR LADYLIKE HEAT,	18	NATURAL DAY	12
ZION			
ZION OF THE WATER BEAD	191	REFUSAL MOURN	8
ZIP			
ZIP ONCE MORE FOR A TRAVELLER	155	RETURN	37
ZODIAC			
HUSK OF YOUNG STARS AND HANDFULL ZODIAC,	138	FIVE & COUNTRY	4
LOOMS THE LAST SAMSON OF YOUR ZODIAC.	161	DEATHS AND ENT	36
ZOO			
THROUGH THE LOUD ZOO OF THE WILLOW GROVES	171	THE HUNCHBACK	22

---- -- 3

	PAGE	TITLE	LINE

AS BELLY, GENITALS, AND ----,	84	LETTER TO AUNT	45
1935			
POET: 1935	46	POET: 1935	T
3			
LOVE'S A DECISION OF 3 NERVES	138	O CHATTERTON	22
3 LITTLE LUSTS SHALL YOUR DOWRY BE,	138	O CHATTERTON	42

COMPONENTS OF HYPHENATED COMPOUNDS

	PAGE	TITLE	LINE
A (5)			
ABRAHAM			
UP ROSE THE ABRAHAM-MAN, MAD FOR MY SAKE, ...	112	NOT FATHER ME	19
AIR			
AND I, CAUGHT IN MID-AIR PERHAPS, ...	9	MINUTE'S HOUR	6
AN AIR-DRAWN WINDMILL ON A WOODEN HORSE, ...	124	TODAY, INSECT	20
ALL			
OR ALL-IN WRESTLING FOR TORN LIMBS TO HEAL, ...	51	OUT OF THE PIT	31
ALL-HOLLOWED MAN WEPT FOR HIS WHITE APPAREL.	111	I, IN IMAGE	102
AND (2)			
APPOINTED			
'REST BEYOND CHOICE IN THE DUST-APPOINTED GRAIN,	146	IF HEAD HURT	26
ARC			
ARC-LAMPED THROWN BACK UPON THE CUTTING FLOOD.	118	ALTARWISE	56
AROUND			
WHEN MY PINNED-AROUND-THE-SPIRIT	151	BELOW A TIME	2
ARROW			
NAKED AMONG THE BOW-AND-ARROW BIRDS	123	FOSTER LIGHT	23
AS			
FOR MAN-BEGETTERS IN THE DRY-AS-PASTE, ...	113	NOT FATHER ME	23
ASH			
KICKED, WITH A CLATTER, ASH-BINS MARKED VERBOTEN,	52	OUT OF THE PIT	57
ASTRAY			
OF THE LED-ASTRAY BIRDS WHOM GOD, FOR THEIR BREAST			
OF WHISTLES, ...	202	SIR JOHNS HILL	43
AT (5)			
ATLAS			
THE ATLAS-EATER WITH A JAW FOR NEWS, ...	117	ALTARWISE	5
AVERTED			
WITH HALF-AVERTED HEADS, AS IF TO LISTEN, ...	40	YOUNG ARE OLD	13
BACKED			
INTO THE MAP-BACKED HILLS WHERE PATHS	44	TO FOLLOW FOX	8
FOR THE CRAB-BACKED DEAD ON THE SEA-BED ROSE	165	LONG-LEGGED	99
ILLUMINATION OF MUSIC! THE LULLED BLACK-BACKED	200	COUNTRY SLEEP	82
BAGGED			
WITH A SAND-BAGGED GARRISON, ...	127	SEED-AT-ZERO	53
BAGPIPE			
THE BAGPIPE-BREASTED LADIES IN THE DEADWEED	119	ALTARWISE	83
BALL			
AT WHOSE BALL-PRYING EVEN DEATH'LL SQUIRM	179	NEW QUAY	22
BARE			
AND COVERING ALL HAS BEEN A QUIETUDE, AND A SINGING			
FROM FLAKE-BARE THROATS.	224	IDYLL UNFORGET	35
BASED			
OR SPRAY-BASED AND ROCK-CHESTED SEA:	145	PLEASURE-BIRD	24
AND OUT OF EVERY DOMED AND SOIL-BASED SHELL	158	INTO HER HEAD	51
BE (1)			
BEARING			
FLEW MAN-BEARING THERE.	157	INTO HER HEAD	6
THE MASSES OF THE INFANT-BEARING SEA	175	FIRE RAID	74
BEATEN			
WITH RAIN-BEATEN HANDS HOLDING THE WHIP, ...	45	PLOUGHMAN GONE	20
BED			
FOR THE CRAB-BACKED DEAD ON THE SEA-BED ROSE	165	LONG-LEGGED	99
BEGETTERS			
FOR MAN-BEGETTERS IN THE DRY-AS-PASTE, ...	113	NOT FATHER ME	23
BEGGARED			
AND WITH NOT ONE FEAR-BEGGARED SYLLABLE	76	LASHED RINGS	10
BELL			
WHO SUCKS THE BELL-VOICED ADAM OUT OF MAGIC, ...	119	ALTARWISE	93

	PAGE	TITLE	LINE
BELL (CONTINUED)			
MY MAST IS A BELL-SPIRE, ...	164	LONG-LEGGED	76
BETHEL			
THAT HYMNING GOOSEBERRY, THAT BETHEL-WORM	179	NEW QUAY	21
BIBLE			
A BIBLE-LEAVED OF ALL THE WRITTEN WOODS	119	ALTARWISE	86
BILLED			
THE DUCK-BILLED PLATYPUS BROODY IN A MILK OF BIRDS.	148	UNLUCKILY FOR	33
BINS			
KICKED, WITH A CLATTER, ASH-BINS MARKED VERBOTEN,	52	OUT OF THE PIT	57
BIRD			
BENT LIKE THREE TREES AND BIRD-PAPPED THROUGH HER			
SHIFT, ...	120	ALTARWISE	103
BECAUSE THE PLEASURE-BIRD WHISTLES	144	PLEASURE-BIRD	T
BECAUSE THE PLEASURE-BIRD WHISTLES AFTER THE HOT			
WIRES, ...	144	PLEASURE-BIRD	1
BIT			
IS MR. JONES THE CAKE, THAT WINKING-BIT, ...	179	NEW QUAY	20
BLACK			
THERE, IN HIS NIGHT, THE BLACK-TONGUED BELLS	92	BOYS OF SUMMER	28
BLACK-TONGUED AND TIPSY FROM SALVATION'S BOTTLE.	118	ALTARWISE	61
ILLUMINATION OF MUSIC! THE LULLED BLACK-BACKED	200	COUNTRY SLEEP	82
BLE			
BUT IF THIS PROVED IMPOSS-I-BLE	84	LETTER TO AUNT	29
BLIND			
AND, CRACKLING INTO THE AIR, LEAVE ME HALF-BLIND.	44	LONGED TO MOVE	14
THESE ONCE-BLIND EYES HAVE BREATHED A WIND OF			
VISIONS, ...	132	I MAKE THIS IN	54
BLOOD			
SLAPPED DOWN THE GUILLOTINE, THE BLOOD-RED DOUBLE	124	TODAY, INSECT	6
THE WOUND-DOWN COUGH OF THE BLOOD-COUNTING CLOCK	141	SAINT TO FALL	9
ALL BLOOD-SIGNED ASSAILINGS AND VANISHED MARRIAGES			
IN WHICH HE HAD NO LOVELY PART	158	INTO HER HEAD	43
BLOWING			
PLUG THE PAPER-BLOWING TUBES;	156	RETURN	79
BLOWN			
TO THE SEA-BLOWN ARRIVAL.	109	I, IN IMAGE	36
TWINE IN A MOON-BLOWN SHELL, ...	129	MY NEOPHYTE	15
BLUE			
WHAT RHUBARB MAN PEELED IN HER FOAM-BLUE CHANNEL	121	ALTARWISE	135
BUT WAILED AND NESTED IN THE SKY-BLUE WALL	153	WAS A SAVIOUR	31
AT HIS THRASHING HAIR AND WHALE-BLUE EYE;	161	LONG-LEGGED	3
TO HAVE KNOWN THEM IN THEIR BLUE-HUED VALIANCE, ...	223	IDYLL UNFORGET	3
AND BLUE-TIPPED BIRDS HAVE RIPPLED IT, ...	224	IDYLL UNFORGET	22
BOARD			
BRED IN THE DARK BEHIND THE SKIRTING-BOARD, ...	28	NO WINGS	21
BOMB			
STRIKE IN THE TIME-BOMB TOWN, ...	142	SAINT TO FALL	35
BONE			
DESTRUCTION, PICKED BY BIRDS, BRAYS THROUGH THE			
JAW-BONE, ...	132	I MAKE THIS IN	36
BONED			
NOR WHEN MY LOVE LIES IN THE CROSS-BONED DRIFT	123	FOSTER LIGHT	22
BONES			
THE HORIZONTAL CROSS-BONES OF ABADDON, ...	117	ALTARWISE	21
BOUND			
TONGUE AND EAR IN THE THREAD, ANGLE THE TEMPLE-BOUND	135	HOW MY ANIMAL	26
BOW			
NAKED AMONG THE BOW-AND-ARROW BIRDS	123	FOSTER LIGHT	23

		PAGE	TITLE	LINE
BOX				
SKIRTING THE ORDERED BEDS OF PAINT-BOX FLOWERS, ...		33	IN GARDENS	3
BOXED				
AND FREE THE TWIN-BOXED GRIEF, ...		108	GRIEF THIEF	20
BREAD				
STILLS SNAPPED BY NIGHT IN THE BREAD-SIDED FIELD,		118	ALTARWISE	54
BREAST				
DIPPED ME BREAST-DEEP IN THE DESCENDED BONE;		118	ALTARWISE	38
BREASTED				
THE BAGPIPE-BREASTED LADIES IN THE DEADWEED		119	ALTARWISE	83
BREATH				
AND THE BREATH-WHITE, CURTAINED MOUTH OF SEED.' ...		132	I MAKE THIS IN	51
THE DEATH-STAGGED SCATTER-BREATH		150	WHEN I WOKE	19
BREEZE				
THE SEA HAS BEEN BREEZE-SERENE SAPPHIRE, ...		224	IDYLL UNFORGET	21
BRIGHT				
THE BRIGHT-EYED WORM ON DAVY'S LAMP, ...		92	BOYS OF SUMMER	35
BROKEN				
LEFT IN THE RECORDS OF LIVING A NOT-TO-BE-BROKEN				
PICTURE, ...		45	PLOUGHMAN GONE	2
BULL'S				
BULL'S-EYE THE OUTLAW THROUGH A EUNUCH CRACK		108	GRIEF THIEF	19
BURIED				
THROUGH THE RIPPLED DRUM OF THE HAIR-BURIED EAR;		157	INTO HER HEAD	4
BUTT				
BUT NOW THERE ARE THE BUTT-ENDS OF SPENT SQUIBS.		52	OUT OF THE PIT	52
BYE				
THEN GOOD-BYE TO THE FISHERMANNED		162	LONG-LEGGED	5
GOOD-BYE TO THE MAN ON THE SEA-LEGGED DECK		162	LONG-LEGGED	18
GOOD-BYE TO CHIMNEYS AND FUNNELS, ...		162	LONG-LEGGED	25
ALWAYS GOOD-BYE TO THE LONG-LEGGED BREAD		165	LONG-LEGGED	94
ALWAYS GOOD-BYE TO THE FIRES OF THE FACE, ...		165	LONG-LEGGED	98
ALWAYS GOOD-BYE, CRIED THE VOICES THROUGH THE SHELL,		166	LONG-LEGGED	121
GOOD-BYE ALWAYS FOR THE FLESH IS CAST		166	LONG-LEGGED	122
GOOD-BYE, GOOD LUCK, STRUCK THE SUN AND THE MOON,		169	LONG-LEGGED	213
CAST				
IS CORNER-CAST, BREATH'S RAG, SCRAWLED WEED, A VAIN		131	I MAKE THIS IN	9
CELL				
AND THE CELL-STEPPED THIMBLE;		111	I, IN IMAGE	76
CHAINED				
TURNS THE MOON-CHAINED AND WATER-WOUND		169	LONG-LEGGED	203
CHARNEL				
RATHER THAN CHARNEL-HOUSE AS SYMBOL		29	LONG, SKELETON	12
CHESTED				
OR SPRAY-BASED AND ROCK-CHESTED SEA:		145	PLEASURE-BIRD	24
CHRIST				
HE HAD BY HEART THE CHRIST-CROSS-ROW OF DEATH.		97	TWILIGHT LOCKS	24
CINDER				
HER MOLTEN FLIGHT UP CINDER-NESTING COLUMNS, ...		132	I MAKE THIS IN	26
CIRCLED				
A THUNDERING BULLRING OF YOUR SILENT AND				
GIRL-CIRCLED ISLAND.		142	SAINT TO FALL	51
CIRCLING				
HEAD TO HEAVEN-CIRCLING HEAD, ...		158	INTO HER HEAD	48
CLERICAL				
OVER A RUMP ON THE CLERICAL-GREY SEASHORE, ...		179	NEW QUAY	25
CLOCKS				
THE WINDER OF THE WATER-CLOCKS		128	MY NEOPHYTE	5
CLOSE				
ONCE CLOSE-UP SMILING IN THE WALL OF PICTURES, ...		118	ALTARWISE	55

	PAGE	TITLE	LINE
CLOSE (CONTINUED)			
FOR HER WHO WALKS WITHIN HER GARDEN-CLOSE.	223	IN DREAMS	7
CLOUD			
BLINDS THEIR CLOUD-TRACKING EYE.	104	WORLD PYRAMID	30
THESE CLOUD-SOPPED, MARBLE HANDS, THIS MONUMENTAL	137	AFTER FUNERAL	36
AND LAID YOUR CHEEK AGAINST A CLOUD-FORMED SHELL:	153	WAS A SAVIOUR	23
AND CLOUD-LIKE.	225	OF ANY FLOWER	3
COCK			
A COCK-ON-A-DUNGHILL	110	I, IN IMAGE	58
FROM THE EMERALD, STILL BELL; AND FROM THE PACING			
WEATHER-COCK	130	SINNERS' BELL	17
COLOURED			
WITH A ONE-COLOURED CALM;	54	WE BY SEASAND	13
TILL THE THREE-COLOURED RAINBOW FROM MY NIPPLES ...	120	ALTARWISE	107
COLUMN			
A FURNACE-NOSTRILLED COLUMN-MEMBERED	158	INTO HER HEAD	28
COLUMNED			
AND THIS WEAK HOUSE TO MARROW-COLUMNED HEAVEN, ...	131	I MAKE THIS IN	8
COME			
THE COME-A-CROPPER RIDER OF THE FLOWER.	128	NOW, SAY NAY	28
CORNER			
IS CORNER-CAST, BREATH'S RAG, SCRAWLED WEED, A VAIN	131	I MAKE THIS IN	9
COUNTING			
THE WOUND-DOWN COUGH OF THE BLOOD-COUNTING CLOCK	141	SAINT TO FALL	9
COUNTRY			
THE COUNTRY-HANDED GRAVE BOXED INTO LOVE, ...	115	A GRIEF AGO	31
CRAB			
FOR THE CRAB-BACKED DEAD ON THE SEA-BED ROSE	165	LONG-LEGGED	99
CRADLE			
TO THE VOICES OF THE WIND CAUGHT IN THE			
CRADLE-PETALS OF THE NIGHT:	223	IDYLL UNFORGET	8
CRISS			
LEAP OVER TO MY CRISS-CROSS RHYTHMS.	33	HELD-OUT HAND	23
CROPPER			
THE COME-A-CROPPER RIDER OF THE FLOWER.	128	NOW, SAY NAY	28
CROSS			
LEAP OVER TO MY CRISS-CROSS RHYTHMS.	33	HELD-OUT HAND	23
HE HAD BY HEART THE CHRIST-CROSS-ROW OF DEATH.	97	TWILIGHT LOCKS	24
THE HORIZONTAL CROSS-BONES OF ABADDON, ...	117	ALTARWISE	21
CROSS-STROKED SALT ADAM TO THE FROZEN ANGEL	119	ALTARWISE	67
NOR WHEN MY LOVE LIES IN THE CROSS-BONED DRIFT	123	FOSTER LIGHT	22
CROW'S			
THAT WIPES AWAY NOT CROW'S-FOOT NOR THE LOCK	95	RUB OF LOVE	23
CULLED			
FAINT ARROWY MOONSTONE ON A TEAR-CULLED CADENCE,	225	SLENDER WIND	3
CURL			
CURL-LOCKED AND ANIMAL CAVEPOOLS OF SPELLS AND BONE,	135	HOW MY ANIMAL	27
CUT			
CUT-TO-MEASURE FLESH BIT, ...	151	BELOW A TIME	3
DAB			
IN THE PEBBLY DAB-FILLED	202	SIR JOHNS HILL	20
DAM			
QUESTION: WHEN SHALL ROOT-DAM DIE?	72	TAKE NEEDLES	61
QUESTION: WHEN SHALL ROOT-DAM GROW?	72	TAKE NEEDLES	63
DANCING			
GLIDING, ROPE-DANCING, IS HIS FANCY, ...	28	NO WINGS	8
DARK			
BY THE SEA'S SIDE HEAR THE DARK-VOWELLED BIRDS. ...	99	OCTOBER WIND	32
FOREVER IT IS A WHITE CHILD IN THE DARK-SKINNED			
SUMMER	130	SINNERS' BELL	19

	PAGE	TITLE	LINE
DARKNESS			
FROM DAMP LOVE-DARKNESS AND THE NURSE'S TWIST	96	RUB OF LOVE	38
DASHED			
HEAR BY DEATH'S ACCIDENT THE CLOCKED AND DASHED-DOWN SPIRE	130	SINNERS' BELL	11
DAY			
TO-DAY, IF ALL MY SENSES ACT, ...	238	MAKES INTERVALS	9
DEATH			
THE DEATH-STAGGED SCATTER-BREATH	150	WHEN I WOKE	19
DECKED			
THE SHEATH-DECKED JACKS, QUEEN WITH A SHUFFLED HEART;	118	ALTARWISE	59
DEEP			
KNEE-DEEP IN VOMIT. I SAW HIM THERE, ...	51	OUT OF THE PIT	43
DIPPED ME BREAST-DEEP IN THE DESCENDED BONE;	118	ALTARWISE	38
DIMENSIONED			
TWO ONE-DIMENSIONED GHOSTS, LOVE ON A REEL, ...	89	EUNUCH DREAMS	12
DOOR			
THE NEXT-DOOR SEA DISPELLED	150	WHEN I WOKE	6
DOWN			
HEAR BY DEATH'S ACCIDENT THE CLOCKED AND DASHED-DOWN SPIRE	130	SINNERS' BELL	11
THE WOUND-DOWN COUGH OF THE BLOOD-COUNTING CLOCK	141	SAINT TO FALL	9
DRAWN			
THE MOON-DRAWN GRAVE, WITH THE SEAFARING YEARS, ...	107	GRIEF THIEF	2
AN AIR-DRAWN WINDMILL ON A WOODEN HORSE, ...	124	TODAY, INSECT	20
DRESSED			
SHE CRIED HER WHITE-DRESSED LIMBS WERE BARE	139	TOMBSTONE TOLD	17
DRIVEN			
DROVE IN THE HEAVEN-DRIVEN OF THE NAILS	120	ALTARWISE	106
DRUG			
CAMPED IN THE DRUG-WHITE SHOWER OF NERVES AND FOOD,	144	PLEASURE-BIRD	8
DRY			
FOR MAN-BEGETTERS IN THE DRY-AS-PASTE, ...	113	NOT FATHER ME	23
DUCK			
THE DUCK-BILLED PLATYPUS BROODY IN A MILK OF BIRDS.	148	UNLUCKILY FOR	33
DUCTED			
THE PLANET-DUCTED PELICAN OF CIRCLES	117	ALTARWISE	17
DUNG			
THAT PRINCE OF PIMPS, THAT DOYEN OF DUNG-LICKERS.	179	NEW QUAY	24
DUNGHILL			
A COCK-ON-A-DUNGHILL	110	I, IN IMAGE	58
DUST			
IT IS THE SINNERS' DUST-TONGUED BELL	130	SINNERS' BELL	T
IT IS THE SINNERS' DUST-TONGUED BELL CLAPS ME TO CHURCHES	130	SINNERS' BELL	1
'REST BEYOND CHOICE IN THE DUST-APPOINTED GRAIN,	146	IF HEAD HURT	26
DWARFED			
CHILD BEYOND COCKCROW, BY THE FIRE-DWARFED	174	FIRE RAID	28
EAGLE			
OH, EAGLE-MOUTHED, ...	232	YOUR VOICE	10
EATER			
LIE ALL UNKNOWING OF THE GRAVE SIN-EATER.	113	NOT FATHER ME	32
THE ATLAS-EATER WITH A JAW FOR NEWS, ...	117	ALTARWISE	5
EATING			
BY THE LIGHT OF THE MEAT-EATING SUN.	143	24 YEARS	5
EDGED			
REHEARSING HEAT UPON A RAW-EDGED NERVE.	95	RUB OF LOVE	19
EMBRACING			
THAT SIN-EMBRACING DRIPPER OF FUN	156	RETURN	88

	PAGE	TITLE	LINE
ENDS			
BUT NOW THERE ARE THE BUTT-ENDS OF SPENT SQUIBS.	52	OUT OF THE PIT	52
EVEN			
THE FRAIL AND DELICATE BREATH OF EVEN-TIME.	222	IN DREAMS	4
EX			
EX-SOLDIERS WITH HORRORS FOR A FACE, ...	41	YOUNG ARE OLD	31
EYE			
BULL'S-EYE THE OUTLAW THROUGH A EUNUCH CRACK	108	GRIEF THIEF	19
AND THE UNDEAD EYE-TEETH, ...	108	GRIEF THIEF	24
EYED			
RAISE UP THIS RED-EYED EARTH?	89	EUNUCH DREAMS	23
THE BRIGHT-EYED WORM ON DAVY'S LAMP, ...	92	BOYS OF SUMMER	35
A THREE-EYED, RED-EYED SPARK, BLUNT AS A FLOWER;	94	IN BEGINNING	15
A THREE-EYED, RED-EYED SPARK, BLUNT AS A FLOWER;	94	IN BEGINNING	15
MY MOTHERS-EYED, UPON THE TOPS OF TREES;	101	FELLOWED SLEEP	9
FADED MY ELBOW GHOST, THE MOTHERS-EYED, ...	102	FELLOWED SLEEP	16
AND THE CAGE FOR THE SCYTHE-EYED RAVEN.	106	ALL ALL AND	21
AND SALT-EYED STUMBLE BEDWARD WHERE SHE LIES	107	GRIEF THIEF	12
THE WOMB-EYED, CRIES, ...	114	SERVANT SUN	32
THEN, PENNY-EYED, THAT GENTLEMAN OF WOUNDS, ...	117	ALTARWISE	7
HE IN A BOOK OF WATER TALLOW-EYED	119	ALTARWISE	72
BY RED-EYED ORCHARDS SOW THE SEEDS OF SNOW, ...	123	FOSTER LIGHT	11
ALL PRAISE OF THE HAWK ON FIRE IN HAWK-EYED DUSK BE			
SUNG, ...	202	SIR JOHNS HILL	27
EYES			
UNSEEN BY STRANGER-EYES	62	EARS IN TURRET	7
FACE			
AFTER A WATER-FACE WALK, ...	150	WHEN I WOKE	18
FACED			
NOW JACK MY FATHERS LET THE TIME-FACED CROOK, ...	108	GRIEF THIEF	15
DRY AS ECHOES AND INSECT-FACED, ...	167	LONG-LEGGED	146
FAIR			
THE TWISTED BRAIN, THE FAIR-FORMED LOIN, ...	32	OUT OF SIGHS	25
FAITHS			
TILL ALL OUR SEA-FAITHS DIE.	91	WHERE ONCE THE	24
FALUTIN			
EMBRACING LOW-FALUTIN	154	RETURN	1
FATHOMED			
AND THE FIVE-FATHOMED HAMLET ON HIS FATHER'S CORAL,	111	I, IN IMAGE	83
FEAR			
AND WITH NOT ONE FEAR-BEGGARED SYLLABLE	76	LASHED RINGS	10
FIFTH			
HIS DRIFTWOOD THIRTY-FIFTH WIND TURNED AGE;	208	POEM ON B'DAY	8
FILLED			
IN THE PEBBLY DAB-FILLED	202	SIR JOHNS HILL	20
FIN			
SUFFER THE SLASH OF VISION BY THE FIN-GREEN STUBBLE,	111	I, IN IMAGE	85
FIRE			
CHILD BEYOND COCKCROW, BY THE FIRE-DWARFED	174	FIRE RAID	28
FISH			
THE SWEET, FISH-GILLED BOATS BRINGING BLOOD	142	SAINT TO FALL	22
THE RAINBOW-FISH BEND IN HER JOYS, ...	163	LONG-LEGGED	34
FIVE			
AND THE FIVE-FATHOMED HAMLET ON HIS FATHER'S CORAL,	111	I, IN IMAGE	83
THIRTY-FIVE BELLS SING STRUCK	209	POEM ON B'DAY	39
FLAKE			
AND COVERING ALL HAS BEEN A QUIETUDE, AND A SINGING			
FROM FLAKE-BARE THROATS.	224	IDYLL UNFORGET	35
FLANKED			
SHALL THE STAR-FLANKED SEED BE RIDDLED, ...	125	SEED-AT-ZERO	16

	PAGE	TITLE	LINE
FLANKED (CONTINUED)			
SHALL THE STAR-FLANKED SEED BE RIDDLED, ...	126	SEED-AT-ZERO	23
WITH A STAR-FLANKED GARRISON, ...	126	SEED-AT-ZERO	46
FROM THE STAR-FLANKED FIELDS OF SPACE, ...	127	SEED-AT-ZERO	51
FLASHING			
OVER THE WAKEWARD-FLASHING SPRAY	164	LONG-LEGGED	73
FLEA			
SWELLING IN FLEA-SPECKED LINEN	154	RETURN	7
FLY			
AND FATHER ALL NOR FAIL THE FLY-LORD'S ACRE, ...	123	FOSTER LIGHT	13
FOAM			
WHAT RHUBARB MAN PEELED IN HER FOAM-BLUE CHANNEL	121	ALTARWISE	135
FOOT			
THAT WIPES AWAY NOT CROW'S-FOOT NOR THE LOCK	95	RUB OF LOVE	23
FOOTED			
AND, WINDING-FOOTED IN THEIR SHAWL AND SHEET, ...	89	EUNUCH DREAMS	4
FOR (2)			
FORMED			
THE TWISTED BRAIN, THE FAIR-FORMED LOIN, ...	32	OUT OF SIGHS	25
AND LAID YOUR CHEEK AGAINST A CLOUD-FORMED SHELL:	153	WAS A SAVIOUR	23
FOUR			
WE SUMMER BOYS IN THIS FOUR-WINDED SPINNING, ...	93	BOYS OF SUMMER	37
SUMMON YOUR SNOWY HORSEMEN, AND THE FOUR-STRINGED			
HILL, ...	122	HOLD HARD	14
BUT GRAFT THESE FOUR-FRUITED RIDINGS ON YOUR COUNTRY;	123	FOSTER LIGHT	9
TWENTY-FOUR YEARS	143	24 YEARS	T
TWENTY-FOUR YEARS REMIND THE TEARS OF MY EYES.	143	24 YEARS	1
FRAMED			
THE TWO-FRAMED GLOBE THAT SPUN INTO A SCORE;	79	LOVE'S FEVER	45
FRESH			
AND THE FRESH-WATER BIRD	231	OUR SANCTITY	24
FRUITED			
BUT GRAFT THESE FOUR-FRUITED RIDINGS ON YOUR COUNTRY;	123	FOSTER LIGHT	9
FRUITFUL			
OF OVER-FRUITFUL SMILES, ...	12	SKY'S BRIGHT	8
FURNACE			
A FURNACE-NOSTRILLED COLUMN-MEMBERED	158	INTO HER HEAD	28
GABBING			
ON THAT CLOUD COAST TO EACH GRAVE-GABBING SHADE;	102	FELLOWED SLEEP	18
GARDEN			
FOR HER WHO WALKS WITHIN HER GARDEN-CLOSE.	223	IN DREAMS	7
ALONG THE BORDERS OF THE GARDEN-WALKS.	223	IN DREAMS	12
GEARED			
OR DRIVE THE NIGHT-GEARED FORTH.	90	EUNUCH DREAMS	26
IN BOTTOM GEAR THROUGH NIGHT-GEARED MAN.	103	I DREAMED MY	12
GESTURED			
OF THE STAR-GESTURED CHILDREN IN THE PARK.	98	OCTOBER WIND	12
GHOST			
HAS SOWN A FLYING GARDEN ROUND THAT SEA-GHOST?	121	ALTARWISE	136
GILLED			
THE SWEET, FISH-GILLED BOATS BRINGING BLOOD	142	SAINT TO FALL	22
GIRL			
A THUNDERING BULLRING OF YOUR SILENT AND			
GIRL-CIRCLED ISLAND.	142	SAINT TO FALL	51
MALE SHAPES, GIRL-LIPPED, BUT CLAD LIKE BOYS:	143	THE MOLLS	2
GIRLS'			
THE FRANK, CLOSED PEARL, THE SEA-GIRLS' LINEAMENTS	131	I MAKE THIS IN	19
GLASS			
OR SAW IN THE LOOKING-GLASS SHELL	139	TOMBSTONE TOLD	7

	PAGE	TITLE	LINE
GLOVED			
COMES LOVE'S ANATOMIST WITH SUN-GLOVED HAND	132	I MAKE THIS IN	44
GLOW			
THE GLOW-WORM LIGHTS HIS DARKNESS, AND	48	POET: 1935	64
AND, BROKEN GHOSTS WITH GLOW-WORMS IN THEIR HEADS,	82	LIGHT BREAKS	4
GOAT			
SO STEAL HER NOT O GOAT-LEGGED WIND	11	AIR BREATHE	7
GOBLIN			
NOR SPROUT ON OWL-SEED LIKE A GOBLIN-SUCKER, ...	123	FOSTER LIGHT	14
GOD			
LOVE-LIES, AND GOD-LIES, AND LIES-TO-PLEASE, ...	36	LET BE KNOWN	2
NO GOD-IN-HERO TUMBLE DOWN	125	SEED-AT-ZERO	4
NO GOD-IN-HERO TUMBLE DOWN	125	SEED-AT-ZERO	11
GOD'S			
AS A HE-GOD'S PADDLING WATER SKIRTS, ...	151	BELOW A TIME	16
GOOD			
THEN GOOD-BYE TO THE FISHERMANNED	162	LONG-LEGGED	5
GOOD-BYE TO THE MAN ON THE SEA-LEGGED DECK	162	LONG-LEGGED	18
GOOD-BYE TO CHIMNEYS AND FUNNELS, ...	162	LONG-LEGGED	25
ALWAYS GOOD-BYE TO THE LONG-LEGGED BREAD	165	LONG-LEGGED	94
ALWAYS GOOD-BYE TO THE FIRES OF THE FACE, ...	165	LONG-LEGGED	98
ALWAYS GOOD-BYE, CRIED THE VOICES THROUGH THE SHELL,	166	LONG-LEGGED	121
GOOD-BYE ALWAYS FOR THE FLESH IS CAST	166	LONG-LEGGED	122
GOOD-BYE, GOOD LUCK, STRUCK THE SUN AND THE MOON,	169	LONG-LEGGED	213
BAY. NO-GOOD IS ABROAD. I UNHARDY CAN	179	NEW QUAY	8
HARDLY BEAR THE DIN OF NO-GOOD WRACKED DRY ON	179	NEW QUAY	9
GRAVE			
ON THAT CLOUD COAST TO EACH GRAVE-GABBING SHADE;	102	FELLOWED SLEEP	18
RANGE FROM THE GRAVE-GROPING PLACE.	127	SEED-AT-ZERO	56
GREEN			
SUFFER THE SLASH OF VISION BY THE FIN-GREEN STUBBLE,	111	I, IN IMAGE	85
AND EYES HAVE BEEN GROVE-GREEN CATCHING MINE FROM THE DEPTH OF THE SILENCE;	224	IDYLL UNFORGET	33
OF THE PALE-GREEN, DELICATE FISHES, SILVER AS SIGHS;	224	IDYLL UNFORGET	39
GREEN-SHADOWED PANOPLY ENVELOPING ALL ITS STRANGENESS AND SOFTNESS OF STEALTH.	224	IDYLL UNFORGET	45
GREY			
DIG NO MORE FOR THE CHAINS OF HIS GREY-HAIRED HEART.	172	DAWN RAID	9
OVER A RUMP ON THE CLERICAL-GREY SEASHORE, ...	179	NEW QUAY	25
GRIEF			
FOR ALL THINGS ARE GRIEF-LIKE	225	OF ANY FLOWER	5
GROPING			
RANGE FROM THE GRAVE-GROPING PLACE.	127	SEED-AT-ZERO	56
GROVE			
AND EYES HAVE BEEN GROVE-GREEN CATCHING MINE FROM THE DEPTH OF THE SILENCE;	224	IDYLL UNFORGET	33
GUNNED			
AND FROM THE WINDY WEST CAME TWO-GUNNED GABRIEL,	118	ALTARWISE	57
GUT			
OVER THE SEA-GUT LOUDENING, SETS A ROCK ALIVE;	122	HOLD HARD	15
HAIR			
THROUGH THE RIPPLED DRUM OF THE HAIR-BURIED EAR;	157	INTO HER HEAD	4
HAIRED			
DIG NO MORE FOR THE CHAINS OF HIS GREY-HAIRED HEART.	172	DAWN RAID	9
HAIRY			
DEATH HAIRY-HEELED, AND THE TAPPED GHOST IN WOOD,	128	NOW, SAY NAY	33
HALF			
WITH THAT HALF-MOULDED MIND I SAID WAS YOURS, ...	10	COOL, OH NO	4
WITH HALF-AVERTED HEADS, AS IF TO LISTEN, ...	40	YOUNG ARE OLD	13
AND, CRACKLING INTO THE AIR, LEAVE ME HALF-BLIND.	44	LONGED TO MOVE	14

	PAGE	TITLE	LINE
HALF (CONTINUED)			
DRY IN THE HALF-TRACKED THIGH.	105	WORLD PYRAMID	60
ALTARWISE BY OWL-LIGHT IN THE HALF-WAY HOUSE	116	ALTARWISE	1
WITH BONES UNBUTTONED TO THE HALF-WAY WINDS, ...	117	ALTARWISE	9
ATLASWISE HOLD HALF-WAY OFF THE DUMMY BAY	121	ALTARWISE	128
HALVED			
THE SEA-HALVED FAITH THAT BLEW TIME TO HIS KNEES,	107	GRIEF THIEF	4
HANDED			
WHEN BLOOD, SPADE-HANDED, AND THE LOGIC TIME	100	RUNNING GRAVE	13
THE COUNTRY-HANDED GRAVE BOXED INTO LOVE, ...	115	A GRIEF AGO	31
HARD			
SPILL THE LANK FOLLY'S HUNTER AND THE HARD-HELD HOPE.	122	HOLD HARD	18
HARP			
THE HARP-WAKED CASANOVA RAKES NO RANGE.	159	TO LEDA	2
HATCHED			
SHAKING THE SEA-HATCHED SKULL, ...	111	I, IN IMAGE	100
HAW			
SEE HOW HE STUMBLES. HALLELUJAH HEE-HAW!	179	NEW QUAY	26
HAWK			
ALL PRAISE OF THE HAWK ON FIRE IN HAWK-EYED DUSK BE			
SUNG, ...	202	SIR JOHNS HILL	27
HE (1)			
HEAD			
OF A LACK-A-HEAD GHOST I FEAR TO THE ANONYMOUS END.	141	I, FIRST NAMED	4
HEADED			
AND HEMLOCK-HEADED IN THE WOOD OF WEATHERS.	117	ALTARWISE	28
HEART			
BUT RAIL WITH YOUR WIZARD'S RIBS THE HEART-SHAPED			
PLANET;	123	FOSTER LIGHT	15
HEAVEN			
DROVE IN THE HEAVEN-DRIVEN OF THE NAILS	120	ALTARWISE	106
HEAD TO HEAVEN-CIRCLING HEAD, ...	158	INTO HER HEAD	48
SHE DELUDES THE HEAVEN-PROOF HOUSE WITH ENTERING			
CLOUDS	169	LOVE IN ASYLUM	6
HEDGED			
THE YEAR-HEDGED ROW IS LAME WITH FLINT, ...	129	MY NEOPHYTE	38
HEE			
SEE HOW HE STUMBLES. HALLELUJAH HEE-HAW!	179	NEW QUAY	26
HEELED			
SO, PLANING-HEELED, I FLEW ALONG MY MAN	101	FELLOWED SLEEP	4
DEATH HAIRY-HEELED, AND THE TAPPED GHOST IN WOOD,	128	NOW, SAY NAY	33
WIND-HEELED FOOT IN THE HOLE OF A FIREBALL, ...	141	SAINT TO FALL	12
HELD			
BRIGHT, WELL-HELD HEAD, ...	14	FOR LEDA	9
UPON YOUR HELD-OUT HAND	32	HELD-OUT HAND	T
UPON YOUR HELD-OUT HAND	32	HELD-OUT HAND	1
SPILL THE LANK FOLLY'S HUNTER AND THE HARD-HELD HOPE.	122	HOLD HARD	18
HEMLOCK			
AND HEMLOCK-HEADED IN THE WOOD OF WEATHERS.	117	ALTARWISE	28
HERO			
NO GOD-IN-HERO TUMBLE DOWN	125	SEED-AT-ZERO	4
NO GOD-IN-HERO TUMBLE DOWN	125	SEED-AT-ZERO	11
SHALL THE HERO-IN-TOMORROW	126	SEED-AT-ZERO	48
SHALL THE HERO-IN-TOMORROW	127	SEED-AT-ZERO	55
HIGH			
OF LAMP-POSTS AND HIGH-VOLTED FRUITS, ...	70	SECRET WIND	16
A STONE LIES LOST AND LOCKED IN THE LARK-HIGH HILL.	159	INTO HER HEAD	62
MAST-HIGH MOON-WHITE WOMEN NAKED	165	LONG-LEGGED	104

	PAGE	TITLE	LINE
HILLED			
LOP, LOVE, MY FORK TONGUE, SAID THE PIN-HILLED NETTLE;	119	ALTARWISE	76
HILLS			
PIN-LEGGED ON POLE-HILLS WITH A BLACK MEDUSA	119	ALTARWISE	68
HOISTED			
THEN THREW ON THAT TIDE-HOISTED SCREEN	129	MY NEOPHYTE	34
HOLLOWED			
ALL-HOLLOWED MAN WEPT FOR HIS WHITE APPAREL.	111	I, IN IMAGE	102
HOUSE			
RATHER THAN CHARNEL-HOUSE AS SYMBOL	29	LONG, SKELETON	12
HUED			
TO HAVE KNOWN THEM IN THEIR BLUE-HUED VALIANCE,	223	IDYLL UNFORGET	3
HUNG			
OF EELS, SAINT HERON HYMNING IN THE SHELL-HUNG DISTANT	202	SIR JOHNS HILL	36
HURT			
LIFT WIT-HURT HEAD FOR SUN TO SYMPATHIZE,	42	A WAR OF WITS	18
HYMEN			
OR RENT ANCESTRALLY THE ROPED SEA-HYMEN,	131	I MAKE THIS IN	12
I			
BUT IF THIS PROVED IMPOSS-I-BLE	84	LETTER TO AUNT	29
ILL			
BETWEEN THE STREET-LAMPS AND THE ILL-LIT SKY,	52	OUT OF THE PIT	61
IMPOSS			
BUT IF THIS PROVED IMPOSS-I-BLE	84	LETTER TO AUNT	29
IN (8)			
INFANT			
THE MASSES OF THE INFANT-BEARING SEA	175	FIRE RAID	74
INSECT			
DRY AS ECHOES AND INSECT-FACED,	167	LONG-LEGGED	146
IRON			
TO MY MAN-IRON SIDLE.	108	I, IN IMAGE	6
JAW			
DESTRUCTION, PICKED BY BIRDS, BRAYS THROUGH THE JAW-BONE,	132	I MAKE THIS IN	36
KILLING			
THE FURIOUS OX-KILLING HOUSE OF LOVE.	168	LONG-LEGGED	200
KNEE			
KNEE-DEEP IN VOMIT. I SAW HIM THERE,	51	OUT OF THE PIT	43
LACK			
OF A LACK-A-HEAD GHOST I FEAR TO THE ANONYMOUS END.	141	I, FIRST NAMED	4
LADLE			
RIP OF THE VAULTS, I TOOK MY MARROW-LADLE	118	ALTARWISE	35
LAMMED			
OR, WATER-LAMMED, FROM THE SCYTHE-SIDED THORN,	114	A GRIEF AGO	3
LAMP			
OF LAMP-POSTS AND HIGH-VOLTED FRUITS,	70	SECRET WIND	16
LAMPED			
ARC-LAMPED THROWN BACK UPON THE CUTTING FLOOD.	118	ALTARWISE	56
LAMPS			
BETWEEN THE STREET-LAMPS AND THE ILL-LIT SKY,	52	OUT OF THE PIT	61
LARK			
A STONE LIES LOST AND LOCKED IN THE LARK-HIGH HILL.	159	INTO HER HEAD	62
LAST			
SPRINKLES IN CHILDREN'S EYES A LONG-LAST SLEEP	56	WHY EAST WIND	13
LEAF			
SLEEP TO A NEWBORN SLEEP IN A SWADDLING LOIN-LEAF STROKED AND SANG	157	INTO HER HEAD	22
FOR ALL THINGS ARE LEAF-LIKE	225	OF ANY FLOWER	2

	PAGE	TITLE	LINE
LEAVED			
A BIBLE-LEAVED OF ALL THE WRITTEN WOODS	119	ALTARWISE	86
THE SUN-LEAVED HOLY CANDLEWOODS	141	SAINT TO FALL	19
LED			
OF THE LED-ASTRAY BIRDS WHOM GOD, FOR THEIR BREAST			
OF WHISTLES, ...	202	SIR JOHNS HILL	43
LEGGED			
AHOY, OLD, SEA-LEGGED FOX, ...	5	PROLOGUE	98
SO STEAL HER NOT O GOAT-LEGGED WIND	11	AIR BREATHE	7
SPARKLING A TWELVE-LEGGED BODY	12	CABARET	19
PIN-LEGGED ON POLE-HILLS WITH A BLACK MEDUSA	119	ALTARWISE	68
BALLAD OF THE LONG-LEGGED BAIT	161	LONG-LEGGED	T
GOOD-BYE TO THE MAN ON THE SEA-LEGGED DECK	162	LONG-LEGGED	18
SPUN ON A SPOUT LIKE A LONG-LEGGED BALL	163	LONG-LEGGED	56
THE LONG-LEGGED BEAUTIFUL BAIT THEIR WIVES.	164	LONG-LEGGED	70
ALWAYS GOOD-BYE TO THE LONG-LEGGED BREAD	165	LONG-LEGGED	94
WHEN HIS LONG-LEGGED FLESH WAS A WIND ON FIRE	168	LONG-LEGGED	195
WITH HIS LONG-LEGGED HEART IN HIS HAND.	169	LONG-LEGGED	216
LICKERS			
THAT PRINCE OF PIMPS, THAT DOYEN OF DUNG-LICKERS.	179	NEW QUAY	24
LIES			
LOVE-LIES, AND GOD-LIES, AND LIES-TO-PLEASE, ...	36	LET BE KNOWN	2
LOVE-LIES, AND GOD-LIES, AND LIES-TO-PLEASE, ...	36	LET BE KNOWN	2
LOVE-LIES, AND GOD-LIES, AND LIES-TO-PLEASE, ...	36	LET BE KNOWN	2
LIGHT			
ALTARWISE BY OWL-LIGHT	116	ALTARWISE	T
ALTARWISE BY OWL-LIGHT IN THE HALF-WAY HOUSE	116	ALTARWISE	1
LIKE			
FOR ALL THINGS ARE LEAF-LIKE	225	OF ANY FLOWER	2
AND CLOUD-LIKE.	225	OF ANY FLOWER	3
FOR ALL THINGS ARE GRIEF-LIKE	225	OF ANY FLOWER	5
AND SHROUD-LIKE.	225	OF ANY FLOWER	6
LILY			
AS THE MOUTH OF THE TIGER-LILY	229	MY RIVER	24
LIMP			
LOST IN A LIMP-TREED AND UNEATING SILENCE, ...	132	I MAKE THIS IN	28
LIPPED			
MALE SHAPES, GIRL-LIPPED, BUT CLAD LIKE BOYS:	143	THE MOLLS	2
FROM SALT-LIPPED BEAK TO THE KICK OF THE STERN	164	LONG-LEGGED	81
LITTLE WHITE-LIPPED FACES HAVE PEERED UP AT ME, ...	224	IDYLL UNFORGET	32
LIT			
BETWEEN THE STREET-LAMPS AND THE ILL-LIT SKY, ...	52	OUT OF THE PIT	61
LOCKED			
CURL-LOCKED AND ANIMAL CAVEPOOLS OF SPELLS AND BONE,	135	HOW MY ANIMAL	27
WINTER-LOCKED SIDE BY SIDE, ...	153	WAS A SAVIOUR	26
LOIN			
SLEEP TO A NEWBORN SLEEP IN A SWADDLING LOIN-LEAF			
STROKED AND SANG	157	INTO HER HEAD	22
LONG			
SPRINKLES IN CHILDREN'S EYES A LONG-LAST SLEEP	56	WHY EAST WIND	13
THE LONG-TAILED STONE	114	SERVANT SUN	18
BALLAD OF THE LONG-LEGGED BAIT	161	LONG-LEGGED	T
SPUN ON A SPOUT LIKE A LONG-LEGGED BALL	163	LONG-LEGGED	56
THE LONG-LEGGED BEAUTIFUL BAIT THEIR WIVES.	164	LONG-LEGGED	70
ALWAYS GOOD-BYE TO THE LONG-LEGGED BREAD	165	LONG-LEGGED	94
AND THE LONG-TAILED LIGHTNING LIT HIS CATCH.	166	LONG-LEGGED	128
WHEN HIS LONG-LEGGED FLESH WAS A WIND ON FIRE	168	LONG-LEGGED	195
WITH HIS LONG-LEGGED HEART IN HIS HAND.	169	LONG-LEGGED	216
LOOKING			
OR SAW IN THE LOOKING-GLASS SHELL	139	TOMBSTONE TOLD	7

	PAGE	TITLE	LINE
LOOPED			
OR LIKE THE TIDE-LOOPED BREASTKNOT REEFED AGAIN ...	131	I MAKE THIS IN	11
LORD'S			
AND FATHER ALL NOR FAIL THE FLY-LORD'S ACRE, ...	123	FOSTER LIGHT	13
ON THE LORD'S-TABLE OF THE BOWING GRASS. FEAR MOST	198	COUNTRY SLEEP	35
LOVE			
BY LOVE-TIP OR MY HAND'S RED HEAT.	19	IMAGES IN AIR	14
LOVE-LIES, AND GOD-LIES, AND LIES-TO-PLEASE, ...	36	LET BE KNOWN	2
FROM DAMP LOVE-DARKNESS AND THE NURSE'S TWIST	96	RUB OF LOVE	38
LOW			
EMBRACING LOW-FALUTIN	154	RETURN	1
LUCK			
FROGS AND SATANS AND WOMAN-LUCK, ...	150	WHEN I WOKE	7
MAD			
SPIED MOON-MAD BEASTS CAROUSING ON THE HILL, ...	50	OUT OF THE PIT	9
MADE			
FROM THE WELL-MADE HAND	241	ADMIT THE SUN	21
MAN			
OF SUNS IN THE MAN-MELTING NIGHT.	102	I DREAMED MY	8
TO MY MAN-IRON SIDLE.	108	I, IN IMAGE	6
UP ROSE THE ABRAHAM-MAN, MAD FOR MY SAKE, ...	112	NOT FATHER ME	19
FOR MAN-BEGETTERS IN THE DRY-AS-PASTE, ...	113	NOT FATHER ME	23
MAN-IN-SEED, IN SEED-AT-ZERO, ...	126	SEED-AT-ZERO	43
MAN-IN-SEED, IN SEE-AT-ZERO, ...	127	SEED-AT-ZERO	50
FLEW MAN-BEARING THERE.	157	INTO HER HEAD	6
MAP			
INTO THE MAP-BACKED HILLS WHERE PATHS	44	TO FOLLOW FOX	8
MARROW			
RIP OF THE VAULTS, I TOOK MY MARROW-LADLE	118	ALTARWISE	35
AND THIS WEAK HOUSE TO MARROW-COLUMNED HEAVEN, ...	131	I MAKE THIS IN	8
MARROWED			
AN OLD MAN'S SHANK ONE-MARROWED WITH MY BONE, ...	95	RUB OF LOVE	32
MAST			
MAST-HIGH MOON-WHITE WOMEN NAKED	165	LONG-LEGGED	104
MASTER			
LAPPING THE STILL CANALS, THE DRY TIDE-MASTER	54	WE BY SEASAND	10
MEASURE			
CUT-TO-MEASURE FLESH BIT, ...	151	BELOW A TIME	3
MEAT			
BY THE LIGHT OF THE MEAT-EATING SUN.	143	24 YEARS	5
MELTING			
OF SUNS IN THE MAN-MELTING NIGHT.	102	I DREAMED MY	8
MEMBERED			
A FURNACE-NOSTRILLED COLUMN-MEMBERED	158	INTO HER HEAD	28
MID			
AND I, CAUGHT IN MID-AIR PERHAPS, ...	9	MINUTE'S HOUR	6
MIDNIGHT			
NOR BLOWS BACK MOON-AND-MIDNIGHT AS SHE BLOWS.	92	BOYS OF SUMMER	30
MILK			
AND MILK-WHITE NAILS.	229	MY RIVER	29
MOON			
SPIED MOON-MAD BEASTS CAROUSING ON THE HILL, ...	50	OUT OF THE PIT	9
NOR BLOWS BACK MOON-AND-MIDNIGHT AS SHE BLOWS.	92	BOYS OF SUMMER	30
THE MOON-DRAWN GRAVE, WITH THE SEAFARING YEARS, ...	107	GRIEF THIEF	2
DAZZLE THIS FACE OF VOICES ON THE MOON-TURNED TABLE,	110	I, IN IMAGE	69
TWINE IN A MOON-BLOWN SHELL, ...	129	MY NEOPHYTE	15
MAST-HIGH MOON-WHITE WOMEN NAKED	165	LONG-LEGGED	104
TURNS THE MOON-CHAINED AND WATER-WOUND	169	LONG-LEGGED	203
MORROW			
O ROME AND SODOM TO-MORROW AND LONDON	168	LONG-LEGGED	191

	PAGE	TITLE	LINE
MORROW (CONTINUED)			
CASTING TO-MORROW LIKE A THORN	180	VISION, PRAYER	25
AND TO-MORROW WEEPS IN A BLIND CAGE	209	POEM ON B'DAY	42
MORROW'S			
TO-MORROW'S DIVER IN HER HORNY MILK,	103	WORLD PYRAMID	4
BIT OUT THE MANDRAKE WITH TO-MORROW'S SCREAM.	117	ALTARWISE	6
HER LOVER'S WINGS THAT FOLD TO-MORROW'S FLIGHT,	159	INTO HER HEAD	57
MOTHERS			
MY MOTHERS-EYED, UPON THE TOPS OF TREES;	101	FELLOWED SLEEP	9
FADED MY ELBOW GHOST, THE MOTHERS-EYED,	102	FELLOWED SLEEP	16
MOULDED			
WITH THAT HALF-MOULDED MIND I SAID WAS YOURS,	10	COOL, OH NO	4
MOUTHED			
OH, EAGLE-MOUTHED,	232	YOUR VOICE	10
MUFFLE			
WINDSHAKE OF SAILSHAPED EARS, MUFFLE-TOED TAP	136	AFTER FUNERAL	2
MUSCLING			
I WOULD NOT FEAR THE MUSCLING-IN OF LOVE	95	RUB OF LOVE	17
NEAR			
SUPER-OR-NEAR MAN	158	INTO HER HEAD	29
NECKED			
EACH ANCIENT, STONE-NECKED MINUTE OF LOVE'S SEASON	131	I MAKE THIS IN	2
NESTING			
HER MOLTEN FLIGHT UP CINDER-NESTING COLUMNS,	132	I MAKE THIS IN	26
NEXT			
THE NEXT-DOOR SEA DISPELLED	150	WHEN I WOKE	6
NIGHT			
WHY NIGHT-TIME RAIN AND THE BREAST'S BLOOD	56	WHY EAST WIND	8
OR DRIVE THE NIGHT-GEARED FORTH.	90	EUNUCH DREAMS	26
IN BOTTOM GEAR THROUGH NIGHT-GEARED MAN.	103	I DREAMED MY	12
TO-NIGHT SHALL FIND NO DYING BUT ALIVE AND WARM	194	CONVERS PRAYER	15
NO (3)			
NON			
STOPPED NON-STOP DANCING TO LET HOT FEET COOL,	51	OUT OF THE PIT	30
NOSTRILLED			
A FURNACE-NOSTRILLED COLUMN-MEMBERED	158	INTO HER HEAD	28
NOT (1)			
OF (1)			
OFF			
I HAD A HANDSOME AND WELL-OFF BOY	149	PAPER & STICKS	13
ON (1)			
ONCE			
THESE ONCE-BLIND EYES HAVE BREATHED A WIND OF VISIONS,	132	I MAKE THIS IN	54
THE CAULDRON'S ROOT THROUGH THIS ONCE-RINDLESS HAND	132	I MAKE THIS IN	55
ONE			
WITH A ONE-COLOURED CALM;	54	WE BY SEASAND	13
TWO ONE-DIMENSIONED GHOSTS, LOVE ON A REEL,	89	EUNUCH DREAMS	12
GRAFTS ON ITS BRIDE ONE-SIDED SKINS OF TRUTH;	90	EUNUCH DREAMS	28
AN OLD MAN'S SHANK ONE-MARROWED WITH MY BONE,	95	RUB OF LOVE	32
AND NO-ONE STIRS AT SHEBA'S SIDE	165	LONG-LEGGED	108
OR (1)			
OUT			
UPON YOUR HELD-OUT HAND	32	HELD-OUT HAND	T
UPON YOUR HELD-OUT HAND	32	HELD-OUT HAND	1
AND OUT-OF-PERSPECTIVE SAILORS,	151	BELOW A TIME	14
OVER			
OF OVER-FRUITFUL SMILES,	12	SKY'S BRIGHT	8
OWL			
ALTARWISE BY OWL-LIGHT	116	ALTARWISE	T

	PAGE	TITLE	LINE
OWL (CONTINUED)			
ALTARWISE BY OWL-LIGHT IN THE HALF-WAY HOUSE	116	ALTARWISE	1
NOR SPROUT ON OWL-SEED LIKE A GOBLIN-SUCKER, ...	123	FOSTER LIGHT	14
OX			
THE FURIOUS OX-KILLING HOUSE OF LOVE.	168	LONG-LEGGED	200
PAID			
MY PAID-FOR SLAVED-FOR OWN TOO LATE	151	BELOW A TIME	6
PAINT			
SKIRTING THE ORDERED BEDS OF PAINT-BOX FLOWERS, ...	33	IN GARDENS	3
OLD PAINT-STAINED TUMBLERS RIDING	154	RETURN	19
PALE			
OF THE PALE-GREEN, DELICATE FISHES, SILVER AS SIGHS;	224	IDYLL UNFORGET	39
PAPER			
PLUG THE PAPER-BLOWING TUBES;	156	RETURN	79
PAPPED			
BENT LIKE THREE TREES AND BIRD-PAPPED THROUGH HER			
SHIFT, ...	120	ALTARWISE	103
PARSLEY			
NUTMEG, CIVET, AND SEA-PARSLEY SERVE THE PLAGUED			
GROOM AND BRIDE	131	SINNERS' BELL	29
PASTE			
FOR MAN-BEGETTERS IN THE DRY-AS-PASTE, ...	113	NOT FATHER ME	23
PENNY			
THEN, PENNY-EYED, THAT GENTLEMAN OF WOUNDS, ...	117	ALTARWISE	7
PERSPECTIVE			
AND OUT-OF-PERSPECTIVE SAILORS, ...	151	BELOW A TIME	14
PETALS			
TO THE VOICES OF THE WIND CAUGHT IN THE			
CRADLE-PETALS OF THE NIGHT:	223	IDYLL UNFORGET	8
PILLARED			
DOWN THE STACKED SEA AND WATER-PILLARED SHADE, ...	132	I MAKE THIS IN	40
PIN			
PIN-LEGGED ON POLE-HILLS WITH A BLACK MEDUSA	119	ALTARWISE	68
LOP, LOVE, MY FORK TONGUE, SAID THE PIN-HILLED			
NETTLE;	119	ALTARWISE	76
THE WORM IS (PIN-POINT) RATIONAL IN THE FRUIT.	159	TO LEDA	3
THE WORM IS (PIN-POINT) RATIONAL IN THE FRUIT.	159	TO LEDA	9
PINNED			
WHEN MY PINNED-AROUND-THE-SPIRIT	151	BELOW A TIME	2
PLANET			
THE PLANET-DUCTED PELICAN OF CIRCLES	117	ALTARWISE	17
PLANING			
SO, PLANING-HEELED, I FLEW ALONG MY MAN	101	FELLOWED SLEEP	4
PLEASE			
LOVE-LIES, AND GOD-LIES, AND LIES-TO-PLEASE, ...	36	LET BE KNOWN	2
PLEASURE			
BECAUSE THE PLEASURE-BIRD WHISTLES	144	PLEASURE-BIRD	T
BECAUSE THE PLEASURE-BIRD WHISTLES AFTER THE HOT			
WIRES, ...	144	PLEASURE-BIRD	1
PLUCKED			
AND FROM THESE TONGUE-PLUCKED SENSES DRAWS HIS TUNE;	76	LASHED RINGS	13
POINT			
THE WORM IS (PIN-POINT) RATIONAL IN THE FRUIT.	159	TO LEDA	3
THE WORM IS (PIN-POINT) RATIONAL IN THE FRUIT.	159	TO LEDA	9
POINTED			
IN THE BEGINNING WAS THE THREE-POINTED STAR, ...	93	IN BEGINNING	1
POLE			
POLE-SITTING GIRLS DESCENDED FOR A MEAL, ...	51	OUT OF THE PIT	29
PIN-LEGGED ON POLE-HILLS WITH A BLACK MEDUSA	119	ALTARWISE	68

	PAGE	TITLE	LINE
POSTS			
OF LAMP-POSTS AND HIGH-VOLTED FRUITS, ...	70	SECRET WIND	16
PRINT			
MOONFALL AND SAILING EMPEROR, PALE AS THEIR TIDE-PRINT, ...	130	SINNERS' BELL	10
PRINTED			
GLINT IN THE STAVED AND SIREN-PRINTED CAVERS, ...	131	I MAKE THIS IN	20
PROGENY			
NO PROPHET-PROGENY OF MINE, ...	150	WHEN I WOKE	26
PROOF			
SHE DELUDES THE HEAVEN-PROOF HOUSE WITH ENTERING CLOUDS	169	LOVE IN ASYLUM	6
PROPHET			
NO PROPHET-PROGENY OF MINE, ...	150	WHEN I WOKE	26
PRYING			
AT WHOSE BALL-PRYING EVEN DEATH'LL SQUIRM	179	NEW QUAY	22
QUARTERS			
AN OLD TORMENTED MAN THREE-QUARTERS BLIND, ...	217	ELEGY	18
RACKED			
TIME'S SHIP-RACKED GOSPEL ON THE GLOBE I BALANCE:	121	ALTARWISE	129
RAIN			
WITH RAIN-BEATEN HANDS HOLDING THE WHIP, ...	45	PLOUGHMAN GONE	20
RAINBOW			
THE RAINBOW-FISH BEND IN HER JOYS, ...	163	LONG-LEGGED	34
RAW			
REHEARSING HEAT UPON A RAW-EDGED NERVE.	95	RUB OF LOVE	19
RED			
COOL AS THE WAX-RED FOUNTAINS OF THE VEINS;	63	WOMAN SPEAKS	5
RAISE UP THIS RED-EYED EARTH?	89	EUNUCH DREAMS	23
A THREE-EYED, RED-EYED SPARK, BLUNT AS A FLOWER;	94	IN BEGINNING	15
BY RED-EYED ORCHARDS SOW THE SEEDS OF SNOW, ...	123	FOSTER LIGHT	11
SLAPPED DOWN THE GUILLOTINE, THE BLOOD-RED DOUBLE	124	TODAY, INSECT	6
RINDLESS			
THE CAULDRON'S ROOT THROUGH THIS ONCE-RINDLESS HAND	132	I MAKE THIS IN	55
RINGED			
THE RINGED-SEA GHOST, RISE GRIMLY FROM THE WRACK.	113	NOT FATHER ME	24
RIPPLE			
FELT THEIR SERENITY OF RIPPLE-WOVEN LOVELINESS; ...	223	IDYLL UNFORGET	4
ROCK			
OR SPRAY-BASED AND ROCK-CHESTED SEA:	145	PLEASURE-BIRD	24
ROOT			
QUESTION: WHEN SHALL ROOT-DAM DIE?	72	TAKE NEEDLES	61
QUESTION: WHEN SHALL ROOT-DAM GROW?	72	TAKE NEEDLES	63
ROPE			
GLIDING, ROPE-DANCING, IS HIS FANCY, ...	28	NO WINGS	8
ROW			
HE HAD BY HEART THE CHRIST-CROSS-ROW OF DEATH.	97	TWILIGHT LOCKS	24
RULED			
WHAT MEANING, VOICES, IN THE STRAIGHT-RULED GRASS,	137	O CHATTERTON	17
SALT			
AND SALT-EYED STUMBLE BEDWARD WHERE SHE LIES	107	GRIEF THIEF	12
FROM SALT-LIPPED BEAK TO THE KICK OF THE STERN	164	LONG-LEGGED	81
SAND			
WITH A SAND-BAGGED GARRISON, ...	127	SEED-AT-ZERO	53
SAWERS			
THE SCALED SEA-SAWERS, FIX IN A NAKED SPONGE	119	ALTARWISE	92
SCALED			
SHAKEN SILKILY FROM STAR-SCALED BOUGHS.	226	SLENDER WIND	5
SCALES			
THE WEIGHING-SCALES, OF MY HAND.	155	RETURN	43

	PAGE	TITLE	LINE
SCATTER			
THE DEATH-STAGGED SCATTER-BREATH	150	WHEN I WOKE	19
SCRAPING			
RANGE ON THE SKY-SCRAPING PLACE.	126	SEED-AT-ZERO	49
SCYTHE			
AND THE CAGE FOR THE SCYTHE-EYED RAVEN.	106	ALL ALL AND	21
OR, WATER-LAMMED, FROM THE SCYTHE-SIDED THORN, ...	114	A GRIEF AGO	3
SEA			
AHOY, OLD, SEA-LEGGED FOX, ...	5	PROLOGUE	98
TILL ALL OUR SEA-FAITHS DIE.	91	WHERE ONCE THE	24
HIS SEA-SUCKED ADAM IN THE HOLLOW HULK, ...	103	WORLD PYRAMID	2
THE SEA-HALVED FAITH THAT BLEW TIME TO HIS KNEES,	107	GRIEF THIEF	4
TO THE SEA-BLOWN ARRIVAL.	109	I, IN IMAGE	36
(TURN THE SEA-SPINDLE LATERAL, ...	110	I, IN IMAGE	67
COME UNTO SEA-STUCK TOWERS, AT THE FIBRE SCALING,	111	I, IN IMAGE	74
SHAKING THE SEA-HATCHED SKULL, ...	111	I, IN IMAGE	100
THE RINGED-SEA GHOST, RISE GRIMLY FROM THE WRACK.	113	NOT FATHER ME	24
AND SIRENS SINGING FROM OUR LADY'S SEA-STRAW.	119	ALTARWISE	70
THE SCALED SEA-SAWERS, FIX IN A NAKED SPONGE	119	ALTARWISE	92
HAS SOWN A FLYING GARDEN ROUND THAT SEA-GHOST?	121	ALTARWISE	136
OVER THE SEA-GUT LOUDENING, SETS A ROCK ALIVE;	122	HOLD HARD	15
OR RENT ANCESTRALLY THE ROPED SEA-HYMEN, ...	131	I MAKE THIS IN	12
THE FRANK, CLOSED PEARL, THE SEA-GIRLS' LINEAMENTS	131	I MAKE THIS IN	19
NUTMEG, CIVET, AND SEA-PARSLEY SERVE THE PLAGUED GROOM AND BRIDE	131	SINNERS' BELL	29
GOOD-BYE TO THE MAN ON THE SEA-LEGGED DECK	162	LONG-LEGGED	18
FOR THE CRAB-BACKED DEAD ON THE SEA-BED ROSE	165	LONG-LEGGED	99
THEY OF THE PALE, SEA-WAN BEAUTY, THEY OF THE HOME	224	IDYLL UNFORGET	38
SEE			
MAN-IN-SEED, IN SEE-AT-ZERO, ...	127	SEED-AT-ZERO	50
SEED			
NOR SPROUT ON OWL-SEED LIKE A GOBLIN-SUCKER, ...	123	FOSTER LIGHT	14
THE SEED-AT-ZERO	125	SEED-AT-ZERO	T
THE SEED-AT-ZERO SHALL NOT STORM	125	SEED-AT-ZERO	1
THE SEED-AT-ZERO SHALL NOT STORM	125	SEED-AT-ZERO	8
MAN-IN-SEED, IN SEED-AT-ZERO, ...	126	SEED-AT-ZERO	43
MAN-IN-SEED, IN SEED-AT-ZERO, ...	126	SEED-AT-ZERO	43
MAN-IN-SEED, IN SEE-AT-ZERO, ...	127	SEED-AT-ZERO	50
SERENE			
THE SEA HAS BEEN BREEZE-SERENE SAPPHIRE, ...	224	IDYLL UNFORGET	21
SET			
STAR-SET AT JACOB'S ANGLE, ...	111	I, IN IMAGE	81
SHADOWED			
GREEN-SHADOWED PANOPLY ENVELOPING ALL ITS STRANGENESS AND SOFTNESS OF STEALTH.	224	IDYLL UNFORGET	45
SHAKEN			
BEFORE THE LUNGE OF THE NIGHT, THE NOTES ON THIS TIME-SHAKEN	203	SIR JOHNS HILL	59
SHAPED			
BUT RAIL WITH YOUR WIZARD'S RIBS THE HEART-SHAPED PLANET;	123	FOSTER LIGHT	15
SHAPING			
IN SHAPING-TIME THE CIRCLE STUNG AWAKE, ...	121	INCARNATE DEVL	3
A SERPENT FIDDLED IN THE SHAPING-TIME.	122	INCARNATE DEVL	18
SHEATH			
THE SHEATH-DECKED JACKS, QUEEN WITH A SHUFFLED HEART;	118	ALTARWISE	59
SHEETS			
DISTURB NO WINDING-SHEETS, MY SON, ...	60	MEAT ON BONES	6

	PAGE	TITLE	LINE
SHELL			
OF EELS, SAINT HERON HYMNING IN THE SHELL-HUNG			
DISTANT	202	SIR JOHNS HILL	36
SHIP			
TIME'S SHIP-RACKED GOSPEL ON THE GLOBE I BALANCE:	121	ALTARWISE	129
THE VANISHING OF THE MUSICAL SHIP-WORK AND THE			
CHUCKED BELLS, ...	141	SAINT TO FALL	8
SHROUD			
AND SHROUD-LIKE.	225	OF ANY FLOWER	6
SIDED			
GRAFTS ON ITS BRIDE ONE-SIDED SKINS OF TRUTH;	90	EUNUCH DREAMS	28
OR, WATER-LAMMED, FROM THE SCYTHE-SIDED THORN, ...	114	A GRIEF AGO	3
STILLS SNAPPED BY NIGHT IN THE BREAD-SIDED FIELD,	118	ALTARWISE	54
SIGNED			
ALL BLOOD-SIGNED ASSAILINGS AND VANISHED MARRIAGES			
IN WHICH HE HAD NO LOVELY PART	158	INTO HER HEAD	43
SIN			
LIE ALL UNKNOWING OF THE GRAVE SIN-EATER.	113	NOT FATHER ME	32
THAT SIN-EMBRACING DRIPPER OF FUN	156	RETURN	88
SIREN			
GLINT IN THE STAVED AND SIREN-PRINTED CAVERS, ...	131	I MAKE THIS IN	20
SITTING			
POLE-SITTING GIRLS DESCENDED FOR A MEAL, ...	51	OUT OF THE PIT	29
SIX			
THE BOAT SWIMS INTO THE SIX-YEAR WEATHER, ...	166	LONG-LEGGED	129
SKINNED			
FOREVER IT IS A WHITE CHILD IN THE DARK-SKINNED			
SUMMER	130	SINNERS' BELL	19
SKIRTING			
BRED IN THE DARK BEHIND THE SKIRTING-BOARD, ...	28	NO WINGS	21
SKY			
RANGE ON THE SKY-SCRAPING PLACE.	126	SEED-AT-ZERO	49
BUT WAILED AND NESTED IN THE SKY-BLUE WALL	153	WAS A SAVIOUR	31
SLAVED			
MY PAID-FOR SLAVED-FOR OWN TOO LATE	151	BELOW A TIME	6
SLEEP			
MAN WAS THE BURNING ENGLAND SHE WAS SLEEP-WALKING,			
AND THE ENAMOURING ISLAND	157	INTO HER HEAD	20
SNAIL			
FROM POLE TO POLE LEAPT ROUND THE SNAIL-WAKED WORLD.	120	ALTARWISE	108
SOFT			
ITS HONEYED CHEEK, SOFT-TALKING MOUTH, ...	35	LIFT UP FACE	16
SOIL			
AND OUT OF EVERY DOMED AND SOIL-BASED SHELL	158	INTO HER HEAD	51
SOLDIERS			
EX-SOLDIERS WITH HORRORS FOR A FACE, ...	41	YOUNG ARE OLD	31
SOPPED			
THESE CLOUD-SOPPED, MARBLE HANDS, THIS MONUMENTAL	137	AFTER FUNERAL	36
SPADE			
WHEN BLOOD, SPADE-HANDED, AND THE LOGIC TIME	100	RUNNING GRAVE	13
SPECKED			
SWELLING IN FLEA-SPECKED LINEN	154	RETURN	7
SPIDER			
THE SPIDER-TONGUED, AND THE LOUD HILL OF WALES) ...	99	OCTOBER WIND	27
SPINDLE			
(TURN THE SEA-SPINDLE LATERAL, ...	110	I, IN IMAGE	67
SPINNING			
BRIGHT AS HER SPINNING-WHEELS, THE COLIC SEASON ...	108	I, IN IMAGE	8
SPIRE			
MY MAST IS A BELL-SPIRE, ...	164	LONG-LEGGED	76

	PAGE	TITLE	LINE
SPIRIT			
THE WATER-SPIRIT MOVES AS IT IS HIDDEN, ...	76	LASHED RINGS	9
WHEN MY PINNED-AROUND-THE-SPIRIT	151	BELOW A TIME	2
TO THE SPRING-SPIRIT	227	SPRING-SPIRIT	T
SPOKEN			
SING THROUGH THE WATER-SPOKEN PROW	164	LONG-LEGGED	78
SPRAY			
OR SPRAY-BASED AND ROCK-CHESTED SEA:	145	PLEASURE-BIRD	24
SPRING			
TO THE SPRING-SPIRIT	227	SPRING-SPIRIT	T
STAGGED			
THE DEATH-STAGGED SCATTER-BREATH	150	WHEN I WOKE	19
STAINED			
AND PRICK THE THUMB-STAINED HEAVEN THROUGH THE THIMBLE.	104	WORLD PYRAMID	27
AND A TEAR-STAINED WIDOWER GRIEF DROOPED FROM THE LASHES	133	MAKE ME A MASK	9
OLD PAINT-STAINED TUMBLERS RIDING	154	RETURN	19
STAR			
OF THE STAR-GESTURED CHILDREN IN THE PARK.	98	OCTOBER WIND	12
STAR-SET AT JACOB'S ANGLE, ...	111	I, IN IMAGE	81
SHALL THE STAR-FLANKED SEED BE RIDDLED, ...	125	SEED-AT-ZERO	16
SHALL THE STAR-FLANKED SEED BE RIDDLED, ...	126	SEED-AT-ZERO	23
WITH A STAR-FLANKED GARRISON, ...	126	SEED-AT-ZERO	46
FROM THE STAR-FLANKED FIELDS OF SPACE, ...	127	SEED-AT-ZERO	51
VENUS LIES STAR-STRUCK IN HER WOUND	166	LONG-LEGGED	117
SHAKEN SILKILY FROM STAR-SCALED BOUGHS.	226	SLENDER WIND	5
STEPPED			
AND THE CELL-STEPPED THIMBLE;	111	I, IN IMAGE	76
STONE			
EACH ANCIENT, STONE-NECKED MINUTE OF LOVE'S SEASON	131	I MAKE THIS IN	2
STOP			
STOPPED NON-STOP DANCING TO LET HOT FEET COOL, ...	51	OUT OF THE PIT	30
STRAIGHT			
WHAT MEANING, VOICES, IN THE STRAIGHT-RULED GRASS,	137	O CHATTERTON	17
STRANGER			
UNSEEN BY STRANGER-EYES	62	EARS IN TURRET	7
STRAW			
AND SIRENS SINGING FROM OUR LADY'S SEA-STRAW.	119	ALTARWISE	70
STREET			
BETWEEN THE STREET-LAMPS AND THE ILL-LIT SKY, ...	52	OUT OF THE PIT	61
STRINGED			
SUMMON YOUR SNOWY HORSEMEN, AND THE FOUR-STRINGED HILL, ...	122	HOLD HARD	14
STROKED			
CROSS-STROKED SALT ADAM TO THE FROZEN ANGEL	119	ALTARWISE	67
STRUCK			
VENUS LIES STAR-STRUCK IN HER WOUND	166	LONG-LEGGED	117
STUCK			
COME UNTO SEA-STUCK TOWERS, AT THE FIBRE SCALING,	111	I, IN IMAGE	74
STUFFED			
AFTER THE FEAST OF TEAR-STUFFED TIME AND THISTLES	136	AFTER FUNERAL	10
SUCKED			
HIS SEA-SUCKED ADAM IN THE HOLLOW HULK, ...	103	WORLD PYRAMID	2
SUCKER			
NOR SPROUT ON OWL-SEED LIKE A GOBLIN-SUCKER, ...	123	FOSTER LIGHT	14
SUN			
COMES LOVE'S ANATOMIST WITH SUN-GLOVED HAND	132	I MAKE THIS IN	44
THE SUN-LEAVED HOLY CANDLEWOODS	141	SAINT TO FALL	19

	PAGE	TITLE	LINE
SUPER			
SUPER-OR-NEAR MAN	158	INTO HER HEAD	29
SYLLABLED			
THREE-SYLLABLED AND STARRY AS THE SMILE;	94	IN BEGINNING	8
TABLE			
ON THE LORD'S-TABLE OF THE BOWING GRASS. FEAR MOST	198	COUNTRY SLEEP	35
TAILED			
THE LONG-TAILED STONE	114	SERVANT SUN	18
BUTT OF THE TREE-TAILED WORM THAT MOUNTED EVE, ...	117	ALTARWISE	32
AND THE LONG-TAILED LIGHTNING LIT HIS CATCH.	166	LONG-LEGGED	128
TALE			
NO TELL-TALE LOVER HAS AN END MORE CERTAIN, ...	125	TODAY, INSECT	24
HILL, TELL-TALE THE KNELLED	202	SIR JOHNS HILL	41
TALKING			
ITS HONEYED CHEEK, SOFT-TALKING MOUTH, ...	35	LIFT UP FACE	16
TALLOW			
HE IN A BOOK OF WATER TALLOW-EYED	119	ALTARWISE	72
TEAR			
AND A TEAR-STAINED WIDOWER GRIEF DROOPED FROM THE LASHES	133	MAKE ME A MASK	9
AFTER THE FEAST OF TEAR-STUFFED TIME AND THISTLES	136	AFTER FUNERAL	10
FAINT ARROWY MOONSTONE ON A TEAR-CULLED CADENCE,	225	SLENDER WIND	3
TEETH			
AND THE UNDEAD EYE-TEETH, ...	108	GRIEF THIEF	24
TELL			
NO TELL-TALE LOVER HAS AN END MORE CERTAIN, ...	125	TODAY, INSECT	24
HILL, TELL-TALE THE KNELLED	202	SIR JOHNS HILL	41
TEMPLE			
TONGUE AND EAR IN THE THREAD, ANGLE THE TEMPLE-BOUND	135	HOW MY ANIMAL	26
THE (1)			
THIRTY			
HIS DRIFTWOOD THIRTY-FIFTH WIND TURNED AGE;	208	POEM ON B'DAY	8
THIRTY-FIVE BELLS SING STRUCK	209	POEM ON B'DAY	39
THREE			
IN THE BEGINNING WAS THE THREE-POINTED STAR, ...	93	IN BEGINNING	1
THREE-SYLLABLED AND STARRY AS THE SMILE;	94	IN BEGINNING	8
A THREE-EYED, RED-EYED SPARK, BLUNT AS A FLOWER;	94	IN BEGINNING	15
TILL THE THREE-COLOURED RAINBOW FROM MY NIPPLES ...	120	ALTARWISE	107
AN OLD TORMENTED MAN THREE-QUARTERS BLIND, ...	217	ELEGY	18
THUMB			
AND PRICK THE THUMB-STAINED HEAVEN THROUGH THE THIMBLE.	104	WORLD PYRAMID	27
THRUSTING THE TOM-THUMB VISION UP THE IRON MILE.	111	I, IN IMAGE	84
TIDE			
LAPPING THE STILL CANALS, THE DRY TIDE-MASTER	54	WE BY SEASAND	10
OF TIDE-TONGUED HEADS AND BLADDERS IN THE DEEP, ...	104	WORLD PYRAMID	16
CARTOON OF SLASHES ON THE TIDE-TRACED CRATER, ...	119	ALTARWISE	71
THEN THREW ON THAT TIDE-HOISTED SCREEN	129	MY NEOPHYTE	34
MOONFALL AND SAILING EMPEROR, PALE AS THEIR TIDE-PRINT, ...	130	SINNERS' BELL	10
OR LIKE THE TIDE-LOOPED BREASTKNOT REEFED AGAIN ...	131	I MAKE THIS IN	11
TIGER			
AS THE MOUTH OF THE TIGER-LILY	229	MY RIVER	24
TIME			
WHY NIGHT-TIME RAIN AND THE BREAST'S BLOOD	56	WHY EAST WIND	8
NOW JACK MY FATHERS LET THE TIME-FACED CROOK, ...	108	GRIEF THIEF	15
IN SHAPING-TIME THE CIRCLE STUNG AWAKE;	121	INCARNATE DEVL	3
A SERPENT FIDDLED IN THE SHAPING-TIME.	122	INCARNATE DEVL	18
STRIKE IN THE TIME-BOMB TOWN, ...	142	SAINT TO FALL	35

	PAGE	TITLE	LINE

TIME (CONTINUED)

BEFORE THE LUNGE OF THE NIGHT, THE NOTES ON THIS
    TIME-SHAKEN 203   SIR JOHNS HILL   59
THE FRAIL AND DELICATE BREATH OF EVEN-TIME. 222   IN DREAMS   4

TIP

BY LOVE-TIP OR MY HAND'S RED HEAT. 19   IMAGES IN AIR   14

TIPPED

AND BLUE-TIPPED BIRDS HAVE RIPPLED IT, ... 224   IDYLL UNFORGET   22

TO (11)

TOED

WINDSHAKE OF SAILSHAPED EARS, MUFFLE-TOED TAP 136   AFTER FUNERAL   2

TOM

THRUSTING THE TOM-THUMB VISION UP THE IRON MILE. ... 111   I, IN IMAGE   84

TOMORROW

SHALL THE HERO-IN-TOMORROW 126   SEED-AT-ZERO   48
SHALL THE HERO-IN-TOMORROW 127   SEED-AT-ZERO   55
FROM YOUR TOMORROW-TREADING SHADE 129   MY NEOPHYTE   41

TONGUE

AND FROM THESE TONGUE-PLUCKED SENSES DRAWS HIS TUNE; 76   LASHED RINGS   13

TONGUED

THERE, IN HIS NIGHT, THE BLACK-TONGUED BELLS 92   BOYS OF SUMMER   28
THE SPIDER-TONGUED, AND THE LOUD HILL OF WALES) ... 99   OCTOBER WIND   27
OF TIDE-TONGUED HEADS AND BLADDERS IN THE DEEP, ... 104   WORLD PYRAMID   16
BLACK-TONGUED AND TIPSY FROM SALVATION'S BOTTLE. ... 118   ALTARWISE   61
IT IS THE SINNERS' DUST-TONGUED BELL 130   SINNERS' BELL   T
IT IS THE SINNERS' DUST-TONGUED BELL CLAPS ME TO
    CHURCHES 130   SINNERS' BELL   1
THE SEAS TO SERVICE THAT HER WOOD-TONGUED VIRTUE   136   AFTER FUNERAL   22

TOPSY

SUFFER, MY TOPSY-TURVIES, THAT A DOUBLE ANGEL 111   I, IN IMAGE   77

TOWER

BY CRANE AND WATER-TOWER BY THE SEEDY TREES 122   HOLD HARD   8

TRACED

CARTOON OF SLASHES ON THE TIDE-TRACED CRATER, ... 119   ALTARWISE   71

TRACKED

DRY IN THE HALF-TRACKED THIGH. 105   WORLD PYRAMID   60

TRACKING

BLINDS THEIR CLOUD-TRACKING EYE. 104   WORLD PYRAMID   30

TREADING

FROM YOUR TOMORROW-TREADING SHADE 129   MY NEOPHYTE   41

TREE

BUTT OF THE TREE-TAILED WORM THAT MOUNTED EVE, ... 117   ALTARWISE   32

TREED

LOST IN A LIMP-TREED AND UNEATING SILENCE, ... 132   I MAKE THIS IN   28

TURNED

DAZZLE THIS FACE OF VOICES ON THE MOON-TURNED TABLE, 110   I, IN IMAGE   69
DOOM ON DENIERS AT THE WIND-TURNED STATEMENT. 119   ALTARWISE   90

TURVIES

SUFFER, MY TOPSY-TURVIES, THAT A DOUBLE ANGEL 111   I, IN IMAGE   77

TWELVE

SPARKLING A TWELVE-LEGGED BODY 12   CABARET   19
BUT STRIP THE TWELVE-WINDED MARROW FROM HIS CIRCLE; 123   FOSTER LIGHT   3
RIPPLING IN TWELVE-WINDED CIRCLES, ... 175   FIRE RAID   64

TWENTY

TWENTY-FOUR YEARS 143   24 YEARS   T
TWENTY-FOUR YEARS REMIND THE TEARS OF MY EYES. 143   24 YEARS   1

TWIN

AND FREE THE TWIN-BOXED GRIEF, ... 108   GRIEF THIEF   20

TWO

THE TWO-FRAMED GLOBE THAT SPUN INTO A SCORE; 79   LOVE'S FEVER   45

		PAGE	TITLE	LINE
TWO (CONTINUED)				
AND FROM THE WINDY WEST CAME TWO-GUNNED GABRIEL,		118	ALTARWISE	57
THE TWO-A-VEIN, THE FORESKIN, AND THE CLOUD.		128	NOW, SAY NAY	35
UP				
ONCE CLOSE-UP SMILING IN THE WALL OF PICTURES, ...		118	ALTARWISE	55
VEIN				
THE TWO-A-VEIN, THE FORESKIN, AND THE CLOUD.		128	NOW, SAY NAY	35
VEINED				
THE WARM-VEINED DOUBLE OF TIME		150	WHEN I WOKE	11
VOICED				
WHO SUCKS THE BELL-VOICED ADAM OUT OF MAGIC, ...		119	ALTARWISE	93
VOLTED				
OF LAMP-POSTS AND HIGH-VOLTED FRUITS, ...		70	SECRET WIND	16
VOWELLED				
BY THE SEA'S SIDE HEAR THE DARK-VOWELLED BIRDS. ...		99	OCTOBER WIND	32
WAKED				
FROM POLE TO POLE LEAPT ROUND THE SNAIL-WAKED WORLD.		120	ALTARWISE	108
THE HARP-WAKED CASANOVA RAKES NO RANGE.		159	TO LEDA	2
WAKEWARD				
OVER THE WAKEWARD-FLASHING SPRAY		164	LONG-LEGGED	73
WALKING				
MAN WAS THE BURNING ENGLAND SHE WAS SLEEP-WALKING,				
AND THE ENAMOURING ISLAND		157	INTO HER HEAD	20
WALKS				
ALONG THE BORDERS OF THE GARDEN-WALKS.		223	IN DREAMS	12
WAN				
THEY OF THE PALE, SEA-WAN BEAUTY, THEY OF THE HOME		224	IDYLL UNFORGET	38
WARM				
THE WARM-VEINED DOUBLE OF TIME		150	WHEN I WOKE	11
WATER				
THE WATER-SPIRIT MOVES AS IT IS HIDDEN, ...		76	LASHED RINGS	9
OR, WATER-LAMMED, FROM THE SCYTHE-SIDED THORN, ...		114	A GRIEF AGO	3
BY CRANE AND WATER-TOWER BY THE SEEDY TREES		122	HOLD HARD	8
THE WINDER OF THE WATER-CLOCKS		128	MY NEOPHYTE	5
DOWN THE STACKED SEA AND WATER-PILLARED SHADE, ...		132	I MAKE THIS IN	40
AFTER A WATER-FACE WALK, ...		150	WHEN I WOKE	18
SING THROUGH THE WATER-SPOKEN PROW		164	LONG-LEGGED	78
TURNS THE MOON-CHAINED AND WATER-WOUND		169	LONG-LEGGED	203
AND THE FRESH-WATER BIRD		231	OUR SANCTITY	24
WAX				
COOL AS THE WAX-RED FOUNTAINS OF THE VEINS;		63	WOMAN SPEAKS	5
WAY				
ALTARWISE BY OWL-LIGHT IN THE HALF-WAY HOUSE		116	ALTARWISE	1
WITH BONES UNBUTTONED TO THE HALF-WAY WINDS, ...		117	ALTARWISE	9
ATLASWISE HOLD HALF-WAY OFF THE DUMMY BAY		121	ALTARWISE	128
WEAR				
WEAR-WILLOW RIVER, GRAVE, ...		203	SIR JOHNS HILL	58
WEATHER				
FROM THE EMERALD, STILL BELL; AND FROM THE PACING				
WEATHER-COCK		130	SINNERS' BELL	17
WEED				
STRUNG BY THE FLAXEN WHALE-WEED, FROM THE HANGMAN'S				
RAFT, ...		110	I, IN IMAGE	65
WEIGHING				
THE WEIGHING-SCALES, OF MY HAND.		155	RETURN	43
WELL				
BRIGHT, WELL-HELD HEAD, ...		14	FOR LEDA	9
I HAD A HANDSOME AND WELL-OFF BOY		149	PAPER & STICKS	13
FROM THE WELL-MADE HAND		241	ADMIT THE SUN	21

	PAGE	TITLE	LINE
WELLS			
ON THE LAST RICK'S TIP BY SPILLED WINE-WELLS	141	SAINT TO FALL	14
WHALE			
STRUNG BY THE FLAXEN WHALE-WEED, FROM THE HANGMAN'S RAFT, ...	110	I, IN IMAGE	65
AT HIS THRASHING HAIR AND WHALE-BLUE EYE;	161	LONG-LEGGED	3
WHEEL			
WHEEL-WINDERS AND FIXERS OF BOLTS.	70	SECRET WIND	18
WHEELS			
BRIGHT AS HER SPINNING-WHEELS, THE COLIC SEASON ...	108	I, IN IMAGE	8
WHITE			
AND THE BREATH-WHITE, CURTAINED MOUTH OF SEED.' ...	132	I MAKE THIS IN	51
SHE CRIED HER WHITE-DRESSED LIMBS WERE BARE	139	TOMBSTONE TOLD	17
CAMPED IN THE DRUG-WHITE SHOWER OF NERVES AND FOOD,	144	PLEASURE-BIRD	8
MAST-HIGH MOON-WHITE WOMEN NAKED	165	LONG-LEGGED	104
LITTLE WHITE-LIPPED FACES HAVE PEERED UP AT ME, ...	224	IDYLL UNFORGET	32
AND MILK-WHITE NAILS.	229	MY RIVER	29
WILLOW			
WEAR-WILLOW RIVER, GRAVE, ...	203	SIR JOHNS HILL	58
WIND			
DOOM ON DENIERS AT THE WIND-TURNED STATEMENT.	119	ALTARWISE	90
WIND-HEELED FOOT IN THE HOLE OF A FIREBALL, ...	141	SAINT TO FALL	12
WINDED			
WE SUMMER BOYS IN THIS FOUR-WINDED SPINNING, ...	93	BOYS OF SUMMER	37
BUT STRIP THE TWELVE-WINDED MARROW FROM HIS CIRCLE;	123	FOSTER LIGHT	3
RIPPLING IN TWELVE-WINDED CIRCLES, ...	175	FIRE RAID	64
WINDERS			
WHEEL-WINDERS AND FIXERS OF BOLTS.	70	SECRET WIND	18
WINDING			
DISTURB NO WINDING-SHEETS, MY SON, ...	60	MEAT ON BONES	6
AND, WINDING-FOOTED IN THEIR SHAWL AND SHEET, ...	89	EUNUCH DREAMS	4
WINE			
ON THE LAST RICK'S TIP BY SPILLED WINE-WELLS	141	SAINT TO FALL	14
WINKING			
IS MR. JONES THE CAKE, THAT WINKING-BIT, ...	179	NEW QUAY	20
WINTER			
WINTER-LOCKED SIDE BY SIDE, ...	153	WAS A SAVIOUR	26
WIT			
LIFT WIT-HURT HEAD FOR SUN TO SYMPATHIZE, ...	42	A WAR OF WITS	18
WOMAN			
FROGS AND SATANS AND WOMAN-LUCK, ...	150	WHEN I WOKE	7
WOMB			
THE WOMB-EYED, CRIES, ...	114	SERVANT SUN	32
WOOD			
THE SEAS TO SERVICE THAT HER WOOD-TONGUED VIRTUE	136	AFTER FUNERAL	22
WOOING			
AND WOULD A-WOOING GO AROUND THE GRAVES.	138	O CHATTERTON	28
WORK			
THE VANISHING OF THE MUSICAL SHIP-WORK AND THE CHUCKED BELLS, ...	141	SAINT TO FALL	8
WORM			
THE GLOW-WORM LIGHTS HIS DARKNESS, AND	48	POET: 1935	64
THAT HYMNING GOOSEBERRY, THAT BETHEL-WORM	179	NEW QUAY	21
WORMS			
AND, BROKEN GHOSTS WITH GLOW-WORMS IN THEIR HEADS,	82	LIGHT BREAKS	4
WOUND			
THE WOUND-DOWN COUGH OF THE BLOOD-COUNTING CLOCK	141	SAINT TO FALL	9
TURNS THE MOON-CHAINED AND WATER-WOUND	169	LONG-LEGGED	203
WOVEN			
FELT THEIR SERENITY OF RIPPLE-WOVEN LOVELINESS; ...	223	IDYLL UNFORGET	4

TABLE OF WORD FREQUENCIES

(4521) THE	(185) NOT	(122) IT	NOR
(1955) AND	(184) OR	(115) DOWN	(68) OLD
(1479) OF	(182) ALL	(113) LIGHT	(67) SKY
(1086) IN	(177) BY	(110) TIME	(66) NOW
(974) A	(174) WHO	(108) SEA	(65) OUR
(662) TO	(167) YOU	(101) WE	(64) WILL
(496) MY	(156) WAS	(100) NIGHT	(63) GREEN
(462) I	(152) ME THIS	(99) DEAD	(61) HAS
(431) ON	(151) BUT LIKE	(92) BLOOD INTO	(60) WATER
(386) WITH	(147) BE HE	(91) DEATH THERE	(59) HAND SHE
(351) THAT	(145) SHALL	(89) ONE THEY	(58) AN
(345) IS	(141) THROUGH	(88) HEART WHERE WIND	(56) HEAD UPON
(333) HIS	(137) AT	(82) OVER UNDER	(55) BEFORE BIRDS
(279) FOR	(136) LOVE	(78) EYES ITS	(54) SEE SO
(274) FROM	(131) HAVE WHEN	(76) LET	(53) BLACK FLESH HOUSE
(267) AS	(130) MAN	(74) UP	(52) STILL THESE
(216) THEIR	(126) ARE	(72) DARK	(51) WORLD
(215) HER	(124) SUN	(69)	(50) AMONG FIRE
(210) NO	(123) OUT		
(205) YOUR			

LIE	BED	BREATH	DYING
MOON	CRY	CHILD	EVERY
O	ONCE	COUNTRY	FEAR
WERE	STONE	DIE	GROUND
	SUMMER	FACE	HAD
(49)	TWO	HOW	LIFE
GRAVE	WOULD	LAND	MAD
THEN		MORE	PRAISE
WHITE	(36)	ONLY	SECRET
	DRY	TONGUE	SWEET
(48)	FALL		WHICH
HIM	THAN	(28)	
SLEEP		BONES	(22)
TREES	(35)	EACH	GREAT
	COME	HERE	HEAR
(47)	DUST	LIVING	LOVE'S
LAST	GO	MADE	MANY
	GOD	ROUND	SEAS
(46)	HANDS	SOUND	SHAPE
DAY	HIGH		
TOO	SPRING	(27)	(21)
		BREAST	BROKEN
(45)	(34)	CHILDREN	COMES
BONE	CLOUD	DEEP	CUT
IF	COULD	GARDEN	GOLDEN
MAKE	FAITH	RED	HALF
VOICE	TILL	SIDE	HOLY
		THEM	MUST
(44)	(33)	TOWN	OWN
GOOD	BLIND		ROOM
	FIRST	(26)	SALT
(43)	HEAVEN	FOOT	SEED
GHOST	LOST	HOLD	SHELL
MEN	TEARS	LIES	SING
NEVER	WHAT	LIPS	UNTIL
	WOUND	PAIN	WAY
(42)		SOME	YET
BIRD	(32)	TREE	
LONG	ALONE		(20)
THOUGH	BACK	(25)	BRAIN
	FLOWER	AGAIN	CLOUDS
(41)	HAIR	BRIGHT	FIELDS
AIR	LEAVES	BURNING	HEARD
		MAY	LEFT
(40)	(31)	OFF	SKULL
AWAY	AM	ROSE	VEINS
CAN	BREAK	SUCH	WEATHER
	RAIN		
(39)	TAKE	(24)	(19)
AFTER	WORDS	AGE	AGAINST
EARTH		COLD	BREAKS
HILL	(30)	GRIEF	MOTHER
KNOW	DO	MORNING	SAND
SAID	EYE	OH	TELL
	LITTLE	SHOULD	TURN
(38)	SNOW		WOMAN
MOUTH	WINGS	(23)	
STARS	YOUNG	ABOUT	(18)
		BODY	AROUND
(37)	(29)	DARKNESS	BOYS

BREAD	EVER	BOAT	TIDE
CROSS	FIND	FROST	TORN
CRYING	FLAME	GIRLS	WOMAN'S
DID	FLOWERS	GLORY	YELLOW
END	HILLS	GODS	
HOME	KISS	HOUR	**(11)**
JOY	LAY	HUNGER	ABOVE
MINE	LIMBS	LAID	ANY
MOVE	LOOK	LOVERS	BAY
TURNED	LOVED	MASK	BEYOND
WALL	MUSIC	MIDNIGHT	BLEW
WHOSE	OPEN	ROCK	BLOW
WOMB	RISE	RUN	BURN
WOMEN	RIVER	SET	CITY
	ROD	SHEET	COUNT
(17)	ROOTS	SILENCE	CRIED
BEGINNING	SAY	STREET	DEW
BEHIND	SINGING	STRUCK	DUSK
BELL	STONES	TOUCH	EMPTY
CANNOT	TURNS	TOWER	EVIL
CAST	VOICES	TREAD	FARM
DROWN	WALKING	WAR	FLOOD
ENOUGH	WATERS	WHILE	GHOSTS
FALLS	WAVE	WHY	GLOBE
FLYING	YEARS	WIDE	GOES
FULL			GOLD
GONE	**(14)**	**(12)**	ICE
LIFT	ACROSS	BEEN	KIND
NEW	ADAM	BENEATH	KING
SAW	ALWAYS	BLOWN	LIGHTNING
STAR	ARMS	BLOWS	LONGER
THOUGHT	BLUE	BRIDE	LOVER
WAVES	BORN	CAME	LYING
WINDS	CALLS	CIRCLE	NAME
WORD	CAUGHT	CRIES	PALE
WORM	DAYS	DEAR	PITY
	DEATH'S	DEVIL	QUICK
(16)	DIED	DOES	RUB
BETWEEN	DROWNED	DROP	SAKE
BOY	EARS	FINGERS	SAME
COLOUR	FALLING	FOOD	SECOND
COOL	FATHER	FOREVER	SHADOW
DUMB	FRUIT	FOUND	SHAPES
GIRL	IMAGE	FOX	SILENT
GRASS	KNOWN	HAIL	SKELETON
HARD	MIGHT	HEADS	SKIES
LEAVE	MORTAL	IT'S	SKIN
LOUD	NERVES	MAKES	SOON
MAN'S	PROUD	NEAR	TELLS
MILK	SHADE	OTHER	THIN
NAKED	SIR	RAGE	THROAT
NOTHING	SMILE	RIDING	TIDES
PLACE	STRONG	ROOT	TOLD
POOR	THINGS	SAIL	WAKE
US	TURNING	SHADES	WITHIN
WINTER	VALLEY	SOFT	
WOOD	WILD	SOUL	**(10)**
		SPIRIT	ALONG
(15)	**(13)**	STREAM	ARM
CATCH	BEAST	THERE'S	AWAKE

BAD	BROKE	SLEEPING	LEADS
BALL	BURNS	SLOW	METAL
BARE	CHANGE	SPACE	MOUNTAIN
BEAUTIFUL	CHILDREN'S	STORM	MUCH
BELLS	CLAY	STREETS	MURDER
BREAKING	CLEAN	STRIKE	NOSE
BREATHE	DOUBLE	TALL	OBLIVION
CALM	FACES	THIGHS	OTHERS
DRIVES	FAIL	THINK	POISON
FEATHER	FAR	TONGUES	PRAY
FIELD	FELLOW	TRUTH	PRIDE
FLY	FEVER	VIRGIN	RAN
FOLLY	FEW	WAITING	RIDE
GAY	FIRES	WALK	RIGHT
GENTLE	FLIGHT	WELL	RIVERS
GIVE	FOLD	WEPT	SAILS
GRAINS	FOLLOW	WHOLE	SHINING
HAWK	FORTH	WINDY	SHIPS
HEARING	FOUNTAIN	WISE	SOIL
HEAVEN'S	FOUR	WORLDS	SONG
HOLLOW	GROW	WOUNDS	SPEAK
HOT	HEEL		STAY
HURT	HELD	**(8)**	STRANGE
LOIN	HERON	ANGER	SUCKED
LOVES	HIDE	ASLEEP	SUFFER
LOVING	HORSES	BECAUSE	TALE
LOW	INCH	BEDS	TELLING
MALE	IRON	BELIEVE	THAT'S
MARROW	ISLAND	BREASTS	THICK
QUIET	KILL	BUILD	THREAD
RING	KNOWS	CARVED	TUNE
SAD	LABOUR	CLOTH	VEIN
SANG	LEARN	COMING	WAYS
SENSES	LIVE	DAWN	WITHOUT
SHARP	LOCKS	DOMINION	
SHUT	MIND	EAR	**(7)**
STAND	MINUTE	EVE	ANGELS
TALES	MOUTHS	FALLEN	ANIMAL
TALK	MOVING	FELL	BEAUTY
TEAR	NEED	FILLED	BEING
THIEF	NONE	FISH	BEST
TRUE	NOTES	FISHES	BLADE
VISION	PAPER	FIVE	BLUNT
WALKED	PARK	FLAMES	BOTH
WALKS	PEACE	FLOW	BRAINS
WHOM	PLAY	FREE	CAGE
WING	PRAYER	GENESIS	CALL
WINGED	PUT	GOING	CHRIST
WORLD'S	RAM	GOOD-BYE	CLIMB
YEAR	RAVEN	GOT	COCK
YOUTH	REST	GREW	COMMON
	RUIN	GROWING	DAMP
(9)	SAINT	GROWS	DELICATE
ALIVE	SEASONS	HEAT	DELIGHT
ANCIENT	SENSE	HONEY	DESIRE
ANSWER	SHELLS	HOURS	DEVIL'S
BEAR	SHOT	IMAGES	DIVINITY
BENT	SIN	INSECT	DOOR
BLESSED	SINCE	I'VE	DREAM
BRANCHES	SINGS	KNEW	DROPPED

DRUM	SMELL	ENEMY	SAYING
EVEN	SOUR	ENTER	SAYS
FAST	SPUN	EVENING	SCALES
FEEL	STRAIGHT	FARMS	SCENE
FLEW	STRENGTH	FATHER'S	SEASON
FLIES	TAIL	FEATHERS	SHADOWS
FOAM	TEETH	FEET	SHAPED
FRIENDS	THOSE	FELT	SHEEP
FUNERAL	THOUGHTS	FIGURES	SHINE
GAVE	THREE	FLED	SHOW
GENTLEMAN	THUNDER	FOOL	SMILES
GOD'S	TIME'S	FOUL	SNAIL
GRAIN	TOUCHED	FRESH	SOLID
HAMMER	UNBORN	FRIEND	SOULS
HANGING	VAIN	GAS	SPINNING
HAPPY	VEIL	GESTURES	SPIRE
HELL	WAKING	GIVES	SPLIT
HOLDING	WATCH	GLASS	STAIRS
HOLE	WHAT'S	GRAVEL	STATEMENT
HORSE	WHISPER	HALVES	STICKS
HUNDRED	WOE	HARBOUR	STIR
I'LL	WONDER	HERO	STIRS
I'M	WOODS	HOPE	SUN'S
KEEP	WRONG	HORN	TAKEN
KINGDOM		INNOCENT	THIGH
LIGHTS	(6)	INSIDE	THROATS
LINES	AGO	IRIS	THROW
LORD	ANCHOR	JOHN'S	THUS
MAKING	ANGEL	KISSED	TICKLED
MARK	ANOTHER	KNIVES	TIMES
MATTER	APPLE	LAUGHTER	TOGETHER
MEAT	ARCHITECTS	LEAPING	TOMB
MIRACLE	ART	LEAVED	TOOK
MOMENT	BAIT	LEAVING	TOWNS
MOST	BEASTS	LIME	TROUBLE
MOTHER'S	BEAT	LONG-LEGGED	TRUMPET
MYSELF	BELIEVES	LOOSE	TWICE
NATURAL	BELLY	LOVELY	WAX
NERVE	BELOW	LUCK	WEATHERS
NEST	BIRTH	MAGGOT	WEED
NOISE	BUD	MEANING	WELCOME
OIL	BURST	MERRY	WINDOWS
PLENTY	BURY	NIGHTINGALE	WISHES
QUESTION	BUSH	NOTE	WORK
RAISE	CADAVER'S	OCTOBER	
RETURN	CALLED	OPENING	(5)
RIBS	CANCER	OWL	ACHE
RICH	CENTRE	PART	ACT
ROCKS	CERTAIN	PAST	ALTHOUGH
RUNS	CHOICE	PATHS	ARMOUR
SAP	CONTENT	PLAGUE	ASK
SAVIOUR	DANCING	PRAISED	AUNT
SHORE	DEATHS	PRAYERS	BARBED
SHROUD	DOG	PRIEST	BEAK
SIGHED	DOOM	PRINT	BETTER
SIGNS	DREAMS	PROCESS	BIRTHDAY
SILVER	DRIFT	PULSE	BIT
SIT	DRIVE	QUEEN	BLESSING
SLOWLY	ENDLESS	REMEMBER	BLOODY
SLY	ENDS	ROUGH	BORE

BOW	GRACE	OAK	STRIP
BROOD	GRIEVE	PATH	STROKE
BROTHER	GULLS	PETALS	SUIT
BROW	GUT	PICKED	SYLLABLES
BURNED	HAIRS	PIECE	THING
CANDLE	HAT	PIGEON	THIRST
CARE	HAY	PLACES	THORN
CHAINS	HEARS	PLAIN	THOU
CHANGED	HEART'S	POINTED	THUMB
CHOIR	HE'LL	PRAYED	TOOTH
CLEAR	HIDDEN	PULLS	TOWARDS
CLIMBING	HOLDS	RAINBOW'S	TOWERS
CLOCK	HOOD	RAISED	TWELVE
CLOSED	HOUSES	REACH	UNDONE
COIL	INNOCENCE	REASON	USE
CONSCIOUS	ISLANDS	REEL	VALES
COUNTRIES	JACK	RIDDLED	VOID
CRACK	KNEES	RINGS	WALES
CRADLE	KNOCKED	RISING	WALLS
CREATURE	LAKES	ROOF	WANTING
CROOKED	LAMP	ROOKS	WATCHING
CROW	LEAD	RULER	WET
CUTS	LEAF	RUNNING	WHISTLES
DAM	LEAP	SAILING	WICKED
DANCE	LEVEL	SCISSORS	WILDERNESS
DEADLY	LIFTED	SEEK	WINE
DESPAIR	LINE	SEEN	WINTER'S
DIES	LINEN	SEES	WISH
DINGLE	LIP	SELF	WITS
DONE	LIT	SENSUAL	WIVES
DOVE	LOCKED	SEVEN	WOODEN
DRAW	LONDON'S	SHAPELESS	WREN
DRINK	LONGED	SHIFT	
DRINKING	LOVER'S	SHONE	(4)
DRUNK	MAGIC	SHOOTING	ACID
EAST	MAIDEN	SHOULDER	ALOUD
EASY	MANNA	SHOULDERS	ALREADY
ECHO	MARRIED	SIDES	AUTUMN
EDEN	MAST	SILK	BABE
EGG	MASTER	SILLY	BARES
ENEMIES	MASTERS	SINGLE	BARREN
ETERNAL	MEET	SISTER	BEACH
FAMOUS	MELTING	SIZE	BEATING
FATHERS'	MESSAGE	SON	BEES
FED	MILLION	SPEAKING	BIG
FELLED	MINUTES	SPEAKS	BINDING
FIERCE	MIST	SPILT	BITS
FINAL	MOCK	SPIN	BLAME
FINGER	MORROW	SPIRAL	BLESS
FLESH'S	MOTION	SPOKE	BLINDING
FLOODS	MOUNTAINS	STARRY	BLINDS
FLOOR	MOURN	STATE	BLOOMS
FOLDED	MOVED	STEPPING	BLOWING
FORGET	MOVES	STEPS	BOATS
FORK	MUD	STICK	BOOK
FORKS	NAY	STOPPED	BOUGHS
FROZEN	NEARLY	STORIES	BOUNCING
GAIETY	NEEDLES	STRANGER	BOWS
GARDENS	NIGHTS	STRANGERS	BREASTED
GLIDED	NOON	STRAWS	BREATHING

BRED	FIXED	LOCK	SHARE
BROWN	FLOWED	LONDON	SHAWL
BRUSH	FLOWS	LONELY	SHIP
BUBBLES	FORCE	LOSS	SHORES
BURIAL	FOREIGN	LUNG	SHORT
BURIED	FOREST	LUST	SHOUT
CARRION	FORSAKEN	MANHOOD	SHY
CATTLE	FORTUNE	MARKED	SICK
CAVERNOUS	FRAIL	MILKY	SIGH
CHALK	FROTH	MINSTREL	SIGHS
CHANT	FURIOUS	MISTER	SIGHT
CHILD'S	FURTHER	MOLTEN	SLAIN
CHILL	GATES	MOON'S	SLEPT
CHURCHES	GLAD	MYSTERY	SLIME
CLASP	GLIDE	NAIL	SMALL
CLAW	GLOVE	NECK	SMOKE
CLOCKS	GOOSE	NEOPHYTE	SNAP
CLOSE	GOSPEL	NEWS	SOMETIMES
COAL	GRAPES	NIGHT'S	SONS
COMFORT	GROVES	OILS	SORROW
COMPANION	GROWN	OUTSIDE	SOUGHT
CONTINENT	GUILT	OWE	SOWN
CORAL	GUTS	OWLS	SPEECH
COUGH	HANG	PACING	SPELLS
CRACKED	HANGS	PALM	SPONGE
CRAFT	HARVEST	PERHAPS	SPOUT
CUP	HEARTS	PIERCED	STAINED
DARKEST	HEAVY	PIT	STALE
DECKS	HEELS	PLAYING	STALKS
DEEPER	HEIR	PLUCK	STANDS
DEER	HERONS	PLUME	STARE
DESTRUCTION	HE'S	POINT	STAR-FLANKED
DILLY	HIDES	POLES	STARS'
DIPPED	HOST	POOL	STEEL
DIRECTION	HOWLING	POT	STEM
DIVE	HUMBLE	PRAYS	STEP
DIVED	HUNG	PRINCE	STERN
DOMES	HUNGRY	PROMISE	STIFF
DOUBT	ILL	RADIANCE	STOOD
DRAMATIC	ILLS	RAGGED	STRAW
DREAMED	INTRICATE	RAMPART	STRING
DREAMING	INVISIBLE	RANG	STUFF
DRENCHED	IVORY	RAVEN'S	SUNDAY
DREW	JORDAN	REGRET	SUNDERED
DRIFTING	JOYS	REMAIN	SWEAT
DRIFTS	JUST	REMAINS	TABLE
DRIP	KINGS	REVOLVING	TASTE
DRIPS	KNOWING	RIDER	TERROR
DROPS	LADIES	ROAD	THIEVES
EAGLE	LAKE	RODE	THIRSTY
ENGINE	LAMB	ROT	THROWN
EYED	LANDS	SAILORS	THUMBS
FADED	LATE	SALTY	THUNDER'S
FAIRY	LEAST	SCARLET	THY
FEAST	LEDA	SEED-AT-ZERO	TINY
FEED	LEVER	SEEDS	TIRED
FEELING	LIDS	SEEDY	TOE
FELLOWS	LIQUID	SENSES'	TOPS
FERN	LISTEN	SERVE	TOSSED
FIST	LIVELONG	SEX	TRACKS

TRAP	BATTLE	COLOURS	FAT
TUMBLE	BEARING	COMB	FATHERS
TURRETS	BECALMED	CONJURED	FEATURES
TURTLE	BIRDS'	CONVERSATION	FEEDING
TWILIGHT	BITE	CORN	FELLOWED
TWIN	BITTER	CORPSE	FEMALE
TWIST	BLAZE	COUNTED	FIERY
TWISTED	BLAZING	COUNTY	FIGHT
UNDEAD	BLEED	COURSE	FILM
UNKNOWING	BLOOM	COVERING	FINDING
UNKNOWN	BOOKS	CRAMP	FINDS
URN	BOTTOM	CRANES	FISHERMAN
VAGUE	BOULDERS	CROSSED	FISHING
VINEGAR	BOUND	CROUCHED	FISTS
VOWS	BOX	CRUEL	FIT
VOYAGE	BRAND	CRUSH	FLAKES
WANTON	BRAVE	CRUST	FLASHED
WARM	BREED	CUPBOARD	FLASHING
WEAK	BREEZE	CURE	FLASK
WEEDS	BRIDES	CURLEWS	FLINT
WEEPS	BRING	CURSES	FLOATING
WHALES	BRITTLE	CURVING	FLOCK
WHEEL	BROUGHT	CYPRESS	FLOCKS
WHISPERED	BUBBLE	DAMNED	FLOWERING
WIFE	BUDS	DAUGHTER	FLOWING
WISDOM	BUILDING	DAUGHTERS	FOG
WITHER	BUSHES	DAZZLING	FOOL'S
WON'T	BUSY	DECAY	FOREHEAD
WORKED	CALF	DELIVER	FORGOTTEN
WORKING	CALVES	DENY	FORKED
WRIST	CANVAS	DEPARTED	FORM
WRITE	CAT	DESCENDED	FOSTER
YARD	CAUL	DESCENDS	FOUNTAINS
YOU'RE	CAVE	DESERT	FOXES
	CELL	DIM	FURIES
(3)	CENTAUR	DIN	FURY
ABSENCE	CHAIN	DIRECTIONS	FUSE
ACRE	CHANNELS	DOING	FUSION
ADAM'S	CHAOS	DOME	GALLERIES
AFRAID	CHAPEL	DRAG	GENIUS
AGONY	CHARMS	DRAWING	GENTLY
AIRY	CHASE	DRAWN	GESTURE
ALMOST	CHEAP	DRIES	GHOSTLY
ALTAR	CHEEK	DRIVEN	GIANT
ANGEL'S	CHIME	DROOPING	GLANCE
ANGLE	CHIMES	DROVE	GLISTENING
ANIMALS	CHOKE	DUG	GLOW
ANSWERS	CHURCH	EDGE	GODHEAD
APART	CINDER	EDGES	GRAIL
ARC	CLEARLY	ELEMENTS	GRAPPLE
ARISE	CLIMBED	ELM	GRAVES
ARK	CLIMBS	EMERALD	GREATER
ARMPITS	CLINGS	ENVELOPING	GREY
ARRIVAL	CLOSER	ERECTED	GRIEVES
ASIA	CLOTHES	ESCAPE	GROOM
ASYLUM	CLOVEN	ESPECIALLY	GULL
BALANCE	COAST	EUNUCH	HABIT
BARLEY	COBBLES	FADE	HACK
BASE	COCKCROW	FAIR	HALF-WAY
BASIN	COLOURED	FANCY	HAMLET

HANGMAN'S	LIMP	PASS	RISES
HARDEN	LISTENING	PASSED	RIVEN
HARDLY	LOFT	PATCH	ROADS
HARM	LONGS	PAVEMENT	ROBBED
HARP	LOSE	PAY	ROCKED
HEATHER	LOVERLESS	PEARL	ROCKING
HEAVENLY	LOVERS'	PEOPLE	ROLLING
HEED	LUMINOUS	PICTURE	ROOTING
HEIGHT	MARBLE	PICTURES	ROPES
HERITAGE	MARKS	PIECES	ROTATING
HEWN	MARRIAGE	PIERCE	ROTTEN
HID	MASSES	PINE	ROUNDS
HIDEOUS	MEANS	PITCH	RULES
HIVES	MEASURE	PLANTED	RUMOUR
HOMES	MEEK	PLANTS	RUNG
HONOURED	MELT	PLAYED	RUSH
HOODED	MERCY	PLOUGHMAN'S	SABBATH
HOPPING	MERMEN	PLUCKED	SACK
HORNS	MIDDLE	PLUMES	SAFE
HOUR'S	MIGHTY	PLUNGE	SAGA
HUNCHBACK	MILD	PLUNGED	SAILED
HUNTING	MILE	POEM	SAILOR
HUSK	MINUTE'S	POET	SANDS
HYMNING	MIRACLES	POLE	SAVE
ICICLE	MIRROR	POSSESSED	SCALDING
I'D	MISERY	POUND	SCALE
IMMORTAL	MOAN	POWER	SCREWS
INCENDIARY	MODERN	PRESS	SCYTHE
ITCH	MONEY	PRINTS	SEASONS'
JACKS	MONSTROUS	PRISON	SEASON'S
JAWS	MONTH	PSALMS	SEEMS
JOURNEY	MOOD	PUFFED	SELVES
JUMP	MOONS	PULLED	SERPENT
KEY	MOONSHINE	PURPOSE	SETS
KEYS	MOTHERS	PURSE	SEWING
KILLED	MOUNT	PYRAMID	SHED
KILLS	MOUSE	QUESTIONS	SHEPHERD
KISSES	MUSCLE	QUICKENING	SHORN
KNEEL	MUTE	RABBLE	SHOTS
KNELT	MYSELVES	RAGING	SHOWS
KNOCKING	NAILS	RAID	SIGNED
KNOWLEDGE	NAMES	RAINING	SIMPLE
LAME	NARROW	RAINY	SKY'S
LAMENTING	NAUGHT	RANGE	SLAP
LANK	NEIGHBOUR	RARE	SLAY
LAP	NEITHER	RATHER	SLEEPER
LARKS	NET	RAVENS	SLEEPERS
LASHED	NIGHTMARE	RAZOR	SLEEPS
LAUGH	NOBLE	READ	SLEEVE
LAUGHING	NURSE	READY	SLEEVES
LEAN	OAT	REBEL	SLENDER
LEANS	ODD	RED-EYED	SLIPS
LEAPT	OFFER	REFUSAL	SMILING
LEARNS	ONTO	REMEMBERED	SMOOTH
LEARNT	ORDERED	RIB	SNAKE
LEG	PACK	RIDES	SNAKES
LENGTH	PAGE	RIND	SNAPPED
LETS	PARADISE	RINGED	SNIPER
LETTER	PARCHED	RIPE	SNOUT
LIGHTLY	PARDON	RIPPLED	SOFTLY

SOMETHING	THRUST	WOOED	BAYONET
SONGS	THUNDERBOLTS	WOVEN	BAY'S
SOUNDS	THUNDERS	WRINGING	BEAKS
SOUTH	TIDY	WRINKLED	BEAMS
SPARK	TIMELESS	WRITTEN	BEARD
SPARROWS	TIMID		BEARDED
SPAT	TIP	(2)	BEARER
SPED	TOES	ABADDON	BEARS
SPELLED	TOILS	ABROAD	BEAUTIFULLY
SPELLING	TO-MORROW	ACHES	BECKON
SPENT	TO-MORROW'S	ACRID	BEDLAM
SPILL	TOP	ACTIONS'	BEGGAR
SPINNEY	TOPPLING	ADD	BEGIN
SPINS	TOUCHING	ADDER	BELLED
SPIT	TRAVEL	ADMIRE	BELLOWING
SPRINGING	TREADS	ADMIT	BELONG
SPRINGS	TREMBLE	ADORE	BELOVED
SPROUT	TRIUMPHANT	ADORED	BEND
SQUARE	TUMBLING	ADVENTURE	BENDS
SQUEAL	TWINED	ADVICE	BERRY
STABLE	UNENDING	AFFECTIONATE	BETRAYAL
STAIN	UNLESS	AGEING	BEWILDERED
STAKED	UNSEEN	AGES	BID
STALKING	UNTO	AIM	BIDING
STAMP	UNWHOLESOME	AISLES	BIRD'S
STARRED	VANITY	ALIGHT	BITES
STEAL	VEGETABLE	ALLOWS	BITTEN
STEPPED	VELVET	ALMANAC	BITTERLY
STIRRED	VENOM	ALSO	BITTERNESS
STOP	VENUS	ALTARWISE	BLACK-TONGUED
STREAMS	VERY	ALTERED	BLADES
STRETCH	VICIOUS	AMBUSH	BLANK
STRIDE	VIGOUR	AMORIST	BLASTED
STRINGS	VILLAGE	ANCHORED	BLASTS
STUMBLE	VILLAGES	ANGELIC	BLEST
SUCK	VIRGINS	ANGUISH	BLINDLY
SUCKS	VOIDS	ANN	BLINDNESS
SUDDEN	WAIT	ANNIVERSARY	BLISS
SUFFERED	WARMTH	ANONYMOUS	BLITHE
SUM	WARRING	ANTIPODES	BLITHELY
SUMMER'S	WARS	APPLES	BLOOD'S
SUNLIGHT	WASTE	ARDOUR	BODY'S
SUNS	WATER'S	ARGUE	BOILING
SURE	WEEP	ARMY	BOLT
SWAM	WEEPING	ARTERIAL	BORDER
SWAN	WEIGHT	ASH	BORED
SWANS	WELSH	ASHES	BOTTLE
SWEETLY	WENDED	ASIDE	BOUGH
SWEPT	WENT	ASTRIDE	BOUNCED
SWING	WEST	BABBLE	BOWED
SWINGS	WHINNYING	BABY	BOWING
SYMBOL	WHISTLED	BABY'S	BOWL
SYMBOLS	WILLING	BACKWARDS	BRACKEN
TAILS	WINDILY	BAPTIZED	BRAMBLES
TAKES	WINDING	BARK	BRANDY
TAKING	WINDMILLS	BARNS	BRASSY
TANGLED	WINDOW	BASES	BRAYS
TAPPED	WINDS'	BATHE	BRILLIANT
TEACH	WITHERED	BATHERS	BROTHERS
THREW	WOKE	BAYING	BRUISING

BUILDINGS	CITIES	CRUMBLE	DOWNED
BULL	CITY'S	CRUMBLED	DOWRY
BURIES	CLACK	CRUMBS	DRAGS
BUSHED	CLASH	CRUMPLED	DRAIN
BUSHY	CLASPED	CRUSHED	DRAINS
BUTTER	CLAWED	CRUSTED	DRANK
BUTTERMILK	CLAWS	CRYSTAL	DREGS
BUTTON	CLEAVING	CUCKOO'S	DRIFTWOOD
BYRES	CLEFT	CUDDLED	DRILL
CABINNED	CLING	CUPPED	DRIVER
CALENDAR	CLOCKWISE	CURLED	DRUID
CAMP	CLOGS	CURLEW	DRUMMED
CANAL	CLOUDY	CURSE	DRUMS
CANDLES	CLOUTED	CURSED	DRUNKEN
CANNONS	CLUCK	CURTAIN	DRUNKS
CAN'T	COBWEB	CURVE	DUCK
CAP	COCKEREL'S	CUTTING	DUCKED
CAPES	COCKS	CYCLONE	DUMBLY
CARED	CODE	DAFT	DUNG
CARING	COFFIN	DAISIES	DUST-TONGUED
CARNAL	COLLAR	DANCED	DWINDLING
CARRIES	COMPLAIN	DANCERS	EARLY
CARRYING	CONCEIVE	DARKER	EARTH'S
CARVEN	CONFESSOR	DARLINGS	EASE
CASTING	CONFUSION	DARTING	EASIER
CASTLE	CONTACT	DAVID	EASILY
CASTS	CONTAGION	DAY'S	EASTERN
CATCHING	CONTAGIOUS	DEAF	EAT
CATHEDRAL	CONTINUAL	DEATHLESS	ECHOES
CATS	COOLS	DECEMBER'S	EELS
CAUSES	CORNER	DECKED	EGGS
CAVES	COSTLY	DECLAIMS	EITHER
CELLS	COTTON	DEEDS	ELBOW
CENTURIES	COUCH	DEEPEST	ELECTRA
CENTURY'S	COUNTING	DELICIOUS	ELECTRIC
CEREMONY	COUNTRYMAN'S	DELL	ELEGY
CERTAINTY	COURSING	DELUDES	ELEMENT
CHAINED	COURTERS'	DENIERS	ELEVATE
CHALKED	CRAB	DEPTHS	ELMS
CHANGES	CRABBED	DERRY	EMPEROR
CHANNEL	CRACKS	DESCENDING	ENCOMPASSED
CHARACTERS	CRANING	DESIGNED	ENDING
CHARMED	CRATER	DESIRES	ENDURE
CHATTERTON	CRAWLING	DESTROYING	ENERGY
CHEEKS	CRAWLS	DIRTY	ENGINES
CHEMIC	CRAZY	DISCORD	ENGLAND
CHERUB	CREATE	DISK	ENGULFING
CHESTS	CREST	DISTURB	ENTERED
CHILDISH	CRIME	DIVIDE	ENTRANCES
CHILLS	CRIPPLED	DIVINELY	ENVY
CHIMNEYS	CROCODILE	DIVING	EVERYTHING
CHIRRUP	CROPS	DIVINING	EXCEEDING
CHORD	CROSSES	DODGING	EXOTIC
CHRISTENS	CROSSING	DOGDAYED	EYELID
CHRISTIAN	CROTCH	DOLL	EYELIDS
CHRIST'S	CROWD	DOORS	FABLE
CHRYSALIS	CROWDS	DOTH	FABLES
CHURN	CROWING	DOUBLED	FABULOUS
CIRCLES	CROWN	DOUBLES	FACED
CIRCULAR	CRUMB	DOUBTS	FADES

FAIRIES	FRUITS	HATCHED	KENNEL
FALSE	FUMED	HAUL	KICK
FAMILIAR	FUNNEL	HAVEN	KICKED
FAMINE	FUNNELS	HAWKS	KILLER
FARMER	FURRED	HAYGOLD	KINDLED
FASTEN	G.	HEAL	KINGLY
FATHERED	GABRIEL	HEARTBONE	KITE
FATHERING	GAIN	HEARTBREAK	KNEELS
FATS	GALES	HEARTH	KNOCK
FEARS	GALLOP	HEARTHSTONE	LABYRINTHINE
FEATHERED	GALLOW	HEARTLESS	LADDER
FEATHERY	GALLOWS	HEAVENS	LADIES'
FENCED	GAME	HEDGEROW	LADY
FERNS	GARAGES	HEDGES	LADY'S
FIBRE	GARRISON	HEELED	LAIN
FIBS	GATHERED	HEIGH	LAIR
FIE	GEAR	HELD-OUT	LAIRS
FIFTH	GEESE	HERD	LANDSCAPE
FIG	GIANT'S	HERO-IN-TOMORROW	LANGUAGE
FILL	GIDDY	HERO'S	LANTERNS
FIN	GIGANTIC	HERS	LAPPED
FINE	GIVEN	HILLY	LAPPING
FINNED	GLASSY	HIMSELF	LAPS
FINS	GLIDES	HISSING	LARGE
FISHES'	GLIDING	HISTORY	LATER
FIX	GLOBES	HO	LAYING
FLAMING	GLOWING	HOISTED	LAYS
FLASH	GOD-IN-HERO	HOLLOWS	LAZARUS
FLAT	GODS'	HOLLY	LEADEN
FLATS	GOOSEBERRY	HONEYED	LEANING
FLAVOURED	GOOSE'S	HOOF	LEAPED
FLEAS	GOSSIPERS	HORIZONTAL	LEAPS
FLEECE	GRAFT	HORNED	LEERED
FLOAT	GRAVEWARD	HORRID	LEGEND
FLOATED	GRAZE	HORROR	LEGENDS
FLOCKED	GREEK	HORSESHOE	LEGION
FLOWERED	GREENWOOD	HOUSED	LEPER
FLOWERS'	GRIEFS	HOWLS	LIFTING
FLUID	GRIEVED	HUGE	LIGHTED
FLUNG	GRIP	HULK	LIGHT'S
FLUTE	GROVE	HULOO	LILACS
FOLDS	GRUMBLE	HUMAN	LILIES
FOLLY'S	GUARD	HUNGERS	LILY
FOND	GULLED	HURRY	LINKED
FONT	GULLY	HUTCH	LION
FOOLISH	GUNS	HYMNED	LIONS
FOOTED	GUTTER	INCARNATE	LION'S
FORCING	GUTTERS	INDEX	LISTENED
FORGED	HACKED	INFANT	LITERARY
FORGIVE	HAGGARD	INFANTS	LIVES
FORMED	HAIR'S	INTANGIBLE	LOADS
FORTRESS	HALTER	INTERVALS	LOCKING
FOSSIL	HANSOM	INWARD	LOG
FOXY	HARBOURS	ISSUE	LONELINESS
FRANK	HARE	ITCHED	LONGING
FRIENDLY	HARK	JACKET	LONG-TAILED
FRO	HARMONY	JAW	LOOKING
FROLIC	HARPS	JERICHO	LOOKS
FRONT	HARPSTRUNG	JESU'S	LOSING
FROSTY	HARSH	KEEPER	LOTH

LOVELINESS	MURDERED	PEELED	RAKE
LOWERED	MUSCLES	PENNY	RANT
LOWLY	MYSTIC	PEOPLE'S	RAPE
LUNAR	NAILED	PERCHED	RARER
LUNGS	NAMED	PERISH	RAT
LUSTS	NAPE	PERISHES	RATIONAL
MACHINE	NATION	PERSON	RAYED
MADDEN	NAVY	PHEASANTS	RAYS
MADHOUSE	NECKS	PHOENIX	RAZED
MADMEN	NEEDLE	PHRASES	REALITY
MAGICAL	NESTED	PICK	REALM
MAGNIFIED	NESTS	PILLAR	REAPED
MAGPIE'S	NETS	PINK	RECORDS
MAID	NETTLES	PIN-POINT	RELIGIOUS
MAIM	NEWBORN	PLAINS	REMARK
MAKER	NIGHT-GEARED	PLANET	REPLY
MANDRAKE	NIGHTINGALES	PLANETS	REWARD
MANES	NIGHTLONG	PLANT	RHYTHM
MAN-IN-SEED	NIGHTLY	PLATE	RIBBED
MANKIND	NIGHTMARE'S	PLEASE	RIBBONED
MANNED	NINE	PLEASURE-BIRD	RICKS
MANTLE	NITRIC	PLUM	RIDERLESS
MANTLED	NO-GOOD	PLUMED	RIDERS
MARE'S	NOSTRILS	POEMS	RIDINGS
MARKING	NOUGHT	POETRY	RIFT
MARROWED	NOVEL	POISE	RIMS
MARVEL	NOWHERES	POISED	RIP
MARY	NUMBERLESS	POLESTAR	RIPENS
MASKED	NUNNERY	POND	RIPPLING
MASTS	NURSERIES	PONDEROUS	RISEN
MAZES	NURSES	PONDS	RITE
MEADOWS	NUT	POSE	ROAR
MEANINGLESS	OBLIVIOUS	POUR	ROARED
MEASURED	OCEAN	POURING	ROARING
MECHANICAL	OCTOPUS	PRAISING	ROB
MEN'S	ORCHARD	PRAYING	ROCKERY
MENTAL	ORCHARDS	PRESENT	ROLL
MERRIEST	ORDER	PRESSED	ROLLED
METRE	ORDINARY	PRETTY	ROMANTIC
MIDWIVES	ORESTES'	PROBE	ROOFED
MILES	ORIGIN	PRODIGAL	ROOK
MILKED	ORIGINAL	PROMISES	ROOT-DAM
MINUS	OUTLAW	PROPHETS	ROSY
MIRRORS	OWL-LIGHT	PROPPED	ROTS
MOANS	OX	PUFFING	ROUNDED
MOISTEN	PADDED	PULL	ROW
MOLE	PAINS	PUNISHES	RUBBISH
MOMENTS	PAINT	PURE	RUDE
MOMENT'S	PAINTED	PUSHED	RULE
MONTHS	PALLOR	PYRE	RUST
MOONLIGHT	PAP	QUARREL	SALMON
MORNINGS	PARCHES	QUARRY	SAMSON
MORNING'S	PARTED	QUARTER	SANCTITY
MOTHERNAKED	PASTURE	QUAY	SANE
MOTHERS-EYED	PAT	QUICKSAND	SANITY
MOUNTED	PATHWAY	QUILL	SAT
MOUNTING	PATIENCE	QUIVERING	SAVED
MOURNING	PATTERNS	RAGS	SAWDUST
MOUTHING	PAVEMENTS	RAILINGS	SCARECROW
MOVEMENTS	PEBBLES	RAISES	SCATTERED

SCENT	SINNERS'	STAVED	TEATS
SCOLD	SINS	STEADILY	TELL-TALE
SCRAPED	SIRE	STEADY	TEMPLE
SCRAWL	SISTERS'	STEALS	TEMPLE'S
SCREEN	SITS	STEEPLE	TEN
SCRUBBED	SITTING	STEEPLES	TENT
SCUDDING	SIX	STILES	TERRIBLE
SCULPTURED	SKIMS	STILTS	TERRIBLY
SCUTTLED	SKIRTS	STIRRING	THEMSELVES
SEAL	SKYSIGNS	STITCH	THIMBLE
SEA-LEGGED	SLANT	STOCK	THINKING
SEAPORTS	SLAPPED	STOLEN	THIRTIETH
SEA'S	SLASHED	STONY	THISTLE
SEASAND	SLEEPY	STOPPING	THISTLES
SEASHORE	SLIDES	STORED	THORNY
SEDGE	SLIGHT	STORMS	THRASHING
SENSITIVE	SLOWS	STORY	THREADS
SENT	SLUMBER	STRADDLE	THRUSTING
SEPARATE	SLUMBERS	STRANGELY	THUMP
SERPENTS	SMACK	STRAPPED	TIDAL
SERPENT'S	SMELT	STRIKES	TILTED
SERVANT	SMOOTHED	STRIPS	TIT
SERVICE	SNIVELLING	STRONGHOLD	TODAY
SETTING	SOAKS	STRUNG	TOLLS
SEWN	SOCK	STRUT	TOM
SHABBY	SOCKET	STUFFED	TOMBS
SHAFT	SOLVE	STUNNED	TOMBSTONE
SHAFTED	SOOTHED	SUBTLE	TONGUED
SHAKEN	SORES	SUFFERING	TORCH
SHAKES	SOVEREIGN	SUFFERS	TOSSING
SHAKING	SOW	SUFFICES	TOWERING
SHAME	SPADES	SULLEN	TOWY
SHAN'T	SPARKLING	SULPHUR	TRACE
SHAPING-TIME	SPEEDED	SULTRY	TRACING
SHEDS	SPELT	SUMMON	TRACK
SHELTER	SPILLED	SUNG	TRADE
SHIELDED	SPINDRIFT	SUNK	TRADES
SHIFTING	SPIRITS	SUNSET	TRAIL
SHINES	SPITTLE	SURFACE	TRAILING
SHIRE	SPLENDOUR	SURGE	TRANSLATING
SHIRES	SPLITTING	SUSPICIOUS	TREMBLING
SHOAL	SPORT	SWEETHEARTS'	TREMENDOUS
SHOOT	SPOTS	SWEETNESS	TRIBE
SHOVEL	SPREAD	SWIFT	TRIBES
SHOWER	SPRINKLE	SWINE	TRICK
SHRILL	SPRUNG	SWORD	TRICKS
SHRINE	SQUIRREL	SWUNG	TRIED
SHUFFLED	STABLES	SYMMETRICAL	TRODDEN
SIGHING	STAGES	TAILOR	TROT
SIGHTS	STAIR	TAILORS	TROUBLED
SIGN	STALK	TAILOR'S	TROUBLES
SIGNAL	STALLION	TALKED	TRUST
SILENCES	STALLS	TALKS	TUFTED
SILENTLY	STAMPS	TAP	TUNNEL
SILKEN	STARING	TAPPING	TURNIP
SILL	START	TASTED	TUSKED
SINEW	STARVED	TAUGHT	TWELVE-WINDED
SINGERS	STATIONS	TAUT	TWENTY-FOUR
SINK	STATUE	TAXIS	TWINE
SINKING	STATUES	TEACHES	TWINING

TWIXT	WHO'LL	AFLAME	APPAREL
UNAGEING	WIDOWS	AFLOAT	APPARELLED
UNDID	WILLOW	AFTERNOON	APPEARS
UNDOER	WINDER	AFTER'S	APPETITE
UNEASILY	WINDLESS	AGAMEMNON	APPLE'S
UNFAILING	WINTRY	AGAPE	APPROACH
UNGOTTEN	WIPE	AGED	APPROACHING
UNIVERSE	WISER	AGELESS	APRIL
UNLOCKED	WIT	AGENT	APRON
UNLUCKILY	WITCH	AGHAST	APT
UNMOVING	WITNESSES	AGLOW	APTITUDE
UNROLLED	WITS'	AGONIZED	ARAN
UNSLEEPING	WOKEN	AGROUND	ARBOUR
UPRIGHT	WOLF	AH	ARCHED
UPWARD	WORDY	AHOY	ARCHES
URCHIN	WORE	AIR-DRAWN	ARCHIVES
USUAL	WORMY	AISLE	ARC-LAMPED
UTTER	WORN	ALBATROSS	ARCLAMPS
UTTERS	WOUNDED	ALBINO	ARCS
VALE	WRAP	ALCOVE	ARCTIC
VALLEYS	YARDS	ALL-HOLLOWED	ARDOUROUSLY
VAN	YEARS'	ALL-IN	AREN'T
VAST	YES	ALLOTMENT	ARGUMENT
VAULT	YOU'LL	ALLOTMENTS	ARISING
VAULTING	YOURS	ALONE'S	ARKS
VEINED	ZODIAC	ALPHABET	ARMIES
VERSE		ALPS	ARMLESS
VICE	(1)	ALTER	ARMOURED
VINE	AARON	AMBASSADOR	AROSE
VIOLET	ABASING	AMBITION	AROUSE
VIPER	ABED	AMBULANCE	ARROW
VISIONS	ABRAHAM-MAN	AMEN	ARROWS'
VISITING	ABSCESSES	AMID	ARROWY
VOLLEY	ABSTRACT	AMPLIFY	ARSE
VOWELS	ABSTRACTED	ANACHRONISTIC	ARTERY
WADING	ACCIDENT	ANAL	ASCEND
WAGES	ACORN	ANATOMIST	ASCENDING
WAGGING	ACORNED	ANATOMY	ASCENSION
WAKES	ACQUAINT	ANCESTRALLY	ASCENT
WANDER	ACQUAINTED	ANCHORGROUND	ASH-BINS
WANT	ACQUAINTING	ANDROGYNOUS	ASHEN
WARNING	ACQUAINTS	ANEMONE	ASHPIT
WAVED	ACRES	ANEW	ASKING
WAX'S	ACRITUDES	ANGELS'	ASKS
WEAPON	ACTIONS	ANGELUS	ASPIRING
WEAR	ACTORS	ANGRILY	ASS
WEARING	ACTS	ANKLING	ASSAILINGS
WEAVE	ADDERS	ANNOUNCED	ASSASSINS
WEB	ADMIRING	ANN'S	ASSEMBLAGE
WEBS	ADMITS	ANOTHER'S	ASSEMBLED
WEEDED	ADOLESCENCE	ANSWERING	ASSEMBLING
WEIGHED	ADORATION	ANTICLIMAX	ASS'S
WE'LL	ADORERS	ANTICS	ASSUMED
WESTERN	ADORNED	ANTISEPTIC	ASSUMING
WHACK	ADORNERS	ANTLERED	ASTONISH
WHEAT	ADORNING	ANTLERS	ASTOUNDED
WHEELS	ADVANCE	ANVILS	ASUNDER
WHIRLED	AEGEAN	ANYTHING	ASYLUMS
WHIRLPOOL	AESOP	APE	ATE
WHISPERING	AFFECTIONS	APOSTLES'	ATLANTIC

ATLAS	BATHER	BIRDMAN	BORDERS
ATLAS-EATER	BATTER	BIRD-PAPPED	BORROW
ATLASWISE	BATTLING	BISCAY	BOSOM
ATONE	BAYS	BISCUIT	BOTTLECORK
ATTENTIVE	BEAD	BISECTED	BOUGHT
ATTIC	BEADS	BISHOP'S	BOULDER
AUCTION	BEAKED	BITCHES	BOUNDED
AUDEN	BEARDING	BITER'S	BOUNDS
AUDEN'S	BEARDLESSLY	BITING	BOW-AND-ARROW
AUSTERE	BEASTHOOD	BLACKAMOOR	BOWELS
AUSTRIAN	BEATS	BLACK-BACKED	BOWER
AUTOCRACY	BECAME	BLACKBERRIES	BOWLER
AUTOMATIC	BECKONED	BLACKBIRDS	BOXED
AUTUMNAL	BEDDED	BLACKED	BOXY
AVALANCHE	BEDFELLOWS	BLACKENED	BOYS'
AVENUES	BEDSITTING	BLACKHEAD	BRACKET
AVIARY	BEDTIME	BLACKNESS	BRAIDING
AVOID	BEDWARD	BLACONY	BRAMBLED
AWAKING	BEECHES	BLADDER	BRANCH
AWARE	BEES'	BLADDERS	BRANDED
AWAY'S	BEETLE	BLANKNESS	BRASS
AWHILE	BEETLES'	BLARED	BRASSILY
AWKWARD	BEGAN	BLASPHEME	BRAWL
AWOKE	BEGGARS	BLAST	BRAWNED
A-WOOING	BEGINS	BLEACHED	BREAD-SIDED
AXE	BEGUN	BLEATING	BREAKERS
AXLE	BEHEADED	BLEEDING	BREAKNECK
AZURE	BELFRIES	BLESSINGS	BREASTBONE'S
BAAING	BELIEVED	BLISTERED	BREAST-DEEP
BABBLED	BELIEVER	BLOCK	BREASTKNOT
BABBLING	BELIEVERS	BLOND	BREAST'S
BABEL	BELIEVING	BLOOD-COUNTING	BREATHED
BABIES	BELLADONNA	BLOODILY	BREATHES
BACKS	BELLBUOY	BLOODRED	BREATH'S
BADINAGE	BELLMETAL	BLOOD-RED	BREATH-WHITE
BADLY	BELLOWED	BLOOD-SIGNED	BREECHES
BAG	BELLOWS	BLOOMING	BREEZE-SERENE
BAGPIPE-BREASTED	BELL-SPIRE	BLOSSOMED	BRETHREN
BAGS	BELL-VOICED	BLOSSOMS	BREVIARY
BALD	BELLYFUL	BLOT	BRIARED
BALLAD	BELT	BLOWCLOCK	BRIDAL
BALL-PRYING	BENEDICTION	BLUE-HUED	BRIDEBAIT
BAMBOO	BENEFIT	BLUE-TIPPED	BRIDGED
BAND	BEQUEATH	BLUFF	BRIDLES
BANDAGE	BEREFT	BLUSH	BRIGHT-EYED
BANDAGED	BESIDE	BOARDS	BRIMMING
BANGED	BETHELS	BOAT'S	BRIMSTONE
BANGS	BETHEL-WORM	BOATSIDE	BRINE
BAPTISM	BETRAY	BOATSIZED	BRINGING
BAR	BETRAYED	BODICE	BRINGS
BARD	BEWILDERMENT	BODIES	BRISKEST
BARED	BIBLE	BODILESS	BROAD
BARENAVELED	BIBLE-LEAVED	BOLTING	BRONZE
BARER	BIDDEN	BOLTS	BROODS
BARKED	BIDE	BONEBOUND	BROODY
BARN	BILLHOOK	BONERAILED	BROOM
BARNROOFS	BILLHOOKS	BONES'	BROOMED
BASKETS	BILLS	BONEYARDS	BROOMSTICKS
BASS	BIND	BONFIRE	BROTHERHOOD
BAT	BIRDLESS	BONY	BROTHERLESS

BROTHERS'	CAMERAS	CELLED	CHRYSOLITH
BROWNS	CAMPED	CELL-STEPPED	CHUCKED
BROWSE	CANALS	CELLULOID	CHUCKLE
BROWSING	CANCEROUS	CEMENTED	CICADA
BRUISES	CANCER'S	CEMENTING	CIGARETTE
BRUIT	CANDLE'S	CENTAUR'S	CIGARETTES
BRUTE	CANDLEWOODS	CENTRAL	CINDER-NESTING
BRYNS	CANKERED	CENTRED	CIPHER
BUBBLED	CANONIZED	CENTRES	CIPHERS
BUCK	CANS	CENTURY	CIRCUMAMBULATE
BUCKLE	CANYONS	CERECLOTH	CIRCUSES
BUCKLEY'S	CAPERS	CEREMENTS	CISTERN
BUCKLING	CAPPED	CERTAINLY	CITIES'
BUCKS	CAPRICORN	CHALLENGE	CIVET
BUGLE	CAPS	CHALLENGED	CIVILIZATION
BUGS	CAPSIZED	CHAMELEON	CLAD
BUILDS	CAPTOR	CHANCE	CLAIM
BUILT	CAPTURE	CHANKLEY	CLAMOUR
BULB	CARBOLIC	CHANTER	CLAN
BULGE	CARCASS	CHAPELS	CLANGOUR
BULLDANCE	CARDBOARD	CHAPTER	CLAP
BULLET'S	CARDIGAN	CHAPTERED	CLAPPED
BULLIES	CARDS	CHARABANCS	CLAPS
BULLOCK	CAREFREE	CHARGE	CLARITY
BULLRING	CARELESSNESS	CHARM	CLATTER
BULLS	CARESS	CHARMINGLY	CLAYFELLOW
BULL'S-EYE	CARGOED	CHARNEL	CLAYFELLOWS
BULLY	CARNAGE	CHARNEL-HOUSE	CLEANEST
BULWARKS	CAROUSES	CHARRED	CLEARER
BUM	CAROUSING	CHARTING	CLENCHED
BUMP	CARPETING	CHASER	CLERICAL-GREY
BUNCHED	CARRIED	CHASES	CLIMATES
BUNTING	CARRY	CHASTE	CLIMBER
BUOYANT	CART	CHASTITY	CLIME
BUOYS	CARTOON	CHATTER	CLINICS
BUOY'S	CASANOVA	CHATTERBOX	CLIPS
BURDEN	CASTAWAYS	CHEAT	CLOAK
BURROW	CASUALTY	CHECK	CLOAKED
BURSTING	CATARACTED	CHERISH	CLOCKED
BURSTS	CATASTROPHE	CHERRY	CLOCKING
BUSHILY	CATCHES	CHIC	CLOISTER
BUSTLING	CATHEDRALS	CHICKEN	CLOSES
BUTT	CATHERINE	CHICKENS	CLOSE-UP
BUTT-ENDS	CATLIKE	CHICKENS'	CLOSING
BUTTERED	CATS'	CHILDLESS	CLOTHESHORSE
BUTTOCK	CAULDRON	CHILDLIKE	CLOTHS
BUY	CAULDRON'S	CHIMED	CLOTTED
BYZANTINE	CAUTIOUSLY	CHIMING	CLOUD-FORMED
CABARET	CAVEPOOLS	CHIP	CLOUD-LIKE
CADAVER	CAVERN	CHIPPED	CLOUDS'
CADAVEROUS	CAVERS	CHOIRS	CLOUD'S
CADENCE	CAWING	CHOKED	CLOUD-SOPPED
CAESARED	CEASE	CHOKING	CLOUD-TRACKING
CAIRO'S	CELEBRATED	CHOPIN	CLOUT
CAKE	CELEBRATES	CHOREOGRAPHED	CLOUTS
CALLIGRAPHER	CELEBRATING	CHOSEN	CLOVE
CALLIGRAPHY	CELERY	CHRISTBREAD	CLOVER
CALLING	CELESTIAL	CHRIST-CROSS-ROW	CLOVES
CALVE	CELIBATE	CHRISTENED	CLOWN
CAMEL'S	CELLAR	CHRISTWARD	CLUB

CLUNG	CONFECTION	COWS'	CUMMINGS
CLUSTERED	CONFESSIONAL	CRAB-BACKED	CUNNING
CLUTCHES	CONFUSED	CRABBING	CUPIDS
COAL-	CONFUSING	CRABS	CURDLE
COASTS	CONGERED	CRACKLING	CURDLERS
COAT	CONJURE	CRADLE-PETALS	CURED
COATS	CONSCIENCE	CRADLE'S	CURELESS
COBBLED	CONSECRATED	CRAGS	CURES
COCKERELS	CONSOLING	CRAMPED	CURFEW
COCKFIGHT	CONSTANT	CRANE	CURIOUS
COCKLED	CONSTRUCTED	CRANNIES	CURLING
COCKLES	CONSUMED	CRANNY	CURL-LOCKED
COCK-ON-A-DUNGHILL	CONSUMPTIVES'	CRASHES	CURRANTS
COCKSHUT	CONTAGES	CRATERS	CURRENCIES
COCKWISE	CONTEMPLATE	CREAM	CURTAINED
CODED	CONTEMPLATED	CREASING	CURTAINS
COGITATIONS	CONTINENCE	CREATED	CURVES
COILED	CONTRARIES	CREATION	CUSS
COILING	CONVENIENT	CREATURES	CUT-TO-MEASURE
COILS	CONVENTION	CREDULITY	CYANIDE
COIN	CONVULSIONS	CREEP	CYPRESSES
COINS	COO	CREEPING	CYST
COITUS	COOED	CREEPS	DABBED
COLDNESS	COOLED	CRESTED	DABBLES
COLIC	COOLER	CREVICES	DAB-FILLED
COLLECTED	COPPERS	CRIB	DAI
COLLECTION	CORALS	CRIER	DAME
COLOSSAL	CORD	CRIERS	DAMS
COLTS	CORE	CRIMES	DANCER
COLUMBUS	CORKSCREW	CRIMSON	DANCES
COLUMN-MEMBERED	CORMORANTS	CRIPPLE	DANDY
COLUMNS	CORNER-CAST	CRISS-CROSS	DANES
COMBED	CORNERS	CROCKED	DANGLER
COMBING	CORPSES	CROCUS	DANGLES
COMBS	CORPSE'S	CROOK	DARKEN
COME-A-CROPPER	CORRAL	CROP	DARKENED
COMERS	CORRECT	CROSS-BONED	DARKENING
COMET	CORRIDOR	CROSS-BONES	DARK-SKINNED
COMETH	CORRIDORS	CROSSLY	DARK-VOWELLED
COMETS	CORROSIVE	CROSS-STROKED	DART
COMIC	CORRUPTED	CROSSTREE	DARTED
COMMAS	CORRUPTING	CROUCH	DASH
COMMIT	CORSET	CROUCHING	DASHED-DOWN
COMMONER	COST	CROWDED	DATED
COMMOTION	COUNTENANCE	CROWED	DAUB
COMMUNAL	COUNTIES	CROW'S-FOOT	DAUBING
COMMUNION	COUNTRY-HANDED	CRUCIFIXION	DAVY'S
COMPANY	COUNTRY'S	CRUDE	DAWNED
COMPASSION	COUNTS	CRUELLER	DAWS
COMPEL	COUPLE	CRUELTY	DAYBREAK
COMPELS	COUPLED	CRUNCHING	DAYED
COMPLETENESS	COURAGE	CRUTCH	DAYLIGHT
COMPOSURE	COURT	CRYPT	DAYS'
COMPRESSED	COVER	CUBBED	DAZZLE
CONCEAL	COVERED	CUCKOO	DAZZLED
CONCEIVING	COVERINGS	CUCKOOING	DAZZLER
CONCERN	COVERS	CUDGEL	DE
CONCRETE	COWARDS	CUDGELLING	DEADROCK
CONDEMN	COWL	CULLED	DEADWEED
CONDENSE	COWPATCHED	CULTURED	DEAN

DEATHBEDS	DIFFERENT	DOUBTFUL	E.
DEATH'LL	DIG	DOUBTING	EAGLE-MOUTHED
DEATH-STAGGED	DING	DOUSING	EAGLES
DECADENT	DINNED	DOVES	EARDRUM
DECAYED	DIP	DOWNFALL	EATING
DECAYING	DIPPING	DOWNS	EAVES
DECEIVED	DIRECTED	DOWNWARD	EBB
DECENCY	DIRECTLY	DOWNY	ECHOING
DECISION	DIRT	DOWSE	ECHO'S
DECK	DIRTBOX	DOYEN	ECSTASY
DECLARE	DIRTIER	DRAGGED	ECSTATIC
DECLENSION	DISAPPOINT	DRAGGING	EEL
DEDICATE	DISCIPLE	DRAGONFLY	EGYPTIAN
DEEPSEA	DISCORDANT	DRAINED	EGYPT'S
DEFACED	DISCOVERED	DRAKED	ELBOWED
DEFEAT	DISCOVERS	DRAWS	ELDER'S
DEFILE	DISCUSSING	DREAD	ELECTRA'S
DEFT	DISEASE	DREADED	ELEGIAC
DEFYING	DISEASES	DREAMLESS	ELEMENTAL
DELIBERATE	DISGUISED	DREAMS'	ELEMENTARY
DELIVERED	DISHEVELLED	DRESS	ELIOT
DELUGING	DISHONOURS	DRESSED	ELMED
DELUSIVE	DISHRAG	DRIED	ELOI
DEN	DISMANTLED	DRIFTLESS	ELUSIVELY
DENIALS	DISPELLED	DRILLED	ELVES
DENIES	DISPLACED	DRINKER	EMASCULATE
DENS	DISSECT	DRINKS	EMBLEM
DENT	DISSOLUTION	DRIPPER	EMBRACE
DEPARTING	DISSOLVED	DRIPPING	EMBRACING
DEPARTURE	DISSOLVING	DRIVELLED	EMETIC
DEPENDING	DISTANT	DRIVING	EMITS
DEPENDS	DISTEMPER	DROOPED	EMPTY'S
DEPTH	DISTURBS	DROPPERS	ENAMEL
DERIDE	DITCH	DROPPING	ENAMELLED
DERIVE	DITCHES	DROP'S	ENAMOURED
DESERTS	DIVER	DROWNS	ENAMOURING
DESERVES	DIVER'S	DRUB	ENCOUNTER
DESIRED	DIVES	DRUG	ENCROACHES
DESIRELESS	DIVIDED	DRUG-WHITE	ENCROACHMENT
DESIRERS	DIVINE	DRY-AS-PASTE	ENCUMBERED
DESIRING	DIVINITIES	DRYER	ENDED
DESOLATE	DIVORCING	DUALIZING	ENDLESSLY
DESOLATION	DOCTOR	DUCK-BILLED	ENDOWED
DESTINATION	DOGS	DUCKS	ENFORCE
DESTINY	DOGS'	DUGS	ENGINE'S
DESTROY	DOG'S	DULL	ENGLISH
DESTROYER	DOLPHINED	DULLED	ENGRAVING
DESTROYS	DOLPHINS	DUMBFOUNDING	ENJOYED
DETECT	DOLPHIN'S	DUMBSTRUCK	ENTERING
DEVELOP	DOMED	DUMMY	ENTERTAINING
DEVILDOM	DOMINIES	DUNCE	ENTICED
DEVILISH	DONG	DUNES	ENTRAIL
DEVOTE	DONKEY	DUNGHILL	ENVIOUS
DEVOTION	DONKEYS'	DUNG-LICKERS	EPITAPH
DEWFALL	DONS	DUNGS	EQUABILITY
DEW'S	DON'T	DUSKY	ERECT
DIAMOND	DOORWAY	DUST-APPOINTED	ERRANDS
DIAPHRAGM	DOORWAYS	DUSTERS	ERROR
DICTATORSHIP	DOUBLECROSSED	DUSTS	ERRORS
DICTIONARY	DOUBLING	DWINDLE	ERSE

ERUPT	FARING	FIREWORKS	FORGETS
ESCAPES	FASTENING	FIRM	FORGIVING
ESQUIRE	FATE	FIRMAMENT	FORGOT
ESTATES	FATHERLESS	FISHERBIRD	FORKING
ESTRANGING	FATHOM	FISHERMANNED	FORSAKE
ETERNITY	FATHOMED	FISHERMEN	FORTUNATE
ETHER	FAULT	FISH-GILLED	FORTUNED
ETHEREAL	FAULTS	FISHTAIL	FORTY
ETNA	FAULTY	FISHWIFE	FOUNTAINHEAD
EUNUCHS	FAWKES	FISTED	FOUR-FRUITED
EVENINGS	FEAR-BEGGARED	FIVE-FATHOMED	FOUR-STRINGED
EVENING'S	FEARING	FIXERS	FOURTH
EVEN-TIME	FEATHERBED	FIXTURES	FOUR-WINDED
EVERGREEN	FEATHERING	FLAGS	FOWLS'
EVERLASTING	FEATHERLANDS	FLAILED	FOX'S
EVERYBODY'S	FEEBLE	FLAILING	FRAGMENTARY
EVILS	FEEDS	FLAKE	FRANKINCENSE
EVIL'S	FEELS	FLAKE-BARE	FREELY
EWE	FEMININE	FLANKS	FREEZE
EXALTATION	FENCE	FLANNEL	FREEZES
EXAMINERS	FENCES	FLARED	FREEZING
EXERCISED	FEND	FLAXEN	FRENCH
EXHALING	FERNED	FLEA	FRESHNESS
EXILED	FEROCIOUS	FLEA-SPECKED	FRESH-WATER
EXODUS	FERRIES	FLEECED	FRIARS
EXPENSIVE	FERRULE	FLEUR	FRIENDS'
EXPLODE	FETCH	FLICK	FRIGHTENED
EXPLORE	FEVERS	FLICKED	FRIGID
EXPOSE	FEVER'S	FLICKERING	FROCK
EX-SOLDIERS	FEWER	FLINGS	FROG
EXULTATION	FIBRES	FLINTSTEPS	FROGS
EXULTATION'S	FIDDLE	FLOGGING	FROZE
EXULTING	FIDDLED	FLOORS	FRUCTIFY
EXULTS	FIDDLES	FLOUNDERS	FULFILL
EYEING	FIDDLING	FLOURISH	FULLNESS
EYE-TEETH	FIEND	FLOWERLY	FUMING
EZRA	FIERCELY	FLOWN	FUN
FABLING	FIFE	FLUCTUANTLY	FURIED
FACING	FIFTY	FLUES	FURLED
FACT	FIGHTING	FLUIDS	FURNACE-NOSTRILLED
FACTORS	FIGS	FLUSH	FURNISH
FACULTY	FIGURE	FLUTTERED	FUSES
FADING	FILE	FLUTTERS	FUTILITY
FAG	FILED	FLY-LORD'S	GAB
FAGGOTS	FILLIES	FOAL	GABBING
FAILING	FILLS	FOAM-BLUE	GABLES
FAINT	FILMED	FOAMED	GAG
FAIR-FORMED	FILMS	FOAMING	GAINSAY
FAITHLESS	FILTHY	FOAMS	GALACTIC
FAITHLESSLY	FINALITY	FOLLOWED	GALE
FAITHS	FINCHES	FOLLOWING	GALED
FAKE	FINGERMAN	FOLLOWS	GALILEE'S
FALLOW	FINGERS'	FOOLISHNESS	GALLANTLY
FALSITY	FINGER'S	FOOTFALL	GALLIC
FAME	FIN-GREEN	FOOTPRINTS	GALLOPS
FAN	FIREBALL	FOOTSTEPS	GAMBO
FANTASTIC	FIRE-DWARFED	FORCED	GANDER
FANTASTICALLY	FIREFLY	FOREHEADS	GANDERS
FARAWAY	FIRELIT	FORESKIN	GANGS
FAREWELLS	FIREWIND	FOREWARNS	GANG'S

GARB	GOBLIN-SUCKER	GROTTOES	HANGAR
GARDEN-CLOSE	GODDESSES	GROUNDS	HANGNAIL
GARDEN-WALKS	GOD-LIES	GROUNDWORKS	HANK
GARLAND	GODLINESS	GROVE-GREEN	HAPPENING
GARMENTS	GONGS	GROWTH	HAPPILY
GARRISONED	GONOCOCCI	GROWTHS	HARBOURING
GASKETTED	GOODNESS	GROYNE	HARDER
GATHER	GOODS	GUARDED	HARD-HELD
GATHERS	GOOSEGIRLS	GUARDIAN	HARDINESS
GAUZE	GOOSEHERD	GUARDING	HARDSHIP
GENDER	GOOSESKIN	GUESSES	HARE-
GENDER'S	GOSSIP	GUEST	HAREBELL
GENEROUS	GOURD	GUIDED	HARING
GENESIS'	GOVERNED	GUIDES	HARKS
GENETIC	GOWN	GUILLOTINE	HARLEM
GENITALS	GOWNED	GUILTLESS	HARMONIES
GENTLEMEN	GRACEFUL	GUILTS	HARMONIOUS
GENTRY	GRACEFULLY	GUILTY	HARNESS
GEOFFREY	GRAFTERS	GULF	HARNESSED
GERANIUM	GRAFTS	GULFED	HARNESSING
GERMY	GRANITE	GULP	HARPIES
GHETTO	GRAPE	GUMS	HARP-WAKED
GIANTS	GRAPE'S	GUN	HARROW
GIBED	GRAPH	GUNMAN	HARSHLY
GIDDILY	GRASSBLADE	GUSHER	HASTENING
GIFT	GRASSES	GUSHERS	HASTENS
GILDERS	GRASSY	GUSTY	HATCH
GILLED	GRATE	GYRATES	HATCHING
GIPSY	GRAVE-GABBING	HADES	HATE
GIRDERED	GRAVE-GROPING	HADES'	HATING
GIRDERS	GRAVELS	HAGS	HATS
GIRDLE	GRAVE'S	HAILING	HATSTAND
GIRL-CIRCLED	GRAVEST	HAIR-BURIED	HAULED
GIRL-LIPPED	GRAVEYARD	HAIRED	HAULS
GIZZARDS	GRAZING	HAIRPINS	HAUNTS
GLADDEN	GREATEST	HAIRY-HEELED	HAVING
GLADE	GREED	HALE	HAVOC
GLADNESS	GREENER	HALF-AVERTED	HAWED
GLAMORGAN	GREENNESS	HALF-BLIND	HAWK-EYED
GLAMORGAN'S	GREEN-SHADOWED	HALFMOON'S	HAWKING
GLAMOUR	GREENSWARD	HALF-MOULDED	HAYBEDS
GLANCING	GREET	HALF-TRACKED	HAYCOCK
GLAND	GREY-HAIRED	HALLELUJAH	HAYCOCKS
GLANDED	GRIEF-LIKE	HALLOWED	HAYRICKS
GLARED	GRIEVERS	HALO	HAYSTACKED
GLASSES	GRIGSON	HALOED	HAZARDOUS
GLASSHOUSE	GRIMACE	HALT	HAZE
GLAZED	GRIMLY	HALTS	HEADED
GLEN	GRIN	HALVED	HEADLANDS
GLINT	GRINDING	HAMLETS	HEADLESS
GLITTER	GRISTED	HANDBAGGED	HEAD'S
GLITTERS	GRISTLE	HANDBELL	HEADSTONE
GLOOM	GRISTLES	HANDFULL	HEALS
GLORIOUS	GROIN	HANDMADE	HEAP
GLORY'S	GROIN'S	HANDPRINT	HEARSE
GLOW-WORM	GROOVE	HAND'S	HEARTBEAT
GLOW-WORMS	GROOVED	HANDSAW	HEARTHS
GNOMES	GROPE	HANDSHAPED	HEART-SHAPED
GOAT-LEGGED	GROPING	HANDSOME	HEATH
GOB	GROSS	HANDY	HEATS

HEAVE	HOIST	HUNCHBACKS	INDULGE
HEAVEN-CIRCLING	HOLIER	HUNGERING	INEXORABLE
HEAVEN-DRIVEN	HOLLER	HUNGER'S	INFANCY
HEAVEN-PROOF	HOLOCAUST	HUNGRILY	INFANT-BEARING
HEAVENS'	HOLT	HUNT	INFINITE
HEDGE	HOMAGE	HUNTER	INFORMED
HEEDING	HOMESTALL	HUNTSMAN	INHALE
HEEDLESS	HONOUR	HURDLES	INHERITS
HEE-HAW	HOO	HURLED	INHOSPITABLE
HE-GOD'S	HOOK	HURLING	INHUMAN
HEIGHTS	HOOKING	HURLS	INMOST
HELLBORN	HOOKS	HURRIED	INSANITY
HELL'S	HOOT	HURRIES	INSECT-FACED
HELPLESSLY	HOOTING	HUSHES	INSECTS
HEMISPHERE	HOOVED	HUSKED	INSIDIOUS
HEMISPHERES	HOOVES	HUT	INSIST
HEMLOCK	HOP	HUTS	INSTRUMENT
HEMLOCK-HEADED	HOPED	HYDRANGEAS	INSTRUMENTAL
HEMMING	HOPHEAD'S	HYENA	INSTRUMENTS
HEMS	HOPING	HYLEG	INTENSE
HEN	HORIZON	HYMN	INTENT
HENNA	HORNING	HYPNOTISED	INTENTIONS
HENRUN	HORNY	ICEBERG'S	INTERLUDE
HENS	HORRIBLE	IDIOM	INTERPRETED
HERALD	HORRIBLY	IDLING	INTIMACIES
HERALDS	HORRORS	IDOL	INTIMATIONS
HERDS	HORSEBACK	IDYLL	INTRICATELY
HERDSMAN	HORSEMEN	ILEX	INVALID
HERMAPHRODITE	HOSANNAS	ILLIMITABLE	INVEIGLERS
HERMITS'	HOSPITAL	ILL-LIT	INVITED
HERODS	HOSTS	ILLUMINATE	INVITERS
HEROIC	HOTHOUSE	ILLUMINATION	INVOKED
HEROINE	HOTTENTOT	ILLUSIONS	INVOLVE
HERONS'	HOUND	IMAGINARY	IRISES
HERRINGS	HOUNDS'	IMAGINED	IRISH
HESPERIDES	HOURGLASS	IMAGININGS	IRONS
HEW	HOURLESS	IMITATE	ISHMAEL'S
HEY	HOURLY	IMMEASURABLE	ISLAND'S
HEYDAYS	HOURS'	IMMEMORIAL	ISLES
HICKORY	HOUSING	IMMENSE	ITEM
HIDER	HOVEL	IMMENSITY	ITSELF
HIDING	HOVER	IMMORTALITY	JACK-
HIGHROAD	HOWL	IMMUTABLE	JACOB
HIGH-VOLTED	HUBBUB	IMPATIENT	JACOB'S
HILLOCK	HUG	IMPLORE	JAILS
HILLOCKS	HUGGED	IMPOSE	JAMES
HILLOCKY	HULKS	IMPOSS-I-BLE	JARRING
HILL'S	HULLABALLOING	IMPRESS	JAWBONE
HINDERED	HUMANITY'S	IMPRINTS	JAW-BONE
HINDERING	HUMBLING	IMPRISONED	JEALOUS
HINGE	HUMILIATE	IMPULSES	JEALOUSY
HINT	HUMMED	IMPULSIVE	JERRYSTONE
HIP	HUMMING	INCESTUOUS	JESTS
HIPS	HUMOUR	INCHES	JEWELLED
HISS	HUMOURED	INCHTAPED	JEYES'
HIST	HUMP	INCISING	JOB'S
HIT	HUMPBACKED	INCONVENIENCE	JOINTED
HIVE	HUMPED	INDIGO	JOINTS
HOBNAIL	HUMPS	INDISTINCT	JOKER
HOGSBACK	HUNCHBACKED	INDUCIVE	JONAH'S

JONES	LADYLIKE	LENDS	LOOSED
JONQUIL	LAGGARDS	LEPERS*	LOOSENS
JOYCE'S	LAKE'S	LESSENS	LOOTED
JOYFUL	LAMBS	LETHAL	LOP
JUAN	LAMENT	LET'S	LOPING
JUDGE	LAMENTS	LETTERED	LOPPED
JUDGING	LAMPED	LETTERS	LOPS
JUDGMENT	LAMPLIGHT	LETTING	LORDING
JUGGERNAUT	LAMP-POSTS	LEVELS	LORDLY
JUGULAR	LAMPS	LEWD	LORD'S
JUICES	LANCE	LIBIDINOUS	LORD'S-TABLE
JUMPING	LANDED	LICE	LOSER
JUMPS	LANDWARD	LICK	LOSSES
JUSTICE	LANE	LIDDED	LOTION
KANGAROO	LANES	LIES-TO-PLEASE	LOTS
KEATINGS	LARK	LIFTS	LOUDEN
KEENLY	LARKED	LIGHTER	LOUDENING
KEEPING	LARK-HIGH	LIGHTNESS	LOUDER
KEPT	LASHES	LIGHTNINGS	LOUSE
KETTLES	LASS'S	LIKENESS	LOUSE'S
KEYHOLES	LASTED	LILTING	LOVEBEDS
KEYLESS	LASTING	LILY'S	LOVE-DARKNESS
KICKS	LASTS	LIMB	LOVELESS
KID	LATCH	LIMIT	LOVE-LIES
KIN	LATCHED	LIMPET	LOVELORN
KINDER	LATERAL	LIMP-TREED	LOVE-TIP
KINDLE	LAUDS	LINEAMENTS	LOWER
KINDLES	LAUGHS	LINENED	LOW-FALUTIN
KINDLING	LAVA	LINGER	LOWLANDS
KINGCRAFTS	LAVA'S	LINGERED	LUBBER
KINGFISHER	LAW	LINNET	LUCID
KINGSLEY	LAWED	LINT	LUCIFER
KISSING	LAWLESS	LIONHEAD'S	LUCKILY
KISSPROOF	LAWN	LIPLESS	LUCKLESSLY
KITCHENS	LAWNS	LIPPED	LUCKY
KNAVE	LAWS	LIVED	LUFF
KNAVES	LAYERS	LIVER	LUGGAGE
KNEADING	LAZY	LIVERY	LULL
KNEE-	LEA	LIZARD	LULLED
KNEE-DEEP	LEAF-LIKE	LO	LULLING
KNELLED	LEAFY	LOAD	LUNGE
KNELLING	LEAGUES	LOAM	LURCHED
KNELLS	LEAK	LOAVES	LURED
KNICKER	LEAKING	LOBSTER	LUSTRELESS
KNICKERS	LEAKS	LOCAL	LYNX
KNIFE	LEANT	LOCKERS	LYS
KNIT	LEAR	LOCKJAW	MACADAM
KNOBBLY	LECHERED	LOCUSTS	MACHINERY
KNOCKS	LED-ASTRAY	LODGED	MACKEREL
KNOT	LEDGES	LOFTY	MADAM
KNOTS	LEECH	LOGIC	MADDENING
KNOWNS	LEECHES	LOGICS	MADMAN
LABORATORY	LEERS	LOIN-LEAF	MADMEN'S
LABOUR'S	LEGAL	LOINS	MAGDALENE
LABYRINTHS	LEGENDARY	LONG-LAST	MAGGOTS
LACED	LEGENDS*	LONGLYING	MAGGOT'S
LACK-A-HEAD	LEGS	LOOKED	MAGICS
LAD	LEISURE	LOOKING-GLASS	MAGNET
LADEN	LEMURAL	LOOMS	MAGNETIZE
LADS	LEND	LOOPED	MAGPIE

MAHOMET	MAZED	MINTED	MOUSE'S
MAIDEN'S	MEADOW	MIRACULOUS	MOUSING
MAIEUTIC	MEADOW'S	MIRE	MOUTHED
MAJESTY	MEAL	MIRRORED	MOUTH'S
MAJORS	MEAN	MISCHIEVOUS	MOVEMENT
MAKER'S	MEASURES	MISGIVING	MOWER
MAMMOTH	MEAT-EATING	MISSED	MR.
MANAGERS	MECHANICALLY	MISSING	MUDDLE
MANALIVE	MECHANICS	MISTAKING	MUFFLED
MAN-BEARING	MEDUSA	MISTS	MUFFLE-TOED
MAN-BEGETTERS	MEDUSA'S	MISVENTURE	MULATTO
MANED	MEETING	MITCHING	MULE
MANHOLES	MEETS	MIX	MULES
MAN-IRON	MELANCHOLY	MIXED	MULTIPLYING
MANMADE	MELODIOUS	MIXES	MULTITUDE
MAN-MELTING	MELTED	MIXTURE	MULTITUDES
MANSEED	MELTS	MNETHA'S	MULTITUDE'S
MANSHAPE	MEMORIAL'S	MOBY	MUMMER
MANSHAPED	MEMORY	MOCKED	MUMMERY
MANSION	MENDED	MOCKERY	MUMMY
MANSIONS	MERCIES	MODEL	MURDERING
MANSOULED	MERCURY	MODERNIST	MURDER'S
MANSTRING	MERIDIAN	MODESTY	MURMUR
MANURING	MERIT	MOIST	MUSCLED
MANWAGED	MERMAID	MOLESTED	MUSCLING
MANWAGING	MERMAIDEN	MOLL	MUSCLING-IN
MANWAX	MESSENGERS	MOLLS	MUSCULAR
MAP-BACKED	METALLIC	MONKEY	MUSHROOM
MAPS	METAMORPHOSIS	MONKEYED	MUSHROOMS
MAR	METAPHOR	MONSTER	MUSICAL
MARCHES	METAPHORS	MONUMENTAL	MUSSEL
MARCHING	METEORS	MOON-AND-MIDNIGHT	MUSTARDSEED
MARE	METICULOUS	MOONBEAM	MUTED
MARRIAGES	METROPOLIS	MOON-BLOWN	MUTTER
MARROW-COLUMNED	MICE	MOON-CHAINED	MUTTON
MARROW-LADLE	MID-AIR	MOON-DRAWN	MUZZLED
MARROWROOT	MIDLIFE	MOONFALL	MYCENAE'S
MARRY	MIDST	MOONLESS	MYSTERIES
MARTYRDOM	MIDWIFE	MOONLIT	MYSTICS
MARVELS	MIDWIVING	MOON-MAD	MYTH
MARYS	MILESTONES	MOONSHADE	MYTHS
MASKER	MILKING	MOONSHOD	NACREOUS
MASKS	MILKMAIDS	MOONSTONE	NAGGING
MASONS	MILKS	MOONSTRUCK	NAMELESS
MASTED	MILK-WHITE	MOON-TURNED	NANSEN'S
MASTERLESS	MILL	MOON-WHITE	NARCOTIC
MASTERY	MILLED	MORALS	NATIVE
MAST-HIGH	MILLING	MORSING	NATRON
MASTIFF	MINCES	MOSSY	NATURE
MATCH	MINDED	MOSTLY	NAVE
MATCHBOARD	MINDS	MOTH	NAVEL
MATCHES	MIND'S	MOTHERED	NAVES
MATE	MINER	MOTHERING	NAVIGATES
MATED	MINERAL	MOTHERLIKE	NAVIGATING
MATERNAL	MINERALS	MOTLEY	NEAT'S
MATTED	MINGLED	MOTOR	NEGATION
MATURED	MINISTERS	MOULDED	NEGATIVES
MAULED	MINNOWS	MOUNTAINOUS	NEGRO
MAULING	MINOTAURS	MOURNS	NEIGHBOURED
MAUVE	MINSTRELS	MOUSEHOLE	NEIGHBOURING

NEIGHBOURS	NUN	OUTSKIRTS	PARKS
NEOPHYTES	NUNNERIES	OUTSPOKEN	PARLIAMENT
NEPTUNE	NURSERY	OUTSTRETCHED	PARLOUR
NESTLING	NURSE'S	OUTWORN	PARNASSIAN
NETTLE	NUTMEG	OVAL	PARSON
NETTLE'S	OAKEN	OVEN	PARTICLE
NEURAL	OAKUM	OVER-FRUITFUL	PARTICLES
NEWSPAPER	OAR	OVERHEAD	PARTING
NEXT	OATH	OVERPOWERING	PASSAGE
NEXT-DOOR	OBEY	OVERWHELMED	PASSAGES
NIBBLE	OBSCURELY	OWL-SEED	PASSES
NIBBLES	OBSERVING	OWNED	PASSION
NICE	OBVIOUS	OX-KILLING	PASTORAL
NICK	OCCURRED	OYSTER	PASTURES
NICKED	OCEANIC	PACE	PATCHWORK
NIGHTBIRD	OCEANS	PACKED	PATIENT
NIGHTBREAK	OCHRE	PACKS	PATIENTS
NIGHTFALL	OCTAGON	PACT	PATROL
NIGHTINGALE'S	OCTOPUSES	PADDING	PATTERN
NIGHTJARS	ODYSSEY	PADDLE	PATTERNED
NIGHTMARISH	OFFENDED	PADDLER'S	PATTING
NIGHTPRIEST	OFFICERS	PADDLES	PAVILIONS
NIGHTSEED	OFFICIAL	PADDLING	PAYING
NIGHT-TIME	OFTEN	PADDOCKS	PAYS
NILE	OGRE	PAGEANT	PEACOCKSTAIN'S
NILLY	OILED	PAGES	PEAKS
NIMBLE	OINTMENTS	PAID-FOR	PEARS
NIMBUS	OLDER	PAIL	PEBBLY
NINEPIN	OLDEST	PAINING	PECK
NINNIES'	OMENS	PAINT-BOX	PECKING
NIPPED	OMIT	PAINTERS	PEDRO'S
NIPPLE	ONCE-BLIND	PAINTINGS	PEERED
NIPPLED	ONCE-RINDLESS	PAINTS	PEERS
NIPPLES	ONE-COLOURED	PAINT-STAINED	PEG
NOAH	ONE-DIMENSIONED	PAIR	PELICAN
NOAH'S	ONE-MARROWED	PALAVERS	PELT
NOBODY	ONES	PALE-GREEN	PELTER
NODDED	ONE-SIDED	PALER	PELTS
NODDING	OPENED	PALLID	PEN
NOISELESSLY	OPIUM	PALMED	PENETRATE
NOISES	ORACLE	PALMS	PENNY-EYED
NOISY	ORACLES	PALSY	PENUMBRA
NONSTOP	ORACULAR	PAN	PERCEIVE
NON-STOP	ORATOR	PANIC'S	PERCEIVES
NO-ONE	ORDURED	PANOPLY	PERCH
NOONS	ORGANPIPES	PANOPTICON	PERCIES
NOOSED	ORGANS	PAPER-BLOWING	PERIL
NORTH	ORNAMENTAL	PAPS	PERILOUS
NOSTRIL	OTTER	PARABLES	PERILS
NOTHINGS	OTTERS	PARABOLA	PERIODIC
NOT-TO-BE-BROKEN	OURS	PARADE	PERISCOPE
NOURISH	OURSELVES	PARADED	PERISCOPES
NOVEMBER	OUTBREAK	PARALLEL	PERISHED
NUDE	OUTCAST	PARCEL	PERPETUAL
NUDGE	OUTCRY	PARCHMENT	PERPETUATE
NUDGING	OUTDO	PARCHS	PERPLEXED
NUISANCE	OUTELBOWED	PARED	PERPLEXION
NUMBED	OUTLINE	PARHELION	PERRINS
NUMBER	OUTLINES	PARIS	PERSONAL
NUMBERED	OUT-OF-PERSPECTIVE	PARISH	PERVERSE

PETAL	PLAYERS	PRINTED	QUICKNESS
PETER	PLAYS	PRISM	QUIETNESS
PETROL	PLEADING	PRISMS	QUIETUDE
PETTICOATS	PLEASING	PRISONER	QUILLED
PETTY	PLEASURE	PRISONERS	QUILTS
PEWS	PLOUGHED	PRIVATE	QUITE
PHANTOM	PLUCKS	PRIZE	QUIVER
PHARAOH	PLUG	PROBLEM	QUOTED
PHARAOH'S	PLUMAGE	PROCESSION	RABBITS
PHOENIX'	PLUMB	PRODIGALS	RACED
PHOSPHORUS	PLUMBED	PRODIGIES	RACK
PHOTOGRAPH	PLUMP	PROFESSIONAL	RACKED
PHOTOGRAPHS	PLUNGING	PROFITS	RACKING
PHRASE	POINTING	PROFLIGATES	RACKS
PICCADILLY	POINTS	PROLOGUE	RADIANT
PICKBRAIN	POKER	PROPER	RADIO'S
PICKERS	POKERS	PROPHET-PROGENY	RADIUM
PICKPOCKET	POLAR	PROSPERED	RAFT
PICKS	POLE-HILLS	PROSTITUTION	RAFTERS
PICKTHANK	POLE-SITTING	PROTRACTED	RAG
PICTURED	POLLEN	PROVE	RAGES
PIERCING	POME'S	PROVED	RAIL
PIETY	POOLED	PROW	RAIN-BEATEN
PIGEONS	POOLS	PROWL	RAINBOW
PIGEON'S	POPEYE	PROWLS	RAINBOW-FISH
PIGMENTS	POPPIED	PRUDE'S	RAINBOWS
PIGS'	POPPY	PSALM	RAINED
PIG'S	PORCHES	PUBLIC	RAINS
PILGRIMAGE	POSITIVE	PUBS	RAISING
PILLARS	POSTER	PUDDLES	RAKES
PILLOW	POSTURES	PUFF	RAKING
PIMPS	POSTURING	PUFFBALL	RAMMED
PIN	POUCH	PULLEYS	RAMPED
PINCERED	POUNCING	PUMPED	RAMSHACKLING
PINCERS	POUNDED	PUNCTUAL	RANGING
PINCH	POUNDS	PUNCTURED	RANKEST
PIN-HILLED	POURED	PUNGENTLY	RANTS
PIN-LEGGED	POURS	PURGE	RAPED
PINNACLE	POUTING	PURIFY	RAPES
PINNED-AROUND-THE-	POVERTY	PURSED	RAPING
SPIRIT	POWDER	PUS	RAPTURE
PINPRICKS	POWERFUL	PUSH	RARENESS
PINS	PRAISES	PUTREFYING	RASCAL
PIN'S	PRANCING	PUTS	RASPED
PINTABLES	PRAYERPIECE	PUTTING	RATTLED
PIOUS	PRAYER'S	PUZZLE	RATTLING
PIPERS	PRAYERWHEEL	PYRAMIDS	RAVAGE
PITCHING	PREACHERS	QUAKED	RAVAGED
PITILESS	PREACHER'S	QUAKING	RAVE
PITS	PRECIPICE	QUARTERED	RAVENED
PIVOT	PREROGATIVE	QUARTERS	RAVES
PLAGUED	PRESENCE	QUAYRAIL	RAVISHMENT
PLAIT	PRETENDER	QUAYSTONE	RAWBONED
PLANET-DUCTED	PRICK	QUELLED	RAW-EDGED
PLANING-HEELED	PRICKED	QUENCH	REACHED
PLANNED	PRIDES	QUENCHED	REACHING
PLANNING	PRIESTED	QUENCHLESS	READYMADE
PLATES	PRIESTS	QUICKEN	REAL
PLATYPUS	PRIEST'S	QUICKENS	REBELLION
PLAYERED	PRIME	QUICKLY	REBORN

RECALL	RHAPSODIC	ROWS	SANK
RECEIVE	RHUBARB	RUBBING	SANSKRIT
RECEIVER	RHYMER	RUFFLED	SAPLESS
RECORDERS	RHYMES	RUFFLING	SAPPHIRE
REDCOATED	RHYTHMS	RUINED	SAP'S
REDEMPTION	RIBBING	RUINS	SARGASSO
REDHAIRED	RICE	RULED	SATANS
REDWOMBED	RICHER	RULY	SATYRS
REEFED	RICK'S	RUMBLING	SAVAGE
REEK	RID	RUMOURS	SAVAGELY
REELS	RIDDEN	RUMP	SAVES
REFLECTED	RIDICULOUS	RUMPUS	SAVOURS
REFLECTION	RIFTED	RUNAWAY	SAWBONES
REFLECTIONS	RIGHTSIGHTED	RUSHES	SAWN
REFUSES	RIM	RUSHING	SCALD
REGARDED	RINGED-SEA	RUSHY	SCALECOPHIDIAN
REGISTER	RINGING	RUSTIC	SCALED
REGULAR	RIPPED	RUSTICATING	SCALING
REHEARSING	RIPPLE-WOVEN	RUSTS	SCALP
REINDEER	RISK	RUSTY	SCALPEL
REINS	RIVALS	RUT	SCALY
REJOICE	RIVER'S	RUTTISH	SCAR
REJOICED	ROADSIDE	S.	SCARVING
REJOICING	ROARER	SABBATHS	SCATTER-BREATH
REKINDLED	ROARER'S	SABLE	SCHOLARS
RELATIONS	ROARS	SABRE	SCHOOL
RELATION'S	ROASTING	SACKCLOTH	SCIATIC
RELEVANT	ROBBERS	SACKED	SCISSORED
RELIC	ROBE	SACRED	SCOLDS
RELIGION	ROBED	SADDEST	SCORE
REMAINED	ROBES	SADDLE	SCORN
REMARKS	ROBIN	SADDLER	SCOUR
REMIND	ROC	SADLY	SCOUTING
REMOVE	ROCKBIRDS	SADNESS	SCRAMS
REND	ROCK-CHESTED	SAFEST	SCRAPE
RENOUNCING	ROCKET	SAGE	SCRAPING
RENT	ROCKETED	SAGS	SCRATCH
REPEAT	ROCKETING	SAHARA	SCRATCHES
REPETITION	RODS	SAILSHAPED	SCRAWLED
REPLIES	ROE	SAINTS	SCREAM
REPLYING	ROISTER	SAINT'S	SCREAMING
REPOSE	ROLLS	SAKES	SCREWED
REPTILE	ROME	SALT-EYED	SCRIBBLED
REQUEST	ROOD	SALT-LIPPED	SCRIPTURE
REQUIEMS	ROOFS	SALTS	SCROLLS
REROBING	ROOFTOPS	SALUTES	SCUD
RESEMBLE	ROOING	SALUTING	SCUDDED
RESEMBLING	ROOKING	SALVAGE	SCUMMED
RESERVOIR	ROOMS	SALVATION'S	SCUMS
RESIN	ROOSTS	SANATORIUM	SCURRY
RESPONSE	ROOTED	SANCTORUM	SCURRYING
RESUFFERED	ROPE	SANCTUM	SCURVY
RESURRECT	ROPED	SANDAL	SCUT
RESURRECTION	ROPE-DANCING	SANDALS	SCYTHED
RETCH	ROSE-	SAND-BAGGED	SCYTHE-EYED
RETREAT	ROUGHLY	SANDCRABS	SCYTHES
REVERENT	ROUNDING	SANDGRAIN	SCYTHE-SIDED
REVOLUTION	ROUNDNESS	SANDGRAINS	SEABEAR
REVOLVED	ROUSED	SANDY	SEABED
REVOLVES	ROUTES	SANGER'S	SEA-BED

SEA-BLOWN	SEPULCHRE	SHOALS	SIZZLING
SEACAVES	SERAPHIC	SHOCKED	SKATED
SEA-FAITHS	SERAPHIM	SHOED	SKEIN
SEAFARING	SERENE	SHOO	SKELETONS
SEA-GHOST	SERENITY	SHOOK	SKELETON'S
SEA-GIRLS'	SERIAL	SHOOTS	SKEWER
SEAGULL	SERMON	SHOP	SKIMMED
SEA-GUT	SERPENTS'	SHORTEN	SKINNING
SEA-HALVED	SERVANTS	SHOULDERING	SKINNY
SEA-HATCHED	SERVES	SHOUTER	SKINS
SEA-HYMEN	SETTLE	SHOVED	SKIN'S
SEALED	SETTLED	SHOWING	SKIPPED
SEALS	SETTLES	SHOWN	SKIRTING
SEA-PARSLEY	SETTLING	SHRAPNEL	SKIRTING-BOARD
SEAR	SEVENTY	SHRINED	SKULKING
SEARCHED	SEVER	SHRIVELLING	SKULKS
SEARCHING	SEVERAL	SHROUDED	SKULLFOOT
SEARING	SEVERERS	SHROUDING	SKY-BLUE
SEA-SAWERS	SEW	SHROUD-LIKE	SKY-SCRAPING
SEASHAKEN	SEWER	SHROUDS	SKYWARD
SEASHELL	SEXTON	SHRUB	SLABS
SEASHORES	SHADOWED	SHRUBBERIES	SLACK
SEASIDE	SHADOWLESS	SHRUBBERY	SLASH
SEASLIDES	SHADOWY	SHUDDERS	SLASHES
SEA-SPINDLE	SHALLOW	SHUFFLING	SLATE
SEA-STRAW	SHAMEFUL	SHUTTERS	SLATES
SEA-STUCK	SHAMES	SHYEST	SLAUGHTERED
SEA-SUCKED	SHANK	SICKENED	SLAVED-FOR
SEATHUMBED	SHANT	SIDEBOARD	SLAVES
SEA-WAN	SHARK	SIDED	SLAVING
SEAWARD	SHARPEN	SIDE'S	SLAYER
SEAWAX	SHARPENED	SIDLE	SLEEK
SEAWEED	SHARPER	SIEVE	SLEEPER'S
SEAWEEDS'	SHATTERED	SIGHTLESS	SLEEPINGS
SEAWEEDY	SHE-	SIGNATURE	SLEEP-WALKING
SEAWHIRL	SHEARWATER	SIGNPOSTS	SLEET
SECONDS	SHEATH-DECKED	SILKILY	SLENDERLY
SECRETLY	SHEBA'S	SILKS	SLEW
SECURE	SHE'D	SILVERFOX	SLID
SEDGES	SHEEPWHITE	SIMMERING	SLIMY
SEDUCER'S	SHELL-HUNG	SIMPLEST	SLIPPED
SEE-AT-ZERO	SHELLING	SIN-EATER	SLIPPERS
SEEDED	SHELTERED	SIN-EMBRACING	SLITS
SEEDLESS	SHELTERS	SINEWS	SLOE
SEEKING	SHEPHERDS	SINGED	SLOPING
SEEPING	SHIELD	SINGEING	SLUG
SEESAW	SHIFTED	SINGINGBIRDS	SLUG'S
SEETHE	SHIFTS	SINGINGS	SLUM
SEETHES	SHINGLE	SINGLY	SLUMMINGS
SEIZING	SHIPPEN	SINGSONG	SLUNK
SEIZURE	SHIP-RACKED	SINGULAR	SLYLY
SELECTED	SHIPS'	SINISTER	SMACKS
SEND	SHIP'S	SINNERS	SMELLING
SENDS	SHIP-WORK	SIPPING	SMILED
SENNA	SHIPWRECK	SIREN-PRINTED	SMIRK
SENSATION	SHIPWRECKED	SIRENS	SMITE
SENSIBLE	SHIPYARDS	SIREN'S	SMOKING
SENTENCE	SHIRT	SIRENSUITED	SMOOTHE
SENTIMENT	SHIRTS	SIXTH	SMOOTHLY
SENTINEL	SHIVER	SIX-YEAR	SMOTHER

SNAILS
SNAIL-WAKED
SNAPPING
SNAPT
SNARED
SNARING
SNARLING
SNARLS
SNATCHED
SNEAK
SNEERS
SNIFF
SNIFFED
SNIPPED
SNIPPING
SNOODS
SNOOP
SNOUTED
SNOWMAN'S
SNOWS
SNOW'S
SNOWY
SNUGGLES
SOAK
SOAKED
SOAKING
SOAR
SOARING
SOBSTUFF
SOCKETS
SODOM
SOFTEN
SOFTER
SOFTEST
SOFTNESS
SOFT-TALKING
SOIL-BASED
SOILED
SOILS
SOILY
SOLDERED
SOLDIER
SOLE
SOLEMNIZING
SOLITARY
SOMBRE
SOMEHOW
SON'S
SOONER
SOOTHE
SORCERER'S
SORE
SORROWS
SOULS'
SOUNDING
SOURCE
SOURS
SOWS
SPADE
SPADE-HANDED

SPADE'S
SPANNED
SPARE
SPARETIME
SPARK'S
SPARROWFALL
SPAVINED
SPEAR
SPECTACLED
SPECTACLES
SPECTRES
SPEECHES
SPELL
SPELLBOUND
SPELLSOAKED
SPEND
SPENTOUT
SPEWED
SPEWING
SPHERE
SPHERES
SPHERES'
SPHINX
SPIDER
SPIDER-TONGUED
SPIED
SPIES
SPIKE
SPIKED
SPINE
SPINNEYS
SPINNING-WHEELS
SPIRE'S
SPITE
SPITTING
SPITTLED
SPLASHED
SPLAY
SPLICE
SPLINTERS
SPLINTS
SPOILERS
SPOKEN
SPONGEBAG
SPOONED
SPOT
SPOUTED
SPRAWL
SPRAY
SPRAY-BASED
SPREADEAGLE
SPREADS
SPRINGFUL
SPRINGSHOOTS
SPRING-SPIRIT
SPRINGTAILED
SPRINGTIME
SPRINKLED
SPRINKLES
SPRINT

SPROUTED
SPUME
SPUMING
SPURNING
SPURNS
SPURT
SPYING
SQUALL
SQUATTERS
SQUAWK
SQUAWKING
SQUEEZE
SQUIBS
SQUIRES
SQUIRM
STABBING
STABS
STACKED
STAGE
STAINING
STAKE
STALKED
STAMMEL
STAMMERED
STANDING
STARBOARD
STARCH
STARER
STARES
STARFISH
STAR-GESTURED
STARLIGHT
STAR-SCALED
STAR-SET
STAR-STRUCK
STARVE
STARVING
STATUARY
STATUED
STATURE
STAYS
STEADIED
STEADIES
STEADYING
STEALER
STEALING
STEALTH
STEALTHY
STEEP
STEEPLED
STEEPLEJACK
STEER
STEERED
STEERS
STEMMED
STENCH
STERILE
STIES
STILLED
STILLS

STILL'S
STILLY
STILT
STING
STINGING
STINGS
STINK
STINKS
STITCHED
STOCKED
STOLE
STOMACHS
STONED
STONE-NECKED
STONING
STOOL
STOOLS
STOOPED
STOPPRESS
STOPS
STORE
STORKS
STORY'S
STOVED
STRAIGHTENS
STRAIGHT-RULED
STRAIT
STRAND
STRANGENESS
STRANGER-EYES
STRANGERS'
STRANGER'S
STRANGLE
STRATA
STRAWBERRIES
STREAK
STREAMED
STREAM'S
STREET-LAMPS
STREETS'
STREW
STREWED
STREWING
STREWN
STRICTURE
STRICTURES
STRIDING
STRIKING
STRINGED
STRIPED
STRIPPING
STRODE
STROKED
STROKES
STROKING
STRONGER
STRUCTURE
STRUGGLE
STRUGGLING
STRUMPET

STRUTTING	SWADDLING	TARRED	THRESHOLD
STUB	SWAG	TASK	THRILL
STUBBLE	SWALLOW	TASSELLED	THRIVE
STUCK	SWALLOWED	TATOOED	THRONE
STUDDED	SWALLOWER	TATTER	THRONG
STUDIES	SWANKED	TAWNY	THRONGED
STUDYING	SWAN'S	TAXED	THROWS
STUMBLED	SWANSING	TAXI	THUD
STUMBLES	SWARD	TEA	THUDDING
STUMBLING	SWARMS	TEAR-CULLED	THUMB-STAINED
STUMP	SWAY	TEARDROPS	THUNDERCLAP
STUMPS	SWEEP	TEAR-STAINED	THUNDERCLAPPING
STUNG	SWEETENS	TEAR-STUFFED	THUNDERING
STY	SWEETER	TELLTALE	THUNDEROUS
STYLUS	SWEETHEARTING	TEMPER	TICKED
SUAVE	SWEETHEARTS	TEMPERED	TICKING
SUBSTANCE	SWELL	TEMPERS	TICKLE
SUBSTANTIAL	SWELLING	TEMPLE-BOUND	TICKLES
SUBWAY	SWELTER	TEMPTER	TIDED
SUCKETH	SWERVE	TENDER	TIDE-HOISTED
SUCKING	SWILL	TENDRIL	TIDE-LOOPED
SUCKLE	SWIM	TENTACLE	TIDE-MASTER
SUCKLED	SWIMMERS'	TERRACE	TIDE-PRINT
SUCKLING	SWIMMING	TERRIFYING	TIDETHREAD
SUCTION	SWIMS	TERRORS	TIDE-TONGUED
SUCTION'S	SWINEHERD	TERRORS'	TIDE-TRACED
SUDDENLY	SWINISH	TESTED	TIE
SUFFERER	SWISS	TESTICLE	TIED
SUICIDES	SWITCHBACK	TETHERED	TIERED
SUITOR	SWITCHED	TEXT	TIGER-LILY
SULKING	SWIVEL	THAMES	TIGERS
SULPHURED	SWOLLEN	THANK	TIGRESS
SULPHUROUS	SWORDFISH	THATCH	TIGRON
SUMMERS	SWORDS	THAT'LL	TILER
SUMMERTIME	SWUM	THEE	TILT
SUMMERY	SYLLABIC	THEFT	TILTING
SUMMONING	SYLLABLE	THEREFORE	TIME-BOMB
SUNCOCK	SYMBOLED	THERE'LL	TIMED
SUNDAYS	SYMBOLISE	THEYD	TIME-FACED
SUNDERING	SYMMETRY	THEY'LL	TIMELESSLY
SUNDOWN	SYMPATHIZE	THEY'RE	TIME-SHAKEN
SUNFLOWERS	SYMPATHY	THICKET	TIN
SUN-GLOVED	SYNAGOGUE	THICKETS	TINGLE
SUNKEN	SYNTHETIC	THINNING	TINNED
SUN-LEAVED	T.	THIRD	TIPS
SUNNY	TABLECLOTH	THIRTY-FIFTH	TIPSY
SUNRISE	TACKLE	THIRTY-FIVE	TIPTOED
SUNSHINE	TACKLED	THISTLEDOWN	TIRELESS
SUPER-OR-NEAR	TAILORS'	THISTLING	TITHINGS
SUPPER	TALE'S	THORNS	TOADS
SUPPOSE	TALKATIVE	THOROUGHFARES	TOCSIN
SURELY	TALKING	THOROUGHLY	TO-DAY
SURNAMES	TALLER	THOUSAND	TODAY'S
SURPLICED	TALLOW	THRASHED	TOEING
SURPRISED	TALLOW-EYED	THREADBARE	TOIL
SURRENDER	TANGLING	THREE-COLOURED	TOLERANCE
SURROUND	TAPE	THREE-EYED	TOLL
SURROUNDING	TAPESTRY	THREE-POINTED	TOLLED
SUSANNAH'S	TAPS	THREE-QUARTERS	TOMMY
SUSPENDED	TAR	THREE-SYLLABLED	TOMORROW

TOMORROW'S	TRUANT	UNCHANGEABLE	UNRAVEL
TOMORROW-TREADING	TRULY	UNCHRISTENED	UNRAVELLER
TOM-THUMB	TRUMP	UNCLAIMED	UNRAVELS
TONGUELESS	TRUMPED	UNCLENCHED	UNREAL
TONGUE-PLUCKED	TRUMPETER	UNCOMPLAININGLY	UNREASON
TO-NIGHT	TRUMPETING	UNCONCEIVED	UNREASONABLY
TONNED	TRUMPETS	UNCOVERED	UNREINED
TONS	TRUNKS	UNCREDITED	UNREMEMBERED
TOOTHLESS	TRY	UNDEFENDED	UNREST
TOPLESS	TRYING	UNDERCLOTHES	UNRETURNABLE
TOPPLE	TUBES	UNDERSTAND	UNRETURNED
TOPSY-TURVIES	TUFT	UNDERTAKER'S	UNRIDDLE
TORE	TUG	UNDESERVING	UNRISEN
TORMENTED	TUGGED	UNDESIRERS	UNRIVALLED
TORRENT	TUMBLEDOWN	UNDIE	UNRULY
TORRID	TUMBLERS	UNDIVIDED	UNSACRED
TORTURE	TUNEFUL	UNDO	UNSAFE
TOSS	TUNES	UNDOING	UNSEEING
TOTTER	TUNICS'	UNDOUBLING	UNSEX
TOTTERS	TUNING	UNDRESS	UNSHACKLED
TOUCHES	TURBINE	UNEARTHLY	UNSHAPED
TOWER'S	TURBULENT	UNEASE	UNSHELVE
TOWY'S	TURNIPS	UNEATEN	UNSHODDEN
TRACED	TURNKEY	UNEATING	UNSKATED
TRACES	TURNTURTLE	UNENTERED	UNSOUNDING
TRAILED	TUSSLE	UNEVEN	UNSOWN
TRAILS	TWELVE-LEGGED	UNFIRED	UNSPENT
TRAMMELLED	TWIG	UNFOLDING	UNSUCKED
TRAMPLING	TWIGS	UNFORGETFULNESS	UNSUCKLED
TRANSLATE	TWILIT	UNFORGETTABLY	UNTHINKING
TRAP'S	TWIN-BOXED	UNFREE	UNTURNING
TRASH	TWINKLING	UNFRIENDLY	UNWASTEABLE
TRAVELLER	TWISTING	UNFRISKY	UNWATERED
TRAVELS	TWITCH	UNHAPPY	UNWAVERING
TRAY	TWO-A-VEIN	UNHARDY	UNWINDING
TREADING	TWO-FRAMED	UNHARMED	UNWORTHY
TREASON	TWO-GUNNED	UNHEALTHILY	UNWRINKLES
TREASON'S	TWOLEGGED	UNHOLY	UNWRINKLING
TREASURES	TYBURN	UNHOUSE	UPCASTING
TREATY	UGLIER	UNHURT	UPCOMING
TREEFORK	UGLY	UNICORN	UPGIVEN
TREES'	ULTIMATE	UNJUDGING	UPHEAVAL
TREE-TAILED	UMBRELLA'D	UNKIND	UPPER
TREMBLED	UNACCUSTOMED	UNLOCKING	UPRISING
TREMBLES	UNALTERED	UNLOVERS	UPROAR
TREMULOUSLY	UNANGLED	UNLOVING	UPROARIOUS
TRESPASSER	UNASHAMED	UNMADE	UPSAILING
TRIANGLE	UNBELIEVING	UNMANLY	UPSIDE
TRIANGLES	UNBENDING	UNMANNINGLY	UPTURNED
TRICKLE	UNBIDDEN	UNMASTERED	UPWARDS
TRIGGER	UNBLESSED	UNMILK	USELESS
TRIM	UNBOLT	UNMINDING	UTTERANCES
TRINITY	UNBOLTS	UNMORTAL	VAGUENESS
TRIOLET	UNBOSOMING	UNMOURNING	VAINLY
TRIPPER'S	UNBROKEN	UNMOVED	VALIANCE
TRITON	UNBUTTONED	UNPACKS	VALUES
TRIUMPH	UNCAGED	UNPIN	VAMPIRE
TROUGH	UNCALM	UNPITIED	VANISHED
TROUNCED	UNCEASINGLY	UNPLANTED	VANISHING
TROVE	UNCERTAIN	UNPRICKED	VANITIES

VAULTED	WALKER	WEAVING	WHIZZBANGS
VAULTS	WALKER'S	WEBBED	WHO'D
VEGETATION'S	WALKETH	WEBFOOT	WHOEVER
VEILED	WALLED	WEDDED	WHOLLY
VENOMS	WALL'S	WEDDING	WHOOPEE
VENOM'S	WALT	WEDDINGS	WICK
VENT	WAND	WEDDINGS'	WICK-
VENUSWISE	WANDERED	WEDS	WICKEDLY
VERBOTEN	WANDERER	WEEK	WIDDERSHIN
VERBS	WANDERING	WEEKS'	WIDOWER
VERGE	WANDERS	WEIGHING-SCALES	WIG
VERMIN	WANTS	WEIGHTLESS	WILDE
VERTICALLY	WARBEARING	WEIGHTS	WILLINGLY
VERTICALS	WARDEN	WEIRD	WILLOWS
VESSEL	WARDS	WELL-HELD	WILLY
VESSELS	WARMED	WELL-MADE	WILLYNILLY
VEST	WARMER	WELL-OFF	WILY
VESTS	WARMING	WELLS	WIN
VIBRATE	WARMS	WELSHING	WIND-
VIBRATIONS	WARM-VEINED	WENDY'S	WINDFALL
VICES	WARN	WE'RE	WIND-HEELED
VICIOUSLY	WARNED	WEST'S	WINDING-FOOTED
VICTORIOUS	WAR'S	WETHER	WINDINGS
VICTORY	WASHING	WETTEN	WINDING-SHEETS
VIEW	WASTED	WHALE	WINDMILL
VILLAS	WASTEFUL	WHALEBED	WINDSHAKE
VINEYARD	WASTERS	WHALE-BLUE	WIND-TURNED
VIOLINS	WASTING	WHALE-WEED	WINDWELL
VIPERISH	WATCHED	WHARVES	WINE-WELLS
VIRGATE	WATCHERS	WHATSOEVER	WINGBEAT
VIRGIL	WATER-	WHEATFIELD	WINGING
VIRGINITY	WATER-CLOCKS	WHEELING	WINKING-BIT
VIRGIN'S	WATERED	WHEELS'	WINKLE
VIRTUE	WATER-FACE	WHEEL-WINDERS	WINNING
VIRTUES	WATERFALLS	WHELPS	WINTERED
VISIONED	WATER-LAMMED	WHENEVER	WINTER-LOCKED
VISITOR	WATER-PILLARED	WHEREON	WINY
VITAL	WATER-SPIRIT	WHERE'S	WIPES
VIXEN	WATER-SPOKEN	WHEREVER	WIRE
VOICED	WATER-TOWER	WHETHER	WIRED
VOICELESS	WATER-WOUND	WHINNY	WIRELESS
VOLES	WATERY	WHIP	WIRES
VOLTS	WAVE'S	WHIPPED	WISECRACKS
VOLUPTUOUS	WAXEN	WHIPS	WISELY
VOMIT	WAXES	WHIRL	WISEMEN
VOWELLED	WAXING	WHIRL-	WISHBONES
VOYAGING	WAXLIGHTS	WHIRLING	WISPS
VULTURED	WAX-RED	WHIRLS	WITCHILIKE
WADED	WAYSIDE	WHIRLWIND	WITCH'S
WAGGED	WEAKEST	WHIRR	WIT-HURT
WAGONS	WEALTH	WHIRRING	WITNESS
WAGS	WEANS	WHISKING	WITNESSED
WAIL	WEARS	WHISKY	WIVING
WAILED	WEAR-WILLOW	WHISPERINGS	WIZARD
WAILING	WEASELS	WHISPERS	WIZARD'S
WAILS	WEATHER-COCK	WHISTLER'S	WIZENED
WAINS	WEATHERCOCKS'	WHISTLING	WOEBEGONE
WAITS	WEATHERING	WHITE-DRESSED	WOLVES
WAKEN	WEATHER'S	WHITE-LIPPED	WOMAN-LUCK
WAKEWARD-FLASHING	WEAVES	WHITES	WOMB-EYED

WOMB'S
WOMEN'S
WOODS'
WOOD'S
WOOD-TONGUED
WOOL
WORD'S
WORKER
WORKS
WORLDED
WORMS
WORSE
WORSHIPPING
WORST
WORTH
WORTHINGTON
WOUND-DOWN
WOUND'S
WOUNDWARD
WRACK
WRACKED
WRACKSPIKED
WRANGLING
WRAPPED
WRAPT
WREATH
WREATHING
WRECK
WRECKED
WRECKS
WRENCHED
WREN'S
WRESTLE
WRESTLED
WRESTLING
WRETCHED
WRING
WRISTED
WRITES
WRITHES
WRITING
WRONGS
WROTE
WYNDS
X
YAWN
YAWNED
YAWNING
YEA
YEAR-HEDGED
YEARN
YEAR'S
YESMAN
YESTERDAY
YIELD
YIELDS
YODEL
YOLK
YOURSELF
YOUTH'S

YOU'VE
ZENITH
ZERO
ZEST
ZION
ZIP
ZOO